WILKINSON'S

ROAD TRAFFIC
OFFENCES

HISTORY OF *WILKINSON*

First Edition	1953	G.S. Wilkinson
Second Edition	1956	G.S. Wilkinson
Third Edition	1960	G.S. Wilkinson
Fourth Edition	1963	G.S. Wilkinson
Fifth Edition	1965	G.S. Wilkinson
Sixth Edition	1970	G.S. Wilkinson and P.J. Halnan
Seventh Edition	1973	P.J. Halnan
Eighth Edition	1975	P.J. Halnan
Ninth Edition	1977	P.J. Halnan
Tenth Edition	1980	P.J. Halnan and J.N. Spencer
Eleventh Edition	1982	P.J. Halnan and J.N. Spencer
Twelfth Edition	1985	P.J. Halnan and J.N. Spencer
Thirteenth Edition	1987	P.J. Halnan and P.S. Wallis
Fourteenth Edition	1989	P.J. Halnan and P.S. Wallis
Fifteenth Edition	1991	P.J. Halnan and P.S. Wallis
Sixteenth Edition	1993	P.S. Wallis and P.J. Halnan
Seventeenth Edition	1995	P.S. Wallis and P.J. Halnan
Eighteenth Edition	1997	P.S. Wallis and P.J. Halnan
Nineteenth Edition	1999	P.S. Wallis and P.J. Halnan
Twentieth Edition	2001	P.S. Wallis and K. McCormac
Twenty-first Edition	2003	P.S. Wallis and K. McCormac
Twenty-second Edition	2005	P.S. Wallis and K. McCormac
Twenty-third Edition	2007	P.S. Wallis and K. McCormac
Twenty-fourth Edition	2009	K. McCormac and P.S. Wallis

WILKINSON'S

ROAD TRAFFIC OFFENCES

Twenty-fourth Edition

VOLUME 1

General Editor

KEVIN McCORMAC, O.B.E., M.A.

of Gray's Inn, Barrister

Consultant Editor

PETER WALLIS

District Judge (Magistrates' Courts)
Recorder of the Crown Court

PHILIP BROWN, M.A., LL.B.   HOWARD RIDDLE

Traffic Commissioner   *District Judge (Magistrates' Courts)*

KATHRYN SWIFT, LL.B.

SWEET & MAXWELL  THOMSON REUTERS

Published in 2009 by
Thomson Reuters (Legal) Limited
(Registered in England & Wales, Company No 1679046.
Registered Office and address for service:
100 Avenue Road, London, NW3 3PF)
trading as Sweet & Maxwell

Tables typeset by Servis Filmsetting Ltd, Manchester

All other typesetting by Sweet & Maxwell Ltd, 100 Avenue Road, London, NW3 3PF
Printed in the UK by CPI William Clowes Beccles NR34 7TL

For further information on our products and services, visit
www.sweetandmaxwell.co.uk

No natural forests were destroyed to make this product; only farmed timber
was used and replanted.

A CIP catalogue record of this book is available from the British Library.

ISBN 978 184 703571 4

Twenty-fourth Edition 2009

CONTENTS

Chapter 2   Procedure

Commencing Proceedings

Chapter 3   Evidence

Chapter 4   Drink/Driving Offences

Chapter 6   Driver Offences

CONTENTS

Chapter 9   Protection of Drivers and Passengers

Chapter 13   Goods and Passenger Vehicles

Chapter 14   Drivers' Hours and Records

Chapter 15   Theft, Taking Conveyances, Aggravated Vehicle-Taking, Criminal Damage and Causing Danger to Road Users

CONTENTS

Chapter 19   Endorsement and Penalty Points

Chapter 20   Disqualification

Chapter 22   Appeals

PREFACE

The law is generally stated as at March 1, 2009, although, as is our custom, we have worked to later dates in some instances.

Since the previous edition, a highly significant event directly affecting road traffic offences has been the creation of the two new offences of causing death by careless driving and of causing death by driving when uninsured, unlicensed or disqualified. These were accompanied both by revisions to the CPS prosecution policy and by the Sentencing Guidelines Council's definitive guidelines on all four of the offences where death was caused by driving. As noted in the Preface to the second supplement to the previous edition, these new offences are significant in the extent to which there may be a substantial gap between the harm caused and the culpability of the offender and, more unusually, that the sanction provided reflects the harm caused to a substantially greater extent than the culpability of the offender. The anticipated difficulties that this will cause for a court when imposing sentence have already started to emerge; this is amply illustrated in the case of *R. v Clifford* (§ 15.54) where a driver (of good character and with a clean driving record but only a provisional licence) had taken a vehicle without authority and had knocked over a child who had stepped into the road; the child died as a result but there was no fault in the offender's driving. A six-month custodial sentence was considered appropriate. Similarly, the gap between the maximum sentence for dangerous driving depending on whether death results or "just" serious injury is becoming more noticeable and there may be a greater use of prosecutions for other offences with higher maximum penalties (such as inflicting grievous bodily harm) as in *R. v Stranney* (§ 5.103).

A further significant event has been the new edition of the *Magistrates' Court Sentencing Guidelines* which became effective in summer 2008. The approach to sentencing for many of the offences in this work must now be based on those guidelines which are more precise than previously in identifying the various types of activity that might constitute a particular offence and in providing both a starting point and range for sentence. Prosecutors and defence advocates can expect a court to anticipate that a case will be presented in a way that assists in identifying the right category for sentencing purposes. These guidelines are also intended to bring greater clarity to mode of trial decisions for those offences triable either way by describing more precisely the types of case requiring sentence beyond the powers of a magistrates' court.

The development with, perhaps, the most wide-ranging influence on the prosecution of road traffic offences has been the growing approach to emphasise the importance of fairness between the parties and the pre-eminent objective of seeking justice. This is seen in the range of cases drawing attention to the overriding objective to do justice as set out in the Criminal Procedure Rules, in the emphasis on defence identification of issues in dispute and in the restrictive approach to abuse of process arguments. In addition, cases around the definition of "accident" for the purpose of determining whether a notice of intended prosecution was required have focused on the underlying purpose of such notices and rejected arguments that sought to evade responsibility for serious offences through technical arguments.

An area of considerable complexity is the admissibility of evidence. The changes in the legislative provisions designed to widen the evidence available to a court have generated substantial case law and the key themes relevant to the offences covered in this edition are set out in Chapter 3. One of the consequences of the changes has been to provide other ways of proceeding where a prosecution witness has not appeared and an application to adjourn has been rejected. As noted from the decision in *Boguslaw Sak v Crown Prosecution Service* (§ 3.19), the defence can no longer assume that successfully opposing a prosecution application to adjourn in such circumstances will mean that the case does not proceed; that is likely to influence the extent to which such applications are opposed.

Finally, the trend to rely on methods beyond prosecution of offences to uphold the law is reflected in the substantial sanctions available to enforcement authorities outside court proceedings. A recent example is seen in the case of *Romantiek Transport v Simms, Allsopp and the Department for Transport* (§ 13.42) which concerned the detention of goods vehicles following unlawful use without an operator's licence.

As always, a great debt of gratitude is owed to the team that supports the production of this work. In particular, the tireless and meticulous work of Kathryn Swift in supporting the editors and in maintaining Volume 2 has continued at an exceptionally high standard and is greatly appreciated.

Kevin McCormac

Worthing

June 2009

TABLE OF CASES

All entries are tabled to paragraph number.

TABLE OF STATUTES

*All entries are tabled to paragraph number. Paragraph numbers in **bold** type indicate where the entry is reproduced.*

TABLE OF STATUTORY INSTRUMENTS

*All entries are tabled to paragraph number. Paragraph numbers in **bold** type indicate where the entry is reproduced.*

TABLE OF EUROPEAN PROVISIONS

*All entries are tabled to paragraph number. Paragraph numbers in **bold** type indicate where the entry is reproduced.*

Decisions

Regulations

TABLE OF INTERNATIONAL CONVENTIONS AND AGREEMENTS

*All entries are tabled to paragraph number. Paragraph numbers in **bold** type indicate where the entry is reproduced.*

WILKINSON SERVICE INFORMATION

Wilkinson's Road Traffic Offences consists of two volumes, 1 Text and 2 Sources, and includes tables and index in both volumes. These volumes are reissued every two years, and are updated by two supplements and *Wilkinson's Road Traffic Law Bulletin* (a bi-monthly newsletter).

Supplements

Two supplements, containing updating material for both volumes, are published during the life of the current edition as part of the *Wilkinson* service. The second supplement is cumulative.

Paragraph numbering

Paragraph numbers appear throughout the text of both volumes of the work. Where reference is made to a particular paragraph in either volume, please check the Wilkinson noter-up in *Wilkinson's Road Traffic Law Bulletin* and, when available, the corresponding paragraph in the current supplement for updating any recent developments on this point.

Publisher note

All suggestions, comments and notices of error should be addressed to the House Editor, *Wilkinson's Road Traffic Offences*, Sweet & Maxwell, 100 Avenue Road, London NW3 3PF.

ABBREVIATIONS

Archbold	*Criminal Pleading, Evidence and Practice*
E. & E. Digest	*English and Empire Digest*
Stone	*Stone's Justices' Manual*
R.T.L.B./W.R.T.L.B.	*Wilkinson's Road Traffic Law Bulletin*

CHAPTER 1

DEFINITIONS

CONTENTS

General

In this book various terms are used which, unless the context otherwise   **1.01**
requires, will generally be used in the sense given in this chapter. It should be
remembered that the meaning of some terms, notably "to permit" and "to use",
varies according to the context of the section of the particular statute in which
they appear. Furthermore, definitions of the same word may vary as between the
Road Traffic Acts and the Vehicle Excise and Registration Act 1994. It is recommended that careful reference is made to the source material in Vol.2 in relation
to the terms defined in this chapter.

The terms immediately below should, in particular, be noted as they are used
throughout this book.

"Magistrates' court"

"Magistrates' court" includes a youth court; but the term includes the Crown   **1.02**
Court only so far as the powers of the Crown Court on appeal are limited to those
of a magistrates' court (see the Supreme Court Act 1981 s.48(4)).

The 1988 road traffic legislation

In 1988 three Acts were passed by Parliament which consolidated road traffic   **1.03**
legislation—the Road Traffic Act 1988 (referred to hereafter as "the 1988 Act")
which deals with the substantive law; the Road Traffic Offenders Act 1988
(referred to hereafter as "the 1988 Offenders Act") which deals with the
consolidation of certain previous legislation relating to the prosecution and
punishment of road traffic offences, including the law relating to fixed penalties;
and the Road Traffic (Consequential Provisions) Act 1988, which makes provi-

sion for repeals, consequential amendments, transitional and transitory matters, following from the enactment of the other two statutes.

MOTOR VEHICLES

"Motor vehicle"

1.04   "Motor vehicle" is defined by s.185 of the 1988 Act for the purposes of that Act and regulations made thereunder. Section 185(1) defines a "motor vehicle" as a mechanically propelled vehicle intended or adapted for use on roads. The Road Traffic Regulation Act 1984 s.136, is in similar terms. This definition does not necessarily apply under the Vehicle Excise and Registration Act 1994, but for many purposes it will be the same. Under the Vehicle Excise and Registration Act 1994 a motor vehicle need not be "intended or adapted for use on a road" (see § 12.03): that Act uses the term "mechanically propelled vehicle" only. It follows that a motor vehicle may require an excise licence when it is kept or used on a public road even though it is not subject to the 1988 Act because it is not intended or adapted for use on a road (e.g. a stock car, a scrambling motor bicycle, a works truck or a digging machine). As to vehicle excise licences for works trucks and digging machines, see §§ 12.14–15. A motor vehicle does not cease to be "used" as a motor vehicle when it is towed by another (*Cobb v Whorton* [1971] R.T.R. 392, § 1.188). The requirement to be licensed applies not only to something that is a mechanically propelled vehicle but also to anything that has been such a vehicle but has now ceased to be (Vehicle Excise and Registration Act 1994 s.1(1B)).

   It should be emphasised that "vehicle" and "motor vehicle" are differently defined for the purposes of drivers' hours and records and tachographs (see Regulation (EEC) 3821/85 art.2, as amended, and Regulation (EEC) 561/2006 art.4).

1.05   Section 192(3) of the 1988 Act and s.142(3) of the Road Traffic Regulation Act 1984 provide that references in the Act to a class of vehicle or traffic must be construed as references to a class defined or described by reference to any characteristics of the vehicles or to any other circumstances whatsoever. The word "category" is also substituted to indicate a class of vehicles however defined or described (Road Traffic (Driver Licensing and Information Systems) Act 1989 Sch.3 para.24).

   The definitions of other terms relating to motor vehicles and classes thereof (which are discussed below) are principally contained in s.185(1) of the 1988 Act and ss.136 and 137 of the Road Traffic Regulation Act 1984.

"Motor car"

1.06   Section 185(1) of the 1988 Act defines "motor car" as follows:

> "In this Act 'motor car' means a mechanically propelled vehicle, not being a motor cycle or an invalid carriage, which is constructed itself to carry a load or passengers and the weight of which unladen—
>
> (a) if it is constructed solely for the carriage of passengers and their effects, is adapted to carry not more than seven passengers exclusive of the driver, and is fitted with tyres of such type as may be specified in regulations made by the Secretary of State for Transport, does not exceed 3050 kilograms;

(b) if it is constructed or adapted for use for the conveyance of goods or burden of any description, does not exceed 3050 kilograms, or 3500 kilograms if the vehicle carries a container or containers for holding for the purpose of its propulsion any fuel which is wholly gaseous at 17.5 degrees Celsius under a pressure of 1.013 bar or plant and materials for producing such fuel;

(c) does not exceed 2540 kilograms in a case not falling within sub-paragraph (a) or (b) above. "

The definition in s.136(2) of the Road Traffic Regulation Act 1984 is similar.

Section 185(1) of the 1988 Act and s.136 of the Road Traffic Regulation Act **1.07** 1984 further define the meanings of "heavy motor car", "motor cycle" (see § 1.12), "invalid carriage" (see § 1.09), "motor tractor", "light locomotive" and "heavy locomotive".

"Hovercraft"

A "hovercraft" within the meaning of the Hovercraft Act 1968 is a motor vehi- **1.08** cle, whether or not it is adapted or intended to be adapted for use on roads, but is treated as not being a vehicle of any of the classes or descriptions specified in s.185(1) of the 1988 Act (s.188(1)). Regulations may modify any of the provisions of the 1988 Act in relation to hovercraft (s.188(2)). Like provisions are in the Road Traffic Regulation Act 1984 s.139.

"Invalid carriage"

An "invalid carriage" is defined by s.185 of the 1988 Act as follows: **1.09**

"In this Act 'invalid carriage' means a mechanically propelled vehicle the weight of which unladen does not exceed 254 kilograms and which is specially designed and constructed, and not merely adapted, for the use of a person suffering from some physical defect or disability and is used solely by such a person. "

The definition in the Road Traffic Regulation Act 1984 s.136(5) is similar save that curiously the expression "physical default" is used in place of "physical defect".

For the purposes of all parts of the 1988 Act, the 1988 Offenders Act and the **1.10** Road Traffic Regulation Act 1984 and of the Road Vehicles (Construction and Use) Regulations 1986 (SI 1986/1078), a carriage for invalids exceeding 254kg in unladen weight is not classified as an "invalid carriage" but is a motor car or, if it has three or less wheels and does not exceed 410kg, a motor cycle; it will also require third party insurance, though one of 254kg or less does not (1988 Act s.143(4)). Otherwise a carriage for invalids over 254kg is again not an "invalid carriage" but comes within whatever category is appropriate for the particular vehicle and these Acts and regulations thereunder will apply, in particular as to insurance, etc.

The description "invalid vehicles" is used in the Road Vehicles (Registration and Licensing) Regulations 2002 (SI 2002/2742) and the weight limit there is 508kg for the purposes of those regulations.

Invalid carriages complying with regs 2–6 of the Use of Invalid Carriages on **1.11** Highways Regulations 1970 (SI 1970/1391) or with regs 4–14 of the like-named 1988 Regulations (SI 1988/2268) are treated for the purposes of the 1988 Acts and the Road Traffic Regulation Act 1984 as not being motor vehicles (Chronically Sick and Disabled Persons Act 1970 s.20). These invalid carriages may also use footways, restricted byways and bridlepaths and only need to show the lights set out in the regulations. There is an exemption from vehicle excise duty under the Vehicle Excise and Registration Act 1994 for certain vehicles for disabled people. This exemption is not limited to vehicles which are "invalid carriages". For the requirements for exemption, see § 12.32 et seq.

"Motor cycle"

1.12   A "motor cycle" is defined by s.185(1) of the 1988 Act as a mechanically propelled vehicle, not being an invalid carriage, with less than four wheels and the weight of which unladen does not exceed 410kg. The definitions in s.136(4) of the Road Traffic Regulation Act 1984 and reg.3(2) of the Road Vehicles (Construction and Use) Regulations 1986 (SI 1986/1078) are similar. This definition may therefore include three-wheelers, motor bicycles, mopeds, certain mowing machines and pedestrian controlled vehicles.

A   *"Three-wheeler cars"*

1.13   A three-wheeler car not exceeding 410kg comes within the definition of "motor cycle". By s.185(1) of the 1988 Act (and s.136(2) of the Road Traffic Regulation Act 1984), a motor vehicle which is a motor cycle is not a motor car (see "Motor car" at § 1.06 above). There are special rules relating to learner drivers of three-wheelers (see § 11.38). Various other provisions apply specifically to three-wheelers.

Motor tricycles weighing up to 550kg fall within Group B1 vehicles for driving test purposes (see the Motor Vehicles (Driving Licences) Regulations 1999 (SI 1999/2864) Sch.2, as amended). Any such vehicles exceeding 410kg will, by definition, be motor cars rather than motor cycles.

B   *"Motor bicycle"*

1.14   A motor bicycle is not defined in the 1988 Act or the Road Traffic Regulation Act 1984. As the prefix implies, a motor bicycle is a form of motor cycle but with two wheels. It is perhaps obvious that the wheels of a side-car are to be excluded. Otherwise a bicycle with a side-car could not be a bicycle. Again there are special rules relating to learner drivers and such vehicles (see §§ 11.29–39). There is a special definition of a motor bicycle in the Motor Cycles (Protective Helmets) Regulations 1998 (SI 1998/1807) reg.4, as amended. Under this a motor bicycle is a two-wheeled motor cycle with or without a side-car and in certain circumstances may include a vehicle with additional wheels. These regulations apply only to such bicycles.

C   *"Side-car"*

1.15   There is no definition of a side-car (that is, a side carriage) as such. A side-car is part of the motor cycle itself and not of its equipment (*Higgins v Feeney* (1954) 88 I.L.T.R. 152). Under the 1988 Act s.186(1) and the Road Traffic Regulation Act 1984 s.137, if the side-car complies with the specified conditions, which are to be found in reg.92 of the Road Vehicles (Construction and Use) Regulations 1986 (SI 1986/1078), it is part of the vehicle and if not it is a trailer. A number of consequences follow. The various restrictions on the use of trailers will apply to trailers and the speed limit for the class of vehicle will be governed accordingly by Sch.6 to the Road Traffic Regulation Act 1984. See also §§ 11.29–39 as to the learner driver provisions.

A flat tubular framework attached to a motor bicycle with a wheel on an axle welded to that framework was held not to be a side-car under the learner driver provisions (*Cox v Harrison* [1968] 3 All E.R. 811). It was said obiter there that a side-car must be capable of carrying a passenger. In *Keen v Parker* [1976] R.T.R. 213 the defendant rode a 500cc motor bicycle with a tubular steel framework attached, designed for the carriage of goods. The framework was roadworthy with a properly sprung wheel. It was held that a roadworthy attachment for the carriage of goods was just as much a "side-car" as one designed for the carriage of a passenger. The obiter dictum of Ashworth J. in *Cox v Harrison* above was disapproved.

D   *"Standard motor cycle"*

A "standard motor cycle" is defined for the purposes of reg.69 of and Sch.9 to   **1.16**
the Road Vehicles (Construction and Use) Regulations 1986 (SI 1986/1078) as a motor cycle which is not a moped. This definition will include some three-wheelers. Motor cycles not exceeding 150cc first used on or after August 1, 1977 and motor cycles not exceeding 125cc first used on or after January 1, 1982 are required to display plates in accordance with this regulation and Schedule. The plates must show whether the cycle is a "standard motor cycle" or a "moped" (Sch.9 para.2, note 1). For this purpose *"moped"* means a moped first used on or after August 1, 1977 (see below). The plates must also give other information designed to show whether the vehicle is a moped (see below) and to enable learner drivers to be restricted to less powerful vehicles. Mowing machines and pedestrian controlled vehicles are not required to carry plates (see reg.69(1)(b) and (c)). It seems that a cycle is still within the definition of standard motor cycle where appropriate even if the plate is not exhibited.

E   *"Learner motor bicycles"*

These are defined by s.97(5) of the 1988 Act. They are either electric motor   **1.17**
bicycles or those which do not exceed 125cc, whose maximum net engine power output does not exceed 11kW.

F   *"Moped"*

A moped is defined in s.108 of the 1988 Act for the purposes of Pt III of that   **1.18**
Act as being *either* a motor vehicle with less than four wheels, with a cylinder capacity not exceeding 50cc, equipped with pedals capable of propelling it and first used before August 1, 1977 *or* such a vehicle first used on or after that date which has a maximum speed not exceeding 50kph and an engine (if an internal combustion engine) not exceeding 50cc. It should be noted that the latter is still termed a moped even though it is not required to be equipped with pedals. It is required to carry a plate (see under "Standard motor cycle" above; the definition of a "moped" in the Road Vehicles (Construction and Use) Regulations 1986 (SI 1986/1078) Sch.9 is also applied to regs 54 and 57 (it sets out some but not all silencer offences: see § 8.73)). It seems that a cycle is still within the definition of moped even if the plate is not exhibited. The Motor Vehicles (Driving Licences) Regulations 1999 (SI 1999/2864) do not further define "moped".

In *G v Jarrett* [1981] R.T.R. 186 a youth was riding a motor cycle which had no footrest on the nearside pedal shaft. Whether it was a moped depended inter alia on whether it was equipped with pedals capable of being propelled. His appeal to the Divisional Court against two convictions stemming from the vehicle being regarded as a motor cycle and not a moped was successful: the vehicle remained a moped.

Other motor vehicles

1.19   "Agricultural motor vehicle" and "dual-purpose vehicle" are defined in the Road Vehicles (Construction and Use) Regulations 1986 (SI 1986/1078) reg.3(2). "Agricultural motor vehicle" is defined as a motor vehicle which is constructed or adapted (see §§ 1.27–31) for use off roads for the purpose of agriculture, horticulture or forestry and which is primarily used for one or more of those purposes, and which is not a dual-purpose vehicle. See also § 6.127 as to "dual-purpose vehicle", § 6.117 as to "passenger vehicles", § 6.120 as to "goods vehicle", and § 12.15 as to "works truck".

A "passenger vehicle" is defined in reg.3(2) of the Road Vehicles (Construction and Use) Regulations 1986 (SI 1986/1078), as a vehicle constructed solely for the carriage of passengers and their effects. If a motor vehicle is constructed or adapted to carry more than eight seated passengers (in addition to the driver) it falls within the definition of a "bus" in reg.3(2); if it is so constructed or adapted to carry more than eight but not more than 16 seated passengers, it falls within the definition of a "minibus" in reg.3(2); and if it is so constructed or adapted to carry more than 16 seated passengers, it falls within the definition of a "large bus" in reg.3(2), as amended. It should be noted that these definitions refer to "seated passengers", and their number is calculated without reference to the driver. Also, that the vehicles may be originally constructed or subsequently adapted to bring them within the terms of these definitions.

1.20   A "coach" is a large bus (see above) with a maximum gross weight (see § 1.68) of more than 7.5 tonnes and with a maximum speed exceeding 60mph (reg.3(2), as amended). "Courtesy coaches" were held to be public service vehicles for the purposes of s.1 of the Public Passenger Vehicles Act 1981 in *Rout v Swallow Hotels Ltd* [1993] R.T.R. 80. The courtesy coaches were used in conjunction with the business of the hotel and at the discretion of the manager. The coaches were part of the hotel business, and the hire or reward was included in the payment of the room or meal by the guest. The drivers of the particular vehicles were required to have a public service vehicles driver's licence or a public service vehicles operator's licence. Another case where the Divisional Court held that a defendant was driving a public service vehicle was *DPP v Sikondar* [1993] R.T.R. 90. Mr Sikondar was carrying 11 schoolgirls, including two of his own daughters and one of his brother's, to school in a minibus rather than them using public transport. This had continued for five months. He had never demanded money, but had been paid sums intermittently. The court found that on the evidence there was plainly a systematic carrying of passengers for reward which went beyond the bounds of social kindness. The matter was remitted to the justices with a direction to convict.

A "motor caravan" is a motor vehicle which is constructed or adapted for the carriage of passengers and their effects and which contains, as permanently installed equipment, the facilities which are reasonably necessary for enabling the vehicle to provide mobile living accommodation for its users (reg.3(2), as amended).

Regulation 3(2), as further amended, also includes definitions for "car transporter" ("a trailer which is constructed and normally used for the purpose of carrying at least two wheeled vehicles") and "engineering equipment" ("engineering plant and any other plant or equipment designed and constructed for the purpose of engineering operations"). See also reg.3(2) for definitions of "low loader", "low platform trailer" and "stepframe low loader".   **1.21**

"Pedal cycles"

Pedal cycles fall into three categories: motor vehicles, certain electrically as-   **1.22**
sisted pedal cycles which despite the motor assistance are excluded from being motor vehicles, and pedal cycles not propelled by mechanical power.

A pedal cycle is defined by the Pedal Cycles (Construction and Use) Regulations 1983 (SI 1983/1176) for those regulations as either a pedal cycle not propelled by mechanical power or an electrically assisted pedal cycle of prescribed type (reg.3(1)).

Electrically assisted pedal cycles

By s.189(1) of the 1988 Act and s.140(1)(c) of the Road Traffic Regulation Act   **1.23**
1984, electrically assisted pedal cycles as specified in the Electrically Assisted Pedal Cycles Regulations 1983 (SI 1983/1168) are not treated as motor vehicles. They must be bicycles or tricycles (reg.3). They must be fitted with pedals by means of which they are capable of being propelled (reg.4(b)). Their electric motor must not be able to propel the vehicle when travelling at more than 15mph (reg.4(c)(ii)). If a bicycle (other than a tandem) it must have a kerbside weight not exceeding 40kg and an electric motor not exceeding 0.2kW (reg.4(a)(i), (c)(i)(A)). If a tandem bicycle or a tricycle (including a tandem tricycle) it must have a kerbside weight not exceeding 60kg and an electric motor not exceeding 0.25kW (reg.4(a)(ii), (c)(i)(B)). A tandem bicycle is defined as a bicycle which is designed to carry two or more persons at least two of whom can propel the vehicle at the same time (reg.2). Reference should be made to the regulations for the full provisions.

The requirement under reg.4(b) of the 1983 Regulations to be fitted with pedals capable of propelling the cycle was considered in *Winter v DPP* [2002] EWCA 1524; [2003] R.T.R. 14. The defendant used a "city bug" electric scooter and was not insured. She was prosecuted for using the vehicle without insurance and the issue had to be resolved as to whether it came within this exemption. The only issue arose from reg.4(b). The scooter had small front pedals capable of powering the front wheel. The Crown Court accepted that the defendant had used the pedals to achieve forward propulsion and had propelled the vehicle a few metres at a time but found as a fact that the vehicle was intended primarily to be powered by an electric motor. Although the scooter could be propelled by the pedals, that was a difficult and precarious exercise that required much practice and it would be impossible for anyone to use the machine safely on the road by relying on pedal power alone. Accordingly, the court found reg.4(b) was not complied with and found the defendant guilty. Her appeal was dismissed. A purposive construction was appropriate to give effect to Parliament's intention.

This had to require the pedals to be capable of propelling the vehicle in a safe manner in its normal day-to-day use. Alternatively, the regulation had to be read with the word "reasonably" inserted before "capable". The critical finding of fact was that it would be impossible to use the vehicle safely if reliance was placed on the pedals alone.

1.24   Electrically propelled vehicles do not however require vehicle excise licences (see § 12.35). As to taking an electrically assisted pedal cycle without consent, see § 15.12.

Goods vehicles

1.25   Note that by s.185(1) of the 1988 Act goods vehicles are "motor cars" if (in most cases) they do not exceed 3,050kg in unladen weight (see § 1.06).

The distinction between heavy and light locomotives and motor tractors on the one hand, and heavy motor cars and motor cars on the other, is that the former are not constructed to carry any load (see further "Loose equipment", § 1.72). In *Thornton v Proudlock*, May 29, 1952, unreported, DC, it was held that a tractor with a transport box is a vehicle "adapted for use for the conveyance of goods". This case was apparently under what is now the Vehicle Excise and Registration Act 1994 and would not necessarily apply under the 1988 Act. A locomotive or motor tractor permanently fitted with a crane, dynamo, etc., does not thereby become a goods vehicle (see 1988 Act s.186(3)); combine harvesters which are self-propelled would be tractors or locomotives (see *William Gwennap Agricultural Ltd v Amphlett* [1957] 2 All E.R. 605). For other cases on the term "goods vehicle", see § 6.122 and §§ 12.21–4 and see the important decision in *DPP v Ryan* (1991) 155 J.P. 456 discussed at § 8.153 below.

"Heavy commercial vehicle"

1.26   "Heavy commercial vehicle" in s.138 of the Road Traffic Regulation Act 1984 for the purposes of that Act and in s.19 of the 1988 Act (prohibition of parking of heavy goods vehicles on verges, central reservations and footways) means any goods vehicle which has an operating weight exceeding 7.5 tonnes. There are identical supplementary provisions in the two Acts (see ss.19 and 20 of the 1988 Act and s.138(2), (4)–(6) of the 1984 Act) to which reference should be made.

"Constructed" and change of use

1.27   Where the use of a vehicle is not immediately apparent, the burden of proof to show that the vehicle is exempt from a construction and use regulation requirement is on the defendant (*Wakeman v Catlow* [1977] R.T.R. 174). The fact that a vehicle is licensed as an "exempt" vehicle is insufficient evidence by itself (*Wakeman v Catlow*, above: jeep licensed as a "land tractor" used on a road with defective tyre; neither prosecution nor defence gave evidence as to whether or not it was a land tractor).

A Mini car fitted with only one seat but designed with space for another seat which could easily be added was held to be constructed for the carriage of more than one person (*Vincent v Whitehead* [1966] 1 All E.R. 917). A vehicle was held to be equipped with means for reversing although the reverse gear was not usable because it had been blanked off (*Baldwin v Worsman* [1963] 2 All E.R. 8).

1.28   "Constructed" in a speed limit case was interpreted as meaning "as originally constructed" (*Hubbard v Messenger* [1937] 4 All E.R. 48) but a motor vehicle can be reconstructed so that it joins another class (*Keeble v Miller* [1950] 1 All E.R. 261: heavy motor car converted to light locomotive). "Constructed" in s.185 of the 1988 Act means "constructed as at the time of the offence" not "originally constructed". The vehicle in *Keeble v Miller* was permanently fitted with a fairground lighting plant. "Constructed" usually means "as constructed when completed" (*Millard v Turvey* [1968] 2 All E.R. 7: a case on a motor vehicle chassis).

Generally it would seem that there must be a major reconstruction before a vehicle changes from one type to another (*Burrows v Berry* (1949) 113 J.P.Jo. 492). The fact that a vehicle happens to be defective does not alter its design and construction unless the defect continues so long that it can be inferred that the defect is intended to remain or there is evidence that a part has been deliberately removed (*G v Jarrett* [1981] R.T.R. 186). Whether there has been a change of type may depend on the circumstances. As is pointed out in a commentary on this case at [1980] Crim. L.R. 652, it may not be possible to discover the type of vehicle by inspecting it. The moped in this case had no footrest on the nearside pedal shaft. Nevertheless, it remained a moped.

"Adapted"

Where the word "adapted" is used disjunctively as an alternative to "constructed" it means "altered so as to make fit", but where it is used on its own, the context will often show that *"adapted"* means "fit and apt" for a purpose without alteration as well as "altered".

1.29

Whether a vehicle is "adapted" is a question of fact. "Adapted" in speed limits legislation was held to mean suitable for the carriage of eight or more passengers whether by original construction or subsequent alteration (*Maddox v Storer* [1962] 1 All E.R. 831). It was also held to mean "fit and apt for the purpose" not merely "altered so as to be apt", although, semble, it can include both vehicles originally constructed to be fit and apt and those subsequently altered so that they then are fit and apt.

In *Taylor v Mead* [1961] 1 All E.R. 626 (a vehicle excise case) the defendant's saloon car was fitted in the rear part of the interior with rails from which dresses were hung, he himself having put in those rails and the screws for their support. When dresses were not hung inside, passengers could sit in the back seats in the normal way. On the question whether the car was adapted for use for conveying goods, the High Court refused to interfere with a finding of magistrates that the car had not been so adapted, but did not say whether they (the judges) would have come to the same conclusion. Lord Parker C.J. said that "constructed or adapted" meant "originally constructed or where the structure is subsequently altered" and approved two earlier cases on the Customs and Inland Revenue Act 1888 s.4, holding that adapting meant some amount of alteration of the original construction. Making a small fitting or attachment involving the boring of holes for screws in the structure would not be altering the structure but fitting stronger springs and widening the wheels would be (*Taylor v Mead* above).

1.30

In *Westacott v Centaur* [1981] R.T.R. 182 four out of 11 seats on a minibus were rendered unusable: two double seats had been placed upside down to block four seats off. A finding of fact by the justices that the minibus was not adapted to fill the additional seats and that therefore the vehicle was not a public service vehicle was upheld. Certain reservations were expressed in the judgment. It was emphasised that the question of permanence did not necessarily arise, but that the primary consideration was the situation at the moment the vehicle was stopped. It was preferable to concentrate on the word "adapted" rather than substituting "suitable". This is clearly a reference to earlier cases such as *Maddox v Storer* [1962] 1 All E.R. 831 and *Wurzal v Addison* [1965] 1 All E.R. 20, where the expression "suitable" was used to interpret "adapted".

1.31   The conclusions to be drawn from the various road traffic authorities on the meaning of "adapted" were set out in *Backer v Secretary of State for the Environment* [1983] 2 All E.R. 1021, a town and country planning case. The court pointed out that "adapted" in the phrase "constructed or adapted for use … solely for the conveyance of any goods" in the context of vehicle licensing was held to mean "altered" in *French v Champkin* [1920] 1 K.B. 76 and *Taylor v Mead* [1961] 1 All E.R. 626. In the former case, Lord Reading C.J. said (at 79): "The justices seem to have treated the word 'adapted' as if it were synonymous with 'suitable' or 'apt', whereas it must be construed as meaning altered so as to make the vehicle apt for the conveyance of goods."

In two other cases it was held that where the word "adapted" appeared by itself it meant merely apt, fit or suitable (*Maddox v Storer* [1962] 1 All E.R. 831 and *Wurzal v Addison* [1965] 1 All E.R. 20). In *Burns v Currell* [1963] 2 All E.R. 297, it was said obiter that "adapted" in the phrase "intended or adapted for use on roads" means merely "apt or fit". The court held in *Backer* that as "adapted" was used in conjunction with "designed", adapted in the context meant "altered".

See also "Removable containers" at § 1.73.

"Vehicle"

1.32   The term "vehicle" usually means one vehicle, not two linked together (*Dixon v BRS (Pickfords) Ltd* [1959] 1 All E.R. 449).

A poultry shed can be a vehicle (see *Garner v Burr* [1950] 2 All E.R. 683), and in *Boxer v Snelling* [1972] R.T.R. 472 a movable stall with tyred wheels was also held to be a "vehicle" for the purposes of what is now the Road Traffic Regulation Act 1984. Where there is no statutory definition of the word "vehicle" a court should consider in a "borderline" case not only the construction or nature or function of the contrivance but also the circumstances in which it is used (*Boxer v Snelling*). In some circumstances, a pram may be a vehicle as may a scooter.

"Mechanically propelled"

1.33   In order that a motor vehicle can be held to come within the definition in s.185 of the 1988 Act or s.136 of the Road Traffic Regulation Act 1984, the vehicle must be "mechanically propelled". The same expression is used in the Vehicle Excise and Registration Act 1994.

The term includes not only petrol-driven and oil-driven vehicles, but also, it seems, steam-driven and electrically driven ones (see *Waters v Eddison Steam Rolling Co* (1914) 78 J.P. 327, where the term interpreted was "locomotive" and the vehicle a steam-roller, and *Elieson v Parker* (1917) 81 J.P. 265, where an electrically propelled bath chair was held to be a vehicle propelled by mechanical power). Schedule 1 Pt IVA (as amended) to the Vehicle Excise and Registration Act 1994 makes special provision as to electric vehicles. Electrically assisted pedal cycles as defined are presumably to be regarded as mechanically propelled but are not treated as motor vehicles for the purposes of the 1988 Act and the Road Traffic Regulation Act 1984 (see further § 1.23). Subject to this, where a pedal cycle is fitted with an auxiliary engine and the engine is connected up, it is a motor vehicle whether the engine is running or not (*Floyd v Bush* [1953] 1 All E.R. 265).

The leaving or keeping of broken-down vehicles on a public road frequently gives rise to prosecutions for offences relating to test certificates, vehicle excise licences, insurance, or defective tyres, brakes or steering. In such cases the question is raised as to whether the particular vehicle can still be said to be mechanically propelled. The test to be followed by a court in deciding the case is *whether the vehicle has reached such a stage that it can be said "there is no reasonable prospect of the vehicle ever being made mobile again"* (*Binks v Department of the Environment* [1975] R.T.R. 318, approving Lord Parker C.J. in *Law v Thomas* (1964) 62 L.G.R. 195 at 196 and also *Smart v Allan* [1962] 3 All E.R. 893). The requirement to be licensed applies not only to something that is a mechanically propelled vehicle but also to anything that has been such a vehicle but has now ceased to be (Vehicle Excise and Registration Act 1994 s.1(1B)). A brief description of the various cases follows. **1.34**

In *Newberry v Simmonds* [1961] 2 All E.R. 318 it was held that a motor car from which the engine had been removed did not thereby cease to be a mechanically propelled vehicle if the evidence admitted the possibility that the engine might shortly be replaced and the motive power restored. Different considerations might apply if the mechanical means of propulsion had been permanently removed; it would be a question of fact and degree in which both the extent to which the power unit and transmission have been removed and the permanence of the removal are matters for consideration (*Newberry v Simmonds* above). Semble the onus of proof that a vehicle had ceased to be mechanically propelled would lie on the defence so long as it resembled an ordinary motor vehicle. See in this connection the parallel argument as to "use" in *Hewer v Cutler* [1974] R.T.R. 155 (as explained by *Eden v Mitchell* [1975] R.T.R. 425, see § 1.187). *Newberry's* case was distinguished in *MacLean v Hall* (1962) 77 Sh. Ct. Rep. 161. In *Lawrence v Howlett* [1952] 2 All E.R. 74, the cylinder, piston and connecting rod had been removed temporarily from the engine of an auto-assisted cycle; it was held that it was a pedal cycle, not a motor vehicle. This case is distinguishable from *Floyd v Bush* above, on the ground that an auto-assisted cycle is capable of use either as a cycle or as a motor vehicle and, on the special facts, it was not only being used as a pedal cycle but was then incapable of use as a motor vehicle; and in *R. v Tahsin* [1970] R.T.R. 88 a defendant pedalling a moped was held to be rightly convicted under what are now ss.4(1) and 5(1) of the 1988 Act. *Floyd v Bush* was applied and at 92 it was explained by Lord Goddard C.J. in that case that the true test as to whether a vehicle is mechanically propelled is "Is the vehicle constructed so that it can be mechanically propelled?" *not* "Has it an engine which is in working order at the relevant time?" In *McEachran v Hurst* [1978] R.T.R. 462 it was held that a moped, being pedalled while the engine did not work and being without petrol, remained (because it had been constructed as a mechanically propelled vehicle) "mechanically propelled" for the purposes of the 1972 Act.

The decision in *Pumbien v Vines* [1996] R.T.R. 37 deserves consideration, **1.35**

because the facts on which the case turned have a familiar flavour to justices applying the road traffic legislation to vehicles at the bargain basement end of the
market. The facts were that Mr Pumbien parked his vehicle on a road at a time
when it was in working order. He cancelled the policy of insurance covering the
use of the vehicle, and some months later the test certificate expired. He had not
driven the vehicle since parking it. No insurance and no MOT were in force on
November 10, the material date. The prosecution alleged that on that date the vehicle was being used on a road without insurance and without a test certificate.
Some three days later the vehicle was removed by a vehicle dismantler to whom
it had been sold after November 10. The case turned on the state of the vehicle. It
was found that the tyres were deflated; the handbrake was on; and the rear brakes
were seized. The gearbox contained no oil because there was a leak in the transmission pipe. It would not have been possible to move the vehicle without first
freeing the brakes, replacing the transmission pipe and oiling the gearbox. No
positive steps had been taken to immobilise the vehicle.

After reviewing the authorities Mitchell J. considered that the two informations should hang or fall together. He did not accept that as between the two provisions the word "use" had a different meaning. Nor did he accept that the distinction between mobility and immobility had any greater relevance to the issue of
"use" in s.47 than it did in s.143 of the Road Traffic Act 1988. In dismissing Mr
Pumbien's appeal by way of case stated, the learned judge stated that the appellant's vehicle was on a road. It was a "motor vehicle" as defined in the 1988 Act,
notwithstanding that one aspect of its condition was reversible immobility. In
such circumstances the appellant was under the obligations imposed on him by
ss.47 and 143.

1.36   The onus of establishing that a vehicle has not reached the point at which there
is no reasonable prospect of its ever being made mobile again is laid on the prosecution; the defence does not have an onus to discharge in this respect (*Reader v
Bunyard* (1986) 85 Cr. App. R. 185). *Smart v Allan* [1962] 3 All E.R. 893 (vehicle without gear box, or with engine in such state that no prospect of vehicle being made mobile, held not a motor vehicle) should be contrasted with *Law v
Thomas* (1964) 62 L.G.R. 195 (broken-down car capable of repair in a matter of
minutes is still a mechanically propelled vehicle). A car is still a motor vehicle
though incapable of being started because of a flat battery (*R. v Paul* [1952] N.I.
61). In *McEachran v Hurst* [1978] R.T.R. 462 the defendant was pedalling a
moped to a friend's house for repair. It was not taxed and there was no current
test certificate. The justices held that it was not a mechanically propelled vehicle,
on the grounds that it was being used as a pedal cycle, the engine did not work
and there was no petrol in the tank. The Divisional Court, reversing the justices,
held that the test to be applied to determine whether a moped was mechanically
propelled was the same as that for any other motor vehicle, namely, on its
construction. If it was *constructed* as a motor vehicle, it remained a mechanically
propelled vehicle unless it could be said (applying the test in *Binks v Department
of the Environment* above) that there was no reasonable prospect of it again being
mechanically mobile.

For the purpose of the Refuse Disposal (Amenity) Act 1978, which relates to
the removal of abandoned vehicles, the term *"motor vehicle"* includes those
which are in an unfit as well as in a fit state for use on the road and a chassis or
body of a motor vehicle with or without wheels and trailers in similar condition
(Refuse Disposal (Amenity) Act 1978 s.11).

"Intended or adapted for use on roads"

The definition of a motor vehicle contained in s.185(1) of the 1988 Act and **1.37**
s.136 of the Road Traffic Regulation Act 1984 requires the vehicle to be "intended
or adapted for use on roads". The use of the word "or" implies that the words are
disjunctive. For "adapted", see § 1.29. The test as to whether a vehicle is intended
or adapted for use on roads is an objective one—would a reasonable person say
that one of its uses would be general use on a road. It depends neither on the
owner's or manufacturer's intention nor, unless there is evidence of regular use
on roads, on its particular use at the time (*Chief Constable of North Yorkshire Po-*
lice v Saddington [2001] R.T.R. 15, following *Avon and Somerset Chief Consta-*
ble v F [1987] R.T.R. 378, applying the dictum of Lord Parker C.J. in *Burns v*
Currell [1963] 2 Q.B. 433 at 440). The cases indicate that "intended" may mean
no more than suitable or apt for use on roads.

A   Go-carts, racing cars, etc.

A motor go-cart was held not to be a motor vehicle where there was no evi- **1.38**
dence of regular use on the road, but it might be otherwise if there was such evidence; the test is whether a reasonable man looking at it would say that one of its
uses would be a road use (*Burns v Currell* above). This test was applied by justices in *O'Brien v Anderton* [1979] R.T.R. 388 when they held an "Italjet" two-
wheeled vehicle resembling a motor cycle with a seat and handlebars but with an
engine capacity of only 22cc was a motor vehicle. The justices' decision was affirmed: they had applied the proper test. A more modern variant was considered
in *Chief Constable of North Yorkshire Police v Saddington* [2001] R.T.R. 15.
The vehicle was a "Go-ped", a motorised scooter, which was sold with specific
instructions that it was not for use on a road. However, the court emphasised that
the test was whether a reasonable person would say that one of its uses would be
use on the roads. That person must consider whether some general use on the
roads must be contemplated and not merely isolated use or use by a man losing
his senses. The court decided that the design and capabilities of the "Go-ped",
and the possibilities it offers, needed to be considered in the context of an assessment of peoples' wish to get quickly through traffic and the pressure of time upon
many people and that the conclusion must be that general use on the roads is to
be contemplated. The distributor's advice would in practice be ignored to a
considerable extent and surrender to the temptation to use it on the roads would
not be an isolated occurrence.

The Divisional Court gave further consideration to the test to be applied when
determining whether an electric scooter is a "motor vehicle" within the definition
contained in s.185 of the Road Traffic Act 1988 in *DPP v King* [2008] EWHC
447; (2008) 172 J.P. 401 where the defendant used a City Mantis electric scooter
on a road. He was disqualified from driving and had no relevant insurance. The
scooter was considered to be unlikely to exceed 10mph; its design limited its use
to smooth and even surfaces and the defendant accepted he would probably use it
on a road or pavement. The district judge found that it was not a motor vehicle
for the purposes of the definition in the 1988 Act, but this decision was overturned
by the Divisional Court. The court referred extensively to *Saddington* above and
to *Chief Constable of Avon and Somerset Constabulary v F* [1987] R.T.R. 378
and drew different conclusions on a number of points from those drawn by the
district judge.

1.39   It had been accepted by the district judge that the maximum likely speed of 10mph was significant, noting the possibility that an electrically assisted pedal cycle had a permitted speed of up to 15mph and the scooter in *Saddington* had a speed of up to 20mph. The Divisional Court did not accept that conclusion; on the contrary, it considered that the fact that the Electrically Assisted Pedal Cycles Regulations 1983 (SI 1983/1168) had been made was indicative that such vehicles were "motor vehicles" and that special provision needed to be made to ensure that, in certain circumstances, riding what would otherwise be a motor vehicle would not be an offence.

The main point at issue was the application of the part of the test which poses the question whether an ordinary person would consider that some general use on a road is something that might well occur. Given the design characteristics, the Divisional Court found it inescapable that the answer is that such a scooter might well be used on a road. The qualification (where such use might be isolated or by a person losing their senses) was considered to be a narrow one. The district judge had also considered that there was a point at which a scooter such as this ceased to be a toy and became a motor vehicle and that he needed to determine whether that point had been crossed. Again, the Divisional Court rejected that approach; a scooter might well be a toy but that would not necessarily prevent a reasonable person from saying that one of its uses might well be on a road.

1.40   In *Nichol v Leach* [1972] R.T.R. 476 a Mini car rebuilt solely for "auto cross" racing was held to have retained its original intended road use character even though the owner never intended it to be used on roads. *Brown v Abbott* (1965) 109 S.J. 437, where the magistrates' finding that a Ford Anglia adapted for stock car racing was not a mechanically propelled vehicle intended or adapted for use on roads was upheld with reluctance by the High Court, was not cited to the court in *Nichol v Leach*. It is submitted that *Nichol v Leach* is the better authority as its reasoning follows that of *Burns v Currell* above, and in particular *Daley v Hargreaves* below, in that the intention of the owner was disregarded.

The same principles would apply to motor cycles used for scrambling. Prosecutions have been successful in magistrates' courts where they have been used on roads even though they were not originally intended for such use. The convictions arise from the actual use and the understandable inference that the intended use is there. The courts also seem to take the view that despite the differences the vehicles are sufficiently close to an ordinary motor bicycle for them to be regarded as adapted for use on roads. The nature of the machine, the degree of adaptation necessary and the extent of the use are factors which have been taken into account.

B   *Dumper trucks, excavators, etc.*

1.41   A diesel dumper used solely for road construction work and not intended to be driven along the parts of the highway open to the public has been held not to be a motor vehicle for insurance purposes (*MacDonald v Carmichael* 1941 J.C. 27). Where there was no evidence whether some dumpers were suitable for being driven on the road in transit or to carry material from one site to another, the High Court, following *MacDonald v Carmichael*, held that they were not intended or adapted for use on the road, but it was said that the High Court might have found differently had there been evidence of such suitability (*Daley v Hargreaves* [1961] 1 All E.R. 552). It was also said that the legislature may have had no particular person's intention in view (e.g. manufacturer, seller, owner or user) as to "intended" for use on the road; "intended" may mean no more than suitable or apt for use. In *Avon and Somerset Chief Constable v F* [1987] R.T.R. 378, Glidewell L.J. applied the test of the view of the reasonable man; he also stated that, once it had been established that a vehicle as manufactured was intended for use on a road, it would require a dramatic alteration before it could be said that the vehicle was no longer "intended or adapted" for use on a road.

In *Chalgray Ltd v Aspley* (1965) 109 S.J. 394, a dumper used on a site was from time to time driven on the adjoining road for short distances. It was held that it was not a motor vehicle as there was no proof of general use on roads as opposed to occasional use. The driver's action could not make, in the absence of further evidence, a dumper into a motor vehicle. The fact that a dumper might emerge on the highway did not alone make it a motor vehicle. On the other hand, in *Childs v Coghlan* (1968) 112 S.J. 175, a Euclid earth scraper which was too big to be transportable and the primary uses of which were to dig up earth on building sites and carry that earth to places away from those sites under its own power was held to be intended for use on roads. There was evidence that it could go at 45mph. It was said that a machine, albeit its primary use was not on roads, which regularly went on roads from one site to another was clearly intended to be used on roads, especially if it had to go under its own power from one site to another.

C *Works' trucks*

A works' truck may be intended for use on roads; an *objective* test should be applied to establish whether a reasonable person looking at the vehicle would say that one of its uses would be use on a road. Account may properly be taken of the actual use to which the vehicle is put to determine what its ordinary use was on the road, so far as such use is relevant to determine whether it was intended for use on roads. In *Percy v Smith* [1986] R.T.R. 252 justices ruled that the defendant company intended to use a fork-lift truck on roads when it suited their business purposes and the Divisional Court upheld the conviction for using the truck with a defective tyre.   **1.42**

Miscellaneous vehicles

By s.189 of the 1988 Act an implement for cutting grass controlled by a pedestrian and not capable of being used or adapted for any other purpose is not, for the purposes of the Act, treated as a motor vehicle. By virtue of s.189(2) the implement must either be constructed or adapted for use only under the control of a pedestrian or, if it is constructed so that it can be controlled either by a pedestrian or someone carried on it, the implement can only be treated as not being a mechanically propelled vehicle so long as it is controlled on foot. This definition must be borne in mind as there are a number of domestic motor mowers on the market with seats for the driver and the verge outside a private home will often be part of the road. Section 140 of the Road Traffic Regulation Act 1984 is in like terms to the 1988 Act. Any other pedestrian controlled motor vehicle otherwise remains a motor vehicle, unless exempt by regulations.   **1.43**

An important decision is Case C–116/91 *Licensing Authority for the South Eastern Traffic Area v British Gas plc* [1992] E.C.R. 1–4071 in which the European Court of Justice gave a preliminary ruling as to whether a derogation contained in Regulation (EEC) 3820/85 applied to a vehicle used by the respondents. The derogation provided that a tachograph did not have to be fitted where vehicles were used for a wide range of general services provided in the public interest. According to art.4(6), these included "gas and electricity services" (now "gas and electricity maintenance services" under art.13(1)(h) of Regulation (EC) 561/2006 which has repealed and replaced the earlier regulation). The respondent's vehicle was stopped while carrying gas cookers, boilers, gas supply meters, gas cylinders, and boxes of rubbish. No tachograph was fitted and criminal proceedings were brought for using for the carriage of goods by road a vehicle not fitted with a tachograph. The magistrates' court stayed the proceedings and referred the question of whether the vehicle was exempt from compliance to the European Court of Justice. That court ruled that the derogation from the requirement to install and use a tachograph applied solely to vehicles used at the relevant time for carriage wholly and exclusively in connection with "the production or distribution of gas, or the maintenance of the necessary installations for that purpose". The court held that the derogation did not apply to vehicles wholly or partly used at the relevant time in connection with the carriage of domestic gas appliances. The narrow interpretation placed by the court on this derogation must not only be logical in law but must also be desirable in terms of public policy when the rationale behind the tachograph legislation is considered.

1.44   In *Swain v McCaul* [1997] R.T.R. 102, the respondents had been acquitted by the justices, who found they had been entitled to claim the benefit of an EC exemption from compliance with certain regulations relating to recording equipment in road transport. The exemption applied to a vehicle "used in connection with ... refuse collection and disposal", and following Case C–116/91 *Licensing Authority for the South Eastern Traffic Area v British Gas plc* above there was a requirement that the service provided by the vehicle concerned was "a general service performed in the public interest". In fact, it was used in the course of a commercial business solely for the delivery and collection of builders' skips. Auld L.J., in giving the judgment of the Divisional Court, stated that the business was the provision of a commercial service to customers whose activities generated large quantities of rubbish. There was no evidence that it was a service which the local authority or any other body responsible for public refuse collection in the area would provide as part of its regular and normally funded collections. The case was remitted to the justices with a direction to convict.

The matter for consideration by the Court of Appeal in the case of *DPP v Hawkins* [1996] R.T.R. 160 was when an ambulance was not an ambulance, and what consequences followed. The defendant was driving a Volvo car which had been adapted as an ambulance and which was fitted with a blue light. When he was stopped, the vehicle was not being used as an ambulance and the blue light was not flashing. He was prosecuted—it being alleged at his trial that if the vehicle was not being used as an ambulance, the blue light should have been covered. The defendant claimed that he was not committing an offence by not covering the light provided the light was not illuminated. The defendant was acquitted and the prosecutor's appeal was dismissed. The Court of Appeal held that a vehicle adapted for the purposes of conveying the sick, and used from time to time for such purposes, was an emergency vehicle for the purposes of reg.16 of the Road Vehicles Lighting Regulations 1989 (SI 1989/1796). Accordingly, the justices were right in deciding that the defendant was not committing an offence by using an emergency vehicle for other purposes when a blue light was fitted but not illuminated.

The term "goods vehicle" is discussed at § 6.120 and § 12.21. The term **1.45** "articulated vehicle" is discussed in relation to "Trailer" below. See also ss.186(2) and 187 of the 1988 Act.

A regulation-making power is given to the Secretary of State as to which sections in the 1984 Act and 1988 Offenders Act should apply to "tramcars", defined to include a carriage used on any road by virtue of an order under the Light Railways Act 1896, or "trolley vehicles", defined as "a mechanically propelled vehicle adapted for use on roads without rails under power transmitted to it from some external source (whether or not there is in addition a source of power on board the vehicle)" (Road Traffic Regulation Act 1984 s.141A and Road Traffic 1988 s.193A).

The Tramcars and Trolley Vehicles (Modification of Enactments) Regulations **1.46** 1992 (SI 1992/1217), in Pt III, list the provisions of the Road Traffic Act 1988 which do not apply to tramcars and trolley vehicles. The following sections apply neither to tramcars nor trolley vehicles: s.40A (using a vehicle in a dangerous condition); s.77 (testing condition of used vehicles in sale rooms); and ss.78 and 79 (weighing of motor vehicles). In addition, the following provisions shall not apply to *tramcars*: s.68 (inspection of public passenger vehicles and goods vehicles); ss.69–73 (prohibition of unfit vehicles); s.75 (vehicles not to be sold in unroadworthy condition or as altered so as to be unroadworthy); s.76 (fitting and supply of defective or unsuitable vehicle parts); s.83 (offences concerning reflectors and tail lamps); s.190 (method of calculating weight of motor vehicles and trailers); and s.191 (interpretation of statutory references to carriages).

As far as *trolley vehicles* are concerned, s.68 of the 1988 Act (inspection of public passenger vehicles and goods vehicles) is to apply to them as if subs.(4) were omitted. That subsection is the penal provision creating an offence where a person obstructs a goods vehicle examiner in the performance of his duty.

Trolley vehicles, trams, bicycles, horse-drawn carts and hand carts are gener- **1.47** ally vehicles and carriages within the meaning of most other Acts and motor vehicles are carriages within the meaning of the Highways, Town Police Clauses, Public Health and other Acts and byelaws (Road Traffic Act 1988 s.191).

A bicycle is a vehicle (*Ellis v Nott-Bower* (1896) 60 J.P. 760) and also a carriage (*Corkery v Carpenter* [1950] 2 All E.R. 745).

"Recovery vehicle"

The text of the current definition of "recovery vehicle" is set out in the Vehicle **1.48** Excise and Registration Act 1994 Sch.1 para.5. It reads as follows:

> "(2) ... 'recovery vehicle' means a vehicle which is constructed or permanently adapted primarily for any one or more of the purposes of lifting, towing and transporting a disabled vehicle.
> (3) A vehicle is not a recovery vehicle if at any time it is used for a purpose other than—
>   (a) the recovery of a disabled vehicle,
>   (b) the removal of a disabled vehicle from the place where it became disabled to premises at which it is to be repaired or scrapped,
>   (c) the removal of a disabled vehicle from premises to which it was taken for repair to other premises at which it is to be repaired or scrapped,

    (d) carrying fuel and other liquids required for its propulsion and tools and other articles required for the operation of, or in connection with, apparatus designed to lift, tow or transport a disabled vehicle, and

    (e) any purpose prescribed for the purposes of this sub-paragraph by regulations made by the Secretary of State.

(4) At any time when a vehicle is being used for either of the purposes specified in paragraphs (a) and (b) of sub-paragraph (3), use for—

    (a) the carriage of a person who, immediately before the vehicle became disabled, was the driver of or a passenger in the vehicle,

    (b) the carriage of any goods which, immediately before the vehicle became disabled, were being carried in the vehicle, or

    (c) any purpose prescribed for the purposes of this sub-paragraph by regulations made by the Secretary of State,

shall be disregarded in determining whether the vehicle is a recovery vehicle

...

(5) A vehicle is not a recovery vehicle if at any time the number of vehicles which it is used to recover exceeds a number specified for the purposes of this sub-paragraph by an order made by the Secretary of State."

1.49   For the meaning of "disabled vehicle", see § 1.56 below. The Recovery Vehicles (Number of Vehicles Recovered) Order 1989 (SI 1989/1226) which has effect as if made under the Vehicle Excise and Registration Act 1994 Sch.1 para.5 defines the maximum number of vehicles a recovery vehicle may be used to recover. The maximum prescribed is two.

    It should be noted that the former definition ("a vehicle which ... is drawing ... apparatus designed for raising a disabled vehicle ...") specifically provided that the apparatus did not have to be mounted on the recovery vehicle itself; the current definition (1994 Act Sch.1 para.5) seems to require it to be so mounted. The mere carriage of a jack would not, it is thought, fulfil the criteria of "constructed or permanently adapted primarily for the purposes of lifting, towing and transporting a disabled vehicle or for any ... of those purposes".

1.50   There are, therefore, two main elements to the test, the vehicle itself—for what purpose has it been constructed or permanently adapted?—and the purpose for which the vehicle is used (Sch.1 para.5(3)). Paragraph 5(3)(e) of Sch.1 provides for other purposes to be prescribed to be included amongst those things that a suitable vehicle can be used for and still remain within the definition of "recovery vehicle". These are contained in Pt I of Sch.7 to the Road Vehicles (Registration and Licensing) Regulations 2002 (SI 2002/2742) and are:

(1) Carrying any person who, immediately before a vehicle became disabled, was the driver of or a passenger in that vehicle, together with his personal effects, from the premises at which the vehicle is to be repaired or scrapped to his original intended destination.

(2) At the request of either a constable or a local authority empowered by or under statute to remove a vehicle from a road, removing such vehicle to a place nominated by the constable or local authority.

(3) Proceeding to a place at which the vehicle will be available for use for either of the purposes specified in para.5(3)(a) and (b) and remaining temporarily at such a place so as to be available for such use.

(4) Proceeding from

     (a) a place where the vehicle has remained temporarily so as to be available for such use;

     (b) a place where the vehicle has recovered a disabled vehicle; or

     (c) any premises mentioned in para.5(3)(b) or (c).

Where a recovery vehicle is being used to recover a disabled vehicle or to **1.51** remove such a vehicle from the place where it has become disabled to a place for repair or for being scrapped, certain uses are permitted which would otherwise take the vehicle outside the definition of a recovery vehicle (see 1994 Act Sch.1 para.5(4)). Paragraph 5(4)(c) of Sch.1 provides for other purposes to be prescribed to be included in those things to be disregarded in determining whether a vehicle is a recovery vehicle. These are set out in Pt II of Sch.7 to the Road Vehicles (Registration and Licensing) Regulations 2002 (SI 2002/2742) and are:

    (1) Repairing a disabled vehicle at the place where it became disabled or to which it has been moved in the interests of safety after becoming disabled.

    (2) Drawing or carrying a single trailer if another vehicle had become disabled whilst drawing or carrying it.

A "locomotive" is defined in the Road Vehicles (Construction and Use) Regulations 1986 (SI 1986/1078) reg.3(2) as a mechanically propelled vehicle which is not constructed itself to carry a load other than water, fuel, accumulators and other equipment used for the purpose of propulsion, loose tools and loose equipment; and the weight of which unladen exceeds 7,370kg. The lifting of the front wheels of a towed vehicle off the ground by means of a hydraulic boom mounted on a recovery vehicle which was a locomotive does not constitute the carriage by that vehicle of a load so as to take it outside the definition of a "locomotive" (*DPP v Yates* [1989] R.T.R. 134).

An interesting decision involving a heavy breakdown recovery vehicle and its **1.52** status as far as the statutory provisions for speeding are concerned is *DPP v Holtham* [1991] R.T.R. 5. The vehicle concerned was equipped with a special boom to assist in the moving and lifting of vehicles. The justices found that the vehicle was so constructed that a substantial part of something else was borne by the vehicle. The question for the court was whether that something was a "trailer" within the definition in s.136(1) of the Road Traffic Regulation Act 1984. The Divisional Court agreed with the justices' interpretation. A broken-down vehicle towed by the arm of a recovery vehicle was a trailer attached to the recovery vehicle so that a substantial part of its weight was taken by the recovery vehicle. The recovery vehicle was therefore deemed to be a vehicle constructed to carry a load and could not therefore be a motor tractor or light or heavy locomotive within s.136(6) and (7). The vehicle was not therefore restricted to a maximum speed of 40mph as provided in Sch.6 to the 1984 Act.

"Breakdown vehicle" and "specialised breakdown vehicle"

A "breakdown vehicle" is defined by the Goods Vehicles (Plating and Testing) **1.53** Regulations 1988 (SI 1988/1478), reg.3 as—

"… a motor vehicle

    (a) on which is permanently mounted apparatus designed for raising one disabled vehicle partly from the ground and for drawing that vehicle when so raised; and

(b) which is not equipped to carry any load other than articles required for the operation of, or in connection with, that apparatus or for repairing disabled vehicles."

The definition of "breakdown vehicle" now needs to be compared with that of "recovery vehicle" in the Vehicle Excise and Registration Act 1994 (see § 1.48). It should be noted that in the current definition of "recovery vehicle" there is a requirement of permanence which was not expressed in the earlier definition. In Case 79/86 *Hamilton v Whitelock* [1988] R.T.R. 23 the European Court of Justice stated that a specialised breakdown vehicle was—

"a vehicle whose construction, fitments, or other permanent characteristics were such that it would be used mainly for removing vehicles that had recently been involved in an accident or had broken down for another reason."

1.54   For the purposes of exemption from the requirements relating to tachographs (see Regulation (EC) 561/2006 art.3(f)), the purpose to which a specialised breakdown vehicle was being put at the particular time was irrelevant, although it must be used within 100km radius of its base.

Community regulations should not be construed as being in an analogous case with national legislation (per Robert Goff L.J. in *Universal Salvage Ltd v Boothby* [1984] R.T.R. 289 at 305). Although the EC legislation in issue in that case differs in some respects from its contemporary counterpart (i.e. Regulation (EEC) 3821/85), the meaning given to a "specialised breakdown vehicle" (at 301) is still applicable:

"a vehicle which is specially built or adapted, and kept, for the purpose of going to the assistance of a broken-down vehicle and which, generally, has the capability for this purpose of raising a broken-down vehicle (wholly or partially) with a view to its recovery either by a conveyance on, or by towing behind, the breakdown vehicle."

1.55   This was said to be a "working definition" which might be refined in the light of experience. The definition was said by Robert Goff L.J. in the *Universal Salvage* case [1984] R.T.R. 289 at 305 to be very similar in meaning (despite having been reached by an entirely different approach) to the definition of "breakdown vehicle" (i.e. the definition before the 1985 amendment) and "recovery vehicle" (in the Vehicle Excise and Registration Act 1994 Sch.1 para.5; see § 1.48). So far as this may be the case, the legality of "one up and one behind" in respect of recovery vehicles (see the *Universal Salvage* case and *Kennet v Holding and Barnes Ltd*, *T.L. Harvey Ltd v Hall*, *The Times*, August 15, 1985) would seem to be applicable to specialised breakdown vehicles.

"Disabled vehicle"

1.56   In *Gibson v Nutter* [1984] R.T.R. 8, it was held that a scrap vehicle was not a broken-down or disabled vehicle (this decision was approved in *Universal Salvage Ltd v Boothby* [1984] R.T.R. 289). However, the Vehicle Excise and Registration Act 1994 s.12(5) provides that, in relation to the conveyance of goods on a vehicle being used under a trade licence, the term "disabled vehicle" includes a vehicle which has been abandoned or is scrap. This amendment has extended the meaning of vehicles which may be recovered by recovery vehicles and applies to the Goods Vehicles (Licensing of Operators) Regulations 1995 (SI 1995/2869) (see Sch.3 Pt I para.9), but not to the Goods Vehicles (Plating and

Testing) Regulations 1988 (SI 1988/1478) Sch.2. Hence, although no operator's licence is required for a "recovery vehicle" recovering abandoned or scrap vehicles under a trade licence, a "breakdown vehicle" engaged on such an operation will fall within the plating and testing requirements (unless otherwise exempt). It remains a question of fact whether a vehicle is recovered or transported. The number of vehicles is still restricted to one up and one behind.

"TRAILER"

Meaning

A "trailer" is defined in s.185(1) of the 1988 Act as a vehicle drawn by a motor   **1.57** vehicle. It is doubtful whether a trailer can be said to be so drawn if it has been detached, particularly if the detachment is for a substantial period of time (cf. the discussion at §§ 1.92 et seq. as to what is meant by "driving"). A "trailer" is differently defined for the purpose of drivers' hours and records when Regulation (EC) 561/2006 applies (see art.4(b) of that regulation).

The term "trailer" includes an empty poultry shed being drawn along by a tractor (*Garner v Burr* [1950] 2 All E.R. 683), and a hut used as an office so drawn (*Horn v Dobson* 1933 J.C. 1). The Road Vehicles (Construction and Use) Regulations 1986 (SI 1986/1078) give certain exemptions for trailers forming part of an articulated vehicle (see § 1.60) or being an agricultural trailer or an agricultural trailed appliance (as defined in reg.3(1) of the regulations). There are also a number of exemptions under the Construction and Use Regulations for trailers manufactured before certain dates. A four-wheeled vehicle being towed with two wheels in the air does not thereby become a two-wheeled trailer (*Carey v Heath* [1951] 2 All E.R. 774). In *Baker v Esau* [1972] Crim. L.R. 559 the justices were held to be "plainly right" in holding that a racing car rigidly placed on a two-wheeled "ambulance trailer" so that its front wheels remained on the road together constituted one trailer, not two. A vehicle and trailer closely coupled together do not thereby become one vehicle (*Dixon v BRS (Pickfords) Ltd* [1959] 1 All E.R. 449). A mobile car jack, i.e. a long towbar with two wheels on a short axle at right angles to the towbar, is a trailer (*Wilkinson v Barrett* (1958) 122 J.P. 349). This case is modified to some extent by item 7 of the table at reg.4(4) of the Construction and Use Regulations. In *Jenkins v Deane* (1933) 103 L.J.K.B. 250 an insurance policy excepted use of the insured vehicle "whilst it has a trailer attached thereto". Towing a broken-down lorry was held not to be within the exception. This case was not cited in the other cases given in this paragraph. Quarter sessions have held that a van inhabited by a family can be a trailer ([1962] Jo.Crim.L. 21). In *Boxer v Snelling* [1972] R.T.R. 472 a movable stall with wheels was held in the circumstances of the case to be a "vehicle". It was said to be a "borderline" case. Where there is no statutory definition of "vehicle", a court should consider in a borderline case not only the construction or nature of the contrivance but also the circumstances in which the contrivance is used (ibid.).

A motor vehicle which is being towed by another motor vehicle both remains a   **1.58** motor vehicle and becomes for the time being a trailer also (*Milstead v Sexton* [1964] Crim. L.R. 474), and there is nothing in the Vehicle Excise and Registration Act 1994 to exempt a mechanically propelled vehicle which is being towed and is for the time being a trailer (*Cobb v Whorton* [1971] R.T.R. 392). The vehicle is "used" for the purposes of insurance while stationary (*Elliott v Grey* [1959] 3 All E.R. 733). A mechanically propelled vehicle does not cease to be "used" on a road when it is towed by another vehicle (*Cobb v Whorton* above; *Nichol v Leach* [1972] R.T.R. 476). The use of the towed vehicle must therefore be covered by insurance, it must be taxed, and it must comply with the Construction and Use Regulations both as a motor vehicle and as a trailer. It would be a trailer only, however, if it had ceased to be mechanically propelled, e.g. if it was a wreck, or if it was not intended or adapted for use on roads, e.g. a high-powered racing car designed for use only on a race track (but not a racing car designed also for ordinary use or even a Mini rebuilt for use in "auto cross" events: see *Nichol v Leach* above). Even the high-powered racing car would be liable to excise duty, however, when on a public road, as the Vehicle Excise and Registration Act 1994 applies to "mechanically propelled vehicles used on public roads" without requiring that they be intended or adapted for such use.

A car supported on roller skates so that its wheels did not touch the road surface was held, nevertheless, to be kept "on" a road for the purposes of s.29 of the 1994 Act (*Holliday v Henry* [1974] R.T.R. 101), nor would it appear to be "on" a trailer (ibid.).

"Semi-trailer", etc.

1.59   A "semi-trailer" is defined in reg.3(2) of the Construction and Use Regulations as a trailer which is constructed or adapted to form part of an articulated vehicle. A "composite trailer" is defined by the same regulation as a combination of a converter dolly (see below) and a semi-trailer. For the purpose of certain Construction and Use Regulations only a "composite trailer" is treated as one trailer (not being a semi-trailer or a converter dolly) only (see reg.3(11)). A "converter dolly" is defined fully in reg.3(2) but broadly speaking is a wheeled chassis between the drawing vehicle and the semi-trailer. A trailer can come within the definition of "converter dolly" even though part of the weight of the semi-trailer is borne by the towing vehicle, provided the trailer in question is used for the purposes of agriculture, horticulture or forestry.

"Articulated vehicle"

1.60   An "articulated vehicle" is still treated as a vehicle and a trailer for the purposes of the 1988 Acts, the Road Traffic Regulation Act 1984 and the Public Passenger Vehicles Act 1981 (see the 1988 Act s.187). The only exception is the articulated passenger vehicle referred to in s.187(2). These are distinguished from articulated vehicles generally by specified structural characteristics. They are classified instead as single motor vehicles thus making them eligible to be treated as public service vehicles. Buses of this type, looking rather like long caterpillars, are occasionally to be encountered on roads.

The drawing unit of an articulated vehicle is a motor car or heavy car, according to its unladen weight without including the trailer's weight (Road Traffic Act 1988 s.185). In *Turberville v Wyer, Bryn Motor Co Ltd v Wyer* [1977] R.T.R. 29 the Divisional Court declined to decide whether the load-carrying part of an articulated lorry which was carrying an insecure load should be described in an information as a trailer. If it was wrongly described in the information, the justices were entitled to ignore the defect under s.123 of the Magistrates' Courts Act 1980 (ibid.).

As to lamps and indicators on drawing vehicles on trailers, see the Road **1.61** Vehicles Lighting Regulations 1989 (SI 1989/1796) and in particular § 8.112 (exemptions from the regulations).

An "articulated vehicle", as defined by reg.3(2) of the Construction and Use Regulations, is a heavy motor car or motor car with a trailer so attached to the drawing vehicle that part of the trailer is superimposed upon the drawing vehicle, and when the trailer is uniformly loaded, not less than 20 per cent of the weight of its load is borne by the drawing vehicle. Under the Construction and Use Regulations articulated buses are expressly excluded (see reg.3(2)). (If the towed vehicle is not superimposed on the drawing vehicle, there is not an "articulated vehicle" (*Hunter v Towers* [1951] 1 All E.R. 349).) The permitted overall length of articulated vehicles is set out in reg.7, Table (as amended) of the Construction and Use Regulations.

For the purposes, however, of speed limits governing certain classes of goods **1.62** vehicles set out in Sch.6 to the Road Traffic Regulation Act 1984 "articulated vehicle" is as defined by the Construction and Use Regulations (see Sch.6 Pt IV para.2 to the 1984 Act). Under these regulations articulated buses are excluded, but in any event the expression "articulated vehicles" is used in Sch.6 only in relation to goods vehicles.

An "articulated goods vehicle" is defined in s.108 of the 1988 Act for the purposes of driving licences as follows:

> "'articulated goods vehicle' means a motor vehicle which is so constructed that a trailer designed to carry goods may by partial superimposition be attached to it in such manner as to cause a substantial part of the weight of the trailer to be borne by the motor vehicle, and 'articulated goods vehicle combination' means an articulated goods vehicle with a trailer so attached. "

This definition also applies in respect of heavy goods vehicle licences (see s.120 of the 1988 Act, as amended).

Drawing of trailers

Regulations 83–86A of the Road Vehicles (Construction and Use) Regulations **1.63** 1986 (SI 1986/1078) restrict the number of trailers which can be drawn by locomotives, motor tractors, heavy motor cars, motor cars, agricultural motor vehicles and motor cycles. As to the difference between side-cars and trailers, see "Side-cars", § 1.15. Whether a recovery vehicle is properly classified as a heavy motor car or a locomotive will determine the number of trailers which it may draw (see the table at reg.83(1) of the Road Vehicles (Construction and Use) Regulations 1986 (SI 1986/1078), and see also *DPP v Yates* at § 1.51).

The trailers which may be drawn by motor cycles are set out in reg.84. As to the meaning of a "side-car", see § 1.15. No motor cycle (whether three-wheeler, combination or motor bicycle) may draw more than one trailer. No motor cycle may draw a trailer carrying a passenger (save trailers which are certain broken-down motor cycles with one passenger). No motor cycle may draw a trailer with an unladen weight exceeding 254kg. This prohibition applies to drawing broken-down motor cycles of such a size.

A solo motor bicycle without a side-car and with an engine capacity of 125cc **1.64** or less may not draw a trailer at all, apart from a broken-down motor cycle. If such a solo motor bicycle exceeds 125cc it may draw a trailer providing certain conditions are fulfilled. These conditions are that (i) the trailer has an overall width not exceeding 1m, (ii) the distance between the rear axle of the motor bicycle and the rearmost part of the trailer does not exceed 2.5m, (iii) the motor cycle is clearly and indelibly marked in a conspicuous and readily accessible position with its kerbside weight, (iv) the trailer is similarly marked with its *unladen* weight, and (v) the *laden* weight of the trailer must not exceed 150kg or two thirds the kerbside weight of the motor bicycle, whichever is the greater (reg.84(1)(e)). Presumably a chalk mark would not suffice. Curiously it is the *laden* weight of the trailer which must not exceed 150kg but the *unladen* weight which must be marked on it. "Kerbside weight" is defined in reg.3(2). The provisions are relaxed for a trailer which is a broken-down motor cycle with one passenger riding it; see reg.84(2).

An invalid carriage or a straddle carrier may not tow a trailer (reg.83(1)). No trailer may be used to convey passengers for hire or reward (reg.90(1)) except for breakdowns as allowed by reg.90(2). (See, however, s.187 of the 1988 Act under which certain passenger vehicles with trailers are classified as single motor vehicles.) Regulation 83 further provides that a trailer may be drawn behind a bus (other than an articulated bus or a minibus) without the trailer being subject to a maximum of 5m in length and without the overall length of the combination being limited to 15m. The overall length of the combination will continue to be restricted, by reg.7 of the Construction and Use Regulations, to 18m.

1.65 The permitted length of a combination of vehicles (towing vehicle and trailer or trailers) is indicated by reg.7. The rearmost trailer must exhibit the drawing vehicle's number, with minor exceptions for works trucks and certain agricultural and other vehicles used on the road to a limited extent (Road Vehicles (Display of Registration Marks) Regulations 2001 (SI 2001/561) regs 5(2) and 8, as amended).

Where a trailer is drawn solely by a rope or chain the distance between the drawing vehicle and the trailer must not exceed 4.5m (reg.86(1)). In effect the measurement is taken between the nearest points on the vehicles (ignoring attachment fittings: see reg.86(2)) when the rope or chain is taut. If the distance between the nearest points of the vehicles (whatever the means of attachment) exceeds 1.5m, steps must be taken to render the means of attachment clearly visible to other road users within a reasonable distance from either side of the vehicle (reg.86(1)). A method commonly used is to tie a piece of cloth to the rope or chain. Regulation 86A prohibits the use of a motor vehicle drawing a trailer on a road where the trailer is not fitted with a device designed to stop the trailer automatically in the event of the separation of the main coupling while the trailer is in motion. Various exemptions and conditions are also contained in the regulation.

1.66 In cases under the Construction and Use Regulations affecting trailers, the regulations themselves should be carefully considered for their definitions and exemptions as to trailers and in particular the definitions of "composite trailer", "converter dolly", "semi-trailer" and "articulated vehicle".

Attendants with special vehicles

1.67 The Road Vehicles (Authorisation of Special Types) (General) Order 2003 (SI 2003/1998) (§ 8.88) requires attendants in certain circumstances in relation to different types of "special vehicle" as defined in the order. The requirements in arts 12(1) 14(1), 15(4), 23(3), 24(5) and 31(3) require there to be one or more attendants in compliance with Sch.6 to the 2003 Order.

"WEIGHT"

Meaning

The provisions of the law relating to weight distinguish between laden and **1.68** unladen weight. The distinction is relevant because there are prohibitions on the total weight which a laden vehicle may transmit to the road surface, while both laden and unladen weights form the criteria by which maximum speed and excise licence duty are computed.

The Road Traffic Act 1988 ss.185 and 190, and the Road Vehicles (Construction and Use) Regulations 1986 (SI 1986/1078) reg.3, provide the code in relation to matters arising under the 1988 Act and those regulations. Section 185 of the 1988 Act classifies motor vehicles by their unladen weight into heavy and light locomotives, motor tractors, heavy motor cars, motor cars, motor cycles and invalid carriages. Section 190 indicates the method of calculating unladen weight for the purposes of the 1988 Act, of the Road Traffic Regulation Act 1984, of the Vehicle Excise and Registration Act 1994, and also for the purposes of any other enactment relating to the use of motor vehicles or trailers on roads. The relevant Construction and Use Regulations are regs 66, 68, 71 and 80. A prosecution under reg.100 for overloading, etc., is not an offence relating to a description of weight (*Hudson v Bushrod* [1982] R.T.R. 87).

Vehicle excise duty under the Vehicle Excise and Registration Act 1994 is **1.69** based on revenue weight.

This is defined to mean (1) where a vehicle has a confirmed maximum weight, that weight; and (2) in any other case, the design weight (determined in accordance with the remaining provisions of s.60A). The meaning of confirmed maximum weight is in s.60A(9). Where a vehicle has a plated gross weight or a plated train weight which is the maximum laden weight at which the vehicle (with or without a semi-trailer) can lawfully be used in Great Britain, that plated weight is the confirmed maximum weight. The meaning of plated gross weight and plated train weight is set out in s.61. Section 60A(3) defines the design weight as:

> "(a) in the case of a tractive unit, the weight which is required, by the design and any subsequent adaptations of that vehicle, not to be exceeded by an articulated vehicle which—
>
> > (i) consists of the vehicle and any semi-trailer capable of being drawn by it, and
> >
> > (ii) is in normal use and travelling on a road laden;
>
> (b) and in the case of any other vehicle, the weight which the vehicle itself is designed or adapted not to exceed when in normal use and travelling on a road laden."

The remainder of s.60A amplifies that definition.

There are definitions in s.108 of the 1988 Act of "maximum gross weight", **1.70** "maximum train weight", "permissible maximum weight", "relevant maximum weight", and "relevant maximum train weight" for the purposes of the provisions of Pt III of the 1988 Act relating to driving licences. See also the Goods Vehicles

(Ascertainment of Maximum Gross Weights) Regulations 1976 (SI 1976/555). For the purposes of Regulation (EC) 561/2006 (drivers' hours), the equivalent of "permissible maximum weight" is "maximum permissible mass" which, by art.4(m), is the maximum authorised operating mass of a vehicle when fully laden. There is a similar but differently worded definition in the AETR agreement (see ibid. art.1(f)).

Section 17(1) of the 1988 Offenders Act provides that in any proceedings for an offence under ss.40A, 41A, 41B or 42 of the 1988 Act (which includes proceedings for an offence under the Construction and Use Regulations relating to weight) if any question arises as to a weight of any description specified in the plating certificate for a goods vehicle and a weight of that description is marked on the vehicle, it is assumed (unless the contrary is proved) that the weight marked on the vehicle is the weight so specified. The complexity of the provisions for defining weight for various purposes was emphasised in *Pritchard and Devenish v Crown Prosecution Service* [2003] EWHC 1851; [2004] R.T.R. 22. The Administrative Court was obliged to consider parts of these provisions in the context of deciding whether a vehicle and trailer was required to be fitted with a tachograph. After reciting the relevant provisions, the court said that "It can hardly be a surprise that these provisions have led to difficulties in this case and no doubt in others. Surely, the time has come when all material should be consolidated into one, hopefully more readily comprehensible, enactment."

1.71   By s.78 of the 1988 Act persons authorised by highway authorities and police officers authorised on behalf of such authorities by a police authority or a chief officer of police may cause vehicles and trailers to be weighed.

The weight of a vehicle which has been registered as being in a heavier class remains at the registered weight in the eyes of the law until it is re-registered as being in another class, though it may be used with a detachable body which, on removal, brings it in fact into that other class (*Scott v Dickson* (1939) 83 S.J. 317).

"Loose equipment"

1.72   As will be seen from the definitions of "motor tractor", "light locomotive" and "heavy locomotive" in the 1988 Act s.185, "loose equipment" is referred to in those definitions as being excepted articles, see s.185(2). Moreover s.190 requires the weight of "loose equipment" to be excluded in any calculation of the unladen weight of a vehicle or trailer. What comprises "loose equipment" is primarily a question of fact: the test is the nature of the superstructure, the use to which it would be put, and the character of its attachment to the vehicle (*Blaikie v Morrison* 1957 S.L.T. 290).

"Loose equipment" does not include loose boards fitted in slots at the side of a lorry and used to enable it to carry a heavier load of coal (*Lowe v Stone* [1948] 2 All E.R. 1076), nor a heavy iron block used for ballast (*London County Council v Hay's Wharf Cartage Co* [1953] 2 All E.R. 34), but does include movable shelves fitted to slide on brackets in a baker's van and used to facilitate the delivery of goods to customers (*Darling v Burton* 1928 J.C. 11, approved in *Lowe v Stone*). Planks and poles to load oil drums on a vehicle fitted with a diesel lighting plant are "loose tools and equipment" (*Keeble v Miller* [1950] 1 All E.R. 261). Side, tail and front boards which, when in use, were fitted inside the vehicle's sides and secured to posts let into the body were held not to be "loose equipment".

Removable containers

For the purposes of calculating a vehicle's unladen weight (s.190 of the 1988 **1.73** Act), regard must be had to the weight of the vehicle inclusive of the body and all parts (the heavier being taken where alternative bodies or parts are used) which are necessary to or ordinarily used with the vehicle when working on a road.

A motor lorry, used to carry cattle and sheep, had superimposed on it a removable "float" or large box secured by ropes, not adapted for use on the lorry alone as a separate body but only in conjunction with the lorry's fixed body. It was held that the float was neither an alternative body nor a part necessary to, or ordinarily used with, the lorry, and should therefore not be included in computing the unladen weight of the vehicle (*McCowan (Donald) v Stewart* 1936 J.C. 36). In *Cording v Halse* [1954] 3 All E.R. 287 the Divisional Court came to a like conclusion in respect of a similar vehicle. In *Mackie v Waugh* 1940 J.C. 49 it was held that a container for transporting sheep, held on a lorry by its own weight and by projections fitted over the platform, removed by a block and tackle and used on the lorry three days a week, was not to be included in its unladen weight. In *Paterson v Burnet* 1939 J.C. 12, however, the court upheld a finding that a liftable container with roof, sides and floor, secured by bolts and rope cleats, was constructed primarily as an additional body and was not a receptacle, and distinguished *McCowan's* case. *McCowan's* case may be compared with *Patterson v Redpath Brothers Ltd* [1979] 2 All E.R. 108. This case was on the question of the meaning of an abnormal indivisible load. The Divisional Court held that a container was a container and not a load. The cases were reviewed in *Brindley v Willett* [1982] R.T.R. 19 where it was held that a container was capable in law of being part of the vehicle. It was immaterial that the container could not be bolted on as it should have been because it had become warped. *Patterson v Redpath Brothers Ltd* and *Brindley v Willett* were followed in *Hawkins v Harold A. Russett Ltd* [1983] 1 All E.R. 215 where O'Connor L.J. at 218 adopted the following test where overall length or overhang are in issue: "Is this vehicle fitted with a body? The body of a vehicle does not cease to be a body because it can be detached with ease, laden or unladen and fitted to a sister chassis. This does not make the body 'a receptacle on or attached to the vehicle …': it is part of the vehicle."

Weight generally

By reg.71 of the Construction and Use Regulations, the unladen weight must **1.74** be painted on the nearside of locomotives, motor tractors and heavy motor cars where the unladen weight is not shown on the Ministry plate. Likewise (but subject to exceptions), every unbraked wheeled trailer must have its maximum gross weight (in kilograms) on its near side. There are certain restrictions on the laden weight of an unbraked wheeled trailer and the drawing vehicle (see reg.87).

The Road Vehicles (Authorisation of Special Types) (General) Order 2003 (SI 2003/1998) indicates the maximum lawful weights for vehicles to which it applies. Where excess weight may be allowed under the order, all the conditions as to attendants, etc., must be fulfilled; if one of them is not, an offence arises under the appropriate regulations of the Construction and Use Regulations (*Siddle C. Cook Ltd v Holden* [1962] 3 All E.R. 984).

Plated weights

1.75   Weights may be shown on the manufacturer's plate or on the Ministry plate issued after testing or on the plate to be fixed in 14 days on new vehicles subject to the compulsory type approval scheme.

Regulation 66(1)(a) of the Road Vehicles (Construction and Use) Regulations 1986 (SI 1986/1078) requires all heavy motor cars and motor cars first used on or after January 1, 1968 (not being passenger vehicles—save as below—or dual-purpose vehicles, agricultural motor vehicles, works trucks or pedestrian controlled vehicles), and every trailer manufactured on or after that date exceeding 1,020kg in weight unladen (save the exceptions mentioned in reg.66(1)(d)) to be equipped with a plate securely attached to the vehicle in a conspicuous and readily accessible position and containing the particulars required by Sch.8, including maximum axle, gross and train weights for vehicles. Buses (whether or not articulated buses) first used on or after April 1, 1982 must also be equipped with such plates (reg.66(1)(b)). Under reg.66(1)(c) there is a similar requirement for wheeled locomotives and motor tractors first used on or after April 1, 1973 (not being agricultural motor vehicles, industrial tractors, works trucks, engineering plant or pedestrian controlled vehicles).

1.76   Regulation 66(1)(e) extends the plate requirement to a "converter dolly" trailer manufactured on or after January 1, 1979 even though it would not otherwise be classified as a trailer needing a plate. In particular, therefore, a "converter dolly" trailer of 1,020kg or less unladen requires a plate. By an apparent oversight the exceptions in reg.66(1)(d) do not apply to such small trailers. Converter dollies are becoming quite common. They are trailers with two or more wheels enabling a semi-trailer to move without any part of its weight being directly superimposed on the drawing vehicle. The converter dolly must not be part of the drawing vehicle or semi-trailer. Regulation 66 provides that alternative plates may be affixed if they comply with specified EC directives (see reg.66(2)(b)). Every agricultural trailed appliance manufactured on or after December 1, 1985 must also be equipped with a plate (see reg.68). All such locomotives, heavy motor cars, motor cars and trailers are still subject to the weight limits laid down in regs 75–80.

Section 17(1) of the 1988 Offenders Act provides that where any proceedings are brought under s.42 of the 1988 Act and any question arises as to a weight of any description specified in the plating certificate for a goods vehicle and a weight of that description is marked on the vehicle, there is a presumption, unless the contrary is proved, that the weight marked on the vehicle is the weight so specified. Save in so far as provision is made by s.17(1) as to this presumption, there is nothing to make the weights marked on a plate affixed pursuant to reg.66 admissible as evidence of the permissible weights. Possibly the plate might be deemed to be an admission at common law by the vehicle owner as to the permitted weights, but this is doubtful as the weights are those fixed by the manufacturer and the owner is merely saying on the plate what the manufacturer has said and this is hearsay. If this evidence were admissible by itself the special provisions of s.17(1) would be unnecessary. The prosecutor should seemingly prove his case by evidence of the actual weight and type of vehicle, though the marking of the unladen weight on a locomotive, tractor or heavy motor car under reg.80, if it had been done by the owner, would be presumably an admission by him.

1.77   A plating certificate has the meaning assigned to it by s.49(2)(a) and (b) of the

1988 Act. Section 49(1) of the 1988 Act refers to the plated particulars under the Goods Vehicles (Plating and Testing) Regulations 1988 (SI 1988/1478). Plated particulars are those shown on a Ministry plate (see the Construction and Use Regulations Sch.10).

By reg.80 of the Construction and Use Regulations the certified weights, which may be less than those allowed by regs 75–79, must not be exceeded and so evidence that the actual weight exceeded the plated weight will suffice. It was held in *William Hampton Ltd v Dixon*, May 22, 1973, unreported, that s.17(1) of the 1988 Offenders Act obviated any necessity for the prosecution to serve a notice on the defendant to produce the plating certificate. Once the prosecution has proved the weight shown on the Ministry plate on the vehicle, it is at once assumed by virtue of s.17(1), in the absence of evidence to the contrary, that the plating certificate shows the same figure (*William Hampton Ltd v Dixon*). The court also held that the weighbridge ticket was admissible under the Criminal Evidence Act 1965 (now see the provisions of the Criminal Justice Act 1988 Pt II) as a trade or business record. See s.17(2) above as to proof of date of manufacture.

In *Wurzal v Reader Bros Ltd* [1973] Crim. L.R. 640 justices were held to be **1.78** wrong in dismissing an information under what is now reg.80 of the Construction and Use Regulations because the traffic examiner did not produce his authority when requiring the vehicle to proceed to a weighbridge under s.224 of the Road Traffic Act 1960. It was held that production of authority was only a prerequisite of prosecutions under what is now s.78 of the 1988 Act and it did not prevent prosecution for an overweight vehicle under what is now reg.80.

"Description of weight"

This expression is to be found in various places in the 1988 Act. See for **1.79** example s.41 (regulations), s.41B(2) (weight defences) and Sch.2 to the 1988 Offenders Act (penalties (as to which, see § 8.100)). It is not defined in the Act or in the Construction and Use Regulations.

Goods vehicles have the advantage for "description of weight" offences contrary to s.41B(1) (construction and use requirements) of the s.41B(2) defence but the disadvantage of an increased maximum fine (see Sch.2 to the 1988 Offenders Act, entry relating to s.41B, column 4). The increased penalty also applies to certain passenger vehicles but without the s.41B(2) defence.

Some of the Road Vehicles (Construction and Use) Regulations 1986 require **1.80** the weight or other relevant information to be displayed and others require the specified weight or weight ratio not to be exceeded. In one sense both are descriptions of weight. The decision in *Hudson v Bushrod* [1982] R.T.R. 87 —a "dangerous use" case—is authority for the proposition that dangerous use is not a description of weight for the purpose of the provisions. Part of the evidence adduced to prove the information in that case related to overloading, and the decision cannot be said to support the proposition that overloading is not a description of weight.

It is submitted that exceeding the maximum weight is a description of weight offence, but it is doubtful whether a contravention of a regulation requiring the weight to be displayed is.

Transmission and ascertainment of weight

Regulation 78 of the Road Vehicles (Construction and Use) Regulations 1986 **1.81**

(SI 1986/1078) refers to "the weight transmitted to the road by one or more wheels … in line transversely". "Transversely" does not mean "obliquely" or "diagonally" and the wheels concerned are (for a four-wheeled vehicle) the two front or the two back wheels, and the measurement is from nearside back to off-side back wheel (or nearside front to offside front wheel) and not from offside front to nearside back wheel (*Thomas v Galloway* 1935 J.C. 27). Regulations 75(1) (item 9 in table) and 78(1) (items 6 and 7 in table) indicate in respect of certain heavy motor cars and motor cars the maximum weights which may be transmitted to the road surface (a) by any one wheel where no other wheel is in the same line transversely, (b) by any two wheels in line transversely, and (c) by all the wheels. Breach of (a) or (b) or (c) is in itself an offence and, in a charge in respect of the weight transmitted by two wheels in line transversely, the prosecution need not also show that excessive weight was transmitted by all the wheels (*Martin v Robertson* (1949) 93 S.J. 19).

The regulations, in limiting the weight transmitted to the road, make no exception with regard to the place at which, or the gradient on which, the weight was ascertained. When a weighing was done on ground which was uneven because of the camber of the road and it was considered by the magistrates that a different weight might be shown on a flat surface, it was nevertheless held by the High Court that, if the weighing on the camber showed an illegal weight, an offence had been committed under what is now reg.75 (*Prosser v Richings* [1936] 2 All E.R. 1627). But a weighing done with the engine still running and on an incline was held not to have been properly done (*McMillan v Caledonian Omnibus Co* (1938) 26 Traff.Cas. 374). In *Thurrock Borough Council v William Blyth & Co Ltd* [1977] R.T.R. 301 it was held to be an unsatisfactory method of weighing an articulated goods vehicle for the tractor and trailer to be weighed separately but while remaining coupled, i.e. tractor weighed on the weighbridge and then driven forward bringing the trailer on to the weighbridge to be weighed separately.

1.82　　　However, many weighbridges will not weigh the whole of large vehicles and the practice is to "double weigh", i.e. to weigh separately front and back and add the totals together. The advised method of cross-checking is by testing a "sample" vehicle and then weighing it on a long weighbridge where it can be weighed in a single operation. The usual error for vehicles over 20 tonnes is less than half of 1 per cent. In view of this summonses should state that the maximum is exceeded, with the actual alleged overload being given in evidence or the statement of facts.

Dynamic axle weighing machines are now in use enabling the axle weights of a motor vehicle or trailer to be ascertained. The limits of presumed accuracy of such machines, the manner in which they are to be used and the form of certificate when used are specified in the Weighing of Motor Vehicles (Use of Dynamic Axle Weighing Machines) Regulations 1978 (SI 1978/1180).

1.83　　　Where in any proceedings in Scotland for a road traffic offence any question arises as to a weight of any description in relation to a goods vehicle, a certificate of, or oral evidence by an inspector of weights and measures as to, the accuracy of the weighbridge or weighing machine used is sufficient evidence of the fact (1988 Offenders Act s.17(4)). If such evidence is not produced, its lack may be fatal to the prosecution (*Grierson v Clark* 1958 S.L.T. 112). This case would not necessarily be followed in England and Wales, however, as evidence of mechanical devices is acceptable without proof of their accuracy if the court thinks fit and the excess weight shown is considerable (cf. *Nicholas v Penny* [1950] 2 All E.R.

89). In any proceedings for an offence under Pt II of the 1988 Act other than ss.47 and 75, the date marked on the vehicle under regulations as the date of manufacture is evidence, in England and Wales, and sufficient evidence, in Scotland, that it was manufactured on the date so marked (1988 Offenders Act s.17(2)).

"Accident"

Meaning

The word "accident" is to be found in several places in the 1988 Act, notably **1.84** in the drink/driving provisions (ss.4–11), particularly s.6(2) (administration of the breath test following an accident); s.170 (failing to stop and failing to report an accident); and s.1 of the 1988 Offenders Act (warning of intended prosecution). In *R. v Morris* [1972] R.T.R. 201 (a case under a similar provision to s.6(2)) an "accident" was said by Sachs L.J. to mean "an unintended occurrence which has an adverse physical result" and it was held that an accident had occurred where two car bumpers had become interlocked while one car was pushing the other. In *Chief Constable of West Midlands Police v Billingham* [1979] R.T.R. 446 (another screening breath test case) it was stated that this attempted definition should be understood in relation to the particular facts of the case.

In *Billingham* the Divisional Court pointed out that there was no definition of **1.85** the word "accident" in what is now the 1988 Act and both judges expressed themselves hesitant to attempt to define the word when Parliament had refrained from doing so: it had different meanings in different statutes according to the mischief against which the Act was aimed. Instead of attempting to give a definition, both judges preferred to suggest that a court, when having to decide whether there was an accident within the meaning of the 1988 Act, should ask itself the question "Would an ordinary man in the circumstances of the case say there had been an accident?" Applying this test the Divisional Court held that there had been an accident. In *Billingham* a police motor vehicle had been damaged as a result of a *deliberate* act of mischief by someone setting the car in motion so that it ran downhill and collided with a telegraph pole.

Billingham was followed in *Chief Constable of Staffordshire v Lees* [1981] R.T.R. 506 (another breath test case) where the defendant deliberately drove at a locked kissing gate, smashing it. Bingham J. said:

> "It would be an insult to commonsense if a collision involving a motor car arising from some careless and inadvertent act entitled a constable to exercise his powers under the Act but a similar result caused by a deliberate anti-social act did not. Previous cases have made it clear that one should look at the ordinary meaning of the word 'accident', and it is relevant to note that in the Oxford English Dictionary, among other meanings, is to be found 'an unfortunate event, a mishap', which definition, it seems to me, is wide enough to include an event not occurring in the ordinary course, of such a nature as in this case."

This approach has been confirmed in another situation. In *R. v Branchflower* **1.86** [2004] EWCA Crim 2042; [2005] 1 Cr. App. R. 10, the court was considering allegations of murder, manslaughter and aggravated vehicle-taking all arising from the same incident. The defendant pleaded guilty to aggravated vehicle-taking and was found guilty of murder, he having seized a momentarily unattended motor car and having driven over and killed the owner in an attempt to get away. He was convicted on both; in order to be convicted of the aggravated vehicle-taking, the court needed to be satisfied that, owing to the driving of the vehicle, an accident occurred by which injury was caused. The defendant appealed on the grounds that a finding of guilt in relation to murder was incompatible with a finding that there had been an "accident". The Court of Appeal referred to *Billingham* and confirmed that a deliberate act does not prevent an occurrence from being an "accident" for these purposes.

It is clear from *Billingham* and *Lees* that there is no need for any other vehicle to be involved. See also *R. v Pico* [1971] Crim. L.R. 500, where a car hit a bank and a gate post injuring the defendant driver and damaging the gate, and *R. v Harling* [1970] R.T.R. 441 (no other vehicle apparently involved).

1.87 A Scottish decision which confirms the view that there does not have to be any form of impact to constitute an "accident" is *Bremner v Westwater* (1993) 1994 S.L.T. 707. For the purpose of determining whether a notice of intended prosecution had to be served, the High Court of Justiciary considered the following facts. A driver had driven his car at excessive speed, without lights during the hours of darkness and at one point had overtaken another vehicle in the face of oncoming traffic, causing the driver of the overtaken vehicle to brake sharply and the driver of an oncoming vehicle also to brake sharply and take evasive action. The evasive action resulted in the oncoming vehicle mounting the nearside verge to avoid a head-on collision. The sheriff had ruled that s.2(1) of the 1988 Offenders Act applied, and that a notice was not required.

The High Court of Justiciary agreed. In dismissing the defendant's appeal, the court held that the occurrence by which the driver by his driving in effect drove the oncoming vehicle off the road onto the verge could properly be described as an "accident". Moreover, the accident had clearly occurred as a result of the presence of the driver's car on the road and the sheriff was accordingly entitled to find that the requirements of s.2(1) were satisfied and that no notice of intended prosecution was required.

1.88 Further consideration has been given by the Court of Appeal in the civil case of *Charlton v Fisher* [2001] EWCA Civ 112; [2001] R.T.R. 33. Personal injury was caused by the defendant when he deliberately drove his car into the rear of a stationary car in which the claimant was sitting in the rear seat. Both cars were in a hotel car park and not "on a road" so the compulsory third party insurance provisions did not apply. The Court of Appeal held that, as a matter of public policy, an insured could not recover for his own benefit under a policy of insurance in respect of loss intentionally caused by his own criminal act. Since the incident occurred otherwise than on a road and use was not required to be covered by insurance, the claimant could not rely on s.151 of the Road Traffic Act 1988 (whereby an insurer must satisfy certain claims on void or cancelled policies) or on the MIB agreements (see § 10.83 below) and had to claim through the defendant. The insurance policy provided cover "in the event of an accident involving … [the] car" and the issue was raised as to whether the commission of a deliberate criminal act could in any case amount to an "accident". Although not necessary to determine the case, a majority held that the term "accident" in this context is wide enough to cover such an event.

"Driver"

Meaning

"Driver" (except for the purposes of s.1 (causing death by dangerous driving)), **1.89**
where a separate person acts as steersman of a motor vehicle, includes that person
as well as any other person engaged in the driving of the vehicle, and the expression "drive" is construed accordingly (Road Traffic Act 1988 s.192). A similar
definition is in the Road Traffic Regulation Act 1984 s.142(1).

Two people may be held to be actually driving the same car at the same time.
In *Tyler v Whatmore* [1976] R.T.R. 83 (following *Langman v Valentine* below) it
was held that a girl in the passenger seat leaning across the person in the driver's
seat with both her hands on the wheel, steering the car, with the ignition switch
and handbrake within her reach, was "actually driving". Her companion in the
driving seat whose view she obstructed and who was controlling the propulsion
of the car but could not control the steering was also driving (*Tyler v Whatmore*,
as above). The degree of control of a passenger must, however, be such as to
amount to driving in the ordinary sense of the word (*Jones v Pratt* [1983] R.T.R.
54). In *Jones v Pratt* the Divisional Court held that the front seat passenger in a
moving car who momentarily grabbed the steering wheel, pushing it in a
clockwise direction, causing the car to leave the road, could not properly be
described as driving the car in the ordinary sense of the word and could not be
convicted of driving with excess alcohol or without due care. A learner driver,
sitting in the driving seat, is a driver, although the instructor who retains simulta-
neous control of the car may also be a driver (*Langman v Valentine* [1952] 2 All
E.R. 803; see also *R. v Wilkins* (1951) 115 J.P. 443 QS). In *Langman's* case the
instructor had his hands on the brake and steering wheel. Where a licensed person
merely sat beside a young boy, who was in the driving seat and, though able to
reach the steering wheel and footbrake, apparently did not have a hand on the
wheel, he was held not to be a driver as he was not in control of the car (*Evans v
Walkden* [1956] 3 All E.R. 64). Where it is not clear which of two persons was
the driver of a vehicle at the relevant time but that whoever had been the passenger must have aided and abetted the commission of the offence, both should
be charged as principals (*Smith v Mellors* [1987] R.T.R. 210). A further variant
on the issue of what makes a person a "driver" was the subject of *Cawthorn
(Jonathan) v DPP* [2000] R.T.R. 45. Mr Cawthorn had stopped his car on a hill
in order to post a letter and had activated the hazard warning lights. Whilst he
was away from the vehicle, it started to roll down the hill and hit a wall that was
damaged. It seemed that the roll was started by a passenger releasing the
handbrake. Mr Cawthorn left the scene and was subsequently convicted of failing
to stop and exchange details and failing to report an accident. The Divisional
Court said that, although there had been a break in the driving, the appellant was
still making his journey as evidenced by the use of the hazard warning lights. The
intervening act by the passenger did not make that passenger the driver.

In allegations involving proof that the defendant was the driver of a vehicle, **1.90**
the burden remains on the prosecution to prove that fact. At no point does it shift
to the defendant. Magistrates dealing with a number of driving offences in *Clarke
v DPP* (1992) 156 J.P. 605 were advised that where it had been shown that the
defendant was the owner of the vehicle concerned (together with any other relevant evidence raising a presumption that the appellant was the driver) the burden

shifted to the defendant—on the balance of probabilities—to show he was not the driver. The Divisional Court held that this was wrong and that in a criminal case the question for decision was, and remained throughout, whether the court was sure that the appellant was the driver. In some circumstances, but in far from all, the presumption might—together with those circumstances—be sufficient to make the sure inference.

A most interesting decision on whether or not a court can infer that an individual was driving from proof of ownership of a vehicle was handed down by the Court of Appeal in *R. v Collins (George)* [1994] R.T.R. 216. The allegation was one of conspiracy to supply drugs. The police observed a box containing drugs transferred to a Saab motor car. The Saab was then driven off by a man wearing dreadlocks. The following week the appellant, who had dreadlocks, was seen driving the Saab. When he stopped he gave a false name, but later he and his brother admitted that they owned the Saab jointly. At the trial of the appellant a submission of no case to answer was rejected. None of the defendants gave evidence. The judge directed the jury that they were entitled to draw the inference that an owner of a vehicle was the driver of that vehicle if he fitted the description of the driver of the vehicle when it was seen at some place in connection with an offence. The appellant appealed against his conviction.

1.91   The appeal was allowed and the conviction quashed. The Court of Appeal held that where a car was owned jointly a jury should not be directed that they could infer that one owner was the driver of the car at the time when it was seen in connection with an offence if he fitted the description of the driver given at that time, without being told that they should bear in mind the possibility that the joint owner had given permission to a third person to drive the car. The submission of no case was wrongly rejected when the trial judge left out of account that the joint owner could have given permission for a third person to drive the car without the defendant's knowledge, and that that third person could have fitted the description of the driver of the car at the relevant time.

Although it might be seen as stating the obvious, the prosecution have to prove the identity of the driver at any given time. In this case it was to prove an essential element in an alleged criminal conspiracy, but it is a requirement in hundreds of road traffic cases prosecuted daily. Inferences may of course be telling, but inferences may only be drawn if it is reasonable under all the circumstances to draw them, and in assessing reasonableness, consideration must be given to other explanations or possibilities. An important "other possibility" was overlooked by the judge in this case and the conviction was thus flawed.

"Driving"

1.92   There are a number of cases on whether a person can be said to be "driving". Some are not easy to reconcile.

In *Saycell v Bool* [1948] 2 All E.R. 83 a person who sat in the driving seat, released the brake and let the vehicle run 100yds downhill was held to "drive it" although there was no petrol in the tank and the engine was not started. In *Ames v MacLeod* 1969 J.C. 1 the High Court of Justiciary in Scotland held that a person "drove" his car which had run out of petrol when he steered it by placing his hand on the wheel while walking beside it as it coasted down a slight incline in the road. In *R. v Munning* [1961] Crim. L.R. 555 a magistrates' court held that pushing a motor scooter was not driving. In *R. v Roberts (No.2)* [1965] 1 Q.B. 85

releasing the brake of a lorry parked on a hill and putting the vehicle in motion so that it ran down the hill was held not to be "driving". In *R. v Kitson* (1955) 39 Cr. App. R. 66 a passenger awoke to find the driver gone and the car moving. He steered it for 200yds until he could safely stop. He was held to be a "driver".

In *Blayney v Knight* [1975] R.T.R. 279 a taxi driver left his taxi which had **1.93** automatic transmission with the engine running. The defendant, who had no intention of driving, sat in the driver's seat. In the course of a struggle with the taxi driver the defendant's foot touched the accelerator causing the taxi to drive along the road, mount the pavement and swerve back to the offside. The defendant was held not to be "driving".

In *R. v MacDonagh* [1974] R.T.R. 372, it was held that a person who pushed a car along a road with both feet on the ground with one arm in the car to control the steering wheel was not "driving" the car and could not be therefore convicted of driving while disqualified. It will be noted that the facts of *Ames v MacLeod* and *R. v MacDonagh* are virtually indistinguishable. *R. v MacDonagh* must be taken as representing the law in England and Wales. The conflict between the two cases may be the reason for a court of five judges in the latter case. A reading of the judgment of Lord Widgery C.J. in *MacDonagh* leads, it is submitted, to the following conclusions:

(1) The primary consideration as to whether a person is "driving" is essentially a question of fact, dependent on the degree and extent to which the person has control of the direction and movement of the vehicle.

(2) One test is whether the accused was "in a substantial sense controlling the movement and direction of the car" (*Ames v MacLeod*, as above). A person cannot be said to be "driving" unless he satisfies this test.

(3) The fact that a person satisfies the test of control in *Ames v MacLeod* is not necessarily exhaustive. It has still to be considered whether the activity in question could fall within the ordinary meaning of the word "driving" in the English language. (See also *McQuaid v Anderton* [1980] 3 All E.R. 540 and *R. v Roberts (No.2)* above.)

Further tests to determine whether a person is driving have been established by **1.94** *Burgoyne v Phillips* [1983] R.T.R. 49 and *Jones v Pratt* [1983] R.T.R. 54.

(4) The essence of driving is the use of the driver's control in order to direct the movement of the vehicle however the movement is produced (*Burgoyne v Phillips* and *Rowan v Merseyside Chief Constable, The Times*, December 10, 1985). (This is in effect a reiteration of tests (1) and (2) above.)

(5) Whether the defendant himself deliberately sets the vehicle in motion is an important factor (*Burgoyne v Phillips* and *Rowan v Merseyside Chief Constable*, as above).

(6) In borderline cases, it is important to consider the length of time the steering wheel or other control was handled (*Jones v Pratt*).

Applying tests (1), (2) and (3) in *MacDonagh* it was held that the defendant was "pushing" rather than "driving". Similarly it was suggested that a person pushing a broken-down motor cycle and walking beside it could not be said to be "driving". On the other hand it was suggested that it would be possible to find as a fact that a person was driving if a motorist pushing the vehicle had one foot in the car in order to make more effective use of the controls.

1.95   In *Burgoyne v Phillips* the defendant was sitting behind the steering wheel of his car. Assuming he still had the keys in the ignition, he let the car roll forward to drive off carefully. He realised he had no keys and put the brakes on quickly. The steering wheel was locked and the engine was not running. The car rolled a distance of 30ft by gravity and collided with another vehicle. The Divisional Court held that the defendant was driving as opposed to attempting to drive and was rightly convicted of driving with excess alcohol.

    The facts of *Burgoyne v Phillips* do not altogether tally with the test used (i.e. test (4) above). The defendant had only limited scope for control. He apparently merely released the handbrake. Releasing the handbrake was held not to be driving in *R. v Roberts (No.2)*. However, unlike the person in that case he was behind the steering wheel and intended to drive. The facts are similar to those in *Saycell v Bool* at § 1.92 above save that *Burgoyne v Phillips* seems to be the first conviction for driving (apart from the "continuing" cases noted below) where there was no control of the steering.

1.96   Further decisions confirm test (1) above. In *Leach and Jeffs v DPP* [1993] R.T.R. 161, an appeal concerning a conviction for wilful obstruction of a constable in the execution of his duty contrary to what is now s.89(2) of the Police Act 1996, the Divisional Court held that a person sitting in the driving seat of a stationary motor vehicle, who switched on the engine, sat erect in his seat and placed his hands on the steering wheel could not per se be a person driving a motor vehicle within the meaning of s.163 of the Road Traffic Act 1988. On the facts of that case, however, the officer was acting in the execution of his duty and the conviction was affirmed.

    A more frightening set of circumstances was considered by three courts in *DPP v Hastings* [1993] R.T.R. 205. The defendant was a front seat passenger in a moving car when he saw a pedestrian, who was a friend of his, walking in the opposite direction along the street. He deliberately pulled the steering wheel towards himself in order to cause the car to veer towards the pedestrian so as to frighten, but not so as to strike, him. The car went out of control and struck and injured the pedestrian. The magistrates convicted the defendant of reckless driving being satisfied that he was "driving". The defendant appealed to the Crown Court successfully. That court found that he could not be said to have been driving. The prosecutor appealed to the Divisional Court. There it was held that whether someone was driving was a matter of fact and degree; that whatever the defendant's motives, his actions had amounted to an act of interfering with the driving of the car rather than the act of driving. On the facts, it had been open to the Crown Court to allow the defendant's appeal. The prosecutor's appeal was dismissed.

1.97   In *Gunnel v DPP* [1994] R.T.R. 151 the appellant was convicted of driving a motor vehicle, a moped, with excess alcohol. When he attempted to start it, the engine did not fire, and he set the moped in motion by sitting astride it and propelling it with his feet in a "paddling" movement. The Divisional Court held that the crucial questions were whether the justices had correctly directed themselves as to the law, and whether there was material before them justifying their conclusion that he was driving. It was the judgment of the court that they had directed themselves as to the law, and there was ample material to justify their conclusion.

    The facts of the Scottish case of *Henderson v Hamilton* 1995 S.L.T. 968 were that a person was found at 11.45pm in the driving seat of a vehicle, but slumped across the passenger seat. The vehicle keys were under the passenger seat and the engine was warm. By a majority, the High Court of Justiciary held that it could properly be inferred that the person—who was capable of driving the vehicle—had driven it to its position in the absence of any competing explanation of how it had got there. Convictions for driving whilst disqualified and using a vehicle without insurance were upheld.

A person may be "driving" even though he is only attempting to control the **1.98** movement of the vehicle. In *Rowan v Merseyside Chief Constable, The Times*, December 10, 1985, the defendant knelt on the driving seat, released the hand-brake and thereafter attempted to re-apply it to stop the movement of the vehicle. He was held to be driving. Nolan J. said that if a defendant caused the vehicle to move on to a road and if he was inside the vehicle trying to control its movement, that was material evidence on which a court could find that he was driving it.

In *Hoy v MacFadyen* 2000 S.L.T. 1060, a car was parked adjacent to a kerb. The appellant opened the driver's door and sat in the driver's seat. A passenger went to the passenger door, opened it, removed something from the car, left the car and returned to a shop. In her absence, the appellant started the engine. Police officers approached, spoke to the appellant and asked him to turn off the engine. This he did, and, at that moment, the car lurched forward slightly since the hand-brake was defective. In order to hold the car on a slope, the appellant had to keep his foot on the footbrake or leave it in gear. The appellant was convicted of driving whilst disqualified and without insurance. On appeal, the court ruled that, in order to prevent movement of the car downhill, there had to be a direct and continuing personal intervention by the person in the driving seat. Having disengaged the gear in order to start the engine, the appellant had to keep his foot on the brake and that had been an act beyond mere preparation for driving. He had commenced driving even though there had been no movement of the car at all until the very end of the incident. The correct test was to look at what the appellant had been doing and not necessarily the result.

A steersman in a motor vehicle towed by a rope or chain can properly be said **1.99** to be driving.

In *Whitfield v DPP* [1998] Crim. L.R. 349, the owner of a tipper lorry which was to be taken for scrap arranged for another lorry to tow the tipper to its destination. The tipper was in a dilapidated condition: its engine would not start, it had no braking system and its electrical system was inoperative. The tipper was towed by means of a tow bar which was free to move at both ends. The owner sat in the tipper whilst it was being towed in order to steer it. During its journey, the tipper became detached from the lorry. The owner was charged with dangerous driving and driving otherwise than in accordance with a driving licence. On appeal, the court stated that the owner clearly had directional control of the vehicle (even though he was not in control of the propulsive force and unable to apply any braking force) and could properly be said to be driving the tipper. Similarly, in *R. (on the application of Traves) v DPP* [2005] EWHC 1482; (2005) 169 J.P. 421 where the appellant was in the driver's seat of his own vehicle which was being towed by another vehicle. The justices accepted that he had been steering and using the brakes to slow the vehicle down for approximately three miles. He was prosecuted for driving the vehicle whilst disqualified and for using it without a valid insurance or test certificate and the issue arose as to whether he was "driving". Unsurprisingly, the justices found that this amounted to "driving" and the Divisional Court agreed. The court cited with approval the statement in

Whitfield that: "The essence of driving is the use of the driver's controls in order to direct the movement, however that movement is produced". Here, movement was produced by the vehicle being towed but the defendant's involvement in both steering and in controlling the movement through the use of the brakes was sufficient. The cases do not decide the position of a vehicle being towed with a rigid towbar, but it is submitted that applying the specified tests a person in the driver's seat of such a car would probably be held not to be driving.

1.100   It is possible, it seems, for a person to be "driving" a motor cycle although he was not riding it at the time. In *McKoen v Ellis* [1987] R.T.R. 26, the defendant had been standing with legs astride a motor cycle and had, for an unspecified distance, been controlling its movement and direction by pushing and steering it while its ignition and lights were on. He was found by the justices to have been "driving" the motor cycle; their decision was upheld by the Divisional Court. The report does not make clear, however, whether the defendant had been "paddling" the motor cycle along with his feet or had merely "walked" it along whilst astride it. *Selby v DPP*, which deals with the question of a person propelling a motor cycle whilst sitting astride it, is the subject of a Note reported at [1994] R.T.R. 157.

An unusual situation arose in *DPP v Alderton* [2003] EWHC 2917; [2004] R.T.R. 23. Following an argument with his wife, the defendant had gone to his car which was parked on the verge outside their house. In order to release his frustration and anger, he had engaged in wheel spinning—having the engine running, putting the vehicle in gear but keeping the handbrake on and then using the accelerator, clutch and steering wheel but with no intention of causing the vehicle to move. Justices found that this was not "driving". The Administrative Court restated the essence of *MacDonagh* as containing two relevant tests—was the defendant in a substantial sense controlling the movement and direction of the car; could the activity fall within the ordinary meaning of the word "driving"? Allowing the prosecutor's appeal, the Administrative Court stated that the action of keeping the handbrake on whilst using the accelerator and the clutch was controlling the movement of the vehicle and it did not matter whether it was the defendant who applied the handbrake or whether he simply left it as set by the previous driver. Referring also to *Hoy v MacFadyen* above, the court reaffirmed that movement is not essential where the acts of the driver have gone beyond preparation for driving to the point where there is active intervention by the driver to prevent the vehicle from moving. Here, there was clearly that intervention and it did not matter that the purpose of the "wheel spinning" was to vent anger.

1.101   An admission that he had driven the motor vehicle is sufficient to establish that a defendant had been driving in order to warrant a conviction under s.5 of the 1988 Act; the prosecution do not have to prove that he drove after drinking; the burden of showing that the defendant consumed alcohol after driving is transferred to the defendant by s.15(3) of the 1988 Offenders Act (*Patterson v Charlton* [1986] R.T.R. 18).

In *Collyer v Dring* [1952] 2 All E.R. 1004, the facts were that a young girl entered a motor car parked in a private forecourt off the road, intending to drive it round the forecourt only and not to go on the road. Through her inexperience she engaged reverse gear and the car went on to the road. On being charged with careless driving and with uninsured use, she contended that she was not driving "on the road" inasmuch as she was on it involuntarily and also that she was not using the car on the road. Her conviction on both charges was upheld by the Divisional Court.

In Pt VI of the Transport Act 1968, which relates to drivers' hours, s.95(3) **1.102** refers to "employee-drivers" and "owner-drivers" and s.103(3) declares that references to a person driving a vehicle are references to his being at the driving controls of the vehicle for the purpose of controlling its movement, whether it is in motion or stationary with its engine running.

The decision in *Richmond LBC v Pinn and Wheeler Ltd* [1989] Crim. L.R. 510 is authority for the proposition that a limited company cannot be convicted of "driving". Informations were preferred against the company under art.3 of the Greater London (Restriction of Goods Vehicles) Traffic Order 1985 (SI 1985/343), which provides that, "no person shall drive or cause or permit to be driven any goods vehicle exceeding 16.5 tonnes ... in any restricted street during the proscribed hours". The company was convicted by the justices, and then successfully appealed to the Crown Court. The prosecutor unsuccessfully appealed to the Divisional Court by way of case stated, it being held that the act of driving a lorry was a physical act which could be performed only by natural persons.

As for attempting to drive and the borderline between "driving" and "attempt- **1.103** ing to drive", see § 1.107.

Continuing driving

The principles given in §§ 1.92–103 only determine whether a person is **1.104** driving. Once it has been determined that a person is driving, the driving may still continue even though the tests laid down in *R. v MacDonagh* cannot be fulfilled. A person may still be driving when he is buying a newspaper or changing a wheel (examples given in *Pinner v Everett* [1969] 3 All E.R. 257 HL) or when he is walking across the forecourt of a garage to take instructions (*Regan v Anderton* [1980] R.T.R. 126). These cases were based on the former s.8(1) of the 1972 Act, since repealed. That section had special features in that it was impossible to take it literally. Nevertheless the cases have a wider significance.

In *Stevens v Thornborrow* [1969] 3 All E.R. 1487 the following propositions were extracted from *Pinner v Everett*:

(1) Whether a person is "driving or attempting to drive" is a question of fact.

(2) It is far easier to find as a fact that a motorist is driving if he is still at the wheel, more difficult if he has dismounted.

(3) The overriding principle, whether or not he is at the wheel, is whether he is doing something connected with driving.

The principles of *Pinner v Everett* and other cases were summarised (so far as **1.105** still relevant) in *Edkins v Knowles* [1973] Q.B. 748 as follows:

(1) The vehicle does not have to be in motion; there will always be a brief interval of time after the vehicle has been brought to rest and before the motorist has completed those operations necessarily connected with driving, such as applying the handbrake, switching off the ignition and securing the vehicle, during which he must still be considered to be driving.

(2) When a motorist stops before he has completed his journey he may

still be driving; an obvious example is when he is halted at traffic lights. Each case will depend upon its own facts, but generally the following questions will be relevant:

(a) What was the purpose of the stop? If it is connected with the driving, and not for some purpose unconnected with the driving, the facts may justify a finding that the driving is continuing although the vehicle is stationary.

(b) How long was he stopped? The longer he is stopped the more difficult it becomes to regard him as still driving.

(c) Did he get out of the vehicle? If he remains in the vehicle it is some indication (although not conclusive) that he is still driving.

(3) If a motorist is stopped and an appreciable time elapses, it will be a question of fact and degree whether the motorist is still to be considered as driving at that time.

(4) When a motorist has arrived at the end of his journey then subject to the brief interval referred to in head (1) above he can no longer be regarded as driving.

(5) When a motorist has been effectively prevented or persuaded from driving he can no longer be considered to be driving.

1.106   The decision in *Edkins v Knowles* [1973] Q.B. 748 would still seem to be applicable to any requirement to produce a driving licence or provide name and address under s.164 or s.165 of the 1988 Act (see also §§ 11.17 et seq.).

Another variant on the question of when a person ceases to be driving was considered in *R. (on the application of Planton) v DPP* [2001] EWHC Admin 450; [2002] R.T.R. 9. A driver was apprehended on suspicion of being drunk in charge of a motor vehicle and subsequently charged with driving that vehicle with excess alcohol. He had been found in his car halfway across a causeway that was tidal. The engine was running, the lights were on, the car was stationary, the defendant's head was against the side window and, when questioned, he said he was "waiting for the tide". The justices found he was waiting for the tide to recede sufficiently to cross the causeway and that he may have dozed or otherwise been distracted. The Administrative Court agreed that the justices were entitled to hold he was driving. Counsel for the driver sought to rely on the absence of movement of the vehicle and the comments of Lord Widgery C.J. in *R. v MacDonagh* (see § 1.93 above) but the Divisional Court reiterated that "it is a question of fact and degree as to whether cessation of movement has been for so long and in such circumstances that it cannot reasonably be said that the person in the driving seat is driving".

"Drives or attempts to drive"

1.107   Section 6(1) of the 1988 Act enables a constable to require a preliminary test not only from a person who is driving or attempting to drive, but also from a motorist who either has been driving or attempting to drive, or is or has been in charge of a motor vehicle. Where two occupants of a motor vehicle are charged, as participants to a joint enterprise, with the principal offence of driving with excess alcohol, it is unnecessary for the prosecution to establish which drove the vehicle and which aided and abetted the driving, provided that it can be proved that each occupant is guilty either because he was driving or because he aided and abetted the driving. In such a case however, it is necessary for the prosecution to establish that both occupants knew, or were reckless, that the other was unfit to drive (*Smith v Mellors* [1987] R.T.R. 210); see further under "Aiding, abetting, counselling and procuring" at § 1.198.

It is submitted that the same principles must be applied to "attempts to drive" as to any other criminal attempt, i.e. there must be an act sufficiently proximate to the commission of the full offence (see § 1.210), in this case, driving.

A drunken person went to the front of a car and turned the starting handle; he **1.108** then opened the offside door, leaned inside and appeared to touch the dashboard instruments. He returned to the starting handle and then sat in the driver's seat; the engine was heard to turn over, but failed to start. The court found that he had the immediate intention of driving and it was held that this was an attempt to drive (*The State (Prendergast) v Porter* [1961] Ir.Jur.Rep. 15). In *Shaw v Knill* [1974] R.T.R. 142 it was held that a motor cyclist could be convicted of attempting to drive while disqualified when he pushed a motor cycle 6yds towards the entrance onto a public road where he was about to ride it. In *Harman v Wardrop* [1971] R.T.R. 127 a motorist gave up his ignition keys to a person whom he mistakenly thought was a police constable. When he realised his mistake he asked for his keys back with the intention of driving the car. He was refused. Lord Parker C.J. doubted whether the motorist would ever be said to be attempting to drive if he merely asked for his keys, although where an unfit driver who had no ignition key sat in the driver's seat attempting to insert other keys into the ignition, he was held to be properly convicted of attempting to drive (*Kelly v Hogan* [1982] R.T.R. 352).

A person was held to "attempt to drive" even though due to a mechanical malfunction the vehicle could not be driven. In *R. v Farrance* [1978] R.T.R. 225 the defendant was held to be "attempting to drive" when found revving the engine of a motor car which in fact could not be driven because the clutch had been burnt out. The different between "driving" and "attempting to drive" is whether or not the vehicle is actually put into motion.

For a persuasive view on the issue of when a defendant can be said to be "at- **1.109** tempting to drive", there is the decision of the High Court of Justiciary in *Guthrie v Friel* (1992) 1993 S.L.T. 899. In that case, police officers found a car in the early hours of the morning stationary at the side of the road. The appellant was asleep seated in the driver's seat and was wearing the seat belt. His head was slumped against the steering wheel. The engine was running and the headlights were switched on in the dipped-beam position. He was charged with attempting to drive when his breath-alcohol exceeded the prescribed limit. He submitted no case on the basis that he could not on those facts be said to have been attempting to drive. The submission failed, and he was convicted of the offence.

The opinion of the High Court was delivered by the Lord Justice-Clerk. He said that the fact that the appellant was asleep or unconscious made a difference. Whether or not a person had reached the stage of attempting to drive depended on the facts. Before a charge of attempting to do something could be established the individual had to have passed from mere preparation to perpetration. The appellant's actions in starting the engine, turning on the headlights and fastening his seat belt might show that he was preparing to drive but fell short of establishing that he was attempting to drive. The case might have been different, he continued, if he had released the handbrake. The court's view was reinforced by the fact that the appellant often slept in his car. The submission of no case to answer should not have been rejected.

"In charge"

1.110   A drink/driving offence may be committed by a person who is "in charge" of a mechanically propelled vehicle (see s.4(2) of the 1988 Act) or a motor vehicle (see s.5(1)(b) of the 1988 Act). The words "in charge" are not defined in the 1988 Act. Whether or not a person is "in charge" of a vehicle is very much a matter of fact and degree.

The concept of being "in charge" within the terms of the drink/driving legislation was considered in *DPP v Watkins* [1989] 2 W.L.R. 966. Taylor L.J., giving the judgment of the Divisional Court, stressed that there could be no hard and fast all-embracing test, but there were broadly two distinct classes of cases:

    (1) If the defendant was the owner or lawful possessor or had recently driven the vehicle, he would be "in charge" and the question would be whether he was still in charge or whether he had relinquished his charge. Usually such a defendant would be prima facie in charge unless he had put the vehicle in someone else's charge. However, he would not be so if in all the circumstances he had ceased to be in actual control and there was no realistic possibility of his resuming actual control while unfit, e.g. if he was home in bed for the night or a great distance from the car or if it was taken by another.

    (2) If the defendant was not the owner, lawful possessor or recent driver, but was sitting in the vehicle or otherwise involved with it, the question for the court was whether he had assumed being in charge of it. In this class of case, the defendant would be in charge if, while unfit, he was voluntarily in de facto control of the vehicle or if, in the circumstances, including his position, his intentions and his actions, he might be expected imminently to assume control. Usually that would involve his having gained entry to the car and having evinced an intention to take control. But gaining entry might not be necessary if he had manifested that intention in some other way, e.g. by stealing the keys of a car in circumstances which showed that he meant to drive it.

1.111   His Lordship continued by saying that the circumstances to be taken into account would vary infinitely, but the following would be relevant:

    (a) whether and where he was in the vehicle or how far he was from it;

    (b) what he was doing at the relevant time;

    (c) whether he was in possession of a key that fitted the ignition;

    (d) whether there was evidence of an intention to take or assert control of the car by driving or otherwise;

    (e) whether any person was in, at or near the vehicle and, if so, the like particulars in respect of that person.

It would be for the court to consider all these factors with any others that might be relevant and to reach its decision as a matter of fact and degree.

Watkins was followed in *Kelso v Brown* 1998 S.L.T. 921. The defendant had been found by police in a deep sleep in the front passenger seat of a car at 4.50am. The key was in the ignition, and the radio and heater were on. The car belonged to his wife who had driven him to his brother's house, where he had had something to drink. His wife later drove him away from the house. A subsequent breath test revealed that the defendant was substantially over the limit. Allowing his appeal against conviction for being in charge, the High Court of Justiciary found that there was nothing in the circumstances to suggest that the defendant had actually assumed control of the car after his wife had left. The court could not be satisfied that he was voluntarily in de facto control of the car. The fact that he had been asleep suggested that he could not have been expected imminently to assume control.

In *DPP v Janman* [2003] EWHC 101; [2004] R.T.R. 31, the defendant was supervising his partner, a provisional licence-holder, who was driving a car. The defendant was himself a provisional licence-holder and not, therefore, entitled as a matter of law to supervise in this way. He failed a breath test and was prosecuted for being in charge of the vehicle. He sought to argue both that he had no need to supervise the driver as she was able to drive and that the prosecution needed to be able to prove that he was entitled to supervise the driver. On appeal against the dismissal of the case by the magistrates' court, the Administrative Court concluded that the act of supervision was a matter of fact and there was no need to prove that the supervisor was qualified under the appropriate regulations to supervise a learner driver. Furthermore, although there might be circumstances in which a supervisor might be able to prove that there was no likelihood of driving, that was likely to be a very difficult task. A supervisor was required because a provisional licence-holder was not yet deemed competent to drive on their own and a supervisor must be prepared at any time to take over responsibility for the vehicle.

1.112

The prosecution is not required to prove that the defendant was likely to drive whilst unfit or over the limit. A defence is provided if the defendant can show that there is no such likelihood (1988 Act s.4(3) or 5(2)). Reversing the Divisional Court, the House of Lords has held that this imposes a legal burden on the defendant but that that is not oppressive. Even if the presumption of innocence is infringed, the provision was directed to a legitimate objective, did not go beyond what was necessary and reasonable and was not arbitrary. Accordingly, the provision did not contravene the European Convention on Human Rights: *Sheldrake v DPP* [2004] UKHL 43; [2005] R.T.R. 2. The way that the 1988 Act is drafted has led to misunderstanding of who needs to prove what and in what order. In *CPS v Bate* [2004] EWHC 2811 the court had found no case to answer having concluded that the prosecution had to prove that the defendant was in charge of the vehicle where he had put forward reasons why he was in the vehicle. It was patently clear that the defendant was in charge of the vehicle but that he may well have been able to satisfy the court that there was no likelihood of him driving whilst over the limit. It seemed to the Administrative Court that the justices had confused the question of whether the defendant was in charge and whether the statutory defence was open to him. The statutory defence required the defendant to prove (on the balance of probabilities) that there was no likelihood of driving whilst he remained unfit. The justices concluded that the intention of the driver not to drive was sufficient to determine that he was not in charge but, as the Administrative Court stated, it is the likelihood of driving not the intention of the defendant that provides the defence. The two may be closely related but they are not the same and it is for the defendant to satisfy the court that the defence has been made out. It was emphasised again in *CPS v Thompson* [2007] EWHC 1841;

[2008] R.T.R. 5 that it is not normally sufficient for the defence to focus on the intent of the driver and that there would usually be other compelling circumstantial evidence or expert scientific evidence. The defendant was well above the prescribed level and stated that he intended to drive when he felt "alright". He had no way of knowing when his blood/alcohol level would fall below the prescribed limit and there was no scientific evidence of when that point might have been reached. In those circumstances, the case was remitted to the justices for further consideration.

"Use" and "driving"

1.113   The distinction between "use" and "driving" was emphasised in *Samuelson v National Insurance and Guarantee Corporation Ltd* [1984] 3 All E.R. 107 (a civil case). The plaintiff was covered for the *use* of a vehicle whilst in the custody or control of a member of the motor trade for its upkeep or repair. He was not covered for *driving* by another person. It was held that he was not covered under the policy when the car was stolen whilst being *driven* by the motor trade repairer to buy spares. Although this decision was reversed by the Court of Appeal ([1986] 3 All E.R. 417), the distinction drawn at first instance between "use" and "driving" would appear to be valid (but cases on drink/driving which extend the concept of "driving" beyond the point when the vehicle is actually in motion would not seem to be applicable to "driving" for insurance purposes).

Pushing and driving

1.114   Proceedings are sometimes brought against persons who have been disqualified from driving or have no driving licence when they have been caught pushing a car or motor cycle, with the engine not running, or against persons pushing a car with someone else at the steering wheel. In the former case the defendant would be "driving" if he was in the driving seat or otherwise in control of the steering and had something to do with the propulsion, e.g. if he was engaged in a common design with his friends who were pushing, if not actually pushing himself (*R. v Roberts (No.2)* [1965] 1 Q.B. 85). If neither he nor his accomplices had any control over the steering, they would not appear to be driving. In the other case (the accomplices pushing from behind or at the side but with no personal control of the steering), it is submitted that they would be aiding and abetting (see §§ 1.198–209) the one in control of the steering if they were all engaged in a common design and could therefore properly be charged (*Shimmell v Fisher* [1951] 2 All E.R. 672). These cases suggest that pushing motor vehicles with control of the steering would be "driving", although sometimes the facts would point also to an attempt to drive. In almost all cases it would be "using" (see § 1.176) by those engaged in the common design whether there was "driving" or not.

See also *R. v MacDonagh* [1974] R.T.R. 373 (§ 1.91).

"Taking a conveyance"

1.115   The offence under s.12 of the Theft Act 1968 involves "taking" a conveyance. It was held in *R. v Bogacki* [1973] R.T.R. 384 that "taking" should not be equated with "using": the word "takes" requires not only an unauthorised taking of possession or control of the vehicle but also some movement of the vehicle however small. Thus taking control of a bus and unsuccessfully trying to start the engine so that the bus did not move could not justify a conviction for "taking" the bus contrary to s.12, only for attempting to do so (ibid.). However, the conveyance does not have to be moved in its own element for an offence to be committed. *P* was convicted of "taking" a rubber dinghy by putting it on a road trailer and driving the trailer away (*R. v Pearce* [1973] Crim. L.R. 321).

The earlier legislation (now repealed) used the expression "taking and driving away" and certain cases on the meaning of this may still be helpful. Where one man held the steering wheel and two others pushed, without the engine being started, all were held to be taking and driving away (*Shimmell v Fisher* [1951] 2 All E.R. 672). Pedalling an auto-assisted cycle without starting the engine was "driving away" (*Floyd v Bush* [1953] 1 All E.R. 265).

"Rider"

The expression "rider" is used in a number of statutory provisions. It will include a pedal cyclist. See, e.g. the Theft Act 1968 s.12(5) (riding a pedal cycle knowing it to have been taken without consent) and the Highway Act 1835 s.72 (wilfully riding on any footpath or causeway by the side of any road). It is an expression which will normally include the passenger who also rides. For instance, such passengers will require protective headgear on motor cycles (see "Motor cycle helmets" at § 9.56). **1.116**

As to what is meant by riding, see *Crank v Brooks* [1980] R.T.R. 441 and the law as discussed at §§ 1.92–103. In particular, note that "riding" is not necessarily to be equated with "driving" a motor cycle (*McKoen v Ellis* (1987) 151 J.P. 61, at § 1.100). Subject to the issue of continuance (see § 1.104) and a person stationary in traffic, etc., riding implies movement. There may be a distinction in this respect between a horse and a vehicle. A horse is not used to serve the purpose of an armchair but a vehicle seat may be. The *Concise Oxford Dictionary* defines "ride" as "sit on and be carried by" including "sit or go or be on something as on a horse especially astride". A magistrates' court (see [1982] Jo.Crim.L. 1) has held a person using a motor bicycle as a seat with the engine off not to be riding. Similarly a girl talking to her boyfriend (or a boy to his girlfriend) may have other things in mind and not be riding even though sitting astride the machine. The issue will be one of fact in each case.

Passenger

A crucial element of the definition of "public service vehicle" in s.1(1) of the Public Passenger Vehicles Act 1981, is the number of passengers for which the vehicle is adapted. The specified number of passengers is nine as the section refers to "more than eight". The criterion in s.1(1)(a) is whether the vehicle is adapted to carry nine or more passengers, not the number in fact carried. Similar expressions are used in many other statutory provisions. **1.117**

Whether the driver should be counted among the passengers is not clear. In Pts I and III of Sch.1 to the Public Passenger Vehicles Act 1981 "driver" is contrasted with "passenger". In Sch.5 to the Road Traffic Regulation Act 1967 (now repealed) the term "passengers" exclusive of the driver was used, which suggests that there he was regarded as otherwise than a passenger. In the equivalent part of the Road Traffic Regulation Act 1984 (Sch.6) the reference is merely to "more than eight passengers" and the definition is now the same as in the 1981 Act. See also s.95(2) of the Transport Act 1968 where again the reference is merely to "passengers". The *Concise Oxford Dictionary* defines "passenger" as "traveller in ... public ... conveyance". A driver in a public conveyance is someone who conveys the traveller on a passage from A to B without wishing to arrive permanently at B himself: it would not be logical to regard Charon, the legendary ferryman over the Styx to Hades, as himself a passenger on a journey to Hell. In *Wurzal v Addison* [1965] 1 All E.R. 20, a finding of magistrates that a Volkswagen minibus seating six passengers behind and with a bench seat seating the driver and two passengers in front was not adapted to carry eight passengers was upheld because the gear lever was in the central position. This implies the driver is not to be included. Lord Parker C.J. said that, in other cases involving similar vehicles, magistrates would, on proper evidence, be almost bound to find that they were adapted to carry eight passengers. (Note that the relevant number is now nine.) It is submitted that eight persons *plus* the driver may be carried before the limit is reached: i.e. the driver is *not* to be regarded as a passenger. In relation to the definition of a bus for the purposes of fixing the rate of excise duty under the Vehicle Excise and Registration Act 1994, reg.44 of the Road Vehicles (Registration and Licensing) Regulations 2002 (SI 2002/2742) provides for the seating capacity of a bus to be taken as the number of persons that can be seated in the bus at any one time (reg.44(1)). That number is calculated by reference to reg.44(2) and (3) which, amongst other things, provides that no account is to be taken of the driver's seat.

Automatism

1.118   The person sitting in the driving seat when the car is in motion is deemed to be the driver and the onus is on him to show that he was incapable of controlling the car by reason of having an epileptic fit or being in a coma or being knocked unconscious by a stone or being under attack by a swarm of bees. Unless he can show that he was temporarily incapable through some such circumstances, he is responsible as the driver (*Hill v Baxter* [1958] 1 All E.R. 193). Automatism connotes in law no wider concept than involuntary movement of a person's body or limbs (*Watmore v Jenkins* [1962] 2 All E.R. 868). There must be evidence to raise a reasonable doubt whether the driver's bodily movements which turned his car hither and thither and kept it moving at a fairly steady speed were wholly uncontrolled and uninitiated by any function of conscious will (*Watmore v Jenkins*, as above). That was a case of dangerous driving where the defendant, a diabetic, was in a state of confusion through his illness but, as he had driven for five miles in that state, a conviction was directed.

A restrictive view has been taken to the defence of automatism. In *Att Gen's Reference (No.2 of 1992)* [1993] R.T.R. 337, the Court of Appeal concluded that the proper evidential foundation had not been laid by the expert evidence available for the defence of automatism to be left to the jury. The condition that faced the driver was described as "driving without awareness". He had been driving a lorry on a long journey, but had taken appropriate breaks. At a point where a motorway narrowed from three to two lanes, he steered apparently deliberately onto the hard shoulder. After driving for some 700m on the hard shoulder, he crashed into a stationary van, which was displaying hazard lights. The prosecution's case was that the driver of the lorry had fallen asleep at the wheel. The defence expert maintained that "driving without awareness" implied a state where the driver's capacity to avoid a collision ceased to exist because repetitive stimuli experienced on long journeys on straight flat featureless motorways could induce a trance-like state in which the focal point for forward vision gradually came nearer and nearer until the driver was focusing just ahead of his windscreen, peripheral vision continued to send signals which were dealt with subconsciously and enabled the driver to steer within highway lanes. The expert said that the condition could occur insidiously without the driver being aware that it was happening. However, usually a driver would "snap out" of the condition in response to major stimuli appearing in front of him. Thus, flashing lights would usually cause him to regain full awareness. The prosecution's expert did not accept that analysis, but the recorder left the defence of automatism as an issue properly open for the jury's consideration.

The Court of Appeal stated that the defence of automatism required that there **1.119** was a total destruction of voluntary control on the defendant's part. Impaired or reduced control was not enough. As the expert witness had accepted, someone driving without awareness within his description retained some control. He would be able to steer the vehicle and usually to react and return to full awareness when confronted by significant stimuli. The recorder ought not therefore to have left the issue of automatism to the jury.

Where a person commits an offence under the influence of epilepsy the strict jury verdict should be "not guilty by reason of insanity" (*R. v Sullivan* [1983] 3 W.L.R. 123 HL). Cases concerning epilepsy must be treated accordingly if tried on indictment.

In *R. v Bailey* [1983] 2 All E.R. 503, the Court of Appeal decided that diabetes **1.120** (unlike intoxication from alcohol or drugs) could provide a defence not only to crimes of specific intent but also crimes of basic intent. The court added that the question was whether the Crown had proved the necessary element of recklessness. Similar principles would appear to apply to epilepsy cases. It is submitted that there can be no defence to a charge of reckless or careless driving if the defendant knew of the risks of epilepsy or knew that he was a diabetic and was aware of the risks of too much or too little insulin.

For a decision on the effect of a hypoglycaemic attack on liability for driving whilst unfit through drugs, see *R. v Ealing Magistrates' Court Ex p. Woodman* [1994] R.T.R. 189 at § 4.107.

For a decision on the effect of the known likelihood of a hypoglycaemic attack **1.121** on a charge of dangerous driving, see *R. v Marison* [1997] R.T.R. 457. In a related issue, the Court of Appeal has considered whether driving ceases when a driver, conscious of the operation of his body, is nonetheless doing something completely different from what he believed he was doing: *Att Gen's Reference (No.4 of 2000)* [2001] EWCA Crim 780; [2001] R.T.R. 27. A driver of a bus with automatic transmission which caused a fatal accident was held to be driving where the most likely explanation was that he pressed the accelerator believing he was pressing the brake.

"ROAD"

Roads and highways generally

"Road" means any highway *and any other road to which the public has access* **1.122** and includes bridges over which a road passes (1988 Act s.192(1)). The definition in the Road Traffic Regulation Act 1984 s.142(1) is virtually the same for England and Wales save that it refers to "any length of highway or of any other road", etc. It is submitted that the use of the word "length" is unlikely to make any material difference. The Vehicle Excise and Registration Act 1994 affects vehicles on "public roads" (i.e. those roads repairable at the public expense).

"Road" has the same meaning under s.58(1) of the Goods Vehicles (Licensing of Operators) Act 1995 as in s.192(1) of the 1988 Act. The Road Traffic Act 1991 adopts, in s.82(1), the definition in s.142(1) of the 1984 Act. For the purposes of the EC provisions on drivers' hours, etc., the term "road" is not defined; but the regulations apply to journeys "made on roads open to the public" (see Regulation (EEC) 3821/85 art.2, as amended, and Regulation (EC) 561/2006 art.4(a)).

1.123   Generally it may be said to be a matter of fact and degree whether it is a "road" or "public place". The onus is on the prosecution to prove that a road is one within the Act (*Williams v Boyle* (1962) 106 S.J. 939), and also to prove that it is a "public place" (*Pugh v Knipe* [1972] R.T.R. 286). A decision where the Divisional Court held that there was "ample evidence" on which justices could conclude that a pavement was a "road" though part of the pavement was in public, and part in private, ownership was *Price v DPP* [1990] R.T.R. 413. The *Concise Oxford Dictionary* defines "road" as a line of communication for use of foot passengers and vehicles. In *Oxford v Austin* [1981] R.T.R. 416 a "road" was said to be a definable right of way for passage between two points.

Trafalgar Square is a road, the Divisional Court decided in *Sadiku v DPP* [2000] R.T.R. 155. The area of Trafalgar Square in question was in the south east corner near where items were sold from a vehicle in order to feed the pigeons. The court considered this to be a thoroughfare that vehicles used from time to time and which was a main route to and from railway and underground stations. Again the court emphasised that it is an issue of fact.

1.124   In *Randall v Motor Insurers' Bureau* [1969] 1 All E.R. 21 a vehicle was deemed on a road when it was partly on the road and partly on private land, and in *Holliday v Henry* [1974] R.T.R. 101 a vehicle was held to be "on" a road when, because a roller skate was interposed between each wheel and the surface of the road, it could not be said to be in actual physical contact with the road.

In relevant cases the test in *Hawkins v Phillips* [1980] R.T.R. 197 may assist. The decision did not relate to a road as such but to a "main carriageway". It was held that a slip or filter road was part of the main carriageway because any vehicle going on to the slip road was committed to proceeding on to the trunk road. This is clearly not sufficient to turn a purely private access drive into a road within the meaning of the 1984 and 1988 Acts. A lay-by was held part of a public road though not maintained by the highway authority as such (*McNeill v Dunbar* 1965 S.L.T.N. 79).

1.125   Normally, a right of way extends to the whole space between the fences, and a grass verge between the pavement and the fence was held to be part of a road in *Worth v Brooks* [1959] Crim. L.R. 855. In *Att Gen v Beynon* [1969] 2 All E.R. 263, it was held that the mere fact that a road ran between fences or hedges did not give rise by itself to a presumption. It was first necessary to decide whether the fences were put up by reference to the highway or for some other reason. If it appeared that the fences had been put up with reference to the highway, a rebuttable presumption of law arose that the highway extended to the whole space between the fences and was not confined to such part as had been made up.

A highway remains a highway though temporarily roped off (*McCrone v Rigby* (1952) 50 L.G.R. 115; see also *Norton v Hayward* (1968) 112 S.J. 767 at § 1.149). If a footpath or a bridleway can properly be described as a "highway" this is sufficient to bring the footpath or bridleway within the definition of "road" in s.192 of the 1988 Act (*Lang v Hindhaugh* [1986] R.T.R. 271). A cycle lane may, like a footway, be part of a road set aside for the purpose.

Section 48(1) of the New Roads and Street Works Act 1991 provides that for **1.126** the purposes of Pt III of the Act, which deals with street works in England and Wales, "street" is defined as:

"the whole or any part of any of the following, irrespective of whether it is a thoroughfare—

(a) any highway, road, lane, footway, alley or passage,

(b) any square or court,

(c) any land laid out as a way whether it is for the time being formed as a way or not."

The subsection also stipulates that where a street passes over a bridge or through a tunnel, references in that Part of the Act include that bridge or tunnel.

The definition of "street" in the Highways Act 1980 s.329(1) has the same meaning as in Pt III of the New Roads and Street Works Act 1991.

"Highway"

The term "highway" is narrower than "road" under the Road Traffic Acts. A **1.127** *full* highway or cartway provides the public with a right of way on foot, riding or accompanied by a beast of burden or with vehicles and cattle (*Suffolk County Council v Mason* [1979] 2 All E.R. 369 at 371 HL). The term "highway" therefore includes public footpaths, public bridleways, public driftways, public carriageways and public footways.

A "Bridleway"

A "bridleway" is a highway over which the public has the following but no **1.128** other rights of way:

(a) a right of way on foot;

(b) a right of way on horseback;

(c) a right of way leading a horse (including in the 1980 and 1981 Acts a pony, ass or mule);

(d) in some cases, a right to drive animals of any description along the way (a drove or driftway); and

(e) a right to ride a pedal cycle providing the cyclist gives way to pedestrians and to persons on horseback, providing also that there is no local authority order or byelaw to the contrary.

(Highways Act 1980 s.329; Wildlife and Countryside Act 1981 s.66(1); Road Traffic Regulation Act 1984 s.142(1); Road Traffic Act 1988 s.192(1).)

B "Carriageway"

A "carriageway" is a way constituting or comprised in a highway, being a way **1.129** (other than a cycle track) over which the public have a right of way for the passage of vehicles (Highways Act 1980 s.329).

C *"Dual carriageway"*

1.130   A dual carriageway is defined for the purpose of speed limits for certain classes of vehicles by the Road Traffic Regulation Act 1984 Sch.6 Pt IV, as a road part of which consists of a central reservation to separate the carriageways (see Sch. para.2). This definition suggests that the dual carriageway does not begin with the hatching markings but only by reference to the physical central reservation itself, because hatching markings are not completely reserved and can be crossed in certain circumstances (see § 6.52). Such dual carriageways may be highways or any other road including a private road to which the public has access. This definition should be contrasted with the definition of a carriageway in the Highways Act 1980 s.329 (see above), which is limited to part of a highway.

D *"Cycle track"*

1.131   A "cycle track" is a way over which the public has a right of way on pedal cycles other than pedal cycles which are motor vehicles under the 1988 Act with or without a right of way on foot (Highways Act 1980 s.329, as amended).

E *"Footpath"*

1.132   A "footpath" is a way over which the public has a right of way on foot only (Highways Act 1980 s.329; Wildlife and Countryside Act 1981 s.66(1); Road Traffic Regulation Act 1984 s.142; Road Traffic Act 1988 s.192). All but the 1984 and 1988 Acts make clear that footways are excluded.

F *"Footway"*

1.133   A "footway" is a way (usually a pavement) comprised in a highway (which also comprises a carriageway) with a public right of way on foot only (Highways Act 1980 s.329).

G *"Walkway"*

1.134   A "walkway" is a way through, over or under a building, created by agreement in accordance with s.35 of the Highways Act 1980 or its earlier equivalent (s.18 of the Highways Act 1971); it may be dedicated by the agreement as a footpath (Highways Act 1980 s.35).

H *"Public path"*

1.135   A "public path" is a highway being a footpath or a bridleway (Wildlife and Countryside Act 1981 s.66(1)).

I *"Byway open to all traffic"*

1.136   A "byway open to all traffic" is defined in the Wildlife and Countryside Act 1981 s.66(1), and for the purposes of s.127 of the Road Traffic Regulation Act 1984 (see below) as a highway over which the public have a right of way for vehicular and all other kinds of traffic, but which is used by the public mainly for the purpose for which footpaths and bridleways are so used. The expression was not previously defined in any of the Acts quoted above. There has been a progression in the terms used, from "cartway" in the earlier Traffic Signs Regulations and General Directions to "road used as a public path" and finally to "byway open to all traffic". These terms have all been attached to similar signs and seem to have similar meanings.

The 1984 Act has effect in relation to any footpath, bridleway or byway as if any reference in the Act to traffic included foot passengers and persons driving, riding or leading horses or other animals of draught or burden, and any reference in ss.2(3) and 14 to foot passengers included such persons also (s.127).

Determining the existence of a highway

A bridleway is a road for the purposes of the offences of dangerous, careless or drunken cycling and carrying two persons on a bicycle (Road Traffic Act 1988 ss.24, 28–30). Section 328 of the Highways Act 1980 includes bridges and tunnels over or through which a highway passes as part of the highway for the purposes of that Act unless the context otherwise requires.   **1.137**

There should be some evidence of permanent dedication of a highway to the public. The maxim is "once a highway, always a highway" and that would not apply to some of the ways held to be "roads". Where a private estate developer purported to convey parking rights on parts of roads on the estate, this was held by a magistrates' court to be an act which was inconsistent with an intention to dedicate those parts of the roads to the public.

Before determining whether a way has been dedicated as a highway, any court   **1.138**
must take into consideration any map, plan, local history or other document tendered in evidence, attaching such weight thereto as it thinks proper (Highways Act 1980 s.32). Such maps are not evidence of the boundaries of the highway (*Webb v Eastleigh Borough Council* (1957) 56 L.G.R. 124). Part III of the Wildlife and Countryside Act 1981 concerns the ascertainment of public rights of way. Under s.56 of the Act certain facts may be established conclusively by the definitive map and statement. Where a footpath is shown, it is conclusive evidence that it was at the relevant date a highway with footpath rights without prejudice to the question of any other rights. Where a bridleway or a road used as a public path is shown, this is conclusive evidence that it was at the relevant date a highway with rights of way on foot and on horseback and leading a horse, without prejudice to the question of any other rights such as a right to drive vehicles or other animals. Part II of the Countryside and Rights of Way Act 2000 converts a "road used as a public path" to a "restricted byway" (2000 Act s.47(2)) and the public have "restricted byway rights" (s.48(1)). Such rights give a right of way on foot, on horseback (or leading a horse) and for vehicles other than mechanically propelled vehicles. The Restricted Byways (Application and Consequential Amendment of Provisions) Regulations 2006 (SI 2006/1177) apply to a restricted byway various provisions in specified Acts and subordinate legislation that apply to a highway. If a "byway open to all traffic" is shown, that is conclusive evidence that it was at the relevant date a highway with a public right of way for vehicles and all other kinds of traffic. *"Relevant date"* means the date specified in the statement or order (s.56(2)). Section 53 of the 1981 Act provides for a duty to keep the definitive map and statement under continuous review.

The 1981 Act contains special provisions for roads used as public paths which must be redesignated. Under s.54 the surveying authority as soon as reasonably practicable is to carry out a review of the definitive map and statement as to roads used as public paths and to modify the map and statement as follows. Every road used as a public path is to be shown as a byway open to all traffic, or a bridleway, or a footpath (s.54(2)).

(1) If a public right of way for vehicular traffic has been shown to exist, it is to be shown as a byway open to all traffic.

(2) If head (1) does not apply and public bridleway rights have not been shown not to exist, it is to be shown as a bridleway (note the double negative).

(3) If neither head (1) nor head (2) exists it is to be shown as a footpath (s.54(3)).

1.139   There are also relevant provisions in the Natural Environment and Rural Communities Act 2006 including s.66, which restricts the creation of new public rights of way, and s.67, which brings to an end certain existing, but unrecorded, public rights of way. In addition, s.70 of the 2006 Act amends s.34 of the Road Traffic Act 1988 (which prohibits the driving of a mechanically propelled vehicle elsewhere than on a road) to allow for driving of vehicles on a road which, immediately before the commencement of s.47(2) of the Countryside and Rights of Way Act 2000, was shown in a definitive map and statement as a public path and used to obtain access to the land by the driving of such a vehicle by a person with an interest in the land (defined in new s.34(7) of the 1988 Act) or as a visitor to the land.

All three (i.e. byways, bridleways and footpaths) are from the operation of the modification order deemed to be highways maintainable at the public expense and each way which under the Countryside Act 1968 Sch.3 Pt III para.9 was so shown shall continue to be so maintainable.

1.140   The position and width, if specified, of a road used as a public path and any specified conditions or limitations affecting the public rights of way may be established by the definitive map and statement.

The absence of a footpath, road or bridleway from the definitive map does not mean that there is not a right of way. Again, as indicated in s.56, where limited rights such as a footpath are shown, further rights may be established. It is always possible for evidence to be called as to the existence of a right of way when it is material in the proceedings.

Under s.56(4) a certified copy of or of any part of a definitive map or statement is receivable in evidence and is deemed, unless the contrary is shown, to be such a copy.

Public access

1.141   The definition of "road" in s.192 of the 1988 Act and s.142(1) of the Road Traffic Regulation Act 1984 includes not only highways but roads other than highways "to which the public have access". The first question is whether it is a road, and the second whether the public have access (*Purves v Muir* 1948 J.C. 122; *Oxford v Austin* [1981] R.T.R. 416). A road is a definable way for passage between two points (ibid.). The majority of cases as to whether a road comes within this definition turn on the second question of whether the public have access to it.

Assuming that the way in question has the nature of a road (see "Car parks and forecourts, 'or other public place'" at § 1.148) a prosecutor will usually have to prove only two things: first, that the general public, and not merely a special class of the general public, has access to the road; and, secondly, that the public has access at least by the tolerance of the owner or proprietor of the road in question

(*Deacon v AT (A Minor)* [1976] R.T.R. 244). The test as to whether the public may be said to have access by the tolerance of the owner was said by Lord Sands in *Harrison v Hill* 1932 J.C. 13 at 17 to be as follows:

> "Any road may be regarded as a road to which the public have access upon which members of the public are to be found who have not obtained access either by overcoming a physical obstruction or in defiance of prohibition express or implied."

This dictum of Lord Sands has been approved and applied in *Houghton v Scholfield* [1973] R.T.R. 239, *Deacon v AT (A Minor)* [1976] R.T.R. 244, and *Cox v White* [1976] R.T.R. 248 *Note*. In *Cox v White* Lord Widgery C.J., at 251, stated: "I think that in ninety-nine cases out of a hundred that direction [i.e. that of Lord Sands] is all the justices need for current purposes". **1.142**

Applying the test of Lord Sands, it is generally a matter of fact and degree whether the public in general have access (*R. v Shaw* [1974] R.T.R. 225; *Blackmore v Chief Constable of Devon and Cornwall, The Times*, December 6, 1984).

The public generally must be shown to have access: it is not sufficient to show that only a restricted class of the public has access. Thus in *Deacon v AT* above the prosecution failed because the prosecutor had not shown that the general public used the road (a housing estate road; there was no proof that it was used by persons other than residents or only visitors to the estate). Lord Clyde, the Lord Justice-General, said in *Harrison v Hill*, as above, at 17: **1.143**

> "I think that, when the statute speaks of 'the public' in this connection, what is meant is the public generally, and not the special class of members of the public who have occasion for business or social purposes to go to the farmhouse or to any part of the farm itself; were it otherwise, the definition might just as well have included all private roads as well as all public highways."

In *Harrison v Hill* a road leading off the public road to a farmhouse was held to be a road to which the public had access. The road had no gate and was maintained by the farmer, who sometimes turned away people using it, but at other times it was used by people with no business at the farm at all.

The test in *Harrison v Hill* was again adopted in *Adams v Commissioner of Police* [1980] R.T.R. 289 at 297. The residents of a private estate sought a declaration that the private road, Aberdeen Park, London N5, was a road to which the public had access within the meaning of what is now s.192(1) of the 1988 Act. The purpose of the proceedings was to secure the enforcement of the road traffic laws. There was evidence of substantial use and the judge agreed with the plaintiffs, although he did not consider a declaration appropriate. It was emphasised (at 298) that signs must be considered as part of the whole picture. Jupp J. also pointed out (at 295) that it did not matter whether the public had access as pedestrians or drivers of motor vehicles as the Act was intended to protect all road users. He quoted *Harrison v Hill* and *R. v Shaw* in support of this principle. Further consideration was given to the definition of "public place" in *R. (on the application of Planton) v DPP* [2001] EWHC Admin 450; [2002] R.T.R. 9. Mr Planton was in his vehicle on a causeway leading to an island. The causeway was sometimes covered by tidal water but was usable for four to five hours twice a day. There was no physical barrier at the entrance to the approach road, but there were signs indicating that it was a private road. There was no evidence of any use of the causeway other than by residents of the island or those visiting as a guest or on business such as making postal deliveries. The Administrative Court found there was no evidence that the causeway was a public place for these purposes. **1.144**

In *DPP v Cargo Handling Ltd* [1992] R.T.R. 318, the Divisional Court was required to determine whether the roads at Heathrow Airport and in the ownership of the British Airports Authority were open to the public for the purpose of Regulation (EEC) 3820/85 (see now Regulation (EC) 561/2006) and thus whether tachograph regulations applied to those roads. The prosecutor's appeal against the acquittal of the respondents by justices was allowed. Leggatt L.J. in his judgment rejected both the respondents' arguments. First, it was submitted that "roads open to the public" meant roads maintainable and manageable at public expense. His Lordship found that as a matter of English the phrase meant roads to which the public had access. Public expense could not be introduced into the concept. Secondly, it was submitted that the public did not have access to the roads at Heathrow as access was limited to those who were going to the airport on business and it was prohibited to use the roads as a short cut. In rejecting that argument too, Leggatt L.J. said that although the roads were subject to various restrictions, thousands of people used them every day and there was evidence that they were open to sightseers. The fact that most visitors were there on business did not mean that they were not members of the public. It was a random selection of people and vehicles who might require business access to the airport. In no sense were the roads private—there were no barriers or obstructions to prevent access by visitors.

1.145   In Scotland, the private drive leading to a house has been held to be a road (*Davidson v Adair* 1934 J.C. 37), but this case will not be followed in England (*Knaggs v Elson* (1965) 109 S.J. 596) and it was doubted in *Hogg v Nicholson* 1968 S.L.T. 265 at 268. In *Harrison v Hill*, a road to a farmhouse from the public road was held to be a road. In *Hogg v Nicholson* a road marked "private road" on an estate served a few houses, but was also used by police cars, visitors and delivery vans. A sub-post office to which people on the estate and from a village a mile away had access as of right was on the road. It was held to be a road to which the public had access. "Private" notices are thus not conclusive. Where there were substantial businesses with premises and no restriction on the public in general coming to those businesses, that was sufficient to show that the public did have access; *Blackmore v Chief Constable of Devon and Cornwall, The Times*, December 6, 1984. *Harrison v Hill* was distinguished in *R. v Beaumont* [1964] Crim. L.R. 665, where an occupation road led to a farm, to a site for 200–250 caravans on that farm, and to a river where anglers went by leave of the farmer and which was also used by picnickers. At the entrance there was an ever-open gate, a 10mph speed limit sign and two "trespassers will be prosecuted" signs. It was held that there was no evidence that the general public used the road and the fact that a large number of persons in a particular class of people used it did not make it a road. In *Knaggs v Elson* above, a cul-de-sac led to 36 houses. There was no gate but there were notices reading "Private Property—No Parking". There was evidence that a motorist not living there had turned his car round there, but this was held to be insufficient to show that the cul-de-sac was a road used by the public in general. Again in *Kreft v Rawcliffe, The Times*, May 12, 1984, use by a police constable, tradesmen, postmen, visitors to a wholesaler's and (rarely) members of the public were not sufficient to make a lane a road. It was necessary to look at the actual access. If only a restricted class of the public is admitted, it is not a road; if only a restricted class is excluded, it will be a road (cf. *R. v Waters* (1963) 47 Cr. App. R. 149). In *Houghton v Scholfield* [1973]

R.T.R. 239 a justices' finding that a cul-de-sac behind some shops was part of a road was upheld because the public had been found there and there was no physical obstruction or prohibition express or implied.

In *Bugge v Taylor* (1940) 104 J.P. 467 a forecourt of an hotel was private property and the public had no access as of right but there was no obstruction of any kind separating the forecourt from High Street, Sutton, and members of the public had in fact used the forecourt not only to reach the hotel but also as a short cut from High Street to another street. On occasions vehicles had been along it. The forecourt was held to be a road. In *Baxter v Middlesex County Council* [1956] Crim. L.R. 561 a forecourt was held on the facts not to be part of the highway. In *R. v Shaw* above a lane on a council estate frequently used by pedestrians as a short cut between two public roads was held to be a road to which the public had access. The footway as well as the carriageway is included in the definition of "road" in the Road Traffic Act 1988 (*Bryant v Marx* (1932) 96 J.P. 383). But a place is not necessarily a road, even if it is not separated by a wall or rail from the highway, and the forecourt of a shop not separated from the street pavement but used only by the customers and not habitually used by the public was held not to be a road (*Thomas v Dando* [1951] 1 All E.R. 1010). Contrast *White v Cubitt* [1930] 1 K.B. 443 and the other cases discussed below as to the meaning of "public place".

1.146

A cul-de-sac can be a road (*Bass v Boynton* [1960] Crim. L.R. 497). Nor does it matter if the road is not made up (ibid.). In *Griffin v Squires* [1958] 3 All E.R. 468 on the facts a car park was held not to be a road. But a conviction was upheld where a jury, on a proper direction, had found a marketplace to be a road (*R. v Waterfield* (1964) 48 Cr. App. R. 42 is the only report on this point). In *Chapman v Parlby* (1964) 62 L.G.R. 150 a road led from the public highway to a government depot and had a solid white line halfway across it from about halfway along. It was held that the part between the highway and the white line was a road, there being no obstacle or prohibition, express or implied, to any member of the public until he reached the white line, and the road being available to the public.

A road in the docks, to which the general public does not have access, either by right or tolerance of the docks authority, is not a road under the Road Traffic Act 1988 (*Buchanan v Motor Insurers' Bureau* [1955] 1 All E.R. 607). A road inside a factory, which only passholders may enter through gates guarded by the police, is not a road to which the public has access (*O'Brien v Trafalgar Insurance Co* (1945) 109 J.P. 107). In *Harrison v Co-operative Insurance Co Ltd* (1968) 118 N.L.J. 910, a road inside factory premises was used by the public to gain access to a weighbridge and to avoid congested highways. A "private road" sign had been removed some time previously. It was held to be a road to which the public had access. A quayside where members of the public were free to walk or motor and where there was no notice or hindrance to stop them was held to be a road in *Newcastle Corporation v Walton* [1957] Crim. L.R. 479. In *Renwick v Scott* (1995) 1996 S.L.T. 1164 it was held that where public access was in practice tolerated on a road owned and occupied by a port authority, byelaws prohibiting unauthorised access and supporting notices did not prevent the dock road from being a "road" for the purposes of the legislation.

1.147

For access by the public to car parks, etc., see § 1.148.

Car parks, forecourts, "or other public place"

There must be a mode of communication which can be described in ordinary

1.148

speech as a road and the mere possibility of vehicular access is not enough: one must first find a road and then ask if it is a road to which the public has access (see §§ 1.141–47). In a case concerning a car park a "road" was described as a definable right of way for passage between two points (*Oxford v Austin* [1981] R.T.R. 416). In *Griffin v Squires* [1958] 3 All E.R. 468 a car park was held not to be a road: the fact that the public has access to it does not of itself make a place a road. Streatfield J. said that no one in the ordinary acceptance of the word "road" would think of a car park as a road.

The approach in *Griffin v Squires* was endorsed by the House of Lords in the joined appeals of *Cutter v Eagle Star Insurance Co Ltd, Clarke v Kato* [1998] 4 All E.R. 417 reversing the wider interpretation given by the Court of Appeal. Whilst it was a question of fact in every case, a road had the physical character of a defined or definable route or way, with ascertained or ascertainable edges, leading from one point to another with the function of serving as a means of access enabling travellers to move conveniently from one point to another along that route. The proper function of a car park was to enable stationary vehicles to stand and wait. Other legislation reinforced the distinction between a road and a car park. In the ordinary use of language, a car park was not a road; they had separate and distinct characters. Where legislation referred to "a road or other public place", the express addition of the words "or other public place" clearly indicates that, where the word "road" stands alone, it bears its ordinary meaning and does not extend to places such as car parks.

1.149   In the case of *Cutter*, the judgment of the House of Lords considered that the Court of Appeal had fallen into the trap of first identifying a road within a car park and then treating the parking bays as integral with the road. Even if the carriageway should be treated as a road, the bays must retain their own integrity. (For a contrasting decision, see *R. v Waterfield* at § 1.146 where a market place was held to be a road.) Following from the decision in *Cutter*, the Motor Vehicles (Compulsory Insurance) Regulations 2000 (SI 2000/726) amended the requirements for compulsory third party insurance so that the cover must extend to the use of the vehicle in public places other than roads.

A courtyard leading off a highway to serve private premises was held not to be a road (*Henderson v Bernard* 1955 S.L.T. (Sh.Ct.) 27), and in *Heath v Pearson* [1957] Crim. L.R. 195 a yard serving several houses was held on the facts not to be a road. A drive-in theatre can be a highway "open to or used by the public" (*Dobell v Petrac* [1961] V.R. 70 (Aus)). A cul-de-sac may be a road (*Bass v Boynton* [1960] Crim. L.R. 497). A justices' finding that a cul-de-sac behind some shops adjoining a road leading to a multi-storey car park was part of a road was upheld in *Houghton v Scholfield* [1973] R.T.R. 239. See also *Bugge v Taylor*, *Thomas v Dando* and *Baxter v Middlesex County Council* (all § 1.146 above) as to forecourts and *Newcastle Corporation v Walton* [1957] Crim. L.R. 479 as to a quayside. The fact that an area is private land does not prevent it from being part of a road (*Norton v Hayward* (1968) 112 S.J. 767).

1.150   A car park attached to a public house may be regarded as a "public place" (see the 1988 Act ss.4 and 5) during general licensing hours, but it may well no longer be a public place outside those hours. In *Sandy v Martin* [1974] Crim. L.R. 258, justices were held to be entitled to acquit after the prosecution had failed to prove that the invitation to the public to use the car park extended one hour after closing time. Unless the point is conceded, the prosecution is put to strict proof that the venue in question is a "public place" for the purposes of the legislation.

In *Elkins v Cartlidge* [1947] 1 All E.R. 829 there was at the side of an inn a well-defined parking ground from which an open gateway gave access to an enclosure. Cars went into this enclosure and parked there. The enclosure was held to be a public place, as being a place to which the public had access in fact; but a car park attached to a club can only be regarded as public if there is evidence of public use of the car park; a public house offers its services to the public but a private club does not (*Pugh v Knipe* [1972] R.T.R. 286, distinguishing *Elkins v Cartlidge* above).

A vacant piece of land used as an overflow car parking ground was held to be a **1.151** public place in *Macdonald v McEwen* 1953 S.L.T. (Sh.Ct.) 26. In *White v Cubitt* [1930] 1 K.B. 443, a case under another statute, a piece of private ground adjoining an inn and separated from the highway only by a level row of stone setts was held to be a public place. The public did not have access to this ground save to enter the inn and it was not a car park.

In *Brewer v DPP* [2004] EWHC 355; [2005] R.T.R. 5, the area concerned was a railway station car park. The allegation was restricted to driving on a "road"; the phrase "or other public place" was not included though it could have been. In addition to the usual use of a car park, this particular one provided an access route to a private staff car park. Justices held that this fell within the definition of a "road" finding that, although its prime function was the parking of cars, it was not its sole function since it was used by both pedestrians and motorists as a through road. Referring to the considerations set out in *Cutter v Eagle Star Insurance Co Ltd*, the Administrative Court allowed the appeal; that use was insufficient to make this car park capable of being a road. The clear moral for prosecutors is to ensure proper drafting of allegations to include the wider category wherever possible.

Magistrates may make use of their general local knowledge in deciding whether a car park is a public place under the 1988 Act s.4 or s.5 (*Clift v Long* [1961] Crim. L.R. 121). But knowledge of one magistrate only need not be accepted by the other magistrates, for the prosecution must prove that the place was a public place at the time of the offence: evidence that it is normally public may not suffice where it is not clear that at the time it was (*Williams v Boyle* (1962) 106 S.J. 939).

The use by magistrates of their general local knowledge was considered by the **1.152** Divisional Court in *Bowman v DPP* [1991] R.T.R. 263. In that case, the magistrates did not accept the defence submission that a National Car Park was not a public place in the early hours of the morning. Although the court dismissed the appeal by the defendant against his conviction, it nonetheless advised that it was always wise for a court to make known to the prosecution and the defence that it was relying on local knowledge, so that legal representatives were given the opportunity of commenting on the knowledge which the magistrates claimed to have had and claimed to use.

A private field to which the public were temporarily invited to watch racing was held to be a public place under the former s.5, although it could be closed at any time and particular persons could be refused admission (*R. v Collinson* (1931) 23 Cr. App. R. 49). In *Montgomery v Loney* [1959] N.I. 171, where a Northern Ireland statutory definition of "road" was considered, it was held that the forecourt of a petrol filling station, with carriageways with unobstructed entrances to, and exits from, the highway, was a "road or other public place". It was said that although the forecourt was open only to those members of the public who wished to do business with the station owner, they were enough to show that the public had access. It was also said that an offence charged as being, "in a road or other public place" was not bad for duplicity.

1.153   In *DPP v Vivier* [1991] 4 All E.R. 18 the prosecution appealed against the acquittal of the respondent for drink/driving in a public place, namely a caravan park. The issue was whether the caravan park was a public place. The justices found that the owners of the privately owned site had taken steps to limit entry, although it was open to a special class of the public. The fact that the special class was large did not make it a public place. On appeal the Divisional Court held that the appeal should be allowed and the case remitted to the justices with a direction to convict. The issue of whether a place was public or private was largely a matter of fact or degree, but the question of whether the justices were entitled to conclude as they had was one of law. After reviewing the authorities, the court found that there was no sufficient segregation or selection of the caravanners or campers passing through the control system at the camp to convert them from members of the general public to a special class. A mere fondness for camping did not have that effect. It was unreal to suggest that some transformation occurred at the gate whereby they altered their legal character, shed their identity as members of the public, and assumed a different status as campers and caravanners.

In *Capell v DPP* (1991) 155 J.P. 361, the appellant was observed by the police getting into his car and the justices found that he was in charge of the car whilst unfit. The car was parked in an "off the road parking bay" adjacent to or forming part of Rickman Drive in the centre of Birmingham. Rickman Drive was itself a public highway, although within a private residential estate. The parking bay joined on to Rickman Drive but was set back from it. There was no physical barrier or impediment between the road and the bay. It was held that the parking bay was a public place at the material time: there was nothing to distinguish the highway from the parking bay in a material respect and nothing to displace the prima facie inference that the bay formed part of the land in public use.

In *R. (on the application of Dunmill) v DPP* [2004] EWHC 1700, a motor car collided with a caravan on a caravan park and the driver was found to have exceeded the prescribed limit. The driver was charged solely with driving on a road; the phrase "or other public place" was not included. The justices found the area to be a road, but the Administrative Court disagreed. The justices had relied on the decision in *DPP v Vivier* above, but, as the Administrative Court made clear, that case was examining the issue of whether a caravan site was a "public place" and could not be applied to the issue of whether part of such a site was a "road". This case emphasises again the need to ensure proper drafting of allegations to include the wider category wherever possible.

1.154   In *DPP v Coulman* [1993] R.T.R. 230, the Divisional Court was required to look at the status of a lane leading from the berth of a cross-Channel ferry through the immigration and docking terminal. Access to it was excluded to all but passengers and certified passholders. Was it a road for the purposes of the Road Traffic Offenders Act 1988? Applying *DPP v Vivier*, Mann L.J. in giving the judgment of the court, stated that it was necessary to inquire whether those having access were there for personal reasons or through characteristics personal to themselves which were not available to the general public. If not, it was a place to which the public had access. His Lordship had no difficulty in finding that the lane was a place to which the public had access. He said that the only reason for being there was for the purpose of disembarkation and that was not capable of conferring on those entering a characteristic or reason for being distinguished from being merely members of the public.

The decisions in *DPP v Vivier* and *DPP v Coulman* above were considered and applied by the Divisional Court in *DPP v Neville* (1996) 160 J.P. 758. The respondent was driving an electric buggy on the "airside" at one of the terminals at Heathrow Airport. He allegedly drove too fast, did not keep a proper look-out and knocked over a child. He was prosecuted for driving without reasonable consideration, but was acquitted, the justices not being satisfied that the place at which the incident had occurred was a "public place" for the purposes of the Road Traffic Acts. The Divisional Court allowed the prosecutor's appeal. Whether or not a place was a "public place" must be settled once and for all. Once it had been decided that it was a public place, by reference to the possibility of a segment of the public gaining access, then it remained a public place, notwithstanding that another segment of the public did not have access. It was held that it was not open to the justices to find that the relevant part of the terminal was not a public place for the purposes of the legislation.

An example of a case where a court also applied the decision in *DPP v Vivier* **1.155** but came to the wrong conclusion on its findings is *Havell v DPP* [1993] Crim. L.R. 621. The appellant was prosecuted for the offence of being in charge of a motor vehicle whilst unfit. The only issue was whether the offence occurred "on a road or other public place". The justices found that he had been in his car, which was parked in the car park of a community centre. The car park was readily accessible from the road and there was no physical obstruction preventing access to it by any member of the public. There were no signs saying—as was the case—that it was private or that there was restricted access. To use the centre's facilities, an individual had first to become a member which required nomination by an existing member. The justices found that the appellant's membership did not give him a special characteristic whereby he lost his identity as a member of the general public. No finding was made, however, as to whether anyone other than a club member was using or ever did use the car park, nor as to the size of the club or whether anyone in the locality was entitled to become a member of it.

The Divisional Court quashed the conviction, and stated that the only conclusion properly to be drawn was that the appellant used the car park as a member of a bona fide club and there was nothing to suggest that the club was of such a size that it was indistinguishable from the public at large in the locality. If someone was a member of a bona fide club and in exercise of that membership used the club's car park, it seemed to the court that he was not using the car park as a member of the general public but was within a category separate to and different from the general public.

It is submitted that the decision in *Havell* follows precisely the tests laid down **1.156** in *DPP v Vivier*, and that on the findings made by the justices—incomplete though they may have been on certain issues—there could have been no conclusion other than that it had not been proved that the appellant's conduct occurred "on a road or other public place".

In *DPP v Greenwood* [1997] C.O.D. 278, justices convicted the appellant of an offence of careless driving. She appealed to the Crown Court asserting that the incident had occurred in a hospital car park and that the car park was not a public place. The Crown Court concluded that it was not a public place, that it was private land and therefore the hospital could expel anyone for trespass if they were making a nuisance of themselves. The prosecutor appealed to the Divisional Court which reviewed a number of authorities including *DPP v Vivier* and *DPP v Coulman* above. It was argued that there was no other reason why anyone would wish to park in the car park other than to visit the hospital and therefore persons visiting the hospital and parking there had a special characteristic which distinguished them from ordinary members of the public. The argument was rejected. The court stated that there appeared to be no special or particular reason which would cause people to visit the car park which distinguished them from ordinary members of the public. The car park would be visited for a variety of reasons, but none would distinguish the users in this way. The Crown Court had been wrong to conclude that the car park was not a public place.

1.157 The vexed issue of whether a car park is a place to which the public have access was again considered, this time by the Court of Appeal, in *R. v Spence* [1999] R.T.R. 353. Mr Spence was convicted by the Crown Court of dangerous driving in a small car park, which consisted of a yard outside a small office building, flanked on three sides by a wall, a hedge and a fence. The fourth side had bollards that prevented access from the road and entrance was through a swing gate which was open by day and closed at night. The car park was used by employees, customers and other business visitors. It led to nowhere other than the door of the office building. There was no evidence of use by members of the public generally just the special class of those with business on the premises. The view of the court (following *DPP v Vivier*) was that, in the absence of evidence of use by the public generally, there was no case to go to the jury. The issue was not whether the public could have access but whether in fact they utilised that access.

Channel tunnel, airfield and Crown roads

1.158 Special legislative provision was made to deal with the opening of the Channel Tunnel. The Channel Tunnel (Application of Road Traffic Enactments) Order 1994 (SI 1994/970), amended by the like-named No.2 Order (SI 1994/1667), provides that road traffic enactments apply to any length of road in the tunnel system to which the public does *not* have access as they apply to a road to which the public have access. This is subject to any exceptions made by the order—see art.5 of the principal order. Article 4 of that order confers powers of local authorities under the Road Traffic Regulation Act 1984 (and under subordinate legislation made under that Act) on the tunnel concessionaires. The principal order came into effect on April 5, 1994 and the No.2 Order on July 22, 1994. The empowering statute, to which reference should be made as to the general status of the tunnel is the Channel Tunnel Act 1987, see particularly s.23(1), (2) and (7).

Section 78(8) of the 1988 Act, which relates to the weighing of motor vehicles (see § 1.68), defines a road for the purpose of that section as including any land forming part of a harbour or adjacent to a harbour and occupied wholly or partly for the purpose of harbour operations.

1.159 The Airports Act 1986 s.65 applies the enactments relating to road traffic, including the lighting and parking of vehicles, and statutory instruments made thereunder, to roads within airports designated for the purpose of s.65 subject to any modifications made by order of the Secretary of State in respect of a particular airport road. Any road or place within an airport in the Metropolitan Police

District is deemed to be a street or place under s.35 of the London Hackney Carriage Act 1831. Section 35 of the London Hackney Carriage Act 1831 provides inter alia that every hackney carriage found standing in any "street or place", and having any of the numbered plates required by that Act to be fixed to hackney carriages, is (unless actually hired) deemed to be plying for hire, even though the hackney carriage is not on any standing or place usually appropriated for the purpose of hackney carriages standing or plying for hire.

A Crown road is defined in s.131 of the Road Traffic Regulation Act 1984 as a "road, other than a highway, to which the public has access by permission granted by the appropriate Crown authority, or otherwise granted by or on behalf of the Crown". Generally, therefore, a Crown road would come within the definition of "road" within the meaning of the Road Traffic Act 1988 s.192, and the Road Traffic Regulation Act 1984 s.142(1). Section 149(1) of the Transport Act 1968 enables the road traffic enactments to be applied by order to Crown roads. The purpose of the section is to enable provisions to be applied to particular Crown roads which, because they might affect the status of the Crown road, could not otherwise be made. It is, therefore, submitted that statutory provisions which apply on roads generally and relate to vehicles and persons and which do not affect the interests of the Crown adversely will apply on Crown roads as they do elsewhere. Thus, a member of the public charged, e.g. with dangerous or careless driving or a drink/driving offence cannot escape liability because the offence took place on a Crown road. This view is strengthened by the judgment in *Kellett v Daisy* [1977] R.T.R. 396, where it was held that the prosecution do not have to prove that the Act creating the offence (s.3 of the 1988 Act) of careless driving which occurred on a Crown road applies to Crown roads. The question is not whether the road was bound by the Act, but whether the defendant was bound by the Act (which he was) (ibid.). It would be different if a question arose regarding whether the Act had affected the Crown or a Crown servant (ibid.). It would therefore appear that once the Crown road comes within the definition of "road" contained in s.192 (above) any member of the public may be prosecuted.

Specified enactments are expressly applied to Crown roads in the royal parks   **1.160**
(as defined), subject to the specified exceptions, adaptations and modifications by the Crown Roads (Royal Parks) (Application of Road Traffic Enactments) Order 1987 (SI 1987/363) art.4 and Schedule. The "royal parks" are defined by art.3(1) of the 1987 Order as all parks, gardens, recreation grounds, open spaces and other land to which the Parks Regulation Act 1872 applies (including all roads deemed by the Crown Estate Act 1961 s.7(5), to be under the management of the Secretary of State). The 1987 Order also applies ss.104–106 of the Road Traffic Regulations Act 1984 to the Crown roads in Hyde Park, Kensington Gardens, Regent's Park, St James's Park and Green Park, as they apply to other roads to which the public has access (art.5).

A statute will necessarily bind the Crown if it is apparent that the Act would be wholly frustrated unless the Crown were bound (*Province of Bombay v Bombay Corporation* [1947] A.C. 58 at 63). As to the application of road traffic legislation to vehicles and persons in the service of the Crown, see § 2.34.

"TO CAUSE", "TO PERMIT", "TO USE"

Meaning

"One may obtain some help from cases in which the construction of similar   **1.161** words in other statutes has had to be considered, but particular care must be taken" (per Edmund Davies L.J. in *Sopp v Long* [1970] 1 Q.B. 518 at 524). The truth of this dictum is particularly apparent when one has to consider the meaning of the phrases "to cause", "to permit" and "to use". Not only has one to construe words in the context of the statute in which they appear but one may have to consider the mischief which the statutory provision is aimed at preventing.

It will be seen that where the statutory provisions create offences by reason of the words "using", "causing" or "permitting to be used" appearing in juxtaposition, as in s.42(b) of the 1988 Act (contravention of the Road Vehicles (Construction and Use) Regulations 1986 (SI 1986/1078) and the Road Vehicles Lighting Regulations 1989 (SI 1989/1796)) and ss.47 (test certificates) and 143 (third party insurance) of the same Act, the words are construed differently where all three phrases do not appear together, e.g. "uses or keeps" in s.29 of the Vehicle Excise and Registration Act 1994, and "causes to be kept" in s.98 of the Transport Act 1968 (drivers' records). Where these three phrases are used in juxtaposition, "to cause" or "to permit" generally requires the prosecution to prove mens rea, while the words "to use" will create an offence of absolute liability. Both the employer and the employee-driver may be convicted of "using" the contravening vehicle if it is used on the employer's business. Where the prosecution is in doubt as to whether a corporate defendant should be charged with "causing" or "permitting" on the one hand or "using" on the other, it should lay charges in the alternative (*Ross Hillman Ltd v Bond* [1974] R.T.R. 279 at 285 and 290). Similarly, as to Scotland see *Smith of Maddiston Ltd v Macnab* 1975 S.L.T. 86 (§ 1.170). In *Ferrymasters Ltd v Adams* [1980] R.T.R. 139 (see § 1.172) the report states the defendant was charged with "causing or permitting" contrary to s.84(2) of the 1972 Act (now s.87(2) of the 1988 Act). The report is erroneous and in fact the defendant company were charged with "permitting" only.

"To cause"

1.162 The offence of "causing" unlawful use requires proof of mens rea in knowledge of the facts rendering the user unlawful: in the case of a limited company such knowledge has to be of someone exercising a directing mind over the company's affairs (*James & Son Ltd v Smee* [1955] 1 Q.B. 78; *Ross Hillman Ltd v Bond* [1974] R.T.R. 279).

In *Ross Hillman Ltd v Bond*, the defendant company was summoned for "causing" one of its vehicles to be used on a road with excess rear axle weight contrary to the former s.40(5)(b) of the 1972 Act. Those responsible for the direction of the company's affairs did not know of the overloading of the vehicle. Following *James & Son Ltd v Smee* above it was held that where the statute makes it an offence to "cause" or "permit" a contravening vehicle to be used on a road as well as the offence of actually "using" the vehicle, the words "cause" or "permit" require proof of mens rea on the part of the defendant and in the case of a corporate defendant, following *Hill & Sons (Botley & Denmead) Ltd v Hampshire Chief Constable* [1972] R.T.R. 29, such guilty knowledge must be knowledge of someone exercising a directing mind over the company's affairs. It was pointed out in *Ross Hillman* that *F. Austin (Leyton) Ltd v East* [1961] Crim. L.R. 119 should not be cited as authority that a company can be convicted of unlawfully causing a motor vehicle to be used in a dangerous condition without proof of mens rea as the point in issue was never argued in that case.

"To cause" involves some express or positive mandate from the person "causing" to the other person, or some authority from the former to the latter, arising in the circumstances of the case (*McLeod v Buchanan* [1940] 2 All E.R. 179 at 187). The general manager of five depots, at each of which there is a vehicle superintendent, is not guilty of causing a vehicle to be on a road in a dangerous condition where he has no knowledge that it is on the road (*Rushton v Martin* [1952] W.N. 258). In *Shave v Rosner* [1954] 2 All E.R. 280 a van was left in a garage for repairs but the garage staff negligently failed to tighten hub nuts on a wheel. The owner of the van then drove the van on the road with the wheel in this defective condition. It was held that the garage proprietor was not guilty of causing the van to be used in a defective condition, as the term "cause" involves some degree of control and direction. Once he had delivered the van to its owner, he ceased to have control and dominion over it and had done nothing which was the active cause of that owner driving it on the road. The owner of a vehicle causes it to be used when he drives it himself as well as when it is driven by another person on his orders (*Baker v Chapman* (1963) 61 L.G.R. 527). Towing a motor vehicle is causing it to be used (*Milstead v Sexton* [1964] Crim. L.R. 474). Where, to the knowledge of a company's transport manager, one of a company's drivers seldom completed the requisite records of hours, the company was not guilty of "causing" the offence under s.97 of the Transport Act 1968 in that the commission of an offence was not the inevitable consequence of sending the driver out (*Redhead Freight Ltd v Shulman* [1988] Crim. L.R. 696). In that case, the proper charge against the company would have been that of "permitting" the commission of the offence.

Where, however, the statute makes it an offence only to "cause or permit" the contravention, without the use of the word "use", an offence of absolute liability without proof of mens rea may be created. Reference was made in *Mounsey v Campbell* [1983] R.T.R. 36 to two river pollution cases on the meaning of causing (*Price v Cromack* [1975] 2 All E.R. 113 and a House of Lords case, *Alphacell Ltd v Woodward* [1972] 2 All E.R. 475). Even where "causing" does not import mens rea it was held in *Price v Cromack* that it requires some positive act and not merely a passive looking on.

In another pollution case, *F.J.H. Wrothwell Ltd v Yorkshire Water Authority* [1984] Crim. L.R. 43, the Divisional Court emphasised that "cause" was to be given its ordinary common-sense meaning. The director of the defendant company was held to have caused the pollution in the stream when he deliberately poured the toxic material into drains even though he believed that the drains would carry the material to the public sewerage works and not to the stream. The case again shows that although a positive act is required, mens rea may not be necessary.

In *Mounsey v Campbell* the defendant parked his van right up against the bumper of a car. The car could have been moved at that time but it was subsequently penned in by a car parked 2ft behind. The defendant refused to move his van and was convicted of causing unnecessary obstruction. He argued that he should have been charged with "permitting" as he had not caused the unnecessary obstruction originally. It was held that he had been rightly convicted. On the facts the van caused an obstruction from the moment it was first parked. There was a positive act by the defendant. Ormrod J. said at 41 "His subsequent refusals to move it could just as well be described as causing an unnecessary obstruction because he could have removed it. It does not seem to me to be properly described, in those circumstances, as 'permitted'."

1.165   Where the statute requires an employer or other person "to cause" something to be done, it may be also held that an absolute offence without proof of mens rea is created. An employer whose driver keeps incorrect records is guilty of failing to cause correct records to be kept, though he had no chance of correcting the entries (*Cox v Sidery* (1935) 24 Traff.Cas. 69). An employer whose driver enters his records in advance is guilty of failing to cause current records to be kept (*Nelson v Coventry Swaging Co* (1936) 25 Traff.Cas. 68). These cases are now modified by s.98(4) of the Transport Act 1968, which allows a defence to an employer charged with failing to cause records to be kept where he can prove he gave proper instructions to the driver and took reasonable steps to secure his instructions were carried out. Section 87(2) of the 1988 Act makes it an offence "to cause or permit" an unlicensed driver to drive (see *Ferrymasters Ltd v Adams* [1980] R.T.R. 139, at § 1.172).

Where the owner of a vehicle is not the employer of the driver, e.g. where the owner hires out a defective vehicle, the owner cannot be said to be "using" the vehicle. In such a case, however, the owner may be charged with "causing" or "permitting" and may be convicted on proof of mens rea (see *Crawford v Haughton* [1972] 1 All E.R. 535, at § 1.186). Similarly, where a vehicle is owned by a partnership, a partner who is not the driver cannot be convicted of using (see *Garrett v Hooper* [1973] R.T.R. 1, at § 1.179), but on proof of mens rea he may be convicted, it is submitted, of "causing" or "permitting" the unlawful use. If uncertain as to whether to charge "causing" or "permitting" on the one hand or "using" on the other, prosecutors should prefer alternative charges (*Ross Hillman Ltd v Bond* [1974] R.T.R. 279). This advice was repeated in *R. v Newcastle JJ. Ex p. Bryce* [1976] R.T.R. 325.

"To permit"

Meaning

1.166   "To permit" is a vaguer term than "to cause". It may denote an express permission, general or particular, as distinguished from a mandate. The other person is not told to use the vehicle in a particular way, but he is told that he may do so if he desires. The word also includes cases in which permission is merely inferred. If the other person is given the control of the vehicle, permission may be inferred if the vehicle is left at the other person's disposal in such circumstances as to carry with it a reasonable implication of a discretion or liberty to use the vehicle in the manner in which it was used (*McLeod v Buchanan* [1940] 2 All E.R. 179 at 187). The statement of *Goodbarne v Buck* [1940] 1 All E.R. 613 at 616, that the only person who can permit the use of a car, in that he can forbid another person to use it, is the owner, is incorrect; any person who has control on the owner's behalf, e.g. a chauffeur or a manager of a company, can permit its use (*Lloyd v Singleton* [1953] 1 All E.R. 291; *Morris v Williams* (1952) 50 L.G.R. 308). Permission is not necessarily revoked by the grantor's death (*Kelly v Cornhill Insurance Co* [1964] 1 All E.R. 321 HL).

"Permitting" means getting someone else to do something and it is wrong to charge a man with permitting himself to do something (*Waddell v Winter* (1967) 202 E.G. 1225, a planning case; *Keene v Muncaster* [1980] R.T.R. 377). In *Keene*

v Muncaster Lord Lane C.J. said that the ordinary use of the word "permit" in what is now reg.101 of the Road Vehicles (Construction and Use) Regulations 1986 plainly envisages that the person requesting permission should request it from another and that a policeman could not therefore give himself permission. A person cannot be said to have permitted a vehicle to be used subject to an express prior condition unless and until that condition is complied with: permission given subject to such a condition which is unfulfilled is no permission (*Newbury v Davis* [1974] R.T.R. 367).

The following propositions as to what constitutes "permitting" are submitted: **1.167**

(1) The context of the statutory provisions requires examination together with the mischief at which the prohibition is aimed. This may result in stricter liability under some statutory provisions than others, e.g. for insurance offences.

(2) A distinction should normally be drawn between knowledge of the use of the vehicle and knowledge of the unlawfulness of its use. Knowledge of the former kind is an essential ingredient of permitting, knowledge of the latter kind may or may not be an essential ingredient.

(3) Normally such knowledge of the unlawfulness of the vehicle's use is required to be proved. "Permitting to be used" in contradistinction to "using" imports mens rea. *Aliter* in the case of insurance offences, where knowledge that the vehicle's use was uninsured does not have to be proved.

(4) Where mens rea is an essential element of the offence of permitting, a limited company can only be convicted if the mens rea can be imputed to the "brains" rather than "hands" of the company.

(5) Mens rea can consist not only of actual knowledge but also of constructive knowledge in the sense that the person concerned wilfully shuts his eyes to the obvious or deliberately refrains from making proper inquiry. Possibly, a failure on the part of an employee can be "permitting" on the part of the employer if it can be shown that the employer left duties to the employee without adequate supervision and in the knowledge that the employee would be employed on work for which he was unskilled.

(6) A prosecutor who is uncertain of being able to prove mens rea may prefer alternative charges of "causing" or "permitting" or "using" (*Ross Hillman Ltd v Bond* [1974] R.T.R. 279, at § 1.162, *R. v Newcastle JJ. Ex p. Bryce* [1976] R.T.R. 325). A summons for "permitting" may be amended to a charge of "using" even though the six-month period for the laying of an information imposed by s.127 of the Magistrates' Courts Act 1980 has expired (see *R. v Newcastle JJ. Ex p. Bryce* above; see also § 2.82). "Using" does not, generally, require proof of mens rea (see § 1.176 and *Green v Burnett* [1955] 1 Q.B. 78 and *Ross Hillman Ltd v Bond* above), but only the employer or employee-driver can be convicted and the former may be appropriate for owners who are not the driver's employers (see *Carmichael & Sons Ltd v Cottle* [1971] R.T.R. 11 and *Crawford v Haughton* [1972] 1 All E.R. 535, at § 1.186).

Cases

A leading case on "permitting" is *James & Son Ltd v Smee* [1954] 3 All E.R.   **1.168**

273. A vehicle belonging to a company had been sent on the road by the company in good condition but, while away from the control of any of the responsible officers of the company, the brakes became defective through the negligence of the vehicle's crew (also company employees) in coupling up the trailer. It was held that the company was not guilty of "permitting" the use of the vehicle with defective brakes contrary to the Construction and Use Regulations, as there was no evidence of any permission *by a responsible officer*, and that the position would be the same whether the owner was a company or an individual. It must be proved that some person for whose criminal act the owner is responsible permitted it, said the court; but this statement, it seems, does not extend to every servant (cf. *John Henshall (Quarries) Ltd v Harvey* [1965] 1 All E.R. 725, where a company was held not guilty of aiding and abetting where the illegal action had been done by a minor servant). Knowledge to constitute permitting can include shutting one's eyes (semble, in the case of a company, the eyes of responsible officers) to the obvious or allowing a servant to do something in circumstances where a contravention is likely, not caring whether it takes place or not (*James v Smee* above, at 278). *Goldsmith v Deaken* (1933) 98 J.P. 4, *Prosser v Richings* (1936) 100 J.P. 390 and *Churchill v Norris* (1938) 158 L.T. 255 were all cited in support of the latter view. In *Grays Haulage Co Ltd v Arnold* [1966] 1 All E.R. 896, it was said that the essence of permitting the commission of an offence is knowledge and, where there was no question of actual knowledge in the defendants, knowledge could not be imputed to them in the absence of prima facie evidence from which it could be said that they had shut their eyes to the obvious or had allowed something to go on not caring whether an offence was committed or not. Even where there has been recklessness in a member of the staff in allowing a vehicle to go on the road in a defective condition, the employing company may not be liable even though it has handed over responsibility to that person: the company is not criminally liable in the absence of knowledge of the facts constituting the offence for the failure of an employee to whom it has delegated a task. The servant is not "the brains of the company" and his knowledge cannot be imputed to a director (*Magna Plant Ltd v Mitchell* (1966) 110 S.J. 349).

The latter case together with *James v Smee* and *Grays Haulage Co Ltd v Arnold* (both above) were all considered in *Hill & Sons (Botley & Denmead) Ltd v Hampshire Chief Constable* [1972] R.T.R. 29. The defendant company was convicted of permitting one of its haulage vehicles to be used with inefficient brakes. Quarter sessions upheld the conviction on the grounds that the managing director was reckless in not ensuring that the vehicle was lubricated more frequently than once every four weeks and also in not ensuring that the four-weekly lubrications were properly carried out. The company's conviction was set aside on the grounds that there was nothing to justify quarter sessions' finding that a four-week interval for lubrication was reckless, nor was it reckless (although it might be negligent) for the managing director not to check up on the foreman fitter, a man of long experience, who was responsible for overseeing the lubrication. Lord Widgery C.J. expressly affirmed *Magna Plant Ltd v Mitchell* (1966) 110 S.J. 349 in that it requires one to look at the minds of those officers of the company who can be described as its "brains" rather than "hands" and that if an employee of the company is shown to be reckless it is not sufficient to impute knowledge of that recklessness unless that person is one who can be fairly described as the "brains" of the company.

It seems that, to make a company liable for permitting, a member of the direct-   **1.169**
ing staff should generally know what is happening, but it is submitted that a
company may still be liable for permitting if it has delegated, through its directors, duties relating to vehicle maintenance, etc., to a subordinate employee,
whom it knows to be unskilled and uninstructed in those duties, e.g. allowing a
junior typist to say if a lorry should go on the road. In such a case could it not be
said that "the brains" of the company were reckless in so doing?

In *Dixon Bool Transport Ltd v Forsyth* [1967] Crim. L.R. 52, a conviction for
permitting was upheld where the company knew that its drivers had been breaking the law by driving for excessive periods and had not taken steps to remedy
this or to acquaint them with the law. *Browning v Watson* [1953] 2 All E.R. 775
is distinguishable. There a company was guilty of permitting a breach of the law
on a motor-coach in the charge of a driver because the company failed to take adequate precautions by instructing its staff by other means to see that the law was
not broken. The decision in *Hutchings v Giles* [1955] Crim. L.R. 784 is not correctly reported. The prosecution need not prove actual knowledge and it may suffice if constructive knowledge is shown, e.g. shutting one's eyes to the obvious
(*Wilson v Bird* (1962) 106 S.J. 880, where there was evidence of actual
knowledge). Knowledge is an essential element in permitting and knowledge is
not imputed by mere negligence but by something more, such as recklessly sending out a car not caring what would happen (*Fransman v Sexton* [1965] Crim.
L.R. 556). In that case the defendant owner had previously hired his car to a
mechanical engineer who told him, on returning it, that the brakes had been tested
and were operating efficiently. In fact they were not and it was held that in those
circumstances the owner was not negligent in failing to take the only steps which
would have revealed the defects.

Following *Ross Hillman Ltd v Bond* [1974] Q.B. 435, the Scottish High Court   **1.170**
of Justiciary held that knowledge was essential for a company to be convicted of
"causing" or "permitting" the use of a vehicle contrary to what is now s.42 of the
1988 Act (*Smith of Maddiston Ltd v Macnab* 1975 S.L.T. 86). Again, where
auctioneers had sold a car and, unknown to them, their employees had given a
bogus cover note to the buyer, who then drove the car uninsured, the auctioneers
did not cause or permit such use by him (*Watkins v O'Shaughnessy* [1939] 1 All
E.R. 385). Assistance in a fraud on an insurance company by the car owner does
not necessarily render the aider liable for permitting uninsured use (*Goodbarne v
Buck* [1940] 1 All E.R. 613).

In some contexts, e.g. permitting a vehicle to be used without third party insurance, the statute imposes an absolute prohibition without proof of mens rea and it
suffices to convict the defendant if he is shown to have permitted use, irrespective
of whether he knew if the vehicle was insured or not (*Tapsell v Maslen* [1967]
Crim. L.R. 53, following *Lyons v May* [1948] 2 All E.R. 1062; *Morris v Williams*
(1952) 50 L.G.R. 308). These cases were not cited to or apparently considered by
the Divisional Court in *Davies v Warne* [1973] R.T.R. 217 where, nevertheless, a
conviction of permitting the use of an uninsured vehicle was upheld where both
the user and permitter genuinely and reasonably believed that the user's use of
the vehicle was covered by insurance.

A person who permits another to use his vehicle on the express condition that   **1.171**
the user first insures the vehicle cannot be convicted of the offence of permitting
because he has not permitted the vehicle to be used while uninsured: permission

given subject to a condition which was unfulfilled is no permission (*Newbury v Davis* [1974] R.T.R. 367). *Newbury v Davis* was followed and applied in *Baugh v Crago* [1975] R.T.R. 453. The defendant, believing him to hold a driving licence, permitted another person to drive his vehicle which was insured for any driver on condition that the driver held a driving licence. The justices were directed to convict: an honest, albeit mistaken, belief that the driver had a licence is no defence. The defendant had not made it a condition of his allowing the vehicle's use by the driver that he was the holder of a licence.

Newbury v Davis* and *Baugh v Crago* were approved in the civil case of *Lloyd-Wolper v Moore* [2004] EWCA Civ 766; [2004] R.T.R. 30. A father had obtained insurance for his son on the basis of a proposal in which it was stated that the son was 17 years of age, held a full licence and that use was restricted to vehicles of no more than 1600cc. An incident occurred when the son was driving. It transpired that the son was aged 16, the licence was not valid because it was based on a test taken when he was under 16 and the car had an engine of 1760cc. The father had believed the licence to be valid having been unaware of his son's precise date of birth. Nonetheless he was found to have permitted the use without insurance. A permission was still a permission even where it is induced by a misrepresentation by the proposed driver. A permission is given where there is an honest, although mistaken, belief about the circumstances of the person permitted to use the vehicle. A permission does not cease to be a permission because the permitter, in good faith, believed wrongly that the use was covered by the policy. This was not a case in which there was any evidence to suggest that the permission had been conditional.

1.172   The decision of *Newbury v Davis* above must be considered with "extreme caution" according to the Divisional Court in *DPP v Fisher* [1992] R.T.R. 93, and it may well be too simplistic a statement of the law to say that permission given subject to a condition which is unfulfilled is no permission. In *DPP v Fisher*, F who owned a car was asked by L to lend him the car for a journey. F knew that L was disqualified and agreed to lend the car provided that L could find a driver who was insured for the journey and held a full valid driving licence. F did not know whom L would ask, and in fact L asked R, a delivery driver, a person not known to F. L did not ask R if he was insured to drive F's car, they both assuming that R would be insured because of his employment as a delivery driver. R drove the vehicle, was involved in an accident, and was uninsured. F was prosecuted for permitting R to drive uninsured. The justices found that F had given conditional permission which extended to R and acquitted F. On appeal to the Divisional Court, it was held that in order to establish a conditional permission, the defendant would have at least to have been found to have given it directly to the would-be driver, regardless of whether the defendant had also given such permission to some other person, such as a would-be passenger in the car. Since the defendant had not given the conditional permission directly to R, the case would be remitted with a direction to convict.

The offence under what is now s.87(2) of the 1988 Act used to be to "employ" an unlicensed driver and it was generally held to be an absolute offence. The Road Traffic (Drivers' Ages and Hours of Work) Act 1976 substituted the words "cause or permit" for the word "employ". In *Ferrymasters Ltd v Adams* [1980] R.T.R. 139 the conviction of the employer for "permitting" his employee-driver to drive unlicensed was upheld on the ground that the employer had failed to adopt any system to ensure that reasonable checks on the employees' driving licences were made and had permitted him to drive, following *Baugh v Crago* [1975] R.T.R. 453. (For a criticism of the case see [1980] Crim. L.R. 187; in addition, see § 10.53.)

In *Sheldon Deliveries Ltd v Willis* [1972] R.T.R. 217 a car delivery firm was held not to have permitted the uninsured use of a car when its delivery driver, contrary to his express instructions, used it on a Sunday and without trade plates. Although the judgments imply that the car delivery firm should not be convicted because knowledge of the fact that the vehicle was uninsured could not be imputed to the company, it was pointed out in *Newbury v Davis* [1974] R.T.R. 367 at 371, that the true ratio decidendi in *Sheldon's* case was lack of knowledge that the vehicle was to be used on the journey in question. Knowledge that a vehicle is used in contravention of the statute is a different matter from knowledge that a vehicle is to be used. The latter is an essential ingredient of permission (ibid.).   **1.173**

The court ought to look at the object of the statute and see whether the principal might be held responsible for the conduct of his agent, though himself unaware of the statute being infringed. If the principal in effect hires out his coach, putting his employee in charge of it and at least leaving it to chance whether it would be used as a stage carriage or not, he permits it to be used as a stage carriage without a licence (*Goldsmith v Deakin* (1933) 98 J.P. 4; *Clydebank Co-operative Society v Binnie* 1937 J.C. 17); a fortiori where he has been warned that it may be so used (*Osborne v Richards* (1933) 96 J.P. 377; *Webb v Maidstone, etc., Services* (1934) 78 S.J. 336). *Browning v Watson* [1953] 2 All E.R. 775 is in accord with these cases as, there, no adequate precautions in instructing the staff or in seeing that the law was obeyed had been taken. But where the owner has no reason to know that his vehicle may be used without the necessary licence, or there are no circumstances which ought to have aroused his suspicion or put him on his guard, he is not guilty of permitting use without a licence for express carriages (*Newell v Cook* [1936] 2 All E.R. 203). Nor is he guilty of permitting use as a stage carriage if he does not know that such use is proposed and does not deliberately refrain from making inquiries or shut his eyes to the obvious (*Evans v Dell* [1973] 1 All E.R. 349). An owner may be liable for permitting overcrowding on a bus when he has appointed a young and inexperienced conductor and has given him no instructions (see *Gough v Rees* (1929) 94 J.P. 53), provided that the regulations justify the use of the word "permit" in the context.

In *Ross Hillman Ltd v Bond* (see § 1.162 above) the defendant company could not be convicted of "causing" its vehicle to be used with excess axle weight because the prosecution was unable to prove guilty knowledge on the part of an officer responsible for directing the company's business. It was said that such mens rea was a necessary ingredient both of the offence of "causing" and of "permitting". *Ross Hillman* was followed and applied in *P. Lowery & Sons v Wark* [1975] R.T.R. 45 where a conviction (under the former s.40, now s.40A of the 1988 Act) of the defendant company for "permitting" its vehicle to be used with a dangerously insecure load was set aside where there was no proof of mens rea on behalf of a person controlling the company.   **1.174**

A corporation can permit an offence for which disqualification is a punishment though not disqualifiable itself (*Briggs v Gibson's Bakery* [1948] N.I. 165). While a person may be guilty of permitting if he fails to take proper steps to prevent something, he is not guilty if he merely fails to take unreasonable steps to prevent it (*Test Valley Investments Ltd v Tanner* [1964] Crim. L.R. 62, a case under another Act).

1.175   A person supervising a learner driver does not necessarily permit the driving. Where the learner was also the owner of the vehicle, the supervisor was not in a position to forbid the use of the vehicle to the owner (*Thompson v Lodwick* [1983] R.T.R. 76). A conviction for permitting no insurance was quashed.

"To use"

Meaning

1.176   Many charges are brought for offences of "using" a motor vehicle without third party insurance or in breach of the Road Vehicles (Construction and Use) Regulations 1986 (SI 1986/1078). The term in such cases usually imports absolute liability (unless there is some special statutory defence such as that given by s.143(3) of the Road Traffic Act 1988 for employees using their master's vehicle in ignorance of the lack of insurance cover) and those responsible for the use of the vehicle can be prosecuted, e.g. the driver and his employer, if the journey was made on the employer's business. An employer may thus find himself charged with an offence of which he himself was quite ignorant and which may have been committed hundreds of miles from his office. However, it was said in *Hart v Bex* [1957] Crim. L.R. 622, where a defect in a braking system (a case of absolute liability) arose unexpectedly and suddenly and the driver was not under a duty to inspect the brakes, that the police should refrain from prosecuting him and, if he was charged, he should be given an absolute discharge. This advice from the High Court, it is submitted, should be considered by all prosecutors and defending advocates in cases where the driver or the owner of the vehicle appears to be morally guiltless and has not been guilty of negligence in relation to the causes of the defect or in carrying on after it has developed.

In this context, practitioners may find useful a reference to *Hickman v Chichester District Council* [1992] R.T.R. 121 in which the Divisional Court was required to consider the "use" of vehicles in any public car park "for any purpose in connexion with trade or business" in determining whether there had been a contravention of a local traffic order made under s.35(4) of the Road Traffic Regulation Act 1984. It was held that a person who places an advertising leaflet under the windscreen wiper of a vehicle in a public car park is using the vehicle for the purpose in connection with trade, etc., and is therefore properly convicted of an offence under the relevant order.

1.177   A rather more important decision on the wide scope of the words "to use" and "using" under the Road Traffic Acts came with the decision of the Divisional Court in *Hallett Silberman Ltd v Cheshire County Council* [1993] R.T.R. 32. The defendant company was prosecuted and convicted for using a vehicle exceeding the maximum permitted laden weight. The vehicle was in fact a heavy motor car drawing a wheeled trailer, the combination of the vehicle and trailer exceeding the relevant permitted weight.

The tractor unit was owned and operated by the driver, a Mr Keeling, but both the tractor unit and the trailer bore in letters the name of the appellants. They appealed contending that they were not using the combination of vehicles specified within the meaning of s.42(b) of the Road Traffic Act 1988. In dismissing the appeal, Beldam L.J. stated that in some regulations the words "a person who uses a motor vehicle" were intended to cover a person whose vehicle was being used for his purposes and on his behalf, under his instruction and control, and that from the many complex factors which a court should take into account in deciding whether a person was using the vehicle on the road, it was too restrictive to isolate the terms of the particular contract under which the driver happened to be engaged to perform the duty of driving, as determining the question. In the instant case, the driver, although self-employed and providing the towing vehicle as part of the combination of vehicles, was not responsible for selecting the route, deciding the load, loading the trailer, deciding which trailer should be used, giving the indemnity or the notice of movement.

The decision in *Hallett Silberman Ltd v Cheshire County Council* above was considered by the Divisional Court in *DPP v Seawheel Ltd* [1993] Crim. L.R. 707. Seawheel had been convicted of using a trailer in a dangerous condition, contrary to reg.100(1) of the Road Vehicles (Construction and Use) Regulations 1986 (SI 1986/1078). It appealed to the Crown Court, and the appeal was allowed on the basis that Seawheel had not been using the trailer. It had hired another company, Transmore, to transport steel pipes between two towns. The pipes were conveyed by an articulated lorry and trailer unit owned by Transmore. They were carried on a bed secured to the skeleton of the trailer and were held in place by stanchions and spansets. The bed, stanchions and spansets were owned by Seawheel. One of the stanchions snapped and the load was shed. There was no finding that Seawheel was in possession of the stanchions, or the trailer. The prosecution appealed by case stated. The Divisional Court held that the Crown Court had been correct. Seawheel's only connection with the trailer was that when it was loaded Seawheel owned part of the whole and that the trailer was being used for the transport of goods owned by it between two towns for the purposes of its business. Mere ownership of the trailer bed, stanchions and spansets as well as the load did not amount to the use of the trailer for the purposes of the regulations, although ownership might be a factor to be taken into account on the facts of a particular case. The ownership of the parts was of little significance where there was no finding either that Seawheel was in possession of the trailer or its parts or that it was in any sense operating the trailer itself.

1.178

Hallett Silberman Ltd v Cheshire County Council was distinguished in *West Yorkshire Trading Standards Service v Lex Vehicle Leasing Ltd* [1996] R.T.R. 70. The Court of Appeal gave a restricted definition of the word "use" when it is found in the same context as "cause" and "permit" in criminal statutes. It was applicable only if a person was the driver or owner of the vehicle, and applied only to the owner if the driver was employed by the owner under a contract of service and at the material time was driving on the owner's business. The decision in *NFC Forwarding Ltd v DPP* [1989] R.T.R. 239 was also distinguished.

The following propositions are submitted:

1.179

(1) Absolute liability for use is imposed by certain statutes and regulations, e.g. use without third party insurance or without most licences or contrary to most of the Construction and Use Regulations, and the fact that the person using is quite unaware of the breach of the law and has not been negligent is immaterial. It is a question of construction in each case whether absolute liability is imposed. (Note § 1.176 above as to uninsured employees. There is also a special defence as to speedometers: see § 8.31.)

(2) An employer may be liable for use by his employee on the employer's business and, if the statute or regulation imposes an absolute prohibition, lack of knowledge or of negligence on the employer's part is no defence, although it may be mitigation. Again, it is a question of construction whether absolute liability for his employee's acts is imposed on the employer. In *Strutt v Clift* (1911) 74 J.P. 471 an employer entrusted a van to his employee to use legally on his (i.e. the employer's) business, but the employee illegally used it for his own pleasure. The employer was held liable in a Revenue prosecution. On the other hand, in *Phelon v Keel* (1914) 78 J.P. 247 "use" in the then regulations relating to trade plates was held to mean use by or on behalf of the holder and not unauthorised use by a trespasser. It is suggested that the very strict liability laid down in *Strutt v Clift* does not necessarily apply in road traffic cases and that it will often be a question of fact whether an employee's deviation from his duty and instructions is sufficiently gross to show that the use of a vehicle was no longer on the employer's business (but see *Richardson v Baker* [1976] R.T.R. 56).

(3) Where the statute creates the offence of "causing" or "permitting" as well as "using", only the driver, a person in the vehicle controlling the driver, a person engaged in a joint enterprise with the driver and the driver's employer, while it is being used on the employer's business, "use" it. An aider and abettor, and an accessory before the fact, should be charged with "permitting" or "causing". Where the only offence is "using" and there is no offence of "causing" or "permitting", as in the Vehicle Excise and Registration Act 1994, then it may be possible for the owner of a vehicle to be charged with using if he caused it to be used by another on his behalf.

(4) Where an employee is driving a vehicle on behalf of a partnership it is normally being used by all the partners (*Passmoor v Gibbons* [1978] Crim. L.R. 498), but it is being used otherwise if it is driven by one of the partners, because one partner is not the employer or employee of another partner (*Garrett v Hooper* [1973] R.T.R. 1; *Bennett v Richardson* [1981] R.T.R. 358).

(5) Where a vehicle and the vehicle's driver is hired out, the person hiring out the vehicle will not normally be held to be "using" the vehicle (although he may be "causing" or "permitting" it to be used) because he is not the employer of the driver (see *Mickleborough v BRS (Contracts) Ltd* [1977] R.T.R. 389 and other cases below).

(6) The cases indicate that a person *driving* a vehicle will normally be *using* it. A person may *use* it by having custody or control of it without *driving* it. There may however be a distinction between "use" and "driving" as was emphasised in *Samuelson v National Insurance and Guarantee Corporation Ltd* [1984] 3 All E.R. 107 (a civil case; the decision was reversed on appeal, but it is thought that the relevance of the distinction between "use" and "driving" to which attention was drawn at first instance remains untainted; see [1986] 3 All E.R. 417 (but cases on drink/driving which extend the concept of "driving" beyond the point when the vehicle is actually in motion would not seem to be applicable to "driving" for insurance purposes)). The plaintiff was

covered for the use of the vehicle whilst in the custody or control of a member of the motor trade for its upkeep or repair. He was not covered for driving by another person. It was held at the trial that he was not covered under the policy when the car was stolen whilst being driven by the motor trade repairer to buy spares; but the Court of Appeal ruled that the car was at the relevant time in the custody or control of a member of the motor trade and hence that no question whether it was being driven by another person arose.

Cases

A person does not use a motor vehicle under s.143 (insurance) of the 1988 Act **1.180** unless there is an element of controlling, managing or operating the vehicle as a vehicle (cited with approval in *Nichol v Leach* [1972] R.T.R. 416); nor does a passenger who is ignorant of the lack of insurance cover and does not procure the making of a journey (*D v Parsons* [1960] 2 All E.R. 493), nor a person sitting in the driving seat, drunk, when the car is stationary and the ignition key and insurance are held by the owner also present in the car (*Fisher v Kearton* (1964) 108 S.J. 258). Passengers have, however, in two insurance cases, been held to be using a motor vehicle when they procured the journey (*Cobb v Williams* [1973] R.T.R. 113) or engaged in a joint enterprise (*Leathley v Tatton* [1980] R.T.R. 21). These cases should be compared with the situation where the passenger has no power of control over the driver and is therefore not using the vehicle (see further §§ 10.34–40). See also *Hamilton v Blair and Meechan*; *Windle v Dunning & Son Ltd*; *Carmichael & Sons v Cottle*; *Crawford v Haughton*; and *Cobb v Williams* (all below).

A driver of a vehicle may be convicted of using it with his load improperly secured, contrary to the Construction and Use Regulations, although the loading was done under the supervision of the hirer's employee and the driver took no part in it (*Gifford v Whittaker* [1942] 1 All E.R. 604). A driver who ought to have known his brakes were defective was also convicted of using his vehicle with defective brakes (*Adair v Donaldson* 1935 J.C. 23). A trade licence issued to a company forbade the carrying of an excessive number of passengers in a vehicle. The company drew its drivers' attention to the licence and ordered them to observe that term. A car driven by an employee carried an excessive number of passengers. The company was convicted of using it and it was said that it would make no difference if the employer had been an individual (*Griffiths v Studebakers* [1924] 1 K.B. 102). However, where a vehicle was used without licence as an express carriage and the illegality arose through the action of some people who were not the vehicle owner's employees or agents, which action was unknown to him, he should not be convicted of using: a person is not guilty if he does an act lawful in itself but which has become unlawful, unbeknown to him, through the actions of such people (*Reynolds v Austin* [1951] 1 All E.R. 606).

A leading case on "using" is *Green v Burnett* [1954] 3 All E.R. 273. In this **1.181** case, an employee used a vehicle with defective brakes. There was some evidence of negligence by the owner's employee in maintaining the brakes but the owner had given him general instructions to take the vehicle to motor engineers whenever he felt it needed maintenance or some defect manifested itself. The vehicle was used on the owner's business and it was held that he (the owner) was guilty of "using", as the Construction and Use Regulations (with a few exceptions) impose an absolute prohibition on use in breach of them, although the owner was quite unaware of the defect. Liability for contravention of an absolute prohibition depends on the fact of contravention and not upon the intention to contravene. Neither mens rea in its true sense of importing a blameworthy mind nor negligence in the form of a failure to take reasonable steps to prevent the offence is relevant save on the question of punishment.

1.182   For the purposes of the Goods Vehicles (Licensing of Operators) Act 1995 (carriage of goods by road, operators' licences, etc.), the driver of a vehicle if he owns it or possesses it under a loan or hire-purchase agreement is deemed to use the vehicle, and in any other case the person whose servant or agent the driver is is the user of the vehicle (Transport Act 1968 s.92(2)). This is, it is submitted, essentially a question of fact. Thus where justices found as a fact that a driver who had been provided for a haulage company by the defendant employment agency was employed by the haulage company and not by the employment agency, the justices' decision of fact could not be impugned (*Alderton v Richard Burgon Associates Ltd* [1974] R.T.R. 422). Nor was the justices' finding reversed when they came to an opposite conclusion, namely that an employment agency employed the driver and not the company to whom the driver was supplied (*Howard v G.T. Jones & Co Ltd* [1975] R.T.R. 150). A further case on this point is *Interlink Express Parcels Ltd v Night Trunkers Ltd* [2001] EWCA Civ 360; [2001] R.T.R. 23. Section 58(2) of the 1995 Act provides that the user of a goods vehicle is the person whose servant or agent the driver was and so it is the employer of that person who needed to hold the operator's licence. In this case, Interlink offered a next day parcel delivery service. The vehicles used were provided by Interlink but some of the drivers were provided by Night Trunkers Ltd. At first instance, the Chancery Division stated that, since on the facts the drivers remained employed by Night Trunkers, that company needed to possess an operator's licence. The Chancery Division did not find the conclusion attractive and could not see why the engagement had to be under a contract of employment and these reservations were shared by the Court of Appeal which overturned the decision. Given that the main purpose of the provision in the 1995 Act was to govern the responsibility of those who controlled the actual use of the vehicle, the Court of Appeal considered that the relevant language was that of tort rather than of contract. In the context of temporary deemed employment, the main test was of control over the activity. In these circumstances the extent of the right to control the various activities raised a strong inference of fact that the claimant had the right to control the way that the drivers operated its vehicles and so those drivers should be regarded as temporary deemed servants of the claimant for the purposes of s.58(2) of the 1995 Act. The absence of a statutory definition in the 1995 Act of the term "servant" allows the court to give it a dynamic meaning and enables the court to keep pace with changes in the nature of employment, including the increasing use of agency workers.

1.183   An owner who hired a vehicle out was held not to be a user of it whilst the hirer had it, and the hirer also, when not in the vehicle, was held not to be using it (*Hamilton v Blair and Meechan* 1962 S.L.T. 69). It was agreed that passengers, including possibly the hirer, were not users in breach of what is now the Public Passenger Vehicles Act 1981. In *Windle v Dunning & Son Ltd* [1968] 2 All E.R. 46, the defendants hired vehicles from a firm of haulage contractors; the drivers, although they spent a lot of time on the defendant's work, were paid by the contractors, and the defendant's employees loaded the vehicles and directed the drivers where to go. The defendant's employees sent them out with overloaded vehicles and it was held that only the drivers and not the defendants were using them as opposed to causing them to be used. "Using" might also cover, it was said, an employer where the driver was about that employer's business.

Where works contractors hired a vehicle plus driver from another company, it was held that the contractors could not be said to be "using" the vehicle which was in contravention of various Construction and Use Regulations, Road Vehicles Lighting Regulations and s.22 of the Vehicles (Excise) Act 1971 (*Balfour Beatty & Co Ltd v Grindley* [1975] R.T.R. 156). The defendant company could have been convicted of causing or permitting the use of the vehicle in contravention of the Construction and Use Regulations (ibid.). Similarly it was held in *Howard v G.T. Jones & Co Ltd* (above) a company could not be held to be "using" a motor vehicle contravening a construction and use regulation if the driver was not employed by the company charged with "using". In *Mickleborough v BRS (Contracts) Ltd* [1977] R.T.R. 389, *Hamilton v Blair and Meechan* 1962 S.L.T. 69 was distinguished first on the grounds that it related to a different provision relating to express carriages and secondly that there was no evidence in that case that the driver was the employee of the owner defendant. In *Mickleborough* the owner was held responsible because the driver was acting in the course of his employer's business, namely that of hiring out motor lorries. The test was stated by Boreham J. to be as follows:

> "['Using'] applies on the authorities to the driver of the vehicle. It ['using'] applies to the owner of the vehicle provided, first, the driver is employed under a contract of service, in other words there is a relationship of master and servant between the owner and the driver; and secondly, that at the material time the driver was driving on his employer's business."

For an analysis by the Divisional Court on the question of "using" for the purposes of reg.100(1) of the Construction and Use Regulations, see *NFC Forwarding Ltd v DPP* [1989] R.T.R. 239.

1.184

The civil case of *Stinton v Stinton* [1995] R.T.R. 167 (and see also § 10.44) confirms that a front seat passenger can in certain circumstances be held to be using a vehicle. The plaintiff went out in a car driven by his brother for an evening's drinking. He knew that his brother was uninsured. An accident took place in which the plaintiff received severe head injuries. The judge dismissed a claim by the plaintiff for a declaration against the Motor Insurers' Bureau that it was liable to satisfy the judgment against the first defendant (the brother), holding that the plaintiff had failed to give notice of the proceedings to the MIB in accordance with the provisions of clause 5 of the 1972 agreement and that he had been a "user" of the vehicle at the relevant time within the terms of the agreement. In the judgment of the Court of Appeal, "being a person using a vehicle" in clause 6(1)(c)(ii) of the agreement was not restricted to a person who was driving the vehicle but included any person controlling, managing or operating it and was wide enough to include a person allowing himself to be carried in pursuance of a joint venture with another. Nourse L.J. stated that in the majority of cases to determine whether a person other than the driver is "a person using the vehicle" the tests of control or management or of joint enterprise will be found to apply. But it should not be thought that those tests will necessarily be exhaustive. A case might arise where a passenger could be said to have been using a vehicle without precisely satisfying either test.

1.185   *Stinton* was distinguished in *Hatton v Hall* [1997] R.T.R. 212 where the Court of Appeal rejected an appeal by the Motor Insurers' Bureau from the decision of a judge at first instance. He had found that the plaintiff, Mr Hatton, who had been a pillion passenger on a motor cycle driven by the first defendant, Mr Hall, on a 10-mile journey to a public house, had not been a user of the motor cycle for the purpose of clause 6(1)(c)(ii) of the 1988 MIB agreement. In the course of giving the judgment of the court, Henry L.J. stated that it was apparent that while every passenger, in ordinary language, "used" the vehicle he was driven in, "use" had to be given a restricted meaning, for if it were not, very many passengers in cars, cabs, and buses had unwittingly but potentially been committing criminal offences in accepting lifts in ignorance of the precise insurance position of the vehicle. In dismissing the appeal, his Lordship said that the judge at first instance had considered and distinguished *Stinton*, and that fundamental to that distinction was his assumption that not all plans shared between driver and passenger gave the passenger sufficient management of the vehicle to make him a user of the vehicle. "That conclusion seemed to be good sense as well as good law". The issue will be one of fact. The extent of the involvement of the putative user will need to be carefully assessed. It may be relevant where the whole venture was one of flagrant criminality: *O'Mahoney v Joliffe* [1999] R.T.R. 245.

    A further case from the civil jurisdiction is *Dunthorne v Bentley* [1996] R.T.R. 428. Mrs Bentley had been driving her car when she ran out of petrol. She parked the car with the hazard lights flashing and stood at the rear of the car. After about 10 minutes she had been seen by a colleague who stopped her car on the opposite side of the road. Mrs Bentley had run across the road and an accident occurred, causing fatal injuries to Mrs Bentley and serious head injuries to the plaintiff. The crucial point was whether his injuries were "caused by, or arising out of" use by Mrs Bentley of her car. The Court of Appeal dismissed an appeal from the decision of the judge at first instance that the accident caused by a person negligently running across a road arose out of that person's use of her motor vehicle. That question was essentially one of fact, and the court held that the judge had been entitled to come to the conclusion he had.

1.186   Where an owner lends his car to a friend on condition that he renews the licence when it expires, the owner does not use the car after expiry of the licence (*Abercromby v Morris* (1932) 96 J.P. 392). It is doubtful, indeed, if a person who lends his car to a friend for social purposes, abandoning all control, uses it at all but, if he knows of defects, he might be liable for aiding and abetting the friend. An unreported case (*Stone v Horton* (1935)) is mentioned at 113 J.P. Jo. 674, however, in which an owner was held to be "using" where he had hired or lent his car to a customer. Apparently, this case was under what is now the Vehicle Excise and Registration Act 1994 and the courts often take a stricter view in Revenue and Customs prosecutions than they do in criminal cases (cf. *Strutt v Clift* (1911) 74 J.P. 471, and see *Hamilton v Blair and Meechan* 1962 S.L.T. 69).

    A further distinction between "using" a vehicle without a licence contrary to the Vehicle Excise and Registration Act 1994 and "using" a vehicle without insurance (s.143 of the 1988 Act) or in contravention of a construction and use regulation (s.42 of the 1988 Act) is that there is no offence of "causing" or "permitting" the use of an untaxed vehicle contrary to s.29 of the Vehicle Excise and Registration Act 1994 (see *Carmichael & Sons v Cottle* [1971] R.T.R. 11, *Crawford v Haughton* [1972] 1 All E.R. 535; and see further as to those cases below). A garage company which lent a car to a customer while his car was being repaired was not guilty of using the lent car when he later drove it with defective tyres, semble even though they may have been defective when the company handed it over (*L.F. Dove Ltd v Tarvin* (1964) 108 S.J. 404). See also *Strutt v Clift* above and *Phelon v Keel* (1914) 78 J.P. 247 as to use without authority.

A vehicle is in use when it is stationary on a road for loading or unloading (*Andrews v Kershaw* [1951] 2 All E.R. 764) and is in use and requires to be insured even where it has been left immobile with an engine which does not work and without petrol and battery, so long as it can be moved, e.g. by pushing or releasing the brake (*Elliott v Grey* [1959] 3 All E.R. 733). Where a vehicle had been left in a gateway of a rural road (but semble on the road) for so long that green grass grew all around, it was held that it was still used on the road for insurance and test certificate purposes (*Another v Howard*, J.P. Jo. Supp., June 11, 1968). A person who had abandoned a car in a lay-by "uses" it and requires a policy of insurance (*Williams v Jones* (1969) W.L.R., March 7, "Recent Points"). It might be that user in breach of other provisions would not necessarily be established in like circumstances. Also, the court said in *Another v Howard* that its finding might be otherwise if the car was totally immobilised by removal of its wheels, i.e. that the vehicle might have ceased to be a "motor vehicle", and, indeed, in *Hewer v Cutler* [1974] R.T.R. 155, for these reasons *Elliott v Grey* was not applied in a case of "using" a motor vehicle without a current test certificate contrary to s.44 of the 1972 Act (now s.47 of the 1988 Act): it was held that a totally immobilised vehicle left on a road could not be said to be "used" for the purposes of s.47. It was doubted, obiter, whether the test as to whether a vehicle is "used" is the same in s.47 as in s.143: in *Elliott v Grey* it was said that "use" for the purpose of s.143 was equivalent to "have the use of the vehicle on the road". But in *Eden v Mitchell* [1975] R.T.R. 425, a car had two defective tyres and was left parked on a road. The owner did not intend to drive it while it had two defective tyres. For this reason the justices dismissed the two charges of using the car with a defective tyre contrary to what is now reg.27 of the Road Vehicles (Construction and Use) Regulations 1986 and s.42 of the 1988 Act. Reversing the justices, the Divisional Court said that "use" (as in *Elliott v Grey*) meant "having the use of" and as the car was capable of being used the justices were directed to convict. *Hewer v Cutler* was explained as being a case where the facts were that the car had been mechanically immobilised and was thus incapable of being driven. It was said that the true test that should be applied in cases of this nature is whether or not steps had been taken to make it impossible for anyone to drive the vehicle. The intention of the defendant as to whether he would drive it is immaterial. *Elliott v Grey* was also followed in *D (A Minor) v Yates* (1984) 148 J.P. 455 (a case on using a CB radio without a licence) where again "use" was held to mean "have the use of" or "have available for use".

However, *D (A Minor) v Yates* above was expressly overruled by the House of Lords in *Rudd v Secretary of State for Trade and Industry* [1987] 1 W.L.R. 786 (a decision on the Wireless Telegraphy Act 1949). Lord Goff of Chieveley with whom Lord Bridge of Harwich, Lord Brandon of Oakbrook, Lord Mackay of Clashfern and Lord Ackner agreed, referred to *Elliott v Grey* [1959] 3 All E.R. 733 and distinguished the position under the Road Traffic Act 1972 provisions from that under the Wireless Telegraphy Act 1949. No shadow is cast over the decision in *Elliott v Grey*.

1.187

1.188

The driver of a towing vehicle causes the towed vehicle to be used and presumably therefore the towed vehicle is also "used" (*Milstead v Sexton* [1964] Crim. L.R. 474). In *Cobb v Whorton* [1971] R.T.R. 392 it was held that a van which was on tow on a road was "used" and if it was untaxed the user, who was in charge of and responsible for the van, was guilty of an offence under what is now s.29 of the Vehicle Excise and Registration Act 1994. It was pointed out that it was inconsistent for the justices, having come to the conclusion that the van was "used" while stationary, then to hold that it ceased to be used the moment it began to be towed (at 395). *Cobb v Whorton* was applied in *Nichol v Leach* [1973] R.T.R. 476. It was held that both the driver of a vehicle being towed by another vehicle and the driver of the towing vehicle could be convicted of "using" whilst uninsured (contrary to what is now s.143 of the 1988 Act) and without an excise licence (contrary to what is now s.29 of the Vehicle Excise and Registration Act 1994). A vehicle does not have to be driven under its own power to be "used" on a road (ibid.).

1.189   Employers can be convicted of "using", contrary to what is now s.42 of the 1988 Act, a vehicle which contravenes a construction and use regulation when the vehicle is being driven as directed by police or a vehicle examiner (*Drysdale v Harrison* [1973] R.T.R. 45). Use of a vehicle by the employer does not cease through an incident of driving such as a police direction to the driver to stop or to take a certain course, or an examiner directing the vehicle to proceed to a weighbridge to be weighed (ibid.). An employer is guilty of "using" an unlicensed vehicle contrary to s.29 of the Vehicle Excise and Registration Act 1994 if the vehicle is used on his business. It is no defence that he did not authorise his employee to take the unlicensed vehicle if in fact the employee used it on the employer's business (*Richardson v Baker* [1976] R.T.R. 56).

1.190   In *Carmichael & Sons Ltd v Cottle* [1971] R.T.R. 11 a company hired out one of their cars to a hirer who was found driving it with a badly worn tyre contrary to what is now reg.27 of the Road Vehicles (Construction and Use) Regulations 1986 (and what is now s.42 of the 1988 Act). The company was convicted of "using" the vehicle in contravention of the regulation but the conviction was set aside on the ground that the only person who could be said to be "using" the vehicle was the driver. It was argued before the Divisional Court that the company could be convicted as an accessory because the tyre must have been in a poor condition when the car was first hired out. This argument was dismissed on the ground that it had not been raised before the justices, but in the course of his judgment Lord Parker C.J. (supported by Ashworth L.J.) suggested that the argument could also be dismissed on the ground that where the words in a statute creating the offence are "using or causing or permitting", the latter words provide for the offences of being an aider and abettor or an accessory, and that if the defendant is an accessory or aider and abettor he should be specifically charged with "causing" or "permitting" the user and not with "using".

The approach above was specifically adopted by Lord Widgery C.J. in *Crawford v Haughton* [1972] 1 All E.R. 535, where the owner of a stock car had been convicted by the magistrates' court of using the vehicle in contravention of seven separate construction and use regulations, using it whilst uninsured, using it without a vehicle excise licence and using it displaying trade plates without being the holder of the trade licence. The convictions were set aside on the ground that he should have been charged with "permitting". Where the statute provides alternative offences of "causing or permitting" the only persons who can be convicted of "using" are the driver or an employer if the vehicle was being on the employer's business by his employee. The Divisional Court refused to extend the meaning of "using" to include the owner where the person driving the vehicle was not his employee even though that person was driving at his specific request on a specific journey. Note that the convictions under the Vehicle Excise and Registration Act 1994 for using the vehicle without an excise licence and displaying trade plates were also set aside, because no distinction had been made in the magistrates' court between these offences and the remainder. Lord Widgery C.J. suggested that different considerations might apply if these two offences had been considered in isolation, as the sections creating the offence do not contain the alternatives of "causing or permitting" the use. It is submitted that, at any rate so far as an offence under s.29 of the Vehicle Excise and Registration Act 1994 is concerned, where a vehicle is driven on behalf of the owner by another on a journey at his request and on his business, the owner may be found guilty of "using". Not only is the Vehicle Excise and Registration Act 1994 a taxation statute where a stricter view is often adopted by the courts, but more importantly there is no offence of "causing" or "permitting" the use of an unlicensed vehicle. Moreover an "aider and abettor" or accessory may be convicted as a principal (Magistrates' Courts Act 1980 s.44; *Du Cros v Lambourne* (1907) 70 J.P. 525). The purpose of the Vehicle Excise and Registration Act 1994 is to tax the person who uses or keeps a vehicle on a road; the Act is silent and uncaring as to who is the driver.

The court applied *Crawford v Haughton* above, and again refused to extend the category of person who can be said to be "using" to a partner when the other partner was driving the vehicle (*Garrett v Hooper* [1973] R.T.R. 1). A partner who is not the driver cannot be said to "use" the vehicle driven by his partner because one partner is not the employee of the other (*Garrett v Hooper*, as above). *Garrett v Hooper* was followed and applied in *Bennett v Richardson* [1980] R.T.R. 358. A blind partner was sitting in the back of a van with no insurance, inefficient brakes, inefficient steering, dangerous rear suspension and defective windscreen washers, driven by the blind defendant's partner. The justices' dismissal of the charges against the defendant because one partner does not "employ" another partner was upheld. (On the other hand if a vehicle belonging to a partnership is driven by an employee of the partners on their business, seemingly each and every partner can be said to be "using".) But in *Cobb v Williams* [1973] R.T.R. 113 it was explained that *Crawford v Haughton* and the other cases supporting it were cases of vicarious liability; a restricted meaning of "use" had been adopted in those cases where the defendant was not himself driving the car. Where a defendant is himself a passenger in his own car driven by a friend directly for the defendant's own purposes, then the defendant is "using" and may be convicted of using the vehicle whilst not insured contrary to s.143 of the 1988 Act (*Cobb v Williams* [1973] R.T.R. 113). *Cobb v Williams* was applied and extended in *Leathley v Tatton* [1980] R.T.R. 21 to a passenger who jointly with another wrongfully took a vehicle.

Employers are often prosecuted for offences under the Construction and Use Regulations because of the defective condition of the vehicle or its load (note the special "defences" as to speedometers in reg.36(2)) and the defence that there is a proper system of maintenance is advanced. Can it prevail? One can only refer to

1.191

the various cases cited: some of them certainly lean strongly towards absolute liability, e.g. in *Gifford v Whittaker* [1942] 1 All E.R. 604, the vehicle had been loaded by experienced men and yet the driver, who had had no hand in it, was convicted. In *Cornish v Ferry Masters Ltd* [1975] R.T.R. 292 a drum fell off a lorry because the pallet upon which it was loaded collapsed due to some extraordinary, unexplained, inherent defect. Both the lorry's owner and driver were directed to be convicted of "using" even though neither was negligent nor at fault. Cases on other (but not all) parts of what is now the Road Traffic Act 1988 establish absolute liability on the employer, and in *Griffiths v Studebakers* (see below) the convicted employers seem to have done all that could reasonably be expected of them to ensure compliance with the law. The regulations can certainly be said to be for the protection of the public and, if there is evidence that a vehicle was sent out on the road by the company's employees in an unlawful condition, the company is liable (*Provincial Motor Cab Co v Dunning* (1909) 73 J.P. 387). In *Churchill v Norris* (1938) 158 L.T. 255 and *Prosser v Richings* (1936) 100 J.P. 390 (both on these regulations), the facts showed that the convicted employers took some risk of the driver's accepting an excessive load, i.e. both could be called slight cases of mens rea. It should also be noted that Parliament has recognised that "using" a vehicle contrary to a construction and use regulation may be an offence of absolute liability by enacting s.48 of the 1988 Offenders Act relating to convictions for offences under s.42 of the 1988 Act, which provides that a person's driving licence cannot be endorsed in respect of construction and use offences relating to brakes, tyres and steering, dangerous condition and insecure load if that person proves that the facts of the case were such that he did not know and had no reasonable cause to suspect that an offence would be committed (see § 8.104).

1.192 Whatever the position may be in law, it is submitted that the justices should inquire carefully into the facts. Rust, loose bolts and other defects are not usually things that come about in a moment, in the twinkling of an eye; they point to defective maintenance. If so, surely the employer is liable, however good he may have imagined his system of maintenance to be (*Provincial Motor Cab Co v Dunning* (1909) 73 J.P. 387). Even if a vehicle goes out in perfect condition and a defect occurs suddenly, e.g. a rod snaps through a fault in the metal, *Griffiths v Studebakers* [1924] 1 K.B. 102 suggests that the employer is still using the vehicle while it continues to be driven on the road although he may have told his drivers to take vehicles off the road immediately such a defect occurs. Indeed, it is hinted at 113 J.P. Jo. 472 that it is difficult to defend a charge of "using" under the regulations and *Green v Burnett* [1954] 3 All E.R. 273 reinforces that view. Whether there should in fact be a prosecution, however, is another matter (see *Hart v Bex* [1957] Crim. L.R. 622, noted at § 1.176).

Is an employer who duly authorises his driver to drive the firm's vehicle on the firm's business liable for using if the driver, without permission, lets some other person drive it on the firm's business? In *Richardson v Baker* [1976] R.T.R. 56 an employer was held to have used an unlicensed vehicle, contrary to s.29 of the Vehicle Excise and Registration Act 1994, when it was used on his business despite the fact that the employer had not authorised the particular lorry to be used anywhere other than in the employer's yard. The judgment of Lord Widgery C.J. in the case seems sufficiently wide to support the proposition that whenever a vehicle is used on the employer's business, the employer should be convicted of "using" even if he had not specifically authorised the employee to undertake such use (per Lord Widgery C.J., at 60). *Aliter* if it were used by a servant "on a frolic of his own" or by a thief (ibid.).

In *J.G. Williams v Harbord*, 1996, unreported (CO/3088/95) a driver and the **1.193** owner of a goods vehicle were prosecuted and convicted by justices of using a goods vehicle exceeding 16.5 tons maximum gross weight in a restricted street. The vehicle had been seen to be driven in the street concerned by an enforcement officer. The facts were not disputed and the driver pleaded guilty. It was argued before the justices that it was wrong in law and in principle, and a misinterpretation of the doctrine of vicarious liability if both the driver and the company were summoned as primary offenders. By charging the company with "using" as opposed to "causing" or "permitting" the prosecutor had deprived the company of a possible defence by establishing a lack of mens rea. The argument failed before the justices and also before the Divisional Court. After reviewing a number of the authorities, the court stated that it was concerned with environmental legislation aimed at noise and pollution in residential areas. The owners were the best persons to keep the driver up to scratch to ensure that such environmental matters were not breached. The Divisional Court held that there had been no error of law on the part of the justices and there had been no abuse of process in charging both the driver and the owner with "using". The appeal was dismissed.

Care needs to be taken to examine the words of the statute. In *Richmond upon Thames London Borough Council v Morton* [2000] R.T.R. 79 the vehicle was being used for the purposes of the registered keeper by a person who was not an employee of the keeper. An offence was alleged contrary to the Greater London (Restriction on Goods Vehicles) Traffic Order 1985 (SI 1985/343). This order differs from many pieces of road traffic legislation both in the provision that "… no person shall use, *drive*, or cause or permit to be driven" and in the presumption contained in art.3(b) that a person who is the registered keeper was the user unless the keeper shows on the balance of probabilities that he was not. The normal line of authorities which required the driver to be employed by the owner under a contract of service before there could be "use" was not applicable, therefore, in the face of the words of the order. In such a case, the nature of the driver's contract was immaterial.

A special defence for persons charged with using a vehicle without insurance **1.194** in the course of their employment is provided by the Road Traffic Act 1988 s.143(3) (see § 10.59).

It should be noted that there is no offence of "using" a vehicle without a number plate contrary to s.42 of the Vehicle Excise and Registration Act 1994. A conviction for this was quashed (*Balfour Beatty & Co Ltd v Grindley* [1975] R.T.R. 156). Section 42 of the 1994 Act makes it an offence only to "drive" or "keep".

The owner is deemed to have been using the vehicle in the absence of contrary evidence (*Watson v Paterson*, noted at 121 J.P. Jo. 336; *Ende v Cassidy* (1964) 108 S.J. 522; but see the qualifications given at § 3.95). On the other hand ownership or proof of ownership is not essential either for proof of "using" a vehicle without being insured under s.143 of the 1988 Act or "using" it without an excise licence contrary to s.29 of the 1994 Act (*Napthen v Place* [1970] R.T.R. 248).

See § 5.64 and *Pawley v Wharldall* [1965] 2 All E.R. 757 as to persons "using" the road under what is now s.3 of the 1988 Act (careless, and inconsiderate, driving).

"AGRICULTURE"

Meaning

1.195   Some statutes and regulations refer to vehicles used "in the business of agriculture" or some such phrase. The Road Traffic Act 1988 and the Road Traffic Regulation Act 1984 contain no general definition; the Vehicle Excise and Registration Act 1994 defines "agricultural tractor, light agricultural vehicle and agricultural engine" in Sch.1, Pt IVA (see *Bullen v Picking* [1974] R.T.R. 46 and the other cases quoted there). "Agricultural motor vehicle", "agricultural trailer" and "agricultural trailed appliance" are defined by reg.3(2) of the Road Vehicles (Construction and Use) Regulations 1986 (SI 1986/1078).

The relevant definition should be consulted in every case, but there have been these decisions. Unprocessed hides imported from abroad are "agricultural produce" (*Scarr v Wurzal* [1951] 1 All E.R. 1014). Taking a pony to a show is not use for hauling agricultural produce (*Henderson v Robson* (1949) 113 J.P. 313). A wholesale greengrocer who buys crops growing in a field does not use a vehicle sent to take them away in the business of agriculture (*Leach v Cooper* (1950) 48 L.G.R. 526). A vehicle licensed as a farm goods vehicle and used to carry furniture from a sale room to a farm worker's cottage is not used solely for the conveyance of articles required for the purposes of agricultural land (*McBoyle v Hatton Estate Co* 1951 S.L.T. (Sh.) 101; certain relevant cases cited are mentioned at [1952] Jo.Crim.L. 170).

1.196   Bricks and a fireplace for installation at a farm worker's cottage are not "articles required for the farm" (*Brook v Friend* [1954] Crim. L.R. 942). Nor is manure produced from racing stables after being produced on a farm as straw (*McKenzie v Griffiths Contractors (Agricultural) Ltd* [1976] R.T.R. 140); nor animal carcasses being taken from a slaughter house to a butcher after being similarly produced on a farm (*Cambrian Land Ltd v Allan* [1981] R.T.R. 109). A market gardener taking vegetables in his car to retail customers uses it in the business of agriculture (*Manley v Dobson* [1949] 2 All E.R. 578). *Fillingham v Hall*, 1935, unreported, deciding that agriculture does not include selling and distributing milk by retail, may be compared so far as farmers so doing are concerned. Moving agricultural implements and furniture from one farm to another is use in the business of agriculture (*Flatman v Poole* [1937] 1 All E.R. 495). See also 117 J.P. Jo. 18 where a decision of the Crown Court is noted accepting that moving furniture to a farm worker's cottage was within the terms of an insurance policy covering agricultural purposes. However, in a Scottish case a policy covering use "solely for agricultural or forestry purposes including the hauling of ... articles required for agriculture" did not cover use of a tractor to convey household furniture of a newly engaged farm servant to the farm (*Agnew v Robertson* 1956 S.L.T. (Sh.) 90). See also *Bruce v Odell* (1939) 27 Traff.Cas. 135, and [1954] Jo.Crim.L. 57.

"Agriculture" seems to include chicken and livestock farmings as well as cultivating the soil (*J.M. Knowles Ltd v Rand* [1962] 2 All E.R. 926) and hatching eggs can be articles required for agricultural land (ibid.). See also *London County Council v Lee* [1914] 3 K.B. 255. Turf can be an agricultural product (*Att Gen (McCloskey) v East* [1964] Jo.Crim.L. 123).

1.197   A finding by justices that a vehicle was an agricultural tractor was upheld by the Divisional Court, as not inconsistent in *DPP v Free's Land Drainage Co Ltd* [1990] R.T.R. 37. The prosecutor's appeal against the decision of justices to acquit the respondent company for using a vehicle without an operator's licence, and without a tachograph being fitted, was dismissed. The vehicle in question was a Unimog, which had been stopped by the police on the M4 motorway. It was towing a composite trailer consisting of a semi-trailer and a converter dolly. The semi-trailer was loaded with a tractor and an attached trailer. The vehicle was being driven to a farm site within a 50km radius from the company's base, and was being used for the carriage of goods for a contract with a farmer to provide drainage on the farm. The vehicle was a transporter to transport machines from site to site and also used for back-filling holes. The respondent company had carried out some non-agricultural work and the company had not been aware that its use of the vehicle had to be confined to agriculture. The justices were of the opinion that the Unimog was constructed and adapted for use off roads for the purposes of agriculture and primarily used for that purpose and was being used on the date in question solely for hauling articles required for farm use by a contractor engaged to do agricultural work. Accordingly, the informations were dismissed.

"AIDING, ABETTING, COUNSELLING AND PROCURING"

Generally

1.198 A person who aids, abets, counsels or procures the commission by another person of an offence commits the like offence although he may be subject to a different penalty. See § 19.15 as to the endorsement of licences and penalty points and § 20.56 as to disqualification of aiders and abettors. Aiding, etc., a summary offence, should in the information be stated to be contrary to s.44 of the Magistrates' Courts Act 1980 which governs the procedure for summary offences. The words aid, abet, counsel and procure do not indicate different offences, but a person cannot be convicted of aiding and abetting alone unless he was present when the offence was committed. It is for this reason preferable to use the complete phrase. Aiding, etc., requires proof of mens rea or guilty intent. Conspiracy to aid and abet is not an offence known to law (*R. v Hollinshead* [1985] 2 All E.R. 769).

A person cannot be guilty of aiding and abetting a crime if it be shown that no crime was committed (*Thornton v Mitchell* [1940] 1 All E.R. 339), but this case is distinguishable where *A* is charged with aiding and abetting the commission of an offence by *B* and it is shown that the offence was committed though not by *B*; cf. *R. v Anthony* [1965] 1 All E.R. 440 and *R. v Humphreys* [1965] 3 All E.R. 689. It seems that a person charged as a principal can be convicted although the evidence shows that he only aided and abetted (*Du Cros v Lambourne* (1907) 70 J.P. 525; *Cooper v Leeke* (1968) 112 S.J. 46).

1.199 The principle in *Thornton v Mitchell* seems to have been followed by the Court of Appeal in *R. v Loukes* [1996] R.T.R. 164 (although the short report does not refer to that authority). There the court of trial had acquitted the driver of a tipper truck of dangerous driving upon the judge's direction, but had then convicted the appellant of aiding and abetting the offence. The facts were that the appellant and his brother were partners in a firm of haulage contractors, and the appellant's role was to oversee the maintenance and servicing by the firm's mechanics of its fleet of vehicles. On the day in question, one of the firm's drivers was driving a tipper truck on the M1 when part of its propeller shaft broke causing the truck to crash into a car killing its driver. In giving the judgment of the Court of Appeal, Auld L.J. stated that the first ground of appeal was that the trial judge having directed the jury to acquit the driver of the principal offence, misdirected the jury by directing that the appellant could be found guilty of the secondary offence. His Lordship said that the effect although not the form of the ruling in regard to the driver of the truck was that there was no evidence of the commission of the actus reus of the principal offence. The actus reus of the offence of dangerous driving had the objective criterion of obviousness to a competent and careful driver, whether or not supplemented by any particular knowledge of the accused driver (s.2A(2) of the 1988 Act as amended). The appeal was allowed on that ground.

The law of aiding and abetting in relation to offences under the Public Order Act 1986 was considered by the Court of Appeal in *R. v Jefferson, Skerritt, Keogh and Readman* (1994) 158 J.P. 76. The court approved the trial judge's direction to the jury and the appeals of each appellant were dismissed.

1.200 The law was also considered in its more usual application to road traffic matters in *R. v Millward* [1994] Crim. L.R. 527. A defendant was convicted of aiding, abetting, counselling and procuring X to cause death by reckless driving. X was acquitted. The prosecution case was that the defendant had given his employee (X) instructions which involved him using one of the defendant's tractors to tow a trailer on a main road. The tractor's hitch was poorly maintained and during the journey the trailer became detached and hit a car causing the death of a passenger. The recklessness alleged was confined to the state of the hitch mechanism and the defendant was alleged to have procured the offence by his instructions to X. Was the defendant correctly convicted following the acquittal of the principal? As the word "reckless" imported a mental element into the actus reus of the offence, did X's acquittal imply that the actus reus had not been committed?

The Court of Appeal dismissed the defendant's appeal. It held: (1) that an accessory can be liable provided that there is the actus reus of the principal offence even if the principal offender is entitled to be acquitted because of some defence personal to him. Procuring does not require a joint intention between accessory and principal. The procuror may therefore be convicted where the principal lacks the necessary mens rea; (2) in the instant case, the actus reus was the taking of the vehicle in its defective condition on to the road so as to cause death (it was procured by the defendant); (3) the authorities cited in argument could be distinguished.

1.201 It should be noted that this decision arose from the old law, and it may be that the position will be much simpler now the "reckless" cases have worked through the system.

Where it is clear that an offence (e.g. a drink/driving offence) has been committed by one of two persons (the one being the driver and the other the passenger, but the circumstances were such that the passenger must have been equally guilty) and each of those persons maintains that the other was the driver, both may be charged as principals on the basis that whoever was the passenger must have been guilty of aiding and abetting the commission of the offence (*Smith v Mellors* [1987] R.T.R. 210).

The Divisional Court considered further the scope of the law relating to aiding **1.202** and abetting under s.44 of the Magistrates' Courts Act 1980 in *DPP v Anderson* [1990] R.T.R. 269. Justices dismissed an information against the respondent which alleged that he had aided and abetted the rider of a motor cycle to drive with excess alcohol. The respondent had been the pillion passenger on the machine at the material time, and it was admitted that the rider had been convicted of the excess alcohol offence. At the trial the prosecution adduced unchallenged evidence of an admission by the respondent to the police of knowing that the motor cyclist at the time when he was driving had consumed half a bottle of wine, half a bottle of cider, and a mixed spirit drink. The respondent also admitted that it was irresponsible of him to encourage the driving but said that he had had a lot to drink and so never thought about telling the motor cyclist not to drive. The Divisional Court, in allowing the appeal, held that in order to establish the offence, the prosecution had to prove that the principal offender had committed the offence; that the respondent was aware that, or was reckless whether, the principal offender had consumed excess alcohol; and that the respondent had aided or abetted, counselled or procured the principal offender to commit the offence.

It is possible to aid and abet an attempt (*R. v Dunnington* [1984] 1 All E.R. 676) although s.1(4) of the Criminal Attempts Act 1981 prevented the creation of the separate offence of attempting to aid and abet the commission of an indictable offence (including an "either way" offence) contrary to s.1(1).

Under s.14(3) of the 1988 Act *only* the person actually breaking the seat belt **1.203** law is guilty of an offence notwithstanding any enactment or rule of law (e.g. aiding and abetting) to the contrary. This provision does not apply to s.15 (drivers to be responsible for the wearing of seat belts or restraining devices by children under 14 in certain circumstances). Only the person driving or riding on a motor cycle in contravention of s.16 of the 1988 Act (crash helmet requirements) is guilty of an offence, notwithstanding any enactment or rule of law (e.g. aiding and abetting) to the contrary (s.16(4)). There is an exception, however, where the principal offender is under 16; the companion of the principal offender may be guilty of aiding and abetting in accordance with ordinary principles (see s.16(4)).

Counselling

It is not implicit in the word "counselling" that there must be a causal connection with the offence, but the offence must be committed within the scope of the authority or advice and not accidentally. So long as there is counselling, and so long as the principal offence has been committed by the one counselled acting in the scope of his authority, the offence is made out (*R. v Calhaem* [1985] Q.B. 808).

Cases

Reference to cases may be helpful. It was suggested by Lord Parker C.J. obiter, with Ashworth J. expressing his agreement, that where the statute creating the offence employs the words "using or causing or permitting" the latter two verbal nouns provide for the offences of being an accessory or aiding and abetting and in such cases the aider and abettor or accessory should be more properly charged with "permitting" or "causing" (*Carmichael & Sons Ltd v Cottle* [1971] R.T.R. 11 at 14, 15). Although Lord Parker C.J. remarked that he did not wish to come to a conclusion to this effect, this reasoning of Lord Parker C.J. and Ashworth J. was specifically approved in *Crawford v Haughton* [1972] 1 All E.R. 535.

If a person knows all the circumstances and those circumstances constitute an offence and he helps in the actions which constitute the offence, that may be enough to convict him of aiding and abetting, although he does not realise that those circumstances constitute an offence (*Ackroyds v DPP* [1950] 1 All E.R. 933). A person who carried on the business of a transport clearing house, hiring lorries to carry goods for other firms, should have inquired whether the A or B licence held by the lorry owner so engaged entitled him to carry the goods in question. If he fails in his duty to see whether the lorry owner can lawfully carry those goods, he abets the lorry owner in failing to comply with a condition of his licence should it be infringed by so carrying the goods (*Carter v Mace* [1949] 2 All E.R. 714). A man who does not know of the essential matters constituting an offence does not aid and abet its commission (*Johnson v Youden* [1950] 1 All E.R. 300). In *Ferguson v Weaving* [1951] 1 All E.R. 412 it was held on the facts that knowledge to constitute aiding and abetting could not be imputed to an employer because his employees know, and in *Cassady v Reg Morris (Transport) Ltd* [1975] Crim. L.R. 398 an employer was held to be rightly acquitted by justices of aiding and abetting his driver to fail to return his record book sheets to him where there was no evidence that the employer had encouraged his driver's failure.

1.206   *Carter v Mace*, above, was distinguished in *Davies, Turner & Co v Brodie* [1954] 3 All E.R. 283. There the defendant had made proper inquiries as to whether goods could be carried in another firm's lorry without contravening the terms of an A licence, but had been given false information. It was held that the defendant was not guilty of aiding and abetting the other firm in the illegal use of the vehicle. In *Smith v Jenner* (1968) 112 S.J. 52 a driving instructor was shown his pupil's then valid driving licence and he told him to renew when necessary. The instructor gave lessons without further inquiry and was charged with aiding and abetting the pupil to drive when unlicensed, the licence having expired. It was held that the instructor should not be convicted. See also *D. Stanton & Sons Ltd v Webber* (1972) 116 S.J. 667 (firm acquitted where there was no actual knowledge that the employee was a learner driver). In *Bateman v Evans* (1964) 108 S.J. 522 where the defendant allowed a disqualified person to drive his car in the belief that he was not disqualified, it was held that he was not guilty but would be if he had shut his eyes to the obvious or perhaps refrained from making the inquiries a reasonably sensible man would have made. Deliberate abstention from obtaining knowledge can constitute aiding and abetting (*Poultry World v Conder* [1975] Crim. L.R. 803).

A person may be guilty of aiding and abetting where he is under a legal duty to act to prevent an offence and he remains passive (*Rubie v Faulkner* [1940] 1 All E.R. 285). A supervisor can be convicted of aiding and abetting the learner driver to drive with excess blood-alcohol. He cannot escape conviction by arguing that he cannot know that the learner driver is above the limit unless and until the blood-alcohol level has been scientifically determined (*Crampton v Fish* (1969) 113 S.J. 1003). The learner driver and supervisor had been out drinking together that evening; the vehicle had hit the bank on three occasions and had been swerving from side to side. In *Carter v Richardson* [1974] R.T.R. 314, a supervisor of a learner driver was similarly convicted of aiding and abetting the learner driver to drive with alcohol in excess of the prescribed limit. It was held that it suffices if the aider and abettor was aware that the principal had had an excessive amount of alcohol or was reckless whether he had done so. The aider and abettor does not have to know the precise amount (*Carter v Richardson*, as above). The supervisor attempted to deceive the police that he had been driving and not his pupil. The justices were entitled to infer from that deception that he knew or believed his pupil had too much alcohol in his blood (per Mackenna J., at 318, *Carter v Richardson* above).

Following an accident, a learner driver walked away from the scene followed **1.207** by his supervisor, who took no steps to ensure that he remained at the scene. Forty minutes later, the two were seen together some two miles away walking towards the scene. The learner driver was convicted of failing to stop and the supervisor of aiding and abetting that offence (*Bentley v Mullen* [1986] R.T.R. 7).

As to the liability of an employer for his employees' acts, contrast *John Henshall (Quarries) Ltd v Harvey* [1965] 1 All E.R. 725 with *National Coal Board v Gamble* [1958] 3 All E.R. 203, where a private firm's lorry went to a Coal Board depot and was loaded with coal there. The Board's employee weighed the loaded lorry at a weighbridge of which he was in charge and found that the laden weight exceeded that allowed by the Construction and Use Regulations. Nevertheless he gave the weight ticket to the driver, who knew of the overweight. It was held, on a charge against the Board of aiding and abetting the use by the firm of an overweight lorry, that the crime of aiding and abetting was committed on proof of a positive act of assistance voluntarily done and a knowledge of the circumstances constituting the offence and that the question of motive was irrelevant. The handing of the weight ticket by the attendant at the weighbridge to the driver with knowledge that an offence was going to be committed made the Board aiders and abettors. A special feature of this case is that the Board called no evidence. In the *Henshall* case it was held that the knowledge of a subordinate employee, who was under the general supervision of a manager, was not enough to make his employer guilty of aiding and abetting an illegal act contributed to by the employee and unknown to the manager: to make the employer, whether a company or an individual, liable the employee should be a responsible officer, part of the "brains" of the company. It might be otherwise if the employer had handed over the effective management to an employee.

In *Pope v Minton* [1954] Crim. L.R. 711, the defendant knew that his friend **1.208** had been disqualified from driving, but told him that he could use his (defendant's) car if he wanted. The defendant was not present when the friend used the car, nor (semble) did he do any more to assist him to take and use it. It was held that the defendant was guilty of aiding and abetting the friend to drive while disqualified, but it would be otherwise if the car owner was genuinely unaware of the disqualification (*Bateman v Evans* (1964) 108 S.J. 522). A bus owner who put an inexperienced conductor in charge of the bus without proper supervision was held guilty of aiding and abetting the conductor in allowing overcrowding (*Gough v Rees* (1929) 94 J.P. 53). A lorry driver employed by a Scottish company set off on a long journey into England with a dangerously worn front offside tyre the condition of which he knew. The state of the tyre was also known to the managing director of the Scottish company. The tyre burst and the lorry crashed into a motor car, killing its occupants. It was held that the company and the managing director were guilty of counselling and procuring the offence of causing death by dangerous driving because the managing director knew of the dangerous state of the tyre (*R. v Robert Millar (Contractors) Ltd and Robert Millar* [1970] 1 All E.R. 577). Moreover, as the crime of the lorry driver was committed in England, and as counselling and procuring was not a crime on its own account but rather participating in a crime, they could be tried in England; an alternative reason for trial in England was that the counselling and procuring was a continuous act and continued as long as the driver drove the lorry with the dangerous tyre.

Evidence that a person charged as an aider and abettor has previously been warned about the same matters is admissible to show that he knew what might be going on (*Duxley v Gilmore* (1959) 123 J.P. Jo. 331). Merely riding in a vehicle, without more, does not show that the rider is aiding and abetting its illegal use; there should be some evidence of a joint enterprise (*D v Parsons* [1960] 2 All E.R. 493). In *Smith v Baker* [1972] Crim. L.R. 25 a passenger in a stolen car was held not to be guilty of aiding and abetting its uninsured use when he had not assisted in its use in any way, even though he had "a fair idea it was stolen" and ran away when the police arrived.

1.209   Surreptitiously lacing a motorist's drink knowing that he will then drive with excess alcohol as a result is "procuring" (*Att Gen's Reference (No.1 of 1975)* [1975] Q.B. 773).

A complex decision involving an alleged "procuring" of a man to drive with excess alcohol is *Blakely v DPP* [1991] R.T.R. 405. The facts contrast nicely with those of *Att Gen's Reference (No.1 of 1975)* above. In the instant case, the appellants laced a man's drinks in the belief that he would be unwilling to drive after drinking excess alcohol and with the hope that he would therefore be unable to return home. Before the appellants informed him that they had laced his drinks he did in fact drive, and was arrested when driving home. The Divisional Court held that the appellants were not on those facts "procuring" the offence. The court quoted with approval the words of Lord Widgery C.J. in the *Reference* that "to procure means to produce by endeavour. You procure a thing by setting out to see that it happens and taking the appropriate steps to produce that happening". McCullough J. said that that passage strongly suggested that the procurer had to be shown to have intended to bring about the commission of the principal offence and that mere awareness that it might result would not suffice. For a commentary on the case, see the article at 155 J.P. 612.

"ATTEMPT"

Generally

1.210   Motoring cases on attempt are discussed under the individual topics to which they relate: see § 4.22 in relation to drink/driving, § 15.27 in relation to theft and taking conveyances.

The Criminal Attempts Act 1981 abolished the common law doctrine that an attempt to commit an offence is itself an offence. By s.1(1) of the 1981 Act it is an offence to attempt to commit an indictable offence (including an "either way" offence). An attempt is defined as with intent doing "an act which is more than merely preparatory to the commission of the offence" (s.1(1)).

1.211   There is no general statutory provision enabling a person to be convicted of an attempt to commit a purely summary offence. It would seem, therefore, unless the wording of the summary offence itself includes attempts within its ambit (e.g. "driving or attempting to drive" with excess blood-alcohol under s.5(1) of the 1988 Act), it is not an offence to attempt to commit a purely summary offence. Section 3 of the 1981 Act provides that for specific statutory offences of attempt a person is guilty of attempt if with intent he does an act more than merely preparatory to the commission of the full offence (s.3(3)). It is not clear, however, whether s.3 applies to attempted offences under ss.4 and 5 of the 1988 Act; the wording of s.3 is obscure, and it is possible that it does not.

It should be emphasised that under the Criminal Attempts Act 1981 s.1(1) and under s.3(3) the defendant must *intend* to commit the relevant full offence. It is submitted that this imports the full mens rea of intent and that recklessness is insufficient. The matter is discussed at [1983] Crim. L.R. 365 and [1984] Crim. L.R. 25.

A person may be guilty of attempt under s.1 (indictable offences) or s.3 (special statutory offences) even though the facts are such that commission of the full offence is impossible (s.1(2) and s.3(4)). A person will still have the intent for the purposes of s.1 or s.3 in certain circumstances despite a misconception as to the facts (s.1(3) and s.3(5)). In *R. v Shivpuri* [1986] 2 W.L.R. 988, the House of Lords confirmed that a person is guilty under s.1 of the Act where, if the facts had been as he believed them to be, the full offence would have been committed by him, even though, on the true facts, the offence he set out to commit was impossible in law. (In reading that decision the House of Lords overruled its decision in *Anderton v Ryan* [1985] A.C. 560, in which reliance had been placed on the distinction between "objectively innocent" and "guilty" acts; in *R. v Shivpuri* the House of Lords stated that such distinction was incapable of sensible application to the law of criminal attempts.) There is still no offence if there is a misconception as to law. **1.212**

Where an unfit driver had no ignition key, but was sitting in the driver's seat attempting to insert other keys into the ignition, the Divisional Court held that he was properly convicted of attempting to drive while unfit through drink or drugs, contrary to s.4(1) of the 1988 Act (*Kelly v Hogan* [1982] R.T.R. 352). The court added that the position was the same as a burglar carrying a jemmy of the wrong size; the facts fell within the fourth category of offences described in *R. v Smith (Roger)* [1975] A.C. 476.

Under the earlier law a person charged with attempting to commit an offence could be convicted even though in law he committed the full offence (*Webley v Buxton* [1977] 2 All E.R. 595). This still seems to be the law. **1.213**

The mode of trial for offences under s.1(1) seems to be the same as for the full offence.

Under s.4 a person convicted of an attempt under s.1(1) incurs "any penalty" to which he would have been liable for the full offence. The effect of s.4 thus seems to be that where the full offence is obligatorily endorsable and carries discretionary disqualification, the attempt to commit that offence under s.1(1) itself becomes endorsable and disqualifiable (e.g. an attempt to drive while disqualified). (Attempted theft or the attempted taking of a motor vehicle carries a discretionary disqualification, but the endorsement of any driving licence with penalty points does not apply to these offences, and thus a penalty points disqualification cannot be imposed for them: see Road Traffic Act 1991 Sch.2 para.32(3).)

1.214   Section 1(1) of the 1981 Act does not apply to conspiracy, aiding, abetting, counselling or procuring the commission of an offence, nor to offences under s.4(1) or s.5(1) of the Criminal Law Act 1967 (s.1(4)). Although s.1(4) prevented the creation of the separate offence of attempting to aid and abet, etc., the commission of an indictable offence (including an "either way" offence) it is possible to aid and abet an attempt (*R. v Dunnington* [1984] 1 All E.R. 676).

Incitement is not affected by the Criminal Attempts Act 1981. The old law applies and it is not possible to incite the impossible if it is impossible (*R. v Fitzmaurice* [1983] 1 All E.R. 189).

"OWNER"

Meaning

1.215   The term "owner", in relation to a vehicle which is the subject of a hiring agreement or hire-purchase agreement, means the person in possession under that agreement (1988 Act, s.192; Road Traffic Regulation Act 1984 s.142(1)). For the purposes of giving information as to insurance under ss.165(1) and 170 the term in relation to a vehicle which is the subject of a hiring agreement includes each party to the agreement (Road Traffic Act 1988 ss.165(7), 171(3); see § 7.41 and § 10.69).

"Owner" is not defined in the Vehicle Excise and Registration Act 1994, and the person who is required to be registered is the person by whom the vehicle is kept (reg.3(1) of the Road Vehicles (Registration and Licensing) Regulations 2002 (SI 2002/2742)) who may or may not be the owner. The expression "ownership" is to be construed similarly (ibid.). "Owner" for the purpose of the vehicle owner liability provisions (Road Traffic Regulation Act 1984 ss.107–109 and Sch.8) is defined as the person by whom the vehicle is kept, and there is a presumption that the owner is the person registered as the keeper of the vehicle at the time (ibid. s.111(3) Sch.8 para.5).

1.216   A wide definition of the word "owner" was approved by the Divisional Court when faced by an application for judicial review in *R. v Parking Adjudicator Ex p. Wandsworth London Borough Council, The Times*, 22 July, 1996 ([1998] R.T.R. 51 records the decisions of the Court of Appeal contrary to the Divisional Court (see below)). The adjudicator had allowed two appeals by an individual, Jane Francis, against notices which had been served on her under the Road Traffic Act 1991 Sch.6 para.1. The facts were that at the relevant time the vehicle was in a garage for repairs. It was parked illegally by the garage and two penalty charge notices were fixed to the vehicle. When the vehicle was returned by the garage to Miss Francis, no mention was made of the notices. In delivering the judgment of the court, Schiemann L.J. stated that in general terms the 1991 Act made the owner liable, but that term was defined in s.82(2) of that Act to mean "the person by whom the vehicle was kept". The adjudicator had decided on appeal that the garage was the "owner". His Lordship said that the crucial question for the court was whether a garage could ever be the "owner", in the sense used by the statute, of the vehicle notwithstanding that it clearly was not the owner in the sense in which one would normally use that word. Having considered the legislation, although the matter was not easy, the adjudicator had been correct in his conclusion that s.82(3) was not an irrebuttable presumption. In essence his

Lordship said that it then became a question of fact. The relief sought by the Council was refused.

However, this decision was reversed by the Court of Appeal, following an appeal by the London Borough of Wandsworth, see [1998] R.T.R. 51. Stuart-Smith L.J., in delivering the principal judgment of the court, stated that the "owner" of a vehicle was defined by s.82(2) as the person by whom the vehicle was kept and that person, by s.82(3), was presumed to be the person in whose name the vehicle was at the time registered under the Vehicle Excise and Registration Act 1994. That presumption of ownership could only be rebutted in the ways mentioned in para.2(4)(a) of Sch.6 to the 1991 Act. The Court of Appeal therefore decided that a garage which accepted a vehicle for repair was not its owner within the meaning of s.82(2) of the Act.

It would seem therefore that it will take a specific statutory provision to remedy the potential for injustice to persons such as Miss Francis who on a broad view bore no culpability whatsoever for the tickets attached to her vehicle. The interpretation of the present law is now clear as a result of the decision of the Court of Appeal. **1.217**

A perhaps rather less important, though nonetheless interesting, case dealing with ownership and whether strict proof is necessary arose in *Sturrock v DPP* [1996] R.T.R. 216. The facts were simple. The defendant was riding a new, expensive cycle fitted with a lock for which he had no key. In interview he had admitted he had taken the cycle, knew it did not belong to him, and failed to give any reason for why he might have had lawful authority for having it in his possession. He was prosecuted under s.12(5) of the Theft Act 1968 that he "without having the consent of the owner or other lawful authority, took a pedal cycle for his own use". He submitted at the close of the prosecution case that he had no case to answer, asserting, in terms, that in the absence of a statement from the owner saying that he had not given consent, etc., it was not possible to prove the case beyond reasonable doubt, or at all. The submission was rejected. The justices found that there was a case to answer relying on the defendant's admissions, the state of the cycle, and the lock, leading by inference to the conclusion that there was an owner of the cycle, even though he had not been called. The defendant then changed his plea to guilty, and appealed by case stated. The Divisional Court gave the appeal short shrift. The justices had been entitled to infer, on the basis of the facts, that the cycle had not been abandoned and did have an owner, even though the owner of the cycle had not been identified. Thus, they were entitled to find that there was a case for the defendant to answer, based on his own admissions concerning the taking and possession of the cycle and in the absence of a formal statement from the loser, first to confirm that there was an owner and thereafter to the effect that consent was not given to anyone to take the cycle. Kennedy L.J. went on to remind justices that there was no obligation whatsoever to state a case where they regarded the request as frivolous!

See also "Proof generally" at § 3.82.

CHAPTER 2

PROCEDURE

CONTENTS

COMMENCING PROCEEDINGS

Generally

2.01   The majority of road traffic prosecutions are begun by summons issued on an information laid before a magistrate or justices' clerk or person authorised by the justices' clerk. The information may, however, be served on the magistrates' court officer by anyone on behalf of the prosecutor (Criminal Procedure Rules 2005 (SI 2005/384) r.2.5(2)). It may be an abuse of the process of the court for a prosecutor to lay an information before deciding whether to prosecute (*R. v Brentford JJ. Ex p. Wong* [1981] Crim. L.R. 339. See further "Refusal to hear a case", § 2.63). The High Court may make a vexatious proceedings order under which the person subject to an order may only pursue proceedings with the leave of the High Court (the Supreme Court Act 1981 s.42).

An information may be oral or in writing (see below, however, for the requirements where a warrant is sought). There is no prescribed form. It should identify the informant and also the defendant (by description if necessary) and give particulars of the offence and statute, etc. It seems that an unincorporated body of persons cannot lay an information charging a criminal offence—see *Rubin v DPP* [1989] R.T.R. 261.

2.02   Section 29 of the Criminal Justice Act 2003 provides a new procedure which enables identified prosecutors to institute criminal proceedings by issuing a written charge together with a requisition, that is, a requirement to appear before a specified magistrates' court to answer the charge. A copy of both the written charge and the requisition must be served on the court. The Criminal Procedure Rules 2005 (SI 2005/384) were amended by the Criminal Procedure (Amendment No.2) Rules 2006 (SI 2006/2636) which apply to these documents the existing rules concerning the form, content and service of summonses. By the same rules, neither requisition nor summons needs to be signed by the person issuing it but the name of that person will be stated within the document. Prosecutors identified by s.29 of the 2003 Act include all those public bodies likely to institute proceedings for the offences described in this work. Where this process is implemented, it will replace the power to lay an information in order to obtain a summons (Criminal Justice Act 2003 s.29(4)). It would appear that the effect of this change is likely to mean that it is the date of the first issuing of the requisition that will be relevant for ascertaining whether an offence has been prosecuted within the required time-limits.

The laying of an information

There is a distinction between laying an information, which is a ministerial act **2.03** by the prosecutor, and issuing process, which is a judicial function for the magistrate or justices' clerk or person authorised by the justices' clerk under the Justices' Clerks Rules 2005 (SI 2005/545): *Hill v Anderton* [1982] 2 All E.R. 963, HL, also reported under the name *R. v Manchester Stipendiary Magistrate* at [1982] R.T.R. 449. The information is laid when it is received at the relevant office. Many informations will be prepared and laid using electronic methods. The need for caution when laying informations electronically was highlighted in *Atkinson v DPP* [2004] EWHC 1457; (2004) 168 J.P. 472. The defendant was prosecuted for carrying an insecure load. The date of the alleged offence was June 16, 2002. The information date printed on the summons was December 10, 2002 (and so within the six-month time-limit). The summons itself was printed on December 20, 2002. On the computer system in use, the police entered initial data and the date of the entry was recorded. A summons would not be issued until that information is "validated" and no record was made of any changes between the original entry and the validation. In that time, it was possible to change the data originally entered including the date given as the information date. The date of validation was not recorded and therefore it was not possible to ascertain any date before the date on which the summons was issued as the date of validation and, therefore, the date of the information. Accordingly, since the summons was issued more than six months after the date of the alleged offence, the magistrates had no jurisdiction.

Factual and legal items common to a number of informations such as the date and place may be set out in a single preamble and incorporated by reference (*Shah v Swallow* [1984] 2 All E.R. 528, HL).

It is quite clear that an information must give sufficient particulars of the of- **2.04** fence being charged. The requirements for a fair hearing in the European Convention on Human Rights (incorporated into domestic law by the Human Rights Act 1998) require defendants to be clearly informed of what is alleged and to have a reasonable time for the preparation of their defence. An illustration of this principle can be found in the decision of the Divisional Court in *Halls Construction Services Ltd v DPP* [1989] R.T.R. 399. The company was convicted of using heavy goods vehicles without holding the appropriate licences. On appeal against conviction, they argued that the informations were defective in that they lacked sufficient particulars of the offences being charged, especially the amount of tax which should have been paid. The appeal was allowed. It was held that the informations did not enable the appellants to appreciate the case they had to meet, nor did they give a clear idea of the maximum penalty. The court also said that notices sent out by the Department of Transport informing the defendants of the penalties and back-duty payable were capable of curing a defective information. However, such notices required study of the legislation—which was being constantly amended—in order to ascertain liability for back-duty and penalties; that was a difficult task even for a lawyer. In view of the requirement for magistrates and defendants to know precisely what sum was payable, it was unacceptable that the appellants had not been informed that the prosecution was seeking to recover penalties and back-duty. The appeal was allowed.

A magistrate (or justices' clerk or authorised person) may not reconsider an application which has already been rejected by a fellow magistrate (or justices' clerk or authorised person) (*R. v Worthing JJ.* [1981] Crim. L.R. 778). It is submitted that this does not preclude a further application at the discretion of the magistrate (or justices' clerk or authorised person) where there is fresh material.

2.05　　Consideration has been given to circumstances in which a decision by the prosecution to expand the number of charges against an offender would be an abuse of process. In *DPP v B (Daniel Paul)* [2008] EWHC 201, the defendant had been charged with a single offence of indecent assault arising from an assault by the defendant on his daughter; the charge referred to a 13-year period during which the offence took place. In interview, the defendant accepted that assaults took place over a seven-year period. He pleaded guilty before a magistrates' court and was committed for sentence. When the case appeared before the Crown Court, the judge took the view that a single charge did not permit the length of sentence that the defendant's criminality might justify and suggested that the prosecution should reconsider its decision on charge. The prosecution subsequently preferred 17 charges. Magistrates accepted the defendant's contention that this was an abuse of process, but this decision was overturned by the Divisional Court. The court stated that "[p]roceedings should only be stayed for abuse of process in exceptional circumstances where it can properly be said that the consequence would be injustice, or where the circumstances giving rise to the proceedings in respect of which the application is made offend one's sense of justice overall": [2008] EWHC 201 at [10]. Whilst the prosecution could properly decline to prefer further charges, it could not be said to be an abuse where they chose to do so. The offender would clearly be at risk of a greater sentence, but he would not be exposed to a sentence other than the proper one for offences established either by his admissions or by trial.

Where an information was required to be laid within two months of the procuring of a sample, unless the magistrate certified that it was "not practicable to do so", the words were to be construed strictly, and the discretion exercised judicially (*R. v Harvey Ex p. Select Livestock Producers Ltd* (1985) 149 J.P. 389).

The issue of a summons

2.06　　The issue of a summons is a judicial act. Certain basic requirements should be fulfilled before the issue, namely that:

    (a)　the allegation is of an offence known to law and the essential ingredients of the offence are prima facie present;

    (b)　the offence alleged is not "out of time";

    (c)　the court has jurisdiction; and

    (d)　the informant has the necessary authority to prosecute.

A proposed defendant has no right to be heard at this stage; he may be heard only at the discretion of the court (*R. v West London JJ. Ex p. Klahn* [1979] 1 W.L.R. 933). The Criminal Procedure Rules 2005 (SI 2005/384) (as amended by the Criminal Procedure (Amendment No. 2) Rules 2008 (SI 2008/3269)) provide in r.7.4(1) that a court may issue (or withdraw) a summons or warrant without giving the parties any opportunity to make representations and without a hearing.

Where a hearing is arranged, it can be in public or in private. In *R. v Clerk to the Bradford JJ. Ex p. Sykes* (1999) 163 J.P. 224, it was held that the person considering the issue of a summons was entitled to make inquiries beyond the information, but was not under a duty to do so.

The question of whether or not an information discloses an offence known to   **2.07**
law is one which should be tackled at the outset, i.e. prior to the issue of a summons; it should not be left in abeyance until the matter comes to trial. A party aggrieved by the issue (or non-issue) of process may apply for judicial review (*R. v Horseferry Road JJ. Ex p. Independent Broadcasting Authority* [1986] 2 All E.R. 666). Magistrates may refuse to issue a summons if they think fit on reasonable grounds. If a summons is unreasonably refused, there may be a judicial review to compel its issue. It was held in *R. v Bury JJ. Ex p. Anderton* [1987] Crim. L.R. 638, that the High Court had jurisdiction to grant relief by way of judicial review to quash a summons where it could be clearly shown that the issue of a summons was an abuse of the process of the court and the allegations which the summons made were oppressive and vexatious. Before exercising their discretion to issue a summons, the person considering the issue is entitled to inquire as to the reasons for delay in laying an information even though the statutory time-limit for the laying of informations has not been breached (*R. v Clerk to the Medway JJ. Ex p. Department of Health and Social Security* [1986] Crim. L.R. 686). In *Wei Hai Restaurant Ltd v Kingston upon Hull City Council* [2001] EWHC Admin 490; (2002) 166 J.P. 185, informations were laid for breaches of food safety provisions virtually at the end of the 12-month limitation period although, the defence alleged, the Council had been in a position to proceed within two to three months of the initial investigation. The deputy district judge found that there had been delay in the proceedings and applied the test of whether that delay had led to prejudice in that the appellants would be denied a fair trial. He found that that was the case in respect of two of the 16 informations and they were stayed. His refusal to stay the other informations was upheld by the Administrative Court which emphasised that the power to stay proceedings was to be exercised "most sparingly" and only when the alleged abuse directly affected the fairness of the trial.

The issue of a warrant

By s.1(4) of the Magistrates' Courts Act 1980 a warrant to arrest a defendant   **2.08**
aged 18 or over in the first instance may not be issued for any offence unless it is indictable or an "either way" offence, or punishable with imprisonment, or his address is not sufficiently established to enable a summons to be served on him. For such a warrant the information must be in writing and substantiated on oath (s.1(3)).

Under s.13 of the Magistrates' Courts Act 1980 (as amended) a warrant may only be issued on non-appearance where the offence is punishable with imprisonment or the court, having convicted the defendant, proposes to disqualify him. Where the defendant is under 18, the requirement is that the offence be punishable with imprisonment in relation to a person aged 18 or over: s.13(3A). There are certain further restrictions on the exercise of this power to issue a warrant on non-appearance which are set out in s.13. If the court has received evidence or convicted the defendant on his pleading guilty the court must think it undesirable to proceed in his absence by reason of the gravity of the offence (s.13(5)). It is submitted that evidence means evidence in the trial and not in respect of a preliminary matter. Any summons issued must have been served and served a reasonable time before the hearing. Apart from this, a warrant may always be issued for a failure to answer bail (Bail Act 1976 s.7(1)).

2.09 A warrant may not be issued unless the condition in s.13(2A) or s.13(2B) has been fulfilled. In s.13(2A), the condition is that it is proved to the satisfaction of the court, on oath or in such other manner as may be prescribed, that the summons was served on the accused within what appears to the court to be a reasonable time before the trial or adjourned trial. In s.13(2B), the condition is that (a) the adjournment now being made is a second or subsequent adjournment of the trial; (b) the accused was present on the last (or only) occasion when the trial was adjourned; and (c) on that occasion the court determined the time for the hearing at which the adjournment is now being made.

The distinction between the position at first instance and following non-appearance will be noted. Some "either way" offences are punishable with imprisonment only on indictment (e.g. forgery of driving licences, insurances, etc., contrary to s.173(1) of the 1988 Act). Although such offences might be regarded as remaining imprisonable after the decision to proceed to summary trial and when being dealt with summarily because of, e.g. the power under s.3 of the Powers of Criminal Courts (Sentencing) Act 2000 to commit for sentence, *R. v Melbourne* [1980] Crim. L.R. 510, see § 16.18 implies the contrary.

2.10 A considerable extension to the powers of the police in cross-border enforcement is provided by ss.136–140 of the Criminal Justice and Public Order Act 1994. Perhaps the most important for readers of this work is s.136, which provides that a warrant for arrest issued in one part of the United Kingdom may be executed in another part and that it may be executed either by an officer from a force within the jurisdiction in which it was issued or by an officer of the jurisdiction within which the arrest takes place, as well as by any other person authorised within the warrant to issue it. Section 140 conveys reciprocal powers of arrest, so that a constable from one jurisdiction and present in another jurisdiction in the United Kingdom, may arrest a person using the police powers applicable to the local jurisdiction.

These provisions must be regarded as unexceptionable, and the flexibility granted by Parliament should enable the police to proceed with fewer encumbrances against alleged offenders who possess much greater mobility than was the case only a few years ago. Consideration is being given to extending these powers to court staff and to approved bodies.

2.11 Unless a statute otherwise requires, a prosecution may be commenced by any person. Exceptions are most prosecutions under Pts II and III of the Public Passenger Vehicles Act 1981 (see s.69), and prosecutions for most of the offences under the Vehicle Excise and Registration Act 1994 (see s.47), and (possibly) for obstruction and other offences under the Town Police Clauses Act 1847 s.28. There is no necessity for a third party prosecutor to prove public interest before being able to initiate proceedings: *R. (on the application of Ewing) v Davis* [2007] EWHC 1730; [2007] 1 W.L.R. 3223. Whilst most prosecutions are initiated by publicly funded bodies or by organisations, a private individual not directly affected by an offence is entitled to lay an information with a view to commencing proceedings for an offence. Where that offence is contrary to a public or general Act of Parliament, that Act would have been enacted for the public benefit and there was no obligation on a prosecutor to demonstrate that the particular prosecution had a public interest benefit. There were sufficient other safeguards arising from the power of the courts in relation to an abuse of process and from the power of the DPP to take over (and discontinue) prosecutions.

The proceedings may be continued notwithstanding the death of the informant prior to the hearing (*R. v Truelove* (1880) 5 Q.B.D. 336), or prior to the appeal if a police informant (*Hawkins v Bepey* [1980] 1 All E.R. 797).

Form of summons

An irregularity or illegality in the mode of bringing a defendant before the court, if not objected to at the hearing, does not invalidate the conviction (*Gray v Customs Commissioners* (1884) 48 J.P. 343).   **2.12**

By r.7.4(2) of the Criminal Procedure Rules 2005 (SI 2005/384) a single summons can be issued on more than one information and r.7.2(4) expressly provides that two or more informations may be set out in one document. The cases where more than one charge has been included in the information should be read with these provisions in mind. See also *Shah v Swallow*, § 2.03 above. As to the particulars in the summons generally, see the Criminal Procedure Rules 2005 r.7.4(3). Examples of insufficient detail in summonses are found in *Stephenson v Johnson* [1954] 1 All E.R. 369 and *Cording v Halse* [1954] 3 All E.R. 287. The summons does not have to show the date of the laying of the information unless there is some question of its being out of time (see *R. v Godstone JJ Ex p. Secretary of State for the Environment* [1974] Crim. L.R. 110). It is perfectly proper for the signature to be affixed by a rubber stamp (*R. v Brentford JJ. Ex p. Catlin* [1975] 2 All E.R. 201). With regard to whether an information is bad for duplicity, practitioners should note the decisions set out at §§ 2.91 et seq.

Under r.7.3(1), every information must contain a statement of the offence (describing it in ordinary language and identifying the legislation that creates it) and enough detail about the conduct to make it clear what is being alleged against the defendant. Under r.7.4(3), a summons must give details of when and where the defendant is required to attend court together with the offence(s) alleged and the person under whose authority the summons is issued. The 2005 Rules are, however, directory and not mandatory because in so far as they conflict with the statute they have to be adapted to meet it (per Ormrod L.J. in *Thornley v Clegg* [1982] R.T.R. 405 at 410). In *Simmons v Fowler* (1950) 48 L.G.R. 623 DC (discussed at 115 J.P.Jo. 322) it was held that the summons should indicate the Act and the regulation. The summons should specify the defects in the parts and accessories but does not need to specify whether the defects are in the parts or in the accessories (*Brindley v Willett* [1981] R.T.R. 19). The requirements for a fair hearing in the European Convention on Human Rights (incorporated into domestic law by the Human Rights Act 1998) require defendants to be clearly informed of what is alleged and to have a reasonable time for the preparation of their defence.   **2.13**

A person cannot be convicted under a repealed statute even if it has been re-enacted with identical words (*Stowers v Darnell* [1973] Crim. L.R. 528). However, the information may be amended. Again, where the statute has been omitted it is possible to amend by inserting it providing the defendant is not misled (*Thornley v Clegg* above, applying s.123 of the Magistrates' Courts Act 1980). See also *Jones v Thomas* [1987] R.T.R. 111 where it was held that an information was not defective and was incapable of misleading where it referred to an alleged offence as being contrary to s.6(1) (now s.5(1) of the 1988 Act) of the Road Traffic Act 1972 "as amended", rather than "as substituted". The Divisional Court considered, however, that the more appropriate form of wording was, " s.6 of the Road Traffic Act 1972 as substituted by s.25 of the Transport Act 1981".

2.14   See § 2.91 as to duplicity and charging alternative offences and § 2.80 as to amending a summons.

Authority to prosecute

2.15   Where the authority of some person or body to prosecute is required, the person before whom the information is laid should satisfy himself that such authority has been duly given before issuing the summons: at the hearing the summons is presumed to have been duly authorised and the prosecutor need take no further steps unless the defence raises an objection. Such an objection should be taken before the prosecutor's case is closed (*Price v Humphries* [1958] 2 All E.R. 725). Where necessary, an adjournment should be granted. A requirement for the consent of a Law Officer of the Crown or the Director of Public Prosecutions for the proceedings to be instituted or carried on by him or them does not prevent the arrest with or without warrant or the remand of the person concerned (Prosecution of Offences Act 1985 s.25). Where any consent or action of the Director is required, the consent given or the action taken by the Crown Prosecutor shall be treated as if made by the Director. The consent signed by the Law Officer, the Director or the Crown Prosecutor is admissible as prima facie evidence (s.26).

Where, however, the defence request proof of compliance with the statutory formalities it is for the prosecution to produce the necessary evidence. In default the justices are entitled to hold that there is no case to answer (*Anderton v Frost* [1984] R.T.R. 106). That case was one of driving a heavy goods vehicle without an HGV licence. Only certain persons, specified in what is now s.3 of the 1988 Offenders Act, may prosecute. The informations were laid in the name of the Chief Constable under a general authority issued by him to his Divisional Chief Officers. The defence required evidence that the informations had been laid by the Chief Constable and this was not forthcoming: cf. *Westminster Coaching Services v Piddlesden* (1933) 97 J.P. 185. The decision in that case was based on what is now s.69 of the Public Passenger Vehicles Act 1981. The statutory provisions were similar to s.3 of the 1988 Offenders Act but it was held that authorisation had been given. A police sergeant laid an information which was signed by an Assistant Commissioner of the Metropolitan Police and by a Superintendent and the Commissioner had given a general authorisation in writing to prosecute. There is an article at (1984) 148 J.P. 521 drawing attention to some of the difficulties inherent in s.69. See also the cases at § 7.26 and § 12.135.

2.16   The limits on the power of a local authority to prosecute were explored in *Middlesbrough Borough Council v Safeer* [2001] EWHC Admin 525; [2002] R.T.R. 3. The Council had initiated proceedings against the defendants for plying for hire as hackney carriages without licences and for using a vehicle without insurance and they had been convicted. On appeal to the Crown Court, it was argued that the Council had no authority to prosecute for the no insurance offences and that, if it did, the word "prosecute" did not encompass initiating proceedings simply allowing the Council to continue proceedings once initiated. The appeals were allowed by the Crown Court and the Council appealed to the

Divisional Court which overturned the decisions of the Crown Court. Section 222 of the Local Government Act 1972 gives wide powers to prosecute proceedings to a local authority where it considers it "expedient for the promotion or protection of the interests of the inhabitants of their area". Section 4 of the Road Traffic Offenders Act 1988 prescribes certain specified offences for which a Council may "institute proceedings"; the offence of no insurance is not among them. The Crown Court allowed the appeals on the basis that s.4 of the 1988 Act provided an exhaustive list of road traffic offences in respect of which a local authority had power to institute criminal proceedings. Section 222 could not, therefore, be relied on by the Council. Rejecting those arguments, the Divisional Court stated that there was nothing in the 1988 Act to justify the conclusion that s.4 provided an exhaustive and comprehensive list and there was no policy reason to read that section as limiting the powers given in the 1972 Act. In the light of the Council's regulatory powers in relation to hackney vehicles there could be no question that the power to prosecute for no insurance was well within the powers given by the 1972 Act. Further, the use of the word "prosecute" in that Act encompassed all steps necessary to pursue a prosecution including the institution of proceedings. Such summonses can be prosecuted in the name of the local authority and do not need to be in the name of a named individual: *Monks v East Northamptonshire District Council* [2002] EWHC 473; (2002) 166 J.P. 592.

Where a certificate may be produced to establish consent and an incorrect certificate has been produced or seemingly has been overlooked, a correct certificate may be produced subsequent to the laying of the information where the lawfulness is challenged: *R. v Clerkenwell Metropolitan Stipendiary Magistrate Ex p. DPP* [1984] 2 W.L.R. 244. The certificate is not the consent but *evidence* (or if the Act so stipulates) *conclusive evidence* of the consent (ibid.).

Where, however, the information has been laid by a person who has not been **2.17** generally or specifically authorised, an authorisation given after the laying of the information would not, it seems, validate the proceedings.

The considerable discretion residing in those taking decisions as to whether or not to institute/continue prosecutions was confirmed by the decision of the Divisional Court in *R. v Chief Constable of Kent Ex p. L*; *R. v DPP Ex p. B* [1993] 1 All E.R. 756. The court would only intervene where it could be demonstrated that the decision was made regardless of settled policy or guidelines. After considering the terms of the relevant Home Office circular on cautioning, Watkins L.J. said that it was difficult to envisage with regard to that policy, a circumstance (fraud or dishonesty apart possibly) which would allow of a challenge to a decision to prosecute or to continue proceedings unless it could be demonstrated, in the case of a youth, that there had been either a total disregard of the policy or, contrary to it, a lack of inquiry into the circumstances and background of that person, previous offences and general character, by the prosecutor and the Crown Prosecution Service. See also *R. v DPP Ex p. C* (2001) 165 J.P. 102.

It is helpful to include at this point the decision in *R. v Tower Bridge Metropol-* **2.18** *itan Stipendiary Magistrate Ex p. Chaudhry* [1994] R.T.R. 113, also reported *sub nom. R. v Metropolitan Stipendiary Magistrate Ex p. Chaudhry* at (1994) 158 J.P. 97. The son of the applicant was killed in an accident. The driver of the vehicle involved was summoned for driving without due care and attention, and for failing to comply with a traffic sign. The case was conducted by the Crown Prosecution Service. The applicant laid an information before a magistrate seeking the issue of a summons alleging an offence of causing death by reckless driving. The magistrate was aware of the proceedings against the driver but unaware of the fact that he intended to plead guilty. He was of the opinion that he was prevented by authority from issuing the summons where the Crown Prosecution Service had conduct of the case, and he refused to issue it. The applicant sought an order of certiorari. Her application failed. The magistrate was not obliged to refuse the summons. He had to consider all relevant circumstances but was not to go so far as to conduct a preliminary hearing. An individual prosecutor did not have the unfettered right to pursue the prosecution to trial. At any time the Director of Public Prosecutions could take over the case and discontinue it. While no suggestion could be made by the court that a magistrate was never to issue a summons for a private person against a defendant who already had to answer one or more informations in respect of the same matter, the magistrate should be very slow to take that step, and should be all the more hesitant when the Director of Public Prosecutions could take over the case. The court stated that it could not and would not interfere with the magistrate's refusal to issue the summons in the exercise of his judicial discretion.

2.19   The decision in *Ex p. Chaudhry* was considered by the Divisional Court in *R. v Macclesfield Magistrates Ex p. Cookson*, February 7, 1996, unreported (CO/737/ 95). A fatal accident had occurred and the police considered that the driver involved in the accident should be prosecuted for causing death by dangerous driving. The Crown Prosecution Service took the view that he should be prosecuted for driving without due care and attention and a summons was issued. The applicant's solicitors applied for a summons for the s.1 offence. The clerk to the justices refused the summons. The driver pleaded guilty to the allegation that he drove without due care and attention, was fined, and had six penalty points endorsed on his licence. Despite the fact that the Chief Crown Prosecutor had informed the applicant in writing that if the parents of the person who had been fatally injured in the accident did start a private prosecution, the Crown Prosecution Service would not take it over, the Divisional Court refused to grant the relief sought. All relevant circumstances of the case had been considered. The clerk knew that the prosecution for driving without due care would be proceeded with; that the Crown Prosecution Service did not intend to take over the prosecution; that there was no bad faith on behalf of the Crown Prosecution Service; and that all relevant circumstances had been considered. The clerk had considered the decision in *Chaudhry* and the representations of the applicant's solicitors. Tribute was paid to the care in which the clerk had addressed the matter and the preparation of notes taken at the time.

JURISDICTION OVER OFFENDERS

Youths

2.20   The principal aim of the youth justice system is set out in s.37 of the Crime and Disorder Act 1998 as the prevention of offending by children and young people. All involved must have regard to that aim: s.37(2). Speed in bringing matters to a conclusion is an important consideration, particularly for persistent young offenders.

Sections 43–45 of the 1998 Act amend s.22 of the Prosecution of Offences Act 1985 to allow for time-limits to be prescribed for the various stages in proceedings affecting young offenders.

The need to avoid adjournments wherever possible is emphasised by s.47(5) of **2.21**
the 1998 Act which provides that a court is not required to adjourn a case just
because another case against the same defendant has been committed for trial or
because a further charge has been preferred. Any case against a young offender
should be dealt with at the earliest possible opportunity.

This and subsequent paragraphs must be read in the light of the implementation of those provisions bringing 17-year-olds within the jurisdiction of what is
now the youth court rather than the adult court. The cases below which, e.g.
determine at what point a youth becomes an adult will continue to provide guiding principles as to when a youth is to be treated as an adult at law, albeit that the
age at which that transition will take place is now 18 rather than 17. In the following text the word "youth" has been used where there was previously a reference to "juvenile".

Subject to the exceptions below, only a youth court may deal with an offence **2.22**
by a youth under 18. Again, subject to the exceptions below, the court cannot
commit the youth for trial at the Crown Court even if the prosecution or the
defence wish to have the charge tried before a jury (Magistrates' Courts Act 1980
s.24). (As to when a youth "appears or is brought" before magistrates for the
purposes of s.24 see below.)

A youth charged with "homicide" or certain offences where a minimum mandatory sentence applies must be committed for trial at the Crown Court if the case
justifies it. Such a charge cannot be tried summarily (s.24(1)).

If the offence is punishable when committed by an adult with 14 years' **2.23**
imprisonment or more (e.g. robbery) or is one of a small number of specified offences, the court may at its discretion commit for trial a youth where of the
opinion that the sentencing court should have available greater powers than those
available to the youth court (s.24(1)(a)). In exercising its discretion, a court does
not have to hear evidence (*R. v South Hackney Juvenile Court* (1983) 77 Cr. App.
R. 294). By virtue of ss.224–229 of the Criminal Justice Act 2003 special sentences are provided for those classified as "dangerous offenders". These provisions only apply to those convicted of "specified offences"—those included in
this work are manslaughter, causing death by dangerous driving and causing
death by careless driving under the influence of drink or drugs. In the case of a
youth, there is already power to commit such an offence to the Crown Court for
trial. Even where a court determines to retain a case for summary trial, there is
now power to commit such a case to the Crown Court for sentence under the
dangerousness provisions.

In the case of "a charge made jointly" against a youth and an adult, the youth
must be sent to a magistrates' court other than a youth court (Children and Young
Persons Act 1933 s.46). There is some uncertainty as to what is meant by
"charged jointly". It may be more restricted than "charged with a joint offence",
so that a youth who is charged with a joint offence but not charged jointly,
because, e.g. the adult has absconded or been dealt with, may nevertheless be
dealt with in a youth court.

Provided the youth is charged jointly with an adult, the magistrates' court may **2.24**
commit them both for trial if the court considers it necessary in the interests of
justice to do so and if the case justifies it (Magistrates' Courts Act 1980
s.24(1)(b)). In *R. v Doncaster Crown Court Ex p. Crown Prosecution Service*
(1987) 85 Cr. App. R. 1, it was held that when justices were considering whether

it was in the interests of justice that a juvenile (youth) should be charged jointly with an adult pursuant to s.24(1)(b) it was necessary that they both appear before the court at the same time; but once that decision had been taken, it was not necessary that they should appear together in subsequent committal proceedings when the case against each individual defendant was being considered. The court in such a case may also commit the youth for trial for any other indictable offence with which he is charged at the same time (whether jointly with the adult or not) if that other offence arises out of circumstances which are the same as or connected with those giving rise to the *joint* offence (s.24(2)) or if the charges for both offences could be joined in the same indictment (s.24(1A)). This section may still mean that the adult is committed for trial on indictable offences connected with other indictable offences with which the youth is charged but for which he cannot be committed for trial. It would be preferable if the youth could be committed on all indictable offences in these circumstances.

Where there is insufficient evidence to commit the adult for trial, he will be discharged and, normally, the youth will be dealt with summarily, unless the offence justifies committal as a "possible severe punishment case". This decision can be taken by a magistrates' court which is not a youth court: *R. v Tottenham Youth Court Ex p. Fawzy* [1998] 1 All E.R. 365. In *R. v Peterborough Magistrates' Court Ex p. Allgood* [1996] R.T.R. 26, an application for leave to apply for judicial review, the interpretation of s.24 of the Magistrates' Courts Act 1980 fell to be considered. In refusing leave, the Divisional Court held that two persons charged respectively with driving and with allowing himself to be carried in a vehicle taken without the owner's consent under ss.12 and 12A of the Theft Act 1968 are properly considered to be charged jointly within the meaning of s.24(1)(b). The word "jointly" in that paragraph does not acquire a restricted meaning, but is to be given its natural meaning.

2.25   Where a youth is before a magistrates' court on an information jointly charging him with an adult in this way and:

    (a) the court does not dispose of the youth's case by way of committal proceedings;

    (b) the adult(s) jointly charged are dealt with by way of committal proceedings or are tried summarily and *plead* guilty;

    (c) the youth pleads not guilty,

the magistrates' court may remit him to a youth court for trial (Magistrates' Courts Act 1980 s.29).

It will be noted that in s.29 the words "information jointly charging him" is specific. They do not mean charged at the same time. It is necessary to watch carefully for the case where the adult has been convicted on an earlier occasion but did not plead guilty. There is no power to remit in these circumstances. This power to remit is not restricted to indictable or "either way" offences. A court committing a youth for trial may do so under s.6 of the Magistrates' Courts Act 1980 (s.24(1)) without consideration of the evidence.

2.26   As stated above, a youth charged jointly with an adult *must* be sent to a magistrates' court (other than a youth court) along with the adult in the first instance. In certain other cases he *may* be tried by a magistrates' court other than a youth court:

    (a) if either the youth or the adult is a principal offender and the other is an aider or abettor of the offence;

(b) if the fact that the defendant is a youth only emerges in the course of the proceedings; or

(c) if the youth is charged with an offence arising out of the circumstances or connected with the circumstances giving rise to an offence for which an adult is charged

(Children and Young Persons Act 1933 s.46; Children and Young Persons Act 1963 s.18).

Section 8 of the Powers of Criminal Courts (Sentencing) Act 2000 provides for a presumption that, where a person aged under 18 is convicted in the Crown Court or a magistrates' court other than a youth court, that court should remit the young person for sentence in a youth court. Where the convicting court is a magistrates' court, it must remit the case to a youth court unless it is required to make a referral order (in which case there is a discretion to remit) or the case can properly be dealt with by an absolute or conditional discharge, a fine or a parental bind over.

Where a young person attains the age of 18 after appearing before a youth   **2.27**
court, that court may (after conviction) remit the young person to a magistrates' court for sentence: 2000 Act s.9. This power should not be used in relation to an offence triable only on indictment since the magistrates' court will have no power to impose sentence.

In *R. v Hammersmith Juvenile Court Ex p. O (A Minor)* (1988) 86 Cr. App. R. 343, the juvenile (youth) had appeared before justices charged with offences of burglary and attempted robbery, had pleaded not guilty and summary trial had been fixed for a later date. On that date the court purported to decline summary trial and commit to the Crown Court. It was held that once the pleas had been taken before the first bench the trial had begun. The decision to commit was quashed, and mandamus issued to direct the justices to hear the cases summarily. Further consideration, however, was given to the circumstances in which a court commencing summary trial in respect of a youth could revert to committal proceedings in *R. (on the application of K) v Leeds Youth Court* [2001] EWHC Admin 177; (2001) 165 J.P. 694. K, aged 17, was charged with robbery and the youth court determined for summary trial after hearing conflicting submissions. The case was adjourned for trial. At the adjourned hearing, on notice, the prosecutor sought to change the mode of trial decision; evidence was called, submissions heard and the youth court decided to discontinue the summary trial. The defendant appealed against that decision contending both that there needed to be a change of circumstances and that the defendant had been given a legitimate expectation that sentence would be constrained by the powers of the youth court. Rejecting both arguments, the Divisional Court emphasised that the power to discontinue summary trial is a discretionary power and so to be exercised judicially which means on some good, proper and relevant reason. A reason that related to the seriousness of the offence would be relevant. A youth court is entitled to keep the mode of trial under review and to change it where that is the appropriate decision. That may arise from a change of circumstances but could also come about where, as the evidence is given, its manner justifies the change. Since the only expectation raised by a decision for summary trial was that any change would be on the basis of lawful principles, there was no justification for any expectation by the defendant as to the more limited powers of sentence of the youth court. Presumably, the only way for the defendant to have capitalised on the earlier decision for summary trial would have been to have entered an immediate guilty plea.

2.28 In England a person attains an age on the day which is the anniversary of his birth (Family Law Reform Act 1969 s.9). For presuming and determining age see s.99 of the Children and Young Persons Act 1933 and s.150(4) of the Magistrates' Courts Act 1980. The procedure under s.12 of the Magistrates' Courts Act 1980 whereby an offender may plead guilty by post only applies to youth courts in limited circumstances (see § 2.145), but s.46(1A) of the Children and Young Persons Act 1933 has the effect of preserving a conviction under that Act of a youth if the magistrates' court had no reason to believe he was a youth. See *R. v Blandford JJ.* [1966] 1 All E.R. 1021 as to accepting pleas of guilty from youths. A court should treat such a plea as a tentative one where, e.g. the youth was not legally represented, was at the younger end of the age spectrum or there was some reason for doubt.

Attaining 18 before the conclusion of proceedings

2.29 Where proceedings in respect of a young person are begun and he attains 18 before the conclusion of the proceedings, the court may deal with the case and make any order which it could have made if he had not attained that age (Children and Young Persons Act 1963 s.29). As to the meaning of when "proceedings are begun" see below. Those who lay informations or charge youths who might soon become 18 should take all reasonable steps to find out exactly when they will become 18 to ensure they would be bailed or summoned to the correct court (*R. v Amersham Juvenile Court* [1981] 2 All E.R. 315). Alternatively, the young person may be remitted to an adult court for the same area for trial or for sentence: Powers of Criminal Courts (Sentencing) Act 2000 s.9. The youth court may proceed if the defendant is found to be 18 during the hearing (Children and Young Persons Act 1933 s.48(1)). Where a defendant crosses a relevant age threshold between the date on which the offence is committed and the date when he is convicted (most likely 17 to 18 but could be 14 to 15 and other thresholds), the point at which the court will start when considering sentence will be that sentence which the defendant would have received if he had been sentenced on the day the offence was committed. There would have to be good reasons to depart from that starting point. It will be very unusual for a court to pass a sentence in such circumstances that is more severe than the maximum applicable to the defendant at the date of the offence: *R. v Ghafoor* [2002] EWCA Crim 1857; (2002) 166 J.P. 601.

Section 29 affords the justices no discretion to overrule the mandatory provisions of s.19(1) or s.24(1) of the Magistrates' Courts Act 1980, in particular as to the right of election of jury for persons aged 18 or over (*R. v Amersham JJ.* above) although this decision was overruled on another point in *Re Daley*. These sections and *Re Daley* are discussed further below.

Commonwealth and foreign servicemen

2.30 Where the defendant is a serviceman of a Commonwealth or allied country, such as the United States of America, the Visiting Forces Act 1952 as extended by the International Headquarters and Defence Organisations Act 1964 will enable magistrates' courts to try him for a road traffic offence, generally speaking, unless it arose out of, and in the course of, his duty (see s.3). Thus, an American army officer driving on manoeuvres would be acting in the course of his duty and would normally not be triable in an English court, but, if he were on a domestic shopping trip with his family, he would not be acting in the course of his duty and would be triable for a road traffic offence by an English court. The Road Vehicles (Construction and Use) Regulations 1986 reg.4, the Road Vehicles Lighting Regulations 1989 reg.7, the Motor Vehicles (Tests) Regulations 1981 reg.6, and the various Motor Vehicles (Type Approval) (Great Britain) Regulations among others give certain exemptions for the vehicles of visiting forces. As to insurance, see § 10.26 and excise licences, § 12.34.

The Visiting Forces and International Headquarters (Application of Law) Order 1999 (SI 1999/1736) applies many provisions of the Road Traffic Acts to vehicles of visiting forces and their drivers when on duty, but offences committed on duty will be tried by the service courts. The general position is that drivers and vehicles of visiting forces are subject to the same provisions of the Road Traffic Acts as persons and vehicles in the service of the Crown (see § 2.34). Section 79 of the Road Traffic Act 1991 specifically provides that nothing in Pt II of the Act (which relates to traffic in London) shall apply to any vehicle which

    (a) at the relevant time is used or appropriated for use for naval, military or airforce purposes;

    (b) belongs to any visiting forces (within the meaning of the Visiting Forces Act 1952); or

    (c) at the relevant time is used or appropriated for use, by any such forces.

2.31 A civil court may not try for the same crime a person already tried by the service court of a visiting force and, where the civil court tries him for a different crime but he has already been tried by the service court wholly or partly for the acts or omissions in respect of which the civil court convicts him, the latter court must have regard to the sentence already passed (Visiting Forces Act 1952 s.4).

Drivers from abroad

2.32 Where a solicitor is instructed in a case relating to the duty payable on, the insurance cover for, or the application of the Construction and Use Regulations to a car brought from abroad or as to the driving licences of overseas visitors, reference should be made, inter alia, to the Motor Vehicles (International Circulation) Order 1975 (SI 1975/1208) as amended. As to driving licences reference should be made to "Drivers from abroad" under "Driving Licences" in Chapter 11. As to excise licences, see § 12.34. He or she may also wish to refer to the Road Vehicles Lighting Regulations 1989 reg.5; the Road Vehicles (Construction and Use) Regulations 1986 reg.4; and the Goods Vehicles (Plating and Testing) Regulations 1988 Sch.2 para.24 as amended. As to the need for a driver from abroad to have a valid test certificate, see "Test Certificates and Testing" in Chapter 8. For drivers' hours and records where the EC international rules apply, see "Drivers' Hours" and "Drivers' Records" in Chapter 14. International passenger services are governed by the Road Transport (International Passenger Services) Regulations 1984 (SI 1984/748). These regulations are made in implementation of EC regulations.

Diplomatic privilege

2.33 By the Diplomatic Privileges Act 1964 Sch.1 arts 31 and 37, members of the diplomatic, administrative and technical staff of a mission and members of the family of such staff forming part of their household are exempt from criminal proceedings, and members of the domestic service staff enjoy like immunity in respect of acts performed in the course of their duties. All such immunities may be waived. Private servants of members of the mission, as opposed to those of the mission itself, are not exempt; nor are members of the family of the diplomatic staff and members of the administrative and technical staff and their families who are British nationals or permanently resident here. By the Diplomatic Privileges (British Nationals) Order 1999 (SI 1999/670), where a person is a member of a mission of a country listed in Sch.1 to the Order (Commonwealth countries and the Republic of Ireland) or a private servant of such a person, and is a citizen both of that country and a British national, he has the same privileges and immunities as he would have if he were not a citizen. Similar privilege may also exist under the International Organisations Act 1968. Consular officers and consular employees, as defined in art.1 of Sch.1 to the Consular Relations Act 1968, are not subject to the jurisdiction of British courts in respect of acts performed in the course of consular functions but such immunity may be waived (Consular Relations Act 1968 Sch.1 arts 43, 45). Where any question of diplomatic or consular immunity arises a certificate should be obtained from the Secretary of State, which certificate is conclusive as to the person's entitlement to immunity.

Diplomatic immunity cannot be successfully pleaded in response to a criminal charge unless the entry into this country has been notified to the Foreign and Commonwealth Office in accordance with art.10 of the Vienna Convention on Diplomatic Relations 1961 (Cmnd.1368), even though art.10 is not reproduced in Sch.1 to the Diplomatic Privileges Act 1964; see *R. v Lambeth JJ. Ex p. Yusufu; R. v Brixton Prison Governor Ex p. Yusufu* [1985] Crim. L.R. 510. A certificate was similarly held to be conclusive in a case of state immunity and could not be challenged by judicial review except on the basis that it was a nullity or was issued outside the scope of the relevant statutory power (*R. v Secretary of State for Foreign and Commonwealth Affairs Ex p. Trawnik, The Times*, April 18, 1985). The waiver of diplomatic privilege must be made by or on behalf of the representative of the country concerned and cannot be made by the defendant himself; until there is due waiver, proceedings are without jurisdiction and are null and void (*R. v Madan* [1961] Crim. L.R. 253).

The Crown

2.34 Parts I, II, III, IV and VII of the 1988 Act apply, to the extent stated in s.183 thereof (as amended), to persons and vehicles in the public service of the Crown. Other Parts of the 1988 Act do not apply to the Crown (*Adair v Feist* 1936 S.L.T.(Sh.) 22). Section 79 of the Road Traffic Act 1991 provides that ss.66, 69–71 of the Act (parking penalties in London, immobilisation of vehicles in parking places, exceptions from s.69, and representations in relation to removal or immobilisation of vehicles) apply to vehicles in the public service of the Crown which are required to be registered under the Vehicle Excise and Registration Act 1994, *except* those exempted because at the relevant time they are used or appropriated for use for naval, military or airforce purposes. Those sections also apply to persons in the public service of the Crown.

Where under the relevant Part of the 1988 Act an offence has been committed in connection with a vehicle in the public service of the Crown, proceedings may be brought in respect of the offence against a person nominated for the purpose on behalf of the Crown and the nominated person may be convicted as well as any person actually responsible for the offence (but without prejudice to proceedings against any person so responsible) (1988 Offenders Act s.94).

Although the nominated person may be convicted, the only order which can be **2.35** made is a fine (1988 Offenders Act s.94(3)). Such an order cannot be enforced and the conviction is to be disregarded for all other purposes except appeal (whether by way of case stated or otherwise).

As to penalty points see the note to Crown servants, § 19.27.

The nominated person will now normally be John Doe, the fictitious litigant of the 17th century, resurrected in *Barnett v French* [1981] R.T.R. 173. The nominated defendant in that case was responsible for 3,500 Crown vehicles and would have been at risk of becoming the citizen with the largest record of motoring convictions ever known. The Divisional Court suggested the use of the name John Doe instead. The name Doe was particularly appropriate in that it comprised the initial letters of the then Department of the Environment.

Drivers of Crown vehicles (including British servicemen on duty) are therefore **2.36** fully responsible for offences of bad or drunken driving, disobeying traffic signs, not reporting accidents, breaches of the Construction and Use and Pedestrian Crossings Regulations, speeding (with certain exceptions) and so on. The position as to insurance is mentioned at § 10.26. The nationalised industries are not Crown emanations (*Tamlin v Hannaford* [1949] 2 All E.R. 327) and the BBC is not a Crown department (*British Broadcasting Corporation v Johns* [1964] 1 All E.R. 923).

A British serviceman may be convicted by court-martial of committing a civil offence of a road traffic type abroad contrary to s.70 of the Army Act 1955 (*Cox v Army Council* [1962] 1 All E.R. 880). The offence in question was careless driving on a road in Germany and it was said that there may be offences under the Road Traffic and Highway Acts which cannot be committed abroad. Where a person subject to the Naval Discipline Act 1957 is acquitted or convicted of an offence by a Naval tribunal, a civil court shall by s.129(1) be debarred from trying him subsequently for the same offence and by s.129(2) acquittal or conviction by a civil court bars subsequent trial by a Naval tribunal. By the s.133 of the Army Act 1955 and the Air Force Act 1955, as amended, where a person subject to military or Air Force law has been tried for an offence by a court-martial or by his commanding officer or had it taken into consideration at a court-martial, a civil court is debarred from trying him subsequently for an offence substantially the same as that offence.

See § 11.65 as to disqualification.

Enactments not specifically naming the Crown

As stated, many of the provisions of the Road Traffic Acts apply to the Crown **2.37** and its servants but the provisions of s.28 of the Road Traffic Regulation Act 1984 (stopping for school crossing patrols) are not mentioned in s.130 of the 1984 Act nor do the Highway Act 1835, the Town Police Clauses Act 1847 and the Highways Act 1980 s.137 (obstruction) contain provisions binding the Crown.

A statute which does not name the Crown does not bind it unless it is an enactment of paramount importance to public safety which requires that Crown servants should be responsible if, in performance of their duties and acting under orders, they contravene its terms (*Cooper v Hawkins* (1904) 68 J.P. 25). It is submitted that the provisions of s.28 of the Road Traffic Regulation Act 1984 and of s.78 of the Highway Act 1835 (relating to school crossing patrols and negligent opening of car doors respectively) are enactments of sufficient importance to public safety to override the rule that Crown servants acting on duty are not liable under them. Even if they do not override that rule, where there is a personal element in a charge against a man under a statute which does not bind the Crown or an individual act by a driver apart from the performance of his duty as a servant of the Crown (per Lord Alverstone C.J. in *Cooper v Hawkins*), or an act by a driver which is his own personal act, e.g. being drunk or in a condition or under circumstances "in which he was not performing a public duty or acting in accordance with superior orders" (per Wills and Channell JJ. ibid.), it is submitted that the driver in such a case cannot claim the benefit of any Crown exemption. Although in *Cooper v Hawkins* above a conviction of an Army driver for exceeding a local speed limit was quashed because he was acting under orders and it was necessary both in the particular circumstances and in the interests of the Army generally that a low speed limit should not be observed, the cited dicta of the judges in the case are, it is argued, sufficient authority for saying that Crown drivers are in the same position as civilian drivers in regard to obeying school crossing patrols and taking precautions before opening car doors, for these are personal matters in the driver's control and save, perhaps, in exceptional circumstances, in no way hinder the performance of the functions of any Crown department. Examples of exceptional circumstances in which a Crown servant might not be liable would be a police officer opening the door of his car as quickly as possible to save life or the driver of an RAF ambulance, under orders to get to a crashed aircraft without delay, ignoring a school crossing patrol's signal. It is submitted that it is only if the driver's personal act is in direct performance of his public duty that the exemption applies.

2.38 As regards obstruction, there is no exemption for the Crown under the Road Vehicles (Construction and Use) Regulations 1986, which relate to motor vehicles and trailers, but it might sometimes be necessary to prosecute Crown drivers and their superior officers under the Highways Act 1980 s.137. Here a defence that it was necessary to leave vehicles near a particular government building for the department's work to be done more efficiently might be successful.

Crown roads are subject to the general statutory provisions which apply to roads generally, it is submitted. Those particular statutory provisions which apply to roads only if particular steps are taken, as by the making of an order, may be applied to Crown roads by order under s.131 of the Road Traffic Regulation Act 1984, e.g. restricted waiting orders, pedestrian crossings, etc.

JURISDICTION OVER OFFENCES

Venue

2.39 The venue for indictable offences is regulated, so far as magistrates' courts are concerned, by s.2 of the Magistrates' Courts Act 1980 (as substituted by the Courts Act 2003 s.44). By s.2(3) magistrates may try summarily an "either way" offence, e.g. theft, which has been committed by a person who appears or is brought before the court, although it has been committed outside their area, provided it is committed in England or Wales or otherwise within their jurisdiction. By s.2(1), a magistrates' court has jurisdiction to try any summary offence.

Trying cases together

An important point on procedure was emphasised in *R. v Bennett* [1980] Crim. L.R. 447. It was stated that it was the obligation of solicitors, counsel and judges to ensure that as far as possible all charges against an individual should be dealt with at the same court by the same judge on a single occasion. Where a solicitor or counsel knows that a defendant is waiting to be dealt with on other charges, there should be an application for the matter to be put back or transferred to the Crown Court centre where the outstanding charges are being tried. This would avoid inconsistency in the sentencing of individuals and the waste of time and money which could result. On the face of it there is no reason why this recommendation should not apply equally to magistrates' courts. It suggests that the practice whereby some courts and some police forces are reluctant to agree to the combination of proceedings may be wrong. Obviously there must be limits and the importance of bringing proceedings to a speedy conclusion must not be overlooked, particularly for youths: Magistrates' Courts Act 1980 s.10(3A). It may well be wrong to combine proceedings which will require witnesses to travel long distances for a disputed case. Again, a case may be so trivial as not to justify the effort.

By virtue of s.27A of the Magistrates' Courts Act 1980 (as inserted by s.46 of the Courts Act 2003), a magistrates' court has power to transfer a case to another magistrates' court. Directions given by the Lord Chancellor (under s.30(5) of the 1980 Act) identify the criteria that will determine the place to which a case might be transferred; these are the local justice area within which the offence was committed, the defendant resides, the witnesses (or a majority of them) reside or where other cases raising similar issues are being dealt with. Guidelines issued by the Justices' Clerks' Society in October 2008 confirm the principles set out in the cases referred to above concerning the need to balance the interests of the parties, victim, witnesses and anyone else with a legitimate interest in the case.

2.40

Limitation of time

For all summary offences, except where expressly provided otherwise by the statute, the information must be laid within six calendar months of the offence (Magistrates' Courts Act 1980 s.127). Section 127 does not prevent a magistrates' court from directing a charge under s.3 of the 1988 Act to be preferred after dismissal of a charge under s.2 (*R. v Coventry JJ. Ex p. Sayers* [1979] R.T.R. 22). In *R. v Haywards Heath JJ. Ex p. White* (2000) 164 J.P. 629, a driver was charged with dangerous driving and careless driving in respect of the same incident. The summons for dangerous driving was dismissed, but the driver was convicted on the lesser charge. The justices retired to consider sentence during which it was drawn to their attention that the summons for careless driving had been issued out of time. They returned to court (before sentence) and set aside the conviction by way of s.142 of the Magistrates' Courts Act 1980. Rejecting the driver's claim that they were they without jurisdiction, they convicted the driver of careless driving as an alternative verdict to the dangerous driving. The

2.41

Divisional Court, noting that the justices had set aside the conviction on the invalid summons and that the alternative verdict on the dangerous driving summons was legitimate, dismissed the application for judicial review.

There is no limit of time in respect of indictable offences unless the statute otherwise provides. Section 127 of the 1980 Act provides that indictable offences triable summarily ("either way" offences) may be dealt with summarily at any time subject only to any time-limit for bringing proceedings for the offence on indictment. See *R. v Dacorum JJ. Ex p. Gardner* (1985) 149 J.P. 677. For confirmation of the principle that an "either way" offence is exempt from the rule relating to the laying of an information for a summary offence within six months (unless otherwise exempted), see *Kemp v Liebherr–GB Ltd* [1987] 1 All E.R. 885.

2.42   Time runs from the commission of the offence, not from its discovery (*Teall v Teall* [1938] 3 All E.R. 349). Provided the information is laid within six months of the offence, the hearing, the issue and service of the summons and the conviction may all be outside that period (*Abraham v Jutson* (1962) 106 S.J. 880; *R. v Fairford JJ. Ex p. Brewster* [1975] 2 All E.R. 757). Nevertheless, justices may decline jurisdiction if they conclude the prosecutor was guilty of an abuse of the process of the court by laying an information without having decided whether to prosecute (*R. v Brentford JJ. Ex p. Wong* [1981] Crim. L.R. 339). On the same principle it may be possible to refuse to hear proceedings because of inordinate delay. See "Refusal to hear a case", § 2.63. The date of the information need not be stated in the summons unless there was some question of its being out of time (*R. v Godstone JJ. Ex p. Secretary of State for the Environment* [1974] Crim. L.R. 110).

Where there is doubt as to whether an information was laid in time, it is for the prosecutor to satisfy the court that it was and the court is entitled to dismiss the case if he fails to do so (*Lloyd v Young* [1963] Crim. L.R. 703). A summons or warrant shall not cease to have effect by reason of the death of the justice or his ceasing to be a justice (Magistrates' Courts Act 1980 s.124). This provision would presumably apply to a summons issued by a justices' clerk or other person authorised by virtue of the Justices' Clerks Rules 2005 (SI 2005/545). The proceedings may be continued notwithstanding the death of the informant prior to the hearing (*R. v Truelove* (1880) 5 Q.B.D. 336), or before the appeal (*Hawkins v Bepey* [1981] 1 All E.R. 797), at least in the case of a police informant. The Divisional Court confirmed in *R. v Clerkenwell Magistrates' Court Ex p. Ewing and Clark, The Times*, June 3, 1987, that there was no breach of the six months' time-limit in which to lay information and to issue summonses in summary cases where proceedings were commenced but were not served, and fresh summonses were issued more than six months after the laying of the original information.

2.43   Section 6 of and Sch.1 to the 1988 Offenders Act lay down a special time-limit for certain offences under the Act. Proceedings may be brought within the period of six months from the date on which sufficient evidence to warrant the proceedings in the opinion of the prosecutor came to his knowledge; and such proceedings may not be brought more than three years after the commission of the offence.

The main offences under the Road Traffic Act 1988 to which s.6 of the 1988 Offenders Act applies are s.99 (driving licence-holder failing to surrender his licence and give particulars when particulars become incorrect), s.103(1)(a) and

(b) (obtaining a driving licence, or driving, while disqualified), s.143 (uninsured use of a motor vehicle), ss.173–175 (forgery, issuing and making false statements in relation to driving licences, test certificates, insurance certificates and certain other documents).

The interpretation of s.6 of the 1988 Offenders Act was considered in *Swan v* **2.44** *Vehicle Inspectorate* [1997] R.T.R. 187. The appellant argued unsuccessfully before the justices that informations laid against him for four offences of driving whilst disqualified and four offences of using a vehicle without insurance were out of time. The offences were discovered by a traffic examiner in May 1995. The following month he submitted a report to the senior traffic examiner who laid informations on a date in November which was outside the six-month limitation period. Therefore although the traffic examiner had sufficient knowledge of the offences more than six months before the beginning of November, the senior examiner did not. Section 6 of course refers to the date on which evidence came to the knowledge of the "prosecutor". Who then was the prosecutor? The justices found as a fact that the traffic examiner was not the prosecutor. He did not have authority to determine whether a person should be prosecuted. That function was conducted by the senior examiner whose decision had fallen within the terms of s.6. Before the Divisional Court, the appellant argued that any person authorised to investigate whether an offence had been committed was a "prosecutor" within the terms of s.6.

That argument was rejected. The court held that the mere fact that someone was investigated for an offence by a person with apparent authority did not mean that the investigator was the "prosecutor". A traffic examiner, employed by the vehicle inspectorate but not authorised to take decisions whether or not to prosecute, was not a "prosecutor" for the purposes of the section.

Detailed consideration as to who is the "prosecutor" for these purposes was **2.45** again given by the Divisional Court in *R. (on the application of Donnachie) v Cardiff Magistrates' Court* [2007] EWHC 1846; [2008] R.T.R. 2. This was a prosecution alleging "clocking" of an odometer. Under the appropriate legislative provisions, the enforcing authorities included the "county council". Issues arose as to whether the offence occurred when the odometer was changed or when the vehicle was sold. The facts of the charge were discovered by an officer of the county council who did not have authority to prosecute. The details were subsequently placed before another officer of the county council with that authority and informations were laid shortly thereafter. The Act required an information to be laid within three years of the commission of the offence or one year of discovery by the prosecutor, whichever is the earlier. The Divisional Court held that, since the county council was a body authorised to initiate proceedings, the relevant date was when sufficient information came to the knowledge of any of its officers. The court distinguished this situation from that in *Swan v Vehicle Inspectorate* above since, under the statutory provisions applicable in that case, prosecution could be initiated only by an individual specifically authorised for that purpose.

A further authority from proceedings other than those concerning road traffic offences may be helpful. In relation to proceedings under the Food Safety Act 1990, time runs from the time the offence is "discovered" and further consideration was given to this issue by the Administrative Court in *Tesco Stores Ltd v London Borough of Harrow* [2003] EWHC 2919; (2003) 167 J.P. 657. Section

34 of the 1990 Act provides that no prosecution shall be begun after the expiry of three years from the commission of the offence or one year from the discovery of it by the prosecutor whichever is the earlier. On February 15, 2001, a purchaser discovered some wire in a bread roll. He notified the prosecutor on February 19, 2001 by leaving a message with an administrative assistant. That message was received the same day by an Environmental Health Officer who confirmed some of the details by telephone with the purchaser's wife but was unable to speak to the purchaser until February 23. The Environmental Health Officer raised the matter with Tesco on February 19, 2001 at a meeting arranged for a different purpose. A report from the public analyst was received on April 23, 2001. An information was laid on February 21, 2002 and the question arose as to whether that exceeded the period of one year from the discovery of the offence by the prosecutor. Finding that the period had expired, the Administrative Court confirmed that "discovery" does not import any investigation; it is simply knowledge of the material facts. The question to be asked is "whether the facts disclosed, objectively considered, would have led a prosecuting authority to have reasonable grounds to believe that an offence may have been committed by some person who has been identified to it. Discovering the offence should be taken to mean discovering sufficient grounds to found a reasonable belief that an offence has been committed. … at that stage, investigation can begin of the primary facts which are then known to the prosecutor".

2.46   With minor alterations s.47 of the Vehicle Excise and Registration Act 1994 is identical in wording to s.6 of the 1988 Offenders Act and applies a similar time-limit to specified offences under that Act, namely, s.29 (using and keeping a vehicle without an excise licence), s.31A (offence by registered keeper where vehicle unlicensed) (when in force), s.34 (misuse of trade licences), s.35A (failing to return licence after cheque dishonoured), s.37 (using a vehicle for a purpose attracting a higher rate of duty), and regulations made in pursuance of the Vehicle Excise and Registration Act. There is a similar limitation for vehicle excise offences in Scotland. The extended time-limits given by s.6 of the 1988 Offenders Act are now otiose so far as prosecutions for "either way" offences are concerned (e.g. fraudulent use of an excise licence contrary to s.44 of the 1994 Act), because under s.127 of the Magistrates' Courts Act 1980 there is no time-limit for "either way" offences unless the statute creating the offence provides otherwise.

If an offence has a special time-limit, the time-limit applies to an aider and abettor of the offence whether the period be longer (*Homolka v Osmond* [1939] 1 All E.R. 154) or shorter (*Gould v Houghton* (1921) 85 J.P. 93).

Where persons have conspired together to evade a statute creating summary offences, they may be tried on indictment for conspiracy even though some of the acts of evasion were more than six months previously (*R. v Blamires Transport Services Ltd* [1963] 3 All E.R. 170), unless the statute itself makes conspiracy to evade it a summary offence (*R. v Barnett* [1951] 1 All E.R. 917).

2.47   Custody time-limits were introduced by the enabling power in s.22 of the Prosecution of Offences Act 1985, as amended, and governed by the Prosecution of Offences (Custody Time Limits) Regulations 1987 (SI 1987/299), as amended. The vast majority of offences falling within the scope of this work will be unaffected by the regulations because they apply solely to offences triable only on indictment, or "either way", and obviously only to defendants who are brought before the court from custody. The present time-limits are 56 days between the first appearance and summary trial; a limit of 70 days from first appearance to committal; and a limit of 112 days from committal to arraignment. If these time-limits are exceeded, the accused must, under the terms of the section, be released on bail. An application may be made to the court to extend the time-limits, and the court may do so if it is satisfied that the need is due to:

(a) the illness or absence of the accused, a necessary witness, a judge or magistrate; or

(b) a postponement caused by the court ordering separate trials of accused persons or offences; or

(c) some other good and sufficient cause; and

(d) the prosecution has acted with due diligence and expedition.

Where a court has to decide whether to extend a custody time-limit, it may **2.48** only extend a limit where satisfied of one of the three qualifying grounds *and* that the prosecution has acted with due diligence and expedition. It will often be the case that all parties to the proceedings could have acted more expeditiously and the court will have to weigh the significance of the prosecution in contributing to the delay. The approach of the court in considering this part of the test will be to ask what was the "real root or principal cause" of the delay, rather than whether anything that the prosecution had done had contributed to the delay: *R. (on the application of Haque) v Central Criminal Court* [2003] EWHC 2457; [2004] Crim. L.R. 298.

The burden of complying with custody time-limits falls on the prosecution, and it would seem that the court dealing with the application should apply the civil standard of proof, i.e. that of the balance of probabilities (*R. v Governor of Canterbury Prison Ex p. Craig* [1990] 3 All E.R. 654).

A development that is likely to affect a wider range of cases has been the **2.49** introduction of case management procedures, in particular those referred to as "CJSSS" (Criminal Justice, Simple, Speedy, Summary). Under this scheme, the prosecutor is expected to make available to the defendant and the court enough information about the case for the defendant to be given proper advice and for the court to make effective case management decisions. The Criminal Procedure Rules 2005 (as amended by the Criminal Procedure (Amendment No.2) Rules 2008 (SI 2008/3269)) provide for the prosecutor to provide initial details of the prosecution at or before the beginning of the day of the first hearing (r.21(2)). Those initial details must include the basis of the prosecution and any previous convictions of the defendant (see further § 2.117 below).

Computing time

The day of the offence is excluded in computing the time (*Radcliffe v Bar-* **2.50** *tholomew* (1892) 56 J.P. 262; *Stewart v Chapman* [1951] 2 All E.R. 613) unless the relevant statute expressly provides otherwise, as in *Hare v Gocher* [1962] 2 All E.R. 763. If an offence is committed at any hour on January 1, the informa-tion may be laid at any hour up to 11.59pm on July 1. A month ends on the day of the next month corresponding in number to that from which the computation begins or, if there is no corresponding one, to the one next before it. Thus where four calendar months ran from midnight September 30, the period expired at midnight on January 30 and an application made on January 31 was out of time (*Dodds v Walker* [1981] 2 All E.R. 609, a unanimous decision of the House of

Lords in a landlord and tenant case). Further examples of how the appellate courts have interpreted the provisions relating to the computing of time arose in *R. v Long* [1960] 1 Q.B. 681 in which it was held that "three days before" means three clear days; and *R. v Turner* [1910] 1 K.B. 346 in which it was held that "Not less than seven days" means not less than seven clear days.

A time-limit expired on a Sunday when the office in question was closed. It was held in *Swainston v Hetton Victory Club Ltd, The Times*, February 11, 1983 CA (a civil case) that Monday was too late. Where notice had to be given it was stated in *Griffiths v Secretary of State for the Environment, The Times*, January 28, 1982 CA, doubting certain earlier cases, that this meant when received and not when sent. The decision was reversed by the House of Lords [1983] 1 All E.R. 439 but on different grounds.

Continuing offences

2.51 Where a regulation requires an action to be done "forthwith", e.g. signing a driving licence, generally this is not a continuing offence and the limitation period runs from the date of the issue of the licence (*A. & E. McLennan (Blairgowrie) Ltd v MacMillan* 1964 S.L.T. 2). For the same reason offences of failing to notify forthwith a change of ownership, etc.,under regs 20–25 of the Road Vehicles (Registration and Licensing) Regulations 2002 (SI 2002/2742) appear not to be continuing offences. It should be noted, however, that the time-limit for these offences is governed not by s.127 of the Magistrates' Courts Act 1980 but by s.47 of the Vehicle Excise and Registration Act 1994, as s.47 applies not only to various offences under the Vehicle Excise and Registration Act, but also to offences under regulations made in pursuance of that Act.

ADVICE, ASSISTANCE AND REPRESENTATION

Grant

2.52 The framework for the statutory scheme for advice, assistance and representation through the Criminal Defence Service is contained in the Access to Justice Act 1999.

Funding is established to provide for giving advice to persons in custody and this may extend to others under investigation (Access to Justice Act 1999 s.13(1)). Under the Police and Criminal Evidence Act 1984 s.58, a person arrested and held in custody in a police station or other premises shall be entitled, if he or she so requests, to consult a solicitor privately at any time. The entitlement does not apply to a person arrested and in custody in the street or in a motor vehicle. In *R. v Samuel, The Times*, December 19, 1987, the Court of Appeal stressed the fundamental right of a person detained to consult a solicitor privately. Justification for denial of that right on reasonable grounds could only be accepted by reference to specific circumstances including evidence about the person detained or the actual solicitor involved. A right to representation may be granted under Sch.3 to the 1999 Act. It is available for binding-over proceedings as well as for any criminal offence: s.12(2).

2.53 The essence of the availability of representation through the Criminal Defence Service in courts dealing with road traffic offences depends on the proceedings being "criminal proceedings" within the terms of s.12(2) of the 1999 Act. Section

12(2)(a) and (b) defines "criminal proceedings" as including proceedings before any court for dealing with an individual accused or convicted of an offence. The revised definition makes it clear that representation may be authorised for applications to remove a driving disqualification since s.12(2)(b) includes within the definition of "criminal proceedings" any proceedings before a court for dealing with an individual convicted of an offence (including proceedings in respect of a sentence or order).

Provided the defendant is financially eligible, the criteria on which the right to representation will be granted will be the interests of justice. Criteria are established in Sch.3 to the Access to Justice Act 1999, which are similar to those previously in force adjusted to take account of case law. These are described more fully below.

An applicant is entitled to the solicitor of his choice (1999 Act s.15(1)) though regulations may restrict this choice.

Application to road traffic offences

By para.5 of Sch.3(5) to the Access to Justice Act 1999 the factors to be taken into account in determining whether it is in the interests of justice for representation to be granted shall include: **2.54**

(a) the risk of loss of liberty or livelihood or serious damage to reputation;
(b) the determination of any matter arising in the proceedings may involve consideration of a substantial question of law;
(c) the accused may be unable to understand the proceedings or to state his own case;
(d) the need for tracing and interviewing of witnesses or expert cross-examination of a witness;
(e) it is in the interests of someone other than the accused that the accused be represented.

The Lord Chancellor is given power to vary the factors under Sch.3 para. 5(3).

Under the previous provisions (which involved similar criteria), one of the criteria was adopted in *R. v Brigg JJ. Ex p. Lynch* (1984) 148 J.P. 214 when it was said that the fact that the applicant's livelihood would be threatened by a conviction ought without more to have led to a grant of legal aid. Legal aid was also appropriate where an applicant was seeking to establish special reasons on the basis that her drink had been laced. A scientific expert would be required to give evidence whether the applicant's explanation was consistent with the scientific facts and to say whether the amount of alcohol that the applicant admitted consuming would have resulted, in any event, in her being over the prescribed limit. In addition, the assistance of a solicitor would be required to find witnesses of the facts, to take proper proofs and to extract the story from those witnesses and from the applicant herself: *R. v Gravesend Magistrates' Court Ex p. Baker* (1997) 161 J.P. 765.

THE HEARING

General

The nature of the conduct of court proceedings is affected by the provisions of **2.55** the Crime and Disorder Act 1998, providing greater emphasis on speed and on early identification and resolution of issues in dispute and those of the Human Rights Act 1998, emphasising fairness, proper time for preparation and equality of arms. In accordance with the Criminal Procedure Rules 2005 (as amended), parties to proceedings are to comply with the overriding obligation to do justice. This was exemplified in *Robinson v Abergavenny Magistrates' Court* [2007] EWHC 2005; (2007) 171 J.P. 683 when the Divisional Court criticised the approach of the defence lawyer. Following speeding charges, technical arguments were raised about whether traffic signs had been in place which was a necessary condition of the relevant orders; however, the nature of the issue in dispute was not brought to the notice of the prosecution in advance and the defence resisted an application for an adjournment. On the defence appeal against the court's granting of that adjournment, the Divisional Court emphasised the effect of the 2005 Rules which included the obligation to notify the court and all parties of any significant failure to take a procedural step and early identification of the real issues in the case. The Divisional Court noted that the approach of the defence was "an exercise which owed more to opportunism and arid technicality than a desire to achieve the overriding objective that the case be dealt with fairly on its merits, properly investigated".

The court

2.56   The hearing must be in public. There are certain statutory exceptions. Otherwise courts should only depart from this practice if, by proceedings in open court, they would frustrate or render impracticable the administration of justice: *R. v Reigate JJ.* (1983) 147 J.P. 385 applying *Scott v Scott* [1913] A.C. 417. This is not a matter of discretion. See also art.6(1) of the European Convention on Human Rights and s.6 of the Human Rights Act 1998.

However, rare circumstances can arise in which part of the proceedings, ancillary in nature, may be held in chambers. These should be exceptional, and are to be discouraged. An example occurred in *R. v Nottingham Magistrates' Court Ex p. Furnell* (1996) 160 J.P. 201. The applicants and two co-accused were charged with affray. In the course of their trial the prosecution agreed that a plea of guilty by one of the co-accused to the lesser charge of obstructing a police constable would be acceptable. The co-accused's solicitor wished to discuss with the stipendiary magistrate whether such a plea could be accepted without the laying of a further information. All the advocates and the clerk went into the magistrate's room, and in the course of his hearing in chambers, the magistrate indicated that he would accept the proposed plea of guilty. There was no satisfactory contemporaneous record of what had happened in the magistrate's room, no shorthand writer was present, and no tape recording made. The trial continued and the applicants were convicted. There was an application for certiorari on the basis of irregularity.

2.57   The Divisional Court refused to grant the relief sought. It held that the inherent discretion of magistrates, whether lay or stipendiary, to permit receiving representations in chambers during the course of a trial should be exercised sparingly and with caution having regard to the role of a magistrate as a fact-finder. Careful consideration should be given to the procedure, with all the parties knowing what was taking place and, save in exceptional circumstances, represented, in chambers. It was important that a contemporaneous note be taken, normally by the clerk.

It is submitted that although it may have been rather cumbersome for the point that arose to be dealt with in open court, there was no reason why it could not have been. In doing so, the issue is made subject to public scrutiny, and the allegation of irregularity made here, though not upheld, could have been avoided.

As to the requirement that justices should not be entitled to remain anonymous when discharging their judicial functions see the judgment of Watkins L.J. in *R. v Felixstowe JJ. Ex p. Leigh* [1987] 1 All E.R. 551. Although justices could decide to sit in camera, it would be an extremely unusual occurrence (and for compelling reasons) to justify a departure from the normal requirement for the proceedings to be conducted in open court. In the connected appeals of *R. v Malvern JJ. Ex p. Evans*; and *R. v Evesham JJ. Ex p. McDonagh* (1988) 152 J.P. 65, the Divisional Court adopted a restrictive approach to justices sitting in camera. Justices were entitled to exercise their discretion in favour of conducting proceedings in camera and thereby prevent the press from reporting those proceedings; nevertheless save where a statute otherwise provided, it was not desirable for justices to adopt that course of action unless there were compelling reasons—the existence of which would be rare—to do so. **2.58**

Wherever possible this course should be avoided, either by handing in an appropriate written statement or by the use of s.4 or s.11 of the Contempt of Court Act 1981 (see below). A single magistrate may sit as an examining justice but, unless expressly provided otherwise by statute, at least two justices must sit to try a case summarily (Magistrates' Courts Act 1980 s.121(1)). Not more than three justices may sit in an adult or youth court. District judges (magistrates' courts) may sit alone. If the justices are equally divided in their findings, the case may be reheard by other justices. **2.59**

A bench of *three* justices who had heard all the evidence in a case were required to proceed to a decision and were not entitled to send the case for rehearing by another bench. If they felt unhappy about convicting a defendant, then their obligation was to acquit: *R. v Bromley JJ. Ex p. Haymills (Contractors) Ltd* (1984) 148 J.P. 363. If necessary a majority decision prevails.

If any evidence is taken, the whole case must be heard by the same justices or two of them, and, if another magistrate joins them, the witnesses must be recalled and testify again (*R. v Manchester JJ. Ex p. Burke* (1961) 125 J.P. 387; Magistrates' Courts Act 1980 s.121(6)). It does not suffice to read their evidence over again to the witnesses who have already given evidence, unless it be a deposition. Thus, if a hearing begins on Monday before three justices, the hearing of the same case on Tuesday must be before them or two of them; if another magistrate sits with the two or one who come again on Tuesday, witnesses called on Monday must be recalled and give their evidence again. A differently constituted court may sentence a person after he has been convicted by another court, provided there is full inquiry into the facts and circumstances of the case (Magistrates' Courts Act 1980 s.121(7)). **2.60**

The functions of a justices' clerk include giving to the justices at their request advice about law, practice or procedure on questions arising, including questions arising when the clerk is not personally attending on them (Courts Act 2003 s.28). He may when he thinks it right bring to their attention any point of law, practice or procedure that may be involved in any such question (ibid.). See also the *Consolidated Criminal Practice Direction*, Pt V.55.

The importance of the clerk advising justices on law, practice and procedure **2.61** openly and the relationship between the clerk to the justices as principal legal adviser, court clerks, and parties to the proceedings is underlined by the decision of the Divisional Court in *R. v Sittingbourne JJ. Ex p. Stickings* (1996) 160 J.P. 801. In the course of a summary trial, there was legal argument about the admissibility of certain evidence which formed part of the prosecution case. The court clerk advised the justices, and one of the clerk's senior colleagues also attended in the courtroom to give advice. The justices excluded the disputed evidence. The hearing was adjourned to be continued on another day. The Branch Crown Prosecutor, who had not been involved in the hearing, subsequently learnt of the ruling and took the view that the advice of the court clerk had been wrong. He telephoned the clerk to the justices to express concern and suggested that he might like to investigate. The clerk to the justices considered that the wrong advice had been given and decided to intervene at the adjourned hearing under the powers in what is now s.28 of the Courts Act 2003. At that hearing, in open court, both parties were given the opportunity to make representations which they declined. The justices were then advised by their clerk and they reversed their earlier ruling on admissibility. The case was then adjourned for retrial. On the hearing of an application for judicial review, the Divisional Court held that there could be circumstances in which a trial court might be entitled to reverse a finding on the admissibility of evidence provided that there was good reason and that no injustice would be done. Use of s.28 to reverse decisions of justices taken on the advice of a court clerk could not occur as a matter of routine, although there could be situations where it would be legitimate for the clerk to the justices, knowing that a legal issue would be raised, to take steps to give further advice to the justices. Pill L.J., in giving the judgment of the court, stated that it was wrong for the Crown Prosecutor to discuss the earlier ruling on admissibility with the clerk to the justices on the telephone between the two hearings. A party wishing to bring matters to the attention of the clerk to the justices before a resumed hearing should normally do so in writing with notice to the other party. His Lordship considered that the unfairness of the reversal tainted the justices' decision at the adjourned hearing. An order was granted prohibiting a fresh trial.

For contempt of court, reference should be made to the Contempt of Court Act 1981. Magistrates' courts have certain powers under s.12 to deal with misbehaviour and wilful interruptions. A right to representation may be granted (s.13) and the criminal provisions are applied. Where there is a possibility of imprisonment, legal advice is desirable although not essential—see *R. v Newbury JJ. Ex p. du Pont* (1984) 148 J.P. 248. The way in which magistrates' courts exercise their powers was the subject of the *Practice Direction (Magistrates' Courts: Contempt)* [2001] 1 W.L.R. 1254; now Pt V.54 of the *Consolidated Criminal Practice Direction*. Justices were required to cease to exercise their powers to bind persons over to be of good behaviour in respect of their conduct in court. The Practice Direction emphasises the importance of offenders being clearly informed of the conduct being complained of and of justices stating their findings of fact. Whenever possible, proceedings should be dealt with on the day the conduct occurred and there is an emphasis on the offender being given every opportunity to apologise and to give undertakings as to his future conduct.

2.62   A court may order the postponement of publication of the proceedings or any part of them if it appears to be *necessary* for avoiding a substantial risk of prejudice to the administration of justice in those proceedings or in any other pending proceedings (s.4). The court should specify the extent of the postponement (see the wording of s.4). Where a court having power to do so allows a name or other matter to be withheld from the public in the proceedings before the court, the court may give necessary directions prohibiting the publication of that name or matter in connection with the proceedings (s.11). The court must first have allowed the name or matter to be withheld from the public during the proceedings or s.11 cannot apply (*R. v Arundel JJ. Ex p. Westminster Press Ltd* [1985] 2 All E.R. 390).

The law relating to the prevention or restriction of publicity by means of an order under s.11 of the Contempt of Court Act 1981 was considered at some length by the Divisional Court in *R. v Dover JJ. Ex p. Dover District Council and Wells* (1992) 156 J.P. 433. In quashing an order made by justices, the court held that the jurisdiction of a court to make an order under s.11 should only be exercised very sparingly and in exceptional circumstances, and only where it could be shown to be necessary.

Refusal to hear a case

Magistrates' courts as well as the higher courts have inherent power to refuse or decline to hear a case on the ground that the proceedings are oppressive or an abuse of process (*R. v Brentford JJ. Ex p. Wong* [1981] Crim. L.R. 339), or where there is some impropriety or *mala fides* (*R. v Grays JJ. Ex p. Graham* [1982] Q.B. 1239). The power to refuse to hear a case is expanded by the Human Rights Act 1998. Magistrates' courts are required to determine issues relating to any of the articles of the European Convention on Human Rights in accordance with the provisions of the Act. However, there are indications that suggest that applications to stay proceedings as an abuse of the process of the court may be better dealt with in the Divisional Court than in either a magistrates' court (*R. (on the application of the DPP) v Croydon Youth Court* (2001) 165 J.P. 181) or the Crown Court (*R. v H (Anthony)* [2002] EWCA Crim 2938; (2003) 167 J.P. 30).

2.63

Proceedings that are vexatious or an abuse of the court can be prohibited summarily by applying to the Divisional Court for judicial review (per *R. v Manchester City Magistrates' Court Ex p. Snelson* [1977] Crim. L.R. 423 and *R. v Horsham JJ. Ex p. Reeves* [1981] Crim. L.R. 566, cases on committal proceedings; and *R. v Cwmbran JJ. Ex p. Pope* (1979) 143 J.P. 638). In the latter case a defendant was acquitted by a jury on an excess alcohol charge on the defence that he was not driving or riding a motor cycle but pushing it. Subsequent proceedings for careless driving were stopped by the Divisional Court on the grounds that the issue was the same and the proceedings would be oppressive. Lord Widgery said in *R. v West London JJ. Ex p. Klahn* [1979] 1 W.L.R. 933 "the magistrate in considering an application for the issue of a summons may and indeed should consider whether the allegation is vexatious: see *R. v Bros* (1901) 8 L.T. 581". An argument that the prosecution had been guilty of abuse of process in preferring more serious charges later failed before the Divisional Court in *R. v Coventry City Magistrates' Court Ex p. M* (1992) 156 J.P. 809. There had been no delay in charging the applicant or in bringing him before the court. There was nothing wrong in bringing a holding charge whilst questions of principle and policy were considered in the light of the applicant's age. Nor was there any culpable delay in the subsequent decision-making by the Crown Prosecution Service in relation to the additional charges.

2.64   The authorities were reviewed in *R. v Canterbury and St Augustine JJ. Ex p. Turner* (1983) 147 J.P. 193 (a case on committal proceedings). McNeill J. said that the decided cases do not show that delay alone is an abuse of process. Drake J. said that one could imagine very extreme cases of delay where delay of itself might constitute an abuse of process. He added that in the decided cases delay had been accompanied either by some deliberate exercise of bad faith or inefficiency or, at its lowest, by an inference that something had gone wrong with the prosecution process.

    In *R. v Canterbury and St Augustines Magistrates' Court Ex p. Barrington* (1994) 158 J.P. 325 an information had been laid at the end of 1988 against the applicant but the summons was not served on him until August or September 1992. The reason was that the applicant had left the only address known to the police and there was no other address known to them at which he could be contacted. Before the magistrates it was asserted that the police had not been especially enterprising or imaginative in their efforts to trace the applicant and in view of the unconscionable delay in serving the summons, it would be an abuse of process to proceed. The justices held that a fair trial would not be seriously prejudiced. The Divisional Court agreed that the justices were entitled to reach the decision they did. There was no obligation for the police to be enterprising in their efforts to trace the applicant by, e.g. combing through the telephone directory to trace the whereabouts of his relatives or checking the community charge register.

2.65   In *R. v West London Stipendiary Magistrate Ex p. Anderson* (1984) 148 J.P. 683 the charge was refusing to supply a laboratory specimen. The defendant was charged on October 28, 1979 and arrested on warrant on December 10, 1982. The magistrate considered that the defendant had made no subsequent inquiries and the police had not acted in bad faith. He decided that the delay did not constitute an abuse of the process of the court. The Divisional Court reversed his decision and prohibited continuance of the proceedings. Substantial delay might be caused by a deliberate act or by inefficiency on the part of the prosecution, and where the defendant had not caused or contributed to it. If the defendant was shown to have suffered prejudice or even if such prejudice was to be inferred from the delay, the justices might exercise their discretion to stop the proceedings. The longer the delay, the more readily might the justices draw the inference of prejudice. Where substantial delay had occurred and that delay could be attributed in part to the prosecution's inefficiency and in part to the defendant's conduct, the justices had to decide whether the substantial delay resulted from the inefficiency of the prosecution and if the defendant had been prejudiced by the delay.

    For an example of a decision in which an abuse of the process of the court was not shown, see *R. v Ealing JJ. Ex p. Keegan, The Times,* November 16, 1987. The Divisional Court refused an order of prohibition, and found that justices had acted correctly, where the latter had refused to exercise their discretion to dismiss four charges similar to those they had previously dismissed for want of prosecution. This decision can be looked at in tandem with that of *R. v Willesden JJ. Ex p. Clemmings* (1987) 152 J.P. 286 in which it was held—on broadly similar facts—that in deciding whether the justices' decision to allow proceedings to recommence subsequent to their earlier dismissal was proper, the applicant had to discharge the high burden of proving that the decision was so untenable and irrational that no bench properly directed could come to the same decision.

Some further decisions on this aspect of procedural law should be noted. The **2.66** principle laid down by Bingham L.J. in *R. v Liverpool City JJ. Ex p. Ellison* [1990] R.T.R. 220 is that the Divisional Court has a duty to intervene if it has cause to suspect that a prosecutor may be manipulating or using the procedures of the court in order to oppress or unfairly prejudice a defendant. This was applied in the interesting decision of *R. v Forest of Dean JJ. Ex p. Farley* [1990] R.T.R. 228. The facts were that the applicant had been drinking with friends and had given two girls a lift in his vehicle. The vehicle had turned over at the bottom of a hill and one of the girls had been killed. The applicant had left the scene and later telephoned the police. He was not breathalysed until the following morning, when his blood-alcohol was just below the statutory limit. The defendant was charged with the indictable only former offence of causing death by reckless driving and with the purely summary offence of driving with excess alcohol. In proceedings before the justices, the prosecution intended to call evidence to show by "back calculation" that the applicant's blood-alcohol would have been above the limit at the time the accident occurred. The applicant's defence would have been that he consumed alcohol after the accident. Although the prosecution was able to adduce some evidence that the applicant had been drinking before the accident, that evidence was insufficient to found a "forward calculation" that the proportion of alcohol in his body at the relevant time would have exceeded the limit.

The prosecution wished to proceed with the summary excess alcohol offence in order to establish that the applicant was driving at the time with excess alcohol. If successful, the charge of causing death by reckless driving would be proceeded with, the recklessness being established by the excess alcohol. The conviction could have been put in at the Crown Court trial under s.74(3) of the Police and Criminal Evidence Act 1984 as evidence of the facts on which it was based, unless the applicant proved to the contrary. The reason the prosecutor wished to proceed in this way was that in the magistrates' court the burden of proving the subsequent consumption of alcohol lay on the accused. In his judgment, Garland J. stated that on the facts, it was in substance a case of double jeopardy which transgressed an accepted principle that offences should generally be prosecuted in decreasing order of magnitude. After reviewing the authorities, his Lordship found that it would be an abuse of the process of the court to proceed in the manner proposed by the prosecution. The prosecution should choose either to proceed with the charge of causing death by reckless driving, and consider bringing the lesser charge if the applicant was acquitted, or to proceed with the excess alcohol charge alone.

In *R. v Bow Street Stipendiary Magistrate Ex p. DPP* (1990) 154 J.P. 237, it **2.67** was held by the Divisional Court that, in criminal proceedings, mere delay which gave way to prejudice and unfairness might, by itself, amount to an abuse of the process of the court. In some circumstances, prejudice would be presumed from substantial delay; in the absence of a presumption where there was a substantial delay, it would be for the prosecution to justify it.

The greater imperative to conclude speedily proceedings against younger offenders (see § 2.20 above) does not mean it need be an abuse of process to continue with cases against adult co-defendants where the proceedings against a co-defendant who was a youth have been stayed for abuse of process on account of delay: *R. (on the application of Knight) v West Dorset Magistrates' Court* [2002] EWHC 2152; (2002) 166 J.P. 705.

2.68   In *R. v Clerkenwell Magistrates' Court Ex p. Bell* (1991) 155 J.P. 669, a stipendiary magistrate was held to have been wrong in refusing to allow the defendant to give evidence on the preliminary issue as to whether the relevant period of delay amounted to abuse of process or not, after he had heard from a police officer on oath that the defendant had not been at his last known address. The refusal had been a breach of natural justice. The Divisional Court also held in *R. v Crawley JJ. Ex p. DPP* (1991) 155 J.P. 841 that, before dismissing a prosecution on the ground of unreasonable delay amounting to an abuse of process, justices should first consider evidence of the course of the proceedings thus far and make themselves aware of the circumstances of the delay, hearing both prosecution and defence.

A case on the subject that has found judicial favour in this country and is of great persuasive authority, particularly in providing five useful criteria which will assist courts in resolving the issue of abuse, is *R. v Jago* (1989) 87 A.L.R. 577. Dean J., sitting in the High Court of Australia, stated that a court should investigate:

(1) the length of delay;

(2) the reasons given by the prosecution to justify it;

(3) the accused's responsibility for the delay and his attitude to it;

(4) the likely prejudice to the accused, i.e. the significance of the passage of time and the fact that witnesses' memories, almost inevitably, will have faded;

(5) the public interest in the disposition of charges of serious offences and in the conviction of those guilty of crime.

2.69   In *R. v Newham JJ. Ex p. C* [1993] Crim. L.R. 130, the Divisional Court refused the applicant an order prohibiting the Newham justices to continue to hear committal proceedings. In the course of the judgment handed down by the court, it was said that in deciding whether a prosecution was an abuse of process because of delay, justices should not attempt a comparison with the facts of another case. Applications to stay proceedings on the ground of abuse of process depended entirely on their own facts. In *R. v Sheffield Stipendiary Magistrate Ex p. Stephens* (1992) 156 J.P. 555, the Divisional Court warned against excessive citing of cases. The principles which were applicable to the exercise of the powers by justices had been authoritatively stated and the excessive citation of cases did nothing to further the cause of justice and should be discouraged.

In *R. v Beckford* [1995] R.T.R. 251, Neill L.J. stated that courts had the power and duty to protect the law by protecting its own purposes and functions. The court has power to stay a criminal prosecution in certain circumstances. The law remained in a state of development and the circumstances of each case required separate consideration. Two main strands could be detected in the authorities:

(1) cases where the court concluded that the defendant cannot receive a fair trial; and

(2) cases where the court concluded that it would be unfair for the defendant to be tried.

2.70   Abuse of process has also been applied to issues arising from the destruction of evidence. In *R. (on the application of Ebrahim) v Feltham Magistrates' Court; Mouat v DPP* [2001] EWHC Admin 130; [2002] R.T.R 7, the defendant (Ebrahim) was stopped by the police and informed he had been speeding. He was taken to the police vehicle, shown a video recording of his car, served with a fixed penalty notice and allowed to drive off. The videotape was reused in the ordinary course of duty of the police officers. The defendant contested the allegation but was convicted in the magistrates' court. He appealed to the Crown Court and sought to have the proceedings stayed as an abuse of the process of the court since, he claimed, the videotape was essential to his defence. The Crown Court dismissed the appeal but that decision was overturned by the Divisional Court. The first issue was to determine whether there was any duty on the police or the prosecutor to obtain or retain material. If there was no duty, then the subsequent trial could not be unfair as a result of the lack of retention. If a duty had been breached, any unfairness that resulted from it should normally be dealt with in the course of the trial and the proceedings should be stayed if the defendant proves (on the balance of probabilities) that the breach of the duty would cause him to suffer serious prejudice and that no fair trial could be had. Here, since a defendant had a period after the issue of a fixed penalty notice to consider whether to contest the allegation, the police were under an obligation to retain the videotape at least until the end of that period. The case was returned to the Crown Court for that court to consider whether it would be possible for a fair hearing to take place. Further guidance was given on the procedure to be adopted where such an allegation is being made. If the complaint of abuse of process is made on appeal from a magistrates' court, the application should be for the conviction to be quashed because the original trial was unfair and because the nature of the unfairness was such that it can not now be remedied rather than for the proceedings to be stayed. Where a decision on such an application is made in the lower court, the court should give its reasons (even if only briefly) and it is the professional duty of the advocates for the parties to take a note of these reasons and provide that note to the High Court. Similarly, if relevant oral evidence is given, an agreed note should be prepared which summarises the effect of that evidence.

In *R. v Sadler* (2002) 166 J.P. 481, the issue was whether the defendant had attacked the victim with a bottle. A bottle neck recovered at the scene was tested for blood and fingerprints but none was found. There was no testing for DNA traces and the bottle neck was destroyed before trial. The defence did not ask to examine the bottle neck at any time but sought to have the trial stayed on a number of grounds one of which was that the destruction of the bottle neck rendered the trial unfair because it was not available for DNA testing. Although the bottle neck should not have been destroyed, the Crown Court held that the police had not acted in bad faith, nor had the defence case been prejudiced. Accordingly, it refused to stay the proceedings. The Court of Appeal agreed. In a case where an application to stay was based on the destruction of exhibits, it had to be considered whether the destruction had resulted from any bad faith on the part of the prosecution and the extent to which, if at all, the conduct of the defence had been prejudiced by the absence of evidence. Significant points were that the absence of blood meant that DNA testing was likely to have little significance and that the defence had not made any request for DNA testing before the start of the trial.

2.71

A further application of the abuse of process argument arose from a consideration of the effect of dismissal by justices elsewhere in the country of a prosecution against the same defendant on substantially the same offences. A defendant was charged with supplying furniture that failed to comply with provisions regarding safety. A prosecution before the Cardiff justices was dismissed. When proceedings came before the Harrogate justices, they acceded to a submission that the proceedings should be stayed as an abuse of the process of the court. This decision was roundly criticised by the Divisional Court in *R. (on the application of North Yorkshire Trading Standards Service) v Coleman* [2001] EWHC Admin 818; (2002) 166 J.P. 76. In the absence of oppression, the acquittal before another magistrates' court was not binding and there may well be reasons why one set of proceedings should lead to a conviction and another to an acquittal. In argument, an example was given of an overweight lorry stopped in the north of England and then continuing its journey and being stopped again in the south. If the proceedings based on the first stopping were dismissed because of, say, faulty weighing, that would not support an argument not to proceed with the other. Similarly, where a supply has continued despite knowledge of illegality.

2.72   Although falling outside the general run of "abuse of process" cases which concern delay leading to express or implied unfairness, *R. v Croydon JJ. Ex p. Dean* [1993] Q.B. 769 and *Dacorum Borough Council v El-Kalyoubi* [2001] EWHC Admin 1052 should be noted. In these cases consideration was given as to how to respond to a situation where proceedings have been instituted in circumstances where a defendant asserted that he had been led to believe that they would not be. In *R. v Croydon JJ. Ex p. Dean* [1993] Q.B. 769 the abuse centred on a promise made by the police to the applicant that he would not be prosecuted. In the event, he was prosecuted and at committal proceedings counsel submitted that there was an abuse because his client had received an undertaking from the police that he would not be prosecuted in connection with a killing. The justices rejected that submission, refused to adjourn the case pending an application for judicial review, and committed the applicant for trial. The committal for trial was quashed by the Divisional Court. The prosecution of a person who had received an undertaking, promise or representation from the police that he would not be prosecuted was capable of being an abuse of the process of the court. It was not necessary that the police had the power to make such a decision or that the case was one of bad faith or something similar. Staughton L.J., at the conclusion of his judgment, did however describe the case as "quite exceptional". That description was supported in *Dacorum Borough Council v El-Kalyoubi*. The defendant had been interviewed by the police after complaints that he had unlawfully evicted a tenant and appropriated his property. The police officer concerned informed the defendant, after interview, that the eviction was a civil matter and the theft a criminal matter. The police did not charge the defendant but, three months later, the Council commenced criminal proceedings alleging unlawful eviction. The defendant sought to have the proceedings stayed as an abuse of process since he had been informed by a public official that no prosecution would be brought against him. Taking into account the three-month delay, the justices stayed the proceedings. Confirming that justices had jurisdiction to stay proceedings where a defendant had been led to believe he would not be prosecuted and had changed his position and would be prejudiced by a prosecution or where allowing the proceedings would bring the system into disrepute, nonetheless, in these circumstances, the Divisional Court allowed the Council's appeal. The power to stay proceedings for this reason should be used very sparingly indeed. Even where some indication had been given, it did not follow automatically that a court should interfere should the prosecutor decide subsequently to proceed. Where that indication had been given by someone with no power to give an assurance, that indication would normally be regarded as of no consequence. The fact that the defendant had mistakenly believed that only the police could bring a prosecution was also irrelevant.

The different problems of justices faced with a constant series of applications **2.73** to adjourn the hearing of an information were considered in *R. v Bristol Magistrates' Court Ex p. Rowles* [1994] R.T.R. 40 (and see further at § 2.100 and § 22.35). The prosecution alleged that the applicant had driven a motor vehicle with excess alcohol. The applicant's defence was post-driving consumption of alcohol. The applicant wanted to call three witnesses in support of his defence, including an expert. The proceedings had been adjourned five times, twice solely at the request of the applicant. On the material date, the applicant was present as was the expert, but of the two other defence witnesses, one was ill and the other absent because he had been threatened with dismissal if he took time off work. The applicant's legal representative was understood by the chairman of the bench to have said that he could go on without them. The application to adjourn was refused, the case went on, and the applicant was convicted. The Divisional Court, in granting certiorari, held inter alia that the justices had proceeded under misapprehensions as to the applicant's ability to proceed with his case in the absence of his witnesses, the applicant's responsibility for the delays, and his apparent failure to take out witness summonses. Despite the difficulties of justices when cases were adjourned again and again, their duty was to examine all the circumstances and decide what was the fair thing to do. Here there had been a breach of natural justice.

Conclusions

The following conclusions are submitted. **2.74**

(1) If an information is properly laid, disclosing an offence for which the magistrates' court has jurisdiction, the magistrates are required to deal with it, and if they decline, they may be compelled to do so by judicial review (Magistrates' Courts Act 1980 s.9(2)).

(2) Magistrates may refuse to hear a case if the proceedings are vexatious or otherwise an abuse of process (*R. v Brentford JJ. Ex p. Wong* [1981] Crim. L.R. 339 and the other cases referred to above) or there is some impropriety or *mala fides* (*R. v Grays JJ.*). It may be an abuse of process if the prosecution have manipulated or misused the process of the court so as to deprive the defendant of a protection provided by the law or to take unfair advantage of a technicality (*R. v Liverpool City JJ.*; *R. v Forest of Dean JJ.*).

(3) In extreme cases, delay itself may amount to an abuse of process if on the balance of probability the defendant has been, or will be, prejudiced in the preparation or conduct of his defence by delay on the part of the prosecution which is unjustifiable; e.g. not due to the complexity of the inquiry and preparation of the prosecution case, or to the action of the defendant or his co-accused, or to genuine difficulty in effecting service.

(4) Substantial delay may amount to an abuse of process if accompanied by some deliberate exercise of bad faith or inefficiency or, at its lowest by an inference that something has gone wrong with the prosecution

process (*R. v Canterbury and St Augustine JJ. Ex p. Turner*; *R. v Canterbury and St Augustine's Magistrates' Court Ex p. Barrington*).

(5) Where there is substantial delay which is due in part to the inefficiency of the prosecution and in part to the conduct of the defence, the justices have to consider whether the substantial delay resulted from the prosecution's inefficiency and whether the defendant has been prejudiced thereby (*R. v West London Stipendiary Magistrate*).

(6) In some circumstances, prejudice would be presumed from substantial delay; in the absence of a presumption where there was a substantial delay, it would be for the prosecution to justify it (*R. v Bow Street Stipendiary Magistrate Ex p. DPP*).

(7) Justices should exercise their discretion in these cases judicially, not dismiss them out of hand (*R. v Birmingham JJ. Ex p. Lamb* [1983] 3 All E.R. 23).

(8) Where the justices exercise their discretion judicially the Divisional Court will not interfere unless the justices have not directed themselves properly in law or they have acted perversely, though it may be preferable for the application to stay proceedings to be heard in the Divisional Court (*R. (on the application of the DPP) v Croydon Youth Court* (2001) 165 J.P. 181).

(9) The Divisional Court (and a fortiori the magistrates' court) has no right to inquire as to the regularity of the proceedings under which a fugitive has been apprehended and given over into custody; see *R. v Plymouth JJ. Ex p. Driver* [1985] 2 All E.R. 681, where the authorities are reviewed. The *Plymouth JJ.* case must now be read in the light of the decision of the House of Lords in *R. v Horseferry Road Magistrates' Court Ex p. Bennett* (1993) 157 J.P. 713.

(10) Finally there is power to refuse to hear a case where there are mutually exclusive informations. It was stated in *R. v Newcastle JJ. Ex p. Hindle* [1984] 1 All E.R. 770 that it would be an abuse of the process to allow the prosecution to proceed with two mutually exclusive cases. The two cases were driving with excess alcohol and obstructing a police constable in the execution of his duty. Neither information could be pursued without necessarily relying on facts which were diametrically opposed. The prosecutor could not justify both informations under s.1 of the Magistrates' Courts Act 1980.

Proof of service; attendance of defendant

2.75 A summons may be served by handing it to the defendant, by leaving it (or sending it) to the "appropriate address for service". For an individual defendant that will be an address where it is reasonably believed that the defendant will receive it; for a corporation that will be the principal office in England and Wales or, if there is none that is readily identifiable, where the corporation carries on its activities or business. Where an individual or corporation is legally represented, it can be the address of the legal representatives' office: Criminal Procedure Rules 2005 (as amended) rr.4.3 and 4.4. If an individual is 17 or under, personal service must be by handing it over to the defendant's parent or other appropriate adult unless no person of that description is readily available: r.4.3(2). Although service through document exchange (DX) or fax is acceptable in relation to some documents, that does not apply to a summons or adjournment notice: r.4.7.

Service may be proved by a signed certificate which explains how and when it was served: r.4.11.

The court has no discretion to require a prosecutor to effect service in any particular one of those ways. In *R. (on the application of Durham County Council) v North Durham JJ.* [2004] EWHC 1073; (2004) 168 J.P. 269, the court had been issued with local guidance that personal service should be effected where a summons did not disclose certain information including the full postal address and date of birth of the defendant. This approach, no doubt, was dictated by the need to have this information in order to enforce successfully any financial order made on conviction. However, the form of service employed by the prosecutor was sufficient to permit the court to proceed in the absence of the defendant and the justices had no power to require the prosecutor to use one method rather than another. **2.76**

By s.14(1) of the Magistrates' Courts Act 1980 the defendant may have the proceedings or an adjudication set aside if he makes a statutory declaration that the summons had not come to his notice until a date specified in the declaration, and within 21 days of the date the declaration is served on the clerk to the justices. The Act also allows a justice (or justices' clerk or person authorised by the justices' clerk), on application by the defendant, to accept service of a statutory declaration outside the 21-day period if he thinks it unreasonable to have expected the defendant to have served the declaration within that period. The declaration sets aside the penalty including any disqualification or endorsement, but only from the time the declaration is lodged. Therefore, a defendant who is disqualified and drives between the time of disqualification and the lodging of the statutory declaration still commits the offence of driving whilst disqualified: *Singh (Jaspal) v DPP* [1999] R.T.R. 424. Similarly, a defendant who successfully appeals against a disqualification, but had not had that disqualification suspended pending the appeal, remains disqualified between the original sentence and the appeal decision: *R. v Thames Magistrates' Court Ex p. Levy* [1997] T.L.R. 394. A fresh summons may be issued on the original information.

Summonses may be served for offences in England on persons who are in Scotland or the Isle of Man under the Summary Jurisdiction (Process) Act 1881. Warrants may also be so issued and executed (Magistrates' Courts Act 1980 s.126). If any such person is in any part of Northern Ireland, the Isle of Man or Channel Islands a warrant may be executed but a summons may not be served under these provisions (ibid.). So far as process between England, Wales, Scotland and Northern Ireland is concerned, these provisions have been largely superseded by Pt X of the Criminal Justice and Public Order Act 1994. A summons for an offence may be served in Scotland or Northern Ireland for the person to appear before a court in England or Wales (Criminal Law Act 1977 s.39). A warrant issued in England or Wales for the arrest of a person charged with an offence may also be executed in Scotland or Northern Ireland (1994 Act s.136). Under the same sections similar provisions are applied vice versa for Scotland and Northern Ireland. **2.77**

If a person is outside the British Isles just named, he cannot be summoned or arrested by warrant save in so far as the procedure relating to fugitive offenders and extradition applies.

2.78   As to certain powers of reopening where the court has convicted or sentenced the defendant through mistake or inadvertence either on the part of the court or on the part of the defendant, see § 2.187. This may well be preferable to the expense of an appeal.

Waiving summons

2.79   The court may deal with a defendant actually before it, though not in answer to a summons, unless he seeks time to prepare his defence. Sometimes, when a defendant has come in answer to a summons, the prosecution desire to prefer a further or alternative charge. The defendant may waive a summons for the new charge and declare himself ready to meet it then and there, and, if he does, the new charge can be proceeded with immediately (*Eggington v Pearl* (1875) 40 J.P. 56). But he is entitled to know exactly the charge and should be told of his right to an adjournment to consider the new charge. Semble a defendant who contends that he has been wrongfully arrested or that his summons is defective may properly object to being tried until proper process summoning him has been issued (*Dixon v Wells* (1890) 25 Q.B.D. 249), but it was remarked in that case that it had been held by some of the judges in *R. v Hughes* (1879) 4 Q.B.D 614 and *R. v Shaw* (1865) 29 J.P. 339 that, if the accused were present and the court had jurisdiction, his protest against any defect in process or wrongful arrest might be of no avail. Semble a summons returnable forthwith, if the time-limit had not expired, could be sought and issued by the magistrates but the defendant should be allowed time to prepare his defence if he wants it.

    An appearance simply to draw attention to an irregularity in service is not a waiver (*Pearks, Gunston & Tee Ltd v Richardson* (1902) 56 J.P. 119). It has long been accepted that a court cannot deal with a defendant who appears under protest, unless the protest be properly overruled. The court must, of course, in every case have jurisdiction to deal with the offence: see §§ 2.39 et seq.

Amending summonses

2.80   Under s.123 of the Magistrates' Courts Act 1980 no objection is allowed to any information or complaint, or to any summons or warrant to procure the presence of the defendant, for any defect in it in substance or in form, or for any variance between it and the evidence adduced on behalf of the prosecutor or complainant at the hearing of the information or complaint. If it appears to a magistrates' court that any variance between a summons or warrant and the evidence adduced on behalf of the prosecutor or complainant is such that the defendant has been misled by the variance, the court must, on the application of the defendant, adjourn the hearing.

    This means in effect that the summons can be amended (per Byrne J. in *Meek v Powell* [1952] 1 All E.R. 347). However, the decisions on the amending of summonses will need to be reviewed in the light of the implementation of the Human Rights Act 1998. In particular, it is necessary that a defendant must be clearly told what offence he is facing and given sufficient time to prepare his case. An allied point was considered by the Divisional Court in *Lewin v Barratt Homes Ltd* (2000) 164 J.P. 174 which was the extent to which the defence can rely on a technical oversight by the prosecution to secure an acquittal after a trial. Although obiter, Newman J. reiterated that, in some instances, justice will not be done where acquittals are secured by pure oversights. It is certainly the case that the burden of proof is generally on the prosecution and the defence is entitled to leave the prosecution to prove the case without drawing attention to any absence of evidence on essential ingredients of the offence. However, there will be areas where the defence, by remaining silent or by not taking a particular course, can be taken to have let points go by default. Particularly in magistrates' courts, it is very important that all points are taken as clearly as possible and at the appropriate time. In this case the defendants sought to rely in the Divisional Court on a point on the wording of the summons that fell well within the discretion contained in s.123 of the Magistrates' Courts Act 1980 and could not have lead to the defendant or the court being misled or put at a disadvantage. See also *Jolly v DPP* [2000] Crim. L.R. 471 quoting with approval *R. v Pydar JJ. Ex p. Foster* (1995) 160 J.P. 87 "justice will not be done if defendants are acquitted purely because of an oversight which was capable of being corrected there and then". This robust approach was continued in *DPP v Short* [2001] EWHC Admin 885; (2002) 166 J.P. 474. A defendant was the subject of an information alleging "use" of a motor vehicle with an excess of alcohol in his blood rather than "driving". The correct section of the Act was contained in the information. Justices acceded to the defence objection to a prosecution application to amend the information after all the evidence had been heard but this was overturned on appeal. Applying *Karpinski v City of Westminster* [1993] Crim. L.R. 606, the court confirmed that the information should be looked at as a whole and this was not such a fundamental error that it could not be cured by amendment.

A crucial amendment cannot be made under s.123 on appeal (*Garfield v Maddocks* [1973] 2 All E.R. 303). However, in *Lee v Wiltshire Chief Constable* [1979] R.T.R. 349, the defect in the original information was merely technical and could not mislead anybody and it was held that in such a case the Crown Court could not dismiss the appeal because the information was defective and could not be amended on appeal. The Crown Court dealing with an appeal from a magistrates' court has no power to amend the information: *R. v Swansea Crown Court Ex p. Stacey* [1990] R.T.R. 183. The information in this case referred to the incorrect date. Nobody noticed at the hearing before magistrates, and the defendant was convicted. He appealed and the error relating to the date was drawn to the attention of the judge at the hearing in the Crown Court. The judge permitted the date to be amended, feeling that it was objectionable to proceed on an information known to be wrong as to date. On an application for judicial review, it was held that the Crown Court had no jurisdiction to amend the information laid before the magistrates' court. The factual situation was that the wrong date in the information was considered to be of no materiality whatsoever; it did not affect the resolution of any of the issues and caused no injustice to the applicant. The decision of the judge to amend was quashed and the Crown Court was ordered to continue the hearing on the unamended information.

2.81

In *R. v Greater Manchester JJ. Ex p. Aldi GmbH & Co KG*; *Aldi GmbH & Co KG v Mulvenna* (1995) 159 J.P. 717 judicial review was allowed to quash the amendment of an information. Justices at Eccles had amended an information brought by Salford Council by substituting Aldi GmbH & Co KG for Aldi Stores Ltd. The Divisional Court applied *Marco (Croydon) Ltd v Metropolitan Police* [1984] R.T.R. 24 in which a distinction had been drawn between those cases where the justices were satisfied the right person had received the summons and knew it was intended for him and was not prejudiced in any way, and a case where the wrong defendant company of a group had been summoned. The latter situation applied in the *Aldi* case. The remedy sought was granted and the amendment quashed. Similarly, in *Sainsbury's Supermarkets Ltd v HM Courts Service and Plymouth City Council* [2006] EWHC 1749; (2006) 170 J.P 690 a decision to permit an amendment was quashed where the wrong company was named and it should have been perfectly obvious to the prosecutor what the correct name was.

2.82   A summons may be amended even if it is outside the six months' time-limit for laying an information imposed by s.127 of the Magistrates' Courts Act 1980 (*R. v Newcastle JJ. Ex p. Bryce* [1976] R.T.R. 325). Justices should, however, exercise their powers under s.123 judicially and so as to do justice between the parties. (Limited company charged with *permitting* its vehicle to be used whilst overloaded, charge amended to the absolute offence of *using* its vehicle whilst so overloaded—held, justices were entitled to allow the amendment, the prosecutor was not introducing new facts.) Again, in an unlicensed sex establishment prosecution, an information was amended from "neglect" to "connivance" even though the amendment was more than technical and made outside the time-limit. No injustice was caused (see *R. v Bow Street Acting Stipendiary Magistrate Ex p. Spiteri, The Times*, October 16, 1984). *R. v Newcastle JJ. Ex p. Bryce* was applied in *R. v Sandwell JJ. Ex p. West Midlands Passenger Transport Board* [1979] Crim. L.R. 56.

     The broad principle in *Garfield v Maddocks* and *R. v Newcastle JJ. Ex p. Bryce* above was summed up by McCullough J. in *Simpson v Roberts, The Times*, December 21, 1984, by stating that *an information which was good enough to enable a defendant to identify the misdoing alleged against him could be amended so long as it continued to allege the same misdoing*. In that case the misdoing was different and an appeal against conviction was allowed.

2.83   The potentially wide discretion allowing a court to amend an information was confirmed by the decision of the Divisional Court in *R. v Scunthorpe JJ. Ex p. McPhee and Gallagher* (1998) 162 J.P. 635. Dyson J. applied *R. v Newcastle JJ.*, and *Simpson v Roberts* and derived the following principles:

     (a) the purpose of the six-month time-limit under s.127 was to ensure that summary offences were charged and tried as soon as was reasonably practicable after their alleged commission;

     (b) where an information had been laid within six months it could be amended after expiry of that period;

     (c) an information could be amended after expiry of that period even to allege a different offence or offences provided that:

        (i) such offence alleged the "same misdoing" as the original offence, and

        (ii) the amendment could be made in the interests of justice.

His Lordship stated that the phrase "same misdoing" was not to be construed too narrowly: it meant that the new offence should arise out of the same, or substantially the same, facts as gave rise to the original offence. Once justices were satisfied that the amended offence did so arise, they had to go on to consider whether it was in the interests of justice to allow the amendment. In exercising their discretion, they should pay particular regard to the interests of the defendant. If an amendment would result in a defendant facing a significantly more serious charge, that should "weigh heavily, perhaps conclusively" against allowing the amendment after the six-month time-limit had expired. In dealing with the possibility of an application for an adjournment where there was a late application to amend, his Lordship considered that the need for an adjournment ought to be "rare" because the amended offence would arise out of the same, or substantially the same, facts as the original offence.

In *R. v Thames Magistrates' Court Ex p. Stevens* (2000) 164 J.P. 233, the original charge was for assault occasioning actual bodily harm on April 1, 1999; the revised charge was for common assault and the application to amend was made on October 15, 1999 outside the six months' time-limit for a summary offence. The amendment was allowed. Dismissing the appeal the Divisional Court confirmed as the key elements that the amended charge arose out of the same facts as the original charge, that the applicant was not prejudiced by the amendment and had not been deprived of any defence to the charge, that the evidence to be adduced was no different and that the effect of the amendment was to reduce the gravity of the charge. However, in *R. (on the application of Fisher) v Weymouth Magistrates' Court*, November 3, 2000, unreported, DC, an amendment out of time was refused where a defendant had pleaded guilty to common assault but the prosecution wanted to adduce an account of actual violence. The defendant objected and the stipendiary magistrate acceded to a request to amend the information out of time to one alleging assault by beating. The Divisional Court drew attention to the fact that assault by beating was more serious and that the defendant had already pleaded guilty to the lesser offence; it was not in the interests of justice to amend the information.

2.84

In *R. (on the application of James) v DPP* [2004] EWHC 1663; (2004) 168 J.P. 596, the defendant was charged with supplying cannabis resin. At the close of the prosecution case, the defence submitted that there was no case to answer since there was no proof of actual supply. The prosecution sought to amend the charge to "attempting to supply" and this was permitted. Dismissing the defendant's appeal, the Administrative Court emphasised not only that no injustice was caused to the defendant but also that the timing of the change did not deprive the appellant of the chance to plead guilty at the earliest opportunity. Further, justices were correct not to restart the mode of trial proceedings.

The principles in *R. v Scunthorpe JJ. Ex p. McPhee and Gallagher* were applied in *Ward v London Borough of Barking and Dagenham* [1999] Crim. L.R. 920. These were proceedings under the Food Safety Act 1990. The original summons described the misdoing so unclearly that it was not possible to identify what was being alleged. In those circumstances the application to amend should have been refused. The power to amend is not a safety net for inexcusably bad drafting.

2.85

R. (on the application of the DPP) v Everest [2005] EWHC 1124; (2005) 169 J.P. 345 is a further example where a refusal to amend an information was upheld. The respondent was prosecuted under the Highways Act 1980 as a result of his lighting of a bonfire. Smoke was alleged to have blown across a road obscuring visibility and an accident occurred. At the close of the prosecution case, the prosecutor sought to amend the information so that a different offence was prosecuted, though under the same Act. The new offence attracted a higher maximum penalty. The magistrates' court declined and the Divisional Court upheld that decision on the grounds that the court had approached the issue correctly. The magistrates' court had recognised that it had discretion to amend even at that stage of the proceedings and after the six-month time-limit had expired. A number of key elements were identified by the Divisional Court as being relevant to such an application, but it may be that it was the final one that was critical! The key elements were:

    (a) This amendment was more than just a simple one to cure a technical defect. It involved a different offence with a new statutory defence. If the change had been allowed, the respondent would have had to prove a statutory defence when he had already established a complete defence to the offence charged.

    (b) To allow the application would have placed an unfair burden on the respondent just before he was to give evidence. This could not have been cured by an adjournment because a rehearing would have been required since the prosecution witnesses had been cross-examined on one basis and were likely to need to be questioned on the statutory defence.

    (c) If the amendment had been allowed, the respondent would have faced a more serious offence with a substantially higher maximum penalty.

    (d) The respondent was unrepresented and so would find it more difficult to adjust to the new offence.

    (e) The "evident, and frankly lamentable, failure of the appellant from the outset to prosecute the right offence, and the failure to review the file or to review it intelligently and to seek an amendment at earlier stages".

2.86   A slightly more surprising decision was *Shaw v DPP* [2007] EWHC 207. The offender had been summoned for having custody of a dog contrary to a disqualification order. Initially the summons described that order (incorrectly) as being made under Dangerous Dogs legislation but it was amended to show (correctly) that it was made under Protection of Animals legislation. The amendment was made after the expiry of the statutory time-limit so no further information could have been laid. The main consequence was that the maximum penalty was three months' imprisonment rather than a fine of level 5 and it was on this ground alone that the Divisional Court quashed the decision to allow the amendment to be made. Given the fact that the defendant could not have been misled or disadvantaged in any way and that the court did not consider that the prosecution was particularly at fault, this is perhaps a decision that should be confined to its own facts. That might also be the correct approach to the decision in *R. (on the application of Thornhill) v Uxbridge Magistrates' Court* [2008] EWHC 508; (2008) 172 J.P. 297. The defendant was charged with four offences, one of which was failing to provide a specimen of breath for analysis. After the expiry of the six-month period, the prosecution made a successful application to amend the charge to one of failure to provide a specimen of urine. That decision was overturned by the Divisional Court which considered that there was a distinct difference between failing to provide a specimen of breath and failing to provide one of urine. One could perhaps understand it if the prosecutor felt aggrieved at this decision; clearly the essence of the offence is failure to provide a specimen for analysis and whether that specimen is of blood, breath or urine seems to be of secondary importance. On the facts of this particular case, there seemed to be common ground that there was a valid reason for the defendant not being required to supply a specimen of breath and so it is very unlikely that the defendant would have been at a disadvantage.

What is now s.123 of the Magistrates' Courts Act 1980 was held to obviate the necessity for a summons to repeat the date upon which the information was laid (*R. v Godstone JJ. Ex p. Secretary of State for the Environment* [1974] Crim. L.R. 110); *aliter* if there was any question as to the information being out of time. In *Atterton v Browne* (1945) 109 J.P. 25, magistrates were held entitled to dismiss the summons altogether for a serious defect, but apparently there were also other grounds for dismissing it. See *Westminster City Council v Peart* [1968] Crim. L.R. 504 for a case where a magistrate was justified in dismissing an insufficiently detailed summons. In *Wright v Nicholson* [1970] 1 All E.R. 12, it was held that the words of what is now s.123(1) of the Magistrates' Courts Act 1980 should not be read literally as meaning that there can be no attack on an information however fundamental the defect. Each case depends on its own merits and circumstances are infinitely variable. It depends in every case whether the variance is of such a character as to require amendment.

If the defendant has been misled or the variance is fundamental so that there **2.87** might be injustice to an accused, an amendment is required. Once an amendment is required s.123(2) operates and requires the court to adjourn if the defence applies. If the defendant does not require an adjournment, the amendment may be made forthwith and the case proceeded with on the amended summons. Thus, where a defendant had been required to provide a specimen of breath by a constable "who had reasonable cause to suspect him of having alcohol in his body", justices cannot convict him on the basis that the constable had reasonable cause to suspect him of having committed a moving traffic offence, without first informing the defendant of the charge and giving him the opportunity of applying for an adjournment under s.123(2) if he had been misled (*Morriss v Lawrence* (1977) 121 S.J. 187).

The variance may be so trivial that no amendment at all is required. In *Darnell v Holliday* [1973] R.T.R. 276the defendant was charged on five informations with using a car in "South Parade". The justices dismissed the case on the grounds that the offences occurred not in South Parade but in an unnamed cul-de-sac opposite. The justices were directed to convict by the Divisional Court as no sort of injustice was suffered by the defendant because of the misnaming of the road. Justices were also held to be entitled in *Turberville v Wyer* [1977] R.T.R. 29 to apply what is now s.123 in respect of an insecure load carried on a "motor lorry" without the necessity of formal amendment when the load was in fact carried on the trailer of an articulated motor lorry.

At the other extreme, one can have a defect that is so fundamental that, far **2.88** from it being required to be cured by amendment, it is in fact incapable of being cured. Thus the summons cannot be amended to a different offence altogether (*Loadman v Cragg* (1862) 26 J.P. 743 —from "drunk and disorderly" to "drunk"; *Lawrence v Fisher* [1947] Jo.Crim.L. 356; *Atterton v Browne* (1945) 109 J.P. 25). Where a defendant is charged with an offence under a repealed statute he cannot be convicted unless the summons has first been amended, even if the statutes are word for word the same. An amendment has been allowed to insert a reference to a statute which had been omitted (*Thornley v Clegg* [1982] R.T.R. 405).

It is proper to amend a summons, subject to the defendant's right to an adjournment if he has been deceived or misled, where the ownership of property maliciously damaged has been wrongly described (*Ralph v Hurrell* (1875) 40

J.P. 119); where the date of the offence has been wrongly stated so long as it is within the six-month period (*Exeter Corporation v Heaman* (1877) 42 J.P. 503); where the defendant appearing in court has been wrongly named in the summons (*Dring v Mann* (1948) 112 J.P. 270); by deleting superfluous words (*Rogerson v Stephens* [1950] 2 All E.R. 144) or where the defendant is charged under the wrong section and the charge is inadequately stated (*Hunter v Coombs* [1962] 1 All E.R. 904).

2.89   Where the defendant is the wrong limited company the summons cannot be amended to show the correct limited company (*Marco (Croydon) Ltd v Metropolitan Police* [1984] R.T.R. 24, see § 2.81 above).

Section 123 can be used after conviction and before sentence (*Allan v Wiseman* [1975] Crim. L.R. 37: defendant convicted in the name of "Jeffrey Thomas Loach"—real name "Jeffrey Thomas Allan"—arrested—name amended to Allan on appearance for sentence). *Allan v Wiseman* was applied in *R. v Eastbourne JJ. Ex p. Kisten* (1984) *The Times*, December 22 (clerical error amended after conviction and before sentence). Where offences are charged in the alternative, the prosecutor must elect at the outset on which he will proceed and it is too late after that to amend the information (*Hargreaves v Alderson* [1962] 3 All E.R. 1019).

2.90   See *R. v Aylesbury JJ. Ex p. Wisbey* [1965] 1 All E.R. 602 as to the amount of information to which a defendant is entitled prior to the hearing. Where the defence asks for further particulars, the prosecution would often be wise to supply them (*Robertson v Rosenburg* (1951) 115 J.P. 128). Justices are not deprived of jurisdiction because a summons is insufficiently detailed (*Neal v Devenish* (1894) 58 J.P. 246); contrast *Stephenson v Johnson* [1954] 1 All E.R. 369, where the particulars of the offence were so lacking that the justices "should not have entertained it". Semble they could at their discretion have adjourned for further and better particulars to be given.

Generally, the later the stage in the proceedings and the more material the amendment, the less desirable it becomes to grant the amendment because of the prejudice to the defendant. One useful test for amending summonses may be to follow the comment of Ormrod L.J. in *Thornley v Clegg* [1982] R.T.R. 405 at 410. This was that if the objection to amendment was an objection of substance and indicated some real injustice, or a risk of injustice being occasioned to the defendant, then the objection might well prevail. Where the prosecutor does not avail himself of his chance to seek amendment of a defective information, a conviction on that information will be bad (*Hunter v Coombs* above). A defendant who disputes the case on its merits is generally deemed to waive objection to unchallenged irregularities in the summons, etc.

A defective summons can be withdrawn and a regular one issued in its place, if within the time-limit and if there has been no adjudication on the first one.

Duplicity

2.91   Rule 7.3(2) of the Criminal Procedure Rules 2005 provides that more than one incident of the commission of an offence may be included in the allegation if they amount to a course of conduct. Whilst a single document may contain more than one information, each information should charge one offence only and, if more than one offence is charged in one information in the alternative, e.g. driving without due care and attention or without reasonable consideration, the court should call on the prosecutor to elect on which charge to proceed (*R. v Surrey JJ. Ex p. Witherick* (1932) 95 J.P. 219; *Fox v Dingley, Ware v Fox* [1967] 1 All E.R. 100). The offence or offences on which he elects not to proceed are struck from the information, and the court proceeds to try the information afresh. If the prosecutor fails to elect, the court is required to dismiss the information forthwith. Where an offence or offences are struck from the information on the prosecutor's election, the court is required to grant the defendant an adjournment where it appears to the court that he has been unfairly prejudiced. The requirement of the European Convention on Human Rights that a defendant be given clear information about the allegation that is faced is likely to lead to prosecuting authorities needing to be even clearer and more precise in the framing of charges and informations.

The test for duplicity is whether the information alleges one or more than one illegal act. In *R. v T* [2005] EWCA Crim 3511; (2006) 170 J.P. 313, the Court of Appeal again emphasised that the rule is to be applied in a practical, rather than strictly analytical, way. It exists to ensure that a defendant is not misled nor left uncertain about the charge that is faced.

In *Shah v Swallow* [1984] 2 All E.R. 528 HL substantial factual and legal ma- **2.92**
terial common to five informations was set out in a preamble and subsequently incorporated by reference. The document was held to be *not* bad for duplicity. In *Kite v Brown* [1940] 4 All E.R. 295 supplying several kinds of rationed food was held to be one illegal act. In *Thomson v Knights* [1947] 1 All E.R. 112 an offence of driving whilst unfit through drink or drugs was held not to be bad for duplicity. In *Mallon v Allon* [1963] 3 All E.R. 843 admitting and allowing to remain in a betting shop was held to be bad for duplicity.

The question has been raised whether it is one offence or more than one offence to fail to produce the various documents specified in s.165(2)(a), (b), (c) of the Road Traffic Act 1988, namely the certificate of insurance, the test certificate and the goods vehicle test certificate, if applicable. This matter was considered in a practical point at (1966) 130 J.P. 543. The answer given there was that this offence is in essence a failure to give to the police constable all the information to which he is entitled.

Support for the answer was also found in the wording of the proviso. It was **2.93**
considered that the use of the phrase "offence under this subsection by reason only of failure to produce" supported the argument that there was only one offence committed however many items of information were withheld. The answer was given in respect of the former section which was in similar terms, although the proviso is now contained in s.165(4). The answer would still seem to be that only one offence is committed by the failure to produce one or more of the relevant documents.

Under s.172(3) of the Road Traffic Act 1988 it is an offence to fail to give information as to the identity of the driver of the vehicle. The circumstances and type of information are specified in s.172(2)(a) and (b) and are varied depending on whether or not the person from whom the information was sought was the keeper of the vehicle. An argument that two offences were created and that a simple allegation under s.172(3) was void for duplicity was rejected in *Mohindra v DPP; Browne v Chief Constable of Manchester* [2004] EWHC 490; [2005] R.T.R. 7. The offence is a failure to comply with the requirement whilst s.172 simply defines the nature of the obligation that has been breached.

For a case where an information under s.170(4) of the 1988 Act (requirement to stop and report) was found not to be bad for duplicity, see *DPP v Bennett* [1993] R.T.R. 175.

2.94   Where there are different constituent elements of an offence such as an offence of theft, assault or careless driving, the various incidents may be included to constitute a single offence contained in a single information. Even though these are not bad for duplicity, there seems to be nothing to prevent the prosecutor including them in separate informations if each can, in its own right, constitute a separate offence.

An information alleging a single offence of driving without due care and attention was not bad for duplicity where the facts revealed two separate incidents separated by a 10-minute interval and two miles in distance witnessed by two different police officers (*Horrix v Malam* [1984] R.T.R. 112). *The test was whether the single count charged more than one activity even though the activity might involve more than one act.* The justices were entitled to take the view that the acts alleged constituted one, continuous, activity, taking into account the time and distance apart and that in each case the appellant was seen to be swerving erratically. A similar test was applied in *Heaton v Costello* (1984) 148 J.P. 688.

2.95   The authorities governing circumstances justifying departure from the normal principle of charging each alleged criminal act as a separate offence were reviewed in *Barton v DPP* [2001] EWHC Admin 223; (2001) 165 J.P. 779. A defendant had been charged with a single count of theft alleging that she had stolen small amounts from a till on 94 occasions over the period of a year. Although it would have been possible to have identified each of the 94 occasions, the magistrates' court considered that the transactions were part of a continuing course of conduct of the same type of dishonesty with no prospect of different defences being raised or of the defendant being prejudiced and declined to reject the information as bad for duplicity. This decision was upheld by the Divisional Court. Drawing attention to the two lines of justification to depart from the normal principle ("general deficiency" and "continuous offence"), and noting the decisions that specimen counts or informations were not possible, the court stated that duplicity is to be applied practically and is a question of fact and degree. Where, as here, there are a number of connected acts of a similar nature which can properly be regarded as being part of the same transaction, they can properly be contained in one count or information where there is sufficient certainty and where the defendant is unlikely to raise different defences for different actions within those connected acts.

There may be one activity but separate issues. There are instances where it is better to charge separate items separately particularly to avoid special findings (*R. v Bristol Crown Court Ex p. Willetts* [1985] Crim. L.R. 219). Again there are instances where the multiplicity of charges may operate unfairly, as e.g. with the single activity of selling a motor vehicle (see below). In such instances the court may approve the combination of issues in a single charge as in *Cullen v Jardine* [1985] Crim. L.R. 668, where the *Willetts* decision was distinguished.

2.96   In *DPP v Dziurzynski* [2002] EWHC 1380; (2002) 166 J.P. 545, on two separate dates, the defendant had attended the premises of a company and been abusive to employees. He was charged with pursuing a course of conduct which amounted to harassment of the employees. The district judge found that the charge was bad for duplicity because it recounted an unknown number of offences and only identified the complainants under the general title of employees of the company. Dismissing the prosecution appeal, the Administrative Court held that only some of the employees had been present on both dates and only some of those had given evidence. Of those giving evidence, only some had been distressed. Accordingly, on the facts, the evidence fell well short of that necessary to support the charges laid. The issue appears to have been the generality of the term used and the outcome may have been different if the charges had identified those concerned with more precision.

The informations should be distinct even though set out in one document. It was decided in *Streames v Copping* [1985] 2 All E.R. 122 that there is a single offence under what is now s.75 of the 1988 Act of selling, etc., an unroadworthy vehicle even though various breaches of the regulations are alleged. Such a charge for a single offence is not bad for duplicity. The decision was obiter but is nevertheless persuasive. It is submitted that selling, supplying, etc., are separate and should still be charged as separate offences.

In *Cross v Oliver* (1964) 108 S.J. 583 a defendant was charged with speeding **2.97** in a road controlled as to part by 1957 regulations and as to part by 1958 ones. The speeding had occurred in both parts and the information alleged one offence of speeding contrary to both regulations. The prosecutor declined to elect to proceed for one offence against one of the regulations only and the conviction was quashed on the ground that the information was bad for duplicity as charging two offences. If a statute forbids the doing of act A or act B, it creates two offences and a conviction of both offences on one information is bad for uncertainty (*Field v Hopkinson* (1944) 108 J.P. 21, but contrast *Davis v Loach* (1886) 51 J.P. 118, where a byelaw forbade the emission of "smoke or steam" and a conviction for emitting "smoke and steam" (they being mingled together) was upheld). But if there is one single incident *R. v Clow* [1963] 2 All E.R. 216 is authority for allowing alternatives to be charged conjunctively. Thus in *Vernon v Paddon* [1972] 3 All E.R. 302 a charge under s.5 of the Public Order Act 1936 of insulting words and insulting behaviour was upheld where it arose out of a single incident.

In *R. v Pontefract Magistrates Ex p. Wright (Heavy Haulage) Ltd*, 1995, **2.98** unreported (CO/3060/95), the Divisional Court considered an application for judicial review after the magistrates had rejected an argument that an information was bad for duplicity. A single information alleged that a motor vehicle and trailer both had specified defects to their braking systems. It was held that the Divisional Court did have a discretion to give leave for judicial review to bring up and quash the determination of the justices in relation to duplicity. The court thought that the simple answer would appear to be for the applicants to plead to the information, but on a specific and clear basis, namely to plead to those elements which related to the motor lorry only (having regard to the instructions given by the applicants to their solicitors, which indicated that they would not in all probability have a defence with respect to the brakes of the tractor unit). It would then be open to the prosecution to invite the justices to deal with the matter on the basis of that plea and that nothing relating to the trailer would be taken into account in sentencing. Alternatively, if the prosecution were to insist that all the elements were taken into account, there would have to be a hearing and it would have to be established beyond reasonable doubt that the braking system of the trailer, in addition to that of the motor lorry, was defective. If the prosecution failed to prove their further contentions, then the court would find itself, by a different route, sentencing in relation to the plea.

The Divisional Court took a practical and enlightened view of the problem recognising that the alternative of judicial review would involve substantial expenditure in costs and would lead to substantially the same situation. Although there may have been factors in the prosecution which were not brought to light in the application to the Divisional Court, it is difficult to see whether there would have been a great deal of difference in sentencing terms if the information had been amended before the magistrates to delete references to the trailer. A practical solution giving effect to the broad justice of the case was much the preferred outcome and the Divisional Court encouraged that to happen.

2.99   The House of Lords considered duplicity in *DPP v Butterworth* [1994] R.T.R. 181. Where a defendant has been charged under s.7(6) of the Road Traffic Act 1988 with failing to give a specimen when required by a constable in the course of an investigation into an offence of being unfit to drive through drink or drugs under s.4 or of having excess alcohol under s.5, it is not necessary to specify in the information whether the charge relates to s.4 or s.5. Lord Slynn, in an opinion with which all of their Lordships agreed, stated that it did not have to be shown that the constable had in his mind a specific offence under one of those sections and that he was investigating that specific offence. It was not therefore necessary to specify in the charge which, if any, specific offence was being investigated by the constable. Lord Slynn dealt with the "separate penalty" point by saying that his reading of s.7(6) was not vitiated by the fact that separate penalties were provided for driving or attempting to drive on the one hand and being in charge on the other. The question whether the person was driving or in charge of the motor vehicle was not part of the inquiry into whether there had been a refusal for the purposes of s.7(6). That question only became relevant after conviction and went to the appropriate penalty. Their Lordships therefore followed the decisions in *Commissioner of Police v Curran* [1976] 1 W.L.R. 87, *Roberts v Griffiths* [1978] R.T.R. 362, and *Shaw v DPP* [1993] R.T.R. 45, but stated that their conclusion was not inconsistent with *R. v Courtie* [1984] A.C. 463 or *R. v Shivpuri* [1987] A.C. 1. Each statute had to be considered separately to decide whether separate offences were created.

However, where the offence is contrary to s.5(1)(a) of the Road Traffic Act 1988 —"If a person drives or attempts to drive a motor vehicle ... after consuming so much alcohol that the proportion in his breath, blood or urine exceeds the prescribed limit ..." it is necessary to show whether the allegation is of attempting to drive or of driving and whether the specimen to be relied on is of breath or blood or urine. If this is not done, the allegation is bad for duplicity and the court is deprived of jurisdiction: *R. v Bolton JJ. Ex p. Khan* [1999] Crim. L.R. 912.

Adjournment

2.100   A single magistrate may adjourn a case and, subject to the consent of both parties, a clerk to the justices (or person authorised by the justices' clerk) may further adjourn a case (Justices' Clerks Rules 2005 (SI 2005/545)).

The power to adjourn has come under increasing scrutiny. Magistrates have been enjoined to examine critically all applications for adjournments with a view to minimising unnecessary delay. Provisions contained in the Crime and Disorder Act 1998 have speeded up the process of bringing matters commenced by charge before the court; and the Criminal Case Management Framework has drawn attention to the need for all concerned in criminal proceedings to work more closely together to improve the speed and effectiveness of the process. This approach needs to be balanced by the obligation under the European Convention on Human Rights to allow proper time for preparation but also to incorporate the need to be conscious of the impact on victims and witnesses of inappropriately extending the time taken to bring a case to conclusion.

Some cases have dealt with specific aspects of the approach to granting an adjournment. **2.101**

In *Smith (George) v DPP, The Times*, July 28, 1999, it was confirmed that, where a person is charged with a road traffic offence (other than motor manslaughter or causing death by either dangerous or careless driving) justices ought not to proceed with a summary trial pending an inquest into the death.

The difficulties faced by justices seeking to make progress in a timely fashion were illustrated in *R. v Ealing JJ. Ex p. Avondale* [1999] Crim. L.R. 840. A defendant had two witnesses available to support his defence. At the first listing of the trial one witness (*E*) attended but the other (*D*) did not because he was on his honeymoon. The second listing was scheduled for 12 noon. *E* had notified the defendant that morning that he could not attend that morning. The case did not come on until 2pm and by then the defendant had time difficulties because of child care responsibilities. Both witnesses were able to give important but different evidence. The bench refused an application to adjourn but this was overturned on appeal. The Divisional Court emphasised that justices should not focus on the perceived irresponsibility of a witness but rather on whether the defendant was the author of the difficulties in question. The fundamental question was whether, in all the circumstances of the case, including the legitimate interests of the prosecution and the court, it was fair to continue the hearing. The Divisional Court expressed considerable sympathy for justices faced with such questions and reaffirmed the propriety of insisting on a hearing in the appropriate circumstances even where a defence witness is unavailable. However, that was a course to be pursued with the very greatest caution if the witness might have significant evidence to give and if the unavailability of the witness was due to no fault on the part of the defendant and his advisers. The Divisional Court applied the principles set out in *R. v Kingston upon Thames JJ. Ex p. Martin* [1994] Imm.A.R. 172:

(1) the importance of the proceedings and their likely consequences to the party seeking the adjournment;

(2) the risk of the party being prejudiced in the conduct of the proceedings if the application were refused;

(3) the risk of prejudice or other disadvantage to the other party if the adjournment were granted;

(4) the convenience of the court;

(5) the interests of justice generally in the efficient despatch of court business;

(6) the desirability of not delaying future litigants by adjourning early and thus leaving the court empty;

(7) the extent to which the party applying for the adjournment had been responsible for creating the difficulty which had led to the application.

The principles in the European Convention on Human Rights will also apply in similar circumstances. Early experience appears to indicate that courts will view the loss of a case to be a disproportionately great penalty for the failure of an important witness to attend. **2.102**

A court faced with an application to adjourn should, therefore, first ascertain the likely substance of the evidence capable of being given by the witness, then ascertain the reasons why the witness has not attended and then apply the principles set out above, balancing the legitimate interests of both parties and the court, to decide whether it was fair to continue the hearing. The importance of doing justice to all involved was emphasised in *R. (on the application of the DPP) v North and East Hertfordshire JJ.* [2008] EWHC 103; (2008) 172 J.P. 193. The defendant was prosecuted for driving with excess alcohol. Issues arose concerning identification, post-incident consumption and the reliability of the sample of blood. An initial trial date was set aside because a new issue raised by the defence required more time than had been allocated. The key prosecution witness was unable to attend the new hearing date at short notice because of adverse weather conditions that both made her own travel difficult and had resulted in unexpected school closures that presented difficulties in arranging for care of a child. The witness was a willing witness who had kept the prosecution and the court fully informed. The court's refusal of the prosecution application to adjourn was overturned by the Divisional Court as being irrational and perverse. The Divisional Court noted that neither the Crown Prosecution Service nor the witness could be said to be at fault and a proper balance needed to be struck between the interests of the defendant (including his legitimate interest in being dealt with promptly) and the general public interest in prosecuting and convicting offenders. Consistent with the overriding objective to do justice, an adjournment is likely to be appropriate where needed to deal with an unmeritorious technical point: *R. (on the application of Taylor) v Southampton Magistrates' Court* [2008] EWHC 3006.

This difficult balancing exercise was further considered in *R. v Al-Zubeidi* [1999] Crim. L.R. 906 in which the Court of Appeal allowed an appeal against a decision of the Crown Court to refuse an adjournment to allow the defendant to instruct fresh counsel where the original counsel had had to withdraw in the light of changed instructions from the defendant. Although conscious of the danger of a defendant rejecting counsel on spurious grounds in order to prolong a trial, this was a case where a foreign national facing a serious charge (robbery) was seeking to run a complex defence.

2.103   In *R. (on the application of Rashid) v Horseferry Road Magistrates' Court*, November 7, 2000, unreported, DC, two defendants were represented by the same counsel who did not receive details of the prosecution case until the day of the trial. Counsel had concerns about whether she ought to represent both defendants on which she sought advice, following which she had about 30 minutes to take proofs from her clients, one of whom needed an interpreter. She sought an adjournment which the stipendiary magistrate refused but which the Divisional Court held should have been allowed. The defendants could not have received a fair trial. The importance of caution in deciding whether to proceed in the absence of a defence witness was again emphasised in *R. v Guildford Crown Court Ex p. Flanighan*, November 3, 1999, unreported (CO/1095/99) DC. Where a defence witness was unavailable through no fault of the defence, the court must be cautious if the witness can give significant evidence, that is, evidence that is plainly material.

Whilst courts have a discretion regarding the decision to adjourn with which an appellate court will not interfere lightly, nonetheless it is imperative that that discretion is exercised judicially. Another element of this sometimes difficult discretion was exposed in *R. (on the application of Irwin) v Sutton Magistrates' Court* [2004] EWHC 1820. After a series of adjournments, a case came before justices on a day set aside for a trial. The defendant attended but there were no prosecution witnesses since they had not been warned to attend. The prosecution was unable to explain why this was the case. The prosecution application to adjourn was opposed by the defence. The magistrates' court acceded to the prosecution request but gave no reasons. The Administrative Court was satisfied that the justices did not know why they were being asked for an adjournment or why they granted it; since this was a non-exercise of discretion, the decision to adjourn was overturned.

The provision of an interpreter was again an issue in *R. (on the application of* **2.104** *Bozkurt) v Thames Magistrates' Court* [2001] EWHC Admin 400; [2002] R.T.R 15. The defendant was a Kurd who spoke little English. He was arrested and taken to a police station where the drink/drive procedure was followed. An interpreter had been called and interpreted throughout. The same interpreter attended the first hearing at the magistrates' court two days later, introduced the defendant to the duty solicitor and interpreted what was said. It was likely that the defendant would plead not guilty and the point was taken that there could not be a fair trial because the prosecution would need to rely on the interpreter to give evidence of the procedure at the police station if that was called into question. Drawing attention to the Guidelines for Interpreters and the emphasis on the importance of there being different interpreters at the police station and the court wherever possible and to the fact that an interpreter is bound by the same rule of privilege as the solicitor, the Divisional Court agreed with the deputy district judge that, since the only questions that could be asked of the interpreter were factual ones about the procedure, that could not be affected by privileged conversation between the solicitor and the client. Although the events which occurred in this case were undesirable because, arguably, they created a perception of unfairness, nonetheless, that perception was dispelled and would be recognised to be dispelled by an objective onlooker aware of the relevant facts. Accordingly there had been no breach of the requirement that there be a fair trial.

Where a case is adjourned part way through one of the party's case, evidence can be adduced at the resumed hearing that was not available at the original hearing: *DPP v Jimale* [2001] Crim. L.R. 138.

The effect of a lengthy delay between the commencement and the conclusion **2.105** of a trial that had to be adjourned was considered in *Khatibi v DPP* [2004] EWHC 83; (2004) 168 J.P. 361. An issue arose regarding the analysis of a specimen of blood at the conclusion of the prosecution case. In the event, the justices adjourned the proceedings to allow the prosecutor to call further evidence. The hearing resumed over four months later and the defendant argued before the justices (and subsequently on appeal) that, inter alia, such a delay meant that a fair trial was not possible. That argument was rejected both by the justices and on appeal. The court and counsel had been able to refresh their memories from notes and no new submissions were made on the substance of the case; in these circumstances, the court was right to continue with the trial.

Guidance for courts faced with a defendant ready to proceed and a prosecutor present but without a prosecution file was given in *DPP v Shuttleworth* [2002] EWHC 621; (2002) 166 J.P. 417. A defendant attended court intending to plead guilty to a charge of driving without due care and attention. The prosecution were present and aware of the case being listed but the file had gone astray. There was no information in the court papers sufficient for the case to proceed. The court gave the prosecutor just over an hour to trace the file. When it was not found, they dismissed the case. Allowing the prosecutor's appeal, the Divisional Court gave three points of general application. First, whilst understanding the frustration of benches faced by the absence of a prosecution file, the power to dismiss the case is not to be used as a punitive or disciplinary provision against the Crown Prosecution Service. Secondly, where an additional hearing is necessary as a result of the fault of the prosecution, magistrates may consider whether there is a costs implication for the defaulting party. Thirdly, whilst it is entirely proper to consider the position of the defendant and the legitimate expectation to have their case dealt with promptly, there is also the general interest in prosecuting and convicting offenders and the particular interest of those personally affected by the offence. Where these interests are in competition with each other, a proper balance must be struck.

2.106   The court does not always have to tolerate the persistent failure of a defendant to attend even in serious cases. In *R. v Ealing Magistrates' Court Ex p. Burgess* (2001) 165 J.P. 82, a defendant charged with harassment secured adjournments on a number of occasions on the basis of letters from himself and his doctor describing nervous exhaustion, anxiety and stress. The defendant had, however, managed to dismiss his solicitor, commence nine private prosecutions against police officers and attend another magistrates' court on three occasions to prosecute other proceedings. On the court having decided to proceed and convict in his absence, the defendant attended later that day to seek the rehearing of the case. Not surprisingly, the Divisional Court rejected his challenge to the decision of the justices. A defendant has to have a "fair opportunity" to be present at his trial—this is not an "unlimited opportunity".

A full review of the authorities touching on the defendant's right to attend his trial was carried out by the Court of Appeal in *R. v Hayward*; *R. v Jones*; *R. v Purvis* [2001] Q.B. 862. Having reviewed the English and European authorities, the Court of Appeal set out six principles to guide a court in relation to the trial of a defendant in his absence. They emphasise the discretion that lies with the court and the importance of fairness to both the defendant and the prosecution. The Court of Appeal certified the following question as one of general public importance "Can the Crown Court conduct a trial in the absence, from its commencement, of the defendant?" and the appeal has been considered by the House of Lords and reported under the name of *R. v Jones (Anthony William)* [2002] UKHL 5; [2003] 1 A.C. 1. Although dismissing the appeal and supporting the checklist promoted by the Court of Appeal as invaluable in the exercise with the utmost care and caution of the discretion to commence a trial in the absence of the defendant, the House of Lords did adjust that checklist in two respects. First, the proposal of the Court of Appeal that the seriousness of the offence was relevant to the exercise of the discretion was not to be applied. The objects were to ensure that the trial was as fair as the circumstances permitted and lead to a just outcome and they were equally important whether the offence was serious or relatively minor. Secondly, even if the defendant had absconded voluntarily, it was generally desirable that he be represented.

2.107   Particular care should be taken where the absent defendant is a youth who will not have the same development and understanding as an adult. Arrest and retention in custody for an unrelated offence was not something over which a young person had control at the time even though he could have avoided it by not committing the offence: *R. (on the application of R) v Thames Youth Court* [2002] EWHC 1670; (2002) 166 J.P. 613.

The defendant must have adequate notice of the adjournment in accordance with s.10(2) of the Magistrates' Courts Act 1980 and with what is now the Criminal Procedure Rules 2005 r.37.11(3) and r.4 as to service (*R. v Seisdon JJ. Ex p. Dougan* (1983) 147 J.P. 177). The full transcript of the judgment makes it clearer that providing it is established that the notice has been properly *served* it is only necessary to establish that the notice has been *received* where required by the rules.

For an example of the principle that one magistrates' court cannot bind another, see the decision of *R. v Horseferry Road Stipendiary Magistrate Ex p. Wilson, The Times*, February 3, 1987. A magistrate had indicated on the adjournment of a case, that because of substantial delay it ought to proceed on the next occasion. On the adjourned date another magistrate further adjourned it. An application for an order of mandamus requiring the magistrate to dismiss the information was rejected. **2.108**

Preliminary points

Preliminary points can be of several kinds. Normally a preliminary point as to jurisdiction, e.g. that the justices cannot try the case because the information is out of time, should be raised at the outset, but nevertheless can be dealt with at any time. On the other hand if there is a point of law or fact in the case which may be decisive (e.g. whether a constable had offered a defendant a part of the specimen of blood in accordance with s.15(5) of the 1988 Offenders Act) it is usually inappropriate for it to be dealt with as a preliminary point (per Lord Widgery C.J. in *Williams v Mohamed* [1977] R.T.R. 12 at 16). However, the increasing complexity of issues being dealt with within magistrates' courts may encourage a different approach. The court has a responsibility to manage the hearing of a case effectively and to ensure that the hearing is conducted fairly and there may be circumstances when a significant issue is best resolved (and any resulting appeal dealt with) before the trial proper gets under way. **2.109**

An issue that presumably may be dealt with as a preliminary point is the validity of a byelaw. In *R. v Reading Crown Court Ex p. Hutchinson and Smith*, and *R. v Devizes JJ. Ex p. Lee* (1988) 152 J.P. 47, it was held by the Divisional Court that when a defendant in summary proceedings wished to challenge the validity of a byelaw under which he had been charged it was open to the justices (and on appeal against conviction to the Crown Court) to hear and determine the issue of its validity. It was not necessary for the defendant to proceed first by way of judicial review. If the court does not accept the legal argument raised in a preliminary point it is not appropriate for the party aggrieved to apply for a case to be stated at the point, but to await the conclusion of the proceedings. See § 22.28, also the decision in *Streames v Copping* [1985] Q.B. 920. That principle applies whether the application for case stated is sought to be made from a decision of a magistrates' court on a preliminary point, or on appeal from a Crown Court hearing and appeal from magistrates—see *DPP v Loade, The Times*, August 29, 1980.

Autrefois acquit or convict and pleas in bar

2.110   Autrefois acquit or convict is a plea in bar on indictment and does not apply in a magistrates' court, but the same principle applies, namely: a defendant cannot be convicted twice of the same offence nor can he be again tried in respect of an offence for which he has been acquitted. The Criminal Justice Act 2003 provides (Pt 10 ss.75–97) for circumstances in which a prosecution can be recommenced despite a previous acquittal for the same offence. It is a power that will apply only to "qualifying offences" as contained in Pt 1 of Sch.5 to the Act. The only offence contained within this work is manslaughter. A further effect of a prior acquittal (autrefois acquit) was considered in *R. v Z (Prior Acquittal)*, *The Times*, December 14, 1999. As well as preventing a second prosecution, a prior acquittal prevents the Crown using the factual circumstances of those allegations as similar fact evidence to support a later prosecution. The onus is, however, on the defendant to show that he has been previously acquitted (or convicted) of the offence. Thus, in *Iremonger v Vissenga* [1976] Crim. L.R. 524, it was held that before dismissing the case against defendants the justices must first hear evidence from the defendants that they had been convicted of a similar offence.

     In *Williams v DPP* [1991] R.T.R. 214 a driver who had provided two samples of breath claimed his right under s.8(2) of the 1988 Act to provide a specimen of blood for analysis. He did so, but despite this, he was charged with driving with excess alcohol in his *breath*. The driver appeared before the justices, and before he entered a plea to the charge his solicitor took the point that once blood had been given under that provision, the specimens of breath could no longer be used. The justices dismissed the charge. A few weeks later the prosecution served a fresh summons charging the driver with an offence of driving with excess alcohol in his blood, together with a certificate of analysis of the specimen of blood. A not guilty plea was entered and at the subsequent hearing, some six weeks later, the defendant was convicted. He appealed to the Divisional Court on two grounds, but unsuccessfully. First, it was asserted that his conviction offended the rule against double jeopardy. The court found against the driver. He had not entered a plea in the original proceedings, and in any event, even if he had done so, s.8(2) of the 1988 Act precluded the admission of evidence of the alcohol level of the defendant's breath. Secondly, he claimed that the certificate of analysis had not been served in accordance with what is now s.16(3) of the 1988 Offenders Act, i.e. "not less than seven days before the hearing". The Divisional Court held that that referred to the hearing at which evidence was to be admitted. The appeal was therefore dismissed.

2.111   The decision in *Williams v DPP* above should be compared with that in *Worsley v DPP* [1995] Crim. L.R. 572. Mr Worsley was charged that he had failed to supply a specimen of "breath/blood/urine" for analysis. This was held by the Divisional Court not to be duplicitous as s.7(6) of the Road Traffic Act 1988 created only one offence.

     Another plea akin to autrefois acquit, which proved unsuccessful in the magistrates' court and again before the Divisional Court was *R. v Truro and South Powder JJ. Ex p. McCullagh* [1991] R.T.R. 374. A man was seen in the driving seat of his car on a garage forecourt. He was not in possession of the ignition key of the car. He was charged with being *in charge* with excess alcohol. At his trial he was acquitted having successfully pleaded the statutory defence that there was no likelihood of his driving, etc. Further police inquiries revealed that he must have driven the car onto the forecourt shortly before the arrival of the police. A second summons was then preferred against him alleging *driving* with excess alcohol. The defendant unsuccessfully raised a plea analogous to autrefois acquit before the justices. It was rejected, and he applied for an order of prohibition. This too was rejected. The test to be applied was whether the acquittal on the first charge necessarily involved an acquittal on the second charge. It did not because the defendant had been acquitted on the first charge on the basis of the statutory defence which was not available to him on the second charge, and because the evidence in relation to the first charge related to a later time than the period during which it was alleged that the applicant had been driving.

Issue estoppel has no application to the criminal law (*DPP v Humphrys* [1976] R.T.R. 339) and in any event could not prevent a charge of perjury being brought where the original determination of the issue had been obtained by fraud (ibid.). (Defendant acquitted of driving while disqualified, subsequently convicted of giving perjured evidence at the original proceedings that he had not driven at all in the year in question.) As to the extent to which courts have a discretion to refuse to hear a case because the proceedings are oppressive or an abuse of process, see § 2.63. **2.112**

There is no double jeopardy where the earlier proceedings were a nullity and the prosecutor may successfully apply for judicial review even though there was a purported dismissal (*Harrington v Roots* [1984] 2 All E.R. 474; *Weight v McKay* [1984] 2 All E.R. 673). *DPP v Porthouse* (1989) 153 J.P. 57 confirms the decisions of these cases. In it the prosecution purported to substitute a properly drafted information for the original which was so defective that the respondent was never in jeopardy on it. The respondent submitted to magistrates that the second information should be dismissed on the autrefois acquit principle as the charges were substantially the same. That submission was accepted and the second information dismissed. On an appeal by the prosecutor, the Divisional Court allowed the appeal, holding that where a totally defective information was replaced by a properly drafted alternative and no evidence was offered on the original information, the defence of autrefois acquit was not a defence to the second information when the original information had been so defective that the respondent could never have been in jeopardy on it. There is no double jeopardy by a foreign conviction unless there is a real risk or danger of punishment (*R. v Thomas* [1984] 3 All E.R. 34). The plea of autrefois convict was held not available to a defendant who had been previously convicted of the same offences in Italy in his absence. He could not be extradited there and would almost certainly never be in jeopardy in that country.

A withdrawal of a summons does not bar subsequent proceedings (*Owens v Minoprio* [1942] 1 All E.R. 30), and in *R. v Bedford and Sharnbrook JJ. Ex p. Ward* (1973) 136 J.P. 40, justices were held to be entitled to hear a charge of driving with excess blood-alcohol against a Mr B.C. Ward who because he had been mistaken for a Colin Ward had been previously told that he would be required no further by the court. A conviction for the former offence of causing death by reckless driving (or semble reckless driving) does not preclude a subsequent conviction for driving whilst unfit (or semble with excess alcohol) arising out of the same incident (*R. v Coventry JJ. Ex p. Wilson* [1982] R.T.R. 177). A conviction for dangerous driving, where the justices have taken into consideration the defendant's speed, bars proceedings for speeding (*Welton v* **2.113**

Tanebourne (1908) 72 J.P. 419); *aliter*, it seems, an acquittal on the graver charge. Section 24 of the Road Traffic Offenders Act 1988 gives considerable scope for both juries and benches of magistrates to return an alternative verdict when they propose to acquit of a graver charge. The alternatives permitted are shown in tabular form opposite the graver offence in the section.

The law generally was reviewed in *Connelly v DPP* [1964] 2 All E.R. 401. A dismissal without a hearing on the merits was held to allow a plea equivalent to autrefois acquit in *British Railways Board v Warwick* [1980] Crim. L.R. 590 and *R. v Swansea JJ. Ex p. Purvis* (1981) 145 J.P. 252. The cases had been dismissed when the prosecution witnesses were not present. The test is not whether there has been a trial on the merits but "whether the defendant has ever been in jeopardy" (ibid.). An excess alcohol information in *Broadbent v High* [1985] R.T.R. 359 was defective in that it referred to a specimen of breath. A second correct information was laid referring to a specimen of blood. The prosecution had elected to proceed on the second correct information and the court had dismissed the first. The defendant unsuccessfully claimed double jeopardy on the authority of *Connelly* and *Purvis*. It was all part and parcel of the same process which resulted in the prosecutor being put to his election. The court indicated that it would have been preferable not to dismiss the first information until after the second had been disposed of. In *R. v Burnham JJ. Ex p. Ansorge* [1959] 3 All E.R. 505, it was said that where two informations, though alleging offences under different enactments, relate to the same facts and a plea of guilty to one information is accepted, the magistrates have jurisdiction to inquire into the matter but, if they find that the facts are the very facts which gave rise to the first conviction, they should proceed no further; if they did convict, appeal would lie. In that case the defendant had been charged with obstruction and breach of a "no-waiting" order and both informations related to the same facts.

2.114   The complicated state of the law as regards autrefois acquit and the need for extreme caution by prosecuting counsel was exemplified in *R. v FG* [2001] EWCA Crim 1215; [2001] 1 W.L.R. 1727. On the date fixed for trial of an indictment, prosecuting counsel sought to amend one of the counts from an allegation of common assault to one of assault occasioning actual bodily harm. It was eventually decided that it would not be permissible to amend the count and so a further count was added and no evidence offered on that relating to common assault on defence counsel undertaking not to pursue an autrefois acquit point. A Not Guilty verdict was entered on that count under s.17 of the Criminal Justice Act 1967. The case was re-listed for trial at a later date when different defending counsel appeared and made a submission of autrefois acquit regarding the assault charge which was rejected. On appeal, the Court of Appeal confirmed that, where the prosecution offered no evidence and a verdict of not guilty was entered under s.17 of the 1967 Act, the defendant was entitled to rely on autrefois acquit in relation to a charge based on the same facts. Prosecutors should therefore be at pains to avoid such situations which have similar application in magistrates' courts as a result of s.27 of the Magistrates' Courts Act 1980. However, a different outcome followed a case where an information had been withdrawn before a magistrates' court after a plea had been entered.

In *Islington LBC v Michaelides* [2001] EWHC Admin 468; [2001] Crim. L.R. 843, the Council obtained a summons against the defendant for failure to comply with an enforcement notice issued under the Town and Country Planning Act

1990. The defendant applied for a certificate of lawful development and the summons was withdrawn in the face of the imminent grant of that certificate. The grant of the certificate was subsequently revoked on the grounds of non-disclosure and misrepresentation and the Council sought to institute fresh proceedings on the same basis as those previously withdrawn. The magistrates' court dismissed that fresh application on the basis of autrefois acquit but the Council's appeal was upheld by the Administrative Court. It was said to be settled law that withdrawal with the consent of the court did not itself bar a further summons in the absence of an adjudication on the merits. Clearly the fact that the earlier withdrawal was secured by misrepresentations by the defendant would have influenced the approach of the Administrative Court. See also the reference to *R. (on the application of North Yorkshire Trading Standards Service) v Coleman* [2002] EWHC 818; (2002) 166 J.P. 76 at § 2.71 above for another imaginative (but unsuccessful) attempt to utilise autrefois convict by way of an argument for abuse of process.

2.115 No person may be convicted of an offence if before proceedings are begun he has paid a fixed penalty. See s.78 of the 1988 Offenders Act. HM Revenue & Customs have wide powers of imposing mitigated penalties under s.152 of the Customs and Excise Management Act 1979. The Secretary of State for Transport may also impose a mitigated penalty in respect of vehicle excise offences under s.6(5) of the Vehicle Excise and Registration Act 1994. As to servicemen and members of visiting forces already dealt with by their own courts, see § 2.31 and § 2.36.

Categories of cases and advance information

2.116 Under the Magistrates' Courts Act 1980 (and as defined in Sch.1 to the Interpretation Act 1978) there are three categories of cases:

(1) those triable only on indictment;

(2) those triable "either way", i.e. either on indictment or summarily; and

(3) those triable only summarily.

The offences with which this book is mainly concerned are categorised as follows:

Triable only on indictment: manslaughter and causing death by dangerous driving (s.1 of the 1988 Act); causing death by careless driving when under influence of drink or drugs (s.3A of the 1988 Act).

Triable "either way": dangerous driving (s.2 of the 1988 Act); causing death by careless or inconsiderate driving (s.2B of the 1988 Act); causing death by driving: unlicensed, disqualified or uninsured drivers (s.3ZB of the 1988 Act); theft (s.1 of the Theft Act 1968); forging, etc., of licences and certain other documents (s.173 of the 1988 Act); causing danger to road users (s.22A of the 1988 Act); most offences of aggravated vehicle-taking under s.12A of the Theft Act 1968.

Triable only summarily: taking, etc., a vehicle without the consent of the owner (Theft Act 1968 s.12), and almost every other offence under the 1988 Act, the Road Traffic Regulation Act 1984 or the Transport Act 1968 comes within this category. A defendant cannot elect trial by jury for any summary offence.

Advance information

2.117 Substantial changes have been made to the procedure for providing information to the defence about the prosecution case, most recently as a result of the initiative described as "Criminal Justice, Simple Speedy, Summary" (CJSSS). Rule 21 of the Criminal Procedure Rules 2005 (as inserted by the Criminal Procedure (Amendment No. 2) Rules 2008 (SI 2008/3269)) provides for the prosecution to give initial details of the case at (or before) the beginning of the day of the first hearing. Where the CJSSS scheme applies, these details need to be served on the court officer and made available to the defendant. The details required include a summary of the evidence on which the case will be based or a statement, document or extract setting out facts or other matters on which the case will be based (or a combination of these). In addition, details of any previous convictions of the defendant must be provided. These provisions apply to summary and "either way" offences.

Where the scheme does not apply, the previous provisions continue. These provide that, where an offence is triable "either way" provision for the disclosure to the defendant of advance information as to the prosecutor's case is made by the Criminal Law Act 1977 s.48 and the Criminal Procedure Rules 2005. For this purpose it is submitted that criminal damage offences of *whatever value* are to be treated as "either way" offences; they are basically classified as such—see the Magistrates' Courts Act 1980 s.17 and Sch.1. The provisions apply to "either way" offences heard in the youth court but by an anomaly not to purely indictable offences heard in such courts. Confirmation that disclosure was not required under these provisions in a summary case was given in *R. v Stratford JJ. Ex p. Imbert* (1999) 163 J.P. 693, which also examined an argument based on art.6 of the European Convention on Human Rights. However, the defence is entitled to know what the allegation consists of.

2.118   The prosecutor is required to give the defendant a written notice as to his right to request disclosure. The disclosure may be in the form of copies of witness statements or a summary. The prosecutor may withhold disclosure if in his opinion its disclosure might lead to the intimidation or to the attempted intimidation of a witness or otherwise to the course of justice being interfered with. Written notice must be given that information is being withheld.

Confirmation of the limited powers of the court where the prosecution fails to comply with its obligations was given in *R. (on the application of AP, MD and JS) v Leeds Youth Court* [2001] EWHC Admin 215; (2001) 165 J.P. 684. The prosecution had been slow in serving advance information. The court granted a further adjournment setting a specific date by which that information should be served on the defence and stating that failure to do so would lead to the case being dismissed on the at the next hearing. That obligation was only partly complied with but further information was available on the hearing day and the court granted a further adjournment to allow the defence to consider that further information. The defence sought judicial review of the decision to adjourn arguing that a legitimate expectation had been raised that the case would be dismissed. Dismissing that application, the Administrative Court confirmed that the consequences of failing to serve advance information were either that the court would proceed in any case or that a further adjournment would be granted. It was only in the most exceptional of circumstances that failure of this type would amount to an abuse of the process of the court. The court should not have threatened to dismiss the case and, since the parties could not expect a court to act unlawfully, no legitimate expectation could have been raised.

Presence of defendant

Minor cases are often dealt with in the absence of the defendant (Magistrates' **2.119**
Courts Act 1980 s.11, as amended). Where a defendant aged 18 or over is not
present, the court is required to proceed in absence unless that would be contrary
to the interests of justice; if it does not proceed in absence, it must give its reasons
in open court and they must be entered in the register (Magistrates' Courts Act
1980 s.11(7)). Whilst a court is not required to proceed in absence if it considers
that there is an acceptable reason for the failure to appear (Magistrates' Courts
Act 1980 s.11(2A)), it is specifically provided that the court is under no obligation to inquire into the reason for the failure to appear (Magistrates' Courts Act
1980 s.11(6)).

A detailed consideration on proceeding in the absence of a defendant has led to
the principles set out by the Court of Appeal in *R. v Hayward; R. v Jones; R. v
Purvis* [2001] EWCA Crim 168; [2001] Q.B. 862, as endorsed and amended by
the House of Lords in *R. v Jones (Anthony William)* [2002] UKHL 5; [2003] 1
A.C. 1, in particular in the judgment of Lord Bingham of Cornhill at [8]–[15].
See also the cases noted at §§ 2.100–8. The practical difficulties faced by a court
were again considered in *R. (on the application of M) v Tower Bridge Magistrates' Court* [2007] EWHC 2766; (2008) 172 J.P. 155. A trial date was fixed for
hearing an allegation that the defendant obstructed a police constable in the execution of his duty. The defendant was not legally represented. About a month
before the date fixed for the trial, the defendant was remanded in custody on
other more serious offences by the same magistrates' court. He did not appear for
the trial and the case proceeded in his absence. A subsequent application to set
aside the trial was refused but that decision was overturned by the Divisional
Court. Applying the principles in *R. v Jones (Anthony William)*, affirming *R. v
Hayward; R. v Jones; R. v Purvis* above, the court considered that too much
weight had been placed on the fault of the defendant in not communicating with
the court and so initiating the process by which he could have been produced.
Whilst relevant, it had been treated as a determinative factor. The test under s.142
of the Magistrates' Courts Act 1980 is whether a rehearing would be in the
interests of justice and it will normally be in the interests of justice for a defendant to be able to defend himself. Unless the evidence indicates that the absence
is "deliberate and voluntary", a rehearing would normally be appropriate. This
case was decided before the change in legislation which has created a presumption in favour of proceeding in absence (see above). No doubt that change will
prompt a further series of appeals.

The defendant may no longer need to be present at committal proceedings. **2.120**
There are special rules for the mode of trial procedure (see § 2.122). The defendant should always be given an adjournment, if he asks for it, when he has had
the summons in insufficient time before the hearing. Save in cases where he is
expressly required to be present by statute or bail, a party represented by solicitor
or counsel is deemed not to be absent (Magistrates' Courts Act 1980 s.122). A
corporation or limited company can plead by a representative or solicitor (see
§ 2.142; the Magistrates' Courts Act 1980 Sch.3, makes provision as to election
for summary trial by a corporation and its committal). A defendant cannot be
sentenced to imprisonment or detention in his absence and he may not be disqualified if absent at the first hearing. In the latter case he must be given the
chance to attend at an adjourned hearing; the notice to him of the adjournment

should show the intention of the court to consider disqualification (Magistrates' Courts Act 1980 s.11(4)).

Save where the defendant is represented by a solicitor who pleads guilty on his behalf, the case must be proved by evidence, if he is absent, and letters to the court or police admitting the offence, if used at all to prove guilt, should only be used to supplement such evidence on proof that such letters are in the defendant's handwriting. No evidence need be given on a plea of guilty (Magistrates' Courts Act 1980 s.9(3)); although, where the defendant disputes the facts, magistrates may call for evidence. If evidence is given in the witness box by way of mitigation on a guilty plea, it follows that the person giving evidence is subject to cross-examination. It must make no difference that the person giving evidence in this way is the defendant himself.

2.121   A defendant cannot be arrested on non-appearance, personally or by solicitor (where this suffices), unless the offence is punishable with imprisonment or, having convicted him, the magistrates propose to disqualify (Magistrates' Courts Act 1980 s.13) (see § 2.08). There are special provisions in this respect relating to the mode of trial procedure—see s.26.

Where a defendant is on bail in criminal proceedings and fails to surrender to custody without reasonable excuse he is guilty of an offence under s.6 of the Bail Act 1976. The means by which a court should deal procedurally with such an offence were reviewed in *Schiavo v Anderton* [1986] 3 All E.R. 10. Some of the complications resulting from the judgment in that case have been eased by the *Consolidated Criminal Practice Direction*, Pt I.13 which should be carefully considered.

Mode of trial procedure

2.122   The restrictions on publicity apply to the mode of trial procedure (Magistrates' Courts Act 1980 s.8(8)). The mode of trial procedure for "either way" offences is set out in ss.18–23 of the 1980 Act. It applies to persons of 18 and over (s.18(1)). The procedure may be before a single justice (s.18(5)) and there may be an adjournment. On such adjournments the defendant must be remanded if he has been previously bailed or remanded or been in custody for the offence (s.18(4)).

The procedure must be "done before any evidence is called" (s.18(2)). It is submitted that this only refers to trial evidence and not evidence on preliminary matters such as bail. These provisions are substantially changed by amendments contained in Sch.3 to the Criminal Justice Act 2003. At the time of writing (March 2009), there is no information as to when the provisions are to be brought into force.

2.123   When in force, amendments to ss.17A–17C of the Magistrates' Courts Act 1980 will permit an adult appearing in a court at which mode of trial is to be determined to give an indication as to whether he will plead guilty. If he indicates that he will plead guilty, the court proceeds to summary trial and the defendant is treated as having pleaded guilty. The court does, however, retain its power to commit the defendant for sentence if the provisions of the sections dealing with committal for sentence are met. The magistrates' court cannot force or require the defendant to give an indication of his plea; whether he does so or not remains a matter solely for the defendant.

If the defendant intimates that he will plead not guilty or fails to give an intimation of plea, the court will adopt the established mode of trial procedure. It must then give the prosecutor and the defendant an opportunity to make representations as to whether summary trial or trial on indictment is more suitable. A note should be made that the defendant was asked if he wished to make representations and of his reply (or that he made no representations) (*R. v Horseferry Road Magistrates' Court* [1981] Crim. L.R. 504). It may be unjust and wrong to add a charge triable only on indictment to ensure trial at the Crown Court (*R. v Brooks* [1985] Crim. L.R. 385). The decision in *R. v Brooks* was referred to and explained in *R. v Redbridge JJ. and Fox Ex p. Whitehouse* (1992) 156 J.P. 293. It was held in the later case that where a defendant was charged with an offence, the fact that the prosecution wished to add to or substitute new charges, either to ensure that the case was tried summarily or to ensure that it was tried in the Crown Court, was not a ground for refusing the issue of a summons or other process *provided* that on the facts disclosed the justices were satisfied that the course proposed by the prosecution was proper and appropriate in the light of the facts put before them. The justices should not agree to the addition of a charge which was triable only on indictment if the facts were incapable of supporting such a charge and the fresh charge could be seen to be a device designed to deprive the justices of their jurisdiction to try the case summarily. In the *Redbridge JJ.* case the decision reached by the justices was held not to be unreasonable.

The much more common situation is where the prosecution seek to prefer an **2.124** offence triable summarily only in substitution for an "either way" offence, often when the defendant has elected trial by jury, thus depriving him of jury trial. It is submitted that the decision in this case is of importance, particularly the five propositions put forward by Neill L.J. in his judgment.

If the prosecution is being carried on by the Attorney General, the Solicitor General or the Director of Public Prosecutions and he applies for committal proceedings, the court must accede (s.19(4)). As far as the Director of Public Prosecutions is concerned, this power shall only be exercised with the consent of the Attorney General. The court next announces its decision as to the mode of trial. If the court decides on summary trial, the defendant must be cautioned as to the right to commit for sentence under s.3 of the Powers of Criminal Courts (Sentencing) Act 2000 on conviction (see § 2.177). The full wording is in s.20(2). The defendant then has a formal right to consent to summary trial or elect trial by jury. In *R. v Warrington JJ.* [1981] Crim. L.R. 629 the defendant elected trial merely to obtain sight of the witness statements. He then applied to revert to summary trial. The justices refused to agree and the Divisional Court disapproved of the defendant's tactics and upheld the justices.

In *R. v Southampton JJ. Ex p. Robins* [1980] Crim. L.R. 440, it was held that **2.125** the justices had a discretion to allow a defendant who had elected summary trial to change his mind at an adjourned hearing and elect trial by jury instead. The need for care in following the mode of trial procedure was emphasised in *R. (on the application of DPP) v Camberwell Green Youth Court* [2003] EWHC 3217; (2004) 168 J.P. 157. A court that has decided for summary trial may change that decision once it has begun trying the information but before the close of the prosecution case: Magistrates' Courts Act 1980 s.25(2). There is no inherent right to change an earlier decision.

There are special provisions as to criminal damage (see § 15.64) and youths (see § 2.20). As regards criminal damage, the statutory figure for the value of the damage at or beneath which an offence is triable summarily is £5,000. This means that an offence where the value of the alleged damage is at or over £5,000 is triable "either way".

2.126 The cases on change of election were reviewed in *R. v Birmingham JJ. Ex p. Hodgson* [1985] 2 All E.R. 193. The defendant's state of mind at the time is crucial and he should not lightly be deprived of the right to trial by jury. The decision was followed in *R. v West London Stipendiary Magistrate Ex p. Keane, The Times,* March 9, 1985. The defendant had elected trial and pleaded guilty when unrepresented. When represented he was allowed to change his plea and the Divisional Court held that he should also have been allowed to change his election. The fact that a defendant was originally unrepresented and did not understand the nature of the election was taken into account in *R. v Highbury Corner Stipendiary Magistrate Ex p. Weekes* [1985] 2 W.L.R. 643. It is not relevant to the *defendant's election* whether the magistrates' court considered itself capable of trying the case (ibid.). This is only relevant for the earlier decision whether summary trial is suitable.

When there is more than one defendant, and one elects trial and the other(s) may wish to be tried summarily. In *Nicholls v Brentwood JJ.* [1992] 1 A.C. 1, the House of Lords stated that it was an irresistible conclusion that in s.20(3) of the Magistrates' Courts Act 1980 the right of election was given to each accused individually, and that the result of it was not intended to be affected by the nature of any different election made by any of his co-accused. The fact that one had elected trial on indictment did not require the justices to commit all the defendants to the Crown Court. It is expected that the court will have greater flexibility in such situations once the changes in the mode of trial procedure contained in Sch.3 to the Criminal Justice Act 2003 are brought into force.

2.127 In *R. v Bourne JJ. Ex p. Cope* (1989) 153 J.P. 161, the Divisional Court held that justices were entitled to refuse a defendant leave to withdraw an election to summary trial if they were satisfied that he had understood the choice between summary and jury trial. Their discretion as to whether leave was granted or not was unfettered. Similarly, in *Revitt v DPP* [2006] EWHC 2266; [2007] R.T.R. 23 the Divisional Court decided that it did not breach a defendant's right to be presumed innocent until proved guilty to refuse to allow the withdrawal of an unequivocal plea of guilty.

In determining whether an "either way" offence should be tried summarily or on indictment, s.19(3) of the Magistrates' Courts Act 1980 requires justices to apply their minds inter alia to the question of whether their powers of punishment would be adequate if they dealt with the case summarily. Section 38 of the 1980 Act, as amended, presently gives justices an unfettered discretion to commit a defendant to the Crown Court for sentence, if, having accepted summary trial, they later decided that their powers were inadequate. However, the justices still have to apply their minds to s.19(3) in deciding to accept summary jurisdiction in the first place.

2.128 The provisions of ss.18–23 governing the mode of trial are mandatory, and failure to comply will lead to the proceedings being quashed as a nullity (*R. v Tottenham JJ. Ex p. Arthur's Transport Services* [1981] Crim. L.R. 180; *R. v Horseferry Road Magistrates' Court* (§ 2.123 above)).

In order to assist in achieving consistency of approach in mode of trial decision, guidelines were issued under the *imprimatur* of the Lord Chief Justice in October 1990. These followed the recommendations of a working party under the chairmanship of Farquharson L.J., and are stated to be for the purpose of "guidance not direction". They apply to adult defendants who face "either way" offences and who have failed to give an intimation of a guilty plea, and first remind courts of the general mode of trial considerations to be found in s.19. The following general observations are then made:

(a) the court should never make its decision on the grounds of convenience or expedition;

(b) the court should assume for the purpose of deciding mode of trial that the prosecution version of the facts is correct;

(c) the defendant's antecedents and personal mitigating circumstances are irrelevant for the purpose of deciding mode of trial;

(d) the fact that the offences are alleged to be specimens is a relevant consideration; the fact that the defendant will be asking for other offences to be taken into consideration, if convicted, is not;

(e) where cases involve complex questions of fact or difficult questions of law, the court should consider committal for trial;

(f) where two or more defendants are jointly charged with an offence and the court decides that the offence is more suitable for summary trial, if one defendant elects trial on indictment, the court must proceed to deal with all the defendants as examining justices in respect of that offence. A youth charged with someone aged 18 or over should only be committed for trial if it is necessary in the interests of justice;

(g) in general, except where otherwise stated, "either way" offences should be tried summarily unless the court considers that the particular case has one or more of the features set out (in the guidelines for particular offences) *and* that its sentencing powers are insufficient.

2.129 The only offence in the guidelines of relevance to this work is dangerous driving. However, this has been superseded by the Magistrates' Court Sentencing Guidelines published by the Sentencing Guidelines Council in May 2008; these guidelines provide starting points and ranges for sentencing in a magistrates' court but also indicate the circumstances in which an offence is likely to require sentence within the powers of the Crown Court. Accordingly, criteria suggesting committal to the Crown Court for trial or sentence are likely to be found in offence specific guidelines rather than in the Mode of Trial Guidelines; those guidelines will be replaced by Sentencing Guidelines Council guidelines when the provisions in Sch.3 to the Criminal Justice Act 2003 are brought into force.

Summary trial: speeches and no case to answer

2.130 The informant may conduct the case for the prosecution and cross-examine witnesses for the defence, and r.37.3 of the Criminal Procedure Rules 2005 gives both the informant and the defendant in a trial the right to address the court. The court is under a statutory duty to assist an unrepresented defendant by ensuring that he understands the charge. The court or the justices' legal adviser may ask a witness questions; in particular, where a defendant is unrepresented, that includes asking any question necessary in the defendant's interests: Criminal Procedure Rules 2005 r.37.4(5). Provisions restricting the right of the defendant to ask certain witnesses questions are contained in ss.36 and 37 of the Youth Justice and

Criminal Evidence Act 1999. Where a defendant was denied her right to address a stipendiary magistrate, her conviction was set aside (*R. v Great Marlborough Street Magistrate Ex p. Fraser* [1974] Crim. L.R. 47). *R. v Great Marlborough Street Magistrate* was followed in *R. v Middlesex Crown Court Ex p. Riddle* [1975] Crim. L.R. 731, where an appellant's application for certiorari quashing his conviction was granted because the Crown Court had refused to allow him a final speech after he had given evidence on his own behalf. However, where a judge of the Crown Court and a lay justice retired to consider an appeal without giving the appellant an opportunity of a final speech, the appellant's application for certiorari was refused. Although a solicitor and a clerk to the justices, he had not protested when the judge retired nor when he returned, and the case was not one in which there was any injustice caused by lack of a final speech (*R. v Knightsbridge Crown Court* [1976] Crim. L.R. 463).

It is clear from the decision in *R. v Milton Keynes JJ. Ex p. DPP* [1991] Crim. L.R. 712 that justices must not dismiss an information without hearing such evidence as may be available from the prosecution. In that case there had been several abortive hearings of a charge of criminal damage. On the date on which the case was set down for trial again a prosecution witness did not attend for the second time. The prosecution sought a further adjournment; the defence applied for the information to be dismissed. The justices dismissed the information without inquiring whether the prosecution were able to proceed with the evidence that was available at court, as in fact they were. The Divisional Court, following *Re Harrington* [1984] A.C. 743, stated that the court must give the opportunity to the prosecution to call such evidence as they had. There was in the case no abuse of process which would have permitted justices to dismiss an information without hearing evidence.

2.131   Where a defendant is representing himself, he may wish to avail himself of assistance from a person who is not a solicitor or barrister—commonly called a McKenzie friend. The history and role was admirably set out by the then Master of the Rolls, Lord Woolf, in *R. v Bow County Court Ex p. Pelling*, July 28, 1999, unreported, CA. Supporting and developing the judgment in *R. v Leicester City JJ. Ex p. Barrow* [1991] 2 Q.B. 260, it was emphasised that the underlying principle is one of fairness to the litigant—a basis that accords with the approach of the Human Rights Act 1998. The 1999 case was set in the context of family proceedings, the *Leicester City JJ.* case in the context of enforcement of community charge. The key points are that the right is that of the party to the proceedings not of the "friend", that a party in person should have the assistance of a McKenzie friend where asked for unless the court considers that fairness and the interests of justice do not require that assistance, reasons should be given for refusing to allow such assistance, the fact that the "friend" is to be paid is unlikely to be of significance, and the assistance can be terminated where it is being provided for a purpose or in a way which prevents the proper and efficient administration of justice (e.g. by causing a party to waste time, advising the introduction of irrelevant issues or the asking of irrelevant or repetitious questions). These principles have been consolidated in guidance from the President of the Family Division dated October 14, 2008. Affirming that (in relation to family proceedings) there is a strong presumption in favour of permitting a McKenzie friend, the guidance makes it clear that that person is not entitled either to address the court or to examine witnesses. However, attention is drawn to the discretionary power of a court to grant rights of audience to unqualified persons in accordance with the Courts and Legal Services Act 1990.

The Crown Prosecution Service was in operation in all parts of England and Wales on October 1, 1986. From that date the police are not permitted to *conduct* criminal or binding-over proceedings other than specified proceedings. Instead it is the duty of the Director of Public Prosecutions and the Crown Prosecutors under him to take over the *conduct* of all such proceedings instituted on behalf of the police (Prosecution of Offences Act 1985 s.3(2)). Anyone else may *conduct* such proceedings unless the Director takes over responsibility (see 1985 Act s.6(2)). Anyone, including the police, may *institute* such proceedings (1985 Act s.6(1)) unless there is a statutory restriction (see, e.g. § 2.15). The institution of proceedings for the purpose of Pt 1 of the Act is defined in s.15 in wider terms than is generally understood for the commencement of proceedings. Both barristers and solicitors may be appointed Crown Prosecutors (1985 Act s.1(4)).

The Director may at any time appoint a barrister on the staff of a public author- **2.132** ity or a solicitor to *institute* or take over the *conduct* of such criminal or binding-over proceedings as the Director may assign to him (1985 Act s.5(1)). Such a person is given all the powers of a Crown Prosecutor in *conducting* the assigned proceedings (1985 Act s.5(2)) but interestingly he is not given any express power in that subsection when *instituting* proceedings, and the general principles of representation would apply. Section 7A of the 1985 Act allows the Director of Public Prosecutions to designate staff who are not solicitors or barristers. Those designated staff have the powers and rights of audience of a Crown Prosecutor in relation to applications relating to bail and the general conduct of certain criminal cases in magistrates' courts.

The procedure to be followed on a trial is set out in the Criminal Procedure Rules 2005 r.37(3). The prosecutor *may* summarise the prosecution case and identify the relevant law and facts but *must* introduce the evidence being relied upon. On conclusion of the prosecution case, the court may acquit on the ground that the evidence is "insufficient for any reasonable court properly to convict"; this may be of its own motion or on application of the defendant, but, in either case, the prosecutor must be given an opportunity to make representations. The next stage is for the defendant who may introduce evidence. Following this, either party has an opportunity to introduce evidence (e.g. in rebuttal), the defendant may make representations about the case and, finally, the prosecutor may make representations about relevant law and the defendant may respond to those representations. The court has a discretion to allow evidence or representations outside the normal sequence.

While the rules make no mention of submitting "No case to answer", this is a **2.133** well-recognised procedure in magistrates' courts and in a criminal case the court should not put a defendant to his election whether to give evidence or rest on a submission of "no case" (*Jones v Metcalfe* [1967] 3 All E.R. 205); evidence may be called if the submission is overruled. It is submitted that the prosecutor may reply to a submission that there is no case to answer since it is a submission of law whatever its basis. Similarly, the justices' clerk may advise the justices. In *R. v Central Criminal Court Ex p. Garnier* [1988] R.T.R. 42 it was held that the trial judge had wrongly exercised his discretion where he had of his own motion adjourned the case to allow the prosecution to obtain further evidence on a defence submission of no case to answer.

Where the defence submit that there is no case to answer, the court should, before ruling, ensure there is no misunderstanding as to whether it is the final speech or a mere submission (*R. v Birkenhead JJ. Ex p. Fisher* [1962] 3 All E.R. 837; *R v Gravesend JJ. Ex p. Sheldon* [1968] Crim. L.R. 506).

2.134   Even where a case has been dismissed on a submission of no case to answer, justices are entitled to reopen the case when it is clear (and agreed by all parties) that they had made their decision on the basis of a mistake: *Steward v DPP* [2004] EWHC 2251; [2004] 1 W.L.R. 592. In these circumstances, both policy and common sense favoured immediate rectification of the mistake without incurring the cost and delay of an appeal. Similarly, the obligation on all professional parties to act fairly was emphasised in *R. v Gleeson* [2003] EWCA Crim 3357; [2004] 1 Cr. App. R. 29 where the defence had waited until the close of the prosecution case to draw attention to an irregularity. The court stated very strongly that a criminal trial was not a game and that its object was to ensure that the guilty were convicted and the innocent acquitted. In the court's view:

> "just as a defendant should not be penalised for errors of his legal representatives in the conduct of his defence if he is unfairly prejudiced by them, so also should a prosecution not be frustrated by errors of the prosecutor, unless such errors have irremediably rendered a fair trial for the defendant impossible. For defence advocates to seek to take advantage of such errors by deliberately delaying identification of an issue of fact or law in the case until the last possible moment is, in our view, no longer acceptable, given the legislative and procedural changes to our criminal justice process in recent years." (at [35])

2.135   In a *Practice Direction (Submission of No Case)* [1962] 1 All E.R. 448 (of which it has been said: "All justices' clerks should keep on their table a copy and make a practice of putting it before the presiding justice for guidance on every submission of no case": per Lord Bridge in *Stoneley v Coleman* [1974] Crim. L.R. 254), the Divisional Court stated that a submission that there is no case to answer may properly be made and upheld: (a) when there has been no evidence to prove an essential element in the alleged offence; or (b) when the evidence adduced by the prosecution has been so discredited as a result of cross-examination or is so manifestly unreliable that no reasonable tribunal could safely convict on it.

Apart from these two situations, the Practice Direction continues, a tribunal should not in general be called on to reach a decision as to conviction or acquittal until the whole of the evidence which either side wishes to tender has been placed before it. If, however, a submission is made that there is no case to answer, the decision should depend not so much on whether the adjudicating tribunal (if compelled to do so) would at that stage convict or acquit but on whether the evidence is such that a reasonable tribunal might convict. If a reasonable tribunal might convict on the evidence so far laid before it, there is a case to answer. The nature of a submission of no case was further considered in *R. v Galbraith* (1981) 145 J.P. 406 and discussed at (1981) 145 J.P. Jo. 690.

2.136   A reminder of the pre-eminent duty of the court to act fairly between the parties to litigation came with the decision of the Divisional Court in *R. v Barking and Dagenham JJ. Ex p. DPP* (1995) 159 J.P. 373. Before entering court at the start of the third day of a summary trial, the justices came to the provisional view that the defendant had no case to answer. In court the prosecution made it clear that their case had been concluded and the defendant's solicitor made it clear that he had no submissions to make, but that he wished to call evidence on behalf of his client. Following a retirement, the justices found that there was no case for the defendant to answer, and they dismissed the charge. The prosecution appealed by way of judicial review. It was held that in circumstances where a magistrates' court was provisionally minded to dismiss an information prior to the start of the defence case (if any) either of its own motion or upon hearing a defence submission to that effect, it should not so rule without first calling upon the prosecution to address the court. The Divisional Court went on to remind courts of the desirability of justices having their attention drawn to the *Practice Direction (Submission of No Case)* (see § 2.135 above) when considering whether or not to conclude that the case go no further. A further reminder of the obligation on the court to act fairly between the parties in the conduct of a trial was given in *Att Gen's Reference (No.2 of 2000)* [2001] Crim. L.R. 842. An unrepresented defendant pleaded not guilty before the Crown Court to a charge of possession of an offensive weapon. The prosecution opened the case to the jury but, before they could call any evidence, the judge directed the jury to acquit. On appeal, the Court of Appeal confirmed that a judge did not have the power to prevent the prosecution from calling evidence simply because he thought a conviction unlikely. Other than where the case was oppressive or vexatious, or some other abuse of the process of the court, the prosecution had a right to present its case.

Convictions were quashed where submissions of no case were mistaken for final speeches in *R. v Birkenhead JJ.* and *R. v Gravesend JJ.*, § 2.133 above, but it is now submitted that if the court has not pronounced sentence, it may, as soon as it realises its mistake, adjourn the case to be reheard by a different bench. The House of Lords in *S v Manchester City Recorder* [1969] 3 All E.R. 1230 held that a magistrates' court is not functus officio until sentence is pronounced. The latter case allowed a defendant to change his plea after it had been accepted and the case adjourned. There is no difference in principle between a defendant being allowed to change his mind and a court being allowed to do so when the court has made a finding of guilt on a mistaken premise. The House of Lords in *S's* case, above, held that magistrates have only one duty, that of carrying a case to its conclusion. This involves a conviction or finding of guilt followed by a further decision as to sentence. Therefore where a magistrates' court mistook a submission of no case for a final speech, announced conviction and did not pronounce sentence, it was held that the case could be reheard *de novo* by a differently constituted bench (*R. v Midhurst JJ. Ex p. Thompson* [1973] 3 All E.R. 1164). If it is argued that a fresh bench cannot hear the case because the defendant has already been convicted, the answer to such a plea of autrefois convict is that the conviction is a nullity because the defendant was given no opportunity of defending the case.

The defendant or his advocate may further address the court on rejection of his **2.137** submission of "No case to answer" (*Disher v Disher* [1963] 3 All E.R. 933, a civil case). The magistrates may still dismiss a case after rejecting a submission of "no case to answer" even though no evidence is given for the defence (*De Filippo v De Filippo* (1964) 108 S.J. 56, a civil case; see also *Rabjohns v Burgar* [1972] Crim. L.R. 46 where the justices' decision was overruled on other grounds).

Disclosure procedures under the Criminal Procedure and Investigations Act 1996

2.138   Part I of the Criminal Procedure and Investigations Act 1996 (as amended by the Criminal Justice Act 2003) provides a statutory scheme of disclosure placing clear and demanding burdens on the prosecution, but also for the first time requiring the defence to disclose the general nature of the defence. The principle of fairness will require the defence to be aware of any relevant or potentially relevant information known to the prosecutor or any other information that could be of use to the defence whether or not the prosecutor intends to rely upon it. The formal rules now need to be read in the light of the obligations under the Criminal Procedure Rules 2005 and the increasingly intolerant line of appeal courts to technical arguments improperly raised. The Criminal Procedure Rules 2005 state that the overriding objective for criminal cases is that they had to be dealt with justly—that includes acquitting the innocent and convicting the guilty (Criminal Procedure Rules 2005 rr.1.1 and 2(a)). This requires the defence properly to alert the prosecution to an issue. Accordingly, in *Malcolm v DPP* [2007] EWHC 363; [2007] R.T.R. 316, the defence was roundly criticised for what was called an "ambush" of the prosecution by raising a technical point in the final speech when it had not been raised in cross-examination of the appropriate witness. The court's decision to allow further evidence in such circumstances was upheld.

The statutory provisions vary considerably depending on whether the case is being tried on indictment or summarily. One of the major differences is that defence disclosure is obligatory if the case is being tried on indictment, but only voluntary in the case of summary trials. Because the vast majority of offences within the scope of this work are likely to be tried summarily, what follows relates solely to that form of trial, i.e.:

(a) a person charged with a summary offence in respect of which a court proceeds to summary trial and in respect of which he pleads not guilty;

(b) a person who has attained the age of 18 is charged with an offence which is triable "either way", in respect of which a court proceeds to summary trial and in respect of which he pleads not guilty;

(c) a person under the age of 18 is charged with an indictable offence in respect of which a court proceeds to summary trial and in respect of which he pleads not guilty.

2.139   The prosecutor, whether an individual or a body, always has obligations under the 1996 Act. His statutory duty under s.3 is to disclose to the defendant any previously undisclosed prosecution material which might reasonably be considered capable of undermining the case for the prosecution against the defendant or of assisting the defendant's case. "Material" means material which is in the prosecutor's possession and came into his possession in connection with the case for the prosecution against the defendant, or which he has inspected in pursuance of a code of practice made under the Act. The prosecutor will also give to the defendant at the same time the schedule of non-sensitive material received by the prosecutor. At this point, in summary trials, the defence having received the prosecution disclosure may make voluntary disclosure by way of a "defence statement", defined as a written statement setting out the nature of the defence and any particular defences to be relied on, indicating the matters on which the defendant takes issue with the prosecution and identifying any points of law to be taken and any authority relied on, and setting out, in the case of each such matter, the reason why he takes issue with the prosecution. In an alibi case, particulars of the alibi must also be disclosed. If such a defence statement is given, the prosecutor must make secondary disclosure which involves any previously undisclosed prosecution material which might reasonably assist the defence as disclosed by the defence statement, or give the defendant a written statement that there is no such material.

In *DPP v Woods, DPP v McGillicuddy* [2006] EWHC 32; (2006) 170 J.P. 177 the defence had, in each case, successfully persuaded a district judge to stay proceedings as an abuse of the process of the court on the ground that the prosecution had failed to disclose relevant material. Issues were taken before the Divisional Court concerning the timing of the prosecution statement that there was no relevant material, the effectiveness of defence statements, the relevance of the material and the power to require disclosure. Whilst emphasising the importance of not being overly particular about the form and content of statements, the Divisional Court stated that "there are real dangers of injustice in treating deficient written defence statements as so wholly ineffective as to be non-existent in reality". As one of the chief purposes of the defence statement is to become the basis for further disclosure, deficiencies can generally be made good during that process. However, the Divisional Court also emphasised the obligation on the defence to provide the basis for disclosure, drawing attention to the comments of Lord Bingham in *R. v H and C* [2004] UKHL 3; [2004] 2 A.C. 134 that: "The trial process is not well served if the defence are permitted to make general and unspecified allegations and then seek far-reaching disclosure in the hope that material may turn up to make them good." In both cases, the defence statement should have been rejected because it was silent as to whether the defendant was the driver or had consumed alcohol or enough to be in excess of the prescribed limits and so did not raise an issue to which reliability or type approval was relevant. They were not free-standing issues.

The most important matter considered was that the material in the hands of Intoximeters UK was not "prosecution material" for the purposes of these provisions. The defence had argued that the company was part of the police or prosecution or investigating team, in part at least because of the contractual relationship which existed between the police and Intoximeters UK. The material would not fall within the terms of s.8(3) and (4) of the Act unless that was accepted. The Divisional Court considered that that could not be accepted. In a strongly worded judgment, it stated (at [43]) that: **2.140**

> "That is an impossible contention. The prosecutor was the CPS. Intoximeters UK is not part of the CPS. There are other provisions which deal with material in the hands of those who are not the prosecutors, and the police and other third parties are dealt with differently. Intoximeters UK is not part of the prosecution team, a concept which itself is misleading and irrelevant in the light of the other specific provisions for disclosure. Intoximeters UK does not become part of the CPS because it has supplied the device to the police force and has certain continuing obligations to the police under that contract. The DJs have lumped together the CPS, the police and third parties who provide and maintain devices for the police to use in the investigation and proof of offences in a way which simply fails to respect the facts or the statutory provisions."

Time-limits are laid down for each stage of the process. Applications may be made to the court by the defendant if he has reasonable cause to believe that there remains undisclosed prosecution material which might reasonably be expected to assist the defence as disclosed in the defence statement; and the prosecution may apply to the court inter alia that material which would otherwise be subject to disclosure should not be, on the grounds that it is not in the public interest to disclose it. The court will rule on such applications as it thinks fit.

2.141   However, two further points can be made. First, the 1996 Act (as amended) places a continuing duty on the prosecution to disclose any prosecution material that meets the test for disclosure. The prosecutor must keep the matter under constant review, and that duty continues until the defendant is acquitted or convicted, or the prosecutor decides not to proceed with the case. Secondly, what happens if the defendant does nothing, or gives late information or inconsistent defences, etc., in the defence statement? The answer is to be found in s.11. The court, or, with the leave of the court, any other party, may make such comment as appears appropriate and the court may draw such inferences as appear proper in deciding whether the defendant is guilty of the offence where there are certain faults with the disclosure. Comment may not be made or inferences drawn where the defendant failed to make a voluntary statement, because, after all, it is voluntary. However, if, e.g. inconsistent defences are set out in the defence statement, or at trial a different defence is put forward than that contained in a defence statement, such comment may be made and inferences drawn. In an echo of the "right to silence" provisions in the Criminal Justice and Public Order Act 1994, s.11(10) of the 1996 Act provides that a defendant cannot be convicted solely on an inference drawn under the section.

Plea of guilty

2.142   A corporation or limited company may enter a plea by a representative appointed pursuant to s.33(6) of the Criminal Justice Act 1925 (Magistrates' Courts Act 1980 Sch.3). The representative need not be a solicitor or barrister but the section is silent on whether the representative may examine and cross-examine witnesses or, indeed, address the court. The extent to which he may do so is, it is submitted, at the discretion of the court (*O'Toole v Scott* [1965] 2 All E.R. 240). Where the defendant appears, s.9 of the Magistrates' Courts Act 1980 requires the court to *ask* him his plea. A plea of guilty by a solicitor on behalf of his client without the question having been put was, for this reason, quashed in *R. v Wakefield JJ. Ex p. Butterworth* [1970] 1 All E.R. 1181 and, similarly, where there was doubt as to whether the charge was properly put, the case was remitted back to the justices for rehearing (*R. v Gowerton JJ. Ex p. Davies* [1974] Crim. L.R. 253), but it was said that if the charge had been properly put, there would be no objection to the plea being given by the solicitor and further that such pleas would be valid even if not justified by the solicitor's instructions if the client did not show dissatisfaction with the pleas at the time. A magistrates' court may allow a defendant to change his plea at any stage up to the moment sentence is pronounced (*S v Manchester City Recorder* [1969] 3 All E.R. 1130). It must be remembered that the court has a discretion to allow a defendant to withdraw his plea; he has no absolute right to do so: see *Revitt v DPP* [2006] EWHC 2266 and § 2.151 below.

     Section 144 of the Criminal Justice Act 2003 provides a statutory framework for the existing judicial practice of allowing defendants credit for a plea of guilty. The use of the power is governed by the Guideline *Reduction in Sentence for a*

Guilty Plea issued initially by the Sentencing Guidelines Council in December 2004 and, in a revised form, in July 2007 (available at *http://www.sentencing-guidelines.gov.uk* [Accessed March 24, 2009]). Every court must have regard to the guideline when it imposes sentence. The guideline emphasises the purpose of the reduction. It is "appropriate because a guilty plea avoids the need for a trial (thus enabling other cases to be disposed of more expeditiously), shortens the gap between charge and sentence, saves considerable cost, and, in the case of an early plea, saves victims and witnesses from the concern about having to give evidence". It is a separate issue from aggravation and mitigation generally and the "sentencer should address the issue of remorse, together with any other mitigating features present, such as admissions to the police in interview, separately, when deciding the most appropriate length of sentence before calculating the reduction for the guilty plea" (Guideline paras 2.1–2.3).

The extent of the reduction will vary with the greatest reduction being given where the plea was entered at the first reasonable opportunity. In such circumstances, the reduction will be a maximum of one third of the sentence that would otherwise have been passed. Where the plea is not entered until the trial is about to begin (or has actually begun), the reduction will not exceed 10 per cent. Whilst the Council considered that the "first reasonable opportunity" will vary from case to case, Annex 1 to the Guideline gives examples to assist consistent interpretation. **2.143**

In common with the wholly welcome and growing requirement for courts to explain their decisions, s.174(2)(d) of the 2003 Act requires courts to state in open court the fact that a less severe sentence has been passed than otherwise would be the case owing to the indication of the defendant of his intention to plead guilty.

Where a defendant has been committed for sentence the case may be remitted by the Crown Court back to the magistrates' court with a direction to enter a plea of not guilty, and unless the Crown Court has exceeded its jurisdiction the magistrates' court may not decline to do so (*R. v Camberwell JJ. Ex p. Sloper* (1979) 123 S.J. 49). The position is otherwise on appeal against sentence (ibid.). **2.144**

Pleading guilty in writing

Section 12 Magistrates' Courts Act 1980 enables pleas of guilty for summary offences to be received in writing in magistrates' courts in the absence of the defendant. This procedure may also be used in youth courts in respect of those defendants who have attained the age of 16 at the time the summons was issued. **2.145**

The Director of Public Prosecutions as head of the Crown Prosecution Service is not responsible for taking over the conduct of the majority of proceedings commenced under s.12 of the Magistrates' Courts Act 1980 *unless* and *until* the court begins to receive evidence in those proceedings. The Prosecution of Offences Act 1985 (Specified Proceedings) Order 1999 (SI 1999/904), as amended, lists as "specified proceedings" proceedings for certain offences if those proceedings are set in train by the prosecution (in this case, the police) by way of the "guilty plea by post" procedure. Such proceedings cease to be specified once the court has decided for whatever reason that evidence must be called; in that event, the Crown Prosecution Service will have to assume responsibility for the further conduct of the proceedings.

With the summons for the offence the defendant is served an explanatory form **2.146** and a statement of the facts of the offence. As an alternative to the statement of facts, the prosecutor may serve a copy of written statements complying with s.9 of the Criminal Justice Act 1967: Magistrates' Courts Act 1980 s.12(3)(b), as amended. This alternative procedure of serving witness statements with the summons instead of the statement of facts was encouraged by the National Audit Office in its report *Criminal Justice: Working Together* published in December 1999. On a plea of guilty, the notification, statement of facts and mitigation are to be read out by the clerk and not the prosecutor. Where s.9 statements are used rather than a statement of facts, the court may allow the statements to be summarised by the clerk. If no plea is submitted, only the prosecutor can present the evidence.

The Divisional Court in *R. v Coventry Magistrates' Court Ex p. DPP* (1990) 154 J.P. 765 held that a claim for costs by the prosecution against the defendant could be notified to the defendant in the same document as that which contained the statement of facts under s.12(1)(b). It did not thereby form part of the statement of facts relating to the offence. If such a claim were so notified it had to be brought to the court's attention by the clerk to the justices, and it was the duty of the court to adjudicate upon it under s.18 of the Prosecution of Offences Act 1985.

2.147   If a court adjourns a case where the s.12 procedure has been adopted, there is no requirement to serve an adjournment notice on the defendant provided the adjournment is for a period of not more than four weeks and the purpose is to hear cases using the s.12 procedure on the next occasion (s.12(11)). This affords greater flexibility to courts in using a list of s.12 cases as "floaters", which if they are not reached because of pressure, e.g. of business, they can be placed in a court list at any time within the next 28 days without the substantial administrative burden of having to give notice of the new hearing date to the defendant.

Where a defendant has been served with the documentation specified in s.12 and submits a plea of guilty by post, but nonetheless appears in court on the date on which the information is to be heard, with the consent of the defendant, the court may proceed as if he were still absent (s.12A(1). That means that the plea of guilty will be indicated and the statement of facts read. However, instead of reading the statement in mitigation, the defendant must be given an opportunity to "make an oral submission with a view to mitigation of sentence". The court will then go on to decide whether the plea is accepted and, if so, sentence is decided and pronounced.

2.148   Another situation may arise where the defendant turns up on the relevant date, but without previously having sent in a guilty plea. If he indicates that he wishes to plead guilty and consents to the procedure being conducted as if under s.12 as before, the court may do so (s.12A(2)). A plea of guilty obviates the need for the indication of guilt that would normally be given in writing and, instead of a written note of mitigation, the defendant must again be given the opportunity to make an oral submission with a view to mitigation of sentence. The procedure is then followed as if he were absent.

Proceedings for certain more serious road traffic offences are not listed as "specified proceedings" even though they may well be commenced under s.12 of the Magistrates' Courts Act 1980; the Crown Prosecution Service will assume responsibility for such proceedings regardless of whether in fact evidence has to be called.

If he wishes to dispute the case, the defendant or his solicitor should notify the **2.149** court in order that a hearing can take place in the usual way with sworn oral evidence or statements under s.9 of the Criminal Justice Act 1967. The statement of facts prepared under s.12 may not be put in evidence at a trial and a witness cannot be cross-examined upon the statement (*Roper v Sullivan* [1978] R.T.R. 181). If he does nothing, the prosecutor, on proof of service of the summons, may prove his case by oral evidence or s.9 statements.

If the defendant or his solicitor writes to the court pleading guilty, then the statement of facts is read aloud to the court and his letter is also read aloud; no oral evidence is allowed to supplement the written statement of facts and the prosecutor may not add anything to the statement (*R. v Malden JJ.* [1966] Crim. L.R. 387; *R. v Liskerrett JJ. Ex p. Child* [1972] R.T.R. 141).

A corporation or limited company may plead guilty in writing signed by a **2.150** director or secretary under s.12 (see Sch.3 to the 1980 Act). The plea must clearly refer to all the offences charged (*R. v Burnham JJ.* [1959] 3 All E.R. 505). If the letter does not amount to a plea of guilty, oral evidence of the offence must be given at an adjourned court. Where a defendant's written statement in mitigation is not read aloud as required (*R. v Oldham JJ.* [1958] 3 All E.R. 559) an application for judicial review may arise; in such a case a declaration that the proceedings and purported conviction are a nullity serves to quash the conviction concerned; it does not, however, act as a bar to the rehearing of the case before justices (*R. v Epping & Ongar JJ. Ex p. C Shippam*; *R. v Same Ex p. Breach* [1987] R.T.R. 233). The Divisional Court did not feel that the result of granting such a declaration should be that defendants would necessarily avoid the consequence of their pleas of guilty.

The defendant's licence may be ordered to be endorsed and penalty points assigned under the s.12 procedure but he may not be disqualified from driving in his absence, where he has pleaded guilty in writing pursuant to that procedure, unless and until the court has given him the opportunity of attending on an adjourned hearing (s.11(4); see *R. v Totton JJ.* [1958] Crim. L.R. 543; *R. v Llandrindod Wells JJ. Ex p. Gibson* [1968] 2 All E.R. 20). If a case under the s.12 procedure has been adjourned without a hearing and the accused has not been required to attend at the adjourned hearing, only the statement of facts served on him may be read out and no witness may be called by the prosecution at the adjourned hearing, unless the accused is present or represented (*R. v Norham JJ.* [1961] 1 All E.R. 455). A notice of adjournment should give the reason for it, e.g. where it is intended that the court will disqualify (ss.12(10) and 11(4)), and if the reason for adjournment was to consider disqualification and this was not stated, the disqualification will be quashed (*R. v Mason* [1965] 2 All E.R. 308).

Equivocal plea and change of plea

It is well established that courts must not accept an equivocal plea. There is a **2.151** clear distinction between the *obligation* not to accept an *equivocal* plea and the *discretion* to permit a change in an *unequivocal* plea of guilty at a later stage until the moment of sentence. This was emphasised in *R. v South Tameside Magistrates' Court* [1983] 3 All E.R. 684. In *Revitt v DPP* [2006] EWHC 2266; (2006) 170 J.P. 729 the Divisional Court confirmed that a court has a discretion where a defendant wishes to rescind an unequivocal plea of guilty. Refusal to do so does not contravene the presumption of innocence until found guilty by a court of law since the entry of the unequivocal plea constitutes that finding of guilt.

On committal for sentence the Crown Court may remit a defendant to the magistrates' court for a plea of not guilty to be entered (*R. v Camberwell JJ. Ex p. Sloper* [1979] Crim. L.R. 264). A Crown Court hearing an appeal has power, however, to investigate itself and should investigate a claim that a plea of guilty had been entered under duress even though the plea had been entered in the magistrates' court (*R. v Huntingdon Crown Court Ex p. Jordan* [1981] Crim. L.R. 641). The same principle applies on appeal where there has been an equivocal plea in the magistrates' court (*R. v Rochdale JJ.* [1981] 3 All E.R. 434). The Crown Court should only remit to the justices if it is satisfied that the original plea was equivocal. There must have been some identifiable information for the court. An issue raised or a mistake of law not apparent is insufficient: *Ankrah v DPP* [1998] R.T.R. 169. Where the Crown Court makes proper inquiry and finds the plea equivocal, it has the right to direct a rehearing by the justices and the justices thereupon have a duty to rehear (*R. v Plymouth JJ. Ex p. Hart* [1986] 2 All E.R. 452). The conviction was for being in charge with excess alcohol contrary to what is now s.5(1)(b) of the 1988 Act and it was apparent that the defendant was raising the statutory defence. The Crown Court should first make proper inquiry as to what happened in the magistrates' court (*R. v Marylebone JJ. Ex p. Westminster City Council* [1971] 1 All E.R. 1025; *R. v Rochdale JJ.* above). A magistrates' court has a discretion to allow the defendant to withdraw his consent to summary trial (*R. v Southampton City JJ. Ex p. Briggs* [1972] 1 All E.R. 573). A mistake in law by a defendant's solicitor does not automatically render a plea of guilty unequivocal and justices still have a discretion to allow a change of plea (*P. Foster (Haulage) Ltd v Roberts*). The court indicated that applications at a late stage by defendants who have at all times been legally represented should be regarded with caution.

Hearing charges together

2.152   Separate counts can be joined in one indictment and a judge has a discretion as to whether or not they should be severed. The content of an indictment must be as set out in r.14.2 of the Criminal Procedure Rules 2005 (as amended). This provides for more than one incident of the commission of an offence to be included in a single count where they amount to a course of conduct. It also provides for an indictment to contain more than one count where the offences are founded on the same facts or are part of a series of offences of the same or a similar character. Whether the judge should sever counts depends on whether there is a nexus between the offences (*R. v Ludlow* [1971] A.C. 29). If there is no connection, counts should not be joined (*R. v Bell (Peter)* [1984] Crim. L.R. 360). It was held in *R. v Bogdal* [1982] R.T.R. 395 that there was insufficient nexus between a dangerous driving charge and a charge of using a driving licence with intent to deceive. The offences were committed on different occasions but in the same car. The judge should have ordered the counts to be severed. They were not a "series of offences of a similar character" within the meaning of what was then r.9 of the Indictment Rules 1971.

In *Clayton v Chief Constable of Norfolk* [1983] 1 All E.R. 984 HL, Lord Roskill at 990–992 set out the principles to be followed when deciding whether there should be a joint trial of defendants or informations. He pointed out that in *R. v Assim* [1966] 2 Q.B. 249, a five-judge Court of Appeal considered at length the circumstances in which it was proper to join separate offenders charged on separate counts in the same indictment. That court had drawn back from laying down exhaustive rules. He quoted at length from Sachs J. at 261. Part of his quotation is as follows:

> "As a general rule it is of course no more proper to have tried by the same jury several offenders on charges of committing individual offences that have nothing to do with each other, than it is to try before the same jury offences committed by the same person that have nothing to do with each other. Where however the matters which constitute the individual offences of the several offenders are upon the available evidence so related, whether in time or by other factors, that the interests of justice are best served by their being tried together, then they can properly be the subject of counts in one indictment and can, subject always to the discretion of the court, be tried together."

Lord Roskill stated in the *Clayton* case that the practice in magistrates' courts **2.153** should henceforth be analogous to the practice prescribed in *Assim* for trial on indictment. In the interests of justice as a whole magistrates should have a discretion.

Where the facts were connected, there was no reason why the justices should not try the informations together if they though fit. When the question arose, the justices would be well advised to inquire of both the prosecution and the defence if there were any objections to hearing the informations together. If consent was forthcoming on both sides there was no problem. If it was not, the justices should consider the rival submissions and, under any necessary advice from their clerk, rule as they thought right in the overall interests of justice. If the defendant was absent or not represented, the justices should seek the views of the prosecution, and again if necessary the advice of their clerk, and then make a ruling in the same way.

Lord Roskill considered that absence of consent, either express or where it was **2.154** necessarily brought about by the absence of the defendant or the absence of representation, should no longer in practice be regarded as a complete and automatic bar, where the facts were sufficiently closely connected to justify joint trial and there was no risk of injustice to defendants by its adoption.

It was impossible to lay down general rules applicable to every case, but if justices always asked themselves the single question—what was the fairest thing to do in all the circumstances in the interests of everyone concerned?—they would be unlikely to err in their conclusion. On the authority of the *Clayton* decision, there is still a discretion to order a joint trial if the facts are connected even though both the prosecution and the defence make representations for separate trials (*R. v Highbury Corner Magistrates' Court Ex p. McGinley* (1986) 150 J.P. 257).

The principles to be applied were set out in *R. v McGlinchey* (1984) 148 J.P. 73 for trials on indictment and they would seem to be similarly applicable to magistrates' courts in view of the *Clayton* decision. They are as follows:

(1) Two offences may constitute a series.

(2) Rule 9 of the Indictment Rules 1971 (see now the Criminal Procedure Rules 2005 r.14) does not mean that joinder of offences can only be sanctioned if they arise out of the same facts or are part of a system of conduct.

(3) A sufficient nexus must exist between the offences.

(4) A sufficient nexus will exist if evidence of one offence would be admissible on the trial of the other, but the rule is not confined to such cases.

    (5) All that is necessary to satisfy the rule is that the offences should exhibit such similar features that they can conveniently be tried together in the general interest of justice, including those of the defendants, the Crown, the witnesses and the public.

    (6) The manifest intention of the Indictments Act 1915 is that charges which either are founded on the same facts or relate to a series of offences of the same or similar character properly can, and normally should, be joined in one indictment and a joint trial of the charges will normally follow, although the judge has a discretionary power to direct separate trials under s.5(3) of the 1915 Act.

    (7) The judge has no duty to direct separate trials under s.5(3) unless in his opinion there is some special feature of the case which would make a joint trial of several counts prejudicial or embarrassing to the accused and separate trials are required in the interests of justice. In some cases the offences charged may be too numerous and complicated so that a joint trial of all the counts is likely to cause confusion and the defence may be embarrassed or prejudiced. In the other cases objection may be taken to the inclusion of a count on the ground that it is of a scandalous nature and likely to arouse in the minds of the jury hostile feelings against the accused.

2.155 Where two defendants are charged with separate offences, e.g. one with using and the other with permitting the use of the same vehicle on the same occasion, and are not tried together, the whole of the relevant evidence must be given in each case, even though most of it is repetition from the first hearing (*Taylor's Central Garages v Roper* (1951) 115 J.P. 445).

The further question of trying charges against *one defendant* of the former offence of reckless and careless driving together is discussed at 112 J.P. Jo. 226 and 305, and 113 J.P. Jo. 201. If the magistrates convict on a charge of dangerous driving and a charge of careless driving, their decision might be open to challenge. It bears some similarity to a court convicting an offender of both murder and manslaughter. If they convict on both and impose a penalty for dangerous driving only, the view used to be that if the defendant successfully appealed to the Crown Court against the conviction of dangerous driving he then escaped all penalty.

2.156 However, the decision in *Dutta v Westcott* [1987] Q.B. 291, which gives considerable flexibility to the appellate court, should be studied. Further (and welcome) flexibility is also given to the trial court by s.24 of the 1988 Offenders Act. Acquittal of the offence charged will allow the court, within the terms of the section, to bring in an appropriate alternative verdict. A considerable range of alternatives is available in particular cases and the table contained in the section lists the alternatives. The clear terms of the section should enable proper verdicts to be entered without some of the procedural difficulties that have attended the earlier, limited provisions dealing with alternatives.

An important case concerning the approach of the court when dealing with two contested informations together, covering similar (although obviously not the same) ground, was *DPP v Gane* [1991] Crim. L.R. 711. Mr Gane was found in the driver's seat of a car with the engine running. He had excess alcohol in his blood. He was prosecuted for driving with excess alcohol and being in charge with excess alcohol. He pleaded not guilty to both matters and was tried by justices. He was convicted of driving with excess alcohol, and in view of that conviction they dismissed the information which alleged he had been in charge. The prosecutor appealed and the Divisional Court allowed the appeal. It was not lawful to dismiss a charge merely because it would have been oppressive to convict the defendant. An appropriate course would have been for the justices to have adjourned the in charge matter sine die pending any appeal. Alternatively, they could have convicted Mr Gane on the lesser charge and imposed a nominal fine and concurrent disqualification.

For a decision on the *listing* of more than one charge against a defendant, see the decision of the Divisional Court in *R. v Weston-super-Mare JJ. Ex p. Shaw* [1987] 1 All E.R. 255 when it was held that it was not unlawful to list all charges, whether related or unrelated, against a single defendant which were set down for hearing on the same day or for the justices to see that list. **2.157**

Where charges against the same defendant are heard separately, the justices should convict or acquit on the first charge before starting on the second, but may postpone sentence (*Hamilton v Walker* (1892) 56 J.P. 583; *R. v Fry* (1898) 62 J.P. 457). Where two defendants are being tried separately on charges arising out of the same facts, e.g. careless driving and causing an accident, the magistrates should announce their finding in the first case before starting to hear the second (*R. v Chambers* (1939) 83 S.J. 439). Where the charge is a joint one, they hear both defendants before coming to a decision. Where defendants on separate charges are being tried together the facts and evidence will normally be so intermingled as to make it desirable to defer any announcement as to findings of guilt or innocence until both defendants have concluded their cases. Where the same defendant is concerned in two cases heard successively it may be proper to offer trial before a different bench in the second case because of the possibility of not approaching the matter in a proper and impartial manner. This is essentially a matter for the discretion of the justices. In *R. v Sandwich JJ. Ex p. Berry* [1982] R.T.R. 332 the defendant had been charged with 16 road traffic offences alleged to have been committed on six different days. He chose separate trials on each of the six sets and then applied for each set to be tried by a different bench, renewing his application at the end of each hearing. The justices refused on each occasion and were upheld by the Divisional Court. It was right that the justices should review their discretion after hearing each case and they had done so.

Duress

The extent of the defence of duress in relation to road traffic offences has been addressed by the courts. For the effect of duress by threats, see *Eden District Council v Braid* [1999] R.T.R. 329 commented on in § 13.246 below. For the consideration of duress by circumstances, see *R. v Cairns* [1999] Crim. L.R. 826 and the commentary on that case. For the defence to be available, the defendant must reasonably believe in the facts alleged to amount to the duress, his belief must have amounted to good cause to fear serious harm and his response must be what could be expected of a person of reasonable firmness. These two cases are at opposite ends of the spectrum of seriousness but the warning in *Braid* should be noted, that this is a defence which can very rarely succeed and its bounds should not be widened. This restrictive approach was again seen in *DPP v Hicks* [2002] EWHC 1638 in which the defendant was charged with driving after having consumed alcohol over the prescribed limit. The police stopped him after he **2.158** had been seen driving erratically. At the police station, he gave a false name. At trial, he relied on a defence of necessity. He submitted that his 19-month-old baby was very sick and that he had been driving to an all-night chemist in order to obtain some medicine for the child. He had not informed the police or the police doctor of that fact. His partner confirmed that the child's condition had been bad but conceded that it had not been so serious as to justify taking her to hospital. The defendant relied on the fact that he did not have access to a telephone and so could not have called for a doctor. Due to the lateness of the hour, he said he did not want to disturb his neighbours. The justices accepted his defence and acquitted him, but the prosecution appeal was allowed. The Administrative Court found that there had been no basis on which a defence of necessity could have been established on the facts found by the justices. There had been no emergency or other circumstance justifying the driving of the vehicle. A reasonable person in the defendant's situation would have asked the neighbours to call a doctor or would have used a public telephone to call the emergency services.

2.159   Further cases have given consideration to aspects of this defence. In *R. v S(D)* [2001] EWCA Crim 1977; [2001] Crim. L.R. 986, the defendant was a former member of the security services charged with breaches of the Official Secrets Act 1989. Issues arose as to the extent of the defences of necessity and of duress of circumstances (as the extended form of duress has become known). The Court of Appeal confirmed that such defences were available for offences such as these but only where a defendant had committed an otherwise unlawful act to avoid imminent peril of danger to life or serious injury to himself or some other person for whom he was responsible. The evil must be directed towards the defendant or some other person for whom he had responsibility and who could be identified by reference to the action threatened. The evil to be prevented must be greater than the evil done which should be no more than reasonably necessary to avoid the harm feared. See the commentary at [2001] Crim. L.R. 987 for an analysis of this judgment. Not all of these tests were satisfied in *DPP v Tomkinson* [2001] EWHC Admin 182; [2001] R.T.R. 38. The defendant had been violently assaulted by her husband after they had returned home from a New Year's Eve party between 2am and 3am. They had only just moved to the area (having only recently married) and her children were still in her former area some 72 miles away. The husband had left the home to go to hospital and warned the wife not to be there when he returned; before leaving he had smashed both the house phone and her mobile phone. The wife was unfamiliar with the area, knew no one in whom she could confide and did not feel she could go to a hotel on that night at that hour. At 6am, frightened for her life and believing she was not over the limit, she left to drive the 72 miles to her former area but was stopped close to her destination and found to be over the limit. She sought to advance the defence of duress and was acquitted by the justices having, unwisely because so much of this aspect of the law has developed in recent years, taken advice from their clerk based on an old edition of *Wilkinson*. The Administrative Court allowed the prosecutor's appeal. Recognising the existence of the defence of duress by circumstances in exceptional circumstances, at the time of arrest the defence had ceased to be available because the defendant was no longer subjected to any effective threat of violence at the hands of her husband. The court also found that that threat did not exist at the time the defendant left the immediate area of her home to commence the journey.

The relevance of a later event to support a defence of duress was considered in **2.160** *R. v Nethercott* [2002] Crim. L.R. 402. The defendant had been charged with dishonest use of a credit card and raised the defence that he was acting under duress, having been threatened by his co-defendant. He sought to adduce evidence that the co-defendant had stabbed him some 12 weeks after the alleged offence, but this was excluded by the trial judge. The Court of Appeal was of the view that the evidence was relevant in the context of this particular case and should, therefore, have been admitted.

In *R. v Snowden* [2002] EWCA Crim 923, the court accepted the admission of a humorous birthday card received by the defendant from his family as evidence relevant to disproving a defence of duress by which the defendant was alleging he was compelled to use his premises to cultivate cannabis. The card was relevant in showing the defendant's state of mind and that he had treated the cultivation as a joke.

The subjectivity of the belief was considered by the Court of Appeal in *R. v* **2.161** *Martin (David)* [2000] 2 Cr. App. R. 42. The circumstances leading to the alleged duress must be taken to be as the defendant honestly believed them to be. A jury should not be told that it needed to be satisfied that there was or may have been in fact an imminent threat: *R. v Safi* [2003] EWCA Crim 1809; [2004] 1 Cr. App. R. 14.

In *DPP v Mullally* [2006] EWHC 3448, the Divisional Court held that the defence of duress was excluded from a driver charged with an offence of driving over the limit contrary to the Road Traffic Act 1988 s.5(1)(a) as it was unreasonable for the driver, who had a genuine fear of violence, to continue to drive once she was aware that police had arrived to deal with the threat of violence. One example of evasive action that is referred to in the authorities which it is expected should be taken is to seek out, and to rely on, the protection of police, if that option is realistically available.

The approach to the defence of duress was considered extensively by the House **2.162** of Lords in *R. v Hasan* [2005] UKHL 22. Having reviewed the authorities, Lord Bingham summarised the key provisions. Having regard to the features of duress set out earlier in the judgment (particularly that it provides a complete defence and, once raised, requires the prosecution to disprove despite the likelihood that all relevant information is within the knowledge of the accused), it was unsurprising that the law should have been developed so as to confine the defence of duress within narrowly defined limits.

To found a plea of duress the threat relied on must be to cause death or serious injury (*R. v Abdul-Hussain* [1999] Crim. L.R. 570). That threat must be directed against the defendant or his immediate family or someone close to him. The relevant tests pertaining to duress have been largely stated objectively, with reference to the reasonableness of the defendant's perceptions and conduct and not, as is usual in many other areas of the criminal law, with primary reference to his subjective perceptions. The defence of duress is available only where the criminal conduct which it is sought to excuse has been directly caused by the threats which are relied upon. The defendant may excuse his criminal conduct on grounds of duress only if, placed as he was, there was no evasive action he could reasonably have been expected to take. This is an important limitation of the duress defence and in recent years it has been unduly weakened. Finally, the defendant may not rely on duress to which he has voluntarily laid himself open.

Conviction

2.163   A great deal more flexibility is granted to courts in finding alternative verdicts by s.24 of the 1988 Offenders Act (as amended by the Road Safety Act 2006 ss.32 and 33). (See also Chapter 5.) Where a person is charged with a particular offence under the 1988 Act and is found not guilty of that offence, he may be convicted of a specified alternative offence in the section provided that the allegations in the indictment or information amount to or include an allegation of an offence under one or more of the offences listed in the second column of s.24(1) of the 1988 Offenders Act. The importance of a finding of "not guilty" was emphasised in *R. v Griffiths* [1998] Crim. L.R. 348. In a trial at the Crown Court, the jury were unable to reach a verdict on a charge of dangerous driving. The judge discharged them from reaching a verdict on that charge and instructed them to consider careless driving as an alternative. On appeal, it was held that there was no power under s.24(1) of the Road Traffic Offenders Act 1988 to return a conviction for careless driving unless the jury had first acquitted the driver of dangerous driving.

    An offence of driving while unfit, carries an alternative of being in charge while unfit; and driving with excess alcohol has the alternative of being in charge with excess alcohol. The offence under s.28 (dangerous cycling) has the alternative of s.29 (careless and inconsiderate cycling).

2.164   The section specifically provides that the provisions of the subsection do not permit that a person charged with an offence under s.3A of the 1988 Act should be convicted of any offence of attempting to drive. But, where a person is charged with either driving while unfit/with excess alcohol (as the case may be) he may be convicted of having committed an offence under the provision in question by attempting to drive.

    To secure a conviction it is not necessary to prove each and every item or particular in a charge providing all the ingredients of the substantive offence are established (*R. v Parker* [1969] 2 Q.B. 248 and *Machent v Quinn* [1970] 2 All E.R. 255). These were cases of theft but it is submitted that the principle is of general application. It is submitted, e.g. that if a charge of careless driving contains two linked incidents of careless driving (as in *Horrix v Malan* [1984] R.T.R. 112), perhaps in two different roads, it is still possible to convict even though only one incident is proved.

2.165   Where, following a plea of guilty, there is a sharp divergence on the facts the court must hear any submissions and, where there is a substantial conflict, either come down in favour of the defendant or call for evidence: *R. v Newton* (1983) 77 Cr. App. R. 13; *R. v Williams* (1984) 148 J.P. 375.

    The approach to be adopted in magistrates' courts when there is an acceptance that the ingredients of the offence are present, and yet there remains a dispute on the facts alleged by the prosecution was outlined in *R. v Telford JJ. Ex p. Darlington* [1988] Crim. L.R. 312. The procedure to be followed is:

      (1) where a defendant pleads guilty and on the facts advanced by the prosecution it appears that the plea involves a clear admission of the whole of the ingredients of the offence charged, the defendant has thereby made an unequivocal plea which the justices have to accept and cause to be entered upon the record;

      (2) the justices then have to turn their minds to, if it exists, any area of

dispute as to facts which do not go to the ingredients of the offence but as to matters affecting sentence;

(3) if summary trial has been decided upon, the justices should hear evidence upon any disputed facts which it is necessary to resolve themselves;

(4) the justices should then proceed to sentence having regard to their findings, and this will include consideration of the power to commit for sentence under s.3 of the Powers of Criminal Courts (Sentencing) Act 2000 in an appropriate case.

The decision of the Court of Appeal in *R. v Kerrigan* (1992) 156 J.P. 889 **2.166** provides a reminder that a tribunal conducting a *Newton* hearing should direct itself to apply the criminal burden and standard of proof.

The importance of any court sentencing on a true factual basis was emphasised further in *R. v Beswick* [1996] 1 Cr. App. R. 427. The Court of Appeal laid down some important guidelines and, although their Lordships were dealing with an appeal from the Crown Court on a criminal matter, the criteria laid down may also be relevant when road traffic cases are dealt with by justices. The principles which may be identified from *R. v Beswick* are:

(a) a court should sentence an offender on a true factual basis; it followed that the prosecution should not lend itself to an agreement with the defence whereby a case was presented to the sentencing judge on an unreal or untrue set of facts concerning the offence to which a guilty plea was to be tendered;

(b) if that occurred, the judge was entitled to direct the trial of an issue so that he could determine the true factual basis on which he had to sentence;

(c) if the judge directed the trial of an issue, that did not entitle the defendant to vacate his plea of guilty to the offence based on agreed facts;

(d) in conducting the trial of an issue the judge was entitled to expect prosecution counsel to assist him in ascertaining the true facts—a prior agreement between the prosecution and defence must therefore be considered as conditional upon the approval of the judge;

(e) it was important that the issues to be tried were clearly identified and that there was an agreement on whether the relevant prosecution witnesses were to be called or their statements could be read.

For a helpful decision on the discretion of a Crown Court to remit to justices **2.167** where there is a dispute as to the facts, in a case where the justices have committed for sentence, see *Munroe v DPP* (1988) 152 J.P. 657, and the commentary at 152 J.P.N. 690. For affirmation of the power of the Crown Court to reach its own conclusions on the facts on an appeal, see *Bussey v DPP* [1998] Crim. L.R. 908.

The normal practice when sentencing co-defendants is to hear all the evidence and submissions relating to sentence in the presence of all of them before passing sentence on any one of them. This practice should only be departed from in exceptional circumstances (*R. v Hall (M.L.)* (1982) 146 J.P. Jo. 281 CA).

Mitigation

Where justices have retired to consider whether to convict or acquit and have **2.168** decided on the defendant's guilt, they should not on their return immediately announce their penalty. After they have announced a conviction, the prosecution should be given an opportunity of citing any previous convictions and making any application for costs, and the court, if it is an endorsable offence, should see the defendant's driving licence and, most importantly, the defendant or his solicitor or counsel should have an opportunity of putting forward any matter in mitigation. If justices find a case proved after a plea of not guilty and pronounce sentence without first giving the defence an opportunity to speak in mitigation of the sentence, their sentence may be set aside (*R. v Southampton JJ. Ex p. Atherton* [1974] Crim. L.R. 108). (The justices decided on the defendant's guilt and immediately announced a fine of £100 without giving the defence counsel an opportunity to speak in mitigation. After remonstrations from the defence counsel they then heard him in mitigation and announced a reduced fine of £80 plus £21 costs. The sentence was quashed and the case was sent back by the Divisional Court for the sentence to be reconsidered by a different bench.) Similarly, a sentence was quashed where justices refused to hear counsel in mitigation after convicting the defendant and before sentencing him (*R. v Billericay JJ. Ex p. Rumsey* [1978] Crim. L.R. 305).

In the course of hearing an appeal against sentence in *R. v Giles (Douglas)* (1991) 155 J.P. 1000, the Court of Appeal stated that it is the duty of both counsel to check the maximum or lawful sentences that are available to the sentencing judge and to stand up and correct him if he falls into error. This obligation was emphasised in *Att Gen's Reference (No.52 of 2003)*; *R. v Webb* [2003] EWCA Crim 3731; [2004] Crim. L.R. 306 and in *R. v Cain* [2006] EWCA Crim 3233. In the context of the Crown Court, it is the duty of prosecuting counsel to draw the attention of the judge to relevant judicial cases and to have copies available for the judge where necessary. A judge must understand that that is the duty of prosecuting counsel and should not take offence at that duty being fulfilled. At a magistrates' court, this function should be undertaken by the legal adviser who is entitled to draw such issues to the attention of the court either on request or on his or her own initiative. Normally, this would be done in open court even where it is also given to the justices or district judge in the retiring room. Prosecutors should nonetheless be alert to be able to tender that information should the court appear to be unaware of it. The Code for Crown Prosecutors (at para.11) reiterates this obligation: see *http://www.cps.gov.uk* [Accessed March 24, 2009].

2.169   It may be wise to support a plea in mitigation by evidence, particularly where the mitigation adduced is of an unusual nature or extraordinary character; in some cases, sworn evidence is essential. e.g. "special reasons" for not endorsing or disqualifying (see §§ 21.60–21.63). By giving sworn evidence a defendant renders himself subject to cross-examination. Where, however, such sworn evidence is required, a statement under s.9 of the Criminal Justice Act 1967 is admissible as evidence to the like extent as oral evidence (s.9(1)). Section 9 statements can be tendered by either party including the defendant. Admissions by the prosecutor may also be obtained (see § 3.80).

The *Consolidated Criminal Practice Direction*, Pt III.28 provides for statements about how a crime has affected them to be made by victims in a way that allows for the statement to be considered and taken into account by a court passing sentence. The personal statement provides a means for the victim to record the impact of the offence upon him or her and is not an opportunity for the victim to offer an opinion as to what the sentence should be. These statements may be particularly pertinent where a road traffic offence has resulted in injury or death.

Defendant's previous convictions

Sections 73, 74 and 75 of the Police and Criminal Evidence Act 1984 deal with **2.170** the methods of proof of previous convictions and acquittals. Convictions and acquittals may be proved in criminal proceedings (see s.82) by certificate if it is established that the person named is the person in question. A certificate duly signed shall be taken to be such unless the contrary is proved (s.73). Other methods of proving convictions and acquittals are not affected (s.73(4)).

A conviction in the United Kingdom of any person other than the defendant is admissible in criminal proceedings to prove that he committed that offence (s.74(1)) and furthermore he is presumed to have committed that offence unless the contrary is proved (s.74(2)). Where the defendant's own UK conviction is admissible in criminal proceedings, he is presumed to have committed that offence unless the contrary is proved (s.74(3)). "Convictions" in s.74 include orders of probation and discharge, and the principles in s.74 apply to service courts outside the United Kingdom.

In *R. v Ireland* [1985] Crim. L.R. 367 the defendant had been convicted of **2.171** driving whilst disqualified and it was sought to prove that he had committed the offence of no insurance on the same occasion. It is suggested in the commentary at p.368 that the evidence of the first conviction would not be admissible under s.74 because it was sought to prove not the conviction or the commission of the first offence but the fact that he was driving. However, it may be that as s.74 makes the conviction admissible as a whole, essential ingredients such as the driving also become admissible by s.74.

There is a presumption in s.74 unless the contrary is proved. It does not therefore constitute issue estoppel. Only subsisting convictions are admissible by s.74 (s.75(4)). "Subsisting" is not defined. "Spent" convictions under the Rehabilitation of Offenders Act 1974 are nevertheless admissible in criminal proceedings subject to certain safeguards. Presumably "spent" convictions therefore still subsist for the purpose of admissibility under s.74.

A restrictive view of the uses of s.74 was taken by the Court of Appeal in *R. v* **2.172** *Robertson*; *R. v Golder* [1987] 3 All E.R. 231. In the course of his judgment, Lord Lane C.J. commented that s.74 was a provision which should be sparingly used; there would be occasions where although the evidence might be technically admissible, its effect was likely to be so slight that it would be wiser not to adduce it.

There are provisions in s.75 for the admissibility of certain documents to establish convictions in accordance with s.74.

Section 42 of the Magistrates' Courts Act 1980 prohibits a justice taking part in trying the issue of a defendant's guilt if the justice has been informed, for the purposes of determining bail, that the defendant has one or more previous convictions.

Previous convictions may not be put forward in the mode of trial procedure for **2.173** the purpose of considering whether the case is more suitable for committal proceedings (*R. v Colchester JJ. Ex p. North Essex Building Co Ltd* [1977] 3 All E.R. 567). However, the authorities stem from a time when the existence of previous convictions did not affect the seriousness of the offence. Since the implementation of s.143(2) of the Criminal Justice Act 2003 it is possible for each previous conviction to aggravate the seriousness of an offence. When implemented, para.5 of Sch.3 to the 2003 Act will introduce a new s.19 to the Magistrates' Courts Act 1980 which will require a court to give the prosecution an opportunity to inform the court of any previous convictions before determining whether to allocate the case to a magistrates' court or to the Crown Court. This does not affect the approach to considering whether justices who have heard such convictions should adjudicate on a subsequent trial, though note should be taken of the powers contained in Pt 11, Chap.1 of the 2003 Act to introduce evidence of "bad character".

Except for s.42 and the *Colchester* decision above it is not necessarily wrong for magistrates to try a defendant when they are aware of his previous convictions but it is usually best avoided. There may be a long-standing relationship, as described in *R. v Metropolitan Stipendiary Magistrate Ex p. Gallagher* (1972) 136 J.P. 80. It would be wrong for them to try a defendant where the previous convictions are disclosed in a way which might lead to bias or a suggestion of bias in the minds of the public (*R. v London JJ. Ex p. South Metropolitan Gas Co* (1908) 72 J.P. 137 and *R. v Birmingham JJ. Ex p. Robinson* (1986) 150 J.P. 1). See also § 2.183.

2.174   Section 4 of the Rehabilitation of Offenders Act 1974 provides that a person shall be treated for all purposes as a person who has not committed, or been charged with, prosecuted for, convicted of, or sentenced for an offence for which he has become rehabilitated (a "spent" offence). The Act does not apply to evidence in criminal proceedings (s.7(2)(a)). Nevertheless no oral evidence in a Crown Court should be given of such a "spent" conviction without the authority of the judge who himself should make no reference to it unless it is necessary to do so for the purpose of explaining the sentence (*Consolidated Criminal Practice Direction*, Pt I.6). Magistrates' courts are similarly enjoined to follow such a practice (Home Office circulars 98 and 130/75). Under the extended system of fixed penalties now embodied in Pt III of the Road Traffic Offenders Act 1988, unpaid penalties are registered for enforcement as if on conviction. They are not previous convictions as such.

Where there was a reference to a previous conviction for dangerous driving during a hearing before magistrates but they announced that they would disregard such reference, and did disregard it, the conviction was upheld (*Cholerton v Copping* (1906) 70 J.P. 484; see also *Barker v Arnold* (1911) 75 J.P. 364). *Aliter* where the High Court is not satisfied that the previous conviction has been disregarded (*R. v Grimsby Borough Quarter Sessions* [1955] 3 All E.R. 300). Where the defendant had been wrongly cross-examined as to a previous conviction, his conviction was quashed, although the magistrates stated that their minds had not been in any way affected by the revelation of his previous court appearance; the cases of *Cholerton v Copping* and *Barker v Arnold* above were not apparently cited (*R. v South Holderness JJ. Ex p. Bonner* [1964] Crim. L.R. 537). A certificate of conviction to prove a disqualification should mention only the offence (or semble one of the offences) for which the defendant was disqualified (*Stone v Bastick* [1965] 3 All E.R. 713). If an endorsed licence is used for this purpose, it is submitted that any other endorsements on it should be covered up before the magistrates see it. Generally, if an irregularity of this kind occurs during a trial and the justices feel that they cannot disregard it, they should adjourn the trial to a different bench (*Elkington v Kesley* [1948] 1 All E.R. 786). It seems to be the better opinion that, where the defendant is absent, previous convictions should not be mentioned on his being convicted unless, perhaps, he has clearly admitted them to a witness. If he is present, he should be asked if he admits them; if he denies them, they must either be strictly proved or ignored. The prosecution, however, may (save in youth courts) use s.104 of the Magistrates' Courts Act 1980. Under it, where a person is convicted by magistrates of a summary offence, then, if it is proved that he has been served personally or by registered post or recorded delivery with a list of previous convictions for summary offences (as defined by Sch.1 to the Interpretation Act 1978) not less than seven days previously, the court may in his absence take account of such convictions. (It should be noted that service of notice to cite previous convictions under s.104 of the Magistrates' Courts Act 1980 may now be effected by sending it by first class post addressed to him at his last known or usual place of abode (Magistrates' Courts (Miscellaneous Amendments) Rules 1992 (SI 1992/729)).) The list of previous convictions, by virtue of the definition in Sch.1 to the Interpretation Act 1978, can show previous traffic offences but not generally crimes of dishonesty.

This procedure may be used whether the case has been established by a written **2.175** plea of guilty under s.12 of the 1980 Act or by evidence in the defendant's absence. His attendance cannot be enforced by warrant, after he has been convicted in his absence, for the mere purpose of proving his record (*R. v Montgomery* (1910) 74 J.P. 110). To get over these difficulties, s.13(3A) and (4) of the 1988 Offenders Act enables details of previous convictions for endorsable offences to be proved to a court in the absence of the defendant and after conviction, usually in the form of a certified computer printout. Section 13 and in particular the period of notice required under it, is discussed further at "Registration particulars and driving licence records", § 3.55.

Particulars of an endorsement on the defendant's licence noted by the police prior to the hearing may be so given in evidence in his absence without a notice to produce it (*Martin v White* (1910) 74 J.P. 106). Where a conviction has to be proved by other means, it can be done by producing a record or extract of such conviction with proof of identity or by fingerprints. Any doubts that existed as to whether a court is entitled to look at a driving licence have been resolved by what is now s.31 of the 1988 Offenders Act which provides that where a person is convicted of an obligatorily endorsable offence, the court may take into consideration particulars of any previous conviction or disqualification or penalty points endorsed on the licence when deciding what order to make in pursuance of the conviction.

The payment of a fixed penalty without prosecution under the 1988 Offenders **2.176** Act, or a mitigated penalty to a council under the Vehicle Excise and Registration Act 1994, does not count as a previous conviction and may not be included in a record of convictions submitted under the Magistrates' Courts Act 1980 s.104. Neither penalty can constitute a previous conviction because neither amounts to a conviction.

In giving the defendant's record after conviction, the police may, in addition to previous convictions, inform the court of matters, whether or not the subject of charges which are to be taken into consideration, which are not disputed by the defendant and ought to be known by the court (*R. v Van Pelz* [1943] 1 All E.R.

36). This seems wide enough to allow them to mention undisputed cautions for motoring offences and also fixed penalty offences.

Committals for sentence

2.177   A magistrates' court has the right to commit a defendant for sentence by the Crown Court for any "either way" offence if of the opinion he should receive greater punishment than the magistrates' court had power to inflict (Powers of Criminal Courts (Sentencing) Act 2000 s.3). The power to commit applies equally to a corporation convicted in the circumstances described, although of course the reference to the committal being "in custody or on bail" does not apply.

This confers a wide discretion—see *R. v North Sefton Magistrates' Court Ex p. Marsh* (1995) 159 J.P. 9 and *R. v Southampton Magistrates' Court Ex p. Sansome* [1998] Crim. L.R. 595—particularly with the increasing use of committal for sentence without mode of trial having taken place: see Magistrates' Courts Act 1980 s.17A and *R. v Warley Magistrates' Court Ex p. DPP* (1998) 162 J.P. 559.

2.178   A defendant on bail prior to committal for sentence would normally have bail continued until sentence even though it was anticipated that the Crown Court would impose a custodial sentence: *R. v Rafferty* (1998) 162 J.P. 353.

An error as to the correct statute in a certificate of committal for trial did not invalidate the committal (*R. v Hall* [1982] 1 All E.R. 75): cf. *R. v Folkestone & Hythe Juvenile Court Ex p. R* [1981] 1 W.L.R. 1501, a committal for sentence. The magistrates' court, when committing the offender for sentence to the Crown Court under s.3, has no power to make any ancillary order, e.g. an order as to costs or compensation, other than an interim order of disqualification (see § 20.68).

2.179   Where an offender has been committed to the Crown Court for sentence under s.3 of the Powers of Criminal Courts (Sentencing) Act 2000, the Crown Court's powers are the same as if the offender had been convicted on indictment before it. The Crown Court has the same powers as a magistrates' court in respect of offences committed under s.6 of the 2000 Act.

Remitting to another magistrates' court for sentence

2.180   Section 10 of the Powers of Criminal Courts (Sentencing) Act 2000 enables one magistrates' court under certain circumstances to remit an offender to another magistrates' court for sentence. The offender must have been convicted of an imprisonable or disqualifiable offence by the remitting court and also have been convicted but not sentenced by the other magistrates' court. The remitting court must obtain the other court's consent to the offender being remitted. The remitting court may remand the offender on remitting him. There is no appeal against an order of remittal. The court to which he has been remitted further under s.10 may remit the offender back to the original court. The power under s.10 is exercisable only in respect of offenders aged 18 or over. The section does not preclude the original court from making a restitution order under s.148 of the 2000 Act. There are separate powers relating to the remittal of youths: 2000 Act ss.8 and 9.

Discontinuance of proceedings

2.181   The Director of Public Prosecutions may give notice of discontinuance for any case he is conducting unless the defendant has been committed for trial or the court has begun to hear evidence in a summary trial (Prosecution of Offences Act 1985 s.23). The defendant may in turn give notice of continuance (presumably to obtain an acquittal and costs against the Director of Public Prosecutions). For the procedure see Pt 8 of the Criminal Procedure Rules 2005. In *DPP v Denning* [1991] 3 W.L.R. 235, it was held that where a notice of discontinuance had been served on justices they still had jurisdiction to make an order for defendant's costs under s.19 of the Prosecution of Offences Act 1985 against the prosecution. The notice of discontinuance merely brought the proceedings to an end in the same way a verdict would have brought them to an end, but it left the normal jurisdiction of the court in the matter of costs unaltered.

Discontinuance does not prevent the institution of fresh proceedings (s.23(9)).

Clarification of the power to discontinue proceedings was provided by the Divisional Court in *Cooke v DPP and Brent JJ.* (1992) 156 J.P. 497. The court confirmed that the power under s.23 of the Prosecution of Offences Act 1985 to serve a notice of discontinuance was additional to pre-existing powers and was not the only way that proceedings could be discontinued. Watkins L.J., in the course of his judgment, stated that it provided, "a most useful pre-hearing procedure, economically beneficial to everyone concerned, which enabled the Crown Prosecution Service, by correspondence and without a court appearance, to dispose of a prosecution which upon further consideration it believed should no longer be proceeded with". **2.182**

A non-technical example of discontinuance (i.e. one that falls outside s.23) was considered in the case of *R. v Grafton* (1992) 184 J.P. 857. In a trial at the Crown Court, the prosecution called two witnesses whose evidence conflicted. After considering the matter and taking further instructions, prosecuting counsel offered no further evidence. The judge strongly resisted such a course and called the remaining prosecution witness himself. The accused was convicted and appealed. After a detailed judgment, the Court of Appeal allowed the appeal. A trial judge was not entitled to refuse to permit the Crown to discontinue a prosecution while the prosecution case was still being presented. Before the completion of the case for the Crown the decision whether or not to continue had to be that of the prosecution.

Irregularity

Where an irregularity occurs during a trial, the court may start the hearing all over again on the same day (*R. v Marsham* (1912) 76 J.P. 284) or permit the summons to be withdrawn and a fresh one issued, if in time (*Davis v Morton* (1913) 77 J.P. 223). If the irregularity prejudices the accused, e.g. disclosure of previous convictions, the case should be adjourned to a fresh bench. Magistrates should not interview a witness privately, either before or after conviction (*R. v Bodmin JJ.* [1947] 1 All E.R. 109), nor allow an informant into their retiring room after retirement (*R. v Stratford-upon-Avon JJ. Ex p. Edmonds* [1973] Crim. L.R. 241), nor a social worker in their retiring room (*R. v Aberdare JJ. Ex p. Jones* (1973) 137 J.P. 57). **2.183**

The House of Lords in *R. v Gough* [1993] A.C. 646, examined the question of bias in a tribunal. Unanimously, it was held that the test to be applied is, having ascertained the relevant circumstances, whether having regard to those circumstances, there was a *real danger of bias* on the part of the relevant member of the tribunal in question, in the sense that he might unfairly regard (or have unfairly regarded) with favour, or disfavour, the case of a party to the issue under consideration by him. In a case concerned with bias on the part of a magistrates' clerk, the court is required to go on to consider whether the clerk has been invited to give the magistrates advice and, if so, whether it should infer that there was a *real danger of the clerk's bias* having infected the views of the magistrates adversely to the applicant. *R. v Gough* has been slightly adjusted in order to ensure compatibility with the European Convention on Human Rights. The question to be asked is whether a fair-minded and informed observer would conclude that there was a "real possibility or real danger, the two being the same, that the tribunal was biased". This is an objective test of the circumstances not an estimate of the likelihood that the tribunal was in fact biased: see *Director General of Fair Trading v Proprietary Association of Great Britain Medicaments and Related Classes of Goods (No.2)* [2001] 1 W.L.R. 700; *Sander v United Kingdom* (2001) 31 E.H.R.R. 44; *Porter v Magill* [2001] UKHL 67; [2002] 2 W.L.R. 37 and the commentaries following *R. v Poole* [2002] EWCA Crim 1406; [2002] Crim. L.R. 242 at 243–244 and *R. v Brown (Robert Clifford)* [2001] EWCA Crim 2828; [2002] Crim. L.R. 409 at 410–411.

2.184 The decision in *R. v Gough* above was, however, applied by the Divisional Court in *R. v Highgate JJ. Ex p. Riley* [1996] R.T.R. 150. The applicant faced two summary road traffic informations before the justices. At the hearing the sole issue was whether he was actually driving the vehicle, as the police constable said he was, or whether he was merely working on it, as he contended. During cross-examination of the constable, defence counsel put it to him that he had not seen the applicant driving the vehicle. The officer asked if he was being called a liar and counsel answered in the affirmative. The chairman then intervened, stating that it was not the practice in that court to call a police officer a liar. The applicant was subsequently convicted, sentenced to three months' imprisonment and disqualified for 12 months. He applied for an order of certiorari to quash the conviction on the grounds of apparent bias. In granting the application, the Divisional Court held that there was a real danger that the chairman was unfairly, though unconsciously, prejudiced in favour of the police officer and that accordingly there was a real possibility that there was not a wholly impartial adjudication of the central dispute of the case. The court also added that the chairman's intervention should have been directed at the officer, who should have been told that it was his duty to answer the questions of counsel himself, since it was counsel's duty to put his case plainly and forthrightly. The need for caution in how to express oneself was again shown in *R. (on the application of Parker) v Warrington Magistrates' Court* [2002] EWHC 1294; (2002) 166 J.P. 563. A district judge criticised the conduct of the claimant's counsel as bordering on sharp practice. The Administrative Court held that it would not be possible to conclude that the proceedings would have the appearance of justice and fairness if the district judge were to continue to hear them.

An important decision on the issue of magistrates, lay or stipendiary, conducting a trial after determining a public interest immunity (PII) application is *R. v Stipendiary Magistrate for Norfolk Ex p. Taylor* (1997) 161 J.P. 773. The magistrate was invited to grant the prosecutor's application that certain unused material should be withheld from the defence. At the hearing, the defendant was not allowed to be present, except through his solicitor. After hearing argument, the magistrate acceded to the prosecutor's request. The defence then submitted that the magistrate should disqualify himself from hearing the case. The magistrate declined to do so as he considered that he could exclude from consideration the unused material that he had seen and read. On appeal, the Divisional Court held that the question of apparent bias should be dealt with in accordance with the test in *R. v Gough* above, i.e. was there a real danger of bias? Normally it was to be expected that the court that ruled on disclosure should also conduct the trial. There might be situations where the material before the court in the PII application was so highly prejudicial that the court should disqualify itself, but they were to be regarded as very unlikely to arise, possibly only as a result of an "extraneous comment or some irrelevant revelation". In such rare situations the court of trial would still need to be appraised of the material not disclosed and the reason for its non-disclosure in order to conduct the trial fairly. In this case, the proper test had been applied by the stipendiary and the appeal would be dismissed.

In *R. (on the application of the Crown Prosecution Service) v Acton Youth Court* [2001] EWHC Admin 402; [2001] 1 W.L.R. 1828, the Divisional Court extensively reviewed the authorities in the light of the enactment of the Human Rights Act 1998 and confirmed the approach set out in *Ex p. Taylor*. In particular, the district judge or justices conducting the PII application, where ex parte as it often will be, has the responsibility of protecting the interests of the defendant. The judge (or justices) also has the final responsibility for ensuring justice is achieved at the trial and if, during the course of the trial, anything occurs which he could not foresee and he has conducted the hearing into the claim for PII, he is still in a position to protect the defendant.

2.185

A robust approach to procedure in a magistrates' court was shown by the Divisional Court in *R. (on the application of McGowan) v Brent JJ.* [2002] EWHC 814; [2002] Crim. L.R. 412. In finding a defendant guilty, justices had given succinct reasons for their decision. Pressed by defence counsel, they initially resisted and then acceded to a request for more detailed reasons and retired for over 90 minutes with their clerk. On giving the reasons, counsel asked the bench whether their reasons had been formulated after the decision to convict and was told by the chairman that they had not been but that the bench had made sure that they had gone over them again. The defence appealed arguing that the initial reasons were inadequate, the time taken to formulate the second set showed that there had been no proper reason for the decision in the first place and the retirement with the clerk gave at least the appearance that he was influencing the decision-making process. The Administrative Court emphasised that the first reasons were adequate and the more elaborate second set were unnecessary, that the chairman's statement after the second set should have been accepted and the point should never have been raised and that the statements of the chairman and the clerk made it clear that the clerk's role was confined to the structuring and formulation of the justices' response. See also the *Consolidated Criminal Practice Direction*, Pt V.55. The importance of giving reasons was again emphasised in *Ritson v Durham Magistrates' Court* [2001] EWHC Admin 519; (2002) 166 J.P. 218. Despite accepting that a defendant would have accepted a fixed penalty and that that ought to have been offered, and despite imposing a fine in the same amount as the fixed penalty, the court ordered the defendant to pay £35 towards the costs of the prosecution in the face of submissions from the defence that no such order should be made. The court was not willing to give reasons and that was criticised by the Administrative Court and the costs order quashed.

2.186   Just when it might have been thought that every kind of possible irregularity to afflict courts had found its way to the Divisional Court, the decision in *R. v Worcester JJ. Ex p. Daniels* (1997) 161 J.P. 121 shows that the scope for relief on this ground is infinite. One of the three magistrates hearing a trial was perceived as not paying attention to the applicant's evidence. That was sufficient to overturn the conviction. The Divisional Court stated that it was not essential that each member of the bench should look at a witness throughout the time she was giving evidence as this might be disquieting. However, a fact-finding tribunal had to be able to assess the credibility of the witness. Whilst there was no obligation to look at a witness all the time, nor to take notes, a complaint that a justice was looking at something else was a different matter. Justices should not be engaged in some other activity inconsistent with the hearing of the evidence before them, at least for any considerable time.

It would appear that as a result of this decision justices should not only manifestly concentrate on the evidence, but be seen to concentrate on the evidence that is being given in front of them.

In the context of irregularity, see also *R. v Nottingham Magistrates' Court Ex p. Furnell* (1996) 160 J.P. 201 at § 2.56 above.

Reopening

2.187   Section 142 of the Magistrates' Courts Act 1980 enables a magistrates' court to reopen the case where the defendant has pleaded not guilty or has been convicted in his absence. The section also enables a court to vary or rescind any sentence or order made by the court, whether the defendant pleaded guilty or otherwise, but there is no power to reopen a case where the defendant has been acquitted (*R. v Gravesend JJ. Ex p. Dexter* [1977] Crim. L.R. 298). The potential breadth of s.142 was apparent in the judgment in *R. v Sheffield City JJ. Ex p. Foster, The Times*, November 2, 1999, where it was held to be wide enough to give a court power to rescind a warrant for overnight detention issued in respect of a default on a financial penalty. See also *R. v Haywards Heath JJ. Ex p. White* (2000) 164 J.P. 629, in which a driver was charged with dangerous driving and careless driving in respect of the same incident. The summons for dangerous driving was dismissed, but the driver was convicted on the lesser charge. The justices retired to consider sentence during which it was drawn to their attention that the summons for careless driving had been issued out of time. They returned to court (before sentence) and set aside the conviction by way of s.142 of the Magistrates' Courts Act 1980. Rejecting the driver's claim that they were then without jurisdiction, they convicted the driver of careless driving as an alternative verdict to the dangerous driving. The Divisional Court, noting that the justices had set aside the conviction on the invalid summons and that the alternative verdict on the dangerous driving summons was legitimate, dismissed the application for judicial review.

2.188   A court—not necessarily of the same composition as that which imposed the sentence or made the order—can act at any time that it appears just to do so up until the time that any appeal, whether to the High Court or the Crown Court, has been determined. The use of the word "determined" implies that a magistrates' court could exercise its powers under the amended section, even though an aggrieved litigant had not only given notice to appeal, but also where an appeal was in the course of being heard by the appellate court. The powers give the courts considerable flexibility in doing justice in a wide range of cases. The scope for its use is almost infinite, but it is a power that needs to be used with care, particularly where it is proposed to make a major change to a sentence for reasons other than a mistake or omission. In *R. (on the application of Holme) v Liverpool City JJ. and the Crown Prosecution Service* [2004] EWHC 3131; (2005) 169 J.P. 306, the defendant was convicted of dangerous driving at a magistrates' court after a trial. A sentence of 50 hours' community service was imposed together with disqualification for 12 months and until a test had been passed. Subsequently, information came to light which gave considerably more detail about the effect of the offence on the victim than had been formally presented to the court when considering sentence. Approximately five months after sentence the Crown Prosecution Service sought (successfully) to persuade the court to reopen the case with a view to reconsidering sentence. Allowing the defendant's appeal against that decision, the Divisional Court concluded both that (even though no specific information was given) the effect of the accident should have been recognised by the court given the nature of the impact between the defendant's vehicle and the victim and that the sentence imposed was about right. Although the requirement to exercise the power within 28 days had been removed by Parliament, it is a power which, in such circumstances, needed to be exercised speedily. A similar power in the Crown Court for correcting sentence (or for commencing an appeal against an unduly lenient sentence) had to be exercised within 28 days. The Divisional Court emphasised that, not least because of the importance of finality, it would only be in very rare circumstances that it would be appropriate to resort to s.142 to consider an increase in sentence, particularly if that increase brought about the possibility of a custodial sentence as opposed to another form of disposal. In *R. (on the application of D) v Sheffield Youth Court* [2008] EWHC 601 it was emphasised that the power was to be regarded as a "slip rule" and should not be extended to cover situations beyond those "akin to a mistake". This case arose from procedures around the determination of mode of trial for a youth appearing in an adult court charged jointly with adult offenders and the strength of the judgment may well be attributable to the facts on which the appeal was based.

Use of the power may well save considerable costs in that rather prosaic category of cases which turn on the production of a motorist's driving documents. Although of no binding authority, it is interesting to note that Home Office circular 66/1995 covering the amendment to s.142 of the 1980 Act envisaged that s.142 would be used in much the same way as before: "where a serious procedural flaw is discovered, or where evidence is produced which conclusively demonstrates a convicted person's innocence".

2.189

A wholly welcome interpretation of s.142 came in the decision of *R. v Newport JJ. Ex p. Carey ; sub nom. R. v Gwent Magistrates' Court Ex p. Carey* (1996) 160 J.P. 613. Mr Carey failed to appear for his trial through his own fault and he was convicted in his absence. He requested the justices to reopen the case under s.142, but they declined to do so. He then applied for judicial review but that relief was refused, the Divisional Court stating that justices had a broad discretion under the section and the way they exercised it did not deprive the applicant of a fair trial. Henry L.J. said that the justices had emphasised, rightly, the inconvenience to witnesses when defendants through their own fault did not attend. He indicated that there was a limit to the court's patience.

2.190   A failure to explain a late arrival should be no bar to the reopening of a serious charge particularly where the defendant was to be dealt with separately for breach of bail. In *R. v Ealing Magistrates' Court Ex p. Satnam Singh Sahota* (1997) 162 J.P. 73, the defendant had been convicted in his absence and had applied 35 days later for the matter to be reheard. The justices rejected the application on the grounds of delay, giving no consideration to other factors such as the defendant's illness on the day of the trial. Garland J. stated that delay was a relevant consideration, but in ignoring other relevant factors the justices had failed to exercise their discretion under s.142. However, the repeal of the 28-day limit is not to be taken as a licence to delay applications and adherence to that limit would be very salutary. Delay was always harmful and the essence of doing justice was that it should be done expeditiously. This decision was followed in *R. (on the application of Blick) v Doncaster Magistrates' Court* [2008] EWHC 2698; (2008) 172 J.P. 651 where a court refused an application to reopen a conviction in absence because the defendant had not acted with all due diligence through not notifying a change of address and failing to attend an earlier hearing. That was held to be the wrong test; the criterion is "the interests of justice".

A defendant in a magistrates' court may have the proceedings or an adjudication set aside if he makes a statutory declaration that the summons had not come to his notice until a date specified in the declaration. The declaration must be made and served within a limited period. See further § 2.75.

2.191   The prosecution may properly be allowed to reopen their case where some formal proof has not been given of, say, a statutory instrument or (subject to what is said below) to hear evidence which owing to mistake or accident or want of foresight has not been given; if the statutory instrument is not immediately available, the court should adjourn (*Duffin v Markham* (1918) 82 J.P. 281; *Palastanga v Solman* [1962] Crim. L.R. 334). Justices have a discretion whether to allow a prosecutor to call evidence, after he has closed his case, to fill a gap and their discretion will not be interfered with by the High Court if they exercise it judicially (*Middleton v Rowlett* [1954] 2 All E.R. 277).

The guiding light is fairness and the emphasis on fairness in the conduct of proceedings is exemplified in a series of cases criticising defence counsel seeking to cause the acquittal of their client on a technicality by not notifying the prosecution or the court of an omission that did not go to the heart of the issue. Where appropriate, the prosecution should be allowed to adduce evidence even after the closure of the defence case (*Jolly v DPP* [2000] Crim. L.R. 471) or an application for amendment to the information allowed (*Lewin v Barratt Homes Ltd* (2000) 164 J.P. 174 noted in relation to § 2.80 above). The test to be applied will assess the interests of justice and whether the defendant has been prejudiced in the sense of affecting the way in which the defence would have been conducted. Rule 37.3(4) of the Criminal Procedure Rules 2005 provides for a party to be able to introduce further admissible evidence following any evidence introduced by the defendant. Whether to allow further evidence is a matter of law (and therefore for the judge alone in the Crown Court when sitting with justices) and a discretion capable of being exercised at any time up to the point at which the bench retires to consider its verdict: *Cook v DPP* [2001] Crim. L.R. 321.

2.192   In *Hammond v Wilkinson* (2001) 165 J.P. 786 the respondent had been charged with failing to dispose of sheep carcasses by a method prescribed by a specified order. After the close of the prosecution case, the respondent submitted that no proof had been offered of the order and the case should be dismissed. The justices did dismiss the case but the Divisional Court held that they were wrong to do so. Where there was a technical deficiency in the prosecution case (such as here), the prosecution should be allowed to reopen the case and remedy the deficiency. The Divisional Court had harsh words for advocates: "[T]his appeal … is a salutary example of an advocate failing to make submissions to a court which properly reflect the reasoning of a case upon which he is relying … We would urge those who are acting on behalf of defendants, in particular before magistrates' courts, to ensure that their submissions are in accordance with authority. It is their obligation to draw relevant authorities to the court's attention and, in particular to ensure that their submission is based upon a proper appreciation and analysis of the reasoning of the case …"

In *James v South Glamorgan County Council* [1992] R.T.R. 312, the Divisional Court held that justices had correctly exercised their discretion to allow the prosecution to reopen their case owing to a unique combination of circumstances. The defendant was alleged to have supplied a motor vehicle in an unroadworthy condition. At the hearing, the person to whom the vehicle was allegedly supplied failed to attend at court to give evidence. At the close of the prosecution case, there was no submission of no case to answer and the defendant was called to give evidence. When his examination-in-chief had finished, the missing witness arrived at court. He had had difficulty getting transport to court, and then locating the courthouse to which the justices had recently removed. The prosecution applied to reopen their case and call the witness. The justices, considering that in the particular circumstances there were good reasons, permitted the prosecution to call the witness. The defendant was convicted, and appealed against his conviction. The Divisional Court held that although the prosecution should normally be precluded from calling further evidence after their case had been closed, courts were entitled in rare circumstances to admit of exceptions. The justices' discretion had been properly exercised.

NOTICES OF INTENDED PROSECUTION

Requirements: Road Traffic Offenders Act 1988 s.1

Section 1 of the Road Traffic Offenders Act 1988 requires that for certain offences: **2.193**

- (a) the defendant must have been warned at the time of the possibility of prosecution for the offence; *or*
- (b) the defendant must have been served with the summons within 14 days of the offence; *or*
- (c) notice of the possibility of the prosecution must have been sent by the prosecutor within 14 days of the offence either to the driver or to the registered keeper of the vehicle (or in cases under s.28 or s.29 of the 1988 Act (dangerous or careless cycling) to the rider of the cycle).

It was held in *Sage v Townsend, The Times,* May 27, 1986 that this requirement will be satisfied when a defendant is charged within 14 days, and given a copy of the charge sheet.

Section 1 applies to inter alia the following offences. The complete list is   **2.194**
contained in Sch.1 to the 1988 Offenders Act:

(1) driving a mechanically propelled vehicle dangerously (s.2), and without due care and attention or without reasonable consideration (s.3);

(2) dangerous or careless riding by cyclists (ss.28 and 29) (in which case the notice is required to be sent to the alleged offender);

(3) offences under s.35 and s.36 (failing to comply with traffic directions and traffic signs) and s.22 (leaving a vehicle in a dangerous position); in *Sulston v Hammond* [1970] 2 All E.R. 830 it was held that what is now s.1 of the 1988 Offenders Act has no application to an offence under s.25 of the Road Traffic Regulation Act 1984 of failing to comply with the requirement of a pedestrian crossing regulation;

(4) aiding and abetting the commission of any of the above-named offences (*The People (Att Gen) v Carroll* [1950] Ir.Jur.R. 20).

It does not apply to any of the offences (1), (3) and (4) above when committed by the driver of a tram or trolley vehicle operated under statutory powers (1988 Act s.193A). It applies to horse-drawn vehicles and other vehicles other than motor vehicles under (3). It does not apply to other road traffic offences by the driver of any vehicle (cf. *Staunton v Coates* (1924) 88 J.P. 193). Nor does it apply to other road traffic offences even if they are similar in character to those enumerated in Sch.1 to the 1988 Offenders Act, e.g. pedestrian crossing offences (see *Sulston v Hammond* above).

2.195   Failure to comply with s.1 means that there cannot be a conviction for the offences to which it applies. It suffices if any one of the requirements of s.1 is fulfilled, e.g. if the defendant was adequately warned at the time, there is no need for a notice (see also *Shield v Crighton* at § 2.204). Many police forces, from abundant caution, do in fact send the notice in all cases although there may have been warning at the time. It will also be noted that, in the case of motor vehicles, the notice can be given to the driver or the registered keeper.

Speeding

2.196   Paragraph 1A of Sch.1 to the 1988 Offenders Act applies the notice of intended prosecution requirements of s.1 of the 1988 Offenders Act to:

(a) speeding offences generally (including temporary minimum speed limits);

(b) speeding offences on motorways; and

(c) temporary speeding restrictions in association with road works.

Offences causing death and courts-martial

2.197   It will be noted that the offences of manslaughter and causing death by dangerous driving do not require a warning or notice. The presumed effect of s.2(4) of the 1988 Offenders Act is that a person charged on indictment with such an offence need not have received a warning or notice if the jury convict him in the alternative either of dangerous driving or of careless driving. Where a charge of dangerous driving under s.2 is reduced pursuant to s.24(3) of the 1988 Offenders Act, notice or warning of the substituted charge need not have been given (1988 Offenders Act s.2(6)). A like provision applies to cyclists.

It would appear that s.1 does apply in favour of a soldier charged at a court-martial with committing a civil offence, namely careless driving, contrary to the

Army Act 1955 s.70. The decision in *R. v Jennings* [1956] 3 All E.R. 429 must be read in the light of comments made by Lord Hodson in *Secretary of State for Defence v Warn* [1968] 2 All E.R. 300.

Waiver

It appears that a defendant may waive a failure to comply with s.1 (see *R. v Hughes* (1879) 4 Q.B.D. 614). **2.198**

Accidents

Section 2(1) of the Road Traffic Offenders Act 1988 exempts the prosecution **2.199** from complying with the requirements of s.1 if, owing to the presence on a road of the vehicle in respect of which the offence was committed, an accident occurred at the time of the offence or immediately thereafter.

It was held by the Inner London Crown Court in *Metropolitan Police v Scarlett* [1978] Crim. L.R. 234 and confirmed in *Bentley v Dickinson* [1983] R.T.R. 356 that a notice of intended prosecution *is* required if an accident occurs of which the defendant is *unaware* and that s.2(1) only applies if the defendant is aware of the accident. For a decision on the question of proof of the motorist's knowledge of an accident, see the commentary on *Selby v Chief Constable of Avon and Somerset* [1988] R.T.R. 216 at § 7.08. However, a gloss on the decision in the *Bentley* case was provided by the Divisional Court in *DPP v Pidhajeckyi* [1991] R.T.R. 136. The defendant had been involved in an accident and had suffered severe injuries including extensive post-traumatic amnesia so that he had no recollection of the incident. An information alleging driving without due care and attention was laid, but no notice of intended prosecution was served. The justices ruled that the trial could not proceed because of the lack of such a notice. The prosecutor's appeal was successful. It was held that in *Bentley*, in which the defendant had not been aware that the accident had occurred, so slight and unnoticeable had it been, the rationale was clearly that if the driver were given no warning within a reasonable time, he would not have the chance to gather evidence for his case. A serious accident was a different situation. The effect of *Bentley* should be restricted to the circumstances in that case.

Section 2(1) will apply to any accident, no matter how trivial, and even if only **2.200** one vehicle is involved. For the meaning of the expression "accident" see Chapter 1. Consideration was given to the meaning of "accident" in *R. v Currie* [2007] EWCA Crim 926; [2007] R.T.R 37. Having been stopped by police officers, the defendant returned to his car when the officer talking to him was distracted and started the ignition. The officer shouted at him to stop and ran towards the vehicle; the vehicle lurched forward and the police officer had to put her hands on the bonnet. Another driver blocked the way forward, the officer grabbed hold of the open passenger door and the defendant reversed up the road causing the officer to lose her grip on the door. On two occasions, the offender nearly hit another vehicle. The offender was subsequently prosecuted for dangerous driving and convicted by the Crown Court after a trial. The trial judge had determined that there had been an accident having considered the contested facts. On appeal, it was argued both that the issue was one of fact to be determined by the jury and that it could not be said that there had been an accident. Since the existence of an accident created an exemption from the requirements, the provisions in s.1(3) did not apply (that applies to proving that the requirements of s.1(1) had not been complied with) and the burden of proof was on the prosecution to prove that an accident had occurred. Having reviewed the authorities, the court was clear that the judge was entitled to find that there was an "accident" in these circumstances. It was emphasised that the purpose of the requirements was to draw the attention of a potential defendant to the possibility of prosecution; in circumstances such as these, the events would have been "sufficiently memorable" for that to be unnecessary.

A similarly expansive interpretation of the provisions was applied in *R. v Myers* [2007] EWCA Crim 599; [2007] R.T.R. 34. Three vehicles were being driven in convoy along a road and aspects of that driving were dangerous. At one point, all the cars dangerously turned around to face the direction from which they had come. As a result, one of those vehicles veered and collided with a parked car. There was no contact between the other two cars and the car involved in the collision which was caused by the manner of the driving of that particular vehicle and the unnecessary use of the handbrake. No warning of prosecution was given and the defendants were prosecuted for dangerous driving. It was argued that the exception did not apply because the accident had not occurred "owing to the presence on a road of the vehicle in respect of which the offence was committed". That argument was rejected in the Crown Court and on appeal. Section 2(1) required there to be a sufficiently causal link between the offence and the accident that the driver did not need to be warned of the risk of prosecution. In the circumstances of this case, there was a sufficient link and the defendants did not need to be warned.

2.201   These decisions appear to be a further manifestation of the low level of tolerance of the courts for unmeritorious technical arguments seeking to avoid conviction where the underlying purpose of the provision has been achieved.

Notwithstanding the wide terms of s.2(1) many police forces continue to comply with s.1 in simple accident cases. It would seem that the fact that a prosecutor endeavoured to comply with the requirement of s.1 but failed to do so will not debar him subsequently from claiming exemption from the requirements of s.1 if the subsection applies.

2.202   The subsection will chiefly apply to dangerous driving and to careless or inconsiderate driving where accidents have occurred. It should be observed, however, that the subsection applies to all offences to which s.1 is otherwise applicable; accidents may occur, e.g. as a result of an offence of failing to comply with a traffic signal (s.36 of the 1988 Act) or causing or permitting a vehicle to remain at rest in a dangerous position, etc. (s.22 of the 1988 Act). The accident must occur "owing to the presence on a road of the vehicle". These words were considered in *Quelch v Phipps* [1955] 2 All E.R. 302 in respect of an offence of failing to report an accident (see § 7.16). The accident must occur "at the time of the offence or immediately thereafter" (s.2(1)).

Presumption of conformity with s.1

2.203   As is clear from s.1(3) of the Road Traffic Offenders Act 1988, it is unnecessary for the prosecution to give any evidence that its requirements have been fulfilled. It is for the defence to allege that they have not, and to call evidence to that effect. This was confirmed in *Offen v Ranson* [1980] R.T.R. 484 where it was emphasised that the burden of proof was on the defendant on the balance of probabilities. In that case the justices were doubtful whether the warning had been understood because it was given on a noisy road by an officer speaking rapidly through the window of a low-slung car. The Divisional Court held that that was the wrong approach. The defendant had not discharged the onus of proof but merely raised a doubt. He had at least to satisfy the justices that he probably did not hear the warning. In *Bee v DPP* [2001] EWHC Admin 812, the defendant was alleged to have exceeded a speed limit. Not having been stopped at the time, the police issued to the defendant a notice of intended prosecution (Road Traffic Offenders Act 1988 s.1) and a notice to the registered keeper (Road Traffic Act 1988 s.172). The defendant completed and returned the s.172 notice but contended at the hearing that there was no proof of the service of the notice of intended prosecution since there was no certificate of posting. He adduced no evidence of non-compliance by the police and the argument was rejected by the district judge on the ground that the requirements of s.1 were deemed to be complied with unless the opposite were proved. The defendant appealed unsuccessfully to the Divisional Court. The burden of proof was on the defendant and, since he had returned the s.172 notice and there was ample evidence from which to infer that the s.1 notice had been served, he had failed to discharge that burden.

The defence must show that the driver and the registered "keeper" of a motor vehicle have not had the notice under s.1(1)(c) and both the driver and the keeper should give evidence to that effect; it is not enough for the defendant alone, when he is not also the keeper, to give evidence that he has not had it (*Sanders v Scott* [1961] 2 All E.R. 403). If the defendant proves that neither he nor the registered "keeper" has had the notice, it is for the prosecutor to prove its posting, if he can, to the last-known address (*Archer v Blacker* (1965) 109 S.J. 113). Semble it would be unnecessary to call the "keeper" if the police were to admit in evidence that no notice had been given to him. See under "Service of notice of intended prosecution", § 2.208, as to non-receipt of a notice sent by post and under "Reasonable diligence", § 2.213, as to excusing non-compliance with s.1.

Warning at the time

A warning under s.1(1) of the Road Traffic Offenders Act 1988 may be oral or **2.204** written. Where an accident occurred at 11.45am, the police arrived at 12.15pm and the defendant was given an oral warning at the scene of the accident at 12.20pm, this was held to be "warning at the time", it having been given at the earliest time reasonably possible after the arrival of the police and while the parties were still at the scene of the accident (*Jeffs v Wells* (1936) 100 J.P. Jo. 406; see also *Shield v Crighton* below). In *Jollye v Dale* [1960] 2 All E.R. 369, a driver was pursued by the police for 30 minutes after an act of dangerous driving and then arrested. An hour later he was medically examined and, very soon after, the first oral warning was given. It was held that the words "at the time of the offence" were not limited to the point of time when the offence was committed and it was a question of fact whether there had been a warning at the time: the High Court refused to interfere with the magistrates' finding that there had been a proper warning under s.1. It was added, however, that where the earliest possible time for warning the driver was several hours later, this would not generally be a warning at the time. After an accident in the country, a car driver took the victim to two hospitals and did not report the accident to the police until four hours after it had occurred; a warning then sufficed (*Sinclair v Clark* 1962 S.L.T. 307). In *Shield v Crighton* [1974] Crim. L.R. 605 it was held that the phrase "at the time" had to be construed "sensibly" and it was held that an oral warning was "at the time the offence occurred" where the constable arrived at the scene of the accident giving rise to the offence 10 minutes after it occurred and gave the oral warning only after having first taken a written statement from the defendant under caution. Whether a warning was given "at the time the offence was committed" was again held to be a question of fact and degree (*R. v Okike* [1978] R.T.R. 489). The test is what is reasonable. It is for the defendant to show that a time lapse between the offence and the warning is unreasonable or unjustifiable and in the absence of evidence to that effect a conviction will stand (ibid.). (The facts were that the defendant was arrested at 12.40am and not warned until 3.05am, during which time, it would appear, the police were investigating whether the defendant was the driver, he having admitted that he was the registered owner of the vehicle but having denied driving it.)

The test in *Okike* was applied in *R. v Stacey* [1982] R.T.R. 20. The defendant was arrested at 11.30pm for driving whilst unfit. He was not charged with any offence relating to drink but just under three hours later he was charged with the former offence of reckless driving. The subsequent conviction was upheld in the Court of Appeal. The court also applied the test in *Sinclair v Clark*: whether or not the chain of circumstances was unbroken and all that took place was connected with the accident. The issue is one for the judge not the jury (*R. v Stacey*).

2.205   The form of words necessary to constitute a warning has been the subject of many decisions. The words, "I think you are exceeding the limit but if (on checking) I find that I am wrong, you will hear no more about it", were held sufficient (*Jessop v Clarke* (1908) 72 J.P. 358; and see *Taylor v Horn* 1929 S.L.T. 600). Is it necessary to state for what offence or offences prosecution may be considered? In *Watt v Smith* 1942 S.C.(J.) 109, it was held that the words, "The circumstances of the accident will be reported to the fiscal for the purpose of considering a prosecution", were insufficient though they were spoken at the scene of the accident; they might have been thought to refer to a common law offence or some other contravention of the Road Traffic Acts. It was also said that the constable need not select the particular offence for which there might be a prosecution, but he must so word his warning as to direct attention to ss.2 and 3 of the 1988 Act. In *Alston v Nurse*, 1933, unreported, the King's Bench Division upheld as a good warning the words, "I will have to report the matter to my superior officer with a view to prosecution"; they gave, it was said, the information which what is now s.1 of the 1988 Offenders Act intends the motorist to have. In *Att Gen v Foley* (1952) 86 I.L.T.R. 30, it was held to be unnecessary to specify for what offences the prosecution would be (see also [1953] Jo.Crim.L. 170). In view of the infinite variety of warning formulae usable, every case must be decided on its facts. In *Parkes v Cole* (1922) 86 J.P. 122, however, it was held that warning of a charge of dangerous driving did not amount to a warning of a charge of exceeding the speed limit.

If a defendant has been orally warned at the time, can he say that the warning was ineffective because he did not or could not take it in? Defendants have successfully so pleaded in Ireland (see [1954] Jo.Crim.L. 275) but here, it is submitted, it would be a question of fact, a heavy onus being on the defendant to show that the warning was ineffective. This submission was approved by Donaldson L.J. in *Gibson v Dalton* [1980] R.T.R. 410 at 413. In that case it was held that the obligation on the prosecutor was to warn the motorist that the question of prosecution would be taken into consideration and not merely to address a warning to him or give a warning. Whether the motorist was in fact warned is a question of fact: prima facie a motorist is warned if, on an objective view, words addressed to him would be expected to be heard and understood by him, but it is still open to him to prove, if he can, that he did not understand or appreciate the words and therefore was not warned. In *Gibson v Dalton* itself the Crown Court found as a fact that the warning to the female motorist did not get through to her and the Crown Court's decision was upheld.

Obviously, bawling formulae into the ear of an unconscious or seriously **2.206** injured man is insufficient. *Gibson v Dalton* still leaves open the position where adequate and proper warning is given, as in that case, but does not get through because of the defendant's own hidden inadequacies of intellect or comprehension. Donaldson L.J. said that the warning must be heard and understood by the person intended to take account of it. If the defendant is apparently in full possession of his faculties, can he plead that because of his own shortcomings or state of anxiety he failed to understand what the police officer said to him? In *Offen v Ranson* [1980] R.T.R. 484 Ackner L.J. said obiter that (if this stage had been reached in that case) there might well have been argument as to whether or not it was his fault he had not heard. In *Day v Harris* (1953) 117 J.P. 313, a civil case on a different statute, it was held that a provision requiring a notice to be read and explained was satisfied if this was done, even if the listener was mentally incapable of understanding it. It might also be argued that a defendant who never took in an oral warning contributed to the failure to comply with what is now s.1 by his own conduct in not listening properly. See also 126 J.P. Jo. 262 and *Wheatley v Lodge* [1971] 1 All E.R. 173 as to stating the reason for arrest to a deaf person. In *Att Gen v Wallace* [1964] I.L.T. 117, a notice written in a language which the defendant did not understand was held to be valid.

Service of summons

For provisions relating to the proof of service of summonses, see § 2.75 above. **2.207**
The rules for the service of summons and other documents allow three methods of service:

    (a) personal service;
    (b) leaving it for the defendant with some person at his last known or usual place of abode;
    (c) sending it by post in a letter addressed to him at his last known or usual place of abode.

Service of notice of intended prosecution

Section 1(1A) of the 1988 Offenders Act provides: **2.208**

"A notice required by this section to be served on any person may be served on that person—
    (a) by delivering it to him;
    (b) by addressing it to him and leaving it at his last known address; or
    (c) by sending it by registered post, recorded delivery service or first class post, addressed to him at his last known address."

This is developed by s.1(2) and (3). The effect is that a notice of intended prosecution sent to a person at his last known address by registered or by recorded delivery post is deemed to be served notwithstanding that the notice was undelivered or was for any other reason not received by him. In other words, there is an irrebuttable presumption of service. In the case of service effected by first class post, however, the requirement is deemed to be complied with unless and until the contrary is proved. This creates a rebuttable presumption of good service. Accordingly, where a notice has been sent by registered post or recorded delivery service to the last known address of the person prosecuted so that it could have been delivered within the 14-day statutory provision, s.1(2) provides that proper service is deemed to have taken place even if the notice is returned undelivered or otherwise not received. Where a notice has been sent by first class post to the last known address of the person prosecuted so that it could have been delivered within the 14-day statutory provision, proper service is deemed to have taken place unless the contrary is proved. The nature of postal services has changed and registered post and the recorded delivery service no longer operate as they did when this provision was enacted. Since this presumption works against a defendant and since the alternative is to assume service unless the contrary is proved, it is submitted that that rebuttable presumption should be applied to service by post whatever type of post is used.

2.209   The notice for the purposes of s.1(1)(c) must be in writing. In *Groome v Driscoll* [1969] 3 All E.R. 1638 the offence occurred on September 4 and the notice of intended prosecution was posted by recorded delivery the following day but was not actually delivered until September 21. The justices dismissed the case, apparently overlooking the proviso to s.1(1)(c), and the Divisional Court directed a conviction. Section 1 is, however, not complied with if a notice arrives outside the 14-day period because it was posted so late—e.g. the 14th day—that the notice could not be expected to arrive within the 14 days in the normal course of post (*Nicholson v Tapp* (1972) 116 S.J. 527). In *Groome v Driscoll* the Divisional Court interpreted the proviso as if the words "in time" were added to the end of the proviso and it was held in *Nicholson v Tapp* that the proviso only applies if the notice was sent at such a time that it could be reasonably expected to arrive in time in the normal course of post. *Stewart v Chapman*, below, although decided before the proviso to s.1(1)(c) was inserted, would therefore still appear to be good law. It was held in *Layton v Shires* [1959] 3 All E.R. 587 that it was good service of a notice if it was sent by registered post to the defendant's address so that it arrived within 14 days after the offence and was taken in there by some person authorised to receive letters on his behalf, e.g. a member of his family or a domestic servant, even if the defendant did not see the notice till over a fortnight after the offence.

A notice may also be served personally, provided it is served within 14 days of the offence. If the defendant and the registered keeper have no fixed abode, it seems that s.2(3) would apply to excuse the police from serving the notice, provided some effort had been made to reach them. Where the notice was handed by a constable to the defendant's wife, who was authorised to accept letters for him, this was held to be valid service (*Burt v Kirkcaldy* [1965] 1 All E.R. 741). In *Burt's* case, it was doubted whether delivery to a hall-porter would be sufficient.

2.210   In *Phipps v McCormick* [1971] Crim. L.R. 541 it was argued (and accepted by the justices) that as the police knew the defendant had been taken to hospital following the accident, the hospital was the correct address for the purposes of what is now s.1(1)(c) as this was his last address that the police knew and that notice should therefore have been sent to the hospital rather than to his home. The Divisional Court overruled the justices and held that "his last known address" for the purposes of s.1 meant the place where the person concerned would normally expect to receive correspondence, an address which had some degree of permanence.

In *Price v West London Investment Building Society Ltd* [1964] 2 All E.R. 318 a case on another statute, it was said that "last known" place of abode means that last known to the person sending the notice and might include a place which the defendant had left if the change was unknown to the sender of the notice.

The notice should be posted within such a time that, in the ordinary course of **2.211** post, it will reach the person to whom it is addressed within the 14 days (*Stewart v Chapman* [1951] 2 All E.R. 613; *Nicholson v Tapp* above). The day of the offence is not counted in computing the 14 days. Thus, if an offence occurs on January 1, the notice should be posted so that it reaches the defendant's address not later than last post on January 15. The state of the postal service near Christmas and the difference in the time of delivery between first class and second class mail should be remembered. A properly addressed letter sent by post will be deemed to have been received, unless the contrary is proved, when it would be delivered in the ordinary course of post (Interpretation Act 1978 s.7); *aliter* where it is wrongly addressed (*Getreide-Import-Gesellschaft mbh v Contimar SA Compania Industrial* [1953] 2 All E.R. 223).

The prosecutor, in cases where non-receipt of a notice is put forward, should always make sure that a warning at the time of the offence was not given as, if it was, it will not matter when the notice was received. He should also remember to ask the defendant expressly, if he has the chance, when the notice was received as it may transpire that, notwithstanding wrong addressing or receipt by another, the defendant did have it within the fortnight. See § 2.203 as to the need for the defendant to prove non-receipt by him and the keeper.

Notice may be either to the defendant or to the person registered as keeper of **2.212** the vehicle at the time of the offence, except in cases of dangerous or careless cycling where it should be given to the defendant. If given to the keeper, the notice need not specify the name of the person to be summoned (*R. v Bolkis* (1932) 97 J.P. 10). The police should, it seems, and generally will, send it to the driver, where he is known; if they serve the keeper, they probably need not show that they did not know who the driver was (*Rogerson v Edwards* (1951) 49 L.G.R. 358 at 360). A notice sent to the owner stating that "you" will be prosecuted for dangerous driving of a lorry is good, although the intention is to prosecute the driver and not (now) the keeper (*Taylor v Campbell* [1956] Crim. L.R. 342). See § 2.215 as to errors in the notice. Delivery at the registered office of a company is good and valid service of a notice to the owner, if the company is the owner, but all that is necessary is that the notice should be in the hands of a responsible officer of the company within the 14 days (*R. v Bilton* (1964) 108 S.J. 880). There, the notice had been brought to the manager at a local office, which was not the registered office; he accepted it after he had consulted the company's solicitors and the notice was in the hands of the assistant secretary and the solicitors within a fortnight of the offence. This was held to be good service.

Reasonable diligence

Section 2(3) of the Road Traffic Offenders Act 1988 provides that the police **2.213** need not have complied with the requirement of s.1(1) of the Offenders Act 1988 if neither the driver's nor the registered keeper's identity could with reasonable diligence be ascertained in time for a summons or notice to be served or sent. A defendant drove on after an accident but his number was taken; it was held that, as the police actually ascertained the owner's identity in time for a notice to be sent to him, the fact that the driver's identity was unknown did not excuse them from so doing and, as no notices had been sent at all, the defendant was acquitted (*R. v Bolkis* above). The question of reasonable diligence is for the judge, not the jury (ibid., confirmed obiter in *R. v Stacey* [1982] R.T.R. 20 at 26). The position seems to be that, if the police have time to find out the identity of, and serve, either the driver or (if he is unknown) the keeper within 14 days, the driver's conduct at the time of the offence does not contribute to their failure to do so. But, if the defendant drives away before his number can be taken, the provisions of subs.(3) excuse the police from complying with the section unless they could have discovered his or the owner's identity with reasonable diligence, or, a fortiori, do discover it within 14 days. It will not suffice if the defendant is interviewed and given an oral warning within that time; a summons must be served or written notice given when he was not warned at the time of the offence. Giving a false address or information or deliberately evading service is conduct contributing to the failure of the police to comply with s.1 and excuses them. Giving an address at which the defendant knows he will not be at the likely time is also such conduct ([1959] Jo.Crim.L. 2).

Where the police made inquiry of the Motor Licences Department (now the DVLA) in good time but were given wrong information, it was held that they had shown reasonable diligence and their failure to send the notice to the correct person was in those circumstances no bar to conviction (*Clarke v Mould* [1945] 2 All E.R. 551; see also *Rogerson v Edwards* above, and *Carr v Harrison*, *The Times*, November 18, 1966, the only report on this point, where it was held that the police in approaching the licensing authority in good time had shown reasonable diligence, though the authority had been slow in supplying the information). This paragraph should be read in conjunction with § 2.199 in cases of accidents.

2.214   Where the police were supplied with the wrong name of the registered keeper at the relevant time and accordingly sent the notice to the wrong person at the wrong address, this failure to send a notice to the registered keeper is no bar to conviction because they will have shown due diligence under s.2(3) (*Haughton v Harrison* [1976] R.T.R. 208). Once the police have established under s.2(3) that their failure to serve a notice is no bar to a conviction, the police are under no duty to serve any further notices as soon as they are told of the correct name and address of the registered keeper (ibid.).

Notice addressed to a firm cannot be regarded as notice to every individual in a firm, and the fact that the owner had caused the vehicle to be registered in the firm's name was not conduct on his part contributing to the police failing to comply with s.1 (*Clarke v Mould* above). There the owner had actually received the notice and, though *Clarke's* case was mentioned in *Rogerson v Edwards* above, it was not distinguished. Notice addressed to a limited company omitting the word "Limited" is good (*Springate v Questier* [1952] 2 All E.R. 21). A notice addressed to "O'Loughlin" was served on the defendant McLoughlin. He signed it and the police officer then put the correct name on it. It was held to be a good notice (*The State (McLoughlin) v The President of the Circuit Court* 1949 I.L.T.R.

130). If a notice is otherwise good and the defendant obviously knows to what incident it relates, a mistake in the number of his car is immaterial (*Att Gen (O'Gara) v Callaman* (1958) 92 I.L.T.R. 74). See also *Taylor v Campbell*, § 2.212. A notice in the name "Hornet" sent to a defendant Horne was held not to have misled him and the error was not sufficient to invalidate the notice (*Camp v Horne*, noted at [1965] Jo.Crim.L. 153).

Errors in the notice

It was said in *Beresford v St Alban's JJ.* (1905) 22 T.L.R. 1 (see below) that the notice for the purposes of s.1(1)(c) is intended to give an idea of the offence of which the defendant will be accused and to guard against the possibility of his being taken unawares (see also *Pope v Clarke* [1953] 2 All E.R. 704), and in *Milner v Allen* (1933) 97 J.P. 111, that the test of the validity of the notice is whether the defendant is in any way prejudiced in his defence by the defect. In *R. v Bilton* (1964) 108 S.J. 880, it was said that the object of the notice is to ensure that the driver is not taken by surprise long after the offence, when his recollection is dulled and witnesses may be difficult to trace. **2.215**

Errors in the nature of the offence

A notice stating that the defendant would be reported for dangerous driving and specifying his conduct, e.g. overtaking and cutting-in, is good although he is subsequently charged with careless driving only (*Milner v Allen* (1933) 97 J.P. 111). The view is advanced at 123 J.P. Jo. 35 that a note specifying a charge of careless driving would suffice for a prosecution for dangerous driving. A notice alleging driving without due care and attention but not specifying the acts of bad driving is good (*Percival v Ball* [1937] W.N. 106). So is a notice stating that it was intended to prosecute the defendant "for an offence against s.12 of the Road Traffic Act 1930 [now s.3 of the 1988 Act] in that you did drive a motor car" at a specified time and place, despite the omission of the words "without due care and attention" or of any alleged acts of bad driving (*Venn v Morgan* [1949] 2 All E.R. 562). In *Venn's* case the car's number was not given. **2.216**

Errors in date, time or place

A notice referred in error to dangerous driving at "1.15pm"; in fact, the accident from which the charge arose was at 11.15am. It was held that the mere fact that the time was wrongly stated made no difference and the notice was valid, for the notice mentioned the place where the accident occurred and the defendant could have been under no doubt that the notice related to it; different considerations might apply where he had had two accidents on the same day or, semble, when the charge was speeding and he had been on the same road more than once that day without being accosted by the police (*Pope v Clarke* [1953] 2 All E.R. 704; *Carr v Harrison* [1967] Crim. L.R. 54, where, although the notice referred to 8.40pm instead of am, the defendant, having been interviewed about the incident and knowing all about it, was not prejudiced by the mistake). In *Walton v Hawkins* [1973] R.T.R. 366 the Divisional Court approved the abandonment of a contention that a notice was bad in that the occurrence took place south of a junction when in fact the road ran east and west, citing *Pope v Clarke*, above. In *Goody v Fletcher* [1962] Crim. L.R. 324, a mistake of one day in stating the date **2.217** was held not to invalidate the notice; the time and place were correctly given in the notice and the defendant was in no doubt as to the incident referred to. A notice cannot be "amended"; if time permits, a fresh notice should be served or sent in lieu of the defective one. It was said obiter in *R. v Budd* [1962] Crim. L.R. 49 that there can be a conviction for dangerous driving only if it occurred in the road named in the warning of intended prosecution. In *Shield v Crighton* [1978] R.T.R. 494 a notice erroneously stated the name of a road some 80yds distant from the road where the offence was committed; it was said obiter that a written document misstating the place could be misleading, but as an oral warning had been given at the scene at the time (see § 2.204), what is now s.1 of the 1988 Offenders Act had been complied with. It is submitted that where an error in the notice is as to the place, it is a question of fact and degree whether the defendant has been misled and that a misstatement is not ipso facto fatal if the defendant has not been misled by the misstatement. The time, apparently, need not be mentioned in a summons. A notice alleging excessive speed "between" two places more than 10 miles apart was held good in *Beresford v St Albans JJ.* (1905) 22 T.L.R. 1, but the then statute did not require, as s.1 does, that the "place" of offence be specified. In Ireland a notice alleging dangerous driving in a road a mile and a quarter long was held to be too vague; there had been no accident (*Duffy v Lovegrove* [1955] Jo.Crim.L. 172). Likewise, in *Young v Day* (1959) 123 J.P. 317, a notice alleging dangerous driving by nearly colliding with a stationary car on the offside in "the Hothfield to Bethersden road" was held insufficient; there had been no accident and the defendant had not been stopped. The High Court said that it was a question of fact for magistrates, using their local knowledge, to decide if a "place" was sufficiently specified. The road named is about four miles long. In the Scottish decision of *Walker v Higson* (1997) 1998 S.L.T. 132, a driver received a notice of intended prosecution in due time, referring to the Road Traffic Act 1988 ss.2 and 3, and expressly referring to driving "recklessly". The point was taken, unsuccessfully, that the notice had wrongly used "recklessly" instead of "dangerously" and the driver appealed. The High Court stated that the notice had informed the driver of the place and date and vehicle with which the possible prosecution was concerned. The objection taken to the use of the word "recklessly" rather than "dangerously" was unfounded. The use of one word rather than the other involved a difference of no substance, having regard to the purpose of the notice.

CHAPTER 3

EVIDENCE

Generally

The operation of the substantive road traffic law in the courts is governed by procedure, dealt with in the preceding chapter, and by evidence. Although there is some overlap between the two, it is felt that each deserves its own identity in this work, not least because each has continued to see major developments at the hands of Parliament and the courts. The law of evidence has not only been radically changed by the enactment of the Police and Criminal Evidence Act 1984 and the sometimes complex provisions of the Criminal Justice Acts 1988 and 2003, but there is also a regular supply of interesting and important decisions from the appellate courts which belie the "subsidiary" status often accorded to the subject. The Human Rights Act 1998 also has affected the rules of evidence, bringing renewed emphasis on fairness in the conduct of proceedings (Sch.1 art.6).   **3.01**

Following the general tenor of this book, the text of this chapter is intended to provide a practitioner's handbook, detailing the more important aspects of the subject which are likely to be of particular relevance to the trial of road traffic offences, the general rules and more important cases rather than a complete overview or academic exposition of the minutiae of the subject. *Cross and Tapper on Evidence* (published by Oxford University Press) and *Phipson on Evidence* (published by Sweet & Maxwell) are two of many works to which recourse might be made for a more substantial study.

Evidence on oath or affirmation

It is the normal practice of a criminal court for all witnesses, whether witnesses for the prosecution or the defence, to be out of court during the hearing until called to give evidence. There is an exception in the case of expert witnesses. There may be other exceptions and it is for the court to decide (*R. v Bexley JJ. Ex p. King* [1980] R.T.R. 49: cf. *Tomlinson v Tomlinson* [1980] 1 All E.R. 593, a Family Division case). If, however, through inadvertence or any other reason the witness is in court, his evidence is admissible with the court making such deductions as to its weight as may be appropriate in the circumstances. Defendants must, save in exceptional circumstances, be allowed to give evidence from the witness box in the same manner as other witnesses. That statutory principle, contained in s.1 of the Criminal Evidence Act 1898, was vigorously reaffirmed by Watkins L.J. in *R. v Farnham JJ. Ex p. Gibson* [1991] R.T.R. 309. Mr Gibson had faced an information alleging that he drove a motor vehicle with excess alcohol. When the time came for him to give evidence, he was required to do so from the dock following the policy of the local justices that all defendants should give evidence from the dock. In quashing the conviction, the learned judge described the justices' explanation for the policy as being "utterly unconvincing".   **3.02**

They were not allowed to direct from where evidence should be given. The exception only arose if there was some reason in relation to the individual defendant for its application. Justice had to be seen to be done.

Witnesses in a trial must normally swear or affirm. The Magistrates' Courts Act 1980 s.98 provides that subject to the provisions of any enactment or rule of law (see below for examples) authorising the reception of unsworn evidence, evidence before a magistrates' court shall be given on oath. The words of the Oaths Act 1978 as to the methods of taking the oath are directory only. Although they should be complied with, failure to do so does not necessarily invalidate the taking of the oath. The efficacy of an oath depends on its being taken in a way binding, and intended to be binding, upon the conscience of the intended witness (*R. v Chapman* [1980] Crim. L.R. 42). In that case the witness failed to take the testament in his hand. The Court of Appeal has considered the validity of the evidence of a witness who had been sworn on the holy book of a religion other than his own. In *R. v Kemble* [1990] 1 W.L.R. 1111, it was asserted that as the appellant's conviction depended on this "evidence"—the witness was the only relevant prosecution witness—the conviction ought to be set aside. It was held that although the witness, a Muslim, had taken the oath on the New Testament, these questions needed to be answered: (a) was it an oath which appeared to the court to be binding on the conscience of the witness?; and, if so, (b) was it an oath which the witness himself considered to be binding on his conscience? The Court of Appeal said that the answer to the first question was in the affirmative and, having received evidence from the witness, it answered the second question similarly. The witness had been properly sworn, there had been no irregularity, and the application for leave to appeal was dismissed.

3.03   A difficult situation arose in the Crown Court in *R. v Mehrban* [2001] EWCA Crim 2627; [2002] 1 Cr. App. R. 40. The defendants were husband and wife and were both Muslims. They were charged with assault on the husband's sister and another family member was the only witness. The defendants and the other family member chose to affirm, the victim took an oath on the Koran. Under cross-examination, the victim said "let her [the female defendant] take her oath on the Koran and tell you what I've said isn't true". Prosecuting counsel then sought leave to ask the three who had affirmed why they had chosen to do so since the jury could have drawn adverse inferences from the failure to swear on the Koran. This leave was granted. The husband gave reasons for affirming, the wife stated she could not take the oath because she was "unclean" at the time and the other family member took the oath having been allowed to ritually wash. In summing up, the jury was told that it was immaterial whether a witness had sworn or taken an oath as each was equally binding and that the fact that the defendants had chosen to affirm was not to be held against them. The defendants were convicted and appealed on the ground that they should not have been allowed to be cross-examined on their religious beliefs. The appeal was dismissed. In the circumstances of the case and because of the assertion made by the victim, the court was entitled to allow the defendants to be cross-examined about the decision to affirm. The questioning had been done in a sensitive and appropriate manner and the directions to the jury were sufficiently clear and precise to negate any misunderstanding that may have existed in the mind of the jury.

Part II of the Youth Justice and Criminal Evidence Act 1999 gives courts flexibility in seeking to ensure that all available evidence is heard in ways that protect the interests of both the witness and the defendant. Sections 53–57 of the 1999 Act provide that everyone is competent to give evidence in criminal proceedings (though the defendant may not give evidence for the prosecution) unless the court is of the opinion that the witness is not able to understand questions to be put to him or to give answers to them which can be understood. The provisions in Pt II enable the court to provide considerable assistance where required to enable witnesses to understand and be understood. It is for the court to determine competence with the onus on the party proposing to call the witness to satisfy the court on the balance of probabilities. If the witness needs to be questioned for this purpose, that questioning will be done by the court and not by the parties.

There is a separate question as to whether a competent witness should be sworn. The procedure is set out in s.55 of the 1999 Act and, again, it is for the court to determine. A witness under 14 will give evidence unsworn. A witness aged 14 or over may not be sworn unless he has "a sufficient appreciation of the solemnity of the occasion and of the particular responsibility to tell the truth which is involved in taking the oath". A witness will be presumed to have that appreciation unless the contrary is proved: s.55(3). A witness who is unable to be sworn will give evidence unsworn. It is an offence to give false unsworn evidence: s.57. Part II of the 1999 Act allows a court to make a special measures direction in relation to vulnerable and intimidated witnesses. A witness under 17 automatically qualifies for assistance in this way. The measures available include screening of the witness, giving evidence by live link, restricting who may be in the court, use of video-recorded testimony and cross-examination through an intermediary. **3.04**

Under the previous legislation, two cases affirmed that it is for the court of trial to carry out the necessary balancing exercise and that receiving evidence by way of video recording can be fair both to the witnesses and to the defendant since it allows the court to hear the whole evidence: *R (on the application of H) v Thames Youth Court and the Crown Prosecution Service* [2002] EWHC 2046; (2002) 166 J.P. 711 and *R. v D and S* [2002] EWCA Crim 1460; (2002) 166 J.P. 792.

The 1999 Act does not require a court to offer the same facilities to a defendant as it offers to a witness. The House of Lords has decided that this does not contravene the provisions of the European Convention on Human Rights: *R. (on the application of D) v Camberwell Green Youth Court* [2005] UKHL 4; [2005] 1 W.L.R. 393. The judgment also suggests that, in appropriate circumstances, a court would be justified in making the same facilities available to a defendant, but the occasions when that is likely to be necessary would be rare. Another practical consequence of providing protection to witnesses was considered in *KL (A Juvenile) v DPP* [2001] EWHC Admin 1112; (2002) 166 J.P. 369. The prosecution made a without notice application for screens to be provided to protect a prosecution witness from intimidation. A further application was made that the justices should disqualify themselves from hearing the trial, having heard the application to use screens. That application was rejected by the justices and the Divisional Court agreed. There was no objection in principle to justices hearing a case after having heard an application for the use of screens.

Exhibits produced by a witness and views of the location are sometimes described as real evidence. Otherwise, all evidence (save where permitted in documentary form) must be given on oath (or affirmation: see below), although a witness producing documents only need not be sworn (for other rare exceptions see § 3.02 above and *Cross and Tapper on Evidence*). **3.05**

Under the Oaths Act 1978 affirmation in lieu of oath is permitted for any person who objects to being sworn. An affirmation is also permitted where it is not reasonably practicable without delay or inconvenience to administer an oath to a person in the manner appropriate to his religious belief. The Children and Young Persons Act 1963 s.28 prescribes the form of oath to be taken by all witnesses in youth courts and by youths in any court and enacts that the proper oath shall be deemed to have been taken although one of the forms prescribed by s.28 has been used instead of the other.

A witness who has given evidence for the prosecution cannot subsequently be called as a witness for the defence (*R. v Kelly*, *The Times*, July 27, 1985). He may be further interviewed with leave of the court. It is submitted that he may also be recalled subject to the normal rules of procedure but that he remains a prosecution witness and should be examined accordingly.

3.06   If a witness gives evidence of a fact directly relevant to the issue, it can be put to him that on some earlier occasion he made a contradictory statement to another person; if he denies it, that other person can be called. This is not possible where the evidence is merely as to credit (*R. v Barking JJ. Ex p. Goodspeed* [1985] R.T.R. 70).

Although a case on the criminal offence of possessing a drug with intent to supply, the importance of *R. v Skinner* (1994) 99 Cr. App. R. 212 is in the guidance given about witnesses discussing evidence in advance of testifying. A police officer accepted he had discussed the case with fellow officers, but not the evidence that was to be given. Mr Skinner's appeal against conviction was dismissed. The Court of Appeal, however, stated that the distinction between discussing the case and discussing the evidence would be hard to apply in practice, because the conversation on one basis would very quickly shade into conversation on the other. It was permissible for police officers to confer together in the making up of their notebooks immediately after events or interviews as an aid to memory, and it was the practice for witnesses to be shown their original statements to refresh their memory immediately before giving evidence. It was nevertheless wrong for a discussion between police officers as to what evidence was to be given by them to take place immediately before they or any of them went into court to give evidence.

3.07   There might be exceptional circumstances where it was necessary to discuss the evidence well in advance of the hearing to ensure what course the prosecution should take in the presentation of its evidence at trial, but that did not apply in a case where witnesses were drawn together immediately before the trial. In the Crown Court, it was a matter for the trial judge to deal with—depending on the circumstances of the case—and it was his duty to draw to the jury's attention any implications which the pre-trial discussion might have on the reliability of the evidence of the witnesses concerned. Similar principles will clearly apply to trials in the magistrates' court.

Enforcing attendance: production of documents

3.08   The attendance of witnesses and the production of documents may be secured by witness summons. Under the Magistrates' Courts Act 1980 s.97, application for a witness summons may be made without oath, but an oath is necessary for a warrant; a reasonable sum must be tendered to the witness for costs and expenses when he is served with the summons. The effect of s.97(2B) and (2C) is to enable a justice to refuse to issue a witness summons in relation to a summary trial if the application is not made as soon as reasonably practicable after the defendant has pleaded not guilty.

Guidance to justices on the issue of witness summonses was given by the Divisional Court in *R. v Peterborough Magistrates' Court Ex p. Willis* (1987) 151 J.P. 785. In an application under s.97 in order to determine whether a witness was likely to be able to give material evidence, the justices had to inquire into the nature of the evidence the witness could give, and whether it was material. See also the decision of *R. v Pollard and Mildenhall JJ. Ex p. Graham*, January 21, 1987, unreported; and the article at 151 J.P.N. 644.

3.09 A witness summons had been issued to secure the attendance of a defence witness to a charge of criminal damage. When the witness failed to attend, the defence solicitor applied for a witness warrant and for the proceedings to be adjourned. The justices refused those applications and the resulting judicial review proceedings are reported at *R. v Nottingham JJ. Ex p. Fraser* (1995) 159 J.P. 612. The justices had taken the view that the witness had no desire to attend court, that the applicant was represented by a solicitor, that his case would be adequately presented to the court, and that further delay would be unfair to the prosecution witnesses. The trial proceeded and the defendant was convicted. It was held by the Divisional Court that the reasons given by the justices for refusing the adjournment were irrelevant. When hearing evidence on oath under s.97(3) of the Magistrates' Courts Act 1980 in relation to an application for a witness warrant, justices should inquire as to whether the witness's evidence really was critical or whether it had been put together for some other purpose.

The procedure for issuing witness summonses, including an application for a summons to produce a document, is now governed by Pt 28 of the Criminal Procedure Rules 2005 (SI 2005/384), as amended. The court can consider the issue of a summons on its own initiative. A hearing under this Part must be in private unless the court otherwise directs. A party who wants the court to issue a witness summons must apply as soon as practicable. The party applying must explain what evidence the proposed witness can give or produce, why it is likely to be material evidence, and why it would be in the interests of justice to issue a summons. The application for a witness summons may be made orally, except that an application for a summons to produce a document must be in writing in the prescribed form. The procedure for issuing an application for a summons to produce a document has been amended to take account of the criticism in *R. (on the application of B) v Combined Court at Stafford* [2006] EWHC 1645; [2007] 1 W.L.R. 1524, when medical records of a child prosecution witness had been sought. The application must be served on the proposed witness and, if the court so directs, on a person to whom the proposed evidence relates. The court must not issue a witness summons under r.28.5 (to produce a document) unless everyone served with the application has had at least 14 days in which to make representations and the court is satisfied that it has been able to take adequate account of the duties and rights, including rights of confidentiality, of the proposed witness and of any person to whom the proposed evidence relates. Rule 28.6 sets out the procedure to be followed when there are objections to the production of the document.

3.10 For an exhaustive review of the law relating to the grant of a witness summons and the relationship between the judicial act of issuing such a summons and the evidence which such a summons seeks to adduce, see the judgment of Lord Taylor C.J. in the House of Lords' decision in *R. v Derby Magistrates' Court Ex p. B* [1996] A.C. 487.

The Divisional Court gave comprehensive guidance about how magistrates should approach the test of materiality (in relation to the production of documents) laid down in s.97 of the Magistrates' Courts Act 1980 in *R. v Reading JJ. Ex p. Berkshire County Council* [1996] 1 Cr. App. R. 239. To fulfil that criterion:

(a) documents must not only be relevant to the issues arising in the criminal proceedings, but also admissible as such in evidence;

(b) documents desired merely for the purpose of possible cross-examination are not admissible in evidence and therefore are not material for the purposes of s.97;

(c) whoever applies for the production of documents must satisfy the justices that the documents are "likely to be material" in the above sense, "likelihood" for this purpose involving a real possibility, although not necessarily a probability;

(d) this procedure must also not be used as a disguised attempt to obtain discovery.

3.11   The mandatory nature of s.97(1) of the Magistrates' Courts Act 1980 was illustrated in *R. v Highbury Corner Magistrates' Court Ex p. Deering* (1997) 161 J.P. 138. A defendant in criminal proceedings wished to call a nine-year-old boy as a witness of fact. He applied to a magistrate for a witness summons. The magistrate found that the boy was likely to be able to give material evidence and would not attend voluntarily. Nevertheless, the summons was refused because the magistrate considered that the obligation to attend court would be detrimental to the boy's welfare and that that factor outweighed the interests of the defendant. The defendant applied for judicial review and the court held that once the criteria for a witness summons contained in s.97(1) of the Magistrates' Courts Act 1980 had been made out, there was no discretion to refuse the issue of the witness summons. It was for the court of trial to balance the harm to the defendant and the interests of a child. The appropriate time for that would usually be when it was desired to call the child. (Note that since the test for the issue of a witness summons has been changed from whether the witness would not attend voluntarily to whether it is in the interests of justice to issue the summons, it is arguable that a different conclusion is now possible.)

Similarly, *Fearnley v DPP* [2005] EWHC 1393; (2005) 169 J.P. 450 was a case where the defence was seeking to call into question one of the types of device used for measuring the level of alcohol in breath. On the first day of a case listed for two days, the defence applied for a witness summons for a Forensic Science Service adviser which was not opposed. It was clear that the witness could give material evidence and would not attend voluntarily. However, the court considered that the calling of the witness was likely to extend the length of the trial and declined the application. The decision was overturned on appeal. It appeared likely that the witness could have attended on the second day of the trial. If that was not possible, the court may have needed to have considered whether to refuse to grant any application for an adjournment but it was not right to refuse the witness summons once the criteria were shown to exist. (See, however, the comment to *Deering* above.)

3.12   Any witness may be committed for up to one month and/or fined up to £2,500 if he refuses to be sworn, give evidence or produce a document, whether he attends on summons or not. Witness process granted when a witness is in England or Wales may be enforced by warrant in any other part of the British Isles under the Magistrates' Courts Act 1980 ss.125 and 126, if he goes there. The attendance of a witness in prison may be obtained by Home Office order (Prison Act 1952 s.22).

Where documents are in the defendant's possession, he cannot be ordered to produce them, but should be given notice to produce them. If he has been given such notice and fails to produce them in court, secondary evidence may be given of their contents. Notice is unnecessary where the summons by its very character puts the accused on notice that a document will be required, e.g. the certificate of insurance on a charge of uninsured driving (*Williams v Russell* (1933) 97 J.P. 128).

Hearsay

The current form of committal prohibits the giving of oral testimony at committal proceedings and ss.5A–5F of the Magistrates' Courts Act 1980 specify the types of evidence which are admissible in committal proceedings. These are written statements, depositions, documentary hearsay and other documents. A magistrate will no longer attend at the bedside of a dangerously ill witness, but that witness will give a witness statement in the usual form, with the usual caution signed by him, or read over to him and signed on his behalf. That statement will form part of the committal bundle. In the case of documentary hearsay, however, the prosecutor is obliged by virtue of s.5D(1)–(4) before the committal proceedings begin to notify the magistrates' court and each of the other parties to the proceedings that he believes that: **3.13**

    (a) the statement might by virtue of what are now ss.116 and 117 of the Criminal Justice Act 2003 be admissible in evidence if the case came to trial; and

    (b) the statement would not be admissible as evidence otherwise than by virtue of what are now ss.116 and 117 of the Criminal Justice Act 2003 if the case came to trial.

The Criminal Justice Act 2003 radically changed the evidential position of hearsay. The previous rule was exclusionary. Now a statement not made in oral evidence in the proceedings is admissible as evidence of the matter stated in the circumstances provided by the Act. A statement is any representation of fact or opinion made by a person by whatever means. If a statement is not hearsay (but is relevant) then it is in principle admissible. If it is hearsay, then the exceptions provided by the Act are sufficiently wide that most relevant hearsay can be admitted either as of right (under ss.116 and 117) or in the interests of justice (s.114). Where it would be unfair to admit hearsay evidence, then the provisions of s.78 of the Police and Criminal Evidence Act 1984 continue to apply. In the Crown Court there is the additional safeguard of s.125, which is the power to stop the case where the hearsay evidence is unconvincing. **3.14**

The courts have shown themselves increasingly prepared to allow the finders of fact, magistrates or jury, to assess for themselves the appropriate weight to place on hearsay evidence. It is therefore essential that the court should be alert to the potential weaknesses of hearsay evidence, the quality of which cannot be tested.

3.15   Often what people say or write is not hearsay, because the purpose is not to cause another person to believe the matter. In those circumstances the statement, if relevant, will be admissible. For example an inquiry as to the availability of drugs was held not to be hearsay in *R. v K* [2007] EWCA Crim 3150; [2007] All E.R. (D.) 48. Similarly the contents of a personal diary, not intended to be read by anyone else, were not hearsay (*R. v N* [2006] EWCA Crim 3309; [2006] All E.R. (D.) 224).

     Where a statement is hearsay, and the identity of the witness is known but he or she is unavailable (dead, unfit, outside the United Kingdom or cannot be found), then the statement is admissible under s.116. Where the witness is in fear the statement is admissible if the court considers that it ought to be admitted in the interests of justice (s.116(4)). Statements produced in the course of a business or trade are potentially admissible under s.117.

3.16   The general rule is that a statement made by a person in a document made or received in the course of trade, etc., or by a person in their capacity as a holder of a paid or unpaid office shall be admissible in criminal proceedings as evidence of any fact of which direct oral evidence by him would be admissible. Where the statement was prepared for the purposes of criminal proceedings, one of the following conditions must be satisfied: that the person who provided the information contained in the statement must be dead or, by reason of his bodily or mental condition, be unfit to attend court; or, that that person is outside the United Kingdom and it is not reasonably practicable to secure his attendance; or, that all reasonable steps have been taken to find that person but he cannot be found; or, that that person will not give oral evidence through fear; or, that that person cannot reasonably be expected (having regard to the time that has elapsed since he made the statement and to all the circumstances) to have any recollection of the matters dealt with in the statement: s.117(4) and (5) and s.116(2).

     By s.116(2), "fear" is to be widely construed. It includes fear of the death of or injury to another person as well as to the person directly concerned. It also includes fear of financial loss. The effect of the fear may be to prevent the person giving evidence at all in the proceedings, to stop him from continuing to give evidence after he has started or to stop him just from giving evidence of the subject-matter of the statement. The court must give leave for the evidence to be given by statement and that leave will only be given where the court considers that the interests of justice require it (s.116(4)). Four factors are listed to which the court must have regard in making that decision. Where the criterion is that the person is not prepared to give evidence on the issue in question through fear, a defendant cannot complain that he has been deprived of a fair trial because the witness was not available for cross-examination: *R. v Sellick* [2005] EWCA Crim 651; [2005] 1 W.L.R. 3257. It was the defendant who had deprived himself of his right to examine the witness where that witness was prevented from giving evidence through fear. There were other procedures in place to offset the disadvantages to the defendant.

3.17   Note also s.116(5) which prevents a person using the benefits of this provision where they themselves have caused the criteria on which they are seeking to rely.

     The defendant in *R. (on the application of the Crown Prosecution Service) v Uxbridge Magistrates* [2007] EWHC 205; (2007) 171 J.P. 279 was charged with actual bodily harm on his wife. She failed to attend to give evidence on the day of his trial. His solicitor told the court and the CPS that she had been sectioned under the Mental Health Act 1983 and admitted to hospital. Subsequent inquiries by the Crown confirmed that, and in those circumstances an adjournment was sought but refused by the bench. Thereafter the CPS sought to admit the evidence of the complainant under the hearsay provisions of the Criminal Justice Act 2003 s.116, on the grounds that the complainant was unfit to be a witness because of her mental condition. That application was also opposed by the defence and also refused. The CPS offered no evidence and the defendant was acquitted. On appeal the CPS contended that the decision of the magistrates' court to refuse to adjourn the trial and to refuse to admit the complainant's evidence as hearsay evidence was perverse and wrong in law. The Divisional Court decided that the decision to refuse an adjournment was within the wide discretion accorded to the justices but added "[i]f, on the other hand, the inevitable result of the adjournment had been that the prosecution must collapse without further ado, I would have taken a different view because there was a strong public interest in the prosecution continuing and no specific prejudice to the defendant" ([2007] EWHC 205 at [8], per David Clarke J.). However, the decision to refuse the hearsay application was held to be plainly wrong. Section 116 of the 2003 Act provides specifically for the admission of a written statement of a witness unavailable through ill health. On such an application the court must consider the matters set out in s.116(4) and (it was said, although there is no statutory requirement to do so) the interests of justice. The court pointed out that the defendant was able to challenge the contents of the statement by giving evidence, and his ability to do that was not hampered.

In *R. v Gyima* [2007] EWCA Crim 429; [2007] Crim. L.R. 89 the witness was **3.18** a child and was abroad. The CPS had made concerted efforts to ensure his attendance but had been unable to do so because the witness's parents were uncooperative. The court confirmed that the correct question is whether it is reasonably practicable to secure attendance, not whether it is reasonably practicable for the witness to attend. This case is also interesting for the dismissal by the Court of Appeal of the argument that to receive evidence under s.116 is unfair because there was no opportunity to cross-examine the witness. See now *Al-Khawaja v United Kingdom* and *R. v Horncastle* mentioned at § 3.21 below.

Hearsay evidence is admissible where all parties agree to it being admissible, and this agreement can be implied by the lack of objection (*Williams v VOSA* [2008] EWHC 849; (2008) 172 J.P. 328). Care should be taken where the defendant is unrepresented.

A statement not made in oral evidence is also admissible if the court is satisfied that it is in the interests of justice for it to be admissible (s.114(1)(d)). The court must have regard to a number of factors in s.114 before exercising its judgment that it is in the interests of justice to admit hearsay under this section (in distinction to the automatic admissibility elsewhere in the Act). When the Crown had made insufficient arrangements to secure the attendance of a witness at court, that witness's statement could nevertheless have been admitted in the interests of justice as it was not really in dispute, even if the defence did not agree to it being read. (In *R. v Adams* [2007] EWCA Crim 3025; [2008] 1 Cr. App. Rep. 35 (p.430), the absent witness gave the only evidence that the defendant was in possession of drugs, but the issue in the case was intention to supply: it was not the defendant's case that he was not in possession.)

In *Boguslaw Sak v Crown Prosecution Service* [2007] EWHC 2886; (2008) **3.19**

172 J.P. 89 the point was taken further. Mr Sak was a Polish national who was convicted of driving whilst unfit. He failed to provide a roadside breath sample, and at the police station was examined by a doctor who concluded that he displayed evidence of intoxication and impaired reaction time. Shortly before the trial date the prosecutor applied to vacate the trial because the doctor was unable to attend court as he could not arrange locum cover for his surgery. That application was successfully opposed by the solicitor acting for the appellant. The prosecutor then successfully applied for the doctor's evidence to be read in accordance with the provisions of s.114 of the Criminal Justice Act 2003. The defendant was convicted and appealed to the Divisional Court against the decision to admit the doctor's statement. It was argued that the evidence of the doctor went to the core of the charge faced by the appellant. The appellant was at a significant disability due to his poor command of English, and the credibility of the doctor's evidence relied not upon his standing as a witness, but on his assessment of the appellant's ability to understand the questions put to him in the tasks asked of him. It was, said the defence, very important that they had the opportunity to cross-examine the witness. The appeal was unsuccessful. It was held that the justices had given proper consideration to the factors set out in s.114 and any other relevant factors. This was not a failed s.116 application and therefore not a case of the prosecution getting around those provisions. With regard to prejudice to the appellant, the issues in the case could be dealt with in a number of ways, including the appellant giving evidence himself of what took place during the examination by the doctor. The Divisional Court said, "It should be noted that the defence can no longer assume, as in the practice of the old days, that the prosecution's unsuccessful application for an adjournment to secure the attendance of an important witness will necessarily mean that the case will not proceed. Such considerations should influence the approach of the defence when considering whether to oppose any such application" ([2007] EWHC 2886 at [18], per Dobbs J.). The observations in the case of *McEwan v DPP* [2007] EWHC 740; (2007) 171 J.P. 308 (that it would be an exceptional case for s.114(d) to be relied upon to rescue the prosecution from the consequences of its own failures) were distinguished. In that case the prosecution had made many mistakes and had been guilty of many failures.

3.20   In practical terms, perhaps the most significant change is that previous inconsistent statements (s.119) and consistent statements (s.120) can be admitted as proof of any matter stated. Thus, even if a witness resiles from or retracts his statement at trial, the magistrates or jury are entitled to decide that the original statement was true (*R. v Joyce and Joyce* [2005] EWCA Crim 1785; [2005] All E.R. (D) 309).

> "In the light of the new statutory provisions in relation to hearsay, in our judgment, it would have been an affront to the administration of justice, on a trial for offences based on this terrifying conduct, if the jury had not been permitted by the judge to evaluate, separately and together, the quality of the three witnesses' oral evidence and to be able to rely, if they saw fit, on the terms of their original statements." ([2005] EWCA Crim 1785 at [27], per Rose L.J.)

The full significance of s.120 may not yet be grasped by all advocates, especially in the magistrates' court. Previous consistent statements are potentially more than just memory-refreshing documents, but can be evidence when the witness cannot reasonably be expected to remember the matters in the statement. A statement that consists of a complaint about an offence can be admissible, in effect to support evidence of recent complaint about any offence. The witness must confirm at trial that he made the earlier statement and that to the best of his belief it is true (s.120(4)).

The prosecution is required to give notice of hearsay evidence (in the magistrates' court at the same time as they purport to comply with the disclosure provisions, and the defendant within 14 days thereafter). However, the court can dispense with the requirement for notice. The Criminal Procedure Rules 2005 apply.

The compatibility of the hearsay provisions with art.6(3) of the European **3.21** Convention on Human Rights (right to a fair trial) has been disputed for some time. The position has been considered by the domestic courts on a number of occasions, e.g. by the Court of Appeal in *R. v Sellick* [2005] EWCA Crim 651; [2005] 1 W.L.R. 3257. In that case the defendants were convicted of murder substantially on hearsay evidence under the pre-2003 provisions. The reasoning used by the Court of Appeal was questioned by the European Court of Human Rights in *Al-Khawaja v United Kingdom* (Application Nos 26766/05 and 22228/06) [2009] All E. R. (D) 132; [2009] Crim. L.R. 352. However, in *R. v Horncastle* [2009] EWCA Crim 964; [2009] All E. R. (D.) 211, the Court of Appeal determined that there was nothing in the judgment of the European Court of Human Rights in *Al-Khawaja* considered in the light of a full analysis of the 2003 Act which led to the conclusion that the Court of Appeal had been wrong in the result it had reached in a number of its decisions in relation to art.6 and art.6(3)(d). Where the hearsay evidence was demonstrably reliable, or its reliability could properly be tested and assessed, the rights of the defence were respected and the trial was fair.

In *R. v Ashford and Tenterden JJ. Ex p. Hilden* [1993] Q.B. 555, it was held that a magistrate could satisfy herself that the witness was not giving evidence through fear by her own observation of the witness's demeanor.

In magistrates' courts the evidence of a witness who has already given evi- **3.22** dence in proceedings on the same issue may be read at the second trial if he is too ill to attend, e.g. where careless driving is tried again because the magistrates could not agree (see *Cross and Tapper on Evidence*). A transcript of evidence of a witness is admissible in evidence in a retrial of a defendant on the named charge when the witness is too ill to travel to court on the second trial (*R. v Thompson* [1982] 2 W.L.R. 603 CA). In the judgment Dunn L.J. referred with approval to statements in *Cross and Tapper on Evidence* (such evidence admissible if the witness was unable to attend through death or illness) and *Phipson on Evidence* (incapable of being called). See also *R. v Lockley* [1995] 2 Cr. App. R. 554 and *Bishop v Hosier*, Guardian, October 11, 1962. On a retrial ordered by the Court of Appeal under the Criminal Appeal Act 1968 evidence may, in the circumstances given in Sch.2, be read from the transcript.

Witnesses abroad

Although the attendance of witnesses from Scotland and Northern Ireland can **3.23** be secured by process, there is no mechanism to secure the attendance of witnesses from the Channel Islands in that way. Witness summonses cannot be served in the Bailiwicks (nor can any summonses) but warrants can be backed and executed (Magistrates' Courts Act 1980 s.126). The greater availability of video links may assist.

Spouses

3.24   The spouse of an accused is competent to give evidence for the prosecution and a co-accused except in those cases when the husband and wife are jointly charged. Moreover, the spouse is competent and compellable to give evidence for the accused. A spouse is not compellable to give evidence for the prosecution against the spouse but will be compellable for or against a co-accused by s.80(2A) of the Police and Criminal Evidence Act 1984. Section 80(3) details the offences, etc., where the spouse is compellable:

(1) assault on, or injury or threat of injury to, the spouse giving evidence or to a person who appears to the court to have been under 16 at the material time;

(2) a sexual offence—see s.80(7)—on a person who appears to the court to have been under 16 at the material time;

(3) attempt or conspiracy to commit, or aiding, abetting, counselling, procuring or inciting any of the above offences.

Section 80(5) deals with the position where the parties have been divorced, in that it provides, "a person who has been but is no longer married to the accused shall be competent and compellable to give evidence as if that person and the accused had never been married". This means that spouses who are separated are still to be treated as spouses for the purposes of the section as a whole. Section 80A retains the well-established rule that the failure of the wife or husband of the accused to give evidence shall not be made the subject of any comment by the prosecution.

3.25   In *R. v Pearce* [2001] EWCA Crim 2834; [2002] 1 W.L.R. 1553, the court was asked to consider whether the European Convention on Human Rights required a court to treat co-habitees and children as competent but not compellable for the prosecution in the same way as a spouse. The defendant was charged with murder of his brother and the prosecution relied on the evidence of the defendant's co-habitee and a child of the relationship. The prosecution successfully sought to have these witnesses treated as hostile and the defendant was convicted. He appealed on the grounds that art.8 of the Convention required the protection against compellability to be extended to these two witnesses. The appeal was dismissed. The extent of the exemption from compellability was clearly defined by statute and could not be extended to embrace a relationship to which it did not apply. The interests of the family need to be weighed against the interests of the community at large; any interference with art.8 was "necessary … for the prevention of … crime" which were words capable of being applied to proceedings after a crime was committed.

Bad character

3.26   The bad character provisions of the Criminal Justice Act 2003 radically changed the circumstances in which bad character can be received as evidence.

> "The 2003 Act completely reverses the pre-existing general rule. Evidence of bad character is now admissible if it satisfies certain criteria (see s.101(1)) and the approach is no longer one of inadmissibility subject to exceptions." (*R. v Somanthan*, one of the cases conjoined in the appeal of *R. v Weir* [2005] EWCA Crim 2866; [2006] 1 W.L.R. 1885 at [35])

Character, including previous convictions, can provide circumstantial evidence that, together with other evidence, points to the guilt or innocence of the defendant. Bad character is misconduct, or a disposition towards misconduct, and means the commission of an offence or other reprehensible behaviour (s.112(1)). Evidence of misconduct which "has to do with the alleged facts" of the offence charged, is excluded from the definition of bad character in s.98, and is therefore admissible if relevant.

In some circumstances the parties agree the introduction of the evidence (s.101(1)(a)) or the evidence is adduced by the defendant himself (s.101(1)(b)). In other circumstances bad character evidence is only admissible with the leave of the court (usually on notice) through s.100 or a s.101 gateway. In practice, probably the most frequent route for admissibility is s.101(1)(g) where the defendant attacks the character of another, in interview or at trial, e.g. by saying the witness attacked him first (as in the defence of self-defence) or is lying. Another frequent route to admissibility is where the evidence is relevant to an important matter in issue (s.101(1)(d)). This includes, but is not confined to, propensity. The relevance of bad character evidence is often not clear until the trial is in progress. Although there is provision in the magistrates' court for a pre-trial binding ruling, such rulings run the risk of being decided on an incorrect assumption of what the matter in issue at trial would be (see *R. v Bullen* [2008] EWCA 4; [2008] 2 Cr. App. R. 25(p.364)). When a defendant denies driving whilst disqualified, the fact that he has similar previous convictions may be relevant if the issue at trial is whether he was driving, but not if the only issue is whether he was in fact disqualified at the material time. Similarly, in a trial for being in charge of a motor vehicle while the proportion of alcohol exceeds the limit, a recent drink/drive conviction may be highly relevant if the defence is the statutory defence that there was no likelihood of him driving while over the limit, but irrelevant if the issue is mistaken identity, or a procedural failure in obtaining the sample. A single conviction for driving while the proportion of alcohol in the blood exceeds the limit would be relevant if the issue is the defendant's invincible repugnance of needles, but not as to the issue of propensity.

In *R. v McKenzie (Mark Anthony)* [2008] EWCA Crim 758; [2008] R.T.R. 22   **3.27** the Court of Appeal advised caution in admitting in an allegation of dangerous driving evidence that the defendant had driven in an aggressive and impatient manner in the past, under s.101(1)(d) of the Criminal Justice Act 2003. In this case, Mr McKenzie was convicted of causing death by dangerous driving on what the Court of Appeal said was formidable evidence. He had pleaded guilty before the jury to careless driving, but denied that he was guilty of dangerous driving. The Crown's case was that the defendant without warning pulled right across the path of an oncoming motor cyclist, with fatal consequences. The jury also heard evidence from two witnesses (a driving instructor and a former girlfriend) that some years earlier the defendant's driving was generally aggressive, risky, or speedy. None of these incidents resulted in a criminal prosecution or conviction. "Many judges would have taken the view that even if such evidence was technically capable of being admitted under the bad character provisions of the Act, they would not admit it because of the risk of the trial and the summing up becoming unduly complicated by collateral issues." However, the court did not consider that it was wrong in principle to conclude that the evidence could be regarded as tending to show that the defendant had a propensity to drive in an aggressive and impatient matter which involved taking dangerous risks (so as to fall within s.103) and that the evidence was relevant to an important matter in issue between the parties, that is whether the prosecution's version of the facts resulting in a fatal accident was to be accepted (so as to be admissible under s.101(1)(d)). Even so, the Court of Appeal said that for several reasons the jury had to be very cautious before using evidence about his driving on other occasions in deciding whether he was guilty of the offences charged. First, they had to be sure that the appellant had taken dangerous risks on the previous occasions. Next, they had to consider whether they could in fairness also be sure that at the time of the fatal accident in April 2006 the appellant was a person who characteristically took dangerous risks when driving. Finally, if the jury were sure that the appellant was someone who had a habit of taking dangerous risks when driving, they must not jump to the conclusion that he was therefore guilty of the offences charged. The evidence of his bad driving was at the most background material which the jury could take into account when assessing the credibility of the direct evidence about a person's driving on the occasion of the fatal accident.

3.28   It is submitted that the best practice is to decide admissibility within the trial process, when the issues are clear. In *R. v Edward Gyima* [2007] EWCA Crim 429; [2007] Crim. L.R. 89, it was said that where it appeared that there might be weaknesses in the prosecution case, it was important to delay the ruling on the admissibility of a defendant's previous convictions until the whole of the prosecution evidence had been adduced:

> "We can entirely understand the practical reason for inviting a judge at the outset of a trial to rule whether a defendant's previous convictions are or are not admissible. There are plainly good reasons for this for the purposes of the administration of justice where there is a prospect that, once the ruling to admit the convictions is made, the defendant will plead guilty. However, in our judgment judges and practitioners should be astute to recognise that there may be cases where it is important to defer such a ruling until the whole of the evidence of the prosecution has been adduced." ([2007] EWCA Crim 429; [2007] Crim. L.R. 89 at [40])

There is no unfairness in following this procedure in the magistrates' court.

> "Where an application is made to adduce bad character evidence before a magistrates' court, the justices will, of necessity, hear details of the conviction in order to rule on the application. If the application fails they will put the conviction out of their mind when they hear the case. The fact that they know the details of previous convictions does not disqualify them from discharging their role as fact finders in the trial." (*R. (on the application of Robinson) v Sutton Coldfield Magistrates' Court* [2006] EWHC 307; [2006] 2 Cr. App. R. 13 (p.208) at [21])

3.29   If a binding ruling is made it cannot be reversed, even if a subsequent bench would have reached a different conclusion, without there being some compelling reason, such as changed circumstances or fresh evidence (*R. (on the application of Crown Prosecution Service) v Gloucester JJ.* [2008] EWHC 1488; (2008) 172 J.P. 506).

The question sometimes arises as to whether the Crown can rely simply on the fact of conviction or must prove the facts underlying the conviction. In the leading case of *R. v Hanson* [2005] EWCA Crim 824; [2005] 2 Cr. App. R. 21 (p.299) the Court of Appeal emphasised that the Crown had to decide, when notice was given of the application, whether it proposed to rely simply upon the fact of a previous conviction or also upon its circumstances. The fact of a conviction might suffice where the circumstances of the offence were sufficiently apparent from its description to justify a finding that it might establish propensity and that the requirements of ss.101(3) and 103(3) could be satisfied. In *R. v Lamaletie* [2008] EWCA Crim 314; (2008) 172 J.P. 249, the court emphasised that there was no rule that full details were necessary in every case where the Crown sought to rely on previous convictions as demonstrating propensity. In that case a mere list of convictions was sufficient because what was relevant was "character" in a broad general sense (the convictions were admissible because Mr Lamaletie's defence was that the person he had assaulted was in fact the aggressor).

Guidance on proving disputed convictions was given in *Pattison v DPP* [2005] EWHC 2938; [2006] R.T.R. 13, reviewing previous authorities, including *R. v Derwentside JJ. Ex p. Heaviside* [1996] R.T.R. 384 DC and other authorities. The court held that when a person was charged with driving while disqualified, it was possible to establish a prima facie case on the basis of the consistency of the details of the accused and those of the person named on the certificate of conviction of the offender. This issue has been further considered in *R. v Burns* [2006] EWCA Crim 617; [2006] 2 Cr. App. R. 16 (p.264), *R. v Lewedon* [2006] EWCA Crim 648; [2006] 2 Cr. App. R. 19 (p.294) and in *DPP v Parker* [2006] EWHC 1270; [2006] R.T.R. 325, where the magistrates' court erred in holding that the memorandum of conviction of the driver of a stolen car did not amount to evidence on a charge against the passenger for having allowed himself to be carried. A record in the police national computer stating that a person had used a particular alias may be proved under s.117 (*R. (on the application of Pierre Wellington) v DPP* [2007] EWHC 1061; (2007) 171 J.P. 497).

A non-defendant's bad character is admissible if the parties agree to the use of **3.30** the evidence (s.100(1)(c)). If not, leave is required (s.100(4)). The test is whether the evidence is important explanatory evidence (s.101(d)) or of substantial probative value (s.100(1)(b) and (3)). Evidence of a non-defendant's bad character extends beyond simply offences which relate to his dishonesty.

Rules about the provision of notice to introduce evidence of bad character are contained in r.35 of the Criminal Procedure Rules 2005, as amended. The circumstances in which the time limit may be extended was considered in *R. (on the application of Robinson) v Sutton Coldfield Magistrates' Court* (quoted at § 3.28 above).

Disclosure of previous convictions of prosecution witnesses

A conviction may be quashed if material previous convictions of prosecution **3.31** witnesses (including "spent" convictions) are not disclosed to the defence (*R. v Paraskeva* [1983] Crim. L.R. 186). Again, a conviction was quashed in *R. v Knightsbridge Crown Court Ex p. Goonatilleke* [1985] 3 W.L.R. 574, where the main prosecution witness deliberately contrived to keep the defendant in ignorance of his bad character and had thereby denied him a valuable plank in his defence.

Expert evidence

The opinion of a witness is inadmissible unless he is an expert giving an **3.32** opinion on matters within his expertise for which he has special knowledge and experience. Taking account of information stemming from the work of others in the same field is an essential ingredient of the nature of expert evidence and is not hearsay (*R. v Abadom* [1983] 1 All E.R. 364).

In *R. v Oakley* [1979] R.T.R. 417 the Court of Appeal upheld a trial judge who admitted a police constable's opinion on theories and conclusions about the accident based upon his considerable experience and expertise in accident investigations. *R. v Oakley* was followed and applied in *R. v Murphy* [1980] R.T.R. 145.

3.33 The court may allow expert witnesses to remain in court while other evidence is given: an exception to the normal practice, discussed in *R. v Bexley JJ. Ex p. King* [1980] R.T.R. 49. The provisions of s.30 of the Criminal Justice Act 1988 should be noted. These allow for an expert report to be admissible as evidence in criminal proceedings, whether or not the person making it attends to give oral evidence in those proceedings. If it is proposed that the person making the report should not give oral evidence, the report is only to be admissible with the leave of the court. An "expert report" is defined to mean a written report by a person dealing wholly or mainly with matters on which he is (or would if living be) qualified to give expert evidence. When admitted, such a report is evidence of any fact or opinion of which the person making it could have given oral evidence. In determining whether or not to give leave, s.30(3) requires the court to have regard:

"(a) to the contents of the report;
(b) to the reasons why it is proposed that the person making the report shall not give oral evidence;
(c) to any risk, having regard in particular to whether it is likely to be possible to controvert statements in the report if the person making it does not attend to give oral evidence in the proceedings, that its admission or exclusion will result in unfairness to the accused or, if there is more than one, to any of them; and
(d) to any other circumstances that appear to the court to be relevant."

3.34 In *R. (on the application of Doughty) v Ely Magistrates' Court* [2008] EWHC 522; (2008) 172 J.P. 259 it was held that magistrates had erred in holding that a former transport police officer did not have sufficient knowledge and expertise to be an expert witness in the trial of a driver charged with speeding as they had relied on matters that went to the weight to be given to his evidence and not to his competence to appear as an expert witness. The expert in this case produced a report raising doubts about the reliability of a specific speed detection device used to provide evidence in the trial of a driver charged with speeding. The fact that he had not operated the device in question since he had been a police officer nine years previously, had not attended recent courses run by the manufacturer of the device and that he had made an error in his report as to the function of the device only went to the weight to be given to his evidence, and not to his competence to appear as an expert witness.

Evidence by the defendant

3.35 In a criminal case a defendant has two choices: to give evidence himself on oath or affirmation when he can be cross-examined (*R. v Paul*; *R. v McFarlane* [1920] 2 K.B. 183); or to say nothing (Criminal Evidence Act 1898 s.1). The defendant's right to remain silent is substantially modified by the provisions of ss.34–39 of the Criminal Justice and Public Order Act 1994. In broad outline only, where before he was charged a defendant on being questioned under caution failed to mention any fact relied on in his defence, or on being charged, etc., failed to mention any such fact, the court may draw such inferences from the failure as appear proper.

A similar provision applies when he has chosen to remain silent at his trial. The court/jury may draw such inferences as appear proper from the failure of the defendant to give evidence or his refusal, without good cause, to answer any question. Similar statutory provisions deal with the situation where he has failed to account for objects, substances or marks, or for his presence at a particular place.

The correct approach when considering whether to draw an adverse inference **3.36** from a defendant's failure to mention a fact relied on in his defence, under the Criminal Justice and Public Order Act 1994 s.34, is to consider: (1) if the defendant has relied in his defence on a fact which he could reasonably have been expected to mention in interview, but did not; (2) if he has, what his explanation is for not having mentioned it, and (3) if that explanation is not a reasonable one, whether the proper inference to be drawn is that he is guilty: *T v DPP* [2007] EWHC 1793; (2007) 171 J.P. 605.

The Youth Justice and Criminal Evidence Act 1999 affects the giving of evidence by a defendant. Section 58 of the 1999 Act modifies ss.34 and 36–38 of the Criminal Justice and Public Order Act 1994. These amendments protect a defendant at an "authorised place of detention" (defined in a new s.38(2A) of the 1994 Act as inserted by s.58(5) of the 1999 Act) who has not been allowed to consult a solicitor.

The 1994 Act also provides for an accused person to be prevented from cross- **3.37** examining in person certain witnesses. This protection is primarily aimed at those who witness the commission of specified offences or a child who is a witness in relation to such an offence. The specified offences are primarily sexual offences, but also included are any offences that involve an assault on, or injury, or threat of injury to, any person. It is certainly possible that some road traffic offences will result in injury; it remains to be seen whether the courts will interpret the provision to include such offences rather than simply those which of necessity involve injury in order to be committed. The principle behind the provision is to protect those who can be made to suffer traumatic events again at the instance of an accused who undertakes questioning in person and it is perhaps unlikely that this will happen in road traffic offences except possibly in instances where death or serious injury is caused by dangerous or careless driving. Legal representation will be arranged to conduct the cross-examination on behalf of the accused: 1994 Act s.38. Even where prohibition is not automatic, the court may prevent the accused from cross-examining a witness in person where it appears that the quality of evidence is likely to be diminished if such cross-examination takes place, would be improved if the accused were prevented from cross-examining and it would not be contrary to the interests of justice to make such a prohibition: 1994 Act s.36.

Section 79 of the Police and Criminal Evidence Act 1984 provides that the de- **3.38** fendant, if giving evidence, must be called before other defence witnesses as to facts unless the court in its discretion directs otherwise. The statute only refers to being *called*. This is not the same as *giving* all the evidence first. The statute only refers to factual evidence and does not prevent character evidence or expert evidence as to opinion being given first.

Trial within a trial

3.39   In a case before a judge and jury, the jury are asked to leave the court while an issue is tried on a matter with which the jury at that stage has no concern, such as the admissibility of evidence, because if the evidence is held to be inadmissible the jury would hear matters which they had no business to hear. In such a case admissions made in a voir dire should not be used against a defendant in the trial (*R. v Brophy* [1981] 2 All E.R. 705 HL). Issues of excessive delay may well be best determined at the outset of the trial. Where, however, the abuse of the court's process is alleged to stem from the conduct of the prosecution, there is no general duty on a judge to conduct a pre-trial inquiry (*R. v Heston-Francois* [1984] 1 All E.R. 795).

   In proceedings before magistrates, there have been several important decisions on this subject; in particular the statutory provisions in s.76 of the Police and Criminal Evidence Act 1984 have been interpreted and the leading case is *R. v Liverpool Juvenile Court Ex p. R* [1987] 2 All E.R. 668. The ruling of Russell L.J. in the Liverpool case repays careful attention, especially for the five points of guidance he laid down in his judgment:

(1) the effect of s.76(2) was that in summary proceedings justices must now hold a trial within a trial if it were presented to them by the defence that a confession had or might have been obtained by either of the improper processes appearing in s.76(2);

(2) in such a trial within a trial the defendant might give evidence confined to the question of admissibility and the justices would not then be concerned with the truth or otherwise of the confession;

(3) therefore the defendant was entitled to a ruling on the admissibility of a confession before or at the end of the prosecution case;

(4) a discretion remained in the defendant as to the stage at which to attack the alleged confession—a trial within a trial would only take place before the close of the prosecution case if it were represented to the court that the confession was or might have been improperly obtained. If no such representation was made the defendant was at liberty to raise admissibility or weight of the confession at any subsequent stage of the trial;

(5) it should never be necessary to call the prosecution evidence relating to the obtaining of a confession twice.

3.40   The Divisional Court held in *R. v Oxford JJ. Ex p. Berry* [1987] 1 All E.R. 1244 that judicial review would lie to quash committal proceedings where justices had refused to entertain an inquiry under s.76(2) into the circumstances of the obtaining of a confession from the defendant, although it was said that it would be rare that the court would quash on that ground alone.

   In *R. v Fulling* [1987] 2 All E.R. 65 the Court of Appeal decided that for the purpose of s.76(2) "oppression" should be given its ordinary dictionary meaning of "exercise of authority or power in a burdensome, harsh, or wrongful manner; unjust or cruel treatment of subjects, inferiors, etc; the imposition of unreasonable or unjust burdens".

Witness statements

In proceedings for committal for trial, no oral evidence can be adduced. The **3.41** defence may make a submission "on the papers", i.e. on the statements and depositions etc., contained in the committal bundle, that there is not sufficient evidence to put the defendant on trial for a proposed charge or charges. Sections 5A–5F of the Magistrates' Courts Act 1980 deal with the types of evidence that are admissible at committal proceedings. For example, s.5B of the 1980 Act prescribes what a written statement must contain. It must purport to be signed by the person making it, it must contain a declaration by that person to the effect that it is true to the best of his knowledge and belief and that he made the statement knowing that, if it were tendered in evidence, he would be liable to prosecution if he wilfully stated in it anything which he knew to be false or did not believe to be true; before the statement is tendered in evidence, a copy of the statement is given, by or on behalf of the prosecutor, to each of the other parties to the proceedings.

In *Chapman v Ingleton* (1973) 137 J.P. 204 it was held that while it was vital for a statement under s.9 of the Criminal Justice Act 1967 to contain the required declaration as to its truth, etc., it did not matter whether the declaration appeared at the head or foot of the statement. In *R. (on the application of Wooldridge) v DPP* [2003] EWHC 1663, a statement tendered under s.9 had been signed after the declaration at the top of the statement but had not been signed at the end. The justices' decision that the statement was admissible was upheld on appeal. It would seem that a child under 10 years of age cannot make such a statement since a child under 10 is not liable to prosecution. Statements would appear to fall within the definition of "instruments" in the Forgery and Counterfeiting Act 1981. The preparation or use of a false statement therefore may constitute an offence under that Act. This view is supported by the decision in *Att Gen's Reference No.1 of 2000* [2001] Crim. L.R. 127 where it was confirmed that a falsified tachograph record was an instrument within the meaning of the 1981 Act. However, see the commentary to the case report which argues powerfully that the decision by which the Court of Appeal considered itself bound was wrongly decided. The use of s.9 statements to obviate the need for police officers to attend in minor cases was recommended in Home Office circular 56/81.

Statements generally

Sections 76 and 77 of the Police and Criminal Evidence Act 1984 provide that **3.42** a confession and wholly or partly adverse admissions (see the definition in s.82(1)) are admissible unless obtained by oppression or in consequence of anything said or done which is likely in the circumstances existing at the time to render them unreliable. If any question of admissibility arises the burden of proof rests on the prosecution to show beyond reasonable doubt that the confession or admission was not so obtained (s.76(2)). Reference may be necessary to the codes of practice.

Facts discovered through inadmissible confessions or admissions may be given in evidence (s.76(4)) but not the method of discovery unless given by the defendant or on his behalf (s.76(5) and (6)). Inadmissible confessions and admissions may be used to show modes of expression used by the defendant (s.76(4)(b)).

Reference should be made to PACE Code C which among other matters deals **3.43** with questioning, cautioning before or during interview, and interviewing. It provides for youths and others at special risk because of mental incapacity, English language difficulties or other disability. Annexes to Code C deal with the conduct of searches, delay in notifying arrest or allowing access to legal advice and written statements under caution.

The PACE codes are admissible in evidence in criminal and civil proceedings and may be taken into account where relevant (s.67(11)). The codes apply to police officers (s.66), and other persons charged with a duty to investigate offences or charge offenders are required in carrying out that duty to have regard to the relevant part of any code (s.67(9A)). The codes therefore apply to Department for Transport examiners and government officers investigating excise offences, but not to persons carrying out an investigation voluntarily. A breach of a code does not of itself render a person liable to civil or criminal proceedings (s.67(10)) but does render a police officer liable to disciplinary proceedings, subject to certain double jeopardy provisions in s.104.

3.44   The defendant's admission that he was driving will suffice to show that he was the driver. Statements by the defendant to the police are admissible in evidence without a caution having been administered and a constable may properly ask a person if he was driving on a particular occasion (*Hennell v Cuthbert* [1962] Crim. L.R. 104). The person's answers will be admissible provided that they were obtained without unfairness (*Berry v Robson* (1964) 108 S.J. 259). Similarly, in *Dilks v Tilley* [1979] R.T.R. 459 justices were held to be wrong in refusing to admit in evidence the answers of the defendant to a constable who had arrived at the scene of an accident and had simply asked the defendant what had happened. The constable at that stage was simply asking for information and could not be thought to have reasonable grounds for suspecting the defendant had committed an offence and thus to be required to administer a caution. But if the defendant has been charged with or informed that he may be prosecuted for an offence or the constable has reasonable grounds for suspecting that he may have committed an offence, then he should first be cautioned. In *Sneyd v DPP* [2006] EWHC 560; [2007] R.T.R. 6, a police officer stopped the appellant's vehicle after he had seen the motorist leaving a public house car park. He did so because he suspected the appellant, who was the driver of the vehicle, had been drinking and wanted confirmation. The appellant was asked whether he had been drinking. His response was that he had consumed three pints. The justices rejected submissions by the defendant that the police were in breach of PACE Code C in failing to caution the defendant before asking him if he had been drinking. The appeal was dismissed. When the constable stopped the defendant outside the public house, though he suspected that the defendant had been drinking, that in itself was not a criminal offence, and, at the point when he asked the defendant if he had been drinking, he did not have grounds to suspect the defendant of an offence. Paragraphs 10 and 11 of PACE Code C were not engaged.

3.45   Where a statement is made without caution in circumstances where compliance with the code of practice on detention, treatment and questioning would necessitate a caution, it is for the judge or magistrates in exercise of their discretion to decide whether the statement should be admitted or not (*R. v Ovenall* [1968] 1 All E.R. 933). Reference should be made to s.67 of the Police and Criminal Evidence Act 1984, which explains the status of the code, and its admissibility in evidence. In *Miln v Cullen* 1967 S.L.T. 35, it was held that the admission of the defendant at the scene of an accident in reply to a question by a constable whether he was the driver may be allowed in evidence if there is no unfairness to him. It was said obiter in *Berry v Robson* above that the question "Are you the driver?" must be answered because of s.171 or s.172 of the 1988 Act but those sections apply only when the constable has been authorised to demand the information by or on behalf of a chief officer of police. It seems that statements made in breach of codes of practice are anyhow admissible at the court's discretion (*Hennell v Cuthbert* above). The admissibility of answers given in response to a s.172 request was considered in great detail by the Privy Council in *Brown v Stott (Procurator Fiscal, Dunfermline)* [2001] 2 All E.R. 97. The impact of the European Convention on Human Rights on the admissibility of information from a driver about his use of the vehicle was given further consideration by the court in *DPP v Wilson* [2001] EWHC Admin 198; [2002] R.T.R. 6. See also § 7.27 below.

Even though a judge or magistrate decides to admit a confession statement as voluntary, the defendant still has the right to challenge the confession statement during the course of the case. It is for the jury to decide whether the statement is true at the end of the case and if the jury consider that the statement was improperly induced it may affect their decision (*R. v McCarthy* [1980] Crim. L.R. 306). The judge or magistrates may reconsider their ruling later in the trial (*R. v Watson* [1980] Crim. L.R. 307).

3.46   The police should supply a copy of the defendant's statement to the defence on request (110 J.P. Jo. 435) and the Home Secretary has said that it is the practice of the police to supply to the solicitor of an accused person on request copies of statements made by him, unless the police think that to do so would impede the course of justice (105 S.J. 133).The police should supply to the defending solicitor, on his request, a list of the defendant's previous convictions, without waiting for the latter's permission. Abstracts of the police report of an accident will generally be supplied on payment of the appropriate charge unless a prosecution is pending. Charges are fixed, from time to time, for interviewing a police officer, for a copy of a witness's statement, a copy of a police report and for photographs.

Witnesses or prospective witnesses may be interviewed before trial by either side, whether or not they have been seen already by the other side; once the defendant has been committed for trial, the defence may still interview the prosecution witnesses but the occasions when such a course is necessary must be rare and, if there is to be an interview after committal, the prosecutor should be invited to attend (*Law Society's Gazette*, February 1963). See also 118 N.L.J. 913. By Home Office circular 82/1969 (issued with the approval of the Lord Chief Justice and the judges of the Queen's Bench Division) witnesses for the prosecution are normally, though not in all circumstances, entitled, if they so request, to be supplied with copies of any statement taken from them by the police.

3.47   An example of the Divisional Court intervening to prevent a potential injustice because of the failure of a party to call witnesses was *R. v Wellingborough Magistrates' Court Ex p. Francois* (1994) 158 J.P. 813. A summary trial was listed for a full day's hearing and the prosecution opened the case on the basis that two witnesses, whose attendance the applicant's solicitor had requested, would be called. After the three prosecution witnesses had given evidence the prosecutor indicated to the court that it was 12.40pm, that she was due to prosecute another case in another court in the afternoon and as the two witnesses did not advance the prosecution case, she would not call them, and closed the prosecution case. The applicant's solicitor objected, and after a short adjournment, the justices stated that they accepted that the prosecution case was closed, that it was for the prosecution to decide which witnesses to call to prove their case, and they wished the defence to continue. The applicant applied for judicial review of his subsequent convictions. The Divisional Court quashed the convictions and ordered a retrial of the case. The following points of principle come from the judgment of McCowan L.J.:

   (a) In a summary trial the discretion of the prosecution to call witnesses or tender them for cross-examination must be exercised in a manner which was calculated to further the interests of justice and at the same time be fair to the defence. In *Francois* there was an improper exercise of discretion by the prosecution.

   (b) Where, in a summary trial, it was shown that the prosecution had acted improperly in not calling a witness, it was open to the justices to invite the prosecution to tender the witness and, if they refused, to call the witness themselves for cross-examination by the defence.

These are clearly matters of the greatest significance for the fair conduct of summary trials.

Editing statements

3.48   The Lord Chief Justice issued a Practice Direction on the subject of editing statements which are to be tendered in evidence by the prosecution at trials or committal proceedings. The responsibility for such editing is that of the Crown Prosecution Service rather than of a police officer (*Consolidated Criminal Practice Direction*, Pt III.24).

Refreshing memory

3.49   By virtue of s.139 of the Criminal Justice Act 2003, a person giving oral evidence in criminal proceedings may refresh his memory from a document made and verified by him at an earlier time providing the witness states in oral evidence that the document records the witness's recollection at that earlier time and that that recollection is likely to have been significantly better at that time than it is at the time of the giving of oral evidence. Similarly, reference may be made to a transcript of a sound recording.

Documentary evidence

3.50   An important case on the approach to take when considering the admissibility of an official document following the introduction of the Criminal Justice Act 2003 is *West Midlands Probation Board v French* [2008] EWHC 2631; (2008) 172 J.P. 617. This case revolves around the admissibility of a document signed by a prison governor, releasing a prisoner on licence with conditions.

The first question when considering the admissibility of such a document is what does the party introducing it wish to prove? The next question to ask is whether the matters identified by the above question constitute "statements not made in oral evidence" within the meaning of s.114 of the Criminal Justice Act 2003. If they are, the document will only be admissible in evidence to prove those matters in criminal proceedings if it satisfies the requirements of one of the paragraphs of s.114(1)(a) to (d). Then the court must consider whether the purpose of making the statements was to cause another person to believe the matters stated or to cause other persons to act on the basis of those matters. If it is, the document, in this case the licence, falls within the definition of s.114 of the Criminal Justice Act 2003. This section, when read with ibid. s.118, abolishes the common law hearsay rules and creates new rules. Statements which fall within the definition set out in ss.114 and 115 are only admissible in criminal proceedings if they can be brought within one of paragraphs (a) to (d) of s.114(1). Thus it was not possible in this case to produce the licence as evidence of the facts stated in it (expressly or impliedly) without considering whether it comes within one or more of paragraphs (a) to (d) of s.114(1).

3.51 The court in *French* considered the preserved common law "rule of law" under which public documents are admissible in criminal proceedings as evidence of the facts stated in them. The document in question must be "public" in three senses: (1) the document must be made by a public officer, that is an officer acting under a public duty when creating the document; (2) the document must be public in the sense of it being created for an official, as opposed to a private, purpose; (3) it must be a public document in the sense of its purpose; it must be made for the purpose of the public making use of it. "Public" does not mean the whole world. It means all those who would have a legitimate interest in the matter that is recorded in the document. In this case it was held that the licence is a public document and therefore admissible. In any event, the court (without making a final decision on whether the licence would also be admissible under s.114(1)(d) of the Criminal Justice Act 2003, in the interests of justice) could see no reason why it should not be admitted under that section.

3.52 By s.11 of the 1988 Offenders Act, in any proceedings for an offence under that Act specified in Sch.1 to the Act, or under any other enactment relating to the use of vehicles on roads, a certificate in the form prescribed by the Evidence by Certificate Rules 1961 (SI 1961/248, as amended), signed by a constable (or a traffic warden acting in discharge of functions authorised under the Functions of Traffic Wardens Order 1970 (SI 1970/1958)) and certifying that a person specified in the certificate stated to him:

(a) that a particular mechanically propelled vehicle was being driven or used by, or belonged to, that person on a particular occasion; or

(b) that a particular mechanically propelled vehicle was used by, or belonged on a particular occasion to, a firm in which that person also stated that he was at the time of the statement a partner; or

(c) that a particular mechanically propelled vehicle was used by, or belonged on a particular occasion to, a corporation of which that person also stated that he was at the time of the statement a director or officer or employee,

shall be admissible as evidence for the purpose of determining by whom the vehicle was being driven or used, or to whom it belonged, as the case may be on that occasion. Nothing in s.11 shall be deemed to make such certificate admissible as evidence in proceedings for an offence except in a case where and to the extent to which oral evidence to the like effect would have been admissible in those proceedings. A copy of the certificate must have been served on the defendant in the manner indicated in r.3 of the Evidence by Certificate Rules 1961 not less than seven days before the hearing and the defendant may require, not later than three days before the hearing, the attendance of the constable who gives the certificate (see s.11(3)). The view is advanced at 122 J.P. Jo. 131 that the certificate of a Scottish constable is admissible under (what is now) s.11 in England. Section 11 applies only to mechanically propelled vehicles and not to pedal cycles.

3.53   Offences under regulations made under any Act mentioned in s.11 are offences under that Act and s.11 applies to such offences (cf. *Bingham v Bruce* [1962] 1 All E.R. 136; *Rathbone v Bundock* [1962] 2 All E.R. 257).

Note the limitations on the matters which can be stated in such certificates, e.g. a constable can certify only that the person interviewed said he was driving a mechanically propelled vehicle on a named occasion and not that that person said that some other person was driving. Although a certificate can be used to show that a particular person was driving, it cannot be used to prove that the vehicle was used or driven on the particular road or place alleged. Sections 11 and 12 of the 1988 Offenders Act are useful to prove ownership of a particular vehicle or to prove that the defendant admitted he was driving it, where the defendant or the owners are interviewed in a town a long way from the court, e.g. when a Durham lorry driver is summoned for an offence in Sussex and his firm, also in Durham, is summoned for permitting the offence. The evidence of the Durham constable who interviewed the defendant and the firm is thus receivable, without his (the constable's) attendance in Sussex, on the matters set out in the sections. It is submitted that the only persons who can answer for a firm or company are those with sufficient authority to make admissions on its behalf.

3.54   Further powers of proving by writing that the defendant was the driver are given by s.12 of the 1988 Offenders Act. On the summary trial of an information for an offence under the 1988 Act or any regulations made or continued thereunder to which s.12 is applied by virtue of Sch.1 to the 1988 Offenders Act, or under any enactment relating to the use of vehicles on roads, if it is proved that a requirement under s.172(2) of the 1988 Act (see § 7.26), to give information as to the identity of the driver of the particular vehicle on the particular occasion to which the information relates, has been served on the defendant by post and a statement in writing, purporting to be signed by the defendant, that he was the driver of the vehicle on that occasion, is produced to the court, that statement may be treated as evidence that he was the driver. In *Mawdesley v Chief Constable of Cheshire*; *Yorke v DPP* [2003] EWHC 1586; [2004] 1 All E.R. 58, forms had been returned showing that the person to whom the form had been sent was the driver. In the case of the offender, Mawdesley, the form was complete apart from the signature and date; in Yorke's case, not all the details were completed nor was it signed. The Administrative Court held that the documents were not admissible under s.12. However, the contents of an unsigned form were a confession (within the meaning of s.82 of the Police and Criminal Evidence Act 1984) and admissible as a document under what was then s.27 of the Criminal Justice Act 1988. The court could properly infer that documents sent to the defendant's address had been completed by the defendant when returned containing relevant information. Section 12 does not apply to committal proceedings or to trials on indictment. It can be used only to prove that the defendant himself was the driver; it cannot be used to prove that he was the owner or that someone else was driving. Section 12 applies to all types of vehicles and, it seems, to riders of cycles (cf. s.172(2) of the 1988 Act). All the above powers are additional to the power to use written statements in evidence under s.5B of the Magistrates' Courts Act 1980 and s.9 of the Criminal Justice Act 1967.

A *Registration particulars and driving licence records*

Section 52 of the Vehicle Excise and Registration Act 1994 and s.13 of the **3.55** 1988 Offenders Act enable evidence as to registration particulars and driving licence records maintained by the Secretary of State for Transport with respect to vehicles to be given by certificate. Section 13 of the 1988 Offenders Act refers to a method of proving previous convictions of endorsable and disqualifiable offences. It is not therefore relevant to the 1994 Act. When a statement is produced to a magistrates' court in proceedings for an offence involving obligatory or discretionary disqualification within the meaning of Pt III of the 1988 Act, for the purposes of s.13(3A) or (4) of the 1988 Offenders Act (establishing previous convictions), the procedure under subs.(4) must be complied with where subs.(3A) does not apply; see s.13(3A)(a). Apart from this instance, there is no procedural provision requiring the other party to be served with a copy of the certificate before the proceedings. As soon as the certificate is produced it proves itself whether or not the defendant is present. Moreover there is no limitation on the nature or type of proceedings for which a certificate may be used. It appears that the sections may be used for any civil or criminal proceedings and are not limited to proceedings under the 1988 Act and the 1994 Act. The only apparent limitation is that the matters for which evidence may be given are only those of a prescribed description (s.13(5) of the 1988 Offenders Act or s.52(1) of the 1994 Act) and that the evidence of any fact is admissible only to the same extent as oral evidence. If, therefore, the certificate contains inadmissible evidence, e.g. hearsay, neither s.52 nor s.13 renders it admissible. The statement will contain details of "previous conviction". It is submitted that this means previous to the date of the statement not to the date of the offence or matter presently before the court.

The Magistrates' Courts (Procedure) Act 1998 introduced a new subs.(3A) to s.13. Unfortunately, another subs.(3A) had already been introduced by the Civil Evidence Act 1995. The later subs.(3A) should be referred to as "subs.(3A) as inserted by s.2 of the Magistrates' Courts (Procedure) Act 1998". The effect of the change is that, where a defendant is convicted of a summary offence under the Road Traffic Acts or the Road Traffic (Driver Licensing and Information Systems) Act 1989 and is not present at the hearing, previous convictions for an offence involving obligatory endorsement (or an order made on conviction) may be proved by means of a printout of the driver record from the DVLA without the need to serve notice (and a copy of the printout) on the defendant.

Reference should be made to reg.3 of the Vehicle and Driving Licences Re- **3.56** cords (Evidence) Regulations 1970 (SI 1970/1997) which prescribes the matters for which certificates may be given under the 1988 Acts.

Where notice of intention to cite previous convictions is required under s.104 of the Magistrates' Courts Act 1980 or s.13 of the Road Traffic Offenders Act 1988, r.37.5 of the Criminal Procedure Rules 2005 allows it to be effected by delivering it to the defendant or by sending it by post in a registered letter or by recorded delivery service, or by first class post addressed to the defendant at his last known or usual place of abode.

If a court convicts and adjourns sentence in order that the prosecution may have an opportunity of serving a notice under s.13(4) of the 1988 Offenders Act, sufficient time must be given to enable the notice to be served "not less than seven days before" the notice is produced, i.e. the notice must arrive in the ordinary course of post so that there are seven clear days between the date of service of the notice and the date of hearing at which the statement is produced. Justices may not adjourn after conviction for a period exceeding four weeks at a time (*R. v Talgarth JJ.* [1973] 2 All E.R. 717) (s.10(3) of the Magistrates' Courts Act 1980), but s.10(3) is directory, not mandatory (*R. v Manchester City JJ. Ex p. Miley and Dynan*, 1977, unreported, but discussed in (1977) 141 J.P. 248). Whether or not the seven-day notice has been served, there is no reason why the contents of a printout including convictions, disqualifications and endorsements should not be put to a defendant who appears and has been convicted.

B   *Weight tickets and timetables*

3.57   A weight ticket given under what is now s.79(1) of the 1988 Act was admitted by magistrates as showing weight, but their decision as to this was not mentioned by the High Court on appeal in *Churchill v Norris* (1938) 158 L.T. 255. See also s.79(4). Obviously, it could be used to refresh the memory of someone who saw the weights shown on the dials.

Timetables, etc., are admissible against employers charged with procuring or inciting their drivers to exceed the speed limit (Road Traffic Regulation Act 1984 s.89(4)). Records of hours of driving kept by a firm's drivers are admissible against the firm on a charge of permitting them to drive for excessive periods contrary to what is now s.96 of the Transport Act 1968 (*Beer v Clench* [1936] 1 All E.R. 449; *Adair v Craighouse* 1937 S.C.(J.) 89). The fact that the numbers on log sheets tally with the numbers of vehicles may suffice to relate the sheets to those vehicles (*Hogg v Burnet* 1938 S.C.(J.) 160). Where letters are sent by a witness to a particular person on a particular matter and an answer is received in due course, there is a presumption that the answer has been written by the person in whose writing (or semble on whose headed letter-paper) it purports to be (see cases in 22 E. & E. Dig. (Blue) 190).

C   *Manufacturers' records and computer evidence*

3.58   Section 117 of the Criminal Justice Act 2003 authorises admissibility in criminal proceedings of a statement in a document as evidence of any fact of which direct oral evidence would be admissible provided that these conditions are satisfied. First, the document must be created or received by a person in the course of a trade, business, profession, or other occupation, or as the holder of a paid or unpaid office; and, secondly, the information contained in the document was supplied by a person (whether or not the maker of the statement) who had, or may reasonably be supposed to have had, personal knowledge of the matters dealt with. The section goes on to state that the main provision applies whether the information contained in the document was supplied directly or indirectly, but if indirectly, only if each person through whom it was supplied received it in a like way, i.e. in the course of a trade, business, etc., or as the holder of a paid or unpaid office.

3.59   In *Brown v Secretary of State for Social Security* [1995] C.O.D. 260, when an earlier, similar, provision was considered, the court held that the "maker" of a statement for the purpose of the section was the person who actually made the statement which it was sought to produce in evidence, rather than the person who supplied the information contained in the statement. The third of the three alternative provisions, which had to be satisfied before the statement in a document, etc., could be admissible, was:

> "the person who made the statement cannot reasonably be expected (having regard to the time which has elapsed since he made the statement and to all the circumstances) to have any recollection of the matters dealt with in the statement."

Collins J. stated that the section drew a distinction between the supplier of information and the maker of the statement. It was "inescapable" as a matter of construction that the maker of the statement was the person who made the statement actually produced rather than the person who had supplied the information contained therein. This decision was not followed in *R. v Derodra* [1999] Crim. L.R. 978. The Court of Appeal considered that the maker of the statement must be the person testifying to the facts represented in the statement not the person who actually created the document.

In *Vehicle and Operator Services Agency v George Jenkins Transport Ltd* **3.60**
[2003] EWHC 2879; *The Times*, December 5, 2003, the defence sought to argue that each document must be produced and spoken to by a witness capable of proving it, including the personal knowledge of the person supplying the information contained in the document. Rejecting this argument, the Administrative Court accepted that the section plainly envisages a process of judgement by inference as one of the methods to be used by a court in deciding whether the second criterion is met. The court recognised Parliament's evident intention to widen the power of the courts to admit documentary hearsay, subject to proper safeguards for the defendant. In this case, it was obvious from looking at the documents that they met the criteria.

Plans, sketches and maps

Plans and sketches are frequently used in careless driving cases—some cases **3.61**
would be incomprehensible without them. It is a common practice not to draw plans to scale but to show distances from a specified location. The resulting sketch may mislead but it enables a correct plan to be drawn to scale if required. A map or plan prepared for the purpose of a trial ought not to contain any reference to transactions and occurrences which are the subject-matter of the investigation before the court and were not existing when the survey was made; if it does *and objection is taken*, the court should not look at it (*R. v Mitchell* (1852) 6 Cox C.C. 82). In *Tarbox v St Pancras Borough Council* [1952] 1 All E.R. 1306 (a civil case), however, particulars of the place where the plaintiff said he was walking, the position of the defendant's servant and the position where the plaintiff fell were ordered to be put on a plan rather than in a statement of claim. If no objection is taken by the other side, a plan or sketch showing both things existing at the time it was made (e.g. traffic lights, white lines, skid marks, piles of mud) and also things surmised by the artist (e.g. the course of a car prior to stopping) can, it seems, be put in evidence, but the other side should first be given a sight of the drawing. Provided that it is made clear to the court that some of it is surmise, that it is for guidance only and that it must be carefully checked with the evidence, a plan or sketch not objected to seems to be no more inadmissible than a sketch made by a magistrate as the case unfolds. If a sketch not to a scale and showing

only things existing and no surmised tracks, etc., is objected to, it would seem that the person who prepared it can still put it in when called as a witness for what it is worth but, if it is such a bad sketch as to be completely out of proportion—as some are—it is submitted that the other side might successfully object to its being put in at all because it is so misleading. If it is a plan to scale, however, and shows only things existing when it is made, it must be admitted when the person who prepared it swears to it in the witness box. Further, by the Criminal Justice Act 1948 s.41 and regulations made thereunder, in any criminal proceedings a plan prepared by a constable, architect, chartered surveyor, civil engineer, municipal engineer or land agent and certified by him to be correctly drawn to a specified scale shall be evidence of the relative position of things shown thereon; the person who prepared the plan need not be called as a witness, but a copy of the plan and certificate must have been served on the defendant at least seven days before the hearing and, not less than three days before the hearing, the defendant can require that person to be called as a witness (see s.41(5)).

It was held in *Hogg v Clark* 1959 S.C.(J.) 7 that a plan could be put by the defence to a prosecution witness although the plan had not at that time been proved.

3.62   Maps, such as the Ordnance Survey, are admissible as to matters deducible from them, such as whether a road is in existence, and distances. A rotameter may be used on a map to show distances travelled. In statutes passed after January 1, 1890 distance is measured in a straight line on a horizontal plane unless the contrary intention appears (Interpretation Act 1978 s.8). Ordnance maps are not in themselves evidence that a forecourt is part of the highway (*Baxter v Middlesex County Council* [1956] Crim. L.R. 561), nor of the boundaries of the highway (*Webb v Eastleigh Borough Council* (1957) 56 L.G.R. 124). The Highways Act 1980 s.32, however, allows maps, plans and local histories to be put in evidence as to the dedication of a highway. Moreover some Ordnance Survey maps show the footpaths, bridleways and roads used as public paths as on a "definitive map" prepared under the National Parks and Access to the Countryside Act 1949 and now under Pt III of the Wildlife and Countryside Act 1981. Section 47(2) of the Countryside and Rights of Way Act 2000 converts references on a definitive map to a road used as a public path to references to a restricted byway. For the implications of this, see § 1.138 above.

Photographs, films, tapes and video tapes

3.63   Photographs are proved by the oath of the person who took them. Photographs of the scene are often of assistance but it should be remembered that distances may appear foreshortened. The police will normally supply a copy of any photograph taken by them on payment of the appropriate fee. It was stated in *R. v Quinn* [1961] 3 All E.R. 88 that a film of a reconstruction of an accident or piece of driving would generally not be admissible. Accident investigation evidence is often based on reconstructions and is often accepted. Obviously such evidence must be approached with care as it is reconstruction only.

It is important to acknowledge the advances that have been made in the recording of police interviews, and a number of cases have been reported concerning the conduct of such interviews and their compliance or otherwise with Code E and Code F of the codes of practice made under the Police and Criminal Evidence Act 1984.

Two interesting decisions on the admissibility of films can profitably be **3.64** considered here. In *R. v Estop* [1976] R.T.R. 493, the defendant at his trial for offences under the former ss.5(1) and 9(3) of the 1972 Act, sought to adduce in evidence a subsequently made film, recording the whole route he had driven showing the hazards of the road, the corners, turns and stopping places from the starting point of his journey to the scene of the collision to establish that, since he had driven without accident before the collision, he could not have been, or was unlikely to have been unfit through drink. The Court of Appeal upheld the decision of the trial judge to permit the jury to see only that part of the film which depicted the sections of the road where the appellant was alleged to have driven dangerously—it helped to illustrate the evidence of the witnesses relating to the manner of his driving. But see also *R. v Thomas (Steven)* [1986] Crim. L.R. 682. A car chase resulted in the defendant being charged with the former offence of reckless driving. The police had followed him for some nine miles. A police technician subsequently made a film of the route and he was accompanied by the same police officers. The purpose of the video was to convey in a helpful and accurate way the picture of the roads involved. The trial judge ruled that the video was admissible in evidence, and that the officers involved in the chase could use the video to present their evidence. It would enable the officer to tie up his notes with the visual presentation of the video. It should perhaps be noted that the defence did not object to the admission of the film.

This is certainly an aspect of the law of evidence where changes can be expected. Previous developments have concerned the admissibility of a photofit of a defendant (see *R. v Cook* [1987] 1 All E.R. 1049 where it was held that such a picture was admissible as part of a witness's evidence and did not breach either the hearsay rule or the rule against the admission of earlier consistent statements; note that *Cook* has been overtaken by s.115 of the Criminal Justice Act 2003: a photofit is now hearsay); and evidence of what was seen on a video recording when the recording itself had been mistakenly erased before the trial (see *Taylor v Chief Constable of Cheshire* [1987] 1 All E.R. 225). Section 71 of the Police and Criminal Evidence Act 1984 provides for the admissibility of enlargements of microfilm copies.

In this context reference should also be made to s.20 of the Road Traffic Of- **3.65** fenders Act 1988 (as amended). This gives authority, subject to the conditions laid down in the section, for the admission in evidence in offences of speeding and failing to conform to a red light signal or bus lane, of a record produced by a prescribed device, and in the same or another document of a certificate as to the circumstances in which the record was produced signed by a police constable, etc. A "prescribed device" is one of a description specified in an order made by the Secretary of State. He may also add to or delete from the offences contained in s.20(2) in respect of which this evidence is admissible.

Section 20(6) states that evidence of a measurement made by a device, or of the circumstances in which it was made, or that a device was of a type approved, or that any conditions subject to which an approval was given were satisfied, may be given by the production of a signed document, which as the case may be, gives particulars of the measurement or of the circumstances in which it was made, or states that the device was of such a type or that, to the best of the knowledge and belief of the person making the statement, all such conditions were satisfied.

3.66   Section 20(8) requires that a copy of the document be served on the defendant not less than seven days before the hearing or trial. The defendant, not less than three days before the hearing or trial, may serve a notice on the prosecutor requiring attendance of the person who signed the document. Clearly, strict procedural requirements attach to the admissibility of evidence produced in such a manner, and the section should be studied in its entirety.

The provisions in s.20 of the Road Traffic Offenders Act 1988, as substituted, must be strictly observed and the prosecution must prove that the device in question has been approved. That is the effect of the decision of the Divisional Court in *Roberts (Colin) v DPP* [1994] R.T.R. 31. In that case, the appellant had been served with a speeding report and a witness statement which alleged that his speed, which had been checked by a radar gun, exceeded the prescribed limit. Before the hearing his solicitor sought to obtain information from the prosecution regarding the radar gun and had done everything reasonably possible before the hearing to alert the prosecution to the fact that the radar gun procedure was in issue. At the hearing in the magistrates' court no evidence was adduced as to the approval of the radar gun and, at the end of the prosecution case, it was submitted on behalf of the appellant that there was no case to answer. The justices ruled that they could take judicial notice of the approval of the radar gun and the appellant was convicted. At the hearing of his appeal in the Divisional Court, it was held that s.20 required the prosecution to prove that the radar gun had been approved by the Home Secretary before its measurement of a driver's speed could be admitted in evidence. In the absence of evidence of approval the conviction could not be sustained.

3.67   The circumstances in which photographs produced by a prescribed device, such as a Gatsometer, can be adduced in evidence were considered again in *Griffiths v DPP* [2007] EWHC 619; [2007] R.T.R. 44. It was decided that the developed film from a negative produced by a Gatsometer is "a record produced by a prescribed device" and therefore admissible under s.20 of the Road Traffic Offenders Act 1988. The provisions in that section must be strictly observed so that, e.g. the photographs served on the defence not less than seven days before the hearing or trial must not be of such poor quality as to be unusable. However, this is not the only method by which photographs can be admitted. In *Griffiths* a witness was able to produce the photographs and did in fact do so. He knew how the machine worked and was able to connect the photographs to the defendant. The Divisional Court confirmed that it is unnecessary in these circumstances either to rely on s.20 or for the prosecution to prove continuity. The photographs are real evidence under the common law. The case also decided that the court is entitled to assume that the timing device on the camera was operating correctly.

It is submitted that where the authorisation of a device is in issue, the prosecution may produce the relevant approval in court or a police officer could give evidence that the device was approved without there being any formal evidence to that effect. In that way the requirements of the section would be satisfied. As to the fact of approval itself, practitioners should refer to § 6.84.

CCTV

3.68   It is obviously of considerable assistance for the court to be able to view good quality CCTV or other film of any disputed incident. Such evidence is real evidence, not hearsay. However, there is nothing special about CCTV, and it must be treated like any other form of material or evidence. Where the Crown does not produce CCTV to the court in evidence or disclose it to the defence under the disclosure provisions, the procedure is the same as for any other material.

The test as to whether CCTV should be seized and retained by the police is set out in *R. (on the application of Ebrahim) v Feltham Magistrates' Court* [2001] EWHC Admin 130; [2001] 1 W.L.R. 1293. If the disclosure officer, having reviewed the relevant footage, decides that it might reasonably be considered capable of undermining the case for the prosecution against the accused or of assisting the case for the accused (Criminal Procedure and Investigations Act 1996, as amended by Pt V of the Criminal Justice Act 2003), it should be disclosed. Disclosure may be by way of provision of copies or by allowing the defendant to inspect the material. If the prosecutor forms the view that the CCTV does not meet the test for disclosure, then in order to obtain disclosure the defence must make a written application under s.8 of the Criminal Procedure and Investigations Act 1996 (and must, therefore, have served a defence statement) before the court can give consideration to whether it should order disclosure of the CCTV. According to the Protocol for the Provision of Advance Information, Prosecution Evidence and Disclosure of Unused Material in the Magistrates' Courts (May 15, 2006, available at *http://www.judiciary.gov.uk/judgment_guidance/protocols/ mags_unused_material.htm* [Accessed May 2, 2009]): "it is improper for courts to make general directions requiring the prosecutor to disclose such material without a proper application and scrutiny of the matter in compliance with the CPIA". Where any CCTV is not in the possession of the police, but may be the property of a third party, then the third party disclosure rules apply. In practice, where the CCTV is in the hands of the police but does not meet the disclosure provisions, the Crown often offers the defence the opportunity to view the item at the police station, in order to avoid dispute.

As CCTV has proliferated, so have abuse of process arguments. In 2008 two **3.69** cases reminded practitioners of the limitations of such arguments. In *R. v C and I* [2008] EWCA Crim 2585 the defendants were accused of robbery. The victim described the clothing worn by the robbers. Shortly before the robbery the defendants had visited the local police station where there was a CCTV camera which would, in the normal course of events, have recorded their visit. A mistake was made in downloading the relevant passage on the CCTV recording. By the time the mistake was discovered the tape had been recorded over so that there was no permanent record by the time of trial. The defendants said that the CCTV would show that they were not wearing clothing of the description described by the victim. The Crown Court judge ruled that the defendants could not have a fair trial and therefore stopped the case as an abuse of process. The prosecution appealed to the Court of Appeal under s.58 of the Criminal Justice Act 2003. In allowing the appeal, the court stated:

> "We should start by saying that it is a considerable problem for courts these days to be faced on a regular basis by applications to stay proceedings as an abuse of process. It does not seem as though proper attention is paid to the fact that it is only in the most exceptional circumstances that a prosecution, otherwise properly brought, should be stayed.
>
> In paragraph 18 of the Divisional Court judgment in Ebrahim [*R. (on the application of Ebrahim) v Feltham Magistrates' Court* [2001] EWHC Admin 1310] the court said as follows: 'the two categories of cases in which the power to stay proceedings for abuse of process may be invoked in this area of the court's jurisdiction are (i) cases

where the court concludes that the defendant cannot receive a fair trial, and (ii) cases where it concludes that it would be unfair for the defendant to be tried.'

It is accepted that this case, if it falls into either category, it falls into the first category. The first category of case is classically one where it is clear that in almost every case the process of trial will be wholly insufficient to deal with the difficulties that may arise out of the fact that evidence, as in this case, has either gone missing or is no longer available.

The Divisional Court in paragraph 24 of its judgment made it plain that this category of case has to be equated to a case where unless the case is stopped there would be a breach of Article 6 of the European Convention of Human Rights. It follows that it is only in the most extreme circumstances that a court should stay proceedings under this heading." ([2008] EWCA Crim 2585 at [13]–[16])

3.70   After this case was heard, but before judgment was published, a similar issue was considered in *Morris v DPP* [2008] EWHC 2788; (2009) 173 J.P. 41. Here the appellant motorist appealed by way of case stated against the dismissal of his appeal against conviction for an offence of driving with excess alcohol in his blood. He claimed that the police had not given the warning of prosecution when requesting the sample as required by the Road Traffic Act 1988 s.7(7). The appellant's submission of abuse of process was based on the failure of the prosecution to provide the CCTV evidence that existed of the custody suite. It was said that the recording may have assisted in determining whether the warning was given. The application was rejected and the appellant was convicted. On a rehearing, the Crown Court concluded that a fair trial was possible in the absence of the CCTV footage and reached the same conclusion as the magistrates' court had done. The Administrative Court held that there was no automatic requirement on the prosecution to retain CCTV evidence where it potentially recorded the administering of the warning under s.7(7), whether or not the defence raised the giving of the warning as an issue before trial. The appeal was dismissed.

Exhibits

3.71   The best evidence rule applies to documents where the original is available but not to chattels generally (*R. v Orrell* [1972] R.T.R. 14 and *Tremlett v Fawcett* (1984) R.T.L.B. 68 and *Hocking v Ahlquist* [1943] 2 All E.R. 722). It is not essential to produce all exhibits (though some, such as statements, must be produced) but the absence of exhibits may be a matter for comment (*Hockin v Ahlquist*). In some instances there are statutory provisions for providing body samples, as for example breath, blood and urine specimens in Pt I of the 1988 Act.

Where there are no statutory provisions there is no need for consent before a sample is taken and produced as an exhibit (*R. v Apicella* [1986] Crim. L.R. 238) and the principles in *R. v Sang* [1979] 2 All E.R. 1222 apply. Where *Sang* applies reference also has to be made to the Police and Criminal Evidence Act 1984 s.78 (see § 3.102). Conversely refusal to provide a sample may constitute corroboration (*R. v Smith (R.W.)* [1985] Crim. L.R. 590).

3.72   Exhibits when produced (or so treated as produced) are the responsibility of the court and the producer. This responsibility was considered in *R. v Lambeth Stipendiary Magistrate Ex p. McComb* [1983] 1 All E.R. 321 where *R. v Lushington* [1894] 1 Q.B. 420 was applied. It is within the power of, and it is the duty of, constables to retain for use in court things which may be evidence of crime, and which have come into their possession without wrongdoing on their part.

When articles have been produced in court by witnesses it is right and necessary for the court, or the constable or person in whose charge they are placed, to preserve and retain them, so that they may be always available for the purposes of justice until the trial is concluded (*Lushington*). It may be right to release the exhibits temporarily for a proper purpose and if so it may be desirable to seek the permission of the court (*McComb*). Even if the exhibit is not produced or treated as produced it is submitted that the court may still have jurisdiction over it.

Inspections

Where vehicles are near the court, the justices may inspect them provided they **3.73** have sworn evidence as to whether they are in a different condition from that at the time of the offence (*Keeble v Miller* [1950] 1 All E.R. 261). Witnesses taking part in a view should be recalled for cross-examination, if desired (*Karamat v R.* [1956] 1 All E.R. 415, where views generally are discussed). In *R. v Knight, The Times*, June 14, 1961, the jury, in a case of taking and driving away a lorry, asked if they could inspect a similar lorry and were allowed to do so. The Court of Criminal Appeal said that applications for inspection should be regarded with great caution, especially when the conditions of the inspection differed.

A conviction was quashed in *R. v Lawrence* [1968] 1 All E.R. 579, where the jury inspected a vehicle after they had retired, but not quashed in *R. v Nixon* [1968] 2 All E.R. 33, where the same had happened but defending counsel had said that he desired the jury to do so. Magistrates were held to be wrong when they took a tyre gauge with them when they retired and carried out a private test on a tyre. Lord Lane C.J. said that the reason why they had carried out this test was objectionable: they were in breach of their duty to hear the whole case in open court (*R. v Tiverton JJ.* (1980) 144 J.P. 747).

There are two instances where there may be a view of a scene; there may be a **3.74** single view of an object or place, or there may be a demonstration with witnesses. The judge should be present in the second instance (the demonstration) (*Tameshwar v R.* [1957] A.C. 476 and *R. v Hunter* [1985] 2 All E.R. 173) and it is recommended that the judge should be present in either instance (*Hunter*).

Where justices decide to view the scene of an alleged offence they should not normally go there without being accompanied by the parties and their legal representatives. Since the parties should be allowed to comment thereafter upon what they saw, the view should take place before the conclusion of the evidence (*Parry v Boyle* [1987] R.T.R. 282). Further guidance was given to courts in cases when it was proposed that there should be a view of the scene of an alleged offence as in *R. v Ely JJ. Ex p. Burgess* (1993) 157 J.P. 484. It is plain from that decision that any appearance of bias must be avoided. For reasons that are not clear, the justices had refused to allow the defendant to be present during the view. The prosecutor had travelled to the view in the same car as the justices and their clerk; on the return journey she had travelled alone with the justices. The Divisional Court held that the view was part of the trial and the presence of the defendant was necessary in the absence of exceptional circumstances. As to ostensible bias, the court adopted the test proposed by Ackner L.J., as he then was, in *R. v Liverpool JJ. Ex p. Topping* [1983] 1 W.L.R. 119, namely:

> "would a reasonable and fair-minded person sitting in court and knowing all the relevant facts have a reasonable suspicion that a fair trial was not possible?"

3.75 In this case for the prosecution to travel with judges of fact would result in a reasonable person having a suspicion that a fair trial was not possible. It follows that in the very small minority of cases where a view is felt to be of assistance, the parties and their legal representatives should be present, and the travelling arrangements to and from the locus must be arranged so that the wholly unsatisfactory circumstances in this case can be avoided.

The danger of a court making a private inspection or view of a locus was illustrated by the decision of the Divisional Court in *Telfer and Telfer v DPP* (1996) 160 J.P. 512, although the court did not—in the event—find anything objectionable or prejudicial in what happened. The chairman of a bench dealing with a trial involving allegations of assault occasioning actual bodily harm made a private visit to the scene of the alleged offence without the knowledge of the clerk and without prior consultation with the parties. The fact of this visit came out before the end of the hearing and the legal adviser, in conduct described by the court as "perfectly sensible", suggested that a further site visit take place with all interested parties present, or that there be a rehearing before a different bench of magistrates, or that the trial continue. Both prosecution and defence advocates opted to continue with the trial. The defendants were in due course convicted and then appealed by way of case stated. The question on which the opinion of the court was sought was the extent to which magistrates were entitled to take into account the view of the parties to the proceedings in deciding whether to continue with the hearing when it was realised that an irregularity had occurred in the conduct of the proceedings.

3.76 It was held that on the assumption that the private view taken by the chairman was an irregularity, since both parties had been legally represented and fully informed of the circumstances, and, given the options referred to, the justices were entitled to treat defence counsel's rejection of those alternatives as strong evidence that no prejudice had resulted from the chairman's irregular private view and to take into account the wishes and representations of the parties for the trial to proceed forthwith. Steyn L.J., who gave the judgment of the court, said:

> "It is always safer for the magistrates to act collectively, to indicate in open court that they plan to have a view, and to make all the appropriate arrangements for the view to take place in a formal way. Much trouble and expense can be avoided if magistrates were to follow this advice."

Local and specialised knowledge

3.77 Where it is a matter of notorious local knowledge that a journey of one and a half miles from point A to point B necessarily involved using several different public roads, the justices were held to be entitled to use this knowledge in rejecting a submission of no case and convicting the defendant where the prosecution had been unable to prove the precise route taken by the offending vehicle (*Borthwick v Vickers* [1973] R.T.R. 390). The Divisional Court gave a warning about the use of local knowledge in *Bowman v DPP* [1991] R.T.R. 263. Magistrates were advised to be "extremely circumspect" when using local knowledge. The court should make the fact known to prosecution and defence that local knowledge was being relied upon and that would afford legal representatives an opportunity of commenting on the knowledge which the magistrates claimed to have had and claimed to have used.

A judge hearing an appeal from magistrates was well acquainted with a road junction on the A25 and A20 and road works being carried on there. He informed the court of this knowledge. The hearing concerned a conviction for driving without reasonable consideration. The judge's use of his knowledge was unsuccessfully challenged in the Divisional Court. The Divisional Court held that local knowledge could not and should not be excluded from the court's mind in drawing inferences (*Chesson v Jordan* [1981] Crim. L.R. 333). The use of local knowledge is implicit in the concept of local magistrates and local justice.

3.78 Justices had no direct evidence that a special constable who required a breath test was in uniform. Evidence was given that another special constable present was in uniform. The defence did not raise the issue in cross-examination. The justices, from their knowledge of the special constabulary, knew that there was no plain-clothes department and the officer having stated that he was on duty they deduced he was in uniform. The Divisional Court held that there was circumstantial evidence whereby the justices could conclude that the officer must have been in uniform (*Richards v West* [1980] R.T.R. 215).

In *DPP v Curtis* [1993] R.T.R. 72 the justices had acquitted the respondent of failing without reasonable excuse to provide two specimens of breath, contrary to s.7(6) of the Road Traffic Act 1988. The prosecutor's appeal by case stated was allowed. In the course of his judgment, Watkins L.J. stated that justices were not entitled to go beyond the evidence before them. There might be occasions where justices could use particular knowledge, such as their knowledge of a locality. However, justices should be wary of using whatever knowledge they had of physical or mental conditions to come to a decision as to what exactly was affecting a motorist when asked to provide a specimen of breath. He continued by saying that justices had to be beware of being gullible, and had to be scrupulous, when deciding whether reasonableness in refusing had been made out, to adhere to the evidence and not rely on experiences of their own which the evidence could not support. The case was not remitted to the magistrates' court.

3.79 A justice with specialised knowledge is entitled to use that knowledge in interpreting or assessing the evidence already before the court and can communicate his views to his fellow justices provided he does not thrust those views upon them. He must not, on the other hand, proceed to give evidence to his fellow justices contradicting the evidence given in court as it is not in open court nor subject to cross-examination (*Wetherall v Harrison* [1976] R.T.R. 125). In *Kent v Stamps* [1982] R.T.R. 273, where the vehicle involved was an elderly lorry, the justices used local knowledge of the location of a speed trap—round a bend and on an upward gradient. The Divisional Court upheld with hesitation their rejection for these reasons of the result of the speed trap equipment.

Admissions

3.80 Admissions by either side before or at the hearing are allowed in the circumstances given in s.10 of the Criminal Justice Act 1967. A defendant may thus be asked to admit in court that he was the driver or what his reply to a constable was; his admission in a magistrates' court must be put in writing and signed by him (Criminal Procedure Rules 2005 r.37.4). Any admission made on behalf of an individual can only be made by a solicitor or barrister. Save so far as admissions are made in advance, each side should be ready to prove its case by ordinary evidence; an admission may only be withdrawn by leave of the court and the side relying on it would no doubt be granted an adjournment to call the necessary evidence. In *R. v Lewis* [1971] Crim. L.R. 414, defending counsel admitted the facts as stated in the prosecutor's opening speech. The Court of Appeal said that it was a practice which should be adopted rarely and with extreme caution. A previous plea of guilty may or may not have some probative value, but before allowing a reference to such a plea it should first be considered whether such probative value as it had would exceed the prejudice induced by its admission (*R. v Rimmer* [1972] 1 All E.R. 604). Admissions made at a pre-trial review should not be used in a trial without the consent of the party making the admission (*R. v Hutchinson* [1985] Crim. L.R. 730). These cases must be reconsidered in the light of the Police and Criminal Evidence Act 1984 s.78, whereby the court has a discretion to exclude *prosecution* evidence if it would be *unfair*. It is submitted that it is likely that similar conclusions would be reached. It may also be necessary to take into account ss.75 and 76 in relation to admissions and whether they are reliable in the circumstances. The power to exclude an admission because admitting it would be unfair will be influenced by the implementation of the Human Rights Act 1998. Early consideration was given in *R. v Kirk (Alfred)* [2000] 1 W.L.R. 567 where an admission was excluded because the suspect was not informed of an event which made the original allegation far more serious until after the admission was made.

3.81   It may be that the practice in relation to admissions will need to be revisited in view of changes of practice, particularly in the magistrates' court, to accommodate the Criminal Procedure Rules 2005. Part 3 of the Rules covers case management. Active case management includes ensuring that evidence, whether disputed or not, is presented in the shortest and clearest way (r.3.2(2)(e)). Some courts are now expecting the parties to agree uncontentious issues by way of admissions at case management hearings. This enables the trial itself to concentrate on the disputed issues. Potential problems arise when the advocate at trial takes points that were conceded, or at least not disputed, earlier. We have discussed above how earlier admissions could be reopened in the interests of justice. Alternatively, it may be in the interests of justice for undisputed facts to be proved by way of hearsay evidence (see §§ 3.13–25 above). What is clear is that the court cannot simply dispense with evidence altogether. In *Mills v DPP* [2008] EWHC 3304, the magistrates had held that they were satisfied beyond a reasonable doubt, given the way in which the case had been managed and run, that the defendant had been disqualified from driving at the material time. The Divisional Court concluded that it was likely that what had occurred was that at the case management hearings it was made clear that the substantive issue before the court was going to be whether or not the defendant was driving the vehicle on the relevant date. It was possible that there was an informal admission at the case management hearing that the defendant was disqualified from driving on that date, but there was no evidence to that effect. The bench was not entitled to convict on the basis of the way the case was managed with regard to the issue of whether the defendant was disqualified. The prosecution had to prove its case. There was no admissible evidence of disqualification and the magistrates were not entitled to convict.

Proof generally

3.82   The owner of a motor vehicle is presumed in law to be the user, in the absence of contrary evidence (*Watson v Paterson*, noted at 121 J.P. Jo. 336). In *Barnard v Sully* (1931) 47 T.L.R. 557, it was held that proof of a defendant being owner of a car was prima facie evidence that it was being driven at the material time by him or his servant or agent. This was a civil case and, in a reference to it in *Ende v Cassidy* (1964) 108 S.J. 522, it was said that there would be a higher standard of proof in criminal cases, but it was held in *Ende's* case that ownership was some evidence that the defendant was responsible for an obstruction with his car, especially as it had been left outside a block of flats where he lived. *Barnard v Sully* was followed in *Baker v Oxford* [1980] R.T.R. 315, see § 4.61 below.

Barnard v Sully and *Ende v Cassidy* were again followed in *Elliott v Loake* [1983] Crim. L.R. 36 where it was held that the justices were justified in finding that the owner of a car was the driver at a time an accident occurred. This prima facie inference was reinforced when the owner told lies. The owner had also not taken any steps to reply to the notice under what is now s.172 of the 1988 Act asking him to state who the driver was and had given no satisfactory explanation for not doing so. This paragraph should now be read subject to the decision in *Clarke v DPP* (1992) 156 J.P. 605 which is included at § 1.90 above and *Brown v Stott (Procurator Fiscal, Dunfermline)* [2001] 2 All E.R. 97.

In *Stickings v George* [1980] R.T.R. 237 justices were directed to continue the hearing of a case of careless driving which they had dismissed on upholding a submission of no case to answer on the ground that none of the prosecution witnesses had identified the defendant. The police had taken a statement from the defendant at the scene and the statement had been put in evidence. Moreover, the defendant, before pleading not guilty, had agreed that she was the person named in the information. **3.83**

In *Scruby v Beskeen* [1980] R.T.R. 420 the defendant admitted owning a blue Range Rover and being at the place in question at the relevant time. The Divisional Court held that this was evidence upon which justices could find that the defendant was the driver of a blue Range Rover which had been driven carelessly at the place in question and upheld a conviction for careless driving.

In *Smith v Mellors* [1987] R.T.R. 210, two occupants of a motor vehicle were charged, as participants to a joint enterprise, with the principal offence of driving after consuming excess alcohol. It was held by the Divisional Court that it was unnecessary for the prosecution to establish which occupant drove the vehicle and which aided and abetted the driving, provided that it could be proved that each occupant was guilty either because he was driving or because he aided and abetted the driving. It was however necessary for the prosecution to establish that both occupants knew or were reckless that the other was unfit to drive. **3.84**

It is difficult to say how far this line of cases will be taken. One has only to consider, as an example, whether a High Court judge would allow the conviction of a car owner for manslaughter where the sole evidence implicating him personally was that he owned the vehicle involved. In seeking proof as to the identity of a driver, the police should remember their powers of requiring the owner or any other person to give information as to this (see § 7.24).

If the name and address of an offending motorist have been obtained from a driving licence produced by the offender at the time of the offence or if the offender has otherwise given a name and address to the constable, the appearance at court of a defendant of that name in answer to the summons is prima facie evidence that he is the driver. In *Cooke v McCann* [1974] R.T.R. 131 it was held that **3.85** justices were not entitled to hold there was no case to answer where a traffic warden was unable to identify the defendant as the driver he had seen driving the wrong way down a one-way street, when the person who had appeared in court bore the name and address he had obtained from the offender's driving licence. Appearance by counsel of a defendant is sufficient prima facie evidence of the identity of the defendant as the driver if the constable gives uncontradicted evidence that the speeding motorist when stopped by him gave the defendant's name and address (*Creed v Scott* [1976] R.T.R. 485). There is no difference for the purpose of proving identity between taking the motorist's name and address from the driving licence produced by him (as in *Cooke v McCann*) and the motorist simply stating to the constable his name and address without production of the licence (ibid.). Bean J. in *Cooke v McCann* quoted with approval Lord Alverstone C.J. in *Marshall v Ford* (1908) 72 J.P. 480, when he said: "When in the course of his duty a constable acting under the Act gets the name of a person who afterwards appears in court that is evidence on which the magistrates may act." An admission by a defendant that he had been driving (without other evidence) is capable of being sufficient evidence to establish driving (*Patterson v Charlton* [1986] R.T.R. 18). The case was for driving with excess alcohol.

These cases were reviewed, as well as a number of similar unreported cases from New Zealand, in the New Zealand case of *Hays v MOT* [1982] 1 N.Z.L.R. 25. *Marshall v Ford*, *Cooke v McCann*, *Creed v Scott* and *Hays v MOT* were all followed in *Allen v Ireland* (1984) 148 J.P. 545, where it was decided that the magistrate was entitled to take judicial notice of the ordinary processes of arrest, charge and bail so as to raise a prima facie case that the person surrendering to bail and answering was the same person who had been arrested, charged and bailed from a crowd of football supporters, although this inference could have been rebutted.

3.86   Where, however, a real question of identity arises, e.g. where a constable sees a person driving the vehicle whom he believes he recognises as a disqualified driver, reference should be made to the appropriate paragraphs in Archbold or *Blackstone's Criminal Practice* and in particular *R. v Turnbull* [1977] Q.B. 224. The practitioner should be aware that in some traffic offence situations *Turnbull* will not necessarily apply fully, e.g. where the issue is whether the defendant or his passenger was the driver.

Where identification is at issue, the requirements of Code D, the relevant code of practice under the Police and Criminal Evidence Act 1984, should be referred to as to the approved methods of identification to deal with any given situation. In *R. v Tiplady* (1995) 159 J.P. 548, an appeal was rejected after argument that there had been various breaches of Code D. In particular, the appellant had been subject to a group identification in the foyer of a magistrates' court. The trial judge ruled that that evidence could be properly admitted without it having an adverse effect on the fairness of the trial. The Court of Appeal stated that the foyer could be an appropriate place for such an identification, and it should not be equated with a police station which was expressly disapproved in para.2.9 of the then Code D. In the public area of a magistrates' court there was much more likely to be a greater coming and going of a greater variety of people than in a police station.

3.87   A definitive decision was handed down by the Divisional Court on the troublesome subject of dock identifications. Those who thought that dock identifications were no longer permitted, as being both unsafe and prejudicial to the defendant, have been proved wrong. In *North Yorkshire Trading Standards Department v Williams* (1995) 159 J.P. 383, the appellant had been charged with a non-arrestable offence, namely the unlawful harassment of a debtor contrary to s.40(1) of the Administration of Justice Act 1970. There had been various unsuccessful attempts to interview him and there was no means—given the status of the offence—to require the appellant to attend an identification parade, or to participate in any of the other forms of identification recognised by the Police and Criminal Evidence Act 1984. The justices refused the prosecutor's application that there be a dock identification. In allowing the prosecutor's appeal, the court stated that the principles that applied were: (1) that although dock identifications were generally undesirable, they were admissible at law; (2) that whether a dock identification should be admitted was for the justices to decide in the exercise of their discretion—each case had to be considered on its own facts and circumstances in order to determine whether the prejudicial value of the evidence outweighed its probative value; (3) if dock identification were admitted, justices would have to be reminded by their clerk of the dangers and potential weaknesses of it in accordance with *R. v Turnbull* [1977] Q.B. 224. It would seem that the *North Yorkshire* decision will have particular relevance in road traffic prosecutions, many of which remain non-arrestable.

In *Karia v DPP* [2002] EWHC 2175; (2002) 166 J.P. 753, the defendant pleaded not guilty to allegations of speeding and failing to produce documents but was convicted. He did not give evidence at his trial nor was the issue of identification raised. On appeal, the driver stated that he did not believe himself to have been the driver when the offences were committed. The Crown Court found as a fact that the driver had not indicated to the prosecution during the trial at the magistrates' court that identification of the driver was in issue, and a dock identification had therefore been made in ignorance of this fact. The Crown Court rejected the submission that the magistrates should not have permitted a police officer giving evidence before them to make a dock identification. The Divisional Court dismissed an appeal from the Crown Court. It was permissible to allow the prosecution to seek and rely upon a dock identification in these circumstances, that is, where there was no prior notification that identity was in issue. It also held that the court had not breached art.6 of the European Convention on Human Rights.

In *Barnes v DPP* [1997] 2 Cr. App. R. 505, the Divisional Court held that it **3.88** was not necessarily unfair for a motorist who had been charged with failing to supply a specimen for laboratory analysis to be identified solely in court by a police officer. It had long been the practice in magistrates' courts for a defendant to be identified by a witness in court. It was impractical to require an identification parade on each occasion of disputed identity.

A registration document states that the registered keeper is not necessarily the legal owner. Its presence proves, or tends to prove, only the identity of the statutory "keeper" (*Beverley Acceptances Ltd v Oakley* [1982] R.T.R. 417 at 432, per Donaldson L.J.—a civil case). The decision was by a majority with Lord Denning dissenting. It should be compared with *R. v South Western JJ. Ex p. Wandsworth LBC* [1983] R.T.R. 425 (a Trade Descriptions Act case). There a vehicle had one owner but five hirers (and therefore registered keepers) under leasing agreements. It was held after reference to the Road Vehicles (Registration and Licensing) Regulations that a reference to one owner was a misleading trade description.

3.89   The court may properly infer that traffic lights work correctly (*Wells v Woodward* (1956) 54 L.G.R. 142). In *Farrell v Feighan* (1961) 76 Sh.Ct.Rep. 141, the owner of a car was found in the road beside it, unconscious; it was held to be sufficient proof that he had been driving but not that he had been driving carelessly. See *Platt v Green* [1965] Crim. L.R. 311 and *Dickens v Smith* [1965] Crim. L.R. 312 for cases where the High Court refused to interfere with convictions in road traffic cases notwithstanding discrepancies in the evidence of identification. The defendant's appearance in court in answer to the summons is not an admission that he was the driver or user at the time of the offence (*Saunders v Johns* [1965] Crim. L.R. 49). In *R. v O'Neale* [1988] R.T.R. 124, a driver had been charged with and convicted of the former offence of causing death by reckless driving. It was held by the Court of Appeal that evidence of the mere fact that he was in breach of the law relating to provisional licence-holders by driving without a qualified supervisor was inadmissible per se. It became admissible only if the lack of supervision could be causally connected with the ensuing accident.

Where several persons are found together in a vehicle, which has been taken without the owner's consent, in suspicious circumstances, that may be prima facie evidence that they were acting in concert and they can all be properly charged with taking it and with using it without insurance (*Ross v Rivenall* [1959] 2 All E.R. 376). The presumption of guilt would be less strong, however, against a passenger where the circumstances were not suspicious (see § 15.23). See also *R. v Baldessare* (1930) 144 L.T. 185.

3.90   In a case where the defendant was found to be driving a car seven miles from a town, it was presumed in the absence of contrary evidence, that he was driving on the same journey and road when three miles from the town shortly before (*Beresford v St Alban's JJ.* (1905) 22 T.L.R. 1).

Where a car collided with a gatepost on private land adjacent to the public highway, it was held by the Divisional Court that it was as "plain as a pikestaff" that the collision could only have occurred because of the vehicle's presence on the road as it drove off either the road or the footpath which formed part of it (*Lewis v Ursell, The Times*, April 23, 1983).

3.91   The prosecution must prove their case. In some road traffic cases it suffices to show that the defendant did the forbidden act without any evidence of a guilty mind: see, e.g. *Hawkins v Holmes* [1974] R.T.R. 436 at § 8.37 (failing to maintain brakes); in others, mens rea must be shown. In dangerous and careless driving cases it is not sufficient to show an accident which may well have occurred through negligence; the defendant's guilt must be established by positive evidence (*Alexander v Adair* 1938 S.C.(J.) 28). But any exception, exemption, proviso, excuse or qualification for a defendant should be proved by him and need not be negatived by police evidence in opening (Magistrates' Courts Act 1980 s.101; see *Baker v Sweet* [1966] Crim. L.R. 51 at § 6.102). The defendant must prove facts peculiarly within his own knowledge, e.g. that he has a licence (*R. v Oliver* [1943] 2 All E.R. 800) or policy of insurance (*Leathley v Drummond* below). This well-established principle was confirmed in *Guyll v Bright* [1987] R.T.R. 104 in which the Divisional Court decided that the offence of keeping a vehicle without an excise licence under what is now s.29 of the Vehicle Excise and Registration Act 1994 provided no exception to the rule under s.101 of the Magistrates' Courts Act 1980. Where it is an offence to do an act without lawful authority, the defendant must prove that he had such authority and the prosecution need not prove its absence (*Williams v Russell* (1933) 97 J.P. 128). On a charge of driving without a licence or insurance, it suffices if the prosecutor proves that the defendant drove a motor vehicle on a road on the day in question and, in law, no further evidence, e.g. that he was asked for, and failed to produce his licence or insurance certificate is required; the onus then shifts to the defendant to show that he had the licence (*John v Humphreys* [1955] 1 All E.R. 793) or insurance policy (*Leathley v Drummond* [1972] Crim. L.R. 227). It would be improper, however, to institute a prosecution on the sole ground that the defendant was seen to drive; the prosecutor should have some reason for thinking that no licence or insurance was in force. In *Howey v Bradley* [1970] Crim. L.R. 223 the court left open the question of whether the onus is on the prosecution to prove that an otherwise valid insurance policy produced by the defendant does not cover the particular use of the vehicle. However, it is suggested that it is for the defendant to prove that the use of the vehicle at the time was in accordance with the insurance in force. This is particularly important as restrictions on use included in insurance policies become more elaborate. See "Speed limits on restricted roads", § 6.103, as to proof that a speed limit applies to a particular road. It should, however, be remembered that where the onus of proof lies upon the defendant, the onus is that of a balance of probabilities—a defendant does not have to prove the matter in question beyond a doubt based on reason (*R. v Carr-Briant* [1943] 2 All E.R. 156).

It is always important for a court dealing with prosecutions under the Road **3.92** Traffic Acts to remind itself that the general burden of proof remains with the prosecution and the standard of proof is "beyond reasonable doubt". So much hardly needs to be stated in a practitioners' reference book, but those tests may not always be straightforward to apply in practice.

In *Rush v DPP* [1994] R.T.R. 268, the appellant was asked whether she wished to exercise her right to provide a specimen for laboratory analysis in place of a breath test. She declined. During the breathalyser procedure a conversation had been held which was not referred to in the record of the procedure. At her trial for driving with excess alcohol, the appellant alleged that an unrecorded conversation had taken place and this had led to her declining the statutory option.

The advice given to the justices was that the driver had to show that the conversation had taken place on the balance of probabilities, but to a high standard. If she satisfied the court on that issue, she then had to satisfy the court— again on the balance of probabilities—that she had been dissuaded from exercising her rights. The justices were satisfied that the conversation had taken place, but ruled that it had not dissuaded her from exercising the statutory option.

The Divisional Court held that if the justices thought (as a result of police evi- **3.93** dence or that of the driver) that the conversation might have taken place and been in the terms alleged by the driver and have dissuaded her from exercising the statutory option, the prosecution would have failed to prove beyond reasonable doubt that the correct procedure had been followed and that the driver should have been acquitted. The alleged conversation did not have to be proved on the balance of probabilities. The convictions were therefore quashed.

Where two defendants each are separately charged with careless driving in a crossroads collision or with certain other offences involving both, it seems that the prosecution can call one defendant to testify against the other, provided they are tried separately; the witness need not answer any questions tending to incriminate him (*Att Gen v Egan* [1948] Ir.R. 433). But a defendant jointly charged with another should not be called for the prosecution and, even where two defendants are charged with separate offences, it is suggested at 109 J.P. Jo. 39 that one should not be called against the other if there is something linking the two offences, e.g. using and permitting. But see *R. v Norfolk Quarter Sessions Ex p. Brunson* [1953] 1 All E.R. 346.

3.94 Any defendant may be called as a witness after he has been sentenced, acquitted or pardoned, or a *nolle prosequi* has been entered. There is no general rule that a defence witness should be sentenced on other pending charges before being called (*R. v Coffey* [1977] Crim. L.R. 45), but it does avoid the allegation that the evidence is being given in a way that seeks to reduce the severity of the sentence on the witness.

Proof in respect of companies, partnerships and employers

3.95 So far as companies are concerned the nature of the proof required will depend on whether the case is one of strict liability when the company will be vicariously liable. If, however, mens rea is required, it will be necessary to show that the requisite knowledge was possessed by the "brains and nerve centre", in other words the directors and manager who represent the directing mind and will of the company and control what it does. The state of mind of these managers is the state of mind of the company and is treated by the law as such. The board of directors may delegate some part of their functions of management giving to their delegate full discretion to act independently of instructions from them. They thereby put such a delegate in their place so that within the scope of the delegation he can act as the company. The various authorities were reviewed in *Essendon Engineering Co Ltd v Maile* [1982] R.T.R. 260, a case on s.171 of the Road Traffic Act 1972 (now s.175 of the 1988 Act) (issue of a test certificate false in a material particular). See also *John Henshall (Quarries) Ltd v Harvey* [1965] 2 Q.B. 233.

This issue may also be relevant if a company is charged with causing, permitting or aiding and abetting (see Chapter 1). Again, in *Edwards v Brookes (Milk) Ltd* [1963] 3 All E.R. 62 it was held that admissions by employees may be used in evidence against their employer when there is prima facie evidence that they are the employer's agents and they have an ostensible status qualifying them to make statements on behalf of the employer; in that case the employee concerned was a depot manager and there was evidence to imply that he had authority. Admissions made by a subordinate employee, however, would not generally be allowed in evidence (*Roberts v Morris* [1965] Crim. L.R. 46; here it was a lorry driver). See § 3.52 as to certificates of admission; it is submitted that the above rules apply to written admissions also. *Watson v Paterson, Ende v Cassidy* and the other cases quoted in §§ 3.82 et seq. show that a vehicle-owner is presumed to be its user and evidence of ownership, if not obtained from the firm's directors, is obtainable from the Department for Transport and from the name and address painted on the vehicle itself (cf. *Martin v White* (1910) 74 J.P. 106). A partner's admissions are evidence against the firm (Partnership Act 1890 s.15). Note also s.10 of the Criminal Justice Act 1967 at § 3.80 which allows admissions before and at the hearing by a defendant or by the prosecution; where the defendant is an individual, only his lawyer may make them for him, prior to the hearing, under s.10. A corporation may make written admissions by its directors, manager, secretary or clerk under s.10.

Evidence generally

In many cases a view of the locus by the advocate is obviously helpful. Skid **3.96** marks and other marks, damage, the visibility and obstructions at corners, the light, the state of the road at the time and mud or other indications where the point of impact was, are all things which may prove very significant at the hearing of a charge of dangerous or careless driving and it should be remembered that the view of a driver from a low, long-bonneted car may differ from that of a tall police officer on foot. The observance or non-observance of the Highway Code may be relied on in any civil or criminal proceedings as tending to establish or negate liability (s.38 of the 1988 Act; see further, however, at § 5.69 where this provision is discussed in the light of decided cases). A table of braking distances based on the diagram of typical stopping distances in the Highway Code appears at the end of this book, along with mileage per hour converted to feet per second. While the diagram of typical stopping distances may be used in cross-examination to prove a breach of the Highway Code, it is otherwise inadmissible by itself to prove speed as it is hearsay (*R. v Chadwick* [1975] Crim. L.R. 105).

While the court can call and recall witnesses itself, it was held in *R. v Owen* [1952] 1 All E.R. 1040 (discussed at [1952] Jo.Crim.L. 249) that this should not be done in jury cases after the summing-up, though this rule may be relaxed for the defence (*R. v Sanderson* [1953] 1 All E.R. 485). But a witness may be recalled at a trial before justices or on appeal from such a trial where no shorthand note is taken, provided that the witness was recalled solely for the purpose of refreshing the court's memory (*Phelan v Back* [1972] Crim. L.R. 104). It is submitted that justices should exercise such a power with extreme caution and should first endeavour to avoid having to do so by seeking agreement from the parties as to what the evidence was. Magistrates have a discretion to admit further evidence at least until the close of the case for the defence, but should not do so after they have retired save in very special circumstances (*Webb v Leadbetter* [1966] 2 All E.R. 114). In *Phelan v Back* [1972] 1 All E.R. 901 following *Webb v Leadbetter* a recorder hearing an appeal was upheld when he recalled a witness for the prosecution to refresh his memory as he had taken no note of his evidence.

The circumstances in which magistrates have a discretion to admit further evidence after the close of the case for the defence, and even after they have retired to consider their verdict, were examined further in *Malcolm v DPP* [2007] EWHC 363; [2007] R.T.R. 27. The position must now be considered in light of the Criminal Procedure Rules 2005, which require the parties actively to assist the exercise by the court of its case management powers, the exercise of which requires early identification of the real issues. It is the duty of the defence to make the real issues clear at the latest before the prosecution closes its case. In this case, the defendant's counsel raised an issue as to the admissibility of the evidence of the analysis of alcohol in the defendant's breath, submitting that there was no evidence of a warning as required by s.7(7) of the 1988 Act that a failure to provide a specimen might render the defendant liable to prosecution, or that any printout of the reading had been served. Before the justices announced that they were accordingly dismissing the case, counsel for the prosecution requested leave to adduce further evidence, which was granted. The defence challenged the decision of the magistrates to allow evidence to remedy the defect in the prosecution case once the magistrates had retired. Stanley Burnton J. said that defence counsel's submissions, which emphasised the obligation of the prosecution to prove its case in its entirety before closing its case, and certainly before the end of the final speech for the defence, had an anachronistic, and obsolete, ring. "Criminal trials are no longer to be treated as a game, in which each move is final and any omission by the prosecution leads to its failure. It is the duty of the defence to make its defence and the issues it raises clear to the prosecution and to the court at an early stage" ([2007] EWHC 363 at [31], per Stanley Burnton J.). Maurice Kay L.J. agreed, and expressed disapproval of an apparent attempt by the defence to ambush the prosecution. He regretted that there are still some advocates who choose to defend a case in the way in which this case was conducted in the magistrates' court. He said the magistrates were to be commended for refusing to succumb to this kind of forensic legerdemain.

This decision was followed in *R. (on the application of Lawson) v Stafford Magistrates' Court* [2007] EWHC 2490. In this case a driver on trial had identified two supposedly crucial issues for the first time during his closing argument. It was held that the magistrates were entitled to adjourn the trial in order to allow the prosecution to adduce further evidence. There was no question of bias on the part of the magistrates and nor would a fair-minded and informed observer have concluded that there was a real possibility of bias.

3.98   A similar firm clear message was given by the Administrative Court in *R. (on the application of Fine) v Abergavenny Magistrates' Court* [2007] EWHC 2005; 171 J.P. 683. Here the two applicants complained that the magistrates had adjourned proceedings on the application of the prosecution. The defence relied on a passage of the judgment of Rose L.J. in *R. (on the application of DPP) v Cheshire Justices* [2002] EWHC 466; [2002] P.N.L.R. 36, where he said at [7], "there was, as it seems to me, no obligation before the justices in relation to a case of this kind to make known to the prosecution in advance what the defence was going to be ... It was for the prosecution to be in a position to deal with whatever defence arises". In the instant case the court said that the conduct of litigation in the magistrates' court has dramatically changed since these observations were made. These observations in *Cheshire JJ.* should not now be relied on by defence advocates. The court was critical of an approach by the defence which "was an exercise which owes more to opportunism and arid technicality than a desire to achieve the overriding objective that the case be dealt with fairly on its merits, properly investigated" ([2007] EWHC 2005 at [29], per Treacy J.).

On indictment the presiding judge has a discretion whether to recall a witness after a submission of "no case" (*R. v McKenna* (1956) 40 Cr. App. R. 65). See also the decision in *James v South Glamorgan County Council* [1992] R.T.R. 312.

3.99   Leading questions may not normally be asked in examination-in-chief save to prove introductory matters but it is a common practice to allow a witness in a criminal case to be led as to matters not actually in controversy. A question may nevertheless be leading even if the witness is presented with a question in an alternative form. The primary test as to whether a question is leading is whether it suggests to the witness what the answer should be. If the court exercises its discretion to allow leading questions, a higher court will not normally interfere (*Ex p. Bottomley* (1909) 73 J.P. 246).

Failure to cross-examine a witness generally amounts to acceptance of his version, but justices were held entitled to convict because they disbelieved the defence witnesses even though the evidence of the defendant and his witnesses had not been challenged (*O'Connell v Adams* [1973] R.T.R. 150). Unlike professional judges, justices are under no obligation to test witnesses in respect of evidence they disbelieve (ibid.). Leading questions should not be asked in re-examination.

The shape of things to come with judges managing cases carefully with an eye **3.100**
to saving public money came in the decision of the Court of Appeal in *R. v Naylor*, February 6, 1995, unreported. The court was hearing an appeal against a criminal conviction for indecent assault. The basis of the appeal was that the trial judge had persistently interrupted counsel whilst she was cross-examining police officers about the procedures adopted in interviewing the 12-year-old complainant. Not only did the Court of Appeal dismiss the appeal, it fired a shot across the bows of those likely to employ "time wasting and argumentative cross-examination". Although the court would always be astute to guard against unfairness, it would "robustly" support judges who intervened to prevent cross-examination of this type. In this case the judge had been "entirely right" in intervening. The Court of Appeal went on by stating that time wasted in one person's defence was court time and legal aid money denied to another. Judges could and should stop time being wasted. The court would in future consider whether to make a wasted costs order.

This was plainly a decision on its own facts from a Crown Court trial and yet the uncompromising language used by the Court of Appeal may be said to have a wider application. Magistrates or district judges (magistrates' courts) must not be deterred in a clear-cut case from intervening to prevent the prolix advocate, nor one who has embarked on a cross-examination which wastes time and/or is argumentative. It is a process that has to be handled with skill and sensitivity but the potential difficulties involved are no good reason for failing to act where it appears just to do so.

As to corroboration in speeding cases, see §§ 6.76–9. It is desirable that the ev- **3.101**
idence of accomplices should be corroborated. See §§ 5.54–7 as to giving evidence in dangerous and careless driving cases when the defendant had been drinking. Evidence of acts of driving some distance away may be given in certain circumstances (see § 5.59).

As to exhibits, see § 3.71 and *R. v Orrell* [1972] R.T.R. 14 and *Tremlett v Fawcett* (1984) 1 R.T.L.B. 68 at § 4.245.

Evidence illegally obtained

Section 78 of the Police and Criminal Evidence Act 1984 imports discretions **3.102**
to exclude *prosecution* evidence if it would be unfair. The court is required to have regard to all the circumstances including the circumstances in which the evidence was obtained. Before the implementation of the Act, evidence (other than admissions or confessions) obtained by illegal means was generally admissible for the prosecution. Reference should be made to the speeches of the Law Lords in *R. v Sang* [1979] 2 All E.R. 1222. There is a useful commentary on the decision in [1979] Crim. L.R. 656.

R. v Sang was followed in *R. v Trump* [1980] R.T.R. 274 CA. In that case a defendant was wrongly arrested because the requirements of the subsection then in force were not fulfilled. While at a police station he provided a blood specimen for analysis after having been warned in accordance with what is now s.7(7) of the Act. The specimen was not obtained with the defendant's consent and was not therefore admissible under s.11(4) of the Act. The defendant was, however, charged with the s.4(1) offence of driving whilst unfit and, applying *R. v Sang*, the Court of Appeal held that the judge had a discretion to admit evidence of the analysis and it would have been improper to exclude it. The court quoted Lord Diplock's statement in *Sang* that "there is no discretion to exclude evidence discovered as the result of an illegal search but there is discretion to exclude evidence which the accused has been induced to produce voluntarily if the method of inducement was unfair".

3.103   *R. v Sang* was explained in *Morris v Beardmore* [1980] R.T.R. 321. Lord Diplock emphasised that there was no general exclusionary discretion. It was confined to the two categories specified in *R. v Sang at* [1979] 2 All E.R. 1222 at 1231A, per Lord Diplock, namely:

"(1) A trial judge ... has always a discretion to refuse to admit evidence if in his opinion its prejudicial effect outweighs its probative value.

(2) Save with regard to admissions and confessions and generally with regard to evidence obtained from the accused after the commission of the offence, he has no discretion to refuse to admit relevant admissible evidence on the ground that it was obtained by improper or unfair means."

The law has been changed in several respects. First, the test of unfairness is different. For instance, the introduction of the evidence may be unfair even though its prejudicial value would not outweigh its probative value. Secondly, the court is given a general *discretion*. This does not mean that improperly obtained evidence will be excluded. The court has first to find that it would be unfair and secondly to decide in its discretion whether to exclude it. In magistrates' courts the decision will be for magistrates, who will have to hear about it and then possibly exclude it.

3.104   Subject to this the principle in *Sang* remains, namely that improperly obtained evidence is admissible unless one of the exceptions applies. The principle in *Sang* was applied in *Fox v Chief Constable of Gwent* [1985] 3 All E.R. 392 HL.

The precise status of s.78 has been underlined in a number of decisions, including *Vel (Kevin) v Chief Constable of North Wales* [1987] Crim. L.R. 496. There the Divisional Court confirmed that the power to exclude unfair evidence conferred by the section did not affect the procedure in the magistrates' court for determining the admissibility of evidence and it did not entitle a defendant to have issues of admissibility settled as a preliminary issue in a trial within a trial *under that* section. *Aliter* if the argument is able to be brought within the terms of s.76. In *Matto v Wolverhampton Crown Court* [1987] R.T.R. 337, the Divisional Court held that the power conferred in s.78 did not reduce a court's discretion to exclude such unfair evidence which the court could have excluded at common law. For further judicial interpretation of this section see the judgment of Watkins L.J. in *R. v Mason (Carl)* [1987] 3 All E.R. 481 CA. A decision where justices were held to have followed the correct principles in refusing to exclude evidence under s.78 of the Police and Criminal Evidence Act 1984 is *Thomas v DPP* [1991] R.T.R. 292. (See § 4.14 below.) Contrast a decision in which justices used s.78 wrongly, abusing the power conferred by the section (*DPP v British Telecommunications plc* (1991) 155 J.P. 869). In considering whether to admit or exclude evidence under s.78 of the Police and Criminal Evidence Act 1984, the court is concerned with substantive issues of fairness and unfairness. Similarly, the European Convention on Human Rights is concerned with substance rather than form. Therefore, where the arrest of a driver had been unlawful because of a matter of form rather than substance, there was no unfairness in allowing the evidence of what occurred at the police station to be admitted: *Harper (Alistair Stewart) v DPP* [2001] EWHC Admin 1071.

The decision in *Vel (Kevin) v Chief Constable of North Wales* above was considered and applied in *Halawa v Federation Against Copyright Theft* [1995] 1 Cr. App. R. 21. At the appellant's trial his counsel raised objection to the admissibility of certain evidence under s.78 of the Police and Criminal Evidence Act 1984. At the end of the prosecution case, the magistrate found that there was a case to answer. Counsel then applied to call his client to give evidence on the admissibility point alone. The magistrate rejected that application and ruled that if the appellant gave evidence he could be cross-examined on any issue in the case. In dismissing his appeal, the Divisional Court stated that justices must either deal with the application when it arises or leave the decision until the end of the hearing with the object of securing a trial which was fair and just to both sides. In securing that objective, justices would be entitled in some cases to allow the defendant to proceed by way of a trial within a trial if he so desired. In most cases of summary trial, since the justices' decision under s.78 had to be determined "having regard to all the circumstances", the better course would be for the whole of the prosecution case to be heard, including the disputed evidence, before any trial within a trial was held. In general, the defendant should, except for good reason, have the opportunity to secure the exclusion of the unfair evidence before he was required to give evidence on the main issues; otherwise his right to remain silent on the main issues would be impaired. In the present case, the appellant had suffered no unfairness and no injustice. **3.105**

A further example of an improper use by a court of s.78 of the Police and Criminal Evidence Act 1984, on facts which may perhaps not be too unusual, came before the Divisional Court in *DPP v Wilson* [1991] R.T.R. 284. Justices were trying an information of driving with excess alcohol, contrary to s.5 of the 1988 Act. They found, inter alia, that as a consequence of an anonymous telephone call, a police officer went to a place where he expected a car to be on the move at any minute, and he could then catch a driver who had been drinking. It was conceded that the police officer was entitled to stop the car, and the issue was whether the justices were correct in their conclusion that the police officer's suspicion was founded on facts wholly unconnected with the defendant's driving. It was argued that it was "oppressive" behaviour by the police officer to act on private information and "lie around the corner" for an offence to be committed. The court remitted the matter back to the justices. The police officer was under a duty to act on information received and when an offence was committed to act appropriately. In *DPP v Corthine*, November 25, 1999, unreported, DC, justices excluded police officers' evidence under s.78 of the Police and Criminal Evidence Act 1984 on the grounds that the officers had seen the defendant before he was to drive and been aware that he intended to drive but did not warn him not to drive. Within a few minutes of him starting to drive he was stopped by those officers in the vicinity. The justices concluded that this course of conduct evinced bad faith and thus constituted malpractice. The Divisional Court disagreed referring to *DPP v Wilson* [1991] R.T.R. 284.

The discretion conferred by s.78 of the 1984 Act was a matter before the Divisional Court in *Sharpe v DPP* [1993] R.T.R. 392. In this case the court **3.106** stressed the fact of discretion which a court was required to exercise judicially. The justices, hearing an information alleging that the appellant drove with excess alcohol, refused to issue witness summonses directed to neighbours of the appellant who would have been able to describe what happened in the driveway of the appellant's house and the constables' alleged oppressive behaviour. The court held, inter alia, that the conduct of the constables in stopping and arresting the appellant in his driveway was relevant to the justices' exercise of their discretion under s.78, and that the justices had not exercised their discretion, for they had in fact stated that whatever the witnesses might have said and however bad the constables' behaviour might have been in the driveway, the justices would still not have excluded the breath analysis evidence. The appeal was allowed, but the case was not remitted to the magistrates' court.

The Criminal Procedure and Investigations Act 1996 Sch.1 Pt 2 makes it clear that, in committal proceedings, evidence of a confession may not be excluded in those proceedings, nor do the provisions of s.78 of the Police and Criminal Evidence Act 1984 apply in those proceedings.

3.107   An important decision on the relationship between exploratory questions and an interview, and the consequent possibility of a breach of one or more of the codes of practice under the Police and Criminal Evidence Act 1984 was that of the Court of Appeal in *R. v Park* (1994) 99 Cr. App. R. 270. Although the appellant's appeal was dismissed on the facts, the principles laid down by their Lordships have widespread application. When the police ask exploratory questions in a roadside inquiry and in due course the answers given lead to a well-founded suspicion that an offence has been committed, then what had started out as an inquiry might become an interview and, if it does, the procedure laid down in the codes of practice under the 1984 Act have to be followed so far as practicable. Although a contemporaneous note is no longer possible, a record should be made as soon as practicable of the earlier questions and answers, the reason for the absence of a contemporaneous note should be recorded and the suspect should be given the opportunity to check the record. If the breaches of the code are significant and substantial they will lead to the exclusion of the relevant parts of the evidence under s.78 of the Police and Criminal Evidence Act 1984.

Section 78 of the 1984 Act was also considered in the linked Court of Appeal decisions of *R. v Smurthwaite; R. v Gill* (1994) 98 Cr. App. R. 437. The court had to determine whether the use of an agent provocateur or entrapment afforded a defence to a criminal charge. The court held that it did not and that s.78 had not altered the substantive rule of law in this regard. However, it went on to find that entrapment, agent provocateur or the use of a trick were not irrelevant to the application of s.78 because the judge had a discretion to exclude the evidence so as to ensure a fair trial. If he considered that in all the circumstances the obtaining of the evidence by those means would have the adverse effect referred to in s.78, he should exclude it. The balance between enforcement agencies acting as undercover agents to investigate criminal activity by gathering evidence or acting as agents provocateurs to incite such activity was considered in *Nottingham City Council v Amin* [2000] R.T.R. 122. The issue surrounded a driver plying for hire in an area different from that in which he was licensed. He was stopped by plainclothes police officers and agreed to convey them to a specified destination for a fare. The Divisional Court reviewed both English authorities and obligations under the European Convention on Human Rights and came to the conclusion that there were no grounds for excluding the evidence of the officers.

Consideration as to the extent and consequences of entrapment was given by **3.108** the House of Lords in *R. v Loosely; Att Gen's Reference (No.3 of 2000)* [2001] UKHL 53; [2001] 1 W.L.R 2060. Both cases arose from the supply of prohibited drugs to undercover police officers. Affirming that entrapment is not a defence in itself but can amount to an abuse of the process of the court, the House of Lords set out the relevant factors in assessing whether an abuse existed. Every court had an inherent power and duty to prevent abuse of its process and it is by recourse to that principle that courts ensured that executive agents of the State did not misuse the coercive, law enforcement functions of the courts and thereby oppress citizens—entrapment is an example of when such misuse may occur. It is not acceptable for the State to lure its citizens into committing forbidden acts and then seeking to prosecute them for doing so. However, what is meant by "lure" is less than precise and there are offences which could never be prosecuted without some active role by the police. This has long been accepted in, for instance, test purchases and the circumstances of *Nottingham City Council v Amin* (see above). When the use of such techniques was acceptable, there were limits. The judicial response to entrapment was based on the need to uphold the rule of law and would assess whether to prosecute in such circumstances would be an affront to the public conscience and would not be fair. The question was whether the police did no more than present the defendant with an unexceptional opportunity to commit the crime. Police conduct of that nature was not to be regarded as inciting or instigating crime or luring a person into committing a crime. It should be realised that proactive techniques were more needed (and hence more appropriate) in some circumstances than in others and that the secrecy and difficulty of detection and the manner in which the particular criminal activity was carried on would be relevant considerations. The greater the inducement held out by the police, the more forceful or persistent the police overtures, the more readily might the court conclude that the police overstepped the boundary and that their conduct may have brought about the commission of a crime by a person who would normally avoid that type of crime. The court must take note of the defendant's circumstances since the significance of an inducement will vary from person to person. In summary, for the police to behave as would an ordinary customer of a trade, lawful or unlawful, being carried on by the defendant would not normally be regarded as objectionable. The appropriate action for a court was to stay the proceedings and the approach had not been changed by the implementation of the Human Rights Act 1998 since there were no appreciable differences between the requirements of art.6 of the European Convention on Human Rights and the English law as it had been developed in recent years. This has been confirmed by the European Court of Human Rights in *Shannon v United Kingdom* [2005] Crim. L.R. 133 and *Eurofinacom v France* [2005] Crim. L.R. 134. In both cases, enforcing authorities had become aware of information suggesting that the defendants were prepared to commit specified crimes. Enforcement officers in one case and investigative journalists in the other in effect made test purchases. The defendants appealed against conviction on the grounds that the right to a fair trial under art.6 had been contravened. Both applications were deemed inadmissible. Whilst admission of such evidence may in certain circumstances be inadmissible, that was clearly not so in these cases.

For a discussion of issues arising from *Loosely* above, see A. Ashworth, "Re- **3.109** drawing the Boundaries of Entrapment" [2002] Crim. L.R. 161–179.

CHAPTER 4

DRINK/DRIVING OFFENCES

CONTENTS

INTRODUCTION

The legislative framework

4.01   The whole of the Road Traffic Act 1972, together with Pt IV of, and Schs 7 and 8 to, the Transport Act 1981 were repealed by the Road Traffic Act 1988 and the Road Traffic Offenders Act 1988 (Road Traffic (Consequential Provisions) Act 1988 Sch.1). Those Acts served to consolidate the previous legislation and apart from some minor stylistic changes and rearrangements in the drafting, faithfully reproduced the repealed provisions. The Road Traffic Act 1988 (referred to hereafter as "the 1988 Act") consolidates provisions relating to road traffic offences whilst the Road Traffic Offenders Act 1988 (referred to hereafter as "the 1988 Offenders Act") amounts to a consolidation of provisions relating to the prosecution and punishment of those, and other, offences.

Section 4 of the 1988 Act (driving a motor vehicle when unfit through drink or drugs, etc.) was amended by Sch.1 to the Road Traffic Act 1991 which replaced the words "motor vehicle" where they appeared in that section with the words "mechanically propelled vehicle". The 1991 Act also inserted a new s.3A in the 1988 Act in order to create with effect from the same date the offence of causing death by careless driving when under the influence of drink or drugs; this offence is dealt with in Chapter 5 below.

4.02   Section 7(3) of the 1988 Act was amended by s.63 of the Criminal Procedure and Investigations Act 1996, which inserted therein a new subs.(bb) enabling police to make full and proper use at police stations of the second generation of stationary breath-alcohol analysers (see § 4.110).

Section 7(4) of the 1988 Act was amended, and a new s.7(4A) inserted, by the Police Reform Act 2002 s.55. The effect of these amendments is to allow registered health care professionals as well as registered medical practitioners to decide that blood specimens should not for medical reasons be extracted from suspects, provided that the opinion of the latter is not contrary to that of the former, and to require the decision as to who is to be asked to take a specimen (if one is to be taken) to be made by the officer making the requirement (see § 4.215).

A new s.7A was inserted in the 1988 Act by the Police Reform Act 2002 s.56, **4.03** in order to provide for the taking of specimens of blood from persons incapable of consenting (see § 4.284).

Section 6 of the 1988 Act was replaced by the Railways and Transport Safety Act 2003 s.107 and Sch.7 para.1, which inserted in its place new ss.6, 6A, 6B, 6C, 6D and 6E in order to provide a statutory regime for the preliminary testing of drivers of motor vehicles for drink or drugs based upon the administration to suspects of three specific kinds of preliminary test; a preliminary breath test, a preliminary impairment test and a preliminary drug test (see §§ 4.35 et seq).

Sections 6D and 7 of the Road Traffic Act 1988 were amended by s.154 of the Serious Organised Crime and Police Act 2005 in order to provide police with a power to undertake evidential breath tests at the roadside (see § 4.37).

The text of the relevant parts of the current legislation is reproduced in full in **4.04** Vol.2.

Where a section of a statute is referred to without its statute being named, the reader may assume that it refers to the Road Traffic Act 1988 ("the 1988 Act").

Offences

The offences dealt with in this chapter are: **4.05**

(1) Driving or attempting to drive a mechanically propelled vehicle while unfit to drive through drink or drugs (s.4(1)).

(2) Being in charge of a mechanically propelled vehicle while unfit to drive through drink or drugs (s.4(2)).

(3) Driving or attempting to drive a motor vehicle on a road or other public place after consuming so much alcohol that the proportion of it in the person's breath, blood or urine exceeds the prescribed limit (s.5(1)(a)).

(4) Being in charge of a motor vehicle on a road or public place after consuming alcohol so that the proportion of it in the person's breath, blood or urine exceeds the prescribed limit (s.5(1)(b)).

(5) Without reasonable excuse, failing to co-operate with a preliminary test (s.6(6)).

(6) Without reasonable excuse, failing to supply specimens of breath, blood or urine for analysis (s.7(6)).

(7) Without reasonable excuse, failing to allow specimen of blood to be subjected to a laboratory test (s.7A).

A summary of these offences is set out in §§ 4.21–7.

Irrelevance of arrest to admissibility of evidence of analysis

In contrast to earlier statutory provisions, the present law entitles a constable to **4.06** require specimens of breath, blood or urine "in the course of an investigation whether a person has committed an offence under section ... 4 or 5 " (s.7(1)). For this reason it was held in three separate cases in the Divisional Court (*Fox v Gwent Chief Constable* [1984] R.T.R. 402, *Anderton v Royle* [1985] R.T.R. 91 and *Bunyard v Hayes* [1985] R.T.R. 348 *Note*) that the fact that the arrest was unlawful (as in *Fox*) or that the officers had failed to prove a valid arrest (as in *Anderton v Royle*) is irrelevant provided that the specimen for analysis was obtained without inducement, threat (other than the statutory warning), trick or other impropriety. In *Bunyard* the defendant refused to supply evidential breath specimens at the police station after having been arrested on suspicion of being the driver involved in an accident (which he was not). It was again held following *Fox* that as there was no misconduct on the part of the police the defendant should be convicted under what is now s.7(6) of refusing specimens for analysis.

The case of *Fox v Gwent Chief Constable* was considered by the House of Lords on appeal ([1985] R.T.R. 337). Their Lordships unanimously upheld the Divisional Court holding that evidence of a specimen of breath obtained at a police station in accordance with the procedure laid down in the Act and without any trick or impropriety was admissible notwithstanding that the accused had been unlawfully arrested. On a proper construction of s.7(1) an arrest or lawful arrest is not an essential prerequisite for the evidence of the breath test result at the police station to be rendered admissible.

Exclusion of evidence of analysis

4.07 It is clear from the unanimous decision of the House of Lords in *Fox* (see § 4.06 above) that evidence or proof of compliance with the requirements of the roadside breath test procedure is no longer an essential prerequirement of proof of an offence under what is now s.5. It was accordingly held in *Gull v Scarborough* [1987] R.T.R. 261. *Note* that, following *Fox*, a magistrate was wrong to dismiss a case under what is now s.5(1) because an arrest for failing to provide a roadside breath specimen was unlawful, the magistrate having found as fact that the police had no reasonable cause to suspect that the accused was driving with an excess of alcohol in his breath. It was further held that there is no distinction in principle between the provision of a breath specimen at a police station, as in *Fox*, and, as was the case in *Gull* where the machine was out of order, the provision of blood.

Although it is not clear from the report what cases were cited to the court in argument, it would appear that the Divisional Court in *DPP v Kay* [1999] R.T.R. 109 drew upon the authority of *Fox* above when advising justices to be slow to exclude evidence of the taking of the substantive specimen of breath because of a technical shortcoming in the roadside procedure. In the case in point the roadside police officer's innocent failure to follow the manufacturer's instructions about allowing a 20-minute gap to elapse from consumption of the last drink to the breath test did not render unlawful the result of the subsequent Intoximeter test at the police station. When weighing the failure to follow the correct procedure at the roadside and its effect on the fairness of proceedings, justices should have in mind that the 1988 Act was enacted to prevent motorists who were over the permitted limit escaping responsibility on technicalities.

4.08 *DPP v Kay* above was considered and applied by the Divisional Court in *DPP v Kennedy* [2003] EWHC 2583; (2004) 168 J.P. 185. A failure to change the mouthpiece on an Alcolmeter SL–400A before a second roadside test on the same suspect could not possibly have distorted the result of that second test. Even if the justices had been correct to hold that the mouthpiece should have been replaced, there would have been no justification, on the authority of *Fox* above, for excluding the evidence of the breath analysis at the police station under s.78 of the Police and Criminal Evidence Act 1984.

A similarly robust course was followed by the court in *Harper (Alistair Stewart) v DPP* [2001] EWHC Admin 1071. Following a forced entry to property in pursuit of a suspected drink/driver, the suspect was arrested by police with the words "I am arresting you on suspicion of driving a motor vehicle on a road whilst over the prescribed limit through drink or drugs". These words were an adequate summary of s.5 of the Road Traffic Act 1988, which did not provide a power of arrest, but were not appropriate to s.4 ibid., which did provide such a power; his arrest, therefore, had been unlawful. The unlawfulness of the arrest had been a matter of form rather than substance, however, and there was no unfairness in allowing the evidence of his refusal to supply a specimen of breath at the police station to be admitted (applying *Fox* above); furthermore, the position was no different under the European Convention on Human Rights, which was concerned with substance rather than form.

It has been further held that, provided there is no malpractice, caprice or opprobrious behaviour on the part of the police, there is no restriction on the stopping of motorists for the purpose of ascertaining whether the drivers have alcohol in their bodies and on the subsequent requirement of a breath test; (what are now) ss.6 and 6A govern the administration of the preliminary breath test and not the stopping of a car; random stopping of cars within these limits is not prohibited, but the police are prohibited from requiring breath tests at random (*Chief Constable of Gwent v Dash* [1986] R.T.R. 41, following *Steel v Goacher* [1983] R.T.R. 98 but disapproving dicta to the contrary in *Such v Ball* [1982] R.T.R. 140) (see further § 4.53)). **4.09**

It should, however, be made clear that while evidence of a breath, blood or urine specimen is normally admissible notwithstanding that there was no arrest or that the arrest was unlawful, the evidential specimen may be inadmissible if it was not obtained in accordance with the procedure for obtaining such a specimen in the police station set out in ss.7, 8 (see further § 4.107).

The principles of *R. v Sang* [1979] 2 All E.R. 1222 (a House of Lords case), to the effect that although a judge has a discretion to exclude evidence of admissions, confessions and evidence obtained from the accused after the commission of the offence, he has no discretion to refuse to admit relevant admissible evidence merely because it has been obtained by improper or unfair means, were to some extent overtaken by statute with the bringing into force on January 1, 1986 of s.78 of the Police and Criminal Evidence Act 1984 (see § 3.102). The section provides that in any proceedings the court may refuse to allow evidence on which the prosecution proposes to rely to be given if it appears to the court that having regard to all the circumstances, including the circumstances in which the evidence was obtained, the admission of the evidence would have such an adverse effect on the fairness of the proceedings that the court ought not to admit it. **4.10**

This statutory provision clearly can apply to statements produced by evidential breath testing machines. The section states that the court has a discretion to exclude the unfairly obtained evidence in any proceedings ("proceedings" are defined as criminal proceedings including courts-martial, etc., s.82 of the 1984 Act). The section would thus seem to be of general application. It will be noted that unlike the doctrine of law in the United States ("the fruit of the poisoned tree") the evidence will not be automatically excluded if obtained illegally or if obtained after an unlawful arrest; instead the court under s.78 has to consider whether the admission of the evidence would have such an adverse effect on the fairness of the proceedings that it ought not to be admitted having regard to all the circumstances, including the circumstances in which it was obtained.

4.11   It was always anticipated that s.78 of the Police and Criminal Evidence Act 1984 would become the subject of case law; that anticipation was fulfilled, albeit to a limited extent and in very unusual circumstances, in the case of *Matto v Wolverhampton Crown Court* [1987] R.T.R. 337 (also reported as *Jit Singh Matto v DPP* [1987] Crim. L.R. 641). Having followed the suspect up a driveway for some 200 or 300yds and been informed by him that they were on private property and could not therefore breathalyse him, the two police officers concerned nevertheless persisted in their request for a breath test and a positive result was obtained. The defendant was arrested and at the police station subsequently provided specimens for an evidential breath test which revealed an alcohol level of 73μg/100ml of breath. He appealed to the Crown Court against his conviction for driving with excess alcohol.

The appeal was conducted by both sides on the basis that the validity or otherwise of the screening breath test was crucial to the determination of the issue. Although the court found that the police *knew* they were acting illegally, it decided not to exercise its discretion to exclude the evidence of the evidential breath test. An appeal to the Divisional Court followed, and in the case stated the Crown Court referred to the screening breath test as having been obtained *voluntarily*.

4.12   The Divisional Court (Woolf L.J. and McCullough J.) interpreted the known facts somewhat differently. Given that the court below had found that at some time after their initial request for a screening breath test the police officers had become aware that their implied licence to be on the property had been terminated, but had nevertheless persisted with their request, the finding that the specimen had been taken voluntarily was, per Woolf L.J., "wholly inconsistent". McCullough J., concurring, stated that he did not think it could properly be said that the appellant in giving the specimen at his house "… was acting voluntarily. It would be almost—not quite, but almost—as logical in the crime of rape to say that the woman who submitted because she believed she had no alternative acted voluntarily".

Having thus established that the police officers were acting *mala fide*, the case could be said to fall within the exceptional category of case envisaged by the House of Lords in *Fox* when they referred to the different view they might have taken had the defendant in that case been lured to the police station by trickery or oppression rather than, as he had been, as the result of a genuine mistake.

4.13   Turning then to s.78 of the 1984 Act, Woolf L.J. observed that he was satisfied that the statute does not reduce the discretion of the court to exclude unfair evidence which existed at common law. Accordingly, given the finding of *mala fides* by the Crown Court, that court "could or might" have exercised its discretion to exclude evidence of the breath-alcohol analysis. The appeal was allowed.

The facts of this case made it an exceptional one, and Woolf L.J. was at pains to point out that in the ordinary way courts will not be concerned with what happened with regard to the screening breath test, but will only be concerned, in accordance with *Fox*, with the procedure at the police station under what are now ss.7, 8.

R. v Sang and *Matto v Wolverhampton Crown Court* above were distinguished **4.14** by the Divisional Court in *R. v Thomas* [1990] Crim. L.R. 269 (also reported as *Thomas v DPP* [1991] R.T.R. 292). Where a police officer unlawfully arrested a motorist for failing to provide a screening breath test (such a specimen not in fact having been requested), but in so doing acted under a misunderstanding rather than in bad faith, there was no reason why evidence of the motorist's subsequent refusal to provide a specimen at the police station should not be admitted. It was clear from the authority of *Fox* that an unlawful arrest was irrelevant to breath test procedures at a police station. A discretion to exclude those procedures rested upon a finding of *mala fides* but in the case in point the justices had specifically found that the police sergeant concerned had acted solely as a result of a misunderstanding. The defendant's appeal against a conviction of an offence under what is now s.7(6) of failure to provide a specimen of breath for analysis was accordingly dismissed.

Thomas v DPP was itself distinguished by the Divisional Court in *DPP v McGladrigan* [1991] R.T.R. 297 and *DPP v Godwin* [1991] R.T.R. 303 in which it was held, applying *R. v Samuel* [1988] QB 615, that the discretion to exclude evidence under s.78 was phrased in general terms and was not dependent upon a finding of *mala fides* on the part of the police.

The case of *Matto v Wolverhampton Crown Court* above was applied by the **4.15** Divisional Court in *Sharpe v DPP* [1993] R.T.R. 392. A defendant whose erratic driving had caused constables to pursue him into his own driveway made it clear to those constables that their presence on his property was unwelcome and that they were trespassers; he was nevertheless led or dragged by them back onto the road where he refused to provide a specimen of breath for a breath test. He was taken under arrest to the police station where he provided specimens for an evidential breath test which revealed an alcohol level of $111\mu g/100ml$ of breath. At the close of the prosecution case the defendant applied for witness summonses for two of his neighbours so that they could give evidence of the constables' oppressive behaviour and also of the normality of the defendant's driving in the vicinity of his home so that the justices would be able to consider exercising their discretion to exclude the breath analysis evidence under s.78 of the Police and Criminal Evidence Act 1984. The justices declined to issue the summonses on the basis that evidence of the defendant's later driving would add nothing material to the case since the constables had given sufficient evidence of earlier erratic driving, and that since the constables had accepted that they were trespassers in the defendant's driveway, any evidence about their exact behaviour would take the matter no further.

Allowing the defendant's appeal against his conviction, the court stated that the conduct of the officers in stopping and arresting the defendant in his driveway was relevant to the justices' exercise of their discretion under s.78 of the 1984 Act. In stating that they would not have excluded the breath analysis evidence whatever the witnesses might have said and however bad the police officers' behaviour might have been, the justices had not exercised their discretion. They therefore erred in excluding the evidence of the neighbours by not issuing the witness summonses and, consequently, in forming the opinion that, whatever the evidence, they would automatically have exercised their discretion in favour of admitting the breath analysis evidence.

4.16   In the course of argument it was submitted on behalf of the defendant that where *mala fides* was established, the discretion under s.78 could only be exercised one way, namely by the exclusion of the evidence of the breath analysis. That "rather extreme" submission (per Buckley J.) was not accepted by the court; the authority of *DPP v McGladrigan* [1991] R.T.R. 297 and in particular *R. v Samuel* [1988] Q.B. 615 cited in that case would appear to contradict, not support, such a submission.

It is important to note that it is not permissible to raise before the Divisional Court the issue of the justices' discretion to exclude evidence under s.78 if that issue was not raised earlier before the justices (*Braham v DPP* [1996] R.T.R. 30). The justices concerned could hardly be criticised for deciding as they did by reference to a power they had not been asked to exercise; accordingly the case did not come in the same category as *Matto v Wolverhampton Crown Court* and *Sharpe v DPP* (both described above).

4.17   The statutory procedure under ss.7 and 8 of the 1988 Act for obtaining specimens for analysis does not constitute an interview for the purposes of Code C of the codes of practice issued under the authority of the Police and Criminal Evidence Act 1984; accordingly the decisions of justices to exclude prosecution evidence under s.78 of the latter Act on the grounds that such evidence was obtained contrary to Code C for the detention, treatment and questioning of persons by police officers were overturned by the Divisional Court in *DPP v D (A Minor)*; *DPP v Rous* [1992] R.T.R. 246.

Where a defendant was presented at the police station with forms telling him that he had a right to see a solicitor "at any time", the court should have considered the possibility of exercising its discretion under s.78 to exclude evidence of his refusal to provide two specimens of breath until he had seen a solicitor. The Crown Court had been wrong in its view that s.78 had no application to breath test procedures. The Divisional Court so held in *Hudson v DPP* [1992] R.T.R. 27 in allowing the defendant's appeal against the rejection of his appeal by York Crown Court. The defendant had spent an hour at the police station before the Intoximeter procedure was begun, during which time the police had been trying to find him a solicitor. When eventually he was asked, he said he would provide the required specimens, but wanted to see the duty solicitor first. A similar reply some 20 minutes later led to the defendant being charged with failure to provide specimens for analysis. Upon looking at the forms given to the defendant it was clear to their Lordships that it was not possible to say that there was no material upon which the court could have exercised its discretion to exclude evidence. In the court's view it would be helpful if in future such forms were to include an indication that the rights referred to therein did not interfere with breath test procedures and gave a suspect no right to delay those procedures.

4.18   The Judicial Committee of the Privy Council in *Brown v Stott (Procurator Fiscal, Dunfermline)* [2003] 1 A.C. 681 overturned the decision of the High Court of Justiciary in Scotland in *Brown v Procurator Fiscal, Dunfermline* 2000 J.C. 328 in which it had been held that the privilege against self-incrimination could not be overridden by the obligation on the registered keeper of a vehicle to supply information which might tend to incriminate the keeper as the driver of the vehicle.

Police officers who attended a superstore to arrest Mrs Brown for shoplifting noted the smell of alcohol on her breath and clothing. When asked how she had travelled to the superstore, she replied that she had driven. As she was leaving to go with the officers to the police station she pointed to a car in the car park and said it was hers. At the police station a set of keys for her car was found in her handbag. Later, and by virtue of the officers' powers under s.172(2)(a) of the 1988 Act, she was required to say who had been driving her car at the time when she would have travelled in it to the superstore car park. She replied "It was me". She was subsequently breathalysed and charged with driving with excess alcohol. Having been so charged, she objected to the admissibility of her admission that she had been the driver of her car at the material time. The issue was whether the admission had been obtained in circumstances that contravened her privilege against self-incrimination, such as would cause the acceptance of that admission into evidence to deny her her right to a fair trial pursuant to art.6 of the European Convention on Human Rights.

It was unanimously held by the Privy Council that neither s.172 itself, nor the admission in evidence at a subsequent trial of the answers given by the defendant to questions posed under s.172, breaches the Convention. Although clearly an implied right under art.6, the privilege against self-incrimination was not an absolute, but rather a qualified right. The need for a fair balance between the general interest of the community and the personal rights of the individual was recognised by the European Court. The high incidence of death and injury on the roads was a very serious problem and the need to address it effectively, for the benefit of the public, could not be doubted. One way in which governments have sought to address it is by subjecting the use of motor vehicles to a regime of regulation and making provision for enforcement by identifying, prosecuting and punishing offending drivers. There being a clear public interest in the enforcement of road traffic legislation, the Committee was of the view that s.172 did not represent a disproportionate response to a serious social problem. In the words of Lord Bingham of Cornhill who delivered the leading opinion: **4.19**

> "If … one asks whether section 172 represents a disproportionate legislative response to the problem of maintaining road safety, whether the balance between the interests of the community at large and the interests of the individual is struck in a manner unduly prejudicial to the individual, whether (in short) the leading of this evidence would infringe a basic human right of the respondent, I would feel bound to give negative answers."

Brown above was applied by the Divisional Court in *DPP v Wilson* [2001] EWHC Admin 198; [2002] R.T.R. 6 when holding that the use in evidence of a defendant's compulsory admission under s.172(2)(b) of the Road Traffic Act 1988 that he was the driver of a vehicle at the time when a road traffic offence was committed, did not infringe his privilege against self-incrimination or right to a fair trial under art.6 of the European Convention on Human Rights. There was no distinction to be drawn between a notice under s.172(2)(a) requiring the vehicle's keeper to identify the driver at the time of the alleged offence, the provision upheld in *Brown*, and a notice under the much wider wording of s.172(2)(b), which enabled the police to require any other person to give information which might lead to the identification of the driver; see further § 7.26. **4.20**

SUMMARY OF OFFENCES

Failing to co-operate with a preliminary test (s.6(6))

4.21   The offence is fully committed when a person fails (and failure includes refusal) to co-operate with a preliminary test when required to do so. The circumstances in which a motorist can be required to do so are set out in §§ 4.35 et seq. The person must have been either driving or attempting to drive or in charge of a motor vehicle on a road or other public place. For special provision for hospital patients, see §§ 4.287 et seq. For procedure, trial and penalties, see §§ 4.316 et seq.

Driving or attempting to drive a mechanically propelled vehicle while unfit through drink or drugs (s.4(1))

4.22   It is an offence under s.4(1) for a person to drive or attempt to drive a mechanically propelled vehicle on a road or other public place while unfit to drive through drink or drugs (see §§ 4.86 et seq.). For procedure, trial and penalties, see §§ 4.316 et seq. For hospital patients, see §§ 4.287 *et seq*. For post-offence consumption of alcohol or drugs, see §§ 4.300 et seq.

In charge of a mechanically propelled vehicle while unfit through drink or drugs (s.4(2))

4.23   It is an offence under s.4(2) for a person to be in charge of a mechanically propelled vehicle on a road or other public place while unfit through drink or drugs (see §§ 4.86 et seq.). It is a defence for the motorist to prove that there is no likelihood of his driving while unfit (see § 4.309). For procedure, trial and penalties, see §§ 4.316 et seq. For hospital patients, see §§ 4.287 et seq.

Driving or attempting to drive a motor vehicle with excess alcohol (s.5(1)(a))

4.24   It is an offence under s.5(1)(a) for a person to drive or attempt to drive a motor vehicle on a road or other public place with excess alcohol (see § 4.165) in his breath (see § 4.107), blood or urine (see § 4.134) as evidenced by a certificate of analysis or printout (see § 4.235). It is not normally a defence that he has not been arrested or validly arrested (see § 4.06) but it may be a defence if the level of alcohol is due to consumption of alcohol after the offence (see §§ 4.300 et seq.). Duress may also be a defence (see § 4.305). Insanity is not a defence (see § 4.307). For special provisions for hospital patients, see §§ 4.287 et seq. For procedure, trial and penalties, see §§ 4.316 et seq.

In charge of a motor vehicle with excess alcohol (s.5(1)(b))

4.25   It is an offence under s.5(1)(b) for a person to be in charge of a motor vehicle on a road or other public place with excess alcohol (see § 4.165) in his breath (see § 4.107) or in blood or urine (see § 4.134) as evidenced by a certificate of analysis or statement (see § 4.235). It is a defence for the motorist to prove that he would be unlikely to drive while above the limit (see § 4.309). For post-offence consumption of alcohol, see §§ 4.300 et seq. For special provisions for hospital patients, see §§ 4.287 et seq. For procedure, trial and penalties, see §§ 4.316 et seq.

Failing to provide a specimen for analysis (s.7(6))

It is an offence for a person who has been required to provide specimens for analysis (see §§ 4.107 and 4.212) to fail without reasonable excuse to do so. The offender is liable to compulsory disqualification if he was driving or attempting to drive but if he was not driving or attempting to drive it is endorsable by 10 penalty points. The police do not have to prove that he was in charge of a motor vehicle. For procedure, trial and penalties generally, see §§ 4.316 et seq. **4.26**

Failing to allow specimen of blood to be subjected to laboratory test (s.7A)

It is an offence under s.7A for a person who has been required to give his permission for a specimen of blood taken from him under that section to be subjected to a laboratory test to fail, without reasonable excuse, to give that permission. The offender is liable to compulsory disqualification if he was driving or attempting to drive but if he was not driving or attempting to drive it is endorsable by 10 penalty points. The police do not have to prove that he was in charge of a motor vehicle. For procedure, trial and penalties generally, see §§ 4.284 et seq. **4.27**

Interaction of the offences

Although the offences under ss.4 and 5 are quite distinct, the two offences are closely inter-related because a person arrested under s.4 will usually have been required to provide a specimen for analysis. (Section 7(1) allows a constable to require specimens for analysis in the course of an investigation whether a person has committed an offence under s.4 or s.5. The word "investigation" on a true construction of s.7(1) requires no greater formality than is normally involved in the plain meaning of the word, namely "inquiring into" (*Graham v Albert* [1985] R.T.R. 352).) For this reason it is usual for a person charged under s.4 to be additionally charged under s.5 if he provides a specimen over the prescribed limit or under s.7(6) (failing without reasonable excuse to provide specimens for analysis) if he fails or refuses to provide specimens. Where a defendant gives only one specimen of breath for analysis instead of the two which the statute requires, he may not be convicted of a s.5(1) offence in addition to one under s.7(6) (*Cracknell v Willis* [1987] 3 All E.R. 801). **4.28**

DEFINITIONS

"Drives or attempts to drive"

For the meaning of "drives or attempts to drive" and "driving" generally, see §§ 1.92–103. **4.29**

"In charge"

For the meaning of "in charge", see § 1.110. **4.30**

"Mechanically propelled vehicle"

Drink/driving offences under s.4 may be committed in respect of a "mechani- **4.31** cally propelled vehicle", a wider category of object than a "motor vehicle". For the meaning of "mechanically propelled", see § 1.33.

"Motor vehicle"

4.32   Drink/driving offences under ss.5, 6 and 7 can only be committed if committed in respect of a "motor vehicle". For the meaning of "motor vehicle", see §§ 1.04–21.

"Road"

4.33   For the meaning of "road", see §§ 1.122–6.

"Or other public place"

4.34   For the meaning of "or other public place", see § 1.148.

PRELIMINARY TESTS

4.35   Somewhat surprisingly given its short title, the Railways and Transport Safety Act 2003 established (by courtesy of s.107 thereof and Sch.7 thereto) a new statutory regime for the testing of drivers of motor vehicles for drink or drugs. In broad terms s.6 of the Road Traffic Act 1988 was replaced with effect from March 30, 2004 by provisions governing the administration to suspects of three specific kinds of preliminary test as follows:

        (a) a preliminary breath test (s.6A);

        (b) a preliminary impairment test (s.6B);

        (c) a preliminary drug test (s.6C).

The legislation followed upon an apparently successful field trial of a fitness test designed to aid police in the detection of drug-related offences. That test has been given statutory form as the "preliminary impairment" test listed at (b) above, but it should be noted that it is designed to indicate whether a person is unfit to drive not solely because of drugs, but through drugs or drink (s.6B). The test referred to in (c) above as a "preliminary drug test" is a more sophisticated procedure based upon the analysis by an approved device of a specimen of sweat or saliva. Practical use of s.6C is dependent upon the availability of a suitable analytical device, and at the time of writing (March 2009) no such device had been approved by the Secretary of State.

4.36   The substituted s.6 of the 1988 Act provides the power to administer each or any of the preliminary tests described above, and its provisions very largely reproduce, albeit in a rearranged form, those of the old s.6 as it applied to what was formerly known as a "breath test". The definition of "breath test" in s.11(2) of the 1988 Act has been removed by the new legislation; definitions, however, of the new terms "preliminary breath test", "preliminary impairment test" and "preliminary drug test" are contained respectively in ss.6A, 6B and 6C.

The powers of arrest and entry in relation to "breath tests" contained in the old s.6 have been re-enacted in a modified form as ss.6D and 6E in order to take account of the new kinds of preliminary test.

4.37   Section 6D of the 1988 Act was amended by s.154 of the Serious Organised Crime and Police Act 2005 in order to provide police with a power to undertake evidential breath tests at the roadside. These provisions were designed to enable admissible evidence to be captured at an earlier stage and hence improve enforcement. It should be noted, however, that at the time of writing (March 2009) no suitable equipment had been approved for roadside use, and the projected cost of any such equipment may in any event prove unattractive to police forces.

The text of the substituted ss.6A, 6B, 6C, 6D (as amended) and 6E is reproduced in full in Vol.2.

Requirement to co-operate

The circumstances in which a constable may require a motorist to co-operate with a preliminary test are dependent on whether the motorist was committing a moving traffic offence, had alcohol or a drug in his body (or was under the influence of a drug) or was involved in an accident. The circumstances under which a preliminary test may be demanded are wide enough to include motorists who are or were in charge of motor vehicles. In addition, the constable's suspicion does not have to arise while the motorist is still driving or attempting to drive. The police may require a preliminary test in respect of a motorist who *has been* driving. **4.38**

It is an offence to refuse to co-operate with a preliminary test (s.6(6)). The offence is endorsable and an offender thus incurs four penalty points. Sentencing and the penalties for the offence are set out in §§ 4.316 et seq.

Preliminary test on suspicion of alcohol, drugs or a moving traffic offence (s.6(2)–(4), (7))

Under s.6(2) a constable (who by s.6(7) must be in uniform) may require a person to co-operate with a preliminary test where he reasonably suspects that person to be driving or attempting to drive or in charge of a motor vehicle on a road or other public place with alcohol or a drug in his body or under the influence of a drug. Under s.6(3) a constable has a similar power where the person has been driving or attempting to drive or in charge on a road or other public place while having alcohol or a drug in his body or while unfit to drive because of a drug and that person still has alcohol or a drug in his body or is still under the influence of a drug. Under s.6(4) a constable may require a preliminary test where he reasonably suspects that the motorist is or has been driving, attempting to drive or in charge on a road or other public place and has committed a traffic offence while the vehicle was in motion. **4.39**

It may be noted that whereas the previous legislation required the constable to have "reasonable cause to suspect" the occurrence of any of the trigger events listed above, the substituted legislation provides that his powers under the section may be exercised if he "reasonably suspects" the occurrence of any such event. It is submitted that in reality this is a distinction without a difference and that existing case law is of continued application to these provisions.

A "Preliminary breath test"

"Preliminary breath test" is defined by s.6A(1) to mean "a procedure whereby the person to whom the test is administered provides a specimen of breath to be used for the purpose of obtaining, by means of a device of a type approved by the Secretary of State, an indication whether the proportion of alcohol in the person's breath or blood is likely to exceed the prescribed limit". **4.40**

Details of the preliminary breath testing devices that have been approved for use can be found at in Vol. 2, § 18.125 of this work (see also *http:// www.police.homeoffice.gov.uk/publications/operational-policing* [Accessed March 16, 2009]). The early machines, Alcotest 80 and 80A, consist of a plastic bag and a glass tube of yellow crystals showing a positive result if the green stain caused by the motorist's breath passes the indication on the tube. Later devices are electronic devices in which a charge is generated proportionate to the amount of alcohol in the breath. Compliance with the manufacturer's instructions in respect of the devices is of importance only in respect of an offence under s.6(6) and the situation of a wrongly administered breath test is discussed under § 4.64. As to approval of the devices by the Home Secretary, see § 4.63.

B   *"Constable in uniform"*

4.41   A preliminary test under s.6(2)–(4) may be administered by a constable only if he is in uniform (s.6(7)).

A "constable" in the section, it is suggested, must refer not to the rank of constable but to any constable of whatever rank and "constable" must refer to any member of any police force within the jurisdiction, including special constables (Police Act 1996 s.30). If the constable omits to state that he was in uniform a court is entitled to assume that he was in uniform when he has stated that he was on duty as a motor patrol officer (*Cooper v Rowlands* [1971] R.T.R. 291). In *Richards v West* [1980] R.T.R. 215 the justices had no direct evidence that a special constable who required a breath test was in uniform. Evidence was given that another special constable present was in uniform. The defence did not raise the issue in cross-examination. The justices, from their knowledge of the special constabulary, knew that there was no plain-clothes department and, the officer having stated that he was on duty, deduced he was in uniform. The Divisional Court held that there was circumstantial evidence whereby the justices could conclude that the officer must have been in uniform. Whether a constable is "in uniform" is a question of fact. In *Wallwork v Giles* (1969) 114 S.J. 36 it was held that a police constable who was not wearing a helmet but who otherwise was in his normal uniform was nevertheless "in uniform". It was said that the object of the provision was to ensure that the constable might be easily identified as a police constable.

4.42   In *Taylor v Baldwin* [1976] R.T.R. 265 this general principle was followed. A police sergeant, wearing his ordinary raincoat over his uniform, driving his private car, was held to have been entitled to require a driver to provide a specimen of breath. It was further held that a constable does not have to be in uniform when the suspicion arises: it is only when the constable requires the specimen of breath that the Act requires him to be in uniform.

A failure to adduce evidence that the constables administering a roadside breath test were in uniform at the relevant time was not fatal to a prosecution for being in charge of a vehicle with excess alcohol, since the requirement to provide samples of breath for analysis can be made in the course of an investigation into whether an offence has been committed under s.4 or s.5 of the 1988 Act. Provided that the procedure under s.7 had been observed, it was not necessary for the procedure under s.6 to have been followed, since a failure to follow the s.6 procedure did not invalidate any subsequent procedure. The High Court of Scotland so held in *Orr v Urquhart* 1993 S.L.T. 406; see also *Fox v Gwent Chief Constable* at § 4.06.

C "May require"

The constable does not have to use any particular formula when he requires the **4.43** motorist to co-operate with a preliminary test. The words "I intend to give you a breath test" were held sufficient in *R. v O'Boyle* [1973] R.T.R. 445, and "I wish to give you a breath test" were held sufficient in *R. v Clarke (Christopher)* (1969) 113 S.J. 428. As long as the language used can fairly be said to be capable of amounting to a requirement, it is purely a question of fact as to whether a constable "required" a motorist to take a breath test (see *R. v O'Boyle* above).

D "Driving or attempting to drive"

It will have been noted that s.6 enables a constable to require a breath test of a **4.44** person who either is *or has been* driving a motor vehicle or who is *or has been* in charge of a motor vehicle.

As to the meaning of "driving or attempting to drive", see § 1.105.

E "Reasonably suspects"

Section 6(2)–(4) gives a constable power to require a person to co-operate with **4.45** a preliminary test where he reasonably *suspects* a moving traffic offence or the consumption of alcohol or drugs. By contrast, s.6(5) gives a constable power to make such a requirement following an accident only where he reasonably *believes* that the person concerned was driving, attempting to drive or in charge at the time of the accident. The distinction between suspicion and belief is a matter of degree and may be important. The circumstances for a constable to be said to have a reasonable belief clearly have to be more definite than the circumstances justifying mere suspicion (see *Johnson v Whitehouse*, § 4.61).

Whether a constable has material upon which to found a reasonable suspicion is a fact, and depends on the circumstances. The cases on earlier statutory provisions as to what circumstances are or are not sufficient will be of help in deciding whether or not an offence under s.6(6) has been committed.

It is clear that the test is not whether the motorist has actually consumed alcohol **4.46** or drugs or actually committed a traffic offence. What matters is whether the constable reasonably suspects consumption of alcohol or drugs or a moving traffic offence. It is for the prosecution to prove that the constable's suspicion was reasonable in all the circumstances, but it may be no defence (nor is it a reasonable excuse) for failing to supply a specimen for analysis that in fact alcohol or drugs may not have been consumed (see *McNicol v Peters* 1969 S.L.T.(J.) 261). If a moving traffic offence is suspected then it is not a defence for failing to supply a specimen for laboratory testing for the defendant to believe that he had not committed a moving traffic offence. All that the prosecution must prove is that the constable reasonably suspected he had committed a traffic offence while the vehicle was in motion (*R. v Downey* [1970] R.T.R. 257).

Nor is it necessary for the constable's ground of suspicion to be first-hand. A constable has been held by the English High Court to have reasonable ground for suspecting a motorist of having consumed alcohol when his only source of knowledge is what he has been told by another constable (*Erskine v Hollin* [1971] R.T.R. 199). The Scottish High Court came to a similar conclusion when it was held that a uniformed officer could have reasonable cause for suspicion when he has been called in for this purpose by plain-clothes police officers (*Copeland v*

McPherson 1970 S.L.T. 87). In *R. v Moore* [1970] R.T.R. 486 it was held that when a police constable received a radio message to the effect that the driver was believed to be drunk it was not possible for it to be argued that the constable had no reasonable cause to suspect alcohol and, although the judge should have left the matter to the jury, the Court of Appeal applied the proviso and dismissed the appeal. *Erskine v Hollin* was applied in *R. v Evans (Terence)* [1974] R.T.R. 232 where it was held that a police patrol officer who had been informed by radio of a foot constable's suspicion of alcohol of a motorist seen driving erratically could thereby himself have reasonable cause to suspect the motorist.

4.47   Can a constable form a reasonable suspicion if his informant is not a police officer? It is submitted that this is primarily a question of fact, not law, and the answer in practice will depend entirely on who was the informant, the precise nature of the information given and all the surrounding circumstances. However, it would be customary for a constable to state the grounds of his suspicion to the motorist before making the requirement and if there is any truth in the allegation either the answer of the motorist or the manner in which the answer is given might well provide sufficient justification for the constable to confirm or negative his suspicions. The facts giving rise to the suspicion must, however, relate to the actual driving of the vehicle on the day in question. In *Monaghan v Corbett* (1983) 147 J.P. 545, neighbours told a constable at about midday that the motorist and his wife had been seen driving off that day and that they habitually went off to a public house at lunchtime on Sunday. The constable, who had smelt alcohol on the motorist's breath the day before, then went to the police station and collected Alcotest equipment, returned to the scene and made a request for a breath test when the motorist returned to his home at 2.30pm It was held that the police officer could not form a reasonable suspicion of alcohol at 2.30pm on the basis that he had smelt alcohol the day before and the neighbours' information about the motorist's Sunday habits.

As a result of an anonymous phone call a police officer lay in wait for, and stopped, a car driven by a man the anonymous caller had alleged to have been drinking. The justices had concluded that the officer's suspicion was founded on facts wholly unconnected with the defendant's driving and that he had acted with *mala fides* in laying a trap for the defendant; they accordingly exercised their discretion under s.78 of the Police and Criminal Evidence Act 1984 to exclude all the evidence following his arrest. They had also found, however, that the defendant had exuded a strong smell of intoxicating liquor whilst sitting in the police car and that second finding was sufficient to provide reasonable cause for suspicion that the defendant had been drinking. In those circumstances their first finding concerning the unconnectedness of the officer's suspicion was untenable in fact and law. The Divisional Court so held in *DPP v Wilson* [1991] R.T.R. 284 when remitting the case to the justices with a direction to continue the hearing. It was further contended on the part of the appellant that the police officer's conduct was oppressive and that accordingly the justices should have exercised their discretion on that ground. Not so, said the Divisional Court; the officer was under a duty to act upon information received, but there was no duty upon him to warn a potential offender of a potential offence.

4.48   A "U" turn in a road, wrong indicator and excess speed do not of themselves indicate a reasonable suspicion of alcohol and if these are the only facts the court will quash a conviction; these facts alone being held insufficient to constitute a suspicion of alcohol (*Williams v Jones* [1972] R.T.R. 5). If it is a matter of fact primarily for the court, a conviction will only be quashed where the evidence as a matter of law could not support reasonable grounds for suspicion (*R. v Fardy* [1973] R.T.R. 268). In considering whether a constable had reasonable grounds for forming a suspicion, regard was to be had to all the circumstances, and the fact that the incident occurred at 3.30am was not to be overlooked (ibid.). In *R. v McGall* [1974] R.T.R. 216 it was again held that all the circumstances had to be considered as to whether a constable had reasonable cause to suspect a motorist of alcohol; abnormally slow driving for no apparent reason late at night with a trafficator unjustifiably repeated after correction could give rise to reasonable suspicion.

A constable under earlier legislation either had to suspect alcohol *or* a moving traffic offence. In practice constables rarely require a preliminary breath test simply on suspicion of a moving traffic offence; they do so only when suspicion of alcohol arises as well. Usually, by definition, suspicion of a moving traffic offence will have arisen while the defendant was still driving but often the constable only begins to suspect alcohol after the defendant has ceased to drive. It was held in a number of cases that the constable was still entitled to require a breath test provided it was made clear that the constable was relying on suspicion of a moving traffic offence (*Timmins v Perry* [1970] R.T.R. 477; *Rickwood v Cochrane* [1978] R.T.R. 218). The alternative ground had to be clearly established on the evidence (*Clements v Dams* [1978] R.T.R. 206) and if the prosecution ran the case on one ground of suspicion, justices were held not to be entitled to convict the defendant on the alternative basis of suspicion of a moving traffic offence (*Morriss v Lawrence* [1977] R.T.R. 205). If justices were considering doing so the defendant should be informed and be allowed to apply for an adjournment if he had been misled.

4.49 Section 6(3) enables a constable to require a person to co-operate with a preliminary test who *has been* driving, attempting to drive or in charge of a motor vehicle if he reasonably suspects that he has been driving, etc., with alcohol or a drug in his body or while unfit to drive because of a drug (s.6(3)(a)) "and still has alcohol or a drug in his body or is under the influence of a drug" (s.6(3)(b)). The circumstances relied upon must therefore be two-fold, namely that the constable has reasonable grounds for suspecting not only that he drove, etc., with alcohol or a drug in his body or whilst unfit through drugs, but also that he still has alcohol or a drug in his body or is still under the influence of a drug.

Section 6(4) entitles a constable to require a person to co-operate with a preliminary test who he reasonably suspects is or *has been* driving, attempting to drive or been in charge of a motor vehicle and *has* committed a traffic offence while the vehicle was in motion.

4.50 It should be noted that while s.6(3) and (4) both refer to motorists who have been driving, it would seem clear that the police have no power of entry to demand a preliminary test. While the police may require a preliminary test "off the road" there is no power of entry on to the defendant's property against his will except in the limited circumstances contained in s.6E (requirement to co-operate with a preliminary test following an accident causing personal injury); see further § 4.79.

F   *"Traffic offence"*

4.51 A traffic offence is defined by s.6(8)(b) as any offence under the 1988 Act except Pt V (which relates to the registration, etc., of driving instructors), any offence under the Road Traffic Regulation Act 1984, any offence under the Road Traffic Offenders Act 1988 (except Pt III, which deals with fixed penalties) and any offence under Pt II of the Public Passenger Vehicles Act 1981.

The traffic offence must have been committed while the vehicle was in motion. Thus driving without lights justifies a test (e.g. *R. v Price* [1968] 3 All E.R. 814), as, it appears, do other moving offences under regulations made under the Acts within the definition (*Bingham v Bruce* [1962] 1 All E.R. 136; *Rathbone v Bundock* [1962] 2 All E.R. 257).

The offence of taking a motor vehicle (now contrary to s.178 of the 1988 Act) was replaced in England and Wales by the Theft Act 1968. It would seem doubtful whether an offence under s.12 of that Act comes within the definition. (Although using a motor vehicle without third party insurance contrary to s.143 of the 1988 Act is within the definition. A joyrider will not usually be insured in respect of the vehicle he has taken.)

G   *"At or near the place"*

4.52   The breath test under s.8(1) of the 1972 Act prior to its amendment by the Transport Act 1981 had to be made "there or nearby". This was held to be a matter of fact and degree in all the particular circumstances of the case and the High Court will regard itself as bound by a finding of fact (*Arnold v Kingston-upon-Hull Chief Constable* [1969] 3 All E.R. 646, where a police station one and a half miles away was held not to be "there or nearby"). Similarly the Divisional Court refused to disturb a finding that 160yds away was not "there or nearby" (*Donegani v Ward* [1969] 3 All E.R. 636).

Sections 6A(2), 6B(4) and 6C(2) require a preliminary test to be administered "at or near the place where the requirement is imposed". This would seem, as in the earlier legislation, to be a matter of fact and degree and similarly, unless the magistrates' finding of fact is so perverse that no reasonable tribunal could come to such a conclusion, the magistrates' finding will not be reversed by the Divisional Court.

Random tests

4.53   The police have a general power to stop a motor vehicle pursuant to what is now s.163 of the 1988 Act. This power was examined in *Beard v Wood* [1980] R.T.R. 454, where it was held that there was nothing in the section which required the prosecutor to prove that a constable stopping a vehicle under what is now s.163 was acting under a common law power; the constable's duty and power came from the section itself. Once a vehicle is stopped, it is possible then for the first time for a constable to suspect the motorist of consuming alcohol. Provided that at the time the constable's suspicions arose the motorist is still "driving or attempting to drive", the constable is lawfully entitled to require the motorist to take a (preliminary) breath test even though the motorist was stopped at random. In *R. v Needham* [1974] R.T.R. 201, the Court of Appeal arrived at the same conclusion on this point, and specifically held there was nothing in the statutory provisions to prevent random stopping; they declined to introduce any further provision as to the circumstances of the stopping of the vehicle which could lead to a lawful demand for a (preliminary) breath test.

The leading case is *Chief Constable of Gwent v Dash* [1986] R.T.R. 41. In that case vehicles were being randomly stopped in order to give a police officer further experience of the breath test procedure under the supervision of her senior. The court held that (what is now) s.6(2) is concerned only with the provision of a specimen of breath; it does not bear upon the circumstances in which a driver may be required to stop. The actions of the police, being neither oppressive, capricious nor opprobrious, did not amount to malpractice; therefore the requirement of a breath specimen and the subsequent procedure were lawful. Random stopping of cars for the purpose of ascertaining whether their drivers have alcohol in their bodies is perfectly permissible; random breath testing, however, is not. In reaching its conclusions the court was assisted by the case of *Steel v Goacher* [1983] R.T.R. 98 (vehicle stopped for random crime check; driver smelling of alcohol; breath test properly required) but disagreed with dicta in *Such v Ball* [1982] R.T.R. 140 to the effect that random stopping by itself amounted to malpractice.

In the light of *Gwent v Dash* cited above the matter may best be summarised **4.54** by saying that the police are not prohibited from random stopping, although they are prohibited from requiring breath tests "at random". It is only if the constable has reasonable cause to suspect under s.6 the motorist of having alcohol or committing a traffic offence while the vehicle was in motion that the constable may lawfully require a (preliminary) breath test (for further authority supporting this view see *Harris v Croson* [1973] R.T.R. 57, *R. v Gaughan* [1974] R.T.R. 195, *Adams v Valentine* [1975] Crim. L.R. 238). In *Winter v Barlow* [1980] R.T.R. 209 it was held that once s.8(1) of the 1972 Act prior to its amendment by the Transport Act 1981 had been complied with it was unnecessary to consider the legality of the police stopping the motorist under what is now s.163, because s.8(1) was a safeguard against arbitrary requests for a breath test. In *Lodwick v Saunders* [1985] Crim. L.R. 210 it was held that what is now s.163 gave a power to a police constable to stop a vehicle and that he may detain the vehicle while he exercised any power he was entitled to exercise in the circumstances.

Although the cases on random testing discussed above were decided at a time when the only preliminary test available was the breath test, it is submitted that the principles they embody will apply with equal force to the administration of preliminary impairment tests or preliminary drug tests.

The power of constables to stop and search persons and vehicles is now **4.55** regulated by ss.1 and 2 of the Police and Criminal Evidence Act 1984. Section 4 of the same statute also makes provision for road checks. A road check under s.4 cannot be used for random checks to see if persons are driving with excess alcohol as these are "traffic offences" and not "indictable offences".

Preliminary test following an accident (s.6(5))

Under s.6(5) a constable may require the co-operation with a preliminary test **4.56** of a motorist who he reasonably believes was driving or in charge of a motor vehicle owing to the presence of which an accident had occurred.

A "Accident"

The wording of the section is such that the police have to prove there has been **4.57** an accident. It is not sufficient to show that the constable had reasonable cause to believe that there had been an accident (*R. v Fardy* [1973] R.T.R. 268; *Chief Constable of the West Midlands Police v Billingham* [1979] R.T.R. 446).

The meaning of the word "accident" was considered in *R. v Morris* [1972] R.T.R. 201. One vehicle was pushing another with its front bumper against the rear bumper of the leading vehicle. The bumpers became interlocked and damage was caused to both vehicles. It was held that there was an "accident", which Sachs L.J. defined as "an unintended occurrence which had an adverse physical result". It was, however, decided in *Billingham* above that it was inappropriate for a definition of the word to be, in effect, written into the 1972 Act (now the 1988 Act) when the Act itself did not define it. The meaning of the word "accident" had different meanings in different statutes. The word in a particular Act should be looked at in the context of the statute and the mischief against which the Act was aimed. The test which should be applied to determine whether there had been an "accident" within the meaning of the word in what is now the 1988 Act was: "Would an ordinary man conclude on the facts of the particular case that there had been an accident?" Applying this test it was held that there was an accident where damage was caused to a police motor vehicle because of a deliberate act of mischief, as a result of which it had rolled away colliding with a telegraph pole and carrying on down an embankment. It was stated that the attempt to define the word in *R. v Morris* above must be understood in relation to the particular facts of the case. The test of what an ordinary man would conclude was also applied in *Chief Constable of Staffordshire v Lees* [1981] R.T.R. 506 where it was held that an accident had occurred where the defendant had deliberately driven through a locked gate. A similar conclusion was reached, applying *Billingham* above, in *R. v Branchflower* [2004] EWCA Crim 2042; [2005] R.T.R. 13 in relation to an aggravated vehicle-taking where there had been a deliberate running over in the course of an attempt to escape arrest.

4.58   No other vehicle need be involved, as in *R. v Pico* [1971] Crim. L.R. 500, where the defendant's car hit the kerb and a gatepost, injuring the defendant and damaging the gate. Similarly in *R. v Harling* [1970] R.T.R. 441, no other vehicle was apparently involved. Where an accident occurs it is not necessary for the defendant's vehicle to be physically involved in the accident, it is only necessary for there to be a direct causal connection between the presence of the defendant's vehicle on the road, and the accident occurring (*Quelch v Phipps* below). So that where a car left the road, and collided with a gate pillar on private land, the accident occurred "owing to" the presence of that car on the road (*Redman v Taylor* [1975] Crim. L.R. 348). *Redman v Taylor* was applied in *M (A Minor) v Oxford* [1981] R.T.R. 246, where it was held that damage caused by a lorry running off a road and colliding with a wall of a house occurred due to an accident "arising out of the presence of a motor vehicle on a road".

The words "owing to the presence of a motor vehicle on a road" were first considered in *Quelch v Phipps* [1955] 2 All E.R. 302 where it was held that there must be some causal connection between the vehicle and the occurrence of the accident. The presence of a vehicle must be a sine qua non and an indirect connection is insufficient (e.g. a pedestrian stepping back to avoid a car and injuring another pedestrian).

4.59   Questions may arise as to how far the presence of a stationary vehicle can be said to cause an accident. Section 6(5) entitles a constable to administer a preliminary test to a person "in charge" at the time of the accident. It would seem clear that a stationary car in the carriageway of a non-residential road might well be the cause of an accident, particularly if at night or unlit, but it would appear doubtful if the car is in a lay-by, or if the car was collided with as a result of a collision between two other vehicles.

B   *"Reasonably believes"*

The constable may require co-operation with a preliminary test solely on the **4.60** fact that he reasonably believes that the motorist was involved in the accident, even if hours before. (It may be noted that earlier legislation required the constable to have "reasonable cause to believe", but it is submitted that in reality this is a distinction without a difference.) It is immaterial that the constable has no reason to believe the motorist had consumed alcohol or drugs, or had driven carelessly or recklessly or had committed any traffic offence. (He cannot, however, be arrested unless he either gives a positive preliminary breath test or if he fails to co-operate with a preliminary test and the constable reasonably suspects that he has alcohol or a drug in his body or is under the influence of a drug (see § 4.84).)

The criteria of a lawful breath test following an accident are:

(a) that there has been in fact an accident owing to the presence of a vehicle on a road (see "Accident" above); and

(b) that the constable had formed a reasonable belief that the defendant was driving, attempting to drive, or in charge of the vehicle at the time of the accident.

Where there had been an accident, and the constable had reasonable cause to **4.61** believe that the defendant drove the vehicle at the time of the accident, and the defendant in fact drove the vehicle away from the scene of the accident, the conviction under what is now s.5(1) was upheld notwithstanding there was doubt if he in fact drove the vehicle at the time of the accident (*R. v Wedlake* [1978] R.T.R. 529). An offence under s.5(1)(a) or s.5(1)(b) requires the prosecution to prove that the defendant drove or attempted to drive or, in the case of s.5(1)(b), was in charge of a motor vehicle. There is no such requirement in respect of a charge under s.7(6) for refusing specimens of breath, blood or urine. A conviction was accordingly directed where a defendant had been arrested because the police believed he had been the driver and had refused at the police station to provide specimens for analysis even though it was subsequently shown he was not the driver (*Bunyard v Hayes* [1985] R.T.R. 348) (see further § 4.252). In *Baker v Oxford* [1980] R.T.R. 315 two men ran away from an abandoned car involved in an accident. One of the two admitted that he was the owner. The justices' finding that the police officer had reasonable cause to believe the defendant was the driver was based on the fact that not only did he admit he was the owner but also that the police computer showed that he was the registered keeper of the vehicle.

The court emphasised in *Baker v Oxford* that the justices appreciated the difference between the words "suspect" and "believe". The circumstances must be stronger before it can be held that a constable has reasonable cause to "believe". Reasonable cause for suspicion alone is insufficient. It was held in *Johnson v Whitehouse* [1984] R.T.R. 38 that the greater force of the word "believe" than "suspect" was an essential part of the law and a breath test following an accident could only be lawfully required if the constable had reasonable grounds for believing that the person concerned was driving at the time of the accident. Where, however, a constable inaccurately uses in evidence the word "suspect" this will not invalidate the requirement for a breath test if in fact the evidence is such that he clearly had reasonable cause to believe the defendant to have been driving (ibid.).

4.62　　The preliminary test following an accident is required in accordance with ss.6A(3), 6B(4) or 6C(2) to be administered "at or near" where the requirement is made (see "At or near the place", § 4.52) or, if the constable thinks fit, at a police station specified by the constable.

Preliminary breath testing devices

4.63　　Details of the preliminary breath testing devices that have been approved for use can be found in Vol. 2, § 18.125 of this work.

A preliminary breath test has to be on a device approved by the Secretary of State (see definition of "preliminary breath test" in s.6A(1)). In *Bentley v Northumbria Chief Constable* [1984] R.T.R. 276 at 280–281 (a case under previous law) it was observed that judicial notice could be taken that the Alcolyser had been approved by the Home Secretary despite the fact that the relevant approval order (the Breath Test Device (Approval) (No.2) Order 1979) was not cited. *Bentley* followed *R. v Jones (Reginald Williams)* [1970] R.T.R. 35 where it was similarly held that judicial notice of the Home Secretary's approval of the Alcotest could be taken. The reason why approval orders were made was to enable the prosecution to avoid having to call an official to give evidence that the Home Secretary had approved the device, production of the order under s.2 of the Documentary Evidence Act 1868 affording prima facie evidence of the Home Secretary's approval (*Hayward v Eames*; *Kirkpatrick v Harrigan* [1985] R.T.R. 12 citing *R. v Clarke* [1969] 2 Q.B. 91).

4.64　　The law on the administration of the Alcotest device was reviewed by the House of Lords in *DPP v Carey* [1969] 3 All E.R. 1662. The justices found that the defendant (contrary to the manufacturer's instructions) had consumed alcohol within 20 minutes of the test, that he had smoked shortly before and neither police officer had instructed him to fill the bag in not less than 10 nor more than 20 seconds and the question that arose in the case was "How far does non-compliance with the manufacturer's instructions invalidate a breath test?". The House of Lords held:

(1) That the manufacturer's instructions supplied with the Alcotest formed no part of the device as approved by the Home Secretary.

(2) That the only manufacturer's instructions which necessarily had to be complied with were those as to the assembly of the device.

(3) That provided there was a bona fide use of the device by the constable subsequent proof of failure to comply with the other instructions would not invalidate the breath test, and in particular:

(a) As to the instructions relating to recent consumption of alcohol, i.e. 20 minutes should elapse between consumption of alcohol and the test: if the constable had no knowledge of or reasonable cause to suspect the consumption of alcohol within 20 minutes preceding the test (if he had he should wait) or recent smoking it was a valid test even if the motorist had consumed alcohol within 20 minutes of the test. Moreover a police officer had no duty to inquire when a motorist last consumed alcohol.

(b) As to the instructions relating to inflating the bag in not less than

10 seconds or more than 20 seconds: a direction to the motorist to take a deep breath and blow in the bag was adequate: the officers could see for themselves whether or not the bag had been inflated in 10 or 20 seconds (and see *Att Gen's Reference (No.1 of 1978)* [1978] R.T.R. 377, § 4.197).

(4) (Per Lord Diplock) the only relevance of non-compliance with any of the instructions for the use of the Alcotest (other than those relating to its assembly) was that it might be evidence from which the *mala fides* of the constable could be inferred.

The above summary of the decision in *Carey* was quoted with approval by the Divisional Court in *Grant v DPP* [2003] EWHC 130; (2003) 167 J.P. 459. A defendant who had been followed by police for four miles but who claimed to have had a drink within the preceding five minutes was clearly lying; accordingly there was no need for the officer to wait a further 15 minutes before administering a preliminary breath test. **4.65**

It is not proposed to discuss further the numerous previous cases on the improper administration of the breath test devices, save to point out that in law a breath test device incorrectly assembled or defective is not in law a breath test. Therefore if a constable realises that the equipment is defective or he has assembled it incorrectly he may reassemble the device or require the test on another device (e.g. *Price v Davies* [1979] R.T.R. 204; *Sparrow v Bradley* [1985] R.T.R. 122). The second point is that a constable has a discretion to administer a second test even if he could have arrested the defendant as a result of the first test. The motorist may be confused or anxious, misunderstand the procedure or make a poor showing on the first occasion (*R. v Broomhead* [1975] R.T.R. 558; *Revel v Jordan*; *Hillis v Nicholson* [1983] R.T.R. 497).

A third reason as to why the cases on the former provisions no longer may apply is that s.11(3) now provides that the motorist must co-operate with a preliminary test "in such a way as to enable the objective of the test ... to be satisfactorily achieved". This latter provision is discussed at § 4.70 where typical manufacturer's instructions for the use of the breath test devices are also set out. **4.66**

The argument that the prosecutor has a responsibility to adduce in evidence the actual reading of the alcohol level revealed by the roadside breath test when the court is dealing with an allegation of driving a motor vehicle having consumed excess alcohol was rejected by the Administrative Court in *Smith v DPP* [2007] EWHC 100; [2007] R.T.R. 36 and also in *Breckon v DPP* [2007] EWHC 2013; [2008] R.T.R 8. Section 15(2) of the Road Traffic Offenders Act 1988 does not apply to preliminary tests under s.6 of the Road Traffic Act 1988 or indeed to preliminary breath tests under its amendment by virtue of s.6A. The purpose of the preliminary test is to obtain an indication of whether the proportion of alcohol was likely to exceed the prescribed limit. It is not to determine whether the limit has in fact been exceeded, which is the function of the specimens taken for analysis under s.7. There is a general duty of disclosure which means that the prosecution would have to disclose roadside breath-test figures which assist the defence or undermine the prosecution case, but that apart there is no obligation upon the Crown to produce the figures.

Radio interference

A warning was issued by the Home Office to police forces that the operation of **4.67** police radio equipment within a few inches of breath testing instruments (including those used for evidential purposes (see § 4.211 below)) may adversely affect their operation (Home Office circular 39/1989).

Failing to co-operate with a preliminary test (s.6(6))

4.68   It is an offence contrary to s.6(6) to fail without reasonable excuse to co-operate with a preliminary test when required to do so in accordance with s.6.

For an offence to be committed the defendant must have failed to co-operate with a preliminary test "in pursuance of a requirement imposed under this section". It would therefore appear that the test must have been provided in accordance with varying circumstances set out in s.6(2)–(5) (see §§ 4.39 and 4.56).

A person may also not be convicted of failing to co-operate with a preliminary test if the police officers were trespassers (see *Fox v Gwent Chief Constable* [1984] R.T.R. 402, and see further § 4.84 below).

4.69   The Alert and Alcolmeter require a breath specimen to be delivered in a manner or at a pressure for which the machine is programmed. The manufacturer's instructions for the Alcotest require the measuring bag to be inflated by one single breath in not less than 10 and not more than 20 seconds. The Alcolyser similarly requires the motorist to take a deep breath and blow steadily until the bag is fully inflated. Section 12(3) of the 1972 Act, prior to its amendment by the Transport Act 1981, stated that references to providing a breath test are references to providing a breath specimen in sufficient quantity to enable the test to be carried out. It was therefore held that if a person did not fully inflate the Alcotest measuring bag, but notwithstanding that the crystals gave a positive result, he had not "failed" to supply a specimen of breath (*Walker v Lovell* [1975] R.T.R. 377; *R. v Holah* [1973] R.T.R. 74). Similarly if the motorist fills the bag in short puffs and the crystals nevertheless turn green he has not "failed" to supply a specimen of breath. In the case of the Alcolmeter apparently it may be capable of giving a positive result even if the motorist does not blow long enough to illuminate light B. Where this happened and the officer did not press the "Read" button it was held in *Fawcett v Tebb* [1984] Crim. L.R. 175, following the same point as in *Walker v Lovell* above, that it could not be said that the defendant failed to supply a specimen of breath, and that the case should therefore be dismissed.

4.70   It was submitted in the twelfth edition and subsequent editions of this work that these and other similar cases might no longer apply because s.11(3) of the 1988 Act provides that not only does the motorist have to provide sufficient breath but that it must also be "provided in such a way as to enable the objective of the test or analysis to be satisfactorily achieved". Those submissions received by implication the support of the Divisional Court (Lord Bingham C.J. and Buxton J.) in *DPP v Heywood* [1998] R.T.R. 1, where attention was focused upon the further amendment of the original legislation by s.59 of the Transport Act 1982, which built in that particular requirement. A motorist undergoing a roadside breath test blew into an Alcolmeter on four occasions, on two of which she managed to illuminate only the "A" light, having failed to illuminate any light at all on the others. On neither occasion when the "A" light was illuminated did the officer press the "Read" button. It was accepted that had she done so, the device (an Alcolmeter S–L2) would have analysed the breath provided and might have given a positive reading; had a positive reading been given it would have been reliable; had a negative reading been given, it would not have been reliable. In other words, there was a risk of the device providing a "false negative". The simple question that arose, therefore, was whether in the circumstances the defendant had provided a specimen of breath which was sufficient to enable the test to be carried out and which was provided in such a way as to enable the objective of the test to be satisfactorily achieved? To that question there was, in the judgment of Lord Bingham C.J., only one possible answer, which was "No". The objective of the test was to establish reliably whether a sample of the defendant's breath had or had not been positive when tested. The defendant had given a specimen in such a quantity or in such a way that it could not be established *reliably* (our italics) whether or not her breath sample was positive. The specimen she had given enabled a reading to be obtained, but the reading might or might not be reliable. It would have been reliable if positive, but not reliable if negative. That put the woman police constable potentially in a quandary. If she had pressed the "Read" button and obtained a positive result, she would have been entitled to arrest the driver under (what is now) s.6D(1) of the 1988 Act. If, however, she had pressed the "Read" button and obtained a negative result, it would have been argued in such a case that no power of arrest would have arisen under (what is now) s.6D at all (despite counsel for the motorist having argued that a power of arrest would have arisen under (what is now) s.6D(2) if a negative result had been obtained). The plain effect of the 1982 amendment of the legislation was the introduction of a new test directed to the satisfying of the objectives of carrying out the test, which was to obtain a reliable reading one way or the other, and not to obtain a reading which was reliable in some circumstances and not in others. The acting stipendiary magistrate whose decision, to the effect that the defendant had no case to answer, was appealed against by the prosecutor had expressed the view in his stated case that if Parliament had wished to make simple failure to illuminate light "B" an offence, it could have said so. Lord Bingham C.J. added that in his judgment it had indeed said so by the amendment which had been made.

The manufacturers of the devices have given instructions as to how the devices should be used. It would seem, therefore, that (to quote s.11(3) once again) "the objective of the test will not be satisfactorily achieved" if the operating instructions are not sufficiently observed.   **4.71**

The instructions for the two following devices are typical of those for the 15 currently approved devices (the twenty-third edition of this work includes manufacturers' instructions for a number of other such devices).

The Alcolmeter

The Home Secretary approved the Alcolmeter device for the purpose of taking breath tests by the Breath Test Device (Approval) (No.2) Order 1979 (as to approval of breath devices, see § 4.63). The operating instructions for the Alcolmeter are as follows: **4.72**

> "*Points to remember*
> Each breath test must be preceded by a satisfactory READY CHECK
> Twenty minutes should elapse between the consumption of alcohol and the use of this instrument.
> Use a new mouthpiece for every test and ensure that the subject blows through the lipped-edge, wide bore end.
> Don't allow the subject to hold the instrument.
> Don't allow tobacco smoke to be blown through the mouthpiece.

Store the unit with the SET button locked in the down position.
Avoid storing the unit in extremes of temperature.
Don't subject the instrument to severe mechanical shock.

Subject breath test—operation checklist
Ready Check. Press 'READ' button and hold down for 10 seconds. Observe display. Only green 'BAT' and 'READY' lights should come on. If amber light comes on depress and lock 'SET' button, wait 2 minutes, repeat Ready Check.
Set. Depress and lock 'SET' button.
Attach mouthpiece. Attach sampling port to hole in the side of a new mouthpiece. Ensure firm connection.
Take sample. Explain the test procedure to the subject. Request subject to fill his lungs and blow one continuous breath through lipped-edge, wide bore end of mouthpiece. He must blow strongly enough to bring on light A and long enough to bring on light B. When light B illuminates, press 'READ' button. Tell subject to stop blowing. If light B does not illuminate, the subject has not provided a satisfactory sample.
Observe reading. To obtain an indication of the subject's blood-alcohol concentration, hold down 'READ' button and observe display lights as they rise to a maximum reading after approximately 40 seconds. Interpret according to table below.
Reset. Note final maximum reading, depress and lock 'SET' button.
Wait. If any light other than the green 'READY' light was illuminated as a result of the test, it may take a few minutes before a satisfactory READY CHECK can be obtained before re-use of the instrument.

Interpretation of display
The highest level shown on the display indicates the blood-level of the subject to be as follows:
RED blood-alcohol above 80mg per 100ml—POSITIVE TEST
RED–
AMBER blood-alcohol between 70 and 80mg per 100ml—NEGATIVE TEST
AMBER blood-alcohol between 5 and 70mg per 100ml—NEGATIVE TEST
GREEN blood-alcohol less than 5mg per 100ml—NEGATIVE TEST"

The Alcolmeter 500

4.73   The Secretary of State Approved the Lion Alcolmeter 500 device with effect from January 15, 2004 for the purpose of taking breath tests by the Breath Test Device Approval 2004. In addition to its function as a preliminary breath-testing instrument so far as road traffic law enforcement is concerned, it also features an optional setting for use in enforcing the lower legal breath-alcohol limit for aircrew (9µg/100ml).

The operator handbook sets out the breath-test procedure on a step-by-step basis:

"**STEP 1— *Preliminary Questions***
Ensure the subject has taken **NOTHING** by mouth for at least **TWENTY** minutes, and has not smoked for at least **TWO** minutes. *If necessary—WAIT*.

STEP 2— *Switch On*
Press FSA (Function Switch A) to the beep, then release. The instrument serial number is displayed.

STEP 3— *Diagnostics*

Allow the **500** to go through its diagnostic sequence. This includes a temperature check, plus verification that the sensor is clear of alcohol from the last test. During these checks the screen flashes: **Please Wait**

STEP 4— *Attach Mouthpiece*

Once the *Diagnostics* sequence has been completed the screen shows: **Fit Mouthpiece: Take Sample**. Push the sampling port on top of the instrument into the small hole in the side of a new mouthpiece, until it locks firmly into place. You may attach it either way round, whichever is more convenient to the circumstances of the test to be carried out ... *BUT* ... **for hygiene reasons do not touch the blowing end of the mouthpiece [the lipped end], other than through the wrapper**.

STEP 5— *Instruct the Subject*

Instruct the subject to take in a deep breath, hold it, form a seal around the lipped end of the mouthpiece with his or her lips; and then blow steadily and continuously until *YOU* say stop.

He or she does *NOT* have to blow *VERY HARD*: a *LONG, MODERATE BREATH* is all that is required.

The subject must keep his or her hands away from the instrument, so as not to cover the display screen from your own view.

If relevant, the subject should also be warned not to try to '*beat or fool the instrument*'. He *must* of course also be warned about the consequences of failure to provide.

STEP 6— *Take Breath Sample*

The subject now blows, *HARD* enough to bring on the display message **Breath Flow** and sound the continuous beep tone (the screen shows **Breath Flow**).

He or she must now continue blowing for *LONG* enough until the sample is taken: (the screen shows **Sample Taken**).

The provision of a satisfactory sample is also indicated by a double beep.

STEP 7— *Take Alcohol Reading*

Wait for the fuel cell to determine the alcohol level. This will take around 20–30 seconds [longer in the cold].

The reading is then shown and held for a pre-set time. There are four possible test results:

	BrAC [µg/100ml]
'Zero'	0–3
'Pass'	4–30
'Warn'	31–35
'Fail'	over 35

If the test result is above the legal limit, the word **FAIL** flashes, with a beep for emphasis.

STEP 8— *Discard Mouthpiece*

When instructed, remove and discard the mouthpiece, with the wrapper. *DO NOT re-use the mouthpiece, on either the same or another subject, except in the case of an* **Incomplete Specimen** (the screen shows **Discard Mouthpiece**).

STEP 9— *Wait [or go to Step 10]*

Depending on how much alcohol was in the last sample, a delay of a minute or so is enforced to allow the unit to clear. *If you wish to run another test leave it switched ON: this hastens recovery time* (the screen shows **Please Wait**).

STEP 10— *Switch Off*

If you do not need to run another test, press FSA and hold down until the triple bleep and switch off. If you do not switch off, the unit will do so itself after a fixed period (the screen shows **Switching Off**)."

Refusal to co-operate with a preliminary test

4.74   By s.11(2) the word "fail" includes "refuse". A person who without reasonable excuse refuses to co-operate with a preliminary test is therefore guilty of an offence under s.6(6).

It was held in *R. v Ferguson* (1970) 54 Cr.App.R. 410 that once a person had been given the opportunity to do something and did not do it, there was a "failure" to do it. Thus where a motorist refused to wait until the Alcotest arrived and suddenly pushed the constable in the chest and knocked him against the side of the car and said, "I am not waiting", it was held by the Divisional Court in *R. v Wagner* [1970] Crim. L.R. 535 that he had refused the test and the constable was thus justified in arresting him. It was also said in the case that a time-lag will often occur between the requirement to take the breath test and its administration. The Alcotest or other approved device (as in *R. v Wagner*) may not be immediately to hand or it may be necessary to wait because of the fact that the constable had reason to believe that the defendant had consumed alcohol less than 20 minutes before. If a defendant shows by his actions, either by running away or otherwise, that he is refusing the test, he may be arrested. If the Alcotest is not available, the time which a motorist can be required to wait is what is reasonable in all the circumstances of the case (*Ely v Marle* [1977] R.T.R. 412). If the motorist did not wait a reasonable time, his action in not waiting amounted to a "failure" to take the test because "failure" indicates refusal (applying *R. v Wagner* above).

4.75   Similarly in *Horton v Twells, The Times*, December 9, 1983 a conviction under earlier legislation was directed where a motorist refused to wait another 10 minutes. He had told the constable that he had last consumed alcohol 10 minutes beforehand, and the constable had arrested him and he refused to wait, knowing that the Alcolmeter should not be operated within 20 minutes of consumption of alcohol. Where police officers were faced with a person who refused to wait they should consider proceeding to arrest for failing to provide a specimen of breath (ibid.).

Defence of reasonable excuse

4.76   Although a person may be said to have "failed" to co-operate with a preliminary test in accordance with s.11(3) when he does not provide breath in the manner or at a pressure for which the machine is programmed, a person cannot be convicted of an offence under s.6(6) if he has a reasonable excuse for failing to do so.

Once the defence of reasonable excuse is advanced, it is for the prosecution to negative the defence (*Rowland v Thorpe* [1970] 3 All E.R. 195 at 197). It is a question of fact as to whether there is a "reasonable excuse" and the court must be satisfied beyond reasonable doubt that the defendant had no reasonable excuse (*R. v Harling* [1970] R.T.R. 441) but whether facts are capable of amounting to a reasonable excuse is a matter of law.

It would seem to be a reasonable excuse if a motorist is bronchitic, asthmatic **4.77** or has a medical or physical condition resulting in loss of lung capacity and for this reason is unable to blow into the bag in one continuous breath, or sufficiently hard to operate the Alert, Alcolmeter or Alcosensor. In *R. v Lennard* [1973] R.T.R. 252, a Court of Appeal case, it was held that a reasonable excuse *must arise out of a physical or mental inability to provide (a specimen) or a substantial risk in its provision.* These criteria would seem to apply equally to preliminary breath tests and to the provision of specimens of breath for evidential purposes at a police station (see § 4.272). In *Dawes v Taylor* [1986] R.T.R. 81, where the defendant found the device difficult to operate, it was held, following *Lennard*, that the fact that a defendant "did his best" to supply a specimen does not of itself amount to a reasonable excuse for a failure to do so (but cf. *Cotgrove v Cooney* [1987] R.T.R. 124, at § 4.273). There was no evidence to suggest that the defendant was physically unable to supply the necessary sample. Clearly a deliberate failure to co-operate precludes a defence of reasonable excuse (*Teape v Godfrey* [1986] R.T.R. 213; see further §§ 4.127 and 4.291).

Although a failure to understand a requirement to co-operate with a preliminary test may in some circumstances amount to a reasonable excuse under s.6(6), it cannot do so where the defendant's refusal is based not upon his lack of understanding but upon his false assertion that he had not been driving (*Chief Constable of Avon & Somerset v Singh* [1988] R.T.R. 107). Lack of understanding may suffice, however, to establish a reasonable excuse where the offence is one under s.7(6); see § 4.249 below.

It is not, however, a reasonable excuse for a defendant to believe that he is not **4.78** "in charge" of the motor vehicle (*Williams v Osborne* [1975] R.T.R. 181) nor that he thought he had not committed a moving traffic offence (*R. v Downey* [1970] Crim.L.R. 287) nor that he had not consumed any alcohol (*McNicol v Peters* 1969 S.L.T.(J.) 261) nor that she was not the driver at the time of the accident (*McGrath v Vipas* [1984] R.T.R. 58). These and other cases on "reasonable excuse" are further discussed in §§ 4.261 et seq.

Powers of entry

In *Fox v Gwent Chief Constable*, below and at § 4.06, it was held that where **4.79** the police were trespassers and administered a breath test the conviction of the defendant under what is now s.6(6) of refusing the preliminary breath test should be set aside, but that the conviction under what is now s.5 of the defendant who had supplied specimens of breath at the police station on the Lion Intoximeter should be upheld. It is only where the evidence of the Intoximeter is obtained by a trick, oppression or inducement that it is possible for the evidence of the printout to be excluded and, normally, the fact that the arrest is unlawful is insufficient (see further § 4.06). It would seem, therefore, that in practice the police will normally be able to obtain a conviction under ss.4, 5 or 7(6) even if it is shown that the police were trespassers and had no power of entry or arrest in the case in question. The relevance of whether or not the police have or have not properly exercised their powers under s.6 will usually be confined in practice to offences of refusing to co-operate with the initial screening breath test under s.6(6).

It would seem that a constable may administer a preliminary test off the road provided that he is not trespassing on the defendant's own property and where the defendant is himself a trespasser.

4.80　　In *Trigg v Griffin* (1969) 113 S.J. 962 the conviction of the defendant was quashed by the Divisional Court on the ground that, although the defendant was a person "driving or attempting to drive", he was not "on a road or public place" because he had driven from the road onto a private forecourt of lock-up garages, one of which was used by him. In *R. v Jones (E.J.M.)* [1970] 1 All E.R. 209 the Court of Appeal disapproved of *Trigg v Griffin*. A motorist cannot, said the Court of Appeal, stultify police action by turning a few feet off the highway. As long as the police have reasonable suspicion of the driver having consumed alcohol or having committed a moving traffic offence, the police may pursue the driver in order to make a breath test requirement. Following the line of decisions relating to arrest and "fresh pursuit", the Court of Appeal in *R. v Jones* ruled that a driver cannot escape the requirement by driving into private property.

The question was raised in *Morris v Beardmore* [1980] R.T.R. 321 whether, if the arresting officer was a trespasser at the time of the breath test requirement, the trespass renders the arrest and subsequent analysis unlawful. The facts were that the officers wished to interview the defendant in connection with an accident. They were let into his house by his son. He then indicated via his son that he was unwilling to discuss the matter and that they were to leave. They went to his bedroom and asked for a specimen of breath. He protested that they were trespassers and refused, whereupon he was arrested under s.8(5) of the 1972 Act prior to its amendment by the Transport Act 1981. As the constable was a trespasser the House of Lords unanimously held that the defendant's detention or arrest following his refusal to give a breath test was unlawful. If Parliament had intended to authorise the tortious act of a police officer, it would have done so expressly. Following on the decision of *Morris v Beardmore* the further question was raised, as to the position where after having properly requested the breath test at the defendant's door, either under s.8(1) of the unamended 1972 Act or s.8(2) ibid., the constable is then refused entry and in the two cases heard together before the House of Lords, *Clowser v Chaplin*; *Finnigan v Sandiford* [1981] R.T.R. 317 it was unanimously held that the constables effecting the arrests being trespassers at the time had no authority to arrest them under s.8(5) of the unamended 1972 Act. While the police have no power to arrest if they are trespassers on the defendant's own property, once a defendant has been lawfully arrested the police are entitled to enter the defendant's property to recapture him. A defendant was initially arrested outside his front door where the police had an implied licence to be; on arrest, a struggle took place with the defendant pulling the constable into the house. It was held that the police had acted lawfully; once an arrest had taken place they were entitled to enter the house to recapture him even if asked to leave (*Hart v Chief Constable of Kent* [1983] Crim. L.R. 117).

4.81　　The arrest or requirement for a breath test is still lawful until the constable becomes a trespasser. Constables, like the general public, have an implied licence to enter on a person's property on lawful business, and go from a person's gate to his front or back door. Until the implied licence is rebutted (e.g. by a notice saying "No admittance to police officers") or revoked, the police officer is not a trespasser (see *Robson v Hallett* [1967] 2 Q.B. 939, in particular Diplock L.J. at 953 and Parker L.J. at 951). Thus in *Pamplin v Fraser* [1981] R.T.R. 494, the defendant, who had driven off the road into an alleyway on his own land, wound up the windows of the car and locked himself inside, was held to be rightly convicted of failing to supply a specimen of breath and of wilfully obstructing a police constable in the execution of his duty, because the constable's implied licence to enter had not been withdrawn. Instances where the implied licence to enter has been withdrawn as a result of which the breath test requirement and arrest became invalid may be found in *Lambert v Roberts* [1981] R.T.R. 113 and *R. v Allen* [1981] R.T.R. 410.

In *Snook v Mannion* [1982] R.T.R. 321 it was held that the implied licence for police officers to enter the defendant's land between his gate and his front or back door must be expressly revoked. The defendant had said "fuck off" to the officers when they caught up with him in his driveway. The justices came to the conclusion that his vulgarity was insufficient to revoke the licence. Their decision was upheld: from the decision in *Gilham v Breidenbach* [1982] R.T.R. 328 it was clear that it was for justices to decide whether "fuck off" was to be taken as terminating a licence to enter or was mere vulgar abuse. In *Faulkner v Willets* [1982] R.T.R. 159 it was held that an invitation to enter private premises could be implied by conduct and need not be orally made. The conviction of refusing to supply a specimen for a laboratory test was upheld. The police officer had gone to the defendant's front door and had explained his reasons to the defendant's wife, whereupon she had opened the door fully and walked back into the house giving the officer the impression it was an implied invitation to follow her. At no time was the officer asked to leave the house.

When considering the new drink/driving law contained in the substituted ss.6–12 of the 1972 Act, the effect of *Morris v Beardmore* and *Clowser* was considered by Parliament and express power of entry, if need be by force, was given by ss.5(6) and 7(6) (now s.6E(1) of the 1988 Act). It may be possible to argue that, except in the circumstances set out in s.6E(1) (where Parliament has given constables express power to enter land), constables, once they are trespassers, have no power to enter land either to breath test the defendant or to arrest him under s.6D. This view is clearly correct where an officer is a trespasser on the defendant's own property. In *Fox v Gwent Chief Constable* [1984] R.T.R. 402 it was held that the police were not entitled to enter the defendant's house under what is now s.6E(1) where the police had no information (and thus had no reason to suspect) that the accident involving the defendant's vehicle had caused any injury to the defendant's passenger, and, therefore, the conviction under what is now s.6(6) of the defendant who had refused a breath test was set aside. While it is clear that the defendant can escape from the requirement of a breath test or arrest once he reaches his own property (except in the circumstances in s.6E(1)) it is still not clear that he can do so by leaving the highway and going on to someone else's private property upon which he as well as the police are trespassers. It is submitted, indeed, that the decision of *R. v Jones*, see § 4.80 above, may apply in such circumstances. In *Morris v Beardmore* itself, every single one of their Lordships stressed that their decision was limited to the case where the police officer was a trespasser on the defendant's own property. It was said by Lord Roskill [1980] R.T.R. 321 at 339: "It by no means follows that a motorist who is himself a trespasser can take advantage of that fact to defeat the intentions of a

4.82

police officer intent upon performing the duties required of him by statute." Lord Scarman at 337 said: "The House is not declaring that every roadside hedge signals to the fugitive motorist the presence of sanctuary from the pursuing officers of the law." Lord Diplock stated (at 328): "Very different considerations may apply to cases of … 'hedge hopping', i.e. where the driver tries to dodge the constable by getting off the road onto adjacent property on which he is also a trespasser."

4.83   The powers of entry in respect of suspected offences in England and Wales under ss.4–11 of the 1988 Act are contained in s.6E(1). Section 6E(2) provides that s.6E does not apply in Scotland and nothing in that subsection affects any rule of law in Scotland concerning the right of entry of a constable in Scotland.

Section 6E(1) enables a constable to enter, if need be by force, any place either for the purpose of imposing upon a person a requirement for a preliminary test or to arrest a person, but only where there has been an accident in which the constable reasonably suspects that injury was involved. There must actually have been an accident; it is not enough for the constable merely to form a reasonable suspicion that there has been an accident. The constable must also reasonably "believe" (not "suspect") that the person was driving, attempting to drive or in charge of the vehicle at the time of the accident (s.6(5)).

Powers of arrest

4.84   An arrest is not a condition precedent to a conviction under ss.4, 5 or 7(6).

The powers of arrest in respect of offences under ss.4–11 are contained in s.6D. (There are also general powers of arrest under s.24 of the Police and Criminal Evidence Act 1984.) Although a constable may arrest under s.6D he is not compelled to do so; the power of arrest is at his discretion. Indeed, it is to be deprecated that in the Metropolitan area and, it is believed, in the great majority of police areas, the individual police officer is not encouraged to use his discretion not to arrest a motorist where there is no apparent need to do so.

Section 6D(1) entitles a constable to arrest if as a result of a preliminary breath test the constable reasonably suspects the proportion of alcohol in the motorist's breath or blood exceeds the prescribed limit. Section 6D(2) alternatively entitles a constable to arrest a motorist who has been required to co-operate with a preliminary test and has failed to do so *and* the constable reasonably suspects he has alcohol or a drug in his body or is under the influence of a drug. It will have been noted that a constable does not have to suspect either alcohol or the commission of a traffic offence to require a breath test from a motorist believed to have been driving at the time of an accident; under s.6D, therefore, he cannot be arrested unless he subsequently provides a positive breath test or if, despite refusal of the test, the constable reasonably suspects he has alcohol or a drug in his body or is under the influence of a drug. It will also be noted that both in s.6D(1) and s.6D(2) the constable does not have to form a reasonable *belief*, only a reasonable *suspicion*.

4.85   The power of arrest under s.6D cannot be exercised where the person is at a hospital as a patient (s.6D(3); see §§ 4.292 et seq.).

The fact that the arrest is unlawful will not normally preclude a conviction under ss.4, 5 or 7(6) (see § 4.09).

DRIVING OR IN CHARGE WHILST UNFIT

Inter-relation of offences

Although the offences under ss.4 and 5 are quite distinct in practice, the two **4.86** offences are closely inter-related because a person arrested under s.4 will usually have been required to provide specimens for analysis. For this reason it is usual for a person charged under s.4 to be additionally charged under s.5 if he provides a specimen over the prescribed limit or under s.7 if he refuses to do so. Similarly, if originally arrested under s.5 he may be charged under s.4, if there is evidence of impairment either because of drugs or a combination of drugs and alcohol.

A certificate of analysis of blood or urine, or a statement and certificate of breath, is admissible both in respect of a charge under s.4 and under s.5.

Offences under s.4(1) (driving or attempting to drive while unfit) and s.4(2) (in **4.87** charge while unfit) must be proved to have occurred on a "road or other public place" in respect of a "mechanically propelled vehicle" and while the defendant was "driving or attempting to drive" or "in charge". The meaning of these basic terms is discussed in detail at §§ 1.04–21, 1.104, 1.110, 1.122.

The offence (s.4(1) and (2))

It is an offence under s.4(1) (as amended by the Road Traffic Act 1991) to drive **4.88** or attempt to drive a mechanically propelled vehicle on a road or other public place whilst unfit to drive through drink or drugs. It is an offence under s.4(2) similarly to be "in charge" of a mechanically propelled vehicle. Prior to its amendment by the 1991 Act offences under this section could only be committed in respect of a motor vehicle. It should be noted that offences under ss.5, 6 and 7 continue to be restricted to motor vehicles.

The meaning of the terms "driving or attempting to drive", "in charge" and "road or other public place" are the same as for the other drink/driving offences and are discussed in detail at §§ 1.104, 1.110 and 1.122. The terms "motor vehicle" and "mechanically propelled" are discussed at §§ 1.04–21. The terms "unfit to drive", "drink" and "drugs" are examined at §§ 4.89–100.

Evidence of impairment

Under s.4(5) a person shall be taken to be "unfit to drive" if his ability to drive **4.89** properly is for the time being impaired. The law before 1962 required that he should be under the influence of drink or drugs to such an extent as to be incapable of having proper control of a motor vehicle, and this is still the standard in respect of cyclists charged under s.30. The fact that the defendant had driven for 200yds in a proper way did not create a presumption of sobriety which medical evidence could not displace in a charge under the old law (*Murray v Muir* 1950 S.L.T. 41). In *R. v Hunt* [1980] R.T.R. 29 a jury was held to be entitled to infer that the defendant's driving was impaired from the facts that (a) he collided with a stationary van which should have been plainly visible to him and (b) his blood-alcohol analysis was nearly two and a half times the prescribed limit.

Impairment of ability to drive properly can be proved by evidence that a car was being driven erratically or had an accident at a spot where there was no hazard for a normal driver, provided, of course, that there is also evidence of drink or drugs. It can be assumed from evidence of the defendant's condition, e.g.

frequently falling asleep or inability to stand or mental confusion, provided, again, that there is some evidence that his condition was due to drink or drugs and not to illness. Following upon an apparently successful field trial of a fitness test designed to aid police in the detection of drink or drug-related offences, s.6B of the 1988 Act gave statutory form to what is now known as a preliminary impairment test. (For the circumstances in which such a test may be administered and the consequences of a refusal to co-operate therewith, see generally above under the heading "Preliminary Tests" at §§ 4.35–7.) Both the relevant standard drink/drugs police pro forma MG DD/F (see § 4.179 below) and the mandatory Code of Practice for Preliminary Impairment Tests published by the Department for Transport in December 2004 set out the specific tests which are to be undertaken, such as pupillary examination, the modified Romberg balance test, the walk and turn test, the one leg stand test and the finger and nose test. The constable, who must have been approved for the purpose of administering such tests, is enjoined by the pro forma to advise the suspect that the results of the preliminary test may be given in evidence.

4.90   As previously mentioned, the test for impairment under s.4(5) is the ability to "drive properly" and the prosecutor need only prove that the defendant could not drive properly. Impairment can also be shown by evidence of the amount of alcohol taken by the defendant as revealed by a test of his blood or urine, if the analysis shows a high blood-alcohol content. It was held in *MacNeill v Fletcher* 1966 S.C.(J.) 18 that even a high blood-alcohol level may still be disregarded by a jury or court in a charge under what is now s.4. It is now, however, submitted that there is increasing evidence, and public awareness, of the fact that a high blood-alcohol level normally will result in substantial impairment of a person's ability to drive properly. Evidence of analysis, whether above or below the limit, always has to be taken into account now (1988 Offenders Act s.15(2), (3)), though the lower the result the more it favours the defence. There are a number of cases where the High Court has held that an analysis, although inadmissible in respect of a charge under earlier legislation, is nevertheless admissible in a charge under what is now s.4(1) or (2).

The 1965 *Report of a Special Committee of the British Medical Association* (which preceded the enactment of the Road Safety Act 1967) recommended that conversion tables should no longer be used to estimate the minimum amount of alcohol which must have been taken by the suspect, because, as is stated in the summary of the Report:

> "the relationship between the amount of alcohol taken and the blood-alcohol concentration varies greatly, both as between different individuals, and in the same individual at different times. It is not possible to give the courts more than a very rough figure and this must often be a gross underestimate. Impairment of driving ability depends primarily upon the concentration of alcohol in the body and not on the amount of alcohol taken, and we recommend that attempts to translate the blood-alcohol concentration into the quantity of alcohol consumed should be limited to the purpose of confirming or rejecting a plea that the suspect has taken little or no alcohol before he was detained. For this purpose detailed conversion tables are not necessary. All that need be said is that a male weighing 11st with a blood-alcohol concentration of 50mg/100ml cannot possibly have taken less than $1\frac{1}{2}$ pints of ordinary beer or 3 single whiskies, and that he has almost certainly had very much more."

4.91   By virtue of the 1988 Offenders Act s.15(1)–(3) a certificate of analysis obtained under s.7 will be admissible where the person faces a charge under s.4. Section 7 enables the police to require the provision of blood, breath or urine for analysis "in the course of an investigation whether a person has committed an offence under section 4 or section 5 " (s.7(1)). The only situation, it is submitted, where a certificate of analysis may be treated as inadmissible is where the specimen for analysis was obtained improperly (see § 4.06).

Section 15(2), (3) of the 1988 Offenders Act provides not only that it shall be assumed that the proportion of alcohol at the time of the offence shall not be less than in the specimen, but also that in proceedings both for s.5 and s.4 offences the certificate "shall be taken into account". Section 15(3) of the 1988 Offenders Act does provide an exception if the defendant can show that he consumed alcohol after the offence (see § 4.300).

Special provision is made where impairment is thought to be due to drugs and is discussed in §§ 4.94–100.

It should be noted that it is usual for the police to charge an offence under s.4 **4.92** together with an offence under s.5 if a specimen of blood, breath or urine is subsequently provided and is above the prescribed limit or together with an offence under s.7 if a specimen is refused without reasonable excuse. A court will often consent to a withdrawal either of the s.5 charge or the s.4 charge if a plea of guilty is tendered to one of the charges under s.4 or s.5. Courts may occasionally be more reluctant to agree to the withdrawal of a s.7(6) charge on a plea of guilty to the s.4 charge on the ground that s.7(6) of necessity includes an element of obstruction of criminal justice.

A witness who is not an expert can give his general impression as to whether a person has taken drink and must decide the facts on which he founds that impression (*R. v Davies* [1962] 3 All E.R. 97; *Sherrard v Jacob* [1965] N.I. 151). He may not, merely because he is an experienced driver, give his impression as to whether such a person was fit to drive (ibid.). Where the court has disregarded opinions as to unfitness to drive given by laymen, a conviction may be upheld (*R. v Neal* [1962] Crim. L.R. 698). Where a driver, before consenting to examination by the police surgeon, has been told that the results of the examination will not be given in evidence, evidence of those results should not be admitted (*R. v Payne* [1963] 1 All E.R. 848). Now a doctor will usually be called to examine a person arrested under s.4. Where a defendant was found by the doctor to be very much under the influence of drink half an hour after his arrest, it was held that the charge should not have been dismissed merely because the doctor's evidence did not relate to the time of the arrest (*Dryden v Johnson* [1961] Crim. L.R. 551).

The evidence of a doctor, police surgeon or not, should be treated as that of a **4.93** professional person giving independent expert evidence with no other desire than to assist the court unless the doctor himself shows that it ought not to be (*R. v Nowell* [1948] 1 All E.R. 794; *R. v Lanfear* [1968] 1 All E.R. 683). In Scotland and Ireland, however, the rule is that the accused's voluntary submission to test and questioning must be proved (*Reid v Nixon* 1948 S.C.(J.) 68; *Gallacher v HM Advocate* 1963 S.L.T. 217; *The State (Sullivan) v Robinson* (1954) 88 I.L.T.R. 169).

Drugs

It was held in *Armstrong v Clark* [1957] 1 All E.R. 433 that a drug means a **4.94** medicament or medicine, something given to cure, alleviate or assist an ailing body. In that case it was held that a diabetic who took a wrong dose of insulin and thereby became incapable of proper control of a car could be charged with driving under the influence of a drug. In *Bradford v Wilson* [1984] R.T.R. 116 it was held that *Armstrong v Clark* was not an authority for saying a substance could only be a drug if it was a medicine; without giving a comprehensive definition, a substance taken into the body which was not a drink and not taken as a food which affected the control of the human body was capable of being a drug (ibid.). Accordingly the defendant, who had inhaled toluene when glue-sniffing, was properly convicted under what is now s.4 (ibid.).

These two cases were decided under the former drink/driving provisions. "Drug" is now defined by s.11 as including "any intoxicant other than alcohol". It would therefore seem that toluene would similarly be held to be a drug. "Intoxicant" in s.11 would seem to mean any substance that affects the self-control of the human body.

4.95   A diabetic, who had administered his normal dose of insulin some 12 hours earlier, suffered a hypoglycaemic attack whilst driving and crashed his car into some trees. He was charged with driving whilst unfit to drive through drugs. Expert evidence indicated that his very low blood-sugar level at the time of the accident could have been produced either by an excessive injection of insulin or by insufficient food intake after normal dosage, and that even a careful diabetic could suffer such attacks. The stipendiary magistrate found that the applicant had acted unreasonably in ignoring medical advice to take more than one injection of insulin and in failing to carry out tests to check his blood-sugar level. He found that the defendant's unfitness to drive was caused by the drug insulin and, accordingly, convicted him.

Quashing his conviction, the Divisional Court held in *R. v Ealing Magistrates' Court Ex p. Woodman* [1994] R.T.R. 189 that, while s.4(1) of the Road Traffic Act 1988 was apt to found the prosecution of a diabetic if it could clearly be shown that his unfitness to drive as a result of a hypoglycaemic attack was the direct result of an injection of insulin, it was not suggested that the injection of insulin administered by this defendant was other than perfectly proper. There was also no evidence before the magistrate as to whether the insulin, or part of it, still remained in the defendant's body at the time of the accident so as to produce the blood-sugar imbalance, and the consequent hypoglycaemic attack, or that either of the defendant's identified failures was itself productive of the attack. Accordingly, the evidence did not entitle the magistrate to be sure beyond reasonable doubt that the injection of insulin was the real effective cause of the defendant's unfitness to drive at the time of the accident.

4.96   It should be noted that certain drugs not only affect the human body but also increase the effect of alcohol. The words "through drink or drugs" in an earlier statute (a predecessor of the 1988 Act) were held to be merely adjectival and accordingly a conviction on a charge of driving while "unfit through drink or drugs" was upheld (*Thomson v Knights* [1947] K.B. 336).

Section 6C of the 1988 Act gives statutory form to what is known as a preliminary drug test. (For the circumstances in which such a test may be administered and the consequences of a refusal to co-operate therewith, see generally above under the heading "Preliminary Tests" at §§ 4.35 et seq.) It is a procedure based upon the analysis by an approved device of a specimen of sweat or saliva. Practical use of s.6C depends upon the availability of a suitable analytical device, and at the time of writing (March 2009) no such device had been approved by the Secretary of State.

Where the police are "in the course of an investigation whether a person has committed an offence under section 4 or section 5 " the police may require the person concerned to supply samples of blood, breath or urine for analysis (s.7(1): see, further, §§ 4.107 et seq.). Section 7(3)(bc) specifically enables a constable to require a specimen of blood or urine where as a result of the administration of a preliminary drug test (see above) he has reasonable cause to believe that the person required to provide the specimen has a drug in his body. **4.97**

The intention of the statutory provisions is to enable the police to obtain the provision of the appropriate type of specimen. Some drugs may be more easily detected in urine, others in blood. The approved evidential breath testing machines are designed to analyse the breath for alcohol levels, not drugs, and if the defendant is at a police station a requirement for a specimen of blood or urine cannot be made unless s.7(3)(a), (b), (bb), (bc) or (c) applies.

Once the preliminary drug test described above has been brought into operational use, there will be two routes leading to the requirement of a liquid sample from a person suspected of a s.4 offence. Where the result of a preliminary drug test gives the constable reasonable cause to believe that the person concerned has a drug in his body, he may require the provision of a specimen of blood or urine (s.7(3)(bc)). Alternatively, s.7(3)(c) provides that a similar requirement may be made where the constable making the requirement has been advised by a medical practitioner that the person's condition might be due to some drug. The constable may require such a specimen even though the person has already provided or been required to provide breath specimens (s.7(3)). Although advice from a medical practitioner is a condition precedent under s.7(3)(c), it would seem that there is nothing in the statutory provisions to prevent a station officer who obtains a negative breath analysis from a motorist from obtaining the advice of a police surgeon if the officer then suspects drugs for the first time. If the doctor then advises the station officer to require the provision of specimens of blood or urine the officer is then legally entitled to do so. (Normally, though, the police will obtain a medical examination of the motorist where an offence under s.4 is suspected and the doctor would presumably at that stage advise the police officer that the motorist may be under the influence of drugs rather than alcohol and advise a requirement of blood or urine depending on the type of drug suspected.) **4.98**

Whilst it may well be desirable where unfitness to drive through drugs is at issue for expert medical evidence to be adduced as to the degree of the defendant's impairment, the lack of such evidence is not necessarily fatal to a prosecution. In *Leetham v DPP* [1999] R.T.R. 29, the Divisional Court upheld a conviction under s.4(1) based upon the defendant's fast and erratic driving, his admitted consumption of cannabis, the presence of cannabis in his blood on subsequent analysis, the known effects of that drug and the evidence of the officers who stopped him that his eyes were red and glazed and that his speech was slow and slurred.

It should be noted that it is necessary at the time of provision of a specimen of blood under s.7(3)(c) for there to have been a clear oral statement by the doctor at the police station to the effect that he believed that drugs were a possible cause of the defendant's condition. The Divisional Court quashed a conviction for failing to provide a specimen of blood for analysis contrary to what is now s.7(6) where **4.99** the doctor had failed to advise the constable of his opinion to that effect (*Cole v DPP* [1988] R.T.R. 224).

Under s.7(4) the police officer requiring a specimen of blood or urine normally decides for himself whether the specimen should be of blood or urine. If, however, he has been advised by the doctor that for medical reasons blood cannot or should not be provided, the police officer is required to ask the motorist to provide a specimen of urine (s.7(4)). Curiously, the Act does not provide the converse; the police can require urine even if the doctor advises that urine cannot or should not be provided. As will be seen from § 4.214, however, the standard police pro forma which is recommended for use by police forces envisages that the station officer will normally require blood under s.7(4) even though the Act gives the police officer requiring specimens of blood or urine under s.7(4) an otherwise complete discretion as to whether it should be blood or urine. (The reason for the pro forma advising the taking of blood specimens may be that it is not uncommon for a defendant who has been required to provide specimens of urine to be unable to provide the second specimen within an hour of the original requirement. If this occurs, a prosecution under s.7(6) will fail unless the police can prove that the defendant had no reasonable excuse for failing to give the second specimen.)

4.100   While a certificate of analysis relating to a drug shall be taken into account under ss.15 and 16 of the 1988 Offenders Act, there is no statutory assumption in the section that the proportion of a drug in the specimen is not less than at the time an offence is committed. It therefore appears necessary for the prosecution to relate the amount of drug shown in the certificate to the amount of drug that would have been shown if the specimen had been provided at the time of the offence. It will also be open to the defence to attack the certificate on the ground that the defendant ingested the drug after the arrest but before he provided the blood or urine sample.

DRIVING OR IN CHARGE ABOVE THE LIMIT

The offence (s.5(1)(a) and (b))

4.101   Under s.5(1)(a) it is an offence if a person drives or attempts to drive a motor vehicle on a road or other public place after consuming so much alcohol that the proportion of it in his breath, blood or urine exceeds the prescribed limit. For the purposes of an offence contrary to s.5(1)(a), the meaning of "consuming" is not limited to drinking; entry into the body other than by mouth is included. The Divisional Court so held in *DPP v Johnson (David)* [1995] R.T.R. 9 in allowing an appeal by the prosecution against the decision of a stipendiary magistrate to acquit the defendant. The magistrate had found that the driver had been injected by a doctor with Kenalog which contained 1.5 per cent benzyl alcohol and had accepted that there was a reasonable possibility that that had affected the Intoximeter reading. The word "consuming" in its usual use did not embrace sniffing or absorbing by way of injection or some patch attached to the body, but was capable of a variety of meanings depending upon its context. Since Parliament intended to diminish the numbers of those who drove with alcohol inside their bodies there was no hiatus in the law whereby the entry of alcohol other than by mouth did not come under the 1988 Act. Accordingly, a court was not entitled to restrict the meaning of "consuming" to the act of drinking and to no other mode of introduction or injection.

A defendant pleaded guilty to an offence alleging that he had driven "a motor vehicle on a road … after consuming so much alcohol that the proportion of it in your breath/blood/urine exceeded the prescribed limit, contrary to s.5(1)(a) of the Road Traffic Act 1988". His appeal was allowed in *R. v Bolton JJ. Ex p. Khan* [1999] Crim. L.R. 912 on the basis that the charge was bad for duplicity. Section 5(1)(a) created six different offences; thus in order to establish an offence under the section, the prosecution had to specify in the charge whether the excess of alcohol was in breath, blood, or urine, as appropriate. The prosecution would always know which would be appropriate and if an error was made in failing to delete from the pro forma charge the otiose words, an amendment could be made without any prejudice to the defendant.

The meaning of the word "breath" in s.5(1) of the 1988 Act is not confined to **4.102** deep lung air and should be given its dictionary definition of "air exhaled from any thing" (*Zafar v DPP* [2004] EWHC 2468; [2005] R.T.R. 18). *Zafar v DPP* was applied by the Divisional Court in *Woolfe v DPP* [2006] EWHC 1497; [2007] R.T.R. 16 when holding that the word "breath" included breath expelled that had been infused with stomach alcohol by way of oesophageal reflux so as to give a reading that did not precisely reflect the blood-alcohol level. Although the Intoximeter EC/IR was designed to make the distinction between deep lung breath and mouth alcohol, such a distinction was not required by s.5, and the word "breath" in that provision did not distinguish between the two meanings. It is therefore not a defence to an allegation under s.5(1) of the Road Traffic Act 1988 that the defendant has regurgitated alcohol from his stomach into his mouth while providing a sample of breath at the police station. One consequence of this is that the standard procedure prescribed in the form MG DD/A (Version 4.3) is no longer appropriate. In *McNeil v DPP* [2008] EWHC 1254; [2008] R.T.R. 359 the appellant gave two specimens of breath into the Intoximeter. They showed readings of between 58 and 59 µg per 100ml. He was then asked, "Before you used the instrument, I asked you whether you have brought up anything from your stomach. Have you brought anything up from your stomach since I asked you that question?" The appellant replied that he had. The form then in use said that in these circumstances a reliable indication of the proportion of alcohol in a person's breath may not have been obtained, and it will be usual to proceed to a requirement for blood or urine. The officer conducting the procedure followed the instructions on the form and requested a sample of blood, which provided a reading of 95mg in blood. On the basis of that result he was convicted of driving with excess alcohol in the blood. The conviction was overturned on appeal by way of case stated. On the facts of the case the cause which the officer thought he had to believe, namely that the breath samples tested on the Intoximeter did not give a reliable indication of the proportion of alcohol in the appellant's breath, was not in law capable of rendering that indication unreliable. In those circumstances the subsequent request for a blood sample was not one which the officer was entitled to make.

The offence requires the offender to be "driving or attempting to drive" a "motor vehicle" on a "road or other public place". These terms are all discussed in detail at §§ 1.04–21, 1.104, 1.110, 1.122 and 1.148.

The circumstances under which a person who is "driving or attempting to **4.103** drive" a motor vehicle may be required to provide a preliminary breath test are discussed at §§ 4.35 et seq. and the circumstances under which he may subsequently be required to provide a specimen of breath, blood or urine for analysis are discussed below.

The "prescribed limit" is defined by s.11(2) as 35µg of alcohol in 100ml of breath, 80mg of alcohol in 100ml of blood or 107mg of alcohol in 100ml of urine, or such other proportion as may be prescribed by regulations made by the Secretary of State. See further § 4.165.

4.104   Analysis of blood or urine specimens is required to be made by an "authorised analyst" and that definition is discussed in detail in § 4.246.

The defendant may challenge the analysis if he proves that he consumed alcohol after the commission of the offence, but before the analysis (see § 4.300).

The defence of duress may, in appropriate circumstances, be available for an offence under s.5(1)(a); see further § 4.305.

Insanity is not available as a defence, since an offence under s.5(1)(a) is one of strict liability for which no mens rea is required; see further § 4.307.

4.105   Under s.5(1)(b) it is an offence if a person is in charge of a motor vehicle on a road or other public place after consuming so much alcohol that the proportion of it in his breath, blood or urine exceeds the prescribed limit. It may be presumed by analogy that as with offences under s.5(1)(a), "consuming" is not limited to drinking, but that entry into the body other than by mouth is included (see *DPP v Johnson (David)* at § 4.113).

As in earlier legislation the offence requires the offender to be "in charge" of a "motor vehicle" on a "road or other public place" and the existing case law on these phrases will be relevant. These are discussed at §§ 1.04–21, 1.104, 1.110, 1.122 and 1.148. The statutory defence to a charge under s.5(1)(b) is discussed at § 4.309 along with the similar defence to a charge under s.4(2).

4.106   It should be noted that the provisions in the Police and Criminal Evidence Act 1984 controlling, defining and restricting police powers in respect of persons detained at police stations do not affect the exercise of ss.7 and 8 of the Road Traffic Act 1988 (Police and Criminal Evidence Act 1984 s.36(6)(d)).

Provision of breath specimens

4.107   The phrase "the constable making the requirement" occurs in a number of places in s.7. Whilst only selected police officers have been trained to operate evidential breath testing machines, there appears to be nothing in the phrase to limit the making of a requirement to a constable who has been trained to operate the machine. It would seem to bear its ordinary meaning, namely the constable, whoever he may be, who makes a requirement under s.7. The only statutory requirement is that it must be a constable. This would seem to include any police constable of any rank including a special constable. There is no requirement for the constable to be in uniform. In practice the constable who usually makes the requirement is the custody sergeant.

4.108   Sections 6D and 7 of the 1988 Act were amended by s.154 of the Serious Organised Crime and Police Act 2005 in order to provide police with a power to undertake evidential breath tests at the roadside. These provisions were designed to enable admissible evidence to be captured at an earlier stage and hence improve enforcement. It should be noted, however, that at the time of writing (March

2009) no suitable equipment had been approved for roadside use, and further that the projected cost of any such equipment may in any event prove unattractive to police forces. Section 7(2), as amended, permits a requirement for an evidential breath specimen to be made at a hospital or at the roadside as well as at a police station. A requirement to provide specimens of breath at the roadside may not be made unless the constable making it is in uniform, or (whether or not in uniform) has required a person to co-operate with a preliminary breath test in circumstances where an accident involving a motor vehicle has occurred and the constable reasonably believes that the person was driving, attempting to drive or in charge of the vehicle concerned at the time of the accident (s.7(2B)). A requirement for an evidential breath specimen may subsequently be made at a police station if, but only if, a device or a reliable device was not available at the roadside or it was impracticable for it to be used there, or the constable making the previous requirement has reasonable cause to believe that the device used has not produced a reliable indication (s.7(2D)).

So far as evidential specimens are concerned, police are compelled to ask for breath rather than blood or urine specimens unless one of the five situations below exists (s.7(3)): **4.109**

"(a) the constable making the requirement has reasonable cause to *believe* [our italics] that for medical reasons a specimen of breath cannot be provided or should not be required, or

(b) specimens of breath have not been provided elsewhere and at the time the requirement is made a device or reliable device of the type mentioned [an approved device; see below] … is not available at the police station or it is then for any other reason not practicable to use … [the machine] there, or

(bb) a device of the type mentioned [an approved device; see below] has been used at the police station or elsewhere but the constable who required the specimens of breath has reasonable cause to believe that the device has not produced a reliable indication of the proportion of alcohol in the breath of the person concerned, or

(bc) as a result of the administration of a preliminary drug test, the constable making the requirement has reasonable cause to believe that the person required to provide a specimen of blood or urine has a drug in his body, or

(c) the suspected offence is one under section 3A, 4 of this Act and the constable making the requirement has been advised by a medical practitioner that the condition of the person required to provide the specimen might be due to some drug."

Subsection (bb) above was inserted by s.63 of the Criminal Procedure and Investigations Act 1996 to enable police to make full use of the second generation of evidential breath testing equipment. This equipment is able to identify and flag up *automatically* certain situations; situations where it is suspected an interfering substance may be present, or the alleged offender produces mouth alcohol, or where (broadly speaking) the difference between the reading for two breath samples is greater than 15 per cent. In such situations the machine will advise the operator and the constable will then be able to require a blood or urine sample as an alternative. **4.110**

Approval orders have been issued in respect of what can be described as second generation machines, and a list of those breath analysis devices approved under s.7(1)(a) of the 1988 Act can be found in Vol.2, § 18.35 of this work (see also *http://www.police.homeoffice.gov.uk/publications/operational-policing* [Accessed March 16, 2009]). The Lion Intoximeter 3000 and Camic Breath Analyser, the first generation machines, have ceased to be approved devices.

4.111   It should be noted that the proviso at the end of s.7(3) "but may then be made notwithstanding that the person required to provide the specimen has already provided or been required to provide two specimens of breath" applies not only to s.7(3)(a) but to s.7(3)(b) (as also to s.7(3)(bb)).

Under s.8(1), (2) if the lower of the two breath specimens is no more than 50µg the motorist may claim that it should be replaced by a specimen under s.7(4), i.e. a specimen of blood or urine: see § 4.134 below.

A   *Reasonable cause to believe that a specimen cannot be provided (s.7(3)(a))*

4.112   It will be seen from the wording of paragraph (a) that although no doubt the constable will accept any medical advice obtainable, there is nothing to prevent the constable believing the motorist's statement that he is chronically short of breath or is bronchitic or asthmatic or for any other reason has not the necessary lung capacity to give two specimens of breath. The first generation machines, the Lion Intoximeter and the Camic Breath Analyser, required the subject to blow at a required pressure for the required length of time. If the motorist failed to blow at the pressure and for the length of time required the cycle of the machine would halt. It is understood that the second generation of evidential breath testing machines (the Camic Datamaster, the lion intoxylizer 6000UK and the Intoximeter EC/IR) are less demanding of breath in terms of pressure and volume than their predecessors, but will nevertheless give an appropriate indication where an inadequate or incomplete sample has been provided. At this stage the constable is in practice presented with a choice of action. He can immediately charge the motorist under s.7(6) with failing to provide specimens for analysis. On the other hand if he has reasonable cause to believe that for medical reasons the person was unable to provide specimens of breath on the machine, he can proceed to require a specimen of blood or urine under s.7(4). (It should be noted that the constable only has to have reasonable cause to believe that medical reasons exist. He does not have to obtain medical advice. If Parliament had intended for a constable to act under s.7(3)(a) and proceed under s.7(4) to require blood or urine only after obtaining medical advice, Parliament would no doubt have done so as in s.7(3)(c) below.)

Where a defendant makes a claim that he has a medical reason for not providing a specimen of breath, the police officer must decide as a layperson whether the claim is capable of being such a condition. The decision is the police officer's alone (although he may, if he wishes, seek professional help); if, on sufficient material, he concludes that the claim is capable of constituting a medical condition, he must then consider whether or not he has reasonable cause to believe that as a consequence of that condition a specimen of breath cannot be provided or should not be required (*Dempsey v Catton* [1986] R.T.R. 194). Where, however, the officer is in some doubt he will be wise to obtain medical advice; see *Horrocks v Binns* below.

4.113   Intoxication by alcohol was capable of amounting to a medical reason for a suspect being unable to provide a specimen of breath for analysis such as would entitle a constable to require the provision of a specimen of blood or urine instead; such a condition had well-known effects on a person's state of control and reason. The Divisional Court so held in *Young v DPP* [1992] R.T.R. 328 when dismissing the defendant's appeal against conviction of an offence of failing to provide a specimen of blood for analysis contrary to s.7(6) of the 1988 Act. The defendant had been unable because of her state of intoxication to provide specimens of breath on the Intoximeter.

It should be particularly noted that s.7(3)(a) requires the constable to have reasonable cause to *believe* that for medical reasons specimens of breath cannot or should not be provided. Belief imports a higher degree of certainty than mere suspicion, and the phrase "reasonable cause to believe" has been contrasted with the phrase "reasonable cause to suspect". These phrases and the contrast between them have been the subject of judicial discussion (*Johnson v Whitehouse* [1984] R.T.R. 38; *Baker v Oxford* [1980] R.T.R. 315). In *Horrocks v Binns* [1986] R.T.R. 202 *Note* it was held that the station officer was not entitled to require a blood specimen where he did not believe the motorist's injury affected his ability to give breath specimens, but was prepared to give the motorist the benefit of the doubt since he felt that the motorist was the best judge of his own injuries. In *Horrocks* it was stated that if a station officer is genuinely in some doubt as to whether or not a driver can blow into the machine he can take the opinion of a doctor.

A different view was taken, however, by the Divisional Court in *White v Proudlock*, a case decided in November 1984 but reported at [1988] R.T.R. 163 *Note*. There it was decided that what was required was not the belief of the officer himself but reasonable cause for such a belief.

The two cases were considered together by the Divisional Court in *Davis v DPP* [1988] R.T.R. 156. Having reviewed the authorities, Mann J. (with whom Bingham L.J. agreed) indicated that he would unhesitatingly choose *White v Proudlock* as correctly representing the law. It would seem, therefore, that when requiring a suspect to provide a specimen of blood for analysis, what must be established is that the officer had reasonable cause (objectively speaking) to believe that for medical reasons a specimen of breath could not, or should not, be taken; the fact that the officer himself did not hold such a belief is quite immaterial. A constable who has reasonable cause to believe that for medical reasons a specimen of breath cannot be provided, and therefore starts the procedure whereby a specimen of blood or urine can be required, can nevertheless charge the defendant with failing to provide a breath specimen without proceeding to obtain a blood or urine sample, given that the officer was later satisfied, on the basis of the doctor's medical opinion, that there was no medical excuse for the defendant's failure to provide breath. This happened in *Longstaff v DPP* [2008] EWHC 303; [2008] R.T.R. 17. Here the defendant's vehicle was involved in a collision as a result of which he was arrested on suspicion of driving a vehicle after consuming excess alcohol. At the police station he was unable to provide a satisfactory sample of breath and said "I cannot breathe properly because of my back pain". The officer conducting the procedure went on to complete section B1 of MG DD/B which is part of the form headed "Breath test device not used/not operating reliably/unreliable indication obtained" (the Form B procedure). The defendant was asked whether or not there was any medical reason why a specimen of blood could not or should not be taken by a doctor and responded in the negative. When the doctor arrived at the police station having been contacted to take a blood sample a discussion with the officers took place. A decision was taken that the doctor would examine the defendant with a view to ascertaining whether there was a medical reason for not providing a sample of breath. After examination the doctor informed the officers that in his opinion there was no

4.114

medical reason for the defendant not supply a sample of breath. The officers did not request the doctor to take a sample of blood or urine. The defendant was charged later that morning with failing to supply a sample of breath. The defendant was convicted and on appeal by case stated that verdict was upheld. The Divisional Court confirmed that the question under s.7(6) is whether, in fact, the defendant had a reasonable excuse for failing to provide a specimen of breath. That is for the justices to decide on all the evidence. The court examined a number of propositions advanced by the defence:

> "... the points sought to be taken by the appellant in this case are utterly without merit and unsustainable. What the appellant has attempted to do, in common with appellants in numerous other cases, is to force the decision-making powers of police officers into a straight jacket which has no basis in the provisions of the statute or established authority. The forensic technique is to seek to refashion the law by reference to the contents of standard forms used by the police. It is a most unattractive development." ([2008] EWHC 303 at [25], per Maurice Kay L.J.)

On the other hand, a constable will not have reasonable cause to believe that an unreliable indication has been obtained from the Intoximeter when a motorist states, in response to the standard question in the form MG DD/A (Version 4.3), that he has brought something up from the stomach (see *McNeil v DPP* [2008] EWHC 1254; [2008] R.T.R. 359, § 4.102).

4.115   It should be borne in mind that if the station officer is over hasty in charging a defendant under s.7(6) for failing to give specimens of breath, the prosecution will not succeed if subsequently it transpires that the defendant might for medical reasons have been unable to give specimens of breath at the pressure and the length of time required by the machine. It is for the prosecution to prove that a defendant charged under s.7(6) has no reasonable excuse to provide specimens for analysis; the onus is not upon the defendant to show that he has. It has, however, been said (per Forbes J. (obiter) in *Teape v Godfrey* [1986] R.T.R. 213 at 221) that if a defendant knows that he suffers from a medical condition which prevents him giving sufficient breath, his duty to provide a specimen must include in those circumstances a duty to inform the police officer making the requirement of that medical condition. Even if a court felt reluctant to regard a defendant as under a "duty" so to inform a police officer of a known medical condition, it might well regard the deliberate concealment of such information as a matter of bona fides which would detract from the reasonableness of such excuse if later raised as a defence to a charge under s.7(6) or s.6(4) (see "Reasonable excuse", §§ 4.261 et seq.).

This issue was considered further in the case of *Piggott v DPP* [2008] EWHC 305; [2008] R.T.R. 16. Here the defendant was arrested on suspicion of driving after consuming alcohol in excess of the prescribed limit. At the police station she agreed to provide specimens of breath for analysis. She made four attempts to do so, but on each occasion failed to provide sufficient breath for analysis. In reply to the police officer conducting the test, she said that there were no medical reasons why she could not provide the specimens. She was convicted by the magistrates of failing, without a reasonable excuse, to provide a breath specimen, contrary to s.7(6) of the Road Traffic Act 1988. The justices heard, and apparently accepted, a report from an expert in respiratory medicine that there was a medical reason for failure to give the breath of specimens, namely that she suffered from asthma and hyperventilation syndrome. In the case stated the magistrates said that "following the case of *Teape v Godfrey* if the appellant knew that she suffered from a medical condition which might affect her ability to provide a sample she was under a duty to inform the officer making the requirement to provide breath specimens of that medical condition. The appellant had not informed PC Henderson of the medical condition and we therefore found her guilty of the offence charged". This conviction was overturned on appeal by case stated. The statutory question is whether there is a reasonable excuse for failing to provide a specimen when required to do so. There is no specific statutory requirement to advance a medical reason for not providing a specimen of breath. This case was distinguished from that of *R. (on the application of Martiner) v DPP* [2004] EWHC 2484; [2005] A.C.D. 65 QBD. In that case the appellant had refused to provide a blood sample. He did not give any medical reason for his refusal when asked for the sample but subsequently produced medical evidence before the district judge that he suffered from a moderate needle phobia. *Martiner* involved a defendant who refused or deliberately failed to provide a specimen, whereas *Piggott* involved a defendant who attempted to give a specimen but failed to do so because of a medical condition. In *Piggott*, the court emphasised that if you fail to mention a medical condition of which you are aware, the justices are likely to conclude that the medical condition is not the reason why the specimen was refused. "They are likely to reject any excuse advanced later for such a failure as being reasonable and are likely to find you guilty" ([2008] EWHC 305 at [24], per Moses J.).

A reason which does not go to a suspect's medical ability to provide a speci-   **4.116**
men of breath may nevertheless be capable of amounting to a medical reason within what is now s.7(3)(a) of the 1988 Act, since that section encompasses not merely inability but also circumstances in which a specimen "should not be required". The Divisional Court so held in *Davies v DPP* [1989] R.T.R. 391 when dismissing an appeal against conviction of an offence contrary to what is now s.7(6). The facts of the case were somewhat unusual. The defendant refused to provide specimens of breath at the police station on the grounds that he was taking a drug called Priadel which a psychiatrist had told him would influence the alcoholic content of his bloodstream. His explanation was accepted and he was asked to provide a specimen of blood. That request he also (with the benefit of legal advice) refused, saying that he suffered from haemophiliac tendencies as evidenced by the fact that a small cut he had received earlier was still bleeding. That explanation was also accepted, and he was asked to provide two specimens of urine instead. In reply to an inquiry as to whether there was any medical reason why he could not supply urine, he stated that whilst there was no such medical reason he was currently taking large doses of various vitamins which would influence the analysis and that he would therefore not provide the specimens. In all the circumstances the officer concerned did have reasonable cause to believe that for medical reasons a specimen of breath should not be required, notwithstanding that the defendant might well have been physically able to provide it.

Davies v DPP above was applied by the Divisional Court in *Webb v DPP* [1992] R.T.R. 299. A female defendant who was of slight build, whose breath smelt of alcohol and who was shaken and upset and apparently in a distressed condition, failed three times to provide a specimen of breath for analysis on a Lion Intoximeter. She was apparently "doing her best". In those circumstances the police officer's conclusion that he had reasonable cause to believe that for medical reasons a specimen of breath could not be provided or should not be required and the conclusion of the justices that she had a medical condition were correct in law. The blood specimen subsequently obtained from her and upon which her conviction of an excess alcohol offence was based had been lawfully required and her appeal was accordingly dismissed.

B Reliable device not available for use (s. 7(3)(b))

4.117 If the calibration check of the machine is not within the permissible limits or if the machine does not satisfactorily purge itself, it would seem that a "reliable device" is not available. It does not matter by how little the machine fails a calibration check; the de minimis rule has no application to this particular statutory provision (*Waite v Smith* [1986] Crim. L.R. 405). If this is the case, or if for any other reason it is not practicable to use the machine, the police constable may proceed to require a specimen of blood or urine under s.7(4). The police, however, are not bound to proceed to require specimens of blood or urine under s.7(4), and there is nothing to prevent the police taking the motorist to another police station where another machine is available, and to require the motorist to provide specimens of breath there (*Denny v DPP* [1990] R.T.R. 417). The machine at Maltby police station diagnosed itself as defective after receiving both the required breath samples; the defendant was then taken to Main Street police station, Rotherham where two further samples were provided by him. In the Divisional Court's view, to suggest that a police officer should be required to ask for a blood or urine sample merely because he had a defective machine was not tenable. Common sense (that most uncommon commodity) dictated that if failure to extract two valid specimens of breath were due to a defect in the machine, then a motorist should be given a second opportunity to provide the same.

Transportation in search of a reliable evidential breath testing machine is not the only option available to the police, however. The Divisional Court has also held, in a case where a reliable Lion Intoximeter was not available and a blood sample was required, but a doctor was not available to extract it at the police station at which the initial request for breath had been made, that it was proper for the defendant to be taken to another police station for the blood sample to be taken. It mattered not that the second police station might have contained a serviceable Intoximeter; the requirement for blood had been lawfully made, and the next step was the taking of the sample (*Chief Constable of Kent v Berry* [1986] Crim. L.R. 748).

4.118 Section 7(3)(b) entitles a police officer to require a specimen of blood or urine if at the time the requirement is made a device or a reliable device is not available or for any other reason it is not practicable to use such a device. It was held in *Cotter v Kamil* [1984] R.T.R. 371 that the words "at the time the requirement was made" refer to the time at which the subsequent requirement to provide blood or urine is made. It was therefore held that where the defendant had provided two specimens of breath on the Lion Intoximeter but before completion of its operation it reached a temperature at which analysis by the machine became unsatisfactory, the police officer in accordance with s.7(3)(b) was entitled to require a specimen of blood. The view of the Divisional Court in *Cotter v Kamil* was reinforced in *Oxford v Baxendale* [1986] Crim. L.R. 631 where the fact that the device had not been functioning reliably was not realised until an hour and three-quarters after the specimens of breath had been provided. Although there was no direct evidence of the reliability or otherwise of the machine at the time when the request for a specimen of blood was made, the justices could have been satisfied by inference and deduction from its earlier unreliability that the machine had continued to be unreliable. It should be noted, however, that the non-availability of a reliable device or the existence of a defect in the device must be proved in court in accordance with the rules of evidence (*Hughes v McConnell* [1985] R.T.R. 244 at 249; *Dye v Manns* [1986] Crim. L.R. 337). Whilst a wide disparity between the readings on the printout in respect of the two specimens might have sufficed to establish the unreliability of a first generation device (*Gordon v Thorpe* [1986] Crim. L.R. 61; *Ross v Allan* 1986 S.L.T. 349), it should be noted that evidential breath testing devices of the second generation will give an automatic indication of unreliability where (broadly speaking) the difference between the reading for two breath samples is greater than 15 per cent, thereby enabling the constable to require an alternative specimen of blood or urine in accordance with s.7(3)(bb) (see § 4.109).

In *Morgan v Lee* [1985] R.T.R. 409 the defendant gave two specimens of breath and the police operator was able to see the readings together with the self-calibration checks on the digital screen but the printout was not expelled from the Intoximeter; the paper was apparently tangled with something inside. The police sergeant thereupon demanded a specimen of blood under what is now s.7(4) (the police sergeant operator was of the opinion that the Lion Intoximeter was inoperative and that he was entitled to do so by virtue of what is now s.7(3)(b)). It was held that there was nothing to show that the machine was unreliable because the police sergeant had been able to see the readings and the self-calibration checks and could have given evidence of them. **4.119**

In *Jones v DPP* [1990] Crim. L.R. 656 a Lion Intoximeter failed to produce a printout because the "modem" switch at the back of the machine was in the "off" position. The operating manual for the machine requires this switch to be checked in the event of printout failure. Since the officer had failed to carry out that check it was not reasonable for him to conclude that the machine was unreliable. Whether a person can blow into the machine is a question of objective fact, and if the machine is in working order it follows that it is practicable to use it (*Horrocks v Binns*, § 4.113 above).

In *Slender v Boothby* (1984) 149 J.P. 405, it was held that "reliable" in the phrase in what is now s.7(3)(b) "a reliable device … is not available" meant "reliable" for the purposes of the Act. Parliament contemplated that the device should have the capacity to produce the correct date and time. Accordingly it was held that a "reliable" device was not available on February 29, 1984 when the machine, because it had not been programmed to cope with a leap year, incorrectly showed the date as March 1, 1984. The station officer was held to be entitled to require the provision of a specimen of blood. **4.120**

In a Scottish case (*Gilligan v Tudhope* 1986 S.L.T. 299) where *Morgan v Lee* was applied, the High Court of Justiciary cast doubt on the decision in *Slender v Boothby* above. The criterion for the reliability of a device was there stated to be the device's ability to perform its analytical function. A failure of the printout mechanism did not reflect upon that ability. This criterion was also applied in *Ross v Allan* 1986 S.L.T. 349, although a differently constituted court there distinguished *Gilligan v Tudhope* on its facts.

In a further Scottish case (*Hodgins v Carmichael* 1989 S.L.T. 514) a Camic **4.121**

Breath Analyser calibrated correctly and disclosed readings of 83μg and 94μg of alcohol per 100ml of breath on its visual display unit, but failed to reproduce any figures on its printout. Noting this apparent defect, the police officer required the defendant to provide a specimen of blood. Later it was realised that the fault in the machine was merely a twisting of the ribbon and paper in its printer. The defect was later remedied and the relevant printout was obtained by courtesy of the machine's memory. The motorist concerned was convicted on the basis of the lower of the two readings on the Camic device (oral evidence of the readings on the visual display unit having been given by the police officers).

The motorist's appeal was dismissed by the High Court of Justiciary. The appellant had argued that the requirement from him of a specimen of blood implied unreliability on the part of the machine, and that its analysis should not be relied upon. The court found, however, that as a matter of fact a reliable machine had been available and had been used. The appellant would not be allowed to escape conviction merely because of an unlawful requirement to provide a specimen of blood, analysis of which in the event could not have been relied upon by the prosecution.

4.122   In *Fawcett v Gasparics* [1986] R.T.R. 375 the Divisional Court held that the fact that a Lion Intoximeter printout stated the correct numerical date but the wrong day of the week might go to the weight or value to be placed upon its contents, but could not undermine its admissibility in evidence; provided that the device functioned and produced the necessary statement and certificate relating to the defendant's specimen, it was to be admitted subject only to criticism or argument as to the *weight* to be attached to it. It was important not to confuse or elide what are now s.7 of the 1988 Act and ss.15, 16 of the 1988 Offenders Act. In an attack upon the admissibility of the printout under ss.15, 16 of the 1988 Offenders Act the court is not in the same way concerned with the reliability of the machine as it is in connection with s.7(3). Noting that the court in *Morgan v Lee* had not had *Slender v Boothby* brought to its attention, Macpherson J. remarked (at 382L) that those particular cases may need to be considered again and together when and if a suitable opportunity presents itself.

Morgan v Lee was distinguished, if not altogether felicitously, by the Divisional Court in *Haghigat-Khou v Chambers* [1988] R.T.R. 95. A Lion Intoximeter at a police station was not functioning correctly with regard to its printout mechanism. The officer concerned formed the view that it was therefore unreliable and accordingly required the appellant to provide a blood specimen; he was in due course convicted on the evidence of that specimen. Drawing upon *Morgan v Lee* counsel for the appellant argued that the defect in the printout mechanism did not of itself render the machine unreliable, since oral evidence of the readout would have been admissible and accordingly evidence of the blood test should have been excluded as it had been unlawfully required.

4.123   In dismissing the appeal the court held that it was not bound by *Morgan v Lee* since in the instant case the defect in the machine was known to the officer at the outset of the procedure whereas in the earlier case the fault was not discovered until after the breath test had been conducted. The court adopted the test of reliability set out in *Thompson v Thynne* (discussed below at § 4.124), namely that "a reliable device" is a device which the officer reasonably believes to be reliable; given that the printout mechanism was clearly malfunctioning, there was evidence to support the officer's conclusion and hence bestow legality upon his subsequent request for blood.

On the face of things it is a little difficult to see how the mere time of detection of a fault which, according to *Morgan v Lee* at least, has no bearing upon the machine's ability to perform its analytical function, can so materially affect assumptions about its reliability. It may be, however, that the adoption of the subjective element in the test of reliability imparted by *Thompson v Thynne* allows the officer concerned considerably more scope in making decisions of this sort, and that his discretion, if reasonably exercised, is less subject to challenge. It should be noted that the subjective test of reliability propounded in *Thompson v Thynne* met with the approval of the Scottish courts in *Burnett v Smith* (1989) 1990 S.L.T. 537. In that case the High Court stated that the provision would be unworkable unless the test was regarded as subjective. The Lord Justice-Clerk (Lord Ross), presiding, added that it was desirable that the provisions be interpreted similarly by the courts of England (and Wales) and Scotland. The subjective approach to the question of reliability was further endorsed by the High Court of Justiciary in *Carson v Orr* (1991) 1993 S.L.T. 362. Two specimens of breath provided by the defendant for analysis by the Camic device revealed respectively 87µg and 58µg in 100ml breath. The calibration checks were all within the acceptable range and the machine had been used on other occasions without any indication of malfunction. Despite the considerable difference between the two readings the police had decided that the device was reliable (an application of the subjective test). The judgment formed by the police was open to question if the decision was one which no police officer acting reasonably could have reached; on the given facts, however, there was nothing to indicate that there was anything wrong with the device and the results were not so absurd that no police officer acting reasonably could properly have regarded them as having been produced by a reliable device.

4.124 A human error which results in an error appearing in the printout will not constitute a malfunction or otherwise render the printout inadmissible (*Toovey v Northumbria Chief Constable* [1986] Crim. L.R. 475, where the appellant's forename was incorrect on the printout; and *Burditt v Roberts* [1986] Crim. L.R. 636, where the appellant's name was spelled "ROGERPBUIURDITTTT" and the word "Station" was also misspelt).

In the cases of *Dye v Manns* and *Oxford v Baxendale* cited at § 4.130 the unreliability of the machine was given a purely objective construction and one which appears to accord with the literal meaning of the words "a device or a reliable device … is not available at the police station" contained in what is now s.7(3)(b). A different view was propounded by the Divisional Court in *Thompson v Thynne* [1986] Crim. L.R. 629 where it was held that the words "a reliable device" are to be given the meaning "a device which [the officer] reasonably believes to be reliable". Since s.7(3)(a) and (c) provide for the officer's decision to depend upon what he "has reasonable cause to believe" or "has been advised", the court found no difficulty in imputing a similar partially subjective element to the ostensibly objective words of s.7(3)(b).

4.125 *Thompson v Thynne* was applied by the Divisional Court in *Haghigat-Khou v Chambers* (discussed at § 4.122 above) and was also cited with approval by the Divisional Court in *Badkin v DPP* [1988] R.T.R. 401. In that case a Lion Intoximeter declined to produce a printout and the operating officer, deciding that the machine might be unreliable, requested a blood sample as he was entitled to do in accordance with what is now s.7(3) and on the authority of *Thompson v*

Thynne. The appellant, however, was not informed of the result of the blood test and the evidence of that test was not relied upon at his trial.

Allowing the appeal, the court held that once a blood sample had been lawfully requested and obtained, any prosecution had to be based upon the blood rather than the breath analysis. Since the officer's belief that the device was malfunctioning was the legitimate excuse for requiring the blood sample, the prosecution had to continue to rely upon that premise and treat the Lion Intoximeter result as unreliable. Even if the prosecution could have succeeded on the basis of the breath test readings, it would still have been necessary for the blood test to have been put in evidence since what is now s.15(2) of the Road Traffic Offenders Act 1988 provides that evidence of alcohol in a specimen of "breath, blood or urine provided by the accused" shall "in all cases" be taken into account.

4.126   *Badkin v DPP* was subsequently applied by the Divisional Court in *McLellan v DPP* [1993] R.T.R. 401 in allowing an appeal against a conviction of a s.5(1) offence based upon a breath analysis where a blood specimen had been provided by the defendant at the request of the police officer conducting the breath test since the Lion Intoximeter appeared to that officer to be unreliable. In the words of Glidewell L.J. in *Badkin v DPP*:

> "If the officer decides that the breath analysis device is not reliable and requires a specimen of blood which is then provided and analysed, any prosecution can thereafter be based only on the analysis of blood and not on that of breath."

In *DPP v Dixon* [1993] R.T.R. 22 the Divisional Court took the opportunity to review the relevant authorities, in particular *Badkin v DPP*, *Morgan v Lee* and *Burnett v Smith* all discussed above and came to the conclusion that the subjective test propounded in *Thompson v Thynne* was the correct one to apply.

4.127   *Badkin v DPP* [1988] R.T.R. 401 (discussed at § 4.126 above) was distinguished by the Divisional Court in *Slasor v DPP* [1999] R.T.R. 432 when deciding that where, as in the case in point, but unlike in *Badkin* and in *McLellan v DPP* [1993] R.T.R. 401 (discussed at § 4.126 above) in which *Badkin* was applied, the prosecution was based on the blood analysis result, nothing in case law or statute prohibits, regardless of its relevance, the admissibility of the breath test result. Following the failure by the Camic machine of its final calibration test, a blood sample was taken from the defendant and divided as is required into two bottles. It was noticed that one of the bottles was cracked and leaking slightly, and using a fresh syringe the police surgeon transferred the blood from the damaged bottle to another one. The defendant at his trial raised the issue of possible contamination of the sample. To meet that issue, the prosecution sought and obtained leave to adduce evidence of the breath test result (102μg/100ml) to show that it was compatible with the blood test analysis (246mg/100ml). Dismissing the defendant's appeal, the court held that, subject to there being some relevant and clearly identified purpose for which it was to be adduced, and subject to the exercise of the court's discretion, evidence of breath test results might properly be admissible in cases where the prosecution was based on the result of a blood-alcohol analysis. The prosecution had to establish beyond reasonable doubt that the blood-alcohol analysis result was reliable and, if the breath test was compatible with, in the sense of broadly equivalent to, the blood analysis result, then, notwithstanding the reason for requiring the defendant to provide blood, such evidence was at least capable of tending to support the reliability of the blood analysis result. That compatibility, however, was not established merely by adducing evidence of the results of the blood and breath tests, and the significance of their relationship must be explained by an expert and not by the police. It was not clear whether in the case in point any such expert evidence had been given, but in any event the justices, having assessed the weight they were prepared to attach to the evidence heard, were perfectly entitled to reach the conclusion that the blood analysis result was a completely reliable one, even without having regard to the evidence relating to the breath test.

The House of Lords (Lord Goff of Chieveley, Lord Mustill, Lord Steyn, Lord Hoffman and Lord Clyde) in *DPP v McKeown*; *DPP v Jones (Christopher)* [1997] R.T.R. 162 unanimously upheld an appeal against the decision of the Divisional Court in *McKeown v DPP*; *Jones v DPP* [1995] Crim. L.R. 69 in which it had been held that the inaccuracy in late July 1992 of the computer clock in the Lion Intoximeter at Widnes Police Station vitiated the convictions of Ms McKeown for driving with excess breath-alcohol and of Mr Jones for failing without reasonable excuse to provide a specimen of breath for analysis. In *Jones*, where the clock was out by 15 minutes, it had been held by the Divisional Court that the Intoximeter concerned was not a reliable device. In *McKeown*, where the clock was 13 minutes slow, it had been held that it had not been shown that the Intoximeter, which was a computer for the purposes of s.69 of the Police and Criminal Evidence Act 1984, was operating properly; accordingly evidence of its visual displays and of the printouts it produced was inadmissible in accordance with s.69(1)(b) of that Act. **4.128**

In view of the fact that s.69 of the Police and Criminal Evidence Act 1984 was repealed with effect from April 14, 2000 when s.60 of the Youth Justice and Criminal Evidence Act 1999 was brought into force, the decision of their Lordships in *McKeown* seems to have been subsumed by events; evidence from computer records is now admissible without conditions relating to the proper use and operation of the computer being shown to be satisfied. Their decision in *Jones*, however, would appear to be of continued application. In that case it was submitted on behalf of the defendant that he could not lawfully be required to provide breath for a Lion Intoximeter with an inaccurate clock. The Lion Intoximeter was an approved device for the purposes of s.7(1) of the 1988 Act, but there was nothing in the statute about the approved device having to have an accurate clock. It was therefore impossible to argue that, by reason of the inaccuracy of its clock, the device at Widnes Police Station could no longer be described as a Lion Intoximeter. Section 7(3)(b) of the 1988 Act clearly contemplated that a device might be "unreliable" and yet of the type approved by the Secretary of State.

Other instances where the device is not reliable are where the calibration checks are outside the limits (see § 4.117 and in particular *Waite v Smith* [1986] Crim. L.R. 405) or where the purge results are other than zero (for sample printouts, see Appendix 1). **4.129**

It should be noted that s.7(3)(b) allows the police to require blood or urine under s.7(4) even if there is a reliable device at the station but nevertheless if "for any other reason [it is] not practicable to use such a device there". The most obvious example of the operation of this provision is where there is no trained police operator at the police station; see *Chief Constable of Avon and Somerset Constabulary v Kelliher* [1986] Crim. L.R. 635 (where the Divisional Court expressly stated that the police were not required to contact other police stations to inquire after the availability of a trained operator before requiring the provision of a specimen for laboratory analysis).

4.130   It is essential from the terms of s.7(3)(b) that the officer who makes a request for a sample of blood or urine must have cause to believe that there is no reliable device available to analyse the driver's breath at the police station. The driver must be made aware of that fact to comply with the requirements of *DPP v Jackson* [1998] R.T.R. 397 (discussed at § 4.147 below). There was, however, no reason to superimpose a requirement that the driver must be informed of that fact by the officer making the request for the sample, since no conceivable prejudice could result if the information was supplied by another officer (in the case in point, the custody officer). The Divisional Court so held in *Bobin v DPP* [1999] R.T.R. 375 when dismissing the defendant's appeal against conviction for failure to supply a specimen of blood.

C   Reasonable cause to believe that the device has not produced a reliable indication of the proportion of alcohol in the subject's breath (s.7(3)(bb))

4.131   A new subs.(3)(bb) was inserted in s.7 of the 1988 Act by s.63 of the Criminal Procedure and Investigations Act 1996. The purpose of this amendment is to enable police to make full use of the second generation of evidential breath testing equipment. This equipment is able to identify and flag up *automatically* certain situations; situations where it is suspected an interfering substance may be present, or the alleged offender produces mouth alcohol, or where (broadly speaking) the difference between the reading for two breath samples is greater than 15 per cent. In such situations the machine will advise the operator and the constable will then, presumably, have reasonable cause to believe that the device has not produced a reliable indication of the proportion of alcohol in the breath of the person concerned and accordingly will be able to require a blood or urine sample as an alternative.

At the time of writing (March 2009) approval orders had been issued in respect of the following second generation machines: the Camic Datamaster, the lion intoxilyzer 6000UK and the Intoximeter EC/IR. The general characteristics and methods of operation of these machines are discussed below at §§ 4.181 et seq.

4.132   Although s.7(3)(bb) was inserted in the 1988 Act with the operation of the second generation of evidential breath testing equipment specifically in mind, it did come under judicial scrutiny in a case involving the use of the new standard drink/drugs police pro forma, form MG/DD/A and B (see § 4.179 below) in conjunction with a machine of the first generation, a Lion Intoximeter 3000. The first specimen obtained showed a breath-alcohol reading of 43µg/100ml; the second showed 33µg/100ml. Those two readings showed a blow difference of some 30.3 per cent. The officer referred to the table of breath difference ranges annexed to the pro forma which suggested that with an old generation device such as the Lion Intoximeter where there is a difference of more than 20 per cent between the lowest and highest readings, the conclusion may be that while the device may be operating reliably, it has not produced a reliable indication. With the benefit of that advice the officer formed the view that the machine had indeed failed to produce a reliable indication and accordingly required the defendant to provide a blood specimen which, when subsequently analysed, revealed a blood-alcohol level of 87mg/100ml. The Divisional Court held in *DPP v Smith (Robert James)* [2000] R.T.R. 341 that the officer had been entitled to exercise his discretion in the way that he had, given that he had had reasonable cause to believe that the Intoximeter had not produced a reliable indication. It would appear that neither the officer concerned nor the court considered the potential impact of s.8(1) of the 1988 Act which provides that of any two specimens of breath provided, that with the lower proportion of alcohol must be used and the other disregarded (see § 4.134). Since in this case the lower specimen revealed a breath-alcohol level below the legal limit, the officer might conceivably have exercised his discretion rather more generously than he did. The Divisional Court did, however, exercise its discretion not to remit the matter for further hearing by the magistrates who had acquitted the defendant in the first instance.

D   *Reasonable cause to believe following preliminary drug test that person has a drug in his body (s.7(3)(bc)); condition of person giving specimen may be due to drugs (s.7(3)(c))*

Because these paragraphs relate to an offence under s.4 (driving, etc., while unfit through drink or drugs) they are discussed in §§ 4.86–100.   **4.133**

A person who is required to give breath is required to give two breath specimens (s.7(1)(a)). By virtue of s.8(1), (2) of any two specimens of breath, that with the lower proportion is to be used and the other shall be disregarded. The breath specimens must be provided "by means of a device of a type approved by the Secretary of State". As to approval of devices, please see further §§ 4.175–8.

Defendant's option to provide blood or urine specimens

If the lower of the two breath specimens is no more than 50µg the person may   **4.134** claim under s.8(2) that it should be replaced by such a specimen as may be required under s.7(4). (Section 7(4) enables a constable to require a specimen of blood or specimens of urine. The defendant cannot choose whether it will be blood or urine, the choice is that of the constable alone; see further § 4.212.)

Section 8(2) refers to "no more than 50 microgrammes". None of the approved devices gives readings of breath in fractions of a microgramme; the readings are in whole numbers. As a result it would appear that a defendant is entitled to opt to give blood or urine instead where the lower of the two breath readings is 50µg.

It was conceded in *Reeves v Enstone, The Times*, February 15, 1985 that the Lion Intoximeter could be inaccurate by two or three microgrammes either way. For this reason the motorist sought to argue that as his lower reading was 51 he was entitled to exercise the option under what is now s.8(2). It was held that the section clearly contemplated the actual reading of the device to be the determining factor and that if the reading exceeded 50 the right to exercise the option did not arise.

If the defendant provides a specimen of blood or specimens of urine, then what   **4.135** is now s.8(2) provides that "neither specimen of breath shall be used". This appears to mean that neither specimen of breath shall be used in evidence (see *Jones v DPP* at § 4.155 and *Yhnell v DPP* at § 4.156 below).

Where a motorist by his own actions frustrated the efforts of a police officer to explain to him his right to choose to provide a blood or urine sample, the prosecution was entitled to rely on the results of his breath test. The Divisional Court so held in *DPP v Poole* [1992] R.T.R. 177. It would appear that the motorist had become extremely agitated and had refused to listen to the police officer who was attempting to explain his rights to him.

Where a motorist provided a specimen of breath for analysis which revealed a level of alcohol low enough to entitle him to offer a sample of blood or urine in its place but, partly because of the alcohol he had consumed, was unable to understand the choice available to him, he could not complain that he had been denied his rights; accordingly evidence of the breath specimen he had provided was admissible against him (*DPP v Berry* (1996) 160 J.P. 707).

4.136　　When offered the option of providing a sample of blood or urine instead of breath the defendant replied: "No, I can't stand the sight of blood". This was interpreted by the police as a refusal. The defendant's conviction was overturned by the Divisional Court in *Surinder Singh Dhillon v DPP* (1992) 157 J.P.N. 420 on the basis that his reply had been at best equivocal and that the police officer ought to have made further inquiry to obtain a clear answer to the question concerning the statutory option.

The failure to obtain the attendance of an appropriate adult before putting a 16-year-old tractor driver to his election as to whether he wished a further sample of blood or urine to be taken did not justify the exercise of the discretion under s.78 of the Police and Criminal Evidence Act 1984 to exclude the evidence provided by the analysis of the prior breath test. On the authority of *DPP v Billington* [1988] R.T.R. 231 and the cases that followed it (see §§ 4.265–70 below) it was not necessary to delay the testing procedure at this stage: *DPP v Evans* [2002] EWHC 2976; [2002] Crim. L.R. 338.

4.137　　The Divisional Court held in *Hope v DPP* [1992] R.T.R. 305 that a motorist who had provided breath specimens analysed at between 40 and 50μg alcohol in 100ml breath might resile from having agreed to provide a specimen of blood; but if he did so resile, he had to accept as a consequence that the prosecution would be able to rely on the breath analysis result.

It was not necessary for the prosecution to prove that an evidential breath testing device was actually working accurately in a case where a defendant was put to his election under s.8(2), since if it was not working properly it was in any event open to the police officer to require a specimen of blood under s.7(3)(b). The Divisional Court so held in *Branagan v DPP* [2000] R.T.R. 235 when refusing an appeal against a conviction based on the blood sample voluntarily provided by the defendant. *Branagan v DPP* was applied by the Divisional Court in *Wright v DPP* [2005] EWHC 1211. In that case the defendant had elected to provide a blood specimen under s.8(2) and was duly convicted of an excess alcohol offence. On appeal to the Crown Court he sought to adduce evidence to show that the Intoximeter used by him had been modified so that it was no longer of the type approved by the Secretary of State. The Crown Court's refusal to allow that evidence was upheld. It was clear from *Branagan* that once an individual had elected to take a blood test the prosecution were not required to prove that the Intoximeter used in breath testing was reliable; by the same token there was no requirement on the prosecution to show that the Intoximeter used in breath testing was of an approved type.

4.138　　It is now clear that if a defendant's lower breath reading is 50μg/100ml or less he may be entitled to be acquitted if:

(a) he is not told of his option (*Anderton v Lythgoe* below); or

(b) he is mistakenly *required* to provide a blood sample (*Wakeley v Hyams* at § 4.154 below); or

(c) he exercises his option and through no fault on his part the blood (or presumably urine) sample cannot be used (*Archbold v Jones* at § 4.155 below); or

(d) he is not given the option of providing urine when he might have a medical reason for not providing a blood sample (*Johnson v West Yorkshire Metropolitan Police* at § 4.157 below); or

(e) improper pressure is exerted on him not to exercise his option to provide a specimen for laboratory analysis (*Green v Lockhart* at § 4.161 below).

The ratio decidendi of *Anderton v Lythgoe* [1985] R.T.R. 395 appears to be that s.8(1) and (2) contemplate two possible ways in which the defendant's guilt or innocence is to be established, normally a breath specimen or at the defendant's election a specimen of blood or urine. Both alternatives have to be made available to the defendant if the plain purpose of the subsection is to be achieved; reliance on a breath specimen alone without the defendant having been informed of his choice is an inadequate performance by the police of the statutory duty imposed by s.8(1), (2).

Provision of specimens for analysis: relationship between ss.7(4) and 8(2)

The House of Lords (Lord Templeman, Lord Roskill, Lord Bridge of Harwich, Lord Goff of Chieveley and Lord Jauncey of Tullichettle) in *DPP v Warren* [1992] 4 All E.R. 865 upheld an appeal against the decision of the Divisional Court in *DPP v Warren* [1992] Crim. L.R. 200 and made it clear that when making a decision under s.7(4) of the 1988 Act as to whether the specimen to be provided should be of blood or urine, the police officer did not have to invite the driver to express his own preference before making that decision. In coming to that conclusion, their Lordships effectively overturned the line of authorities inaugurated by *Hobbs v Clark* [1988] R.T.R. 36. That case marked the genesis of what is described in the speech of Lord Bridge as the doctrine of "driver's preference" and which came to full fruition in the case of *DPP v Byrne* [1991] R.T.R. 119. (*Hobbs v Clark* and the cases which followed it were discussed at length in the fifteenth edition and supplements thereto.) The doctrine was based (as the editors of this work have argued in previous editions) upon a misreading of a few words in the judgment of Nolan J. in *Anderton v Lythgoe* above. **4.139**

The defendant in *Warren* provided two specimens of breath as requested at Vine Street police station, but the calibration system of the machine was found not to be functioning correctly. The Lion Intoximeter being thus defective, the officer said (in the words of Metropolitan Police pro forma Book 116): "... Accordingly, I require you to provide an alternative specimen ... The specimen may be of blood or urine, but it is for me to decide which ... If you fail to provide a specimen you may be liable to prosecution. Are there any reasons why a specimen of blood cannot or should not be taken by a doctor?" The defendant replied "No". The officer asked "Will you provide a specimen of blood?" to which the defendant replied "Yes". It was submitted on behalf of the defendant that he had no case to answer since the officer's words did not convey to him that the required sample might be of blood or urine; neither did they give him any opportunity to consider which he would prefer if he had the choice, nor an opportunity to give reasons for any expressed preference. The magistrate upheld the submission and his decision was affirmed by the Divisional Court.

On the authorities, particularly that of *DPP v Byrne*, neither the magistrate nor **4.140**

the Divisional Court had any option but to decide as they did. Although it was
true that *Byrne* was a case (unlike the instant one) where the s.7(4) procedure
came into play, not for any of the reasons specified in s.7(3), but because the
driver was entitled under s.8(2) to exercise his option to have the breath
specimens he had given replaced by "such specimen as may be required under
s.7(4) ", previous decisions had also laid it down that the identical procedure was
to be followed in both cases. Hence it was the inevitable application of the law as
stated by Bingham L.J. in *Byrne* which effectively determined the case in point in
the courts below and it was the law as so stated which the appellant prosecutor
sought to challenge as an unwarranted judicial gloss upon the statutory language,
as opposed to a legitimate construction of it.

On the face of the statute, their Lordships could see nothing in the language
which would justify a procedural requirement in either a s.7(3) or s.8(2) case that
the driver should be invited to express his own preference for giving blood or
urine, subject only to the right to object to giving blood on medical grounds. In
Anderton v Lythgoe Nolan J. had stated that s.8(2) contemplated:

> "… two possible ways in which guilt or innocence are to be established. One is by
> the breath sample. The other—if the subject so chooses—is by the sample of blood or
> urine. The alternatives must both be made available to the subject …."

4.141   It was important to note that when Nolan J. spoke of the alternatives which
"must both be made available to the subject" he was clearly referring to the
alternative on the one hand of allowing the breath specimen to stand and on the
other hand of exercising the right to have it replaced by a specimen of blood or
urine in accordance with s.7(4). If he had been intending to say that, in the situation which he was considering, the alternatives of giving either blood or urine
"must both be made available to the subject", this was simply wrong. However,
in *Hobbs v Clark* May L.J. rejected a submission that the language used by Nolan
J. bore the meaning their Lordships had indicated they thought it was intended to
bear, which implied that he read the judgment as authority for the proposition
that in a s.8(2) case the alternatives of giving either blood or urine "must both be
made available to the subject". The judgment of Roch J carried the matter a step
further:

> "[The police officer's] decision … must be an informed decision. It cannot be an
> informed decision unless the person who has provided the specimens of breath knows
> that there are two possible specimens which can be substituted for them and has been
> given the opportunity of making representations as to which of the two types of speci-
> men it should be."

4.142   That reasoning could only be intended to give effect to the language of Nolan
J., interpreted in the same sense by Roch J. as by May L.J.. Here was the genesis
of the doctrine of "driver's preference" which came to full fruition in the judgment of Bingham L.J. in *Byrne*, all based on a misreading of a few words in an
earlier judgment (*Anderton v Lythgoe*) as enunciating a proposition which simply
could not stand with the statutory language.

Hobbs v Clark was considered and followed in *DPP v Magill* [1988] R.T.R.
337 and *Regan v DPP* [1990] R.T.R. 102, but neither of those cases in their Lordships' view provided any independent support for the doctrine of "driver's
preference". In *DPP v Gordon* [1990] R.T.R. 71 it was held that *Hobbs* applied
not only to driver's option cases but also to obligatory s.7(4) cases and that was

followed in *Paterson v DPP* [1990] R.T.R. 329. The essential reasoning in those two cases was that s.7(4) could not bear two different constructions depending upon the route by which it was reached, and in their Lordships' view that was an indisputable proposition.

Having examined the decided cases, their Lordships had found nothing which **4.143** caused them to depart from their view as to the appropriate procedure to be followed under s.7(3) and s.8(2) considered simply on the basis of the statutory language. In summary, in a case where the necessity to require a specimen of blood or urine under s.7(4) arose for one of the reasons specified in s.7(3), what was required was no more and no less than the formula used in the instant case or words to the like effect. In a case where the driver's option fell to be explained to him under s.8(2), the driver should be told that if he exercised the right to have a replacement specimen taken under s.7(4), it would be for the officer to decide whether that specimen was to be of blood or urine. If the officer intended to require a specimen of blood to be taken by a medical practitioner, the driver should be told that his only right to object to giving blood and to give urine instead would be for medical reasons to be determined by the medical practitioner. In neither case was there any need to invite the driver to express his preference for giving blood or urine. In the light of the above, much of the reasoning in the judgments following *Hobbs v Clark* and in particular the summary of the law given by Bingham L.J. in *DPP v Byrne* had now to be considered unsound.

It was subsequently held by the Divisional Court (Rose L.J. and Pill J.) in *Edge* **4.144** *v DPP* [1993] R.T.R. 146 that the passage in the speech of Lord Bridge in *DPP v Warren* above, wherein he stated that if a constable decided to require a specimen of blood he must ask the motorist if there were any reasons why a specimen could not or should not be taken from him by a doctor, was of general application. Although it might well be for the medical practitioner to reach a view as to the validity of any reason for not giving a particular type of specimen, the words of Lord Bridge, in relation to that which a constable must do when requesting a specimen, were clear and binding on the court. Thus where the officer when faced with a malfunctioning Intoximeter required the defendant to provide a specimen of blood or urine, warned him that failure to provide a specimen would make him liable to prosecution and asked, "Will you provide such a specimen?", but failed to inquire about the existence or otherwise of any reasons which might prohibit the taking of such a specimen by a doctor, the defendant's conviction of a s.5 offence had to be quashed. A similar conclusion was reached by an identically constituted Divisional Court in *Meade v DPP* [1993] R.T.R. 151. In the context of these cases it may be noted that police forces now have available to them a standard pro forma (as approved by the Association of Chief Police Officers) to assist them in conducting the s.7 procedure. Although designed principally to cope with the introduction at police stations of the second generation of evidential breath testing machines, this pro forma was drafted with the requirements enunciated in *Warren* very much in mind (see further §§ 4.179 et seq.).

The defendant provided two specimens of breath for analysis at a police station. The result obtained entitled him to claim under s.8(2) that it should be replaced by a specimen of blood or urine. The police sergeant conducting the procedure and reading from a form used by the Northumbria Police informed him that he might claim replacement of the specimen by a specimen of blood or urine; that the decision whether it was to be blood or urine would be made by the sergeant although the defendant would be given an opportunity to make representations about his preference; that his only right to object to giving blood and to give urine instead would be for medical reasons to be determined by a medical practitioner, and that if the defendant provided a specimen of blood or urine neither specimen of breath would be used. Without being informed that any blood specimen would be taken by a medical practitioner, the defendant was asked whether he wished to replace the breath specimen with a specimen of blood or of urine. He answered "No", and was duly charged with, and convicted of, an offence under s.5(1).

4.145   Dismissing his appeal against conviction, which was mounted on the basis that in order to comply with the requirements of ss.7(4) and 8(2) of the 1988 Act the police officer should have informed him that a specimen of blood, if selected, would be taken by a doctor, the Divisional Court (Lord Bingham C.J. and Moses J.) held in *Fraser v DPP* [1997] R.T.R. 373 that where the right of election arose under s.8(2) the statutory provisions required a motorist to be informed of a number of matters, but they did not require him to be informed of all of them at the outset. The provisions only required him to be told that if he exercised his right under s.8(2) it would be for the officer to decide, pursuant to s.7(4), whether the replacement specimen should be of blood or urine and, if the former, that his only right to object would be for medical reasons to be determined by a doctor. The officer was not required to tell the defendant at the outset in terms that a specimen of blood, if selected, would be taken by a doctor; accordingly there had been a sufficient compliance with the statutory provisions and the defendant had been properly convicted. The form of words used by the Northumbria Police was closely modelled on, and accorded with, the summary of the procedure set out by Lord Bridge of Harwich in *DPP v Warren* (discussed above); that summary contained everything that the statute itself required a driver to be told at the outset.

During the course of his judgment in *Fraser* Lord Bingham C.J. made reference to a number of (as then) unreported cases. One of those, now reported sub nom. *Gorman v DPP*; *DPP v Arnup* at [1997] R.T.R. 409, was of particular interest as it contained a review of a not inconsiderable number of cases decided in the wake of *DPP v Warren* above. Rose L.J. (with whom Maurice Kay J. agreed) acknowledged the five criteria relevant to the s.8(2) procedure which were derived from the speech of Lord Bridge in *Warren* and conveniently set out by Kennedy L.J. in *DPP v Charles (Note—1994)* [1996] R.T.R. 247:

1. the lower of the specimens of breath provided by the driver exceeds the statutory limit but does not exceed 50μg alcohol per 100ml breath;

2. in these circumstances he may claim to have the specimen replaced by one of blood or urine if he wishes;

3. if he does so it will be for the constable to decide whether the replacement specimen is to be of blood or urine;

4. if the constable requires a specimen of blood it will be taken by a doctor unless the doctor considers that there are medical reasons for not taking blood, when urine may be given instead;

5. if the constable intends to require a specimen of blood to be taken by a medical practitioner the driver should be told that his only right to object to giving blood and to giving urine instead will be for medical reasons to be determined by the medical practitioner.

Turning then to the many decisions subsequent to *Warren* on the interpretation **4.146**
of s.8(2) and s.7(4), Rose L.J. stated that the following principles could be gleaned
from the authorities:

(1) The statutory requirements must be strictly complied with because an
accused is being asked to provide evidence against himself (*Murray v
DPP* [1993] R.T.R. 209 (§ 4.249)).

(2) The requirements enunciated by Lord Bridge in *Warren* concerning the
procedure to be followed by police when offering a s.8(2) option are
not the words of a statute to be analysed as such (*Hayes v DPP* [1993]
Crim.L.R. 966 (§ 4.163) and *DPP v Charles (Note—1994)* [1996]
R.T.R. 247). They are to be complied with to the extent that Lord
Bridge's guidance represents "a reproduction of the statutory
requirements. To the extent that they exceed the strict requirements of
the statute, they fall into the category of guidance only" (*DPP v
Ormsby (Note)* [1997] R.T.R. 394), an important gloss on what was
said in *R. v Cheshire JJ. Ex p. Cunningham (Note)* [1995] R.T.R. 287).

(3) Although the statutory provisions, as interpreted in *Warren*, must be
complied with "it is also important to have regard to the overall intention of Parliament when the statute was enacted. The relevant provisions were intended to enable a driver to provide a replacement specimen in a situation in which, as Lord Bridge has pointed out, he faces
conviction on the basis of a specimen already provided. The provisions
were not intended to provide a series of hazards for police officers
which if not skilfully negotiated with complete precision would enable
drivers to escape conviction entirely" (*DPP v Charles (Note—1994)*
[1996] R.T.R. 247).

(4) Failure precisely to follow the particularly long procedure does not
necessarily mean that non-compliance with the statutory procedure
renders inadmissible a specimen obtained in consequence of it (*DPP v
Ormsby (Note)* [1997] R.T.R. 394).

(5) The fundamental question to be determined has been expressed in different cases in different ways. For example, whether "failure to give
the full formula deprived the driver of the opportunity to exercise the
option or caused him to exercise it in a way that he or she would not
have done had everything been said" (*DPP v Charles (Note—1994)*
[1996] R.T.R. 247). What is required is that "the driver is fairly and effectively exposed to all of the information and choices identified in
Lord Bridge's speech" (*R v Burton on Trent JJ. Ex p. Woolley* [1995]
R.T.R. 139 (§ 4.294)), "so long as the option given by the statute is
explained fairly and properly so that the driver can make an informed
decision, the requirements of justice and the efficacy of the driver's option given by the statute under s.8(2) are ensured" (*Baldwin v DPP*
[1996] R.T.R. 238).

(6) In addition to the observation in *Ormsby* already referred to, the general tenor of the more recent decisions is best exemplified by Simon
Brown L.J. in *Baldwin*:

"I cannot accept that the decided authorities now so encrust and gloss the
statute so as to require not merely adherence to the procedure laid down in …

Lord Bridge's speech in *Warren*, but the slavish adoption of a form of words which, in terms, involves stating to the defendant at the earlier stage that he has 'a right to object'."

(7) To comply with the statutory requirements, a driver must be asked whether there are reasons why a specimen of blood should not be taken (*Ogburn v DPP* [1994] R.T.R. 241 (§ 4.294)). A driver must consent to the taking of blood by a doctor and therefore, it seemed to the court, a driver must be specifically told that, if he consents, a doctor will take blood and he must be asked whether there are reasons why blood should not be taken.

(8) Criterion 5 was derived from the end of Lord Bridge's speech in *Warren*. It was recognised in *DPP v Charles (Note—1994)* [1996] R.T.R. 247 as being a reformulation of criterion 4 as set out earlier in that speech.

(9) Failure to comply with that criterion is not in itself fatal to the admissibility of a previously obtained breath sample (*Robinson (Dena) v DPP (Note)* [1997] R.T.R. 403).

(10) It is not necessary for an officer to refer to medical reasons when inquiring whether there are reasons why a blood sample should not be taken by a doctor (*Baldwin v DPP* [1996] R.T.R. 238).

4.147　　*Fraser v DPP* [1997] R.T.R. 373 (discussed above) was applied by the Divisional Court in *DPP v Donnelly* [1998] R.T.R. 188. A driver who had been properly required (in the absence of a serviceable Lion Intoximeter) to provide a specimen for laboratory analysis was not advised that any specimen of blood would be taken by a doctor; nor was he asked whether there was any medical or other reason why blood should not be taken. Allowing the prosecutor's appeal against acquittal by the magistrate, the court stated that the principle in *Fraser v DPP* to the effect that there was no requirement for the defendant to be informed at the outset that any specimen of blood would be taken by a doctor was equally applicable to a case such as this. It would seem that the court was also of the view that the failure to ask at that initial stage whether there were any reasons why a specimen of blood should not be provided was not fatal to the procedure. If he had agreed to provide a liquid specimen, he would have been asked (in accordance with the Cheshire police pro forma) whether there were any objections to his supplying blood and advised that a sample of blood would be taken by a doctor; his refusal, however, had obviated the provision of that information.

4.148　　It should be noted, however, that a differently constituted court in *Jackson v DPP* [1998] R.T.R. 141 found itself in opposition to *DPP v Donnelly* [1998] R.T.R. 188 (discussed above) on the question of the information to be provided in a s.7(4) case to a suspect on a request to supply a specimen for laboratory analysis. Buxton J. (with whom Lord Bingham C.J. agreed) said that the procedure laid down in *DPP v Warren* [1992] 4 All E.R. 865 required that the police officer should ask whether there were "any reasons" why a specimen of blood should not be taken by a doctor and in *Jackson's* case the officer had qualified his inquiry as to "any reasons" by immediately restricting the reasons to medical ones. The use of the expression "medical reasons" was appropriate to driver's option cases under s.8(2), but not to the mandatory cases under s.7(4); its use in a s.7(4) case was in breach of the *Warren* guidelines. Although the court would have been inclined, in the absence of binding authority to the contrary, to follow the decision in *DPP v Donnelly* that decision could not stand with the rule laid down in *Warren*. The court expressed the hope that the matter would be the subject of early reconsideration by the House of Lords, and certified for their Lordships' House a question in the following wide terms:

> "To what extent, if at all, should the guidance given by the House in *DPP v. Warren* as to the procedure to be followed when a request is made for a sample of blood under the provisions of section 7(4) of the Road Traffic Act 1988 be applied beyond the issue arising in the case of whether the driver should be invited to express a preference for giving blood or urine? If that guidance does not apply other than in respect of that issue, what on the true construction of the Road Traffic Act 1988 is the procedure to be followed when a request is made under sections 7(3), 7(4) and 8(2) of that Act ?"

The conflicting lines of authority referred to in *Jackson* above came in due course before the House of Lords (Lord Slynn of Hadley, Lord Griffiths, Lord Lloyd of Berwick, Lord Steyn and Lord Hutton) for resolution in *DPP v Jackson; Stanley v DPP* [1998] R.T.R. 397. The unanimous decision of the House is set out in the speech of Lord Hutton, who said that much of the argument in the instant conjoined appeals related to the effect of the speech of Lord Bridge in *DPP v Warren* where the issue was whether, when a driver was requested under s.7(3) of the 1988 Act to provide a specimen of blood or urine, the police officer was required to ask him whether he had a preference for giving blood or urine. The ratio of that decision was that the Act imposed no such requirement. But in order to give guidance as to the appropriate procedures to be followed by the police in a s.7(3) case and a s.8(2) case, Lord Bridge stated certain requirements as to what the officer should tell or ask the driver. It had been hoped that that would have settled the law on the vexed topic of the procedures to be followed by the police, but unfortunately that had not been achieved.

4.149

The principal difficulty which arose was that different approaches had been taken in two lines of cases to the question whether the requirements stated by Lord Bridge were mandatory so that failure to observe a requirement must lead to an acquittal, or whether a breach of a requirement was not necessarily a bar to conviction. In considering the issues raised by these two lines of cases it was necessary to have regard to the respective functions of the police officer and the doctor under the 1988 Act. Section 7(4) provided that if a specimen other than a specimen of breath was required it was for the police officer to decide whether that specimen would be blood or urine. But s.11(4) provided that the specimen of blood was to be taken by a doctor. In addition, the police officer's right to choose whether the specimen would be blood or urine was subject to the qualification that if a medical reason was raised why a specimen of blood could not or should not be taken, the issue was to be decided by a doctor and not a police officer. An offence of failure without reasonable excuse to provide a blood or urine specimen when required to do so or an offence of driving while over the prescribed limit proved by a breath specimen where the driver had not claimed under s.8(2) to replace it with a blood or urine specimen, was an unusual offence in that the driver had a choice to make in the police station prior to being charged. It was because the driver had those choices and because a doctor had a role to play both in the taking of blood and in deciding the validity of a reason advanced by the driver as to why blood should not be taken that Lord Bridge said in *Warren* that the driver:

"should be fully informed of the nature of the option open to him and what will be involved if he exercises it."

4.150 However, in this area of the law there were a number of disadvantages if formulae stated by an appellate court for use by the police, which were based on the need for fairness to the driver but which were not required by the express words of the Act, were regarded as mandatory requirements. One disadvantage was that the facts of individual cases and the exchanges between a driver and a police officer in the police station and within the confines of the procedures laid down by the Act may vary considerably, so that one prescribed form of words might not be appropriate in every case. Another disadvantage was that there was no unfairness and no resultant injustice if a driver was convicted notwithstanding that one of the *Warren* requirements had not been observed. It was submitted on behalf of the respondent to the first appeal, Mr Jackson, that if the *Warren* guidelines were regarded as being guides to fairness rather than as mandatory, there would be uncertainty as to the law and the administration of that branch of it would be brought into disrepute because exactly the same facts would lead to an acquittal in one part of England and to a conviction in another.

His Lordship did not accept that submission because the many decisions in the Divisional Court showed how different were the precise facts which came before the justices. Moreover, justices and judges in a criminal trial frequently had to give a ruling on fairness in the particular circumstances of the case and that did not cause uncertainty or bring the law into disrepute. His Lordship said that the requirements stated by Lord Bridge in *Warren* were, with three exceptions, not to be treated as mandatory but as indicating the matters of which a driver should be made aware so that whether in a s.7(3) case or a s.8(2) case, he could know the role of the doctor in the taking of a specimen and in determining any medical objections which he might raise to the giving of such a specimen. The three exceptions which should be regarded as mandatory were:

    (1) in a s.7(3) case the warning as to the risk of prosecution required by s.7(7);

    (2) in a s.7(3) case the statement of the reason under that subsection why breath could not be used: and

    (3) in a s.8(2) case the statement that the specimen of breath which the driver had given containing the lower proportion of alcohol did not exceed 50µg in 100ml of breath.

4.151 As well as complying with those three mandatory requirements police officers, in order to seek to ensure that a driver would be aware of the role of the doctor, should continue to use the formula in a s.7(3) case and the formula in a s.8(2) case as set out by Lord Bridge in *Warren* or words to the same effect. What was necessary was that the driver should be aware, whether or not he was told by the police officer, of the doctor's role so that he did not suffer prejudice. Therefore, if the driver appreciated that a blood specimen would be taken by a doctor and not by a police officer, the charge should not be dismissed by the justices because the police officer had failed to tell the driver that the specimen would be taken by a doctor. The first issue for the justices to decide would be whether the matters set out in the *Warren* formula had been brought to the driver's attention by the police officer. If the answer was "No", the second issue was whether, in relation to the non-mandatory requirements, the police officer's failure to give the full formula deprived the driver of the opportunity to exercise the option or caused him to exercise it in a way which he would not have done had everything been said. If the answer to the second issue was "Yes", the driver should be acquitted. But if the answer to the second issue was "No" the police officer's failure to use the full formula should not be a reason for an acquittal. It would only be in exceptional cases that the justices would acquit on the ground that the driver suffered prejudice, without having heard evidence from the driver himself raising the issue that he had suffered prejudice. Both issues were questions of fact and therefore, if the justices, having heard the driver's evidence, were not satisfied beyond a reasonable doubt that he was not prejudiced, they should acquit. There was nothing in the wording of the relevant sections and no considerations of fairness which required a police officer to ask a driver if there were any non-medical reasons why a specimen of blood should not be taken. If there was some non-medical reason which would support a reasonable cause for failure to provide a specimen when requested to do so, that was a matter for the justices to decide. In a s.8(2) case, in addition to telling the driver that a specimen of blood "will be taken by a doctor unless the doctor considers that there are medical reasons for not taking blood", the officer should ask the driver if there were any medical reasons why a specimen could not or should not be taken by a doctor. The driver should be told of the doctor's role at the outset before he had to make the decision to give blood. It was a question of fact whether a statement by a driver (as in the instant cases) that he did not like needles raised a potential medical reason for not providing a blood specimen and the court was entitled to find on the facts that the officer was not obliged to investigate further. Mr Jackson had made it entirely clear that he was not going to give a specimen of blood or urine and therefore he suffered no prejudice; the prosecutor's appeal against the decision of the Divisional Court in *Jackson v DPP* discussed above was accordingly upheld. In Mr Stanley's case it was a question of fact whether the statement raised a medical issue which required further inquiry from the officer and it was open to the court to conclude from the evidence that it did not amount to a medical reason; Mr Stanley's appeal against the upholding by the Crown Court of his conviction by justices was accordingly dismissed.

In a case the nature of which was described in the judgment as "exceptional", **4.152** the Divisional Court (Lord Woolf C.J. presiding) in *Joseph v DPP* [2003] EWHC 3078; [2004] R.T.R. 21 upheld an appeal against conviction for an excess alcohol offence on the basis of an incorrect interpretation by the police officer of the requirements of the statutory procedure under s.7(4) and s.8(2). Before the officer could make his choice as to which liquid specimen should be provided, the defendant made it clear that he was not prepared to provide a specimen of blood as it was against his beliefs as a Rastafarian. The officer told the defendant that if he did not give blood he would have no option but to charge him with driving with excess alcohol. Before the Divisional Court it was conceded by the prosecution that the officer had considered that if there was no medical reason for not choosing blood, he was required to choose blood. In the court's view this was a misunderstanding of the position. It was not challenged that the defendant genuinely believed he should not give a blood sample. That was something which the officer, in exercising his discretion, should have considered before deciding whether to require blood or urine. He did not do so because he did not appreciate that he had a discretion, albeit not a discretion which would have required him to investigate the wishes of the driver whom he was testing. Where there was no reason for not choosing urine in preference to blood, and a valid reason was put forward why urine should be the choice instead of blood, the officer was obliged at least consider whether blood or urine should be the choice. If he concluded that it should be the one to which the suspect objected, without any basis for doing so, the decision could be categorised as perverse; or alternatively, as in the case in point, it might be said that the officer had misunderstood the legal position and accordingly the statutory procedure had not been validly gone through.

It is essential from the terms of s.7(3)(b) that the officer who makes a request for a sample of blood or urine must have cause to believe that there is no reliable device available to analyse the driver's breath at the police station. The driver must be made aware of that fact to comply with the requirements of *DPP v Jackson* (discussed at § 4.149 above). There was, however, no reason to superimpose a requirement that the driver must be informed of that fact by the officer making the request for the sample, since no conceivable prejudice could result if the information was supplied by another officer (in the case in point, the custody officer). The Divisional Court so held in *Bobin v DPP* [1999] R.T.R. 375 when dismissing the defendant's appeal against conviction for failure to supply a specimen of blood.

4.153   A police pro forma was found not to be defective in the terms of *DPP v Warren* (discussed above) by the Divisional Court in *DPP v Hill-Brookes* [1996] R.T.R. 279. The defendant was informed of the statutory option to provide an alternative sample of blood or urine which he could exercise under s.8(2) of the Road Traffic Act 1988, but that information was prefaced by the following words: "As the breath specimen with the lower proportion of alcohol shows an alcohol content of between 40 and 50 microgrammes inclusive of alcohol in 100 millilitres of breath ...". It was argued on behalf of the defendant that the procedure laid down in *Warren* had not been followed because he had not been expressly told that the specimen with the lower proportion of alcohol exceeded the statutory limit. That argument was rejected by the court. Telling a driver that the preconditions for the existence of the option had been fulfilled could have no effect upon his being fully informed either of the nature of the option or what would be involved in its exercise. Accordingly, it could not affect the driver if he was told of the precondition by the words "the specimen of breath which you have given containing the lower proportion of alcohol exceeds the statutory limit", or by being told that the alcohol content of his breath was in a bracket which in fact established that the statutory limit had been exceeded.

DPP v Hill-Brookes above was applied by the Divisional Court in *Chatelard v DPP* [1997] R.T.R. 362. The defendant, a Frenchman, provided two specimens of breath for analysis, each of which contained 46μg of alcohol per 100ml of breath. He was informed in the terms of the relevant constabulary's standard forms of his right under s.8(2) of the 1988 Act to claim that his breath specimen be replaced by one of blood or urine. He complained, inter alia, of the officer's failure to tell him that he was over the limit. The court held, applying *DPP v Hill-Brookes*, that it was necessarily implicit in his being told that if he accepted the Lion Intoximeter breath reading he would be prosecuted, that his reading was in excess of the statutory limit. (The court further noted when dealing with this point that *DPP v Hill-Brookes* had also been applied, and to similar effect, in *DPP v Ormsby (Note)* [1997] R.T.R. 394.)

In *Wakeley v Hyams* [1987] R.T.R. 49 a defendant's breath specimens both re-   **4.154**
vealed an alcohol content of 50μg/100ml, but he was mistakenly informed by a
police officer that he was therefore *required* to provide a blood sample. The
Divisional Court ruled, following (inter alia) *Anderton v Lythgoe* above, that the
evidence of the breath specimens and the blood sample was inadmissible because
of the failure to comply with the procedure of what is now s.8(1), (2) by which he
should have been informed of his right (not his duty) to provide the blood sample.

A defendant whose lower Lion Intoximeter breath-alcohol reading showed
44μg/100ml was told of her right to have that specimen replaced by a specimen
of blood. She asked whether it would make any difference and was told "probably not". She appealed to the Divisional Court on the grounds that her choice was
vitiated by the officer's words. Not surprisingly, the Divisional Court gave that
argument short shrift. In the words of Watkins L.J. it was "a pity that a point such
as this (was) taken, for it palpably has no validity". The officer's remark was
merely an expression of opinion and could not possibly be said to have affected
the appellant's rights in the matter (*Sharp v Spencer* [1987] Crim. L.R. 420).

In *Archbold v Jones* [1985] Crim. L.R. 740 it was held that what is now s.8(1),   **4.155**
(2) is mandatory in precluding the use of the breath specimen if a blood specimen
was provided. Accordingly where the defendant had provided a blood specimen
but through no fault of his own it could not be used, he was entitled to be
acquitted. The breath specimen cannot be held in reserve if the blood specimen is
spilt or lost or is otherwise unusable (ibid.).

In *Jones v DPP* [1990] Crim. L.R. 656 a defendant who provided two
specimens of breath which measured 50 and 45μg respectively on the Lion Intoximeter screen claimed his right to replace the breath specimens with a specimen of urine (he being scared of needles). The officer then observed that the
machine had failed to produce a printout, concluded that it was unreliable and
proceeded under s.7(3)(b) (see § 4.117 above). In fact the machine's failure to
disgorge a printout was due to the "modem" switch at the back being in the "off"
position. The operating manual for the machine requires this switch to be checked
if a printout fails to appear; since the officer failed to carry out that check it was
not reasonable for him to conclude that the machine was unreliable. It was argued
on behalf of the defendant that the justices should not admit the evidence of the
urine sample as it had been improperly obtained. Not so, said the Divisional
Court; since the defendant had claimed that the breath sample should be replaced
by a urine sample and had provided such a sample, the requirements of s.8 had
been fulfilled. Had he changed his mind prior to the provision of that sample,
problems under s.7 might well have arisen; but there was no finding that that was
the case.

A defendant who provided breath samples with readings respectively of 42   **4.156**
and 43μg decided to take advantage of his option to provide a specimen of blood.
The prosecution analysis of their part of the specimen revealed a blood-alcohol
content of 97mg/100ml. The defendant, however, by injecting his part of the
sample with alcohol-free blood managed to obtain an analysis result showing
only 74mg of alcohol per 100ml of blood. At his trial the justices admitted evidence of the breath test results on the grounds that it was necessary as evidence to
justify the requirement of blood and that it would have no prejudicial effect. The
defendant contended, to the contrary, that what is now s.8(2) prohibits the use of
the breath specimens once blood has been provided and that their admission was

indeed prejudicial. The Divisional Court held in *Yhnell v DPP* [1989] Crim. L.R. 384, when dismissing the defendant's appeal, that what is now s.8(2) does not prohibit the prosecution from adducing evidence which they are required to adduce in order to satisfy the requirement that the procedure must be strictly gone through in order to establish their right to rely upon the blood sample. It was clear from the case stated that the justices had based their findings upon the results of the analysis of the blood sample provided to the prosecution and had accepted that the lower reading obtained from the defendant's sample was due to his having tampered with it. They had not taken into account the breath specimen readings and therefore those specimens had not been "used" in the sense contemplated by the statute.

Yhnell v DPP above was applied by the Divisional Court in *Carter v DPP* [2006] EWHC 3328 where the district judge had perfectly properly used the evidence of the breath test, together with other material, as a means of helping her to determine whether the defendant's evidence of how much alcohol he had consumed was capable of belief. Section 8(2) was not worded in such a way as to preclude its use in that context.

4.157   In *Johnson v West Yorkshire Metropolitan Police* [1986] R.T.R. 167, the defendant provided two specimens of breath, the lower of which was less than 50µg/100ml. He chose to exercise his option and in accordance with the local police force's practice he was then offered only blood, which the defendant declined as he "did not like needles", having fainted years earlier after a blood test. The Divisional Court upheld his acquittal. Although the choice as to whether blood or urine should be given is that of the police officer, it is subject to medical constraint in that the police officer must not usurp the function of the medical practitioner in deciding whether the reason given for declining blood was valid or not. The defendant was denied the full benefit of his choice and, following *Anderton v Lythgoe*, the condition for making the breath specimen admissible was not fulfilled. *Johnson v West Yorkshire Metropolitan Police* was followed by the Divisional Court in *R. v Epping JJ. Ex p. Quy* [1998] R.T.R. 158. A defendant who apparently declined to provide a replacement specimen of blood under s.8(2) on the basis of his fear of needles offered to provide instead a specimen of urine; his offer was rejected by the police officer conducting the procedure who insisted that the replacement sample should be of blood. The court held, quashing the conviction, that the defendant had given what was capable of being a medical reason. This did not necessarily mean that a doctor had to be called, however. The applicant had not given a reason for his fear. If he had been asked for his reasons, it might have been established that his fear was unfounded and, applying *Johnson*, the officer would have been entitled to act as he did. Alternatively, the need to call a medical practitioner might have been established.

Johnson v West Yorkshire Metropolitan Police was also applied by the Divisional Court (albeit with a different result in the light of the particular facts) in *Andrews v DPP* [1992] R.T.R. 1. The defendant's lower breath specimen revealed 45µg alcohol in 100ml breath. Upon being offered the statutory option he indicated that he wished to provide a specimen of urine as he was "petrified of the needle". The police officer conducting the procedure obtained a medical opinion by telephone to the effect that such a fear did not amount to a medical reason for not supplying blood. The defendant declined to supply a specimen of blood and was convicted of a s.5(1)(a) offence on the evidence of his breath-alcohol analysis. Dismissing the defendant's appeal against conviction, the court held that the constable had complied with the requirement imposed by s.7(4) to obtain a medical opinion and whether that opinion was right or wrong was irrelevant.

Johnson v West Yorkshire Metropolitan Police was further applied by the **4.158** Divisional Court in *DPP v Wythe* [1996] R.T.R. 137 and *Wade v DPP* [1996] R.T.R. 177. In *DPP v Wythe* a motorist was asked, in the absence of a functioning Lion Intoximeter, if there were any reasons why a specimen of blood should not be extracted from him. He replied that he was a diabetic with an aversion to needles being used on him by others. The police officer, observing that he had pierced ears and tattoos, required him to supply a specimen of blood. He replied that he would only allow such a specimen to be taken from his finger. The constable referred to a police surgeon the question whether there was a medical reason why a specimen of blood could or should not be taken. Crucially, there was no evidence adduced as to the surgeon's opinion on the question referred to him. In a case such as this where a medical objection had been raised, albeit an unconvincing one, it was not for the constable to substitute his own opinion for that of a medical practitioner unless the reasons advanced were so "obviously frivolous" that they could not possibly amount to a medical condition providing significant reasons for refusing to provide a specimen. The defendant had accordingly been rightly acquitted of failure to provide a specimen for analysis, since the requirement was, in the circumstances, an unlawful one.

In *Wade v DPP* a motorist was required, in the absence of a serviceable Lion Intoximeter, to provide a liquid sample for analysis and was asked whether there were any reasons why a specimen of blood could not or should not be taken. He replied "I do take tablets". A specimen of blood was thereupon taken and the driver was subsequently convicted of driving with excess alcohol. Allowing his appeal, the Divisional Court held that the motorist's reply relating to the taking of the tablets should have been taken as a representation as to which specimen should be taken. There was no evidence that the officer had taken account of that representation or had given any consideration to whether it should have been treated as a medical reason. Far-fetched though it might seem, the taking of tablets might have affected the analysis of the specimen, or it might have made the taking of the specimen medically unwise. The officer should have inquired further, and, if left in a state of doubt thereafter, should have sought the views of a medical practitioner before proceeding to make the requirement.

Wade v DPP above was distinguished by the Divisional Court in *DPP v Gib-* **4.159** *bons* [2001] EWHC Admin 385; (2001) 165 J.P. 812 on a factual basis. A motorist arrested for public order matters refused to consent to a medical examination. The police surgeon opined that the suspect's obstructive attitude could be attributed to the influence of drugs. The police officer accordingly required a specimen of blood for analysis, with the proviso that the specimen could be of urine if there was a medical reason why blood should not be taken. The suspect replied, "You are not going to examine me". He gave no reason for his refusal to consent, nor any medical reason as to why he should not supply a specimen of blood. At his trial the justices, relying inappropriately upon *Wade v DPP*, concluded that the police surgeon's opinion as to the reason for the suspect's behaviour and his lack of consent, which precluded the taking of a blood sample, together constituted a medical reason necessitating the officer to go on to require a specimen of urine from him.

In the court's view this case was clearly distinguishable from *Wade v DPP*, since there was a medical practitioner present throughout and the motorist's statement to the effect that he was not going to submit to a medical examination did not offer any possible medical reason as to why a specimen of blood could or should not be taken. A refusal to be examined (without more) could not possibly amount to such a medical reason. Whether the specimen is to be of blood or urine is to be decided, in accordance with the procedure set out in *DPP v Warren* (discussed above) by the police officer and not dictated by the preference of the suspect.

4.160   *Wade v DPP* was also found to be inapplicable by the Divisional Court in *Steadman v DPP* [2002] EWHC 810; [2003] R.T.R. 2 since that case was concerned with the supplying of blood specimens under s.7(4) of the 1988 Act rather than, as in the case in point, the provision of evidential breath specimens. That section made specific provision for a medical practitioner's opinion, as the taking of blood was more invasive than the taking of breath or urine. The mere fact that the defendant took sleeping pills and had one on him could not have given the officer reasonable cause to believe in the terms of s.7(3)(a) ibid. that the defendant should not have been required to provide specimens of breath. The defendant had told the officer that he had not in fact taken any drugs that evening and had made no assertion that the sleeping pills would have had any impact upon the reliability of the results obtained from the evidential breath testing machine. Nothing in s.7(3)(a) suggested that an officer should be required to take medical advice. If Parliament had intended otherwise it would have said so, as in s.7(4).

Wade v DPP was again distinguished, and correctly so, by the district judge who tried the matter at first instance, in *Kinsella v DPP* [2002] EWHC 545. In *Wade* it had been made clear to the officers that there were grounds why the taking of a blood specimen might be inappropriate because of medical considerations. In the case in point, however, the defendant had specifically said that there were no such reasons, and had not sought to say that the spray and tablets in his possession gave rise to a medical reason. There was in those circumstances no obligation upon the officer to consult a doctor before deciding that blood should be provided.

4.161   In *Green v Lockhart* 1986 S.L.T. 11, a nervous defendant was advised of his statutory right to provide a specimen of blood or urine. He suggested a specimen of urine, but a police officer emphatically stated that the specimen must be of blood. The police tried successfully to dissuade the defendant from providing a specimen for laboratory analysis and the High Court of Justiciary found that improper pressure had been exerted, resulting in a miscarriage of justice which necessitated the conviction (based on evidence of the breath tests) being quashed. That decision may be contrasted with *Woodburn v McLeod* 1986 S.L.T. 325, where the defendant hummed and hawed after being told of his statutory right; he was (improperly) offered gratuitous advice by a police officer not to bother with a blood test; but in the event he made up his own mind not to exercise his right and no miscarriage of justice occurred.

The effective exercise by a defendant of his option to provide a specimen of blood or urine precludes the admission of evidence of the analysis of breath by prosecution or defence, even in relation to a plea of special reasons (*Smith v Geraghty* [1986] R.T.R. 222). It is otherwise, however, if the exercise of the option is rendered ineffective by subsequent events. In *DPP v Winstanley* [1993] R.T.R. 222 it was held that where a police officer informed the defendant that any specimen given to replace the breath specimen would have to be of blood and it then became apparent that no doctor was available, the officer was entitled to ask the driver to provide a specimen of urine instead. The driver exercised his option to provide a replacement specimen consisting of the latter substance but, through no fault of his own, was unable to provide the same. In those circumstances the prosecution were entitled to rely on the breath specimen previously provided.

DPP v Winstanley was considered and approved by the Divisional Court in **4.162** *Hayes v DPP* [1993] Crim. L.R. 966 when shutting with some firmness a door left slightly ajar by the House of Lords in *DPP v Warren* [1992] 4 All E.R. 865 (see § 4.139). In that case their Lordships had said that if a driver exercised his option to provide replacement specimens, but then failed to provide the same, the sanction against him would be the use in evidence of his breath specimen. In such cases there would be no need, although it might be theoretically possible, to prosecute for a failure to provide a replacement specimen. The appellant in *Hayes*, who had not been warned that failure to provide a replacement specimen might render him liable to prosecution, argued that, if there were a theoretical possibility of prosecution, then the statutory warning under s.7(7) would be mandatory, and failure to give it would render inadmissible the evidence obtained. The court held, however, that the proper construction of ss.8(2) and 7(7) of the 1988 Act was that the statutory warning had to be given where a person was *required* under s.7(7) to provide a specimen of blood or urine. A person who had *elected* to provide an alternative specimen under s.8(2) was not required to do so. He was at liberty to change his mind about providing such a specimen; if he did so, the only sanction would be that the breath specimen would be used as evidence. There was no duty upon the police to give the statutory warning because a failure to provide a replacement specimen under s.8(2) did not render a driver liable to prosecution.

DPP v Winstanley was further approved and applied by the Divisional Court in **4.163** *Hague v DPP* [1997] R.T.R. 146, when dismissing an appeal against conviction of an excess alcohol offence. Two samples of breath, the lower showing an alcohol level of not less than 68µg/100ml breath, were provided by the appellant but the officer operating the machine believed that it had failed to calibrate properly and required the appellant to give a sample of blood. This he refused to do. It was then discovered that the machine had been working correctly and had given an accurate reading. The court said that it was agreed that there had been nothing wrong with the machine. It had been held in *Winstanley* that in the event of the replacement liquid sample not being forthcoming, the original breath specimen was admissible. In the view of the court it would be surprising if the opposite result pertained in the instant case. A breath sample remained potentially admissible unless and until replaced by an admissible blood or urine sample.

A defendant when exercising his option is not under a "requirement" to provide blood or urine and thus precluded by virtue of what is now s.7(3) from providing it at a police station (*Sivyer v Parker* [1986] Crim. L.R. 410).

If the defendant, after opting, fails to provide a specimen of blood or urine under s.7(4) he does not commit any offence, but if for whatever reason the defendant fails or refuses to provide the blood or urine, the breath specimen may still be used in evidence against him in respect of an offence under s.5 or s.4.

4.164   Where a suspect initially declined to provide an optional blood specimen after a breath test but later changed his mind and did provide one, the justices were entitled to disregard the blood specimen and admit evidence only of the breath specimen (*Smith v DPP* [1989] R.T.R. 159). In the case in point some 63 minutes had elapsed between the initial offer and the defendant's subsequent acceptance of it. The police officer concerned had kindly allowed the defendant to change his mind; it was, however, for the justices rather than the police officer to decide whether the statutory procedure had ended and the justices had clearly been right to decide as a matter of fact that it had.

     The Secretary of State can by regulation substitute another proportion of alcohol in the breath in place of the 50µg level (s.8(3)).

Alcohol levels

4.165   Section 11(2) of the Road Traffic Act 1988 lays down the following as the prescribed limits:

       (a) 35 microgrammes of alcohol in 100 millilitres of breath; or

       (b) 80 milligrammes of alcohol in 100 millilitres of blood; or

       (c) 107 milligrammes of alcohol in 100 millilitres of urine.

     The Secretary of State may by regulation alter the prescribed levels (s.11(2)). (To convert µg alcohol per 100ml of breath to equivalent of mg of alcohol per 100ml of blood, multiply the breath-alcohol figure by 2.3 and round up or down to the nearest whole number; to convert to urine multiply by 3.06.) A conversion chart is set out in Appendix 1, "Alcohol concentration".

     The police are entitled therefore to proceed against a person under s.5 where the level is 36µg in breath, 81mg in blood and 108mg in urine (s.5 states that the prescribed levels must be exceeded), and it was held in *Delaroy-Hall v Tadman* [1969] 2 Q.B. 208 that the fact that the defendant's blood-alcohol was "not less than 81mg" was not a special reason for not disqualifying. In practice, however, a motorist whose breath reading is 39µg or less will not be charged under s.5. Chief Constables are independent of the Home Office, but usually are careful to follow the advice given by the Home Office and in Home Office circular 46/1983 it is stated:

> "To cater for those occasions where the machine may be reading high, albeit within this range [i.e. 32–38µg inclusive] the police will not proceed against the offender with a result less than 40µg. This will ensure that the offender prosecuted will have a result in excess of the prescribed limit. This allowance is comparable with the allowance currently subtracted from specimens analysed in the laboratory."

4.166   (The allowance currently subtracted from specimens of blood analysed in the laboratory is 6mg from all averages of 100mg or less and 6 per cent from all averages exceeding 100mg.) No proceedings will be instituted in Scotland on the basis of breath-alcohol readings of less than 40µg; see the letter from the Crown Agent to the Law Society of Scotland reproduced in the report of *Lockhart v Deighan* 1985 S.L.T. 549.

     Note that the Act requires the defendant's blood, breath or urine/alcohol level to "exceed" the prescribed level. A metropolitan stipendiary magistrate refused to accept a plea of guilty where the defendant's blood had been analysed at "not less than 80 milligrammes". The Metropolitan Police Solicitor subsequently withdrew the proceedings.

Back calculation

Section 15(2) of the 1988 Offenders Act states that it shall be assumed that the **4.167** proportion of alcohol in the accused's breath, blood or urine was "not less" than in the specimen. This wording prevents a defendant challenging the analysis as being too high on the ground that because he had only recently imbibed alcohol, the alcohol level in his breath, blood or urine had risen since the time he was stopped by the police. That the statutory presumption is irrebuttable has been emphasised by the Divisional Court in *Beauchamp-Thompson v DPP* [1988] Crim. L.R. 758. It has also been held in *Parker v DPP* [2001] R.T.R. 16 that that irrebuttable presumption does not infringe a suspect's rights under art.6(2) of the European Convention on Human Rights (the presumption of innocence) having regard to the context of the legislation, concerned as it was with preventing consumption of quantities of alcohol which impaired the ability of a driver to drive.

The cases of *Beauchamp-Thompson v DPP* and *Parker v DPP* discussed above were followed and applied in *Griffiths v DPP* [2002] EWHC 792; (2002) 166 J.P. 629. The defendant had sought to argue that the proportion of alcohol to breath at the time he had provided a sample was still rising, and that it would have been lower than the prescribed limit at the time he was driving. On the proper construction of s.15(2) of the 1988 Act as it had been held to be in the two cases cited, however, the expert evidence to that effect which he wished to adduce was irrelevant and therefore inadmissible. Furthermore, the statutory presumption was a proportionate response to what is in effect reprehensible conduct on the part of any person who takes a car on to the road having consumed alcohol and did not amount to an infringement of a defendant's right to a fair trial under art.6 of the European Convention on Human Rights. (The expert evidence in question was similarly incapable of use to found special reasons since it related to the offender rather than to the offence.)

Beauchamp-Thompson above was also approved by the Divisional Court **4.168** (Watkins L.J. and Nolan J.) in *Millard v DPP* [1990] Crim. L.R. 601. The defendant, who had consumed a bottle of wine with his sandwiches during an extended lunch break, left his office at 5.30pm and drove to a public house. Soon after 5.45pm he drank nearly all of a large whisky. He then left the pub to move his car to another parking place. He returned to the public house and drank most of a pint of beer. At that point the police arrived, spoke to the defendant and invited him outside. He was positively breathalysed at the roadside and subsequently (at about 7.15pm) provided breath samples for the Lion Intoximeter which showed an alcohol level of 56μg/100ml of breath. Almost an hour later he provided a blood sample which on analysis revealed 97mg of alcohol per 100ml of blood.

The defendant sought to adduce expert evidence concerning the effects of the whisky drunk before driving and the beer drunk afterwards; the justices were of the opinion that by virtue of what is now s.15(2) of the 1988 Offenders Act and the decision in *Beauchamp-Thompson* they were able to allow evidence concerning the beer, but not the whisky. Their opinion was correct, said the Divisional Court; the statutory presumption was irrebuttable. To hold otherwise would be to make what is now s.15(2) a partially nonsensical provision.

On the other hand, the definition would seem to allow the police to call evi- **4.169** dence that at the time of the commission of the offence, the defendant's alcohol

level was higher than shown in the analysis or printout. This is most likely to occur where there has been a considerable lapse of time between the time of the offence and the time of the defendant's apprehension and subsequent provision of
specimens for analysis. Depending on the rate of ingestion, the alcohol level will
continue to rise for a short while after consumption but will thereafter decline.
The rate of decline and the consequential back calculation depends on a great
number of factors, all of which may have a major effect on the calculation; the
factors include the individual's personal physiology, the time of day or night at
which the alcohol was consumed, the rate at which it was consumed, whether the
alcohol was on an empty stomach, or taken with a meal, and the amount and type
of alcohol. The prosecution would additionally have to prove that the defendant
had not consumed alcohol after the offence had occurred and before the provision
of the specimen.

     The principle of back calculation to ascertain the alcohol level at an earlier
point in time than the time when the specimen is taken ("backtracking") for forensic purposes received the qualified approval of the Divisional Court in *Smith v
Geraghty* [1986] R.T.R. 222, a case on special reasons. In the words of Glidewell
L.J. (at 232):

> "Going back to the level of alcohol in the blood at the time of driving is clearly
> permissible but only practicable ... provided that there is reasonably clear, straightfor-
> ward and relatively simple evidence to show it. In other circumstances ... I would take
> the view that justices ought not to be drawn into any detailed scientific calculation."

4.170   Following a conviction by the Birmingham justices in a drink/driving case in
which the alcohol in the defendant's body at the time of an incident was
calculated by reference to a subsequent breath test and backtracked to the time of
the incident (see (1986) 3 R.T.L.B. 51), the Minister of State at the Home Office
told the House of Commons on July 2, 1986 that the Government had no intention of restricting the discretion of the courts in relation to the admission of such
evidence. The conviction by justices was subsequently upheld by the Birmingham Crown Court on appeal (as reported in a news item in *The Times*, November
19, 1986). As had been widely predicted, the case arrived in due course before
the Divisional Court and was dealt with, together with a companion case, by
Watkins L.J. and Mann J. as *Gumbley v Cunningham; Gould v Castle* [1987] 3
All E.R. 733. In each case the defendant had been convicted on the basis of back
calculation from "below the limit" specimens of blood and breath respectively
provided in the first case 4 hours 20 minutes and in the second case 3 hours 47
minutes after being involved in road traffic accidents.

     Mann J., giving the judgment, confirmed the view that what is now s.15(2) of
the 1988 Offenders Act does not preclude the admission of evidence other than
that of the specimen itself to show a greater level of alcohol than that revealed by
the specimen, although, subject to the "hip flask" defence, the specimen would
always provide a "not less than" or base figure.

4.171   Such a conclusion meant that those who drove with excess alcohol could not
necessarily escape punishment because of the lapse of time. However, it also
meant that in such cases justices might find themselves confronted by complicated
scientific evidence. Drawing upon the cautionary words of Glidewell L.J. in
Smith v Geraghty [1986] R.T.R. 222 concerning the undesirability of justices being drawn into "detailed scientific calculation" (quoted above), Mann J. emphasised the court's view that the prosecution should not rely on such evidence

except where that evidence was easily understood and clearly persuasive of the presence of excess alcohol at the time of driving.

Furthermore, justices had to be careful not to convict unless they were *sure* on the basis of the scientific and other evidence presented that the defendant had been over the limit at the time of the alleged offence. Gumbley's appeal was dismissed on the basis that the justices had been so satisfied; in the other case, however, the appeal was allowed since the justices had accepted evidence that the defendant was "likely" to have been over the prescribed limit at the time of the accident. In the court's view that was not the equivalent of being satisfied so as to be sure of guilt.

The House of Lords was in due course asked to adjudicate upon the matter,   **4.172**
and in *Gumbley v Cunningham* [1989] R.T.R. 49 their Lordships unanimously upheld the Divisional Court's decision. Specific approval was also expressed by Ackner L.J. (delivering judgment) for the advice given by the Divisional Court (see immediately above) concerning the caution to be exercised by prosecutors and justices alike in such cases.

As regards such "back calculation" the 1965 *Report of a Special Committee of the British Medical Association* noted:

"It is inevitable that some delay will occur between the time when the alleged offence was committed and the time when a sample is obtained for analysis. It takes between 15 and 90 minutes for the peak concentration in blood to be reached following a drink of alcohol, and in most cases little more than 30 minutes. If, as must generally be the case, the motorist is detained by the police after the peak concentration has been reached, the delay in obtaining a sample will be in his favour, as the sample will yield a lower concentration than when the offence was alleged to have been committed. In this connection we advise strongly against the court permitting any 'back calculation' to determine how much higher the blood alcohol concentration must have been at the material time. In fact the rate of elimination of alcohol, both between different individuals and in the same individual at different times, varies to some extent and an exercise of this kind cannot, in our opinion, be justified, although we are aware that it is the accepted practice in some other countries. Conversely, if the suspect is known to have taken alcohol just prior to being detained the possibility must be borne in mind that the blood alcohol concentration was still rising at the time the sample was taken."

The mean elimination rate in respect of blood-alcohol appears to be 11–21mg   **4.173**
per hour, but Dubowski ("Unsettled Issues and Practices in Chemical Testing for Alcohol" in *Alcohol and Road Traffic*, London, British Medical Association, 1963) states:

"Numerous recent studies confirm the extreme variability of the blood clearance rate … with most investigations disclosing significant numbers of individual clearance rates which exceeded or trailed the average by factors of 2–4, and some extremes differing by factors of 8."

Further scientific evidence concerning rates of elimination of alcohol from the body is contained in the *Report on Breath Alcohol Measuring Instruments* (P.G.W. Cobb and M.D.G Dabbs with a foreword by Sir William Paton, F.R.S., HMSO, 1985). The modal range of elimination of the varied section of the population who provided the data was 8–9μg/100ml per hour (corresponding to a value for blood of 18–21mg/100ml per hour), a figure rather higher than the previously oft-quoted average rate for blood of 15mg/100ml per hour. An even more significant finding, however, was that 5 per cent of the persons concerned had an elimination rate exceeding 14µg/100ml per hour (32mg/100ml per hour in blood), while five people had rates exceeding the equivalent of 40mg/100ml per hour in blood (further reference should be made to the tables in the report and tables A16, A17 and A34 in particular).

4.174   Not only has it been shown that the rate at which alcohol is eliminated from the body can vary greatly from individual to individual, but it should also be noted first that an individual does not eliminate alcohol at a steady rate and secondly that a person's alcohol level may in fact continue to rise for some time after the ingestion of alcohol. Factors such as these make any back calculation based on the average rate of alcohol elimination a very imprecise calculation. To quote again from Glidewell L.J. in *Smith v Geraghty* [1986] R.T.R. 222 at 232:

> "... as a generality, it is in my view most undesirable that justices should be drawn into or allow themselves to be drawn into considering detailed calculations with all the variations which necessarily have to be built into such calculations, with the margins of error which there are. And I say that even if those calculations are put before them by way of expert evidence. Such a course is even less desirable in my judgment without the aid of expert evidence."

It should further be noted that a defendant only has to establish special reasons on a balance of probabilities. If the prosecution seek to rely on back calculations to prove that the defendant was above the prescribed limit, they have to prove that he was so that the court can feel sure, beyond reasonable doubt, that he was above the limit at the material time.

Evidential breath test devices

A   *Approval of devices*

4.175   Section 7(1)(a) requires the type of device to be approved by the Secretary of State. In order to avoid the police having to call evidence from someone on behalf of the Home Secretary, the Lion Intoximeter 3000 and Camic Breath Analyser were approved by the Home Secretary by the Breath Analysis Devices (Approval) Order 1983 made on April 18, 1983. As a result of the introduction to service of the more sophisticated second generation evidential breath test devices described below, the Camic Breath Analyser and Lion Intoximeter 3000 have ceased to be approved devices.

Although the first generation evidential breath test devices can no longer be used at police stations, a substantial proportion of the accumulated case law in relation to those devices is likely to continue to be of application with regard to the machines of the second generation. An account of cases which are believed to be of continuing relevance has accordingly been retained in the text.

4.176   Section 7(3) of the 1988 Act was amended by the Criminal Procedure and Investigations Act 1996 s.63, in order to allow for the installation at police stations of the next generation of evidential breath testing equipment (see § 4.110). A list of the breath analysis devices approved under these provisions can be found in Vol. 2, § 18.35 of this work (see also *http://www. police.homeoffice.gov.uk/publications/operational-policing* [Accessed March 16, 2009]). The application of the excess alcohol provisions of ss.4–11 of the Road Traffic Act 1988 to tramcars, etc., is discussed at § 13.233.

A Welsh language version of the software which forms part of the lion intoxilyzer 6000UK, version 2.34, was approved for use in England and Wales by the Breath Analysis Device Approval 1999. The Approval covers use not only under s.7 of the Road Traffic Act 1988 but also in accordance with s.31 of the Transport and Works Act 1992.

In *Hayward v Eames*; *Kirkpatrick v Harrigan* [1985] R.T.R. 12 it was held that **4.177** the terms of what is now s.7(1) plainly implied that the Home Secretary had both the power and the duty to approve such type of device as he thought fit and the fact that his approval was given two weeks before the relevant provisions came into force did not mean the approval was ineffective. The approval order merely meant that the fact of the approval became a matter of easy proof under s.2 of the Documentary Evidence Act 1868 by simple production of the order. Following *Hayward v Eames* it was held in *Chief Constable of Northumbria v Browne* [1986] R.T.R. 113 that a reference to the wrong manufacturing company in the Breath Analysis Devices (Approval) Order 1983 regarding the Camic simulator and the Camic breath analyser did not invalidate the approval order since the material part of the order simply provided that the Secretary of State had to approve a type of device.

Chief Constable of Northumbria v Browne above was approved and applied by the High Court of Justiciary in *Brown v Gallagher* 2002 S.L.T. 756 (also reported as *Brown (Gary) v Procurator Fiscal, Falkirk* at [2003] R.T.R. 17) when dealing with a challenge to the admissibility of the evidence provided by a machine of the second generation, an Intoximeter EC/IR, installed at the Falkirk Police Office. It had been manufactured by Alcotek Inc., a separate legal entity to Intoximeters Inc. The court held that where a type of device had been approved for measuring the proportion of alcohol in a specimen of breath, the identity of the manufacturer of the device was not a defining or a necessary part of the approval. The approval order in question, the Breath Analysis Devices (Scotland) Approval 1998, refers to "types" of device and the use of the word "type" necessarily connotes that devices used in police stations must have the same characteristics in terms of build and function as the device specified in the schedule to the approval. There was no requirement that such devices be of common manufacture with those which were subject to the approval process.

The current approval order for the Intoximeter EC/IR specifies software ver- **4.178** sion 5.23. Guidelines on type approval procedures produced by the Home Office Operational Policing Policy Unit state that where there is a change to a component which is actually specified in the approval order, a new order is needed. So far as evidential breath analysers are concerned, the software version is specified, so any upgrade to a new software version requires, in the view of the Home Office, a new approval order. A district judge has held, not at all unreasonably in the circumstances, that a machine whose software had been upgraded to version 5.26 without benefit of a fresh approval order had thereby ceased to be an approved device and accordingly that any evidence produced by it was inadmissible, regardless of its actual accuracy or reliability. It is perhaps unfortunate, therefore, that in a case reported subsequently, namely *DPP v Memery* [2002] EWHC 1720; [2003] R.T.R. 18 (see further § 4.201 below), a submission by the respondent that an Intoximeter EC/IR had lost its approval as a result of alterations to its software and alcohol profile was not in the event considered by the court. It would appear, however, that an answer to the question as to the effect of a software change upon the approval of a device may now be found (albeit obiter) in a passage in the judgment of Burnton J. in *Richardson v DPP* [2003] EWHC 359. After citing the description of the Intoximeter EC/IR which appears in the schedule to its approval order, he says: "On the face of it, therefore, it would seem that a device ... the software version of which was not UK5.23, but some significantly different version, would not be an approved device." He goes on to say that it does not follow from that that every modification to an Intoximeter would take it out of the approval. The alteration would have to be such that the description in the schedule to the order no longer applied to the device.

The question of whether an Intoximeter EC/IR device is an approved device was considered again in *Breckon v DPP* [2007] EWHC 2013; [2008] R.T.R. 8. It was argued at trial that there was insufficient evidence that the machine used in this case was an approved device. Reliance was placed upon the fact that the Guide to Type Approval relating to the device provided that the "gas delivery system shall comprise an automatic change-over valve", whereas the device in question had a manual change-over valve. The Administrative Court concluded that the device which is approved is set out in the schedule to the approval document dated February 25, 1998. As there is no reference, express or implied, in this schedule to either the agreement with the manufacturer or to the Guide, then there is no reason why those documents should be incorporated within the approval or why the approval should be read as being subject to them. The definition of the device stands by itself in the schedule to the approval and does not admit of further identification or specification. The court said that there must be room to make sensible modifications without having to seek a new approval every time this is done. The test is whether after such modification or alteration the machine remains one to which the description in the schedule still properly applies. If it does not, then the device is no longer an approved device; but if the description does still properly apply to the device it will remain an approved device even though modifications or alterations have been made. Thus the removal of one cylinder, which did not affect the operation of the device, did not take it out of the approval. Nor did the supply of a device with a manual change-over valve rather than an automatic change-over valve, when the machine had two cylinders, render it no longer an approved device. (See also the section on general serviceability and type approval at §§ 4.197 et seq. below.)

B   *Standard drink/drugs police pro forma*

4.179   Standard drink/drugs police pro forma are available for use by police forces throughout England and Wales. The pro forma in question (available at *www.homeoffice.gov.uk/operational-policing/road-traffic.html* [Accessed March 16, 2009]) is subdivided into five parts. Part A (Form MG DD/A) is entitled "Drink/Drugs Station Procedure—General" and deals with the procedures for the obtaining of breath specimens on both first and second generation devices. It includes a space for the attachment of the printout obtained from the instrument. Part B (Form MG DD/B) is headed "Drink/Drugs Station Procedure—Specimens/ Impairment" and covers the procedures for the obtaining of samples of blood or urine where an evidential breath testing device is not used, or is not operating reliably, or has produced an unreliable indication. It also deals with procedures concerned with the statutory driver's option where the reading given by the evidential breath test machine is 40–50µg per cent inclusive, as well as for the statutory option where the reading is 39µg per cent or less and back calculation is being considered (see further §§ 4.167 et seq.); additionally, as its heading would suggest, this part of the pro forma provides guidance on the correct procedures to be followed where unfitness to drive through drink or drugs (impairment) is suspected. Part C (Form MG DD/C) bears the title "Drink/Drugs Hospital Procedure" and deals, unsurprisingly, with procedures for the obtaining of specimens at a hospital. Part D (Form MG DD/D) is headed "Alcohol Technical Defence Form" and assists in the compilation of relevant information for use by forensic science laboratories and subsequently in court in "hip flask" or "laced drink" cases. Part E (Form MG DD/E) is the "Drug Sample Information Form" and is designed to accompany the drug sample to the laboratory where it is to be analysed. Part F (Form MG DD/F) is the "Impairment Assessment" form which was first developed for use in the field trial of a fitness test designed to aid police in the detection of drink or drug-related offences; that test now has statutory form as the preliminary impairment test (see further §§ 4.35 et seq.).

Forms MG DD/A and B described above came under judicial scrutiny in *DPP* **4.180** *v Smith (Robert James)* [2000] R.T.R. 341 (see further § 4.132 above). The pro forma was described therein as the "plain man's guide" to a simple understanding of the procedures provided by the 1988 Act to ensure, in a practical way, that those called upon to operate the procedures do not omit a relevant step; that at stages where there is a choice of steps, they appreciate that such a choice exists, and it also offers quite clearly common-sense guidance as to the way in which choices should be exercised when they fall to be made. There was no obligation upon the prosecution to call evidence as to the provenance of the form, since it merely conveys common-sense *advice* to the operator of the procedure and in no way *instructs* him as to what he should do.

DPP v Smith above came under consideration in *DPP v Coulter* [2005] EWHC 1533. During the procedure for the obtaining of a breath specimen at a police station the suspect, when asked if he had eaten anything, replied that he might have had a "tic-tac". The officer, unaware of guidelines recommending that in the event of consumption of food by a suspect a period of 20 minutes should be allowed before continuing, pressed on with the procedure. It was held by the Divisional Court that there was nothing in s.7 of the 1988 Act to indicate that a requirement to produce a breath specimen would be rendered unlawful by a failure to observe police guidelines. Although it was possible that in certain circumstances a failure to follow the guidelines could affect the reliability of a specimen, that was not relevant in the case in point as no specimen of breath had been provided.

C Description of devices

The second generation evidential breath testing machines referred to above **4.181** (see § 4.176) share a common ability, as predicated by s.7(3)(bb) of the 1988 Act, as amended (see § 4.109), to provide, in appropriate circumstances, an automatic indication of their inability to produce a reliable indication of the proportion of alcohol in the breath of the subject and of the reasons for that inability. They are possessed of considerably greater specificity than their predecessors and are thus able to differentiate with accuracy between ethanol (ethyl alcohol) and other organic contaminants which may be present in a breath sample. The method by which this end is achieved, however, is not common to all three machines. The Camic Datamaster and the lion intoxilyzer 6000UK both rely solely upon infrared spectroscopy, using the absorption of infrared light by ethanol in order to determine its concentration, and make no use of secondary sensors such as semiconductors or fuel cells. Specificity is achieved in the lion intoxilyzer, for instance, by the use of selective optical filtering. The Intoximeter EC/IR, on the other hand, uses a fuel cell sensor which is specific for alcohol in combination with a multi-filter infrared detector offering "real time" analysis of the breath sample. It is beyond the competence of the editors of this publication to enter into discussion of the relative merits of the competing systems; suffice it only to say that all three machines have met the requirements for government approval and have been duly approved. The first generation of evidential breath testing equipment at police stations (the Lion Intoximeter 3000 and the Camic Breath Analyser) was entirely replaced by December 31, 1999.

In addition to their ability to differentiate between ethyl alcohol and other organic contaminants, the current machines are equipped to recognise the presence of mouth alcohol in a breath sample. A true measurement of the concentration of alcohol in a person's body can only be obtained from breath if the breath which is analysed is "deep lung air", since only this breath has been in close contact with the blood of the subject. If a subject takes a drink of alcohol, or regurgitates alcohol from stomach to mouth, an artificially high level of breath alcohol is produced immediately afterwards. As the subject continues to blow, however, any mouth alcohol rapidly evaporates and the level of alcohol starts to decrease. By monitoring in real time the level of alcohol in the breath as the subject is blowing (employing a technique known as "slope detection") the fall in alcohol level which indicates the presence of mouth alcohol can be detected.

4.182   The presence of mouth alcohol, or indeed of an interfering substance, in a sample of breath is indicated to operators of these machines by means of an "error message" and the production of an appropriate printout. Error messages and accompanying printouts are also produced where, for instance, the breath difference revealed by the analysis of the first and second samples provided exceeds 15 per cent of the lower figure and the numerical difference between them exceeds 5µg/100ml (per the lion intoxilyzer 6000UK Operator Handbook), or where either of the two specimens is "out of range", i.e. exceeds 220µg/100ml (lion intoxilyzer 6000UK and Intoximeter EC/IR) or 230µg/100ml (Camic Datamaster). Where an interfering substance has been detected or a "breath difference" message appears, the police officer conducting the test will be entitled to resort in accordance with s.7(3)(bb) of the 1988 Act to the requirement of a blood or urine sample since he will clearly have reasonable cause to believe that the device concerned has not produced a reliable indication of the proportion of alcohol in the breath of the subject. Where both specimens are "out of range", the officer will similarly have to invoke his powers under s.7(3)(bb); but where the lower of them is within range, that specimen would appear to be admissible in evidence in accordance with s.8(1) of the 1988 Act. Where mouth alcohol has been detected, operators of the Intoximeter EC/IR and lion intoxilyzer 6000UK are advised to refer to prevailing police procedures; the Operators Manual for the Camic Datamaster, however, is silent on that particular issue. The standard drink/drugs police pro forma MG DD described above offers the officer conducting the test the choice of proceeding to require a laboratory specimen (of blood or urine) in accordance with s.7(3)(bb), or of taking no further action. It is submitted that in the majority of cases the former is a likelier outcome than the latter. It is also submitted, though with some caution, that if the reason for the presence of mouth alcohol in the specimen can be determined, as, e.g., where the subject has been less than accurate in stating the time at which he or she last consumed alcohol, it would not appear to be improper for a second breath testing cycle to be conducted after an appropriate period of time has elapsed.

In addition to the error messages described above, which are of relevance to the invocation of police powers under s.7(3)(bb) of the 1988 Act, the current machines also give appropriate indications of unreliability of the more basic kind envisaged by s.7(3)(b) ibid., where, e.g., a simulator error is detected, or where alcohol or similar vapours are present in the room air which is used to purge the machine before and after each specimen is provided. Needless to say, a failure by a breath test subject to provide either or both of the required samples of breath will also result in the production of an error message and an appropriate printout.   **4.183**

It was held in *Jubb v DPP* [2002] EWHC 2317; [2003] R.T.R. 19, distinguishing *Tobi v Nicholas* [1988] R.T.R. 343 discussed at § 4.241, that an error message printout of the "breath difference" variety was admissible in evidence as part of the circumstances that gave the police officer concerned reason to believe that an unreliable indication had been given by the machine, notwithstanding that no copy of that printout had been served upon the accused. The requirements as to service imposed by s.16 of the 1988 Offenders Act applied only where the printout was being relied upon to establish that the proportion of alcohol in the sample was in excess of the prescribed limit.

D   *Calibration of devices*

In addition to its relevant software, each machine works in conjunction with a gas or gas delivery system for calibration checking purposes. The practical advantage of a gaseous rather than a liquid simulator is understood to be its longevity, in that the "shelf life" of the former is measured in weeks whereas that of the latter is restricted to a number of days. In each case a compressed mixture of alcohol vapour in air set at 35µg/100ml is supplied by the "gas simulator" to the machine; if a reading outside the range 32–37µg/100ml is obtained during the first simulator check the test cycle will be aborted. Where, however, the first check is satisfactory but the second simulator check, at the end of the breath test procedure, is outside the required range, an "error message" will be displayed and an appropriate printout will be produced by the machine. Such a message will invalidate for evidential purposes the breath measurements obtained during that cycle (see *R. v Kingston upon Thames JJ. Ex p. Khanna* [1986] R.T.R. 364 below), but will enable police in accordance with s.7(3)(b) to require blood or urine under s.7(4).   **4.184**

The apparent asymmetry of the acceptable calibration range is explained by the fact that the top thereof represents 37.9µg/100ml, which is shown on the machines as 37µg/100ml (as indeed it was on machines of the first generation). It would appear that the decided cases which bear upon the evidential and procedural significance of self-calibration checks will continue to be of some relevance to the new machines (see, e.g. *Oldfield v Anderton*, *Mayon v DPP* and *Waite v Smith* below).

Where a self-calibration check is outside the limit, the evidence of the readings is inadmissible and should not be led (*R. v Kingston upon Thames JJ. Ex p. Khanna* [1986] R.T.R. 364).   **4.185**

Proof of proper calibration is essential if a conviction is to be obtained, and where a case stated failed to indicate that calibration had taken place the conviction of an offence under what is now s.5(1) had to be quashed (*Mayon v DPP* [1988] R.T.R. 281).

The fact (elicited in cross-examination) that the constable operating a Camic Datamaster did not know the correct calibration limits of the machine had no bearing upon the question as to whether the machine was operating correctly. There was no other challenge to her knowledge and expertise. The operator was a trained operator and had given evidence that the machine was working properly; furthermore the machine was self-calibrating and had produced a printout with appropriate readings, the lower of which was above the prescribed limit (*Haggis v DPP* [2003] EWHC 2481; [2004] 2 All E.R. 382).

4.186   Although evidence of the self-calibration checks being within the limit is required where it is sought to put in evidence a breath reading given by the device, there is no such requirement where the defendant is charged under what is now s.7(6) with failing to provide breath specimens; in such a case what matters is whether the defendant failed or refused to provide specimens (*Oldfield v Anderton* [1986] Crim. L.R. 189).

If the two check results are not within the prescribed figure or if the machine does not satisfactorily purge itself, the police are entitled in accordance with s.7(3)(b) (see above) to require blood or urine under s.7(4) (see §§ 4.212–24). In this context it matters not that the final calibration check registers a temperature of a mere 0.1° above the maximum permitted; the de minimis rule has no application to this provision (*Waite v Smith* [1986] Crim. L.R. 405).

All the current machines produce at the conclusion of the sequence a printout incorporating the statement and certificate as defined by s.16(1) of the 1988 Offenders Act. (As to proof and production, etc., of the statement and certificate, see §§ 4.235–47.) The certificate will be signed by the operator and in England and Wales the subject will also be invited to sign; it would appear that no such invitation is issued to subjects in Scotland. The person is under no legal obligation to sign; if he does not sign, the operator usually writes "refused" in the space for the subject's signature and makes a note in the appropriate place on the pro forma.

E   *Operation of devices*

4.187   As may be seen from the specimen printouts set out in Appendix 1 below, the operational sequence for what may be described as a "regular" breath test for the second generation machines is as follows:

(1) Purging with clean air ("Blank").

(2) Injection of simulator gas to check calibration ("Simulator Check 1").

(3) Purging with clean air ("Blank").

(4) Subject provides first breath sample ("Breath Specimen 1").

(5) Purging with clean air ("Blank").

(6) Subject provides second breath sample ("Breath Specimen 2").

(7) Purging with clean air ("Blank").

(8) Injection of simulator gas to check calibration ("Simulator Check 2").

As with the previous generation of machines, the subject is allowed three minutes in which to provide his first specimen and a further three minutes in which to provide a second one. It is stated in the Operator Handbook for the lion intoxilyzer 6000UK that up to five attempts should be possible within each three-minute period. A horizontal bar on that machine's display unit provides a representation of the volume of breath which has been blown and of the amount of breath still required. According to the manufacturers the subject does not have to blow hard, but must continue to blow until he has brought the horizontal bar to the end of the stop. The volume of air that has to be exhaled by the subject in order for deep lung air to be reached and the specimen analysed is dependent upon the size of that person's lungs: the larger the lungs, the more the air that has to be blown.

Each machine is equipped with a keyboard and a visual display panel upon which messages and prompts appear, and with a printer unit. Each is also fitted with a clock. The Intoximeter EC/IR and the lion intoxilyzer 6000UK clocks are self-adjusting between Greenwich Mean Time and British Summer Time; the clock fitted to the Camic Datamaster, however, requires re-setting twice a year. **4.188**

The Operator Manuals for the Camic Datamaster and the Intoximeter EC/IR provide operating instructions in shortened form for ease of reference; these are reproduced, together with specimen standard printouts, in Appendix 1 below. There is no such short form instruction list in the Operator Handbook for the lion intoxilyzer 6000UK; its operational sequence may be gleaned, however, from perusal of its specimen standard printout (also to be found in Appendix 1).

F *Admissibility of specimens of breath*

A considerable volume of case law accumulated in connection with the admissibility or otherwise of specimens obtained from evidential breath testing machines of the first generation (the Lion Intoximeter 3000 and the Camic Breath Analyser). Many of the decided cases continue to be of relevance so far as the current machines are concerned, and reference may be made generally to the cases described below. **4.189**

Section 7(1)(a) requires a defendant to provide two specimens of breath on the approved device and s.8(1) provides that of any two such specimens that with the lower proportion of alcohol shall be used and the other disregarded. Where the alcohol levels for the two specimens are identical, the reading relating to either specimen may be adduced in evidence (*R. v Brentford Magistrates' Court Ex p. Clarke* [1986] Crim. L.R. 633). In *Howard v Hallett* [1984] R.T.R. 353 the operator neglected to ask the motorist for a second specimen. On realising his mistake he restarted the machine and obtained two further specimens. The prosecution relied on the second printout of the two later specimens and on cross-examination it was admitted that the first breath specimen was lower than the second or third specimens. The Divisional Court held that on a proper construction of what is now s.15(2), (3) of the 1988 Offenders Act only evidence of the proportion of alcohol in a person's breath, blood or urine which had been obtained in accordance with the statutory procedure in what is now s.7 was to be taken into account and accordingly directed the defendant's acquittal.

In *Stewart v DPP* [2003] EWHC 1323; [2003] R.T.R. 35 the defendant provided two specimens of breath for analysis at a police station, but the difference between the two readings was in excess of 15 per cent; they were therefore an unreliable indication of the amount of alcohol in his breath. The police officer thereupon invited the defendant to choose between providing two further **4.190** specimens of breath or a sample of blood. He chose to provide two more breath specimens. The lower of these formed the basis of his conviction for driving with excess alcohol. On appeal it was argued that the police officer had exceeded his powers, hence the evidence of alcohol in his breath had been unlawfully obtained and was inadmissible. Not so, said the Divisional Court (Lord Woolf C.J. presiding), in dismissing the appeal. Whilst s.7(3)(bb) entitled a police officer to require a specimen of blood or urine in the event of an unreliable indication being obtained from the breath specimens, nothing in the section stated that in such a case the officer was *obliged* (our emphasis) to require blood or urine and that a further breath test could not be offered. In addition, on any sensible interpretation of s.11(3)(b) ibid. each of the defendant's first two breath specimens did not "enable the objective of the … analysis to be satisfactorily achieved" and, therefore, once it was accepted that effectively no specimen of breath had been provided, there was nothing to prevent the officer requiring further specimens of breath. In any event, the officer concerned had invited the defendant to choose between providing further breath samples or a specimen of blood, and in such circumstances it was artificial to speak of a *requirement* (our emphasis) to provide breath specimens. The officer had acted lawfully and the analysis of the second breath test was admissible.

Stewart v DPP above was considered and approved by the Divisional Court in *Edmond v DPP* [2006] EWHC 463; [2006] R.T.R. 18. The readings obtained from the two specimens of breath provided by the defendant revealed an excessive breath difference. The officer conducting the test concluded that the test was unreliable and *invited* (our emphasis) the defendant to provide two further specimens of breath. The defendant agreed to do so. He was not warned a second time pursuant to s.7(7) that a failure to provide such specimens might render him liable to prosecution. He had been so warned at the outset when he was first required to provide a specimen of breath, and in the court's view there was no need for a further warning when *invited* rather than *required* to provide further specimens since failure to do so could not render him liable for prosecution. The only consequence of that failure was that the officer would be entitled to *require* a specimen to be given, whether that specimen be of breath, blood or urine.

4.191   The principle that a conviction under what is now s.5(1) may be supported by evidence relating only to a single specimen of breath no longer subsists. *Duddy v Gallagher* [1985] R.T.R. 401 and *Burridge v East* [1986] Crim. L.R. 632 were both overruled by the unanimous decision of the House of Lords (Lord Keith of Kinkel, Lord Brandon of Oakbrook, Lord Griffiths, Lord Oliver of Aylmerton and Lord Goff of Chieveley) in *Cracknell v Willis* [1988] R.T.R. 1. Lord Griffiths drew specific attention to the statutory safeguards provided for the motorist's protection, amongst which was the requirement for two specimens of breath to be taken, for the specimen containing the lower proportion of alcohol to be used and the other to be discarded (what are now s.7(1) and s.8(1), (2)). That precaution was clearly intended to give a suspect the benefit of the doubt in the case of any variability in the performance of the machine. It had to follow, therefore, that it was not intended that a defendant should be convicted on the basis of a single specimen of breath.

However, in assessing the penalty to be imposed for what is now the s.7(6) offence of refusing to provide a breath specimen, justices were entitled to take into account any evidence indicative of the defendant's alcohol consumption, including the result of the analysis of the first (and only) breath specimen provided. Thus the concern of the Divisional Court (as expressed in *Duddy v Gallagher*) that a defendant who, on seeing that his first specimen is high in alcohol, refuses to provide a second specimen, will prevent the justices dealing with what is now a s.7(6) offence from knowing just how intoxicated he was, has been rendered unnecessary. (The reports make no reference to the case of *Denneny v Harding* [1986] R.T.R. 350 discussed in the thirteenth edition, but it is nevertheless to be presumed that in so far as it was authority for the proposition that a defendant may be convicted of an offence under what is now s.5(1) on the evidence of one specimen of breath only, it too has been overruled.)

In *Chief Constable of Avon and Somerset Constabulary v Creech* [1986] R.T.R. **4.192** 87 the defendant provided one breath specimen of 95µg/100ml but because of her nervous state the time for giving the second specimen elapsed before she could give it. The police operator thereupon restarted the machine and she then gave two further breath specimens. The prosecution conceded that there was no power to require more than two specimens and relied on the oral evidence of the police operator as to the readings of the first two specimens. The justices dismissed the case on the ground that for two specimens to be admissible they have to be given during the same cycle of the machine. Allowing an appeal, the Divisional Court held that what is now s.15(2), (3) of the 1988 Offenders Act is to be construed as referring to specimens validly taken in accordance with s.7, that only two specimens may be required, and that any deviation from the operating procedures sufficient to question the accuracy of any measurement will invalidate the analysis. But they said that as there was no evidence that the accuracy of the first operation was compromised by the omission of the second specimen, the prosecutor was entitled to put in evidence the first and second specimens actually given, following *Howard v Hallett* above, *Morgan v Lee* [1985] R.T.R. 409 above and *Owen v Chesters* [1985] Crim. L.R. 156 where it was held that oral evidence may be given of breath specimen readings.

Chief Constable of Avon and Somerset Constabulary v Creech discussed above was followed and applied in *Mercer v DPP* [2003] EWHC 225; [2004] R.T.R. 8. Breath specimens were taken from a suspect using a lion intoxilyzer 6000. Before the first specimen was taken the machine correctly calibrated itself. After the second specimen, however, the machine recorded "interfering substance" on its display and the cycle was aborted without a second self-calibration. Having no reason to suppose that the machine was working other than properly, the officer took a further two samples, the machine performing its self-calibration checks in the proper manner both before the first sample and after the second one. At trial the prosecution relied, as they were entitled to do on the authority of *Creech*, upon the first specimen taken in the first cycle and the first taken in the second cycle and prosecuted on the basis of the lower of those two. There was nothing in the statute to say that the two specimens must be part of the same cycle, and the defendant's contention that the law now required calibration before and after specimens had been received in any one cycle did not find favour with the court.

Where a person has failed to supply a specimen of breath for analysis when **4.193** duly required to do so, there is no reason why the police should not make a further request for a specimen of breath (*Owen v Morgan* [1986] R.T.R. 151 (applying *Revel v Jordan*, *Hillis v Nicholson* [1983] R.T.R. 497); see also *Reid v Tudhope* 1986 S.L.T. 136).

Oral evidence may be given of the printout levels of the defendant's breath specimens (*DPP v Parkin* [1989] Crim L.R. 379 where the printout had been lost by the police). In *Thom v DPP* [1994] R.T.R. 11 it was explained that s.16(1) of the 1988 Offenders Act was permissive and provided for one method by which the proportion of alcohol in a specimen of breath might be proved (the Lion Intoximeter printout) and did not, either expressly or impliedly, prevent any other admissible evidence from being relied on. The results of the self-calibration of the device are vital to establish the reliability of the machine. However, evidence of the officer that he checked the machine to make sure it was working correctly is sufficient. It is unnecessary for the officer to deal expressly with the calibration figures, or the purging process, at least in the absence of a direct challenge by the defence (*Sneyd v DPP* [2006] EWHC 560; [2007] R.T.R. 6, similarly *Greenaway v DPP* [1994] R.T.R. 17).

4.194   A motorist whose breath specimen revealed a level of alcohol (47μg/100ml) which entitled him to exercise his option under s.8(2) of the Road Traffic Act 1988 to have that specimen replaced by one of blood or urine was subsequently convicted of driving with excess alcohol on the basis of the alcohol level of the specimen of blood (91mg/100ml) which he provided. He appealed on the grounds that no evidence of the accuracy of the calibration of the Lion Intoximeter had been produced; neither had its printout. In those circumstances, it was submitted, the breath specimen was not lawfully obtained and what followed was invalid. Not so, said the Divisional Court in *Prince v DPP* [1996] Crim. L.R. 343. The appellant's reliance upon *Greenaway v DPP* [1994] R.T.R. 17 (referred to above) was misplaced, since there had been no attempt by the prosecution in the instant case to prove the offence by means of the breath specimen. The obtaining of that specimen was merely the precondition for the obtaining of the blood specimen; accordingly there was no need for evidence to be given as to the calibration of the Lion Intoximeter.

As it is well known that the Camic Datamaster is, in common with other currently approved evidential breath testing machines, self-calibrating, the fact that its operator was ignorant of the correct calibration limits of the machine did not cause her to cease to be a trained operator, and as there was no evidence of any malfunction of the machine its analysis of the defendant's breath was properly admissible against him; *Haggis v DPP* [2003] EWHC 2481; [2004] 2 All E.R. 382.

4.195   The breath printout will not be used if the result was 50μg or less and the defendant chose to provide blood or urine instead (see §§ 4.134–8). It should be noted, however, that a breath sample remains potentially admissible unless and until replaced by an admissible blood or urine sample (*Hague v DPP* [1997] R.T.R. 146; see further § 4.163).

Challenging the evidential breath testing machines

4.196   Although the machines of the first generation, the Camic Breath Analyser and the Lion Intoximeter 3000, ceased to be approved devices at the end of 1999, a substantial proportion of the accumulated case law in relation to those devices is likely to continue to be of application with regard to the machines of the second generation. An account of cases which are believed to be of continuing relevance has accordingly been retained where appropriate in the text.

A *General serviceability and type approval*

Where the accuracy of the analysis is challenged on the grounds of non-compliance with the instructions as to its use, it would seem that the onus will be on the defence to show that the instructions have not been complied with, and that, that being so, the non-compliance is unduly favourable to the prosecution (*Att Gen's Reference (No.1 of 1978)* [1978] R.T.R. 377). In *Black v Bickmore* [1982] R.T.R. 167 the principle of the *Att Gen's Reference* was applied to the Alcolmeter and it would seem applicable to evidential breath test devices in the same way as to screening breath devices. **4.197**

Defendants wishing to challenge the accuracy of the machine were denied by the High Court the use of witness summonses to investigate the Lion Intoximeter log, service repair reports and test records. It was said that it was up to police forces to consider whether a more uniform practice was desirable and whether in the light of the Metropolitan Police experience a policy of voluntary disclosure should be more widely adopted. There was no discovery of documents in the magistrates' court or Crown Court and a witness summons must not be issued as a disguised attempt to obtain discovery (*R. v Skegness Magistrates' Court Ex p. Cardy*; *R. v Manchester Crown Court Ex p. Williams* [1985] R.T.R. 49). It was held similarly in *R. v Coventry Magistrates' Court Ex p. Perks* [1985] R.T.R. 74 that a magistrates' court should not have issued a witness summons for production of a Lion Intoximeter's log book since it was in the nature of a fishing expedition to determine the reliability of the machine and there was no general power of discovery in magistrates' courts. On November 19, 1985 the appeal committee of the House of Lords refused leave to appeal in the case of *R. v Skegness Magistrates' Court.*

That there is no general power of discovery in magistrates' courts was once again emphasised by the Divisional Court in *R. v Tower Bridge Magistrates' Court Ex p. DPP* [1989] R.T.R. 118 when quashing a stipendiary magistrate's order issuing a witness summons requiring the production of the service record of a Lion Intoximeter. An application for such a summons by the defence could be regarded as a fishing expedition and was not a matter to be decided by the magistrate in advance of the hearing. **4.198**

R. v Skegness Magistrates' Court Ex p. Cardy above was expressly applied and reaffirmed by the House of Lords in *DPP v McKeown*; *DPP v Jones* [1997] R.T.R. 162. The justices in that case had been right to reject the defence's application for discovery of design documents and circuit diagrams for the Lion Intoximeter. The defence had made no attempt to lay a foundation for their application by evidence of how such documents and diagrams might demonstrate that, contrary to the prosecution expert's empirical observations, the inaccuracy of the machine's clock did in fact have some effect on the breath analysis.

A defendant provided specimens of breath for analysis by a Lion Intoximeter 3000; a breath-alcohol reading above the prescribed limit was the outcome. During the course of the hearing on a charge of driving with excess alcohol, it was revealed by an expert witness for the prosecution that the device concerned had previously received minor modifications. The defence sought (not altogether surprisingly, it may be thought) to cross-examine the witness in order to discover whether by virtue of its modifications the machine had ceased to be an "approved device" in the terms of the Breath Analysis Devices (Approval) Order 1983. The **4.199** justices disallowed the cross-examination and convicted the defendant. The conviction was quashed on appeal to the Divisional Court in *Young v Flint* [1987] R.T.R. 300 (Watkins L.J. and Mann J.). The defendant had been denied his fundamental right to cross-examine a prosecution witness on a relevant matter and accordingly the court had no alternative but to quash the conviction, "exceedingly fortunate" though he may have been.

Young v Flint above was referred to in *Grant v DPP* [2003] EWHC 130; (2003) 167 J.P. 459 as authority for the proposition that alterations to a device can be so fundamental that they cause the device to be such that it is no longer the device approved. Furthermore, per Clarke L.J. (albeit obiter), once the issue is sufficiently raised the burden is on the prosecution to prove beyond reasonable doubt that the device is an approved device. In the case in point, however, the Crown Court had formed the view that the evidence put forward to suggest that the device had been altered was to a significant extent founded upon speculation, and had been entitled to reject it on that basis.

4.200   Even if expert evidence had been given that the Lion Intoximeter was working erratically and unpredictably, if the effect of the defect was to make the readings too low, the justices were still entitled to rely on the printout as the error was entirely in the motorist's favour (*Wright v Taplin* [1986] R.T.R. 388 *Note*).

The Divisional Court in the conjoined cases of *DPP v Brown*; *DPP v Teixeira* [2001] EWHC Admin 931; [2002] R.T.R. 23 dispatched beyond the boundary a notably unmeritorious challenge to the admissibility of the evidence of breath alcohol obtained by use in each case of an Intoximeter EC/IR. Each defendant had provided a breath sample which was in excess of the prescribed limit. A team of experts had subsequently visited the respective police stations and had tested the machines installed there by swilling a diluted alcohol solution without swallowing it and then providing specimens of breath for analysis. In some instances the machines failed to register the presence of mouth alcohol in the proportion of deep lung alcohol in the breath. Before the magistrates it was successfully contended in each case that a failure to detect mouth alcohol took the device outside the required specification standard, and that the device was not therefore to be treated as "a device approved by the Secretary of State"; accordingly its use was unlawful and evidence derived from it inadmissible.

4.201   The court held that where the presumption that an intoximeter is reliable is challenged, magistrates should only concern themselves with the particular intoximeter device used. It was no part of their function to consider whether the Intoximeter EC/IR should have received the approval of the Secretary of State. Any representations to the effect that an intoximeter device is generally unreliable should be addressed to the Secretary of State (*R. v Skegness Magistrates' Court Ex p. Cardy* [1985] R.T.R. 49; see § 4.197). The court should examine carefully whether the presumption as to the reliability of the machine has been challenged by any *relevant* evidence. If, as in the cases in point, it was common ground that there would not have been mouth alcohol, or alcohol vapour generated by regurgitation or eructation in the dead-space of the upper respiratory tract of the defendant, a challenge to the reliability of the device based upon evidence as to the effect upon the device of mouth alcohol or alcohol vapour was a challenge founded upon irrelevant evidence where the court was satisfied that the device was otherwise reliable. (It should be borne in mind that it is standard police procedure in accordance with Form MG/DD/A (see § 4.179) for a suspect to be asked whether he has consumed any alcohol within the previous 20 minutes. The purpose of that question is specifically to ensure that any specimens provided will not be contaminated by mouth alcohol (which according to expert opinion generally decays within 10 minutes) and a truthful answer by the suspect should protect him from any erroneous readings produced by that substance.

DPP v Brown; *DPP v Teixeira* discussed above and *Brown v Gallagher* 2002 S.L.T. 756; [2003] R.T.R. 17 (discussed at § 4.177 above) were both cited with approval by the Divisional Court in *DPP v Memery* [2002] EWHC 1720; [2003] R.T.R. 18 when allowing an appeal by the prosecution against the decision of the Crown Court at Warrington to allow an appeal against conviction for driving with excess alcohol. The fact that a device for measuring the proportion of alcohol in a specimen of breath could not detect mouth alcohol did not deprive it of type approval. The question posed to the court was whether it was open to the Crown Court to find that the Secretary of State in approving the device had acted unlawfully and/or *Wednesbury* unreasonably (*Associated Provincial Picture Houses Ltd v Wednesbury Corp* [1948] 1 K.B. 223 CA); the answer to that question was "No". When looking at the procedural safeguards relating to inaccurate readings due to mouth alcohol, the approval of the device was not irrational; and in the circumstances the ability of the device to detect mouth alcohol was wholly irrelevant to the reliability of the evidence as its accuracy was not doubted by the experts.

DPP v Brown; *DPP v Teixeira* above was applied by the Divisional Court in *Fernley v DPP* [2005] EWHC 1393; (2005) 169 J.P. 450. At trial the defendant disputed the accuracy of the breath analysis on the grounds that the Intoximeter EC/IR could not detect mouth alcohol and produced higher readings than the other two types of approved device. He did not, however, adduce any evidence that the software installed in the device was otherwise than as specified in the approval order; accordingly the justices were entitled to rely upon the general presumption that the device used was an approved device. **4.202**

In *Breckon v DPP* [2007] EWHC 2013; [2007] R.T.R. 8 it was said that when the device was approved because it fell within the definition in the schedule to the approval order, then it follows that expert evidence about Intoximeter design was not relevant or therefore admissible.

A case to be treated with the utmost caution is *Kemsley v DPP* [2004] EWHC 278; (2005) 169 J.P. 148 as it turns solely and only upon the form in which the case stated was drafted. The only permissible reading of that case was that the district judge had accepted expert evidence to the effect that the device used, the Intoximeter EC/IR, was not an approved device, by virtue of its having been modified and altered to such an extent as to fall outside the Secretary of State's approval, a finding fatal to the admissibility of the evidence that that device had produced. The court was at pains to point out, however, that the instant case does not decide anything about breathalyser cases in general, and should not be cited as any more than a decision on the particular evidence that was before the court. Those who wished to argue that the EC/IR had been changed so as to be outwith its approval would be well advised to be in a position to demonstrate how and in what respects the machine is different from that approved, and whether that difference is sufficient to make it a different type. The mere fact that there are *some* (our emphasis) differences does not mean that the machine is of an unapproved type.

4.203   Proceedings were stayed as an abuse of process in two separate cases before district judges because of the failure of the prosecution to comply with orders made under s.8 of the Criminal Procedure and Investigations Act 1996 for the disclosure of material concerning the Intoximeter EC/IR which was in the possession of the manufacturers, Intoximeters UK Ltd, and not in possession of the police or the Crown Prosecution Service. It was held by the Divisional Court in *DPP v Wood*; *DPP v McGillicuddy* [2006] EWHC 32; (2006) 170 J.P. 177 that those proceedings should not have been stayed for two reasons. First, the lawfulness of type approval was not a matter which could be raised as a defence to an excess alcohol charge. Where the contention was that the device which was originally type approved had been altered in such a way as to take it outwith its approval, and disclosure was sought to further that contention, the court would require more than the asserted fact of unapproved modification to justify disclosure. There would have to be some material which explained how the alteration could go to loss of type approval and how disclosure could advance that point. On the facts of the instant case there was no material sufficient to justify the disclosure orders that had been made.

    The second question was whether, if otherwise justified, disclosure should have been ordered of the material which was all in the hands of Intoximeters UK. The issue was whether the material was prosecution material within s.8(3) and (4) of the 1996 Act. The court held that in each case the prosecutor was the Crown Prosecution Service. Intoximeters UK Ltd was not part of that service and it did not become part of that service because it had supplied the device to the police force and had certain continuing contractual obligations to the police. Accordingly disclosure of material in the company's hands could not be ordered under s.8.

4.204   In the absence of any evidence at all suggesting that the software installed in an Intoximeter EC/IR was not that which it ought to have been, namely version 5.23, it was permissible for a court to assume that the software within the approved device was correct. There was an evidential burden upon the defendant to make good what was otherwise mere assertion, and that burden the defendant had failed to discharge; *Skinner v DPP* [2004] EWHC 2914.

B   *Comparative specimens*

4.205   It was not possible to challenge the reliability of the Lion Intoximeter by calling expert evidence that the Intoximeter's analysis was unreliable on the ground that the defendant, after providing specimens of breath on the machine, would not have been able to provide within so short a time a negative result on the Alcolmeter or the Alcotest (R) 80 before being allowed to leave the police station. Both the Alcolmeter and the Alcotest were screening devices only, while the Intoximeter was an approved device for the detailed and evidential analysis of the content of alcohol (*Snelson v Thompson* [1985] R.T.R. 220). It is submitted, moreover, that the expert evidence in this case should be viewed with caution in the light of the scientific findings of the *Report on Breath Alcohol Measuring Instruments*. While the average hourly rate of alcohol elimination may be 18–21mg/100ml of blood, the evidence disclosed in the report showed that 5 per cent of the persons tested eliminated alcohol at a rate exceeding 32mg/100ml and that there were even some who exceeded 40mg/100ml.

    Where a motorist had provided a sample of blood for analysis which proved positive, yet minutes later provided a sample of breath which proved negative, he was entitled to an adjournment in order to seek expert evidence of the rate of alcohol metabolism in order to challenge the accuracy of the blood sample: *Parish v DPP* [2000] R.T.R. 143; *The Times*, March 2, 2000. Although the report does not make it clear, it is presumed from the reference by the Divisional Court to *Snelson v Thompson* (discussed above) that the breath testing device used was a roadside rather than an evidential one. The court stated that there was nothing to indicate that such evidence was inadmissible, or if admissible should be ignored; accordingly the view of the justices that the evidence sought would be of no value to the defendant was wrong, and they should not have refused his adjournment request.

It was possible to challenge the result of the Lion Intoximeter if the analysis of a blood or urine sample voluntarily provided by the defendant threw sufficient doubt upon the Intoximeter result (*Lucking v Forbes* [1985] Crim. L.R. 793). In *Lucking* the defendant sought to challenge the reading of 58µg/100ml on the Intoximeter by his behaviour at the police station and the fact that the blood sample he gave (pursuant to the now defunct blood/urine option experiment described below) was analysed on behalf of the police as 87mg/100ml while an analysis of the sample of blood retained by the defendant showed a mean reading of 80.5mg/100ml. The justices' dismissal of the case on the ground of the unreliability of the Lion Intoximeter was upheld; although the defendant's behaviour could not be relied on to show any inaccuracy of the Intoximeter the justices were entitled to hold, on the evidence before them, that the blood sample results were inconsistent with the Intoximeter reading. Although the blood/urine option experiment in respect of readings in excess of 50µg/100ml of breath, which led to the publication of the *Report on Breath Alcohol Measuring Instruments* referred to above and last discussed in the eighteenth edition, was discontinued in 1989, there would appear to be nothing to prevent the astute and not over-inebriated defendant from calling a doctor at his own expense to take samples from him for analysis with a view to adducing them, in the event of the results of the analysis being favourable to his cause, as evidence with which to challenge the evidential breath machine readings.

4.206

C   *Amount of alcohol consumed*

The cases of *Hughes v McConnell* [1985] R.T.R. 244 and *Price v Nicholls* [1985] Crim. L.R. 744 were both overruled by the unanimous decision of the House of Lords (Lord Keith of Kinkel, Lord Brandon of Oakbrook, Lord Griffiths, Lord Oliver of Aylmerton and Lord Goff of Chieveley) in *Cracknell v Willis* [1988] R.T.R. 1.

The Divisional Court in the overruled cases had been of the opinion that it was not open to a defendant to challenge the reliability of the Lion Intoximeter by adducing (oral) evidence of the amount of alcohol he had consumed (although in *Lucking v Forbes* above it had been accepted, not surprisingly, that the evidence of analysis of a blood sample voluntarily provided by the defendant would, in appropriate circumstances, be capable of mounting such a challenge). In reaching its view the Divisional Court had (in *Price v Nicholls*) drawn attention to the wording of what is now s.15(2) of the 1988 Offenders Act that "evidence of the proportion of alcohol ... in a specimen of breath ... provided by the accused shall, in all cases ..., be taken into account, and it shall be assumed that the

4.207

proportion of alcohol in the accused's breath ... at the time of the alleged offence was not less than in the specimen ...".

4.208 The House of Lords, however, did not consider that the statutory provisions pointed to only one type of evidence being admissible to challenge the reliability of a breath testing device. The assumption in what is now s.15(2) of the 1988 Offenders Act was not an assumption that the device was functioning correctly; it was an assumption that the proportion of alcohol in the relevant specimen was not less than the proportion of alcohol at the time of the offence. Before making that assumption justices would have to be satisfied, in the case of a blood or urine specimen, that they could rely on the analysis of the specimen, and they might have to choose between conflicting prosecution and defence analyses of portions of the same specimen. In the case of a breath specimen there was, of course, a presumption that the machine was working correctly; but if that presumption was challenged by relevant evidence, justices would have to be satisfied before making the assumption that the machine's reading was one on which they could rely. To paraphrase the words of Lord Griffiths, was a teetotal motorist to be convicted without the opportunity of calling two bishops with whom he had dined as witnesses to the fact that he had drunk nothing that evening and inviting the justices to infer that the machine must have been unreliable when it, to his astonishment, showed very high readings? If Parliament wished to provide that the presumption in favour of the machine's reliability was irrebuttable, or that it could only be challenged by a particular kind of evidence, then it had to take the responsibility of so deciding and spell out its intention in clear language. In the meantime, evidence was admissible which, if believed, led to a reasonable inference that the machine was unreliable.

Lord Griffiths expressed the hope that good sense on the part of justices and an awareness on the part of the motoring public that approved machines are proving reliable would combine to ensure that few defendants would seek to challenge a breath analysis by spurious evidence of their alcohol consumption. His optimism in this regard was not shared by Lord Goff, however, who referred to the well-known "industry" devoted to assisting motorists to defeat charges brought under what is now s.5 and implied that the court's decision would be likely to lead to renewed activity. It was to be expected that the responsible authorities would keep the situation under careful review in order to consider whether further strengthening legislation might be necessary in the public interest.

4.209 A motorist provided two specimens of breath for analysis by a Lion Intoximeter; the lower of the readings obtained recorded 46μg of alcohol. Before justices it was successfully contended on his behalf that the machine must not have been working properly as he had only drunk half a pint of lager. He worked at a nightclub (which would account for the smell of alcohol upon him) and was not allowed to drink while on duty. Remitting the case to the justices with a direction to convict, the Divisional Court in *DPP v Hill* (1992) 156 J.P. 197 distinguished *Cracknell v Willis* above and pointed out that while the statutory presumption that the proportion of alcohol in the accused's breath was not less than the specimen could be challenged, it was impossible on the facts of the case in point to come to the conclusion that the machine was not reliable.

DPP v Hill above was distinguished, and *Cracknell v Willis* above applied, by the Divisional Court in *DPP v Spurrier* [2000] R.T.R. 60. An acquittal by justices on the basis of the presumed unreliability of a Lion Intoximeter 3000, a conclusion on the facts which they had reached without the benefit of any expert evidence, was not overturned, although the court did say that the defendant's case "bumped up against the borderline" at which it became perverse for the inference of unreliability to be drawn in the absence of such evidence. The defendant's evidence was that she had taken no alcohol in the 12 hours prior to her arrest, but had prior to that consumed two cans of lager and a quarter of a bottle of whisky. The breath-alcohol reading revealed by her breath sample was 143µg/100ml. Although her breath smelt of alcohol, she was not unsteady on her feet and her eyes were not glazed.

Where a defendant challenged the accuracy of the Intoximeter analysis by as- **4.210** serting that he had only drunk a certain amount and that accordingly the reading should not have been what it was (see *Cracknell v Willis* above), it was open to the prosecution to rebut that by any relevant evidence. The result of the (presumably positive) roadside breath test was admissible for that purpose, but in considering the weight to be given to such evidence it should be remembered that the roadside device was not as accurate as the Lion Intoximeter. The Divisional Court so held in *Lafferty v DPP* [1995] Crim. L.R. 429 when dismissing an appeal against conviction of an offence of driving with excess alcohol. Leave to appeal to the House of Lords was refused.

D *Radio interference*

A warning was issued by the Home Office to police forces that the operation of **4.211** police radio equipment within a few inches of breath testing instruments (including those installed at police stations and used for evidential purposes) may adversely affect their operation. Forces are recommended to incorporate a warning to the effect in the pro forma used in police stations to record action taken in drink/driving cases (Home Office circular 39/1989).

Provision of blood or urine specimens

A person may only be required to provide specimens of blood or urine at a po- **4.212** lice station or a hospital (s.7(3)). But a person may be required to provide blood or urine at a police station instead of breath only if one of the five situations set out in s.7(3)(a), (b), (bb), (bc) or (c) exists (see § 4.109). If one of these situations exists, he may be required to provide blood or urine specimens notwithstanding that he "has already provided or been required to provide two specimens of breath" (s.7(3)).

Under s.7(4) only the police officer requiring a specimen of blood or urine decides whether to require the suspect to provide a specimen of blood or specimens of urine, and he is under no obligation to consult the accused. His discretion is virtually absolute; whether it shall be blood or urine "shall be decided … by the constable making the requirement". If, however, a medical practitioner or registered health care professional (whose opinion may be subject to overruling by a medical practitioner) is of the opinion that for medical reasons a specimen of blood cannot or should not be taken, the constable is then, and only then, restricted to requiring urine (s.7(4A)). Although the doctrine of "driver's preference" as to sample provision was firmly laid to rest by the House of Lords in *DPP v Warren* [1992] 4 All E.R. 865 (see further § 4.139), there remains a procedural requirement for the police officer to make reference to the possible alternative of giving urine (per Lord Bridge at 875a).

4.213   According to the High Court of Justiciary in *Simpson v McClory* 1993 S.L.T. 861 the reason why Lord Bridge referred in *DPP v Warren* above to the continuance of the procedural requirement for the police officer to make reference to the possible alternative of giving urine may well have been that the police in that case had used the Metropolitan Police pro forma which expressly referred to the two types of specimen and to the matter of choice between them (as indeed did the Tayside police pro forma used in *McLeod v MacFarlane* (1992) 10 W.R.T.L.B. 56 in which *Warren* was followed). In *Simpson's* case, however, the pro forma used by the Northern Constabulary made no reference to any possibility of the motorist supplying a specimen of urine, nor to the fact that the police made the choice between blood and urine. In dismissing the defendant's appeal against conviction the court held that there was no legal obligation upon a constable in a case where the specimen was mandatorily required under s.7(3) to tell a motorist that he was required to give a specimen of blood or urine but that the decision as to which was a matter for the constable; it was sufficient for the constable merely to state that he required the motorist to provide a specimen of (for argument's sake) blood. Given that he had no right to express any preference as to the type of specimen to be supplied, there did not appear to be any reason why the motorist should have to be told that he was required to give a specimen of blood or urine, but that the police would choose which specimen was to be given. In relation to the statutory option to provide a replacement specimen under s.8(2) (see §§ 4.134–8), the Lord Justice-Clerk (Lord Ross) contrasted (obiter) the need to inform the motorist of his right to claim that the specimen of breath should be replaced by a specimen of blood or urine (and that the constable would choose which) with the lack of any need (when the actual requirement to provide a specimen for analysis is made) to refer to the possible alternatives.

4.214   In practice, the officer under s.7(4) will almost invariably require blood. The standard police pro forma (as approved by the Association of Chief Police Officers) encourages him to do so and only suggests that he require urine when he is advised by a medical practitioner not to require blood. The reason for this may perhaps be that it is not uncommon for a person who has been required to provide specimens of urine to be unable to provide a second specimen of urine within one hour of requirement. It should also be noted that an invalid but unproductive request for a specimen of blood to be provided does not render evidence of a subsequent correctly taken specimen of urine inadmissible (*DPP v Garrett* [1995] R.T.R. 302). The defendant in that case had not been given an opportunity to object to the taking of a blood sample. In the event the attempt to obtain blood was abandoned on medical grounds, and a sample of urine was requested instead. The officer's right to change his mind as to the type of specimen he required continued until the defendant complied with the requirement in s.7(1).

Blood specimens

4.215   Section 15(4) of the 1988 Offenders Act provides that a specimen of blood will be disregarded unless either it was taken from the accused by a medical practitioner (or, with effect from April 1, 2003, by a registered health care professional) with his consent, or he has subsequently given permission for a sample taken from him by a medical practitioner without his consent under s.7A of the 1988 Act to be laboratory tested.

     Section 11(4) of that Act states that a person provides a specimen of blood if and only if he consents to it being taken wherever it is so taken by a medical practitioner, or in a police station by either a medical practitioner or a registered health care professional.

Under art.18(4) of the Road Traffic (Northern Ireland) Order 1995 (SI 1995/ **4.216** 2994), legislation based upon, and virtually identical to the equivalent English legislation (s.7(3) of the 1988 Act), a requirement to provide a specimen of blood or urine may only be made at a police station or a hospital. It was not necessary, however, according to the House of Lords in *Russell (RUC Superintendent) v Devine* [2004] UKHL 24; [2003] 1 W.L.R. 1187, for the specimen actually to be taken at a police station or a hospital. Attention was to be drawn to s.15(4) of the 1988 Offenders Act which stated in effect that a blood specimen might be taken by a doctor at a place other than a police station or a hospital. On the facts of the case in point the requirement for the taking of a specimen had been properly made at the police station and the fact that due to the doctor's commitments the specimen had had to be taken by the doctor at the health centre where he was alone on duty did not render inadmissible the certificate of analysis relating to that specimen.

Where a person accused of drink/driving had given a constable his consent to a sample of his blood being taken, it nevertheless required to be shown that he had also given his consent to the medical practitioner taking the sample at the time that that was done. The High Court of Justiciary, sitting as the Court of Criminal Appeal, so held in *Friel v Dickson* [1992] R.T.R. 366. The onus was upon the prosecution to establish, beyond reasonable doubt, that the defendant had given his consent to the taking of blood by the surgeon.

Under earlier legislation it was clear that if consent was obtained improperly **4.217** the defendant could not be said to consent and a conviction would be quashed. In *R. v Palfrey; R. v Sadler* [1970] 2 All E.R. 12 the Court of Appeal made it clear that if there was some real substance in the assertion that the specimen of blood or urine was improperly taken against the will of the defendant or without his true consent, it was for the defendant to raise the issue, and show that there was some substance in it, and the court then had a discretion to exclude the results. The court referred to *R. v Payne* [1963] 1 All E.R. 848 (a s.5 case) where the results of a medical examination were excluded after the defendant before consenting to a medical examination was told by the police surgeon that the results of the examination would not be given in evidence (see also § 4.07).

With the notable exception of samples taken under s.7A of the 1988 Act from persons incapable of consenting (see §§ 4.284 et seq.), a blood sample can only properly be taken with the true and unconditional consent of the defendant. But where the defendant so conducts himself that the medical practitioner reasonably believes that the defendant has not given unconditional consent to the taking of the sample, the court will not allow the defendant later to complain that the sample was not taken and that his statutory right under what is now s.8(2) was accordingly lost (*Rawlins v Brown* [1987] R.T.R. 238, where the magistrate found that the defendant had in practice given true and unconditional consent to the taking of the sample although the doctor had reasonable grounds to believe otherwise).

It is for the doctor or registered health care professional to say how the blood **4.218** specimen should be taken. The defendant cannot insist on the blood being taken from a particular part of his anatomy (*Solesbury v Pugh* [1969] 2 All E.R. 1171) nor can he insist on giving capillary blood instead of intravenous blood (*Rushton v Higgins* [1972] Crim. L.R. 440). Under previous legislation it was possible for the defence to establish the analysis to be incorrect because the sample of blood or urine was placed in a dirty or contaminated container, or a container not empty of material, or that a proper specimen was not taken. This is a matter of fact to be decided by the court. In *Rowlands v Harper* [1972] R.T.R. 469 a police sergeant contrary to instructions assembled the syringe needle and capsules for the taking of the blood specimen. The justices had doubts as to whether a true specimen was taken. Upholding the justices' decision, the Court of Appeal said that the true ratio decidendi is that the prosecution have to prove beyond reasonable doubt that the sample has been properly taken.

In *R. v Bolton Magistrates' Court Ex p. Scally* [1991] R.T.R. 84 the Divisional Court decided that it could grant certiorari to quash convictions of motorists who had pleaded guilty to driving with excess alcohol in their blood without being aware that the blood tests on which the prosecution relied had been taken using cleansing swabs impregnated with alcohol. Manchester police surgeons were provided with a standard kit including skin cleansing swabs, called medical cleansing towelettes, which contained no alcohol. In February 1987, however, the towelettes were replaced with Medi-prep swabs which were found in November 1988 to contain about the same alcohol concentration as beer. Although no dishonesty was involved, the process leading to conviction had been corrupted in a manner which was unfair and analogous to fraud, collusion or perjury.

4.219   Although the onus is on the prosecution if the defence have not required the presence of the analyst or medical practitioner, the burden of proof that it was properly taken is sufficiently discharged by the production of the certificates. Even where the doctor gives evidence, a court may infer the specimen was properly taken even where the evidence is very scanty. In *Braddock v Whittaker* [1970] Crim. L.R. 112 the defendant was held to be rightly convicted, even though the sample produced in court was not identified by the doctor and the cups into which the samples of blood taken from the specimen were placed contained crystals which the doctor assumed contained anti-coagulant crystals without any evidence as to what the crystals actually were.

Urine specimens

4.220   Section 9(5)(b) of the 1972 Act prior to its amendment by the Transport Act 1981 required the defendant to provide two specimens of urine within one hour of the request and s.9(6) ibid. provided that the first specimen was to be disregarded. Section 7(5) of the 1988 Act states that "a specimen of urine shall be provided within one hour of the requirement for its provision being made and after the provision of a previous specimen of urine".

It would appear in the light of the decision of the Divisional Court in *Nugent v Ridley* [1987] Crim. L.R. 641 that there is in fact a practical difference between the former s.9(5)(b) and (6) and what is now s.7(5). In that case a doctor requested a suspect to provide a specimen of urine in order to ascertain whether he could satisfactorily provide such a specimen. The test, as it were, was successful, and the defendant went on to provide two further specimens, the second of which on analysis indicated an alcohol level above the prescribed limit. The defendant's appeal against conviction of what is now a s.5(1) offence on the grounds that the specimen analysed was the third taken from him and accordingly had been taken otherwise than in accordance with the requirements of the statute was dismissed by the court. Provided that the analysed specimen was furnished after the provision of a previous specimen and within one hour of the initial request for a specimen of urine, what is now s.7(5) was complied with; the fact that it was the third (or even later) specimen taken was not relevant.

A suspect who had exercised his option under s.8(2) of the 1988 Act to supply a sample of blood or urine, his breath specimen having revealed an alcohol level of 50µg/100ml breath, was requested on medical grounds to provide a specimen of urine rather than blood, but was not given an opportunity to provide such a specimen until 30 minutes after the request had been made. His failure to provide a second specimen within the one-hour period from the time of the request as required by s.7(5) led to his prosecution for driving with alcohol in excess of the prescribed limit. It was successfully argued on his behalf in *Robertson v DPP* [2004] EWHC 517 that given the delay between the request for a urine sample and the first opportunity that he had had to supply one, he had not been permitted the prescribed period of one hour between the two required urine tests and accordingly was not in breach of s.7(5) such that the prosecution could rely on the earlier breath test.   **4.221**

Where the defendant supplies a specimen of urine the analyst is not required to make a further calculation to show what would be the equivalent blood-alcohol level: *McGarry v Chief Constable of Bedfordshire* [1983] R.T.R. 172.

Although the previous and present statutory provisions lay down that the requirement to provide a second specimen is to be made within one hour, in two cases on the former provisions it was held that analyses of second specimens obtained more than one hour after the first were admissible (*Roney v Matthew* [1975] R.T.R. 273; *Standen v Robertson* [1975] R.T.R. 329). A similar conclusion was reached under the current provisions in *DPP v Baldwin* [2000] R.T.R. 314 where it was again held that a specimen of urine which was not provided by a motorist within one hour of a request, contrary to s.7(5) of the 1988 Act, was nevertheless admissible in evidence on a charge of driving with excess alcohol. The only purpose of s.7(5) was to make finite the length of time in which a driver was required to provide a sample, and if he did not provide it within that time, he could be charged under s.7(6) with failing to provide a specimen. A police officer was not obliged to extend that time, but if he did, the sample analysis would not thereby be rendered inadmissible.   **4.222**

Unlike blood specimens, specimens of urine are not required to be taken by a medical practitioner. They are usually taken by the police officer who made the initial requirement, but the statutory provisions are silent as to who may take them. Occasionally the specimens may be taken by the police surgeon if he is present. Where the person is a woman the specimen will be taken either by the police surgeon or by a woman police officer.

There is nothing in the previous or present statutory provisions requiring the person giving specimens to empty his bladder when giving the first specimen nor do the provisions require the first or second specimen to be of any particular quantity. A conviction was upheld in *R. v Radcliffe* [1977] R.T.R. 99 even though the defendant on the doctor's advice may not have fully emptied his bladder when giving the first specimen. Similarly where a defendant had of his own free will given a second specimen one minute after the first, a conviction was directed   **4.223** as it was clear that two distinct specimens had been given (*Over v Musker* [1985] R.T.R. 84). But where a station officer initially took a specimen of the defendant's urine, told him to stop and then to "continue urinating" the whole process taking no more than two minutes, justices were upheld in finding that the urine obtained was all one specimen and that the analysis was therefore inadmissible (*Prosser v Dickeson* [1982] R.T.R. 96).

Evidence has to be given to prove that the correct specimen of urine was sent for analysis. If there is any doubt raised as to whether the analyst's certificate relates to the correct specimen, it is submitted that it is for the prosecution to prove that it was. See *Dickson v Atkins* [1972] R.T.R. 209 and *R. v Orrell* [1972] R.T.R. 14.

4.224   As in the case of a blood sample (see *Rowlands v Harper*, § 4.218 and *R. v Bolton Magistrates' Court Ex p. Scally*, § 4.218), analysis of a urine sample may be successfully challenged if it is shown that the specimen as analysed may have been contaminated. Where an analyst stated that a urine sample was found to be contaminated by micro-organisms capable of producing alcohol but that it was unlikely that the organisms present would have significantly contributed to the alcohol in the specimen unless the defendant suffered from diabetes, it was held that in the absence of any evidence as to whether or not the defendant had diabetes, the court could not be satisfied so that they could be sure of the defendant's guilt (*Collins v Lucking* [1983] R.T.R. 312).

Results of laboratory analysis

4.225   A defendant may properly challenge the accuracy of the analysis of blood or urine by giving evidence of the analysis of his sample and challenging the accuracy of the sample analysed by the forensic laboratory. In *R. v Kershberg* [1976] R.T.R. 526 the Court of Appeal quashed a conviction because of a lingering doubt as to the correctness of official analysis (official analysis of urine 108mg, defendant's sample's analysis 70mg—defendant gave a negative breath test after supplying specimen of urine). The analysis must "exceed" the prescribed limit (s.5(1)).

Earlier legislation required the alcohol in the defendant's blood to be ascertained from the laboratory test and from no other source. A high blood-alcohol level could therefore be proved by no other method. Under the present law a certificate of analysis is no longer a sine qua non to a successful prosecution under s.5. Oral evidence of the lower breath reading on the visual display of the Lion Intoximeter can be sufficient (see § 4.193).

4.226   It was held under previous legislation that there was no requirement for the prosecution to prove beyond doubt a particular figure as to the blood or urine-alcohol level, only that the level exceeded the prescribed limit (*R. v Coomaraswamy* [1976] R.T.R. 21; dicta to different effect in *R. v Boswell* [1974] R.T.R. 273 were not followed). *R. v Coomaraswamy* was followed in *Gordon v Thorpe* [1986] Crim. L.R. 61 where it was held that the same principles apply to the present law and all that the prosecution must prove is that the relevant limit was in fact exceeded.

If there is a dispute between the prosecution's and defendant's analysts, the court is entitled to prefer the prosecution's analyst in the same way as it is entitled to accept or reject any other evidence. The court is entitled to act on the opinion of one expert in preference to another; so long as it is satisfied beyond reasonable doubt that the expert it relies on is right, it does not have to explain the difference between the two opinions (*R. v Elliott* [1976] R.T.R. 308; *R. v Sodo* [1975] R.T.R. 357; *R. v Marr* [1977] R.T.R. 168). In *Walker v Hodgins* [1983] Crim. L.R. 555 the police analyst had followed the usual practice of deducting 6mg for a margin of error while the defendant's analyst had not. The police analyst then gave a figure of 96 and the defendant's analyst 83. The justices were upheld in acquitting the defendant; it was held that they were entitled to have regard to the normal laboratory practice of deducting 6mg, and had acted perfectly properly in deciding that they could not be satisfied beyond reasonable doubt that the defendant's blood-alcohol content exceeded the limit when the defence analyst had acted in good faith and used unimpeachable methods.

Although it is customary to deduct 6mg of alcohol in the blood-alcohol level to allow for a margin of error in analysis, there was no requirement further to round down anything less than a whole milligram of blood-alcohol content in the results of that analysis when given in evidence (*Oswald v DPP* [1989] R.T.R. 360). Where a laboratory split a sample of blood into a number of sub-samples for analysis, it was lawful to use the average result and not necessary to use the lowest result (*DPP v Welsh* (1997) 161 J.P. 57).   **4.227**

Where two types of laboratory testing had been used to determine the proportion of alcohol in a blood specimen and the results obtained thereby differed, magistrates were entitled to prefer one set of results to the other on grounds of the reliability of the respective methods employed (*Stephenson v Clift* [1988] R.T.R. 171). The justices had decided that the prosecution tests using the gas chromatography method were more accurate than those obtained by the defence using the ICMA system. The question was wholly one of fact (per McNeill J.).

A 4ml blood sample was evenly divided by the police surgeon into two vials, each with a maximum capacity of 6ml. Faced with unchallenged expert evidence to the effect that with less blood in the vial than its maximum capacity there would be too much fluoride preservative present for an equilibrium to occur when the blood was heated, which would cause the analytical result to show a blood-alcohol level that was too high by some 8 per cent, the Crown Court had fallen into error in excluding that evidence on the basis that it was purely theoretical; it was in fact based upon incontrovertible facts and was accordingly admissible opinion evidence which seriously called into question the reliability and accuracy of the blood-alcohol analysis (*Gregory v DPP* [2002] EWHC 385; (2002) 166 J.P. 400).   **4.228**

Absent any evidence to the contrary, a court would be entitled to assume that the procedures laid down for the preservation of blood samples for analysis had been correctly carried out (*Carter v DPP* [2006] EWHC 3328; [2007] R.T.R. 22, applying *Dhaliwal v DPP* [2006] EWHC 1149).

Supply of specimen of blood or urine to the defendant

While the accused has to be given a part of the specimen of blood or urine *if he asks for it* there is neither any obligation on the part of the constable to remind him when requesting a specimen of blood or urine that he is entitled to a sample, nor does that sample have to be offered to him in a "suitable container". Defendants have to rely on the standard police pro forma being followed. If the words of the statute are strictly followed the defendant cannot escape conviction on the ground that he was not reminded that he could ask to be supplied with a   **4.229** sample, nor can he argue that he was not supplied with a suitable container to contain his sample of blood or urine. However, in *Anderton v Lythgoe* [1985] R.T.R. 395 it was held by the Divisional Court that a driver is entitled to be told of his statutory option to provide blood or urine where his lower breath specimen is no more than 50μg, and where the police omitted so to inform him it was held that a court has a discretion to exclude evidence of the printout. By analogy, if the High Court are prepared to follow the reasoning of *Anderton*, it may be that the High Court may hold that there is a similar discretion to exclude the analysis of the blood or urine sample where the defendant is not told of his right to have a sample of his own for independent analysis, particularly if the official analysis is only just above the prescribed limit. It would appear from the decision of Pitchford J. sitting as an Administrative Court of the Queen's Bench Division in *Campbell v DPP* [2003] EWHC 559 that such a discretion may well exist in circumstances where a defendant wished to challenge the admissibility of a sample and had suffered prejudice as a result of a failure to tell him of his right to part of the specimen. There was, however, no statutory or common law right for an accused to be informed of his right to part of such a specimen.

4.230   The specimen of blood is required to be divided into two parts at the time it was provided, and the part not sent to the police laboratory supplied to the accused (1988 Offenders Act s.15(5)). Where a specimen of blood has been taken from the accused without his consent under s.7A of the 1988 Act (see further §§ 4.284 et seq.), the specimen is also required to be divided into two parts at the time it was taken, and any request to be supplied with the other part which was made by the accused when he gave his permission for a laboratory test must be complied with (1988 Offenders Act s.15(5A)). The requirement that the sample be divided "at the time" meant, in the view of the Divisional Court in *DPP v Elstob* [1992] R.T.R. 45, that the division had to be closely linked in time and to be part of the same event; that was a question of fact and degree. After a sample of blood had been provided, the doctor had left the room and divided the specimen out of the view of the defendant. He was apparently absent for about two minutes. On those facts the justices had been wrong to decide that as division of the sample had not taken place "at the time", the requirements of s.15(5)(a) of the 1988 Offenders Act had not been fulfilled. Desirable though it was that the division should take place in the presence of the accused, if Parliament had deemed his presence to be essential it would doubtless have said so in so many words. Where a police officer advised the defendant that a part specimen of blood handed to her was not suitable for analysis because it had not been placed in a signed, sealed envelope, her subsequent conviction based on the laboratory analysis of the other part of that specimen was quashed by the Divisional Court (*Perry v McGovern* [1986] R.T.R. 240). Where, however, the wrong name had been written on the container label and an analyst declined on that basis to analyse the sample, *Perry v McGovern* did not apply since the sample was nonetheless capable of analysis and had been supplied for the purposes of s.15(5) of the 1988 Offenders Act (*Butler v DPP* [1990] R.T.R. 377). It is no longer possible for two specimens of blood to be taken from the accused, one specimen being analysed by the laboratory and the other specimen supplied to the accused for analysis by him.

4.231   *Perry v McGovern* and *Butler v DPP* above were both considered by the Divisional Court in *DPP v Snook* [1993] Crim. L.R. 883 when upholding the prosecutor's appeal against dismissal of an information charging an excess alcohol offence and remitting the case for retrial. The facts were that the defendant's blood specimen was divided in two and he was given a sealed container containing his blood. He was also given a brown envelope. The usual practice of placing the container in the envelope was not followed. In the course of a telephone conversation with an analyst the defendant was given to understand that because the phial had not been supplied sealed in the envelope the result of any analysis would be of little value in court proceedings.

In the court's view the statutory requirement in s.15(1)(a) of the 1988 Offenders Act was quite straightforward. The supply of the divided sample in an envelope was but a gloss on the basic procedure and not any part of the statutory requirement. The defendant was unable to rely on *Perry v McGovern* because whereas in that case the defendant had been misled by the prosecutor into thinking that she did not have a specimen capable of being submitted for independent analysis, in the instant case what the analyst may have told the defendant was nothing to do with the prosecution or the police. It might well be, however, that when the matter was remitted to the justices the defendant could argue under s.78 of the Police and Criminal Evidence Act 1984 that it would be unfair for the prosecution sample to be used in evidence where the defence has been frustrated through no fault of its own in its attempt to secure its own analysis (see also §§ 4.07 *et seq.*).

Following a failed breath test, a blood specimen was taken and divided into **4.232** two samples. The defendant was asked which of the two samples she wanted. She pointed to one of the samples, but never physically took hold of it. Both were sealed and placed in a refrigerator in the presence of the defendant. She did not ask to take the sample with her when she left the police station. It was argued on her behalf in *Jones (Elaine) v CPS* [2003] EWHC 1729; (2003) 167 J.P. 481 that her pointing to the sample was an implied request for it to be supplied to her, and that as thereafter there was no such supply, the evidence of analysis was inadmissible against her. The Divisional Court held that on these facts the defendant had not "asked" to be provided with part of the sample. But even if she had, the combined effect of the offer of one of two samples and of the defendant pointing to a sample specimen amounted to a tendering of the sample to her. If she did not immediately take up the offer and take hold of her chosen specimen, or take it with her when she left the police station, or return shortly afterwards to collect it, she could not later be heard to say that it was not supplied to her (applying *Walton v Rimmer* [1986] R.T.R. 31 discussed at § 4.235 below).

It should be noted that if s.15(5) or (5A) (as appropriate) of the 1988 Offenders Act is not strictly complied with, the certificate is not admissible and a prosecution under s.5 of the 1988 Act will fail unless the prosecution can by other means show that the defendant's alcohol level was above the prescribed limit. Thus, e.g., where the portion of the specimen of blood supplied to the defendant had been mixed with a portion, admittedly minimal, of blood taken from the defendant some time earlier, the portion of blood retained by the police, and its analysis, were inadmissible against the defendant (*Dear v DPP* [1988] Crim. L.R. 316).

It should be noted also that a certificate of analysis is also not admissible if the charge is one under s.4 of the 1988 Act, and s.15(5) or (5A) (as appropriate) of the 1988 Offenders Act has not been complied with. As the section states that the certificate is not admissible, it would seem that the court has no discretion and must exclude it, save that a defendant if properly advised may presumably waive the benefit of the subsection where it has been complied with and agree to evidence of the analysis being given.

4.233   Where the defendant intends to argue that s.15(5) (or (5A), presumably) of the 1988 Offenders Act has not been properly complied with, objection must be taken during the prosecution case to the admissibility of the prosecution's analysis (*Hudson v Hornsby* [1973] R.T.R. 4).

Section 15(5) applies where the defendant asked for the sample at the time of the provision of the specimen, but not where he asks for it afterwards. Whether he has been supplied with it is a question of fact (*R. v Jones (Colin)* [1974] R.T.R. 117). While it is a wise and proper practice to supply the part of the specimen to the accused before he leaves the police station, it need not necessarily be supplied to him before he does leave, so long as it is supplied within a reasonable time; the court should review all the circumstances, including the reason why the police did not give it to him before he left (e.g. he was too drunk to accept it) and the question whether he was prejudiced by the failure to get it when he left and whether the time when he did get it was within a reasonable time (*R. v Sharp* [1968] 3 All E.R. 182).

4.234   There have been a large number of cases on whether, in accordance with earlier legislation, the part of the specimen given to the defendant is adequate. The cases may be summarised as follows:

(1) Each part of the specimen including the part given to the defendant must be of a quality and quantity to be capable of analysis by the use of ordinary equipment and ordinary skill by a reasonably competent analyst (*Smith v Cole* [1971] 1 All E.R. 200; *Nugent v Hobday* [1972] Crim. L.R. 569).

(2) The part when handed to the defendant must also be capable of remaining suitable for analysis within a reasonable time (*Thompson v Charlwood* (1969) 113 S.J. 1004; *Ward v Keene* [1970] R.T.R. 177; *R. v Wright (John)* [1975] R.T.R. 193).

(3) The adequacy of the sample is a question of fact, not law, and must be decided by the court on the evidence presented to it. The burden of proof of the adequacy of the sample is on the prosecution, although the fact that the prosecution's sample which was chosen at random was capable of analysis was evidence, but not conclusive evidence, that the defendant's was also capable of analysis (*Crankshaw v Rydeheard* (1969) 113 S.J. 673; *Ward v Keene* and *Smith v Cole* above, *Kierman v Willcock* [1972] R.T.R. 270).

Defendants anxious to obtain an analysis of the part specimen can obtain advice as to how to keep the sample, and where and to whom it should be sent for analysis, from the Royal Society of Chemistry, Burlington House, Piccadilly, London W1J 0BA (telephone 020 7437 8656, website *http://www.rsc.org/* [Accessed March 20, 2009]).

Certificates of analysis and printouts, etc.

4.235   Evidence of the proportion of alcohol or a drug in a specimen of breath, blood or urine and that a specimen of blood was taken from the accused with his consent by a medical practitioner can be proved in proceedings for offences under ss.4 and 5 by the production in court of the following documents:

(1) a statement as to analysis of breath automatically produced by an approved evidential breath testing device with the certificate signed by the constable that the statement relates to a specimen provided by the accused at the date and time shown in the statement; and

(2) a certificate signed by an authorised analyst as to the proportion of alcohol or any drug found in a specimen of blood or urine identified in the certificate; and

(3) a certificate purporting to certify that a specimen of blood was taken from the accused with his consent by a medical practitioner purporting to be signed by a medical practitioner.

In a case involving alleged driving with excess alcohol, blood sample analysis **4.236** evidence by an analyst who was not an "authorised analyst" within the meaning of the Road Traffic Offenders Act 1988 s.16(7), which had been submitted by way of a witness statement and served pursuant to the Criminal Justice Act 1967 s.9, was admissible: *R. (on the application of Crown Prosecution Service) v Sedgemoor JJ.* [2007] EWHC 1803; [2007] All E.R. (D.) 24.

By virtue of s.16(3)(a), (b), (4) of the 1988 Offenders Act a statement as to breath analysis produced by the approved device with the accompanying certificate signed by the constable can *only* be produced if a copy of it either was handed to the accused when the document was produced by the machine, or was served on him not later than seven days before the hearing. If not served not later than seven days before the hearing the copy must be handed to the motorist. It is not sufficient to place copies on the counter of the station with no indication that one was for him to take away (*Walton v Rimmer* [1986] R.T.R. 31), but the Act could not be construed so that a defendant could render the copy inadmissible by refusing to take the document handed to him (ibid.). In this context "handed" can be regarded as "tendered", there being no obligation upon the defendant to keep the printout.

Walton v Rimmer above was applied, and the commentary upon it therein expressly approved, by the Divisional Court in *McCormack v DPP* [2002] EWHC 173; [2002] R.T.R. 20. A driver who had provided specimens of breath for analysis was offered a copy of the printout and advised to take it, but refused to do so. The court held that s.16(3)(a) of the Road Traffic Offenders Act 1988 had been duly complied with by the offer to the driver of a copy of the printout, even in the absence of the physical transfer of possession of a copy to him. The court was referred to a contrary decision on the same point made north of the border in *McDerment v O'Brien* 1985 S.L.T. 485 in which "handed to" was interpreted as meaning more than "tendered", but preferred the interpretation advanced in *Walton v Rimmer*, albeit that that would result in the words of the statute being construed differentially on either side of Hadrian's Wall.

The printout is in fact one document (although s.16(1) of the 1988 Offenders **4.237** Act envisages that it might consist of two documents) and consists of a "statement automatically produced by the device by which the proportion of alcohol in a specimen of breath was measured" (s.16(1)) and "a certificate signed by a constable ... that the statement relates to a specimen provided by the accused at the date and time shown in the statement" (also s.16(1)).

Where a defendant pleads guilty to driving with excess alcohol, there is no duty upon the prosecution to produce to the court the original Intoximeter printout; the best evidence of the defendant's guilt is his guilty plea. The

Divisional Court so held in *R. v Tower Bridge Metropolitan Stipendiary Magistrate Ex p. DPP* [1988] R.T.R. 193. It had apparently become the practice of the magistrates' court in question to ask to see the original document in order to check that the calibration and readings were correct. This procedure had its good qualities, particularly where a defendant was unrepresented, but as a matter of law it was unnecessary for either the original printout or a copy thereof to be produced. Accordingly where a stipendiary magistrate (before whom the prosecution had been unable to produce the original printout on a guilty plea) ordered a change of plea, refused a further adjournment and dismissed the charge, the court's discretion had been improperly exercised.

4.238   By way of contrast, the Divisional Court held in *Hasler v DPP* [1989] R.T.R. 148 that a failure by the prosecution to produce an Intoximeter printout which had been available in court was a failure to adduce evidence, and accordingly a conviction for driving with excess alcohol fell to be quashed. Although no mention of the defendant's plea appears in the report, it is to be hoped that it would be safe to assume that it was one of "not guilty".

In *Chief Constable of Surrey v Wickens* [1985] R.T.R. 277, the constable signed the original certificate but had served an unsigned copy on the defendant. It was held that an unsigned copy was a copy for the purposes of what is now s.16(3) of the 1988 Offenders Act and that if the legislature had intended the copy as well as the original to be signed it would have said so. There was no question in the present case of the defendant's interests having been prejudiced. Section 16(1) of the 1988 Offenders Act envisages that the certificate signed by the constable will either be a certificate separate from the printout or "statement automatically" produced by the approved device or on the printout itself. As will be seen from Appendix 1 the approved devices automatically provide on the printout itself such a certificate to be signed by the police officer. Section 16(3) only requires the statement and certificate to be handed to the accused at the time the document was produced. In *Beck v Scammell* [1985] Crim. L.R. 794 the police officer altered the time on the copy printout handed to the defendant from 03.52 to 04.52 and added to the police copy "British Summer Time and not GMT". The lines of deletion were not identical on each printout. The justices dismissed the case on the ground that the document was not an automatically produced statement within the meaning of what is now s.16(1) of the 1988 Offenders Act and, because of the amendments, was not a "copy" within the meaning of s.16(3) ibid. It was held that the document was not altered in a material respect and remained a statement automatically produced for the purposes of s.16(1) of the 1988 Offenders Act and was a "copy" for the purposes of s.16(3) ibid.

There is no requirement that the accused sign the printout nor is there any requirement that the accused need accept it when handed to him. The standard police pro forma advises that the additional printout be attached with the others in the space provided in the pro forma, and a note made as to whether the accused accepted or refused to accept the printout when handed to him.

4.239   The prosecution must normally rely on the printout itself for evidence as to the measurement of the breath specimens provided by the motorist. It is inadmissible for the constable to give oral evidence of the defendant's breath specimens only because the printout also gives the result of the self-calibration checks which are vital to establishing the reliability of the device (*Owen v Chesters* [1985] Crim. L.R. 156 and see *Morgan v Lee* [1985] R.T.R. 409, at § 4.119).

In *Gaimster v Marlow* [1984] R.T.R. 49 justices refused to admit in evidence the printout produced by a Lion Intoximeter, on the ground that the test record produced by the machine was unintelligible. The justices further held that they should refuse to allow the police operating the machine to explain its meaning. It was unanimously held by the Divisional Court presided over by the Lord Chief Justice that the whole of the document including the certificate signed by the constable was admissible and that the document which contained both the statement and the certificate should be construed as a whole. The test record was such a statement and if it was unintelligible, which their Lordships doubted, it could be explained by the police officer provided the police officer is shown to be a trained operator of the machine.

The offence in *Gaimster v Marlow* was an offence contrary to what is now **4.240** s.5(1) of the 1988 Act. Sections 15 and 16 of the 1988 Offenders Act apply to proceedings for offences contrary to ss.4 and 5 (1988 Offenders Act s.15(1)). Where a defendant is charged with an offence under s.7(6) of the 1988 Act of refusing without reasonable excuse to supply specimens for analysis, s.15 of the 1988 Offenders Act cannot be relied on as authority for the production of the printout. In *Castle v Cross* [1985] R.T.R. 62, justices refused to admit the printout in evidence in proceedings for an offence under what is now s.7(6) on the ground that the printout was a statement made by a machine akin to a computer, that the Lion Intoximeter contributed to its own knowledge and that the printout was therefore inadmissible. Reversing the justices, the Divisional Court held that the printout was admissible. An Intoximeter was a tool, albeit sophisticated, operated by a police officer trained in its use. The printout was a product of the machine and fell into the category of real evidence as the recordings did in *The Statue of Liberty* [1968] 1 W.L.R. 739. It should be observed that the Divisional Court in *Castle v Cross* specifically observed that there was no challenge in the particular case to the efficiency of the machine and no finding that it was defective. It would appear, therefore, that it is still open to the defence in an appropriate case to challenge the admissibility of the printout on the ground that the machine did not work or did not work properly or was unreliable.

The omission of the police officer's signature from the printout of an approved device does not affect its admissibility and nothing in what is now s.16(1) of the 1988 Offenders Act prevents a police officer from giving oral evidence of the results of the breath tests. The purpose and effect of that section was to permit a printout to be tendered without the necessity of anyone being called to prove it. The Divisional Court so held in *Garner v DPP* [1989] Crim. L.R. 583. The printout was real evidence and as such was admissible at common law (following *Castle v Cross* above).

Section 16(3) of the 1988 Offenders Act provides that the other certificates (i.e. **4.241** certificate of analysis or the taking of blood specimens by a medical practitioner) may only be produced in court in evidence if they have been served on the accused "not later than seven days before" the hearing. That this requirement is mandatory and not subject to waiver was confirmed by the Divisional Court in *Tobi v Nicholas* [1988] R.T.R. 343 when allowing an appeal by Mr Tobi against conviction by a stipendiary magistrate of offences under what are now ss.4 and 5 of the 1988 Act. The defendant had not been served with a copy of the doctor's certificate. If not "handed" to the defendant at the time s.16(3) provides that the printout and certificate signed by the constable may also be admissible if it is served on the accused "not later than seven days before the hearing". "Not later than seven days before" seems to mean seven clear days between the date of service and the date of hearing.

Tobi v Nicholas discussed above was distinguished as to its facts by the Divisional Court in *Louis v DPP* [1998] R.T.R. 354. Where the prosecution in a case of driving with excess alcohol complied with the statutory requirement for service of a doctor's certificate of analysis of a blood specimen within seven days, the defendant's waiver of strict proof of service could not render the document inadmissible. It was of course accepted in accordance with *Tobi v Nicholas* that the requirement as to service of the document under s.16(3) of the Road Traffic Offenders Act 1988 was statutory and could not be waived. In the case in point it was discovered that there was no signature on the certificate of service. No submission was made, however, that the analyst's certificate was not admissible for failure to comply with s.16. The stipendiary magistrate was not dealing with whether there had been service, but whether a certificate of service had been signed. All that was in issue was the certificate of service and not service itself. The defendant had waived the requirement of strict proof of service and the document was duly admitted.

4.242   If the defendant is legally represented not only is service of the certificate, etc., on the solicitor most convenient, but it is legally untenable to hold that the document has not been properly served under s.16(3) of the 1988 Offenders Act because it has been served on the solicitor instead of the defendant personally: *Anderton v Kinnard* [1986] R.T.R. 11. The copies may be served personally or sent by registered post or recorded delivery (1988 Offenders Act s.16(6)). Proof of proper service of the document either in person or by post may be proved by production of a certificate purporting to be signed by the person who posted to or served the certificate or document on the accused (Criminal Procedure Rules 2005 r.4.11). In this regard a certificate of service by an acceptable method of delivery and within the required time under what is now s.16(6) of the 1988 Offenders Act by the person dispatching the document will satisfy the requirements of that rule (*Hawkins v DPP* [1988] R.T.R. 380).

Section 7 of the Interpretation Act 1978 provides that service will be deemed to have been effected when it would have arrived in the normal course of post.

The accused can secure the attendance at court of the person who signed any of the documents (i.e. the police officer who signed the certificate relating to the printout, the medical practitioner or the authorised analyst) if the accused has served the prosecutor personally by registered post or recorded delivery a notice to that effect "not later than three days before the hearing or within such further time as the court may in special circumstances allow" (1988 Offenders Act s.16(4)).

4.243   The effect of the service of a notice by the defendant is to require the attendance at court of the police officer who signed the certificate. The notice renders the "certificate" inadmissible (so that the police officer has to give evidence that the "statement" relates to the defendant at the date and time shown in the statement), but it does not render the "statement" itself inadmissible. Accordingly where justices had decided otherwise they were held to be wrong (*Temple v Botha* [1985] Crim. L.R. 517).

In *Anderton v Kinnard* [1986] R.T.R. 11 the defendant gave breath specimens the lower of which was 50µg/100ml and then exercised his option to give blood;

the police did not serve the resulting medical practitioner's and analyst's certificates on the defendant as required by what is now s.16(3) of the 1988 Offenders Act. His solicitors then requested copies of them from the police, and on receiving them the solicitors replied that they did not wish their attendance for cross-examination. The case was dismissed by the justices because the certificates had not been served in accordance with what is now s.16(3). Allowing the prosecutor's appeal, the Divisional Court held that notwithstanding the reference to personal service in s.16(3), service on an authorised agent of the defendant in the circumstances in which the solicitors had waived the attendance of the witnesses was good service for the purpose of s.16(3). Service may even be effected in certain circumstances on counsel on behalf of the defendant, but counsel always has the right to decline to accept service (*Penman v Parker* [1986] R.T.R. 403, where counsel who had conduct of the case and had accepted service in the absence of the defendant and his solicitor was held to have been validly served on behalf of his lay client).

It would seem that if the prosecution has not complied with the requirements **4.244** of s.16(3) of the 1988 Offenders Act they are entitled to call the person in question as a witness in court whether that person be the registered medical practitioner, the authorised analyst, or the police officer who certified the printout (as to oral evidence of the approved device see *Owen v Chesters* above, *Morgan v Lee* at § 4.119 and *Oldfield v Anderton* at § 4.186).

There have been a number of cases on the previous legislation (which corresponds to the present s.16(1) of the 1988 Offenders Act) as to whether or not a certificate of analysis can be proved to relate to the actual specimen of blood or urine taken from the accused. It should be noted that both in the previous legislation and the present s.16(1) the specimen of blood or urine may be identified in the certificate. It is submitted that in practice the production of the certificate bearing on it the name of the accused, and the labelling of the specimen container of the sample of blood or urine with the time, date and place as to when and by whom the specimen was taken, is usually sufficient for a court to infer that the analysis is of the specimen taken from the accused. That submission received judicial support in *Khatibi v DPP* [2004] EWHC 83; (2004) 168 J.P. 361. It had been reasonable to infer that the label bearing the defendant's name had been created contemporaneously with the taking of the sample, that it had been created by a police officer in the course of his work and that the information contained in the label had therefore been supplied by a person who had had personal knowledge of the matters dealt with. The magistrates had been entitled to conclude on the evidence of the police officer, the medical examiner, the defendant herself and the details on the label, that there was evidence upon which they could have found that the blood analysed by the forensic scientist was that of the defendant.

It should also be noted that the police officer at the station is usually required to **4.245** give corresponding evidence of the labelling of the specimen after referring to the standard police pro forma (Form MG DD/B). Difficulties can arise where there are typographical errors either on the certificate or in the labelling of the specimen. It is submitted that, as in *Dickson v Atkins* [1972] R.T.R. 209, what it is necessary for the prosecution to prove is:

(a) that the specimen taken from the accused was sent to the analyst; and

(b) that the analyst's certificate refers to that specimen.

If the prosecution can satisfy the court on (a) and (b) above, it matters not that the certificate or label show typographical errors (ibid.). Similarly in *R. v Orrell* [1972] R.T.R. 14 it was held by the Court of Appeal that it was sufficient for the prosecution to prove by written markings on the sample bottle of urine that the sample of urine taken from the defendant was that received by the laboratory and analysed by the analyst. In *Tremlett v Fawcett* (1984) 1 R.T.L.B. 68 it was held that there was no need for the prosecution to prove specifically that a sample of urine had been sent from the police to the laboratory for analysis. In that case the sample had been marked and placed in an envelope signed across the seal by the police officer with the envelope bearing the name of the defendant. The analyst had certified that he had received the specimen in a sealed container.

4.246   A sample of blood was taken from a defendant at the police station by a doctor. The police sergeant completed self-adhesive labels with the defendant's name, the force, division, station, time, and the name of the officer in the case. The doctor signed the labels and they were affixed to two sample bottles of the defendant's blood, one for retention by the police, and one for the defendant. The police sample was placed in a sealed bag. According to the police pro forma the sergeant wrote his own initials on the bag, but in evidence the sergeant said he had written the initials "JVR" on the bag. The statement of another officer which was admitted in evidence revealed that that other officer had removed a bag marked "JVR 1" from the refrigerator the following morning and sent it by recorded delivery to the forensic science laboratory. There was also evidence from the forensic scientist that he had received by recorded delivery a sample attributed to the defendant bearing the same receipt number as that sent by the officer. The defendant's appeal against conviction for driving with excess blood alcohol on the basis that there was insufficient evidence that the samples were the same, having regard to the discrepancies in the evidence as to the initials marked on the bag, was firmly dismissed by the Divisional Court in *Gregson v DPP* [1993] Crim. L.R. 884. There was overwhelming evidence that the sample examined by the forensic scientist was the sample taken from the defendant. The court added that unmeritorious points of this kind should not be taken.

Analyses of blood or urine specimens are required to be made by an "authorised analyst". The term "authorised analyst" is defined in s.16(7) of the 1988 Offenders Act as persons possessing the qualifications prescribed by regulations made under the Food Safety Act 1990 for appointment as public analysts together with any other person authorised by the Home Secretary to make analyses for the purposes of s.16. Such latter authority has been given by the Home Secretary to various named persons at the police forensic laboratories. It was held in *R. v Rutter* [1977] R.T.R. 105 that although the certificate has to be given by the analyst, there is nothing in the section which requires the analysis to be made by the analyst himself; it suffices if the analysis was carried out under his control and supervision.

4.247   Section 15(2), (3) of the 1988 Offenders Act provides that a defendant can rebut the assumption as to the level of alcohol in his blood, breath or urine as evidenced by the specimen provided by him if he proves that he consumed alcohol after he had ceased to drive, attempt to drive or be in charge and before he provided the specimen. This is dealt with and discussed in § 4.300. The defendant is also entitled, if he asks for it, to a sample of any specimen of blood or urine provided by him. This has been dealt with in § 4.229, above.

Warning of prosecution

Section 7(7) of the 1988 Act places a duty upon the constable when requiring a   **4.248**
specimen of breath, blood or urine under s.7 to warn the defendant that failure to
provide it may render him liable to prosecution.

That the requirement to administer a warning under what is now s.7(7) is
mandatory, not directory, so far as offences of failing to provide a specimen for
analysis contrary to what is now s.7(6) are concerned was made plain by the
Divisional Court in the case of *Simpson v Spalding* [1987] R.T.R. 221. Possibly
the fact that the defendant was a police officer might have led the investigating
officer to omit the statutory warning of the penal consequences of failure to
provide a specimen; in any event his neglect of the requirements of (what is now)
s.7(7) was, by a logical extension of the principle in *Howard v Hallett* [1984]
R.T.R. 353, fatal to the prosecution and the defendant ought to have been
acquitted. In delivering judgment, Ralph Gibson L.J. remarked obiter that on the
facts found, the fact that the appellant was a police officer did not serve to imply
that he was conversant with the excess alcohol procedure.

The position with regard to the effect of failure to give a warning upon offences   **4.249**
under what is now s.5 of the 1988 Act where the defendant, despite the absence
of such a warning, actually provides specimens, is now clear as a result of the decision of the Divisional Court in *Murray v DPP* [1993] R.T.R. 209, a case in
which the statutory warning was not given. Watkins L.J., who gave the judgment
of the court, said that the effect of the decision in *Howard v Hallett* was that the
results of a breath, blood or urine test were only admissible if the procedural
requirements of ss.7 and 8 of the 1988 Act had been fully complied with. It mattered not that the defendant had suffered no prejudice as a result of the failure to
warn him. On a proper construction of s.15(2) of the 1988 Offenders Act, the
admission in evidence of the results of tests was dependent upon the statutory
procedures having been carried out; it was impossible to carve out an exception
for those cases where the breach of procedure caused no prejudice. Although that
decision meant that unmeritorious defendants might sometimes be acquitted, it
had to be remembered that the legislation, contrary to the general traditions of the
criminal law, but for good and pressing social reasons, compelled a suspected
person to provide evidence against himself. It was therefore not surprising that a
strict and compulsory code had to be complied with in order to render that evidence admissible. The defendant's appeal against his conviction of a s.5 offence
was accordingly upheld.

It is a reasonable excuse for a defendant if he was unable to understand because
of his limited command of English the purpose of a requirement to provide laboratory specimens, or to appreciate the penal consequences of a refusal (*Beck v
Sager* [1979] Crim. L.R. 257). See also *Spalding v Paine* [1985] Crim. L.R. 673
and *Chief Constable of Avon & Somerset v Singh* [1988] R.T.R. 107, at § 4.282.

Detention at the police station

Section 10 of the Road Traffic Act 1988 provides that after a person has been   **4.250**
required to provide a specimen of breath, blood or urine he may thereafter be
detained at a police station until it appears to a constable that he would not be
committing an offence under s.4 or s.5 of the Act if he were then to drive, but a
person may not be detained if it appears to a constable that there is no likelihood

of his driving or attempting to drive whilst his ability to drive properly is impaired or whilst the proportion of alcohol is above the prescribed limit. If there is any question of a person's ability to drive being affected through drugs, the constable is required to consult a doctor and act on his advice (s.10(3)).

These provisions replaced earlier legislation which enabled a person to be detained until he gave a negative breath test. Section 10 is silent on how a constable should form his opinion as to whether the defendant is or is not likely to be above the limit. In cases where the accused may still be suffering the effects of alcohol it is the practice in many police stations to detain the car rather than the driver and to allow the accused to be driven home by taxi or by a friend. The section specifically recognises this practice and requires the constable to release him if it appears to the constable there is no likelihood of his driving while impaired or above the limit.

4.251 It may be noted that s.10 of the 1988 Act was amended with effect from March 30, 2004 in order to extend the power of detention to a person who has been required to give permission for a laboratory test of a specimen of blood taken from him without his consent under s.7A of the 1988 Act. (discussed at §§ 4.284 et seq. below).

FAILING TO PROVIDE A SPECIMEN

The offence (s.7(6))

4.252 A person who without reasonable excuse fails to provide a specimen when required to do so in pursuance of s.7 is guilty of an offence (s.7(6)).

A person can be lawfully required to provide specimens of blood, breath or urine "in the course of an investigation whether a person has committed an offence under section 4 or section 5 " (s.7(1)). There is therefore no requirement for the person to have been arrested, nor will the legality of an arrest following a roadside breath test be an issue. In *Bunyard v Hayes* [1985] R.T.R. 348, it was held following *Fox v Gwent Chief Constable* that the fact that a person may possibly have been wrongly arrested does not preclude him being convicted of failing to provide specimens of breath. (*Fox* went in due course to the House of Lords who unanimously upheld the Divisional Court's decision: [1985] R.T.R. 337.) It should also be noted that it is not a prerequisite for an offence under s.7(6) that an offence under s.4 or s.5 has been committed; a bona fide investigation as to whether such an offence has been committed empowers a constable (as the editors would suggest s.7(1) so clearly indicates) to require a suspect to provide specimens of blood, breath or urine. Hence the dismissal of a charge under s.4 on the basis that the car park where the vehicle had been driven was not a public place is no bar to a conviction of a s.7(6) offence (*Hawes v DPP* [1993] R.T.R. 116).

4.253 Detention under s.136 of the Mental Health Act 1983 does not of itself give rise to any legal bar to the administration of the breath test procedures in accordance with s.7 of the 1988 Act (*Francis v DPP* [1997] R.T.R. 113). The defendant had been detained under s.136 of the 1983 Act, which empowers a constable to remove a person who appears to him to be suffering from mental disorder and to be in need of care or control to a place of safety and there detain him for up to 72 hours. The police surgeon was not able to be at the police station and the officer, being satisfied that the driver understood the position, required him to provide specimens of breath for analysis. He declined to do so. The defendant's argument that his detention under s.136 invalidated the breath-test procedure was rejected by the court. Provided that the police were satisfied that the driver was capable of understanding the breath-test procedure, they were entitled to proceed.

As in earlier legislation, it would seem that in certain circumstances an offence can be committed of failing to supply specimens even if it subsequently transpires that the offender was neither driving nor attempting to drive nor in charge of a motor vehicle. A police officer who had reasonable cause to believe that one of three suspects was the driver of a vehicle and that each had consumed alcohol was entitled to require each to provide specimens of breath for analysis in accordance with what is now s.7. The Divisional Court so held in *Pearson v Commissioner of Police of the Metropolis* [1988] R.T.R. 276 when dismissing two appeals against conviction for failing to provide specimens of breath contrary to what is now s.7(6).

The Divisional Court (Watkins L.J., Macpherson J. and Roch J.) held in *Shaw v DPP* [1993] R.T.R. 45 that s.7(6) creates one offence rather than two and that the decision to the contrary in *DPP v Corcoran* [1992] R.T.R. 289 was erroneous and reached per incuriam since the court had not had the case of *Commissioner of Police of the Metropolis v Curran* [1976] 1 W.L.R. 87 cited to it. Although the maximum punishment for the offence is higher when the specimen was required from a person driving or attempting to drive a vehicle, an information charging an offence under s.7(6) without specifying in which circumstances the specimen was required does not contain two offences and is not bad for duplicity. There was unquestionably a single course of conduct which constituted the offence, namely the failure without reasonable excuse to provide the specimen. *Shaw v DPP* was followed, and *DPP v Corcoran* again disapproved, by the Divisional Court in *DPP v Butterworth* [1994] R.T.R. 181. In view of continuing attempts to persuade lower courts that *Corcoran* was still good law, however, the court certified that a point of law of general public importance was involved in the decision, although leave to appeal to the House of Lords was refused. The matter came in due course before their Lordships as *Butterworth v DPP* [1994] R.T.R. 330, where the decision of the Divisional Court was unanimously upheld. It was clear that the substance of the offence was the refusal to provide a specimen in the course of an investigation as to whether an offence under s.4 or s.5 had been committed. Which offence it was said was committed was only relevant to the appropriate penalty. (See further § 2.99.)

4.254

For the present offence under s.7(6) there are only two sets of penalties, (a) where the offender was driving or attempting to drive, and (b) all other cases, i.e. where the offender was not driving or attempting to drive, whether or not he was in charge. Where the offender was driving or attempting to drive, the offence under s.7(6) is obligatorily disqualifiable in accordance with Pt I of Sch.2 to the 1988 Offenders Act. Justices should state clearly upon which basis they were sentencing a defendant. They were not bound by the wording of the information even if it charged driving or attempting to drive. If they came to the conclusion that he was only in charge of the motor vehicle they should sentence accordingly; *Crampsie v DPP* [1993] R.T.R. 383.

On the other hand, where the offender was not driving nor attempting to drive, the offence is no longer obligatorily disqualifiable (see paragraph (b) in columns

4.255

4 and 5 of the entry relating to s.7(6) in Pt I of Sch.2 to the 1988 Offenders Act) and an offender incurs 10 penalty points in accordance with column 7 ibid. No doubt in the majority of cases where the offender is not driving or attempting to drive it can be shown that he was in charge, but even if he is neither proved to be in charge nor driving or attempting to drive he will still be liable to the full range of penalties in accordance with (b) in columns 4 and 5 of the entry relating to Sch.2 to the 1988 Offenders Act. It should be noted, however, that in *McCormick v Hitchins* [1988] R.T.R. 182 *Note* special reasons were found for not endorsing the defendant's licence with the obligatory 10 penalty points where the defendant:

(a) had no intention of driving on the vehicle, and

(b) could not have been a danger on the road.

In *Bunyard v Hayes* (above) the defendant was held to be rightly convicted under what is now s.7(6) where he refused without reasonable excuse to provide specimens of breath for analysis, the police officers having taken the defendant to the police station after forming the suspicion that he had been the driver of a vehicle involved in an accident, although it subsequently transpired that he was not the driver.

A   *"Fails"*

4.256   The cases on the former section show that a person cannot be convicted of failing to supply a specimen for analysis if he has consented to supply a specimen and provided it. Thus in *R. v Rothery* [1976] R.T.R. 550 a defendant was acquitted of failing to supply a specimen where after providing a specimen of urine he stole it before leaving a police station; he could only be convicted of theft (ibid.). The defendant in *Ross v Hodges* [1975] R.T.R. 55 was held not to have provided a specimen when the jar containing the specimen fell out of his hand as he handed it to the police officer. If the second specimen of urine is in fact so small as to be incapable of analysis, it cannot be said that the defendant has provided a specimen (*R. v Coward* [1976] R.T.R. 425). See also *MacDougall v MacPhail* (1990) 1991 S.L.T. 801 where a second specimen consisting of a mere three drops of urine was held to be insufficient to be divided into two parts and therefore insufficient in law.

Where a Lion Intoximeter did not record any sample as having been provided by the defendant, the Divisional Court directed a conviction under what is now s.7(6); justices must assume that the Intoximeter was in good working order in the absence of any evidence to the contrary (*Anderton v Waring* [1986] R.T.R. 74). That case was followed in *Dawes v Taylor* [1986] R.T.R. 81, but Kennedy J. expressly drew attention to the fact that *Beck v Sager* [1979] Crim. L.R. 257 had not been drawn to the court's attention in *Anderton v Waring*. Oral evidence of the defendant's failure to provide specimens of breath as recorded on the printout may be given; in a case under s.7(6) evidence of the self-calibration checks is unnecessary (*Oldfield v Anderton* [1986] Crim. L.R. 189). It should be noted in this context that s.11(3) requires the specimen of breath "to be provided in such a way as to enable the objective of the test or analysis to be satisfactorily achieved".

B   *"Refuses"*

4.257   As in earlier legislation the word "fails" includes "refuses" (s.11(2)), and the cases on the previous law would appear relevant.

It was held under earlier legislation that once the defendant has refused all three requests, breath, urine and then blood, the offence is complete. In *Procaj v Johnstone* [1970] Crim. L.R. 110 the accused changed his mind before being charged, and it was held that it was then too late to do so. In *Muat v Thynne, The Times*, May 28, 1984, the defendant failed to supply specimens of blood or urine in accordance with s.9 of the 1972 Act (prior to its amendment by the Transport Act 1981). His conviction under s.9 was upheld by the Divisional Court even though he subsequently supplied a blood sample for the purpose of determining whether an offence under what is now s.4 had been committed. It would seem that in the present law once a defendant has been properly required to provide a specimen in accordance with the procedure under s.7 he can be charged even if he subsequently changes his mind. The circumstances surrounding the defendant's change of mind, however, are clearly material to the court's determination. A motorist, when asked to provide specimens of breath for analysis, said "No"; five seconds or so later he said he wanted to change his mind. The only conclusion that the Divisional Court in *Smyth v DPP* [1996] R.T.R. 59 felt able to draw, having regard to all his words and conduct, was that he had not refused to provide a specimen.

In a highly fact-specific case (*Plackett v DPP* [2008] EWHC 1335; (2008) 172 J.P. 455) the motorist successfully appealed his conviction in the magistrates' court for failing to provide a specimen of breath for analysis under s.7(6) of the Road Traffic Act 1988. He initially refused to provide two specimens, but then left the room to speak to the duty solicitor. On his return he expressed the wish to take the test, and the officer by his conduct agreed to the request. However, the operating cycle of the breath analysis machine had started while the appellant was out of the room and he had only one minute, instead of the usual three, to provide two samples. His first two attempts were unsuccessful and the machine stopped. It was held that the appellant had not been afforded a proper opportunity to provide a specimen of breath for analysis.

4.258 In *Hussein v DPP* [2008] EWHC 901; [2008] R.T.R. 30, the appellant was convicted of failing to provide a specimen of breath for analysis contrary to s.7(6) of the Road Traffic Act 1988. He had provided earlier samples, but they were not reliable, because, apparently, of machine failure. Approximately an hour later, at another police station, he refused to provide breath specimens when requested. As the specimens of breath provided at the first police station did not constitute valid specimens for the purpose of s.11(3) of the Road Traffic Act 1988, a police officer was entitled to require two further specimens of breath. The Divisional Court held that the appellant's refusal to do so constituted the offence of which he was convicted.

If a defendant, after giving a lower breath specimen of 50µg or less, opts to give a specimen of blood or urine instead under s.7(4), he cannot be convicted under s.7(6) of failing or refusing to supply a specimen if he then fails to provide a specimen. The only effect of his failure in such circumstances is that the original breath specimen can be used in evidence against him (see further §§ 4.134–8).

4.259 A motorist whose breath smelt of alcohol was required to take a screening breath test; he said, and presumably did, nothing. At the police station to which he was subsequently taken he was arrested and cautioned (and therefore informed of his right to remain silent). On three occasions he was asked whether he agreed to provide specimens under what is now s.7 on the Lion Intoximeter in the adjoining room (to which the defendant was not taken). On each occasion he made no reply. He was charged and convicted of an offence contrary to what is now s.7(6). It was contended on his behalf before the Divisional Court that having been cautioned he was not required to reply and that as the device had not been presented to him he had neither the opportunity to provide specimens nor to refuse to do so. In dismissing his appeal against conviction, the court in *Campbell v DPP* [1989] R.T.R. 256 held that whilst a person could not fail to do that which he had no opportunity to do, the defendant in this case had been given an opportunity to provide breath specimens for he had clearly been asked so to do and he could reasonably be expected to have known that an Intoximeter was present and readily available; in those circumstances there was no need for the defendant actually to be shown the machine. Further, the defendant's failure to reply following the caution had no bearing upon the statutory requirement to supply a specimen under what is now s.7.

Where a motorist refused to supply a specimen of blood but offered to supply a urine sample instead, he committed the offence of failing to provide a specimen contrary to what is now s.7(6) of the 1988 Act. Furthermore, there was no obligation upon the police to ask why the blood sample was being refused or to arrange for a medical practitioner to attend to determine whether a sample of blood could not or should not be provided if there was nothing to put the police on inquiry as to any possible medical reasons for the defendant's refusal (*Grix v Chief Constable of Kent* [1987] R.T.R. 193).

4.260   By s.7(1) a defendant is required to provide two specimens of breath for analysis. Where, therefore, a defendant only provides one specimen, he is guilty of refusing a specimen for analysis under s.7(6) (*Cracknell v Willis* [1987] 3 All E.R. 801, *Stepniewski v Commissioner of Police of the Metropolis* [1985] Crim. L.R. 675). In the latter case the single specimen of breath gave a reading below the prescribed limit. The court held that in such circumstances a court could and should mitigate the penalty which would otherwise be imposed. The court also stated that prosecuting authorities should consider very carefully indeed whether a defendant should be prosecuted in such circumstances.

C *"Reasonable excuse"*

4.261   The offence is only committed if the defendant fails or refuses "without reasonable excuse". Once the defence of reasonable excuse is advanced it is for the prosecution to disprove it (*Rowland v Thorpe* [1970] 3 All E.R. 195 at 197). It is a question of fact as to whether a defendant has a reasonable excuse and the court must be satisfied beyond reasonable doubt that the defendant had no reasonable excuse before he can be convicted (*R. v Harling* [1970] R.T.R. 441; *McKeon v DPP* [2007] EWHC 3216; [2008] R.T.R. 14). But whether facts are capable of amounting to a reasonable excuse is a matter of law; if it is capable in law of amounting to a reasonable excuse, then it becomes a matter of fact and degree whether it does so or not, with the burden being on the prosecution to negative it (*Law v Stephens* [1971] R.T.R. 358).

It was established in the case of *DPP v Thomas* (1993) 157 J.P. 480 (also reported as *DPP v Thomas (Elwyn Kenneth) (Note—1992)* at [1996] R.T.R. 293) that there is no obligation upon a police officer to warn a motorist who has been required to provide specimens of breath for analysis that he must provide those specimens within the three minutes which the machine allows for the completion of its testing cycle. Thus where a motorist was not told of the necessity of providing the required specimens within a total period of three minutes until after his first unsuccessful attempt at providing a specimen, he could not claim to have had a reasonable excuse for not providing those specimens. The Divisional Court so held in *DPP v Coyle* [1996] R.T.R. 287, but added that the matter might have been viewed differently if there had been evidence that the failure to warn the defendant had actually affected his compliance with the request.

A similar, but not identical, point to that raised in *DPP v Coyle* above was adjudicated upon by the Divisional Court in *Cosgrove v DPP* [1997] R.T.R. 153 with a similar result. The appellant had argued that since the Lion Intoximeter provided a three-minute period before it shut down, then in every case a person must be given the full three minutes before it could be said that there had been an unreasonable refusal. Not so, said the court. Although the machine provides a three-minute period, there is no principle of law that a person must necessarily be allowed the three minutes nor be told he has three minutes at any stage of the procedure. If the officer concludes that the motorist is failing to provide a specimen, he may stop the procedure before the three minutes have elapsed. His decision may, of course, be subsequently challenged in court, but as a matter of law he is entitled to take that course. **4.262**

Following a road traffic accident in the small hours of the morning, a defendant of good character who had been wrongly suspected by police of being a burglar was arrested, forcibly handcuffed and taken to a police station; there he was dragged by the handcuffs into a cell and was later taken before a sergeant to whom the defendant stated that he wished to complain about his treatment. The sergeant required him to provide specimens of breath for analysis; the defendant refused to co-operate until he could make a complaint and see a doctor and a solicitor. Justices dismissed a charge under what is now s.7(6) on the basis that his state of mind as a result of his treatment was such that he could not understand the consequences of his refusal to provide specimens. Allowing the prosecutor's appeal, the Divisional Court in *Chief Constable of Avon and Somerset Constabulary v O'Brien* [1987] R.T.R. 182 held that the justices had been wrong to infer that the defendant had a reasonable excuse for failure within what is now s.7(6); the facts pointed not so much to an agitated and confused state of mind as to an expressed desire to see a doctor and solicitor before providing a specimen. In remitting the case to the justices with a direction to convict, the court did indicate that the defendant might seek to advance special reasons under what is now s.34(1) of the 1988 Offenders Act as to why he should not be disqualified.

Chief Constable of Avon and Somerset Constabulary v O'Brien above was considered and applied by the Divisional Court in *Salter v DPP* [1992] R.T.R. 386 where the defendant stated that he would not supply a specimen until he had seen a solicitor. There being not the slightest hint of confusion, anxiety, incomprehension or mental stress on his part, the facts as found were not capable of amounting in law to a reasonable excuse for not providing a specimen. **4.263**

A defendant was advised by his solicitor to refuse a lawful request at the police station for him to provide two specimens of breath for analysis. That such bad advice cannot amount to a reasonable excuse for failure to provide a specimen has been emphasised by the Divisional Court in *Dickinson v DPP* [1989] Crim. L.R. 741. To have held otherwise would have been to defeat the entire purpose of the statute.

4.264   A mistaken or even genuine belief on the part of the defendant is usually incapable of amounting to a "reasonable excuse"; e.g. that he had not consumed alcohol (*McNicol v Peters* 1969 S.L.T.(J.) 261); that he did not believe he had committed a moving traffic offence (*R. v Downey* [1970] Crim. L.R. 287); that he did not believe that he was "in charge" of a motor vehicle (*Williams v Osborne* [1975] R.T.R. 181); that he did not think the officer was acting bona fide (*McGrath v Vipas* [1984] R.T.R. 58); that he thought he had not failed the breath test (*Mallows v Harris* [1979] R.T.R. 404).

    A prior alleged assault at the roadside upon a motorist by the police officers arresting him could not amount to a reasonable excuse for failure to supply specimens of breath when safely ensconced in the secure environment of a police station (assuming, of course, that the provision of such specimens would not be injurious to his health). The High Court of Justiciary so held in *Gallacher v Scott* 1989 S.L.T. 397 when dismissing the motorist's appeal against conviction. A different view might well be taken, however, if the result of an assault was damage sufficient to render the suspect incapable of providing a specimen.

4.265   Upon being asked to provide a blood sample a defendant had replied: "In view of the danger of AIDS I would rather not give blood". The Divisional Court in *DPP v Fountain* [1988] R.T.R. 385 held that the defendant's belief was not capable of amounting to a reasonable excuse for not providing a specimen for analysis. A refusal accompanied with a reason was a refusal nonetheless, and whether a reasonable excuse for the refusal could be said to exist was a matter of law. A belief, whether mistaken or genuine, had never in law constituted a reasonable excuse. Where, however, medical evidence established the existence in the defendant's mind of a genuine phobia (on the particular facts a long-standing obsession with his health and a genuine but unreasonable fear of contracting AIDS from the Intoximeter's mouthpiece), that might amount to a reasonable excuse *De Freitas v DPP* [1992] Crim. L.R. 894.

    An agreement subject to an unreasonable condition is treated as no acceptance and amounting to a refusal, e.g. an agreement only to provide a specimen when his solicitor was present (*Pettigrew v Northumbria Police Authority* [1976] R.T.R. 177; *Payne v Diccox* [1980] R.T.R. 83). Although the police have a discretion to allow a solicitor to be present, they are under a duty to end their concession if it appears to be a delaying tactic or creates too great a delay. The Divisional Court held in *DPP v Billington* [1988] R.T.R. 231 that s.58 of the Police and Criminal Evidence Act 1984 giving an arrested person in custody the right to see a solicitor as soon as was practicable did not require the police to delay taking samples for analysis in accordance with what is now s.7(1) of the 1988 Act until after the suspect had consulted a solicitor; neither did it provide the suspect with a reasonable excuse under what is now s.7(6) ibid. for failing to provide a specimen until he had seen a solicitor. All that the Act and the codes of practice made thereunder required was that the defendant be permitted to see a solicitor as soon as practicable. (A similar conclusion was also reached in *Grennan v Westcott* [1988] R.T.R. 253, a case decided by the Divisional Court some six months earlier.)

4.266   Lloyd L.J., giving the judgment in *DPP v Billington*, was relieved to reach the result concerned for two reasons; first, it was important for procedures under what is now s.7 to be conducted as quickly as possible and, secondly, it would be undesirable for there to be a difference between the rights of an arrested person and one who had gone to the police station voluntarily.

DPP v Billington above was applied by the Divisional Court in *DPP v Cornell* [1990] R.T.R. 254 when deciding that the right of a suspect to read inter alia the relevant code of practice (issued under the authority of the Police and Criminal Evidence Act 1984) dealing with the detention, treatment and questioning of persons detained by the police did not confer upon him a right to delay the breath test procedure. He should accordingly have been convicted of failure to provide a specimen for analysis contrary to what is now s.7(6) since he had no reasonable excuse for not providing one. The case was remitted to the magistrate with a direction to convict. In an apparently rather similar case it was held by the Divisional Court that a mistaken belief by a defendant that he was entitled to read the codes of practice issued under the 1984 Act before acceding to a police officer's proper requirement for the provision of a specimen of breath for analysis could not amount to a reasonable excuse for failure to supply such a specimen, notwithstanding that he might in some degree have been confused or misled by what the officer said to him about his right to see those documents. Since the defendant understood what was being asked of him, there could be no reasonable excuse for non-compliance in the absence of a physical or mental reason which would entail a substantial risk to health (*DPP v Whalley* [1991] R.T.R. 161, applying *R. v Lennard* [1973] R.T.R. 252 discussed below and *Grennan v Westcott* above and following in particular *DPP v Cornell*).

4.267 *DPP v Billington* and *Grennan v Westcott* above were unsurprisingly followed by the Divisional Court in *DPP v Varley* [1999] Crim. L.R. 753. Having been informed of his right to contact a solicitor, the defendant refused to provide two specimens of breath for analysis until he had sought legal advice. He was warned of the consequences of failure to provide the required specimens. He had not in any way been misled by the police (an officer had said, "I'm not prepared to wait until the duty solicitor rings") and the facts found did not constitute a reasonable excuse. A similar conclusion was reached in *DPP v Noe* [2000] R.T.R. 351 in which it was held that the defendant's refusal to provide specimens unless given prior access to a law book could not amount to a reasonable excuse. Although these cases do not add a great deal to the existing law, they do serve to illustrate the narrow scope of the concept of "reasonable excuse".

It was held by the Divisional Court in *Campbell v DPP* [2002] EWHC 1314; [2004] R.T.R. 5 that *DPP v Billington* above is still good law despite its apparent incompatibility with art.6(3) of the European Convention on Human Rights. That article did not provide a blanket requirement that each time a person was detained legal advice had to be obtained before he could be asked to do or say anything. In each case a balancing exercise had to be carried out between the protection of the individual on the one hand and the interests of the community at large on the other. The restriction on any right in relation to art.6(3) had to be proportionate to the aim sought to be achieved. The interests of the community in the suppression of drink/driving in order to save lives and prevent serious injury to its members were self-evident, as was the fact that even a short delay in obtaining a specimen would be prejudicial to that aim. It was entirely proportionate to allow a police officer to require a member of the community to provide a specimen albeit that legal advice had not been obtained.

4.268 A similar conclusion was reached in *Kennedy v DPP* [2002] EWHC 2297; [2004] R.T.R. 6, applying *Billington* and *Campbell*, where a defendant requested to speak to a solicitor prior to the breath test procedure, but contact with the duty solicitor call centre was deferred until immediately after that procedure. In a matter of this kind the public interest required that the obtaining of breath specimens should not be delayed to any significant extent in order to enable a suspect to take legal advice.

Kennedy v DPP above was applied by the Divisional Court in *Kirkup v DPP* [2003] EWHC 2354: [2004] Crim. L.R. 230. According to the code of practice (Code C) issued under authority of the Police and Criminal Evidence Act 1984, the obligation upon the custody officer to secure the provision of legal advice for a suspect could only sensibly arise after the formalities of authorising detention had been carried out. The actual delay in the case in point amounted to a mere seven minutes, a period so short as to occasion the most minor breach of Code C. It was neither a significant delay nor a substantial one and the justices' decision not to exclude under s.78 of the 1984 Act the evidence of the request for specimens of breath could not be faulted.

4.269   *Kennedy v DPP* above was further considered and approved by the Divisional Court in *Whitley v DPP* [2003] EWHC 2512; [2004] Crim. L.R. 585. A suspect's request to speak to a solicitor as soon as practicable led to his being told that the breath-test procedure could not be delayed for him to obtain legal advice. It was submitted on his behalf on appeal that certainty was required and that custody officers ought to know, as a matter of principle, whether, if they were asked by a suspect for legal advice they should contact the duty solicitor call centre before the breath-test procedure was started. The court held, however, that what was practicable had to be considered from the point of view, and the state of knowledge, of those then present at the police station, not from the point of view of those who had had the opportunity to reflect upon the matter with some care and the benefit of hindsight. It was important, given the enormous variety of circumstances which might confront a custody officer, that he should be given flexibility to respond to the demands of the particular case. As the court had said in *Kennedy*, it was a question of fact and degree in any given case whether the custody officer had acted without delay to secure the provision of legal advice, and whether the person held in custody had been permitted to consult a solicitor as soon as was practicable.

Kennedy v DPP was also cited and followed by the Divisional Court in *R (on the application of Forde) v DPP* [2004] EWHC 1156. In that case the appellant, after a number of refusals to provide a specimen, had simply said that he did not want to take a blood test before he had spoken to a solicitor. It would be putting too great an onus on the police officer who was carrying out the procedure, even assuming it had not been completed, to be expected to infer from such a comment that he ought to give the suspect an immediate opportunity to contact a solicitor. (In the earlier case of *Myles v DPP* [2004] EWHC 594; [2005] R.T.R. 1 which was also cited in *Forde*, it had been held, applying *Kennedy*, that the appellant's argument that for a short, defined period, namely 15 minutes, it should be permissible to delay the sample-taking process for the purpose of obtaining legal advice, ran counter to the clear principle as expressed in *Kennedy* that the process should not be delayed to any significant extent.)

4.270   It was held by the Divisional Court in *Causey v DPP* [2004] EWHC 3164; (2005) 169 J.P. 331, following the long line of cases headed by *Kennedy v DPP* above, that there is no general duty upon the police to delay the taking of a specimen at the police station until a suspect has obtained legal advice. Magistrates had been entitled on the facts of the instant case to conclude that a delay of 15 minutes between a request to speak to a solicitor and an attempt to contact that solicitor was neither significant nor substantial. As the law on this issue had been clear for some time the court stated that appeals should not be made which raised the question of the principles to be applied in such cases, save in exceptional circumstances. Despite this, the position had to be restated in *Gearing v DPP* [2008] EWHC 1695; [2009] R.T.R. 7. Having reviewed the authorities, the Divisional Court summarised the position as follows. Someone who asks for legal advice must be permitted to consult a solicitor as soon as is practicable, and indeed the officer must act under PACE Code C 6.5 without delay in seeking that advice. But having said that, it is also clear that there can be no significant delay because of the important public interest in those who have in fact failed a roadside breath test being tested promptly. It is only in circumstances such as where there is a duty solicitor there and present who can be spoken to for a couple of minutes, or where the individual wishes to speak to his or her own solicitor or the duty solicitor, and that solicitor in question is known to be immediately available that there would be no significant delay. It is emphasised that anything other than a very, very short period will amount to a significant delay. The example given is "a couple of minutes" or "immediately available". If it is apparent that legal advice can be readily made available, in a couple of minutes or so, then it would be appropriate to balance the rights and the obligations in question by requiring the police to delay the breath test at the least for that short time. If it is anything greater than that, then it is not a requirement that the police should delay the giving of the breath test simply for that reason.

It is clear from *DPP v Billington* above that the right to consult a solicitor under s.58 of the Police and Criminal Evidence Act 1984 does not require the police to delay taking samples for analysis in accordance with s.7(1) of the Road Traffic Act 1988. The Divisional Court, in *DPP v Ward* [1999] R.T.R. 11, decided that similar principles apply in a case where a motorist provides a breath specimen containing no more than 50μg of alcohol in 100ml of blood and accordingly may claim under s.8(2) of the 1988 Act that it should be replaced by a specimen of blood or urine (see § 4.134). Since there was no logical distinction between the procedures of s.7 and s.8, a suspect had no right to legal advice when making a decision under s.8(2).

Where the defendant's own doctor is present, the defendant will not be held to have refused if he consents to the blood specimen being taken only by his own doctor (*Bayliss v Thames Valley Police* [1978] R.T.R. 328). There is, however, no general right for a defendant to insist that the blood specimen be taken by his own medical practitioner. The Divisional Court so held in *DPP v Smith (Alan)*, *The Times*, June 1, 1993 and pointed out that *Bayliss v Thames Valley Police* was a special case on its own facts in that there the defendant's own medical practitioner had in any event been present at the police station at the relevant time. The defendant cannot insist on the blood specimen being taken only from a particular part of his anatomy, or of capillary instead of intravenous blood. Once a doctor has asked to take a specimen in accordance with ordinary medical practice, an offer for it to be taken only in a different way is a refusal (*Solesbury v Pugh* [1969] 2 All E.R. 1171; *Rushton v Higgins* [1972] Crim. L.R. 440; *R. v McAllister* [1974] Crim. L.R. 716).

A constable is justified in treating the refusal to sign a form of consent for a

4.271

specimen of blood to be taken by a medical practitioner as a refusal where the defendant had previously refused to supply a blood specimen (*R. v McAllister*). A driver was however held *not* to have refused when he insisted on reading the consent form before signing it, although it appeared to the police to be a delaying tactic (*Hier v Read* [1978] R.T.R. 114).

4.272   In *R. v Harling* [1970] R.T.R. 441 a defendant lost confidence in a doctor after three unsuccessful efforts to obtain blood, and it was observed that he might have had a reasonable excuse to refuse to supply blood. In *Rowland v Thorpe*, § 4.271 above, the court may have been prepared to hold as a reasonable excuse for refusing to supply urine that there was no woman police officer present to take the specimen, as the defendant was a woman. Mental incapacity can amount to a reasonable excuse. In *R. v Harding* [1974] R.T.R. 325 a conviction was set aside where a jury might have found the defendant was so afraid of a hypodermic needle as to be incapacitated from submitting to it. In most cases, fear of providing blood must be supported by medical evidence (ibid.). *Harding* was applied in *Alcock v Read* [1980] R.T.R. 71 where justices were upheld in finding the defendant had a reasonable excuse because of an "invincible repugnance" to giving blood. Evidence was given that he had twice passed out after giving blood and was terrified of blood being taken. Where the defendant threw an apparent fit when a doctor tried to obtain a blood specimen, the justices' finding that the fit could have been genuine was held to justify an acquittal. *R. v Lennard* [1973] R.T.R. 252 and *Harding* were applied in *Sykes v White* [1983] R.T.R. 419 where it was held that fear of blood so that the defendant became light-headed and had to sit down and fear of fainting so that he could not provide urine could not amount to a reasonable excuse, nor could an irrational belief that discomfort at providing blood would be misinterpreted as incapacity to drive a motor vehicle. The possibility of the defence establishing a phobia of machines as a reasonable excuse for not supplying a specimen of breath was considered in *Dempsey v Catton* [1986] R.T.R. 194. The issue was left open by the Divisional Court; but it is clear that, at best, such a defence would be difficult to establish.

In *DPP v Mukandiwa* [2005] EWHC 2977; [2006] R.T.R. 24, it was held that a defendant who had refused to provide a blood specimen on the grounds that the sight of blood was apt to drive him into a trance, in which state he could become violent to himself and those around him, did not have a reasonable excuse for his failure to provide such a specimen. There was a material difference between the *sight* of blood and the *taking* of blood; an obvious way for the defendant to have avoided the sight of blood was for him to close his eyes or look away. (This case was obviously a sub-editor's delight, appearing as it does under the singularly apposite headline "taking blood may not mean seeing red".)

4.273   It was said in *R. v Lennard* above that a reasonable excuse "*must arise out of a physical or mental inability to provide one or a substantial risk to health in its provision*". Under the present law the prosecution are less likely to succeed in negativing a reasonable excuse based on a physical inability to provide a specimen, particularly where the specimens required to be provided are breath. Both first generation evidential breath testing devices, the Lion Intoximeter 3000 and the Camic Breath Analyser, required the subject to blow for a given interval at a given pressure and under s.11(3) a specimen of breath has to be "provided in such a way as to enable the ... analysis to be satisfactorily achieved". A defendant was therefore entitled to advance as a reasonable excuse that he had not the lung capacity or physical ability to blow sufficiently hard and long to provide a specimen which the Camic or Lion was able to analyse. In *Cotgrove v Cooney* [1987] R.T.R. 124, the Divisional Court held that justices were not wrong in law in dismissing an information alleging failure to provide specimens of breath for analysis where they were satisfied that the defendant had tried as hard as he could, albeit unsuccessfully, to provide the same. (It should be noted in this context, however, that the second generation machines currently approved for the analysis of evidential breath specimens are designed to be less demanding of breath than their predecessors (see § 4.280 below) and that the task of negativing a reasonable excuse based upon physical inability may be less onerous than it used to be for the prosecution. See also subsequent cases below.)

Making every effort to provide breath samples when requested to do so could **4.274** not of itself amount to a reasonable excuse for failure; some additional evidence of inability was necessary. Such evidence would normally be furnished by a medical practitioner, although it could in appropriate circumstances come from the defendant himself. The Divisional Court so held in *Grady v Pollard* [1988] R.T.R. 316, following the authority of *R. v Lennard* [1974] R.T.R. 252. The appellant's conviction by justices had properly been upheld by the Crown Court, which court had not on the facts presented felt it necessary to consider whether the appellant would have had a defence to the charge had he been able to satisfy the court that he had blown as hard as he could. The facts were that the appellant had failed in his attempt to provide a screening breath test and subsequently failed at the first attempt to provide a specimen on the Lion Intoximeter; he then refused to undertake a second test. He said that he was trying as hard as he could and that he was not suffering from any chest complaint or other ailment. The Divisional Court did not feel called upon to decide whether or not *Cotgrove v Cooney* [1987] R.T.R. 124 had been wrongly decided since the court in that case had been faced with a finding of fact by the justices that the defendant *had* tried as hard as he could, that there was no wilful refusal and that reasonable excuse could be raised on his behalf. *Grady v Pollard* was applied by the Divisional Court in *Smith (Nicholas) v DPP (Note—1989)* [1992] R.T.R. 413 where justices had rightly held that a motorist who had "done his best" had no reasonable excuse for his failure; although he had been nervous, there was no finding that his nervousness had been the cause of that failure.

Further doubt was cast upon the decision in *Cotgrove v Cooney* [1987] R.T.R. **4.275** 124 by the Divisional Court (Watkins L.J. and Nolan J.) in *DPP v Eddowes* [1991] R.T.R. 35. Justices should be careful not to be so gullible as to accept as a defence the argument that a defendant was under too much stress following an accident to be able to provide a specimen of breath for analysis. The defendant had apparently succeeded in his first attempt to provide a specimen but had failed to provide further specimens. Given the undesirable way in which the case had been drafted (a recital of the evidence given rather than a series of findings of fact) it was impossible to deduce precisely which facts had been found by the justices, but they appeared to have concluded that the defendant had a reasonable excuse for not providing the required specimens despite the lack of any evidence of mental or physical disability. It seemed to their Lordships, however, that the question as to whether a reasonable excuse had been provided did not arise since no excuse whatsoever had been given. Many motorists had to provide specimens after being involved in accidents and if "post-accident stress" were to provide an automatic reasonable excuse the whole purpose of the statute would be defeated. Having thus distinguished the instant case from *Cotgrove v Cooney* the potential conflict with that earlier case was avoided; however, Watkins L.J. did say obiter that he would be prepared to say that the observations in that case should not be followed and that the court should turn for guidance to *R. v Lennard* above.

4.276   The observations of Watkins L.J. in *Eddowes* to the effect that justices should follow the guidance of Lawton L.J. in *R. v Lennard* [1973] R.T.R. 252 were specifically approved by the Divisional Court in *DPP v Ambrose (Jean-Marie)*, *The Times*, November 7, 1991 (also reported as *DPP v Ambrose* at [1992] R.T.R. 285). In that case it was held that stress caused by self-precipitated agitation did not amount to a reasonable excuse for failing to provide a breath specimen when required to do so. In the absence of medical evidence (which in such cases would almost invariably be required), the justices were wrong to have embarked upon an investigation of their own. Their assumption about the defendant's distressed state was not evidentially based and accordingly their decision was fatally flawed.

    DPP v Eddowes was applied by the Divisional Court in *DPP v Daley* [1992] R.T.R. 155 in allowing an appeal by the prosecutor against a dismissal by justices of charges under ss.6(4) and 7(6) of the 1988 Act. There was no suggestion made to the justices that the defendant was under any form of stress and no evidence of any medical incapacity or physical inability to do that which any normal person could, without much effort, do; accordingly the defendant had no excuse whatsoever, let alone a reasonable excuse, for failing to provide a specimen. (In fairness to the justices, *Eddowes* was not reported until the day after they made their decision.) (It may also be noted in passing that *DPP v Daley* was revisited by the Divisional Court in *DPP v Daley (No.2)* [1994] R.T.R. 107 when dealing with a misguided attempt by the Crown Court to reuse for "special reasons" purposes a factually unsustainable finding arising from the original case; see further, § 21.46.)

4.277   The warning given by Watkins L.J. in *Eddowes* that justices should take great care not to be gullible in these cases was re-emphasised by the Divisional Court in *DPP v Pearman* [1992] R.T.R. 407 (although the court was able to distinguish the earlier case on the basis of very different facts). The defendant in *Pearman* had succeeded in providing a first sample for analysis, but thereafter declined into a distraught state, sobbing continuously and becoming unable to breathe properly. Although the case was on the borderline in view of her having been able to provide the first specimen, it was nevertheless open to the justices to find that the defendant had been physically incapable of providing the second one. Although it was clear from *Grady v Pollard* [1988] R.T.R. 316 that medical evidence would normally be required to establish a reasonable excuse, there were nevertheless circumstances such as these in which the evidence of the defendant alone might suffice.

    DPP v Pearman above was applied by the Divisional Court in *DPP v Crofton* [1994] R.T.R. 279. The justices' conclusion that the defendant's inability to provide two specimens of breath for analysis was due to breathlessness caused by pre-existing depression and was not self-precipitated, and accordingly afforded him a reasonable excuse for his failure, was sustainable even in the absence of medical evidence. The important matters for their consideration, namely the need for evidence of physical or mental incapability to provide the specimen, the normal requirement of medical evidence in support of such a claim and the existence of a necessary causative link between the physical or mental conditions and the failure to provide the specimen had all been addressed by the justices. Having believed the defendant on those issues by unimpeachable findings of fact, the court which had not seen the witnesses was unable to overturn such a clear assessment.

DPP v Pearman above was also referred to, and applied, in *DPP v Falzarano* **4.278** [2001] R.T.R. 14 where it was held that justices were entitled to conclude from the defendant's demeanour during her trial that she had suffered a panic attack at the police station during which she was unable to provide a breath specimen and therefore had a lawful excuse for failure to provide such a specimen. According to the evidence of her general practitioner the slightest source of stress would result in her suffering extremes of agitation requiring chemical intervention. They found as a fact that she had not taken the medication which helped control her panic attacks for seven to ten days prior to her arrest. Although they had received medical evidence that a panic attack would not have prevented the defendant from understanding what people were saying to her and that there would have been nothing physical or mental to prevent her from providing the breath specimens, they nonetheless concluded that she had done her best to provide those specimens and had provided a reasonable excuse for not doing so. The justices had been led by the demeanour of the accused to accept the evidence that when upset she was very short of breath, and they were entitled to so conclude. There were findings that led the justices to conclude that there was a causative link between a physical and mental condition of the defendant and her failure to provide a specimen. The court could not go behind those findings or castigate them as being illogical or perverse.

The significance of medical evidence in such cases was re-emphasised by the Divisional Court in *DPP v Brodzky (Note—1994)* [1997] R.T.R. 425. A motorist provided a positive roadside breath test, was arrested and conveyed to a police station. Whilst waiting there in the custody suite he was subjected to threatening behaviour by the custody sergeant. He attributed his subsequent failure (despite his best endeavours) to provide a specimen of breath for analysis to the mental anguish caused by the sergeant's behaviour. The justices found that this amounted to a reasonable excuse for failure to provide such a specimen. Overturning that decision, the court held that in the absence of medical evidence to support the defendant's claim there was insufficient evidence to justify the justices' conclusion that there was a causative link between the physical or mental condition alleged and the failure to provide a specimen.

A defendant was held not to have a reasonable excuse when he had difficulty in **4.279** breathing through his nose, but was not physically unable to provide breath specimens nor would doing so entail substantial risk to his health (*Woolman v Lenton* [1985] Crim. L.R. 516). Clearly a deliberate failure to provide a specimen of breath (e.g. by blowing round rather than into the tube) will preclude a defence of reasonable excuse under s.7(6) and also under s.6(4) (*Teape v Godfrey* [1986] R.T.R. 213).

Where a motorist deliberately failed to provide two specimens of breath for analysis (by blowing around rather than into the tube) and later found that for medical reasons he would have been unable to provide a proper specimen, he did not have a reasonable excuse for failing to provide a specimen. The Divisional Court so held in *DPP v Furby* [2000] R.T.R. 181, applying *Teape v Godfrey* above. A person who was unaware of an impediment (in the case in point, a reduced lung capacity) could not rely upon it as an excuse unless he made a genuine attempt to provide a specimen. There had to be a direct relationship between the excuse relied on and the failure to provide a sample. The fact that the motorist subsequently discovered that, had he made a genuine attempt, he would not have been able to provide a specimen was, for the purposes of s.7 of the 1988 Act, irrelevant. That approach was fortified by s.7(3)(a) ibid.; if a person such as the motorist made an attempt to provide a specimen and did what he could (or if he explained that he was unable to provide any specimen because of his condition) the police would be able to require a specimen of blood or urine; if a suspect did not so conduct himself the provisions of s.7(3)(a) would be nullified. The need for a causative link between the physical or mental condition and the failure to provide the specimen had also been correctly identified in *DPP v Crofton* [1994] R.T.R. 279 (see § 4.277 above).

4.280   A useful article by Dr Jocelyn Morris on the difficulties of satisfying the Lion Intoximeter 3000's appetite for breath appeared at 151 J.P.N. 249. It seemed to be the case that blowing too hard increased quite considerably the acceptable minimum volume for analysis required by the machine and thus multiplied the subject's difficulties. It should be noted, however, that according to the Operator Manuals for the approved evidential breath testing devices of the second generation, the provision by a subject of satisfactory breath specimens for such machines should be an easier task than with their predecessors. So far as the Camic Datamaster is concerned, e.g., it is said that "... unlike the previous breath analysers there is now no minimum breath volume requirement. The breath analyser will automatically monitor the blowing rate and the alcohol level of the breath sample and determine whether a satisfactory sample has been provided." The Handbook for the lion intoxilyzer 6000UK exhorts the subject to "... exhale continuously through the mouthpiece to make the beeper sound and bring up the vertical and horizontal bars in the display". In order to achieve that objective "... he does not have to blow hard", and the volume of breath which must be provided is just 1.2 litres. In the event of any alcohol being detected in the sample, however, the subject must continue to blow until deep lung air is reached. The Manual for the Intoximeter EC/IR instructs the subject to "... take a deep breath and blow into the mouthpiece as steadily and long as possible". No minimum volume or pressure is specified.

A physical inability is capable of amounting to a reasonable excuse, e.g. bronchitis or asthma if breath is demanded, or haemophilia if blood is required. A potential inability should be communicated to the officer conducting the breath test, but see the case law and commentary in § 4.115 above. The religious beliefs of a person precluding the giving of blood were held, however, *not* to amount to a reasonable excuse (*R. v John* [1974] R.T.R. 332). In *John*, while following *R. v Lennard*, it was said that the language of *Lennard*, if construed too strictly, might result in an "over rigid approach", but that a distinction must be drawn between some physical or mental condition of a person which might preclude the giving of specimens, and his beliefs, which although sincere could not preclude the giving of specimens.

4.281   A genuine physical inability to provide a second specimen of urine within an hour of the successful provision of a first specimen can in appropriate circumstances amount to a reasonable excuse (*McGregor v Jessop* 1988 S.L.T. 719, following *R. v Lennard*). There would appear to be nothing, however, to prevent the police in such circumstances from applying *Hall v Allan* 1984 S.L.T. 199 and requiring a specimen of blood for analysis. Some small comfort may be derived by the defendant in a marginal case from the passing of at least an hour before the provision by him of a definitive specimen.

McGregor v Jessop above was distinguished as to its facts by the High Court of Justiciary in *McGuckin v O'Donnell* (2000) 2001 S.L.T. 768. Having successfully provided a first specimen, the defendant had failed to provide a second specimen of urine within the one hour allowed. On being charged with failure to provide a specimen without reasonable excuse, his response was "I can't provide it, I'm not ready for one". On the facts of the case there was nothing in the defendant's attitude to the requirement made of him to suggest that there was any reasonable excuse for his failure to provide a specimen, because he had made no attempt even to pass a specimen when asked to do so on a number of occasions during the hour. In the light of the fact that there was nothing in the way of a medical condition or physical incapacity to prevent, at the very least, an attempt being made to pass urine during the specified period, the sheriff had been entitled to reach the view that the driver was in effect refusing to provide a specimen when required to do so.

One circumstance that may amount to a reasonable excuse is if the defendant **4.282** does not understand the statutory warning that he will be prosecuted if he fails or refuses to supply specimens for analysis (*R. v Dolan* [1970] R.T.R. 43; see further § 4.249). In *Beck v Sager* [1979] Crim. L.R. 257 it was held to be a reasonable excuse that the defendant was unable to understand because of his limited command of English the purpose of the requirement to provide a laboratory specimen or to appreciate the penal consequence of a refusal. *Beck v Sager* was explained in *Spalding v Paine* [1985] Crim. L.R. 673 in the terms of the definition of "reasonable excuse" by Lawton L.J. in *Lennard* above in that the defendant in *Beck*, because of a lack of English, was "mentally unable" to understand both what was required and the penal nature of failing to comply with the requirement. In *Spalding* the defendant was found in the driving seat of an illegally parked car with a half bottle still containing some whisky on the front passenger seat. At the police station she repeatedly said she wanted to die. The justices' finding that because of her emotional distress she had a reasonable excuse in that she had not heard or been aware of the requirement was upheld on the ground that it came within the principle as explained in *Beck v Sager*; the court distinguished the situation of self-induced intoxication rendering the defendant unable to appreciate the request being made to him. The principle of *Beck v Sager* was reiterated by the Divisional Court in *Chief Constable of Avon & Somerset v Singh* [1988] R.T.R. 107. There was doubt as to the respondent's ability to understand anything more than simple English; accordingly he could not be regarded as having understood the nature of the warning read to him at the police station and in those circumstances should have been acquitted of the charge under what is now s.7(6).

As indicated in *Spalding v Paine* above, an inability to understand the breath **4.283** test procedure as a result of self-induced intoxication cannot amount to a reasonable excuse for failure to provide a specimen for analysis. The Divisional Court so held in *DPP v Beech* [1992] Crim. L.R. 64, when remitting the case to justices with a direction to convict. To have held otherwise would have been to defeat the purpose of the legislation.

FAILING TO ALLOW SPECIMEN TO BE LABORATORY TESTED

The offence (s.7A)

4.284   A person who, without reasonable excuse, fails to give his permission for a laboratory test of a specimen of blood taken from him without his consent under s.7A is guilty of an offence (s.7A(6)).

By virtue of s.7A(1) a police officer may request a medical practitioner to take a specimen of blood from a person irrespective of whether that person consents if:

    (a) the person concerned is a person from whom the officer would (absent any incapacity or objection under s.9 (protection of hospital patients)) be entitled under s.7 to require the provision of a specimen of blood for a laboratory test;

    (b) it appears to that officer that the person concerned has been involved in an accident that constitutes or is comprised in the matter under investigation or the circumstances thereof;

    (c) it appears to that officer that the person concerned is or may be incapable (whether or not he has purported to do so) of giving a valid consent to the taking of a specimen of blood; and

    (d) it appears to that officer that that person's incapacity is attributable to medical reasons.

4.285   A request under s.7A may not be made to the medical practitioner who has clinical care of the person concerned (s.7A(2)(a)). It will normally be made to a police medical practitioner (as defined in s.7A(7)), but provision is made for any other registered medical practitioner to be pressed into service if necessary (s.7A(2)). In any event a specimen of blood taken by a medical practitioner in accordance with s.7A will be lawfully taken, and the practitioner concerned may provide a sample to the police (s.7A(3)).

A specimen taken in accordance with s.7A may not be subjected to a laboratory test unless the person from whom it was taken has subsequently been informed of its taking, has been required to give his permission for it to be laboratory tested, and has done so (s.7A(4)). A person who is required to give permission for a laboratory test must be warned by the officer making the requirement that a failure to give the permission may render him liable to prosecution (s.7A(5)).

4.286   As with the offence of failing to provide a specimen under s.7(6) (see §§ 4.252 et seq.), there are two sets of penalties; (a) where the offender was driving or attempting to drive, and (b) all other cases, i.e. where the offender was not driving or attempting to drive, whether or not he was in charge. Where the offender was driving or attempting to drive, the offence under s.7A is obligatorily disqualifiable in accordance with Pt I of Sch.2 to the 1988 Offenders Act, as amended. On the other hand, where the offender was not driving or attempting to drive, the offence is subject to discretionary disqualification (see paragraph (b) in columns 4 and 5 of the entry relating to s.7A in Pt I of Sch.2 to the 1988 Offenders Act) and an offender incurs 10 penalty points in accordance with column 7 ibid. No doubt in the majority of cases where the offender is not driving or attempting to drive it can be shown that he was in charge, but even if he is neither proved to be in charge nor driving or attempting to drive, he will still be liable to the full range of penalties set out in the Part of Sch.2 to the 1988 Offenders Act referred to above. In *McCormick v Hitchins* [1988] R.T.R. 182 where the offence concerned was failing to provide a specimen contrary to s.7(6), special reasons were found for not endorsing the offender's licence with the obligatory 10 penalty points where he had had no intention of driving the vehicle and could not have been a danger on the road. It would appear that in appropriate circumstances this case may be of application to an offence under s.7A.

As with the offence of failing to provide a specimen contrary to s.7(6), the word "fails" includes "refuses" (s.11(2)). The offence is only committed if the defendant fails or refuses "without reasonable excuse". It has long been held with regard to s.7(6) offences that once the defence of reasonable excuse is advanced it is for the prosecution to disprove it (*Rowland v Thorpe* [1970] 3 All E.R. 195 at 197). Furthermore, it is a question of fact as to whether a defendant has a reasonable excuse and the court must be satisfied so that it is sure that the defendant had no reasonable excuse before he can be convicted (*R. v Harling* [1970] R.T.R. 441; *R. v Knightley* [1971] 2 All E.R. 1041). But whether facts are capable of amounting to a reasonable excuse is a matter of law; if it is capable in law of amounting to a reasonable excuse, then it becomes a matter of fact and degree whether it does so or not, with the burden being on the prosecution to negative it (*Law v Stephens* [1971] R.T.R. 358). There would appear to be no reason why these cases should not be equally applicable to offences contrary to s.7A.

HOSPITAL PATIENTS

Introduction

The present law, like earlier legislation, contains special provisions for the protection of hospital patients.   **4.287**

Section 9 of the Road Traffic Act 1988 states that while a person is *at a hospital as a patient* he cannot be required to co-operate with a preliminary test or provide a specimen for a laboratory test, or have taken from him without his consent a specimen of blood, or be required to give his permission for a sample so taken to be subjected to laboratory testing, unless *the medical practitioner in immediate charge of his case* has been notified of the proposal to take the specimen or make the requirement concerned. The medical practitioner may object either to the requirement being made or the specimen being taken (s.9(1), (1A)). The grounds upon which the doctor may object are that the requirement, the actual provision or the warning under s.7(7), or in the case of a sample of blood taken without consent under s.7A that the actual taking, the requirement or the warning under s.7A(5) would be prejudicial to the proper care and treatment of the patient.

The terms of s.9 of the Road Traffic Act 1988 are mandatory, not merely good practice (*R. v Bryan* [2008] EWCA Crim 1568; [2009] R.T.R. 4).

"At a hospital"

"Hospital" is defined in s.11(2) as an institution which provides medical or surgical treatment for in-patients or out-patients. Whether an institution is a hospital seems to be a simple question of fact. Both private and NHS hospitals come within the definition. The protection afforded by s.9(1) depends on whether the person is a patient "at" the hospital. Under earlier legislation, for this reason,   **4.288** someone in an ambulance on his way to hospital was held not to be "at a hospital" (*Hollingsworth v Howard* [1974] R.T.R. 58). A person is, however, "at a hospital" if he is anywhere within the precincts of the hospital, e.g. the hospital car park (*Att Gen's Reference (No.1 of 1976)* [1977] R.T.R. 284).

"As a patient"

4.289   A person may be at a hospital, but the protection of the statute only applies to a person who can be said to be at the hospital "as a patient". That this is usually a simple question of fact was confirmed by the Divisional Court in *Askew v DPP* [1988] R.T.R. 303. The defendant had been discharged from hospital with some painkilling tablets and the casualty doctor told the police that those tablets would not in any way affect any breath-test procedure. He provided a positive breath test in the hospital car park. The following day he was readmitted to the hospital when it was discovered that he was suffering from broken ribs. On those facts the justices could only sensibly conclude (as they had done) that the defendant was not a patient at the time that the request for a breath test had been made. The word "patient" clearly includes both in-patients and out-patients in view of the definition of "hospital" above. Hospitals usually have a strict routine as to the keeping of records and once a person is admitted as a patient he will be regarded by the hospital as a patient until discharged by a doctor or by himself. If he discharges himself against medical advice the hospital will normally record this fact. The purpose of the law was held to be the protection of patients and the avoidance of a collision between doctors trying to treat their patients and the police endeavouring to require a breath test. In the *Att Gen's Reference (No.1 of 1976)* [1977] R.T.R. 284 it was held that where a person attended hospital to seek treatment he ceases to be a patient as soon as the treatment on the occasion of his visit is complete, even if he is required subsequently to return for further treatment (e.g. for the removal of stitches). It was also suggested that "treatment" should be given a wide interpretation (e.g. if he was told "sit down for half-an-hour before you go", then the subsequent half hour would be included). In *Watt v MacNeill* [1988] R.T.R. 310, however, and on very different facts, the High Court of Justiciary declined to follow *Att Gen's Reference (No.1 of 1976)* when holding that a patient who had received treatment, but who nevertheless at the relevant time was still upon a hospital trolley naked from the waist up and minus his shoes and had not then discharged himself, could legitimately be regarded as continuing to be in hospital as a patient. Clearly the primary consideration for a court in assessing the defendant's status is the particular facts and circumstances of the case concerned.

4.290   In *Webber v DPP* [1998] R.T.R. 111 it was held that where a suspect whilst a patient at a hospital was lawfully required to provide a specimen of blood, that requirement was not varied or discharged by the fact that the patient left the hospital before she could comply with it. It remained valid when the discharged patient was subsequently arrested under s.6 of the Road Traffic Act 1988 and taken to a police station where a breath analysis machine was available. There was nothing in the statute to say that the locus was so vital that the specimen had to be provided at the hospital. The defendant had refused to take a preliminary breath test at the hospital; she was therefore required to provide a blood sample, but was discharged before she could comply. The lawful requirement for the provision of a blood specimen set in train a procedure backed up by the sanction of s.7(6) of the 1988 Act. Once set in train that course could not be discharged by an irrelevant change of locus. As long as the s.9(1)(a) procedure was started in hospital and not abrogated, it continued after the patient left hospital. Only if an officer, following the patient's discharge, set in train the s.7(1)(a) procedure, making it abundantly plain that the procedure previously in course was no longer in course, could there be an abrogation. In the instant case there was no such indication.

"Medical practitioner in immediate charge of his case"

This phrase was also included in the former law. It was held that the police do **4.291** not have to produce medical lists to prove that the person is a medical practitioner, nor do they have to call the doctor himself and check that no objection is made. In *Jones v Brazil* [1970] R.T.R. 449 it was agreed that if the police said M appeared to be the casualty officer with nurses and others in attendance, this was sufficient to raise a prima facie case that M was the "medical practitioner in immediate charge of his case".

A constable may give evidence that the doctor did not object; this is not hearsay (*Burn v Kernohan* [1973] R.T.R. 82).

Preliminary tests

While a person is at a hospital as a patient he cannot be required to co-operate **4.292** with a preliminary test, which in practice is likely to be a preliminary breath test, until the doctor has been notified of the proposal and the doctor does not object. It was held in respect of a requirement under earlier legislation that a patient did not have to be out of earshot of the doctor when the police officer is notifying the doctor of his proposal (*Oxford v Lowton* [1978] R.T.R. 237). (That decision was approved and followed under the current legislation in *Butler v DPP* [2001] R.T.R. 28, with regard to a request for a blood specimen.)

The doctor may object not only to the administration of a preliminary test but also to "the requirement". The condition of a patient may be such that a doctor may consider it prejudicial to the proper care of his patient's treatment merely to be asked to co-operate with a preliminary test.

In practice the doctor is frequently asked simultaneously by the constable if he objects to the requirement to co-operate with a preliminary test, the requirement to provide specimens of blood or urine, the actual provision of specimens and the accompanying warning of the consequence of failure to provide specimens for analysis; in *Ratledge v Oliver* [1974] R.T.R. 394 it was held that there was no objection to such a course.

Once the requirement to co-operate with a preliminary test is made the patient is guilty of an offence if he fails or refuses to so co-operate (see further § 4.68). The preliminary test must be administered "at the hospital"; it cannot be administered elsewhere or, seemingly, at another hospital (s.9(1)(a)).

The patient, while a patient at the hospital, cannot be arrested whether or not he provides a positive preliminary breath test or fails or refuses to co-operate with a preliminary test (s.6D(3)).

Blood or urine specimens

None of the approved evidential devices can be used at a hospital. Section 7(2) **4.293** only allows a requirement for specimens of breath for evidential purposes to be made at a police station.

Although in most cases the police will only require the provision of blood or urine specimens after the patient has been required to co-operate with a preliminary test, which in practice is likely to be a preliminary breath test, the police can apparently require the provision of blood or urine notwithstanding the fact that the patient has not been asked to co-operate with a preliminary test. Section 7 entitles a constable to require specimens for analysis "in the course of an investigation whether a person has committed an offence under section 4 or section 5 ". If, therefore, the doctor has objected to a breath test but does not object to the warning and the requirement for the provision of a blood or urine specimen, a specimen of blood or urine may be required.

4.294　　　The procedure governing the provision of specimens of blood or urine from a suspect at a police station in England and Wales has been established by the House of Lords in *DPP v Warren* [1992] 4 All E.R. 865 (see §§ 4.139 et seq. above); the procedure applicable in Scotland would appear to be somewhat different in the wake of *Simpson v McClory* 1993 S.L.T. 861 (see § 4.213 above). The Divisional Court in *Ogburn v DPP* [1994] R.T.R. 241 addressed itself to a situation not considered in *Warren*, namely the provision of a specimen of blood or urine from a suspect at a time when he was a hospital patient. The court concluded that the procedure laid down in *Warren* was, with some modifications, of equal application in that situation. The appropriate procedure in cases involving a patient in hospital should begin with the officer telling the patient that a breath specimen for analysis could not be taken as breath specimens could be taken only at a police station; it should then continue as set out by Lord Bridge in *Warren* and as applied by the Divisional Court in *Edge v DPP* [1993] R.T.R. 146 and *Meade v DPP* [1993] R.T.R. 151 (both discussed at § 4.144 above).

A quite contrary view was taken, however, by the Divisional Court (Beldam L.J. and Buxton J.) in *R. v Burton upon Trent JJ. Ex p. Woolley* [1995] R.T.R. 139, in which *Ogburn v DPP* (referred to throughout the report as *Williams v DPP*) was reviewed and disapproved. It was apparent to their Lordships that *Warren* was not a "hospital" case and that Lord Bridge did not there specifically address the particular requirements that existed in such cases. The court in *Ogburn* had clearly seen itself as applying the general requirements identified by Lord Bridge to the example of hospital cases, without seeking to add of its own motion to the elements found within Lord Bridge's speech. Such an application was not in the court's view justified by the 1988 Act and the elucidation of the requirements of that Act by the House of Lords in *Warren*. In hospital cases, there was no obligation for the constable to inform an injured driver why a specimen of breath could not be taken, but at some stage during the process at the hospital the constable had to ask the driver whether there was any reason why a specimen of blood should not be taken. There was no obligation for the constable to ask specifically whether there was any such reason based on medical grounds. (Although in the light of these conflicting decisions of the Divisional Court the law cannot be stated with certainty, it is nonetheless submitted with all due respect that *R. v Burton upon Trent JJ. Ex p. Woolley* presents a cogent view of the statutory requirements and is likely to be followed.)

4.295　　　Our opinion that *R. v Burton upon Trent JJ. Ex p. Woolley* above presented a cogent view of the statutory requirements governing the provision of specimens in a hospital and was likely to be followed was reinforced by the decision of the Divisional Court in *Jones (Vivian) v DPP* [2004] EWHC 3165; [2005] R.T.R. 15. Having refused a preliminary breath test, the defendant agreed to provide a specimen of blood. The specimen was duly divided into two canisters, one of which was placed in the defendant's handbag by the constable. The defendant's submission that the evidence of analysis should be excluded on the grounds that the constable had failed to tell her why she could not provide a specimen of breath pursuant to s.7 of the 1988 Act and that she had been prejudiced in that she had not had a sample of blood to analyse since due to her drowsiness at the time she had no recollection of receiving the sample and never found it was rejected by the justices, and rightly so. As the procedure had been carried out from first to last at a hospital, there was under s.7(2) (as it then was) no power to take a specimen of breath for analysis from the defendant. There was therefore no conceivable good reason to require the police to explain why a breath test could not be taken and such a requirement would offer no proper or legitimate protection to the individual. Furthermore, the justices had been entitled to find that the defendant had been supplied with a sample of her blood when the constable offered her the sample and subsequently placed it into her handbag.

R. v Burton upon Trent JJ. Ex p. Woolley above was distinguished by the Divisional Court in *Butler v DPP* [2001] R.T.R. 28, on different, though related, facts. The defendant when at the police station earlier had stated that he was suffering from an "immune system breakdown"; that information had not been conveyed by the police to the medical practitioner in immediate charge of his case at the hospital. Whilst it would be otiose if the legislation required the police officer to make in hospital a general medical inquiry when the medical practitioner might be expected to make that and other inquiries, it would not be otiose if the legislation required a police officer, who knows that the patient has articulated a potential medical reason for not taking a specimen of blood, to tell the medical practitioner in the hospital of the potential medical reason. There was, in the court's view, a difference between making an unnecessary general inquiry and passing on potentially relevant specific knowledge. Accordingly the procedure required by the legislation had not been followed, and the blood specimen obtained from the defendant should not have been admitted in evidence.

The safeguards for the provision of a blood or urine specimen are similar to those under earlier legislation. The doctor has to be notified of the proposal to make the requirement and may object if the requirement, the warning under s.7(7) or the provision of blood or urine would be prejudicial to the proper care and treatment of his patient.   **4.296**

Section 9(1)(b) states that if the doctor objects, "the requirement shall not be made". At first sight this would seem to preclude any requirement being made if the doctor raises a partial objection, e.g. an objection to blood but not to urine. The purpose of s.9 is the proper protection of patients and a strict and careful analysis does not seem to require s.9 to be interpreted in such a way that an objection to the taking of one type of specimen has the effect of forbidding the constable to require the taking of the other.

As under earlier legislation the doctor may object not only to the requirement but also to the warning required to be given to the patient should he refuse or fail to give specimens for analysis. It was held in *Baker v Foulkes* [1975] R.T.R. 509 that there was no obligation on the police to notify the doctor that the warning   **4.297** would be given or to obtain his consent to the warning; nor is there any obligation on the police to ensure that the patient is out of earshot when the police notify the doctor (*Oxford v Lowton* and *Butler v DPP* at §§ 4.292 and 4.295 above). The warning required under s.7(7) is simply that "failure or refusal to supply a specimen may render you liable to prosecution" and is thus less frightening and less likely to be objected to than the warning under the former law ("failure to provide a specimen may make you liable to imprisonment, fine and disqualification").

The requirement will be to provide specimens either of blood or urine. The patient will not have a choice: the constable making the requirement shall decide whether the specimen required shall be of blood or urine save that if a medical practitioner is of the opinion that for medical reasons a specimen of blood cannot or should not be taken the specimen shall be a specimen of urine (s.7(4)). When informed by a constable at a hospital that she was required to produce one or other of a blood or urine sample, and that the constable had the right to elect which it should be but that she could make representations to him as to the decision, the defendant replied: "No, no, no". The constable did not go on to the next stage of the procedure and choose the kind of sample he was requiring and to put the request again. Her conviction for failure to provide a specimen was upheld by the Divisional Court in *Burke v DPP* [1999] R.T.R. 387. In order to prove the offence under s.7(6) of the 1988 Act, the prosecutor had to prove that the defendant was required to provide a specimen in pursuance of s.7, and whether the defendant was so required was a matter of fact. In order to prove the making of a requirement, it was not essential for the constable either to specify which category of specimen, blood or urine, he required or to ask the defendant whether she was willing to provide that specimen. There was evidence on which the justices could be satisfied that the defendant had refused without reasonable excuse to provide a specimen.

4.298　　Difficulties have arisen in the past where a person either ceases to be a patient at the hospital or absconds (*Bosley v Long* [1970] R.T.R. 432; *Bourlet v Porter* [1973] R.T.R. 293; *Cunliffe v Bleasdale* [1972] Crim. L.R. 567; *Edwards v Davies* [1982] R.T.R. 279), but in practice the present law does not seem to provide as many difficulties as earlier legislation. Cases will no doubt arise where a patient absconds from hospital after being required to co-operate with a preliminary test or having to provide blood or urine specimens. If he absconds after being required to co-operate with a preliminary test, he can be dealt with under s.6, as he will by definition no longer be a patient at a hospital. If he absconds after being required to provide either a specimen of blood or of urine, he will have failed to provide a specimen as soon as he absconds, contrary to s.7(6).

Where the person does not abscond but ceases to be a patient at the hospital because his treatment is complete (see § 4.289) s.9 does not require the person to remain a patient by the time he actually provides the specimen. The only requirement of s.9 is that if a person is a patient at a hospital, the specimen must be provided at the hospital. If the person concerned has not been required to provide a breath test before he ceases to be a patient, there seems no reason why he should not be required to provide a breath test under s.6(2), nor if he is still at the hospital does there seem to be any reason precluding the police from requiring him to provide blood or urine under s.7 for analysis.

4.299　　A defendant, in hospital with a broken pelvis after a traffic accident, supplied a blood sample for hospital purposes. Having ascertained that there were no medical reasons to prevent the taking of a further blood sample, a constable, during the course of an investigation as to whether an offence under what is now s.4 or s.5 had been committed, required the defendant to provide a specimen for laboratory analysis. He failed to do so and was charged with an offence under what is now s.7(6). In his defence he put forward as a reasonable excuse for not providing the specimen the fact that he had already provided the hospital with a sample of his blood. The justices were of opinion that, although he was in some pain, he understood the requirement made of him, and the excuse he proffered did not relate to his physical or mental capacity to supply the specimen; they convicted him. The conviction was upheld by the Divisional Court in *Kemp v Chief Constable of Kent* [1987] R.T.R. 66. Whether or not circumstances were capable of providing the defence of reasonable excuse was a matter of law; whether or not circumstances did provide such an excuse, however, was a question of fact for the justices, and on the particular facts of the case they were plainly entitled to decide as they did.

POST-OFFENCE CONSUMPTION OF ALCOHOL OR DRUGS

Alcohol

A certificate of analysis obtained in accordance with s.7 of the Road Traffic **4.300** Act 1988 shall be "taken into account" in respect of offences under s.4 and s.5 of the 1988 Act, and may be evidence of the proportion of alcohol or any drug in a specimen of breath, blood or urine (1988 Offenders Act s.15). Section 15(2) of the 1988 Offenders Act further provides that it shall be assumed that the proportion of alcohol at the time of the offence is not less than that contained in the certificate of analysis.

It is also provided by s.15(3) of the 1988 Offenders Act that this statutory assumption that his alcohol level was not less than that of the certificate will not apply if the accused proves that he (a) had consumed alcohol after he had ceased to drive, attempt to drive or be in charge, and before he provided the specimen and (b) that had he not done so the proportion of alcohol would not have been such as to impair his ability to drive properly or, in the case of s.5 offences, above the prescribed limit. It should be noted that the onus of proof that he consumed alcohol is on the defendant, and it is for the defendant to establish by properly admissible evidence that he had consumed alcohol after the relevant time. In *Patterson v Charlton* [1985] R.T.R. 18 there was evidence by admission that the defendant had driven the car but no evidence that he had driven it after drinking. The justices dismissed the case but were directed by the Divisional Court that once the sample showed excess alcohol what is now s.15(3) of the 1988 Offenders Act operated to transfer the burden of proof on to the defendant to show that he consumed alcohol after he ceased to drive; there is no requirement for the prosecution to prove that drink was taken before the defendant drove. *Patterson v Charlton* was applied by the Divisional Court in *DPP v Williams* [1989] Crim. L.R. 382. It was unfortunate, said the court in remitting the case for the hearing to be continued, that the justices had had neither that case nor the provisions of what is now s.15(3) of the 1988 Offenders Act drawn to their attention. Had that happened, they would doubtless have appreciated that the defendant's admission of having driven his car that night had effectively shifted the burden of proof in his direction.

4.301   The compatibility or otherwise with the European Convention on Human
Rights of the statutory provisions relating to the "hip-flask" defence was
considered by the Court of Appeal in *R. v Drummond* [2002] EWCA Crim 527;
[2002] R.T.R. 21. The judge at first instance had declined to accept a submission
from the defence that s.15(3) of the 1988 Offenders Act should be "read down"
so that it imposed only an evidential and not a persuasive burden and accordingly
that the ultimate burden of proof remained upon the prosecution. In the court's
view he had been right to do so. Not all apparently persuasive burdens had to be
"read down" to be evidential burdens. It was necessary to look at the legislation
as a whole to determine whether Parliament intended to impose a persuasive
burden and whether such a burden was justifiable. The offence of driving whilst
over the legal limit did not require the court to ascertain the intent of the accused
at all. Conviction followed after an exact scientific test and if the accused drank
after the event it was *he* (our emphasis) who defeated the aim of the legislature
by doing something which made the scientific test potentially unreliable.
Furthermore, the relevant scientific evidence to set against the result obtained
from the specimen of breath or blood was all within the knowledge (or means of
access) of the accused rather than the prosecution. The legislative interference
with the presumption of innocence in s.15 of the 1988 Offenders Act amounted to
the imposition of a persuasive burden on the defendant and such interference was
not only justified but was also no greater than was necessary.

   As the onus of proof is on the defence, it would seem that as in other criminal
statutes where Parliament has placed an onus of proof on the defendant it will be
held that the onus is only that of a balance of probabilities.

4.302   Where the offence is under s.4 the defendant merely has to show that but for
the added alcohol, his ability to drive properly would not have been impaired.
Where the offence is under s.5 the defendant has to show that his alcohol level
would not have been above the prescribed limit. In this connection, the comments in the 1965 *Report of a Special Committee of the British Medical Association* as to the translation of blood-alcohol concentration into quantity of alcohol
consumed should be noted (see § 4.172). It will also usually be necessary for the
defence to give expert evidence of the rate at which the defendant would have
eliminated alcohol from his body, and in this connection it is important to bear in
mind the degree of potential variance between individuals identified by the *Report
on Breath Alcohol Measuring Instruments* (HMSO, 1985) (see § 4.173)).

   Courts are advised to adopt a similar approach as in the "laced drink" case of
Pugsley v Hunter [1973] R.T.R. 284, namely that unless it is obvious to a
layperson that the post-offence consumption of alcohol explained the excess, the
defendant must call medical or scientific evidence to prove that he would not
otherwise have been above the prescribed limit (*Dawson v Lunn* [1986] R.T.R.
234 *Note*, where the dicta of Lord Widgery in *Pugsley v Hunter* were said to be
equally applicable to the defence under what is now s.15(3) of the 1988 Offenders Act where the facts were not obvious from the non-expert evidence). Courts
should beware, however, of being drawn into detailed scientific calculation except
where there is "reasonably clear, straightforward and relatively simple evidence"
from which they may determine the level of alcohol at the time of driving (per
Glidewell L.J. in *Smith v Geraghty* [1986] R.T.R. 222, a case on special reasons).
Where justices had received clear expert evidence as to the amount of alcohol
necessary to cause a particular driver to exceed the prescribed limit and had been

given plausible evidence as to the quantity of alcohol consumed after an accident, it was open to them, notwithstanding a discrepancy concerning the amount of post-accident alcohol indicated by the defendant to police as having been consumed by him, to find that the defendant had established a defence under s.15(3) of the 1988 Offenders Act. The Divisional Court so held in *DPP v Lowden* [1993] R.T.R. 349, distinguishing *DPP v Singh* [1988] R.T.R. 209 on the basis that in that earlier case the justices had had no expert guidance from which they could have drawn the conclusion that the defendant had discharged the burden of proof placed upon him by s.15(3). The Divisional Court in *DPP v Tooze* [2007] EWHC 2186 provided a useful reminder that in cases of post-offence consumption of alcohol the burden of proof is on the driver to prove that the alcohol he had drunk after driving had been responsible for his being over the legal limit. Here the defendant had been acquitted by the magistrates despite producing no scientific evidence to prove that it was the alcohol consumed after driving that meant he was over the legal limit. As the magistrates had in any event concluded that it was likely that the defendant was over the limit when he drove, the case was remitted with a direction to convict.

Section 15(3)(a) of the 1988 Offenders Act requires the defendant to show that **4.303** he consumed alcohol "after he had ceased to drive, attempt to drive or be in charge of a motor vehicle on a road or other public place". That the "or"s in this subsection are disjunctive rather than conjunctive has been established by the Divisional Court in *Rynsard v Spalding* [1985] Crim. L.R. 795. If a person is charged with "driving" he must show consumption of alcohol after he has ceased to drive; if charged with "attempting to drive", he must show the consumption was after ceasing to attempt to drive; if charged with "being in charge", he must show consumption after he ceased to be in charge (ibid.).

Drugs

It should be noted that while a certificate of analysis showing the proportion of **4.304** a drug in a specimen can be "taken into account" under s.15(2) of the 1988 Offenders Act, there is no statutory assumption in the section that the proportion of a drug in the specimen is not less than that at the time the offence is committed. Section 15(2) refers only to the proportion of *alcohol*. Moreover, the proviso in s.15(3)(a), (b) of the 1988 Offenders Act also refers only to alcohol. It would therefore appear that it is first necessary for the prosecution to relate the amount of a drug shown in the certificate to the amount of the drug that would have been shown if the specimen had been provided at the time of the offence. Secondly, it will be open to the defence to attack the certificate of analysis on the ground that he had ingested the drug after the time of the offence, but before he provided the specimen of blood or urine.

DEFENCE OF DURESS

The line of cases headed by *R. v Willer* [1987] R.T.R. 22 (see § 5.81), in which **4.305** it was held that duress was available as a defence to a charge of reckless driving, has been extended to include a case where that defence was made out in respect of a charge of driving with excess alcohol. In *DPP v Bell* [1992] Crim. L.R. 176 the Divisional Court held that it was clear that duress was made out where fear engendered by threats caused a person to lose complete control of his will. The facts were that the defendant had been out drinking with some friends. Some trouble broke out which caused him to run back to his car pursued by others who were less than well disposed towards him. Fearing serious physical injury, he drove off for some distance in a state of terror. The fact that he drove only for some distance down the road and not all the way home was of significance, since in *DPP v Jones* [1990] R.T.R. 33 the defence of duress was held not to have been established where the defendant, having driven off to escape the immediate danger, continued to drive to his home some two miles away without checking whether or not he was being pursued. In the instant case, however, the defence of duress continued to avail the defendant and had not been negated by the prosecution.

Two cases which on their facts did not meet the requirements for the establishment of the defence of duress were dealt with together by the Divisional Court in *DPP v Davis*; *DPP v Pittaway* [1994] Crim. L.R. 600. Although the defence of duress was subjective, it also had objective elements to it, namely whether there was good cause to fear death or serious injury would occur unless the defendant acted as he had done, and whether a sober person of reasonable firmness, sharing the defendant's characteristics, would have responded in the same way. In *Davis* the defendant had fled from the flat of a male acquaintance in order to escape from an unwelcome homosexual advance and had driven two miles before being stopped. In *Pittaway* the defendant ran 200yds home from a party outside which she had been the subject of angry words and unspecified threats from a man with whom she had formed a relationship, hid in her car for five minutes and then drove 200yds before being stopped. The man she was seeking to avoid was not in the vicinity at the time. In the court's view the justices had neglected to apply the objective limb of the test, since there was no evidence in either case of a threat of death or serious bodily injury. Both cases were remitted to the magistrates with a direction to convict.

4.306   Following a New Year's Eve party, the defendant was violently assaulted by her husband, who also injured himself and then departed in a taxi for hospital having left her without a phone, but saying that police were on their way and that she had better leave before he returned home. The police having failed to arrive, she left her house at about 6am to drive to her former home (where her children were) some 72 miles away. She was stopped by police about 9.30am and when breathalysed was found to be over the prescribed limit. She was acquitted by justices on the basis of duress. It was held by the Divisional Court, however, in *DPP v Tomkinson* [2001] R.T.R. 38 that the defence of duress did not avail her; she was no longer subjected to any effective threat of violence when she left the immediate area of her home in her car to commence the long journey from Harrogate to Sale, and there was no basis for the justices' conclusion that a sober woman of reasonable firmness would or might have responded to the situation as the defendant did and drive 72 miles over the Pennines. It was similarly held in *DPP v Mullally* [2006] EWHC 3448 that duress could not be established where the defendant, despite becoming aware of the arrival of police to deal with the threat of violence from her sister's partner at her sister's address, continued to drive to her own residence. In *Crown Prosecution Service v Brown* [2007] EWHC 3274; [2007] All E.R. (D.) 330 the Divisional Court concluded that the justices had been wrong to accept a defence of duress of circumstances in relation to an offence of driving with excess alcohol. Mr Brown said that he had driven to avoid a violent confrontation following a threatening phone call. At the time he was stopped there was no evidence that the threat was continuing or that he reasonably believed he was being pursued. The case was remitted to the magistrates' court with a recommendation to convict. The court did not have to resolve the question of whether or not the defence was available at the time he got into the car as it was not available when he was stopped.

INSANITY

Notwithstanding that the common law defence of insanity might be available to a defendant in a summary trial, it could only be raised where guilty intent was an essential element of the offence. Therefore, because a charge of driving with excess alcohol was a strict liability offence for which no mens rea was required, insanity was not available as a defence. The Divisional Court so held in *DPP v Harper* (1997) 161 J.P. 697 when remitting the case to the justices with a direction to convict.   **4.307**

NON-INSANE AUTOMATISM

The High Court of Justiciary held in *Finegan v Heywood* 2000 J.C. 444; 2000 S.L.T. 905 that where a person whose conscious mind was not controlling his actions because of parasomnia (in lay terms, sleepwalking) drove a vehicle whilst the proportion of alcohol in his breath exceeded the prescribed limit, the defence of automatism was not available to him if he knew that previous incidents of such sleepwalking had been preceded by his consuming alcohol. The defendant had been aware that at least three of his prior experiences of the condition had been preceded by his consuming approximately the same amount of alcohol as he had consumed on the occasion in question. The defence of automatism could not be established on proof of a transitory state of parasomnia resulting from, and induced by deliberate and self-induced intoxication.   **4.308**

DEFENCES TO "IN CHARGE" OFFENCES

Defences under s.4(2) and s.5(1)(b)

A person charged under s.4(2) of the 1988 Act with being in charge of a mechanically propelled vehicle while unfit to drive through drink or drugs is deemed not to be in charge of a mechanically propelled vehicle if he proves that at the material time the circumstances were such that there was no likelihood of his driving it so long as he remained unfit to drive through drink or drugs. Similarly s.5(2) of the 1988 Act gives a defence to a charge under s.5(1)(b) (in charge with excess alcohol level) if he proves that, at the time he is alleged to have committed the offence, the circumstances were such that there was no likelihood of his driving the vehicle whilst the proportion of alcohol in his breath, blood or urine remained likely to exceed the prescribed limit. The question whether the reverse onus of proof imposed by s.5(2) needed to be read down under s.3(1) of the Human Rights Act 1998, in order for it to be compatible with the presumption of innocence enshrined in art.6(2) of the European Convention on Human Rights, so that it imposed only an evidential burden of proof on the   **4.309** accused was considered by the House of Lords in *Sheldrake v DPP* [2004] UKHL 43; [2005] R.T.R. 2. Their Lordships unanimously held that in the case of the 1988 Act it was not necessary to read down the onus in s.5(2) as an evidential burden. Section 5(2) was plainly directed to a legitimate object: the prevention of death, injury and damage caused by unfit drivers. The provision met the tests of acceptability identified in the Strasbourg jurisprudence. The burden placed on the defendant could not be regarded as beyond reasonable limits or in any way arbitrary. It was not objectionable to criminalise a defendant's conduct in those circumstances without requiring a prosecutor to prove criminal intent. The defendant had a full opportunity to show that there was no likelihood of his driving, a matter so closely conditioned by his own knowledge and state of mind at the material time as to make it much more appropriate for him to prove on the balance of probabilities that he would not have been likely to drive than for the prosecutor to prove, beyond a reasonable doubt, that he would. The imposition of a legal burden did not go beyond what was necessary. If a driver tried and failed to establish a defence under s.5(2), the resulting conviction could not be regarded as unfair.

Sheldrake is also important for the analysis in the Divisional Court ([2003] EWHC 273, especially Clark L.J. at [54]–[63]) and the House of Lords ([2004] UKHL 43, especially Lord Bingham at [38]–[40] and Lord Carswell at [82]–[85]) of the nature of the offence and the defence in s.5(2) of the 1988 Act. "Likelihood" means real risk, a risk that ought not to be ignored. Thus the defendant must satisfy the court that there is no risk that he would drive while over the limit. The contrast is between a real risk and a fanciful risk. It is important to note that the intention of the accused not to drive is only one factor in deciding whether there is a risk that he may drive while over the limit. "A man's intention may change, especially at night when influenced by alcohol" ([2003] EWHC 273 at [62]).

> "There is ... an obvious risk that if a person is in control of the car when unfit he may drive it ... The defendant can exonerate himself if he can show that the risk which led to the creation of the offence did not in his case exist ... The offence does not require proof that the defendant is likely to drive ... This is not ... an oppressive outcome, since a person in charge of a car when unfit to drive it may properly be expected to divest himself of the power to do so (as by giving the keys to someone else) or put it out of his power to do so (as by going well away)." ([2004] UKHL 43 at [40])

4.310   The statutory defence under s.5(1)(b) was considered again in the case of *Crown Prosecution Service v Thompson* [2007] EWHC 1841; [2008] R.T.R. 5. The defendant was found by police officers asleep in his van in a car park. The keys were in the ignition and the heater fan was working, but the engine was not running. At the police station the defendant provided two samples of breath, with a lower reading of 106µg/100ml. The defendant disclosed to police that the vehicle was a company van in which he often slept due to the nature of his employment. To facilitate this, the van contained a homemade mattress and a sleeping bag (although these had not been used on the occasion in question). No expert evidence was adduced to show when the proportion of alcohol in the defendant's breath/blood would have fallen below the prescribed limit. The justices accepted that the defendant had no intention of driving the vehicle either at the time he entered the vehicle or at the time he was awoken by the police officers. They dismissed the case, and the prosecutor appealed. The appeal was allowed.

The burden of proof was on the defendant to prove the statutory defence on the balance of probabilities. The question to be addressed was whether the defendant had shown that there was no likelihood of his driving the vehicle whilst the alcohol in his body remained likely to be above the prescribed limit. The justices were wrong to focus on the defendant's intention at the time he entered the vehicle or the time he was awoken by the police officers. The defendant's subjective intention could not be decisive in circumstances where he was affected by drink, well above the prescribed limit, intended to drive when he felt "alright", had no way of knowing when he would be below the prescribed limit and had put forward no scientific evidence to indicate when that point might be reached.

The presence of a wheel clamp on a motor vehicle could not be discounted by the court when considering, under s.5(2) of the 1988 Act, the likelihood of the person in charge of the vehicle being able to drive it while over the limit. The Divisional Court so held in *Drake v DPP* [1994] Crim. L.R. 855 when allowing an appeal by way of case stated against the dismissal by the Crown Court of the defendant's appeal against his conviction by justices of a s.5(1)(b) offence. He had refused to pay the fee to have the wheel clamp on his car removed and had then attempted to remove it with a claw hammer. In those circumstances there was no likelihood of his driving the vehicle.

There are semantic differences between the two defences. In s.4 the person is **4.311** deemed not to be in charge if he establishes the statutory defence, in the s.5 offence "it is a defence" if he establishes the statutory defence; in s.4, the defendant has to establish the defence that there was no likelihood of his driving "at the material time", while in s.5 the material time is described as "the time he is alleged to have committed the offence". It is submitted that these differences between the statutory defences are purely semantic. It is difficult to discern a difference in meaning albeit that slightly differing words are used.

The only material difference between the two defences is that in s.4 the defendant has to show there is no likelihood of his driving while unfit and in s.5 that there is no likelihood of his driving while above the prescribed proportion of alcohol in his body.

It is submitted that in practice it may be easier to establish a defence under s.4 **4.312** that there is no likelihood of his driving while unfit than to establish the defence under s.5. In *Northfield v Pinder* [1968] 3 All E.R. 854 the defendant was accused of being in charge with more than 80mg of alcohol in his blood; the certificate of analysis showed that he had 240mg. He was found by his car at 9.14pm and the magistrates considered that he was at that time so hopelessly drunk as to be incapable of driving his car or even of finding it or walking to it, so they dismissed the charge. The High Court quashed their decision and directed a conviction, saying that he must show that there was no likelihood of his driving whilst his level exceeded 80mg and that there had been no evidence that he would not have driven when the worst effects of the drink had worn off. Medical evidence would probably be needed to show when his level would decrease to 80mg but other evidence such as arranging for someone else to drive it or taking a bedroom at a hotel nearby would prove the "unlikelihood" better. A very material factor in almost every case will be the level of alcohol in the blood as found by the analyst. If the level is only just over the limit, the defendant's blood-alcohol level will comparatively quickly recede below 80mg. If, on the other hand, the blood-alcohol level is grossly above the limit, medical evidence may be required even if the defendant can show that he had arranged overnight accommodation. It is perfectly possible for a person to be still over the prescribed limit the morning after the night before, particularly if the night before involved a very large amount of alcohol.

In *Pugsley v Hunter* [1973] R.T.R. 284 it was held that it was only if it were obvious to a layperson that the "lacing" of the defendant's drink accounted for the defendant being above the limit that expert evidence is not required to be called by the defence. That test was commended as the appropriate one to apply by the Divisional Court in *DPP v Frost* [1989] R.T.R. 11. Whereas the question of unfitness was one upon which a layperson might reasonably be expected, in appropriate circumstances, to form a view without expert help, the position under what is now s.5 was quite different. The question of the rate of decline of alcohol in the body was one which, in a case where the defendant was more than marginally over the legal limit and the time interval before his intended resumption of driving was not long, required clear cogent expert evidence on the rate of alcohol destruction. It should be noted that in *Dawson v Lunn* [1986] R.T.R. 234 *Note* the dicta of Lord Widgery in *Pugsley v Hunter* were held to be similarly applicable to a defence under what is now s.15(2), (3) of the 1988 Offenders Act (see § 4.315).

4.313   It is provided by s.4(4) that a court in determining whether there was any likelihood of the defendant driving whilst unfit *may* disregard any injury to him and any damage to his vehicle. Section 4(4) is in identical terms to a similar proviso in s.5(3). It was held by the Divisional Court in *Drake v DPP* [1994] Crim. L.R. 855 (discussed at § 4.310 above) that the application of a wheel clamp could not constitute damage to the vehicle under s.5(3) of the 1988 Act as there had been no intrusion into the integrity of the vehicle.

It should be noted that the word *may* in both subsections imparts a discretion as to the exercise of which the Act gives no assistance. The intention would appear to be to prevent a driver from relying on the defence where, had it not been for the purely fortuitous intervention of an accident, he would have continued to drive or remained in charge.

4.314   A drunken supervisor of a learner driver may be held to be "in charge" of the motor vehicle and in *Sheldon v Jones* (1969) 113 S.J. 942, the prosecution sought to argue that it was impossible for a supervisor to establish that there was no likelihood of his driving since at any moment he might have to take over the driving. The justices found as a fact that there was no such likelihood, and the Divisional Court, although stating that they themselves might have come to a different conclusion, felt unable to disturb the justices' finding to that effect. It is, however, submitted that a supervisor will usually have a difficult task in demonstrating that there was no likelihood of his driving. It is submitted that momentarily taking over control of the steering or of the engine may well amount to "driving" as one of the main duties of a supervisor of a learner driver is to take control of the car in an emergency, as the cases below suggest.

4.315   A man was supervising his wife when she was driving under a provisional licence. He had consumed alcohol in excess of the prescribed limit and was charged with an offence under s.4(2) of the Road Traffic Act 1988. He accepted that he had been in charge of the vehicle but claimed that there was no likelihood of his driving the vehicle whilst in that state. His appeal against conviction was dismissed by the High Court of Justiciary in Scotland in *Williamson v Crowe*

1995 S.L.T. 959 on the basis that the sheriff's finding that the man might have taken control of the vehicle as a last resort was sufficient to preclude him from running the s.5(2) defence.

It was only in extraordinary circumstances that a s.5(2) defence of no likelihood of driving based on competence could be made out because the very purpose of the statutory requirement for supervision was that a provisional driver was, by statute, not competent to drive alone: *DPP v Janman* [2004] EWHC 101; [2004] R.T.R. 31. Whilst there could be circumstances where a supervisor could show the defence (per *Sheldon v Jones* discussed above) the court agreed with the submission above to the effect that any supervisor would have a difficult task in demonstrating that it was not the case that he might take control at any time. In any ordinary case, if a learner was driving, the person supervising would be in control of the vehicle. That was the obvious and normal consequence of the requirement for supervision. The instant case did not raise the particular facts required to draw any contrary conclusion; furthermore there was no requirement for the prosecution to prove that the defendant was a driver qualified to supervise a learner within the meaning in reg.17 of the Motor Vehicles (Driving Licences) Regulations 1999 (SI 1999/2864) (see § 11.40 below).

SENTENCING, PROCEDURE AND TRIAL

Procedure and trial

The drink/driving offences dealt with in this chapter are all triable only summarily. Where the offence is under s.7(6) (refusing or failing without reasonable excuse to provide a specimen) or under s.4(1) or (2) (driving or in charge while unfit), some police forces, following an arrest, immediately charge the offender and either bail him to appear at the magistrates' court under s.43 of the Magistrates' Courts Act 1980 or, if not bailed, produce him as soon as reasonably practicable. Some police forces similarly charge and bail where the police are able to rely on a statement as to the proportion of breath being above the limit. In all other cases the police either bail under s.43(3) to come back to the police station when the certificate of analysis of blood or urine is available or else proceed by way of summons.

4.316

In *R. v McKenzie* [1971] 1 All E.R. 729 (a decision of first instance at Durham Assizes) it was held that the former provisions of the 1972 Act prior to its amendment by the Transport Act 1981 only allowed the arrest and detention of a motorist for the purpose of supplying a specimen of blood or urine for laboratory testing and that the police only had power to detain him thereafter under s.11 ibid. Therefore, it was held, the police had no power to require a recognisance under what is now s.43(3) and bail him to appear at the police station or court. It was widely believed that what is now s.10 of the 1988 Act, albeit re-enacted in slightly different terms, had not resolved the difficulty brought to light by *McKenzie*. The uncertainty was removed, however, by the coming into force of the Police and Criminal Evidence Act 1984; it would appear that a person arrested under the Police and Criminal Evidence Act 1984 may be bailed under s.38 of that Act because s.34(6) specifically provides that an arrest under what is now s.6D of the 1988 Act constitutes an arrest for an offence.

4.317

Drink/driving: penalties

Offence	Section	Imprisonment	Fine *	Disqualification	Penalty points	Endorsement code	Sentencing guideline
Driving or attempting to drive while unfit	s.4(1)	6 months	level 5*	Obligatory	(3–11)†	DR20 (drink): DR80 (drugs)	
Driving or attempting to drive with excess alcohol	s.5(1)(a)	6 months	level 5*	Obligatory	(3–11)†	DR10	See Appendix 3‡
In charge while unfit	s.4(2)	3 months	level 4*	Discretionary	10	DR50 (drink): DR90 (drugs)	See Appendix 3
In charge with excess alcohol	s.5(1)(b)	3 months	level 4*	Discretionary	10	DR40	See Appendix 3
Failing to co-operate with a preliminary test	s.6(6)	—	level 3*	Discretionary	4	DR70	See Appendix 3
Failing or refusing to supply an evidential specimen when "driving or attempting to drive"	s.7(6)	6 months	level 5*	Obligatory	(3–11)†	DR30	See Appendix 3
Failing or refusing to provide an evidential specimen when not "driving or attempting to drive"	s.7(6)	3 months	level 4*	Discretionary	10	DR60	See Appendix 3
Failure to allow specimen to be subjected to laboratory test when "driving or attempting to drive"	s.7A	6 months	level 5*	Obligatory	(3–11)†		

Offence	Section	Imprisonment	Fine *	Disqualification	Penalty points	Endorsement code	Sentencing guideline
Failure to allow specimen to be subjected to laboratory test when not "driving or attempting to drive"	s.7A	3 months	level 4*	Discretionary	10		

* As to the current levels of maximum fines, see § 18.07.

† No points may be imposed when offender is disqualified (see further § 4.324).

‡ For conversion of breath-alcohol to blood/urine alcohol see Appendix 1, "Alcohol concentrations".

Sentencing guidelines

4.318   On August 4, 2008, new Magistrates' Court Sentencing Guidelines became effective; the revised guidelines are summarised in § 18.05 below and the guidelines for road traffic offences are set out in Appendix 3 below. The full text can be found at *http://www.sentencing-guidelines.gov.uk* [Accessed March 16, 2009].

As always, the guidelines are for a first-time offender convicted after trial. The guideline for Excess alcohol (drive/attempt to drive) (p.1237 below) has four levels of sentence depending on the level of alcohol. The lowest level, 36 to 59µg of alcohol in breath, has a starting point and range of a Band C fine with a disqualification of between 12 and 16 months. The next level is from 60 to 89µg in breath which also carries a starting point and range of a Band C fine and a disqualification ranging from 17 to 22 months. It will be noted that a B and C fine is within the range of 125 per cent to 175 per cent of income. There is therefore likely to be a higher fine for a higher reading as well as a longer period of disqualification. The next level is 90 to 119µg in breath with a medium level community order as the starting point within a range of low level community order to high level community order and a disqualification from 23 to 28 months. Once the level of alcohol is 120 and above the custody threshold is reached, with a starting point of 12 weeks' custody in a range of a high level community order to 26 weeks' custody, and a disqualification of 29 to 36 months.

4.319   The guideline for Unfit through drink or drugs (drive/attempt to drive) (p.1245 below) mirrors that set out above for Excess alcohol (drive/attempt to drive). The lowest level is where there is evidence of a moderate level of impairment and no aggravating factors. The next band is where there is evidence of a moderate level of impairment and presence of one or more aggravating factors listed in the box at p.1245 below. The next band is where there is evidence of high level of impairment and no aggravating factors. The custody threshold is passed when there is evidence of high level of impairment and presence of one or more of the aggravating factors listed.

The guideline for Excess alcohol (in charge) (p.1247 below) again has four levels of sentence depending on the level of alcohol. The starting point and range for 36 to 59µg of alcohol in breath is a Band B fine with 10 penalty points. The starting point and range for 60 to 89µg of alcohol in breath is again a starting point of Band B fine with 10 penalty points or consider disqualification. For 90 to 119µg of alcohol in breath the starting point is a B and C fine within the range of B and C fine to medium level community order and consider disqualification up to 6 months or 10 penalty points. The starting point for 120 to 150µg of alcohol in breath is a medium level community order with a range of low level community order to six weeks' custody and disqualification of 6 to 12 months.

4.320   The guideline for Unfit through drink or drugs (in charge) (p.1247 below) mirrors that for Excess alcohol (in charge) above and uses the same four bands as set out above for Excess alcohol (drive/attempt to drive).

The guideline for Fail to provide specimen for analysis (drive/attempt to drive) (p.1241 below) specifies three levels of sentencing. For a defendant who refused a test when he had an honestly held but unreasonable excuse, the starting point and range is a Band C fine with a disqualification of from 12 to 16 months. For deliberate refusal or deliberate failure, the starting point is a low level community order with a range of B and C fine to high level community order and disqualification from 17 to 28 months. For deliberate refusal or deliberate failure where there is evidence of serious impairment, the starting point is 12 weeks' custody within a range of high level community order to 26 weeks' custody and disqualification from 29 to 36 months.

The guideline for Fail to provide specimen for analysis (in charge) is set out at p.1242 below. The starting point and range for a defendant who refused a test when he had an honestly held but unreasonable excuse is a Band B fine with 10 penalty points. For a deliberate refusal or deliberate failure, the starting point is a Band C fine with a range of B and C fine to a medium level community order and consider disqualification or 10 penalty points. For deliberate refusal or deliberate failure where there is evidence of serious impairment, the starting point is a medium level community order within the range of a low level community order to six weeks' custody and disqualification from 6 to 12 months. **4.321**

Obligatory disqualification

On conviction of an offence under s.4(1) (driving or attempting to drive while unfit), s.5(1)(a) (driving or attempting to drive with excess breath, blood, or urine/alcohol levels) s.7(6) (failing to supply specimens for analysis when driving or attempting to drive) or s.7A (failing to allow a specimen to be subjected to laboratory test when driving or attempting to drive) a court is obliged to disqualify for *at least* 12 months unless the court for *special reasons* orders him not to be disqualified or disqualifies him for a shorter period (see Chapter 21). **4.322**

Where a motorist was arrested for failing to provide a specimen for analysis and the prosecution was conducted on the basis that the specimen had been required to ascertain whether the defendant had been drunk *in charge* of a vehicle when arrested, it was not open to the court of trial to conclude that it had in fact been required to ascertain his ability to drive and therefore to impose a mandatory disqualification; to act in such a manner would be contrary to the justice of the proceedings (*George v DPP* [1989] R.T.R. 217).

A similar conclusion was reached by the Divisional Court in *Gardner v DPP* [1989] R.T.R. 384. The investigating constable had indicated that he had cause to suspect that the appellant was in charge of a motor car; accordingly his offence contrary to what is now s.7(6) was subject to discretionary rather than mandatory disqualification and the case was remitted to the justices for reconsideration (they having erroneously concluded that the appellant was subject to mandatory disqualification). **4.323**

Section 11(4) of the Magistrates' Courts Act 1980 prohibits a court from disqualifying a person in his absence unless the court has previously adjourned under s.10(3) of the Magistrates' Courts Act 1980. The notice of adjournment must include notice of the reason for the adjournment (Magistrates' Courts Act 1980 s.11(4)). Where a magistrates' court, without first adjourning under (what is now) s.10(3) of the Magistrates' Courts Act 1980, convicted and disqualified a defendant in his absence for driving with excess blood-alcohol, the disqualification (but not the conviction) was quashed (*R. v Bishop's Stortford JJ. Ex p. Shields* [1969] Crim. L.R. 201).

Penalty points disqualification

Where a court imposes an obligatory disqualification upon an offender the **4.324** licence is required to be endorsed but no penalty points may be imposed in respect of the offence concerned. Nor, as a result of the amendment of s.29 of the 1988 Offenders Act by the Road Traffic Act 1991 (see § 20.37), is the court required to take into account the 3–11 points attributable to an obligatorily disqualifiable offence; thus the perils of double disqualification for a single offence are avoided.

The offences under s.4(2) and s.5(1)(b) of being in charge while unfit or with excess alcohol incur 10 penalty points and the offence of refusing a preliminary breath test involves four penalty points.

For discussion as to endorsement of these penalty points and any resulting penalty points disqualification see §§ 20.33–36.

Obligatory disqualification for at least three years

4.325 Where a defendant is convicted of driving or attempting to drive whilst unfit (s.4(1)) or with excess alcohol levels (s.5(1)(a)) or refusing to supply a laboratory specimen (s.7(6)) when driving or attempting to drive at the relevant time or failing to allow a specimen to be subjected to laboratory test (s.7A) when similarly driving or attempting to drive and has been previously convicted of any such offence within a period of 10 years, the minimum period for which a court is obliged to disqualify is increased to three years (1988 Offenders Act s.34(3)).

Previous convictions under the provisions of the Act in respect of being *in charge* of a motor vehicle do not count as previous convictions for the purpose of increasing the obligatory disqualification to three years on conviction of a drink/drive offence. (Although it would seem that a person convicted of driving with excess alcohol or unfit who on the earlier occasion was not disqualified because of "special reasons" will nevertheless be liable to the minimum period of three years' disqualification if he commits another such offence within the three-year period; s.34(3) merely refers to a person being "convicted". That this is so was confirmed by the Divisional Court in *Boliston v Gibbons* [1985] R.T.R. 176 where it was held that a court can only take account of special reasons which relate to the *later* offence; in reaching its decision the court (per Forbes J. at 180E) expressly approved a passage to the like effect in the eleventh edition of this work. Some sympathy was felt for the defendant in these circumstances and it was observed that the appellant might after due time make application under what is now s.42 of the 1988 Offenders Act for the removal of disqualification (see § 20.99).)

4.326 It should be particularly noted that the wording of s.34(3) of the 1988 Offenders Act makes it clear that the 10-year period has to be calculated from the date of the *commission* of the subsequent offence back to the date of the *conviction* of the earlier offence. This has a number of consequences; a person appearing before a court charged with two offences committed on different dates is only liable to a minimum of 12 months on each as he will not necessarily have been convicted for the earlier offence when he committed the second offence. Similarly if, e.g., an offender commits an offence on December 1, 2008 of driving while unfit contrary to s.4(1), and commits an offence of driving with excess alcohol on February 28, 2009, he will not be liable to the minimum three years' disqualification when he is dealt with for the February 28 offence unless he was convicted of the December 1 offence before February 28.

The method of calculating the 10-year period in accordance with s.34(3) of the

1988 Offenders Act can, however, also work to the disadvantage of the defendant. Thus if the later offence occurred on January 1, 2009 and the earlier offence was committed in December 1998, for which the defendant was convicted on February 1, 2009, he is liable to the three-year compulsory disqualification. (Quaere in such a case whether the disqualification cannot be reduced to less than three years for "special reasons". It would seem not. To do so would seem to involve the proposition that the words of s.34(3) of the 1988 Offenders Act do not mean what they say.)

A motorist who has been disqualified for the three-year obligatory period may, despite the fact that it is a minimum period of three years, apply for removal of the disqualification under s.42 of the 1988 Offenders Act after two years: *Damer v Davison* [1976] R.T.R. 45 (but see the remarks of Lord Widgery C.J. in that case, noted at § 20.99). **4.327**

The Secretary of State for Transport will not automatically issue a licence at the conclusion of his latest period of disqualification to an offender who has been disqualified twice for drink/driving offences within the relevant 10-year period (see below).

Reduction of disqualification

The Drink-Drive Rehabilitation Scheme which was piloted in certain court areas from July 1992 to December 1999 was made permanent by means of the Courses for Drink-Drive Offenders (Experimental Period) (Termination of Restrictions) Order 1999 (SI 1999/3130) and since January 1, 2000 the referral of drink/driving offenders to a rehabilitation course has been an option available to all courts in Great Britain. Drink/driving offenders may be able to obtain a reduction in the period of disqualification imposed upon them by satisfactorily completing a rehabilitation course designed to influence attitudes by retraining and thereby reduce the risk of further offending. The reduction obtainable is not less than three months nor more than one quarter of the total period of disqualification originally imposed. **4.328**

For details of the scheme, see further §§ 20.92–3.

Alcohol ignition interlocks

Section 15 of the Road Safety Act 2006 (if and when in force) inserts new ss.34D–34G and 41B into the 1988 Offenders Act in order to give courts the power in certain circumstances to offer offenders the opportunity to participate, at their own not inconsiderable expense, in an "alcohol ignition interlock programme". Successful participation will result in a reduction of the overall period of the disqualification. To qualify for the scheme the offender must have *committed* (not, as with s.34(3), been *convicted* of) a relevant drink/driving offence within a period of 10 years ending with the date of the instant conviction; must have been disqualified for not less than two years (a curious choice, given that the minimum period under s.34(3) for a second relevant conviction is *three* years); and further the court must make no order under s.34A concerning a drink-drive rehabilitation course (see above). The central feature of the scheme is that after the end of the reduced period of disqualification and until the end of the entire period of disqualification originally imposed the offender may only drive a motor vehicle fitted with an alcohol interlock device designed to prevent the **4.329** vehicle being driven until a specimen of breath has been given in which the proportion of alcohol does not exceed a specified amount (currently 9μg of alcohol in 100ml of breath). Section 16 of the 2006 Act provides for an experimental period for the testing of the programme (until the end of 2010 unless extended by order) and for certain court areas to be designated for the purpose of the experiment. At the time of writing (March 2009) no indication had been given as to a likely date for implementation of these provisions.

Problem drinkers

4.330   The Committee on Drinking and Driving (the "Blennerhasset Committee") in 1976 was concerned with the problem posed by those whom the committee referred to as "high risk offenders". Statistics show that there is a category of offender who repeatedly commits drink/driving offences with high blood-alcohol content—so high in fact that much expert evidence is of the opinion that such offenders usually are among the class of persons with an alcohol problem. The Government accordingly decided, with effect from May 6, 1983, to introduce special arrangements as to the issue of licences after the expiration of the court's order of disqualification in respect of offenders who came within one of the three following categories:

(1) Those disqualified twice within 10 years for driving or attempting to drive when on both occasions their alcohol level was more than two and a half times the prescribed limit.

(2) Those disqualified twice within 10 years, once for driving with more than two and a half times the prescribed limit, and once for failing to provide a specimen of breath, blood or urine for analysis when required to do so.

(3) Those disqualified twice within 10 years for failing to provide a specimen for analysis where police evidence suggests that there are reasonable grounds for suspecting that the driver has an alcohol problem.

The Minister for Roads and Traffic announced in reply to a parliamentary question on December 1, 1988 that the Government intended to modify the scheme covering high risk offenders to include (in addition to the categories listed above) all offenders convicted of driving whilst two and a half times over the prescribed limit, thus moving the threshold to the level recommended by the Blennerhasset Committee. It was further proposed that offenders be required to pay an administrative charge to meet the costs of the new scheme. Regulations to effect these changes would be made under the authority of the Road Traffic (Driver Licensing and Information Systems) Act 1989. It was anticipated that these measures would be implemented in June 1990.

4.331   In the event the changes as implemented turned out to be more far-reaching than had been anticipated. So far as convictions entered on or after June 1, 1990 are concerned, drivers will be regarded as high risk offenders if they fall within any of the following categories:

(1) Those disqualified for driving whilst two and a half times over the prescribed limit.

(2) Those disqualified twice for drink/driving offences within 10 years.

(3) Those disqualified for refusal to supply a specimen for analysis.

(See now the Motor Vehicles (Driving Licences) Regulations 1999 reg.74.)

The administrative charge for the issue of a new licence to a "high risk offender" is set as from May 1, 2007 at £85.

After a relevant conviction an offender will be advised by the DVLA (formerly DVLC) that when he re-applies for a licence on the expiry of his disqualification, consideration will be given to whether the conviction indicates a medical disability and, if so, whether he has managed to bring the drinking problem under control. He will be advised to seek such help and advice during the period of disqualification.

Four months before the end of the disqualification the Medical Advisory **4.332** Branch of the Department for Transport will send him an application form for renewal of his licence together with a letter explaining that his licence will not be renewed unless he can satisfy the Secretary of State that he does not have an alcohol problem.

Once an application is received at DVLA the offender will be invited to attend a special examination centre where he will be taken through an interview and given a medical examination. Following the interview the offender will be referred to a local hospital for a blood sample which will be analysed on behalf of the Secretary of State.

The results of the interview and blood analysis will determine the Secretary of State's decision as to whether or not to refuse to issue the licence. Borderline cases will be referred to a consultant psychiatrist specialising in alcohol problems.

Legal position

The powers of the Secretary of State to revoke or to refuse a licence are **4.333** contained in s.92 of the 1988 Act and he has no choice but to refuse if on inquiry he is satisfied that the person concerned is suffering from a "relevant disability". These include not only the various diseases or disabilities set out in reg.71 of the Motor Vehicles (Driving Licences) Regulations 1999 but also "any other disability likely to cause the driving of a vehicle by him ... to be a source of danger to the public" (s.92(2), (3)). "Relevant disability" includes persistent misuse of drugs or alcohol, whether or not such misuse amounts to dependency. If after the inquiries set out above the Secretary of State refuses to issue a licence by virtue of s.92, the applicant has a right of appeal under s.100 of the 1988 Act to the magistrates' court acting for the petty sessions area in which he resides, or, if he resides in Scotland, to the sheriff within whose jurisdiction he resides. The decision of the court is binding on the Secretary of State.

On appeal to the magistrates' court it would seem to be a matter of fact for the court to decide in accordance with the medical and other evidence before it as to whether the applicant has or has not an alcohol or drugs problem so that it can be said he *is* suffering from a disability or disease "likely to cause the driving of a vehicle by him to be a source of danger to the public". It is relevant that a person can be cured of an alcohol or drugs problem and presumably the court when considering the appeal will have to decide not whether he *had* such a problem but whether the alcohol or drugs problem of the defendant is such that at the time of the hearing he still has an alcohol or drugs problem and therefore it *is* "likely to cause the driving of a vehicle by him to be a source of danger to the public".

OTHER OFFENCES INVOLVING DRINK OR DRUGS

Riding a cycle whilst unfit

4.334　　Section 30(1) of the 1988 Act provides that it is an offence for a person to ride a bicycle, tricycle or cycle having four or more wheels, not being a motor vehicle, on a road or other public place, whilst unfit to ride it through drink or drugs. By s.30(1) "unfit to ride" means being under the influence of drink or drugs to such an extent as to be incapable of having proper control. The offence is punishable with a fine of level 3 on the standard scale.

So far as England and Wales are concerned, s.30 contains no specific power of arrest; a constable may, however, arrest a suspect under s.24 of the Police and Criminal Evidence Act 1984, as substituted by s.110 of the Serious Organised Crime and Police Act 2005, if the constable reasonably suspects him to be committing, or about to commit an offence of whatever kind. With regard to Scotland, s.30(2) provides a specific power for a constable to arrest without warrant a person committing a s.30 offence. There are no provisions importing the procedures under what are now ss.6, 6A, 6B, 6C, 7 and 9 of the 1988 Act and s.15 of the 1988 Offenders Act into offences involving cyclists; and the police have therefore no power to require a cyclist to provide a specimen of breath, blood or urine. Nor can the prosecution rely on any refusal by the cyclist to provide any specimen of blood or urine as support for its case. But if the cyclist in fact provides a specimen, its analysis will presumably be admissible.

4.335　　The offence may be committed not only on a public highway, but also on footpaths or footways forming part of a road. It will also be committed upon a private road to which the public has access.

Section 5 of the 1988 Offenders Act exempts any person liable to be charged under s.30 from any charge under s.12 of the Licensing Act 1872 (see below) or the equivalent Scottish enactment. As this exemption only applies to a person liable to be charged with "riding" a cycle, the appropriate charge for a person attempting to ride, or in charge of, a cycle whilst drunk may be under s.12 of the Licensing Act 1872.

In charge of a carriage, horse or cattle, when drunk

4.336　　Section 12 of the Licensing Act 1872 makes it an offence to be in charge of any carriage, horse or cattle on any highway or other public place when drunk. The penalty is a fine of level 1 on the standard scale or one month's imprisonment. The section applies to cyclists (*Corkery v Carpenter* [1951] 1 K.B. 102) and semble barrows ([1939] Jo.Crim.L. 338). "Cattle" generally includes housed domestic animals, horses, asses, pigs and sheep.

The prosecution must establish that the defendant was not merely under the influence of drink, but "drunk".

CHAPTER 5

DANGEROUS, CARELESS AND INCONSIDERATE DRIVING, ETC.

CONTENTS

INTRODUCTION

The offences with which this chapter is mainly concerned are now contained in ss.1–3A of the Road Traffic Act 1988, as amended by the Road Traffic Act 1991, and are as follows: **5.01**

   (a) causing death by dangerous driving (ss.1, 2A);

   (b) dangerous driving (ss.2, 2A);

   (c) careless and inconsiderate driving (s.3); and

   (d) causing death by careless driving when under the influence of drink or drugs (s.3A).

The 1988 Act is further amended by ss.20 and 21 of the Road Safety Act 2006 (which came into force on August 18, 2008) and created two new offences as follows:

   (a) causing death by careless, or inconsiderate, driving (s.2B);

   (b) causing death by driving whilst unlicensed, disqualified or uninsured (s.3ZB).

This chapter also deals with the related offences of dangerous, careless and inconsiderate cycling in ss.28 and 29 of the 1988 Act, as amended by the Road Traffic Act 1991, and other related offences in the 1988 and other Acts, including "motor manslaughter". The penalties and sentencing for all the above offences are dealt with at §§ 5.114 et seq. **5.02**

DANGEROUS DRIVING

Abolition of reckless driving, etc.

The offences of causing death by driving, and driving, in a manner dangerous **5.03** or at a speed dangerous to the public were repealed in 1977. The principal reason for their abolition was the lack of any sufficiently established distinction between dangerous driving and the offence of careless driving under s.3 of the 1972 Act. Problems continued to be experienced, however, with the remaining offences of reckless driving and causing death thereby, particularly in the light of the importation of the concept of recklessness enshrined in *R. v Caldwell* (1981) 73 Cr. App. R. 13 into road traffic law by the House of Lords in *R. v Lawrence* [1981] R.T.R. 217. The difficulty of proving a subjective mental element as well as a more obvious physical one (the nature of the driving) probably led to many seriously errant motorists being convicted of careless driving where prosecution for a more serious offence might well have appeared desirable in the public interest.

Section 1 of the Road Traffic Act 1991 amended the Road Traffic Act 1988 by replacing ss.1 and 2 of that Act with new ss.1, 2 and 2A. Those substituted sections abolished the concept of driving recklessly and replaced it with one of driving dangerously. Section 1 provides that a person who causes the death of another person by driving a mechanically propelled vehicle dangerously on a road or other public place shall be guilty of an offence. Section 2 provides in similar terms that it shall be an offence for a person to drive a mechanically propelled vehicle dangerously on a road or other public place.

What is dangerous driving?

5.04   Section 2A(1) of the 1988 Act provides that a person is to be regarded as driving dangerously if:

    (a) the way he drives falls far below what would be expected of a competent and careful driver, and

    (b) it would be obvious to a competent and careful driver that driving in that way would be dangerous.

The determination of what amounts to driving dangerously is thus by means of a test which concentrates upon the nature of the driving rather than the defendant's state of mind. The first limb of the test (s.2A(1)(a)) requires the driving to fall "far below what would be expected of a competent and careful driver" and the second limb (s.2A(1)(b)) requires the dangerousness of such driving to be "obvious to a competent and careful driver". Since Scottish courts had not experienced under the previous legislation the difficulties of proof of a subjective mental element which had so beset the English courts in the wake of *R. v Lawrence* [1981] R.T.R. 217, it is probably no accident that this wording follows as closely as it does the test for recklessness laid down by the High Court of Justiciary in *Allan v Patterson* [1980] R.T.R. 97:

> "Judges and juries will readily understand ... that before they can apply the adverb 'recklessly' to the driving in question they must find that it fell far below the standard of driving expected of the competent and careful driver and that it occurred either in the face of obvious and material dangers which were or should have been observed, appreciated and guarded against, or in circumstances which showed a complete disregard for any potential dangers which might result from the way in which the vehicle was being driven."

5.05   So far as the standard of driving is concerned, the test to be applied is clearly objective in nature, albeit that it employs the sense and senses of a familiar fictional character, the "competent and careful driver". (In this age of personalised transport the man on the Clapham omnibus appears finally to have given way to his more affluent successor, the man on the North Circular.) The intention of Government as expressed in the White Paper which preceded the legislation was that the standard of driving should be judged in absolute terms, taking no account of factors such as inexperience, age or disability (though such factors would be relevant in sentencing). It was not intended that the driver who merely makes a careless mistake of a kind which any driver might make from time to time should be regarded as falling *far* below the standard expected of a competent and careful driver. There is thus a clear qualitative distinction to be drawn between the standard of driving required for offences under ss.1, 2 ("*far* below what would be expected of a competent and careful driver") and that for offences of careless driving contrary to s.3 ("below the standard of a reasonable, prudent and competent driver"); see further "The difference between dangerous and careless driving", § 5.42.

The entirely objective nature of the test to be applied to determine whether or not a course of driving is dangerous in the terms of s.2A(1) was re-emphasised by the Court of Appeal in *R. v Collins (Lezlie)* [1997] R.T.R. 439 when upholding the conviction of a police officer of two charges of causing death by dangerous driving. In the course of a pursuit at high speed he had successfully negotiated two junctions where access had been controlled by other police cars and he had had reasonable visibility of the approach roads. At the third junction, however, visibility of cars approaching from one side was obscured. The appellant erroneously concluded from the presence of a parked police car in the mouth of the road at the other side that access to this junction had also been controlled. He went over a red light and collided with a motorist crossing from the obscured road; that motorist and the appellant's police observer were both killed.

It was argued on behalf of the appellant that the jury should have been told of **5.06** his genuine belief that as he approached the junction, police were controlling it, and that that was a factor they ought to consider in deciding how a competent and careful driver would have reacted in those circumstances; or alternatively that there were clear circumstances of fact founding that belief which should have been put to the jury (such as the presence of the police car, the appellant's knowledge of police practice concerning the blocking of junctions, the fact that the previous junctions had been blocked and the lack of apparent traffic as he approached the junction). Those arguments were rejected by the court; the test of whether or not the standard of driving is "far below" that to be expected of a competent and careful driver is a purely objective one, and the offender's belief, whether genuine or not, is not a relevant factor. The trial judge had fully and properly directed the jury on the law, had thoroughly reviewed the evidence and had correctly pointed out the issues for them to decide.

Some helpful guidance on the subject of what is, or rather what on the facts of the case in point was not, dangerous driving has been provided by the Court of Appeal in *R. v Conteh* [2004] R.T.R. 1. The defendant moved his car into a bus lane on his left in which there was no traffic, just before a pelican crossing at which the lights for him were green, with a view to turning left into a side road just after the crossing. On his nearside were two pedestrians waiting for the lights to change so that they could cross. In the offside lane a van had stopped to let two pedestrians cross from the central reservation, even though the lights were against them. The defendant did not and could not have seen them until one of the pedestrians walked past the van into the front offside of his car as he drove over the crossing whilst the lights were still green for him. Although he had been travelling at only about 20mph, the collision proved fatal for the pedestrian. He was convicted of causing death by dangerous driving. Allowing his appeal, the court held that it was important to keep firmly in mind, however tragic the outcome, the high threshold that s.2A of the 1988 Act established for the commission of such an offence. In this instance, whether the circumstances were taken in combination or individually and in combination, the case for the prosecution, at its highest, was well below the statutory threshold, and, if the pedestrian had not died it was unlikely that the prosecution would have considered a charge of dangerous driving. Accordingly, the judge had been wrong to refuse to uphold the submission of no case to answer and should have removed the charge from the jury. A conviction for careless driving was substituted.

5.07   It was held in *Att Gen's Reference (No.4 of 2000)* [2001] EWCA Crim 780; [2001] R.T.R. 27 that the fact that a driver had pressed the accelerator unintentionally, when he had meant to press the brake, was no defence to a charge of dangerous driving. The offence was intended to cover cases in which a driver had made a mistake with tragic consequences; but the fact that the offence was due to a mistake went only to mitigation, not guilt.

Although the offence of driving at a speed dangerous to the public was abolished by s.50 of the Criminal Law Act 1977 (see § 5.03), the High Court of Justiciary in Scotland would appear to have come perilously close to recreating that offence in non-statutory form by its decision in *Trippick v Orr* (1994) 1995 S.L.T. 272. A driver travelled at a recorded speed of 114mph on a dual carriageway subject to a 70mph limit. In the court below the sheriff stated that there was nothing inherently dangerous in the manner of driving, apart from the speed. Visibility was excellent, the driver's car was in excellent condition, the road surface was dry and the weather was good. There were, however, potential hazards, including other vehicles turning on to the carriageway at the two road junctions which lay ahead, a tyre burst, loose chippings damaging the car's windows and deer crossing the road. The sheriff found, presumably in the light of the driver's apparent disregard of these potential hazards, that the requirements of s.2A(1)(a) and (b) of the Road Traffic Act 1988 had been met. The High Court found that the sheriff had been satisfied that there were potential dangers on the stretch of road concerned which ought to be taken into account; what remained was a question of fact and degree, which was the process of assessing their significance in the light of the grossly excessive speed. The decision was not one which was not open to the sheriff on the facts; accordingly the driver's appeal was dismissed.

5.08   Further steps down the road towards the reconstitution in all but name of the former offence of driving at a speed dangerous to the public were taken by the High Court of Justiciary in *McQueen v Buchanan* (1996) 1997 S.L.T. 765 when dismissing the appeal against conviction for dangerous driving of an offender who had driven at 114mph on a single carriageway road subject to the normal 60mph limit when traffic in both directions was light. The court stated (obiter) that driving at grossly excessive speed in itself might in certain circumstances give rise to such obvious risks that the test of dangerous driving set out in s.2A(1) of the 1988 Act might be satisfied without the need to conduct a minute examination into the layout of the road and the presence or otherwise of other traffic in the vicinity.

A not dissimilar conclusion was reached by the High Court of Justiciary in *Howdle v O'Connor* (1997) 1998 S.L.T. 94. A motorist drove at 119mph on a stretch of motorway where a number of hazards (such as debris, broken-down vehicles and straying animals) were known to arise from time to time, albeit that none of those potential risks had materialised on the occasion in question. He was charged with dangerous driving, but convicted by the sheriff of careless driving. Substituting a conviction for dangerous driving as originally charged, the court said that the driving had fallen far below what was expected of a competent and careful driver and it should have been obvious that driving in that way would be dangerous. Whilst excessive speed alone was no basis for convicting of dangerous driving, where the speed was grossly excessive and the vehicle was driven at such speed on a stretch of road with other cars, especially when the other drivers would not readily anticipate the speed of the offending vehicle, the proper conclusion was that the driving was dangerous.

5.09 *McQueen v Buchanan* and *Howdle v O'Connor* (both discussed above) were considered by the Divisional Court in *DPP v Milton* [2006] EWHC 242; [2006] R.T.R. 21. The defendant, a police officer and grade 1 advanced driver, was charged with dangerous driving and five alternative charges of speeding whilst on duty. His normal vehicle was out of commission and he was given instead a high performance car with which he was unfamiliar. The district judge who tried the case at first instance found as facts that the defendant had decided to practise his driving skills on this unfamiliar vehicle, as he had been instructed to do in the course of his police training. Honing his skills in this way entailed his driving at speeds grossly in excess of the relevant speed limits (at average speeds of 148–149mph on a motorway and at a maximum of 91mph in a 30mph limit). At the time the weather was fine, visibility was good and the roads were more or less deserted, and there was no evidence that any other road user was in fact endangered by the manner of the defendant's driving. He was extremely familiar with the roads concerned, he was in control of his vehicle at all times and his driving was of a high standard. The district judge dismissed all the charges on the basis that the defendant's driving did not fall below the standard expected of a competent and careful driver and that, in exceeding the speed limit the defendant was driving for police purposes in accordance with s.87 of the Road Traffic Regulation Act 1984 (see § 6.71).

Allowing the prosecutor's appeal, the court held that under s.2A of the 1988 Act the test of whether driving was dangerous for the purposes of s.2 was to be judged objectively as being what would have been obvious to the independent bystander. It appeared that in considering whether the defendant's driving was dangerous, the district judge had taken into account in the defendant's favour the defendant's own knowledge of his driving skills. In so far as he had thereby imported a subjective element into the test of dangerous driving, he had been wrong in law to have done so. Furthermore, it was a failing on his part not to have taken into account the effect on other road users of somebody coming up behind them, or across their path, at speeds of the kind at which the defendant was driving and with no warning. While speed alone was not sufficient to found a conviction for dangerous driving, driving at the speeds attained by the defendant on public roads without any warning, however good and skilled the driver, amounted to a prima facie case of dangerous driving.

5.10 So far as the speeding offences were concerned, the court declined obiter to find that a police officer who drove at speeds as excessive as those in the case in point could not possibly come within the exemption for police purposes, save when in hot pursuit of a dangerous criminal. It was a matter of fact and degree for the tribunal of fact.

The case was remitted to a differently constituted court for rehearing, where he was convicted of dangerous driving and in turn appealed to the Divisional Court. It was explicitly decided that the fact that the driver is a grade 1 advanced police driver is a circumstance to which regard must be had, pursuant to s.2A(3) of the Road Traffic Act 1988, as amended by the Road Traffic Act 1991. Taking circumstances known to the accused into account does not detract from the objectivity of the test. The court said it could not accept that the statute requires that a circumstance relating to a characteristic of the individual accused driver should be taken into account if it is unfavourable to him but cannot be taken into account if it is favourable. The court was clearly mindful of the "floodgates" argument. It said that it will only be the extremes of "special skill" and "almost complete lack of experience" that will be such as could affect the mind of the decision maker. "The mere fact that the driver has driven for 30 years without an accident will not be relevant" ([2007] EWHC 532 at [28], per Smith L.J.). Gross J. stated:

> "Having regard to the objective test of 'driving dangerously', there will, in the nature of things, be relatively very few circumstances known to the accused capable of having a bearing on the competent and careful driver's consideration of the driving in question. It is likely that there will be fewer still which do in fact serve to alter the result to which the court would otherwise have come, though that is a matter for the tribunal of fact. The subjective views of the accused are irrelevant, for the reasons given in *Director of Public Prosecutions v Milton* [[2006] EWHC 242; [2006] R.T.R. 21]. It is therefore inherently likely that only circumstances known to the driver and capable of objective proof will need to be taken into consideration. Applied in this way, s.2A(3) should not be unduly burdensome. It would of course be most undesirable if straightforward cases were extended or complicated by background evidence as to the driver which, sensibly considered, took matters no further—and nothing said in this case should prevent tribunals from being astute to discourage such a course." ([2007] EWHC 532 at [34(vii)])

5.11   Section 2A(2) provides that "A person is also to be regarded as driving dangerously ... if it would be obvious to a competent and careful driver that driving the vehicle in its current state would be dangerous". This extension of the ambit of dangerous driving is wider in its scope than the principle established by the case of *R. v Robert Millar (Contractors) and Robert Millar* [1970] 2 Q.B. 54 to the effect that a driver who knowingly drives a defective vehicle is guilty, where danger results, of dangerous driving, since actual knowledge of the defect is not required if the "current state" of the vehicle speaks sufficiently clearly for itself. (To make matters worse for the accused, actual knowledge on his part of a dangerous defect which would not have been obvious to a careful and competent driver must be taken into account when determining what would be expected of, or obvious to, that fictional person; see s.2A(3) discussed below.)

The Court of Appeal held in *R. v Marchant; R. v Muntz* [2003] EWCA Crim 2099; [2004] R.T.R. 15 that the safe use on the road of an inherently dangerous agricultural vehicle which was nevertheless authorised for such use would not normally attract a prosecution for causing death by dangerous driving after a fatal accident. In the course of his employment by Mr Muntz, a farmer, Mr Marchant was driving a loading machine which had attached to its front a boom and a grab with forward-pointing spikes on both the upper and lower jaw. Whilst waiting on the correct side of the road to turn into a farm entrance, with the boom and grab in the position recommended by the manufacturers for travel on the road, a motor cyclist travelling fast in the opposite direction collided with part of the lower jaw of the grab and later died from his injuries. The loading machine was an agricultural vehicle authorised by the Secretary of State for use on public roads and the offence of using a vehicle in a dangerous condition (1988 Act s.40A) was consequently disapplied to it; the offence of causing death by dangerous driving, however, on the basis that it would be "obvious to a careful and competent driver that driving the vehicle in its current state would be dangerous" (ibid. s.2A(2)), was not. The court was of the view that, whilst there would be cases where the condition of a vehicle was such that, even if specifically authorised by the Secretary of State for road use, it would nonetheless be appropriate to prosecute for offences under s.1 or 2, those cases would almost always involve an allegation that the driver had so manoeuvred the vehicle as to create a danger additional to that created by its mere presence on the road. A driver who manoeuvred dangerously could not escape prosecution simply because the Secretary of State had exempted the vehicle from prosecution under s.40A. Where, however, the allegedly obvious dangerous condition of a vehicle stemmed purely from its inherent design rather than from lack of maintenance or positive alteration, particular care had to be taken in deciding whether it was appropriate to prosecute the user of such a vehicle at all. The convictions were accordingly quashed.

In *R. v Strong* [1995] Crim. L.R. 428 the Court of Appeal allowed an appeal **5.12** against a conviction for dangerous driving based upon the driving of a vehicle in a dangerously defective condition where it had never been suggested by the Crown that the appellant was *aware* of the corrosion which made his vehicle dangerous; the case had been put on the basis that the defect would have been *obvious* to a competent and careful driver in the terms of s.2A(2) of the 1988 Act. Evidence was given by a vehicle examiner retained by the police that only by going underneath the car, or by getting someone with some mechanical knowledge to look at it, would the defect have become apparent. On behalf of the prosecution it was submitted that any careful and competent driver knowing that there was some corrosion in this vehicle, as he must have done given its age and recorded mileage, would hardly have driven it on a road without having it inspected properly. Such an inspection would have been bound to reveal that the car was in a state of collapse and that it was dangerous to drive it. In the court's view, however, that would not be the proper test. What has to be shown is whether there is evidence such as would have made it obvious to a competent and careful driver that it would be dangerous to drive that vehicle in its current state. Evidence, in other words, that it would be obvious to that driver in the sense that it could be "seen or realised at first glance, evident" to him (that definition being drawn from the *Oxford Dictionary*). Since there was no evidence from the vehicle examiner or any other reliable evidence that anyone looking at the car from a layperson's point of view would be aware of its dangerous condition, the case should have been withdrawn from the jury.

The definition of obviousness set out in *R. v Strong* above was adopted by the Court of Appeal in *R. v Roberts and George* [1997] R.T.R. 462 when dealing with the appeals against conviction of causing death by dangerous driving of a tipper truck driver and his employer. A wheel of the tipper became detached and hit another vehicle, killing its driver. The prosecution argued that the truck was in a dangerous condition because of lack of proper maintenance, and that should have been obvious to both men. The defence argued that the design of the wheel assembly was inherently dangerous and that the wheel could come off without there being any indication that anything was wrong. In accordance with his employer's instructions, the driver undertook a daily visual inspection of the wheels and a weekly physical check of the wheel nuts. Allowing the appeals, the court stated that more might be expected of a professional driver than an ordinary motorist. Where a driver was an employee, it would be important to consider the instructions given by the employer. Generally speaking it would be wrong to expect him to do more than he was instructed to do, provided that the instructions were apparently reasonable. In the instant case the driver could not have been expected to have done more than he was told to do by his employer, since there was no evidence before the jury which could have entitled them to conclude that he should have appreciated that his instructions were inadequate.

5.13   *R. v Strong* above was further commented upon by the Court of Appeal in *R. v Marsh (Michael)* [2002] EWCA Crim 137 when dealing with an appeal against conviction and sentence for an offence of causing death by dangerous driving based on the state of the vehicle concerned. The appellant had been driving a lorry fitted with a loading crane. The lorry was equipped with outriggers and legs for stabilising the crane when in use. As a result of his failure properly to secure those devices prior to setting off, one of the outriggers swung out from the lorry when it was on the move and struck two children, one of whom subsequently died. In his summing-up the judge at first instance had adopted the definition of "obvious" used in *R. v Strong*, and in response to a jury question had elaborated upon the meaning of the word "glance" from that definition. The court opined that *R. v Strong* was not attempting to lay down a form of words to be used in every case; the word "obvious" was an English word which had no special meaning in the context of s.2A(1) and judges would be well advised not to define it further. Although the conviction was upheld, the Court of Appeal reduced the term of imprisonment from two years to one on the basis that the driver had not in fact known of the danger his vehicle posed, albeit that he ought to have done.

Section 2A(3) provides that the word "dangerous" in subss.(1), (2) refers to danger of either physical injury or serious damage to property, terms not dissimilar to those contained in the model direction to English and Welsh juries laid down by the House of Lords in *R. v Lawrence* [1981] R.T.R. 217 when dealing with cases of the former offence of reckless driving. It would appear that any contemplated injury would suffice, however slight, but there may well be room for argument as to what degree of damage is represented by *serious* damage and what resemblance it may or may not bear to the concept of *substantial* damage to property familiar from *Lawrence*. In any event it is not incumbent upon the prosecution to establish that any person or property was *actually* endangered; it will suffice that the nature or circumstances of the driving were such as would make the dangerousness of it obvious to the competent and careful driver.

Section 2A(3) further provides that in determining what would be expected of, and obvious to, a competent and careful driver, regard must be had not only to the circumstances of which he (i.e. North Circular Man) could be expected to be aware, but also to any circumstances shown to have been within the knowledge of the accused. Thus if the defendant decides to drive a vehicle which, whilst not obviously in a dangerous condition, is nevertheless known to him to possess a dangerous defect, he runs the risk of being convicted on the basis of that knowledge. This importation of an element of subjectivity into an otherwise objective test may well pose some practical problems for the prosecution when it comes to establishing evidentially the existence or extent of the defendant's guilty knowledge.

According to the Court of Appeal in *R. v Marison* [1997] R.T.R. 457 the driving of a vehicle where it was the *driver* who was in a dangerously defective state rather than the vehicle was capable of amounting to dangerous driving in terms of the definition of dangerous driving in s.2A of the 1988 Act. The facts of the case were that a diabetic driver, who was aware that there was a real risk that he would suffer a sudden hypoglycaemic attack, nevertheless started to drive his car. Such an attack occurred, resulting in his car veering off course and crashing into an oncoming vehicle, killing its driver. His full awareness of his proneness to hypoglycaemic attacks without warning constituted "circumstances of which he could be expected to be aware" and of which he also had knowledge (s.2A(3)). In *R. v Woodward (Terence)* [1995] R.T.R. 130 (discussed at § 5.55) the Court of Appeal had pointed out that it would be strange indeed if Parliament intended to make driving a vehicle in a dangerously defective state an offence under the section, but not driving when the driver was in a dangerously defective state due to drink. Drink did not arise in the instant case, but on the evidence the appellant was in a dangerously defective state due to diabetes. There was no difference in principle involved. The crucial issue was whether the driver in question had knowledge of the circumstances in question, which this driver undoubtedly did. **5.14**

Section 2A(4) provides that in determining the state of a vehicle for the purposes of s.2A(2), regard may be had to "anything attached to or carried on or in it and to the manner in which it is attached or carried". This extension of the definition of a vehicle in a dangerous state to cover such appendages as trailers and loads and the manner of their attachment and carriage enshrines in statutory form the decision of the Court of Appeal in *R. v Crossman* [1986] R.T.R. 49 in which it was held that a lorry driver rightly pleaded guilty to the then offence of causing death by reckless driving, when his load fell off and killed a pedestrian after he had decided to drive the vehicle knowing there was a risk of the load falling off and thereby killing or injuring another road user.

Scope of the offence

All offences of dangerous and careless driving (and cycling) apply to servants of the Crown (1988 Act s.183). **5.15**

The offences of dangerous driving and causing death thereby may be committed not merely on roads but also in other public places, such as car parks and forecourts (see § 1.148). This extension of the ambit of these offences brings them sensibly into line with drink/driving offences under ss.4 and 5 of the 1988 Act (see Chapter 4).

It should also be noted that offences under ss.1 and 2 may be committed in a "mechanically propelled vehicle", a wider category of object than the "motor vehicle" referred to in the previous legislation (see § 1.04). Whilst all motor vehicles are mechanically propelled vehicles, the converse is not necessarily the case; e.g. stock cars, scrambling motor cycles, dumpers and digging machines are not motor vehicles as they are not "intended or adapted for use on a road", and electrically assisted pedal cycles, whilst specifically excluded from the category of motor vehicle by s.189 of the 1988 Act (see § 1.23), are nonetheless "mechanically propelled" (see § 1.33). Spreading the net more widely in this way may be seen as being fairer as between one road user and another, since the amount of danger which can be caused by a vehicle is not necessarily bound up with its intended use or exact means of propulsion.

Procedure

5.16   Dangerous driving contrary to s.2 of the 1988 Act is an "either way" offence within the meaning of the Magistrates' Courts Act 1980, as amended by the "plea before venue" provisions of s.49 of the Criminal Procedure and Investigations Act 1996. If the defendant indicates a guilty plea, he loses his right to be tried at the Crown Court, although he may still be committed to that court for sentence. If he indicates a not guilty plea, or fails to indicate his plea, the established mode of trial procedure applies; the defendant must consent to any summary trial and accordingly may insist on trial by jury (see Chapter 2, Mode of trial procedure). Careless or inconsiderate driving contrary to s.3 may only be tried summarily (although a jury may convict a defendant of careless or inconsiderate driving if acquitted of a charge of causing death by dangerous driving contrary to s.1 or of dangerous driving contrary to s.2). If dangerous driving is heard on indictment it is a Class 3 offence and thus will ordinarily be heard at the most convenient location of the Crown Court (see *Practice Direction (Criminal Proceedings: Consolidation)* [2002] 3 All E.R. 904, as amended (hereafter "the *Consolidated Criminal Practice Direction*")).

It was held in *R. v McBride* [1962] 1 Q.B. 167 that a charge of driving under the influence of drink might be tried along with one for dangerous or careless driving. It would seem that a s.4 or s.5 charge may similarly be tried along with dangerous or careless driving (see *R. v Thorpe* [1974] R.T.R. 465) as there seems to be no distinction between the former offence of dangerous driving and the present s.2 offence in this context. It should be noted, however, that the drink/driving offences under ss.4 and 5 can no longer be tried on indictment. It should also be noted, though, that where a defendant is committed for trial for an "either way" offence (such as dangerous driving) he may also be committed in respect of any imprisonable or endorsable offence arising out of the same or similar circumstances. The Crown Court may deal with him for such an offence if he pleads guilty, but not otherwise (Criminal Justice Act 1988 s.41). Thus where a defendant who had been committed for trial at the Crown Court on alternative charges of reckless and careless driving (the latter under s.41) pleaded not guilty to the charge of reckless driving but guilty to careless driving, the Crown Court had no jurisdiction to sentence him for that offence once he had been acquitted of reckless driving. Only if he was convicted of an "either way" offence could the Crown Court determine whether the considerations under s.41(1) applied to the summary offence; otherwise it must send back the summary offence for trial by the magistrates' court which was deemed by that section to have adjourned it (*R. v Foote* [1991] Crim. L.R. 909). It is submitted that evidence proving the commission of an offence under s.4 or s.5 may be admissible in a charge of dangerous driving tried on indictment (see § 5.54).

5.17   Careless or inconsiderate driving can only be tried by magistrates. It is for the court to decide, having heard representations from both sides, whether or not more than one information based on connected facts should be tried together (*Clayton v Chief Constable of Norfolk* [1983] 1 All E.R. 984, HL; see further § 2.152).

It is for the prosecutor, not the magistrates, to decide at the first instance whether the charge shall be under s.2 or s.3 and the magistrates should not refuse to issue a summons for careless driving if he applies for that only (*R. v Nuneaton JJ.* [1954] 3 All E.R. 251).

See § 2.152 as to trying together charges against separate defendants or a number of charges against one defendant.   **5.18**

A member of the armed forces may properly be tried by court-martial for dangerous or careless driving on a road abroad on a charge of committing a civil offence contrary to the Army Act 1955 s.70 (*Cox v Army Council* [1962] 1 All E.R. 880).

Warning of intended prosecution is required for offences under ss.2 and 3 unless an accident occurred (see Chapter 2).

Section 24 of the Police and Criminal Evidence Act 1984 enables a constable   **5.19** to arrest without warrant anyone who is committing, or is about to commit an offence of whatever kind, or whom the constable reasonably suspects to be committing, or about to commit an offence. It should be noted, however, that for this power to be exercisable the constable must have reasonable grounds for believing that an arrest is necessary in order, inter alia, to enable a person's name or address to be ascertained or to prevent any subsequent prosecution from being hindered by the disappearance of the person in question.

Section 127(1) of the Magistrates' Courts Act 1980 requires an information for a s.3 offence to be laid within six months. This time-limit does not apply to dangerous driving because s.2 is an "either way" offence and s.127(1) does not apply to indictable and "either way" offences (Criminal Law Act 1977 s.64(1)).

As to venue, see § 2.39.

Alternative verdicts

Although under previous legislation there were some statutory provisions al-   **5.20** lowing a person acquitted of a more serious bad driving offence to be convicted of a lesser one, those provisions did not deal with all situations and they differed as between England and Wales and Scotland. The North Committee's recommendation that the scope of what is now the 1988 Offenders Act be extended so that throughout the two jurisdictions it would always be possible, where appropriate, to convict of a less serious bad driving offence where a more serious one was charged was accepted by the Government of the day and is now embodied in s.24 of the 1988 Offenders Act as substituted by s.24 of the Road Traffic Act 1991. The implementation of ss.31 and 33 of the Road Safety Act 2006 on September 24, 2007 extended the list of alternative verdicts to include alternatives for motor manslaughter and extended the list of alternatives for s.3A of the 1988 Act (causing death by careless driving when under the influence of drink or drugs).

In paraphrased form, s.24(1) provides that where a person charged with an offence under the Road Traffic Act 1988 specified in the first column of the table set out in that section is found not guilty of that offence, but the allegations amount to or include an allegation of an offence under one or more of the provisions specified in the corresponding entry in the second column, he may be convicted of that offence or one of those offences. So far as the offences dealt with in this chapter are concerned, the relevant parts of the table are set out below, and have been adapted to include the amendments made by the Road Safety Act 2006, as mentioned above.

Offence charged	Alternative
Motor manslaughter	Section 1 (causing death by dangerous driving)
	Section 2 (dangerous driving)
	Section 3A (causing death by careless driving when under the influence of drink or drugs)
	Section 35 Offences Against the Person Act 1861 (furious driving)
Section 1 (causing death by dangerous driving)	Section 2 (dangerous driving)
	Section 3 (careless, and inconsiderate, driving)
Section 2 (dangerous driving)	Section 3 (careless, and inconsiderate, driving)
Section 3A (causing death by careless driving when under the influence of drink or drugs)	Section 3 (careless, and inconsiderate, driving)
	Section 4(1) (driving when unfit to drive through drink or drugs)
	Section 5(1)(a) (driving with excess alcohol in breath, blood or urine)
	Section 7(6) (failing to provide specimen)
	Section 7A(6) (failing to give permission for laboratory test)
Section 28 (dangerous cycling)	Section 29 (careless, and inconsiderate, cycling)

5.21   In the absence of a verdict of not guilty of the more serious offence originally charged, there is no power to convict of a lesser alternative offence; see *R. v Griffiths* [1998] Crim. L.R. 348 at § 5.22 below. Where, however, an allegation of dangerous driving tried summarily is dismissed on the basis that there is no case to answer, that dismissal is analogous to an acquittal and accordingly there is power to convict of the lesser offence of careless driving; see *DPP v Smith (Roger)* [2002] EWHC 1151; [2002] Crim. L.R. 970 at § 5.23 below.

Where a person is charged with a s.3A offence, s.24(1) of the 1988 Offenders Act, as substituted, does not authorise his conviction of any offence of attempting to drive (s.24(2)).

The Crown Court when convicting a person of a summary offence has the same powers and duties as a magistrates' court would have (s.24(4)). Similar provisions are made for Scottish courts (s.24(5)).

Section 24 has effect without prejudice to certain other statutory provisions principally concerning alternative verdicts on trial on indictment (such as s.6(3) of the Criminal Law Act 1967; see § 5.34) (s.24(6)).

It should be noted that failure to comply with s.1(1) of the 1988 Offenders Act (warning of intended prosecution) is not a bar to conviction of a lesser offence in accordance with s.24 (1988 Offenders Act s.2(4)).

Section 3 creates two separate offences and a conviction for driving without **5.22** due care or reasonable consideration is bad (*R. v Surrey JJ.* (1932) 95 J.P. 219). In *Hutton v Casey* (1952) 116 J.P. Jo. 223, however, convictions under both limbs of s.3 not in the alternative were upheld in respect of an act of driving lasting only a few seconds. In Scotland, it seems, a charge under both limbs of s.3 in the alternative is good (*Archibald v Keiller* [1931] J.C. 34). As s.3 consists of two separate offences, it would seem necessary for a jury to be directed as to which of the two s.3 offences they should find the defendant guilty of. It would seem that a person driving without reasonable consideration is also driving without due care. On the other hand a person driving without due care and attention is not necessarily driving without reasonable consideration for other road users (see § 5.45). For this reason a direction to the jury that they may find the defendant guilty of driving without due care or attention if they find a charge under s.1 or s.2 not proved may usually be correct, but a direction to find him guilty of driving without reasonable consideration for other road users may not be if there is no evidence of lack of consideration for actual road users. The separateness of the two offences under s.3 was re-emphasised by the Court of Appeal in *R. v Griffiths* [1998] Crim. L.R. 348. A judge in his summing-up to the jury in a case of dangerous driving gave only passing mention to the possibility of an alternative verdict under s.3 of careless and inconsiderate driving. The jury was unable to reach a verdict, despite a majority direction. The judge discharged them from reaching a verdict on the count of dangerous driving and asked them to consider an alternative count of careless driving. The accused was subsequently convicted of driving without due care and attention. His appeal against conviction was upheld because first in the absence of a verdict of not guilty on the count of dangerous driving there was no power under s.24(1) of the 1988 Act for the jury to return a verdict of guilty of careless driving, and secondly the jury were in any event insufficiently directed in respect of the alternative verdict, bearing in mind that s.3 dealt with two offences rather than one, namely the offences of driving without due care and attention and driving without reasonable consideration for other road users, which were not to be treated either as a composite offence or as necessarily equivalent or interchangeable, even though a given set of facts might well justify a charge under either limb.

R. v Griffiths above was distinguished by the court in *DPP v Smith (Roger)* **5.23** [2002] EWHC 1151; [2002] Crim. L.R. 970. Where an allegation of dangerous driving tried summarily is dismissed on the basis that there is no case to answer, the effect of that dismissal is analogous to an acquittal (per Magistrates' Courts Act 1980 s.27); accordingly the defendant may by virtue of s.24(1) of the 1988 Offenders Act be convicted, if the evidence warrants it, of the lesser offence of careless driving.

It was not open to a jury to return an alternative verdict for a lesser offence (driving whilst unfit through drink or drugs) under s.24(1) of the 1988 Offenders Act where they had been discharged from returning a verdict on the more serious offence (causing death by careless driving under the influence of alcohol) following the grant of a stay of proceedings in respect of the latter offence (*R. v Khela*; *R. v Smith* [2005] EWCA Crim 3446; [2006] Crim. L.R. 526).

CAUSING DEATH BY DANGEROUS DRIVING

The offence (s.1)

5.24   Section 1 of the 1988 Act provides that "a person who causes the death of another person by driving a mechanically propelled vehicle on a road or other public place is guilty of an offence". The phrase "the death of another person" does not relate only to the death of a person who was in life at the time of the dangerous driving; where, therefore, the injuries causing death were inflicted upon a foetus *in utero* who was later delivered alive by Caesarean section but who died the following day from those injuries, a charge under s.1 would lie against the person whose (reckless) driving caused those injuries. The High Court of Justiciary so decided in *McCluskey v Her Majesty's Advocate* [1989] R.T.R. 182 in refusing an appeal against the sheriff's decision to the like effect.

The statutory offence of causing death by dangerous driving on a road or other public place is also manslaughter (see *R. v Governor of Holloway Ex p. Jennings* [1983] A.C. 624, § 5.38). Manslaughter will normally only be charged in a very grave case; see further § 5.38. It should also be noted that it is not possible to charge a person with causing death by dangerous driving if the offence was not on a "road or other public place" or the vehicle was not a "mechanically propelled vehicle" within the meaning attributed to these words (see further Chapter 1).

Evidence and procedure

5.25   The prosecution must prove that the defendant caused the death by driving dangerously. As to what amounts to dangerous driving see "What is dangerous driving?", §§ 5.04–14.

Evidence of the mere fact that a person charged with the former offence of causing death by reckless driving was in breach of the law relating to provisional licence-holders by driving without qualified supervision was inadmissible per se; it only became admissible if it could be shown that the lack of supervision was causally connected with the ensuing accident (*R. v O'Neale* [1988] R.T.R. 124).

5.26   The prosecution must also prove that the defendant caused the death of another person, who may be a passenger in the defendant's vehicle. In *R. v Curphey* [1957] Crim. L.R. 191 (a case of causing death by dangerous driving) it was held that a jury might properly be directed to convict if they considered the defendant's driving was the *substantial* cause of death but not the sole one. In *R. v Gould* [1963] 2 All E.R. 847 a jury were directed that they might convict if the defendant's dangerous driving was *a* substantial cause and not *the* substantial cause. These cases were reviewed by the Court of Appeal in *R. v Hennigan* [1971] 3 All E.R. 133. The defendant's car was driven in a restricted area at estimated speeds of up to 80mph. It crashed into another car which was astride the centre of the road having emerged from a minor road. The defendant was going dangerously fast but it might be held that the other driver was substantially to blame as she was clearly at fault in emerging from the minor road. The jury were directed that they could convict even if the defendant was only a little more than one fifth to blame. The Court of Appeal ruled that this was an incorrect approach. The proper way for a jury to be directed is for them to be told to consider whether the defendant's driving is *a* cause, and it no longer has to be a *substantial* cause, Lord Parker C.J. stated (at 135):

"the court would like to emphasise that there is nothing in the statute which requires the manner of the driving to be a substantial cause or a major cause or any other description of cause, of the accident. So long as the dangerous driving is *a* cause and something more than de minimis, the statute operates."

Questions of causation were raised in *R. v Pagett, The Times*, February 4, 1983, and in *R. v Mitchell* [1983] Crim. L.R. 549. In the former case a conviction for manslaughter of a pregnant girl was upheld where the defendant shot at armed police and used the pregnant girl as a shield who was killed by the police. In the latter case the defendant hit an elderly man who fell against an elderly woman who subsequently died; his conviction for manslaughter of the elderly woman was also upheld. In *Pagett* Robert Goff L.J. said "the question whether an accused person can be guilty of homicide … of a victim the immediate cause of whose death is the act of another person must be determined on the ordinary principles of causation". These words were cited with approval in *Mitchell*. Causing death by dangerous driving is a statutory form of manslaughter (see *R. v Governor of Holloway Ex p. Jennings*, § 5.38). The statement of Parker L.J. in *R. v Hennigan* above would seem to be in general accord with these two cases. If *A* drives recklessly (dangerously) as a result of which he collides with *B*'s vehicle which as a result then collides with *C*'s vehicle killing *C*, surely *A* can be convicted of causing death by reckless (dangerous) driving, of *C*?

The consequences of the driving of a vehicle in a dangerous condition, with particular reference to the issue of causation and remoteness, were considered by the Court of Appeal in *R. v Skelton* [1995] Crim. L.R. 635. A heavy goods vehicle driver took his vehicle back on to the road despite being warned by another lorry driver, from whom he had requested assistance at a motorway service area, that his air pressure gauges were not registering and that he should call a mechanic. Some time later he smelled burning and pulled on to the hard shoulder. Investigation revealed nothing, so he set off again. Very soon thereafter, the loss of air pressure caused the hand brake system to be activated. The driver tried to get back on to the hard shoulder, but came to a halt with his trailer unit blocking the nearside lane of the motorway (albeit with hazard warning lights in operation). Although several vehicles managed to avoid the obstruction, some 12 minutes later a lorry drove into the back of the trailer. That lorry caught fire and its driver was killed. It was argued on behalf of the defendant both at his trial and before the Court of Appeal that if, as in the event the jury considered was the case, there had been an act of dangerous driving in taking the vehicle back on to the road in a state which it would have been obvious to a competent and careful driver was dangerous, that act was nevertheless spent by the time the fatal crash occurred. What caused the death of the unfortunate lorry driver was an obstruction in the highway and his failure to see it. In dismissing the appeal, the court set out the two principles of law to which the criminal courts should have regard in this context. Beyond those two principles, the questions are questions of fact and degree. First, the dangerous driving must have played a part, not simply in creating the occasion of the fatal accident, but in bringing it about. Secondly, on the authority of *R. v Hennigan* [1971] 3 All E.R. 133 (discussed above at § 5.26), there is no particular degree of contribution to the death, beyond a negligible one, which is required. Within that framework it could not be said that the consequences of the appellant's driving were on any view spent and the accident either the sole fault of the deceased in failing to see the obstruction, or at best a pure

5.27

accident. The evidential point at which the dangerous driving, although established, was too remote from the supervening death to have been the cause of it, had by no means been reached in the instant case.

5.28   *R. v Hennigan* mentioned above was also referred to and applied by the Court of Appeal in *R. v Kimsey* [1996] Crim. L.R. 35 when dealing with the appropriateness or otherwise of a recorder's direction to a jury on the question of causation in a case of causing death by dangerous driving where it was for them to decide the extent, if any, to which the defendant's driving had contributed to the death of the driver of another car with which the defendant had been racing. The recorder had told the jury that they did not have to be sure that his driving "was the principal, or a substantial, cause of the death, as long as you are sure that it was a cause and that there was something more than a slight or trifling link". In the court's view the recorder's reference to a "slight or trifling link" was a permissible and useful way to avoid the term "de minimis" and his direction was faithful to the logic of *Hennigan*.

The common law rule that death must occur within a year and a day in homicide was abolished by the Law Reform (Year and a Day Rule) Act 1996. Two important safeguards against inappropriate prosecutions are, however, contained in the Act. The Attorney General's consent to prosecute is required where either the injury alleged to have caused the death was sustained more than three years before the death occurred, or the prospective defendant has already been convicted of an offence committed in circumstances alleged to be connected with the death. The Act applies inter alia to manslaughter and other offences of which one of the elements is causing a person's death.

5.29   For the purposes of s.1, "driver" does not include a separate person acting as steersman (s.192(1)) but such a person might, if the facts warrant, be prosecuted for aiding and abetting an offence under s.1.

The offence can be committed only on a "road" (as defined in the 1988 Act: see Chapter 1) or other public place (see also Chapter 1) and relates only to mechanically propelled vehicles. Carters, drivers of "fours in hand" and pony traps, and cyclists may be charged with manslaughter.

Spouses are competent and compellable witnesses in the Crown Court against each other where the victim was under 16 years of age (Police and Criminal Evidence Act 1984 s.80) as "bodily injury" in s.80(3)(a) must include a fatal injury.

5.30   By s.38 of the 1988 Act non-observance of the Highway Code may tend to establish liability for the offence (for a discussion of the Highway Code as to offences of dangerous or careless driving, see Highway Code, §§ 5.69–73).

In *R. v Bogdal* [1982] R.T.R. 395 it was held that a charge of dangerous driving and one of using a licence with intent to deceive were in the circumstances of the case not a "series of offences of a similar character" within the meaning of what was then r.9 of the 1971 Indictment Rules and should not have been tried together (October 20 licence suspended and defendant ordered to produce his licence in seven days under what is now s.7 of the 1988 Offenders Act, October 24 seen driving by constable to whom he produced licence, November 27 seen by same constable driving dangerously).

5.31   It is no longer possible for a case of driving under the influence of drink or drugs (s.4(1)) or with excess blood-alcohol (s.5(1)) to be tried on indictment, but it is submitted that evidence of drink is only admissible if "the amount of drink taken was such as would adversely affect a driver or alternatively the driver was in fact adversely affected" (see *R. v Woodward (Terence)* and other cases under "Drink", § 5.55). A novel attempt to circumvent the evidential problems engendered by the fact that driving with excess alcohol contrary to s.5(1) of the 1988 Act is not triable on indictment was firmly repulsed by the Divisional Court in *R. v Forest of Dean JJ. Ex p. Farley* [1990] R.T.R. 228. The prosecution had sought to proceed summarily against a defendant for driving with excess alcohol with a view to a conviction on that charge being used to found a further prosecution for causing death by reckless driving in which the only recklessness alleged would be the fact of having driven after drinking. In the view of the court such a manner of proceeding would be oppressive and unfair, since on the facts it was in substance a case of double jeopardy; accordingly the justices were ordered not to proceed with the trial. (See further § 2.66.)

Causing death by dangerous driving is triable only on indictment at the Crown Court. It is a Class 3 offence in accordance with the *Consolidated Criminal Practice Direction*. So far as Class 3 offences are concerned, the magistrates' court which commits or sends the defendant for trial should specify the most convenient location of the Crown Court.

Warning of intended prosecution is not required for offences under s.1 nor does s.1 of the 1988 Offenders Act prevent a jury bringing in alternative verdicts under s.2 of dangerous driving or s.3 of careless or inconsiderate driving (1988 Offenders Act s.2(4)). **5.32**

The proceedings will be commenced by summons or arrest, with remand on bail or in custody, to the magistrates' court where the defendant will in due course be committed or sent for trial to the Crown Court (see Chapter 2).

So far as powers of arrest are concerned, s.24 of the Police and Criminal Evidence Act 1984 enables a constable to arrest without warrant anyone who is committing, or is about to commit an offence of whatever kind, or whom the constable reasonably suspects to be committing, or about to commit an offence.

A youth court may not try homicide (Magistrates' Courts Act 1980 s.24). The legal dictionaries define homicide as "killing a person" and do not limit it to murder and manslaughter. Homicide thus includes any offence an essential element of which is that the accused caused the death of another person. Causing death by dangerous driving contrary to s.1 of the 1988 Act satisfies this test as well as the more usual forms of homicide such as murder, manslaughter or infanticide. It is therefore submitted that a youth charged with causing death by dangerous driving can only be tried at the Crown Court. **5.33**

Alternative verdicts

By virtue of s.24(1) of the 1988 Offenders Act a jury on a charge under s.1 may convict the defendant of dangerous driving under s.2 or of careless or inconsiderate driving under s.3 (see further §§ 5.20–3). Since s.24 has effect without prejudice to s.6(3) of the Criminal Law Act 1967, it would seem possible that a jury may alternatively convict the defendant of causing bodily harm by furious driving under s.35 of the Offences Against the Person Act 1861 (see §§ 5.101–3). In *R. v Thompson* [1980] R.T.R. 387 the defendant pleaded not guilty to the former offence of reckless driving but guilty to careless driving. The prosecution was not prepared to accept the plea and the matter proceeded to trial. The jury acquitted the defendant of reckless driving. The judge thereupon, on the **5.34** basis of the original plea, sentenced the defendant for careless driving. The sentence was set aside as a complete nullity. The judge had not, as he could have done, directed the jury as to an alternative verdict of careless driving should they find the reckless driving not proved.

If a judge in his summing-up wishes to leave to the jury the alternative verdict of careless or inconsiderate driving and the possibility of doing so has not previously been canvassed, the judge should first mention the matter to counsel in the jury's absence in order that counsel can make submissions to the judge on the matter and, more importantly, address the jury on the issues raised by the alternative charge. Where a judge directed a jury on the alternative verdict of careless driving in his summing-up without warning and without counsel being afforded an opportunity of addressing the jury, this was held to amount to a serious irregularity in the course of the trial and the resulting conviction for careless driving was quashed (*R. v Hazell* [1985] R.T.R. 369).

5.35   A defendant charged with the former offence of causing death by reckless driving submitted that, on the basis of the evidence that he and his witnesses had presented, the alternative of careless driving ought to be left to the jury. The trial judge directed the jury that they were not dealing with a case of careless or inconsiderate driving, but only of reckless driving. The defendant was convicted (by a majority verdict) of causing death by reckless driving. On appeal, the Court of Appeal held in *R. v Fairbanks* [1986] R.T.R. 309 that the interests of justice required that lesser alternatives should be left to the jury where the evidence was such that it would be wrong for the defendant to be acquitted altogether merely because the jury could not be sure that he was guilty of the greater offence. His conviction was quashed and a verdict of guilty of the lesser offence of careless driving substituted.

R. v Fairbanks was referred to by the Divisional Court in *R. v Jeavons* [1990] R.T.R. 263 where it was held on the facts to be perfectly proper for the trial judge not to have acceded to a submission that the alternative of careless driving should be left to the jury. According to the prosecution, the appellant and a friend were racing each other when the friend's motor car struck and killed a pedestrian on a crossing. Although the appellant did not give evidence, self-exculpating answers he had given to the police were read to the court in evidence. The issue was a relatively straightforward one. If the prosecution's allegations of racing failed there was no basis for any charge of careless driving. The conviction was neither unsafe nor unsatisfactory.

Inquests

5.36   Section 16 of the Coroners Act 1988 requires the coroner, in the absence of reason to the contrary, to adjourn the proceedings when he is notified by the clerk of the magistrates' court of a charge under ss.1, 2B, 3ZB or s.3A of the 1988 Act or of murder, manslaughter, corporate manslaughter, infanticide, aiding and abetting a suicide or causing or allowing the death of a vulnerable adult. The coroner is also similarly required to adjourn the proceedings where requested to do so by the Director of Public Prosecutions where a person has been charged with any offence other than those set out above committed in circumstances connected with the death of the deceased. The clerk of the magistrates' court is required to notify the coroner of the result of the committal proceedings, and the appropriate officer of the Crown Court of the results of the proceedings before that court (Coroners

Act 1988 s.17). Where the coroner has been requested by the Director of Public Prosecutions to adjourn the proceedings, the Director is required to notify the coroner of the offence selected by him and the result of the proceedings.

A motor cyclist was involved in a collision with a car driven by the defendant, and died as a result of his injuries. He was charged with driving without due care and attention, contrary to s.3 of the 1988 Act. An inquest into the motor cyclist's death was opened, but was not concluded until two years later. In the meantime the defendant came to trial before the justices. The prosecution sought an adjournment on the ground that two witnesses to the collision had recently been traced but were not in court to give evidence. The justices, who were aware that the motor cyclist had died but were unaware that an inquest had been opened, refused the adjournment and the defendant was acquitted. The father of the deceased appealed as an aggrieved party against the justices' decision not to grant the adjournment. The Divisional Court in *Smith v DPP* [2000] R.T.R. 36 dismissed the appeal and held that, when criminal proceedings had been commenced relating to an incident regarding which an inquest had been opened, and it was not a case in which the coroner was required by s.16 of the Coroners Act 1988 to adjourn the inquest pending the conclusion of the criminal proceedings, as a matter of practice, justices ought not to proceed with the case until the inquest had been held. There was, however, no absolute rule of law requiring justices to adjourn such a case pending an inquest, and in all the circumstances of the case the justices had been entitled in the exercise of their discretion to refuse the adjournment.

MOTOR MANSLAUGHTER

Constituents of the offence

Manslaughter, whether committed by an adult or a youth, is a Class 2 offence **5.37** (see directions of the Lord Chief Justice) triable at the Crown Court. It need not have been committed on a road or other public place.

The offence is an obligatorily disqualifiable offence (Pt II of Sch.2 to the 1988 Offenders Act). By s.38 of the 1988 Act non-observance of the Highway Code may tend to establish liability for the offence (for a discussion as to the effect of s.38(7) on careless and dangerous driving offences, see §§ 5.69–73).

Section 23 of the 1988 Offenders Act (alternative verdicts in Scotland) is **5.38** amended by s.32 of the Road Safety Act 2006 (from September 24, 2007) to provide for alternative verdicts of causing death by dangerous driving, dangerous driving and causing death by careless driving when under the influence of drink or drugs on an unsuccessful culpable homicide prosecution. Section 24 ibid. is amended by s.33 of the 2006 Act (from September 24, 2007) to provide for alternative verdicts of any of the three offences listed above, with the addition of the offence of furious driving (Offences Against the Person Act 1861 s.35), on an unsuccessful manslaughter prosecution. By s.23(1) in its unamended form, juries in Scotland may bring in an alternative verdict of dangerous driving if they find a motorist not guilty of culpable homicide; by s.24(1) ibid., they may convict a person charged with the statutory offence of causing death by dangerous driving of either of the lesser offences of dangerous driving or careless driving (see § 5.20). In addition to these statutory alternative verdicts it appears to have been the practice in Scotland (at least since the case of *Dunn v HM Advocate* 1960 J.C.

55) to prosecute on one charge of culpable homicide, or alternatively of the (former) statutory offence of causing death by reckless driving, leaving the jury (if it decides to convict) to decide whether to do so on the first or second alternative. In England and Wales, however, the House of Lords in *R. v Seymour (Edward)* [1983] R.T.R. 455 has stated (per Lord Roskill at 465L) that there should not be a joinder of the charges of manslaughter and what is now causing death by dangerous driving on a single indictment and if any such joinder should occur it is incumbent on the trial judge to require the prosecution to elect on which of the two counts they wish to proceed and not to allow the trial to proceed on both events (at 466A–B).

The House of Lords has further held (*R. v Governor of Holloway Ex p. Jennings* [1983] R.T.R. 1) that, while prosecuting authorities today would only prosecute for manslaughter "in a very grave case" (per Lord Roskill at 19G–H), the offence of "motor manslaughter" was not abolished by implication either by the creation of the offence of causing death by reckless or dangerous driving in 1956 or by the amendment of that offence (Criminal Law Act 1977 s.50) restricting it to a single offence of causing death by reckless driving (now causing death by dangerous driving).

5.39   It was held by the Court of Appeal (Lord Taylor C.J. presiding) in *R. v Pimm* [1994] R.T.R. 391 that the elements of the offence of manslaughter by motor vehicle and the former offence of causing death by reckless driving were not in law the same; accordingly, the sentencing powers of the court for manslaughter were not limited by relation to the maximum sentence for the former statutory offence. The court also emphasised, applying *R. v Seymour* as explained by the Privy Council in *Kong Cheuk Kwan v R.* (1985) 82 Cr. App. R. 18, that the more grave offence should only be charged where on the facts there was a very high risk of death.

So far as sentencing is concerned, the guidance on sentencing in cases of what is now causing death by dangerous driving given in *R. v Cooksley* [2003] R.T.R. 32 (see §§ 5.131 et seq.), although of relevance, does not fully cover offences of motor manslaughter, since the driver's blameworthiness may well be aggravated by his hostile motivation (*R. v Mitchell* [1989] R.T.R. 186).

See § 5.36 as to inquests and as to notifying the coroner of committal (or transfer).

Hit-and-run drivers

5.40   It is submitted that there may be one other instance where manslaughter might possibly be committed by a motorist. One of the purposes of Parliament when enacting the duty to stop after an accident and to report that accident now contained in s.170 of the 1988 Act was, it was submitted, the saving of life. If therefore a motorist, knowing serious injury and the risk of death if not medically attended, fails to stop or fails to report the accident and as a result of that failure the person whom he has hit with his motor vehicle dies, it could be argued that his deliberate or reckless failure to comply with the positive duty placed upon him by s.170 might be sufficient to warrant a charge of manslaughter even if there is no evidence of the manner of the defendant's driving. It should be noted that the duty to stop means to stop sufficiently long to exchange particulars with anyone requiring the same (*Lee v Knapp*, § 7.09). The duty of reporting an accident is required to be exercised "as soon as reasonably practicable". As was held in *Bulman v Bennett* [1974] R.T.R. 1, this means exactly this; it does not mean that the motorist has 24 hours within which to report the accident.

DANGEROUS, CARELESS AND INCONSIDERATE DRIVING

The Road Safety Act 2006

With effect from September 24, 2007, the Road Safety Act 2006 brought into being a new offence of causing death by careless driving. This offence is discussed at §§ 5.96–8 below. In conjunction with the introduction of that offence, the Government also saw fit to provide, for the first time, a statutory definition of careless or inconsiderate driving (1988 Act s.3ZA, as inserted by s.30 of the 2006 Act). A person is to be regarded as driving without due care and attention if (and only if) the way he drives falls below what would be expected of a competent and careful driver (s.3ZA(2)). In determining what would be expected of a careful and competent driver, regard must be had not only to the circumstances of which he (the competent and careful driver) could be expected to be aware, but also to any circumstances shown to have been within the knowledge of the accused (s.3ZA(3)). A person is to be regarded as driving without reasonable consideration for other persons only if those persons are inconvenienced by his driving (s.3ZA(4)).

5.41

Since s.3 of the 1988 Act is in terms all but identical to s.12 of the Road Traffic Act 1930, it would seem that the courts have already had ample opportunity to decide upon the meaning of careless and inconsiderate driving, as evidenced by the considerable body of case law discussed below. It is submitted that in reality there is no measurable difference between the "competent and careful" driver envisaged by the statute and the "reasonable, prudent and competent" driver hallowed by so many years of judicial consideration. What is slightly more significant, however, is the requirement for regard to be had, as in the test for dangerous driving (s.2A(3)), to circumstances shown to have been within the knowledge of the accused.

The difference between dangerous and careless driving

The distinction to be drawn between careless and dangerous driving is a qualitative one based primarily upon the standard of driving displayed by the alleged offender. It is essentially a matter of fact and degree.

5.42

In simple terms, the actus reus of offences under ss.1 and 2 is driving in a manner which falls far below what would be expected of a competent and careful driver in circumstances in which it would be obvious to such a competent and careful driver that driving in that way (or driving the vehicle at all in its current state) would be dangerous. In this connection "dangerous" refers to a danger either of personal injury or of serious damage to property. The actus reus of a charge under s.3 is, since the implementation of s.30 of the Road Safety Act 2006, driving in a manner that falls below what would be expected of a careful and competent driver. This may merely cause annoyance or show lack of consideration, with little risk of injury or serious damage. Thus the difference between the two types of offence is the extent to which the offender's driving falls below the required standard; namely "*far* below" for ss.1 and 2, but merely "below" for s.3.

5.43   Both offences are absolute in the sense that it is unnecessary to show that the defendant's mind was conscious of the consequences of his actions; it is only necessary to show that he was conscious of what he was doing. However, it is important to note that for both dangerous driving and, since the implementation of the 2006 Act, careless driving, in determining what would be expected of a careful and competent driver regard shall be had not only to the circumstances of which he could be expected to be aware but also to any circumstance shown to be within the knowledge of the accused (s.2A(3) and s.3ZA(3)). So, if an offender drives a vehicle which, whilst not obviously in a dangerous condition, is nevertheless known by him to possess a dangerous defect, that guilty knowledge may lead to his conviction of a s.1 or s.2 offence. It should also be noted that in the view of the Court of Appeal a s.1 or s.2 offence may be committed where it is not the vehicle but the *driver* who is in a dangerously defective state, whether through drink (*R. v Woodward (Terence)* [1995] R.T.R. 130; see § 5.55) or diabetes (*R. v Marison* [1996] Crim. L.R. 909; see § 5.14). In the great majority of cases, however, it will be the nature of the defendant's driving viewed objectively which will determine whether or not a dangerous driving offence has been committed, and proof of mens rea will not be required.

In December 2007 the Crown Prosecution Service introduced new guidance on what constitutes dangerous driving, from the point of view of charging standards (*Policy for Prosecuting Cases of Bad Driving*, available at *http:// www.cps.gov.uk/publications/prosecution/pbd_policy.html* [Accessed March 21, 2009]). Under the revised policy dangerous driving includes: racing or competitive driving; disregarding warnings from passengers; reading a newspaper or map; and aggressive driving. Careless driving includes driving inappropriately close to another vehicle; turning on a radio; and selecting and lighting a cigarette. Inconsiderate driving includes flashing lights to force other drivers to give way unnecessarily; remaining in the overtaking lane; driving with undipped headlights; splashing pedestrians by driving through puddles; and driving a bus in a way that alarms passengers. Annex A to the Sentencing Guidelines Council Definitive Guideline to Causing Death by Driving (Appendix 4, p.1284 below) sets out examples of dangerous and careless driving.

Summary of careless and inconsiderate driving

5.44   Section 3 of the 1988 Act, as amended by the Road Traffic Act 1991, provides that it is an offence for a person to drive a mechanically propelled vehicle on a road or other public place "without due care and attention, or without reasonable consideration for other persons using the road or place". The amendments effected by the 1991 Act amount to the replacement of "motor vehicle" by "mechanically propelled vehicle" and the extension of the ambit of the offence to include "other public places" as well as roads. The significance of these changes is discussed at §§ 5.15 above.

The prosecutor has to prove beyond reasonable doubt that the motorist is "at fault", i.e. had departed from the standard of a competent and careful driver in all the circumstances of the particular case. This is primarily a question of objective fact. An acquittal by magistrates on the facts will normally not be set aside by the High Court unless the facts are such that no reasonable tribunal could possibly have acquitted. Normally the justices are the best judges as to the actual facts. The Highway Code is a good guide to whether the motorist has departed from the required standard of driving, but breach of the code is not necessarily conclusive. If the facts are such that in the absence of an explanation put forward by the defendant the only possible conclusion is that he was careless, he should be convicted. Unless there is evidence before them for it, magistrates should refrain from theorising and advancing an explanation for the behaviour of the defendant's vehicle. However, once a possible explanation is put forward the prosecution are required to prove it untrue beyond reasonable doubt. It is a defence that the vehicle had a sudden defect of which the defendant neither knew nor should have been expected to know. On the other hand, if a defendant drives knowing of the defect, he is guilty of careless or, more likely, dangerous driving. Similarly automatism is a defence, but if the defendant knows that he is suffering from an illness likely seriously to affect his control of the car and drives, he is guilty. For an offence under s.3 (also ss.1 and 2) to be committed the prosecution must show that the defendant "drove". The meaning of the word is discussed in Chapter 1. In *Jones v Pratt* [1983] R.T.R. 54 it was held that a front seat passenger was not "driving" when he momentarily grabbed the steering wheel of the car causing it to go off the road when he saw a small animal running across the road.

The difference between careless and inconsiderate driving

Careless and inconsiderate driving under s.3 of the 1988 Act, as substituted by the 1991 Act s.2, means driving without due care and attention, or without reasonable consideration for other persons using the road or place. Since the implementation of the Road Safety Act 2006 a person is to be regarded as driving without due care and attention if (and only if) the way he drives falls below what would be expected of a competent and careful driver (s.3ZA(2)). It follows that a person who drives without reasonable consideration for other road users can be convicted of driving without due care and attention, because a competent and careful driver would not drive without reasonable consideration for others. However, the corollary does not apply. A person may be convicted of driving without reasonable consideration for other persons using the road or place only if other persons are inconvenienced by his driving (s.3ZA(4), confirming earlier case law). **5.45**

Examples of careless driving might include: overtaking on the inside or driving inappropriately close to another vehicle; inadvertent mistakes such as driving through a red light or emerging from a side road into the path of another vehicle; or short distractions such as tuning a car radio. Examples of inconsiderate driving might include: flashing of lights to force another driver to give way; misuse of any lane to avoid queuing or gain some other advantage over other drivers; driving that inconveniences other road users or causes unnecessary hazards such as unnecessarily remaining in an overtaking lane, unnecessarily slow driving or braking without good cause, driving with undipped headlights which dazzle oncoming drivers or driving through a puddle causing pedestrians to be splashed.

A typical piece of careless driving may be that it is a momentary negligent error of judgment or a single negligent manoeuvre, so long as neither falls so far below the standard of the competent and careful driver as to amount to dangerous driving.

Objective standard of care

The test as to whether a defendant is guilty of careless driving is an objective **5.46** one (*McCrone v Riding* below). What the prosecution have to prove is *that the defendant has departed from the standard of a competent and careful driver in all the circumstances of the case*. (It is submitted that this is essentially the same test as that of the *reasonable, prudent and competent driver* that prevailed in the case law before 2007, and that the cases below remain good law.) This is primarily a question of fact. The standard of care demanded by the criminal law cannot be higher than that demanded by the civil law of negligence (*Scott v Warren* [1974] R.T.R. 104).

If the defendant fails to exercise due care, he is guilty whether or not his failure is due to his inexperience (*McCrone v Riding* [1938] 1 All E.R. 157: learner driver guilty) and whether or not it was a deliberate act or an error of judgment (*Taylor v Rogers* (1960) 124 J.P. 217). *McCrone v Riding* was followed in *R. v Preston JJ. Ex p. Lyons* [1982] R.T.R. 173, where the Divisional Court refused an order of mandamus requiring the justices to state a case. The applicant, an "L" driver, had been instructed by his driving instructor to execute an emergency stop. He had not looked in his mirror and a motor cyclist had driven into the back of his vehicle. The justices convicted the defendant, ordered an absolute discharge and did not endorse his licence, holding the test of whether a person had driven carelessly to be objective. A criticism of the case is contained in an article by Martin Wasik [1982] Crim. L.R. 411–418. The commentator to the report in the *Criminal Law Review* also criticised the case as unjust ([1982] Crim. L.R. at 451). It is submitted that the underlying ratio of the decision, namely the necessity for an objective standard of driving to be maintained, is correct (see also the letter from the prosecutor ([1982] Crim. L.R. at 620)). It was held in *R. v Bristol Crown Court Ex p. Jones; Jones v Chief Constable of Avon and Somerset Constabulary* [1986] R.T.R. 259 that a driver suddenly confronted by an emergency should not be judged by hindsight; the test in such circumstances as to whether he is guilty of careless driving is, "Was it reasonable for him to have acted as he did?". The facts of the case were that the defendant was driving an articulated lorry at 52–57mph on a motorway at night when all his lights suddenly failed without warning. He immediately pulled onto the hard shoulder and had the misfortune of colliding with an unlit parked vehicle of which he could not have been aware. His conviction was accordingly quashed on the ground that his action was reasonable in the circumstances.

5.47   Knowledge of the defendant's carelessness is not an essential element of careless driving. A lorry driver who was not aware that he had hit a stationary vehicle was held to be rightly convicted of careless driving, although his conviction for failing to report the accident was quashed because he did not know of the accident (*Hampson v Powell* [1970] 1 All E.R. 929).

If a driver does not exercise the necessary degree of care and attention he is guilty whether or not he is committing an error of judgment (*Simpson v Peat* [1952] 1 All E.R. 447, discussed at 102 L.J. News 146, 213 L.T. News 176 and 121 J.P. Jo. 591). Where magistrates had dismissed a charge of careless driving because they thought that the driver must have had a dizzy spell or been hit by a stone or a bird, there being no evidence before them to that effect, they were directed to convict, it being said that their doubt was fanciful and not reasonable (*Oakes v Foster* [1961] Crim. L.R. 628). See also *Johnson v Fowler, Rabjohns v Burgar, Gubby v Littman* under "Res ipsa loquitur", at §§ 5.50–1 below. If the charge is one of driving without reasonable consideration for other road users, it is submitted that the test here would also be objective. One can have a situation where a whole enterprise was reckless and yet have an incident within the chain of reckless events which can properly be described as careless driving (*M (A Minor) v Oxford* [1981] R.T.R. 246). It is submitted that a person is guilty of careless driving once it is proved that he has departed from the required standard of driving. It matters not whether this was due to his negligence, incompetence, inexperience, recklessness, or even his deliberate intent: the only mens rea required in a case of careless driving is (per Lord Diplock in *R. v Lawrence* [1981] R.T.R. 217 at 220) "simply to show that the prohibited physical act (actus reus) done by the accused was directed by a mind that was conscious of what his body was doing".

In another sense the test as to what is careless driving is subjective. Although   **5.48** careless driving objectively depends on whether the defendant departed from the standard of what might be expected of a competent and careful driver in all the circumstances of the case, the particular circumstances of each case must be considered subjectively. What may amount to careless driving in one situation may be wholly prudent in a different situation. What may be careless driving on a road in the rush hour may not be at 10 o'clock on a Sunday morning. It is primarily a question of fact whether the particular circumstances of the case do, or do not, show that the defendant departed from the standard to be expected.

The best judges as to what is or what is not careless driving are the justices who know the district (see *Walker v Tolhurst* [1976] R.T.R. 513). Each case is unique. Thus while a motorist who collides with a cyclist at night or collides when emerging from a side turning into a main road will usually be convicted, not all such cases invariably lead to a conviction because the facts and road situation in each case will differ (see some of the cases cited under " Highway Code ", §§ 5.69–73).

A wrong action in the agony of the collision will not suffice alone to prove an offence under s.3 (*Simpson v Peat* above), if the defendant had been driving properly beforehand and his actions prior to the time when the collision became imminent had been those of a prudent driver.

Automatism

In certain very limited circumstances it may be possible for a defence of au-   **5.49** tomatism to be raised to charges under ss.1, 2 and 3 of the 1988 Act. The law on the subject was reviewed by the Court of Appeal in *R. v Hennessy* [1990] R.T.R. 153. This and other relevant cases are discussed in Chapter 1 (see §§ 1.118 et seq.).

Res ipsa loquitur

Frequently the only evidence which the police are able to bring is evidence of   **5.50** the defendant's vehicle leaving the road and a collision occurring with a wall or a pole or the vehicle ending up in a ditch or upside down in a field. In the absence of any explanation by the defendant, if the only conclusion which it is possible to draw is that the defendant was negligent or had departed from what a competent and careful driver would have done in the circumstances, a court should convict. The doctrine of res ipsa loquitur is a rule of evidence applicable to the tort of negligence and as such has no application to the criminal law. But the fact that res ipsa loquitur has no application to criminal law does not mean that the prosecution have to negative every possible explanation of a defendant before he can be convicted of careless driving where the facts at the scene of an accident are such that, in the absence of any explanation by the defendant, a court can have no alternative but to convict. Thus in *Rabjohns v Burgar* [1972] Crim. L.R. 46 the defendant's car on a dry road collided with the concrete wall of a bridge on a fine clear day with no other vehicle apparently involved. There were two skid marks behind the car. There were no witnesses to the accident and the defendant gave no explanation as to how the accident occurred. The justices found that there was sufficient evidence for the defendant to be required to answer the prosecution's case but, on the defendant declining to give or call any evidence, ruled that there was insufficient evidence to convict. The Divisional Court held that the facts were so strong that the defendant should be convicted and pointed out that the prosecution did not have to show there was nothing wrong with the steering as the defendant had not raised the matter. A magistrates' court was directed to find that there was a case for the defendant to answer in *Watts v Carter* [1971] R.T.R. 232, where the defendant's car was found to have hit a Post Office support pole 2ft 9in from the edge of the road and his suggestion that there was something wrong with the steering was shown to be wrong. This case was applied in *Wright v Wenlock* [1972] Crim. L.R. 49, where the defendant's vehicle hit a telegraph pole near to the road's edge. In the absence of any explanation of the accident, the justices were directed by the Divisional Court to find that there was a case for the defendant to answer. Similarly in *Bensley v Smith* [1972] Crim. L.R. 239 justices were directed to convict a defendant who had crossed a central white line and collided with a car coming in the opposite direction. Crossing a white line was itself evidence of careless driving and in the absence of explanation the justices must convict (ibid.). It would appear that, despite its age, *Bensley v Smith* is still good law, as it was followed by the Administrative Court in *R. v Warwickshire Police Ex p. Manjit Singh Mundi* [2001] EWHC Admin 448 when holding that crossing a central white line without explanation was, in itself, evidence of careless driving.

5.51   However, if an explanation, other than a fanciful explanation, is given by the defendant it is for the prosecution to disprove it and unless it is disproved the defendant is entitled to the benefit of the doubt (see *R. v Spurge*, § 5.60). Thus in *Butty v Davey* [1972] Crim. L.R. 48 the defendant's car, after negotiating a sharp bend, failed to negotiate a slight left-hand bend and slid on to the wrong side of the road and collided with an oncoming lorry. The defendant contended that he could only have done so because of some unexpected slipperiness of the road due to rain. The justices were upheld in dismissing the case as the defendant's explanation was not fanciful. It was also said that it was not incumbent on a defendant in a criminal case to show that he had skidded without fault (although it should be noted that in this particular case the defendant had given an explanation which was upheld by the justices). In *Lodwick v Jones* [1983] R.T.R. 273 the defendant skidded on an icy patch and collided with a motor cyclist. The justices dismissed the case on the ground that the prosecution had not proved that ice could reasonably have been expected on the road. It was held that the justices' conclusion was not shown to be perverse, although there was frost on the windscreen of the car when the defendant had set out that morning this did not give rise to an irresistible inference that there was ice on the road, moreover the motor cyclist had ridden on the road without difficulty. Where a vehicle takes a dangerous course and there is an accident, magistrates should refrain from theorising about its causes in the absence of any evidence and should not assume that the steering column must have broken just before the accident, when there is evidence that the vehicle was in good condition prior to the accident (*Johnson v Fowler* [1959] Crim. L.R. 463). In *Griffin v Williams* [1964] Crim. L.R. 60 a conviction was directed where a car went out of control and there was no evidence of any defect. In *Hougham v Martin* (1964) 108 S.J. 138, a car inexplicably veered off its course and collided with another vehicle: it was said that magistrates were not entitled to assume, without evidence, that, because it was a modern, mass-produced car, it was prone to mechanical defects. There must be properly admissible evidence of a mechanical defect. Justices dismissed a case of careless driving on the supposed ground that the defendant was unaware that brand new tyres do not have the holding qualities of ones which had run a few hundred miles, causing him to go onto the wrong side of the road when rounding a bend thus causing an accident. The evidence as to this supposed lack of holding qualities of brand new tyres consisted of a suggestion to this effect from an otherwise unqualified police officer who had interviewed the defendant and the production by the defendant's solicitor of a leaflet issued by the British tyre industry without either the leaflet's author being called or any expert evidence adduced to show any inherent risk involved when running in brand new tyres. The justices were directed to reconsider the case on the basis that there was no evidence of hazard in new tyres (*Gubby v Littman* [1976] R.T.R. 470). See *Oakes v Foster*, § 5.47.

On the other hand, it should perhaps be emphasised that the facts must be so strong that in the absence of any evidence of mechanical defect, illness or other explanation that is given, the facts must give rise to an inference that the defendant was guilty of careless or dangerous driving. The facts have to be such as to show beyond reasonable doubt that the defendant's standard of driving was less than that required of a competent and careful driver in all the circumstances of the case (see §§ 5.69–73 and in particular *Scott v Warren* [1974] R.T.R. 104 following car hitting car in front which had made an emergency stop; and also *Jarvis v Fuller* [1974] R.T.R. 160 colliding at night with cyclist without lights). **5.52**

Falling asleep

A driver who allows himself to be overcome by sleep, so that the car mounts the pavement or goes to the wrong side, is guilty at least of careless driving, for he should have stopped when he felt sleep overtaking him (*Kay v Butterworth* (1945) 110 J.P. 75; (1945) 61 T.L.R. 452; *Henderson v Jones* (1955) 119 J.P. 304). **5.53**

Drink

Where there is no charge of driving under the influence of drink and the accused is being tried for dangerous or careless driving only, evidence that he was at the time adversely affected by drink is of probative value and admissible and its admissibility is not limited to rebuttal of such a defence as that he was not in control through no fault of his own. Such evidence must tend to show that the amount of drink taken was such as adversely to affect a driver or that he was in **5.54** fact adversely affected, but the court has an overriding discretion to exclude such evidence where its prejudicial effect outweighs its probative value (*R. v McBride* [1962] 2 Q.B. 167). Ashworth J. said that no general rule could be laid down as to the way in which the discretion could be exercised, as each case must be considered on its own particular facts, but, if such evidence is introduced, it should at least appear of substantial weight (ibid. at 172). Cases where such evidence has been allowed are *R. v McBride* above (enough drink taken to justify a charge of driving under the influence of drink); *R. v Richardson* [1960] Crim. L.R. 135 (visits to public houses before driving); and *R. v Fisher* [1981] Crim. L.R. 578 (ibid.: practically the whole day spent in public houses prior to driving). In *R. v Thorpe* [1972] R.T.R. 118, following *R. v McBride* above, evidence that the defendant was guilty of an offence of having more than the prescribed blood-alcohol level contrary to what is now s.5 of the 1988 Act was held to be admissible on a charge of causing death by dangerous driving because a blood-alcohol level of over 80mg per 100ml was such that it could tend to prove that it could affect a driver even if, for a particular driver, it might or might not affect his ability to drive. The test of whether evidence of drink is admissible was said in *R. v Thorpe* to be (quoting Ashworth J. in *R. v McBride* above, at 172, with approval) that "such evidence must tend to show that the amount of drink taken was such as would adversely affect a driver or alternatively that the driver was in fact adversely affected". Thus evidence merely that the driver's breath smelled of drink or that he had been in one bar for a short while would not, it is submitted, generally be of sufficient probative value to justify its admission. As stated, the court has a discretion to exclude any such evidence, and the test to be applied is that already quoted.

5.55   It was held by the Court of Appeal (Lord Taylor C.J. presiding) in *R. v Woodward (Terence)* [1995] R.T.R. 130 that the principle laid down in *R. v McBride* was still good law in relation to the new offence of dangerous driving or causing death by dangerous driving. In the case in point the prosecution evidence went no further than to show that the appellant had been seen with a glass in his hand and had been drinking. In accordance with *R. v McBride* that would not have amounted to relevant evidence. Mere consumption of alcohol in itself was insufficient. The jury would have had to be satisfied that the appellant had consumed such a quantity of alcohol as might adversely affect a driver, and of that there simply was no evidence.

R. v Woodward (Terence) above was followed by the Court of Appeal in *R. v Ash* [1999] R.T.R. 347 when ruling that evidence of a *single* specimen of blood revealing a level of alcohol well in excess of the statutory limit (in point of fact 128mg/100ml) was properly admissible against a defendant charged with an offence of causing death by dangerous driving since it would be open to the jury to conclude that the amount of drink taken was such as adversely to affect the quality of the defendant's driving. The provisions of s.15 of the 1988 Offenders Act dealing with the division of such a specimen into two parts and the supply of one part thereof to the accused (see § 4.230) were limited to proceedings under s.3A, 4 or 5 of the 1988 Act and could not be extended to offences under s.1 thereof.

5.56   The Court of Appeal held in *R. v Millington* [1995] Crim. L.R. 824 that in applying the appropriate test as to whether a defendant charged with causing death by careless driving when under the influence of drink had in fact driven without due care and attention, the jury was entitled to look at all the circumstances of the case, including evidence that the defendant had been affected by drink or that he had taken such an amount of drink as would be likely to affect a driver. Although the principle laid down in *R. v McBride* [1962] 2 Q.B. 167 and applied in *R. v Woodward (Terence)* [1995] R.T.R. 130 (both discussed above) related to causing death by dangerous driving, there was no reason why the same should not apply in a case of causing death by careless driving when under the influence of drink. The defendant in the instant case had consumed sufficient alcohol to take him close to twice the legal limit for driving, having been drinking in a public house for some two hours. The jury was well able to judge what the likely effect of such a quantity of alcohol would be.

It would seem that like principles might apply where it is alleged that the defendant's driving was affected by his having taken a drug or even by severe pain or emotional upset, if such evidence is of substantial weight. The relevance or otherwise of the ingestion of cocaine to the issue of dangerous driving was considered by the Court of Appeal in *R. v Pleydell* [2005] EWCA Crim 1447; [2006] 1 Cr. App. R. 12. It was held that, in contrast to perhaps modest consumption of alcohol, the jury had been entitled to view the consumption of cocaine per se as relevant to that issue. If the jury had been persuaded that the defendant had been adversely affected by drugs, that he *had* been so affected would have been relevant to the issue as to whether he had driven dangerously. The evidence adduced by the prosecution indicated that the defendant had taken cocaine shortly before the accident, had lied about the timing of that taking, and that the drug, whilst short lasting, had a tendency or a capacity to impair driving ability. Quantification of the precise amount of cocaine consumed would not have taken the matter any further.

A like rule as to admissibility of evidence of drinking applies in Scotland (*Burrell v Hunter* 1956 S.L.T.(Sh.) 75).   **5.57**

A charge of driving under the influence of drink or drugs may be tried along with one of dangerous or careless driving (*R. v McBride* above), provided that in a magistrates' court the parties consent.

The fact that dangerous driving is caused by drink is an aggravating feature; see §§ 5.140.

Speed

In order to comply with the requisite standard of care (i.e. that of a reasonable, prudent and competent driver) a driver had to drive at such a speed as to be in a position to maintain control of his vehicle whilst, e.g., steering away from the centre of the road in order to leave more room for a vehicle passing in the opposite direction (*Blake v DPP* [2002] EWHC 2014). Opinion evidence as to the defendant's speed given by the driver of the oncoming vehicle was admissible as part of his overall evidence as to the manner of the defendant's driving, notwithstanding that it would have been insufficient on the authority of *Crossland v DPP* [1988] 3 All E.R. 712 (see § 6.78) to found a conviction for speeding. It was not necessary for the defendant's precise speed to be determined in these circumstances, since what needed to be decided was whether the defendant had lost control of his car because he was driving too fast for the conditions, and had accordingly driven carelessly.   **5.58**

Evidence of previous driving

Evidence of dangerous driving a few minutes before but two miles from the   **5.59** scene of the accident was held to be admissible in *Hallett v Warren* (1929) 93 J.P. 225; and in *R. v Taylor* (1927) 20 Cr. App. R. 71, evidence of reckless driving five miles away was given. It is submitted, however, that the evidence of the earlier acts of driving must have some relevance to those charged, e.g. fast driving in the Strand is not necessarily relevant on a charge of careless driving in Piccadilly if the only allegation in Piccadilly is that the defendant, while driving slowly was frequently glancing at shop windows as he drove. Indeed, evidence that the defendant was driving fast at a place where it was not unsafe to drive fast seems irrelevant and might be unfairly prejudicial, and it is submitted that only acts of dangerous or careless driving within a reasonable distance and time should be allowed in evidence. It seems to be in order to charge the offence as having been committed in all the roads where the defendant drove dangerously or carelessly. If the charge relates to driving in the last road only and evidence is tendered of driving in other roads so that the defendant is misled or taken by surprise, he should be granted an adjournment, if he asks for it (*Hallett v Warren* above). That case suggested that, if dangerous driving within the jurisdiction was proved, the court should convict even if there was no proof of an offence on the road actually charged as the scene of the offence, e.g. a charge of dangerous driving in Piccadilly should not be dismissed even if there was no evidence of dangerous driving there, so long as there is proof of dangerous driving in Trafalgar Square and Lower Regent Street. The prosecutor, however, would be wise to name all the roads in his information, as *Hallett v Warren* above may yet be distinguished and it was said obiter in *R. v Budd* [1962] Crim. L.R. 49 that there can be a conviction for dangerous driving only if it occurred in the road named in the warning of intended prosecution under what is now s.1 of the 1988 Offenders Act. In *Horrix v Malam* [1984] R.T.R. 112 a conviction for careless driving was confirmed. The Divisional Court held that the information was not bad for duplicity when it referred to two incidents of swerving separated by a 10-minute interval and two miles in distance witnessed by two different police officers. The test in such a case is whether the charge or information involves only one activity even though that activity might involve more than one act (*R. v Jones* [1974] I.C.R. 310). It was, however, said in *Coles v Underwood*, *The Times*, November 2, 1983 that evidence of previous driving may be admissible but justices must be extremely circumspect in having regard to what took place at some distance from the event which is the subject of the charge.

Mechanical defects

5.60   It was a defence to the former charge of dangerous driving under the Road Traffic Act 1972 prior to its amendment by the Criminal Law Act 1977 and also to careless driving that if the driver, without fault of his own, was deprived of control of his vehicle by a mechanical defect therein of which he did not know and which was not such as he should have discovered if he had exercised reasonable prudence and, once there is some evidence of such a defect, the accused should be acquitted if his explanation leaves a real doubt in the minds of the jury or magistrates (*R. v Spurge* [1961] 2 All E.R. 688). It would appear similarly to be a defence to an allegation of dangerous driving as currently constituted that the manner of his driving was caused by a mechanical defect provided that as a result of the defect the vehicle was not in such a state as to render the dangerousness of its use obvious to a careful and competent driver (1988 Act s.2A(2)) and further provided that the accused had no actual knowledge of the defect (1988 Act s.2A(3)). For the defect to pass the test of being "obviously dangerous" there must be evidence that it would be obvious to the competent and careful driver in the sense that it could be "seen or realised at first glance, evident" to him (*R. v Strong* [1995] Crim. L.R. 428; see § 5.12). In *Spurge* the conviction was upheld because, although a defect causing the car to pull to its offside was proved, the driver knew of this defect and yet continued to drive in a manner which was dangerous in those circumstances. Where a lorry driver knew that a tyre was dangerously worn and drove, his conviction for the former offence causing death by dangerous driving was upheld after the tyre had burst, causing the lorry to swerve and kill the occupants of an oncoming car (*R. v Robert Millar (Contractors) Ltd and Robert Millar* [1970] 1 All E.R. 577, following and approving the principle of *R. v Spurge*). The scope of the dangerous driving offences as presently enacted is wider still, since actual knowledge of the defect is not required if the "current state" of the vehicle speaks sufficiently clearly for itself. The principle in *R. v Spurge* is that if the danger was created by a sudden loss of control in no way due to any fault on the part of the driver, the defendant should be acquitted. Once there is evidence of a mechanical defect which the driver neither knew of nor ought to have known of, "the onus of disproving [it] undoubtedly rests on the prosecution" (per Salmon J. at 692, expressly cited with approval by the Court of Appeal in *R. v Gosney* [1971] 3 All E.R. 220). Once it has been found as a fact that the motorist knows or ought to have known of the mechanical defect, he cannot avail himself of the defence even if the car has been subsequently serviced by a garage (*Haynes v Swain* [1975] R.T.R. 40). Where a car has been serviced by a garage all that can be assumed is that the car has been serviced, nothing else (ibid.).

The converse of the principle that an unexpected mechanical defect is a defence is that if the motorist drives a car having a dangerous mechanical defect of which he knows (or ought to know given that the state of the vehicle would render obvious to a competent and careful driver the dangerousness of its use in terms of injury to any person or serious damage to property), he should be convicted of dangerous driving. Presumably where the degree of risk inherent in the defect does not pass the test of being "obviously dangerous" in the eyes of the competent and careful motorist, but where in fact danger results, a conviction for careless driving would be appropriate, for no reasonable, prudent and competent driver will knowingly drive a defective vehicle. *R. v Spurge* was expressly upheld not only in *R. v Gosney* above but also in *R. v Atkinson* [1970] Crim. L.R. 405, where a motorist's conviction was quashed when he had not even been allowed to call evidence to rebut the prosecution's evidence that he should have known his brakes were defective.   **5.61**

The court should not assume, without evidence, that a vehicle must have developed defects: see *Rabjohns v Burgar, Johnson v Fowler, Bensley v Smith* and *Gubby v Littman*, §§ 5.50–1.

Cases on careless driving

It is emphasised that the following cases of careless driving do not lay down principles of law but are of use principally in illustrating what facts can amount to careless driving. A slight variation in the facts of a particular case, e.g. visibility, amount of traffic or geography, may make a difference. Whether a person should be convicted of careless driving is primarily a question of fact not of law.   **5.62**

Mounting the verge and hitting a pole nearly 3ft from the edge of the road is prima facie evidence of careless driving, unless explained, e.g. a skid (*Watts v Carter* [1971] R.T.R. 232). A driver who signals that he will turn right and then turns left without taking any precautions to see if anything is coming behind is guilty of careless driving (*Pratt v Bloom* [1958] Crim. L.R. 817). Failing to stop and look at a "T" junction was held to be careless driving in *Baker v Spence, The Times*, May 27, 1960. The driver's duty is not confined to making signals: he must see, so far as he can, that they have been understood and he may be guilty of careless driving if he drives on after making one without so seeing (*Sorrie v Robertson* [1944] S.C.(J.) 95). The High Court reluctantly upheld a conviction of a motorist who edged from a park on to a road when his view of it was obstructed by parked vehicles (*O'Connell v Fraser* (1963) 107 S.J. 95). A defendant who gave misleading signals that he was going to turn but did not in fact turn was held guilty of careless driving (*Another v Probert* [1968] Crim. L.R. 564). It is submitted that this case is not necessarily an authority for the view that a driver who is, without negligence, unaware that his indicators are flashing is therefore guilty of careless or inconsiderate driving. A conviction was directed when a car was driven at 25mph past an obscured halt sign, and though the driver must have seen the white lines to mark the junction, he failed to see a car on the main road (*Spencer v Silvester* (1963) 107 S.J. 1024). Crossing a central white line is itself evidence of careless driving in the absence of an explanation (*Bensley v Smith* [1972] Crim. L.R. 239; *R. v Warwickshire Police Ex p. Manjit Singh Mundi* [2001] EWHC Admin 448). A metropolitan magistrate convicted a driver who was reading a newspaper and the case was likened to a driver who kept kissing his passenger ([1954] Jo.Crim.L. 204). A driver of a bus who is reversing and relying on his conductor's signals must satisfy himself that the conductor is so positioned that he can see what he ought to see; if that person is not so positioned, the driver may be guilty of careless driving (*Liddon v Stringer* [1967] Crim. L.R. 371).

5.63   On a right-hand bend the rear of a lorry swung anti-clockwise and then clockwise into the path of an oncoming vehicle, with which it collided. There was no evidence of mechanical defect nor of anything on the road surface that would be likely to affect the lorry's performance. The tachograph, however, revealed that immediately prior to impact the defendant had braked heavily, probably (according to expert evidence) causing the wheels to lock. The defendant accepted that applying the brakes after the anti-clockwise movement would "make matters worse". The justices were entitled, as they did, to find that the braking was not the action of a reasonable, prudent and competent driver and accordingly to convict the defendant of careless driving (*R. (on the application of Bingham) v DPP* [2003] EWHC 247; (2003) 167 J.P. 422).

Although a distraction (children emerging from a car stalled in the outside lane) could operate as a defence to careless driving, a driver who allowed himself to be distracted for too long a period of time for the speed at which he was travelling was driving carelessly (*Plunkett v DPP* [2004] EWHC 1937).

Cases on inconsiderate driving

5.64   Drivers have been prosecuted for driving without reasonable consideration for other road users where they have had brilliant headlights which they have not dipped for oncoming traffic, or they have driven through puddles at speed, drenching pedestrians (129 J.P. Jo. 338). In *Saville v Bache, The Times*, February 28,

1969, a civil case, it was said by the Court of Appeal that, if a motorist drove with undipped headlights in circumstances where he should know that they might dazzle an oncoming driver, it was for the former motorist to disprove his prima facie negligence in doing so by giving evidence of a good reason for not dipping. See § 5.107 as to driving with uncorrected defective eyesight. A conviction was directed where the only road users affected were passengers in the defendant's vehicle; "other road users" include persons in or outside the vehicle (*Pawley v Wharldall* [1965] 2 All E.R. 757). Semble it must be proved that there actually were other road users; there is no reference in the current legislation to persons who might reasonably be expected to be on the road. The defendant in *Pawley's* case had driven a bus in a way which scared the passengers. It may be necessary on this charge to show that the defendant was knowingly acting without consideration for others; his acts or omissions will often establish a prima facie case to this effect. A motorist who kicked out at a pedal cyclist was held not guilty of this offence as there was no evidence that his machine came near enough to the pedal cycle to constitute the offence (*Downes v Fell* (1969) 113 S.J. 387).

Civil cases

The standard of driving required by the criminal law cannot be greater than that imposed by the tort of negligence (*Scott v Warren* [1974] R.T.R. 104).   **5.65**

A skid is not necessarily evidence of negligence (*Laurie v Raglan, etc., Co* [1941] 3 All E.R. 332), and in *Custins v Nottingham Corporation* [1970] R.T.R. 365 a bus driver was found not to be negligent in allowing his bus to get out of control on an icy road. But in *Richley v Faull* [1965] 3 All E.R. 109 an unexplained and violent skid was said to be in itself evidence of negligent driving.

Stopping suddenly is not necessarily evidence of negligent driving (*Parkinson v Liverpool Corporation* [1950] 1 All E.R. 367). Automatic stop lights may not be in themselves sufficient warning to following traffic (*Croston v Vaughan* [1937] 4 All E.R. 249). Hitting an unlit obstruction in the road does not necessarily show that the driver is negligent (*Tidy v Battman* [1934] 1 K.B. 319), and in *Hill v Phillips* (1963) 107 S.J. 890, it was said that persons driving along country roads with dipped headlights should keep an especially careful look-out, as the presence of unlit obstructions should be anticipated there. In *Grange Motors (Cwmbran) Ltd v Spencer* [1969] 1 All E.R. 340 it was held that a driver is not necessarily negligent in acting on the signals of another person, here a postman driver as opposed to a casual onlooker. In *Clarke v Winchurch* [1969] 1 All E.R. 275 the Court of Appeal said that flashing headlights could mean "come on", notwithstanding r.96 of the 1969 Highway Code which said it means merely advising other road users of one's presence. If a driver is proceeding slowly and carefully where his view is obstructed, it is a counsel of perfection to require him to stop and look again when his bonnet is 1ft out (ibid.), but Russell L.J. dissented where the situation was potentially dangerous. It should be noted that *Clarke v Winchurch* has twice been suggested not to have laid down any principle of law (*Garston Warehousing Company Ltd v O.F. Smart* [1973] R.T.R. 377 and *Worsfold v Howe* [1980] R.T.R. 131).   **5.66**

A pedestrian crossing a road junction was struck and injured by a car which had entered the junction against a red traffic light. It was held in *Tremayne v Hill* [1987] R.T.R. 131 that the driver was guilty of serious careless driving and that the pedestrian did not owe any specific duty of care to the driver; accordingly any   **5.67** possible failure by the pedestrian to keep a good look-out could not amount to contributory negligence. It would appear that the pedestrian had chosen not to make use of a nearby light-controlled pedestrian crossing. It was stated per curiam that a pedestrian has no duty in law to use such a crossing; he is entitled to cross wherever he likes, provided he takes reasonable care for his own safety.

A driver on a major road must still take precautions as to traffic emerging from minor roads and take due care to avoid colliding with it or endangering it (*Lang v London Transport Executive* [1959] 3 All E.R. 609) and it is a question of fact whether he has been negligent in regard to it. While entitled to assume that drivers on the minor road will behave properly, he must take precautions if it is apparent they will not (*Browne v Central SMT Co* 1949 S.C. 9). It was said in *Butters v J.H. Fenner & Co, The Times*, February 6, 1967 that a driver on a major road must still watch minor roads. It may be negligent to enter another road without ensuring that there is no traffic hidden by other vehicles in that road (*Harding v Hinchliffe, The Times*, April 8, 1964).

5.68   It was a dark and stormy night and a lorry was being backed into a car park: it was at right angles to the carriageway and totally obstructed it and it showed no lights to the side. The plaintiff, driving along the road, collided with it and it was held that there was negligence by the lorry driver (*Barber v British Road Services, The Times*, November 18, 1964). Similarly in *Jordan v North Hampshire Plant Hire* [1970] R.T.R. 212 the driver of an articulated lorry was held to be negligent to drive, in the dark, his 35ft long lorry out of a drive and across a fast stretch of road where there were double white lines and a gradual bend. It was said to be a most dangerous manoeuvre despite the fact that the sides of the lorry were not required by law to be lit. It is submitted that both in *Barber* and in *Jordan* either defendant could be charged with driving without reasonable consideration. If a driver is in doubt whether he has room to pass a stationary vehicle or obstruction, he should stop and check up (*Randall v Tarrant* [1955] 1 All E.R. 600). To drive a motor vehicle along a country road when the driver knows that the vehicle has no front light is negligent (*Dawrant v Nutt* [1960] 3 All E.R. 681). A motorist who disregards a white line at an uncontrolled road junction is not negligent (*Homewood v Spiller* (1962) 106 S.J. 900) but per Pearson L.J. it might indicate a junction where extra care is needed. Now, under reg.25(2) of the Traffic Signs Regulations and General Directions 2002, double broken lines at a road mouth mean that the driver must take precautions. It may therefore be that *Homewood v Spiller* is now of less authority. Driving at a speed of 25–30mph in a quiet residential road on a Sunday and not sounding a horn or slowing down when passing a large coach parked on the nearside is not negligent (*Moore v Poyner* [1975] R.T.R. 127). Deceleration without warning to following traffic is not an act of negligence, even on a motorway, but a driver should signal his intention to make a sudden heavy stop (*Jungnickel v Laing* (1967) 111 S.J. 19), and in *Goke v Willett* [1973] R.T.R. 422 a driver was held to be negligent in relying solely on his indicator and stop lights when slowing down in the centre lane of a three-lane busy trunk road to turn right into a service station.

Highway Code

5.69   The best *guide* for those engaged in dangerous and careless driving cases is the Highway Code itself; its non-observance can be relied on as tending to establish liability in such cases, but failure to observe a provision of the Highway Code will not of itself render that person liable to criminal proceedings of any kind (1998 Act s.38(7)). The fifteenth edition of the Highway Code was published in 2007 and is available online at *http://www.direct.gov.uk/en/TravelAndTransport/ Highwaycode/DG_070190* [Accessed March 21, 2009]. As the introduction to the Highway Code states, it is essential reading for everyone. The introduction goes on to point out that the most vulnerable road users are pedestrians, particularly children, older or disabled people, cyclists, motor cyclists and horse riders. The section on road users requiring extra care runs from r.204 to r.225 and provides advice on, e.g. driving near schools. Rule 90 reminds drivers that they must report to the DVLA any health condition likely to affect driving. The next rule warns that driving when tired greatly increases the risk of collision. There is a reminder (r.110) not to flash headlights to convey any message other than to let other road users know you are there. There is a similar reminder (r.112) never to sound the horn aggressively and that it is illegal to use the horn while stationary on the road or when driving in a built-up area between the hours of 11.30pm and 7am except when another road user poses a danger. Rule 149 states that it is an offence to use a hand-held mobile phone, or similar device. It also points out that using hands-free equipment is also likely to distract your attention from the road. There is a similar warning in r.150 about the danger of driver distraction being caused by in-vehicle systems such as satellite navigation systems, congestion warning systems, PCs, multimedia, etc. Rule 154 advises motorists of the need to take extra care on country roads and the necessity of being able to stop within the distance that can be seen to be clear. Rule 157 confirms that certain motorised vehicles, including most types of miniature motor cycles, must not be used on roads.

Rule 95 provides general information on the effects of alcohol upon a driver **5.70** and advises the road user on wheels not to drink and drive and prohibits driving with a breath or blood-alcohol level which exceeds the statutory limit. Rule 96 prohibits driving under the influence of drugs or medicine and gives general information about the potential dangers to road users which may flow from the use of such substances.

While the typical stopping distances diagram accompanying r.126 of the Highway Code (see the end of this volume for a table of stopping distances) may be used in cross-examination to prove a breach of the Highway Code, it is otherwise inadmissible by itself to prove speed as it is hearsay (*R. v Chadwick* [1975] Crim. L.R. 105).

Prosecutions occasionally are brought on the basis that because a defendant is **5.71** in breach of a provision of the Highway Code, he should automatically be convicted of careless driving in the absence of any other explanation. The facts of the case may, of course, be so overwhelming that in the absence of any explanation the defendant should be convicted (see "Res ipsa loquitur", § 5.50), but the mere breach of a provision of the Highway Code by itself is not sufficient (s.38(7)). In *Scott v Warren* [1974] R.T.R. 104 the defendant driving in a line of moving traffic was unable to avoid hitting a piece of metal which had fallen off a lorry in front of the van. The magistrates dismissed the case and it was suggested on the hearing of the case stated before the High Court that if a driver did not leave sufficient space between himself and the vehicle in front to avoid a collision, then the defendant was prima facie guilty of careless driving as he would be in breach of what is now r.126 of the Highway Code. The Divisional Court disagreed, holding that whether a person has driven carelessly is primarily a matter of fact: the duty of a driver following another vehicle was, as far as reasonably possible, to take up such a position and to drive in such a fashion as to be able to deal with all traffic exigencies reasonably to be expected (applying *Brown and Lynn v Western SMT Co Ltd* 1945 S.C. 31). Another case where the justices' dismissal of a careless driving charge was upheld by the High Court where the defendant was in breach of the Highway Code is *Jarvis v Fuller* [1974] R.T.R. 160. The defendant drove at 50mph in drizzle at night with dipped headlights and failed to avoid hitting a pedal cyclist wearing dark clothing whose rear light was probably not working. The Divisional Court again emphasised that whether a defendant was driving carelessly is primarily a question of fact. *Jarvis* was followed in *Webster v Wall* [1980] Crim. L.R. 186 where the High Court refused to disturb the justices' acquittal of careless driving of a motor cyclist who had collided at night with an unlit stationary vehicle on a wet road in conditions of poor visibility. It was impossible to say that the decision was perverse: the question was whether the justices' decision could have been reached by a reasonable bench of justices.

5.72   In *Hume v Ingleby* [1975] R.T.R. 502 a defendant was acquitted of careless driving. He entered his van, which was parked off the main carriageway on an unlit road at night, he looked in his rear view mirrors, looked round as far as he could and reversed, thereby colliding with a car parked facing away from him and causing slight damage to the car and his van. The Divisional Court refused to hold that the acquittal of the motorist by the justices was perverse: a motorist who reverses and collides with something behind him is not ipso facto guilty of careless driving despite what is now r.202 of the Highway Code ("You should ... check there are no ... obstructions in the road behind you").

By way of contrast to *Hume v Ingleby* above, the High Court of Justiciary upheld the conviction for careless driving of a motorist who when reversing a mobile shop into a cul-de-sac where he knew that children were wont to play, collided with and killed a 16-month-old child (*McCrone v Normand* (1988) 1989 S.L.T. 332). Although it had been argued before the court that the driver had done all that could reasonably have been expected of him to ensure that no danger was caused by his manoeuvre, the sheriff had properly had regard to what is now r.202 of the Highway Code. Clearly each case falls to be determined very much on its own facts, always bearing in mind that although failure to observe a provision of the Highway Code may tend to establish liability for careless driving, it cannot of itself render a person liable to criminal proceedings (see § 5.69 above).

5.73   It may be "bold" for justices to acquit a motorist of careless driving who emerged into a high street with trafficators working and hit a cyclist riding along the high street. It was 5.50pm on a dark January evening. The street lights were not lit and it was raining. The Divisional Court observed that, more often than not, colliding with another vehicle on the main road on emerging from a side road must amount to careless driving, but the decision of the justices must be a subjective one on the facts. The case was not strong enough for it to be said that the justices' decision was perverse (*Walker v Tolhurst* [1978] R.T.R. 513). A breach of the Highway Code is, in accordance with s.38(7) of the 1988 Act, only evidential in its effect. On the other hand, the evidential effect of a failure to observe the Highway Code may be strongly relied on to prove carelessness, dangerous or potentially dangerous driving. In *Trentham v Rowlands* [1974]

R.T.R. 164, the Divisional Court relied inter alia on r.116 of an earlier edition of the Highway Code ("overtake only on the right ... never move to a lane on your left to overtake") in holding that it was potentially dangerous and thus dangerous driving for a motorist to overtake another on the outside lane at 70mph by moving over to the inner lanes to do so, particularly having regard to the obligation imposed by r.114 on the driver being overtaken to return to the inside lane. It should be noted that under s.38(7) only a *failure* to observe the Highway Code is of evidential value. The fact that a defendant or prosecution witness has complied with the Highway Code does not mean that that person cannot have been careless or negligent. In *Goke v Willett* [1973] R.T.R. 422, a driver who gave no hand signal but relied only on his indicator and stop lights to show he was slowing in the middle lane of a three-lane trunk road to turn right, was held to be negligent even though the Highway Code can be read as indicating that if trafficators and stop lights are both fitted and are in good working order, hand signals need never be used. In so far as the Highway Code indicated that hand signals need never be used, this is unwise advice (ibid., per Edmund Davies L.J. at 425). Rules 103–112 of the most recent edition set out the current position as regards signals.

Visibility

Where a driver finds himself unexpectedly blinded by headlights or the sun, or for any reason he cannot see properly or control the car, then, unless the loss of vision or control immediately ceases, he should stop at once. If during the literal second or two while he has not proper vision or control an accident occurs which is due entirely to that loss of vision or control, it is submitted that he is not guilty of careless driving. But if the accident occurs more than two seconds after the loss of vision or control began and the driver has not done anything about reducing speed or stopping, he should, it is submitted, generally be found guilty of careless driving at least, not so much for running into something because he could not see it but rather for continuing to drive when he could not see or control the car properly. In *S v Lombard* [1984] (4) South African L.R. 346 it was held that if a horsefly or any insect which could perhaps cause trouble flies in at the window, a reasonable driver will immediately apply his brakes and stop. Again, the driver should keep his eyes on the road, but must occasionally look aside to watch his dashboard or pedestrians or police signals from the pavement or to observe direction signs. It is submitted that no criminal liability should attach to a driver for not keeping a proper look-out during the second or two while he necessarily glances away from the road ahead provided he is driving at a reasonable speed. If he is travelling at a speed of 30mph, a glance away for even four seconds may be dangerous, certainly gazing up at signposts while approaching a busy road junction could be, and a driver's failure to stop or slow down might amount to careless driving. The late author recalled a very experienced solicitor advising a driver to plead guilty to a charge of careless driving where the latter had reversed a few yards from a stationary position and collided with something because she had not made sure that the road behind was clear (in *Hume v Ingleby* the defendant looked in his mirrors—see § 5.72). Somewhat similar cases are reported at [1954] Jo.Crim.L. 120 and 121 J.P. Jo. 421. A driver who intends to reverse and cannot see from the driving seat whether he safely can, should, it is submitted, alight and satisfy himself that the road will be clear. If there are children about, even that might not suffice, and he should wait until some reliable

5.74

person can be found to signal him. It was held in *S v Lalla* [1964] (4) South African L.R. 320 that the reasonable driver who intends to reverse out of his garage or backyard where small children are or may be playing in close proximity to his line of travel knows that he must not begin to reverse before satisfying himself that no child has walked or crawled behind the car, for he is alive to that possibility and to the fact that he may not observe such a child by merely looking behind him from the driver's seat. (Reference should now be made to r.202 of the current edition of the Highway Code which requires a motorist to ensure there is nothing behind him when reversing, and if he cannot see to get someone to guide him.)

Use of headlights

5.75   It is obviously dangerous to drive at night with sidelights only on an unlit road, and by reg.25 of the Road Vehicles Lighting Regulations 1989 it is an offence if the street is not illuminated by street lamps. The Court of Appeal in *Hill v Phillips* (1963) 107 S.J. 890 (a civil case) held that, when driving with dipped headlights on country roads, motorists should drive so that they could see unlighted obstructions the presence of which might be anticipated, e.g. cycles without lights or people in dark clothes. But whether the defendant who collides or fails to see something at night or in conditions of poor visibility is like any other case guilty of careless driving is primarily a question of fact (see *Jarvis v Fuller, Webster v Wall* and *Hume v Ingleby*, §§ 5.71–2).

Two offences from one incident

5.76   The police sometimes charge a driver with both careless driving and disobedience to traffic lights or a "stop" sign in respect of the same incident. It is submitted that it is proper to convict on the major charge only where there has been some carelessness over and above the disobedience to the sign, e.g. approaching the junction too fast or not keeping a proper look-out for approaching traffic; the other charge can be marked "no adjudication" or "adjourned sine die " if there is a conviction on the graver offence, so as to preserve, if desired, the position on appeal. Alternatively, if there is no likelihood of appeal or there has been a plea of guilty to the major charge, the lesser charge, it is submitted, may properly be dismissed. If the adjudication on the lesser charge has been adjourned, it may in any event be dismissed once the time for appeal has expired. Like principles would apply where there are charges of failing to accord precedence on a crossing and of careless driving from one incident or of crossing double white lines and careless driving from one incident. If there is nothing more to the case than disobedience to the red light (or other minor charge) and the driver has otherwise been careful, it is submitted that a conviction on the lights charge suffices and the careless driving one can properly be dismissed. Similarly, it is also submitted that if the only carelessness is to fail to observe the lights or traffic sign, conviction on the graver charge only is sufficient. *R. v Parker* (1957) 41 Cr. App. R. 134 is not overlooked, but it is submitted that to convict on both is oppressive, especially as it can lead to two endorsements and two penalties for one incident which might properly have been charged as a traffic light offence at the start. Cf. *R. v Burnham JJ.* at § 2.113.

   The above paragraph was considered by the Divisional Court in *Theobald (J.)*

(Hounslow) Ltd v Stacy [1979] R.T.R. 411 and given qualified approval (see Lord Widgery C.J. at 416B–D). See also *Welton v Taneborne* at § 2.113.

Aiders and abettors and supervisors

In *Du Cros v Lambourne* (1906) 70 J.P. 525, it was held that a person charged **5.77** with dangerous driving could be convicted although the evidence might show only that he was aiding, abetting, counselling and procuring, and the actual driver had not been summoned (see also [1953] Jo.Crim.L. 173). In that case the lower court had found it unnecessary to decide whether the defendant had been driving: he had been sitting in the front of the car, and, being its owner, could control the manner of its driving. Two persons pursuing a common purpose may be guilty of criminal negligence in driving, although only one of them drives (*R. v Baldessare* (1930) 22 Cr. App. R. 70). In that case the jury found that the passenger joined in responsibility with the driver for the way in which the vehicle was driven, but the doctrine of joint responsibility should not be applied indiscriminately where it is not clear who drove or whether the passenger was joined in responsibility for the way it was driven (*Webster v Wishart* 1955 S.L.T. 243). A managing director of a haulage company, together with the haulage company in Scotland, were held to be rightly convicted of aiding and abetting causing death by dangerous driving in England where the defendant lorry driver had been sent on a journey from Scotland into England when the managing director knew that the lorry had a dangerously worn tyre (*R. v Robert Millar* [1970] 2 Q.B. 54).

The defendant, who had not been drinking, offered his co-accused and another man a lift home. At some point during the journey he permitted the co-accused, who had been drinking all day, to drive. The co-accused drove erratically and at excessive speed. The vehicle left the road and one of the passengers was thrown out and killed. The co-accused pleaded guilty to causing death by dangerous driving; the defendant was charged with aiding and abetting that offence. At trial the prosecution sought to prove firstly that the defendant knew it was dangerous to permit the co-accused to drive because of his state of intoxication and, secondly, that the defendant appreciated during the journey that the defendant was driving at a dangerous speed and that he ought to have intervened but failed to do so. The judge's summing-up reflected those alternative bases. The defendant was convicted.

Allowing his appeal, the Court of Appeal in *R. v Webster* [2006] EWCA Crim **5.78** 415; [2006] R.T.R. 19 held that although the evidence that the co-accused had been drinking before driving was relevant and admissible, it did not determine whether the way in which he drove was dangerous as defined by s.2A of the Road Traffic Act 1988. In order to establish secondary liability against the defendant it was necessary to prove that he foresaw the likelihood that the co-accused would drive in a dangerous manner, and the more drunk the co-accused appeared to be, the easier that would be to prove. In directing the jury, however, the trial judge had failed to distinguish between the question of whether it was obvious to the defendant that it would be dangerous to allow the co-accused to drive and the question of whether the defendant recognised that, because of his drunken state, the co-accused was likely to drive dangerously. Furthermore, the jury should have been directed that it was necessary to prove that the defendant did recognise the danger, not merely that he ought to have recognised it. Since those issues, had they been laid before the jury correctly, would not inevitably have been resolved against the defendant, the verdict was unsafe.

With regard to the alternative way in which the prosecution had put its case, it was incumbent upon the prosecution to prove that there was an opportunity for the defendant to intervene when he knew that the co-accused was driving dangerously, and that the defendant's failure to exercise his right as owner of the car demonstrated his encouragement or assistance. The judge had failed to leave to the jury the question of whether, at the time the defendant recognised that the co-accused was driving at a dangerous speed, he had an opportunity to intervene but failed to take it. Since that was a matter for the jury to assess, a conviction on the second basis was not inevitable and the appeal had therefore to be allowed.

5.79   The supervisor of a learner driver may be found guilty of aiding and abetting careless driving by the learner if he has failed to supervise him properly (*Rubie v Faulkner* [1940] 1 All E.R. 285). He must not be passive where his supervisory duties require him to be active and he must advise the learner what to do to avoid accidents and risks (ibid.). If he does so advise and takes other available steps to avoid danger, it is submitted that the supervisor should not be found guilty merely because there has nevertheless been an accident because of the learner's failure to heed his advice, or because of a sudden and unexpected action. Driving test examiners are there to observe the driver's mistakes and are not in the position of a driving instructor or supervisor (*BSM Ltd v Simms* [1971] R.T.R. 190).

Public emergencies

5.80   There is no exemption for police, fire-engine or ambulance drivers from prosecution for dangerous or careless driving and prosecutions are reported at 113 J.P. Jo. 374, 114 J.P. Jo. 54 and [1961] Jo.Crim.L. 1. See also *R. v Lundt-Smith* [1964] 2 Q.B. 167, § 21.50 and *R. v O'Toole* (1971) 55 Cr. App. R. 206 (two cases of ambulance drivers driving dangerously in an emergency). In *Gaynor v Allen* [1959] 2 All E.R. 644, a civil case, it was held that a police officer driving in the course of his duty owes the same duty as a civilian driver to the public to drive with due care, and in *Wardell-Yerburgh v Surrey County Council* [1973] R.T.R. 462 it was held that the driver of a fire tender responding to an emergency call owed to the public the same duty of care as any other driver. In *Wood v Richards* [1977] R.T.R. 201 the conviction of a police officer driving without due care and attention was upheld for the same reason. Responding to an emergency, the police patrol driver drove along the hard shoulder of a motorway and collided with a stationary lorry. It was again held that it was impossible to say that a special standard should be applied to a police officer and in *Marshall v Osmond* [1983] 2 All E.R. 225 it was again emphasised that a police officer driving a vehicle in accordance with his duty owed the same duty of care as he owed to anyone else in all the circumstances of the case. The officer was pursuing someone who bore the appearance of someone engaged in an arrestable criminal activity and that fact was one of the circumstances of the case which must be borne in mind in deciding whether or not the constable had been negligent. Any sympathy with a police officer driving in such a situation is best expressed when the court comes to consider the penalty (*Wood v Richards* above). See also Chapter 21 as to "special reasons".

Defence of necessity or duress

5.81   In *Wood v Richards* above it was held that the defence of necessity was not justified in that case. In *Buckoke v GLC* [1971] 2 All E.R. 254 there was no such defence available to a firefighter who jumped a red light in order to attend an emergency.

As a result of a succession of Court of Appeal cases decided between 1986 and 1988 it was established that necessity could only be a defence to a charge of reckless driving where the facts, viewed objectively, established "duress of circumstances". Such a defence would appear to be equally applicable to dangerous driving under current legislation. The first case to be decided was *R. v Willer* [1987] R.T.R. 22 in which it was held that duress was available as a defence to a charge of reckless driving when a motorist mounted a pavement to drive away from a gang of youths who were shouting: "I'll kill you", and one of whom had entered the car and was fighting with a passenger in the rear seat and was still there, fighting, when the motorist drove to a police station to make a complaint. Watkins L.J. delivering judgment pointed out that although the defendant had sought in vain before the Crown Court to put forward the defence of necessity, the appropriate defence for the defendant to have raised in the particular circumstances of his case was duress. The court did not feel bound in view of that finding to decide whether or not necessity might similarly have been available to the defendant as a defence.

The Court of Appeal then held in *R. v Denton* [1987] R.T.R. 129 that any possible defence of necessity to a charge of reckless driving must be excluded where the defendant asserts that he did not take risks and drove carefully throughout. The defendant's case was that having been approached by a large man, he fled in his car in fear and panic and continued to flee when he found himself being followed by two unmarked police cars. According to him, his driving throughout his flight was safe and proper, not reckless. The police account, which the jury apparently preferred, was that he had driven at a speed dangerous for the conditions, had skidded on bends, had narrowly missed a pedestrian and had reversed intentionally into one of the police cars. **5.82**

Denton and *Willer* both fell to be considered by the court in *R. v Conway* [1989] R.T.R. 35. The appellant, when approached by police officers, drove off at speed at the instigation of his passenger, a man who was wanted by the police. On an earlier occasion (to the appellant's knowledge) this particular passenger had been in a vehicle when another man was shot; he himself was chased and escaped but narrowly. It was for fear of another potentially fatal attack that the appellant drove as he did, namely at excessive speeds. The court accepted that the case with which they were dealing could be distinguished from *Denton* since the defendant accepted that his driving had been excessively fast, but felt bound in relation to duress by *Willer*. The conclusion to be drawn was that necessity could only be a defence to a s.2 offence where the facts established "duress of circumstances", and that such a defence was only available if, from an objective standpoint, the defendant could be said to be acting in order to avoid a threat of death or serious injury.

R. v Conway was applied by the Court of Appeal in *R. v Martin* [1989] R.T.R. 63, a case involving a defendant who drove whilst disqualified in the belief that his wife would commit suicide if he did not drive. It was said per curiam that there was no distinction between offences of reckless driving and driving whilst disqualified so far as the application of the defence of necessity is concerned (see further § 11.65 below). The defence has also been found to apply to an offence of **5.83** driving with excess alcohol under s.5 of the 1988 Act (*DPP v Bell* [1992] Crim. L.R. 176; see further § 4.305 above). It would seem in the light of the decision of the High Court of Justiciary in *Moss v Howdle* 1997 S.L.T. 782 that the defence of necessity may also apply, in appropriate circumstances, to the offence of speeding; see further § 6.74 below.

R. *v Martin* above was applied by the Court of Appeal in *R. v Cairns* [2000] R.T.R. 15. One of a group of young people had climbed onto the bonnet of the appellant's car. When he came to a speed hump he braked, causing the young man to fall off in front of the car and be run over. The appellant was charged inter alia with dangerous driving. There was evidence at the trial that the young people who had been following the car had been shouting and gesturing in an effort to prevent the victim from behaving as he did. The appellant's defence was one of accident and of duress of circumstances in that he had been afraid that the young people were hostile towards him. The judge directed the jury in relation to duress that what the appellant did had to be actually necessary to avoid the evil in question and that it would not assist him that he believed or might have believed what he did to have been necessary. Allowing his appeal, the court held that nowhere in the direction suggested in *R. v Martin* does it appear that the threat perceived by a defendant relying on the defence of duress of circumstances had to prove to be an actual or real threat. The question for determination was the defendant's perception of the threat with which he was confronted and whether he acted reasonably and proportionately in responding to that perceived threat; accordingly, the question of whether or not there was actually a threat to justify his response was immaterial.

5.84   The driver of an unmarked police car, covertly following a vehicle carrying persons believed to be planning to carry out an armed robbery, went through a red traffic light in order to maintain contact with the suspects. In doing so, he collided with another vehicle. He contended that his actions had arisen from necessity and that he was not therefore guilty of driving without due care and attention. In upholding the prosecution's appeal against an acquittal by justices, the Divisional Court in *DPP v Harris* [1995] Crim. L.R. 73 held that the driver could not rely upon the common law defence of necessity in such circumstances, because the care due from the driver was specifically provided for by (what is now) reg.36 of the Traffic Signs Regulations and General Directions 2002 (see further § 6.26). The regulation allows the driver to cross the stop line against the red light, but requires him not to do so (broadly speaking) in such a way as to cause danger to any other vehicle. The care due would have involved waiting for a couple of seconds at the junction or edging slowly forward, being prepared to stop if there had been a vehicle in the lane crossing the junction. This the driver in the case in point had failed to do. In the court's view the same principles would apply on a charge of reckless (now dangerous) driving where, (what is now) reg.36 applying, the driver had gone through a red light.

Some doubt has been cast upon the decision of the Divisional Court in *DPP v Harris* discussed above by the Court of Appeal in *R. v Backshall* [1998] R.T.R. 423. The appellant, whilst fleeing in an attempt to escape pursuit by a man who had previously attacked his car with a hammer, reversed from a side street into a major road and stopped, facing the wrong direction in traffic. He was charged with dangerous driving, but convicted of the alternative offence of careless driving. He appealed on the basis that the recorder had failed to direct the jury that necessity or duress of circumstances was a possible defence to careless driving. The court in *Harris* had been divided on the question whether the defence of necessity or duress of circumstances could never apply to a charge of driving without due care and attention, but their Lordships in the instant case were prepared to hold that the view of Curtis J. that it would be anomalous for the defence to be available on a charge of the more serious offence, but not on the lesser alternative offence, was in fact correct. The contrary view expressed by Mc-Cowan L.J. in *Harris* was to the effect that because the charge was one of driving without due care and attention then necessarily the court was required to take account of all the surrounding circumstances to the offence. In other words, a separate defence of necessity was unnecessary. Even on that view, however, it would be necessary in summing up to include an explanation of the fact that the jury was entitled to take account of the circumstances in deciding whether the driving was careless or not. Without such a direction the jury might think it sufficient to take an objective view of the driving itself without taking account of the reasons for it. Their Lordships accordingly held that it was better to take the view that necessity was available as a defence so that the position would be plain to the jury or fact-finding tribunal.

It should be noted that the court in *Harris* certified a question of general public importance, namely whether a driver who was otherwise guilty of driving without due care and attention could rely on the defence of necessity or duress of circumstance, but refused leave to appeal to the House of Lords. It is to be hoped that an opportunity may in due course present itself for a definitive answer to the question to be given.   **5.85**

It was stated by three of the Law Lords in *Lynch v DPP* [1975] 1 All E.R. 913 that there is no logical distinction between the principles of necessity and duress. There must be a relationship between the need or the duress and the act, i.e. the need or duress must justify the act.

Where the defence of necessity or duress is not available or is not accepted the circumstances may still amount to special reasons for not endorsing or not disqualifying (see Chapter 21).

Defence of reasonable force to assist in arrest of offenders

Where the acts of a defendant charged with dangerous driving also amount to reasonable force for the purpose of assisting in the arrest of an offender, he may take advantage of the defence afforded by s.3(1) of the Criminal Law Act 1967 (*R. v Renouf* [1986] 2 All E.R. 449). The successful appellant in that case had been pursuing a Volvo containing persons who had committed an arrestable offence and had "edged it off the road" in order to ensure that the car and its occupants would still be on the scene when the police arrived. On those somewhat unusual facts the appellant's defence should have been left to the jury.   **5.86**

CAUSING DEATH BY CARELESS DRIVING WHEN UNDER THE INFLUENCE OF DRINK OR DRUGS

The offence (s.3A)

Section 3A of the 1988 Act created an entirely new offence of causing the death of another person by driving carelessly or without reasonable consideration   **5.87** whilst either unfit to drive through drink or drugs, or with excess alcohol, or subsequently failing without reasonable excuse to provide a specimen for analysis. Section 31 of the Road Safety Act 2006 (implemented in September 2007) provides that it shall additionally be an offence under s.3A of the 1988 Act for a person to cause the death of another person by driving carelessly, etc. and subsequently to fail to give permission for a laboratory test of a specimen of blood taken from him under s.7A of that Act.

The first element of the offence to be considered is that the driving of the vehicle must have caused the death concerned (s.3A(1)). So far as the degree of causation is concerned, existing case law would appear to be as applicable to this offence as to a s.1 offence; thus although the driving does not have to be the sole cause of death, nor even a *substantial* one, it does have to be *a* cause (*R. v Hennigan* [1971] 3 All E.R. 133, § 5.26). The phrase "the death of another person" may include a foetus *in utero* subsequently born alive but dying thereafter from injuries received as a result of the defendant's driving; see *McCluskey v Her Majesty's Advocate* [1989] R.T.R. 182, § 5.24.

5.88   The second element of the offence requires the offender to have driven either carelessly or without reasonable consideration for other users of the road or place (s.3A(1)). Since the words chosen by the draftsman are drawn from s.3 of the 1988 Act (as amended), it may with some confidence be presumed that existing case law on the subject of careless and inconsiderate driving will continue to be of application. Thus where carelessness is alleged the prosecution will need to prove that the defendant departed from the standard of care and skill that in the particular circumstances of the case would have been exercised by a competent and careful driver (see § 5.46); where lack of reasonable consideration is alleged it will additionally be necessary to establish that other users of the road or place were actually inconvenienced (*Dilks v Bowman-Shaw* [1981] R.T.R. 4).

The third element of what can with some justification be described as a "hybrid" offence relates to the physical condition of the driver and his alleged intake of alcohol and/or other drugs. In order to gain a conviction the prosecution must establish either:

(a) that he was *unfit* to drive through drink or drugs; or

(b) that the proportion of alcohol in his breath, blood or urine exceeded the prescribed limit; or

(c) that within 18 hours of the driving he failed when required to provide a specimen for analysis; or

(d) that he failed to give permission for a laboratory test of a specimen of blood taken from him.

5.89   Dealing first with unfitness to drive (s.3A(1)(a)), it should be noted that the draftsman has sensibly plundered s.4 of the 1988 Act in the interests of consistency between offences. The description of the offending driver as "unfit to drive through drink or drugs" (s.3A(1)(a)) is word for word the same as the corresponding passage in s.4 of the 1988 Act and the test of unfitness propounded in s.3A(2) ("ability to drive properly … impaired") is drawn directly from s.4(5) of that Act. Existing case law pertinent to those provisions would appear to be of application to the more recent offence (see §§ 4.89 et seq.).

Turning next to the case of the driver whose alcohol level exceeds the prescribed limit (s.3A(1)(b)), it may be observed that the crucial words "so much alcohol that the proportion of it in his breath, blood or urine ... exceeds the prescribed limit" are drawn directly from s.5(1) of the 1988 Act. In order to determine the amount of alcohol in the driver's body a specimen will be required for analysis; accordingly para.42 of Sch.4 to the Road Traffic Act 1991 amended s.7 of the 1988 Act ("provision of specimens for analysis") to incorporate references wherever appropriate to s.3A. Paragraph 44 of Sch.4 to the 1991 Act similarly amended s.11 of the 1988 Act (the interpretation section) to ensure that the "prescribed limit" of alcohol has the same significance for this offence as for the familiar excess alcohol offence contained in s.5 of the 1988 Act (i.e. 35μg/100ml breath, 80mg/100ml blood or 107mg/100ml urine; see § 4.165).

Section 15 of the 1988 Offenders Act ("use of specimens in proceedings for an **5.90** offence") was also amended (by para.87 of Sch.4 to the 1991 Act) to incorporate references to the s.3A offence. Thus the statutory presumption that the proportion of alcohol in the defendant's body at the time of the alleged offence was not less than in the specimen applies (s.15(2); see § 4.167), as does its rebuttal if the defendant proves (on a balance of probabilities) that he consumed alcohol after the time of the alleged offence and before he provided the specimen, and that had he not done so the proportion of alcohol in his body would not have exceeded the prescribed limit or, where unfitness is alleged, his ability to drive properly would not have been impaired (s.15(3); see § 4.300).

The third qualifying category of potential offender is the motorist who, subsequently to the alleged course of driving, fails without reasonable excuse to provide a specimen for analysis when required to do so (s.3A(1)(c)). It should be particularly noted, however, that for the offence to be established the requirement must be made within *18 hours* of the time at which he drove. It should also be noted that this time-limit is of relevance only to cases which fall under this particular subheading and is without prejudice to the use in other appropriate circumstances (where a specimen *is* provided) of the process of "back calculation" which was given qualified approval by the House of Lords in *Gumbley v Cunningham* [1989] R.T.R. 49 (see § 4.172).

The fourth category was introduced in September 2007 by the implementation **5.91** of s.31(2) of the Road Safety Act 2006. The law already made provision for the taking of specimens of blood from persons incapable of consenting (1988 Act s.7A). However, where a specimen is taken under this section, it shall not be subjected to a laboratory test until the person from whom it was taken has given his permission. It is an offence to refuse to give permission without reasonable excuse, and now in appropriate circumstances it can be a constituent part of the more serious offence of causing death by careless driving when under the influence of drink or drugs.

Scope of the offence

It is to be noted that here as in the s.1 offence of causing death by dangerous **5.92** driving, the criminality of the conduct extends beyond roads to include "other public places" (e.g. public car parks and other public places to which the public has access).

Section 3A(3) provides that the offence can only be committed by a person driving a mechanically propelled vehicle *other than a motor vehicle* (e.g. a stock car, scrambling motor cycle, dumper, digging machine or electrically assisted pedal cycle) if the driver is found to have been unfit to drive; offences which fall within the "excess alcohol" or "failure to provide specimen for analysis" categories can only be committed in a motor vehicle. (Section 4 of the 1991 Act amended s.4 of the 1988 Act in order to replace all references therein to a "motor vehicle" with references to a "mechanically propelled vehicle"; see § 1.04.)

Procedure and evidence generally

5.93   The offence of causing death by careless driving when under the influence of drink or drugs is, by virtue of Sch.2 to the 1988 Offenders Act (as amended by Sch.2 to the 1991 Act), triable only on indictment. It is a Class 3 offence in accordance with *Practice Direction (Criminal Proceedings: Consolidation)* [2002] 3 All E.R. 904 (as amended). So far as Class 3 offences are concerned, the magistrates' court which commits or sends the defendant for trial should specify the most convenient location of the Crown Court. A jury acquitting a defendant of a s.3A offence may in the alternative convict him of one of a number of lesser offences under the 1988 Act, namely careless or inconsiderate driving (s.3), driving whilst unfit through drink or drugs (s.4(1)), driving with excess alcohol (s.5(1)(a)), failing to provide a specimen (s.7(6)) or failing to give permission for a laboratory test (s.7A(6)) (1988 Offenders Act s.24(1)), but not of any offence of attempting to drive (ibid., s.24(2)); see further § 5.20.

It should also be noted that failure to comply with s.1(1) of the 1988 Offenders Act (warning of intended prosecution) is not a bar to conviction of a lesser offence in accordance with s.24 (1988 Offenders Act s.2(4)).

5.94   The proceedings will be commenced by summons or arrest, with remand on bail or in custody, to the magistrates' court where the defendant will in due course be committed or sent for trial to the Crown Court (see Chapter 2).

The provisions relating to arrest without warrant and for the trial of youths at the Crown Court apply to s.3A offences as they do to offences under s.1.

See § 5.36 as to inquests and as to notifying the coroner of committal.

Spouses are competent and compellable witnesses in the Crown Court against each other where the victim was under 16 years of age (Police and Criminal Evidence Act 1984 s.80) as "bodily injury" in s.80(3)(a) must include a fatal injury.

5.95   By s.38 of the 1988 Act non-observance of the Highway Code may tend to establish liability for the offence (for a discussion of the Highway Code as to offences of careless driving, see Highway Code, § 5.69).

ROAD SAFETY ACT 2006; NEW OFFENCES

Causing death by careless, or inconsiderate, driving

5.96   Section 20 of the Road Safety Act 2006 (brought into force with effect from August 18, 2008) inserted a new s.2B into the 1988 Act to create the new offence of causing death by driving a mechanically propelled vehicle on a road or other public place without due care and attention, or without reasonable consideration for other persons using the road or place.

There is also now a statutory definition of careless or inconsiderate driving (1988 Act s.3ZA, inserted by s.30 of the 2006 Act). A person is to be regarded as driving without due care and attention if (and only if) the way he drives falls below what would be expected of a competent and careful driver (s.3ZA(2)). In determining what would be expected of a careful and competent driver, regard must be had not only to the circumstances of which he (the competent and careful driver) could be expected to be aware, but also to any circumstances shown to have been within the knowledge of the accused (s.3ZA(3)). A person is to be regarded as driving without reasonable consideration for other persons only if those persons are inconvenienced by his driving (s.3ZA(4)).

So far as causation is concerned, it is submitted that the principles to be applied to the new offence should not differ from those established in respect of offences under s.1 and s.3A of the 1988 Act; thus although the driving does not have to be the sole cause of death, nor even a *substantial* one, it does have to be *a* cause (*R. v Hennigan* [1971] 3 All ER 133, § 5.26). The phrase "the death of another person" may include a foetus *in utero* subsequently born alive but dying thereafter from injuries received as a result of the defendant's driving: see *McCluskey v Her Majesty's Advocate* [1989] R.T.R. 182, § 5.24.   **5.97**

Provision is made by means of amendments to s.24 of the 1988 Offenders Act for conviction of an offence under s.2B to be a possible alternative verdict where a prosecution for an offence under s.1 (causing death by dangerous driving) or s.3A (causing death by careless driving when under the influence of drink or drugs) of the 1988 Act has been unsuccessful. It is further provided that conviction of an offence under s.3 (careless or inconsiderate driving) may be an alternative to conviction of an offence under s.2B (2006 Act s.20(2)).

Causing death by careless driving contrary to s.2B of the 1988 Act is an "either way" offence within the meaning of the Magistrates' Courts Act 1980 and is subject to the mode of trial procedure (see Chapter 2, Mode of trial procedure, § 2.122). The offence is punishable on conviction on indictment with up to five years' imprisonment, or a fine, or both, and on summary conviction by six months' imprisonment or the statutory maximum fine, or both. It is subject to mandatory disqualification and endorsement.   **5.98**

The Sentencing Guidelines Council has issued a guideline for the sentencing of this offence (see Appendix 4, p.1281).

Causing death by driving: unlicensed, disqualified or uninsured drivers

Section 21 of the Road Safety Act 2006 (in force from August 18, 2008) inserted a new s.3ZB into the 1988 Act to create a new offence committed where a person causes the death of another person by driving a motor vehicle on a road and, at the time when he is driving, the circumstances are such that he is committing an offence under s.87(1) (driving otherwise than in accordance with a licence; see further Chapter 11), s.103(1)(b) (driving while disqualified; see further Chapter 11) or s.143 (using motor vehicle while uninsured; see further Chapter 10) of the 1988 Act.   **5.99**

The question of causation may well prove problematical in practice for both the courts and prosecuting authorities. It would appear from the way in which the statute has been framed that the nature and quality of the driving concerned is irrelevant; it is the very act of driving a motor vehicle on a road (but not on any other public place) which constitutes the first element of the offence. Whilst a disqualified driver may generally speaking be presumed to be aware of the criminality of his actions when deciding to drive, it is not hard to envisage circumstances in which due to inadvertence, or ignorance of the actions of other parties such as banks or insurance companies (or indeed the DVLA), an otherwise law-abiding motorist who despite driving perfectly properly is involved in an accident which leads to the death of another person may be faced with the prospect of prosecution and potential incarceration for an offence under this legislation.

5.100   Causing death by driving while unlicensed, disqualified or uninsured contrary to s.3ZB of the 1988 Act is an "either way" offence within the meaning of the Magistrates' Courts Act 1980 and is subject to the mode of trial procedure (see Chapter 2, Mode of trial procedure, § 2.122). The offence is punishable on conviction on indictment with up to two years' imprisonment, or a fine, or both, and on summary conviction by six months' imprisonment or the statutory maximum fine, or both. It is subject to mandatory disqualification and endorsement.

The Sentencing Guidelines Council has issued a guideline for the sentencing of this offence (see Appendix 4, p.1282).

RELATED OFFENCES

Causing bodily harm by furious driving, etc.

5.101   Section 35 of the Offences Against the Person Act 1861 is still occasionally used, particularly where the driving complained of did not take place on a road or other public place within the meaning of the 1988 Act. Section 35 reads as follows:

> "Whosoever having the charge of any carriage or vehicle, shall, by wanton or furious driving or racing, or other wilful misconduct, or by wilful neglect, to do or cause to be done any bodily harm to any person whatsoever, shall be guilty of an offence."

An offence under s.35 is only triable on indictment (unless committed by a youth). It should be noted that s.35 creates a number of separate offences. Section 35 applies to pedal cycles as well as to other vehicles (*R. v Parker* (1859) 59 J.P. 793). Where the victim is under 16, spouses are competent and compellable witnesses for the prosecution against each other (Police and Criminal Evidence Act 1984 s.80). Quarter sessions have held that, on a charge under s.35, the Crown must prove a degree of lack of care which would amount to dangerous driving: "wanton driving" indicates a positive lack of care and "wilful neglect" implies something of a negative nature ([1954] Crim. L.R. 137). In *R. v Philip Cooke* [1971] Crim. L.R. 44 the charge under s.35 was that the defendant having charge of a motor vehicle caused bodily harm by "wilful misconduct". The jury at quarter sessions were directed that there was no need for the prosecution to prove an intention to cause injury or bodily harm. If the defendant's driving was intended it was "wilful" and if it fell below the normal standard so that it could be called "misconduct" it sufficed if the "wilful misconduct" amounted to a substantial cause of the injury. Failure to have a light at night on a horse-drawn vehicle can be "wilful neglect" under s.35 (*Att Gen v Joyce* (1956) 90 I.L.T.R. 47). A conviction under s.35 was upheld where the jury had found that the defendant was driving in a wanton way by reason of the amount of liquor he had taken; there was also evidence of reckless driving (*R. v Burdon* (1927) 20 Cr. App. R. 60). In *R. v Mohan* [1975] R.T.R. 337 the defendant drove his motor car at a police constable, who leapt out of his way and avoided being struck. He was charged with attempting by wanton driving to cause bodily harm to the constable. It was held that mens rea was an essential element of the common law offence of attempting to commit an offence under s.35 of the Offences Against the Person Act 1861 and a specific intent on the part of the defendant to commit the offence had to be proved.

The inherent difficulties of defining ancient offences in modern terms are amply **5.102**
illustrated in *R. v Okosi* [1997] R.T.R. 450. After a disagreement about a fare, a
minicab driver drove off with his erstwhile passenger hanging on to his car; the
resultant dragging along the road caused bodily harm to that hanger-on. The trial
judge directed the jury that the term "wanton" could apply to someone driving a
motor vehicle in an irresponsible or reckless manner. Having defined recklessness, he continued by telling them that if they thought the actions of the driver in
driving along with a person hanging on to the door, with the driver not stopping,
knowing that that was going on, that would amount to wanton furious behaviour
(*sic*) and the driver would be guilty of the offence. He was convicted and appealed inter alia on the ground that the judge's direction was wrong, in that he
had directed the jury on objective recklessness, whereas the jury should have
been directed that they had to be satisfied that the driver had been aware of the
risk but had nevertheless gone on and taken it. In dismissing his appeal, the Court
of Appeal held that assuming, but not deciding, that the correct approach to s.35
required recklessness, namely foresight of harm, but of a subjective and not an
objective character, the direction given by the judge had amply warned them of
the need to be sure that the defendant had been fully alive to the risk to which he
was subjecting the hanger-on, before they could convict.

It is not clear from the report of *Okosi* above just why it was thought appropriate for a charge under s.35 to be preferred. The facts as quoted indicate that the
incident complained of took place on a road, but are silent as to whether or not a
notice of intended prosecution was given. What can be said with some force,
however, is that the only useful purposes of s.35 now seem to be for dealing with
horse-drawn vehicles and cyclists and as a reserve charge for motorists who cannot be prosecuted for dangerous driving either because notice of intended prosecution was not given or the offence was not committed on a road or other public
place within the meaning of the 1988 Act.

An offence under s.35 carries a maximum of two years' imprisonment or a **5.103**
fine. Offences committed after September 24, 2007 in respect of a mechanically
propelled vehicle are subject to discretionary disqualification and obligatory
endorsement with 3–9 penalty points.

Section 35 refers to causing "bodily harm" and not to causing "grievous bodily
harm". In cases where extremely serious harm had been caused recklessly by
dangerous driving, there is nothing to prevent the Crown from preferring charges
under s.20 of the 1861 Act. Where that happened there is no principle that would
require the courts to ignore the statutory maximum for the s.20 offences. This
was the decision of the Court of Appeal in *R. v Stranney* [2007] EWCA Crim
2847; [2008] 1 Cr. App. R. (S.) 104. In that case the appellant pleaded guilty to
two counts of unlawfully inflicting grievous bodily harm, contrary to s.20 of the
Offences against the Person Act 1861, and one count of dangerous driving. The
appellant had driven dangerously down a cobbled road at high speed and negotiated bends at high speed. His female passengers were thrown around in the back
seat of the car and asked him to slow down. The appellant drove at high speed
over speed humps, causing the car to take off and land heavily. After driving over
one speed hump, the appellant lost control of the car, which collided with railings
and traffic light poles. One of the women sustained severe injuries and her left
arm was left permanently disabled. The second woman suffered a fractured pelvis.
After arrest, the appellant failed to provide a specimen of breath for analysis. In

all the circumstances, and bearing in mind the defendant's plea of guilty, the appropriate sentence was two-and-a-half years' imprisonment concurrent. It follows that the court was not constrained by the maximum penalty of two years' imprisonment for dangerous driving: *Stranney* above, preferring *R. v Bain* [2005] EWCA Crim 7; [2005] 2 Cr. App. R. (S.) 53 to *R. v Bridle* [2002] EWCA Crim 908; [2003] 1 Cr. App. R. (S.) 3. But see criticism in *Criminal Law Week*, Issue 08, 2008, p.7.

Where a motor vehicle is deliberately used as a weapon and serious harm is caused it may be appropriate for a charge to be brought under s.18 of the Offences Against the Person Act 1861.

Motor racing on highways

5.104   It is an offence to promote or take part in a race or trial of speed between motor vehicles on a public way (s.12 of the 1988 Act).

The offence must be committed on a "highway". This expression is not defined. It seems narrower than a "road" within the meaning of s.192 of the 1988 Act (see § 1.122), since the definition would seem to exclude a private road to which the public has access. At common law a highway is by definition public, i.e. it is a right of way upon which the public are entitled to pass and repass.

5.105   It would seem that timekeepers, stewards and possibly passengers as well as promoters can be convicted under s.12: anyone who "takes part in" a race or trial of speed commits a s.12 offence. It has been held by the Crown Court that an offence is committed even when different routes are taken by each vehicle starting from a common starting point to a finishing point. The offence must consist of a race or trial between vehicles. No offence is committed under this section where one vehicle races and is not in competition with another vehicle. In *Hunter v Frame* 2004 J.C. 81; 2004 S.L.T. 697 two drivers, both travelling at speeds considerably in excess of a speed limit, were seen to drive for short distances abreast of one another, with one then slowing down to fall in behind, then overtaking, the other. Their convictions under s.12 were overturned by the High Court of Justiciary. The expression "to race" meant a competition as to speed and as one car had driven in parallel with, then deliberately fallen behind the other, this was not racing within its ordinary meaning and there was insufficient material to found a conviction on the basis that either driver was promoting a race.

There is no necessity for a prior arrangement to race in order for the offence to be committed; a spontaneous contest or competition of speed, albeit without any particular beginning or end, will suffice (*Ferrari v McNaughton* 1979 S.L.T.(N.) 62).

5.106   The offence is triable summarily only. For penalty see § 5.114.

It is similarly an offence to promote or take part in a race or trial of speed between cycles unless authorised or conducted in accordance with regulations (s.31).

Driving with uncorrected defective eyesight or refusing to submit to an eyesight test

5.107   It is an offence under s.96(1) of the 1988 Act for a person to drive a motor vehicle on a road while his eyesight is such that he cannot comply with the prescribed requirement. The offence is committed if the defective vision either is not or cannot be sufficiently corrected by glasses. It is also an offence under s.96(3) for a driver to refuse to submit to an eyesight test when required to do so by a constable who suspects he may be committing an offence under s.96(1). The requirement as to eyesight mentioned in s.96 is that the driver, whether wearing glasses or not, can read a car's number plate at a distance of 20.5m (20m for new style, smaller plates) in good daylight (12.3m (12m for new style, smaller plates) for mowing machines or pedestrian controlled vehicles) (Motor Vehicles (Driving Licences) Regulations 1999). Inability to comply with this requirement (with the aid of glasses if worn) is a prescribed disability preventing the holding of a driving licence (reg.72(1)). There is a question to this effect on driving licence application forms and a person who knowingly makes a false answer to this question commits an offence under s.174 of the 1988 Act.

The Secretary of State, by virtue of s.94(5)(b) of the 1988 Act, can require a licence-holder or applicant for a licence whom he believes may have defective eyesight to submit to an examination. Section 96 makes it clear that, if he needs glasses to read the plate at 20.5m (20m for new style, smaller plates) and he was not wearing them when he was driving, he is guilty and that he is to be tested in the same state as to wearing or not wearing them as when he was driving. It is submitted that the police may require the motorist under s.96(2) to take an eyesight test subsequent to the occasion which gave rise to the constable's suspicions. A person may be seen driving at night or in conditions of poor visibility and the prescribed test as to eyesight has to be taken in good daylight.

If the defendant's eyesight has not been corrected by spectacles or is incapable **5.108** of being corrected by spectacles, a court would seem to be under a duty under s.22 of the 1988 Offenders Act to notify the Secretary of State with a view to the licence being revoked. Additionally, the court may consider disqualifying the defendant under s.36(1) of the 1988 Offenders Act until he passes a test.

For penalties for offences under s.96, see § 5.114.

Driving to the common danger, etc.

Offences akin to dangerous and careless driving arise also under the Highway **5.109** Act 1835 s.78, the Metropolitan Police Act 1839 s.54, and the Town Police Clauses Act 1847 s.28. These Acts would apply to motor vehicles, cycles and horse-drawn vehicles and (except for s.28) to equestrians, mahouts, cameleers and outward-bound ladies from Riga (*Williams v Evans* (1867) 41 J.P. 151) but see 119 J.P. Jo. 746. As to Crown drivers, see § 2.34.

The only value of these Acts so far as cases against motorists and cyclists are concerned is that warning of intended prosecution need not have been given (see Chapter 2).

DANGEROUS, CARELESS AND INCONSIDERATE CYCLING

The offences (ss. 28 and 29)

Sections 28 and 29 of the 1988 Act contain provisions similar to those of ss.2 **5.110** and 3 in respect of dangerous or careless riding of bicycles, tricycles and (s.192) cycles having four or more wheels.

It would seem that dangerous cycling should be interpreted in the same manner as dangerous driving, and similarly careless or inconsiderate cycling is interpreted in the same manner as careless or inconsiderate driving.

Whereas the criminality of dangerous driving has been extended to include "other public places", dangerous cycling remains confined to roads. It should be noted that a cycle lane may be part of a road set aside for the purpose of cycling (see § 1.125).

5.111   An auto-assisted cycle may be a cycle for the purposes of ss.28 and 29 if its engine is disconnected and essential parts have been removed (*Lawrence v Howlett* [1952] 2 All E.R. 74). Otherwise, it is a motor vehicle whether the engine is running or not, and the definition of "cycle" contained in s.192 specifically excludes cycles which are motor vehicles (but it may nevertheless be a pedal cycle for the purpose of s.12(5) of the Theft Act 1968, see § 15.12).

The *Concise Oxford Dictionary* defines "ride" as "sit on and be carried by", including "sit or go or be on something as on a horse, especially astride". It is not clear whether a cyclist who is propelling himself by standing with one foot on the pedal and by touching the ground occasionally with the other "rides": it can certainly be said that he is being "carried by" his machine. In *Crank v Brooks*, § 6.165, it was observed obiter that a cyclist having one foot on the pedal was "riding" if she was thereby using the cycle as a scooter. In that case the cyclist was pushing the cycle with both feet on the ground and was held to be a foot passenger for the purpose of the "Zebra" Pedestrian Crossings Regulations. By contrast, s.35 of the 1988 Act (drivers to comply with traffic directions) refers to persons "driving or propelling vehicles".

Offences contrary to ss.28 and 29 are only triable summarily.

5.112   So far as powers of arrest are concerned, s.24 of the Police and Criminal Evidence Act 1984 enables a constable to arrest without warrant anyone who is committing, or is about to commit an offence of whatever kind, or whom the constable reasonably suspects to be committing, or about to commit an offence. It should be noted, however, that for this power to be exercisable the constable must have reasonable grounds for believing that an arrest is necessary in order, inter alia, to enable a person's name or address to be ascertained or to prevent any subsequent prosecution from being hindered by the disappearance of the person in question.

The provisions of s.1 of the 1988 Offenders Act (notices of intended prosecution: see Chapter 2) apply to offences under ss.28 and 29.

5.113   A court acquitting a defendant of dangerous cycling may in the alternative convict him of careless cycling (1988 Offenders Act s.24(1); see § 5.20).

It is an offence contrary to s.31 of the 1988 Act for a person to promote or take part in a race or trial of speed of cycles (not being motor vehicles) on public highways (note that the offence is confined to "public highways"). This is a different definition from the definition of "road" under s.192 of the 1988 Act (see Chapter 1). It would seem not to include roads to which the public have access which are not public highways (see further Chapter 1).

For penalties for offences contrary to ss.28, 29 and 31, see § 5.114.

5.114

Table of penalties

Offence	Mode of trial	Section	Imprisonment	Fine	Disqualification	Penalty points	Endorsement code	Sentencing guideline
Manslaughter** or, in Scotland, culpable homicide	Only on indictment	Common law	Life	Unlimited	Obligatory (minimum 2 years) Compulsory retest	3–11*	DD60	—
Causing death by dangerous driving	Only on indictment	s.1	14 years	Unlimited	Obligatory (minimum 2 years) Compulsory retest	3–11*	DD80	See Appendix 4
Dangerous driving	a) On indictment	s.2	2 years	Unlimited	Obligatory Compulsory retest	3–11*	DD40	—
	b) Summarily	s.2	6 months	Level 5†	Obligatory Compulsory retest	3–11*	DD40	See Appendix 3
Causing death by careless or inconsiderate driving	a) On indictment	s.2B	5 years	Unlimited	Obligatory (minimum 12 months) Discretionary retest	3–11*	CD80	See Appendices 3 and 4

Offence	Mode of trial	Section	Imprisonment	Fine	Disqualification	Penalty points	Endorsement code	Sentencing guideline
	b) Summarily	s.2B	6 months	Level 5†	Obligatory (minimum 12 months) Discretionary retest	3–11*	CD80	See Appendices 3 and 4
Careless or inconsiderate driving	Summary	s.3	—	Level 5†	Discretionary	3–9	CD10 careless driving CD20 inconsiderate driving; CD30 in Scotland (both offences)	See Appendix 3
Causing death by driving unlicensed, disqualified or uninsured	a) On indictment	s.3ZB	2 years	Unlimited	Obligatory (minimum 12 months) Discretionary retest	3–11*	CD90	See Appendices 3 and 4
	b) Summarily	s.3ZB	6 months	Level 5†	Obligatory (minimum 12 months) Discretionary retest	3–11*	CD90	See Appendices 3 and 4

Offence	Mode of trial	Section	Imprisonment	Fine	Disqualification	Penalty points	Endorsement code	Sentencing guideline
Causing death by careless driving when under influence of drink or drugs, etc.	Only on indictment	s.3A	14 years	Unlimited	Obligatory (minimum 2 years)‡	3–11*	CD40 (unfit; drink) CD50 (unfit; drugs) CD60 (excess alcohol) CD70 (fail provide specimen)	See Appendices 3 and 4
Causing bodily harm by furious driving, etc.	Only on indictment	s.35 Offences Against the Person Act 1861	2 years	Unlimited	—	—	—	—
Motor racing	Summary	s.12	—	Level 4†	Obligatory	3–11*	MS50	—
Driving with uncorrected sight, or refusing to submit to an eyesight test	Summary	s.96(1)	—	Level 3†	Discretionary	3	MS70	—
	Summary	s.96(3)	—	Level 3†	Discretionary	3	MS80	—
Dangerous cycling	Summary	s.28	—	Level 4†	—	—	—	—

Offence	Mode of trial	Section	Imprisonment	Fine	Disqualification	Penalty points	Endorsement code	Sentencing guideline
Careless or inconsiderate cycling	Summary	s.29	—	Level 3†	—	—	—	—

* No penalty points may be imposed if the offender is disqualified.

** A mandatory life sentence may be required in certain circumstances for manslaughter: see § 5.115.

† For current maxima for the standard levels of fine, see § 18.07.

Mandatory life sentence for manslaughter

Section 2 of the Crime (Sentences) Act 1997 (repealed and replaced by s.109 **5.115** of the Powers of Criminal Courts (Sentencing) Act 2000) was brought into force on October 1, 1997. Section 2(5) thereof defined and listed certain offences as "serious offences" for the purposes of that section; manslaughter (which may be taken to include motor manslaughter) is one of the offences so listed. Where a person aged 18 or over at the time of his offence was convicted after October 1, 1997 of a "serious offence", and that person had a previous conviction for a "serious offence", he was liable, in the absence of exceptional circumstances relating either to him or to his offences, to a mandatory sentence of imprisonment for life.

It should be noted that s.109 of the 2000 Sentencing Act was repealed by the Criminal Justice Act 2003, and replaced by new provisions concerning what are referred to in that Act as "dangerous offenders", in turn amended by the Criminal Justice and Immigration Act 2008 (please see further Chapter 18).

Compulsory driver retesting

A court which disqualifies a person under s.34(1) of the 1988 Offenders Act **5.116** (obligatory disqualification) on conviction of any of the offences listed in s.36(2) of that Act must also order him to be disqualified until he passes an extended driving test (s.36(1) ibid.). The offences are:

(a) manslaughter, or in Scotland culpable homicide;

(b) causing death by dangerous driving;

(c) dangerous driving;

(d) causing death by careless driving when under the influence of drink or drugs (where the offence was committed on or after January 31, 2002; see the Driving Licences (Disqualification until Test Passed) (Prescribed Offence) Order 2001 (SI 2001/4051)).

Despite the fact that the requirement in s.36(1) of the 1988 Offenders Act for the compulsory retesting of drivers convicted of certain offences is a mandatory one, the Court of Appeal in *R. v Cully* [2005] EWCA Crim 3483; [2006] R.T.R. 32 saw fit to remove an order for an extended retest of an appellant convicted of dangerous driving.

Period of obligatory disqualification

Offenders convicted of motor manslaughter, causing death by dangerous driv- **5.117** ing (s.1) or causing death by careless driving when under the influence of drink or drugs (s.3A) must be disqualified (unless special reasons are found; see Chapter 21) for not less than two years (1988 Offenders Act s.34(4)). For those convicted of dangerous driving (s.2) the minimum period is 12 months.

The offence of causing death by careless driving when under the influence of drink or drugs, etc. (s.3A) is included in the category of drink/driving offences for which a further offence within 10 years of a previous similar conviction entails a minimum disqualification period of three years (1988 Offenders Act s.34(3); see further § 4.325).

Careless or inconsiderate driving

The offence is endorsable with 3–9 penalty points unless special reasons are **5.118** found. For the penalty points system, see § 19.20. It is submitted that the criterion for the number of penalty points is primarily the degree of carelessness or lack of consideration; see further "Variable penalty points", § 19.30.

Section 23 of the Road Safety Act 2006 increased the maximum fine for a s.3 offence from level 4 on the standard scale to level 5. The new penalty applies to offences committed on or after September 24, 2007.

Alternative verdicts: sentencing

5.119   The Crown Court when sentencing an offender convicted of an offence triable only summarily has the same powers and duties as to sentencing as a magistrates' court (1988 Offenders Act s.24(4)).

Driving to the common danger, etc.

5.120   The offences under s.78 of the Highway Act 1835 are punishable by a fine of level 1 on the standard scale and under s.54 of the Metropolitan Police Act 1839, by a fine of level 2 on the standard scale.

Offences contrary to s.28 of the Town Police Clauses Act 1847 are punishable by a fine of level 3 on the standard scale.

Disqualification and endorsement cannot be ordered for these offences.

SENTENCING GUIDELINES

Generally

5.121   The landscape of sentencing guidelines for offences covered by this chapter changed dramatically in 2008. The definitive guideline on causing death by driving came into force for offences where death results for offenders aged 18 and over who are sentenced on or after August 4, 2008. This guideline is set out in full in Appendix 4. The Magistrates' Courts Sentencing Guidelines apply to a wide range of offences, including the most common road traffic offences that are sentenced in the magistrates' courts. These guidelines also apply to allocation (mode of trial) decisions, but are not binding on a Crown Court where the defendant has elected trial by jury.

As the courts must have regard to these guidelines when sentencing, all previous guidelines and guideline cases (including those of the Court of Appeal) must be treated with considerable caution. For that reason we are not reproducing here the cases that have guided the courts over recent years, except those that set out general principles that are unchanged. It is almost certain that the new guidelines will soon be illuminated by decisions of the higher courts, and those will be published in forthcoming supplements to this work.

Motor manslaughter

5.122   There are no guidelines issued by the Sentencing Guidelines Council specifically for this offence. That may be because it is rarely prosecuted and because the few cases that fall to be sentenced are so different from each other as to mean that guidelines would provide little help. It is likely that courts will nevertheless bear in mind the guidelines for causing death by dangerous driving, but adjust for the different level of culpability.

It is submitted that in the worst cases, where culpability is very high, the courts will not necessarily be constrained by the maximum sentence for the statutory offence. The following cases are illustrative of that principle. However, the sentences passed in the pre-guideline cases provide no guidance in themselves: the maximum sentence and, with it, the guideline starting points for the most serious cases have increased since these cases were heard.

It should be noted that manslaughter is a serious specified offence for the purposes of ss.224–236 of the Criminal Justice Act 2003. This means that an offender convicted of such an offence committed after April 4, 2005 is liable, if certain conditions are specified to a mandatory life sentence. This topic is covered more fully in Chapter 18 (§ 18.15).

It was held by the Court of Appeal (Lord Taylor C.J. presiding) in *R. v Pimm* **5.123** [1994] R.T.R. 391 that the elements of the offence of manslaughter by motor vehicle and the former offence of causing death by reckless driving were not in law the same; accordingly the sentencing powers of the court for manslaughter were not limited by relation to the maximum sentence for the former statutory offence. The appellant, who at the time of the offence was aged 17, had been sentenced to nine years' detention in a young offender institution for manslaughter. The deceased had been unsuccessfully attempting to prevent him from driving off in a previously stolen van and had been fatally injured when thrown off the roof of that van as a result of its violent swerving. The appellant's conduct had been appalling, combining repeated theft, excess alcohol, attempts to escape lawful apprehension and gross disregard for human life and limb. Despite his youth, the sentence was wholly justified.

An offender had knocked down and killed a woman with whom he had formerly had a relationship by driving a van at her as she walked away and colliding with her as she attempted to cross the road. He pleaded guilty to manslaughter and causing death by careless driving when under the influence of drink and was sentenced to nine years' imprisonment for the former offence and four years' (concurrent) for the latter. He appealed against sentence on the basis that the offence of manslaughter when committed with a vehicle ought to be equated with other offences of causing death by driving, such as those contrary to ss.1 and 3A of the Road Traffic Act 1988. The Court of Appeal in *R. v Gault* [1996] R.T.R. 348 considered that, whilst the sentence of nine years was excessive, a different approach was justifiable and proper when the offender was convicted of manslaughter rather than one of the statutory offences. There was an element of hostility in the offence committed by the appellant which imparted a gravity to the offence which exceeded that of the statutory offences. The sentence of nine years would be reduced to six; the sentence of four years for the s.3A offence would be quashed and replaced with no separate penalty.

R. v Gault above was applied by the Court of Appeal in *R. v Dwyer* [2005] **5.124** Crim. L.R. 320 when re-emphasising the legitimacy of a different approach to sentencing where an offender was convicted of manslaughter rather than one of the statutory offences. The defendant in the instant case had been sentenced on the basis that she had driven off knowing that the deceased was on the bonnet of the car, had known that he had fallen off as she swerved from lane to lane of a busy multi-lane road and had then driven through a red light and driven away from the scene without stopping. The sentencing judge had been right to take a serious view of the case, albeit that his starting point was too high; accordingly the sentence would be reduced from seven to five years' detention in a young of-fender institution.

The element of hostility which may lead to the selection of manslaughter rather than any of the statutory offences as the appropriate charge (see *R. v Gault* above) may also amount to a very significant aggravating factor where the offence in fact charged is one of causing death by dangerous driving. Thus where a driver used his car in a hostile manner towards a cyclist, who suffered injuries from which he died, such an action was regarded as very grave even where there were no other aggravating features. The Court of Appeal so held in *R. v Dickinson* [1998] R.T.R. 469. The appellant, a taxi driver, had had an argument with a cyclist whilst wait-ing at traffic lights. As they moved off the cyclist appeared to be trying to keep up with the taxi and made a sudden unexplained movement towards it. The taxi then swerved violently towards the cyclist before accelerating away. There was no contact between the vehicles, but the cyclist fell to the ground and suffered fatal head injuries. The fact that the appellant's driving was deliberately hostile was regarded by the court as very grave, even if, as was suggested, he had been provoked by the cyclist's aggressive manner. It was not acceptable for a person to lose his temper while driving and to act upon it. Nevertheless, the proper sentence in the case was three and a half years' imprisonment rather than the four and a half years originally imposed.

Causing death by dangerous driving, causing death by careless driving when under the influence of drink or drugs, causing death by careless driving, and causing death by driving: unlicensed, disqualified or uninsured drivers

5.125   The Sentencing Guidelines Council has published a Definitive Guideline entitled Causing Death by Driving (set out in full at Appendix 4 below). This guideline applies to the two existing offences of *causing death by dangerous driving* and *causing death by careless driving under the influence of alcohol or drugs* as well as to the two new offences of *causing death by careless driving* and *causing death by driving: unlicensed, disqualified or uninsured drivers*. The guideline applies to the sentencing of offenders convicted of any of the offences dealt with in the guideline who are sentenced on or after August 4, 2008. The two new offences created by the Road Safety Act 2006 were implemented on August 18, 2008 (see §§ 5.01, 5.96 and 5.99 above), so all such offences will fall to be sentenced under the guideline.

The Crown Prosecution Service's *Policy for Prosecuting Cases of Bad Driv-ing* (see § 5.43 above) sets out the approach for prosecutors when considering the appropriate charge based on an assessment of the standard of the offender's driving. This has been taken into account when formulating the guideline.

5.126   Because the principal harm done by these offences (the death of a person) is an element of the offence, the factor that primarily determines the starting point for sentence is the culpability of the offender. Accordingly, for offences other than causing death by driving: unlicensed, disqualified or uninsured drivers, the central feature should be an evaluation of the quality of the driving involved and the degree of danger that it foreseeably created. The guideline draws a distinction be-tween those factors of an offence that are intrinsic to the quality of driving (referred to as "determinants of seriousness") and those which, while they ag-gravate the offence, are not.

The levels of seriousness in the guidelines for those offences based on dangerous or careless driving alone have been determined by reference only to determinants of seriousness. Aggravating factors will have the effect of either increasing the starting point within the sentencing range provided or, in certain circumstances, of moving the offence up to the next sentencing range. The outcome will depend on both the number of aggravating factors present and the potency of those factors. Thus, the same outcome could follow from the presence of one particularly bad aggravating factor or two or more less serious factors.

The determinants of seriousness likely to be relevant in relation to causing death by careless driving under the influence are both the degree of carelessness and the level of intoxication. The guideline sets out an approach to assessing both those aspects but giving greater weight to the degree of intoxication since Parliament has provided for a maximum of 14 years' imprisonment rather than the maximum of five years' imprisonment where the death is caused by careless driving only.

Since there will be no allegation of bad driving, the guideline for causing death **5.127** by driving: unlicensed, disqualified or uninsured drivers links the assessment of offender culpability to the nature of the prohibition on the defendant's driving and includes a list of factors that may aggravate an offence.

There are five factors that may be regarded as determinants of offence seriousness, each of which can be demonstrated in a number of ways. Common examples of each of the determinants are: awareness of risk; effect of alcohol or drugs; inappropriate speed of the vehicle; seriously culpable behaviour of the offender; and victim. Alcohol/drugs, avoidable distractions, and vulnerable road users are considered in more detail in the guideline. Aggravating and mitigating factors, again considered in more detail in the guideline, are that more than one person was killed; the effect on the offender; and actions of others. Personal mitigation is also considered and it is said that evidence that an offender is normally a careful and conscientious driver, giving direct, positive assistance to the victim and genuine remorse may be taken into account as personal mitigation and may justify a reduction in sentence.

The guideline tables apply, as always, to a first-time offender aged 18 or over convicted after trial, who has not been assessed as a dangerous offender.

For causing death by dangerous driving, level 1 is for the most serious offences **5.128** and encompasses driving that involved a deliberate decision to ignore (or a flagrant disregard for) the rules of the road and an apparent disregard for the great danger being caused to others. Level 1 is that for which the recent increase in maximum penalty was aimed primarily. The starting point is eight years' custody with a sentencing range of 7 to 14 years' custody. Level 2 is driving that created a substantial risk of danger and carries a starting point of five years' custody within a range of four to seven years' custody. Level 3 is driving that created a significant risk of danger and has a starting point of three years' custody within a range of two to five years' custody.

For causing death by careless driving when under the influence of drink or drugs or having failed without reasonable excuse either to provide a specimen for analysis or to permit the analysis of a blood sample the guideline is based both on the level of alcohol or drug consumption and on the degree of carelessness. At the top end of the scale is careless/inconsiderate driving falling not far short of dangerousness with 71µg or above of alcohol in breath/high quantity of drugs *or* deliberate non-provision of specimen where evidence of serious impairment exists. At this top level the starting point is eight years' custody in a range of 7 to 14 years' custody. At the lowest level of the scale is careless/inconsiderate driving arising from momentary inattention with no aggravating factors where there is 35–50µg of alcohol/a minimum quantity of drugs *or* test refused because of an honestly held but unreasonable belief. Here the starting point is 18 months' custody within a sentencing range of 26 weeks to 4 years' custody.

5.129   The new offence of causing death by careless or inconsiderate driving carries a maximum sentence of five years' imprisonment. As a result, the sentence ranges are generally lower for this offence than for the offences of causing death by dangerous driving or causing death by careless driving under the influence, for which the maximum sentence is 14 years' imprisonment. However, it is unavoidable that some cases will be on the borderline between dangerous and careless driving or may involve a number of factors that significantly increases the level of seriousness of an offence. As a result, the guideline for this offence identifies three levels of seriousness, the range for the highest of which overlaps with ranges for the lowest level of seriousness for causing death by dangerous driving.

The three levels of seriousness are defined by the degree of carelessness involved in the standard of driving. The most serious level for this offence is where the offender's driving fell not that far short of dangerous. Here the starting point is 15 months' custody within a range of 36 weeks to 3 years' custody. The least serious group of offences relates to those cases where the level of culpability is low, e.g. in a case involving an offender who misjudges the speed of another vehicle, or turns without seeing an oncoming vehicle because of restricted visibility. The starting point for careless or inconsiderate driving arising from momentary inattention with no aggravating factors is a community order (medium) within a range of community order (low) to community order (high). (In other words, custody does not fall within the range for this lowest level of offence, and it can be assumed that such offences will normally be tried in the magistrates' court.) This offence is therefore also covered by the revised Magistrates' Court Sentencing Guidelines, which also became effective on August 4, 2008. The guidelines are summarised in § 18.06 below and the guidelines for road traffic offences are set out in full in Appendix 3 below. Other cases will fall into the intermediate level for which the starting point is 36 weeks' custody within the range of community order (high) to two years' custody.

5.130   The new offence of causing death by driving: unlicensed, disqualified or uninsured drivers has a maximum penalty of two years' imprisonment and is triable "either way". Culpability arises from the offender driving a vehicle on a road or other public place when, by law, not allowed to do so; the offence does not require proof of any fault in the standard of driving. A fine is unlikely to be an appropriate sentence for this offence; where a non-custodial sentence is considered appropriate, this should be a community order. Since driving whilst disqualified is more culpable than driving whilst unlicensed or uninsured, a higher starting point is proposed when the offender was disqualified from driving at the time of the offence. Where the offender was disqualified from driving *or* the offender was unlicensed or uninsured plus two or more aggravating factors from the list provided, then the starting point is 12 months' custody with a range of 36 weeks to 2 years' custody. When the offender was unlicensed or uninsured plus at least one aggravating factor from the list provided, the starting point is 26 weeks' custody within a range of community order (high) to 36 weeks' custody. Where the offender was unlicensed or uninsured with no aggravating factors a community order will normally be the appropriate penalty. Again the offence is also covered by the Magistrates' Court Sentencing Guidelines (see Appendix 3 below).

The following cases, although recent, nevertheless predate the new guideline and should be considered with appropriate caution. In *R. v Mazour* [2008] EWCA Crim 1427; [2008] 1 Cr. App. R. (S) 34 it was said that whilst the offender's good character was certainly a matter which the court could and should take into account, the extent to which it could do so in cases involving seriously bad driving is bound to be tempered by the fact that this is an offence committed on many occasions by those with impeccable characters. *R. v Herbert* [2007] EWCA Crim 3034; [2008] Crim.L.R. 314 is an example of sentencing a 17-year-old for an offence towards the top end of the range. Here the defendant youth (who was on bail and disqualified from driving, with convictions for vehicle-taking, aggravated vehicle-taking and assault occasioning actual bodily harm) stole a car and drove it with two young female passengers. He was chased by police at speeds of up to 70mph in a 30mph zone, drove dangerously over a prolonged period before losing control, hit the central reservation, crossed into the other carriageway and hit an oncoming vehicle. His two female passengers were killed and two of the occupants of the other car were injured. The offender, who had suffered only minor injuries, denied that he had been driving the car and then fled the scene. Because it was possible to conceive of a somewhat worse case, 12 years' imprisonment was the appropriate starting point, to be reduced to eight years by the offender's guilty plea, youth and remorse. Since young offenders may change and mature in a shorter time than adults the offender, being relatively young, might lose his fixation for cars over some years, and so an extended sentence under s.228 of the Criminal Justice Act 2003 (rather than detention for public protection under s.226) would be adequate protection for the public. The driver in *R. v Smith* [2007] EWCA Crim 2539; [2008] 2 Cr. App. R. (S) 1 was convicted of causing death by careless driving whilst under the influence of alcohol or drugs. Driving a stolen car, she failed to see a line of cars in front of her, swerved into the wrong side of the road to avoid them and collided with a car travelling in the opposite direction. The four passengers, all children including two of her own children, were killed. The offender had amphetamine in the blood which was two to three times the average dose for an amphetamine user. Nine years' imprisonment was held not to be manifestly excessive.

The revised sentencing guidelines for causing death by dangerous driving set out in the guideline case of *R. v Richardson* [2006] EWCA Crim 3186; [2007] R.T.R. 29 (itself superseded by the new guideline) apply to sentences for offences that occurred after the maximum penalty was raised in February 2004, whether or not the offence occurred before the guidelines were established; *R. v Payne* [2007] EWCA Crim 157; [2007] 2 Cr. App. R. (S.) 45. Mr Payne was driving a seven-and-a-half ton lorry approaching a motorway junction where there was a warning that queues ahead were likely. Because he was using his mobile phone he failed to notice the queue in time and collided with the rear vehicle, causing the death of one person. The Court of Appeal ruled that the reassessed relevant starting point for causing death by dangerous driving, given the highly dangerous use of the mobile phone, was four-and-a-half years' imprisonment.

5.131

Another case falling into the most serious sentencing bracket is *R. v Bradley Barney and Marcus Barney* [2007] EWCA Crim 3181. Over the course of 15 minutes in the seven miles from the start of their journey to the point of the fatal accident, the appellant brothers drove in a highly dangerous matter. They were racing or driving competitively at high speed over a prolonged period. They engaged in reckless and aggressive overtaking of vehicles, at speed, on blind bends in contravention of double white lines. They forced oncoming traffic to take evasive action. During one such manoeuvre Marcus Barney drove into the opposite carriageway to overtake a bus on a sweeping bend. Bradley Barney followed. The deceased, who was a young lady due to be married in four days time, was driving towards them in the correct carriageway. She applied emergency braking to avoid a collision. Her vehicle rotated 190° and collided with the bus. She was killed instantly. Both vehicles were destroyed by fire but the bus driver and passengers escaped with minor injuries. Bradley Barney failed to stop. Neither reported the accident and both attempted to cover their tracks, initially inventing stories, saying they had not been there or were unaware of the collision. Marcus Barney had no insurance. Bradley Barney had one prior conviction for dangerous driving. The Court of Appeal confirmed the starting points of 10 years' imprisonment for Bradley Barney and nine years' imprisonment for his brother (subject to an appropriate discount for guilty pleas).

5.132   Cases do not always fit comfortably into any of the brackets identified in *R. v Cooksley* [2003] EWCA Crim 996; [2003] R.T.R. 32, as revised in *R. v Richardson* above, or of course by the subsequent guidelines. In *R. v Featherstone* [2007] EWCA Crim 208; [2007] 2 Cr. App. R. (S.) 57 the driver allowed three youths to be towed on their mini-scooters as he drove his van at 15mph out of a car park onto a public road (with them holding onto various parts of the van). As he did so, one of the youths hit a kerb, fell to the ground and was run over by the van. The offence involved a grave error by the offender in his failure to recognise the great dangers involved in what he was doing. As such, although there were no aggravating factors, the offence did not fall within the lowest culpability bracket (12 to 24 months) but in the intermediate culpability bracket (two to four-and-a-half years) albeit not at the top of that bracket. In *Att Gen's Reference (No.146 of 2006) (R. v Vandermeulen)* [2007] EWCA Crim 570; [2007] 2 Cr. App. R. (S.) 470 an experienced lorry driver with no convictions fell asleep at the wheel when driving on a motorway without proper rest (but not driving for excessive hours). He collided with a car stopped on the hard shoulder, killing the driver and seriously and permanently injuring a young child. The sentencing judge was correct to conclude that the case fell into the "higher culpability" bracket identified in the then guideline case of *R. v Cooksley*. The aggravating factors were the injury to the child, the offender's failure to resist pressure from his employers to drive without adequate rest and his disregard of the regulations relating to rest periods. The appropriate starting point was five years' imprisonment, to be reduced to take account of the plea and personal mitigation.

Where death had occurred as a result of a momentary error and dangerous driving that could not be described as reckless, a sentence of 12 months' imprisonment was not unduly lenient. However, the court should not have suspended sentence: *R. v Legrys* [2007] EWCA Crim 1605; [2008] 1 Cr App. R. (S.) 66.

5.133   The case of *R. v Green* [2007] EWCA Crim 2172; [2008] 1 Cr App. R. (S.) 97

provides a reminder that the court will need to consider the dangerousness criteria as set out in the Criminal Justice Act 2003 when the defendant is to be sentenced for causing death by careless driving when unfit. Mr Green was sentenced to imprisonment for public protection with a minimum term of three years for this offence. Because he had a conviction for wounding contrary to s.20 of the Offences Against the Person Act 1861 the presumption of dangerousness arose. The fact that this was a quite different kind of offence and one which, by itself, was not likely to be repeated in such a way as to cause serious harm to members of the public was not an argument against the assumption of dangerousness. It was held that once a defendant has been convicted of a serious offence within the meaning of the Act, whatever the facts and nature, it is perfectly possible for a finding of dangerousness to be made on the basis of material which has no close relationship to the actual offence for which sentence is being passed. Although the dangerousness provisions have altered since this case was determined (see Chapter 18) the principle in *R. v Green* remains.

The position of dangerous young offenders was considered (before the revisions to the provisions of the Criminal Justice Act 2003 ss.224–236 introduced by the Criminal Justice and Immigration Act 2008) by the Court of Appeal in *R. v Herbert* [2007] EWCA Crim 3034; [2008] 2 Cr. App. R. (S.) 28. The 17-year-old appellant had been on bail (for handling) and was disqualified from driving when he took a car, drove dangerously (and indeed recklessly), and crashed, causing the death of his two passengers and injuries to the occupants of another vehicle. The trial judge imposed a sentence of detention for public protection on each count of causing death by dangerous driving. The appeal court confirmed that the sentencing judge had to consider whether the defendant was a dangerous offender within the meaning of the Criminal Justice Act 2003. After "anxious consideration" the Court of Appeal decided that an extended sentence under s.228 would be adequate to protect the public from the appellant and substituted such a sentence for the original sentence under s.226. The court considered what had been said in *R. v Lang* [2005] EWCA Crim 2864; [2006] 2 Cr. App. R. (S.) 3 about the fact that young offenders might mature and change. In the current case the appellant would be nearly 30 before his total sentence expired, by which time, it was said, he should have matured sufficiently for the public to be protected.

In *R. v Z* [2008] EWCA Crim 753; [2008] 2 Cr. App. R. (S.) 623 the defendant **5.134** was even younger, 14 at the time of the offence and 15 at the time of his appeal against sentence. Z took a jeep and drove it around a residential estate one afternoon. There were adults and children passing by. Z was showing off to his co-accused (of a similar age), although he had little driving experience to speak of. He drove erratically, swerved and accelerated harshly. He drove too fast for the conditions. As he accelerated while trying to turn a corner he lost control of the vehicle, mounted the pavement, hit a tree which snapped and fell on a buggy carrying two babies. One of the babies, Billy, 19 months old, died of multiple injuries. The other children and their mother were uninjured. On a late plea of guilty he was sentenced to 42 months' detention for causing death by dangerous driving and 18 months' detention concurrent for aggravated vehicle-taking. He was also disqualified from driving for 10 years. The sentence was upheld on appeal.

R. v Akinyeme [2007] EWCA Crim 3290; [2008] R.T.R. 20 is an example of a case of causing death by dangerous driving that fell to be sentenced in the upper part of the old higher culpability bracket. In the light of the new guidelines, cases such as this that were sentenced before August 4, 2008 are of limited assistance. The defendant, who had no driving licence and had never taken a driving test, suffered from very bad epilepsy. It appeared that he had had an epileptic seizure while driving a high-performance car, and struck a cyclist, who died as a result of his injuries. The defendant, who had a considerable record of vehicle-related offences, pleaded guilty to causing death by dangerous driving. He accepted that, knowing that he was subject to frequent epileptic fits, he had driven the car when he had not taken his medication for several days. On the material available, there was an insufficient basis for finding a significant risk that the defendant would behave in the same way as he had done on the occasion in question and thereby cause another death by dangerous driving. Accordingly, the conditions for an indeterminate sentence were not satisfied. By reason of the aggravating factors of the defendant's failure to take his prescribed medication and his offending record, the case fell in the upper part of the higher culpability bracket, though not right at the top of that bracket, with a starting point of six years' imprisonment. With full credit for an early plea of guilty, a sentence of four years' imprisonment was appropriate.

5.135   Significant changes in the law relating to dangerousness were introduced by the Criminal Justice and Immigration Act 2008, which apply to everyone sentenced on or after July 14, 2008 under ss.224–236 of the Criminal Justice Act 2003. The Sentencing Guidelines Council has published a supplement to its Sentencing Guidelines Compendium which seeks to describe the law as it currently stands and to apply the judgments to those provisions as appropriate (*Dangerous Offenders: Guide for Sentencers and Practitioners*, available at *http://www.sentencing-guidelines.gov.uk* [Accessed March 21, 2009]). Caution should be applied to cases sentenced before July 14, 2008, as they may fall to be sentenced differently now the changes have taken effect.

Dangerous and careless driving

5.136   A guideline for these offences is now included in the Magistrates' Court Sentencing Guidelines which became effective on August 4, 2008. The revised guidelines are summarised at § 18.05 below and the guidelines for road traffic offences are set out in full in Appendix 3 below. The full text can be found at *http://www.sentencing-guidelines.gov.uk* [Accessed March 21, 2009]. The guidelines apply to cases sentenced in the magistrates' courts, to allocation (mode of trial) decisions, and to appeals against sentence by magistrates heard in the Crown Court. They do not apply to cases tried in the Crown Court, and there is no specific guideline for the more serious cases of dangerous driving heard in the Crown Court.

For dangerous driving (p.1234 below) the starting point in the guidelines where there is a single incident with little or no damage or risk of personal injury is a medium level community order. The starting point for incident(s) involving excessive speed or showing off, especially on busy roads or in a built-up area; *or* a single incident where there was little or no damage or risk of personal injury but the offender was a disqualified driver is 12 weeks' custody. For prolonged bad driving involving deliberate disregard for the safety of others; *or* incidents involving excessive speed or showing off, especially on busy roads or in a built-up area, by a disqualified driver; *or* driving while being pursued by police, the case is normally too serious to be sentenced in the magistrates' court and will carry a sentence of between six months' imprisonment and two years' imprisonment (the maximum sentence) in the Crown Court. This more serious category will therefore continue to include cases such as *R. v Watson* [2007] EWCA Crim 1595; [2008] 1 Cr. App. R. (S.) 55 where it was said that the sentencing bracket for cases of road rage, where no injury in fact results, where there is no consumption of alcohol, and where the evidence demonstrates furious driving in a temper with intent to cause fear and possible injury, was between 6 and 12 months' imprisonment. In this case 12 months' imprisonment was appropriate where the defendant, a 53-year-old chauffeur with minor traffic convictions, reacted to being given a ticket by a traffic warden by chasing the warden up the road, throwing a stone at him, driving at the warden, mounting the kerb with both nearside wheels, speeding up and deliberately swerving towards the warden, forcing him to jump out of the way. The offender returned to the scene two minutes later, again speeding towards the warden and swerving at him when he ran over to the other side of the road and again when he crossed back. In *R. v Gray* [2008] EWCA Crim 336; [2008] 2 Cr. App. R. (S) 72, the defendant was an 18-year-old who was not travelling at excessive speed but straddled the white line in the middle of the road whilst driving round a bend. He collided with a motor cyclist who was severely injured (one leg amputated and indefinite pain and arthritis in his other leg), was wheelchair bound and in need of constant care from his wife. The victim's family were concerned about their ability to cope financially. The defendant pleaded guilty on the day of trial and his sentence was reduced on appeal to eight months in a young offender institution. Although the consequences were appalling, the criminality of the driving itself was at the lower end of the scale and a difficult balance had to be struck between the consequences on the one hand, and the culpability and mitigation on the other.

In *R. v Nunn* [1996] Crim. L.R. 210 the Court of Appeal held that as a general principle, the opinions of the victim or his surviving close relatives as to the propriety of a sentence do not provide any sound basis for its reassessment. The irrelevance of their opinions as to what the sentence should be is re-emphasised in para.28 of the *Practice Direction (Criminal Proceedings: Consolidation)* [2002] 3 All E.R. 904 which deals with victim personal statements. What may be relevant, however, is the consequences of the offence upon such persons.

In *R. v Tomkins* [2004] EWCA Crim 2792; (2004) 168 J.P.N. 861 a disquali- **5.137** fied driver drove off when approached by police officers (hitting and injuring one of them as he did so), drove through a "no entry" sign and crashed into another car, injuring both the other driver and himself and badly damaging both vehicles. He had previous convictions for driving offences. He pleaded guilty to dangerous driving and was sentenced to 18 months' imprisonment. On appeal it was argued on his behalf that the sentence was manifestly excessive given the two-year maximum penalty. The Court of Appeal held that the sentence was not manifestly excessive since he had used the car as a weapon and had shown disregard for the law.

For careless driving (driving without due care and attention) the maximum penalty is now a level 5 fine and the guideline is set out in the Magistrates' Court Sentencing Guidelines (see p.1230 below). For a momentary lapse of concentration or misjudgement at low speed the starting point is a Band A fine with three to four penalty points. Where there is loss of control due to speed, mishandling or insufficient attention to road conditions, or carelessly turning right across oncoming traffic the starting point is a Band B fine with five to six penalty points. Where there is an overtaking manoeuvre at speed resulting in a collision of vehicles or driving bordering on the dangerous the starting point is a Band C fine and consider disqualification or seven to nine penalty points.

5.138   In the past, magistrates were sometimes faced with the dilemma caused by sentencing where careless driving has resulted in death. Until recently many considered that the sentence should be determined solely by the level of culpability (in other words the quality of the driving) without regard to the harm. Moreover the maximum penalty was a level 4 fine until September 24, 2007, when it rose to level 5. However, careless driving after August 18, 2008 that results in death will now presumably be charged as the new offence of causing death by careless driving (see § 5.96 above), with a maximum sentence of five years' imprisonment and a guideline (Appendix 4 below). Although the guideline may well assist the court in deciding sentence, it cannot solve the central dilemma: it is impossible to find a level of punishment that both fairly reflects the culpability of the offender and satisfies the friends and family of the deceased that their loss has been adequately reflected. While it is clear that harm must to some extent be reflected in cases where a death has occurred (because the new offence and guideline say so explicitly), the issue will continue to be raised where this is injury, perhaps very serious injury, but not death. Here the maximum penalty where the driving is careless as opposed to dangerous remains a level 5 fine. It is submitted that the modern view is that the harm caused must now be a factor in sentencing, even though the penalty cannot in most cases adequately reflect the suffering of the victim.

Views of the victim or victim's family

5.139   The *Consolidated Criminal Practice Direction* Pt III.29 sets out how victims may have a formal opportunity to say how a crime has affected them, by making a personal statement to a police officer that will later be drawn to the attention of the sentencing court. The Practice Direction says that: "The court must pass what it judges to be the appropriate sentence having regard to the circumstances of the offence and the offender, taking into account, as far as the court considers it appropriate, the consequences to the victim. The opinions of the victim or the victim's close relatives as to what the sentence should be are therefore not relevant, unlike the consequence of the offence on them" (Pt III.29.2c).

Alcohol/drugs

5.140   In the past there has been discussion as to whether the consumption of alcohol or drugs is an aggravating feature of an offence where the presence of alcohol or drugs is not an element of the offence. The Sentencing Guidelines Council guideline on causing death by driving says (see Appendix 4, p.1270) that in these circumstances, where there is sufficient evidence of driving impairment attributable to alcohol or drugs, the consumption of alcohol prior to driving will make an offence more serious. Where the drugs were legally purchased or prescribed, the offence will only be regarded as more serious if the offender knew or should have known that the drugs were likely to impair driving ability. Unless inherent in the offence or charged separately, failure to provide a specimen for analysis (or to allow a blood specimen taken without consent to be analysed) should be regarded as a determinant of offence seriousness.

Disqualification

Section 34(4) of the 1988 Offenders Act provides that a minimum mandatory period of disqualification of two years with compulsory driver retesting applies to an offender convicted of:

(a) manslaughter, or in Scotland culpable homicide, or

(b) causing death by dangerous driving, or

(c) causing death by careless driving while under the influence of drink or drugs.

5.141

An offender convicted of dangerous driving is subject to a 12-month minimum period of disqualification (ibid. s.34(1)) and a compulsory retest provision. A driver convicted of causing death by careless or inconsiderate driving (Road Traffic Act 1988 s.2B) or the offence of causing death by driving: unlicensed, disqualified or uninsured drivers (Road Traffic Act 1988 s.3ZB) must be disqualified for a minimum of 12 months with a discretionary retest provision.

The Sentencing Guidelines Council guidelines for causing death by driving point out that for the relevant offences, disqualification is a mandatory part of the sentence (subject to the usual (very limited) exceptions), and therefore an important element of the overall punishment for the offence. In addition, an order that the disqualification continues until the offender passes an extended driving test is compulsory for those convicted of causing death by dangerous driving or by careless driving when under the influence, and discretionary in relation to the two other offences. Any disqualification is effective from the date on which it is imposed. When ordering disqualification from driving, the duration of the order should allow for the length of any custodial sentence in order to ensure that the disqualification has the desired impact. In principle, the minimum period of disqualification should either equate to the length of the custodial sentence imposed (in the knowledge that the offender is likely to be released having served half of that term), or the relevant statutory minimum disqualification, whichever results in the longer period of disqualification.

A disqualification for a period longer than the appropriate minimum is a matter for the discretion of the court and (per James L.J. in *R. v Lobley* [1974] R.T.R. 550 at 553) "… in the end each case has to be visited with a period of disqualification which is appropriate to the facts of that particular case".

5.142

A period of disqualification should be fixed without regard to the right of a defendant to apply for its removal under what is now s.42 of the 1988 Offenders Act (*R. v Lobley* [1974] R.T.R. 550).

Where the offender is young, the principle that young offenders should normally not be disqualified for very long periods applies to s.1 offences. Nevertheless, in an appropriately serious case a lengthy period of disqualification will be upheld (see e.g. *R. v Marshall* [1976] R.T.R. 483: an 18-year-old, "showing off", driving at 50mph in a 30mph area, unable to avoid hitting an 81-year-old; disqualification for five years upheld). In *R. v Farrugia* [1979] R.T.R. 422 (a case of "preventative disqualification") the defendant having a bad driving record was disqualified for seven years for a bad case of causing death by reckless driving.

The Court of Appeal reduced the period of disqualification to five years: it was said a long sentence of disqualification can be counter-productive particularly for men in their twenties. In *R. v Hudson* [1979] R.T.R. 401 a period of disqualification was reduced from five years to three because of the defendant's loss of employment. In *R. v Midgley* [1979] R.T.R. 1 despite not having asked for a reduction, the period of disqualification of seven years was reduced to four. In *R. v Russell (Ian) (Note)* [1993] R.T.R. 249 an offender was disqualified for seven years for reckless driving. He had used his vehicle as a weapon by driving it at another man; as luck would have it, the victim was only struck a glancing blow. The Court of Appeal reduced his disqualification to a period of five years on the basis that the court below had failed to give sufficient weight to the undoubtedly profound adverse effects that such a lengthy disqualification would have on the driver's prospects of effective rehabilitation on his release from custody.

5.143   Disqualification for life is a highly exceptional course, but might be appropriate in a case where the danger represented by the offender was an extreme and indefinite one; a case perhaps such as *R. v Noble* [2002] EWCA Crim 1713; [2003] R.T.R. 6.

Section 36(1) of the 1988 Offenders Act provides that in addition to the mandatory disqualification which must be imposed under s.34 of that Act, an offender convicted of manslaughter (or in Scotland culpable homicide), or causing death by dangerous driving, or dangerous driving must also be disqualified until he passes an extended driving test (see further § 5.116). So far as offences of causing death by careless driving while under the influence of drink or drugs and careless and inconsiderate driving are concerned, where any such offence is committed on or after January 31, 2002, the court must similarly order the offender to submit to a further, and extended, driving test (see the Driving Licences (Disqualification until Test Passed) (Prescribed Offence) Order 2001 (SI 2001/4051)). So far as offences of careless and inconsiderate driving are concerned, the court has a discretionary power to order an offender to submit to a further "ordinary" driving test (see below). In determining whether to make an order disqualifying the offender until he has passed such a test, the court must have regard to the safety of road users (ibid. s.36(6)).

5.144   A retest can be ordered at the discretion of the court on conviction if causing death by careless driving (1988 Act s.2B) or causing death by driving: unlicensed, disqualified or uninsured drivers (1988 Act s.3ZB).

CHAPTER 6

DRIVER OFFENCES

CONTENTS

SIGNS AND SIGNALS

Generally

Offences against traffic signs and police signals are dealt with in ss.35, 36, 37 **6.01**
and 163 of the Road Traffic Act 1988. The use of traffic signs is regulated by Pt V
of the Road Traffic Regulation Act 1984.

The expression "traffic sign" is defined in s.64 of the 1984 Act and the colour,
size and type of traffic signs are prescribed by the Traffic Signs Regulations and
General Directions 2002 (SI 2002/3113). Those regulations consolidated, with
substantial amendments, the Traffic Signs Regulations and General Directions
1994 and their amending instruments, which in their turn had consolidated the
eponymous regulations of 1981. The earlier regulations were accordingly revoked
(reg.2). Traffic signs erected under the 1994 and 1981 Regulations and continuing to comply with those regulations are to be treated as prescribed by the new
regulations; deadlines, however, have been imposed on the replacement of signs
rendered obsolete by those regulations (reg.3).

A general saving for the powers of the Secretary of State, the Scottish Ministers **6.02**
and the National Assembly for Wales to authorise traffic signs of a character not
prescribed by the regulations is contained in reg.8 and reg.9 makes it clear that
nothing in the regulations is to have effect to authorise anyone to place signs on
or near a road to indicate a temporary obstruction. The relevant regulations for
this purpose are the Traffic Signs (Temporary Obstructions) 1997 (SI 1997/3053);
see further § 6.04 below.

The 2002 Regulations were amended with effect from March 1, 2003 by the
Traffic Signs (Amendment) General Directions 2003 (SI 2003/393) to provide
that approvals for road studs given under direction 50 of the revoked Traffic
Signs General Directions 1994 are to be treated (until January 31, 2005) as

having been given under direction 58(1) of the 2002 Directions. The 2002 Regulations were further amended with effect from August 21, 2006 by the Traffic Signs (Amendment) Regulations 2006 (SI 2006/2083) to insert new diagrams to indicate quiet lanes in England. Quiet lanes may be designated by local traffic authorities in England in accordance with the Quiet Lanes and Home Zones (England) Regulations 2006 (SI 2006/2082). With effect from September 15, 2008, the Traffic Signs (Amendment) Regulations 2008 (SI 2008/2177) amended the 2002 Regulations to provide improvements to the signing of safety cameras. The amendments are designed to assist drivers in recognising and complying with the speed limit on roads where camera enforcement is in place.

6.03   Section 65 of the 1984 Act authorises the traffic authority to place traffic signs on or near any road. In s.65, "traffic authority", by s.80 includes any person, not being a traffic authority, responsible for the maintenance of a road and therefore includes persons responsible for private roads which are nevertheless roads within the definition of the 1984 Act (see Chapter 1). Section 66 of the same Act authorises constables, or any person acting under the instructions (general or specific) of a chief officer of police, to place on any highway or on any structure on a highway authorised signs relating to certain special traffic regulations, orders and directions.

By s.67 of the 1984 Act constables, or any person acting under the instructions (general or specific) of a chief officer of police, may place on a highway or on a structure on a highway authorised signs to prevent or mitigate congestion or obstruction of, or danger to or from traffic in consequence of extraordinary circumstances, but such signs by s.67(1) may not be maintained for longer than seven days.

6.04   Flat traffic delineators, road vehicle signs, traffic cones, traffic pyramids, traffic triangles, keep right signs and warning lamps used in conjunction with those signs may be placed on roads in accordance with the Traffic Signs (Temporary Obstructions) Regulations 1997 (SI 1997/3053) to warn traffic of a temporary obstruction, other than road works, on the road. Such an obstruction may be caused, e.g., by a stationary vehicle, including an emergency or breakdown vehicle. At least four flat traffic delineators, traffic cones or traffic pyramids must be set out, and not more than one warning lamp may be placed in conjunction with each of the other signs. The traffic triangle must be placed at least 45m away from the obstruction.

The offences under ss.35, 36 and 163 of the 1988 Act are considered below, and matters relating to particular signs are dealt with thereafter. Proceedings and penalties for the offences will be found at §§ 6.60–5.

Failing to comply with a sign

6.05   It is an offence under s.36(1) of the 1988 Act to fail to comply with the indication given by a sign if it indicates a statutory prohibition, restriction or requirement or if it is expressly provided by or under any provisions of the Act that s.36 applies to that sign or type of sign. Section 36(2) is curiously worded in that it says that a sign shall not be deemed to have been "lawfully placed" unless it indicates the statutory prohibition, etc., or it is expressly provided that s.36 applies to the sign; it does not expressly say that it is not an offence to disobey any other sign. The term "statutory prohibition, restriction or requirement" means, it is submitted, one having effect pursuant to a public or local Act of Parliament and does not extend to signs, such as "No Waiting", having effect under an order or regulation (see below): cf. the meaning of "enactment" in s.172 of the 1988 Act (see § 7.31).

Regulation 10 of the Traffic Signs Regulations and General Directions 2002 provides that s.36 applies to the signs listed in that regulation, so that it is an offence under s.36 to fail to comply with such a sign. The list of signs is a formidable one and includes inter alia "Stop" (at junctions of major roads), "Give Way" (at junctions of major roads or at certain open railway level crossings), "Stop" (at road works), the straight arrow to indicate that traffic is to proceed in a particular direction, the diagonal arrow for "keep left" or "keep right", the right-angled arrow indicating that traffic must turn ahead in the direction indicated, the opposed arrows indicating that priority must be given to vehicles from the opposite direction, the mini-roundabout, mandatory height limits, the yellow box markings at junctions and level crossings which prohibit entry in a manner which causes any part of a vehicle to remain at rest within the marked area due to the presence of stationary vehicles, bus stop clearway signs, red traffic lights (including certain motorway flashing red signals and the flashing red lights at railway automatic level crossings), green arrow traffic light signals, the double white lines (either both unbroken or continuous/broken line), the zig-zag lines at a Toucan or equestrian crossing facility, the round red sign with the white band meaning "No Entry" and the "Drivers of Large or Slow Vehicles Must Phone" sign at automatic level crossings.

Temporary signs erected by the police in the exercise of the powers conferred **6.06** on them by s.67 of the 1984 Act are expressly included in the category of signs to which what is now s.36 applies by virtue of s.67(2). The signs most often used by the police when exercising their powers of placing temporary signs under s.67 in order to prevent obstruction at public events are "no waiting" cones. The cones, as such, do not appear to be authorised by the 2002 Regulations; the opinion is held, however, that provided the cone bears the sign shown in diagram 636 and its dimensions are within the permissible limits, a motorist may be convicted under s.36 of failing to conform with the sign, as the structure upon which the sign is allowed to be displayed is not prescribed.

As to signs at census points, see § 6.48.

Is it an offence under s.36 to fail to comply with any other sign prescribed by **6.07** the regulations such as "One Way Traffic", "No Waiting", or "No Right Turn"? It is submitted that disobedience to any such sign should be prosecuted under s.5(1), s.8(1) or s.53(5) or (6) of the 1984 Act in respect of the particular traffic regulation order whereby waiting in, entry to the street, etc., is forbidden and not under s.36. If any sign indicates a "statutory prohibition, restriction or requirement" (see s.36(2)(a)), then reg.10, which as noted above sets out certain signs to which s.36 does apply, is completely unnecessary. The signs in reg.10 have effect under the Traffic Signs Regulations and General Directions 2002 just as other signs have effect under the 2002 Regulations and (usually) some other order as well. Indeed, if a person stopped to unload goods in a "No Waiting" area where unloading was allowed, to charge him with contravention of the "No Waiting" sign might be to deprive him of the benefit of the unloading exemption unless it can be said that the latter part of s.36(2) preserves his rights.

Although contravention of a sign which is not referred to in reg.10 can seemingly not be dealt with under s.36, such a contravention may amount to evidence of dangerous, careless or inconsiderate driving, e.g. a driver who crosses from a minor into a major road disobeying double broken transverse lines at the junction. It has been suggested that such contraventions may be offences contrary to what is now s.91 of the 1988 Offenders Act. This section provides generally, subject to certain exceptions, for a maximum fine of level 3 for contraventions of regulations made under the Traffic Acts where no offence is provided elsewhere. The 2002 Regulations are made under the 1984 Act and it is submitted that any prosecution would be under this Act if at all. However, many of the signs are advisory or informatory and it is doubtful for similar reasons whether a contravention amounts to an offence under s.91 any more than under s.36 unless it is expressly specified to be one by virtue of reg.10 or otherwise. Penal provisions are construed strictly. If it were to be an offence merely to contravene the sign, the various exemptions might be lost.

Cyclists, other vehicles and equestrians

6.08   Section 36 applies to cyclists, trams, trolley vehicles, horse-drawn vehicles and hand carts as well as to motor vehicles, but not to equestrians. Section 36 applies to Crown vehicles. For many years there has been an advanced stop line for cyclists in Oxford in the cycle lane at the junction of Broad Street (commonly called "the Broad") and Parks Road with the result that Oxford undergraduates have had a flying start. It would appear that this benefit may now be available to all thanks to a new reg.43 of the Traffic Signs Regulations and General Directions 2002 and a new road marking depicted in diagram 1001.2 in Sch.6 to the 2002 Regulations, which together prescribe and define the component parts and layout of a junction incorporating an advanced stop line for pedal cyclists.

As to persons pushing cycles, see 114 J.P. Jo. 160. A person who pushed a lorry to try to make it start was held to be guilty of taking and driving it away (*Shimmell v Fisher* [1951] 2 All E.R. 672) and so it can be argued that persons pushing bicycles and hand carts are guilty of an offence if they disobey a traffic sign. On the other hand, there is the argument that "Stop" signs and traffic lights do not apply to persons pushing pedal cycles and hand carts because, presumably, such signs are not meant to affect pedestrians, who can walk into main roads and against traffic signs at their pleasure. If a pedestrian can do that, cannot a pedestrian pushing a pram, or a child with a scooter, do the same? And if a pram-pusher can, why should not a cycle-pusher? A counter-argument is that the mischief aimed at by s.36 is to prevent any type of vehicle being in a major road in disobedience to the sign or going against the red light and that it is immaterial whether such a vehicle arrives there by mechanical or muscular power, the offence being "driving or propelling" a vehicle. Compare *McKerrell v Robertson* at § 6.165 —woman and go-cart which she was pushing held to be one entity under the Pedestrian Crossings Regulations, and *Crank v Brooks* [1980] R.T.R. 441. In the latter case, a cyclist pushing a cycle using both feet on the ground was held to be a foot passenger for the purpose of the "Zebra" Pedestrian Crossings Regulations; *aliter* if the person had one foot on the pedal and was using the cycle as a scooter.

Conformity of signs

6.09   A traffic sign placed on or near a road shall be deemed to be of the prescribed size, colour and type or of another character authorised by the Secretary of State and to have been lawfully so placed, unless the contrary is proved (1988 Act s.36(3)). See § 6.58 as to defective signs. See also *Woodriffe v Plowman* at § 6.32.

Traffic lights are presumed to be working properly (see *Wells v Woodward* at § 6.32).

An order under s.1 of the Road Traffic Regulation Act 1984 (or s.6 in respect **6.10** of Greater London) may provide that a part of the road, or the times at which a part of the road is controlled, may be identified by the placing of a traffic sign. For the purposes of the order any such traffic sign is deemed to be lawfully placed unless the contrary is proved (ss.4(1) and 7(1)).

Illumination of signs is dealt with below in respect of particular signs and by regs 18–21 of the Traffic Signs Regulations and General Directions 2002.

Defences

It is no defence that the defendant did not see the sign; mens rea is not essential **6.11** (*Rees v Taylor*, 1939, unreported, cited in Stone in the notes to what is now s.36(1)(b); *Hill v Baxter* [1958] 1 All E.R. 193).

In *R. v Spurge* [1961] 2 All E.R. 688 it was held that it is a defence to a charge of what was then dangerous driving if it occurred owing to a defect in the vehicle of which the driver did not know and which he could not previously have discovered by the exercise of reasonable prudence, and in *Burns v Bidder* [1966] 3 All E.R. 29 it was said that being pushed by another vehicle on to a crossing or a latent defect might afford a defence to a charge of not according precedence on a pedestrian crossing. The same principles presumably apply as defences to charges of disobeying police signals and traffic signs.

Neglecting or refusing to comply with directions given by police or traffic wardens

By the Police and Criminal Evidence Act 1984 Pt I the police have powers to **6.12** carry out searches including vehicle searches and road checks, but these do not apply to minor road traffic offences. For the power of search, see §§ 15.32–4.

By s.35 of the 1988 Act it is an offence if any person driving or propelling a vehicle of any kind (including a pedal cycle) neglects or refuses to stop the vehicle or make it proceed in or keep to a particular line of traffic when directed so to do by a constable or traffic warden engaged in regulating traffic on a road; the vehicle itself need not be on a road. By s.163 of the 1988 Act, a person driving a mechanically propelled vehicle and a person riding on a road a cycle (i.e. a bicycle, tricycle or any other form of cycle) shall stop on being so required by a constable in uniform.

A "road check" under s.4 of the Police and Criminal Evidence Act 1984 is an **6.13** exercise of the power contained in s.163 of the 1988 Act (see s.4(2)) to stop all vehicles or vehicles selected by any criterion to check whether a person has committed, is about to commit or is a witness to an offence (other than a road traffic or vehicle excise offence) or is unlawfully at large. Section 163 is limited so far as constables are concerned to constables in uniform; as to "in uniform", see § 4.41

Before a s.4 road check is carried out, authorisation must be recorded in writing with the specified details and, except in urgent cases, must be given by a superintendent or person of higher rank. He must have reasonable grounds for *believing* (see § 4.48) that the offence is an indictable offence (see Police and

Criminal Evidence Act 1984 s.24) and he must also have reasonable grounds for *suspecting* (again see § 4.48) that where an offender or escapee is being sought he is in the locality.

6.14   In effect, s.4 precludes *general* road checks for all offences except road traffic and vehicle excise offences. Road traffic offences are not defined and the meaning may be wider than the Road Traffic Acts if the legislation in question relates to road traffic. The s.163 power to stop individual vehicles and to carry out checks of any kind for road traffic and vehicle excise offences is unaffected and authorisation is not necessary.

The reference is to the exercise of the s.163 power. Where a person fails to stop for a s.4 road check properly carried out, he will therefore commit the s.163 offence (provided, of course, that the constable is in uniform and that the vehicle concerned is a motor vehicle or cycle). The exercise of a power under the 1984 Act gives the constable a right to use reasonable force if necessary in the exercise of that power (s.117). This applies to s.4 road checks, and to s.163 offences generally, if committed on or after October 1, 2002, as a result of amendments made with effect from that date by the Police Reform Act 2002 s.49. From that same date constables are given the power of arrest for offences contrary to s.163 (1988 Act s.163, as amended), and powers of entry and search for the purpose of effecting such an arrest (1984 Act s.17, as amended).

6.15   It is an offence under s.37 of the 1988 Act for a pedestrian to fail to comply with a direction to stop given by a constable in uniform in the execution of his duty. Section 169 gives to constables (and traffic wardens) the right to require names and addresses from offenders against s.37.

It is an offence under s.59 of the Police Reform Act 2002 to fail to comply with an order given by a constable in uniform to stop a motor vehicle in motion where the constable has reasonable grounds for believing that the vehicle is being used in a manner which contravenes s.3 or 34 of the 1988 Act (careless and inconsiderate driving and prohibition of off-road driving) and is causing, or is likely to cause, alarm, distress or annoyance to members of the public (s.59(6)). In addition to the power to order vehicles to stop, constables are empowered to seize and remove the vehicle concerned and may, in the exercise of their powers of stop and seizure, enter, with reasonable force if necessary, any premises on which they have reasonable grounds for believing the motor vehicle to be (s.59(3)).

6.16   Vehicles seized in pursuance of the powers conveyed by s.59 are to be dealt with in accordance with the provisions of the Police (Retention and Disposal of Motor Vehicles) Regulations 2002 (SI 2002/3049). A seizure notice must be served as soon as reasonably practicable upon the owner or apparent owner of the vehicle, who may obtain its release on payment of charges in respect of its removal (£105) and retention (£12 per day). The charges may be waived where the use which led to the seizure was not that of the owner and where he neither knew of, consented to, or could have prevented that use.

"Constable" and "traffic warden"

6.17   Section 30 of the Police Act 1996, as amended, allows a constable and/or a special constable to act as a constable throughout England and Wales. Under ss.37 and 163 of the 1988 Act, offences arise only if the constable is in uniform; under s.35 he need not be in uniform but, if he is not, it must be proved that the defendant knew him to be a constable. On the other hand, it can be argued that the liability under s.35 is absolute, so that it is unnecessary to prove that the defendant knew a person in plain clothes to be a constable and his ignorance is no defence: cf. *Kenlin v Gardiner* [1966] 3 All E.R. 931 at 934, where it was said that, on a charge of assaulting a police officer, knowledge that he was one is not necessary.

Traffic wardens appointed under the Road Traffic Regulation Act 1984 s.95 are not constables but by virtue of the Functions of Traffic Wardens Order 1970 (SI 1970/1958) and s.96 of the 1984 Act references to a constable in ss.35 and 37 of the 1988 Act include traffic wardens. If a motorist ignores a traffic warden's direction under s.35, he can thus be prosecuted and convicted exactly as if a constable had been on duty. Moreover the traffic warden is empowered (also by virtue of the Functions of Traffic Wardens Order and s.96) to demand the offending motorist's name and address under s.165(1). The traffic warden (unlike a constable) cannot, however, demand to see the offending motorist's driving documents, as reg.3(3) only applies s.165(1) so far as it relates to "the furnishing of names and addresses". A traffic warden can demand the production of a driving licence and require in the prescribed circumstances a statement of the date of birth (see reg.3(4)) in a different context (certain functions regarding the custody of vehicles, e.g. at a car pound).

A motorist failing to comply with a traffic warden's directions and contravening s.35 is liable to have his licence endorsed (see § 6.63). **6.18**

"Engaged in the regulation of traffic"

It will be noted that offences under s.35 arise only where the constable (or traffic warden) is engaged in regulating traffic, and there is no such limitation under **6.19** s.163. The *Concise Oxford Dictionary* gives one definition of "traffic" as "coming and going of persons or goods by road", etc. This implies that for s.35 the *purpose* must be more than stopping a single vehicle even though only one vehicle may be stopped. Section 35 refers to "regulation" and to various forms of traffic while s.163 refers only to stopping when required.

"In the execution of his duty"

In both ss.35 and 163 of the 1988 Act, before an offence can be said to have **6.20** been committed, the constable must have been acting in execution of his duty. Section 35(1) explicitly so states and it was held in *R. v Waterfield* [1963] 3 All E.R. 659 that what is now s.163 does not confer statutory power on a police constable improperly to detain a vehicle where a constable would not have power under the common law to do so. *Waterfield* was distinguished in *Beard v Wood* below, also a case on what is now s.163, but was applied to what is now s.35 in *Hoffman v Thomas* [1974] R.T.R. 182 where it was held that the power of a constable to regulate traffic in execution of his duty stems from the constable's duty and right at common law to act in protection of life and property and that a constable has no right to regulate traffic for personal motives or other extraneous reason; his right and duty solely arise because of the danger to life and limb which unregulated traffic can present. The conviction under what is now s.35 of a motorist who refused to proceed to a census point in accordance with the direction of a constable who was engaged in selecting vehicles at random on a motorway and directing the selected vehicles to a census point was accordingly set aside. Conducting a traffic census is not part of a constable's duty to regulate traffic in execution of his right to protect life and property (ibid.) (but see now s.36(4) and "Census points", § 6.48). *Hoffman v Thomas* was followed in *Johnson v Phillips* [1976] R.T.R. 170, where a conviction for obstructing a police in the execution of his duty was upheld. The defendant refused to obey a constable who requested him to reverse his car the wrong way down a one-way street in order to avoid his car obstructing the removal of injured persons and the possible arrival of other ambulances. Each case depends on its own facts: a constable has no general discretion to disobey traffic regulations or to direct other persons to disobey them (ibid.). However, in accordance with the special facts of the case the constable was entitled and indeed under a duty to give such instructions if it was reasonably necessary for the protection of life and property. Refusal to obey them in these circumstances was obstructing the constable in the execution of his duty.

6.21   *Waterfield* and *Hoffman v Thomas* were distinguished as invalid exercises of the power given by what are now ss.163 and 35 in *Beard v Wood* [1980] R.T.R. 454. In that case it was stated that the police constable derives his duty as well as his power to stop vehicles from the terms of s.163 itself. It was suggested that a different conclusion might have been reached if the constable had not been acting bona fide. In *Steel v Goacher* [1983] R.T.R. 98, Griffiths L.J. at 103 doubted dicta of Ashworth J. in *Waterfield* (adopted by Wien J. in *Beard v Wood*) that what is now s.163 confers a power to stop drivers of motor vehicles. Griffiths L.J. said that nothing in s.163 gives any power to a constable to stop a motorist. Once a motorist has stopped he can, thereafter, challenge the constable's right to stop him. Griffiths L.J. pointed out however that under *Winter v Barlow* [1980] R.T.R. 209 and *Such v Ball* [1982] R.T.R. 140 the police could still proceed to administer a breath test despite a mistaken view as to the power to stop. With the assistance of *Steel v Goacher* the Divisional Court determined in *Chief Constable of Gwent v Dash* [1986] R.T.R. 41 that the random stopping of motor vehicles under what is now s.163 is permissible and is not malpractice, even though the purpose is to ascertain whether administering a breath test is justified. The suspicion of alcohol and the other justifications relate to the breath testing and not the stopping. See further §§ 4.45–7.

The powers of the constable under what is now s.163 were reviewed in the important case of *Lodwick v Sanders* [1985] 1 All E.R. 577. It was again stated that the authorities were inconsistent with the proposition that s.163 conferred upon a constable a power physically to detain a motor vehicle. It was also stated that the driver was under a duty to stop when required and having stopped was under a similar duty to remain at a standstill while the officer exercised whatever power he sought to exercise.

As to constables at census points, see § 6.48.

"Stop"

6.22   See above and § 7.09 for further cases on the meaning of "stop". It is suggested that "stop" in these sections means both "bring to a halt" and "remain at rest". The requirement to stop may be a verbal one as well as by hand signal.

Notwithstanding the reference in s.28(2) of the Road Traffic Regulation Act 1984 to starting up again after being required to stop by a school crossing patrol, it is submitted that a driver who has stopped at a constable's signal may not start again until he has been signalled or otherwise permitted to proceed. If the constable is still holding up his hand, the driver offends in the second after he has started again by not stopping; in other cases, the constable will often in fact have made a second signal to him.

The Divisional Court has stated that the offence under what is now s.35 is com- **6.23** mitted when a driver who has stopped then proceeds in defiance of a command to remain stationary (*Kentesber v Waumsley* [1980] R.T.R. 462). This does not mean that the driver has to remain stationary until ordered to proceed. Each case has to be decided on its merits. In *Kentesber v Waumsley* there was no evidence that the driver was required to remain stationary by a traffic warden and the driver was acquitted although she had proceeded after stopping.

Defences

Is it a defence that the defendant in any of the above cases never saw the **6.24** constable's signal? In *R. v Ellis* [1947] 1 W.W.R. 717, a Canadian case, it was held that a driver could not be guilty of failing to stop at a junction when "signalled" to do so by a police officer unless the signal was consciously received by him, although his failure to see it was due to the fact that he was not keeping a proper look-out in the direction in which he was going. In *R. v Barber* [1963] 3 South African L.R. 700, a defendant who had not in fact seen the constable's signal was held to have been properly acquitted, after reference to English cases including *Harding v Price* below. On the other hand, it may be thought that a signal can be made without necessarily being seen and it is no defence here that a driver failed to see a traffic sign (*Rees v Taylor* at § 6.11). It can be argued, however, that traffic signs are placed in positions where they can easily be seen and at places, such as road junctions, where a driver would expect to find them, and it is a different matter where a driver without negligence and in conditions of bad visibility fails to see a police officer's signal from a crowded footpath or in an ill-lit street. There was once no offence in like circumstances under the Pedestrian Crossings Regulations (*Leicester v Pearson* [1952] 2 All E.R. 71: see § 6.167) and the law does not call on persons to perform a duty on an event happening un- less they know that the event has happened (*Harding v Price* [1948] 1 All E.R. 283 and cases there cited: see § 7.07). Magistrates in a case reported at 119 J.P. Jo. 659 dismissed a charge of failing to stop in response to a lamp signal given by a police officer at night where the motorist had not understood the meaning of the signal. In *Keane v McSkimming* 1983 S.C.C.R. 220 the police officer's signal to stop was not recognised by the driver. The charge was dismissed on a submission of no case to answer, implying that the onus is on the prosecution. The decision was upheld on appeal by the High Court. The view is advanced at [1956] Jo.Crim.L. 192 that a defendant may be excused if he does not see a constable's signal through no fault of his own, but the onus of proving his lack of negligence lies on him. Dicta in *Harding v Price* also support this view.

See "Absolute liability of a driver", § 6.166 as to defects in the vehicle making compliance with a signal impossible.

Horse riders

The 1988 Act contains no provision requiring equestrians, mahouts and other **6.25** riders of animals to obey police signals. If an accident occurs or might occur because of a horse rider's disregard of a constable's signal, it might be that this would be obstructing the police in that an accident could be a breach of the peace (cf. *Duncan v Jones* (1936) 99 J.P. 399). Also, he might be charged, if the facts warrant, with interrupting by negligence or by misbehaviour the free passage of another person or of a vehicle (Highway Act 1835 s.78; see *Baldwin v Pearson* at § 6.257).

Traffic lights

6.26   Regulations 33–52 of the Traffic Signs Regulations and General Directions 2002 deal with light signals for traffic and pedestrians. Regulation 36(2) requires drivers passing signals to proceed with due regard for the safety of other road users and subject to the directions of any uniformed constable or other duly authorised person engaged in the regulation of traffic. For the purposes of reg.36, the expressions "vehicle" and "vehicular traffic" do not include tramcars (reg.36(3)). Traffic wardens may regulate traffic and so be duly authorised persons (see § 6.17).

    In *Joseph Eva Ltd v Reeves* [1938] 2 All E.R. 115 (a civil case) it was held that a driver who has the green light in his favour owes no duty to traffic entering a crossing in disobedience to the lights save that, if he actually sees such traffic, he must take all reasonable steps to avoid a collision. (See, however, the terms of reg.36(2).)

6.27   The 2002 Regulations exempt a vehicle from compliance with traffic lights if the vehicle is being used for "fire brigade or, in England or Wales, fire and rescue authority, ambulance, bomb or explosive disposal, national blood service or police purposes" and the observance of the red light is "likely to hinder the use of that vehicle for the purpose for which it is being used". Where for such a purpose a red light is disregarded the driver is required, in effect, to treat the red signal as a "Give Way" sign, i.e. he must not enter the road in such a manner or at such a time as to be likely to cause danger to any other driver on the road or so as to necessitate a change of course or speed by that driver in order to avoid an accident. It was held in *DPP v Harris (Nigel)* [1995] R.T.R. 100 that the driver of a vehicle being used for police purposes who failed to stop at a red traffic light could not rely on a common law defence of necessity to a charge of driving without due care and attention, since the degree of care required in such circumstances was specifically provided for by what is now reg.36(1)(b). The care due would have involved waiting for a couple of seconds at the junction or edging slowly forward, being prepared to stop if there had been a vehicle in the lane crossing the junction. The ambulance, police or fire-engine driver is further required not to endanger "any person", which expression presumably includes pedestrians, equestrians, etc. It may be observed that the regulation does not expressly require the vehicle to be an ambulance, fire-engine or police vehicle. It would seem that any vehicle comes within the exemption conferred by the regulation if the vehicle is used for fire brigade or, in England, fire and rescue authority, ambulance or police purposes and observance of the traffic lights would hinder the purpose for which the vehicle was used on that occasion.

6.28   By reg.36(1)(c) of the 2002 Regulations the amber-with-red signal shall not alter the prohibition conveyed by the red signal. By reg.36(1)(e) the amber-alone signal shall convey the same prohibition as the red signal, namely that vehicular traffic (other than tramcars) shall not proceed beyond the stop line, except that, as respects any vehicle (other than a tramcar) which is so close to the stop line that it cannot safely be stopped without proceeding beyond the stop line, it shall convey the same indication as the green signal or green arrow signal which was shown immediately before it. Regulation 10 does not provide that disobedience to the amber-alone signal is an offence against what is now s.36 of the 1988 Act. A metropolitan magistrate, however, dismissed a case under what is now s.36 of crossing on amber alone ([1959] Jo.Crim.L. 87). It is also doubtful whether there is an offence contrary to s.118 of the Road Traffic Regulation Act 1984. For the arguments see "Failing to comply with a sign", §§ 6.05–11. The driver might still be liable for careless driving. The position with regard to the amber-alone signal may be compared with the steady amber light and flashing amber light provisions in the Zebra, Pelican and Puffin Pedestrian Crossings Regulations and General Directions 1997 (see §§ 6.171–9).

Regulation 36(1)(a) of Pt I of the 2002 Regulations describes the significance of the red light as follows:

"… the red signal shall convey the prohibition that vehicular traffic shall not proceed beyond the stop line."

The prohibition on passing over the stop line applies to any part of the vehicle **6.29** when the red light is showing; if the front of a vehicle has already crossed that line when the light goes red, it is an offence under what is now s.36 for it to proceed further (*Ryan v Smith* [1967] 1 All E.R. 611).

Regulation 43(1) of the 2002 Regulations defines the term "stop line" in relation to light signals as the road marking placed on a carriageway in conjunction with those signals and further provides that where no stop line is provided or the stop line is not visible, references to the stop line in a case where the "When red lights shows wait here" sign is placed in conjunction with the light signals (e.g. at a road works) are to be treated as references to that sign, and in any other case as references to the post or other structure on which the primary signals are mounted.

Where lights have apparently stuck at red, a district justice held that a driver **6.30** who has waited a reasonable time for them to change in his favour may then proceed with caution against them ([1959] Jo.Crim.L. 222). The case was heard in the Dublin District Court. In effect the justice held that a reasonable belief that the lights had failed would be a defence. This decision was criticised in [1959] Jo.Crim.L. 222 at 224. A prosecution against a careful driver in such circumstances would rightly be condemned but he might have no defence in particular in a civil case. It is submitted that if the lights have, in fact, failed a motorist may ignore the lights because the lights, having failed, no longer comply with the regulations. The onus is, however, on the defendant to show that the lights are out of phase.

There may be problems where some of the traffic signals are working and some are not. The situation is covered to some extent by reg.43(4) which states that:

"a reference … to light signals, to the signals or to a signal of a particular colour, is, where secondary signals as well as primary signals have been placed, a reference to the light signals displayed by both the primary and secondary signals or, as the case may be, by the primary signals operating without the secondary signals or by the secondary signals operating without the primary signals."

This implies that an offence may be committed where the secondary lights are **6.31** working but the primary lights are not and vice versa. It is relevant only where secondary lights have been erected as well as primary lights. It leaves open the position where primary or secondary lights alone respectively are relied on and one of the sets is not working. The wording of reg.43(4) seems to imply that either *both* the primary signals or *both* the secondary signals must be working where there is more than one. "Primary" and "secondary signals" are defined in reg.43(5)(a) and (b). The definitions make clear that both nearside and offside signals are included as appropriate but does not help further. It may still be the case therefore that no offence is committed where reliance is on the primary lights alone or the secondary lights alone and one of them is not working. It is always possible for the other working set to be obscured or hidden from view. The offence arises from the prohibition conveyed by the red light or possibly the amber light. Subject to the comments above about the inter-relationship of the primary and secondary signals, if the relevant red light (or possibly amber light) is not working it is submitted that there can be no prohibition and no offence.

6.32   A temporary light signal for road works is, it seems, presumed to have been lawfully placed and it is not necessary to prove that it was lawfully maintained; s.67 of the Road Traffic Regulation Act 1984, relating to emergency signs, does not apply (*Woodriffe v Plowman* (1962) 60 L.G.R. 183). Regulation 35 of the 2002 Regulations requires portable light signals to be of the size, colour and type shown in diagram 3000.1 in Sch.8 to the regulations and further requires their sequence of illumination to be the same as that of permanent lights, namely red, then red and amber together, then green, then amber and so on.

If the lights are showing green for east–west traffic, magistrates are entitled to infer, unless the contrary be shown, that they are red for north–south traffic (*Wells v Woodward* (1956) 54 L.G.R. 142; *Pacitti v Copeland* 1963 S.L.T. (Notes) 52). Intermittent red signals under reg.39(1) (which are for use at automatic level crossings) convey the prohibition that a vehicle shall not proceed beyond the stop line (reg.40).

Motorway and dual carriageway traffic lights

6.33   The four intermittent red signals under reg.37(1) displayed at the side of a motorway or dual carriageway convey the prohibition that vehicular traffic shall not proceed beyond those lights. When placed over the carriageway they operate similarly on the appropriate traffic lane (reg.38(3)). Vehicles being used for "fire brigade or, in England or Wales, fire and rescue authority, ambulance or police purposes" (for the meaning of this see above) are not within reg.38 and these intermittent red lights are to have no significance to them (ibid.) (at least in law). As already indicated, it is an offence under s.36 to contravene these lights.

It is not an offence under s.36 to ignore a motorway or dual carriageway matrix sign or hazard warning (other than the light signals depicted at diagrams 6031.1 and 6032.1 conveying the requirement not to proceed beyond those signals generally or in respect of the lane below the signal as appropriate), because those signs (as prescribed in Sch.11 to the 2002 Regulations) are not included in reg.10. Proceedings may possibly arise for driving dangerously, carelessly or without consideration.

Detection of offences

6.34   Section 95A of the Highways Act 1980 empowers a highway authority in England and Wales to install, on or near a highway, structures and equipment for the detection of traffic offences. Section 40 makes similar provision for Scotland by means of the insertion of s.49A of the Roads (Scotland) Act 1984. So far as traffic light signals are concerned, the equipment takes the form of a camera which automatically photographs the rear of a motor vehicle detected by the equipment in the process of infringing the 2002 Regulations in order that it may be identified by means of its registration plate. Section 20(1) of the 1988 Offenders Act (as substituted by s.23 of the 1991 Act) enables evidence to be given in the form of a documentary record produced by the prescribed device, accompanied by a certificate as to the circumstances in which that record was produced.

The Light Signals (Detection of Offences) Devices Approval 1992 approved the Gatsometer BV Type 36 and Traffiphot IIIG Red Light Monitor devices for use. Offences of disobeying light signals at level crossings are also capable of automatic detection by photographic or other image recording equipment; see further § 6.46 below.

A device known as RedGuard, manufactured by Monitron International Ltd of Kiddderminster, Worcestershire, was approved with effect from May 20, 2003 by the Light Signals (Detection of Offences) Devices Approval (No.2) 2003 for the purpose of the detection of light signal offences. **6.35**

A device known as RedSpeed, also manufactured by Monitron International Ltd, was approved with effect from May 20, 2003 by the Road Sensors Speed Measuring and the Light Signals (Detection of Offences) Devices Approval 2003 for the purpose of the detection of both speeding offences) and red light offences.

It should be noted that consequent upon Monitron International Ltd changing its name to Redspeed International Ltd, the two machines described above were re-approved with effect from November 3, 2004.

"Stop" signs at major roads

The octagonal "Stop" sign is prescribed by diagram 601.1 in the 2002 Regula- **6.36** tions and it is an offence under reg.10 to disobey it. The sign is required to be 750, 900 or 1200mm in width (for tolerances see reg.12). By direction 36 the temporary "Stop" signs may only be used where one-way working is necessary owing to a temporary closure of a part of the width of the carriageway. By direction 17 a "Stop" sign may be used on a road only in conjunction with the road marking of solid transverse lines to indicate the position beyond which vehicles must not proceed (diagram 1002.1) and with the painted letters "Stop" on the carriageway (diagram 1022), save where road works temporarily require their removal or the "Stop" sign itself was erected temporarily because of road works. The post may be of any single colour (direction 41). The back of the sign shall be grey, black or in a non-reflective metallic finish (direction 42), but as the back of the sign is not the side designed to give the indication and guidance for which it was erected, presumably the High Court would hold that the sign would not be invalidated if it were painted a different colour (see *Sharples v Blackmore* [1973] R.T.R. 249, where it was held that a speed limit sign was not invalidated by its back not being painted grey).

The requirement of this "Stop" sign is that every vehicle shall stop before crossing the transverse line or, if that line is not clearly visible, before entering the major road and shall not proceed past that line or, if it is not clearly visible, enter the major road so as to be likely to cause danger to the driver of or any passenger in any other vehicle on the major road or to cause such a driver to change the speed or course of his vehicle so as to avoid an accident (reg.16(1) item 1).

6.37   Presumably an offence is committed if any part of the vehicle stops on or over the line or enters the major road in breach of the regulation (*Ryan v Smith* [1967] 1 All E.R. 611, at § 6.29). There must be a likelihood (and not a mere possibility) of danger to the driver and not merely to the vehicle. Many cases are based on the second part (changing speed or course, etc.). The accident avoided need not necessarily be with the vehicle entering from the minor road.

The "Stop" sign presumably requires that a vehicle subject to it be brought to a standstill; it was so held in relation to the former "Halt" sign (*Tolhurst v Webster* [1936] 3 All E.R. 1020), where it was also said that the vehicle should stop (see reg.16(1)) at the major road or line provided and not the sign itself. Justices were directed to convict where a driver had stopped at the sign and not at the major road (*Brooks v Jefferies* [1936] 3 All E.R. 232).

For a case where the word "Stop" painted on the carriageway was partially invisible, see *Skeen v Smith* at § 6.59.

"Give Way" signs

6.38   The "Give Way" sign is No.602 in the 2002 Regulations and it is an offence under reg.10 to disobey it. It is an inverted white triangle and its measurements are 600, 750, 900, 1200 or 1500mm (for tolerances see reg.12); its borders are red and the lettering black and, by reg.13, the size of the letters is proportionate. By direction 17 the "Give Way" sign may be used only in conjunction with the road marking of broken transverse lines (diagram 1003) and the triangle painted on the road (diagram 1023), save where road works temporarily require the removal of the lines and triangle. By reg.16(1) item 3 the requirement conveyed by the "Give Way" sign is that no vehicle shall cross the transverse line nearest to the major road or, if that line is not clearly visible, enter that major road so as to be likely to cause danger to the driver of or any passenger in any other vehicle or to cause such a driver to change the speed or course of his vehicle so as to avoid an accident.

As to this wording see the comments under "'Stop' signs at major roads", §§ 6.36–7. It may be noted that the regulation requires the emerging vehicle not to affect in the manner specified not only a vehicle on the nearside of the main road but also a vehicle on the far side of it.

6.39   The wording under reg.16(1) item 4 is similar where a "Give Way" sign is used at an open level crossing.

"One Way", "No Right Turn", "Access Only", etc., orders

6.40   It is submitted that disobedience to signs having effect under traffic regulations or designation orders should be prosecuted under s.5(1), s.8(1), s.53(5) or (6) of the 1984 Act and not under s.36 (see §§ 6.05–11).

Where defendants are charged under s.5, s.8, or s.53 with using a vehicle, or causing or permitting a vehicle to be used (for "using, causing or permitting", see §§ 1.161 et seq.) or for any other offence in contravention of a traffic regulation order, the defence may properly insist on production of the relevant order. If the order has not been published in accordance with regulations made under what is now Pt III of Sch.9 to the 1984 Act no offence will have been committed (*James v Cavey* [1967] 1 All E.R. 1048). If the prosecution, even after notice from the defence, omits to prove proper publication, the court should normally grant the prosecution an adjournment to do so, it is submitted, as such evidence is of a formal nature (see *Royal v Prescott-Clarke* [1966] 2 All E.R. 366 where the High Court similarly interpreted comparable regulations made under s.72(5) of the Road Traffic Regulation Act 1967 in respect of motorways).

In *Wright v Howard* [1973] R.T.R. 12 the High Court considered the effect of a **6.41** "No Right Turn" order. The relevant order prohibited motorists emerging from Turl Street, Oxford, from "making a right hand turn into" High Street (commonly called "the High"). The right-hand kerb of Turl Street was in line with the left-hand kerb of Alfred Street. The defendant therefore had to veer slightly to the right across High Street to enter Alfred Street. The Divisional Court held that no offence was committed; giving importance to the word "into" it was held that making a right turn "into" meant proceeding right "into" High Street, not virtually going straight across High Street and veering slightly right to enter Alfred Street.

Whether a person turns right (or left) is a question of fact. Justices were entitled to find as a fact that a motorist did not turn right who drove a motor car along a lane, passed "No Right Turn" signs before and at its junction with a bypass, and then turned *left* into the bypass and drove along it for some 60 yards before executing a "U" turn and returning as if he had turned *right* (*Gouldie v Pringle* [1981] R.T.R. 525).

One sign in common use is the sign prohibiting entry for motor vehicles save **6.42** for access. Reference should in all cases be made to the relevant order as under many orders the access must be to adjacent premises. Under such an order a magistrates' court has convicted a person who entered to park in the road, and who did not visit any adjoining premises.

"Keep Left" signs and arrows

It is an offence under what is now s.36 of the 1988 Act by virtue of reg.10 of **6.43** the 2002 Regulations to disobey the white arrow on a blue circle, with white border (diagram 606—proceed in direction indicated by arrow), the right-angled white arrow on a blue circle, with white border (diagram 609—vehicular traffic must turn left or right) and the diagonal white arrow on a blue circle, with white border (diagram 610—keep left or right). The dimensions are 270, 300, 450, 600, 750, 900, 1200 or 1500mm (for diagrams 606 and 610) and 450, 600, 750, 900 or 1200mm for diagram 609 (as to variations see reg.12(1)). Sign 606 may be used only on the central island of roundabouts, with the dual-carriageway sign (diagram 608) or to indicate the effect of an order, regulation, byelaw or notice (direction 7). The illumination of signs 606 and 610 is prescribed by reg.18(1) and Sch.17. By reg.19(2) both signs must otherwise be illuminated by reflecting material.

A roundabout bore a "Keep Left" sign but a motorist approaching made a "U" **6.44** turn in the road 62ft short of it. It was held that in those circumstances he had not committed an offence of disobeying the sign (*Brazier v Alabaster* [1962] Crim. L.R. 173). Semble, if he had been very close to the sign, he would have had to obey it and go round the roundabout in order to turn back.

Automatic level crossings

The sign requiring drivers of abnormally large or slow vehicles (abnormal **6.45** transport units) to telephone the railway signalman to obtain permission to cross at automatic railway level crossings is diagram 784.1 and is governed by reg.16(1) item 6 of the regulations. The person who must telephone is the actual driver of the vehicle; if there is more than one driver, the driver of the foremost vehicle forming part of the vehicle must telephone. The railway signalman can impose terms on the driver before allowing the vehicle to cross and if the terms are not complied with the regulation is contravened (reg.16(1) item 6(c)). Note the proviso at the end of the regulation which requires a driver who does not receive an answer to try for not less than two minutes to telephone the signalman unless the line is dead and only to cross the crossing during the times shown near the telephone during which trains do not normally travel. If no such times are exhibited, the driver has no alternative but to wait until the signalman answers the telephone and gives him permission to cross.

"Abnormal transport units" are defined as motor vehicles or vehicle combinations which, inclusive of any load, 61ft 6in. (18.75m) in length or 9ft 6in. (2.9m) in width or with a maximum gross weight exceeding 44 tonnes, or which are incapable of proceeding or unlikely to proceed over such crossings faster than 5mph.

6.46   The approaches to many railway level crossings (whether or not they are automatic) are marked by double white lines. These double white lines are not part of the signs of an automatic level crossing. Regulation 26 governs all double white lines whether at railway level crossings or elsewhere, and prosecutions for failing to conform to double white lines at level crossings will be by virtue of that regulation and not reg.16. Similarly a driver who disobeys the red lights at the automatic level crossing will contravene reg.40 and not reg.16: the offence is contrary to s.36. The red lights consist of two horizontal red lights with an amber light below the centre point between the two red lights. The sequence of lights (amber followed by red), the flashing of the red lights (one must be on while the other is off), the rate of flashing and dimensions are set out in reg.39(1), (2).

The Light Signals (Detection of Offences) Devices Approval 1999 approved two devices for use for the purpose of detection of offences specified in s.20(2)(e) of the 1988 Offenders Act: Interface for railway level crossing signals, manufactured by Peek Traffic Ltd, for use only with the CE approved version of the Traffiphot IIIG Red Light Monitor; and Interface for railway level crossing signals, manufactured by B.I.C. Electronics Ltd, for use only with the CE approved version of the Gatsometer BV Type 36. As may be deduced from the wording of the approval, these new interfaces when used in conjunction with equipment previously approved for use at traffic light signals have the effect of facilitating the automatic detection of offences committed in respect of light signals at automatic level crossings.

6.47   The Light Signals (Detection of Offences) Devices Approval (No.3) 2003 approved a device named the "Level Crossing Camera", manufactured by Peek Traffic Ltd, for use with effect from November 1, 2003 for the purpose of the detection of light signal offences, but only when used with the CE approved version of the Traffiphot IIIG Red Light Monitor.

Census points

6.48   Section 22A of the 1972 Act (now s.36(4) of the 1988 Act) was passed as a result of the decision in *Hoffman v Thomas* [1974] R.T.R. 182 (see § 6.20) where it was held that a constable was not acting in execution of his duty of regulating traffic in selecting vehicles at random from a motorway to go to a census point. A motorist who refused to comply with the constable's signal directing him to stop and proceed to the census point was not guilty of an offence under what is now s.36 of the 1988 Act. It was also held that the sign "Stop at Census Point" was informatory only in its effect, and non-compliance with it could also not give rise to an offence contrary to s.36.

Section 36(4) reverses the decision of *Hoffman v Thomas*. The census signs (830, 830.1, 831: "Stop at Census Point", "Census Stop If Directed", and "Slow— Census Point") now appear to be mandatory by virtue of s.36(4). It is also made an offence by s.35(2) to fail to comply with traffic directions given by a constable for the purpose of a traffic census. The section gives a wide definition of a "traffic direction" for this purpose and provides that a motorist commits an offence not only if he neglects or refuses to stop or make the vehicle proceed in, or keep to, a particular line of traffic as directed but also if he fails "to proceed to a particular point". Parliament was anxious that motorists should not be compelled to give census information and that any information should only be given voluntarily. Not only is it not an offence to refuse to supply information for the purposes of a survey (see definition of "traffic direction" in s.35(2)(b)), but also the power to give a traffic direction must, in accordance with s.35(3), be exercised so as not to cause unreasonable delay to a person who indicates he is unwilling to participate in the census. Nevertheless it would seem that a motorist who is unwilling to participate in the census must comply with traffic directions unless and until he indicates he is unwilling to furnish information. On the other hand it would seem that a constable will not be acting in execution of his duty and a conviction under s.35 will be set aside if the power to give a traffic direction is exercised in contravention of s.35(3). Although a traffic direction for the purpose of a traffic census is treated as a direction by a police constable in the execution of his duty, a constable may not be said to be acting in execution of his duty if he acts in contravention of the wishes of Parliament as enacted in s.35(3).

Contravention of a traffic direction for the purpose of a traffic census or of the sign is an offence contrary to s.35 or s.36 as appropriate and is punishable accordingly. **6.49**

The census signs (diagrams 830, 830.1, 831 and 832) may be used only for a traffic census approved by the highway authority and the chief constable and approved by or on behalf of the Secretary of State for Transport (direction 39(6)).

Other signs

A portable sign of an authorised nature requiring a vehicle to stop must be obeyed although the person using it is not a police officer in uniform (*Langley Cartage Co v Jenks* [1937] 2 All E.R. 525). Such signs are now only the round red "Stop" signs used at road works (diagram 7023 in the 2002 Regulations). Sign 7023 may be used only where one-way driving is necessary owing to temporary closure of part of the width of the carriageway of the road (direction 39(1)). **6.50**

White lines and double white lines

By the Road Traffic Regulation Act 1984 s.64, lines or marks on roads may be **6.51** traffic signs if they indicate a warning, prohibition, restriction or requirement prescribed or authorised under s.64. It had been held previously in *Evans v Cross* [1938] 1 All E.R. 751 that a white line on a bend or down the centre of a road was not a traffic sign. Single white lines, if disobeyed, create no offence under s.36 of the 1988 Act, although a charge of careless driving may be justified for a central white line (see *Bensley v Smith* and *R. v Warwickshire Police Ex p. Manjit Singh Mundi* at § 5.50), but reg.25(2) specifically provides that the transverse lines at the mouth of a minor road (diagram 1003), where it enters a major road, whether or not used with the "Give Way" sign (602), create the requirement that no vehicle shall pass them into the major road in such a manner or at such a time as is likely to cause danger to a vehicle on the major road or to cause it to change speed or course to avoid it. A driver who disobeys this requirement seemingly offends against s.36, since reg.10 now specifically applies s.36 to that road marking (diagram 1003).

Double white lines

6.52　　Regulation 26 of the 2002 Regulations deals with the double white lines (diagrams 1013.1 and 1013.3). Double white lines consist either of two continuous white lines or one continuous white line together with a broken white line. Two continuous white lines require vehicles in either direction at all times to keep to the nearside of the nearest continuous line, and a broken line with a continuous white line requires a vehicle to keep to the nearside of the continuous white line when the continuous white line is the nearer of the two lines to his vehicle. In diagram 1013.1 five different methods of marking are indicated. The second of the five consists of two continuous white lines with hatching between them. It is not always appreciated that the double white line regulation (and thus s.36) applies to them. See below, however, as to the need for an approach arrow.

Regulation 10 applies so that contravention of the requirements of reg.26(2) becomes an offence contrary to what is now s.36.

6.53　　It is an offence to stop on *either* side of a road within a double white line system, whether the lines are both continuous or only one of the two lines is continuous. It is also a requirement that the driver must keep his moving vehicle in a position on a road governed by a double white line system so that at all times the offside of the vehicle is on the nearside of the white lines while both white lines are continuous or where the nearside white line is continuous and the offside line is broken. On the other hand if the broken line of a double white line is nearest to the vehicle viewed in the direction of travel, the double line may be crossed if it is seen to be safe to do so (reg.26(7)); if it was crossed when unsafe, the charge should not be under s.36, for reg.10 does not apply to breach of reg.26(7), but careless driving. Stopping is permitted by reg.26(3)–(5) to enable a person to board or alight from the vehicle or to load or unload goods, for building operations, road and public utility works, for vehicles used for fire or, in England or Wales, fire and rescue authority, ambulance or police purposes (as to this see the comments at §§ 6.26 et seq. as to the traffic lights exemption), for pedal cycles without side-cars, whether or not auto-assisted, for exigencies of traffic, to avoid an accident or with the permission of a constable in uniform or when directed by a traffic warden. It is an offence to drive on the wrong side of double white lines when both lines are continuous or only the nearside is continuous even if it is perfectly safe to do so.

Defences are set out in reg.26(6). These allow a vehicle to cross or straddle the **6.54** continuous line in order to obtain access to side roads or land or premises adjoining the road; to pass a stationary vehicle; to avoid an accident or in circumstances beyond the driver's control; to pass a road maintenance vehicle moving at a speed not exceeding 10mph; to pass a pedal cycle moving at a speed not exceeding 10mph; to pass a horse that is being ridden or led at a speed not exceeding 10mph; or to comply with the direction of a uniformed police constable or traffic warden. In *R. v Blything (Suffolk) JJ. Ex p. Knight* [1970] R.T.R. 218 the justices were advised by their clerk that what is now reg.26(6) only gave a defence where the vehicle actually crossed or straddled the white lines and therefore the defendant, who was on the offside of the road before the double white lines began, could not avail himself of the defence contained in the regulations. It was held that this was wrong and that "crossing or straddling" did not have this restricted meaning. On the facts the Divisional Court held that the defendant, who had commenced overtaking two vehicles before the double white lines, could not have a defence under what is now reg.26(6). *R. v Blything* was explained in the unreported case of *Hillyer v Hooper* heard in the Divisional Court on March 20, 1984. It was held in the latter case that the position depended on the facts as to whether the act or omission of a third party or parties enabled the person to bring himself within the defence of circumstances beyond the driver's control. The decision in *Blything* was that where in the circumstances a man chose to overtake and then for one reason or another—connected with the ordinary experience in the course of driving vehicles on the highway—found it impossible to get back, that was not a statutory defence.

The lines must, by reg.11(1), be white and, by reg.31(3), illuminated by reflecting material and studs incorporating reflectors between the two lines. The variations in dimensions allowed by reg.12 apply.

The lines must comply with the regulations and if they do not a person **6.55** contravening them commits no offence even if the lines are readily recognisable as double white lines (*Davies v Heatley* [1971] R.T.R. 145, where the lines were not in accordance with diagram 1013 under the 1964 Regulations in so far as an intermittent white line had been placed between two continuous white lines and the continuous lines were too far apart). In *Walton v Hawkins* [1973] R.T.R. 366 it was held that diagram 1013 of the 1964 Regulations was not one unit but consisted of three separate markings each having a different purpose and the sequence in which they were imposed was a matter for the highway authority to suit the requirements of the road in question. *Aliter*, seemingly, if the markings or the arrows have been correctly marked even though they are partially invisible (cf. *Skeen v Smith* at § 6.59), providing their meaning is clear.

A trivial departure from the requirements of regulations will not however provide immunity from prosecution (*Cotterill v Chapman* [1984] R.T.R. 73). In that case for some 30m distance the gap between the double white lines was 87mm instead of the 90mm minimum. The error had arisen following repainting.

Under the 2002 Regulations a warning arrow (diagram 1014) is mandatory **6.56** (see direction 48). More than one (in line) is permissible. No approach distance is specified. The proposition in the fourteenth edition that a prosecution for a failure to comply with a double white line system should fail if there is no warning arrow received judicial support in the Divisional Court case of *O'Halloran v DPP* [1990] R.T.R. 62. Direction 42 of Pt II of the Traffic Signs Regulations and

General Directions 1981 (SI 1981/859) was mandatory, and accordingly a system of double white lines which did not include an arrow preceding it was not a system lawfully placed. The justices' conclusion that although the warning arrows were mandatory at a sequence of double white lines, what was then direction 42 of the 1981 Regulations did not require arrows at every series of double solid white lines was erroneous, and the appellant's conviction had to be quashed.

Non-conforming and damaged signs

6.57   The colours, sizes, dimensions, proportions and forms of letters and numerals are dealt with by regs 11–14, illumination of signs by regs 18–21 and Sch.17, and the variations by reg.12. The dimensions of all signs are metricated.

All existing permanent regulatory signs under the 1994 and 1981 Regulations are preserved until divers dates by reg.3(2).

6.58   Where a "no waiting" order or other traffic regulation order, e.g. a clearway, has been made, normally it must be indicated by traffic signs which conform with the 2002 Regulations, even though the local authority have a discretion whether to erect such signs. If it is not so indicated or the signs do not conform, *MacLeod v Hamilton* 1965 S.L.T. 305 seems to be authority for the proposition that there might be no offence against the order. In *Power v Davidson* [1964] Crim. L.R. 781 it was held in relation to former push button pedestrian crossing regulations of 1954 that where the studs were not in compliance with the regulations no offence was committed. *Davies v Heatley* [1971] R.T.R. 145 is authority for the proposition that, because by s.64(2) of the Road Traffic Regulation Act 1984 traffic signs shall be of the size, colour and type prescribed by regulation, if a sign the contravention of which is an offence contrary to s.36 is not as prescribed by the regulation, no offence is committed if the sign is contravened even if the sign is clearly recognisable to a reasonable man as a sign of that kind (but see *Sharples v Blackmore* below). The facts of *Davies v Heatley* were that a single intermittent line had originally been placed in the centre of the road. Double white lines were subsequently placed on the road but the intermittent line was insufficiently defaced. Although the court might possibly have been able to hold that the old line could be subtracted from the existing double lines and thus form no part of them, in any event the existing double lines were more widely spread than was permitted by the regulation.

A trivial departure, however, from the regulation requirements will not provide immunity from prosecution (see *Cotterill v Chapman* [1984] R.T.R. 73 under "Double white lines", §§ 6.52–6). *Cotterill v Chapman* was applied in *Canadine v DPP* [2007] EWHC 383 when holding that the fact that the black casing around an illuminated speed limit sign was visible on close frontal examination did not render it non-prescribed in accordance with s.64(1) of the 1984 Act. There was no question of road users being misled or misinformed, and any deviation from the prescribed form was so minor that it fell to be disregarded under the de minimis principle.

6.59   In *Skeen v Smith* 1979 S.L.T. 295 the "Stop" sign on the pole was in order, but the word "Stop" painted on the road was not fully visible. The Appeal Court directed the magistrates to convict. This was not a case of an initial and continuing failure to comply with the regulations: the markings had been in order at one time and were still partially visible.

In *Sharples v Blackmore* [1973] R.T.R. 249 the Divisional Court held that the colour of the back of a speed limit sign was immaterial as it was the front of the sign which of course conveyed the warnings to the motorist. Where, therefore, a speed limit sign's back was painted black instead of grey, the sign was nevertheless held to be a sign prescribed under the Traffic Signs (Speed Limits) Regulations and General Directions 1969 (SI 1969/1487). It would seem that a sign not complying with direction 42 of the 2002 Directions which requires the back of signs to be grey or black or in a non-reflective metallic finish (or black in the case of signs mounted on traffic lights) would, following *Sharples v Blackmore*, be held to comply with the 2002 Regulations and Directions, where the back of the sign is immaterial for its purpose of regulating traffic. *R. v Priest* (1961) 35 C.R. 31, a decision of the Ontario Court of Appeal that a non-conforming stop sign was binding on the driver providing he could have seen it if he was keeping a proper look-out, was distinguished in *Davies v Heatley* above on the ground that the Canadian legislation did not make it an offence to comply with a "prescribed stop sign" but only with a stop sign.

SIGNS AND SIGNALS: PROCEEDINGS AND PENALTIES

Warning of intended prosecution

Warning of intended prosecution (see Chapter 2) is required for all offences **6.60** under ss.35, 36 of the 1988 Act (1988 Offenders Act s.1 and Sch.1), whether committed by the driver of a motor vehicle or by the rider or propeller of any other type of vehicle, including pedal cyclists and tricyclists, or by the driver of a horse-drawn vehicle, unless s.2(1) of the 1988 Offenders Act applies in the particular case. In *Walton v Hawkins* [1973] R.T.R. 366 at 369, it was argued that the notice of intended prosecution did not comply with the statutory requirements in that the failure to observe double white lines according to the notice occurred south of a junction when in fact the road ran east and west; this contention was abandoned by the appellant with the approval of the court as the appellant had not been prejudiced by the error (following *Pope v Clarke* [1953] 2 All E.R. 704).

Proceedings generally

An information under what is now s.35 is not bad because it uses the word **6.61** "fail" instead of "neglect" (*Pontin v Price* (1933) 97 J.P. 315).

Where a court has taken into consideration disobedience to traffic signs on convicting for dangerous or careless driving, the conviction would seem to be a bar to further proceedings under s.36 (cf. *Welton v Taneborne* (1908) 72 J.P. 419) but it would be otherwise if there had been an acquittal under s.2 or s.3. See § 5.76 as to convicting for both offences.

Penalties

A table of penalties for offences involving traffic signs and signals is set out at **6.62** § 6.65 below.

It should be noted that the phrase "traffic red light signals" which appears in the table includes motorway flashing red lights, the flashing red lights at automatic level crossings and the portable red lights at road works. The phrase "double white lines" includes any contravention of double white lines, whether by stopping within the system or driving a vehicle on the wrong side of double lines or the wrong side of a continuous line if it is on the nearside of the road.

6.63   The decision in *Rumbles v Poole* [1980] R.T.R. 449 that a motorist convicted of failing to conform to a traffic warden's directions does not commit an endorsable offence has been reversed, as what is now column 5 of Sch.2 to the 1988 Offenders Act includes reference to "traffic warden" as well as "constable" in relation to s.35 offences.

It should further be noted that s.27 of the Road Safety Act 2006 (amending Sch.2 to the 1988 Offenders Act) increases the maximum fine for a s.163 offence involving a motor vehicle from level 3 on the standard scale to level 5. The new penalty applies to offences committed on or after September 24, 2007.

Sentencing guidelines

6.64   On August 4, 2008, new Magistrates' Court Sentencing Guidelines became effective; the revised guidelines are summarised in § 18.05 below and the guidelines for road traffic offences are set out in Appendix 3 below. The full text can be found at *http://www.sentencing-guidelines.gov.uk* [accessed March 31, 2009]. The Magistrates' Court Sentencing Guidelines include guidelines relating to offences of failing to comply with traffic signs and signals (see p.1250 below). With the exception of the guideline for Fail to stop when required by police constable (Band B), the starting point is a Band A fine.

Signs and signals: penalties

Offence	Mode of trial	Section *	Imprisonment	Level of fine	Disqualification	Penalty points	Endorsement code	Sentencing guideline †
Traffic red light signals	Summary	s.36	—	3	Discretionary	3	TS10	Fine band A
Traffic light green arrows	Summary	s.36	—	3	Discretionary	3	TS10	Fine band A
Double white lines	Summary	s.36	—	3	Discretionary	3	TS20	Fine band A
"Stop" sign	Summary	s.36	—	3	Discretionary	3	TS30	Fine band A
Disobeying police constable directing traffic	Summary	s.35	—	3	Discretionary	3	TS40	Fine band A
"No entry" sign	Summary	s.36	—	3	Discretionary	3	TS50	Fine band A
Mandatory height restrictions	Summary	s.36	—	3	Discretionary	3	TS50	Fine band A
"Give way" sign, "Keep left" signs and temporary traffic signs	Summary	s.36	—	3	—	—	—	Fine band A
Failing to stop for police constable	Summary	s.163	—	5	—	—	—	Fine band B
Pedestrian disobeying police constable	Summary	s.37	—	3	—	—	—	—

Offence	Mode of trial	Section *	Imprisonment	Level of fine	Disqualification	Penalty points	Endorsement code	Sentencing guideline †
Large or slow vehicle not obtaining level crossing permission	Summary	s.36	—	3	Discretionary	3	TS50	—
Contraventions of traffic regulation	Summary	ss.5, 8, 53 RTRA 1984	—	3	—	—	—	—

* Road Traffic Act 1988 unless otherwise specified.
† **Note**: Fine bands "A", "B" and "C" represent respectively 50%, 100% and 150% of relevant weekly income. A timely guilty plea should attract a discount. See Appendix 3.

SPEED LIMITS

Generally

Offences of exceeding the speed limit are contained in the Road Traffic Regula- **6.66**
tion Act 1984 and fall into four classes, namely:

(a) exceeding the limit on a road restricted to 20, 30, 40 or 50mph;

(b) exceeding the temporary limits of 70, 60 and 50mph on roads other than motorways;

(c) exceeding on any road the limit applicable to the class of vehicle; and

(d) exceeding the limits of speed applicable to motorways only.

Heavy lorries, for example, are subject to speed limits under all four; ordinary passenger motor cars and motor cycles with pneumatic tyres, not drawing trailers, are subject to a limit only on a restricted road and to the overall maxima of 70mph on dual-carriageway roads and motorways, 60mph on single-carriageway roads, or such lesser speed as may be specified in respect of certain specified stretches of road under the Temporary Speed Limit Order.

The limit of 30mph on restricted roads is imposed by the Road Traffic Regula- **6.67**
tion Act 1984 s.81; s.84 of that Act allows the proper authorities to fix other speed limits for designated roads in all areas. The Road Traffic Regulation Act 1984 (Amendment) Order 1999 (SI 1999/1608) removes, from the orders for which the consent of the Secretary of State would otherwise be required by para.13 or 14 of Sch.9 to the Road Traffic Regulation Act 1984, any order made under s.84 of that Act which contains a provision applying to any road a speed limit of 20mph.

The Road Traffic Regulation Act 1984 s.88, authorises certain temporary or experimental speed limits and minimum speed limits on specified roads. Temporary speed limit orders made under s.88 can be made in respect of all types of road other than motorways (s.88(6)). A temporary speed restriction may also be imposed under the Road Traffic Regulation Act 1984 s.14, where a speed restriction is required because of roadworks.

The offences in relation to the class of vehicle on all roads and on motorways **6.68**
fall under the Road Traffic Regulation Act 1984 s.86, and the limits for the various classes are indicated in Sch.6 to the 1984 Act.

There may also be some speed limits of local application, e.g. in Royal Parks. Section 199(4) of the Port of London Act 1968 has the effect of imposing a speed limit of 30mph on all vehicles in the Port of London Authority area.

Offences of contravening speed limits are punishable under s.89 of the Road Traffic Regulation Act 1984 and Sch.2 to the Road Traffic Offenders Act 1988, except that contravening a motorway speed limit (other than the motorway speed limits for special classes of vehicle) is punishable under s.17(4) of the 1984 Act and Sch.2 to the 1988 Offenders Act; offences against orders under s.88(1)(b) imposing minimum speed limits are punishable under s.88(7) of the 1984 Act and Sch.2 to the 1988 Offenders Act and offences against s.14 of the 1984 Act (temporary speed restrictions for road works, etc.) are punishable under s.16(1) of the 1984 Act and Sch.2 to the 1988 Offenders Act.

The four classes of offences are considered in more detail at §§ 6.103–9 after **6.69**
evidential matters, and the proceedings and penalties for the offences will be found at §§ 6.139–43.

Application

6.70   Section 141A of the Road Traffic Regulation Act 1984 allows the Secretary of State to apply provisions of that Act to tramcars and trolley vehicles. The Tramcars and Trolley Vehicles (Modifications of Enactments) Regulations 1992 (SI 1992/1217) apply speed limits and restrictions to such vehicles. Speed limits under the above sections apply only on roads (as defined in Chapter 1). Save as mentioned at §§ 6.71–3, the limits apply to vehicles of the Crown and visiting forces.

Exemptions

6.71   Vehicles being used for fire and rescue authority, ambulance or police purposes are not subject to any speed limit either on a restricted road or by virtue of their class if observance of the limit would be likely to hinder their use for the purpose for which they are being used on that occasion (Road Traffic Regulation Act 1984 s.87), but are otherwise not exempt from any speed limit. A private person who is trailing a police car with a view to obtaining evidence to prosecute its driver for speeding cannot plead what is now s.87 as a defence (*Strathern v Gladstone* 1937 S.L.T. 62). If, in a particular case and a particular set of special circumstances, it is established that, solely in order to enable a police purpose to be performed, or solely to ensure that a police purpose requiring to be performed is not frustrated, use must be made of a vehicle and the use being made of it would be hindered by observance of the provisions restricting the speed at which vehicles can travel, then in such circumstances what is now s.87 excuses the offence of travelling too fast (*Aitken v Yarwood* [1964] 2 All E.R. 537). In that case, the car taking a police officer to court to give evidence broke down and it was held that in those circumstances he was entitled to exceed the limit in order to get to court in time. Normally, however, a constable should start for court in time to get there without exceeding the limit and it would only be in unforeseen circumstances, e.g. a breakdown or stopping to give first aid at an accident, that he would be entitled to exceed the limit. Like considerations apply to fire and rescue authority and ambulance vehicles; they may exceed the limit only if it would hinder the relevant use on the particular occasion, e.g. the chief fire officer in his car must obviously get to the fire as quickly as possible but there is no need to hurry home on going off duty. Semble a car taking a casualty to hospital in an urgent case is being used for ambulance purposes but it is doubtful if a doctor hurrying to an urgent case is using his car for ambulance purposes; an ambulance, according to the *Oxford Dictionary*, is a vehicle for taking sick or injured people to or from hospital.

It was stated obiter in *DPP v Milton* [2006] EWHC 242; [2006] R.T.R. 21 that it was not necessarily the case that a police officer who drove at grossly excessive speeds could not possibly come within the exemption for police purposes, save when in hot pursuit of a dangerous criminal. It was a matter of fact and degree for the tribunal of fact (see further § 5.09).

6.72   The Motor Vehicles (Variation of Speed Limit) Regulations 1947 (SR & O 1947/2192), as amended, provide that what is now Sch.6 to the 1984 Act shall have effect as though it imposed no speed limits in relation to certain types of vehicles owned by the Secretary of State for Defence and used for naval, military or air force purposes or which are so used whilst being driven by persons subject to the orders of a member of the armed forces of the Crown. There is a similar exemption (by the 1954 Regulations) for like vehicles in the service of a visiting force (see § 2.30). The types of vehicles so exempted are ones constructed or adapted for combative purposes or training in connection therewith, for conveyance of personnel, for use with or to carry or draw guns and machine guns, certain track-laying vehicles, fire tenders and ambulances. Vehicles used for salvage purposes pursuant to Pt IX of the Merchant Shipping Act 1894 are also exempt from Sch.6 under the 1947 Regulations and so are vehicles used in the conduct of experiments or trials for road improvements (see Pt IV, para.1 of Sch.6).

6.73 The 1947 Regulations only exempt the vehicles referred to therein from the provisions of Sch.6. The regulations do not confer exemption on these vehicles in respect of roads subject to restricted speeds. Section 87 would seem to confer exemption from such restrictions in respect of service ambulances and fire and rescue authority vehicles, and (possibly) service police vehicles if it can be argued that military, naval or air force police purposes come within "police purposes" in s.87.

It should be noted that s.19 of the Road Safety Act 2006 (if and when in force) replaces s.87 of the 1984 Act with new provisions enabling the Secretary of State to prescribe, by regulations, other purposes (in addition to the familiar fire and rescue authority, ambulance or police or Serious Organised Crime Agency purposes) for which vehicles may be exempt from speed limits. Any such exemption will not apply unless the driver concerned has successfully completed a course of training in the driving of vehicles at high speed, or is driving as part of such a course.

Defence of necessity

6.74 A passenger in a car being driven on a motorway suddenly cried out in pain. The driver, fearful for the health of his passenger, drove at a speed in excess of 100mph to the nearest service station (his mobile phone being inoperative at the time due to a run down battery). When he got there, the passenger told him that he had suffered an attack of cramp. The driver was charged with speeding and, despite pleading necessity, was convicted. He appealed to the High Court of Justiciary (*Moss v Howdle* 1997 S.L.T. 782). The court referred to a number of decisions, including *R. v Conway* [1989] R.T.R. 35 (§ 5.82), *R. v Willer* [1987] R.T.R. 22 (§ 5.81) and *R. v Martin* [1989] R.T.R. 63 (§ 5.83) in satisfying itself that the defence of necessity (or coercion or duress) was applicable to road traffic offences. It further ruled that such a defence was not limited to occasions caused by deliberate threats from a third party, but might include a contingency such as natural disaster or illness; also the defence was available where the threatened danger was not to the accused but to another person, in this case his passenger. However, as in English law (cf. *R. v Conway*) the defence was not available where the circumstances did not constrain the accused to act in breach of the law. In this case, the driver had an alternative to driving at speed to the nearest service station; he could (and should) have driven on to the hard shoulder and inquired what was troubling his passenger. Had he taken that alternative course of action, he would have discovered that there was no need for driving on at excessive speed. His appeal was accordingly dismissed.

Driving at a dangerous speed

6.75 Dangerous driving under what is now s.2 of the 1988 Act and promoting or taking part in a race or speed trial between motor vehicles (1988 Act s.12) are dealt with in Chapter 5. (It may be noted here in passing that the High Court of Justiciary in Scotland would appear to have come perilously close to recreating the offence of driving at a dangerous speed in non-statutory form by its decisions in *Trippick v Orr* (1994) 1995 S.L.T. 272, *McQueen v Buchanan* (1996) 1997 S.L.T. 765 and *Howdle v O'Connor* (1997) 1998 S.L.T. 94; see further §§ 5.07–8 above.)

Evidence and corroboration

6.76   By the Road Traffic Regulation Act 1984 s.89(2), a person prosecuted for driving a motor vehicle at a speed exceeding the limit imposed by or under any enactment shall not be convicted solely on the evidence of one witness to the effect that, in the opinion of the witness, the defendant was driving at a speed exceeding that limit. A like provision applies to offences of not attaining minimum speed limits (1984 Act s.88(7)).

These corroboration requirements do not apply to motorway speeding offences contrary to s.17(4) of the 1984 Act (overall speed limit on motorways) as s.17(2) is specifically excluded from the effects of s.89 by s.89(3) but they do apply to the motorway speed limits for special classes.

6.77   The corroborative witness must speak as to speeding at the same moment of time as the first witness, so one police officer who saw the defendant on one part of the road did not corroborate another who saw him some moments later at a place further along the same road (*Brighty v Pearson* [1938] 4 All E.R. 127). Corroboration is usually provided nowadays by the speedometer of a police vehicle, radar equipment, or Vascar or by the speed testing device being used. In *Nicholas v Penny* [1950] 2 All E.R. 89 it was held that a person could be convicted on the evidence of one police officer supported by evidence by him of the reading of a speedometer or other mechanical means, even though there was no evidence that the speedometer had been tested. In that case the defendant was said to be going 10mph in excess of the limit and the court commented on the amount of the excess; had the speed been only, say, 2mph in excess of the limit, they might have called for evidence of the accuracy of the speedometer. In any case, it is in the discretion of the magistrates to accept or reject evidence tendered in speeding as in all other cases. Applying *Nicholas v Penny* it was held in *Swain v Gillett* [1974] R.T.R. 446 that for the purposes of s.89(2) a speedometer reading was capable of amounting to corroboration of a police officer's opinion evidence about the speed of a vehicle without proof of testing of the accuracy of the speedometer. The magistrates, who had dismissed a case of speeding on accepting a submission of no case to answer on the ground that the officer's evidence as to speeding was not corroborated by a speedometer for which no evidence as to its accuracy had been produced, were directed to continue the hearing of the case.

Similarly a radar gun reading can amount to reliable or proper corroboration of the opinion of a police officer even though the gun has not been checked against the known speed of a vehicle fitted with a calibrated speedometer (*Collinson v Mabbott*, *The Times*, October 6, 1984). The principles established by *Nicholas v Penny* and *Swain v Gillett* above were also applied by the Divisional Court in *Darby v DPP* [1995] R.T.R. 294 when holding that the police constable's evidence as to the speed of a vehicle was capable of being corroborated by a technical device (the GR Speedman speed trap), the accuracy of which had not been proved. The still photographs produced by a Laser LT1 20/20 speed measuring device are capable of corroborating a police officer's opinion as to the defendant's speed: *Barber v DPP* [2006] EWHC 3137; [2007] R.T.R. 25. This case also confirmed that an officer who had four years' experience using this device could give expert evidence as to how the word "Timeout" might affect the validity of the stills produced in evidence (it was, said the officer on oath, not an indication of any error in the operation of the device).

In the light of the decision of the High Court of Justiciary in *Hogg v MacNeill*   **6.78** (2000) 2001 S.L.T. 873, it may be necessary in certain circumstances where an offence of speeding is alleged for the prosecution to adduce admissible evidence that the marked out distance on a road used for calibrating speed measuring equipment was indeed the exact distance it was indicated to be, particularly where that marked out distance was used to check the accuracy both of police vehicle speedometers and of Vascar-type equipment (see § 6.95). In such a case any error in the marking of the fixed distance would not necessarily come to light as it would be a common factor in the calibration of each of the devices. Since in the case in point the distance between the two painted marks on the road had not been shown to have been measured as being half a mile, the fact that it was half a mile could not be inferred from past use of that marked distance when calibrating other equipment or speedometers.

Factual evidence, such as skid marks and damage sustained by a vehicle, may amount to corroboration sufficient to justify a conviction for speeding based upon the opinion of a single police officer. The Divisional Court so held in *Crossland v DPP* [1988] 3 All E.R. 712, a case in which the evidence for the prosecution amounted to a reconstruction of an incident drawn from objectively determinable phenomena, namely tyre burns, skid marks and damage to the vehicle driven by the defendant. The court indicated that it would be good practice if, as had happened in the case under consideration, the prosecution alerted the defence to the fact that speed had been calculated from observations and measurements of skid marks and made disclosure of the details of any calculations made therefrom. A certificate that the decision involved a point of law of general public importance was granted, but leave to appeal was refused.

The evidence of two police officers independently forming an opinion about   **6.79** the speed of an offending vehicle is sufficient as a matter of law to constitute corroboration as required by s.89(2), but it is for the magistrates as a tribunal of fact to consider how much weight should be attached to the evidence adduced.

In *Houston v Leslie* 1958 S.L.T. 109, a variation between the evidence of two constables as to the vehicle's position behind another vehicle was held enough to justify a doubt as to the proving of the case, on its particular facts. In *Gillespie v Macmillan* 1957 S.L.T. 283, a conviction was upheld where a constable, on a measured length of road, had started a stopwatch when a car passed; another constable further along the same length had started his watch when the car passed him and, on the watches being stopped when the car was stopped, a comparison of the two watches showed a speed of 52mph.

Speed check equipment

The general approach to the use of speed check equipment is indicated by the   **6.80** comments of Ormrod J. in *Kent v Stamps* [1982] R.T.R. 273 at 278 in relation to the Truvelo electronic trip wire equipment.

"The basic principle must be that the reading on the machine is evidence. It is very cogent evidence indeed, and in the vast majority of cases one would suppose that it was conclusive evidence. But we have not reached the stage when the reading on such a piece of apparatus as this has to be accepted as absolutely accurate and true, no matter what. There are all kinds of things in a case like this which might have gone wrong .... The reading on the machine is, as I have said before, strong and should in most cases be conclusive evidence of the fact that the vehicle was travelling at a speed in excess of the limit. The justices would be, and should be, extremely reluctant to reject that finding, although there must be situations in which they are entitled to doubt it. They will be very few and far between, and the justices must be very careful not to allow somebody to run away with their judgment on these matters."

6.81   The decision in *Kent v Stamps* should be compared with that in *Burton v Gilbert* [1984] R.T.R. 162. The court held that the mere opinion of a driver as to his speed provided no evidential basis to cast doubt on the reading provided by the speed testing equipment. The decision is not easy to follow in that the court apparently accepted a similar opinion by the police officer as to the speed and regarded the radar machine as corroborating it.

Enforcement and technology

6.82   The Road Traffic Law Review (the North Report) (HMSO, 1988) set great store by the use of technology to aid the detection of offences. The deployment in other countries of automatic speed sensing devices in conjunction with cameras in order to detect offences and identify offending vehicles commended itself to the Review body, as did the use of automatically operated cameras at traffic lights to detect offences of a signal kind (see further § 6.34).

Their recommendation that such technology be brought into use in this country bore fruit in the shape of s.23 of the Road Traffic Act 1991, which replaced s.20 of the 1988 Offenders Act with an altogether grander version entitled "Speeding offences etc: admissibility of certain evidence". It enables evidence to be given in the form of a documentary record produced by a prescribed device, accompanied by a signed certificate as to the circumstances in which that record was produced (s.20(1)). That document gives particulars of the measurement made by the device or of the circumstances in which that measurement was made (s.20(6)). These provisions apply presently to traffic light signal offences, speeding offences generally, motorway speeding offences, speed restrictions in association with road works and temporary minimum speed limits (s.20(2)), but the list may be added to, or subtracted from, by order (s.20(3)). The Road Traffic Offenders (Additional Offences and Prescribed Devices) Order 1997 (SI 1997/384) added to that list offences under the Road Traffic Regulation Act 1984 of failing to comply with a bus lane or a route for use by buses only. A record produced or measurement made by such a device is only admissible in evidence if the device concerned is of an approved type and is operated subject to any conditions imposed upon its approval by the Secretary of State (s.20(4), (5)). A copy of the record must be served on the defendant not less than seven days before the trial; the defendant may, by service of notice upon the prosecution not less than three days before the hearing, require the attendance at court of the person who signed the document (s.20(8)).

6.83   It was held by the Divisional Court in *DPP v Thornley* [2006] EWHC 312; (2006) 170 J.P. 385, following *Garner v DPP* [1989] Crim. L.R. 583 (see further

§ 3.71), that, properly constructed, s.20(1) and (8) of the Road Traffic Offenders Act 1988 was permissive and allowed a record produced by a prescribed device to be adduced as real evidence without the necessity of a witness being called. A defendant who was disadvantaged by a failure by the prosecution to comply with the notice requirements of the section might well be allowed an adjournment if he wished to consider the record produced by the machine, or have it subjected to scientific examination.

Prescribed devices

Under s.20(9) of the 1988 Offenders Act a "prescribed device" means a device **6.84** of a description specified in an order made by the Secretary of State. A considerable number of prescribed devices have been approved and these are listed in the note to s.20 in Vol.2 of this work. Prescribed devices include: a device designed or adapted to record the presence of a vehicle on an area of road which is a bus lane or a route for use by buses only; radar speed measuring devices; devices designed or adapted for recording a measurement of the speed of motor vehicles activated by means of sensors or cables on or near the surface of the highway, and also by a light beam or beams; a device designed or adapted for recording a measurement of the speed of motor vehicles by (a) capturing by means of unattended cameras images of the motor vehicle at each of two predetermined positions on the road, (b) digitally recording each image and the time at which it is captured, and (c) calculating the average speed of the motor vehicle over the distance between the above-mentioned two positions by reference to the above-mentioned times.

An addition to the prescribed devices was made by the Road Traffic Offenders (Prescribed Devices) Order 2008 (SI 2008/1332), which came into force on June 16, 2008. The order approves a manually activated device designed or adapted for recording the measurement of the speed of a motor vehicle ("Vehicle A") from another motor vehicle ("Vehicle B") by:

   (a) measuring the time taken by Vehicle A to pass two positions on the road either directly or by reference to the time taken by Vehicle B to pass the same two positions on the road;

   (b) recording the distance between the two positions by counting the odometer pulses from Vehicle B as it travels between the two positions; and

   (c) calculating the average speed of Vehicle A over the distance between the two positions by reference to the time recorded in sub-paragraph (a) and the distance either calculated in accordance with sub-paragraph (b) or measured manually.

This means that devices of this type can be approved by the Secretary of State and the record produced from those approved devices can then be adduced as evidence in proceedings for certain road traffic offences when accompanied by an appropriately signed certificate as to the circumstances of its production. The order permits the use of devices that record the time it takes for a vehicle to travel between two points on a road by manual activation and which are capable of measuring the distance between those two points by means of the odometer pulses of the vehicle to which they are fitted.

Radar speed meters

The Home Office Scientific Research and Development Branch has produced a **6.85** report on fixed radar speed detection devices. It is entitled *The Evaluation of the Gatso Radar Speedmeter* by R.J. Harris, D.S. Keen and S.J. Amos (Home Office Publication 17/84). The report makes certain recommendations and examines the value of the Gatso devices.

6.86 It should be noted that it is incumbent upon the prosecution in a speeding case to prove that the Secretary of State has approved the use of the radar gun in question before the measurement of speed given by it can be admitted in evidence. Thus where the procedure for use of the device was in issue in its entirety, and the defence had given due warning of that fact, the justices were not entitled to take judicial notice that the device had been approved for use merely from the evidence of the police officer that he regularly used it. The approval of the device should not be taken for granted but should be established evidentially; the relevant approval could be produced in court or the officer could give evidence as to its approval (*Roberts v DPP* [1994] R.T.R. 31).

In *DPP v Mura Deva Bharat* (2000) 19 W.R.T.L.B. [73] it was held that *Roberts v DPP* above had been misapplied by justices who had upheld a submission of no case to answer on the basis of the failure of the prosecution to prove that the LTI 20.20 was an approved device "by the production of a document which is signed" (per s.20(6) of the 1988 Offenders Act) and by service of a copy thereof upon the defendant seven days before the hearing (per s.20(8) ibid.). The justices had had the benefit of the evidence of the officer to the effect that to his knowledge the device *had* been approved by the Home Secretary, and had been referred to the first two sentences of (what is now) § 6.93 of "Wilkinson's Road Traffic Offences" (*q.v.*). It was submitted on behalf of the prosecution that the justices could and should have found that the 20.20 device was approved. There were indeed two alternative bases for such a finding. First, the police officer's own oral evidence to that effect; secondly, the justices' entitlement to take judicial notice of the approval by reference to the authoritative statement in *Wilkinson*. The court was in no doubt that those submissions were soundly based. When the issue was raised at trial, the prosecution had been able to deal with the matter then and there, first by inviting the court to take judicial notice based on the quoted passage in *Wilkinson*, and secondly by recalling the police officer to give the necessary evidence orally. It was not in those particular circumstances necessary for the matter to have been dealt with by the production of a formal document in accordance with s.20 of the 1988 Offenders Act. That, no doubt, would be necessary in the case of a device whose approval had not become widely known, e.g. before it found its way into *Wilkinson*, and it might be necessary if the defendant gave advance notice that an approval was to be contested. This, however, was not such a case.

6.87 In *Farrell v Simpson* 1959 S.L.T. (Sh. Ct.) 23 there is a good example of the type of evidence given in a straightforward case. A sheriff convicted on the evidence of a reading of such a meter by two constables, who also gave their opinion that the car was exceeding 30mph. The evidence showed that the road was straight and level for a long distance, that the car was the only vehicle about, that the meter had been tested that day and that the speed of 42mph recorded on the meter had been shown thereon for over two and a half seconds.

Evidence of mechanical devices such as speedometers and stopwatches is acceptable in English courts (*Nicholas v Penny* [1950] 2 All E.R. 89) and, where radar is used, it is a question of fact for the magistrates whether or not its evidence on the particular facts before them should be accepted. Such cases and opinions as have been reported or given seem to show that meters are very accurate if working under good conditions and operated by experienced constables. Such cases as are dismissed by magistrates are almost invariably dismissed, not because the magistrates are not satisfied as to the accuracy of the radar meter, but because they are not satisfied as to the accuracy of the evidence of the police officers operating the radar trap. Instances have occurred where the police officer has been unable to satisfy the magistrates that either he had read the radar meter correctly or the meter reading he has given in evidence referred to the defendant's motor vehicle. Radar traps are usually operated so that one constable is stationed by the radar set observing the speed of the vehicle as it passes through the radar beam, and another constable is stationed considerably further down the road to stop an offending vehicle. The constable stopping an offending vehicle will usually be told by radio of that vehicle's registration number and the type of vehicle; occasionally magistrates have dismissed a case where they have not been satisfied that the correct vehicle was stopped, either because of a possible error on the part of the constable at the radar set in identifying the vehicle, or an error on the part of the constable responsible for stopping the vehicle.

Radar detection devices

The Divisional Court held in *R. v Knightsbridge Crown Court Ex p. Foot* **6.88** [1999] R.T.R. 21 that microwave radio emissions from police radar speed guns did not constitute a "message" for the purposes of s.5(b)(i) of the Wireless Telegraphy Act 1949, even within the extended meaning of "message" given by s.19(6) of that Act. Accordingly, the use by a motorist of an electrical field meter to detect the presence of such emissions was not an offence under s.5(b)(i) since the device was not used "to obtain information as to the contents, sender or addressee of any message". A police officer beaming emissions to and receiving information from an inanimate moving object was not exchanging messages with the motor car. There could be no reception of a message save between two human operators. Tempting though it was to outlaw the anti-social use of such devices, now that they were no longer banned under s.1(1) of the 1949 Act, to do so would be to stretch the language of s.5(b)(i) to breaking point.

Hand-held radar guns

Most police forces have now introduced hand-held radar guns which also oper- **6.89** ate by means of a radar beam. They may be operated by a single constable and the machine itself is capable of providing corroboration when required by law.

These machines work on the doppler effect. The gun is pointed by the constable at the moving vehicle. A radar beam strikes the vehicle and the frequency of the beam reflected back to the gun is changed proportionate to the speed of the vehicle. The gun measures this change and gives the speed of the vehicle on a digital display which may be retained in the machine by pressing a button or similar mechanism. The guns have a range of 500yds or more.

There are at least five ways the guns can give a false reading: through low batteries; poor contact through car lighter sockets; radio or similar interference; reflection of the beam off a metal object (such as a lamppost or postbox) on to some other moving object; or measurement of the speed of some other object in the wide beam. A test on a smaller nearer vehicle might pick up a reflection from a larger more distant one behind. Usually in such instances the reading would not be steady and would jump from one vehicle to another. The Home Office study *Measurements on Police Hand Held Radar Speedmeters* (Home Office Publication 28/84) did not indicate any likelihood of false readings from aircraft, birds, insects, powerlines or a movement *behind* the radar gun.

6.90   The training manual for one of the machines warns against using a device within a quarter of a mile of powerful VHF radio or UHF TV transmitters; within 100yds of high voltage overhead power cables; near large rotating fans or signs; near large rotating radar equipment; or within 30yds of smaller transmitters.

The procedure to be followed by police officers was recommended in the Home Office study to be as follows. A position by the road should be selected with a clear view. The battery indicator should be checked but if this is not fitted the later checks should confirm the battery state. The range switch should be pointed at the sky and turned slowly through 360°. During this test the display should be examined for several seconds to see that it is clear and there is no radio interference, and that the meter is working and the battery is not flat. This procedure should be repeated at intervals between speed measurements. Any test buttons should also be checked.

6.91   A tuning fork should then be struck and vibrated in front of the aerial. The reading on the machine should correspond with the reading on the fork. A written note should be kept of the speed of the vehicle used to test the radar gun.

The means of carrying out a radar check should be as follows. When, in the opinion of the officer, a vehicle is considered to be exceeding the speed limit, the speedometer should be pointed at the vehicle and a reading taken. The reading should be observed for at least three seconds and during that period the reading should be steady. An erratic series of numbers would indicate that an erroneous reading had been taken, and that the measurement was invalid. If the reading is considered correct, the trigger in the handle of the meter can be squeezed, and the speed reading fixed on the display. The reading can then be shown to the offending motorist although there is no legal requirement to do so. When the button is squeezed again the reading is lost and the meter is ready to make another measurement.

6.92   In practice many courts have shown a reluctance to convict where these recommendations and procedures have not been carried out adequately, and a doubt is established as to the speed recorded. As with other radar equipment, if operated correctly, radar guns normally have a high standard of accuracy but it may be possible to challenge the accuracy of the police officer or suggest the radar beam struck the wrong vehicle or another object. In cases of doubt the defence representative should question the prosecution carefully on any of the points mentioned above which may have affected the accuracy of the reading, in particular inquiring whether there was a parked car or other metal object nearby.

Laser speed measuring equipment

6.93   The hand-held LTI 20.20 TS/M speed detection device has been approved by the Secretary of State for the purposes of s.20 of the Road Traffic Offenders Act 1988. Judicial notice may be taken that the LTI 20.20 is an approved device by the reference to it in *Wilkinson*; see *DPP v Mura Deva Bharat* at § 6.86 above. The LTI 20.20 determines speed by measuring the time of flight of very short pulses of infrared light. Since the speed of light is a constant, the time it takes the laser pulse to travel to the target and back is directly proportional to the distance to the target. By firing two pulses a known time apart, two distances can be calculated; the change in distance divided by the time interval between the two pulses gives the speed of the target. Whilst in theory it is possible to make a speed measurement using only two pulses of light as described, in practice this would be prone to errors such as a shift of the aiming point between pulses. To eliminate the possibility of such errors, the device applies a number of independent tests to the pulse data and failure of any one of those tests will result in an error message being displayed.

On the front face of the device are two lenses which transmit the laser beam and receive the return signal. Mounted on the top of the device is a sighting scope; that scope contains within it a red dot which is aligned with the beam and in use is placed by the operator on the target vehicle. Having sighted the target the operator presses the trigger and activates a short burst of pulses which strike the target and provide a return signal. In that burst there will be approximately 60 pulses which take a series of measurements in as many milliseconds. The software within the device then constructs a profile of those measurements and makes comparisons to ensure consistency. If the measurements are consistent the device will provide a speed and range reading within 0.3 seconds of its actuation. If any inconsistencies are found the software will trap the error and display only an error reading. It will not display a spurious or false reading. The error reading will indicate to the operator that he should try again (which he may do almost immediately given the rapidity with which a reading is obtained).

6.94 The laser technology employed by the device offers the particular benefit of a narrow beam width (120cm at a range of 400m) in order to allow accurate targeting of individual vehicles amongst traffic; whether in single or multiple lanes. The equipment will read and display ranges up to 1km, and experience has shown that with average skill and practice an operator can regularly capture targets at 700–800m. The LTI 20.20 is not subject to interference in the same way as radar-based equipment, and cannot be fooled by rotating or vibrating objects. It can also discriminate between approaching and departing targets. During its pre-approval testing procedures the device was found to have a theoretical accuracy in its laser speed measuring mode of plus or minus 0.35km/h (which in any practical operational sense equates to plus or minus 0mph!).

A bewildering array of laser speed measuring equipment is now available for use by police forces for the detection of speeding offences. A list of currently approved devices is set out in tabular form in the note to s.20 of the 1988 Offenders Act in Vol.2.

Vascar

6.95 Some police forces have equipped traffic police vehicles with Vascar (visual average speed computer and recorder). Like radar meters, Vascar is technically extremely accurate. Unlike radar meters which record the vehicle's speed in the fraction of a second it takes a vehicle to pass through the radar beam, the Vascar device records the speed as averaged by the vehicle over the distance recorded; but like radar meters, it will usually be extremely difficult to obtain an acquittal on a charge of speeding on technical grounds where Vascar is used. The degree of training required of a police constable for the proper operation of Vascar is, if anything, rather more than that required for radar, and it is believed most forces require a constable to pass a stringent test programme before allowing the constable to operate the device for the purposes of prosecution. The proper operation of Vascar depends on the police constable accurately operating the switches and being able to satisfy the court that there has been no mistake in relation to the identification of the offending vehicle and no misjudgment of the exact moment the vehicle passed the relevant landmark used in its operation sufficient to render unreliable the speed as recorded by the device. However, in February 2009, there was a report that the Association of Chief Police Officers in Scotland had ordered forces to stop using Vascar speed detection equipment because of the risk of radio interference (CrimeLine Updater, reporting the BBC). This was considered a significant development by the reporter, but at the time of writing (March 2009) it has not proved possible to determine how significant this development may be.

Police Pilot

6.96   The Metropolitan Police have equipped their traffic vehicles with the Police Pilot PD2601S. Like Vascar (see § 6.95), this device measures distance and time by the operation of two switches and then computes the average speed of the vehicle being checked. The instrument may be used while the police vehicle is in motion or while parked. It may be used at night or in the daytime, and in foul or fair weather. It is not necessary for the police vehicle to be travelling in the same direction as the target vehicle, nor to follow that vehicle at an even distance, nor to pursue it.

The instrument is electronic and has at its heart a simple computer. It emits no signal and does not interfere with radio transmissions or reception. Only an electrical failure in the vehicle in which it is installed can affect its working or accuracy. The equipment is recalibrated once a month, and checked daily either by driving over a set distance and comparing the distance readout with the known distance travelled, or by comparing the speed readout in standby mode with the vehicle's certified speedometer.

Electric trip wire equipment

6.97   The electronic equipment used by the police in *Kent v Stamps* [1982] R.T.R. 273 is called Truvelo equipment. Two wires are stretched across the carriageway at a fixed distance apart, the distance being 1.5m. It was stated in that case that the normal police practice is to set the wires 1.55m apart so as to leave a margin of error in favour of the driver. The wires consist of co-axial cables which are sensitive to pressure. When a vehicle is driven over the first one and then the other, a pulse or electrical charge is created, and these pulses or charges are conveyed to a computer, which then calculates from the time taken to compress first one cable and then the other the actual speed in miles per hour of the vehicle.

In *Kent v Stamps* the justices rejected the result of the equipment even though they apparently accepted that it was in working order and had been checked and used correctly. The rejection was because of the age of the lorry and their knowledge of the location—round a bend and on an upward gradient. With some hesitation the Divisional Court agreed that they were entitled to wonder whether the machinery had worked accurately and to reach the decision they did.

Warnings of speed traps: obstruction

6.98   In *Bastable v Little* [1907] 1 K.B. 59 the defendant gave warnings of a speed

trap. He was acquitted of obstruction on the ground that he was preventing offences because the drivers of other vehicles slowed down. The decision was
strongly criticised in *Green v Moore* [1982] 2 W.L.R. 671, where the Divisional
Court said that until overruled it should be strictly confined to its own facts.

Bastable v Little and *Green v Moore* above were both considered by the
Divisional Court in *DPP v Glendinning* [2005] EWHC 2333; (2005) 169 J.P.
649. As he approached a police speed trap the defendant was observed making a
slowing down signal with his hand to drivers behind him. He was convicted of
obstruction. Video evidence shown to the Crown Court on appeal revealed that
none of the drivers were travelling in excess of the speed limit and that they had
not reacted to the defendant's signals by slowing down. The issue was whether,
for there to be an obstruction of a police constable acting in the execution of his
duty by warning other motorists of the presence of a speed trap, it was necessary
for the prosecution to prove that those warned were either exceeding the speed
limit or were likely to do so at the location of the speed trap. The Crown Court
upheld the defendant's appeal on the basis that such proof was necessary, and the
Divisional Court concurred. It is understood, however, that the matter is likely to
proceed in due course to the House of Lords.

Accident investigation

Sometimes charges of speeding are brought following an accident. The **6.99**
estimate of speed is based on tyre marks and other factors and presumably the
various technical factors involved must constitute corroboration of each other.
For a report of a successful appeal against a speeding conviction on such evidence see (1977) 141 J.P. 403 in which the judge commented on the lack of
safeguards for a defendant when presented with such technical evidence. Reference should also be made to a letter commenting on the report at ibid., p. 463.
See also *Crossland v DPP* at § 6.78 above.

Evidence generally

Timetables, schedules and directions issued by an employer may be produced **6.100**
as evidence in a prosecution of the employer for procuring or inciting his drivers
to exceed a speed limit imposed under any enactment, where they show that the
driver is bound to exceed the limit if he is to comply with the document issued to
him (Road Traffic Regulation Act 1984 s.89(4); and see *Newman v Overington*
(1928) 93 J.P. 46).

Measurement of a distance on a map by a rotameter, to show the distances
given in the driver's records could not be covered without exceeding the limit,
was held admissible in *Morrison v McCowan* [1939] S.C.(J.) 45.

The opinion of any witness as to speed is receivable (*Cross and Tapper on* **6.101**
Evidence). Magistrates have convicted on the evidence of police officers on foot
alone, without stopwatches or speed meters, in a case of exceeding the limit on a
restricted road, for, while it is unwise to accept such evidence as to what a
vehicle's speed was, it is relatively easy to accept that a vehicle which is going
very fast is going in excess of 30mph (118 J.P. Jo. 105 and 104 S.J. 20) but it is in
their discretion whether or not to accept such evidence.

A person may refresh his memory from a contemporaneous record compiled
by another provided it was checked at the time by him and adopted as his own.

The constable who had observed the speed recorded by the radar meter of an offending vehicle checked and countersigned a record compiled by the constable responsible for later stopping the offending vehicle; he was held to be entitled to refresh his memory from the other constable's record of the offence (*Groves v Redbart* [1975] Crim. L.R. 158). See further § 3.49 as to refreshing memory.

6.102   In *Baker v Sweet* [1966] Crim. L.R. 51 a temporary speed limit order restricted speeds on all roads save motorways and dual carriageways; on the hearing of a charge of exceeding the limit, the order was not produced and no evidence was given that it applied to the road in question and it was held that it was for the defendant to show, pursuant to what is now s.101 of the Magistrates' Courts Act 1980, that the order did not apply to the road. As the order was not even published as a statutory instrument, this is an unsatisfactory decision in that magistrates seem to be expected to take their law from what they have read about speed limits in the newspapers or from the *ipse dixit* of the prosecutor.

Speed limits on restricted roads

6.103   The term "built-up", which appeared in former Acts, is still an expression which is commonly used but it is not used in the Road Traffic Regulation Act 1984; s.81 of that Act makes it an offence to drive a motor vehicle on a "restricted road" at a speed exceeding 30mph. Where a limit has been imposed under s.84 of the 1984 Act (generally a limit other than 30mph), such a road is not deemed to be a restricted road for the purposes of s.81 (s.84(3)). By s.82 a "restricted road" is a road where there is provided a system of street lighting furnished by means of lamps placed not more than 200yds apart or a road in respect of which the relevant authority has made a direction that it shall be a restricted road notwithstanding the absence of such street lighting. In the following paragraphs the term means roads subject to speed limits whether of 30mph or otherwise.

In *Hood v Lewis* [1976] R.T.R. 99 a speeding motorist failed to see the 30mph signs as his vision of them was obscured by bushes and posts and a lorry which he was overtaking. Since street lamps not more than 200yds apart were plainly to be seen, the justices were directed to convict. It was also said that it is no possible answer to prosecution on a charge of speeding if a motorist driving into a built-up area plain for all to see chooses to follow closely behind or overtake a lorry so that he fails to see the 30mph signs (nor can it be a special reason for not endorsing if the 30mph signs are obscured if there is a system of street lamps not more than 200yds apart: see *Walker v Rawlinson*, at § 21.55). In fact, in order to prove that a motorist was guilty of exceeding a speed limit contrary to s.81(1) of the 1984 Act on a road that was a restricted road by virtue of the provision on it of a system of street lighting, it was not necessary for the prosecution to prove that the relevant traffic authority had complied with its duty to provide traffic signs warning motorists what the prescribed speed limit was. The Divisional Court in *Humber v DPP* [2008] EWHC 2932; [2008] All E.R. (D.) 154 said that it is clear from the opening words of s.85(4) that the absence of traffic signs had no bearing on liability where a system of road lighting as mentioned in s.82 was provided. In principle it was, said the court, for a motorist to know where he stood regarding the prescribed speed limit by observing whether the road on which he was travelling was lit, and whilst that might not be as well known as it might be, it was explicitly referred to in the Highway Code.

6.104   Where a lamp is temporarily missing, e.g. it has been knocked down, so that at one place two lamps are more than 200yds apart, it is suggested that a "system of street lighting" is still provided as above (see 114 J.P. Jo. 627). Where there is a direction in force imposing a limit under what is now s.82 on a road without the requisite lampposts, the presence of the speed limit signs is prima facie evidence that the speed limit applies to that road, and the police need not call evidence to prove the direction unless the defence call evidence that the road is not restricted (*Boyd-Gibbins v Skinner* [1951] 1 All E.R. 1049). A conviction was upheld where a defendant had exceeded the limit on a road on which there were four lamps, two of which were 201½yds apart and the others 200yds apart (*Briere v Hailstone* (1968) 112 S.J. 767); the de minimis principle was applied. It might be otherwise if all or nearly all the lamps were more than 201yds apart. Indeed, it is respectfully submitted that the *Briere* case was not really a correct application of the de minimis rule; part of the road in question there had the relevant system of street lighting and it was thus relevant that the limit was also exceeded on a part where the lamps were more than the prescribed distance apart. It may also be pointed out that s.82 refers to a "system" of street lighting furnished by lamps placed not more than 200yds apart. If some of the gaps between lights are slightly more than 200yds it is possible to argue that there is still a "system" of street lighting if the number of lights is such that the gaps average less than 200yds.

In *Spittle v Kent County Constabulary* [1985] Crim. L.R. 744 it was confirmed that whether there is the relevant system of street lighting is a question of fact. It was immaterial that one lamp was in a state of disrepair. The facts were that there were 24 lamps set on average 95yds apart but between two lamps the distance was 212yds. The Divisional Court applied the de minimis principle in *Briere v Hailstone* above and upheld the conviction.

In *Roberts v Croxford* (1969) 113 S.J. 269 magistrates, on inspecting a road, **6.105** found that the system of street lighting was for lighting a promenade nearby and not for lighting the road; their action in inspecting and their finding that the road had not the necessary system was upheld.

By the Road Traffic Regulation Act 1984 s.85(5), if a road has the relevant system of street lighting, evidence of the absence of derestriction signs shall be evidence that it is deemed to be a road which is restricted. If the road has not the relevant system of street lighting but is restricted, a person shall not be convicted unless there are the necessary restriction signs (s.85(4)). The signs must not only be present, but must be erected and maintained in such a way as to provide adequate guidance to motorists as to the speed limit to be observed (s.85(1)). The signs should indicate the limit to an approaching driver in sufficient time for him to reduce from a previous lawful speed to a speed within the new limit. Thus where the signs indicating the limit had only become visible at the point at which the defendant had driven past them because until that point they had been obscured by overgrown hedgerows, the statutory requirements had not been met and the defendant should not have been convicted; *Coombes v DPP* [2006] EWHC 3263; [2007] R.T.R. 31.

Where different lengths of one road are governed by different regulations applying to one length only, even though imposing the same limit, an information **6.106** alleging an offence against both regulations is bad for duplicity; there should either be separate, fresh informations for each length or the prosecution should have elected on the original information to proceed in respect of one length only (*Cross v Oliver* (1964) 62 L.G.R. 501).

The required regulatory signs for speed limits are now contained in Sch.2 to the Traffic Signs Regulations and General Directions 2002 (SI 2002/3113) (diagrams 670–675). The regulations allow for variations in the dimensions of the overall diameter of the circular signs pictured at diagrams 670–673. Speed limit signs should be illuminated by lighting where so required by Sch.17, item 10, or by lighting or by "retroreflecting material" where not so required (ibid., item 11). Retroreflecting material is defined by reg.4 as material which reflects a ray of light back towards the source of that light. Direction 11 of the 2002 Directions requires that repeater signs be placed "at regular intervals". There is a saving for signs which conform to previous regulations and directions, but note s.85(5) (above) as to roads which have not the necessary lamps. Where some lamps were more than 200yds apart and there were no intermediate repeater signs as required by the then relevant Traffic Signs (Speed Limits) Regulations and General Directions, a conviction for exceeding the limit was quashed (*Mackereth v Madge* (1968) 66 L.G.R. 69). The erection of repeater signs in a 30mph area governed by a system of street lighting is specifically prohibited by the 2002 Regulations. It is submitted that where there are such illegal repeater signs, a conviction for exceeding 30mph will not be invalidated. Only the converse applies (see s.85(4) and (5) of the 1984 Act).

6.107   It is a common complaint that there are no repeater signs indicating restricted roads. In fact the reference to the relevant system of street lighting is designed to obviate the need for such repeater signs. Were they to be used on some roads it would be argued that they should be used on all the vast number of restricted roads which have the relevant system of street lighting.

As special limit signs must, in accordance with s.85 and s.64(1), (2) and (3), be the "prescribed" traffic signs it would appear that, if the sign is not in accordance with the regulations, the defendant is entitled to be acquitted unless the offence took place in an area restricted to 30mph by reason of a system of street lamps not more than 200yds apart. Under reg.18 of, and Sch.17 to, the regulations, signs not illuminated by external lighting must be illuminated by "retroreflecting material", but by reg.19(4) no retroreflecting material is to be applied to any part of the sign coloured black.

6.108   The only signs which are required to be illuminated are those "terminal" signs erected on a trunk or principal road where there is an electrical street lamp within 50m. Such "terminal" signs are required either to be continuously illuminated through the hours of darkness, or illuminated while the street lamp is lit providing the sign is also illuminated by retroreflecting material (defined at § 6.106 above). A "terminal" sign is defined by reg.4 as those required at the beginning and end of the speed limit in accordance with direction 8 or 9, as appropriate. Where a terminal sign required to be illuminated under what is now reg.18 was in such a condition that it could not be illuminated, justices dismissed a case of speeding during daylight hours on the ground that as the sign could not comply with (what is now) reg.18 it did not comply with s.54(2) of the Road Traffic Regulation Act 1967. The justices were directed to convict where the speeding took place in daylight: the requirement that the sign should be illuminated was not contravened, as there was no requirement that during daylight hours the sign should be in a state fit for illumination in the dark (*Stubbs v Morgan* [1972] R.T.R. 459).

Direction 42 of the Traffic Signs Regulations and General Directions 2002 provides that the back of speed limit signs shall be grey, black or in a non-reflective metallic finish. So far as speeding offences are concerned, however, the colour of the back of a sign is immaterial since the requirements of s.85 of the Road Traffic Regulation Act 1984 only apply to the front of the prescribed sign (*Sharples v Blackmore* [1973] R.T.R. 249). The colour of the back of a sign (which no driver sees until he passes it and only then if he turns round) does not make an otherwise restricted road into an unrestricted road (ibid.).

In *Burgess v West* [1982] R.T.R. 269, the finding was that there was no 30mph **6.109** speed limit sign. The rightness of the conviction was not canvassed. The defendant believed he was in a 40mph area. The absence of the sign was a fact and not a mere mistaken belief (see *Jones v Nicks* at § 21.55). Because the belief was induced by the fact of the absence of the sign it was a reason special to the offence and the justices were entitled at their decision to find it a special reason for not endorsing. See further §§ 21.54–5.

Interestingly the actual speed was 46mph. The defendant contended that the police would not have prosecuted for a 6mph excess and the court did not comment on this—and did not use it as a ground for overturning the special reason finding. Clearly it is not a ground for an acquittal.

Temporary speed limits

Temporary maximum and minimum speed limits may be imposed by orders **6.110** made under s.88(1)(a) and (b) respectively of the 1984 Act. Temporary speed restrictions may also be imposed by orders under s.14 of the 1984 Act because of road works.

Temporary maximum speed limits

The 70mph, 60mph and 50mph (Temporary Speed Limit) Order 1977 is **6.111** deemed to be made under s.88 of the Road Traffic Regulation Act 1984 and applies to all roads other than motorways in England, Wales and Scotland. For motorway speed limits see § 6.135. Unless a lower limit is specified for any particular road or stretch of road either by Sch.1 or 2 to the order, as varied, unrestricted dual-carriageway roads are limited to 70mph and all unrestricted single-carriageway roads are limited to 60mph.

Section 88(5) of the Road Traffic Regulation Act 1984 provides that where a temporary speed limit is imposed on all roads, on all roads of any class specified in the order or on all roads other than roads of any specified class, s.85 (which requires speed limit signs to be displayed) does not apply. The effect of s.88(5) of the Road Traffic Regulation Act 1984 seems to be that speed limit signs need not be displayed in respect of the overall limits of 70 and 60mph. Those lengths of dual or single-carriageway roads specified in Sch.1 to the order and limited to 50mph together with the dual-carriageway roads specified in Sch.2 limited to 60mph are required to have signs displayed.

See *Baker v Sweet* at § 6.102 as to proof of the Temporary Speed Limit Order.

Temporary minimum speed limits

These may be imposed for specified roads by orders under the Road Traffic **6.112** Regulation Act 1984 s.88(1)(b) and are punishable under s.88(7) and Sch.2 to the 1988 Offenders Act, not s.89. By s.88(5) signs must be displayed where the limit is for a specific road. The relevant order, when made, should be consulted for any exception allowing lower speeds for safety reasons.

Temporary speed restrictions for road works, etc.

6.113   A traffic authority may impose a temporary speed restriction under the Road Traffic Regulation Act 1984 ss.14–16 because of road works or works near the road or because of the likelihood of danger to the public or of serious damage to the highway. Such restrictions cannot remain in force for longer than 18 months without the approval of the Secretary of State. It is an offence to contravene, or use or permit the use of a vehicle in contravention of a restriction. As to "use" and "permit", see Chapter 1. Such a speed restriction may be imposed in respect of any road. This therefore includes a motorway, a view supported by a "Question and Answer" at (1979) 143 J.P. 212. It was emphasised in *Platten v Gowing* [1983] Crim. L.R. 184 that this is a speed *restriction* and not a speed *limit* (but see § 6.138 below).

The speed limit on a particular stretch of road was not invalidated by the placing of the restriction signs so as to indicate that the length of the restriction was greater than that actually imposed by a speed restriction order. The Divisional Court in *Wawrzynczyk v Chief Constable of Staffordshire Constabulary, The Times,* March 16, 2000 held that although wrongfully positioned, the signs gave adequate guidance as to the speed limit to be observed on the part of the road properly subject to the order and did not invalidate that order. The report is very brief, but it is presumed from the reference therein to a restriction order made under s.14 of the Road Traffic Regulation Act 1984 that the speed limit concerned was a temporary one.

Speed limits applicable to particular classes of vehicle

6.114   Certain vehicles are restricted as to speed, whether on restricted roads or not, by the Road Traffic Regulation Act 1984 Sch.6; see Vol.2. There are different limits for motorways, dual-carriageway roads other than motorways, and other roads. A dual carriageway is defined in Pt IV of Sch.6 as a road part of which consists of a central reservation to separate the carriageways. This definition suggests that the dual carriageway does not begin with the hatching markings but only with the physical central reservation itself.

Certain vehicle speed limits were amended by the Motor Vehicles (Variation of Speed Limits) Regulations 1986 (SI 1986/1175). The speed limit for passenger vehicles, motor caravans, car derived vans or dual-purpose vehicles which are drawing one trailer was increased from 50 to 60mph on a motorway or dual carriageway; the speed limit for an articulated goods vehicle not exceeding 7.5 tonnes maximum laden weight or for a motor vehicle (other than a car derived van) towing a single trailer where the maximum laden weight of the combination does not exceed 7.5 tonnes was increased to 60mph on a dual carriageway; and a speed limit of 40mph was introduced for agricultural motor vehicles on all roads. These changes have been noted where appropriate in the lettered sections dealing with particular classes of vehicle (see below).

6.115   The terms "light (and) heavy locomotive", "motor tractor" and "invalid carriage" used in this Schedule are defined in s.136 of the Road Traffic Regulation Act 1984 in similar terms to s.185 of the 1988 Act. The definition of an "articulated vehicle" where the expression is used in Sch.6 under "goods vehicle" is the same as in the Road Vehicles (Construction and Use) Regulations (see Chapter 1 and in particular *Hunter v Towers* at § 1.60, and under "Goods vehicles" below). The definitions of "passenger vehicle", "dual-purpose vehicle", "industrial tractor" and "works truck" are also as in those regulations.

See §§ 1.27 and 1.29 as to "constructed" and "adapted". A vehicle can be reconstructed so that it joins another class (*Keeble v Miller* [1950] 1 All E.R. 261). Adaptation, seemingly, is insufficient to change a goods vehicle to a passenger one, however; there must be a major reconstruction (*Fry v Bevan* (1937) 81 S.J. 60). Fitting a different body could be a major reconstruction (*Burrows v Berry* (1949) 113 J.P. Jo. 492). Fitting a container to a tractor or locomotive would not convert it to a goods vehicle and, in view of para.4, Pt IV of Sch.6, it seems doubtful if such an adaptation would allow such vehicles to go at the same speed as goods vehicles. See *Plume v Suckling* below.

Weight is calculated pursuant to s.190 of the 1988 Act (see that section and **6.116** Chapter 1), even though this may result in a vehicle being of a different unladen weight under the Vehicle Excise and Registration Act 1994.

A   *Passenger vehicles and motor caravans*

Ordinary, i.e. passenger-carrying, motor cars of an unladen weight not exceed- **6.117** ing 3.05 tonnes and motor cycles and motor cycle combinations, provided they are adapted to carry not more than eight passengers exclusive of the driver, and motor caravans are not subject to any special speed limit applicable to the class, unless drawing trailers. The speed limits for other passenger-carrying vehicles are indicated in Sch.6 to the Road Traffic Regulation Act 1984. Passenger vehicles, motor caravans and dual-purpose vehicles with an unladen weight exceeding 3.05 tonnes or adapted to carry more than eight passengers exclusive of the driver are subject to a 70mph limit on motorways. At present this makes no material difference as this is the overall maximum. They are subject to a 60mph limit on dual carriageways and 50mph on other roads. If they exceed 12m in overall length they are subject as well to a 60mph limit on motorways. Unlike goods vehicles and car-derived vans the reference is to unladen weight.

If they are drawing one trailer they (and also car-derived vans) are subject to a 60mph limit on motorways and dual carriageways and a 50mph limit on other roads and if more than one trailer to 40mph on motorways and 20mph on all other roads including dual carriageways.

The distinction between a vehicle being used under a PSV operator's licence **6.118** and a passenger vehicle being used otherwise has been abolished.

"Passenger vehicle" is defined by the Construction and Use Regulations for this purpose as a vehicle "constructed solely for the carriage of passengers and their effects". As to "constructed", "passenger" and "trailer", see Chapter 1. A goods vehicle adapted to carry passengers is not so "constructed". Further, a vehicle must be constructed "solely" to carry passengers and a utility vehicle made to carry passengers or goods is not constructed "solely" to carry passengers even if goods are never in fact carried (*Hubbard v Messenger* [1937] 4 All E.R. 48). Unless, as will often be the case now, it is a dual-purpose vehicle, as defined in the Schedule, a utility vehicle will generally be classed as a goods vehicle; cf. *Taylor v Thompson* [1956] 1 All E.R. 352.

In *Plume v Suckling* [1977] R.T.R. 271 a coach adapted to carry six passengers, **6.119** kitchen equipment and a stock car was held to be a "goods vehicle" and restricted to 40mph. The defendant had converted the coach to carry his family, kitchen equipment and a stock car at weekends, which the justices had held to constitute "passengers and their effects". Eveleigh J. stated that "passenger effects are things which one would readily and normally recognise as accompanying a passenger. A stock car is not such" (ibid. at 275J).

B   *Goods vehicles*

6.120   Goods vehicles by Pt IV of Sch.6 to the 1984 Act have the same meaning as in s.192(1) of the 1988 Act. They are therefore vehicles constructed or adapted for use for the carriage of goods or burden of any description. As to "constructed or adapted", see §§ 1.27 and 1.29 and also below. Car-derived vans (see below) are treated separately and it is necessary therefore to check first that the goods vehicle is not a car-derived van.

Goods vehicles (not drawing trailers) having a maximum laden weight of 7.5 tonnes or less are not subject to any special speed limits on motorways and may therefore travel at up to 70mph. They are subject to a 60mph limit on dual carriageways and 50mph on other roads.

6.121   All goods vehicles drawing one trailer where the maximum laden weight of goods vehicle and trailer together is 7.5 tonnes or less and all articulated vehicles of whatever weight up to 7.5 tonnes are subject to a 60mph limit on motorways and dual carriageways and to 50mph on other roads.

All goods vehicles (whether or not drawing a trailer) with an aggregate maximum laden weight exceeding 7.5 tonnes and all articulated vehicles again with an aggregate maximum laden weight exceeding 7.5 tonnes are subject to a 60mph limit on motorways, 50mph on dual carriageways and 40mph on other roads. Goods motor vehicles carrying more than one trailer are subject to a 40mph limit on motorways and 20mph on all other roads including dual carriageways.

6.122   There are special limits for vehicles which have a wheel or wheels not fitted with pneumatic tyres and for track-laying vehicles. Motor cycles with side-cars made to carry goods may be goods vehicles and therefore subject to goods vehicle limits when drawing a trailer. See also under "car-derived vans" below. Works trucks and industrial tractors are restricted to 18mph on all roads. Other motor tractors, light locomotives and heavy locomotives are restricted (with or without one trailer) to 40mph on motorways and 30mph on all other roads including dual carriageways, if they (including any trailer) have the springs and wings specified in Pt IV of Sch.6. If not or if drawing more than one trailer, they are limited to 20mph on all roads including motorways.

It will be seen that motor tractors are now subject to stringent limits including limits on motorways. A motor tractor is defined by s.136 of the Road Traffic Regulation Act 1984 as a motor vehicle which is not constructed itself to carry a load, other than excepted articles as there specified and of which the weight unladen does not exceed 7,370kg.

6.123   The limits apply whether the vehicle is carrying goods or not and whether it has a goods vehicle licence or not and whatever its unladen weight, save that dual-purpose vehicles, as defined below, are treated in the same way as passenger vehicles. The speed limit for tower wagons, sound-recording vans, breakdown lorries and vehicles fitted with a special appliance or apparatus is discussed at 121 J.P.Jo. 479; such items are by s.137(3) not goods or burden. Generally, such vehicles will carry goods also and can be found to be goods vehicles. A chassis, while remaining a motor vehicle, was held not to be subject to any limit, as it did not come within any of the types there specified (*Millard v Turvey* [1968] 2 All E.R. 7). This still seems to be the position. A vehicle constructed solely to carry passengers and their effects and not adapted to carry goods will remain a passenger vehicle and subject only to the limits (if any) prescribed for such vehicles even though it carries goods which are not the "effects" of the passengers. Dual-purpose vehicles (below) are also treated on the same basis as passenger vehicles.

Goods vehicles must comply with speed limits at all times, whether or not they are carrying goods, because the test is not whether goods are actually carried but whether the vehicle is constructed or adapted for the carriage of goods or burden of any description, not including dual-purpose vehicles. In *Bryson v Rogers* [1956] 2 All E.R. 826, a farmer's Austin pick-up van, which did not conform to the definition of dual-purpose vehicle, as defined below, was held to be subject to a goods vehicle speed limit although it was not carrying goods. A van adapted to carry passengers and with no shelves for goods was held not to be a goods vehicle (see *Tait v Odhams Press*, a case on goods vehicles licensing, and other cases noted at § 13.45). In *Levinson v Powell* [1967] 3 All E.R. 796, a taxi was held not to be a goods vehicle, though it may be a dual-purpose one.

"Goods" is not confined to goods for sale or delivery; it includes a window-cleaner's ladders, rags and buckets (*Clarke v Cherry* [1953] 1 All E.R. 267) and effluent (*Sweetway Sanitary Cleansers v Bradley* [1961] 2 All E.R. 821); in *Bourne v Norwich Crematorium Ltd* [1967] 1 W.L.R. 691 at 695 (a tax case), it was held that corpses are not "goods", though it was argued that coffins and shrouds might be and reference was made to a case where dogs were held to be goods. **6.124**

C Car-derived vans

The restrictions on goods vehicles do not apply to car-derived vans. "Car-derived vans" by Sch.6, Pt IV are goods vehicles which are constructed or adapted as a derivative of a passenger vehicle and which have a maximum laden weight not exceeding 2 tonnes. Strangely enough despite the use of the word "van", this definition is wide enough to include a motor cycle constructed or adapted to carry goods. Although it will be a question of fact, such a vehicle might well be regarded as being derived from a passenger vehicle. **6.125**

The only restrictions on these vehicles as a class are when drawing one trailer (60mph on motorways and dual carriageways, 50mph on other roads) and when drawing more than one trailer (40mph on motorways and 20mph on dual carriageways and other roads).

As to "constructed" and "adapted" see §§ 1.27 and 1.29. It will be noted that the reference is to *laden* weight. Car-derived vans have been omitted from item 1 of the Table in Sch.6. This would only be material in the unlikely event of a car-derived van being both a goods vehicle and at the same time a vehicle adapted to carry more than eight passengers exclusive of the driver but not within the narrower definition of a dual-purpose vehicle. Such a car-derived van would not be subject to the item 1 limits. **6.126**

D Dual-purpose vehicles

"Dual-purpose vehicle" has the same meaning as in the Road Vehicles **6.127**

(Construction and Use) Regulations 1986 reg.3(2). All dual-purpose vehicles must not exceed 2,040kg in unladen weight. The reference to unladen weight should be contrasted to goods vehicles where the position depends on maximum laden weight for the purposes of Sch.6. They must be "constructed or adapted", etc., and this expression is interpreted differently from and should be contrasted with the expression "constructed solely" which is used in the definition of passenger vehicles and to "adapted" by itself used for dual-purpose vehicles in Sch.6, item 1. As to the meaning of "constructed or adapted" see §§ 1.27 and 1.29.

Dual-purpose vehicles are treated exactly the same in Sch.6 as passenger vehicles and motor caravans and not as goods vehicles regardless of whether or not they are carrying goods.

6.128   They are basically exempt from speed limits relating to the type of vehicle. In effect these limits will only apply if they are adapted to carry more than eight passengers excluding the driver or if they are drawing one or more trailers. As to "passengers" see § 1.117.

They include shooting brakes and utility vehicles. Vehicles so constructed or adapted that the driving power of the engine is, or by the appropriate use of the controls can be, transmitted to all the wheels are also included providing the unladen weight does not exceed 2,040kg and there are an increasing number of such vehicles. Examples are Range Rovers, Land Rovers, Jeeps, certain similar Japanese vehicles and those designed to go over rough ground as well as on roads, not being track-laying vehicles; and they are dual-purpose vehicles whether or not they comply with the conditions as to construction specified in the Construction and Use Regulations, e.g. rigid roofs, transverse seats, etc. (*Kidson v Swatridge* [1957] Crim. L.R. 193). Shooting brakes and utility vehicles without four-wheel drive must comply with those conditions to obtain the relevant exemptions from speed limits when not on restricted roads. A van had been adapted to be a "dual-purpose vehicle" by adding windows, but its windows were covered by panels of wood screwed into the windows so as to obscure them entirely. It was held that the van had been adapted to become a dual-purpose vehicle and that it was not subject to any limit as a goods vehicle (*Popperwell v Cockerton* [1968] 1 All E.R. 1038). In *Levinson v Powell* [1967] 3 All E.R. 769 a taxi was held to be a dual-purpose vehicle, but each vehicle would have to be inspected to see if it did fall within the definition in the regulations.

6.129   Four-wheel-drive vehicles are excluded from the definition of "dual-purpose vehicle" in respect of the Type Approval Regulations (see § 8.09). This provision in the Type Approval Regulations does not appear to affect in any way the meaning of the expression in Sch.6 or the definition in the Construction and Use Regulations.

If a vehicle, though constructed or adapted to carry goods and passengers, does not come within the definitions given, because its unladen weight exceeds 2,040kg or it has a non-rigid roof or its seats run lengthways and not transversely, it will under the regulations be a goods vehicle, whether or not it is carrying goods (*Bryson v Rogers* [1956] 2 All E.R. 826).

E   Articulated vehicles and trailers

6.130   The lower limits laid down when a vehicle draws a trailer will be noted. The limits for these vehicles have been set out above under the various types. In effect the requirements for passenger vehicles, motor caravans, dual-purpose vehicles, car-derived vans, articulated vehicles not exceeding 7.5 tonnes maximum laden weight and motor vehicle (excluding a car-derived van) and single trailer combinations not exceeding 7.5 tonnes are now the same, i.e. restricted to 60mph on motorways and dual carriageways and 50mph on other roads. 50mph trailer plates are no longer needed. Other goods vehicles and articulated goods vehicles have lower maximum speed limits depending on the circumstances.

Passenger vehicles, motor caravans, dual-purpose vehicles, car-derived vans and goods vehicles (unless having a lower maximum limit) are all limited when drawing more than one trailer to 40mph on motorways and 20mph on other roads including dual carriageways.

An articulated goods vehicle is defined for the purpose of Sch.6 to the 1984 **6.131** Act by reg.3(2) of the Road Vehicles (Construction and Use) Regulations 1986 and is not treated as a vehicle drawing a trailer but as a single vehicle. Articulated buses are excluded.

This definition is somewhat different from and less comprehensive than that in ss.186(2) and 187 of the 1988 Act and ss.137(2) and 136 of the 1984 Act and this could give rise to problems.

The only specific reference to articulated vehicles in Sch.6 is under goods **6.132** vehicles and the definition in the Construction and Use Regulations applies to such goods vehicles. Other vehicles including buses may be articulated and the Construction and Use Regulations' definition of an articulated vehicle will not apply, and the definition in ss.137(2) and 136 will normally apply instead. Such vehicles are again treated as one vehicle.

A vehicle and trailer closely coupled together, not being an articulated vehicle, do not thereby become one vehicle (*Dixon v BRS (Pickford) Ltd* [1959] 1 All E.R. 449). A car towing a two-wheeled caravan with the aid of a "van dolly", i.e. a small chassis with two wheels, is towing a four-wheeled trailer (*Brown v Dando* (1954) 118 J.P.Jo. 319). A trailer and car amalgamated into one four-wheeled rigid unit is one trailer not two (*Baker v Esau* [1972] Crim. L.R. 559).

A heavy breakdown recovery vehicle equipped with a special boom to assist in **6.133** the lifting and moving of vehicles was not a motor tractor, light locomotive or heavy locomotive under s.136(6) and (7) of the Road Traffic Regulation Act 1984 and thus was not restricted to a maximum speed of 40mph under Sch.6 to the Act. The Divisional Court so held in *DPP v Holtham* [1990] Crim. L.R. 600 when dismissing the prosecution's appeal against an acquittal by justices of a defendant charged with driving a Volvo F12 recovery vehicle at a speed greater than 40mph on the M40. The case involved a short point on the construction of s.137(2) of the Act having regard to s.136(1). A broken-down vehicle towed by the arm of a recovery vehicle was a trailer attached to the recovery vehicle so that a substantial part of its weight was taken by the recovery vehicle. The recovery vehicle was therefore deemed to be a vehicle constructed to carry a load and could not be a motor tractor or light or heavy locomotive within s.136(6) and (7). (See further § 1.48.) Many caravans are drawn by passenger or dual-purpose vehicles and as trailers come under Sch.6 Pt 1.

F Agricultural vehicles

A speed limit of 40mph applies to agricultural vehicles on all roads (Motor **6.134** Vehicles (Variation of Speed Limits) Regulations 1986 (SI 1986/1175)).

Motorway speed limits

6.135   The motorway speed limits for certain classes of vehicle have been set out above, §§ 6.114–34, under the various classes. See Sch.6 to the 1984 Act in Vol.2. Where there is an overall lower maximum motorway speed limit (see below) this maximum will apply instead.

For the vehicles which may lawfully travel on a motorway see § 6.144.

6.136   The temporary speed limits of 50, 60 and 70mph do not and could not apply to motorways as the enabling section of the Act under which the order was made does not apply to motorways (Road Traffic Regulation Act 1984 s.88). Vehicles not already subject to a lower speed limit by virtue of Sch.6 are subject to an overall maximum limit of 70mph on motorways by virtue of the Motorways Traffic (Speed Limit) Regulations 1974 (SI 1974/502). These regulations provide for an overall motorway limit of 70mph and also special overall limits of 50 and 60mph on particular stretches of various motorways as set out in Schedules to the order as amended. The 1974 Regulations are not temporary or limited in time and were made by virtue of s.13 of the Road Traffic Regulation Act 1967. See also "Temporary speed restrictions for road works, etc.", § 6.113.

SPEED LIMITS: PROCEEDINGS AND PENALTIES

Warning of intended prosecution

6.137   When the 1988 Offenders Act first appeared it did not take commentators long to notice that s.1 of that Act (requirement of warning of prosecutions for certain offences) did not apply to speeding offences, even though the previous legislation which the 1988 Acts replaced specifically required notice of intended prosecution to be given to persons accused of such offences. Schedule 1, para.2 of the Road Traffic Act 1991 repaired that apparently unintentional omission by inserting a new para.1A in Sch.1 to the 1988 Offenders Act in order to apply the requirements of s.1 of that Act to:

(a) speeding offences generally (including temporary minimum speed limits);

(b) speeding offences on motorways; and

(c) temporary speeding restrictions in association with road works.

Temporary speed restrictions for road works, etc.

6.138   The court in *Platten v Gowing* [1983] Crim. L.R. 184 drew a distinction between *temporary speed restriction* under ss.14–16 and the more *general speed limits*. A temporary speed restriction must always be lower than the relevant speed limit. If the speed limit is contravened as well a person will commit two offences and the prosecuting authorities may proceed for the contravention of the speed limit offence, if they so wish. This issue was discussed in *DPP v Wells and Halliwell* [2007] EWHC 3259; [2008] R.T.R. 23 where the Divisional Court did not consider itself bound by *Platten*. Burton J. stated:

> "It is, in my judgment, a much more straightforward answer, rather than saying that both offences could be charged in appropriate cases, simply to say that both offences are available to be charged as alternatives. But it is plainly tidier and more sensible to deal with all questions of speeding under s.89 where there is, in any event, the express

protection of the motorist by virtue of the need for corroboration." ([2007] EWHC 3259 at [28])

It should be noted that an offence contrary to s.16(1) of the Road Traffic Regulation Act 1984 (contravention of temporary prohibition or restriction, e.g. a temporary speed restriction in connection with road works) is endorsable with 3–6 points (or 3 only if dealt with by way of fixed penalty): Road Traffic Act 1991 Sch.2 para.2; see further § 6.140 below.

As to two convictions from one incident see below.

Proceedings generally

In *Welton v Taneborne* (1908) 72 J.P. 419 a conviction for driving in a danger-ous manner, where the court had taken into consideration the defendant's speed, was held to bar a subsequent prosecution for exceeding the speed limit. In that case both summonses had been preferred together, but the dangerous driving charge was heard first and upon the conviction being announced, the police desired to proceed on the speeding charge also. It would seem, however, that, if there had been an acquittal on the graver charge, this would not necessarily bar the speeding one. See also "Two offences from one incident" at § 5.76.

6.139

Fixed penalties and penalty points for speeding

In the course of looking at the number of penalty points allocated to particular offences under the then existing legislation, the Road Traffic Law Review (the North Report) (HMSO, 1988) found itself compelled to the conclusion that, in re-lation to speeding, 3 points was an "inadequate response" to a bad case. On the other hand, a range of points would be impracticable to administer within the confines of a fixed penalty system. Their solution to the problem, namely the cre-ation of a range of points for use by courts running side by side with a fixed number of points for an offence dealt with by way of fixed penalty is embodied by amendments to s.28 of, and Sch.2 to, the 1988 Offenders Act made by s.27 of, and Sch.2 to, the Road Traffic Act 1991. The combined effect of these amend-ments is that a fixed penalty speeding offence continues to attract 3 points, whereas such an offence dealt with in court is endorsable with 3–6 points. The additional incentive that that arrangement provides towards accepting a fixed penalty if one is offered is probably not altogether unintentional. On the other hand, given that the range of points for use by courts was introduced ostensibly to enable them to deal more effectively with *bad* speeding offences, it ought to be possible to argue that a defendant who has been offered, but not accepted, a fixed penalty should not have more than 3 points endorsed upon his licence, since had his offence been in the eyes of the reporting officer a *bad* one, the fixed penalty would not have been offered in the first place. The extra cost to the public purse of a court hearing might be appropriately dealt with by an order for costs against the defendant if he is convicted.

6.140

It should be noted that s.17 of the Road Safety Act 2006 (if and when in force) amends Pt I of Sch.2 to the 1988 Offenders Act to extend the range of penalty points which may be imposed for speeding offences (including motorway speed-ing offences) from "3–6 or 3 (fixed penalty)" to "2–6 or appropriate penalty points (fixed penalty)". Provision will thus be made for a more graduated arrangement of fixed penalties in respect of these offences (see further Chapter 17). At the time

6.141

of writing (March 2009) no indication had been given as to a likely implementation date for these provisions.

Sentencing guidelines

6.142   On August 4, 2008, new Magistrates' Court Sentencing Guidelines became effective; the revised guidelines are summarised in § 18.05 below and the guidelines for road traffic offences are set out in full in Appendix 3 below. The full text can be found at *http://www.sentencing-guidelines.gov.uk* [Accessed March 31, 2009]. The Magistrates' Court Sentencing Guidelines include guidelines for speeding offences (see p.1244 below). There is a starting point and range of either a Band A fine or Band B fine depending on how far the motorist has exceeded the speed limit. Similarly, the number of points and period of the disqualification goes up depending on by how far the speed limit has been exceeded.

Speed limits: penalties

Offence	Mode of trial	Section *	Imprisonment	Level of fine	Disqualification	Penalty points	Endorsement code	Sentencing guideline
Exceeding general speed limit for road	Summary	s.89	—	3	Discretionary	3–6	SP30	See Appendix 3
Exceeding speed limit for goods vehicles	Summary	s.89	—	3	Discretionary	3–6	SP10	See Appendix 3
Exceeding speed limit for type of vehicle	Summary	s.89	—	3	Discretionary	3–6	SP20	See Appendix 3
Exceeding speed limit for passenger vehicles	Summary	s.89	—	3	Discretionary	3–6	SP40	See Appendix 3
Exceeding overall speed limit for motorway	Summary	s.17(4)	—	4	Discretionary	3–6	SP50	See Appendix 3
Exceeding lower speed limit for vehicle on motorway	Summary	s.89	—	3	Discretionary	3–6	SP10, SP20 or SP40 as appropriate	See Appendix 3

Offence	Mode of trial	Section *	Imprisonment	Level of fine	Disqualification	Penalty points	Endorsement code	Sentencing guideline
Temporary speed restriction for roadworks, etc.	Summary	s.16(1)	—	3	Discretionary	3–6	SP60	See Appendix 3
Minimum speed limit	Summary	s.88(7)	—	3	—	—	—	—

* Road Traffic Regulation Act 1984.

MOTORWAYS

Generally

The only vehicles which may lawfully use the motorways at all times are those **6.144** in Classes I and II in Sch.4 to the Highways Act 1980.

Class I vehicles are heavy and light locomotives, heavy motor cars, motor cars and motor cycles with engine or cylinder capacity not less than 50cc which comply with the Construction and Use Regulations and satisfy various conditions. Class II vehicles include motor vehicles and trailers authorised to carry abnormal indivisible loads; certain motor vehicles and trailers constructed for the purposes of the armed forces or defence purposes.

The remaining classes may only use a motorway in accordance with reg.15 of **6.145** the Motorways Traffic (England and Wales) Regulations 1982 (SI 1982/1163), as amended. Class III consists of motor vehicles controlled by pedestrians and Class IV of all motor vehicles (other than invalid carriages and motor cycles less than 50cc) not comprised in Classes I–III. "Abnormal indivisible load" in Class II has the same meaning as in the Road Vehicles (Authorisation of Special Types) (General) Order 2003 (SI 2003/1998).

Curiously a 50cc motor cycle may be used on a motorway even though it may be classified as a moped (see § 1.18). As to invalid carriages, certain vehicles are treated as invalid carriages *for certain purposes* (see § 1.09), e.g. carriages for invalids exceeding 254kg but not exceeding 10cwt are treated as invalid carriages for the purpose of Pt III of the 1988 Act (driving licences and driving tests). As expressions in Sch.4 to the Highways Act 1980 have the same meaning as in the 1988 Act, it is submitted that such invalid carriages are *not* therefore excluded from motorways.

The use of a motorway by a vehicle of a class or type excluded from motor- **6.146** ways is an offence contrary to s.17 of the Road Traffic Regulation Act 1984.

Special speed limits for certain classes of vehicles on motorways are prescribed by Sch.6 to the Road Traffic Regulation Act 1984 but the law relating to speed limits generally is otherwise applicable (see the previous section on Speed Limits).

Contravention of the red flashing motorway signs is dealt with in the section relating to traffic lights at § 6.33, "Motorway and dual carriageway traffic lights".

Certain of the cases in Chapter 5 relate to motorways (see notably *Trentham v Rowlands* at § 5.72).

Where the prosecution omitted before closing their case to prove that a motor- **6.147** way was a "special road" in accordance with the Special Roads (Notice of Opening) Regulations 1962, made under what is now s.17(2) of the Road Traffic Regulation Act 1984, and also to prove the regulations, the justices were directed that they had a discretion to allow the prosecution to reopen their case and should exercise their discretion in favour of the prosecution as the evidence was purely of a formal nature (*Royal v Prescott-Clarke* [1966] 2 All E.R. 366), despite the fact that the defence had given the prosecution notice prior to the hearing that formal proof of these matters would have to be given.

The use of the carriageway by pedestrians is restricted by reg.15(1)(b) of the 1982 Regulations and s.17(1) of the Road Traffic Regulation Act 1984, as amended. In *Reed v Wastie* [1972] Crim. L.R. 221 it was held that it was also wilful obstruction of a highway contrary to what is now s.137 of the Highways Act 1980, and that a constable could therefore lawfully arrest a person who was standing on the carriageway causing danger to himself and others and who had refused to move when requested to do so.

6.148   The Motorways Traffic (England and Wales) Regulations 1982 were amended by the like-named Amendment Regulations 1992 (SI 1992/1364), principally to take account of the coming into force on that date of the Road Traffic Act 1991. The regulations contain many prohibitions and the appropriate regulation should in each particular case be referred to. The definitions include specific definitions of "carriageway", "hard shoulder" and "verge". Carriageway is no longer that part constructed with a surface suitable for the regular passage of motor vehicles, but that part provided for them. It has been suggested that the change is merely an acceptance of reality. The definitions are such that the hard shoulder is not part of the carriageway and is no longer part of the verge. The verge in turn means "any part of a motorway which is not a carriageway, a hard shoulder, or a central reservation".

Regulation 7 contains restrictions on stopping on carriageways, and where a vehicle has to stop on a motorway by reason of an emergency or other circumstances set out in reg.7(2), it is required to be driven or moved onto a hard shoulder. Regulation 9 makes it an offence for a vehicle to be driven or to stop on a hard shoulder unless the circumstances set out in reg.7(2) or (3) exist.

6.149   One of the grounds set out in reg.7(2) justifying a motorist stopping on the hard shoulder is "by reason of any accident, illness or other emergency" (reg.7(2)(b)). A motorist, when a mile from a motorway, began to feel drowsy but reached the slip road to the motorway before he saw a place to park his car. Knowing that the next motorway intersection was 10 miles further on he parked his car at the side of the slip road. It was held that the element of suddenness was not to be emphasised in the meaning of "emergency" in reg.7(2)(b) but the emergency must arise after the defendant had entered the motorway system and he should therefore be convicted as he felt drowsy before he reached the motorway slip road (*Higgins v Bernard* [1972] R.T.R. 304). The conviction of a defendant praying in the direction of Mecca who had stopped his vehicle on a motorway is reported in *The Times* on February 8, 1980.

Other offences contained in the regulations are reversing (reg.8), using the central reservation or verge (reg.10), driving by learner drivers (reg.11). The learner drivers excluded under reg.11 do not include LGV (large goods vehicle) and PCV (passenger-carrying vehicle) licence learners, nor those with provisional entitlement to drive motor cars with trailers, trucks and vans between 3.5 and 7.5 tonnes and buses with between nine and 16 passenger seats (regardless of whether the passengers are carried for hire or reward), provided they have passed a test for at least a category B licence (motor cars).

6.150   Vehicles now excluded from the outside lane of a motorway with three or more operational lanes are listed in reg.12, as amended. The prohibited vehicles are goods vehicles with a maximum laden weight exceeding 7.5 tonnes, goods vehicles with a maximum laden weight exceeding 3.5 tonnes but not exceeding 7.5 tonnes if required to be fitted with a speed limiter, passenger vehicles constructed or adapted to carry more than eight seated passengers in addition to the driver with a maximum laden weight exceeding 7.5 tonnes, passenger vehicles constructed or adapted to carry more than eight seated passengers in addition to

Motorways: penalties

Offence	Mode of trial	Section *	Imprisonment	Level of fine	Disqualification	Penalty points	Endorsement code	Sentencing guideline †
Driving in reverse	Summary	s.17(4)	—	4	Discretionary	3	MW10	Fine band C on main motorway Fine band B on slip road
Driving in wrong direction	Summary	s.17(4)	—	4	Discretionary	3	MW10	Fine band C on main motorway Fine band B on slip road (consider disqualification)
Driving off carriageway	Summary	s.17(4)	—	4	Discretionary	3	MW10	Fine band B on central reservation or on hard shoulder
Driving on slip roads against "no entry" sign	Summary	s.17(4)	—	4	Discretionary	3	MW10	Fine band B
Making "U" turn	Summary	s.17(4)	—	4	Discretionary	3	MW10	Fine band C
Learner driver or excluded vehicle	Summary	s.17(4)	—	4	Discretionary	3	MW10	Fine band A

Offence	Mode of trial	Section *	Imprisonment	Level of fine	Disqualification	Penalty points	Endorsement code	Sentencing guideline †
Stopping on hard shoulder	Summary	s.17(4)	—	4	—	—	—	Fine band A on main motorway or on slip road
Stopping on carriageway	Summary	s.17(4)	—	4	Discretionary	3	MW10	—
Exceeding overall speed limit for motorway	Summary	s.17(4)	—	4	Discretionary	3–6	SP50	As appropriate for speeding (see Appendix 3)
Exceeding lower speed limit for vehicle	Summary	s.89	—	3	Discretionary	3–6	As appropriate for speeding	As appropriate for speeding (see Appendix 3)

* Road Traffic Regulation Act 1984.

† **Note**: Fine bands "A", "B" and "C" represent respectively 50%, 100% and 150% of relevant weekly income. A timely guilty plea should attract a discount. See Appendix 3.

PEDESTRIAN CROSSINGS

Generally

Section 25 of the Road Traffic Regulation Act 1984 empowers the Secretary of **6.154** State to make regulations as to pedestrian crossings. The Zebra, Pelican and Puffin Pedestrian Crossings Regulations and General Directions 1997 (SI 1997/2400) contain not only all relevant regulations and directions with regard to Zebras and Pelicans, animals with which road users are doubtless familiar, but also add a new creature to the menagerie, namely the Puffin. In this age of superabundant acronyms, "Puffin" (Pedestrian User-Friendly Intelligent crossing) deserves reasonably high marks for ingenuity, if hardly for orthography. The "intelligence" possessed by Puffins (but not, it would seem, by Pelicans in this context) is provided by the incorporation of a sensor which delays vehicular traffic as long as is necessary to enable pedestrians to cross, but will not delay traffic when there are no pedestrians on the crossing. A further significant difference between Pelicans and Puffins is that the light signals for the latter include a red with amber phase to indicate to vehicular traffic an impending change to green.

The traffic signs and road markings which indicate these three types of crossing are prescribed by reg.5 of, and Schs 1–4 to, the 1997 Regulations; the marking of give-way lines, stop lines and controlled areas is governed by reg.6 and Schs 1 and 4 ibid. Where those requirements have not been complied with in every respect, the crossing (or controlled area) will nevertheless be treated as complying with the regulations if the non-compliance does not materially affect the general appearance of the crossing or controlled area as may be, does not (in the case of a Pelican or Puffin crossing) affect the proper operation of its vehicular and pedestrian signals, and does not relate to the size of the controlled area (reg.10). The significance of vehicular light signals at Pelican and Puffin crossings is described at regs 12 and 13 respectively, and the significance of give-way lines at Zebra crossings at reg.14.

The stopping of vehicles on crossings is, as under previous regulations, **6.155** prohibited, but with some exceptions (reg.18). One of those exceptions has been redrafted, however. Whereas under the previous regulations a driver was permitted to stop if it was necessary for him to do so in order to avoid *an accident*, he is now allowed to do so in order to avoid *injury or damage to persons or property*. The stopping of vehicles other than pedal cycles in controlled areas is prohibited as heretofore (reg.20); here again the exception relating to the avoidance of an accident has been redrafted as in reg.18 (reg.21). Regulation 22 contains further exceptions to the prohibition on stopping conveyed by reg.20; these rehearse the exceptions contained in the previous regulations, but are set out more cleanly and tidily than before. Vehicles must not proceed across Pelican or Puffin crossings when the vehicular red light signal is displayed (reg.23). Vehicles are prohibited from overtaking within the limits of a controlled area if proceeding towards the crossing (reg.24). Vehicles must accord precedence to pedestrians on Zebra crossings (reg.25) and on Pelican crossings when the flashing amber vehicular signal is displayed (reg.26).

It may be noted that direction 8(3) of the General Directions part of the 1997 Regulations was amended by the Pelican and Puffin Pedestrian Crossings General (Amendment) Directions 1998 (SI 1998/901) so as to add the colour black to the colours which may be used for posts to mount vehicular light signals, pedestrian light signals, indicators for pedestrians and pedestrian demand units. It would seem that the colour black was inadvertently omitted from the original list of permissible colours.

6.156   The crossings described above fall into two basic categories; "uncontrolled" crossings ("Zebra" crossings) and "controlled" crossings, i.e. controlled by pedestrian-operated push buttons ("Pelican" and "Puffin" crossings). Each category is described in greater detail below.

By s.25(6) of the 1984 Act, a crossing shall be deemed to be duly established and indicated unless the contrary be proved.

Zebra crossings

6.157   Zebra crossings are now regulated by the Zebra, Pelican and Puffin Pedestrian Crossings Regulations and General Directions 1997 (SI 1997/2400). The regulations prescribe the road markings for the crossing, the controlled areas and the appropriate traffic signs together with the various offences (see Sch.1).

The regulations apply to drivers of motor vehicles, trams, trolley vehicles and horse-drawn vehicles and to the riders of motor cycles and cycles (save as indicated in reg.20) but not to equestrians. Save as provided in reg.21, there is no exemption for fire-engines, ambulances or police cars. The regulations apply to Crown vehicles (s.130 of the 1984 Act).

6.158   By reg.5(1) every crossing and its limits shall be indicated in accordance with the provisions of Sch.1. This means that every crossing shall be indicated by two lines of studs placed across the roadway in accordance with Pt 2 of Sch.1. There the distances apart, the colour, size, shape and permitted projection of the studs are prescribed. The crossing must also be indicated by black and white stripes on the crossing (para.6). Paragraph 8(1) allows the omission of black painted stripes where the surface of the road provides a reasonable contrast to the white stripes. By para.12, a Zebra crossing or a Zebra controlled area shall not be deemed to have ceased to be indicated by reason only of the discolouration or partial displacement of any of the prescribed road markings, so long as the general appearance of the pattern of the lines is not impaired.

Paragraph 1 of Pt I of Sch.1 requires the crossing also to be indicated by yellow globes mounted on posts or brackets. Although there must be a yellow globe at or near each end of the crossing, there need not be globes on any central reservation or street refuge but such globes *may* be placed there. If globes are not placed on a central reservation, the crossing would appear to be sufficiently indicated. The globes are required to be illuminated by flashing lights or, where so authorised by the Secretary of State, by a constant light. By para.4, a crossing shall not be taken to have ceased to be properly indicated by reason only of the imperfection, disfigurement or discolouration of any globe or post, or the failure of illumination of any of the globes. Paragraphs 1 and 2 prescribe the limits of dimensions of the globes, their height above ground, and the alternate black and white horizontal stripes on the posts. Where a globe is mounted on a bracket, the bracket does not have to be striped. It is only posts specially provided for the purpose of bearing globes which are required to be painted black and white. Paragraph 3 enables beacons to be fitted with backing boards to improve their conspicuity, with shields to prevent the scattering of light to adjoining properties, and with a light to illuminate the crossing.

6.159   Part II of Sch.1 contains provisions prescribing the manner in which the Zebra controlled area and "give way" lines are to be indicated. A broken white line (the "give way" line) must be placed 1,100–3,000mm each side of the crossing and two or more longitudinal white lines ("zig-zag" lines) must be placed on each side of the crossing indicating the controlled area. The Schedule prescribes the dimensions of the signs and reg.7 prescribes the permitted variations in the dimensions. By para.12 a controlled area shall not be deemed to have ceased to be properly indicated by reason only of the discolouration or partial displacement of any of the prescribed road markings, so long as the general appearance of the pattern of the lines is not impaired.

The proviso in para.12 preserves the legal status of the crossing or controlled area "so long as the general appearance of the pattern of the lines is not impaired"; if it is submitted that no offence can be committed (cf. *Power v Davidson* (1964) 62 L.G.R. 320 at § 6.58 and see. "Non-conforming and damaged signs", §§ 6.57–9).

The Road Traffic Regulation Act 1984 s.25(4), allows special provisions to be made in regard to particular crossings (note also the provisions as to variation contained in Pt II of Sch.1). **6.160**

The "limits" of a Zebra crossing

The "limits" of a Zebra crossing referred to in Sch.1 to the regulations are defined by the studs across the road on each side of the black and white stripes (Sch.1 Pt II para.6), and a vehicle has not come "within the limits of a crossing" under para.6 if it has come within the zig-zag lines marking the approach to the crossing but has not reached the studs bordering the black and white stripes (*Moulder v Neville* [1974] R.T.R. 53, a case on the 1971 Regulations, following *Hughes v Hall* [1960] 2 All E.R. 504, a similar decision on the 1954 Regulations). A pedestrian is seemingly outside the limits of the crossing if he is outside the studs but within the "give way" line which is 1,100–3,000mm away. It seems that the effect of the "give way" line is not to extend the limits of the crossing but to indicate to the motorist where he should stop to accord precedence to a pedestrian who is on the black and white stripes of the crossing. **6.161**

Note the provision in reg.25 as to the parts of a Zebra crossing on each side of a street refuge or central reservation being treated as separate crossings for the purposes of that regulation.

According precedence at Zebra crossings

This is dealt with by reg.25 of the 1997 Regulations. If the crossing is for the time being controlled by a police officer in uniform or by a traffic warden the provisions relating to pedestrians being accorded precedence cease, but vehicles and pedestrians must obey the police officer's or traffic warden's signals (see further below) and failure to do so may result in prosecution under s.35, s.37 or s.163 of the 1988 Act. **6.162**

Liability under reg.25 arises only if the pedestrian is on the carriageway within the limits of the crossing before the vehicle or any part of it has come on the carriageway within those limits, i.e. the black and white striped area inside the innermost lines of studs. See above as to the "limits" of a crossing. A pedestrian waiting on the kerb or walking along the roadway towards the crossing is thus not within reg.25. It is essential not to be confused between the "limits" of the crossing and the "Zebra controlled area", i.e. the area of carriageway, bordered by zig-zag lines both sides of the actual crossing (see § 6.171 as to the Zebra controlled area). Justices who dismissed a case of failing to accord precedence under what is now reg.25 because they were not certain whether the motorist reached the beginnings of the Zebra controlled area before the pedestrian stopped on the actual crossing were directed to convict the motorist (*Moulder v Neville* [1974] R.T.R. 53); a case can only be dismissed under reg.25 if the prosecution fail to prove that the foot passenger stepped onto the actual crossing before the car reached the actual limits of the crossing, i.e. the black and white striped area.

6.163   Regulation 14 requires the motorist to stop at or before the "give way" line, which is 1,100–3,000mm from the limits of the crossing, in order to accord the pedestrian precedence, and he will offend against reg.25 if he does not do so.

Where there is a central reservation or street refuge in a crossing, the parts on each side of the reservation or refuge are treated as separate crossings (reg.25). A motorist approaching a crossing on the left-hand side of a road thus owes no duty under reg.25 to a pedestrian who is walking from the right-hand kerb towards a central reservation.

6.164   If a Zebra crossing is for the time being controlled by a police officer or traffic warden, again reg.25 will not apply, and the driver or rider of a vehicle must obey the police officer's signals. The reason for this provision seems to be that pedestrians who themselves disobey the warning gestures of a police officer thereby put themselves in peril, and to cast a double duty on a motorist of both obeying a police officer and according precedence to a pedestrian would be unfair. A High Court decision noted at (1966) 130 J.P. Jo. 759 is that a crossing is not controlled by a police officer when the latter is standing on the pavement at the crossing but has not begun controlling the traffic, even if he is about to do so. A police officer was on a school crossing patrol at a pedestrian crossing. He only stopped the traffic when children or sometimes the elderly wanted to cross. When he did so other adults crossed the road. At other times he allowed the traffic to continue and a motorist driving across at this time was convicted of failing to accord precedence to a pedestrian. The motorist thought the pedestrian should have waited for the police officer to indicate that he should cross. A Crown Court judge sitting with justices at the Inner London Crown Court dismissed an appeal against conviction by magistrates but found special reasons for not endorsing as the motorist had been misled. The Crown Court held that the crossing was not controlled all the time and was not controlled when his vehicle passed. The decision is not binding: whether a crossing is controlled is very much a question of fact.

In *Kayser v LPTB* [1950] 1 All E.R. 231, a case on the pre-1951 regulations, it was held that, where a driver is satisfied that persons on the crossing are out of danger from him, he may proceed at a reasonable speed. Compare *Wishart v McDonald* at § 6.170 below.

6.165   In *McKerrell v Robertson* 1956 S.L.T. 290 it was held that precedence must be accorded to a woman pushing a go-cart when the go-cart is on the crossing, although she is still on the pavement: she and the go-cart are one entity. The case is discussed at 125 J.P. Jo. 341 of a pedestrian on a crossing who does not wish to cross.

A magistrates' court has held that a child on roller-skates is not a "foot passenger". It is submitted that this decision is correct. In the absence of a definition a "foot passenger" must mean someone on foot. Cyclists who push their cycles across uncontrolled pedestrian crossings are pedestrians (*Crank v Brooks* [1980] R.T.R. 441). "[A person] with both feet on the ground, so to speak, is clearly a foot passenger. If for example she had been using [the bicycle] as a scooter by having one foot on the pedal and pushing herself along, she would not have been a foot passenger" (per Waller L.J., at 443).

Absolute liability of driver

Subject to the limited exceptions given in *Burns v Bidder* below, the duty of **6.166** the motorist, cyclist or other driver to accord precedence is absolute.

In *Neal v Reynolds* (1966) 110 S.J. 353, it was said that magistrates should not approach these prosecutions on the basis whether the defendant driver was negligent or not. In *Burns v Bidder* [1966] 3 All E.R. 29, the cases were all reviewed again and James J. said:

> " Regulation 4 must be read 'subject to the principle of impossibility' ... In my judgment the regulation does not impose an absolute duty come what may, and there is no breach [of it] in circumstances where the driver fails to accord precedence to a pedestrian solely because his control of the vehicle is taken from him by the occurrence of an event which is outside his possible or reasonable control and in respect of which he is in no way at fault. [He instanced the driver being stung by bees or having an epileptic fit or his vehicle being propelled forward by being hit from behind as illustrations of the vehicle's being taken out of the driver's control, so that his failure then to accord precedence would be no offence, and continued] ... a sudden removal of control over the vehicle occasioned by a latent defect of which the driver did not know and could not reasonably be expected to know would render the resulting failure to accord precedence no offence, provided he is in no way at fault himself. But beyond that limited sphere, the obligation of the driver under the regulations can properly be described ... as an absolute one."

This case settled the law fairly conclusively as to reg.4 of the 1954 Regulations. **6.167** Regulation 25 of the 1997 Regulations does not differ materially from reg.4 and it is submitted that *Burns v Bidder* still expresses the law. Similar factors were mentioned in *R. v Bell (David)* [1984] Crim. L.R. 685 (a reckless driving case) and it was held that an excuse of being driven on by God was not in that category. Running out of petrol is not a latent defect (*Oakley-Moore v Robinson* at § 6.171).

In *Gibbons v Kahl* [1955] 3 All E.R. 645 it was said that it is the duty of a driver to be able to stop before he gets to a crossing unless he can see that there is no one on it. If he cannot see if there is anybody on it, he must drive in such a way that he can stop if there is a person on it masked from him by other traffic. In the *Gibbons* case, the defendant overtook a bus, which had stopped at a crossing to allow pedestrians to proceed; the pedestrians were hidden from the defendant by the bus and he did not see them until they had passed in front of the bus. He was then too near the crossing to stop and he was held guilty of not according precedence. This case was followed in *Lockie v Lawton* (1960) 124 J.P. 24, where it was said that a driver approaching a crossing must drive in such a way that he can stop if there is a pedestrian on the crossing, although his view of the crossing may be blocked by other vehicles until he is right on it. In *Hughes v Hall* [1960] 2 All E.R. 504 it was said that there was an absolute duty under the regulations, and it is immaterial whether there is any evidence of negligence or failure to take care by the driver. In *Scott v Clint, The Times*, October 28, 1960, a driver was approaching a crossing at 15–20mph and, when he was 10yds from it, two children stepped on it without looking. He swerved but could not avoid hitting one of them. It was held that he was guilty but that it was a proper case for an absolute discharge. The case of *Leicester v Pearson* [1952] 2 All E.R. 71, holding that a driver could be excused if he was driving reasonably and with care in bad visibility, no longer seems to be of authority. In *Hughes v Hall* above the driver was approaching the crossing at a proper speed and had passed or partly passed over the approach studs when a pedestrian stepped on the crossing without looking and walked 9 or 10ft before being hit by the car, which was rapidly pulling up. As stated, the driver was held guilty, and unless the High Court is prepared to draw a distinction between the cases cited above and cases where a pedestrian steps practically in front of a slow-moving car when it is a foot or so from the crossing, it seems that the driver must always be found guilty if he had not in fact accorded precedence, although an absolute discharge is often justifiable, where the driver is not negligent, and "special reasons" could be found.

6.168 The meaning of the term "accord precedence" was considered by two metropolitan magistrates, whose views are reported at [1952] Jo.Crim.L. 105 and 110, but should now be read in the light of the cases cited in the last paragraph. In one case the defendant drove between two pedestrians on a Zebra crossing; he was driving cautiously and neither pedestrian was endangered. Sir Wilfred Bennett dismissed the charge, holding that "according precedence" meant much the same as "not interrupting the free passage of a pedestrian", the term in the pre-1951 regulations. He said that the new regulation required that a driver must not cause a pedestrian to stop once he has started to cross. The expression "accord precedence" is still used in the current regulations. In the other case, the facts accepted were that the pedestrians were on the crossing but so far away from the defendant's car that he could not have interrupted their crossing. Mr T.F. Davis apparently did not agree that the law had not been altered and, save for "suicide cases" (semble people who stepped practically in front of a fast moving car), held that a motorist who could reasonably stop must stop if there are pedestrians on the crossing. In *Rhind v Irvine* [1940] 2 W.W.R. 333, a Canadian case, it was held that the motorist's duty to "yield the right of way" to a pedestrian on a crossing did not give a pedestrian a right to walk into or against an obstructing car or to walk over the crossing with his eyes shut. In *Wishart v McDonald* (1962) 78 Sh.Ct.Rep. 3, a driver passed over a crossing while a blind pedestrian was walking over it, the pedestrian being neither impeded by the car nor even aware of it; the sheriff acquitted the driver of not according precedence. The sheriff rejected the view that the regulation means that the pedestrian shall go first over the crossing before the vehicle goes over it. Precedence, he said, means "go before" or "in front of" and the regulation means that the vehicle shall not prevent a foot passenger from crossing; the issue of precedence would arise only where there was a likely encounter between vehicle and pedestrian.

6.169 A New Zealand regulation required the motorist when approaching a pedestrian crossing to "yield the right of way" to a pedestrian on it. It was held that a motorist approaching a crossing on which there was a pedestrian must surrender to the latter any priority in passage ahead which he might otherwise have had whether or not a collision might seem likely or however far the pedestrian might be on the crossing to his left and that a pedestrian who had begun to cross and then paused and stopped was still within the protection of the regulation (*Torok v Lake* [1964] N.Z.L.R. 824). In *Kozimor v Adey* [1962] Crim. L.R. 564, a civil case, Megaw J. said that the only way a motorist can be certain of avoiding a breach of the regulations is to approach the crossing at such a low speed that he can stop in the event of any conceivable use of the crossing by any conceivable pedestrian except a suicidal one who deliberately walked in front of a car. If, therefore, a motorist driving in the centre of a wide street sees a pedestrian step off the kerb, the motorist, it is submitted, must stop if there is any reasonable possibility that the pedestrian might get in the car's path; the fact that the pedestrian is walking so slowly that it is unlikely that he will get in the car's path would not necessarily be an excuse, for he might panic and break into a run.

If a pedestrian signals a car to come on and himself stops, it still seems that the driver should accord him precedence as a matter of strict law (*Neal v Bedford* [1965] 3 All E.R. 250), though no doubt it would be strong mitigation if the driver accepted the pedestrian's signal to him to proceed and then the pedestrian dashed forward. In that case pedestrians had stopped to allow a car ahead of the defendant's car to pass in front of them; they moved on when the first car had passed and the defendant's car also came on and struck one of them. The High Court said that reg.4 of the 1954 Regulations imposed an absolute duty to accord precedence and whether the defendant genuinely thought that the pedestrians would let him pass was irrelevant; they had not waived their precedence by signalling to him to pass but had started walking. A conviction was directed. However, in most cases it will turn out to be a question of fact and a motorist, even if he is held to have broken the law, may still have many matters to urge in mitigation of penalty.

Defence of mechanical failure, etc.

See *Burns v Bidder* above, where it was said that it would be a defence if a vehicle went on to a crossing because of the driver's excusable loss of control, through being stung or being pushed forward by a vehicle behind or through a latent defect in the brakes of which the driver could not reasonably be expected to know, so long as he was in no way at fault himself. As to running out of petrol, see *Oakley-Moore v Robinson* below. **6.170**

Stopping in the Zebra controlled area

Regulation 18 relates to stopping on crossings: circumstances beyond the **6.171** driver's control and stopping to avoid injury or damage to persons or property are defences. Regulation 19 also forbids pedestrians to loiter on the crossing. Regulation 20 forbids the driver of a vehicle to stop in the Zebra controlled area. Note the definition of "Zebra controlled area" in reg.3(1). It is the area bordered by zig-zag lines as required by reg.6(1) and not for instance the crossing itself, a point emphasised in *Wright v Hunt, The Times*, May 12, 1984. Note Pt II of Sch.1 and reg.7 as to variations and in particular para.12 of Sch.1 as to imperfections. Bicycles are exempted from the regulation even if additional means of propulsion are attached. The bicycle must not, however, have a side-car. It should be noted that the controlled area normally extends to both sides of the crossing, and unlike the former regulations, it is an offence to stop on the further side to the crossing, as well as on its approach.

Regulations 21 and 22 contain various exemptions from reg.20: fire and rescue, ambulance and police purposes, building works, road works, emergencies, etc. Stopping for the purpose of turning right or left is exempted. Public service vehicles are also exempted for the purpose of picking up or dropping passengers on the far side of the crossing but not on the approach to the crossing. Stopping for reasons beyond a driver's control or to avoid injury or damage to persons or property is also exempted. In *Oakley-Moore v Robinson* [1982] R.T.R. 74 a motorist brought his car to rest within the approach limits of a Pelican crossing, thinking he had run out of petrol. He claimed that he was prevented from proceeding by circumstances beyond his control. The Divisional Court upheld the justices' finding that this was a matter within his control: it was not a latent defect. The same principle would seem to apply to a Zebra pedestrian crossing. It was suggested (ibid.) that the burden of proof regarding circumstances beyond the driver's control and stopping to avoid injury or damage to persons or property remained on the prosecution throughout, although no doubt the defendant would raise the matter in the first instance. This suggestion must be treated with some reserve. It was accepted in the judgment but the point was not argued. The regulations forbidding stopping in the area controlled by a Zebra crossing apply even if the crossing is for the time being controlled by a police officer or traffic warden.

Overtaking in the Zebra controlled area

6.172   It is an offence when approaching a Zebra crossing to overtake a moving motor vehicle (reg.24(1)(a)) or a stationary vehicle (reg.24(1)(b)) in the area controlled by the crossing. It is not an offence to overtake a vehicle in the controlled area on the further side of the crossing. It is also not an offence where the passing vehicle is on the crossing itself at the moment at which it passed ahead of the foremost part of the other vehicle, because the passing vehicle had by then passed one of the limits of the crossing and because the crossing itself was not part of the controlled area (see *Wright v Hunt, The Times*, May 12, 1984 on this point).

    Regulation 24(1) is phrased in such a way that a vehicle "overtakes" another once any part of the vehicle passes ahead of the foremost part of the other vehicle. It would appear, therefore, that an offence is committed even if the overtaking vehicle subsequently drops back. However, it is only an offence if the vehicle overtaken is either the only other vehicle on the approach to the crossing or, if there is more than one, it is the nearest vehicle to the crossing.

6.173   The vehicle being overtaken may be either moving or stationary, but if it is stationary the overtaking is only an offence if the vehicle overtaken "is stationary for the purpose of complying with reg.25 " (see reg.24(1)(b)). It was held in *Gullen v Ford; Prowse v Clark* [1975] R.T.R. 303 that "stopped for the purpose of complying with [(what is now) reg.25] " did not mean that the stationary vehicle must have stopped because a pedestrian had a foot on the crossing and the driver would thus have committed an offence under reg.25 if the car had not stopped. Stopping for the purpose of reg.25 includes a car which had stopped out of courtesy to a pedestrian who was waiting to cross but who had not actually placed his foot on the carriageway. It was said obiter by Lord Widgery C.J. that he was concerned in the case of very long crossings when no danger was caused by reason of a technical breach of (what is now) reg.24(1)(b). He suggested that the prosecution in such a case should refrain from prosecuting on a purely technical charge when no danger of any kind was created. *Gullen v Ford* above was followed in *Connor v Paterson* [1977] R.T.R. 379. A Mini had stopped at a crossing to give precedence to pedestrians using the crossing; the defendant's van had pulled alongside the Mini and then passed in front of it over the crossing at a time when no pedestrians were using it. It was held that an offence contrary to what is now reg.24 had been committed. "Stopped for the purpose of complying with [(what is now) reg.25] " meant stopped not only when pedestrians were on the crossing, or likely to be there (as in *Gullen v Ford* above) but also when the overtaken vehicle had stopped to allow pedestrians to move away, but had not moved after having stopped to allow them to cross.

A further distinction between the offence under reg.24(1)(a) of overtaking a moving motor vehicle and under reg.24(1)(b) of overtaking a stationary vehicle is that an offence is only committed in overtaking a moving vehicle if the vehicle which is overtaken is a motor vehicle. An offence under reg.24(1)(b) on the other hand is committed if the vehicle overtaken is any type of vehicle including a bicycle (see "Vehicle", § 1.32 and also § 1.43).

Pelican crossings

The Zebra, Pelican and Puffin Pedestrian Crossings Regulations and General Directions 1997 (SI 1997/2400) made under the authority of s.25 of the Road Traffic Regulation Act 1984 are set out in full in Vol.2. **6.174**

The traffic signs and road markings which indicate a Pelican crossing are prescribed by reg.5(2) of, and Schs 2 and 4 to the 1997 Regulations; the marking of stop lines and controlled areas is governed by reg.6(2) and Sch.4 ibid. Where those requirements have not been complied with in every respect, the crossing (or controlled area) will nevertheless be treated as complying with the regulations if the non-compliance does not materially affect the general appearance of the crossing or controlled area as may be, does not affect the proper operation of its vehicular and pedestrian signals, and does not relate to the size of the controlled area (reg.10). The significance of vehicular light signals at Pelican crossings is described at reg.12.

The stopping of vehicles on Pelican crossings is, as under previous regulations, prohibited, but with some exceptions (reg.18). One of those exceptions has been redrafted, however. Whereas under the previous regulations a driver was permitted to stop if it was necessary for him to do so in order to avoid *an accident*, he is now allowed to do so in order to avoid *injury or damage to persons or property*. The stopping of vehicles (other than pedal cycles without side-cars) in controlled areas is prohibited as heretofore (reg.20); here again the exception relating to the avoidance of an accident has been redrafted as in reg.18 (reg.21). Regulation 22 contains further exceptions to the prohibition on stopping conveyed by reg.20; these rehearse the exceptions contained in the previous regulations, but are set out more cleanly and tidily than before. Regulations 18, 20, 21 and 22 apply equally to Pelican and to Zebra crossings; they are discussed at greater length at § 6.171 above. **6.175**

Vehicles must not proceed across Pelican crossings when the vehicular red light signal is displayed (reg.23).

Vehicles are prohibited from overtaking within the limits of a controlled area if proceeding towards the crossing (reg.24). (Regulation 24 applies equally to Pelican and to Zebra crossings; its significance is discussed in detail at §§ 6.172–3 above.)

Vehicles must accord precedence to pedestrians on Pelican crossings when the flashing amber vehicular signal is displayed, but not where the pedestrian is on a **6.176** central reservation which forms part of a system of staggered crossings (reg.26). This regulation mirrors in large part reg.25, which deals with the precedence of pedestrians over vehicles at Zebra crossings. That regulation, together with the case law adhering to it and its predecessor regulations is discussed in depth at §§ 6.162–5 above.

Provision has been made for both "primary" and "secondary" vehicular light signals at Pelican crossings, and the prohibition on proceeding (red light) and the requirement for precedence for pedestrians (flashing amber light) apply even when one set of lights is operating without the other (regs 12, 23 and 26); the signals concerned are defined in reg.3(1). If the stop line is not visible, and a red or steady amber light is exhibited, vehicles are prohibited from proceeding beyond the post or other structure on which the primary signal is mounted (regs 12(1)(c), (d), (3) and 23).

Puffin crossings

6.177   The Zebra, Pelican and Puffin Pedestrian Crossings Regulations and General Directions 1997 (SI 1997/2400) contain not only all relevant regulations and directions with regard to Zebra and Pelican crossings, but also introduce a type of crossing called the "Puffin" (**P**edestrian **U**ser-**F**riendly **In**telligent) crossing. The "intelligence" possessed by Puffins is provided by the incorporation of a sensor which delays vehicular traffic as long as is necessary to enable pedestrians to cross, but will not delay traffic when there are no pedestrians on the crossing. A significant difference between Pelicans and Puffins is that the light signals for the latter include a red with amber phase to indicate to vehicular traffic an impending change to green.

The traffic signs and road markings which indicate a Puffin crossing are prescribed by reg.5(3) of, and Schs 3 and 4 to the 1997 Regulations; the marking of give way lines, stop lines and controlled areas is governed, as it is for Pelican crossings, by reg.6 and Sch.4 ibid. Where those requirements have not been complied with in every respect, the crossing (or controlled area) will nevertheless be treated as complying with the Regulations if the non-compliance does not materially affect the general appearance of the crossing or controlled area as may be, does not (in the case of a Pelican or Puffin crossing) affect the proper operation of its vehicular and pedestrian signals, and does not relate to the size of the controlled area (reg.10). The significance of vehicular light signals at Puffin crossings is described at reg.13.

6.178   The stopping of vehicles on crossings is, as under previous regulations in respect of Zebra and Pelican crossings, prohibited, but with some exceptions (regs 18, 21 and 22). The stopping of vehicles (other than pedal cycles without sidecars) in controlled areas is prohibited (reg.20). Regulations 18, 20, 21 and 22 apply equally to Puffin and to Zebra crossings; they are discussed at greater length at §§ 6.171 and 6.174 et seq.

Vehicles must not proceed across Puffin crossings when the vehicular red light signal is displayed (reg.23).

6.179   Vehicles are prohibited from overtaking within the limits of a controlled area if proceeding towards the crossing (reg.24). (Regulation 24 applies equally to Puffin and to Zebra crossings; its significance is discussed in detail at §§ 6.172–3 above.)

Provision has been made for both "primary" and "secondary" vehicular light signals at Puffin crossings, and the prohibition on proceeding (red light) applies even when one set of lights is operating without the other (regs 13 and 23); the signals concerned are defined in reg.3(1). If the stop line is not visible, and a red or steady amber light is exhibited, vehicles are prohibited from proceeding beyond the post or other structure on which the primary signal is mounted (regs 13(1)(c), (d), (3) and 23).

PEDESTRIAN CROSSINGS: PROCEEDINGS AND PENALTIES

Generally

What is now s.1 of the 1988 Offenders Act requiring warning of intended prosecution (see Chapter 2) does not apply to an offence in respect of a Pelican crossing (*Sulston v Hammond* [1970] 2 All E.R. 830). It would appear that s.1 of the 1988 Offenders Act does not apply to an offence committed in respect of a Zebra crossing either. **6.180**

The penalty for a breach of the Zebra, Pelican and Puffin Crossings Regulations and General Directions 1997 is a fine of level 3 (Road Traffic Regulation Act 1984 s.25(5), and Sch.2 to the 1988 Offenders Act). However the penalty for a breach of a regulation made under s.64 (e.g. the steady amber light) is by s.118 and Sch.2 to the 1988 Offenders Act a fine of level 3 also but without the power to endorse, disqualify or order penalty points.

Section 112 of the 1984 Act (information as to identity of driver or rider), s.11 of the 1988 Offenders Act (evidence by certificate) and s.12 ibid. (proof of identity of driver) apply to s.25 offences. Section 25 of the 1984 Act applies to vehicles and persons in the public service of the Crown, as does s.64 (see s.130). **6.181**

As a result of the amendment of the Functions of Traffic Wardens Order 1970 by the like-named Amendment Order 1993 (SI 1993/1334), traffic wardens may be employed to enforce the law with respect to offences of causing vehicles to stop on pedestrian crossings in contravention of pedestrian crossing regulations.

Pedestrian crossings: penalties

Offence	Mode of trial	Section *	Imprisonment	Level of fine	Disqualification	Penalty points	Endorsement code	Sentencing guideline †
Pedestrian crossing regulation (moving vehicle)	Summary	s. 25(5)	—	3	Discretionary	3	PC20	Fine band A
Pedestrian crossing regulation (stationary vehicle)	Summary	s. 25(5)	—	3	Discretionary	3	PC30	Fine band A

* Road Traffic Regulation Act 1984.

† **Note**: Fine bands "A", "B" and "C" represent respectively 50%, 100% and 150% of relevant weekly income. A timely guilty plea should attract a discount. See Appendix 3.

Proceedings for other offences

It is not uncommon, particularly where a pedestrian has been injured on a **6.183** Zebra, Pelican or Puffin crossing, for the prosecution to bring proceedings for careless or even dangerous driving in addition to the pedestrian crossing offence.

A conviction for the more serious offence, i.e. dangerous or careless driving, together with the imposition of a penalty, would generally afford a good ground for not convicting or sentencing for the pedestrian crossing offence (see "Two offences from one incident" at § 5.76). An acquittal for the offence of careless or dangerous driving would be no bar, however, to the proceedings in respect of the pedestrian crossing offence.

EQUESTRIAN AND TOUCAN CROSSINGS

Generally

An equestrian crossing is, as its name suggests, and as defined by reg.4 of the **6.184** Traffic Signs Regulations and General Directions 2002 (SI 2002/3113), a place on the carriageway of a road where provision is made for equestrian traffic to cross the carriageway and whose presence is indicated by a combination of traffic light signals and road markings.

A Toucan crossing is a crossing designed for use by both pedestrians and pedal cyclists; hence the chosen acronym which indicates that "two can" cross. Its definition in reg.4 of the 2002 Regulations is in similar terms to that of the equestrian crossing discussed above.

Regulations 27 and 28 of the 2002 Regulations provide that zig-zag lines when placed at a signal-controlled crossing facility, such as an equestrian or a Toucan crossing, shall in effect have the same meaning and significance as the zig-zag lines prescribed by the Zebra, Pelican and Puffin Pedestrian Crossing Regulations and General Directions 1997 (SI 1997/2400); see §§ 6.154 et seq. The vehicular light signals to be installed at these crossings are prescribed by reg.33 of the 2002 Regulations, and their significance is set out in reg.36 ibid.; see further §§ 6.26 et seq. where traffic lights are discussed at some length.

Regulation 10(1) of the 2002 Regulations provides that s.36 of the 1988 Act **6.185** applies to the zig-zag road markings and the vehicular light signals which are constituent parts of each of these crossings; failure to comply with such signs should accordingly be prosecuted under that section. By virtue of reg.10(2) ibid., offences in respect of these particular markings and signals are made subject to obligatory endorsement and discretionary disqualification. As with other controlled crossings, stopping within the controlled area is prohibited, but with some exceptions which mirror those which apply to other controlled crossings (reg.27(3)); overtaking is similarly prohibited within the controlled area (reg.28). The penalty for either offence, as well as for disobedience to the vehicular light signals, is a level 3 fine and 3 penalty points.

SCHOOL CROSSINGS AND STREET PLAYGROUNDS

Generally

Sections 26, 28 and 29 of the Road Traffic Regulation Act 1984 contain provi- **6.186** sions as to school crossings and street playgrounds.

School crossings

6.187   Under s.26 of the Road Traffic Regulation Act 1984, authorities (principally the councils of London Boroughs, the Common Council of the City of London and county councils or metropolitan district councils outside Greater London) are empowered to arrange the patrolling of crossings used by children on their way to or from school or on their way from one part of a school to another. Section 28 of the Act lays down the circumstances under which vehicles can be required to stop and to remain stationary by the school crossing patrol.

A person required to stop by the school crossing patrol sign must "cause the vehicle to stop before reaching the place where the children are crossing or seeking to cross and so as not to stop or impede their crossing" (s.28(2)(a)) and must not put it in motion again to reach that place while the sign continues to be exhibited (s.28(2)(b)). It should be noted that before a person may be convicted under s.28(2)(a) or s.28(2)(b) he must first have been required to stop in accordance with s.28(1).

6.188   In *Franklin v Langdown* [1971] 3 All E.R. 662 a party of children with two or three adults were crossing a road under the protection of a school crossing patrol sign. When the last of the children had passed over the crown of the road, the defendant drove out of a side turning and passed behind the last of the adults, causing her to hasten her steps. At the time of so doing, the sign continued to be exhibited. The magistrates' court dismissed the case because they were of the opinion that a conviction under what is now s.28(2)(a) could only be obtained if the motorist acted so as to stop or impede the children crossing. The justices were directed to convict and it was held that the words "and so as not to stop or impede their crossing" were merely descriptive of the manner in which a motorist is required to stop (see further below). In *R. v Greenwood* [1962] Crim. L.R. 639 a motorist was acquitted where there were no children on the crossing and none, apparently, seeking to cross. This decision, which was criticised in *Franklin v Langdown* above, may possibly be explained on the ground that the motorist in that case had not been lawfully required to stop under what is now s.28(1) because, when he was required to do so, there were no children crossing or seeking to cross and the school crossing patrol could not therefore display his sign in accordance with the section. Nevertheless, the case was again criticised in *Wall v Walwyn* [1974] R.T.R. 24, where following *Franklin v Langdown* justices were again directed to convict a motorist whom they had acquitted because the children had not been impeded. Lord Widgery in *Wall v Walwyn* at 27, repeated his view as to the duty of a driver as he expressed it in *Franklin* in the following terms:

> "In my judgment the reference to 'and so as not to stop or impede their crossing' in section 25(1)(a) is merely descriptive of the manner in which the driver should stop. My reading of the section, therefore, is that once the sign has been properly exhibited in accordance with section 25(1) the driver must stop, unless indeed by the time he reaches the crossing the prescribed sign had already been removed. Of course, if he approaches slowly and the patrol had taken the sign down before the driver gets there, naturally he can proceed. But if the sign is still exhibited there is in my judgment an obligation to stop, which obligation cannot be released until section 25(2)(b) has been satisfied, namely, that the sign no longer continues to be exhibited."

6.189   Under the 1984 Act s.28 is in equivalent terms to s.25. It is submitted that the liability under s.28 is absolute and that a driver must stop even if it is very difficult for him to do so because of the lateness of the signal; compare the cases on according precedence at §§ 6.162–5. Where it is desired to exempt drivers from an absolute duty to stop, the regulations say so, e.g. as to amber lights. The sign must be exhibited by the school crossing patrol in such a way that the approaching driver can see the words on the sign but it need not be full face to oncoming traffic (*Hoy v Smith* [1964] 3 All E.R. 670). The sign has been altered from "Stop: Children Crossing" to "STOP: Children", but *Hoy v Smith* seems as applicable to the new signs as to the old.

Section 28(2)(b) creates a separate offence of again putting the vehicle in motion so as to reach the place while the sign continues to be exhibited. It should be noted that this is a separate offence from s.28(2)(a) and that an information charging both offences would be bad for duplicity. It would appear that an offence can only be committed under s.28(2)(b) after the motorist has stopped. If he does not stop at all he should be charged with not stopping contrary to s.28(2)(a). It may also be noted that the vehicle may move sufficiently "so as to reach the place in question", i.e. the place where children are crossing or seeking to cross, before having to stop.

By s.28(5) signs are presumed to be of the prescribed size, colour and type and **6.190** to have been illuminated as prescribed.

The sign is prescribed by the School Crossing Patrol Sign (England and Wales) Regulations 2006 (SI 2006/2215). Warning lights may be erected giving motorists advance warning of the school crossing patrol. The warning lights are governed by reg.50 of the Traffic Signs Regulations and General Directions 2002 (SI 2002/3113). The erection of warning lights is discretionary and it would seem that their absence or non-illumination would not affect a conviction under s.28. Of the directions only direction 42 (relating to the colour of the back of signs) appears to relate to school crossing patrols. It is submitted that even if the colour of the back of the sign were incorrect, this would not invalidate a conviction (see § 6.108 and *Sharples v Blackmore* noted there).

By s.28(1) the school crossing patrol must wear the approved uniform. The **6.191** uniform worn is deemed to be approved by the Home Secretary unless otherwise proved (s.28(4)). No statutory instrument approving any uniform has been found, but by Home Office circular 3/89 the approved uniform for a school crossing patrol is a peaked cap, a beret or a yellow turban and a white raincoat, dustcoat or other white coat. The coat may be covered on the upper half or any part by fluorescent material. It seems that this means that a fluorescent overgarment may be worn or the fluorescence may be applied. Alternatively, a high visibility raincoat or dustcoat complying with BS6629 may be worn. Having regard to the presumption contained in s.28(5)(b), it is not necessary for the prosecution to prove that the Home Secretary's approval has been given to the uniform. The prosecution only has to prove that the school crossing patrol is wearing a uniform. Semble the defence would succeed if the school crossing patrol did not wear a white dustcoat or raincoat, but it is submitted that the wearing of the cap or beret is not essential (see *Wallwork v Giles*, § 4.41, as to a police constable in "uniform"). (As to traffic wardens acting at school crossings, see below.)

"School" is not defined and the term seems to include private and nursery schools and Sunday schools as well as those of education authorities. Section 28(1), as amended by s.270 of the Transport Act 2000, enables crossing patrols to stop traffic for any pedestrians and not just for those who are school children or are accompanying a school child. Furthermore, the former 8am to 5.30pm time restriction no longer applies to the provision of school crossing patrols.

6.192   On the analogy of *Burns v Bidder*, cited at § 6.166, the inability of a motorist or cyclist to stop because of a latent defect in his brakes, undiscoverable on a reasonable examination, or because he was pushed forward by a vehicle colliding with his vehicle's rear, or because he lost control under attack by a swarm of bees, would probably be a defence.

"Road" has the same meaning as elsewhere in the 1988 Act (see further Chapter 1).

Section 28 applies to all vehicles, including trams, trolley vehicles and cycles, but not seemingly to equestrians. See also *Crank v Brooks* at § 6.165.

6.193   The term "children" is not defined for the purposes of s.28. While a child under the Children and Young Persons Act 1933 means one under the age of 14, it is submitted that for the purposes of s.28 the definition should not exclude children of 14 or above but should at least extend to all children of compulsory school age, and that it would be within the spirit and object of s.28 if it extended to all pupils at secondary schools, whether above or below compulsory school age.

"Child", in the context of s.28, it is submitted, means any child of any age who goes to school.

6.194   Sometimes the school crossing patrol displays his sign for the benefit of children cycling to school. There appears to be nothing in s.28(1) to limit the protection given by the school crossing patrol to children on foot only and it is submitted that a motorist can be lawfully required to stop whether the children are crossing the road on foot or on bicycles.

Traffic wardens appointed under the Road Traffic Regulation Act 1984 s.95 may act as school crossing patrols (see Functions of Traffic Wardens Order 1970 (SI 1970/1958)) and when so doing it is not essential for them to wear the white coat prescribed in the Home Office circular 3/89, but they must when so doing exhibit the prescribed sign and be wearing the approved traffic warden's uniform (see Home Office circular 57/1997). A traffic warden may under para.1(5) of the Schedule to the 1970 Order be engaged in a school crossing patrol or by para.1(6) engaged in the general regulation of traffic. The corresponding prosecution will be under s.28 of the 1984 Act or s.35 of the 1988 Act respectively. The two main differences between s.28 and s.35 are the required exhibition of the sign under s.28 and the application of s.1 of the 1988 Offenders Act (notices of intended prosecution) to s.35 offences, but not to s.28 offences.

6.195   If the traffic warden is operating a school crossing patrol and has the sign, it is submitted that prosecutions should be brought under s.28 and he should exhibit the pole bearing the sign. He is presumably operating under para.1(5). Motorists would be watching the sign and might otherwise be seriously misled. If he does not have the sign, the question arises whether he is operating incorrectly under para.1(5) or under para.1(6). This will be a question of fact and impression but it may be possible to regard him as operating under s.35 of the 1988 Act.

Nothing in s.28 prevents proceedings being taken against motorists and cyclists for dangerous or careless driving or riding or against drivers or riders of any vehicles and equestrians for driving or riding to the common danger under the Highway Act 1835 (but see "Two offences from one incident" at § 5.76).

6.196   Section 28 does not apply to vehicles and persons in the public service of the

Crown. It is nevertheless submitted that a Crown vehicle driver may be prosecuted for dangerous, careless or inconsiderate driving if he recklessly or negligently fails to observe a school crossing patrol's sign and endangers or inconveniences other road users or children as a result.

Street playgrounds

Local traffic authorities are empowered by s.29 of the Road Traffic Regulation **6.197** Act 1984 (as substituted by the New Roads and Street Works Act 1991) to make orders prohibiting or restricting roads from use by vehicles to enable them to be used as a street playground. Any such order is required to make provision for permitting reasonable access to premises on or adjacent to the street.

It is an offence by virtue of s.29(3) for a person to use, or cause or permit a vehicle to be used in contravention of a street playground order (for "using", "causing" or "permitting" see Chapter 1).

Section 31 of the 1984 Act allows local traffic authorities to make byelaws for street playgrounds.

Section 29 does not apply to vehicles or persons in the public service of the Crown.

SCHOOL CROSSINGS, ETC.: PENALTIES

Table of penalties

Offence	Mode of trial	Section *	Imprisonment	Level of fine	Disqualification	Penalty points	Endorsement code	Sentencing guideline
Not stopping at school crossing	Summary	s.28(3)	—	3	Discretionary	3	TS60	—
Contravention of street playground order	Summary	s.29(3)	—	3	Discretionary	2	MS30	—
Contravention of street playground order (Greater London)	Summary	s.29(3)	—	3	Discretionary	2	MS30	

* Road Traffic Regulation Act 1984.

OBSTRUCTION, PARKING, ETC.

Generally

Obstruction and parking offences are contained in a number of Acts including **6.199** the Highways Act 1980, the Road Traffic Regulation Act 1984 and the 1988 Act. The 1984 Act regulates the provisions of parking places and the making of traffic regulation orders (see Pt IV). The various offences are considered below and the penalties for the offences will be found at § 6.267. Parking within the limits of a pedestrian crossing is considered under the section on "Pedestrian Crossings" (see § 6.171 and §§ 6.175 et seq.). The Highways (Road Humps) Regulations 1996 (SI 1996/1483) have been made under the Highways Act 1980 as amended, and road humps may be set up on any highway which is subject to a 30mph speed limit. Note should be taken of s.50 of the Road Traffic Act 1991, which empowers the Secretary of State by order to designate any road in London as a priority route (in popular parlance, a "Red Route"). Section 50(2) envisaged the establishment by such orders of a network of priority routes with a view to improving the movement of traffic in London.

The functions, powers and duties of uniformed parking attendants are discussed at § 6.273 below.

Nuisance parking

Two new offences were created by ss.3 and 4 of the Clean Neighbourhoods **6.200** and Environment Act 2005. The first of these, punishable on summary conviction by a fine not exceeding level 4, is exposing vehicles for sale on a road. The use of the plural is deliberate as for an offence to be committed two or more vehicles must have been left parked, on a road or roads, within 500m of each other (s.3(1)). A person is not to be convicted if he proves (presumably on a balance of probabilities) that he was not acting for the purposes of a business of selling motor vehicles (s.3(2)).

The second offence, also punishable by a level 4 fine, is that of repairing vehicles on a road (s.4(1)). A person is not to be convicted if he establishes evidentially that the works were not carried out in connection with a business or for gain or reward (s.4(3)). Emergency repairs to a broken-down or accidentally incapacitated vehicle within 72 hours of the accident or breakdown may also provide an exemption from conviction (s.4(5)).

Also on the statute book in relation to England only are ss.6–9 of the Act which provide local authorities with the power to issue fixed penalty notices in respect of offences under ss.3 and 4. The fixed penalty is presently set at £100.

Obstruction

Proceedings for obstructing the highway can be brought under the Highways **6.201** Act 1980 s.137 (wilfully obstructing the free passage of a highway), the Town Police Clauses Act 1847 s.28 (wilfully causing an obstruction in any public footpath or public thoroughfare), and reg.103 of the Road Vehicles (Construction and Use) Regulations 1986 (causing or permitting (see Chapter 1) a motor vehicle or trailer to stand on a road so as to cause any unnecessary obstruction of the road). The regulations extend to the whole of Great Britain and the Highways Act to

England and Wales, including London (London Government Act 1963 s.16(2)). (See below as to the 1847 Act.)

The regulations apply to a "road" as defined in Chapter 1. The Highways Act applies to ways over which all members of the public are entitled to pass and repass. A decision of quarter sessions under s.31(1) of the National Parks and Access to the Countryside Act 1949, since repealed, was a judgment in rem and binding on a magistrates' court. An owner was held not to be able therefore to dispute the status of a public path declared to be such by quarter sessions when prosecuted under the Highways Act for wilful obstruction (*Armstrong v Whitfield* [1973] 2 All E.R. 546) (but see § 1.122).

6.202   The Town Police Clauses Act 1847 s.28, other than the provisions relating to hackney carriages, seems now to apply to all districts, whether they were formerly boroughs, urban districts or rural districts (s.171 of the Public Health Act 1875 and para.23 of Sch.14 to the Local Government Act 1972).

An obstruction under the 1847 Act must be shown to have been to the obstruction, annoyance or danger of the residents or passengers in the street.

Regulation 103 applies to trams and trolley vehicles (see s.193A of the 1988 Act) as well as to motor vehicles generally. The Acts apply to all vehicles.

The position as to the application of the Highways and Town Police Clauses Acts to Crown vehicles is discussed at § 2.34. The regulations apply to Crown vehicles.

What amounts to obstruction

6.203   Obstruction can be caused by actual physical obstruction of an essential line of traffic, e.g. taking up half of a narrow, busy road, so that single-line working has to be employed. Or it may be unreasonable use of the right of stopping even though there is plenty of room for other traffic to pass. An example of the former is *Wall v Williams* [1966] Crim. L.R. 50, where a vehicle making a forbidden "U" turn in a very crowded street held up the traffic for 50 seconds; the conviction under (what is now) reg.103 of the Construction and Use Regulations was upheld.

In *Mounsey v Campbell* [1983] R.T.R. 36, the defendant parked his van right up against the bumper of a car. The car could have been moved at that time but it was subsequently penned in by a car parked 2ft behind. The defendant refused to move his van and was convicted of causing unnecessary obstruction contrary to reg.122 of the former 1978 Regulations. He argued that he should have been charged with "permitting" as he had not caused the unnecessary obstruction originally. It was held that he had been rightly convicted, because on the facts the van caused an unnecessary obstruction from the moment it was first parked. The case does not cover the situation where the defendant parks his car a reasonable distance in front and the blockage is caused by the unreasonable way the car behind is parked subsequently (always assuming there is no refusal to move). There is clearly an obstruction but it is submitted it might be held to be neither "wilful" nor "unnecessary" on the part of the defendant.

Parking in a bus bay for five minutes was held not to be unnecessary obstruction in *Brown v Cardle* 1983 S.L.T. 218 in the absence of any evidence of a bus trying to park during that time. The bus bay was held to be simply part of the road. The same principle would apply to parts of the road set aside similarly for other purposes. Obviously the position would be different if a bus had tried to park.

The public were fully entitled to the use of the whole footpath available to **6.204** them and an intrusion of some 9ft on to the highway at weekends for the purpose of displaying produce for sale could not be a mere technical obstruction which was to be disregarded under the de minimis principle. The Divisional Court so held in *Hertfordshire County Council v Bolden* (1987) 151 J.P. 252 when upholding the prosecutor's appeal against dismissal by justices.

While there is obviously an offence if there is a serious obstruction in fact, unreasonable use of the highway calculated to obstruct and whereby persons might be obstructed may suffice for a conviction without evidence that anyone has actually been obstructed (*Gill v Carson* (1917) 81 J.P. 250, a case under the Town Police Clauses Act 1847 s.28). In *Nagy v Weston* [1965] 1 All E.R. 78 parking a van for five minutes in a wide, busy street near a bus stop and refusing to move was held to be an obstruction under what is now s.137 of the Highways Act 1980. Lord Parker C.J. said:

> "While there must be proof of unreasonable use, whether or not user amounting to an obstruction was or was not unreasonable use was a question of fact, depending on all the circumstances, including the length of time the obstruction continued, the place where it occurred, the purpose for which it was done and whether it caused an actual as opposed to a potential obstruction."

These words were expressly approved by Ashworth J. in *Evans v Barker* [1971] **6.205** R.T.R. 453 at 456, where it was held, following *Solomon v Durbridge* below, that leaving a car for a reasonable time, although amounting to an obstruction, did not amount to an unnecessary obstruction within the meaning of what is now reg.103 of the Construction and Use Regulations. The facts were that the defendant had left his car on a Wednesday, which was the market day, between 2.45pm and 4pm in Welsh Walls, Oswestry, leaving 20ft of the width of the road clear. The justices' finding that this was not an "unnecessary" obstruction was upheld by the Divisional Court. It is primarily a question of fact, applying a test such as is adduced by Lord Parker as quoted, whether the circumstances in which a car is left are "unreasonable". If the obstruction is "unreasonable" it would appear to be "unnecessary" within the meaning of reg.103.

It was again emphasised in *Wade v Grange* [1977] R.T.R. 417 that what amounts to obstruction is primarily a question of fact and that the Divisional Court is only concerned with correcting mistaken applications of the law.

The test of reasonableness or unreasonableness was applied in *Lewis v Dickson* [1976] R.T.R. 431 where the defendant was charged with wilful obstruction **6.206** under what is now s.137 of the Highways Act 1980. The defendant, who was a security officer on duty at a large factory, caused continuous lines of employees' vehicles to build up in both directions on the main road due to his stopping every vehicle at the factory gate to check it. The case was sent back to the justices who were directed that the proper test for them to apply in deciding the case was whether the defendant's action in all the circumstances at the time was a reasonable method of admitting the cars to the works. In *Nelmes v Rhys Howells Transport Ltd* [1977] R.T.R. 266 the definition of obstruction (as quoted above in *Nagy v Weston*) was again followed in a case contrary to what is now reg.103 where the defendants had used a road for parking four or five of their trailers for which they had no room in their yard. The justices found the defendants had no case to answer as the prosecution had adduced no evidence of actual obstruction. The case was sent back to the justices; in considering whether or not the obstruction was unreasonable, one of the factors is the purpose for which it was done, and it should be borne in mind when considering the purpose of the obstruction that the highway was intended to provide for the requirements of people in transit and that the highway was not a store (ibid.). In *Absalom v Martin* [1974] R.T.R. 145 a bill poster parked his van with two wheels on a footpath and the other two on the roadway while posting a bill. The justices found as a fact that the obstruction was not an unreasonable use of the highway and their dismissal of a charge under s.121(1) of the Highways Act 1959 was upheld by the High Court who again cited with approval the words of Lord Parker C.J. in *Nagy v Weston* set out above. The court reserved for a future occasion whether it is more difficult to justify reasonable use when parking on a footpath rather than on the carriageway (see also *Worth v Brooks* below). In *Pitcher v Lockett* (1966) 64 L.G.R. 477 it was held that it was not a reasonable use of the highway to park a van on a busy road to sell hot dogs from it. It was also said that, normally, if what is done is nothing to do with the passage to and fro, this is not making a use of the highway which is reasonable, but that a milkman on his rounds was making a reasonable use of the road even though he might occasionally sell a bottle of milk. This view was applied in *Waltham Forest LBC v Mills* [1980] R.T.R. 201 where it was held that selling refreshments from a parked mobile snack bar in a highway lay-by was an unreasonable use of the highway in itself and an offence contrary to what is now s.137. The decision is of considerable importance in view of the prevalence of the practice.

6.207   Whether particular facts amount to an unreasonable use would depend very much on the magistrates' local knowledge of the importance of the particular road; a long stay may not be out of order in a quiet residential side road, but it would be otherwise in a busy shopping street. An obstruction only comes into existence if there is an unreasonable use of the right of stopping (*Nagy v Weston* above), and it is a matter of degree (*Dunn v Holt* (1904) 68 J.P. 271). In *Gill's* case a vehicle had been left unattended for five minutes in such a position as to block one out of four lines of traffic in a street carrying a tram route, and the High Court held that those facts showed no evidence of unreasonable use of the highway; it added, however, that, had the vehicle been left for a long period, there would have been an obstruction. In *Dunn's* case, where there was an acquittal, no one was obstructed and the vehicle, though stationary for several hours, took up less than 3ft in a carriageway 30ft wide. It is doubtful how far *Dunn's* case is still of authority in relation to obstructions lasting several hours. In *Absalom v Martin*, where the nearest public car park was several hundred yards away, the defendant parked partly on the carriageway and partly on the footpath and was endeavouring to carry on his business of bill posting in such a way as to cause the least inconvenience to pedestrians and other road users. A defendant who sold fruit from a barrow for 15 minutes, the barrow taking up 5ft in a 24ft road and customers causing further obstruction, was held to have been rightly convicted, as continuous selling does not mean that the barrow was not standing longer than was necessary (*Whiteside v Watson* 1952 S.L.T. 367). In *Bego v Gardner* 1933 S.L.T. 110 the conviction was upheld of a man who sold ices from his van parked in a cul-de-sac frequented by the public.

Leaving a car unattended for three hours, which was found to cause danger to the public and annoyance to the residents but which was not specifically found to cause an obstruction, was held to constitute the offence of leaving a car unattended for longer than was necessary to load or unload it (*Henderson v Gray* [1927] S.C.(J.) 43). A motorist parked his car in a line of cars in a street and left it there for five hours. He argued that, as he parked in a line of cars, he was not causing an unnecessary obstruction. The High Court held that he clearly caused one (*Solomon v Durbridge* (1956) 120 J.P. 231). In *Gelberg v Miller* [1961] 1 All E.R. 291 at 295–296, it was said that to leave a car for the luncheon period in Jermyn Street, London, was plainly an obstruction. Parking for five hours on a grass verge between the footpath and the wall was held to cause an unnecessary obstruction in *Worth v Brooks* [1959] Crim. L.R. 885, but in *Police v O'Connor* [1957] Crim. L.R. 478, quarter sessions held that it was not an unreasonable use of the highway to park a large vehicle outside the driver's own house in a cul-de-sac. In *Worth's* case it was said that, if a car was immobile through a breakdown, the obstruction might be "necessary".

In *Redbridge LBC v Jaques* [1971] 1 All E.R. 260 it was held that the fact that **6.208** a street trader had for many years sold from a fruit stall erected on the back of his stationary vehicle without objection from the local authority and without inconveniencing the public use of the highway was not a reason for dismissing a charge of wilful obstruction under what is now s.137 of the Highways Act 1980. This case was applied in *Cambridgeshire County Council v Rust* [1972] 3 All E.R. 232, where it was held not to be a "lawful excuse" for a person, prosecuted under what is now s.137 for setting up a stall on the highway, to believe he could lawfully do so because he made reasonable inquiries and had paid rates on the stall to the district council. Once a highway always a highway, and a council cannot grant a licence to perform an unlawful act.

The principle that the payment of rates for the operation of a stall, and its operation in the same position for a number of years, does not impliedly constitute lawful authority to cause an obstruction under s.137 of the Highways Act 1980 was reaffirmed by the Divisional Court in *Pugh v Pidgen; Same v Powley* (1987) 151 J.P. 644. The court further held that the fact that the stall operators had tried to ensure that their customers queued on private land rather than the pavement did not of itself amount to a defence. Nevertheless in the particular circumstances of the case the justices were entitled, as they did, to dismiss the case against the operators of a mushroom and fruit stall in The Mall, Bromley.

It was held in *Arrowsmith v Jenkins* [1963] 2 All E.R. 210, a case of causing a **6.209** crowd to collect, that, if a person intentionally by exercise of his will does something which causes an obstruction of a highway, this constitutes wilful obstruction under what is now s.137 and it is no defence that the person believes that he has genuine authority to do what he is doing if he has not lawful authority or reasonable excuse.

The judgment of the sheriff-substitute in *Macmillan v Gibson* 1966 S.L.T.(Sh.) 84 suggests that, when there is no actual physical obstruction, a conviction should follow only if it has been brought to the motorist's attention, e.g. by a police warning or by a notice or sign, that there is a regulation against the stopping of vehicles in the particular street, i.e. that the obligation imposed on the driver is not absolute but the prosecutor should show mens rea. That case concerned parking in breach of byelaws, not of what is now reg.103, and *Watson v Ross* 1920 1 S.L.T. 65, on which reliance was placed, concerned a charge of standing longer than necessary.

6.210   In *Seekings v Clarke* (1961) 59 L.G.R. 268, a case under what is now s.137 not involving a motor vehicle, it was said that anything which substantially prevented the public from passing over the whole of the highway (including the footway) and which was not purely temporary was an unlawful obstruction, subject to an exception on the de minimis principle. This case is discussed in *Wolverton UDC v Willis* [1962] 1 All E.R. 243.

It was held in *Waite v Taylor* (1985) 149 J.P. 551 that juggling with fire sticks in a pedestrian precinct in Bath amounted to wilful obstruction of the highway notwithstanding that people were free to move along the street and the justices considered the use of the highway was not unreasonable. The defendant had a cap on the ground to invite donations. The Divisional Court held that the stopping was not merely ancillary to exercising the right of passing and repassing and directed a conviction.

6.211   In *Hirst and Agu v Chief Constable of West Yorkshire* [1987] Crim. L.R. 330, the Divisional Court held on the leading modern authority of *Nagy v Weston* above that where a court was satisfied that a person had without lawful authority wilfully or deliberately caused an obstruction in his use of the highway, the court was not entitled to convict him of obstruction without being further satisfied that his use of the highway was unreasonable. The Crown Court in the case in point acting in its appellate jurisdiction had failed to turn its mind to the question of reasonableness of user, and accordingly the convictions of the appellants were quashed.

A useful article on the conflict between free passage along the highway and free public protest may be found at 151 J.P.N. 39.

6.212   The driver of a slow vehicle does not "negligently interrupt the free passage" of overtaking vehicles merely because they have to go to the offside of the road to pass him (*Sleith v Godfrey* (1920) 85 J.P. 46). In a case noted at 85 J.P. Jo. 500, the High Court upheld the conviction for obstruction where a lorry driver refused to draw into his nearside but drove along the centre of the road so that traffic could not overtake him. Obstruction of the footway can be an offence under the regulations (*Bryant v Marx* (1932) 96 J.P. 383). On a charge of having deposited without lawful authority or excuse anything on a highway in consequence whereof a user of the highway was injured or endangered, it is no defence that it was commercially convenient to do so (*Gatland v Metropolitan Police Commissioner* [1968] 2 All E.R. 100 —hopper, 6ft wide, left at night on 43ft road, only place where it could conveniently be placed). Builders' skips have subsequently become subject to control by what are now ss.139 and 140 of the Highways Act 1980 (see §§ 6.254–6).

The right of an occupier of premises abutting on a highway to make use of it for the purpose of obtaining access to his premises and of loading and unloading goods there is subject to the right of the public to use the highway (*Vanderpant v Mayfair Hotel Co* (1930) 94 J.P. 23, a civil case). In *Trevett v Lee* [1955] 1 All E.R. 406, a civil case, a landowner laid a small hosepipe across the road to other land; it was held that whether or not he was obstructing the highway was to be judged by reasonableness both from his point of view and from that of other members of the public. In *Marr v Turpie* [1949] Jo.Crim.L. 416, the High Court of Justiciary upheld the conviction of a motorist who had left his car for 30 minutes outside his own premises in a narrow street. The question whether a moving vehicle can be said to "stand" on a road within the meaning of reg.103 of the Construction and Use Regulations was raised but not decided in *Carpenter v Fox* (1929) 93 J.P. 239; Lord Hewart C.J. thought, however, that it was not a very strong argument to say that a moving vehicle was not "standing". The fact that someone is left in charge of a vehicle does not prevent there being an offence of obstruction if there is in fact an obstruction (*Hinde v Evans* (1906) 70 J.P. 548).

An act which in fact causes an obstruction cannot be justified by the motive or purpose which inspires or induces its commission (*W.R. Anderson (Motors) Ltd v Hargreaves* [1962] 1 All E.R. 129). It is submitted, however, that to constitute an offence the obstruction must be unlawful, and whether or not obstruction is unlawful depends on whether the action of the person was, or was not, reasonable in all the circumstances at the time (see *Lewis v Dickson*, above). **6.213**

When lorries were parked on a grass verge and the drivers went to a café to get meals, it was held that they did not obstruct the highway merely by a temporary call for a legitimate purpose provided that they did not stop in a place where the mere presence of a stationary vehicle would create an obstruction (*Rodgers v Ministry of Transport* [1952] 1 All E.R. 634). But to leave a large roller on the highway, even when it belongs to the owner of the land on each side, is not a reasonable use of the highway (*Wilkins v Day* (1883) 48 J.P. 6). (As to the parking of vehicles on verges now see ss.19, 19A and 20 of the Road Traffic Act 1988, at §§ 6.240–2.) In *Baxter v Middlesex County Council* [1956] Crim. L.R. 561, a forecourt was held on the facts not to be part of the highway; it was used as a display park for cars. A claim by an innkeeper for standing his guests' vehicles on the highway cannot be supported, even though it has been so used for more than 20 years (*Gerring v Barfield* (1864) 28 J.P. 615); once a highway always a highway (see *Cambridgeshire CC v Rust* above). If a local authority has designated part of a street as a parking place, no offence of unnecessary obstruction is committed by leaving vehicles in that part during the period allowed by the order and the motive in leaving them there, e.g. to relieve congestion in the owner's premises, is irrelevant (*W.R. Anderson (Motors) Ltd v Hargreaves* [1962] 1 All E.R. 129); but it is submitted that if the vehicle is parked in such a way as to cause a physical obstruction in a busy street where proper parking would not cause it, then the offender could properly be charged notwithstanding the street's designation for parking. If a vehicle breaks down and causes an obstruction, there is no wilful obstruction, it seems, if the driver does his best to get it moved out of the way within a reasonable time (*Original Hartlepool Collieries v Gibb* (1877) 41 J.P. 660). A van driver who stops it to sell ices has not "pitched a stall on the highway" contrary to what is now s.148 of the Highways Act 1980 (*Divito v Stickings* [1948] 1 All E.R. 207). *Divito v Stickings* was distinguished in *Waltham Forest LBC v Mills* [1980] R.T.R. 201 where parking a mobile snack bar in a lay-by was held to be "pitching a stall". The snack bar was a "stall" since it could be removed from the towing vehicle, and it had been "pitched" on the lay-by, being always in the same place for extended periods. The defendant was convicted not only under what is now s.148 but also under what is now s.137 of the 1980 Act. A bus driver who left a bus in the road and went off duty without giving its charge to any other person caused an obstruction under what is now reg.103 (*Ellis v Smith* [1962] 3 All E.R. 954).

It was held by the Divisional Court in *Scott v Mid-South-East JJ.*, March 25, 2004, unreported; (2004) 21 W.R.T.L.B. [85], applying *DPP v Jones* [1999] 2 W.L.R. 625, a House of Lords decision on the nature of trespassory assembly **6.214** under s.14A of the Public Order Act 1986, that the justices had not erred in holding that the defendant had a reasonable excuse for the wilful obstruction of a highway by the operation of a fast food outlet from a large parked van on an industrial estate where the minimal amount of traffic was in fact generated by the van itself. On the authority of *Jones* it was a matter of fact and degree in each case whether or not a person had a reasonable excuse for an obstruction; given that a criminal prosecution was involved, the justices had been entitled to find that the user may have been reasonable and to acquit the defendant.

Arrest

6.215   Under the Police and Criminal Evidence Act 1984 a constable may arrest without warrant any person whom he sees obstructing the highway contrary to s.137(2) of the Highways Act 1980 provided that one of the conditions precedent to an arrest under s.24 of the 1984 Act apply. The section is set out in full in Vol.2.

Parking meters

6.216   The Road Traffic Regulation Act 1984 ss.45–56 deal with parking on the highway and parking meters. It is necessary to obtain information about orders designating parking areas locally from the police or local authority.

The Road Traffic Regulation (Parking) Act 1986 amended s.45(2) of the 1984 Act to give local authorities the flexibility to charge or not to charge various categories of persons (e.g. residents and permit holders) for parking on the highway. It also substituted s.51 of the 1984 Act so as to clarify that in-car parking devices are lawful (e.g. to avoid the use of parking meters in areas of outstanding natural beauty).

6.217   The Parking Act 1989 amended s.47 of the 1984 Act to allow for the use (where mechanically appropriate) of bank notes, credit cards or debit cards with parking apparatus. It also amended s.51 above in similar fashion.

"Parking places" are provided on the highway, marked with lines, and some may accommodate several vehicles. Each driver, on putting the appropriate coin in the meter, may park there for a specified time but no longer; if the vehicle stays for longer than that time, an excess charge must be paid to the local authority. If it is there for more than four hours, an offence is committed. A motorist may not put more money in the meter to extend his period, unless the order permits. He may go to another "parking place" but may not return to his original one or sometimes one within the same zone until he has been gone from it for a prescribed period. The cited provisions are taken from one particular order and other orders differ. The police or council may prosecute for offences.

6.218   Section 47(1) specifies a number of offences and s.47(2) makes the driver who first left the vehicle generally responsible. One example which has been quoted is a driver who was responsible even though it was his mother-in-law who by mistake put the money in the wrong meter. The spouse who drove the vehicle thus would be responsible even though it was the other spouse who arrived late to drive it away.

By s.48(1) acceptance of the excess charge bars proceedings for failing to pay an initial charge. A defendant accused of failing to pay an excess charge may in the circumstances given in s.47(6) be convicted of failing to pay an initial charge.

An excess charge levied by a local authority for the non-payment or non-display of parking tickets or for overstaying in a car park is not unlawful or unreasonable even if it includes operating costs such as recovering excess charges from non-payers in civil proceedings (*Crossland v Chichester District Council* [1984] R.T.R. 181). In that case the district council had fixed £20 as the excess charge but had also fixed a lower sum of £8 by way of discount for prompt payment.

Orders usually contain exemptions for loading and unloading. A case under an order of two vehicles parking in one space is reported at [1959] Jo.Crim.L. 98. The case was heard at Bow Street magistrates' court. It was held that there was no breach of the requirement to pay the initial charge as the time was unexpired. Whether any offence is committed will depend upon the wording of the relevant order.   **6.219**

An order regulating the use of a parking place may make provision for treating the indications given by a meter or ticket as evidence of such facts as may be provided by the order (s.46(2)).

By s.124(1)(f) and Sch.9 Pt VI of the 1984 Act, a designation order, setting aside parking places on the highway, may not be challenged in any legal proceedings, save that it allows a challenge in the High Court only for a period after the order has been made. These provisions are extended to certain other orders under the 1984 Act by the same Schedule.

If a motor vehicle is left in a parking bay, no time is allowed for delaying the insertion of the coin in the meter unless it be merely to alight from the car and walk to the meter. Payment must be made as soon as the car is left in the bay, whether the driver stays in it or not, and he must not go off looking for change if he does not have the right coin on him (*Strong v Dawtry* [1961] 1 All E.R. 926). In *Riley v Hunt* [1981] R.T.R. 79 it was held that the latest time for paying the initial charge payable under the Mendip District Council (Off-street Parking Places in Street) Order 1976 was before the person parking his car left the car park. Justices were directed to convict the defendant who had arrived at the car park without the appropriate coin and had gone off shopping with the intention of returning and paying the charge afterwards. The relevant order should always be scrutinised, however, to see if it contains exemptions not in the order considered in *Strong's* case, where the High Court expressed surprise that a motorist who had left his car for only a minute or so to get change for the meter had been fined at all.   **6.220**

A motorist parked her car at a meter showing unexpired time. After the expiry of that time she returned to insert coins which would have allowed additional parking time. According to the Divisional Court in *Beames v DPP* [1989] Crim. L.R. 659 she was rightly convicted of inserting an additional coin into a parking meter postponing the time after which an excess charge was incurred, contrary to arts 8 and 15 of the Parking Places and Controlled Parking Zone (Manchester) Order 1971 and ss.45 and 47 of the Road Traffic Regulation Act 1984. Article 25(1) of the 1971 Order made it quite clear that an initial charge paid by one motorist who has left with time still unexpired on the meter is regarded as having been made by the second motorist who parks and takes advantage of that unexpired time. The appellant's options were therefore two-fold: she could either take advantage of the unexpired time provided she moved her car before its expiry, or, by virtue of art.7(4), she could use the unexpired time to enable her to make a reduced payment for the total period of time for which she wished to park. What she could not do was both, since the options were alternatives.

6.221   In *Roberts v Powell* (1966) 64 L.G.R. 173 it was held, on the terms of a particular order, that where a meter had been temporarily suspended or removed by the local authority a prosecution under the order failed. *Roberts v Powell* was followed in *Wilson v Arnott* [1977] 2 All E.R. 5, where it was held that while the placing of a red bag over the meter suspended the bay from normal use, the bay nevertheless remained a designated parking place within the meaning of the local order and "waiting" in the bay as distinct from "using" the bay was not suspended. The conviction of the defendant was set aside as he was entitled under the local order to "wait" in the parking bay for not more than 30 minutes for loading or unloading.

Where tickets were issued by a machine for use in an unattended car park and had to be fixed to the vehicle parked, the fact that the machine *might* be out of order was not a defence to a charge of not fixing a ticket (*Rawlinson v Broadley* (1969) 113 S.J. 310).

"Bank holiday" in a parking order means an official public holiday, not a day when the banks have shut pursuant to a royal proclamation (*O'Neill v George* (1969) 113 S.J. 128).

"No Waiting" streets

6.222   "No Waiting" and other traffic regulation orders are made under ss.1–8 of the Road Traffic Regulation Act 1984. Offences against such orders are under s.5(1) and Sch.2 to the 1988 Offenders Act (outside Greater London) and s.8(1) and Sch.2 to the 1988 Offenders Act (Greater London). For the purpose of s.2(3) there is a widened definition of pedestrian in s.127.

The power to make orders is exercisable by the London Borough Councils and the Common Council of the City of London. Under s.9 of the London Local Authorities Act 1995, the London Borough Councils (other than Tower Hamlets) may by notice impose temporary waiting restrictions (up to three days in duration) at times when "special events" (as defined) are held. Such restrictions are enforceable as if contained in an order under s.6 of the 1984 Act. The notice concerned must be prominently displayed in the relevant vicinity for the duration of the restriction and for at least one day previously.

6.223   Section 2(4) of the 1984 Act as amended by the New Roads and Street Works Act 1991 enables local traffic authorities to make orders specifying through routes for heavy commercial vehicles and prohibiting or restricting their use in specified zones or on particular roads. As to the definition of "heavy commercial vehicles", see § 1.26.

By s.3(1), relating to places outside Greater London, an order may not prevent access to premises adjoining the road at any time for persons on foot and for no more than eight hours out of every 24 in respect of vehicles; if it does, presumably it is ultra vires to that extent. "Preventing access" in s.1(5) was held to mean precluding access and not merely hindering it (*Corfe Transport Ltd v Gwynedd County Council* [1984] R.T.R. 79). Section 3(1) has to be read subject to s.3(2) which allows orders to restrict vehicle access provided that the order states that the traffic authority is satisfied that such restriction is necessary to avoid danger, to prevent danger arising or damage to the road or buildings on or near it, to facilitate passage of vehicles on the road, or to preserve or improve amenity by restricting or prohibiting the use of heavy commercial vehicles.

6.224   An exemption from waiting restrictions in respect of hackney carriages using an authorised hackney carriage stand was inapplicable where a licensed hackney carriage was waiting there for purposes other than of operating as a hackney carriage. The Divisional Court so held in *Rodgers v Taylor* [1987] R.T.R. 86 when interpreting art.5(1)(c) of the City of Gloucester (Eastgate Street) (Waiting Regulation) Order 1982. An offence under s.5(1) of the 1984 Act was accordingly committed when the vehicle in question was left locked and unattended at the hackney carriage stand for approximately one hour.

Signs

If signs to indicate the effect of a "No Waiting" order have not been erected or signs have been erected not conforming to s.64 of the Road Traffic Regulation Act 1984 and the Traffic Signs Regulations and General Directions 2002 (SI 2002/3113), no offence against the "No Waiting" order is committed (*MacLeod v Hamilton* 1965 S.L.T. 305). See also *Davies v Heatley* at § 6.55. Further confirmation (if confirmation were needed) that the absence of a sign specifying the prescribed hours of restricted parking in a road marked with a single yellow line is fatal to a successful prosecution for a no waiting offence has been provided by the Divisional Court in *Hassan v DPP* [1992] R.T.R. 209. **6.225**

A single yellow line supplemented by the authorised indication of the duration of the prohibition is sufficient indication that parking is prohibited on a Sunday as well as working days, and a conviction will be directed if the local order so prohibits parking on a Sunday (*Derrick v Ryder* [1972] R.T.R. 480). In *James v Cavey* [1967] 1 All E.R. 1048 a motorist parked at 6am, when the sign indicated that parking was permitted under an "alternative day waiting" order. At 9am the sign was changed to forbid parking. It was held that, as the sign did not forbid parking when he left his car, he committed no offence under the order by waiting after 9am.

The placing of signs to mark the effect of no parking orders was formerly discretionary in London and mandatory elsewhere. For this reason the absence of yellow lines on a street in the City of London was held not to be fatal to a prosecution (*Cooper v Hall* (1967) 111 S.J. 928). The regulations relating to traffic orders in the Metropolis were brought into line with those applying outside London by a series of measures and are now governed by the Local Authorities' Traffic Orders (Procedure) (England and Wales) Regulations 1996 (SI 1996/2489). Although many if not all of the current London Traffic Orders were made before 1972, the absence of yellow lines in London may, it is submitted, notwithstanding *Cooper v Hall* above, afford a defence. **6.226**

Direction 25 of the Traffic Signs Regulations and General Directions 2002 requires all parts of a controlled zone not allocated to parking bays to be marked with yellow lines. This obligation is quite specific.

In *Macmillan v Gibson* 1966 S.L.T.(Sh) 84 a person parked his vehicle in breach of byelaws made under the Roads and Bridges (Scotland) Act 1878; as there were no notices to warn him of the byelaws and no evidence that he knew of them, he was acquitted. **6.227**

In *Kierman v Howard* [1971] Crim. L.R. 286 it was held that a local authority had erected signs near the road "… where parking was allowed" in accordance with reg.17(1)(f) of the Local Authorities' Traffic Orders (Procedure) (England and Wales) Regulations 1969 (SI 1969/463), when the only signs they had erected informing motorists of a disc parking scheme were at the entrances to and exits from the zone. "Near" should be interpreted in the light of all the circumstances and in the case of a zone or area could be aptly treated as meaning at the entrance to the zone or area (ibid.). The procedure to be followed by local authorities in England and Wales (including London) when making orders under the 1984 Act is now laid down by the Local Authorities' Traffic Orders (Procedure) (England and Wales) Regulations 1996 above.

Exemptions for loading, etc.

6.228   Local Acts and orders sometimes permit vehicles to stop in "No Waiting" streets while loading or unloading goods. The question was raised but not decided in *Kirkland v Cairns* 1951 S.C.(J.) 61 whether the goods must be limited to those not sold from the vehicle; in that case fish and chips were sold from the vehicle. In *Whiteside v Watson* 1952 S.L.T. 367 it was doubted if selling to customers is "unloading". "Unloading" was held by a metropolitan magistrate to include taking a large sum of money from a car into a bank ([1952] Jo.Crim.L. 193). Money in bulk can be "goods" (112 J.P. Jo. 49, QS). It is not "loading goods" to put a small parcel in a private car, but it might be if an object not easily portable was put in a car, e.g. a laundry basket or several chairs (*Sprake v Tester* (1955) 53 L.G.R. 194). In *Richards v McKnight* [1977] R.T.R. 289 it was held by a majority that, in accordance with a local order in Manchester, a motorist was not exempted from parking restrictions when collecting £695 for his employees' wages which he was able to carry on his person. The exemption was held to cover the collection and delivery of goods *in a vehicle*, but not the mere collection and delivery of goods by a person who happens to be in a vehicle, i.e. if a vehicle is needed for collection or delivery of the goods, the vehicle is exempted; but otherwise if the goods to be collected can be carried on the driver's person, e.g. a fountain pen or pair of shoes, or (as in *Boulton v Pilkington* [1981] R.T.R. 87) a Chinese takeaway meal. It is submitted that, on the authority of these cases, the need of a vehicle may depend on the physical capabilities of the persons in it.

6.229   A metropolitan magistrate has held that, where a van is left in a restricted street for 18 minutes and during most of that time the driver is not engaged in loading or unloading, he is not within an exemption for delivering or loading, etc. The van must be engaged, as distinct from the driver, in loading or delivering during the whole time. Further, the regulations in question required the driver to be with the van all the time (102 S.J. 358). In *Macleod v Wojkowska* 1963 S.L.T. (Notes) 51 it was held that an exemption in an order for loading and unloading goods extended to taking goods from the vehicle into premises and depositing them there. Similarly, in *Bulman v Godbold* [1981] R.T.R. 242 it was held permissible to unload frozen fish into a hotel refrigerator. Where an order permits waiting "while loading", the defendant must show that his actions were covered by the latter words; if he had merely been asking customers if they had goods for loading but no goods had been loaded, he was not within the permission (*Holder v Walker* [1964] Crim. L.R. 61). A metropolitan magistrate has held that waiting in expectation of a load is not within the exemption ([1963] Crim. L.R. 706). In *Chafen v Another*, Supplement to the *Justice of the Peace and Local Government Review*, March 21, 1970, it was held that an exemption for the loading or unloading of goods did not extend to leaving a vehicle for so long as might be necessary for the goods to be located. No criticism could be made of a finding that 35 minutes' parking was unreasonable.

It was held in *Hunter v Hammond* [1964] Crim. L.R. 145 to be no defence to a **6.230** charge of waiting for longer than the permitted period that the defendant was delayed by having to dry his coat, when coffee had been spilt upon it. Nor is it a defence to a charge of breach of a "No Waiting" order that a taxi driver would otherwise find it very difficult to carry on his legitimate business (*Levinson v Powell* [1967] 3 All E.R. 796). Orders forbade waiting in roads *A* and *B* but exempted unloading; a driver unloaded goods outside premises in *A* and then moved to *B* to park there, as *B* was a wider road. He was held guilty, as the unloading was finished even though the business connected with it was not; on the facts the High Court recommended leniency (*Pratt v Hayward* [1969] 3 All E.R. 1094).

When an order in respect of a "No Waiting" street forbade a vehicle to wait but continued an exemption for waiting "for so long as may be necessary to enable any person to board or alight from the vehicle", it was held that this allowed a car to stop for only so long as necessary to allow someone to get in or out; taking parcels into a nearby house and returning, all within five minutes, was not within the exemption (*Clifford-Turner v Waterman* [1961] 3 All E.R. 974). In *Kaye v Hougham* (1964) 62 L.G.R. 457 it was likewise held not to be within that exemption where a taxi driver went to get change for a £5 note from his fare at the end of the fare's journey, but it was said that prosecutions should not be brought in such circumstances. The relevant order should always be scrutinised to see the precise form of exemption.

For a case of a constable purporting to give herself permission to park in a "No **6.231** Waiting" area, see 131 J.P. 627. In *Keene v Muncaster* [1980] R.T.R. 377 Lord Lane C.J. said that the ordinary use of the word "permit" in what is now reg.101 of the Road Vehicles (Construction and Use) Regulations 1986 (parking after dark) plainly envisages that the person requesting permission should request it from another and that a police officer could not therefore give himself permission. The position would depend on the wording in the order and whether the word "permit" is used. A constable who parked in a place reserved for disabled drivers in order to visit a nearby jewellers to take a statement as to a recent robbery was held to be performing a statutory power or duty in a police force vehicle and thus exempted by art.11 of the Borough of Reading (Parking Places for Disabled Drivers) Order 1955 (*George v Garland* [1980] R.T.R. 77).

The prosecution need not show that the defendant's conduct in parking did not fall within any of the exemptions, such as unloading; it is for the defendant to establish that the waiting was for a permitted purpose (*Funnell v Johnson* [1962] Crim. L.R. 488).

Exemptions for disabled drivers

Disabled persons' badges may be issued by local authorities under the Chroni- **6.232** cally Sick and Disabled Persons Act 1970 (as amended by the Road Traffic Act 1991) for motor vehicles driven by, or used for the carriage of, disabled persons (s.21). The Local Authorities' Traffic Orders (Exemptions for Disabled Persons) (England) Regulations 2000 (SI 2000/683) provide for exemptions in favour of a vehicle displaying a disabled person's badge. The regulations apply, in England, to orders made by a local authority (other than a London local authority) under ss.1, 9, 35, 45 and 46 of the Road Traffic Regulation Act 1984 and to orders made by a London local authority under ss.6, 9, 45 and 46 of the Act; they do not apply, however, to orders relating to the Cities of London and Westminster, the

Royal Borough of Kensington and Chelsea or to any part of the London Borough of Camden south of, and including, Euston Road. These areas have their own regulations and exemptions, each individual to the area concerned. In broad terms the regulations provide that all limited waiting and (provided loading and unloading is permitted) "No Waiting" traffic orders and also parking place orders made under the sections of the Act listed above must contain an exemption in respect of vehicles displaying a disabled person's badge. The exemptions to be included in orders made under the Act relate to parking on streets and highways and do not extend to off street parking. These are minimum exemptions which *must* be contained in the orders and all orders should be consulted as they may contain additional exemptions. Off street parking orders may also contain their own exemptions. (For regulations and exemptions applying to Wales, see SI 2000/ 1785.)

In the case of on street parking meters there is no charge or time-limit. In the case of limited waiting orders there is no time-limit. In the case of "No Waiting" orders (where loading and unloading is permitted) the maximum waiting period for disabled persons is three hours, and the time disc issued for use with disabled persons' badges in such circumstances must also be set and displayed in addition for the exemption to apply.

6.233   It should be emphasised that the exemptions conferred on disabled persons' badge holders are only in respect of orders made under the specific provisions of the 1984 Act and do not extend to other provisions of road traffic law, so that displaying the disabled persons' badge does not, e.g., permit a person to cause an obstruction.

There are two situations in which the provisions of the 1970 Act operate: where the disabled person is the driver and where he is the passenger. If he is the passenger, it is immaterial whether he or his driver stays with the vehicle when it is parked, providing the vehicle "is being used to convey him" (s.21(1) and (2)). There is no reason why the vehicle should not be used by an able-bodied driver or passenger providing it is being used as indicated by the disabled persons' badge holder.

6.234   The disabled persons' badge must be displayed on the dashboard or facia so as to be legible from outside the vehicle, or if none is fitted, in a conspicuous position from which it is legible from outside the vehicle. Under s.21(1) of the 1970 Act, a disabled persons' badge issued in one local authority area must be valid in other such areas subject to the provisions of the regulations. If the conditions relating to the badge, including its display and, where appropriate, the display of the time disc are not complied with, the driver and in certain circumstances the owner commit the underlying parking offence.

Badges are issued in England in accordance with the Disabled Persons (Badges for Motor Vehicles) (England) Regulations 2000 (SI 2000/682) (as amended) and in Wales under the Disabled Persons (Badges for Motor Vehicles) (Wales) Regulations 2000 (SI 2000/1786). The Welsh regulations provide for appeals to the National Assembly rather than the Secretary of State and omit provisions in the earlier regulations specifically referring to further appeal to magistrates' courts. As might be expected, the regulations also provide for the circumstances in which a badge may be displayed when the vehicle is being driven or is parked.

6.235   The regulations prescribe the descriptions of persons to whom a badge may be issued and the cases where a local authority may refuse to issue a badge, or require its return. These cases include where in relation to a badge misuse on at least three occasions has led to a relevant conviction. "Relevant conviction" means:

(a) the conviction of either the holder of a disabled person's badge, or any other person using a disabled person's badge with the holder's consent, of an offence of using or causing or permitting a vehicle to be used arising—

    (i) under ss.5, 8, 11 or 16(1) of the Road Traffic Regulation Act 1984 if the offence consisted of the unlawful parking of the vehicle, or

    (ii) under ss.35A(1) and (2), 47(1), 53(5), 53(6) or 117(1) of the 1984 Act; and

(b) the conviction of any person other than the holder of a disabled person's badge of an offence under s.117(1) of the 1984 Act where the badge was displayed on the vehicle with the consent of the holder at any time during which the offence was being committed.

Where a badge is refused or recalled because of misuse there is a right of appeal to the Secretary of State (or National Assembly) within 28 days of the date on which the notice is issued. There is no right of appeal under the regulations for a refusal on other grounds. It will be noted that the relevant convictions may be of persons other than the badge holder and it is the use or display as appropriate of the badge with the holder's consent which is specified and not the commission of the offence with the holder's consent. Some of the appeals may turn on whether this consent to the use or display was in fact given.

The provisions in the regulations regarding misuse were made as a consequence of ss.21(7A)–(7E) of the Chronically Sick and Disabled Persons Act 1970 inserted by s.68 of the Transport Act 1982. See the provision in s.21(7B) as to the service of notices by post. **6.236**

Public disquiet about misuse of the disabled persons' badge scheme, particularly by able-bodied people, led to the undertaking of a major review of the scheme by the Department for Transport. One particular problem was identified as the practical difficulty of enforcing the offence provisions of s.117 of the 1984 Act which required the offender to have committed an offence under a provision of the 1984 Act other than s.117 ("the first offence") and to have done so whilst fraudulently using a disabled person's parking concession. The identification of such wrongdoers could not be described as straightforward. A package of proposals was accordingly brought forward by the review, including the introduction of a new passport-style badge with photograph and the creation of a new offence of displaying a disabled person's badge when driving a motor vehicle on a road except where the badge is issued and displayed in accordance with regulations.

Section 35(4) of the Road Traffic Act 1991 amended s.21 of the Chronically **6.237** Sick and Disabled Persons Act 1970 (badges for display on motor vehicles used by disabled persons) in order to provide for the new offence described above by means of the insertion in that section of new subss.(4A), (4B) and (4C). Section 35(6) of the 1991 Act amended s.117 of the Road Traffic Regulation Act 1984 in order to put the offence under that section (wrongful use of disabled person's badge) into a more easily understood and enforceable form. A person who commits a parking offence under the 1984 Act and at the same time makes improper use of a disabled persons' badge also commits an offence under s.117(1) ibid.: see the provisions of that section, as amended, in Vol.2.

Offences against s.35A(1) (breach of order as to off street parking or on street parking without payment) and against s.47(1) (contraventions relating to designated parking places) are committed in an aggravated form and carry a heavier maximum fine where the person parks in a place reserved for disabled persons' vehicles without qualifying (see the entries in Sch.2 to the 1988 Offenders Act referring to these offences).

6.238   In the unanimous decision of the House of Lords in *R. v Courtie* (1984) 78 Cr. App. R. 292, Lord Diplock said at 300 (in relation to a different statute) that the much more suitable way is to put into separate counts in an indictment charges which include allegations of factual ingredients which attract different maximum punishments. It is suggested therefore that where the allegation is of an aggravated offence, this should be specified and set out in an information separate from that for an unaggravated offence. Sections 21A–21C of the Chronically Sick and Disabled Persons Act 1970 provide for the recognition in England and Wales of disabled persons' badges issued outside Great Britain and affords the same parking concessions to holders of such badges as are allowed to holders of domestic disabled persons' badges.

Clearways

6.239   The Various Trunk Roads (Prohibition of Waiting) (Clearways) Order 1963 (SI 1963/1172) is made under s.1 and 6 of the Road Traffic Regulation Act 1984 (see §§ 6.222–4 as to the provisions of these sections). It forbids vehicles to stop on the main carriageways of certain named roads unless with police permission, for building, road or public utility works, fire and rescue authority, ambulance or police purposes, postal collections and deliveries, local authority cesspool and refuse vehicles, to close gates and barriers, to avoid accidents or in circumstances beyond the driver's control. "Main carriageway" means any carriageway of that road primarily used by through traffic and excludes lay-bys. A slip road was held to be within the definition of "main carriageway" in *Hawkins v Phillips* [1980] R.T.R. 197 because any vehicle going on to the slip road was committed to go on the main road. It is submitted that parking on a grass verge is not included within the definition in that the verge is not a carriageway. A vehicle may not wait on a lay-by or verge of any such clearway for the purpose of selling goods from that vehicle unless they are at once delivered to premises adjacent to that vehicle. Other clearways orders have been made and the wording of each order should be referred to in each case.

Parking on verges, footpaths and central reservations

6.240   Section 19 of the Road Traffic Act 1988 prohibits the parking of heavy commercial vehicles on verges, footpaths or central reservations of roads.

For the definition of a heavy commercial vehicle, in relation to s.19 although contained in s.20, see § 1.26. Under s.20(5) the Secretary of State for Transport may by regulation amend this definition.

The prohibition under s.19 applies to "the verge" of the road, "any land which is situated between two carriageways ..." of the road and any "footway", i.e. a way over which the public have a right on foot only and which is comprised in a highway consisting of a carriageway (see s.329 of the Highways Act 1980).

6.241   Mr Wolman regularly parked his motor cycle on the pavement at locations near his home and place of work. He would either rest the motor cycle with its centre stand on the pavement and both wheels clear of the ground or with one wheel resting against his own property and the other suspended above the surface of the pavement. Two local authorities each issued penalty charge notices against him for parking his motor cycle on an urban road other than a carriageway in contravention of the Greater London Council (General Powers) Act 1974 s.15, as amended by the London Local Authorities Act 2000 s.15(2). He commenced proceedings against the local authorities claiming damages for, amongst other things, wrongful interference with his motor cycle. He argued that as a matter of ordinary language the word "on" in this context connoted some degree of physical contact, direct or indirect, between the wheels and the pavement. The Court of Appeal held in *Wolman v Islington London Borough Council* [2008] EWCA Civ 823; [2008] R.T.R. 6 that by parking his motor cycle on its stand on the pavement with its body and one or both of its wheels on or over the pavement he was in contravention of s.15 of the 1974 Act, and was accordingly liable to a penalty charge. However, a motor cycle parked in the road with one wheel extending over, but not touching, the pavement would not be in contravention of the Act. Although the legislation is specific to London, this point is likely to have more general relevance.

Provided it is not left unattended, it is a defence to a charge under the section if the vehicle was parked for loading or unloading on the footway or verge and the loading or unloading could only be satisfactorily performed by being so parked. It is also a defence if the vehicle was parked with police permission or for life saving, fire fighting or in a like emergency.

Evidence may be given by way of certificate under s.11 of the 1988 Offenders **6.242** Act (see § 3.50) and proof of identity of the driver may be given by s.12 ibid. (see § 3.54).

Immobilisation of vehicles illegally parked

The immobilisation of vehicles illegally parked is provided for by ss.104–106 **6.243** of the Road Traffic Regulation Act 1984. Details of the areas covered and approved immobilisation devices can be found in Vol.2 in the note to s.104 of the 1984 Act. Although a wheel clamp device could originally only be fixed by or under the direction of a constable, it should be noted that the powers of a constable to immobilise vehicles illegally parked were extended to traffic wardens by the Functions of Traffic Wardens (Amendment) Order 1993 (SI 1993/1334) which amends the Functions of Traffic Wardens Order 1970 (SI 1970/1958) and is incorporated therein. With the device an appropriate notice must also be fixed to the vehicle. The notice includes information as to how the release of the vehicle may be secured. Subject to this, release may be obtained by payment of the prescribed charge. The police still retain the power to remove such illegally parked vehicles. Interference with the notice is an offence (s.104(5)) carrying a maximum penalty of a fine of level 2. It is also an offence to remove or attempt to remove the device without authorisation; the maximum penalty for this is a fine of level 3 (s.104(6)).

There are exemptions for vehicles displaying a current disabled person's badge (s.105). However, under s.105(5) and (6) it is an offence for an able-bodied person to use the badge illegally in the immobilisation area. The maximum penalty is a fine of level 3. It is also not possible to use the device on vehicles parked for up to two hours after the expiry of the initial parking meter charge (including "borrowed time"). However, the device may be used where there have been other contraventions.

6.244   By s.72 of the Transport Act 1982, ss.53 and 54 apply to vehicles and persons in the public service of the Crown.

Private wheel clamping; criminal damage to wheel clamps

6.245   The Divisional Court has held in *Lloyd v DPP* [1991] Crim. L.R. 904 that a motorist who ignored clear warnings that unauthorised vehicles would be wheel clamped and parked without permission in a private car park consented thereby to the risk of his car being clamped and had no lawful excuse for damaging the clamp. (The court was not deciding whether clamping in such circumstances was lawful; that was a matter for Parliament or the civil courts.) Put at its worst, what the defendant had suffered was a civil wrong, the remedy for which would have been payment of the £25 penalty for the vehicle's release and a subsequent civil action for its recovery.

So far as the legality (or otherwise) of private wheel clamping is concerned, it should be noted that the High Court of Justiciary in Scotland has held that such activity can amount to extortion and theft: *Black v Carmichael, The Times*, June 25, 1992.

6.246   *Lloyd v DPP* above was approved and *Black v Carmichael* distinguished by the Court of Appeal in *Arthur v Anker* [1996] R.T.R. 308. A motorist who trespassed by parking his car on private property, having seen a warning notice there that a vehicle parked without proper authority would be wheel clamped and released on payment of a fee, was to be taken to have consented to the effect of the notice, provided that the release fee was reasonable, the vehicle was released without delay when the motorist tendered the fee and there were means by which the motorist might communicate his offer of payment. Where, therefore, those conditions were satisfied the wheel clamper's activity was neither tortious nor criminal. So far as tort was concerned, the maxim of volenti fit injuria applied; the motorist, by voluntarily accepting the risk that his car might be clamped, also accepted the risk that the car would remain clamped until he paid the reasonable cost of clamping and declamping. He consented not only to the otherwise tortious act of clamping but also to the otherwise tortious act of detaining the car until payment. So far as crime was concerned, *Lloyd v DPP* made it clear that the motorist was not on any showing entitled to convert the clamps and padlocks belonging to the clampers. *Black v Carmichael*, where wheel clampers, although held to be not guilty of extortion, were held to have been guilty of theft, fell to be distinguished since an intention to deprive the owner permanently of the goods was not a necessary ingredient of the offence of theft in Scots law.

Lloyd v DPP and *Arthur v Anker* (both discussed above) were referred to by the Court of Appeal in *Vine v Waltham Forest London Borough Council* [2000] R.T.R. 270 but distinguished as to their facts since in the instant case there was a clear finding of fact that the motorist had not seen a sign warning her that cars parked in that place without permission were liable to be clamped. In such circumstances she could not be taken to have consented to the risk of clamping and accordingly the clamping amounted to a trespass to her property.

6.247   *Lloyd v DPP* above was followed by the Court of Appeal in *R. v Mitchell*

[2003] EWCA Crim 2188; [2004] R.T.R. 14 when dismissing an appeal against conviction for criminal damage to a wheel clamp. Although the defendant had considered that his vehicle was lawfully parked, the fact that he had altered the date on his parking permit and had stated the time of parking as "1000" rather than "2200" (use of the 24-hour clock being expected) had led the clamping company reasonably to believe that the vehicle was unlawfully parked. The defendant refused to pay the £60 fee required and cut the chain securing the clamp with an electric cutter. Applying *Lloyd*, it was clear that self-help of the kind employed by the defendant was not his only reasonable remedy. He could have paid the £60 and then sought to recover it via the clamping company's appeal process or through the civil courts.

Abandoning vehicles

By s.2(1) of the Refuse Disposal (Amenity) Act 1978 any person who, without **6.248** lawful authority, abandons on any land in the open air, or on any other land forming part of a highway, a motor vehicle or anything which formed part of a motor vehicle and was removed from it in the course of dismantling the vehicle on the land commits an offence. By s.2(2), a person who leaves anything on any land in such circumstances or for such a period that he may reasonably be assumed to have abandoned it or to have brought it to the land for the purpose of abandoning it there, shall be deemed to have abandoned it there or, as the case may be, to have brought it to the land for that purpose unless the contrary is shown. Proof of the contrary seems to be on the defendant. The offence may be prosecuted by any person, e.g. an aggrieved landowner. In view of the wording of s.2(2), it may be that the time-limit for proceedings runs from the date of the leaving of the vehicle and that the offence is not a continuing one; cf. *R. v Boulden* (1957) 41 Cr. App. R. 105; *Vaughan v Biggs* [1960] 2 All E.R. 473. "Motor vehicle" is widely defined in s.11(1) of the Act as including trailers and contraptions which have ceased to be motor vehicles under the 1988 Act.

By ss.3 and 4 of the Act power is given to local authorities to remove vehicles appearing to have been abandoned on any land in the open air or on any other land forming part of a highway, to dispose of abandoned vehicles and to recover their expenses.

"Abandon", according to the *Concise Oxford Dictionary*, means to give up **6.249** completely or desert or leave permanently; it is not "abandoning children in a manner likely to cause them unnecessary suffering" to leave them in Chatham Juvenile Court whilst in session (*R. v Whibley* [1938] 3 All E.R. 777).

Driving on the footway and on common or private land

Under the Highway Act 1835 s.72, it is an offence wilfully to ride or drive on **6.250** the footway, even though the driving may last for only a few seconds (*McArthur v Jack* 1950 S.C.(J.) 29). The offence will apply to pedal and motor cyclists. Driving across the footway to get to a private park was held to be an offence in the absence of proof of long user or of its being a way of necessity (*Curtis v Geeves* (1930) 94 J.P. 71) but in *Vestry of St Mary, Newington v Jacobs* (1871) L.R. 7 Q.B. 47 the owner of land adjoining the highway was held to be entitled to convey machinery on trolleys over the pavement into his premises. "Wilfully" under this section means purposely; see *Fearnley v Ormsby* (1879) 43 J.P. 384, and a magistrates' court has acquitted a defendant who drove on the footway in ignorance that it was part of the footway. On the same principle a defendant who drove on the footway accidentally should be acquitted.

Section 28 of the Town Police Clauses Act 1847 also prohibits the drawing or driving of a carriage upon any footway of a street. Both the 1847 and the 1835 Acts refer to "carriages", which expression includes motor vehicles and trailers (1988 Act s.191). Not all police forces take active steps to enforce these sections, but many more are now doing so in order to prevent subsequent parking on the pavement. Quaere whether there is a common law right to divert on to the pavement in cases of necessity when the carriageway is blocked.

6.251   Section 34 of the Road Traffic Act 1988 prohibits the driving of mechanically propelled vehicles on footpaths, bridleways, restricted byways, common land, moorland or other land not part of a road, with an exception for parking within 15yds of a road or for emergencies. Section 34(2A) provides a further exception enabling persons with an interest in land, or visitors to it, to drive on a road if immediately before the commencement of the 2000 Act it was defined as a road used as a public path and was in use for obtaining access to the land by the driving of mechanically propelled vehicles. The substituted provisions refer expressly to "mechanically propelled vehicles" (other than as described in s.189(1)(a)–(c) of the 1988 Act) , a wider category of objects than the "motor vehicles" of the previous legislation. As to the definition of "mechanically propelled", see § 1.33.

The effect of s.34, it is submitted, is that a motorist may drive on common or moorland off a public road for 15yds, so long as he intends to park; if he goes more than 15yds, he commits an offence whether he parks or not. If he goes on private land, he commits no offence so long as he parks there and does not go more than 15yds, even though the landowner does not consent to the vehicle going on the land; the landowner should sue for trespass. If the motorist parks, say, 20yds from the road on private land, he commits an offence under s.34 and he also commits an offence if he drives less than 15yds on private land for the purpose of turning his car round. Quaere if a defence of de minimis could be raised for a move lasting four or five seconds only 3ft up a private drive. It seems to be an offence to drive on private land under s.34, unless within the exceptions; consequently, motoring trespassers can be prosecuted if, say, they drive up the approach to a country house or a farm purely from motives of curiosity and with no intention of visiting the occupant. The motorists' passengers could be charged if aiding, abetting, counselling and procuring can be proved. Persons coming to a house on lawful business, however, have an implied licence to go through an unlocked gate (if motorists, perhaps not to open a closed gate) and up to the door (*Robson v Hallett* [1967] 2 All E.R. 407) but not, it is suggested, to deviate from a driveway or roadway on to grassland. The opinion is advanced that s.34 extends to any private land and that such land need not be ejusdem generis with a common or moor land—it could be a factory yard or private car park as well as a field—the words "other land of whatsoever description" being wide enough to exclude the ejusdem generis rule.

6.252   The Court of Appeal in *Massey and Drew v Boulden* [2002] EWCA Civ 1634; [2003] 11 E.G. 154 emphasised that the prohibition conveyed by s.34 was unambiguous and that the words "or land of any other description" meant what they said. They applied to a track over a village green, unless it could be said to form part of a road as defined in s.192(1) of the 1988 Act (see § 1.122). For the definition to be satisfied, however, the public must have access to the track in the sense of using it as a road; it would not be sufficient that members of the public using the green would walk over the track if they were not walking on it qua road.

The question discussed at 125 J.P. Jo. 251 is whether what is now s.34 applies to all footpaths, both those at the side of carriageways and those ways for pedestrians and cyclists only. It is submitted there, following earlier opinions cited, that what is now s.34 is aimed at persons who drive mechanically propelled vehicles on footpaths, bridleways and restricted byways which are not at the side of a carriageway and that the section applies to such ways for foot passengers and cyclists in towns as well as in the country but not those adjoining a carriageway. For a contrary view that s.34 applies also to footways adjoining a carriageway, see an article at (1981) 145 J.P. Jo. 697. The Highway Act 1835 s.72 refers to footpaths at the side of a road.

The Law of Property Act 1925 s.193(4) provides that any person who without **6.253** lawful authority draws or drives upon any metropolitan common, manorial waste, common wholly or partly within a borough or urban district, or any land subject to rights of common to which the section may be applied under s.193(2), any carriage, cart, caravan, truck or other vehicle or who camps or lights a fire thereon commits an offence.

Depositing builders' skips on the highway

The Highways Act 1980 s.139(1) and (3) makes it an offence to be the "owner" **6.254** (see definition below) of a builder's skip which has been deposited on the highway without permission of the highway authority. It was said in *York City Council v Poller* [1976] R.T.R. 37 that the Act does not contemplate blanket permits and any permission has to be in writing. It is also an offence for the owner to fail to comply with a condition imposed by the permission or to fail to secure that the skip is properly lighted at night, to fail to remove the skip as soon as practicable after it has been filled and to fail to secure that the skip is clearly and indelibly marked with his name and address or telephone number.

Section 139(11) defines a "builder's skip" as a container designed to be carried on a road vehicle and to be placed on a highway or other land for the storage of builders' materials, or for the removal and disposal of builders' rubble, waste, household and other rubbish or earth. "Owner" is defined as the hirer where the skip is hired for not less than one month or is hired under a hire-purchase agreement.

The skip must under s.139(4) also comply with the marking regulations. The **6.255** Builders' Skips (Markings) Regulations 1984 (SI 1984/1933) provide that each end of a builder's skip, part of which is placed on any part of a highway except a footway or verge, must be marked with a specified marking. Every such marking must be clean and efficient and clearly visible for a reasonable distance to persons using the highway. The only exception is a door required to be open for loading or unloading. Accidentally leaving the door open would not be an exception; the door must be required to be open for the purpose of loading or unloading. The markings may be fixed to plates riveted to skips or they may be attached directly to skips. Painted markings are illegal. The requirement for owners to ensure that they are properly lit during the hours of darkness remains.

The s.139(1) offence is wide enough to include leaving a skip for a number of days after permission had expired; *Craddock v Green* [1983] R.T.R. 479. Under s.139(5) proceedings may be taken against any other person whose act or default resulted in the offence being committed whether or not proceedings are also taken against the owner (*PGM Buildings Co Ltd v Kensington LBC* [1982] R.T.R. 107). It is only if some other person's act or default resulted in the offence that proceedings may be taken against a person other than the owner (see, e.g. *York City Council v Poller* above).

6.256   It is a defence to a charge under s.139 that the commission of the offence was due to the act or default of another and that the defendant took all reasonable precautions and exercised all due diligence to avoid the commission of the of- fence (s.139(6)). To avail oneself of the defence notice has to be given to the prosecutor seven clear days before the hearing of such information identifying or assisting in the identification of the other person as is then in one's possession (s.139(7)). It is not necessary to identify the other person if it is not possible to do so (*PGM Buildings Co Ltd v Kensington LBC* above). If notice has not been given or seven days' notice is not given, the defence may be relied on with the leave of the court. A defendant giving notice under s.139(7) identifying that other person has to give as full information as he is able honestly to provide in accor- dance with the facts in his possession at the time he gives the notice (*Barnet London BC v S & W Transport Ltd* [1975] Crim. L.R. 171). It was held in *Lam- beth London BC v Saunders Transport Ltd* [1974] R.T.R. 319 that the owner of a skip who had hired it out could avail himself of the defence as he had taken all reasonable precautions and had used due diligence to see that the hirers were aware of their duties as to lighting it. The purpose of s.139(6) was to provide a defence for owners of skips who were accustomed to hire out skips and took the necessary steps to see that the hirers complied with their duties such as lighting (ibid.).

A constable in uniform has powers under s.140(2) of the Highways Act 1980 to require the removal of a builder's skip from the highway, and failure to remove the same when required to do so constitutes an offence contrary to s.140(3) ibid. In order to secure a conviction, however, it is necessary for the constable to ap- pear in person to make the requirement of the defendant; a request by telephone is insufficient (*R. v Worthing JJ. Ex p. Waste Management Ltd* [1988] Crim. L.R. 458).

Negligent opening of car doors

6.257   It is convenient to mention here prosecutions of motorists and their passengers who suddenly open a car door and strike a passing cyclist or pedestrian. The po- sition is now covered, so far as motor vehicles and trailers are concerned, by reg.105 of the Road Vehicles (Construction and Use) Regulations 1986, discussed below. Prosecutions may still be brought under the Highway Act 1835 s.78, however, and persons on cycles and in horse-drawn vehicles who cause hurt can only be charged under that Act. They should not be charged under the limb of s.78 of the Highway Act 1835 which deals with drivers on the highway causing hurt by negligence; that limb is concerned with negligence in driving and not with things done after the vehicle has stopped (*Shears v Matthews* [1948] 2 All E.R. 1064). But the driver or any passenger who opens a car door in a negligent way may be convicted of interrupting by negligence the free passage of a person or vehicle on the highway under another limb of s.78 (*Watson v Lowe* [1950] 1

All E.R. 100). Where a defendant had taken precautions to see if traffic was coming and nevertheless an accident occurred when he opened the door, it was held on those facts that he should not be convicted of "wilful obstruction" (*Eaton v Cobb* [1950] 1 All E.R. 1016). It may be that the "interrupting by negligence" limb of s.78 covers cases where cigarette ash is carelessly flicked into a cyclist's face causing him to have an accident. "Car door" accidents, if a person or animal is injured or another vehicle damaged, should be reported to the police by the driver where s.170 of the 1988 Act applies (*Jones v Prothero* [1952] 1 All E.R. 434). See § 7.12.

A passenger may properly be convicted of hindering the free passage of a person on the highway by negligently opening a car door (*Baldwin v Pearson* (1958) 122 J.P. 321).

Regulation 105 of the Road Vehicles (Construction and Use) Regulations 1986 **6.258** makes it an offence to cause or permit any door of a vehicle to be opened on a road so as to injure or endanger any person.

The regulation applies to any person, e.g. a commissionaire, as well as to people in the vehicle. It applies only on a road (see Chapter 1). Regulation 125 of the 1978 Regulations referred to "motor vehicle or trailer", whereas the new reg.105 which replaces it refers only to "vehicle". However, since "trailer" is defined in the table set out in reg.3(2) as "a vehicle drawn by a motor vehicle" (as it also is in s.185(1) of the 1988 Act), it is submitted that the new regulation also applies to caravans and other trailers, but only whilst they are attached to a motor vehicle (see under "Trailer" in Chapter 1).

The words "cause injury or danger" in the former regulation have been replaced by the words "injure or endanger"; it is submitted that the change is one of semantics rather than substance and that such case law as was engendered by the old wording will apply equally to the new.

In *R. v Cowley* [1971] C.L.Y. 10145, a case at Middlesex Quarter Sessions, the **6.259** words "cause injury or danger" in reg.125 of the previous 1978 Regulations were held to be merely descriptive and the summons was thus not held to be bad for duplicity. Quaere whether the defendant is liable to conviction if he has not been negligent. While there is a presumption that mens rea is required for all offences, this can be displaced by the subject-matter with which the regulation deals. Normally, unless mens rea is clearly or by necessary implication ruled out, proof of it is required (*Brend v Wood* (1946) 110 J.P. 317). On the other hand, it can be argued that it is the duty of every door opener to satisfy himself that no cyclist or other person can possibly be endangered and to make allowance for blind spots in his view behind, e.g. by using another door, so that an almost undischargeable burden is on the defendant; support for this strict view may come from the need to suppress the mischief at which reg.105 is obviously aimed, as decisions establishing absolute liability often arise from statutes which strike at an evil affecting the public welfare. But in *Sever v Duffy* [1977] R.T.R. 429, justices dismissed a charge brought under the former reg.125 on the ground that there was an element of doubt whether the defendant caused danger to other road users in that they considered he had done all that was reasonable in all the circumstances and that the car overtook the defendant's stationary vehicle too closely. The justices' dismissal was upheld: this was a factual decision they were entitled to make (ibid.). It was unnecessary to decide whether the offence involved an element of mens rea as it did not arise on the facts found by the justices (ibid.). It would seem that justices are entitled to find as a fact that the act of opening a car door did not cause danger, if the driver of the stationary car took all reasonable precautions and the danger was caused by the overtaking vehicle.

See § 2.34 as to drivers in Crown service committing these offences.

Leaving vehicle in dangerous position

6.260   Section 22 of the 1988 Act prohibits causing or permitting a vehicle or trailer to remain at rest on a road so as to involve a danger of injury to other persons using the road. This includes not only leaving a vehicle just around a blind corner, but also leaving one in a position which is safe while it is at rest but dangerous if it moves (*Maguire v Crouch* (1940) 104 J.P. 445: driver leaving a vehicle without setting the brake so that it ran away).

Section 22 refers to danger of injury to *other persons using the road*. It does not extend, therefore, to danger to persons who are not using the road but are, e.g. in adjoining buildings. A stipendiary magistrate has accordingly dismissed a case where the defendant's vehicle so blocked a road that fire-engines and ambulances were unable to reach premises further along the road. The danger had been to persons in the premises and not persons using the road.

6.261   Warning of intended prosecution (see Chapter 2) is required (1988 Offenders Act s.1) for all vehicles; s.22 applies to Crown vehicles, trams and trolley vehicles operated under statutory powers, cycles and carts as well as to motor vehicles on roads but not off them.

Parking or driving on cycle tracks

6.262   A person who drives or parks a mechanically propelled vehicle wholly or partly on a cycle track without lawful authority commits an offence, contrary to s.21 of the Road Traffic Act 1988, as amended by the Countryside and Rights of Way Act 2000. The amended provisions extended the prohibition to "mechanically propelled vehicles" (other than as described in s.189(1)(a)–(c) of the 1988 Act), a wider category of objects than the "motor vehicles" of the previous legislation. As to the definition of "mechanically propelled", see § 1.33; "cycle track" is as defined in the Highways Act 1980 (see also § 1.131). The offence does not apply to trailers. Electrically assisted pedal cycles as defined in Chapter 1 are allowed to use such tracks, but pedal cycles which are motor vehicles under the 1988 Act are excluded.

Parking at night

6.263   By reg.101 of the Road Vehicles (Construction and Use) Regulations 1986, no person shall cause or permit a motor vehicle to stand on any road between sunset and sunrise otherwise than with its left or near side as close as may be to the edge of the carriageway. The main exceptions are:

    (a) permission of a police officer in uniform;

    (b) fire and rescue, police, defence and ambulance vehicles but only in such circumstances that compliance with this regulation would hinder or be likely to hinder the use of the vehicle for the purpose for which it is being used on that occasion;

    (c) vehicles on building work, repair work or road work (see 118 J.P. Jo.

101), or removing traffic obstructions, but only if compliance with the regulations would hinder or be likely to hinder the use of the vehicle, etc.;

(d) one-way streets; and

(e) car parks, taxi stands and bus stops.

A case is discussed at 131 J.P. Jo. 627 of a policewoman in uniform purporting to give herself leave to park in a "No Waiting" area; vehicles used for police purposes may be exempt under what is now reg.101. It is submitted that it is primarily a question of fact whether a vehicle is used for police purposes. In *Keene v Muncaster* [1980] R.T.R. 377 it was held as a matter of construction that "permission" in what is now reg.101(1) envisaged permission being requested by one person from another and that a police officer could not therefore give himself permission. It was not contended that the exemption under what is now reg.101(2) (police vehicles) applied. Although the officer's vehicle was used for police purposes it could not be said that compliance with the regulation would hinder its use for police purposes.

Depositing mud and other matter on highways

Byelaws are in force in some areas prohibiting the dropping of mud from a vehicle upon the highway (see [1954] Crim. L.R. 213). See Local Government Act 1972 s.238 for proof of byelaws. **6.264**

It is an offence for a person without lawful authority or excuse to deposit any thing whatsoever whereby a user of the highway is injured or endangered (Highways Act 1980 s.161(1)). The prosecution must prove injury or danger caused by the matter deposited (*Gatland v Metropolitan Police Commissioner* [1968] 2 Q.B. 279). It is also an offence for a person without lawful authority or excuse to allow any filth, dirt, lime or other offensive matter to run or flow on to a highway from adjoining premises (Highways Act 1980 s.161(4)).

There are further "depositing" offences in s.148 of the Highways Act 1980. In *Remet Co Ltd v Newham LBC* [1981] R.T.R. 502 it was held that no offence was committed under this section if the depositing was unintentional. It was suggested that the position might be different if a consistent practice of loading were adopted whereby material was likely to fall on the highway. The decision appears to cover the wording of s.161(1) also. For a case where depositing tubs of flowers in a London mews was held to be unreasonable and therefore without lawful excuse and contrary to s.148 see *Putnam v Colvin* [1984] R.T.R. 150.

Section 161(2) of the Highways Act 1980 provides that lighting a fire on or over a carriageway or discharging a firearm or firework within 50ft of the centre thereof and consequently injuring, interrupting or endangering a user of the highway will constitute an offence punishable by a fine of level 3. Section 161A further provides that a person who lights, or directs or permits to be lit, a fire on land *not* forming part of a carriageway, and in consequence causes a user of a carriageway to suffer injury, interruption or danger as a result of the smoke therefrom, commits an offence punishable by a fine not exceeding level 5. A statutory defence is provided in the form of satisfaction on reasonable grounds that danger, etc., would be unlikely to result from the fire in question or its concomitant smoke, and that either all reasonable steps were taken both before and after the event to prevent such danger, etc., or that there was reasonable excuse for not taking such **6.265** steps. Doubtless the arguments about the merits of stubble burning will continue in other quarters, but the passing motorist ought to benefit substantially from this particular legislative innovation.

OBSTRUCTION, PARKING, ETC.: PENALTIES

Generally

6.266   A number of the offences listed in the table of penalties at § 6.267 below, particularly parking offences, are fixed penalty offences by virtue of Sch.3 to the Road Traffic Offenders Act 1988 (see Chapter 17). For such offences the opportunity to pay a fixed penalty may be offered as an alternative to prosecution. It is submitted that magistrates, when deciding on the amount of the fine, should take into consideration whether the defendant has had such an opportunity. Regard should also be had in appropriate cases to whether the defendant has had to pay a removal fee (see § 6.269 below) after having had his vehicle towed away.

Obstruction, parking, etc.: penalties

Offence	Mode of trial	Section	Imprisonment	Level of fine	Disqualification	Penalty points	Endorsement code	Sentencing guideline*
Obstruction of highway	Summary	s.137 Highways Act 1980	—	3	—	—	—	—
Obstruction of road	Summary	s.42 RTA 1988 and Construction and Use Regs	—	4	—	—	—	—
Obstruction of street	Summary	s.28 Town Police Clauses Act 1847	14 days	3	—	—	—	
Contravention of traffic regulation order	Summary	s.5 RTRA 1984	—	3	—	—	—	—
Contravention of traffic regulation order (Greater London)	Summary	s.8 RTRA 1984	—	3	—	—	—	

Offence	Mode of trial	Section	Imprisonment	Level of fine	Disqualification	Penalty points	Endorsement code	Sentencing guideline*
Contraventions of parking places	Summary	ss.35A(1), 47(1) RTRA 1984	—	2	—	—	—	—
Contraventions of parking places reserved for disabled vehicles	Summary	ss.35A(1), 47(1) RTRA 1984	—	3	—	—	—	—
Improper use of disabled person's badge	Summary	s.117 RTRA 1984	—	3	—	—	—	—
Driving on footpaths, etc.	Summary	s.34 RTA 1988	—	3	—	—	—	—
Illegal parking on verges, etc.	Summary	s.19 RTA 1988	—	3	—	—	—	—
Driving on commons, etc.	Summary	s.193(4) Law of Property Act 1925	—	1	—	—	—	—
Depositing builders' skips illegally on highway	Summary	s.139(1), (3) Highways Act 1980	—	3	—	—	—	—
Negligent opening of car doors	Summary	s.42 RTA 1988 and reg.105 Construction and Use Regs	—	4	—	—	—	—

Offence	Mode of trial	Section	Imprisonment	Level of fine	Disqualification	Penalty points	Endorsement code	Sentencing guideline*
Negligent opening of car doors	Summary	s.78 Highway Act 1835	—	1	—	—	—	—
Leaving vehicle in dangerous position	Summary	s.22 RTA 1988	—	3	Discretionary	3	MS 10	Fine band A
Pedestrian crossing—illegal parking	Summary	s.23 RTRA 1984	—	3	Discretionary	3	PC 30	Fine band A
Improper parking at night	Summary	s.42 RTA 1988 and reg.101 Construction and Use Regs	—	4	—	—	—	—
Parking or driving illegally on cycle track	Summary	s.161(1) Highways Act 1980	—	3	—	—	—	—
Depositing mud, etc., on highway	Summary	s.161(1) Highways Act 1980	—	3	—	—	—	—
Annoyance by playing games on highway	Summary	s.161(3) Highways Act 1980	—	1	—	—	—	—

Offence	Mode of trial	Section	Imprisonment	Level of fine	Disqualification	Penalty points	Endorsement code	Sentencing guideline*
Abandoning vehicles	Summary	s.2(1) Refuse Disposal (Amenity) Act 1978	3 months or £1,000 or both		—	—	—	—

* **Note**: Fine bands "A", "B" and "C" represent respectively 50%, 100% and 150% of relevant weekly income. A timely guilty plea should attract a discount. See Appendix 3 below.

Removal of illegally parked and abandoned vehicles

The power to remove illegally parked vehicles is given to the police by ss.99– **6.268**
102 of the Road Traffic Regulation Act 1984, and by the Removal and Disposal
of Vehicles Regulations 1986 (SI 1986/183). As from June 1, 1993, the same
power was extended to traffic wardens under reg.4A of the Removal and Disposal
of Vehicles Regulations 1986 (as inserted by the like-named 1993 Amendment
Regulations (SI 1993/278)). With effect from December 2, 2002, that power was
further extended (in England only) to persons designated or accredited by chief
officers of police under the Police Reform Act 2002 (Removal and Disposal of
Vehicles) (Amendment) (No.2) Regulations 2002 (SI 2002/2777)). See also the
Removal and Disposal of Vehicles (Loading Areas) Regulations 1986 (SI 1986/
184).

The Removal and Disposal of Vehicles Regulations 1986 have been further
amended by the like-named 2002 Amendment Regulations (SI 2002/746). When
an abandoned vehicle is in such condition that it ought to be destroyed, the period
which must elapse after an appropriate notice has been fixed to the vehicle before
it may be destroyed has been reduced with effect from April 9, 2002, from seven
days to 24 hours. From the same date the amendment regulations reduced the
time allowed to the owner to reclaim the vehicle from custody from 21 days to
seven days.

A Schedule to the Removal and Disposal of Vehicles Regulations 1986 lists **6.269**
the enactments breach of which enables an offending vehicle to be removed, and
includes virtually every statutory provision enabling orders to be made prohibiting waiting of motor vehicles. The powers of removal under s.99 include vehicles
which have broken down, and vehicles causing obstruction, danger or potential
danger (s.99(1)). The Removal and Disposal of Vehicles (Traffic Officers)
(England) Regulations 2008 (SI 2008/2367), made under s.99, came into force on
October 1, 2008 and confers power on traffic officers to require the removal of, or
to remove, vehicles from the relevant road network. Non-compliance is not an
offence as such, but wilful obstruction of a traffic officer in the execution of his
duties is a summary offence under s.10 of the Traffic Management Act 2004.

Section 102(4) of the Road Traffic Regulation Act 1984 entitles the police or
local authority to retain custody of the vehicle until the removal fee is paid. From
October 1, 2008 charges for the removal, storage and disposal of a vehicle are as
set out in the Removal, Storage and Disposal of Vehicles (Prescribed Sums and
Charges) Regulations 2008 (SI 2008/2095). The charges in relation to the removal of vehicles vary according to the vehicle position and condition, and the
weight. For a vehicle that is upright and not substantially damaged (or any two-
wheeled vehicle whatever its condition) weighing less than 3.5 tonnes the charge
is £150. At the other end of the scale the charge rises to £6,000 for a laden vehicle, either not upright or substantially damaged or both, weighing over 18 tonnes.
Storage charges vary from £10 a day to £35 a day, according to weight and type
of vehicle. There is also a charge for the disposal of vehicles.

It was held that dismissal of proceedings for the contravention for which the **6.270**
vehicle was towed away was a bar to proceedings for recovery of the removal fee
(*Metropolitan Police Commissioner v Meller* (1963) 107 S.J. 831). Quaere in
such circumstances whether the vehicle owner may recover a fee which he has
paid in order to repossess his vehicle.

The theft of a vehicle during the absence on holiday of its owner was reported to police by a friend of hers. The vehicle was found the following day by a police officer, who arranged for its removal to a garage where it was retained, efforts to contact the owner's friend by telephone prior to the vehicle's removal having proved fruitless. The owner was subsequently invoiced by the garage for removal and storage charges in respect of the vehicle. The owner's friend, contending that the vehicle had not been abandoned for the purposes of s.99 of the Road Traffic Regulation Act 1984, applied to the county court in his own name for the immediate return of the vehicle. His application was rejected on the basis that the police officer had acted lawfully in arranging for the vehicle's removal and that in any event the only person entitled to recover the vehicle was its owner on payment of the charges for its removal and storage. It was held in *Clarke v Chief Constable of West Midlands Police* [2002] R.T.R. 5, dismissing his appeal, that the legislative purpose of s.99(1) of the 1984 Act and reg.4 of the 1986 Regulations was to enable swift action by police to remove and protect vehicles. The issue raised was not whether the vehicle had in fact been abandoned but whether, in the wording of reg.4, it had been left in such a position as to appear to a police constable to have been abandoned. In the absence of any evidence to show that it did not appear to the police officer who found the stolen car that the vehicle had been abandoned, its removal was lawful. Furthermore, in accordance with s.101 of the 1984 Act, charges for the removal and storage of the vehicle were only payable by the owner of the vehicle.

6.271   The proper construction of the term "obstruction" in reg.3(1)(a) of the Removal and Disposal of Vehicles Regulations 1986 received the scrutiny of the Court of Appeal in *Carey v Chief Constable of Avon and Somerset* [1995] R.T.R. 405. The plaintiff parked his coach, which served him as a family home, by the kerbside of a road in a residential area for several weeks. A number of other large vehicles were similarly parked for similar periods of time by other persons for living, storage or repair purposes. Police officers acting under the presumed authority of regs 3(1)(a) and 4 of the 1986 Regulations had the plaintiff's coach towed away for causing an obstruction to other road users. The plaintiff sued in the county court in respect of damage allegedly caused to the vehicle whilst being towed away and claimed that the removal of his vehicle was unlawful as it had not caused any obstruction. The judge rejected his claim on the basis that the plaintiff's coach had been parked unreasonably and had caused an obstruction. The plaintiff placed reliance in his subsequent appeal upon an apparent distinction between reg.3 which focused upon persons being obstructed from using the road and s.137 of the Highways Act 1980 and reg.103 of the Road Vehicles (Construction and Use) Regulations 1986 which created offences in connection with the obstruction of highways and roads. Allowing his appeal, the court held that whereas an offence of obstruction under s.137 of the Highways Act 1980 or reg.103 of the Construction and Use Regulations was established by proof that any part of the highway had been wilfully and without lawful excuse obstructed so as to deny access by persons to that part and so constitute an unreasonable use of the highway, reg.3(1)(a) of the Removal and Disposal of Vehicles Regulations 1986 provides for its application to a vehicle which has "been permitted to remain at rest on a road in such a position or in such condition or in such circumstances as to cause obstruction to persons using the road or as to be likely to cause danger to such persons". The words "position", "condition" and "circumstances" in that regulation qualified "obstruction" and had no reference to user of the highway and, in the absence of any qualification as to reasonableness, "obstruction" in reg.3 did not have the same meaning as obstruction in s.137 of the 1980 Act or reg.103 of the Construction and Use Regulations 1986 but meant obstruction to the use of the road by persons who were using or might be expected to use it. The essential requirement for the exercise of the power of removal under reg.4 of the Removal and Disposal of Vehicles Regulations 1986 was that the vehicle should not merely be occupying part of the highway, and thus impeding the free access of members of the public to every part of the highway, but should be considered to be obstructing the passage of road users along the highway, hindering or preventing them from getting past. On the evidence, the plaintiff's vehicle was not a vehicle which had been permitted to remain at rest on a road in such a position or in such condition or in such circumstances as to cause obstruction to persons using the road; accordingly the removal of the vehicle by police officers was unlawful and could not be justified.

A person convicted under s.2(1) of the Refuse Disposal (Amenity) Act 1978 **6.272** may in addition to a penalty be ordered to pay the proper charges in respect of the removal of the vehicle under s.102 of the Road Traffic Regulation Act 1984 or under s.5 of the Refuse Disposal (Amenity) Act 1978.

Parking attendants

Section 63A(4) of the Road Traffic Regulation Act 1984 allows certain func- **6.273** tions to be performed by parking attendants in London when they are wearing uniform. Under the authority of the Parking Attendants (Wearing of Uniforms) (London) Regulations 1993 (SI 1993/1450) they may remove vehicles under s.99 of the 1984 Act, fix and give penalty charge notices under s.66 of the Road Traffic Act 1991 (as extended by s.77 ibid.), and may immobilise vehicles under s.69 or 77 of that Act. Various Civil Enforcement of Parking Contraventions Designation Orders are providing similar powers to civil enforcement officers in different parts of England and Wales. By reg.5A of the Removal and Disposal of Vehicles Regulations 1986, where a vehicle has been permitted to remain at rest or has broken down and remained at rest on a road in Greater London in contravention of certain specified provisions, a parking attendant may (subject to certain restrictions) arrange for the removal of the vehicle from the road, provided that it has been in position illegally for at least 15 minutes. Under the Removal, Storage and Disposal of Vehicles (Prescribed Sums and Charges) (Amendment) (England) Regulations 2008 (SI 2008/3013) the Secretary of State can recover charges for the storage and disposal of vehicles removed by traffic officers. The regulations came into force on December 17, 2008.

It should be noted that reg.5A of the 1986 Regulations was amended by the Greater London Road Traffic (Various Provisions) Order 2001 (SI 2001/1353) to install Transport for London as the relevant London authority.

CHAPTER 7

ACCIDENTS AND FURNISHING INFORMATION

CONTENTS

ACCIDENTS INVOLVING INJURY

Production of certificates (s.170(5))

7.01   Under s.170(5) and (6) of the Road Traffic Act 1988, where, owing to the presence of a motor vehicle (other than an invalid carriage: see further § 1.09) on a road or public place, an accident occurs involving personal injury to another person and the driver does not at the time produce his certificate of insurance to the police or to some person who has on reasonable grounds required its production, the driver shall, as soon as practicable and in any case within 24 hours of the accident, report it to the police and thereupon produce his certificate, provided that he may within seven days after the accident cause it to be produced at such police station as he specifies at the time of reporting (s.170(7)). Note that the driver does not have to produce the certificate in person to avail himself of the defence in s.170(7) (as also under s.165: see § 10.70). The extended time-limit for production and the defences of reasonable impracticability which are provided for certain offences (including offences under s.165) do not apply to s.170(5) offences.

In *Tremelling v Martin* [1971] R.T.R. 196 the defendant produced his driving licence and certificate of insurance at a police station. The clerk was called to the telephone before the documents could be examined. The defendant did not wait and walked out of the station. Directing a conviction under both sections, the Divisional Court held that the purpose of producing driving licences was to enable the police to ascertain the name and address of the holder of the licence, the date of issue and the authority that issued it, and the purpose of s.165 was to enable a constable to inspect the certificate of insurance and see that it was a proper certificate. The case would appear to apply to s.170(5) also, because the object of the section appears to be similar to that of s.165.

7.02   The requirements under s.170(5), which only arise on an accident involving personal injury to another person, must be obeyed although the driver has given his name and address to some person reasonably requiring it under s.170(2) (see below). The section would not apply where the driver was quite unaware of the accident, or the injury (*Harding v Price* [1948] 1 All E.R. 283). In *Hampson v Powell* [1970] 1 All E.R. 929 a lorry driver was held not to be guilty under what is now s.170(2) and (3) of failing to stop and failing to report an accident of which he was not aware, although he was convicted of careless driving as the evidence, although insufficient to show that he knew of the accident, was sufficient to show that he drove the vehicle without due care and attention. The section would seem to apply where a passenger was injured and it could be particularly important now that passenger liability is compulsorily insurable.

It would seem, following *Bulman v Bennett* [1974] R.T.R. 1 (see § 7.13), a case on the predecessor to s.170(6), that the driver does not have 24 hours to obey the section, he must do so "as soon as possible".

It is an offence under s.165 to fail to produce the certificate to a police consta-   **7.03**
ble at the time (subject to the same seven days of grace as above), but no offence to fail to produce it to any other person. If the driver has no certificate of insurance, he does not "produce" one and so must report to the police. Note that the "driver" has the obligation, not the owner or anyone else, save so far as he may aid and abet the driver's failure.

Section 170 does not apply to drivers of trams and trolley vehicles operated under statutory powers (s.193 and Sch.4). Nor does it apply to Crown vehicles.

ACCIDENTS TO PERSONS, ANIMALS, VEHICLES OR PROPERTY

Stopping and reporting: requirements of ss.170(1)–(4), (6) and 168

Section 170(1) and (2) of the 1988 Act (as amended) requires a driver to stop   **7.04**
his vehicle if an accident has occurred owing to the presence of a mechanically propelled vehicle on a road or other public place, in which *either* personal injury is caused to someone other than the driver of the vehicle, *or* damage is caused to a vehicle (excepting the defendant's own vehicle or a trailer drawn by the driver's vehicle), or to an animal (excepting an animal in the driver's vehicle or trailer), or to any property attached to land on which the road is situated or adjacent to the road. If so required by a person having reasonable grounds, the driver must give his own name and address, those of the owner of the vehicle and the identification marks of the vehicle (s.170(2)). The address must be one through which the driver can be contacted but may not necessarily be his home address. In *DPP v McCarthy* [1999] R.T.R. 323, a driver gave the address of solicitors that he instructed. The court considered that, in the circumstances of the case, this met the purpose of s.170(2) to enable reasonably swift and easy communication between the parties, both for the purposes of identification and post-accident negotiations. If the driver (in such circumstances) does not give his name and address to any such person he must report the accident at a police station or to a constable as soon as reasonably practicable and, in any case, within 24 hours (s.170(3)). A prosecution under s.170 of the Road Traffic Act 1988 fell to be considered by the Divisional Court in *DPP v Bennett* [1993] R.T.R. 175. The court allowed a prosecutor's appeal against a decision of the Crown Court which found that s.170(2) created two possible factual situations and that an information reciting both was bad for duplicity. Beldam L.J. held that the Crown Court had erred in its view. In order to comply with s.170(2) it was necessary for the driver to fulfil both the duty of stopping and giving his name and address to anyone who reasonably required it.

It is also an offence under s.168 of the 1988 Act for a person alleged to have committed an offence of dangerous or careless driving or cycling (ss.2, 3, 28 and 29 of the 1988 Act) to refuse, on being so required by any person having reasonable ground to do so, to give his name and address to that person, or to give a false name and address. The offence under s.168 does not require there to have been an accident. Section 168 applies to drivers of mechanically propelled vehicles and riders of cycles. The person asking his name and address must have reasonable ground for so asking from the other person who is alleged to have committed dangerous or careless driving or cycling.

7.05   The obligations of s.170 arise only where there has been injury to a person or an animal (i.e. any horse, cattle, ass, mule, sheep, pig, goat or dog: see s.170(8)) or damage to another vehicle, mechanically propelled vehicle or not, or to the road or roadside property as particularised in s.170(1)(b)(iii). The words of the section make it clear that it does not apply where the only damage is to the mechanically propelled vehicle concerned or its trailer or an animal therein or the only person injured is the driver himself. It applies where a passenger is injured. Note that the term "animal" does not include cats or any other beast not mentioned in s.170(8) or birds. See § 4.336 as to the meaning of "cattle".

A bicycle is a vehicle (*Ellis v Nott-Bower* (1896) 60 J.P. 760). Trams and trolley vehicles are also vehicles within the meaning of s.170 where damage is caused *to* them by a mechanically propelled vehicle. Horse-drawn carts are, too. It may be that "vehicle" in s.170 means one normally used on the carriageway as opposed to the footway. However, this may not be wholly sufficient. A dictionary definition is "a thing used for transporting people or goods on land" (*Oxford English Dictionary*). This could include a pram, pushchair or scooter.

7.06   The section formerly applied only where there had been injury or damage to another vehicle or person or animal (as defined in s.170(8)). Damage to property growing in, constructed on, fixed to or forming part of the land of the road or land adjacent thereto now gives rise to the obligations contained in s.170(2) and (3). The words "growing in" quite clearly bring damage to trees, crops and plants within the ambit of the section. The amendment does not include property not fixed, etc., on the road or roadside, and it would therefore appear that if the damage was, e.g. only to the load of another vehicle, or to the clothing only of a pedestrian, he being unhurt, s.170 as amended would not apply. If a traffic sign or other roadside property is damaged, there will usually be no one to whom the driver can reasonably be required to give his name and address, and in such a case he will therefore be under an obligation to report the accident to the police (see *Peek v Towle* at § 7.15).

The driver is under the obligations imposed by s.170 even though the accident may have been caused entirely by the fault of someone else.

Knowledge of driver

7.07   It is the "driver" who has the duties under s.170, not the owner or anyone else save so far as the latter may aid, abet, counsel or procure the driver's failure. The requirement imposed by the provisions of s.170 only applies if the defendant knows that an accident has occurred (*Harding v Price* [1948] 1 All E.R. 283). The judges held in *Harding v Price* that there was a positive duty—something more than a mere prohibition—imposed by the statute to report and the driver could not discharge that duty unless he had knowledge of the accident. When the case was decided, "knowledge" was thought to include wilfully shutting one's eyes to the obvious. This view is nowadays not put forward quite in this form: "knowledge" refers also to the situation where the driver really knows that there has been an accident but deliberately chooses to put it out of his mind. Usually the prosecution can show either that the defendant actually knew of the accident or that he ought reasonably to have known of it, e.g. by there being a severe jolt or a loud crash at the time. Once the damage or injury has been proved, the burden of proof is on the defence to produce some evidence of the defendant's genuine unawareness of them. Unlike the original section in the Motor Act 1903, the current section does not require the prosecution to prove knowledge. In *Harding v Price* the judges held, in view of this, that the absence of knowledge in the statute had the effect of shifting the burden of proof.

It is for the defendant to prove absence of knowledge. Where such a burden is placed on the defendant, the proof is on the balance of probabilities (*R. v Carr-Briant* [1943] 2 All E.R. 156). If, after hearing all the evidence, the court is in doubt whether or not the defendant knew that he was involved, he should be acquitted.

The principle of *Harding v Price* was applied in *Hampson v Powell* [1970] 1   **7.08** All E.R. 929, where convictions of a lorry driver for failing to stop and failing to report an accident were quashed. In this case it was held that the knowledge of the driver was a "necessary ingredient" of the offence. No damage could be seen on the lorry; when the driver was seen by the police he admitted he was in the relevant area at the time but denied all knowledge of an accident.

The commentary in the relevant paragraph of a previous edition of this work was approved in *Selby v Chief Constable of Avon and Somerset* [1988] R.T.R. 216. The defendant had been charged with an offence of failing to report an accident under s.25 of the 1972 Act. The justices found that the defendant was the driver of the vehicle involved and that there was a rebuttable presumption that he knew he had been involved in the accident. On appeal, Schiemann J. approved the proposition established by *Harding v Price* that the absence of any reference to the defendant's knowledge in the statute had the effect of shifting the burden of proof on to the defendant once damage or injury was proved. The learned judge preferred that authority to *Hampson v Powell* above because the argument in the latter case did not appear to be directed to the question of whether the burden of proof shifted to the defence.

Meaning of "stop", "driver", "injury" and "accident"

In *Lee v Knapp* [1966] 3 All E.R. 961 it was held that "stop" in s.170(2) means   **7.09** stop and remain at the scene of the accident for such a time as in the prevailing circumstances, having regard in particular to the character of the road or place in which the accident happened, would provide a sufficient period to enable persons who had a right so to do, and reasonable ground for so doing, to require of the driver direct and personally the information which might be required under the section. It does not suffice if an employee or agent of the driver waits at the scene (ibid.). It was also held in *Ward v Rawson* [1978] R.T.R. 498 that to "stop" means to remain near the vehicle for a sufficient period to allow a person having reasonable grounds for doing so to ask for the driver's name and address. (The defendant collided with a depot fence, inspected the damage, left his vehicle at the scene and ran off, not wanting to be breathalysed.) The driver does not have to wait indefinitely (*Norling v Woolacott* [1964] S.A.S.R. 377: accident involving an unattended vehicle, no other people or houses near).

It is submitted that a person must *stop* in accordance with the specific requirement of the section even though the driver is in the middle of nowhere and there can be no question of exchanging information. In *Hallinan v DPP* (1999) 163 J.P. 651, the appellant was a bus driver. In the course of a journey, his bus halted sharply and a passenger sustained injury. He failed to stop, despite being informed by other passengers that the passenger had been injured and despite their requests to him to stop. It was held that, where an accidental injury had been sustained by a passenger on a bus, with no damage to anything outside the bus or injury to another person, the scene of the accident for the purpose of s.170 of the Road Traffic Act 1988 was not the bus itself, but the point in the road where the accident occurred. The driver's duty to stop arose immediately. If he failed to do so immediately, he failed to satisfy the requirements of s.170(2) of the 1988 Act.

7.10   While the decision is not binding, a magistrates' court has convicted a driver who in the early hours collided with and damaged a wall and drove on without stopping because there was no one in the vicinity. The driver was granted an absolute discharge. In such a situation the stopping may need only to be for a minimal period—see the cases noted above.

In common with other summary offences, a person may be arrested by a constable without a warrant only if the conditions are met as set out in s.24 of the Police and Criminal Evidence Act 1984. Section 24, as substituted, replaces the previous provisions which were dependent upon whether or not an offence was an arrestable offence.

7.11   In *Jarman v Walsh* [1936] S.A.S.R. 25, a case on an Australian statute requiring a driver to stop and, if required, give his name and address, it was held that a driver who had gone on for 300yds and then returned to the scene of the accident had not complied with the statute. In *McDermott v DPP* [1997] R.T.R. 474, driving on for about 80yds, then stopping and returning to the other vehicle was not sufficient and the defendant was properly convicted of failing to stop after the accident. However, in *R. v Criminal Injuries Board* [1981] R.T.R. 122, a driver started to move away with the intention of leaving. The offence of failure to stop was held not yet to be complete.

There is nothing in the statute to require a person to go around knocking on doors or seeking by other means to discover whether there is anybody who might have the necessary right to ask the questions envisaged by the section: *Mutton v Bates (No.1)* [1984] R.T.R. 256. This would be particularly true when the time (as in that case) is 2.30am.

7.12   "Driver" in s.170(2) means the person who takes the vehicle out on the road; he remains the driver until he finishes the journey, although he may have stopped and switched off the engine some minutes before (*Jones v Prothero* [1952] 1 All E.R. 434 —driver convicted for not reporting accident to cyclist knocked over by a car door opening suddenly; he was still in the car); see § 1.89. Following an accident a learner driver walked away from the scene followed by his supervisor who took no steps to ensure he remained at the scene. Some 40 minutes later the two were seen together two miles away walking towards the scene. The learner driver was convicted of failing to stop and the supervisor of aiding and abetting (*Bentley v Mullen* [1986] R.T.R. 7).

"Injury" has been held by a stipendiary magistrate to include shock, citing *Hay (or Bourhill) v Young* [1943] A.C. 92 (115 J.P. Jo. 250) . A hysterical and nervous condition can be "actual bodily harm" (*R. v Miller* [1954] All E.R. 529). In *Clements v Gill* [1953] S.A.S.R. 25, an Australian case, a pedestrian was struck and thrown to the ground by a motor vehicle. Evidence was given that he was shaken and dazed, but there was no evidence of any actual physical injury. It was held that the evidence was insufficient to prove that injury had been caused to him. For the meaning of the word "accident", see § 1.84.

Duty to exchange names or report

If the driver for any reason has not given his name and address to any person who has reasonable grounds for requiring it, s.170(3) requires him to report the accident at a police station or to a police constable "as soon as reasonably practicable and in any case within twenty-four hours". Unlike s.170(2), s.170(3) only refers to the driver's name and address. "As soon as reasonably practicable" was held to mean precisely what it says: a driver who did not report the accident as soon as it was reasonably practicable for him to do so was held to have committed the offence even though he made admissions about the accident within 24 hours to a constable who came to interview him (*Bulman v Bennett* [1974] R.T.R. 1). The additional words "and in any case within 24 hours" do not qualify the obligation to report as soon as reasonably practicable and thus give a driver the right to wait 24 hours before reporting; the words "in any case" were held to be equivalent to "without prejudice to the foregoing" (ibid.). It is thus clear that: **7.13**

    (a) the driver must report as soon as reasonably practicable (and this, it is submitted, is a matter of fact for the court to determine depending on the particular circumstances of each case); and

    (b) the driver must in any event report it within 24 hours, seemingly, even if not reasonably practicable to do so within that time.

Similarly, in *DPP v Hay* [2005] EWHC 1395; [2006] R.T.R. 3, the defendant was seen by a police officer to collide with a traffic island and then hit a stone wall. The driver was rendered unconscious and it was not possible for the officer to speak to him either at the scene or at the hospital to which the driver was taken. The driver was recognised by the police officer. A magistrates' court upheld the defence submission that there was no obligation to report an accident where the police were on the scene throughout. Upholding the prosecution appeal, the Divisional Court confirmed the plain meaning of the statutory provision. There was no express exception where the accident was observed by the police and none should be implied.

Forbes J. in *Mutton v Bates (No.1)* [1984] R.T.R. 256 emphasised the difference between "as soon as reasonably practicable" and "as soon as reasonable". **7.14**

The test as to whether an offence is made out is not, "Is it reasonable for the defendant to have reported the accident earlier?" but, as in the statute, "Did the defendant report the accident 'as soon as reasonably practicable'?" In *Bulman v Lakin* [1981] R.T.R. 1 the defendant had had an accident at 1.10am and at 11am, after a police constable had fruitlessly called three times at the home of the defendant, called in and reported the accident at the police station. At the hearing of the charge of failing to report the accident the defendant made an unsworn statement but did not explain why he had not reported the accident earlier. The case was dismissed by the justices because they were of the opinion that it was not reasonable to expect the defendant to have reported the accident earlier. The Divisional Court held that the offence was made out. The justices had not asked themselves the right question: no reasonable tribunal would have done other than come to the conclusion, in the absence of an explanation to the contrary, that the defendant had not reported the accident as soon as was reasonably practicable.

7.15   It has also been held that if the driver refuses his name and address to a person reasonably requiring it, he commits an offence although he reports to the police within 24 hours (*Dawson v Winter* (1932) 49 T.L.R. 128). If he does give his name and address, etc., to such a person, he need not report to the police (*Adair v Fleming* [1932] S.C.(J.) 51; *Green v Dunn* [1953] 1 All E.R. 550), unless there has been personal injury and the insurance certificate has not been produced, so that s.170(5) applies. It should be emphasised that if an accident occurs and the driver does not give his name and address, etc., because no one asks for it (e.g. because the driver was clearly not responsible for the accident) or because there is no one at the scene, or for any other reason, he must still report to the police (*Peek v Towle* [1945] 2 All E.R. 611).

     In *DPP v Drury* [1989] R.T.R. 165, the respondent had been driving his car which also contained a passenger. There was music playing in the car, and neither he nor his passenger was aware of a minor collision with another car in a narrow country lane, although they appreciated that the cars had passed very close. On arrival at their destination some 15 minutes later both the respondent and his passenger noticed a small rubber mark on the driver's side. They both assumed there must have been a minor collision. The respondent did not report the accident. He was acquitted of the offence of failing to report the accident, but the prosecutor's appeal to the Divisional Court was successful. That court held that a driver who was not aware of an accident at the time it occurred, but subsequently became aware of it, had a duty to report it (under s.170(3)) provided that he became so aware within 24 hours.

7.16   The strict obligation to report an accident under what is now s.170(3) where the driver has not complied with the immediately preceding subsection was again emphasised in *R. v Crown Court at Kingston-Upon-Thames Ex p. Scarll* [1990] Crim. L.R. 429. A driver was involved in an accident causing injury to a young girl. He was known to the girl's parents who soon arrived at the scene of the accident. He did not give them his name and address or report the accident at a police station. He contended that the duty to report did not arise because he had met substantially the requirements of s.170(2) by telling the father what had happened and because he was known to him. It was held in the Divisional Court that the father of the girl had not required the driver to provide his name and address, but s.170(3) required the driver to report the accident if for any reason he had not complied with s.170(2). Therefore there had been a breach of s.170(3).

     The words "owing to the presence of a motor [now mechanically propelled] vehicle on a road or other public place" were considered in *Quelch v Phipps* [1955] 2 All E.R. 302. It was held that there must be some direct causal connection between the vehicle and the occurrence of the accident and the section applied where a passenger jumped off a moving bus and hurt himself. The presence of the vehicle must be more than a mere sine qua non and an indirect connection is insufficient, e.g. a pedestrian stepping back to avoid a car and injuring another pedestrian. The section is not limited to collisions. Questions can arise as to how far the presence of a stationary car can be said to cause an accident; its presence probably does where a cyclist runs into it but it might be otherwise if he swerved to avoid it and fell off his machine; often the driver will not have been in the car so that in that case there might be no duty on him.

7.17   It can be argued that the defendant driver's vehicle need not even have been involved in the accident if his driving has been the primary cause of collision between two other vehicles, if such accident would never have happened but for the defendant's own bad driving. In such a case the prosecutor would have to prove that the defendant knew both that there had been a collision and that injury or damage had been caused. On the other hand, it could be said that, if the collision of the pedestrians need not be reported (see above), nor need the collision of two other vehicles by a third driver whose conduct caused it.

For a helpful Scottish case on the issue of whether or not there was an "accident" in deciding whether or not a notice of intended prosecution needed to be served, see *Bremner v Westwater* (1993) 1994 S.L.T. 707. The decision may be of assistance in examining the rather wider definition in s.170, "... owing to the presence of a mechanically propelled vehicle on a road or other public place, an accident occurs ...".

In this case a driver drove his vehicle without lights during the hours of darkness and at an excessive speed. He overtook one vehicle in the face of oncoming traffic, causing the driver of the overtaken vehicle to brake sharply and the driver of the oncoming vehicle also to brake sharply and take evasive action, namely mounting the nearside kerb to avoid a head-on collision. This conduct was held by the High Court of Justiciary to be an "accident", which had occurred as a result of the presence of the driver's car on the road.   **7.18**

It would be surely to fly in the face of common sense if this were not so and, provided requirements of the remainder of s.170 were made out, the driver would be guilty of the failing to stop/report offences if the same facts were proved in England and Wales rather than in Scotland. See also § 1.84–8 and § 2.199.

The onus of proof that a driver failed to report to the police does not seem to lie on the police; it is a matter peculiarly within the driver's own knowledge whether he did so.   **7.19**

The obligation under s.170(3) is to report "at" a police station or "to" a constable; this means that the driver must report in person at a police station or personally make the report to a constable—telephoning a police station or police constable is insufficient (*Wisdom v Macdonald* [1983] R.T.R. 186).

There might be circumstances in which the driver would be well advised to telephone if there were practical difficulties in attending in person. Although that would not fulfil the statutory obligations, it would bring the accident to the notice of the police and could be a relevant matter to be taken into account in deciding whether or not there had been a report as soon as reasonably practicable and in deciding whether or not to prosecute (ibid.).   **7.20**

The question of the driver's obligation to report an accident to the police as soon as reasonably practicable was considered by the High Court in Scotland in *Hornall v Scott* (1992) 1993 S.L.T. 1140. The court upheld the appeal by a motorist holding that the onus was on the Crown to prove that it would have been reasonably practicable for the driver to have reported the accident to the police sooner than he in fact did. The Crown had not made out such a case and the appeal was allowed.

The facts should be given in full because the circumstances described are commonplace in prosecutions on both sides of the border. The driver was driving on a motorway early in the morning when he collided with a barrier. The barrier was damaged and the car was extensively damaged. The driver used his carphone to arrange for a breakdown vehicle to tow his car away. He then rang his wife and arranged for her to collect him from the scene of the accident. His wife arrived   **7.21** and took him home before the breakdown vehicle arrived. The police arrived at the scene before the breakdown vehicle had taken the damaged car away. The driver arrived home at 2.15am and the police arrived about one hour later. The driver sustained a fracture of the collar bone in the accident. He did not become aware of this until some time later, but by the time the police arrived he was in such pain that he could not sign his name. The driver was convicted before the sheriff, finding that as the driver was not aware of his injury his wife might have taken him to a police station on his way home to report the accident, or he could have waited until the breakdown vehicle arrived and travelled with it to the police station. At the High Court, the Lord Justice-Clerk stated that the court was not persuaded that, had the driver done as was suggested, he would in fact have reported the accident any earlier. In fact two of the local police stations were closed at that time of night and the driver might have found some difficulty in communicating with a police station to telephone through information regarding the accident.

If this reasoning is followed in decisions in England and Wales, it opens up rather greater flexibility in interpreting the phrase "as soon as reasonably practicable".

7.22   Sections 164 and 165 specifically empower a constable to require a driver whom he has reasonable cause to believe was involved in an accident to produce his driving licence, insurance certificate, etc., and one of the purposes of these sections is seemingly to enable a police officer to require a driver reporting an accident to produce these documents. Forbes J. however in *Mutton v Bates* was disposed to accept obiter that the object of s.170 was to obtain details for the other parties and had nothing to do with whatever powers the police might have to investigate possible infringements of proper driving procedures.

If either element of s.170(2) is missing, i.e. if a person fails to stop but later gives his particulars or if he stops but refuses those particulars, an offence is committed (*North v Gerrish* (1959) 123 J.P. 313).

One offence or two?

7.23   A person is guilty of an offence under s.170(4) of the 1988 Act if he fails to comply with either s.170(2) or s.170(3). He is guilty of two offences if he fails to comply with both (*Roper v Sullivan* [1978] R.T.R. 181). It is an offence under s.170(2) of the 1988 Act to fail to stop and give particulars. If a person fails to stop but later gives particulars, or if he stops but fails to give particulars, an offence is committed (*North v Gerrish* (1959) 123 J.P. 313). To fail to give a name and address is not bad for duplicity and an offence is committed if only the name or part of the name or only the address or a material part of the address is omitted or false. See further "Duplicity", § 2.91 and *DPP v Bennett*, § 7.04 above.

In *Johnson v Finbow* [1983] 1 W.L.R. 879 it was held that a driver who failed to stop after an accident contrary to s.170(2) and who subsequently failed to report the accident contrary to s.170(3) committed two offences but on the same occasion for the purpose of penalty points (see § 19.38), because their commission arose from the same accident (see also § 7.04).

FURNISHING INFORMATION

Generally

7.24   The duty to give information as to the driver of a vehicle arises under s.172 of the 1988 Act, s.112 of the Road Traffic Regulation Act 1984 and s.46 of the Vehicle Excise and Registration Act 1994. There are also other instances when information may be required of owners and drivers, and these are discussed below, § 7.42 and § 7.43. As to the duty to state the ownership of a vehicle for fixed penalty offences and excess meter charges and the fixed penalty provisions in Pt III of the Road Traffic Offenders Act 1988, see Chapter 17.

The Police and Criminal Evidence Act 1984, Pt I gives the police additional powers of search and carrying out road checks but not for minor motoring offences.

7.25 In *City of Rochester upon Medway v Derbyshire* (1997) 17 W.R.T.L.B. [247], the appellant was convicted by the magistrates' court of failing to give information as to the driver of a car. The argument relied on was that the car was in such a state that it could not be driven and ipso facto could not have a driver. The Crown Court dismissed the appeal. It is not difficult to understand how that conclusion was reached.

Driver alleged to be guilty of a specified offence

7.26 By s.172(2) of the 1988 Act, where the driver of a vehicle (whether a motor vehicle or not) is alleged to be guilty of an offence to which the section applies:

 (a) the person keeping the vehicle shall give such information as to the identity of the driver as he may be required to give by or on behalf of a chief officer of police; and

 (b) any other person shall if required as stated above give any information which it is in his power to give and may lead to the identification of the driver.

As to whether a demand for information is made "by or on behalf" of a chief officer of police, see *Record Tower Cranes Ltd v Gisbey* [1969] 1 W.L.R. 148, *Nelms v Roe* [1969] 3 All E.R. 1379 and *Pamplin v Gorman* [1980] R.T.R. 54 at § 7.40.

7.27 Whether the obligation to provide information under s.172 of the 1988 Act infringed the right to a fair trial under the European Convention on Human Rights by requiring an individual to incriminate himself was subject to a full judgment by the Privy Council in another Scottish case, *Brown v Stott (Procurator Fiscal, Dunfermline)* [2003] 1 A.C. 681. The case concerned a woman who was required to say who had been driving her car at a certain time. When asked, she was already a suspect in relation to a drink/driving charge. No caution was given. She admitted she was the driver and the prosecution wished to adduce that evidence as part of the case against her. It was argued that adducing the evidence would contravene the right to silence and the right against self-incrimination and thereby infringe art.6(1) of the European Convention on Human Rights. (Although art.6(1) does not refer directly to a right against self-incrimination, it is widely accepted that such a right exists. The covenant on which the Convention was founded states that "in the determination of any criminal charge against him" everyone shall be entitled "not to be compelled to testify against himself or to confess guilt". In *Funke v France* (1993) 16 E.H.R.R. 297, the court recognised that a fair trial within art.6 includes the right of anyone charged with a criminal offence to remain silent and not to contribute to incriminating himself.) The High Court upheld this submission and took the view that s.172(2) could be read in a manner compatible with Convention rights if read as meaning that the Crown had no power to lead evidence of her reply at her trial. The court accepted that a right not to incriminate oneself at the trial must include the same right during the investigation since otherwise the right to silence at trial could be evaded by questioning during the investigation and then the leading of the answers during the trial. However, the Privy Council allowed the prosecutor's appeal holding that reliance on such an admission was not a breach of the right to a fair trial. Powerful judgments from Lord Bingham and Lord Hope explored the background and concluded that s.172 provided for the putting of a single, simple, question the answer to which could not of itself incriminate the suspect since it was not, by itself, an offence to drive a car. The decision was applied by the Divisional Court in *DPP v Wilson* [2001] EWHC Admin 198; [2002] R.T.R 6. A district judge had excluded an admission of driving given in pursuance of s.172 of the Road Traffic Act 1988 by virtue of s.78 of the Police and Criminal Evidence Act 1984. The prosecutor's appeal was allowed. To admit answers given as a result of such a request was neither unfair nor contrary to the provisions of the European Convention on Human Rights. This approach has been confirmed by the European Court of Human Rights. In *O'Halloran and Francis v United Kingdom* (2008) 46 E.H.R.R. 21; [2007] Crim. L.R. 897 the court ruled that the nature of the information that was sought destroyed neither the right to remain silent nor the privilege against self-incrimination. Accordingly, neither the degree of compulsion exercised through the sanction for failure to comply nor the attempt to obtain evidence in this way violated the right to a fair trial. Those who choose to keep and drive cars could be taken to have accepted certain responsibilities and obligations including, within the legal framework of the United Kingdom, the obligation in certain circumstances to inform the authorities of the identity of the driver. That judgment was applied in *Luckhof and Spanner v Austria* [2008] Crim. L.R. 549. The European Court of Human Rights unanimously found there to be no violation of art.6(1) in requiring the owner of a vehicle to give details of the person driving the vehicle at a particular time and the imposition of a financial penalty in default.

7.28   The issue of self-incrimination was also considered by the House of Lords in *R. v Hertfordshire County Council Ex p. Green Environmental Industries Ltd* [2000] 2 W.L.R. 373. Under the Environmental Protection Act 1990, a waste regulation authority may require a person to give information some or all of which could be used against them in a prosecution. Failure to comply with the request is an offence. When a request was made to the company, solicitors sought an assurance that the answers would not be used in any prosecution, which was not forthcoming. Proceedings for failure to provide the information requested were subject to judicial review. The House of Lords held that the issue of whether potentially incriminating answers should be excluded from the evidence was for the trial judge exercising the discretion provided under s.78 of the Police and Criminal Evidence Act 1984 and therefore the request for information had to be complied with. The privilege of self-incrimination during pre-trial investigations was designed to inhibit abuse of power by investigatory authorities but there were exceptions most of which had been created by statute. Whether a particular statute excluded the privilege against self-incrimination was a question of construction. In this case, the investigatory powers were for the broad purpose of protecting public health and the environment, not simply to enable the authorities to obtain evidence against an offender. The questions asked were all requests for factual information and none invited any admission of wrongdoing. There was no express provision that the answers were to be admissible in criminal proceedings and so the discretion of the court to exclude evidence under s.78 of the Police and Criminal Evidence Act 1984 was unimpaired.

A further attempt to demonstrate that these provisions are incompatible with the principles against self-incrimination was made in *Hayes v DPP* [2004] EWHC 277. The court robustly dismissed the argument emphasising again that the privilege against self-incrimination is not an absolute right. **7.29**

The veritable explosion of litigation on the provision of information in accordance with s.172 has continued. The most significant decision is that in *Francis v DPP* [2004] EWHC 591; (2004) 168 J.P. 492. The defendant had returned a form without giving identification details of the driver and without signing it. In a comprehensive judgment, the court considered and rejected a range of arguments. Section 172 requires the keeper of a vehicle to give "such information as to the identity of the driver" as required by the police. Section 12 of the Road Traffic Offenders Act 1988 permits a statement in writing, signed by the accused, in response to such a request to be acceptable as evidence that the accused was the driver. It was argued that, as a criminal sanction is attached to failure to comply, the provision must be restrictively construed. Since nothing is said about how a person should respond to the request for the information, and there is no requirement to sign anything, it could not be said that an offence was committed when information was given in another way or not signed. Further, that, as there were grounds for suspecting the keeper of an offence, in order to comply with the requirements of Code C of the PACE Codes of Practice, a caution should have been incorporated in the request for information (it was recognised in putting that argument that there was a tension between making a demand which had to be complied with in order not to commit a criminal offence and advising that nothing needed to be said).

In rejecting both arguments, the court referred to *Boss v Measures* [1990] **7.30** R.T.R. 26 (as long as the person requesting the information makes reasonable requests as to how and when the information is to be provided, that is lawful); *DPP v Broomfield* (below) (stressing that since the requirement is designed to produce a document acceptable as evidence, it cannot be said that responding in another way complies with the requirement): *Mawdesley v Chief Constable of Cheshire*; *Yorke v DPP* [2003] EWHC 1586; [2004] 1 All E.R. 58 (unsigned form not admissible under s.12 but admissible as a confession); and *Jones v DPP* [2003] EWHC 1729; [2004] R.T.R. 21 (accused returned form not completed but accompanied by a signed letter giving the information). The court concluded that:

> "... section 172(2) empowers a chief officer of police to require that certain information be given. Section 172(7) enables him to make that requirement by means of a written notice, and by implication he is entitled to make reasonable requirements prescribing how the person to whom the notice is addressed shall respond. So the chief officer can require that the response be in writing ... and that it be signed. The application of a signature is not giving information beyond the scope of section 172(2). It is in the first place a normal form of authentication by the vehicle keeper of the written information which he provides, but it is also something that it is clear from section 12(1) that Parliament envisaged being part of a written response to a notice sent to a vehicle keeper pursuant to section 172(2). The fact that section 172 and section 12 are in different statutes

is of no relevance bearing in mind that both statutes were enacted at precisely the same time, that they both deal with the same subject matter, and that section 12(1) expressly refers to section 172(2). "

Regarding the need for a caution, the court was clear that none was required.

It is not sufficient to indicate that it could have been the owner or one other person but neither could recollect driving the vehicle at the time. There is an obligation to give details of the driver or any information that might lead to the identification of the driver: *R. (on the application of Flegg) v Southampton and New Forest JJ.* [2006] EWHC 396; (2006) 170 J.P. 373.

7.31   Section 172(5) deals with the situation where a body corporate is guilty of an offence under the section and the offence is proved to have been committed with consent/connivance/neglect of a director, manager, secretary, etc. That individual as well as the body corporate is guilty of that offence, and is liable to be proceeded against and punished accordingly. The "reasonable diligence" defence provided in subs.(4) is disapplied where the alleged offender is a body corporate, or where proceedings are brought under subs.(5), unless in addition to the matters mentioned in subs.(4) the alleged offender shows that no record was kept of the persons who drove the vehicle, and that the failure to keep a record was reasonable. Section 172(7)–(10) deals with the service of notices under the section, and provides definitions. In this respect it has been held that a requirement to supply information under s.172 of the Road Traffic Act 1988 made against a limited company does not have to satisfy the requirements of s.725 of the Companies Act 1985 (now s.1139 of the Companies Act 2006), with regard to the service of documents on companies; a requirement made of the company secretary will suffice (*Blake v Charles Sullivan Cars Ltd, The Times*, June 26, 1986).

The section extends to any offence under the 1988 Act, other than offences under Pt V (registration of driving instructors), and ss.13, 16, 51(2), 61(4), 67(9), 68(4), 96, 120. It also extends to offences against any other enactment relating to the use of vehicles on roads and to any offence under ss.25, 26, 27 of the 1988 Offenders Act. See below as to s.172 extending to regulations. In Scotland, s.172 extends to offences under s.178 (taking and driving away) also; it is submitted that, by virtue of the Interpretation Act 1978 s.17(2), it extends also to offences under s.12 of the Theft Act 1968 (taking conveyances) in England and Wales.

7.32   The offence under s.172 carries as a maximum a fine of level 3, but in addition, a compulsory endorsement of the offender's licence with six penalty points, and discretionary disqualification. Unsurprisingly, the power to endorse/disqualify does not apply when the offence has been committed by a body corporate.

Section 112 of the Road Traffic Regulation Act 1984 is in like terms to s.172 (although there are minor differences) and extends to offences under ss.1–111 of that Act, save those under ss.43, 52, 88(7), 104, 105, 108, including s.108 as modified by s.109(2) and (3), and s.35A(5) in its application to England and Wales. Neither s.112 of the 1984 Act nor ss.171 and 172 of the 1988 Act apply to persons and vehicles in the public service of the Crown.

7.33   There is no time-limit in s.112 of the 1984 Act for the provision of information. The Divisional Court held in *Lowe v Lester* [1986] Crim. L.R. 339 that it meant providing the information forthwith or as soon as reasonably practicable. A request to supply the information in 14 days was held in that case to be reasonable.

Section 46 of the Vehicle Excise and Registration Act 1994 is also in like terms to s.172 of the 1988 Act and extends to offences under ss.29, 34, 37 and 43A. In relation to offences of using a vehicle in contravention of these sections, both the driver and the person using the vehicle shall be treated as the persons concerned whose identities are required to be given, and, where the offence alleged is keeping a vehicle, the person whose identity has to be given is the person keeping it. The person who can demand information under s.46 is the chief officer of police or the Secretary of State for Transport. Section 46 does not extend to Crown drivers.

The cases cited below with reference to s.172 presumably apply to s.171 and in principle also to s.112 of the 1984 Act and s.46 of the 1994 Act.

There are two types of case which can arise under s.172 (or indeed under s.46 **7.34** of the 1994 Act or s.112 of the 1984 Act above). The first and more usual situation is that once a good notice under the section has been served or sufficient requirement made, the person to whom the demand is made is then under the statutory obligation to give further information; once he is told of the fact that the vehicle in question was seen at a particular place at a particular time, the police do not have to prove the offence alleged or, indeed, any further information about the allegation (*Pulton v Leader* [1949] 2 All E.R. 747; *Jacob v Garland* [1974] R.T.R. 40). If the person fails to give the information required he may only escape conviction if he can avail himself of the defence in s.172(4) if he is the owner or if the other person referred to in s.172(2)(b), that it is not in his power to give the information. (The owner can properly be summoned under s.172(2)(b) as well as (a) (*Hodgson v Burn* (1966) 110 S.J. 151).) The other type of case which can arise under s.172 is where the person from whom the information is demanded denies that the vehicle in question was at the place at the time alleged, and accordingly refuses to give the information required on the ground that it is impossible for him to do so as the vehicle was elsewhere at the time. In this case, the police are required to prove that the vehicle was at the place at the time specified in the notice (*Neal v Fior* [1968] 3 All E.R. 865; *Jacob v Garland* above).

Proof of the posting of the requirement has to be given in each case by rules made under s.69 of the Courts Act 2003. Rule 4.11 of the Criminal Procedure Rules 2005 is the relevant rule.

In *Record Tower Cranes Ltd v Gisbey* [1969] 1 W.L.R. 148, inquiring of only **7.35** 12 out of 25 drivers was said not to show due diligence under what is now s.172(4). It is not a condition precedent to the owner being required to give information that the driver should previously have refused his own name and address (*R. v Hankey* (1905) 69 J.P. 219). The person who was the offending driver must give the required information if it is demanded under s.172(2)(b) and cannot claim the privilege of not incriminating himself, see §§ 7.26–7 above. It would seem, similarly, that the keeper of the vehicle if he is also the driver likewise cannot claim the privilege of not incriminating himself when required to disclose who the driver was under s.172(2)(a).

The reference in s.172(2) to "in his power to give" is in para.(b) only, but by s.172(4) the person keeping the vehicle required to give information under (a) is not guilty if he shows that he did not know and could not with reasonable diligence have ascertained who the driver was. The obligation under s.172(2)(b) to give any information "which it is in his power to give" applies to a doctor who has the information as a result of a professional consultation. He cannot say that by reason of the ethics of the medical profession it is not within his power to give the required information (*Hunter v Mann* [1974] R.T.R. 338). The court (per Lord Widgery C.J. at 345) cited with approval the *BMA Handbook* which states:

> "A doctor should refrain from disclosing to a third party information which he has learnt professionally or indirectly in his professional relationship with a patient ... subject to (the following exceptions) ... where the information is required by law."

7.36   The court in *Hunter* accordingly upheld a conviction under s.172 of a doctor who had refused to disclose the identity of a man and a girl who had been treated by him following an accident in which a motor car which had been taken without the owner's consent had been involved. In *Hawkes v Hinckley* (noted at 120 J.P. Jo. 642) the High Court held that the obligation to give information continues even after the person from whom it is required has himself been summoned for dangerous driving. The police may thus use s.172 to obtain information as to the identity of a driver at any time. The obligation imposed by s.172 on the person keeping the vehicle is a personal one and cannot be discharged by some other person, such as a solicitor, giving the information on his behalf (*Hodgson v Burn* (1966) 110 S.J. 151). A person becomes owner of a vehicle on hire purchase when he takes possession on the signing of the agreement; he must then answer questions under s.172 in respect of matters before that date, when he had in fact had possession of it (*Hateley v Greenough* [1962] Crim. L.R. 329).

The obligation is to respond within the time and in the manner required by the notice. In *DPP v Broomfield* [2002] EWHC 1962; [2003] R.T.R. 5, a defendant successfully persuaded the Crown Court that giving the information orally by telephone had discharged the obligation imposed. However, the Divisional Court agreed with the magistrates' court that that was not sufficient. The information must be given in the way required by the notice. That notice specified how the information was to be given and that requirement was reasonable since having the information in writing and signed enabled it to be accepted as evidence of the identity of the driver of the vehicle. In *Mawdesley v Chief Constable of Cheshire*; *Yorke v DPP* [2003] EWHC 1586; [2004] 1 All E.R. 58, forms had been returned showing that the person to whom the form had been sent was the driver. In the case of the offender, Mawdesley, the form was complete apart from the signature and date; in Yorke's case, not all the details were completed nor was it signed. The Administrative Court held that the documents were not admissible under s.12 of the Road Traffic Offenders Act 1988. However, the contents of an unsigned form were a confession (within the meaning of s.82 of the Police and Criminal Evidence Act 1984) and admissible as a document under what was then s.27 of the Criminal Justice Act 1988. The court could properly infer that documents sent to the defendant's address had been completed by the defendant when returned containing relevant information.

7.37   In the case of offences under the Road Traffic Regulation Act 1984 s.47, in relation to parking places, and s.35A(5) (plying for hire on parking places), the power to require information may be exercised as well by the local authority, but must be in writing. Section 172(2) would generally extend to offences under regulations made under any provisions of the 1988 Act mentioned in s.172(1), e.g. the Pedestrian Crossings Regulations, the Construction and Use Regulations, etc. (*Bingham v Bruce* [1962] 1 All E.R. 136; *Rathbone v Bundock* [1962] 2 All E.R. 257), and now by the substituted s.172(1) of the 1988 Act to any offence against any other enactment relating to the use of vehicles on roads. Section 112 of the 1984 Act would likewise extend to offences under orders and regulations made under that Act.

"Use" includes leaving a vehicle stationary (*Elliott v Grey* [1959] 3 All E.R. 733) (but see "using" for the purposes of a requirement under s.46 of the 1994 Act above).

It seems that the police can make more than one duly authorised demand, e.g. **7.38** where a person says on Monday that he can ascertain by Friday who the driver was and fails to give the information when demanded again on Friday, he can be summoned for the Friday offence. If a person duly required to give information under s.172, s.112 or s.46 knowingly gives false information, he seems to be guilty of an offence against the section because he has failed to give "information which he is required to give" and which it is "in his power to give". He is likewise guilty if he pretends not to know the answer to the questions put.

Sections 172 and 112 apply where the "driver" and to a certain extent riders of a vehicle are alleged to be guilty of an offence. Semble it does not extend to inquiries as to offences by persons in other categories, e.g. to the supervisor of a learner. The extension to "riders" in s.172 is only to riders of cycles which are not mechanically propelled vehicles and in s.112 only to riders of bicycles and tricycles which are not motor vehicles and not multi-wheeled cycles to be seen at seaside resorts. It will not apply to other riders that are not mentioned in s.172.

Place of offence

The issue has been raised as to whether the offence is committed in the place to **7.39** which the reply should be sent or at the place from which it should be sent but has not been sent. In *Kennet District Council v Young* [1999] R.T.R. 235 it was held that the offence was certainly committed in the place to which the information should have been sent and may well be committed where the request for information was received.

"By or on behalf of a chief officer of police"

It seems that a constable may not use s.172 on his own initiative; he must be **7.40** authorised by or on behalf of his chief constable and the prosecution should prove this (*Osgerby v Walden* [1967] Crim. L.R. 307, where the silence of the defendant was held on the particular facts to amount to an admission as to this). Where information was demanded in writing on a form signed by a police sergeant and there were added after his signature the words "on behalf of the Commissioner" this was held not to be proof that the sergeant had the necessary authority (*Record Tower Cranes Ltd v Gisbey* [1969] 1 W.L.R. 148), but this case was distinguished in *Nelms v Roe* [1969] 3 All E.R. 1379, where evidence was given that the inspector who made the request was authorised to do so, by his sub-divisional police superintendent. Although it was held that the Commissioner of Police was not in the position of a Minister of the Crown who can act through an officer of the department of the Crown, the Commissioner of Police in entrusting the superintendence of the sub-division to the police superintendent impliedly authorised the superintendent to act on his behalf through a responsible officer in the sub-division. It was therefore held that the superintendent's delegation to the inspector of the power to make the request was done with the implied authority of the Commissioner of the Metropolitan Police. This principle would seem to apply also to the delegation by chief constables of provincial police forces to their divisional officers. In *Pamplin v Gorman* [1980] R.T.R. 54, the notice was also signed by a police superintendent and it stated that he was so authorised by the chief officer of police for the county. The justices rejected the defence submission that the notice was invalid because the prosecution had not proved that the superintendent had been so authorised by the chief officer of police. Upholding the justices the Divisional Court held that the notice having been produced from an official source and having every appearance of authenticity, the justices could infer from the document itself in the absence of contrary evidence that the superintendent was so authorised. It has been held in Scotland that statements obtained by constables not authorised under s.172 may be inadmissible (*Foster v Farrell* 1963 S.L.T. 182), but this decision was distinguished in *Miln v Cullen* 1967 S.L.T. 35, on the question of admissibility in other proceedings of statements made. One should distinguish between the admissibility in other proceedings of statements made pursuant to requests purporting to be made under s.172 or s.112, whether intra vires or ultra vires the requesting constable, and the commission of an offence under those sections by refusing to answer. "Chief officer of police" is now defined in s.101 of the Police Act 1996 as the Commissioner of the City or Metropolitan Police or the chief constable of a county force but does not, it seems, include the chief constable of a special force such as a Ministry of Defence Police Force or the British Transport Police. Compare *Westminster Coaching Services v Piddlesden* at § 13.207 as to delegation by the chief officer of police on a differently worded section and also compare "Authority to prosecute", § 2.15.

Vehicle driven without insurance

7.41   It is the duty of the owner of a motor vehicle under penalty to give such information as he may be required by or on behalf of a chief officer of police to give for the purposes of determining whether the vehicle was or was not being driven in contravention of s.143 of the 1988 Act (no insurance), on any occasion when the driver was required to produce his certificate of insurance (1988 Act s.171). "Owner", in relation to a vehicle which is the subject of a hiring agreement, includes each party to the agreement (1988 Act s.171(3)); and see § 1.215.

Other instances

7.42   A person who refuses information or to give his name and address to the police is not guilty of obstructing the police (*Gelberg v Miller* [1961] 1 All E.R. 291), but it may be obstructing the police to give false information as to the identity of an offender (*R. v Field* [1964] 3 All E.R. 269 at 280).

Section 164 of the 1988 Act enables the police when requiring the driver to produce his driving licence to require him also in certain circumstances to state his date of birth (see §§ 11.17–23). Likewise where a person is convicted of an endorsable offence, the court, unless his date of birth is known, is required to order the defendant to state his date of birth (1988 Offenders Act s.25(1)). Where a person has stated his date of birth either to a constable or to a court, the Secretary of State may serve a notice on the person requiring him to verify the date of birth (1988 Offenders Act s.25(5); 1988 Act s.164(9)).

7.43   Section 165 of the 1988 Act also confers powers on constables, whether authorised by a superior officer or not, to require information as to drivers, owners and insurance in the case of accidents and suspected offences (see §§ 11.17–23).

PROCEEDINGS AND PENALTIES

Penalties for failure to stop and report

The possible seriousness of offences under s.170 has been reflected in the **7.44** maximum penalty for each offence of six months' imprisonment and/or a fine of level 5 (Road Traffic Act 1991, Sch.2, para.29(a)). The range of penalty points the court is obliged to impose is within the range 5–10 (Road Traffic Act 1991, Sch.2, para.29(b)). As far as the offences of failing to stop and report are concerned, the Magistrates' Court Sentencing Guidelines provide three levels of seriousness based either on the degree of damage caused or on the extent to which the offender had complied with the obligations to stop and/or report. A court will be looking to sentence within level 1 where the damage or injury caused is minor or where the offender stopped at the scene of the accident, but did not exchange particulars or report the accident. An offence will fall within level 2 if there was moderate injury or damage or the offender failed both to stop and to report. An offence will fall within the most serious level, level 3, where there was serious damage or injury and/or evidence of bad driving. Care will need to be taken to avoid double counting where there is a separate offence arising from the bad driving.

For level 1, the starting point is a fine in Band B (100 per cent of relevant weekly income) within a range of Band B (75–125 per cent of relevant weekly income) and 5–6 penalty points; for level 2, the starting point is a fine in Band C (150 per cent of relevant weekly income) within a range of Band C (125–175 per cent of relevant weekly income), 7–8 penalty points and consideration of disqualification from driving; and, for level 3, a starting point of a high-level community order within a range of Band C fine to 26 weeks' custody accompanied by disqualification for 6–12 months or, where disqualification is not ordered, 9–10 penalty points.

The place of the starting point within a range will be affected by the various **7.45** aggravating and mitigating factors; those identified as particularly relevant to these offences include aggravating factors of there being evidence of drink or drugs having been consumed or evasion of a likely test to see whether they were present, knowledge or suspicion that personal injury had been caused, leaving an injured party at the scene or giving false details. Mitigating factors include a belief by the offender that his or her identity was known, a genuine fear of retribution if he or she had remained at the scene or the later reporting of the accident.

The custody threshold is likely to be crossed within the third level where there are aggravating factors present including such statutory factors as the existence of relevant previous convictions.

Where a custodial sentence is imposed and the offender is also disqualified from driving, courts are now encouraged to take into account the time to be spent in custody and to fix the length of the disqualification so that the period that the court considers appropriate is served after the expected time of release.

Endorsement of a defendant's licence may not be ordered if there are special **7.46** reasons and a useful example of what has been held to be capable of amounting to a special reason is contained in the unreported case of *Leeman v Walton* (judgment given on October 8, 1984). A bus driver pleaded guilty to failing to give his name and address. The bus was a corporation bus with a route service number and the driver had his identity disc in a prominent position attached to his uniform. The Divisional Court indicated that there was sufficient information available to be capable of amounting to a special reason for not endorsing. The driver had not sought to conceal his name, and his identity and the name and registration marks of the vehicle concerned were plainly exhibited and obviously intelligently recorded. The case was accordingly sent back to the justices to consider whether the special reason should be found to justify them in not endorsing. The court emphasised that no general rule was being laid down to this effect where the identification was obvious.

The court may order the defendant to be disqualified until he passes a test (1998 Offenders Act s.36) and in determining whether to order such a disqualification the court is required to have regard to the safety of road users (s.36(6)) (see § 20.69).

The penalty for an offence under s.168 is a fine of level 3.

Penalties for refusal to give information, etc.

7.47   It is submitted that refusal to give information is not a continuing offence and that the six months' limitation period starts with each demand (see generally § 2.41). It is submitted also that an information for failing to give both name and address is not bad for duplicity (see §§ 2.91 and 7.04).

In *Mohindra v DPP* [2004] EWHC 490; [2005] R.T.R. 7, the court rejected the argument that where a person had failed to reply at all, the prosecution (in order to avoid duplicity) needed to lay two informations since the offence could have been committed in two different ways. The court was clear that s.172(3) creates only one offence; all the prosecution had to prove was that the notice was sent and was not returned.

7.48   The penalty for an offence under s.171 of the 1988 Act is on level 4. Offences under s.172 of the 1988 Act, s.112 of the Road Traffic Regulation Act 1984, and s.46 of the Vehicle Excise and Registration Act 1994, carry a fine of level 3. In addition an offence under s.172 is subject to obligatory endorsement of six penalty points and discretionary disqualification. The Magistrates' Court Sentencing Guidelines include a guideline for the offence of failing to give information of driver's identity as required. The starting point is a fine in Band C (150 per cent of relevant weekly income). By virtue of the Fixed Penalties Offences Order 2003 (SI 2003/1253), a contravention of s.172 is a fixed penalty offence.

Accidents and furnishing information: penalties, etc.

Offence	Mode of trial	Section *	Imprisonment	Level of fine	Disqualification	Penalty points	Endorsement code	Sentencing guideline †
Failing to stop after accident	Summary	s.170(4)	6 months or level 5 or both		Discretionary	5–10	AC10	Fine band B for each offence; if serious consider disqualification
Failing to report after accident	Summary	s.170(4)	6 months or level 5 or both		Discretionary	5–10	AC20	—
Failing to produce insurance, etc., after injury accident	Summary	s.170(7)	—	3	—	—	—	—
Refusing to give or giving false name and address in case of dangerous, careless or inconsiderate driving or cycling	Summary	s.168	—	3	—	—	—	—
Failure of owner of motor vehicle to give police information as to insurance	Summary	s.171	—	4	—	—	—	—

Offence	Mode of trial	Section *	Imprisonment	Level of fine	Disqualification	Penalty points	Endorsement code	Sentencing guideline †
Failure of keeper of vehicle and others to give information as to driver, etc.	Summary	s.172	—	3	Discretionary if committed otherwise than by virtue of s.172(5) or (11)	6	—	Fine band C
Failure of keeper of vehicle and others to give information as to driver, etc.	Summary	s.112 RTRA 1984	—	3	—	—	—	—
Failure of keeper of vehicle and others to give information as to driver, etc.	Summary	s.46 Vehicle Excise and Registration Act 1994	—	3	—	—	—	—

* Road Traffic Act 1988 unless otherwise specified.

† **Note**: See Appendix 3.

CHAPTER 8

VEHICLE OFFENCES

CONTENTS

CONSTRUCTION AND USE

Generally

The two main sources are the Road Vehicles (Construction and Use) Regula-   **8.01**
tions 1986 (SI 1986/1078) and the Pedal Cycles (Construction and Use) Regulations 1983 (SI 1983/1176). The lighting regulations, some of which are made
under s.41 of the 1988 Act and deal with the fitting, maintenance and use of
lamps, etc., are dealt with separately, see §§ 8.112 et seq.

The 1986 Regulations have been much amended. They are divided into two
main parts; the part governing the construction and equipment of motor vehicles
and trailers, and the part governing their use. It may be that causing danger is in a
category of its own in applying both to maintenance and use (regs 100 et seq.).

The "construction" part of the regulations is being gradually superseded by the
system of type approval (see § 8.09). It is essential therefore when any "construction" regulation is in issue to check whether the type approval system applies
instead of the construction regulation. For this purpose reference should be made
to reg.6 (Compliance with Community Directives and ECE Regulations) and
Sch.2 to the 1986 Regulations. The position normally depends on the date of
manufacture and date of first use. The definition of "Community Directives"
includes directives issued by the European Parliament and the Council of the EU
as well as those adopted by the Council of the Commission of the European
Communities.

Certain of the "use" regulations depend on the "construction" regulation. If the   **8.02**
"construction" regulation does not apply then the "use" regulation will not apply
either. A use or maintenance offence will sometimes be a contravention of the basic construction regulation and sometimes of the type approval or approval mark
requirement (see, e.g. regs 35 and 36 (speedometers) and 18 (brakes)). It is necessary for the prosecution to choose the correct provision and for the defence to
ensure that they have done so. A practical test as to whether the vehicle is subject
to type approval may be whether there is a type approval certificate.

The Construction and Use Regulations and the type approval schemes are
considered below. Matters relating to particular regulations are then dealt with
together with the penalties for all offences.

The Construction and Use Regulations

8.03   Regulation 3 contains the definitions, and definitions in the 1988 Act also apply where the regulations do not have a specific one. The case of *Wakeman v Catlow* [1977] R.T.R. 174 is of importance where a court has to decide whether a vehicle comes within a specified class of vehicle. The defendant drove a jeep with two defective tyres. It was licensed under what is now the Vehicle Excise and Registration Act 1994 as a "land tractor" (as defined in the 1978 Regulations). A "land tractor" is exempted from the requirements of the former reg.99 relating to defective tyres. The justices without considering the definition of "land tractor" and in particular whether the jeep was used "primarily for work on land" dismissed the case. Sending the case back to the justices, the Divisional Court held that the nature of the excise licence alone is insufficient to establish the category of the vehicle and the onus of proof to show that a vehicle comes within an exempt category is on the defendant. Where the category of a vehicle depends not only on its physical characteristics but also on the use to which the vehicle is put, the defence must produce evidence to show that the vehicle was used for that purpose. It will be noted that many of the definitions contained in reg.3 require a vehicle to be used for a certain purpose, e.g. "industrial tractor", "works trailer" and "works truck". There is no definition of the phrase "land tractor" in the 1986 Regulations. The phrase used is "agricultural motor vehicle". The principle in the *Wakeman* case would appear to be applicable to the new definition, however.

A living van is defined in reg.3(2) as a vehicle which is used primarily as living accommodation and which is not also used for the carriage of goods or burden which are not needed for the purpose of residence in the vehicle. For the interpretation of this the decision in *Plume v Suckling* [1977] R.T.R. 271 may assist. A coach had been converted to carry six passengers, kitchen equipment and a stock car. The stock car was held not to be goods needed for the purpose of residence, but it is submitted that not every luxurious item of goods or burden would take the vehicle out of the definition.

8.04   The regulations and definitions are detailed and should always be carefully consulted. Offences under the regulations are generally for "using" or "causing" or "permitting" use: see Chapter 1 as to these expressions. Of the cases there cited, many were on these regulations.

Some of the regulations refer to vehicles "first used on or after a specified date" e.g. reg.15. What is meant by "first used" is set out in reg.3(3). An exemption is provided for a vehicle first used on or after the specified date where that vehicle was manufactured at least six months before that date: reg.4(2). This acknowledges the inevitable gap for most vehicles between construction and use. Similarly, where an exemption applies to a vehicle first used before a specified date, e.g. reg.15, it will also apply to a vehicle first used on or after that date if it was manufactured at least six months before that date: reg.4(3). Other provisions apply to vehicles manufactured before or after a certain date (e.g. reg.15). In that case, no further extension is given.

8.05   The regulations normally apply to both wheeled and track-laying vehicles: reg.4(1). However, reg.4(4) contains exemptions from specified regulations for certain vehicles, including certain track-laying vehicles, such as vehicles in the service of a visiting force or of a headquarters, vehicles going to a port for export and vehicles on test. Motor vehicles and trailers brought temporarily into Great

Britain are also exempted from some of the regulations. "Temporarily" means "casually" and does not include a trailer brought intermittently but regularly into this country (see *BRS v Wurzal* [1971] 3 All E.R. 480). Some regulations specifically exempt certain vehicles. For instance, "works trucks" are exempted from reg.63 (wings). A works truck is defined in reg.3. One part of the definition is use in "the immediate neighbourhood" of the premises. It was held that "in the immediate neighbourhood" had to be construed with reference to the amount of use on the roads involved. Land adjacent or nearly adjacent to the main premises may not be in the "immediate neighbourhood" if it nevertheless involves having to travel a considerable distance on a public road (*Hayes v Kingsworthy Foundry Co Ltd* [1971] Crim. L.R. 239). This case was followed in *Lovett v Payne* [1980] R.T.R. 103, a case of the nearest weighbridge. "Nearest" was held not to be as the crow flies but the nearest suitable road route (i.e. suitable for the vehicle in question). Regulation 4(4) and (5) qualifies the case of *Wilkinson v Barrett* (1958) 122 J.P. 349 (see § 1.57, meaning of "trailer").

8.06 Regulation 4 confers other exemptions from some of the regulations for certain motor vehicles in addition to those mentioned. It may therefore be worthwhile to refer to reg.4 (as amended) in an appropriate case.

The regulations apply to wheeled vehicles, not being tram or trolley vehicles operated under statutory powers (see powers contained in the Road Traffic Act 1988 s.193A), and additional obligations are imposed by the Public Service Vehicles (Conditions of Fitness, Equipment, Use and Certification) Regulations 1981 (SI 1981/257), as amended, and the Minibus (Conditions of Fitness, Equipment and Use) Regulations 1977 (SI 1977/2013) (see further § 13.171 and § 13.212). Generally, the 1986 Regulations would seem to apply only to roads and only to motor vehicles and trailers while used on a road as defined in Chapter 1; strange results would follow if they applied to them off the road. See s.42 of the Road Traffic Act 1988.

The regulations apply to Crown vehicles and drivers and (with the exceptions detailed in reg.4) to vehicles and drivers of visiting forces.

8.07 Provisions are included in the regulations about the construction of minibuses, which are defined in reg.3(2) as motor vehicles constructed or adapted to carry more than eight but not more than 16 seated passengers in addition to the driver. Regulations 41–44 (as amended) and Sch.6 to the 1986 Regulations are relevant here. It is noteworthy that none of the requirements relates to "a vehicle manufactured by Land Rover UK Limited and known as the Land Rover". Nor do the provisions in the Schedule relating to the construction of minibuses relate to vehicles constructed or adapted for the secure transport of prisoners.

Failure to comply with the regulations is an offence: Road Traffic Act 1988 ss.41A, 41B and 42. The summons should indicate that it is contrary to the appropriate section of the 1988 Act and the particular regulation (*Simmons v Fowler* (1950) 48 L.G.R. 623, discussed at 115 J.P. Jo. 322). The prohibition on "use" (as opposed to causing or permitting use) in s.42(b) is absolute in the sense that no mens rea, apart from user, need be shown unless a regulation is so worded as to show that the exercise of proper care and absence of knowledge are defences, as in the regulations on speedometers and excessive noise (*James v Smee; Green v Burnett* [1954] 3 All E.R. 273). Where, however, the charge is causing or permitting, this normally requires prior knowledge of the unlawful user on the part of the person causing or permitting (see *Ross Hillman Ltd v Bond* [1974]

R.T.R. 279 and other cases cited in §§ 1.161 et seq.). But where a regulation casts a duty only upon the vehicle-owner, it may be that use by another is not an offence (126 J.P. Jo. 93), save so far as it is aiding and abetting.

8.08   As to the various provisions relating to weighbridges, ascertainment and transmission of weight, plated weights and defences to weight prosecutions, see §§ 1.68–83. As to unnecessary obstruction (reg.103) see §§ 6.201 et seq.; as to opening car doors (reg.105) see § 6.257; as to the use of lights in conditions of seriously reduced visibility, see § 8.138 and as to lights generally, see §§ 8.112 *et seq.*

TYPE APPROVAL SYSTEM

Vehicles subject to type approval

8.09   The construction of motor vehicles in Great Britain hitherto has been controlled by manufacturers being required to ensure that their vehicles are constructed in accordance with the Construction and Use Regulations. One result of the accession by the United Kingdom to the European Community and the consequent acceptance and implementation of the EC's common transport policy is that, in time, the construction of motor vehicles and their parts will be controlled by type approval schemes based on uniform conditions applying throughout the Community in accordance with EC directives or regulations.

Whether a vehicle is subject to "type approval" usually depends on the date of manufacture and the date of first use (which often means the first registration under the Vehicle Excise and Registration Act). There is a time between EC decisions being incorporated in the type approval regulations and in turn in the exemptions in the Construction and Use Regulations. The law so far as it affects Great Britain is contained in ss.54–65A of the 1988 Act and the regulations made thereunder. Using, or causing or permitting to be used on a road, a vehicle subject to the type approval requirements without a certificate of conformity is an offence against s.63(1) of the 1988 Act.

The optional EC type approval scheme

8.10   The relevant regulations are the Road Vehicles (Approval) Regulations 2009 (SI 2009/717). For agricultural and forestry vehicles, see the Tractor etc. (EC Type-Approval) Regulations 2005 (SI 2005/390), as amended, which apply to agricultural and forestry tractors, their trailers and interchangeable towed machinery together with their systems, components or separate technical units. In addition, there are the Motor Cycles etc. (EC Type Approval) Regulations 1999 (SI 1999/2920).

Application may be made to the approval authority (the Secretary of State) for EC type approval for light passenger vehicles and components (2009 Regulations reg.12). In relation to an EC type approval certificate or an EC certificate of conformity, it is an offence for a person, with intent to deceive, to forge, alter or use such a document, or to lend or allow such a document to be used by another person or to make or have a document so closely resembling such a document as to be calculated to deceive. The maximum punishment is, on summary conviction, a fine not exceeding the statutory maximum and, on indictment, two years' imprisonment and/or an unlimited fine. It is a summary offence to make false statements in connection with the supply of information or documents under the regulations: 2009 Regulations reg.33.

The European Court of Justice has given consideration to the extent of a classification given to a vehicle under the EC type approval scheme. In *Voigt v Regierungsprasidium Karlsruhe-Bretten* [2006] R.T.R. 36, a driver had been driving a vehicle on a motorway in Germany on which different speed limits applied depending on whether the vehicle was a passenger vehicle or a goods vehicle. The vehicle in question was designated a passenger vehicle under the type approval scheme but a goods vehicle by German law relating to speed limits. Accordingly, it was subject to a lower speed limit. The court confirmed that the purpose of the directive on which the scheme is based was to remove obstacles to the free movement of goods; that was achieved by the harmonisation of requirements and technical characteristics but does not go beyond that. Accordingly, it does not introduce consequences that relate to the application of national road traffic rules governing the speed limits that apply to different categories of vehicle. **8.11**

Where either a type approval certificate has been issued by the Secretary of State or a certificate of conformity by the manufacturer (see, e.g. the Motor Vehicles (Type Approval) (EEC Manufacturers) Regulations 1981 (SI 1981/493)) reg.6 of and Sch.2 to the Road Vehicles (Construction and Use) Regulations 1986 exempt from the regulations specified in the table the motor vehicle or trailer or its component part.

The following points may be emphasised. The application of the 2009 Regulations and reg.6 of the Road Vehicles (Construction and Use) Regulations 1986 is not obligatory. The exemption therefore only exists where the conditions in reg.6 apply. The burden of proof of establishing the exemption is therefore on the defendant on the balance of probabilities (Magistrates' Courts Act 1980 s.101, and *R. v Carr-Briant* [1943] 2 All E.R. 156). Under the 1980 Regulations, the type approval certificate is issued by the British Secretary of State. Regulation 6 of the 1986 Regulations also exempts motor vehicles, trailers and component parts manufactured abroad with either a type approval certificate from a member country or a certificate of conformity with such a foreign type approval certificate. By reg.6 the scheme applies to trailers. **8.12**

The compulsory British type approval scheme

The relevant regulations are the Motor Vehicles (Type Approval) (Great Britain) Regulations 1984 (SI 1984/981), as amended, and the Motor Vehicles (Type Approval for Goods Vehicles) (Great Britain) Regulations 1982 (SI 1982/1271), as amended. The Motor Cycles Etc. (Single Vehicle Approval) Regulations 2003 (SI 2003/1959) introduced a scheme for approving the design, construction, equipment and marking of mopeds (diesel or electric as well as other mopeds), motor cycles, motor tricycles and quadricycles (all as defined and limited in the regulations) and providing for those vehicles to be examined for the purposes of obtaining an approval certificate. Exceptions are provided in reg.13. Regulation 2 defines those vehicles that fall within the described types to which the regulations apply. **8.13**

The 1984 Regulations make provision on a national basis for certain classes of motor vehicles and their components manufactured on or after October 1, 1977 to be compulsorily subject to conformity with type approval schemes. The main **8.14** category to which the 1984 Regulations apply is (subject to reg.3(2)) every motor vehicle (and parts of such vehicles) which was manufactured on or after October 1, 1977 and not first used before August 1, 1978 which is *either* constructed solely for the carriage of passengers and their effects *or* a dual-purpose vehicle, and which is:

    (a) adapted to carry not more than eight passengers (exclusive of the driver) and either has four or more wheels or has only three wheels and is of more than 1,000kg gross weight, or

    (b) has three wheels (not being a motor cycle with or without side-car), falls below the specified maximum gross weight and falls within a specified design speed or engine capacity.

For the meaning of "adapted", "dual-purpose vehicle", etc., see Chapter 1.

8.15   The 1982 Goods Vehicles Regulations similarly provide that certain classes of motor vehicles and their components manufactured on or after October 1, 1982 and not first used before April 1, 1983, or six months after manufacture as the case may be, shall be compulsorily subject to conformity with type approval schemes. The main category to which the regulations apply is motor vehicles which have three or more wheels and are either goods vehicles, tractor units of articulated vehicles or bi-purpose vehicles (reg.3(1)). A "bi-purpose vehicle" means a vehicle constructed or adapted for the carriage of both goods and not more than eight passengers, not being a vehicle to which the 1984 Regulations apply nor a motor ambulance or a motor caravan which are also excluded separately (reg.2(1)). Regulation 3(2) contains a large number of exemptions. They include vehicles brought temporarily into Great Britain which comply with certain requirements and which display a registration mark mentioned in reg.5 of the Motor Vehicles (International Circulation) Regulations 1985 (SI 1985/610). The exemptions also include certain vehicles for export, visiting forces' vehicles, vehicles formerly in the public service of the Crown, prototype vehicles not intended for general use on roads, motor tractors, light locomotives and heavy locomotives (see the definitions in Chapter 1); engineering plant, pedestrian con- trolled vehicles, straddle carriers, works trucks and track-laying vehicles, all as defined in reg.3(2) of the Road Vehicles (Construction and Use) Regulations 1986.

8.16   The Motor Vehicles (Approval) Regulations 2001 (SI 2001/25) revise the system for approving the construction of single vehicles before they enter service. They apply to vehicles to which the 1984 Regulations apply and to certain vehicles to which the 1982 Regulations apply (reg.4 of the 2001 Regulations).

Pt III of the 2001 Regulations provides for an approval certificate to be issued by the Secretary of State. There are two sets of requirements, basic and enhanced (reg.5). Special classes of vehicle are defined in Sch.2 to the regulations and those need only comply with the basic requirements. Equivalent approvals granted in other EEA states will be recognised (reg.5(8)(c)).

8.17   Regulation 3 of the Motor Vehicles (Type Approval) (Great Britain) Regula- tions 1984, as amended, now applies to motor ambulances, motor caravans, personally imported passenger vehicles and amateur-built passenger vehicles which had previously been excluded. This means that in future such a vehicle may either be type approved in accordance with the 1984 Regulations or may be granted single vehicle approval in accordance with the 2001 Regulations.

Section 63 of the 1988 Act makes it an offence to use, cause or permit to be used on a road (for the meaning of these words, see Chapter 1) a vehicle subject in whole or in part to type approval unless it appears from one or more certificates in force that the vehicle or its parts comply with the type approval. Type approval contraventions will be contrary to s.63.

The following points may be emphasised. As stated, the scheme is compulsory. **8.18** Presumably, therefore, proof of the type approval scheme and the certificate will be a matter for the prosecution to establish. At present the regulations do not apply to trailers as such but only to motor vehicles and component parts. The scheme is limited to certificates issued by the Secretary of State backed up where appropriate by certificates of conformity.

Both the 1982 and the 1984 Regulations prohibit the first issue of a vehicle excise licence in respect of a vehicle subject to type approval unless the application is accompanied by evidence showing that the vehicle conforms with the type approval requirements.

Approval marks

Vehicles showing designated approval marks are exempted from certain brak- **8.19** ing regulations. The Motor Vehicles (Designation of Approval Marks) Regulations 1979 (SI 1979/1088), as amended, are based on ECE Regulations, i.e. regulations prepared by the United Nations Economic Commission for Europe annexed to the Agreement of 20 March 1958 as amended (Cmnd. 2535 and 3562) relating to conditions for approval for motor vehicles equipment and parts (see s.80 of the 1988 Act).

Sale of vehicles and parts without required certificate

If a goods vehicle or parts are sold without the certificate of conformity or Sec- **8.20** retary of State's approval certificate required by the compulsory type approval scheme being in force an offence is committed under s.65 of the 1988 Act. The person who supplies or offers to sell or supply or exposes for sale such goods vehicles or parts similarly will also commit an offence.

Section 65(3) exempts vehicles for export. It also exempts a person who had reasonable cause to believe that the vehicle (or part when fitted) would not be used on a road in Great Britain or at least until it had been certified or that it would be used within the terms of prescribed exemptions.

SPECIFIC CONSTRUCTION AND USE REGULATIONS

Agricultural trailed appliance

The term "land implement" was deleted from reg.3 of the Construction and **8.21** Use Regulations and replaced by "agricultural trailed appliance" which is defined there. The definition includes a number of elements. One element requires it to be a trailer which is an instrument constructed or adapted (see § 1.27) for use off roads for the purpose of agriculture, horticulture or forestry and which is only used for one or more of these purposes. The wording of the last part of the definition (b(ii)) is complicated but appears to mean that an agricultural implement is not an agricultural trailed appliance even though it is rigidly mounted on a vehicle and supported by its own wheels, unless the mounting is permanent or unless part of its weight is supported by its own wheel or wheels and the greater part of it is capable of swivelling horizontally in relation to the rear part of the carrying vehicle. Regulation 3 also defines an agricultural trailed appliance conveyor.

Opinions as to the former definitions of "land implement" and "crop sprayer" appear at 125 J.P. Jo. 314 and 341. An elevator capable by adaptation of being worked by belt and pulley from a tractor but designed to be run and driven by its own engine and having rubber wheels was held not to be a land implement (*Hockin v Reed & Co (Torquay) Ltd* (1962) 60 L.G.R. 203). A trailer, in this instance a Webb Masterspread, was able to fall within the definition of "land implement" in the former reg.3 irrespective of the manner in which it was drawn and it could be within the exemptions given by the old regulations whether or not it was for the time being used with a land locomotive or land tractor (*Amalgamated Roadstone Corporation v Bond* [1963] 1 All E.R. 682).

8.22　　A vehicle excise licence is insufficient evidence to show that a vehicle is an "agricultural motor vehicle". The defendant must show that the vehicle is used for the purpose specified in reg.3(2) (see *Wakeman v Catlow* at §§ 1.27, 8.03). It would seem that an agricultural trailed appliance under reg.3 does not include a machine used for scraping earth and carrying it from one place to another; it must be connected with agriculture and use with an agricultural motor vehicle is confined to farming and forestry land and does not cover engineering work on building sites (*Markham v Stacey* [1968] 3 All E.R. 758).

Length, width, height and overhang

Length

8.23　　The meaning of "overall length" is set out in reg.3(2) with the limits contained in reg.7. "Overall length" includes all the parts of a vehicle, any receptacle of a permanent character and any fitting attached to the vehicle unless excepted by the rest of the definition in reg.3(2). Exceptions make provision for a wide range of equipment from snow ploughs to tailboards to receptacles containing indivisible loads of exceptional length to rear buffers of resilient material.

In relation to trailers and semi-trailers, towing equipment and other parts not extending the load carrying space are also excepted.

The permitted lengths of different types of vehicle are set out in a table in reg.7(1). These lengths are qualified for some vehicles by reg.7(2)–(8). Some of the qualifications use measurements of length other than the overall length of the vehicle, e.g. reg.7(5A). By reg.7(9), it is illegal for a trailer with an overall length exceeding 18.65m to be used on a road unless the police have been notified and an attendant employed.

8.24　　In reg.7(3), (3A) and (5)(b) the word "normally" has its ordinary meaning and is used in contradistinction to abnormal or exceptional; where a vehicle carried exceptionally long loads on 46 journeys out of 177, it was held that these 46 journeys could not be said to be exceptional or abnormal (*Peak Trailer & Chassis Ltd v Jackson* [1967] 1 All E.R. 172). The exemption in the proviso did not therefore apply. An "indivisible" load is not of "exceptional" length if it would go in a vehicle of standard length (*Cook v Briddon* [1975] Crim. L.R. 466). The actual use of an articulated vehicle on the day in question is not the governing factor. In deciding whether the regulation applies the justices should consider whether

(a) the vehicle is "constructed" for the conveyance of indivisible loads of exceptional length and, if this is proved, then

(b) whether the defendant can also show that the articulated vehicle was "normally used" for this purpose (*Kingdom v Williams* [1975] R.T.R. 333).

As to "constructed", see § 1.27.

By the Road Vehicles (Authorisation of Special Types) General Order 2003 **8.25** (SI 2003/1998) and regs 81, 82, and Sch.12 to the Construction and Use Regulations, where a vehicle carries long or wide loads or a combination of vehicles exceeds certain lengths or there are certain projections, an attendant must be carried, at least two clear working days' notice to the police must be given and projections must be marked. "Working day" in the Schedule means a day which is not a Sunday, a bank holiday (as further defined), Christmas Day or Good Friday. A movable cattle-container on an articulated vehicle does not make it a vehicle constructed to carry indivisible loads under reg.7(3) (*Fellside Transport v Hyde*, 1962, unreported). See also *Patterson v Redpath Brothers Ltd* [1979] 2 All E.R. 108, to the same effect. In that case Griffiths J. said that "indivisible load" refers to the contents of the container and not the container itself.

In *Hawkins v Harold A. Russett Ltd* [1983] 1 All E.R. 215 it was held, following *Patterson v Redpath Bros Ltd*, that to determine overhang and overall length, the "body" of the vehicle should be taken into account. It was immaterial that it was detachable. The exemption conferred by the wording in reg.3(iii) of the 1978 Construction and Use Regulations did not apply. The wording of the exemptions is now substantially different. The court distinguished the expression "body" from "container". In the course of his judgment, O'Connor L.J. said at 218:

> "It is obvious that parts of a vehicle which are detachable do not cease to be parts of the vehicle, for example the wheels. The fact that the body of a vehicle is detachable does not justify referring to it as a 'container'. When overall length or overhang are in issue in a case such as the present, I think that the correct question to ask is: 'Is this vehicle fitted with a body?' The body of a vehicle does not cease to be a body because it can be detached with ease, laden or unladen and fitted to a sister chassis. This does not make the body 'a receptacle on or attached to the vehicle...': it is part of the vehicle. On the facts of the present case as found by the justices, coupled with the sketch and photograph of the vehicle, the correct question can only receive one answer: 'This vehicle was fitted with a body'. It was not carrying a container; its body was loaded with jam etc; the overhang was excessive."

Width

The meaning of "overall width" is set out in reg.3(2) with the limits contained **8.26** in reg.8. "Overall width" includes all the parts of a vehicle, any receptacle of a permanent character and any fitting attached to the vehicle unless excepted by the rest of the definition in reg.3(2). Exceptions make provision for a wide range of equipment from driving mirrors to tyre distortions made by the weight of the vehicle to sideboards to sheeting for covering a load. The permitted widths of different types of vehicle are set out in a table in reg.8(1). An exception is provided for a broken-down vehicle being towed because it is broken down: reg.8(2).

Height

The meaning of "overall height" is set out in reg.3(2) with the limits contained **8.27** in regs 9–10C. "Overall height" is the distance from the ground to the highest point of the vehicle with tyres suitably inflated, the vehicle at its unladen weight and the ground reasonably flat. The power collection equipment on the roof of a trolley bus is not included in this measurement.

Regulation 9 places a limit of 4.57m on the overall height of a bus. Regulations 10–10C provide for warnings to be given to drivers of vehicles above 3m "overall travelling height", defined by reg.10A as the height of the vehicle, its equipment and load. This height is extended to 4m for vehicles or trailers put into circulation in an EEA state and used in international traffic: reg.10(8). Where the overall travelling height exceeds 3m, a notice to that effect must be clearly displayed where it can be read by the driver. No other notices which would be mistaken for a description of height should be displayed where they could be read by the driver: reg.10(2). The content of this notice is set out in reg.10(3). The notice need not be displayed:

(1) where it is highly unlikely that the driver will have less than 1m clearance of any overhead structure along any roads likely to be used. Account must be taken of the possibility of unforeseen diversions and of the driver losing his way: reg.10(4);

(2) where the driver has a prescribed "safe" route set out in documents easily accessible to the driver on the vehicle and the driver is either on that route or off it only by reason of a diversion that could not have been foreseen at the beginning of the journey: reg.10(5);

(3) where the driver has within easy reach documents giving details of the height of structures under which he could or could not pass and which, in the light of the journey to be taken, would be enough to enable the driver safely to fulfil the purpose of the journey: reg.10(6) and (7).

8.28   Special provisions apply to vehicles first used on or after April 1, 1993 (subject to exceptions: reg.10B(2) and (3)) containing high-level equipment, that is, equipment capable of being raised by a power operated device which would affect the overall travelling height. Generally, these vehicles must have a visible warning device for the driver if the height of the equipment exceeded the overall travelling height by a predetermined limit while the vehicle was being driven.

Overhang

8.29   The meaning of "overhang" is set out in reg.3(2) with the limits contained in reg.11. The measurement starts with the rearmost point of the vehicle (with some exclusions) and goes forward to a point defined by reference to the number or nature of the axles of the vehicle.

Even where a vehicle complies with the regulations as to overhang there might be a prosecution for a dangerous load under reg.100 (see § 8.43). Where an exhaust system protruded laterally from a car window, conviction under reg.100 was justified as the justices had found that there was a danger. This was despite the fact that a different offence would also have been committed because of the excessive projection. Under reg.100 the court has to find that there was a potential danger (or presumably, where appropriate, a nuisance) regardless of the extent of the projection (*O'Connell v Murphy* [1981] R.T.R. 163).

Rear markings

8.30   Motor vehicles with a maximum gross weight exceeding 7,500kg and trailers with a maximum gross weight exceeding 3,500kg are required to display rear markings by virtue of the Motor Vehicles (Rear Markings) Regulations 1982 (SI 1982/430). See also the International Carriage of Dangerous Goods (Rear Markings of Motor Vehicles) Regulations 1975 (SI 1975/2111). Regulation 3 of the 1982 Regulations exempts certain vehicles. Regulation 4 prescribes which rear markings are fitted to which type of vehicle, while reg.6 and Pts I and II of the Schedule prescribe their size and colour. Pt III of the Schedule details their position. Regulation 7 modifies Pt III and enables rear markings to be fitted to the load of a vehicle instead when the load projects beyond the rear of the vehicle so as to obscure any rear markings which the vehicle might have. It is an offence not to maintain in a clean and efficient condition rear markings fitted under reg.4 (or reg.5) while the vehicle is in use on a road.

The International Carriage of Dangerous Goods (Rear Markings of Motor Vehicles) Regulations 1975 apply when the vehicle is carrying dangerous goods on a journey "some part of which has taken place, or will take place, outside the United Kingdom".

Speedometers

Regulation 35 requires a speedometer, as defined, to be fitted to every motor **8.31** vehicle first used on or after October 1, 1937 except agricultural motor vehicles not driven at more than 20mph, invalid carriages, works trucks, motor cycles with engines not exceeding 100cc, and certain other vehicles of low speed except that invalid carriages, works trucks and motor cycles with engines not exceeding 100cc first used on or after April 1, 1984 must be fitted with a speedometer. The margin of accuracy provision which appeared in previous construction and use regulations in which the speedometer was required to be plus or minus 10 per cent when the speed was in excess of 10mph has not been carried forward into the present regulations. Regulation 35 merely refers to every motor vehicle being "fitted with a speedometer … capable of indicating speed in both miles per hour and kilometers per hour". If a car has no speedometer but a revolution counter, it is doubtful if it would comply (*Sellwood v Butt* [1962] Crim. L.R. 841), especially as, under reg.36, the instrument must be "easily read".

The speedometer equipment of motor vehicles which complies with Directive 97/39/EC was brought within the Motor Vehicles (Type Approval) Regulations 1980 (SI 1980/1182) and if the vehicle complies with the directive or with ECE Regulation 39, it does not have to comply with reg.35: reg.35(3). A further exemption exists for a vehicle to which a passenger approval certificate has been issued under the Motor Vehicles (Approval) Regulations 1996 (as replaced and revised by the like-named 2001 Regulations (SI 2001/25)) and which complies with or is exempt from the approval requirements relating to speedometers: 1980 Regulations Sch.2A para.5.

Regulation 36 requires speedometers to be maintained which are fitted in ac- **8.32** cordance with reg.35 (construction requirements), which are exempted from reg.35, or which have the marking specified in reg.35(2)(h) (certain approval marks). The designated approval marks system, where applicable, replaces the normal construction requirement in reg.35. The exemption from the construction requirement also applies to both compulsory and voluntary tachograph vehicles: reg.36(1)(b).

There are two types of designated approval marks for speedometers: those for "ordinary" speedometers and those for "tachograph" (recording equipment) speedometers. Failure to maintain under reg.36 is an offence in respect of an "ordinary" speedometer. It is also an offence under reg.36 to fail to maintain a voluntary tachograph speedometer. Failure to maintain a compulsory tachograph speedometer is not an offence under reg.36 but an offence contrary to the amended s.97(1)(a) of the Transport Act 1968 where applicable. Reference should therefore be made to § 14.114 and §§ 14.119 et seq as there are certain defences.

8.33   The exemption from the construction requirement only applies to tachograph equipment if the equipment complies with reg.35(2)(h). Nevertheless it is submitted that a temporary defect in maintenance of a tachograph speedometer would not bring it, for the time being, within the construction requirements of reg.35(1) and the maintenance requirements consequent thereon (i.e. in the case of compulsory equipment the maintenance requirements not otherwise applicable and in the case of voluntary equipment different maintenance requirements). Any other conclusion could lead to a number of strange and unforeseen consequences (e.g. while a vehicle was under repair) and the wording of reg.35 is not appropriate.

Regulation 36 requires the speedometer to be at all material times maintained in good working order and free from obstruction, but it is a defence that

(a) the defect occurred in the course of a journey during which the contravention was detected or

(b) at the time of detection steps had already been taken to have the defect remedied with all reasonable expedition.

See the similar provisions in the Lighting Regulations at § 8.127. The burden of proof on the defence is on the balance of probabilities (*R. v Carr-Briant* [1943] 2 All E.R. 156). The wording of (b) is such that some step must have actually been taken. The regulation does not specify by whom the steps have to be taken (presumably it could be an employer or employee), nor their extent. It has been held by a magistrates' court that the defence in (a) includes a round journey but not the return journey from a fixed destination when the defect occurred in the course of the outward journey.

8.34   Certain vehicles must be fitted with a speed limiter: regs 36A and 36B. If the vehicle is a coach (defined in reg.3(2)), depending on when it was first used, the speed will be limited to 112.65km/h (70mph) or 100km/h (60mph): reg.36A(1) and (2). If the vehicle is a goods vehicle, the speed will be limited to 90km/h (56mph) or 85km/h (53mph) depending on the date of first use and on weight: reg.36B(1) and (2). Defences are provided where the vehicle is being taken to a place where the limiter is to be installed, calibrated or repaired or where the vehicle is completing a journey during which the limiter has accidentally stopped working (coaches and goods vehicles) or a goods vehicle is being used for certain military, fire brigade or, in England and Wales, fire and rescue authority, or ambulance purposes or in moving between land in the occupation of the keeper of the vehicle providing it is not used on public roads for more than six miles in a week: regs 36A(13) and 36B(14).

Brakes

8.35   Regulations 15–18 of and Sch.3 to the Construction and Use Regulations apply. Regulation 15 provides that vehicles first used on or after various specified dates and trailers manufactured on or after various specified dates, must comply with specified EC directives. Exemptions are provided in reg.15(2)–(3B). Alternatively, vehicles may comply with certain specified ECE Regulations (reg.15(4)–(5A)). The Road Vehicles (Construction and Use) (Amendment) (No.4) Regulations 2001 (SI 2001/3208) introduced two further exemptions from the requirements concerning anti-lock braking systems contained in reg.15(1E) and (5B). Those vehicles which have a maximum design weight of 7,500kg and which are purpose built, designed and used for street cleansing do not have to have such a system fitted. Vehicles used by a police authority and authorised by a chief constable for use in undertaking accident reconstructions are exempt from the prohibition on the use of isolation switches which allow the system to be disengaged. Regulation 5 of the 2001 Regulations amends reg.15 of the Construction and Use Regulations and extends the category of vehicles to be fitted with such a system at the point of manufacture. The new categories are vehicles with more than eight passenger seats in addition to the driver and all vehicles and trailers over 3,500kg first used on or after April 1, 2002.

Regulation 16 provides for vehicles to which reg.15 does not apply. However, a vehicle to which reg.16 applies may instead choose to comply with reg.15 (see provisos to reg.15(1)–(1D) and reg.16(2)). The other exemptions for reg.16 are contained in reg.16(3) and (5)–(7). Vehicles to which reg.16 applies must comply with the applicable requirements of Sch.3 set out in the table following reg.16(4). Regulation 18 relates to maintenance of brakes and is widely drawn so as to apply to all maintenance whether the construction is governed by the Construction and Use Regulations, the type approval system or the approval mark system. It is advisable that prosecutors choose the right provision and defendants should ensure that they have done so. The standard of efficiency to which the service braking system (defined in reg.3(2)) is to be maintained is set out in a table at reg.18(3) providing percentage efficiencies as against the braking efficiency (defined in reg.3(2)) of the vehicle. Extended definitions apply to goods vehicles and to buses: reg.18(4) and (4A).

Every part of every braking system fitted to the vehicle and the means of operation, must be maintained in good and efficient working order and properly adjusted. In *Kennett v British Airports Authority* [1975] Crim. L.R. 106 justices who had dismissed a charge because the overall braking system of a car was efficient, were directed to convict the defendant because the disc braking on one wheel was badly worn. Justices on a charge of this nature should examine every part of the braking system as it applied to each wheel (ibid.); but a conviction for bad maintenance under reg.18 cannot be sustained if a condition of bad maintenance of the brakes was "probably" present prior to an accident. The degree of proof required to show that the vehicle was not so maintained as required by the regulation is proof beyond reasonable doubt (*Bailey v Rolfe* [1976] Crim. L.R. 77). The regulation contains a number of other requirements. It seems that the fact that the brakes failed to work on one occasion does not prove that the braking system is improperly constructed and in such a case a prosecution should be brought under reg.18 for bad maintenance (*Cole v Young* [1938] 4 All E.R. 39). Similarly, where the brakes do not comply with Pt II but they are properly maintained, it is wrong to charge under reg.18 (*Unwin v Gayton* (1949) 93 S.J. 72). A missing handbrake ratchet can be a defect of construction, as well as of maintenance (*Smith v Nugent* 1955 S.L.T.(Sh) 60).

8.36

The method of calculating the number of wheels on which a braking system is deemed to operate under reg.18 was considered in *Langton v Johnson* [1956] 3 All E.R. 474; see the relevant regulations now as to the inclusion of front wheels in calculating the wheels on which a braking system operates. The prosecution should prove that a trailer exceeds the specified unladen weight where its brakes are defective (*Muir v Lawrence* 1951 S.L.T.(Sh.) 88). A brake drum for the purposes of the regulations is part of the wheel and not of the braking system (reg.3(6)).

8.37   The obligation to maintain the brakes in good and efficient working order is an absolute one (*Green v Burnett* [1954] 3 All E.R. 273); it is not a defence that the defendant ensured that the brakes were regularly maintained or that he had done all he could to see his brakes were in order (*Hawkins v Holmes* [1974] R.T.R. 436), otherwise the exemption from endorsement conferred in what is now s.48 of the 1988 Offenders Act would not be necessary (ibid.). All that a driver can assume after a car has been serviced by a garage is that it has been serviced. He cannot assume it is in good mechanical order; per Park J. in *Haynes v Swain* [1975] R.T.R. 40 at 44. Cases on motorscooter brakes are at [1957] Crim. L.R. 709 and [1965] Jo.Crim.L. 155. It is suggested at the latter place that in the case of vehicles to which Sch.4 to the former regulations applied (see now regs 15–18 and Sch.3 to the 1986 Regulations), the prosecutor had to show both that the brakes were not in good and efficient working order and properly adjusted and also that they did not have the efficiency required by the relevant regulations. The case in question was decided by the former Chief Metropolitan Stipendiary Magistrate, Sir Kenneth Barrowclough, at Bow Street Magistrates' Court. But it may be that breach of either requirement suffices (cf. *Butterworth v Shorthouse* (1956) 120 J.P.Jo. 97). Tests on stationary vehicles are also discussed.

The fact that brakes are inefficient does not have to be proved as a result of a test by an authorised examiner. In *Stoneley v Richardson* [1973] R.T.R. 229 a constable, with the permission of the defendant, was able to push the defendant's car along the road with the handbrake fully applied; the justices were directed to convict even though the constable was not an authorised examiner. It is submitted that whether or not brakes are maintained in good and efficient working order is a simple question of fact, albeit in some cases technical evidence may be necessary. Normally, evidence improperly obtained is nevertheless admissible (see § 3.102, in particular *R. v Sang*). In *Stoneley* there was no suggestion that the evidence was improperly obtained, as the test was made with the defendant's consent.

8.38   The decision of the Divisional Court in *DPP v Young* [1991] R.T.R. 56 in interpreting reg.18(1) confirms that the requirement that brakes on a motor vehicle should be maintained in efficient working order applies to any trailer fitted with brakes even if that trailer was not required to have brakes. The court decided that the decision of *Muir v Foulner*, referred to in the text as *Muir v Lawrence* 1951 S.L.T. (Sh.) 88, was wrongly decided.

The respondent succeeded in a submission of no case to answer before justices because the prosecution had adduced no evidence that the trailer exceeded 750kg in gross axle weight and was therefore of such a weight that it was required to be fitted with brakes. In allowing the prosecutor's appeal, Leggatt L.J. stated that in the regulation the expression "motor vehicle" included a trailer and thus every part of every braking system fitted to the trailer had to be maintained in good working order. If brakes were fitted, anyone not in the habit of using the trailer would expect the brakes to work. It was "absurd" that defective brakes could not be prosecuted unless it was established that the trailer in question weighed in excess of 750kg.

What is now s.43(2) of the 1988 Act provides that no provision in the regula-   **8.39**
tions imposing or varying requirements in respect of the brakes with which a motor vehicle must be equipped shall be taken to relate to the construction of vehicles. The reason is explained in *Hansard*, July 27, 1960, cols 1734–1738.

Regulation 107 is not a regulation as to the condition of brakes but as to a failure to apply them: for this reason an offence under reg.107 is not endorsable (*Kenyon v Thorley* [1973] R.T.R. 60). It is submitted that, for the same reason, offences under regs 19 and 89 as to the application of trailer brakes are not endorsable. See further § 8.93.

Designated approval marks

Further important exemptions from the Road Vehicles (Construction and Use)   **8.40**
Regulations 1986 are conferred by regs 3 and 6. The explanatory note to the regulations clarifies that recognition of compliance with European vehicle standards as an alternative to national standards has been made more comprehensive by the insertion of appropriate references in Pt II which are interpreted in accordance with regs 3 and 6. Whereas, under the 1978 Construction and Use Regulations, the fact that a vehicle had been marked or certified when new to show that it complied with a European standard for a particular system or component meant that it was totally exempted from the substantive regulation dealing with that system or component, now, in the case of regulations dealing with systems or components which are liable to deteriorate or be replaced while the vehicle is in use, only continued compliance with the European standard is accepted as an alternative to compliance with the national standard. Particular reference should be made therefore to the Motor Vehicles (Designation of Approval Marks) Regulations 1979 (SI 1979/1088, as amended), and regs 3, 6, and Sch.2 to the 1986 Regulations. These exemptions mark another step in the departure from the construction regulations.

Under s.80(2) of the 1988 Act any person who applies an approval mark without being authorised by the competent authority as defined in that section or applies a mark so nearly resembling an approval mark as to be calculated to deceive is guilty of an offence under the Trade Descriptions Act 1968.

Pedal cycles

The Pedal Cycles (Construction and Use) Regulations 1983 (SI 1983/1176)   **8.41**
were made under s.81 of the 1988 Act. They make separate provisions as to pedal cycles (including tricycles and other forms of pedal cycles) which are and are not respectively electrically assisted. For the definition of electrically assisted pedal cycles, see Chapter 1. The police are given powers of testing.

For electrically assisted pedal cycles the regulations require them to be fitted with a plate showing certain particulars, brakes as specified, a battery which does not leak and a device to control the operation of its motor. These brakes, battery and motor device and the pedals and motor must be in efficient working order. For ordinary pedal cycles the regulations refer only to brakes. An offence is committed if a person rides or causes or permits to be ridden on a road a pedal cycle in contravention of the regulations under s.91 of the 1988 Offenders Act. For "causes" or "permits" see § 1.161 et seq. For "rides" see § 1.116. Magistrates have held parents liable under the similarly worded earlier regulations in respect of their children's cycles (99 S.J. 602). The offence with regard to the maintenance of the motor appears harsh in that in the event of a breakdown it is not permitted to use the ordinary pedals to ride home without committing an offence.

8.42   Under s.81(6) it is an offence to sell, supply or offer to sell or supply a cycle in contravention of the regulations unless it is sold, etc., for export or in the belief that it would not be used on a road in Great Britain until it had been put in a condition complying with the regulations. The offence under s.81(6) is imposed by the 1983 Regulations in respect of brakes on electrically assisted pedal cycles and on and after August 1, 1984 on other pedal cycles unless it is a pedal cycle without a braking system specifically designed for off-road racing on enclosed tracks.

The regulations add the words "for delivery" after supply. These words are not to be found in s.81(6) and it is not clear whether they add anything. The Pedal Bicycles (Safety) Regulations 2003 (SI 2003/1101) were made under s.11 of the Consumer Protection Act 1987 regarding the supply of bicycles.

Vehicle or load in dangerous condition

8.43   Section 40A of the 1988 Act provides express statutory authority for dealing with the use, etc., of vehicles in a dangerous condition. Under the section, a person is guilty of an offence if he uses, causes or permits another to use a motor vehicle or trailer on a road when either—

    (a) the condition of the motor vehicle or trailer, or of its accessories or equipment; or

    (b) the purpose for which it is used; or

    (c) the number of passengers carried by it, or the manner in which they are carried; or

    (d) the weight, position or distribution of its load, or the manner in which it is secured,

is such that the use of the motor vehicle or trailer involves a danger of injury to any person.

8.44   An illustration of an unsuccessful prosecution for an offence of using a vehicle when the number of passengers in it or the manner in which they were carried was such as to involve a danger of injury, contrary to s.40A(c) of the 1988 Act, was the Scottish decision of *Akelis v Normand* 1997 S.L.T. 136. A passenger was carried in the rear of a van, in addition to two passengers in the front. The passenger in the rear was lying on the floor with his head at one side of the van and his feet at the other. There was no seat or restraint of any kind in the rear of the van. The driver was summoned for the s.40A(c) offence and was convicted. He appealed to the High Court. It was held that whether or not there was a breach of the section depended on the facts of the case. But where passengers were carried in the rear of a van, the possibility of injury to a person depended (in part at least) on the speed at which the van was driven. Although speed was not the only consideration it was material to the issue of whether the manner in which passengers were carried was such as to involve a danger of injury. Although there had been no specific finding as to the speed of the van, the court noted that the police had stated that it had not been travelling at excessive speed. On the particular facts, the charge had not been made out and the appeal was allowed. Further consideration was given to the manner of carriage of a passenger in *Gray v DPP* [1999] R.T.R. 339. Mr Gray carried his seven-year-old son on a short journey in central London in the open back of a Jeep. The boy sat on a flat piece of metal covering the wheel arch holding on to a roll bar and stood up from time to time. He was prosecuted under s.40A(c) of the 1988 Act and convicted. The Divisional Court upheld the conviction. The test is not what the driver (or user) of the vehicle may have believed, however genuine the belief may have been but rather an objective one. The court has to decide on the evidence whether it is satisfied that there was a danger of injury to any person having regard to the way in which passengers were being carried. Much may depend on the circumstances in which the vehicle was being driven but the section is directed at the danger of injuries which might occur as a result of the ordinary problems of driving such as sudden braking, or having to swerve, pull out, turn or stop. Here, it was significant that Mr Gray's son did not remain seated, as was the relative size of his grip and the diameter of the roll bar.

8.45 The original offence in the Construction and Use Regulations arises under reg.100. The different wording of paras (1), (2) and (3) of reg.100 should be carefully noted. The relevant words in these paragraphs read:

100(1): "such that no danger is caused or is likely to be caused";

100(2): "neither danger nor nuisance is likely to be caused"; and

100(3): "cause or be likely to cause danger or nuisance".

Charges contrary to reg.100(1) and (2) in effect contain a double negative and it may be misleading to try and simplify this by turning it round into a positive. Remote possibility of danger is not enough. Magistrates acquitted a defendant of using a Mini without a front grille: the possibility of danger by a person touching the revolving fan on a transverse engine was considered to be unlikely. Defendants have, however, been convicted by magistrates in such circumstances when the fan was at the front. While these decisions are not binding, they are persuasive and illustrate the application of reg.100. Paragraph (2) unlike the other paragraphs refers only to the situation where danger (or nuisance) is "likely" to be caused. This distinction may be material as indicated below. In *Bennington v Peter, R. v Swaffham JJ. Ex p. Peter* [1984] R.T.R. 383 "likely" in different regulations was construed as something more than a bare possibility but less than a probability. In *DPP v Potts* [2000] R.T.R. 1 an agricultural tractor was being driven in a rural locality on a C class road with its front link arms lowered. An oncoming car crossed the path of the tractor and collided with it. The driver of the car was killed. The justices' dismissal of the charge was upheld on appeal. The Divisional Court emphasised that the facts had been properly considered and that the decision was within the scope of an acceptable decision but ought not to be taken as implying that such a use would always be acceptable.

8.46 Paragraphs (2) and (3) (but not para.(1)) refer to "nuisance". In *St Albans Sand and Gravel Co Ltd v Minnis* [1981] R.T.R. 231 it was held that an information alleging "danger or nuisance" is not bad for duplicity. This decision gives rise to certain sentencing problems (see § 8.97 below). This decision should be compared with that in a Scottish case where it was held that reg.100(1) creates three separate offences in respect of condition, of passengers and of load, and all three should not be charged in one information (*Dickson v Brown* 1959 S.L.T.

207). The court in the *St Albans* case was apparently not referred to this case although they were referred to other cases on duplicity. The House of Lords in *R. v Courtie* (1984) 78 Cr. App. R. 292 in a decision on a different statute implied that offences should be treated as separate where there was a different penalty. The summons should specify the defects in the parts and accessories (*Simmons v Fowler* (1950) 48 L.G.R. 623), but need not specify whether the defects relate to the parts or to the accessories (see *Brindley v Willett* [1981] R.T.R. 19 at § 8.50 below).

8.47   Regulation 100 consists of three separate paragraphs (see *Dickson v Brown* above), and the prosecution should be careful to bring their case under the correct paragraph. Thus in *Leathley v Robson's Border Transport Ltd* [1976] R.T.R. 503 an articulated lorry shed its load of bundles of paper while negotiating a bend. The defendants were charged under reg.100(1). The justices dismissed the case on the ground that there was no evidence to show that the weight distribution, etc., of the load was not such that no danger was caused. In upholding the dismissal, the Divisional Court observed that on the face of it there would have been no defence if the charge had been brought under reg.100(2). See also the important case of *McDermott Movements Ltd v Horsfield* [1983] R.T.R. 42 below. In *Turberville v Wyer, Bryn Motor Co Ltd v Wyer* [1977] R.T.R. 29, justices were held to be entitled to apply what is now s.123 of the Magistrates' Courts Act 1980 in convicting the defendants of a breach of reg.100(2) even though the information might have been defective in that the load was described as being carried on a motor lorry instead of on the trailer of an articulated motor vehicle. It was also held that the justices were entitled to convict, in the absence of any explanation, once the driver had admitted that the load had fallen from the vehicle while he was driving it. In *Cornish v Ferry Masters Ltd* [1975] R.T.R. 292 a drum fell off a lorry onto the road because the pallet upon which it was loaded collapsed due to some extraordinary, unexplained, inherent defect. The lorry's owners and driver were both charged with "using" and the justices dismissed the charges against both defendants as both were neither at fault nor negligent. The High Court directed both to be convicted: the offence of "using" is an absolute offence, the defendants' knowledge or lack of knowledge of the defect is irrelevant. The likelihood or otherwise of danger being caused was to be adjudged according to the factual circumstances as they were, regardless of the knowledge of the person using the vehicle (see also *Keyse v Sainsbury* [1971] Crim. L.R. 291). On the other hand where an employer is charged with "permitting" a vehicle with an insecure load contrary to reg.100(2) the prosecution must prove that a director or "brain" of the company knew of the contravention (*P. Lowry & Sons Ltd v Wark* [1975] R.T.R. 45, applying *Ross Hillman Ltd v Bond* at § 1.162 and § 1.170).

8.48   Where crates fall off a lorry when going round a sharp bend, an offence arises and the driver may be convicted though the crates were loaded by another person (*Gifford v Whittaker* [1942] 1 All E.R. 604). Where trees protruded 32ft beyond the back of a trailer, an offence against reg.100 arose. There was a conviction under this regulation where the blades of a bulldozer being carried on a vehicle projected 3ft beyond the offside of the vehicle; the blades being detachable, the bulldozer was not an "indivisible" load (*Newstead v Hearn* (1950) 114 J.P. Jo. 690). It was stated in *Andrews v Kershaw* [1951] 2 All E.R. 764 at 768, that, if a large van was driven with the tailboard down, this might be an offence under reg.100. But evidence merely that many milk cans rattled on a lorry and made a great noise does not suffice to show that their loading or adjustment was faulty (*Re Scottish Farmers' Dairy Co* (1934) 98 J.P.Jo. 848). An interesting decision on reg.100(1) and the importance of considering defects to a trailer separate from the motor vehicle as a whole is *NFC Forwarding Ltd v DPP* [1989] R.T.R. 239.

Regulation 100(1) is absolute in terms and the vehicle must at all times on the road be in such condition that no danger is caused or is likely to be caused to road users; if it is not in such condition, an offence arises even though the dangerous condition is due to a latent defect (*F. Austin (Leyton) Ltd v East* [1961] Crim.L.R. 119). The fact that a defect was a latent defect and there was no negligence is a mitigating circumstance, however (*F. Austin (Leyton) Ltd v East* above). The dangerous condition in reg.100(1) does not necessarily have to arise through lack of maintenance; where a motor cyclist added extension pieces to his exhaust to a height of 2ft 8in causing danger in that passers-by could be burnt if they touched the exhaust or found the exhaust fumes directed at their faces, it was held that the motor cyclist should be convicted of an offence under reg.100(1) (*Reeve v Webb* [1973] R.T.R. 130).

The decision in *Wood v Milne, The Times,* March 27, 1987 puts beyond doubt **8.49** that reg.100 relates to a vehicle in its manufactured condition and not merely to its maintenance. A prosecution under reg.97(1) of the 1978 Regulations led to the conviction of a defendant who drove a mechanical digger on a road with its bucket lowered so that unguarded two inch spikes protruded from it. His appeal against conviction was dismissed, the Divisional Court holding that the regulation applied to a vehicle which in its manufactured condition was inherently likely to cause danger, as well as to vehicles which had become dangerous through defective maintenance.

The regulation applies to both the *number* of passengers and the *manner* in which they are carried. There is a difference in the sentencing between the two (see § 8.91 below). So far as the *number* of passengers is concerned, reg.100(1) contains special provisions for public service vehicles.

Where an examiner found excessive play in the steering joint and pivot of the **8.50** steering arm due to wear, causing one third free play in the steering wheel, it was held that the charge was not improperly brought under reg.100 (dangerous condition) rather than under reg.29 (defective steering) (*Bason v Eayrs* [1958] Crim. L.R. 397). Similarly, where an exhaust system protruded laterally from a car window a conviction under reg.100(1) was justified as the justices found there was a danger, despite the fact that a different offence would have been committed by reason of the excessive projection (*O'Connell v Murphy* [1981] R.T.R. 163).

Regulation 100(1) refers to a motor vehicle, every trailer drawn thereby and all *parts* and *accessories* of such vehicles and trailers. In *Brindley v Willett* [1981] R.T.R. 19, decided on the earlier regulations with like wording, it was held that a container was capable in law of being a part of a vehicle. (See also the other cases noted under "Removable containers" in Chapter 1, § 1.73.) It was immaterial that the container could not be bolted on as it should have been because it was warped. In the course of the judgment, Donaldson L.J. observed that the prosecuting authority tied themselves to the proposition that the container was part of the vehicle. He said that he could see no reason why prosecuting authorities should make an advance election. There was no injustice to the accused provided the object in question was clearly specified.

8.51   In *Jenkins v Dean* (1933) 103 L.J.K.B. 250, an insurance case, a tow chain was held not to be part of the vehicle and a condition of the policy in respect of driving "in an unsafe condition" was not breached by using a defective chain to tow another vehicle, and in *Keyse v Sainsbury* [1971] Crim. L.R. 291, a heavy weight of concrete and steel attached by two hooks to a steel bar at the back of a tractor were held not to be part of the tractor as such and the charge, which was so framed that it related solely to the condition of the tractor, was held to be rightly dismissed.

Even if parts and accessories are in good repair, they must also be in proper working order; where, e.g. a tow bar was of good construction and in good repair but became uncoupled because someone failed to ensure it was properly engaged, the user of the vehicle was guilty under reg.100 (*O'Neill v Brown* [1961] 1 All E.R. 571).

8.52   Regulation 100(1) makes it an offence if the "weight, distribution, packing and adjustment of the load" are dangerous; reg.100(2) provides that "the load carried ... shall at all times be so secured and be in such a position" that no danger is caused. It may be thought that "securing" and "carrying" a load are often akin to "packing" and "adjustment" and that it will be difficult to judge whether the offence is under reg.100(1) or reg.100(2). It is submitted that, where a load is not adequately tied by ropes or kept from falling overboard by other means, it is not "secured" and that if it is placed on the edge of the vehicle or on top of it and is likely to bounce off, it is not "carried in a [safe] position". If it is packed in such a way that parts of it burst out of the packing and fall on the road or if it is distributed in such a way that heavier parts push other parts off the vehicle or if it is adjusted in such a way as to import a dangerous bias to one side, then reg.100(1) applies.

The above paragraph and submission were quoted with approval (from the tenth edition of this book) in *McDermott Movements Ltd v Horsfield* [1983] R.T.R. 42. In that case a load of tubular steel was too high and slipped. The prosecution was brought under reg.100(1) as to the packing and adjustment. The Divisional Court held that the prosecution should have been brought under reg.100(2). The load was properly adjusted and packed and it would not have been too high if it had been properly secured. It was not properly secured as required by reg.100(2). The court also emphasised that under reg.100(2) it is sufficient if the load or part of it moves—it need not be shed.

8.53   The *Oxford Dictionary* defines "adjustment" as including "settling, harmonising or properly disposing" and "putting in proper order". "Packing" is defined as including "the putting of things together compactly as for transport ... the fitting (of a receptacle) with things so put in". Reference, in cases of doubt, should also be made to *Leathley v Robson's Border Transport Ltd* at § 8.47 above. It would seem that if the load has been shed or partly shed or has moved, the prosecutors would usually be wise to prosecute under reg.100(2). *McDermott's* case demonstrates the importance of choosing the right paragraph.

An offence under reg.100(2) (insecure load, etc.) and reg.100(3) (unsuitable use) is committed even if the insecure load or unsuitable use is likely to cause only nuisance and not danger. This difference from reg.100(1) should be carefully noted; the word "nuisance" is not to be found in paragraph (1).

8.54   It should be noted that reg.100(2) requires a *likelihood* of danger or nuisance only (contrast reg.100(1)). Therefore one can have the rare situation that if danger is in fact caused but the load was so secured or in such a position that danger was *unlikely* to be caused, a prosecution under reg.100(2) might fail. In *Friend v Western British Road Services Ltd* [1976] R.T.R. 103 a charge was dismissed because there was no requirement that the load should be secured and it was in such a position that no danger was likely to be caused. The load consisted of three coils of sheet steel weighing 17 tons, and due to an unexpected and unexplained phenomenon known as "slow roll" the articulated lorry negotiating a roundabout shed the steel, causing danger. The dismissal of the charge under the former wording of reg.100(2) was upheld because the load was in such a position as to be unlikely to cause danger. It will be noted that the load is now required both to be secured "if necessary by physical restraint other than its own weight" *and* to be in such a position that no danger is likely to be caused.

Friend v Western British Road Services Ltd above was explained in *Dent v Coleman* [1978] R.T.R. 1 as a defect not in the securing of the load or the fastening of the load but in the vehicle itself. In *Dent v Coleman* justices were directed to convict the defendant, who had been charged with using, contrary to reg.100, with an insecure load. The load consisted of three coils, one of which fell from the vehicle after its straps had come loose at the joints. Although the case of *Friend v Western British Road Services Ltd* has not been overruled or distinguished, we understand that there is a body of expert opinion that is sceptical of the "slow roll" phenomenon. It may be that an opportunity will present itself for the theory to be tested further in some future appeal. *Cornish v Ferry Masters Ltd*, § 8.47 above, was again applied, the court stating that the offence under reg.100 was an absolute offence as explained in that case.

A conviction for an offence under reg.100(2) was affirmed by the Divisional **8.55** Court despite a novel argument by the appellants. In *Walker-Trowbridge v DPP* [1992] R.T.R. 182 two vats were loaded on to a vehicle and adequately secured by straps. The vehicle was driven under a bridge, one of the vats was struck and knocked off the vehicle. The owners and driver were convicted of the offence under reg.100(2) and appealed. It was argued on their behalf that the load had not fallen because it had been inadequately secured, rather that it had been knocked off the vehicle by the bridge. It was held that the term "falling" embraced not only things that fell off a vehicle but things that were knocked off. In considering the security of the loading it was necessary to have regard to the nature of the journey, the way in which the load was secured, the way in which it was positioned, and the journey to be taken. What might be "secure" for a journey in fine weather on good roads might not be so in poor weather on less good roads. The question was whether, in the conditions, danger was likely to be caused. In the instant case, when one looked at the route the danger had been inevitable as the load was too high to pass under the bridge and the contravention of reg.100(2) had been made out.

Finally it should be noted that reg.100(2) includes the likelihood of danger or nuisance to property as well as persons.

Regulation 100(3) forbids a motor vehicle to be used for any purpose for which **8.56** it is unsuitable so as to cause or be likely to cause danger. In *Hollis Brothers Ltd v Bailey*; *Buttwell v Bailey* [1968] 1 W.L.R. 663 a lorry's load was badly stacked, causing it to topple over; the conviction was set aside; the fact that the load was unsuitably stacked did not necessarily cause the vehicle to be unsuitable to carry that load. This case may be contrasted with *British Road Services v Owen* [1971]

2 All E.R. 999, in which a lorry was loaded with two forklifts which were too high to go under a footbridge, causing a collision. The load was properly secured and stable, and the lorry mechanically sound. The lorry was held to be unsuitable for the purpose, as when assessing the purpose for which a vehicle is to be used regard must be had to the nature and features of the route to be taken by that vehicle. A further decision on the interpretation of reg.100(3), which is in line with the decisions of *Hollis Brothers v Bailey* and *British Road Services v Owen* is *Young and C.F. Abraham (Transport) Ltd v DPP* (1991) 155 J.P. 738. The Divisional Court allowed an appeal against the decision of justices to convict both appellants. It was held that a trailer which was designed for the purpose of carrying goods and could carry the goods without danger when properly loaded was suitable for its purpose and did not become "unsuitable" within the meaning of reg.100(3) merely because it had been badly loaded.

A case of note dealing with loads was *R. v Crossman* [1986] R.T.R. 49. The driver of a goods vehicle was held guilty of causing death by reckless (now dangerous) driving when, knowing there was a serious risk that the vehicle's heavy load might fall off and kill or injure another road user, he nevertheless ran that risk. Presumably an employer aware of the risk might be guilty of aiding and abetting (cf. *R. v Robert Millar (Contractors)* [1970] 2 Q.B. 54).

Quitting vehicles, etc.

8.57   By reg.107 it is an offence for a person to leave or cause or permit to be left a motor vehicle on a road unattended by a person duly licensed to drive it unless the engine has been stopped and the brake set or it is a fire-engine at work or a gas-driven vehicle or being used for police or ambulance purposes. A motorist who leaves a vehicle without setting the brake may also be convicted under s.22 of the 1988 Act (see § 6.260) if the vehicle is on a slope so that it runs away and causes a danger of injury (*Maguire v Crouch* (1941) 104 J.P. 445). A motorist was charged with not stopping his engine and not setting the brake but the magistrates found that he had stopped the engine. He argued that the information was bad for duplicity and that reg.107 required both failures to be proved. The High Court upheld his conviction (*Butterworth v Shorthouse* (1956) 120 J.P. Jo. 97). It is submitted at 119 J.P. Jo. 262 that a person offends against this regulation if the vehicle has run on to the road from private land. In *Davidson v Adair* [1934] J.C.(J.) 37, a judge did say obiter that the offence of quitting a vehicle without setting the brake under what would now be reg.107 could be committed on a common or public seashore; another judge, however, disagreed. The prosecution must show that the defendant caused or permitted the offence, and this would not be the case if the handbrake were released or the engine were started by a third person acting independently. From *Maguire v Crouch* and from the wording of the regulations an offence is committed if a vehicle is left unattended *off the road* with the engine running or the handbrake not set and the vehicle subsequently runs away of its own motion *on to a road*.

For a car to be "attended", there must be a person able to keep it under observation, see any attempt to interfere with it and have a reasonable prospect of preventing interference (*Starfire Diamond Rings Ltd v Angel* (1962) 106 S.J. 854, followed in *Ingleton of Ilford Ltd v General Accident, etc., Co* [1967] 2 Lloyd's Rep. 179, where a van was deemed unattended when the driver was in a place where he could not see it and had no reasonable prospect of being able to reach it in time). Donaldson L.J. described the test as being whether there is a person "in it or in close attendance on it" (*Bulman v Godbold* [1981] R.T.R. 242). In *Attridge v Attwood* [1964] Crim. L.R. 45 the defendant had left a taxi in the street and taken the ignition key with him; the taxi was in his view from the building nearby, where he was. His conviction, for leaving the taxi without someone proper to take care of it under the Town Police Clauses Act 1847 s.62 was upheld. On other terms of a policy, a vehicle was deemed to be "not unattended" when the driver was in it, asleep (*Plaistow Transport Ltd v Graham* [1966] 1 Lloyd's Rep. 639).

Regulation 107 is not a construction and use regulation as to the condition of **8.58** brakes but as to their application and for this reason an offender against it cannot be disqualified nor have his licence endorsed (*Kenyon v Thorley* [1973] R.T.R. 60). Similarly, it would seem that an offender against reg.89 (detached trailer to have one wheel braked or otherwise secured) would also be exempt from disqualification or endorsement (see further § 8.95).

Regulation 98 requires the engine to be stopped when the vehicle is stationary, so far as may be necessary for the prevention of noise; there are exceptions for examination, working for another purpose and gas-propelled vehicles.

Tyres

Section 41A of the Road Traffic Act 1988 provides that an offence is commit- **8.59** ted if a person contravenes or fails to comply with a construction and use requirement as to brakes, steering gear or tyres.

Using a vehicle with defective tyres means "having the use of" (see *Eden v Mitchell* [1975] R.T.R. 425 at § 1.187). The "use" is the use the vehicle is being put to at the time. It is not necessary to keep the tyre inflated so as to be fit for some possible or even probable future use (*Conner v Graham* [1981] R.T.R. 291). Magistrates were held to be wrong when they took a tyre gauge with them when they retired and carried out a private test on a tyre. The magistrates were in breach of their duty to hear the whole case in open court (*R. v Tiverton JJ.* (1980) 144 J.P. 747). Where there is a question of whether a vehicle is exempt from the requirements of reg.27 by reason of it being an "agricultural motor vehicle" the onus of showing that the vehicle comes within the exemption is upon the defendant (see *Wakeman v Catlow* [1977] R.T.R. 174 at §§ 1.27, 8.03).

Regulation 27(1) specifies eight different types of defect in sub-paras (a)–(h). **8.60** In *Saines v Woodhouse* [1970] 2 All E.R. 388 it was held that there must be a separate information in respect of each tyre which is alleged to contravene any of the sub-paragraphs. The justices had dismissed an information in respect of the rear offside tyre under one sub-paragraph after they had convicted the defendant in respect of the rear nearside tyre under a different sub-paragraph. Their reason was that the former reg.107(5) (which itself reproduced the wording of former regulations) required one information in respect of all the tyres of the vehicle. That regulation is now replaced by reg.27(1)(h) of the 1986 Regulations, under which it is unlawful for a tyre not to be maintained in such a condition as to be fit for the use to which the vehicle or the trailer is being put or has a defect which might in any way cause damage to the road surface or to persons on or in the vehicle, or other road users. In *Goosey v Adams* [1972] Crim. L.R. 49 it was held that, although close-coupled wheels are required by reg.3(7) to be treated as one wheel, this has no application to tyres, and that each tyre on a close-coupled wheel should be looked at in isolation to see whether it complies with what is now reg.27(1)(g).

Regulation 27(1)(f) creates an offence where the base of any groove which showed in the original tread pattern of the tyre is not clearly visible. This means that a bald patch where the base of the original groove in the tread pattern is no longer clearly visible is illegal. It follows that a bald inner or outer edge caused by a tracking defect will be illegal even though it does not extend to one quarter of the breadth of the tread.

8.61   As any baldness in the tread pattern is caught by reg.27(1)(f), reg.27(1)(g) prohibits tyres which are not bald, but where the tread pattern is not of the required depth. Seemingly the fact that a tyre is partially bald would not preclude a prosecution being brought where the other requirements of this sub-paragraph are fulfilled. Regulation 27(1)(g) requires the grooves of the tread pattern of the tyre to have a depth of at least 1mm throughout a continuous band measuring at least three quarters of the breadth of the tread and round the entire outer circumference of the tyre. There is a special provision for tyres with a tread pattern covering only part of the tread. Where the original tread pattern of the tyre does not extend beyond three quarters of the breadth of the tread, the base of any *groove* which showed in the original tread pattern must have a depth of at least 1mm. The entire outer circumference of the tyre means that part of the tyre normally in contact with the road surface; it does not include the outer walls and shoulder of a tyre which is not normally in contact with the road (*Coote v Parkin* [1977] R.T.R. 61). See also the definition of breadth of tread below.

Sub-paragraphs (f) and (g) are disapplied to passenger motor cars other than motor cars constructed or adapted to carry more than eight seated passengers in addition to the driver, and to goods vehicles with a maximum gross weight which does not exceed 3,500kg and also to light trailers first used on or after January 3, 1933: reg.27(4). A "light trailer" is a trailer with a maximum gross weight not exceeding 3,500kg. The requirement, based on EC specifications, is that the grooves of the tread pattern of every tyre fitted to the vehicles in question must be of a tread pattern of a depth of at least 1.6mm throughout a continuous band situated in the central three quarters of the breadth of the tread and round the entire outer circumference of the tyre. This is rightly seen as a more stringent requirement than the one it replaces. Sub-paragraphs (f) and (g) of reg.27(1) will, of course, continue to apply to categories of vehicle not specifically mentioned.

8.62   "Tread pattern", "original tread pattern", and "breadth of tread", are all defined in the regulations: reg.27(6). Tread pattern includes both plain surfaces and grooves but it should be emphasised that tie bars and tread wear indicators (as defined) are excluded, and also features designed to wear out substantially before the rest of the pattern under normal conditions. Such tie bars and wear features are found particularly on goods vehicle and lorry tyres and have led to acquittals when it has been established that these were the only parts below the legal limits. "Breadth of tread" means the breadth of that part of the tyre which can contact the road under normal conditions of use measured at 90 degrees to the peripheral line of the tread. "Contact the road under normal conditions" would not seem to include that part which only comes into contact on skidding or turning. This view is supported by *Sandford v Butcher* [1978] R.T.R. 132 although that decision is outdated following revisions in the regulations.

In *Renouf v Franklin* [1971] R.T.R. 469 a tyre had a V-shaped tear producing a triangular flap of rubber which could be lifted by the finger, exposing the tyre cord. A conviction under what is now reg.27(1)(e) was set aside, because for a tyre to have the "ply or cord structure exposed" meant exposed to view. The word "structure" no longer appears in the regulation but this does not appear to affect the decision. The court indicated that in such a case if the dimensions of the cut were sufficient sub-para.(c) would have been the appropriate sub-paragraph; on the other hand, if the tyre had a worn patch exposing the cords, sub-para.(e) would be appropriate.

Regulation 27(1)(a) deals with mixing tyres generally but reg.26 prohibits the mixing of types of tyre on the same axle and restricting it on different axles. **8.63**

For a case where a lorry driver was held guilty of causing death by dangerous driving, and his employers guilty of aiding and abetting, when he knowingly drove a lorry with an unsafe tyre, see *R. v Robert Millar (Contractors)* [1970] 2 Q.B. 54.

Whether a tyre complies with the regulations is a question of fact; it does not matter that the constable who examined the tyre and gave evidence as to its condition is not an authorised examiner (*Phillips v Thomas* [1974] R.T.R. 28, following *Stoneley v Richardson*, § 8.37).

Informations were laid alleging that a tyre contravened what is now **8.64** reg.27(1)(c), (d) and (e) of the 1986 Regulations. The informations referred to the tyre as the "rear nearside tyre". At the trial the police officer gave evidence that the tyre in question was the "rear offside tyre". The justices allowed an amendment to the informations notwithstanding that a fresh information would have been prohibited by reason of what is now s.127 of the Magistrates' Courts Act 1980. An application for an order prohibiting the justices from further hearing and adjudicating on the amended informations was dismissed by the Divisional Court. There was only one tyre involved, the defendants knew which it was and no injustice had been caused by its misdescription (*R. v Sandwell JJ. Ex p. West Midland Passenger Transport Board* [1979] Crim. L.R. 56).

The Motor Vehicles Tyres (Safety) Regulations 1994 (SI 1994/3117), as amended, govern the consumer protection aspect of tyre sale and supply, in relation to the vehicles specified. Offences committed under the regulations are punishable on summary conviction by s.12(5) of the Consumer Protection Act 1987 with imprisonment for up to six months and/or a fine not exceeding level 5 on the standard scale.

The 1994 Regulations create the offence of supplying a tyre (other than a **8.65** retreaded or part-worn tyre) designed to be capable of being fitted to a wheel unless the tyre is marked with an approval mark in accordance with the relevant ECE regulations or Directive 92/23/EEC. Corresponding provisions relating to motor cycle tyres (reg.5) were implemented on January 1, 1998. Regulation 6 deals with retreaded tyres and reg.7 with part-worn tyres. Exemptions from these requirements (reg.10) came into force on June 1, 1995. Certain tyres are exempt from the general prohibition. A tyre is supplied in "exempt circumstances" (reg.8) if certain conditions are met, including the condition that the supplier reasonably believes that the tyre will not be used in this country. An offence is committed under reg.12 if any indication given by an approval mark, etc., is false. By reg.13 for the purposes of the regulations a reference to any standard adopted or recognised by a contributing party to the agreement on the European Economic Area may be substituted for any reference to a British Standards specification. The regulations represent an attempt to tighten substantially the controls on the supply of potentially unsafe tyres and seek to apply similar standards throughout the EU.

8.66   It should be noted that none of the 1994 Regulations applies to motor bicycles and some unsafe tyres are used on motor bicycles on roads (see "Knobbly tyres", below).

Regulation 25 of the 1986 Regulations deals with tyre loads and speed ratings, defining the strength of tyres by reference to both load and maximum speed of the vehicle.

Knobbly tyres

8.67   A number of cases are being brought regarding knobbly tyres. These are special tyres used on scrambling motor bicycles. They are also found on bicycles used by farmers around their farms. The knobbly design is to give them a better grip over rough country.

These tyres are usually clearly marked "not for Highway Use" or in a similar fashion. At speed the knobs will distort and the bicycle will become unstable. The tyres are not designed for use on roads because the adhesion of the rubber on the road is greatly reduced.

8.68   The charge usually brought regarding them is one contrary to reg.27(1)(a) of the 1986 Regulations, namely that the "tyre is unsuitable having regard to the use to which the motor vehicle or trailer is being put".

Some magistrates' courts have convicted and some have acquitted. Some have taken the view that these tyres are completely unsuitable for use on roads. In other courts the defendant has emphasised the words "having regard to the use to which the motor vehicle ... is being put". Evidence has been given that the motor cycle is being driven slowly and with extra care or for a short distance for access purposes.

Mirrors

8.69   The requirements as to the fitting of mirrors on motor vehicles (not being road rollers) are stipulated in reg.33 of the 1986 Regulations. Different requirements exist depending on the type of vehicle, and the table to that regulation sets out the detail. In accordance with reg.33(5) and (6), certain vehicles may alternatively comply with earlier requirements. In some cases, that is dependent upon the date the vehicle was first used. In virtually every case (items 1–7 and 8 in the table), the mirror so fixed must remain steady under normal driving conditions, and each exterior mirror must be visible to the driver through a side window or the part of the windscreen swept by the windscreen wiper. If the bottom edge of the mirror is less than 2m from the road, the mirror must not project more than 20cm beyond the overall width of the vehicle (or trailer, if wider). This is extended to 25cm for mirrors which comply with Directive 2003/97/EC or 2005/27/EC or with ECE Regulation 46.02. Both an interior mirror and an exterior mirrors on the driver's side of the vehicle have to be capable of being adjusted by the driver whilst in the driving position. Most vehicles will come within items 3–6 or 8 in the table which cover most goods vehicles, buses and ordinary motor cars. Motor cycles are covered by item 7. In each case, the table specifies the directive or regulation to be complied with as applicable to the need to have fitted mirrors or other devices for indirect vision and the requirements for such a mirror or device. Motor vehicles, other than two-wheeled motor cycles first used on or after June 1, 1978 (but before January 26, 2010) are required to have both an interior rear view mirror and an exterior offside rear view mirror. There are slightly different dates for Ford Transits. There are provisions for the alternative of rear view mirrors on the rear and offside where an interior mirror would not be adequate.

Mascots

The term means something supposed to bring luck ([1957] Crim. L.R. 563). **8.70** On this basis insignia would be exempt, particularly where used for identification purposes. Presumably it is a question of fact when objects such as lions and unicorns cease to be exempt insignia and are regarded instead as lucky mascots. It should be noted that under reg.53 of the 1986 Regulations, the definition of mascot is extended and includes "mascot, emblem, or other ornamental object". Compliance with Directive 74/483/EEC or 79/488/EEC or with ECE Regulation 26.01 exempts a vehicle from compliance with the regulation.

A stipendiary magistrate has held that a manufacturer's fitting on the top of the bonnet is an item of construction. As reg.100 of the 1986 Regulations is aimed at maintenance, the fitting could not constitute an offence contrary to reg.100 as being dangerous ([1957] Crim. L.R. 562). See, however, the comments in the section on offences of dangerous conditions, § 8.43.

Wings

The requirements in respect of wings are now contained in reg.63. Heavy mo- **8.71** tor cars, motor cars, motor cycles, invalid carriages, trailers, and agricultural motor vehicles driven at more than 20mph must be equipped with wings to catch, so far as practicable, mud or water thrown up by the rotation of their wheels or tracks. Various vehicles are exempted by reason of their type in reg.63(4); and compliance with Directive 78/549/EEC exempts a vehicle from compliance with the regulation.

Emissions

Regulation 61 controls the construction, maintenance and use of vehicles so as **8.72** to prevent avoidable emissions. The reference in reg.61 to the emission of oily substances, etc., covers not only the actual discharge but dripping which follows it (*Tidswell v Llewellyn* [1965] Crim. L.R. 732).

Regulation 61 makes requirements as to the precise levels of noxious emissions such as carbon monoxide, and maximum percentage levels are prescribed. There are variations between the type of engine and the time when it was first used. The measurement of exhaust emissions is in accord with Sch.7B to the 1986 Regulations. This refers to "the emissions publication" currently in its fourteenth edition.

Silencers, noise and warning instruments

Regulations 55–59 relate to noise and noise measurement. Regulations 54 and **8.73** 57 relate to silencers and regs 37 and 99 to the use of audible warning instruments. Any instrument on a vehicle first used on or after August 1, 1973 has to be continuous and uniform and not strident. Use of two-toned horns, gongs, bells, sirens, or instruments making similar sounds, other than by users authorised in reg.37, is prohibited by reg.99.

The use of a warning instrument of a stationary vehicle is prohibited by reg.99 at any time other than times of danger due to another moving vehicle on or near the road. The use of a warning instrument is prohibited, even where there is danger, between 11.30pm and 7am in the case of a motor vehicle in motion on a restricted road. It would seem that a person can use his horn with impunity under reg.99 provided the vehicle is not on a road. Thus one can sound one's horn coming out of one's driveway up until one reaches the road. There are various exemptions to reg.99 for theft alarms (which must not be able to sound for more than five minutes continuously: reg.37(8)), public service vehicles, authorised two-toned horns and vehicles with goods for sale. This last group may sound an instrument or apparatus whilst stationary between 12 noon and 7pm to inform the public that it is conveying goods for sale: reg.99(6).

8.74   There is no offence of failing to maintain a warning instrument. Where a horn is defective, a prosecution is usually brought under reg.37. This refers to a motor vehicle being fitted with an instrument capable of giving audible and sufficient warning of its approach or position. The reasoning is not entirely satisfactory but it is based on the argument that the warning instrument must be both fitted and capable. Prosecutions are usually brought under s.42 of the Road Traffic Act 1988 alleging contravention of one of the relevant regulations.

Regulation 54 requires every vehicle propelled by an internal combustion engine to be fitted with an exhaust system including a silencer whereby exhaust gases pass through the silencer into the atmosphere. The system and silencer are to be maintained in good and efficient working order and are not to be altered after the date of manufacture to increase the noise made by the escape of such gases (reg.54(2)). Compliance with one or another of a number of EC directives absolves the vehicle from compliance with reg.54(1).

8.75   Noise is controlled by regs 55–59. Regulations 55 and 55A provide the framework for motor vehicles generally and regs 57–57B provide for motor cycles. Regulation 55 provides for vehicles first used on or after October 1, 1983 subject to certain exemptions set out in regs 55 and 59. Regulation 55A provides for vehicles first used on or after October 1, 1996. Both regulations provide standards for the construction of vehicles referred to.

Regulation 57 makes provisions for noise limits in the construction of mopeds and motor cycles first used on or after April 1, 1983. Depending on the date of its first use on the road it must comply with the requirements of one or other of the "items" of the Table in Pt 1 of Sch.7A to the 1986 Regulations. Alternatively it must comply with one or more of the EC directives mentioned in the regulation.

8.76   Regulation 57A makes extensive provision relating to exhaust systems for motor cycles and lays down standards for original and replacement silencers forming part of the exhaust systems. Regulation 57B deals with noise limits and maintenance requirements for motor cycles. The prohibition created is novel in its wording. No person may use (or cause or permit to be used) a motor cycle to which reg.57 applies, if three conditions are all fulfilled. The conditions are:

    (a) that the vehicle does not meet the noise limit requirements;

    (b) that any part of the vehicle is not in good and efficient working order, or the vehicle has been altered; and

(c) that the noise made by the vehicle would have been materially less if all the parts of the vehicle were in good and efficient working order, or if the vehicle had not been altered.

The Motor Cycle Silencer and Exhaust Systems Regulations 1995 (SI 1995/ **8.77** 2370) lay down the standards that must be met for this type of motor cycle equipment and mean that it will be an offence for a person to supply, offer or agree to supply, or expose or possess for supply a silencer or exhaust system comprising a silencer for a motor cycle, motor scooter or moped, unless it meets the standards of the appropriate EC directive or British Standard; or that is marked "not for road use" or words to that effect; or is marked "pre 1985 MC only". The regulations also impose requirements as to packaging, labelling and instructions.

Scrambling motor cycles may fall outside these provisions depending on their intended or adapted use. See § 1.04.

Fuel tanks

By reg.39 every fuel tank fitted to a wheeled motor vehicle shall at all times be **8.78** so maintained that

(a) if it contains petroleum spirit, the tank is reasonably secure against it being damaged, and

(b) leakage of liquid or vapour from the tank is adequately prevented.

The wording of this regulation appears to be absolute. The tank, if containing petroleum spirit, must be made only of metal, except in the case of a motor cycle first used on or after February 1, 1993: reg.39(3A). Regulation 39 provides that instead of complying with these requirements as to construction, the vehicle may comply with the requirements of Directive 70/221/EEC (in so far as they relate to fuel tanks), or ECE Regulation 34 or 34.01, or, if the vehicle is an agricultural motor vehicle, of Directive 74/151/EEC.

Televisions and videos

By reg.109 no person shall drive, or cause or permit to be driven, a motor vehi- **8.79** cle with television receiving apparatus (defined in reg.109(2)) if the screen is partly or wholly visible (directly or reflected) to the driver whilst in the driving seat. A television set which was designed to receive television signals but which was connected without modification to a video recorder rather than an aerial was television receiving apparatus and caught by the regulation (*Target Travel (Coaches) Ltd v Roberts* [1986] R.T.R. 120). Coach owners who used such a set to transmit a video recording in a coach in such a position that it might distract other drivers had been properly convicted. Certain uses are exempt including use to display information to assist the driver to reach his destination: reg.109(1)(d).

Mobile telephones

By reg.110, three main offences are created in relation to the use of a mobile **8.80** telephone: use by the driver, causing or permitting the use by the driver and supervising a provisional licence-holder whilst using. The offences are punishable under s.41D of the Road Traffic Act 1988 with a maximum financial penalty of level 4 if committed in respect of a goods vehicle adapted to carry more than eight passengers and of level 3 otherwise, obligatory endorsement (three penalty points) and discretionary disqualification. The offences are fixed penalty offences.

The first offence is committed by a person who *drives* a *motor vehicle* on a *road* whilst *using* a *hand-held mobile telephone* or a hand-held device of a kind specified in reg.110(4). A mobile telephone or other device is deemed to be hand held if it is actually held or must be held at some point during he course of making or receiving a call or of performing any other *interactive communication function*: reg.110(6)(a). An interactive communication function is not defined conclusively but it does include sending or receiving messages, faxes or pictures or providing access to the internet: reg.110(6)(c). Defining it in this way should enable the provision to survive beyond technological change!

8.81   The hand-held device which is not a mobile telephone is one which is not a two-way radio but which performs an interactive communication function by transmitting or receiving data: reg.110(4). A two-way radio is a wireless telegraphy apparatus (see reg.110(6)(e)) defined by reference both to its purpose (transmitting and receiving *spoken* messages (i.e. not written ones)), and by the frequency on which it operates: reg.110(6)(d)(ii).

The second offence is committed by a person causing or permitting a person to drive a motor vehicle on a road whilst using a hand-held mobile telephone or specified device.

The third offence is committed by a person supervising a provisional licence-holder who is required to be supervised as a condition of his licence: reg.110(3) and (6)(b). As with drivers themselves, the supervisor may not use a hand-held mobile telephone or hand-held device as specified in reg.110(4).

8.82   In the case of each type of offence, there is an exemption if the person using the mobile telephone or device fulfils three criteria—that the call is to an emergency service using 112 or 999, that the caller is acting in response to a genuine emergency and that it is unsafe or impracticable to cease the driving (either of the person making the call or the supervised provisional licence-holder) in order to make the call. All three of these criteria must be met. It will be interesting to see whether there is any distinction drawn between an "emergency" and a "genuine emergency". It is likely the use of the word "genuine" simply reinforces the fact that this is an objective element and it seems very unlikely that the first and third criteria could be met but not the second.

For the meaning of *drive, causing or permitting, motor vehicle, road, use*, see Chapter 1. There are no additional restrictions on these definitions. This may mean that use of a mobile telephone whilst stationary in a traffic jam will come within the ambit of the offence. However, the purpose of the legislation is one of safety—the distraction caused by the use of a mobile telephone is considerable—and so it is anticipated that prosecution would not follow from use in circumstances where the vehicle is clearly not going to be moving for some time.

Sale of unroadworthy vehicles and parts

8.83   Section 75 of the 1988 Act makes it an offence to supply, or cause or permit to be supplied, a motor vehicle or trailer in such a condition that its use on a road would be unlawful, by regulations under s.41 of the 1988 Act as to brakes, steering or tyres or as to construction, weight or equipment or maintenance of vehicles, their parts and accessories, or in such a condition that its use on a road would involve a danger of injury to any person. "To supply" includes to sell, offer to sell or supply or expose for sale: s.75(2). Judicial consideration to the meaning of "supply" in this context was given by the Divisional Court in *Devon County Council v DB Cars Ltd* [2001] EWHC Admin 521; [2002] Crim. L.R. 71. A car owner took his car to a garage for repairs to the suspension to be done to enable it to pass the MOT test. Those repairs were done and the repairer successfully presented the car for testing and then returned it to the owner. Just over two months later, the suspension collapsed and the matter was referred to the Trading Standards Department of the County Council who prosecuted the garage which had undertaken the repairs for "supplying a motor vehicle in an unroadworthy condition". The garage contended that the word "supply" was being stretched too far, particularly as the owner had remained the owner throughout the transaction. The justices agreed but the Divisional Court did not. In upholding the prosecution appeal, the Divisional Court said that "supply" had to be given its ordinary meaning and involved nothing more than the transfer of physical control from one person to another in order to provide that person with something that other wanted or required. Here, the garage had provided the owner with what he required, a vehicle which had been repaired and which had passed its MOT test and so a "supply" had taken place within the meaning of the section.

It is also an offence to alter a motor vehicle or trailer so as to render its condition such that its use on a road would be unlawful under provisions relating to construction, weight or equipment by regulations under s.41 or would involve a danger of injury to any person. It was decided in *Streames v Copping* [1985] 2 All E.R. 122 that there is a single offence under what is now s.75 of selling, etc., an unroadworthy vehicle even though various breaches of the regulations are alleged. Such a charge for a single offence is not bad for duplicity. The decision was obiter but is nevertheless persuasive. It is submitted that selling, supplying, etc., are separate and should still be charged as separate offences. **8.84**

In *R. v Nash* [1990] R.T.R. 343, it was held in the Court of Appeal that the fact that proceedings might properly on the facts be instituted against a defendant for the sale of an unroadworthy vehicle under the section, did not inhibit a prosecutor from instituting proceedings against the defendant for applying a false trade description to a vehicle and for supplying a vehicle with a false trade description. This was so even though the offences under s.1 of the Trade Descriptions Act 1968 (unlike that under s.75 of the 1988 Act) were triable on indictment and were punishable with a custodial sentence.

An auctioneer does not offer to sell the goods auctioned, he invites those present to make offers to buy. Accordingly auctioneers of an unroadworthy vehicle which was driven away by the successful bidder cannot be convicted of an "offer to sell" contrary to s.75 (*British Car Auctions Ltd v Wright* [1972] Crim. L.R. 562: for criticism of the case see ibid. at 568). **8.85**

The liability of a seller under s.75 is absolute and, unless he has a statutory defence, he is guilty if he sells or supplies a vehicle in breach of it, whether or not he had guilty knowledge (*Sandford Motor Sales v Habgood* [1962] Crim. L.R. 487).

Section 75(6) provides that a defendant shall not be convicted if he proves (presumably on a balance of probabilities): **8.86**

   (a) that the vehicle or trailer was sold, supplied, etc., for export from Great Britain; or

   (b) that he had reasonable cause to believe that the vehicle or trailer would not be used on a road in Great Britain without it first being put into a roadworthy condition.

Section 75(6A) disapplies the statutory defence in s.75(6)(b) from a person acting in the course of a trade or business, who:

(a) exposes a vehicle or trailer for sale, *unless* he also proves that he took all reasonable steps to ensure that any prospective purchaser would be aware that its use in its current condition on a road in Great Britain would be unlawful; or

(b) offers to sell a vehicle or trailer, *unless* he also proves that he took all reasonable steps to ensure that the person to whom the offer was made was aware of that fact.

Whether the steps he took were reasonable or not are a matter for the court. In *R. (on the application of Newcastle upon Tyne City Council) v Le Quelenec* [2005] EWHC 45; *The Times*, January 13, 2005, justices had to consider the extent of s.75(6)(b). The defendant had sold a trailer which had unserviceable brakes and a corroded chassis and, if used on a road as a heavy braked trailer carrying a load, would contravene reg.100. It was known that the purchaser would tow the trailer away and would not use it loaded until it was fit for purpose. During the journey away, the axle snapped and a wheel came off and hit a passing car. Justices accepted the proposition that if at the relevant time the trailer was not carrying a load, it was not unroadworthy. The Divisional Court confirmed that that was a conclusion the justices were entitled to reach.

8.87 It is an offence under s.76 for a person to fit or cause or permit a vehicle part to be fitted, if by reason of that part being fitted the use of the vehicle on a road would thereby involve a danger of injury to any person or constitute a contravention of or a failure to comply with *any* of the construction and use regulations. It is similarly an offence under s.76(3) for a person to sell, supply, offer to sell or supply a vehicle part, or to cause or permit a vehicle part to be sold, supplied or offered for sale or supply when he has reasonable cause to believe it will be fitted to a motor vehicle so as to give rise to a contravention of or non-compliance with a construction and use regulation.

Subsections (2) and (5) of s.76 set out statutory defences to offences under s.76(1) and (3) respectively. In each case it is for the defence to prove that the statutory defence exists, presumably on a balance of probabilities.

Special types of vehicles

8.88 The Road Vehicles (Construction and Use) Regulations 1986 are qualified as to particular types of vehicles by the Road Vehicles (Authorisation of Special Types) (General) Order 2003 (SI 2003/1998). The Order relates to the use on roads of four types of vehicle—vehicles for moving abnormal indivisible loads, mobile cranes, engineering plant and road recovery vehicles. Where these vehicles (or the projections of any load that is carried on them) exceed certain specified lengths, widths or weights then notifications must be given to the police (in accordance with Sch.5), to the Secretary of State (Sch.7) and the authorities responsible for the maintenance of roads and bridges on which the vehicle is to be used (Sch.9, Pt 1). The Schedules contain detailed requirements relating to the construction and use of each of the vehicles and vehicle-combinations. Part 4 of the Order groups together a number of provisions authorising five different categories of vehicle in respect of which notifications must be given to various authorities or attendants provided. These are vehicles carrying loads of exceptional width, local excavation vehicles, vehicles for test, trials and non-UK use, track-laying vehicles and straddle carriers. Part 5 lists a number of miscellaneous special vehicles. If the conditions are not fulfilled, an offence may arise under the general law (for instance, under the Construction and Use Regulations) but no offence would arise under the Special Types Order.

Abnormal indivisible load

An abnormal indivisible load is a load which cannot be divided into two or more loads for the purpose of carriage on roads, without undue expense or risk of damage, and which is either too large or too heavy to be carried on a vehicle fully complying with the Road Vehicles (Construction and Use) Regulations 1986: Road Vehicles (Authorisation of Special Types) (General) Order 2003 Sch.1 para.2. **8.89**

In deciding whether a load cannot without undue expense or risk of damage be divided into two or more loads, the only undue expense or risk of damage to which the court may have regard is that likely to be incurred in dividing the load; any additional expense or risk involved in carrying the load in two vehicles is irrelevant (*Sunter Bros Ltd v Arlidge* [1962] 1 W.L.R. 199). The load in that case was two steel plates loaded on one vehicle for convenience. A like decision is *Siddle C. Cook Ltd v Arlidge* [1962] 1 W.L.R. 203, where the magistrates had found that a load of 10 steel boxes could have been divided without undue expense or risk of damage. A vehicle carried a hopper, which was an abnormal indivisible load in the main, but valves, etc., had been detached from the hopper and left in the vehicle; the total weight exceeded that allowed by the former reg.87 of the Construction and Use Regulations. It was held that the exemption for an abnormal load did not apply, as the hopper was divisible in respect of the valves, so that the carriage of the valves was not allowed; it was suggested that tarpaulins and plant battens might be allowed as being "in connection with the carriage" of the load (*Crabtree v McKelvie & Co* (1964) 62 L.G.R. 192). In *Smith v North-Western Traffic Area Licensing Authority* [1974] R.T.R. 236 it was similarly held that 12 separate prestressed concrete beams could not constitute an abnormal indivisible load; as the load was capable of being reduced into 12 separate beams, the company were accordingly rightly convicted of exceeding the plated train weight of the vehicle contrary to reg.80 of the Construction and Use Regulations (see also § 8.24 and the decision in *Kingdom v Williams*). If the conditions are not fulfilled, an offence may arise under the general law (for instance, under the Construction and Use Regulations) but no offence would arise under the Special Types Order.

In *Patterson v Redpath Brothers Ltd* [1979] 2 All E.R. 108, it was held that a container was not an indivisible load of exceptional length. The purpose of the container was to hold livestock and the livestock could have been separated and carried as two loads. Griffiths J. said that "indivisible load" refers to the contents of the container and not the container itself. Lord Widgery C.J. said that it cannot have been the intention of the legislature to allow the provisions of the regulations to be circumvented merely by packing goods into a larger receptacle. **8.90**

CONSTRUCTION AND USE: PENALTIES

Generally

Offences involving breach of the 1986 Regulations carry different levels of **8.91** penalty depending on the statutory provisions in the substituted sections of the 1988 Act. An offence under s.40A (use involving a danger of injury) carries a maximum fine of level 4, but a fine of level 5 if committed in respect of a goods vehicle or a vehicle adapted to carry more than eight passengers. Where a person convicted of an offence under this section has a previous such conviction recorded within the three years prior to the commission of the current offence, the court is obliged to disqualify the offender for at least six months (subject to special reasons in the usual way).

Exactly the same penalty, a maximum fine of level 4, but a fine of level 5 in respect of a goods vehicle, etc., is applicable for a breach of s.41A for contravention or failure to comply with a construction and use requirement as to brakes, steering gear or tyres, or where an offender uses, causes or permits to be used on a road a motor vehicle or trailer which does not comply with such a requirement.

8.92 For offences under s.41B of the 1988 Act, dealing with breach of a requirement as to weight in respect of goods vehicles or motor vehicles or trailers adapted to carry more than eight passengers, the maximum penalty is a fine of level 5 on the standard scale. Under s.42, which governs all breaches of construction and use regulations not falling within s.41A(a) or s.41B(1)(a), a defendant is liable on summary conviction to a fine not exceeding level 4 if the offence is committed in respect of a goods vehicle or a vehicle adapted to carry more than eight passengers, and a fine of level 3 in any other case.

As to brakes on pedal cycles and the various "selling and supplying", etc., offences, see §§ 8.109 and 8.110. A table of penalties is provided at § 8.111.

Endorsement

8.93 Limited powers of endorsement and disqualification are given by Sch.2 to the 1988 Offenders Act. Endorsement must be ordered, unless there are "special reasons" (see Chapter 21) or the defendant did not know *and* had no reason to suspect that an offence was being committed (see § 8.104 below), for an offence contrary to s.40A, s.41A or s.41D.

Section 40A is a freestanding section not dependent on the Construction and Use Regulations.

Section 41 is the authority for making the Construction and Use Regulations. Section 41A deals with breach of construction and use requirements as to brakes, steering gear or tyres. Offences under that section carry a discretionary disqualification and an obligatory endorsement with three points. Section 41B deals with breach of construction and use requirements as to weight, etc. Contraventions of this section are neither disqualifiable, nor endorsable.

8.94 Section 42 deals with breach of other construction and use requirements. Contraventions of this section too are neither disqualifiable nor endorsable.

It follows that the particular section under which the conduct is charged/summoned is the determining feature as to whether disqualification/endorsement should follow. If a breach of reg.100 is alleged, the proceedings must be brought under s.42 and on conviction no disqualification/endorsement may follow. If the prosecution is brought not within reg.100/s.42, but under s.40A the consequences on the defendant's conviction will be discretionary disqualification and obligatory endorsement as mentioned above. Where the offence is committed within three years of a conviction for another offence under s.40A, the disqualification is obligatory. The minimum period of disqualification will be six months: see 1988 Offenders Act s.34(4B).

An offence under reg.107 of leaving a vehicle unattended without setting the **8.95** brake does not carry endorsement because it is not an offence as to use of the vehicle but as to the duties of the driver and also because it would be anomalous if this did carry endorsement while the offence under the same regulation of not stopping the engine did not (*Kenyon v Thorley* [1973] R.T.R. 60) (see § 8.58). For a similar reason it would appear that an offence contrary to reg.19 (driver of a trailer to be in a position to operate a brake) or reg.89 (application of brake to wheel of detached trailer) is neither endorsable nor disqualifiable.

"Trailer" is defined by s.185(1) of the 1988 Act as a "vehicle", so it is submitted that offences of use, etc., of trailers in a dangerous condition, with defective brakes, etc., attract compulsory endorsement and optional disqualification and penalty points.

Description of weight offences

The words "description of weight" are to be found in s.41B(1)(a) and (2) of the **8.96** Road Traffic Act 1988 as inserted by s.8 of the 1991 Act. The offence is punishable with a maximum fine of level 5, but is neither endorsable nor disqualifiable.

In *Hudson v Bushrod* [1982] R.T.R. 87 the defendants had been prosecuted under reg.100(1) in connection with a grossly overloaded goods vehicle. The Divisional Court upheld the decision of the justices that this was not an offence relating to a description of weight and congratulated them on their analysis of the provisions. The court drew attention to the absence (prior to the 1991 amendments) of "any description of weight" in columns 5 and 6 of Sch.2 to the 1988 Offenders Act. It follows that there is no power to endorse or disqualify or order penalty points for a description of weight offence.

Loads causing nuisance

Under reg.100(2) and (3) offences may be committed if the load or unsuitable **8.97** use causes nuisance as well as danger. An information alleging both danger and nuisance is not bad for duplicity (*St Albans Sand and Gravel Co Ltd v Minnis* [1981] R.T.R. 231). Despite this, however, it is submitted that where an offender is convicted under reg.100(2) or reg.100(3) and causes nuisance but no danger the court has no power to endorse or disqualify or order penalty points since the offence is punishable by virtue of s.42 of the 1988 Act. Otherwise if prosecuted under s.40A.

Weight prosecutions

For breach of requirement as to descriptions of weight for goods vehicles and **8.98** passenger vehicles adapted to carry more than eight passengers see s.41B of the Road Traffic Act 1988. The potential commercial gain from overloading vehicles is considerable as are the risks to public safety and the condition of the roads. Courts are entitled to expect prosecutors to draw attention to the advantages to the operator of overloading vehicles and to take that into account in assessing the appropriate penalty. As to the meaning of "description of weight", see § 1.79. Maximum weights for vehicles are provided in regs 75–80 of and Schs 11 and 11A to the 1986 Regulations. Further restrictions for certain categories of vehicles are contained in the Road Vehicles (Authorised Weight) Regulations 1998 (SI 1998/3111) (as amended) though, by regs 4 and 5, these are subordinate to the 1986 Regulations, where appropriate.

The question whether there can be offences simultaneously of excess axle weight and excess overall weight has been determined by *J. Theobald (Hounslow) Ltd v Stacy* [1979] R.T.R. 411. The defendants were before the court for exceeding the overall gross weight, for exceeding the maximum weight on the first axle and for exceeding the maximum weight on the second axle. It was unsuccessfully argued that the three summonses were oppressive. The Divisional Court confirmed that convictions could be recorded on each summons. The case of *Martin v Robertson* (1949) 93 S.J. 19 (see § 1.81) also seems to be in point. The question was further considered by the Divisional Court in *Travel-Gas (Midlands) Ltd v Reynolds, Myers v Licensing Authority for the North Eastern Traffic Area* [1989] R.T.R. 75. The court held that it was not duplicitous so to proceed. MacPherson J. said that the difference in the wording between reg.80(1) of the 1986 Regulations and its predecessor in the 1978 Regulations, which specifically created separate offences, had cast doubt on whether more than one information could still be preferred in respect of excess weight offences by a single vehicle on the same occasion. In His Lordship's judgment, the later regulation did no more than set out the previous regulation and it had only been sought to compress the words used. The Divisional Court considered the wording of reg.80(1) and (2) in *DPP v Marshall and Bell* (1990) 154 J.P. 508. It held that the two paragraphs did not create distinct offences and the offence would be committed under para.(1).

8.99   All overloading offences may affect the steering and the braking power and cause damage to the road surfaces. It should be remembered that while the regulations prohibiting excess axle weight are designed primarily to prevent damage to the surfaces and foundations of roads, the regulations prohibiting excess overall weight are designed to ensure that a vehicle does not exceed the weight for which it is designed and constructed to carry loads and is able to pull up within the distance for which its brakes were designed.

Defences to weight prosecutions

8.100   Section 41B(2) of the 1988 Act reads:

"In any proceedings for an offence under this section in which there is alleged a contravention of or failure to comply with a construction and use requirement as to any description of weight applicable to a goods vehicle, it shall be a defence to prove either—

    (a) that at the time when the vehicle was being used on the road—

        (i) it was proceeding to a weighbridge which was the nearest available one to the place where the loading of the vehicle was completed for the purpose of being weighed, or

        (ii) it was proceeding from a weighbridge after being weighted to the nearest point at which it was reasonably practicable to reduce the weight to the relevant limit, without causing an obstruction on any road, or

    (b) in a case where the limit of that weight was not exceeded by more than 5 per cent—

        (i) that that limit was not exceeded at the time when the loading of the vehicle was originally completed, and

        (ii) that since that time no person has made any addition to the load."

A prosecution brought under reg.100 of the Road Vehicles (Construction and **8.101**
Use) Regulations 1986 (overloading, etc.) is not an offence relating to a description of weight (*Hudson v Bushrod* [1982] R.T.R. 87). It follows that the defence
in s.41B(2) does not apply to reg.100 offences. See also § 1.79.

The "nearest" weighbridge is the nearest in road distance that the particular vehicle can go (*Lovett v Payne* [1980] R.T.R. 103). From a transcript of the judgment it may be noted that the test "nearest weighbridge to which the lorry can
go" should be applied in a practicable and sensible sense, i.e. a route would not
be the nearest if it involved the lorry going on a road which was not suitable or
practicable for that lorry. The "practicable and sensible" test does not allow the
choice of another weighbridge which is more convenient or which involves no
element of danger. The vehicle must proceed to the nearest if it is available (*Hal-
liday v Burl* [1983] R.T.R. 21). It is the nearest weighbridge that was actually
available to the driver rather than the nearest of which the driver was aware. Thus
the test would not be satisfied where a driver was on the way to a weighbridge,
but there was a nearer one that was available of which the driver was unaware:
Vehicle and Operator Services Agency v F. & S. Gibbs Transport Services Ltd
[2006] EWHC 1109; [2007] R.T.R 17.

The burden of proof of establishing a defence under s.41B(2) is upon the de- **8.102**
fendant and the standard is that of a balance of probabilities. Thus in *Thurrock
DC v L.A. & A. Pinch Ltd* [1974] R.T.R. 269 a magistrates' court was held to be
wrong in dismissing charges on the ground that, because they were in doubt
whether or not the vehicles were proceeding to a weighbridge to be weighed, the
defendant was entitled to the benefit of that doubt. Local knowledge as to the location of weighbridges may be important in cases under s.41B(2)(a). Semble if
the paragraph is interpreted literally, a defendant driver who is on his way to a
weighbridge which he genuinely believes to be the nearest one, but which in fact
is not, will be unable to set up the defence, but there is obvious mitigation. The
weighbridge to which a driver is proceeding must be the "nearest available" one
and it is submitted that, when the driver leaves the place of loading, he must, to
avail himself of the defence, believe that there is a weighbridge open within a
reasonable distance. A driver who starts on a long journey late in the evening,
when the weighbridges are all shut, should not be able to say in his defence that
he is on the way to the nearest available weighbridge which is perhaps 150 miles
and several hours' driving away. If he does and it is shown that he could not reasonably have believed that there was a weighbridge open within a reasonable
distance, on this argument he could be convicted. The standard of proof on him
is, no doubt, that of balance of probabilities. When he is coming from the weighbridge after being weighed and found overweight, he must, to avail himself of the
defence under the second part of s.41B(2)(a), be going to the nearest practicable
unloading point. Often, there may be no such place available, e.g. because the
yard where he loaded is shut for the evening. It is suggested that he may then
proceed on his journey but should take the vehicle off the highway, or, at least,
stop driving until the yard opens or some of the excess load can be put into other
vehicles.

There is no requirement that evidence of weight obtained from a weighbridge **8.103**
should be supported by a certificate of accuracy relating to that weighbridge. In
Kelly Communications Ltd v DPP [2002] EWHC 2752; (2003) 167 J.P. 73, a
driver of a van suspected to be overweight was taken to a weighbridge which

confirmed that it was overweight. The police gave unchallenged evidence that the weighbridge was a public weighbridge available for the weighing of vehicles and that they had carried out basic checks of the weighbridge for reliability. No documentary proof of the accuracy of the weighbridge was presented to the court. The defendant argued that the court could not rely on the evidence of weight since there was no evidence as to accuracy but was convicted. On appeal, the Administrative Court held that the effect of the submission would be to import into the 1988 Act a requirement of a certificate of accuracy for every weighbridge. The statute did not expressly require this and it was not possible to describe exactly the evidence that would be required in every case. Although production of a certificate was a sensible course of action, it was not essential and the court had been entitled to convict.

The "5 per cent addition" under s.41B(2)(b) was originally enacted primarily to deal with cases where snow or petrol, etc., have increased the weight, but the plain words of the subsection are not so limited (see e.g. *Thurrock Borough Council v William Blythe & Co Ltd* [1977] R.T.R. 301). By s.70 of the 1988 Act, powers of immediately prohibiting the use on the road of overweight vehicles are conferred; and by s.17(3) of the 1988 Offenders Act, if any question arises whether a weight has been reduced to the permitted limit in proceedings under s.70, the burden of proof is on the accused. Where the burden of proof lies on a defendant, the standard of proof is only on a balance of probabilities (*R. v Carr-Briant* [1943] K.B. 607).

Penalty points and exemptions from endorsement

8.104   All endorsable offences under the Construction and Use Regulations carry three penalty points. Section 48 of the 1988 Offenders Act provides that where a person is convicted of a contravention of s.40A of the Road Traffic Act 1988 (using a vehicle in a dangerous condition, etc.) or of s.41A of that Act (breach of requirement as to brakes, steering gear or tyres), the court must not:

    (a) order him to be disqualified or

    (b) order any particulars or penalty points to be endorsed on the counterpart of any licence held by him or on his driving record, if he proves certain facts to the court.

In the case of s.40A, he must prove that he did not know, and had no reasonable cause to suspect, that the use of the vehicle involved a danger of injury to any person. In the case of s.41A, he must prove that he did not know and had no reasonable cause to suspect that the facts of the case were such that the offence would be committed. The effect of this is to exempt from endorsement, driving test and disqualification, including the penalty points disqualification (but not from conviction and fine), a driver who shows that he had taken out his vehicle in reliance on his foreman's or its owner's assurance that the brakes, steering, etc., were in order or in reliance on the load being properly packed by his firm's loaders; likewise it will exempt an employer who sends out his drivers with properly maintained vehicles and proper instructions to take them off the road if defects appear but whose drivers disobey those instructions, so that the employer, though physically absent, is charged with using defective brakes, etc. It may well exempt sons and daughters who drive their parents' cars on the assumption that they are in good running order.

8.105   It will be a question of fact in each case whether the defendant has any reasonable cause to suspect that there was anything wrong with the brakes, steering or tyres.

The provision will certainly exempt those who drive defective vehicles relying on the owner's assurance that they are in good condition and those who drive vehicles which have just come back from a check at a garage, provided that in these and the earlier cited cases they do not go on driving after the defect has become obvious, or otherwise had no reasonable cause to suspect the defect to exist. The defendant's evidence will always be required and he must show not only that he did not know of the defect but also that he had no reasonable cause to suspect it. The test of reasonableness is, it is submitted, subjective; the test is not whether there is reasonable cause to suspect (that would be an objective test) but whether *he* has reasonable cause. The standard of knowledge expected of the driver of the Clapham omnibus will be higher than that of the man on it, when driving his own car, unless he is in the motor trade, but there must come a time when it is obvious to anyone that something is wrong. A motorist who genuinely believes his steering to be in order, having just had it repaired, but finds it fails in Piccadilly Circus, may claim the benefit of the exception if he stops at once but he cannot avoid responsibility if, knowing the defect, he continues to drive into Trafalgar Square. It will also exempt a lorry driver convicted of using the lorry with an insecure load which has been caused by a latent defect of which he neither knew nor could have known (e.g. situations such as arose in *Cornish v Ferry Masters Ltd* at § 8.47 and *Keyse v Sainsbury* at § 8.47).

8.106 Endorsement need not be ordered in any event if there are special reasons (see Chapter 21). This is discretionary and should be compared with the specific statutory provisions contained in s.48 of the 1988 Offenders Act detailed above.

Disqualification

8.107 Disqualification for any period and a driving test may be ordered for any offence for which endorsement is obligatory but not for any other offence under the regulations. Penalty points disqualification applies to all offences under the Construction and Use Regulations which are endorsable. The penalty points disqualification would not apply if the defendant proves that he had no reason to suspect that an offence would be committed (see "Penalty points and exemptions from endorsement", § 8.104 above).

Endorsement code

8.108 The endorsement codes for offences contrary to the Construction and Use Regulations are set out in the table of penalties at § 8.111.

Brakes on pedal cycles

8.109 The offence of riding, or causing or permitting to be ridden, a pedal cycle on the road in contravention of the Pedal Cycles (Construction and Use) Regulations is punishable under s.91 of the 1988 Offenders Act on summary conviction with a fine of level 3. Endorsement, disqualification and penalty points may not be ordered, even if the pedal cycle is an electrically assisted pedal cycle (see § 1.23 and § 8.41).

Selling, etc., unroadworthy vehicles and parts

8.110 Offences of selling, supplying, etc., motor vehicles and trailers in an unroadworthy condition under s.75 of the 1988 Act, or without a certificate of conformity or type approval certificate under s.65, and for fitting or causing or permitting to be fitted parts which would render the vehicle unroadworthy under s.76(1) are all punishable with a fine of level 5. The maximum fine for offences contrary to s.76(3) (sale, etc., of such parts) is a fine of level 4. For the similar offence in relation to cycles under s.81 the penalty is a fine of level 3. Similar types of offences to those under s.75 of the 1988 Act (selling unroadworthy parts) are prosecutable under the Consumer Protection Act 1987. Thus, the Road Vehicles (Brake Linings Safety) Regulations 1999 (SI 1999/2978) create offences of supplying or fitting brake linings containing asbestos. The maximum fine under the Consumer Protection Act 1987 s.10 for supplying, etc., illegal tyres is a fine of level 5 or six months' imprisonment or both. It is triable only summarily. There are similar defences to those applicable for the sale of inadequate crash helmets (see § 9.65). Endorsement, disqualification and penalty points may not be ordered for these offences.

Construction and use: penalties

Offence	Mode of trial	Section *	Imprisonment	Fine	Disqualification	Penalty points	Endorsement code	Sentencing guideline ††
Using vehicle in dangerous condition, etc.	Summary	s.40A	—	a) Level 5 if committed in respect of a goods vehicle or a vehicle adapted to carry more than eight passengers b) Level 4 in any other case	Obligatory if committed within 3 years of a previous conviction under s.40A; otherwise discretionary. May not disqualify where the offender proves that he did not know, had no reasonable cause to suspect, that the use of the vehicle involved a danger of injury to any person	3	CU20	Up to 3.5 tonnes Fine band B If in the course of business or over 3.5 tonnes Driver or owner-driver¶ Fine band B Owner-company Fine band C

Offence	Mode of trial	Section *	Imprisonment	Fine	Disqualification	Penalty points	Endorsement code	Sentencing guideline †‡
Load likely to cause danger because of its insecurity or position	Summary	s.40A		a) Level 5 if committed in respect of a goods vehicle or a vehicle adapted to carry more than eight passengers b) Level 4 in any other case	Obligatory if committed within 3 years of a previous conviction under s.40A; otherwise discretionary. May not disqualify where the offender proves that he did not know, had no reasonable cause to suspect, that the use of the vehicle involved a danger of injury to any person	3	CU50	Up to 3.5 tonnes Fine band B If in the course of business Driver or owner-driver¶ Fine band A Owner-company Fine band B Over 3.5 tonnes Driver or owner-driver¶ Fine band B Owner-company Fine band C

Offence	Mode of trial	Section *	Imprisonment	Fine	Disqualification	Penalty points	Endorsement code	Sentencing guideline ††‡
Breach of requirements as to brakes/steering gear/or tyres	Summary	s.41A	—	a) Level 5 if committed in respect of a goods vehicle or a vehicle adapted to carry more than 8 passengers b) Level 4 in any other case	Discretionary except where the offender proves that he did not know, and had no reasonable cause to suspect, that the facts of the case were such that the offence would be committed	3	CU10/ CU40/CU30	Up to 3.5 tonnes Fine band B If in the course of business or over 3.5 tonnes Driver or owner-driver¶ Fine band B Owner-company Fine band C

Offence	Mode of trial	Section *	Imprisonment	Fine	Disqualification	Penalty points	Endorsement code	Sentencing guideline †††
Breach of requirement as to weight	Summary	s.41B	—	5	—	—	—	Up to 3.5 tonnes Fine band A If in course of business Driver or owner-driver¶ Fine band A Owner-company Fine band B Over 3.5 tonnes Fine band B If in course of business Driver or owner-driver¶ Fine band B Owner-company Fine band C Where overload exceeds 10%, increase fine by 10% for each 1% overload

Offence	Mode of trial	Section *	Imprisonment	Fine	Disqualification	Penalty points	Endorsement code	Sentencing guideline ††
Breach of requirements as to control of vehicle, mobile telephones, etc.	Summary	s.41D	—	a) Level 4 if committed in respect of a goods vehicle adapted to carry more than 8 passengers b) Level 3 in any other case	Discretionary	3	CU80	Fine band A (mobile telephones only)
Breach of other construction and use requirements	Summary	s.42	—	a) Level 4 if committed in respect of a goods vehicle or a vehicle adapted to carry more than 8 passengers b) Level 3 in any other case	—	—	—	—

Offence	Mode of trial	Section *	Imprisonment	Fine	Disqualification	Penalty points	Endorsement code	Sentencing guideline †‡
Pedal cycles (construction and use)	Summary	Pedal Cycles (Construction and Use) Regs and s.91 RTOA 1988	—	3	—	—	—	—
No type approval certificate of conformity	Summary	s.63(1)	—	4	—	—	—	—
Selling unroadworthy vehicle, etc.	Summary	s.75	—	5	—	—	—	—
Fitting defective or unsuitable parts	Summary	s.76(1)	—	5	—	—	—	—
Selling defective or unsuitable parts	Summary	s.76(3)	—	4	—	—	—	—
Selling, etc., wrongly made tail lamps or reflectors	Summary	s.83	—	5	—	—	—	—

Offence	Mode of trial	Section *	Imprisonment	Fine	Disqualification	Penalty points	Endorsement code	Sentencing guideline ††
Selling, etc., without required type approval certificate	Summary	s.65	—	5	—	—	—	—
Selling pedal cycle in contravention of regulations	Summary	s.81	—	3	—	—	—	—
Supplying, etc., illegal tyres	Summary	s.12(5) Consumer Protection Act 1987	6 months or level 5 or both		—		—	

* Road Traffic Act 1988 unless otherwise specified.

† **Note**: Fine bands "A", "B" and "C" represent respectively 50%, 100% and 150% of relevant weekly income. A timely guilty plea should attract a discount. See Appendix 3.

‡ In all cases, a court will take safety, damage to roads and commercial gain into account. Where an offence is "commercially motivated", higher fines can be expected.

¶ Where "owner-driver", consider 25% uplift.

Lighting

The Road Vehicles Lighting Regulations

8.112   The law as to lighting of vehicles is contained in the Road Vehicles Lighting Regulations 1989 (SI 1989/1796), as amended, made under s.41 of the 1988 Act in respect of all vehicles save cycles not being motor vehicles. The regulations in respect of cycles not being motor vehicles are made under s.81 of the 1988 Act. The regulations correspond with the Road Vehicles (Construction and Use) Regulations also made under s.41 in that they are divided into equipment, maintenance and use.

     What used to be called side lights are now more accurately called front position lamps. Headlamps are still so described and include main-beam and dipped-beam headlamps. In some places the regulations merely refer to headlamps and in other places specify main-beam or dipped-beam headlamps.

8.113   Dim-dip lighting devices provide for intermediate strength headlights for when a vehicle is about to start. They will only apply to motor vehicles with three or more wheels not being a motor bicycle with a side-car, capable of exceeding 25mph on the level and only to vehicles manufactured on or after October 1, 1986 and first used on or after April 1, 1987. It is important to note that under the regulations these dim-dip lights will not fulfil the headlamp requirements or the seriously reduced visibility in daytime requirements.

     Under the 1989 Regulations the day is divided into two periods, "between sunrise and sunset" and "between sunset and sunrise", which should prove somewhat simpler and clearer than the former definitions of "daytime hours" and "hours of darkness". Those old definitions are still applicable, however, in the provisions of the regulations relating to the use of headlamps or front fog lamps. "Daytime hours" is defined as meaning the time between half an hour before sunrise and half an hour after sunset. "Hours of darkness" means the time between half an hour after sunset and half an hour before sunrise. "Sunset" means sunset according to local, not Greenwich, time (*Gordon v Cann* (1899) 63 J.P. 324).

8.114   Regulation 3A allows the requirement of compliance with British Standards in respect of lamps, retro reflectors and rear markings to be widened to include "corresponding standards" as an alternative. The "corresponding standards" are those laid down or recognised in any Member State of the European Economic Area. In some ways this resembles the trend in type approval (see §§ 8.10 et seq.) where a compulsory British Standard runs in parallel with the optional European Standard. The logic is to have agreed standards throughout the EU.

     From April 1, 1995 it has been an offence to use, or cause or permit to be used, a bus for the purpose of carrying children under the age of 16 years to or from school without there being prescribed signs fitted to the front and rear of the bus. These have in recent years become as common in this country as they have been for rather longer in Europe. The signs depict two young schoolchildren in black against yellow retroreflective material.

Application

8.115   The 1988 Act s.41 and the regulations made under s.41 apply to vehicles of the Crown (s.183 of the 1988 Act) but see § 2.34. Section 81 in theory also applies to

Crown vehicles, but the offence section for s.81 is s.91 of the 1988 Offenders Act and this section does not apply to Crown vehicles (see s.183). The regulations therefore apply to Crown vehicles save that no offence is committed in respect of a cycle which is not a motor vehicle. Regulation 7 makes special provision as to vehicles of the home forces and of visiting forces. Section 41 and therefore the material regulations do not apply to trolley vehicles or trams.

Offences

A defendant who causes or permits a vehicle to be used in breach of the 1989 **8.116** provisions is guilty of an offence under s.42(b).

Exemptions from the 1989 Regulations

Nothing in the regulations requires any lamp or reflector to be fitted between **8.117** sunrise and sunset to a vehicle which does not have a front or rear position lamp, incomplete vehicles proceeding to a works for completion, pedal cycles, pedestrian controlled vehicles, horse-drawn vehicles, vehicles drawn or propelled by hand or combat vehicles (defined in reg.3(2)). Such vehicles are exempt from all such requirements during that period. Horse-drawn vehicles include vehicles drawn by any animal!

With regard to the exemption for vehicles not fitted with front or rear position lamps such a lamp is not to be treated as fitted if it is so painted over or masked that it is not capable of being immediately used or readily put to use, or if the lamp is an electric lamp which is not provided with any system of wiring by which it is or can readily be connected with a source of electricity. There is a difference between readily used and readily connected. A paper mask means that a lamp cannot be readily used, but merely a loose wire still means that the electricity can be readily connected.

There are also certain exemptions for invalid carriages (reg.8), visiting **8.118** vehicles, temporarily imported vehicles and vehicles proceeding to a port for export (reg.5). Hand drawn or propelled vehicles are exempt if they are 800mm or less wide including any load if used close to the nearside or left-hand edge of the carriageway or to cross the road (reg.9).

Parts II and III of the Road Vehicles Lighting Regulations 1989 govern the fitting, maintenance and use of lamps, reflectors, rear markings and devices. Use by a vehicle examiner is exempt from the provisions of Pts II and III where the use of the vehicle is to submit it for examination at a vehicle-testing station in order to make sure that the examination carried out there is in accordance with the required testing standards or to remove it after completion of the examination. Two requirements must be met: the vehicle examiner must have been authorised in writing by the Secretary of State for these purposes and must reasonably believe that any defects in the vehicle do not give rise to a danger of injury to any person while it is being used for this purpose (reg.4A(2)).

Vehicles towing or being towed

Rear lamps are only required for drawing vehicles and front lamps, etc., for **8.119** trailers in the case of new vehicles, that is motor vehicles first used on or after April 1, 1986 and trailers manufactured on or after October 1, 1985. Trailers manufactured before October 1, 1990 are exempt from stop lamps and indicators if one indicator at least on each side and the stop lamp(s) on the drawing vehicle are visible to an observer from 6m behind the trailer whether loaded or not.

Broken-down vehicles are also exempt from fitting and maintenance of lamps, reflectors or rear markings save that rear position lamps and rear reflectors must be fitted between sunset and sunrise.

Fitting of lamps, etc.

8.120   Part II of the regulations (regs 11–22) governs the fitting of lamps, reflectors, rear markings and devices. It is an offence to use, cause or permit to be used on a road a vehicle specified in Sch.1 not fitted with lamps, reflectors, rear markings and devices of the type specified in the Schedule and which comply with the described installation and performance requirements. Schedule 1 is divided into seven tables. They deal respectively with motor vehicles having three or more wheels not being vehicles applicable to any of the other tables; solo motor bicycles and motor bicycle combinations; pedal cycles; pedestrian controlled vehicles, horse-drawn vehicles and track-laying vehicles; vehicles drawn or propelled by hand; trailers drawn by a motor vehicle and trailers drawn by a pedal cycle. Each table is divided into three columns, the first dealing with the type of lamp, etc, the second with the Schedule in which the relevant installation and performance requirements are specified, and the third, any exceptions.

The colour of light to be shown by lamps and reflectors is governed by reg.11, their movement by reg.12, restrictions on flashing lights by reg.13, restrictions on the fitting of warning beacons, special warning lamps and similar devices by reg.16, obligatory warning beacons by reg.17, and reg.22 governs the requirement for additional side marker lamps for vehicles or combination of vehicles with an overall length (including any load) exceeding 18.3m or in certain circumstances 12.2m. Regulation 20 requires that every specified optional lamp, reflector, rear marking or device fitted to a vehicle must comply with the provisions in column 3 of the table to that regulation. (For a decision on the interpretation of reg.16 of the 1989 Regulations, see *DPP v Hawkins* [1996] R.T.R. 160, considered at § 1.44 above.)

Projecting trailers and projecting and overhanging loads

8.121   Regulation 21 governs projecting trailers and projecting and overhanging loads and reference should be made to the regulation for the full requirements.

It is an offence by reg.21 to use, cause or permit to be used on a road a vehicle during the hours of darkness or seriously reduced visibility in contravention of the requirements. In effect a sideways projection of more than 400mm from the outermost part of the relevant position lamp has to be lit by an additional lamp or the original lamp moved. The projection may consist of a load or equipment or it may be a trailer without front lights projecting sideways more than 400mm from the front position lamp on any preceding vehicle. The same applies to a projection more than 1m to the rear (more than 2m in the case of agricultural vehicles and vehicles carrying fire escapes). The installation and performance requirements for rear position lamps do not apply to such rearward projection lamps.

8.122   If a load projects either laterally or beyond the rear of a vehicle, it must be fitted with reflectors in addition to lamps. In addition, where a vehicle carries a load or equipment which projects beyond the *front* of the vehicle more than 1m (2m in the case of an agricultural vehicle, or a vehicle carrying a fire escape) the vehicle is required to be fitted with an additional front lamp capable of showing white light to the front and a white reflecting device, both visible from a reasonable distance.

In effect as seriously reduced visibility may occur at any time, it will be necessary to provide for reg.21 to be complied with accordingly.

Headlamps—requirements

The specifications for headlamps are set out in Schs 4 and 5. All vehicles must have two save solo motor bicycles, motor bicycle combinations, and certain old or small three-wheeler motor vehicles. (All these may have one only, though see in each Schedule para.2(ii)(A)(ii).) Certain old large passenger vehicles may have two main-beam and one dipped-beam headlamps. Pairs must be matched and must switch on or off simultaneously. The colour must be white or yellow. At first sight the intensity does not appear in all cases to be specified but this will be governed either in the specification or by the approval or BS mark. New requirements contained in Sch.4 (dipped-beam headlamps) include those for the alignment of such lamps, and an indication of the downward inclination of such lamps must be shown on a motor vehicle first used after April 1, 1991. In Sch.5 (main-beam headlamps), optional main-beam headlamps fitted to motor vehicles first used after April 1, 1991 must bear an approval mark. **8.123**

Position lamps—requirements

The specifications for front position lamps are set out in Sch.2 and for rear position lamps in Sch.10. All vehicles must have two front position lamps save pedal cycles with less than four wheels and without a side-car, solo motor bicycles, handcarts with an overall width (including any load) not exceeding 1250mm and invalid carriages (all one lamp only). Motor cycle combinations with a headlamp on the motor cycle may have one front position lamp only on the side-car. Apart from this and trailers manufactured before October 1, 1985, the two must form a pair, but on each front side. They must be white or, if incorporated in a headlamp which is capable of emitting *only* a yellow light, yellow. In this context it may be argued that a headlamp with a yellow mask for a continental journey is not capable of emitting *only* a yellow light, so that the use of an incorporated front position lamp masked yellow is illegal in this country. **8.124**

All vehicles must have two red rear position lamps save pedal cycles with less than four wheels and without a side-car, solo motor bicycles, handcarts, trailers drawn by pedal cycles, trailers of 800mm width or less drawn by motor bicycles including combinations (in this instance there is no reference to the width of the load) and certain old large passenger vehicles (all one position lamp only). Certain motor vehicles and trailers drawn by them which cannot comply with the full requirements as to position and angles of visibility must have four.

Rear registration plate lamps

As well as being included in these regulations, there is also the offence relating to the failure to illuminate the rear index plate. This is also an offence of using, causing or permitting. The offences under the two different sets of regulations are compared at § 12.130. **8.125**

Maintenance

8.126   Part III of the Regulations (regs 23–27) governs the maintenance and use of lamps, reflectors, rear markings and devices. Regulations 23 governs maintenance. It is an offence to use, cause or permit the use on a road of a vehicle if every front position lamp, rear position lamp, headlamp, rear registration plate lamp, side marker lamp, rear fog lamp, retro reflector, end-outline marker lamp and rear markings required and every stop lamp and indicator fitted (required or not) is not in clean and good working order (reg.23(1)). As noted, the law applies additionally to optional stop lamps and indicators if fitted. From the wording it again seems that there is a single offence of not having the lamps, etc., as required, and using, causing or permitting offences arise accordingly.

Exemptions—maintenance

8.127   The main exemption from reg.23(1) is for a defective lamp or reflector fitted to a vehicle in use on a road between sunrise and sunset if such lamp or reflector became defective during the journey in progress or if arrangements have been made to remedy the defect with all reasonable expedition (reg.23(3)). It must be necessary to have made some arrangements even if garages are closed or it is a Bank Holiday. Arrangements with a garage are not stipulated and presumably arrangements through a relative or an employer or employee might be sufficient. It may be reasonable expedition to await an insurance company's permission even though the company is not as prompt in replying as one would wish.

These exemptions are applicable during daytime and therefore during seriously reduced visibility but not during the hours of darkness even though the defect arose in the middle of nowhere in the course of the journey. It has been held by a magistrates' court in respect of the similarly worded speedometer exemption (see §§ 8.31–4) that the defence would include a round journey, but not the return journey from a fixed destination when the defect occurred in the course of the outward journey.

8.128   There is an exemption in reg.23(3) from the maintenance of rear fog lamps on motor vehicles drawing trailers and on vehicles which are part of a combination of vehicles any part of which is not required to have rear fog lamps. There is also an exemption for lamps, reflectors and rear markings between sunrise and sunset fitted to combat vehicles (also reg.23(3)).

See also the exemption noted at § 8.118 above in relation to use by a vehicle examiner.

Further maintenance offences

8.129   Regulation 23 adds further that the lighting equipment, if fitted, has to be in good working order and, in the case of a lamp, clean. They must be so maintained that their aim will not cause undue dazzle or inconvenience to other persons using the road: reg.27.

Headlamps—keeping lit during darkness or seriously reduced visibility

8.130   It is an offence by reg.25 to use, cause or permit to be used on a road a vehicle fitted with obligatory dipped-beam headlamps unless every such lamp is kept lit during the hours of darkness (except on roads restricted for the purpose of s.81 of the Road Traffic Regulation Act 1984 with street lamps *actually illuminated* not more than 200yds apart (see further §§ 6.104 et seq.)) and in seriously reduced visibility.

Dim-dip lights do not satisfy reg.25.

Exemptions

Exemptions are provided where the main-beam headlamp(s) or the fog lamps are lit, where the vehicle is being towed or where the vehicle is being used to propel a snow plough: reg.25(2). Parked vehicles are also exempted, but see reg.24 (§ 8.134 below) regarding lighting of such vehicles, and reg.27 creating an offence of lighting certain lamps whilst a vehicle is parked. **8.131**

By reg.27 it is an offence to use or cause or permit to be used on a road a vehicle with a headlamp (dipped or main) (a) so as to cause undue dazzle or discomfort to other road users or (b) when parked. Parked must mean something more than merely stationary—see reg.24 and in particular reg.24(1)(b).

Position lamps, etc.—keeping lit during darkness or seriously reduced visibility

By reg.24 it is an offence to use, cause or permit to be used on a road any vehicle between sunset and sunrise or any vehicle which is in motion between sunrise and sunset in seriously reduced visibility unless every front position lamp, rear position lamp, rear registration plate lamp and side marker lamp required is kept lit and unobscured. **8.132**

It is also an offence to allow or cause or permit a vehicle to remain at rest on a road between sunset and sunrise unless these lamps are kept lit. For parking exemptions see below.

Trailers by themselves must have front position lamps fitted and lit and a solo motor bicycle must have a front position lamp fitted and lit in these circumstances, even though not otherwise required for these vehicles. Similarly a motor cycle combination with a front position lamp on the side-car must have a pair fitted and kept lit (reg.24(3)). From the wording it again seems that there are single offences of not having the various lamps lit and using, causing or permitting offences arise accordingly. **8.133**

Exemptions for parked vehicles

Exemptions for parked vehicles from the need to illuminate position lamps, rear registration plate lamps and side marker lamps are contained in reg.24(3), (5) and (9). In prescribed circumstances, parked vehicles are not required to display lights provided that the road in question is subject to a speed limit of 30mph or lower. The exemption only applies if the vehicle is parked so that its left or nearside is as close as may be, and parallel to, the edge of the carriageway. Where the street is one way only, the regulations allow the vehicle to be parked so that either its left or nearside is as close as may be to the left edge of the carriageway or its right or offside is as close as may be to the right edge of the carriageway. **8.134**

The exemption from lights only applies to passenger vehicles constructed or adapted to carry not more than eight passengers exclusive of the driver, goods vehicles having an unladen weight not exceeding 1,525kg, invalid carriages, motor cycles and pedal cycles (or tricycles). Front and rear lights must be displayed if the vehicle has an overhanging or projecting load to which reg.21 applies. Lights also must be displayed on vehicles to which a trailer is attached.

8.135 The exemption for a parked vehicle only applies if no part of the vehicle is within 10m of a junction whether that junction is on the same side of the road as the parked vehicle or not.

Schedule 22 to the 1989 Regulations (applied by reg.24(6)) provides a helpful diagram showing where unlit parking is not permitted near a junction. See also *Bunting v Holt* [1977] R.T.R. 373 and *R. v Derby Crown Court Ex p. Sewell* [1985] R.T.R. 251.

8.136 Regulation 24(5)(b) allows an exempted vehicle to park without lights in a recognised parking place or in a lay-by. Such places are:

(a) places set aside as parking places under an enactment or instrument;

(b) lay-bys indicated in accordance with diagram 1010 in Sch.6 to the Traffic Signs Regulations and General Directions 2002 (SI 2002/3113) (this diagram shows a longitudinal line to indicate the edge of the carriageway at a lay-by (or road junction although this is not material in this context));

(c) lay-bys where the surface is of a colour or texture which is different from that of the part of the carriageway of the road used primarily by through traffic; and

(d) lay-bys where the limits are marked out by a continuous (but not a dotted) strip of surface of a different colour or texture from that of the surface of the remainder of the carriageway of the road.

A vehicle is not exempted from showing lights in a parking place ((a) above) if it is parked "in a manner" which contravenes the provisions of an enactment or instrument relating to the parking place. The meaning of "manner" in this context may give rise to argument. It is possible that parking for an excess period would not be a contravention of the manner of parking. The purpose presumably is that the vehicle should be visible without lights and should therefore be parked in the normal way. There would be a contravention of the Lighting Regulations if the vehicle were parked in a different way from that specified in the instrument.

8.137 The earlier regulations which allowed parking lights to be displayed on one side of the vehicle have been revoked. The effect of this is that where lights are required by the regulations to be displayed on a parked vehicle, that vehicle is required to display all four lights, front and rear.

The above exemptions for parked vehicles only apply to vehicles in an area of 30mph or lower. They do not apply to lay-bys on other roads. A further exemption is provided in reg.24(9)(c), and is perhaps an obvious and appropriate one. It is where a vehicle is parked in an area on part of a highway on which roadworks are being carried out and which is bounded by amber lamps and other traffic signs so as to prevent the presence of the vehicle, its load or equipment being a danger to persons using the road.

Seriously reduced visibility

8.138 The seriously reduced visibility offences together with the exemptions have been incorporated in reg.24 and reg.25.

"Seriously reduced visibility" is not defined and seems to be essentially a question of fact. Examples will be fog, mist, snow storms, heavy rain storms, spray conditions, badly overcast weather. It is not restricted to poor weather conditions and might for instance include a poorly illuminated tunnel or a smoke cloud.

Earlier regulations referred to poor visibility conditions. In *Swift v Spence* [1982] R.T.R. 116, a case on the earlier regulations, the Divisional Court accepted a finding of justices that visibility down to between 20yds and 75yds in icy fog amounted to poor visibility conditions. The justices considered that, having regard to the nose-to-tail line of very slow and frequently stationary traffic, failure to use headlights was, in the particular circumstances, not a hazard and acquitted. (The defendant's car had sidelights on.) The Divisional Court held that there ought to have been a conviction as there was "no way under this regulation whereby it can be said that in some conditions there is an obligation to have sidelights on but not dipped headlights. It is dipped headlights or nothing." It is submitted that while the decision is correct this statement may be misleading, as both the former and the present regulations permit either a main beam or a dipped beam on headlamps for this purpose. **8.139**

In conditions of seriously reduced visibility the driver may use instead of his headlamps two front fog lights so fitted that the outermost part of the illuminated area of each lamp in the pair is not more than 400mm from the outer edge. One fog lamp may be used as an alternative to headlamps where only one headlamp is fitted or in the case of solo motor bicycles or motor bicycle combinations even though fitted with a pair of headlamps.

Fog lamps

The requirements for, and exceptions regarding, rear fog lamps are in Schs 1 and 11 to the 1989 Regulations. Most vehicles first used on or after April 1, 1980 must have at least one rear fog lamp. Where front fog lamps are fitted, they must comply with Sch.6. **8.140**

A front or rear fog lamp may not be used, etc., on a vehicle on a road other than in conditions of seriously reduced visibility (as to this see § 8.130 above) nor when a vehicle is parked, nor so as to cause undue dazzle or discomfort to other persons using the road. Any contravention will constitute offences under reg.27. It will be an offence therefore to use these fog lamps during daylight or darkness unless the exceptional visibility conditions exist. Presumably there will be no contravention in continuing to use them where the adverse visibility conditions exist but in a patchy form, providing there is no undue dazzle or discomfort.

Improper use of lamps, etc.

By reg.27 it is an offence to use, cause or permit to be used on a road any vehicle on which a lamp hazard warning signal or warning beacon is used in a manner prohibited by column 3 of the table to the regulation. In particular, in addition to the headlamps and fog lamps prohibitions already set out under these headings above, hazard warning signals may only be used: **8.141**

    (a) to warn persons using the road of a temporary obstruction when the vehicle is at rest;

    (b) on a motorway or unrestricted dual carriageway, to warn following drivers of a need to slow down due to a temporary obstruction ahead; or

(c) in the case of a bus, to summon assistance for the driver or any person acting as a conductor or inspector on the vehicle or, where a school bus has the prescribed signs fitted, to indicate that children are in the process of entering or leaving that bus.

Reversing lamps may only be used, etc., for the purpose of reversing.

LIGHTING: PROCEEDINGS AND PENALTIES

Generally

8.142   The Road Vehicles Lighting Regulations 1989 are made under s.41 of the 1988 Act in respect of all vehicles save cycles not being motor vehicles and the maximum penalty for a contravention is a fine of level 4 if committed in respect of a goods vehicle or a vehicle adapted to carry more than eight passengers. For other vehicles, the maximum fine is level 3: s.42(b).

In respect of cycles not being motor vehicles the 1989 Regulations are made under s.81 of the 1988 Act and the maximum penalty for a contravention is a fine of level 3. As to the definition of cycles not being motor vehicles, see § 1.22; this definition seems to include electrically assisted pedal cycles.

8.143   The maximum penalty for an offence under reg.9 of the Road Vehicles (Display of Registration Marks) Regulations 2001 (SI 2001/561) (lighting of rear registration plates) is a fine of level 3.

Lighting: penalties

Offence	Mode of trial	Section *	Imprisonment	Level of fine	Disqualification	Penalty points	Endorsement code	Sentencing guideline ‡
Driving without lights	Summary	Road Vehicles Lighting Regs and s.41	—	4 if goods vehicle or vehicle adapted to carry more than 8 passengers: otherwise 3	—	—	—	Fine band A If in course of business Driver or owner-driver¶ Fine band A Owner-company Fine band B
Other lighting offences (including number plate lamps)	Summary	Road Vehicles Lighting Regs and s.41	—	4 if goods vehicle or vehicle adapted to carry more than 8 passengers: otherwise 3	—	—	—	—
Lighting offences (cycles not being motor vehicles)	Summary	Road Vehicles Lighting Regs and s.81	—	3	—	—	—	—

Offence	Mode of trial	Section *	Imprisonment	Level of fine	Disqualification	Penalty points	Endorsement code	Sentencing guideline ‡
Lighting of rear registration plates	Summary	Road Vehicles (Display of Registration Marks) Regs and ss.22, 57 Vehicle Excise and Registration Act 1994	—	3†	—	—	—	—

* Road Traffic Act 1988 unless otherwise specified.

† As to how this is arrived at, see § 12.116.

‡ **Note:** Fine bands "A", "B" and "C" represent respectively 50%, 100% and 150% of relevant weekly income. A timely guilty plea should attract a discount. See Appendix 3.

¶ Where "owner-driver", consider 25% uplift.

Test Certificates and Testing

Generally

Sections 45–48 of the Road Traffic Act 1988 (as amended) contain provisions **8.145**
as to test certificates for vehicles, and ss.67–73 and the Road Traffic (Foreign
Vehicles) Act 1972 as to the roadside testing of vehicles. These are discussed
below, and the penalties for offences under these provisions will be found at the
end of the section.

Test certificates

Section 47 of the 1988 Act requires every motor vehicle first registered more **8.146**
than three years before the time at which it is being used on the road to pass a test
under s.47. Motor vehicles used for the carriage of passengers and with more
than eight seats excluding the driver's seat, taxis as defined and ambulances as
specifically defined, must be tested after one year. This will apply to many minibuses. Section 47 ensures that vehicles manufactured abroad more than three
years before their use on a road also require test certificates once they are brought
into the United Kingdom and registered here. Sections 47 and 48 bind the Crown
(s.183).

The Motor Vehicles (Tests) Regulations 1981 (SI 1981/1694) as amended apply and regulate the procedure, etc. There are exemptions listed in reg.6 from the
operation of s.47, for inter alia locomotives, motor tractors, track-laying vehicles,
agricultural motor vehicles, goods vehicles with a design gross weight exceeding
3,500kg, articulated vehicles (other than articulated buses), works trucks, pedestrian controlled vehicles, invalid vehicles of less than 306kg (if a Government
supplied invalid vehicle, one which does not exceed 510kg), certain hackney carriages in London and some other towns, licensed private hire cars, vehicles for
export or belonging to a visiting force or certain United Kingdom personnel,
certain Northern Ireland vehicles, certain police vehicles and certain vehicles
temporarily in Great Britain. Vehicles on certain small islands and vehicles where
minimal use of the road is established are also exempt. There are further exemptions for the use of special types authorised under s.44, the use of vehicles
imported into Great Britain driven to the importer's or driver's residence, the
towing away of abandoned vehicles under the Refuse Disposal (Amenity) Act
1978, or illegally parked vehicles by the police or local authority under the Road
Traffic Regulation Act 1984, or the detention or seizure of vehicles by the police
or HM Revenue & Customs. Motor traders may also use a vehicle under or after
repair by them.

Schedule 2 to the 1981 Regulations deals with the prescribed statutory require- **8.147**
ments as to the carrying out of tests. The manner and conditions of carrying out
tests will in future be the subject of instructions and guidance given administra-
tively to authorised examiners. Speed limiters are now testable items in respect of
coaches to which they are required to be fitted.

Under the 1981 Regulations public service vehicles are not exempt from tests.
A person authorised by the Secretary of State may issue a temporary exemption
certificate for up to three months for certain unexpected emergencies other than
vehicle breakdowns or mechanical defects or non-delivery of spare parts, in the
case of a public service vehicle adapted to carry more than eight passengers:
s.48(4) of the 1988 Act. As to "adapted" and "passengers", see §§ 1.29 and 1.117.

8.148   Section 47(2)(b) requires a vehicle manufactured more than three years ago and used on roads in the United Kingdom to have a test certificate whether or not it has been registered in Great Britain and whether or not it was manufactured in Great Britain. However, reg.6(1)(xi) exempts vehicles from the requirement for a test certificate if they are temporarily in Great Britain and displaying a registration mark mentioned in reg.5 of the Motor Vehicles (International Circulation) Regulations 1971 (SI 1971/937). The exemption applies where less than 12 months have elapsed since the vehicle was last brought into Great Britain. Apart from the other exemptions for imported vehicles referred to above there are no other exemptions for imported vehicles and no reciprocal arrangements for recognising EC or foreign tests.

The most common exemption relied on by defendants charged with using a vehicle without a certificate is that the vehicle was proceeding to or from a test (reg.6(2)(a)). It is sometimes argued by a defendant that he is exempted because he is taking his car to a testing station garage "by previous arrangement" under reg.6(2)(a)(i) even though he has not made a previous arrangement because the garage has advertised to the effect that tests can be given without prior notice. Where such an argument is put forward, many magistrates' courts have nevertheless convicted, taking the view that "previous arrangement" requires the car owner to have previously contacted the testing station to confirm the test for his car.

8.149   Schedule 2 to the 1981 Test Regulations sets out the prescribed requirements for the testing of motor vehicles. Test certificates under s.47 are issued annually but if a vehicle is retested within the last month of an existing test certificate s.48(2) allows the new test certificate to expire on the anniversary of the expiry of the old certificate. Similarly, a certificate issued in the month before one is first needed is treated as if issued on the due date: s.48(1A). For public service vehicles adapted to carry more than eight passengers, the one-month period in s.48(2) and s.48(1A) is extended to two months: s.48(5).

Test certificates are obtainable only from "authorised examiners" and other inspectors set out in s.45(3) (as amended). Where a test certificate is refused the tester is required to issue a notification of refusal stating the grounds of refusal and a person aggrieved may appeal to the Secretary of State, who shall cause a further examination of the vehicle and either issue a test certificate or his own notice of refusal (s.45(4)). Evidence from records of vehicle examinations will be admissible in evidence for certain purposes: new s.46B as inserted by s.4 of the Road Traffic (Vehicle Testing) Act 1999.

8.150   A person who uses, or causes or permits a vehicle to be used without a test certificate commits an offence under s.47(1). No offence arises from mere failure to submit the vehicle to a test. It is use on the road which gives rise to an offence.

In a case at quarter sessions *Elliott v Grey* [1960] 1 Q.B. 367 was applied to a vehicle which was left in a cul-de-sac without rear wheels and a rear axle and the defendant's conviction of "using" the vehicle without a test certificate was upheld, but in *Hewer v Cutler* [1974] R.T.R. 155 it was held that a car parked on a road with disconnected gearbox linkage so that the car could be neither driven nor moved did not require a test certificate. *Elliott v Grey* was distinguished and it was doubted whether the test as to whether a car requires a test certificate is the same as the test to be applied in determining whether an insurance certificate is required. But in *Eden v Mitchell* [1975] R.T.R. 425 *Hewer v Cutler* was explained as a case where the car had been completely immobilised and thus was incapable of being driven. Reversing the justices who had acquitted the defendant of "using" a motor vehicle with defective tyres because he had said he had not intended to drive it, the court said that the true test that should be applied in the case of a stationary vehicle left on the highway was whether steps had been taken to make it impossible for a driver to drive the vehicle (see further as to the terms "using", "causing" or "permitting" a vehicle to be used, Chapter 1).

Sections 173 and 175 (forging and issue of false documents, see Chapter 16) apply in respect of test certificates. By s.165 (which extends to Crown drivers) test certificates must be produced to constables. It is no defence to a charge under s.165 that the driver would find it difficult if not impossible to obtain the test certificate from the owner (*Davey v Towle* [1973] R.T.R. 328), but this decision must now be read bearing in mind the amendment now enacted in s.165(4)(c) of the 1988 Act. **8.151**

The amendment extends the period for production to seven days and also provides a defence:

(a) if the test certificate is produced at the specified police station as soon as is reasonably practicable or

(b) if it is not reasonably practicable for it to be produced at the specified police station before the day on which proceedings are commenced.

For this purpose the commencement of proceedings is specifically defined as the laying of the information. This presumably means not until the charge is presented to the court or court office even though the defendant has been charged at a police station.

What is reasonably practicable is a question of fact. The same expression is used in the failing to report an accident provisions and the cases noted at §§ 7.13 et seq. may assist. While it is not binding, a magistrates' court has held that awaiting a duplicate document may amount to a defence under the section if it has only recently been lost, but not if it has been lost for some time. A person should keep the documents in a safe place available for production and should take immediate action to replace a lost document in order to bring himself within the "reasonably practicable" defence. Section 101 of the Magistrates' Courts Act 1980 applies and the onus of proving the defence will be on the defendant on the balance of probabilities (*R. v Carr-Briant* [1943] K.B. 607). **8.152**

Goods vehicles

Unlike the testing of vehicles under ss.45 and 46 of the 1988 Act, the testing and plating of goods vehicles under ss.49–53 is carried out by the Secretary of State for Transport at government testing stations. The principal regulations are the Goods Vehicles (Plating and Testing) Regulations 1988 (SI 1988/1478, as amended). Under the regulations, after the first examination vehicles must be submitted for test annually. Schedule 2 to the regulations lists the vehicles which are exempt from the necessity of plating and test certificates. Included are tower wagons as defined in the Vehicle Excise and Registration Act 1994 Sch.1 para.8 or ibid. Sch.2 para.17. In *Anderson and Heeley Ltd v Paterson* [1975] R.T.R. 248 a van fitted with an extendible high loader was held not to be a tower wagon as it could and did carry a load contrary to one of the requirements of the definition in what is now the 1994 Act. **8.153**

The exemption in Sch.2 does not extend to dual-purpose vehicles which are constructed or adapted to form part of an articulated vehicle unless otherwise exempt. The exemption for engineering plant extends to motor vehicles and trailers; which are not engineering plant, but are movable plant or equipment especially designed and constructed for the special purposes of engineering operations. They must presumably be both designed and constructed. The paragraph specifies that they must not be constructed primarily to carry a load. The decision of the Divisional Court in *DPP v Ryan* (1991) 155 J.P. 456 is important in that it relates to a number of different aspects of the law relating to goods vehicles. In so far as the text of this paragraph is concerned, it suffices to say that the "engineering plant" exemption exempting such vehicles from the requirements of the Goods Vehicles (Plating and Testing) Regulations 1988 did not apply. The vehicle in question did not have inter alia a goods vehicle plating certificate. It was used solely for winch and lifting work in connection with the respondents' business of drilling water wells. It carried two winches, a small one at the front which was fixed to the chassis and a larger one at the back attached to the vehicle. The rear of the vehicle had been modified to give a tailboard which dropped flat in order to provide a working platform. Although the large winch could only be powered from an external source it could only be used in conjunction with the lorry as modified.

8.154 Regulation 3 of the 1988 Regulations applied the definition of "engineering plant" found in the Road Vehicles (Construction and Use) Regulations 1986, namely:

> "(a) movable plant or equipment being a motor vehicle or trailer specially designed and constructed for the special purposes of engineering operations, and which cannot, owing to the requirements of those purposes, comply with all the requirements of these Regulations and which is not constructed primarily to carry a load other than a load being either excavated materials raised from the ground by apparatus on the motor vehicle or trailer or materials which the vehicle or trailer is specially designed to treat while carried thereon ..."

8.155 Otton J., in the course of a long and detailed judgment, stated that the proper approach is to consider whether the degree of alteration was so great as to bring the vehicle outside the definition of a vehicle constructed for the carrying of goods and within the definition of engineering plant "specially designed and constructed for the special purposes of engineering operations". If the vehicle has been constructed for carrying goods it will require very substantial and dramatic alteration for it to lose its original identity as a HGV. His Lordship continued by saying that the alterations, although considerable, could not be categorised as substantial or dramatic. The attachment of the two bars for the use of a pulley and clock, the attachment of the winches and the modification of the tailboard did not cause the vehicle to lose its initial identity. At best the vehicle had undergone modifications to enable it to be used for the sole purpose of drilling and maintenance of water wells, and still required an external source of power to operate the large winch. It could not be said to have been "especially [*sic*] designed or constructed for the special purpose of engineering operations". There was no evidence to show that in its condition it could not be equipped with a Ministry plate securely fixed to the vehicle in the cab, or undergo or pass a goods vehicle test for the purpose of certification. It was held therefore that the justices were incorrect in ruling that the vehicle was within a class to which the exemption provision applied.

In *DPP v Derbyshire (Derek)* [1994] R.T.R. 351 the facts were that a two-axled rigid bodied vehicle with a gross design weight of 16,260kg had a boiler attached to its chassis and was used for conveying molten asphalt to sites where the asphalt was distributed on to floor surfaces by means of buckets. The user of the vehicle claimed that it was exempt from the 1988 Regulations, asserting that the exemption contained in Sch.2, para.4 of the 1988 Regulations applied, namely: **8.156**

> "... plant, not being engineering plant, which is movable plant ... being a motor vehicle ... (not constructed primarily to carry a load) especially designed and constructed for the special purposes of engineering operations."

The justices found that the vehicle had been constructed for two purposes: transporting asphalt and laying floors. The Divisional Court hearing an appeal from their decision found that some of their findings were inconsistent, but had they considered the question whether the primary purpose for which the vehicle had been constructed was that of carrying a load, they would have inevitably answered in the affirmative. That would have concluded the matter, as the vehicle would be seen to have fallen outside the terms of the exemption.

A scrap vehicle is not a disabled vehicle, so a goods vehicle used to transport a scrap vehicle is not a breakdown vehicle exempted by Sch.2 (*Gibson v Nutter* [1984] R.T.R. 8). As to the meaning of "breakdown vehicle", see § 1.53. **8.157**

Section 49(5) provides that tests may be prescribed where recording instruments (tachographs) are required to be installed.

Using a goods vehicle on a road, or causing or permitting it to be so used, without the necessary test certificate and using, etc., a goods vehicle without a plating certificate are offences under s.53(2) and (1) respectively. It is also an offence to use a goods vehicle on a road, or cause or permit it to be so used, with an alteration to the vehicle or equipment without the Secretary of State for Transport having been notified of the alteration as required by the regulations (s.53(3)). It is a defence to s.53(3) that the alteration was not specified in the relevant plating certificate (s.53(4)).

Section 173 applies in respect of goods vehicle test certificates and plating certificates, and s.174(2) applies to the supply of information or documents for the purposes of ss.53–60 and s.63 (see Chapter 16). **8.158**

The display of the Ministry plate issued under ss.51–53 is governed by reg.70 of the Road Vehicles (Construction and Use) Regulations 1986. However, under that regulation the plate in the case of vehicles to which the Motor Vehicles (Type Approval for Goods Vehicles) (Great Britain) Regulations 1982 (SI 1982/1271) apply must be fixed 14 days after issue. This is because the plate will be issued as part of the certification under these regulations and not as a result of the first examinations under ss.51–53.

Roadside tests

Section 67 of the 1988 Act enables an authorised examiner to make a roadside test of a motor vehicle as to its brakes, silencer, steering gear, tyres, emission of smoke or fumes and lighting equipment and reflectors and noise. "Authorised examiner" for the purposes of this section may include both a constable appointed as such by his chief constable and a person appointed by the police authority for **8.159** the purposes of this section acting under the directions of the chief constable and a traffic warden: Functions of Traffic Wardens Order 1970 (S1 1970/1958). The driver may elect for the test to be deferred unless the constable thinks that the vehicle is so defective that the test should be carried out forthwith or that the vehicle has caused an accident (s.67(8)). The option extends to him only and not to the owner, nor need the examiner tell the driver of his option (*Brown v McIndoe* 1963 S.L.T. 233). Failing to comply with the requirements of the section or obstructing an examiner is an offence.

Prosecution for contravention of a construction and use regulation as to tyres or brakes does not depend on whether the evidence as to the contravention has been obtained as a result of a test by an authorised examiner (*Stoneley v Richardson* [1973] R.T.R. 229; *Phillips v Thomas* [1974] R.T.R. 28). Similarly, production of a traffic examiner's authority is not a prerequisite of a conviction of being overweight contrary to reg.80 of the Construction and Use Regulations (*Wurzal v Reader Bros Ltd* [1974] R.T.R. 383).

8.160   The statutory authority for vehicle examiners is contained in s.66A of the Road Traffic Act 1988. The Secretary of State appoints such examiners as he considers necessary for carrying out functions under the 1988 Act Pt II, the Goods Vehicles (Licensing of Operators) Act 1995, the Public Passenger Vehicles Act 1981, the Transport Act 1968, and any other enactment. An examiner may test a motor vehicle to ascertain whether the following requirements are complied with:

> "(i) the construction and use requirements, and
> (ii) the requirement that the condition of the vehicle is not such that its use on a road would involve a danger of injury to any person."

In order to test a vehicle, the examiner may require the driver to comply with his reasonable instructions, and may drive the vehicle.

8.161   As well as the power to test a vehicle on a road given to an authorised examiner, the narrower category of vehicle examiner may inspect at any time a goods vehicle, a public service vehicle or a motor vehicle not a public service vehicle but adapted to carry more than eight passengers. A vehicle examiner or a constable in uniform may require such a vehicle to be taken to a place where it can be inspected as long as that place is not more than five miles away. The requirement is to a person in charge of the vehicle and the vehicle must be stationary on a road at the time: s.68(4). For some of the vehicles, the examiner may also enter the premises where the vehicle is kept: s.68(1)(b) and proviso to s.68(6). It is an offence to obstruct an examiner using his powers under s.68(1) or to refuse or neglect to comply with a requirement under s.68(4).

Where a vehicle is tested, either as part of the formal testing programme or on the road, power is given to prohibit its further use: s.69 of the 1988 Act. This may be exercised by a vehicle examiner if, owing to any defects in the vehicle, it is, or is likely to become, unfit for service. The power may be exercised by an authorised constable if, owing to any defects in the vehicle, continuing use would involve a danger of injury to any person.

8.162   The prohibition on the use of a vehicle may be:

> (a) absolute; or
> (b) for a specified purpose; or
> (c) except for a specified purpose.

The examiner or constable must give immediate written notice of the extent of the prohibition which will take effect immediately where driving the vehicle would involve a danger of injury to any person. A similar provision applies where a goods vehicle or a motor vehicle adapted to carry more than eight passengers has been weighed and found to be in breach of various descriptions of weight regulations: s.70. The power to prohibit use may be exercised by a vehicle examiner, or by an authorised constable or by an person authorised by a highway authority for this purpose. It is an offence to drive a vehicle contrary to a notice under s.69 or s.70, or to cause or permit a vehicle to be so driven: s.71. It is also an offence to fail to comply with a direction given to remove an overweight vehicle given in connection with the exercise of the s.70 power: s.70(3) and s.71.

Foreign goods vehicles

The Road Traffic (Foreign Vehicles) Act 1972 (as amended) gives additional powers to examiners, authorised inspectors and authorised persons (defined in s.7) to issue prohibition orders in respect of foreign goods vehicles and foreign public service vehicles. Where the examiner, authorised inspector or authorised person exercise any function listed in Sch.1, he may issue a prohibition order should there be *any* contravention of any of the regulations or enactments in Sch.2 to the Act. Schedule 2 includes the whole of the Construction and Use Regulations, and certain requirements relating to lights on vehicles, operators' licences, drivers' hours and tachograph records, and regulations under s.57 of the Goods Vehicles (Licensing of Operators) Act 1995.   **8.163**

A prohibition order may also be made if the driver obstructs the examiner, authorised inspector or authorised person or fails to comply with requirements made by the examiner, etc.: s.1(2)(a), (3)(a). A prohibition order may also be made to prohibit the driving of goods vehicles not complying with the requirements of the Goods Vehicles (Community Authorisations) Regulations 1992 (SI 1992/3077): Goods Vehicles (Community Authorisations) (Modification of the Road Traffic (Foreign Vehicles) Act 1972) Regulations 2002 (SI 2002/1415).

Any person who drives a vehicle or causes or permits one to be driven in contravention of such a prohibition or does not comply with the direction made as a result of a prohibition order commits an offence (s.3(1)), and can be arrested by a constable without warrant if falling within s.24 of the Police and Criminal Evidence Act 1984. The constable is also given powers of impounding a vehicle where he suspects an offence under s.3(1). He may authorise an appropriate person to remove the vehicle for that purpose (s.3(3)–(6)).   **8.164**

A foreign goods vehicle or foreign public service vehicle is one brought into the United Kingdom and not registered in the United Kingdom (s.7), and any vehicle not displaying a licence or trade plates issued under the Vehicle Excise and Registration Act 1994 shall be presumed unless the contrary be proved not to be registered in the United Kingdom (s.7(4)).

Regulation (EC) 1100/2008 has, with effect from November 14, 2008, repealed and replaced Regulation (EEC) 4060/89. It codifies the previous Regulation and provides for the elimination of controls formerly performed at the frontiers of the Member States in the field of road transport, etc. Such controls may however still be applied as part of normal control procedures within a Member State. The annex to the 2008 Regulation contains a list of the relevant controls.   **8.165**

TEST CERTIFICATES: PENALTIES

Generally

8.166   Using, or causing or permitting a vehicle to be used, without a test certificate contrary to s.47 is punishable by a fine of level 3 save that the maximum penalty for s.47 offences in the case of a vehicle adapted to carry more than eight passengers is a fine of level 4. This will include some private vehicles and many minibuses. As to "adapted" and whether "passengers" includes the driver, see § 1.29 and § 1.117. It is submitted there that it does not in the case of public service vehicles. The position for private vehicles is less certain but there seems to be a tendency to distinguish between drivers and passengers. It is not punishable by imprisonment, nor may disqualification, endorsement or penalty points be ordered. The Magistrates' Court Sentencing Guidelines are set out in the table at § 8.168 (see further Appendix 3).

By virtue of the Fixed Penalty Offences Order 2003 (SI 2003/1253), a contravention of s.47 is a fixed penalty offence. Using a goods vehicle on a road, or causing or permitting it to be so used, without the necessary test certificate (s.53(2)) is subject to a fine of level 4 and using, etc., a goods vehicle without a plating certificate (s.53(1)) to a fine of level 3. Using, etc., a goods vehicle with an alteration not notified to the Secretary of State for Transport (s.53(3)) is punishable with a fine of level 3. None of the offences under s.53 carries endorsement or disqualification.

8.167   The offence of obstructing an examiner carrying out a test is punishable with a fine of level 3 (s.67). Driving a goods vehicle in contravention of a prohibition order under s.71 or refusing to proceed to a place of inspection is punishable with a fine of level 5, and any person who drives a vehicle or causes or permits one to be driven in contravention of a prohibition under s.3(1) of the Road Traffic (Foreign Vehicles) Act 1972 or does not comply with the direction made as a result of a prohibition order is liable on summary conviction to a fine of level 5. There is no power to order endorsement, disqualification or penalty points for any of these offences.

An offence against s.165 of the 1988 Act (production of certificates) is punishable with a fine of level 3.

Test certificates: penalties

Offence	Mode of trial	Section *	Imprisonment	Level of fine	Disqualification	Penalty points	Endorsement code	Sentencing guideline †
No test certificate (using, causing or permitting)	Summary	s.47	—	3	—	—	—	Up to 3.5 tonnes Fine band A If in course of business Driver or owner-driver‡ Fine band A Owner-company Fine band B
No test certificate (using, causing or permitting) for vehicle adapted to carry more than 8 passengers	Summary	s.47	—	4	—	—	—	—
No goods vehicle test certificate (using, causing or permitting)	Summary	s.53(2)	—	4	—	—	—	Driver or owner-driver‡ Fine band B Owner-company Fine band C

Offence	Mode of trial	Section *	Imprisonment	Level of fine	Disqualification	Penalty points	Endorsement code	Sentencing guideline †
Failing to produce test certificate or goods vehicle test certificate	Summary	s.165	—	3	—	—	—	Fine band A
No goods vehicle plating certificate (using, causing or permitting)	Summary	s.53(1)	—	3	—	—	—	Driver or owner-driver‡ Fine band A Owner-company Fine band B
Goods vehicle with alteration not notified to Secretary of State (using, causing or permitting)	Summary	s.53(3)	—	3	—	—	—	—
Obstructing test by authorised examiner or failing to comply with requirement	Summary	s.67	—	3	—	—	—	—

Offence	Mode of trial	Section *	Imprisonment	Level of fine	Disqualification	Penalty points	Endorsement code	Sentencing guideline †
Driving vehicle in contravention of prohibition or failing to proceed to place of inspection, etc.	Summary	s.71	—	5	—	—	—	
		s.3(1) Road Traffic (Foreign Vehicles) Act 1972	—	5	—	—	—	

* Road Traffic Act 1988 unless otherwise specified.

† **Note**: See Appendix 3.

‡ Where "owner-driver", consider 25% uplift.

CHAPTER 9

PROTECTION OF DRIVERS AND PASSENGERS

CONTENTS

GENERALLY

9.01   Offences for adults not wearing seat belts arise under s.14 of the Road Traffic Act 1988 (as amended) and regulations made thereunder. The current regulations are the Motor Vehicles (Wearing of Seat Belts) Regulations 1993 (SI 1993/176) (as amended). These provisions are considered first, followed by those concerning children under 14. With regard to the wearing of seat belts or other restraints by children under 14, the offences arise under s.15 of the 1988 Act, as amended. There are separate statutory provisions depending on whether the child is in the front or the rear of the motor vehicle. This complication means that each has to be considered separately. The Motor Vehicles (Wearing of Seat Belts) Regulations 1993 also regulate children under 14 in the rear (see, in particular, Pt III). Section 15(3A) protects certain vulnerable children by prohibiting the carrying of small children in the rear without wearing seat belts or restraints if they are available in the front. The Motor Vehicles (Wearing of Seat Belts by Children in Front Seats) Regulations 1993 (SI 1993/31) regulate children under 14 in front seats. Although it is not altogether logical, the provisions are considered in this sequence, as it is easier to follow the regulations in this order. Clarity is not assisted by the duplication of some provisions in both regulations.

In all cases the regulations provide for various exemptions. As there are exemptions depending on availability, it is also necessary to ascertain which seats have to be fitted with seat belts or an equivalent restraint. Failure to have these fitted where required will normally be an offence under the Construction and Use Regulations. These aspects, including definitions, are considered after the discussion of the offences and the exemptions. All the seat belt offences apply at present only for motor vehicles and not for other vehicles but different provisions apply to different vehicles as described in the text and it is always important to check this aspect.

9.02   Offences relating to motor cycle helmets and other motor cycle head-worn safety appliances arise under ss.16 and 17 of the 1988 Act and regulations made thereunder. Offences relating to the carrying of passengers on motor cycles, other than breaches of the learner driver provisions, arise under s.23 of the 1988 Act. All these offences together with certain linked safety legislation are considered after the seat belt provisions. Procedures and penalties are dealt with at the end of the chapter.

SEAT BELTS

Wearing of seat belts by persons of 14 and over

Section 14 of the 1988 Act provides for the making of regulations for the wearing of seat belts. The regulations are the Motor Vehicles (Wearing of Seat Belts) Regulations 1993 (SI 1993/176) (as amended) which are made thereunder.   **9.03**

In relation to a person aged 14 or over, it is an offence under s.14(3) (applying reg.5 of the Wearing of Seat Belts Regulations 1993) to *drive a motor vehicle* without wearing an adult seat belt. It is an offence under the same provisions to *ride* in a *front or rear seat* of a *motor vehicle* without wearing an adult seat belt.

While the decision is not binding, a magistrates' court has found that "wearing" includes "having properly fastened". Compare the protective helmet regulations where there is an express requirement that the helmet must be securely fastened. The first sentence of this paragraph was quoted to the court in *DPP v Shaw* [1993] R.T.R. 200. The facts in that case were that the defendant had fastened the belt which was of the inertia type laterally across his chest but he had purchased and fitted a clip to the belt near to the top anchor point on the door pillar which allowed the belt to be worn loosely, hanging down vertically to the waist before crossing to the fixed point. The justices had acquitted the defendant. The prosecutor before the Divisional Court accepted that the clip would not have been illegal if it had merely adjusted the tension by an inch or two, but maintained that in this case the way it was used impeded the belt from being worn properly.   **9.04**

The court said that it did not accept the argument that the belt had to be worn properly in what was described as the approved manner. The question was: as it was worn, was it a belt intended to be worn by a person in a vehicle and designed to prevent or lessen injury to its wearer in the event of an accident. If in fact it were the case that a clip was employed which did not prevent the belt coming into operation so preventing or lessening injury, then the court could not see anything wrong with its use. It was essentially a matter of fact.

As to the nature of an "adult belt", see "Definitions", below.   **9.05**

Aiding and abetting

Notwithstanding any enactment or rule of law (e.g. aiding and abetting) only the principal offender, i.e. the person actually breaking the s.14 seat belt law relating to the wearing of seat belts by persons of 14 and over, is to be guilty (s.14(3)). If the driver and front seat passenger are both not wearing seat belts, both may be prosecuted as principals but cannot be prosecuted for aiding and abetting each other. If the front seat passenger is not wearing a belt, the driver cannot be prosecuted under s.14(3) if he himself is wearing a belt. Compare the position under s.15 where, if the passenger is under 14 and not wearing a belt the driver commits an offence under s.15(1) (front seats) or s.15(3) (rear seats) and a child of 10 or more years of age can in theory be prosecuted for aiding and abetting. However, any prospect of the prosecution of a child would be likely to be theoretical because of the advice against such prosecutions under the principle in *R. v Tyrell* [1894] 1 Q.B. 710, which is to the effect that prosecutions should not be brought for aiding and abetting where the alleged offender is the vulnerable child the statute sets out to protect.   **9.06**

Persons 14 and over: non-availability of seat belts

9.07   The seat belt requirements do not apply if there is no adult belt provided for the driver's seat, or available for persons of 14 and over riding in the front or the rear respectively (see reg.6(3)). This means in effect that a driver need only wear one if it is fitted. So far as passengers are concerned, the wording is such that if there is an adult belt available in the front, a front passenger must move across to use it and similarly a rear passenger must move across if there is one available in the rear, but there is no need for a person to transfer to the front or to the rear. Front fittings were introduced before rear fittings.

Under the existing legislation, while there are special provisions for children, there is nothing in law, in view of the wording of reg.6(3), to prevent extra passengers being carried in either the front or the rear unless perhaps it could be said that an offence has been committed of carrying a dangerous number of passengers or carrying passengers in a dangerous manner contrary to s.40A of the 1988 Act. Subject to this a large group of persons over 13 will not be prevented from travelling together simply because there are more people than seat belts. It will be for the occupants to decide who should be protected. A failure to wear a seat belt may however have consequences in civil legal proceedings.

9.08   The meaning of the non-availability exemption is further elaborated in Sch.2 to the Wearing of Seat Belts Regulations 1993, covering both adults and children. In summary, the seat must be unavailable because it is otherwise properly occupied in accordance with the legal requirements, that is, by a person properly wearing a belt or appropriate child restraint, or medically exempt, or there is an inappropriate child restraint in the way which cannot be removed without tools, or the seat is specially designed to be adjusted and has been adjusted for goods or personal effects, preventing the seat belt use, and it would not be reasonably practicable for the items to be carried in the vehicle without the adjustment. A seat belt is not available if it would not be practicable for the person in question to wear the relevant belt by reason of his disability (Sch.2, para.3(e)).

Persons 14 and over: non-compliance seat belts exemption

9.09   A seat is regarded as provided with an available adult seat belt if the belt is fixed so that it can be worn by the occupier. By reg.2(7) of the Wearing of Seat Belts Regulations 1993, a seat is not regarded as so provided if it is an inertia belt locked by a steep incline or if the adult belt of any kind does not comply with reg.48 of the Road Vehicles (Construction and Use) Regulations 1986 (maintenance of seat belts and anchorage points). There is no such exemption where the anchorage point does not comply; reg.48, by para.1, applies to reg.47 seat belts.

In some instances, seat belts have been deliberately made difficult to wear, either by pushing them behind the seat or by damage. If the seat belt is not maintained, an offence is committed contrary to reg.48 of the Road Vehicles (Construction and Use) Regulations 1986. If it can be worn, even with difficulty, it is submitted that the person is obliged to do so or the "failure to wear" offence will be committed. A seat is to be regarded as provided with an adult seat belt (subject to the provisions of reg.2(7)), if it is so fixed that it can be worn (reg.2(6)). One problem is that in the case of persons of 14 and over, those responsible for causing the difficulty cannot be prosecuted as aiders and abettors.

Persons 14 and over: general exemptions from wearing seat belts

9.10 There are a number of general exemptions from the seat belt requirements for persons of 14 and over (see regs.5 and 6 of the Wearing of Seat Belts Regulations 1993, as amended). There is no requirement for persons riding on two-wheeled motor cycles with or without a side-car (reg.5). The exemptions under reg.6 include delivery persons, persons reversing, taxi and private hire vehicle drivers, police (and persons in vehicles being used for prisoner escort purposes), fire-fighters, driving test examiners in certain circumstances and persons *riding* in vehicles under trade plates investigating or remedying mechanical faults and *riding* in processions. The wording should be studied in each case (see below).

The delivery exemption applies only to vehicles constructed or adapted (see Chapter 1) for carrying goods. It applies to the driver and to any passenger, but it only applies while on a journey not exceeding 50m. That journey must be being undertaken in order to deliver or collect any thing. The previous requirement of a "round" has gone and been replaced by the short journey limit. If any stages in that journey exceed 50m, then the exemption will not apply at that time only to the times when the journey between stops does not exceed 50m.

9.11 The reversing exemption applies to a person who is driving a vehicle. It also applies to a qualified driver supervising a learner driver who is performing a manoeuvre which includes reversing. As the exemption refers to the person who is driving, it would not extend to any other passenger (except the supervisor of a learner driver) even though the passenger were assisting and giving advice regarding clearance or other aspects of the manoeuvre. The exemption covers a "manoeuvre which includes reversing". It is not therefore limited to when the vehicle is in reverse and it would be a question of fact as to when the manoeuvre began and ended.

The taxi exemption only applies while the taxi is on hire business and the equivalent private hire vehicle exemption only when the vehicle is being used to carry a passenger for hire. Note the definitions of taxi and private hire vehicle and the different exemption applicable to each. A taxi is, by the Transport Act 1985 s.13(3), a vehicle licensed under s.37 of the Town Police Clauses Act 1847, s.6 of the Metropolitan Carriage Act 1869, or any similar enactment, or s.10 of the Civic Government (Scotland) Act 1982. These statutes are in effect all statutes licensing vehicles to ply for hire.

9.12 A person conducting a driving test under the Motor Vehicles (Driving Licences) Regulations 1999 is exempt if wearing a seat belt would endanger himself or any other person. The proviso is worded in terms which are awkwardly restrictive and it might be argued how and when the dangerous circumstances could arise. The examiner might become painfully aware of the risks only as the test progressed!

Persons are exempt when driving or riding in a vehicle while it is being used for Serious Organised Crime Agency (SOCA) powers, for police or fire brigade, or, in England and Wales, fire and rescue authority, purposes. It will be noted that the exemption is not in its wording limited to police, SOCA or fire-fighting vehicles or personnel. There is also an exemption for those driving or riding in a vehicle when it is being used for carrying a person in lawful custody, including the prisoner. This exemption would cover private escort contractors under the agency schemes.

9.13   One special exemption is for *passengers* riding in vehicles taking part in processions organised by or on behalf of the Crown or held to mark or commemorate an event if either the procession is one commonly or customarily held in that police area or notice in respect of that procession has been given under s.11 of the Public Order Act 1986. These vehicles are not likely to be driven at anything but slow speeds. The exemption does not extend to the driver. Interestingly the exemption appears to remain valid, even though the procession is subsequently banned under s.13 of the Public Order Act.

Exemption on medical grounds

9.14   There is also an exemption in reg.6 for those holding a medical certificate as specified signed by a doctor to the effect that it is inadvisable on medical grounds for him or her to wear a seat belt. There has been some discussion about whether this applies to a person who is able to wear a seat belt when on but who cannot put the belt on or take it off. Clearly such a person can wear a seat belt just as an invalid can wear clothes in such circumstances. It is submitted, however, that a doctor may be justified in certifying that it would be *inadvisable* on medical grounds for such a person to wear a seat belt. From the wording the prosecution cannot go behind a medical certificate on the basis that there were no medical grounds for it to have been issued save conceivably by judicial review. As from January 1, 1995, the certificate must specify its period of validity and bear the exemption symbol shown in the regulations.

Following a police warning of prosecution, the medical certificate may be relied on only if:

    (a) it is produced at the time to a constable, or

    (b) it is produced within seven days to a specified police station, or

    (c) it is produced at the specified police station as soon as is reasonably practicable, or

    (d) it is not reasonably practicable for it to be produced at the specified police station before the day on which the proceedings are commenced (1988 Act s.14(4)).

9.15   For the purpose of this defence the "commencement of proceedings" is defined as the "laying of the information", or, in Scotland, the service of the complaint on the accused. As to "reasonably practicable", see § 7.13. As to "laying an information" and beginning proceedings, see Chapter 2.

Section 101 of the Magistrates' Courts Act 1980 applies and the onus of proving the defence will be on the defendant on the balance of probabilities (*R. v Carr-Briant* [1943] K.B. 607).

9.16   It is submitted that the wording does not require production in person of the certificate. (Compare the wording of ss.170, 164 and 165 of the 1988 Act discussed at §§ 7.13 et seq. and §§ 11.19 et seq.)

Wearing of seat belts, restraints, etc., by children in rear of motor vehicles

9.17   Section 15(3) and (4) of the Road Traffic Act 1988 make it an offence for a person without reasonable excuse to drive on a road a motor vehicle to which is fitted any seat belt in the rear of the vehicle when there is in the rear of the vehicle a child of or over the age of three but under the age of 14 who is not wearing a seat belt in conformity with the regulations. It is an offence if the child is *anywhere* in the rear of the vehicle and not wearing a seat belt, even if the child is *standing up*. It should be emphasised that, in relation to a child aged from 3 to 13 years inclusive, the provisions only apply where a seat belt, etc., is actually fitted in the rear. A child under three years in the rear must always be wearing an appropriate seat belt.

As noted previously, there is generally no requirement for passengers of 14 and over to move between the front and the rear to take advantage of seats with seat belts. Parliament has however taken special action to protect children. In particular it has protected small children by making it an offence under s.15(3A) and (4) for a person to drive a passenger car on a road without reasonable excuse when there is a child who is both under 12 and less than 135cm tall in the rear when there is *no* seat belt *fitted* in the rear and there is an unoccupied seat in the front provided with a seat belt. The penalty is the same as for other offences of failing to ensure that children in the rear wear seat belts or restraints, namely a fine of level 1. As to "passenger car", see "Definitions", below.

Section 15(3A) differs from s.15(3) in that s.15(3A) in its terms is limited to small children; it refers to the situation where *no* seat belt *is fitted* in the rear; and under it carriage in the rear is prohibited unless the small child moves to certain occupied as well as unoccupied seats. Conversely s.15(3) applies (in relation to a child aged from 3 to 13 years inclusive) where seat belts/restraints *are fitted* in the rear.   **9.18**

These principal offences are committed by the driver but a person (unlike the general provisions) may be convicted of aiding and abetting. This could in theory include the child in question provided he is at least 10 years old, but see further § 9.06. Note the defence of "reasonable excuse": see § 4.261.

In addition the Motor Vehicles (Wearing of Seat Belts) Regulations 1993 (SI 1993/176) (as amended) have been made under s.15.   **9.19**

As to "road", "driving", see Chapter 1. "Seat belt" by s.15(9) includes any description of restraining device for a child. Further definitions are contained in reg.2 of the Wearing of Seat Belts Regulations 1993, including further information on when a seat belt is "appropriate" for a child under 14. By reg.2, "rear seat" means a seat not being the driver's seat, a seat alongside the driver's seat or a specified passenger seat. This means that a rear seat as defined may not necessarily be right at the rear.

"Child restraint" means a seat belt for the use of a young person which is designed either to be fitted directly to a suitable anchorage or to be used in conjunction with an adult seat belt and held in place by therestraining action of that belt, and which has been marked in accordance with reg.47(7) of the Construction and Use Regulations (which refer to British Standard Marks and Designated Approval Marks). A "child restraint" may be alternatively, in certain circumstances, a type approved by the authority of another EU Member State for use by a child, provided the corresponding legal requirements would be met if it were to be worn by a child travelling in that vehicle in that state.   **9.20**

Children under 14 in rear: description of belts to be worn as required by s.15(3)

A child under 14 in the rear is by reg.2(8) and (9) and reg.8 regarded as wear-   **9.21** ing a conforming seat belt for the purposes of s.15(3) if and only if he is wearing a child restraint of a description specified for a child of his height and weight or, in the case of a large child, an adult belt.

A large child (and for this purpose, a large child is defined as a child aged either 12 or, if under 12, 135cm or more in height) must wear in the rear an adult seat belt or a child restraint suitable to his weight and height in accordance with the indication shown on the marking required under reg.47(7) of the Construction and Use Regulations (reg.2(8) and reg.8).

9.22   A child who is both under 12 and under 135cm in height (defined as a small child) must wear a similar restraint or a restraint which would meet the corresponding legal requirements of another EU Member State.

A small child of three years or more may as an alternative wear an adult belt in the rear in the situations set out in reg.10 (see below).

Children in rear: non-availability exemption

9.23   A large child does not have to comply and there is an exemption from the s.15(3) offence if there is no appropriate seat belt available for the child (regs 2(9), 10(4) and Sch.2), or, in other words, where every child or adult in the rear or front for whom an appropriate seat belt is available is wearing such a belt and there are other children in the rear without a seat belt available for them.

The meaning of non-availability is further elaborated in Sch.2. Apart from modifications for children's belts, the exemption is basically the same as the non-availability exemption for persons of 14 and over (see § 9.07), but this has to be read subject to the provisions of reg.10(2), (3), (4) and (4A) (relating to s.15(3)) and reg.10(5) (relating to s.15(3A)), which are described separately below.

9.24   There is a rear seat exemption from the s.15(3) rear seat offence for a child aged under three if there is no appropriate seat belt available in the rear seat of a small bus, but otherwise the prohibition will apply (reg.10(2)). In the case of a small child aged three or more, there is a rear seat exemption if there is neither an appropriate seat belt or an adult belt available for him in the front or rear of the small bus (reg.10(3) and (3A)). For a large child there is a rear seat exemption in any vehicle if no appropriate seat belt is available to him in the rear (reg.10(4)). The requirements under s.15(3) do not apply to a small child riding in a small bus being used to provide a local service in a built-up area or on which standing is permitted (reg.10(4A)).

Adult seat belts which do not comply with reg.48 of the Construction and Use Regulations and certain locked inertia reel mechanism belts are by reg.2(7) not regarded as being available for the child.

9.25   Child restraints which are available in or on the vehicle and not being appropriately worn and which can be fixed on the seat without tools are treated as being provided for the seat for the purposes of Sch.2 (availability).

Children in rear of motor vehicles: vehicle exemptions

9.26   Vehicles which are large buses are exempted by reg.9 from the requirements of s.15(3) and (3A).

Licensed taxis and licensed hire cars within the meanings given by s.13 of the Transport Act 1985 in which (in each case) the rear seats are separated from the driver by a fixed partition are also exempt (reg.9). The view is presumably that the partition provides protection. There is no equivalent exemption for passengers of 14 and over. See the definition of "rear seat" noted above at § 9.19.

Section 13 defines a licensed hire car as a vehicle licensed under s.48 of the **9.27** Local Government (Miscellaneous Provisions) Act 1976 or s.7 of the Private Hire Vehicles (London) Act 1998 and a licensed taxi as, in England and Wales, a vehicle licensed under s.37 of the Town Police Clauses Act 1847, or s.6 of the Metropolitan Public Carriage Act 1869, or under any similar enactment and, in Scotland, a taxi licensed under s.10 of the Civic Government (Scotland) Act 1982.

Children in rear of motor vehicles: other exemptions

The medical exemption applies as with the other seat belt medical exemptions **9.28** where there is a medical certificate for the child to the effect that it is inadvisable on medical grounds for that child to wear a seat belt (reg.10(1)(a) and Sch.1). As from January 1, 1995, the medical certificate for a child, as for a person of 14 or more, must specify its period of validity and bear the exemption symbol shown in the regulations. The provisions of s.15(7) and (8) as to the production of certificates and the defence for non-production apply similarly as under s.14(4) and (5). A disabled child is exempt if wearing a disabled person's seat belt (reg.10(1)(g)).

There are further exemptions provided in reg.10(1) (as amended) in relation to a small child. The prohibitions in both s.15(3) and (3A) do not apply:

(a) to a small child aged under three years riding in a licensed taxi or hire car if there is no appropriate seat belt available in the front or the rear (reg.10(1)(b));

(b) to a small child of any age in a vehicle being used for the purposes of police, security or emergency services where that enables the proper performance of their duty (reg.10(1)(e));

(c) to a small child aged three or over in a licensed taxi or hire car or in a small bus (though see also the further exceptions in reg.10(3) and (4A) above) who is wearing an adult seat belt and there is no appropriate seat belt available in the front or rear of the vehicle (reg.10(1)(c));

(d) to a small child aged three or over wearing an adult seat belt in a passenger car (as defined) or a light goods vehicle (as defined) where there are two children in child restraints in the rear preventing the use of an appropriate seat belt in the rear and no appropriate seat belt is available in the front (reg.10(1)(d)); or

(e) to a small child aged three or over wearing an adult seat belt who, because of an unexpected necessity, is travelling a short distance in a passenger car or light goods vehicle where no appropriate seat belt is available (reg.10(1)(f)). What constitutes an "unexpected necessity" or a "short distance" will need to be decided in each case but is likely to be interpreted narrowly given the safety concerns that have prompted the legislation. Comparison with the approach to "duress" may be of some assistance: see § 2.158.

In each case, whether an appropriate seat belt is "available" is determined in **9.29** accordance with Sch.2 to the regulations.

Section 15(3A) offence: driver not moving unprotected small child to the front—summary of requirements and exemptions

9.30   As noted and discussed above, it is an offence under s.15(3A) for a person to drive a passenger car on a road without reasonable excuse when there is a child who is both under 12 and less than 135cm tall in the rear when there is no seat belt fitted in the rear and there is an unoccupied seat in the front provided with an appropriate seat belt (s.15(3A) and reg.10(5)). The exemptions in reg.10(1) apply to the s.15(3A) offence as to the s.15(3) offence.

Section 15(3A) refers to an unoccupied seat, but this does not read easily with reg.10(5). Regulation 10(5) states that the prohibition in s.15(3A) does not apply if no appropriate seat belt is available (see Sch.2 to the Wearing of Seat Belts Regulations 1993) in the front. This is not easy to follow because it is a double or even a triple negative! "Appropriate seat belt" is as defined in reg.2(1) and reg.8 of those regulations (see above). However Sch.2 contains what is in effect yet another negative. Sub-paragraphs (a)–(d) of para.3 inclusive are excluded by para.4 for the purposes of reg.10(5). The apparent result is that a seat belt or restraint is to be regarded as available for the small child in the front even though another person, adult or child, is wearing it (para.3(a) and (b)) or a disabled person with a disabled person's belt (para.3(d)) or a person with a medical exemption certificate (para.3(c)) is occupying the seat. In other words the presence of such a person in the front will not provide an excuse for the small child to be carried unrestrained or unbelted in the rear.

9.31   From this the s.15(3A) result may be summarised as follows. It applies where no belts are fitted in the rear. If there is a suitable restraint in the front but no seat belts fitted in the rear, the small child must be moved to the available restraint in the front (s.15(3A)). If there are no restraints but an adult seat belt is available in the front, a child over two may and should wear it if the child is to be driven. In the instances given, it will be immaterial that the front seats are otherwise occupied.

Wearing of seat belts by children in the front of motor vehicles

9.32   The Motor Vehicles (Wearing of Seat Belts by Children in Front Seats) Regulations 1993 (SI 1993/31) (as amended) are made under s.15 of the 1988 Act. They relate to children in the *front* of motor vehicles. Under s.15(1) and (2) it is an offence without reasonable excuse to drive a motor vehicle on a road when there is in the front of the vehicle a child under 14 who is not wearing a seat belt in conformity with the regulations. Section 15 applies subject to these 1993 Regulations which specify the seat belts to be worn by children, provide definitions and set out exemptions. Other provisions in s.15 concern children in the *rear* and these therefore have been discussed separately above.

As stated it is an offence where there is a child under 14 *in the front of the vehicle* not wearing a seat belt or other child restraint, etc. An offence would therefore be committed where there is a child in the front *standing up*. "In the front" is defined for the purpose of s.15 and these regulations as every part of the vehicle forward of the transverse vertical plane passing through the rearmost part of the driver's seat (reg.4), excluding any part of an upper deck, even if it is over the driver's head. "Rear seat" means any seat which is not the driver's seat, a seat alongside the driver's seat or a specified passenger seat. Section 15(1A) requires any air bag to be "deactivated" where a child is being carried in the front of a motor vehicle (other than a bus) in a rear-facing child restraining device. "Deactivated" includes adaptation or design to prevent the air bag from inflating in a way that would cause harm to a child in such a device (s.15(9A)). It is an offence under s.15(2) to drive a vehicle on a road in such circumstances without reasonable excuse without such an air bag being deactivated.

The principal offence is committed by the driver but a person (unlike the general provisions for persons over 14) may be convicted of aiding and abetting. This could in theory include the child in question provided he is at least 10 years old, but see further § 9.06. Note the defence of "reasonable excuse": see § 4.261. **9.33**

For "road", "driving", see Chapter 1. "Seat belt" in s.15 includes any description of restraining device for a child and any reference in s.15 to wearing a seat belt is to be construed accordingly (s.15(9)).

Children in the front: description of belts to be worn as required by s.15(1) and the regulations

A child in the front is by reg.2(9) and reg.5 regarded as wearing a conforming seat belt for the purposes of s.15(3) if and only if he is wearing an appropriate belt of a description specified for a child of his height and weight. **9.34**

A large child as defined must wear in the front an adult seat belt or a child restraint suitable to his weight and height in accordance with the indication shown on the marking required under reg.47(7) of the Construction and Use Regulations (reg.5).

A child who is both under 12 and under 135cm in height (defined as a small child) must wear a similar restraint or a restraint which would meet the corresponding legal requirements of another EU Member State.

A small child of three or more may as an alternative wear an adult belt in the front but only if the situation falls within the exemptions in reg.7 (see below). **9.35**

These provisions correspond closely to those applying to children in the rear of motor vehicles.

Children in the front: description of vehicles

Section 15(1) applies to motor vehicles, but by reg.7(2) the children in front provisions do not apply to a bus which is being used to provide a local service within the meaning of the Transport Act 1985 in a built-up area or is constructed or adapted for standing passengers and where the operator (as defined) permits standing. The provisions do not apply to two-wheeled motor cycles with or without side-cars (reg.6). **9.36**

Children in the front: exemptions

The prohibition in s.15(1) does not apply to a large child if no appropriate seat belt is available in the front (reg.7(3)). Additional large children may therefore be carried unfastened in the front in these circumstances. There is however no similar exemption for small children and it follows that the s.15(1) offence will be committed if a small child is carried unfastened anywhere in the front. Unless the use falls within the very limited circumstances set out in reg.7(1), as amended, the only exceptions for a child under the age of three are where there is a medical **9.37** certificate or the child is disabled and wearing a disabled person's belt. These also apply to an older child. There is a further (but again limited) exemption for a small child aged three or more who is riding in a bus and is wearing an adult seat belt if there is no appropriate seat belt available for that child in the front or rear of the bus. "Available" is to be determined in accordance with Sch.2.

Specified motor vehicles and vehicle exemptions generally

9.38   The motor vehicles in which persons have to wear seat belts are as follows. The requirements for persons of 14 and over to wear seat belts apply by reg.5 of the Wearing of Seat Belts Regulations 1993, to persons driving or riding in the front or rear seats of motor vehicles other than, in each case, a two-wheeled motor cycle with or without a side-car. The requirements relating to children under s.15, namely children in the front, in the rear and in certain circumstances requiring them to be transferred to front fastenings before the vehicle is driven, all by that section apply to persons riding in motor vehicles, subject to the excepted vehicles. Vehicles which are large buses are exempted from the prohibitions in s.15(3) and (3A) regarding the carriage of children in the rear (Wearing of Seat Belts Regulations 1993 reg.9(a)). Licensed taxis and licensed hire cars in which in each case the rear seats are separated from the driver by a fixed partition are also excepted for children in the rear and from the s.15(3A) requirement to move to the front (Wearing of Seat Belts Regulations 1993 reg.9(b)). In the case of children in the front, there is a further exception for a bus which is being used to provide a local service within the meaning of the Transport Act 1985 in a built-up area or is constructed or adapted for standing passengers and where the operator (as defined) permits standing (reg.7(2)).

Section 15B to the 1988 Act places an obligation on the operator of certain buses in which any of the passenger seats are fitted with a seat belt. That obligation is to take reasonable steps to ensure that every passenger is notified of the requirement to wear the seat belt fitted when the bus is in motion. The means of notification are prescribed and set out in s.15B(2) as an official announcement (including by audio visual means) when (or soon after) the passenger joins the bus or a sign prominently displayed at each seat equipped with a seat belt. The requirement does not apply to a bus being used to provide a local service in a built-up area, that is, where the entire route consists of restricted roads. The requirement also does not apply to a bus constructed or adapted for the carriage of standing passengers and on which the operator permits standing (s.15B(6)). It is the operator who is liable; by s.15B(7) this is defined as the owner of the bus or other person in possession of it under a hire, hire purchase, conditional sale, loan or other similar agreement. It is a summary offence punishable by a maximum fine of level 4.

Definitions

"Motor vehicle"

9.39   References to "motor vehicle" in the Road Traffic Act 1988 and the seat belts regulations made under it will be as defined in s.185 of the Act.

"Bus", "large bus", "small bus"

9.40   A "bus", by s.15(9), is a motor vehicle that has at least four wheels, is constructed or adapted for the carriage of passengers, has more than eight seats in addition to the driver's seat and has a maximum design speed that exceeds 25kph.

A "large bus", by reg.2 of the Wearing of Seat Belts Regulations 1993, is a bus with a maximum laden weight (as defined) exceeding 3.5 tonnes.

A "small bus" is a bus with a maximum laden weight not exceeding 3.5 tonnes. **9.41**

"Passenger car" and "light goods vehicle"

A "passenger car" by s.15(9) means a motor vehicle which is constructed or **9.42** adapted for use for the carriage of passengers and is not a goods vehicle, has no more than eight seats in addition to the driver's seat, has four or more wheels, has a maximum design speed exceeding 25kph and has a maximum laden weight not exceeding 3.5 tonnes.

A "light goods vehicle" by reg.2 of the Wearing of Seat Belts Regulations 1993 means a goods vehicle which has four or more wheels, a maximum design speed exceeding 25kph and a maximum laden weight not exceeding 3.5 tonnes.

"Large child", "small child", "front", "rear"

The definitions of "large child", "small child", "front" and "rear" may be found **9.43** in the paragraphs covering children above, e.g. §§ 9.17–18.

"Adult belt"

"Adult belt" is separately (but identically) defined in both the 1993 Seat Belts **9.44** Regulations. In summary, adult seat belts are a three-point belt or a lap belt which has been marked in accordance with reg.47(7) of the Construction and Use Regulations, a seat belt which falls within reg.47(4)(c)(i) or (ii) of those regulations (certain British Standard seat belts), or a type approved by the authority of another EU Member State for use by persons who are over 12 or of 135cm or more in height, provided the corresponding legal requirements would be met if it were to be worn by persons in those categories travelling in that vehicle in that Member State. A seat is to be regarded as provided with an adult seat belt if it is fixed in such a position that it can be worn by an occupier, but not if it does not comply with the requirements of reg.48 of the Construction and Use Regulations or has an inertia reel mechanism which is locked because of a steep incline. These exceptions have been discussed above.

"Child restraint"

"Child restraint" and "restraint system" have the same definition in both the **9.45** Seat Belts Regulations 1993 (*q.v.*). Under those regulations, "seat belt" includes a "child restraint", but an adult seat belt obviously does not.

"Seats", and various "seat belts"

"Disabled person's belt", "lap belt", "seat", "specified passenger seat" and **9.46** "three-point belt" all have under the 1993 Seat Belts Regulations the meanings given by reg.47(8) of the Construction and Use Regulations. The same definitions are also adopted in reg.48 of the Construction and Use Regulations (maintenance of seat belts and anchorage points) (see reg.48(6)). "Seat" is defined to include any part of a bench seat if that part is designed for one adult.

"Front seat"

"Front seat" in the Motor Vehicles (Wearing of Seat Belts by Children in Front **9.47**

Seats) Regulations 1993 means a seat which is wholly or partially in the front of the vehicle and "rear seat" means any seat which is not a front seat (reg.2(1)). These regulations also define "front" in some detail for the purpose of the regulations (see reg.4).

"Rear seat"

9.48   "Rear seat" in the Wearing of Seat Belts Regulations 1993 means a seat not being the driver's seat, a seat alongside the driver's seat or a specified passenger seat (reg.2(1)). This means that a rear seat as defined here may not necessarily be right at the rear, and in theory at least might not be the same as under the Children in Front Seats Regulations 1993.

"Specified passenger seat"

9.49   The "specified passenger seat" in the 1993 Seat Belts Regulations has the same meaning as in reg.47(8) of the Construction and Use Regulations. Where there is one forward facing front seat alongside the driver's seat it is that seat. Where there is more than one such seat it is the one furthest from the driver. Where there is normally no such seat alongside, it is the foremost forward facing front passenger seat furthest from the driver's seat unless there is a fixed partition between it and the space in front alongside the driver's seat.

Other definitions

9.50   Other definitions can be found in reg.3(2) of the Construction and Use Regulations and the Seat Belts Regulations 1993. For "riding" see Chapter 1.

Provision of seat belts

9.51   The vehicles which must be fitted with seat belts, the types of belts and the seats which have to have belts fitted are specified in reg.47 and the vehicles which must be provided with anchorage points are specified in reg.46 of the Construction and Use Regulations, as amended, or equivalent EC directives. Regulation 47 is to some extent based on reg.46. Parliament has been continually extending the fitting requirements in anticipation of extensions to the wearing requirements. Reference should be made to Vol.2 of this work for these provisions.

     The original fitting requirements were for the driver's seat and for the specified front passenger's seat (if any). This is still the requirement for any vehicle first used before April 1, 1981. Regulation 46 makes provision for anchorage points and reg.47 for the provision of seat belts.

9.52   Regulation 46 specifies the type of anchorage points required for all vehicles used after specified dates (reg.46(1)) unless these vehicles are excepted (reg.46(2)). The seats for which mandatory anchorage points are required and the technical and installation requirements are set out in a table in reg.46(3). Non-mandatory anchorage points must, nonetheless, comply with the requirements applicable to mandatory anchorage points (reg.46(5)).

     Regulation 47 specifies the type of belt required for different seats in the various vehicles covered by the regulation. Increasingly, more vehicles are required to have belts of the prescribed types.

Maintenance of seat belts

9.53   Regulation 48 of the Construction and Use Regulations deals with the maintenance of seat belts and anchorage points. Words used in reg.48 and defined in reg.47 have the same meaning. Regulation 48(1) refers to the anchorages, fastenings, adjusting device and retracting mechanism (if any) of every such seat belt. This implies that all these are part of the seat belt. Note that there is a distinction between anchorages and anchorage points. The latter are specified separately in regs.46 and 48.

There are two exceptions in reg.48(5) —

(1) where the requirement ceased to be complied with (i.e. the fault arose) after the start of the journey and

(2) where steps have been taken for compliance with all reasonable expedition.

As to the meaning of similarly worded defences for speedometers and lights, see Chapter 8. Here the word "defence" is not used but it is submitted that it is nevertheless a qualification, etc., within the meaning of s.101 of the Magistrates' Courts Act 1980 so that the burden of proof remains on the defendant on the balance of probabilities.

SAFETY EQUIPMENT FOR CHILDREN IN MOTOR VEHICLES

Section 15A of the Road Traffic Act 1988 enables regulations to be made as to equipment designed for use by a child that is conducive to safety in the event of an accident in prescribed motor vehicles. **9.54**

If a person sells or offers for sale or lets on hire or offers to let on hire equipment not of the type prescribed, or contravening the regulations for children or vehicles not of the class prescribed, offences will be committed contrary to s.15A(3) and (4) respectively.

There is a defence that the equipment was sold or offered for sale for export. Also, Sch.1 to the 1988 Act is applied and certain warranty defences are added. **9.55**

MOTOR CYCLE HELMETS

Wearing of helmets

Section 16 of the 1988 Act empowers the Secretary of State to make regulations requiring persons driving or riding motor cycles of any class specified in the regulations to wear protective headgear, and by s.16(4) any person who drives or rides on a motor cycle in contravention of such regulation is guilty of an offence. **9.56**

Regulations treated as if made under s.16 are the Motor Cycles (Protective Helmets) Regulations 1998 (SI 1998/1807), as amended.

The regulations limit the necessity of wearing protective headgear to persons riding or driving a motor *bi* cycle as defined in the regulations. A "motor bicycle" is defined, for the purpose of the regulations, by reg.4, as "a two-wheeled motor cycle, whether or not having a side-car attached" (any wheels the centres of which in contact with the road surface are less than 460mm apart to be counted as one wheel). This definition has been examined in relation to the BMW C1 motor cycle: *DPP v Parker* below. Magistrates found that it was a motor cycle within the definition in s.185 of the Road Traffic Act 1988.

The regulations do not apply to certain motor mowers which may otherwise come within the definition of "motor bicycle" in the regulations (reg.4(2)(a)). As to the definition of "motor cycle" generally, see Chapter 1. **9.57**

It will be seen that protective headgear does not have to be worn by a driver or rider whilst the motor bicycle is being propelled by a person on foot (reg.4(2)(b)). In *Crank v Brooks* [1980] R.T.R. 441 Waller L.J. said that if a person had been using a bicycle as a scooter by having one foot on the pedal and pushing herself along she would not have been a foot passenger. This referred to a pedal cycle. If the same principle were applied to a motor cycle such a person would presumably not be on foot and so a helmet should be worn. The person on foot propelling the motor bicycle need not be the driver or rider. Thus, a child sitting on a motor bicycle being pushed by another person would not need to wear protective headgear.

9.58   Regulation 4 requires every person driving "or riding on" a motor bicycle to wear protective headgear. Thus both the driver and a pillion passenger are required to wear helmets. In *DPP v Parker* [2004] EWHC 1248; *The Times*, June 29, 2004, the vehicle in question was a BMW C1 motor cycle. The C1 is not a conventional motor cycle or scooter having passive safety features developed from automobile technology—a rigid rider cell, front and side crash elements, roll-over hoops and shoulder protection bars. It also has a safety belt system and an ergonomically designed seat. Unless the seat belts are engaged, it cannot be driven. On a prosecution for not wearing a helmet, magistrates found that the word "on" applied to both "driving" and "riding" and, as they found the driver to be "in" what was essentially an enclosed vehicle, they acquitted the defendant. The prosecutor's appeal was allowed. Drawing attention to the statement at the beginning of this paragraph, the court confirmed that a passenger would be "riding on" a motor cycle, the person in control would be "driving" and the word "on" would not be attached to the word "driving". It was acknowledged that it was not common to refer to the person in control of a motor cycle as the "driver"; indeed, in these cases the summonses alleged "riding". The court emphasised that the legislation had nonetheless drawn that distinction and that it would be prudent for summonses to put the allegation by reference to a person "driving" a motor cycle rather than "riding" it where the subject of the summons was the person in control. See below as to aiding and abetting. Persons riding "in" a side-car are exempt (see s.16(1)). For the meaning of "side-car" and "riders", see § 1.15 and § 1.116.

By s.16(2) a requirement imposed by regulations made or treated as made under s.16 does not apply to any follower of the Sikh religion while he is wearing a turban. For a report where a defendant appeared in court in a flowing gown and turban seeking to claim to be a follower of the Sikh religion, but subsequently pleaded guilty, see the *Daily Telegraph* of January 8, 1987. The exemption by its wording applies to followers of the religion and not to members of the Sikh community.

9.59   The helmets required to be worn must either conform to one of the British Standards specified in reg.5 and Sch.2, subject to any amendments to that standard at the date of manufacture, and be marked with the number of the British Standard and the certification mark of the British Standards Institution; or not only give a similar or greater degree of protection than a British Standard helmet but also be of a type manufactured for motor cyclists (reg.4(3)). The regulations also provide that if the helmet is worn with a chin cup, it must be provided with an additional strap under the jaw for securing the helmet (see reg.4(3)(b)).

The definition of protective headgear makes it clear that if the helmet is worn unfastened or improperly fastened, an offence is committed reg.4(3)).

Section 16 applies to vehicles and persons in the public service of the Crown. **9.60**

Aiding and abetting

Only the person driving or riding on a motor cycle in contravention of s.16 **9.61**
(crash helmets) is to be guilty notwithstanding any enactment or rule of law (e.g.
aiding and abetting) to the contrary (see the proviso in s.16(4)). The Act makes
an exception where the person actually committing the offence is under 16. "Actually committing" must mean the principal offender.

By way of example, where a person aged 18 and a person aged 15 are both on
a motor bicycle without a side-car and neither has a crash helmet, the 18-year-old
can be guilty of the principal offence in respect of himself and the aiding and
abetting offence in respect of the 15-year-old but the 15-year-old can only be
guilty of the principal offence in respect of himself. If both were 18 each would
only be responsible for the principal offence in respect of himself and could not
be guilty of aiding and abetting.

Section 16 should be compared with the seat belt provisions in s.14 and s.15 **9.62**
(see § 9.06). Section 14 is in similar terms but s.15 refers to children under *14*
and in that instance the driver can be responsible *and* the child can be guilty of
aiding and abetting.

The restricting aiding and abetting provisions apply to s.16 but not to s.18 (eye
protectors, etc.—see below).

Eye protectors

The Motor Cycles (Eye Protectors) Regulations 1999 (SI 1999/535) are made **9.63**
under s.18 of the 1988 Act. Anyone who drives or rides on a motor bicycle as
defined in the regulations on a road otherwise than in a side-car and uses an eye
protector not as prescribed is guilty of an offence (s.18(3)). As to "drive" and
"ride", see Chapter 1.

It should be emphasised that these provisions do not require the *use* of the eye
protectors in any specified circumstances. Section 18(3) of the 1988 Act applies
to persons in the public service of the Crown, but there are certain exemptions.

Under reg.4(4) of the 1999 Regulations there are exemptions for mowing **9.64**
machines; for machines for the time being propelled by a person on foot; for
vehicles brought temporarily into Great Britain by persons resident outside the
United Kingdom which have not remained in the United Kingdom for more than
one year from the date the vehicle was last brought into the United Kingdom and
for persons on duty in the armed forces of the Crown and wearing an eye protector supplied as part of their service equipment.

Sale, etc., of helmets

It is an offence under s.17(2) of the 1988 Act for a person to sell, offer for sale, **9.65**
let on hire or offer to let on hire, a helmet for affording protection from injury in
the event of accident for persons driving or riding on or in motor cycles if the
helmet is either not of a type prescribed by the regulations (see above) or, if a
type authorised by the regulations, sold or offered for sale, etc., subject to any
conditions prohibited in the authorisation. By s.17(5) "helmet" includes any
head-dress. Topees together with hats worn at Ascot are thus included in the

definition. A person may not be convicted if he proves (semble on the balance of probabilities) that the helmet was sold or offered for sale for export from Great Britain.

An offence under s.17(2) of selling, etc., an illegal helmet is committed even though the helmet is sold for off-road use only (*Losexis Ltd v Clarke* [1984] R.T.R. 174); a case under a repealed enactment in similar terms.

9.66   Section 17 applies to vehicles and persons in the public service of the Crown.

"Third party" proceedings

9.67   A person charged with selling or offering for sale, etc, under s.17(2), a helmet which does not conform with a type set out in the regulations may himself summon the person actually responsible for the offence in the same proceedings by following the procedure set out for the purpose in Sch.1. Paragraph 2 of Sch.1 gives the prosecutor the right to proceed directly against a person whose act or default gave rise to the offence and thus proceed in an appropriate case directly against the wholesaler or manufacturer instead of the retailer.

Sale, etc., of eye protectors

9.68   As with helmets, there is an offence of selling, etc., an eye protector which is not of the prescribed type (s.18(4)). Similarly the defendant will escape conviction if he proves (semble on the balance of probabilities) that it was sold, etc., for export from Great Britain (s.18(5)). The third party procedure in Sch.1 is also available (s.18(6)). Presumably the principle in *Losexis Ltd v Clarke* above will apply (see § 9.65).

Section 18(4) applies to vehicles and persons in the public service of the Crown.

Helmets, eye protectors and child safety equipment: warranty offences

9.69   By paras 6 and 7 in Sch.1 to the 1988 Act, it is an offence for a person in any proceedings for an offence under ss.15A, 17 or 18(4) wilfully to apply to equipment, information, a helmet or, as the case may be, an appliance a warranty not given in relation to it (para.6(1)). It is also an offence for a person in respect of equipment, a helmet or an appliance sold by him or information provided by him in respect of which a warranty might be pleaded under paragraph 5, to give to the purchases a false warranty in writing unless he proves that when he gave the warranty he had reason to believe that the statement or description contained in it was accurate (para.6(2)).

MOTOR CYCLE PASSENGERS

Carrying passengers

9.70   Section 23 of the 1988 Act as amended makes it an offence to carry more than one passenger on a motor bicycle. It is also an offence under the section to carry a passenger on such a motor bicycle otherwise than sitting astride the bicycle and on a proper seat securely fixed behind the driver's seat. Note that only the driver commits an offence under s.23(3) although any person carried in contravention of s.23 may be convicted of aiding and abetting. For definition of "driver", see

Chapter 1. For the meaning of "carry", the definition of "rider", also in Chapter 1, may assist. It is submitted that "carry" implies some movement from A to B.

Section 23 applies to vehicles and persons in the public service of the Crown (s.183).

PENALTIES AND PROCEEDINGS

Seat belts (ss.14 and 15)

Both s.14 and s.15 apply to the drivers and riders of Crown vehicles. See also **9.71** § 2.34.

The adult front and rear seat belt offences applicable to persons of 14 and over are contrary to the Motor Vehicles (Wearing of Seat Belts) Regulations 1993 and s.14 of the 1988 Act and the maximum fine under Sch.2 to the Road Traffic Offenders Act 1988 is of level 2. The offence of driving with a child in the front without a seat belt/restraint as required is contrary to s.15(1) and (2) of the 1988 Act and the Motor Vehicles (Wearing of Seat Belts by Children in Front Seats) Regulations 1993 and carries a maximum fine of level 2 as is that for having a child in a rear-facing child restraint in a front seat with an active air bag. The offence of driving with a child in the rear without a seat belt/restraint is contrary to s.15(3) and (4) and the Motor Vehicles (Wearing of Seat Belts) Regulations 1993 and carries a maximum fine of level 2. The offence of driving with a small child in the rear without a seat belt fitted in the rear when there is a suitable belt/restraint in the front is contrary to s.15(3A) and (4) and the Motor Vehicles (Wearing of Seat Belts) Regulations 1993 and also carries a maximum fine of level 2. Failing to notify bus passengers of the requirement to wear seat belts is an offence contrary to s.15B of the 1988 Act and carries a maximum fine of level 4. For a table of penalties, see § 9.77.

Motor cycle helmets (ss.16 and 17)

For the "third party" procedure for selling, etc., offences, see § 9.67. **9.72** For a table of penalties, see § 9.77.

Motor cycle passengers (s.23)

The offence is obligatorily endorsable in the absence of "special reasons" (see **9.73** Chapter 21) and carries three penalty points. Disqualification may be ordered (see Chapter 20). Section 35 of the Road Traffic Offenders Act 1988 (penalty points disqualifications) applies (see §§ 20.33 et seq.). The court has power to disqualify until the defendant passes a test under s.36 of the 1988 Offenders Act.

See also the table of penalties at § 9.77.

Eye protectors (s.18)

For the "third party" procedure for selling, etc., offences, see § 9.67. **9.74** For a table of penalties, see at § 9.77.

By virtue of the Fixed Penalty Offences Order 2004 (SI 2004/2922), a contravention of s.18(3) is a fixed penalty offence.

Helmets, eye protectors and child safety equipment: warranties

Schedule 1, para.6(3) of the Road Traffic Act 1988 provides an extended juris- **9.75** diction for para.6(2) warranty offences. In relation to offences under s.15A, 17 or 18(4), court proceedings may be taken where the item was procured, where the information, or any of it, to which the warranty relates, was provided or where the warranty was given. There is no extension of jurisdiction for para.6(1) offences.

Subject to the regulations, s.15A will apply to vehicles and persons in the public service of the Crown, as do the Sch.1, para.6 offences.

9.76   Offences contrary to s.15A(3) or (4) (selling, etc., equipment as conducive to the safety of children in motor vehicles) is triable only summarily with a maximum fine of level 3. Offences of applying a warranty to a protective helmet, appliance or child safety equipment in defending proceedings under s.15A, 17 or 18(4) where no warranty was given (para.6(1)) or applying a false warranty (para.6(2)) are triable only summarily with a maximum fine of level 3.

Protection of drivers and passengers: penalties

Offence	Mode of trial	Section *	Imprisonment	Level of fine	Disqualification	Penalty points	Endorsement code	Sentencing guideline
Not wearing seat belt (14 and over)	Summary	Motor Vehicles (Wearing of Seat Belts) Regs 1993 and s.14(3)	—	2	—	—	—	Fine band A
Driving with child in front not wearing seat belt	Summary	s.15(1), (2) and Motor Vehicles (Wearing of Seat Belts by Children in Front Seats) Regs 1993	—	2	—	—	—	Fine band A
Driving with child in rear not wearing seat belt or child restraint	Summary	s.15(3), (4) and Motor Vehicles (Wearing of Seat Belts) Regs 1993	—	2	—	—	—	Fine band A

Offence	Mode of trial	Section *	Imprisonment	Level of fine	Disqualification	Penalty points	Endorsement code	Sentencing guideline
Driving with small child in rear without seat belt fitted in rear when suitable belt available in front	Summary	s.15(3A), (4) and Motor Vehicles (Wearing of Seat Belts) Regs 1993	—	2	—	—	—	Fine band A
Selling, etc., child safety equipment not as prescribed, etc.	Summary	s.15A(3) and (4)	—	3	—	—	—	—
Failing to notify bus passengers of requirement to wear seat belts	Summary	s.15B	—	4	—	—	—	—
No crash helmet as required	Summary	Motor Cycles (Protective Helmets) Regs and s.16	—	2	—	—	—	—
Selling, etc., helmet not as prescribed	Summary	Motor Cycles (Protective Helmets) Regs and s.17	—	3	—	—	—	—

Offence	Mode of trial	Section *	Imprisonment	Level of fine	Disqualification	Penalty points	Endorsement code	Sentencing guideline
Carrying passenger on motor cycle incorrectly	Summary	s.23	—	3	Discretionary	3	MS 20	—
Breach of eye protector regs	Summary	Motor Cycles (Eye Protector) Regs and s.18(3)	—	2	—	—	—	—
Selling, etc., eye protector not as prescribed	Summary	Motor Cycles (Eye Protector) Regs and s.18(4)	—	3	—	—	—	—

* Road Traffic Act 1988 unless otherwise specified.

Chapter 10

INSURANCE

Contents

Introduction

10.01   The principal offence relating to insurance of motor vehicles, using a motor vehicle without insurance, is contained in s.143 of the 1988 Act and is discussed in detail below. When in force, ss.144A–144D (as inserted by s.22 of the Road Safety Act 2006) create a new offence of keeping a vehicle which does not meet insurance requirements. This offence avoids the need to prove use of the vehicle.

Other insurance offences of failing to produce insurance certificates and forgery, etc., of insurance certificates are in ss.165, 166, 171 and 173–175 of the 1988 Act and are discussed in Chapter 16. These latter offences apply also to other documents.

THIRD PARTY INSURANCE POLICIES

Generally

10.02   Subject to exceptions, s.143(1) of the 1988 Act requires every person who uses, or causes or permits another person to use, a motor vehicle on a road or other public place to have a policy of insurance (or a security) in respect of third party risks in accordance with Pt VI of that Act in relation to the user of the vehicle by the person using it. Section 145(2) prescribes the conditions with which such policies must comply, including a requirement that they be issued by authorised insurers.

It is, perhaps, worth emphasising that a person commits an offence contrary to s.143 of using, etc., a vehicle without insurance, notwithstanding the fact that a policy of insurance has been effected, if an insurance certificate in the prescribed form has not been first delivered to the assured (s.147(1): see § 10.11). Section 147(2) makes a similar provision that, where security is given, such security is of no effect until a "certificate of security" has first been given. The police do not always prosecute in such cases providing they are satisfied that the insured person would be regarded by the insurance company as being "on risk", but they are entitled to do so. Any person submitting him or herself to a driving test must sign a declaration before taking the test that the vehicle to be used is properly insured: Motor Vehicles (Driving Licences) Regulations 1999 (SI 1999/2864) reg.38(5).

There is nothing inherently objectionable in construing a contract of insurance in such a way as to put the insurers on and off risk at short and recurring intervals: *Samuelson v National Insurance and Guarantee Corporation Ltd* [1986] 3 All E.R. 417, CA.

10.03

A cover note was issued at 6.30pm on March 25 expressed to cover from 6.45pm and later the policy was issued stating that the insurance commenced on March 25. It was held that the insured was not covered at 6.05pm on that day (*Smith v Alexander* [1965] 1 Lloyd's Rep. 283).

If a general or continuing permission is given by one person to another to use a motor vehicle and the vehicle is not insured, a separate offence of permitting the uninsured use is committed on each occasion the vehicle is so used (*Barnet v Fieldhouse* [1987] R.T.R. 266). All authorised insurers in Great Britain are required to be members of the Motor Insurers' Bureau. This requirement is now set out in s.145(2), (5) and (6) of the 1988 Act. Section 145(6) contains certain residuary requirements should an insurer cease to be a member and accordingly cease to be authorised.

10.04

For the special defence for persons using vehicles in the course of their employment in ignorance of lack of cover, see § 10.59.

Nature of the insurance

The nature of the insurance required by s.143 is set out in s.145(3).

10.05

Under s.145(3)(a) of the 1988 Act it is necessary for the policy to cover any liability which may be incurred in respect of the death of, or bodily injury to, any person or damage to property caused by, or arising out of, the use of the vehicle on a road or other public place in Great Britain. The extension to damage to property implements Council Directive 84/5/EEC. Under s.145(3)(aa), as inserted by the Motor Vehicles (Compulsory Insurance) Regulations 1992 (SI 1992/3036), the policy cover for a vehicle normally based in another EU Member State must cover any civil liability which may be incurred from an event relating to the use of the vehicle in Great Britain if higher cover would be required in corresponding circumstances in that territory.

Section 145(4) of the 1988 Act sets out six exceptions to s.145(3)(a). Cover is not required:

10.06

(1) to cover liability in respect of the death, arising out of and in the course of his employment, of a person in the employment of a person insured by the policy or of bodily injury or damage to property sustained by such a person arising out of and in the course of his employment, but only if the person is otherwise covered by insurance in fact provided under a requirement of the Employers' Liability (Compulsory Insurance) Act 1969 (s.145(4)(a) as affected by subs.(4A) which was inserted by the Motor Vehicles (Compulsory Insurance) Regulations 1992); or

(2) to provide insurance for more than £250,000 in respect of all such liabilities as may be incurred in respect of damage to property caused by, or arising out of, any one accident (see below) involving the vehicle; or

(3) to cover liability in respect of damage to the vehicle; or

(4) to cover liability in respect of damage to goods carried for hire or

reward in or on the vehicle or in or on any trailer (whether or not coupled) drawn by the vehicle; or

(5) to cover any liability of a person in respect of damage to property in his custody or under his control; or

(6) to cover any contractual liability.

Section 145(4)(b) refers to "one accident". Under the Interpretation Act 1978 s.6 the singular includes the plural unless the contrary intention appears. The reference to "one" clearly indicates a contrary intention. However, under s.161(3) of the 1988 Act (Interpretation of Pt VI of the 1988 Act) any reference in Pt VI to an accident includes a reference to two or more causally related accidents. It follows that there will be corresponding changes in the liability of the Motor Insurers' Bureau.

10.07 In addition the policy must in the case of a vehicle normally based in Great Britain insure in respect of any liability arising out of the use of the vehicle and of any trailer, whether or not coupled, in the EU Member States other than Great Britain and Gibraltar, according to the law on compulsory insurance against civil liability in respect of the use of vehicles of that state where the event occurred, or if the British cover for a corresponding event would be higher, equivalent higher cover (s.145(3)(b) as amended by the Motor Vehicles (Compulsory Insurance) Regulations 1992). As to trailers generally, see § 10.32. The policy must also insure payments for emergency treatment (s.145(3)(c)).

Reading s.145(3) with s.143 it is clear that the use of only motor vehicles (and not trailers) in Great Britain has to be covered by law, whereas the use of both motor vehicles and trailers in other EU Member States (excluding Gibraltar) is required to be covered by s.145(3)(b). Obviously if a trailer is used with a motor vehicle it may be within the scope of the use of the motor vehicle.

10.08 The inter-relationship between s.143 and s.145(3) in the similarly worded earlier legislation and the meaning of "any person" in s.145(3) was considered in *Cooper v Motor Insurers' Bureau* [1985] 1 All E.R. 449, CA (a civil case). It was held that "any person" did not in the context include the policy-holder or the person the policy-holder caused or permitted to use the vehicle. *K* permitted *C* to use a vehicle to test it. *K* was negligent in that the vehicle was defective. *C* was seriously injured. *C* was not a third party within the meaning of s.143 and s.145(3), and *K* did not have to be insured against risks to *C*. The exclusion of the driver has been confirmed in *R. v Secretary of State for Transport Ex p. National Insurance Guarantee Corporation plc, The Times,* June 3, 1996.

Where a policy covered an authorised driver as well as the policy owner who owned the car, it was held that where damages were awarded against the driver in favour of the policy-holder, the driver was entitled to be indemnified under the policy even though the benefit was to the policy-holder: *Digby v General Accident Fire & Life Assurance Corporation Ltd* [1943] A.C. 121; *Richards v Cox* [1942] K.B. 139.

The Motor Insurers' Bureau

10.09 The operation of the Motor Insurers' Bureau (MIB) is based on a series of agreements between the Bureau and the Secretary of State. The purpose of the MIB is to provide compensation where the victim of a road accident may be left without other remedy: that is, first, when the person responsible is uninsured;

secondly, when the person responsible is untraced (as in a hit-and-run case); and, thirdly, where the insurance company has gone into liquidation without funds to meet claims. Up to December 31, 1988 the MIB only met claims arising from death or bodily injury. A more extensive MIB agreement was signed on December 21, 1988 which became operative from December 31, 1988 and covered damage to property. By including damage to property by uninsured drivers, the 1988 agreement implemented the provisions of Directive 84/5/EEC (see also § 10.28). Whether the agreement adequately gives effect to the directive was argued, but not resolved, in *Evans v Motor Insurers' Bureau, The Times*, October 12, 1998, CA. A further agreement was signed on August 13, 1999, which applies to accidents occurring after October 1, 1999.

The current agreement providing for the compensation of victims of untraced drivers was signed and came into operation on February 14, 2003. The agreement applies to applications for compensation in respect of death, bodily injury or damage to property. The MIB scheme provides for compensating a victim of a road traffic accident where there is no other remedy. However, art.1(4) of Directive 84/5/EEC requires the scheme to be as effective as that applicable under national law where the driver had been insured. Whilst the MIB scheme provides for claims to be made within three years, a claim in tort for a young person could be made at any time prior to the 21st birthday. In this respect the scheme fails to comply with the Directive: *Byrne v Motors Insurers' Bureau* [2008] EWCA Civ 574; [2008] R.T.R. 26.

10.10 The Bureau operates from Linford Wood House, 6–12 Capital Drive, Linford Wood, Milton Keyes MK14 6XT (website: *http://www.mib.org.uk* [Accessed March 31, 2009]). A summary of the current scheme is set out in §§ 10.83–86 together with its effect on compensation orders.

Certificates and policies

10.11 By s.147(1) of the 1988 Act, a policy is of no effect unless and until the insurer delivers to the assured a certificate in the prescribed form. For a conviction for using a vehicle contrary to s.143 under the earlier corresponding legislation because the certificate had not been delivered, see *Starkey v Hall* [1936] 2 All E.R. 18, a case on special facts. Correspondence at (1990) 7 W.R.T.L.B. 47 draws attention to the practice of some reputable insurance companies whereby they sell "instant cover" motor insurance over the telephone. Section 147(1) refers to the delivery of the certificate by the insurer "to the person by whom the policy is effected". The letter points out that the Association of British Insurers claims that the delivery criterion is achieved by the instant delivery to a separate insurance company which acts as an agent for the insured. It is suggested by the correspondent that the terms of the subsection are not fulfilled because the certificate is not delivered to the *person* by whom the policy is effected. The writer adds that correspondence with the Minister of Transport indicates that he is unsure as to what interpretation the courts would adopt. Some insurance brokers similarly appear to consider that delivery to them is sufficient as agents on behalf of the insured. It may be helpful to compare the position under other legislation such as under ss.164 and 165 of the 1988 Act, and the cases discussed at §§ 7.13 et seq. It is submitted that the tests are whether an agency is in fact created and whether there is an indication in s.147 that delivery to the person, personally, is required. It is the practice of some brokers to deliver a certificate and then reclaim it to hold against the payment of instalments, or retain it for that purpose, claiming that delivery to them is sufficient, as the agent for the insured. However reprehensible this practice may be, it would not seem to be illegal, if the delivery requirements are fulfilled. Nor can it be said that the certificate has been "lost", so as to entitle the insured to obtain a fresh certificate.

The Motor Vehicles (Third Party Risks) Regulations 1972 (SI 1972/1217) as amended prescribe the forms of certificate. A certificate may be produced on any suitable material provided it has a white background. Form B in the Schedule to the regulations is in such a form that the registered number of the vehicle does not have to be shown. By reg.10 (as amended) every company issuing a policy or security is required to keep a record as to specified details of the policies and of any certificate issued therewith and all such companies are required without charge to furnish to the Secretary of State or any chief officer of police any particulars of such records and may provide them, in electronic form only, to the MIB. The companies must keep the records for seven years from the date of expiry of the policy. Defendants before the courts often have difficulty in obtaining copies of insurance policies, cover notes and other certificates from their insurance brokers or sometimes even from the insurance company, especially when their copy has not been lost because they were never supplied in the first place with a copy to keep. Use of the police power to obtain a copy free of charge under this regulation can be effective and can save considerable time although the police are understandably reluctant to undertake additional work. Regulation 13 requires an insurance company to issue on demand a fresh certificate to the loser if they are satisfied it has been lost or destroyed. Benefits arising from developments in IT may now enable an insurer to agree with the Secretary of State to allow verification of a policy from an insurer's database.

10.12 By s.161(1) "policy of insurance" includes a cover note. Every such policy in the form of a cover note has to bear a certificate (Form C in the Schedule) that it satisfies the requirements of the relevant law in Great Britain (reg.5(3) of the regulations above).

Occasionally in the past different certificates have been issued under one policy to cover different vehicles (e.g. where one is a sports car) without the vehicle being specified on the certificate. It would be an offence to use such a certificate for the wrong vehicle with intent to deceive (see s.173 of the 1988 Act). These differences might not necessarily be revealed by an examination of the policy or the certificates. Generally it is now the practice to specify individual vehicles on individual certificates unless the policy is a group policy covering all the vehicles of a certain type, such as all those used by a motor trader in the course of his business or all those used by employees of a particular firm.

10.13 While it may be desirable that the policy should be seen, it need not be seen if the court is satisfied that all the required information can be obtained from the certificate (*Borders v Swift* [1957] Crim. L.R. 194). In *Leathley v Drummond* [1972] R.T.R. 293 a case was remitted to the justices who had dismissed it on a submission of no case after only a certificate of insurance but no policy had been produced; it was for the defendants to prove that the use of the vehicle in question was covered by insurance (ibid.). The policy overrides the certificate where there is inconsistency between the two (*Biddle v Johnston* (1965) 109 S.J. 395); not only cannot the certificate override the policy but the certificate itself is not a policy (*Roberts v Warne* [1973] R.T.R. 217).

With regard to the issuing of a cover note and the timing of cover, see *Smith v Alexander* at § 10.03 above.

Green Card Scheme

By international agreement the Green Card is recognised in many European **10.14** and other countries as evidence that a motorist has insurance to cover the minimum insurance requirements of that country. The equivalent Green Card for visitors entering Great Britain is governed by the Motor Vehicles (International Motor Insurance Card) Regulations 1971 (SI 1971/792), as amended. A valid Green Card held by a visitor is to be regarded under these regulations as if it were a policy of insurance complying with the relevant requirements of the 1988 Act.

So far as EU countries are concerned it is not essential to hold a Green Card as the necessary cover must be provided under the British insurance in accordance with s.145(3)(b) of the 1988 Act (as amended by the Motor Vehicles (Compulsory Insurance) Regulations 1992). See § 10.05.

Social and business purposes

Policies often refer to use for social, domestic and pleasure purposes: this does **10.15** not cover a trip by the proprietor of a business to negotiate a contract (*Wood v General, etc., Assurance Co* (1949) 65 T.L.R. 53). A car lent to a friend for a pleasure trip, the friend paying the owner for the petrol in it, is being used for social and domestic purposes and is not "hired" (*McCarthy v British Oak Insurance Co* [1938] 3 All E.R. 1). A policy limited to use "in the assured's business" does not cover him when he and another member of his firm are using the car on their respective businesses (*Passmore v Vulcan, etc., Insurance Co* (1935) 52 T.L.R. 193). But giving a lift out of courtesy to a person on business rounds is use for social purposes (ibid.), and in *DHR Moody (Chemists) v Iron Trades Mutual Insurance Co* [1971] R.T.R. 120 it was held that a council in trying to encourage contacts with a foreign town were using a car for a social purpose even if the driver, who was the clerk of the council, was fulfilling a duty to his employers by driving the car for that purpose. Carrying furniture, without payment, for a friend is use for "social, domestic and pleasure purposes" (*Lee v Poole* [1954] Crim. L.R. 942). Use of a tractor to convey household furniture of a newly engaged farm servant to the farm was not within a policy covering use "solely for agricultural or forestry purposes including the haulage of articles required for agriculture" (*Agnew v Robertson* 1956 S.L.T.(Sh.) 90, a Scottish case). Carrying cattle food for cows is not use for domestic purposes though it might be otherwise if it was food for a pet dog or canary (*Whitehead v Unwins (York) Ltd* [1962] Crim. L.R. 323). The court reserved its opinion whether lending a lorry to a person out of friendship would be for "social" purposes even where the borrower's employee was driving. In *Att Gen (McCloskey) v East* (1964) 98 I.L.T.N. 33, a farmer loaded his vehicle with turf and was taking it to a neighbour to use as fuel; his policy permitted carriage of agricultural produce and it was held in Ireland that he was insured. When a car owner allowed the foreman of a garage, where his car had been left for certain work, to use the car on a condition and the foreman used it in breach of that condition, the insurers, on the terms of the policy, were held not liable (*Browning v Phoenix Assurance Co* [1960] 2 Lloyd's Rep. 360).

10.16 If a car is insured in respect of use on the owner's business and that business is specified in the policy, use for another business which he also carries on would not be covered (*Jones v Welsh Insurance Co* [1937] 4 All E.R. 149). Where a vehicle is used for two purposes and one of the purposes is outside the terms of the cover, the insurance will not be valid; *Seddon v Binions* [1978] 1 Lloyd's Rep. 381. In that case (a civil case) a father used his son's car to go to the site and help his son who was a carpet fitter. The father was not employed and his use was for social, domestic or pleasure purposes. The son's employee was ill and when the father went for lunch, he drove the employee home in the son's car. On the way there was a serious accident. The employee's journey in the son's car was held to be for a business purpose and as one of the dual purposes was outside the clause, therefore the use was not covered. The court referred to the decision in *Passmore v Vulcan, etc., Insurance Co* above and emphasised the point made in that case that if the carriage had been a mere act of social kindness, it would have been within the cover, but the facts went beyond that. In *Keeley v Pashen* [2004] EWCA Civ 1491; [2005] R.T.R. 10, the driver was a taxi driver. After he had dropped off his last fare (four passengers), he reversed his car in order to frighten his former passengers, one of whom was killed. The driver was convicted of manslaughter and a subsequent civil claim was made by the widow in which the extent of the insurance cover was relevant. The court held that, having dropped his final fare, the driver was using the vehicle for social, domestic or pleasure purposes. Even though there was a deviation (by reversing towards the four passengers in order to frighten them), that could not be described as a separate journey.

10.17 It is submitted that the activities of charity workers, magistrates and elected councillors receiving reimbursement of expenses only would normally be acts of social benefaction and could not be classified as business use. Different issues might arise when financial loss allowances were paid to cover earnings. In view of the special nature of an insurance contract, full disclosure is always to be recommended.

Car sharing; hire or reward

10.18 Most standard form insurance policies specifically exclude, unless specifically included, the use of the insured's vehicle when it is used for hiring or for "hire or reward", or for purposes of a business or commercial character. As to the meaning of hire or reward, see § 13.49.

It was nevertheless considered important that car sharing should be encouraged in order to reduce road congestion, particularly in commuter journeys to and from work.

10.19 To avoid any resulting illegality, it is provided by s.150 of the 1988 Act that certain forms of car sharing must be covered by any insurance policy issued to fulfil the requirements of s.145, even though passengers are carried at separate fares. Fares and separate fares have the same meaning as in s.1(4) of the Public Passenger Vehicles Act 1981, in relation to public service vehicles. It is immaterial how the exclusion or restriction clauses in the policy or security are worded.

There are certain conditions set out in s.150(2) which must be fulfilled. The vehicle must not be adapted to carry more than eight passengers and must not be a motor cycle. As to "adapted", "passengers", and "motor cycle", see Chapter 1. The fare or aggregate of the fares paid for the journey must not exceed the amount of the running costs of the vehicle for the journey. For this purpose the running costs can include an appropriate amount for depreciation and general wear. The arrangements for payment by separate fare passengers must have been made before the journey began.

Employees and agents

Where a policy covered the assured "or his paid driver" this was held to cover **10.20** a driver who was driving for the assured and was paid as a driver, though not necessarily being paid by, or being in the general employment of, the assured (*Bryan v Forrow* [1950] 1 All E.R. 294). An agent employed by the assured under a contract of service and using the car to try to sell it for him was held to be in his employment (*Burton v Road Transport, etc., Insurance Co* (1939) 63 Lloyd's Rep. 253). Where an employee had the option of using his employer's vehicle to return from a job and was injured while so riding in it, this injury did not arise out of and in the course of his employment under a policy but he was nevertheless being carried on the vehicle by reason or in pursuance of his contract of employment (*McSteen v McCarthy* [1952] N.I. 33; cf. the English workmen's compensation cases). A garage proprietor driving a lorry to the assured's premises after effecting repairs is not a person "in the assured's employment" (*Lyons v May* [1948] 2 All E.R. 1062). If a policy covers employees, driving by one in an unauthorised manner, if within the scope of his employment, will normally be covered (*Marsh v Moores* [1949] 2 All E.R. 27). A garage proprietor with whom an owner has left his car is not in the owner's employment (*Lyons v May* above).

A vehicle owner had frequent business deals with the defendant and one day asked him to drive the vehicle home and collect the owner next day to go on a business journey; the defendant deviated from the quickest way home to give a girl a lift. It was held that the defendant was in the owner's employment and was not on a frolic of his own in going two and a half miles more with the girl (*Ballance v Brown* [1955] Crim. L.R. 384).

The principle in *Marsh v Moores* will not protect someone completely outside **10.21** the scope of his employment. In *Sands v O'Connell* [1981] R.T.R. 42, for the purpose of the relevant clause in the policy the hirer of a car and any person driving the vehicle was deemed to be in the employment of the policy-holder (the hiring company) under a contract of service. One of the conditions of hire was that drivers had to be aged between 21 and 70. The hirer allowed a 20-year-old woman to drive. It was held that she was not driving on the orders or with the permission of the hiring company. In view of her age the hirer was acting in a wholly unauthorised manner in allowing her to drive. Accordingly, since the policy did not extend to indemnify her she was rightly convicted of having no insurance.

Driving licence condition

A common form of policy allows driving, with the permission of the insured **10.22** person, by any person "who holds or has held a driving licence" and is not disqualified, or any person "who holds or has held a driving licence". The exact wording should always be checked. With that form of wording, if the driver has once held a driving licence, he will be covered even though it may have expired and even though it was only provisional. A driving licence would normally include a provisional driving licence (1988 Act s.108) and in *Rendlesham v Dunne*

[1964] 1 Lloyd's Rep. 192 it was held in a county court that the policy still covered use by a learner driver although he was driving in breach of the terms of his provisional licence. It will depend on the terms of the policy whether he is covered if his licence extends to certain classes of motor vehicle and the insured vehicle is not in one of those classes. An unusual situation arose in *Sedgefield BC v Crowe* [2008] EWHC 1814; [2009] R.T.R. 10. The defendants operated a taxi service; they held an insurance policy covering any "private motor car or licensed taxi" for which they were leally responsible. A proviso restricted cover to a person who "holds a licence to drive the vehicle". A person who did not have a licence to drive a hackney carriage (but held an ordinary driving licence) drove one of the taxis to deliver forms to the office of the local authority; these forms related to the business. He was prosecuted for using a motor vehicle without insurance on the basis that he did not hold a hackney carriage licence and so fell outside the proviso. The driver had pleaded guilty to the offence of driving a hackney carriage without being the holder of a hackney carriage licence. The dismissal of the no insurance offence by justices was upheld on appeal; the proviso did not require the driver to hold a hackney carriage licence.

If a person who does not hold a licence commits an offence and the court lawfully orders his licence to be endorsed, a licence subsequently obtained by him is of no effect if he did not disclose particulars of the endorsement (1988 Offenders Act s.45(3)). Consequently he might not be covered by a policy if it requires him "to hold" a licence. In regard to policies which allow driving by a person "who holds a driving licence", it is submitted that this includes a foreign driving licence, unless the terms of the policy make it clear that it does not. Persons are permitted to drive in Great Britain on foreign and international licences, and insurance companies must know that such people may well drive the insured vehicle with the policy-holder's permission, particularly if he is himself a foreigner. Moreover, a policy will normally be construed against the insurer. In *Kinsey v Herts County Council* [1972] R.T.R. 498, a 16-year-old was held not to "hold" a driving licence which had been issued to him a month before his sixteenth birthday, to come into effect on his birthday. (The minimum age for driving the vehicle in question was raised to 17 between the date of issue and his birthday.)

10.23   Where a person obtains insurance by concealing the fact that he is disqualified the insurance will nevertheless be valid for the purpose of s.143 until declared void (*Adams v Dunne* [1978] R.T.R. 281, discussed at § 10.52). It is suggested at (1980) 144 J.P. Jo. 591 that a person who obtained such an insurance would nevertheless not be covered if the contract of insurance included a term requiring the person to be someone who "is not disqualified for holding or obtaining a driving licence".

Subsequently, a case has been considered where a clause in an insurance policy specified that the policy-holder must hold a licence to drive the motor vehicle or must have held and not be disqualified from holding or obtaining such a licence. Such clauses are increasingly common. A defendant obtained the insurance without disclosing that he had been disqualified. While the decision is not binding, a stipendiary magistrate held that while the policy was obtained by a fraudulent misrepresentation, it was voidable and therefore still otherwise valid until avoided, but that the breach of the specific condition in the clause referred to did invalidate it, so that the defendant was using the vehicle without insurance. The difference was between the validity of the policy generally and the breach of the particular condition which invalidated the cover. This is in accordance with the suggestion in (1980) 144 J.P. Jo. 591 above, but not every minor breach of condition would necessarily lead to the same result.

This point has been confirmed and developed in a Scottish case. In *Barr v Carmichael* 1993 S.L.T. 1030 three persons seeking insurance wrongly stated that none of them had a motoring conviction in the previous five years. One of those persons had convictions in that period. The wrong information was given both orally to a clerk in the office of the insurance agent who was asked to arrange the insurance and on the form of application. The High Court was of the opinion that it was plain from the facts that the policy was void and not merely voidable. The High Court may have been assisted in this conclusion by the insured persons written acceptance of a proposition from the insurer that the policy was void and by the acceptance of the return of the premium paid for the insurance. On the facts the High Court considered it unnecessary to express a preference between the decision in *Adams v Dunne* above and *Guardian Assurance Co Ltd v Sutherland* [1939] 2 All E.R. 246 (§ 10.52 below). **10.24**

A disqualified driver may still require insurance to cover the use of the vehicle on the road and its driving by someone else. He would be well advised to check the terms of the certificate and the policy and confirm the position with the insurance company. He will in any case be under a duty to disclose his disqualifications to the insurance company in view of the special nature of an insurance contract.

"Disqualified from holding or obtaining a driving licence" means "disqualified by order of a court", and a person who has been refused renewal of a driving licence because he is mentally defective is not "disqualified" within the meaning of the policy (*Edwards v Griffiths* [1953] 2 All E.R. 874). But a person is "disqualified from holding a licence" if he is, under s.101 of the 1988 Act, prohibited from driving by reason of his age (*Mumford v Hardy* [1956] 1 All E.R. 337; *R. v Saddleworth JJ.* [1968] 1 All E.R. 1189). **10.25**

Where a person is disqualified until he passes a test under s.36 of the Road Traffic Offenders Act 1988 it would appear that he does not become uninsured because s.37(3) of that Act allows him to take out a provisional licence.

Public authorities and other special cases

It seems that s.143 does not apply to Crown vehicles, because s.183 of the 1988 Act does not mention s.143, and Crown vehicles, it is gathered, are in fact not insured. But a government employee who uses a government vehicle for purposes other than the public service of the Crown without being insured offends against s.143 (*Salt v MacKnight* 1947 S.C. (J.) 99). A metropolitan magistrate has held that a postman not employed to drive who drives a mail van on post office business without authority offends against s.143 ([1946] Jo.Crim.L. 168). (Note, however, that the Post Office is in any event no longer a Department of the Crown.) Reference to s.144 shows that that section contains special exemptions for the vehicles of, inter alia, local and police authorities, for those of persons who have deposited £500,000, or such sum as may be prescribed, in the Supreme Court and for merchant navy salvage vehicles. Section 143 applies to motor vehicles, defined in s.185 as a mechanically propelled vehicle intended or adapted for use on roads. It does not apply to vehicles which are not mechanically propelled vehicles intended or adapted for use on roads, such as dumpers, or **10.26** which have ceased to be such vehicles or to pedestrian controlled grass cutting implements or electrically assisted pedal cycles of a prescribed class: s.189. See further Chapter 1.

The use of motor vehicles of visiting forces (see § 2.30) on duty need not be covered by insurance, but members of such forces, when off duty, must comply with s.143 (Visiting Forces and International Headquarters (Application of Law) Order 1999 (SI 1999/1736)). The Motor Vehicles (International Motor Insurance Card) Regulations 1971 (SI 1971/792) as amended relate to the insurance of vehicles brought here temporarily by visitors. See § 10.14 (the Green Card Scheme).

10.27 The exemption in s.144 for police authorities extends to a police officer using his own vehicle for police purposes: *Jones v Bedfordshire Chief Constable* [1987] R.T.R. 332. By comparison, the local authority exemption is more narrowly worded and extends only to vehicles owned by the authority at a time when the vehicle is being driven under the authority's control.

Void conditions

10.28 By s.148(5) of the 1988 Act, a condition in a policy that liability shall not arise or shall cease because of something done or omitted after the event giving rise to a claim is void, but a condition in a policy that pillion passengers should not be carried is valid and is not made void by s.148(2) if such a passenger is carried (*Bright v Ashfold* (1932) 96 J.P. 182). But see § 10.30 below. Further, by s.148(1), so much of a third party policy as purports to restrict the insurance by reference to:

(a) the age or physical or mental condition of persons driving the vehicle; or

(b) the condition of the vehicle; or

(c) the number of persons that the vehicle carries; or

(d) the weight or physical characteristics of the goods that the vehicle carries; or

(e) the times at which or the areas within which the vehicle is used; or

(f) the horse power or cylinder capacity or value of the vehicle; or

(g) the carrying on the vehicle of any particular apparatus; or

(h) the carrying on the vehicle of any particular means of identification other than any means of identification required to be carried by or under the Vehicle Excise and Registration Act,

is of no effect as respects the liabilities to be covered by s.143 of the Act. The principle behind these provisions is also included in European Council directives designed to reduce disparities between laws of Member States regarding compulsory cover. Under those directives it is possible to exclude persons in some situations which they had brought upon themselves (persons entering a vehicle which they knew to have been stolen) or where compensation could be claimed elsewhere but an insurer is not entitled to avoid civil liability on the ground that the driver was intoxicated although the insurer may provide in such circumstances to claim an indemnity from the driver: Case C–129/94 *Criminal Proceedings against Bernaldez (Rafael)* [1996] E.C.R. I–1829.

10.29 It is suggested, however, that it is lawful for an issuer to restrict the nature of the use of the vehicle in circumstances other than those set out above. Thus, if the insurance for a driver plying a trade as a private hire vehicle is restricted to use for passengers previously booked, that is a valid condition and use for picking up passengers without prior booking would not be covered by the insurance policy.

A person holding a policy which contains a condition rendered void by s.148 and using the insured vehicle in breach of that condition only may have a good defence to a prosecution under s.143 (but see a contrary opinion at 110 J.P. Jo. 498) and, even if he has not, s.148 provides good grounds for arguing lenient treatment in cases to which it applies. Section 148(2)(d), relating to the physical characteristics of the goods carried, does not prevent the insurers limiting the policy to cover goods carried for the assured's business only (*Jones v Welsh Insurance Co* [1937] 4 All E.R. 149). A term in a policy that only steady and sober drivers should be employed is not one restricting it by reference to the physical or mental condition of persons driving the vehicle within s.148(2)(a) (*National Farmers' Insurance Society v Dawson* [1941] 2 K.B. 424).

Quaere if a condition that a pillion passenger shall not be carried on a motor cycle or combination is rendered void by s.148(1) in that it is a condition "as to the number of persons that the vehicle carries". The importance of this condition has been increased in that passenger liability was made compulsorily insurable from December 1972. It is submitted that if a policy purports to exclude liability when a passenger is carried this may be held to be a void condition in that it restricts the number of persons carried if the vehicle is constructed or adapted to carry one or more passengers. On the other hand, if a motor cycle does not, e.g. have a pillion seat, a condition in a policy that the motor cycle should not be adapted for the carriage of a passenger would appear to be lawful. This is because it would be a condition more as to the manner of carriage than as to the numbers carried. **10.30**

A policy which prohibits the carrying of a load in excess of that for which the vehicle was constructed refers to the weight-load specified for lorries and vans and is not infringed by carrying excess passengers (*Houghton v Trafalgar Insurance Co* [1953] 2 All E.R. 1409). An overloaded vehicle can be in an "unsafe and unroadworthy condition" within the meaning of an exception clause and this condition can be permanent or temporary (*Clarke v National Insurance and Guarantee Corporation* [1963] 3 All E.R. 375 CA). "Maintaining a car in an efficient condition" generally means that it should be capable of doing what is normally and reasonably required of it (*McInnes v National Motor, etc., Union* [1963] 2 Lloyd's Rep. 415). A policy required the insured to take all reasonable steps to maintain the vehicle in an efficient condition; this means in roadworthy condition. The tyres had no tread and this was obvious to anyone looking at them; it was held that the vehicle was not maintained in an efficient condition (*Conn v Westminster Motor Insurance Association Ltd* [1966] 1 Lloyd's Rep. 407).

Under a somewhat similar Irish statute, a side-car was held not to be "equipment" of a motor cycle but part of the motor cycle itself (*Higgins v Feeney* (1954) 88 I.L.T.R. 152). **10.31**

Trailers

Reading s.145(3) with s.143 it is clear that only the use of motor vehicles and not trailers in Great Britain has to be covered by law, whereas the use of both **10.32** motor vehicles and trailers in other EU Member States (excluding Gibraltar) is required to be covered by s.145(3)(b). Obviously if a trailer is used with a motor vehicle it may be within the scope of the use of the motor vehicle. In *NFC Forwarding Ltd v DPP* [1989] R.T.R. 239, the offence of using a defective trailer contrary to the Construction and Use Regulations was held to be an offence distinct from that of using a defective motor vehicle. In that instance the wording specifically referred to using a "motor vehicle or trailer" thus creating the distinction. It is submitted that for insurance purposes it is necessary to determine whether the use of the trailer is integral so that there is a clear use of the motor vehicle or whether the use of the trailer is distinct. By way of another example under different statutory provisions, it was held in *James v Davies* [1952] 2 All E.R. 758, a vehicle taxation case, that the haulage by a dual-purpose vehicle, a Land Rover, of a trailer laden with goods on the owner's business was a conveyance of goods and that it was immaterial that the towing vehicle held no goods. This example of the inter-relationship between the towing vehicle and the trailer may assist although the principles of a vehicle taxation case might not necessarily be applied in the same way in an insurance case. See also § 1.57 where trailers are discussed generally and where the position regarding uncoupled trailers is considered.

10.33   A policy which excepts from cover any use while drawing more trailers than is permitted by law is avoided where the vehicle is so used, and the driver offends against s.143 (*Kerridge v Rush* [1952] 2 Lloyd's Rep. 305). Use when drawing a trailer is an offence if the policy expressly does not cover use with a trailer (*Robb v M'Kechnie* 1936 S.C.(J.) 25). But a policy which insures against the consequences of negligent driving is valid under s.143 although it may permit the vehicle to be used illegally by drawing laden trailers (*Leggate v Brown* [1950] 2 All E.R. 564). See also *Jenkins v Deane* at § 1.57. A charge of using "a motor vehicle and trailer" in breach of s.143 is bad; the reference to the trailer should be deleted (*Rogerson v Stephens* [1950] 2 All E.R. 144).

A motor vehicle which is being towed remains a motor vehicle and its use on the road must be covered by insurance (*Milstead v Sexton* [1964] Crim. L.R. 474). See generally § 1.57. A motor cycle side-car is not a trailer (s.186(1)).

LIABILITY OF INSURERS

General conditions of liability

10.34   Section 151 of the Road Traffic Act 1988 sets out the duty of insurers to satisfy judgments and includes certain limits to that duty. The difference between being under a duty to satisfy judgments and legally providing cover under the insurance contract may be significant. For instance, in *Motor and General Insurance Co Ltd v Cox* [1991] R.T.R. 67 PC, a certificate of insurance was not in force at the time of an accident but was subsequently issued and backdated to cover the relevant time. Under legislation similar to s.151, the Judicial Committee of the Privy Council held the insurers liable to satisfy the judgment. This was despite s.147 which states that a policy is of no effect until the certificate has been delivered and the fact that in these circumstances the offence of using without insurance would therefore have been committed.

While the position will depend on the wording of the contract and the policy, it was held in *Kelly v Norwich Union Fire Insurance Society Ltd* [1990] 1 W.L.R.

139 that the policy in question did not provide cover for loss or damage for an insured peril which occurred prior to the period covered by the policy even though the consequent damage occurred during the insured period.

The policy is the document which the court must consider and, where a policy **10.35** clearly does not cover the risk, an offence is committed although the insurers may be willing, as an act of grace, to accept liability (*Egan v Bower* [1939] 63 Lloyd's Rep. 266, where it was also held that a letter from the insurers should be disregarded). But where there was a question before magistrates whether a vehicle in its particular state was covered by the policy and evidence was given on behalf of the insurers that they regarded themselves as still liable on the policy, such being a reasonable interpretation thereof, the magistrates' dismissal of a charge under s.143 was not upset by the High Court (*Carnill v Rowland* [1953] 1 All E.R. 486). On the other hand, an offence will be committed where a policy does not cover a risk notwithstanding that the insurers accept liability on a mistaken view of the law (*Mumford v Hardy* [1956] 1 All E.R. 337). It is the policy of insurance that matters; if there is no insurance policy covering the use of the vehicle by the defendant, rights at law under contract, whether between the defendant and another or with the insurance company, cannot make good the deficiency of a policy (*Roberts v Warne* [1973] R.T.R. 217).

A car-hire firm held a policy which excluded publicans from driving hired cars. The defendant, who was a publican, completed the firm's form for hirer-driving insurance by giving his occupation as a printer. It was held that he was guilty of uninsured use in driving a car hired from the firm (*Evans v Lewis* [1964] Crim. L.R. 472): there was no question of false representation being made to the insurance company by the publican; the policy was effected between the insurance company and the garage and therefore there was no question of s.151 applying. The problem is being compounded now that persons more often have several occupations.

A policy covering use of "any farm implement or machine not constructed or **10.36** adapted for the conveyance of goods" means "any farm implement or farm machine" and does not cover a cement mixer, as that is not a farm machine (*JRM (Plant) Ltd v Hodgson* [1960] 1 Lloyd's Rep. 538).

If a policy of insurance is in force covering the use of the vehicle, a policy covering the personal liability of the driver is not required (*Marsh v Moores* [1949] 2 All E.R. 27, a case which also deals with questions of driving within the scope of employment). An exceptions clause in a policy relating to persons who "to the knowledge of the assured" were unlicensed means that the assured must have actually known that; the fact that the assured was reckless in not making inquiries does not mean that he actually had knowledge, and it was held that he was covered by the policy (*Ellis v Hinds* [1947] 1 All E.R. 337). A policy which did not cover driving by an unlicensed person was held to cover driving of a car by such a person where a licensed person sat by her and retained effective control (*Langman v Valentine* [1952] 2 All E.R. 803); it would be otherwise if the licensed person gave merely passive supervision (*Evans v Walkden* [1956] 3 All E.R. 64).

General conditions of liability: criminal acts

The cover required by s.143 includes cover against intentional criminal acts **10.37** (*Hardy v Motor Insurers' Bureau* [1964] 2 All E.R. 742 confirmed by the House of Lords in *Gardner v Moore* [1984] 1 All E.R. 1100). Where the defendant has a policy covering the driving of any car by him, stipendiary magistrates have held that this covers driving of a car which he has illegally taken without the owner's consent (*The Times*, May 25, 1954 and March 28, 1961); at 124 J.P. Jo. 109 quarter sessions apparently reached a like conclusion. In *Police v Bishop* [1956] Crim. L.R. 569 a policy covering motor vehicles not belonging to the defendant was held to cover a vehicle which the defendant had taken without the owner's consent. But many policies cover only driving with the leave of the other car owner. See 125 J.P. Jo. 108 where there is a useful article on taken motor vehicles, no insurance and joint enterprises.

In *Singh v Rathour* [1988] R.T.R. 324 it was held that third party insurers were not liable to provide indemnity where a person borrowed a vehicle with the owner's consent subject to an implied (but known) limitation as the purpose for which it was to be driven when he drove it outside the terms of that limitation. It was held that the vehicle was not driven with the owner's consent because the owner only gave consent subject to the implied limitation.

10.38   In *Singh v Rathour*, May L.J. said that the situation was different from that in *Whittaker v Campbell* [1984] Q.B. 318 where a general consent to take a motor vehicle was held to be consent for the purposes of s.12(1) of the Theft Act 1968, even though the vehicle had been procured by fraud. Neither *Whittaker v Campbell* nor *R. v Peart* [1970] Q.B. 672 dealt with a consent which was limited as to time, place or purpose. For a discussion of these cases, see §§ 15.15–16. A further example of the consequences of a deliberate criminal act were considered in *Charlton v Fisher* [2001] EWCA Civ 112; [2001] R.T.R. 33; see discussion at § 1.88 above. As a matter of public policy, an insured should not be permitted to benefit from insurance in respect of his own intentional criminal act. The majority of the Court of Appeal was satisfied that "accident" could include the deliberate act of the insured.

General conditions of liability: temporary cover on renewal

10.39   Where cover has run out and the insurers give an extended cover note, the defendant must accept that cover note before he is validly insured under it and, if he is shown not to have relied on it, e.g. by later insuring with another company and never paying the first company, that cover note will not insure him (*Taylor v Allon* [1965] 1 All E.R. 557).

The importance of *Taylor v Allon* is often not appreciated by prosecutors. When insurance cover runs out many such expired certificates include a certificate of insurance for the following 15 days. The significance of this is that it was decided in *Taylor v Allon* that this constitutes an offer of insurance which has to be accepted to be effective. Presumably it could be accepted in writing or orally and possibly by conduct. The position may depend on the terms and whether the cover is dependent on renewal with the same company. In the course of the judgment Lord Parker C.J. said "It may be, although I find it unnecessary to decide in this case, that there can be an acceptance of such an offer by conduct and without communication with the insurance company. It may well be that if a man took his motor car out on to the road in reliance on this temporary cover, albeit there had been no communication of that fact to the insurance company, there would be an acceptance, and that the contracts so created would contain an implied promise by the insured to pay" either in the renewal premium when paid or for the temporary period.

This extended cover on renewal is often not as comprehensive as the policy **10.40**
and may be for minimum risks only.

General conditions of liability: disposal and acquisition

It used to be considered that, where a policy covers a named vehicle and "any **10.41**
other vehicle not belonging to or hired by" the assured, the policy lapsed on the
sale of the named vehicle, unless rights of user of it are retained (*Boss v Kingston*
[1963] 1 All E.R. 177; and see *Smith v Ralph* below). But a policy for third party
risks only may not lapse on the sale of the vehicle, unless the terms of the policy
show that it does (ibid.). Many policies now make specific provision for the
acquisition by the policy-holder of a new car. The cases quoted above must be
read subject to any such specific provision in the policy. See also *Tattersall v
Drysdale* [1935] 2 K.B. 174 and *Rogerson v Scottish Automobile, etc., Insurance
Co* (1931) 48 T.L.R. 17, as to vehicles being used "instead of" the insured car.
However, although each policy must be considered on its own terms, the
presumption is now in favour of the cover continuing: *Dodson v Peter H. Dodson
Insurance Services (A Firm)*, *The Times*, January 24, 2001.

A policy which covers persons driving a vehicle by the order, or with the
permission, of the assured does not extend to a purchaser from him even though
the purchase price has not been paid in full (*Peters v General, etc., Assurance Co*
[1938] 2 All E.R. 267). Where the assured's business was taken over by a
company in which she was the chief shareholder, a policy in her name did not
insure the company's vehicles (*Levinger v Licences, etc., Insurance Co* [1936] 54
Lloyd's Rep. 68).

Permission to drive given by a policy-holder cannot extend beyond the time **10.42**
when he ceases to have an insurable interest because he has sold the car (*Smith v
Ralph* [1963] 2 Lloyd's Rep. 439).

General conditions of liability: death of insured

Permission to drive granted by the policy-holder is not necessarily revoked by **10.43**
his death (*Kelly v Cornhill Insurance Co* [1964] 1 All E.R. 321 HL).

Meaning of "use" generally

"Use" under s.143 means that there must be an element of controlling, manag- **10.44**
ing or operating the vehicle as a vehicle: the term "use" does not include the relationship of a passenger to a vehicle or part of it (*Brown v Roberts* [1963] 2 All
E.R. 263). A wider interpretation was applied in the context of civil proceedings
turning on the word "use" in the MIB agreement (*Stinton v Stinton* [1995] R.T.R.
167; for details of this case see § 1.184 above). However, such an extension appears neither necessary nor desirable in the context of criminal proceedings,
particularly where the possibility exists of prosecuting those who aid and abet,
but see §§ 10.48–51 for circumstances where the definition of "use" has been
extended on the particular facts.

Further consideration was given to the meaning of "use" in clause 6 of the
MIB 1988 agreement (see now clause 6.1 of the 1999 agreement) in *Hatton v
Hall* [1997] R.T.R. 212. In this context, the Court of Appeal held that "use" had
to be given its usual meaning in road traffic legislation and not its everyday
meaning. Therefore, the concept of joint enterprise (see *Stinton v Stinton* above)

had not itself widened the concept of "use" in this context. *Brown v Roberts* above remains good law and not all plans shared between a driver and passenger gave the passenger sufficient management over the vehicle to justify the application of "use" to that passenger.

10.45   The test of "an element of controlling, managing or operating the vehicle as a vehicle" was adopted and applied in *Thomas v Hooper* [1986] R.T.R. 1. The defendant was held not to be using a vehicle on tow when the steering was locked, there was no key, the brakes were seized, many parts needed replacing and the engine could not be started. The facts were said to be most unusual. The court said that the defendant could not be in control and in many ways this was not a vehicle at all but an inanimate hunk of metal. *Thomas v Hooper* was distinguished in *Pumbien v Vines* [1996] R.T.R. 37. A vehicle had been parked on a road at a time when it was in working order and covered by an insurance certificate. That certificate was subsequently cancelled and by the time of the allegation of using the vehicle without insurance, the condition of the vehicle had deteriorated so that the tyres were deflated, the handbrake was on and the rear brakes had seized and the gearbox contained no oil because there was a leak in the transmission pipe. It was not possible to move the vehicle (other than by dragging it) without freeing the brakes, replacing the transmission pipe and oiling the gearbox. It was held that the test of user was the same for offences relating to both test certificates and insurance and that in these circumstances the vehicle was a "motor vehicle" even though one aspect of its condition was reversible immobility.

A vehicle is in use on the road even when it is stationary and unattended, and it must be insured (*Elliott v Grey* [1959] 3 All E.R. 733, followed in *Adams v Evans* [1971] C.L.Y. 10361, a case at quarter sessions where the vehicle had no rear axle or rear wheels and was parked in a cul-de-sac):

10.46   An employer, whether or not in a vehicle as a passenger, would normally retain control, management or operation of the vehicle when it was being used on his business with his permission and would therefore be using it for the purposes of s.143 as well as the driver. (For the special defence for employees, see § 10.59.) As to the meaning of "use" generally and in particular as to the special position of employers, partners and hirers, see §§ 1.176–9.

The distinction between "use" and "driving" was emphasised in *Samuelson v National Insurance and Guarantee Corporation Ltd* [1986] 3 All E.R. 417 (a civil case). The plaintiff was covered for the *use* of a vehicle whilst in the custody or control of a member of the motor trade for its upkeep and repair. He was not covered for *driving* by another person. He was accordingly not covered under the policy when the car was being driven by a motor trade repairer to buy spares. The car became on risk again as soon as the car repairer parked it to make the purchase. The repairer was in charge for the purpose of repairing it and the insurers were liable when the car was stolen from the parked position.

10.47   The court considered the meaning of driving in the particular context. The parking was not for the purpose and incidental to the driving, but for the purpose of the journey—to effect a repair.

Use by passengers

10.48   An owner (as well as an employer) sitting by the driver would normally retain control of his vehicle and so would be a user under s.143 along with the driver. In

Carmichael & Sons v Cottle [1971] R.T.R. 11 it was suggested that the only person who could be said to "use" a vehicle was either the driver or an employee when driven on the employer's business. This suggestion was followed in *Crawford v Haughton* [1972] R.T.R. 125, where the court declined to extend the "user" to include the owner of a car when it was driven by another at his request. In such cases he should be charged with "causing" or "permitting", which was said in *Carmichael's* case to provide for the offences of aiding and abetting or being an accessory (see § 1.176). But where the owner was actually in his motor vehicle as a passenger, and the vehicle was driven for him by a friend, it was held that the owner was "using" the vehicle (*Cobb v Williams* [1973] R.T.R. 113).

Passengers engaged in a joint enterprise with the driver have been held to be using the vehicle under s.143. Passengers in a car who know that it is being used without insurance may be guilty under s.143 (*Ross v Rivenall* [1959] 2 All E.R. 376, where there was evidence of all the car's occupants having been concerned together in unlawfully taking it) but not, it seems, if they are ignorant of the lack of cover and do not procure the use of the vehicle (*D v Parsons* [1960] 2 All E.R. 493 and other cases cited at § 15.24).

10.49 In *Leathley v Tatton* [1980] R.T.R. 21 it was held that a defendant who sat in the passenger seat of a vehicle to see how the vehicle performed with a view to purchase was "using" it. The fact that a passenger in a motor vehicle runs away on seeing the police does not justify on its own the inference that he was knowingly helping the driver to commit the offence of no insurance, and a conviction of aiding and abetting the driver's uninsured use was set aside (*Smith v Baker* [1971] R.T.R. 350).

Other than in these instances passengers who have no power of control over the driver will not be users under s.143 and, it is submitted, will not cause or permit his uninsured use merely by letting themselves be driven even if they know of the lack of insurance unless they have procured the making of the journey. For example, a passenger who said, "I accede to your unsolicited invitation to drive me to London in your uninsured car" would not offend against s.143 or, in the absence of any form of procurement or assistance, cause or permit but he would cause or permit if he said to the driver, "Please take me to London in your uninsured car". It is appreciated that the number of persons who would use such language is probably small.

10.50 In *Fisher v Kearton* (1964) 108 S.J. 258 it was held that a passenger, found drunk in the driving seat, was not a user under s.143 when a policy and the ignition keys were held by another person in the car.

In *B (A Minor) v Knight* [1981] R.T.R. 136 the defendant was given a lift in a van. During the course of the drive he learned that it had been taken without the owner's consent. It was held that he should not be convicted of using the van without insurance; aliter if the taking had been a joint enterprise (cf. *Ross v Rivenall* and *Leathley v Tatton* above). The defendant was, however, convicted of knowingly allowing himself to be carried contrary to s.12 of the Theft Act 1968. See also §§ 15.23–4.

10.51 A person supervising a learner driver does not necessarily permit the driving. Where the learner was also the owner of the vehicle, the supervisor was not in a position to forbid the use of the vehicle to the owner (*Thompson v Lodwick* [1983] R.T.R. 76). A conviction for permitting no insurance was quashed. While valuable, the test adopted in that case of forbidding the use is a negative one and may not therefore supply an answer in every case.

Policy obtained by misrepresentation

10.52   A policy obtained by a false and material representation remains valid so far as the criminal liability under s.143 is concerned, unless the insurers have taken steps to avoid it; it makes no difference whether it is void or voidable (*Durrant v MacLaren* [1956] Crim. L.R. 632). It had already been held that a voidable policy satisfied s.143 unless and until it was avoided (*Goodbarne v Buck* [1940] 1 All E.R. 613). In neither case, however, was reference made to *Guardian Assurance Co v Sutherland* [1939] 2 All E.R. 246, where it had been held that a policy obtained by a false and material representation insured no one and was not a policy within s.145(3).

The case of *Adams v Dunne* [1978] Crim. L.R. 365 seemed to have resolved the uncertainty in favour of validity. A defendant concealed the fact of his disqualification from an insurance company, who issued him a cover note. The justices dismissed a charge under what is now s.143 of the 1988 Act of using the vehicle without insurance as no steps had been taken by the insurance company to void the cover note. Applying *Durrant v MacLaren*, the Divisional Court upheld the justices. However, a Scottish case (*Barr v Carmichael* 1993 S.L.T. 1030) shows that there will be circumstances in which a false and material representation will make a policy void (see § 10.24).

Absolute Liability: Using, Causing and Permitting

Generally

10.53   The offence under s.143 arises if a person "uses" a motor vehicle on a road or "causes" or "permits" any other person to use it on a road while uninsured. Subject to the special defence for employees, it was expressly held in *Tapsell v Maslen* [1967] Crim. L.R. 53, following *Morris v Williams* (1952) 50 L.G.R. 308 and *Lyons v May* [1948] 2 All E.R. 1062, that s.143 imposes an absolute prohibition on using an uninsured vehicle or causing or permitting it to be used on a road. A conviction must follow if it be shown that a defendant used it or caused or permitted its use, irrespective of whether he knew or not that the vehicle was uninsured (unless the special defence under s.143(3) of the 1988 Act (§ 10.59) applies). But a person does not "permit" a vehicle to be used uninsured if he allows another to use it only on the express condition that that person will first insure it. When the borrower used the vehicle without having insured it it was held that as he was using it without having insured the vehicle as required by the owner, he was using it without the owner's permission and thus the owner could not be convicted of "permitting" (*Newbury v Davis* [1974] R.T.R. 367).

10.54   The test in *Newbury v Davis* was adopted in *Baugh v Crago* [1975] R.T.R. 453 with a different conclusion. The defendant had a policy of insurance covering the use of his vehicle by any driver who was the holder of a driving licence. He permitted another person who did not hold a driving licence to use his vehicle, honestly believing that that person was the holder of a driving licence. The Divisional Court directed the justices to convict the defendant of the charge of "permitting" use without insurance. Honest and genuine belief that the vehicle was insured is no defence; it is only a defence if he had made it a prior condition of permission that the driver was the holder of a licence. *Newbury v Davis* and *Baugh v Crago* were approved in the civil case of *Lloyd-Wolper v Moore* [2004]

EWCA Civ 766; [2004] R.T.R. 30. A father had obtained insurance for his son on the basis of a proposal in which it was stated that the son was 17 years of age, held a full licence and that use was restricted to vehicles of no more than 1600cc. An incident occurred when the son was driving. It transpired that the son was aged 16, the licence was not valid because it was based on a test taken when he was under 16 and the car had an engine of 1760cc. The father had believed the licence to be valid having been unaware of his son's precise date of birth. Nonetheless he was found to have permitted the use without insurance. A permission was still a permission even where it is induced by a misrepresentation by the proposed driver. A permission is given where there is an honest, although mistaken, belief about the circumstances of the person permitted to use the vehicle. A permission does not cease to be a permission because the permitter, in good faith, believed wrongly that the use was covered by the policy. This was not a case in which there was any evidence to suggest that the permission had been conditional.

Although the circumstances of giving permission to another to drive who is **10.55** subsequently discovered to be uninsured may not be sufficient to avoid conviction, it may allow special reasons to be found to avoid endorsement of the permitter's licence. In the Scottish case of *Gordon v Russell* 1999 S.L.T. 897, the defendant gave permission to drive to another on the mistaken belief that the use would be covered by the other person's insurance. He had earlier been told by the other person that his policy was fully comprehensive and, by his own parents, that comprehensive policies allowed use of another's vehicle. The sheriff declined to find special reasons for not endorsing the permitter's licence on the ground that he had not made sufficient inquiry as to the cover. Applying *Marshall v Macleod* 1998 S.L.T. 1199, the High Court allowed the appeal. The permitter had a genuine belief that the driver would be covered based on information given by the driver and his own parents.

Lyons v May and *Tapsell v Maslen* above were distinguished in *Newbury v Davis* above for the reason that in both those cases it was not disputed that the defendants had given permission for the respective vehicles to be used. The question in both those cases was as to whether it was also necessary to prove that the defendants knew there was no insurance covering the permitted use. *Sheldon Deliveries v Willis* [1972] R.T.R. 217 was explained in support of the view that no one can be convicted of permitting a vehicle to be used unless that person has allowed the vehicle to be used. In *Sheldon*, a car delivery firm were held not to have permitted the uninsured use of a vehicle being delivered by them, when their delivery car driver had, contrary to instructions and unknown to the delivery company, driven the car on a Sunday for his own purposes and without the trade plates. It was held in *Sheldon* that the car delivery firm could not be convicted of permitting as they had no knowledge, actual or constructive, of the unauthorised use of the car. In *Newbury v Davis* above it was pointed out that a distinction must be drawn between lack of knowledge of the fact that a vehicle was being used as in *Sheldon* and lack of knowledge of the fact that when a vehicle was being used it was in contravention of s.143 because it was uninsured (*Lyons v May*; *Tapsell v Maslen*).

Newbury v Davis above was distinguished in the important case of *DPP v* **10.56** *Fisher* [1992] R.T.R. 93. The defendant in *Fisher* was charged with permitting driving without insurance. He had granted the permission to *L* who was disqualified, provided *L* found someone else to drive who was insured and had a valid driving licence. *L* broke the condition of the permission by asking *R* who was not insured. *L* did not check with *R* because he assumed that *R* was covered by his own employment. As a result of the driving by *R* there was a collision with the consequence that a person in the other vehicle had to have a leg amputated. *R* was convicted of driving without insurance and the issue was whether the defendant owner, *F*, should be convicted of the permitting offence.

The Divisional Court held that *Newbury v Davis* should be regarded with extreme caution and that it was only capable of application in extreme circumstances. They distinguished it on the ground that in *Fisher* there was no direct communication between the owner and the driver and that the owner could not know and had not ensured that his conditional permission had been passed on. The appeal was allowed and a conviction for permitting was directed.

10.57   The decision is criticised in the commentary on the case in [1991] Crim. L.R. at 787 where it is pointed out that the absolute liability for offences of permitting no insurance is in itself an exception. Providing the permission is given with the condition adequately conveyed, it could be argued that it is immaterial whether it was given directly or indirectly. The reasoning behind the decision is apparently that it was given both indirectly and inadequately. (See also § 1.171 where *Newbury v Davis* and the other cases are discussed in relation to the meaning of "to permit".)

In *British School of Motoring Ltd v Simms* [1971] 1 All E.R. 317 it was held to be an implied term of a contract between a driving school and a pupil that the vehicle provided by the school for the pupil to take the test should be insured. It is submitted that criminal liability under s.143 for "permitting" would also attach. Note the current requirement to declare proper insurance on submitting to a driving test (see § 10.02).

10.58   Any person using a vehicle in breach of s.143 offends against it, whether he be its owner or not (*Williamson v O'Keeffe* [1947] 1 All E.R. 307), and in *Napthen v Place* [1970] R.T.R. 248 it was held that ownership or proof of ownership of a vehicle was not essential to proof of an offence under s.143. The test is whether the prosecution can prove that the defendant "used or permitted the use of it" (see § 10.44). But it will be a defence if the employer is covered by his policy of insurance in respect of his employee's driving, even if the employee-driver himself is not covered because of his age (*Ellis Ltd v Hinds* [1947] 1 All E.R. 337). The strictness of the test to be satisfied for an owner to be liable for "using" a vehicle driven by an employee was again considered in *Jones v DPP* [1999] R.T.R. 1. The three-fold test is that the defendant owned the vehicle, that the driver was at the material time employed by him and that the driver was acting in the course of his employment. In this case the only evidence that the driver was employed by the defendant came from a statement by a police officer that the driver had said that he was employed by the defendant. As the statement was inadmissible, the prosecution failed. A person may "permit" though he is not the owner (*Lloyd v Singleton* [1953] 1 All E.R. 291). On a charge of permitting the use of a car without insurance the defendant's counsel submitted that since the defendant was not the registered owner he could not be convicted of the offence. The prosecuting inspector referred to p.202 of the fifth edition of this textbook, where it was stated: "A person may permit though he is not the owner", citing *Lloyd v Singleton*. Counsel persuaded the justices that unless the inspector could produce

Lloyd v Singleton they could not refer to this book. In remitting the case back to the justices for the hearing to be continued, Lord Parker stated: "In my judgment that is wholly wrong. They are entitled to and should look at the textbook; and if they then feel in doubt they should, of their own motion, send for the authority and, if necessary, adjourn for it to be obtained" (*Boys v Blenkinsop* [1968] Crim. L.R. 513).

A passenger who is ignorant of the lack of cover and does not procure the making of the journey should not be prosecuted (*D v Parsons* [1960] 2 All E.R. 493). See "Use by passengers", § 10.48 above.

Special defence for persons using vehicles in the course of their employment

Section 143(3) provides a special defence for employees using vehicles in the course of their employment in ignorance of the lack of cover (see the wording of the provision itself). The burden of proof will be on the defendant on the balance of probabilities (*R. v Carr-Briant* [1943] 2 All E.R. 156). The acquittal of an employee pursuant to s.143(3) does not prevent the conviction of his employer for causing or permitting under s.143(1) (*Att Gen v Downes* (1959) 93 I.L.T.R. 121), or, presumably, using the vehicle.   **10.59**

The wording of the defence is such as to demand the fulfilment of each and every requirement for it to be established. The person must prove that the vehicle did not belong to him, that it was not in his possession under a contract of hiring or loan, that he was using the vehicle in the course of his employment and that he neither knew nor had reason to believe that insurance, etc., was not in force.

A   *"Belonging"*

The extended definition of "belonging" in ss.1 and 5 of the Theft Act 1968 does not apply to s.143 but the meaning may be wider than ownership.   **10.60**

B   *"In the course of his employment"*

The subsection refers to "in the course of his employment" and not to "employee".   **10.61**

The expression is not restricted to employment by the person to whom the vehicle belongs; the defence might well apply to a driver who was hired out with his vehicle by an independent contractor to work for someone else.

The question has been raised in a magistrates' court whether the defence can be available to a person who is "self-employed", but using a vehicle belonging to someone else. The *Shorter Oxford English Dictionary* gives both meanings for "employment", i.e. occupation and the provision of services. In the context, "employment" may be more likely to mean when one is employed under a contract of employment or similar arrangement and not merely working for oneself.

As the defence only applies to use "in the course of his employment" it cannot apply to purely private use. A person may be acting in the course of his employment even though he is not working at the particular moment. The position of persons travelling to and from work in their employer's vehicle will depend on the facts existing at the time. See also Chapter 1 on the meaning of "to cause, to permit, to use" and § 10.20 above.   **10.62**

C   *"Neither knew nor had reason to believe that there was not in force"*

The interpretation of "believe" in drink/driving offences may assist—see   **10.63**

Chapter 4. The requirement includes a double negative and it may be misleading to try and simplify this by turning it round into a positive.

KEEPING VEHICLE NOT MEETING INSURANCE REQUIREMENTS

10.64   Section 22(1) of the Road Safety Act 2006 (when in force) creates a new offence by the insertion of a new s.144A into the Road Traffic Act 1988. If a registered vehicle does not meet the insurance requirements, the person in whose name it is registered is guilty of an offence. A series of exceptions are set out in new s.144B which incorporates those set out in s.144 but also provides for circumstances where the person shown as the registered owner is no longer the keeper of the vehicle and has complied with notification requirements or where the vehicle has been stolen and notification requirements have again been complied with. The maximum penalty for an offence contrary to s.144A is a fine up to a maximum of level 3 (£1,000). It is not endorsable.

Liability

10.65   The offence is committed where the vehicle does not meet the "insurance requirements" (s.144A(1)). Those requirements are set out in the following subsections and require that the vehicle is covered by a policy of insurance (or security) and either the vehicle is identified in the policy by its registration mark or the policy (or security) covers unidentified vehicles owned by the person who owns the vehicle in question.

Exemptions

10.66   Where the vehicle does not meet the insurance requirements an offence is committed unless one of the conditions set out in s.144B are satisfied. The defendant must adduce sufficient evidence to raise the issue but, having done so, it is for the prosecution to prove beyond reasonable doubt that the exception does not apply (s.144B(9)). The conditions incorporate those set out in s.144(1) and (2) (see § 10.26 above) and provide for three further situations where the registered keeper has transferred the vehicle or has kept the vehicle off the road (or other public place) or where the vehicle has been stolen. In each case, there will be requirements regarding notification which are expected to be in regulations made under s.144B(7).

Penalty

10.67   This offence may lead to the issuing of a fixed penalty notice; if so, this will be in the sum of £100 (new s.144C). Subject to regulations, there is likely to be power to immobilise vehicles where it appears that an offence under s.144A is being committed (new s.144D).

If prosecuted, the maximum penalty is a fine of level 3; it is not an endorsable offence.

EVIDENCE AND PROCEDURE

Burden of proof

10.68   Section 101 of the Magistrates' Courts Act 1980 has the effect of placing the burden of proof of insurance cover on the defendant and requiring him to produce a certificate of insurance or policy to show that he was insured (see also *Williams v Russell*; *Leathley v Drummond*; and *Davey v Towle*, *DPP v Kavaz* and the other cases noted at § 10.69 below). Once he has done this and produces what on the face of it is a valid policy or certificate covering the use in question, it is submitted that the evidential burden of proof may shift to the prosecution to prove that that policy does not cover the use of that particular vehicle on that particular occasion because of an exception clause in the policy or for some other reason. In *Howey v Bradley* [1970] Crim. L.R. 223 the Divisional Court left open the question whether, once a policy of insurance is produced which purports to cover the use of the vehicle, the burden is on the prosecution to show that the use of the vehicle is not within the uses covered by the policy.

It is possible that arguments will be raised that situations where the burden of proof is on the defendant contravene the right for everyone charged with a criminal offence to be presumed innocent until proven guilty according to law: art.6(2) of the European Convention on Human Rights. European jurisprudence appears to recognise the legitimacy of circumstances where a defendant has to prove certain facts to avoid conviction and also of offences of strict liability. However, it is interesting to note the growing trend for Government to establish access to records enabling confirmation of the existence of insurance and test certificates as well as vehicle excise licences (see, e.g. the Disclosure of Vehicle Insurance Regulations 2005 (SI 2005/2833)).

Evidence

Notice to produce the policy is not required and evidence of its terms may be **10.69** given by a police officer who saw the insurance certificate, if the defendant does not produce it in court (*Williams v Russell* (1933) 97 J.P. 128; *Machin v Ash* (1950) 94 S.J. 705). However, the usual statutory demand or request for the relevant documents is desirable and evidence of that should be before the court. Since there is scope for abuse of the procedure, it is open to a court to inquire more fully into the circumstances where the formal request had not been made: *DPP v Kavaz* [1999] R.T.R. 40. The onus of proving possession of a policy is on the defendant once it is shown that he has used a motor vehicle on a road (*Philcox v Carberry* [1960] Crim. L.R. 563, following *John v Humphreys* [1955] 1 All E.R. 793). In *Leathley v Drummond, Leathley v Irving* [1972] R.T.R. 293 it was again affirmed that the onus is on the defendant, once it has been shown that a vehicle has been used on a road, to show that the use of the vehicle was covered by insurance. The onus is on the defendant to show that the vehicle's use in question was covered by an insurance policy, even though he is not the owner. A driver charged with using a vehicle without insurance must still show that the vehicle's use was insured even though, because he is not the owner, he might find it difficult to obtain the owner's certificate of insurance or insurance policy (*Davey v Towle* [1973] R.T.R. 328). See also *Howey v Bradley* above.

Production of certificates

Section 165 of the 1988 Act makes provision for the production of insurance **10.70** certificates to the police by drivers and suspected drivers and offenders. No offence is committed if the certificate is produced within seven days at a named police station by the person concerned or on his behalf. Section 165(4) does not require production within seven days in person by the person concerned. In *Tremelling v Martin* [1971] R.T.R. 196 it was held that production for this purpose must be long enough to enable the police to inspect it and see that it is a proper certificate of insurance. The Motor Vehicles (International Motor Insurance Card) Regulations 1971 (SI 1971/792), as amended, apply this provision to such cards (reg.6(1)). Section 165 requires the giving of names and addresses both of the persons interrogated and of the vehicle-owners. The term "owner", in relation to a vehicle which is the subject of a hiring agreement, includes all parties to the agreement (s.165(7)).

In order to improve the access of the police to records showing whether or not the use of a vehicle is covered by insurance, s.153 of the Serious Organised Crime and Police Act 2005 provides a regulation-making power to enable the Secretary of State to make provision for the disclosure of information relating to the insurance status of a vehicle. The Disclosure of Vehicle Insurance Regulations 2005 (SI 2005/2833) provide for the Motor Insurers' Information Centre to supply information to what is now the National Policing Improvement Agency. This may be used to assist a police officer in deciding whether to use the power under s.165 of the Road Traffic Act 1988 to require a person who is (or may have been) driving a vehicle to produce evidence that the use of the vehicle is insured. Further regulations may be made extending that requirement to others who may be prescribed under a new s.159A to the 1988 Act inserted by s.22(2) of the Road Safety Act 2006 (when in force).

10.71   There is a further power to seize and retain a vehicle where the evidence is not produced (1988 Act ss.165A and 165B).

Production of certificates—defence

10.72   Section 165(4) of the 1988 Act also provides a defence:

      (a) if the certificate is produced at the specified police station as soon as is reasonably practicable, or

      (b) if it is not reasonably practicable for it to be produced at the specified police station before the day on which the proceedings are commenced.

For the purpose of this defence commencement of proceedings is defined as the "laying of the information" or, in Scotland, the service of the complaint on the accused. As to "reasonably practicable" see § 7.13. As to "laying an information" and beginning proceedings, see Chapter 2, in particular §§ 2.03–5. Section 101 of the Magistrates' Courts Act 1980 applies and the onus of proving the defence will be on the defendant on the balance of probabilities (*R. v Carr-Briant* [1943] K.B. 607).

Production of certificates—other provisions

10.73   As to the duty of the owner of a motor vehicle under s.171 of the 1988 Act to give such information regarding insurance as may be required by or on behalf of a chief officer of police and as to the duties after an accident, including the duty under s.170 to produce insurance after personal injury accidents, see Chapter 7.

PROCEEDINGS AND PENALTIES

Limitation of time

10.74   By s.6 of the Road Traffic Offenders Act 1988 proceedings may be brought for an offence under s.143 within six months from the date on which the offence came to the prosecutor's knowledge subject to an overall time-limit of three years from the commission of the offence. A certificate signed by or on behalf of the prosecutor as to when evidence of the offence came to his knowledge is conclusive evidence of that fact. A certificate purporting to be so signed shall be deemed to be so signed unless the contrary is proved. The offence can only be tried summarily.

The extent of challenge to such a certificate was considered in the unreported case of *R. v Haringey Magistrates' Court Ex p. Amvrosiou*, June 13, 1996 where it was sought to allege that sufficient information had come to the attention of the prosecutor in advance of the date given in the certificate. The view of the Divisional Court was that the purpose of the provision was to provide certainty and that there could be no challenge to the certificate unless, perhaps, it was inaccurate on its face or fraud could be shown. For consideration of the powers of a local authority to institute and continue proceedings, see § 2.16 above recording the decision in *Middlesbrough Borough Council v Safeer* [2001] EWHC Admin 525; [2002] R.T.R. 3.

Penalties

Endorsement of the offender's driving licence must be ordered on his convic- **10.75** tion under s.143 unless there are special reasons (see below). The offence carries 6–8 penalty points. As to variable points, see § 19.30. By virtue of the Fixed Penalty Offences Order 2003 (SI 2003/1253), contravention of s.143 is a fixed penalty offence.

Section 35 of the Road Traffic Offenders Act 1988 (penalty points disqualification) applies to offences under s.143 (see §§ 20.33 et seq.). Where two vehicles were being used by the defendant outside his home for stripping parts from one vehicle to repair the other, it was held that the two offences of using the vehicles without insurance were committed on the same occasion for the purpose of penalty points (see *Johnston v Over* [1985] R.T.R. 240).

Disqualification for any period may at the court's option be ordered on a first **10.76** or subsequent conviction under s.143. The court may also disqualify an offender until he passes a test (1988 Offenders Act s.36). Where there is deliberate uninsured use, an absolute or conditional discharge should be given only in exceptional circumstances (*Taylor v Saycell* [1950] 2 All E.R. 887). Where a defendant is conditionally or absolutely discharged, his licence, in the absence of "special reasons", is obliged to be endorsed and he may also be disqualified (1988 Offenders Act s.46). For a table of penalties, see § 10.88.

The Magistrates' Courts Sentencing Guidelines (see Appendix 3) incorporate a system of seriousness indicators for certain offences, including offences of no insurance. The guidelines provide that the starting point is a fine in Band C (150 per cent of relevant weekly income) within a range of Band C (125–175 per cent of relevant weekly income) and up to 12 months' disqualification. It is no longer possible to impose a community order for this offence since it is not imprisonable: Criminal Justice Act 2003 s.150A (as inserted by the Criminal Justice and Immigration Act 2008 s.11(1)).

The guidelines also identify factors likely to increase or decrease the serious- **10.77** ness of an offence. Those likely to increase seriousness include that the offender had never passed a driving test, the giving of false details, the driving of vehicles in certain circumstances where there is higher risk such as a goods vehicle or public service vehicle or where the vehicle was being driven for hire or reward or where there is evidence of sustained use. An offence is also likely to be more serious where the vehicle was involved in an accident particularly where that results in injury. Lower culpability is likely to arise where there was a genuine misunderstanding about the insurance cover, where the responsibility for insurance rested with another person, where there was a recent failure to renew insurance or to update it on change of vehicle or where the vehicle was not being driven.

The court should carefully consider the option to disqualify. In relation to endorsement or disqualification, the guidelines propose consideration of a range from seven penalty points to two months' disqualification where the vehicle was being driven and there was no evidence that the offender has held insurance and of disqualification from 6 to 12 months where there is evidence of sustained use without insurance or there has been an accident.

Special reasons

10.78   There are a number of instances where special reasons have been found for not endorsing in respect of no insurance offences (see Chapter 21, with particular reference to § 21.12).

Ignorance of the limited cover provided by a policy of insurance does not normally constitute a special reason for not endorsing a licence (*Rennison v Knowler* [1947] 1 All E.R. 302, also reported as *Knowler v Rennison* [1947] K.B. 488). Where there is a particular explanation for that ignorance, such as recent personal injuries preventing the policy-holder from acting prudently to check the terms of his policy, a court may properly find a special reason (*East v Bladen* [1987] R.T.R. 291). In that case a defendant who had recently been seriously injured was carried as a passenger in his own car driven by a friend on a non-emergency trip to hospital. His policy did not cover that friend to drive, despite the defendant's genuinely and honestly held belief that it did.

10.79   Courts have also found special reasons in other instances where there is a belief in the existence of cover and a particular explanation for ignorance of the lack of cover. See the examples at § 21.12.

Magistrates' courts have often found a special reason where it would be right for a child to rely on a parent who had arranged to provide cover, or for a subordinate to rely on a person in authority. Compare the special *defence* for persons using vehicles in the course of their employment set out in § 10.59.

10.80   In *Barnet v Fieldhouse* [1987] R.T.R. 266 a father gave a general continuing permission to his son to use a car. The father was convicted of permitting the use without insurance on a certain day and again two days later. During this period the father was on holiday. The Divisional Court held that the conviction for the separate use on the second day was correct in law. The court indicated, however, that the fact that the father was on holiday and out of touch might constitute a special reason for not endorsing and therefore not assigning separate penalty points for the second separate occasion.

Compensation and insurance

10.81   As to the award of compensation generally and in particular in respect of vehicles stolen or taken without consent, see Chapter 18 and the general principles and overall statutory limits set out there. There is power to award compensation for injuries, loss (apart from death) or damage resulting from offences due to accidents not involving motor vehicles (e.g. pedal cycles) and due to accidents occurring off the roads whether or not involving motor vehicles, independent of whether or not there was insurance cover: Powers of Criminal Courts (Sentencing) Act 2000 s.130.

Compensation may in addition be awarded by a criminal court in respect of any injury, loss or damage (other than loss suffered by a person's dependants in consequence of his death) which was due to an accident arising out of the presence of a motor vehicle on a road if the offender was uninsured in relation to the use of the vehicle (but should have been—see s.130(8) of the 2000 Sentencing Act) and compensation was not payable under any arrangements to which the Secretary of State is a party (i.e. under the Motor Insurers' Bureau agreements, see § 10.09). It should be noted that the word used is "payable" and not "paid". The compensation order may include the whole or part of any "no claims" discount lost as a result of the accident.

10.82 Section 144 of the 1988 Act provides for certain exemptions from insurance. Section 130(8) of the 2000 Sentencing Act ensures that such vehicles are not to be treated as uninsured for compensation purposes.

As to the meaning of "the presence of a motor vehicle on a road", see *M (A Minor) v Oxford* [1981] R.T.R. 246. "Motor vehicle" is not defined in the 2000 Sentencing Act and the meaning may differ from the restricted definition in the Road Traffic Act 1988 (see Chapter 1).

10.83 The MIB agreements, which provide the means for compensating a victim of a road traffic accident where there is no other remedy, have been described above (see § 10.09). The MIB has also been designated as the compensation body for the United Kingdom by the Motor Vehicles (Compulsory Insurance) (Information Centre and Information Body) Regulations 2003 (SI 2003/37) implementing Directive 2000/26/EC relating to the insurance against civil liability in respect of the use of motor vehicles. A person resident in the United Kingdom may claim compensation from the MIB where loss or injury has arisen from an accident caused by another vehicle in a public place in an EEA state other than the United Kingdom or in a country subscribing to the Green Card scheme. Prior to doing so, the claimant must have sought compensation from the liable insurer who must have failed to make a reasoned reply within three months. A claim may also be made where the vehicle or insurer cannot be identified.

It is necessary to establish which claims the MIB is liable for. Compensation may be awarded against the uninsured offender only in respect of the remainder.

10.84 Under the extended provisions in the 1999 uninsured drivers agreement compensation may be awarded by the criminal courts in the following instances:

(1) The agreement provides reimbursement for all injuries in such cases (apart from the exceptions noted below) but not for the first £300 (£175 for accidents before October 1, 1999) of property damage nor for any property damage in excess of £250,000 per accident. Compensation may be awarded accordingly for property damage not covered by the MIB. It is likely that compensation will frequently be ordered for property damage up to the £300 maximum. An award of the excess over £250,000 is somewhat less probable!

(2) The agreement does not cover damage to a victim's motor vehicle or losses arising therefrom if, at the time of the accident, the victim was himself not insured to the extent required by the 1988 Act and the claimant knew or ought to have known that that was the case. In many such instances it might be unjust for the criminal courts to fill the gap despite the victim's own insurance lapse and award compensation for this damage, but in some instances it might be reasonable to do so. The £300 limit does not apply because the MIB will not be liable at all.

(3) The agreement does not cover any injury, death, or damage suffered by a person allowing himself at the time of the accident to be carried in or on the vehicle if he knew or ought to have known either that the vehicle had been stolen or unlawfully taken or that insurance was not in force as required by the 1988 Act to cover the use. The MIB will only reject liability if the person knew or ought to have known this either before the commencement of the journey in the vehicle, or after the commencement if he could reasonably have been expected to have alighted from the vehicle.

The meaning of "knew or ought to have known" was considered by the House of Lords in *White v White* [2001] UKHL 9; [2001] R.T.R. 25. It was held that an injured passenger was not debarred from claiming against the MIB by mere carelessness or negligence as to whether the driver had been insured. *B* had been a passenger in a car driven by his brother, *S*, who had lost control on a bend and the car had crashed. *S*'s driving had been at fault. *B* had been very seriously injured. Neither *S* nor the car had been insured. *S* had not passed a driving test and, moreover, was disqualified from driving. At the time of the accident, *B* had not known that *S* was unlicensed and thus uninsured, but he had known in the past that *S* had driven without a licence. The European Court of Justice had stressed repeatedly that exceptions were to be construed strictly. Here, a strict and narrow interpretation of what constituted knowledge was reinforced by the subject matter. Proportionality required that a high degree of personal fault must exist before it would be right for an injured person to be deprived of compensation. In its context, knowledge that a driver was uninsured meant primarily possession of information from which the passenger drew the conclusion that the driver was uninsured. Most obviously, that occurred where the driver told the passenger so, but the information might be obtained in other ways, as where the passenger knew that the driver had not passed his test. Knowledge of that character was often labelled actual knowledge. There was one category of case so close to actual knowledge that the law generally treated a person as having knowledge. That was where, as applied in the present context, a passenger had information from which he had drawn the conclusion that the driver might well not be insured but had deliberately refrained from asking lest his suspicions should be confirmed. He had wanted not to know. Such a passenger as much colluded in the use of an uninsured vehicle as one who actually knew. They should be treated alike. The directive should be construed accordingly. However, his Lordship was in no doubt that "knew" in the directive did not include what could be described broadly as carelessness or negligence. Typically, that would cover the case where the passenger had given no thought to the question of insurance, even though an ordinary prudent passenger in his position and with his knowledge would have made inquiries. A passenger who was careless in that way could not be treated as though he knew of the absence of insurance.

The exception in clause 6.1(e)(ii) of the MIB agreement had been intended to carry through the provisions of the directive. It was apt to include knowledge that an honest person who entered the vehicle voluntarily would have. It included the case of a passenger who deliberately refrained from asking questions. It was not apt to include mere carelessness or negligence. A mere failure to act with reasonable prudence was not enough.

The wider wording of this provision should be noted and in particular the reference to injury and the unrestricted nature of the damage (compare (2) above).

Under the wording of the agreement this exception only applies where the claimant was allowing himself to be carried in a vehicle owned or used by the offender incurring liability.

In these instances it is likely that it would be unjust for the criminal courts to fill the gap and award compensation for injury or damage in view of the passenger's criminal participation even though they have power to do so under the 2000 Sentencing Act. The £300 damage limit does not apply to the courts in these circumstances because the MIB will not meet the claim at all.

The converse is that the MIB does accept liability under the agreement despite the criminal behaviour of the claimant passenger where the uninsured offender is a third party not owning or using the vehicle in which the passenger is carried. Before awarding compensation in such instances (e.g. up to the £300 damage maximum), the criminal courts would no doubt take into account the criminal behaviour and consider carefully the merits of the case.

(4) Following a line of cases excluding from the agreement those who were participating in the criminal or other activity that led to the claim, the following clause, applying to accidents on or after October 1, 1999, was included in the 1999 agreement. It will, however, make it more difficult for the court considering compensation to be sure whether the issue falls within or outside the scheme. As compensation orders are intended for use in straightforward cases, it may be prudent to leave the issue to the civil courts where it is not reasonably clear.

> " **6.1** ...
>
> (e) a claim which is made in respect of a relevant liability described in paragraph (2) by a claimant who, at the time of the use giving rise to the relevant liability was voluntarily allowing himself to be carried in the vehicle and, either before the commencement of his journey in the vehicle or after such commencement if he could reasonably be expected to have alighted from it, knew or ought to have known that—
>
> i. the vehicle had been stolen or unlawfully taken,

    ii. the vehicle was being used without there being in force in relation to its use such a contract of insurance as would comply with Pt VI of the 1988 Act,

    iii. the vehicle was being used in the course or furtherance of a crime, or

    iv. the vehicle was being used as a means of escape from, or avoidance of, lawful apprehension.

6.2 The relevant liability referred to in paragraph (1)(e) is a liability incurred by the owner or registered keeper or a person using the vehicle in which the claimant was being carried.

6.3 The burden of proving that the claimant knew or ought to have known of any matter set out in paragraph (1)(e) shall be on MIB but, in the absence of evidence to the contrary, proof by MIB of any of the following matters shall be taken as proof of the claimant's knowledge of the matter set out in paragraph (1)(e)(ii) —

    (a) that the claimant was the owner or registered keeper of the vehicle or had caused or permitted its use;

    (b) that the claimant knew the vehicle was being used by a person who was below the minimum age at which he could be granted a licence authorising the driving of a vehicle of that class;

    (c) that the claimant knew that the person driving the vehicle was disqualified for holding or obtaining a driving licence;

    (d) that the claimant knew that the user of the vehicle was neither its owner nor registered keeper nor an employee of the owner or registered keeper nor the owner or registered keeper of any other vehicle.

6.4 Knowledge which the claimant has or ought to have for the purposes of paragraph (1)(e) includes knowledge of matters which he could reasonably be expected to have been aware of had he not been under the self-induced influence of drink or drugs."

(5) Crown vehicles do not require insurance and are therefore by s.130(8) of the 2000 Sentencing Act not treated as uninsured. No claim for a compensation order should therefore arise against the offender where the offender is using a Crown vehicle. Where damage is caused to a Crown vehicle by an uninsured person using a vehicle that is not a Crown vehicle, the maximum compensation order that a court may make is £300. In *R. v Austin* [1996] R.T.R. 414, the appellant took a motor cycle without permission and committed offences of aggravated vehicle-taking, dangerous driving and using a vehicle whilst uninsured. During the course of his offending, he caused damage valued at £3,462 to a police motor car, a Crown vehicle. It was held that the damage to the police vehicle was not excluded from the scope of the MIB agreement as the appropriate clause of the agreement related to the vehicle which caused the damage, not the damaged vehicle. Therefore, compensation for damage in excess of £175 (now £300) was covered by the agreement and there was no power to make a compensation order in excess of that sum.

10.85   With regard to category (3) in *Stinton v Stinton* [1995] R.T.R. 167, a civil case, a passenger who was in a car which was being driven by a driver whom he knew to be uninsured and who was involved in a joint enterprise with the driver was held to be a person using the vehicle for the purposes of the MIB agreement of 1972 and not entitled to claim compensation from the MIB under that agreement (see also § 10.44). A further case considering the circumstances in which a person was a "user" is *O'Mahoney v Joliffe* [1999] R.T.R. 245. The injured claimant was a pillion passenger on a motor cycle of which the driver lost control. Although the passenger had not actively procured the journey for her own ends, it was a jointly conceived plan to combine periods of illicit joyriding with intervals of dalliance between. Both the driver and the passenger were well aware that the law was being breached. However, subsequent to the incident which led to the judgment in *White*, a further MIB agreement included the presumptions set out in para.6.3 of the agreement (see above) which, whilst confirming that proof of an exception is on the MIB, certain matters, once proved, are to be taken as proof of the matters required including the knowledge that the use of the vehicle was not covered by insurance. One of those matters is that the claimant was the owner of the vehicle or had caused or permitted its use. To that extent, the effect of the judgment in *White* is now more limited: *Phillips v Rafiq* [2007] EWCA Civ 74; [2007] R.T.R. 33.

Further consideration to a related issue was given in *McMinn v McMinn* [2006] EWHC 827; [2006] R.T.R. 33. Under the terms of s.151(4) of the 1988 Act, an insurer could exclude liability for injury to a person who "knew or had reason to believe" that the vehicle had been stolen or taken unlawfully. In interpreting "reason to believe", the High Court held that the insurers did not need to prove that the injured person actually so believed but that he had the information which would have given him good reasons had he applied his mind to the issue. This may be of some assistance when interpreting the terms of the MIB agreement.

The effect of the MIB scheme on the compensation powers of courts has been **10.86** a contentious issue which has been resolved by the Divisional Court in *DPP v Scott* [1995] R.T.R. 40. A motor accident had occurred as a result of which damage valued at £1,407.42 had been caused. The defendant, *S*, was convicted of driving without due care and attention and without insurance. After full inquiry, the Salisbury Justices were satisfied that there was no reason why the MIB should not accept liability in due course, subject to the loser fulfilling the requirement of the scheme to obtain judgment against *S*. The justices concluded that they were only entitled to order compensation of the amount for which the MIB would not be liable, that is, the first £175 (now £300). This interpretation of the law was found to be correct by the Divisional Court. Since this has been an issue for some time the arguments and judgment of the Divisional Court are reproduced in some detail below from the judgment of Smith J. (at 44, 46 and 47):

> "... the appellant's main contention ... is that section 35(3) [now s.130 of the 2000 Sentencing Act] permits the court to make an unlimited order of compensation where ... no judgment has been obtained against the tortfeasor and where the MIB were not under an immediate obligation to satisfy judgment. In other words, they invited the court below, and invite this court, to place a narrow construction on the words 'compensation is not payable' under the MIB arrangements. In effect, they invite the court to say that 'payable' means immediately payable as an immediate obligation. In this case, no judgment had been obtained against the tortfeasor, so compensation was not payable under the MIB agreement. Therefore, says the appellant, the condition at section 35(3)(b)(ii) was satisfied and a compensation order could have been made in the full amount.
>
> The contrary view ... is that compensation under the MIB agreement may be said to be payable at any time after the accident has occurred, and it is seen that the tortfeasor was at fault, has caused damage to the victim, was uninsured and that none of the exceptions set out under clause 6 of the agreement apply. For that construction to be right, the word 'payable' in subsection (3)(b)(ii) must not only mean payable

immediately, it must also be capable of meaning payable immediately or at some time in the future.

... it appears to me that the intention of Parliament is that the victim of the road traffic accident should be compensated for losses which he or she will not be able to recover from elsewhere, either from the insurer of the tortfeasor, or from the Motor Insurers' Bureau.

... In the real world, courts will almost always make compensation orders long before judgment in a civil claim has been obtained, and inevitably, therefore, before the Motor Insurers' Bureau is obliged to satisfy the judgment. The Act allows for review if the facts turn out differently from that which was envisaged. If it is recognised that a section 35 compensation order will be made before judgment in the civil claim, it must in my view also be anticipated that the order will be made before the MIB are under an immediate obligation to pay. It is, therefore, in my view, clear that section 35(3)(b)(ii) refers to the compensation which will become payable at a future time. I conclude, therefore, that a sum which is payable within this section is not only a sum due for immediate payment, but also a sum which will fall to be due to be paid at some future time.

As the Motor Insurers' Bureau will never pay out in respect of the first £175 [now £300] of any claim it must always be said that compensation is not payable in respect of £175.

I conclude, therefore, that the justices were correct in attempting to determine the question of compensation when it involved consideration of the agreements between the Secretary of State and the MIB. That was the first question which they posed for the consideration of this court.

The second was whether they were correct in concluding that their power to order compensation was restricted to £175. In my judgment, they were.

I would add only that, in attempting to determine the question of compensation where it involves consideration of the agreements between the Secretary of State and the Motor Insurers' Bureau, magistrates should only act in clear cases. They were right to do so in this case because the facts were clear. Justices should not in my view attempt to resolve any disputed issues of fact. If they are in doubt, no order should be made under this subsection.

In my judgment also, they were right in concluding that their powers were limited to making an order of £175 and for those reasons I would be in favour of dismissing this appeal."

10.87   The MIB has indicated that it accepts that if a person using a Crown vehicle sustained injury, etc., as a consequence of the negligent action of a different uninsured vehicle, that person using the Crown vehicle would still be entitled to claim against the MIB (see also § 10.84).

The extent to which loss not covered by the MIB agreement was covered by the Criminal Injuries Compensation Scheme was considered in *R. v Criminal Injuries Compensation Board Ex p. Marsden* [2000] R.T.R. 21. A 10-year-old boy was walking along a works access track when he was struck and seriously injured by a motor cyclist who was uninsured. As the accident had not occurred on a road, the MIB agreement was not applicable. The Criminal Injuries Compensation Scheme para.11 excludes compensation for personal injury attributable to traffic offences except where they arose from a deliberate attempt to run the victim down. However, on the basis of advice from the Home Office in the past, the Board had made awards of compensation where there was no insurance and the MIB agreement did not apply. Despite acknowledging that the scheme was not legislation and not subject to the same strict rules of construction, the court took the view that the wording was extremely clear and the claim could not be allowed.

10.88

Insurance: penalties

Offence	Mode of trial	Section *	Imprisonment	Level of fine	Disqualification	Penalty points	Endorsement code	Sentencing guideline †
No insurance	Summary	s.143	—	5	Discretionary	6–8	IN10	Fine band C
Failing to produce insurance certificate	Summary	s.165(1)	—	3	—	—	—	Fine band A

* Road Traffic Act 1988.

† **Note**: Fine bands "A", "B" and "C" represent respectively 50%, 100% and 150% of relevant weekly income. A timely guilty plea should attract a discount. See Appendix 3.

CHAPTER 11

DRIVING LICENCES

CONTENTS

PROVISIONS AND OFFENCES

Generally

The Motor Vehicles (Driving Licences) Regulations 1999 (SI 1999/2864), as **11.01** amended, made under the Road Traffic Act 1988, apply.

Council Directive 91/439/EEC on driving licences is implemented. A complete list of the categories of vehicles for licensing and testing purposes is contained in Sch.2 to the 1999 Regulations. A distinction is drawn between driving competencies for different sizes/types of vehicles, and provisional entitlement for larger vehicles has been "staged" and depends on the possession of a licence to drive smaller vehicles. A similar provision stages the entitlement with regard to larger motor cycles, which are defined (somewhat technically) to mean those which have 25kw net power output or power to weight ratio exceeding 0.16kw/kg. Provisional entitlement depends on the possession of a licence to drive smaller motor cycles. Regulations 64 and 65 together provide that there must be compulsory basic training in the form of an approved training course conducted only by a certified direct access instructor. That person will not be authorised unless he holds a full driving licence to drive large motor bicycles, has held that licence for a specified period, is a certified instructor, and has successfully completed the licensing authority's assessment course for certified direct access instructors. An interpretative communication on Community driving licences (O.J. No.C77, March 28, 2002) provides background information to Community driving licences and also "legal interpretation" of specific provisions of Directive 91/439/EEC on driving licences with a view to consistent application of those provisions throughout the Community.

Separate tests must be passed by those with a full driving licence in category B **11.02** (motor cars and small goods vehicles) before the holders are entitled to drive medium-sized goods vehicles and small buses (categories C1 and D1), although they are still able to drive vehicles in categories F (agricultural or forestry tractors), K (mowing machines, etc.), and P (mopeds) without passing further tests.

There is a two-stage test (the *theory* test and the *practical* test) for those intending to drive cars and for those wishing to drive medium-sized and large goods and passenger-carrying vehicles. Schedules 7 and 8 to the 1999 Regulations outline the syllabuses for both the theory and the practical tests, and although in broad terms they cover similar matters there are some variations depending on the category of vehicle for which the tests are to be conducted.

The theory test must normally be passed before the candidate presents himself **11.03** for the practical test. The theory test will consist of two parts. The first part will consist of a number of multiple choice questions covering such headings as:

(a) road traffic regulation, which includes road signs, signals and speed limits;

(b) the driver, which includes alertness, attitudes to other road users, judgment and changes in driver behaviour;

(c) the road, which includes safe distances between vehicles, road conditions, characteristics of various types of road;

(d) other road users, which includes lack of experience of other road users, and the vulnerable;

(e) general rules and regulations, which includes administrative documents for vehicles, how a driver should behave in the event of an accident, etc.;

(f) road and vehicle safety, which includes mechanical aspects of the vehicle with a bearing on road safety, use of safety equipment, including seat belts, etc.;

(g) environmental matters, which includes appropriate use of horns, moderate fuel consumption, limitation of emissions, etc.

The second part will be a hazard perception test based on film clips.

11.04   The practical test covers six main headings which will be familiar: eyesight; vehicle safety checks; preparation to drive; technical control of the vehicle; behaviour in traffic; and alighting from the vehicle. The candidate must satisfy the examiner that he can carry out properly the activities specified and perform competently, without danger to and with due consideration for other road users, the manoeuvres listed under those headings.

The Motor Vehicles (Driving Licences) (Amendment) (No.4) Regulations 2003 (SI 2003/2003), inter alia, introduced the vehicle safety check to the practical test. The like-named 2003 (No.5) Regulations (SI 2003/3313) further amend the 1999 Regulations by including a requirement for a candidate undertaking a unitary test for a licence to drive vehicles in vehicle categories F, G, H or K to be able to demonstrate on one occasion and describe on another, a safety check on a component of a class of vehicle in respect of which he is applying for a licence.

11.05   There is some specification of vehicles which are used for tests (e.g. a car used for a test in category B must be four-wheeled and capable of a speed of at least 100kph). With regard to driving instructors, motor cars provided by candidates for the purpose of the driving ability fitness test, the instructional ability and fitness test and the test of continued ability in fitness to give instruction must have a seat belt, head restraint and (where appropriate) an additional rear view mirror available for use by the examiner (see the Motor Cars (Driving Instruction) Regulations 2005 (SI 2005/1902)).

More significantly, before taking a practical or unitary test, candidates are required to sign a declaration to the effect that he or she meets the necessary residence requirements and, except in relation to the armed forces, the only evidence that will be accepted for verification purposes is a valid passport (see the Motor Vehicles (Driving Licences) (Amendment) (No.2) Regulations 2005 (SI 2005/2717)).

11.06   With regard to the permitted forms of identification for those taking the examination of ability to give instruction in the driving of motor cars, candidates are no longer permitted to give evidence of proof of his or her identity by producing a cheque guarantee or credit card bearing his or her photograph and signature. Regulation 4 of the Motor Cars (Driving Instruction) Regulations 2005 (SI 2005/1902) as amended by the like-named 2006 Amendment Regulations (SI 2006/252) states that the only forms of identification in all cases are a photocard licence and its counterpart or a licence in a form other than a photocard and a current passport. For the instructional ability and fitness test, a candidate may alternatively provide a licence in a form other than a photocard and a licence issued under the Road Traffic Act 1988 s.129(2).

The 2005 Regulations give the examiner of the instructional ability and fitness test the discretion to play two of three specified roles to conduct the test, one of which is a role as a qualified driver undertaking driver development training.

As regards arrangements for taking tests, both theory and practical, the period **11.07** of time that must elapse between the date an instructor supplies an applicant's details to the examiner and the test day itself is reduced to one clear working day, which includes a Saturday (see the 2005 Amendment (No.2) Regulations regs 5 and 6).

The already strict provisions relating to medical fitness in the primary legislation are modified in regs 70–73 to create different requirements depending on the type of vehicle one is licensed to drive (see § 11.49 below for the full legal requirements as to the physical fitness of drivers). Two groups have been created. Group 1 includes the smaller or slower vehicles contained within categories A, B, B+E, F, G, H, K, L and P. Group 2 includes the remaining categories (subject to reg.75(2) and (3)) and thus includes medium-sized and large goods vehicles and all passenger carrying vehicles. Apart from enhanced standards in respect of the drivers of Group 2 vehicles, stricter eyesight tests for drivers of Group 2 vehicles are also required.

It should be noted that the passing of a test on automatic transmission cars only **11.08** confers exemption for other classes of vehicles which also have automatic transmission (see reg.45(2)). It should also be noted (see "Learner drivers", § 11.29) that the holder of a "full" licence does not need to take out a provisional licence in respect of certain vehicles for which he has not passed a test. A full licence confers provisional licence entitlement for certain vehicle classes not otherwise covered by the full licence. Reference should be made to the licence, to s.97 of the 1988 Act and to the regulations. A provisional licence-holder may not drive a motor bicycle with an engine capacity exceeding 125cc "not being a vehicle having three wheels" (see "Learner drivers", § 11.29).

Driving permits issued by HM Forces are not driving licences (121 J.P. Jo. 732). Permits issued by visiting forces may be valid as licences in respect of the holder but do not qualify him to be the "qualified driver" to accompany a learner (*Urey v Lummis* [1962] 2 All E.R. 463). See further under "Qualified drivers", § 11.40, "Drivers from abroad", § 11.58, and "Exchangeable driving licences", § 11.63.

The Road Traffic (New Drivers) Act 1995 provides that drivers who obtain six **11.09** penalty points on their licences within two years of passing their first driving test lose their entitlement to drive—except as learners under provisional driving licences—until they pass a further test.

Section 1 defines the probationary period for a new driver as two years from the date when he became a qualified driver by passing a driving test. Section 6 and Sch.1 apply a similar provision to those who have passed their test but who have at the material time not exchanged their provisional licence for a full licence. Production of the test certificate in these cases is evidence of the date of becoming a qualified driver, and it is the certificate rather than the licence which will be revoked.

11.10   Section 2 of the 1995 Act provides that where six or more penalty points have been endorsed on the licence of a driver following an offence committed during the probationary period, the court or the appropriate person (as the case may be) on endorsing the licence must send it to the Secretary of State for revocation. "Licence" includes a Northern Ireland licence. The Secretary of State revokes the licence, and may not issue any further licence reviving entitlement in the revoked licence until the person in question has passed a further test in the category, or one of the categories, of vehicles he was previously entitled to drive. Once he has passed such a test he is eligible for a licence equivalent to the one revoked. Section 5 requires the Secretary of State to restore entitlement to drive in a case where there is an appeal against a court decision that led to the attachment of penalty points. This will be a temporary restoration pending the hearing of an appeal. The procedure is contained in the New Drivers (Appeals Procedure) Regulations 1997 (SI 1997/1098). If the appeal is successful in that the number of penalty points is reduced below six, the restoration is permanent.

The aim of the measure is to protect the public from incompetent new, though not necessarily young, drivers. Research has shown that although accidents among learner drivers are rare, newly qualified drivers are among the highest risk groups. Certainly 42 per cent of drivers who had received a fixed penalty notice or summons in the first year after passing their test had been involved in an accident.

11.11   Different European states have tackled the perceived problems of new drivers in different ways, some by requiring the display of special precautionary plates on vehicles, some in imposing a speed limit much lower than the general speed limit applying in that state. The solution in the 1995 legislation—rightly or wrongly—is to set a higher standard for new drivers than the average motorist, or to be more accurate to set precisely the same standard, but to penalise more rigorously departures from that standard.

A case which considered the provisions of the Road Traffic (New Drivers) Act 1995 and the Road Traffic Offenders Act 1988 was *Adebowale v Bradford Crown Court and the Secretary of State for Transport* [2004] EWHC 1741. The claimant sought to challenge decisions of the Bradford Crown Court to uphold his conviction for speeding offences and also the decision of the Driver and Vehicle Licensing Agency (DVLA) on behalf of the Secretary of State for Transport to revoke his licence in the light of his conviction. In December 2000 the claimant, who at that time held a provisional licence to drive motor vehicles, was stopped when committing a driving offence. He passed his driving test in March 2001 and thus became a probationary driver for a period of two years. In October 2001 he appeared before a magistrates' court in respect of the incident of December 2000, and he was convicted of driving otherwise than in accordance with the terms of his licence. He was fined and his licence was endorsed with six penalty points. In July 2002 he was detected by a speed camera allegedly travelling in a 30mph restricted area at a speed exceeding the speed limit. He appeared before another magistrates' court in April 2003 in respect of that offence. Having pleaded not guilty he was convicted, fined and five penalty points were endorsed on his licence. On appeal against that conviction and sentence, the Crown Court (which heard the appeal on October 30, 2003) dismissed the appeal save that the number of penalty points was reduced from five points to four points and the fine was reduced. In November 2003 the DVLA revoked the claimant's licence by letter dated November 18, which was to take effect after five days. The claimant commenced the proceedings in December 2003 challenging the Crown Court's dismissal of his appeal and the decision of the DVLA. Following the claimant's failure to succeed with his claim against the decision of the Crown Court, the Divisional Court was left to consider the 1995 Act in the context of the convictions recorded against the claimant. The Divisional Court concluded that at the time of his appearance before the magistrates' court in April 2003 the claimant had committed an offence during the probationary period of his full driving licence. It was therefore obliged to notify the Secretary of State of its order that the licence be endorsed, and it had to send to the Secretary of State on production to it, the licence and its counterpart. This event, by virtue of s.3(1) of the 1995 Act, obliged the Secretary of State to revoke the licence. The claimant's contention that when the magistrates' court in April 2003 was dealing with the matter, it was required by the statute to disregard the six penalty points which were ordered to be endorsed in October 2001 was simply impossible to be read into the statute. The application for judicial review was, therefore, dismissed.

The provisions as to driving licences and the offences connected therewith are **11.12** discussed below. The offence of driving whilst disqualified is considered separately afterwards, and proceedings and penalties for the offences will be found at the end of the chapter.

Renewal of licences and pending applications

Full licences are granted until the holder attains the age of 70 (in the absence **11.13** of any disease or disability). After 70 years of age the licence is renewable every three years. Where the licence is in the form of a photocard, that photocard must be surrendered no less often than every 10 years. It will be reissued free of charge, allowing for the provision of a more current photograph. Applications for the grant of a licence may be received and dealt with at any time within two months before the date on which the grant is to take effect. "Grant" includes grant by way of renewal (1988 Act ss.97 and 98).

Section 39 of the Road Safety Act 2006, when in force, creates a new s.98A of the Road Traffic Act 1988. The new section makes provision for the Secretary of State to make an order requiring the holders of old-form driving licences to surrender them. By s.98A(7) of the 1988 Act, the holder of a licence who fails to surrender the licence and counterpart commits a summary offence which is punishable by a fine not exceeding level 3 on the standard scale.

It is the duty of the licence-holder to renew the licence on expiry and it is no **11.14** excuse that no reminder has been sent to him (*Caldwell v Hague* (1914) 79 J.P. 152). A person is unlicensed if he has no licence at 11am even though he takes one out later the same day (*Campbell v Strangeways* (1877) 42 J.P. 39; and cf. *Wharton v Taylor* (1965) 109 S.J. 475). There are no "days of grace" for renewing driving licences. It was held in *Nattrass v Gibson* (1968) 112 S.J. 866 that a vehicle is not licensed even if the cheque and application for a licence or renewal have been sent to the licensing authority so long as the licence has not been issued, but the position as to driving licences is now altered by virtue of s.88(1) and (2) of the 1988 Act (as amended). The position may be summarised by saying that a person may drive notwithstanding he has not received his licence provided either that the licence has been surrendered in one of a number of specified circumstances or that a valid application for the grant or renewal of the licence has been received by the DVLA at Swansea except:

(a) where the application is for a first provisional licence (in which case the person concerned cannot drive until the licence is issued);

(b) where the application is to drive further classes of motor vehicle for which the existing licence carried no full or provisional licence entitlement (again, he cannot drive until the licence is issued);

(c) the applicant has in effect rendered himself ineligible to obtain a licence by stating on his application form that he is suffering from a relevant disability (s.92).

If a person applies for a driving licence indicating that a disability has ceased, the question arises whether the applicant is entitled to obtain a licence. The cessation may be a question of fact but it is submitted that such a person making a genuine application is prima facie eligible (see (c) above) even though the authority proposes to make further inquiries.

11.15   The scope of s.88(1) and (2) is extended by s.88(3) and (4) which allows the Secretary of State to make regulations extending the benefit of s.88(1) and (2) in similar circumstances to a person who has not previously held a licence to drive vehicles of the relevant class.

The exemption under s.88 is subject to certain conditions:

(a) the application must have been received by the Secretary of State; and

(b) the legal conditions under s.97(3) or 98(2) or 99(7B) must have been complied with.

Where a person has been disqualified by the court he is (if such is the case) a person who "has held and is entitled to obtain" a licence when the disqualification expires. It is submitted that by s.88 and the regulations thereunder such a disqualified person may drive immediately the disqualification expires providing the application has been received and the conditions are fulfilled. This interpretation of the law was adopted by the Divisional Court in *Crawley Borough Council v Crabb* [1996] R.T.R. 201. Under the Local Government (Miscellaneous Provisions) Act 1976 s.51(1)(b), a local authority is required to grant a licence to drive a private hire car, unless inter alia the applicant has not for at least 12 months been, and is not at the date of the application for the licence, the holder of a licence under Pt III of the Road Traffic Act 1988 (other than a provisional licence). Carnwath J. held that that subsection did not require an applicant for a licence to drive a private hire vehicle to have been in possession of a driving licence for 12 months before making his application, and that a driver who had been disqualified from driving could apply shortly after the period of disqualification ended.

11.16   An applicant who is only disqualified until he passes a test of competence to drive under s.36 of the 1988 Offenders Act may immediately apply for a provisional driving licence (see 1988 Offenders Act s.37(3)), and may therefore drive once the application has been received.

If the relevant conditions are not fulfilled a driver will commit the offence of driving otherwise than in accordance with a licence because he will no longer be protected by s.88(1). In addition a person disqualified until a test is passed will commit the offence of driving whilst disqualified (see *Hunter v Coombs* [1962] 1 All E.R. 904).

Production of licences

See § 19.42 as to production of licences to the court under ss.7 and 27 of the 1988 Offenders Act. **11.17**

Section 99(2A) of the 1988 Act requires a holder of a photocard licence to surrender it no less often than every 10 years and s.99(4) requires a licence-holder to surrender his driving licence forthwith to the Secretary of State on a change of name or address; failure to do so is an offence: s.99(5). Under s.99(3) and (3A) the Secretary of State may revoke a licence and require the holder by service of a notice to deliver it up where it was granted in error or there is an error or omission either in the licence particulars or in respect of any endorsement. It shall be the duty of that person to comply with the requirement. On surrender of a licence under s.99(2A), s.99(4) or s.99(3), the DVLA will deliver a new and correct licence free of charge unless the error or omission under s.99(3) was attributable to the licence-holder. Evidence may be required of a name or address: s.99(7B).

In *DPP v Hay* [2005] EWHC 1395; [2006] R.T.R. 3, the Administrative Court held that it is for a defendant to show that he held a driving licence and was insured once the prosecution had established that he had been driving a motor vehicle on a road and that the driver of a vehicle involved in an accident must report that accident to the police within the prescribed time under s.170(3) of the Road Traffic Act 1988, regardless of the fact that the accident had been observed by the police. In this case the defendant, although convicted of dangerous driving before a magistrates' court, was acquitted of driving without a driving licence and without third party insurance on the basis that no evidence had been produced by the prosecution to establish the commission of those offences because the defendant had discharged himself from hospital before the police were able to make a request for the production of driving documents. The offences of failing to produce a driving licence and insurance were remitted to the justices for a rehearing and on the charge of failing to stop and report an accident (in respect of which the defendant had also been acquitted), the matter was remitted to the magistrates' court with an order for it to convict the defendant. **11.18**

Licences not produced pursuant to a requirement under s.27 of the 1988 Offenders Act are suspended and a person who fails to produce such a licence or to send it to the court after being so required commits an offence punishable by a fine of level 3 unless he satisfies the court that he has applied for a new licence and not received it (s.27(4)). The requirement to produce is a formal one and many courts make discreet inquiries as to whether there is a good reason for non-production before making the formal requirement leading to suspension. It is submitted that this is both reasonable and valid. If, after being required to produce the licence, he drives without having produced the licence to the court, he commits the offence of driving without a licence. In *R. v Bogdal* [1982] R.T.R. 395 a driver who produced to the police a licence he knew to be suspended under s.27 was convicted of using a driving licence with intent to deceive contrary to s.173 of the 1988 Act.

By s.164 of the 1988 Act the police may demand production of driving **11.19** licences; this power extends to Convention, Community and British Forces' driving licences (Motor Vehicles (International Circulation) Order 1975 (SI 1975/1208) Sch.3). Powers to seize revoked licences and to require the production of licences obtained by false statements are also given by the same section.

The power to require production of a driving licence under s.164(1) (or insurance or test certificates under s.165 which is in similar terms save as to personal production) applies s.164(1) to:

    (a) a person driving a motor vehicle on a road;

    (b) a person whom a constable or vehicle examiner has reasonable cause to believe was the driver of a motor vehicle involved in an accident;

    (c) a person whom the constable or vehicle examiner has reasonable cause to believe has committed an offence in relation to the use of the motor vehicle on a road; and

    (d) a person who is supervising a learner driver or whom the constable or vehicle examiner reasonably believed was supervising when an accident occurred or an offence was suspected.

11.20   It will be noted that paras (a) and (b) of s.164(1) are in similar terms to s.6(1) and (2) of the 1988 Act ("driving or attempting to drive") although closer still to those provisions before amendment, and in *Boyce v Absalom* [1974] R.T.R. 248 the question arose for consideration as to whether a person who had ceased driving at the time of the constable's request could be validly required to produce his driving licence under s.164 or test or insurance certificate under s.165. Following *Edkins v Knowles* [1973] R.T.R. 257 it was held that the test of the word "driving" in what is now s.164(1)(a) and s.165(1)(a) should be the same as in that case and as it was agreed that the defendant had ceased driving when the request was made, the dismissal of the charge was upheld. See also "Continuing driving", § 1.102. On the other hand where there was a suspicion of a traffic offence under s.164(1)(c), the test is whether there has been a continuous chain of events from the suspicion to the requirement, and the fact that the driving has then ceased is irrelevant. It would seem that where the requirement is based on suspicion of the vehicle having been involved in an accident under s.164(1)(b) the requirement may be made at any time.

Under s.164(5), where a person has been required under s.27 of the 1988 Offenders Act to produce a licence to the court and fails to do so, a constable may require him to produce it and, upon its being produced, may seize it and deliver it to the court. Under s.164(6) if "a person required under the foregoing provisions of this section to produce a licence ..." fails to do so, he commits an offence. Section 164(5) fulfils the requirements of a "foregoing provision". Section 164(8), however, gives a further seven days for production of the licence in person at a specified police station. Section 164(5) is not clear as to whether one constable may seize on behalf of another. The section gives no right of entry to private property. Section 164(6) also makes it an offence where a person is required to produce his certificate of completion of a training course for motor cycles and fails to do so.

11.21   Where a driver fails to produce his licence and names a police station at which he wishes to produce it within seven days under s.164(6), it is unnecessary for the police to call any witnesses from that police station to show that he did not, for the obligation is on the defendant to show that he produced the licence. Section

164(8) provides a further defence in circumstances where the licence is not produced within seven days if the document or evidence is produced at the specified police station as soon as is reasonably practicable or if it is not reasonably practicable for it to be produced at the specified police station before the day on which proceedings are commenced.

In *Tremelling v Martin* [1971] R.T.R. 196 it was held that in order to avail himself of the defence of producing his licence at the police station, a person must produce it at a police station for a sufficient time for the constable to ascertain the matters set out in s.164(1), namely that person's name and address, the date of issue of the licence and the authority that issued it. The court also held that the similar proviso to s.165 as to the production of a certificate of insurance requires the defendant to produce the certificate of insurance for a sufficient time to enable the police to examine it.

A police constable, when he makes a requirement for production of a driving **11.22** licence, may additionally under s.164 require the motorist to state his date of birth under any of the following circumstances: when he does not produce his licence forthwith, or where the constable has reason to suspect that the licence was not granted to the motorist, was granted in error or has been altered with intent to deceive (1999 Regulations reg.83). A constable may also request the motorist to state his date of birth where the driver number on the licence has been altered, removed or defaced or where the person is supervising a learner driver and the constable has reason to suspect he is under 21 years of age.

In a case where the facts did not disclose that a police officer had required a motorist to produce his driving licence and evidence of insurance for any reason other than the statutory purposes set out in s.164 of the Road Traffic Act 1988, a magistrates' court was entitled to convict a defendant for failing to produce the required documentation (*Nembhard v DPP* [2009] EWHC 194).

Section 164(8) makes it clear that the fact that a person produces a driving licence at the police station in seven days is only a defence to a charge of not producing the licence, it is not a defence to a charge under the section of not stating his date of birth.

It may be that the time-limit for an offence under s.164 or s.165 does not begin **11.23** to run until the seven days have expired. However, the wording of s.164(8) that "... it shall be a defence to show ..." indicates that the offence is committed when the requirement is made and not complied with. See 115 J.P. Jo. 254 and § 2.50.

In *Ex p. Jefferson, The Times*, November 5, 1966, the High Court declined to interfere with the conviction of a man who had spelt out the letters of his name one at a time and had taken an inordinate time in giving his name under s.164.

The driver must produce his licence "in person" at the police station. He cannot, seemingly, avail himself of the defence if it is produced by someone else on his behalf. A constable may not be able to ascertain the name and address of the holder under s.164(1) if it is not produced in person and, following *Tremelling v Martin* above, this is the purpose of its production. Moreover, s.164(8) may be contrasted with the parallel provisions as to production of a certificate of insurance contained in s.165(4) and s.170(7) where, clearly, the sections allow the certificate of insurance to be produced by someone on behalf of the driver. Compare reporting an accident discussed at § 7.04 and the seat belt medical certificate production discussed under seat belt offences, at § 9.14.

Driving otherwise than in accordance with a licence

11.24   Section 87(1), as amended, provides that it is an offence for a person to drive on a road a motor vehicle of any class otherwise than in accordance with a licence authorising him to drive a motor vehicle of that class.

A dispute about the likely interpretation of the amended s.87 has been drawn to our attention, in circumstances where a person too young to hold any type of licence drives a motor vehicle. Paragraph 19 of Sch.2 to the Road Traffic Act 1991 provides that an obligatory endorsement with points in the range three to six, and a discretionary disqualification, will follow "in a case where the offender's driving would not have been in accordance with any licence that could have been granted to him". As a driving licence could not be granted to a 16-year-old, it is argued that such an offence would not be endorsable. Although the provision may have to be interpreted by the Divisional Court, it is submitted that this is somewhat tortuous reasoning. The "totally unlicensed" driver, which includes those too young to hold, or to have held, a licence are surely in the same position as those who have a licence, but have failed to comply with the conditions thereof. It is difficult to see any logic in an alternative interpretation.

11.25   On a charge of driving without a driving licence, the prosecutor need in law prove only the act of driving a motor vehicle on a road and the defendant must prove he had the licence (*John v Humphreys* [1955] 1 All E.R. 793). The same principle applies to driving otherwise than in accordance with a licence.

The Tramcars and Trolley Vehicles (Modification of Enactments) Regulations 1992 (SI 1992/1217) provide that s.87 of the 1988 Act applies to tramcars. A licence authorising a person to drive a motor vehicle in Category B within the meaning of the 1999 Regulations shall be regarded as authorising that person to drive a tramcar.

Employing an unlicensed driver

11.26   The wording of s.87(2) of the 1988 Act, as amended, makes it an offence for a person to cause or permit another person to drive on a road a motor vehicle of any class otherwise than in accordance with a licence authorising that other person to drive a motor vehicle of that class.

It is not clear whether the words "cause or permit" require the prosecution to prove that an employer knew that his employee driver was unlicensed. The words "cause or permit" in s.81 of the Act formerly in force seem to have been held to import strict liability (see "'To cause', 'to permit', 'to use'", §§ 1.161 et seq.). It would seem that an employer is under a duty to see that his employee driver has a current licence when he takes him into his employment and to take reasonable steps to ensure that the licence is renewed. In *Ferrymasters Ltd v Adams* [1980] R.T.R. 139 the employers were convicted of permitting their employee to drive unlicensed. Although they had checked that he had a driving licence when he was taken into their employment, they failed to adopt any system to check that their employee drivers renewed their licences. For this reason they were convicted by the justices. Upholding the justices, the Divisional Court held that the case was indistinguishable from *Baugh v Crago* (at § 10.54). The ratio decidendi in *Ferrymasters* is inconsistent with other cases on "causing" or "permitting". The commentator in [1980] Crim. L.R. 187 at 188 is critical. However, the conclusion of the court is consistent with the importance of the issue and, it is submitted, is right in principle and in law.

Aiding and abetting imports mens rea; an employer cannot be convicted of **11.27**
aiding and abetting his employee not to display "L" plates and to drive
unsupervised when the employer had no knowledge that the employee was a
learner driver only and had not shut his eyes to the fact (*D. Stanton & Sons Ltd v
Webber* (1972) 116 S.J. 667).

Driving under age

The under-age driver will be prosecuted for driving otherwise than in accor- **11.28**
dance with a licence contrary to s.87 of the Road Traffic Act 1988, as amended.
See § 11.24 above. Although an under-age person is disqualified from holding a
licence (s.101), they do not commit the offence of driving whilst disqualified if
they drive on a road: s.103(4).

Section 101 of the 1988 Act sets out in tabular form the minimum ages for the
driving of specified classes of motor vehicles. Regulation 9 of the 1999 Regulations deals with minimum age requirements for driving specific vehicles or
combinations of vehicles.

Learner drivers

Part V of the 1988 Act (ss.123–142, as amended) provides for the registration **11.29**
of persons engaged in giving instruction in the driving of motor vehicles and for
instruction for payment being given only by registered instructors. The sections
require driving instructors to be registered and provide for the examination of
persons applying to be registered. It is only the driving instruction given for
money or money's worth that is controlled. Provided neither money nor money's
worth is given, any unregistered person may give driving instruction, but free
driving instruction given by someone engaged in the business of buying and selling motor cars shall be deemed to be for the payment of money if given in connection with the supply of a motor vehicle (s.123(3)).

Paragraph 2 of Sch.6 to the Road Safety Act 2006 substitutes a new s.123 of
the Road Traffic Act 1988 in relation to instruction in the driving of motor cars. A
system of registration of instructors and instruction businesses is introduced. A
new s.123A creates offences in relation to the contravention of s.123. Exemptions
from registration are set out in s.124 and s.125 allows regulation to be made for
the establishment and maintenance of a register of those persons and businesses
which are registered. Conditions of registration are set out in a new s.125ZA.
There are three amendments to the duration of registration (s.126), the extension
of registration (s.127) and the termination of registration by a Registrar (s.128).
In due course the Registrar will have power to give direction as to further applications (s.128A). At the time of writing (March 2009) the amendments set out
in para.2 of Sch.6 to the 2006 Act were not in force.

The question of what constitutes payment for the purposes of driving instruc- **11.30**
tion by a registered driving instructor was considered in *Mahmood v Vehicle
Inspectorate* (1998) 18 W.R.T.L.B. [163]. A registered driving instructor gave
instruction to a learner driver, but the learner driver failed to make payment in
full to him. In November 1995, the instructor's name was removed from the register of driving instructors. On two occasions in May 1996 the instructor gave
driving instruction to the learner driver, the learner and the instructor agreeing
that in consideration for the instruction in May 1996 she should pay the instructor

the money which she already owed him. At this time she had paid him £40. The driving instructor was convicted by a magistrates' court of an offence under s.123. In the Divisional Court, it was argued that the money paid in May 1996 had been money which was already owed to him and there was no fresh consideration. The court rejected the argument. The purpose of s.123 was to ensure that driving instruction was only given commercially by registered or licensed persons. The court must look at the issue in the context of s.123. The test was whether the arrangement had a commercial flavour and, in applying this test, the reaction of the man in the street to the particular set of circumstances might be borne in mind. Exemption is given to police driving instructors giving instruction under the authority of a chief officer of police under arrangements made by him or a local authority.

Provisional licences (apart from Group A) and most other licences last until the 70th birthday and in this respect there is no difference between full licences and provisional licences. After 70 years of age is reached they have to be renewed every three years. Provisional licences for motor bicycles or mopeds normally run for two years. Such licences are not normally renewable within one year of expiry, etc. There are special provisions for licences surrendered, revoked and exchanged and for short period licences granted on health grounds. During the gap year it would become necessary to rely on a different Group licence. If a person did not want the two-year period to run out and, e.g. was going abroad, he could surrender his licence and save the balance of the period. Similarly if a person is disqualified, the disqualification period would not count as his licence would be revoked. A disqualification until a test is passed is unlikely in such circumstances, but if such a person obtained the permitted provisional licence the period would start to run again. A person who drove a motor cycle in the gap year would commit the endorsable offence of driving otherwise than in accordance with a licence (see s.87(1) of the 1988 Act and Sch.2 to the 1988 Offenders Act). After the gap year expired the similar offence would not be endorsable if he displayed "L" plates, because he would be entitled to a provisional licence. It is pointed out in an article at (1984) 148 J.P.N. 212 that the one-year rule will not affect the holder of a full licence who is treated as if a Group A provisional licence-holder.

11.31   The effect of s.97(3)(d) of the 1988 Act is to restrict motor cycle learner drivers to:

    (a) learner motor bicycles (see § 1.17);

    (b) motor cycles first used before January 1, 1982 and not exceeding 125cc (for "first used" see reg.3(2) of the Construction and Use Regulations 1986);

    (c) motor cycles with side-cars where the power to weight ratio is less than or equal to 0.16kw/kg.

Mopeds may not be driven under a provisional licence unless the rider has passed a test of competence or is undergoing training on an approved course: s.97(3)(e) 1988 Act.

Subject to certain exceptions (for motor cycle licences over 125cc) full and provisional licences are for certain groups treated as provisional licences for certain other groups. Reference should be made to the licence, to s.97 and to the regulations. It is submitted that this still may be the case even though a person is at first ineligible—e.g. a 16-year-old who becomes 17 will when 17 have a provisional licence entitlement in respect of motor cars.

Subject to the statutory exceptions, a provisional licence-holder (or the holder **11.32** of a full licence who is driving a vehicle for which he has only a provisional licence entitlement and who is treated as a provisional licence-holder for the vehicle in question) must when driving a vehicle covered by the provisional licence be under the supervision of a qualified driver and must ensure that the prescribed distinguishing mark is displayed on the vehicle; further, he may not (save in the case of agricultural tractors and articulated vehicles) use the vehicle to draw a trailer nor (in the case of a motor bicycle without a side-car) may the vehicle carry any person other than a qualified driver (see reg.16 of the Motor Vehicles (Driving Licences) Regulations 1999). The general rule relating to provisional licence-holders is that they:

> "shall not drive a vehicle of a class which he is authorised to drive by virtue of that licence—
>
> (a) otherwise than under the supervision of a qualified driver who is present with him in or on the vehicle,
>
> (b) unless a distinguishing mark in the form set out in Part 1 of Schedule 4 is displayed on the vehicle in such manner as to be clearly visible to other persons using the road from within a reasonable distance from the front and from the back of the vehicle, or
>
> (c) while it is being used to draw a trailer."

(see reg.16(2)).

A number of exceptions are provided to the condition in reg.16(2)(a), and, for the avoidance of doubt, reg.16(3) exempts compliance when the holder of the provisional licence is riding a motor bicycle, whether or not a side-car is attached, certain other vehicles constructed for only one person, or certain vehicles driven on an exempted island (defined in reg.16(13)).

Moreover, the regulation also provides (reg.16(6)(b)) that a provisional **11.33** licence-holder shall not drive or ride a moped or a motor bicycle not having attached thereto a side-car, while carrying on it another person. Thus not only does the provisional licence-holder for mopeds or motor cycles not have to have a supervisor with him on the vehicle, he is expressly prohibited from doing so: reg.16(6). However, there are extensive regulations requiring supervision by instructors prior to appropriate tests being passed (e.g. reg.16(7)).

A driver from abroad who takes out a provisional licence may be exempt from the above requirements (see *Heidak v Winnett* [1981] R.T.R. 445 at § 11.58).

A person who has never held a provisional licence or whose provisional licence **11.34** has expired and who drives without supervision or "L" plates commits only one offence, namely driving otherwise than in accordance with a driving licence, contrary to s.87, but it is more serious because of his non-compliance with the conditions which would otherwise apply to him. Endorsement in such a case must be ordered (see "Endorsement, disqualification and penalty points", § 11.82). Only persons actually holding a current driving licence at the time of the offence can be charged under reg.16. A learner driver who drives a solo motor bicycle, without a side-car, the engine capacity of which exceeds 125cc does not offend against any of the 1999 Regulations; the effect of s.97(3)(d) is that he is only guilty of an offence contrary to s.87 of driving otherwise than in accordance with a licence. Endorsement must also be ordered in such a case (see § 11.82). The age for taking out a licence to drive motor cycles (except most large motor cycles) is 17 save that it is 16 for mopeds of up to 50cc (see s.101 and reg.9).

Supervision of learner drivers

11.35   The supervisor's duties were considered in *Rubie v Faulkner* [1940] 1 All E.R. 185. It is his duty, when necessary, to do whatever can reasonably be expected to be done by a person supervising the acts of another to prevent that other from acting unskilfully or carelessly or in a manner likely to cause danger to others, and to this extent to participate in the driving. It would be a question of fact in each case whether the position and actions of the qualified driver were such that the learner was under his supervision. If the learner was not, he could be charged with driving when not under supervision and the supervisor with aiding and abetting him. A supervisor may also be convicted of aiding and abetting the learner driver to drive with excess blood-alcohol, contrary to s.5 of the 1988 Act. It is not a defence that he did not know that the defendant had consumed too much, because no one can know until his blood has been analysed. The justices were directed to convict the supervisor when the evidence was that the vehicle had been swerving from side to side, that it had hit the bank on three occasions, and that the supervisor had told the police that he and the learner driver had been out drinking together that evening (*Crampton v Fish* (1969) 113 S.J. 1003). It was similarly held in *Carter v Richardson* [1974] R.T.R. 314 that to convict a supervisor of aiding and abetting the learner driver to drive with an excess blood-alcohol level, it is sufficient for the justices to be satisfied that he knew the learner driver had an excessive amount of alcohol, even though he could not know the precise alcohol content of his blood.

One of the learner driver conditions requires supervision by a qualified driver who must be *present* with the learner *in or on* the vehicle. This would preclude a supervisor standing beside the vehicle helping with an awkward manoeuvre. It is suggested at (1985) 149 J.P. 608 that it would be surprising for a supervisor in the back seat of a car to be sufficient to comply with the condition. He would not be in a position to take over the controls. The condition is, however, not so limited.

11.36   Following an accident a learner driver walked away from the scene followed by his supervisor who took no steps to ensure he remained at the scene. Some 40 minutes later the two were seen together two miles away walking towards the scene. The learner driver was convicted of failing to stop and the supervisor of aiding and abetting (*Bentley v Mullen* [1986] R.T.R. 7). As to careless driving by a learner driver, see § 5.46, and in particular *McCrone v Riding* and *R. v Preston*.

It has been argued that a driving examiner has not the duties of a supervisor, and in *BSM Ltd v Simms* [1971] R.T.R. 190, a case of civil negligence, it was held that an examiner was not a driving instructor or a passenger supervising a learner driver. His duty is to examine the applicant and see if he passes the test. This means that sometimes he must not interfere in the driving in order to see if the applicant makes a mistake. A supervisor who has ascertained that his pupil has a valid provisional licence and has warned him to renew it is not under a duty to see that the licence is valid every time they go out together (*Smith v Jenner* (1968) 112 S.J. 52).

11.37   Requirements with regard to the giving of driving instruction by disabled persons were introduced by the Road Traffic (Driving Instruction by Disabled Persons) Act 1993 which inserted new provisions into the Road Traffic Act 1988; see particularly ss.125A–125B and ss.133A–133D. Regulation 17 of the 1999

Regulations, as amended by the Motor Vehicles (Driving Licences) (Amendment) (No.2) Regulations 2005 (SI 2005/2717), broadens the categories of vehicles in which disabled drivers may supervise a provisional licence-holder to include not only cars, but other vehicles such as coaches, buses and lorries.

Learner drivers and unqualified passengers

A provisional licence-holder cannot carry any passenger on a motor cycle or **11.38** moped: reg.16(6). If he is driving a motor car, as defined in Chapter 1, he must be accompanied by a qualified driver, and if the car is so constructed that there is no room for the supervisor, and is not exempted under reg.16, it must not be used by a learner driver. If he is driving a tractor, road roller or track-laying vehicle (see Chapter 1) he should be under supervision unless the vehicle is made so as to accommodate the driver only. If he is driving a motor tricycle (i.e. not exceeding 410kg in unladen weight) he should be accompanied by a qualified driver unless the vehicle is so constructed that there is no room for one; such a vehicle is not a "motor bicycle" under reg.16(3), as that means a two-wheeled machine, though it is a "motor cycle" under s.185 (*Brown v Anderson* [1965] 2 All E.R. 1).

In *Vincent v Whitehead* [1966] 1 All E.R. 917, a learner driver was in a Mini car fitted with only one seat but the vehicle was designed with space for another seat, which could easily be added. It was held that the vehicle was constructed to carry more than one person and that the driver should have been accompanied by a qualified driver under what is now reg.16 of the 1999 Regulations.

Aiding and abetting

It is submitted that the mere presence of an unqualified person in a car or on **11.39** the pillion of a motor bicycle driven by a provisional licence-holder does not show that the former is guilty of aiding and abetting the latter's offence. There must be some knowledge of the illegality shown by the prosecutor. In *D. Stanton & Sons Ltd v Webber* (1972) 116 S.J. 667 it was held that a limited company was rightly acquitted of aiding and abetting their employee, who only held a provisional licence, to drive without "L" plates and without supervision of a full licence-holder, when there was no evidence that the company knew of the absence of a full licence or that they had deliberately shut their eyes to that fact.

Qualified drivers

"Qualified driver" is defined in reg.17 of the Motor Vehicles (Driving **11.40** Licences) Regulations 1999. Generally, it extends to the holder of a full United Kingdom licence or a Community licence covering the class of vehicle, defined as a relevant licence-holder. Where a person with certain disabilities is the supervising driver, they must be able to take control of the steering and braking functions in an emergency. A supervising driver must either be a member of the armed forces of the Crown acting in the course of his duties or be at least 21 years of age and have held a relevant licence referred for at least three years. The three-year requirement does not apply to a person supervising the driver of a large goods or passenger carrying vehicle of any class.

The 1999 Regulations have been amended by the Motor Vehicles (Driving Licences) (Amendment) Regulations 2006 (SI 2006/524). Regulation 3 of the 2006 Amendment Regulations concerns the minimum period for which a qualified driver who supervises a provisional licence-holder must hold a licence authorising the driving of a category of vehicle in the same category as the vehicle driven by the provisional licence-holder. The principal regulations introduced a requirement that this must be for a minimum three-year period. The 2005 Amendment (No.2) Regulations (SI 2005/2717) amended this requirement by widening the categories of vehicles in respect of which any person supervising a provisional licence-holder driving, broadly a passenger-carrying vehicle or goods vehicle, may hold a licence so that in some circumstances such a qualified driver need not hold such a licence for a minimum three-year period. However, the 2005 Amendment (No.2) Regulations inadvertently removed the minimum three-year requirement in respect of other categories of vehicle. Regulation 3 of the 2006 Amendment Regulations amends reg.17 of the principal regulations so as to restore this requirement in respect of such other vehicles.

11.41   Regulation 17 of the principal regulations is also amended by reg.3 of the 2006 Amendment Regulations as regards the requirements for a qualified driver supervising a provisional licence-holder driving passenger-carrying vehicles or goods vehicles in the same class as the vehicle being driven by the provisional licence-holder. Such a person must have held a licence of a type specified for a minimum period of three years provided that licence also authorises the driving of vehicles in the same category as the vehicle being driven by the provisional licence-holder and he has held that entitlement for a minimum period of one year. A person supervising a provisional licence-holder driving a vehicle in category C could, e.g. hold a licence which authorises the driving of category C vehicles which he has held for a minimum period of one year and which authorises the driving of category D vehicles which he has held for a minimum period of three years.

It is insufficient to be the holder of a provisional licence and a certificate of passing the relevant test. The holder of a United States Forces' driving permit is not a qualified driver under reg.17 for the purposes of supervising a learner (*Urey v Lummis* [1962] 2 All E.R. 463). British international driving permits provide no authority to drive in this country. Driving permits issued by HM Forces are not driving licences (see 121 J.P. Jo. 732). See further "Drivers from abroad", § 11.58.

11.42   By reg.80 of the 1999 Regulations certain persons holding certain foreign and international driving permits, British Forces driving licences and British external licences granted in the Isle of Man, Jersey or Guernsey are to be treated as the holder (for 12 months after they become resident in Great Britain for the purpose of s.87) of a licence allowing the classes of small vehicle, motor bicycle or moped authorised by the permit. A holder of a British external licence granted in the Isle of Man, Jersey or Guernsey authorising the driving of large and medium-sized goods vehicles or passenger carrying vehicles is also similarly authorised for those vehicles. This authorisation only applies if the driver is not disqualified for holding or obtaining a licence in Great Britain. It is submitted that reg.80 as presently drafted is not wide enough for drivers to be treated as licence-holders generally so that they are drivers qualified to supervise learners. There is power to draft the regulations in wider terms (see s.88(5) and (6)) but this power has not as yet been exercised.

Miscellaneous offences

11.43   Anyone who is a qualified driver can supervise and teach a provisional licence-holder. What the supervisor cannot do, however, is to give the learner instruction in the driving of the motor car for money or money's worth unless the supervisor is registered or licensed under Pt V of the 1988 Act. Instruction in connection with the supply of a motor car in the course of business is deemed to be a given for the payment of money: 1988 Act s.123(3).

Part V of the 1988 Act only applies to "motor cars" as defined by s.185 of the Act (see § 1.06). Thus it is possible, e.g., for non-registered instructors to be paid for teaching learners to ride motor cycles or to drive heavy goods vehicles.

Section 123(1) is drafted widely so as to make it clear that no instruction can **11.44** be given if it either is or will be given for payment of money or money's worth. Moreover, the payment of money or money's worth may be made by or "in respect of" the person to whom the instruction is given. Thus it is no defence for the instructor to argue that payment was made by a third party or that the instructor did not himself receive the payment. See also § 11.29. It is only instruction "in the driving of a motor car" that is prohibited. This phrase is not defined.

By s.123(2) the motor car must have exhibited and fixed to it a certificate showing that the instructor is in the register or is a licence-holder. The certificate has to be fixed and exhibited in the manner and in the form as prescribed by the regulations (see the Motor Cars (Driving Instruction) Regulations 2005 (SI 2005/1902) reg.20). For amendments to the prescribed manner of fixing and exhibiting the certificate or a licence in accordance with reg.20, see the Motor Cars (Driving Instruction) (Amendment) Regulations 2008 (SI 2008/419).

As a result of the enactment of the Road Traffic (Driving Instruction by Dis- **11.45** abled Persons) Act 1993 s.125A was inserted into the 1988 Act providing for the registration of disabled persons as instructors.

By s.123(4) the person who gave instruction contrary to s.123(1) is guilty of an offence and if that person is employed by another to give that instruction that other person is guilty of an offence as well. It is a defence to a charge under s.123(4) for the defendant to prove (presumably on a balance of probabilities) that he did not know that his name or his employee's name was not in the register at the material time (s.123(5)).

The instructor also commits an offence by virtue of s.123(6) if the motor car does not have fixed to it and exhibited the prescribed certificate. By s.18 of the 1988 Offenders Act a certificate purporting to be signed by the Registrar is evidence of whether a person is or is not in the register or a licence-holder, etc.

For an example of a prosecution under s.123 of the 1988 Act, which led to an **11.46** appeal to the Divisional Court, see *Toms v Hurst*; *Toms v Langton* [1996] R.T.R. 226. The matters on which the appeal turned concerned sufficiency of evidence and its assessment rather than on the interpretation of the section. For that reason the facts are unimportant. Indeed, the Divisional Court ruled that the case be remitted to the justices to resume the hearing. Perhaps the only significance for practitioners and those advising justices came in the following *per curiam* remarks:

> "Justices might find it helpful to remind themselves that, when they are deciding questions of fact such as those involved in the present case, it is necessary, first, to find the primary facts and then to consider whether there are necessary and proper deductions to be made from the primary facts and then go on, lastly, to evaluate the worth of those deductions."

Note the prospective substitution of s.123 providing for a new system of registration of instructors and instruction businesses and also the creation of new offences in relation to paid driving instruction introduced by new s.123A of the 1988 Act, when in force (Road Safety Act 2006 Sch.6 para.2). See § 11.29 above.

11.47   By s.138 where a corporation is guilty of an offence under Pt V of the 1988 Act a director, manager, secretary or other similar officer may also be convicted of the offence if the offence is proved to have been committed with that person's consent or connivance or is attributable to his neglect (this provision is similar if not identical to other statutory provisions; see e.g. the Theft Act 1968 s.18(1)).

Offences contrary to s.123(4) are triable summarily only and are punishable by a fine of level 4; those contrary to s.123(6) are punishable by a fine of level 3. None of the offences are endorsable nor are they punishable with imprisonment.

11.48   Magistrates have been criticised for allegedly inadequate fines. It is suggested that magistrates can properly have regard, among other considerations, to the commercial benefit obtained by an offender.

Disease or disability

11.49   Section 100 of the 1988 Act gives a right of appeal against the refusal or revocation of a licence (under s.92) or a decision to grant a full licence for three years or less (under s.99(1)(b)). These sections relate to the physical fitness of drivers.

Regulation 71 of the Motor Vehicles (Driving Licences) Regulations 1999 sets out the diseases and disabilities justifying refusal of a licence: severe mental disorder, epilepsy (but see below), sudden attacks of disabling giddiness or fainting (including liability to such attacks by reason of a heart condition or that a person has a heart pace-maker implanted in his body), and persistent misuse of drugs or alcohol. Any one of the disabilities set out is described in s.92 of the 1988 Act as a "relevant disability". Further disabilities relating to respectively Group 1 and Group 2 licences (defined in reg.70) are listed in regs 72 and 73, as amended. By s.92, a licence may be refused because of other diseases or physical disabilities which would make the applicant a source of danger to the public, e.g. deafness (*Woodward v Dykes* (1968) 112 S.J. 787). Section 92(2) defines "disability" as including a "disease".

11.50   Section 92(10) provides that a person who holds a licence authorising him to drive a motor vehicle of any class and who drives a motor vehicle of that class on a road is guilty of an offence if the declaration included in accordance with s.92(1) as to physical fitness in the application on which the licence was granted was one which he knew to be false.

As to revoking a licence because of physical unfitness, see s.93.

A person who is refused a licence because of defective eyesight which he had himself disclosed on his application form cannot appeal to a magistrates' court under s.100 (*R. v Cumberland JJ. Ex p. Hepworth* (1931) 95 J.P. 206). But, if a licence is refused because of information disclosed otherwise than on the form which the applicant has completed, e.g. from inquiries made by the authority, the applicant may appeal to the magistrates against refusal (*R. v Cardiff JJ. Ex p. Cardiff City Council* [1962] 1 All E.R. 751). He may likewise appeal against revocation under s.100 or, save for certain disabilities, demand a test on revocation. Licensing of drivers is the responsibility of the Secretary of State. The regulations allow a licence to be revoked if a holder suffers from "sudden attacks of disabling giddiness or fainting". A person had attacks which allowed sufficient warning for her to stop and park the car; it was held that these, being attacks which came on unexpectedly, were "sudden attacks" (*Swift v Norfolk CC* [1955] Crim. L.R. 785).

11.51 A case before the Sheriff Court in Kilmarnock (*Carruth v Advocate General* 2006 S.L.T. (Sh. Ct.) 33) considered the revocation of a driving licence by DVLA. The pursuer in this case, although seen by a psychiatrist on behalf of the DVLA, was not physically examined. DVLA made no further inquiries as the pursuer's fitness to drive and revoked the driving licence. The pursuer had learned to live with her condition and had approached her driving responsibly. She was able to anticipate when it would be unwise for her to drive in view of her state of health and would not drive when she felt unwell. She had been driving for 20 years. There was no evidence that she had ever driven a car in a careless or unsafe manner and she relied heavily on being able to drive her car. Given that s.100(2) of the Road Traffic Act 1988 gave the court a wide discretion to make any order it saw fit, the court could not accept the decision of DVLA to revoke the pursuer's licence was a correct one, or indeed a reasonable one. In those circumstances the appeal against the revocation of the licence was allowed.

A person had suffered from periodic epileptic fits, the last being about two years ago. He claimed that, so long as he continued to take the necessary drugs, the chance of another attack was practically eliminated. It was held that he should be refused a licence, for, so long as drugs were necessary to prevent the manifestation of the disease, the disease remained (*Devon County Council v Hawkins* [1967] 1 All E.R. 235), but by virtue of s.92 an epileptic may now obtain a Group 1 driving licence if he satisfies the conditions prescribed by reg.72(2) and (2A) to comply with directions from his medical practitioner regarding treatment and check-ups (and, if required, to provide a declaration to the Secretary of State that he will do so). The Secretary of State will also need to be satisfied that the driving of a vehicle by the person in question is not likely to be a source of danger to the public.

11.52 More stringent provisions relating to epilepsy and Group 2 licences are contained in reg.73(8).

As to the duty of the court to notify the Secretary of State under s.22 of the 1988 Offenders Act where the defendant may suffer from a disease or disability, see § 20.88. See § 5.107 as to driving with defective eyesight.

Under s.94 if at any time a licence-holder becomes aware that he is suffering from a "relevant disability", a "prospective disability", or that an existing disability has become more acute he must notify the Secretary of State of that fact unless the disability is one which the licence-holder has not previously suffered and he has reasonable grounds for believing that it will not extend more than three months.

11.53 The Secretary of State may impose conditions to be attached to a driving licence restricting the classes or categories of vehicle which, in view of the licence-holder's disability, he can properly drive. If the disabled driver drives a vehicle which is not within the class or category of vehicle to which his licence is restricted, he offends against s.87(1) (driving otherwise than in accordance with a licence). Section 192(3) of the Act provides that references in the Act to a class of vehicle shall be construed as references to a class defined by reference to any characteristics of the vehicle or to any other circumstances whatsoever.

In *McKissoch v Rees-Davies* [1976] R.T.R. 419, a licence was issued to a one-armed driver with a condition that the licence was restricted to "a motor car with all controls correctly and conveniently operated without the use of the right arm". The Divisional Court held that this condition, as worded, did not prevent the licence-holder from driving an unadapted, standard model, car which had a central floor-mounted manual gear lever and central floor-mounted hand brake.

11.54　　In *Ogilvie v O'Donnell* 1983 S.C.C.R. 257 a licence was issued to a driver without a right arm on condition that "all the controls (including direction indicators and stop lights)" were "so fitted that they can be correctly and conveniently operated despite loss of right arm". The switches for the lights, windscreen wipers and washers were on the right-hand side. It was held that he was in breach of the condition in that they were controls which could not be correctly and conveniently operated. There had been a conviction under s.87(1) for the former offence of no driving licence and the Scottish court accepted this without comment.

Section 94(3A) of the 1988 Act deals with the provision of information about disabilities. It is an offence for a person who holds a licence authorising him to drive a motor vehicle of any class and who drives a motor vehicle of that class on a road, if at an earlier time while the licence was in force he was required by s.92(1) to notify the Secretary of State but has failed without reasonable excuse to do so.

11.55　　A more serious offence, where imprisonment is an option for the convicting court, is provided under s.94A. An offence is committed if a person drives a motor vehicle of any class on a road otherwise than in accordance with a licence authorising him to drive a motor vehicle of that class, if:

(a) at any earlier time the Secretary of State has in accordance with s.92(3) refused to grant such a licence, or has under s.93(1) or (2) revoked such a licence, and

(b) he has not since that earlier time held such a licence.

Appeal

11.56　　Now that most licences normally last until the age of 70 and are not renewed periodically, increasing use is being made by the Secretary of State of the power to revoke licences by reason of disability. Consequently there is an increasing use of the right of appeal under s.100 of the 1988 Act. The procedure is by way of complaint in accordance with Pt II of the Magistrates' Courts Act 1980.

Before a person may appeal under s.100 against the refusal or revocation of his licence to the magistrates' court acting for the local justice area in which he resides, he is required to be a "person aggrieved". It was held in *R. v Cumberland JJ.*, at § 11.50, that the applicant could not be said to be a "person aggrieved" where the disability which he himself disclosed on his application form was such that the authority had no choice but to refuse his application. The appellate court has no greater authority to grant a licence than has the Secretary of State. *R. v Cumberland JJ.* was followed in *R. v Ipswich JJ. Ex p. Robson* [1971] 2 All E.R. 1395. On appeal the magistrates' court is not entitled to entertain any question of the applicant's competence to drive if the examiner has declared that he failed the test (s.100(3)). It would seem that the burden of establishing that he is entitled to a licence or that the test was wrongfully conducted is on the appellant. He who asserts must prove. The power of the Secretary of State to revoke or refuse licences in the case of, inter alia, problem drinkers is considered in full at § 4.330. As far as convictions entered on or after June 1, 1990 are concerned drivers will be regarded as high risk offenders if they fall within any of the following categories:

(a) those disqualified for driving whilst two and a half times over the prescribed limit;

(b) those disqualified twice for drink/driving offences within 10 years;

(c) those disqualified for refusal to supply a specimen for analysis.

Electrically assisted pedal cycles

An electrically assisted pedal cycle as defined (see § 1.23) is not to be treated **11.57** as a motor vehicle (although it will be a mechanically propelled vehicle) for the purposes of the 1984 and 1988 Acts. No driving licence is therefore required. If a person under 14 drives such a pedal cycle or if a person knowing or suspecting that another person is under the age of 14 causes or permits him to drive such a pedal cycle, he commits an offence contrary to s.32 of the Road Traffic Act 1988.

As to "drives", "pushing and driving", "causes", and "permits" see Chapter 1. "Knowing" imports mens rea. The offence of dishonest handling contrary to s.22 of the Theft Act 1968 requires "knowledge" or "belief" and some of the cases on that section may assist. "Suspect" is a lower "standard" than "believe". See also § 4.45 and § 15.02.

Drivers from abroad

Regulation 80 of the Motor Vehicles (Driving Licences) Regulations 1999 **11.58** provides that a person who holds a "relevant permit" (see reg.80(6)) and who becomes resident in Great Britain and is not disqualified from holding a licence in Great Britain will be entitled to drive on his permit in this country for a period of one year. His foreign licence will entitle him to take a driving test within that period to obtain a full driving licence. If a year has passed and he has not taken and passed a driving test he must then obtain a British provisional licence, and comply with the usual conditions of that licence. On a purely practical basis, there is nothing to prevent a driver from abroad obtaining a provisional driving licence within the first year after becoming resident. It has the advantage of ensuring continuity, however, in that the driver who waits until the end of the year before applying for a provisional licence will not be able to drive if the application for the provisional licence takes some time to process. The simplest practical advice is for the foreign driver who becomes resident here to make arrangements to take his driving test with due diligence. Note as well reg.18 which provides that a visitor or new resident in Great Britain who is entitled to drive by virtue of a relevant permit who, during that period, acquires a provisional licence is exempt from compliance with reg.16.

Where a driver who was still exempt took out a provisional licence under the 1988 Act, he did not have to comply with the learner driver conditions because he could rely on his exemption (*Heidak v Winnett* [1981] R.T.R. 445). If he is disqualified for holding or obtaining a driving licence by an English court, his right to drive ceases.

A judgment of the European Court of Justice on a reference for a preliminary **11.59** ruling (Joined Cases C–329/06 and Case C–343/06 *Arthur Wiedemann v Land*

Baden-Württemberg, Peter Funk v Stadt Chemnitz, June 26, 2008, Third Chamber) determined that on a proper construction of Council Directive 91/439/EEC on driving licences, as amended, it is contrary to those provisions for a Member State to refuse to recognise in its territory the right to drive stemming from a driving licence subsequently issued by another Member State beyond any period in which the person concerned is forbidden to apply for a new licence. It is not contrary to those provisions for a Member State to refuse to recognise that right to drive if it is established that when the licence was issued its holder had been the object of a measure withdrawing an earlier licence. In effect the European Court of Justice ruled that Germany was entitled to refuse to recognise licences obtained by German drivers who had been disqualified and applied for and obtained replacement licences in the Czech Republic. They were not normally resident in the Czech Republic when those licences were issued.

Article 3 of the Motor Vehicles (International Circulation) Order 1975 (SI 1975/1208, as amended) deals with visiting forces and their dependants.

Persons between the ages of 18 and 20 may drive in certain circumstances even though they would otherwise be disqualified by being under 21. Further, ss.173, 174 of the 1988 Act and s.13 of the 1988 Offenders Act (forgery of documents, etc., false statements and withholding material information, and admissibility of evidence) now apply to British international driving permits.

11.60   It would seem that a United Kingdom citizen cannot drive in the United Kingdom on an international driving permit issued to him, but it would seem that he may drive on his international driving permit outside the United Kingdom even if he is disqualified by an English court. Although the Secretary of State can do so, there is no provision requiring him to revoke the international driving permit; nor can it be said that an international driving permit is a licence issued under Pt III of the 1988 Act.

A Community licence (defined in s.108(1)) holder may drive a motor vehicle in Great Britain of any class which he is authorised to drive by his Community licence providing he is not disqualified from obtaining a British licence: s.99A. Controls exist to equate Community licences to national licences for prescribed classes of goods vehicles and passenger-carrying vehicles: ss.99A(3), (4) and 99B–99E.

11.61   A judgment of the European Court of Justice on a reference for a preliminary ruling (Case C–476/01 *Criminal Proceedings against Felix Kapper*, April 29, 2004, ECJ) dealt with the mutual recognition of driving licences and the residence requirement under Directive 91/439/EEC. The case concerned the effects of the withdrawal or cancellation of a previous driving licence and the recognition of a new driving licence issued by another Member State. It was decided that art.1(2), 7(1)(b) and 91 of the directive, taken together, must be interpreted as meaning that they preclude a Member State from refusing to recognise a driving licence issued by another state, on the ground that, according to the information available for the first Member State, the holder of the licence had, on the date on which it was issued, taken up normal residence in that Member State and not in the Member State in which the licence was issued. Further, the European Court of Justice held that the provisions of arts 1(2) and 8(4) of Directive 91/439/EEC, taken together, must be interpreted as meaning that they precluded a Member State from refusing to recognise the validity of a driving licence issued by another Member State on the ground that its holder had, in the first Member State, been subject to a measure withdrawing or cancelling the driving licence issued by that Member State, where a temporary ban on obtaining a new licence with which the measure was coupled, had expired on the date of issue of the licence issued by the other Member State.

Council Directive 2006/126/EC on driving licences recasts the provisions of Directive 91/439/EEC and provides for a fuller harmonisation of the driving licence regime within the European Union. The 2006 Directive covers the introduction of a "model" Community driving licence and the mutual recognition of licences (arts 1 and 2). Article 3 deals with anti-forgery measures, while art.4 contains provisions relating to categories of licence, definitions and the minimum ages required to drive certain categories of vehicle.

In the preamble to the 2006 Directive, there is also reference to enforcement **11.62** provisions and the establishment of minimum standards concerning access to the profession of examiner and examiner training requirements.

The main provisions of the directive entered into force on January 19, 2007, although certain articles do not apply until January 19, 2009.

Holders of licences issued in EU countries, entitling them to drive motor cars, will be permitted to apply for a licence to drive taxis or private hire cars and to drive small buses for charitable purposes.

Exchangeable driving licences

The 1988 Act allows licences of other countries or territories to be exchanged. **11.63** The country or territory must be so designated by statutory instrument. See the various Driving Licences (Exchangeable Licences) Orders from 1984 onwards and the references and definitions in s.108(1) and (2) of the 1988 Act. The countries designated include Australia, Barbados, British Virgin Islands, Canada, Cyprus, Falkland Islands, the Faroe Islands, Hong Kong, Japan, Republic of Korea, Malta, Monaco, New Zealand, Singapore, South Africa, Switzerland and Zimbabwe. A licence granted in either of those countries to a person who has passed a test there or by exchange with a licence granted in any EEA state or any country listed in the Schedule to the order and which authorises driving of a class of vehicle specified in the regulations may be exchanged for a United Kingdom licence. The classes of vehicle covered are mopeds, motor cycles, motor cars and small goods vehicles up to 3.5 tonnes, tractors, pedestrian controlled vehicles and mowing machines though not all countries are designated to the same extent. For instance, motor cycle licences granted in the Republic of Korea are not exchangeable whereas car licences are. If the test was on a vehicle with automatic transmission, the United Kingdom licence will only authorise driving of such vehicles even if the original licence also allowed driving of vehicles with manual transmission.

It was held in Case C–193/94 *Criminal proceedings against Skanavi (Sofia) and Chryssanthakopoulos (Konstantin)* [1997] R.T.R. 344 that if the person failed to exchange his driving licence within one year he should not have been liable to sanctions appropriate to a person who had been driving without a licence.

Subject to satisfying the other requirements of Pt III of the 1988 Act (e.g. age, **11.64** physical fitness, not disqualified) a person may under s.89 of the 1988 Act exchange his exchangeable driving licence (other than a United Kingdom licence) for a corresponding British Pt III licence if he has become normally resident in

Great Britain (or, where the exchangeable licence is a Community licence, the United Kingdom) but has not been so resident for more than a year. The right to exchange does not apply to learner exchangeable licences (see s.89(8)). It does not apply when the Community licence has already been obtained by exchange for a non-Community licence (see s.108(1)).

Section 89(8) specifies that for the purpose of this s.89 exchange application the exchangeable licence must be for the time being valid at the time of application. It must also be valid for the purpose of s.88(1) (ibid.) which is to apply. This apparently means that the exchangeable licence must be valid at the time of the application for the Pt III licence but the applicant may drive (even though the exchangeable licence expires in the meantime) under and subject to the s.88(1) conditions until the application is dealt with. For Pt III renewals, by contrast, it is immaterial that the licence has already expired at the time of application providing the applicant "*has held*" such a licence (see s.88(1)). Similarly, a driving licence can be granted in the United Kingdom if the person applying holds a full British external licence providing the Secretary of State has designated the law under which the licence was granted as making satisfactory provision. British external licences may be granted in the Isle of Man and in the Channel Islands.

DRIVING WHILE DISQUALIFIED

The offence (s.103)

11.65   Putting it at its simplest, it is an offence under s.103, if a person, while disqualified for holding or obtaining a licence (a) obtains a licence, or (b) drives a motor vehicle on a road. The section goes on to say (in subs.(2)) that a licence obtained by a person who is disqualified is of no effect (or where the disqualification relates only to vehicles of a particular class, is of no effect in relation to vehicles of that class). A constable in uniform may arrest without warrant any person driving a motor vehicle on a road whom he has reasonable cause to suspect of being disqualified. Section 103(4) excludes "under-age drivers" from the effects of the section, and they will be prosecuted under s.87 for driving "otherwise than in accordance with" a licence.

The offence of driving while disqualified is one of strict liability. It is no defence that the offender did not know of the disqualification; knowledge of the disqualification need not be proved (*Taylor v Kenyon* [1952] 2 All E.R. 726). In *R. v Bowsher* [1973] R.T.R. 202, the court upheld a conviction, following *Taylor v Kenyon*, where the defendant had had his licence returned to him in error by the licensing authority. In *R. v Miller* [1975] R.T.R. 479, it was held that the fact that the offender thought that the place on which he was driving was not a road could not provide a defence. In *R. v Martin* [1989] R.T.R. 63, a motorist drove a motor vehicle on a road whilst disqualified from driving. He was indicted under the former s.99(b) (now s.103(b)). At his trial, the judge made a preliminary ruling on the application of counsel that a defence of necessity was not available in law, but that the facts alleged might go to mitigation of the offence. Martin pleaded guilty and was sentenced. The facts were that Martin's wife had suicidal tendencies, and on a number of occasions had attempted to take her own life. On the day in question, her son had overslept to the extent that he was bound to be late for work thereby risking his employment. The wife was distraught and threatened suicide. A doctor's opinion said that it was likely Mrs Martin would have attempted suicide unless Martin had driven the son to work. It was held by the Court of Appeal that in extreme circumstances a defence of necessity was recognised and could arise from duress of circumstances, namely objective dangers threatening the accused and others. Viewed objectively, it was available only if the accused could be said to be acting reasonably and proportionately in order to avoid a threat of death or serious injury. Mr Martin's conviction was therefore quashed.

There have been a number of important decisions which are declaratory of the **11.66** existing law, but which have caused something of a stir in police prosecution departments and the courts. It has always been the law that the offence of driving while disqualified requires the prosecution to prove that the defendant was driving and that at the time he was disqualified. It is not disputed that the second element may sometimes cause evidential difficulties. In *R. v Derwentside JJ. Ex p. Heaviside* [1996] R.T.R. 384 the applicant for judicial review had been convicted on the basis of evidence that he had been seen driving by a police officer who knew him to be disqualified. No evidence was given of the disqualification, save that an entry in the court register was produced showing that someone of the same name and with the same date of birth as the applicant had been disqualified for three years, up to and including the date of the alleged offence. The applicant applied for an order of certiorari to quash his conviction on the ground that there was no evidence before the court of an essential element of the offence of driving whilst disqualified, namely the disqualification. The Divisional Court held that proof of a conviction, pursuant to s.73 of the Police and Criminal Evidence Act 1984, required strict proof of the identity of the person convicted, by admission, by fingerprints, or by evidence of a person present in court at the time of the conviction to identify the defendant. The mere matching of personal details of the defendant with those of the convicted person was not sufficient proof of identity. In this case, no sufficient evidence of identity had been put before the magistrates' court.

A differently constituted Divisional Court in *R. v Derwentside Magistrates' Court Ex p. Swift*; *R. v Sunderland Magistrates' Court Ex p. Bate* [1997] R.T.R. 89, whilst of course adopting what was said in the *Heaviside* case, explained that the three methods of providing the identity of the person disqualified was not an exhaustive list. Whether the evidence, e.g. took the form of an admission made by the defendant to a witness or a statement of a police officer admitted under s.9 of the Criminal Justice Act 1967, it was always for the justices to determine whether they were satisfied by evidence that the previous conviction did indeed relate to the defendant before the court. Both applications for judicial review were dismissed.

In *DPP v Mooney* [1997] R.T.R. 434, the defendant was seen by a police of- **11.67** ficer driving a vehicle and stopped. The police officer asked if he was banned from driving and he replied that he was. He was cautioned and arrested for driving whilst disqualified. When subsequently charged with that offence, he said that he was guilty. At the hearing before the justices, the defendant submitted that, following *Heaviside*, strict proof that the defendant was a disqualified driver was required in one of three ways and as there was no such evidence before the justices, they dismissed the case. The Divisional Court allowed the prosecutor's appeal. It held that the three methods of proof listed in *Heaviside* were not exclusive and that cogent evidence should not have been ignored merely because it did not fall into one of the three categories. The admissions which the defendant had made to the police, although not formal admissions under s.10 of the Criminal Justice Act 1967, confirmed the evidence in the certificate of conviction in the court record that he was the person so disqualified by the court at that time. The justices, having admitted that evidence, should have convicted and, accordingly, the case would be remitted with a direction to convict. In *Bailey v DPP*, *The Times*, July 30, 1998, the appellant was convicted by justices on November 11, 1997 for driving whilst disqualified. On December 6, 1996, a person with a name and date of birth identical to the appellant's and the address of the appellant's sister, where the appellant had been living temporarily, had been convicted of driving (*sic*) without insurance and disqualified from driving for nine months. The appellant said he had no recollection of those proceedings and that the memorandum of conviction did not prove that the conviction related to him. The justices found that the appellant and the Colin Richard Bailey referred to in the memorandum of conviction were one and the same and convicted.

11.68   In allowing the appellant's appeal and quashing the conviction, Simon Brown L.J. said that the link between the certificate of conviction and the defendant had to be proved beyond reasonable doubt. That was plain from the second limb of s.73(1) of the Police and Criminal Evidence Act 1984. The means of proving that link were not limited to those listed in *Heaviside* and other measures could be envisaged. In his Lordship's judgment, there had to be some evidence that the previous conviction in the defendant's name was not explicable by reference to some other person having given the defendant's details and name to the police and the court in respect of the earlier offence. He added that the fact that the address given at the earlier proceedings was that of the appellant's sister and relatively few people knew that he was living there, was not sufficient evidence. It is to be hoped that the introduction of the photocard driving licence will reduce the occasions when this issue will be a significant problem. In *Moran v Crown Prosecution Service* (2000) 164 J.P. 562, a driver appealed against his conviction for driving whilst disqualified basing his appeal on the fact that his earlier conviction had not been proved by a certificate of conviction in accordance with s.73(1) of the Police and Criminal Evidence Act 1984. At his trial, the driver had admitted that, in the course of a police interview, he had admitted his earlier conviction. The court pointed out that proof of conviction under s.73(1) was stated expressly by s.73(4) to be in addition to and not to the exclusion of any other authorised manner of proving a conviction. In *Heaviside*, the court had recognised that convictions could be proved in a number of different ways and the court could think of no stronger way of proving a conviction than by admission by the driver in interview and repeated by him in evidence. The appeal was dismissed.

A further case dealing with the issue of whether a defendant has been disqualified has been considered by the Administrative Court (see *R. (on the application of Howe) v South Durham Magistrates' Court* [2004] EWHC 362; (2004) 168 J.P. 424). When interviewed by the police, the defendant had not admitted to being disqualified. The prosecution sought a witness summons in order to compel the attendance to give evidence of the solicitor who represented the defendant in the earlier proceedings and was representing him in the current proceedings. The magistrates' court issued the witness summons, accepting that the only evidence that the solicitor could be expected to give was of what happened in the courtroom; anything covered by legal professional privilege would be excluded. That decision was upheld by the Administrative Court. The permissible questions did not infringe legal professional privilege since they were solely about the identity of the person disqualified earlier and the fact that that was the same person as the defendant in the current proceedings. This did not enter into the territory of solicitor and client communication. Whilst the effect would be to prevent the solicitor acting for the defendant in the current proceedings, the right to a lawyer of one's own choice was not an absolute one and may be overridden where that is necessary in the interests of justice.

The state of the law is that strict proof remains necessary to show that the driver before the court was the same individual who was previously disqualified; the matter is primarily one of sufficiency of evidence; there are a number of ways in which such proof may be adduced. **11.69**

It will be noted that "driving", as discussed in Chapter 1, must be proved. If the defendant is merely in charge, without any attempt at driving, there is no offence. The offence requires the vehicle to be driven "on a road". For the meaning of "road", see Chapter 1.

A person disqualified under s.36 of the 1988 Offenders Act until he passes a test commits an offence under s.103 if after taking out a provisional licence he fails to comply with a provisional licence condition (*Scott v Jelf* [1974] R.T.R. 256). The wording of the provisions poses the problem which test or tests have to be passed to bring the disqualification to an end. The earlier driving licence will have been revoked. It is understood that following such a disqualification the DVLA will not issue a full licence covering any group unless the relevant test has been passed for that group.

A further evidential issue arose in the case of *DPP v Barker* [2004] EWHC **11.70** 2502; (2004) 168 J.P. 617. The respondent had been disqualified from driving for 12 months and further disqualified until he passed an extended driving test. At the time of the alleged offence of driving whilst disqualified, although the 12 months' disqualification had expired, he was still subject to the requirement to pass an extended driving test. The justices dismissed an information for an offence of driving whilst disqualified, because although the respondent had admitted in interview that he had no authority to drive a motor vehicle, the prosecution had failed to show that the respondent had driven in breach of the conditions under which a provisional licence was held, irrespective of whether he had applied for and been granted a provisional licence. In allowing the prosecutor's appeal by way of case stated, the Divisional Court confirmed that in such cases, the burden of proof lay with the respondent to show that he not only had a provisional licence but was driving in accordance with the conditions of such a licence. Once the court was satisfied that he was the driver, it should have convicted him. (*Scott v Jelf* [1974] R.T.R. 256 applied.) Collins J. stated that the existence of a burden on the respondent to establish that he was entitled to drive at the time when he was seen to be driving was wholly proportionate and was to be accepted.

For a number of years, imaginative attempts have been made to persuade courts that the prosecution has not satisfied its obligation to prove that the person before the court is the person disqualified from driving. In *Ellis v Jones* [1973] 2 All E.R. 893, this led the court to describe the defence submission as "another example of submissions made by advocates for the defence in circumstances which are wholly inappropriate and which give rise to a great deal of waste of time and money".

11.71   In *Pattison v DPP* [2005] EWHC 2938; (2006) 170 J.P. 51, the Divisional Court took the opportunity to conduct an extensive review of the legal provisions and the authorities. It concluded that:

> "The principle that emerges from the cases is that it will normally be possible to establish a prima facie case on the basis of consistency of details between the accused and the person named on the memorandum of conviction. If the accused calls no evidence to contradict that prima facie case, it will be open to the court to be satisfied that identity is proved."

The court set out a number of principles able to be extracted from the cases. It emphasised that it was for the prosecution to prove to the criminal standard that the accused was a disqualified driver but it could do so by any admissible means including a non-formal admission. *Heaviside* identifies three clear ways but there are no prescribed ways. An example of another way is where there is a match between the personal details of the accused and those recorded on the certificate of conviction. Even where the personal details (such as name) are not uncommon, a match will be sufficient for a prima facie case. In the absence of evidence contradicting this prima facie case, the evidence will be sufficient for the court to find identity proved. If the accused does not give evidence in rebuttal, that is a matter that the court can take into account. If it is proper to do so (and provided a warning has been given), that can also give rise to an adverse inference (Criminal Justice and Public Order Act 1994 s.35(2)). See also *West Yorkshire Probation Board v Boulter* [2005] EWHC 2342; [2006] 1 W.L.R. 232, in which a person subject to a community rehabilitation order was brought before a magistrates' court on a warrant for breaching the order. The proceedings were adjourned. The defendant did not attend subsequent hearings but was legally represented. The justices accepted defence submissions that the prosecution had failed to prove that the person summoned to appear was the person made subject to the order and that the coincidence of names, date of birth and address was insufficient to prove identity beyond a reasonable doubt. The Divisional Court upheld the prosecution appeal:

> "When magistrates have evidence that the person before them has the same name, date of birth and address as the person previously convicted, it was open to them to draw an inference that he is the same person. Whether that inference is to be drawn in any particular case depends on all the facts of that case."

11.72   Where all three of those personal details coincided, it was to be expected that justices would draw such an inference unless there was some other factor which cast doubt on the inference.

In s.103 (and in all other sections of Pt III), "licence" means a licence to drive a motor vehicle granted under Pt III (applicable only to England, Wales and Scotland).

11.73   A person from abroad who is disqualified under s.103 of the 1988 Act by a court in Great Britain may not drive here though he may hold a driving licence or permit of his own country; s.103 forbids driving while disqualified for holding or obtaining a "licence" (which means a licence issued under Pt III of the 1988 Act). If a "relevant permit" is held and produced to the court, it must be sent to the Secretary of State and returned only on request on leaving the country or the disqualification ending: 1988 Offenders Act s.47(2). A disqualified person may not, in Great Britain, drive on a road any motor vehicle (including a trolley vehicle) even though he may have joined HM Forces and have been issued with a service driving licence. He may drive outside Great Britain, e.g. Northern Ireland, the Isle of Man or the Channel Islands unless also prohibited by the laws of the foreign country. The converse is also true, namely that a person disqualified in Northern Ireland or in another country outside Great Britain is not thereby disqualified under s.103 and therefore does not commit the offence of driving while disqualified contrary to s.103 if he drives in Great Britain. He may commit the offence of driving otherwise than in accordance with a licence. The position will depend on the effect of the disqualification according to the law of the country issuing the driving licence.

Allowing a person who is known to be disqualified to drive can amount to aiding and abetting this offence (*Pope v Minton* [1954] Crim. L.R. 711), but it is otherwise where the car owner allows a disqualified person to drive in ignorance of the disqualification and after making inquiries which a reasonable man should make (*Bateman v Evans* (1964) 108 S.J. 522).

Applying for a licence whilst disqualified

Before a disqualified driver can drive after the period of his disqualification has **11.74** expired he must apply for a driving licence, as his previous licence is treated as revoked by reason of the order of disqualification (1988 Offenders Act s.37(1)). If the formerly disqualified driver drives without a driving licence he commits an offence under s.87.

A disqualified person who applies for a licence to be issued to operate during the currency of a disqualification may commit an offence under s.174(1) of the 1988 Act of knowingly making a false declaration to obtain a driving licence.

When a person has been disqualified by the court, he is nevertheless (if such is **11.75** the case) a person who in the wording of s.88(1) of the 1988 Act "has held and is entitled to obtain" a licence when the disqualification expires. It is submitted that by s.88(1) a disqualified person may drive immediately the disqualification expires providing the application has been received and the conditions are fulfilled.

A person only disqualified until he passes a test of competence to drive may immediately apply for a provisional licence (1988 Offenders Act s.37(3)). He may therefore drive once the application has been received.

Obtaining a licence whilst disqualified

If a person disqualified for holding or obtaining a licence obtains a licence **11.76** while so disqualified, he commits an offence (1988 Act s.103(1)(a)). This must be read in conjunction with the comments at § 11.74 above. "Licence" means a licence to drive a motor vehicle granted under Pt III of the 1988 Act. Presumably "licence" in this context means a current licence. Applications for the grant of a licence may be dealt with within two months before the date the licence is to take effect (Motor Vehicles (Driving Licences) Regulations 1999, reg.10). Licences are sometimes sent out in advance of the commencement date, particularly for young drivers close to the driving age. It is submitted that this does not constitute an offence under s.103(1)(a).

Section 103(1)(a) must be read in conjunction with s.102. By this a person is disqualified for obtaining a Pt III licence for any motor vehicle class so long as he is the holder of another Pt III licence for that class, whether it is suspended or not. The result of this is that it is possible to commit the s.103(1)(a) offence of obtaining a licence whilst disqualified without, by driving, committing the offence of driving whilst disqualified, as the first licence is valid or only in suspense.

Disqualification quashed on appeal

11.77   It was held in *R. v Lynn* [1971] R.T.R. 369 that a person may still commit the offence of driving whilst disqualified even though the conviction imposing the disqualification is subsequently quashed on appeal. Presumably the same principle would apply to a person obtaining a licence whilst disqualified. The decision in *R. v Lynn* was followed by the Divisional Court in *R. v Thames Magistrates' Court Ex p. Levy* [1997] T.L.R. 394. On June 17, 1996, the applicant was disqualified from driving. He appealed against his conviction but made no application to have his disqualification suspended. On July 18, 1996 he was stopped by police officers on two separate occasions and charged with driving whilst disqualified. On September 25, 1996, the appeal against conviction for the original offences was allowed. On October 26, 1996, it was submitted to the bench dealing with the offences of driving whilst disqualified that the applicant's successful appeal against the conviction which led to his disqualification meant that the disqualification was nullified ab initio. The argument was rejected and the applicant was convicted. On application for judicial review, the Divisional Court held that not only *R. v Lynn*, but good sense and justice led inevitably to the conclusion that the applicant's argument was misconceived and unsustainable. The court stated that it would be odd if a person who had been disqualified could drive pending an appeal, it being unknown to him, the police or his insurers, whether or not he was committing an offence. Similarly, a defendant who successfully appeals against a disqualification, but had not had that disqualification suspended pending the appeal, remains disqualified between the original sentence and the appeal decision: *R. v Thames Magistrates' Court Ex p. Levy* above.

Power of arrest

11.78   The offence of driving whilst disqualified created by s.103(1)(b) of the Road Traffic Act 1988 is an indictable offence: Police and Criminal Evidence Act 1984 ss.24 and 24A.

A civil claim for false imprisonment was rejected in *McCarrick v Oxford* [1983] R.T.R. 117 on the ground that a constable acted reasonably in arresting an accused for driving whilst disqualified under the previous power and in declining to go to his home to see a letter from the Crown Court suspending the disqualification pending appeal.

The power of arrest by a police constable is limited to a person "driving" whom the constable has reasonable cause to suspect of being disqualified and the alternative "or attempting to drive" has been excluded as has reasonable suspicion of having been the driver: *DPP v Swann* (1999) 164 J.P. 365.

Attempts

11.79   One of the results of the reclassification of the offence of driving whilst disqualified as summary only by s.37 of the Criminal Justice Act 1988 is that the Criminal Attempts Act 1981 ceases to have any application. The 1981 Act applies to any offence which, if it were completed, would be triable in England and Wales as an indictable offence. As offences triable "either way" are technically indictable offences, the 1981 Act was the authority prior to the implementation of the 1988 Act for charging offences of attempted driving whilst disqualified, as driving whilst disqualified was then an "either way" offence. This is no longer the case. The better view is that as a result, there is no longer an offence of attempted driving whilst disqualified.

There is no offence in s.103(1)(a) of the 1988 Act of attempting to obtain a driving licence whilst disqualified: the principal offence is purely summary and the Criminal Attempts Act 1981 does not therefore apply. However, the offence of making a false statement for the purpose of obtaining a licence may have been committed: 1988 Act s.174(1).

PENALTIES AND PROCEEDINGS

General offences

A table listing offences, penalties and the relevant Magistrates' Court Sentenc- **11.80** ing Guidelines is provided at § 11.90 below.

The maximum penalty on summary conviction for the offence of driving otherwise than in accordance with a licence (s.87) is a fine of level 3. The offence remains unendorsable where the fully licensed driver has lost or misplaced his licence, but where an offender's driving is not in accordance with any licence that could have been issued to him, the offence carries obligatory endorsement of penalty points within the range three to six, and discretionary disqualification (1991 Act Sch.2 para.19).

Driving after a false declaration as to physical fitness (s.92(10)) is triable sum- **11.81** marily with a maximum penalty of a fine of level 4. It carries an obligatory endorsement with penalty points within the range three to six and discretionary disqualification. The penalty for an offence under s.94(3A) (driving after failure to notify Secretary of State) is the same as that for an offence under s.92(10).

The more serious offence under s.94A (see § 11.55) is punishable on summary conviction with a maximum of six months' imprisonment or a fine of level 5, or both. The offence also carries obligatory endorsement with points within the range three to six and discretionary disqualification.

Endorsement, disqualification and penalty points

Endorsement, disqualification and penalty points may be ordered for any of the **11.82** general offences set out in the table at § 11.90 except:

(1) an offence under s.87(1) committed by driving a motor vehicle in a case where either no licence authorising the driving of that vehicle could have been granted to the offender (e.g. an under-age driver or a learner driver riding a solo motor cycle with an engine exceeding 125cc) or, if a provisional (but no other) licence to drive it could have been granted to him, the driving would not have complied with the conditions thereof; or

(2) the offence of a learner driver failing to comply with a condition of his provisional licence or of a full licence-holder likewise failing to comply with a provisional licence condition when the vehicle he drives is not

covered by his full licence but, instead, confers a provisional licence entitlement.

Thus, a person of any age who has not passed a test to drive the particular type of vehicle in use, or is not otherwise qualified to drive, is liable to disqualification if he drives unaccompanied by a competent driver or without "L" plates. The holder of a provisional licence who drives unaccompanied or without "L" plates may also be disqualified. A disqualification and endorsement was quashed where a person with a lapsed provisional driving licence drove complying with the learner driver conditions (*R. v Reading JJ.* [1982] R.T.R. 30). Semble endorsement must, and disqualification may, be ordered if a provisional licence-holder or a person who holds no licence and has not passed a test drives a solo motor bicycle with an engine of a cylinder capacity exceeding 125cc. Endorsable driving licence offences carry penalty points within the range three to six.

11.83   The endorsement codes for driving licence offences are set out in the table of penalties at § 11.90. Endorsement under s.44 of the 1988 Offenders Act must be ordered for endorsable offences unless there are special reasons (see Chapter 21).

Disqualification may be imposed for any endorsable offence and s.35 of the 1988 Offenders Act (the penalty points disqualification) applies to such offences (see §§ 20.33 et seq.). For "mitigating circumstances" justifying a court not imposing the compulsory penalty points disqualification, see Chapter 21.

Endorsement, disqualification and penalty points may thus not be ordered for an offence of driving otherwise than in accordance with a licence if the offender has omitted to renew it, so long as that licence would have covered driving the class of motor vehicle which he was driving. Nor may they be ordered for causing or permitting an unlicensed driver to drive contrary to s.87(2) even though such orders are made in respect of the driver himself. In the case of an expired provisional licence, as stated, the driver of a motor car must be accompanied by a competent driver and show "L" plates to avoid liability to disqualification and endorsement. An order of disqualification until the passing of a driving test may be made for any of the above offences for which disqualification may be ordered. It would seem that a full licence-holder, when relying on his provisional licence entitlement to drive a vehicle not covered by his full licence, will not only have his licence endorsed if he fails to comply with a provisional licence condition, but may also be ordered to be disqualified until he passes another test. The effect of such an order will be that his full licence is revoked, and that he has to take out a provisional licence for all groups.

Driving while disqualified

11.84   By s.6 of the 1988 Offenders Act, proceedings for an offence under s.103, as amended, may be brought within a period of six months from the date on which sufficient evidence of the commission of the alleged offence came to the knowledge of the prosecutor, provided that no proceedings may be brought more than three years after the commission of the offence. All offences under s.103 alleged to be committed in England and Wales are summary only and the defendant has no right of election for trial by jury.

The maximum penalty on conviction is a fine of level 5 and/or six months' imprisonment. Obligatory endorsement carries six penalty points and the offence is subject to discretionary disqualification. Reference should be made to Appendix 3 below for revised Magistrates' Court Sentencing Guidelines dealing with this offence.

Proof of the order of disqualification may be by the endorsement (see s.31 of **11.85** the 1988 Offenders Act), by a certified statement under s.13 of the 1988 Offenders Act or by certificate of conviction or extract from the magistrates' court register, with identification of the defendant (*Stone v Bastick* [1965] 3 All E.R. 713, where there was a certificate of quarter sessions to which the defendant had been committed for sentence and which had disqualified him, after conviction by magistrates). Only the offence for which he was disqualified should appear in the certificate or extract; if he was disqualified for more than one offence, it seems that only a conviction involving one of the current disqualifications should be shown (ibid.). Semble if there were consecutive disqualifications, it might be necessary to show more than one. If the defence are not disputing the disqualification, an admission under s.10 of the Criminal Justice Act 1967 can be used to avoid the magistrates or jury looking at a certificate or extract which shows more than is necessary. It would also be possible to prove an order of disqualification by certificate under s.11 of the 1988 Offenders Act (see § 3.52). In *Holland v Phipp* [1983] R.T.R. 123 it was held that the justices were bound by a certified extract as to the duration of disqualification periods even though it showed an error of law on the face of it. The conviction for driving whilst disqualified after the end of the period shown on the certified extract was accordingly quashed. Unless the defendant accepts that he is the person named in the memorandum of conviction, etc., the prosecution must prove that *that* individual was the person disqualified. Proof of the same name and similar details may be insufficient, see *R. v Derwentside JJ. Ex p. Heaviside* [1996] R.T.R. 384 at § 11.66 and the comment at 159 J.P.N. 238.

Concerns about the extent to which persons who are disqualified continue to drive have resulted in the growing use of the imposition of anti-social behaviour orders (ASBOs) in addition to the sentence for the offence. One of the issues that has needed to be resolved has been the extent to which an ASBO should prohibit something which is already a criminal offence. This is particularly significant where the maximum penalty for the offence is less than for a breach of an ASBO—this is the case for driving whilst disqualified which carries a maximum of six months' imprisonment compared with a maximum of five years for a breach of an ASBO. In *R. v Hall* [2004] EWCA Crim 2671; [2005] 1 Cr. App. R. (S) 118, the defendant had an appalling driving record and had committed other serious offences. The court concluded that the regularity of the defendant's offending demonstrated total disregard for the law and imposed an unlimited ASBO prohibiting the defendant from driving any mechanically propelled vehicle on a public road in the United Kingdom without being the holder of a valid driving licence and certificate of insurance. A primary purpose was to increase the sentencing powers of any court faced with dealing with a further offence. Whilst requiring the ASBO to be for a set period, the Court of Appeal considered that the order was not wrong in principle in these circumstances. It was precise and capable of being understood by the appellant.

In *R. v Lawson* [2005] EWCA Crim 1840; [2006] 1 Cr. App. R. (S.) 59, the ap- **11.86** pellant drove a car while under the influence of drink at high speed through a city centre. An accident occurred in which a driver of the other car was injured, as were the appellant's passengers. Having pleaded guilty before a magistrates' court to dangerous driving, driving with excess alcohol, driving whilst disqualified and driving without insurance, and having been committed to the Crown

Court for sentence, the appellant was made subject to an order which forbade him from owning, borrowing or occupying the driving seat of any motor vehicle on a road or any public place until further order. The appellant was disqualified for six years and sentenced to a total of 18 months' imprisonment. The Court of Appeal reduced the period disqualification from driving to four years on the basis that the period of disqualification imposed in the court below was too long. The ASBO was quashed since it was unjustified and disproportionate. (*R. v Kirby* [2005] EWCA Crim 1228; [2006] 1 Cr. App. R. (S.) 26 followed.)

In *R. v Williams* [2005] EWCA Crim 1796; [2006] R.T.R. 4 the Court of Appeal held that s.1C of the Crime and Disorder Act 1998 provided that an ASBO may be made on conviction of a relevant offence where the offender had acted at any time since the commencement date in an anti-social manner, and the court considered that an order was necessary to protect persons from further anti-social acts by him. Where there was a beach of an ASBO it would be open to the court to impose a sentence of imprisonment of up to five years, whereas for driving whilst disqualified the maximum sentence available to the magistrates' court was six months' imprisonment. In this case, the Court of Appeal followed the principles set out in *Kirby* (above), since having appeared before the Crown Court for driving whilst disqualified and driving with excess alcohol, and having breached a community rehabilitation order, the imposition of an ASBO was unwarranted in this case. Accordingly the order was quashed.

11.87   See also *R. v Boness, R. v Bebbington* [2005] EWCA Crim 2395; [2006] 1 Cr. App. R. (S.) 120. Before an order can be made, the court must be satisfied both that the offender had acted in an anti-social manner and that an order was necessary to protect persons in England and Wales from further anti-social acts by him.

The penalty for obtaining a licence while disqualified (s.103(1)(a)) is a fine of level 3. Endorsement, disqualification, penalty points and a driving test cannot be ordered. As stated above, the penalty for driving while disqualified (s.103(1)(b)) is a fine of level 5 or six months' imprisonment or both. Magistrates' courts have power to order detention in a young offender institution where appropriate.

An order of endorsement must be made for the offence of driving whilst disqualified, unless there are special reasons. The offence carries six penalty points.

Disqualification

11.88   It was said in *R. v Phillips* (1955) 119 J.P. 499, that when disqualification and imprisonment are imposed together, the period of disqualification should be sufficiently long to ensure that the greater part of it will not have expired by the time the defendant is released, but it is suggested that regard should also be had to the danger of imposing long periods of disqualification, particularly if it is likely to cause the offender to drive while disqualified or is likely to hinder him in leading an honest life. A defendant sentenced to 12 months' imprisonment and disqualified for three years had the disqualification reduced to 12 months by the Court of Appeal on the ground that the period of imprisonment was the deterrent and he would face financial difficulties when leaving prison, strengthening the temptation to drive while disqualified (*R. v Pashley* [1974] R.T.R. 149).

R. v Zindani [2006] EWCA Crim 3176, the Court of Appeal reduced a period of 10 years' disqualification for dangerous driving and driving whilst disqualified to five years on the basis that, as the appellant had also been ordered to take an extended driving test, and being mindful of the need to protect the public by giving him the chance to feel that he could get back into driving, it was right to reduce the disqualification.

The offence of obtaining a driving licence whilst disqualified under s.103(1)(a) **11.89** of the 1988 Act does not carry endorsement or disqualification. The offence of driving whilst disqualified carries the power for courts to impose a discretionary disqualification under s.34(2) of the 1988 Offenders Act provided the penalty points to be taken into account number fewer than 12. If, however, the defendant is due for "totting up" he will be disqualified for the appropriate period under s.35 unless the court is satisfied having regard to all the circumstances that there are grounds for mitigating the normal consequences of the conviction. In an appropriate case the court may also exercise its powers under s.36 to order disqualification until the defendant has passed a driving test. In deciding whether or not to exercise its discretion the court is required to have regard to the safety of road users.

Driving licences: penalties

Offence	Mode of trial	Section *	Imprisonment	Level of fine	Disqualification	Penalty points	Endorsement code	Sentencing guideline †
Driving otherwise than in accordance with licence	Summary	s.87(1)	—	3	Discretionary if offence is committed by driving a motor vehicle in a case where either no driving licence for driving that vehicle could have been granted to offender, or where offender is under age, or unsupervised in vehicle as "L" driver, or without "L" plates as an "L" driver, or a learner motor cyclist carrying a passenger	3–6	LC20	Fine band A Aggravating factor if no licence ever held

Offence	Mode of trial	Section *	Imprisonment	Level of fine	Disqualification	Penalty points	Endorsement code	Sentencing guideline †
Causing or permitting a person to drive otherwise than in accordance with driving licence	Summary	s.87(2)	—	3	—	—	—	—
Failure to deliver licence revoked by virtue of s.92(7A) to Secretary of State	Summary	s.92(7C)	—	3	—	—	—	—
Driving after making false declaration as to physical fitness	Summary	s.92(10)	—	4	Discretionary	3–6	LC30	—
Failure to deliver revoked licence to Secretary of State	Summary	s.93(3)	—	3	—	—	—	—
Driving after failure to notify Secretary of State	Summary	s.94(3A)	—	3	Discretionary	3–6	LC40	—
Driving after refusal of licence under s.92(3) or revocation under s.93	Summary	s.94A	6 months or level 5 or both		Discretionary	3–6	LC50	—

Offence	Mode of trial	Section *	Imprisonment	Level of fine	Disqualification	Penalty points	Endorsement code	Sentencing guideline †
Failing to sign licence	Summary	Motor Vehicles (Driving Licences) Regs and s.91 RTOA 1988	—	3	—	—	—	—
Failing to produce driving licence, etc., or state date of birth	Summary	s.164	—	3	—	—	—	—
Failing to produce licence to court	Summary	s.27 RTOA 1988	—	3	—	—	—	—
Failing to produce Northern Ireland licence to court	Summary	s.109	—	3	—	—	—	—
Failing to give date of birth	Summary	s.25 RTOA 1988	—	3	—	—	—	—
Applying for or obtaining a licence without disclosing current endorsement	Summary	s.45 RTOA 1988	—	3	—	—	—	—

Offence	Mode of trial	Section *	Imprisonment	Level of fine	Disqualification	Penalty points	Endorsement code	Sentencing guideline †
Failing, etc., to surrender licence on change of name or address	Summary	s.99(5)	—	3	—	—	—	—
Failing to notify Secretary of State of disability	Summary	s.94	—	3	—	—	—	—
Driving an electrically assisted pedal cycle while under 14 (or causing or permitting)	Summary	s.32(2)	—	2	—	—	—	—
Obtaining driving licence whilst disqualified	Summary	s.103(1)(a)	—	3	—	—	—	—
Driving whilst disqualified	Summary	s.103(1)(b)	6 months or level 5 or both		Discretionary	6	BA10	See Appendix 3

* Road Traffic Act 1988 unless otherwise specified.
† **Note**: Fine bands "A", "B" and "C" represent respectively 50%, 100% and 150% of relevant weekly income. A timely guilty plea should attract a discount. See Appendix 3.

CHAPTER 12

EXCISE AND TRADE LICENCES

CONTENTS

Generally

12.01   The Vehicle Excise and Registration Act 1994 (as amended each year by the relevant Finance Act) endeavours to set out the provisions in a logical and easy to follow form. Pt I relates to vehicle excise duty and licences; Pt II to registration of vehicles; Pt III to offences; Pt IV to legal proceedings; and Pt V to supplementary matters. Schedule 4 paras 1–5 preserve previously made regulations unless specifically revoked. The 1994 Act applies to the whole of the United Kingdom.

Vehicle excise duty is payable on a mechanically propelled vehicle which is either registered under the 1994 Act or, if it is not registered, is used or kept on a public road in the United Kingdom. The licence must be taken out either by the person registered or the keeper (1994 Act s.1(1C)). Where a vehicle is not registered, it is the keeper who is liable to take out the licence (1994 Act s.1(1D)). In addition, any thing that has been, but is no longer, a mechanically propelled vehicle which is either registered under the 1994 Act or used or kept on a public road in the United Kingdom remains liable for duty, again removing possible defences around ceasing to be a mechanically propelled vehicle (new 1994 Act s.1(1A)). For the purposes of the 1994 Act, the term "vehicle" is redefined to include both a mechanically propelled vehicle and any thing (whether or not it is a vehicle) that has been, but is no longer, a mechanically propelled vehicle.

12.02   The fact that a vehicle is taxed under the 1994 Act as a particular class of motor vehicle is not necessarily evidence that it is the same or a similar type of vehicle for the purpose of the 1988 Act, the Transport Act 1968 or the Road Traffic Regulation Act 1984 (e.g. *Wakeman v Catlow*, § 1.27).

This chapter is arranged so as deal with the provisions in four main sections— applications generally, registration marks, trade plates and special provisions governing the conduct of proceedings under the 1994 Act. Since being brought into force, the Act has experienced a range of significant changes.

VEHICLE EXCISE DUTY AND LICENCES

12.03   Vehicle excise duty is charged in respect of every mechanically propelled vehicle used or kept on a public road in the United Kingdom. Duty is also chargeable in respect of everything that has been a mechanically propelled vehicle but has since ceased to be if it is either registered under the 1994 Act or used or kept on a public road in the United Kingdom even though not registered. It is of no consequence if this thing has not only ceased to be a mechanically propelled vehicle but has also ceased to be a vehicle at all. If a vehicle is no longer to be taxable, it will need to have its registration cancelled and it must not be kept or used on a public road (1994 Act s.1(1)). Where the vehicle is registered, the licence is to be taken out by the person in whose name the vehicle is registered or the keeper if different. Where the vehicle is not registered, the licence is to be taken out by the keeper of the vehicle: 1994 Act s.1(1D).

For the meaning of mechanically propelled vehicle, see Chapter 1. Note that if a mechanically propelled vehicle is in fact used on a public road, duty will be chargeable, unless the Act itself exempts it, whether or not the vehicle is "intended or adapted for use on a road".

Practically all the offences under the Act and regulations are limited to matters **12.04** arising on "public roads", i.e. roads which (in England, Wales and Northern Ireland) are repairable at the public expense (1994 Act s.62(1)), a definition narrower than that in the 1988 Act (see § 1.122). In Scotland, "public road" means the same as in the Roads (Scotland) Act 1984. A road which came into existence after 1835 will not normally be publicly repairable unless the procedure of Pt IV of the Highways Act 1980 (or its statutory predecessor) has been followed (*Alsager UDC v Barratt* [1965] 2 Q.B. 343) unless there is proof that it has become publicly repairable some other way, e.g. under the Private Street Works Act 1892 or the Public Health Act 1875. Some roads may be privately owned by the highway authority and may be repaired by the authority in a private capacity.

It suffices in law for the prosecutor to show that the defendant used or kept the vehicle on a public road. The burden of proving the purpose of the use rests on the defendant (s.53 of the 1994 Act). It is for the defendant to show that it was licensed (s.101 of the Magistrates' Courts Act 1980 confirmed in *Guyll v Bright* [1987] R.T.R. 104). Presumably the burden will be on the balance of probabilities (see § 12.142).

Duty is chargeable on mechanically propelled vehicles kept or used on public **12.05** roads, even though they are never driven (1994 Act s.1(1)). It is also chargeable on anything that is or has been a mechanically propelled vehicle (1994 Act s.1(1A)–(1D)). A motor vehicle separated from the road surface by roller skates is nevertheless "on" a road (*Holliday v Henry* [1974] R.T.R. 101). A person "keeps" a vehicle on a road if he causes it to be on a road when not in use, no matter how short the period may be (s.62(2), nullifying the effect of *Dudley v Holland* [1963] 3 All E.R. 732).

It is submitted, therefore, that the mere sight of a vehicle stationary and unattended on a public road is sufficient evidence of its being kept there. Ownership or proof of ownership is not essential to proof of the offence of "keeping" or "using" (*Napthen v Place* [1970] Crim. L.R. 474). Section 1(1)–(1D) of the 1994 Act now removes the need for debate about whether or not a vehicle is a mechanically propelled vehicle. The obligation to licence a vehicle will arise if anything that has at some time been a mechanically propelled vehicle is registered whether or not it remains a mechanically propelled vehicle. Even if it is not registered, the liability still arises if anything which is or has been a mechanically propelled vehicle is used or kept on a public road. If it is an issue whether a vehicle is a mechanically propelled vehicle, then it is a question of fact in each case whether the vehicle remains a "mechanically propelled vehicle" (see Chapter 1); removal of most of its essential parts might cause it to cease to be, but a vehicle which resembles a car is presumed still to be a mechanically propelled vehicle, even though essential parts have been removed, if there is a possibility of their replacement in a reasonable time (see *Newberry v Simmonds* [1974] 2 Q.B. 345; *aliter* if there is no conceivable prospect of it being made mobile: see *Smart v Allan* [1963] 1 Q.B. 291). These and other cases are considered at § 1.34. In *Binks v Department of the Environment* [1975] Crim. L.R. 244, a vehicle without an engine was held to be mechanically propelled because it was the intention of the owner to make it mobile again.

12.06   If it is shown that anything that should have been licensed has been used without an excise licence, the case must not be dismissed even though the breach of the law is highly technical and trivial and there are mitigating circumstances as well. The defendant must be found guilty but the penalty may properly be small in such a case (*Patterson v Helling* [1960] Crim. L.R. 562). And see *Nattrass v Gibson* at § 12.57 (no defence that cheque in post).

Where an employed driver is found using a vehicle on his employer's business and the proper duty has not been paid, generally the employer and not the driver should be summoned (*Carpenter v Campbell* [1953] 1 All E.R. 280). Applying *James & Son v Smee* [1955] 1 Q.B. 78 (see § 1.168) it was held that where an unlicensed vehicle is driven by an employee on his employer's business, the vehicle is "used" by the employer even though the vehicle had been taken without the employer's knowledge or authority (*Richardson v Baker* [1976] R.T.R. 56). Once it is shown that it is used on the employer's business, it is used on the employer's business for the purposes of s.29 of the Vehicle Excise and Registration Act 1994 (ibid.). As to using, generally, see Chapter 1.

12.07   If a vehicle is used on the road, there is a presumption that the use is by or on behalf of the registered owner and he may properly be summoned if the driver's identity is unknown (*Watson v Paterson* (1957) 121 J.P. Jo. 336); though the person summoned may still show that he knew nothing of the use and so be not guilty. See the discussion on proof of ownership at § 3.82.

The rates of duty are set out in Sch.1 to the Vehicle Excise and Registration Act 1994, as amended. The method for calculating the rates where duty charged is in respect of keeping the vehicle rather than using it is contained in s.2(2)–(7) of the 1994 Act. In particular, the new provisions provide for situations where a vehicle is liable to duty because it is registered but is not being used on a public road within the United Kingdom. Regulation-making power has been provided to enable supplements to be charged where a vehicle licence is not renewed on time (1994 Act ss.7A and 7B). Licences for any vehicle may be taken out for a period of 12 months (s.3(1)). Where the annual rate of duty exceeds £50, a licence may be taken out for six months (s.3(2)). In both cases, the period will run from the beginning of the month in which the licence first has effect. The Secretary of State may make regulations changing these periods within limits prescribed in the 1994 Act s.3. The Vehicle Licences (Duration of First Licences and Rate of Duty) Order 1986 (SI 1986/1428) allows first licences to run from the tenth, seventeenth or twenty-fourth day of the preceding month in addition to the six or 12-month period. An additional amount of duty is payable in respect of the additional days.

Where a licence is taken out for six months, the duty is 55 per cent of the annual rate. Fractions of 5p are to be disregarded unless they exceed 2.5p in which case they are to be regarded as 5p (1994 Act s.4). **12.08**

By s.5 of the Vehicle Excise and Registration Act 1994, certain vehicles are exempt from duty. The rates of duty are contained in Sch.1 and eight broad categories of vehicle are provided for. Exempt vehicles are contained in Sch.2 and 13 broad categories are provided for. Even though they are exempt from duty, most of these vehicles are nil licence vehicles and they must obtain a nil licence which must be displayed in the same way as one which attracts duty: Road Vehicles (Registration and Licensing) Regulations 2002 (SI 2002/2742) reg.33.

RATES OF DUTY

The rates of duty are regularly changed in the Finance Acts. The latest Finance Act should therefore always be checked. **12.09**

General

Part I of Sch.1 to the 1994 Act provides a general rate for those vehicles not otherwise provided for in the Schedule. It is often substantially amended by the Finance Acts. The power to introduce lower rates of duty for vehicles with lower polluting emissions has been applied to vehicles first registered on or after March 1, 2001. There are four different levels of emissions with differing rates depending on whether the engine is powered by alternative fuel, by petrol or by diesel. Differing rates also apply to goods vehicles satisfying reduced pollution requirements. **12.10**

In some circumstances, the rate of duty will be affected by the cylinder capacity of the vehicle. The method of calculation of that cylinder capacity is to be in accordance with regulations made by the Secretary of State (1994 Act Sch.1 para.1(2B)). Paragraph 1(2B) widened the regulation-making power in para.2(4) of Sch.1 which related only to motor cycle engines. Although para.2(4) was repealed, regulations made under it continue to be in force and are deemed to have been made under para.1(2B): see Finance Act 2002 s.20(3). The appropriate regulation is reg.43 of the Road Vehicles (Registration and Licensing) Regulations 2002.

Motor cycles

A motor cycle is defined as a motor bicycle or motor tricycle, both of which are themselves defined in the 1994 Act Sch.1 para.2(3). The motor cycle must not exceed 450kg in weight unladen (Sch.1 para.2(1)). The duty varies according to the cylinder capacity of the engine. The method of calculation of the cylinder capacity is set out in reg.43 of the Road Vehicles (Registration and Licensing) Regulations 2002. **12.11**

Buses

A bus is a public service vehicle (see Public Passenger Vehicles Act 1981 s.1) which is not an excepted vehicle. Excepted vehicles are those with seating capacity under nine or community buses (defined in Sch.1 para.3, as amended), or **12.12** vehicles used under permits granted to educational and other bodies under the Transport Act 1985 s.19. The annual rate of duty varies with the seating capacity of the bus (1994 Act Sch.1 para.3, as amended). The method of calculating seating capacity for this purpose is set out in reg.44 of the Road Vehicles (Registration and Licensing) Regulations 2002. Unsurprisingly, it is the number of persons that may be seated in the bus at any one time, but that raises a number of questions as to how this is calculated. Regulation 44 provides that, where a separate seat is provided for each person, that counts as one seat. Where it is a continuous seat, it is counted as one seat for each 410mm. Arms that can be folded back are not taken into account, nor is the driver's seat.

Special vehicles

12.13   A special vehicle is:

(a) a vehicle which has a revenue weight exceeding 3,500kg and is a digging machine, a mobile crane, a mobile pumping vehicle, a works truck or a road roller;

(b) a vehicle designed or adapted for use to convey goods or burden of any description but either not so used or not so used for hire or reward or in connection with any trade or business; or

(c) a vehicle designed or adapted for use with a semi-trailer attached but is either not so used or, if it is so used, the semi-trailer is not used to carry goods or burden of any description.

The annual rate of duty is the basic goods vehicle rate. These provisions are in the 1994 Act Sch.1 para.4, as amended.

"Digging machines" and "mobile cranes"

12.14   "Digging machines" and "mobile cranes" are vehicles designed, constructed and used for trench digging, shovelling and excavating and vehicles designed and constructed as mobile cranes, provided they are used on public roads only for work of excavating, etc. (or, if cranes, for work on a site in the immediate vicinity), or for proceeding to and from the place of work, and carry no load other than that necessary for their propulsion or equipment. The definition of "mobile crane" was considered in an appeal against the decision of a VAT and duties tribunal. In *Nationwide Access Ltd v Commissioners of Customs and Excise* [2001] V. & D.R. 31; *The Times*, March 22, 2000 it was confirmed that the essence of the definition was what the vehicle did, not how it did it. The tribunal had excluded a vehicle because the lifting operations undertaken were effected by a hydraulic telescopic lifting arm and not by rope and pulley. This was overturned on appeal. The essence of a crane was that it was a machine that lifted objects and moved them to a radius. Although the traditional method was by rope and pulley, there had been technological advances and operation by such means was not an essential feature.

"Works truck"

12.15   Paragraph 4 of Sch.1 defines "works truck" in similar terms to those contained in reg.3(1) of the Construction and Use Regulations (see §§ 8.03–8), save that the vehicle must be a "goods vehicle" as defined in s.62(1), it must be used on a *public* road and that the definition refers to "the immediate vicinity" instead of "the immediate neighbourhood". It was held in *Hayes v Kingsworthy Foundry Co Ltd* [1971] Crim. L.R. 239 that a vehicle was not a "works truck" within the meaning of the Construction and Use Regulations where the vehicle had to travel six tenths of a mile along a road even though the two sites were very close together. "Immediate neighbourhood" had to be measured by reference to the amount of user of the road involved, not in relation to the distance which the two sites are apart "as the crow flies". Similarly, a journey between two premises two miles apart by road was held not to be "in the immediate neighbourhood" (*G. Greaves & Son Ltd v Peam* [1972] R.T.R. 146, applying *Hayes* above). A similar principle was followed in *Lovett v Payne* [1980] R.T.R. 103, a case on the nearest weighbridge. "Nearest" was held to be not as the crow flies but the nearest road route suitable for the vehicle in question. The same conclusion was reached in *North Western Traffic Area Licensing Authority v Flood* [1992] Crim. L.R. 509. The distance in *Flood* was between a building site and a tip. It was 860m by road and 380m as the crow flies and this was held to be too far to be in the immediate vicinity. Many works trucks are subject to vehicle excise duty under the 1994 Act although they are not subject to most of the Road Traffic Acts' provisions.

Recovery vehicles

For the current definition of a "recovery vehicle", see Chapter 1. Note the restrictions on use for other purposes and on who may be carried on the vehicle: Sch.1 para.5(2)–(5). If these restrictions are breached, an offence under s.37 will be committed if the use was such that a higher rate of duty was payable. The rate of duty is assessed as a proportion of the basic goods vehicle rate calculated in relation to the revenue weight of the vehicle (1994 Act Sch.1 para.5, as amended). **12.16**

Vehicles used for exceptional loads

A heavy motor car used to carry exceptional loads or a heavy locomotive, light locomotive or motor tractor used to draw trailers carrying exceptional loads is subject to a separate category of duty (1994 Act Sch.1 para.6, as amended). The definitions in s.185 of the Road Traffic Act 1988 are applied and so define "heavy motor car", "heavy locomotive", "light locomotive" and "motor tractor". An exceptional load is defined in Sch.1 para.6(3), as amended, as a load too big to be carried by a heavy motor car and/or trailer or too heavy to be carried by a heavy motor car and/or trailer having a laden weight of not more than 41,000kg. In both circumstances the heavy motor car and trailer against which the nature of the load is tested must comply with regulations made under s.41 of the Road Traffic Act 1988 (the Construction and Use Regulations). Vehicles used for exceptional loads may be specially authorised under s.44 of the Road Traffic Act 1988. A vehicle which comes within para.6 is liable for duty at the heavy duty tractive unit rate as set out in Sch.1 Pt VIII para.11 except where it is used on public roads, but not for the carriage of exceptional loads (1994 Act Sch.1 para.16(2)). **12.17**

Haulage vehicles

By Sch.1 para.7, haulage vehicles are vehicles constructed and used on public roads solely for haulage, such as tractors, and not constructed and used to carry or have superimposed on them loads other than necessary for their own propulsion and equipment. This haulage category does not include vehicles which fall **12.18** into certain other categories described separately, namely special vehicles, recovery vehicles and exceptional load vehicles. The rate varies depending on whether the vehicle is a showman's vehicle (see § 12.19 below).

A tractor fitted with a winch, jib and anchor used for loading tree trunks on a trailer drawn by it, the tractor being incapable of carrying any goods, is constructed and used for haulage solely under para.7 and is not a goods vehicle under para.8 (*T.K. Worgan & Sons v Gloucestershire County Council* [1961] 2 All E.R. 301). In *London County Council v Hay's Wharf Cartage Co* [1953] 2 All E.R. 34, a Scammell heavy duty tractor, used for towing, was held, on the facts, to be a haulage vehicle and it did not become a goods vehicle merely because such things as tools, blocks and ballast were carried by it to render it more fit for haulage work. In *Att Gen (Croke) v O'Sullivan* (1958) 92 I.L.T.R. 21 it was held that a tractor adapted to carry sacks by fitting a detachable wooden platform was "hauling" goods, so as to attract the rate of duty for a goods vehicle.

Showmen's vehicles

12.19   By s.62(1) of the 1994 Act, a "showman's vehicle" is a vehicle registered under the Act in the name of the person following the business of a travelling showman and used solely for the purposes of his business and for no other purpose. Different rates apply for a showman's *goods* vehicle (also defined in s.62(1)).

A showman hired out a circus tent and an electrical generator for a music festival. It was held in *Creek v Fossett* [1986] Crim. L.R. 256 that the vehicle was not being used solely for the business of a travelling showman. The Divisional Court indicated that it might well be that the words "travelling showman" should not be construed too narrowly but that it was not possible to construe them so widely as to embrace the business of hiring equipment to enable a third party to stage a music festival. A conviction was directed for the offence of no goods vehicle operators' licence. A travelling commercial exhibition and sales point was held not to be a showman's goods vehicle in *R. v Department of Transport Ex p. Lakeland Plastics (Windermere) Ltd* [1983] R.T.R. 82: such a vehicle is a vehicle used in the entertainment industry. By virtue of the wording of the definition in s.62(1) "showman's vehicle" will be interpreted similarly. Again, in *Bowra v Dann Catering Co Ltd* [1982] R.T.R. 120 a company which specialised in providing portable lavatories for travelling showmen was held (at 125) not to be a "travelling showman". A conviction under s.18(1) and (4) of the 1971 Act (now s.37 of the 1994 Act) for under-payment of duty was directed.

12.20   Although the decision is not binding, a showman appeared before a magistrates' court after he had used a showman's vehicle to go to a show site for show business purposes. It was used for sleeping accommodation but not to provide a display on that occasion. The magistrates acquitted him, holding that he was within the exemption. The vehicle was constructed to display novelties to be disposed of by lotteries. It was held in the same case to be a showman's goods vehicle.

Goods vehicles

12.21   Schedule 1 Pt VIII (as amended) provides for rates of duty for goods vehicles. However, not all goods vehicles are specified. Any that are not are covered by

Sch.1 Pts I, II, IV, IVA, V or VII as appropriate (1994 Act Sch.1 para.16). Rates of duty are provided for rigid goods vehicles and for tractive units. The actual rate is determined in relation to the revenue weight of the vehicle and the number of axles (1994 Act Sch.1 Pt VIII, as amended) and also the extent to which pollution requirements are met. Special provision is made within those rates for certain categories such as showmen's goods vehicles, island goods vehicles and goods vehicles used loaded only in connection with a person learning to drive the vehicle or taking a driving test. "Loaded" in this context means used for the conveyance of goods or burden of any description (1994 Act Sch.1 paras 9(2) and 11(2), as amended). Definitions appear in ss.60A, 61 and 62 of the 1994 Act.

Many of the old cases set out below have been retained in the text as they may still help to determine differences between private and goods use. They will usually no longer be of assistance for the types of vehicle in question because of the merger of private and light goods vehicles. Difficulties over the difference between private and goods vehicles are less likely to arise with larger vehicles.

Meaning of "goods vehicle"

"Goods vehicle", by s.62(1) of the 1994 Act, means a mechanically propelled   **12.22**
vehicle constructed or adapted for use *and* used for the conveyance of goods or burden of any description, whether in the course of trade or otherwise. Thus, a private car, not constructed or adapted for the conveyance of goods, is still taxable at the private rate although it may carry goods in the course of trade (see *Taylor v Mead* [1961] 1 All E.R. 626 and generally the definitions of "constructed" and "adapted" in Chapter 1).

Lord Parker C.J. said in *Taylor v Mead* that "constructed or adapted" in what is now s.62(1) meant "originally constructed or where the structure is subsequently altered" and approved two earlier cases on the Customs and Inland Revenue Act 1888 s.4, holding that adapting meant some amount of alteration of the original construction. Making a small fitting or attachment involving the boring of holes for screws in the structure would not be altering the structure but fitting stronger springs and widening the wheels would be (ibid.). The question whether an adaptation is such as to make a passenger vehicle into a goods vehicle is resolved by assuming that it had originally been constructed in its altered condition and then deciding whether as such it would be a passenger or goods vehicle; actual use is irrelevant (*Flower Freight Co v Hammond* [1962] 3 All E.R. 950).

Where the director of a firm of photographers carried photographic equipment   **12.23**
in a shooting-brake on the firm's business, it was held that the vehicle was a goods vehicle and taxable accordingly; the exclusion provisions did not apply as it was used to carry goods or burden for a trade business (*Taylor v Thompson* [1956] 1 All E.R. 352). A shooting-brake is now almost certain to be in the private/light goods category. Carriage of personal luggage or farm produce for the owner's own use would not attract the "basic goods vehicle rate" duty. In *Armitage v Mountain* [1957] Crim. L.R. 257, use of a farmer's goods vehicle to carry the furniture of a newly engaged farm-labourer as an act of kindness and not for payment was held not to be use for the farmer's trade or business. The term "goods vehicle" in the 1988 Act and the Transport Act 1968 is discussed at §§ 1.25 and 13.45. The term "hire or reward" is discussed at § 13.49.

In *James v Davies* [1952] 2 All E.R. 758 it was held that haulage by a Land Rover, itself empty, of a trailer laden with goods on the owner's business was a conveyance of the goods and that it mattered not that the towing vehicle carried no goods. The Land Rover was a vehicle constructed for the conveyance of both goods and passengers and was therefore itself within the definition of "goods vehicle". In *Pearson v Boyes* [1953] 1 All E.R. 492, however, an empty van towing an empty caravan was held not to be carrying goods or burden; the court pointed out that the Act seemed to differentiate between hauling and towing on the one hand and carriage on the other, and stressed that clear words imposing a higher rate of taxation must be used to authorise it. By s.17(2), if duty has been paid under Pt VIII of Sch.1, higher duty is not payable on goods vehicles substantially used to carry loads if also used to carry employees of the owner of the loads.

12.24   A tractor unit was used by a motor repairer and tester in the course of his business. The use in question was the collection and return of empty trailers for repair and testing. The Divisional Court held that the justices were entitled to find that the tractor unit was a goods vehicle being used to haul goods in connection with the defendant's trade or business. The justices were entitled to hold that a vehicle excise licence was required and that the defendant could not rely on trade plates: *Booth v DPP* [1993] R.T.R. 379. Although the court was referred to the fifteenth edition of this work, there is no specific reference in the judgment in *Booth* to the comments made by the court in *Pearson v Boyes* above. It should be emphasised that the defendant in *Booth* was in effect conveying goods by hauling the empty trailers as part of his regular business and it was not in any sense a completed or "idle" activity. The court also upheld a decision that a goods vehicle operator's licence was required under the Transport Act 1968, but s.92 of that Act expressly defines "carriage of goods" as including the "haulage of goods".

Trailers

12.25   By Sch.1 para.17 of the 1994 Act, as amended, the term "trailer" in Pt VIII does not include appliances to apply loose gritting material onto roads, or snow ploughs. The term "trailer" has been held to include an empty poultry shed being drawn by a tractor (*Garner v Burr* [1950] 2 All E.R. 683) and a hut used as an office towed along the highway (*Horn v Dobson* 1933 S.C.(J.) 1).

    A mechanically propelled vehicle can be both a "mechanically propelled" vehicle and a trailer. There is nothing in the 1994 Act to exempt a mechanically propelled vehicle from taxation when it is being towed on a publicly repairable road. Where, therefore, a van was towed without its having been licensed, the justices were directed to convict the defendant even though the towing vehicle was itself licensed (*Cobb v Whorton* [1971] Crim. L.R. 372). It is only if the vehicle is in such a condition that it can no longer be said to be mechanically propelled that no licence is needed (see meaning of "mechanically propelled" in Chapter 1).

Taxation of goods vehicles

12.26   A summary of the position may be helpful:

Goods vehicles not exceeding 3,500kg laden weight

12.27   These vehicles are taxed at a flat rate under the 1994 Act Sch.1 para.1 whether used to carry goods or not and are merged together with private class vehicles in a duty class (private/light goods).

Goods vehicles over 3,500kg laden weight

12.28 These vehicles will be subject to duty under the 1994 Act Sch.1 Pt VIII unless they come within one of the other categories listed in Sch.1 para.16. Separate provisions apply depending on whether they are rigid vehicles or tractive units. "Rigid vehicles" and "tractive units" are defined in s.62(1). Lower rates apply where pollution requirements are met.

(a) *Rigid vehicles*. These will be subject to duty according to the vehicle's revenue weight defined in s.60A.

(b) *Rigid vehicles drawing trailers*. A rigid goods vehicle over 12,000kg revenue weight drawing a trailer which is being used for conveying goods or burden and which has a plated gross weight exceeding 4,000kg will have to pay supplementary duty. The supplement will depend on the plated gross weight of the trailer. See further under § 12.25 above.

(c) *Tractive units (articulated vehicles)*. An articulated vehicle will be subject to duty as a combination according to the revenue weight.

Showmen's and island goods vehicles

12.29 Special rates for island and showmen's goods vehicles apply to all the categories. These are contained in the 1994 Act Sch.1 paras 9 and 11, as amended. The category of "island goods vehicle" was introduced by the Finance Act 1995. Such a vehicle is defined in Sch.1 para.18 to the 1994 Act. The islands to which the exemption applies and the extent of the exemption are set out in para.18 and in orders issued by the Secretary of State the most recent of which included islands in the Orkney Islands, the Outer Hebrides and the Shetland Islands. The rates of duty closely follow those applied to showmen's goods vehicles, but are not identical.

Exceptional load vehicles

12.30 The duty category for vehicles used for carrying exceptional loads which do not comply with the Construction and Use Regulations, but which are specially authorised for road use under s.44 of the 1988 Act, is the heavy duty tractive unit rate (1994 Act Sch.1 para.6, as amended).

Ascertainment of weight of vehicles

12.31 Any reference in Sch.1 to the plated gross weight of goods vehicle or trailer is a reference to the plated weight or maximum laden weight (s.61(1)). The plated weight is that within the meaning of Pt II of the 1988 Act, i.e. the maximum gross weight in Great Britain. The definition of plated train weight is similar and refers to the maximum gross weight including drawn vehicles trailers. Plated weight will include a compulsory type approval certificate plate and any other plate such as a certificate of conformity plate having the same effect as a "Ministry plate". By s.60A(3) "design weight" means the weight which a vehicle is designed or adapted not to exceed when in normal use and travelling on a road laden. As to "designed or adapted", see Chapter 1. The weights set out on the goods vehicle's manufacturer's plate should normally include what is in effect the design weight applicable until the goods vehicle is plated and tested unless exempt from plating under the type approval system. Revenue weight is defined in s.60A of the 1994 Act.

A vehicle with a detachable body is treated as being of the heavier weight unless it is re-weighed and re-registered (*Scott v Dickson* (1939) 83 S.J. 317, a case on the Road Traffic Act). See generally as to "weight", Chapter 1.

Exemptions from duty

General

12.32   By s.5 of the Vehicle Excise and Registration Act 1994 certain vehicles or certain uses are exempt from vehicle excise duty.

In proceedings for an offence under s.29, 34, 37 or 45 (see §§ 12.51, 12.59, 12.83, 12.142), the burden of proof that an exemption exists is on the accused (1994 Act s.53: see § 12.142).

12.33   The details of the exemptions are contained in Sch.2 to the Vehicle Excise and Registration Act 1994, as amended. Vehicles exempted from duty include:

    (a) vehicles used on tram lines;

    (b) electrically assisted pedal cycles;

    (c) vehicles neither constructed nor adapted for use for the carriage of a driver or passenger;

    (d) vehicles used for police purposes;

    (e) fire-engines (whether kept by a public authority or other person);

    (f) vehicles kept by a fire and rescue authority for the purpose of its fire and rescue service;

    (g) ambulances for humans or animals;

    (h) vehicles used solely as mine rescue vehicles or for conveying or drawing emergency winding-gear at mines;

    (i) lifeboat haulage vehicles;

    (j) vehicles not exceeding 508kg unladen specially adapted for invalids;

    (k) other vehicles kept by disabled persons in certain circumstances;

    (l) vehicles (other than ambulances) used for the carriage of disabled people by a body for the time being recognised by the Secretary of State for the purpose of this exemption;

    (m) vehicles used only for agricultural, horticultural or forestry purposes which only travel on public roads for no more than 1.5km to pass between different areas of land occupied by the same person;

    (n) other vehicles including agricultural tractors and off-road tractors, light agricultural vehicles used off roads, agricultural engines, and mowing machines;

    (o) steam-powered vehicles;

    (p) electrically propelled vehicles;

    (q) vehicles used as snow ploughs and gritters;

    (r) vehicles being used in certain circumstances in connection with an attempt to obtain a test certificate or its equivalent, a reduced pollution certificate or vehicle weight test;

(s) light passenger vehicles with low CO_2 emissions;

(t) exemption is given for vehicles zero-rated for value added tax with a view to being taken abroad by an overseas resident, but duty is payable if they are not taken abroad;

(u) certain vehicles constructed before January 1, 1973.

The Secretary of State may extend the scope of an exemption and has done so for certain former members of the armed forces by the Motor Vehicles (Exemption from Vehicles Excise Duty) Order 1985 (SI 1985/722).

Vehicles are exempt from duty where imported by members of the armed **12.34** forces of specified countries by members of specified international headquarters and organisations. A list of countries is contained in para.3 of Sch.5 to the Road Vehicles (Registration and Licensing) Regulations 2002 (SI 2002/2742), as amended. Paragraph 4 of Sch.5 to the 2002 Regulations lists the relevant headquarters and organisations. See also § 2.30 and the Visiting Forces and International Headquarters (Applications of Law) Order (SI 1999/1736). The vehicle becomes an exempt vehicle for 12 months from the date of issue of a nil licence. During the period of the exemption the owner or keeper of the vehicle must comply with the provisions as to the licensing and registration of vehicles and the display of licences and the form and display of registration marks (see 2002 Regulations reg.32). The exemption is lost if during the 12 months' period the person who imported the vehicle becomes liable to pay any duty or tax in respect of its import.

Electrically propelled vehicles

Electrically propelled vehicles are exempt vehicles (1994 Act Sch.2 para.20G). **12.35** Electrically assisted pedal cycles are also included in the list of exempt vehicles (1994 Act Sch.2 para.2A). The Secretary of State may make regulations prescribing requirements for such vehicles and the requirement specified in reg.4 of the Electrically Assisted Pedal Cycles Regulations 1983 (SI 1983/1168) has been applied for the purpose of defining those electrically assisted pedal cycles which are exempt: 2002 Regulations reg.4. Exempt electrically assisted pedal cycles do not need to display a nil licence: 2002 Regulations reg.33.

Trams

Any vehicle used on tram lines is an exempt vehicle. It is not required to have **12.36** a nil licence: 2002 Regulations reg.33.

Police vehicles

A vehicle being used for police purposes is an exempt vehicle (1994 Act Sch.2 **12.37** para.3A).

Fire-engines, etc.

By Sch.2 para.4(2) of the 1994 Act, a fire-engine is defined as a vehicle **12.38** constructed or adapted for use for purposes in relation to which a fire and rescue authority under the Fire and Rescue Services Act 2004 has functions (whoever uses it for those purposes). By Sch.2 para.5 any vehicle kept by a fire and rescue authority is an exempt vehicle but only when it is being used or kept on a road for the purposes of the authority's functions.

"Fire and rescue authority" is not defined, but as the exemption is not limited to Fire and Rescue Services Act engines, it is submitted that fire-engines maintained by private organisations for a body of staff for firefighting and/or salvage would be exempted. As with mine rescue vehicles, the restrictive nature of the requirement for sole use should be noted. The position of unaltered museum or vintage engines is doubtful, but it is submitted that they would no longer be in use and used for the purposes of a fire and rescue authority. There are in any event special taxation provisions for certain vintage vehicles.

Ambulances

12.39   An ambulance is an exempt vehicle. Schedule 2 para.6(2) defines "ambulance" as a vehicle which is constructed or adapted for, and used for no other purpose than, the carriage of sick, injured or disabled persons to or from welfare centres or places where medical or dental treatment is given; and is readily identifiable as such a vehicle by being marked "Ambulance" on both sides. A similarly worded definition is included for veterinary ambulances which are also exempt (Sch.2 para.9).

A vehicle is exempt when it is being used or kept on a road by a health service, or health and social services body, or a National Health Service, an NHS foundation trust, the Commission for Healthcare Audit and Inspection, a Primary Care Trust or other stipulated body.

Mine rescue vehicles

12.40   This exemption is available only for vehicles used solely for the purpose prescribed (1994 Act Sch.2 para.10).

Lifeboat vehicles

12.41   Again the vehicle must be used for no other purposes than those prescribed (1994 Act Sch.2 para.11).

Vehicles for disabled people

12.42   Schedule 2 para.18 of the 1994 Act provides exemption for vehicles specially adapted and used or kept on a road for an invalid provided the vehicle does not exceed 508kg in weight unladen. Other vehicles used or kept for use by, or for the purposes of, a disabled person may be exempt. Each disabled person may have no more than one exempt vehicle registered in his or her name under this category or the related one in Sch.4 para.7 (Sch.2 para.19(1)). In order to obtain the exemption, the vehicle must be registered in the name of a disabled person who has received or obtained:

  (1) a disability living allowance by reason of entitlement to the mobility component at the higher rate (this is made more flexible by Sch.2 para.19(2A)), or

  (2) a mobility supplement, or

  (3) a grant under certain National Health Service Acts in relation to the vehicle (or is eligible for such a grant) (Sch.2 para.19(2)).

Where a person satisfies (1) or (2) above, the vehicle may be registered in the name of an appointee (as defined in Sch.2 para.19(4)) instead of in the name of the disabled person. Further exemptions are contained in Sch.4 para.7 where a vehicle is suitable for (and registered in the name of) a person having a particular disability that so incapacitates them in the use of their limbs that they have to be driven and cared for by a full-time constant attendant.

Regulation 33 of the 2002 Regulations, as amended, provides that the informa- **12.43** tion relating to the payment of the mobility supplement of the war pension and the higher rate mobility component of disability living allowance, and to the suspension of an entitlement to receive the latter, is prescribed for the purpose of the Vehicle Excise and Registration Act 1994 s.22ZA. Information so prescribed may be disclosed by the Secretary of State to another Secretary of State in order to verify entitlements to exemption from vehicle excise duty by virtue of the keeper or user of a vehicle being entitled to receive such benefit.

Vehicles used for the carriage of disabled people

By Sch.2 para.20 of the 1994 Act such a vehicle (other than an ambulance as **12.44** defined in Sch.2 para.6) used by a body recognised by the Secretary of State for the purposes of this paragraph is an exempt vehicle. The Secretary of State must recognise a body if, on application in the prescribed manner, it appears to him that the body is concerned with the care of disabled people.

Vehicles used between different parts of land

A vehicle is exempt that is only used for purposes relating to agriculture, **12.45** horticulture and forestry, is used on public roads only in passing between different areas of land occupied by the same person and the distance it travels on public roads in passing between such areas does not exceed 1.5km (1994 Act Sch.2 para.20A).

Other exempt vehicles

These include agricultural or off-road tractors (paras 20B and 20C), mowing **12.46** machines (para.20E), steam powered vehicles (para.20F), snow ploughs (para.20H) and gritters (para.20J).

Vehicles being tested

By the 1994 Act Sch.2 para.22 (as amended) a vehicle is exempt from duty **12.47** (and is not required to obtain a nil licence: 2002 Regulations reg.33) when proceeding to and from a previously arranged compulsory, reduced pollution or vehicle weight test or re-examination, or, where the test is failed, to and from the place where relevant work is to be carried out on the vehicle by previous arrangement. In all cases, the arrangement must be specific as to both time and date. As with other exemptions, this one is restricted to vehicles being solely used for the purpose for which the exemption is granted. Thus, an impecunious Londoner is prevented from arranging a test in Penzance in order to use his car untaxed to carry his family on holiday to Cornwall.

In *Secretary of State for Transport v Richards* [1998] R.T.R. 456, the Divisional Court considered an appeal by DVLA against a decision of the Crown Court regarding the extent of this exemption. The defendant, Mr Richards, was travelling to a pre-arranged test. He stopped to buy petrol, then he stopped for cigarettes at a shop and talked to the shop owner for about 10 minutes. While his car was parked, it was seen by the police and Mr Richards was reported for using a vehicle without a licence. The conviction at the magistrates' court was overturned on appeal by the Crown Court. The Crown Court decision was upheld by the Divisional Court and Gage J. is reported as saying "on the facts of this case, I would regard it as ridiculous if a driver could not stop to get petrol on the way. I would regard it as flying in the face of common sense if some short stop cannot be made by a defendant for whatever purpose providing he is on his way to the test station." It is a question of fact and degree in every case.

Exemption is also given to an authorised person (defined in Sch.2 para.22(7)) who uses the vehicle in the course of a compulsory test solely to convey the vehicle to or from a place where part of the test is to be carried out or, indeed, to carry out the test (Sch.2 para.22(2)) including use solely to warm up the engine (Sch.2 para.22(2A)).

"Compulsory test" is defined in Sch.2 para.22(4)–(6). It is the normal, so-called MoT test, under s.45 of the Road Traffic Act 1988 or other examinations in connection with goods vehicles compliance with construction and use regulations or with type approval requirements. "Reduced pollution test" is defined in Sch.2 para.22(6AA). "Relevant work" in this context is defined by Sch.2 para.22(10) as being work necessary to remedy the defects identified.

Old vehicles

12.48   A vehicle constructed before January 1, 1973 is exempt unless it comes within any of the descriptions specified in Sch.2 para.1A(2). Those descriptions are:

    (a) a vehicle for which an annual rate is specified in Sch.1, Pt III (buses), Pt V (recovery vehicles), Pt VI (vehicles used for exceptional loads), Pt VII (haulage vehicles) and Pt VIII (goods vehicles);

    (b) a special vehicle (Sch.1, Pt IV) which is not a digging machine, mobile crane, works truck or road roller but which is either designed or adapted for use for the conveyance of goods or burden of any description, is put to commercial use on the road but not used to convey goods or burden or is designed or adapted for use with a semi-trailer attached, is put to commercial use on a public road but, where that use is with a semi-trailer attached, the semi-trailer is not used to convey goods or burden.

Collection of duty

12.49   By s.6 of the Vehicle Excise and Registration Act 1994, duty is levied by the Secretary of State who, together with his officers and authorised agents, have the same powers and duties as HM Revenue & Customs and their officers in respect to matters other than those relating only to duty on imported goods. This extends to punishments and penalties (s.6(3)) but is subject to the provisions of the Vehicle Excise and Registration Act 1994 (s.6(4)). It does extend to mitigated penalties and to remission, for which see §§ 12.145–6.

Subject to the prescribed regulations, when in force (see 1994 Act Sch.4 para.9), s.20 of the 1994 Act allows an application to be made by the holder of a vehicle excise licence for a rebate of duty, where a goods vehicle is transported between the nearest suitable rail points in Great Britain in the course of the combined transport of goods between Member States. The goods vehicle must have a plated gross weight, a plated train weight or if not plated, a design weight exceeding 3,500kg. The rebate will only apply where the vehicle itself is transported by rail.

Vehicle licences

12.50   Sections 7–10 of the Vehicle Excise and Registration Act 1994 (as amended) control the issue, transfer and surrender of licences. Section 9 allows the Secretary of State to issue a temporary licence instead of the licence asked for. Such a licence may be renewed if necessary. Duplicates may be obtained where a licence has been stolen, destroyed, damaged or become illegible and the licence-holder is under an obligation to seek such a duplicate in these circumstances: 2002 Regulations reg.8. Where, during the currency of a licence, the vehicle is used in a way that subjects it to a higher rate then that higher rate becomes chargeable (s.15). This includes situations where a vehicle is used in breach of conditions imposed and entitling the owner or keeper to pay a lower rate of duty (s.15(3)). It also includes situations where the vehicle attracted a lower rate of duty because it satisfied the reduced pollution requirements, but subsequently failed to satisfy those requirements: s.15(2A). Where a higher rate becomes chargeable, the licence may be exchanged for a new licence which will commence on the day on which the new rate became chargeable and last for the balance of the term of the original licence (s.15(4)).

Certain exemptions are provided in respect of goods vehicles by ss.16 and 17. By s.16, tractive units (defined in s.62(1)) which obtain a licence in three specified circumstances avoid being liable for a different rate of duty if they are used only in one alternative way each. In each circumstance, a tractive unit licensed on the basis of use with semi-trailers with a certain number of axles may be used with semi-trailers with a lesser number of axles provided certain weight restrictions are adhered to. By s.17(2), where duty has been paid under paras 8–17 of Sch.1 (goods vehicles) and the vehicle is to a substantial extent being used to carry goods or burden belonging to a particular person (who may or may not be the keeper of the vehicle), then higher rate does not become chargeable simply by use of the vehicle to carry, without charge and in the course of their employment, employees of the person to whom the goods or burden belong.

OFFENCES IN RESPECT OF LICENCES

Using or keeping a vehicle on a public road without a licence

The Vehicle Excise and Registration Act 1994 provides that a person who uses **12.51** or keeps on a public road a vehicle for which a licence is not in force shall be liable:

(1) to whichever is the greater of the following penalties, namely:
    (a) an excise penalty on level 3; or
    (b) an excise penalty equal to five times the amount of duty chargeable (s.29(3)); and
(2) to back-duty (s.30: see § 12.67 below),

unless the vehicle is exempt from duty under the Act or any other enactment. Sections 29 and 30 of, and Sch.2A to, the 1994 Act have been amended so as to impose additional liability for the offences if using or keeping an unlicensed motor vehicle (see Finance Act 2008 Sch.45 paras 2–8).

Almost all exempt vehicles are nil licence vehicles and, as such, are required to have a nil licence in force for it: 2002 Regulations reg.33. Using or keeping such a vehicle on a public road without a nil licence being in force will be an offence under s.43A punishable by a fine (not an excise penalty) of level 2. Those exempt vehicles which are not nil licensable vehicles are registered Crown vehicles (2002 Regulations reg.30(4)), trams, electrically assisted pedal cycles, vehicles not intended to carry a driver or a passenger, those being tested and those for export: 2002 Regulations reg.33(1).

12.52   Further offences were created by ss.31A–31C in respect of the person in whose name the vehicle is registered where that vehicle is unlicensed. Section 31A provides that the offence does not apply in respect of exempt vehicles which have complied with any obligation to have and display a nil licence and that a licence ceases to apply on the transfer of the vehicle to another person unless the licence is delivered to the other person with the vehicle.

Section 31A of the 1994 Act shall not apply to a person in whose name a vehicle is registered before December 19, 2003, if before that date that person has sold, disposed of or permanently exported that vehicle or it has been stolen and not recovered.

12.53   Section 31B provides for four conditions which avoid the registered person committing an offence. The first condition is that he is not the keeper of the vehicle. However, if he was previously the keeper of the vehicle, this condition will only avoid the offence if he has complied with requirements under s.22(1)(d) of the 1994 Act to notify change of ownership. The second condition applies where the person registered is the keeper but the vehicle is neither kept nor used on a public road and the relevant requirements of s.22(1D) of the 1994 Act have been complied with. The third condition applies where the vehicle has been stolen and not recovered at the time of the alleged offence (the "relevant time") and the registered person has complied with conditions prescribed in regulations to be made by the Secretary of State under s.31B(6). The fourth condition is that the relevant time is within a prescribed period (called "grace days") and a licence is in fact taken out within the limit of the grace days and covers them.

These conditions may be changed or added to by regulations made by the Secretary of State (s.31B(7)).

It is for the registered person to adduce sufficient evidence to raise an issue with regard to the existence of one of those conditions but, having done so, it is for the prosecution to prove beyond reasonable doubt that this exception does not apply (s.31B(8)).

12.54   As regards penalty, there is the usual provision for an excise penalty of up to level 3 or five times the amount of annual duty whichever is the greater but there is also provision for an additional, substantial, penalty with the minimum prescribed by statute as well as the maximum. New s.31C(1) provides for the standard penalty but also for an additional amount where s.31C(3) applies, that is, where, when the proceedings commenced he was the person in whose name the vehicle was registered and, also, the vehicle was unlicensed from the time of the offence to the start of the proceedings. The minimum additional penalty will be the greater of the maximum normal penalty (level 3 or five times annual duty) or the supplement payable for non-renewal. The maximum additional penalty is either the same as the minimum or 10 times the annual duty whichever is the greater (new s.31C(2)).

By s.22 (as amended), the Secretary of State may by regulations allow the making of a declaration that a vehicle will not be kept or used on a public road during a specified period. If the vehicle is used or kept on a public road during that period, the reference to level 3 as the maximum penalty is increased to level 4 (s.29(3A).

By s.32A and Sch.2A, power is given to the Secretary of State to make regulations extending the use of wheel clamps to suspected offences under s.29(1).

Proceedings under s.29 may be brought within six months of evidence sufficient in his opinion to justify the proceedings coming to the knowledge of the prosecutor, subject to an overriding time-limit of three years from the date of the offence (s.47(2), (3)). Proceedings may only be brought by the Secretary of State or a constable with his approval (see s.47(1), § 12.135). **12.55**

Proceedings under s.29 are specified offences under the Prosecution of Offences Act 1985 (Specified Proceedings) Order 1999 (SI 1999/904) for the purpose of s.3 of the Prosecution of Offences Act 1985. This means that the DPP and under him the Crown Prosecutor is not obliged to take over from the police s.29 proceedings issued with the written plea of guilty procedure in s.12 of the Magistrates' Courts Act 1980 unless and until a magistrates' court begins to receive evidence.

Because the punishment for non-payment is expressed as a penalty and not as a fine imposed as a punishment for an offence, the various provisions of the Customs and Excise Acts apply where they have not been expressly excluded. (See in particular § 12.147 below.) It should be remembered that, although rarely exercised, under s.147(3) of the Customs and Excise Management Act 1979 the prosecutor has a right of appeal to the Crown Court against any decision of a magistrates' court in proceedings for an offence to which that Act applies. **12.56**

It may be relevant that the defendant has been given the opportunity to pay a mitigated penalty and has either not availed himself of the opportunity or has declined it wishing instead to mitigate the offence before a magistrates' court or to plead not guilty (see § 12.145 below).

If use without payment of duty is established, the defendant must be found guilty, however trivial the case (see *Patterson v Helling* at § 12.06). Ownership or proof of ownership of the vehicle is not essential to proof of the offence of "keeping" or "using" (*Napthen v Place* [1970] Crim. L.R. 474). In *Secretary of State for the Environment, Transport and the Regions v Holt* [2000] R.T.R. 309, no vehicle excise licence was displayed on an unattended vehicle stationary on a road. At some previous date, the registered keeper of the vehicle had notified the Secretary of State that he had disposed of the vehicle. A notice under s.46 of the Vehicle Excise and Registration Act 1994 was sent to the registered keeper requesting the name and address of the person responsible for the vehicle but the registered keeper did not reply. An information charging the registered keeper with keeping a mechanically propelled vehicle in respect of which no licence was in force was dismissed but an appeal allowed. The burden of proof under s.29 remains on the prosecution throughout. If it was shown merely that the defendant was the registered keeper of the vehicle, the burden of proving that the registered keeper was in fact the keeper on the day in question might not have been discharged. Although s.46 created a separate offence of non-compliance, a failure to respond to that notice gave rise to an adverse inference which, coupled with the fact of the registration as the keeper of the vehicle, discharged the burden of proof on the prosecution. The case was remitted with a direction to convict. It is no defence that a cheque has been posted to the licensing authority prior to the use of the vehicle on the road (*Nattrass v Gibson* (1968) 112 S.J. 866). By s.29(2) a vehicle is unlicensed if no licence is in force in respect of the vehicle. However, these problems are more likely to be met by prosecutions under ss.31A–31C (see § 12.52 above). **12.57**

12.58   Section 29(1) and (2) read together refers to a person using, etc., a vehicle "for which a licence is not in force". A licence is, presumably, "in force" as soon as it is issued or granted. The time at which a licence is issued or granted is not the time at which it is received but the time at which it is granted by or on behalf of the Secretary of State. The tax disc will usually be stamped with the date of issue. However, a licence is void from the time it is granted if it is paid for by a cheque that is dishonoured where a notice has been sent by post to the licence-holder informing him that the licence is void as from when it was granted (1994 Act s.19A). The Secretary of State may issue licences to those who have agreed to pay in a manner provided for in the agreement (s.19B). If the duty is not paid and the Secretary of State sends a notice by post that the licence is void from the time it was granted then the licence is so void (s.19B(2)). Alternatively, the Secretary of State may send a notice specifying a time within which an overdue payment has to be made. If payment is still not made and a further notice is sent as under s.19B(2), the licence is void from the time it was granted (s.19B(3)).

Section 34 imposes like penalties on a holder of a trade licence or licences who uses on a public road at any one time a greater number of vehicles than he is authorised to use by virtue of that or those licences. The same time-limit applies under s.47.

12.59   The maximum penalty under s.29(3) is calculated as five times the annual rate of duty applicable to the vehicle at the date of the offence (s.29(6), (7)). In the case of a continuing offence, the offence shall be deemed to have been committed on the date or latest date to which the conviction relates (s.29(8)). Where, in the case of a vehicle kept on a road, the rate of duty at the date of the offence differs from the annual rate by which the vehicle was chargeable, namely that applicable at the date of issue of its last licence, the duty shall be calculated at the latter rate (s.29(7)). Any duty actually paid by the defendant would seem not to alter the maximum penalty; only the amount of any back-duty payable under s.30 would be affected (see below). Where a licence has not been taken out at all, the defendant cannot plead that he would have licensed the car for a shorter period and that the quintuple duty should be calculated for that period only.

The court may mitigate the penalty to whatever extent it wishes (Customs and Excise Management Act 1979 s.150), but not the back-duty (see § 12.67).

The burden of proof that the vehicle was licensed rests on the defendant (s.101 of the Magistrates' Courts Act 1980, confirmed in *Guyll v Bright* [1987] R.T.R. 104). Presumably the burden will be on the balance of probabilities—see § 12.142. The burden of proof as to purpose of use, etc., is thrown on the defendant by s.53 (§ 12.142) in proceedings under s.29.

12.60   Fourteen days of grace are, in practice, allowed for the renewal of licences (other than trade licences) providing the earlier licence has expired immediately before but, if a licence is not taken out after they have passed, it is proper to charge unlicensed use during them (*Sly v Randall* (1916) 80 J.P. 199). It is the duty of the licence-holder to renew it when it expires and it is no defence that he has not been given a reminder by the authorities (*Caldwell v Hague* (1914) 79 J.P. 152). Regulation-making power has been provided to enable supplements to be charged where a vehicle licence is not renewed on time (1994 Act ss.7A and 7B). This power was exercised and the Road Vehicles (Registration and Licensing) (Amendment) (No.3) Regulations 2003 (SI 2003/2981) inserted a new reg.9A into the 2002 Regulations. Failing to renew within one month (or to comply with the requirements of Sch.4 to the 2002 Regulations (statutory off-road notification, see below)) will lead to a supplement being required which will be halved if paid within 28 days of demand.

A person who is detected using an unlicensed vehicle on a public road at any time commits an offence and cannot plead as a defence that he took out a licence five minutes later (*Campbell v Strangeways* (1877) 42 J.P. 39; *Wharton v Taylor* (1965) 109 S.J. 475), nor that a cheque had been posted to the licensing authority before the vehicle was used on the road (*Nattrass v Gibson* (1968) 112 S.J. 866).

In *Flack v Church* (1918) 82 J.P. 59, it was held that the fact that in a particular **12.61** year a person had been convicted of keeping a dog without a licence did not prevent a further conviction for keeping the same dog without a licence on another day later in the same year. Liability under taxing statutes can sometimes be strict. In *Strutt v Clift* (1911) 74 J.P. 471, a master sent his servant out in a carriage on lawful business; the servant used it for a frolic of his own in an unlawful way which attracted higher duty. The master was held liable. In *Stone v Horton* (1949) 113 J.P. Jo. 674, an owner was likewise held liable where he had hired or lent the car to a customer. On the other hand, it was held in *Abercromby v Morris* (1932) 96 J.P. 392 that an owner who lends his car to a friend for a period, on the understanding that the friend will renew the licence, is not liable for unauthorised use by the friend on expiry of the licence. And see *L.F. Dove Ltd v Tarvin* (1964) 108 S.J. 404 and *Carmichael & Sons Ltd v Cottle* [1971] R.T.R. 11, and cases on the Construction and Use Regulations.

Use in contravention of the statutory off-road notification (SORN)

The Road Vehicles (Registration and Licensing) Regulations 2002 (SI 2002/ **12.62** 2742) prescribe what is to be done by a person who surrenders a vehicle licence, does not renew a licence or keeps an unlicensed vehicle: reg.26 and Sch.4. Breach of these regulations is an offence punishable under s.59(2)(a) of the 1994 Act with a fine up to level 3. One of the consequences of the regulations is that s.29(3A) of the 1994 Act is activated whereby an offender who has made a declaration under Sch.4 para.2 of the 2002 Regulations and then takes the vehicle on a public road whilst the statutory off-road notification (SORN) is in force becomes liable to the higher (level 4) penalty in respect of the s.29 offence. Exempt vehicles coming under Sch.2 paras 2, 2A, 3, 23 and 24 of the 1994 Act are excluded but other exempt vehicles (e.g. police vehicles (Sch.2 para.3A), fire-engines (Sch.2 para.4) and ambulances (Sch.2 para.6)) are not excluded. Also excluded are unlicensed vehicles which are off the road on January 31, 1998 which will not be included in the scheme until after a vehicle excise licence is taken out or they are used or kept on a public road after January 31, 1998 (reg.4(b)).

The provisions apply to a vehicle which is registered in the Great Britain re- **12.63** cords and kept in Great Britain unless exempted from the application of the provisions as described above. Such a vehicle is referred to as a relevant GB vehicle. Similar provisions apply to vehicles registered and kept in Northern Ireland. A person surrendering a licence, not renewing a licence or keeping an unlicensed vehicle must make a declaration to the Secretary of State that (except for use under a trade licence) he does not for the time being intend to use or keep the vehicle on a public road and will not do so without first taking out the appropriate licence: 2002 Regulations Sch.4 para.1(1). That declaration must be accompanied by details of the registration mark, make and model of the vehicle and, if asked for, the address where the vehicle is kept: 2002 Regulations Sch.4 paras 1(1) and 2(2). The provisions apply differently to person who is a relevant vehicle trader (as defined in Sch.4 para.1(4) which applies the definition by reference both to the occupation of the person concerned (e.g. holder of a trade licence, auctioneer of vehicles, motor dealer) and also to the circumstances in which the vehicle is in his possession (e.g. temporarily in the course of his business as an auctioneer/ motor trader)).

12.64   Where a licence is surrendered after January 31, 1998 the declaration must be made and the particulars given unless the vehicle is no longer kept by the licence-holder or the licence-holder is a relevant vehicle trader (2002 Regulations Sch.4 para.3). The words "relevant vehicle trader" are defined in Sch.4 para.1(4) by reference both to the occupation of the person concerned and the circumstances in which the vehicle is in his possession.

Where a licence ceases to be in force on or after January 31, 1998 and a further consecutive licence is not taken out, the keeper of the vehicle must make the declaration and furnish the particulars not later than the day following the day on which the licence expired unless the keeper is a vehicle trader in which case the obligation has to be discharged within three months starting from the day following the day on which the licence expired (2002 Regulations Sch.4 para.4).

12.65   Subject to the exemption referred to above, a person keeps an unlicensed vehicle and 12 months has elapsed during which the vehicle has been kept (not necessarily by the current keeper) in Great Britain either unlicensed or without a nil licence being in force but neither the declaration or the particulars have been given, then, unless a licence is taken out to start from the end of that 12 months, the keeper of the vehicle must make the declaration and give the particulars not later than the day following the expiry of the 12 months (2002 Regulations Sch.4 para.5).

For the purposes of this provision, where the 12 months starts to run with the surrender of a licence the vehicle is deemed to be unlicensed from the beginning of the month in which the licence was surrendered (2002 Regulations Sch.4 para.5(2)). Where there is a change of keeper of an unlicensed vehicle, the new keeper must take out a licence or make a declaration and give the particulars not later than the day following the day on which the change takes place (2002 Regulations Sch.4 para.6(b)) or, if the new keeper is a relevant vehicle trader, within three months beginning with the day following the day on which the change took place (2002 Regulations para.6(b)).

Effect of failure to transfer licence

12.66   A licence may be delivered to the new keeper of vehicle when a change of keeper occurs: Road Vehicles (Registration and Licensing) Regulations 2002 reg.20(2). However, if a licensed vehicle is transferred by the holder of the licence to another person without the licence being handed over at the same time, any use of that vehicle on a public road is deemed by s.29(4) of the Act to be an unlicensed use. Quaere if the vehicle becomes re-licensed, as it were, once the licence has been delivered; it is arguable on the wording that it still remains unlicensed, especially from the omission of "and until" after "unless". On the other hand, this subsection imposes a taxing burden in making duty payable possibly twice and it can be said that only clear words can justify such an interpretation against the transferee.

Calculation of back-duty

By s.30 of the Vehicle Excise and Registration Act 1994, where a person **12.67** convicted of an offence of using or keeping an unlicensed vehicle is the person by whom that vehicle was kept at the time of the offence, the court is obliged to order him to pay, in addition to any penalty, back-duty calculated in accordance with ss.30 and 31; this provision applies also where the defendant is discharged absolutely or conditionally (see s.32). Similarly, if the registered keeper is convicted under s.31A(1) (see § 12.52 above), the registered keeper will be liable to be ordered to pay the back duty.

The amount of back-duty is an amount equal to one twelfth of the annual rate of duty for each calendar month or part of a calendar month in the relevant period. "The relevant period", by s.31, is one ending with the date of the offence and beginning:

(a) if the defendant has before that date notified the licensing authority of his acquisition of the vehicle, with the date of receipt of that notification or, if later, with the expiry of the licence last in force for the vehicle, or

(b) in any other case, with the expiry of the licence last in force for the vehicle before the date of the offence or, if there has not at any time before that date been a licence in force for the vehicle, with the date on which the vehicle was first kept by that person.

By s.31(4), if a person has been previously ordered to pay back-duty for the **12.68** same vehicle, the relevant period begins with the month following that in which the first offence was committed. Again if a person has been previously ordered to pay back-duty under s.36 in respect of a void licence for the same vehicle, those months are to be excluded (s.31(6)).

Section 31(5) (as amended) reads:

"(5) Where the person convicted proves—

(a) that throughout any month or part of a month in the relevant period the vehicle in question was not kept by him, or

(b) that he has paid duty due ... in respect of the vehicle for any such month or part of a month,

any amount which the person is ordered to pay under s.30 is to be calculated as if that month or part of a month were not in the relevant period."

A more extensive liability applies to a registered keeper convicted as such under s.31A. As regards penalty, there is the usual provision for an excise penalty of up to level 3 or five times the amount of annual duty whichever is the greater but there is also provision for an additional, substantial, penalty with the minimum prescribed by statute as well as the maximum. Section 31C(1) provides for the standard penalty but also for an additional amount where s.31C(3) applies, that is, where, when the proceedings commenced he was the person in whose name the vehicle was registered and, also, the vehicle was unlicensed from the time of the offence to the start of the proceedings. The minimum additional penalty will be the greater of the maximum normal penalty (level 3 or five times annual duty) or the supplement payable for non-renewal (see § 12.10 above). The maximum additional penalty is either the same as the minimum or 10 times the annual duty whichever is the greater (s.31C(2)).

12.69   The defendant is no longer entitled to escape back-duty by showing that the vehicle was off the road or that the vehicle was not used or kept by him on a public road or even by showing that the vehicle was not chargeable with duty. It is unfortunate that this liability for back-duty may arise even though the vehicle was not subject to tax during the relevant period in question. This result leads to complaints of injustice even though the liability is designed to deter offences and punish offenders. It does not mean that the law-abiding citizen should have to pay if he puts a vehicle on the road after a period off the public roads. He can put the vehicle on a public road without committing an offence by first ensuring that the vehicle is properly taxed. He will then not incur any back-duty liability while the vehicle was off the public roads or while the vehicle was not chargeable with duty.

The change is only designed to catch those who put the vehicle back on public roads without first obtaining the vehicle excise licence.

12.70   Defendants will be more likely to seek to avail themselves of the escape clause in s.31(5)(a) that the vehicle was not kept by the defendant himself but by someone else, such as a relative or acquaintance, during the relevant period. The defendant will himself escape the back-duty if he establishes this on the balance of probabilities and no doubt the courts will be asked to examine such claims carefully.

It is also possible that defendants will more frequently claim in mitigation that the vehicle excise licence application was in the post and that the licence should have been issued for an earlier date. The date stamp on the licence will normally establish the day of issue.

12.71   Note that s.30 applies only to the person convicted under s.29 and only if he was the person by whom the vehicle was kept at the time of the offence. Thus if *A*'s son uses *A*'s unlicensed car, the son cannot, on conviction under s.29, be made to pay back-duty under s.30 of the 1994 Act. If *A* has been convicted of aiding and abetting his son's unlicensed use, *A* has, it is submitted, been himself "convicted of an offence" under s.29; s.44 of the Magistrates' Courts Act 1980 says that an aider and abettor is "guilty of the like offence". Then *A* must be ordered to pay back-duty. However, it is more likely that *A* will be prosecuted under s.31A(1) as the registered keeper in which case he will be liable for even higher maximum penalties.

A puzzling case has been reported from Scotland. In *Peacock v Hamilton* 1996 S.L.T. 777 a driver was charged with using a vehicle without a licence contrary to s.29(1) and pleaded guilty. Part of the sentence was an order for back-duty. This was quashed on appeal on the grounds that the driver had not been charged as keeper of the vehicle, only as user. This decision appears to fly in the face of the plain meaning of s.30. Although it can never be assumed that a user is the keeper, nonetheless the order for back-duty can be made where the person convicted of *an* offence under s.29 is the person by whom the vehicle was kept at the relevant time.

12.72   See s.18 as to the back-duty on vehicles zero-rated for VAT because they are to be taken abroad, and then becoming chargeable with duty because not taken abroad.

Section 52 of the 1994 Act enables evidence of prescribed matters to be given by the production of a document authenticated by a person authorised in that behalf by the Secretary of State (see § 3.55). Details in respect of vehicle excise licences are held in the DVLA centralised computer at Swansea, and evidence of the existence or non-existence of such a licence may therefore be established in this way.

Summary as to proceedings for payment of back-duty, etc.

The provisions of s.30 as to back-duty apply only where there is a conviction **12.73** under s.29 of the Vehicle Excise and Registration Act 1994 for using or keeping an unlicensed vehicle on a public road; if the conviction is under s.34 (trade licences), the Act does not apply in respect of back-duty; in these circumstances back-duty is recoverable as a civil debt. With regard to s.15 (alteration of use of vehicle) there are in s.38 separate back-duty provisions. There are also separate back-duty provisions in s.36 for void cheque offences; see § 12.81 below.

If, however, there is a conviction (including an order of absolute or conditional discharge) under s.29, the court has a discretion as to the amount of the penalty but must order the full back-duty, however great the financial hardship to the defendant and however impecunious he is, unless the defendant can show that for some or all of the relevant period he was not the keeper of the vehicle or that the relevant back-duty has in fact been paid.

Back-duty is not a pecuniary penalty or forfeiture or pecuniary compensation. **12.74** It is simply the sum which ought to have been paid by way of excise licence fee. Section 32(2) states that the back-duty provisions in s.30 are to have effect subject to the provisions (modified as appropriate) of any enactment relating to the imposition of fines by magistrates' courts and may be recovered and applied as a fine. Despite this, any such provision conferring a *discretion as to amount* is not applied. This means that unlike a fine there is no power to mitigate the back-duty in accordance with s.34 of the Magistrates' Courts Act 1980 or to take into account the defendant's means under s.35 of the same Act. Section 35 must be read in conjunction with s.34 which plainly confers a discretion. *The full amount* must be ordered unless one of the s.30 exceptions applies. This was confirmed in *Chief Constable of Kent v Mather* [1986] R.T.R. 36.

The effect of s.85(2) of the Magistrates' Courts Act 1980 is that, although a court after non-payment of a fine or inquiring into the offender's means may ordinarily remit the whole or part of a fine because of a change in his circumstances, this power of remission cannot be exercised either in respect of orders for the payment of back-duty under s.30 or in respect of any penalties imposed under s.29, 34 or 37 as these do not come within the definition of "fine" in s.85(2). Courts sometimes achieve the same result by ordering one day's detention in default of the penalty, costs and back-duty.

The statement of facts normally indicates the amount of back-duty claimed **12.75** and the Department for Transport should know when any was last paid. It has been emphasised that the basis on which the defendant is said to be liable to pay back-duty and the penalties should be clearly set out by the prosecution in the back-duty notice (*Halls Construction Services Ltd v DPP* [1989] R.T.R. 399). A defendant who seeks to prove that he was not the keeper during any part of the relevant period should adduce evidence to that effect; the then owner of the vehicle may give evidence as to this but is in danger of incriminating himself both for not notifying the change and for not paying duty. Members of the defendant's household or neighbours can often help on this point.

The defendant may also show that he has paid duty for the relevant period or some of it and in this case the period is calculated as if the month or part of a month for which he has paid were not comprised in the relevant period (s.31(5)). Or it may be shown that he has already been ordered to pay back-duty for the same vehicle on a previous conviction, in which case the back-duty now payable by him begins to run with the month following the previous conviction. The defendant may, possibly, appeal to the Crown Court against the amount ordered (see further on this point, § 22.15).

Examples

12.76   Some examples may assist:

(1) *X* has kept his motor vehicle off the public road between January 1, and June 2, 2009. His last vehicle excise licence expired on December 31, 2008. On June 1, 2009 he sends off the tax application correct in all aspects for the licence to commence from June 1, 2009. The application is delayed in the post and does not arrive until June 4, 2009. In the meantime he is caught using the vehicle on a public road on June 3, when no tax is in force. Even though the vehicle was not on a public road from January to May 2009 the court will still have to order the back-duty for those five months.

(2) The circumstances of *Y* are identical but his application is not delayed in the post and arrives on June 2, 2009. The tax disc is stamped with that date and is in force from then. *Y* will commit no offence if he puts the vehicle on a public road on June 3, and no back-duty liability at all will follow.

(3) *A* commits the offence of using a motor vehicle on a public road on March 18, 2009. The licence ran out on December 31, 2007 and *A* calls no evidence to suggest he was not the keeper of the vehicle during 2008–09. In addition to the fine, the amount of which is at the magistrates' discretion, he must be ordered to pay full back-duty for the 12 months of 2008 and three months of 2009. The duty to be claimed, by s.30(3), is the annual rate applicable to it at the beginning of each month, or part.

(4) The same facts but *A* notified the licensing authority that he had become the owner on June 22, 2008. Then he is liable to pay back-duty only for the months commencing June 1, 2008. It seems on the wording of s.31(2)(a) that it is only notification by the person convicted that counts; a notification by the previous owner does not although the prosecution would no doubt in practice not pursue the claim if satisfied of the date of acquisition. Notification must be before the offence, not the conviction. See, however, the dual notification requirements in regs 22–24 of the 2002 Regulations placing the onus on the disposer of a vehicle to obtain details of the new keeper and send them to the Secretary of State.

(5) The same facts but *A* proves to the court that he did not acquire the motor vehicle until June 22, 2008 and did not keep it until that date. Again he will be liable to pay back-duty only for the months commencing June 1, 2008.

(6) The same facts but it is established that the vehicle was exempt from

duty between January 1, 2008 and June 22, 2008. If the offence is committed, it is not possible for the defendant to escape the back-duty liability by proving that the vehicle was not chargeable with duty. *A* is liable in law to pay the full back-duty for the 15 months, and the exempt period is ignored. The position is similar to the person who keeps the vehicle off the public roads but who is penalised by the obligatory order of back-duty for the full period because he has failed to ensure that the vehicle is taxed and the law complied with before the vehicle is put on the public road. These exempt situations do not arise often in practice.

(7) The same facts but *A* shows that he has in fact paid the back-duty before he came to court, e.g. he had sent a cheque off to the DVLA a fortnight before he came to court. Then no back-duty is orderable by the court; if he paid only part of the back-duty, the court should order payment of the part unpaid.

(8) *B*'s last licence expired on June 30, 2008; he commits the offence of using his car on a public road on March 21, 2009, and is later convicted of it at Oxford. He proves to the Oxford court that he was convicted of a like offence committed at Cambridge in January 2009 and that the Cambridge court ordered him to pay back-duty for July to December 2008 and for January 2009. The Oxford court should order him to pay back-duty for February and March 2009 under s.31(4).

Supposing the defendant commits the offence on March 1; should back-duty **12.77** be ordered for the month of March? By s.31(1) the relevant period is one "ending with the date on which the offence was committed". Does that period "end" at 00.01 hours on March 1, so that no back-duty can be ordered or at 23.59 on that day or at the time of the offence so that the payment for the full month of March is due? A taxing statute is construed against HM Customs & Revenue and the licensing authority can always obtain payment of unpaid duty by other means, but logic would suggest that as in other circumstances a back-duty order can be made and that a purposive construction means the relevant time on the date in question.

In all the examples given above where an offence is committed the court should order a penalty or absolute or conditional discharge in addition to the back-duty. By s.30(4) a vehicle is deemed to have belonged to the same duty-class throughout, unless otherwise proved; the prosecution may elect to treat it as being in the class in which it was when a licence was last taken out. The back-duty paid must be the back-duty "appropriate to the vehicle" under s.30(2).

Failing to display licence

By the Vehicle and Excise Registration Act 1994 s.33(1) and (1A), it is an of- **12.78** fence to fail to fit to and exhibit on a vehicle a licence which is in force for the vehicle. The Secretary of State may regulate to prohibit the exhibition on a vehicle liable to duty of anything either intended to be or which could reasonably be mistaken for a valid licence (s.33(4), as amended). This prohibition is contained in reg.7 of the Road Vehicles (Registration and Licensing) Regulations 2002; it applies to vehicle licences, nil licences and trade licences. If there is no licence for the vehicle, the user may be prosecuted and incur the excise penalty under s.29 for using the vehicle without a licence and may also be fined for the offence of not exhibiting a licence under s.33(1) (*Pilgram v Dean* [1974] R.T.R. 299). The Department for Transport and the Crown Prosecution Service usually only prosecute one of these charges to conclusion, but are entitled to prosecute both. The offence of failing to display a vehicle excise licence may be dealt with by means of a fixed penalty under the Road Traffic Offenders Act 1988 fixed penalty provisions. Failure to pay the fixed penalty may mean that other proceedings ensue, if, as is usually the case, the "vehicle owner liability" provisions are used. The only defence is that provided by reg.6 of the 2002 Regulations, which provides that, where a licence (including a nil licence) has been delivered to the Secretary of State with an application for a replacement then no licence needs to be shown on the vehicle until that replacement is obtained. The terms of this regulation are a little different from its predecessor in that it refers to a replacement licence being sought rather than a new licence though this is unlikely to make a difference in practice. Regulation 6 prescribes how and where the licence is to be fixed. It must be in a holder; that holder must be sufficient to protect the licence from the weather to which, in the absence of the holder, it would be exposed: reg.6(3). It must be fixed where prescribed by reg.6(4); this is so that the information on the licence is clearly visible in daylight from the near side of the road (reg.6(5)).

12.79   Specific amendments have been made to s.33 of the 1994 Act by the Finance Act 2008 in relation to a failure to exhibit a licence during a "period of grace" (2008 Act s. 147).

A New Zealand regulation read: "No person shall permit a motor vehicle to be on a road ... unless there is carried on the vehicle a current warrant of fitness". A car exhibited the necessary warrant on the windscreen and the owner left the car for a short time; when he returned, he found that a trespasser had removed the warrant and that a traffic-offence notice had been stuck to the windscreen. It was held, after considering *Halsbury's Laws* and *Russell on Crime*, that the owner was not guilty as the omission to carry the warrant was not within his conduct, knowledge or control (*Kilbride v Lake* [1962] N.Z.L.R. 590).

This New Zealand case was considered in *Strowger v John* [1974] R.T.R. 124. It was held that the offence was absolute and no mens rea was required. A motorist left his car locked and while away the plastic holder containing the licence fell from the windscreen out of sight on to the floor of the car; the justices were directed to convict the motorist in that the car and its accessories were at all times under his control (ibid.). *Kilbride* was distinguished because in *Kilbride* the removal of the licence was totally unexplained—it had disappeared from the car. Lord Widgery C.J. in *Strowger*, at 130, specifically reserved for future consideration whether a driver would have a defence if the car is broken into and the licence stolen.

12.80   The offence may only be committed when a vehicle is used or kept on a public road. Bexley London Borough Council purported to make an order that a penalty was payable if a car was parked on off-street parking without a valid licence being displayed. The Divisional Court held that this order was ultra vires as the 1994 Act only applied to vehicles without licences on a public road: *R. v Parking Adjudicator Ex p. Bexley London Borough Council* [1998] R.T.R. 128.

An offence under s.33(1) or (1A) is punishable by a fine not exceeding level 1. Where the failure to exhibit is without fault or blame on the part of the defendant an absolute discharge may be the appropriate penalty. In *Strowger v John* above, the Divisional Court remitted the case back to the recorder of the Crown Court to enable him to give "(with a clear lack of discouragement) the opportunity of imposing an absolute discharge as the only possible penalty".

Void cheques: failure to deliver up excise licences

Where an excise licence, including a trade licence, is paid for by cheque and **12.81** the cheque is dishonoured, the licence may be void as from the time it was granted (1994 Act s.19A). For the licence to be void, the Secretary of State must first send a notice to the licence-holder informing him that the licence is void from the time it was granted. This notice may be sent once the cheque is dishonoured (s.19A(2)) or it may follow a notice giving a further opportunity to pay (s.19A(3)). Provision to allow formal arrangements to regulate payment in arrears in certain circumstances is contained in s.19B. It contains similar provisions to those in s.19A(2) and (3) where a payment is not made.

The notice under s.19A or s.19B may require the licence-holder to deliver up the licence within a specified and reasonable period and, if appropriate, to pay the amount due for the period for which the licence has been in the possession of the licence-holder: s.35A(3)–(7). Failure to comply is an offence under s.35A. The penalty is an excise penalty (not a fine) of either level 3 or an amount equal to five times the annual rate of duty that was payable on the grant of the licence or would have been payable if it had been taken out for 12 months, whichever is the greater. The effect of ss.47(1) and (2) and 55 are applied to proceedings under s.35A.

Where a person is convicted under s.35A in relation to a vehicle or trade **12.82** licence, in addition to the penalty for the offence, the court must order the equivalent of back-duty (1994 Act s.36(1)). The period of liability commences with the day on which the licence was to have effect and ends with the earliest of the date of the end of the month in which the court order is made, the date on which the licence applied for was due to expire, the end of the month in which the licence was in fact delivered up or the end of the month preceding that in which a new licence took effect (s.36(4), (4A)). There is a saving provision to avoid double payment where back-duty is also ordered in respect of the same period under s.30 (s.36(5)) or where payment has been made as a result of a requirement in the notice to deliver the licence to the Secretary of State (s.36(6)).

Under-payment of duty

By s.37(1) it is provided that an offence is committed where a licence has been **12.83** taken out for a vehicle at a certain rate, the vehicle is at any time so used on a public road that duty at a higher rate becomes chargeable under s.15 (see § 12.50) and that higher rate was not paid before the vehicle was so used. By s.37(2), the person so using the vehicle will be liable to whichever is the greater of the following penalties, namely:

    (a) an excise penalty of level 3; or

    (b) an excise penalty of an amount equal to five times the difference between the duty actually paid and the amount of duty at that higher rate (calculated semble at the annual rate: see § 12.59).

A magistrates' court may, however, mitigate the penalty to such extent as it thinks fit (Magistrates' Courts Act 1980 s.34). The burden of proof as to the characteristics of the vehicle or the purpose for which it is used is laid on the defendant in proceedings under s.37 (see s.53). See also s.154 of the Customs and Excise Management Act 1979, at § 12.143. An information specifying an offence of under-payment must itself or by means of the accompanying notice give sufficient particulars of the provisions under which the offence is being charged and the amount of duty which should have been paid. The information should give a clear idea of the maximum penalty and back-duty and must enable the defendant to appreciate the case he has to meet: *Halls Construction Services Ltd v DPP* [1989] R.T.R. 399.

12.84　　Under Sch.4 to the Finance Act 2000, the Secretary of State may make regulations providing for particulars to be furnished on applications for licences and to be supported by documentary or other evidence. Where any licence is issued where the application states that the vehicle falls within specified parts of Sch.1 to the 1994 Act and duty falls to be paid at a higher rate, the enforcement provisions of Sch.4 para.4 to the 2000 Act apply. The Secretary of State may send by post notice to the person to whom the licence was issued stating that the licence is void ab initio (Sch.4 para.5) or may (by notice by post) require that person to pay the additional duty payable within a reasonable and specified period and (if compliance does not follow) may send notice by post that the licence is void ab initio (Sch.4 para.6). In either of these two cases, the Secretary of State may require the return of the licence within a reasonable and specified period (Sch.4 para.7) or may both require the return and/or payment of the monthly duty shortfall (as defined) for each month or part of a month in the relevant period (as defined in Sch.4 para.11) (Sch.4 para.8). Any person who fails to return a licence when requested is liable on summary conviction to a fine of level 3 or five times the annual duty shortfall calculated by reference to the rates in force at the beginning of the relevant period (Sch.4 para.9). In addition, a person convicted may also be required to pay the arrears (Sch.4 para.10(1)).

Section 15(4) makes provision as to the payment of extra duty when, because of a change of use, a licence has to be exchanged (see § 12.50).

12.85　　The time-limit for proceedings under s.37 is six months from the date when evidence sufficient to justify the proceedings comes to the knowledge of the authorised prosecutor, subject to an overriding time-limit of three years from the commission of the offence (see s.47 at § 12.137). A prosecution may be instituted only by the Secretary of State for Transport or by a constable with his approval (ibid.).

A court is obliged by s.38 to order payment of the appropriate additional back-duty where the keeper is convicted for under-licensing under s.37. It applies to all motor vehicles. The amount to be paid will vary according to the case type. It will be an amount equivalent to one twelfth of the difference between the rate at which the licence was taken out and the relevant higher rate in relation to the vehicle for each month or part of a month in the relevant period (s.38(2)). The relevant higher rate is defined in s.39 and the relevant period in s.40. By s.39 there are five different methods of calculating the appropriate higher rate. By s.40 the relevant period is:

> (1) in cases where the vehicle has been replated after the current licence was taken out the period starting from the date on which the vehicle was replated at the higher weight and ending with the date of the offence (s.40(1), (2));

(2) in other cases the period starting from the date on which the current licence was taken out and ending with the date of the offence (s.40(1), (3)).

Ancillary provisions state that:

(a) a vehicle is deemed to have been chargeable at the higher rate throughout the relevant period unless it is proved to have fallen within some other description for the whole or part of any month in that period (s.38(3));

(b) where a person is convicted of more than one offence under s.37 in relation to the same vehicle, the amount of back-duty on each is reduced to avoid double payment (s.38(4));

(c) an absolute or conditional discharge for the offence under s.37 is a conviction for the purposes of s.38 (s.41(1)).

Information as to user

By s.46 of the 1994 Act, keepers and other persons are required, under penalty **12.86** of a fine of level 3, to furnish information to the police or the Secretary of State as to the identity of drivers or users of a vehicle, where it is alleged that a vehicle has been used, etc., in contravention of s.29, 34, 37 or 43A (see the discussion at §§ 7.24–40). Users may be required to give information available to them as to the identity of the keeper of the vehicle (s.46(3)). Any person may prosecute under s.46 and the time-limit is six months. There is a defence available to a keeper of a vehicle if they can satisfy the court that they did not know, and could not reasonably have found out, the driver or user in question (s.46(6)).

The Secretary of State has power under s.22 to make regulations requiring information to be supplied by those by, through or to whom a vehicle has been sold or disposed of or who is surrendering or not renewing a vehicle licence or who is keeping an unlicensed vehicle.

Section 46A(2) permits the Secretary of State to require such persons to **12.87** provide certain information. Failure to comply is an offence (s.46A(3)) punishable on summary conviction by a fine not exceeding level 3 (s.46A(4)). Section 51A provides the same evidential opportunity as presently extended to s.46 (see § 12.140 below).

Immobilisation, removal and disposal of vehicles

By Sch.2A to the 1994 Act (as amended) the Secretary of State may make **12.88** regulations in respect of the immobilisation, removal and disposal of vehicles where an authorised person has reason to believe that an offence under s.29(1) (using or keeping an unlicensed vehicle on a public road) is being committed. The regulations may also make provision for the same purposes as provided for in s.19A and s.36 and for disputes arising as a result of the regulations to be dealt with in a magistrates' court (Sch.2A paras 7 and 8). The Schedule provides for a number of offences.

The regulations currently in force are the Vehicle Excise Duty (Immobilisation, Removal and Disposal of Vehicles) Regulations 1997 (SI 1997/2439), as amended. They give various authorities to an "authorised person". By reg.3, authorised persons are persons authorised by the Secretary of State for the purpose of these regulations. An authorised person may be a local authority, an employee of a local authority, a member of a police force or any other person: reg.3(2).

Immobilisation, removal and disposal

12.89   Where an authorised person has reason to believe that an offence is being committed anywhere in England and Wales under s.29(1) of the Vehicle Excise and Registration Act 1994 in respect of a vehicle which is stationary in a relevant place (which is defined in reg.2 as "a place to which Schedule 2A to the 1994 Act applies"), an authorised person or a person acting under his direction may enter that place and clamp that vehicle: reg.5. Clamping may take place where the vehicle is, or the vehicle may be moved to another relevant place and clamped there: reg.5(2). Release may only be obtained by paying the prescribed charge and producing evidence that no offence under s.29(1) of the 1994 Act was being committed when the immobilisation device was fixed or the vehicle moved is produced; a surety payment; a vehicle licence for the vehicle, which is in force; or a declaration that—(i) an appropriate licence was in force for the vehicle at the time when the immobilisation device was fixed or the vehicle moved; (ii) save in the case of a vehicle stationary on a public road, a relevant declaration was in force for the vehicle at that time; or (iii) at that time the vehicle was an exempt vehicle which was not one in respect of which regulations under the 1994 Act require a nil licence to be in force: reg.6. The clamping does not prejudice the institution of proceedings for an offence under s.29(1). The regulations also provide for such vehicles to be removed and disposed of whether or not they have been clamped: reg.9. Various offences are provided for:

> (a) unauthorised removal of an immobilisation notice or interference with it (reg.7(1))—summary, fine, level 2 (reg.7(2));
>
> (b) unauthorised removal or attempt to remove the clamp (reg.7(3))—summary, fine, level 3 (reg.7(3));
>
> (c) making a false declaration that the vehicle is an exempt vehicle (see below) in order to secure the release of the vehicle from the clamp (reg.8(2))—"either way" offence: summary—fine, statutory maximum; indictment—two years' imprisonment, fine or both (reg.8(3));
>
> (d) making a false declaration that the vehicle is an exempt vehicle in order to secure the release of a removed vehicle (reg.13) —"either way": summary—fine, statutory maximum; indictment—two years' imprisonment, fine or both (reg.13(2)).

Offences relating to vouchers

12.90   Regulations may provide that certain conditions need to be met before a vehicle is released. These include either production of a valid licence or in specified situations, the making of a surety payment to secure the release of a vehicle (whether clamped or removed) in place of the vehicle licence. A voucher will be issued to the payer which will be a good defence to a charge under s.29(1) for 24 hours (reg.15). In specified circumstances, the payer will be able to obtain a refund for the voucher (reg.15(6)). Various offences are created:

> (1) knowingly making a declaration which is false or materially misleading to obtain a voucher or a refund on the voucher—"either way" offence: summary—fine, statutory maximum; on indictment—two years' imprisonment and/or a fine;
>
> (2) forging a voucher or fraudulently using or allowing another to use a

voucher—"either way" offence: summary—fine, statutory maximum; on indictment—two years' imprisonment and/or a fine (reg.16).

The regulations may also provide for making the voucher void if issued against a cheque which is dishonoured. Various further offences are provided in the 1994 Act:

(a) contravening regulations controlling the delivery up of void vouchers—fine, level 3 (1994 Act Sch.2A para.6(1));

(b) contravening regulations controlling the delivery up of licences obtained using a void voucher—fine, greater of level 3 or five times the annual rate of duty plus back-duty (1994 Act Sch.2A para.6(2) and 6(3));

(c) knowingly using a void voucher to defray an amount of vehicle excise duty due—fine, level 6 (1994 Act Sch.2A para.5(4)).

Appeals against refusal to refund

Under reg.17 of the 1997 Regulations, where there is a dispute over the making of a refund of a payment made to secure the release of a vehicle, there is an appeal against the refusal to refund to an authorised person (reg.17(2)). There is a further right of appeal to an appropriate court (reg.17(5)). **12.91**

A claimant who has made an appeal to an authorised person under reg.17(2) may make a further appeal if either his appeal is rejected under reg.17(4) and the further appeal is made within 28 days of the claimant being served with notification to that effect under reg.17(4)(b) or the authorised person has not notified the claimant of the outcome of his appeal and 56 days have elapsed since he appealed. By reg.17(6), the authorised court is provided for. Where the vehicle was stationary in a relevant place in England and Wales, appeal is to a magistrates' court by way of complaint; if in Scotland, to a sheriff by way of summary application; if in Northern Ireland, to a court of summary jurisdiction. If either of the grounds in reg.17(1)(a) is established, the appropriate court must order the Secretary of State to refund the disputed charge.

Exemptions

By reg.4, the following vehicles are exempt from the provisions of the regulations: **12.92**

(a) vehicles displaying current disabled person's badge;

(b) vehicles displaying a British Medical Association car badge;

(c) vehicles appearing to have been abandoned;

(d) vehicles which are a PSV and being used for the carriage of passengers;

(e) vehicles being used by a public utility or a universal service provider in relation to the provision of a postal service;

(f) vehicles stationary at a time when less than 24 hours have elapsed since release from immobilisation or removal.

Northern Ireland and Scotland

The principal regulations were extended to Northern Ireland and Scotland by the like-named amendment regulations, SI 1997/3063 and SI 1998/1217. **12.93**

Trade Licences

Generally

12.94   A motor trader or vehicle tester (or person intending to commence business as such) may, on payment of the appropriate rate of duty, apply to the Secretary of State for a trade licence under the Vehicle Excise and Registration Act 1994 s.11.

By s.62(1) of the 1994 Act a motor trader is defined as:

     (a) a manufacturer of vehicles, or

     (b) a repairer of vehicles, or

     (c) a dealer in vehicles, or

     (d) anyone else who carries on a business prescribed for this purpose by the Secretary of State in regulations—a prescribed category is the business of modifying or valeting vehicles (Road Vehicles (Registration and Licensing) Regulations 2002 reg.35).

A person is treated as a dealer if his business is wholly or mainly collecting and delivering vehicles and does not include any other activities except as a manufacturer, repairer or dealer in vehicles (s.62(1)).

12.95   A vehicle tester is a person other than a motor trader who regularly in the course of business engages in testing on roads of vehicles belonging to other persons (s.62(1)).

The effect of the licence varies with the category of person to whom it is granted and may be subject to conditions prescribed in regulations which can require compliance after the licence has been issued (s.11(1), as amended). A licence issued to a motor trader who is a manufacturer of vehicles is a licence for:

     (1) all vehicles which from time to time are temporarily in his possession in the course of his business as a motor trader;

     (2) all vehicles kept and used by him solely to conduct research and development in the course of his business as a manufacturer;

     (3) all vehicles submitted to him from time to time by other manufacturers for testing on the roads in the course of his business as a manufacturer (s.11(2)).

12.96   A licence issued to any other motor trader will cover all mechanically propelled vehicles which are from time to time temporarily in his possession in the course of his business as a motor trader (s.11(3)).

A licence issued to a vehicle tester will cover all mechanically propelled vehicles which are from time to time submitted to him for testing in the course of his business as a vehicle tester (s.11(4)).

Limitations on use of trade licences

12.97   By s.12 of the Vehicle Excise and Registration Act 1994, a trade licence does not entitle the holder to use more than one vehicle at any one time. However, there is nothing to prevent a person holding two or more licences (s.14(1)). A licence may be surrendered at any time to the Secretary of State (s.14(2)). The Secretary of State must make regulations restricting the purpose for which a vehicle is used under a trade licence and may regulate the circumstances in which a vehicle can be kept on a road if it is not being used (s.12(2)(b), (1)(c)). It is not possible to use a vehicle under a trade licence to carry goods or burden of any description except in the circumstances set out in s.12(3). In summary, the circumstances in which a load may be carried are:

(a) a load carried solely for the purpose of demonstrating or testing the vehicle;

(b) where the vehicle is being delivered or collected, a load which is another vehicle used or to be used for travelling to or from the place of delivery or collection;

(c) a load built into the vehicle or permanently attached to it;

(d) a load of parts, etc., designed to be fitted to the vehicle and of necessary fitting tools;

(e) a load consisting of a trailer other than one which is for the time being a disabled vehicle.

For the purposes of subs.(3), a vehicle and trailer are deemed to be a single vehicle where a substantial part of the weight of the trailer is carried by the vehicle (s.12(4)). A disabled vehicle includes one which is abandoned or is scrap (s.12(5)). **12.98**

Where an application for a trade licence is refused by the Secretary of State, the applicant may request a review of the decision and the Secretary of State must conduct that review (s.14(3)). Regulations prescribe the period within which that review must be requested.

The Road Vehicles (Registration and Licensing) Regulations 2002 Pt VII and Sch.6, have been made to prescribe the conditions subject to which trade licences are issued and the purposes for which the holder of a trade licence may use a vehicle under the licence. Regulation 35 extends the definition of motor trader (see above), reg.36 prescribes 28 days as the period for requesting review of a decision refusing a trade licence, Sch.6 para.1 requires the holder to notify the Secretary of State of any change in the name or address of his business and in such a case also to forward his trade licence for amendment, regs 40 and 41 prescribe the issue and replacement of trade plates, and Sch.6 paras 2–4 forbid the alteration or mutilation of trade plates or the exhibition of anything which might be mistaken for a trade plate. Regulation 42 relates to the exhibition of trade plates and licences, regs 37 and 38 and Sch.6 restrict the use of trade plates and licences and prescribe the conditions for which a vehicle may be used under a trade licence. For each trade licence issued, the Secretary of State must issue to the licence-holder a set of trade plates appropriate to the class of vehicles for which the licence is to be used: reg.40(1). Each of those plates must carry the general registration mark which will be issued to the licence-holder under reg.39: reg.40(2). One of those plates must include a device allowing the trade licence itself to be fixed to the plate: reg.40(2). **12.99**

Duration of licences

A trade licence may be taken out for one year, for a period of six months beginning with the first day of January or July or, if the applicant is a person who intends to commence business as a motor trader or vehicle tester and does not hold a trade licence, for a period of seven, eight, nine, ten or eleven months beginning with the first day of any month other than January or July and ending no later than December 31, of that year for licences taken out in February to June inclusive or June 30, of the following year for licences taken out in August to **12.100**

December inclusive (s.13(1), as amended). There is a further provision in para.8 of Sch.4 to the 1994 Act that restricts the duration to the first two options. This provision will come into force on a date to be decided by the Secretary of State.

Improper use of vehicles under a trade licence

12.101   It is an offence under s.34(1) of the Vehicle Excise and Registration Act 1994 for a person holding a trade licence or licences to use on a public road by virtue of that licence or those licences—

(1) a greater number of vehicles at any one time than he is authorised to use under the licence(s); or

(2) any vehicle for any purpose other than such purposes as may have been prescribed by regulations made under s.12(2)(b).

It is also an offence if he uses the licence(s) for the purpose of keeping on a road a vehicle which is not being used on that road except in circumstances permitted by regulations made under s.12(1)(c). It will be seen that in effect s.34(1) creates three different offences.

For the meaning of "using" and "keeping", see the definition of "use" in Chapter 1 and also §§ 12.03 et seq.

A *"Public road"*

12.102   The offences are only committed if the vehicle is on a public road. This is also true of most offences under the regulations. For the meaning of "public road" see the comments on vehicle excise licence offences at §§ 12.03 et seq.

B *"Holder of a trade licence"*

12.103   The offences can be committed only by the holder of a trade licence. Generally speaking the offences under the Act and the regulations are worded as absolute offences so that the trade licence-holder may be liable without guilty knowledge, for instance for the act of an employee. In cases of difficulty reference to the employer/employee cases noted at §§ 1.161–94 may assist. A non-licence-holder may be convicted as an aider and abettor but mens rea will be required. See Chapter 1. The non-licence-holder may also be liable for use without a licence (see, e.g. reg.34). The regulations should be studied carefully as some apply only to the holder of a licence and others apply generally (see *Waugh v Paterson* (1924) 68 S.J. 52).

C *Purposes for which a vehicle is used*

12.104   The vehicle must be used for a business purpose as prescribed by regulations made under the Vehicle Excise and Registration Act 1994 s.12(2)(b) (by virtue of Sch.4 to the 1994 Act, these are the Road Vehicles (Registration and Licensing) Regulations 2002, and, in particular, Sch.6) or an offence is committed.

If an offence is committed by contravening the provisions of reg.37 and Sch.6, a defendant should be charged under s.34(1), since the purpose of the regulation is to define and delimit s.34 in accordance with s.12, rather than for a breach of the regulations.

A trade licence may only be used for one of the purposes set out in Pt II of Sch.6 to the 2002 Regulations. There are three stages to the definition of the purpose for which such a licence must be used: Sch.6 para.10. It must first be a business purpose (defined in Sch.6 para.11), then it must be a para.12 purpose (Sch.6 para.12) and, finally, the purpose must not include the carriage of anything other than "specified goods" (as defined in Sch.6 para.13). There are further provisions applying to vehicles kept by a motor trader for research and development in the course of his business as a manufacturer of vehicles (Sch.6 para.14) and to vehicles used by a vehicle tester since a vehicle tester does not fall within the definition of motor trader as such (Sch.6 para.15).

Business purposes

Schedule 6 para.11 defines a business purpose as use for the purpose of a motor trader's business for the undertakings described in s.62(1) of the 1994 Act (see § 12.94 above).   **12.105**

Paragraph 12 purposes

These set out in more detail the circumstances within that business purpose for which a trade licence will authorise use. They include testing or trying out the vehicle or its accessories or equipment for a variety of specified reasons (including for the benefit of prospective purchasers), delivering it to where the purchaser intends to keep it and moving it between showrooms.   **12.106**

Specified loads

Schedule 6 para.13 sets out what may be carried in a vehicle being used by virtue of a trade licence. These include those items built in as part of the vehicle or permanently attached to it and "test loads" as further defined by para.13(2). This further definition again has three elements, the purpose for which the vehicle is being used, the purpose for which the load is being carried and a restriction on the circumstances in which the load can be removed from the vehicle before it is returned to the place where it was loaded. It should be noted that there is also a limit to the people who may be carried on a vehicle used by virtue of a trade licence: Sch.6 para.9—see § 12.114 below).   **12.107**

Research and development

Schedule 6 para.14 provides for a further category of use by a motor trader who is a manufacturer of vehicles. This applies to vehicles kept solely for the purpose of carrying out research and development as part of his business as a manufacturer and allows the use of the vehicle under a trade licence for that purpose. The only loads that can be carried are those which are part of the vehicle and those carried solely for testing purposes and not removed during the use unless necessary to test it or because of an accident.   **12.108**

Vehicle testers

Although not within the definition of motor trader in s.62(1) of the 1994 Act, a vehicle tester may be issued with a trade licence by virtue of s.11 of that Act. A vehicle tester is defined in s.62(1) of the 1994 Act as a person other than a motor trader who regularly in the course of his business engages in the testing on roads of vehicles belonging to other persons. The purpose for which a vehicle tester may use a vehicle under the trade licence is set out in Sch.6 para.15. It is restricted to testing it and the load that can be carried is restricted to that necessary for the purposes.   **12.109**

12.110   One case on "business purpose" under the former regulations may be helpful by way of example. In *Murphy v Brown* [1970] Crim. L.R. 234 the defendant was the holder of trade plates issued for use in his business as a repairer and dealer in motor vehicles. He bartered a vehicle for a pony and towed the pony to pony rides in a trailer, making use of the trade plates. It was held that the process was unauthorised and the defendant was guilty. The use must be in connection with the defendant's business (in this case as repairer or dealer). It was not sufficient that the use was in general connected with the business (ibid.).

     In the previous regulations the term "prospective purchaser" included a possible purchaser (*Hilson v Barnard* 1922 S.L.T. 40), and this decision would appear to apply to para.12(c) of Sch.6 to the 2002 Regulations.

     As indicated, the business purposes are specified and an offence is committed if the vehicle is used for any other purpose, business or otherwise. It is immaterial that the vehicle is also being used for a specified business purpose (see wording of s.34(1)(b) of the 1994 Act).

D   *"Vehicles temporarily in his possession"*

12.111   It should be noted that, except for vehicles used by motor manufacturers under Sch.6 para.14 of the 2002 Regulations solely for the purpose of research and development, a vehicle may not be used under trade plates unless it is temporarily in the possession of the motor trade (1994 Act s.11(2) and (3)). A motor trader who carries on the business of collecting and delivering vehicles may legitimately use trade plates for this purpose (see 2002 Regulations Sch.6 para.12(j)), but where part of the business of the motor trade was to collect and deliver trailers from one factory where they were partly assembled to another factory where the trailers were completed, a magistrates' court has held that the motor trader could not use trade plates on the vehicles which towed the trailers unless the towing vehicles as well as the trailers were temporarily in the possession of the motor trade. The provision (now 2002 Regulations Sch.6 para.8), which requires the towing vehicle and trailer to be treated as one vehicle, could not be construed in such a way that the towing vehicle could therefore be said to be temporarily in the possession of the motor trader merely because the trailer was.

E   *"Workshops"*

12.112   Schedule 6 para.12(h) of the 2002 Regulations allows a trade licence to be used for a vehicle proceeding to or returning from a workshop in which a body or a special type of equipment or accessory is to be or has been fitted to it or in which it is to be or has been painted; valeted or repaired. In *Bowers v Worthington* [1982] R.T.R. 400 a vehicle was used under trade plates to carry six container bases. Each in turn was to be built up on the vehicle in question in the workshop. It was held that the purpose was not that of having the bases fitted to the particular vehicle and the use was not covered by the trade plates. Ormrod L.J. at 404 said that, looking at the relevant provision in its context, what was contemplated was a vehicle being taken to a workshop to be fitted, more or less permanently, with either a body or some special type of equipment. It could not mean the vehicle standing as a kind of dummy.

Display of trade plates

12.113   For each trade licence issued, the Secretary of State must issue to the licence-holder a set of trade plates appropriate to the class of vehicles for which the licence is to be used: reg.40(1). Each of those plates must carry the general registration mark which will be issued to the licence-holder under reg.39: reg.40(2). One of those plates must include a device allowing the trade licence itself to be fixed to the plate: reg.40(2). When a vehicle is used by virtue of the plate, the trade plate must be displayed in the same way as if it were an ordinary registration mark, that is, as near vertical as is reasonably practical and so that each character is distinguishable in normal daylight for the prescribed distance: reg.42(2) applying regs 5 and 6 of the Road Vehicles (Registration and Licensing) Regulations 2002 (see § 12.131 below). Similarly, the trade licence must be displayed on the front of the vehicle in a way that is clearly visible by daylight by being fixed to the trade plate: reg.42(3) and (4).

Offences under the regulations

The restrictions in Sch.6 on the use of trade plates and trade licences by persons **12.114** other than licence-holders, on the conveyance of goods and burden and the widely drawn restrictions on the carriage of passengers should be particularly noted as should the obligations on the licence-holder to control the use of the trade plates and to ensure they are in good condition in Pt I of Sch.6.

The holder of the trade licence must ensure that the licence and the trade plates are not used other than on a vehicle being used for the purposes of the holder in accordance with the licence: Sch.6 para.5. That vehicle must fall within the prescribed classes of vehicle (see 1994 Act s.11(2)–(4)) and must be used for one of the prescribed purposes as set out in Sch.6. This will prohibit the loan of trade plates to a friend unless the friend drives the vehicle and it is being used for the licence-holder and for a prescribed purpose. An independent contractor or a hirer may similarly drive providing the use is that of the licence-holder.

Schedule 6para.9 limits the ability to carry people in a vehicle being used **12.115** under a trade licence on a public road. No one may be carried in the vehicle or on a trailer drawn by it unless they are being carried in connection with the purpose authorising the use of the vehicle except a person carried in connection with a purpose for which the holder of the trade licence may use the vehicle. This will normally preclude the carrying of hitch-hikers, spouses, children and friends as passengers.

TRADE LICENCES: PROCEEDINGS AND PENALTIES

Generally

The penalty for an offence under s.34(1) of the 1994 Act is an excise penalty of **12.116** level 3 or five times the annual duty chargeable on the offending vehicle (s.34(2)). A vehicle bearing trade plates for which their use is unlawful will usually not have a current vehicle excise licence. In such a case a prosecution under s.29 may be brought, particularly if the user was not the holder of the trade plates.

Offences may be tried by magistrates only. Any person may prosecute for an offence under the regulations where the prosecution is by virtue of s.59 of the 1994 Act. For offences under s.34 or s.59 the time-limit is six months from the date on which evidence sufficient to justify the proceedings came to the knowledge of the prosecutor, subject to an overriding time-limit of three years from the date of the offence (s.47(2)). Only the Secretary of State for Transport or a constable with his approval may prosecute under s.34 (see § 12.135). Contraventions of the regulations which are not an offence under s.34 are liable to prosecution by virtue of s.59 of the 1994 Act with a maximum fine of level 3.

12.117   Magistrates cannot remit payment wholly or partly of a penalty under s.34(2) on a means inquiry as the penalty is not a "fine": *aliter* a fine for breach of the regulations (see § 12.147).

Because the punishment under s.34(2) is expressed as a "penalty" and not as an "offence" punishable with a fine, the various provisions of the Customs and Excise Acts apply where they have not been expressly excluded (see § 12.147 as to other aspects arising as a consequence).

As to the prosecutor's right of appeal to the Crown Court, see § 12.138. For a table of penalties, see § 12.118.

12.118

Trade licences: penalties

Offence	Mode of trial	Section *	Imprisonment	Level of fine	Disqualification	Penalty points	Endorsement code	Sentencing guideline
Improper use of trade licence	Summary	s.34(2)	—	Excise penalty of level 3 or five times annual duty, whichever is greater	—	—	—	—
Trade licence regulations	Summary	s.59(2)(a)	—	3	—	—	—	—
Trade licence regulations	Summary	s.59(2)(b)	—		—			

* Vehicle Excise and Registration Act 1994 unless otherwise specified.

EXCISE LICENCES: REGISTRATION

Registration

12.119   The provisions regarding registration of vehicles are contained in ss.21–28 of the Vehicle Excise and Registration Act 1994 (as amended) and regulations made or deemed to be made under them. The Secretary of State is required to register a vehicle on the first issue of either a vehicle licence or a nil licence (as defined in s.62(1), as amended) (s.21(1), as amended). Regulation-making powers are contained in s.22, as amended.

The relevant regulations are the Road Vehicles (Registration and Licensing) Regulations 2002 (SI 2002/2742), as amended.

Amongst other things the regulations relate to the production of registration documents (reg.12) and to the duty of vendors and purchasers of motor vehicles to notify the registration authority of the sale and of changes of address (regs 21–25). They also set out the duty to notify any alteration to the vehicle (reg.16), any change of address of the keeper (reg.18), the destruction or permanent export of the vehicle (reg.17), and details as prescribed of vehicles exempt from duty.

12.120   The Road Vehicles (Registration and Licensing) Regulations were further amended by the Road Vehicles (Registration and Licensing) (Amendment) Regulations 2004 (SI 2004/238). The 2004 Regulations introduce a fee in certain circumstances for persons who require a new vehicle registration document to be issued; introduce a fee where an application is made for a replacement registration certificate because the previous registration document has been, or may have been, lost, stolen, destroyed or damaged, or its particulars have become illegible; introduce a fee where an application is made for a new registration document because the previous document is inaccurate or incorrect, but the previous document cannot be produced; introduce a fee where an application is made for a new registration document because there has been a change in the keeper's name or address, but the previous document cannot be produced; place an obligation on a new keeper to apply, with a fee, for a new registration document where all or the relevant part of the previous document has been, or may have been, lost, stolen or destroyed. Where the new keeper can produce the part of the document which has to be given to a new keeper, a fee is not payable.

The 2002 Regulations also provide for the registration of Crown vehicles though such vehicles are exempt from duty: reg.30. Regulations 20–25 provide a detailed scheme governing obligations where there is a change in the keeper of a vehicle. These obligations apply also to Crown vehicles even where the change in keeper is from one government department to another: reg.30(5). The only variation from the main scheme is where a vehicle's body work has been so damaged that the cost of being repaired commercially would be greater than the value of the vehicle once repaired and either the keeper is not insured for that damage or the keeper is an insurer (defined in reg.3). In such a case, the keeper must surrender the registration document to the Secretary of State or, if the keeper is an insurer, may destroy the document: reg.20(5). This will require a new keeper to apply for a new registration document which will prompt the necessary inquiries.

12.121   In other circumstances, there are two factors which provide for variations in the basic scheme. The first factor is the date of issue of the current registration document. A different scheme applies if that document was issued before March

24, 1997. The second factor is whether or not the new keeper is a vehicle trader as defined in reg.20(6).

Registration document issued before March 24, 1997

12.122 This scheme applies whether or not the new keeper is a vehicle trader. The registered keeper must, if he has the registration document, give the part relating to a change of keeper to the new keeper: reg.21(2)(a). He must also notify the Secretary of State immediately of the date of transfer of the vehicle with details of the new keeper and of the vehicle in question: reg.21(2)(b). The new keeper must notify the Secretary of State of his name and address whether or not he intends to use or keep the vehicle on a public road unless he intends to use the vehicle on a public road solely under a trade licence. In those circumstances, the new keeper must notify the Secretary of State of that intention no later than three months from when he became the new keeper or the date of any subsequent change of keeper whichever is the earlier: reg.21(4).

Change on or after March 24, 1997 and new keeper not a vehicle trader

12.123 Again, the registered keeper must give the relevant part of the registration document to the new keeper if that document is in his possession. The remainder is to go to the Secretary of State from the registered keeper and will include not only the date of transfer and the details of the new keeper but also signed declarations by both the registered keeper and the new keeper as to the correctness of the details given: reg.22.

Change on or after March 24, 1997 and new keeper is a vehicle trader

12.124 In these circumstances, the registered keeper must give the relevant part to the vehicle trader but must send the rest to the Secretary of State with details of the transfer and signed declarations verifying the transfer from both the registered keeper and the vehicle trader: reg.23. For the purposes of these provisions, a vehicle trader is defined in reg.20(6). It may be the holder of a trade licence of a person carrying on a business as a dealer or auctioneer or dismantler of motor vehicles or may be a finance company which has acquired the vehicle in question under an order for repossession or an insurer acquiring the vehicle in satisfaction of a total loss claim. The vehicle trader must separately notify the Secretary of State of the transfer to him

(1) on or before the day he first uses the vehicle on a public road other than under a trade licence;

(2) on or before the day he first keeps the vehicle on a public road; or

(3) the day after three months have expired since the vehicle was last kept by a person who was not a vehicle trader, whichever is the earliest: reg.24(3).

12.125 It is not possible to accumulate the periods of three months by transferring from one vehicle trader to another. The start of the period is the day after the date when the vehicle was last kept by a person who was not a vehicle trader: reg.24(3)(c). If, however, there is a transfer to another vehicle trader within the three months, the registration document must be passed on: reg.24(4). Where the vehicle is transferred to a person who is not a vehicle trader, the vehicle trader transferring the vehicle must send to the Secretary of State details of the transfer and the new keeper together with declarations signed by both the vehicle trader and the new keeper as to the accuracy of the details.

Failure to notify the registration authority is not a continuing offence and time runs from a day or two after the change of ownership (*A. & C. McLennan (Blairgowrie) Ltd v MacMillan* 1964 S.L.T. 2). See s.29(4) at § 12.66 as to the effect of non-delivery of the licence on transfer.

By s.23 to the 1994 Act, the Secretary of State is required to assign a registration mark to a vehicle on registration under s.21(1) which will indicate the registered number of the vehicle. Regulations may be made regarding the fixing, characteristics and display of these marks (s.23(3), (4)). The Road Vehicles (Display of Registration Marks) Regulations 2001 (SI 2001/561), as amended, apply.

12.126   By s.42 of the 1994 Act it is an offence if a registration mark is not fixed to a vehicle. The offence is committed by the relevant person, defined in s.42(3) as the person driving the vehicle or, where it is not being driven, the person keeping it. By s.62(2) a person keeps a vehicle on a public road if he causes it to be on such a road for any period, however short, when it is not in use there. The maximum penalty is a fine of level 3 (s.42(2)). A defence is provided where the accused can prove that he had no reasonable opportunity to register the vehicle which was being driven for the purpose of being registered (s.42(4)). It is also an offence to drive or keep a vehicle with the registration mark obscured or rendered or allowed to become not easily distinguishable (s.43(1)). A defence is provided where the accused can prove that he took all reasonable steps which it was reasonably practicable to take to prevent the mark being obscured or rendered or allowed to become not easily distinguishable (s.43(4)). There is no requirement for knowledge for the offence to be committed. The maximum penalty is a fine of level 3 (s.43(2)).

Using an incorrectly registered vehicle

12.127   Section 43C of the Vehicle Excise and Registration Act 1994 creates an offence of using an incorrectly registered vehicle. A person will be guilty of an offence if a vehicle is used on a public road to which the 1994 Act applies and where the name and address of the keeper are not recorded in the register or any of the particulars recorded in the register are incorrect. The provisions are applicable to a vehicle where vehicle excise duty is chargeable in respect of it or it is an exempt vehicle, in respect of which regulations require a nil licence to be in force. The police are given powers to require production of vehicle registration documents and to seize vehicles driven without both a licence and insurance. A person found guilty of the offence is liable to a maximum fine of level 3.

Sale and transfer of registration marks

12.128   Part 2 of the Vehicles (Crime) Act 2001 requires registration plate suppliers to be registered and gives powers to make regulations requiring them to keep certain records and to obtain information from prospective purchasers. With effect from August 1, 2008, the Vehicles Crime (Registration of Registration Plate Suppliers) Regulations 2008 (SI 2008/1715) make provision for the registration of registration plate suppliers which extends to the whole of the United Kingdom. The regulations include provisions relating to exemptions from the definition of sale under s.17 of the Vehicles (Crime) Act 2001 where the seller is a dealer and has arranged first registration (reg.3), prescribe particulars which must be contained in the register (reg.4) and the requirements for a registration application and a fee (reg.5). They further provide the requirement that a seller must obtain and verify information from a prospective purchaser before selling a plate (reg.6 and the Schedule) together with a provision for the keeping of records by registered persons (reg.7). Section 24(4) of the 2001 Act applies to reg.7 so if an offence is committed, the offender is liable to a fine of level 3.

Visitors from abroad

The Motor Vehicles (International Circulation) Regulations 1985 (SI 1985/ **12.129** 610) (as amended) require persons resident outside the United Kingdom who bring a visiting vehicle into Great Britain to produce on requirement at any reasonable time a certificate of insurance or security or an insurance card and any registration document or card to the registration authority, and any registration document similarly to a police officer or person acting on behalf of the Secretary of State for Transport (reg.4).

Regulation 17 and Sch.2 apply to the issued registration mark if it is in Roman letters or ordinary European numerals or both. If not, a special registration mark has to be assigned (regs 5 and 8) though see § 12.131 below.

Sections 129 and 130 of the Local Transport Act 2008 insert new ss.49A and 49B into the Road Safety Act 2006, which relate to the disclosure of information in respect of foreign registered vehicles and the use of that information.

Rear number plate lamps

The fitting, maintenance, keeping lit and use of rear registration plate lamps is **12.130** governed by the Road Vehicles Lighting Regulations 1989 (SI 1989/1796). See Chapter 8. There is also an offence under reg.9 of the Road Vehicles (Display of Registration Marks) Regulations 2001 (SI 2001/561) of using on a road between sunset and sunrise any vehicle (other than those excepted by reg.9(1)) without the rear registration plate being lit as required by reg.9(3) or (5). The 1989 Regulations concentrate on the lamps themselves and the 2001 Regulations concentrate on the provision of illumination. Nevertheless there is some overlap and the penalties are different. The 1989 Regulations also apply in seriously reduced visibility, but reg.9 of the 2001 Regulations only applies during the hours of darkness. Where there is in effect only one failure it is submitted that two convictions should not be recorded.

The defence in s.43(4) of the 1994 Act applies to reg.9 offences but not to offences under the Lighting Regulations. The case of *Printz v Sewell* (1912) 76 J.P. 295 was a case on an unlit mark under a predecessor regulation to reg.9 of the 2001 Regulations and would still seem to be applicable.

Display of registration marks

The Road Vehicles (Display of Registration Marks) Regulations 2001 (SI **12.131** 2001/561), as amended, relate to the exhibition, position, lighting and content of registration marks. All vehicles other than works trucks, road rollers and agricultural machines (defined in reg.2) registered on or after the relevant date (October 1, 1938—reg.2) must have a registration plate fixed to the rear and front of the vehicle (regs 5 and 6). The placing of that plate is prescribed (regs 5(3)–(6) and 6(3)–(5)). Qualifying vehicles first registered before the relevant date must also display registration marks but the placing provisions are less prescriptive (reg.7). Similarly for works trucks, road rollers and agricultural machines (reg.8).

The sizing of the registration plate is prescribed with different provisions applying to vehicles first registered on or after September 1, 2001 (or replacement plates applied on or after that date), to those registered on or after January 1, 1973 but before September 1, 2001 and to those registered before January 1, 1973 (reg.10). The material of the plate must not make it difficult to photograph (reg.11(1) and (2)) and the method of fixing the plate to the vehicle must not be such as to change the appearance or the legibility of the registration mark or to affect adversely any photographic image (reg.11(4)). Contravention of the regulation is an offence under s.59(2)(a) of the 1994 Act attracting a maximum penalty of level 3.

12.132 The 2001 Regulations are very prescriptive about the sizing and spacing of letters and numbers on the registration plate. The size of each character is prescribed in reg.14(1)–(3) (subject to reg.12(2)), the width of each character is prescribed in reg.14(4)–(5) (again subject to reg.12(2)), and the spacing between any two characters is prescribed by reg.14(6)–(11) (subject to reg.12(3)). Layout of the mark on the plate is prescribed by reg.13. A partial exemption is provided for vehicles imported into the United Kingdom which do not have EC type approval (see § 8.10 above) and have been made in a way that prevents a plate being fixed that complies with reg.14: reg.14A. In such circumstances, reg.14A(2) provides for a different height, width and spacing requirement, almost, but not quite, identical to those applicable to motor cycles.

The style of characters used is prescribed by reg.15. Those plates affixed on or after September 1, 2001 must be in the prescribed font (defined in reg.2) (reg.15(1)). Those affixed between January 1, 1973 and September 1, 2001 must be in the prescribed font or something similar and must be easily distinguishable (reg.15(2)). Certain ways of forming characters are specifically prohibited such as fonts that are not vertical or ones that make a character look like a different character (reg.15(2)–(4)).

12.133 A registration plate may not contain anything other than the registration mark except the international distinguishing sign of the United Kingdom (reg.16, as amended). This must comply with the appropriate EC Regulation (see Regulation (EC) 2411/98 in Vol.2).

These provisions do not apply to a vehicle first registered before January 1, 1973 or to other exempt vehicles (regs 3 and 18). Optional specifications are provided for vehicles registered before January 1, 1973 by Sch.2 Pt III to the 2001 Regulations.

There is likely to be substantial prosecutions and enforcement activity as the creativity of those who imaginatively construct personalised number plates is put to the test. The regulations are made under ss.23 and 57 of the 1994 Act. Offences regarding the fixing of the registration mark are punishable under s.42 of the 1994 Act, others are punishable under s.59 of the 1994 Act.

EXCISE LICENCES: PROCEEDINGS AND PENALTIES

Fines for breach of the 2002 Regulations

12.134 The Road Vehicles (Registration and Licensing) Regulations 2002 (SI 2002/1/800)

2742) are deemed to be made under the 1994 Act. The maximum fine for a breach of these regulations under the 1994 Act is therefore under s.59 of *level 2*, save where an increase has been prescribed.

An increase to *level 3* has been prescribed by Sch.8 to the 2002 Regulations in respect of the following regulations:

16(1)	(Notification of alteration of vehicles)
17	(Notification of destruction or permanent export of vehicle)
18(1)	(Notification of change of name or address of keeper of vehicle)
19(1)	(Notification of change of name or address by holder of trade licence)
21–25	(Notification of change of keeper)
26	(Statutory off-road notification)
40(5)	(Return of trade plates)
42	(Exhibition of trade plates and licences)

For a table of penalties, see § 12.149.

Who may prosecute and authorisation to do so

Section 2 of the Magistrates' Courts Act 1980, granting magistrates' courts jurisdiction to try summary offences, is an overriding provision and confers jurisdiction on a magistrates' court to try an offence under what is now s.29 of the Vehicle Excise and Registration Act 1994 committed by a "privileged tinner" who claimed trial by a county court which had inherited the jurisdiction of the Stannaries Court (*R. v East Powder JJ. Ex p. Lampshire* [1979] 2 All E.R. 329). Under s.6 of the 1994 Act, the Secretary of State and his officers including authorised agents have equivalent powers with regard to vehicle excise duty as those given to HM Revenue & Customs save for those relating to imported goods.   **12.135**

Summary proceedings for an offence under ss.29, 31A, 34, 35A, 37 and 43C of the 1994 Act may be instituted in England and Wales by the Secretary of State for Transport or a constable (severally referred to as "the authorised prosecutor") within six months from the date on which sufficient evidence (in the opinion of the authorised prosecutor) came to his knowledge to warrant the proceedings (s.47(2)). No such proceedings may be instituted more than three years after the commission of the offence (s.47(3)). The extended time-limit also applies to proceedings for an offence under the regulations (s.47(2)(b)). Proceedings under ss.29, 31A, 34, 35A and 37 may only be instituted in England and Wales by the authorised prosecutor; and no such proceedings may be instituted by a constable except with the approval of the Secretary of State (s.47(1)). As to "Authority to prosecute", see Chapter 2. The Crown Prosecutor is not an authorised prosecutor under s.47, although he has the power and in some cases the duty to take over proceedings and the other powers given him by s.3 of the Prosecution of Offences Act 1985.

If the information is laid by an official and not by a constable and it alleges that the proceedings are instituted by that official on behalf of the Secretary of State, it seems that this is sufficient proof that they are so instituted unless the contrary is proved (*Dyer v Tulley* (1894) 58 J.P. 656; Customs and Excise Management Act 1979 s.148). A certificate in due form stating the approval by the Secretary of State to the institution of specified proceedings by a constable is conclusive evidence of that approval (s.47(4)). The justices' clerk, person authorised by a   **12.136** justices' clerk or justice issuing a summons to a constable should satisfy himself by the production of that certificate that the proceedings are brought by the constable with the approval of the Secretary of State. There is no need for the prosecutor to take any further step to prove authorisation in open court unless the defence object that it has not been proved. Such objection by the defence should be taken before the close of the prosecution's case, and if objection is made the prosecution should be given the opportunity to prove the consent (*Price v Humphries* [1958] 2 All E.R. 725); if necessary, an adjournment can properly be granted. It is submitted that as the matter is of a technical or formal nature, the adjournment should be granted almost as a matter of course (see, e.g. *Royal v Prescott-Clarke* [1966] 2 All E.R. 366). Where an information is laid by an officer who has not been generally or specially authorised to take those proceedings, an authorisation given after the laying of the information would not, it seems, validate the proceedings.

Limitation of time

12.137   Offences of failure to notify change of ownership are not continuing offences. As to time-limits for bringing charges, see Chapter 2. It should be noted that the special time-limit in s.47 of the 1994 Act only applies to the particular offences specified. The period of six months runs from the date of the discovery by the prosecutor of sufficient evidence of the offence although the overriding limit of three years runs from the date of the commission of the offence.

Where a police officer discovered facts that led him to believe a motorist to be committing an offence under what is now s.29 and informed the Secretary of State accordingly, the six-month period for the institution of proceedings under the provisions of s.47 ran from the date on which evidence sufficient in the opinion of the Secretary of State to warrant the proceedings came to his knowledge and not from the date on which the police officer became aware of the facts. The Divisional Court so held dismissing an appeal against conviction in *Algar v Shaw* [1986] Crim. L.R. 750.

12.138   It may also be noted that a certificate of the authorised prosecutor shall be conclusive evidence of the date of discovery of the offence by him and the approval of the institution of proceedings by the Secretary of State for Transport. This may be contrasted with the signature of the certificate, which is deemed to be signed on behalf of the Secretary of State "unless the contrary is proved" (s.47(6)). By s.49 a person authorised for these purposes by the Secretary of State may appear in any proceeding under the Act in a magistrates' court or before a district judge in a county court.

A right of appeal by the prosecutor to the Crown Court is given by the Customs and Excise Management Act 1979 s.147(3). This power exists in relation to any decision of a magistrates' court in proceedings for an offence under the Customs and Excise Acts. This extends to both mode of trial and sentence: *R. v Commissioners of Customs and Excise Ex p. Wagstaff* [1998] Crim. L.R. 287, *Commissioners of Customs and Excise v Brunt* [1998] All E.R. (D.) 565.

12.139   In *R. v Godstone JJ. Ex p. Secretary of State for the Environment* [1974] Crim. L.R. 110 it was held that a summons which did not bear the date upon which the information was laid was not ineffectual. It is only where there is some question as to whether the information was laid in time that it is material. It is submitted that if there is any question whether the information was laid in time, it is the duty of the prosecution to give proof of the date of laying of the information because an information for a purely summary offence laid out of time renders the proceedings a nullity.

Evidence

By s.51 of the Vehicle Excise and Registration Act 1994 where a prosecution is for an offence under s.29 (using or keeping without a licence), s.34 (misuse of trade licence), s.43A (use without a nil licence) and by s.51A for offences under regulations made by virtue of s.22(1)(d), (dd) and (1D), the court may accept as evidence a statement that the accused was the driver, user or keeper of the vehicle where that statement is in writing and purports to be signed by the accused and has been made after a notice requiring information had been served on the accused under s.46(1) or (2), or s.46A. Note the requirement that the notice must have been served on the accused and the admission must also purport to be signed by the accused. By s.52 statements contained in records maintained by the Secretary of State as part of his functions under this Act are admissible as evidence of any fact stated in it with respect to matters prescribed by regulations. The appropriate regulation is reg.46 of the Road Vehicles (Registration and Licensing) Regulations 2002 (SI 2002/2742).

12.140

Venue

Section 28A of the Customs and Excise Management Act 1979 appears to apply to offences under the 1994 Act and regulations made thereunder. Consequently, proceedings may also be taken where the offender resides or is found in any part of England in cases where the offence was committed in England (similarly in Scotland: see [1958] Jo.Crim.L. 269) as well as where the offence was committed. The view is, however, held in some authoritative circles that s.148 applies only to offences which are "excise offences", i.e. where payment of duty is in issue, and not, e.g., to failing to illuminate a number plate or to display an excise licence. This view is based on s.6 of the 1994 Act, which applies the Customs and Excise Act in relation to "duties of Excise" and punishments and penalties in connection therewith. See *McMillan v Grant* 1924 J.C. 13.

12.141

Where a false statement was knowingly made in one jurisdiction in an application for a licence and it was sent by post to the licensing authority in another jurisdiction, it was held in Scotland that the locus for the offence could only be where it was received (*Gibb v Hill* [1948] Jo.Crim.L. 185). Under the regulations various offences arise of failing to notify change of ownership; such defaulters can be prosecuted either where they are when they make default or where the offices which should be notified are, see *Kennet District Council v Young* [1999] R.T.R. 235. The general rules as to venue set out in Chapter 2 supplement the above provisions.

Burden of proof

By s.53 it is provided that if, in proceedings under s.29 (using and keeping vehicles without a licence) or under s.31A (offence by registered keeper where vehicle unlicensed), or under s.34 (breach of trade licence), or under s.37 (not paying duty at higher rate), or under s.45 (false or misleading declarations and information), any question arises:

12.142

    (a) as to the number of vehicles used, or

    (b) as to the character, weight or cylinder capacity of a vehicle, or

    (c) as to the number of persons for which a vehicle has seating capacity, or

    (d) as to the purpose for which any vehicle has been used,

the burden of proof in respect of the matter in question shall lie on the defendant. The section was discussed in *McCrone v J. & L. Rigby (Wigan) Ltd* (1952) 50 L.G.R. 115, and it should be noted that it applies only to certain proceedings; in summary proceedings under other sections, the normal rule as to the burden of proof applies. Generally, a defendant must prove facts peculiarly within his own knowledge, e.g. that he has a licence: *Guyll v Bright* [1987] R.T.R. 104 applying s.101 of the Magistrates' Courts Act 1980 under which any exception, exemption, proviso, excuse or qualification for a defendant should be proved by him and need not be negatived by the prosecution in opening. The defendant's burden under s.53 may be discharged by evidence for the defence or by precise admissions made by the witnesses for the prosecution (*McCrone v Rigby* above) and is less than that on a prosecutor generally to prove a criminal charge; he may satisfy the court of the probability of what he alleges (*R. v Carr-Briant* [1943] 2 All E.R. 156).

12.143   The nature of a burden of proof as a balance of probabilities was specified in *R. v Swaysland*, *The Times*, April 15, 1987. Proof on a balance of probabilities means that the court or jury has to be satisfied that it is more likely than not or more probable than not that a fact is made out. The Court of Appeal emphasised that the defendant had to tip the balance but no more. The Court of Appeal quashed a conviction where the test had been merely described as on the balance of probabilities without explanation.

    By the Customs and Excise Management Act 1979 s.154, where in any proceedings relating to excise any question arises as to whether duty has been paid on any goods or as to whether any goods or other things whatsoever are of the description or nature alleged in the information, the burden of proof lies on the defendant.

Written plea of guilty procedure

12.144   By far the majority of cases under s.29 and s.35A of the Vehicle Excise and Registration Act 1994 will be brought under the procedure set out in the Magistrates' Courts Act 1980, by which a defendant may plead guilty by post. Section 55 of the 1994 Act adapts the procedure to allow the prosecutor to serve with the summons a notice stating that, in the event of the defendant being convicted, he will be required to pay the amount of back-duty specified in the notice unless he states it is inappropriate. If he pleads guilty and does not state that the amount is inappropriate s.55(5) requires the court to order payment of the back-duty. Frequently, defendants delete on the form the wrong alternative, leaving the other alternative: "I do not wish to challenge the accuracy of the amount alleged to be due ...", and then proceed to write as mitigating circumstances a statement that the vehicle has only just been purchased, or some other statement showing that the amount of back-duty is inappropriate. It is submitted that the court can and should adjourn such cases to give the defendant an opportunity of disputing the back-duty. Section 55(5), it is submitted, only requires the court to order payment of back-duty where the defendant unequivocally accepts the amount of back-duty or does not answer at all regarding the back-duty.

Under the written plea of guilty procedure (and only when the written plea of guilty procedure is being applied by the court) the prosecutor's statement of facts, relating to the charge, can be read by the magistrates' legal adviser. The back-duty details would seem to be facts relating to the charge so that they can also legitimately be read out by the legal adviser, together with written details of any costs sought.

Mitigated penalties

12.145 The Secretary of State is, by s.6 of the Vehicle Excise and Registration Act 1994, given the same powers of mitigation and remission of penalty as are possessed by HM Revenue & Customs in respect of offences under the Customs and Excise Acts.

The power conferred by s.6(5) to offer a mitigated penalty is used by the Secretary of State in a very large number of cases under s.29 of using a vehicle without an excise licence. The offender is sent a letter offering him the opportunity of paying a mitigated penalty within a set period, usually 14 or 21 days if he would like to avoid being prosecuted. This procedure is used only where the vehicle has been unlicensed for 12 months or less and may not be used at all where a specific campaign has been used to target offenders.

12.146 The mitigated penalty is calculated by the formula of: Back-duty lost $\times$ $1^{1}/_{2}$ + £10.

If the offender does not pay within the period allowed he is prosecuted either by the Department for Transport or by an authorised police officer.

It is submitted that it may be proper for a court to be informed after the conviction of the amount of the mitigated penalty offered to a defendant by the prosecution.

Remission of fine or penalty

12.147 By reason of the restricted definition of "fine" contained in s.85(4) of the Magistrates' Courts Act 1980, on an inquiry into a defendant's means after non-payment of a fine where there has been a change in the defendant's circumstances magistrates may remit the whole or part of a fine imposed but not any penalties imposed under ss.29 (no excise licence), 31A–31C (offence by registered keeper where vehicle unlicensed), 37 (using a vehicle without paying a higher rate of duty), 35A or 102(3) of the Customs and Excise Management Act 1979 (void licence offences), any order for payment of back-duty under these offences, namely 30, 31C, 38 or 36, and any penalty under 34 (trade licence offences).

It may be worthwhile to note that the distinction between an "offence" punishable with a fine and a contravention punishable with a "penalty" generally means that the Customs and Excise Management Act 1979 applies to the latter but probably not to the former. It should be remembered that under s.147(3) of the Customs and Excise Management Act 1979 the prosecutor has a right of appeal to the Crown Court against any decision (including sentence: see § 12.138 above) of a magistrates' court in proceedings for an offence to which that Act applies.

12.148 The penalties for offences with regard to vehicle excise licences are set out at § 12.149.

12.149

Vehicle excise licences: penalties

Offence	Mode of trial	Section *	Imprisonment	Level of fine	Disqualification	Penalty points	Endorsement code	Sentencing guideline ‡
No vehicle excise licence	Summary	s.29	—	Excise penalty of level 3 or five times the annual duty chargeable, whichever is greater (and back-duty—see § 12.67)	—	—	—	Fine band A (where unpaid duty 1–3 months) Fine band B (where unpaid duty 4–6 months) Fine band C (where unpaid duty 7–12 months)
Offence by registered keeper where vehicle unlicensed	Summary	s.31A	—	Excise penalty of level 3 or five times annual duty chargeable whichever is the greater (and additional penalty—see § 12.67)	—	—	—	—

Offence	Mode of trial	Section *	Imprisonment	Level of fine	Disqualification	Penalty points	Endorsement code	Sentencing guideline ‡
Vehicle use when liable at higher vehicle excise rate	Summary	s.37	—	Excise penalty of level 3 or five times the difference calculated at annual rate, whichever is greater (and back-duty—see § 12.67)	—	—	—	—
Failure to fix, etc., registration mark (index plate)	Summary	s.42	—	3	—	—	—	—
Failure of keeper of vehicle and others to give information as to driver, etc.	Summary	s.46	—	3	—	—	—	—
Failure to display licence	Summary	s.33	—	1	—	—	—	—

Offence	Mode of trial	Section *	Imprisonment	Level of fine	Disqualification	Penalty points	Endorsement code	Sentencing guideline ‡
Using an incorrectly registered vehicle	Summary	s.43C	—	3	—	—	—	—
Breach of 2002 regulations other than those made under s.24, s.26, s.27 or s.28 †	Summary	s.59	—	3 (if regs 16(1), 17, 18(1), 19(1), 21–25, 26, 40(5), 42 otherwise level 2)	—	—	—	—
Breach of regulations made under s.24	Summary	s.59	—	1	—	—	—	—
Breach of regulations made under s.28	Summary	s.59	—	3	—	—	—	—

Offence	Mode of trial	Section *	Imprisonment	Level of fine	Disqualification	Penalty points	Endorsement code	Sentencing guideline ‡
Failure to deliver up void excise licence following dishonoured cheque	Summary	s.102(3) Customs and Excise Management Act 1979 or s.35A	—	Excise penalty of level 3 or five times the annual duty chargeable whichever is greater and back-duty	—	—	—	—

* Vehicle Excise and Registration Act 1994 unless otherwise specified.

† For more detail on the regulations and the penalties for breach of them, see § 12.119.

‡ **Note:** Fine bands "A", "B" and "C" represent respectively 50%, 100% and 150% of relevant weekly income. A timely guilty plea should attract a discount. See Appendix 3.

CHAPTER 13

GOODS AND PASSENGER VEHICLES

CONTENTS

DRIVER LICENSING: LARGE GOODS VEHICLES, HEAVY GOODS VEHICLES, PASSENGER-CARRYING VEHICLES AND PUBLIC SERVICE VEHICLES

Generally

13.01   The unified licensing requirements for large goods vehicle (LGV) and passenger-carrying vehicle (PCV) drivers, together with the transitional licensing arrangements for heavy goods vehicle (HGV) drivers and public service vehicle (PSV) drivers which they replaced, are outlined below with detailed treatment of certain features. This is followed by the provisions for the licensing of goods vehicle operators and other aspects of goods vehicle operations including the conveyance of dangerous substances, international haulage authorisations and the international carriage of perishable foodstuffs. Despite the replacement, the meaning of a public service vehicle will remain relevant also for PSV operator licensing and related topics, which are next described. The chapter ends with taxi and private hire vehicle licensing.

LGV and PCV drivers' licences

13.02   A driving licence issued under Pt III of the Road Traffic Act 1988 is required to cover the driving of LGVs and PCVs respectively on a road, but there are certain transitional arrangements for HGV and PSV drivers' licences. In so far as it covers these vehicles, the Pt III licence is by s.110 of the 1988 Act subject to Pt IV of the Act as well. The regulations are the Motor Vehicles (Driving Licences) Regulations 1999 (SI 1999/2864), as amended. The Driving Licences (Community Driving Licence) Regulations 1996 (SI 1996/1974) make provision regarding LGV and PCV community licences (see § 13.23).

A unified driving licence has been issued since April 1, 1991 under Pt III of the Road Traffic Act 1988, as amended, incorporating for new licences the different categories of authorisation, including the ordinary entitlement and in addition the descriptions of large goods vehicle and passenger-carrying vehicle driving. Applications for these uniform licences are made to the Secretary of State through the DVLA under Pt III as amended and the substituted s.110 of the 1988 Act and the regulations, and not to the traffic commissioner, although the commissioner still exercises his functions under s.111 as substituted over the conduct of those holding or applying for LGV and PCV authorisation.

It is an offence under s.87(1) of the 1988 Act to drive on a road a motor vehicle **13.03** of any class otherwise than in accordance with a driving licence authorising the driving of a motor vehicle of that class. It is also by s.87(2) an offence to cause or permit another person to drive on a road a motor vehicle without being similarly authorised. As to driving licences generally, see Chapter 11. These offences would apply to those who drive vehicles which require a particular LGV or PCV driving licence authorisation without being licensed for that class and also to those who hold existing HGV or PSV licences which do not cover the particular class driven.

It is a separate offence punishable summarily with a maximum fine of level 3 either contrary to s.114(1) to fail without reasonable excuse to comply with conditions of LGV or PCV licences, being provisional licences or full licences issued to persons under 21, or, contrary to s.114(2) knowingly to cause or permit persons under 21 to drive them in contravention of the conditions.

An applicant for a driving test must sign a declaration that a policy of insur- **13.04** ance is in force for the vehicle in which the test is to be carried out (Motor Vehicles (Driving Licences) (Large Goods and Passenger-Carrying Vehicles) (Amendment) Regulations 1994 (SI 1994/639)).

A "large goods vehicle" is defined as a motor vehicle (not being a medium-sized goods vehicle within the meaning of Pt III of the 1988 Act) which is constructed or adapted to carry or to haul goods and the permissible maximum weight of which exceeds 7.5 tonnes. A "passenger-carrying vehicle" means either a large or a small passenger-carrying vehicle as defined. A "large passenger-carrying vehicle" is a vehicle used for carrying passengers which is constructed or adapted to carry more than 16 passengers. A "small passenger-carrying vehicle" is a vehicle used for carrying passengers for hire or reward which is constructed or adapted to carry more than eight but not more than 16 passengers. In either case, the definition includes a combination of such a vehicle and a trailer. See the interpretation section, s.121 of the 1988 Act, as amended. For further discussion as to the interpretation of the wording of these definitions, see Chapter 1 and § 13.126 onwards. In particular, the expression "for hire or reward" is used only for small PCVs and not large ones and as to the meaning of "hire or reward", see § 13.130. The definition of a PCV seems designed to tie in with the definition of a PSV in the Public Passenger Vehicles Act 1981, but the definition of a PSV in that Act is wider—see § 13.113.

In respect of the driving test for heavy goods vehicles and buses, it should be **13.05** noted that the Motor Vehicles (Driving Licences) Regulations 1999 (SI 1999/2568) were substantively amended by the Motor Vehicles (Driving Licences) (Amendment) (No.4) Regulations 2008 (SI 2008/1435), which replace the existing theory test with a new one consisting of two parts (a large vehicle test of driving theory and a large vehicle test of hazard perception) with the additional requirement to pass a practical test (this is now a three-part driving test).

Certificates of professional competence

13.06   Council Directive 2003/59/EC on the initial qualification and periodic training of drivers of certain road vehicles for the carriage of goods or passengers has been implemented by the Vehicle Drivers (Certificates of Professional Competence) Regulations 2007 (SI 2007/605). The directive requires such drivers to take an initial practical and theoretical driving test which is valid for five years, together with 35 hours of periodic training every five years.

The competent authority in Great Britain is the Secretary of State; in Northern Ireland, it is the Department of the Environment (reg.2).

In general terms, the categories of driver to which the regulations apply are those who drive buses and heavy goods vehicles (reg.3). Exceptions from the requirement include those who drive emergency vehicles, vehicles used by the police or armed forces or vehicles used for training or testing purposes (reg.3(2)).

Any new driver is prohibited from driving a public service vehicle on or after September 10, 2008 or a heavy goods vehicle on or after September 10, 2009 on a public road unless that driver has passed a theory and practical driving test, which is referred to as an "initial CPC test" (reg.4).

13.07   The test is more extensive than the current driving test and may be taken at the same time as that driving test. Drivers who are undergoing a vocational training course may be exempted for up to 12 months from taking that test by the competent authority. Those drivers who already hold a PCV or LGV driver's licence before the relevant implementation date (known as "acquired rights") are also exempt from the initial CPC test.

Initial CPC tests may be organised by the competent authority or a person approved by it. Fees will be charged for the initial CPC test and these are in addition to any fee that an applicant must pay for a driving test (reg.5).

There is a prohibition against anyone driving a bus or a heavy goods vehicle unless that person has passed the initial CPC test within the previous five years or has completed 35 hours of periodic training within that period. Drivers with acquired rights must complete 35 hours of periodic training by the relevant date (September 10, 2013 for PCV licence-holders and September 10, 2014 for LGV licence-holders) (reg.9).

It is an offence punishable by a fine up to level 3 on the standard scale if a person drives without a CPC as required by the regulations (reg.10).

13.08   A driver who is required to hold a CPC or who is exempt because he is undergoing an approved national training course must carry evidence of that entitlement while driving and to produce it on demand by a police constable or traffic examiner. It is an offence punishable with a fine up to level 3 on the standard scale in the case of a failure to do so (reg.11).

A new driver qualification card or a document authorising driving whilst undergoing approved national vocational training may be issued by the competent authority if the card or document contains any errors. If the name on the card ceases to be correct or the error was the card-holder's fault, a fee of £25 is payable. In all other cases a new card is free of charge. Failure to surrender a card or document with errors is an offence punishable with a fine up to level 3 on the standard scale (reg.12).

It is an offence for a person to forge or make false statements with respect to any document which purports to evidence a CPC entitlement or a training exemption. It is an "either way" offence, summary conviction carrying a fine up to the statutory maximum on conviction on indictment up to two years' imprisonment, a fine or both (reg.13).

Police officers and traffic examiners may seize any documents in respect of which an offence concerning evidence of CPC entitlement or a training exemption may have been committed under the regulations (reg.14).

The Motor Vehicles (Driving Licences) Regulations 1999 are amended by **13.09** reg.15 with the result that the new minimum age requirements in the directive apply to PCV and LGV licence-holders who have passed the initial CPC test. Generally, the age of 21 is substituted by the age of 18 for the drivers of buses and coaches and heavy goods vehicles provided that, in the case of passenger-carrying vehicles, the driver is carrying passengers on a route which does not exceed 50km or does not carry passengers at all. For other bus drivers, age 20 is substituted for 21.

Apart from reg.15, which extends to Great Britain only, these regulations extend to the United Kingdom. Regulation 15 came into force on September 10, 2008 in respect of PCV drivers' licences and on September 10, 2009 in respect of LGV drivers' licences. All other regulations came into force on March 27, 2007.

With effect from April 1, 2008, the Vehicle Drivers (Certificates of Professional Competence) (Amendment No.2) Regulations 2008 (SI 2008/1965) amend the Motor Vehicles (Access to Driving Licensing Records) Regulations 2001 (SI 2001/3343) and the Vehicle Drivers (Certificates of Professional Competence) Regulations 2007. Regulation 5 of the 2008 Amendment Regulations amends reg. 4 of the 2007 Regulations to make provision for applying to the competent authority for an NVT certificate, including the charging of a fee of £25. In addition, reg.6 of the 2008 Amendment Regulations amends reg.5 of the principal regulations requiring a practical test to be passed not more than 24 months after passing the theoretical test and makes provision for an increase in certain fees. New reg.5A requires proof of identify for persons taking the initial CPC test.

Offences are created for those who fail to comply with the regulations.   **13.10**

Nationals of Member States who work in the United Kingdom can also attend a periodic training course (2008 Amendment Regulations reg.8(b), amending reg.6 of the principal regulations) and a new reg.6A is inserted into the principal regulations to provide for appeals to the appropriate tribunal. Approved persons will be subject to a fee calculation when they notify completion of a periodic training course; and the driver qualification card rules are amended by the insertion of a new reg.8A to permit other persons to apply for a driver qualification card upon payment of a fee.

Fitness of LGV and PCV licence applicants and holders

These LGV and PCV driving licence authorisations may under the substituted **13.11** s.112 only be granted if the Secretary of State is satisfied, having regard to his conduct, that the applicant is a fit person to hold the licence. The issue may be referred to the traffic commissioner. "Conduct" means the conduct (including conduct in Northern Ireland) of a LGV licence-holder or applicant as a *driver* of a motor vehicle and of a PCV licence-holder or applicant both as a driver of a motor vehicle and in any other respect relevant to his holding a PCV driving licence (s.121, as amended). The same test applies to LGV or PCV community licence-holders. This could include references to convictions and also conduct even though an acquittal resulted. The Rehabilitation of Offenders Act 1974 is not excluded; spent convictions need not be admitted. In *Secretary of State for Transport, Local Government and the Regions v Snowdon* [2003] R.T.R. 15 DC the North Shields Justices had decided that Mr Snowdon was a fit person to hold a passenger-carrying vehicle driver's licence despite his convictions for indecent assault on a girl travelling on a school trip. The appeal was dismissed. The Divisional Court held that conviction for a sex offence did not automatically disqualify a bus driver from holding a passenger-carrying vehicle driver's licence. Fitness to hold such a licence should be determined by taking all personal circumstances into account.

A magistrates' court dismissed an appeal by a claimant against the Secretary of State's refusal to grant him a Group 2 driving licence which would permit him to drive large goods vehicles and passenger-carrying vehicles. Under ss.92 and 97 of the Road Traffic Act 1988 an application had to be granted, although the standards prescribed for the grant of Group 2 licences were set out in Directive 91/439/EEC. The directive precluded the claimant from holding such a licence because he did not have binocular vision. His appeal to the magistrates' court was dismissed because the district judge concluded that the terms of the directive were binding on him. On appeal by way of case stated, the Divisional Court held (*R. (on the application of Irving) v Secretary of State for Transport* [2008] EWHC 1200) that Directive 91/439/EEC should bear its ordinary natural meaning and on that basis the claimant did not meet the standard required by the directive. In this case, the aim of both the domestic legislation and the European directive was at least, in part, to promote road safety. Words could be read into the statute or the regulations or by interpreting s.92(2)(b) of the 1988 Act so that if the driver of a vehicle failed to satisfy the standards required by the directive, then he suffered from a disability likely to cause the driving of vehicles by him to be a danger to the public.

13.12   There are, in Pt IV of the 1988 Act as substituted, powers of revocation, suspension and disqualification from driving LGVs and PCVs. In the case of LGV licence-holders under 21 the disqualification is in certain circumstances obligatory—see below. It is under s.118 an offence to fail without reasonable excuse to surrender a revoked or suspended LGV or PCV licence after due notice. The offence is triable summarily with a maximum fine of level 3.

A person aggrieved by a refusal or failure to grant a LGV or PCV licence under s.112 or s.113(4) or its suspension or revocation under s.115 or s.116(4) or disqualification under s.117(2) of the 1988 Act, as substituted, may appeal to a magistrates' court under s.119. The appellant must first give notice to the Secretary of State and any traffic commissioners to whom the matter has been referred who are to be treated as respondents (s.119(2)). The court may make such order as it thinks fit. However, a court considering an appeal against the revocation of a licence by the Secretary of State has no greater discretion than the Secretary of State had: *Secretary of State for the Environment, Transport and the Regions v Elsy* [2000] R.T.R. 29. An LGV licence-holder who was under 21 acquired more than three points on his licence and thus came within the Road Traffic Act 1988 s.115(1), which required the Secretary of State to revoke his LGV licence. He appealed against that revocation and the justices took into account the profound effects of the disqualification on both the licence-holder and his employer and allowed the appeal. Overturning that decision, the Divisional Court confirmed that the Secretary of State was acting under a mandatory duty with no discretion whatsoever. Although s.119 of the 1988 Act allowed justices on appeal to make such order as is thought fit, that did not entitle them to consider discretionary matters where the Secretary of State had already carried out a mandatory revocation. The procedure will now be by way of complaint in accordance with the Criminal Procedure Rules 2005 made to the magistrates' court (or in Scotland the sheriff's court).

The holder of a PCV driver's licence appealed to a magistrates' court against a **13.13** decision of a traffic commissioner to revoke his entitlement to hold such a licence. The traffic commissioner had taken into account the considerations set out in s.112(1) of the Road Traffic Act 1988 and had made his decision in accordance with the provisions of ss.115–117 of that Act. The traffic commissioner had also disqualified the appellant from holding or obtaining a PCV driver's licence indefinitely pursuant to s.117(2) of the 1988 Act. The vocational licence-holder's appeal to the magistrates' court was dismissed and having been requested to give reasons for their decision, the justices noted the applicant's previous convictions for assault and for failing to surrender to bail. Whilst noting that a community rehabilitation order had "gone well", they added that the appellant was still suffering from depression and that as vocational entitlement could only be achieved by demonstrating fitness, the justices had regard to the claimant's conduct and found that he was not a fit person to hold a PCV driver's licence. The Administrative Court (*R. (on the application of Stace) v Milton Keynes Magistrates' Court* [2006] EWHC 1049) decided to accept a claim for judicial review on the basis that the provision of reasons by the justices made it unnecessary for the appellant to ask the magistrates' court to state a case in order to find out the nature of the justices' reasons. In granting the application for judicial review, it was held that justices had to look not only at the appellant's convictions, but his other conduct as well, including his failure to appear at either of the hearings before the traffic commissioner and the way that he had responded positively to the community rehabilitation order. The convictions recorded against the appellant should not be looked at in a vacuum and had to be considered in the context of whether conduct of the particular kind might affect fitness of drivers of passenger-carrying vehicles. The justices had to consider the seriousness of the appellant's conduct, the risks of any repetition of violence, and the way in which his propensity for violence impinged upon his abilities as a driver. Also relevant was the extent to which he may have been a risk to those passengers with whom he had come into contact. The justices had only referred to the community rehabilitation order in their reasoning and it was unclear whether they had thought that it was inappropriate for someone suffering from depression to hold a PCV driver's licence. Accordingly, their decision was flawed since they had taken into account an irrelevant consideration (the fact that the community rehabilitation order was still in place) and failed to put a relevant consideration (the appellant's depression) in its proper context. They did not appear to have looked at the conduct in the context of whether conduct of that particular kind might affect fitness to drive PCVs. The justices' decision dismissing the driver's appeal was quashed and the matter was remitted to the magistrates' court to be heard by a differently constituted bench.

13.14   Traffic commissioners have agreed guidelines in respect of the effect of disqualifications from driving when consideration is being given to a driver's "conduct" in the context of the grant, revocation or suspension of a vocational driving licence. These guidelines stress that the conduct of each driver must be considered on its merits but give indications of the likely effect of disqualifications and of aggravating features. Details of these and of principles followed by the Transport Tribunal in hearing similar appeals from disciplinary decisions of traffic commissioners are usefully set out in a short article at 159 J.P.N. 604. An example of the courts' response to this type of approach is seen in the case of *Wathan v Traffic Commissioner for South Wales*, October 12, 1994, unreported. The traffic commissioner had disqualified Mr Wathan from driving heavy goods vehicles for two years. In addition to concerns about defective eyesight, Mr Wathan had been convicted of two offences of driving without due care and attention. On the second occasion he had been disqualified under the totting-up provisions. The Divisional Court upheld the magistrates' court's rejection of Mr Wathan's appeal.

   The most recent guidelines issued by traffic commissioners in respect of driver conduct, are set out in Traffic Commissioners' *Practice Direction No.3* effective from November 2008.

13.15   It would appear that the burden of proof to show that he is entitled to hold a licence is on the appellant. He who asserts must prove (semble on the balance of probabilities).

   The magistrates' court has no greater power than the licensing authority and cannot grant on appeal a LGV or PCV licence which the licensing authority could not grant, nor may the applicant be a "person aggrieved" if he has been deprived of something the licensing authority could not grant (*R. v Ipswich JJ. Ex p. Robson* [1971] 2 All E.R. 1395). A magistrates' court may determine whether a test for a licence has been properly conducted in accordance with the regulations and, if it is found not to have been so conducted, the court may order the applicant to be allowed another test.

The LGV and PCV regulations

13.16   The Motor Vehicles (Driving Licences) Regulations 1999 (SI 1999/2864) apply.

   Applications for a LGV or PCV licence are made under Pt III of the 1999 Regulations and the 1988 Act. The nature of the driving tests, classes and categories of vehicles and relevant fees are also set out in the regulations. More stringent disability restrictions are prescribed in regs 70–75. Learner driver provisions are in regs 15–19. A driver's licence issued as a provisional licence carries the conditions prescribed by reg.16, i.e. displaying the learner marks, and driving only when under the supervision of the holder of a full LGV, HGV, PCV or PSV licence as the case may be. That licence does not have to have been held for three years or more (reg.17(3)). In the case of PCVs there is a condition restricting passengers (reg.16(8)). Failure to comply with a provisional licence condition without reasonable excuse is an offence under s.114(1) and punishable with a fine of level 3. There is a special scheme for LGV trainee drivers' licences for persons under 21 (reg.54) with more stringent conditions. The scheme is operated by employers registered for training and by registered training schools. The other conditions are the same. The Motor Vehicles (Driving Licences) (Amendment

No.2) Regulations 2004 (SI 2004/1519) amended the definitions in reg.54(5) relating to LGV trainee drivers' licences in consequence of the Young LGV Driver Training Scheme approved in February 2004.

The age limits applicable to various types of vehicle are set out in the Road **13.17** Traffic Act 1988 s. 101. If a person holds a LGV licence and is under 21, reg.55 provides that if his licence or counterpart records more than three penalty points or he is disqualified by a court, his LGV authorisation will be revoked under s.115(1)(a) of the 1988 Act and he must be disqualified either indefinitely or for a limited period as determined at least until 21 (regs 55(3) and (4)).

Court disqualification until test passed

By reg.56 of the Motor Vehicles (Driving Licences) Regulations 1999 where **13.18** the holder of a LGV or PCV licence is disqualified from driving by an order of a court, the licensing authority may also order that person to be disqualified from holding or obtaining a LGV or PCV licence for such period as the authority thinks fit. The authority may require the licence-holder to be disqualified until a test is taken. Disqualifications under these provisions may be removed by the authority on the application of the licence-holder in a way similar to that applicable to disqualifications imposed by a court (reg.57). In such cases, the licensing authority is usually the traffic commissioner for the area in which the holder of the relevant licence resides.

Disqualification with revocation when LGV driver under 21

Under s.115(1)(a) of the 1988 Act and reg.55 of the 1999 Regulations, if a **13.19** LGV driver under 21 accumulates more than three penalty points or is disqualified by an order of a court, he must be disqualified indefinitely by the licensing authority from LGVs or for such period at least until reaching the age of 21 as the Secretary of State may determine.

Duration of licence authorisation

The LGV or PCV licence will normally remain in force until the driver's 45th **13.20** birthday or for five years whichever is the longer, but between that age and 65 for five years or until 66 whichever is the shorter. After a person reaches 65, the licence authorisation has to be renewed annually. Licences granted to persons with relevant or prospective disabilities will last for between one and three years (1988 Act s.99(1A)).

Exemptions from the LGV and PCV licensing requirements and from the regulations

By reg.50 certain classes of vehicle are exempted from Pt IV of the 1988 Act **13.21** and from regs 54–57. However, a disqualification from driving LGVs or PCVs under s.117 of the 1988 Act will apply to all LGVs and PCVs whether or not exempted. Exempted vehicles are those vehicles included in categories F (agricultural or forestry tractor), G (road roller) or H (track-laying vehicle steered by its tracks) or sub-category C1 + E (8.25 tonnes), any PCV more than 30 years old provided it is not driven for hire or reward or to carry more than eight passengers, any PCV driven by a constable to remove or avoid an obstruction or protect life or property, etc., and vehicles which are exempted goods vehicles or exempted military vehicles as prescribed by reg.51. Exempt vehicles by reg.51 include steam-propelled goods vehicles, certain road construction vehicles, engineering plant, works trucks, industrial tractors, agricultural motor vehicles, digging machines, certain vehicles only used for short distances on public roads, lifeboat vehicles, a mobile project vehicle, certain recovery vehicles and certain forces vehicles.

Other exemptions and special provisions

13.22   No additional PCV authorisation is required for a person to drive a small PCV, that is, a vehicle carrying up to 16 passengers, excluding the driver, providing it is not used for hire or reward. They must be covered by an ordinary driving licence held for at least two years and must be over 21 (reg.7(6)).

A person who, for at least two years, has held a full licence to drive category C vehicles may also drive a motor vehicle used for carrying passengers with more than eight seats excluding the driver's if it is not being used to carry anyone not connected with the operator and is either damaged or defective and being driven to a place of repair or being road tested following repair (reg.7(1)). The purpose of this is to allow LGV and HGV drivers in these categories to drive large buses for repair and testing. As to the favourable licensing treatment of the drivers of tramcars, see § 13.147.

LGV and PCV drivers' licences: exemptions for persons from abroad

13.23   Under the Motor Vehicles (International Circulation) Order 1975 (SI 1975/1208), as amended, and the Motor Vehicles (Driving Licences) Regulations 1999 (SI 1999/2864) reg.80, it is lawful for a person resident outside the United Kingdom who is temporarily in Great Britain, who holds a Convention driving permit as defined, a foreign domestic driving permit or a British Forces driving permit as defined, a foreign domestic driving permit or a British Forces driving licence to drive or for any person to cause or permit such a person to drive in Great Britain during a period of 12 months from the date of his last entry into Great Britain a LGV or PCV brought temporarily into Great Britain which he is authorised by that permit to drive even though he is not the holder of a corresponding Pt III licence. In addition, if such a person is resident in a Member State of the EU or holds a British external licence granted in the Isle of Man, Jersey or Guernsey, he may drive any LGV or PCV during the 12 months, whether or not the vehicle is temporarily brought into Great Britain. There is also a provision under which such qualified persons even though between the ages of 18 and 21 may drive such vehicles providing the vehicle is registered in a Convention country as defined.

The Driving Licences (Community Driving Licences) Regulations 1996 (SI 1996/1974) make further changes affecting holders of driving licences issued by states which are contracting parties to the European Economic Area Agreement. Holders of such licences will not generally be obligated to exchange that licence for a British one after a year but will become subject to the same standards of health, etc. Resident Community licence-holders entitled to drive certain classes of goods and passenger-carrying vehicles will be obliged to submit certain details to the Secretary of State within one year of becoming resident. The right to be licensed to drive a taxi, private hire vehicles or small buses for charitable and similar purposes is also extended to holders of Community licences.

The appropriateness of a fine or imprisonment as a sanction for failing to obtain **13.24** the exchange of a licence was considered in Case C–193/94 *Criminal proceedings against Skanavi* [1997] R.T.R. 344. The European Court of Justice considered that this issue related directly to the freedom of movement within the EU and the sanction should be proportionate to the offence and should not be equated with the sanction for those who did not hold a licence.

LGV AND PCV DRIVERS' LICENCES: PROCEEDINGS AND PENALTIES

Generally

The evidential provisions in s.11 of the 1988 Offenders Act (evidence by cer- **13.25** tificate) are applied to offences contrary to s.114(1) and (2) of the 1988 Act and in s.12(1) (proof of identity of driver) to s.114(1) offences.

Offences of driving without LGV or PCV authorisation are in effect offences of driving a class of vehicle not in accordance with a driving licence for that class contrary to s.87(1) of the 1988 Act, and that of causing or permitting the driving contrary to s.87(2). Driving offences under s.87(1) may carry endorsement, 3–6 penalty points and discretionary disqualification in certain circumstances—see Chapter 11 and also the Magistrates' Court Sentencing Guidelines in Appendix 3. The number of penalty points to be assigned for s.87(1) offences will vary depending on the seriousness of the offence. As to variable points, see Chapter 19. Where a fixed penalty is accepted the penalty points will be restricted to the lowest in the range, that is, three. Section 87(2) offences and breaches of LGV and PCV learner licence conditions are not subject to endorsement or disqualification. All these offences carry a maximum fine of level 3.

LGV drivers under 21 are subject to special conditions. In particular this **13.26** entitlement under their licence is to be revoked if they incur more than three penalty points. The risk of this is that much the greater with the possibility of between three and six variable points for speeding offences dealt with by the courts. There is an incentive to accept any offered fixed penalty as the points for endorsable fixed penalty cases are limited to three.

For a table of penalties, see § 13.27.

Large goods and passenger-carrying vehicles: driving licence penalties

Offence	Mode of trial	Section	Imprisonment	Level of fine	Disqualification	Penalty points	Endorsement code	Sentencing guideline*
Driving a class of motor vehicle not in accordance with driving licence for that class (see Chapter 11)	Summary	s.87(1) RTA 1988	—	3	Discretionary if offence is committed by driving a motor vehicle in a case where either no driving licence for driving that vehicle could have been granted to offender or, if a provisional licence only to drive it could have been granted, the driving would not have complied with the conditions. Otherwise no disqualification	3–6, if disqualifiable	LC10	Fine band A where eligible for a licence that would have covered the driving Fine band A Aggravating factor if no licence ever held

Offence	Mode of trial	Section	Imprisonment	Level of fine	Disqualification	Penalty points	Endorsement code	Sentencing guideline*
Causing or permitting a person to drive class of motor vehicle not in accordance with driving licence for that class	Summary	s.87(2) RTA 1988	—	3	—	—	—	—
Failing to comply with conditions of LGV or PCV licence	Summary	s.114(1) RTA 1988 as substituted	—	3	—	—	—	—
Knowingly causing or permitting person under 21 to drive LGV or PCV in contravention of conditions	Summary	s. 114(2) RTA 1988 as substituted	—	3	—	—	—	—
Failing to surrender revoked or suspended LGV or PCV licence	Summary	s.118 RTA 1988 as substituted by RT (DL & IS) Act 1989, Sch.2	—	3	—	—	—	—

Offence	Mode of trial	Section	Imprisonment	Level of fine	Disqualification	Penalty points	Endorsement code	Sentencing guideline*
Contravention of regs made under RTA 1988 s.120(5) about LGV or PCV licences which is declared by regs to be an offence	Summary	s.120(5) RTA 1988	—	3	—	—	—	—

*Note: Fine bands "A", "B" and "C" represent respectively 50%, 100% and 150% of relevant weekly income. A timely guilty plea should attract a discount. See Appendix 3.

GOODS VEHICLE OPERATORS' LICENCES

Generally

The licensing of the operator of a goods vehicle for the carriage of goods for **13.28** hire or reward or for or in connection with a trade or business comes under the Goods Vehicles (Licensing of Operators) Act 1995, the Goods Vehicles (Licensing of Operators) Regulations 1995 (SI 1995/2869), the Goods Vehicles Operators (Qualifications) Regulations 1999 (SI 1999/2430) and the Goods Vehicles (Licensing of Operators) (Fees) Regulations 1995 (SI 1995/3000). The key provisions are referred to below.

An operator's licence is required under s.2 of the 1995 Act from the traffic commissioner (see s.1) for the use on a road of a goods vehicle for the carriage of goods (a) for hire or reward, or (b) for or in connection with any trade or business carried on by the applicant. No operator's licence is needed for certain vehicles: see § 13.59. Provision is made by ss.3 and 46 of the 1995 Act and reg.30 of the 1995 Regulations as to operators' licences in respect of holding companies and subsidiaries.

The definitions section is s.58. The procedure for applying for a goods vehicle **13.29** operator's licence is contained in the 1995 and 1999 Regulations.

By s.23, environmental conditions can be attached on grants and variations. The question of road safety was held under the previous provisions not to be an environmental matter but one of suitability as to the premises. If the traffic commissioner was not satisfied as to road safety, the problem could not therefore be solved by the imposition of an environmental condition and the proposed premises were unsuitable and the application had to be refused: *Surrey County Council and Mole Valley District Council v Norman Marshall Ltd* (1991) Transport Tribunal Appeal Nos 1991 C9 and C10.

The 1995 Regulations additionally allow the making of a condition regulating **13.30** the means of entry to and exit from the operating centre (reg.14(d)) and s.21 permits the making of conditions to prevent vehicles causing a danger to the public.

Notice of applications for operators' licences and applications for variations (except for certain trivial applications) has to be published in a local newspaper circulating in the locality in which the operating centre will be located, for the benefit of persons who have statutory rights of objection and of persons who are entitled to make representations, in each case subject to certain governing requirements and time limits.

Types of operator's licence

Further provisions have been adopted by the EU Council on the admission to **13.31** the occupation of road haulage and road passenger operator and on the mutual recognition of qualifications within the EU (Directive 96/26/EC, May 23, 1996 extended by Directive 98/76/EC). These provisions aim to facilitate the freedom of establishment in both national and international transport operations. They have been incorporated through the 1999 Regulations.

The 1995 Act provides for two types of licence, a standard licence and a restricted licence.

Standard operator's licence

13.32   Under this licence, goods vehicles may be used either for hire or reward or for or in connection with a trade or business carried on by the holder of the licence. This type of licence is further divided in that it may cover the carriage of goods for hire or reward on both international and national transport operations (sometimes called an international standard operators' licence) or may cover such carriage on national transport operations only (sometimes called a national standard operators' licence).

Restricted operator's licence

13.33   Under this licence, goods vehicles may only be used for or in connection with a trade or business carried on by the holder of the licence other than that of carrying goods for hire or reward.

In general the provisions of the 1995 Act apply to both types of operator's licence, but by s.11 and Sch.3 (as amended or replaced by the 1999 Regulations) the provisions are made more stringent with regard to the repute, financial standing and professional competence of applicants for standard operators' licences. There are special arrangements for holding companies and subsidiaries under Sch.2 to the 1995 Regulations.

Professional competence, financial standing, etc.

13.34   New entrants to the industry seeking a standard operator's licence have to qualify as to good repute, appropriate financial standing and professional competence (s.11 and Sch.3, as amended). The traffic commissioner is obliged to revoke a standard licence, subject to due notice and the due procedures, if it appears to that authority that these requirements are no longer satisfied by the holder (ss.26–29). With effect from January 1, 2005, the Goods Vehicles (Qualifications) (Amendment) Regulations 2004 (SI 2004/3222) amended para.6(2) of Sch.3 to the Goods Vehicles (Licensing of Operators) Act 1995, which prescribe the requirements which an applicant for, or holder of, a standard operator's licence must meet in order to be of appropriate financial standing. The amendment by the 2004 Amendment Regulations applied prescribed minimum amounts for capital reserves to all standard licences, national as well as international whereas the former regulations did not apply to national operations. Full details of the statutory requirements with regard to the test of financial standing are to be found in Traffic Commissioners' *Practice Direction No.1* effective from January 1, 2005 (available at *http://www.vosa.gov.uk* following the "Publications" link [Accessed April 7, 2009]).

In *Muck It Ltd v Secretary of State for Transport* [2005] EWCA Civ 1124; [2006] R.T.R. 9, the Court of Appeal, when allowing appeals by operators in part, held that an applicant for an operator's licence bears the burden under the Goods Vehicles (Licensing of Operators) Act 1995 s.13, of satisfying the traffic commissioner that the applicant fulfils the relevant requirements. When the traffic commissioner is considering making a direction such as revocation of an operator's licence using discretionary powers under s.26 of the 1995 Act or under the mandatory requirements set out in s.27, it was the traffic commissioner who had to be satisfied of the existence of a ground for revocation, and not the licence-holder who has to satisfy the traffic commissioner to the contrary. The operator should be informed of any evidence to be put before the traffic commissioner prior to the public inquiry.

The meaning and method of proof of professional competence are set out in **13.35** Sch.3 to the 1995 Act, as amended. In s.58(1) "transport manager" is defined in relation to a business as an individual who is in, or who is engaged to enter into, the employment of the holder of a standard licence and who, either alone or jointly with one or more others, has continuous and effective responsibility for the management of the transport operations of the business in so far as they relate to the carriage of goods. References to professional competence are to the professional competence of an individual and a company satisfies the requirement as to professional competence if and so long as it has a transport manager for its road transport undertaking or such number of them as the licensing authority may require who or each of whom is of good repute and professionally competent (Sch.3, as amended). Traffic commissioners have issued guidance to the industries as to the approach which they will take when assessing whether a person satisfies the requirements of professional competence when acting as a transport manager for an operator.

When a partnership applies for a standard licence, all of the partners must under the regulations as amended be of good repute, the partnership firm must satisfy the requirements of appropriate financial standing and in addition if a partner is the manager of the road transport business, he must be professionally competent or if an employee is the manager, he must be both professionally competent and of good repute. There is nothing in this wording to suggest that the professionally competent partner must spend a substantial proportion of his working time on the transport operation. This conclusion was reached by the Transport Tribunal in *Baker and Baker* (1984) Appeal 1984 No.U 19 on the different wording of the former sub-paragraph of the regulation (overruling the licensing authority (now traffic commissioner) on that point) but seems still to be applicable. It was held sufficient (even if the professionally competent partner had another full-time job) if he spent enough time on it to carry out the work satisfactorily.

With the company holder of a standard licence, the issue of good repute will be **13.36** the good repute of the company or any of its officers, servants, agents or directors. Obviously the ill repute of the directors or senior officials may blacken the repute of the company and convictions will be material.

Good repute

When the traffic commissioner considers whether an applicant is of good **13.37** repute, he is required under para.1(1)(a) of Sch.3 to the 1995 Act to have regard to "relevant convictions" (as defined in Sch.3 para.1(3)). "Relevant conviction" means any conviction mentioned in para.5 of Sch.2 to the 1995 Act or corresponding Northern Ireland or foreign convictions or any serious or road transport offence (defined in paras 3 and 4, as amended, of Sch.3) which is not "spent" under the Rehabilitation of Offenders Act 1974.

The traffic commissioner is required by para.1(1)(b) also to have regard to any other information in his possession which appears to relate to the applicant's fitness to hold a licence. Under para.1(1)(b), the commissioner should properly have regard to any conviction not falling within the term "relevant conviction" (as defined) provided that it is not "spent" under the 1974 Act and it relates to the question of the applicant's good repute (*Batch (trading as AJB Motor Services) v Hampshire Constabulary* (1988) Appeal 1988 No.Z 4, Transport Tribunal). When considering these other convictions, the commissioner has to decide whether they are material to the applicant's fitness to operate vehicles under a licence and if so to what extent. Unlike "relevant convictions", these convictions are not conclusively taken into account and have to be weighed in the light of any other factors. Consideration was given to the use of spent convictions in a Scottish case, *O'Doherty v Renfrewshire Council* (1997) 1998 S.L.T. 327. The Court of Session endorsed the dictum of Sedley J. in *R. v Hastings JJ. Ex p. McSpirit, The Times*, June 23, 1994, that spent convictions should stay spent unless, in the classes of case where it is permissible to do so, the party applying to put in the spent conviction can satisfy the judicial authority that there is no other way of doing justice. This appears to follow the approach set out in relation to applications for taxi and private hire licences in *Adamson v Waveney District Council*: see § 13.275.

13.38   A traffic commissioner is *obliged* to hold that an individual is not of good repute if he has been convicted of more than one serious offence or has been convicted of road transport offences (Sch.3 para.2, as replaced by reg.2 of the 1999 Regulations). A serious offence for this purpose is any offence under any United Kingdom law for which a sentence of imprisonment for a term exceeding three months, a fine exceeding level 4 on the standard scale or a community order for more than 60 hours was imposed and any foreign offence for which a corresponding punishment was imposed (Sch.3 para.1). Sentence of imprisonment includes any form of custodial sentence or order other than one under the mental health enactments (Sch.3 para.3). A road transport offence in this context is defined as a United Kingdom offence relating to road transport, including in particular drivers' hours and rest periods, the weights and dimensions of commercial vehicles and road and vehicle safety and any corresponding foreign offence, offences relating to the protection of the environment and offences concerning professional liability (Sch.3 para.4, as amended). The Transport Tribunal has decided that the phrase "road traffic offence" should be read as if the word "serious" appeared before it: *Clark (Brian)* (2002) Appeal No.74/2001. This reflects the fact that such a conviction obliges the Commissioner to hold that the individual is not of good repute and therefore the operator's licence would be revoked.

An example of application of the test of good repute is to be found in an appeal to the Transport Tribunal: *Roadway Transport Ltd* (2000) Appeal 1999 No.L 67; (2000) 19 W.R.T.L.B. [109]. An applicant for an operator's licence was a company with a single director. The company had been convicted on four occasions within seven months for illegal use of a vehicle. The traffic commissioner approached the issue as if it had been made by an individual thus obliging him to hold that the applicant was not of good repute. This approach was endorsed on appeal.

13.39   In deciding whether a company is of good repute, the traffic commissioner is required by para.1(2) of Sch.3 to the 1995 Act to have regard to "all the material evidence". Under ss.8 and 9 of the 1995 Act an applicant, on request, must disclose certain information to the traffic commissioner, including information regarding the notifiable convictions (see paras 1 and 4 of Sch.2 to the 1995 Act) of any relevant person (see Sch.2 paras 2 and 4). Non-endorsable fixed penalties are not convictions but if repeated may be taken into account in determining good repute: *MacPherson & Colburn Ltd* (1992) Appeal 1992 No.D 16, Transport Tribunal.

Two cases show the tough stance adopted by tribunals fully aware of the commercial pressures that apply to operators. Offences of falsifying tachograph records were committed by goods vehicle operators who fitted and used interrupter switches which bypassed the tachograph heads in their vehicles. In breach of a condition of their licences, they failed to report their convictions to the licensing authority. After a public inquiry, the licensing authority (now traffic commissioner) revoked their licences and disqualified them from holding an operator's licence for 12 months (one of the operators had a "renewal" application refused). The operators' appeal to the Transport Tribunal on the ground that the decision had been too harsh was dismissed (*Featherstone, Featherstone and Hammond* (1994) Appeal 1993 No.E 40). There had been a calculated, deliberate and persistent breach of the rules relating to drivers' hours and the licensing authority had been fully entitled to conclude that it had not been an isolated incident. Even though the consequences of the revocation and disqualification were disastrous, the licensing authority had not misdirected himself. It was said that suspension of licences would have given the wrong message to other operators and that the disqualification both properly marked the gravity of the operators' conduct and made it clear that they would not recover their good repute after a relatively short period of time.

In *R., B. & D. Smith Ltd* (1994) Appeal 1993 No.E 36 the licensing authority **13.40** (now traffic commissioner) (relying exclusively on tachograph records) found that the operator company had treated speed limits with contempt as a matter of policy in order to deliver goods within time-limits. The occasions were not simply matters of wandering over speed limits without realising it; three drivers had deliberately driven at high and illegal speeds in order to meet deadlines. Although the operator's record was otherwise impeccable and although there had been no conviction of any driver for exceeding the speed limit, the licensing authority concluded that the operator's licence should be revoked for loss of good repute. The appeal to the Transport Tribunal on this point was fruitless. The tribunal had little sympathy for arguments that neither the operator not the drivers could, in the circumstances, have been prosecuted for speeding offences. The Transport Tribunal endorsed the view of the licensing authority that suppliers or customers who encouraged hauliers to break speed limits, either because of the terms of their contracts or because they loaded the haulier late and then failed to take responsibility for that failure, might find that they were guilty of aiding and abetting or counselling and procuring offences committed by the haulier in his attempts to deliver on time.

Traffic commissioners are concerned to ensure that they receive details not only of offences committed but also of circumstances where financial penalties ordered by a court remain outstanding after the due payment date. Traffic commissioners have indicated that failure to pay a fine is likely to lead to loss of financial standing leading to immediate revocation of the operator's licence. The commissioners would not expect an operator to need to a pay a fine by instalments.

The type of conduct which can justify a finding that an operator is no longer of **13.41** good repute was considered in *Crompton v Department of Transport North Western Area* [2003] EWCA Civ 64; [2003] R.T.R. 34. The court emphasised that, whilst the revocation of an operator's licence would be compatible with the

European Convention on Human Rights in pursuance of a legitimate aim, it needed to be proportionate. The revocation of an operator's licence by a traffic commissioner on the basis of the operator's behaviour following an earlier hearing when he behaved in a threatening and abusive way was challenged and the Court of Appeal reinstated the operator's licence. In this case it was stated that the issue had to be the fitness of the operator to hold the licence.

Good repute was also considered by the Transport Tribunal in *Byran Haulage* (Case TT 217/2002) where it was stated that the test of good repute which must be applied by a traffic commissioner was "does this operator deserve to be put out of business?".

13.42   As to the powers of traffic commissioners to take action against non-compliant operators generally, see *Romantiek BVBA v Simms, Allsopp and the Department for Transport* [2008] EWHC 3099 in which a claim against a traffic commissioner for malfeasance in public office failed.

Authorised vehicles

13.43   The vehicles which are authorised to be used under an operator's licence are specified in s.5 of the 1995 Act (as amended by s.263 of the Transport Act 2000, when in force). Section 5(4) restricts the authorisation of vehicles to vehicles whose operating centres are for the time being within the area of the traffic commissioner by whom the licence was granted (or outside that area if the operating centres have not been there for a period of more than three months).

Note that by s.5(8) a motor vehicle can be specified in only one licence. Semble if two licences are issued for one vehicle, the second one may be void and any conditions attached to the second one issued in point of time may be void also, so that it may not be an offence to fail to comply with a condition of the second one. Under s.5(2) the traffic commissioner can specify different types of motor vehicles or trailers and specify the maximum numbers for each type.

Using a goods vehicle without an operator's licence

13.44   Section 2 subject to exceptions (see s.2(2) and Sch.1), requires any user of a goods vehicle on a road for the carriage of goods for hire or reward or for or in connection with any trade or business carried on by him to hold an operator's licence. A person who uses a vehicle in contravention of the section commits an offence (s.2(5), as amended by Transport Act 2000 s.261).

A   *"Goods vehicle"*

13.45   Only goods vehicles, i.e. vehicles and trailers constructed or adapted to carry goods, need licences under the 1995 Act. By s.58(1) goods-carrying trailers are included and trams and trolley vehicles operated under statutory powers excluded.

A van adapted for the carriage of passengers and used only to carry samples to the owner's place of business was held not to be a goods vehicle in *Tait v Odhams Press* (1937) 26 Traff.Cas. 80, where certain exempting regulations were also in point. Where a passenger vehicle has been altered to carry goods, the test whether the vehicle is a goods or passenger one is whether it would, if it had been constructed in its altered condition, still be regarded as a vehicle used to carry passengers and their effects (*Flower Freight Co v Hammond* [1962] 3 All E.R.

950). Passengers' effects are not goods (ibid.). A shooting-brake or other utility vehicle would be within the Act if used to carry goods for reward or in connection with a trade or business (cf. *Taylor v Thompson* [1956] 1 All E.R. 352), but many will be exempt as being under 1,525kg (Sch.1 to the 1995 Act). The term "goods vehicle" includes a van used only for carrying a window cleaner's ladders, rags and buckets, as these are goods (*Clarke v Cherry* [1953] 1 All E.R. 267). A decision of magistrates that a car adapted to carry dresses hung on rails at the back was not adapted to carry goods was upheld in *Taylor v Mead* [1961] 1 All E.R. 626. It is submitted that, as in s.58(1) the term "adapted" is contrasted with "constructed", the former means "altered physically so as to make fit for the purpose" (*Maddox v Storer* [1962] 1 All E.R. 831) (see further Chapter 1 and in particular the definitions of "adapted" and "constructed" at §§ 1.27–31).

In *Vehicle Operator Services Agency v Law Fertilisers Ltd* [2004] EWHC **13.46** 3000; [2005] R.T.R. 21 it was held that there was an exemption from the requirement under the Goods Vehicles (Licensing of Operators) Act 1995 for an operator's licence in respect of goods carried on a vehicle but not in respect of goods on a trailer hauled by a vehicle. There was nothing to support the proposition that where an agricultural engine was used on a public road for carriage or haulage it became a goods vehicle that required a licence under the Vehicle Excise and Registration Act 1994.

An essential ingredient of the offence of using a vehicle without an operator's licence under s.2 of the 1995 Act is that the vehicle is carrying goods at the relevant time (*Robertson v Crew* [1977] R.T.R. 141). "Carriage of goods" is defined in s.58(1) of the 1995 Act as including "haulage of goods". In *Booth v DPP* [1993] R.T.R. 379 it was held that justices were entitled to find that a licence was required where a tractor unit was used by a motor repairer and tester, in the course of his business, to collect and return empty trailers for repair and testing. The tractor unit was a goods vehicle used to haul goods in connection with the defendant's trade and business.

In *Cleansing Service Group Ltd v Vehicle and Operator Services Agency* **13.47** [2006] EWHC 662; [2007] R.T.R. 15 the appellant company was convicted of unlawfully using a goods vehicle on a road for the carriage of goods without an operator's licence contrary to s.2(1) and (5) of the Goods Vehicles (Licensing of Operators) Act 1995. The issue which was central to the case was whether the appellant company was "... a contractor employed to do agricultural work on the farm by the occupier of the farm". The justices found that the appellant company was not employed by the occupier of the farm in question to carry out agricultural work on the farm and they determined that the use of the vehicle in question (which was not specified on the company's operator's licence) at the time and date of the alleged offence did not fall within the exemption set out in the Goods Vehicles (Licensing of Operators) Regulations 1995 Sch.3 Pt II para.2. The Administrative Court held that if possible, para.2 must be interpreted in such a way as to give effect to each and every word in that paragraph. There had to be a direct contractual relationship between the occupier of a farm and the person employed to do agricultural work on that farm for the exemption from the need for a standard national goods vehicle operator's licence to apply. In the instant case there had been no such relationship, and the exemption in para.2 had not applied. The Administrative Court was of the view that some system of regulating haulage operators was clearly required in order to protect public safety. It was not a question of giving the exceptions a broad or a narrow interpretation. The ordinary and natural meaning of a contractor being employed by someone to do something is that there is some contractual nexus between them. In this case there was no such nexus. Whilst the work was carried out by the appellant company at the direction of the farmer, it was an incident of a haulage contract between the appellant and a third party.

B *"Use"*

13.48   Note that an offence under s.2 can only be committed by a person who "uses" in contravention of s.2; any person who is not a "user" can be charged only with aiding and abetting use. By s.58(2) the driver, if he is the owner or is in possession under a hire-purchase agreement, etc., and in any other case the person whose servant or agent the driver is, is deemed to be the user; normally therefore an employed driver should not be charged under s.2 and the High Court said in *Carpenter v Campbell* [1953] 1 All E.R. 280 that, where it is the employer's duty to get the licence, the driver should not be prosecuted. For a case in which an employment agency who introduced drivers to haulage companies were held not to be the employers of the drivers and thus could not be prosecuted by virtue of what is now s.58(2) when a client haulage company had no operator's licence, see *Alderton v Richard Burgon Associates Ltd* [1974] R.T.R. 422. In *Interlink Express Parcels Ltd v Night Trunkers Ltd* [2001] EWCA Civ 360; [2001] R.T.R. 23, Interlink offered a next-day parcel delivery service. The vehicles used were provided by Interlink but some of the drivers were provided by Night Trunkers Ltd. Night Trunkers decided which driver should drive on any of the particular routes assigned to it and were responsible for the wages, discipline and holiday entitlement of the drivers. There was also a clause in the agreement between the two companies that, should it come to a premature end, Interlink would employ Night Trunker's staff. At first instance, the Chancery Division concluded that since, on the facts, the drivers remained employed by Night Trunkers, that company needed to possess an operator's licence. However, on appeal, the Court of Appeal decided that, given that the main purpose of the provision in the 1995 Act was to govern the responsibility of those who controlled the actual use of the vehicle, the relevant language was that of tort rather than of contract. In the context of temporary deemed employment, the main test was of control over the activity. In these circumstances the extent of the right to control the various activities raised a strong inference of fact that the claimant had the right to control the way that the drivers operated its vehicles and so those drivers should be regarded as temporary deemed servants of the claimant for the purposes of s.58(2) of the 1995 Act. The absence of a statutory definition in the 1995 Act of the term "servant" allows the court to give it a dynamic meaning and enables the court to keep pace with changes in the nature of employment, including the increasing use of agency workers. See Chapter 1 as to the meaning of "use".

It is very doubtful whether a lorry returning from a place where it has carried goods for hire or reward or going to a place where it will carry goods for hire or reward can be said at such times to be used on the road for carriage of goods for hire or reward (per Lord Parker C.J. in *Roberts v Morris* [1965] Crim. L.R. 46). By the definition in s.58(3) of the 1995 Act, "authorised vehicle" means one authorised to be used under an operator's licence whether or not it is for the time being in use for a purpose for which an operator's licence is required.

C   *"Hire or reward"*

The leading case on the meaning of "hire or reward" is *Albert v Motor Insur-*   **13.49**
ers' Bureau [1971] 2 All E.R. 1345. This was not a case on an operator's licence
but on s.203(4) of the Road Traffic Act 1960, which exempted a driver of a motor
vehicle from being required to insure against passenger liability provided the
passengers were not carried for "hire or reward". The House of Lords disapproved *Coward v Motor Insurers' Bureau* [1962] 1 All E.R. 531, where it was
held that "hire or reward" meant a monetary reward legally recoverable under a
contract express or implied, and held that the test as to whether a vehicle was being used for "hire or reward" was whether there had been a systematic carrying
of passengers for reward which went beyond the bounds of mere social kindness.
It was immaterial that no contractual relationship was intended. The words "hire
or reward" must be read disjunctively.

A garage proprietor who used a converted bus only for the purpose of transporting a stock car to stock car race meetings where it competed for modest prizes
was acquitted of using the converted bus without an operator's licence for goods
vehicles, contrary to what is now s.2 (use of vehicle for hire or reward or in connection with a trade or business) (*Stirk v McKenna* [1984] R.T.R. 330). It was
conceded that in the light of *Customs and Excise Commissioners v Lord Fisher*
[1981] 2 All E.R. 147 and *Blackmore v Bellamy* [1983] R.T.R. 303, neither
competing for prize money nor the receipt of money from sponsorship was sufficient to constitute a connection with a trade or business for the purpose of what
is now s.2.

A defendant trained horses for reward and it was his duty to see that they   **13.50**
reached the racecourses; he carried a horse to a race meeting in an unlicensed
vehicle. It was at the owner's discretion whether he paid the defendant for the
transport and in fact he was not paid. The defendant was held not guilty under a
corresponding Irish statute (*Att Gen v Brogan* (1953) 87 I.L.T.R. 181). A
company owning a vehicle with a restricted licence agreed for an unexpected
reward to arrange for the transport of goods from London to Northumberland; a
vehicle belonging to another firm, with an A licence, was to take them from East
London to Northumberland but the company's vehicle took them from North
London to the starting point. A metropolitan magistrate held this journey to be
part of the whole journey for arranging which the company was being paid and
convicted the company of carrying goods without an A or B licence ([1954]
Jo.Crim.L. 219). Where a vehicle was used at a standard charge to empty a septic
tank and dumped the effluent emptied from the tank on farmland some distance
away, it was held that the effluent was "goods" and that it was a carriage for
reward (*Sweetway Sanitary Cleansers Ltd v Bradley* [1961] 2 All E.R. 821).

A licence allowed the holder to use the vehicles for or in connection with any
trade or business carried on by him but not for carrying goods for hire or reward.
The vehicles were used to remove surplus excavated earth at an agreed price
from a building site for the builders (third parties). The vehicle-owner paid someone else to tip it. It was held that, as a large part of the payment was for the carriage of the rubbish, the vehicles were used to carry goods for reward, it being
immaterial that the property in the earth passed to the vehicle owners when it was
loaded (*Spittle v Thames Grit and Aggregates Ltd* [1937] 4 All E.R. 101). This
case was distinguished by a metropolitan magistrate in *Metropolitan Traffic
Commissioner v Alexander Thomson & Co* [1952] Jo.Crim.L. 194, where the

vehicle-owners were themselves also the contractors who did the work of laying cables as well as removing the surplus earth. He held that this was not carrying goods for hire or reward but was use in connection with the company's trade or business and was covered by their restricted licence. The prosecution did not appeal by case stated.

13.51   A firm of sand and gravel merchants excavating those materials from a pit were required by a planning condition to fill up the parts excavated. To do this, they took rubbish from a building site, the builder paying them 8s. 6d. per cubic yard of rubbish. The House of Lords held that, by virtue of s.164(5)(a) of the Road Traffic Act 1960, the rubbish was being used in the course of the sand merchant's business and was not being carried for reward (*Hammond v Hall and Ham River Ltd* [1965] 2 All E.R. 811, overruling *Corbett v Barham* [1965] 1 W.L.R. 187).

A lorry owner went from *C* to *B* in Ireland to borrow some planks. The plank owner agreed to lend them but said they were at *F* and asked the lorry owner, when bringing them to *C*, to take some scaffolding for him at the same time. The lorry owner, when charged with carrying the scaffolding "for reward", pleaded that he did so merely to oblige and he was found not guilty (*Att Gen (Holland) v Hurley* [1960] Jo.Crim.L. 59, where conflicting views are discussed). In *Stewart v McFadyen* 1958 S.L.T.(Sh.) 7 it was held that a licence to carry building materials included granite chips for road making, as being road building materials. A stipendiary magistrate acquitted a coal merchant who had loaded his vehicle with scrap iron to see if it was likely in the future to be fit for use for carrying coal ([1958] Crim. L.R. 693).

13.52   An incorporated society, consisting of miners at one colliery, delivering coal to one of its members at a charge to be deducted from his wages, uses the vehicle for hire or reward; *aliter* where it is an unincorporated society delivering to a member (*Wurzal v Houghton Main Home Delivery Service Ltd* [1936] 2 All E.R. 311).

A reference to "hire and reward" in relation to the carriage of passengers may assist. See §§ 13.130–3.

Conditions attached to licences

13.53   By s.22(1) of the 1995 Act conditions as to notifying certain matters may be attached to an operator's licence. By s.22(2) certain conditions must be attached to a standard licence. Section 22(6) makes it an offence for any person to contravene any condition attached under s.22 to a licence of which he is the holder.

The conditions which a traffic commissioner may attach under s.22(1) may require the holder to inform him:

    (a) of any change, of a kind specified in the conditions, in the organisation, management or ownership of the trade or business in the course of which vehicles are used under the licence;

    (b) where the holder of a licence is a company, of any change, or of any change of a kind so specified, in the persons holding shares in the company;

    (c) of any other event of a kind so specified affecting the holder of the licence which is relevant to the exercise of any powers of the traffic commissioner in relation to the licence.

By s.22(2), it is obligatory on the traffic commissioner on the issue of a stan- **13.54** dard operator's licence to attach conditions requiring the licence-holder to inform the commissioner of any event which could affect the holder of the licence satisfying the requirements of good repute, appropriate financial standing and professional competence and to notify any similar event affecting the transport manager (save as to appropriate financial standing). In the case of the transport manager the reference to professional competence is to anything relied on by him to satisfy that requirement. The notification must be within 28 days of the event or, in the case of a transport manager, within 28 days of the event coming to the knowledge of the licence-holder. A refusal to renew a standard national operator's licence on the grounds of relevant previous convictions and a failure to notify them within 28 days was upheld by the Transport Tribunal in *Batch (trading as AJB Motor Services) v Hampshire Constabulary* (1988) Appeal 1988 No.Z 4.

The duty only refers to the licence-holder and only concerns events affecting him and the transport manager and not other directors or employees, unless the happening is such as to reflect on the holder or transport manager himself. The duty on the face of it extends to the notification of convictions for dishonesty and relevant road traffic and transport convictions.

In the case of a company, it is not necessary for the holder to notify a share- **13.55** holding change unless the control of the company passes (s.22(4)). The exact meaning of a change in control is defined for this purpose by s.22(5).

Note that by s.5(8) a motor vehicle can be specified in only one licence. Semble if two licences are issued for one vehicle, the second one may be void and any conditions attached to the second one issued in point of time may be void also, so that it may not be an offence to fail to comply with a condition of the second one.

As well as under s.22 (notifications), there is power to attach conditions to an operator's licence to secure road safety (s.21) and as to the use of operating centres (s.23 and reg.14 of the 1995 Regulations).

Operating centres

Sections 7 and 23 of the 1995 Act and Pt IV of the 1995 Regulations set out **13.56** the provisions for operating centres. "Operating centre" in relation to any vehicle means the base or centre at which the vehicle is normally kept, and references to an operating centre of the holder of an operator's licence are references to any place which is an operating centre for vehicles used under the licence (s.7(3)). The base or centre at which the vehicle is normally kept covers where the vehicle is normally parked when not being driven as well as where the vehicle is to be parked and maintained. The control of operating centres is governed by ss.21 and 23. A person who uses (see Chapter 1) a place as an operating centre for authorised vehicles under an operator's licence which is not specified in the licence commits an offence which carries a maximum fine of level 4 (s.7(2)). It is necessary to advertise applications in the period 21 days before the date of application to 21 days after (s.11). There is provision for objections. There is power to attach conditions (ss.21 and 23). Maintenance might well affect the suitability and the environmental factors. It is possible for a condition to be attached that no routine maintenance or servicing should be carried out at the centre.

Environmental control

Section 23(6) of the 1995 Act makes it an offence for any person to contravene **13.57** any condition attached under s.23 to a licence of which he is the holder. The conditions which may be attached to the use of an operating centre are set out in s.23(2) and reg.14 of the 1995 Regulations.

They are conditions regulating:

(a) the number, type and size of authorised vehicles which may at any one time be at any operating centre of the holder of the licence in the area of the traffic commissioner for the purposes of maintenance and parking;

(b) the parking arrangements to be provided for authorised vehicles at or in the vicinity of every such operating centre;

(c) the time between which there may be carried out at every such operating centre any maintenance or movement of any authorised vehicle and the times at which any equipment may be used for any such maintenance or movement; and

(d) the means of ingress to and egress from every such operating centre for any authorised vehicle.

In *W.R. Atkinson (Transport) Ltd* (1987) Appeal 1987 No.X 30, the Transport Tribunal held that a condition prohibiting traversing a road at particular times was ultra vires. The Transport Tribunal substituted a condition as to the means of ingress and egress at a particular times.

13.58   The power of the traffic commissioner to impose conditions on the grant of an operator's licence under s.23 is restricted to conditions relating to vehicles authorised under the licence: *C Smith (trading as A1 Demolition)* (1968) Appeal 1986 No.X 1. In the case cited, the Transport Tribunal also stated that the power to impose conditions regulating inter alia the number of vehicles at an operating centre did not empower the traffic commissioner to attach conditions regulating the number of vehicles in the vicinity of the operating centre at any one time. The Transport Tribunal further stated in that case that it was wrong in principle for a traffic commissioner to impose an obligation on an operator to negotiate parking arrangements with the local planning authority.

A traffic commissioner may refuse a licence if he thinks that the parking of vehicles under the licence would cause adverse effects on the environmental conditions in the vicinity of the operating centre (see s.14(2)). In this context, the term "parking" applies only to vehicles which are stationary after the necessary manoeuvres to arrange them in position have been completed (*D. & A. Transport Ltd v Lancashire CC* (1968) Appeal 1985 No.W 23). This does not extend to requiring the operator to plant a screen to "hide" the operating centre: *Conwy County Borough Council v Murphy* (1998) Appeal 1998 No.K 13, Transport Tribunal.

Exemptions

13.59   By s.2(2) of the 1995 Act an operator's licence is not required in cases specified in the regulations for the use of a "small goods vehicle" or for the use of a goods vehicle for international haulage by a haulier established in a Member State or in Northern Ireland but not established in the United Kingdom/Great Britain. "Small goods vehicle" is defined in Sch.1 to the 1995 Act as being, in the case of a lone vehicle without a trailer, one with a plated (i.e. laden) weight of 3.5 tonnes or less or, if it has no plated weight, with an unladen weight of 1,525kg or less; see Sch.1 para.5 as to the term "relevant plated weight" and Sch.1 para.4 as to the definition of "small goods vehicle" in relation to an articulated vehicle or Sch.1 para.3 for a goods vehicle linked with a trailer or trailers. Basically for the 3.5 tonnes or 1,525kg limits to apply, the aggregate weight of all the vehicles and trailers in a vehicle combination must be below that limit (excluding any small trailer) but for articulated vehicles only the aggregate weight of the combination (i.e. the drawing vehicle and superimposed trailer) must be below that limit, and other drawn trailers are not taken into account. Under reg.33 and Sch.3 para.24 to the 1995 Regulations, a vehicle first used before January 1, 1977 which has an unladen weight not exceeding 1,525kg, and for which the maximum gross weight on the Construction and Use Regulations exceeds 3.5 tonnes but does not exceed 3.5 tons, is exempt from the requirement of an operator's licence.

Regulation 33 of the 1995 Regulations, together with Sch.3, exempts a further 28 classes of vehicle from the necessity of obtaining operators' licences. These include dual-purpose vehicles (as defined in reg.3(2) of the Road Vehicles (Construction and Use) Regulations 1986), farm and forestry haulage tractors, etc., vehicles used for police, fire brigade or, in England and Wales, fire and rescue authority, or ambulance purposes, showmen's goods vehicles and trailers drawn thereby and vehicles used for the purposes of funerals. In this context "showmen's goods vehicle" means a vehicle as defined in s.62(1) of the Vehicle Excise and Registration Act 1994 (1995 Regulations Sch.5 Pt I para.24 and reg.3(2)). Clearly use for private purposes would not mean that an operator's licence would be required. See further "Showmen's vehicles" at § 12.19; in *Bowra v Dann Catering Co Ltd* noted there, convictions for both no operator's licence and under-payment of vehicle excise duty were directed and in *Creek v Fossett* also noted there, a conviction for no goods vehicle operator's licence was again directed.

One of the exemptions in Sch.3 to the 1995 Regulations is for any vehicle **13.60** constructed or adapted primarily for the carriage of passengers and their effects, and any trailer drawn by it, while being so used (no.4). The exemption would not therefore apply if the vehicle were being used for goods other than the passengers' effects. Another exception exists for recovery vehicles (no.27). "Recovery vehicle" has the same meaning as in Pt V of Sch.1 to the Vehicle Excise and Registration Act 1994, as amended. A goods vehicle not within the recovery vehicle definition may therefore become subject to the goods vehicle operators' licensing requirements even though it is used for recovery purposes. The meaning of "recovery vehicle" was considered in *Vehicle Inspectorate v Richard Read Transport Ltd* [1998] R.T.R. 288. The alleged offence took place in 1994 and the relevant legislation has subsequently been amended by two Finance Acts. However, the case re-emphasises the strictness of the limits of the definitions leading to exemption and also discounts an argument that subsidiary use as a recovery vehicle was sufficient. The primary purpose of this particular vehicle was as a workshop on wheels not to lift a disabled vehicle, even though, from time to time, the vehicle may have been used for that purpose.

There is an exemption for vehicles proceeding to or from a testing station established under s.45 of the 1988 Act, for examination under that section, provided that the only load carried is a load required for the purposes of the examination, and is being carried at the request of the Secretary of State (no.29).

Another exemption is for vehicles being used for snow clearing, or for the **13.61** distribution of grit, salt or other materials on frosted, ice-bound or snow-covered roads or for going to or from the place where the vehicle is to be used for this purpose or for other directly connected purposes (no.28). This exemption now applies to any vehicle used for the purpose and not merely to local authority vehicles. The farm or forestry tractor haulage exemption includes hauling contrivances for clearing snow (Sch.3 Pt II). The registered keeper may also haul within 15 miles of the farm or forestry estate occupied by him agricultural or woodland produce of that farm or estate, and material to be spread on roads to deal with frost, ice or snow. This last exemption, while more clearly covering preparatory work, appears to overlap with the more general bad weather exemption described above which has no distance limit. In the 1995 Regulations, "farm" includes a "market garden" (reg.3(2)). Tractors registered in the names of local authorities are additionally exempt when hauling soil for landscaping or similar works and mowing machines.

Exemption no.26 relates to a vehicle being held ready for use in an emergency by an undertaking for the supply of water, electricity, gas or telephone services. The extent of this exemption was considered in *Wing v T.D. & C. Kelly Ltd* [1998] R.T.R. 297. "Ready for use in an emergency" connoted a vehicle being held by its owners for the purpose of use in an emergency. The exemption applied only to one of the specified undertakings and not, presumably, to others who may be utilised by those undertakings.

13.62   Another of the exemptions is for vehicles fitted with a machine, appliance, apparatus or other contrivance which is a permanent or essentially permanent fixture, provided that the only goods carried on the vehicle are such as are required for use in connection with it or the running of the vehicle or to be mixed by the machine, etc., for certain purposes or which have been swept up from the road surface (no.15).

In *North West Traffic Area Licensing Authority v Post Office* [1982] R.T.R. 304, the Post Office used a goods vehicle with a machine for drilling telephone pole holes. The justices found that the vehicle carried in addition goods for erecting the poles, a kettle and the poles themselves. The Divisional Court directed a conviction. The telegraph poles were not for use in connection with the machine but for the operation in which the machine was going to be used. They were not therefore within the exemption proviso and an operator's licence was required. The court made no comment about the kettle.

13.63   The decision was followed in *British Gypsum Ltd v Corner* [1982] R.T.R. 308. There the vehicle carried a water bowser and pipes for use in connection with a drill. An operator's licence was required as the drill was mounted on another vehicle.

These cases were followed in *DPP v Scott Greenham* [1988] R.T.R. 426 where a tractor unit and semi-trailer were fitted out permanently to carry on the trailer either a crane jib or the crane counterweights. These would be put together from that and another vehicle to operate from the vehicles as a crane at the site. Neither vehicle could operate in isolation. It was held that these were not goods required in connection with any permanent fixture on the trailer.

13.64   A different conclusion was reached in *DPP v Howard* [1991] R.T.R. 49. The defendant was using a cement mixer vehicle also carrying sand and cement to be mixed on site. The Divisional Court held that the goods in this case were processed by the machine and used in connection with it and no operator's licence was needed.

A temporary exemption may be granted by the traffic commissioner for an emergency or temporary need for national transport operations in favour of a person engaged exclusively in those operations if they have only a minor impact on the transport market because of the nature of the goods carried or the short distance (1995 Act s.4).

Exclusions or modifications for certain foreign and Northern Ireland vehicles

Where a goods vehicle is being used for international carriage by a haulier   **13.65**
established in an EU Member State other than the United Kingdom but not established in the United Kingdom or for international carriage by a haulier established in Northern Ireland but not established in Great Britain, the requirement to have an operator's licence is excluded (1995 Act s.2(2)). In effect therefore the operator licensing requirements and the Temporary Use in Great Britain Regulations modifications (see below) are excluded for these goods vehicles of EU Member States (other than British vehicles) when used for international carriage, and in particular when used in the United Kingdom. In this context, international carriage has the same meaning as in Regulation (EEC) 881/92 art.2, set out in Vol.2. International carriage by these EU vehicles will instead be subject to the international haulage authorisation system dealt with later in this chapter.

The Goods Vehicles (Licensing of Operators) (Temporary Use in Great Britain) Regulations 1996 (SI 1996/2186) modify the relevant sections of the 1995 Act in respect of certain other foreign and Northern Ireland goods vehicles. Regulation 3 defines a "foreign goods vehicle" as a goods vehicle:

"(a) which is operated by a person who is not established in the United Kingdom and has been brought temporarily into Great Britain;

(b) which is not being used for international carriage by a haulier established in a Member State other than the United Kingdom;

(c) which is engaged in carrying goods by road on a journey some part of which has taken place, or will take place, outside the United Kingdom; and

(d) which, except in the case of use under a Community cabotage authorisation, is not used at any time during the said journey for the carriage of goods loaded at one place in the United Kingdom and delivered at another place in the United Kingdom."

The word "temporarily" was construed as "casually". If the vehicle is brought   **13.66**
regularly although intermittently, into Great Britain it is not "temporarily" in Great Britain (*BRS v Wurzal* [1971] 3 All E.R. 480). The regulations make special provision for foreign goods vehicles used for the carriage of goods in Albanian, Austrian, Bulgarian, Channel Islands, Cypriot, Czech, Estonian, Faroese, Hungarian, Jordanian, Latvian, Lithuanian, Manx, Moroccan, Polish, Roumania, Slovak, former Soviet Union, Swiss, Tunisian, Turkish, Ukrainian, Macedonian, Moldovan, Georgian, Croatian and Slovenian goods vehicles by dispensing with the need for them to have operators' licences, substituting a requirement in certain circumstances for the carrying of other permits or documents, and modifying (as set out in various Schedules to the regulations) various sections of the 1995 Act. The regulations also provide for alterations to the 1995 Regulations in relation to foreign goods vehicles temporarily in Great Britain and fulfilling the terms of the

definition and make special provisions for the goods vehicles of Northern Ireland hauliers.

In *Romantiek Transport BVBA v Vehicle and Operator Services Agency* [2008] EWCA Civ 534; *The Times*, June 3, 2008, the Court of Appeal held that the detention of goods vehicles owned by Belgian companies on the basis that they were being used without an operator's licence was lawful because their use in the United Kingdom was not temporary. Their activity was not cabotage, meaning that the exemption of the need for an operator's licence set out in the Goods Vehicles (Licensing of Operators) Regulations 1995 Sch.3 para.23 did not apply. Various operators which were based in Belgium had appeared to be operating vehicles and trailers in the United Kingdom without a valid British operator's licence. Following VOSA's impounding of a number of vehicles and trailers, the applicants applied to the traffic commissioner for the return of those vehicles and trailers under the Goods Vehicles (Enforcement Powers) Regulations 2001 (SI 2001/3981) (see § 13.71 below) on the basis that the operation was exempt from a domestic licence since it constituted cabotage. The traffic commissioner refused to return the vehicles and trailers in question and the Transport Tribunal agreed, on appeal, that the vehicles should not be returned to the applicants. The Court of Appeal ruled that host Member States were entitled to impose regulations in relation to cabotage transport operations in that state, and penalties could be imposed on non-resident carriers who had committed infringements. Where there was no cabotage operation, the relevant Regulation became inapplicable. Paragraph 23 of Sch.3 could not apply to exempt a road haulier from the need for an operator's licence in such circumstances. In terms of the detention of the vehicles and trailers in question, the relevant contravention of s.2 of the Goods Vehicles (Licensing of Operators) Act 1995 was the absence of a licence.

GOODS VEHICLE OPERATORS' LICENCES: PROCEEDINGS AND PENALTIES

Offences of breaches of conditions

13.67   Offences under s.21 (road safety conditions), s.22 (notification conditions) and s.23 (environment conditions) can be committed only by the holder of an operator's licence or by a person who aids and abets him. Some knowledge of the fact that the condition is being breached or possibly a wilful shutting of eyes to it is generally needed to prove aiding and abetting.

As the licence-holder will almost always know of the matters to be notified, when they arise, it seems unnecessary to discuss whether his liability is absolute or not; see § 2.51 as to whether this would be a continuing offence.

Proceedings and penalties: generally

13.68   The following offences carry a maximum fine of level 4: use of a goods vehicle contrary to s.2 of the Goods Vehicles (Licensing of Operators) Act 1995 without an operator's licence (s.2(5)) (maximum level 5 for offences committed on or after February 1, 2001); breach of the conditions of an operator's licence (ss.21–23), breach of the requirements as to the maximum number of vehicles (s.6), using as an operating centre a place other than one specified in an operator's licence (s.7), knowing failure to notify a notifiable conviction arising between the dates of application and determination of an application for an operator's licence (s.9) and applying for an operator's licence whilst disqualified from holding one (s.28(2)). Regulations 23(3), 23(4), 25, 26, 27(1), 27(3), 28(1)–(4), and 30(6) of the 1995 Regulations all carry a maximum fine of level 1 by s.57(9) of the 1995 Act. Using a goods vehicle to carry goods for hire or reward under a restricted licence or using a goods vehicle for carrying goods for hire or reward on international transport operations under a standard licence restricted to national operations both carry a maximum fine of £500 (s.3(6) and (7)).

Section 26 of the 1995 Act empowers the licensing authority to revoke, suspend, or curtail an operator's licence.

13.69 In deciding how to use its powers to suspend an operator's licence, a licensing authority may properly take into account the need for a deterrent message to be given to other operators. In *Yuill v Dodds Ltd* (1993) Appeal 1993 No.E14, Transport Tribunal, the operator of goods vehicles had been called to a public inquiry following a number of convictions relating to false records and breach of drivers' hours provisions. The inquiry did not lead to any adverse finding in relation to the good repute of the operator, but the licence was suspended for one week (leading to the possible loss to the operator of some £30,000 in contracts), the licensing authority (now traffic commissioner) declaring that the decision was in part a deterrent message to other operators. The appeal on this point was dismissed. The authority had properly sought to counter the temptation for hard-pressed contractors to accept work from powerful customers on terms set by those customers when professional experience informed the contractors that those terms could not be lawfully met.

Any operator's licence obtained by a disqualified person in breach of the disqualification is of no effect and a person who applies for or who obtains a licence in breach of an order of disqualification commits an offence punishable on summary conviction by a fine of level 4 (s.28(2)).

13.70 The time-limit for all offences under the 1995 Act and 1995 Regulations is six months. The court has no power to endorse or disqualify or to revoke, suspend or curtail the operator's licence, but a relevant conviction may be brought to the attention of the licensing authority.

Regulation-making power has been granted to allow for the detention, removal and disposal of goods vehicles where s.2 of the 1995 Act appears to have been contravened (1995 Act Sch.1A as inserted by the Transport Act 2000 s.262).

13.71 The Goods Vehicles (Enforcement Powers) Regulations 2001 (SI 2001/3981) have been made. Regulation 3 gives to an "authorised person" power to detain a vehicle believed to be being used in contravention of s.2 of the 1995 Act. Where a vehicle has been detained, an immobilisation device may be fixed to it which must be accompanied by an "immobilisation notice" warning that the device has been fixed. It is an offence (summary conviction: maximum penalty a fine up to level 2) to remove or interfere with the notice or (fine to level 3) to remove or to attempt to remove the device: reg.6. It is also an offence (fine to level 3) to intentionally obstruct an authorised person exercising his powers under reg.3 or reg.8 (removal and delivery of property detained). The authorised person may release the vehicle from the immobilisation device. If a person makes a declaration in order to secure the return of the vehicle that the vehicle was not being used (or had not been used) in contravention of s.2 of the 1995 Act and the person knows the declaration to be false or to be misleading in a significant way, then an "either way" offence is committed under reg.21 punishable on indictment by two years' imprisonment or a fine or both and on summary conviction to a fine up to level 5. If the authorised person does not release the vehicle, an application for release can be made by the owner of the vehicle to a traffic commissioner: reg.10. An appeal from that decision can be made to the Transport Tribunal: reg.13. However, where there is a dispute arising from the return or disposal of the contents of a vehicle in such circumstances or from the application of the proceeds of the sale of a vehicle or its contents, the claimant may apply in writing to the Secretary of State for a determination. An appeal against that determination can be made to the "appropriate court" which is the magistrates' court or the sheriff court for the local justice area or sheriffdom in which the claimant resides (if an individual) or where the principal or last known place of business is situated (in the case of a partnership) or where the registered or principal office is situated (in the case of an incorporated or unincorporated body): reg.19. The appeal must be lodged within 21 days of the claimant being notified by the Secretary of State of the rejection of his application or within or where 56 days have elapsed since the application was made and the claimant has not been notified of the outcome. If the grounds of appeal are established, the court will order the authorised person to pay to the claimant the amount due to him.

For a table of penalties, see § 13.72.

Goods vehicle operators' licences: penalties

Offence	Mode of trial	Section *	Imprisonment	Level of fine	Disqualification	Penalty points	Endorsement code	Sentencing guideline §
No GV operator's licence	Summary	s.2 1995 Act	—	4† 5‡	—	—	—	Fine band B Driver Fine band B Owner-driver Fine band C Owner-company
Breach of condition of operator's licence	Summary	ss.21–23 1995 Act	—	4	—	—	—	—
Using operator's centre for vehicles not specified in operator's licence	Summary	s.6 1995 Act	—	4	—	—	—	—
Restricted operator's licence improperly used for hire or reward	Summary	s.3(6) 1995 Act	—	£500	—	—	—	—

Offence	Mode of trial	Section *	Imprisonment	Level of fine	Disqualification	Penalty points	Endorsement code	Sentencing guideline §
Standard operator's licence limited to national operations improperly used for hire or reward on international transport	Summary	s.3(7) 1995 Act	—	£500	—	—	—	—
Other regulations	Summary	regs 23(3), 23(4), 25, 26, 27(1), 27(3) 28(1)–(4), 30(6), 1995 Act	—	1	—	—	—	—

* Goods Vehicles (Licensing of Operators) Act 1995 or Goods Vehicles (Licensing of Operators) Regulations 1995.

† If offence committed before February 1, 2001.

‡ If offence committed on or after February 1, 2001.

§ **Note**: Fine bands "A", "B" and "C" represent respectively 50%, 100% and 150% of relevant weekly income. A timely guilty plea should attract a discount. See Appendix 3.

CARRIAGE OF GOODS, ETC.

Carriage of controlled waste

The unsightly practice of unauthorised "fly-tipping" of waste from vehicles **13.73** has led to limited control through registration with local authorities. The Control of Pollution (Amendment) Act 1989, as amended, makes it an offence by s.1 punishable with a fine of level 5 for a person who is not a registered carrier to transport controlled waste to or from any place in Great Britain in the course of any business of his or otherwise with a view to profit. The registration is of the carrier not of the vehicle. Thus, where a vehicle operated by an unregistered company was used under the direction and authority of a registered carrier, that complied with the requirements of the 1989 Act: *Cosmick Transport v Bedfordshire County Council* [1997] R.T.R. 132. The 1989 Act provides that a magistrate may on sworn information in writing order the seizure of a vehicle (s.6) and there are further provisions as to its subsequent disposal.

The Carriage of Dangerous Goods and Use of Transportable Pressure Equipment Regulations 2007 (SI 2007/1573) impose requirements and prohibitions in relation to the carriage of goods by road or rail and the use of transportable pressure equipment. The regulations apply three European directives and also make other provisions. As far as road transport is concerned, the regulations apply Directive 94/55/EC on the approximation of the laws of Member States with regard to the transport of dangerous goods by road, as amended. The directive applies the European Agreement concerning the international carriage of dangerous goods by road (ADR) signed at Geneva on September 30, 1957, as amended. The current edition of the ADR became applicable as from January 1, 2009 for international transport, with a six-month transitional period, and on July 1, 2009 for domestic traffic for Member States of the European Union. This European Agreement restates the aim of increasing the safety of the international transport of dangerous goods by road. Dangerous goods are classified according to their physical and chemical properties. All parts of the agreement are fully updated. The 2007 Regulations also apply Directive 1999/36/EC concerning transportable pressure equipment, as amended. The regulations consolidate existing legislation and abolish many of the previous regulations which governed control of waste.

The Controlled Waste (Registration of Carriers and Seizure of Vehicles) **13.74** Regulations 1991 (SI 1991/1624) set out the procedure for registration. Registration may be revoked for prescribed convictions, if it also seems undesirable for the carrier to continue to be registered. The Act gives rights of appeal to the Secretary of State against refusal or revocation of registration and also where consideration of an application is delayed (see s.4 for the full wording).

The Controlled Waste Regulations 1992 (SI 1992/588) define various forms of waste including what is and what is not household waste. Seaweed was held not to be controlled waste within the meaning of s.3(2) of the Control of Pollution Act 1974: *Thanet DC v Kent County Council, The Times*, March 15, 1993.

The European Court of Justice has confirmed that the system of supervision and control over waste is intended to cover all objects and substances discarded by their owners even if they have a commercial value and are collected on a commercial basis for recycling, reclamation or re-use: Case C–304/94 *Criminal proceedings against Tombesi* [1997] All E.R. (E.C.) 639.

Regulation (EEC) 259/93, as amended, regulates the shipment of waste materi- **13.75** als for recovery. Waste materials are assigned to a green, amber or red list depending on the level of environmental problem caused. Differing degrees of regulatory control are assigned to the different lists. The impact of carrying a mixture of goods all of which fell within the green list was considered by the High Court in *R. v Environment Agency Ex p. Dockgrange Ltd* [1997] Env.L.R. 575.

The Environment Agency had sought to apply the more stringent red list, but the court emphasised the need for more flexibility, consistent with the objects of Regulation (EEC) 259/93 to organise the supervision and control of shipments of waste so as to preserve, protect and improve the quality of the environment.

13.76   A person is not guilty of an offence where the controlled waste is transported for certain imports and exports or within the same premises (s.1(2)).

Where a person appears to them to be or to have been engaged in transporting controlled waste, s.5 gives authorised officers and constables certain powers of stopping the person, requiring the production of the authority for transportation, searching the relevant vehicle, testing and sampling. This section gives no power to anyone save a constable in uniform to stop a vehicle on a road (s.5(2)). Powers to obtain entry and information are given by s.7.

Offences

13.77   In addition to the principal offence under s.1 of the 1989 Act of transporting without being registered, there are further offences: the intentional obstruction of any authorised officer or a constable in exercising any power under a s.6 seizure warrant (s.6(9)); a similar intentional obstruction when s.5 powers are being exercised (s.5(4)(a) and (7)); failing without reasonable excuse to comply with any requirement under the regulations to provide information to the Secretary of State or the authority (s.7(3)(a) and (4)), or, in complying, providing information known to be false in a material particular or recklessly providing information false in a material particular (s.7(3)(b) and (4)). If a person fails without reasonable excuse to comply with a requirement imposed in the exercise of a s.5(1) power, he commits an offence contrary to s.5(4)(b) and (7), but he is only guilty if it is shown that the waste was controlled waste and that he did transport it to or from a place in Great Britain (s.5(5)).

Exemptions

13.78   There are certain exemptions from registration in reg.2. Exemptions include waste collection, disposal and regulation authorities for the purpose of Pt II of the Environmental Protection Act 1990, certain forms of disposal at sea, charities and certain voluntary organisations; also exempt are producers of the controlled waste in question except where it is building or demolition waste which is defined as waste arising from works of construction or demolition including waste from preparatory work. It is submitted that in any event a DIY producer of waste working on his own home would not normally be working in the course of business or even with a view to profit, if he transported his own waste, even though the home improvement incidentally enhanced the value of his property.

Defences

13.79   There are defences in s.1(4) where the waste was transported in an emergency, notice of which was given as soon as practicable afterwards to the authority in whose area the emergency occurred; where the defendant neither knew nor had reasonable grounds for suspecting that it was controlled waste and took all reasonable steps for ascertaining whether it was such waste, or where he acted under instructions from his employer. The burden of proving these defences will be on the defendant on the balance of probabilities. What is meant by an "emergency" is defined in s.1(6). The wording of s.1(4) is such that it may be difficult for a defendant to establish the defence of ignorance. The defence of obedience to an employer's instructions may be more commonly put forward. The defendant will have to establish the instruction and to show this, he may have to set out in some detail his relationship with his employer.

Where the expression "without reasonable excuse" is used in s.5(4)(b) and s.7(3)(a), the burden of proving this rests on the defendant. This is specifically enacted for Scottish proceedings as well as in England and Wales. The burden of proof will be on the balance of probabilities.

Carriage of controlled waste: proceedings and penalties

Proceedings can be instituted against directors, managers, etc., in appropriate cases (s.7(6)) and against third parties when the offence is due to their act or default (s.7(5)). **13.80**

The maximum penalties for offences contrary to ss.1 (unregistered carriage of controlled waste), 5(4)(b) and (7) (failing to comply with s.5 requirement), 5(4)(a) and (7) (intentional obstruction where s.5 power being exercised), 6(9) (seizure warrant—intentional obstruction), 7(3)(a) and (4) (failing to provide information under regulations), 7(3)(b) and (4) (providing false information) are in each case a fine of level 5. They are triable summarily only.

Conveyance of dangerous substances generally

National provisions implementing Directive 94/55/EC on the approximation of national laws on the transport of dangerous goods by road were to be enacted and in force by January 1, 1997 (art.10(1)). On that date, Directive 89/684/EEC on vocational training for drivers carrying dangerous goods by road was to be repealed, subject to savings for certificates already issued (art.11). Effect was given to this directive by the Road Traffic (Training of Drivers of Vehicles Carrying Dangerous Goods) Regulations 1992 (SI 1992/744). The current provisions with regard to driver training are contained in reg.38 of the Carriage of Dangerous Goods and Use of Transportable Pressure Equipment Regulations 2007 (SI 2007/1573). **13.81**

Directive 94/55/EC applies to the transport of dangerous goods by road both within and between Member States. Vehicles used by the armed forces are specifically excluded from the scope of the directive (art.1(1)) as are certain matters where Member States' laws respect EC law (art.1(2)). Each state may authorise the transport by road within its boundaries of dangerous goods duly classified, packaged and labelled for maritime or air transport (art.6(1)). It may also retain existing laws (subject to compatibility) relating to vehicles registered with its own authorities and operating within its boundaries (art.4). Certain other national laws (other than those relating to safety during transport) may also be retained on certain grounds (art.5(1)). Vehicles constructed before 1997 may be allowed to continue in use within the boundaries of the state where they are registered even if they do not comply with the directive, provided that they are maintained to the required standard (art.5(3)). Subject to art.6, dangerous goods must not be transported by road where prohibited by Annexes A and B to the directive (art.3(1)). Where such goods may be transported by road, conditions are imposed as to packing and labelling of the goods and as to the construction, equipment and proper use of the vehicles (art.3(2)).

13.82   Directive 95/50/EC harmonises checks on the transport of dangerous goods by road. It applies to dangerous goods transported by road within the territory of a Member State or entering it from a third country but does not apply to vehicles of the armed forces. It requires a proportion of consignments of dangerous goods to be subjected to random checks carried out at places where there is no danger to safety by reason of remedying faults or immobilising vehicles. Immobilisation may be effected in addition to other penalties available. Subject to provisions on market access, if the transport complies with the ADR, vehicles from non-Member States will be permitted to carry dangerous goods within the EU on international journeys.

The Carriage of Dangerous Goods and Use of Transportable Pressure Equipment Regulations 2007 consolidated the previous regulations and apply to the transport of dangerous goods by road.

13.83   The 2007 Regulations impose requirements contained within ADR with regard to interpretation (reg.2), their application (reg.8), exceptions (regs 9–13) and derogations (regs 14–34). The regulations implement Council Directive 94/55/EC as adapted to technical progress for the sixth time by Commission Directive 2006/89/EC.

Part 4 of the 2007 Regulations imposes the requirements of Directive 1999/36/EC with regard to placing transportable pressure equipment on the market and using it at work (regs 72–74), reassessing the conformity of existing transportable pressure equipment (reg.75), periodic inspection (reg.76), notified and approved bodies for inspecting transportable equipment (regs 77 and 78) and conformity marking (reg.80).

13.84   It is an offence to contravene regulations made under the Health and Safety at Work, etc. Act 1974. Under the 2007 Regulations, the responsibility for compliance is placed in the person who is conducting an international transport operation for the carriage of goods, including carriage, by more than one mode of transport, from consignor to consignee where that carriage takes place in more than one state.

The requirement for hazard warning panels and labels with signs indicating the type of danger are perhaps the most familiar aspects of the 2007 Regulations and are contained in Sch.7.

13.85   Offences are not limited to road journeys; provided it is for the purpose of carriage by road, it is immaterial whether or not the vehicle is on a road (as defined in s.192 of the Road Traffic Act 1988) because for the purpose of carriage by road, both the road tanker and the tank container carried on a vehicle, if loaded empty, are deemed to be engaged in the carriage from the time of commencement of loading with the dangerous goods. If the tank container is pre-loaded with the dangerous goods before being placed on the vehicle, it is deemed to be engaged in the carriage when the tank container is placed on the vehicle for the purpose of the carriage. The carriage is deemed to last until the time of the removal of the tank container or alternatively the time the road tanker or tank container has been so cleaned or purged that any of the goods or any vapour which remains therein is not sufficient to create a risk to the health or safety of any person (see Directive 94/55/EC, as applied by the 2007 Regulations).

Definitions are contained in reg.2 of the 2007 Regulations and Annex A of Directive 94/55/EC.

In summary, dangerous goods must not be consigned for carriage by road un- **13.86** less the goods have been classified in accordance with any general requirements applicable to the goods in question, in accordance with any class specific requirements applicable to the goods in question, or using the test methods applicable to the goods in question as set out in the ADR.

With regard to the use of packaging, there is an obligation to ensure that goods are packed in accordance with any general packing provisions, packing instructions, special packing provisions, or special packing provisions as set out in ADR in relation to the carriage of goods by road (2007 Regulations reg.51).

Defences and exemptions

Regulations 35–37 of the 2007 Regulations provide for circumstances when **13.87** exemptions do not apply.

Defences are provided in reg.93. In any proceedings for an offence for contravention of any of the provisions of the 2007 Regulations, it shall be a defence for the person charged to prove that (a) the commission of the offence was due to the act or default of another person, not being one of his employees and (b) he took all reasonable precautions and exercised all due diligence to avoid the commission of the offence.

The defence is not available without leave of the court unless the person charged has served on the prosecutor a notice in writing giving such information identifying or assisting the identification of the other person, as was then in his possession, at least seven days before the court proceeds to hear mode of trial (or, in Scotland, before the trial).

Carriage of dangerous goods: training

Regulation 38 of the 2007 Regulations requires a person involved in the car- **13.88** riage of goods by road to ensure that he and those of his employees whose responsibilities are concerned with carriage, receive training which complies with and is documented in accordance with the requirement of ADR. There is an obligation upon any carrier carrying dangerous goods by road to ensure that drivers receive training which complies with the ADR which is relevant to the goods, person, and type of vehicle in question, including any special training required by ADR. The appropriate certificate must be obtained by the driver concerned.

Conveyance of dangerous substances: carriage of explosives

The carriage of explosives comes within the jurisdiction of the 2007 **13.89** Regulations. Special provisions apply to the armed forces (reg.10).

Conveyance of dangerous substances: radioactive material

The Radioactive Material (Road Transport) Act 1991 enables the Secretary of **13.90** State to make regulations under s.2 of that Act regarding the road transport of radioactive material, and also ancillary matters. The Radioactive Material (Road

Transport) (Definition of Radioactive Material) Order 2002 (SI 2002/1092) lowers the level of activity required to fall within the definition of "radioactive material" thus widening that definition.

The Radioactive Material (Road Transport) Regulations 2002 (SI 2002/1093) give effect to an international agreement on the level of control of the radiation, criticality and thermal hazards associated with the transport of radioactive material. Subject to specified exceptions (reg.5), the regulations apply to the transport of a consignment where a journey by road starts after the regulations come into force and is either a Great Britain journey, an ADR journey or a non-ADR journey (as defined). The regulations control the packaging and labelling of consignments, the need to take proper care and the need to have a proper programme of quality assurance established and operating. Consignors and carriers are responsible for the acts and omissions of their employees and of any agents or other persons whose services they use to transport such material provided those persons are acting within the scope of their employment (reg.47). For liability for offences committed by a body corporate, see s.6(1) of the 1991 Act. Offences under the regulations are punishable on conviction on indictment by a fine and/or imprisonment for a term not exceeding two years or, on summary conviction, by a fine not exceeding the statutory maximum and/or imprisonment not exceeding two months.

Amendments to s.2 of the 1991 Act are made by s.57 of the Road Safety Act 2006 concerning the regulations for preventing injury or damage from transport by road of radioactive material. The amendments relate to the keeping and production of records, the provision of information, facilities and assistance (s.2(2)(d), (e) and (f)). Provision is also made for the imposition of requirements by examiners (s.2(3)(za)). At the time of writing (March 2009) no date had been fixed for the coming into force of these amendments.

13.91   Section 3 of the 1991 Act contains provisions allowing an inspector or examiner to prohibit the driving of the vehicle and at his discretion (under s.3(4)) to direct the vehicle's removal. Any person who contravenes a prohibition under s.3 or fails to comply with a direction under s.3(4) commits an offence contrary to s.3(8).

If an inspector is of the opinion that any person is failing or is likely to fail to comply with regulations made under s.2 which make provision for regulating the manufacture, or requiring the maintenance, of packaging components, he may serve a s.4 notice on that person. Any person who fails to comply with a s.4 notice commits an offence, contrary to s.4(3).

Section 5 gives inspectors and examiners certain powers to enter vehicles and, in the case of inspectors, premises, and allows magistrates on sworn information in writing to issue search warrants for vehicles and premises. Any person who intentionally obstructs any person exercising any s.5 power or warrant commits an offence. The need for the prosecution to establish the necessary intent should be noted.

Codes of practice, regulations etc.: use in evidence

13.92   The Health and Safety Commission previously published approved codes of practice, see the Approved Carriage List (Third Edition) and approved requirements. The Approved Carriage List is no longer published. Instead reference should be made to the Carriage of Dangerous Goods and Use of Transportable Pressure Equipment Regulations 2007, the ADR and to the *Dangerous Goods Emergency Action Code List 2005* (July 2005, TSO, ISBN 0113413041).

In *West Cumberland By Products Ltd v DPP* [1988] R.T.R. 391 the prosecution had examined what was then the approved code of practice to the earlier Dangerous Substances Regulations made in consultation between the Health and Safety Commission and the Secretary of State. The prosecution had found in the code matters on which it wished to rely but which it had not specified. The correct approach to the use of the code of practice in evidence was described by the Divisional Court. The provisions of the code were in the first instance only of an *evidential* nature. The code could not impose a *duty* on a party. A duty could only be specified in the regulations or the section. Subject to this the provisions of the code became good and complete *evidence* of an offence under the regulations or the section, unless the court was satisfied that a requirement or prohibition had been complied with by the defence otherwise than by way of the code.

Conveyance of dangerous substances: proceedings

For the procedure generally, reference should also be made to the Health and Safety at Work, etc., Act 1974 which contains a number of special provisions. **13.93**

Section 36 of that Act provides that where the commission by any person of an offence under any health and safety regulations or under the relevant statutes is due to the act or default of some other person, that other person shall be guilty of the offence and may be charged and convicted whether or not proceedings are taken against the first-mentioned person. The special provisions for enforcement in the 1974 Act include extended time-limits and restrictions on prosecution. Other items covered include venue, bodies corporate, evidence, remedial action and forfeiture and reference should be made to the specific wording.

Radioactive material: proceedings and penalties

Where an offence under the Radioactive Material (Road Transport) Act 1991 has been committed by a body corporate and is proved to have been committed with the consent or connivance of, or to be attributable to any neglect on the part of, any director, manager or secretary or other similar officer of the body corporate or any person who was purporting to act in any such capacity, he, as well as the body corporate, is deemed to be guilty of that offence and liable to be proceeded against and punished. **13.94**

Offences contrary to ss.2(4) (breach of regulations), 3(8) (breach of prohibition or direction) or 4(3) (breach of s.4 notice) are all "either way" offences punishable on indictment by two years' imprisonment or a fine or both and on summary conviction by two months' imprisonment or the statutory maximum fine or both.

The court by or before which a person is convicted of an offence under s.2(4) or 3(8) in respect of any radioactive material may order the material to be destroyed or disposed of and any expenses reasonably incurred in connection with the destruction or disposal to be defrayed by that person (s.6(4)). An offence of international obstruction contrary to s.5 carries a maximum fine of level 3. **13.95**

Conveyance of dangerous substances: penalties

The regulations are all made under the Health and Safety at Work, etc., Act **13.96**

1974. The offences are "either way" offences and the maximum penalty for a contravention is a fine of the statutory maximum on summary conviction and an unlimited fine on indictment (1974 Act s.33 and Sch.3A).

Concerns have been expressed that fines imposed by magistrates' courts for health and safety offences are too low and offences relating to the conveyance of dangerous substances are closely linked to health and safety matters. In *R. v Howe and Son (Engineers) Ltd* (1998) 163 J.P.359 the Court of Appeal sought to set out some helpful indicators whilst accepting that it was impossible to lay down a tariff or to relate the fines to turnover or net profit. It would often be helpful to assess how far short of the appropriate standard the defendant fell in failing to meet the "reasonably practicable" test. Generally, when death results it should be treated as an aggravating feature. Other aggravating features include a failure to heed warnings, deliberately profiting financially from failing to take necessary health and safety steps and specifically running a risk to save money. Mitigating features could include prompt admission of liability, a timely plea of guilty, taking remedial steps after the deficiencies came to notice, and a good safety record. Any fine should reflect the means of the offender (whether corporate or individual) but also needed to be large enough (where the defendant was a company) to bring home to both managers and shareholders the purpose of the legislation which is to create a safe environment.

International carriage

13.97   The various statutory provisions use expressions such as "international journeys", "international carriage" and "international operations" depending on the circumstances, sometimes with reference to particular countries. The meaning is also discussed at §§ 14.21–2 where the cases noted may be of assistance. Sometimes the statutory provision defines or indicates what is meant by "international". For example in Regulation (EEC) 881/92 international carriage is defined in detail in art.2. In summary, it covers international vehicle journeys starting or finishing in an EU Member State or passing through a Member State regardless of intervening countries, together with empty journeys in conjunction with such carriage.

International haulage authorisations/permits

13.98   International haulage authorisations and permits are governed by the Goods Vehicles (Community Authorisations) Regulations 1992 (SI 1992/3077) made under the European Communities Act 1972 s.2(2) and the International Road Haulage Permits Act 1975.

A Community authorisation is required within the EU for the international carriage of goods by road for hire or reward. The provisions of Regulation (EEC) 881/92 are *directly applied* by the 1992 Regulations for this purpose.

13.99   Any non-resident road haulage contractor who holds one of the Community authorisations under Regulation (EEC) 881/92 is, by Regulation (EEC) 3118/93, allowed to operate also, on a temporary basis and without quantitative restrictions, national road services for hire or reward (cabotage operations) in another Member State, without any need to have a registered office or other establishment in that State (arts 1(1) and 12(3)).

Regulations (EEC) 881/92 and (EEC) 3118/93 were amended by Regulation

(EC) 484/2002. Where goods may be carried by road only under a Community authorisation under Regulation (EEC) 881/92 or a cabotage authorisation under Regulation (EC) 3118/93, the driver will need to be attested.

All these cabotage transport operations must be undertaken (except where **13.100** otherwise provided by EC regulations) in accordance with the national operation requirements relating to rates and conditions of the transport contract, weights and dimensions of road vehicles, requirements as to the carriage of certain categories of goods (particularly dangerous goods and perishable foodstuffs, and live animals), driving and rest time and VAT on transport services (art.6(1)). Vehicles must meet the technical standards of construction and equipment for vehicles used for international transport (art.6(2)).

Member States are empowered to impose warnings or a temporary ban on cabotage operations within their territories on these non-resident carriers if they contravene Regulation (EEC) 3118/93, EC law or national transport legislation in the course of their operations (art.8(2) and (3)) and this power is without prejudice to the taking of criminal proceedings (ibid.). A falsified cabotage authorisation may be confiscated immediately (art.8(3)).

These provisions should all be compared to the provisions previously **13.101** introduced (see § 13.201) which allow passenger vehicle operators authorised for international journeys to carry out also certain further national passenger transport (cabotage) operations.

An EU haulier possessing a Community authorisation issued under Regulation (EEC) 881/92 who fails to pay a fine incurred in the United Kingdom in relation to the use of one of his vehicles runs the risk of losing his authorisation. To enforce a fine against an EU haulier who has left the country, a court should notify the Road User Safety Division of the Department for Transport, 76 Marsham Street, London SW1P 4DR. The Department would notify the authorities in the haulier's Member State which, depending on the seriousness of the offence, may lead to withdrawal of the Community authorisation. This would prevent the haulier from carrying out all international work.

"International carriage" is more widely defined under art.2 of Regulation **13.102** (EEC) 881/92 as summarised at § 13.97 above. "Vehicle" is also defined by art.2 to mean a motor vehicle registered in a Member State including those which are part of coupled combinations, but only if the vehicles are used exclusively for the carriage of goods.

These authorisations in the form prescribed by Annex 1 of Regulation (EEC) 881/92 (valid for five years, renewable and with rights of appeal) are issued in this country by the traffic commissioner to hauliers with operating centres in Great Britain. Hauliers are entitled to an authorisation if they are holders of an international standard operator's licence. The holder must retain the original authorisation and a certified copy must be kept on each goods vehicle being used for international carriage and produced to authorised inspecting officers on demand (art.5 and Annex I). In Great Britain the officers authorised are police constables and traffic examiners (1992 Regulations reg.8). There are a number of significant exemptions to Regulation (EEC) 881/92 in Annex II. Reference should be made to the details of the requirements and exemptions in the regulation set out in Vol.2.

A person who uses a vehicle in the United Kingdom in contravention of art.3(1) **13.103** of Regulation (EEC) 881/92 (requirement for Community authorisation) commits an offence (1992 Regulations reg.3). There are further offences of failing to return authorisations and certified copies (1992 Regulations reg.9) and failing to supply information (1992 Regulations reg.10) in each case without reasonable excuse. A person who uses a vehicle in the United Kingdom under a Community authorisation and who without reasonable excuse fails to comply with any of the conditions governing its use under the Regulation (EEC) 881/92 commits an offence. All these offences carry a maximum fine of level 4.

Under s.1 of the 1975 Act it is an offence to use a goods vehicle or trailer on an international journey as prescribed by regulations without an international haulage permit. The wording of the Act is such that the international journey commences as soon as the journey starts. An offence may thus be committed before the vehicle leaves the United Kingdom and while passing through the United Kingdom.

13.104   Section 1(2) of the 1975 Act requires the permit to be produced to a goods vehicle examiner. Refusing or failing to produce the permit without reasonable excuse or otherwise failing to comply with a requirement under s.1(2) without reasonable excuse or wilfully obstructing an examiner is an offence.

Under s.2 of the 1975 Act there is power to issue a prohibition notice in relation to permit requirements and any person who, without reasonable excuse, removes a goods vehicle or trailer out of the United Kingdom in contravention of a prohibition notice, or causes or permits a goods vehicle or trailer to be removed out of the United Kingdom in contravention of such a prohibition, commits an offence.

13.105   For offences referring to "vehicle" or "trailer" reference should be made to *NFC Forwarding Ltd v DPP* [1989] R.T.R. 239 and § 1.184 and § 10.32. For "using", "causing", "permitting" see Chapter 1.

Sections 173, 174 and 176 (forgery, false statements, etc.) of the Road Traffic Act 1988 include international permits within their ambit but have not yet been amended to include international haulage authorisations. See Chapter 16.

For a table of penalties, see § 13.106.

International haulage authorisations/permits: penalties

Offence	Mode of trial	Section / regulation	Imprisonment	Level of fine	Disqualification	Penalty points	Endorsement code	Sentencing guideline
Using vehicle in UK in contravention of art.3(1) of Regulation (EEC) 881/92 (requirement for Community authorisation)	Summary	reg.3 *	—	4	—	—	—	—
Using vehicle in UK under Community authorisation and without reasonable excuse failing to comply with conditions	Summary	reg.7 *	—	4	—	—	—	—
Failing to return authorisations/ certified copies without reasonable excuse	Summary	reg.9 *	—	4	—	—	—	—
Failing to supply information	Summary	reg.10 *	—	4	—	—	—	—
Using goods vehicle or trailer contrary to regulations	Summary	s.1(3) †	—	4	—	—	—	—

Offence	Mode of trial	Section / regulation	Imprisonment	Level of fine	Disqualification	Penalty points	Endorsement code	Sentencing guideline
Refusing or failing to produce permit without reasonable excuse	Summary	s.1(4) †	—	3	—	—	—	—
Wilfully obstructing examiner	Summary	s.1(4) †	—	3	—	—	—	—
Contravention of prohibition notice	Summary	s.2(6) †	—	4	—	—	—	—

* Goods Vehicles (Community Authorisations) Regulations 1992.
† International Road Haulage Permits Act 1975.

International carriage of perishable foodstuffs

International carriage of perishable foodstuffs is governed by specific laws. **13.107** The International Carriage of Perishable Foodstuffs Act 1976, as amended provides for issue of a certificate of compliance in respect of transport equipment for such carriage based either on an examination or on type approval. Alternatively a certification plate may provide evidence of compliance. The International Carriage of Perishable Foodstuffs Regulations 1985 (SI 1985/1071), as amended, are in operation.

For the meaning of "international carriage" reference should be made to the definition in s.19 of the 1976 Act and the application of the 1985 Regulations (see reg.3). Presumably it includes that part of the journey which takes place in this country (cf. *Paterson v Richardson* [1982] R.T.R. 49 noted at § 14.22). "Transport equipment" is defined in s.19 to include goods vehicles, which are also defined in s.19 (and see Chapter 1). For "perishable goods" and other expressions see also s.19. For "use", "cause", "permit" see Chapter 1.

"Transport equipment" is as prescribed by the ATP Agreement on the **13.108** International Carriage of Perishable Foodstuffs and the Special Equipment to be used for Such Carriage as concluded in Geneva on September 1, 1970 (Cmnd. 8272) as amended (available at *http://www.unece.org/trans/main/wp11/atp.html* [Accessed April 7, 2009]).

The 1985 Regulations apply to "transport equipment" used or intended to be used for the "international carriage" of "perishable foodstuffs" where the journey is or is to be effected by road or rail or by a sea crossing of less than 150km (93.75 miles) or by any combination of them (reg.3).

Certificates of compliance and certification plates may be issued after examination, testing or on the basis of type approval. It is an offence contrary to s.7 of the 1976 Act to use, cause or permit to be used transport equipment for the international carriage of perishable foodstuffs:

(a) without a certificate of compliance in force or a valid certification plate affixed in accordance with the regulation;

(b) without exhibiting the designated mark (see reg.22); or

(c) contravening the regulations.

There is a defence in s.7(3) if the person charged proves that he is the carrier **13.109** for hire or reward and it is a term of the contract for the carriage that he does not undertake to comply or secure compliance with the regulation to which the charge relates.

The regulation relating to the affixing of designated marks is reg.22. They must be affixed to transport equipment relying on a certificate of compliance. For a table of penalties, see § 13.110.

13.110

International carriage of perishable foodstuffs: penalties

Offence	Mode of trial	Section	Imprisonment	Level of fine	Disqualification	Penalty points	Endorsement code	Sentencing guideline
Using, causing or permitting transport equipment for the international carriage of perishable foodstuffs a) without certificate of compliance or a valid certification plate affixed, b) without exhibiting designated mark, or c) breach of regulations	Summary	s.7 International Carriage of Perishable Foodstuffs Act 1976	—	3	—	—	—	—

PUBLIC SERVICE VEHICLES

Generally

The law as to the operation of public service vehicles (PSVs) is contained in **13.111** the Public Passenger Vehicles Act 1981 (referred to as the 1981 Act) as amended and the Transport Act 1985 (referred to as the 1985 Act). The system of public service licensing contained in Pt III of the 1981 Act has been abolished and the whole of Pt III repealed. A separate system exists for London—see Pt IV of the Greater London Authority Act 1999. In the rest of England, Wales and Scotland no licence is required and only local services have to be registered.

The 1981 and 1985 Acts extend to Scotland except for ss.10 (immediate hiring of taxis at separate fares) and 11 (advance booking of taxis and hire cars at separate fares) of the 1985 Act. The provisions as to PSV operators' licences and discs are in Pt II of the 1981 Act. This system is similar to that for goods vehicle operators' licences.

The following sections deal with the definition and classifications of PSVs, **13.112** which services are local services and therefore require registration, which services are London local services and therefore require licences, PSV operators' licences, conditions applied to them and fitness requirements and the various offences which may arise. Special types of service subject to special provisions are then considered followed by proceedings and penalties. The conduct of drivers, conductors and passengers on PSVs is considered separately at the end of the chapter. Driver licensing requirements were considered at the beginning of this chapter as part of the unified driver licensing system.

PSVs: DEFINITION AND CLASSIFICATION

"Public service vehicle"

Section 1(1) of the Public Passenger Vehicles Act 1981 defines a "public ser- **13.113** vice vehicle" for the purposes of the Act as a motor vehicle (other than a tramcar) which:

    (a) if adapted to carry more than eight passengers, is used for carrying passengers for hire or reward; or

    (b) if not so adapted, is used for carrying passengers for hire or reward at separate fares in the course of a business of carrying passengers.

A vehicle is used for this purpose if it is being so used or if it has been permanently discontinued (s.1(2)). The exclusion of tramcars should be noted in view of the introduction of tramway systems.

Local or stage services and express services are carriages at separate fares; contract carriages (that is vehicles hired as a whole) are not. It follows that s.1(1)(a) of the 1981 Act relates to all these but s.1(1)(b) relates only to local or stage services and express services.

In *Vehicle and Operator Services Agency v Johnson* [2003] EWHC 2104; **13.114** (2003) 167 J.P. 497, the magistrates' court had to decide whether a stretch limousine carrying nine passengers was a public service vehicle. The justices concluded that the carriage of passengers was only one factor to be taken into account when deciding whether the vehicle had been adapted to carry more than eight passengers. Despite the fact that there were nine passengers aboard the vehicle in question, the justices decided that given the normal use of the vehicle and because of the "L" shaped bench layout and intended generosity of the seating space, it was not practicable for the vehicle to carry a ninth passenger and that the limousine was not a public service vehicle. The allegations of using a public service vehicle without a certificate of initial fitness or a public service vehicle operator's licence (together with one of permitting the driver of the vehicle to drive a public service vehicle without a passenger-carrying vehicle driver's licence) was dismissed. On appeal by the prosecution, it was held that whilst the design of seating space and the number of seatbelts were relevant considerations they could seldom be determinative of the issue of the suitability of the vehicle for a given number of passengers. Pitchford J. held that the justices had exercised sound judgement and common sense in deciding that the vehicle was not designed and laid out to carry more than eight passengers. The prosecutor's appeal was dismissed.

A public service vehicle which is adapted to carry more than eight passengers must not be used on a road in plying for hire as a whole (Transport Act 1985 s.30(1)) or an offence is committed contrary to s.30(2).

Hiring of taxis at separate fares

13.115   Section 10 of the Transport Act 1985 provides for a special scheme for taxis whereby the licensing authority may set up such a scheme to allow the immediate hiring of taxis for the carriage of passengers for hire or reward at separate fares without them becoming a public service vehicle. The procedure for setting up a scheme under s.10 is contained in the Taxis (Schemes for Hire at Separate Fares) Regulations 1986 (SI 1986/1779).

Section 11 of the same Act allows the advance hiring of taxis and private hire cars for the carriage of passengers for hire or reward at separate rates without them becoming a public service vehicle. The Secretary of State may make modifications under s.13 to the provisions of ss.10, 11 or 12.

13.116   For taxis being hired at separate fares in accordance with ss.10 and 11 of the 1985 Act, see the Licensed Taxis (Hiring at Separate Fares) Order 1986 (SI 1986/1386) and the Licensed Taxis (Hiring at Separate Fares) (London) Order 1986 (SI 1986/1387). These orders modify and to some extent disapply the taxi code as defined in s.13(3) of the 1985 Act.

As to a special form of operators' licence for taxis, see § 13.163.

Local, express and contract services

13.117   Public service vehicles may be used for different forms of service commonly distinguished by being described as local or stage services, express services and contract services respectively. The purpose of the 1985 Act was to relax controls on local or stage services, and remove the *service licensing* requirements for express services. The 1985 legislation did not intend that the expressions "express services" and "contract services" should be used for the future. The purpose was to distinguish between local services (still subject to certain controls) on the one hand and other services, whether express or contract, which are uncontrolled (controls still remain for PSV operator licensing and PCV/PSV driver licensing for all three types of service). Nevertheless the expressions "express services" and "contract services" still offer a useful "shorthand" description and have been used in the text. The full meaning is shown by the new definitions of these terms.

By Sch.1 para.16 of the 1985 Act the following definitions apply instead in any instrument or enactment made before January 6, 1986:

"Stage carriage" means a public service vehicle being used for local service (see § 13.120).

"Stage carriage service" means a local service (see § 13.120).

"Express carriage" means a PSV being used to carry passengers for hire or reward at separate fares other than for a local service.

"Express carriage service" means a service for the carriage of passengers for hire or reward at separate fares which is neither a local service nor one to which Pt III of Sch.1 to the 1981 Act applies (see § 13.138).

"Contract carriage" means a PSV being used to carry passengers for hire or reward otherwise than at separate fares.

"Local service" has the same meaning as in the Transport Act 1985 (see s.82(1) of the 1981 Act as amended by Sch.1 to the 1985 Act) and this meaning is defined and described in §§ 13.120–3 below.

13.118 The difference between a local or stage service and an express service depends on the length of journey and not on the minimum fare. An express service is where the passenger journey is of 15 miles or more. The definition in s.2 of the 1985 Act means that a local or stage service is provided by an ordinary bus picking up and setting down passengers along a local route, e.g. the bus along the Strand, and an express carriage is a bus on a regular service, perhaps from Exeter to London, picking up passengers from towns on the way, but 15 miles or more apart.

If two stopping places en route are less than 15 miles apart (e.g. Yeovil and Sherborne) that part would be a local service and would have to be registered, but the rest (if the stopping places were 15 miles or more apart) would not be a local service and need not be registered.

13.119 Local (or stage) and express services are those for which passengers each pay separate fares, though not necessarily to the vehicle owner. A contract service is where a public service vehicle is hired by one person or body, the cost falling entirely on the hirer, e.g. a football club hiring a coach for the football team where the club meets the whole cost of the hire, or a philanthropist hiring a motor coach to give a free outing to the blind. Where the head of a family hires a taxi for the family and pays the whole cost, this would be in the nature of a contract carriage, but normally the vehicle will be adapted for eight or fewer passengers and not a public service vehicle.

Local services

13.120 "Local service" has the same meaning in both the 1981 and 1985 Acts (s.82(1) and the 1981 Act as amended by Sch.1 to the 1985 Act).

A "local service" is defined by the Transport Act 1985 s.2. "Local service" means a service using one or more public service vehicles for the carriage of passengers by road at separate fares (see § 13.134), unless excluded.

The following PSV services are excluded from being local services. A service is not a "local service" if the conditions set out in Sch.1Pt III to the 1981 Act (see

§ 13.138) are met in respect of each vehicle journey and such a service need not be registered.

13.121   A service is not a local service if every vehicle is used under a s.19 permit (permits for certain educational and other bodies) (see § 13.173) and such PSV services which are excluded again need not be registered from being local services.

A service is not a local service if (save in an emergency) every passenger is set down at a place 15 miles or more (measured in a straight line) from the place where he is picked up, or some point on the route between those places is 15 miles or more measured in a straight line from either of these places. Where this is satisfied in part, *that part* is to be treated as a separate service and therefore *that part* is not a local service. There are similarities between this last exclusion and the former definition of an express carriage, and reference should be made to § 13.125.

13.122   Local services must be registered with the traffic commissioner for the appropriate area. No offence is specifically committed by operating without registering under Pt I of the 1985 Act.

Local services in London are dealt with separately in Pt IV of the Greater London Authority Act 1999.

Local service: traffic regulation conditions

13.123   If he is asked by the traffic authority, the traffic commissioner may attach traffic regulation conditions in respect of a local service to a PSV operator's licence or to a community bus service permit (Transport Act 1985 ss.7 and 8). The traffic regulation condition must be required to prevent danger to road users or to reduce severe traffic congestion. The condition may, among other matters, specify the route, the stopping places and the length of stop. Conditions may also regulate the roads to be used, the manoeuvres to be performed when turning a vehicle, limiting the number of vehicles which may be used or limiting the frequency at which vehicles may be operated. These conditions may affect along all the route or only part of it and may apply either generally or at specified times or periods (Public Service Vehicles (Registration of Local Services) Regulations 1986 (SI 1986/1671), as amended). There is a right of appeal to the Secretary of State (s.9). For the offence of breach of a PSV operator's licence condition see § 13.160 and § 13.203. For the offence of breach of a community bus service permit see § 13.184.

Other definitions

A   "Excursion or tour"

13.124   "Excursion or tour" means a service for the carriage of passengers (see Chapter 1) by road (see Chapter 1) at separate fares (see § 13.134) on which the passengers travel together on a journey with or without breaks, from one or more places to one or more other places and back (1985 Act s.137).

B   "Stopping place"

13.125   "Stopping place" means in relation to any service or part of a service, a point at which passengers are (or in a proposed service are proposed to be) taken up or set down in the course of that service or part (1985 Act s.137).

"Used for carrying passengers"

This expression is used in both limbs of s.1(1) of the 1981 Act. It is pointed out **13.126** at (1981) J.P. Jo. 107 that the definition does not say habitually or normally used. It is suggested there that where a mechanic was road testing a coach it was not being used as a public service vehicle and therefore was not to be classified as such. It seems that this conclusion, however desirable, is not in accordance with the extended definition in s.1(2) set out above ("has been used" ... "and that use has not been permanently discontinued"). The arguments are set out at (1981) 145 J.P. 107 and 352. See also Chapter 1 as to the meaning of "use" and also compare *Roberts v Morris* [1965] Crim. L.R. 46 noted at § 13.48. The doubts expressed appear to have been accepted because the holder of a full LGV licence to drive category C vehicles is now permitted to drive as well a passenger vehicle with more than 16 seats excluding the driver provided it is not being used for hire or reward or for carrying more than eight passengers. The purpose of this is to allow these drivers to drive large buses for repair and testing.

"Adapted"

"Adapted" is discussed at § 1.29. The cases on the meaning of "adapted" in **13.127** s.117(1) of the Road Traffic Act 1960 would seem still to be relevant to the definition of "public service vehicle" in s.1(1) of the 1981 Act.

Whether a vehicle is "adapted" is a question of fact. *Westacott v Centaur* [1981] R.T.R. 182 noted at § 1.30 was a case relating to public service vehicles. In that case four out of 11 seats on a minibus were rendered unusable: two double seats had been placed upside down to block four seats off. A finding of fact by the justices that the minibus was not adapted to fill the additional seats and that therefore the vehicle was not a public service vehicle was upheld.

The word "adapted", according to the judgment in *Traffic Commissioner for* **13.128** *South Wales Traffic Area v Snape* [1977] Crim. L.R. 427, must, however, be read in conjunction with reg.28(1)(b) of the Public Service Vehicles (Conditions of Fitness, Equipment, Use and Certification) Regulations 1981 (SI 1981/257) as amended, which provides subject to certain qualifications that "a length of at least 400mm measured horizontally along the front of each seat shall be allowed for the accommodation of a seated passenger". The folding arms of continuous seats are to be ignored. This case was in fact decided on an earlier similarly worded regulation which referred to 1ft 4in in place of 400mm. It was held following *Wurzal v Addison* [1965] 1 All E.R. 20 (see § 1.30) that as the vehicle was used for hire or reward and no factor other than the length of the seats was relevant in the case and the minibus had three seats together with a bench 7ft 4in long, it was thus suitable and, therefore, "adapted" as a public service vehicle. A tantalising problem has arisen with the emergence of the "stretch limo". These are often designed to provide generous accommodation but for no more than eight passengers. However, the generosity of the seating space allowed is such that far more than 400mm is given for each seat. Seat belts may be provided for only eight passengers. The question arises as to whether this is a public service vehicle. It is submitted that the nature of the use to which this vehicle is put and the requirements regarding seat belts (which have changed since the decision in *Snape*) combine to exclude such vehicles from the definition.

With regard to the definition of "adapted" as to whether a "stretch limo" was a

PSV, see *Vehicle and Operator Services Agency v Johnson* above at § 13.114. It should be emphasised that courts need to take care to prevent operators circumventing the plain purpose of the legislation which is to encompass vehicles adapted for more than eight passengers, by relying on the style rather than the substance of the accommodation provided.

"More than eight passengers"

13.129　　A crucial element of the definition of "public service vehicle" in s.1(1) of the 1981 Act is the number of passengers for which the vehicle is adapted. The specified number of passengers is nine as the section refers to "more than eight". The criterion in s.1(1)(a) is whether the vehicle is adapted to carry nine or more passengers, not the number in fact carried.

Whether the driver should be counted among the passengers is not clear. In Pts I and III of Sch.1 to the 1981 Act "driver" is contrasted with "passenger". The problem is one which arises under a number of statutory provisions and the question is discussed with the relevant cases at § 1.115. For the purpose of s.1(1)(a) and (3) and Sch.1 Pts I and III, it is submitted that eight persons plus the driver may be carried before the limit is reached: i.e. the driver is not to be regarded as a passenger.

"Hire or reward"

13.130　　The expression "hire or reward" is found in both s.1(1)(a) and s.1(1)(b) of the 1981 Act and also in Sch.1 to that Act. Its meaning is discussed at § 13.48. Here the meaning is extended by s.1(5). The same expression "hire or reward" again as extended by s.1(5) is by s.137(3) of the 1985 Act also to be used in that Act. Section 1(5) reads as follows:

> "(5) For the purposes of this section, ... and Schedule 1 to this Act —
>
> (a) a vehicle is to be treated as carrying passengers for hire or reward if payment is made for, or for matters which include, the carrying of passengers, irrespective of the person to whom the payment is made and, in the case of a transaction effected by or on behalf of a member of any association of persons (whether incorporated or not) on the one hand and the association or another member thereof on the other hand, notwithstanding any rule of law as to such transactions;
>
> (b) a payment made for the carrying of a passenger shall be treated as a fare notwithstanding that it is made in consideration of other matters in addition to the journey and irrespective of the person by or to whom it is made;
>
> (c) a payment shall be treated as made for the carrying of a passenger if made in consideration of a person's being given a right to be carried, whether for one or more journeys and whether or not the right is exercised."

13.131　　Paragraphs (a), (b) and (c) of s.1(5) are in like terms to s.118(3)(a), (b) and (c) of the Road Traffic Act 1960. Section 118(3)(d) which is not reproduced in the 1981 Act used to catch within the meaning of "hire or reward" the carriage of passengers for hire or reward otherwise than in the course of a business of carrying passengers. This is no longer necessarily the case.

A group of parents acquired a minibus jointly which carried more than eight passengers. They ran it as a joint enterprise without profit to take their children to school. They took it in turns to drive. No fares were collected and each met his own expenses. There was no question of hire or reward in the normal sense. The question was whether there was a reward within the extended definition of s.1(5)(a). The parents argued that it was a joint enterprise and on the facts there was no payment for matters which included the carrying of passengers, between one member of the group and another. The police and the traffic examiners decided not to prosecute. In view of the wording of s.1(5)(a), however, the position cannot be regarded as settled.

The meaning was considered in *DPP v Sikondar* [1993] R.T.R. 90. The defen- **13.132** dant regularly used his privately owned motor vehicle to carry girls to school, receiving petrol money. He was stopped when carrying 11 girls, for eight of whom payment had been made. It was held on the facts that he was undertaking a systematic carrying of passengers for reward which went beyond mere social kindness. The decision was based on the meaning of "reward" and not on the s.1(5) extended meaning. Indeed the defence pointed out that the girls for whom payment was made were given no right to be carried. The Divisional Court adopted the test in *Albert v Motor Insurers' Bureau* [1971] 2 All E.R. 1345, HL, at § 13.48, and as also applied in *Motor Insurers' Bureau v Meanen* [1971] 2 All E.R. 1372, pointing out that in the latter case, the arrangement for transport was completely informal without any binding obligation, without any definite terms and without the driver taking any definite steps with regard to their carrying out. It was held unnecessary in *Sikondar* for the prosecution to establish the existence of a legally enforceable agreement. A conviction was directed for the offence of using a PSV without a PSV operator's licence. The problem with the decision is that although there was a payment, it is difficult to describe it as a reward because the driver was probably "rewarded" with a loss on the transaction. The decision still gives no final answer for the situation described in the example of the parents' joint enterprise, described above, where there was no payment at all. It might be argued that in that example there was a mutual carriage and that the arrangements went beyond social kindness.

The decision in *Sikondar* and the other cases was followed in *Rout v Swallow* **13.133** *Hotels Ltd* [1993] R.T.R. 80. In the *Swallow Hotels* case, a courtesy coach and a minibus were provided without charge to run between the hotels and points of arrival and departure and places of entertainment. The vehicles could be used not only by persons staying at or visiting the hotels but also by friends. No one was given any right to travel. The Divisional Court held that the vehicles were public service vehicles carrying passengers for hire or reward. The vehicles were a part of the hotel business and the hire or reward was included in the payment by the guest for the room or the meal.

"Separate fares"

The expression "separate fares" appears in s.1(1)(b) of the 1981 Act (definition **13.134** of "public service vehicle" (see § 13.113)) and in s.2 of the 1985 Act (definition of "local services" (see § 13.117 and § 13.120)). Section 1(5)(a), (b) and (c) of the 1981 Act extends the meaning of "payment" and "fare" for the purposes of s.1 and Sch.1 to the 1981 Act (public service vehicles). Section 1(5)(b) and (c) extends the meaning of "fare" in s.2 of the 1985 Act (s.2(5)) in relation to "local services" (for "local services" see § 13.117 and § 13.120). Section 1(5)(a) is not strictly relevant to the meaning of a fare. The cases as to the meaning of "separate fares" which follow were decided on the old law and the 1960 Act (now repealed). What is now s.1(5) of the 1981 Act makes more stringent provision as to the payment of separate fares. The cases should be read in the light of it.

13.135   A bus proprietor hired a bus out to a football club and it stood in a street awaiting any passengers who might come along; there was no question of a private party. Each passenger paid a separate fare, which went to the club secretary. It was held to be used as a stage carriage, as what is now s.1(5) makes it immaterial to whom the fares are paid (*Osborne v Richards* (1932) 96 J.P. 377). A railway company ran excursions to a certain station, where the defendants' buses met the passengers and conveyed them to a chocolate factory, the railway company receiving an inclusive fare from each excursionist; the railway company afterwards paid to the defendants a sum exceeding 1s. for each passenger carried in the buses. It was held that the buses were express carriages, it being immaterial, in view of what is now s.1(5), that the excursionists paid nothing to the defendants (*Birmingham, etc., Omnibus Co v Nelson* (1932) 96 J.P. 385). Where a company hired a bus to take employees to work and the employees made payments to the company, this was held to be carriage at separate fares although the passengers paid nothing themselves to the owner of the bus (*Wurzal v Wilson* [1965] 1 All E.R. 26). "Separate fares" simply means payments for a carriage by individual passengers and it is immaterial whether there is a firm arrangement as to the amount of payment or a tariff of payments (*Aitken v Hamilton* 1964 S.L.T. 125). Tips unsolicited by the driver were held on the facts not to be separate fares (*Maclean v Fearn* 1954 S.L.T.(Sh.) 37). Coaches hired from the defendants by a stadium proprietor picked up casual passengers at several points and took them to the stadium; the passengers paid nothing for their rides and were free not to go into the stadium, if they wished, the charge for admission being the same for them as for anyone else. It was held that the coaches were stage, not contract carriages, as the passengers were carried in consideration of separate payments made by them to the stadium proprietor and were thus caught by what is now s.1(5) (*Westminster Coaching Services v Piddlesden* (1993) 97 J.P. 185). A lorry owner who used his lorry to carry other people's goods to market and also carried as passengers the people whose goods were in the lorry was held to be running an express carriage although he contended that the payments were for carriage of the goods only (*Drew v Dingle* (1934) 98 J.P. 1). Public advertisement of a trip can convert what would otherwise be a trip for which authorisation is unnecessary, under Sch.1 to the 1981 Act, into one which would now require registration, or in London a licence, if it constituted a local service (*Evans v Dell* [1937] 1 All E.R. 349; and see *Goldsmith v Deakin* (1933) 98 J.P. 4). A car owner regularly drove three fellow-employees to work at a factory and back; the expenses of oil and petrol were shared by each paying 5s. per week. It was held that the friends were carried in consideration of separate payments (*East Midlands, etc., Commissioners v Tyler* [1938] 3 All E.R. 39). A club hired a taxi to take members to work regularly and each member made separate payments, covering both transport charges and other purposes; it was held that, under s.118(3)(d), these were separate fares (*Hawthorn v Knight* 1962 S.L.T. 69).

13.136   Where a hirer of a minibus agreed to pay to its owner a daily sum to take her and her fellow workers to work, however many were carried, and she herself collected separate fares from the other passengers, it was held that, under what is now s.1(5), there was a payment of separate fares (*Wurzal v Addison* [1965] 1 All E.R. 20). An arrangement was made whereby 15p was paid for each journey during the week by each of seven passengers going to a factory. If a regular passenger could not travel on a particular day that passenger would have to pay for that day but her place could be taken free of charge by a fellow workmate. At the end of the week all the money was collected by the passenger sitting nearest the driver and paid over to him. It was contended by the defendant, who owned and operated the vehicle, that it was not an express carriage because he received the same amount of money each week and did not separately charge the passengers. Following *Wurzal v Addison* it was held that under what is now s.1(5)(b) there was a payment of separate fares (*Vickers v Bowman* [1976] R.T.R. 165). In this last case the vehicle might now presumably be within s.1(1)(b) of the 1981 Act (not adapted for more than eight passengers and not used in the course of a passenger-carrying business). If so it would not now be a public service vehicle. The principle, however, remains.

For special provisions as to special fares and the hiring of taxis, see § 13.115.

"In the course of a business of carrying passengers"

The expression "in the course of a business of carrying passengers" is found in **13.137** s.1(1)(b) and also in s.1(3) of the 1981 Act (certain vehicles fulfilling the conditions of Pts I and III of Sch.1 not to be treated as public service vehicles). The expression does not include, for the purposes of s.1, passenger journeys for separate fares where the total running costs (including depreciation and general wear) are not exceeded and the fare arrangements were made before the journey began (s.1(4)). This subsection seems designed to exempt works buses and similar non-profit-making journeys in vehicles adapted for eight passengers or less. As the word "including" indicates that the list of running costs given is not exhaustive, it is submitted that a "safety margin" or "windfall" profit would not necessarily therefore turn the venture into a business.

It should be noted that s.1(1)(b) and (3) only relate to vehicles adapted for eight or less passengers. Where a vehicle is adapted for more than eight passengers, it will be caught by s.1(1)(a) and the test will be merely "hire or reward", as extended by s.1(5).

Certain PSVs not treated as such

A public service vehicle carrying passengers at separate fares in the course of a **13.138** business of carrying passengers, but doing so in circumstances where the conditions of Pt I or III of Sch.1 to the 1981 Act are fulfilled shall be treated as not being a public service vehicle unless it is adapted to carry more than eight passengers (s.1(3)). Pt II of Sch.1 has been repealed.

The conditions in Pts I and III may be summarised by saying that, in general, vehicles which would otherwise be public service vehicles by reason of s.1(1)(b) will not be public service vehicles if they are adapted to carry eight passengers or less and the journey is not organised by the driver or owner or person making the vehicle available or receiving any remuneration in respect of the arrangements. The journey must also be made without previous advertisement to the public. Under Pt I the service may be advertised where, in England and Wales, a county council, metropolitan district, London borough or City of London council, or, in

Scotland, a regional or islands council, has approved the arrangements as designed to meet the social and welfare needs of one or more communities. Otherwise the only advertisements permitted are those which, by virtue of the supplemental provisions of Pt IV, are not regarded as advertisements. Pt IV applies to advertisements relating to places of worship, work places and club or association premises. Several announcements taken together can constitute an advertisement (*Poole v Ibbotson* (1949) 113 J.P. 466).

13.139   Section s.79 of the Public Passenger Vehicles Act 1981, as amended, provides that a vehicle which is not a public service vehicle because of s.1(3) or (4) of the 1981 Act is nonetheless to be treated as one in order to exclude it from regulation as a private hire vehicle. Section s.79A provides that a vehicle with not more than eight passenger seats, which is provided for hire together with the services of a driver and which carries passengers other than at separate fares, must generally be licensed as a private hire vehicle.

A bus hired to take people back after a dance went to their various homes; it was held that this was not a "journey to a particular destination" under what is now para.7 (in Pt III) of Sch.1 (*Clark v Dundee Council* 1957 S.L.T. 306).

Certain PSV services not to be regarded as local services

13.140   Where the conditions of Pt III of Sch.1 (see above) are fulfilled a service provided by a public service vehicle will not be regarded as a local service even though passengers are carried at separate fares and even though it otherwise would be (1985 Act s.2(4)).

Registration of PSV services

13.141   No licence is required for the provision by public service vehicles of local, or stage services, save in London. As to the definition of PSVs, see §§ 13.113 et seq. and as to the definition of local services, see § 13.117 and § 13.120. Instead the local service must be registered under s.6 of the 1985 Act with the traffic commissioner for the appropriate area. The procedure for registration is set out in the Public Service Vehicles (Registration of Local Services) Regulations 1986 (SI 1986/1671), as amended.

The application is made to the traffic commissioner for the traffic area in which the stopping places are (1985 Act s.6(2)). Applications for registration for services which have stopping places in more than one area are to be made to the traffic commissioner for the area in which the service will start (1986 Regulations reg.3(1)). No registration is required for express or contract services. As to the meaning of express and contract services, see § 13.117.

13.142   The particulars of the local services which have to be registered under s.6 of the Transport Act 1985 are specified in the Schedule to the 1986 Regulations. In specified circumstances, reg.9 allows local services to be varied without varying the registration. One such circumstance was an increase in the number of vehicles used where the existing timetable was followed as closely as possible. In 1994 that provision was qualified by a requirement that, from February 1, 1995, before deploying extra vehicles, an operator must have reasonable grounds to expect (owing to special circumstances) that the normal number of vehicles would be insufficient at the relevant time (Public Service Vehicles (Registration of Local Services) (Amendment) Regulations 1994 (SI 1994/3271)).

Under the Schedule appropriate adjustments have to be made for excursions and tours. The registration requirements under s.6 do not apply to excursions or tours except to excursion or tour services operated at least once a week for six consecutive weeks (1986 Regulations reg.10). For the meaning of "excursions or tours", see § 13.124. Registration with the traffic commissioner would accordingly be necessary for regular tourist sight-seeing excursions or tours, operated outside London, in this way for at least six consecutive weeks, as for example in the summer season.

13.143 Under the 1986 Regulations, except when the PSV is used under a special licence or for an excursion or tour (see above), the PSV operator must during such time as a vehicle is being used to provide a service cause a fare table and a timetable to be displayed in the vehicle and also a notice clearly visible from the exterior indicating the destination (if any) and the route of the service. The fare table and timetable must be displayed in a manner clearly legible to the passengers or must be available on the vehicle to them on request.

The liability only arises when the vehicle is being used to provide a service. Whether a vehicle has been put into service or taken out of service and whether a vehicle is being used to provide a service will be a question of fact. It is submitted that a PSV waiting and collecting passengers at the starting point may well be "being used to provide a service".

13.144 The various definitions in the 1981 and 1985 Acts may assist as to "service" although they concentrate on the types of service and service vehicles, rather than the meaning of service itself. As to "passengers" see Chapter 1. The expression may not be wide enough to include intending passengers who have not yet boarded the vehicle. As to "special licences" see § 13.163 and the 1986 Regulations, as amended.

Certain failures to operate local services may by s.8(6) of the 1985 Act be ignored in particular circumstances. The period prescribed for the purposes of s.8(6) is 28 days (1986 Regulations reg.11).

The 1986 Regulations are made under various subsections of the 1981 and 1985 Acts, in particular, s.60(1)(f) of the 1981 Act (documents, plates and marks to be carried) and s.6(9) of the 1985 Act (provision of information).

Penalties

13.145 The maximum penalty for contraventions of the 1986 Regulations (including in particular the regulations as to fare tables, timetables and destination notices) is contained in s.67 of the 1981 Act (see § 13.213 and § 13.216). As to the defence of reasonable excuse under s.68(1) of the 1981 Act, see § 13.212.

No offence is specifically committed by operating without registering under s.6 and Pt I of the 1985 Act. Control is instead by sanctions applied to the holding of a PSV operator's licence (see § 13.149).

There is power to fix conditions which must be met in the provision of registered local services. These conditions are fixed in accordance with ss.7–9 of the 1985 Act and the Public Service Vehicles (Traffic Regulation Conditions) Regulations 1986 (SI 1986/1030), as amended (see also § 13.123). Certain restrictions may be imposed on operators who apply to register a local service under s.6 of the Transport Act 1985 in an area where a quality partnership scheme, containing registration restrictions, has been made and processes set out in the Public Service Vehicles (Registration Restrictions) (England and Wales) Regulations

2009 (SI 2009/443) apply to such cases in circumstances specified in those regulations and the Local Transport Act 2008.

London local services

13.146   It is an offence to provide a London local service other than in accordance with the provisions of the Greater London Authority Act 1999. Only the operator commits the offence which is contrary to s.180(2) of the 1999 Act. See "Offences", § 13.203 below. Another person may be guilty of aiding and abetting the operator. As to the definition of PSVs, see § 13.113 and, as to the definition of local services, see § 13.117 and § 13.120.

Responsibility for the provision of London local services is with Transport for London.

PSV LICENSING AND FITNESS REQUIREMENTS

Transport systems including tramways

13.147   A tramcar is not included in the definition of a public service vehicle in s.1(1) of the Public Passenger Vehicles Act 1981. No PSV operators' licence will therefore be required and operators will be separately authorised. The Road Traffic Act 1991 repealed s.193 of and Sch.4 to the 1988 Act, which exempted trams and trolley vehicles from certain provisions of the Road Traffic Acts, including Pt III of the 1988 Act (driver licensing). Section 46 of the Road Traffic Act 1991 instead inserted s.193A in the 1988 Act allowing the Secretary of State to make regulations applying specific sections of the 1988 Act and the 1988 Offenders Act with or without modifications to tram and trolley vehicles. The regulations may also amend special Acts.

The Tramcars and Trolley Vehicles (Modification of Enactments) Regulations 1992 (SI 1992/1217) exclude and modify certain provisions of the 1988 Act and also of the Road Traffic Regulation Act 1984 in relation to tramcars and trolley vehicles and reference should be made to the regulations. In particular, while s.87 of the 1988 Act (driver licensing, including PCV driving authorisation), applies to tramcars and trolley vehicles, an ordinary category B licence within the meaning of the Motor Vehicles (Driving Licences) Regulations 1999 also authorises a person to drive a tramcar (see s.87(3)). Regardless of this requirement, there is an exemption in that a person may drive or cause or permit a person to drive a tramcar if the driver was employed on duties which required the driving of tramcars on roads at any time during the one year ending immediately before July 1, 1992 (s.87(4) as added).

13.148   The Transport and Works Act 1992 enables the Secretary of State to make orders regarding the operation of transport systems including tramways, trolley vehicles and guided transport. These orders may apply, modify or exclude any statutory provision and may under Sch.1 provide for the charging of fares, including penalty fares, and the creation of summary offences in connection with non-payment or a person's failure to give his name and address with reference to a penalty fare. They may also deal with the making and enforcement of byelaws, including the creation of summary offences. The summary offences created by these orders may carry a maximum fine not exceeding level 3; they must not carry imprisonment (s.5(5)).

Each transport system including the long existing Blackpool tramway system will need individual consideration. For further provisions regarding trams, including the wide-reaching excess alcohol enactments, see "Conduct on tramcars, etc.", § 13.232 below.

PSV operators' licences

The *operator licensing* requirements as to PSVs apply to PSVs as defined in **13.149** this chapter and are subject to the relaxations and exemptions discussed below. The reference to PSVs remains despite the *driver licensing* change to PCVs in place of PSVs.

PSV operators' licences are required for operators of all PSVs used on a road for carrying passengers for hire or reward no matter what type of service provided (1981 Act s.12(1)). It is an offence to use a PSV on a road whether for local (stage) services, long distance (express) services or contract services without such an operator's licence. As to "use" and "road" see Chapter 1. As to "hire or reward" see § 13.130. The offence is only committed by the operator of the vehicle, but another person may be guilty of aiding and abetting him. See further "Offences", § 13.203 below.

In addition to the commission of an offence for operating without a PSV **13.150** operator's licence, s.47 of the Local Transport Act 2008 inserts new s.12A and Sch.2A into the 1981 Act which provide for a new regime for the detention of certain public service vehicles used in contravention of the operator licensing requirements.

A PSV operator's licence may be held by an individual, a company or a **13.151** partnership. The 1981 and 1985 Acts are modified in certain respects as far as partnerships are concerned (see the Operations of Public Service Vehicles (Partnership) Regulations 1986 (SI 1986/1628, as amended)). Persons in partnership are specified by these regulations as eligible for the grant of a PSV operator's licence or a London local service licence.

A PSV operator's licence is obtained from the traffic commissioner for the area where the operating centre, or one of the operating centres, is situated (1981 Act s.12(2)). The Public Service Vehicles (Operators' Licences) Regulations 1995 (SI 1995/2908) and the Public Service Vehicles (Operators' Licences) (Fees) Regulations 1995 (SI 1995/2909) refer to the procedure for applications and specify the fees. Under s.14A of the 1981 Act the police or local authority may enter objections to the grant of an operator's licence (other than a special licence (see § 13.163)) on the ground that the requirements in s.14(1) or (3) (see below) are not met. The onus of proof rests on the police or local authority (1981 Act s.14A(3)).

The licence may be of one of two kinds: a standard licence or a restricted licence (1981 Act s.13(1)). The provisions are somewhat similar to those requiring standard and restricted operators' licences for goods vehicles (see § 13.32 and § 13.33). The environmental requirements applicable to goods vehicle operators' licences have not been extended to PSV operators' licences, although there have been suggestions that they should be.

Standard PSV operator's licence

A standard licence authorises the use of any public service vehicle for both **13.152** international and national transport operations or national transport operations only.

Restricted PSV operator's licence

13.153   A restricted licence authorises the use (whether in national or international operations) of public service vehicles:

    (a) not adapted to carry more than eight passengers; and

    (b) not adapted to carry more than 16 passengers when used:

        (i) otherwise than in the course of a business of carrying passengers (and this includes local and public authority passenger vehicles unless used for the authority PSV undertaking); or

        (ii) by a person whose main occupation is not the operation of public service vehicles adapted to carry more than eight passengers (1981 Act s.13(3) and (4)).

Provision (b) (ii) may be of some use as a sideline or by way of reserve to an operator running services with comparatively small vehicles.

A transport tribunal has held that the word "occupation" in s.13(3) means the occupation by which a person ordinarily seeks to get his or her livelihood (*Day* (1987) Appeal 1987 No.Y 11).

13.154   Before a standard or a restricted licence may be granted the traffic commissioner must be satisfied that the applicant is of good repute and of appropriate financial standing and in the case of a standard licence of professional competence (s.14(1)). These requirements are further elaborated in Sch.3 to the 1981 Act and the Public Service Vehicles (Operators) (Qualifications) Regulations 1990 (SI 1990/1851), as amended. The commissioner must also be satisfied as to arrangements for maintenance and for securing compliance with the law relating to the driving and operation of those vehicles (s.14(3)).

The qualifications necessary for obtaining a standard operator's licence are contained in the Public Passenger Vehicles Act 1981 Sch.3. Certain of these provisions have been amended by the Public Service Vehicle Operators (Qualifications) Regulations 1999 (SI 1999/2431) which implement Council directives on the admission to the occupation of road passenger transport operator in national and international transport operations.

13.155   The provisions regarding financial standing and professional competence were amended by regs.3 and 4 of the 1999 Regulations. Regulation 4 of the 1999 Regulations amends Sch.3 para.6 of the 1981 Act by permitting written examinations which may be supplemented by an oral examination organised by the approved body as defined and by requiring a certificate to be issued.

The Public Service Vehicle Operators (Qualifications) (Amendment) Regulations 2004 (SI 2004/3223) amended para.2 of Sch.3 to the 1981 Act by prescribing the requirements which an applicant for, or a holder of, a PSV operator's licence must meet in order to be of appropriate financial standing. The amendment applies the prescribed minimum amounts for capital and reserves to standard PSV operators' licences, national as well as international. Full details can be found in Traffic Commissioners' *Practice Direction No.1*, effective January 1, 2005 (available at *http://www.vosa.gov.uk* following the link "Publications" [Accessed April 7, 2009]).

13.156   In relation to "good repute", reg.2 of the 1999 Regulations replaces para.1(3)

and (5) of Sch.3 to the 1981 Act. The amended para.1(3) removes the requirement for "repeatedly convicted of road transport offences" and replaces it by
"convicted of road transport offences". The definition is still in the plural but the
uncertainty of "repeatedly" is removed. This accords with a general tightening of
the approach to operators convicted of relevant offences. A "road transport offence" is defined in the amended para.1(5) of Sch.3 which is expanded to include
both offences relating to the protection of the environment and any offence
concerning professional liability.

Section 16A of the Public Passenger Vehicles Act 1981, as inserted by reg.5 of
the 1999 Regulations, requires a traffic commissioner to insert a condition into
any standard licence issued that requires the licence-holder to notify the commissioner of any event which could affect the fulfilment by the licence-holder of any
of the requirements of s.14(1) or by a relevant transport manager (defined in
s.16A(2)) of any of the requirements under s.14(1)(a) or (c) of the 1981 Act. Failure to comply with this condition is an offence punishable on summary conviction by a fine not exceeding level 4: s.16A(3).

Transitional provisions in the 1999 Regulations protect from the changes those
with a licence or a certificate of competence granted or issued before October 1,
1999.

Compare the requirements for goods vehicle operators' licences and see **13.157**
§ 13.34 and § 13.37 as to professional competence, good repute, etc., as those
provisions are in similar terms.

Under ss.14, 14A and 17 the traffic commissioner may refuse, suspend or
revoke a PSV operator's licence. Before the traffic commissioner refuses,
suspends or revokes a PSV operator's licence, the holder of the licence should be
given the requisite notice in accordance with the regulations, warning him in
advance, including providing adequate information as to the grounds (*Russell*
(1990) Appeal 1990 No.B 40, PSV, Transport Tribunal). A person should be
made aware of any possibility of disqualification, so that he has an opportunity to
make representations. The commissioner has power to disqualify PSV operators
when revoking an operator's licence (1985 Act s.28). There is a right of appeal
(see s.50 of the 1981 Act as substituted by s.31 of the 1985 Act).

Where a vehicle is being used where a PSV operator's licence is required, a **13.158**
PSV operator's disc must be fixed and exhibited on the vehicle as prescribed
(1981 Act s.18(1)). The Public Service Vehicles (Operators' Licences) Regulations 1995 prescribe the manner in which operators' discs are to be fixed and
exhibited and provide for the production of licences and discs for examination.
Contravention of s.18(1) is an offence (s.18(4)), but it can only be committed by
the operator of the vehicle. It is an offence under s.65 of the 1981 Act to forge,
alter, use, etc., such a disc with intent to deceive (see Chapter 16).

Applicants for PSV operators' licences and the holders of such licences are
obliged under the 1981 Act to give the traffic commissioners certain information
regarding relevant convictions (s.19 and Sch.3) and as to vehicles (s.20), and the
traffic commissioners may require certain information themselves. The applicant
and anyone who aids or abets him commits an offence if he fails to comply
(ss.19(5) and 20(4)). What are relevant convictions are specified in detail in
reg.17 and the Schedule to the 1995 Regulations and reference should be made to
the goods vehicles operators' licence provisions which contain similar terms.

A person who under s.20(3) of the 1981 Act supplies information which he **13.159** knows to be false or does not believe to be true commits a more serious offence (s.20(5)). For the s.68 defence available, see § 13.212.

PSV operators' licences: conditions

13.160   The system of licensing the operation of services has been removed save in London. Outside London the control of specified misconduct, improperly provided or neglected services and inadequate maintenance (see s.26 of the 1985 Act for the full wording) is achieved by the imposition of conditions either on the initial grant of the operator's licence or at a later stage (ss.26 and 27 of the 1985 Act). The condition may prohibit the operator from using vehicles to provide local services (see § 13.117 and § 13.120) of a specified description or of any description and where appropriate arrange for the cancellation of the registration. There are rights of appeal to the Transport Tribunal under ss.50 and 51 of the 1981 Act.

The effect of this is to make more important the offence of contravening a condition attached to an operator's licence. Contravention of any such condition is made an offence by s.16(7) of the 1981 Act but only by the holder of the licence. Another person may be guilty of aiding and abetting him. See further "Offences", § 13.203 below. The wording of s.16(7) refers to any condition attached to a licence. This seems wide enough to include a condition attached under s.26 and s.27 (see above) of the 1985 Act as well as those attached under s.16 of the 1981 Act. It would have been preferable if the wording had expressed the position more clearly.

13.161   As noted above further conditions may be attached under s.16. It is obligatory for the traffic commissioner to attach conditions specifying the maximum number of vehicles which may be used under an operator's licence (1981 Act s.16(1)). Section 16(1A) limits the maximum number which may be specified for a restricted licence. The traffic commissioner has a discretion to attach further conditions for restricting or regulating the use of vehicles under the licence being conditions of any prescribed description (s.16(3)) (see § 13.123). Again a breach of the condition is an offence committed by the holder of the licence or any person aiding and abetting him (s.16(7)).

Amendments made by the Public Service Vehicles (Traffic Regulations Conditions) (England and Wales) Regulations 2004 (SI 2004/2682) allow traffic commissioners to determine traffic regulation conditions for the purposes of regulating the emission levels of vehicles that provide local bus services and of regulating the noise pollution levels created by loudspeaker systems or other public address systems used in those vehicles. Only one such application has been made to a traffic commissioner. This resulted in the Traffic Commissioner for the Western Traffic Area attaching traffic regulation conditions to tourist buses in the city of Bath upon an application by Bath and North East Somerset Council in May 2006.

13.162   Where the traffic commissioner is satisfied that the operator of a local service has without reasonable excuse failed to operate a local service registered under s.6 or operated a local service in contravention of s.6 he may in addition to imposing conditions impose a penalty of up to £550 per vehicle based upon the maximum number of vehicles authorised to be used on the operator's licence in accordance with s.155 of the Transport Act 2000. Judicial guidance on the imposition of penalties is set out in the Court of Appeal case of *Ribble Motor*

Services Ltd v Traffic Commissioner for the North Western Traffic Area, The Times, March 8, 2001 and the Transport Tribunal has also commented on the approach taken by traffic commissioners when considering the imposition of penalties in appeals, see *Andrews Sheffield Ltd and Others* (2003/300/301/302). Guidance on the imposition of penalties is to be found in Annex B to Traffic Commissioners' *Practice Direction No.4* (effective January 1, 2005).

Special licences (restricted PSV operators' licences)

A taxi licence-holder or a private hire licence holder may apply under s.12 of **13.163** the Transport Act 1985 (as amended by the Local Transport Act 2008 s.53) to the appropriate traffic commissioner for a restricted PSV operator's licence (a special licence) if he states in the application that he proposes to provide a local service. This allows taxi and private hire proprietors to register to run the equivalent of local bus services.

Such applications must be granted and the prerequisites in s.14 of the 1981 Act for the grant of a PSV operator's licence do not apply. In effect the applicant will be qualified by the taxi licence or licensed hire car without the taxi or hire car becoming a PSV. "Taxi licence" means a taxi licence under the Town Police Clauses Act 1847 or similar enactment, the Metropolitan Public Carriage Act 1869 s.6 or the Civic Government (Scotland) Act 1982. These statutes are all statutes licensing vehicles to ply for hire. A "licensed hire car" is defined as a vehicle licensed under s.48 of the Local Government (Miscellaneous Provisions) Act 1976 or s.7 of the Private Hire Vehicles (London) Act 1998.

The traffic commissioner may attach conditions to the special licence under **13.164** s.16 of the 1981 Act. He must attach a condition under s.16 and under s.12(7) of the 1985 Act that the maximum number used under the special licence must be the number for which for the time being relevant licences are held. He must also attach conditions under s.12(5) of the 1985 Act that every vehicle used under the special licence must be covered by a taxi or a private hire licence and must be used under the special licence only for providing a local service (see § 13.120) with one or more stopping places in the area of the authority which granted the relevant licence for that vehicle. "Local services" in this context do not include excursions or tours (s.12(6)) and a special licence cannot therefore be used to authorise tours or excursions. A separate special licence may be held for a different traffic area.

The following provisions do not apply to special licences or to vehicles used under such licences: the Public Passenger Vehicles Act 1981 s.16(1A) and (2) (conditions), s.17(3)(d) (revocation, suspension, etc., of a restricted licence on the ground of no longer satisfying the requirement to be of good repute or of appropriate financial standing), s.18 (duty to exhibit operator's disc), ss.19 and 20 (duty to inform traffic commissioner of certain matters), and s.26 (control of number of passengers), and the Transport Act 1985 s.26(5) and (6) (conditions following lack of maintenance or certain avoidance arrangements).

Relaxations and exemptions from the PSV requirements

There has been an increasing tendency to relax the laws relating to public ser- **13.165** vice vehicles and in particular for small and socially beneficial operations.

Under s.46 of the 1981 Act education authorities may use school buses, when being used to provide free school transport, to carry also fare paying passengers. They may also use school buses belonging to the authority, when not being used to provide free school transport, to provide local stage carriage services. In both cases no PCV driver's licence or PSV operator's licence is required where the school bus belongs to the authority.

13.166   As to exemptions in relation to services by certain educational and other bodies under s.19 of the 1985 Act permits and as to community bus services under s.22 of the 1985 Act, see below. There are also special provisions relating to British PSVs on international journeys (see below) and foreign PSVs. Other exemptions are noted above in the context of requirements to which they relate.

Examples

13.167   It may be helpful to explain the PSV licensing requirements by examples. As to eight or more passengers, see § 1.117. It is submitted there that the driver is excluded, making the demarcation point nine seats or less (including the driver's seat) and 10 seats or more.

Smith owns an eight-seater car and carries on business as a taxi and private hire proprietor with an appropriate licence for it. Smith will not require a PSV operator's licence for carrying passengers for hire or reward otherwise than at separate fares (formerly called contract carriage), whether locally or otherwise or for any use which falls within s.37 and the subsequent sections of the Town Police Clauses Act 1847 (taxi licensing), the Local Government (Miscellaneous Provisions) Act 1976 (private hire licensing) or Pts I and III of Sch.1 to the 1981 Act, even though separate fares are paid by his passengers. If he takes not more than eight passengers on any journey at separate fares and does not previously advertise the journey save as permitted and otherwise complies with Pts I and III he is exempt from having a PSV operator's licence. But if he takes two or more passengers at separate fares and advertises other than as permitted or otherwise fails to comply with Pt I or III he will require such a licence.

13.168   If a scheme is in force in the area under s.10 of the Transport Act 1985, Smith will on an immediate hiring be able to carry passengers for hire or reward at separate fares without the taxi becoming a public service vehicle, providing he complies with the terms of the scheme. In any event under s.11 of the same Act Smith will be able to take an advance booking for the carriage of passengers for hire or reward at separate fares without becoming a public service vehicle. Each of the passengers must have consented when booking his journey to share the use of the vehicle on that occasion with others on the basis that a separate fare would be payable by each passenger for his own journey. Presumably a parent may pay separately as agent for a child.

Smith may apply for a restricted PSV operator's licence (a special licence) under s.12 of the Transport Act 1985 so that he can register to provide local bus services at separate fares. He may not obtain authorisation by this means to operate local tours or excursions at separate fares and for tours and excursions he would have to operate under his taxi licence or in accordance with Pt I or Pt III or s.10 or 11. If he fails to comply, his vehicle will become classified as a public service vehicle.

13.169   Jones similarly owns an eight-seater car and takes passengers on similar journeys for separate fares. He does not carry the passengers in the course of a passenger-carrying business. The car will not therefore be classified as a PSV. He will not require a PSV operator's licence and Sch.1 to the 1981 Act will not concern him.

Brown owns a 24-seater motor coach. He will require a PSV operator's licence for carrying passengers for hire or reward whether or not at separate fares. He will require to be registered before he can provide local bus services or in London he will need to obtain a local service licence.

Robinson owns a 12-seater minibus. He does not have a s.19 permit (formerly known as a minibus permit) and is not operating a community bus service. He carries passengers for payment. He will be in exactly the same position as Brown. This will be so even if the "hire or reward" or the "payment" is merely implied within the terms of s.1(5)(a), (b) or (c). In some circumstances, however, Robinson may be eligible for a *restricted* PSV operator's licence or to be authorised for a community service bus.

13.170

If Brown or Robinson fulfils the conditions of Pt III of Sch.1, local service registration or in London a local service licence will not be required.

If the conditions of any Part of Sch.1 applicable to the journeys of the vehicles of Smith, Brown or Robinson are not complied with, a licence under s.12 (PSV operators' licence) may become necessary and offences may arise. An offence might be committed in respect of a Pt I or Pt III trip if it were publicly advertised.

Fitness of PSVs

A PSV operator's licence can only be granted for a vehicle adapted for eight or more passengers if a certificate of initial fitness is in force in accordance with s.6(1) of the 1981 Act. Alternatively, by s.6(1) there may be a type approval certificate under s.10 of the 1981 Act, or an equivalent type approval certificate under s.54 of the Road Traffic Act 1988. An offence under s.6(2) is committed by the operator of the vehicle if a vehicle is used in contravention of s.6(1). See further "Offences", § 13.203 below.

13.171

The fitness requirements are specified in Pt II of the Public Service Vehicles (Conditions of Fitness, Equipment, Use and Certification) Regulations 1981 (SI 1981/257) as amended. The requirements of these regulations are additional to those of the Construction and Use Regulations. Part II (fitness) only applies to vehicles adapted to carry eight or more passengers (reg.3(1)). Part IV (use) does not apply to Crown vehicles or vehicles in the service of a visiting force or of a headquarters (reg.4).

The Public Service Vehicles (Conditions of Fitness, Equipment, Use and Certification) (Amendment) (No.3) Regulations 2005 (SI 2005/2986) provide that the requirements set out in the 1981 Regulations may alternatively be met by a vehicle satisfying such of the Annexes of Directive 2001/85/EC relating to special provisions for vehicles used for the carriage of passengers comprising more than eight seats in addition to the driver's seat as may apply to it. The Public Services Vehicles Accessibility (Amendment) Regulations 2005 (SI 2005/2988) modify the requirements of the Public Services Vehicles Accessibility Regulations 2000 (SI 2000/1970) which prescribe wheelchair accessibility requirements and general accessibility requirements for single-deck and double-deck buses and coaches to offer compliance with Directive 2001/85/EC, as art.2 of the directive requires that the United Kingdom may not refuse or prohibit sale or entry into

13.172

service of a vehicle, or bodywork intended to be part of the vehicle (which may be type approved separately), if the requirements of the directive and its Annexes are met.

The 1981 Regulations are further amended by the Public Services Vehicles (Conditions of Fitness, Equipment, Use and Certification) (Amendment) (No.4) Regulations 2005 (SI 2005/3128). They allow a steam-powered vehicle manufactured before January 1, 1955 to be eligible to be issued with a certificate of initial fitness.

There are widely drawn powers to prohibit absolutely or conditionally the driving of unfit vehicles generally in ss.69–72A of the 1988 Act, as inserted by ss.12–15 of the 1991 Act. Additional power is given to prohibit the driving of overloaded motor vehicles if adapted to carry more than eight passengers (presumably excluding the driver, see Chapter 1, "Passengers") (s.70, as amended). As to these powers of prohibition generally, see further Chapter 8.

Services by certain educational and other bodies

13.173   Certain vehicles used by bodies for educational and other public purposes are exempted by ss.19–21 of the Transport Act 1985 from the PSV licensing requirements of the Act even though passengers are carried for hire or reward. Section 19 permits must be held instead. Section 19 of the 1985 Act has been amended by the Local Transport Act 2008 ss.57 and 58 so that public service vehicles with fewer than nine passenger seats can be used under a section 19 permit. As a result, there are two classes of permit: a large bus permit, which authorises the use of a vehicle adapted to carry more than 16 passengers, and a standard permit, which authorises the use of a small bus (defined as a vehicle adapted to carry more than eight, but not more than 16, passengers) or a public service vehicle other than a bus (a vehicle adapted to carry fewer than nine passengers).

Vehicles operated by permit holders are defined as "public service vehicles" and a requirement is introduced to ensure that proper records are kept in respect of the issue of permits in relation to the use of public service vehicles by educational and other bodies. Section 23A of the Transport Act 1985, as inserted by the 2008 Act s.60A, provides for a power to allow for the making of regulations to limit such permits to five years. The requirement to keep records about such permits is vested in the traffic commissioner.

"Hire or reward" in ss.19–21 has the same extended meaning as in s.1(5) of the 1981 Act (1985 Act s.137(3)). See § 13.49 and § 13.130.

13.174   Sections 19–21 apply to vehicles which:

    (a) come within the definition of a public service vehicle (a large bus, a small bus, or public service vehicle other than a bus);

    (b) are specified in a s.19 permit;

    (c) are used by the body to whom the permit is granted;

    (d) are not used for the carriage of members of the public at large;

    (e) are not used with a view to profit;

    (f) are not used incidentally to an activity which is itself carried on with a view to profit;

    (g) are used in accordance with the conditions of the permit;

    (h) are not used in contravention of regulations made under s.21.

The meaning of (e) and (f) above was considered in *R. v Secretary of State for the Environment, Transport and the Regions Ex p. Thomas's London Day Schools (Transport) Ltd*, November 11, 1999, unreported (CO/1703/99) DC. The company was established to provide transport services for schools owned and operated by a partnership, Thomas's London Day Schools, of which the partners in this company were also partners, together with other members of the Thomas family. The transport company was not carried on with a view to making a profit; in fact it made losses each year which were made good by the partnership. The partnership was operating the schools with a view to profit. The company argued that it was a distinct entity from the partnership and, as it was not being run for profit, it should be entitled to a permit.

However, to qualify for a permit the vehicle must be used by a body "concerned   **13.175**
with education". It was clear on the facts that the use of the vehicle was incidental to the activities of the partnership which were carried on with a view to profit. Indeed, this was the only way to bring the company within the criterion of being concerned in education. Accordingly, the company was not entitled to a s.19 permit.

So long as requirements (a)–(h) above are satisfied, s.12(1) (PSV operators' licences) and the driver who drives a large bus whilst it is being used under a permit satisfies the conditions set out in reg.3 of the Section 19 Permit Regulations 2009 (SI 2009/365), although the vehicle will still be a public service vehicle (1981 Act s.18). So long as the same requirements are satisfied small buses will not be treated as being public service vehicles for these purposes (s.18) even if they otherwise would be.

Under s.19(4), s.19 permits may be issued in respect of public service vehicles other than large buses by the traffic commissioner, to any body appearing to him to be concerned with education, religion, social welfare, recreation or other activities of benefit to the community, if it appears to him that the relevant activity is to be carried on in his area.

Section 19 permits may also be granted in respect of a small bus, or a public   **13.176**
service vehicle other than a bus, under a standard permit by a body designated for this purpose in an order made under s.19(7) of the 1985 Act. In this instance the permits are not issued by the traffic commissioner but by the designated body either to itself or to another body as specified in the order. So far as large buses are concerned s.19 permits may only be granted by the traffic commissioner (s.19(5)). The grant must be to a body which assists and co-ordinates the activities of bodies within his area which appear to him to be concerned with education, religion, social welfare or other activities of benefit to the community. This wording implies that a body has to be some form of umbrella organisation in order to be eligible. In this subsection there is no reference to recreation but this would seem to make little difference as non-profit-making recreation would normally appear to be an activity of benefit to the community and therefore eligible.

The traffic commissioner must not grant a permit for the use of a large bus unless satisfied that there will be adequate facilities or arrangements for maintaining the bus or buses in a fit and serviceable condition (s.19(6)).

Under s.20(2) there is power to grant a permit to a named individual on behalf   **13.177**
of the body. "Body" means a body of persons whether corporate or incorporate (1985 Act s.137). The wording of this seems to preclude an application by an individual person. Section 6 of the Interpretation Act 1978 provides that the plural

includes the singular unless the contrary intention is shown. An individual cannot be a body of persons and it seems therefore that there is a contrary intention.

Under s.20(4) there are powers to impose conditions and under s.20(5) there are certain powers to vary or revoke a permit.

13.178   The Section 19 Permit Regulations 2009 provide that permits granted on or after April 6, 2009 must be granted for a period not exceeding five years (reg.8). A corresponding disc, with an identical serial number, must be issued with every permit and must be displayed in the vehicle which is being used to provide a service under a permit, and contain the prescribed information (reg.9(1) and (2)). A legible disc must at all times be affixed to the inside of the vehicle in such a position that it does not interfere unduly with the driver's view and can easily be seen and read in daylight from outside the vehicle (reg.9(5)).

The conditions to be fulfilled by the driver of a small bus if the driver does not hold a PCV driver's licence, a PCV Community licence or a Northern Ireland equivalent are set out in reg.4 of the 2009 Regulations. Regulation 5 of the 2009 Regulations sets out the conditions to be fulfilled by a driver of a public service vehicle other than a bus.

13.179   The conditions of fitness for use of a small bus are set out in reg.6 of the 2009 Regulations. A small bus used under a section 19 permit must comply with regs 41–43 of the Road Vehicles (Construction and Use) Regulations 1986 or alternatively if the vehicle was first used before April 1, 1988, regs 6–33, 35–44 and 45A of the Public Service Vehicles (Conditions of Fitness, Equipment Use and Certification) Regulations 1981 (SI 1981/257).

Offences

13.180   There is no offence provided for a breach of s.19 itself. In the case of small buses the effect is that if there is a breach of the s.19 requirements, the vehicle may be treated as a public service vehicle so that there may be an offence accordingly. In the case of large buses, if there is a similar breach of the s.19 requirements, the exemptions (see s.18) from ss.12(1) (PSV operators' licences) and the PCV driver licensing requirements will cease to apply so that there may be offences accordingly.

Under the earlier legislation it was submitted that a breach of the regulations would not necessarily be such as to take the vehicle outside the definition of a small or large bus and therefore outside the protection of s.18. This has now been corrected in that by s.19(2) the s.18 exemption ceases to apply if the bus is used in contravention (however slight) of any provision of s.21 regulations.

13.181   The Minibus (Conditions of Fitness, Equipment and Use) Regulations 1977 (as amended) are by the Interpretation Act 1978 to be treated as if made under s.21 of the 1985 Act and s.41 of the 1988 Act. The Section 19 Permit Regulations 2009 are also made under s.21 but not under s.41. The penalty for a breach of regulations made under s.21 is contained in s.67 of the 1981 Act. See § 13.188, § 13.215 and § 13.216 for the s.67 penalty and § 13.212 as to the defence available for a breach of regulations made under s.21.

The maximum penalty in Sch.2 to the Road Traffic Offenders Act 1988 for a breach of regulations made under s.41 is a fine of level 5 or level 4 depending on the circumstances. See the penalty provisions under the section on the Construction and Use Regulations in Chapter 8. Section 41A of the 1988 Act as inserted by the 1991 Act refers to breaches of a "construction and use requirement" as to brakes, steering gear and tyres and a "construction and use requirement" under s.41A is defined by s.41(7) as a requirement imposed under s.41. Certain offences under the 1977 Regulations are to be treated as under s.41A (brakes and steering) and on this basis carry endorsement and discretionary disqualification. These offences will carry three penalty points. A defendant will escape endorsement if he proves that he did not know and had no reasonable cause to suspect that the facts of the case were such that the offence would be committed (see Chapter 8).

Community bus services

Sections 22 and 23 of the 1985 Act provide for the grant of community bus **13.182** permits for the provision of community bus services. "Community bus service" under s.22 (as amended by the Local Transport Act 2008 s.59) is defined as a local service (see § 13.120) by vehicles adapted to carry more than eight passengers. As with s.19 permits, the power is introduced to limit permits issued under s.22 to five years (Transport Act 1985 s.23A, inserted by the Local Transport Act 2008 s.60) and there is now a requirement placed on traffic commissioners to keep records about such permits (Transport Act 1985 s.126, as amended by the Local Transport Act 2008 s.61). As to "adapted" and "passengers" see Chapter 1.

The service must be provided by a body of persons (whether corporate or unincorporate—see the definition in s.137(1) of the 1985 Act) who are concerned for the social and welfare needs of one or more communities (s.22(1)). The wording of this seems to preclude an application by an individual person. Section 6 of the Interpretation Act 1978 provides that the plural includes the singular unless the contrary intention is shown. An individual cannot be a body of persons and it seems therefore that there is a contrary intention. The service must also be non-profit-making (s.22(1)) either on the part of the body or anyone else.

Community bus permits are granted under s.22 for the use of public service **13.183** vehicles for community bus services, or for such services and in addition for carrying passengers for hire or reward where it will directly assist the provision of the community service by providing financial support for it. This means that excursions may be provided to subsidise the local service but not vice versa.

The extended meaning of "hire or reward" in s.1(5) of the 1981 Act applies in the 1985 Act (s.138(5)). As to "hire or reward" see § 13.49 and § 13.130. The vehicles must be only those adapted to carry more than eight passengers (s.22(1)). The meaning of "adapted" and the question of whether "passengers" includes the driver is discussed in Chapter 1.

Section 23(2) specifies the conditions which apply to the use of any vehicle **13.184** under a community bus permit. Failure to comply with a condition is an offence contrary to s.23(5), see "Offences", § 13.203 below. Section 59 of the Local Transport Act 2008 relaxed the restrictions which apply to the provision of community bus services in two respects:

(a) the restriction on the use of vehicles adapted to carry more than 16 passengers was removed, thus allowing services to be provided under a community bus permit using either a small bus (a vehicle adapted to carry more than eight but not more than 16 passengers) or a large bus (a vehicle adapted to carry more than 16 passengers);

(b) the removal of the prohibition on certain drivers of such vehicles from being paid.

The Community Bus Regulations 2009 (SI 2009/366), which came into effect on April 6, 2009, prescribe further conditions which must be met by the drivers of small buses and large buses when used under such a permit (regs 3 and 4).

Regulation 5 of the 2009 Regulations prescribes the conditions of fitness to be satisfied by a small bus used under a permit. No such conditions of fitness are prescribed for a large bus. A large bus must hold a certificate of initial fitness and thereby satisfy the requirement of s.6 of the Public Passenger Vehicles Act 1981.

Regulation 6 of the 2009 Regulations empowers a traffic commissioner to attach conditions to permits restricting the use of any large bus, or large bus of a specified description, under a permit.

13.185   Under the 2009 Regulations, a community bus service disc must be displayed in accordance with reg.10(4).

The 2009 Regulations contain provisions relating to permits. These include procedures for permits to be returned to a traffic commissioner for the purposes of the imposition of conditions (reg.7), the fee to be paid for the grant of a permit (currently £55) (reg.8) and the information which a permit must contain. The Local Transport Act 2008 amended the 1985 Act to empower the Secretary of State to limit the validity of community bus permits to a period not exceeding five years. Regulation 9(1) provides for all permits granted on or after April 6, 2009 to be so limited. The procedure to be followed when a permit or disc is lost or needs to be returned to the traffic commissioner is set out in regs 11–13. It should be noted that any permit or disc granted or issued before April 6, 2009, if lost or destroyed, will be revoked and a five-year validity limit placed on any new permit. The 2009 Regulations also revoke the Community Bus Regulations 1986 (SI 1986/1254, as amended) (reg.14).

13.186   It should be stressed that it is the holder of the permit who commits an offence contrary to s.23(5) if a condition is contravened while any person may commit an offence by a breach of the Community Bus Regulations 2009 (see "Offences" below).

Offences

13.187   No offence is expressly provided for use without a community bus permit. As is made clear from s.18, if the use is outside the terms of the permit, the vehicle may be a public service vehicle so that there may be an offence contrary to s.12(5) (no PSV operator's licence) or s.87 of the 1988 Act (no PCV driver's licence).

Contravention of a condition attached to a community bus permit is an offence under s.23(5) punishable on summary conviction with a fine of level 3. The offence is committed by the holder of the permit. Another person may be guilty of aiding and abetting, see Chapter 1. The defence in s.68(3) (due diligence) of the 1981 Act applies—see § 13.212.

The Community Bus Regulations 2009 are made under the 1981 Act ss.52(1) and 60, the 1985 Act ss.23(2), (3) and (8), 23A(1) and 134 and the Local Transport Act 2008 s.60(2) and (7). The penalty is therefore that provided by s.67 of the 1981 Act. Section 67 (by s.127(3)) has effect as if Pts I and II of the 1985 Act (which include ss.22 and 23) were contained in the 1981 Act. Section 67 breach of regulations offences carry a maximum fine of level 2. The defence under s.68(1) (reasonable excuse) is available—see § 13.212.

13.188   If a breach of the regulations is charged under the 1981 Act, the penalty section is s.67 and the maximum fine is of level 2. For the defence of reasonable excuse available for offences under s.67, see s.68(1) and § 13.212. If a breach of any of the regulations is charged as an offence contrary to s.41 of the 1988 Act, the maximum penalty is a fine of level 5 or level 4 depending on the circumstances. See the penalty provisions under the section on the Construction and Use Regulations in Chapter 8. Section 41A of the 1988 Act as inserted by the 1991 Act refers to breaches of a "construction and use requirement" as to brakes, steering gear and tyres and a "construction and use requirement" under s.41A is defined by s.41(7) as a requirement imposed under s.41. Certain offences to be treated as under s.41A (brakes and steering) on this basis carry endorsement and discretionary disqualification and three penalty points. A defendant will escape endorsement if he proves that he did not know and had no reasonable cause to suspect that the facts of the case were such that the offence would be committed (see § 8.104).

International passenger services

British vehicles on international passenger journeys, such journeys by vehicles **13.189** from EU Member States and certain journeys by passenger vehicles from third countries are controlled by the Road Transport (International Passenger Services) Regulations 1984 (SI 1984/748), as amended. These regulations are to be treated as made under s.60 of the Public Passenger Vehicles Act 1981 and s.41 of the 1988 Act. They extensively modify the 1981 and 1985 Acts in relation to public service vehicles on international journeys and, as they are complicated, reference should be made to the specific regulations. The regulations refer to EC regulations and the current EC regulation is 684/92, as amended. The procedure in the Netherlands Regulations for the authorisation of such services was considered in Case 88/86 *Bovo Tours BV v Minister of Transport, Water Control and Construction* [1989] R.T.R. 222. The case concerned services between Amsterdam and London.

Part II of the 1984 Regulations (regs 4–6) provides for vehicles registered in the United Kingdom; Pt III (regs 7–12) for vehicles registered abroad. The regulations do not make provision for vehicles registered in Northern Ireland when used in Great Britain on services running between Northern Ireland and Great Britain but not outside the United Kingdom. Provision for them is made in the Road Transport (Northern Ireland Passenger Services) Regulations 1980 (SI 1980/1460).

The Public Service Vehicles (Conditions of Fitness, Equipment, Use and Cer- **13.190** tification) Regulations 1981 (SI 1981/257), as amended, do not apply to non-British vehicles (to which Pt III of the 1984 Regulations applies instead), or to vehicles registered in Northern Ireland (to which Pt II applies instead).

Where appropriate British vehicles must comply with British law as well.

By reg.2 of the 1984 Regulations "public service vehicle" has the same meaning as in s.1 of the 1981 Act.

The 1984 Regulations refer to "Community regulated" services and to "regu- **13.191** lar", "shuttle" and "occasional" services. "Community regulated" services are those to which Regulation (EEC) 684/92 applies; they are defined by art.1 of Regulation (EEC) 684/92. They are services for the international carriage of passengers by coach and bus within the EU by carriers for hire or reward or own account carriers established in an EU Member State using vehicles which are registered in that Member State and which are suitable, by their construction and equipment for carrying more than nine persons (specifically including the driver) and intended for that purpose, when both the departure and the arrival are within the EU. Also included are the empty movements of these vehicles in connection with the carriage and, if the appropriate agreement is reached, those parts of journeys between Member States and third countries which take place within the EU.

13.192   Community regulated services may be "regular", "special regular", or "occasional" services, or own-account transport operations, all as defined by art.2, as amended. The nature of a regular service was considered by the European Court of Justice in Case C–47/97 *Criminal Proceedings against E. Clarke and Sons (Coaches) Ltd* [1998] R.T.R. 333. The company was prosecuted for failing to keep tachograph records. It relied on the exemption in art.4(3) in its defence. The term "regular service" is defined in art.2 of Regulation (EEC) 684/92 primarily as services which provide to carry passengers at specified intervals along a specified route with the passengers being taken up and set down at predetermined stopping points. Amendments to this regulation by Regulation (EC) 11/98 do not affect this decision. A regular service is to be open to all subject, where appropriate, to compulsory reservation (art.2(1.1). There is a further provision for "special regular services" for those services which operate under the conditions of art.2(1.1) but provide for specified categories of passengers to the exclusion of other passengers (art.2(1.2)). Examples given include carriage of workers between home and work and carriage of school pupils and students to and from an educational institution. In this case, one of the company's coaches was used by a tour operator to convey tourists between the airport and the hotel with occasional stops at tourist attractions. Each component part of the journey was less than 50km. The meaning of "regular service" as set out in art.2 to Regulation (EEC) 684/92 requires that the service be provided at "specified intervals". This means that the frequency had to be specified with precision and had to be regular. Here, it was the needs of the tour operators that determined the use and that depended on reservations made by customers. It was not "regular". A further requirement is that there are specified routes, which means precisely defined routes. Article 2 envisages stopping points along the route at which passengers could be taken up and set down. People concerned had to know the route to be taken and the stopping points. It was not sufficient merely to know in advance the points of departure and arrival.

13.193   Finally, the term "specified categories of passengers" in art.2(1.2) meant passengers sharing the same status. It did not cover a group of passengers whose only common feature was that they had made reservations for a journey with the same tour operator.

A special regular service is a service for a regular category of persons such as workers or schoolchildren or the carriage of soldiers and their families between their state of origin and their barracks. An occasional service is one that does not meet the definition of a regular service and which carries groups of passengers assembled on the initiative of the customer or the carrier.

13.194   Own-account transport operations are carried out for non-commercial and non-profit-making purposes by a natural or legal person. The transport activity must be an ancillary activity and the vehicles must be owned (including hire-purchase and long-term leasing) by the natural or legal person and must be driven by a staff member or by the natural person himself. Special regular services, occasional services and own-account transport operations do not require authorisation (art.4, as amended). Own-account transport operations are subject to a system of certificates (art.13(1)).

PSVs registered in Northern Ireland

Regulations 4, 5 and 6 of the 1984 Regulations provide exemptions for **13.195** Northern Ireland vehicles. Regulation 4 provides that where a public service vehicle, registered in Northern Ireland, is being used for the Community regulated carriage of passengers, providing the vehicle is used in accordance with the applicable requirement of the Council regulations (see reg.2 and Sch.1), the following sections of the 1981 Act s.6 (certificate of initial fitness), s.12 (PSV operators' licences), and s.18 (exhibition of operators' discs) do not apply to those vehicles on such journeys through Great Britain. Also excluded was s.22 (PSV drivers' licences). Presumably this should be interpreted as excluding the re-enacted driver licensing requirements for PCVs in Pts III and IV of the 1988 Act. If there is a breach of the Council regulations, it would seem that the relevant 1981 Act offence would be committed.

In respect of PSVs registered in Northern Ireland, used for non-Community regulated international carriage of passengers on regular, special regular or shuttle services, reg.5 provides that ss.6, 12 and 18 (PSV operators' licences, etc.) and s.22 (PSV drivers' licences) (now to be read as the equivalent Pt III licence) do not apply to them on such journeys through Great Britain. But presumably if the appropriate authorisation is not in force, the offence of not having the appropriate s.12 or Pt III licences will be committed. In addition a varied s.6 of the Transport Act 1985 (requirement for international passenger transport authorisation) is substituted so that an offence may be committed accordingly.

In respect of occasional services by vehicles registered in Northern Ireland be- **13.196** ing used for the international carriage of passengers by road (which are Community regulated by art.2(3.1) of Regulation (EEC) 684/92 or regulated by the Agreement on the International Occasional Carriage of Passengers by Coach and Bus (Interbus Agreement or, before January 1, 2003, its similarly named predecessor, the ASOR Agreement: see § 13.197 below) or otherwise are public service vehicles or services as described in art.2), reg.6 provides that, in addition, ss.6, 12 and 18 (PSV operators' licences, etc.) and s.22 (PSV drivers' licences) (presumably now to be read as the equivalent Pt III licence) do not apply to them on such journeys through Great Britain.

PSVs registered abroad

No public service vehicle operator's licence is needed in Britain in the in- **13.197** stances described below. These are affected by two similarly named agreements, the Agreement on the International Occasional Carriage of Passengers by Coach and Bus (Interbus Agreement) and the Agreement on International Carriage of Passengers by Road by means of Occasional Coach and Bus Services (ASOR). The Interbus Agreement is effective from January 1, 2003 for those contracting states that have ratified it—the European Community, Albania, Bosnia and Herzegovina, Bulgaria, the Czech Republic, Hungary, Lithuania, Latvia, Macedonia, Moldova, Montenegro, Romania, Slovenia and Turkey. The ASOR Agreement continues in force for journeys before January 1, 2003 or for journeys involving those who have ratified ASOR, but not the Interbus Agreement. By virtue of the Interpretation Act 1978, it is submitted that references in the 1984 Regulations to ASOR also apply to the Interbus Agreement. No licence is needed for:

(a) certain temporary visits to Britain of three months or less by public service vehicles which are for nine or less passengers (specifically including the driver) (reg.7);

(b) Community regulated services, providing the use is in accordance with the appropriate Council or Commission regulations (reg.8—from June 11, 1999, Regulation (EEC) 684/92 is further amended to provide for Community licences to be issued in order to carry out international passenger transport operations by coach and bus (art.3A));

(c) non-Community regulated services, providing the vehicle is used by or on behalf of a person who is authorised as appropriate in the country of registration (reg.9);

(d) certain Community regulated occasional services under art.2(3.1) and certain Interbus Agreement/ASOR occasional services under art.2(3.1) (subject to the requirements as to waybills) (reg.10);

(e) certain non-Community regulated occasional services, described in art.2(3.1), by vehicles registered in states which are members of the European Conference of Ministers of Transport (ECMT) excluding EU and Interbus Agreement/ASOR states for temporary visits of three months or less, provided the vehicle is used by or on behalf of a person who is authorised as appropriate in the country of registration (reg.11);

(f) certain occasional services of whatever kind (i.e. under art.2(3.1)) by vehicles not registered in an EU Member State or a country not otherwise mentioned above for temporary visits of three months or less (subject to the same proviso) (reg.12).

13.198   In cases (c), (d), (f) and, in certain circumstances, (e), a person who causes or permits such a public service vehicle to be used on a road for the international carriage of passengers without an international passenger transport authorisation in force and carried on the vehicle commits an offence. In case (e) (in certain circumstances) a slightly different s.12 of the 1981 Act is substituted. In this case the document which must be carried on the vehicle is one issued by the competent authority of the country in which the vehicle is registered and it must be in the form set out in Sch.3 to the regulations and duly completed.

Further requirements

13.199   Regulations 15–18 of the 1984 Regulations contain provisions as to authorisations, certificates, waybills, etc.

It is an offence contrary to reg.19(1) if a person without reasonable excuse uses a vehicle for the Community regulated carriage of passengers by road, or causes or permits such a vehicle to be used to provide regular, special regular, shuttle, or worker services, without or not in accordance with the appropriate authorisation or without the appropriate certificate for worker services. He commits an offence contrary to reg.19(2) if without reasonable excuse he uses a vehicle for the Community regulated or Interbus Agreement/ASOR regulated carriage of passengers by road or causes or permits a vehicle to be so used to provide occasional services when there is not duly and correctly completed for the vehicle a passenger waybill or when the top copy of the waybill is not kept on the vehicle as required.

A person commits an offence contrary to reg.20 who: **13.200**

  (a) without reasonable excuse contravenes or fails to comply with a requirement imposed by or under regs 15(4) or (5), 16(2)(a), 17(1) or (2) or 18(4) or (5), or by or under any provision of Interbus Agreement/ ASOR or the Council or Commission regulations referred to in any of these provisions; or

  (b) obstructs an examiner in the exercise of his powers under regs 16(2), 17(1) or (2) or 18(5) or (6) or under any provision of Interbus Agreement/ASOR or the Council or Commission regulations referred to in any of these provisions.

Non-regular national passenger services to be permitted by EU Member States

On June 11, 1999, Council Regulation (EC) 12/98 came into force and was   **13.201**
implemented by the Road Transport (Passenger Vehicles Cabotage) Regulations 1999 (SI 1999/3413). A carrier operating road passenger services for hire or reward and holding a Community licence under Regulation (EEC) 684/92 art.3A (see § 13.197), is able, temporarily, to operate national passenger services for hire or reward in a Member State other than one where the carrier is established. In Regulation (EC) 12/98, these are referred to as cabotage transport operations. However, these services will be restricted (art.3) to special regular services which are operated under a contract between the organiser and the carrier, occasional services, and regular services which are provided in the course of a regular international service. Urban and suburban services are excluded. Many of these terms are defined in arts 2 and 3. National laws will continue to apply in most respects, particularly drivers' hours. The EC regulations provide for certain key documents to be kept on the vehicle and available for inspection and continue to allow the host state to take action against operators who infringe the regulations. These may be by administrative penalty under art.11 or by summary offence under the 1999 Regulations. "Vehicles" are defined as motor vehicles which, by virtue of their type of construction and equipment, are suitable for carrying more than nine persons—including the driver—and are intended for that purpose. Compare the definitions in Chapter 1.

Without prejudice to any criminal proceedings, the host country may by art.11(3) of Regulation (EC) 12/98 impose a temporary ban on cabotage passenger transport operations by the non-resident carrier within the host state territory in the event of serious or frequent infringements of Regulation (EC) 12/98 or of Community or national transport regulations within its territory on the occasion of a cabotage passenger transport operation. Note that infringements of these laws in the course of other transport operations will not qualify.

Penalties

The penalty for a breach of Interbus Agreement/ASOR, council or Commis   **13.202**
sion regulations, by reg.19 is a fine of level 3. The penalty for a breach of regs 15(4) or (5), 16(2)(a), 17(1) or (2), 18(4) or (5) or (relating to the obstruction of examiners) regs 16(2), 17(1) or (2) and 18(5) or (6) of the Road Transport (International Passenger Services) Regulations 1984 —or the regulations referred to in any of them—is a fine of level 3 also (reg.20). The regulations have effect as if made under the 1981 Act and under s.67 of that Act the penalty regarding the remaining regulations is a fine of level 2.

Section 65 of the 1981 Act (forgery, etc., of licences and documents) is applied by reg.21 of the 1984 Regulations to authorisations, certificates and other documents required by the Council or Commission regulations or the 1984 Regulations. The offence contrary to s.65 is an "either way" offence triable in accordance with ss.18–23 of the Magistrates' Courts Act 1980. The maximum penalty on indictment is two years' imprisonment or an unlimited fine or both and the maximum penalty on summary conviction is £5,000. See further §§ 13.203 and 13.208 below and Chapter 16.

Offences

13.203   The principal offences under the 1981 Act have been referred to in context above. However, in each case the relevant section should be closely consulted as to the persons who may be liable and the defences available. These and other matters are discussed below.

Section 12(5) (no PSV operator's licence) refers to a vehicle being "used". The previous equivalent section was differently worded and many of the earlier cases are therefore no longer applicable. The liability now seems to be absolute without any need for a guilty intent. See below, however, for defences available. As to "using" see Chapter 1. A person may "use" through his agent or employee. He may not be "using" if the vehicle is hired to another. See, however, below for certain modifications as to hirings with regard to the meaning of "operator of a vehicle".

13.204   In addition to prosecution, PSV operators who use certain PSVs without a PSV operator's licence may have their vehicles detained by virtue of provisions introduced by s.47 of, and Sch.3 to, the Local Transport Act 2008 which inserts s.2A and Sch.2A into the Public Passenger Vehicles Act 1981. Regulations will make provision for applications to be made to a traffic commissioner for the return of detained vehicles.

Cases

13.205   The cases on the road service licence provisions now repealed may still be relevant for breaches of conditions and for the London local service requirements. A road service licence was not required for a service provided under a scheme by the British Transport Commission or its agent; where the Commission itself hired a bus and gave all the directions as to its movements, it was held to provide the transport itself (*Railway Executive v Henson* (1949) 113 J.P. 333).

If an employee disobeyed a term of his master's road service licence, e.g. by diverting from the authorised route, the master might be liable (*G. Newton Ltd v Smith* [1962] 2 All E.R. 19). In that case, the charge was failure to comply with a condition of the licence and it was held that liability was imposed on a master for a failure by him or his servant to comply with the conditions of the licence, provided the driver acted willfully or negligently.

13.206   In *Carpenter v Campbell* [1953] 1 All E.R. 280 it was stated that where it is an employer's duty to obtain a licence and he fails to do so, the driver should not be prosecuted. Many prosecutions are now restricted to specified defendants in any event, but it is possible that a prosecution might be considered against a driver for aiding and abetting where it can be established that he is aware of the lack of a licence.

Under the old law there was no liability when a trip was made illegal by the action, unknown to the defendant, of a person not subject to his control (*Reynolds v Austin* [1951] 1 All E.R. 606). See below as to the defences available in any event.

Where an offence is committed by a company under Pt II of the 1981 Act, certain responsible officers of the company will also be liable to prosecution (s.74).

Section 1(5) of the 1981 Act makes special provisions as to arrangements between a society and its members or between members for transport being deemed a carriage for hire or reward; otherwise, a member of an unincorporated society could be said to be using his own vehicle if the society owned it. The principle laid down in *Wurzal v Houghton Main Home Delivery Service Ltd* at § 13.45 therefore seems inapplicable.   **13.207**

Many of the regulations provide that no PSV operator's licence or PCV driver's licence need be held if certain requirements are fulfilled. If these requirements are not fulfilled and if no other offence is substituted it is submitted that the offence is committed of not having the licence authorisation.

Section 65 of the 1981 Act provides for offences of forgery and misuse of documents, etc. By s.65(3) as amended by s.12 of the Forgery and Counterfeiting Act 1981 "forges" means "makes a false document or other thing in order that it may be used as genuine". This is a different and simpler definition from that used in the Forgery and Counterfeiting Act itself. Section 66 provides for offences in relation to false statements to obtain licences, etc. Sections 65 and 66 are worded similarly to ss.173 and 174 of the 1988 Act, and reference to Chapter 16 where these sections are discussed may be helpful. Sections 65 and 66 apply to permits under s.19 (for educational and similar bodies) and s.22 (community bus services) of the 1985 Act and also to London local service licences. Section 67 provides for offences for breach of regulations made under the Act (see § 13.188).   **13.208**

"Operator of the vehicle"

Certain offences are committed only by the "operator of the vehicle", e.g. s.12(5) of the 1981 Act (no PSV operator's licence). The offence under s.30(2) of the Transport Act 1985 (plying for hire as a whole with a PSV adapted to carry more than eight passengers) is committed by the operator of the vehicle. Certain other offences can only be committed by the "operator of the service", e.g. s.35(1) and (6) of the 1985 Act (providing a London local service without a licence).   **13.209**

The "operator of the vehicle" for the purposes of the 1981 Act and the 1985 Act (see s.137 of that Act) means (1981 Act s.81(1)(b)):

   (a) the driver, if he owns the vehicle; and

   (b) in any other case, the person for whom the driver works (whether under a contract of employment or any other description of contract personally to do work).

This seems to be wide enough to include a self-employed person who hires himself out.

This definition may be modified in the case of hiring arrangements: for a modification in the case of hiring between holders of PSV operators' licences, see the PSV (Operators' Licences) Regulations 1995 reg.22. Under these regulations the holder from whom the vehicle is hired is still regarded as the operator if   **13.210** under the hiring the hirer is not entitled to keep the vehicle in his possession for a total period of more than 14 days (reg.22(a)). There must be a gap of at least 14 days between such hirings to the same hirer (reg.22(b)). The purpose of this is presumably to prevent long-term arrangements being disguised by short breaks, but there seems to be nothing to prevent a hiring of a different vehicle to the same hirer for 14-day periods. The reference in reg.22(a) and (b) is to the vehicle. This point has now to some extent been covered by s.26(5) of the 1985 Act which allows the traffic commissioner to attach a restrictive condition to the PSV operator's licence if it appears to him that the operator has been involved in arrangements with any other operator for the use of each other's vehicle with a view to hindering enforcement of any requirements of the law relating to the operation of these vehicles. The disc of the person making the hiring must be displayed when required. If this is not done, reg.22 ceases to apply (reg.22(c)) and seemingly the hirer will be operating the vehicle without a PSV operator's licence. These provisions as to hiring arrangements do not apply to special licences (see § 13.163).

"Operator of the service"

13.211   By s.137(7) of the 1985 Act for the purposes of that Act the operator of a service is the person providing the service. For those purposes the operator of a vehicle being used on a road for the carriage of passengers for hire or reward at separate fares shall be taken to be providing the service in question unless he proves that the service is or forms part of a service provided not by himself but by one or more other persons. The burden is placed on the operator of the vehicle in these circumstances to prove on the balance of probabilities that he is not providing the service (*R. v Carr-Briant* [1943] K.B. 607).

Defences

13.212   Defences contained in s.68 are available for many of the offences under the 1981 Act. The defence of reasonable excuse in s.68(1) is available for offences contrary to ss.19(5), 20(4), 24(2) and (3), 25(3), 26(2), 67 and 70(3) and so much of s.22(9) as relates to contravention of s.22(1)(a). It should be noted that s.67 (penalty for breach of regulations) applies to regulations made under Pts I and II of the 1985 Act, such as the Public Service Vehicles (Registration of Local Services) Regulations 1986, and also the Community Bus Regulations 2009 which are made under that Act (see s.127(3) of the 1985 Act). The defence in s.68(1) will be available accordingly.

The defence in s.68(3) that the defendant took all reasonable precautions and exercised all due diligence to avoid the commission of any offence under that provision is available for offences contrary to ss.6(2), 9(9), 12(5), 16(7), 18(4), 26(2), 27(2) and so much of s.22(9) as relates to contravention of s.22(1)(b). The s.68(3) defence also applies to s.35(6) and s.38(7) of the 1985 Act (London local services offences) and to s.30(2) of that Act (PSVs adapted to carry more than eight passengers plying for hire as a whole). The most important of these are s.12(5) (no PSV operator's licence) and s.16(7) (breach of condition of PSV operator's licence). For the meaning of "all due diligence" see § 14.185 and for "reasonable excuse" refer to § 4.261. The defences will be judged on the balance of probabilities and it will be for the defendant to establish them.

PSV LICENSING: PROCEEDINGS AND PENALTIES

Generally

The following sections of the 1981 Act apply to offences under Pt I or II of the **13.213** Transport Act 1985 as they apply to offences under Pt II of the 1981 Act, namely s.69 (restriction on proceedings and authority to prosecute), s.70 (duty to give information as to identity of driver), s.71 (evidence by certificate), s.72 (proof of identity of driver) and s.74 (offences by companies).

By s.69 of the 1981 Act proceedings for an offence under s.12 (PSV operators' licences) or any other provisions in Pt II of the Act or any regulations made thereunder shall not in England be instituted except by or on behalf of the Director of Public Prosecutions or by a person authorised in that behalf by commissioners of a traffic area, a chief officer of police or the council of a county or district. This does not apply to regulations under s.25 (conduct of passengers) or s.26 (control of number of passengers).

Where a police sergeant laid an information which was signed by an Assistant **13.214** Commissioner of the Metropolitan Police and by a superintendent and the Commissioner had given a general authorisation in writing to prosecute, it was held in *Westminster Coaching Services v Piddlesden* (1933) 97 J.P. 185, that the sergeant had authority to take proceedings under what is now s.69. Contrast *Record Tower Cranes v Gisbey* [1969] 1 W.L.R. 148 and *Nelms v Roe* [1969] 3 All E.R. 1379 noted at § 7.40, "By or on behalf of a chief officer of police" and see generally "Authority to prosecute", in Chapter 2. There is an article on authority to prosecute at (1984) 148 J.P. 521 which discusses the difficult wording in s.69.

As to evidence by certificate, see s.71, and as to proof of a driver's identity, see s.72. Sections 71 and 72 are worded similarly to ss.11 and 12 of the Road Traffic Offenders Act 1988. These sections are discussed at § 3.52. Section 70 (duty to give information as to identity of driver) has similarities to s.172 of the Road Traffic Act 1988 and reference to § 7.24 where that section is discussed may assist.

The offence of using a PSV without an operator's licence contrary to s.12(5) **13.215** carries a maximum fine of level 4. The offence of driving without a PSV or PCV driver's licence is in effect contrary to s.87(1) of the 1988 Act and that of causing or permitting the driving contrary to s.87(2). Section 87(1) offences (driving otherwise than in accordance with licence) may carry endorsement, 3–6 penalty points and discretionary disqualification in certain circumstances. Section 87(2) offences (causing or permitting driving otherwise than in accordance with licence) and breaches of PCV and PSV learner driver licence conditions and other conditions and the other offences set out there are not subject to endorsement or disqualification.

Note that the s.67 penalty applies also to regulations made under Pts I and II of the 1985 Act such as the Public Service Vehicles (Registration of Local Services) Regulations 1986 and the Community Bus Regulations 2009 (1985 Act s.127(3)). The s.67 penalty is not subject to endorsement of driving licences, disqualification or penalty points.

For a table of penalties, see § 13.216.

13.216

Public service vehicles operators' licences, etc.: penalties

Offence	Mode of trial	Section *	Imprisonment	Level of fine	Disqualification	Penalty points	Endorsement code	Sentencing guideline
No PSV operator's licence	Summary	s.12(5)	—	4	—	—	—	Fine band B Owner-driver Fine band C Owner-company
Breach of PSV operator's licence conditions	Summary	s.16(7)	—	3	—	—	—	—
Failing to fix and exhibit operator's disc	Summary	s.18(4)	—	3	—	—	—	—
Offences of failing to give information to traffic commissioner	Summary	s.19(5), 20(4)	—	3	—	—	—	—
False information	Summary	s.20(5)	—	4	—	—	—	—
False statement to obtain licence	Summary	s.66	—	4	—	—	—	—
Breach of regulations under Act	Summary	s.67	—	2	—	—	—	—
No certificate of fitness	Summary	s.6(2)	—	4	—	—	—	—

Offence	Mode of trial	Section *	Imprisonment	Level of fine	Disqualification	Penalty points	Endorsement code	Sentencing guideline
Forgery and misuse of documents	a) On indictment b) Summary	s.65	2 years or unlimited fine or both 6 months or statutory maximum or both					
Holder of community bus permit breaching condition	Summary	s.23(5) Transport Act 1985	—	3	—	—	—	—
Operator of PSV adapted to carry more than 8 passengers plying for hire as a whole	Summary	s.30(2) Transport Act 1985	—	3	—	—	—	—
Providing London local service other than in accordance with the 1999 Act	Summary	s.180(2) Greater London Authority Act 1999	—	3	—	—	—	—

Offence	Mode of trial	Section *	Imprisonment	Level of fine	Disqualification	Penalty points	Endorsement code	Sentencing guideline
Breach of certain international passenger service regulations— regs 15(4) or (5), 16(2)(a), 17(1) or (2), 18(4) or (5) and 19, or, relating to obstruction of examiners, regs 16(2), 17(1) or (2) and 18(5) or (6)	Summary	Road Transport (International Passenger Services) Regs 1984, reg.20, and 1981 Act	—	3	—	—	—	—

* Public Passenger Vehicles Act 1981 unless otherwise stated.

CONDUCT ON PUBLIC SERVICE VEHICLES AND TRAMCARS, ETC.

Generally

The behaviour of drivers, conductors and passengers on public service vehicles **13.217**
(other than trams) is regulated by the Public Service Vehicles (Conduct of Drivers, Inspectors, Conductors and Passengers) Regulations 1990 (SI 1990/1020), as amended made under ss.24(1), 25(1) and (4), and 60 of the Public Passenger Vehicles Act 1981 and ss.23(2)(b), 134(1) and 137(1) of the Transport Act 1985. Conduct on tramcars, etc., is discussed separately at §§ 13.232–4.

Definitions are contained in reg.3 of the 1990 Regulations. "Driver" means a person who is the holder of a licence and who is for the time being responsible for driving the vehicle. Compare this definition with the other "driver" definitions discussed under "Driver" in Chapter 1. "Licence", subject to the transitional provisions for PSV licences, means a licence to drive under Pt III of the Road Traffic Act 1988 and a PSV is to be construed for the purposes of ss.24–26 inclusive as meaning a PSV being used on a road for carrying passengers for hire or reward (s.24, as amended). "Conductor" means a person, not being the driver, who is authorised by the operator to act as a conductor on the vehicle, but does not include an inspector. "Vehicle" means any vehicle used as a PSV as defined in the 1981 Act (see § 13.113) but excluding any vehicle used under a s.19 permit (services by certain educational and other bodies—see § 13.173).

For cases on the term "passengers" including intending passengers, see [1952] **13.218**
Jo.Crim.L. 102, and 116 J.P.Jo. 280. What is meant by "entering" and "alighting" a public service vehicle was considered at [1952] Jo.Crim.L. 116 in the light of certain magistrates' courts' decisions which are not binding. It was held that a person on the platform had already entered. The driver was under a duty to act as if at a bus stop even though he had stopped at a request stop because of the traffic and without any request being made.

Conduct of drivers, inspectors and conductors

Regulations 4–5 of the 1990 Regulations deal with the conduct of drivers, **13.219**
inspectors and conductors.

The provisions in the former regulations that the driver and conductor behave in a civil and orderly manner and do not deceive or refuse to inform any passenger as to the destination, route or fare have been omitted. The requirements that the driver and conductor should not cause the vehicle to remain stationary longer than reasonably necessary except at permitted places have not been repeated. Another desired result of the original regulation was to prevent buses bunching gregariously and this sanction no longer remains. Following the repeal of s.3(4) of the Road Traffic Regulation Act 1984 traffic regulation orders made by local authorities under the 1984 Act may impose prohibitions or restrictions on waiting by PSVs.

Under reg.4(1) a driver must not, when a vehicle is in motion, hold a **13.220**
microphone or any attachment thereto unless it is necessary for him to speak into it, either in an emergency or on grounds of safety. Under reg.4(2) a driver must not, when a vehicle is in motion, speak to any person either directly or by means of a microphone unless obliged to do so by reason of an emergency or on grounds of safety; he may also speak to a relevant person (defined in effect as the operator

or an employee of the operator) in relation to the operation of the vehicle provided that he can do so without being distracted from his driving of the vehicle. In addition the driver of a relevant service may make short statements from time to time indicating the location of the vehicle or on operational matters, again provided he is not similarly distracted. For this purpose, a relevant service is a service for the carriage of passengers for hire or reward at separate fares (see §§ 13.126, 13.130 and 13.134) which is neither an excursion or tour (see § 13.124) within the meaning of s.137(1) of the Transport Act 1985, nor any other service the primary purpose of which is sightseeing.

There is nothing in reg.4(2) to overrule the prohibition in reg.4(1) against holding a microphone. On this basis, a microphone may only be held to speak on the emergency or safety grounds. If a microphone is to be used otherwise than in accordance with reg.4(2), it would seem that it would have to be a fixed and not a hand-held microphone.

13.221   Regulation 5(1) requires a driver and conductor to take all reasonable precautions to ensure the safety of passengers who are on, or who are entering or leaving the vehicle. A driver must, when picking up or setting down passengers, stop the vehicle as close as is reasonably practicable to the left or nearside of the road.

In *Steff v Beck* [1987] R.T.R. 61 the conviction of a driver was upheld by the Divisional Court for failing to take reasonable precautions for the safety of a passenger contrary to the former regulations. Lloyd L.J. emphasised that the standard is one of reasonableness but that each case depends on its circumstances. In *Steff v Beck* the driver was driving a single decker one man operated bus. He knew that it was not possible to start this bus without a jerk and that the passenger was a pensioner who had not yet sat down.

13.222   Lloyd L.J. added that there was no rule of law by which a driver or conductor was liable to prosecution under the former regulations whenever a bus started with a passenger standing in the aisle and that passenger was injured. Otherwise London buses would be brought to a standstill during every rush hour.

For a case where the justices' finding of fact that the prosecutor had not proved that a defendant coach driver had failed to take all reasonable precautions to ensure the safety of his passengers contrary to reg.4 of the former regulations was upheld, see *Edwards v Rigby* [1980] R.T.R. 353.

A conductor should not open the door for passengers to alight until the vehicle has stopped (*Nicholson v Goddard* [1954] Crim. L.R. 474, a prosecution). Where a Mrs Entwistle fell off a bus and the conductress was charged with failing to take reasonable precautions for the safety of the passengers contrary to reg.4(c) of the former regulations, it was held that whether "reasonable precautions" had been taken was a question of fact for the court and it was immaterial that the regulations do not define them (*Marshall v Clark* 1958 S.L.T. 19).

13.223   In *Reid v MacNicol* 1958 S.L.T. 42, the driver of a bus was charged with failing to take precautions for the safety of passengers entering it contrary to reg.4(c) of the former regulations in that he did not halt at a bus stop and a person stumbled on boarding the bus. It was held that the regulations only imposed a duty towards persons entitled to enter the bus and no person was entitled to enter a moving bus.

In *Askew v Bowtell* [1947] 1 All E.R. 883, a tram conductor was charged with endangering the safety of a passenger by negligence contrary to the Stage Carriages Act 1832 s.48. The conductor was on top of the tram as it approached a compulsory stop and the driver slowed to a speed of 1mph. A lady began to get off when the driver accelerated and she was thrown. The conductor was unaware that she wished to alight. It was held that the conductor was entitled to assume that the driver would stop at the compulsory stop and that passengers would not alight before the tram halted; the conductor was therefore not guilty of negligence. It was also said that, if the tram had stopped, it would be his duty to see that passengers were safely off and on before it started again. This Act has been repealed but the case may still be of assistance in interpreting the regulations.

A driver, inspector or conductor must under reg.5(3) give his name and that of **13.224** the person by whom he is employed if requested by a constable or other person having reasonable cause. A driver must also if similarly requested give particulars of his driver's licence. Regulation 5 also restricts smoking by drivers, inspectors and conductors.

A driver, inspector and conductor must under reg.5(2) take all reasonable steps to ensure that the provisions of these regulations relating to the conduct of passengers (see below) are complied with. One passenger could bring this regulation into play by complaining about another passenger, but the steps to be taken are only such as are reasonable.

Following the introduction by the Public Service Vehicle Accessibility Regula- **13.225** tions 2000 (SI 2000/1970) of accessibility requirements to buses and coaches, reg.5 of the 1990 Regulations was amended to add a requirement that, subject to there being suitable space available, a disabled person accompanied by an assistance dog, guide dog or hearing dog (all defined in reg.3 of the 1990 Regulations, as amended) shall not be prevented from boarding the bus or coach with the dog. Regulation 6 of the 1990 Regulations, as amended, allows for the presence of an assistance dog, guide dog or hearing dog and obliges a disabled person to comply with instructions to remove the dog from a gangway. Part IV was added to the 1990 Regulations to govern provision in buses and coaches for wheelchair users including obligations to display route numbers and/or destinations. Regulation 17, as substituted, defines the extent of the duty on the driver or conductor, essentially one of reasonable care but with no obligation to take any steps if, on reasonable grounds, he considers there to be a risk to the health, safety or security of anyone or to the safety and security of the vehicle: reg.17(2)(b).

The regulations are not intended to deal with traffic offences by a driver, e.g. where he had driven without reasonable consideration for his passengers (*Pawley v Wharldall* [1965] 2 All E.R. 757).

Conduct of passengers

Regulations 6–9 of the 1990 Regulations (as amended) deal with the conduct **13.226** of passengers.

Regulation 7 covers tickets and the payment of fares. Under reg.7(1), passengers on a vehicle being used for the carriage of passengers at separate fares must not use any ticket which has been altered or defaced, which has been issued for use by another person on terms that it is non-transferable or which is expired. The reference to reasonable excuse is not retained. Any ticket issued must be retained for the rest of the journey.

Under reg.7(2) and (3), where the driver has no conductor the fare must be **13.227** paid immediately on boarding to the driver or, where appropriate, by insertion in any fare-collection equipment provided. Alternatively it must be paid as otherwise directed by the driver, an inspector or a notice displayed on the vehicle. In this case permission may be given for payment to be deferred. From the wording, these provisions are wide enough to give power to require production of the exact fare. If there is a conductor the fare must be paid to him immediately on request.

Any passenger who fails to meet his fare as required or does not have with him a ticket issued to him beforehand for the journey must pay the fare to the driver, inspector or conductor on request and in any case before he leaves the vehicle unless otherwise agreed by one of the three (reg.7(4)).

13.228   Under reg.7 where a passenger uses a ticket which has been altered or defaced it is not necessary for the prosecution to prove that he did so with intent to avoid payment of a fare. Nor does the prosecution have to prove an intent to avoid payment of a fare where an expired period or season ticket is produced; nor where a passenger leaves or attempts to leave the bus without having paid the fare. The passenger is under an obligation to pay the fare as directed. Where a passenger travels beyond the distance for which he has paid a fare, he may be required to pay the additional fare or leave the public service vehicle.

13.229   Regulation 6 deals with the conduct of passengers generally. Under reg.6(1)(a) passengers must use the proper door in accordance with any notice unless otherwise directed or authorised by a driver, inspector or conductor. The provision specifically referring to "entering" is reg.6(1)(b) which states that no passenger shall put at risk or unreasonably impede or cause discomfort to any person travelling on or entering or leaving the vehicle, or a driver, inspector, conductor or employee of the operator when doing his work on the vehicle. This could make it an offence to queue jump if the result was to impede unreasonably someone in front who was entering or the conductor on the bus if supervising entry.

The legal position as to boarding buses between stops is discussed at 119 J.P. Jo. 98. The decision of a metropolitan stipendiary magistrate is noted there to the effect that a bus was available to the public and could be boarded anywhere en route when it was standing in a street. This will be subject to any byelaw or provision or order to the contrary. The decisions of magistrates' courts are not binding but this decision is supported in the article. Another magistrates' court has held that it is not entering a bus when the person is on the platform. In such circumstances the person was found to have already entered. Regulation 6(1)(g) prohibits speaking to the driver except on three grounds—in an emergency, for reasons of public safety or to give directions as to the stopping of the vehicle. SI 1995/186 replaced "on grounds of safety" by the more narrowly defined "for reasons of public safety".

13.230   One provision which may be controversial is that in reg.6(1)(l). This provides that no passenger on a vehicle shall play or operate any musical instrument or sound reproducing equipment to the annoyance of any person on the vehicle or in a manner which is likely to cause annoyance to any person on the vehicle.

Under regs 8 and 9, any passenger on a vehicle who is reasonably suspected by the driver, inspector or conductor of contravening any provisions of the regulations must give his name and address to him on demand (or in Scotland to a police constable). This power is not necessary for a police constable in England and Wales because of the Police and Criminal Evidence Act 1984.

Carrying capacity

13.231   The number of passengers to be carried in a public service vehicle is regulated by the Public Service Vehicles (Carrying Capacity) Regulations 1984 (SI 1984/1406) made under ss.26 and 60 of the 1981 Act. Special provision is made as to children. A bus owner, who had appointed a young and inexperienced conductor and had not provided for adequate inspection, was convicted of aiding and abetting the conductor to allow overcrowding, although the owner was not present on the bus at the material time (*Gough v Rees* (1929) 94 J.P. 53). The offences under the regulations include driving, causing or permitting to be driven on a road a vehicle with seated passengers in excess of the number specified. There is a similar offence regarding standing passengers. There are also prohibitions against standing in certain places including the upper deck and the steps leading to it. Any person may prosecute under them.

Power is given to prohibit the driving of overloaded motor vehicles if adapted to carry more than eight passengers (presumably excluding the driver, see Chapter 1, "Passengers") (s.70 of the 1988 Act, as amended). As to powers of prohibition generally, see Chapter 8.

Conduct on tramcars, etc.

13.232 Tramway systems have been introduced in Manchester and elsewhere. The legal position for each system should be checked individually.

Section 193A of the Road Traffic Act 1988 allows the Secretary of State to make regulations applying specified sections of the 1988 Act and the 1988 Offenders Act with or without modifications to trams and trolley vehicles. The regulations may also amend special Acts.

The Tramcars and Trolley Vehicles (Modification of Enactments) Regulations 1992 (SI 1992/1217) modify or disapply certain of the provisions of the Road Traffic Regulation Act 1984 and the Road Traffic Act 1988 in relation to tramcars and trolley vehicles and make transitional arrangements. Both Acts will however apply to duobuses. A duobus is a trolley vehicle able to operate either by overhead wires or by a power source on board, as defined in detail in these regulations.

Section 67 of the Transport and Works Act 1992 defines "tramway", "guided transport" system, "operator" and other terms.

13.233 Section 61 of the Transport and Works Act 1992 amends ss.24 and 25 of the Public Passenger Vehicles Act 1981 so that regulations regarding the conduct of drivers, inspectors and conductors and passengers respectively can be made to apply to tramcars. Section 61 also amends s.60(1)(j) and (k) of the 1981 Act so that regulations regarding the carriage of luggage and goods and custody of property, respectively, can be made similarly for tramcars. There is power to amend or exclude local enactments covering the same subject-matter.

Chapter I of Pt II of the 1992 Act enacts offences equivalent to the road traffic excess alcohol and unfit through drink or drugs legislation applying to persons working on public passenger tramways. Section 39 of the 1992 Act inserted a new s.192A in the Road Traffic Act 1988 which excluded the drink and drugs provisions in ss.4–11 of the 1988 Act when these provisions apply. So far as guided transport systems are concerned the Secretary of State is empowered to make regulations applying ss.4–11 with any appropriate modifications. These offence relating to tramways apply not only to drivers but also to guards, conductors, signalmen, maintenance workers, including supervisors and look-outs. Maintenance is widely defined. Reference should be made to the full wording in the statute, which includes equivalent provisions for arrest and testing for alcohol.

If an individual commits the offence under s.27 of working on a tramway transport system when unfit through drink or drugs, not only is he guilty of an offence under s.27(1) but the responsible operator or other employer is also guilty under s.28 unless he has exercised all due diligence to prevent the commission of the offence on the system. As this is an exception from conviction, the burden of proof rests on the defendant on the balance of probabilities. As to "due diligence", see § 14.185.

Conduct on tramcars: proceedings and penalties

13.234   Proceedings may be brought in England and Wales only by or with the consent of the Secretary of State or the Director of Public Prosecutions for an offence under Pt II of the Transport and Works Act 1992 (s.58). Certain officers of corporate bodies and persons purporting to act as such and certain other members of the body may be guilty of a Pt II offence as well as the body itself (s.59). There are further provisions for Scotland (see s.59(3)).

The penalty under s.36 of the 1992 Act for the excess alcohol and unfit offences is six months' imprisonment or a level 5 fine or both. A person who without reasonable excuse fails to provide a preliminary specimen of breath when required is liable on conviction under s.29(5) and s.36(2) of the 1992 Act to a maximum fine of level 3. For these offences, reference to Chapter 4, "Drink/Driving Offences" may assist.

13.235   The Statute Law (Repeals) Act 1981 (c.19) repealed the Stage Carriages Act 1832 save that it retained the Act in force specifically only for the Blackpool Tramway system, and neither the 1991 nor the 1992 Acts refer to it. The 1832 Act will not apply to other systems in the absence of statutory amendment or statutory enactment for that purpose.

CONDUCT ON PSVs: PROCEEDINGS AND PENALTIES

Generally

13.236   Proceedings for an offence by a passenger may be instituted by any person, but those for an offence by a driver, inspector or conductor only by a person mentioned in s.69 of the 1981 Act (see § 13.213 and "Authority to prosecute", in Chapter 2), so far as the regulations are concerned. Offences under the regulations may be prosecuted within six months (*Orr v Strathern* 1929 S.C.(J.) 30).

A constable is able to arrest without warrant a person if he reasonably suspects him to be committing, or about to commit, an offence of whatever kind in the circumstances specified in s.24 of the Police and Criminal Evidence Act 1984.

13.237   The 1984 Act does not apply to Scotland and Northern Ireland. For this reason regs 8 and 9 of the 1990 Regulations give extra powers to Scottish police constables for obtaining the names and addresses of passengers.

The penalty for offences contrary to s.24(2) of the 1981 Act is a fine of level 2 in respect of offending inspectors, drivers or conductors. If the convicting court thinks fit, particulars of the conviction of such an offence may be endorsed on the licence of an offending driver. The penalty for failing to produce the licence within a reasonable time under s.24(3) is a fine of level 3. The penalty for offending passengers under s.25(3) is a fine of level 3. The penalty under the Carrying Capacity Regulations 1984 is under two different sections depending on the circumstances (s.26—control of number of passengers) and s.67 (other regulations) but the maximum penalty is the same—a fine of level 2 in each case. In view of s.31 of the Criminal Law Act 1977 the maximum penalty under the Stage Carriage Act 1832 is a fine of level 1. All such offences are triable by magistrates only.

There is no power to disqualify from driving or to endorse a driving licence or order penalty points.   **13.238**

As to the defence of reasonable excuse under s.68(1) of the 1981 Act, which is available for offences contrary to ss.24(2) and (3), 25, 26 and 67 including the regulations made thereunder, see § 13.212.

The defence under s.68(3) of the 1981 Act (all due diligence) is also available for offences contrary to s.26 regulations. See also § 13.212.   **13.239**

For a table of penalties, see § 13.240.

13.240

Conduct on PSVs: penalties

Offence	Mode of trial	Section *	Imprisonment	Level of fine	Disqualification	Penalty points	Endorsement code	Sentencing guideline
Conduct of inspectors, drivers or conductors	Summary	s.24(2)	—	2	—	—	—	—
Failing to produce PSV licence	Summary	s.24(3)	—	3	—	—	—	—
Conduct of passengers	Summary	s.25(3)	—	3	—	—	—	—
Control of numbers of passenger	Summary	s.26	—	2	—	—	—	—
Other regulations	Summary	s.67	—	2	—	—	—	—

* Public Passenger Vehicles Act 1981.

TAXIS AND PRIVATE HIRE VEHICLES

Generally

Section 37 of the Town Police Clauses Act 1847 provides for the licensing **13.241**
outside London by local authorities of hackney carriages for plying for hire in a
street, that is acting as taxis. Section 15 of the Transport Act 1985 requires the
licensing system to apply throughout the whole of a district council area in
England and Wales. There is, however, a separate system in London in the area
where the Metropolitan Public Carriage Act 1869 applies. As a result of the creation of the Greater London Authority, changes (effective from April 1, 2000)
have been made to the boundary of the Metropolitan Police which will have an
effect on some of the licensing regimes. In relation to the licensing of hackney
carriages and private hire vehicles, responsibility transfers to the district councils
of those areas newly outside the Metropolitan Police district by virtue of s.255 of
the Greater London Authority Act 1999. Transitional and consequential provisions are contained in the Greater London Authority Act 1999 (Hackney Carriages and Private Hire Vehicles) (Transitional and Consequential Provisions)
Order 2000 (SI 2000/412).

Sections 53 and 54 of the Road Safety Act 2006 abolish the "contract exemp-
tion" set out in s.75(1)(b) of the Local Government (Miscellaneous Provisions)
Act 1976 and amend the definition of "private hire" vehicle in s.1(1)(a) of the
Private Hire Vehicles (London) Act 1998 by removing the words "to the public".
These changes bring operators and drivers who are currently providing a service
to an identified group or organisation but not to the public at large within the
London private hire licensing regime.

In the legislation taxis are described as hackney carriages and vehicles which **13.242**
do not ply for hire as private hire vehicles. The 1847 Act is to be read as one with
the like-named 1889 Act. There are a wide range of regulatory offences in the
taxi code contained in ss.37–68 of the 1847 Act and the police as well as the local
authority are entitled to prosecute. The maximum penalty for driving, standing or
plying for hire without a taxi licence or not displaying the licence number all
contrary to s.45 is a fine of level 4.

In *Brentwood BC v Gladen* [2004] EWHC 2500; *The Times*, November 1,
2004, the Administrative Court held that on a proper construction of the legislation it was not necessary for the operator of licensed hackney carriages used by
licensed hackney carriage drivers as private hire vehicles also to hold an
operator's licence for private hire vehicles under the Local Government (Miscellaneous Provisions) Act 1976 s.55.

In *Chauffeur Bikes v Leeds City Council* [2005] EWHC 2369; [2006] R.T.R. 7, **13.243**
the Divisional Court held that it was inconceivable that Parliament did not intend
that, when granting a private hire licence, the safety of the vehicle for use as a
private hire vehicle was to be taken into account. A vehicle may be in a safe
condition for a vehicle of its type, size and design (as in this case which concerned
a motor cycle) but for safety reasons the vehicle could be judged to be unsuitable
in type, size or design for private hire use. The decision of the Crown Court was
not unreasonable given the statutory considerations set out in s.48(1)(a)(i) and
(iv) of the 1976 Act.

In considering an appeal in connection with a taxi licence, the Administrative

Court held that the application for a taxi licence could be dealt with by the local authority on the basis of the conditions which obtained when the application was made, rather than the new conditions imposed sometime later (but before the local authority had made its decision). The Crown Court had been entitled to draw this conclusion. (See *R. (on the application of Leeds City Council) v Taxi Centre (Newcastle Upon Tyne) Ltd* [2005] EWHC 2564.)

13.244 The requirement by a local authority that the respondent pass a Driving Standards Agency taxi test before it would consider renewing his hackney carriage licence was not a condition attached to the grant of the vehicle but a request for information. The Administrative Court so ruled in *Darlington BC v Kaye* [2004] EWHC 2836. It was reasonably necessary for the local authority to request such information in order to assess whether the respondent was a fit and proper person to hold a licence.

A hackney carriage will ply for hire *in a street*. The authorities were reviewed governing the situation where a taxi was stationed off a street but attracting custom from a street in *Eastbourne Borough Council v Stirling and Morley* [2001] R.T.R. 7. Drivers of private hire vehicles were waiting at a taxi rank on a railway forecourt which was not a street. The Divisional Court held that there was no difficulty in construing the expression "plying for hire in a street" as covering a situation in which a vehicle was in a prominent position just off the street and the public were in numbers on the street. Here, the taxi rank was immediately adjacent to a public street in a busy part of the town where pedestrian traffic was high and drivers were likely to attract custom from the public using the adjoining streets. The decision of the stipendiary magistrate was overturned.

13.245 The meaning of "hackney carriage" was explored in *R. v Cambridge City Council Ex p. Lane* [1999] R.T.R. 182. Section 47(1) of the Local Government (Miscellaneous Provisions) Act 1976 gave the local authority (as the licensing authority under the Act) additional powers to attach conditions to the grant of licences in respect of "hackney carriages" as defined in the Town Police Clauses Act 1847 s.38 ("Every wheeled carriage, whatever may be its form or construction, used in standing or plying for hire in any street within the prescribed distance … shall be deemed to be a hackney carriage …"). A trishaw plainly falls within the definition but it was argued that it also fell within the proviso to s.38 ("Provided … that no stage coach used for the purpose of standing or plying for passengers to be carried for hire at separate fares … shall be deemed to be a hackney carriage within the meaning of this Act "). This was rejected. Accordingly, the 1976 Act licensing regime applied to trishaws and both an operator's licence and a relevant driver's licence for a hackney carriage were required.

The question of whether a bicycle rickshaw was a hackney carriage within the meaning of the Metropolitan Public Carriage Act 1869 s.4 or a stage carriage was considered by the Administrative Court in the case of *Oddy v Bugbugs Ltd* [2003] EWHC 2865. It was held that such vehicles were stage carriages, as passengers were charged separate and distinct fares for their respective places. The defendant's drivers had not solicited persons to hire the rickshaws as they had made no form of invitation to prospective clients. Pedalled rickshaws, therefore, had no need to undergo licensing procedures. It was however stated by Pitchford J. that a licensing regime for such vehicles was likely to be prepared in the coming months.

13.246 A difficult situation was considered by the Divisional Court in *Eden District*

Council v Braid [1999] R.T.R. 329. The council had made a byelaw that the driver of a hackney carriage should not carry more passengers than the number specified on the plate affixed to the carriage. Mr Braid was licensed for six passengers. At about 11pm during a local horse fair known to attract travelling people and drunken and disorderly behaviour, Mr Braid was called to a social club to collect a fare. On arrival, the customer and nine other people, all gypsies or travelling people, some of whom smelt strongly of alcohol, got into the taxi. Mr Braid attempted to persuade them to reduce the number but they refused in an aggressive manner and, although no threat of violence was made, Mr Braid feared that he would suffer injury unless he took them all together. Despite seeing that he was being followed by a local authority enforcement officer, he drove them to their destination. On arrival, the enforcement officer was subjected to confrontational behaviour by the passengers and withdrew. Mr Braid was prosecuted and pleaded duress.

The justices dismissed the information and that dismissal was upheld by the Divisional Court. Confirming that the defence of duress is available also for offences of strict liability, if the only reason a defendant does an act proscribed by law is that he was subjected to a threat of serious personal injury which he reasonably thought would be carried out in circumstances where a reasonable person of ordinary firmness with the same apprehension might act in the same way, there is no reason why the defence of duress should not be available. The Divisional Court particularly pointed out the high quality of advice that the justices received from their clerk. The court also indicated that this defence will only rarely succeed and that its bounds should not be widened. There is a Judicial Studies Board specimen direction on duress by threats and circumstances which will also assist courts when this defence is raised (available at *http://www.jsboard.Couk/criminal_law/cbb/index.htm* [Accessed April 7, 2009]).

Further consideration to the defence of duress was given by the Court of Appeal in *R. v Martin (David)* [2000] Crim. L.R. 615. The subjective nature of the test where the basis of the defence is duress by circumstances was emphasised. Where, as in *Braid*, the defence is duress by threats, there is more of an element of the reasonable person and the reasonable belief, but it would be appropriate for the court to take the circumstances in which the threats were offered as the defendant honestly believed them to be. See also § 2.161 above.

13.247

Section 16 of the Transport Act 1985 provides that the 1847 Act, as incorporated into any enactment whenever passed, has effect as if it provides that the grant of a hackney carriage licence may be refused for the purpose of limiting the number of hackney carriages in respect of which licences are granted if, but only if, the council is satisfied that there is no significant demand for the services of hackney carriages (within the area to which the licence would apply) which is unmet.

Different approaches to s.16 were taken by the Divisional Court in two separate cases: in *R. v Reading Borough Council Ex p. Egan* [1990] R.T.R. 399, where it was emphasised that s.16 obliged councils which did not feel satisfied that there was no unmet need to issue taxi licences without limit of number, and in *Ghafoor v Wakefield Metropolitan District Council* [1990] R.T.R. 389. In *Ghafoor*, the later case, the Divisional Court held that nothing in s.16 prevented an authority from advising itself about the number of taxis which would have to be licensed to meet all significant demand. Having granted licences up to that

13.248

number, the authority was not prevented from refusing the next applications unless the circumstances had changed so that the authority, given the total number of licences then issued, could no longer be satisfied that there was no significant unmet demand.

The burden of proof was on the authority to establish that no unmet demand existed and the standard of proof was civil, that is, on the balance of probabilities (*Ghafoor*). In the Scottish case of *Coyle v City of Glasgow Council* 1998 S.L.T. 453, an applicant for a new taxi operator's licence was refused on the grounds of no significant unmet demand. In 1991, the licensing committee had determined a number which they had never reconsidered. The court held that the assessment had to be made in relation to the situation when the application fell to be considered. Where an authority had carried out an exercise to determine the level of demand, all that was required was for the matter to be kept under review by an official who had the information to judge whether demand had increased since the matter was last considered. If the officer informed the committee prior to the meeting that there had been no change in the level of demand, the committee could be satisfied that there was no significant unmet demand.

13.249   The Divisional Court had also indicated a cautious approach when considering s.16 in *R. v Great Yarmouth Borough Council Ex p. Sawyer* [1989] R.T.R. 297 (a case of judicial review). Hardship to individual taxi drivers is not a ground for intervention. Deferment by a council for a short period of a decision as to a taxi licence pending a survey to determine whether there was an unmet demand does not amount to a refusal: *R. v Middlesbrough District Council Ex p. I.J.H. Cameron (Holdings) Ltd*, *The Times*, November 19, 1991.

Although a vehicle with an ordinary hackney carriage licence has an enhanced value, it is not possible to sell it but retain ownership of the licence plate. The plate is issued by the council under s.35 of the Local Government (Miscellaneous Provisions) Act 1976 and remains the property of the council. Consequently an offence was committed contrary to s.40 of the Town Police Clauses Act 1847 when the defendant stated in a requisition signed by him for the purpose of renewing the licence that he was the proprietor of a hackney carriage when he had sold it without the plate: *Challoner v Evans*, *The Times*, November 22, 1986.

13.250   Such conditions as the council considers reasonably necessary may be attached under s.47 of the Local Government (Miscellaneous Provisions) Act 1976 to taxi licences granted under s.37 of the 1847 Act. The council may require any licensed taxi to be of such design or appearance or bear such distinguishing marks as shall clearly identify it as a hackney carriage. A taxi driver wishing to ply for hire on railway premises needs to have not only the licence but also permission under the British Railways Board byelaws: *Hulin v Cook* [1977] R.T.R. 345.

The extent of the discretion of a local authority was further considered in *R. v City and County of Swansea Ex p. Jones*, November 28, 1996, unreported. The Divisional Court was of the opinion that a local authority had power (probably under s.37 of the Town Police Clauses Act 1847) to adopt a policy in relation to conditions to be attached to a licence. A local authority is charged with statutory responsibility for the licensing of hackney carriages and, where it sees fit to impose high standards in order to achieve the statutory objectives, a policy adopted to achieve those objectives cannot be said to be unlawful provided the authority is prepared to hear each case on its merits. On this occasion the policy was that a new licence would only be issued in respect of a vehicle that was new.

Other decided cases have approved policies to licence only London type cabs, to require vehicles to be adapted to take wheelchair bound passengers, to licence for the first time only vehicles less than three years old and normally to refuse licences to men over 65 years.

The Divisional Court was concerned to ascertain that the local authority had **13.251** considered the case on its merits and that the policy was not unreasonable or irrational.

Proprietors' licences for private hire vehicles are obtained under s.48 of the 1976 Act and under that section such conditions as the council considers reasonably necessary may again be attached, including conditions requiring or prohibiting the display of signs on or from the vehicle. In addition to proprietors' licences for private hire vehicles under s.48, operators' licences for private hire vehicles are obtained under s.55 and private hire drivers' licences under s.51 of the same Act.

Section 61 of the Local Government (Miscellaneous Provisions) Act 1976, as amended, provides that licensing authorities in England and Wales outside London may suspend or revoke a hackney carriage or private hire vehicle driver's licence with immediate effect where it is the interests of public safety.

A private hire vehicle is under s.80(1) of the 1976 Act, for the purposes of Pt II **13.252** of that Act and unless the subject or context otherwise requires, a motor vehicle constructed or adapted to seat fewer than nine passengers (other than a hackney carriage, a public service vehicle or a tramcar) which is provided for hire with the services of a driver for the purpose of carrying passengers. The reference to tramcars was inserted by the Transport and Works Act 1992.

The Private Hire Vehicles (Carriage of Guide Dogs etc.) Act 2002 makes it an offence under a new s.37A of the Disability Discrimination Act 1995 for the operator of a private hire vehicle to refuse to accept a booking by a disabled person on the ground that that person wishes to be accompanied by an "assistance dog" (as defined) or to make an additional charge in respect of that booking. Similarly a refusal by the driver to carry out that booking is an offence. The maximum penalty is a fine of level 3 (Disability Discrimination Act 1995 s.37A(4)). The licensing authority may grant a certificate of exemption to a driver if appropriate on medical grounds. To be effective, that certificate must be displayed on the vehicle to which it relates.

Section 80(2) of the 1976 Act provides that in Pt II of the Act, references to a **13.253** licence are to a licence issued by the council for the district concerned. This means that the private hire vehicle operator licensed under s.55, the vehicle and the driver all have to have separate licences issued by the same council for the controlled district where the operations took place: *Dittah v Birmingham City Council* [1993] R.T.R. 356. It was not possible for a private hire vehicle operator licensed by the city council to use private hire vehicles and drivers licensed in Solihull.

Taxi drivers' licences granted under the Town Police Clauses Act 1847 and private hire drivers' licences granted under s.51 of the Local Government (Miscellaneous Provisions) Act 1976 last for up to three years. Either licence must under s.53(3) of the 1976 Act be produced for inspection at the request of an authorised officer of the council or of a constable either forthwith or before the expiration of five days beginning with the day following that on which the request was made. In the case of the council authorised officer, it must be produced at the principal offices of the council and, in the case of a constable, it must be produced at any police station within the area of the council and nominated by the driver when the request was made. It is an offence to fail to produce it without reasonable excuse. For the procedure, a reference to Chapter 7 may assist. The maximum penalty is a fine of level 3 under s.76 of the 1976 Act.

13.254 One of the conditions for the grant of a licence to drive private hire vehicles contained in s.51 of the 1976 Act, as amended, is that the applicant must hold (and must have held for at least 12 months) a full driving licence. In *Crawley Borough Council v Crabb* [1996] R.T.R. 201 it was held that this 12 months need not be the 12 months immediately preceding the making of the application. It was sufficient for the applicant to have held a licence for 12 months in the past and to hold a licence at the date of the application even though there was no continuity between the two periods.

A vehicle which is licensed as a hackney carriage by a local authority is not for that reason prevented from being licensed as a private hire vehicle in another area: *Kingston upon Hull City Council v Wilson, The Times*, July 25, 1995.

Section 75 of the 1976 Act contains certain exemptions which are from the requirements of the whole of Pt II (ss.45–80 inclusive). These exemptions include use for weddings and funerals. The burden of proof to establish a s.75 exemption rests on the defendant on the balance of probabilities: *Leeds City Council v Azam* [1989] R.T.R. 66.

13.255 If any person be found driving, standing, or plying for hire with any carriage within the prescribed distance for which a taxi licence is required but has not been obtained, an offence is committed contrary to s.45 of the Town Police Clauses Act 1847. A minicab was not licensed as a taxi under s.37. It was marked phonetically on the side not "phone" but "Fon-a-car". The driver was approached by two plain-clothes police officers who asked "Are you free?" He replied "Yes". The Divisional Court held that at that stage when he had entered into hire negotiations, he was plying for hire and had been rightly convicted of the offence of being unlicensed contrary to s.45: *Nottingham City Council v Woodings* [1994] R.T.R. 72. A further case where a licence-holder was prosecuted for plying for hire out of area is *Nottingham City Council v Amin* [2000] R.T.R. 122. The defendant had been stopped by plain-clothes police officers and agreed to convey them for a fare. He was not in the area for which he was licensed nor was the light on his cab illuminated. The stipendiary magistrate declined to admit the evidence of the police officers after argument based on the powers under s.78 of the Police and Criminal Evidence Act 1984 and art.6(1) of the European Convention on Human Rights but the Divisional Court returned the case with a direction to convict.

The offence has to be committed on a street, defined for the purpose of the 1847 Act by s.3 as extending to and including "any road, square, court, alley, and thoroughfare or public passage". It was held in *Young v Scampion* [1989] R.T.R. 95 that a taxi rank at an airport was not a street for the purpose of the Act as it was private property to which the public had no right of access. The Divisional Court added that the legislation did not prevent a taxi duly licensed in one area from driving through another unlicensed area when carrying a fare.

13.256 A hackney carriage will ply for hire *in a street*. The authorities were reviewed governing the situation where a taxi was stationed off a street but attracting custom from a street in *Eastbourne Borough Council v Stirling and Morley* [2001]

R.T.R. 7. Drivers of private hire vehicles were waiting at a taxi rank on a railway forecourt which was not a street. The Divisional Court held that there was no difficulty in construing the expression "plying for hire in a street" as covering a situation in which a vehicle was in a prominent position just off the street and the public were in numbers on the street. Here, the taxi rank was immediately adjacent to a public street in a busy part of the town where pedestrian traffic was high and drivers were likely to attract custom from the public using the adjoining streets. The decision of the stipendiary magistrate was overturned.

In *Darlington Borough Council v Thain* [1995] C.O.D. 360, the owner of a licensed hackney carriage drove his vehicle for a family purpose and with no intention to ply for hire but with its light lit and the plate number displayed. His hackney carriage driver's licence had not been renewed. It was decided by the Divisional Court that the holder of a hackney carriage driver's licence may not drive his own vehicle for a private purpose if that vehicle is a licensed hackney carriage and gives the appearance of such a carriage.

The principle behind the reasoning in the case of *Darlington Borough Council v Thain* was applied in *Benson v Boyce* [1997] R.T.R. 226. The defendant drove a minibus containing his employer's son and eight friends on a trip in the prosecutor's controlled district. The defendant held a hackney carriage licence but not a private hire licence. He was charged with acting as driver of a private hire vehicle without having a current licence contrary to s.46(1)(b) of the Local Government (Miscellaneous Provisions) Act 1976 and convicted. In upholding the conviction, the Divisional Court confirmed that s.46(1)(b) of the 1976 Act applied to all driving in a controlled district of a vehicle which s.80(1) of the Act characterised as a private hire vehicle whatever the particular reason for the vehicle being used at the time in question. The wording "provided for hire" in s.80(1) related to the nature of the vehicle not the activity and the prosecutor did not have to prove an actual hiring. **13.257**

In *Reading Borough Council v Iftekhar Ahmad, The Times*, December 4, 1998, a driver used a licensed private hire car in a controlled district to collect friends under an arrangement whereby no money changed hands and was charged with acting as the driver of a private hire car (which he had borrowed) without holding a current licence under the 1976 Act. The justices had accepted the driver's submission that he did not realise that he needed a private hire vehicle's driver's licence to drive the vehicle in a private capacity when no fare was paid noting the use of the expression "knowingly contravenes" in s.46(2).

The Divisional Court said that, in order to establish that an offence under s.46(1)(b) had been committed, it was necessary for the prosecution to show that the driver knew that he was in a controlled district, that he knew that the vehicle had been licensed for private hire and that he knew that he did not hold a driver's licence for a private hire vehicle. In respect of those matters, the knowledge that an offence was being committed was immaterial; any finding as to the driver's state of mind was irrelevant to whether or not he had contravened s.46(1)(b). **13.258**

Under s.80 of the Local Government (Miscellaneous Provisions) Act 1976, the definition section, "'operate' means in the course of business to make provision for the invitation or acceptance of bookings for a private hire vehicle". The defendant was licensed under s.55 as the operator of private hire vehicles. Unexpectedly he was short of staff and on two occasions arranged for his wife to carry out bookings. She had no private hire driver's licence and used vehicles which were unlicensed. On the defendant's instructions she made no charge and accepted no tip. The Divisional Court held that the defendant was acting in the course of his business and was operating the vehicles as private hire vehicles. The bookings were fulfilled, the customers remained customers and he was not engaged in a purely domestic arrangement but was fulfilling his contractual obligation. He was therefore guilty of the offences of operating a private hire vehicle without either the vehicle or the driver being licensed: *St Albans District Council v Taylor* [1991] R.T.R. 400.

13.259   A private hire operator whose offices were in Slough outside the controlled district of Maidenhead did not operate under s.80 within the controlled district merely by advertising in a directory which circulated in Maidenhead as well as Slough: *Windsor and Maidenhead Royal Borough Council v Khan (Trading as Top Cabs)* [1994] R.T.R. 87. The court held that s.80 did not relate to the places an invitation might reach but the places where provision was made to deal with it. The defendant had made the advertised provision for the acceptance of bookings in Slough and not in the other areas where the directory circulated.

In *Adur District Council v Fry* [1997] R.T.R. 257 it was confirmed that "operate" has a more restricted meaning than "use". Thus, where a booking was accepted at a licensed operator's base in Hove, there was no offence where the journey took place wholly within an adjoining area (in which the driver and vehicle were unlicensed) even where during the course of the journey, the initial passenger asked the driver to collect another person from her destination and convey that person to another destination which the driver did. The need for the driver and vehicle to be licensed in the other area is obviated by s.75(2) of the 1976 Act and, on the facts, there was no "operation" of the vehicle. The Divisional Court indicated that activity taking place outside an operator's premises could be envisaged as coming within the definition of "operate" in s.80(1), but no such activity had taken place in this case.

13.260   In *East Staffordshire Borough Council v Rendell* (1995) *Independent*, November 27, 1995, the holder of an operator's licence for a private hire vehicle in one controlled district redirected his calls from that controlled district to a telephone on premises in an adjacent controlled district for which he held no licence. It was held that he had committed an offence contrary to s.46(1)(d) of the 1976 Act since he had arranged to accept bookings in an area for which he did not hold a licence.

In *DPP v Computer Cab Co Ltd* [1996] R.T.R. 130, the defendant company provided services including bookings to licensed cab drivers, by subscription. Drivers received bookings by radio whilst in the area for which they were licensed, but were to collect the fare in an area for which they were not licensed. On receiving the call and accepting the booking the cab driver started the meter and was obligated to the company to carry out the hiring. It was held that no offence had been committed since, once the position had been reached within the licensed area that nothing further remained to be agreed between the driver and the fare, it was proper to find that the hiring had taken place in the licensed area where the cab was when receiving the booking call and not in the unlicensed area where the fare was collected.

Where a parking order allowed a hackney carriage to wait at an authorised hackney carriage stand, parking was only permitted for the purpose of operating as a taxi. It was an offence contrary to s.5(1) of the Road Traffic Regulation Act

1984 to leave it unattended for an hour when the driver was not plying for hire: *Rodgers v Taylor* [1987] R.T.R. 86.

London

The Private Hire Vehicles (London) Act 1998 provides for the licensing and **13.261** regulation of private hire vehicles (not licensed taxis or public service vehicles or vehicles whose use as a private hire vehicle is limited to use in connection with weddings and funerals), their drivers and operators, within the metropolitan police district and the City of London.

By virtue of the Transport for London Act 2008, some vehicles which were previously exempt are now required to hold a private hire licence in order to operate in London. Vehicles with fewer than nine passengers and which are made available for hire with a driver now require a private hire licence to operate. Amendments made to the 1998 Act (see Transport for London Act 2008 ss.23–25) bring minicabs, community transport vehicles and non-emergency ambulances within the range of private hire vehicles which need licences. Both vehicles and drivers which fall within the revised definition will require a private hire licence and any body corporate that hires out such vehicles and drivers will need to hold a private hire vehicle operator's licence. An exemption applies if the vehicle is being hired for self-drive or has nine or more passenger seats.

As a consequence of the transfer to Transport for London of the functions of **13.262** the then Secretary of State for the Environment, Transport and the Regions in relation to the licensing of London cabs, the London Cab Order 1934 (Modification) Order 2000 (SI 2000/1666) amended the 1934 Order to treat references to the Assistant Commissioner, the Commissioner of Police and the Secretary of State as references to Transport for London.

The 1998 Act creates an offence for anyone who makes provision for the invitation or acceptance of private hire bookings or who accepts such a booking who is not the holder of a private hire vehicle's operator's licence for London (a London PHV operator's licence): s.2. Failure to comply is a summary offence punishable by a fine not exceeding level 4. "Private hire booking" is defined as a booking for the hire of a private hire vehicle for the purpose of carrying one or more passengers (including a booking to carry out as sub-contractor a private hire booking accepted by another operator): s.1(4).

The holder of a London PHV operator's licence must not accept in London a **13.263** private hire booking except at an operating centre specified in his licence. The operator must ensure that any vehicle used to carry out a private hire booking is either a vehicle for which a London PHV licence is in force driven by a driver holding a London PHV driver's licence or is a London cab driven by a London cab driver's licence-holder. The operator must keep records of the bookings accepted by him. Each journey booked must be recorded before it is commenced. Failure to comply is a summary offence punishable by a fine not exceeding level 3: s.4. A defence of due diligence is provided: s.4(6). The Act also controls subcontracting by a London PHV operator to another operator: s.5(1). Failure to comply is a summary offence punishable by a fine not exceeding level 3: s.5(2).

The procedure for obtaining a London PHV operator's licence is set out in s.3 and provides for application to Transport for London. An applicant may appeal to a magistrates' court against a decision not to grant a licence, a decision not to specify a proposed address as an operating centre or a condition attached to the licence other than one prescribed under s.3(4).

13.264   A vehicle may only be used as a private hire vehicle on any road in London if there is a private hire vehicle licence in force (s.6). This licence is defined in s.6(6) as a London PHV licence or, if the booking was accepted outside London, an equivalent licence. This provision does not apply where the journey began in an area of England and Wales which is not a controlled district: s.6(7). Failure to comply is a summary offence punishable by a fine not exceeding level 4: s.6(5). A defence of due diligence is provided: s.6(4).

    The procedure for applying for a London PHV licence is set out in s.7. An applicant may appeal to a magistrates' court against refusal of the licence or the imposition of discretionary conditions: s.7(7).

13.265   The owner of a licensed vehicle may be required to present his vehicle for inspection and testing by Transport for London and must report to Transport for London as soon as reasonably practical (and in any case within 72 hours) any accident to the vehicle materially affecting the safety, performance or appearance of the vehicle or the comfort or convenience of persons carried in the vehicle. If ownership of the vehicle changes, the former owner must notify the Secretary of State, within 14 days, of the change and the name and address of the new owner. Failure to comply is a summary offence punishable by a fine not exceeding level 3: s.8(5).

    A constable or authorised officer can inspect and test a licensed vehicle to ascertain its fitness. If not satisfied, the owner can be required to make the vehicle available for further testing or the licence can be suspended until the constable or authorised officer is satisfied of its fitness.

13.266   If the licence is still suspended after two months have elapsed the constable or authorised officer may notify the owner that the licence is revoked. An owner may appeal to a magistrates' court against a notice of suspension or of revocation: s.9(6).

    Transport for London will issue a disc or plate for each vehicle licensed and no vehicle may be used unless that is exhibited in the prescribed manner: s.6. Failure to comply will be a summary offence punishable by a fine not exceeding level 3: s.10(7). A defence of due diligence is provided. The offence may be committed by the driver, by the operator and by the owner of the vehicle.

    A vehicle to which a London PHV licence relates may not be equipped with a taximeter (as defined). Failure to comply will be a summary offence punishable by a fine not exceeding level 3: s.11(2).

13.267   No vehicle may be used as a private hire vehicle on a road in London unless the driver holds a private hire vehicle driver's licence. This is defined similarly to a private hire vehicle licence. It is an offence for an operator or driver to use a vehicle in contravention and for the owner of the vehicle to permit its use. Failure to comply is a summary offence punishable by a fine not exceeding level 4: s.12(5). This provision does not apply where the journey began in an area of England and Wales which is not a controlled district: s.12(7).

    Application for a London PHV driver's licence is to Transport for London who will grant the licence if satisfied that the applicant is 21 or over, is (and has been for at least three years) authorised to drive a motor car and is a fit and proper person to hold this licence. Transitional provisions have been made to safeguard the position of an "existing driver": Private Hire Vehicles (London) (Transitional and Saving Provisions) Regulations 2003 (SI 2003/655). Such a driver must have registered with Transport for London no later than June 1, 2003. The Private Hire

Vehicles (London) (Transitional and Saving Provisions) Regulations 2003 were amended by the Private Hire Vehicles (London) (Transitional and Saving Provisions) (Amendment) Regulations 2006 (SI 2006/584) to enable Transport for London to issue temporary permits (which last for three months) to any existing driver or to an applicant for a London private hire vehicle driver's licence, before January 1, 2007, who meets all the requirements of Transport for London under the 1998 Act and who pays the prescribed fee. For applications for a driver's licence received on or after April 1, 2003, Transport for London must require applicants to show that they possess an appropriate level of knowledge of all or part of London and of general topographical skills. An applicant may appeal to a magistrates' court against the refusal of a licence or against any condition imposed on it: s.13(6).

Transport for London will issue a badge to a person granted a driver's licence **13.268** which must be worn so as to be plainly and distinctly visible. The badge must be produced for inspection, when requested (s.14(3)). Failure to comply is a summary offence punishable by a fine not exceeding level 3: s.14(5).

Transport for London may suspend or revoke a London PHV operator's, vehicle or driver's licence if no longer satisfied that the vehicle is fit for such use or that the licence-holder is fit and proper or if the licence-holder has failed to comply with any obligation under the Act. The holder of the licence or the vehicle-owner may appeal to a magistrates' court against such a decision: s.17(4).

A London PHV operator may apply to Transport for London to vary the **13.269** operator's licence by changing the description of the operating centre. Appeal against refusal lies to a magistrates' court: s.18(5). Transport for London may suspend or vary an operator's licence if no longer satisfied that the centre meets any of the requirements prescribed or for any other reasonable cause. The licence-holder may appeal to a magistrates' court: s.19(5). The exercise of the power to suspend under equivalent legislation in Scotland was considered in *Ward v City of Dundee Council* 1999 S.L.T. 56. A licence was suspended on the basis of irresponsibility on behalf of the licence-holder resulting in the poor condition of the vehicle. However, the sheriff found that the operator had acted entirely responsibly, entrusting the maintenance of the vehicle to a reputable and independent garage whose failures had been unexpected and contrary to the normal course of dealing between it and the licence-holder. There had to be an element of culpability on the part of the operator before he could be declared no longer to be a fit and proper person.

Licences must be produced at the request of a constable or authorised officer. The vehicle-owner must also produce a certificate of insurance on request. A document required to be produced must be produced forthwith or within six days starting with the day on which the request is made. Failure to comply without reasonable excuse is a summary offence punishable by a fine not exceeding level 3: s.21(4).

A licence-holder must return an expired or revoked licence within seven days **13.270** of the date the expiry or revocation takes effect. Failure to comply without reasonable excuse is a summary offence punishable by a fine not exceeding level 3 and up to £10 a day for each day on which the offence continues after conviction: s.22(6).

It is an offence to wilfully obstruct a constable or authorised person acting under this Act punishable on summary conviction by a maximum fine of level 3:

s.27(1). It is an offence to fail, without reasonable excuse, to comply with any requirement properly made by a constable or authorised person or to fail to give other assistance or information reasonably required. Failure to comply is a summary offence punishable by a fine not exceeding level 3: s.27(2).

13.271   It is an offence knowingly to make a false statement to a constable or authorised officer acting in pursuance of the Act. Failure to comply is a summary offence punishable by a fine not exceeding level 5: s.27(3).

The Act allows for regulations to be made controlling what may be displayed in London on or from vehicles other than licensed taxis and public service vehicles: s.30. Failure to comply will be a summary offence punishable by a fine not exceeding level 4: s.30(3).

The Act controls certain advertisements relating to private hire vehicles. Failure to comply is a summary offence punishable by a fine not exceeding level 4: s.31(4). Defences are provided by s.31(5).

13.272   Where there is an appeal to a magistrates' court, s.25 provides for that to be by way of complaint for an order which must brought within 21 days of the date on which the notice of the decision was served on the appellant. Either party to the appeal may appeal further to the Crown Court: s.25(6).

Notices served under the Act may be served by post. Any notice to an operator is properly addressed if sent to him at any of his operating centres in London. Any notice to an owner is deemed to be effective if sent to the last person notified to the Secretary of State as owner: s.34(3). Section 35 prescribes that the owner of a vehicle is the person by whom it is kept. There will be a presumption that the registered keeper is the owner (s.35(2)) but both the defence and the prosecution may show to the contrary: s.35(3).

TAXIS AND PRIVATE HIRE VEHICLES: PROCEEDINGS AND PENALTIES

Proceedings generally

13.273   It will be for the applicant to establish the grounds of his licence application on the balance of probabilities, such as whether he is a fit and proper person. In seeking to rebut such a contention, the local authority was required to satisfy only the civil standard of proof, even if the substance of what it sought to prove was a criminal offence. For this purpose the authority was entitled to go behind the facts of an applicant's acquittal on a charge of indecent assault: *R. v Maidstone Crown Court Ex p. Olson, The Times*, May 21, 1992 (an appeal against a refusal to renew a taxi licence).

In considering an offence under s.54(2)(b) of the Local Government (Miscellaneous Provisions) Act 1976, for not displaying a private hire vehicle driver's badge for the purposes of that section, mere forgetfulness, of itself and without more, could not as a matter of law amount to a reasonable excuse. That was not to say, however, that forgetfulness could not be a relevant factor, in conjunction with other relevant circumstances, as to whether there could be a reasonable excuse (*Reading Borough Council v Hussain* [2006] EWHC 1198).

13.274   In *McCool v Rushcliffe Borough Council* [1998] 3 All E.R. 889, the Divisional Court considered the admissibility of hearsay evidence in deciding whether to grant a private hire licence. The court stated that s.51(1) of the Local Government (Miscellaneous Provisions) Act 1976 made it clear that a local authority had a mandatory obligation to grant a licence but was prohibited unless satisfied that the applicant was a fit and proper person. The onus of satisfying the authority or the justices (on appeal) that the applicant was a fit and proper person was on the applicant on the balance of probabilities. The licensing regime was intended to ensure that licensed drivers were suitable, safe drivers with a good record, sober, honest and not the type to take advantage of their employment to assault passengers. A decision-maker might take account of hearsay evidence provided it was thought worthy of credence although it might not be evidence which would stand scrutiny in a formal court of law. Both a local authority and justices are entitled to rely on any evidential material which "might reasonably and properly influence the making of a responsible judgment in good faith on the question in issue".

Councils which are licensing authorities are given a discretion to send to the chief officer of police for the area a copy of the application for a licence to drive a taxi or private hire vehicle, together with a request for observations. On receipt of the request, the police are required to respond. (See s.47 of the Road Traffic Act 1991, which inserted s.51(1A) after s.51 (licensing of drivers of private hire vehicles) and s.59(1A) after s.59 (qualifications for drivers of taxis) in the 1976 Act.) These two sections are in identical terms and similar provision again is made by s.47 where any local Act contains a provision requiring a district council to be satisfied as to the fitness of an applicant for a licence to drive a hackney carriage or private hire vehicle.

The 1991 Act amendments reflect concern about drivers being licensed who **13.275** have previously been found guilty of serious sexual and other offences. Applicants for these licences are not excepted from the Rehabilitation of Offenders Act 1974 and are not obliged to disclose spent convictions, but the inserted provision should allow the police to make appropriate observations and offer some degree of safeguard.

The approach to deciding whether to admit spent convictions was set out in *Adamson v Waveney District Council* [1997] 2 All E.R. 898. The first stage was to be clear about the issue to which such convictions would relate if admitted. The second stage was for those presenting the material to give their own professional consideration to the question whether any of the spent convictions were capable of having a real relevance to the issue. When the matter was before justices, that was for the advocate for the local authority; when it was before the local authority, it was for the chief constable. It is wrong to put in everything automatically and let the tribunal decide. The third stage was for the tribunal to decide whether to admit the convictions. In a magistrates' court, this would be done by the local authority advocate indicating the class of offence, the age of the offence and, perhaps, in broad terms the apparent seriousness of the offence gauged by penalty. The justices, having heard anything the applicant wished to say, would then decide whether to admit any of the spent convictions. Even if admitted, the applicant may still argue in support of his appeal that they should not jeopardise his application. In deciding whether to admit spent convictions, the judicial authority will come to its own dispassionate conclusion on the information it is given having in mind not only the interest of the applicant as a person with spent convictions but also the interests of the public in whose interests the powers are being exercised.

Rights of appeal: taxis and private hire vehicles

13.276   Under all the licensing provisions there is a right of appeal by way of formal complaint to a magistrates' court by a person aggrieved by the refusal of a licence or by the imposition of any conditions. Who is a person aggrieved by a condition imposed on a private hire licence was considered in *Swansea City and County Council v Davies* [2001] R.T.R. 6. Mr Davies was the holder of a hackney carriage licence. The council imposed a condition on the holders of private hire licences against which Mr Davies wished to appeal. The magistrates' court agreed that, in the circumstances, he was a person aggrieved and could appeal to the court. The Divisional Court agreed. Although the class of persons was not limitless, the statute was widely drawn.

A much narrower definition was applied by Silber J. in the Divisional Court in *Peddubriwny v Cambridge City Council* [2001] EWHC Admin 200; [2001] R.T.R 31. In this case, the relevant condition complained of was the requirement for a police check. Again, the appellant had not been the subject of an application for a private hire licence but had suffered loss in relation to a delay in completing the police check which had caused his hackney carriage licence to lapse for over three weeks. The requirement for a police check was also a condition for the grant of a private hire licence and it was against that condition that the appeal was lodged. The appellant had never applied for such a licence. Silber J. agreed with both the magistrates' court and the Crown Court that this appellant did not come within the definition of a "person aggrieved". "A potential applicant for a licence does not ... have the standing to bring an appeal under section 52. ... The legislature has made the position quite clear and the stark fact is that a person has to have made an application before he can have the right to bring an appeal under section 52(2)." The only recourse for a person in the position of the appellant was to seek judicial review. However, the wording of s.52(2) of the Local Government (Miscellaneous Provisions) Act 1976 (the appeal provision in this case) and that in s.48(7) of the 1976 Act (the appeal provision in the *Swansea* case above) is virtually identical and Munby J. in the *Swansea* case took the view that Parliament could easily have drawn the category of persons entitled to appeal much more narrowly if it had chosen (as it had elsewhere in the Act). That was indicative of Parliament's intention to enable a wider category of persons to appeal. The critical factual difference is that, in the *Swansea* case, the appellant (a hackney carriage licence-holder) was seeking to demonstrate that conditions imposed on a private hire licence (which he had not applied for) led to potential confusion between private hire vehicles and hackney carriages in contravention of a statutory obligation on the Council contained in s.48(1) of the 1976 Act. It was, therefore, an application in which it was easier to conclude that the appellant had a legitimate interest than in the *Cambridge* case. Nonetheless, there are now two apparently conflicting decisions on the extent to which a person can appeal against conditions imposed on a licence for which he has not applied. The resolution of the conflict may well be that the categories of persons are wider than just an applicant for, or direct beneficiary of, a licence but are limited to a person whose interests are affected by the condition.

13.277   The need to use this avenue of appeal where available was emphasised in *R. v Blackpool Borough Council Ex p. Red Cab Taxis Ltd* [1994] R.T.R. 402 which was an appeal against conditions. The Divisional Court considered the conditions to be outside the powers given by the 1976 Act, but refused the application for judicial review. The condition could be amended in the magistrates' court to which the parties had a right of appeal. Further consideration was given to the availability of judicial review where a right of appeal to a magistrates' court is provided in *R. v Falmouth and Truro Port Health Authority Ex p. South West Water Services* (1999) 163 J.P. 589. Confirming the general rule that matters should be dealt with by way of appeal, it was held that the circumstances of this case were an exception in that they centred on an issue that could probably not have been raised on appeal and on a complex issue as to the meaning of a key word.

In *R. (on the application of Kelly) v Liverpool Crown Court* [2006] EWCA Civ 11, the Court of Appeal determined that a judge had erred in refusing to grant judicial review of a decision of the Crown Court, after protracted proceedings, to refuse the claimant's appeal against the local authority's refusal to grant him hackney carriage licences on the basis of a change in policy. In all the circumstances, neither delay nor the change in policy that had occurred in that intervening period were a complete answer to the claimant's case and the court would substitute an order of its own, granting the applicant some licences, subject to conditions.

Appeals are by way of rehearing. Although it is not binding, the view was taken in a Crown Court taxi appeal that the facts should be considered as they existed at the time of the appeal and not at the time of the original hearing (*Murray v Knowlsley Borough Council* (1990) 154 J.P. 617). It seems that hearsay evidence may be admitted in these civil proceedings, although the weight of the evidence will be a matter for the court (cf. *Westminster City Council v Zestfair Ltd* (1989) 153 J.P. 613 (rehearing in magistrates' court) and *Kavanagh v Devon and Cornwall Chief Constable* [1974] Q.B. 624 (rehearing in Crown Court)). **13.278**

In *Kelly v Wirral Metropolitan Borough Council, The Times*, May 13, 1996, it was confirmed both that an appeal against the withholding of a licence could be made where the local authority had failed to determine an application and that, on an appeal against the refusal by a local authority to grant a hackney carriage vehicle licence, a Crown Court which concluded that there was significant unmet demand in the area for taxis could determine the extent of that demand and how it was to be matched or remit the matter to the local authority for consideration.

Following an appeal to a magistrates' court, the Divisional Court held in *Solihull Metropolitan Borough Council v Silverline Cars* [1989] R.T.R. 142 that the plate design on a private hire vehicle was entirely a matter for the council under the statutory provisions. The council is required to issue a disc under s.48(5) and under s.48(6) a person commits an offence, subject to an exemption in s.75(3), if he uses or permits the use of a private hire vehicle licensed under the section in a controlled district as a private hire vehicle unless the plate or disc is exhibited on the vehicle. The condition under s.48 merely related to the manner of exhibition and there was no right to appeal under the statute in respect of the size or design of the plate or disc. **13.279**

Under s.77 of the 1976 Act, the appeal provisions in ss.300–302 inclusive of the Public Health Act 1936 apply to appeals under the 1976 Act. Under these provisions the appeal must be brought within 21 days from the date on which notice of the decision was served and the notice must state the right of appeal. The procedure in respect of such an appeal will be by way of complaint. There is under s.301 a further right of appeal to the Crown Court.

A taxi driver appealed against a council decision to revoke the taxi driver's licence. The council was held in *Cook v Southend Borough Council* [1990] 1 All E.R. 243 to be a person aggrieved (in other than criminal cases) for the purpose of the statutory provisions.

Penalties

13.280   For a table of penalties for the main offences, see § 13.281.

Taxis and private hire vehicles: penalties

Offence	Mode of trial	Section *	Imprisonment	Level of fine	Disqualification	Penalty points	Endorsement code	Sentencing guideline
Driving, standing or plying for hire without a taxi licence or not displaying licence number	Summary	s.45 Town Police Clauses Act 1847	—	4	—	—	—	—
Proprietor of vehicle other than licensed taxi knowingly using or permitting it to be used in a controlled district as private hire vehicle without s.48 phv licence	Summary	ss.46(1)(a) and (2) and 76	—	3	—	—	—	—
Knowingly acting as driver of phv in a controlled district without s.51 phv driver's licence	Summary	ss.46(1)(b) and (2) and 76	—	3	—	—	—	—

Offence	Mode of trial	Section *	Imprisonment	Level of fine	Disqualification	Penalty points	Endorsement code	Sentencing guideline
Proprietor of licensed phv knowingly employing driver without s.51 phv driver's licence for purpose of being hired by any person	Summary	ss.46(1)(c) and (2) and 76	—	3	—	—	—	—
Knowingly operating vehicle as a phv in a controlled district without s.55 phv operator's licence	Summary	ss.46(1)(d) and (2) and 76	—	3	—	—	—	—

Offence	Mode of trial	Section *	Imprisonment	Level of fine	Disqualification	Penalty points	Endorsement code	Sentencing guideline
Licensed operator knowingly operating vehicle as a phv in a controlled district (1) without s.48 phv licence (2) without driver having s.51 phv driver's licence	Summary	ss.46(1)(e) and (2) and 76	—	3	—	—	—	—
Failing to produce driver's licence for taxi or private hire vehicle within specified time without reasonable excuse	Summary	ss.53(3) and 76	—	3	—	—	—	—

* Local Government (Miscellaneous Provisions) Act 1976 unless otherwise stated.

CHAPTER 14

DRIVERS' HOURS AND RECORDS

CONTENTS

INTRODUCTION

Generally

14.01　This chapter contains a general introduction setting out the application of the legislation with a summary of the applicable EC law and defining and describing the various forms of transport. This is followed by definitions of general application.

　The drivers' hours rules are considered separately for goods and passenger vehicles with the application of the AETR agreement (see § 14.05 for full title), offences, proceedings and penalties at the end. The tachograph and written records requirements are then considered similarly for goods and passenger vehicles, again with the application of the AETR agreement, offences, proceedings and penalties at the end.

14.02　The applicable Community rules (see § 14.16) as to hours of work and driving periods on national and international journeys are now contained in Regulation (EC) 561/2006 of the European Parliament and of the Council of March 15, 2006 on the harmonisation of certain social legislation relating to road transport. This Regulation repeals and replaces Regulation (EEC) 3820/85, which provided common Community rules for maximum driving times and minimum rest periods for all drivers of road haulage and passenger transport vehicles. In the preamble to Regulation (EC) 561/2006 it is stated that by amending Council Regulations (EEC) 3821/85 and (EC) 2135/98 and repealing (EEC) 3820/85 a clearer and simpler set of rules is introduced which will be "more easily understood, enforced, interpreted and applied" by the road transport and the enforcement authorities (para.(4)). The arrangements regarding driving hours and rest periods required modification in view of the introduction of the digital tachograph pursuant to Regulation (EC) 2135/98 and Regulation (EC) 561/2006 provides for an arrangement based upon the existing system, but removing those elements which make correct calculation difficult. Paragraph (3) of the preamble states that difficulties have been encountered in interpreting, applying and enforcing and monitoring the provisions of Regulation (EEC) 3820/85 relating to driving time, break and rest period rules. Accordingly, arts 6, 7 and 8 provide revised rules in this regard. The regulation is also intended to incorporate those changes made necessary by the developments which have taken place since Regulation (EEC) 3820/85 was adopted. Examples include Directive 2002/15/EC on the organisation of working time of persons performing mobile road transport activities, Commission Regulation (EC) 422/2004 (which amended Council Regulation 3821/85 on recording equipment), and Council Directive 88/599/EEC on standard checking procedures for the implementation of Regulation (EEC) 3820/85. Provisions are also laid down with regard to crew, liability of the undertaking, exceptions, and control procedures and penalties.

With effect from July 2, 2007, the Community Drivers' Hours and Recording Equipment Regulations 2007 (SI 2007/1819) facilitate compliance with Regulation (EC) 561/2006. The 2007 Regulations revoke the Community Drivers' Hours and Recording Equipment (Exemptions and Supplementary Provisions) Regulations 1986 (SI 1986/1456) (see "Exemptions" at § 14.71 below) and also make consequential amendments to Pt VI of the Transport Act 1968, which sets out the drivers' hours enforcement penalties in relation to both the EC and domestic drivers' hours rules.

By art.2, Regulation (EC) 561/2006 applies to the carriage of goods by road of **14.03** vehicles where the maximum permissible mass of the vehicle, including any semi-trailer, exceeds 3.5 tonnes, or of passengers by vehicles which are constructed or permanently adapted for carrying more than nine persons including the driver, and are intended for that purpose (art.2(1)). The regulation applies to vehicles, irrespective of their country of registration, which undertake carriage by road exclusively within the Community or between the Community, Switzerland and the countries which are party to the Agreement on the European Economic Area (art.2(2)).

The AETR agreement (see below) applies instead of Regulation (EC) 561/2006 to international road transport operations undertaken in part outside the areas mentioned in art.2(2) to:

(a) vehicles registered in the Community or in countries which are contracting parties to the AETR, for the whole journey, and

(b) vehicles registered in a third country which is not a contracting party to the AETR, only for the part of the journey on the territory of the Community of countries which are contracting parties to the AETR.

Article 6 of Regulation (EC) 561/2006 provides for a maximum daily driving time of nine hours, which may be extended to a maximum of 10 hours on two occasions during the week. Daily and weekly rest periods are dealt with in art.8. A regular daily rest period of 11 hours is stipulated, although this may be reduced to nine hours on up to three times between weekly rests. In any two consecutive weeks, a driver must take at least one uninterrupted weekly rest period of 45 hours and at least one other weekly rest. There are also requirements to give compensation for any reduced weekly rests, all of which are set out in art.8 of Regulation 561/2006. Tachographs will enable the activities of a driver over a 28-day period to be recorded electronically on the driver's own driver card which will make for more rapid and comprehensive roadside checks than is currently possible. Regulation (EC) 561/2006 entered mainly into force on April 11, 2007.

14.04   The exceptions to the enforcement date of April 11, 2007 relate to art.10(5) (which deals with vehicles used which are already fitted with recording equipment that complies with Regulation (EEC) 3821/85) and other formal amendments to Regulation (EEC) 3821/85 and Regulation (EC) 2135/98, which are set out in arts 26(3) and (4) and 27. These latter provisions entered into force on May 1, 2006.

There is some uncertainty as to whether the applicable Community rules can be said to be still applied when there are limited exemptions—see § 14.16. It is an offence under s.96(11A) of the Transport Act 1968, as amended, to contravene the Community rules as to periods of driving or distance driven or periods on or off duty. The EC regulation applies to most commercial drivers of goods vehicles over 3.5 metric tonnes.

14.05   Contraventions of the applicable parts of Regulation (EEC) 3821/85 (tachograph), as amended, are punishable under s.97(1) of the 1968 Act. Section 97(1) provides that it is an offence to use, cause or permit to be used a vehicle to which the tachograph provisions apply without recording equipment which has been installed in accordance with Regulation (EEC) 3821/85, which complies with Annexes I and II of that regulation and which is being used as provided by arts 13–15 of that regulation. The requirement for a vehicle to use a tachograph is dependent on the type of vehicle, not on the purpose of the vehicle's journey. The Administrative Court so held in *Vehicle and Operator Services Agency v North Leicester Vehicle Movements Ltd* [2003] EWHC 2638; (2004) 168 J.P. 285 where a tractor was taken to docks for export. It was not used on that journey for carriage of goods or people. Failing to return tachograph record sheets to the employer as specified and failing to secure their return is an offence contrary to what is now s.97C of the 1968 Act. Further tachograph offences are contained in other provisions of Pt VI of the 1968 Act.

It may also be necessary to refer to the European Agreement concerning the Work of Crews of Vehicles engaged in International Road Transport (the AETR agreement) (see §§ 14.87–93).

14.06   There are separate provisions for drivers excepted from the EC regulations. These provisions are known as domestic driving or work. Contraventions of the domestic drivers' hours code are offences contrary to s.98(11) of the 1968 Act and contravention by domestic drivers and others of the manual records provisions are offences contrary to s.98(4) of the same Act.

British law as to drivers' hours and records is governed primarily by Pt VI of the Transport Act 1968. The purpose of the law is set out in s.95(1) of the Act. This states:

> "This Part of this Act shall have effect with a view to securing the observance of proper hours or periods of work by persons engaged in the carriage of passengers or goods by road and thereby protecting the public against the risks which arise in cases where the drivers of motor vehicles are suffering from fatigue."

14.07   The legal requirements for drivers' hours and conditions of work and the keeping of records are complicated, and in particular complicated by the application of the Community rules. The Passenger and Goods Vehicles (Community Recording Equipment Regulation) Regulations 2006 (SI 2006/3276) amend existing legislation to bring up to date the definition of "Community Recording Equipment Regulation" so as to ensure that the drivers' hours and tachograph requirements can be enforced in accordance with the current version of Regulation (EEC) 3821/85. As regards the application of the Community rules generally, the recommended approach is to apply a process of elimination. First, it must be ascertained whether the vehicle in question is subject to Pt VI of the Transport Act 1968. If it is, the classification of the particular journey or work must then be established. There are four classes of journeys or work:

(a) international journeys or work;

(b) national journeys or work;

(c) domestic journeys or work; and

(d) "mixed" driving, i.e. journeys or work falling partly in one of the above classes and partly in another.

It is then necessary to determine whether the journey is by a goods vehicle or a passenger vehicle as there are distinct provisions, each of which is discussed separately. It should be noted that for certain purposes drivers of goods vehicles are only to be treated as such if at least half of their driving in a working period as defined is spent driving goods vehicles. See "Mixed journeys", § 14.85. Finally, it is necessary to consider relevant exemptions.

Application

Part VI of the Transport Act 1968, by s.95(2), as amended, applies to: **14.08**

(a) passenger vehicles, i.e.:

  (i) public service vehicles; and

  (ii) motor vehicles (other than public service vehicles) constructed or adapted to carry more than 12 passengers;

(b) goods vehicles, i.e.:

  (i) heavy locomotives, light locomotives, motor tractors and any motor vehicle so constructed that a trailer may by partial superimposition be attached to the vehicle in such a manner as to cause a substantial part of the weight of the trailer to be borne by the vehicle; and

  (ii) motor vehicles (except those mentioned in (a) above) constructed or adapted to carry goods other than the effects of passengers.

(c) vehicles (as now defined in art.4 of Regulation (EC) 561/2006) not included in (a) or (b) and which are not exempt.

The Vehicle and Operator Services Agency (VOSA) interprets "more than twelve passengers" as including the driver for enforcement purposes. The provisions apply to both employee-drivers and owner-drivers: s.95(3).

The nature of a motor vehicle so constructed that a trailer might by partial **14.09** superimposition be attached to the vehicle in such a manner as to cause a substantial part of the weight of the trailer to be borne by the vehicle was considered in *DPP v Free's Land Drainage Co Ltd* [1990] R.T.R. 37. It was held by the Divisional Court that a substantial part of the weight of the trailer was being borne by the intervening converter dolly. There was no evidence before the court that a substantial part of the weight was being borne by the drawing vehicle. The vehicle did not therefore require a tachograph and the defendant had been rightly acquitted of the tachograph offence. The drawing vehicle was by type a Unimog; it was accepted that at the time by reason of its special use, it was not a locomotive or a motor tractor or otherwise within Pt VI.

The combination of vehicle and trailer was again considered by the Divisional Court in *National Trailer and Towing Association Ltd v DPP* [1999] R.T.R. 89. The driver was driving a vehicle weighing 2,550kg towing a trailer weighing 2,600kg carrying a car. It was being used for commercial purposes. The justices found that the vehicle was a goods vehicle (in that the combined weight exceeded 3,500kg) and should have been fitted with recording equipment. The Divisional Court appears to have been severely constrained by the lack of findings of fact in the case stated by the justices but rejected the prosecution's contention that the attachment of the trailer turned the towing vehicle into a vehicle adapted to carry goods within the meaning of s.95(2)(b)(ii) of the Transport Act 1968. The Divisional Court addressed two ancillary points. It emphasised that it was incumbent on prosecuting authorities to ensure that they addressed their minds to the correct sections of the Act and correct regulations and, if necessary, called expert evidence. It also noted that the justices had been referred to Regulations (EEC) 3821/85 and 3820/85. In the absence of findings to the contrary, it was a possible inference that the justices had confused the EC Regulations with the Act and had drawn on definitions from the regulations rather than concentrating on the definition of a goods vehicle in the Act. This arrangement would now be brought within s.95(2)(c) of the 1968 Act.

14.10   The application of Pt VI to the Crown, military, police and fire brigade vehicles is indicated in s.102 of the 1968 Act. See also "The Crown", § 2.34.

Finally it may be relevant whether the use is for private purposes or a commercial operation. All these matters are discussed in greater detail below.

EC law: summary

14.11   As a result of the United Kingdom's accession to the Treaty of Rome and the consequent enactment of the European Communities Act 1972, the law relating to drivers' hours and records in respect of both British and foreign vehicles is to a substantial extent governed by EC law.

Under the European Communities Act 1972, EC regulations have a direct and binding effect on United Kingdom law save and so far as they are expressly excluded or modified (see s.2). The EC regulations may be implemented by statutory instrument or Order in Council (s.2(2)). The penalty for breach is to be provided by the member countries (but see Sch.2 for certain maximum limitations). Action may be taken against a member country in the European Court of Justice for failing to give effect to such regulations. For example, in the *Commission of the European Communities v United Kingdom* [1979] R.T.R. 321 the European Court of Justice on the application of the Commission declared that the United Kingdom had failed to fulfil its obligations under the EEC Treaty by not implementing the EEC tachograph regulation as required. The United Kingdom was ordered to bear the costs of the hearing.

14.12   Article 70 (ex 74) EC requires member countries to work towards a common transport policy and art.71 (ex 75) EC is directed towards the establishment of common rules for international transport. Substantial progress had been made towards harmonisation at the time of the United Kingdom's accession to the Treaty of Rome, and the European Communities Act 1972 accordingly amended the relevant provisions of the Transport Act 1968.

The major and striking result is that, as will be seen, the majority of journeys in this country, whether the vehicles be registered in this country or in the EU or elsewhere, will be governed by Regulation (EC) 561/2006 so far as the driving hours of a driver or a driving mate are concerned and by the tachograph provisions (which incorporate and to some extent directly apply Regulation (EEC) 3821/85, as amended) so far as the keeping of records is concerned.

The imposition of strict criminal liability by a Member State on an employer in respect of a breach by his employee of the EC regulations was held by the European Court of Justice to be valid providing it is proportionate to the offence and to similar offences in the same country; Case C–326/88 *Anklagemyndigheden v Hansen & Son I/S* [1990] E.C.R. I–2911. The case concerned driving and rest periods. **14.13**

The tachograph rules govern the keeping of records, and are contained in ss.97, 97AA, 97B and 97C of the 1968 Act (as amended). These statutory rules incorporate and to some extent make directly applicable the EC tachograph regulation (Regulation (EEC) 3821/85, as amended). A tachograph is a compulsory requirement for virtually every transport operation subject to Regulation (EC) 561/2006 (drivers' hours and rest periods) (see s.97(6) and art.3 of Regulation (EEC) 3821/85).

There is an exemption for vehicles used for the carriage of passengers on regular national services on routes exceeding 50km. (The EC rules do not apply at all to routes of 50km or less and these are subject to the domestic code.) Drivers and driving mates of services on routes exceeding 50km do not have to keep records but have to comply with art.16 of Regulation (EC) 561/2006 (control procedures and sanctions) if no tachograph is fitted. This exemption also applies to certain short regular international passenger services operated in border areas but apart from the Channel Tunnel operating and being available to road as well as rail transport, this exemption is not likely to be material in British law. **14.14**

Reference may also be necessary to the European Agreement concerning the Work of Crews of Vehicles engaged in International Road Transport (the AETR agreement) where foreign vehicles are operating in the United Kingdom and where United Kingdom vehicles set out in the United Kingdom on a journey to, or return from, a country which is subject to the AETR agreement but which is not an EU country. This agreement is summarised at § 14.87.

Contraventions of Regulation (EC) 561/2006 (the applicable Community rules) as to hours of work, etc., on both international and national journeys are punishable under s.96(11A) of the Transport Act 1968 as amended by the 1976 Act. **14.15**

Applicable Community rules

"Applicable Community rules" in s.96 (11A) of the 1968 Act means any directly applicable Community provision for the time being in force about the driving of road vehicles (s.103(1) of the 1968 Act as amended). Such rules are discussed in the text as they apply individually. **14.16**

Section 96(11A) refers to applicable Community rules as to periods of driving or distance driven or periods on or off duty. This wording is not apt to include the requirements of art.5 of Regulation (EC) 561/2006 as to the age or experience of drivers. These requirements are covered in British law by the driving licence requirements described in Chapters 11 and 13. The art.5 provisions may have to be complied with abroad on international journeys.

Persons completely excepted from and outside the scope of Regulation (EC) **14.17**

561/2006 and Regulation (EEC) 3821/85 (the applicable Community rules) are subject to the domestic drivers' hours code (see §§ 14.78–83).

There has been some argument as to whether drivers who are subject generally to the applicable Community rules, but who are exempted from the particular drivers' hours or records provisions of those rules, become instead subject to the domestic drivers' hours code and manual record requirements. The argument in favour of this is that if a person does not have the Community rules as to hours and records applied to him, he then becomes subject to the domestic drivers' hours code and records regulations.

14.18   The argument turns on whether "applicable Community rules" means generally applicable or applicable in any particular instance. In this context the wording of s.96(11) of the Transport Act 1968 (which refers to the domestic drivers' code), s.96(11A) (which refers to hours and records and contraventions of "applicable Community rules") and the definition in s.103(1) of "applicable Community rules" are relevant.

Department for Transport guidance has taken the view that where goods vehicles are exempted from EC regulations, as allowed for under those regulations, they nevertheless become subject to the domestic drivers' hours code (discussed at §§ 14.78–83). There are arguments in favour of this view. If particular Community rules do not apply then they cannot be said to be applicable. The Drivers' Hours (Goods Vehicles) (Modifications) Order 1986 (SI 1986/1459) refers to drivers subject to Pt VI of the Transport Act 1968 — Pt VI is generally worded, relating to drivers and others subject both to the EC provisions and the domestic provisions. In the interests of road safety, the domestic code should apply if no other rules apply.

14.19   There are difficulties over the Department for Transport interpretation. Regulation 2 of the Drivers' Hours (Harmonisation with Community Rules) Regulations 1986 (SI 1986/1458) categorically states that, subject to the provisions of this regulation, the domestic drivers' hours code shall not apply in relation to any Community driving or work of a driver of a vehicle to which Pt VI of the 1968 Act applies. The reference to the provisions of the 1986 Regulations is not material in this context as the provisions relate to mixed driving.

The Community rules have to be applied by the English legislation and remain applicable in general terms and it may be argued that the person is carrying out Community driving or work even though there is a particular exemption. The definitions and general principles of the Community rules would continue to apply; in some circumstances the definitions in the Community rules differ from the domestic code legislation. Some exemptions are under British legislation, while others are under the applicable Community rules; some are partial exemptions and some are for emergency situations. It would be difficult to imagine the domestic drivers' hours code coming into operation in some of these circumstances. An exemption is an exemption, and it may be thought strange that it was intended in the absence of clear wording to catch the driver again, once granted exemption. The provisions are penal and would have to be interpreted in favour of the driver.

14.20   The same query arises in relation to exemptions from the tachograph provisions. The Drivers' Hours (Goods Vehicles) (Keeping of Records) Regulations 1987 (SI 1987/1421) by reg.4 apply where the applicable Community rules do not apply.

National and international journeys

National and international journeys or work are subject to Regulation (EC) **14.21**
561/2006 as to hours and conditions of work of drivers and driving mates, and to
the tachograph provisions as to records. There are certain total or partial *exemptions* but despite this the classification of national or international journeys or
work may still apply. There are also *exceptions* from the Regulation (EC) 561/
2006 and from the tachograph provisions. These exceptions are contained in art.3
and are also exceptions from the compulsory tachograph provisions (art.3 of
Regulation (EEC) 3821/85: the tachograph regulation). The art.3 exceptions are
classified as domestic journeys or work, and are discussed separately below.

A convention applied to carriage between two different countries. It was held
in *Chloride Industrial Batteries Ltd v F & W Freight Ltd* [1989] R.T.R. 125,
confirmed by the Court of Appeal ([1989] 3 All E.R. 86), that a country's
dependencies were to be regarded as being part of that country. For the purpose
of the convention, Jersey was not a different country from the United Kingdom.
A contract of carriage between Manchester and Jersey was not for international
carriage. Generally, the nature of international journeys or work is self-evident.
(As to non-EC international journeys, see the AETR agreement, discussed at
§§ 14.87 et seq.) It should be noted that the AETR agreement and not primarily
the EC regulations may also cover EC *journeys* which take place in part through
a third country. The issue has been referred to the European Court of Justice (see
§ 14.90). The AETR agreement is apparently enforced through Regulation (EC)
561/2006.

International journeys or work include that part of the journey which takes **14.22**
place in this country (quoted and confirmed as correct in *Paterson v Richardson*
[1982] R.T.R. 49). The Divisional Court in *Paterson* also quoted as persuasive
authority for the meaning of an international operation an EEC Commission
opinion of May 16, 1974 addressed to the Irish Government. The intention of the
Irish Government had been to draft regulations basing the journey on the driver,
rather than on the vehicle plus the load and driver. The opinion stated:

> "The Irish Government's interpretation of the term 'international transport operations' which appears in Article 19(2) of Council Regulation (EEC) No 543/69 is, admittedly, not defined in the Regulation, but this is because it is generally considered to be
> self-explanatory. The Community has always understood international transport to be
> all transport between the beginning of a journey and the destination. What the transport
> world generally considers international transport to be appears clearly from the following definitions taken from two high-level international agreements:
>
>> General agreement on the economic regulation of international road transport, 17
>> March 1954 …: 'International goods transport is transport carried out by means of
>> a vehicle employed in the transport of goods, the point of departure and the
>> destination being located in two different countries.'
>
>> European agreement concerning the work of crews of vehicle engaged in
>> international road transport (AETR) of 1 July 1970: 'For the purposes of the present Agreement the expression "international road transport" means road transport
>> which involves the crossing of at least one frontier.'"

In *Paterson v Richardson* the driver drove a vehicle to the docks at Dover. An- **14.23**
other driver drove the vehicle on to the continent. It was held that the first driver
was engaged in an international transport operation.

In *Paterson* the vehicle left the country. The Department for Transport has previously expressed the view in a booklet on tachographs that this is necessary and that therefore merely taking a load to the docks and unloading it for shipment is not an international journey or work. While this view is not authoritative, it is submitted that it is correct (cf. the Community opinion quoted in *Paterson* and the definition of "carriage by road" at § 14.42).

14.24   Regulation (EEC) 543/69 has been revoked and replaced by an altered regulation, but the principle remains. The point is of importance for drivers making dock journeys because of the different provisions for national and international transport operations respectively and because there are additional exemptions from the Community rules for certain national operations. It is submitted therefore that a dock journey where the vehicle is not transported abroad is a national transport operation.

National journeys or work are those national operations which are not excepted from Regulation (EC) 561/2006 by art.3 and not outside the scope of the applicable Community rules.

Domestic journeys

14.25   Domestic journeys or work are those which are outside the scope of Regulation (EC) 561/2006. The exceptions from Regulation (EC) 561/2006 (which therefore primarily become domestic journeys or work) are set out in art.3 of that regulation. As to other transport operations which may be classified as domestic journeys, see § 14.17.

Domestic journeys or work under the art.3 exceptions are where the carriage is by the following types of vehicle: vehicles used for the carriage of passengers on regular services where the route covered by the service in question does not exceed 50km; vehicles with a maximum authorised speed not exceeding 40kph; vehicles owned or hired without a driver by the armed services, civil defence services, fire services, and forces responsible for maintaining public order when the carriage is undertaken as a consequence of the tasks assigned to these services and is under their control; vehicles, including vehicles used in the non-commercial transport of humanitarian aid, used in emergencies or rescue operations; specialised vehicles used for medical purposes; specialised breakdown vehicles operating within a 100 km radius of their base; vehicles undergoing road tests for technical development, repair or maintenance purposes, and new or rebuilt vehicles which have not yet been put into service; vehicles or combinations of vehicles with a maximum permissible mass not exceeding 7.5 tonnes used for the non-commercial carriage of goods; commercial vehicles, which have a historic status according to the legislation of the Member State in which they are being driven and which are used for the non-commercial carriage of passengers or goods.

14.26   One of the exceptions in art.3(f) is for "specialised breakdown vehicles" operating within 100km radius of their base. As a working description a "specialised breakdown vehicle" should be regarded as a vehicle which is specially built or adapted, and kept, for the purpose of going to the assistance of a broken-down vehicle and which, generally, has the capability, for this purpose, of raising a broken-down vehicle (wholly or partially) with a view to its recovery either by conveyance on, or by towing behind, the breakdown vehicle: *Universal Salvage Ltd v Boothby* [1984] R.T.R. 289. The EC regulation and the British statutory instruments had different origins and were not necessarily to be interpreted in the same way although in fact a like result was reached in that case. Perhaps unfortunately, the British statutes and statutory instruments have been changed to give a different definition. See § 1.53 and § 1.56. The EC definition is unaltered. In that case it was held that a vehicle used to collect broken-down vehicles from garages was in effect a transporter and not a breakdown vehicle.

The definition of a "specialised breakdown vehicle" was further considered by the European Court of Justice in *Hamilton v Whitelock* [1988] R.T.R. 23. The court held that it was apparent from the very words of the relevant provisions that the derogation in question was conditional only on the nature of the vehicle as a "specialised breakdown vehicle", regardless of the kind of transport operation carried out.

14.27 The fact that, by contrast with the wording of other derogations, no condition regarding use was laid down in respect of "specialised breakdown vehicles" led to the conclusion that the application of the exemption laid down for such vehicles did not depend on the use actually made of them.

Having regard, on the one hand, to the guidance provided by the judgment of the court in Case 133/83 *R. v Scott (Thomas) and Sons (Bakers) Ltd* [1984] E.C.R. 2863, see § 14.72 where this case is discussed, and, on the other hand, to the ordinary meaning of the word "breakdown", the expression "specialised breakdown vehicle" was to be understood as meaning a vehicle whose construction, fitments or other permanent characteristics were such that it would be used mainly for removing vehicles that had recently been involved in an accident or had broken down for another reason.

14.28 The size of that type of vehicle should enable it to be distinguished from vehicles mainly used for merely transporting other vehicles and not for providing a breakdown service.

On those grounds the European Court of Justice (Third Chamber) ruled that the expression "specialised breakdown vehicle" in art.4(9) of Regulation (EEC) 543/69 (now art.3(f) of Regulation (EC) 561/2006) meant a vehicle whose construction, fitments or other permanent characteristics were such that it would be used mainly for removing vehicles that had recently been involved in an accident or had broken down for another reason. Such a vehicle was subject to the exception from the EC regulations as to drivers' hours, records and the tachograph, whatever use was actually made of it by its owner.

14.29 At the original hearing before the Scottish court, a motor repairer had a vehicle converted for use as a breakdown vehicle. At the material time he was using it without a tachograph to transport unroadworthy vehicles from a car auction to his trade premises for repair and resale. He was acquitted, the use being immaterial.

For the meaning of "specialised vehicles used for medical purposes", reference to §§ 14.72 et seq. may assist.

14.30 Domestic journeys or work are still covered by the United Kingdom legislation, in particular Pt VI of the Transport Act 1968 (see the definition in the Drivers' Hours (Harmonisation with Community Rules) Regulations 1986 (SI 1986/1458)). Where records are concerned, the relevant provisions are the Drivers' Hours (Goods Vehicles) (Keeping of Records) Regulations 1987 (SI 1987/1421). Hours and conditions of work are covered by the domestic drivers' hours code. This code is defined by s.96(13) of the Transport Act 1968, and means the provisions of s.96(1)–(6) inclusive, modified as appropriate. Section 96(13) was added by s.2 of the Road Traffic (Drivers' Ages and Hours of Work) Act 1976.

EC law: definitions

14.31 Some basic definitions in art.4 of Regulation (EC) 561/2006 differ from those in the Road Traffic Act 1988 and the Road Traffic Offenders Act 1988, e.g. "vehicle" and "trailer". The same definitions in Regulation (EC) 561/2006 apply also in Regulation (EEC) 3821/85 (the tachograph regulation) (see art.2, as amended, of that regulation).

"Motor vehicle" under art.4(b) means any self-propelled vehicle travelling on the road (other than rails), and normally used for carrying passengers or goods. The inter-relationship of "carriage by road" and "motor vehicle" in art.1 of Regulation (EEC) 3820/85 was considered in *British Gypsum Ltd v Corner* [1982] R.T.R. 308. It was held that the words "on the road" were not to be added by implication to the last part. In *British Gypsum* the lorry was normally used for carrying goods and it was immaterial that it was not normally used on roads. It did circulate on a road and was therefore within the EC definition. In interpreting "normally used" the court followed *Peak Trailer & Chassis Ltd v Jackson* [1967] 1 All E.R. 172 noted at § 8.24.

14.32 "Driver" is defined in art.1 as meaning "any person who drives the vehicle, even for a short period, or who is carried in the vehicle as part of his duties to be available for driving if necessary". The offence in s.96(11A) as amended (breach of applicable Community rules as to hours and rest periods) is limited to drivers (and employers, etc.) and is not extended from drivers to others being carried. By contrast s.97 and s.97AA (installation and use of tachograph) and s.98(4) (manual, i.e. non-tachograph records) refer to "any person". In any event the tachograph driver carried as passenger may not be liable under Regulation (EEC) 3821/85 (the tachograph regulation). Section 97C (failing to return tachograph record sheets to employer and allied offences) requires drivers to return paper records. Article 15(2) of Regulation (EEC) 3821/85 states that drivers must use the record sheets every day on which they are driving, starting from the moment they take over the vehicle. In *Vehicle Inspectorate v Anelay* [1998] R.T.R. 279, the Divisional Court decided that "take over the vehicle" applied to any driver present in a vehicle who was to drive that vehicle for some part of the journey. The defendant was one of two drivers employed to take a coach overseas. Although he had not yet started to drive, his obligation to begin keeping his record had started and did not apply only to the person driving at the material time.

14.33 Further consideration was given in *Vehicle Inspectorate v Southern Coaches Ltd* [2000] R.T.R. 165. The company was sending two coaches on an extended day trip from the south of England to Belgium. Three drivers were employed to achieve this. One of the drivers was a passenger in one of the coaches whilst not driving. That driver was not expected to be available to take over the driving whilst travelling as a passenger (although he would have done if necessary), was not obliged to be on the coach at all and could have made his own way to where he was to take over the driving and was not guaranteed a place on the coach if it was full with passengers. The magistrates concluded that the mere presence of the individuals in the vehicle in these circumstances did not make them drivers. The Divisional Court extensively reviewed the provisions and authorities and, indicating that it had been a difficult issue, allowed the appeal of the Vehicle Inspectorate. As well as considering the definition of "driver", the court considered when a driver "took over a vehicle" and so was required to start to use record sheets under Regulation (EEC) 3821/85 and the meaning of a rest period. In a thorough judgment, the court considered that the passenger/driver was not at rest as he was not free to go about his own business and was in the tachograph vehicle whilst it was in motion. Applying Case C–394/92 *Criminal Proceedings against Michielsen and Geybels Transport Service NV* [1994] E.C.R. I–2497 and *DPP v Guy* [1999] R.T.R. 82, the court considered that the time as a passenger was a time of availability under art.15 of Regulation (EEC) 3821/85 and records needed to be kept. However, for a suggestion that the conclusion of the reasoning could have been different, see the commentary to the case at [2000] Crim. L.R. 596.

In *DPP v Woods, trading as W.T. Coaches* (1992) *Road Law* 77, a case heard **14.34** at Liverpool Crown Court on April 12, 1991, before Judge Clark on appeal from Makerfield Magistrates' Court, it was held that a driver who was carried as a passenger to be available for the separate return journey had not taken over the vehicle on the outward journey and therefore did not have to keep tachograph records as a driver at that stage. It may be that the driver in *Woods* was during the outward journey a passenger and not intended to be available for driving at all. However, the point made in the case, which is not binding, is that there may be a distinction between being available for driving and the stage where the vehicle is taken over within the meaning of art.15(2).

References in Pt VI of the 1968 Act to a person "driving" a vehicle are references to "his being at the driving controls of the vehicle for the purpose of controlling its movement, whether it is in motion or is stationary with the engine running" (s.103(3)). Clearly a driving mate who in fact drives may be subject to Pt VI offences as a driver. A person who is carried to be available for driving but also does not in fact drive will be a driver for the purposes of the EC regulations but will not be within the Pt VI definition. He may not therefore be liable for contraventions of s.96(11A) committed by him although he may be liable under ss.97, 97AA, 97C and 98(4).

The s.96 provisions as to hours and rest periods for domestic journeys apply to **14.35** drivers only and the offence under s.96(11) refers to drivers only in addition to employers, etc.

The AETR agreement refers to crew members. "Crew members" in that agreement include drivers, extended in the same way to include driving mates and also includes non-driving mates and conductors. Offences under the AETR agreement are apparently contrary to s.98(4) although this issue has been referred to the European Court (see "AETR agreement, Enforcement", § 14.92) and the wording of s.98(4) is wide enough to include a crew member. The question was raised (but not answered) in *Pearson v Rutterford* [1982] R.T.R. 54 whether an HGV instructor was a crew member. It is doubtful whether he could come within either of the extended definitions of "driver" referred to above as he would normally be carried in the vehicle to give instruction and not to drive.

There is a derogation from the daily rest period provisions set out in art.8(2) of **14.36** Regulation (EC) 561/2006 for drivers engaged in multi-manning. Multi-manning is defined in art.4 as the situation where, during each period of driving between any two consecutive rest periods, or between a daily rest period and a weekly rest period, there are at least two drivers in the vehicle to do the driving. For the first hour of multi-manning the presence of another driver or drivers is optional, but for the remainder of the period it is compulsory.

For "specialised breakdown vehicles" excepted by art.3(f) of Regulation (EC) 561/2006, see *Universal Salvage Ltd v Boothby* at § 1.54 and *Hamilton v Whitelock* at § 1.53 and § 14.26.

14.37   In Case C–394/92 *Criminal Proceedings against Michielsen and Geybels Transport Service NV* above, the European Court of Justice (applying *van Swieten*, see § 14.40 below) held that the term "daily working period" as used in Regulation (EEC) 3821/85 art.15(2) (which requires drivers to use record sheets every day on which they are driving and which prohibits, without authorisation, the withdrawal of a record sheet from a tachograph before the end of the daily working period), comprised the driving time, all other periods of work, the period of availability, breaks in work and (where a driver divided the daily rest entitlement between two or three separate periods) such a period of rest, provided that it did not exceed one hour. The daily working period commenced when the driver activated the tachograph following a weekly or daily rest period, or (where the daily rest period was divided into separate periods) following a rest period, of at least eight hours' duration. The daily working period ended at the beginning of a daily rest period or (where the daily rest period was divided into separate periods) at the beginning of a rest period extending over a minimum of eight consecutive hours. The court also held that the term "day" used in Regulation (EEC) 3820/85 (drivers' hours) and Regulation (EEC) 3821/85 (tachographs) must be understood as having the same meaning as the term "period of 24 hours" which referred to any period of that duration which commenced at the time when the driver activated the tachograph following a weekly or daily rest period.

In *DPP v Guy* [1998] R.T.R. 82, the Divisional Court held that, given that art.15(2) unequivocally stated that the daily work period started from the moment a driver took over the vehicle and given the public safety objectives under the legislation, the conclusion has to be that the work period under art.15(2) did not finish until, at the earliest, the driver ceased driving the tachograph vehicle. Driving home in that vehicle at the end of the working day was within the daily working period.

14.38   Similarly, time spent by coach drivers getting from their homes to the pick-up point for the vehicles had to be recorded on the vehicle's tachograph: Case C–297/99 *Criminal Proceedings against Skills Motor Coaches Ltd* [2001] R.T.R. 21. As part of their work, drivers employed by a passenger coach operator could be called on to pick up coaches at a point away from either the company base or their home and they were free to choose how to reach the place specified. On several occasions, drivers travelled by car to the point at which they were to take over a vehicle which was subject to tachograph requirements but the time spent in doing so was not recorded in the tachograph sheets. It was alleged that that time should have been recorded as "other periods of work". The defendants contended that a driver who travelled from home to the pick-up point for a vehicle, freely choosing how he travelled, could freely dispose of his time, with the result that the time thus spent was to be regarded as rest time. The court could not accept that argument. A driver who went to a specific place, other than the undertaking's operating centre, indicated to him by the employer in order to take over and drive the vehicle was satisfying an obligation towards his employer. One of the aims of the regulation was to ensure that driving times and rest periods alternated so that drivers did not remain at the wheel so long as to cause tiredness and thus jeopardise road safety. Time spent by a driver to reach the place where he took over the tachograph vehicle was liable to have a bearing on his driving in that it would affect his state of tiredness. Accordingly, in light of the aim to improve road safety, such time was to be regarded as forming part of "all other periods of work" within art.15 of Regulation (EEC) 3821/85. The defendants argued that it was to be inferred from *Michielsen and Geybels* (above) and *Van Swieten* (below) that no period had to be entered on record sheets until the vehicle had been taken over. However, in those cases the court was considering a situation where the vehicle was driven immediately after a rest period. It could not be taken that the exclusion should apply to work periods of actual activity occurring between the end of the rest period and the time when the vehicle was taken over. The driver was performing a task required of him by virtue of his employment relationship and so he did not freely dispose of his time. On a proper construction of art.15 of Regulation (EEC) 3821/85, a driver's obligation to record all other periods of work extended to:

(a) time which a driver necessarily spent travelling to take over a vehicle subject to the obligation to install and use a tachograph and which was not at the driver's home or the employer's operational centre, regardless of whether the employer gave instructions as to when and how to travel or whether that choice was left to the driver; and

(b) periods of driving spent by a driver while performing a transport service falling outside the scope of Regulation (EEC) 3821/85 before taking over a vehicle to which that regulation applied.

"Week" in Regulations (EC) 561/2006 and (EEC) 3821/85 means the week **14.39** from midnight at the beginning of Monday. "Working week" has the same meaning in Pt VI of the 1968 Act (s.103(1)). Reference was made to the European Court of Justice as to the meanings of "previous week" and "the last day of the previous week" (Case C–158/90 *Public Prosecutor v Nijs*; *Public Prosecutor v Vanschoonbeek–Matterne NV* [1991] E.C.R. I–6035). The first question was whether the "last day of the previous week on which he drove" in art.15(7) of Regulation (EEC) 3821/85 meant the last calendar day, the last working day or the last driving day of that week. The second question was whether "previous week" meant the week directly preceding the inspection or any week preceding that inspection in which the driver drove a vehicle subject to the relevant EC regulations. The "last day of the previous week" was held to refer to the last driving day of the last week before the current week, during which the driver concerned drove a vehicle subject to Regulations (EEC) 3820/85 and 3821/85. (Article 15(7), as amended by Regulation (EC) 561/2006, substitutes a reference to "the previous 15 days" for the "last day of the previous week", see § 14.137 below.)

The day referred to in art.6(1) of Regulation (EEC) 3820/85 (ibid. Regulation (EC) 561/2006) was interpreted as meaning successive periods of 24 hours beginning with the driver's resumption of driving after his last weekly rest period. In other words the day is to be construed as a rolling day: *Kelly v Shulman* [1989] R.T.R. 84, per Hutchison J. The magistrates in the case cited were held to be wrong in finding that the 24-hour day commenced at midnight. The magistrates had justified their conclusion by reference to the definition of week in art.1 of Regulation (EEC) 3820/85 (now art.4(i) of Regulation (EC) 561/2006) but Hutchison J. found no support in that definition. The fact that the regulations were dealing with an activity which proceeded by day and night militated in favour of the rolling-day construction.

14.40   The meaning of the four and a half hours' maximum driving period in art.7 of
Regulation (EEC) 3820/85 was held by the European Court of Justice in Case
C–116/92 *Re Charlton* [1994] R.T.R. 133 to be a rolling period (see now art.7 of
Regulation (EC) 561/2006). The driver was not permitted to drive continuously
for more than four and a half hours.

In Case C–313/92 *Criminal Proceedings against van Swieten BV* [1994]
E.C.R. I–2177 the European Court of Justice ruled that the reference to "each period of 24 hours" in art.8(1) of Regulation (EEC) 3820/85 (driver's entitlement to
daily rest period; see now art.8(2) of Regulation (EC) 561/2006) meant any period of 24 hours commencing at the time when the driver activated the tachograph following a daily or weekly rest period. When the daily rest period was
taken in two or three separate periods, the calculation of the 24-hour period must
commence at the end of a rest period of at least eight hours.

The time recorded is the time which agrees with the official time in the country
of registration of the vehicle (art.15(3) of the tachograph regulation). Tachographs should not therefore be adjusted on the continent to show continental time
and a time allowance may have to be made for foreign vehicles in Great Britain.

14.41   Section 96(11A) offences are expressly restricted to offences in Great Britain;
ss.97 and 98(4) do not contain a similar restriction. There is a wide jurisdiction
given by s.103(7) (see § 14.190).

The tachograph regulation refers to "employers" but both Regulation (EC)
561/2006 and the AETR agreement refer to "undertakings". The meaning of
"undertaking" was considered by the European Court of Justice in *Auditeur du
Travail v Dufour* [1978] R.T.R. 186. It was held that responsibility rested with
the undertaking rather than the agency so far as compliance with the former
regulation was concerned. There is no reason why the decision should not be of
more general application. Compare *Alcock v Griston Ltd* at § 14.182. The meaning of the word "undertaking" in art.15 of Regulation (EEC) 3820/85 was
considered by the European Court of Justice in Case C–7/90 *Public Prosecutor v
Vandenne* [1991] E.C.R. I–4371. It meant an autonomous natural or legal person
carrying on a transport business and empowered to organise and control the work
of drivers and crew members. See now the definition of "transport undertaking"
at art.4(p) of Regulation (EC) 561/2006.

Definitions: "carriage by road"

14.42   "Carriage by road" is defined as "any journey made entirely or in part on roads
open to the public by a vehicle, whether laden or not, used for the carriage of passengers or goods" (art.4(a)). As stated, this also applies to the tachograph regulation (art.4(a) of that regulation).

The decision in *DPP v Cargo Handling Ltd* [1992] R.T.R. 318 concerned the
carriage of cargo on the private roads at Heathrow Airport, owned by the British
Airports Authority. Despite the private nature of the roads, there was substantial
public access by members of the unselected general public. A conviction was
directed against the company for using an uncalibrated tachograph on a road, as
defined by arts 1(1) and 2 of Regulation (EEC) 3820/85. However, the United
Kingdom has been authorised to grant an exemption from the regulation to
vehicles which travel exclusively within the boundaries of airports provided that
they are used in connection with the operation of airports and that they are not
authorised or "technically approved" for travel on public roads outside airports
(Commission Decision 94/451/EC art.1(1)).

In *DPP v Ryan* (1991) 155 J.P. 456, the defendants were acquitted by the justices of tachograph offences, contrary to s.97(1). The acquittal was upheld by the Divisional Court on two grounds. The first was that the exception for vehicles used for water services includes private commercial vehicles used for this purpose as well as public authority vehicles. On this basis the vehicle would be subject instead to the domestic journeys rules. The second ground was that the vehicle was not a goods vehicle as described in the definition of "carriage by road" under the EC regulations, although it was held to have been constructed as a goods vehicle and therefore a goods vehicle as defined under the Road Traffic Acts. The vehicle was used solely for winch and lifting work in connection with the respondents' business of drilling water wells. It carried two winches, a small one at the front which was fixed to the chassis and a larger one at the back attached to the vehicle. The rear of the vehicle had been modified to give a tailboard which dropped flat in order to provide a working platform. Although the large winch could only be powered from an external source it could only be used in conjunction with the lorry as modified. **14.43**

DRIVERS' HOURS

Generally

The main provisions as to drivers' hours and conditions of work so far as national and international journeys or work (defined at § 14.21) are concerned are contained in arts 5–15 of Regulation (EC) 561/2006 and (in appropriate contexts) in s.96 of the Transport Act 1968 and are described in this section. The regulation applies in full to both national and international journeys. **14.44**

Domestic journeys or work are excepted as they are outside the scope of the applicable Community rules. Section 96 in an earlier form applies to domestic journeys or work. These subss.(1)–(6) of s.96 are known as the domestic drivers' hours code and are discussed at § 14.78. So far as domestic journeys or work are concerned, s.96 applies in a modified form for goods vehicles and in a more extensively modified form for certain light vans and in a yet differently modified form for passenger vehicles. The definition of domestic journeys or work and the uncertainty over the meaning of "applicable Community rules" have been discussed at § 14.18 and § 14.25.

Regulation (EC) 561/2006 applies to all goods and passenger vehicles, subject to the exceptions and exemptions stated therein and also subject to Pt VI of the 1968 Act, in particular s.95(2) which specifies the vehicles to which Pt VI of the Act applies. Section 96 applies to public service vehicles, passenger vehicles constructed to carry more than 12 passengers and goods vehicles, all as defined in s.95(2) which relates to drivers' records and tachographs as well as to drivers' hours. The application of these sections to Crown, military, police and fire brigade vehicles is indicated in s.102. **14.45**

The EC regulation will normally apply not only to British vehicles on national and international journeys or work but also to vehicles from other EU countries on any international journey in Great Britain. For journeys to, from or through a third country (i.e. a non-EU country), see the AETR agreement, discussed at §§ 14.87–90, on whether or not the third country is a party to the AETR agreement and whether or not the journey is to, from or through an EU country. Certain of these aspects have been referred to the European Court of Justice, as noted at

§§ 14.89–90. The AETR agreement is apparently enforceable through Regulation (EC) 561/2006.

14.46   Definitions are to be found in s.103 of the 1968 Act and in art.4 of the EC regulation as described at § 14.31. It should be noted that the EC regulation definitions do not always correspond and reference should be made where appropriate to the exact wording.

The offences of breach of the EC regulation and the domestic drivers' hours code are set out in s.96(11A) and (11) respectively. Various other offences relating to the inspection of records and other documents under s.99 are considered there.

DRIVERS' HOURS: GOODS VEHICLES

National and international journeys

14.47   The provisions of Regulation (EC) 561/2006 as regards hours and rest periods for drivers of *goods* vehicles on national and international journeys or work are summarised in Table 1. (As to *passenger* vehicles, see §§ 14.94 et seq.) The first column shows the position under s.96 of the Transport Act 1968 which applies to domestic journeys or work. The second column shows the position under the EC regulation. The relevant articles for national and international journeys or work are arts 6 and 7 (driving periods) and 6, 7 and 8 (rest periods).

The key to understanding the interaction between arts 6 and 8 of Regulation (EC) 561/2006 is to appreciate that, whereas restrictions on daily driving are expressed in terms of the maximum length of driving periods between daily rests, the requirements as to daily rests are expressed in terms of minimum daily rest periods in 24 hours: *Kelly v Shulman* [1989] R.T.R. 84, per Hutchison J. However the meaning of certain aspects has been referred to the European Court of Justice; see Definitions.

The provisions are as follows:

Daily driving period (art.6)

14.48   Article 6 restricts the daily driving period so that it cannot exceed nine hours save that it may be extended twice in one week to ten hours.

Maximum driving period (art.7(1))

14.49   There is a four and a half hours maximum driving period (art.7(1)).

Rest breaks

14.50   After four and a half hours' driving, the driver must observe a rest break of at least 45 minutes unless he begins a rest period. This rest break of 45 minutes may be replaced by a break of at least 15 minutes followed by a break of at least 30 minutes, each distributed over the period in such a way as to comply with the provisions of the first paragraph of art.7.

Daily rest period (art.8)

14.51   In each 24-hour period a driver must take a daily rest period of 11 consecutive hours (art.8(1)). This may be reduced to a minimum of nine consecutive hours not more than three times. A "daily rest period" is defined in art.4(g) as the daily period during which a driver may freely dispose of his time and covers "a regular daily rest period" and "reduced daily rest period". "Regular daily rest period" means any period of rest of at least 11 hours. Alternatively this regular daily rest period may be taken in two periods, the first of which must be an uninterrupted period of at least three hours and the second an uninterrupted period of at least nine hours. "Reduced daily rest period" means any period of rest of at least nine hours but less than 11 hours.

Within each period of 24 hours after the end of the previous daily rest period or weekly rest period a driver shall have taken a new daily rest period. If the portion of the daily rest period which falls within that 24-hour period is at least nine hours but less than 11 hours, then the daily rest period in question shall be regarded as a reduced daily rest period (art.8(2)). A daily rest period may be extended to make a regular weekly rest period or a reduced weekly rest period (art.8(3)). A driver may have at most three reduced rest periods between any two weekly rest periods (art.8(4)).

The daily rest period may be taken in a vehicle as long as there are suitable sleeping facilities for each driver and the vehicle is stationary.

Weekly rest period (art.8)

A weekly driving time of 56 hours is specified. Within six 24-hour periods **14.52** from the end of the last weekly rest period, a driver will extend a daily rest period into either a regular weekly rest period of at least 45 hours, or a reduced weekly rest period of less than 45 hours but at least 24 hours.

In any two consecutive weeks, a driver shall take at least two regular weekly rest periods, or one regular weekly rest period and one reduced weekly rest period of at least 24 hours. The reduction shall be compensated by an equivalent period of rest taken en bloc, before the end of the third week following the week in question.

When a driver takes weekly rest periods away from base, they may be taken in **14.53** a vehicle provided that there are suitable sleeping facilities for each driver and the vehicle is stationary.

A weekly rest period which begins in one week and continues into the following week may be attached to either of those weeks, but not in both. Detailed consideration to this issue was given by the Divisional Court in *Vehicle Inspectorate v York Pullman Ltd* [2001] R.T.R. 18. One of the defendant's drivers, B, started work on Tuesday May 5 having had a rest period of 84 hours 30 minutes. He drove for 11 driving periods on 11 consecutive days and then took a rest of 61 hours 30 minutes on a Saturday and Sunday before driving for another eight driving periods. He took a rest period of 34 hours 25 minutes midweek and drove for a further four periods on four successive days. The company was prosecuted for permitting B to drive having failed to take a weekly rest period after the twelfth day. The company was convicted by the justices but its appeal to the Crown Court was allowed. The prosecutor successfully appealed to the Divisional Court. The prosecution contended that the Saturday and Sunday rest period should have been at least 72 hours since the rest period for the first week should have been 36 hours but was postponed to the end of the second week when it had to be added to the 36 hours due for the second week. The defence contended that at least 36 hours of the rest period before B commenced work on Tuesday May 5 could be allocated as the rest period for the first week and therefore the total rest period at the end of the second week was only 36 hours which had been taken. It was accepted that the period of rest where there had been 11 or 12 driving periods had to be the aggregate of the two weekly rest periods and so the issue was whether that obligation had been fulfilled. The prosecution argued that, if the object and purpose of Regulation (EEC) 3820/85 was to be met, then there must be a mandatory obligation to take the weekly rest after driving. The Divisional Court agreed. The provision in art.8(4) that a weekly rest period which begins in one week and continues into the following week may be attached to either of those weeks (on which the defence had relied) was acknowledged to cause some problems in application but the court considered it unnecessary to seek to resolve those problems since it concluded that the meaning and purpose of art.6 clearly required the rests to be taken after the driving.

14.54   The total driving period must not exceed 90 hours in any two consecutive weeks.

Where a driver accompanies a vehicle which is transported by ferry or train, and takes a regular daily rest period, that period may be interrupted not more than twice by other activities not exceeding one hour in total. During the regular daily rest period the driver shall have access to a bunk or couchette (art.9(1)). Any time spent travelling to a location to take charge of a vehicle falling within the scope of art.9, or to return from that location, when the vehicle is neither at the driver's home nor at the employer's operational centre where the driver is normally based, shall not be counted as a rest or break unless the driver is on a ferry or a train and has access to a bunk or couchette (art.9(2)). Any time spent by a driver driving a vehicle which falls outside the scope of art.9 to or from the vehicle within the scope of the Regulation which is not at the driver's home or at the employer's operational centre where the driver is normally based, shall count as other work.

TABLE 1

GOODS VEHICLES: HOURS AND REST PERIODS

14.55	*Nature of provision*	*Domestic journeys or work*	*National and international journeys or work*
	Continuous driving period	—	$4^1/_2$ hours (art.7)
	Daily driving period	10 hours (s.96(1))	9 hours (art.6) (or 10 twice in one week)
	Rest breaks	—	At least 45 minutes after maximum permitted continuous period of driving, but may be 1 × 15 mins and 1 × 30 mins (art.7)
	Weekly driving limit	—	56 hours (art.6)
	Fortnightly driving limit	—	90 hours (art.6)

Nature of provision	Domestic journeys or work	National and international journeys or work
Daily rest period	—	Normally 11 hours but may be reduced to 9 hours not more than three times a week between any two weekly rest periods. May be split into two periods, but must total 12 hours
Weekly rest period	—	A rest period of at least 45 hours taken by means of two regular weekly rest periods or one weekly rest period and one reduced weekly rest period of at least 24 hours. There must be compensation by an equivalent period of rest taken en bloc before the end of the third week following the week in question. Weekly rest period to start no later than at the end of six 24-hour periods from the end of the previous weekly rest period.
Daily hours of duty limit (spread over)	11 hours (s.96(3)(a))	—
Weekly hours of duty limit	—	

Definitions

Article 4 contains definitions. The principal definitions are discussed at § 14.31. **14.56**
The European Court of Justice in Case C–116/92 *Re Charlton* [1994] R.T.R. 133
ruled on the definition of the four and a half hours maximum driving period in
art.7 of Regulation (EEC) 3820/85 (now Regulation (EC) 561/2006). The court
held that art.7 was to be interpreted as prohibiting drivers to which it applied
from driving continuously for more than four and a half hours. However, where a
driver had taken 45 minutes' break, either as a single break or as several breaks
of at least 15 minutes during or at the end of a four and a half hours driving period, the calculation was to begin afresh, without taking into account the driving
time and breaks previously completed by the driver. This calculation began at the
moment the driver set in motion the tachograph recording equipment, or its equivalent, and began driving.

The day referred to in the former art.6(1) of Regulation (EEC) 3820/85 was
held to mean successive periods of 24 hours beginning with the driver's resumption of driving after his last weekly rest period. The day is a rolling day: *Kelly v
Shulman* [1989] R.T.R. 84. It follows from the judgment and from the wording of
the regulation that the rolling period interpretation also applied in art.8: "each period of 24 hours"; "each period of 30 hours".

The position was summarised in *Kelly v Shulman* as follows: **14.57**

"1 The term 'day' in article 6(1) meant successive periods of 24 hours beginning
    with the driver's resumption of driving after his last weekly rest period.
 2 Every driver had to have a weekly rest period, as defined in article 8, once in every

week, that is, in the period between midnight on Sunday and midnight the following Sunday.

3 In certain circumstances the weekly rest period fell to be taken earlier. Thus:

    (a) any driver who, in the course of six consecutive driving periods since his last weekly rest had driven in the aggregate not less than the maximum number of hours permitted by the regulations in six such periods had to begin a weekly rest immediately on the conclusion of the sixth period; but

    (b) any such driver who in those six driving periods had driven for an aggregate of less than the maximum number of hours permitted by the regulations could postpone the commencement of his weekly rest period until the end of the sixth day and drive during the period of postponement provided he did not by so doing increase the aggregate of the hours driven since his last weekly rest to a figure exceeding the maximum number of hours permitted by the regulations in six consecutive daily driving periods."

14.58   See also Case C–394/92 *Criminal proceedings against Michielsen and Geybels Transport Service NV* [1994] E.C.R. I–2497, referred to in § 14.37, confirming that "day" had the same meaning as "period of 24 hours" which is any period of that duration commencing when the driver activated the tachograph following a weekly or daily rest period (though see also § 14.37 above).

    In Case C–313/92 *Criminal proceedings against van Swieten BV* [1994] ECR I–2177 the European Court of Justice ruled that since the reference to "each period of 24 hours" in art.8(1) of Regulation (EEC) 3820/85 (driver's entitlement to daily rest period) meant any period of 24 hours commencing at the time when the driver activated the tachograph following a daily or weekly rest period, when the daily rest period was taken in two or three separate periods, the calculation of the 24-hour period must commence at the end of a rest period of at least eight hours.

14.59   The "week" is the period of time between 00.00 on Monday and 24.00 on Sunday (art.4(i)). It is submitted that the definition of "maximum permissible mass" in art.4(m) has a similar meaning to the definition of "permissible maximum weight" in s.108 of the Road Traffic Act 1988. In effect it means the total permissible maximum weight of the vehicle combination and any trailers drawn. "Driver" includes any person carried to be available for driving. For provisions relating to multi-manned vehicles, see § 14.36 above.

Exceptions and exemptions

A   *Exceptions*

14.60   The journeys or work excepted by art.3 of Regulation (EC) 561/2006 are domestic journeys or work (see § 14.25) and are altogether outside the scope of the Community rules.

B   *Exemption for safety purposes (art.12) applicable to both national and international journeys*

14.61   Article 12 of Regulation (EC) 561/2006 provides an exemption for the driver (see § 14.32) for the purposes of safety. This exemption applies to both national and international operations and is from all the EC regulation provisions. It is to the extent necessary to ensure the safety of persons, of the vehicle and of its load.

Road safety must not be jeopardised and it is only to enable the driver to reach a suitable stopping place. The driver must indicate the nature and reasons for breach manually on the record sheet of the recording equipment or on a printout from the recording equipment or in his duty roster.

The cases of emergency are:

(a) events which cause or are likely to cause such—

    (i) danger to life or health of one or more individuals or animals, or

    (ii) a serious interruption in the maintenance of public services for the supply of water, gas, electricity or drainage or of telecommunication or postal services, or

    (iii) a serious interruption in the use of roads, railways, ports or airports, as to necessitate the taking of immediate action to prevent the occurrence or continuance of such danger or interruption; and

(b) events which are likely to cause such serious damage to property as to necessitate the taking of immediate action to prevent the occurrence of such damage.

14.62 The European Court of Justice (in criminal proceedings alleging a departure from the restrictions upon driving times in arts 6, 7 and 8 of Regulation (EEC) 3820/85 (driving periods, breaks and rest periods)) considered whether, where a driver has satisfied the preconditions of art.12 and the court is satisfied that road safety has not been jeopardised (bearing in mind the obligation of a transport undertaking under art.15 to organise a driver's work in such a way that he is able to comply with the regulation), a driver is entitled to take advantage of art.12 if the need to depart from the provisions of arts 6, 7, and 8 was known before the particular journey commenced. The decision was that art.12 only applies to unforeseen events which render compliance with the other provisions of the EC regulation impossible and could not be invoked if the particular events were known before the journey commenced. The art.12 derogation is intended to ensure the safety of persons, the vehicle and the load. It is for the driver to decide whether it is necessary and to record the necessary details. The European Court of Justice held that it was clear that the possibility of derogating from the EC regulation was only enjoyed by the driver and did not extend to the driver's employer. Further, that, as part of the overall context of art.12, this provision required transport undertakings to organise work in such a way that drivers were able to comply with the regulation. (Case C–235/94 *Bird v Vehicle Inspectorate* [1996] E.C.R. I–3933.)

C   *National territory exemptions (which may also be extended by agreement to other EU Member States)*

14.63 Article 13(1) of Regulation (EC) 561/2006 allows EU Member States to grant exemptions in respect of transport *within its own territory* or, with the agreement of the states concerned in respect of transport on the territory of another Member State. There appears to be a distinction between national transport operations and what are here described as operations in the national territory, which could include the national part of an international operation.

The *exemptions* are from all the EC regulation requirements save those in art.5 (minimum ages for drivers). It should be emphasised that despite the *exemptions* the operations remain classified as international or national operations. Cf. the complete *exception* by art.3 for domestic journeys or work. The exemptions may be summarised as follows.

Various exemptions (art.13)

14.64   Some of the exceptions are considered in more detail below, but they mainly reflect the exceptions set out in the earlier regulations, with one or two deletions and additions.

Agricultural, etc., vehicles (art.13(1)(c))

14.65   There is an exemption for vehicles being used by an agricultural, horticultural, forestry or fishery (but see below) undertaking to carry goods within 100km radius of the place where the vehicle is normally based, including local administrative areas the centre of which is situated within that radius. The effect seems to be that operations are also exempt which are carried out within the administrative areas, i.e. the town or city, etc., the centre of which (i.e. presumably geographical centre) is situated within the radius of 100km even though parts of the town or city are outside that radius. This radius could cover two or more such centres. The fishery exemption only applies to the carriage of live fish or the carriage of a catch from the place of landing to the place of processing.

Also exempt is any tractor used exclusively for agricultural and forestry work. As to agricultural use, see Chapter 1.

Goods vehicles carrying working materials and equipment (art.13(1)(d))

14.66   There is an exemption for vehicles or combinations of vehicles used for the carriage of goods providing the maximum permissible mass does not exceed 7.5 metric tonnes. The vehicles must be those used by universal service providers to deliver items (such as postal articles) as part of the universal service, or vehicles used for carrying materials, equipment or machinery for the driver's use in the course of his work within a 50km radius of the vehicle's normal base. Driving the vehicle must not constitute the driver's main activity. The exemption would be available for a local builder but it would not be available if the person were employed basically as a driver. The material or equipment must be for the driver's use and not for someone else's use. The 50km radius is a strict limit and there is no administrative centre extension. In *Vehicle Inspectorate v Norman* [1999] R.T.R. 366, a vehicle whose use would otherwise fall within the item 7 description was being driven to auction carrying only the vehicle's registration document. The justices dismissed informations for failing to use the tachograph, but this was overturned on appeal by the Divisional Court. The justices had been referred to the interpretation of "material or equipment" contained in this paragraph but declined to follow the interpretation. However, the Divisional Court considered that interpretation to be correct, relying as it did on *DPP v Aston* [1989] R.T.R. 198. The registration document could not, therefore, bring the use of the vehicle within the exemption.

In Case C–128/04 *Criminal Proceedings against Raedonck* [2005] R.T.R. 25 (reference for a preliminary ruling), the European Court of Justice (Third Chamber) ruled on March 17, 2005 that the terms "materials or equipment" in art.13(1)(g) of Regulation (EEC) 3820/85 must, in the context of the exemption scheme provided for in art.3(2) of Regulation (EEC) 3821/85, be construed as covering not only "tools and instruments" but also the goods, such as building materials or cables, which are required for the performance of the work involved in the main activity of the driver of the vehicle concerned.

Electric and gas driven vehicles (art.13(1)(f))

Also exempt up to a permissible maximum weight of 7.5 metric tonnes are **14.67** vehicles used for the carriage of goods within a 50km radius from the base of the undertaking and propelled by natural or liquefied gas or electricity.

Island exemption (art.13(1)(e))

There is an island exemption for vehicles which operate exclusively on an **14.68** island which does not exceed 2,300 square km in area and which is not linked to the rest of Great Britain by a bridge, ford or tunnel for motor access.

Driving instruction (art.13(1)(g))

There is an exemption for vehicles being used for driving instruction and ex- **14.69** amination with a view to obtaining a driving licence or a certificate of professional competence provided that they are not being used for the commercial carriage of goods or passengers. This could include instruction for LGV authorisation. It is submitted that this means that goods can be carried to demonstrate how the vehicle handles when loaded but not for business purposes at the same time.

Public authorities (art.13(1)(a))

The exemption applies to vehicles owned or hired, without a driver, by public **14.70** authorities to undertake carriage by road which do not compete with private transport undertakings. The public authorities concerned are health authorities providing NHS ambulance or general services, local authority social services departments providing services for the old or physically or mentally handicapped, coastguard lighthouse or harbour authorities, airport authorities within the perimeter of the authority airport, certain authorities for railway maintenance, and British Waterways for maintaining navigable waterways.

D Exemptions for exceptional circumstances (art.13(3)) applicable to both national and international journeys

Certain exemptions for exceptional circumstances are contained in Pt 2 of the **14.71** Schedule to the Community Drivers' Hours and Recording Equipment Regulations 2007 (SI 2007/1819). The exemptions in the 2007 Regulations are for vehicles being used by the RNLI for hauling lifeboats, vehicles manufactured before January 1, 1947 and vehicles propelled by steam.

As the above exemptions are under art.13(3), the exemptions are from all the requirements of the EC regulation, whether national or international, save those in art.5 (minimum age for drivers).

Regulation (EC) 561/2006 refers to both "specialised vehicles" and "specially **14.72** fitted" vehicles. Nevertheless the cases on the former expression "specialised vehicles" (see §§ 1.53–5) may be of assistance in determining the meaning of "specially fitted". The expression "specialised vehicles" is also to be found in arts 3 and 13 of Regulation (EC) 561/2006.

The leading case on the meaning of "specialised vehicles" is Case 133/83 *R. v Scott (Thomas) and Sons (Bakers) Ltd* [1984] E.C.R. 2863. This is a decision of the European Court of Justice following a reference by the House of Lords. The European Court of Justice held that "specialised" referred to the vehicle and was intended to cover exclusively vehicles whose construction, fitments or other permanent characteristics guaranteed that they were used primarily for the operation in question. This conclusion was applied by the court to those specialised for door-to-door selling, mobile banking or the trading of books or records, but there is no reason why the same principle should not be applied to the other named operations such as cultural events and mobile exhibitions. The court indicated that modification of the vehicle was insufficient. It is submitted that a modification to provide a permanent characteristic could be sufficient.

14.73   The vehicle in question in the case had been specially adapted for the transport of bread and cakes by means of plastic interlocking trays held by clips moved up and down by metal rods fitted to the side of the vehicle. It did not have a specialised engine such as that normally used in a milk float where door-to-door selling required constant stopping and starting, nor was it so arranged as to enable the potential customer to inspect within the vehicle the goods offered for sale. It was not so constructed or adapted as to render the constant loading and unloading envisaged in the concept of door-to-door sales particularly more convenient to the salesman. It had been held not to be a specialised vehicle (see the earlier report at [1983] R.T.R. 369). It may be however that a bread van adapted in this way would be regarded as "specially fitted" within the requirement of the revised regulation.

The decision in *R. v Scott (Thomas) and Sons (Bakers) Ltd* was applied when a similar decision was reached in *Hamilton v Whitelock* [1988] R.T.R. 23 (referred to in more detail at §§ 14.26 and 14.27) as to the meaning of a "specialised breakdown vehicle". See also §§ 1.53–5.

14.74   The earlier cases have to be reconsidered in the light of these decisions but they may still be of some assistance. In a Scottish case, *Stewart v Richmond* 1983 S.L.T. 62 the High Court of Justiciary held that a flat-bottomed lorry used for coal deliveries was not specialised in any respect. For an instance where a specially constructed and adapted coal lorry was held to be "specialised", see *Re British Fuel Co Ltd* noted at [1983] Crim. L.R. 747. In another Scottish case *Struthers (Lochwinnoch) Ltd v Tudhope* 1982 S.L.T. 393 the vehicle had been provided with a platform designed to carry only soft drinks and was held to be specialised.

As to "door-to-door selling" the court stated that it did not matter whether the selling was to individuals, to wholesalers or to other customers provided that the activity of selling was characterised by frequent stops. It could consist of calls on potential wholesale customers, such as shops, works canteens, old people's homes or supermarkets providing that the activity of selling is characterised by frequent stops by the specialised vehicles. In *Struthers (Lochwinnoch) Ltd v Tudhope* above on the day in question delivery and collection was being made of a whole load and this was held not to be door-to-door selling. The court considered it important to examine the nature of the transport operation and not whether the vehicle was commonly used for door-to-door selling. In *DPP v Digby* [1992] R.T.R. 204 the defendant drove an autobagger lorry to deliver concessionary coal to miners or retired miners. He was paid by his company but received no payment from those to whom he delivered. The Divisional Court held that while it was a door-to-door activity, the vehicle was not used for door-to-door selling. The acquisition of the coal was not by way of sale but by reference to the miner's employment or former employment and the consideration was their present or past service. The exemption did not apply.

Many door-to-door transactions consist of taking an express or implied order   **14.75**
for a future week coupled with delivery under a previous order, e.g. a milk round
or the delivery of bread and other foods. In the *British Fuel Co Ltd* case above it
was stated that door-to-door selling did not cease to be so because the commodity
had been pre-ordered. This was a Crown Court decision on appeal from a magistrates' court and is not binding. However, in the judgment of the lower court in
Oxford v Scott (Thomas) and Sons (Bakers) Ltd [1984] R.T.R. 337 a distinction
was drawn between a delivery vehicle and a sales vehicle. It is submitted on the
authority of this remark in *Oxford v Scott (Thomas) and Sons (Bakers) Ltd* that
deliveries to order made previously at the door would be within the expression
"door-to-door" selling. It would not include delivering goods door-to-door
against sales not made door-to-door but made beforehand by different means.

The meaning of "local market" was considered in *DPP v Sidney Hackett Ltd*
[1985] R.T.R. 209. It was a decision of the European Court of Justice. The court
interpreted "local market" as meaning the market which, having regard to
geographical circumstances, was the nearest to a particular farm and at which it
was possible to buy or sell, as the case might be, according to the needs of the
normal, average-sized farms which might be considered typical of the area in
question.

A horsebox would seem to be a specially fitted vehicle and it has been sug-   **14.76**
gested that the use of a horsebox to attend a gymkhana or even a hunt would be
attendance at a "cultural event". In *Creek v Fossett* [1986] Crim. L.R. 256, the
use of a circus tent for a musical event was held to be for a cultural event. The
exemption for specialised vehicles for cultural events or "mobile exhibitions"
was not considered in *Bowra v Dann Catering Co Ltd* at § 12.19. Nevertheless,
the decision is justified on the facts (portable lavatories being conveyed to a public house under renovation). A conviction under the former Regulation (EEC)
543/69 was directed, as the circus and fun-fair equipment exception in art.4 did
not apply. What is a cultural event is a matter of taste and could apply to the
specially fitted props vehicles of both the English National Opera and a pop star
with his entourage.

There is no exemption for dumper trucks or works trucks as such if they are
otherwise subject to the EC regulation but they are likely to be within one of the
exemptions. Although the above transport operations may be partially exempt, it
must be stressed that such operations still remain subject to the EC regulation.
These *exemptions* should be compared with the *exceptions* which clearly take the
transport operations in question altogether outside the scope of the EC regulation
so that they become domestic journeys or work. Whether these partially exempt
operations become instead subject to the domestic drivers' hours code is
discussed at §§ 14.16–20.

The exemptions discussed above may be compared with the exemptions for   **14.77**
drivers on domestic journeys or work contained in the Drivers' Hours (Goods
Vehicles) (Exemptions) Regulations 1986 (SI 1986/1492), see § 14.84. It seems
that the exemptions from the EC regulation apply whether or not the tachograph
is being correctly operated (see § 14.153 and § 14.156).

Domestic journeys

Regulation (EC) 561/2006 does not apply to domestic journeys or work. These   **14.78**
are journeys or work which are excepted by art.3 from the terms of the EC regula-

tion and to which Pt VI of the Transport Act 1968 applies instead. This definition of domestic journeys or work is in reg.2(6) of the Drivers' Hours (Harmonisation with Community Rules) Regulations 1986 (SI 1986/1458). What constitutes domestic journeys or work is set out in detail at § 14.25.

See "Mixed journeys", § 14.85, where the driver undertakes both EC regulated journeys or work as well as domestic journeys or work.

14.79   The provisions of s.96 of the Transport Act 1968 will continue to apply to journeys or work excepted from the EC regulation unless there is an exemption from the requirements of s.96 also. Section 96(1)–(6) is known as the domestic drivers' hours code (s.96(13)). Section 96 is basically but not completely (see s.96(1)) a code of working hours for drivers rather than a code of driving hours.

It may be a suitable approach to apply a process of elimination. First it is necessary to confirm that the transport is a domestic operation, considering the description at § 14.25 and whether any of the exemptions at § 14.84 below apply. Then it is necessary to decide whether it is a goods or passenger operation, also bearing in mind the special provisions for mixed journeys noted at § 14.85. Finally it is necessary to decide whether it is an ordinary goods vehicle operation or whether the special provisions for light goods vehicles apply.

14.80   In this context only but in relation to all domestic journey goods vehicles a different definition of working day is substituted in s.103(1) of the Transport Act 1968 by the Drivers' Hours (Goods Vehicles) (Modifications) Order 1986 (SI 1986/1459). The wording is complicated but the effect is that it means any work period or the total working periods on duty in any 24-hour period.

The definition of "working week" in s.103(1) is a week beginning at midnight between Sunday and Monday, but note the power of a traffic commissioner to vary the commencement time on application (s.103(5)).

14.81   Section 103(4) explains references to a driver being on duty, so that he is deemed to be on duty for purposes other than driving when engaged in the course of his employment by his employer; there is special provision as to owner-drivers. See also § 14.105 and in particular *Carter v Walton* at § 14.110.

Orders have been made under s.96(12) modifying s.96 in respect of both goods vehicles and passenger vehicles. The order relating to goods vehicles is the Drivers' Hours (Goods Vehicles) (Modifications) Order 1986. The effect of the modifications apply differently to goods vehicles generally and to certain light goods vehicles as defined.

14.82   Where during any working day (as defined, see above) a driver spends all or the greater part of the time when he is driving vehicles to which Pt VI of the 1968 Act applies in driving goods vehicles of any type, that Pt of that Act shall have effect, as respects that driver and that working day, as if—

    (a) subss.(2), (3)(b), (4)–(6) and (8)(b) of s.96 were omitted;

    (b) for the words "subss.(1), (2) and (3)" in subs.(7) of that section there were substituted the words "subss.(1) and 3(a)";

    (c) for the words "subss.(2) and (3)" in subs.(8)(a) of that section there were substituted the words "subs.(3)(a)".

Section 96 in its form amended for this purpose is set out in Vol.2 and it may be easier to see what is meant by looking at it there. In effect however only subss.(1) and (3)(a) remain operative for goods vehicles generally which are subject to the domestic drivers' hours code and the domestic journey provisions in Pt VI. Those provisions of s.96 which remain applicable are a maximum driving period in a working day (see above) of 10 hours (s.96(1)) and a maximum working day (see above) of 11 hours (s.96(3)(a)). As to when a person is to be regarded as on duty, see §§ 14.105–13.

There is an additional modification for certain light goods vehicles. These are **14.83** dual-purpose vehicles or goods vans which have a permissible maximum weight as defined in s.108 of the Road Traffic Act 1988 not exceeding 3.5 tonnes. The effect of the modifications is that drivers of those vehicles used for professional purposes (doctors, dentists, midwives, nurses or vets) or for services of maintenance, repair, inspection, installation, cleaning or fitting, or by commercial travellers, or by employees of the, e.g. AA or RAC, RASC or by a person carrying on for himself or for his employer the business of cinematography (motion pictures), radio or television broadcasting are exempted from all the provisions of s.96 other than the requirement in s.96(1) not to drive for more than 10 hours a day.

The operation of a video amusement game was held by the House of Lords not to constitute "an exhibition of moving pictures" for the purpose of the cinematograph licensing requirements then in force: *British Amusement Catering Trades Association v Westminster CC* [1988] 1 All E.R. 740 reversing the decision in the Court of Appeal. In so far as the decision is applicable to this context, the implication is that a person engaged in the video amusement game business is not entitled to the benefit of the modification.

Exemptions for the drivers of goods vehicles in cases of emergency

Exemptions for the drivers of goods vehicles in cases of emergency are set out **14.84** in the Drivers' Hours (Goods Vehicles) (Exemptions) Regulations 1986 (SI 1986/ 1492). The exemptions are from the requirements of s.96(1) (maximum daily driving period) and (3)(a) (maximum daily duty). These are the only requirements as to hours and driving which apply to those engaged in goods vehicle domestic journeys or work. However the person must not spend more than 11 hours on duty in aggregate during the working day apart from time spent to deal with the emergency (reg.2). "Emergencies" are defined as events which cause or are likely to cause danger to the life or health of a human being or an animal, serious interruption to public water, gas, electricity, drainage, telecommunication or postal services, serious interruption in the use of roads, railways, ports or airports, or serious damage to property so as to necessitate the taking of immediate action. (Note the similarity with the safety exemption under the EC regulation described at § 14.61.) The 1986 Exemptions Regulations refer to "on duty" so that the principle in *Carter v Walton* (see § 14.110) may apply to exclude "rest breaks" in the calculation of the overall period.

Note s.96(9) as to drivers engaged in agricultural, forestry, quarrying or road construction operations. The section applies to empty vehicles of the types specified in s.95 as well as to loaded ones.

Mixed journeys

Domestic journeys or work to take into account national and international journeys or work

The Drivers' Hours (Harmonisation with Community Rules) Regulations 1986 **14.85** (SI 1986/1458) make special provision for mixed driving, that is, where drivers perform journeys or work which are partly international, or national or both, and partly domestic. These special provisions are contained in reg.2 of the above 1986 Regulations. The regulations require any time spent on national or international driving or work to be taken into account and regarded as domestic driving or work for the purpose of applying the limits in the domestic drivers' hours code on periods of driving or length of working day or calculating periods of driving for the purposes of s.96(7) of the 1968 Act. Conversely any time spent on national or international driving or work is not to be regarded as constituting or forming part of an interval for rest, etc., for the purposes of the domestic drivers' hours code. The purpose is to prevent drivers on domestic journeys or work from escaping the restrictions by interposing national or international journeys or work.

The regulations refer to "applicable Community rules"; for the meaning of this, see § 14.16. "Working day" and "working week" for the purpose of domestic code journeys are defined in s.103(1) of the 1968 Act. In effect "working day" in this context means any work period or the total work periods in any 24-hour period.

Goods vehicles' and passenger vehicles' drivers

14.86   Where a person during any working day (see above) drives both goods vehicles and other vehicles he is not to be treated for the purpose of the domestic rules as a goods vehicle driver unless at least more than half the time is spent driving goods vehicles (Drivers' Hours (Goods Vehicles) Modifications Order 1986 (SI 1986/1459) art.2). It is only when the greater part of his driving time is spent driving goods vehicles in any working day (see above) that he is entitled to the benefits of the 1986 Modifications Order.

The AETR agreement

Generally

14.87   The Member States of the EU have ratified or acceded to the European Agreement concerning the Work of Crews of Vehicles engaged in International Road Transport (AETR), Cmnd. 7401 (as amended). The United Kingdom ratified the agreement on February 17, 1978. The agreement did not become operative for the United Kingdom immediately on ratification, but is now operative and has been amended. It becomes operative for a country 180 days after it deposits its instrument of ratification or accession (art.16(5)). Those countries who have ratified or acceded to the AETR agreement are shown at the end of the agreement (see Vol.2). As will be seen below, however, its effect is not applicable only to those countries.

Amendments to the AETR agreement introducing the digital tachograph entered into force on June 16, 2006. The countries have four years to implement them.

Provisions

14.88   Article 2 indicates that the AETR agreement applies to the whole of the journey. This implies that a journey to the docks is included if the vehicle is embarked even though the driver does not. This view is supported by *Paterson v Richardson* [1982] R.T.R. 49. See § 14.21.

The most recent amendments mean that the requirements under the agreement are broadly the same as under Regulations (EC) 561/2006 and 3821/85. The AETR agreement refers to crew members. "Crew members" in that agreement includes drivers, extended to include driving mates and also non-driving mates and conductors. Offences under the AETR agreement are apparently contrary to ss.96(11A) and 98(4) of the Transport Act 1968 (see below). The wording of s.98(4) is wide enough to include a crew member. The EC regulations are more restrictive and s.96(11A) refers only to driver (and employer, etc.). See § 14.31. The result is that it may be possible to prosecute mates who do not in fact drive for a breach of s.98(4) but not for a breach of s.96(11A).

Application

Article 2 of the AETR agreement provides that the agreement shall apply in **14.89** the territory of each contracting party to all international road transport by any vehicle registered in the territory of the said contracting party or in the territory of any other contracting party. There are certain exceptions which are largely the same as the EC regulation exceptions.

The AETR agreement applies to international road transport (art.2). This must, however, be read subject to the EC regulation which itself covers international road transport within the EU and specifies in art.2(3) the extent of the international road transport operations to which the AETR agreement is to apply. The application is much wider than might at first be thought.

Article 2(3) of Regulation (EC) 561/2006 provides that the AETR agreement **14.90** shall apply to international road transport operations to and/or from third countries which are contracting parties to that agreement, or in transit through such countries, for the whole of the journey where such operations are effected by vehicles registered in a Member State or contracting party. Article 2(3)(b) provides that the AETR agreement shall apply to "vehicles registered in a third country which is not a contracting party to the AETR, only for the part of the journey on the territory of the Community or of countries which are contracting parties to the AETR". In effect, therefore, the AETR agreement applies to these third country transport operations. In particular it will be noted that it applies to vehicles registered in a third country which is *not a contracting party* to the agreement. A "third country" is a country that is not an EU Member State.

However, where a vehicle is registered in a Member State, no express provision is made in respect of journeys which start or finish within a country which is neither a Member State nor a party to the AETR. In such cases, the practice of the Netherlands authorities had been to apply national law, but the European Court of Justice has held (partly relying on the wording of corresponding earlier legislation) that the regulation (and not the AETR or national law) applies to all road transport journeys within the EU undertaken by vehicles registered in a Member State in the course of journeys to or from third countries which are not parties to the AETR or in transit through such countries (Case C–313/92 *Criminal proceedings against van Swieten BV* [1994] E.C.R. I–2177).

Exemption for emergencies

Article 9 of the AETR agreement provides partial exemptions in cases of **14.91** emergency. The wording and effect of the emergency exemption in art.12 of Regulation (EC) 561/2006 is similar (see § 14.61). The driver must indicate the nature and reasons for the breach on the record sheet or in his duty roster.

Enforcement

14.92 The AETR agreement has not been directly enforced by United Kingdom legislation. A spokesperson for the Department for Transport has stated that the Department regards the AETR agreement as being enforceable under s.96(11A) and s.98(4) of the Transport Act 1968 in the same way as the EC regulation is enforceable. This is based on a belief that art.2(3) of Regulation (EC) 561/2006 has incorporated the AETR agreement by reference. This link is rather tenuous, especially as ss.96 and 98 refer to "applicable Community rules" and the AETR is not a Community rule but an international agreement or rule in a wider sense. EU countries are only contracted to it on an individual basis.

The incorporation by reference propounded by the Department for Transport is achieved as follows. The effect of art.2(3) of the EC regulation is to disapply it to certain AETR journeys (see above) and to substitute the AETR agreement instead. Article 2 is in wide terms and, as shown above, includes the third country transport operations (including AETR and non-AETR operations) specified therein. Article 2 also states that Regulation (EC) 561/2006 applies to all carriage by road. Contraventions of the AETR rules are thereby contraventions of ss.96(11A) and 98(4). It appears that it is for the national court to determine on the facts whether it is appropriate to apply the provisions of what is now Regulation (EC) 561/2006 or those of the AETR: Case C–439/01 *Kvasnicka v Bezirkshauptmannschaft Mistelback*, European Court of Justice , January 16, 2003.

14.93 The penalties for breach of these sections are set out at § 14.194 and §§ 14.197 and 14.198.

DRIVERS' HOURS: PASSENGER VEHICLES

Generally

14.94 The provisions of Regulation (EC) 561/2006 as regards the hours and conditions for drivers of passenger vehicles on national and international journeys or work are summarised in Table 2. The first column shows the position under s.96 of the Transport Act 1968 as modified which applies to domestic journeys or work. The second column shows the position under the EC regulation for national operations. The third column shows the position for international operations under the EC regulation. As to on and off duty and whether the required breaks are part of the duty periods see § 14.105 and in particular *Carter v Walton* at § 14.110.

National and international journeys

14.95 Both the national and international journeys or work of drivers of passenger vehicles are governed by Regulation (EC) 561/2006. Article 3 of the EC regulation sets out the *exceptions* to the regulation. They are detailed at § 14.25 and include carriage by certain passenger vehicles. These exceptions are completely outside the EC regulation and are known as domestic journeys or work. Pt VI of the Transport Act 1968, and in particular s.96 as modified, continues to apply to them.

TABLE 2

PASSENGER VEHICLES: HOURS AND REST PERIODS

Nature of provision	Domestic journeys or work	National journeys or work	International journeys or work
Continuous driving period	5¹/₂ hours *working* period (s.96(2)) (but see s.96(2) as modified for certain variations)	4¹/₂ hours (art.7)	As national
Daily driving period	10 hours (s.96(1))	9 hours (or 10 hours twice in one week) (art.6)	As national
Rest breaks	30 mins (s.96(2))	Period of at least 45 mins after maximum permitted continuous period of driving but may be 1 × 15 mins and 1 × 30 mins instead (art.7) (certain urban variations allowed)	As national but no urban variations
Weekly driving limit	—	56 hours (art.6)	As national
Fortnightly driving limit	—	90 hours (art.6)	As national
Daily rest period	10 consecutive hours during the 24-hour period preceding working time, but may be reduced to 8¹/₂ hours three times a week (s.96(4))	11 consecutive hours but may be reduced to 9 hours three times a week. May be split as in art.8(1) if not reduced, but this must be for 12 hours	As national

Nature of provision	Domestic journeys or work	National journeys or work	International journeys or work
Weekly rest period	24 hours per fortnight from Sun midnight to Sun midnight not necessarily preceded or followed by a daily rest period (s.96(6))	45 consecutive hours including daily rest period immediately before or after. May be reduced to not less than 36 hours if taken at base or 24 hours if taken elsewhere but only if an en bloc rest period making up the reduction is granted during the next three weeks. The weekly rest period must be taken after any consecutive 6 days' or 56 hours' driving (arts 4 and 8). For non-regular national services—may be postponed as for international (Community Drivers' Hours and Recording Equipment Regulations 2007)	As national but for non-regular services weekly rest period may be postponed. Lost period must then be made up before end of third week (arts 4(4) and 8(6))
Daily hours of duty limit (spread over)	16 hours (s.96(3))		
Weekly hours of duty limit	—		

Exemptions

14.97   The Community Drivers' Hours and Recording Equipment Regulations 2007 (SI 2007/1819) revoke the Community Drivers' Hours and Recording (Exemptions and Supplementary Provisions) Regulations 1986 (SI 1986/1456). The 2007 Regulations give effect to those discretionary national derogations contained in Regulation (EC) 561/2006 that have been adopted in Great Britain. They also continue to exempt certain operations that were exempted after a special authorisation was granted by the EC in 1997 (see reg.2).

The 2007 Regulations define "historic status" for the purpose of a new automatic exemption in Regulation (EC) 561/2006 for commercial vehicles which have a historic status according to the legislation of the Member State in which they are being driven and which are sued for the non-commercial carriage of passengers or goods (reg.3).

14.98   Certain other exemptions set out in Pt 1 of the Schedule apply to passenger vehicles as well as goods vehicles. One of these is the use of any vehicle with not more than 17 seats, including the driver's seat, used exclusively for the non-commercial carriage of passengers (Schedule item 9). There is also an exemption for certain islands which do not exceed 2,300km and are not linked to the rest of Great Britan by a bridge, ford or tunnel open for use by motor vehicles (Schedule item 5 and see § 14.68 above). Item 7 of the Schedule also provides an exemption for vehicles being used for driving instruction and examination for obtaining a driving licence or certificate of professional competence.

The above exemptions are under art.13 of Regulation (EC) 561/2006 and as noted are restricted at present to territorial, i.e. United Kingdom operations. Other exemptions have been granted under art.13 and these are from all the EC regulation requirements, whether national or international, save those in art.5 (minimum ages for drivers).

Part 2 of the Schedule to the 2007 Regulations adds to the exemptions under **14.99** art.13(3) vehicles being used by the RNLI for hauling life-boats, vehicles manufactured before January 1, 1947 and vehicles propelled by steam.

Burden of proof of exemption

The burden of establishing an exemption under the 2007 Regulations rests on **14.100** the defendant on the balance of probabilities (*Gaunt v Nelson* [1987] R.T.R. 1).

Provisions

In general the rest periods are set out in Table 2, at § 14.96 above. The weekly **14.101** rest period for drivers of passenger vehicles on non-regular international services may be postponed to the thirteenth consecutive day (i.e. after 12 days) or until the maximum 12 daily driving periods are complete. In any event the maximum driving period in a fortnight is 90 hours (art.6(3)). The lost period must then be made up.

A coach driver who decided to postpone his weekly rest period to the following week had to take two weekly rest periods, consecutively and without any break between them, in that week: Case C–193/99 *Criminal Proceedings against Hume* [2001] R.T.R. 10. By art.6(1) of Regulation (EEC) 3820/85, coach drivers were required to take a weekly rest period after no more than 12 daily driving periods. That period could be postponed until the following week and added onto the second week's weekly rest (art.8(5)). The defendant coach driver worked without a weekly rest period between July 16 and 24, 1995 and then took a rest period from July 24 to 26. On August 3 he began a further rest period. He was prosecuted for having failed to take two weekly rest periods back to back. He disputed that the periods had to be taken in that way and stated that the rest period taken from July 24 to 26 was by way of postponement (art.8(5)) of the period due during the week beginning July 17 and the rest period starting on August 3 was by way of postponement (again art.8(5)) of the period due in the week beginning July 24. In its judgment, the European Court of Justice held that, in all the language versions of art.8(5), the term rendered in the English version as "added on to" had the meaning that the postponed weekly rest period had to be taken together with the rest period for the following week. That literal interpretation was in conformity with the aims of the regulation amongst which was to improve working conditions and road safety. The reasoning in *Hume* was considered and applied by the Divisional Court in *Vehicle Inspectorate v York Pullman Ltd* [2001] R.T.R. 18: see § 14.53 above.

14.102   The EC regulation has certain special provisions as to the daily rest period in relation to transportation by ferry boat or train. These have been described in the section on goods vehicles at §§ 14.47–55, and the same provisions apply to passenger vehicles.

As to the meaning of the 24-hour day and other definitions reference should be made to §§ 14.47 et seq.

Domestic journeys

14.103   Domestic journeys or work by passenger vehicle drivers are still governed by s.96 of the Transport Act 1968 in an extensively modified form unless otherwise exempt. The modifications were effected by the Drivers' Hours (Passengers and Goods Vehicles) (Modifications) Order 1971 (SI 1971/818).

The definition of "working day" in s.103 is also modified in relation to passenger vehicles by the substitution of "ten hours" for "eleven hours" and "eight and a half hours" for "nine and a half hours" in respect of the rest periods which conclude a working day.

There are certain exemptions, in particular for certain emergencies (see the Drivers' Hours (Passenger Vehicles) (Exemptions) Regulations 1970 (SI 1970/145) as amended).

Mixed journeys

14.104   Under the Drivers' Hours (Harmonisation with Community Rules) Regulations 1986 (SI 1986/1458) reg.3, where the driver of a passenger vehicle engages in mixed driving or work, the periods spent on Community regulated national or international transport are to count towards the periods specified under the domestic rules in s.96(1)–(7) (periods of driving or duty or length of working day) for passenger drivers performing domestic journeys or work. This applies similarly to goods vehicles.

Where a person on any working day drives both passenger and goods vehicles, he is not to be treated for the purpose of the domestic rules as a goods vehicle driver unless more than half the time is spent driving goods vehicles. See the Drivers' Hours (Goods Vehicles) (Modifications) Order 1986 (SI 1986/1459). As to "working day", which is defined differently in s.103(1) for domestic journeys or work as a result of amendments by the above regulations, see §§ 14.80 and 14.85.

DRIVERS' HOURS: PROCEEDINGS

Offences and proceedings; driving and duty periods

14.105   Criminal liability for a breach of the applicable Community rules for international or national transport is cast by s.96(11A) of the Transport Act 1968 on any "driver" (see § 14.32 for difficulties in interpreting the various meanings) and any other person, being the offender's employer or a person to whose orders that offender was subject, who caused or permitted the contravention. See also the decision in *Coggins* noted below. The breach must be of a rule as to periods of driving, or distances driven, or periods on or off duty. The requirements of art.5 of Regulation (EC) 561/2006 as regards age or experience of drivers are covered in British law by the driving licence requirements described in Chapters 11 and 13. The art.5 provisions may have to be complied with abroad on international journeys. Criminal liability is limited to offences in Great Britain (see s.96(11A)), although periods of driving or work abroad may be taken into account.

The possibility of any exemption or defence should always be considered. Punishment imposed by a Member State on an employer for a breach by his employee of the EC regulations was held by the European Court of Justice to be valid even though it was not attributable to an intentional or negligent failure, providing it was proportionate to the offence and analogous to punishments for similar offences in the same country: Case C–326/88 *Anklagemyndigheden v Hansen & Son I/S*, [1990] E.C.R. I–2911. The case concerned the validity of a Danish law imposing strict liability for breaches of driving and rest period requirements.

Payments to wage-earning drivers, including any person carried to be available for driving, are prohibited by art.10 of Regulation (EC) 561/2006, even in the form of bonuses or wage supplements, if they relate to distances travelled and/or the amount of goods carried, unless these payments are of such a kind as not to endanger road safety.   **14.106**

Reference to "Liability of employers for staff defaults", § 14.148 and § 14.181, in relation to tachograph and manual records may assist.

Criminal liability under s.96 or for breach of the domestic drivers' code is similarly cast by s.96(11) on the driver and on any other person, being that driver's employer or a person to whose orders that driver was subject, who caused or permitted the contravention. Consequently a transport manager might be liable for causing or permitting. "Permitting" in s.96(11) requires proof of knowledge; despite the defence it is not an absolute offence (*Licensing Authority for Goods Vehicles in Metropolitan Traffic Area v Coggins, The Times*, February 28, 1985). This knowledge can be found to exist where a transport manager takes insufficient disciplinary action against offending drivers (*Light v DPP* [1994] R.T.R. 396). Aiding and abetting can also be charged. Cases on causing and permitting will be found in Chapter 1.

In *Knowles Transport Ltd v Russell* [1975] R.T.R. 87 knowledge of the ir-   **14.107**
regularities was held to be an essential requisite before an employer could be said to have "caused" or "permitted" contravention of the regulations. Where the defendant is a corporation, such guilty knowledge must be imputed to a "responsible officer" of the corporation, i.e. "one whose duty included some measure of control of the company's business" (per Melford Stevenson J., at 93). Two checking clerks could have detected the excessive hours worked by the company's drivers when they checked the drivers' time sheets and calculated their wages, but as there was no evidence that the matter was brought to the attention of a responsible officer of the company or that any matter came to his notice which should have put him on inquiry, the company's conviction was set aside. In *Nuttall v Vehicle Inspectorate* [1999] R.T.R. 264 HL (Divisional Court judgment reported under the name of *Vehicle Inspectorate v Shane Raymond Nuttall (trading as Redline Coaches)* [1998] R.T.R. 321), coach drivers employed by the defendant had exceeded the permitted hours and the defendant (the employer) was charged with causing or permitting contravention of the applicable Community rules by the drivers. The employer had received but not checked the tachograph records. The

prosecution argued that this amounted to a reckless disregard of the situation, bordering on negligence, which could constitute implied knowledge. Agreeing, the Divisional Court held that the duty under art.15 of Regulation (EEC) 3820/85 to conduct periodic checks to ensure compliance with all provisions had to be read with art.14 of Regulation (EEC) 3821/85, thus making it a requirement that periodic checks be made on tachograph charts. Even though the employer had had no reason to consider that breaches had occurred, in the light of the responsibility under art.15, failure to check the tachograph charts amounted to a reckless shutting of the company's eyes to what had taken place. Although setting aside the judgment of the Divisional Court on an unrelated point, the House of Lords confirmed that "permit" in this context had its wider meaning of not taking reasonable steps to prevent something in one's power. The offence is not one of strict liability; nothing less than wilfulness or recklessness is sufficient. Evidence that the employers had not examined the records over the relevant period was capable of amounting to a prima facie case. This was further considered by the Divisional Court in *Yorkshire Traction Co Ltd v Vehicle Inspectorate* [2001] EWCA Admin 190; [2001] R.T.R. 34. The company was prosecuted for permitting a driver to driver without taking the required break. Justices found that the company's schedules were tight, that an adequate system of monitoring drivers' hours was not in place and that the company had failed to notice the problem over a three-week period although it checked the tachographs weekly. Considering this to be reckless, the justices convicted. The company appealed contending that the effectiveness of its monitoring system was limited by legislation since art.15(7) of Regulation (EEC) 3821/85 required drivers to be able to produce the current week's tachograph sheet and the last tachograph sheet from the previous week and what was then s.97A of the 1968 Act gave drivers 21 days in which to return those sheets. Allowing the appeal, the Divisional Court, applying *Nuttall v Vehicle Inspectorate*, accepted that argument and also noted that the justices had failed to consider the necessary causal relationship between the driver's breach and the company's conduct and had not identified who represented the "brains" of the company.

14.108   In *P. Foster (Haulage) Ltd v Roberts* [1978] 2 All E.R. 751 a solicitor entered a plea of guilty on behalf of the company to 48 offences under s.96 of the Transport Act 1968 of permitting its drivers to work excessive hours. The solicitor was under the mistaken impression that the offence was an absolute offence and that lack of knowledge provided no defence. The solicitor informed the magistrates' court accordingly. The magistrates made their own inquiries and were satisfied that the company must have known the true position. The Divisional Court held that this was an unequivocal plea of guilty. However, if the plea had been equivocal the justices would have been called upon to intervene even though the defendant was represented.

The defence under s.96(11)(i) as to unavoidable delay applies to all types of journeys or work (see also s.96(11B)(a) which stipulates this) and to any person, driver or not.

In *Whitby v Stead* [1975] R.T.R. 169, a driver was delayed for an hour while attempting to deliver some goods and again delayed while helping in an accident to other vehicles. He was charged with exceeding the working day of 14 hours and driving for a period exceeding 10 hours, because by s.103(1)(b) his two periods of driving became aggregated, since they were not separated by an interval of rest of at least 11 hours. The justices acquitted because of unavoidable delay under s.96(11)(i). The Divisional Court directed a conviction because the problems caused to the defendant by the delays could have been avoided by the defendant starting his second period of driving later. The defence of unavoidable delay is not available to excuse a failure to have an interval of 11 hours' rest (ibid.).

In *Green v Harrison* [1979] R.T.R. 483 a minibus driver took a party to York   **14.109** races and back. He was delayed on the outward journey by a puncture to his vehicle. On the return journey several hours were spent in a café and leisure centre and as a result the round trip took more than the permitted 16 hours. The justices concluded that the puncture had caused an unavoidable delay and dismissed the case. The Divisional Court directed the justices to convict. Neill J. said that "the circumstances which caused the delay on the outward part of the journey did not lead to delay 'in the completion of the journey' and indeed had nothing to do with the journey at all". The defence under s.96(11)(ii) or s.96(11B)(b) applies to all types of journeys or work and applies to employers, transport managers and other directing staff. In such a case the defendant must show not only that he was unaware that a driver had been driving otherwise than in his employment with the defendant's firm but also that the defendant could not reasonably have become aware of that fact. This suggests that employers and transport managers may have some duty to instruct their drivers to report to them if the drivers have been driving outside their employment. It seems to be no defence under s.96(11) or (11A) (assuming a defence is not available under s.96(11)(ii) or (11B)(b)) if the driver had been on duty in his employer's business for an excessive period even though directly against his master's orders: the master should supervise properly, but it may be a defence if he did supervise properly and his orders were still disobeyed unknown to him (*Gray's Haulage Co Ltd v Arnold* [1966] 1 All E.R. 896). Some of the cases are concerned with driving and some with duty and rest periods. Clearly, different criteria may apply. As stated in *Carter v Walton* below the question must be one of fact in each case.

Where a driver is engaged in canvassing and delivering during a journey, this   **14.110** was held under the old law to be time spent in driving (*McCallum & Son v Adair* 1937 S.C.(J.) 114) and clearly is time on duty under s.96 of the Transport Act 1968 (see s.103(4)(a)). By s.103(4), time spent on other "employment under the person who is his employer" is time spent on duty, as is time spent in the employment as a driver. Subject to the comments below, it may be that time spent on work for another employer does not count and, since questions may arise as to who is the employer, e.g. where there are several sub-contractors on a site, the common law cases as to who is the employer may be of relevance.

The phrase "on duty" appears in s.96(11A) as well as in the domestic drivers' hours code. The restrictive definition of "on duty" in s.103(4) should be compared with the definition of "carriage by road" in art.4 of Regulation (EC) 561/2006. In *Carter v Walton* [1985] R.T.R. 378, it was said that whether statutory breaks for rest and recreation, whether paid or unpaid, should be considered "off duty" breaks and be deducted in arriving at the length of a working day for the purpose of s.96(3)(a) of the 1968 Act was a question of fact in each case. The court allowed an appeal against the defendant's conviction for exceeding working hours. Watkins L.J. said that there was nothing in the relevant legislation or EC regulations which led to the conclusion that the whole of the legislation assumed that when a driver was taking a statutory break he was still on duty. If that was the implication some provision would appear in the Act that that was the effect of a driver taking a break. A driver might be on a break away from his lorry without being under any duty to his employer. Although it applies to s.96(3)(a) the principle cannot apply to s.96(3)(b) because off duty periods are by the wording clearly included in s.96(3)(b). In other words the break may have to be excluded from the s.96(3)(a) 11 hours, but must be included in the s.96(3)(b) 12½ hours. The provisions of s.96(3)(b) now appear to be otiose because of the relaxations contained in the Drivers' Hours (Goods Vehicles) (Modifications) Order 1986, but the principle remains. It is a question of fact in every case as to whether a lorry driver who took statutory breaks was off duty (*Carter v Walton* above). The cases below should be read subject to this so far as s.96(11) and s.96(11A) are concerned.

14.111 It was held in *Beer v Fairclough* (1937) 101 J.P. 157 on the old law that provided employers allowed their driver proper time for resting they did not have to see that he actually spent it in resting and they committed no offence if he did not, but it might be otherwise if he had, to their knowledge, to spend part of his rest period in travelling to the place at which he had orders to resume work. This rule is not expressly reversed by s.96, but s.96(11)(b) and s.96(11B)(b) suggest that an employer or transport manager might be liable if a driver had been working for someone else to the defendant's knowledge and would therefore be driving for the defendant for an excessive period or would not have enough rest. See also *Pearson v Rutterford* below.

A driver, after driving a goods vehicle for the maximum permitted period, used his employers' car to get home; sometimes he drove it and sometimes he was a passenger in it, but his employers gave him a genuine option to stay overnight at the place where he left his goods vehicle. It was held that, in view of this option, he had been given his rest period and no offence was committed if he chose to use the car (*Witchell v Abbott* [1966] 2 All E.R. 657 at 659), but this case was distinguished in *Potter v Gorbould* [1969] 3 All E.R. 828. The defendant was allowed by his employer, when he had finished his normal day's work, to earn overtime by cutting up scrap in his employer's scrap yard if he wished. As a result the defendant had less than the period for rest required. It was held that, as what was being done was not purely for the benefit of the driver but equally for the benefit of the employer and he was bound by the terms of his employment to obey the employer's directions and it was within the general terms of his employment, it could not be held that he had been given his period of rest.

14.112 A driver for employer *A* also worked as an HGV driving instructor on behalf of employer *B*. This was to the knowledge of employer *A*. The court held that the work for employer *B* should be regarded as a period of attendance at work so far as employer *A* was concerned and not put down as a daily rest period. The driver should have been convicted of keeping false records contrary to s.99(5) and of failing to take the daily rest periods required by art.8 of Regulation (EEC) 3820/85 (*Pearson v Rutterford* [1982] R.T.R. 54). (The question was also raised but not answered whether an HGV driving instructor was a crew member.)

Where the driver's records show that he was working for a particular period and that period exceeds the permitted period of work, there is a prima facie case against him and against his employers for permitting him to work excessive hours; he or his employers must show that he was in fact resting or off duty (*Smith*

v All-Wheel Drive Co Ltd, Guardian, February 12, 1962). The magistrates should
not infer that it was unlikely that he was working without such evidence (ibid.).

The records of the driver's hours are admissible against his employer in a   **14.113**
charge under s.96 (s.98(5)). They appear to be admissible anyhow at common
law against the driver himself and possibly against the transport manager, if the
court holds that the latter has the duty of seeing that his firm's drivers obey the
requirements of s.96. Under s.97B similarly tachograph entries are admissible
and in Scotland are sufficient evidence. Under s.97B also any entries made
thereon for the purposes of art.17(2), (3) or 18(2) (temporary records) of the EC
tachograph regulation may be admitted in evidence. If the manager is charged
with aiding and abetting the employer, it could be argued that, by s.44 of the
Magistrates' Courts Act 1980, the manager is "guilty of the like offence", so that
evidence admissible against the employer is likewise admissible against the
manager; on the other hand, there are cases every day where evidence against one
defendant is not admissible against another. Certainly, if the manager is charged
as the principal offender, it can be said that, as against him, the driver's records
are hearsay and not admissible. The prosecutor might be wise to call the driver to
give oral evidence or submit his written evidence under s.9 of the Criminal Justice
Act 1967, the driver refreshing his memory from his records (*R. v Bryant* (1946)
110 J.P. 267) . Relevant cases are *Beer v Clench* and *Adair v Craighouse & Co* at
§ 14.189; see *Hogg v Burnet* (also at § 14.189) as to a vehicle number on a record
identifying it.

As to penalties and proceedings generally, see §§ 14.187 et seq.

DRIVERS' RECORDS

Generally

The provisions relating to the installation and use of recording equipment ("ta-   **14.114**
chographs") are contained in ss.97, 97B and 97C of the Transport Act 1968, as
amended. These statutory rules incorporate and to some extent make directly applicable Regulation (EEC) 3821/85 (the current tachograph regulation) as
amended.

A tachograph is a cable-fed combination of a speedometer, an odometer and a
24-hour clock. The expression used in the statutory provisions and the EC regulation is "recording equipment" but "tachograph" is the commonly used name.

Tachograph provisions became applicable for national and international   **14.115**
transport operations (defined at § 14.21) from January 1, 1982. The tachograph
provisions apply to all the vehicles specified in s.95(2) subject to the exceptions
and exemptions set out at § 14.139. There are special provisions for certain regular passenger services.

Domestic journeys or work excepted from Regulation (EC) 561/2006 are also
excepted from the tachograph regulation by art.3. (See the definition of domestic
journeys or work at § 14.25.) They are instead subject to s.98 of the 1968 Act
and, where appropriate, to the Drivers' Hours (Goods Vehicles) (Keeping of Records) Regulations 1987 (SI 1987/1421), made thereunder.

Section 98 and the 1987 Regulations apply also to certain responsibilities of   **14.116**
employers and may apply where there are tachograph exemptions—see § 14.17.
Despite the exception in art.13(d) of Regulation (EC) 561/2006 by which they

are excluded from being subject to the EC regulations and become subject instead to the domestic journeys and work rules, certain vehicles used for carrying postal articles are required to comply with Regulation (EEC) 3821/85 (the tachograph regulation). Breaches in respect of these post-carrying vehicles will be contraventions of ss.97(1) and 97C of the 1968 Act (s.97(6) and art.3(4) of Regulation (EEC) 3821/85).

14.117　　Tachographs may also be used voluntarily on vehicles which are excepted or exempted from the tachograph provisions (see § 14.153). Where "conforming" tachographs are used handwritten records need not be kept (see § 14.153).

Definitions are contained in s.103 of the 1968 Act and art.4 of Regulation (EC) 561/2006 (applied by art.3 of the tachograph regulation). See § 14.31.

Contraventions of the tachograph provisions are offences under ss.97(1) and 97C(5) of the 1968 Act. Contraventions of the manual record provisions are offences contrary to s.98(4) of the 1968 Act.

The application of these sections to Crown, military, police and fire brigade vehicles is indicated in s.102 of the 1968 Act.

14.118　　In *Vehicle and Operator Services Agency v Jones* [2005] EWHC 2278; [2006] R.T.R. 6, the defendant admitted driving a heavy goods vehicle on two occasions when the tachograph on the vehicle had been interfered with. The interference resulted in a false reading on the tachograph record. The driver admitted that he had opened the tachograph cover because his speedometer was not working properly. Before the magistrates' court, the justices acquitted the defendant on the basis that he did not withdraw the record sheet from the tachograph casing although it could no longer make a record. On appeal by the prosecutor, the Divisional Court held that if a driver interferes with tachograph equipment with the result that it does not function properly, then whatever the drivers' motive, an offence is committed under s.97(1)(a)(iii) of the Transport Act 1968, unless he can rely upon one of the specific defences set out in the Act. The action of lifting the record sheet from the styli before the end of the daily working period could be regarded as withdrawal of that record since such an action withdrew the record sheet from such part of the mechanism so far as to prevent its proper functioning. (*Birkett v Vehicle Inspectorate* [1998] R.T.R. 264 applied.)

Drivers' Records: Tachographs

Goods vehicles on national and international journeys

Provisions

14.119　　Most of Regulation (EEC) 3821/85, as amended, is specified directly or indirectly by ss.97, 97B and 97C of the Transport Act 1968. The parts of the regulation which are specifically applied, and contraventions of which therefore constitute an offence are, under s.97(1)(a), as substituted and amended.

Under s.97(1)(a), as amended, it is an offence to use, cause or permit to be used (as to these expressions see Chapter 1) a vehicle to which the tachograph provisions apply without recording equipment:

　　(i) which has been installed in accordance with the regulation;

　　(ii) which complies with the relevant Annexes (requirements for construction, testing, installation and inspection; approval mark and certificate); and

(iii) is being used as provided by arts 13–15.

It is submitted that it is possible to charge (i), (ii) and (iii) separately if so **14.120**
desired. See "Duplicity", Chapter 2.

In *Pritchard and Devonish v Crown Prosecution Service* [2003] EWHC 1851;
[2004] R.T.R. 22, the issue was whether a piece of heavy equipment towed behind
a vehicle was a trailer for the purposes of assessing the weight of the vehicle and,
thus, the requirement to have a tachograph fitted and used. Appeals against
conviction were dismissed on the basis that there could be no difference in the
concept between a goods carrying trailer and a piece of heavy equipment towed
behind a vehicle. The legislation was directed at the driving of heavy vehicles
and their attachments on the road.

The phrase "recording equipment in use according to arts 13 and 15" was **14.121**
considered in *Birkett and Naylor v Vehicle Inspectorate*; *Vehicle Inspectorate v
Dukes Transport Ltd* [1998] R.T.R. 264. It was held to extend to record sheets
which had been used in a machine and removed as well as those currently inside
it. Therefore, coach drivers unable to produce record sheets from a previous day
were guilty of an offence contrary to s.97.

Under s.97(1)(b) it is an offence to use, cause or permit to be used, a vehicle to
which s.97 applies in which there is recording equipment which has been repaired
(whether before or after installation) otherwise than in accordance with the Community Recording Equipment Regulation (Regulation (EEC) 3821/85). From the
wording, although the repair may be incorrect before installation, the offence
only arises when the illegally repaired tachograph has been installed in the vehicle and the vehicle has been used.

A person commits an offence under s.97AA(1) of the Transport Act 1968 who, **14.122**
with intent to deceive, forges, alters or uses any seal on recording equipment
installed in, or designed for installation in, a vehicle to which s.97 of the Transport
Act 1968 applies.

A person forges a seal within the meaning of s.97AA in its application to
England and Wales if he makes a false seal in order that it may be used as genuine (s.97AA(3)). See also Chapter 16, Forgery, etc., and the cases discussed
there.

This offence under s.97AA may be committed in respect of a seal on tacho- **14.123**
graph equipment designed for installation and therefore before the equipment has
been installed. It will still be necessary for the prosecution to prove that the tachograph equipment is for installation in a vehicle to which s.97 applies and not for
instance in a vehicle for which a tachograph is not necessary but where it is to be
used on a voluntary basis. The prosecution's task will be easier if the equipment
is in or has come from and is to be returned to a vehicle to which s.97 applies but
the position depends not only on the type of vehicle but also on the use to which
it is put.

The other parts of the tachograph regulation which are applied and are material
are as follows:

(i) art.16(2) is relevant for the defence in s.97(3)(b), which relates to keeping temporary records when the recording equipment breaks down;

(ii) art.3 contains certain exemptions; and

(iii) any expression used in s.97, 97B or 97C which is also used in the
regulation has the same meaning as in that regulation (s.97(6)).

14.124   By Pt III of Annex I a tachograph must include visual instruments showing the distance travelled, the speed and the time, instruments for recording the distance travelled, speed and time and a marking device showing on the record sheet each opening of the case containing that sheet. A common form of tachograph record consists of a waxed circular disc placed on a rod and marked by three styli, one stylus showing automatically the distance by a line going to and fro, one similarly showing the speed and one manually set by means of a "mode key" showing the current activity of the driver. This form of tachograph record is, however, not obligatory and Annex I makes it clear that the recording sheet may be in the form of a strip as well as a disc.

Part II of Annex I provides that the tachograph must be capable of recording the following activities:

    (a) distance travelled;

    (b) speed;

    (c) driving time;

    (d) other periods of work or of availability;

    (e) breaks from work and daily rest periods;

    (f) opening of the case containing the record sheet;

    (g) (for new vehicles from January 1, 1996 and for type approval from July 1, 1991), interruptions in the electrical power supply (except illumination) to the distance and speed sensor. (Note that from January 1, 1996, Regulation (EC) 2479/95 enabled electronic monitoring to be used to prevent manipulation of tachographs as an alternative to the protection required for the cables connecting the recording equipment to the transmitter.)

14.125   Where there are two drivers, the equipment must be capable of recording simultaneously but distinctly and on two separate sheets the items at (c), (d) and (e) above, i.e. the driving time, other periods of work or of availability, and breaks from work and daily rest periods.

Regulation 4 of the Passenger and Goods Vehicles (Recording Equipment) Regulations 1979 (SI 1979/1746), as amended, provides for the approval of fitters and workshops for installation and repair and the nomination of bodies for carrying out checks and inspections. The inspection of the equipment must be every two years and the inspection as to maximum tolerances (i.e. a calibration check) must be every six years. Apart from transitional arrangements these dates begin with the date shown on the installation plaque. These inspections are in accordance with requirements in Annex I. The offence is created by s.97 which requires the recording equipment to comply with Annex I. If the equipment has not been inspected as required can it be said not to comply? It is submitted that an offence is created although the wording is rather tenuous.

14.126   A number of offences are occurring because these two-year inspections have not been carried out or because the full six-year inspection and calibration requirement has been overlooked or ignored. The dates of the inspections and the dates of the six-year calibration checks are similarly shown by a plaque (or plaques) on the vehicle.

Article 13 stipulates that the employer and the drivers (see § 14.31) are responsible for seeing that the equipment functions correctly. Article 14(1) provides that the employer shall issue a sufficient number of record sheets and that the sheets must be of an approved model, and art.14(2) that the employer must retain record sheets and printouts, whenever printouts have been made to comply with art.15(1), in chronological order and in a legible form for at least a year after their use and shall give copies to the drivers concerned who request them. The employer must also give copies of downloaded data from the driver cards to the drivers concerned who request them and the printed papers of these copies. The record sheets, printouts and downloaded data must be produced or handed over at the request of any authorised inspecting officer.

There is a requirement in art.14(1) and (2) for the employer of a driver to man- **14.127** age the tachograph discs. Where a vehicle is hired out without a driver and the driver is supplied by the company by which the vehicle is hired, it is that company which must manage the discs, not the owner of the vehicle: Case C–228/01 *Bourasse v Minister Public, Ministère Public v Perchicot* [2003] R.T.R. 24.

Article 15 contains the detailed obligations of the drivers. Article 15 was amended from May 1, 2006 by Regulation (EC) 561/2006 art.26(4). Article 15 provides that drivers shall not use dirty or damaged record sheets or driver cards. The sheets must be adequately protected on this account. There are also requirements for drivers to give not less than 15 days' notice of intention to renew a driver card and where a driver card or record sheet is damaged it must not be withdrawn but provide details which enable the driver to be identified and information required by art.15 relating to the recording of time on the sheet which agrees with the official timetable of the country of registration of the vehicle and the use of the mode switch and the signage to be used to indicate driving time, other work, availability and breaks in work and daily rest periods. Drivers must use record sheets or driver cards every day on which they are driving starting from the moment they take over the vehicle. The record sheet or driver card shall not be withdrawn before the end of the daily working period unless its withdrawal is otherwise authorised. No record sheet or driver card may be used to cover a period longer than that for which it is intended. When as a result of being away from the vehicle, a driver is unable to use the equipment fitted to the vehicle, the periods of time referred to which relate to the "other work", "availability" and "breaks in work and daily rest periods" shall be entered on to the record sheet or on to the driver card using the manual entry facility provided in the recorded equipment. Which method of recording is used will depend upon the type of recording equipment fitted in the vehicle (art.15(2), (3)).

A new art.15(3)(b) defines "other work" as any activity other than driving and **14.128** also any work for the same or another employer within or outside the transport sector, and must be recorded under the appropriate sign.

From the wording of the EC regulation it seems that the tachograph sheets and cards are personal to the drivers and driving mates rather than to the vehicle. Under s.97(1)(a)(i) it is an offence for an employed driver or driving mate to fail without reasonable excuse to return any record sheet which relates to him to his employer within 21 days of completing it. Where he has two employers he must notify each of the name and address of the other (s.97A(1)(b)).

Record books need not be kept where a tachograph is used. Section 98(2A) **14.129** provides that where s.97(1)(a)(ii) (compliance with tachograph regulation) applies to a vehicle, the regulations under s.98 regarding the driving of a vehicle (in particular as to manual record books) cease to apply. See further § 14.153.

As the tachograph records the speed of the vehicle, the record can be used as evidence in a speeding prosecution by either the prosecution or the defence. It may also be material evidence for other prosecutions, e.g. dangerous or careless driving.

Digital tachographs: general provisions

14.130   Sections 99ZA–99ZF of the Transport Act 1968 contain detailed enforcement provisions which apply where tachographs, whether analogue or digital, are used or documents are required under Community Rules. A digital tachograph is one which complies with Annex 1B to Regulation (EEC) 3821/85 (as inserted by Regulation (EC) 1360/2002). The enforcement powers are conferred on officers who are examiners from the Vehicle and Operator Services Agency or the police.

Section 99ZA gives officers the power to require the production of records and the driver cards used with digital tachographs. They may copy the electronic data.

14.131   Powers of entry are conferred upon officers by virtue of s.99ZB. Officers may enter vehicles required to be fitted with tachographs, inspect equipment and other things on and in the vehicles, copy data and retain evidence. Officers may also enter premises. A time-limit of six months is imposed by s.99ZC on the retention powers, unless the retained items are required for proceedings.

It is an offence under s.99ZD, not to comply with an officer's requirements or to obstruct an officer. The maximum penalty is a fine at level 5 on the standard scale.

Offences in respect of false records and data, destruction of records and data and failure to make relevant records are provided for in s.99ZE. The offences extend to those causing or permitting the actions as well as those actually carrying them out. The maximum penalty on summary conviction is the statutory maximum; the maximum penalty on the conviction on indictment is two years' imprisonment or a fine.

14.132   The Passenger and Goods Vehicles (Recording Equipment) (Fitting Date) Regulations 2006 (SI 2006/1117) amend s.97 of the Transport Act 1968 to set the date from which the new digital tachograph must be fitted to a new vehicle which requires a tachograph.

The digital tachograph as provided for by Regulation (EC) 2135/98, which amended Regulation (EEC) 3821/85 and specified the date from which vehicles first put into service were to be fitted with digital tachographs, was amended by art.27 of Regulation (EC) 561/2006. The new date is included in the definition of "the relevant Annexes" as substituted, i.e. May 1, 2006.

With effect from August 21, 2006, the Passenger and Goods Vehicles (Recording Equipment) (Tachograph Card) Regulations 2006 (SI 2006/1937) make provision in relation to the cards used with digital tachographs. The regulations prohibit the use by a person of more than one driver card, of a driver card of which he is not the holder, of a forged or altered card and of a card issued as a result of an incorrect application. Making a false statement in an application for a card is also prohibited. Breach is an offence—the penalty depending upon the nature of the breach (reg.3). Similarly, offences are created in relation to the use of more than one workshop card and there are other provisions in relation to the use of a personal identification number and the use of forged or altered cards (reg.4). There are also provisions requiring written notification of lost or stolen cards to the Secretary of State and offences are created for the non-return of damaged or malfunctioning cards (reg.5). There are similar requirements in regs 6 and 7 in relation to the notification of details on the card requiring correction and a requirement to surrender cards which have been falsified or which have been issued as a result of a false application.

The Passenger and Goods Vehicles (Recording Equipment) (Downloading and **14.133** Retention of Data) Regulations 2008 (SI 2008/198) complete the implementation of Regulation (EC) 561/2006 in Great Britain by making provision in respect of the downloading of data from digital tachograph recording equipment and record retention. The regulations amend Pt VI of the Transport Act 1968.

Regulations 2 and 4(c) of the 2008 Regulations repeal s.97A of the 1968 Act and replace it with a new provision (s.97C) requiring drivers to return paper records held by them to the transport undertaking(s) for which they have been working within 42 days of the records having been created.

Article 10(5)(a) of Regulation (EC) 561/2006 is implemented by reg.2 of the **14.134** 2008 Regulations through the insertion of the following provisions into the Transport Act 1968:

(a) New ss.97D and 97E require transport undertakings to download data held electronically on a vehicle unit and a driver card whenever that is necessary to ensure that data are not over-written or otherwise lost to the undertaking and in any event before the expiration of specific periods according to the data concerned. In the case of data stored on the vehicle other than detailed speed data, a period of 56 days computed in accordance with s.97D(3) is prescribed. Where data are stored on the driver card, the period is 28 days computed in accordance with s.97E(3).

(b) Transport undertakings are required to download any data held electronically on a vehicle unit or driver card where an enforcement officer has reason to believe that an offence under the Road Traffic Regulation Act 1984, the Road Traffic Act 1988, the Road Traffic Offenders Act 1988, or Pt VI of the Transport Act 1968 has been committed (see new s.97F).

(c) New offences are created in new ss.97G and 97H of failing to download or to retain data and provide for the making of data which has been downloaded accessible to enforcement officers. Offences committed under s.97G or 97H are punishable on summary conviction with a fine not exceeding level 5 on the standard scale.

New ss.102B and 102C are inserted into the 1968 Act by reg.3 of the 2008 Regulations. They make provisions in respect of criminal proceedings against transport undertakings which are unincorporated bodies such as partnerships and offences committed by a corporate or unincorporated body with the consent or connivance of a director or other officer of that body. Broadly, they make provision for proceedings to be brought in the name of a partnership or an unincorporated association and provide for the criminal liability of a body corporate where an offence is committed by an officer of that body.

Miscellaneous amendments are also made to the 1968 Act by reg.4. The regula- **14.135** tion implements art.20(3) of Regulation (EC) 561/2006 by making it an offence if a driver who works for two or more transport undertakings fails to provide each of them with sufficient information to enable them to discharge their obligations in relation to drivers' hours (1968 Act s.96(11D)). The offence is punishable by a fine not exceeding level 4 on the standard scale.

Definitions

14.136   Article 2 of Regulation (EEC) 3821/85, as amended, provides that for the purposes of the tachograph regulation the definitions in art.4 of Regulation (EC) 561/2006 (driver's hours and rest periods) shall apply. For the definitions in art.4, see § 14.31. Any expression in the tachograph regulation which is also used in s.97, 97B or 97C of the 1968 Act has the same meaning in the Act as in the regulation (s.97(6)). "Driver" wherever it is used in the EC regulations means any person who drives the vehicle even for a short period, or who is carried in the vehicle to be available for driving if necessary. This extended meaning will not include a non-driving mate or a conductor. The expression "driver and driving mate" has accordingly been used. The liability of a driver's mate may however be restricted by the limitation contained within art.15(2) which pertains to when a driver takes over the vehicle. See the cases at §§ 14.31 et seq.

    Section 97 refers to any person but ss.97B and 97C refer to drivers.

14.137   The time recorded on a tachograph must be the time which agrees with the official time in the country of registration of the vehicle (art.15(3)). Tachographs should not therefore be adjusted on the continent to show continental time and time allowance may have to be made for foreign vehicles in Great Britain.

    Article 15(7) has been inserted in Regulation (EEC) 3821/85 by Regulation (EC) 561/2006. In summary, where a driver drives a vehicle fitted with recording equipment in conformity with Annex 1 of Regulation (EC) 3821/85, whenever an inspecting officer so requests, the driver must produce the record sheets for the current week and those used by the driver in the previous 15 days, the driver card if he holds one, and any manual record and printout made during the current week and the previous 15 days as required under both the 1985 and 2006 Regulations. After January 1, 2008, the time periods relating to the production of record sheets and driver cards shall cover the current day and the previous 28 days. Where the driver drives a vehicle fitted with recording equipment in conformity with Annex 1B to the tachograph regulation, the driver must be able to produce when requested his driver card together with any manual record and printout made during the current week and the previous 15 days. He must also produce record sheets corresponding to the same period. Again, after January 1, 2008, manual records must cover the current day and previous 28 days. Authorised inspecting officers may check compliance with Regulation (EC) 561/2006 by an analysis of the record sheets, printed data or driver card. If none of these options are possible, any other supporting document that justifies non-compliance may be analysed, e.g. a duty roster.

14.138   The first part of Annex I defines, for the purpose of the annex, "recording equipment", "record sheet", the "constant" of the recording equipment, the "characteristic coefficient" of the vehicle and the "effective circumference" of the wheel tyres. The definition of "recording equipment" is differently worded from the definition in s.97(7) for the purposes of Pt VI of the 1968 Act. In s.97(7) and s.103(1)(b) it means "equipment for recording information as to the use of a vehicle". In Annex I it is defined as equipment "intended for installation in road vehicles to show and record automatically or semi-automatically details of the movement of those vehicles and of certain working periods of their drivers".

Exceptions and exemptions

14.139   Tachographs need not be installed or used in the vehicles referred to in art.3 of

Regulation (EC) 561/2006. The journeys or work *excepted* by art.3 (see "Domestic journeys", § 14.25) are altogether outside the scope of the Community rules.

Article 3(2) and (3) of the tachograph regulation allows member countries to make certain *exemptions* in respect of national and certain international transport operations. Under reg.4 of the Community Drivers' Hours and Recording Equipment Regulations 2007 (SI 2007/1819), as amended, the exemptions including the emergency exemptions are the same as from the drivers' hours provisions. There is, however, an additional exemption, but only from all the tachograph requirements, for vehicles being used for collecting sea coal. The exemption is under the 2007 Regulations, art.3(2) of Regulation (EEC) 3281/85 and art.13 of Regulation (EC) 561/2006. This exemption applies to both national and international operations.

14.140 See further § 14.61 and § 14.63 where the exemptions are set out in detail and the cases described. Note also the discussion on "applicable Community rules" at § 14.16. The question is whether the exemptions are complete or only from the EC regulations, so that manual records may have to be kept instead in accordance with the Drivers' Hours (Goods Vehicles) (Keeping of Records) Regulations 1987 (SI 1987/1421).

The burden of establishing an exemption rests on the defendant on the balance of probabilities (*Gaunt v Nelson* [1987] R.T.R. 1). That case concerned the meaning of a specialised vehicle and the exemption under the regulations from the fitting and use of a tachograph.

14.141 The AETR agreement has been amended to reflect and reproduce relevant provisions of Regulation (EEC) 3281/85.

There are certain exemptions for regular passenger services.

Proceedings

14.142 Records and other documents which are required to be kept for inspection under s.99 of the Transport Act 1968 include any record sheet or hard copy of electronically stored data which a person is required to retain or to be able to produce (s.99ZA). As to this and the penalties for contravening s.97 and s.97C, see § 14.198.

Defences

14.143 Article 1 refers to tachographs which as regards construction, installation, use and testing "comply" with the requirements of Regulation (EEC) 3821/85 and of Annexes I and II thereof which form an integral part of the tachograph regulation. Annex IB sets out the technical requirements for the construction, testing, installation and inspection of tachographs. Recording equipment for the purposes of the principal regulation is equipment which complies with Annex I or IB or with Annex II (see art.1). By Regulation (EC) 1360/2002, the technical specifications of Annex IB have been adapted to technical progress, with particular regard to the overall security of the system and the inter-operability between the recording equipment and the driver cards. Where an obligatory tachograph has been installed but for one reason or another does not conform to Annex I or II an offence will be committed under s.97(1).

A defence was created for s.97(1) (tachograph installation, use and repair) offences by the Passenger and Goods Vehicles (Recording Equipment) Regulations 1989 (SI 1989/2121), by the insertion of s.97(1A) in the Transport Act 1968.

Section 97(1A) provides that a person shall not be liable to be convicted under s.97(1) if he proves that he neither knew nor ought to have known that the tachograph had not been installed or repaired in accordance with the tachograph regulation.

14.144   The defence will be available for all s.97(1) offences including the defective repair offence in s.97(1)(b). There is no reference to "use" in s.97(1A), but it is submitted that the defence will nevertheless be available for a "use" offence attributable to defective installation or repair.

Section 97(2), (3), (4) and (4A) provide defences for s.97(1)(a) offences where:

(a) a vehicle is proceeding to a place where the recording equipment is to be fitted in accordance with the EC regulation requirements (s.97(2));

(b) in the case of defective recording equipment, it had not become reasonably practicable for the equipment to be repaired by an approved fitter or workshop *and* the requirements of art.16(2) (temporary records) were being complied with (s.97(3));

(c) in the case of broken seals, breaking or removal could not have been avoided *and* it had not become reasonably practicable for the seal to be replaced by an approved fitter or workshop *and* in all other respects the equipment was being used as provided by arts 13–15 (s.97(4));

(d) in the case where a driver card has not been used with the recording equipment, the defendant proves to the court that the driver card was damaged, malfunctioning or stolen, that art.16(2) and (3) (apart from the last paragraph) of Regulation (EEC) 3821/85 were being complied with, and in all other respects the recording equipment was being used in accordance with arts 13 and 15 of that regulation (s.97(4A)).

14.145   Both the wording of the statute and the sense imply that (b) and (c) respectively are cumulative. In other words the defendant must prove *both* limbs of (b) above before that defence applies and the three limbs of (c) above before that defence applies.

Section 97(3) of the 1968 Act provides that a person shall not be convicted under s.97(1)(a) (installation of conforming tachographs and their use) if the tachograph installed is not in working order if he proves that approved repairs were not reasonably practicable and that the requirements of art.16(2) were being obeyed. Article 16(2) requires that where the tachograph is unserviceable or operating defectively, temporary records must be kept instead. The failure to keep temporary records under art.16(2) or otherwise to comply with the tachograph regulation will mean that the defence in s.97(3) cannot be made out. Compare the defence under s.98(4A), discussed at § 14.156–7, relating to the voluntary use of tachographs. Compare also the exception in s.98(2A), discussed below, which covers the inter-relationship between the tachograph and the Drivers' Hours (Goods Vehicles) (Keeping of Records) Regulations 1987 but which does not refer to applicable Community rules.

14.146   Section 97(4) of the 1968 Act provides a further statutory defence to a charge of not using a tachograph as required in that, in the case of broken seals, breaking or removal could not be avoided, it had not become reasonably practicable for the seal to be properly replaced and in all other respects the equipment was being properly used. The extent of this defence was considered by the Divisional Court in *Vehicle Inspectorate v Sam Anderson (Newhouse) Ltd* [2001] EWHC Admin

893; [2002] R.T.R. 13. A driver for the defendant company had been stopped on October 6 and the Inspector had noticed that the plastic cover over the switches came away when finger pressure was applied. The Inspector formed the view that the seal to the cover had been tampered with and that part of the plastic was missing. There was no evidence that the switches had been tampered with and the tachograph was being used properly in all other respects. The vehicle had been inspected by an authorised dealer on September 21 and by the company's own workshop on September 24 and on neither occasion had any fault been observed, nor had the driver reported one. The court heard that the nature of the seals in use differ considerably from those in use when the regulations were made and the employer has to rely on visual inspection by looking down from above from which perspective it would not have been possible to have seen the missing plastic and removal was not permitted. At trial, the defendant argued that the break could not have been avoided, it had not become reasonably practicable to replace it and the tachograph was being properly used in all other respects. Before the justices, it was successfully submitted that the statutory defence now had to be considered in the context of the working environment in which the newer type of seal is used and that it should be construed widely to cover situations where it could be shown that the defendant could have done no more to prevent the seal being broken, that he had no knowledge of the break and that there was a system of checks designed to identify failures when they occurred. Disagreeing with that argument, the Divisional Court emphasised that the statutory defence did not say "could not be avoided by the defendant" simply "could not be avoided". Since it was self-evident on the facts that the interference was deliberate, it could have been avoided by the person who did it. Public policy requires a strict interpretation and lack of knowledge on the part of the defendant and its system of checking are matters that properly go to sentence.

It should be emphasised that the defences in s.97(2), (3) and (4) only apply to **14.147** s.97(1)(a) with the three paragraphs (i), (ii) and (iii) and the references in s.97(2), (3) and (4) to s.97(1) have been altered to references to s.97(1)(a) to correspond. They do not apply to s.97(1)(b) (the defective repair offence), whereas the s.97(1A) defence noted above applies to both s.97(1)(a) and s.97(1)(b).

Defences under s.97(4A) were inserted by the Passenger and Goods Vehicles (Recording Equipment) Regulations 2005 (SI 2005/1904) and provide for cases where a person shall not be guilty under s.97(1)(a) if he proves to the court that a driver card was damaged, malfunctioning, lost or stolen, that the main requirements in art.16 of Regulation (EEC) 3281/85 were being complied with and that in all other respects the recording equipment was being used in accordance with arts 13–15 of that regulation.

These defences will be on the balance of probabilities (*R. v Carr-Briant* [1943] 2 All E.R. 156) and the burden of proof will be on the defendant (see s.101 of the Magistrates' Courts Act 1980).

Liability of employers for staff defaults

An employer may be liable generally for using or causing or permitting to be **14.148** used a vehicle to which s.97 of the 1968 Act applies where the tachograph is not installed, used or repaired as specified (s.97(1)). (For "using", "causing" and "permitting" see Chapter 1. Unlike the "using" offence, "causing" and "permitting" both require proof of mens rea.)

Clearly the employer may be vicariously liable where an employee is *using* the vehicle without a tachograph being *installed* or repaired as required. The question is whether he can be vicariously liable where the employee is *using* the vehicle without *using* the tachograph as required. This is something which is very often completely outside the control of the employer. Nevertheless, it seems that the wording is wide enough to make him vicariously liable (cf. the other examples under "To use" at §§ 1.176 et seq.). It has been argued that, as no obligation is placed on the *employer* by art.15, an *employer* cannot use the vehicle where there is a failure by the employee to comply with art.15 without the knowledge of the employer. It is submitted that this argument is not valid. The relevant part of s.97(1) of the Transport Act 1968 provides that no person shall use a vehicle unless there is equipment which is being used as provided by arts 13–15. There appears to be ample authority to construe "use" to include the situation described: see §§ 1.176 et seq. The key phrase in s.97(1) is "is being used". The articles in the EC regulations place different obligations, some on the employer, some on the driver, some on both. However, it is s.97 that creates the offence.

14.149   As an example of the absolute nature of the using offence, a stipendiary magistrate convicted a limited company for using a vehicle without a tachograph sheet inserted. The transport manager had orally warned the driver, given him a written warning and sacked him for the offence. The comment of the transport manager in court was: "He's a young man who simply will never learn he's got to do as he's told; he will always go his own sweet way." The manager's comments out of court have not been quoted. The company received an absolute discharge. The defence in s.98(4) does not apply as this was a contravention not of s.98(4) but s.97 and the defence in s.98(4) only applies to employers "liable to be convicted under this subsection".

There is a limited defence under s.97(1A) to any s.97(1) offence where the employer can prove that he neither knew nor ought to have known that the tachograph had not been installed or repaired in accordance with the regulation. There seems to be no reason why this defence should not be available for a "using" offence attributable to defective installation or repair.

14.150   The employer should always check carefully whether there is any exemption or defence available. Punishment imposed by a Member State on an employer for a breach by his employee of the EC regulations was held by the European Court of Justice to be valid even though it was not attributable to an intentional or negligent failure, providing it was proportionate to the offence and analogous to punishments for similar offences in the same country: Case C–326/88 *Anklagemyndigheden v Hansen & Son I/S*, [1990] E.C.R. I–2911. A Danish law imposing strict liability for breaches of driving and rest period requirements was upheld.

The nature of "causing" in this context was considered in *Redhead Freight Ltd v Shulman* [1989] R.T.R. 1. In that case, a company was charged with two offences contrary to s.97 of the Transport Act 1968, of causing an employee to use a goods vehicle fitted with a tachograph which was not being used as required.

14.151   The company either knew that one of its employees was failing to fill in his tachograph records, except on isolated occasions, or at least through its transport manager deliberately shut its eyes to the failure. Nevertheless it was held that the employer company could not be said to have *caused* the offence contrary to s.97(1). The company did not cause the employee not to use the vehicle recording equipment.

The word "cause" implies that it must be an inevitable consequence of sending out the driver that the tachographs would not be filled in. This was not the situation in the *Redhead* case. Although there was acquiescence in the record-keeping failure which could amount to the offence of permitting, it fell short of a positive mandate or any other sufficient act for the offence of "causing".

The responsibilities of an employer under arts 13 and 14 have already been described at §§ 14.126–7.   **14.152**

An employer commits an offence who fails without reasonable excuse to secure that employee crew members comply with s.97A(1)(a), i.e. failing without reasonable excuse to return any record sheet relating to the employee to the employer within 21 days of completing it (s.97A(2)). As to the meaning of "without reasonable excuse", compare § 4.261 and § 13.211.

An employer may be convicted of aiding and abetting an employee or of conspiracy to contravene a Pt VI offence (see *R. v Blamires Transport Services Ltd* [1963] 3 All E.R. 170).

Tachograph records replacing handwritten records

Where a person is a driver or driving mate of a vehicle using a "conforming" tachograph, the requirements of art.16 (timetables and duty rosters) of Regulation (EC) 561/2006 cease to apply. The wording is such that it is immaterial whether the use is compulsory or voluntary.   **14.153**

Section 98(2A) of the Transport Act 1968 states that regulations under this section (i.e. the Drivers' Hours (Goods Vehicles) (Keeping of Records) Regulations 1987 (SI 1987/1421)) are not to apply as respects the driving of a vehicle "to which Section 97 of this Act [the tachograph provisions] applies and in relation to which subsection (1)(b) of that section has come into force". It is clear from this that for the purpose of s.98(2A) it is immaterial that the tachograph is not installed as required or does not conform. It should be noted that all relevant regulations and Pt VI of the Transport Act 1968 have been amended to take account of the digital tachograph.

The wording of s.98(2A) is such that only the vehicles subject to the tachograph rules, i.e. where the tachograph is compulsory, are excluded from being subject to the 1987 Regulations. Section 98(2A) refers to the "driving" of a compulsory tachograph vehicle. There is no suggestion that any other applicable Community rules are to be applied instead where the tachograph rules do not apply. At first sight therefore the 1987 Regulations continue to apply to employers with compulsory tachograph vehicles as they are not "driving". This may not be the intended interpretation and it seems that there is nothing for employers of compulsory tachograph vehicle crew members to comply with under the 1987 Regulations. Similarly, there will be nothing for them to comply with when there is a complete exemption from keeping records.   **14.154**

The 1987 Regulations specifically state that they are not to apply in relation to a journey made or work done by a driver which is subject to the applicable Community rules. As to the uncertainty over the meaning of "applicable Community rules" and whether exemptions from them but under them leave the 1987 Regulations applicable instead, see § 14.16.

Where the tachograph breaks down and the required alternative temporary written records are not kept instead, then the requirements of the 1987 Regula-   **14.155** tions for employers are not resurrected so far as the driving is concerned. The temporary record is not a record book as specified in the 1987 Regulations, but a record sheet as specified under Regulation (EEC) 3821/85, and the employer's liability will therefore be under that regulation and under ss.97, 97B and 97C of the 1968 Act (see in particular "Defences" at § 14.143).

Voluntary use of the tachograph

14.156   Drivers of vehicles excepted or exempt from the compulsory tachograph requirements may instead rely on a tachograph as a voluntary alternative to keeping manual records if the vehicle is suitably equipped. The voluntary use of a tachograph will therefore be appropriate as an alternative to complying with the relevant legislation. It will be appropriate for vehicles within the classification of domestic journeys or work or within the AETR provisions.

Section 98(4A) of the 1968 Act provides that, in effect, a person may rely on the tachograph rules instead of keeping manual records, and if so, no offence will be committed under s.98(4) (failing to keep records, etc.). The burden of establishing this rests on the defendant on the balance of probabilities. Section 98(4) relates to manual record contraventions whether under the former Community rules, the AETR agreement, or regulations made under s.98. There is therefore a complete exemption from s.98(4) records offences for drivers, drivers' mates and employers relying voluntarily on a tachograph in this way.

14.157   The wording of s.98(4) is such that if a person is relying on the voluntary use of a tachograph instead of fulfilling the manual records legal requirements and the tachograph breaks down, the standard tachograph defences will apply to him also. If, however, he is unable to establish the tachograph defence, there will be (per s.98(4A)) a contravention of s.98(4) (the manual records offence). Section 98(4A) is curiously worded in that it refers to proving "there would have been no contravention of the provisions of this Part of this Act so far as they relate to the use of such vehicles". In fact the only "use" offences under Pt VI are the s.97(1) tachograph "use", etc., offences.

If a person is using a tachograph on a *purely voluntary* basis and not instead of keeping records then it is submitted the legal tachograph rules cannot bind him.

Passenger vehicles

14.158   Basically the same tachograph rules and regulations apply to passenger vehicles as to goods vehicles. Section 95(2) of the 1968 Act applies the provisions to *all* public service vehicles and other motor vehicles constructed and adapted to carry more than 12 passengers. It is not clear whether this includes the driver, but it is submitted that it does not (see § 1.117).

Passenger vehicles: exceptions—domestic journeys or work

14.159   Article 3 of Regulation (EC) 561/2006 (see § 14.25) which also applies to the tachograph regulation (see art.3 of that regulation) excepts vehicles (i.e. public service vehicles) which in construction and equipment are suitable for carrying not more than nine persons including the driver and are intended for that purpose. Also excepted are passenger vehicles on regular services not exceeding 50km. These become primarily subject to the domestic journeys or work rules and therefore in certain instances of mixed driving subject to the manual records requirements of the Drivers' Hours (Goods Vehicles) (Keeping of Records) Regulations 1987, as amended.

The meaning of "regular service" was considered by the European Court of Justice in Case C–47/97 *Criminal Proceedings against E. Clarke and Sons (Coaches) Ltd* [1998] R.T.R. 333. The company was prosecuted for failing to keep tachograph records. It relied on the exemption in art.4(3) of Regulation (EEC) 3820/85 in its defence. The term "regular service" is defined in art.2 of Regulation (EEC) 684/92, primarily as services which provide to carry passengers at specified intervals along a specified route with the passengers being taken up and set down at predetermined stopping points. Amendments to this regulation by Regulation (EC) 11/98 do not affect this decision. A regular service is to be open to all subject, where appropriate, to compulsory reservation (art.2(1.1)). There is a further provision for "special regular services" for those services which operate under the conditions of art.2(1.1) but provide for specified categories of passengers to the exclusion of other passengers (art.2(1.2)). Examples given include carriage of workers between home and work and carriage to and from an educational institution of school pupils and students.

In this case, one of the company's coaches was used by a tour operator to **14.160** convey tourists between the airport and the hotel with occasional stops at tourist attractions. Each component part of the journey was less than 50km. The meaning of "regular service" as set out in art.2 to Regulation (EEC) 684/92 requires that the service be provided at "specified intervals". This means that the frequency had to be specified with precision and had to be regular. Here, it was the needs of the tour operators that determined the use and that depended on reservations made by customers. It was not "regular". A further requirement is that there are specified routes, which means precisely defined routes. Article 2 envisages stopping points along the route at which passengers could be taken up and set down. People concerned had to know the route to be taken and the stopping points. It was not sufficient merely to know in advance the points of departure and arrival.

Finally, the term "specified categories of passengers" in art.2(1.2) meant passengers sharing the same status. It did not cover a group of passengers whose only common feature was that they had made reservations for a journey with the same tour operator.

Passenger vehicles: exemptions

A tachograph need not be installed or used in passenger vehicles on regular **14.161** national services exceeding 50km or short regular international services in the border areas of Member States (see art.3(1) of Regulation (EEC) 3821/85 and art.16(1) of Regulation (EC) 561/2006). These remain subject to the Community rules. Service timetables and duty rosters must be drawn up and carried for such operations (art.16(2)). Each driver and driving mate assigned to such a regular service must carry an extract from the duty roster and a copy of the service timetable. Article 16(3) contains certain further requirements as to the roster.

In Case C–387/96 *Criminal Proceedings against Sjöberg* [1998] E.C.R. I–225, Sjöberg was convicted under a Swedish regulation corresponding to art.14 of Regulation (EEC) 3820/85 imposing obligations to carry an extract from the duty roster and a copy of the service timetable. He appealed on the ground that the exemption in art.13(1)(b) of Regulation (EEC) 3820/85 applied, that is, "vehicles used by public authorities to provide public services which are not in competition with professional road hauliers". Alternatively, that art.14 was satisfied by the carrying of duty roster extracts limited to one day. The company had successfully tendered to operate exclusively certain public road passenger services under three to five-year contracts. The European Court of Justice dismissed the appeal on both counts. The absence of competition is a condition of the exemption in art.13(1)(b). This is to be assessed both when the contract was awarded as well as during its performance. There was competition at the tendering stage and, inevitably, during the contract given that the successful tenderer would wish to obtain renewal. Accordingly the exemption did not apply.

14.162   Regarding the carrying of the duty roster, since, in the case of regular passenger services, the extract from the duty roster and the copy of the service timetable replaced the recording equipment, they must be equally effective in monitoring compliance with controls of driving time and rest periods. Under the tachograph provisions, Regulation (EEC) 3821/85 provides by art.15(7) for a driver to be able to produce record sheets for the current week and those used by the driver in the previous 15 days and where a vehicle is fitted with recording equipment, the driver card. Accordingly, art.16 of Regulation (EC) 561/2006 requires more than the duty roster extract for that day alone.

The exemption provisions for passenger vehicles under the Community Drivers' Hours and Recording Equipment Regulations 2007 (SI 2007/1819), as amended, are similar in content to those for goods vehicles under those regulations. Reference should be made to § 14.60 where the goods vehicles exemptions are described, to § 14.97 where passenger vehicles exemptions relating to drivers' hours, etc., are given and to § 14.139 where goods vehicles exemptions relating to tachograph records are discussed. The exemptions under art.13 of Regulation (EC) 561/2006, and the regulations (which may also arise from the tachograph requirements), may apply to national territory operations (thus covering the national part of an international journey) or with the agreement of the states concerned in respect of transport in the territory of another Member State. The 2007 Regulations make no reference to any such agreement. Exemptions under art.13(2) and the 2007 Regulations (exceptional circumstances) may apply to both international and national operations.

14.163   The national territory operations exemptions (see § 14.97 and also § 14.139) include the use of vehicles which are constructed and equipped to carry not more than 17 persons including the driver. It seems that the occasional use of such a vehicle with more than 17 persons may not affect the exemption providing the vehicle has only 17 seats. This exemption should be compared with the exception for passenger vehicles used for domestic journeys or work (see § 14.25). One of these domestic journeys, etc., exemption items is worded "vehicles which in construction and equipment are suitable for carrying not more than nine persons including the driver and are intended for that purpose". Regular use with an excessive number of passengers may be evidence of the appropriate intent.

The above exemptions are *national territory* exemptions under art.3(2) of Regulation (EEC) 3821/85 and art.13 of Regulation (EC) 561/2006 and the 2007 Regulations. With the agreement of the states concerned, they may be extended in certain circumstances to other Member States, but the 2007 Regulations make no mention of any such extension.

14.164   There are also exemptions under art.3(3) of Regulation (EEC) 3821/85 and art.13(3) of Regulation (EC) 561/2006. These exemptions apply to both *national* and *international* operations. The exemption most likely to be material to passenger vehicles is that for vehicles manufactured before January 1, 1947 (2007 Regulations. Other art.13(3) exemptions are for vehicles propelled by steam and vehicles used by the RNLI for hauling lifeboats.

Passenger vehicles: summary

The records requirements for passenger vehicles are set out in Table 3. **14.165**

Reference should also be made where necessary to the inter-relationship of the tachograph and handwritten records at § 14.153. There may also be voluntary reliance on the tachograph (see § 14.156).

TABLE 3

PASSENGER VEHICLES: TACHOGRAPHS AND RECORDS

14.166

Class of transport operation	*Class of vehicle*	*Records requirements*
International journeys or work	PSVs for 10 or more passengers including the driver (s.95(2) and art.4(2) of Regulation (EEC) 3820/85)	Tachograph required (art.3(1) of Regulation (EEC) 3821/85 and s.97(1)). No timetables or duty rosters required
	Other passenger vehicles for more than 13 passengers including the driver (s.95(2))	
	Above vehicles on certain short regular international border services	No tachograph required (art.3(1) of Regulation (EEC) 3821/85). Timetables and duty rosters required (art.16 of Regulation (EC) 561/2006)
National journeys or work	All passenger vehicles (including PSVs) for 17 or more passengers including the driver (see Community Drivers' Hours and Recording Equipment Regulations 2007)	Tachograph required (art.3 and s.97(1)). No timetables or duty rosters required

Class of transport operation	Class of vehicle	Records requirements
National journeys or work *ctd*	Above vehicles on regular services exceeding 50km	No tachograph required (art.3(1) of Regulation (EEC) 3821/85). Timetables and duty rosters required (art.16 of Regulation (EC) 561/2006)
	PSVs for from 10 to 17 passengers including the driver (s.95(2) and art.4(2))	No tachograph, records, timetables or duty rosters required (Community Drivers' Hours and Recording Equipment Regulations 2007)
	All passenger vehicles (other than PSVs) for 16 or 17 passengers including the driver (s.95(2) and art.4(2))	No tachograph, records, timetables or duty rosters required (Community Drivers' Hours and Recording Equipment Regulations 2007)
Domestic journeys or work	All PSVs and other passenger vehicles for 14 or more passengers including the driver on regular services of 50km or less (s.95(2) and art.4(3))	No tachograph required (art.4). Drivers' Hours (Goods Vehicles) (Keeping of Records) Regulations 1987 may apply to a limited extent although primarily concerning goods vehicles
	All PSVs for 9 passengers or less including the driver (s.95(2) and art.4(2))	
—	Passenger vehicles (other than PSVs) for 13 passengers or less including the driver (s.95(2))	No tachograph, records, timetables or rosters required (outside Pt VI: s.95(2))

Notes
1. A tachograph may be used on a voluntary basis to replace record-keeping.
2. This table must be read subject to other exceptions or exemptions where applicable.
3. As to passengers "including the driver" for the purposes of s.95(2), see further §§ 1.117 and 14.06. In all the other provisions mentioned the inclusion of the driver is specified.

DRIVERS' RECORDS: MANUAL RECORDS

Generally

The Drivers' Hours (Goods Vehicles) (Keeping of Records) Regulations 1987 **14.167**
(SI 1987/1421), as amended, apply in the following instances:

(1) They govern the manual records to be kept by goods vehicles drivers in respect of journeys or work where the applicable Community rules do not apply (reg.4).

(2) They govern the employers' responsibilities generally (including owner-drivers) for the keeping of drivers' manual records for goods vehicles in respect of journeys or work to which the applicable Community rules do not apply (reg.4).

(3) They similarly govern to an extent the responsibilities of certain passenger vehicle drivers who also drive such goods vehicles. The 1987 Regulations apply in respect of goods or passenger related journeys or work to which the applicable Community rules do not apply. This is subject to the exemption in reg.12(3) for certain "mixed" driving of this kind (see below).

These provisions, their application and exemptions from them and the relevant cases are discussed in greater detail below. As to when the applicable Community rules do not apply, see § 14.16 where this is considered fully and also see below.

Definitions

"Working day" is as defined in s.103 of the Transport Act 1968. There is no **14.168**
modification effected by the 1987 Regulations. Compare the modification in the meaning of "working day" for the purpose of the drivers' hours, etc., legislation governing drivers similarly not subject to the applicable Community rules noted at § 14.82. For further definitions, see § 14.31.

When the manual records requirements apply

A *Domestic journeys*

Domestic journeys or work are defined at § 14.25. Domestic journeys, etc., are **14.169**
excepted from the applicable Community rules by art.3 of Regulation (EEC) 3821/85 (tachograph recording equipment) and art.3 of Regulation (EC) 561/2006 (drivers' hours, etc.). Goods vehicle drivers and certain passenger vehicle drivers in this category and subject to the domestic drivers' hours code still have to carry and complete records in accordance with the 1987 Regulations unless they are otherwise exempt. (For these exemptions from the 1987 Regulations, see reg.12 discussed below.) If the 1987 Regulations are applicable, they apply equally to the relevant goods and passenger vehicles as defined in s.95(2) of the Transport Act 1968 and to employee-drivers and owner-drivers as defined in s.95(3). It is recommended that the process of elimination suggested in §§ 14.04–5 be adopted.

B   *Where the Community rules are not applicable*

14.170   The 1987 Regulations apply in relation to goods vehicles and certain passenger vehicles subject to Pt VI of the Transport Act 1968 apart from journeys or work to which the applicable Community rules apply (reg.4). There has been some uncertainty over the exact meaning of "applicable Community rules" and whether this means applicable generally or applicable in particular circumstances. The question is relevant as to whether vehicles subject to the applicable Community rules generally but exempt from the tachograph requirements become instead subject to the 1987 Regulations. It should be remembered that a person keeping temporary manual records under the tachograph regulation because the tachograph has broken down will be doing so under the applicable Community rules and will not become subject to the 1987 Regulations. There are various limited exemptions from the tachograph regulation including the possibility of temporary exemptions for up to 30 days in urgent cases such as weather emergencies. The position is discussed at § 14.16.

C   *Universal service providers and the domestic rules*

14.171   Despite the exception in art.3 by which domestic operations are excluded from being subject to the EC regulations and become instead subject to the domestic rules, art.3(4) of Regulation (EEC) 3821/85 allows Member States to require the installation and use of tachograph equipment for national operations. In accordance with this, certain vehicles used for carrying articles for universal service providers (such as post) are required to comply with Regulation (EEC) 3821/85. On this basis, tachograph breaches in respect of these vehicles will by s.97(6) be contraventions of ss.97(1) and 97C of the Transport Act 1968 and reference should accordingly be made to the tachograph provisions. The tachograph provisions require that if the tachograph breaks down, certain temporary manual records must be kept instead pending repair.

There is a corresponding exemption (by reg.12(4)) for these vehicles from reg.7 (entries in the drivers' record books) and from reg.10 (drivers' books to be carried by drivers).

Manual records: exemptions from the 1987 Regulations

14.172   Regulation 12(1) exempts vehicles which do not require an operator's licence or Crown vehicles which would otherwise be exempt from the operator's licence requirements. As to operators' licences, see Chapter 13. This exemption does not apply if the driver also drives a non-exempt vehicle during any working day. As to "working day", see § 14.168 above.

Regulation 12(2) exempts also where the driver does not drive for more than four hours nor outside a radius of 50km from the vehicle's operating centre. For the purpose of this four-hour, etc., exemption the time is to be ignored which is spent driving off the road on agriculture, forestry or quarrying operations, building construction, alteration or maintenance, etc., or fixed works of construction or civil engineering. Where this work is for the improvement or maintenance of a road and is on that road, the vehicle shall be treated as being driven elsewhere than on a road (reg.12(2)(b)). It should be noted that this provision in effect extends the time but does not extend the distance.

Where such vehicles are subject to the tachograph requirements as noted above, there is an exemption (by reg.12(4)) from reg.7 (entries in the drivers' record books) and reg.10 (drivers' record books to be carried by driver). **14.173**

There is a further exemption relating to mixed goods and passenger vehicle driving—see below.

The burden of proving an exemption would seem to be on the defendant on the balance of probabilities. Cf. *Gaunt v Nelson* [1987] R.T.R. 1, a case on a tachograph exemption.

Mixed driving

There is by reg.12(3) an exemption from regs 7 and 10 of the 1987 Regulations where during any working day (see § 14.168 above) the driver does not spend all or the greater part of the time (i.e. more than 50 per cent) driving goods vehicles to which the 1987 Regulations would otherwise apply when driving vehicles to which Pt VI of the Transport Act 1968 applies. In other words it is necessary to ascertain first what part of the working day he spends driving vehicles to which Pt VI applies and then to divide that part into goods and non-goods vehicle driving time respectively to see whether he has spent more than 50 per cent driving goods vehicles. If, e.g., he drove passenger vehicles subject to Pt VI for 50 per cent of his driving time during a working day he would be exempt from the requirements of the 1987 Regulations for that working day. A vehicle might be subject to Pt VI under either the domestic code or under the applicable Community rules. **14.174**

Subject to this, reg.7 (entries in drivers' record books) and reg.10 (drivers' record books to be carried by drivers) apply to a driver who in any working week (i.e. starting Sunday midnight/Monday morning) drives both goods and passenger vehicles (reg.13(1)). The goods vehicle employer and not the passenger vehicle employer will be responsible for issuing the record book (reg.13(2)). A passenger vehicle employer may be liable for a breach of reg.7(4) (certain entries in the record book) in addition to the possibility of aiding and abetting offences.

Provisions of the regulations and cases

Regulation 7 of the 1987 Regulations is perhaps the most important; it requires the driver to record and the employer of an employee-driver to cause him to record in his record book the information required. Regulation 12 exempts drivers from keeping records in specified circumstances (see above). **14.175**

The contents of the record book are specified in reg.5 and the Schedule to the regulations. Regulation 8(1) requires an employee-driver to deliver the driver's record book to the employer within seven days from the date of completion of the weekly record sheet or earlier if required. The employer must examine the weekly record sheet and sign it and its duplicate, detach the duplicate sheet and return the book to the driver before he is next on duty (reg.8(2)).

An owner-driver must deliver the duplicate sheet to the undertaking's address within seven days from the date of completion of the weekly record sheet (reg.8(4)). There is a defence for the employee and the owner-driver if he can **14.176** show that it was not reasonably practicable to comply and that the duplicate of the weekly record sheet was delivered as soon as reasonably practicable (reg.8(5)). Presumably the burden of proof will be on the balance of probabilities.

When all the weekly record sheets have been used the driver must retain the record book for 14 days from the date the record book was last returned to him under reg.8(2) and must then return it to his employer as soon as reasonably practicable. This is so that it can be available for inspection.

14.177   Regulation 6 covers the issue of record books and also makes special provision where a driver has two or more employers for whom he drives. The issuing employer is the goods vehicle employer (see reg.13(2)) for when the driver first acts in the course of his employment (reg.6(2)). Regulation 9 requires the second or subsequent employer to require production of the current record book and to enter on the front sheet the name, address, telephone number and stamp (if any) of the employer. The employee-driver must produce the current record book to any employer whenever required (reg.9(2)).

A driver must have his current driver's record book (including all unused record sheets) in his possession at all times when he is on duty (reg.10).

14.178   It was held under the former regulations that an employer should not be convicted of aiding and abetting a breach by his driver unless the employer knowingly encouraged such a breach in some way (*Cassady v Reg Morris (Transport) Ltd* [1975] Crim. L.R. 398). While the *Cassady* case is still good law, charges of aiding and abetting will rarely be brought against employers now in view of the express provisions in the regulations.

Regulation 11 requires employers to "preserve … intact" a driver's record book for one year. Under earlier regulations an employer issued a book to one employee who duly completed the required records on the first five pages and then returned it to his employer, who then reissued it to another driver, who used it and produced it to a police officer when stopped. It was held in *Blakey Transport v Casebourne* [1975] R.T.R. 221 that the employer did not preserve the book intact in accordance with what is now reg.11 by reissuing the book to another employee for use by him; nor in such a case is it a "new" book as is required by what is now reg.6 (*Cassady v Ward & Smith Ltd* [1975] Crim. L.R. 399). However, a used record book may be reissued to a different driver so that he can use the remaining daily sheets and weekly reports (*Lackenby v Browns of Wem Ltd* [1980] R.T.R. 363). The prosecution in *Lackenby* was for a breach of what is now reg.7 of the 1987 Regulations. Griffiths J. pointed out that in neither the Transport Act nor the EC regulation is there any specific requirement that the book should be issued in an unused condition. *Cassady v Ward & Smith Ltd* relates to reg.6 and Griffiths J. was not prepared to read a similar obligation into reg.5 (now reg.7). He added that he could see a powerful argument for construing "new" as "another" in the context of reg.6. This dictum must cast some doubt on this aspect of the decision in *Cassady*. The record book in *Lackenby* should not have been issued, but should have been kept for 12 months in accordance with what is now reg.11. Griffiths J. pointed out that as it was issued in breach of what is now reg.11, it was not issued in conformity with the regulations. This point was never taken or argued before the justices and was therefore ignored in reaching a decision.

The cases which follow were decided on the Transport Act 1960 and regulations thereunder and may still be of relevance. A fitter was employed to do running repairs to vehicles broken down in the highway; it was held that, when he drove to that work, he was a part-time driver and should keep records (*Mackie v MacLeod* 1956 S.L.T. 116). In *Gross Cash Registers Ltd v Vogt* [1965] 3 All E.R. 832 a salesman was free to do his travelling in any way he chose—on foot, by bus or in the firm's van; if he chose the van, he was allowed to drive it and did so; it was held that, when he drove it in the course of his employment, he was a part-time driver and should keep records. **14.179**

Under the old regulations, no licence-holder needed to keep records in respect of driving by him of a licensed vehicle on journeys which were in no way connected with any trade or business carried on by him, and there was no duty to keep records outside the scope of an employed driver's work. The court should ask itself whether the driver was working in an irregular and unauthorised manner or was acting wholly outside the scope of his employment. In the latter case the employer was not liable for not keeping records (*Jack Motors Ltd v Fazackerly* [1962] Crim. L.R. 486). It was held proper to charge a defendant, where appropriate, with "failing to keep or to cause to be kept" the necessary records in one information (*Field v Hopkinson* (1944) 108 J.P. 21). Compare "enter or secure that there is entered on the front sheet the information specified", etc., in reg.7.

The AETR agreement

The AETR agreement now incorporates requirements for a control device similarly to Regulation (EEC) 3821/85. As noted at § 14.87 the AETR rules are apparently to be treated as if applicable Community rules. **14.180**

Liability of employers for staff defaults: generally

The hours and conditions of work of *drivers and* (where applicable) *driving mates* are governed mainly by the Community rules. The tachograph rules govern for the most part the keeping of records, particularly for national and international journeys or work, and affect *drivers, driving mates and employers*. The employer's liability for breaches of the tachograph rules is dealt with at § 14.148. An employer may be convicted of aiding and abetting an employee in breach of these rules or conspiracy to contravene them (see *R. v Blamires Transport Services Ltd* [1963] 3 All E.R. 170). In respect of domestic journeys or work and generally where the Community rules do not apply the duties and responsibilities of *employers* are still governed by the Drivers' Hours (Goods Vehicles) (Keeping of Records) Regulations 1987. These relate to the employers of British goods and passenger vehicle drivers where the Community rules *do not* apply (that is, employers of drivers subject to the domestic drivers' hours code). Despite the title of the 1987 Regulations, they affect certain passenger vehicle operations as well where "mixed" goods and passenger vehicle driving occurs. **14.181**

In *R. v J.F. Alford Transport Ltd* [1999] R.T.R. 51, the Court of Appeal considered the liability of a company, its managing director and its transport manager all of whom were charged with aiding and abetting the falsification of tachograph records. The prosecution case was that, as the individuals charged were personally involved in the management of what was a small company, they must have known and accepted (if not actively encouraged) what the drivers were doing. At the trial, there had been no evidence that either individual had checked any tachograph chart against any driver's time sheet. No analysis of the charts alone would have disclosed any offence. The summing-up to the jury gave three stages—proof that the driver concerned had committed an offence, proof that the individuals knew full well what the driver was doing and proof that at least one of the individuals charged gave positive encouragement to the driver to act illegally. Although knowledge could be inferred where a defendant shuts his eyes to the obvious, that could not be proved in this case. The Court of Appeal was of the view that, if knowledge could have been shown on the part of either of the individuals concerned, the jury could legitimately have inferred that he had positively encouraged the commission of the offence.

14.182   "Employer" for the purposes of Pt VI of the 1968 Act is defined by s.103(1) of the Act as meaning, in relation to an employee-driver, the employer of that driver in the employment by virtue of which that driver is an employee-driver. Interpreting this subsection, Kilner Brown J. said in *Alcock v G.C. Griston Ltd* [1981] R.T.R. 34: "It is perfectly plain having regard to the definition of employer that whilst he was driving for the firm which required him to drive he was an employee driver in relation to that firm." The company obtained the part-time services of a driver from an employment agency which continued to pay his wages. He failed to keep records as required by the former Regulation (EEC) 543/69 and Pt VI of the 1968 Act. The Divisional Court held that the company was his employer and had been wrongly acquitted by the justices.

The meaning of "undertaking" was considered by the European Court of Justice in *Auditeur du Travail v Dufour* [1978] R.T.R. 186. In that case an employment agency supplied a driver to a transport undertaking. It was held that the responsibility rested with the undertaking rather than the agency so far as compliance with art.14(7) and (8) of Regulation (EEC) 3820/85 was concerned. The meaning of the word "undertaking" in art.15 of Regulation (EEC) 3820/85 was referred to the European Court of Justice in Case C–7/90 *Public Prosecutor v Vandenne* [1991] E.C.R. I–4371. The conclusion of the European Court of Justice may provide useful comparisons. It defined an "undertaking" as an autonomous natural or legal person, irrespective of legal form, regularly carrying on a transport business and empowered to organise and control the work of drivers and crew members.

14.183   Article 10 of Regulation (EC) 561/2006 prohibits payments to wage-earning drivers and driving mates, even in the form of bonuses or wage supplements, related to distances travelled and/or the amount of goods carried, unless these payments are of such a kind as not to endanger road safety. If enforceable at all this would presumably be enforceable under s.96(11A) of the 1968 Act. However, although in wide terms, it is not clear that s.96(11A) is wide enough to cover this provision. Defendants would no doubt put forward the defence in the last part of art.10 although it is likely that bonuses or like payments related to distances would endanger road safety by encouraging speeding and inducing fatigue. Similarly bonuses or like payments as to the amount carried would be likely to endanger road safety by encouraging overloading. The exemptions from Regulation (EC) 561/2006 would apply (see § 14.139).

A limited company was held liable for the acts and omissions of its transport manager who permitted various drivers' hours offences even though he was self-employed, acting under a contract for services (*Worthy v Gordon Plant (Services) Ltd* [1989] R.T.R. 7. The court referred to him acting as the transport manager appointed under the former Goods Vehicle (Operators' Licences, Qualifications and Fees) Regulations 1984. This may mean that the same conclusion might not be reached where this is not the case.

Certain of the cases noted in Chapter 1 under "use", "cause", "permit" and **14.184** "aiding and abetting" may assist as to the existence or otherwise of an employer-employee relationship. See also "Proof in respect of companies, partnerships and employees", § 3.95.

The employer of a driver engaged in domestic journeys or work or subject to the AETR agreement has the defence in the proviso to s.98(4), that he had given proper instructions to his employees and from time to time has taken reasonable steps to secure that those instructions are being carried out; the onus is on the employer and the prosecution do not have to disprove this in advance. This defence for s.98(4) offences applies to manual records. Compare the absolute responsibility of employers with very limited defences for user tachograph offences contrary to s.97(1) discussed at § 14.148. In deciding whether "reasonable steps" have been taken, the tough stance of the Divisional Court in *Light v DPP* [1994] R.T.R. 396 may be informative. The case concerned permitting breaches of drivers' hours regulations shown on tachograph records.

Presumably these defences are on the balance of probabilities and the burden **14.185** is on the defence (see s.101 of the Magistrates' Courts Act 1980). It is for the court to say, after hearing the employer, whether he has given "proper" instructions and taken "reasonable steps" from time to time.

Under the previous law it was a defence if an employer had been able to show "due diligence" in seeing that the law had been complied with. The expression "due diligence" still appears in s.24 of the Trade Descriptions Act 1968, s.21 of the Food Safety Act 1990 and in other statutes. The meaning of the expression does not seem to be very different from the words used in s.98(4). The leading case on the meaning of "due diligence" in s.24, etc., is *Tesco Supermarkets v Nattrass* [1971] 2 All E.R. 127. In the case of a large-scale organisation the owner, whether it be a limited company or an individual, cannot personally supervise the activities of all his servants, and it would be consistent with the taking of reasonable precautions and the exercise of all due diligence to institute an effective system to prevent the commission of offences under which superior servants were instructed to supervise inferior servants whose acts might otherwise lead to the commission of an offence. It is submitted that the approach to the problem posed under the Trade Descriptions Act shown by the House of Lords in *Tesco* is of relevance in considering whether a defence under s.98(4) is made out. It is submitted that whether the employer has given "proper" instructions and taken "reasonable steps" is essentially a question of fact and degree.

It should be noted that the defence of "due diligence" under s.24 of the Trade **14.186** Descriptions Act, as amended, has been further refined by reg.11 of the Business Protection from Misleading Marketing Regulations 2008 (SI 2008/1276). The defence must prove that the commission of an offence was due to mistake, reliance on information supplied by another, the act or default of another, an accident, or another cause beyond the defendant's control. The requirement to satisfy the court that all reasonable precautions have been taken and the exercise of due diligence to avoid the commission of the offence is also stipulated.

DRIVERS' HOURS AND RECORDS: PROCEEDINGS AND PENALTIES

Proceedings

14.187   A traffic examiner or police officer is empowered under the Transport Act 1968 s.99(1) and s.99ZA to require the production for inspection of various documents to which the Act or regulations made under the Act refer. He is given power under s.99(2), (3) and s.99ZB to enter vehicles and premises in the course of his duties and he may detain a vehicle to inspect the vehicle and recording equipment in or on it. For new powers and offences introduced by ss.97ZA–99ZE, see §§ 14.190–3 below. Any person who fails to comply with a requirement under s.99(1) or who obstructs an officer in the course of his duties under s.99(2) or (3) commits an offence (s.99(4)). Clarification around procedures on prosecutions connected with record sheets was given in *Murfitts Transport Ltd v Department of Transport*; *Department of Transport v Murfitts Transport Ltd* [1998] R.T.R. 229. The company was prosecuted both for failing to produce records and for failing to keep records. In the right circumstances this is permissible. An employer would be in breach of s.99ZD of the Transport Act 1968 if he failed to produce records that ought to have been in his possession in compliance with art.14(2) of Regulation (EEC) 3821/85 whether or not he had them in his possession and regardless of the reason for not having them.

14.188   A company argued that the requirement in s.99(1) of the Transport Act 1968 to produce records did not require them to hand them over, simply to make them available for inspection. That argument was rejected by the Divisional Court in *Cantabrica Coach Holdings Ltd v Vehicle Inspectorate* and by the House of Lords [2001] UKHL 60; [2002] R.T.R. 8. The Divisional Court agreed with the Hemel Hempstead Justices that there was no express power under s.99 of the 1968 Act requiring the defendant to hand over tachograph sheets to the Vehicle Inspectorate except where the Inspectorate had reason to believe the records had been falsified. However, the Divisional Court also agreed that the 1968 Act had been amended as a result of Regulation (EEC) 3821/85, in particular the obligation in art.14(2) to produce or hand over the documents on request. It was for the authorised officer to decide where to inspect the documents. It was implicit in that power that the operator should be permitted to take copies of any record proposed to be taken away unless that was not reasonably practical, perhaps because the operator was obstructive or unco-operative. The House of Lords agreed with the Divisional Court. On its true construction, s.99(1) of the Transport Act 1968 authorised an officer to insist that record sheets that had been required to be kept by art.14(2) of Regulation (EEC) 3821/85 should be handed over on demand in order that they can be examined and analysed at the premises of the Inspectorate without prior notice. Taking away the records for effective and thorough examination in the office of the Inspectorate was within the ambit of the power of inspection given. The objective of the legislation was to protect the public from tired drivers of goods and passenger vehicles. The careful checking and examination of tachograph records was a necessary part of the procedure and such checking would on occasions require the records to be taken to an office of the Inspectorate where the necessary specialised equipment and the requisite number of staff would be available. The powers of a VOSA officer to inspect documents is now expressly contained in s.99ZA of the Transport Act 1968.

In *John Mann International Ltd v Vehicle Inspectorate* [2004] EWHC 1236;

[2005] R.T.R. 8, it was held that a failure by the holder of a goods vehicle opera-tors licence to produce tachograph records pursuant to s.99(1) of the Transport Act 1968 was not a continuing offence. In this case a traffic examiner had served three notices on the operator to produce tachograph record sheets and informa-tions were laid within six months of the date of compliance with the third notice. An appeal against conviction for failure to comply with that notice was dismissed.

In relation to offences under this section, an information referring to several **14.189** lapses was not duplicitous. Any person who knowingly falsifies tachograph entries under s.97 or entries kept for the purposes of regulations under s.98 or under applicable Community rules is guilty of an offence (s.99(5)). Doubts are expressed at (1982) 146 J.P. Jo. 186 as to whether certain parts of s.99 (including parts of s.99(2)(b) and (3)) have come into force. It is submitted that the better view is that these subsections were merely, to some extent, kept "on ice" and came fully into force with s.99(2)(a). A tachograph record is an "instrument" for the purposes of the Forgery and Counterfeiting Act 1981 and proceedings may be brought under that Act also: *Att Gen's Reference No.1 of 2000* [2001] Crim. L.R. 127, though see the commentary which is critical of the reasoning and the conclusion.

Records are admissible in evidence against the employers, whether on charges under s.98 or otherwise (*Beer v Clench* [1936] 1 All E.R. 449; *Adair v Craig-house Cabinet Works & Co* 1937 S.L.T. 499). When the number of a vehicle ap-pears in the record, that may suffice to identify that vehicle (*Hogg v Burnet* 1938 S.C.(J.) 160). Such records were not made admissible previously by any statute but are now made specifically so by s.98(5), when entered by an employee-driver, in proceedings under Pt VI against his employer whether for contravening Regulation (EC) 561/2006 or the AETR agreement or the 1987 Regulations. Under s.97B similarly tachograph entries are admissible and in Scotland are suf-ficient evidence. Under s.97 also any entries made thereon for the purposes of arts 15(2), (5) or 16(2) of Regulation (EEC) 3821/85 may also be admitted in evidence. It is submitted that these provisions do not cut down the admissibility of such records generally under the cases just cited.

By ss.99A–99C of the 1968 Act an authorised officer may prohibit the driving **14.190** of a United Kingdom vehicle where the driver obstructs the exercise of powers under s.99(2) or (3) or there are other breaches relating to hours or recording of hours. It is an offence under s.99C to fail to comply. Section 103(7) of the Transport Act 1968 was substituted by s.3 of the Road Traffic (Drivers' Ages and Hours of Work) Act 1976. The amendment overrules the decision in *R. v Hitchin JJ. Ex p. Hilton* [1974] R.T.R. 380. It extends the jurisdiction of the courts with very wide terms when dealing with offences under Pt VI. It states that an offence under Pt VI may be treated for the purpose of conferring jurisdiction on a court, without prejudice to any other jurisdiction, as having been committed in the place where the person charged was driving when evidence first came to the attention of a constable or vehicle examiner; in the place where that person resides or is believed to reside or be at the time when proceedings are commenced; or in the place where at that time that person, or, in the case of an employee-driver, that person's employer or, in the case of an owner-driver, the person for whom he was driving, has his place or principal place of business or his operating centre for the vehicle in question. Prosecutors have suggested that the wording is such as to enable prosecutions to be brought in Great Britain for offences committed on the continent when the defendant has been found in this country. It should be noted, however, that s.96(11A) specifies that contraventions of applicable Community rules caught by that subsection must be in Great Britain. Sections 97(1) and 98(4) are not so limited. It should also be noted that s.103(7) relates to *any* offence under Pt VI of the Transport Act 1968, whether relating to the observance of hours or the keeping of records or any other provision in Pt VI.

14.191   An indictable charge at common law of conspiracy to contravene these provisions may properly be brought (*R. v Blamires Transport Services Ltd* [1963] 3 All E.R. 170). In that case a haulage company's conviction on indictment of conspiring with the company's drivers to make false records under the 1960 Act was upheld on appeal.

Under s.97(1)(a), as amended, it is an offence to use, cause or permit to be used a vehicle to which the tachograph provisions apply without recording equipment: (i) which has been installed in accordance with the regulation, (ii) which complies with the relevant Annexes, and (iii) is being used as provided by arts 13–15. One purpose of the change to Regulation (EEC) 3821/85 as already noted seems to have been to combine items (i), (ii) and (iii) into a single offence. It is submitted that it is still possible to charge them separately if so desired. See "Duplicity", § 2.91. As to "using", "causing" and "permitting", see §§ 1.161 et seq.

14.192   Under s.99ZD of the Transport Act 1968 it is an offence to fail to comply with any requirements imposed by an officer under ss.99ZA–99ZC of the 1968 Act relating to the officer's power to inspect records or of obstructing an officer in the exercise of his powers.

The offences of knowingly making false records, altering records with intent to destroy records or recording equipment, or failing to make a record or making false record entries, producing false records or destroying such records are set out in s.99ZE of the Transport Act 1968.

14.193   New offences created by the Passenger and Goods Vehicles (Recording Equipment) (Tachograph Card) Regulations 2006 (SI 2006/1397) came into force on August 21, 2006. They make provision in relation to company cards, control cards, driver cards and workshop cards used with digital tachographs which comply with Regulation (EEC) 3821/85. The 2006 Regulations prohibit the use by a person of more than one driver card, of a driver card of which he is not the holder, of a forged or altered card and of a card issued as the result of an incorrect application. Making false statement in the application for a card is also prohibited. Breach is an offence triable summarily except in cases where there is an element of deception, false statements or forgery (see reg.3 (driving card) and reg.4 (work shop cards)). Offences in the latter category are triable either way. Failure to give written notification of lost or stolen cards to the Secretary of State and a failure to return damaged cards or malfunctioning cards is an offence which is triable summarily. A similar offence is created in relation to the return of cards issued incorrectly for correction. Similarly, a failure to surrender a card which identifies another person as the holder, which has been falsified or which has been issued as a result of a false application is also a summary offence.

On January 30, 2009 the European Commission adopted a directive which established a common grading of the most common infringements to the "social rules" in the road transport sector (those that govern driving hours and rest periods for professional drivers in the EU). The categorisation distinguishes three levels of infringements: minor infringements, serious infringements and very serious infringements. The severity of infringement depends on its influence on road safety. In the "very serious" category are actions that make monitoring compliance with social legislation impossible, such as fraud. The common categorisation is designed to facilitate the exchange of information between Member States (Regulation (EC) 68/2009, adopting for the 9th time to technical progress Council Regulation (EEC) 3821/85).

Penalties

The penalty for breach of s.96(11) or (11A) for contravening drivers' hours or **14.194** for breach of s.97(11C) for failing to take steps to comply with rules as to contractually agreed transport time schedules is a fine of level 4. Offences can be tried by magistrates only. There is no power to endorse, disqualify or order penalty points.

The maximum fine for offences contrary to s.97(1)(a) (tachograph installation and use), s.97(1)(b) (incorrect repair) and s.99ZD (failing to produce, etc. records) is of level 5. The new offences which are created by the Passenger and Goods Vehicles (Recording Equipment) (Tachograph Card) Regulations 2006 (SI 2006/1397) relating to the use of more than one driver card or the wrong driver card or workshop cards, contrary to reg.3(1)(a) and (b) and reg.4 (1)(a), (b), (c) and (g) of the 2006 Regulations, are also punishable with a maximum fine at level 5 on the standard scale. The maximum fine for s.97C offences (failing to deliver tachograph records) is at level 4.

Contraventions of the 1987 Regulations as to manual records, required, e.g. for domestic journeys and contraventions of Regulation (EC) 561/2006 as to records on AETR journeys are punishable under s.98(4) on conviction with a maximum fine of level 4.

The forgery, falsification, etc., offences under s.97AA, s.99(5) and s.99ZE are **14.195** "either way" offences triable in accordance with ss.18–23 of the Magistrates' Courts Act 1980. Similar offences under the 2006 Tachograph Card Regulations are also triable either way. The defendant can insist on trial by jury. On summary conviction there is a statutory maximum fine of £5,000 and on indictment the maximum penalty is two years' imprisonment or unlimited fine or both. There is no time-limit as these are "either way" offences (1980 Act s.127). It may be helpful to note the level of sentence considered appropriate on a conviction for falsifying records, failing to use the tachograph and failing to take daily rest periods. In *R. v Potter (David)* [1999] 2 Cr.App.R. (S.) 448, the owner-driver of a goods vehicle had fitted a device to allow him to switch off the tachograph. This was discovered and the records inspected revealed offences as listed above to which he pleaded guilty. Reducing the sentence of nine months' imprisonment to one of three months' imprisonment, the Court of Appeal noted his previous, positive, good character and that he had not persuaded employees to break the law. In *R. v Saunders* [2001] EWCA Crim 93; [2002] R.T.R. 4 CA, the defendants were employed by a haulage company to drive lorries. They made journeys to collect items that they failed to record correctly. Their conduct was discovered because of police inquiries at the haulage company on unrelated matters. They were charged with numerous offences of making a false record contrary to s.99 of the 1968 Act and pleaded guilty. Two defendants were of previous good character and one had previous convictions but not for similar offences. All were sentenced to eight months' imprisonment and these sentences were upheld on appeal. The

Court of Appeal confirmed that it was appropriate in principle to pass a custodial sentence of significant length for offences such as these which involved the use of heavy vehicles on the roads in a way that concerned public safety and had potentially serious consequences. In this case, there was a financial motive for the defendants' actions and, whilst they had not received the profit of their actions, they had received increased wages because of the false entries. Although there is a distinction between wage earning and profiteering from such acts, there were a considerable number of offences committed over a considerable period of time and members of the public were put in considerable danger by the defendants' conduct.

14.196   A traffic commissioner is empowered to revoke, suspend or curtail an operator's licence if the licence-holder or his servant or agent has been convicted in the preceding five years of an offence under, or conspiracy to contravene, Pt VI of the 1968 Act in relation to a goods vehicle (Goods Vehicles (Licensing of Operators) Act 1995 s.26(1)(c)). Such offences also have to be declared by applicants for operators' licences (1995 Act ss.8 and 9). In *Yuill v Dodds Ltd* (1993) Appeal 1993/E 14, the transport tribunal upheld a licensing authority's decision to suspend an operator's licence as a deterrent to other operators. This operator had been convicted of offences relating to false records and breaches of the provisions relating to drivers' hours. The licensing authority subsequently suspended the operator for a week. In dismissing the appeal on this point, the tribunal confirmed the propriety of the suspension because of the temptation for hardpressed contractors to accept work from powerful customers on terms set by those customers when professional experience informed the contractors that the terms could not be lawfully met.

For tables of penalties, see § 14.197 and § 14.198. See also Appendix 3, Magistrates' Courts Sentencing Guidelines.

Drivers' hours: penalties

Offence	Mode of trial	Section *	Imprisonment	Level of fine	Disqualification	Penalty points	Endorsement code	Sentencing guideline
Breach of domestic drivers' code	Summary	s.96(11)	—	4	—	—	—	—
Breach in Great Britain of applicable Community rules	Summary	s.96(11A), (11C)	—	4	—	—	—	—

* Transport Act 1968.

Drivers' records: penalties

Offence	Mode of trial	Section *	Imprisonment	Level of fine	Disqualification	Penalty points	Endorsement code	Sentencing guideline †
Tachographs—installation or use	Summary	s.97(1)(a)	—	5	—	—	—	Fine band B Driver / Fine band B Owner-driver / Fine band C Owner-company
Tachographs—incorrect repair	Summary	s.97(1)(b)	—	5	—	—	—	—
Failing to return or receive tachograph records	Summary	s.97C	—	4	—	—	—	—
AETR or regulations as to domestic journeys	Summary	s.98(4)	—	4	—	—	—	—
Offences of production of documents, obstruction, etc.	Summary	s.99(4)	—	3	—	—	—	—
Failing to comply with prohibition order	Summary	s.99C	—	5	—	—	—	—

Offence	Mode of trial	Section *	Imprisonment	Level of fine	Disqualification	Penalty points	Endorsement code	Sentencing guideline †
Failing to comply with requirements of officer with regard to production, etc. of records/equipment	Summary	s.99ZD	—	5	—	—	—	—
Forgery, altering, etc., tachograph seals	a) On indictment	s.99AA	2 years' imprisonment or unlimited fine or both		—	—	—	—
	b) Summary	s.99AA	—	Statutory maximum		—	—	
Falsification of tachograph or documents, etc.	a) On indictment	s.99(5)	2 years' imprisonment or unlimited fine or both		—	—	—	Fine band C Owner-company Fine band B Owner-driver
	b) Summary	s.99(5)	—	Statutory maximum		—	—	

Offence	Mode of trial	Section *	Imprisonment	Level of fine	Disqualification	Penalty points	Endorsement code	Sentencing guideline †
Falsification, forgery, etc. of records	a) On indictment	s.99ZE	2 years' imprisonment or unlimited fine or both		—	—	—	—
	b) Summary	s.99ZE	—	Statutory maximum	—	—	—	—
Using, etc. more than one driver card or wrong driver cards/workshop cards	Summary	Tachograph Card Regs 2006 reg.3(1)(a), (b) reg.4(1)(a), (b), (c), (g)	—	5	—	—	—	—
Forgery, etc. of document/making false statements to obtain driver cards/workshop cards	a) On indictment	Tachograph Card Regs 2006 reg.3(1)(c) reg.4(1)(d)	2 years' imprisonment or unlimited fine or both		—	—	—	—
	b) Summary		3 months' imprisonment/statutory maximum or both		—	—	—	—

Offence	Mode of trial	Section *	Imprisonment	Level of fine	Disqualification	Penalty points	Endorsement code	Sentencing guideline †
Use or possession of false, or falsely obtaining driver card/workshop card	a) On indictment	Tachograph Card Regs 2006 reg.3(1)(d), (e) reg.4(1)(e), (f)	2 years' imprisonment or unlimited fine or both		—	—	—	—
	b) Summary			Statutory maximum	—		—	—

* Transport Act 1968.

† **Note**: Fine bands "A", "B" and "C" represent respectively 50%, 100% and 150% of relevant weekly income. A timely guilty plea should attract a discount. See Appendix 3.

ROAD TRANSPORT (WORKING TIME) REGULATIONS 2005

14.199   The Road Transport (Working Time) Regulations 2005 apply to "mobile workers" who drive, or are otherwise involved in operations which are subject to the EU drivers' hours rules (Regulation (EC) 561/2006). They include own-account drivers and agency drivers. Department for Transport guidance indicates that anyone in a vehicle that is required by EU rules to have a tachograph is affected by the regulations. Those workers who are only occasionally undertaking activities covered by the EU drivers' hours rules are regulated by the Working Time Regulations 1998 (SI 1998/1833, as amended) rather than the Road Transport (Working Time) Regulations 2005.

The Road Transport (Working Time) (Amendment) Regulations 2007 (SI 2007/853) amend the principal regulations so as to replace references to Regulation (EEC) 3820/85 with corresponding references to Regulation (EC) 561/2006.

14.200   A mobile worker is any worker forming part of the travelling staff such as drivers and crew (including trainees and apprentices) who are in the service of an undertaking which operates road transport services for passengers or the movement of goods. Mobile workers include drivers who work for hire and reward companies or companies with own-account operations. The 2005 Regulations also extend to those road transport operations which require additional non-driving crew members to be carried in the vehicle, e.g. in household removals, conductors on inter-urban buses and security staff in high-value goods and cash transport operations. Mobile workers who do not participate in road transport activities covered by EU drivers' hours rules and staff who are excluded from the definition "mobile workers", together with self-employed drivers and workers who only occasionally carry out work within the scope of the EU drivers' hours rules, are not subject to the 2005 Regulations.

In general terms, the working time of a mobile worker shall not exceed 60 hours in a week. In any "reference period" as defined by reg.4(3), a mobile worker's working time shall not exceed an average of 48 hours for each week. A formula is set out in reg.4(5) for the purposes of calculating a mobile worker's average weekly working time during a reference period.

14.201   Periods of availability are defined in reg.6. Whilst they exclude periods where the mobile worker does not know before the start of the relevant period about that period of availability and its reasonably foreseeable duration, time spent by a mobile worker who is working as part of a team, travelling in, but not driving a moving vehicle as part of that team shall be a period of availability for that mobile worker. Rests or breaks are not included. The provisions relating to breaks are set out in reg.7 and deal with the entitlement of mobile workers to take a minimum break. The length of the break will depend upon the number of hours worked. Regulation 8 applies the provisions of Regulation (EEC) 3821/85 relating to daily and weekly rest. Obligations are placed upon employers to take reasonable steps to ensure that there is compliance with these provisions.

The enforcement provisions are set out in regs 16–19 and Sch.2. Inspectors are to be appointed to carry out investigations for the purposes of compliance with the regulations and their powers include the right to ask questions and the inspection and copying of entries in records for the purposes of any examination or investigation. Where an inspector concludes that a person is contravening one or more of the regulations or has contravened one or more of the regulations in circumstances that make it likely that the contravention will be repeated, an "improvement notice" may be served upon that person requiring that person to remedy the contravention, or as the case may be, the matter occasioning it within such period as may be specified in the notice. In addition, inspectors may serve a prohibition notice in cases where an inspector concludes that the activities carried out, on, by or under the control of a person being investigated involve or, as the case may be, will involve a risk of serious personal injury. There is a right of appeal against an improvement or a prohibition notice to an employment tribunal.

Offences

By reg.17, any person who fails to comply with any of the relevant require-   **14.202**
ments commits an offence. A person found guilty of an offence under reg.17(1) will be liable on summary conviction to a fine not exceeding the statutory maximum, or on conviction on indictment to a fine. Schedule 2 provides for enforcement and reg.17(3) sets out the basis of criminal liability for any person who commits offences in contravention of improvement notices or prohibition notices, or who intentionally obstructs an inspector in the execution or performance of powers, uses or discloses any information in contravention of Sch.2, or makes a false statement in purported compliance with a requirement to furnish information.

Regulation 18 deals with offences which are due to the fault of another person. It provides that where the commission by any person of an offence is due to the act or default of some other person, that other person will be guilty of the offence, and a person may be charged with the commission of the offence by virtue of reg.18 whether or not proceedings are taken against the first-mentioned person.

Regulation 19 applies to offences by bodies corporate so that where an offence   **14.203**
committed by a body corporate is proved to have been committed with the consent or connivance of, or to have been attributable to any neglect on the part of any director, manager, secretary or other similar officer of the body corporate or a person who was purporting to act in any such capacity, he as well as the body corporate will be guilty of that offence and shall be liable to be proceeded against and punished accordingly.

Regulation 22 permits a court to order the cause of any offence to be remedied within a specified time either in addition to or instead of imposing any punishment.

CHAPTER 15

THEFT, TAKING CONVEYANCES, AGGRAVATED VEHICLE-TAKING, CRIMINAL DAMAGE AND CAUSING DANGER TO ROAD USERS

CONTENTS

Generally

15.01   This chapter deals with the offences of theft and taking conveyances in ss.1 and 12 of the Theft Act 1968 and with aggravated vehicle-taking in s.12A ibid. Thereafter the related offences of interfering with vehicles (Criminal Attempts Act 1981 s.9), tampering with and getting on vehicles (Road Traffic Act 1988 ss.25 and 26), criminal damage (Criminal Damage Act 1971 s.1) and causing danger to road users (Road Traffic Act 1988 s.22A) are considered.

THEFT AND TAKING CONVEYANCES

The offences (ss.1 and 12)

15.02   As to theft generally, see the standard textbooks.

The offence of taking a conveyance without consent is to be found in s.12 of the Theft Act 1968. A person commits an offence under s.12 who, without having the consent of the owner or other lawful authority, takes any conveyance (as defined in subs.(7)) for his own or another's use *or* who, knowing that any such conveyance has been taken without such authority, drives it or allows himself to be carried in or on it.

15.03   The provisions of s.12 do not apply to Scotland, where s.178 of the 1988 Act applies. This section is a re-enactment, almost word for word, of s.217 of the Road Traffic Act 1960, as amended by s.44 of the Road Traffic Act 1962. The section relates to motor vehicles only. Some of the cases cited below were on s.217 of the 1960 Act.

Section 12 was primarily designed to deal with people who took cars for "joyrides" and then abandoned them, thus escaping a charge of theft on the ground that there was no intention permanently to deprive the owner of them.

15.04   A person who enters a building as a trespasser with intent to take a conveyance does not commit burglary under s.9 of the Theft Act because offences under s.12 are not comprised in s.9(1) or (2). By s.25(5) of the Theft Act 1968, the offence of having an article for use in connection with theft is, however, specifically applied to offences under s.12(1); a person who had with him (otherwise than at his place of abode) a set of car keys or a car park attendant's uniform with a view to facilitating an offence under s.12 would be guilty—see s.25(3) as to burden of proof. This does not apply to persons equipped to take pedal cycles.

Belief by a defendant to a charge under s.12 that he had lawful authority or would have had the owner's consent had the owner known of his action and the circumstances of it constitutes a statutory "defence" to the charge: see s.12(6) discussed at §§ 15.18–21, although in fact where the issue is raised the onus is on the prosecution to establish lack of belief on the criminal standard of proof.

15.05 The belief of the accused that he had authority need not be reasonable and the onus is not on him to prove it; the offence is complete if the defendant "takes" not "takes and drives away" the conveyance (see *R. v Bogacki, R. v Pearce* and *R. v Bow* below, and also, in relation to employee-drivers, *McKnight v Davies* at § 15.26).

The section extends to ships, rubber dinghies, aircraft, vehicles whether mechanically propelled or not, e.g. carts, trams, trolley vehicles, railway rolling-stock, and, as indicated in s.12(5), cycles; the *Concise Oxford Dictionary* defines "cycle" as including a bicycle, tricycle or similar machine. The definition of "conveyance" in s.12(7) suggests that there is no offence if a person takes a remotely controlled aircraft or vehicle (see *R. v Roberts (No.2)* at § 15.22). The conveyance must be constructed or adapted for the carriage of a person or persons, so that a goods trailer, milkfloat or porter's trolley or hand-barrow is not covered. Presumably, the presence of a seat for the driver shows that a conveyance is constructed for the carriage of "a person"; otherwise it would not be an offence to take a lorry. It is submitted that an excavator or bulldozer which has a seat for the driver is constructed or adapted for the carriage of a person and so is a conveyance under s.12. In *R. v Bow* below it was said that the vehicle must be used as a means of transport.

15.06 A horse is not a "conveyance" (*Neal v Gribble* [1978] R.T.R. 409). Moreover, even if a horse could be said to be a conveyance, which it is not, it cannot be said to be "adapted" for the conveyance of the rider by the putting of a bridle on it: a bridle, halter or saddle does not "adapt" the horse but simply makes it easier to ride (ibid.).

In *R. v Bogacki* [1973] R.T.R. 384 it was held that "take" as expressed in s.12 of the Theft Act was not equivalent to "use", nor could it consist of a mere assumption of possession adverse to the rights of the true owner; to constitute the offence of taking, there must be an unauthorised taking possession or control of the conveyance adverse to the rights of the true owner or person otherwise entitled to such possession or control coupled with some movement of the conveyance no matter how small. *Bogacki* was followed and applied in *R. v Miller* [1976] Crim. L.R. 147, where it was held that the charge of allowing oneself to be carried requires movement of the conveyance while carried. With regard to proof of taking, the Divisional Court held in *Chief Constable of Avon and Somerset v Jest* [1986] R.T.R. 372 that magistrates were entitled to take the view that the defendant's left thumb print on the internal rear-view mirror of a motor car was insufficient evidence of possession of the vehicle to found a case under s.12.

15.07 *Bogacki* was further considered in *R. v Bow* [1977] R.T.R. 6 where it was held that for a vehicle to be taken for "his or another's use", the vehicle had to be used as a conveyance, namely, as a means of transport. The vehicle in *Bow* was a gamekeeper's Land Rover obstructing the poachers' escape route. One of the poachers entered the Land Rover and coasted it down hill, without using the engine, for 200yds. The conviction under s.12 was affirmed as the Land Rover was in fact used as a conveyance. It was, however, said that pushing an obstructing vehicle out of the way for a yard or two would not involve the use of the vehicle as a conveyance and that the facts involved in the removal of an obstructing vehicle must be examined in each case ([1977] R.T.R. 6 at 11C).

The need to take as a conveyance was again emphasised in *R. v Stokes* [1983] R.T.R. 59. In that case the car belonged to a former girlfriend. The car was pushed around the corner as a practical joke. It was held following the decision in *Bow* that "use" involved use as a conveyance and the defendant was acquitted. It is submitted that the intent to use it as a conveyance is sufficient, providing it is moved (compare *R. v Pearce* below) without anyone actually travelling in it. On the other hand in *Bow* the Land Rover was in fact used as a conveyance even though the purpose of the poacher was not to be conveyed but to remove an obstruction. Although it is not a binding decision further support for the view that the taking must be for use as a conveyance may be derived from the direction to the jury in *R. v Dunn and Derby* [1984] Crim. L.R. 367. A motor bicycle had been taken and wheeled 40yds to look at it by a porch light but not for use as a conveyance. An acquittal was directed.

15.08   Where a conveyance taken without consent and then abandoned is subsequently taken, an offence under s.12(1) may be constituted. An offender was seen driving a car which had earlier been taken without consent from a car park. When stopped by police he ran away. He had not been responsible for the original taking. He claimed he was merely moving the car prior to notifying the police of its whereabouts. The Crown Court on appeal found that the moving was for the offender's own use but he was not the original taker and he could not be convicted on the basis of the subsequent removal. The Divisional Court in *DPP v Spriggs* [1994] R.T.R. 1 allowed the prosecutor's appeal against the decision of the Crown Court. The car was taken and possession of it was abandoned. There was then a fresh assumption of possession and taking within the language of s.12(1). Offences under that subsection are not limited only to facts where there has been one taking either by a single person or by his acting jointly with another. The test to be applied is that the defendant must have taken control of the vehicle and caused it to be moved and he must have done so for his own or another's use.

Accidentally putting a foot on the accelerator of an automatic drive vehicle which had the engine running with the result that the vehicle drove all over the road, is not "taking" for the purpose of s.12 (*Blayney v Knight* [1975] Crim. L.R. 237). The construction placed on "drive" in s.12(7) does not mean that the movement of the conveyance has to be in the element in which the conveyance is designed to travel; thus, in *R. v Pearce* [1973] Crim. L.R. 321 a defendant's conviction was upheld for taking an inflatable rubber dinghy from a lifeboat depot, and putting it on a trailer which he then drove away.

15.09   *R. v Miller* was applied in *R. v Diggin* [1981] R.T.R. 83. A defendant allowed himself to be carried in a vehicle taken without the owner's consent by his brother and a Mr Zubal. Because of drink and because the vehicle was of the same year and manufacture as one he knew was owned by Mr Zubal, he thought he was in that vehicle. The car stopped at a motorway service area, and before the car could move off, the police approached. The defendant asserted that only then did he re-alise the vehicle had been taken without consent. The Court of Appeal held that, for the offence under s.12 of allowing oneself to be carried knowing it to have been taken without authority, there must have been some movement of the vehi-cle after the defendant had knowledge of its unlawful taking.

Although not otherwise adverted to, it should be noted that the second part of s.12(1) and (5) of the Theft Act refers to "knowing" that the conveyance or pedal cycle has been taken without authority. There has been no reported decision adverting to the contrast between s.12 and s.22 of the Theft Act, namely that the mens rea on a charge of handling stolen goods under s.22 is stated as "knowing or believing" the goods to be stolen, whereas the mens rea in s.12 is stated as "knowing" only. It would seem that the prosecution under s.12 has to prove knowledge of the unauthorised taking of the vehicle; belief would seem to be insufficient. An article on the mental element in s.12 offences appears at [1980] Crim. L.R. 609.

The difference between theft (s.1) and taking a conveyance (s.12)

Sometimes a person who takes a car or motor vessel is accused of stealing the **15.10** petrol also but it is submitted that he should not be punished for both offences (see [1968] Crim. L.R. 282; *R. v Burnham JJ. Ex p. Ansorge* [1959] 3 All E.R. 505; and "Two offences from one incident" at § 5.76). A person charged under s.12 may still, it is submitted, be convicted even if the facts show that he is guilty of theft because he dishonestly took the conveyance with the intention of permanently depriving the owner of it. It was held to be no defence to the previ-ous offence of driving or allowing oneself to be carried, when not a party to the original taking, that the defendant knew that the vehicle had been *stolen* and not just taken (*Tolley v Giddings* [1964] 1 All E.R. 201).

While a jury may convict a defendant charged with theft of taking under s.12 (s.12(4)), a magistrates' court cannot do so unless he has been additionally charged in the alternative.

One distinction between theft and taking is that the offence of theft is required **15.11** to be dishonestly committed and requires proof of mens rea; an offence under s.12(1) does not require proof of an intention to commit it, but it does require knowledge and mens rea in this respect (see *R. v Diggin* above). On the other hand s.12(1) requires the vehicle to be physically moved (*R. v Bogacki* above), and the offence of theft is complete once the vehicle has been dishonestly ap-propriated; "appropriation" does not require the vehicle to be physically moved. It is necessary to prove intent to use as a conveyance or actual use for convey-ance (see *R. v Stokes* and *R. v Pearce* above). This is not essential to establish theft. An offence of theft also requires proof on the part of the defendant of an intention permanently to deprive the owner of the vehicle; under s.12 no such intention is required.

Pedal cycles

Section 12(1) does not apply to pedal cycles even though they are conveyances. **15.12** Section 12(5) creates the separate offence of taking a pedal cycle without consent. The wording is similar to s.12(1) save that the reference is to riding instead of driving or allowing oneself to be carried, etc. The maximum penalties are less severe. As to riding, see § 1.116. The expression is wide enough to include a passenger, whether carried legally or illegally. The defence in s.12(6) of belief in lawful authority or owner's consent applies to s.12(5) offences as does, it is submitted, the law generally relating to the taking of conveyances and movement of pedal cycles only for the purpose of conveyance. The s.25 offence of going equipped applies by s.25(5) to s.12(1) offences, but not to pedal cycles.

The Divisional Court in *Sturrock v DPP* [1996] R.T.R. 216 dismissed an appeal by the defendant against a ruling that there was a case for him to answer on a charge of taking a pedal cycle without the consent of the owner contrary to s.12(5) of the Theft Act 1968. The defendant had admitted that the cycle did not belong to him and that he did not have the consent of the owner to take it. On the facts as found, the justices had been entitled to infer that the cycle had not been abandoned. It was not necessary that there should be before the court a statement from the owner of the cycle as to his ownership and that he had not consented to its being taken by the defendant.

15.13   Section 12(5) states specifically that s.12(1) shall not apply to pedal cycles and the issue is not whether the vehicle is a motor vehicle but whether it is a pedal cycle. If a s.12(5) charge is used it will be for the prosecution to establish to the criminal standard of proof that it is a pedal cycle. If a s.12(1) charge is used, the pedal cycle provision would seem to be an exception, so that under the Magistrates' Courts Act 1980 s. 101, the onus of proof is on the defendant to establish that it is a pedal cycle and that the s.12(1) offence does not therefore apply.

15.14   The standard of proof will be on the balance of probabilities (*R. v Carr-Briant* [1943] 2 All E.R. 156). Whether a vehicle is a pedal cycle is a question of fact. Most auto-assisted motor vehicles (including electrically assisted pedal cycles) are not really designed to be driven extensively with pedals although they are capable of being propelled by them. Nevertheless it is submitted that they are also pedal cycles (as, e.g. is indicated by the expression electrically assisted pedal cycles) and that prosecutions should be under s.12(5) and not s.12(1). Penal provisions should be construed strictly.

Consent of owner

15.15   If the owner's consent were obtained by intimidation seemingly this would not be "consent" under s.12 (*R. v Hodgon* [1962] Crim. L.R. 563). In *R. v Peart* [1970] 2 All E.R. 823 it was held that consent of the owner as to the use of the car by another was not vitiated by the fact that the defendant obtained the owner's consent by falsely pretending that he needed the car to go to Alnwick when in fact he went to Burnley instead. The court held that when s.12 was enacted there was no intention by Parliament to create a new offence of taking conveyances by false pretences. If therefore the owner's consent is obtained by means of a false pretence either as to the destination or purpose of the journey, no offence under s.12 appears to be committed. The court, however, reserved for a future occasion the legal position where the consent of the owner was obtained by a fundamental misrepresentation, as, e.g. where *B* pretended to the owner that he was *C*.

This was partly answered by the important case of *Whittaker v Campbell* [1983] 3 All E.R. 582, which held, following *R. v Peart*, that fraud did not vitiate consent. The defendants had used another's driving licence to hire a car, representing that one of them was that person. It is immaterial that B thought C was someone else such as a famous film star as in *Lewis v Averay* [1971] 3 All

E.R. 907 referred to in the *Whittaker* case. The position should be compared with *R. v Phipps*; *R. v McGill* [1970] R.T.R. 209, a case under the Road Traffic Act 1960 where *M* obtained permission to borrow the car to go to the railway station. He did not return and used it next day to go to Hastings. It was held that, since he had once failed to return the car, his use was unlawful unless he reasonably believed that the owner in the circumstances would have given his consent if asked. It seems that if the defendant in *Peart* had in fact gone to Alnwick and then on to Burnley he would be guilty in accordance with *Phipps*. For further criticism of *Peart* see [1970] Crim. L.R. 480. It should also be noted that *Phipps* was followed and applied in *McKnight v Davies* (see § 15.26). The distinction between a person obtaining permission to use a vehicle for a limited purpose and going beyond that purpose and therefore being held guilty of an offence under s.217 of the 1960 Act or s.12 of the 1968 Act (*Phipps*) and a person obtaining permission for a different purpose from the one he actually used it for (*Peart*) is a fine one. *Peart* was cited in argument to the court in *McKnight v Davies* but there is no mention of it in the judgment. (*Phipps*, contrary to the statement in the judgment of *McKnight v Davies* [1974] R.T.R. 4 at 7G, was a case under s.217 of the 1960 Act, not s.12 of the Theft Act.)

15.16 *Whittaker v Campbell* and *R. v Peart* were both distinguished as to their facts by the Court of Appeal in *Singh v Rathour* [1988] R.T.R. 324, a civil case involving the liability (or otherwise) of an insurance company to indemnify a defendant in respect of damages for negligence in respect of a motor accident. Neither of the earlier cases dealt with a consent limited as to time, place or purpose. In the instant case, however, where a person had borrowed a vehicle subject to an implied (but known) limitation as to the purpose for which it was to be driven, he did not have the consent of the owner when driving it outside the terms of that limitation and was accordingly uninsured when so driving it.

Evidence

15.17 It was held in a Crown Court case, *R. v Francis (Ronald)* [1982] Crim. L.R. 694, applying *R. v Hulbert* (1979) 69 Cr. App. R. 243 (a receiving case contrary to s.22 of the Theft Act 1968) that the fact that the defendant had said that his companion the driver of the car had told him that he had "nicked it" was not evidence upon which the prosecution could rely to prove that the car had been taken without consent. The comment may be evidence to show the defendant's state of mind. Neither that nor the surrounding circumstances were such that the jury could properly infer that the owner had not, as a matter of fact, consented.

Defences: belief of lawful authority or owner's consent (s.12(6))

15.18 Unlike the former offence in England and Wales, and the present offence in Scotland under s.178 of the 1988 Act, the onus of proving that the accused did not believe under s.12(6) that he had lawful authority to take the conveyance or that he would have had the owner's consent if the latter knew of his doing it and the circumstances of it is on the prosecution.

Section 12(1) and (5) refer to the owner's consent or *other* lawful authority. Section 12(6) refers to lawful authority *or* the owner's consent. This distinction may imply that there may be a valid belief in the owner's consent even though there is an unlawful element.

15.19 It was held in *R. v McPherson* [1973] R.T.R. 157 that if an issue arises as to whether a defendant under s.12(6) had a belief of lawful authority, etc., the onus is on the prosecution to prove that the defendant had no such authority or consent. On the other hand the prosecution do not have to prove a specific intent on the part of the defendant to take the vehicle (ibid.). Thus where the defendant was drunk (but not so drunk as to raise the defence of insanity) a judge was entitled to direct the jury that self-induced drunkenness was no defence, and that, unless an issue under s.12(6) was raised, the only matters that the jury had to be satisfied about were (a) that the vehicle was taken by the defendant and (b) that it was without the owner's consent. (It should be noted that although the offence of unlawful taking under s.12(1) is triable only summarily, it is a constituent part of the "either way" offence of aggravated vehicle-taking under s.12A (see §§ 15.47–50) and accordingly may come from time to time within the purview of judges and juries.)

A conviction for taking a motor vehicle without consent was quashed, following *McPherson*, by the Court of Appeal in *R. v Briggs* [1987] Crim. L.R. 708 on the grounds that when asked by the jury to define "lawful authority" the judge failed to direct the jury in the course of his summing-up as to the statutory defence under s.12(6).

15.20   It is clear from *McPherson* above that the onus of disproving the defendant's belief of lawful authority is on the prosecution where such an issue arises. The reported facts of *Briggs*, however, give some cause for doubt as to whether that issue was ever raised. When stopped by police the appellant said that he was repairing the motor cycle for a friend, and he gave his friend's name and address. At the trial he neither gave evidence nor called witnesses. In those circumstances it may be wondered whether any kind of lawful authority (actual or believed) other than the owner's consent was in issue. Be that as it may, it is clearly incumbent now upon judges to make specific reference to the s.12(6) defence when summing up to juries in such cases.

McPherson was again applied by the Divisional Court in *R. v Gannon* [1988] R.T.R. 49. On the facts of the case, however, the appellant had not raised the issue of believed authority under s.12(6) since he had been unable to produce evidence that he held such a belief. After consuming a considerable amount of alcohol at a dance he had got into a car similar to his own (which, incidentally, he had not taken with him that evening) and had been involved in an accident which put him in hospital for four days and effectively erased his memory of events between leaving the dance and subsequently regaining consciousness. The evidence about the similarity of the cars and the fact that his keys fitted it was equivocal and it could not be argued that, because he was drunk, he must or might have believed the car to be his. In these circumstances there was nothing for the prosecution to disprove, and the jury would have had to be directed that the only verdict open to them was one of guilty.

15.21   Magistrates' courts have acquitted where it has been established that the defendant mistook the vehicle believing it to be his own on the basis that as it was his own he believed he had lawful authority. There is a well-known story of a junior barrister who drove off from a golf club in a Mini belonging to a senior judge. The judge's Mini was identical to his own. There was another incident where a person took a police vehicle after dark and parked it in his garage leaving behind his own similar white Ford Escort. No prosecution followed.

The statute does not apparently require the defendant's belief under s.12(6) that he had lawful authority or consent to be reasonable. The very absurdity of some factors for the belief can show that he did not really hold it, but it need not be reasonable. A follower of an obscure religion might have some literally fantastic belief but, if the prosecution do not disprove that he had such a belief, it seems to be a defence. It is a question of fact even though the defendant has no driving licence and no insurance (*R. v Clotworthy* [1981] Crim. L.R. 501). Magistrates acquitted a defendant who took a car in the belief that the owner, a friend, would have consented; the owner testified that, while normally he would have consented, he would not have done so on that occasion as the fanbelt was broken ([1968] Jo.Crim.L. 3). Moving a motor vehicle simply for one's own convenience, e.g. because it is blocking a doorway, is not normally an offence under s.12 (*Shimmell v Fisher* [1951] 2 All E.R. 672; see also *R. v Bow* at § 15.07).

"Driving away"

In *Shimmell v Fisher* [1951] 2 All E.R. 672 three men approached a parked **15.22** lorry and the handbrake was released; two of the men pushed it and the third held the steering wheel and they tried unsuccessfully to start the engine. On a charge under s.217 of the Road Traffic Act 1960 of taking and driving away the lorry, it was held that "driving away" means causing the vehicle to move from the place where it was standing and that a vehicle could be said to be driven if one man pushed and another steered. It is submitted that under s.12 all three would be joint offenders engaged in a common purpose and should be convicted if they intended to use it as a means of transport (see *R. v Bow* at § 15.07). But merely releasing the brake of a lorry, so that it ran downhill driverless, is not taking and driving away (*R. v Roberts (No.2)* [1964] 2 All E.R. 541). It can be argued that letting a vehicle run downhill unattended or a vessel drift away unmanned is likewise not "taking" it under s.12 and that there should be some measure of control by the accused over it. The case of *R. v Roberts*, however, turned partly on the question whether what the defendant did was "driving away" and it was suggested in the judgment of Lord Parker C.J. that this might be taking. The taking, by s.12(1), must be for "the use of" the defendant or another; letting a vehicle run away is hardly for anyone's use, and it would now seem from *R. v Bow* (see § 15.07) that the unauthorised possession or control of the conveyance for purposes of transport is the essential element in such cases. Letting a vehicle run downhill or a boat downstream unattended would not constitute transport, but otherwise if the offender was in the driving seat or on the boat.

Passengers

In *R. v Baldessare* (1930) 22 Cr. App. R. 70, two persons engaged in a com- **15.23** mon purpose were both held guilty of criminal negligence in driving though one only drove. Passengers are, it seems, aiders, abettors, counsellors and procurers of the offence by the driver if they act together in taking the car, and they can all properly be convicted along with him. The matter is put beyond doubt by the second part of s.12(1), which extends to a person who, "knowing that any conveyance has been taken without [the owner's consent or other lawful] authority, drives it or allows himself to be carried in or on it". Where any such driver or passenger was not a party to the original taking and the charge is contrary to this second part of s.12(1) (knowingly, etc.), the prosecution must prove that the driver or passenger knew that the vehicle had been taken without consent or other lawful authority. The passenger must also be carried in the conveyance while it is in motion (*R. v Miller* and *R. v Diggin* at § 15.06 and at § 15.09). There is a clear case to answer against passengers as well as against the driver where a car is found at 2 am without petrol and the passengers give an unsatisfactory explanation to the police of the reason for their presence in the car (*Ross v Rivenall* [1959] 2 All E.R. 376) but Donovan J. (as he then was) doubted if mere presence in a car as a passenger, without any suspicious circumstances, was enough (ibid.). It does not matter whether the driver or a passenger took the car, so long as they were acting in concert, or even if they had it from another person (*R. v Richardson* [1958] Crim. L.R. 480), but to convict a passenger of taking there must be some evidence to show that each accused was a party to the taking or knew of the unlawful taking; entering a car after it has been taken, without evidence that the passenger was a party to or knew of the taking, is not enough (*R. v Stally* [1959] 3 All E.R. 814).

In *Boldizer v Knight* [1980] Crim. L.R. 653 the defendant was given a lift in a van. During the course of the drive he learned that it had been taken without the owner's consent. It was held that he should not be convicted of using the van without insurance; *aliter* if the taking had been a joint enterprise (cf. *Ross v Rivenall* above). The defendant was, however, convicted of knowingly allowing himself to be carried contrary to s.12 of the Theft Act 1968. (See also under Chapter 10, "Insurance".) Compare *R. v Diggin* at § 15.09, where the passenger also did not learn that the vehicle had been taken without consent until after the beginning of the journey. Here there was no evidence of movement or of being carried after the discovery and an acquittal was directed.

15.24   The conviction of the driver for an offence under s.12 of the Theft Act 1968 was admissible and raised a strong prima facie case that the vehicle in which the defendant was a passenger had been taken without the consent of the owner: *DPP v Parker* [2006] EWHC 1270; [2006] R.T.R. 26.

If evidence is produced to show that a passenger was a party to the taking, it need not be shown that he was present at the taking (ibid.). It was said in *R. v Pearce* [1961] Crim. L.R. 122 that it was not correct to say that there was a new taking and driving away every time the car was moved. Convictions were quashed where there was no evidence to show that a passenger was concerned in the original taking (*D v Parsons* [1960] 2 All E.R. 493; *A v Bundy* (1960) 125 J.P. 89), but see now the express reference in s.12(1) to knowledge that a conveyance has been taken without authority. A person not a party to the taking who, knowing that a motor vehicle had been *stolen*, drives or travels in it commits an offence (*Tolley v Giddings* [1964] 1 All E.R. 201).

Employees and hirers

15.25   It was held that a van driver, in lawful possession of his employer's van, who drove it on a frolic of his own, committed no offence in *Mowe v Perraton* [1952] 1 All E.R. 423. It would be otherwise if he had put the vehicle back into his employer's possession, e.g. by leaving it in the employer's garage, and then took it out of such possession without leave. The reason for the decision was that an employee, being in lawful possession of his employer's vehicle whilst on duty, cannot "take" what he already has, but this reasoning was inconsistent with *R. v Phipps*; *R. v McGill* [1970] R.T.R. 209, and the latter case was followed in preference to *Mowe v Perraton* in *McKnight v Davies* below.

In *R. v Wibberley* [1965] 3 All E.R. 718, the defendant, a truck driver, was supposed to return the truck to his employer's premises at the end of the day's work but, instead, he took it home and parked it outside his house for two hours. He then drove it away for a purpose of his own. The employers would not have objected to him parking outside his house for the night and taking the truck to work next morning. His conviction for taking it for his own purposes, after he had parked it, was upheld, as he had no authority to use it, after parking it outside his home, until the next day's work began. There was a distinction between deviation from employment during working hours, when he still intended to carry out his instructions to drive the vehicle to his employer's premises, and taking it after working hours with no such intention and after an interruption in time.

In *McKnight v Davies* [1974] R.T.R. 4 a lorry driver returning to his employer's   **15.26**
depot struck a low bridge with the roof of his lorry. He was not permitted to use the lorry for his own purposes, but, being scared on seeing the damage to the lorry's roof, he drove to a public house and had a drink, then drove three men to their homes and returned to the centre of the city, had a drink at another public house and drove home leaving his lorry nearby, in all driving 30 miles in excess of his proper delivery route. *R. v Wibberley* above and *R. v Phipps* [1970] R.T.R. 209 were followed in preference to *Mowe v Perraton*, which was held to be inconsistent in particular with *Phipps*. (In *Phipps* it was held that where a defendant had been given permission to take and use a vehicle for a limited purpose, and thereafter used it for another purpose, he was guilty of the offence; see also § 15.15.) The court went on in *McKnight v Davies* to consider to what extent the unauthorised use by an employee of his employer's vehicle could in law amount to a "taking" for the purposes of s.12. Not every brief unauthorised diversion from his proper route would necessarily involve a "taking" for use (*McKnight v Davies* [1974] R.T.R. 4 at 8); if, however, he returned the vehicle and parked it for the night and drove off on an unauthorised errand (as in *R. v Wibberley*) that would be a sufficient "taking" (ibid.). It was suggested that to constitute a "taking" of the vehicle during his working day or while he had authority to use the vehicle, he must have appropriated it in a manner which repudiated his employer's true rights. In other words he had altered the character of his control over the vehicle so that he no longer held it as employee but assumed possession of it in the legal sense. In the opinion of the court, the defendant "took" the vehicle not when he first went to a public house, but when he left it to drive the three men home.

R. v Phipps and *McKnight v Davies* above were both applied by the Divisional Court in *McMinn v McMinn* [2006] EWHC 827; [2006] 3 All E.R. 87. Where an employee, who was permitted to drive a vehicle owned by his employer, allowed a third party to drive the vehicle (with himself as a passenger), the employee would be guilty of taking the vehicle without authority if it could be said that he had appropriated the vehicle for use in a manner which repudiated the owner's rights and showed that he had assumed control of the vehicle for his own purposes; to which end, the question would be whether he knew or believed that his employer would not have permitted the third party to drive the vehicle.

A person who takes away a conveyance on hire purchase with the hirer's consent but without the consent of the dealer or finance company which owns it does not offend against s.12 because, by s.12(7)(b), "owner", in relation to a vehicle which is the subject of a hiring agreement or hire-purchase agreement, means the person in possession of the vehicle under that agreement (*R. v Tolhurst* [1962] Crim. L.R. 489).

Attempts

15.27   See "Attempt" at § 1.210 and the cases at § 1.108 as to attempting to drive. The definition of "attempt" offences is now to be found in the Criminal Attempts Act 1981, and the cases below must be read in the light of that Act, and the definition contained therein, although they may well still be of assistance.

In *R. v Cook* [1964] Crim. L.R. 56 it was held that a man who was found in the front seat of a car fiddling with the ignition, the dashboard being lit, and who later said that, if not caught, in another minute he would have got away with the car, could properly be convicted of an attempt to take it. In *R. v Bogacki* (see § 15.06) the defendants acting in concert entered a bus with the intention of driving it away; one of them turned the engine over with the starter, but the engine never started and the bus did not move; their conviction of attempting to take the bus was quashed because the jury were wrongly directed as to the meaning of the word "take", but it is clear from the judgment of the Court of Appeal that if the jury had been properly directed there was ample evidence to constitute an attempt. The act of endeavouring to open a car door is capable of amounting to an attempt to take and drive it away without authority; in deciding if such an equivocal act does amount to an attempt, the court should take into consideration any evidence of the defendant's actual intention, including any statement made by him (*Jones v Brooks* (1968) 52 Cr. App. R. 614).

15.28   A person charged with attempting to commit an offence can be convicted of the attempt even though in law he committed the full offence. In *Webley v Buxton* [1977] Crim. L.R. 160 the defendant, who had been charged with attempting to take a motor cycle without the owner's consent, was seen astride the motor cycle with his hands on the handlebars and using his feet to push it 8ft across a pavement towards a motorway. The magistrates convicted him as charged, i.e. attempting to commit the offence, even though they were satisfied he had committed the full offence. It was held by the Divisional Court that the justices were entitled to do so. It is submitted that this decision is unaffected by the Criminal Attempts Act 1981.

As to the offences with which a defendant may be charged where the offences under s.1 or s.12 are incomplete, see "Interfering with vehicles", §§ 15.57–61 and "Tampering with vehicles", §§ 15.62–3.

THEFT AND TAKING CONVEYANCES: PROCEEDINGS AND PENALTIES

Generally

15.29   Offences of theft under s.1 and any attempt to commit them are "either way" offences triable at the Crown Court and may be tried by magistrates pursuant to ss.18–23 of the Magistrates' Courts Act 1980. If the defendant indicates a guilty plea, he loses his right to be tried at the Crown Court, although he may still be committed to that court for sentence. If he indicates a not guilty plea, or fails to indicate his plea, the established mode of trial procedure applies; the defendant must consent to any summary trial and accordingly may insist on trial by jury. Offences of unlawful taking under s.12(1) are triable only summarily (s.12(2), as amended by the Criminal Justice Act 1988 s.37). Taking a pedal cycle, etc., is a summary offence only (s.12(5)). There is no offence under s.1 of the Criminal Attempts Act 1981 of attempting to commit a purely summary offence such as this.

Section 12 of the Theft Act 1968 was amended by s.37 of the Vehicles (Crime) Act 2001 in order to provide that the time-limit for commencing prosecution of offences under s.12(1) is, subject to an overall limit of three years from the date of the offence, six months from the date on which sufficient evidence to justify the proceedings comes to the knowledge of the prosecutor (ss.12(4A)–(4C), as inserted). These provisions apply to offences committed on or after October 1, 2001.

If the accused, being of the age of 17 or over, has a firearm or imitation firearm in his possession when committing an offence under s.1 of the Theft Act or attempting such an offence, or uses one with intent to resist arrest, he must be sent for trial at the Crown Court (Firearms Act 1968 Sch.6 Pt II para.3; Theft Act 1968 Sch.2). This provision no longer applies to offences under s.12(1) and does not apply where a pedal cycle, etc., is taken.

15.30 It is submitted that a vehicle taken in breach of s.12 is not stolen goods so that a person who dishonestly receives one which he knows to have been so taken is not guilty of handling under s.22 of the Theft Act.

Where an offence under s.1 or s.12 is committed, attempted, abetted or procured by a member of a visiting force (see § 2.30) in respect of a conveyance which belongs to that force or to a member, or dependant of a member, of that force, he may not be tried by a British civil court, save where the visiting force consents (Visiting Forces Act 1952 s.3). "Dependant" does not include a person who is a British citizen or ordinarily resident here.

15.31 Offences and attempts to commit offences under s.1 or s.12(1) would be an "unlawful purpose" within s.4 of the Vagrancy Act 1824 relating to persons found in certain buildings or enclosed places, and this applies in respect of taking pedal cycles also. This part of s.4 has not been repealed.

Search

15.32 Under s.1 of the Police and Criminal Evidence Act 1984 a constable has power to search for or seize stolen or prohibited articles. He must follow the codes of practice and in particular Code A. As to the codes of practice, see § 3.43. "Prohibited articles" are defined in s.1(7) and (8) of the 1984 Act as (in addition to offensive weapons) articles made, adapted or intended for use in burglary, theft, deception under s.15 of the Theft Act 1968 and s.12 offences (taking motor vehicles and other conveyances without authority). No offence is created for non-co-operation but there may be an obstruction of the constable in the execution of his duty contrary to s.89(2) of the Police Act 1996. A constable may use reasonable force if necessary (1984 Act s.117).

The power only arises if the constable has "reasonable grounds for suspecting" that he will find such articles (s.1(3)). The subsection refers to articles in general, but the nature of the article may be relevant where the existence of reasonable grounds for suspicion is in question. "Reasonable grounds for suspicion" is described in Code A, paras 2.2–2.11 (see "Reasonable cause to believe", §§ 4.60–2). "Suspect" is less strong than "believe".

15.33 The power to search would apply to a key to be used for a stolen or unlawfully taken vehicle but in theory not for the offence of interfering with vehicles (see §§ 15.57–61). In practice in such a case the constable would have a reasonable suspicion of the s.12 offence.

The power is to search any person, any vehicle or anything which is in or on the vehicle. The person or vehicle may be detained for the purpose. The word "detain" must imply an initial holding or stopping. See also s.2(9)(b) of the 1984 Act which states that nothing in these provisions authorises a constable to *stop* a vehicle if he is not in uniform. The power extends to public places as defined in s.1 (see also § 1.148) and other places to which people have ready access. It does not extend to dwellings and buildings and land occupied and used with the dwelling, unless the constable has reasonable grounds for believing that the person does not reside there and does not have the express or implied permission of a resident. Here the word is "believe" and not "suspect" (see above). What is "ready access" is a question of fact, but it is submitted that it may include a place adjoining the road where a person drives while trying to escape. The constable may use reasonable force, if necessary, in order to search, detain or seize as the case may be.

15.34   Before a constable commences the search, he has to produce documentary evidence that he is a constable if he is not in uniform and give certain other information including the grounds for the search. This is to the person concerned or the person in charge of the vehicle. If the vehicle is unattended a notice must be left in accordance with s.2(6) of the 1984 Act. The search must be recorded in writing in accordance with s.3 of the 1984 Act and the person or the owner of the vehicle at the time may request a copy within 12 months of the search date.

The constable may search a vehicle for a stolen article. The question arises as to the position if the vehicle itself is stolen or taken without consent. It is difficult to argue that he can search a vehicle for the vehicle itself. If, in the course of a search, the constable discovers an article which he has reasonable grounds for considering to be a stolen or prohibited article, he may seize it. This may allow him to seize a car if he has reasonable grounds for considering it to be stolen, but not normally if merely taken without consent. He would, however, have a power of arrest in any event and it is submitted that this would give him certain rights and responsibilities regarding property in the arrested person's possession (see *Liepens v Spearman* [1986] R.T.R. 24).

Arrest

15.35   Section 24 of the Police and Criminal Evidence Act 1984 enables a constable to arrest without warrant anyone who is committing, or is about to commit, an offence of whatever kind, or whom the constable reasonably suspects to be committing, or about to commit an offence.

Penalties generally

15.36   A person found guilty of a s.1 offence by, or who indicates a plea of guilty to such an offence before, magistrates may be committed to the Crown Court for heavier sentence under s.3 of the Powers of Criminal Courts (Sentencing) Act 2000 (hereafter referred to as "the 2000 Sentencing Act"). Magistrates should not order disqualification and endorsement before committing for sentence (see the 2000 Sentencing Act ss.6, 7) but leave that to the Crown Court; they may order an interim disqualification (see §§ 20.79).

If under the age of 18, an offender under s.12(1) may be sentenced to a detention and training order (15 to 17 years old; 12 to 14 years old if a persistent offender) or community punishment (16 years old if a community punishment scheme is in operation in the area) by a youth court. When the relevant provisions of the Criminal Justice and Immigration Act 2008 are in force (at the time of writing (March 2009) anticipated as autumn 2009) the current various community penalties will be replaced by a single generic order, the youth rehabilitation order. If convicted by a magistrates' court an offender must be remitted to the youth court for sentence if this is thought appropriate; this applies if he was under 18 at the time proceedings were commenced (see § 2.20), even if he has subsequently attained that age; if he has attained the age of 18, magistrates may sentence him to detention in a young offender institution. A referral order is available in the adult and youth courts where a defendant under the age of 18 pleads guilty and has no previous convictions.

The Court of Appeal in *R. v Evans (Brandon)* [1996] R.T.R. 46 has provided   **15.37** some guidance on the subject of the appropriate level of sentencing for those involved in the "ringing" of motor cars by their theft, handling, disguising and subsequent disposal. A ringleader who pleaded not guilty to such sophisticated criminal activity might expect to receive a prison sentence of four to five years on conviction. For a "lieutenant", as the appellant in the instant case might appropriately have been described, a sentence of three years on a plea of not guilty might be appropriate. Allowing the appropriate discount for a guilty plea, the sentence of three years which the appellant had received was quashed and a sentence of 27 months was substituted.

On August 4, 2008, new Magistrates' Courts Sentencing Guidelines became effective, see Appendix 3 below. The guideline for taking a vehicle without consent sets out three levels of seriousness, all of which have a community order as the starting point. New guidelines for theft and burglary (other than burglary in a dwelling) took effect for offences sentenced on or after January 5, 2009. Although there is no offence guideline specific to motor vehicles, the general principles of assessing seriousness are nevertheless relevant in such cases.

Compensation may be ordered, on conviction of any offence in respect of   **15.38** personal injury, loss or damage resulting from that offence, of up to £5,000 if convicted by magistrates or of an unlimited amount if convicted on indictment (2000 Sentencing Act s.130). The court is required to have regard to an offender's means, so far as they are known, in fixing the amount of compensation (s.130(11)). No application by or on behalf of the loser is necessary. When making an order the court is to give preference to compensation over a fine although it may impose a fine as well. Compensation is to be of such an amount as the court considers appropriate, having regard to any evidence and to any representations that are made by or on behalf of the accused or the prosecution. The court must also give reasons when not making a compensation order in a case where it is empowered to do so (s.130(3)).

Courts are now empowered by virtue of s.130(6) of the 2000 Sentencing Act to make compensation orders in respect of injury, loss or damage due to an accident arising out of the presence of a motor vehicle on a road, where either:

    (a) the damage is treated as having resulted from an offence under the Theft Act 1968; or

    (b) the injury, loss or damage involves the uninsured use of a motor vehicle by the offender, and compensation is not payable under any arrangements to which the Secretary of State is a party (i.e. the Motor Insurers' Bureau);

and the amount of compensation to be ordered may include an amount in respect of the loss of a "no claims" bonus. It should be noted that "payable" in this context means "liable to be paid at some time", not "immediately owing": *DPP v Scott* [1995] R.T.R. 40. Accordingly the justices were right in concluding that their powers were limited to making an order of £175 (the sum in respect of which compensation would never be paid by the Motor Insurers' Bureau—now a figure of £300) (see further § 10.86). *DPP v Scott* above was applied by the Court of Appeal in *R. v Austin* [1996] R.T.R. 414 when reducing to £175 an order for compensation totalling £3,642 made in the Crown Court in respect of damage inflicted upon a police car by an uninsured offender charged inter alia with aggravated vehicle-taking.

15.39   If the offence is under the Theft Act and the property is recovered any damage occurring to the property while out of the owner's possession shall be treated as resulting from the Theft Act offence no matter who caused the damage or how it occurred (s.130(5)). Thus if a person is convicted of stealing or taking a vehicle, driving it knowing it to have been taken, or allowing himself to be carried on or in it under the Theft Act and it is damaged, whether in a road accident or any other way, that person can be ordered to pay compensation for that damage. Since a person who steals a vehicle or takes one without consent is almost by definition uninsured, s.130(6)(b) would appear to allow courts to make compensation orders in respect of other damaged vehicles as well as the one unlawfully taken. Compensation may be awarded not only in respect of an offence for which the defendant is convicted but also an offence taken into consideration (in such a case a magistrates' court is still limited to a maximum sum of £5,000 for each offence for which the offender is *convicted* (see further §§ 18.26 et seq.).

15.40   In *R. v Donovan* [1982] R.T.R. 126 the defendant hired a car for two days but kept it for some two and a half months. He was ordered to pay £1,388 compensation based on loss of use. The compensation order was quashed by the Court of Appeal. Eveleigh L.J. said that:

> "The amount of such damages is notoriously open to argument, and this case is therefore not one of the kind for which a compensation order is designed. A compensation order is designed for the simple, straightforward case where the amount of the compensation can be readily and easily ascertained."

More recently it is possible to detect a greater willingness to order compensation even when the exact amount may not be easy to quantify. The Magistrates' Court Sentencing Guidelines say that "in cases where it is difficult to ascertain the full amount of the loss suffered by the victim, consideration should be given to making a compensation order for an amount representing the agreed or likely loss" (Magistrates' Court Sentencing Guidelines, p.165 at *http://www.sentencing-guidelines.gov.uk* [Accessed April 8, 2009]).

Endorsement and disqualification

15.41   Offences under s.1 or s.12 are subject to discretionary disqualification but are not endorsable with penalty points. These provisions apply to anyone convicted under s.1 or s.12 as well as to drivers, provided in all cases the offence was in respect of a motor vehicle. It is appropriate to disqualify the passenger as well as the driver in a joint venture (*R. v Reed* [1975] R.T.R. 313; *R. v Saunders* [1975] R.T.R. 315). It was said by the Court of Appeal in *R. v Earle* [1976] R.T.R. 33 at

36E, that the object of giving a court the discretionary power of disqualification for taking vehicles without consent was to ensure that vehicles may not be used for criminal offences. One other reason might be to punish joyriders. In *R. v Callister* (1992) 156 J.P. 893 it was held that the punishment of disqualification should generally be restricted to cases involving bad driving, persistent motoring offences or the use of vehicles for the purposes of crime.

It seems that a person convicted of burglary or robbery involving theft of a motor vehicle is liable to discretionary disqualification. Column 1 of Sch.2 Pt II to the 1988 Offenders Act does not specify a section of the Theft Act and refers simply to "stealing or attempting to steal". Contrast ibid., the references in column 1 to offences contrary to ss.12 and 25 of the Theft Act.

Scotland

The punishment under s.178 of the 1988 Act is three months' imprisonment or   **15.42**
a fine of £5,000 on summary conviction, or both. On indictment the maximum is an unlimited fine or 12 months' imprisonment or both. The offence or attempted offence under s.178 carries discretionary disqualification but is not endorsable with penalty points.

For a table of penalties for offences contrary to ss.1 and 12, see § 15.56.

AGGRAVATED VEHICLE-TAKING

The offence (s.12A)

The Aggravated Vehicle-Taking Act 1992 inserted a new section (s.12A) into   **15.43**
the Theft Act 1968 in order to create an aggravated form of the offence of taking, etc., a conveyance without consent. It should be noted at the outset, however, that it applies only to mechanically propelled vehicles and not to conveyances generally. "Aggravated vehicle-taking" is defined by s.12A(1) as the commission of an offence under s.12(1) in relation to a mechanically propelled vehicle (the "basic offence"; see §§ 15.02–09 above) where, after its taking but before its recovery, the vehicle is driven, or injury or damage is caused, in certain specified circumstances. Those circumstances are:

(a) that the vehicle was driven dangerously on a road or other public place;

(b) that an accident occurred (owing to the driving of the vehicle) by which injury was caused to any person or damage was caused to any property (other than the vehicle); or

(c) damage was caused to the vehicle (s.12A(2)).

The words "owing to the driving of the vehicle, an accident occurred by which   **15.44**
injury was caused to any person" in s.12A(2)(b) of the Theft Act 1968 do not import a requirement of fault in the driving of the vehicle. The Court of Appeal so held in *R. v Marsh (William)* [1997] R.T.R. 195 when dismissing an appeal against conviction of a s.12A offence, a guilty plea having been entered at the Crown Court following a preliminary ruling on a point of law. The accident in question had involved injury to a pedestrian, but the Crown had not relied on any evidence of fault in the appellant's driving. In the court's view the ordinary meaning of the words in s.12A(2)(b) was simple and pointed to a requirement of a causal connection between the driven vehicle and the accident. No word suggest-

ing fault appeared. Accordingly the judge had construed the subsection correctly. Although s.12A(2)(c) of the 1968 Act was not adverted to by the court, its wording is materially identical ("owing to the driving of the vehicle, an accident occurred by which damage was caused ...") and it is submitted that the decision in *Marsh* is of equal application to that subsection. It will be a defence to such a charge for the defendant to prove (presumably on the balance of probabilities) that the driving, accident or damage referred to in the charge occurred before the basic offence of taking without consent was committed, or that he was neither in the vehicle nor in its immediate vicinity when the driving, accident or damage took place (s.12A(3)).

15.45   It would appear from the above that any person who commits the "basic offence" (whether as driver or passenger) is liable to be convicted of an aggravated offence where, following the taking of the vehicle (whether by that person or another) and before its recovery, any of the aggravating circumstances listed above occurs and the second limb of the s.12A(3) defence cannot be established. It should be noted that the aggravating circumstances are not of themselves offences which need to be proved against individual defendants; nor is it necessary for the prosecution to establish that any particular defendant was directly responsible for the aggravation concerned. It is to be presumed, however, that it is incumbent upon the prosecution to prove beyond reasonable doubt that the necessary aggravating circumstances were present, e.g. that the vehicle was driven dangerously or that an injury-causing accident occurred.

An offender was arrested when he was detained by automatic activation of the door locks inside a motor vehicle specially adapted by the police as a trap. In attempting to escape from his lawful arrest the offender caused damage to the vehicle. The Divisional Court held in *Dawes v DPP* [1994] R.T.R. 209, when dismissing his appeal against conviction of an offence of aggravated vehicle-taking, that the provisions of s.12A were onerous. There was a high degree of liability on those who took motor vehicles. In s.12A(2)(d) damage done to a vehicle was left unqualified. For the purposes of that subsection it was sufficient that damage had been done to the vehicle in the escape attempt before the vehicle was retrieved by the police.

15.46   For the purposes of s.12A, dangerous driving is defined in the same language as is used in the Road Traffic Act 1988, as amended by the 1991 Act (s.12A(7); see § 5.04).

Section 12A does not apply to offences committed, or driving, injury or damage occurring, before April 1, 1992.

AGGRAVATED VEHICLE-TAKING: PROCEEDINGS AND PENALTIES

15.47   Offences under s.12A are generally triable "either way" and therefore subject to the "plea before venue" procedure (see Chapter 2); where, however, the only aggravating element is damage to the vehicle and/or other property, the offence is triable only summarily if the value of the damage does not exceed the relevant sum under s.22 of the Magistrates' Courts Act 1980 (see § 15.72). There is no power for magistrates in such a case to commit an offender to the Crown Court for heavier sentence (*R. v Kelly* [2001] R.T.R. 45). In the case of damage to the vehicle involved in the offence, the calculation of the value of that damage is based upon the market cost of repair or the market value of the vehicle before it was unlawfully taken, whichever is the less, or, where the vehicle is beyond repair, its market value before its unlawful taking (s.2).

The driver and passenger of a motor vehicle which had been taken without consent, who were charged in separate informations with aggravated vehicle-taking, were to be regarded as jointly charged; accordingly a passenger who was under the age of 18 could be committed for trial to the Crown Court with the adult driver (*R. v Peterborough JJ. Ex p. Allgood* [1996] R.T.R. 26) (see Chapter 2).

A person found not guilty of a s.12A offence may (in appropriate circum-**15.48** stances) be convicted of an offence under s.12(1) (the "basic offence") (s.12A(5)). If the convicting court is the Crown Court, that court has the same powers and duties as a magistrates' court would have had on convicting him of such an offence (s.12A(6)).

It was confirmed in *R. (on the application of H) v Liverpool City Youth Court* [2001] Crim. L.R. 487 that the power to convict of an offence under s.12(1) as an alternative to an offence under s.12A is fully exercisable by magistrates' courts as well as the Crown Court. There was nothing in s.12A(5) to indicate that it did not apply to magistrates' courts. The only purpose of s.12A(6) was to prevent the Crown Court from having larger powers in relation to sentencing than those possessed by a magistrates' court. The application for judicial review of a stipendiary magistrate's decision to continue with a trial of the lesser offence, following acceptance by him of a submission of no case to answer in respect of the aggravated offence, was accordingly dismissed.

Offences under s.12A are punishable on conviction on indictment by up to two **15.49** years' imprisonment; where, however, the aggravation relates to an injury caused to any person as a result of an accident and the accident causes the death of that person, the maximum penalty rises to 14 years' imprisonment (s.12A(4), as amended by the Criminal Justice Act 2003 s.285). The Court of Appeal in *R. v Sherwood; R. v Button* [1995] R.T.R. 60 has held, applying the reasoning adopted by the House of Lords in *R. v Courtie* [1984] A.C. 463 (see § 6.238), that s.12A creates two offences: one with a maximum penalty of two years' imprisonment and a second more serious one, if the facts under s.12A(2)(b) (see § 15.43 above) are proved and death results, where the maximum is (now) 14 years. It is essential that the indictment makes clear, by setting out in short form the facts which constitute its necessary ingredients, which offence it is that is being charged. The indictment in the case in point referred only to the dangerous driving element of a s.12A offence, and made no reference to death which had occurred or its causation; in those circumstances it was not open to the judge to pass the sentence of three years' imprisonment, richly deserved though it was.

Section 12A offences are subject to obligatory disqualification (minimum 12 months) and endorsement with 3–11 penalty points where, for special reasons, disqualification is not imposed (see Chapter 21). Where a person is convicted of a s.12A offence, the fact that he did not himself drive the vehicle in question cannot amount to a special reason for him not to be disqualified (1988 Offenders Act s.34(1A)). As with the basic offence under s.12(1), both passengers and driver are equally liable.

It should be noted that ss.224–236 of the Criminal Justice Act 2003, with effect **15.50** from April 4, 2005, establish a new regime for dealing with what the Act describes as "dangerous offenders". Significant changes in the law relating to dangerousness were introduced by the Criminal Justice and Immigration Act 2008, which apply to everyone sentenced under these provisions on or after July 14, 2008. The Sentencing Guidelines Council has published a supplement to its Sentencing Guidelines Compendium which seeks to describe the law as it currently stands and to apply the judgments to those provisions as appropriate (*Dangerous Offenders: Guide for Sentencers and Practitioners*, available at *http://www.sentencing-guidelines.gov.uk* [Accessed April 8, 2009]). Caution should be applied to cases sentenced before July 14, 2008, as they may fall to be sentenced differently now the changes have taken effect. A person aged 18 or over convicted of a serious specified offence, which category includes aggravated vehicle-taking involving an accident which caused the death of any person, is liable, if certain conditions are satisfied, to a mandatory indeterminate sentence for public protection (please see further Chapter 18).

Sentencing guidelines

15.51   The Court of Appeal (Lord Taylor C.J. presiding) availed itself of an early opportunity to provide some guidance for sentencers in the case of *R. v Bird (Simon)* [1993] R.T.R. 1 (also reported as *R. v Bird* at [1993] Crim. L.R. 85). In judging the gravity of a case of aggravated vehicle-taking, the most important of the statutory circumstances set out in s.12A(2) was the circumstance that the vehicle was driven dangerously on a road or other public place because that concerned the culpability of the driver, whereas the other circumstances were, to some extent, matters of chance. Despite that, however, the higher maximum sentence where death was involved showed that the extent of the physical harm done was an aggravating factor, if only to reflect public reaction to maiming or death caused by bad driving.

In general terms, aggravating features of the offence would be primarily the overall culpability of the driving: how bad and how long, and to a lesser extent, how much injury and/or damage was caused. Where drink was involved, no doubt that would affect the dangerousness of the driving. If drink was a major factor, it would often be the subject of a separate charge.

15.52   As in other cases, a guilty plea showing contrition would be a mitigating feature. The youth of a defendant, however, would be less significant in mitigation than in other cases because s.12A was aimed primarily at young offenders, amongst whom such activity had become so prevalent.

In the case in point the appellant's driving had been appallingly dangerous for 18 miles. Apart from the high speed at which the car had been driven, there were numerous and varied incidents of dangerous driving, such as going through red lights and driving on the wrong side of the road at or in close proximity to a chasing police car (which was damaged, and the police officer in it injured). The injury to the police officer was minor but the driving could well have resulted in much more serious injury, not only to the officer but at any time during the 18 miles of the car's erratic course. As the law stood at the time the sentence was passed, 15 months' detention in a young offender institution was in no way excessive. The powers of the court, however, had been cut down by s.63(4) of the Criminal Justice Act 1991, which came into force on October 1, 1992. Had that Act applied, the maximum sentence on the appellant (who was aged 17) would have been 12 months. Solely in those circumstances, the sentence would be reduced to 12 months. (It may be noted here in passing that a single new custodial sentence for 12–17-year-olds, namely the detention and training order, is now in operation and that the maximum sentence under such an order is 24 months; see further Chapter 18.)

The Court of Appeal in *R. v Ore and Tandy* [1994] Crim. L.R. 304 has also **15.53** provided specific guidance in sentencing both driver and passenger offenders convicted of aggravated vehicle-taking where death has been caused. The defendant driver lost control of the car during a race with another car, hit a parked car and veered onto the pavement, striking and killing a boy who was walking there. Each defendant was sentenced to four years' detention in a young offender institution. Upholding the sentences, the court pointed out that the essence of the offence of aggravated vehicle-taking was the occurrence of dangerous driving or injury to others, or the other specified matters set out in s.12A(2), when a vehicle had been taken unlawfully. Driving and being carried in the vehicle were comparably criminal acts; the offence pays regard to the effect on others, rather than to who was actually at the wheel. On the facts of the case, both defendants were equally guilty. The maximum sentence for the offence had been fixed at five years for the very worst cases. The sentence must obviously stay within the bounds set by the legislature, but how far within those bounds was not to be determined in every case by simply discounting from the maximum in order to leave room for still worse cases. If the sentences of four years served to deter one young person from a similar escapade, and protected one other person from death or maiming, they would have served their purpose.

The Court of Appeal in *R. v Woolley* [2005] EWCA Crim 2853 endorsed submissions of counsel for the appellant to the effect that there were seven different ways in which the offence of aggravated vehicle-taking resulting in death could be committed. They were, in descending order of gravity:

(1) Where the offender is driving and death results from persistent dangerous driving.

(2) Where persistent dangerous driving causes the death but the deceased was a passenger in the vehicle and was encouraging the driver in driving dangerously.

(3) Where the offender is a passenger in such a dangerously driven vehicle, but is either neutral as to the manner of driving, or seeks to discourage bad driving.

(4) Where there is careless driving by an offender which causes death.

(5) Where there is careless driving causing death when the offender was a passenger rather than the driver.

(6) Where the offender, albeit the driver, did not drive dangerously so as to cause the death.

(7) Where the offender was a passenger in a vehicle where the driver was not driving dangerously so as to cause the death.

Whilst the court did not say that the ways were necessarily limited to the seven identified above, it did accept that the most significant feature in relation to sentence is usually likely to be the degree of culpability of the driving of the offender.

A 43-year-old man of good character and with a clean driving record drove a **15.54** car which he was not permitted to drive (holding only a provisional licence) and whilst driving (not dangerously and below the speed limit) hit and killed a seven-year-old boy who had stepped into the road. The victim could not have been seen by the offender, whose driving did not contribute to or cause the accident and who would in any event have been unable to avoid him. The defendant pleaded guilty and showed deep remorse. Although the maximum sentence for causing death by aggravated vehicle-taking has now been increased from five years' imprisonment to 14, none of the frequently occurring aggravating factors was present, and there was significant mitigation. In the circumstances a sentence of six months' imprisonment was held to be appropriate (*R. v Clifford* [2007] EWCA Crim 2442; [2008] 1 Cr. App. R. (S) 100). Note that it is likely that in future a case on these facts would be charged as causing death by driving: unlicensed, disqualified or uninsured drivers for which there is a Sentencing Guidelines Council guideline (see Appendix 4 below). *R. v Kirby* [2007] EWCA Crim 3410; [2008] 2 Cr. App. R. (S.) 46 is an example of a defendant being entitled to a discount for pleading guilty, even where the case (aggravated vehicle-taking, dangerous driving, driving while disqualified) could hardly have been more serious, and even where the prosecution case was overwhelming. (Two years' imprisonment reduced to 22 months by the Court of Appeal.)

Some helpful general hints on the approach to be adopted with regard to the sentencing of drivers and passengers convicted of s.12A offences have been provided by the Court of Appeal in cases dealing with the problems of disparity, both apparent and real. In *R. v Harper* [1995] R.T.R. 340 it was stated that, all other things being equal, a passenger in a case of aggravated vehicle-taking could ordinarily expect to receive a lesser sentence than the driver. Similarly in *R. v Gostkowski* [1995] R.T.R. 324 it was held so far as disqualification was concerned that the disqualification imposed on the passenger ought to have been something in the order of half the disqualification imposed upon the driver. In *R. v Wiggins* [2001] R.T.R. 3, following *Harper* and *Gostkowski* above, both a sentence of imprisonment and a disqualification were reduced for a passenger who had no convictions for bad driving (*sic*) and who had made attempts to prevent the co-accused driving in the manner complained of.

15.55   On August 4, 2008, new Magistrates' Court Sentencing Guidelines became effective (see Appendix 3 below). The guideline where damage is caused to property other than the vehicle in accident or damage caused to the vehicle sets out three levels of seriousness, depending on the nature of the taking and the degree of damage (p.1228 below). The guideline where there is driving or accident causing injury also has three levels of seriousness, but it varies with the nature of the bad driving (see p.1229 below).

Theft, taking conveyances and aggravated vehicle-taking: penalties

Offence	Mode of trial	Section *	Imprisonment	Level of fine	Disqualification	Penalty points	Endorsement code	Sentencing guideline
Theft or attempted theft of motor vehicle	a) On indictment	s.1	7 years or unlimited fine or both		Discretionary	—	UT20	—
	b) Summary	s.1	6 months or level 5 or both		Discretionary	—	UT20	—
Taking, etc., motor vehicle without consent	Summary	s.12(1)	6 months or level 5 or both		Discretionary	—	UT40	See Appendix 3
Driving, etc., or allowing oneself to be carried in taken vehicle	Summary	s.12(1)	6 months or level 5 or both		Discretionary	—	UT40	—
Aggravated vehicle-taking	a) On indictment	s.12A	2 years (14 if death caused) or unlimited fine, or both		Obligatory	3–11†	UT50	See Appendix 3
	b) Summary	s.12A	6 months or level 5 or both		Obligatory	3–11†	UT50	See Appendix 3
Taking pedal cycle without consent	Summary	s.12(5)	—	3	—	—	—	—
Going equipped to steal or take a motor vehicle	a) On indictment	s.25	3 years or unlimited fine or both		Discretionary	—	UT30	—
	b) Summary	s.25	6 months or level 5 or both		Discretionary	—	UT30	—

* Theft Act 1968.

† No points may be imposed when offender is disqualified.

OTHER RELATED OFFENCES

Interfering with vehicles

15.57   Where a potential offender is caught before he has done anything amounting to the complete offence or an attempt under s.1 or s.12 of the Theft Act 1968, he may be charged with interfering with a vehicle contrary to s.9 of the Criminal Attempts Act 1981. A person commits the offence if he interferes with a motor vehicle or trailer or with anything carried in or on a motor vehicle or trailer with the intention to commit, by himself or some other person, the offence of:

"(a) theft of the motor vehicle or trailer or part of it;

(b) theft of anything carried in or on the motor vehicle or trailer; [or]

(c) an offence under s.12(1) … (taking and driving away without consent)."

The reference to taking and driving away is a strange reference to the law before it was changed by the Theft Act 1968. Presumably it is a general reference to s.12(1) offences and the obsolete reference is therefore immaterial. The concept of "taking and driving away" still applies in Scotland (see § 15.03) but the 1981 Act (apart from a minor reference to service personnel) does not apply to Scotland. Presumably the reference to s.12(1) therefore includes the offences of driving or allowing oneself to be carried, etc. Unlike s.12(1) in offence (c) above, s.1 is not specified in offence (a) or (b). By reason of the wording of s.9 of the 1981 Act, "theft" will seemingly include burglary and robbery.

15.58   The offence does not apply to s.12(5) (pedal cycles). Nor does it apply to other forms of conveyance such as a yacht, whereas s.12(1) does. As to the nature of a pedal cycle see § 1.22 and §§ 15.12–14. An electrically assisted pedal cycle is not a motor vehicle under the 1988 Act (see Chapter 1) and is therefore not a motor vehicle for the purposes of s.9(2)(a) or (b). It might be a trailer although this is unlikely. Other auto-assisted cycles are motor vehicles and therefore within s.9(2)(a) and (b), but as noted at §§ 15.12–14 all pedal cycles are not within s.12(1) and therefore not within s.9(2)(c).

If it is shown that a person intended that one of the specified offences should be committed, it is immaterial that it cannot be shown which it was (s.9(2)). It is not therefore necessary for the prosecutor to select which specified offence providing he alleges the intention that an offence specified in s.9(2) shall be committed. Nevertheless, it is submitted that if the prosecutor does select, and if both the prosecutor and the defendant base their cases on that selection, it may be wrong to convict on a completely different basis. Up to a point it may be possible to amend (see § 2.80).

15.59   "Motor vehicle" and "trailer", by s.9(5), have the meanings assigned to them by s.185(1) of the 1988 Act (see Chapter 1). "Trailer" under s.185(1) means a vehicle drawn by a motor vehicle. It is doubtful whether a trailer can be said to be so "drawn" if it has been detached, particularly if the detachment is for a substantial period of time. It is submitted therefore that the offence is not committed where the trailer has been detached and left for unloading, e.g. in a dock or factory yard. A poultry shed can be a trailer and an office hut also (*Garner v Burr*, *Horn v Dobson*, both noted § 1.57), but it is hardly likely that this offence extends to interfering with a poultry shed in the middle of a field in order to steal the chickens in the shed.

The offence extends to interfering with anything carried in or on the motor vehicle or trailer. The intent to commit the specified offence must, however, still be established (s.9(1)). This includes the theft of the "motor vehicle or trailer or part of it". It is not clear whether "part of it" refers to part of the motor vehicle as well as part of the trailer but it is submitted that it does (e.g. the theft of a car wheel). It also includes the theft of anything carried in or on the motor vehicle or trailer.

Merely looking into vehicles is not interfering with them (*Reynolds and Warren v Metropolitan Police* [1982] Crim. L.R. 831). It clearly may be supportive evidence if there is evidence of interference. It was said in the same case that merely touching car door handles did not amount to interference. It might have been different if the defendants had been seen to apply pressure. The decision was that of a Crown Court hearing an appeal from Acton Magistrates' Court. The decision is not satisfactory, in that the members of the court seem to have had different reasons for acquittal, and is not binding. The commentary in the *Criminal Law Review* is rightly critical and it is submitted that touching car doors in this way is capable of constituting interference. **15.60**

While in many cases it will be desirable for the prosecution to show more than one act of interference, a single act seems sufficient in law under s.9.

The maximum penalty for an offence against s.9 is a fine of level 4 or three months' imprisonment or both. It is triable only summarily. There is no power to order disqualification or endorsement or penalty points. **15.61**

Tampering with vehicles; getting on vehicles

Where a potential offender is caught before he has done anything amounting to the complete offence or an attempt under s.1 or s.12 of the Theft Act 1968 and a charge of interference cannot be established or is not thought appropriate, he may instead, if the facts warrant, be charged under s.25 of the 1988 Act with getting on a motor vehicle or tampering with the brake or other part of its mechanism without lawful authority or reasonable cause. It is submitted that, as the brake alone is mentioned and no other category of equipment, the ejusdem generis rule is excluded and "other part of its mechanism" includes parts nothing to do with the brakes. This offence arises only if the vehicle is on a road or on a parking place *provided by a local authority*. It is submitted that the term "local authority" includes parish councils as well as county and district councils and London boroughs (cf. Local Government Act 1972 s.270). It seems that it need not be a parking place open to the public; if a local authority provides a parking place for its employees' cars, that is within s.25. Car parks provided by government departments and public utility boards are not within s.25. **15.62**

It is also an offence under s.26 of the 1988 Act for a person otherwise than with lawful authority or with reasonable cause to take or retain hold of or get on to a motor vehicle or trailer while in motion on a road for the purpose of being carried. An offence can only be committed under s.26 if the person got on or took or retained hold of the vehicle while it was in motion on a road. If it was stationary and a motor vehicle, he may be charged under s.25, if appropriate. Section 25 refers only to motor vehicles, not trailers. Section 26(1) and (2) refer to trailers as well. The trailer must be drawn by a motor vehicle (1988 Act s.185(1)). "For the purpose of being carried" (s.26(1)) should be compared with the offence in s.26(2) of taking or retaining hold of a motor vehicle or trailer while in motion on a road "for the purpose of being drawn". There is no reference to lawful authority or reasonable cause in s.26(2).

15.63   The penalty under s.25 is a fine of level 3 and under s.26, a fine of level 1. Disqualification and endorsement may not be ordered for these offences.

Criminal damage

15.64   By s.1(1) of the Criminal Damage Act 1971 it is an offence either intentionally or recklessly to destroy or damage property and by s.1(2) it is an aggravated offence if there is an intention of endangering life or recklessness as to whether someone else's life would be endangered. By ss.28 and 30 of the Crime and Disorder Act 1998 an offence of criminal damage may be racially aggravated if motivated by racial hostility, or if racial hostility was demonstrated towards the victim either at the time of committing the offence, or immediately before or after committing it.

The offence under s.1(1) is committed if the defendant either had an intention to destroy or damage property or was reckless as to whether the property would be destroyed or damaged. It should be noted that the intention relates to the destruction or damage not of the particular property intended to be damaged but of any property belonging to another, and therefore the fact that the defendant may not have intended to damage or destroy the particular property that was in fact destroyed is not a defence. The prosecution only has to prove either an intention to destroy or damage property of another or that the defendant was reckless in that regard. As to proof of recklessness, see *Metropolitan Police Commissioner v Caldwell* (1981) 73 Cr. App. R. 13. The meaning of the first limb of the definition of recklessness used in the *Caldwell* case was further considered in *R. v Miller* [1983] 1 All E.R. 978, HL and *Elliott v C* [1983] 2 All E.R. 1005, CA. The "obvious risk" in the first limb means that the risk is one which must have been obvious to a reasonably prudent man and not necessarily to the particular defendant if he or she had given thought to it.

15.65   An attempt under the auspices of art.6 of the European Convention on Human Rights to impugn the decision in *Caldwell* as to the meaning of recklessness was rebuffed by the Court of Appeal in *R. v G and R*, *The Times*, August 1, 2002 on the basis that art.6 is concerned with the fairness of procedural law, not with the fairness of the substantive rules of criminal law.

It would seem from *R. v Smith (DR)* [1974] 1 All E.R. 632 that a person who honestly believes, whether it is a justifiable belief or not, that the property he damages is his own, cannot be convicted under the Criminal Damage Act 1971. But as long as it is property belonging to another, the identity of the person is irrelevant (*Pike v Morrison* [1981] Crim. L.R. 492).

"Property" includes any property of a tangible nature, real or personal (s.10), but not the flowers, fruit or foliage of a plant growing wild on any land.

Causing danger to road users

15.66   Although it was on the very fringes of its terms of reference, the Road Traffic Law Review (the North Report) addressed the serious problem of the danger caused to road users by obstructions put or thrown onto the roads which either hit vehicles or into which they ran. The Government of the day accepted the Review body's conclusion that there was a need (in England and Wales at least) for legislation to be introduced to make it a criminal offence intentionally to obstruct a road or interfere with devices for the regulation of traffic. Section 6 of the Road

Traffic Act 1991 created such an offence by inserting a new s.22A in the 1988 Act.

Section 22A(1) provides that a person is guilty of an offence if he intentionally and without lawful authority or reasonable cause:

> "(a) causes anything to be on or over a road, or
> (b) interferes with a motor vehicle, trailer or cycle, or
> (c) interferes (directly or indirectly) with traffic equipment,
>
> in such circumstances that it would be obvious to a reasonable person that to do so would be dangerous."

Section 22A(2) defines "dangerous" as referring to danger either of injury to **15.67** any person while on or near a road, or of serious damage to property on or near a road. It goes on to state that in determining what would be obvious to a reasonable person in a particular case, regard must be had not only to the circumstances of which that reasonable person could be expected to be aware but also to any circumstances shown to have been within the knowledge of the accused.

It should be noted at the outset that this offence can only be committed *intentionally*; recklessness (as in criminal damage) or negligence will not suffice. The intentional act or acts, however, must be committed in circumstances that would render the dangerousness of the act obvious to a reasonable person. The concept of the reasonable man is not exactly unfamiliar in the criminal law and ought not to cause undue difficulty. Although not necessarily a motorist, our reasonable man may be presumed to have some knowledge of the likely consequences of acts as various as causing traffic lights to work out of sequence by electrical or electronic interference or heaving blocks of concrete off motorway bridges onto vehicles travelling below.

Our contention that the "reasonable person" predicated by s.22A(1) of the **15.68** Road Traffic Act 1988 was not necessarily a motorist has received judicial endorsement. An offender had placed a metal road sign in one lane of a single carriageway road that was subject to a 50mph limit. Some time thereafter a car travelling at excessive speed had crashed into the sign, with fatal consequences for its occupants. Evidence was adduced at trial that the sign had been visible from up to 100m away, that the overall stopping distance for a car travelling at 70mph was 96m and that a number of other road users had passed the sign safely. The district judge held that in determining whether, for the purposes of s.22A(1), it would be obvious to a reasonable person that placing the sign in the road was dangerous, it was appropriate to consider whether danger would be obvious to a reasonable, prudent, straightforward and careful motorist driving at the correct speed. The Divisional Court held in *DPP v D* [2006] EWHC 314; [2006] R.T.R. 38 that this was the wrong approach. The appropriate test was not whether the danger would be obvious to a reasonable and prudent motorist driving at the correct speed but whether a reasonable bystander, whether he was a motorist or not, would consider that the act in question represented an obvious danger. A reasonable person would doubtless be aware that not all motorists drive carefully and well. A reasonable person should realise that the placing of a sign as in the instant case could cause an accident, notwithstanding that the primary factor of such an accident was excessive speed.

In assessing what "dangerous" means in s.22A(1) above, s.22A(2) sets out a test to be applied which essentially equates to the method of determining what is dangerous so far as the dangerous driving offences are concerned (see further Chapter 5). Thus the danger must be either of injury to a person or of serious damage to property; and the objective assessment of the obviousness of the danger may be coloured with subjectivity by matters shown to have been within the accused's actual knowledge.

It should be noted that the class of conveyance to be safeguarded from unlawful interference is a wide one, embracing as it does not only motor vehicles but also cycles and trailers (s.22A(1)(b)).

15.69   Section 22A(3) defines "traffic equipment" as anything lawfully placed on or near a road by a highway authority, or a lawfully placed traffic sign, or any fence, barrier or light lawfully placed on or near a road in pursuance of legislation providing for guarding, lighting and signing in connection with street works, or placed there by a constable or other person acting under the instructions of a chief police officer.

For the purposes of s.22A(3) anything placed on or near a road shall, in the absence of proof to the contrary, be deemed to have been lawfully placed there (s.22A(4)).

15.70   For the purposes of s.22A, "road" does not include a footpath or bridleway (s.22A(5)).

Section 22A does not extend to Scotland (s.22A(6)) (presumably because the Scottish common law offence of reckless conduct is deemed for the moment to be adequate to deal with such behaviour).

OTHER RELATED OFFENCES: PROCEEDINGS AND PENALTIES

Generally

15.71   For penalties for offences under s.9 of the Criminal Attempts Act 1981 and ss.25 and 26 of the 1988 Act, see §§ 15.56–61 and § 15.62–3 respectively.

As for s.1(1) and (2) of the Criminal Damage Act 1971, where there is a reliance in the alternative on specific intent and recklessness, it was said in *R. v Hardie* [1984] 3 All E.R. 848, CA, that the alternatives should be made the subject of separate counts for the jury. The extent to which this practice is applicable to magistrates' courts and is adopted there remains to be seen.

15.72   Subject to certain exceptions, if the amount of damage does not exceed £5,000, the offence under s.1(1) is triable only summarily and the penalty is a fine of level 4 and/or three months' imprisonment. If the amount of damage exceeds the relevant sum the offence is an "either way" offence and therefore subject to the "plea before venue" procedure. If the defendant indicates a guilty plea he loses his right to be tried at the Crown Court, although he may still be committed to that court for sentence. If he indicates a not guilty plea, or fails to indicate his plea, the established mode of trial procedure applies; the defendant must consent to any summary trial and accordingly may insist on trial by jury. If he consents to summary trial, he will be subject to a maximum penalty of £5,000 and/or six months' imprisonment. Where two or more such offences are charged and they appear to the court to be part of a series, any reference in s.22 of the Magistrates' Courts Act 1980 to the "value involved" shall be construed as a reference to the *aggregate* of the values involved. If the value of the damage cannot be ascertained, the offence remains an "either way" offence but if the defendant then indicates a guilty plea or consents to summary trial the penalty to which he is subject on summary conviction is the same as if it were a summary offence, i.e. level 4 and/or three months' imprisonment (Magistrates' Courts Act ss.22 and 33). However, when the criminal damage is by fire (arson) the offence is triable "either way" regardless of the value of the damage caused. The maximum penalty when tried summarily is a level 5 fine and/or six months' imprisonment. The maximum penalty when tried on indictment is life imprisonment. An offence of racially aggravated criminal damage is also triable "either way" regardless of the amount of the damage and the maximum penalty on summary conviction is a fine of £5,000 and/or six months' imprisonment (see further § 15.64).

Where a prosecuting authority was in difficulties establishing the value of damage caused by one of a number of defendants it was entitled to prove the minimum amount of damage caused (*R. v Salisbury JJ. Ex p. Mastin* [1986] Crim. L.R. 545). The facts of the case were unusual to say the least. A farmer's crop valued at £5,800 had been damaged by about 30 motor vehicles driven into a field. One of the vehicles was driven by the appellant. The prosecution had assessed the value of damage by measuring the distance between the stationary vehicles in the field and the point at which they had entered the field so that the minimum distance could be proved. On that basis the damage to the crops was calculated at between £16 and £117 per vehicle, and accordingly in the absence of a joint enterprise the right of trial by jury did not arise for any individual defendant.

There is also a right of election (subject to the "plea before venue" procedure described above) where, even if the value of the damage does not exceed the prescribed sum (*R. v St Helens JJ. Ex p. McClorie* (1983) 147 J.P. 456), the offence appears to the court to constitute or form part of a series of two or more offences of the same or similar character (Magistrates' Courts Act 1980 s.22(7)). There are a number of authorities as to the meaning of the words, not all of which are easy to reconcile. **15.73**

In *R. v Hatfield JJ. Ex p. Castle* [1980] 3 All E.R. 510 it was held that for offences to be of the same or similar character:

(a) they must bear a similarity of fact and law;

(b) one of the essential characteristics of similarity in law that must be present is that the other offence or offences are also triable "either way";

(c) the offences must form part of a series of two or more offences.

For a discussion of this and other cases, see the commentary at [1980] Crim. L.R. 580.

In *R. v Leicester JJ. Ex p. Lord* [1980] Crim. L.R. 581 it was held that, provided there was sufficient nexus, offences could be of the same or similar character even if under differing sections of different Acts. **15.74**

In *R. v Tottenham JJ. Ex p. Tibble* (1981) 145 J.P. 269 in the Divisional Court, Lord Lane C.J., resolved the dilemma after considering the various cases by following the decision in the *Hatfield* case. It is submitted therefore that principles (a), (b) and (c) above should be applied.

The mode of trial procedure for criminal damage is set out in ss.22 and 23 of the Magistrates' Courts Act 1980 and the penalties in ss.32 and 33. Schedule 2 to that Act applies the same principles to aiding, abetting, inciting and attempting. The penalties for offences of racially aggravated criminal damage are set out in **15.75** s.30 of the Crime and Disorder Act 1998; see further § 15.64. The Criminal Justice Act 1988 (Reviews of Sentencing) Order 2003 (SI 2003/2267) added (inter alia) the offence of racially aggravated criminal damage to the list of "either way" offences which may be referred to the Court of Appeal by the Attorney General in accordance with Pt IV of the Criminal Justice Act 1988 where he considers that a sentence imposed in the Crown Court was unduly lenient. The 2003 Order came into effect on October 13, 2003 and applies to sentences imposed on or after that date.

In *R. v Canterbury and St Augustine JJ. Ex p. Klisiak*; *R. v Ramsgate JJ. Ex p. Warren* [1981] 3 All E.R. 129 it was held that where a court was directed by s.22(1) to consider whether the value exceeded £400 (then the relevant sum) "having regard to any representations made by the prosecutor and the accused", "representations" meant something less than evidence. Justices could at their discretion hear evidence but were not bound to do so.

15.76   Even though justices are required to deal with the offence (unless racially aggravated; see § 15.72) as if it were a summary offence if the value does not exceed £5,000, it remains an indictable offence for other purposes.

The offence under s.1(2) (destroying or damaging property either intending another's life to be endangered or reckless in that regard) can only be tried on indictment, the maximum punishment being life imprisonment.

15.77   There is no power to order disqualification, endorsement or penalty points for either offence.

Under s.130 of the Powers of Criminal Courts (Sentencing) Act 2000 compensation up to £5,000 may be ordered to be paid by the defendant to the person whose property was damaged. The court has power to award compensation of its own motion under s.130 and its power to do so does not depend on an application by the loser. The court must also give reasons when not making a compensation order where it is empowered to do so (s.130(3)). Compensation is payable under the Act in respect of loss or damage due to an accident arising out of the presence of a motor vehicle on a road (s.130(6)) if it is as a result of an offence under the Theft Act 1968 or if the offender's use of a motor vehicle was uninsured and compensation is not payable by the Motor Insurers' Bureau (see §§ 18.26–30).

15.78   The offence of causing danger to road users is triable "either way" (see Chapter 2). It is subject when tried on indictment to a maximum penalty of seven years' imprisonment or a fine, or both. It is not subject to either endorsement or disqualification.

On August 4, 2008, new Magistrates' Court Sentencing Guidelines became effective (see Appendix 3 below). The guideline for vehicle interference specifies three levels of seriousness according to whether entry was gained to the vehicle, and whether damage was caused (see p.1225 below). The guideline for arson (criminal damage by fire) relates to the severity of the damage caused (see p. 1223 below). The guideline for criminal damage (other than by fire) includes five levels of seriousness depending on the nature and value of the damage (see p.1224 below).

Other related offences: penalties

Offence	Mode of trial	Section	Imprisonment	Level of fine	Disqualification	Penalty points	Endorsement code	Sentencing guideline
Interfering with vehicle	Summary	s.9 Criminal Attempts Act 1981	3 months or level 4 or both		—	—	—	See Appendix 3
Causing danger to road users	a) On indictment	s.22A RTA 1988	7 years or unlimited fine or both		—	—	—	—
	b) Summary	s.22A RTA 1988	6 months or level 5 or both					
Tampering with motor vehicles	Summary	s.25 RTA 1988	—	3	—	—	—	—
Getting onto or holding vehicle in motion in order to be carried	Summary	s.26 RTA 1988	—	1		—	—	—
Criminal damage value not exceeding £5,000 and otherwise triable summarily only	Summary	s.1(1) Criminal Damage Act 1971	3 months or level 4 or both		—	—	—	—

Offence	Mode of trial	Section	Imprisonment	Level of fine	Disqualification	Penalty points	Endorsement code	Sentencing guideline
Criminal damage triable "either way"	a) On indictment	s.1(1) Criminal Damage Act 1971	10 years* or unlimited fine or both (arson—life imprisonment)		—	—	—	—
	b) Summary	s.1(1) Criminal Damage Act 1971	6 months or level 5 or both		—	—	—	—

* 14 years if racially aggravated; see § 15.64.

CHAPTER 16

FORGERY, FRAUDULENT USE AND FALSE STATEMENTS

CONTENTS

Introduction

This chapter deals with forgery and fraudulent use under the Vehicle Excise   **16.01**
and Registration Act 1994 and with forgery and fraudulent applications under the
Road Traffic Act 1988.

FORGERY AND FRAUDULENT USE

Generally

It is an offence under s.44 of the Vehicle Excise and Registration Act 1994 for   **16.02**
a person to *forge* or *fraudulently* alter, use, lend or allow to be used a number
plate, trade plate, vehicle or trade licence or registration document. It is an "either
way" offence punishable summarily with a fine of £5,000, or on indictment with
an unlimited fine or two years' imprisonment or both. If the defendant indicates a
guilty plea before magistrates, he loses his right to be tried at the Crown Court,
although he may still be committed to that court for sentence. If he indicates a not
guilty plea, or fails to indicate his plea, the established mode of trial procedure
applies; the defendant must consent to any summary trial and accordingly may
insist on trial by jury. The Court of Appeal held in *R. v Johnson (Tony)* [1995]
R.T.R. 15 that exhibiting an altered vehicle excise licence on a vehicle parked on
private land could not amount to fraudulent use of the licence contrary to what is
now s.44 of the Vehicle Excise and Registration Act 1994. That offence could
only be committed where there was evidence that the vehicle was being or had
been used on a public road while displaying the offending licence. The intention
to use the vehicle in the future with that licence was not enough.

R. v Manners-Astley [1967] 3 All E.R. 899 and the other earlier cases about the
meaning of "fraudulently" were overturned by the House of Lords in *R. v Terry*
[1984] 1 All E.R. 65. It is not necessary for the prosecution to prove an intent to
avoid payment; it is sufficient to prove that the defendant's purpose was to deceive
a person responsible for a public duty and that the intended means of achieving
this purpose was dishonest.

The cases noted below on the meaning of "forge" are unaffected.   **16.03**

The word "forge" as it appears in s.44(1) is not there defined, but it is
comprehensively defined in s.1 of the Forgery and Counterfeiting Act 1981 as
"making a false instrument with the intent ... to induce somebody to accept it as

genuine and by reason of so accepting it to do or not to do some act to his own or any other person's prejudice". It will be noted that this differs from the simplified definition provided by s.12 of the same Act for what is now s.173(3) of the 1988 Act and s.65(3) of the Public Passenger Vehicles Act 1981. The position is further complicated by the gloss on the interpretation of s.1 of the Forgery and Counterfeiting Act 1981 in ss.8–10 of that Act. In *Clifford v Bloom* [1977] Crim. L.R. 485 "forge" within the meaning of what is now s.44 was considered. It was defined as the making of a false document or a mark on a number plate with the intention that it should be regarded as genuine. The defendant had altered the number plates from YYR 798H to YYR 798K. His conviction was upheld. Although the number plate did not tell a lie about itself, it could not be treated in isolation. For the purposes of what is now s.44 the mark, the plate to which it should be fixed and the motor vehicle were to be treated and regarded as a whole (ibid.).

16.04   *Clifford v Bloom* was followed in *R. v Clayton* (1980) 72 Cr. App. R. 135 where a disabled driver entitled to a vehicle licence exempt from duty altered his tax disc and number plates from GWK 923N to GWK 923R. His conviction under what is now s.44 of forging the tax disc was upheld; an intention to deceive was sufficient for the purposes of what is now s.44. The court made use of the definition of forgery in s.1 of the Forgery Act 1913 in reaching its decision. It was pointed out in the judgment that there was a tendency to approach these cases as if there was a hard and fast dividing line between intent to defraud and intent to deceive. The truth was that they overlapped and ran into each other. Section 44(1) refers separately to "forges" and "fraudulently".

The changed definition of forgery in s.1 of the Forgery and Counterfeiting Act 1981 received the scrutiny of, and was drawn upon by, the Court of Appeal in *R. v Macrae* [1994] Crim. L.R. 363. The defendant had displayed on June 4, a photocopied altered tax disc whilst his application for an excise licence was (genuinely) in the post. It was submitted on his behalf that he had no intention of passing off the photocopied disc as a tax disc, but did not want to draw attention to his car, having once been cautioned for putting "tax in the post" on his vehicles. It was submitted by the prosecution that although the car was taxed from June 1, the police had a duty to enforce the law and the defendant intended them to accept the licence as genuine and to act, or not to act, on that basis. The defendant was in the court's view rightly convicted, since the offence under what is now s.44 was committed if:

(a) he made a false licence;

(b) with the intent that he or another should use it to induce another (in this case the police) to accept it as genuine; and

(c) by reason of so accepting it to do or not to do some act to his own or another's prejudice as a result of such acceptance of the false licence as genuine in connection with the performance of any duty.

16.05   The term "licence" in the section is not defined but in *Taylor v Emerson* (1962) 106 S.J. 552 it was held to include an expired licence. Compare *Aziz v Knightsbridge Gaming and Catering Services and Supplies Ltd* (1982) 79 L.S. Gaz. 1412 where an instrument drawn on a fictitious bank was nevertheless held to be a cheque.

False declarations

16.06   It is an offence under s.45 of the Vehicle Excise and Registration Act 1994 if a person, in connection with an application for an excise licence, makes a declaration which to his knowledge is false or, in any material respect, misleading. It is an "either way" offence punishable summarily with a fine of £5,000, or on indictment with an unlimited fine or two years' imprisonment or both. If the defendant indicates a guilty plea before magistrates, he loses his right to be tried at the Crown Court, although he may still be committed to that court for sentence. If he indicates a not guilty plea, or fails to indicate his plea, the established mode of trial procedure applies; the defendant must consent to any summary trial and accordingly may insist on trial by jury.

The onus of proving the truth of his declaration is cast on the defendant by s.53 to the extent set out therein. As s.45 requires that the declaration be false or misleading "to the knowledge" of the declarant, such knowledge must be shown, subject to s.53, and it does not suffice to convict merely on proof of the falsity; *R. v Cummerson*, at § 16.13, is not applicable. A defendant who signed an application form completed by his daughter and failed to read it and thus notice that it contained a false declaration was not guilty of making a declaration which to his knowledge was false (*Bloomfield v Williams* [1970] Crim. L.R. 292). It was said obiter by Donaldson J. that if someone signs an application he impliedly says that he knows what is in the particulars and he must be guilty of making a declaration which to his knowledge is misleading (another offence under the subsection) if he has not bothered to check. With respect, it is submitted that "knowledge" is the same for the offence of making a false declaration as it is for making a declaration "in any material respect misleading". "Knowledge" in this context means either actual knowledge or second degree knowledge "where a man deliberately shuts his eyes to information which he fears will give him knowledge he does not wish to acquire" (per Devlin J. in *Roper v Taylor's Central Garages (Exeter) Ltd* [1951] 2 T.L.R. 284 at 288, referred to in *Bloomfield v Williams* [1970] Crim. L.R. 292).

16.07 The declaration on the application form in *Bloomfield v Williams* used words to the effect that "I declare that all the information I have given in this application is correct." The present declaration on the application form has been expanded and contains the words "I declare that I have checked the information given in this application and that to the best of my knowledge it is correct." With such a declaration the defendant in *Bloomfield* might well have been convicted.

Section 45 extends to applications for trade licences.

FORGERY AND FRAUDULENT APPLICATIONS

Generally

16.08 Sections 173, 174 and 175 of the 1988 Act respectively penalise a person who:

(1) with intent to deceive, forges or alters or uses or lends or allows the use of a document or thing or makes or has in his possession a document so closely resembling a certificate as to be calculated to deceive, or

(2) makes a false statement or withholds any material information for the purpose of obtaining such a certificate, or

(3) issues one knowing it to be false in a material particular.

Forgery

16.09   "Forges" in s.173 means making a false document or other thing in order that it may be used as genuine (s.173(3)).

Under ss.1 and 3 of the Forgery and Counterfeiting Act 1981 forgery carries no ingredient of dishonesty (*R. v Campbell (Mary)*, *The Times*, July 31, 1984; *Horsey v Hutchings*, *The Times*, November 8, 1984). The same would seem to be true for s.173. Compare the offence under s.65 of the Public Passenger Vehicles Act 1981 of forging, altering, using, etc., a PSV operator's disc with intent to deceive.

16.10   Section 173 applies to certificates of insurance, test certificates, plating certificates, certificates of conformity, driving test certificates, international road haulage permits, British international driving permits and other documents, which are set out or referred to in s.173(2).

Under s.173(1)(a) of the 1988 Act it is an offence for a person to use, with intent to deceive, a document to which the section applies. Alternatively it is an offence under s.173(1)(c) for a person with intent to deceive to have in his possession any document "... so closely resembling a document ..." to which the section applies as to be calculated to deceive. In *Holloway v Brown* [1978] R.T.R. 537 the defendant used a forged international permit and was convicted by justices of an offence under what is now s.173(1)(a). The conviction was set aside because, as the document was forged, it could not be said to be "a document ... to which this section applies". Per curiam, the justices could have convicted the defendant, applying s.123 of the Magistrates' Courts Act 1980, of an offence under what is now s.173(1)(c). *Holloway v Brown* was distinguished in *R. v Pilditch* [1981] R.T.R. 303. A Ministry of Transport test certificate form which had been stolen and which bore a false stamp and had been completed by someone other than an authorised vehicle examiner was nevertheless held to be a test certificate and therefore "a document ... to which this section applies". It was further held that the statute had to be construed so as to give a sensible and unstrained meaning to all the words, including the word "forges". In *Pilditch*, however, the document was nevertheless a true original and although the decision in *Holloway v Brown* may now be regarded as doubtful, it has still not been overruled. See also on this point the *Aziz* decision noted at § 16.05.

16.11   The case of *R. v Cleghorn* [1938] 3 All E.R. 398 is sometimes cited as showing that a certificate of insurance which was once valid but has ceased to be so because of the cancellation of a policy is a document so closely resembling a certificate as to be calculated to deceive. "Calculated to deceive" seems to mean "likely to deceive" as well as "intended to deceive" (82 J.P. Jo. 447, and see Stroud's *Judicial Dictionary*). In *R. v Davison* [1972] 1 W.L.R. 1540 "calculated to deceive" in the House to House Collections Act 1939 was held to mean "likely to deceive". This interpretative approach was bolstered by the Court of Appeal in *R. v Aworinde* [1996] R.T.R. 66, in which it was held that blank bogus certificates of insurance could constitute documents so closely resembling genuine insurance certificates as to be calculated to, in the sense of likely to, deceive in the terms of s.173(1) of the 1988 Act. In addition to a police officer who might have legitimate reason for examining certificates of insurance, such forms might well be likely to deceive anyone seeking insurance cover for a motor vehicle, and in that sense, if produced to such a person, would clearly be likely to deceive.

An expired certificate would still seem to be a certificate under s.173 (cf. *Taylor v Emerson* (1962) 106 S.J. 552). Under a similarly worded provision in another context, it was held that, on a charge of possessing documents resembling clothing coupons with intent to deceive, it sufficed if the prosecutor established the intent to deceive and he was not also put to proof that the defendant knew of the falsity of the documents (*R. v Greenberg* [1942] 2 All E.R. 344), but the defendant may set up the defence that he acted in good faith (*Brend v Wood* (1946) 110 J.P. 317).

False statements, etc.

The documents to which s.174 applies are set out in that section. **16.12**

The question was posed in (1976) 140 J.P. 270 whether a person may be convicted under what is now s.174 of making a false statement for the obtaining of a certificate of insurance, if, in answer of the question whether he has been convicted of an offence for which an order of endorsement has been made, he states that he has not been so convicted on the ground that the conviction has become "spent" as a result of the operation of the Rehabilitation of Offenders Act 1974. Whether an endorsement is a disability within the meaning of that Act is discussed in an article at (1980) 144 J.P. Jo 542. It was submitted in previous editions of this work that the opinion set out in (1976) 140 J.P. 270 was correct, namely an order of endorsement was a "disability" and thus only became "spent" when it might be lawfully removed from a driving licence (i.e. 4 or 11 years as the case might be). The Court of Appeal in *Power v Provincial Insurance plc* [1998] R.T.R. 60, however, held (by a majority) that an endorsement was not a "disqualification, disability, prohibition or other penalty" for the purposes of s.5(8) of the Rehabilitation of Offenders Act 1974; accordingly a motorist who had been fined and disqualified on July 30, 1986 for an offence of driving whilst unfit through drink or drugs was entitled to treat himself as a rehabilitated person when completing a proposal for insurance on September 5, 1991. The words "disability" and "prohibition" had been given too wide an interpretation by the judge in the court below by construing them as including an order for endorsement; further, although an endorsement constituted a threat of a future penalty and had unpleasant consequences for a motorist, it was no more than a record of the particulars of the conviction and was not a "penalty" within the meaning of the statute. The rehabilitation period in this case, therefore, was that which was appropriate to the fine and disqualification, namely five years, rather than the period of effectiveness of the endorsement as set out in s.45(5) of the Road Traffic Offenders Act 1988 (11 years: see § 19.47). Since there was no other disability, prohibition or penalty extending the rehabilitation period beyond five years, the conviction had become spent before the motorist completed the insurance proposal form, and he was entitled to answer "No", as he had done, to the question whether he had at any time been disqualified from driving for any motoring offence.

It is immaterial, in a charge under s.174 of making a false statement, that no **16.13** gain accrued to the defendant from it (*Jones v Meatyard* [1939] 1 All E.R. 140). The offence under s.174(5) of making a false statement for the purpose of obtaining the issue of a certificate of insurance is an absolute offence and consciousness by the defendant of the statement's falsity need not be shown, so long as it was false; the offence of withholding material information for the same purpose may, however, predicate a conscious withholding on his part (*R. v Cummerson* [1968] 2 All E.R. 863). It is doubtful how far, if at all, the Criminal Justice Act 1967, s.8 (proof of criminal intent) applies a subjective test as to what a defendant intended or foresaw in these cases.

A person who commonly uses a name other than his proper name may be guilty of an offence if in completing a proposal form for insurance he uses the adopted name and does not reveal his real one (*Clark v Chalmers* 1961 S.L.T. 325). It might be otherwise if he had lawfully changed his name (ibid.). On a charge against a car owner of making a false declaration that a car had not been used within a particular period, it was held not sufficient for the prosecutor to show that some unidentified person was seen to use it within the period and rely on the presumption that a car is being used by its owner (*Att Gen (Connor) v Shorten* (1959) 93 I.L.T.R. 168).

Issue of false documents

16.14   Section 175 applies to the documents referred to in that section.

On a charge under s.175 of issuing a certificate which is to the knowledge of the defendant false, the prosecutor must show not only that it was false but also that the defendant knew it to be so (*Ocean Accident, etc., Co v Cole* (1932) 96 J.P. 191).

Test certificates

16.15   Sections 173 and 175 (forging and issue of false documents) apply in respect of test certificates. In *R. v Pilditch*, § 16.10, a test certificate form which bore a false rubber stamp and the signature of a person who was not an authorised examiner was nevertheless held to be a test certificate. The material date for deciding if a test certificate is false in a material particular contrary to s.175 is the date of issue, even though the examination may have taken place earlier (*R. v Evans (No.2)* [1964] 3 All E.R. 666). A test certificate which has been backdated is false in a material particular (*Murphy v Griffiths* [1967] 1 All E.R. 424).

Under a s.175 prosecution it is necessary to prove that the defendant knew that the certificate was going to be issued false in a material particular. In *Essendon Engineering Co Ltd v Maile* [1982] R.T.R. 260, a certificate was issued by an employee while the sole director was away on holiday. The court reviewed the authorities on whether the knowledge of the employee could be imputed to the company—see further "Proof generally", § 3.82.

Driving licences

16.16   A false answer on the application form for a driving licence is an offence whether or not the question asked is intra vires (*Woodward v Dykes* (1968) 112 S.J. 787). These sections extend to badges of, and applications to become, approved driving instructors. Use of a licence with intent to deceive means use in connection with driving or attempted driving and not merely sending it for renewal (ibid.) but this decision of quarter sessions is respectfully doubted as putting too narrow a meaning of "use". For a case of conspiracy by impersonation at a driving test, see *R. v Potter* [1958] 2 All E.R. 51. The term "licence" would include an expired licence (*Taylor v Emerson* (1962) 106 S.J. 552) and possibly a forged licence—see the *Aziz* decision at § 16.05.

In *R. v Bogdal* [1982] R.T.R. 395 CA, it was held that there was insufficient nexus between a charge of using a driving licence with intent to deceive contrary to what is now s.173 and a dangerous driving charge committed on different occasions but in the same car. The two charges were in the circumstances not a "series of offences of a similar character" within the meaning of r.9 of the 1971 Indictment Rules. The deception charge evidence prejudiced the dangerous driving charge. The judge should have ordered the severance of the counts and the conviction for dangerous driving was quashed. In *Bogdal* the defendant had produced a driving licence to the police which he knew had been suspended under what is now s.27(3) of the 1988 Offenders Act pending its production for the court. The conviction for using a driving licence with intent to deceive was upheld.

PROCEEDINGS AND PENALTIES

Generally

Offences under s.173 are "either way" offences triable in accordance with **16.17** ss.18–23 of the Magistrates' Courts Act 1980, as amended by the Criminal Procedure and Investigations Act 1996 s.49. Offences under s.174 committed on or after January 29, 2004 are similarly triable "either way". If the defendant indicates a guilty plea before magistrates, he loses his right to be tried at the Crown Court, although he may still be committed to that court for sentence. If he indicates a not guilty plea, or fails to indicate his plea, the established mode of trial procedure applies; the defendant must consent to any summary trial and accordingly may insist on trial by jury.

An extended time-limit, i.e. within six months from the time when the offence came to the prosecutor's knowledge but not more than three years from its commission, is provided by the 1988 Offenders Act s.6 and Sch.1 for ss.174(1), (5) and 175. As a result of the coming into force of s.286 of the Criminal Justice Act 2003, however, offences under s.174 are now "either way" offences. There is no time-limit for "either way" offences (Magistrates' Courts Act 1980 s.127) and it would seem, therefore, that the provisions of s.6 of, and Sch.1, to the 1988 Offenders Act no longer apply to s.174 offences even though those provisions have not been repealed. The limit given in s.6 of the 1988 Offenders Act continues to apply to s.175 offences, but offences under ss.173 and 174 (in the latter case only if committed on or after January 29, 2004) are not time limited.

By s.176 power of seizure of documents contravening ss.173–175 is given to **16.18** the police.

A person convicted under s.173(1) by a magistrates' court may be committed for sentence if the magistrates' court considers its power of punishment is inadequate (see "Committals for sentence", § 2.177). As the offence cannot be punished summarily by imprisonment, it would seem that magistrates may commit him for sentence if they consider the offender should be sent to prison even for a short period or even where a suspended prison sentence, community service order or other order dependent on the power to imprison is considered appropriate. In *R. v Melbourne* [1980] Crim. L.R. 510 it was held that since the defendant had been convicted summarily of such an offence (an offence under the Trade Descriptions Act 1968 s.14 (since repealed)), he could not be said to have been convicted of an offence punishable with imprisonment as was required by (what are now) ss.119 and 120 of the Powers of Criminal Courts (Sentencing) Act 2000 (power to activate suspended sentences).

16.19   As a result of the coming into force of s.286 of the Criminal Justice Act 2003, offences under s.174 committed on or after January 29, 2004 are "either way" offences and persons convicted by magistrates may be committed to the Crown Court for sentence. Unlike s.173 offences, which are not imprisonable on summary conviction, offences under s.174(1) or (5) committed on or after January 29, 2004 are punishable on summary conviction with up to six months' imprisonment.

On August 4, 2008, new Magistrates' Court Sentencing Guidelines became effective (see Appendix 3 below). The guideline for vehicle licence/registration fraud has three levels of offence seriousness (see p.1226 below).

Forgery, fraudulent use and false statements: penalties

Offence	Mode of trial	Section	Imprisonment	Level of fine	Disqualification	Penalty points	Endorsement code	Sentencing guideline
Forgery or fraudulently altering, using, etc.	a) On indictment	s.44 Vehicle Excise and Registration Act 1994	2 years or unlimited fine or both		—	—	—	—
	b) Summary	s.44 Vehicle Excise and Registration Act 1994	—	5	—	—	—	See Appendix 3
False declaration, etc.	a) On indictment	s.45 Vehicle Excise and Registration Act 1994	2 years or unlimited fine or both		—	—	—	—
	b) Summary	s.45 Vehicle Excise and Registration Act 1994	—	5	—	—	—	—
Forgery, etc., of licences, test certificates, etc.	a) On indictment	s.173(1) RTA 1988	2 years or unlimited fine or both		—	—	—	—
	b) Summary	s.173(1) RTA 1988	—	5	—	—	—	—

Offence	Mode of trial	Section	Imprisonment	Level of fine	Disqualification	Penalty points	Endorsement code	Sentencing guideline
False statement, etc., offences	a) On indictment	s.174(1), (5) RTA 1988	2 years or unlimited fine or both		—	—	—	—
	b) Summary	s.174(1), (5) RTA 1988	6 months or level 5 fine or both		—	—	—	—
		s.174(2), (3), (4) RTA 1988	—	4	—	—	—	—

Chapter 17

FIXED PENALTIES

Contents

Introduction

The extended system of fixed penalties originally enacted as Pt III of the **17.01** Transport Act 1982 and now embodied in Pt III of the Road Traffic Offenders Act 1988 came into force in England and Wales on October 1, 1986 (SI 1986/1326). As will be seen from the detailed analysis of the system set out below, for the initiation of the procedure there is required either the physical presence of the driver to whom a notice may be handed, or the presence of a stationary vehicle to which a notice may be affixed. At the conclusion of the procedure an unpaid fixed penalty may be treated as though it were a fine imposed on conviction and collected under the normal court enforcement procedures. The motorist's lack of response to the notice(s) served upon him raises the presumption of his guilt. The end result of his inactivity will be what has been aptly described as a "conviction by inertia".

Those parts of Pt III of the Transport Act 1982 which related to Scotland were brought into force when the Procurator Fiscal and Fixed Penalty Scheme came into effect on June 30, 1983 and were subsequently re-enacted as ss.75–77 of the 1988 Offenders Act. Under those provisions procurators fiscal were empowered to send a "conditional offer" of a fixed penalty through the post to an alleged offender. Inertia by the recipient led not to the enforcement of the unpaid penalty as if it were a fine, but merely to the possibility of criminal proceedings in respect of the offence concerned.

The introduction by the Road Traffic Act 1991 of automatic devices for the **17.02** detection of speeding and traffic light offences (see Chapter 6) had implications for the fixed penalty system in England and Wales, in that the existing arrangements for endorsable offences such as those required the presence of the offender at the time at which the fixed penalty was imposed. Section 34 of the 1991 Act solved the problem by replacing ss.75–77 of the 1988 Offenders Act with three new sections which extended the "conditional offer" scheme throughout Great Britain. Under this scheme the police in England and Wales and Scotland (as well as procurators fiscal in Scotland) may send a notice offering a fixed penalty (the "conditional offer") to an alleged offender through the post.

Although the conditional offer scheme is designed to be available for all fixed penalty offences, it was anticipated that its use (initially at least) would be limited in England and Wales to offences detected by the new automatic devices. The Revised Home Office Fixed Penalty Notice Guidance issued in April 2006 encourages the greater use of the conditional offer scheme where a fixed penalty cannot be issued at the time of the offence. The guidance also allows for the issue of up to three fixed penalty notices per occasion, with the proviso that only one of those relates to an endorsable offence. The system is discussed in rather more detail at §§ 17.80–4.

17.03   A number of local authorities in England, Scotland and Wales took part in a pilot scheme under the auspices of the Road Traffic (Vehicle Emissions) (Fixed Penalties) Regulations 1997 (SI 1997/3058) which empowered them to issue fixed penalty notices to users of vehicles which produced unlawful emissions and to drivers of vehicles who left their engines running whilst stationary. Those 1997 Regulations have been revoked and replaced so far as England is concerned by the Road Traffic (Vehicle Emissions) (Fixed Penalty) (England) Regulations 2002 (SI 2002/1808), which came into force on July 18, 2002, and so far as Scotland and Wales are concerned by the Road Traffic (Vehicle Emissions) (Fixed Penalty) (Scotland) Regulations 2003 (SI 2003/212) and the Road Traffic (Vehicle Emissions) (Fixed Penalty) (Wales) Regulations 2003 (SI 2003/300), in force on March 21, 2003 and May 1, 2003 respectively. Under the 2002 Regulations a local authority in England may apply to the Secretary of State for designation. A local authority so designated may use fixed penalty notices to enforce offences of the kind described above within its area. The scheme and its operation is described in more detail at §§ 17.85 et seq.

With effect from March 31, 2009, s.5 of, and Sch.1 to the Road Safety Act 2006 amend Pt III of the 1988 Offenders Act to enable vehicle examiners to issue both fixed penalty notices and conditional offers. The system will operate along similar lines to the existing fixed penalty system, save that it will be administered by the Secretary of State through the medium of the Vehicle and Operator Services Agency (VOSA).

17.04   Section 11 of the 2006 Act (which came into force on January 5, 2009) inserts a new s.90A into the 1988 Offenders Act to give constables and vehicle examiners power to impose a requirement for the payment of a deposit (a "financial penalty deposit") by a person believed to have committed an offence in relation to a motor vehicle who does not provide a satisfactory address in the United Kingdom at which it is likely that he can be found. The deposit would be used to pay any uncontested fixed penalty notice or be offset against any fine imposed in subsequent court proceedings. In the event either of a court verdict of not guilty or the case not going to court within a year (or, if shorter, any period after which prosecution for the offence would be time barred), the deposit would be refunded, with interest. The powers conferred by these provisions are now exercisable by the Road Safety (Financial Penalty Deposit) Orders 2009 (SI 2009/491; SI 2009/492; SI 2009/498) which came into force on March 31, 2009. There are detailed tables setting out the amount of the deposit for fixed penalty offences with the amount varying according to the provision that creates the offence. A new s.90D enables the police or vehicle examiners to prohibit the moving of the vehicle if the deposit is not paid immediately. That prohibition will continue in force until the deposit or fixed penalty is paid, the driver is charged with the offence or informed he will not be prosecuted or payment is made, or the time-limit for prosecution is reached, whichever occurs first. Failure to comply with the prohibition will be a summary offence liable to a fine of level 5. Schedule 4 to the 2006 Act provides for the immobilisation, removal and disposal of prohibited vehicles. The powers conferred by this provision are now exercisable by the Road Safety (Immobilisation, Removal and Disposal of Vehicles) Order 2009 (SI 2009/493) which came into force on March 31, 2009.

The bulk of this chapter is devoted to the fixed penalty system which has operated in England and Wales since October 1, 1986 and which is contained in ss.51–74 and ss.78–90 of the 1988 Offenders Act. It may be assumed, unless the contrary is stated, that any references hereafter to the fixed penalty system will appertain to that system and to that jurisdiction. Where a section of a statute is referred to without its statute being named, the reader may assume that the reference is to the Road Traffic Offenders Act 1988 ("the 1988 Offenders Act").

Crown roads and royal parks

As a result of the coming into force on April 1, 1987 of the Crown Roads **17.05** (Royal Parks) (Application of Road Traffic Enactments) Order 1987 (SI 1987 No 363), the fixed penalty provisions of what is now Pt III of the Road Traffic Offenders Act 1988 apply to Crown roads in the royal parks as they do to other roads to which the public has access. The term "royal parks" is defined in the regulations as all parks, gardens, recreation grounds, open spaces and other land to which the Parks Regulation Act 1872 applies (i.e. all "parks, gardens, recreation grounds, open spaces and other land vested in, or under the control and management of", the Secretary of State for Environment, Food and Rural Affairs: Parks Regulation (Amendment) Act 1926 s.1) and includes all roads deemed to be under the management of the Secretary of State by virtue of the Crown Estate Act 1961 s.7(5).

DEFINITIONS

"Fixed penalty"

Section 53 of the Road Traffic Offenders Act 1988 provides that the "fixed" **17.06** penalty for an offence shall be such amount as the Secretary of State may by order prescribe, or one half of the maximum fine to which a person committing that offence would be liable on summary conviction, whichever is the less.

The Fixed Penalty Order 2000 (SI 2000/2792) came into effect on November 1, 2000. It provides for the following fixed penalty levels:

£60 for offences involving obligatory endorsement;

£60 for illegal parking on a "Red Route";

£40 for illegal parking in London outside the "Red Routes";

£30 for illegal parking elsewhere and for all other non-endorsable offences.

Since none of the offences listed in Sch.3 to the 1988 Offenders Act as fixed penalty offences is punishable on summary conviction by a maximum fine of less than £120, £80 or £60 as appropriate, the above levels apply to offences committed on or after November 1, 2000. For the purposes of these levels London is defined as the Metropolitan Police District together with the City of London, the Inner Temple and the Middle Temple. There is thus a uniform approach to penalties within those areas.

17.07   The Fixed Penalty Order 2000 referred to above was amended with effect from June 1, 2003 by the Fixed Penalty (Amendment) Order 2003 (SI 2003/1254) by the insertion therein of a new fixed penalties table. Three offences and their penalties were added thereto. The fixed penalty offences concerned are:

    (a) using a motor vehicle without the required test certificate (£60);

    (b) using a motor vehicle without insurance (£200); and

    (c) failure to give information as to the identity of the driver of a vehicle (£120).

In addition, the existing fixed penalty for failure to exhibit an excise licence (a non-endorsable offence) was raised from £30 to £60.

The amendments described above apply to offences committed on or after June 1, 2003.

17.08   The Fixed Penalty Offences Order 2004 (SI 2004/2922) specifies as a fixed penalty offence the offence under s.18 of the Road Traffic Act 1988 of driving or riding a motor cycle while using eye protectors if the eye protectors are not of a type prescribed by the relevant regulations or they are used in contravention of such regulations. The order came into force on December 1, 2004 and applies to offences committed on or after that date.

The Fixed Penalty Offences Order 2009 (SI 2009/483), which came into force on March 31, 2009, adds a significant number of offences to the list of fixed penalty of offences for the purposes of Pt III of the Road Traffic Offenders Act 1988.

"Graduated fixed penalties"

17.09   It should be noted that s.53 of the 1988 Offenders Act is amended by s.3 of the Road Safety Act 2006 from January 5, 2009 in order to enable the Secretary of State by order to prescribe different levels of fixed penalty for offences depending on the circumstances surrounding them, including (in particular):

    (a) the nature of the contravention or failure constituting the offence;

    (b) how serious it is;

    (c) the area, or sort of place, where it takes place; and

    (d) whether the offender has committed any other prescribed offences during a prescribed period (s.53(2), as substituted).

"Fixed penalty notice"

17.10   Section 52(1) defines "fixed penalty notice" as a notice offering the opportunity of the discharge of any liability to conviction of the offence to which the notice relates by payment of a fixed penalty.

"Suspended enforcement period"

17.11   Section 78(1) provides that proceedings shall not be brought against any person

for the offence to which a fixed penalty notice relates until the end of the
"suspended enforcement period"; that is to say, the period of 21 days following
the date of the notice or such longer period (if any) as may be specified in the notice (s.52(3)(a)). It is understood that in accordance with advice given in Home
Office circular 92/1985 28 days is the period specified by police forces throughout
England and Wales.

"Owner"

Section 68(1) provides that for the purposes of Pt III of the 1988 Offenders Act **17.12**
the owner of a vehicle shall be taken to be the person by whom the vehicle is
kept. It is further provided that for the purposes of determining ownership in the
course of proceedings brought under s.63 of the Act (effect where fixed penalty
notice is affixed to a vehicle) it shall be presumed that the owner was the
registered keeper of the vehicle at the material time. Section 68(2) provides that
notwithstanding the above presumption it shall be open to the defence to prove
that the registered keeper was not the person by whom the vehicle was kept at the
relevant time, and to the prosecution to prove that it was kept by some other
person at that time.

"Relevant person" and "appropriate person"

Originally a fixed penalty notice could be issued only by a constable in **17.13**
uniform. As stated above at § 17.03, s.5 of, and Sch.1 to, the Road Safety Act
2006 amend from March 31, 2009 Pt III of the 1988 Offenders Act to enable vehicle examiners to issue both fixed penalty notices and conditional offers. The
system will operate along similar lines to the existing fixed penalty system, save
that it will be administered by the Secretary of State through the medium of the
Vehicle and Operator Services Agency (VOSA).

The term "relevant person" was introduced to cover the dual enforcement procedure following the issue of a fixed penalty notice, and means (Road Traffic Offenders Act 1988, as amended by the Road Safety Act 2006 Sch.1) s.63(2A) (service of notice to owner if penalty not paid) and, in a slightly expanded form,
s.66(8) (hired vehicles) and s.70(2A) (registration certificates):

    (a) if the fixed penalty notice was fixed by a constable, the chief officer of
        police, and

    (b) if it was fixed by a vehicle examiner, the Secretary of State.

However, in relation to s.73(4A) (notices affixed to vehicles: when registration **17.14**
invalid) the relevant person means:

    (a) if the fixed penalty notice concerned was fixed by a constable, the fixed
        penalty clerk, and

    (b) if it was fixed by a vehicle examiner, the Secretary of State.

Moreover, under s.70(3A) (registration certificates) the appropriate person
means:

    (a) if the fixed penalty notice in question was given or fixed by a constable
        or given by an authorised person, the fixed penalty clerk, and

    (b) if it was given or fixed by a vehicle examiner or given by the Secretary
        of State, the Secretary of State.

"Notice to owner"

Section 63(1), (2) and (3), provides that where a fixed penalty notice has been **17.15** affixed to a vehicle and the fixed penalty has not been paid within the suspended enforcement period, and no person has given notice requesting a hearing in respect of the offence, a "notice to owner" may be served by the relevant person upon any person who appears to be the owner of the vehicle. The notice must:

    (a) give particulars of the alleged offence and of the fixed penalty concerned;

    (b) state the period allowed for response to the notice (21 days or longer if so specified);

    (c) indicate that if the fixed penalty is not paid before the end of that period, the person on whom the notice is served is asked to furnish before the end of that period to the relevant person a "statutory statement of ownership".

"Statutory statement of ownership"

17.16   Part I of Sch.4 to the 1988 Offenders Act provides that for the purposes of Pt III of the Act, a "statutory statement of ownership" is a statement on an official form signed by the person furnishing it and stating whether he was the owner of the vehicle at the time of the alleged offence and, if he was not the owner of the vehicle at that time, whether:

    (a) he was never the owner; or

    (b) he ceased to be the owner before, or became the owner after, that time;

and in a case within paragraph (b) above, stating, if the information is in his possession, the name and address of the person to whom, and the date on which, he disposed of the vehicle, or similar particulars of the person from whom, and the date on which, he acquired it.

"Statutory statement of facts"

17.17   Part II of Sch.4 to the 1988 Offenders Act provides that a "statutory statement of facts" is a statement on an official form, signed by the person furnishing it, to the effect that the person furnishing it was not the driver of the vehicle at the time of the alleged offence, and further stating the name and address (at the time when the statement is furnished) of the person who was the driver of the vehicle at the time of the alleged offence.

FIXED PENALTY PROCEDURE: AN OUTLINE

17.18   It should be noted at the outset that the procedure to be followed varies in accordance with the circumstances in which the fixed penalty notice was issued. The object of this introductory section is to set out a brief and, it is hoped, manageable guide to the system. Later sections will deal in greater detail with its procedural elements.

As an aid to rapid familiarisation, terms whose definitions are contained in the previous section will make their first appearance in *this* section in italic script.

Person present

17.19   A constable in uniform or a vehicle examiner who has reason to believe a fixed penalty offence is being or has been committed may give the person concerned a *fixed penalty notice* (s.54(1), (2)).

If the offence is endorsable, the constable or vehicle examiner can only give a fixed penalty notice to a person if:

(a) the person produces a driving licence;

(b) the penalty points to be incurred for the offence will not bring the total on the licence to 12 or more; and

(c) the person surrenders his licence to the constable or vehicle examiner (s.54(3)).

If the offence is endorsable and the person concerned is travelling without his **17.20** licence, the constable may give him a notice to be produced within seven days together with the driving licence at a police station of the person's choice (in England and Wales). In similar circumstances the vehicle examiner may give him a notice to produce his licence within 14 days at the place specified in the notice (s.54(4A)).

If the person concerned delivers both notice and licence in accordance with s.54(4A) within the time allowed to him, and if:

(a) the penalty points to be incurred for the offence will not bring the total on the licence to 12 or more; and

(b) the licence and its counterpart are delivered to be retained,

he shall be given a fixed penalty notice (s.54(5)).

An amended s.54(5A) provides (from March 31, 2009) circumstances where **17.21** the fixed penalty notice procedure can be applied to a person who is not the holder of a licence. Here the constable or vehicle examiner must be satisfied, on accessing information held on his driving record, that the person would not be liable to be disqualified if the penalty points to be incurred for the offence will not bring the total on his record to 12 or more. In those circumstances the procedure to be followed is as described above in relation to a driver who has a licence, save of course that no licence is required to be delivered to be retained (ss.5A, 5B, 5C, 5D and 5E).

If the fixed penalty is paid before the end of the *suspended enforcement period* no proceedings may be brought against any person in respect of the offence concerned (s.78(2)).

In the case of an endorsable offence, where the fixed penalty is paid before the end of the suspended enforcement period the person to whom it is paid must endorse the licence and return it to its holder (s.57(3)).

If, before the end of the suspended enforcement period, the recipient of the **17.22** fixed penalty notice gives notice requesting a hearing in respect of the offence concerned his case may be tried summarily in due course (s.55(2)).

If, by the end of the suspended enforcement period, the recipient has not given notice requesting a court hearing, and the fixed penalty has not been paid, a sum equal to the fixed penalty plus one half of the amount of that penalty may be registered for enforcement against the recipient as a fine (s.55(3)).

The registration certificate must be sent to the designated officer for a local justice area (in England and Wales) in which the defaulter appears to reside (s.70(4)(a)). The term "defaulter" includes an unincorporated person (*R. v Clerk to Croydon JJ. Ex p. Chief Constable of Kent* [1991] R.T.R. 257).

The designated officer must register the sum for enforcement as a fine (or pass **17.23** the certificate on to the appropriate designated officer if the defaulter appears to reside in another local justice area) (s.71(1), (2), (4), (5)). The designated officer who registers the sum for enforcement must send notice of the registration to the defaulter (s.71(6)).

If the offence concerned is endorsable, the designated officer who registers the sum for enforcement must notify the fixed penalty clerk of the registration. On being so notified, the person to whom the fixed penalty is required to be paid must endorse the licence and (unless s.2(4) of the Road Traffic (New Drivers) Act 1995 applies; see § 17.52) return it to its holder. If that person is himself the officer who registers the sum for enforcement he must endorse and return the licence upon registration of the sum (s.57(4)).

17.24   The registered sum is enforceable in all respects as if it were a fine imposed by the registering court on the conviction of the defaulter on the date of registration (s.71(7)).

The recipient of a notice of registration may within 21 days of receipt of that notice make and serve a statutory declaration to the effect that:

    (a) he was not the person to whom the fixed penalty notice was given; or

    (b) before the end of the suspended enforcement period he gave notice requesting a hearing (s.72(1), (2)).

In broad terms, such a declaration invalidates both the registration and any licence endorsement which may have taken place, and in case (b) above also serves as a notice requesting a hearing in respect of the alleged offence.

Stationary vehicle

17.25   A constable or vehicle examiner who has reason to believe that a non-endorsable fixed penalty offence is being or has been committed in respect of a stationary vehicle may affix a fixed penalty notice to that vehicle (s.62(1)).

If the fixed penalty is paid before the end of the suspended enforcement period no proceedings may be brought against any person in respect of the offence concerned (s.78(2)).

17.26   If before the end of the suspended enforcement period any person gives notice requesting a hearing and states in that notice that he was the driver at the time of the alleged offence, his case may be tried summarily in due course (s.63(3)).

Where the fixed penalty has not been paid before the end of the suspended enforcement period and no person has in that time requested a hearing in accordance with s.63(3) above, the relevant person may serve a *notice to owner* upon the person who appears to be the owner of the vehicle (s.63(2)). The procedure which follows the service of such a notice varies in accordance with the nature of the response (if any) elicited by that notice.

Nil response

17.27   If there is *no response whatsoever* within the time allowed by the notice to owner, and the fixed penalty remains unpaid, the relevant person may register a sum equal to the fixed penalty plus 50 per cent thereof for enforcement as a fine against the person on whom the notice was served (s.64(2)). The term "person" includes an unincorporated body (*R. v. Clerk to Croydon JJ. Ex p. Chief Constable of Kent* [1991] R.T.R. 257). The procedure for registration is the same as that for a non-endorsable offence where the fixed penalty notice has been given to a "person present" (§§ 17.19–24). The recipient of a notice of registration is similarly protected by the power to make a statutory declaration of a specified kind (s.73(1), (2)). The statutory declaration provisions of the Act are discussed in detail later in this chapter (§§ 17.64–5).

Person served requests hearing

If the person on whom the notice to owner was served gives notice requesting **17.28** a hearing in respect of the offence concerned within the period allowed for response to the notice, proceedings may be brought against him in due course (ss.64(1), (3), 65(2)). For the purposes of instituting and conducting such proceedings it is to be conclusively presumed (subject to the exception immediately below) that the person on whom the notice to owner was served was the driver of the vehicle at the time of the alleged offence (s.64(3)).

Section 64(6) provides that the above presumption will not apply if it is proved that at the time of the alleged offence the vehicle was in the possession of some other person without the consent of the accused.

Person served not the owner

A person on whom a notice to owner is served will escape liability for the of- **17.29** fence concerned if he was *not* the owner of the vehicle at the time of the alleged offence and he furnishes a *statutory statement of ownership* to that effect within the time allowed for response to the notice (s.64(4)).

Person served not the driver

If the person on whom a notice to owner is served was not the driver at the **17.30** time of the alleged offence, and the person purporting to be the driver wishes to have a court hearing, the person served may furnish within the time allowed for response to the notice both a statutory statement of ownership and a *statutory statement of facts* identifying the driver at the time of the alleged offence. The latter document has effect as a notice by the driver requesting a hearing in respect of the offence concerned (s.63(6)).

Schedule of Fixed Penalty Offences

Description of offences

Section 51(1) of the 1988 Offenders Act provides that subject to any limitation **17.31** or exception mentioned in the "description of offence" column of the Schedule, any offence in respect of a vehicle committed or punishable under an enactment specified in column 1 of Sch.3 to the Act is a fixed penalty offence.

Section 51(2) provides that an offence under an enactment so specified is *not* a fixed penalty offence if it is committed by *causing or permitting* a vehicle to be used in contravention of any statutory provision, restriction or prohibition. It would seem, therefore, that whilst the driver of a vehicle being used, e.g., in breach of a construction and use regulation, may take advantage of the convenience and relative cheapness of a fixed penalty, a permissive owner or employer may not. There would appear to be nothing (other, perhaps, than a sense of equity) to prevent the latter person being prosecuted in the normal way. It is to be hoped, however, that where any question of causing or permitting an offence arises, the relevant person concerned will use the discretion vested in him by the Act and report the offence(s) disclosed for prosecution rather than offer or issue a fixed penalty notice. Similarly, although the Act does not specifically exclude the offence of aiding, abetting, counselling or procuring the commission by another person of a summary offence, and notwithstanding the fact that an aider and abettor may be charged with, and convicted of, the principal offence, it is submitted that the better course would be for both principal and accessory to be reported for prosecution.

17.32   Although s.54 of the Act (which deals with the issue of fixed penalty notices at the roadside and subsequently at a police station) refers to "fixed penalty offence" in the singular, applying the Interpretation Act 1978, s.6, there would appear to be no reason why more than one notice should not be issued at the same time if more than one fixed penalty offence is being or has been concurrently committed. It is understood, however, that in the light of guidance received police forces are limiting themselves to one fixed penalty notice per defendant per occasion. (For a discussion of the procedure to be followed where some endorsable offences have been dealt with by fixed penalty and others have been prosecuted in the "normal" way, see § 17.71.)

In the table of fixed penalty offences set out below, "E" in the endorsement column means that the offence is subject to obligatory endorsement, and "E*" means that the offence is endorsable if committed in the circumstances described in Sch.2 to the 1988 Offenders Act.

17.33   It is to be noted that the Secretary of State may by order provide for offences to become, or (as the case may be) to cease to be, fixed penalty offences (s.51(3)). The Fixed Penalty Offences Order 1999 (SI 1999/1851) added a number of offences to the list of those offences which may be dealt with by a fixed penalty in England and Wales. The offences in question are:

(a) overtaking a moving or stationary vehicle on a Zebra, Pelican or Puffin crossing;

(b) failing to fix a registration mark to a vehicle;

(c) driving on the footway;

(d) carrying more than one person on a pedal cycle; and

(e) cycling on the footway.

The offences listed in (a) above are endorsable and therefore liable to a fixed penalty of £60; the remainder are subject to a penalty of £30. The offences listed in (a), (b) and (c) above may also be dealt with by way of fixed penalty in Scotland.

17.34   The Fixed Penalty Offences Order 2003 (SI 2003/1253) and the Fixed Penalty (Amendment) Order 2003 (SI 2003/1254) together made provision inter alia for additional offences to be brought within the ambit of the fixed penalty system. With effect from June 1, 2003 the offences of having no insurance, having no MoT certificate and failing to give information as to the identity of the driver of a vehicle became liable to fixed penalties of £200 (with six penalty points), £60 and £120 respectively, and the fixed penalty for failing to display an excise licence was increased from £30 to £60.

The Fixed Penalty Offences Order 2004 (SI 2004/2922) specifies as a fixed penalty offence the offence under s.18 of the Road Traffic Act 1988 of driving or riding a motor cycle while using eye protectors if the eye protectors are not of a type prescribed by the relevant regulations or they are used in contravention of such regulations. The order came into force on December 1, 2004 and applies to offences committed on or after that date.

The Fixed Penalty Offences Order 2009 (SI 2009/483), which came into force **17.35** on March 31, 2009, adds a significant number of offences to the list of fixed penalty offences for the purposes of Pt III of the Road Traffic Offenders Act 1988. The offences relate to drivers' hours, public service and goods vehicles' authorisations, certificates of professional competence and trade licences.

The Secretary of State has also exercised his powers under s.53(1)(a) of the Act to vary the amounts of fixed penalties. The operative levels for offences committed on or after November 1, 2000 in England and Wales are set out at § 17.06.

Graduated fixed penalties

It should be noted that s.53 of the 1988 Offenders Act was amended by s.3 of **17.36** the Road Safety Act 2006 from January 5, 2009 in order to enable the Secretary of State by order to prescribe different levels of fixed penalty for offences depending on the circumstances surrounding them, including (in particular):

(a) the nature of the contravention or failure constituting the offence;

(b) how serious it is;

(c) the area, or sort of place, where it takes place; and

(d) whether the offender has committed any other prescribed offences during a prescribed period (s.53(2), as substituted).

Provision is also made (by means of amendments to s.28 of the Offenders Act effected from March 31, 2009 by s.4 of the 2006 Act) for the Secretary of State by order to prescribe appropriate numbers of penalty points ("graduated fixed penalty points") for a fixed penalty offence depending upon the circumstances (as particularised above).

TABLE OF FIXED PENALTY OFFENCES

Section	Offence	Endorsement	Penalty points
RTRA 1984			
s.5(1)	Using vehicle in contravention of traffic regulation order outside Greater London	—	—
s.8(1)	Breach of traffic regulation order in Greater London	—	—
s.11	Breach of experimental traffic order	—	—
s.13	Breach of experimental traffic scheme regulations in Greater London	—	—
s.16(1)	Using vehicle in contravention of temporary prohibition or restriction of traffic in case of execution of works, etc.	E*	3
s.17(4)	Wrongful use of special road (motorway offences)	E*	3

17.37

Section	Offence	Endorsement	Penalty points
s.18(3)	Using vehicle in contravention of provision for one-way traffic on trunk road	—	—
s.20(5)	Driving vehicle in contravention of order prohibiting or restricting driving vehicles on certain classes of roads	—	—
s.25(5)	Breach of pedestrian crossing regulations, except an offence in respect of a moving motor vehicle [other than a contravention of regs 23, 24, 25 and 26 of the Zebra, Pelican and Puffin Crossings Regulations and General Directions 1997 (SI 1997/2400)]	E*	3
s.29(3)	Using vehicle in contravention of street playground order	E*	2
s.35A(1)	Breach of order regulating use, etc., of local authority parking place, but only where offence committed in relation to parking place on road	—	—
s.47(1)	Breach of parking place designation order and other offences committed in relation to a designated parking place, *except* offence of failing to pay an excess charge within the meaning of RTRA 1984 s.46	—	—
s.53(5)	Using vehicle in contravention of parking place designation order having effect under RTRA 1984 s.53(1)(a) (inclusion of certain traffic regulation provisions, e.g. directions for proceeding or waiting and loading restrictions)	—	—
s.53(6)	Breach of parking place designation order having effect under RTRA 1984 s.53(1)(b) (use of any part of a road for parking without charge)	—	—
s.88(7)	Driving vehicle in contravention of minimum speed limit order under RTRA 1984 s.88(1)	—	—
s.89(1)	Speeding offences	E	3

VE & RA 1994

Section	Offence	Endorsement	Penalty points
s.33	Using or keeping vehicle on public road without exhibiting excise licence in prescribed manner	—	—

Section	Offence	Endorsement	Penalty points
s.42	Driving or keeping vehicle without required registration mark or hackney carriage sign	—	—
s.43	Driving or keeping vehicle with registration mark or hackney carriage sign obscured, etc.	—	—
s.59	Failure to fix prescribed registration mark to vehicle	—	—
RTA 1988			
s.14	Breach of regulations requiring wearing of seat belts	—	—
s.15(2)	Breach of restriction on carrying children in the front of vehicles	—	—
s.15(4)	Breach of restriction on carrying children in the rear of vehicles	—	—
s.16	Breach of regulations relating to protective headgear for motor cycle drivers and passengers	—	—
s.18	Breach of regulations relating to eye protectors for use on motor cycles	—	—
s.19(1)	Parking heavy commercial vehicle on verge or footway	—	—
s.22	Leaving vehicle in dangerous position	E*	3
s.23	Carrying *more* than one passenger on motor cycle or carrying *one* such in an unlawful position	E	3
s.24	Carrying more than one person on a pedal cycle	—	—
s.34	Driving vehicle elsewhere than on a road	—	—
s.35	Failure to comply with traffic directions	E*	3
s.36	Failure to comply with traffic signs	E*	3
s.40A	Using vehicle in dangerous condition	E	3
s.41A	Breach of requirement as to brakes, steering gear or tyres	E	3
s.41B	Breach of requirement as to weight: goods and passenger vehicles	—	—
s.41D	Breach of requirement as to control of vehicle, mobile telephone, etc.	E	3
s.42	Breach of other construction and use requirements	—	—
s.47	Use motor vehicle without test certificate	—	—

Section	Offence	Endorsement	Penalty points
s.87(1)	Driving otherwise than in accordance with requisite licence	E*	3
s.143	Using a motor vehicle without insurance	E	6
s.163	Failure to stop when required by constable in uniform	—	—
s.172	Failure to give information as to the identity of the driver of a vehicle	E	3
Greater London Council (General Powers) Act 1974			
s.15	Parking vehicle on footways, verges, etc.	—	—
Highways Act 1980			
s.137	Obstructing highways (by means of vehicle)	—	—
Highways Act 1835			
s.72	Driving on the footway	—	—
s.72	Cycling on the footway	—	—
Roads (Scotland) Act 1984			
s.129(5)	Driving on the footway	—	—

* Endorsable if committed in the circumstances described in Sch.2 to the 1988 Offenders Act.

FIXED PENALTY NOTICE

Issue of a fixed penalty notice

Driver present; offence endorsable

17.38   A police constable in uniform or a vehicle examiner who has reason to believe that an endorsable fixed penalty offence is being or has been committed may, provided that certain requirements are fulfilled, give the person concerned a fixed penalty notice. The requirements are that:

(a) the person concerned produces his driving licence for inspection;

(b) the constable or vehicle examiner is satisfied that the addition of the appropriate number of penalty points for the offence concerned will not bring the total of points on the licence to 12 or more and thus render the holder liable to disqualification under s.35(1) of the 1988 Offenders Act;

(c) the person concerned surrenders or delivers his driving licence to the constable or vehicle examiner (s.54(1), (2)).

It is to be noted that the term "constable" in the context of an endorsable offence can only include a traffic warden if the offence was committed while the vehicle concerned was stationary (s.86(1)). It should also be noted that in determining whether a person would be liable to disqualification under s.35(1) of the 1988 Offenders Act it shall be assumed that in the case of an offence which is subject to a range of points, the number of points to be attributed to it would be the lowest in the range (s.54(10)).

If a constable makes a mistake in calculating the total number of penalty points **17.39** which will appear on the licence as a result of the fixed penalty endorsement, and the driver is in fact liable to a penalty points disqualification, s.61 of the Act enables the fixed penalty clerk to retrieve the situation by sending the licence unendorsed to the police. A prosecution through the courts may subsequently be embarked upon. Presumably such a mistake is unlikely to happen in the procedure to be followed when a fixed penalty notice is issued by a vehicle examiner. The methods of rectifying mistakes are discussed at §§ 17.62–3.

The holder of the licence who surrenders or delivers it either at the roadside or at a police station must be given a receipt for it (s.56(1)). This initial receipt will be valid for one month (beginning with the date of issue) or such longer period as may be prescribed (s.56(3)(a)). In this connection a period of two months has been prescribed by reg.11 of the Fixed Penalty (Procedure) Regulations 1986 (SI 1986/1330). A new receipt may be obtained on request from the fixed penalty clerk to whom the licence will have been sent by the police (ss.56(2) and 54(7)). Such a receipt will be valid for as long as specified therein by the fixed penalty clerk (s.56(3)(b)).

Section 27(4) of the 1988 Offenders Act provides a defence to a charge under **17.40** s.27(3) ibid. (failure to produce licence to court for endorsement) and further provides that the requirement in s.27(3) for the licence to be suspended until produced shall not apply if the licence-holder satisfies certain conditions (see below). Section 26(4) provides a defence to a charge under s.26(3) of the Act (failure to produce licence to court making order for interim disqualification). Section 164(7) of the Road Traffic Act 1988 provides a similar defence to a charge under s.164(6) ibid. (failure to produce licence to constable). In order to avail himself of any such defence the person concerned must produce a current receipt for the licence in the manner in which the licence itself was required to be produced and must subsequently produce the licence "immediately on its return". It is submitted that in this context "immediately" means "as soon as is reasonably practicable".

Section 93(4) of the Road Traffic Act 1988 provides that a person who has surrendered his licence on receipt of a fixed penalty notice shall not be taken to be in breach of any duty under that section (revocation on disability, etc.) to deliver his licence forthwith to the Secretary of State if he delivers the licence immediately on its return.

Driver present; offence not endorsable

A police constable in uniform or a vehicle examiner who produces his author- **17.41** ity who has reason to believe that a non-endorsable fixed penalty offence is being or has been committed may give the person concerned a fixed penalty notice (s.54(1), (2)). The Functions of Traffic Wardens (Amendment) Order 1986 (SI 1986/1328) provides that for the purposes of such parking offences, etc., as are fixed penalty offences for the purposes of Pt III of the Act, traffic wardens may exercise the functions conferred upon constables by Pt III.

The question of whether a parking attendant had been prevented from issuing a penalty charge notice was considered by the Administrative Court in *R. (on the application of Transport for London) v Parking Adjudicator* [2007] EWHC 1172; [2007] R.T.R. 39.

17.42   Section 66(1) of the Road Traffic Act 1991 provides:

> "Where, in the case of a stationary vehicle ... a parking attendant has reason to believe that a penalty charge is payable with respect to the vehicle, he may—
>
> > (a) fix a penalty charge notice to the vehicle or
> >
> > (b) give such a notice to the person appearing to him to be in charge of the vehicle."

Section 5(1) of the London Local Authorities Act 2000, as amended by the Transport for London (Consequential Provisions) Order 2005 (SI 2005/56), provides:

> "Where a parking attendant attempts to issue a penalty charge notice in accordance with section 66(1) of the Act of 1991 but is prevented from doing so by any person—
>
> > (a) Transport for London, if the attendant was acting on its behalf; or
> >
> > (b) in any other case the council on whose behalf the attendant was acting,
>
> may serve a penalty charge notice on the person appearing to it or them to be the owner of the vehicle."

A driver had stopped his car on double red lines. A parking attendant saw the car and began to write down some details prior to writing out a parking ticket and putting it on the windscreen or handing it to the driver. As he was doing so, the driver got into the car, said "I am going now", and drove off. Because the parking attendant had been unable to fix a ticket on the windscreen or to hand it to the driver, the claimant, Transport for London, sent a penalty charge notice to the keeper of the car. The court decided, interestingly, that as there is a well-established understanding among the parking authorities and adjudicators that, if a driver drove away before a ticket was actually put on the windscreen, through the window of the car or into his hands, and no violence or threat of violence was inflicted on the attendant, that did not amount to preventing the issue as a penalty charge notice for the purposes of s.5(1) of the London Local Authorities Act 2000. It was therefore not appropriate for the court to make a declaration which reversed that understanding. The court was told that such clarification is important because regulations similar to those in force in London are in the near future apparently to be issued in respect of all those authorities, and they represent the majority in the country, which have decriminalised parking conventions.

Driver absent

17.43   Where a police constable or vehicle examiner comes upon a stationary vehicle and has reason to believe that a non-endorsable fixed penalty offence is being or has been committed in respect of it, he may affix to that vehicle a fixed penalty notice (s.62(1)). This function with respect to such parking offences, etc., as are fixed penalty offences may also be carried out by a traffic warden (Functions of Traffic Wardens Order 1970).

The fixed penalty procedure cannot be used in the absence of the driver if the offence concerned is an endorsable one (s.62(1)) since the constable or vehicle examiner will have no way of ascertaining whether or not the offender is liable to fall foul of the totting-up provisions of s.35 of the Act. Difficulties may conceivably arise in respect of, e.g., construction and use offences which become endorsable if the conditions as to their commission set out in Sch.2 to the Act are satisfied. There would not appear to be any machinery within the Act for correcting the error if a fixed penalty notice is issued in the mistaken belief that the offence concerned is not endorsable.

Section 62(2) provides that it is an offence for a notice affixed to a vehicle as above to be removed or interfered with except by or under the authority of the driver or person in charge of the vehicle, or the person liable for the offence in question. It is punishable on summary conviction by a maximum fine of level 2.

Contents of a fixed penalty notice

A fixed penalty notice must give such particulars of the circumstances alleged to constitute the offence to which it relates as are necessary for giving reasonable information about the alleged offence, and must specify the suspended enforcement period in respect of the offence, the amount of the fixed penalty and the person to whom and the address at which the fixed penalty may be paid (s.52(2), (3)). Both the date of contravention and the date of the notice have to be stated on a penalty charge notice: *R. (on the application of Barnet London Borough Council) v Parking Adjudicator* [2006] EWHC 2357; [2007] R.T.R. 14. It must also specify the manner in which notice may be given requesting a court hearing in respect of the offence. The contents of such a notice (and that of the "provisional fixed penalty notice" to be issued under s.54(4) to a driver travelling without his licence where an endorsable fixed penalty offence is alleged to have been committed) have been prescribed by the Secretary of State in the exercise of his powers under s.84. Two visually distinct forms have been developed for use respectively in "driver present" and "driver absent" cases. **17.44**

SUSPENDED ENFORCEMENT PERIOD

Provisions of ss.78 and 52(3)(a)

Section 78(1) provides that proceedings shall not be brought against any person for the offence to which a fixed penalty notice relates until the end of the "suspended enforcement period"; that is to say, the period of 21 days following the date of the notice or such longer period (if any) as may be specified in the notice (s.52(3)(a)). It is understood that in accordance with advice contained in Home Office circular 92/1985 a period of 28 days has been specified for this purpose by police forces throughout England and Wales. **17.45**

A motorist was stopped whilst driving by police officers who informed him that he had been exceeding a speed limit. They took him to their vehicle where they showed him a video recording which showed their speed and his car in front of them. He was given a fixed penalty notice. He did not pay the fixed penalty, but requested a court hearing. The video tape was reused in the ordinary course of police duties. On appeal to the Crown Court against his conviction by justices it was contended on his behalf that the proceedings should be stayed as an abuse of process as the destruction of the recording meant that he could not have a fair trial, since that recording was essential to his defence of duress.

It was held inter alia by the Divisional Court in *R. (on the application of Ebrahim) v Feltham Magistrates' Court; Mouat v DPP* [2001] EWHC Admin 130;

[2002] R.T.R. 7 that the defendant had been entitled to consider during the suspended enforcement period whether he wished to contest his liability in court, and the police were under a duty under the Code of Practice published pursuant to ss.23 and 25 of the Criminal Procedure and Investigations Act 1996 to retain the video tape until after that period had expired, at the very least.

17.46   Payment of the fixed penalty before the end of the suspended enforcement period is an absolute bar to proceedings being brought against any person in respect of the offence concerned (s.78(2)). If the offence for which the fixed penalty has been paid is endorsable, the person to whom it is paid must endorse the licence and return it to its holder (s.57(3)).

Payment may be made (without prejudice to payment by any other method, e.g. in person) by post to the fixed penalty clerk specified in the fixed penalty notice or to the Secretary of State and, in the absence of proof to the contrary, shall be deemed to have been made at the time at which the letter concerned would be delivered in the ordinary course of post (s.69(1A), (2), (3)). In any proceedings for the offence, a certificate purporting to be signed by the person to whom the fixed penalty was required to be paid, stating whether or not payment of a fixed penalty was received by a date specified in the certificate, or stating that a letter containing an amount sent by post in payment of a fixed penalty was marked as posted on a specified date, shall be evidence of the facts stated (s.80).

Requests for court hearings

Driver present

17.47   Where a fixed penalty notice has been given to an alleged offender, no proceedings shall be brought against the recipient for the offence concerned unless before the end of the suspended enforcement period he has requested a hearing in the manner specified in the notice (s.55(2)).

Driver absent

17.48   Where a fixed penalty notice has been affixed to a stationary (and presumably unoccupied) vehicle, the "notice to owner" procedure (see § 17.55 below) may not be embarked upon if before the end of the suspended enforcement period any person has requested a hearing in the manner specified in the notice and has further stated in his notice that he was the driver of the vehicle at the time of the alleged offence (s.63(2), (3)).

Events subsequent to the suspended enforcement period

The consequences of inertia

17.49   It is to be expected that in at least a proportion of cases the suspended enforcement period will expire without either payment being made or a court hearing being requested. The procedure to be followed in such circumstances depends upon the method by which the fixed penalty notice was issued.

Driver present

17.50   If by the end of the suspended enforcement period the recipient of a fixed penalty has not given notice requesting a court hearing, and the fixed penalty has not been paid, a sum equal to the fixed penalty plus one half of the amount of that penalty may be registered for enforcement against the recipient as a fine (s.55(3)).

The procedure for registration is governed by ss.70 and 71. The relevant person may issue a certificate in respect of any sum payable in default (i.e. the fixed penalty plus 50 per cent thereof) for enforcement against the defaulter as a fine (s.70(2)). Having issued such a certificate (known as a registration certificate), he must cause it to be sent to the designated officer for the local justice area in which the defaulter appears to reside (s.70(4)). The certificate must inter alia give particulars of the offence to which the fixed penalty relates and state the name and last-known address of the defaulter and the amount of the sum payable in default (s.70(5)). With regard to a body corporate, the place where that body resides shall be either that body's registered or principal office, or the address which, with respect to the vehicle concerned, appears in the record kept under the Vehicle Excise and Registration Act 1994 as that body's address (s.71(9)). Provided that the defaulter does indeed reside within his local justice area, the designated officer who receives the registration certificate must register the sum concerned for enforcement as a fine in his court by entering it in the court register (s.71(1)). If by chance the defaulter resides in another local justice area, he may send the certificate without registering it to the designated officer in whose area the defaulter appears to him to reside. Assuming that he correctly locates the area in which the defaulter lives, the recipient designated officer will be responsible for registering and enforcing the sum payable (s.71(4), (5)).

The designated officer who registers the sum payable in default for enforce- **17.51**
ment as a fine must thereupon give notice of the registration to the defaulter, specifying inter alia the amount payable and the particulars of the offence contained in the registration certificate forwarded by the relevant person (s.71(6)).

Once registered, the sum payable in default is enforceable in all respects as if it were a fine imposed by the registering court on the conviction of the defaulter on the date of registration (s.71(7)).

"Defaulter" within the meaning of what is now s.70 of the 1988 Offenders Act means any "person" and thus includes an unincorporated body. The Divisional Court so held in *R. v. Clerk to Croydon JJ. Ex p. Chief Constable of Kent* [1991] R.T.R. 257 when allowing an application for judicial review against the refusal of the Clerk to the Croydon Justices to accept as valid fixed penalty registration certificates issued against an unincorporated body. By virtue of s.5 of, and Sch.1 to, the Interpretation Act 1978, "… 'person' includes a body of persons corporate or unincorporate ". The practical difficulties of enforcement against unincorporated bodies were, however, appreciated. It appeared that the DVLC (now DVLA) was prepared to issue excise licences in the names of unincorporated associations, e.g., business names or partnerships, and to register such "persons" as owners. Whether or not that practice was sanctioned by law was not argued before the court, but obviously it would be easier for the purposes of enforcement if either a natural person or a corporate body was registered.

In the case of an endorsable fixed penalty offence, the designated officer who **17.52**
registers the sum for enforcement is under a duty to notify the relevant person of the registration. Upon receipt of such notification the relevant particulars must be endorsed upon the licence and it must be returned to the licence-holder. If the relevant person is himself the designated officer who registers the sum for enforcement as a fine, he must endorse and return the licence upon registration of that

sum (s.57(4)). Where, however, the penalty points to be taken into account by the appropriate person number six or more, and it appears to him that the offence concerned was committed within the offender's probationary period (two years beginning on the day on which he became a qualified driver), he must not return the licence to its holder but must instead send it to the Secretary of State for revocation (Road Traffic (New Drivers) Act 1995 s.2(3), (4)). These provisions apply to any person whose first driving test was passed on or after June 1, 1997 (s.1 ibid.; see further § 11.09).

Driver absent; notice affixed to vehicle

17.53   If by the end of the suspended enforcement period the fixed penalty has not been paid, and no person has given notice requesting a court hearing in respect of the offence, a notice to owner may be served by or on behalf of the relevant person upon any person who appears to him (or his authorised officer) to be the owner of the vehicle (s.63(2)). It is provided by s.68(1) that the owner of a vehicle shall be taken to be the person by whom the vehicle is kept. It is further provided that, for the purposes of determining ownership in proceedings for the offence concerned, it shall be presumed that the owner was the registered keeper of the vehicle at the material time.

Section 68(2) provides that notwithstanding the above presumption it shall be open to the defence to prove that the registered keeper was not the person by whom the vehicle was kept at the relevant time, and to the prosecution to prove that the vehicle was kept by some other person at that time. The notice to owner must give particulars of the alleged offence and of the fixed penalty concerned, must state the period allowed for response (21 days or such longer period as may be specified therein), and must indicate that, if the fixed penalty is not paid before the end of that period, the person served is asked to furnish to the relevant person a statutory statement of ownership (s.63(4)). It must also indicate that the person on whom it is served may, within the period allowed for response, either:

(a) give due notice requesting a hearing in respect of the offence; or

(b) if he was not the driver at the time of the alleged offence, and the person purporting to be the driver wishes to give notice requesting a hearing, furnish together with a statutory statement of ownership a statutory statement of facts identifying the actual driver (s.63(6)).

17.54   In order to preserve their right subsequently to bring proceedings in respect of the offence against the person served, if that person requests a hearing within the time allowed for response, the relevant person must ensure that the notice is served before the end of the period of six months beginning with the day on which the fixed penalty notice was affixed to the vehicle (s.64(1), (3)).

SERVICE OF NOTICE

Procedure following service of notice to owner

17.55   The procedure which follows the service of a notice to owner is governed by the nature of the response (if any) which the notice produces.

Payment during the period allowed for response

17.56   It is provided by s.65(3) that payment of the fixed penalty before the end of the period allowed for response to a notice to owner is an absolute bar to proceedings being brought against any person identified as the driver of the vehicle in a statutory statement of facts furnished in response to that notice. Proceedings against the person properly served with a notice to owner may only be brought if he has requested a hearing in due time and form (s.65(2)) and the fixed penalty has not been paid before the end of the period allowed for response to the notice (s.64(1)(b), (3)); it is clear, therefore, that payment during the time allowed for response is also an absolute bar to proceedings against the person served with the notice to owner.

Nil response

If the notice to owner provokes nothing in the way of a response within the **17.57** time it allows for response, and if the fixed penalty remains unpaid, the relevant person may issue a certificate in respect of the sum payable in default (i.e. the amount of the fixed penalty plus 50 per cent thereof) for enforcement against the person on whom the notice to owner was served, as a fine (s.64(2)). The procedure for registration is similar to that which applies in the case of a non-endorsable offence where the fixed penalty notice was given to a driver who was present at the time (see "Driver present", §§ 17.50–52). Once such a sum has been registered for enforcement as a fine against the person on whom the notice to owner was served, no proceedings may be brought against any other person in respect of that offence (s.65(4)).

Person served requests a hearing

If the person on whom the notice to owner was served gives notice requesting **17.58** a hearing in respect of the offence concerned in the manner indicated, and within the time allowed, by the notice to owner, proceedings may be brought against him in due course (ss.4(1), (3), 65(2)). It is to be noted that in order to commence proceedings an information must be laid within 12 months of the time the offence was committed (s.64(7)).

For the purposes of instituting proceedings against the person on whom the notice to owner was served, and in the course of any proceedings so brought, it shall be presumed (subject to the exception in s.64(6) discussed immediately below) that the person on whom the notice to owner was served was the driver of the vehicle at the time of the alleged offence, and the acts or omissions of the driver will be imputed to him (s.64(6)). Section 64(6) provides that the above presumption will not apply if it is proved that, at the time of the alleged offence, the vehicle was in the possession of some other person without the consent of the accused.

Person served not the owner

A person on whom a notice to owner is served will not be liable for the offence **17.59** concerned if he was *not* the owner of the vehicle at the time of the alleged offence and he furnishes a statutory statement of ownership to that effect within the time allowed for response to the notice (s.64(4)). A statutory statement of ownership is a statement on an official form signed by the person furnishing it and stating whether he was the owner of the vehicle at the time of the alleged offence and, if he was not the owner of the vehicle at that time, whether:

(a) he was never the owner; or

(b) he ceased to be the owner before, or became the owner after, that time;

and in a case within paragraph (b) above, stating, if the information is in his possession, the name and address of the person to whom, and the date on which he disposed of the vehicle, or similar particulars of the person from whom, and the date on which, he acquired it (Sch.4 para.1(1)).

Person served not the driver

17.60   If the person on whom a notice to owner is served was not the driver at the time of the alleged offence, and the person purporting to be the driver wishes to give notice requesting a court hearing, the person served may furnish within the time allowed for response to the notice both a statutory statement of ownership and a statutory statement of facts identifying the driver at the time of the alleged offence. The latter document, provided it is countersigned by the purported driver, has effect as a notice given by the driver requesting a hearing in respect of the offence concerned (s.63(6), Sch.4 para.3(2)). This incidentally, is the only means by which proceedings in respect of the offence concerned can be brought against any person other than the person served with the notice to owner (s.65(1)).

If the person served with a notice to owner furnishes a statutory statement of facts as described above, any notice requesting a hearing which he may purport to give on his own account shall be of no effect. In addition, a sum in default may not be registered against him unless no summons in respect of the offence in question is served on the purported driver within the two months immediately following the end of the period allowed for response to the notice to owner (s.63(7)).

False statements in response to notice to owner

17.61   In order to discourage unlawful attempts to escape liability for the consequences of a fixed penalty offence, s.67 and Sch.2 provide that any person who in response to a notice to owner furnishes a statement which is false in a material particular, and does so recklessly or knowing it to be false, commits an offence punishable on summary conviction by a maximum fine of level 5. Subject to an overall time-limit of three years from the date of commission of the offence, proceedings may be brought within six months from the date on which evidence, sufficient in the opinion of the prosecutor to warrant the proceedings, came to his knowledge (s.6(1)).

RECTIFICATION OF MISTAKES

Driver liable to penalty points disqualification

17.62   It will be recalled that one of the conditions which must be fulfilled before a constable or vehicle examiner may issue a fixed penalty notice for an endorsable offence is that the penalty points to be added for the offence concerned will not bring the total number of points on the licence of the driver concerned to 12 or more and thus render him liable to disqualification under s.35(1) of the 1988 Offenders Act. It is inevitable that from time to time miscalculations of points will be made and fixed penalty notices will be issued when they should not have been. In such circumstances all is not necessarily lost for the prosecution, provided that the fixed penalty clerk spots the mistake.

Section 61 provides that, in circumstances where the licence was sent to the fixed penalty clerk, having discovered on inspecting the licence that the holder thereof would be liable to a penalty points disqualification if the penalty points for the fixed penalty offence were added to those already endorsed upon it, the fixed penalty clerk may not endorse the licence but must instead send it to the police (s.61(1), (2)). Proceedings may thereafter be brought for the offence concerned, provided that those proceedings are commenced within six months of the date on which the fixed penalty notice was erroneously issued (s.61(3)). If proceedings are commenced, the fixed penalty notice is treated in all respects as if it had never been issued, and any action previously taken in respect of it (e.g. registration and enforcement) is regarded as void (s.61(4), (5)).

There is no provision in the Act, however, for rectification of a mistake made **17.63** in the opposite direction, as it were. For example, a police officer at the roadside may conclude erroneously from an inspection of the licence that an offender would be liable to a penalty points disqualification and hence will feel obliged not to issue a fixed penalty notice.

A police officer subsequently inspecting a licence at a police station in a case where a "provisional" fixed penalty notice has been issued by another officer at the roadside may similarly err. In each case it is to be presumed that the offender will be reported for prosecution in the normal way. It is submitted that the fact that the offender has mistakenly been denied the opportunity to discharge his liability for the offence by payment of a fixed penalty amounts to a mitigating factor which the court ought properly to consider when passing sentence.

Statutory declarations

It is inevitable with procedures as complicated as those introduced by the Act **17.64** that from time to time matters will go awry. Identities will be mistaken, documents will go astray, and errors may not be discovered until a notice of registration of a sum payable in default is served upon an alleged offender, or proceedings to enforce that sum are taken against him. Sections 72, 73 and 74 of the Act are intended to provide adequate safeguards for the innocent victims of such mistakes. The machinery of the sections is modelled upon the statutory declaration provisions of the Magistrates' Courts Act 1980 s.14. It is designed to cater for any of three sets of circumstances in which an error has occurred. The first of these is where the operation of the fixed penalty procedure has failed (for whatever reason) to advise a person before registration of his liability to pay a fixed penalty. The second is where registration has taken place despite the driver's request for a court hearing in respect of the offence. The third is where due to impersonation (possibly accompanied by the fraudulent use of a driving licence) the wrong person has been made liable to a fixed penalty and the error has not been detected until receipt of a registration certificate.

As will be seen in due course, the nature and content of a statutory declaration made under ss.72, 73 vary in accordance with the manner in which the fixed penalty notice concerned was issued. Certain aspects of the procedure, however, are common to all cases.

The declaration must be made and served within 21 days of receipt of a notice **17.65** of registration upon the proper officer for the court which issued that notice (ss.72(1)(b), 73(1)(b) and 74(5), (6)). It may be delivered to him, left at his office or sent to him by registered or recorded delivery post (s.74(4)). There is provision for the court (which for this purpose may consist of a single justice) to accept late service in circumstances where it would be unreasonable to expect service within the normal time limit (s.74(2)). In order to cater for cases where the notice of registration does not find its target, s.74(5), (6) provides that a person shall be taken as receiving notice of registration when he receives notice either of the registration as such or of any enforcement proceedings in respect of the sum registered.

Procedure where fixed penalty notice given to offender

17.66   In this case the declaration must state either:

    (a) that the declarant was not the person to whom the relevant fixed penalty notice was given; or

    (b) that he gave notice requesting a court hearing in the time allowed and the manner prescribed by the notice

(s.72(2)).

In case (a) above, the effect of the declaration is to render void the fixed penalty notice, the registration and any enforcement proceedings already taken (s.72(3)). In such a case, where the actual recipient of the fixed penalty notice has surrendered the declarant's driving licence, any endorsement of that licence which may have been made will also be void (s.72(4)).

17.67   In case (b) above, the registration, any enforcement proceedings already taken and any endorsement of the declarant's driving licence will be made void, and the declarant will be treated as if he had given notice requesting a hearing in respect of the offence (s.72(5)). For the purposes of subsequent proceedings for that offence, the six months' time-limit for the initiation of proceedings for summary offences (Magistrates' Courts Act 1980 s.127(1)) runs from the date on which the declaration was served rather than the date of commission of the alleged offence (s.74(1)).

Procedure where fixed penalty notice affixed to stationary vehicle

17.68   In this case the declaration must state either:

    (a) that the declarant did not know of the fixed penalty or any notice issued in respect of it until he received the notice of registration; or

    (b) that he was not the owner of the vehicle at the time of the alleged offence and that he has a reasonable excuse for failing to comply with the relevant notice to owner; or

    (c) that he gave notice requesting a court hearing in the time allowed and the manner prescribed by the notice to owner

(s.73(2)).

In cases (a) and (b) above, the relevant notice to owner, the registration and any enforcement proceedings already taken will be void, but without prejudice in case (a) to the service on the declarant of a further notice to owner (irrespective of whether the original notice to owner was properly served) (s.73(3)).

17.69   In case (c) above, no proceedings may be brought for enforcing payment of the sum registered for a period of 21 days following the date of the declaration; if during that period a fresh notice to owner is served, enforcement proceedings will be further suspended until the end of the period allowed for response to that notice (s.73(4)). If no such notice is served, or if a notice is served and the recipient supplies a new statutory statement of ownership as requested, the registration and any enforcement proceedings already taken will be void, and the case will be treated (after certain amounts of time have passed) as one in which the declarant has asked for a court hearing in respect of the alleged offence (s.73(5)). In a case where no new notice to owner has been served, the time which must elapse is 21 days following the date of the declaration; in a case where a new statutory statement of ownership has been furnished, it is 21 days following the time when the statement was furnished (s.73(6)). It is to be noted that in the event of non-compliance with a new notice to owner served as above, the original registration and any associated enforcement proceedings do not become void; in such a case, enforcement may get under way again after the time allowed for response to the notice has expired.

Protection from unauthorised actions

The provisions of ss.72, 73 and 74 described above do not in any way preju- **17.70**
dice any other rights of redress a person may have as a result of the invalidity of any action purportedly taken in pursuance of the fixed penalty procedure but not in fact authorised by the Act (s.74(7)).

Miscellaneous Provisions

Penalty points: modification where fixed penalty also in question

It may very well arise in practice that whereas one, or possibly more than one, **17.71**
endorsable offence is dealt with by way of fixed penalty, other and possibly more serious offences may be reported for prosecution in the normal way. It is more than likely, e.g., that a driver travelling without his driving licence (or, for that matter his insurance certificate) will be issued with a Form HO/RT/1 requiring production of any missing documents at the same time as he is given a "substantive" or "provisional" fixed penalty notice for any concurrently committed fixed penalty offence. In such circumstances he may find himself liable both to a fixed penalty and to a summary prosecution.

Section 30 provides that where a person is convicted of an endorsable offence, and the court is satisfied that his driving licence has been or is liable to be endorsed without a court hearing by a fixed penalty clerk in respect of an offence committed on the same occasion, the appropriate number of penalty points for the offence of which he is convicted shall be the number of penalty points to be attributed to that offence *less* the number of points required to be endorsed in respect of the "connected" fixed penalty offence.

Special provisions for hired vehicles

In order to protect car hire firms from some of the indiscretions of their custom- **17.72**
ers, s.66 makes provision for dealing with the problems of fixed penalty notices affixed to hired vehicles.

It applies to hiring, but not hire-purchase, agreements which provide for a fixed period of hire of less than six months (whether or not that period is extendable by agreement) (s.66(7)). In any case where a hire firm is served with a notice to owner, the firm concerned may escape liability for a fixed penalty offence if at the time of the alleged offence the vehicle concerned was let to another under a qualifying hiring agreement, and if within the time allowed for response to the notice it serves certain documents upon the relevant person (s.66(1)). These documents are as follows:

    (a) a statement signed by or on behalf of the firm to the effect that the vehicle was hired under a hiring agreement at the time of the alleged offence;

    (b) a copy of the hiring agreement; and

    (c) a copy of a statement of liability signed by the hirer under that agreement indicating his acceptance of liability as the "owner" of the vehicle for fixed penalty offences committed during the currency of the hiring agreement (s.66(2), (3)).

17.73   It is to be noted that the relevant person may, at any reasonable time within six months of service of the notice to owner, require the firm to produce the originals of the hiring agreement and statement of liability in question (s.66(5)). Such production would obviously be necessary if any question arises as to the authenticity of the copy documents originally produced in response to the notice to owner. Failure to produce the original documents when so required results in the firm losing the protection of s.66 and becoming liable in the same way as a person who has been served with a notice to owner and has failed to furnish the statutory statement of ownership in response to it.

    In normal circumstances, however, the copy documents will suffice, and s.66(4) provides that where such documents have been served the default procedure appropriate in the case of a fixed penalty notice affixed to a stationary vehicle will apply as if reference to "owner of vehicle" and "statutory statement of ownership" were references to "hirer" and "statutory statement of hiring" respectively.

OPERATION OF THE FIXED PENALTY SYSTEM

Conclusions and practical problems

17.74   One of the bugbears of the old fixed penalty system was a considerable degree of inconsistency in the use made of it from area to area. In an attempt to introduce a measure of consistency and conformity in the use to be made of the present system throughout England and Wales, the Secretary of State was obliged by s.87 to issue guidance to chief officers of police throughout the jurisdiction in respect of the operation of Pt III of the Act, with the objective, so far as possible, of working towards uniformity.

    Another area of concern in the operation of the system is the strain and potential points of breakdown inherent in the complexity of its procedures. The sheer volume of paperwork which must be handled is daunting. With at least 10 categories of official notice, to say nothing of driving licences, to be processed, it is inevitable that some documents will go astray. To take but one trivial example, the driver who elects to produce his provisional fixed penalty notice at a police station in Ashford, Newcastle, Newport or St Ives may unwittingly be the source of some confusion. An overall impression of the complexity of the system may be gleaned from the "flow charts" which appear at §§ 17.77–9.

17.75   One source of potential difficulty to fixed penalty clerks, police and public alike is the problem of late payments, most particularly in the case of a fixed penalty notice affixed to a stationary vehicle. The opportunity to pay the fixed penalty lapses at the end of the suspended enforcement period, but is revived when the notice to owner is issued. In the possibly protracted fallow period between these two events, the fixed penalty clerk has no authority to receive a payment. It is clearly unfortunate that in such circumstances the police will be obliged to embark upon the costly and time-consuming "notice to owner" procedure even if the offender attempts, albeit belatedly, to pay the fixed penalty, but given the way in which the Act was drafted, no obvious solution has presented itself.

FLOW CHARTS

Explanation and key

17.76

The flow charts set out on the next few pages are designed to illustrate in simple terms the procedure to be followed in the cases of "driver present" fixed penalty offences (endorsable and non-endorsable) and "stationary vehicle" non-endorsable offences where the fixed penalty notice has been affixed to the vehicle in question by a constable. In March 2009, a parallel but different process was introduced for situations where the notice has been fixed by a vehicle examiner (see § 17.03).

The symbols used are as follows:

= A question

= An instruction, item of information or procedural step

= An outcome

The abbreviations used are as follows:

DL = driving licence	FPN = fixed penalty notice
FP = fixed penalty	SEP = suspended enforcement period
FPC = fixed penalty clerk	SSoF = statutory statement of facts

"Driver present"—endorsable offence

17.77

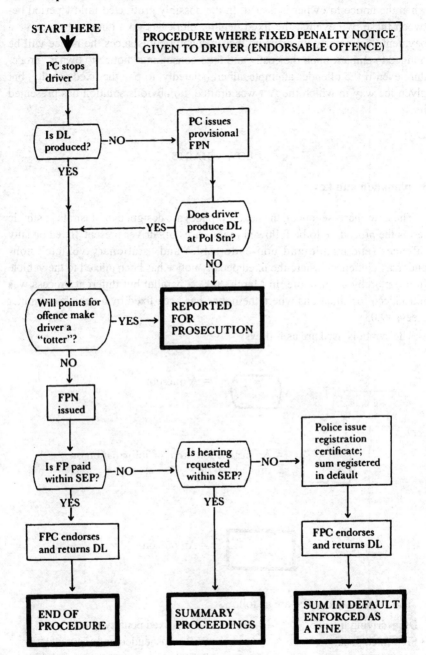

START HERE

PROCEDURE WHERE FIXED PENALTY NOTICE
GIVEN TO DRIVER (ENDORSABLE OFFENCE)

PC stops driver

Is DL produced? —NO→ PC issues provisional FPN

YES

Does driver produce DL at Pol Stn?

YES

NO

Will points for offence make driver a "totter"? —YES→ REPORTED FOR PROSECUTION

NO

FPN issued

Is FP paid within SEP? —NO→ Is hearing requested within SEP? —NO→ Police issue registration certificate; sum registered in default

YES

YES

FPC endorses and returns DL

FPC endorses and returns DL

END OF PROCEDURE

SUMMARY PROCEEDINGS

SUM IN DEFAULT ENFORCED AS A FINE

"Driver present"—non-endorsable offence

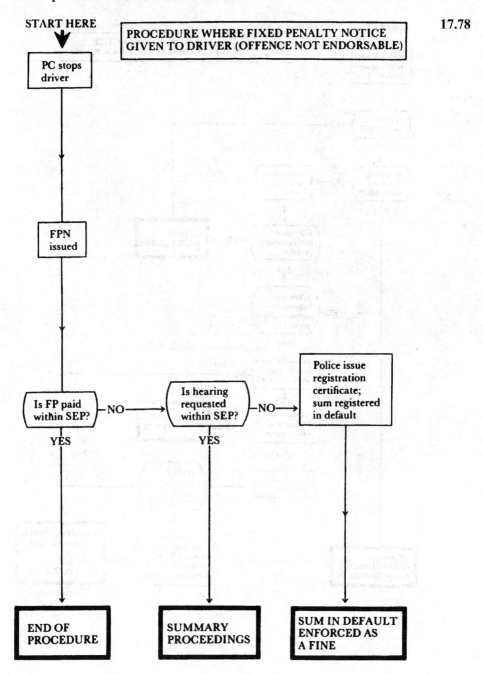

"Stationary vehicle"—non-endorsable offence

17.79

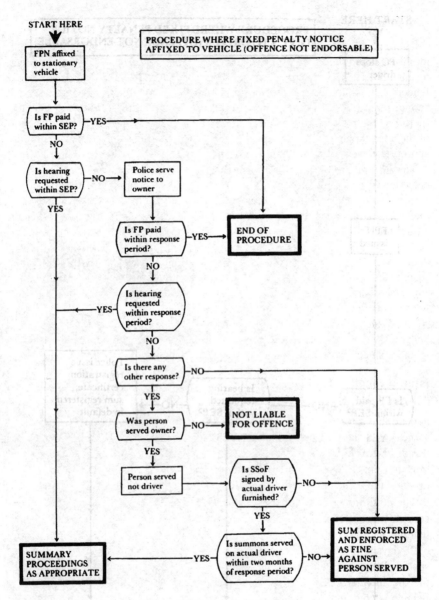

START HERE

FPN affixed to stationary vehicle

PROCEDURE WHERE FIXED PENALTY NOTICE AFFIXED TO VEHICLE (OFFENCE NOT ENDORSABLE)

Is FP paid within SEP? —YES→

NO

Is hearing requested within SEP? —NO→ Police serve notice to owner

YES

Is FP paid within response period? —YES→ **END OF PROCEDURE**

NO

Is hearing requested within response period? ←YES—

NO

Is there any other response? —NO→

YES

Was person served owner? —NO→ **NOT LIABLE FOR OFFENCE**

YES

Person served not driver → Is SSoF signed by actual driver furnished? —NO→

YES

SUM REGISTERED AND ENFORCED AS FINE AGAINST PERSON SERVED

Is summons served on actual driver within two months of response period? —NO→

←YES— **SUMMARY PROCEEDINGS AS APPROPRIATE**

CONDITIONAL OFFER OF FIXED PENALTY

Introduction

Those parts of the Transport Act 1982 which related to Scotland were brought **17.80** into force when the Procurator Fiscal and Fixed Penalty Scheme came into effect on June 30, 1983 and were subsequently re-enacted as ss.75–77 of the 1988 Offenders Act. Under those provisions procurators fiscal were empowered to send a "conditional offer" of a fixed penalty through the post to an alleged offender. Inertia by the recipient did not lead as in England and Wales to the enforcement of the unpaid penalty as if it were a fine, but rather to the subsequent initiation in appropriate cases of criminal proceedings in respect of the offence concerned.

The introduction by the Road Traffic Act 1991 of automatic devices for the detection of speeding and traffic light offences (see Chapter 6) had implications for the fixed penalty system in England and Wales, in that the existing arrangements for endorsable offences such as those required the presence of the offender at the time at which the fixed penalty was imposed. Section 34 of the 1991 Act addressed that problem by substituting ss.75–77 of the 1988 Offenders Act in order to extend the "conditional offer" scheme throughout Great Britain. Under this scheme the police in England and Wales and Scotland (as well as procurators fiscal in Scotland) may send a notice offering a fixed penalty (the "conditional offer") to an alleged offender through the post.

Although the conditional offer scheme is designed to be available for all fixed **17.81** penalties, its use would appear presently to be limited in England and Wales to offences detected by the automatic devices described above.

Issue of conditional offer

Where in England and Wales a constable or vehicle examiner has reason to **17.82** believe that a fixed penalty offence has been committed, a notice (described by s.75(5) as a "conditional offer") may be sent to the alleged offender by or on behalf of the chief officer of police or the Secretary of State. Such a notice may only be sent, however, where a fixed penalty notice was neither given to the driver at the scene nor at a police station nor affixed to the vehicle (s.75(1), (1A)).

The conditional offer must give particulars of the circumstances alleged to constitute the offence, must state the amount of the fixed penalty and must indicate that proceedings for the offence cannot be commenced until the end of the period of 28 days following the date of issue of the offer or such longer period as may be specified therein (s.75(7)). It must also indicate that if payment is made within the specified period and (if the offence concerned is endorsable) the offender's licence is contemporaneously delivered and he is not liable to disqualification under s.35 of the Act, any liability to conviction of the offence shall be discharged (s.75(8)).

The failure of a conditional offer of fixed penalty to state that proceedings **17.83** could not be commenced against the alleged offender in respect of the offence concerned until the end of the period of 28 days (or such longer period as might have been specified) following the date on which the conditional offer was issued, as required by s.75(7)(c) of the Road Traffic Offenders Act 1988, was not a bar to proceedings being brought against the alleged offender provided that those proceedings were not commenced before the end of the minimum period specified in s.75 (i.e. 28 days); *DPP v Holden* [2006] EWHC 658; [2007] R.T.R. 5.

If the offender within the time allowed for response to the notice (generally 28 days) sends both payment and his licence to the appropriate person, and assuming that he is not liable to a penalty points disqualification, his licence will be duly endorsed and returned to him (ss.76(3), 77(1)). If, however, it is discovered on inspection of the licence that a liability for disqualification under s.35 exists, the unendorsed licence and the payment will both be returned and proceedings may in due course be commenced. Similarly proceedings may be commenced if the alleged offender fails to make payment and to deliver his licence within the specified period.

17.84   In the event that the penalty points to be taken into account by the appropriate person number six or more, and it appears to him that the offence concerned was committed within the offender's probationary period (two years beginning on the day on which he became a qualified driver), he must not return the licence to its holder but must instead send it to the Secretary of State for revocation (Road Traffic (New Drivers) Act 1995 s.2(3), (4)). These provisions apply to any person whose first driving test was passed on or after June 1, 1997 (s.1 ibid.; see further § 11.09).

If a cheque tendered in payment of a fixed penalty is dishonoured, the endorsement remains effective (s.77(3)). If the offender is subsequently prosecuted for the original offence, the court must order the removal of the fixed penalty endorsement; if it finds the offender guilty, however, a fresh endorsement may be ordered (s.77(4)).

VEHICLE EMISSIONS

17.85   The Road Traffic (Vehicle Emissions) (Fixed Penalty) Regulations 1997 were made under the authority of s.87 of the Environment Act 1995 and came into force on December 26, 1997. These regulations permit participating local authorities to issue fixed penalty notices to users of vehicles within their area who contravene, or fail to comply with, reg.61 of the Road Vehicles (Construction and Use) Regulations 1986 (emission of smoke, vapour, gases, oily substances, etc.) and to drivers of vehicles who contravene, or fail to comply with reg.98 of the 1986 Regulations (stopping of engine when stationary). The fixed penalty is £60 in the case of unlawful vehicle emissions and £20 for leaving the engine of a stationary vehicle running.

The Road Traffic (Vehicle Emissions) (Fixed Penalty) Regulations 1997 described above have been revoked and replaced (so far as England is concerned) with effect from July 18, 2002 by the Road Traffic (Vehicle Emissions) (Fixed Penalty) (England) Regulations 2002 (SI 2002/1808). References to specific regulations in the text which follows are, unless specified otherwise, references to the 2002 Regulations. In relation to Wales, the 1997 Regulations were revoked and replaced by the Road Traffic (Vehicle Emissions) (Fixed Penalty) (Wales) Regulations 2003 (SI 2003/300), which came into force on May 1, 2003. (In Scotland, see now the Road Traffic (Vehicle Emissions) (Fixed Penalty) (Scotland) Regulations 2003 (SI 2003/212), which came into force on March 21, 2003.) Under the 2002 Regulations a local authority in England may apply to the Secretary of State for designation. A local authority so designated may use fixed penalty notices to enforce offences of the kind described above within its area.

As with other fixed penalty legislation, payment of the fixed penalty within the period fixed for payment discharges any liability to conviction for the offence (reg.17(4)). No proceedings will be instituted against the alleged offender until the payment period has expired unless the person concerned has requested a hearing in respect of the offence concerned (reg.17(3)). The time-limit for the service by the alleged offender of a notice requesting a hearing must be specified in the fixed penalty notice (reg.18(1)). Where such a notice is served, the fixed penalty notice may be treated as an information for the purposes of the prosecution (reg.18(2)(b)).

Where the fixed penalty remains unpaid after the period allowed for payment **17.86** and no notice requesting a hearing has been served, the penalty is increased to £90 for vehicle emission offences and £40 for leaving an engine running. The outstanding sums are enforceable in England and Wales through the county court (2002 and 2003 (Wales) Regulations, reg.21), and in Scotland in like manner as an extract registered decree arbitral bearing a warrant of execution issued by the sheriff court of any sheriffdom in Scotland (2003 (Scotland) Regulations, reg.22).

A number of authorities were listed in the interpretation section (reg.2) of the 1997 Regulations as participating in what was initially a pilot scheme. Amongst those authorities were the City Council of Glasgow and the Council of the City and County of Swansea, and their continued participation is presumed under the auspices of the 1997 Regulations. Persons authorised by designated authorities in England under the 2002 Regulations have power to require the disclosure by a driver of his name, address and date of birth (for vehicle emissions under reg.11(1) and for stationary engine running offences under reg.14(1)); failure to comply with such a requirement is punishable on summary conviction with a fine of level 3. A fixed penalty notice may be withdrawn if the appropriate authority determines it ought not to have been issued or ought not to have been issued to the person named as the person to whom it was issued (reg.20).

CHAPTER 18

CUSTODIAL AND OTHER PENALTIES

CONTENTS

INTRODUCTION

The legislative framework

18.01   The Powers of Criminal Courts (Sentencing) Act 2000 (generally referred to hereafter in this chapter as the 2000 Sentencing Act) consolidated earlier enactments relating to the powers of courts to deal with offenders and defaulters and to the treatment of such persons. It gathered together in one place most, if not all, of the statutory provisions then governing the sentencing of offenders by the criminal courts.

Some (but not all) of the 2000 Act has been replaced by the Criminal Justice Act 2003; Pt 12 of which (ss.142–305) is devoted to sentencing. Some of these provisions have been amended, most significantly, by the Criminal Justice and Immigration Act 2008.

18.02   The Criminal Justice Act 2003 (generally referred to hereafter as the 2003 Act) created the Sentencing Guidelines Council. Every court in sentencing an offender must have regard to any guidelines issued by the Council as are relevant to the case (s.172).

The Court of Appeal in *R. v Oosthuizen* [2005] EWCA Crim 1978; [2005] Crim. L.R. 979 pointed out that this does not mean that the guidelines must necessarily be followed slavishly. The statutory provisions (particularly 2003 Act s.174(2)(a) ibid.) recognise that the sentencer may depart from a guideline if there is good and sufficient reason to do so, provided that the court's reasons are clearly stated. The sentencing court, however, is not permitted simply to disregard the guideline because it disagrees with it.

18.03   Section 142 of the 2003 Act lists the purposes of sentencing, to which the sentencing court must have regard, as the punishment of offenders, the reduction of crime (including by deterrence), the reform and rehabilitation of offenders, the protection of the public and the making of reparation by offenders to persons affected by their offences. Section 143 of the 2003 Act provides that in determining the seriousness of an offence, the court must consider the offender's culpability and the harm which the offence caused, was intended to cause or might foreseeably have caused. Where an offender has one or more previous convictions, the court must treat each previous conviction as an aggravating factor where it is reasonable to do so having regard in particular to the nature of the offence to which the conviction relates, its relevance to the current offence and the time that has elapsed since conviction. The fact that an offence was committed whilst on bail must also be treated as an aggravating factor.

Discount for guilty plea

It has long been custom and practice for courts to reduce the sentence where an **18.04** offender has entered a timely guilty plea. Sections 144 and 174 of the 2003 Act require a court when sentencing an offender who has pleaded guilty to take into account the stage in the proceedings at which the offender's intention to plead guilty was indicated, and the circumstances in which that indication was given. If, as a result of taking those matters into account the court imposes a punishment less severe than it would otherwise have imposed, it must state in open court that it has done so.

A definitive guideline, "Reduction in Sentence for a Guilty Plea", was issued by the Sentencing Guidelines Council in July 2007. The guideline provides for the greatest reduction where a plea was entered at the "first reasonable opportunity". Annex 1 to the guideline notes that that is a question of judgement and gives examples of when that opportunity is most likely to be. In most cases, it is likely to be the first time a defendant appears before a court and has the opportunity to plead guilty. A reduction of one third is recommended for such a plea reducing to one quarter for a plea after a trial date has been set and to one tenth for a plea "at the door of the court" or after a trial has begun. Since the purpose of giving a reduction is to encourage guilty pleas and so avoid the need for a trial (not least because of the benefit that brings to any victim and to witnesses), there is a presumption in favour of the reduction even where the prosecution case is overwhelming. However, the guideline recognises that there will be situations where the fact that the prosecution case was overwhelming (without relying on admissions from the defendant) justifies a departure from the guideline and, in such circumstances, the recommended reduction for a guilty plea at the first reasonable opportunity reduces to 20 per cent. All Sentencing Guidelines Council guidelines are available at *http://www.sentencing-guidelines.gov.uk* [Accessed April 8, 2009].

The Magistrates' Court Sentencing Guidelines

A revised edition of the Magistrates' Court Sentencing Guidelines has been **18.05** published by the Sentencing Guidelines Council (available at *http:// www.sentencing-guidelines.gov.uk* [Accessed April 8, 2009]). The new guidelines are a further evolution from previous editions and incorporate relevant material from other Sentencing Guidelines Council guidelines and appeal court decisions. The structure will be immediately recognisable with offence specific guidelines complemented by explanatory material. In relation to the more serious offences where a number of different sentencing outcomes are possible, the offence specific guidelines follow the style of other Sentencing Guidelines Council guidelines and provide several descriptions of different types of activity within the general definition of the offence followed by a starting point and a sentencing range for each. The approach of a sentencing court will be to identify the description that most closely matches the offence before the court and then to move up or down within the range depending on the aggravating or mitigating factors present.

Combinations of aggravating factors may suggest a sentence above the range; combinations of mitigating factors or the effect of any reduction for a guilty plea may take the sentence below the range. Wherever a sentence is imposed that is outside the range provided, the court is obliged to give its reasons. In relation to other offences where a fine or discharge is most likely to be appropriate, the guidelines tend to provide a starting point alone. Where an offence can be committed by the owner or the driver, the guidelines tend to provide three starting points, one for the driver, one for an owner-driver and one where the owner is a company.

Explanatory material gives greater guidance than at present. As well as giving further guidance on the approach to the assessment of a financial penalty, the guidelines include a section on road traffic offences drawing attention to the approach to the different types of disqualification—obligatory, discretionary and until a test is passed. Guidance is given suggesting that the opportunity to reduce a period of disqualification by completion of a rehabilitation course should be considered for all convicted for the first time of a relevant offence; a court should also be willing to consider offering the opportunity to attend a second course unless there is good reason not to do so. However, it will not usually be appropriate to give the opportunity to attend a third time.

In relation to the circumstances in which a court should exercise its power to disqualify a driver not present before the court, the guidelines state that the power should not normally be exercised unless "the court is sure that the offender is aware of the hearing and the likely imposition of disqualification".

18.06   Under the relevant legislation, a "new driver" who accumulates six points in the two years following passing the driving test will suffer automatic revocation of the licence. It is possible to avoid this revocation where the court disqualifies the offender and courts have sometimes been asked to proceed in this way in order to do so. The guidelines suggest that that is "inappropriate since it would circumvent the clear intention of Parliament". The guideline sentences are based on a first-time offender convicted after pleading not guilty. Relevant guidelines in respect of road traffic offences are set out in full in Appendix 3 below.

The fines in the guidelines are given as one of three bands, "A", "B" or "C". The bands represent respectively (in ascending alphabetical order) 50 per cent, 100 per cent and 150 per cent of the defendant's "relevant weekly income". In essence, this is net income. However, where that income is £100 per week or less or the offender is primarily in receipt of benefit, the relevant weekly income is deemed to be £100 per week. Where there is no reliable information on which a court can rely, provision is made for a deemed income of £350 per week. Where a defendant is to be fined for several offences and his means are limited it may be better to fix the relevant level for the most serious offence and order "no separate penalty" on the lesser matters.

Fines

Generally

18.07   Section 32(9) of the Magistrates' Courts Act 1980, as amended, provides that the maximum fine on summary conviction of an offence triable "either way" (the "prescribed sum") is £5,000. The standard scale of fine levels is as follows:

Level on the scale	Maximum
1	£200
2	£500
3	£1,000
4	£2,500
5	£5,000

The assessment and imposition of fines

18.08 Courts are required by s.164 of the Criminal Justice Act 2003 to inquire into the financial circumstances of the offender (if he is an individual) before fixing the amount of a fine. The amount of the fine shall be such as, in the opinion of the court, reflects the seriousness of the offence. In fixing the amount the court must take into account the financial circumstances of the offender (whether an individual or otherwise) so far as they appear or are known and shall do so whether taking those circumstances into account has the effect of *increasing* or *reducing* that amount. Whenever a court is imposing a fine, it must also impose a "victims surcharge"—currently £15. If the offender has insufficient means to pay both the victims surcharge and the fine, then the fine must be reduced. A compensation order continues to take priority over both a victims surcharge and a fine where the means of the offender are insufficient (2003 Act s.161A).

Section 162 of the 2003 Act empowers a court dealing with a convicted person to make what is described as a "financial circumstances order" in respect of him before proceeding to sentence. A like order may also be made in respect of a person who has signified his intention to plead guilty by post. Such an order requires the offender to furnish the court with a statement of his financial circumstances. Where despite its best endeavours the court finds itself with insufficient information to make a proper determination of the offender's financial circumstances, it may make such determination as it thinks fit (s.164(5)). Section 165 of the 2003 Act allows courts to remit all or part of fines discovered subsequently to have been set at too high a level.

18.09 The application of a rigid formula in the assessment of fines, even for a single offence, is not right; to apply it to each of 10 offences and add up was clearly wrong. The Divisional Court so held in *R. v Chelmsford Crown Court Ex p. Birchall* [1990] Crim. L.R. 352 in reducing fines totalling £7,600 for excess weight offences to a total of £1,300. Courts had to consider all the circumstances and apply the principles of sentencing (in particular the "totality" principle) which were well known.

A speeding driver attempted to pay a fixed penalty of £60 and have his licence endorsed with three penalty points but his attempt was thwarted by the fact that he produced what was classified as a "foreign" licence (a Northern Ireland driving licence). He was prosecuted and fined £180 and received five penalty points. His appeal against sentence was upheld by the High Court of Justiciary in *Stockton v Gallagher* 2004 S.L.T. 733 on the basis that it would be unjust and oppressive to penalise him more harshly than was provided for in the fixed penalty notice. The Magistrates' Court Sentencing Guidelines provide (at p.189) that an offender unable to pay a fixed penalty for reasons outside his or her control should not be disadvantaged; the starting point would normally be what the fixed penalty would have been.

18.10   Magistrates have power to mitigate a pecuniary penalty for any road traffic of-fence, including excise licence ones, however many the previous convictions (Magistrates' Courts Act 1980 s.34), unless the statute otherwise provides. It is to be noted, however, that the sum recoverable in addition to any penalty imposed for an offence of using or keeping a vehicle without an excise licence is *back-duty*, not a pecuniary penalty; what is now s.19 of the 1991 Act therefore does not apply, and courts have no discretion to mitigate the sum payable (*Chief Constable of Kent v Mather* [1986] R.T.R. 36).

As to the fixed penalty procedure for certain offences, see Chapter 17. As to mitigated penalties offered by the Department for Transport, see § 12.145.

Fines, costs and compensation imposed on youths

18.11   Section 137 of the 2000 Sentencing Act provides that so far as persons aged under 18 are concerned, courts should order the parent or guardian to pay the fines, etc., imposed upon the young person unless that parent or guardian cannot be found or to make such an order for payment would be unreasonable in the cir-cumstances of the case. The Act further provides that a local authority having parental responsibility for a child or young person in its care or accommodated by it shall be treated as a parent or guardian (s.137(8)). So far as the financial cir-cumstances of an offender are concerned, where the court makes an order for payment of fines, etc., by a parent or guardian, it is the financial circumstances of that person which have to be considered (s.138).

Notwithstanding the maximum fine levels for particular offences committed by persons aged 18 or over, there is an overriding maximum fine level of £250 in re-spect of offences committed by offenders aged 10 to 13, and an overall fine level of £1,000 in respect of offenders aged 14 to 17.

IMPRISONMENT AND OTHER CUSTODIAL SENTENCES

Statutory restrictions on imposition of discretionary custodial sentences

18.12   Section 152(2) of the Criminal Justice Act 2003 prevents a court from impos-ing a custodial sentence upon an offender unless it is of the opinion that the of-fence, or the combination of the offence and one or more offences associated with it, was "so serious that neither a fine alone nor a community sentence can be justified". Section 153 of the 2003 Act stipulates that the custodial sentence must be for the shortest term that in the court's opinion is commensurate with the seriousness of the offence, or the combination of the offence and one or more of-fences associated with it.

The court must obtain a pre-sentence report before forming the opinion referred to above (s.156(3)), unless the court is of the opinion that it is unnecessary to obtain such a report (s.156(4)). In the case of offenders under the age of 18, however, a court may only dispense with the requirement to obtain a report if it has considered an existing pre-sentence report on the offender concerned (s.156(5)). Failure to obtain a report in accordance with s.156(3) does not invalidate a custodial sentence, but such a report must (subject to s.156(7) described below) be obtained by the court which deals with an appeal against sentence. Section 156(7) enables the appeal court to dispense with a pre-sentence report if of opinion that the court below was justified in concluding that such a report was unnecessary, or if of opinion that although the court below was not so justified, the circumstances of the case at the time it is before the court render such a report unnecessary.

The 2003 Act does not attempt a definition of the expression "so serious that **18.13** only such a [*custodial*] sentence can be justified". Guidance is gradually being issued by the Sentencing Guidelines Council indicating the circumstances in which a particular offence is likely to have passed the statutory threshold thereby enabling (but not compelling) such a sentence to be imposed. Many of the offences included in this work are incorporated into the revised Magistrates' Court Sentencing Guidelines (see § 18.06 above and Appendix 3 below). Further specific guidelines relating to the four offences of causing death by driving were published by the Sentencing Guidelines Council in July 2008 (see Appendix 4 below). All documents published by the Sentencing Guidelines Council can be found at *http://www.sentencing-guidelines.gov.uk* [Accessed April 9, 2009]. Sentencing Guidelines Council guidelines describe the circumstances in which an offence is likely to be sufficiently serious to cross a threshold. Other than where a sentence under the "dangerous offender" provisions is necessary, a sentence must not exceed that which the seriousness of the offence permits. However, in many cases, there will be mitigating factors relating to the offender that lead a court to determine that a lesser sentence could be justly imposed.

A custodial sentence may also be imposed upon an offender if he refuses to consent to a proposed community sentence which requires his consent (s.152(3)).

Section 83 of the 2000 Sentencing Act forbids a court to sentence an offender **18.14** to prison or detention, unless:

(a) he is legally represented; or

(b) he has been granted a right to representation, but the right has been withdrawn because of his conduct; or

(c) he has been offered and has refused or failed to apply for such representation; or

(d) he has been previously sentenced to immediate imprisonment or detention as the case may be.

Length of custodial sentences

As noted above, a discretionary custodial sentence shall be for such term as is **18.15** (in the opinion of the court) commensurate with the seriousness of the offence (or of the offence and one or more offences associated with it). It should be noted, however, that ss.224–236 of the Criminal Justice Act 2003, as amended, have established a new regime for dealing with what the Act describes as "dangerous offenders". A person aged 18 or over convicted of a serious specified offence, which for the purposes of this work means manslaughter, causing death by dangerous driving, causing death by careless driving when under the influence of drink or drugs or aggravated vehicle-taking involving an accident which caused the death of any person, is liable, if certain conditions are satisfied, to either a life sentence (for manslaughter), indeterminate sentence for public protection or an extended sentence (for any of the other listed offences). The conditions which must be satisfied are that the court is of the opinion that there is a significant risk to members of the public of serious harm occasioned by the commission by the offender of further specified offences. The specified offences concerned are listed in Sch.15 to the Act. Generally, such a sentence will only be imposed where the offence is sufficiently serious to justify a determinate custodial sentence of four years or more.

Young offenders and youths; custodial sentences

18.16   Section 96 of the 2000 Sentencing Act provides that where a person aged at least 18 but under 21 qualifies for a custodial sentence under what is now s.152 of the 2003 Act, the sentence that the court is to pass is a sentence of detention in a young offender institution. The maximum term of detention which may be imposed for an offence is the same as the maximum term of imprisonment for that offence.

The custodial sentence for young offenders is a detention and training order. Such orders may be imposed on a child or young person who is aged 12 and under 18 at the time of sentence (2000 Sentencing Act s.100(1)), but in the case of an offender under the age of 15 at the time of conviction, only if he is a "persistent offender" (s.100(2)(a)). The Court of Appeal in *R. v Smith* [2000] Crim. L.R. 613 was satisfied that a 14-year-old offender was a "persistent offender" in the light of the offences to which he had pleaded guilty, a series of crimes (robbery, possession of an offensive weapon and false imprisonment) committed over a period of two days, even though he had no previous convictions. It was also held by that court in *R. v D* [2000] Crim. L.R. 867 that a 14-year-old who had only one previous conviction but who had received three formal cautions was a "persistent offender" for the purposes of the legislation. In *R. v B* [2001] Crim. L.R. 50 it was further held that in addition to cautions, a court may also look at offences committed after the offence in respect of which the detention and training order was made as well as offences committed before the offence for which the order was made. It was not necessary that before a person could be categorised as a "persistent offender" he should have been committing a string of offences either of the same or similar character, or that his failure to address his offending behaviour was established by his failure to comply with previous orders of the court. The question of whether or not a given offender had achieved that degree of persistence in his offending to qualify as a "persistent offender" was best left (as Parliament intended) to the good sense of the court which was called upon to sentence in any given case.

18.17   Detention and training orders are for terms of 4, 6, 8, 10, 12, 18 or 24 months (s.101(1)) and may be imposed by magistrates' courts and the Crown Court, provided that the term of such an order does not exceed the maximum term of imprisonment that the Crown Court could impose upon an offender aged 21 or over for the offence (s.101(2)). Detention and training orders may be made consecutive to one another provided that the overall term does not exceed 24 months (s.101(4)). Within that overall limit courts may impose consecutive sentences which may result in an aggregate sentence which does not correspond with one of the statutory periods specified in s.101(1), provided that it adds up to any even number of months between four and 24 (*R. v Norris* [2001] Crim. L.R. 48). When brought into force (anticipated to be in November 2009), the Criminal Justice and Immigration Act 2008 will additionally require a court, before imposing custodial sentence, to be satisfied that a youth rehabilitation order with intensive supervision and surveillance or with fostering cannot be justified.

Suspended sentences

Sections 189–192 of the Criminal Justice Act 2003, implemented with some **18.18** modifications on April 4, 2005, and applying only to offences committed on or after that date, established a new regime for the imposition of suspended sentences of imprisonment. A court which passes a sentence of imprisonment for a term of at least 14 days but not more than 12 months (in a magistrates' court, six months) may order the offender to comply during a specified "supervision period" with one or more of the requirements which normally form part of a community order (unpaid work, supervision, etc.), and order that the sentence of imprisonment is not to take effect unless either the offender fails to comply with any such requirement, or commits another offence (whether or not punishable with imprisonment) during the "operational period" (s.189(1)). The "supervision period" and the "operational period" must each be a period of not less than six months and not more than two years beginning with the date of the order (s.189(3)).

Detention in police cells, etc.

Section 135 of the Magistrates' Courts Act 1980 allows a court to order an of- **18.19** fender found guilty of an offence carrying imprisonment to be detained in the courthouse or at any police station until such hour as the court may direct being not later than 8pm.

Deferment of sentence

Sections 1 and 2 of the 2000 Sentencing Act, as substituted, allow a court to **18.20** defer passing sentence for a period of up to six months for the purpose of enabling the court in determining the sentence to have regard to the defendant's conduct during the period of deferment, including the making of reparation for his offence and any change in the defendant's circumstances. The substituted provisions require an offender to undertake to comply with any requirements as to his conduct during the period of deferment that the court may impose, and provide for the court to appoint a probation officer or any other person to supervise him in that endeavour. A breach of any such undertaking may result in his being sentenced before the end of the deferment period. The court can only defer sentence if the defendant consents (s.1(3)(a)); the court must be satisfied, having regard to the nature of the offence and the character and circumstances of the offender, that it would be in the interests of justice to defer sentence (s.1(3)(c)). Consent must be obtained for the defendant personally: *R. v Gilbey* [1975] Crim. L.R. 352. The use of the power to defer sentence is subject to guidelines issued by the Sentencing Guidelines Council, *New Sentences: Criminal Justice Act 2003*, Section 1 Part 2. The guidelines identify three purposes likely to be achieved by deferring sentence, testing the commitment of the offender not to reoffend, giving the offender an opportunity to do something where progress can be shown in a short period and providing an offender with opportunity to behave (or refrain from behaving) in a particular way relevant to sentence. The guideline concludes that the use of a deferred sentence "should be predominantly for a small group close to a significant threshold" in circumstances where by his or her conduct, the defendant can give a court grounds for imposing a lesser sentence. The Sentencing Guidelines Council emphasises the need for clarity in the terms of the deferral both for the benefit of the defendant and any court subsequently called upon to impose sentence. It would not seem normally appropriate for a court to defer sentence for an obligatorily disqualifiable offence, because the main penalty, that of disqualification, could not be altered after any deferment; the disqualification is mandatory unless "special reasons" exist and such special reasons are limited to the offence and cannot include "the character and circumstances of the defendant" or "his conduct during the period of deferment" (see s.1). It is bad practice and contrary to the statute to impose an order of disqualification and then defer sentence (*R. v Fairhead* [1975] Crim. L.R. 351).

The power of a court to pass sentence when the sentence has been deferred extends to committing the offender to the Crown Court for sentence (2000 Sentencing Act s.1D(2)(b)).

18.21　　If sentence is deferred and the offender is subsequently convicted of another offence during the period of deferment, the court which convicts him of the new offence may also sentence him in respect of the offence for which sentence was deferred (save that a magistrates' court cannot subsequently sentence an offender in respect of an offence for which a Crown Court deferred sentence) (2000 Sentencing Act s.1C(3)(a)). In considering the sentence of an offender after deferment, the Court of Appeal will normally look at two matters: first how the offender had behaved during the period of deferment, and secondly whether the sentence imposed was excessive having regard to the actual offence (*R. v Smith* [1977] Crim. L.R. 234).

A deferred sentence is a sentence for the purposes of ss.35 and 36 of the Criminal Justice Act 1988 and may as such be referred to the Court of Appeal by the Attorney General in pursuance of his powers to refer thither cases of "unduly lenient" sentencing in the Crown Court (*Att Gen's Reference No.22 of 1992 (Thomas)* [1993] Crim. L.R. 227).

Non-Custodial Sentences

Community sentences

18.22　　In relation to offenders aged 18 or over, s.177 of the Criminal Justice Act 2003 provides for a single community order incorporating court specified requirements inter alia for unpaid work, supervision, curfew, specified and prohibited activities, accredited programmes, drug rehabilitation and alcohol treatment. The court may impose more than one requirement under a community order, provided that the requirements are compatible with one another. Such an order may be imposed only in respect of an offence for which imprisonment could be imposed by the court passing sentence. For the small number of offences punishable by imprisonment in the Crown Court, but not in a magistrates' court, this will mean that, where a community order is the appropriate sentence, the case will have to be committed to the Crown Court for sentence.

Section 148 of the 2003 Act establishes three common principles governing the passing of community sentences. These are:

(1) that the offence (or the combination of the offence and one or more offences associated with it) is *serious enough* to justify such a sentence (s.148(1));

(2) that the particular requirement or combination of requirements to be

imposed by the court is the *most suitable* for the offender (s.148(2)(a)); and

(3) that the restrictions on liberty implicit in the order are *commensurate with the seriousness* of *all* the offences for which the offender is being dealt with (s.148(2)(b)).

18.23 A community order must specify a date, not more than three years after the date of the order, by which all the requirements it contains have to be complied with; and if two or more different requirements are imposed, an earlier date or dates may be specified for compliance with any one or more of them (s.177(5)).

An unpaid work requirement under a community order must be, in the aggregate, for not less than 40 and not more than 300 hours (s.199).

A supervision requirement in relation to a community order subsists for the period for which the community order concerned remains in force (s.213). The approach when imposing a community order is set out by the Sentencing Guidelines Council in its guideline *New Sentences: Criminal Justice Act 2003* and in the Magistrates' Court Sentencing Guidelines at pp.160–162.

Absolute or conditional discharge

18.24 Where a court thinks it inexpedient to inflict punishment, the offender may be given an absolute discharge. The *only* condition of a conditional discharge is that, if the offender commits a further offence during the period of the order (up to a maximum of three years), the court may sentence for the original offence as if the defendant had just been convicted of it.

An order for compensation or costs may be coupled with an order for conditional or absolute discharge. Section 46 of the 1988 Offenders Act requires a court to disqualify and endorse for an obligatorily disqualifiable offence and to endorse with a discretion to disqualify for any offence for which the court is obliged to endorse.

18.25 A court may not impose a fine and an order of conditional discharge for one offence (*R. v McClelland* [1951] 1 All E.R. 557). An offence for which an offender is given an absolute or conditional discharge is deemed to be a conviction only for the purposes of the proceedings for which the conditional or absolute discharge was made (2000 Sentencing Act s.14(1)); however, orders of absolute or conditional discharge are to be treated as convictions for the purposes of s.143 of the Criminal Justice Act 2003, which enables a sentencing court to take into account any previous convictions of the offender when assessing the seriousness of any offence.

Before making an order of conditional discharge the court is required to explain the effect of an order of conditional discharge in ordinary language: for this reason it would appear that an order of conditional discharge cannot be made in a defendant's absence.

Compensation

18.26 Compensation of up to £5,000 by a magistrates' court (unlimited for a Crown Court) may be ordered under s.130 of the 2000 Sentencing Act to be paid by any person convicted of an offence.

Where a person has inadequate means to pay what would otherwise be the appropriate fine together with the appropriate amount of compensation, the court is required to give preference to the order of compensation (s.130(12)). Moreover an order of compensation is a sentence in its own right; s.130 allows a court to make an order of compensation instead of dealing with the offender in any other way.

18.27 Compensation is not limited to any damage which has been incurred but includes compensation for any personal injury, loss or damage resulting from the offence for which the offender was convicted or any other offence taken into consideration by the court. A compensation order may include payments for funeral expenses or bereavement where death results from an offence, other than a death due to an accident arising out of the presence of a motor vehicle on a road (s.130(1)(b)). The court must also give reasons when not making a compensation order in a case where it is empowered to do so (s.130(3)). In deciding how much compensation to award, the court is required to have regard to the defendant's means. No application for compensation need be made by the loser to the court; the court may award compensation on its own motion. In the case of an offence under the Theft Act 1968 (or now the Fraud Act 2006) where the property in question is recovered, any damage which occurred while it was out of the owner's possession shall be treated as having resulted from the offence, howsoever and by whomsoever the damage was caused (s.130(5)).

18.28 Courts are empowered by s.130(6), (7) of the 2000 Sentencing Act to make compensation orders in respect of injury, loss or damage due to an accident arising out of the presence of a motor vehicle on a road, where either:

    (a) the damage is treated as having resulted from an offence under the Theft Act 1968 (or Fraud Act 2006); or

    (b) the injury, loss or damage involved the uninsured use of a motor vehicle by the offender, and compensation is not payable under any arrangements to which the Secretary of State is a party (i.e. the Motor Insurers' Bureau);

and the amount of compensation to be ordered may include an amount in respect of the loss of a "no claims" bonus. The power to make a compensation order arises only where the offender is uninsured; accordingly in a case where the offender's use of a motor vehicle was in fact insured there was no jurisdiction to make such an order (*McDermott v DPP* [1997] R.T.R. 474). It should be noted that "payable" in this context means "liable to be paid at some time", not "immediately owing" *DPP v Scott* [1995] R.T.R. 40. Accordingly the justices were right in concluding that their powers were limited to making an order of £175 (the sum in respect of which compensation would never be paid by the Motor Insurers' Bureau—this figure is now £300) (see further § 10.86). *DPP v Scott* was followed and applied by the Court of Appeal in *R. v Austin* [1996] Crim. L.R. 446 when reducing to £175 an order for compensation totalling £3,462 made in the Crown Court in respect of damage inflicted upon a police car by an offender charged with aggravated vehicle-taking, dangerous driving and using a vehicle whilst uninsured.

18.29 The accident does not have to be on the road, it merely has to arise out of the presence of a motor vehicle on the road. The following remarks of Bridge J. in *Redman v Taylor* [1975] Crim. L.R. 348 were quoted with approval in *M (A Minor) v Oxford* [1981] R.T.R. 246:

    "Any accident resulting from such driving on a road as resulted in the vehicle running off the road and then colliding with some stationary object was clearly an accident which occurred 'owing to the presence of a motor vehicle on a road' within s.8(2) [of the 1972 Act] notwithstanding that the vehicle was off the road before the impact occurred."

Compensation may be awarded where the offence is under the Theft Act 1968. The effect is that if a vehicle has been taken without the owner's consent or has been stolen, the thief or person convicted under s.12 may be ordered to pay compensation in respect of any damage to the owner's vehicle, including damage that has occurred in respect of a road accident before the vehicle was recovered. Since a person who steals a vehicle or takes one without consent is almost by definition uninsured, s.130(6) would appear to allow courts to make compensation orders in respect of other damaged vehicles as well as the one unlawfully taken.

Compensation can be ordered to be paid jointly and severally by co-defendants, but in view of the difficulties which ensue as to accountability and enforcement, such an order should not be made (*R. v Grundy* [1974] 1 All E.R. 292). Nor should compensation be ordered unless the claim is simple and straightforward (*R. v Daly* [1974] 1 All E.R. 290), nor if the amount ordered would take a number of years to repay (ibid.). Compensation should not be ordered in respect of costs for a parallel civil claim (*Hammertons Cars Ltd v Redbridge LBC* [1974] Crim. L.R. 241). Compensation orders should not be made without careful inquiry into the defendant's ability to pay. Any period allowed for time to pay should not be excessive. The Crown Court should always have in mind that it will be the magistrates' court which will have to enforce any order it makes; if the circumstances are such that it is not realistic for an instalment order to be made there and then, the matter of rate of payment should be left to the magistrates (*R. v Scott, The Times*, April 2, 1986).

The effect of a compensation order on a subsequent award in civil proceedings is dealt with in s.134 of the 2000 Sentencing Act. A person in whose favour a compensation order has been made shall not be entitled to receive any amount due to him until (disregarding leave to appeal granted out of time) there is no further possibility of an appeal being made (s.132(1)), but the court is nevertheless entitled to receive, and account for, payments made during the period of "suspension" (s.132(2)). **18.30**

Magistrates may not order compensation on committing a person to the Crown Court for sentence (*R. v Blackpool JJ. Ex p. Charlson* [1972] 3 All E.R. 854; *R. v Brogan, The Times*, February 6, 1975).

Compensation may be awarded for any offence taken into consideration (s.131).

Forfeiture of property used for criminal purposes

The power of forfeiture of property under what is now s.143 of the 2000 Sentencing Act has frequently been used in respect of motor vehicles used for criminal purposes, since "property" must clearly include a motor vehicle. Where an order is made under s.143 the offender is deprived of all right to the property and it is required to be taken into police possession (if not already in their possession) (s.143(3)). By s.144(1) and (2) a person claiming ownership may apply under the Police (Property) Act 1897 within six months of the order but cannot succeed in his application unless he satisfies the magistrates' court that either he did not consent to the offender having possession or he did not know and had no reason to suspect that it would be used for criminal purposes. **18.31**

The power to deprive an offender of property used for the purposes of crime applies to any offence of which he is convicted (s.143(1)). Before making any such order, however, the court must have regard to the value of the property and the likely financial effects upon the defendant of the court's sentence *in toto*. Thus in *R. v Highbury Corner Magistrates' Court Ex p. Di Matteo* [1991] R.T.R. 234 it was held that whilst the use of a car to commit the offence of driving whilst disqualified came within the ambit of the amended section, a failure to take sufficient account of the financial consequences for the defendant meant that the magistrates' forfeiture order had to be quashed. A forfeiture order was similarly quashed in *R. v Ball* [2003] 2 Cr. App. R. (S.) 18 where a Mercedes estimated to be worth £19,000, bearing a personalised number plate which had an unascertained value of its own, was taken from a defendant who had stolen goods worth £3,000 from a department store. The sentencing judge had given no warning of his intention to make such an order, and had declined to change his mind when counsel addressed him on the effect of the order; furthermore, he had not made a fair estimate of the value of the property prior to its making.

18.32   The court, whether it is the Crown Court or a magistrates' court, must be satisfied that the property was in his possession or under his control at the time of his apprehension (i.e. either physical possession or an entitlement to an immediate right to possession): for this reason an order was quashed where the car was detained by the police at the time of the offence but the offender was not arrested until some days later (*R. v Hinde* [1977] R.T.R. 328).

An order should only be made if the property was used for the purpose of committing or facilitating the commission of the offence (s.143(1)(a)), or intended to be used by that person for that purpose (s.143(1)(b)). For this reason an order of deprivation of a motor car was quashed in *R. v Lucas* [1976] R.T.R. 235. An order was set aside on appeal in respect of a motor car used to convey the appellant and co-accused from the scene of a robbery on the grounds that the robbery was committed on the spur of the moment and the order of forfeiture of a £1,600 motor car was too heavy an additional punishment (*R. v Miele* [1976] R.T.R. 238 *Note*). In *R. v Tavernor* [1976] R.T.R. 242 *Note* a defendant was ordered to be deprived of a car used to transport drugs in a burglary; the order was quashed as the car was bought out of compensation moneys for physical injuries and it would be too heavy an additional penalty to deprive him of the car which he had still to use as a means of transport because of his injuries. On the other hand, although the power of forfeiture is an additional penalty, the legislature intended it to be such and where a car was used as an integral part of an offence of handling stolen property ("the reason why the thieves had come to him, was because he had a motor car suitable for transferring the goods"), the order depriving the handler of the £250 Jaguar was upheld (*R. v Lidster* [1976] R.T.R. 240).

18.33   Positive encouragement towards the use of forfeiture orders in appropriate cases may be found in the Court of Appeal case of *R. v Stratton*, *The Times*, January 15, 1988. Where a car was used to facilitate the commission of an offence (in the case in point, domestic burglary), it was "extremely appropriate" for the court to take advantage of the powers under (what is now) s.143 to bring home to the offender the serious consequences of his conduct. The car in question was worth between £1,500 and £2,000 and the Crown Court had quite properly ordered its forfeiture; indeed, it was perhaps a power which courts should consider more frequently when considering what was the appropriate penalty.

Section 143(6) of the 2000 Sentencing Act provides that where a person commits an offence listed in s.143(7) of that Act by driving, attempting to drive, or being in charge of a vehicle, or failing to provide a specimen for analysis when required to do so, or failing to allow a specimen to be subjected to laboratory test, or failing, as the driver of a vehicle, to stop after or report an accident, the vehicle shall be regarded as used for the purpose of committing the offence (and therefore liable to forfeiture). The offences listed in s.143(7) are as follows:

(a) manslaughter (involving a vehicle), and

(b) wanton and furious driving (contrary to s.35 of the Offences Against the Person Act 1861), and

(c) any offence under the 1988 Act which is punishable with imprisonment.

18.34 Like compensation orders, orders requiring forfeiture should only be made in simple, uncomplicated cases. Difficulties arise where the defendant does not have individual ownership of the property. Accordingly, an order was quashed in respect of a tipper lorry which was owned jointly by the defendant with his business partner (*R. v Troth* [1980] R.T.R. 389). The problems may be even more acute if the property to be forfeited does not belong to the defendant at all. In *R. v Maidstone Crown Court Ex p. Gill* [1986] Crim. L.R. 737, a father had lent two motor cars to his son without any reason to suppose that they would be used for other than lawful purposes; they were in fact used by the son in the course of illegally supplying heroin. The forfeiture orders made by the trial judge were accordingly quashed (see also § 22.41).

18.35 A rather different view of the significance of ownership has been taken, however, north of the border. Under Scottish legislation comparable to what is now s.143 of the 2000 Sentencing Act a disqualified driver was ordered (inter alia) on conviction of driving whilst disqualified to forfeit the vehicle he had been driving, even though it had been paid for by and was registered in the name of his wife. She applied to the High Court of Justiciary to quash that order of forfeiture on the ground that it was oppressive and unjust (*Re Donald (Linda)* (1995) 1997 S.L.T. 505). Having reviewed the facts, the court held that it could not quash the order in the absence of evidence of the wife having taken appropriate and effective steps to ensure that under no circumstances could her husband drive the car while he was disqualified.

Section 145 of the 2000 Sentencing Act empowers courts when dealing with an offender convicted of an offence which has resulted in a person suffering personal injury, loss or damage, or when taking any such offence into consideration, to make an order that any proceeds (not exceeding a sum specified by the court) arising from the disposal of property forfeited as above be paid to the person concerned. The court may only make an order, however, in circumstances where but for the defendant's inadequate means it would have made a compensation order of an amount not less than the specified amount (as to compensation orders, see §§ 18.26–30 above).

18.36 Where an order is made under s.143 depriving a defendant of his rights in respect of a motor vehicle, the proper course for a third party who claims in respect of it is to apply to the magistrates' court under s.1(1) of the Police (Property) Act 1897 within six months of the order being made (see s.144(1)). In *R. v Chester JJ. Ex p. Smith* [1978] R.T.R. 373, justices were compelled by order of mandamus to hear such an application.

COSTS

Award of costs against the accused

18.37   Convicted defendants and unsuccessful appellants or applicants for leave to appeal to the Court of Appeal or the House of Lords may be ordered by magistrates' courts, the Crown Court or the Court of Appeal as appropriate to pay to the prosecutor such costs as the court considers just and reasonable (Prosecution of Offences Act 1985 s.18(1), (2)); the actual amount to be paid, however, must be specified in the court's order (s.18(3)). The defendant's financial circumstances are clearly a relevant consideration when deciding to order the defendant to pay costs (*R. v Wright* [1977] Crim. L.R. 236). It would also be wrong in principle to order a defendant to pay more than he could reasonably cope with in about a year (*R. v Nottingham JJ. Ex p. Fohmann, The Times,* October 27, 1986).

     The Divisional Court in *R. v Northallerton Magistrates' Court Ex p. Dove* [1999] Crim. L.R. 760 provided a helpful restatement of the principles to be applied when making an order under s.18 for the payment by a defendant of the costs of the prosecution. The primary consideration should be the defendant's ability to pay, and the total payable in fines and costs should be kept within his means. Although there was no requirement for the amounts concerned to stand in any arithmetical relationship with one another, in the ordinary way the amount of costs ordered should not be "grossly disproportionate" to the fine. The fine should be determined first, then the costs application. If the total arrived at exceeded that which the defendant could reasonably be ordered to pay, it was preferable to achieve an acceptable total by reducing the costs order. It was for the defendant to provide evidence of his means, and in the absence of such disclosure the court would be entitled to draw reasonable inferences as to his means from the evidence and all the circumstances of the case.

18.38   A defendant pleaded not guilty to a charge of careless driving, but guilty to a substituted charge of driving on a footpath; the prosecution offered no evidence in relation to the charge of careless driving, which was dismissed. The justices imposed a fine equivalent to the fixed penalty which the defendant said he would have paid had it been offered to him (£40), but further ordered him to pay prosecution costs (£35). On an application for judicial review of the costs order (*Ritson v Durham Magistrates' Court* [2001] EWHC Admin 519; (2002) 166 J.P. 218) the court held that the magistrates having found that the driver would have paid a fixed penalty if that option had been offered to him, it was incumbent upon them either not to award any costs or to give a reason for awarding costs in the circumstances. They did not pursue either course, and to that extent they had erred; the order for costs was accordingly quashed.

     A magistrates' court shall not order a person convicted of an offence to pay any costs where it has ordered a sum not exceeding £5 to be paid as a fine, penalty, forfeiture or compensation for that offence unless in the particular circumstances of the case it considers it right to do so (s.18(4)).

18.39   In the case of a defendant under 18, the costs ordered by a magistrates' court in the event of his conviction shall not exceed the amount of any fine imposed on him (s.18(5)).

     There would appear to be no appeal against a magistrates' order for costs alone, but in view of the Crown Court's power to vary a sentence on appeal by a defendant, an appeal against a sentence might result in the costs ordered being reduced (Magistrates' Courts Act 1980 s.108).

Particulars as to costs do not have to be stated in the particulars of a conviction endorsed on a person's licence (Criminal Procedure Rules 2005 r.55.1).

Awards of costs in other circumstances

Where one party to criminal proceedings has incurred costs as a result of an **18.40** unnecessary or improper act or omission by, or on behalf of, another party to the proceedings, a magistrates' court, the Crown Court or the Court of Appeal (as appropriate) may, after hearing the parties, order that all or part of the costs so incurred by that party shall be paid to him by the other party (Costs in Criminal Cases (General) Regulations 1986 reg.3). The amount to be paid must be specified in the court's order. In the case of a convicted defendant under 17 years of age, the amount of such an order must not exceed the amount of any fine imposed upon him. Subject to that proviso, such an order may be made at any time during the proceedings.

Regulations 3A, 3B, 3C and 3D of the 1986 Regulations, as amended, make provision for the payment of wasted costs orders to be borne by legal or other representatives in criminal proceedings. All or part of the wasted costs may, after allowing representations to be made, be disallowed or ordered to be paid by the court. The amount disallowed or ordered to be paid must be specified by the court (reg.3B); failure to so specify is a fatal flaw (*Wasted Costs Order (No.1 of 1991)* (1992) 95 Cr. App. R. 288). In that case the Court of Appeal also indicated that a court should consider first of all whether there had been an improper, unreasonable or negligent act or omission; secondly whether any costs had been incurred by any party as a result thereof; and thirdly whether the making of an order was an appropriate exercise of its discretion.

The order may be appealed by notice in writing given within 21 days (reg.3C). **18.41**

In addition to the above powers, the Supreme Court (which includes the Crown Court) may in the exercise of its inherent jurisdiction order a solicitor to pay costs thrown away by reason of some improper act or omission on his part or that of his staff. That jurisdiction, however, arises from conduct which involves a *serious dereliction* on the part of the solicitor of his duty to the court. It is not available in cases of mistake, error of judgment or mere negligence. The Court of Appeal so held in *McGoldrick & Co v Crown Prosecution Service, etc., The Times*, November 15, 1989 when dealing with a number of appeals by firms of solicitors against costs orders made against them.

The regulations also provide for the payment from central funds of the expenses of witnesses (professional and otherwise), interpreters and qualified medical practitioners reporting orally or in writing to the court.

CHAPTER 19

ENDORSEMENT AND PENALTY POINTS

ENDORSEMENT

Summary

19.01   The principles of endorsement now contained in the Road Traffic Offenders Act 1988 (as amended by the Road Traffic Act 1991) are summarised below; their detailed application is discussed in the subsequent sections of this chapter.

(1) Unless an offence is one which is described in Sch.2 to the 1988 Offenders Act and shown there to involve "obligatory endorsement" (an "endorsable" offence) a court has no power to order the endorsement of the offender's licence.

(2) Every endorsable offence carries penalty points and, on conviction, unless the offender is disqualified, the licence must be endorsed with the appropriate number of penalty points.

(3) A court may only refrain from endorsing the offender's licence on conviction if:

(a) "special reasons" for not doing so are found by the court (see Chapter 21); or

(b) the offence is in respect of a contravention of the Construction and Use Regulations and the defendant is able to show that he did not know and had no reasonable cause to suspect that the facts of the case were such that an offence would be committed (see § 8.104).

(4) Where a licence is ordered to be endorsed, particulars of the endorsement are recorded on the licence and are also recorded (following notification by the court) centrally at the Driver and Vehicle Licensing Authority (DVLA) at Swansea, formerly DVLC.

(5) Endorsable offences are divided into two classes: those involving obligatory disqualification (an "obligatorily disqualifiable offence", e.g. causing death by dangerous driving, driving with excess alcohol, etc.); and the remainder, for which the court has a discretion whether to disqualify.

(6) Offences contrary to ss.1, 12 and 25 of the Theft Act 1968 and s.178 of the 1988 Act are not endorsable if committed on or after July 1, 1992; they remain subject, however, to discretionary disqualification.

(7) Speeding offences committed on or after July 1, 1992 are subject to a

range of points (three to six) if dealt with by a court but to a fixed number of points (three) if dealt with by way of fixed penalty.

Sections 8, 9 and 10 of, and Schs 2 and 3 to, the Road Safety Act 2006 (if and when they are all in force) together provide for a new system for the endorsement of driving licences. Section 8 inserts a new s.97A into the 1988 Offenders Act in order to introduce the concept of a record held by the Secretary of State (a "driving record") designed for the endorsement of particulars of offences committed under the Traffic Acts. Section 9 and Sch.2 introduce a system of endorsement of driving records for unlicensed and foreign drivers who do not have counterpart licences. Sections 8, 9 and Sch.2 came into force on April 1, 2009. Section 10 and Sch.3 (not in force as of March 2009) introduce the new system of endorsement of driving records for all drivers, with the result that counterparts will no longer have any function. Once up and running the system will enable fixed penalty notices to be given to drivers who do not have counterpart licences, and in the fullness of time will presage the abolition of the counterpart itself. Given the resource implications of converting from paper counterparts to electronic records it would seem that a staggered implementation schedule is inevitable.

Table of endorsable offences

The following table sets out all the endorsable offences, their penalty points value, and whether or not they are obligatorily disqualifiable.   **19.02**

Offence	Legislative provision	Number of penalty points	Disqualification
Manslaughter (or in Scotland culpable homicide) by driver of a motor vehicle	(common law)	3–11[1]	Obligatory
	1988 Act		
Causing death by dangerous driving	s.1	3–11[1]	Obligatory
Dangerous driving	s.2	3–11[1]	Obligatory
Causing death by careless or inconsiderate driving	s.2B	3–11[1]	Obligatory
Careless or inconsiderate driving	s.3	3–9	Discretionary
Causing death by driving unlicensed, disqualified or uninsured	s.3ZB	3–11[1]	Obligatory
Causing death by careless driving when under influence of drink or drugs	s.3A	3–11[1]	Obligatory
Driving or attempting to drive when unfit through drink or drugs	s.4(1)	3–11[1]	Obligatory
Being in charge when unfit through drink or drugs	s.4(2)	10	Discretionary

Offence	Legislative provision	Number of penalty points	Disqualification
Driving or attempting to drive with excess alcohol	s.5(1)(a)	3–11[1]	Obligatory
In charge with excess alcohol	s.5(1)(b)	10	Discretionary
Failing or refusing to provide breath for preliminary test	s.6(4)	4	Discretionary
Failing or refusing to provide specimens for analysis when driving or attempting to drive	s.7(6)	3–11[1]	Obligatory
Failing or refusing to provide specimens for analysis when not driving or attempting to drive	s.7(6)	10	Discretionary
Failing to allow specimen to be subjected to laboratory test when driving or attempting to drive	s.7A	3–11[1]	Obligatory
Failing to allow specimen to be subjected to laboratory test when not driving or attempting to drive	s.7A	10	Discretionary
Motor racing or speed trials on highway	s.12	3–11[1]	Obligatory
Leaving motor vehicle in dangerous position	s.22	3	Discretionary
Carrying passenger on motor cycle other than astride and on a seat	s.23	3	Discretionary
Failing to comply with traffic directions or signals in respect of motor vehicle[2]	ss 35, 36	3	Discretionary
Using vehicle in dangerous condition	s.40(A)	3	Discretionary
Breach of requirement as to brakes, steering gear or tyres	s.41A	3	Discretionary
Breach of requirement as to control of vehicle, mobile telephones, etc.	s.41D	3[6]	Discretionary
Driving otherwise than in accordance with a licence[3]	s.87(1)	3–6	Discretionary
Driving after making false declarations as to physical fitness	s.92(10)	3–6	Discretionary
Driving after failure to notify disability	s.94(3A)	3–6	Discretionary
Driving after refusal or revocation of licence	s.94A	3–6	Discretionary

Offence	Legislative provision	Number of penalty points	Disqualification
Driving with uncorrected defective eyesight	s.96(1)	3	Discretionary
Refusing eyesight test	s.96(3)	3	Discretionary
Driving while disqualified by court order	s.103(1)(b)	6	Discretionary
Using motor vehicle whilst uninsured	s.143	6–8	Discretionary
Failing to stop after accident	s.170(4)	5–10	Discretionary
Failing to give particulars or report accident	s.170(4)	5–10	Discretionary
Failure to give information as to identity of driver[4]	s.172	3	Discretionary
Taking, etc., a motor vehicle in Scotland without authority	s.178		Discretionary
Theft Act 1968			
Stealing or attempting to steal a motor vehicle	s.1		Discretionary
Taking or attempting to take, etc., a motor vehicle without authority	s.12		Discretionary
Aggravated vehicle-taking	s.12A	3–11[1]	Obligatory
Going equipped for stealing or for taking motor vehicles	s.25		Discretionary
RTR Act 1984			
Contravention of temporary speed restriction	s.16(1)	3–6 or 3 (fixed penalty)	Discretionary
Motorway offences[5]	s.17(4)	3–6 or 3 (fixed penalty) if speeding, otherwise 3	Discretionary
Pedestrian crossing offence in respect of motor vehicle	s.25	3	Discretionary
School crossing patrol offence in respect of motor vehicle	s.28	3	Discretionary
Street playground offence in respect of motor vehicle	ss.29, 30	2	Discretionary
Speeding offences	s.89	3–6 or 3 (fixed penalty)	Discretionary
RTO Act 1988			
Aiding and abetting, etc., an obligatorily disqualifiable offence	s.28(1)(b)	10	Discretionary

Offence	Legislative provision	Number of penalty points	Disqualification
Aiding or abetting, etc., an endorsable offence	(§ 19.18)		
Attempting to commit an endorsable offence	(§ 19.15)		

[1] No penalty points may be imposed when the offender is disqualified; see § 19.37.

[2] Certain traffic signs only; see § 6.65.

[3] As to when the offence is endorsable, see § 11.80.

[4] As to when the offence is endorsable, see § 7.32.

[5] As to when motorway offences are endorsable, see § 6.153.

[6] For offences committed on or after February 27, 2007.

Requirement to endorse

19.03   Section 44(1) of the 1988 Offenders Act requires a court to order the defendant's driving licence to be endorsed with particulars of the conviction whenever he is convicted of an offence carrying obligatory endorsement and with particulars of the disqualification also if he is ordered to be disqualified from driving as well, unless:

(a) there are special reasons justifying non-endorsement (see Chapter 21); or

(b) the Mental Health Act 1983 s.37(3), applies; or

(c) the offence was under the Construction and Use Regulations as to brakes, steering, tyres, dangerous condition or load, etc., and the court finds that he did not know and had no reasonable cause to suspect that the facts were such that an offence would be committed (see § 8.104).

Any special reasons under head (a) above for not endorsing or disqualifying should be stated in open court and, in the case of a magistrates' court, entered on the court register (1988 Offenders Act s.47(1)); the finding is valid, however, if they are not stated aloud (*Brown v Dyerson* [1969] 1 Q.B. 45).

19.04   If the defendant is discharged absolutely or conditionally in England or Wales, his licence must be endorsed unless there are special reasons (1988 Offenders Act s.46(1)).

The phrasing of s.44 of the 1988 Offenders Act is such that "any" licence of which the defendant is the holder is required to be endorsed. The court is required to make such an order (in the absence of "special reasons") whether or not the defendant actually has a licence. A "licence" in the context of s.44 means a licence issued under Pt III of the Road Traffic Act 1988 (s.108 ibid.), and a court cannot therefore actually endorse particulars of a conviction on an international driving permit, a foreign licence, a driving permit issued under the Visiting Forces Act 1952, or a heavy goods vehicle licence. Although holders of foreign driving licences and driving permits will not have their licences or permits actually endorsed, any order of endorsement counts towards a penalty points disqualification. Moreover, should a British driving licence be taken out in the future, the applicant will have to disclose any previous orders of endorsement;

and the endorsements will be entered on the British licence unless it is outside the period after which the endorsement may be removed (see § 19.47).

It used to be thought that a fine or imprisonment or other order should always **19.05** accompany endorsement. However, in *Bell v Ingham* [1962] 2 All E.R. 333 it was said obiter that endorsement can truly be described as "part of the penalty". This statement, taken with *R. v Bignell* (1967) 111 S.J. 773 (that there need be no penalty when disqualification is ordered), suggests that endorsement on its own may be ordered as the sole penalty. While a court on convicting should normally proceed to judgment, it is not clear whether there is precise authority that the "judgment" must include a custodial sentence or a fine or probation or absolute or conditional discharge; convictions followed by recognisances only (which the relevant statutes allowed) were held to be valid in *R. v Miles* (1890) 24 Q.B.D. 423 and *R. v Blaby* [1894] 2 Q.B. 170. It is submitted, however, that endorsement should not be ordered on its own as the sole penalty. As was said in *Bell v Ingham* above, it is "part of" the penalty; the court in the absence of special reasons is obliged to order endorsement if it is an obligatorily endorsable offence. Moreover, by r.55.1 of the Criminal Procedure Rules 2005, particulars of the sentence of the court are required to be included, and it is difficult to regard as a sentence an order under s.44 of the 1988 Offenders Act that particulars of the conviction, which must include the sentence, are to be endorsed on the licence. On the basis of all the foregoing it has been submitted in previous editions that in order to avoid these problems and such circular arguments, that the court should order an absolute discharge where the court considers an endorsement by itself is sufficient punishment. As a result of the coming into force on October 12, 1988 of s.156 of the Criminal Justice Act 1988, however, the position now appears to be somewhat different. The section, which amended s.48 of the Supreme Court Act 1981, is understood to have been designed to give statutory effect to the decision of the Divisional Court in *Dutta v Westcott* [1986] 3 All E.R. 381 (see § 22.24). That case decided that where a defendant convicted of a number of offences committed on the same occasion appealed only in respect of the offence meriting the highest number of penalty points, the Crown Court was nevertheless empowered on a broad interpretation of s.48 as it then was to deal with the whole of the decision made by the justices and not merely the decision appealed against; therefore penalty points could be imposed as appropriate for other subsisting offences. The amendment introduced by the 1988 Act replaces the words "the decision appealed against" in s.48(2) with the words "any part of the decision appealed against, including a determination not to impose a separate penalty in respect of an offence". It would seem in the light of this amendment that by a process of retrospective inference, authority may be gleaned for the practice which has in any event become more common in magistrates' courts in recent years of imposing no separate penalty in appropriate cases, but nevertheless endorsing the defendant's licence where so required by statute. It should also be noted that the *DVLA Court Guidelines on Driver Notifications* now contain a specific sentence code for the adjudication "no separate penalty", namely "I"; see Appendix 2 below.

Although it is submitted that an endorsement is "part of the penalty" for the **19.06** purposes adverted to in *Bell v Ingham* above, the Court of Appeal in *Power v Provincial Insurance plc* [1998] R.T.R. 60 held, disapplying *Bell v Ingham* in this context, that an endorsement was not a "penalty" for the purposes of s.5(8) of the Rehabilitation of Offenders Act 1974; therefore there was no obligation upon an applicant for motor insurance to disclose a previous disqualification after the rehabilitation period appropriate to the fine and disqualification imposed upon him had expired (see further § 16.12).

Where a court orders endorsement, the particulars to be endorsed include the name of the court, the date of the offence, the date of the conviction and (where different) the date on which sentence is passed, particulars of the offence and particulars of the sentence (including the number of penalty points and the period of any disqualification); but not, any longer, particulars relating to any order for costs.

Omission to order endorsement

19.07   If the chairman omits to say "licence endorsed" on a conviction where there are no special reasons, the prosecutor can seek mandamus from the High Court to require endorsement. Moreover if the magistrates' court does not make an order of endorsement it is required to state its reasons for not doing so in open court (1988 Offenders Act s.47(1)). If the omission is caused by a slip of the tongue there can be no doubt, it is submitted, that the court may repair the omission (see, e.g. *R. v Newcastle upon Tyne JJ. Ex p. Swales* [1972] R.T.R. 57). Section 142(1) of the Magistrates' Courts Act 1980 allows a magistrates' court to vary a sentence or other order made by it when dealing with an offender. This power seems sufficiently wide to include the power to order endorsement which was originally omitted and which the court was obliged to make by virtue of what is now s.44 of the 1988 Offenders Act.

Endorsement as evidence

19.08   Particulars of any conviction, disqualification, or penalty points, endorsed on a driving licence which is produced on conviction of an endorsable offence are prima facie evidence of such particulars (1988 Offenders Act s.31(1)). Endorsement of a licence is especially important as it is only convictions to be endorsed that count as the "qualifying" ones leading to obligatory disqualification under s.35 of the 1988 Offenders Act. A court after conviction is bound to require its production (see the 1988 Offenders Act s.7) and is entitled to take into consideration particulars of any convictions endorsed upon it (see the 1988 Offenders Act s.31(1)(b)).

Notification of endorsement

19.09   By s.47(2) of the 1988 Offenders Act, the court ordering endorsement must notify the central licensing department at the DVLA, Swansea. The notification to the central licensing department is in code form and the endorsement of licences issued from Swansea is in the same code (see Appendix 2). The court may either notify the DVLA and send the driving licence back to the defendant after endorsement, or send the licence itself after endorsement to the DVLA (1988 Offenders Act s.47(2)). If disqualification for 56 days or more is ordered, the court must send the licence to the DVLA. In the event that the penalty points to be taken into account under s.29 of the 1988 Offenders Act number six or more, and it appears to the court that the offence concerned was committed within the offender's probationary period (two years beginning on the day on which he became a qualified driver), the licence must not be returned to its holder but must instead be sent to the DVLA for revocation (Road Traffic (New Drivers) Act 1995 s.2(1), (2)). These provisions apply to any person whose first driving test was passed on or after June 1, 1997 (s.1 ibid.; see further §§ 11.09 et seq.). Courts are also required to notify particulars of the motorist's sex and date of birth, in addition to the other particulars prescribed. The court when making an order of endorsement is required to order the defendant to state in writing his sex and date of birth, if not already known. If a person knowingly fails to comply with such an order he is guilty of a summary offence punishable with a fine of level 3 on the standard scale (1988 Offenders Act s.25(3)). Where a person has stated his date of birth to a court, the Secretary of State can require him to produce evidence to verify that date of birth, and where he has changed his name, his name at the date of his birth. Non-compliance with the Secretary of State's order is similarly punishable (1988 Offenders Act s.25(6)). (It may be remarked that the subsection places adopted persons in a difficulty. An adopted person usually knows only the names given to him on adoption. Presumably the Secretary of State would be content with production of the adoption certificate.)

To enable particulars of the conviction to be recorded on the central computer at Swansea by the DVLA, courts are required to notify many of the particulars in code form. Particulars are endorsed on the licences in the same form.   **19.10**

The endorsement and sentence code is set out in Appendix 2 at the end of this volume.

Committal for sentence

Where a magistrates' court commits a defendant to the Crown Court for sentence the magistrates' court may disqualify him until he is dealt with at the Crown Court. The magistrates' court has no power of endorsement if they do so (see § 20.79).   **19.11**

Remittal for sentence

Where a magistrates' court remits a defendant to another magistrates' court to be sentenced in accordance with s.10 of the Powers of Criminal Courts (Sentencing) Act 2000 for an offence involving obligatory or discretionary disqualification, the remitting court may order him to be disqualified until he has been dealt with by the other court (1988 Offenders Act s.26(1)(b)). The remitting court has no power of endorsement if it does so (s.26(10) ibid.).   **19.12**

Deferment of sentence

Where a court defers passing sentence on an offender in respect of an offence involving obligatory or discretionary disqualification, it may order him to be disqualified until he has been dealt with in respect of the offence. There is no power of endorsement at the time of deferment (1988 Offenders Act ss.26(2)(a), (10), as amended).   **19.13**

Adjournment for sentence

Where a court adjourns after convicting an offender of an offence involving obligatory or discretionary disqualification, it may order him to be disqualified   **19.14** until he has been dealt with in respect of the offence. There is no power to order endorsement when adjourning (1988 Offenders Act ss.26(2)(b), (10), as amended).

Attempts

19.15   The 1988 Offenders Act gives no power to endorse for an attempt to commit an endorsable offence save for:

    (a) attempting to drive when unfit through drink or drugs or with more than the permitted amount of alcohol in the blood; or

    (b) refusing evidential specimens under s.7(6) of the 1988 Act when attempting to drive at the relevant time; or

    (c) failing to allow a specimen of blood to be laboratory tested under s.7A(6) of the 1988 Act when attempting to drive at the relevant time.

In these excepted cases the 1988 Offenders Act gives express power to endorse for the attempt. Otherwise, for attempting to drive while disqualified or attempting to commit any other offence specified in what is now Sch.2 to the 1988 Offenders Act, there was no power to endorse (*Bell v Ingham* [1968] 2 All E.R. 333), but see the Criminal Attempts Act 1981 below.

19.16   Although *Bell v Ingham* above remains authority for the proposition that unless the 1988 Offenders Act gives express power to endorse and disqualify for an attempt there is no such power, it would seem that by virtue of the Criminal Attempts Act 1981 where the attempted offence is an indictable offence or an "either way" offence the person convicted of attempting to commit the offence is now liable to exactly the same penalties as if he had been convicted of the actual offence. Section 4(1)(b) of the 1981 Act provides that if the offence is indictable a defendant convicted on indictment under s.1 of attempting to commit an offence shall be liable to "any" penalty to which he would have been liable if convicted on indictment of the offence which he attempted to commit. Section 4(1)(c) similarly provides that a person summarily convicted under s.1 of an attempt to commit an offence is liable on summary conviction to "any" penalty to which he would have been liable on summary conviction of the "either way" offence. Section 1 does not apply to offences triable only summarily.

19.17   A defendant charged with attempting to commit an offence may be convicted of the attempt although the magistrates' court is satisfied he had committed the full offence (*Webley v Buxton* [1977] Crim. L.R. 607). It would seem that if an offender is charged with attempting to commit an offence for which the attempt is not endorsable he will escape endorsement even if the justices are satisfied he committed the full offence because he may be convicted of the offence charged, namely an attempt.

Where an attempt is endorsable, the offender will have his licence endorsed in accordance with the endorsement code as if he had been convicted of the full offence and will incur the appropriate number of penalty points for the full offence.

Aiders and abettors

19.18   A person convicted of aiding, abetting, counselling and procuring an offence is, by s.44 of the Magistrates' Courts Act 1980, "guilty of the like offence" and is thus liable to the same penalties as the principal offender. An aider or abettor who aids or abets an endorsable offence must therefore have his licence endorsed and may be disqualified. If not disqualified, his licence will be endorsed with the same number of penalty points as if he had been convicted of the principal offence; but if the offence is obligatorily disqualifiable, an aider and abettor of that offence is not liable to obligatory disqualification, but will incur 10 penalty points if not disqualified (1988 Offenders Act ss.34(5) and 28(2)). But he is liable, like a principal offender, to an obligatory disqualification under s.35 of the 1988 Offenders Act if the offence for which he is an aider or abettor is an endorsable offence and brings the total number of penalty points to 12 or more. The only effect of s.34(5) of the 1988 Offenders Act is that if the principal offence is an obligatorily disqualifiable offence, an aider or abettor is not liable to obligatory disqualification for the offence itself, but he is still liable to obligatory endorsement. It was held in *Ullah v Luckhurst* [1977] Crim. L.R. 295 that what is now s.34(5) of the 1988 Offenders Act did not exempt an aider or abettor from the former "totting-up" provisions of s.93(3) of the 1972 Act. Similarly, if a person has a previous conviction for aiding and abetting a drink/driving offence and is subsequently convicted of a drink/driving offence he is liable to the minimum period of three years' disqualification under the 1988 Offenders Act s.34(3) (*Makeham v Donaldson* [1981] Crim. L.R. 570).

If endorsement of the driving licence of an aider and abettor is required, then it may be avoided if "special reasons" are found (see Chapter 21) or the provisions as to certain offences under the Construction and Use Regulations apply (see § 8.104).

19.19 The DVLA endorsement code (see Appendix 2) provides that an aider and abettor of an endorsable offence is distinguished in that the last numeral 0 of the code is replaced by 2. For a person convicted of inciting an offence, the 0 is changed to 6. Thus a conviction of no insurance is shown as IN 10, one of aiding and abetting such an offence as IN 12 and one of inciting such an offence as IN 16. The 0 is changed to 4 in respect of a person convicted of "causing or permitting".

As to attempts, see §§ 19.15–17 above.

PENALTY POINTS

Summary

19.20 The penalty points system is principally contained in ss.28, 29 and 35 of, and Sch.2 to, the 1988 Offenders Act, as amended by the Road Traffic Act 1991. These statutory provisions are briefly summarised below, as is the endorsement of penalty points; penalty points disqualification is discussed at §§ 20.33 et seq.

Endorsement

19.21 A person convicted of any existing endorsable offence in addition to the previous particulars has endorsed on his licence the number of penalty points allocated to the offence unless there are "special reasons" for not endorsing his licence.

Number of points to be endorsed

19.22 The number of penalty points for most offences is a fixed number, but for a minority of offences the number of points has to be decided by the court within an indicated range. As a further complication, speeding offences committed on or after July 1, 1992 are subject to a range of points (three to six) if dealt with by a court but to a fixed number (three) if dealt with by way of fixed penalty (see Chapter 17). The number of penalty points for each offence is set out in the table at Column 7 of Sch.2 to the 1988 Offenders Act and in § 19.02 above.

Where a person is convicted of a number of offences committed on the same occasion, the number of penalty points to be imposed is normally the number of points in respect of the offence which incurs the highest number of points.

19.23   Where the court disqualifies the offender the court may not impose any penalty points for his offence. Neither is he liable to have points endorsed upon his licence in respect of any other offence of which he is convicted on the same occasion (*Martin v DPP* [2000] R.T.R. 188; see further § 20.40).

Disqualification

19.24   A person is liable to disqualification if he incurs a total of 12 relevant points. Relevant points are points incurred in respect of offences *committed* within a period of three years, other than offences which are "wiped off" as a result of a previous penalty points disqualification.

"Wiping the slate clean"

19.25   Only a disqualification for accumulating 12 or more penalty points has the effect of "wiping the slate clean", i.e. removing all existing penalty points from the licence; all other disqualifications leave them undisturbed.

Period of disqualification

19.26   The minimum period of disqualification is six months, but is increased to one year if the defendant has been previously disqualified for 56 days or more within three years immediately preceding the commission of the latest offence in respect of which penalty points have been taken into account. If there are two such orders of disqualification the period is two years. Where a person is convicted on the same occasion of more than one offence not more than one disqualification under s.35(3) of the 1988 Offenders Act may be imposed.

Crown servants

19.27   Section 92 of the 1988 Offenders Act applies "the provisions connected with the licensing of drivers" to vehicles and persons in the public service of the Crown. Part II of the 1988 Act deals with the licensing of drivers and vehicles and is applied to Crown servants by s.183 of that Act. It would appear, therefore, that the penalty points system applies to such persons and vehicles (as to vehicles and persons in the service of the Crown generally see § 2.34).

Number of points to be endorsed

19.28   A court is required to endorse the number of penalty points set out in Sch.2 to the 1988 Offenders Act unless the court either finds "special reasons" for not endorsing or imposes a penalty points disqualification upon the offender. Where "special reasons" are found the court cannot impose a lesser number of points: it must either endorse the appropriate number of points or decide, because of "special reasons", not to endorse at all.

Schedule 2 sets out either a fixed number or a variable number of points for each offence. The penalty points for each offence are indicated in the table at § 19.02 and also in Chapters 4–16 where the penalties for each offence are discussed.

Attendance on courses

Section 34 of the Road Safety Act 2006 (if and when in force) inserts new ss.30A–30D into the 1988 Offenders Act in order to enable courts to offer persons convicted of careless driving, speeding or failing to comply with traffic signs the opportunity of reducing the number of penalty points to be taken into account under s.29 of the 1988 Offenders Act by successfully completing a retraining course. In order to qualify for the scheme there should be at least seven and no more than 11 points to be taken into account at the time of the conviction. The consequence of successful completion of the course within a specified time is that 12 months after the conviction three points (or fewer if fewer were endorsed) will cease to be taken into consideration under s.29, thus providing some relief from the rigours of the "totting-up" provisions of s.35 ibid. This opportunity will not be offered to anyone who has completed such a course within the preceding three years; nor will it be available to a person convicted during his probationary period under the Road Traffic (New Drivers) Act 1995. It should be noted, however, that at the time of writing (March 2009) no indication had been given as to any likely date for implementation of these provisions. **19.29**

Variable points

The penalty points to be attributed to certain offences were varied in respect of offences committed on or after July 1, 1992 by the Road Traffic Act 1991 Sch.2. In addition, some offences which were previously fixed points offences were made subject to a range of points, and several new variable points offences were created. The changes are set out below: **19.30**

Offence	Former value	Present value
Failure to stop after accident	8–10	5–10
Failure to report accident	8–10	5–10
Contravention of temporary speed restriction	—	3–6
Speeding generally (including motorways)	3	3–6
Driving otherwise than in accordance with a licence	2	3–6
Driving after false declaration as to fitness	—	3–6
Driving after failing to notify disability	—	3–6
Driving after refusal or revocation of licence	—	3–6

It should be noted that the offence of driving otherwise than in accordance with a licence will only be endorsable with 3–6 penalty points where the offender's driving would not have been in accordance with any licence that could have been granted to him (see further § 11.24).

19.31   With regard to variable points offences, problems both of sentencing and practice arise. The fundamental question as to sentencing is the criteria by which a court should decide the number of penalty points. Should a court have regard primarily to the facts of the offence in fixing the number of points or should it take into account the previous motoring record of the offender? The Transport Bill as originally introduced contained a fixed number of points for all offences, but as a result of amendments by both Houses variable points were introduced because of the opinion expressed that the gravity of these particular offences varied so much. Although *Hansard* cannot be used in the interpretation of an Act of Parliament, it is submitted that the Act requires a court to have regard primarily to the gravity of the offence in deciding the appropriate number of points. The record of the offender, it is submitted, is of little relevance. Parliament intended, it is submitted, the previous convictions of an offender to be dealt with by the accumulation of penalty points and consequent risk of disqualification under s.35(1) of the 1988 Offenders Act. What is most relevant, it is submitted, in deciding the number of points is the gravity or otherwise of the facts of the offence. For example, in careless driving cases the primary criterion is the degree of carelessness; was it on the one hand a case of momentary inattention, or did the offender deliberately take a risk? In insurance cases, did the offender deliberately use the car knowing it to be uninsured, or did he have an insurance policy but was ignorant of the fact that its terms did not cover the particular use on the day in question?

19.32   It is stated that a court should have regard primarily to the gravity of the offence in deciding the appropriate number of points in respect of a variable points offence. Some commentators have gone so far as to suggest that this is the only criterion and for this reason a court should not look at the licence before deciding the number of points.

This, it is submitted, is wrong. Not only does s.31 of the 1988 Offenders Act implicitly require the court to look at the driving licence before sentencing the defendant, but the gravity of an offence can also be affected by a previous conviction of a *similar* offence. For example, it may be relevant to know whether the defendant has previously been convicted of another case of careless or inconsiderate driving. Otherwise previous convictions of endorsable offences which are different from the instant offence will usually be of little relevance in deciding the appropriate number of points. Moreover a court should be careful not to give the impression, when it hears of the number of penalty points already on a licence, that it is increasing the number of points in order to be able to impose a penalty points disqualification, or, on the other hand, decreasing the number of points it would otherwise impose in order to avoid having to impose a penalty points disqualification.

19.33   The above submission to the effect that the gravity of an offence is not the *only* criterion which a court should use when assessing the appropriate number of penalty points to be endorsed for a variable points offence received the support of the High Court of Justiciary in Scotland in *Nicholson v Westwater* 1995 S.L.T. 1018. A motorist had the maximum of six points endorsed upon his licence for a speeding offence as this was his third such offence in a period of two years. He appealed on the basis that it was unfair that penalty points should be awarded by reference to previous convictions rather than by reference to the gravity of the particular offence before the court. The High Court was not satisfied that s.28 or s.31 of the 1988 Offenders Act restricted the view of the court when awarding penalty points to the particular case. The motorist's appeal was accordingly dismissed.

Nicholson v Westwater above was followed and applied by the High Court of Justiciary in *Urquhart v Lees* (1999) 2000 S.L.T. 1109 when dismissing an appeal against sentence of a driver made subject to a penalty points disqualification. He had pleaded guilty to careless driving. It was noted by the sheriff that this was a case involving excessive speed and bad, though not the very worst, driving and that some eight days before the event the driver had been convicted of speeding. With that in mind he decided that nine penalty points, the maximum for the offence of careless driving, were appropriate to be endorsed. The appellant argued the same point as had been litigated in *Nicholson v Westwater*, namely that the gravity of the particular offence should be the only consideration in ordering penalty points. The court declined to overrule *Nicholson v Westwater*, which had not been questioned either side of the border, and held that the sheriff had been fully entitled to take the earlier conviction for speeding into account, and that his decision was in accord with s.31 of the 1988 Offenders Act.

Fixed penalties and penalty points

In the course of looking at the number of penalty points allocated to particular **19.34** offences under the then existing legislation, the Road Traffic Law Review (the North Report) found itself compelled to the conclusion that, particularly in relation to speeding, three points was an "inadequate response" to a bad case. On the other hand, a range of points would be impracticable to administer within the confines of a fixed penalty system. The solution to the problem, namely the creation of a range of points for use by courts running side by side with a fixed number of points for an offence dealt with by way of fixed penalty is embodied in amendments made by the Road Traffic Act 1991 to s.28 of, and Sch.2 to, the 1988 Offenders Act. The combined effect of these amendments (which came into effect on July 1, 1992 and apply to offences committed on or after that date) is that a variable points offence when dealt with by way of fixed penalty is endorsable with a fixed number of points (either as specifically indicated in Sch.2 by the addition of the words "fixed penalty" or, where not so marked, the lowest number in the range shown), whilst the same offence dealt with in court is subject to the full range of available points. Thus by way of illustration, a fixed penalty speeding offence (including speeding on a motorway) attracts three points, whereas such an offence dealt with in court is endorsable with 3–6 points. The additional incentive that that arrangement provides towards accepting a fixed penalty if one is offered is probably not altogether unintentional. On the other hand, given that the range of points for use by courts was introduced ostensibly to enable them to deal more effectively with *bad* speeding offences, it ought to be possible to argue that a defendant who has been offered, but not accepted, a fixed penalty should not have more than three points endorsed upon his licence, since had his offence been in the eyes of the reporting officer a *bad* one, the fixed penalty would not have been offered in the first place. The extra cost to the public purse of a court hearing might be appropriately dealt with by an order for costs against the defendant if he is convicted.

It should be noted that s.17 of the Road Safety Act 2006 (if and when in force) amends Pt I of Sch.2 to the 1988 Offenders Act to extend the range of penalty

points which may be imposed for speeding offences (including motorway speeding offences) from "3–6 or 3 (fixed penalty)" to "2–6 or appropriate penalty points
(fixed penalty)". Provision will thus be made for a more graduated arrangement
of fixed penalties in respect of these offences (see further Chapter 17). At the time
of writing (March 2009) no indication had been given as to a likely implementation date for these provisions.

Fixed points offences

19.35   Some of the fixed points offences deserve specific comment.

The offence of failing to comply with traffic signs or directions is in some cases
endorsable and in others not. Failing to comply with the directions of a traffic
warden is expressly made endorsable by the entry in Column 5 of Sch.2 to the
1988 Offenders Act and the offender will thus incur penalty points. If the offence
is not endorsable, then no penalty points are incurred (for a list of traffic signs
contravention of which involve endorsement, see § 6.65).

19.36   It should be noted that offences contrary to ss.1, 12 and 25 of the Theft Act
1968 and s.178 of the 1988 Act are not endorsable if committed on or after July
1, 1992; they remain subject, however, to discretionary disqualification.

A person may be convicted of refusing to supply a specimen for analysis even
when he was neither driving or attempting to drive nor in charge of a motor
vehicle. On conviction his licence must be endorsed with 10 penalty points or he
may be disqualified (see § 4.255).

Penalty points for obligatorily disqualifiable offences

19.37   Where a person is disqualified for any obligatorily disqualifiable offence, the
court may not impose penalty points in respect of that offence (1988 Offenders
Act s.44(1)). The Inter-Departmental Working Party whose report led to the creation of the penalty points system by the Transport Act 1981 recommended that
in cases where for "special reasons" disqualification was not imposed, courts
should have discretion to award such number of points, if any, as the justice of
the particular case required. The Government of the day, however, decided that
the penalty points to be awarded ought to equate with one endorsement under the
old "totting-up" provisions, i.e. four points.

The Road Traffic Law Review (the North Report) came to the conclusion that a
range of penalty points would be preferable, since the "special reasons" found
could cover a wide variety of circumstances and in many instances the fixed
figure of four points was unrealistically low bearing in mind the seriousness of
the offences concerned. The suggestion in the Report that points in the range of
3–11 should be imposed was taken up by the Government and Sch.2 to the Road
Traffic Act 1991 effected the necessary changes by means of amendments to
Sch.2 to the 1988 Offenders Act. If, therefore, "special reasons" are found for not
disqualifying for the obligatorily disqualifiable offence the courts are obliged to
impose between 3 and 11 penalty points. Because "special reasons" are narrowly
defined (see Chapter 21) a court, if it thinks the imposition of points would be
unjust, may in such circumstances consider whether the facts constituting the
reasons for not disqualifying are also sufficient to constitute "special reasons" for
not endorsing.

It should also be noted that as a result of the amendment of s.29 of the 1988

Offenders Act by s.28 of the 1991 Act, courts are no longer required to take into account the penalty points they would have imposed for a particular offence had they not disqualified the defendant for the offence concerned (see further § 20.37).

Offences committed on the same occasion

Section 28 of the Road Traffic Offenders Act 1988, as substituted, provides **19.38** that where a number of offences are committed on the same occasion, courts shall have a discretion to impose penalty points for more than one of them.

Section 28(4) provides that where a person is convicted (whether on the same occasion or not) of two or more offences committed on the same occasion and involving obligatory endorsement, the total number of penalty points to be attributed to them is the number or highest number that would be attributed on a conviction of one of them (so that if the convictions are on different occasions the number of penalty points to be attributed to the offences on the later occasion or occasions shall be restricted accordingly). The bracketed parts of the paraphrased subs.(4) above safeguard the defendant from any detriment which might otherwise accrue to him as a result of offences which were committed on the same occasion being dealt with on different occasions. Unless it decides to exercise the discretion provided by s.28(5) (see below), the "later" court will have to take due note of the "earlier" court's award of points. It would appear, therefore, that if Court A dealt with a six-point offence and Court B had only a three-point offence to deal with, Court B would not normally endorse any points. If the position were reversed, however, Court B would presumably wish to endorse an additional three points to bring the offender up to the six points merited by his most serious offence.

Section 28(5) enables a court to depart from the normal procedure described **19.39** above and instead order the endorsement of points for more than one offence committed on the same occasion; the result for the defendant will be a greater aggregate of points on his licence which will assuredly take him nearer the 12-point level and its concomitant disqualification. The Road Traffic Law Review recommended this measure for use by courts both to reflect the seriousness of multiple offending and to serve as a powerful deterrent to future offending. Experience would seem to suggest, however, that the courts have not greeted this procedure with any enthusiasm and that the power to aggregate points in this way has seldom been exercised, if at all.

In the light of the above it is anticipated that in the vast majority of "multiple offence" cases, the number of points to be endorsed will continue to be "the number or highest number that would be attributed on a conviction of one of them" (1988 Offenders Act s.28(4)). At first sight the phrase "the number or highest number" seems confusing and might appear to allow a court to take the absurd course of arbitrarily selecting the number of any one of the various offences committed on the same occasion whether that offence has the highest points or not. It is, however, submitted that the correct interpretation of the phrase is that the court is required to impose the number of points for any one of those offences if all those offences have the same number, or if the offences have differing numbers of points, the court is required to impose the number appropriate to the offence which has the highest number of penalty points. It should be remembered that in many instances all the offences committed will incur the same number of points. Moreover, it cannot have been Parliament's intention to allow a court to impose a lower number of points simply because the offender has committed another offence on the same occasion, which, by definition, is the more serious.

19.40   A further difficulty of interpretation occurs where one of the offences has a variable number of points. Should the court automatically impose the highest number of points within the range of points for that offence if that offence is committed on the same occasion as other offences? For example, if a person commits the offence of failing to comply with a traffic sign and on the same occasion also drives while uninsured, should the court automatically impose eight points (the highest number of points for the insurance offence)? It is submitted that the court is not required to do so. The proper approach for a court is first to consider the circumstances of the variable points offence and then decide the appropriate number of points for that offence and if the number so decided is then the highest of the offences, that is the number that should be endorsed.

It should be noted that s.28(4) of the 1988 Offenders Act refers to offences which were "committed on the same occasion". It is clear that offences committed on differing dates will not have been committed on the same occasion (unless, perhaps, the occasion was spread over midnight). It is also clear that the court may be required to add up points if the offences were committed on separate occasions even if committed on the same day (e.g. speeding on the way to work in the morning and speeding home after work). Whether offences are committed on the same occasion is a question of fact: the offences do not have to be committed simultaneously, they can be committed one after another, but they must be linked in some way so that it can be said that all were committed on the same occasion. This seems to have been the approach adopted by the court in *Johnson v Finbow* [1983] 1 W.L.R. 879 where it was held that a motorist who failed to stop after an accident, contrary to what is now s.170(4) of the 1988 Act, and who subsequently failed to report that accident to the police contrary to that section was to be treated as having committed both offences on the same occasion because their commission arose from the same accident. In *Johnston v Over* [1985] R.T.R. 240, it was held by the Divisional Court that where two vehicles were used by the defendant for stripping parts from one vehicle to repair the other and the defendant was not insured for either vehicle, the two offences of using the vehicles without insurance were committed on the same occasion for the purpose of endorsing penalty points. It was again observed that whether two or more offences were, or were not, committed on the same occasion is a matter of fact and not of law.

19.41   In *McKeever v Walkingshaw* (1995) 1996 S.L.T. 1228 the High Court of Justiciary held that it would be wrong to construe the phrase "on the same occasion" as meaning "arising out of a single course of driving". A driver whose speeding offence had been detected by radar was subsequently chased for about one and three quarter miles by police; during the course of that pursuit he was seen to cross a double white line. On the facts those two offences had not occurred on the same occasion for the purposes of s.28(4). *McKeever v Walkingshaw* was followed by the High Court of Justiciary in *Cameron v Brown* (1996) 1997 S.L.T. 914 and further doubt was cast upon the decision in *Johnson v Finbow* above. A driver stopped his car within the limits of a Pelican crossing controlled area. He was approached by police officers who suspected he had been drinking and who required him to take a roadside breath test, which proved positive. He subsequently refused to supply a specimen of breath for analysis at the police station. He was charged with both a pedestrian crossing offence and an offence of failing to provide specimens of breath for analysis (presumably on the basis of having been in charge of the vehicle at the material time in the light of the number of points subsequently endorsed upon his licence). The sheriff in the court below ordered his licence to be endorsed with three penalty points in respect of the first offence and with 10 points in respect of the second offence; the points were then added together and the driver was disqualified for 12 months (presumably under s.35 of the 1988 Offenders Act). The High Court took the view that the incident at the police station leading to the breath test offence was wholly separate from that relating to the Pelican crossing offence (although the two had an obvious connection with each other). Where as in this case the offences were separate (in the sense of not being contemporaneous with each other) they could not be said to have been committed on the same occasion. It was clear to the court that the English and Scottish authorities were not obviously reconcilable, and that the time may have come for the decision in *Johnson v Finbow* to be revisited.

PROCEDURE ON CONVICTION

Production of driving licence for endorsement

Sections 27(1) and 31(1) of the Road Traffic Offenders Act 1988 make clear **19.42** beyond doubt the power of the courts to call for the licence following conviction of an obligatory endorsable offence in order to discover what previous convictions are endorsed on the licence. The position, therefore, is that a person prosecuted for an offence involving obligatory endorsement must deliver his driving licence to the court or send it by registered or recorded delivery post or produce it at the hearing (1988 Offenders Act s.7). If he is not convicted of the offence, he commits no offence if he has not sent or produced his licence to the court. If he is convicted of the offence, the court must require the licence to be produced to it and, if the court does not know his date of birth, must also require him to state his date of birth (s.25(1)). Section 27 allows no suspension of the requirement for production of the licence and, if it has not been sent or is not produced on conviction for an endorsable offence, it is suspended from the time of the making of the order for production. Under s.164(3) of the 1988 Act where a person has been required under s.27(1) to produce his licence to the court and has failed to do so a constable may require him to produce it and upon it being produced may seize it and deliver it to the court. It would appear that if a defendant fails to produce the licence to the constable after being so required he commits an offence under s.164(6) of the 1988 Act unless he subsequently produces it at a police station of his choice within seven days of the requirement (but see further § 11.18 for defences to such a charge).

Section 31(1) of the 1988 Offenders Act in England, Wales and Scotland makes it clear beyond any doubt that the court is entitled to look at any endorsement on the licence and take it into account in determining sentence. In *Dyson v Ellison* [1975] Crim. L.R. 48 (a case on s.101 of the Road Traffic Act 1972 before its amendment by the 1974 Act and its subsequent re-enactment as s.31 of the 1988 Offenders Act) it was held that the court should call for the licence after conviction in order to look at the licence to see if any convictions were endorsed upon it.

On convicting a motorist of a road traffic offence, justices are entitled to **19.43** consider his record of previous convictions, whether or not evidenced by "old" endorsements no longer effective by virtue of what is now s.45(4), (5) of the 1988 Offenders Act (*Chief Constable of West Mercia Police v Williams* [1987] R.T.R. 188). The facts of the case were somewhat unusual. On conviction of a road traffic offence, the defendant had produced to the court a clean, but forged, licence created by him. His true licence would have revealed endorsements in respect of convictions entered more than four years previously. He was charged with an offence under s.3 of the Forgery and Counterfeiting Act 1981. The justices erroneously concluded that they would not have been entitled to have sight of those endorsements and dismissed the charge on a submission of no case to answer. Allowing the prosecutor's appeal, the Divisional Court remitted the case to the justices with a direction to continue the hearing.

A court is entitled to adjourn after conviction under s.10(3) of the Magistrates' Courts Act 1980 and may quite properly do so for the production of the licence. Where a court does so adjourn it should not be for a period of longer than four weeks at a time (*R. v Talgarth JJ. Ex p. Bithell* [1974] R.T.R. 546). Moreover s.10(3) requires that the court shall not have sentenced or dealt with the defendant on the first occasion; where the court fined the defendant in his absence and then adjourned under s.10(3) and disqualified him on the adjourned hearing, the disqualification was set aside on the ground that the magistrates had acted in excess of their jurisdiction (ibid.). If a court is minded to adjourn, it should adjourn the whole question of sentencing and disposal and deal with the whole of the sentencing process at the adjourned hearing (ibid.). But in *R. v Manchester JJ. Ex p. Miley*, February 16, 1997, unreported, it was held that s.10(3) was directory and not mandatory; a sentence will not be quashed because it was passed after an adjournment of more than four weeks in breach of s.10(3) (ibid.).

19.44   On a conviction for an endorsable offence being announced, the court should look at the defendant's licence, if it has been sent to the court or the defendant voluntarily produces it, before deciding whether to endorse and disqualify; if the defendant is present and will not produce it voluntarily, an order for its production must be pronounced and then an offence arises under s.27(3) of the 1988 Offenders Act if it is not produced. If the defendant has not got it with him or he has not sent it, the court may adjourn so that it may be inspected at the adjourned hearing to see if there are previous convictions; on non-production, the court should order it to be produced and adjourn for not more than four weeks. During this period inquiries may be made of the DVLA at Swansea and previous endorsements may be proved in accordance with s.13 of the 1988 Offenders Act, as amended. The police may require the defendant to produce the licence and seize it under s.164(3) of the 1988 Act (see above).

The above provisions as to production of a driving licence to the court appear to apply to Northern Irish driving licences (1988 Act s. 109(2)), but not to international driving licences, visiting forces' drivers' permits or foreign domestic driving licences (Motor Vehicles (International Circulation) Order 1975 (SI 1975/1208)) unless disqualification is ordered.

19.45   If the court has not received the offender's driving licence when the order for production is made, he is liable by s.27(3) of the 1988 Offenders Act to a fine of level 3 on the standard scale and his driving licence is suspended and of no effect until it is produced to the court. An offender who drives a motor vehicle on a road after conviction and prior to the production of the licence appears to offend against s.87 of the 1988 Act (driving otherwise than in accordance with a licence) in addition to being liable to a fine under s.27(3), but not, it is thought, under s.103 of the 1988 Act for driving whilst disqualified. (Section 27(3) only "suspends" the licence; the holder is not disqualified for "holding or obtaining a licence".) In certain circumstances, however, the defendant may be prosecuted for using a licence with intent to deceive, contrary to s.173 of the 1988 Act. The Court of Appeal held the defendant to be "clearly guilty" of this offence in *R. v Bogdal* [1982] R.T.R. 395 when he had been required under what is now s.27(3) to produce a licence within seven days and within this period had been seen driving by a constable who had thereupon stopped him and asked for his licence which was then produced as a valid licence.

In any prosecution for disobedience to s.27(3) or under s.87 of the 1988 Act (as a result of the suspension of the licence for non-production to the court), presumably the prosecution must prove that the defendant was aware that he had been summoned for the offence. In proving that the defendant had received the summons, the Interpretation Act 1978 s.7, provides that a properly addressed letter is deemed to have been received, unless the contrary is proved, when it would be delivered in the ordinary course of post. Posting may be proved by the certificate endorsed on the duplicate summons. Rule 4.11 of the Criminal Procedure Rules 2005 specifically allows proof of the posting, etc. by such a certificate. Must the prosecution prove that the defendant had been informed that his licence was required for production? Although most summonses refer to his duty to produce it, the duty does not arise until he is convicted and an order for its production is made, and the prosecutor would be wise to prove that notice to produce it after conviction was duly given to the defendant, though, as disqualification is deemed effective as soon as it was ordered by the court (*Taylor v Kenyon* [1952] 2 All E.R. 726), the making of the order for production alone might suffice where the defendant claimed never to have been told of it. The duty to produce falls on "the holder of a licence" (see s.27(3)); if he does not hold one or his licence expired before the conviction without prior production, seemingly he commits no offence of non-production. It will be seen from the text of s.27(3) (see Vol.2) that an offender is not guilty of an offence under the section nor is his licence suspended if his failure to produce the licence is caused by the fact that "he has applied for a new licence and has not received it"; nor if he produces a receipt for his driving licence when it has been surrendered on receipt of a fixed penalty notice under Pt III of the Road Traffic Offenders Act 1988, provided that he produces the licence to the court "immediately on its return" (see s.27(4) of the 1988 Offenders Act).

19.46   Where the name or address on a licence-holder ceases to be correct, the licence-holder is required by s.99(4) of the 1988 Act forthwith to surrender the licence and furnish particulars of the alteration. On surrender of the licence, the Secretary of State may then furnish the person who has surrendered his licence with "a new licence" (1988 Act s.99(7)). The opinion is given in a "Practical Point" in (1977) 141 J.P. Jo. 74, that a surrender for a new licence under what is now s.99(4) as described does not amount, in law, to an application for a new licence for the purposes of s.27(3) of the 1988 Offenders Act and that, therefore, a person who complies with s.99(4) of the 1988 Act and does not receive his new licence back in time to produce it to court commits an offence under s.27(3) and, if he drives, is guilty of the offence of driving otherwise than in accordance with a

licence. It is submitted that although it is possible to argue that this might technically be a possible interpretation of the relevant statutory provisions, this interpretation of s.27(3) and s.99(4) is wrong. Both s.99(7) of the 1988 Act and s.27(3)
of the 1988 Offenders Act refer to a "new licence", and the purpose of the defence
to s.27(3) is to prevent the conviction of a person who genuinely cannot produce
his licence because he is awaiting a new licence.

The court cannot require the production of a driving licence to inspect it for
endorsements if the offender is convicted of an offence which does not carry
endorsement.

REMOVAL OF ENDORSEMENT

Application for removal of endorsement

19.47   Once an endorsement ceases to be effective, the licence-holder is entitled to
apply to the DVLA for a new licence free from the endorsement on payment of
the prescribed fee and on the surrender of the subsisting licence (Road Traffic Offenders Act 1988 s.45(4)).

The periods are laid down by s.45(5) of the 1988 Offenders Act as follows:

    (a) if an order is made for the disqualification of the offender, until four
years have elapsed since the *conviction*;

    (b) if no order of disqualification is made, until either four years have
elapsed since the *commission* of the offence or an order of disqualification under s.35 ibid. (penalty points disqualification) is made;

    (c) if the offence is causing death by dangerous driving or dangerous driv-
ing, the endorsement in any event must remain effective until four years
have elapsed since the *conviction* of the offence; and

    (d) if the offence is causing death by careless driving when under the influ-
ence of drink or drugs (1988 Act s.3A) or driving or attempting to
drive while unfit (1988 Act s.4(1)) or driving or attempting to drive
with excess alcohol (1988 Act s.5(1)(a)) or refusing to provide
evidential specimens of breath, blood or urine (1988 Act s.7(6)) while
driving or attempting to drive, until 11 years have elapsed after the
conviction (a close analysis of s.45(5) of the 1988 Offenders Act leads
to the conclusion that the period of 11 years applies to any conviction
for these offences even if a disqualification was not imposed for
"special reasons"). (See further *Boliston v Gibbons* [1985] R.T.R. 176
at § 20.32.)

The offence of failing to allow a specimen of blood to be laboratory tested
when driving or attempting to drive, contrary to s.7A(6) of the Road Traffic Act,
was originally omitted from the list of offences for which application for removal
of endorsement could be made but has now been included by s.14 of the Road
Safety Act 2006 (by statutory instrument in September 2007).

19.48   Although the period of effectiveness of an endorsement for any of the offences
listed in (d) above is 11 years, the rehabilitation period following conviction of
such an offence is governed for the purposes of the Rehabilitation of Offenders
Act 1974 by the sentence imposed, the endorsement not being a "penalty" for
those purposes (*Power v Provincial Insurance plc* [1998] R.T.R. 60; see further
§ 16.12).

It was held in *R. (on the application of Pearson) v Driver and Vehicle Licensing Agency* [2002] EWHC 2482; [2003] R.T.R. 20 that the fact that a job applicant had to disclose the continued existence of an endorsement on a driving licence for a drink/driving offence beyond the period during which the conviction for the offence became spent in accordance with the Rehabilitation of Offenders Act 1974, was not a breach of the right to privacy guaranteed by art.8 of the European Convention on Human Rights. It was the case that Parliament had considered what was appropriate to provide an effective system for the provision of information relevant to sentencing. If there was an interference with art.8 rights it was minimal because it had temporal limitations and arose only in contingent circumstances in relation to which there were statutory safeguards. Even if art.8(1) was engaged, the interference was justified under art.8(2).

CHAPTER 20

DISQUALIFICATION

CONTENTS

GENERAL PRINCIPLES

Introduction

20.01   The principles of disqualification contained in the 1988 Offenders Act (as amended by the Road Traffic Act 1991) are summarised below; their detailed application is discussed in the subsequent sections of this chapter.

Obligatory orders of disqualification

20.02   (1) A court is obliged to disqualify an offender for at least 12 months when he is convicted of an "obligatorily disqualifiable offence" (see § 20.26 et seq.) unless the court is able to find "special reasons" (see Chapter 21) for not doing so. The minimum period of disqualification rises to two years where:

(a) the offender is convicted of manslaughter (or, in Scotland, culpable homicide), causing death by dangerous driving or causing death by careless driving while under the influence of drink or drugs; or

(b) more than one disqualification for a fixed period of 56 days or more has been imposed upon him within the three years immediately preceding his offence.

(2) A court is obliged to disqualify an offender for at least six months when he is convicted of offences totalling 12 or more penalty points (see §§ 20.33 et seq.) unless the court is able to find "mitigating circumstances" for not doing so (see Chapter 21).

(3) A court is obliged to disqualify an offender until he passes an extended driving test on convicting him of an offence of manslaughter (or, in Scotland, culpable homicide), causing death by dangerous driving, dangerous driving or causing death by careless driving when under the influence of drink or drugs (see § 20.68 et seq.).

Discretionary orders of disqualification

20.03   (1) A court may disqualify for any endorsable offence provided that the offender is not also liable for a penalty points disqualification (see § 20.56).

(2) The Crown Court may disqualify an offender under s.147 of the Powers of Criminal Courts (Sentencing) Act 2000 where a motor vehicle has been used for crime in respect of *any* indictable offence punishable with imprisonment of two years or more (see § 20.58).

(3) Any court may disqualify under s.147 of the Powers of Criminal Courts (Sentencing) Act 2000 a person convicted of common assault or of any other offence involving an assault if the offence was committed by driving a motor vehicle (see § 20.58).

(4) Any court may disqualify an offender until he passes a test of competence to drive on convicting him of any endorsable offence (see § 20.69). An offender convicted of an offence involving obligatory disqualification or disqualified because of the accumulation of 12 or more penalty points will have to pass an extended driving test (see § 20.70).

(5) A magistrates' court may disqualify an offender who has been convicted of an endorsable offence when committing him for sentence to the Crown Court (see § 20.79).

(6) A court may disqualify an offender convicted of an offence of stealing or attempting to steal a motor vehicle or taking, etc., a motor vehicle without consent or going equipped for stealing or taking motor vehicles (see § 20.57).

Period and commencement of disqualification

All orders of disqualification commence immediately and cannot be postponed (except when suspended pending the hearing of an appeal; see §§ 22.08–14) and cannot be made consecutive to any other order of disqualification. **20.04**

Escaping disqualification by deception

Where a court is deceived regarding any circumstances that were or might **20.05** have been taken into account in deciding whether or for how long to disqualify an offender when dealing with him for an endorsable offence, then if the deception constituted or was due to an offence committed by that person, on conviction of that offence the court has the same powers and duties regarding an order of disqualification as the original court, but must take into account any order made on his conviction of the original endorsable offence (see § 20.86).

Notification of disease or disability

A court must notify the Secretary of State if an offender suffers from any **20.06** prescribed disease or disability which may render his driving a source of danger to the public (see §§ 20.88–91).

Probationary period for newly qualified drivers

Drivers who accumulate six or more penalty points within two years of first **20.07** passing a driving test taken on or after June 1, 1997 will have their full licences automatically revoked and will have to pass another driving test in order to restore their previous entitlements (see § 20.95).

Removal of disqualification

Application may be made to the court for the removal of any order of **20.08** disqualification for a period of more than two years (see §§ 20.99 et seq.).

Scope and effect of disqualification

20.09   A person may be disqualified without any other sentence, such as a fine, being passed on him for the offence (*R. v Bignell* (1968) 52 Cr. App. R. 10). *R. v Surrey Quarter Sessions Ex p. Commissioner of Police* [1963] 1 Q.B. 990, which is to the contrary, was not cited to the court in *Bignell* but it is nevertheless considered that unless and until *Bignell* is reconsidered by the Court of Appeal it may be relied on. It is, however, submitted that if a court does not wish to impose any penalty other than disqualification, it is proper to make an order of absolute discharge. Alternatively, it now seems possible in the light of s.48(2) of the Supreme Court Act 1981 as amended by the Criminal Justice Act 1988 s.156 for an order of no separate penalty to accompany a disqualification (see further § 19.05).

A person who holds a foreign driving licence, an international driving licence or a visiting forces' driving permit is, if disqualified by a court in Great Britain, forbidden to drive on roads in Great Britain even though this foreign licence is still valid (Motor Vehicles (International Circulation) Order 1975 (SI 1975/1208) art.2(4)); moreover s.103(1)(b) of the 1988 Act forbids a person to drive when disqualified for holding or obtaining a licence issued under the 1988 Act.

20.10   The effect of a disqualification is that the defendant may not drive in Great Britain a motor vehicle of any type on a road which is a highway or to which the public have access during the period of disqualification, but he may drive on private land or on places which are not "roads". If a disqualified farmer drives straight across the highway on a tractor from one field to another he commits an offence, though the brevity of the journey and lack of any other vehicles when he crosses might possibly be a "special reason" (see *Coombs v Kehoe* and other cases at "Shortness of distance driven", §§ 21.39–43). At the time of writing (March 2009) a British disqualification does not forbid driving abroad, although the driver must of course comply with the relevant foreign law as to licences. That position will change, however, so far as states within the European Union are concerned when Pt 3 of the Crime (International Co-operation) Act 2003 is fully implemented (see "Mutual recognition of disqualifications", §§ 20.13–15).

There is no power to limit disqualification to the type of vehicle in use at the time of the offence. If disqualification is imposed, the defendant is disqualified from driving all types of motor vehicle and for all purposes.

20.11   "Disqualified" in a policy was held to mean "disqualified by order of the court" and not to cover the case of a person who had been refused renewal of his driving licence because of mental deficiency (*Edwards v Griffiths* [1953] 2 All E.R. 874). Although s.101 of the 1988 Act provides that a person is disqualified for holding or obtaining a licence to drive a motor vehicle if he is under the minimum age specified for the particular class of motor vehicle, s.103(4) ibid. excludes under-age driving from the effects of s.103(1) ibid. which creates the offence of driving whilst disqualified. Under-age drivers are accordingly liable for prosecution for the lesser offence under s.87 of the 1988 Act of driving otherwise than in accordance with a licence (see § 11.24).

Where the holder of a licence is sentenced to disqualification for a period of 56 days or more by order of a court, the licence shall be treated as having been revoked from the beginning of the period of disqualification or, if suspended, from the day on which the suspension ceases (1988 Offenders Act s.37). One effect is that, before an offender may drive after a period of disqualification has ceased, he must apply for a new driving licence. If he drives after the period of disqualification without doing so he commits the offence of driving without holding a licence contrary to s.87 of the 1988 Act.

Where the offender is disqualified for a fixed period of less than 56 days or is made subject to an order of interim disqualification imposed in any of the circumstances predicated by s.26 of the 1988 Offenders Act (see § 20.75), his licence is not revoked but will have effect again at the end of the period of disqualification. **20.12**

Mutual recognition of disqualifications

The Council of the European Union on June 17, 1998 drew up a Convention on Driving Disqualifications (reproduced in Vol.2 at §§ C12.01 et seq.) concerning the mutual recognition within the European Union of disqualifications imposed by Member States. Effect is given to that Convention so far as the United Kingdom is concerned by Pt 3 of the Crime (International Co-operation) Act 2003, which at the time of writing (March 2009) remains largely unimplemented. The Mutual Recognition of Driving Disqualifications (Great Britain and Ireland) Regulations 2008 (SI 2008/3010) have been made under Pt 3 of the Act, which provides for mutual recognition of driving disqualifications between Member States of the European Union. Part 3 will be commenced in relation to Ireland on a date to be appointed, which will be advertised and will also be notified on the Department for Transport website (*http://www.dft.gov.uk/* [Accessed April 9, 2009]). The relevant provisions of the Act (ss.54–79) are reproduced in Vol.2. **20.13**

Chapter 1 (ss.54–75) is headed "Convention on Driving Disqualifications". Sections 54 and 55 deal with road traffic offences committed in the United Kingdom by an individual normally resident in a Member State other than the United Kingdom. Where such an individual is convicted of an offence listed in Sch.3, no appeal is outstanding and the driving disqualification condition is met (s.54(2); see below), notice must be given to the authorities of the Member State in which the individual is normally resident of a driving disqualification imposed in the United Kingdom. Sections 56–58 set out broadly similar powers and duties in respect of the conviction and disqualification in another Member State of an individual normally resident in the United Kingdom.

The United Kingdom offences to which the above provisions apply are listed in the two Parts of Sch.3. Part 1 is headed "Offences where order of disqualification for a minimum period unnecessary" and contains the following offences: manslaughter or culpable homicide by the driver of a motor vehicle; exceeding a speed limit; causing death by dangerous driving or by careless driving when under the influence of drink or drugs; dangerous driving; careless and inconsiderate driving; driving, or being in charge, when under influence (*sic*) of drink or drugs; driving, or being in charge, with alcohol above prescribed limit; failing to provide a specimen of breath for a breath test; failing to provide a specimen for analysis or laboratory test; motor racing on public ways; driving while disqualified; failure to stop after accident and give particulars or report of (*sic*) accident. Part 2 is headed "Offences where order of disqualification for minimum period necessary" and comprises any offence mentioned in Pt 1 of Sch.2 to the 1988 Offenders Act or the equivalent Northern Ireland legislation which is not included in the list of offences set out in Pt 1 (see above). So far as offences committed in Member States apart from the United Kingdom are concerned, reference should **20.14** be made to the list of offence types set out in the Annex to the Driving Disqualifications Convention (see §§ C12.21–22 in Vol.2). Broadly speaking, that list describes conduct not dissimilar to that of the offences listed in Sch.3.

The driving disqualification condition mentioned above is met in relation to a United Kingdom offence listed in Pt 1 of Sch.3 if any order of disqualification is made, regardless of its length. With regard to Pt 2 offences, however, the disqualification must be for not less than the minimum period; that period is normally six months, but may be for less than that where the state in which the offender normally resides has prescribed a shorter period for that purpose. So far as disqualifications imposed in other Member States are concerned, similar rules apply.

20.15   Sections 59–62 make provision for a person disqualified in another Member State by virtue of s.57 above to appeal against that disqualification to his local magistrates' court in England and Wales, sheriff court in Scotland or court of summary jurisdiction in Northern Ireland. Sections 63 and 64 deal with the production of licences following disqualification and create offences punishable by a fine of level 3 for those in Great Britain (s.63(6)) and Northern Ireland (s.64(6)) who fail to do so within 21 days. Where the holder of a Community licence is disqualified under s.57, particulars of the licence-holder and the disqualification must be sent to the licensing authority in the Member State which issued the licence (s.65). Section 66 provides that where a person is disqualified under s.57, his national licence is to be treated as revoked with effect from the beginning of the disqualification, and s.67 lays down a rule for determining the end of the period of disqualification. Sections 68 and 69 provide respectively for particulars of the disqualification to be endorsed on the counterpart of the national licence in Great Britain or Northern Ireland. Sections 70–75 deal with general matters, including interpretation (s.74).

Chapter 2 (ss.76–79) is headed "Mutual Recognition within the United Kingdom etc.". Section 76 by the insertion of a new s.102A into the Road Traffic Act 1988 effectively provides for recognition in Great Britain of disqualifications imposed in Northern Ireland, the Isle of Man, the Channel Islands or Gibraltar. Section 77 inserts a new s.109A in the 1988 Act to provide for the endorsement of counterparts issued to holders of Northern Ireland licences. It also inserts new ss.91ZA and 91ZB into the Road Traffic Offenders Act 1988 to enable the application of various provisions of that Act to Northern Ireland licences, and for the effect of endorsement on Northern Ireland licence holders. Section 78 establishes a prohibition on holding or obtaining Great Britain and Northern Ireland licences (by amendments to ss.97, 99 and 102 of the 1988 Act). Section 79 contains additional amendments to the 1988 Act relating to Northern Ireland (revocation of authorisation conferred by Northern Ireland licence because of disability or prospective disability (new s.109B) and information relating to disabilities, etc. (new s.109C)).

The mutual recognition of driving disqualifications between Great Britain and Northern Ireland described above was extended with effect from May 23, 2005 to include the Isle of Man. Thus if a driver receives a disqualification on or after that date in Great Britain, Northern Ireland or the Isle of Man it will apply in all three jurisdictions for the period of the disqualification.

Undertaking not to drive

20.16   Sometimes a defendant will give an undertaking to the court that he will not drive again, and the court may refrain from disqualifying in reliance on this undertaking. Should he then drive again, "vows, etcetera, deriding", the books on criminal law do not mention such a breach as being the crime of contempt, but breaches of an undertaking to the courts in general are mentioned in 9 *Halsbury's Laws* (4th ed.) 44, para.75 as being contempts. It is suggested that, in such a case, the matter should be reported to the Director of Public Prosecutions.

If the defendant has surrendered his licence, after having given such an undertaking, he may be prosecuted for driving without a licence because, having given up his licence to the Department for Transport, he is no longer the holder of it.

Period and commencement of disqualification

Every order of disqualification must commence from the moment the order is pronounced; it cannot be ordered to run consecutively to any other order of disqualification or to an order of imprisonment (*R. v Meese* [1973] R.T.R. 400; *R. v Higgins* [1973] R.T.R. 216; *R. v Bain* [1974] R.T.R. 213; *R. v Graham* below).   **20.17**

The usual minimum periods in the absence of special reasons are six months for a penalty points disqualification and 12 months for an obligatorily disqualifiable offence. These periods and when the minimum periods are increased are discussed at § 20.33 and §§ 20.53–5, respectively.

In all cases disqualifications should be for a specified period and not for an indefinite one (*R. v Fowler* [1937] 2 All E.R. 380). Offences for which disqualification is a proper penalty should not be taken into consideration when sentence is being passed for a different offence (*R. v Collins* [1947] 1 All E.R. 147), but it is permissible to take into consideration another offence of a similar kind (*R. v Jones* [1970] 3 All E.R. 815). Disqualification is effective as soon as it is ordered by the court (*Taylor v Kenyon* [1952] 2 All E.R. 726) and a disqualification expressed to run from the day of release from prison is void (*R. v Graham* [1955] Crim. L.R. 319). It was said that when it is imposed along with imprisonment, the period of disqualification should not be so short that most of it will have expired on release from prison (*R. v Phillips* (1955) 119 J.P. 499). However, in *R. v Pashley* [1973] R.T.R. 149, a defendant sentenced to 12 months' imprisonment and disqualified for three years had the disqualification reduced to 12 months on the ground that the imprisonment was the deterrent and he would face financial difficulties when leaving prison, strengthening the temptation to drive while disqualified. In reducing a driving disqualification from four years to 18 months, the court in *R. v Chalcraft* [2007] EWCA Crim 1389 reiterated earlier authority in which it was said: **20.18**

> "This is a man whose living is based upon his driving. He works in the docks in relation to the importation of cars. He has to drive to carry on that job. There is an important principle in respect of the imposition of periods of disqualification that they should not, except in exceptionally severe cases, be so long as to impair prospects of rehabilitation, with the impact that that can have on the family of the offender as well as on him." (*R. v Chivers* [2005] EWCA Crim 2252 at [12], per David Clarke J.)

It is submitted that the correct sentencing policy is not to impose a very lengthy period of disqualification unless the public needs to be protected from the defendant being allowed to drive.   **20.19**

This principle may be modified if the Coroners and Justice Bill comes into force in its current (March 2009) form. Clause 119 of and Sch.14 to the Bill insert a new section, s.35A, into the Road Traffic Offenders Act 1988. Section 35A provides for an extension in the length of the period of a driving disqualification imposed under ss.34 and 35 of that Act where a custodial sentence is also imposed for the offence. The court must, under the proposed provisions, determine the appropriate discretionary period of disqualification and then add on the appropriate extension period.

20.20   The extent to which existing cases on this topic remain relevant will need to be reconsidered if and when the Coroners and Justice Bill comes into force. For example, in *R. v Gibbons* [1987] Crim. L.R. 349, a disqualification for four years imposed upon a young man, who had pleaded guilty to (inter alia) reckless driving, driving whilst disqualified and taking a vehicle without consent and been sentenced to 12 months' youth custody, was upheld by the Court of Appeal on the grounds that the defendant had shown himself to be a complete menace on the roads from whom the public needed to be protected. A long period of disqualification in his case would allow him the opportunity to mature.

In an attempt to avoid apprehension by police, a 23-year-old offender drove a stolen car at excessive speed and dangerously in busy streets on an August evening, causing damage to another vehicle. He was convicted of dangerous driving and aggravated vehicle-taking and sentenced to 18 months' concurrent imprisonment on each offence. For the offence of dangerous driving he was disqualified from driving for five years, but due to a judicial oversight he was not disqualified pending passing an extended driving test as he should have been pursuant to s.36(1) of the 1988 Offenders Act (see further § 20.68). The Court of Appeal in *R. v Callum* [1995] R.T.R. 246 held that whilst the driving offences were very bad, they had been duly punished with a substantial period of imprisonment. The appellant was of an age where a long period of disqualification might well have a serious effect on his prospects of employment and he might be unduly tempted to flout the disqualification. On the facts the five-year disqualification in addition to the prison sentence was excessive and unnecessary; the proper period of disqualification was two years, which was accordingly substituted. The offender was additionally ordered to be disqualified until he had passed the appropriate driving test, since the requirement to so disqualify in accordance with s.36(1) of the 1988 Offenders Act was a mandatory one.

20.21   In *R. v McLaughlin* [1978] R.T.R. 452 the Court of Appeal, after observing that very long periods of disqualification may be said to be counter-productive, upheld a 20-year period of disqualification where the defendant had a drink problem, did not recognise that he had a problem, and had previous convictions and where in the opinion of the court there was a serious risk that he would injure or kill someone if allowed to drive. In *R. v Bowling* [2008] EWCA Crim 1148; [2008] Crim. L.R. 726 the appellant pleaded guilty to two counts of engaging in sexual activity in the presence of a child. The offences occurred while he was driving his car. He was sentenced to 22 months' imprisonment, with a sexual offences prevention order under the Sexual Offences Act 2003 and was disqualified from driving for four years under the Powers of Criminal Courts (Sentencing) Act 2000 s.147. He appealed against the length of the disqualification. It was accepted on his behalf that the sentencing judge had jurisdiction under s.147 to make the order disqualifying him from driving. The question that arose on appeal was whether the disqualification should extend beyond the period the appellant would be required to spend in custody. It was said that the general principle is that if a defendant is given a custodial sentence, and the court imposes a period of disqualification from driving under s.147, it would normally do so for a period equal to or slightly in excess of the period the offender would spend in custody. The policy behind this general principle is that the court should not impose a period of disqualification that would inhibit the offender from rehabilitating himself. This is particularly so in cases where the offender is dependent on the ability to drive for his livelihood. In this case the question was whether the nature of the offences committed by the appellant was such that in the public interest those general principles should not apply. The appellant had worked as a self-employed roofer before the offences, and would continue to pursue that trade on his release. The sentencing judge had made a sexual offences prevention order, providing that the appellant could not work with children and could not go within 100m of school premises. The court could see that there might be cases involving offences of this type where the period of disqualification should be significantly longer than the period during which the offender was in custody, but the court did not think that that was appropriate in the present case. The period of disqualification was reduced to 24 months. A commentary by Dr Thomas in the *Criminal Law Review* ([2008] Crim. L.R. 726 at 727) points out that a disqualification from driving under s.147 can only be general, prohibiting driving on any occasion and in any circumstances. In the instant case a sexual offences prevention order could be tailored to include the restrictions necessary in the circumstances of the individual case.

Unless its minimum period be limited by statute, the disqualification can be for such period, long or short, as the court orders. Obligatory orders of disqualification have minimum periods, but no maximum periods.

The court should decide on the period of disqualification which is appropriate **20.22** to the facts of the case; it is wrong for the court in pronouncing sentence to advert to the fact that the defendant after the appropriate period can apply for restoration of his licence under s.42 of the 1988 Offenders Act (*R. v Lobley* [1974] R.T.R. 550). *R. v Lobley* was applied by the Divisional Court in *R (on the application of Corner) v Southend Crown Court* [2005] EWHC 2334; (2006) 170 J.P. 6. The Crown Court had declined to reduce on appeal a four-year disqualification imposed by magistrates for an offence of driving with excess alcohol, the defendant's blood alcohol having been four times the legal limit, on the basis that he would be entitled to apply after two years for the period of disqualification to be reduced or terminated under s.42 of the 1988 Offenders Act. The Crown Court had clearly erred in law by regarding as pertinent the ability of the defendant to make such an application. A period of two years disqualification was accordingly substituted, the circumstances of the original offence being extremely unusual in that the defendant, who some three years earlier had suffered serious head injuries as a result of a violent assault, had tried to drive his car over a cliff but had instead crashed into a fence.

Disqualification for life was upheld in *R. v Wallace* [1955] N.I. 137 and in *R. v Tunde-Olarinde* [1967] 2 All E.R. 491, but the policy of the Court of Appeal is increasingly to discourage disqualification for life or for very long periods, particularly where the offender is young. Thus in *R. v Ward* [1971] Crim. L.R. 665, a "bad case of dangerous driving" by a person sentenced to borstal, disqualification was varied from life to five years. Likewise in *R. v Lee* [1971]

Crim. L.R. 177 a disqualification for another young man sentenced to borstal was reduced from 10 to three years. Indeed in *R. v North* [1971] R.T.R. 366 (applied in *R. v Ward* above) it was said that "unless there were unusual circumstances a disqualification for life is wrong in principle". A driver pleaded guilty to reckless driving. Following an argument with his wife he had driven straight at a police car in which she was a passenger. The policewoman driver sustained a whiplash injury and damage to the extent of £2,300 was caused to the car. The driver's alcohol level was two and a half times the prescribed limit. He was sentenced to nine months' imprisonment and disqualified for life. In reducing the period of disqualification to five years, the Court of Appeal in *R. v Scott* [1989] Crim. L.R. 920 emphasised that it was wrong in principle to impose disqualification for life in addition to a custodial sentence on a man with no previous complaint of bad driving and no previous disqualification. Furthermore, the judge had given no prior intimation of his intentions with regard to disqualification so that counsel had had no opportunity to make submissions on the point; that was also wrong. (See further the discussion of *R. v Ireland* [1989] Crim. L.R. 458 at § 20.57 below.) In *R. v Tantrum* (1989) 11 Cr. App. R. (S) 348 the Court of Appeal stated that disqualification for life should be imposed only in very exceptional circumstances as very long periods of disqualification tended to inhibit the rehabilitation of the offender. In *R. v Rivano (Frank)* (1993) 158 J.P. 288 that court allowed an appeal against an order for disqualification for life of a 30-year-old man who had driven very badly and who had a terrible record. Although the court agreed that the driver was at that time an absolute menace to other people, it was not convinced that there were such very exceptional circumstances requiring disqualification for life, or that it should conclude that the driver would be a danger to the public indefinitely. His contempt for the law was properly marked by the sentence of six months' imprisonment that had been imposed, but for a man of his age disqualification for life was not appropriate. Accordingly his disqualification was reduced to a period of 10 years.

20.23   The Court of Appeal held in *R. v Charles Harrison* [2004] EWCA Crim 1527 that in circumstances where a driving licence had been revoked by the DVLA due to a medical condition (insulin-dependent diabetes), and the dangerous driving complained of had arisen from that medical condition but with no moral blame attaching to the defendant, there was no reason for a court to impose a lifetime disqualification. The starting point was that the defendant should be prevented from driving for a period long enough to protect the public; when and if he could show he was no longer a risk he should be allowed to drive. The issue should be left in the hands of the DVLA.

Disqualification starts to run on the day on which the order of disqualification is made, even though that day is later than the day of conviction, e.g. because there has been an adjournment (see below). The day on which the order is made counts as one full day of the period of disqualification and the defendant may not drive from the moment when the court pronounces the order; someone else must drive his vehicle away from the court unless notice of appeal in writing is given and the court suspends the disqualification. Thus, a disqualification for 12 months imposed on the afternoon of January 1, will expire at midnight on December 31. Time during which the disqualification was suspended is disregarded (Road Traffic Offenders Act 1988 s.43). There is no power to disqualify from the driving of any type of vehicle other than a motor vehicle or trolley vehicle.

Where an offender who has been made subject to an order of interim disquali-   **20.24**
fication under s.26 of the 1988 Offenders Act is subsequently sentenced, any period of disqualification imposed by the court shall be treated as reduced by the
period during which he was disqualified by virtue of that order (s.26(12); see further § 20.77).

Attempts

Whether there is power or a duty on a court to disqualify depends primarily on   **20.25**
whether an attempt to commit the offence is itself endorsable (see § 19.15). It
should be noted, however, that although as a result of amendments made by the
Road Traffic Act 1991 to Sch.2 to the 1988 Offenders Act offences of attempting
to steal a motor vehicle or taking a motor vehicle without consent, etc., committed on or after July 1, 1992 are no longer endorsable, they remain subject to
discretionary disqualification.

OBLIGATORY DISQUALIFICATIONS

Obligatory disqualification

On conviction for an offence involving obligatory disqualification (see the   **20.26**
table at § 19.02), the offender must (save as mentioned below) be disqualified for
holding or obtaining a licence to drive a motor vehicle for not less than 12 months
(1988 Offenders Act s.34(1)). Section 34(4) ibid. (as substituted by the Road
Traffic Act 1991) provides for a minimum two-year period of obligatory
disqualification for certain offences and for certain offenders with a bad driving
record. The offences concerned are:

(a) manslaughter, or in Scotland, culpable homicide;

(b) causing death by dangerous driving; and

(c) causing death by careless driving while under the influence of drink or
drugs (s.34(4)(a)).

So far as offenders are concerned, s.34(4)(b) applies the increased minimum
period of disqualification to a person on whom more than one disqualification for
a fixed period of 56 days or more has been imposed within the three years immediately preceding the commission of the offence concerned. The qualification
for a two-year minimum disqualification set out in the latter subsection thus appears to be the commission of an offence subject in the normal course of events to
obligatory disqualification for not less than 12 months (e.g. driving with excess
alcohol) by an offender whose past record includes two or more previous
disqualifications, each of at least eight weeks' duration and each imposed within
the three years prior to the commission of the obligatorily disqualifiable offence.

It is provided by the inserted s.34(4A) that certain other disqualifications are to   **20.27**
be disregarded for the purposes of subs.34(4)(b) above. They are:

(a) interim disqualification;

(b) disqualification where vehicle used for purpose of crime;

(c) disqualification for stealing or taking a vehicle or going equipped to
steal or take the same.

See § 20.32 below as to the three-year compulsory disqualification for committing within 10 years of a previous conviction a second drink/driving offence.

The requirements of s.34(1) of the 1988 Offenders Act apply on first or subsequent conviction. Semble, under s.46(2) of the 1988 Offenders Act, if a defendant in England or Wales was absolutely or conditionally discharged, this counts as a conviction, if it was endorsed.

20.28   There cannot be a disqualification in the defendant's absence unless the case has been adjourned to give him an opportunity to be present and he has been warned in the notice of adjournment of the intention to disqualify (Magistrates' Courts Act 1980 s.11(4)). The Magistrates' Court Sentencing Guidelines published in 2008 recommend (p.186) that the court should avoid exercising this power wherever possible unless it is sure that the offender is aware of the hearing and the likely imposition of disqualification.

The court may only refrain from imposing the 12-month, two-year or three-year disqualification for any offence involving obligatory disqualification or impose a shorter period of disqualification:

(a) if there are special reasons (see Chapter 21), when the court may either not disqualify at all or disqualify for less than the appropriate minimum period;

(b) if the offenders are aiders and abettors, counsellors or procurers of an obligatorily disqualifiable offence, when they need not be disqualified (s.34(5)) but otherwise incur 10 penalty points (see § 19.18);

(c) where, under the Mental Health Act 1983 s.37(3), the court is satisfied as to the offence and makes a guardianship or hospital order "without convicting him", when, presumably, there can be no disqualification or endorsement at all as there is no "conviction".

20.29   An obligatory disqualification counts as a disqualification for the purpose of any increase in the minimum period of a penalty points disqualification (see §§ 20.53–5).

In England and Wales, an offender must be disqualified, unless there are special reasons, on the granting of an absolute or conditional discharge for an offence for which disqualification is obligatory (Road Traffic Offenders Act 1988 s.46(1); *Owen v Imes* [1972] R.T.R. 489).

The disqualification imposed under s.34(1) must be imposed even if the court is obliged also to impose a penalty points disqualification as a result of another offence or other offences being dealt with at the same time (see § 20.38).

20.30   The court may at its discretion disqualify for a longer period than the obligatory period of 12 months, two years or three years (as appropriate).

Any order of disqualification, whether it be discretionary or obligatory, must run from the moment it is pronounced (*R. v Higgins* [1973] R.T.R. 216; *R. v Bain* [1973] R.T.R. 213); likewise, it seems, a penalty points disqualification or, indeed, any other order of disqualification. Thus where a defendant was disqualified for two and a half years on one count of causing death by dangerous driving and two and a half years on another count of driving with excess blood-alcohol, the order of the trial judge that the two periods of disqualification should run consecutively was set aside by the Court of Appeal, who ordered them to run concurrently (*R. v Meese* [1973] R.T.R. 400). Where an offender was liable to both an order of obligatory disqualification for an offence and an order of disqualification for penalty points, the Court of Appeal made one order of disqualification only in *R. v Elliott* (*R. v Boswell* [1984] 1 W.L.R. 1047).

Where the court does not disqualify in a case under s.34(1) of the 1988 Of- **20.31**
fenders Act or disqualifies for a shorter period, the "special reasons" must be
stated in open court and, if a magistrates' court or, in Scotland, a court of summary jurisdiction, entered in the register (1988 Offenders Act s.47(1)), but failure
to state them aloud does not invalidate the decision (*Brown v Dyerson* [1968] 3
All E.R. 39).

Second conviction for drink/driving, etc., offences

A previous conviction in the 10 years preceding the commission of a second **20.32**
such offence for causing death by careless driving when under the influence of
drink or drugs, for driving or attempted driving when unfit through drink or drugs,
for driving or attempted driving with alcohol concentration above the prescribed
limit, for refusing to give a specimen for analysis or a laboratory test or for failing to allow a specimen to be subjected to laboratory test when the accused had
been driving or attempting to drive at the relevant time brings a three-year minimum obligatory disqualification on subsequent conviction for any one of those
four offences (1988 Offenders Act s.34(3)). It should be noted that the 10-year
period is calculated from the date of *commission* of the second offence back to
the date of *conviction* of the earlier offence. An offender just within the 10-year
period cannot therefore avoid his liability to a three-year disqualification by
obtaining an adjournment. These provisions do not apply where the conviction is
for being in charge or refusing to supply a specimen while in charge at the relevant time, but do apply where the previous conviction was for aiding or abetting
a drink/driving offence (*Makeham v Donaldson* [1981] R.T.R. 511). It should
also be noted that offenders convicted of attempting to drive are liable to three
years' disqualification whether the first or second offence (or both) was only attempting to drive.

It should be noted that a second offender is liable to the three-year minimum
disqualification even if he escaped disqualification for the first offence (*Boliston v
Gibbons* [1985] R.T.R. 176; see further § 4.325).

Summary of penalty points disqualification

The penalty points system came into operation on November 1, 1982. Every **20.33**
endorsable offence attracts a fixed or variable number of penalty points. The
number of points to be imposed for the particular offences is set out in a table at
§ 19.02 and discussed in detail at §§ 19.20 et seq. The system is set out in ss.28,
29 and 35 of, and Sch.2 to, the Road Traffic Offenders Act 1988.

A penalty points disqualification is not additional or consecutive to any other
order of disqualification. Like any other type of disqualification, unless suspended
pending the hearing of an appeal, it takes effect from the moment it is made and
cannot be postponed to take effect at a later date or to be made consecutive to any
other order of disqualification. Where an offender is dealt with on the same occasion by a court in respect of a number of endorsable offences, the court is required
to make only one order of penalty points disqualification (see § 20.54).

Where an offender appears before the court for one or more offences which **20.34**
were not *committed* on the same occasion, each of the offences committed on different occasions incurs the imposition of penalty points (see § 19.39). It should
also be noted that as a result of the amendment of s.29 of the 1988 Offenders Act

by the Road Traffic Act 1991, courts now have a discretion to impose penalty points for more than one offence where a number of offences are committed on the same occasion (see § 19.38).

Where a penalty points disqualification is imposed the court (as with any other order of disqualification) is required to notify the DVLA. The code used for a penalty points disqualification is TT99.

20.35   A penalty points disqualification (unlike other orders of disqualification) removes from the defendant's licence any previous penalty points (see § 20.50) and counts (provided it was for a fixed period of 56 days or more) as a disqualification for the purpose of increasing the period of a subsequent penalty points disqualification (see § 20.54).

A court is obliged to impose the minimum period of a penalty points disqualification unless "having regard to all the circumstances there are grounds for mitigating the normal consequences of the conviction". Certain mitigating circumstances are, however, specifically excluded (see Chapter 21).

20.36   A court is required (in the absence of "mitigating circumstances"; see Chapter 21) to impose a penalty points disqualification under s.35 of the 1988 Offenders Act when an offender is convicted of any endorsable offence when the number of penalty points for that offence and others which have to be taken into account under s.29(1), (2) of the 1988 Offenders Act amount to 12 or more.

Penalty points required to be taken into account

20.37   With regard to the operation of the penalty points system generally, the Road Traffic Law Review (the North Report, HMSO, 1988) commented upon the unsatisfactory nature of the "wiping the slate clean" provisions of what is now the 1988 Offenders Act whereby virtually any disqualification, however short and whysoever imposed, had the effect of presenting the offender with a clean licence upon the expiry of his disqualification. Concern was also expressed about the "double disqualification" which arose where, e.g. the notional four points then attached to an obligatorily disqualifiable offence when added to the points already endorsed upon the licence meant that an offender had to be disqualified twice over (albeit concurrently).

Section 28 of the Road Traffic Act 1991 rectified these two problems by replacing s.29 of the 1988 Offenders Act with a considerably revised version. This provides that where a person is convicted of an offence involving obligatory endorsement, the penalty points to be taken into account on that occasion are:

(a) any that are to be attributed to the offence(s) of which he is convicted, disregarding any offence in respect of which the defendant is disqualified under s.34 of the Act (obligatory or discretionary disqualification for an offence), and

(b) any that were on a previous occasion ordered to be endorsed, except that:

     (i) no points will be taken into account if since that occasion and before the conviction the offender has been disqualified under s.35 of the Act (penalty points disqualification) (see § 20.50); and

     (ii) points will not be added to each other where any of the offences in respect of which points were imposed was committed more than three years before another.

The Divisional Court in *Learmont v Crown Prosecution Service* [1994] R.T.R. **20.38**
286 confirmed (if confirmation were needed) that "double disqualification" for a
single offence is no longer possible under s.29 of the 1988 Offenders Act, as
substituted by the Road Traffic Act 1991. The court accepted, however, that two
periods of disqualification may be imposed on the same occasion in respect of
different offences.

Although the revised s.29(1)(a) paraphrased at (a) above eradicates the
mischief at which it was aimed, namely double disqualification for a single offence, it does not appear to, and was probably not intended to, ameliorate the position of an offender who, e.g., commits an offence punishable with obligatory
disqualification and also commits other endorsable offences on the same occasion, since the only points to be disregarded are those attributable to the offence
for which disqualification must be ordered under s.34(1) of the 1988 Offenders
Act. Thus a drinking driver with six points already on his licence who drives
whilst uninsured would appear to run the risk of being disqualified under both
s.34(1) and s.35. He might derive some consolation, however, from the fact that
the s.35 disqualification would have the effect of removing from the licence the
points previously endorsed upon it, whereas had he committed only the excess
alcohol offence, those points would continue (subject to the effluxion of time) to
be recorded against him; see § 20.50 below.

Further problems relating to multiple offences must also be addressed. Taking **20.39**
again as an example the offender convicted of driving with excess alcohol and
uninsured use of a vehicle, what should happen if he produces a licence with no
more than three points already endorsed upon it? Section 19 of the Transport Act
1981 which dealt with the endorsement of licences provided that particulars of an
offence, including penalty points, should be endorsed where the court did not order the offender's disqualification *whether on that or any other conviction*. When,
however, that Act was repealed and consolidated by the 1988 Offenders Act,
those helpful words of clarification disappeared from the legislation. Their loss
was not greatly felt since the penalty points system as then enacted provided that
most kinds of disqualification had the effect of "wiping the slate clean" and courts
did not generally feel disposed to indulge in the otiose exercise of endorsing
points which would be destined for instant erasure.

In the light of the amendments to the penalty points system made by the Road **20.40**
Traffic Act 1991, however, the position appeared to be somewhat different. The
endorsement of licences was, and is, controlled by s.44 of the 1988 Offenders Act
which provides that where a person is convicted of an offence involving obligatory endorsement, the court must endorse particulars of that conviction, including
penalty points, upon the licence if it does not order him to be disqualified. In the
absence of the words "whether on that or any other conviction" there was
considerable debate as to whether the obligation arose in respect of each and
every endorsable offence committed by the offender. If it did, then in addition to
disqualifying our exemplary uninsured drink/driver for the excess alcohol offence, the court would have been under a duty to endorse his licence with the appropriate number of points in respect of the insurance matter. The judicial
clarification was provided by the Divisional Court in *Martin v DPP* [2000] R.T.R.
188 in which it was held that where a court convicted a person for driving with
excess alcohol and ordered obligatory disqualification for that offence, it could
not endorse his licence with penalty points in respect of other offences of which

he had been convicted on the same occasion. The court had very much in mind the presumption that consolidating legislation did not change existing law without a clear indication of an intention to do so, as well as the principle against construing enactments as extending penal sanctions when the legislature's intention to do so was doubtful. The court drew also upon the persuasive authority of the decision of the High Court of Justiciary in Scotland in *Ahmed v McLeod* [2000] R.T.R. 201 to the effect that by the consolidation effected by s.44(1) of the 1988 Offenders Act, Parliament was presumed not to have intended to change the substance of the provision, but to have intended that s.44(1) should operate in the same way as the legislation it replaced, so that a court could not order penalty points to be endorsed if it ordered the offender to be disqualified in respect of any offence of which he had been convicted on that occasion. The words "if the court orders him to be disqualified" in s.44(1) had to be given a broad interpretation and applied to disqualification for any offence of which he had been convicted on that occasion, and not just for the particular offence resulting in the disqualification.

20.41 A different, but almost equally disturbing, complication so far as the amended provisions are concerned arises from the fact that s.29(1)(a) should be read in conjunction with s.34(2) of the 1988 Offenders Act which provides that a *discretionary* disqualification may only be imposed if the offence concerned is not endorsable (e.g. offences under s.1, 12 or 25 of the Theft Act 1968), or if the penalty points to be taken into account on that occasion number fewer than 12. Whether or not the court has power to disqualify in these circumstances depends upon the points to be taken into account; but the number of points to be taken into account depends on whether or not the court disqualifies. It is suggested that the circularity inherent in these provisions is logically inescapable; but see further § 20.56 and the case of *Jones v DPP* [2001] R.T.R. 80 discussed there.

As can be seen, the above rules are not exactly uncomplicated and it may assist if a number of examples of their operation are given.

Example 1

20.42

Offence	Date of offence	Sentence
Tyre	1.1.07	3 points
Speeding	1.9.08	3 points
Careless driving	1.7.09	5 points
Speeding	1.12.09	(Instant offence)

In this example the court is required to consider disqualifying as soon as he has been convicted of all the offences. It will be noted that all the offences took place within three years of each other and he was not disqualified for any of them.

Example 2

20.43

Offence	Date of offence	Sentence	Date of conviction
Tyre	1.1.07	3 points	2.4.07
Careless driving	1.7.07	5 points	4.9.07
No insurance	1.9.08	Disqualified 6 months (penalty points)	2.11.08

Offence	Date of offence	Sentence	Date of conviction
Speeding	1.12.09	(Instant offence)	

In this case it will be noted that the court is not obliged to disqualify: although all the offences were committed within three years of each other, the penalty points disqualification imposed on November 2, 2008 "wiped the slate clean" (see § 20.50).

Example 3

Offence	Date of offence	Sentence	Date of conviction	20.44
Tyre	1.1.07	3 points	4.3.07	
Careless driving	1.7.07	6 points	12.9.07	
In charge with excess alcohol	1.8.07	Disqualified 6 months (penalty points)	1.9.07	
No insurance	1.12.09	(Instant offence)		

In this case the court is obliged to consider disqualifying because despite the defendant receiving a penalty points disqualification on September 1, 2007 the careless driving points were not "wiped clean" because they were ordered after the occasion on which that disqualification was imposed.

Example 4

Offence	Date of offence	Sentence	Date of conviction	20.45
Tyre	1.1.07	3 points	4.3.07	
Speeding	1.7.08	Disqualified 3 months (for offence)	12.9.08	
Careless driving	31.3.09	6 points	29.6.09	
Tyre	1.12.09	(Instant offence)		

In this instance the court is obliged to consider disqualifying because the disqualification for the speeding offence committed on July 1, 2008 did not "wipe clean" the points imposed for the earlier tyre offence (see § 20.50).

Example 5

Offence	Date of offence	Sentence	Date of conviction	20.46
Tyre	1.1.08	3 points	1.4.08	
Careless driving	1.7.09		(10.10.09)	
No insurance	1.9.09	7 points	1.10.09	

It would seem that where an endorsable offence committed before another is dealt with after a later offence was dealt with, the court is usually required under s.29 of the 1988 Offenders Act to take into account the number of points imposed in respect of the later offence when the court comes to deal with the earlier offence. Assuming the sentence for careless driving is dealt with on October 10, 2009, the court is then obliged to consider a penalty points disqualification.

Example 6

20.47

Offence	Date of offence	Sentence	Date of conviction
Tyre	1.1.06	3 points	1.9.06
Speeding	1.4.06	3 points	1.12.06
No insurance	30.3.08	(6) points	(1.12.09)
Street playground offence	2.2.09	2 points	1.10.09

Where, however, the earliest offence and the latest offence are more than three years apart and the offence for which the court is sentencing the offender took place between the dates of the earliest offence and the latest offence, the points for the earliest offence and the latest offence cannot both be included in the total computation. In such a case some commentators suggest the wording of the proviso in s.29(2) of the 1988 Offenders Act requires the court not to take into account the points in respect of both offences.

In this example the court have fixed six as the appropriate number of points to be imposed in respect of the insurance offence being dealt with on December 1, 2009. It is submitted that the court is obliged to impose a penalty points disqualification.

20.48   Some commentators have argued that a strict interpretation of the proviso in s.29(2) requires the court to ignore the points for the earliest offence and only take into account the points of the latest offence. This seems to be wrong. The proviso only requires them not to be added to each other. It may nevertheless be argued that s.29 should be interpreted in the same way as s.35(2) where the relevant periods are much more clearly expressed. This would involve interpreting the words "the other" at the conclusion of s.29(2) as meaning "the other or others". The Interpretation Act 1978 requires the singular to include the plural unless the context otherwise requires. If this latter interpretation is correct it will result in a defendant in an example similar to that given being able to avoid a penalty points disqualification by virtue of his having committed a subsequent offence. This cannot have been the intention of Parliament.

Attendance on courses

20.49   Section 34 of the Road Safety Act 2006 (when in force) inserts new ss.30A–30D into the 1988 Offenders Act in order to enable courts to offer persons convicted of careless driving, speeding or failing to comply with traffic signs the opportunity of reducing the number of penalty points to be taken into account under s.29 of the 1988 Offenders Act by successfully completing a retraining course. In order to qualify for the scheme there should be at least seven and no more than 11 points to be taken into account at the time of the conviction. The consequence of successful completion of the course within a specified time is that 12 months after the conviction three points (or fewer if fewer were endorsed) will cease to be taken into consideration under s.29, thus providing some relief from the rigours of the "totting-up" provisions of s.35 ibid. This opportunity will not be offered to anyone who has completed such a course within the preceding three years; nor will it be available to a person convicted during his probationary period under the Road Traffic (New Drivers) Act 1995. It should be noted, however, that at the time of writing (March 2009) no indication had been given as to a likely date for implementation of any of these provisions.

"Wiping the slate clean"

Whereas prior to the amendment of the 1988 Offenders Act by the Road Traffic **20.50** Act 1991 any disqualification under s.35 or s.34 of the former Act had the effect of "wiping the slate clean", s.29(1)(b) (as substituted) provides that so far as offences committed on or after July 1, 1992 are concerned, only a disqualification for accumulating 12 or more penalty points will remove existing points from the licence; disqualification for a specific offence will leave them undisturbed. Two road safety benefits ensue from this change of approach: courts ought to feel encouraged to make greater use of short periods of disqualification; and drivers returning to the road after disqualification should be cautioned as to their future behaviour by the points remaining on their licences.

The substantive reason for doing away with "double disqualification" for a single offence (s.29(1)(a); see § 20.38) is, of course, s.35 of the 1988 Offenders Act, which provides that the minimum period of a penalty points disqualification becomes two years if there were two or more disqualifications within the three years prior to the latest effective point scoring offence; where only one such disqualification was imposed, the minimum period is but one year. The triggering of the greater penalty as a result of concurrent disqualifications simultaneously imposed for the same offence was an arguably unintentional and unfortunate side effect of the earlier legislation and its passing should not be lamented.

It should be noted that it would seem that if a person commits two offences on **20.51** different occasions and the earlier offence is dealt with after the later offence, the defendant's licence is not wiped clean if the court convicts and imposes a penalty points disqualification as a consequence of the later offence before the earlier offence has been dealt with (see Example 3 above). When an offender was disqualified by virtue of the accumulation of penalty points which fell to be taken into account under s.29 of the 1988 Offenders Act, the relevant date for the purpose of "wiping the slate clean" under s.29(1)(b) was the date sentence was imposed, not the date the offence was proved against him. The Divisional Court so held in *R. v Brentwood JJ. Ex p. Richardson* [1993] R.T.R. 374 when dealing with a problem which had arisen as a result of a delay between verdict and sentence. During that delay the defendant had been disqualified by different justices applying the "totting-up" procedure when imposing sentence for a different offence. The original justices had not realised that and when his case came back for sentence they disqualified him again, totting up the same penalty points with the additional ones they were imposing.

Parliament could not have intended that result. The date of "conviction" under s.29 had to be construed as being the date sentence was imposed, not the date of the verdict. In addition, the phrase "on that occasion" in s.29(1) had to refer to sentencing, which necessitated a wide construction of the term "conviction". Penalty points were not taken into account until sentence was considered and therefore the term "conviction" had to include the sentencing process.

Section 29(2) of the 1988 Offenders Act states that penalty points for an of- **20.52** fence must not be added to penalty points for another if the former offence was committed "more than three years" before the other. It would seem therefore that if the earlier offence was committed on January 1, 2006 and the later offence on January 1, 2009, the court is not required to consider the disqualification because although the earlier offence was committed three years before the later offence, it was committed "more than" three years before the other; the relevant period would seem to include the last day and exclude the first day (as to earlier offences being dealt with later than subsequent offences, see Examples 5 and 6 above).

Period of disqualification

20.53   The statutory period of a penalty points disqualification is a *minimum* period of six months. It is concurrent with any other period of disqualification and, it would seem, like any order of obligatory disqualification under s.34(1) of the 1988 Offenders Act or discretionary disqualification under s.34(2) ibid., cannot be ordered to be consecutive (*R. v Higgins* [1973] R.T.R. 216; *R. v Bain* [1974] R.T.R. 213). It is submitted that the absence of a specific statutory provision allowing or requiring a penalty points disqualification to be made consecutive was deliberate and that, as in other orders of disqualification, a penalty points disqualification must commence from the moment it is pronounced. The only circumstances where this is not the case is where an order is suspended pending an appeal (see §§ 22.08–14).

It will also be noted that s.35(2) of the 1988 Offenders Act refers to six months as the "minimum period". It is submitted that a court, when determining a period of disqualification, should take into account the amount of points that will be wiped clean and the extent to which the penalty points would be exceeded if he were not disqualified. The period under s.35(2) is a minimum period and should not become the tariff period, it is submitted.

20.54   Section 35(2) (as amended by the Road Traffic Act 1991) provides that the minimum period shall be 12 months if there has been a previous disqualification for a fixed period of 56 days or more imposed within the three years immediately preceding the latest offence in respect of which penalty points are taken into account. The subsection further provides that the minimum period shall be two years if there have been two such previous disqualifications. It seems clear from a reading of the subsection (particularly when one refers to s.35(5)) that the word "disqualification" in s.35(2) refers not only to a previous penalty points disqualification under s.35(1), but also to any disqualification imposed under s.34 of the 1988 Offenders Act and, indeed, one imposed under s.49 ibid. (see § 20.86). Like the period in s.29 (see above) the period of three years referred to in s.35(2) would seem to include the last day and exclude the first day.

The Divisional Court held in *Learmont v Crown Prosecution Service* [1994] R.T.R. 286 that a "double disqualification" for a single offence imposed prior to the amendment of s.29 of the 1988 Offenders Act by the Road Traffic Act 1991 (see § 20.37 above) should count as *one* period of disqualification rather than two for the purposes of calculating the minimum period applicable to a penalty points disqualification. The justices in the case in point had been of the view (unsurprisingly, since it was a view widely held and supported literally by the statute) that the defendant was liable to a minimum period of disqualification of two years as a result of a previous relevant conviction containing a disqualification for 18 months for an excess alcohol offence and a concurrent disqualification for six months imposed on the same occasion under s.35.

20.55   Section 35(3) requires a court, when an offender is convicted on the same occasion of more than one offence involving discretionary or obligatory disqualification, to take into account in determining the period of disqualification "all the offences". The subsection further states that no more than one order under s.35(1) shall be made, but for the purposes of appeal the order shall be treated as being made on the conviction of each of the offences. As already stated, although no express statutory provision has been made (other than s.35(3)) requiring a court when determining a period of disqualification to have regard to the number of points already imposed, it is submitted that, by reason of the "wiping the slate clean" provisions and the fact that the period under s.35(1) is expressed as a "minimum" period, a court should, whenever imposing a penalty points disqualification, have regard to the number, if any, of penalty points that will be wiped off by reason of the disqualification and also the number of points which the offender would incur but for the disqualification. A court must distinguish one offender from another and do justice as between offenders. It is submitted therefore that where, for example, an offender who already has 10 or 11 points is then convicted of, e.g., being in charge of a motor vehicle with excess alcohol (which itself carries 10 points), he normally should be disqualified for a longer period than an offender who commits offences the total points value of which only just reaches 12.

DISCRETIONARY DISQUALIFICATIONS

Exercise of discretionary power

Section 29 of the Road Traffic Act 1991 amended s.34 of the 1988 Offenders **20.56** Act in order to limit the circumstances in which a discretionary disqualification may be imposed upon an offender in respect of offences committed on or after July 1, 1992. Prior to that date s.34(2) provided an unfettered power of disqualification as a matter of discretion for any offence for which endorsement was obligatory but which did not involve obligatory disqualification under s.34(1). The amended s.34(2) provides that where a person is convicted of an offence involving discretionary disqualification, and either—

(a) the penalty points to be taken into account on that occasion number fewer than 12, or

(b) the offence is not one involving obligatory endorsement,

the court may order him to be disqualified for such period as the court thinks fit.

It will be seen from (a) above that a person who is liable to disqualification under s.35 of the 1988 Offenders Act as a result of accumulating 12 or more penalty points cannot additionally be disqualified for the offence he has committed if that offence is subject to discretionary rather than mandatory disqualification; if he is to be disqualified at all in those circumstances it has to be under the auspices of s.35. Thus the perils of "double disqualification" for a single offence are avoided (see § 20.37 above). A rather more serious problem remains, however. In order to ascertain the number of penalty points to be taken into account, reference must be made to s.29(1)(a) which requires the court to disregard any offence in respect of which an order under s.34 (i.e. obligatory or *discretionary* disqualification) is made. Thus whether or not the court has power to disqualify as a matter of discretion depends upon the penalty points to be taken into account; but the number of points to be taken into account depends upon whether or not the court exercises its discretion to disqualify. The circularity of these provisions requires a robust approach on the part of the court if an escape is to be effected. An answer to this long-standing conundrum has been provided by the Divisional Court (Buxton L.J. and Penry-Davey J.) in *Jones v DPP* [2001] R.T.R. 80. The appellant, who already had 11 points on his licence, had been convicted of speeding at between 94 and 101mph on a road subject to a 60mph limit; the magistrates (unsurprisingly, it may be thought) disqualified him for six months under s.35. It was contended, inter alia, on his behalf that the magistrates should have first considered whether to impose a discretionary disqualification for the index offence. Observing the lack of any prior authority on this issue, the court approached the matter on the basis of first principles. The amendments to the 1988 Offenders Act brought about by the Road Traffic Act 1991 were intended primarily to avoid double disqualification (as discussed above). In the court's view the proper approach of magistrates faced with an apparent choice between a totting-up disqualification and a discretionary disqualification would be to consider first the exercise of their powers under s.34(2), but in the light of a defendant's whole record; and if they came to the conclusion that he should have a longer disqualification because of his record, they could bring that about by not disqualifying under s.34(2), thus rendering him liable to disqualification under s.35. The court recognised that such an approach would produce what might be argued to be an anomaly in that, in a case where the instant offence was not regarded as sufficiently serious in itself to merit disqualification at all, a totting-up liability would nonetheless arise; but in truth that would not be an anomaly, because the offender's "offence" in such circumstances would be his prolonged record of instances of committing offences that attract penalty points. In the court's view it was unlikely that there would be many cases which potentially fell within the totting-up provisions where the magistrates would not conclude that those provisions should apply, bearing in mind the intention and the objective of them, which was to impose a reasonably substantial period of disqualification on people who have shown that they persistently offend against the road traffic laws. The statute does not make that compulsory; but simply gives the magistrates a discretion that they ought carefully to exercise in the circumstances of the offender's whole record in deciding which course to take.

20.57   A person who commits only an offence which does not involve obligatory endorsement (e.g. an offence of stealing or taking a vehicle or going equipped to steal or take the same) is always liable to be disqualified (if disqualification is deemed appropriate) under this section; since these offences carry no penalty points, they cannot of themselves contribute to an accumulation of points sufficient to trigger the mechanism of s.35.

Where the court is empowered to disqualify under s.34(2) it is entirely a matter for the court whether or not to order disqualification, and, if so, for how long, subject to these qualifications:

(1) In England and Wales an offender may be disqualified at the court's discretion on ordering an absolute or conditional discharge (1988 Offenders Act s.46).

(2) A person who has pleaded guilty in writing under s.12 of the Magistrates' Courts Act 1980 may not be disqualified in his absence unless he has been given the opportunity of attending at an adjourned hearing (see s.11(4) of the 1980 Act). The notification of the adjourned hearing must indicate the reason for the adjournment, i.e. that the magistrates are considering disqualification (*R. v Mason* [1965] 2 All E.R. 308;

s.11(4)). Disqualification may be ordered in his absence if he has been duly notified and does not attend. The same rule was held to apply in "totting-up" cases under s.93(3) of the 1972 Act (*R. v Llandrindod Wells JJ. Ex p. Gibson* (1968) 112 S.J. 218) and, no doubt, applies to all other types of disqualification as s.11(4) of the 1980 Act is general in its terms.

Where the procedure of the 1980 Act for a plea of guilty in his absence has not been used for the first hearing but the defendant has been summoned and fails to attend he may not be disqualified in his absence at that first hearing, but the case should be adjourned to give him the opportunity of attending and the notice of adjournment given to him should give the reason for the adjournment (1980 Act s.11(4)). Any disqualification imposed in a defendant's absence in breach of what is now s.11(4) of the 1980 Act is invalid notwithstanding that the disqualification was mandatory and that the defendant knew that he might be disqualified (*R. v Bishop's Stortford JJ. Ex p. Shields* (1968) 113 S.J. 124). If he fails to attend at the adjourned hearing he may then be disqualified. An absent defendant represented by counsel or solicitor is deemed not to be absent (1980 Act s.122).

(3) An aider and abettor of an offence involving obligatory or discretionary disqualification may be disqualified, but the court is not obliged to do so (1988 Offenders Act s.34(5); *Ullah v Luckhurst* [1977] Crim. L.R. 295). As to persons convicted of attempts, see § 20.25.

(4) Where the Mental Health Act 1983 s.37(3), applies, disqualification may not be ordered.

(5) Where the defendant has been convicted of a Construction and Use Regulation offence as to dangerous condition, dangerously unsuitable use, insecure load, or brakes, steering or tyres, etc. (see § 8.104), he may not be disqualified if he did not know and had no reasonable cause to suspect that the facts of the case were such that that offence would be committed (1988 Offenders Act s.48, offences contrary to ss.40A and 41A of the 1988 Act).

(6) The whole of the sentence, including any order of disqualification, should normally be imposed on the same occasion (*R. v Talgarth JJ. Ex p. Bithell* [1973] R.T.R. 546; *R. v Fairhead* [1975] Crim. L.R. 351), but the Crown Court was able to adjourn a question of disqualification for possible "totting-up" disqualification when neither the defendant's licence nor details of previous endorsements were available. Under these circumstances the Crown Court might have sentenced immediately and postponed the question of disqualification (*R. v Annesly* [1976] R.T.R. 150).

(7) A discretionary disqualification, like a disqualification where vehicle used for crime (see § 20.58), should not be imposed without prior warning and an opportunity to address the court being given to the defence (*R. v Ireland* [1989] Crim. L.R. 458).

Disqualification where vehicle used for crime

The Criminal Justice Act 1972 introduced two new orders where motor **20.58** vehicles are used for the purposes of crime. The first was an order entitling a court to deprive the offender of his property rights in a motor vehicle which had been used for the purposes of a crime (see now s.143 of the Powers of Criminal Courts (Sentencing) Act 2000). (This power is described at §§ 18.31 et seq.) The second is a power of disqualification for driving or holding or obtaining a driving licence. This power of disqualification is now contained in s.147 of the 2000 Act. It enables the Crown Court to disqualify a person convicted on indictment of an offence punishable on indictment with imprisonment for a term of two years or more or, having been convicted of such an offence, is committed to the Crown Court for sentence by a magistrates' court under s.3 of the 2000 Sentencing Act, where the court is satisfied that a motor vehicle was used for the purpose of committing, or facilitating the commission of, the offence concerned. Section 147(2), (4) extends that power to *any* court dealing with an offence of common assault or any other offence involving an assault if the court is satisfied that the assault was committed by driving a motor vehicle.

Section 39 of the Road Traffic Act 1991 provides Scottish courts with a primary power to disqualify a person convicted of an offence committed on or after July 1, 1992 (other than one triable only summarily) if satisfied that a motor vehicle was used for the purpose of committing, or facilitating the commission of, that offence.

20.59   The court is under a duty to require the person disqualified to produce his licence to the court. If he does not do so he commits an offence under s.27(3) of the 1988 Offenders Act (see § 19.42) of failing to produce a licence (2000 Sentencing Act s.147(5)). An order of disqualification under the section may be removed, like any other disqualification, under s.42 of the 1988 Offenders Act (s.44(3); for s.42 see § 20.99). It would seem that an order under s.44 may be suspended pending the hearing of an appeal under s.39(1) of the 1988 Offenders Act, as s.39(1) does not seem to be limited to an order of disqualification made under the Act. The order of disqualification in *R. v Ackers* [1977] R.T.R. 66 was suspended by a single judge pending the hearing of the appeal by the full Court of Appeal.

The court cannot order the licence to be endorsed, because the power of endorsement only applies to the offences referred to in Sch.2 to the 1988 Offenders Act. For this reason a conviction of an offence for which the defendant is disqualified under s.147 does not count as a conviction for the purpose of a penalty points disqualification under s.35 of the 1988 Offenders Act. Neither does such a disqualification count as a disqualification so that the minimum period of a penalty points disqualification is increased (1988 Offenders Act s.35(5)).

20.60   The court is obliged to send notice of the disqualification (code NE) to the Department for Transport (1988 Offenders Act s.47).

It will be noted that the motor vehicle does not have to be actually used in the course of the crime; it merely has to have been used for the purposes of committing or facilitating the offence. Note also the very wide definition of "facilitating" in s.147(6) of the 2000 Sentencing Act. Moreover the offender does not have to be the person driving the vehicle; the only requirement is that the person be convicted of an offence in respect of which the motor vehicle was used. An order cannot be made under this provision unless the prosecution can prove that the vehicle was used in connection with the actual offence charged (*R. v Parrington* [1985] Crim. L.R. 452). However, s.146 of the same Act could be applied (see § 20.65 below).

An offender allowed himself to be carried as a passenger in a motor vehicle to **20.61** 10 separate banks, at each of which he drew £30 on a stolen cheque. While he was in the bank, an accomplice in the car prepared a duplicate cheque-book for use at the next bank to be visited. It was held that the motor vehicle was used by the defendant for the purpose of facilitating the commission of offences (*R. v Mathews* [1975] R.T.R. 32).

Although the section is in very wide terms, the provision seems primarily designed to enable the courts to disqualify "the motor man", the driver of the getaway car, in a serious crime such as a wages snatch or bank robbery. In *Mathews* above, the Court of Appeal, although holding that the trial judge was legally entitled to disqualify the offender, allowed his appeal against the sentence of disqualification, since the vehicle was not used as a getaway car. Moreover, as the offender was sentenced to prison for five years, it was unnecessary and undesirable that he should have the additional penalty of disqualification when he was released, which could hinder him in earning an honest living. On the other hand, where an offender was paid £50 to drive a vehicle containing carpets worth £33,000 stolen from a warehouse, his disqualification for two and a half years, together with an order under what is now s.143 depriving him of the car, were upheld (*R. v Brown (Edward)* [1975] R.T.R. 36 *Note*). In *R. v Thomas (Derek)* [1975] R.T.R. 38 *Note* a disqualification of six years was reduced to five; the defendant was sent to prison for five years for driving another man to a car park to steal jewellery worth £20,000 from the boot of a parked car belonging to a jeweller. In *R. v Ackers* [1977] R.T.R. 66 the appellant had used his heavy goods vehicle licence for the purpose of hiring a van and lorry to enable stolen tyres to be disposed of. He was disqualified under what is now s.147 for 12 months. The order of disqualification was upheld on appeal because the use of the appellant's licence by him was an integral part of the offences.

An offender used his car as a weapon to damage property with intent to **20.62** endanger life by driving it deliberately at 20 to 30mph into another car which contained two adults and four children. He was sentenced to six years' imprisonment and disqualification for life. The Court of Appeal in *R. v King (Philip)* [1993] R.T.R. 245 reduced the period of disqualification to five years on the basis that it was inappropriate to impose a lifetime disqualification in the absence of psychiatric evidence or of evidence of many previous convictions indicating that the defendant would be a danger to the public indefinitely if allowed to drive. The court should also have had regard to the effect of disqualification for life upon the defendant's prospects of effective rehabilitation. (In the light of the defendant's antecedents and the circumstances of the case, the length of the prison sentence he had received was also excessive; it was accordingly reduced to three years.)

An offender pleaded guilty to wounding with intent to cause grievous bodily harm. He was driving in his car when another car pulled out from a side road ahead of him. He drove close behind that other car whilst flashing his lights; a passenger in the other car made gestures in his direction. When both cars stopped at a traffic light, the appellant got out armed with a gear lever lock and went to the passenger side of the other car. The appellant shouted at the passenger to get out of the car, and as the passenger did so, he struck him in the face. There was evidence that the appellant had driven in an attempt to stop the other car before it reached the traffic light. He was sentenced to nine months' imprisonment, disqualified from driving for three years under what is now s.147 of the 2000

Sentencing Act and further ordered to take an extended driving test. The Court of Appeal held in *R. v Rajesh Patel* [1995] R.T.R. 421 that on those facts the use of the car could properly be described as "facilitating the commission of the offence" and that accordingly there was jurisdiction for the making of an order under s.147. Three years was too long, however, in the light of the probably adverse effects of such a disqualification upon the offender's employment prospects upon release; the period was therefore reduced to one of 12 months. The order to take a further driving test was, however, without jurisdiction, since there was no power to order an offender to take such a test where the disqualification was imposed under s.147. (Section 36 of the Road Traffic Offenders Act 1988 applies only to the offences specified in subs.(1) thereof, or to offences involving obligatory endorsement (s.36(4)); see §§ 20.68 et seq.)

20.63   A disqualification from driving for five years imposed under what is now s.147 of the 2000 Sentencing Act upon an offender sentenced to four months' imprisonment for evading excise duty on imported alcohol and tobacco was unsurprisingly held to be manifestly excessive by the Court of Appeal in *R. v Liddey* [1999] Crim. L.R. 340. As had been made clear in *R. v Wright (Desmond Carl)* [1979] R.T.R. 15, the sentencing court should take account of the effect of a disqualification upon an offender's employment prospects on his release from custody. A disqualification for 12 months was substituted. Similarly in *R. v Skitt* [2004] EWCA Crim 3141; [2005] Crim. L.R. 252 the Court of Appeal reduced disqualifications imposed upon three excise duty evaders from five years, three years and eighteen months to two years, twelve months and six months respectively.

It is important that in any case where a court is considering exercising the power to disqualify under what is now s.147, it should indicate to the defence that it may be so minded so that considerations which might make that course of action inappropriate may be brought to its attention (*R. v Lane* [1986] Crim. L.R. 574; see also *R. v Money* [1988] Crim. L.R. 626). Failure to afford the defence such an opportunity may result (as in the cases cited) in the disqualification being quashed.

20.64   There is no power to make an order of disqualification under what is now s.147 of the 2000 Sentencing Act for the offence of conspiracy to steal (*R. v Riley* [1984] R.T.R. 159). Where, however, a vehicle was used for the purpose of avoiding arrest for conspiracy to rob, a disqualification under what is now s.147 was upheld; the definition of "facilitating" in what is now s.147(6) of the 2000 Sentencing Act includes steps taken to avoid apprehension after the commission of the offence (*R. v Devine* [1990] Crim. L.R. 753).

Disqualification for any offence or for the enforcement of fines

20.65   Section 146 of the 2000 Sentencing Act provides courts with the power to order disqualification for driving for such period as is thought fit in respect of *any* offence (regardless of its nature) in addition to, or, in specified instances, instead of dealing with an offender in any other way. Courts are obliged by s.146(4) ibid. to require the offender to produce his driving licence and its counterpart or his Community licence and its counterpart (if any). There is no power to endorse the licence, but the DVLA needs to be notified of the order of disqualification using offence code NE98.

Section 301 of the Criminal Justice Act 2003 empowers courts to order the disqualification for a period not exceeding 12 months of fine defaulters instead of issuing a warrant of commitment or, in the case of young offenders, making an appropriate order under s.81 of the Magistrates' Courts Act 1980. Payment of the whole of the outstanding sum will cause the order of disqualification to cease to have effect; payment of part of the sum outstanding will reduce the disqualification proportionately. Specific notification from the Secretary of State of the availability of the power is a condition precedent to its use by a court.

The Court of Appeal in *R. v Cliff* [2004] EWCA Crim 3139; [2005] R.T.R. 11 **20.66** confirmed (if confirmation were needed) that the power to disqualify an offender under s.146 above was not limited to any particular offence and that it was not necessary that the conviction should be connected in any way with the use of a motor vehicle. It was emphasised by the Court of Appeal in *R. v Sofekun* [2008] EWCA Crim 2035; [2009] 1 Cr. App. R. (S.) 78 that comments in *Cliff*, above, should not be interpreted as having created any restriction on the exercise of that power. It is plain that s.146 is an additional punitive power and is available whether or not the defendant has committed a driving-related offence.

Following a positive roadside breath test, an offender who had been previously disqualified for an excess alcohol offence ran off and evaded capture until the following day, by which time he had avoided the possibility of providing an evidential breath specimen at the police station which might well have led to a prosecution for driving with excess alcohol. His disqualification under s.146 of the 2000 Sentencing Act for 18 months for escaping from lawful custody was upheld by the Court of Appeal in *R. v Waring* [2005] EWCA Crim 1080; [2006] 1 Cr. App. R. (S.) 9. The judge had been right to ensure that the offender had obtained no benefit from escaping, and the disqualification was entirely merited.

Parallel provisions to s.146 of the 2000 Sentencing Act and s.301 of the Crim- **20.67** inal Justice Act 2003 discussed above are to be found in the Criminal Procedure (Scotland) Act 1995 ss.248A and 248B, which do not apply to offences committed before January 1, 1998. As with the English and Welsh legislation, courts in whom these powers are to be vested will be prescribed by order. The Disqualification from Driving (Prescribed Courts) (Scotland) Order 1997 prescribes for these purposes, and with effect from January 1, 1998, the sheriff courts of Paisley and Perth.

Disqualification pending passing a driving test

The Road Traffic Law Review recommended in their report (the North Report, **20.68** HMSO, 1988) that legislation should be introduced to provide that a court should be required to order an offender to take a further driving test prior to restoration of his licence to him in any case where it disqualified him for 12 months or more, and that it should have an unfettered discretion to make such an order in the case of endorsable offences generally. The Review further recommended that such retests should be twice the length of the normal driving test and should include (wherever possible) a period of driving on an unrestricted dual carriageway.

The Government's legislative response did not initially go quite so far as these proposals, although powers for the subsequent extension of the retesting scheme have been provided. Section 32 of the Road Traffic Act 1991 replaced s.36 of the 1988 Offenders Act with an entirely new section, which applies to offences committed on or after July 1, 1992. Section 36(1) provides that where that subsection applies to a person, the court must order him to be disqualified until he passes the appropriate driving test. Section 36(2) applies s.36(1) to a person who is disqualified under s.34 of the 1988 Offenders Act on conviction of:

    (a) manslaughter, or in Scotland culpable homicide;

    (b) causing death by dangerous driving;

    (c) dangerous driving.

20.69   Although the catchment area for compulsory "retestees" is initially limited by s.36(2) above to those disqualified for one of three very serious road traffic offences, s.36(3) allows the Secretary of State by order to extend that area to take in persons disqualified either as a matter of discretion or by virtue of the "totting-up" provisions in whatever circumstances and for whatever period he may determine; he may indeed go even further and apply the retesting requirements to persons convicted of such endorsable offences as may be thought fit. He has exercised his powers under s.36(3) in order to add (effectively rather than literally) the offence of causing death by careless driving while under the influence of drink or drugs, contrary to s.3A of the 1988 Act, to those listed in s.36(2); where any such offence is committed on or after January 31, 2002, the court must similarly order the offender to submit to a further, and extended, driving test (see the Driving Licences (Disqualification until Test Passed) (Prescribed Offence) Order 2001 (SI 2001/4051)).

    Section 36(4) preserves the pre-existing *discretionary* power to make orders of "disqualification until test passed" upon conviction of any endorsable offence (whether or not the offender has previously passed a driving test), but subs.(6) provides for the first time some statutory guidance in the use of that power. It requires the court when determining whether to make such an order to have regard to the safety of road users. Thus the principle enunciated in cases such as *R. v Donnelly* [1975] 1 W.L.R. 390 and *R. v Banks (John)* [1978] R.T.R. 535 to the effect that disqualification of this kind ought to be treated as a road safety measure rather than as a punishment, even though its effect tended to be punitive, is now enshrined in statute. The power to disqualify under s.36(4) is thus best used, it is submitted, where the offender is aged, infirm or inexperienced and where the circumstances of the offence or the offender are such that it is in the public interest that the offender pass a driving test before he again drives on a full licence. The Court of Appeal in *R. v Miller* [1994] Crim. L.R. 231, when dismissing an appeal against an order disqualifying until test passed a defendant convicted of careless driving, re-emphasised the significance of s.36(6) of the 1988 Offenders Act so far as the use of the power to disqualify "until test passed" is concerned. There was an abundance of evidence (not least in his demonstrated inability to adhere to speed limits or to negotiate corners without skidding) to show that the driver in question was grossly incompetent, and had moreover shown a wanton disregard of the rights of other road users. In making its order the court below had properly had regard, as it was required to by the statute, to the safety of road users.

20.70   Section 36(5) defines the two types of test ("extended driving test" and "test of competence to drive") to which an offender may be compelled to submit and provides that it is the new extended test which will be required of those convicted either of obligatorily disqualifiable offences or as a result of the accumulation of 12 or more penalty points; in any other case, the appropriate test will be the test of competence to drive. The Court of Appeal held in *R. v Bradshaw, The Times*, December 31, 1994 (also reported as *R. v Bradshaw; R. v Waters (Note—1994)* at

[2001] R.T.R. 41) that when sentencing a defendant for an offence of aggravated vehicle-taking where the allegation was that he was a passenger in the car rather than the driver, it was not appropriate to order him to take an extended driving test at the end of a period of disqualification. *R. v Bradshaw* was applied by the Court of Appeal in *R. v Wiggins* [2001] R.T.R. 3 when quashing a similar order imposed in similar circumstances.

It should be noted that s.36(5) is amended by s.37 of the Road Safety Act 2006 (when in force) by the substitution of a new definition of "appropriate driving test". The new definition will enable the Secretary of State to prescribe by secondary legislation when the appropriate test is to be an extended test. It is understood to be the Government's intention that repeat drink/drive offenders should in due course be made subject to mandatory retesting; the amended s.36(5) will circumvent the present requirement for such a test to be an extended one.

Section 36(7) provides that where an order for an extended driving test is made, any earlier order to retake the "ordinary" driving test lapses; it also prohibits the making of further orders under this section while the extended test order remains in force.

An order made under s.36(1) does not come into effect until the period of oblig- **20.71** atory disqualification imposed by the court under s.34 of the 1988 Offenders Act has come to an end. An order made under s.36(4) may take effect immediately or on the expiration of a period of complete disqualification if the court also orders the latter. Where the order takes effect immediately, the offender may drive as soon as he obtains a provisional licence (1988 Offenders Act s.37(3)) but, of course, must comply with the conditions of a provisional licence. If a person is disqualified for a period and also disqualified until he passes a driving test, he cannot take out a provisional licence until the period of ordinary disqualification has elapsed.

A person who has been disqualified from driving until he has passed the test offends against s.103 of the Road Traffic Act 1988 (driving while disqualified) if he drives after having taken out a provisional licence and fails to comply with a provisional licence condition (e.g. not displaying "L" plates, driving while not accompanied by a qualified driver, etc.) (*Scott v Jelf* [1974] R.T.R. 256); but the law is different in Northern Ireland (*McGimpsey v Carlin* [1968] Jo.Crim.L. 221, showing the resident magistrate's decision to have been upheld by the Court of Appeal). Such a disqualification expires as soon as evidence of passing the test is produced to the licensing authority (1988 Offenders Act s.36(8)).

The effect of the above provisions is that, if Jehu is disqualified from driving **20.72** for 12 months on July 1, 2008 and further disqualified until he passes a driving test, he is disqualified from that moment and may not drive at all until July 1, 2009. On and from July 1, 2009 (provided he takes out a provisional licence) he may drive only as a learner driver, i.e. with "L" plates and accompanied in a car by a duly qualified person, until he passes the test.

A court cannot impose a condition that the applicant take and pass a driving test when considering an application for removal of disqualification under what is now s.42 of the 1988 Offenders Act (*R. v Bentham* [1982] R.T.R. 357).

A compulsory order of disqualification until the extended test is passed made **20.73** under s.36(1) of the 1988 Offenders Act, as amended by the Road Traffic Act 1991, cannot be removed under s.42 of the 1988 Offenders Act; the person must pass the test (s.42(6)). It would appear that s.42 was not amended (as it should have been) by the 1991 Act in order to take account of discretionary orders of disqualification until test passed made under s.36(4), and so there is no specific reference in s.42 to such orders; logic would suggest, however, that they should be similarly treated. Section 42(6) does not prevent a person who was disqualified for five years and who was also disqualified until he passed a test from applying for the removal of the five-year disqualification (*R. v Nuttall* [1971] R.T.R. 279). The two orders are separable. When a term of disqualification expires or is removed under s.42 of the 1988 Offenders Act, the applicant may then take out a provisional licence and on passing the test may obtain a full licence.

The duty imposed upon a court to disqualify until test passed an offender convicted of an offence to which s.36(1) of the 1988 Offenders Act applies (see § 20.68 above) is a mandatory one, and it is submitted that such an order must be made even where the offender is disqualified for life under s.34 of that Act. A person disqualified for life may apply for the removal of that disqualification after five years (see § 20.99); if the sentencing court were dissuaded on grounds of apparent incompatibility from exercising its mandatory duty, a successful applicant would escape the consequences required by s.36(1). That cannot have been what Parliament intended.

20.74 Although the requirement under s.36(1) of the 1988 Offenders Act to disqualify until appropriate test passed an offender convicted of an offence of dangerous driving is a mandatory provision, it is, unfortunately, sometimes overlooked. The Court of Appeal so held in *R. v Callum* [1995] R.T.R. 246 when rectifying just such an omission (see further § 20.20). It is perhaps equally unfortunate to have to report that despite the mandatory nature of the requirement in s.36(1) for the compulsory retesting of drivers convicted of certain offences, the Court of Appeal in *R. v Cully* [2005] EWCA Crim 3483; [2006] R.T.R. 32 saw fit to remove an order for an extended retest of an appellant convicted of dangerous driving.

There is no endorsement code for an order disqualifying an offender pending passing a test. Instead the court notifies the DVLA of the order on form D20.

Interim disqualification

20.75 It has long been the case that a magistrates' court on committing an offender to the Crown Court for sentence for an endorsable offence has had the power to disqualify such a person pending his appearance at the Crown Court (see § 20.79). Section 25 of the Road Traffic Act 1991, by substituting s.26 of the 1988 Offenders Act, extended the powers of courts in England and Wales to allow for the imposition of an order of interim disqualification in any of the following circumstances (s.26(1), (2)):

(a) where a magistrates' court remits an offender to another magistrates' court to be sentenced in accordance with s.10 of the Powers of Criminal Courts (Sentencing) Act 2000;

(b) where a court defers passing sentence on an offender; or

(c) where a court adjourns for sentence after convicting an offender.

Section 26(3) provides powers similar to the above for Scottish courts.

20.76 An order of interim disqualification expires at the latest after six months (or at the end of the period of deferral in Scotland where that period may exceed six months) (s.26(4), (5)).

Section 26(6) provides that only one order of interim disqualification can be made in respect of any offence or set of offences and thus ensures that the six months' limit cannot be circumvented by the making of successive orders under the section.

It should be noted that the power to impose interim disqualification applies not only to offences which carry mandatory disqualification but also to those for which disqualification is discretionary. It is anticipated, however, that courts will be more ready to use their new powers when the eventual disqualification is inevitable than when it is optional.

It is also important to note that credit will be given for time spent under order **20.77** of interim disqualification when it comes to the imposition of sentence; s.26(12) ensures that the eventual disqualification for the offence is treated as reduced by the length of the period during which the offender has been prevented from driving by an order under this section. Thus if Joe Bloggs, who was convicted on April 1, 2009 and placed under interim disqualification for an excess alcohol offence, appears on April 29, 2009 for sentence and is disqualified then by the court for 12 months, his disqualification will end at midnight on March 31, 2010.

A driving licence is not revoked by an order of interim disqualification (1988 Offenders Act s.37(1A)). There is no power for the court to order the endorsement of particulars of the disqualification upon the offender's licence; the DVLA must, however, be notified of the order on form D20. If the court which finally deals with the offender decides in the event not to disqualify him under s.34 or s.35, notice of the determination of the interim disqualification must similarly be sent to the DVLA (s.26(10)).

The defendant must produce his licence to the court when an order of interim **20.78** disqualification is made and if he does not do so he is guilty of an offence (s.26(7), (8)).

Disqualification on committal for sentence

By ss.6 and 7 of the Powers of Criminal Courts (Sentencing) Act 2000, where **20.79** a magistrates' court commits an offender to the Crown Court for sentence under s.3 of that Act, the Crown Court may or shall disqualify him and shall order endorsement of his licence, as required, whether or not a custodial sentence is imposed. By s.26(1) of the 1988 Offenders Act, a magistrates' court committing for sentence, in custody or on bail, may order the defendant to be disqualified, if he has been convicted of an endorsable offence, until the Crown Court deals with him; by s.26(12) any period of disqualification imposed by the Crown Court on any such person committed for sentence shall be treated as reduced by any period he was disqualified by reason only of an order made under s.26(1).

The provisions above and in § 20.81 below extend to committal to the Crown Court for offences occurring during the currency of a conditional discharge order, offences committed by released prisoners during currency of original sentences, offences committed during a suspended sentence and offenders committed for sentence under the Vagrancy Act 1824.

A court may not impose an interim order of disqualification on committal for **20.80** trial. Section 26 only allows an order to be made where the offender has been committed for sentence. On committal for trial the offender, by definition, will not have been convicted.

It is possible to make it a condition of bail that a defendant does not drive, but such a condition should not be imposed where it would cause injustice (*R. v Kwame* [1975] R.T.R. 106). Following the enactment of the Bail Act 1976, it is generally accepted that a condition of bail may only be imposed if one of the grounds for refusal of bail may exist, e.g. likelihood of commission of further offences.

20.81   By s.6(3) of the 2000 Sentencing Act, where a magistrates' court has convicted a person of an offence or offences which carry compulsory or optional disqualification, whether a summary offence or one triable summarily or on indictment, and commits him to the Crown Court for another offence under s.3 of that Act or under the powers mentioned in § 20.79 above, the magistrates may commit him in respect of the first-mentioned offences also, notwithstanding that they are not triable on indictment. By s.7(1), the Crown Court may deal with him for such offence or offences in any way in which the magistrates could have dealt with him and, in particular, may disqualify and endorse. Thus if *A* is convicted by magistrates of stealing a car, driving it carelessly and using it without insurance and the magistrates commit him for sentence for the first of those offences under s.3, they may, by s.6(3), commit him to the Crown Court for the other two offences also, so that the Crown Court may fix the total amount of disqualification and will not be hampered by any decision of the magistrates as to disqualification. The effect of s.7(1) and (3) is that magistrates have no power to sentence or otherwise deal with him (other than by interim disqualification); the magistrates' powers and duties are vested in the Crown Court which in an appropriate case may be required to disqualify the offender (*R. v O'Connor* [1976] R.T.R. 414).

The Criminal Justice Act 1988 extended the range of circumstances in which the Crown Court may find itself dealing with summary offences. Section 41, as amended, provides that where a magistrates' court commits for trial a person charged with an "either way" offence, it may also commit him for trial for an offence punishable with imprisonment or subject to endorsement which arises out of circumstances the same as, or connected with, the "either way" offence. So far as sentencing is concerned, however, the Crown Court may deal with him in a manner in which a magistrates' court could have dealt with him.

20.82   Magistrates may by s.26(1) of the 1988 Offenders Act disqualify for a summary offence committed for sentence until it is dealt with by the Crown Court.

These powers under s.6(3) of the 2000 Sentencing Act of committing summary, etc., offences for sentence extend to summary offences punishable with imprisonment as well as to those for which disqualification may or must be ordered.

An order of disqualification under s.26 does not wipe off any penalty points on the offender's licence (see § 20.50), nor does it count as an order of disqualification so as to increase the minimum period of a penalty points disqualification (see § 20.54) (1988 Offenders Act s.35(5)).

20.83   The defendant must produce his licence to the magistrates' court on conviction and if he does not do so is guilty of an offence (1988 Offenders Act s.26(7), (8)). The magistrates' court shall send the licence to the Crown Court.

Disqualification from driving for non-payment of child support

20.84   Section 16 of the Child Support, Pensions and Social Security Act 2000 amends the Child Support Act 1991 by the insertion therein of new ss.39A and

40B. The combined effect of those sections is that the Child Support Agency may apply to a magistrates' court in England and Wales or a sheriff court in Scotland for an order disqualifying a non-resident parent from driving as a way of enforcing unpaid child support. The court must inquire in his presence as to:

    (a) whether he needs a driving licence to earn his living;

    (b) his means; and

    (c) whether there has been wilful refusal or culpable neglect (to pay) on his part.

If, but only if, satisfied as to wilful refusal or culpable neglect, the court may disqualify him for a period not exceeding two years, or may make a disqualification order, but suspend its operation until such time and on such conditions as it thinks fit.

There will be no endorsement of any kind, but those disqualified will be **20.85** required to surrender their driving licences for onward transmission by the court to the DVLA. The court may substitute a shorter period of disqualification or revoke its order of disqualification if part of the amount due is paid, and must revoke the order if it is paid in full.

The law regarding disqualification from driving for non-payment of child support will be governed by s.30 of the Child Maintenance and Other Payments Act 2008, when in force. An amended s.40B of the Child Support Act 1991 sets out the circumstances in which the Child Maintenance and Enforcement Commission may apply to the court for an order disqualifying a person for holding or obtaining a driving licence for unrecovered child maintenance. On such an application the court shall (in the presence of the liable person) inquire as to:

    (a) whether the liable person needs a driving licence to earn a living;

    (b) the liable person's needs; and

    (c) whether there has been wilful refusal or culpable neglect on the part of the liable person.

The court shall not question the liability order or the maintenance calculation. If, but only if, the court is of the opinion that there has been wilful refusal or culpable neglect on the part of the liable person, it may either make a disqualification order against the liable person or make such an order but suspend its operation until such time and on such conditions (if any) as it thinks just.

MISCELLANEOUS MATTERS

Escaping disqualification by deception

Section 49 of the 1988 Offenders Act provides that where a court was deceived **20.86** regarding any circumstances that were or might have been taken into account in deciding whether or for how long to disqualify an offender when dealing with him in respect of an endorsable offence and the deception constituted or was due to an offence committed by him, then if he is convicted of that offence the court shall have the same power and duties of disqualification as the original court. The court must take into account any order of disqualification by the original court.

This provision does not appear as yet to have been much used by the courts. It may be noted, however, that where a court has been deceived and as a result the offender escaped an obligatory disqualification, whether it is under the penalty points system or "totting-up" provisions, or in respect of an obligatorily disqualifiable offence, the court subsequently dealing with the offender is under the same obligation to consider disqualifying the offender as the original court, except in so far as the original court disqualified him on the earlier occasion. An offender may, e.g., obtain a duplicate licence free from endorsement relating to a previous drink/driving offence in order to produce it when subsequently convicted of another drink/driving offence. If he is then disqualified for only one year and subsequently convicted for knowingly making a false statement in obtaining the duplicate driving licence (under s.174 of the 1988 Act), the court convicting him is then under an obligation to disqualify him for at least two years (i.e. the obligatory three years less the 12-month disqualification originally imposed).

20.87   It should be noted that the prosecution may not have to prove that the offender deceived the court, only that the court was deceived due to the offence committed by the defendant.

Where a court disqualifies an offender under s.49 of the 1988 Offenders Act the court is under an obligation to notify the Secretary of State of the order of disqualification (s.47(2)), and as the court "shall have the same powers and duties regarding an order of disqualification as had the court which dealt with him for the endorsable offence" it would seem that the court should endorse the offender's licence and notify the DVLA as if the court had originally disqualified the offender. It would seem to count as a disqualification for the purpose of increasing the minimum period of disqualification of a subsequent penalty points disqualification as it is not amongst the disqualifications specifically excluded for this purpose by s.35(5) of the 1988 Offenders Act.

Notification of disease or disability

20.88   Section 22 of the 1988 Offenders Act requires a court to notify the Secretary of State for Transport if in any proceedings for an offence committed in respect of a motor vehicle it appears to the court that the accused may be suffering from any relevant disability or prospective disability within the meaning of Pt III of the Road Traffic Act 1988.

The section requires the court to notify the Secretary of State in such manner and containing such particulars as are required, and for the notification to be sent to such address as the Secretary of State may determine. No such determination has yet been made.

20.89   It should be noted that a court has no discretion whether to notify the Secretary of State or not. The terms of the section are such that once it "appears" to the court that the accused *may* be suffering from a notifiable disability the court must send notification to the Secretary of State. It does not appear necessary for the accused always to be convicted. The offence may be committed but because of the defendant's notifiable disease or disability he may not be guilty of the offence, e.g. the defendant suffered unknowingly from blackouts and drove in a state of automatism. In such a case the defendant may be acquitted but it is submitted that the court is required to notify under s.22.

"Relevant disability" for the purposes of Pt III of the 1988 Act (in particular s.92) is any disability or disease likely to cause the driving of a vehicle by the person concerned to be a source of danger to the public together with any "prescribed" disability. The "prescribed" disabilities are those prescribed by reg.71 of the Motor Vehicles (Driving Licences) Regulations 1999 (SI 1999/

2864). These include epilepsy, severe mental disorder, sudden attacks of disabling giddiness or fainting and persistent misuse of drugs or alcohol (see § 11.49). A "prospective" disability is one which while not a relevant disability is one which because of its intermittent or progressive nature may become in the course of time a relevant disability.

When notified under s.22 the Secretary of State will make inquiries and if **20.90** satisfied that the defendant is suffering from a relevant disability may either revoke the licence outright or substitute a licence subject to conditions depending on the nature or extent of the disease or disability. Where the offender is subject to a prospective disability the Secretary of State will revoke the licence and may grant a licence of limited duration.

Once it "appears" to a court that a defendant "may" be suffering from a relevant disability or disease, s.22 states that a court "must" notify the Secretary of State. The purpose of s.22 is to enable the Secretary of State to inquire whether the person concerned is, or is not, suffering from the disease or disability. Moreover, it should be noted that the Secretary of State will not automatically reissue a driving licence to a "high risk offender" (see §§ 4.330–2).

An authorised insurer (i.e. a company empowered to issue insurance policies **20.91** for the use of motor vehicles under s.145 of the 1988 Act) is required to notify the Secretary of State under s.95(1) of the 1988 Act if he refuses to issue a motor insurance policy on the grounds that the health of the proposer is unsatisfactory or on grounds which include that ground.

Courses for drink/drive offenders

The Drink-Drive Rehabilitation Scheme established by ss.34A, 34B and 34C **20.92** of the 1988 Offenders Act has been made permanent and since January 1, 2000 the referral of drink/drive offenders to a rehabilitation course has been an option available to all courts in Great Britain. The courses are designed to influence attitudes by retraining and thereby reduce the risk of further offending. Research carried out on behalf of the then DETR during the experimental period which ended on December 31, 1999 suggested that those who attend rehabilitation courses are three times less likely to reoffend than those who do not.

The scheme applies to persons disqualified for 12 months or more for any of the following offences under the Road Traffic Act 1988:

(a) causing death by careless driving when under the influence of drink or drugs (s.3A) (see Chapter 5);

(b) driving or in charge whilst unfit through drink or drugs (s.4) (see Chapter 4);

(c) driving or being in charge with excess alcohol (s.5) (see Chapter 4); or

(d) failing to provide a specimen for analysis (s.7) (see Chapter 4).

The reduction of disqualification obtainable on satisfactory completion of an **20.93** approved course is not less than three months and not more than one quarter of the total period originally imposed; thus a "standard" 12 months' disqualification will be reduced to nine months. As a further example, the range of reduction for a two-year disqualification will be from three months to six months; the length of the period of reduction (within the prescribed limits) is a matter within the discretion of the court, as, indeed, is the decision whether or not to offer the offender the opportunity of participating in the scheme in the first place. The offender, who must be 17 or over, must consent to attend the course and must pay in advance any fees associated with it. Upon satisfactory completion of the course the course organiser will issue a certificate to that effect; upon receipt of that certificate the clerk of the supervising court will send the appropriate notice to the DVLA so that the offender's driver record may be updated. If on the other hand the course organiser decides not to issue a certificate of completion he must give the offender written notice of his decision within 14 days of the end of the course; the offender may then apply to the supervising court for a declaration that the organiser's decision was contrary to the requirements of the statute.

Reduced disqualification period for attendance on course; other offences

20.94   Section 35 of the Road Safety Act 2006 (when in force) substitutes ss.34A–34C of the 1988 Offenders Act and inserts therein a new s.34BA in order to extend the principle of the Drink-Drive Rehabilitation Scheme to offenders disqualified for 12 months or more for any of the following offences:

   (a) failing to allow a specimen of blood to be laboratory tested (Road Traffic Act 1988 s.7A(6)) (see Chapter 4);

   (b) careless or inconsiderate driving (1988 Act s.3) (see Chapter 5);

   (c) failing to comply with traffic signs (1988 Act s.36) (see Chapter 6);

   (d) motorway offences (Road Traffic Regulation Act 1984 s.17(4)) (see Chapter 6);

   (e) speeding offences (1984 Act s.89(1)) (see Chapter 6).

As with the existing drink/drive scheme, the reduction of disqualification obtainable on satisfactory completion of an approved course will be not less than three months and not more than one quarter of the total period originally imposed. This opportunity will not be offered to anyone who has completed such a course within the preceding three years; nor will it be available to a person convicted during his probationary period under the Road Traffic (New Drivers) Act 1995 (see below). It should be noted, however, that at the time of writing (March 2009) no indication had been given as to a likely date for implementation of any of these provisions.

Probationary period for newly qualified drivers

20.95   The Road Traffic (New Drivers) Act 1995 established a two-year probationary period for newly qualified drivers and applies to any person who first passes a driving test taken on or after its commencement date (June 1, 1997). The accumulation of six or more penalty points by such a driver before the end of a period of two years beginning on the date on which he first passed a driving test will result in the revocation of his licence and a requirement for him to pass another driving test in order to restore his previous entitlements (see further §§ 11.09–11). Penalty points acquired before the first driving test was passed will be included in the calculation if they fall to be taken into account in accordance with s.29(1), (2) of the 1988 Offenders Act (see § 20.37). Clear support for that interpretation of the legislation was provided by the Administrative Court in *Adebowale v Bradford Crown Court* [2004] EWHC 1741. Under s.2 of the Road Traffic (New Drivers) Act 1995 where a probationary driver had six or more points on his licence "on that occasion", including by virtue of s.29 of the 1988 Offenders Act any points that had on a previous occasion been ordered to be endorsed, the court was required to send the licence to the Secretary of State for revocation. It was impossible to read the statute in a way that disregarded the points previously awarded.

It matters not whether the points concerned were acquired by a court conviction or by payment of a fixed penalty. Points will also be counted where the date of the offence is within the probationary period even though the date of conviction or sentence for that offence falls outside that period. Whilst there is no right of appeal against the revocation of a licence in accordance with s.3 of the Road Traffic (New Drivers) Act 1995, s.5 of that Act provides that where a person has appealed against a conviction or endorsement which was the basis (or part of the basis) of the revocation, his full entitlements must be restored to him pending the result of that appeal.

Although the revocation of a licence under the 1995 Act is not a disqualifica- **20.96** tion as such, its effects mimic those of disqualification pending passing a driving test under s.36 of the 1988 Offenders Act (see § 20.68), save that a person who, after revocation, continued to drive without holding the appropriate provisional licence or without observing the conditions attaching to such a licence would be committing an offence under s.87(1) of the Road Traffic Act 1988 (driving otherwise than in accordance with a licence) rather than under s.103 of that Act (driving while disqualified).

The interaction of revocation under these provisions with disqualification imposed under ss.34, 35 or 36 of the 1988 Offenders Act merits some consideration. It should be noted that since it is provided by s.37(1) of the 1988 Offenders Act that one of the effects of a disqualification is that the licence concerned is treated as revoked, the licence cannot at the same time be revoked under s.3 of the 1995 Act. Nor can it be so revoked if further points are ordered to be endorsed (in relation to another offence) before the end of the disqualification period. Where, however, the offender accumulates six or more penalty points *after* his disqualification has expired but *before* the probationary period has ended, his licence will be revoked. This may be illustrated thus:

29.6.09	Offender first passes driving test
11.7.09	Fixed penalty for speeding—three points
10.9.09	Convicted of careless driving—disqualified for three months pursuant to s.34(2) of the 1988 Offenders Act
22.1.10	Fixed penalty for speeding—three points—licence revoked.

The successful negotiation of a retest will have no effect upon the points our **20.97** offender has acquired thus far. If further points are accumulated, either before or after a retest has been passed, so as to total 12 or more, our offender will be liable in the usual way for a penalty points disqualification under s.35 of the 1988 Offenders Act. The illustrative process may be continued thus:

9.3.10	Fixed penalty for speeding as provisional licence-holder—three points
18.5.10	Retest passed
13.6.10	Commits further speeding offence
1.9.10	Receives penalty points disqualification for six months.

At the end of the above period of disqualification he regains his full licence; further retesting is not required, since s.7 of the 1995 Act provides that the probationary period comes to an end when the retest is successfully negotiated. It should be borne in mind, however, that the court which imposed the s.35 disqualification would have had the additional power to disqualify our notional offender until test passed under s.36(4); had it exercised that power, the offender would have been required to pass an *extended* driving test (see § 20.70).

20.98   In the event that a person whose licence has been revoked under s.3 of the 1995 Act becomes subject to an order of disqualification under s.36 of the 1988 Offenders Act *before* he has passed the relevant retest, s.4 of the 1995 Act operates to obviate the double jeopardy of the same person being required to take two retests; the order under s.36 takes priority.

The process of revocation only applies where the offence which causes the points to be taken into account under s.29 of the 1988 Offenders Act to number six or more is committed during the offender's probationary period. Thus a driver who has acquired six or more "live" penalty points *before* first passing a driving test may acquire and retain his full entitlements provided that he commits no "triggering" offence during his probationary period. By the same token, a person who has suffered a penalty points disqualification whilst a provisional licence-holder and accordingly had his "slate wiped clean" (see § 20.50) is in no worse position than a newly qualified driver with an unblemished record so far as the 1995 Act is concerned, and is considerably better placed than the newly qualified driver who has acquired three points for a minor speeding offence committed just prior to his driving test.

REMOVAL OF DISQUALIFICATION

Application for removal

20.99   By s.42 of the 1988 Offenders Act a person disqualified may apply for removal of his disqualification:

     (a) if the disqualification is for less than four years, when two years from the date on which it was imposed have expired;

     (b) if the disqualification is for less than 10 years but not less than four years, when half the period of disqualification has expired;

     (c) in any other cases, i.e. 10 years or more or for "life", when five years have expired from the date of disqualification.

Thus, a person disqualified for two years or less cannot apply at all for removal of his disqualification; his only course is to appeal to the Crown Court in the hope of a reduction of the period.

An offender disqualified for three years or more because of a second drink/driving offence may nevertheless apply under s.42 (*Damer v Davison* [1976] R.T.R. 44). Lord Widgery C.J. observed, however, at 94:

> "I would only add that justices ... may if they think fit regard a mandatory disqualification as one which they are somewhat less ready to remove than a discretionary disqualification.

20.100   On the other hand in *Boliston v Gibbons* [1985] R.T.R. 176, where it was held that a person was still liable to the three-year minimum disqualification for a second drink/driving offence even if he had escaped disqualification for the first offence because of special reasons, both judges expressed sympathy with the defendant and observed that he could apply for removal of the disqualification under what is now s.42 (see also § 4.327).

An order of disqualification under s.147 of the 2000 Sentencing Act (disqualification for using a vehicle for criminal purposes (see § 20.58)) may, seemingly, be removed under s.42 (but is, of course, subject to the time-limits set out above).

There is no power to remove a disqualification imposed under s.36 of the 1988 Offenders Act, i.e. a disqualification until a driving test is passed (see § 20.68). Section 42 of that Act does not apply to such a disqualification (s.42(6)). In *R. v Nuttall* [1971] R.T.R. 279 the applicant was disqualified for five years for the offence of causing death by dangerous driving and also disqualified until he passed a test of competence to drive. In view of what is now s.42(6) some doubt had been expressed whether the five years' disqualification could be removed in view of the additional order of disqualification pending a test. Bridge J., in hearing the case, considered the matter, held that he had power to do so and granted the application on its merits.

Procedure for removal

If the application is refused, another application may not be entertained until **20.101** three months thereafter (1988 Offenders Act s.42(4)). Rule 55.2 of the Criminal Procedure Rules 2005 requires an application to a magistrates' court under s.42 to be made by way of complaint and for a summons to be issued to the chief officer of police to show cause why an order shall not be made. "Chief officer of police" would seem to be the Chief Constable or in the Metropolitan area, the Commissioner. Can a complaint be made for the issue of a summons before the relevant period under s.42 has elapsed? It is submitted it can, provided that the date upon which the summons is returnable is after the period has expired. Section 42 only prohibits application being made to the court before the period has expired. The complaint for the summons is made to a magistrates' court for a summons to be issued and is a matter of procedure not of substance. The application is made when heard.

The court may, if it thinks proper having regard to the applicant's character, his conduct subsequent to his conviction, the nature of the offence and any other circumstances of the case, remove the disqualification. The magistrates' court officer on the granting of an application notifies the Department for Transport of the removal of the disqualification.

Where the disqualification was imposed by a Crown Court, the application **20.102** should be made to the location of the Crown Court where it was originally made (*Practice Direction (Criminal Proceedings: Consolidation)* [2002] 3 All E.R. 904, para.33.10). Where the disqualification was imposed by the Crown Court, the applicant should get in touch with the Crown Court offices at the location specified in the Practice Direction (see above). It is said at 111 J.P.Jo. 699 that, where a juvenile court (now the youth court) has disqualified a young person, any application to remove the disqualification should be made to the juvenile court (the youth court), although the defendant may have since become an adult.

If a disqualification is "for life", it is submitted that five years must elapse before the first application to remove can be made.

It is submitted that a magistrates' court cannot refuse to issue a summons for removal of a disqualification, whatever it may think of the applicant's chances, provided the application is not less than three months after any previous one and not before the expiry of the period after which the applicant may first apply (see above); the reason for this view is that r.55.2 of the Criminal Procedure Rules 2005 says that the magistrates "shall" issue a summons to the police, thus taking away the normal discretion whether or not to issue one.

20.103   The application need not be heard by the same judge or justices as imposed disqualification, so long as the same court hears it, but, where a disqualification period is varied on appeal to the Crown Court, it seems that the magistrates' court can hear an application to remove (*The Times*, February 4, 1931; [1956] Crim. L.R. 41; for a contrary view see [1955] Crim. L.R. 767 and [1956] Crim. L.R. 110). It is submitted that the correct view is that given at 121 J.P.Jo. 819, namely that in view of the latter part of s.110 of the Magistrates' Courts Act 1980, declaring that a decision of quarter sessions on appeal has effect as if it is made by the magistrates' court, it should be the magistrates' court which hears an application to remove a disqualification imposed or confirmed by quarter sessions on appeal. The Courts Act 1971 (see now the Supreme Court Act 1981) made no difference to the legal position save to substitute the Crown Court for quarter sessions. However, in *Sherrard v Woods* [1958] N.I. 13, where a like Northern Irish statute was under consideration, it was said that, while the magistrates' court was the proper tribunal to remove a disqualification imposed there and upheld by sessions on appeal without alteration, it might be otherwise if the magistrates' order had been varied or sessions had imposed a disqualification and the magistrates had not. No doubt the magistrates can obtain leave by letter from the Crown Court to deal with the application if in doubt as to their powers; see generally 120 J.P.Jo. 294 and 374. There is no appeal from a refusal to remove the disqualification or against a removal save in either case to the High Court on a point of law. The applicant may be ordered to pay costs, whether successful or not (s.42(5)), and by the Magistrates' Courts Act 1980 s.64, the person opposing removal may be ordered to pay costs if the disqualification is removed (see the Criminal Procedure Rules 2005 r.55.2, declaring such applications to be by complaint and making the police, in effect, the respondent). The Divisional Court has held in *R. v Recorder of Liverpool Ex p. McCann, The Times*, May 4, 1994 (also reported as *R. v Liverpool Crown Court Ex p. McCann* at [1995] R.T.R. 23) that applications for the removal of a disqualification from driving are within the definition of "criminal proceedings" in s.12(2) of the Access to Justice Act 1999; therefore there is jurisdiction for a competent authority to exercise its discretion under Sch.3 to that Act to grant a right to representation for such an application (see further Chapter 2).

20.104   It seems that, in computing the time after which a person may apply for removal of a disqualification, any time after the conviction during which it was suspended or he was not disqualified shall be disregarded.

It seems that the court must either remove the disqualification altogether or refuse the application altogether; a disqualification cannot be varied under what is now s.42 (*R. v Cottrell (No.2)* [1956] 1 All E.R. 751), but a court may remove the disqualification "from such date as may be specified in the order" (s.42(2)). There seems nothing to prevent a court, therefore, granting the application for removal to come into effect, say, in one year's time from the date of the hearing of the application. A person was disqualified in April 1954 for three years. In May 1955 the court removed the disqualification as from April 1956. He applied in August 1955 for its immediate removal. It was held that the magistrates were not estopped by their May decision from hearing the August application (*R. v Manchester JJ. Ex p. Gaynor* [1956] 1 All E.R. 610).

Where a licence is restored under s.42 the court is required to endorse **20.105** particulars of the order on any licence previously held by the applicant (s.42(5)), except where the order of disqualification which is removed is an order under s.147 of the 2000 Sentencing Act (disqualification for using a vehicle for criminal purposes; see § 20.58). The court is obliged to notify the Department for Transport of an order under s.42 (whether it is an ordinary order of disqualification or one under s.147 of the 2000 Sentencing Act).

CHAPTER 21

SPECIAL REASONS AND MITIGATING CIRCUMSTANCES

CONTENTS

Introduction

21.01 In Chapters 19 and 20, the offences carrying obligatory endorsement or disqualification were described in detail. The first part of this chapter is concerned with the reasons upon which a court may refrain from disqualifying in respect of an obligatorily disqualifiable offence or to refrain from endorsing in respect of an endorsable offence. The reasons are commonly referred to as "special reasons".

Advocates should be careful to distinguish between special reasons for not disqualifying or endorsing, and the circumstances in which a court, under a very much wider discretion, may refrain from disqualifying when considering a penalty points disqualification. The latter are usually referred to as "mitigating circumstances" and are dealt with at §§ 21.64–7.

21.02 It is important to remember that neither special reasons nor mitigating circumstances automatically enable the defendant to escape disqualification or endorsement. Where special reasons or mitigating circumstances are found it merely means that the court has a discretion to disqualify the offender for a lesser period or not at all; the court is not bound to exercise its discretion and in an appropriate case will not do so. Indeed in *Vaughan v Duff* [1984] R.T.R. 376 it was said (per Robert Goff L.J., at 381J, following Lord Widgery C.J. in *Taylor v Rajan* [1974] R.T.R. 304, an "emergency" case) "the exercise of the discretion [of special reasons] should only be exercised in clear and compelling circumstances". This should be contrasted with the provision made for defendants convicted of offences under the Construction and Use Regulations. If such a defendant proves that he did not know and had no reasonable cause to suspect that the facts of the case were such that an offence would be committed, the court cannot order endorsement or disqualification (see § 8.104).

Special reasons cannot be found to impose a lesser number of penalty points for an endorsable offence. If, however, the court is persuaded by special reasons to exercise its discretion not to endorse, then there is no power to endorse the licence with penalty points.

SPECIAL REASONS

Definition and criteria

Where special reasons are found for not endorsing in respect of an offence for **21.03** which penalty points are incurred, the court may decide either that the special reasons are sufficient not to order endorsement, or that the reasons are insufficient, in which case the appropriate number of points must also be endorsed. A court cannot find special reasons for not imposing a lesser number of points than those set out in Sch.2 to the 1988 Offenders Act: it must either endorse the appropriate number of penalty points or decide because of special reasons not to endorse at all.

It may be particularly important from an advocate's point of view for special reasons to be found by a court for refraining also from ordering endorsement where special reasons have already been found enabling an offender to escape disqualification in respect of an obligatorily disqualifiable offence. If the offender has already incurred nine penalty points, in such a case although the offender will have escaped disqualification for the offence, the court will be obliged to impose a penalty points disqualification if an order of endorsement is made (see § 19.35).

The phrase "special reasons" is not statutorily defined. But in *R. v Crossen* **21.04** [1939] 1 N.I. 106, the King's Bench Division of Northern Ireland held:

> "A 'special reason' within the exception is one which is special to the facts of the particular case, that is special to the facts which constitute the offence. It is, in other words, a mitigating or extenuating circumstance, not amounting in law to a defence to the charge, yet directly connected with the commission of the offence and one which the court ought properly to take into consideration when imposing punishment. A circumstance peculiar to the offender as distinguished from the offence is not a 'special reason' within the exception."

This passage was approved by Lord Goddard in *Whittal v Kirby* [1946] 2 All E.R. 552, and it remains the basic definition of the phrase. In *R. v Wickens* (1958) 42 Cr. App. R. 236 four minimum "criteria" were laid down: to amount to a "special reason" a matter must:

(1) be a mitigating or extenuating circumstance;

(2) not amount in law to a defence to the charge;

(3) be directly connected with the commission of the offence; and

(4) be one which the court ought properly to take into consideration when imposing sentence.

In Scotland, the courts have adopted the same approach (see *Adair v Munn* **21.05** 1940 S.C.(J.) 69).

Curiously, in none of these cases was the court's attention apparently drawn to s.11(3) of the Road Traffic Act 1930 which entitled the court to refrain from disqualifying "having regard to the lapse of time since the date of the previous or last previous conviction, or for any *other* special reason". Whether or not full consideration of all the contexts in which the phrase "special reasons" (or indeed "special circumstances", a phrase which has been held to have an identical meaning) appeared in the various Road Traffic Acts prior to the Road Traffic Act 1960 would have produced the same judicial opinion is now academic. In *R. v Steel* (1968) 52 Cr. App. R. 510, it was said that it was too late to challenge the decision in *Whittal v Kirby*. And in *R. v Anderson* [1972] Crim. L.R. 245 the Court of

Appeal expressly declined to redefine "special reasons", and stated that *Whittal v Kirby* remained good law and should be followed.

21.06   But the application of *Whittal v Kirby* causes considerable difficulties in practice. The triviality of an offence could appear to meet all four criteria. Indeed in Scotland, the High Court of Justiciary held that a very minor degree of blameworthiness on the part of a defendant convicted of driving without due care and attention could amount to a special reason: see *Smith v Henderson* 1950 S.C.(J.) 48. It was there suggested that the mischief at which the provisions relating to endorsement and disqualification were aimed was the element of danger to the public, and that where that element was absent, special reasons could be found.

In *Reay v Young* [1949] 1 All E.R. 1102, Lord Goddard applied a similar test when upholding a finding of special reasons where an uninsured driver merely held the wheel of a car for a distance of 150yds on an open moorland road on which "there was no traffic". Again in *James v Hall* [1968] Crim. L.R. 507, a finding of special reasons was upheld where a driver, whose blood-alcohol level was above the prescribed limit, drove his car a few yards off the road into a friend's driveway (but see § 21.39).

21.07   However, in *Nicholson v Brown* [1974] R.T.R. 177, Lord Widgery, disapproving *Smith v Henderson*, said:

> "I would not accept the proposition that if a man is guilty of driving without due care and attention, he can be excused endorsement of his licence on the basis of special reasons merely because it was not a bad case, or merely because the degree of blameworthiness was slight. I think that the line must be drawn firmly at guilt or innocence in those cases. If the defendant is guilty, then the consequences of endorsement of the licence must follow, unless there is some special reason properly to be treated as such, not such a matter as that the offence was not a serious one."

In *Delaroy-Hall v Tadman* [1969] 2 Q.B. 208, Lord Parker declined to find special reasons where the analysis of a defendant's blood-alcohol level showed that he was only just above the prescribed limit. In doing so, he stated that there may be some overriding reason to be found in the legislation constituting the offence, which precludes a court from considering as a special reason something which at first sight might appear to fall within the principle of *Whittal v Kirby*.

21.08   In *Marks v West Midlands Police* [1981] R.T.R. 471 it was held that while a special reason could never be constituted by the fact that the breach of the law was small, the minor nature of the offence could not be totally ignored: the lack of an intention to commit an offence had to be weighed against the problem faced by the defendant. In that case the defendant exceeded a motorway speed limit of 70mph by 10mph. He was worried by his blind, incontinent, 80-year-old passenger becoming ill and was thereby not aware of exceeding the limit, being anxious to reach the nearest motorway service area.

It is axiomatic that a circumstance peculiar to an offender as distinguished from an offence cannot amount to a special reason. Thus an offender's ignorance of the fact that a motorised scooter (a "Go-ped") was in law a mechanically propelled vehicle intended for use on roads could not amount to a special reason so far as the offences of driving with excess alcohol or without insurance were concerned (*DPP v Murray* [2001] EWHC Admin 848).

21.09   These decisions cannot easily be reconciled into a coherent set of principles which can be applied to future circumstances. There is, undoubtedly, a strong public policy element in the decisions. But so long as *Nicholson v Brown* remains good law, the principle often appears to be that a special reason has to be found outside the facts which constitute the mischief of the offence itself.

Because of the difficulty in practice of identifying what the court will accept as a special reason, the most useful approach is by analogy with previous decisions. Set out below are a number of examples first under a general heading and then divided by reference to the offence in question.

EXAMPLES OF SPECIAL REASONS

Generally

The following are capable of amounting to special reasons: **21.10**

The fact that the defendant drove for a short distance and in circumstances such that he was unlikely to be brought into contact with other road users: *Reay v Young* (above), *James v Hall* [1968] Crim. L.R. 507 (§ 21.39 below) as qualified by *R. v Mullarkey* [1970] Crim. L.R. 406 and *Coombs v Kehoe* [1972] R.T.R. 224 (see "Shortness of distance driven", § 21.39 below).

The fact that the defendant unintentionally committed the offence or was misled, without negligence, into committing it; see below under "Insurance", "Drink/driving" and "Speed limits". (§§ 21.12–17, 21.18–30 and 21.54–5.)

The fact that the defendant's breath sample included regurgitated alcohol which caused the readings recorded by the Intoximeter to exceed the prescribed limit: see below under "Drink/driving" (§ 21.22).

The fact that the defendant committed the offence whilst coping with a true emergency: see below under "Insurance", "Drink/driving", "Reckless and careless driving" and "Speed limits".

The following have been held *not* to be capable of amounting to special **21.11** reasons:

The fact that the defendant is of good character, has a good driving record, or that he, his family or employees, will suffer personal, financial or other hardship, however severe: *Whittall v Kirby* (see § 21.04).

The fact that the defendant is a doctor, or has some other employment of benefit to the public, for the proper discharge of which a licence is important or vital; *Gordon v Smith* [1971] Crim. L.R. 173; *Holroyd v Berry* [1973] R.T.R. 145.

The fact that, as a condition of bail prior to trial, the defendant was not permitted to drive: *R. v Kwame* [1975] R.T.R. 106. Such a condition is lawful, but could produce injustice of which a court should be made aware whenever it considers imposing this condition. Since the enactment of the Bail Act 1976 it is generally considered that a condition of bail may only be imposed where one of the grounds for refusal of bail exists, e.g. likelihood of commission of further offences. The defendant's redress in the event of the condition being imposed is to apply to a High Court judge in chambers for a variation of the conditions of bail.

The fact, by itself, that the offence was trivial (see *Nicholson v Brown, Delaroy-Hall v Tadman* and *Marks v West Midlands Police* at § 21.07 and § 21.08 above).

Insurance

21.12 Prior to 1965, disqualification or, at one time, imprisonment was obligatory for using a motor vehicle without insurance, or causing or permitting such use. A substantial number of early decisions on the application of *Whittall v Kirby* (see above) are in respect of convictions for this offence.

There are numerous examples of cases in which the court has held that the defendant was misled into committing the offence, and that this was capable of amounting to a special reason, e.g.:

> A garage proprietor applied for full cover, but was issued with a named-driver policy without the difference being pointed out to him by the insurance company: *Labrum v Williamson* [1947] 1 All E.R. 824.
>
> The owner of a lorry requested the proprietor of the garage at which it was repaired to drive it to his premises, assuming that the garage proprietor would, as in normal commercial circumstances he should, have been covered by his own insurance. He was not, and did not inform the owner: *Lyons v May* [1948] 2 All E.R. 1062.
>
> An employer told his employee to take a vehicle onto the road. It was reasonable for the employee to assume that he would be insured: *Blows v Chapman* [1947] 2 All E.R. 576. (The employee would now have a defence under s.143(3) of the 1988 Act: see § 10.59.)
>
> A perusal of the words of the policy by a layperson would suggest that the use of the vehicle was covered by the policy: *Boss v Kingston* [1963] 1 All E.R. 177 and *Carlton v Garrity* [1964] Crim. L.R. 146.

21.13 But the defendant must show that he was in some way misled. An honest, but groundless, belief that the policy covered a particular use cannot amount to a special reason: *Rennison v Knowler* [1947] 1 All E.R. 302.

A defendant who had recently been seriously injured was carried as a passenger in his own car driven by a friend on a non-emergency trip to hospital; his policy did not cover that friend to drive, despite the defendant's genuinely and honestly held belief that it did. In finding that there were special reasons for not endorsing the defendant's licence, the justices were of the opinion that his injuries had so acted upon his mind as to reduce his ability to behave with the standard of prudence normally expected of a policy-holder.

21.14 The Divisional Court, distinguishing *Rennison v Knowler* on the grounds that on the facts as presented the defendant had, as a result of his injuries rendering him less aware of the contents of his policy, reasonable grounds for his belief that he was covered, upheld the justices when dismissing an appeal by the prosecutor against a finding of special reasons (*East v Bladen* [1987] R.T.R. 291).

Although in *Reay v Young* (at § 21.06) the shortness of a journey was held, in the particular circumstances, to be capable of amounting to a special reason, the facts were unusual; and its application is likely to be rare in practice: see *Milliner v Thorne* [1972] Crim. L.R. 245. In *Gott v Chisholm* (1950) 114 J.P.Jo. 212, the court refused to find special reasons where an unskilled, unsupervised driver drove only a short distance, but caused an accident in the process.

Justices found special reasons for not endorsing the licence of a defendant who **21.15** had driven an uninsured vehicle onto the road outside his house and had left it parked there. Perhaps not surprisingly, the prosecution appealed against that finding on the basis that the use of the vehicle complained of had not been the driving of it but the leaving of it on the road and that the shortness of the distance it had been driven could not constitute special reasons in such circumstances. The Administrative Court in *DPP v Heritage* [2002] EWHC 2139; (2002) 166 J.P. 772 declined to interfere with the justices' finding; the driving of the vehicle onto the road, the parking of it there and the subsequent running into it by another vehicle had all occurred within a relatively short period on the same day, and the justices were entitled to look at these matters as a whole. It was not wrong for them to have found special reasons on the basis of the shortness of the distance driven where the prosecution case had been founded solely on the basis that the vehicle had been left parked on a public road.

Following repairs to his four-year-old son's toy motor cycle, which was generally pushed to a field some one and a half miles from the family home and used there by his son, the defendant "drove" the vehicle for test purposes at no more than 2mph across a narrow road by sitting astride it with the engine switched on and kicking it along with his feet. When halfway across the road he was hit by a Volvo motor car which was damaged in the collision. He pleaded guilty to (inter alia) careless driving, driving without insurance, driving without "L" plates, without a helmet and without a registration mark. The justices had accepted that the defendant had reasonably concluded that the road traffic legislation did not apply and found special reasons for not endorsing his licence. The prosecutor appealed against that ruling to the Divisional Court in *DPP v Powell* [1993] R.T.R. 266.

On appeal it was conceded by counsel for the defendant that the justices' find- **21.16** ing of special reasons with regard to the offence of careless driving simply could not be sustained. With regard to the other offences, however, the court said that the justices had obviously not regarded the defendant as someone who in the ordinary way would so much as have contemplated using the toy cycle on a road in the manner of an ordinary motor cycle. On the authorities they had reasonably concluded that in relation to the insurance and "L" plates offences the defendant was reasonable in not regarding himself in the circumstances as under an obligation to obtain insurance or to display "L" plates. The appeal was allowed only in so far as it related to the offence of careless driving.

The defendant's ignorance of the law cannot be a special reason: *Swell v McKechnie* [1956] Crim. L.R. 423. Nor is the fact that the defendant made several attempts to obtain a policy, was not conversant with insurance practice and was not deliberately or intentionally trying to evade the law: *Surtees v Benewith* [1954] 3 All E.R. 261.

Swell v McKechnie above was followed, and *DPP v Powell* above explained **21.17** and distinguished, in *DPP v Murray* [2001] EWHC Admin 848. Ignorance of the law as to the nature of a motorised foot scooter was, as explained in *Swell v McKechnie*, a circumstance peculiar to the offender and accordingly could not amount to a special reason; furthermore, the facts of the instant case were very different from those in *DPP v Powell*, the offender having used the motorised scooter as an alternative to his other motor vehicles in order to drive home from a public house.

Drink/driving

21.18   The circumstances which have been held to be capable of amounting to special reasons can be divided into three groups:

> (1) those explaining how the defendant became unfit to drive, or had excess alcohol in his body;
>
> (2) those explaining why the defendant drove in such a condition; and
>
> (3) miscellaneous circumstances relating to the offence.

A clear distinction must be drawn between the cases involving charges under s.4 of the 1988 Act (unfitness to drive) and those involving charges under s.5 of the 1988 Act (having excess alcohol). In the latter, Parliament has set a clear dividing line between guilt and innocence, and an obligatory penalty in the event of guilt. There is no room for arguing special reasons simply because the blood-alcohol level is marginally too high (*Delaroy-Hall v Tadman* at § 21.07) or because the defendant's driving ability was in no way impaired (*R. v Jackson* [1969] 2 All E.R. 453) or because the defendant's ability to drive was impaired, not by the alcohol even though over the limit, but by disease or drugs (*R. v Scott* [1969] 2 All E.R. 450 and *Goldsmith v Laver* (1970) 134 J.P.Jo. 310) but there is room for arguing that when the blood-alcohol level is below the limit, special reasons can be found for refusing to supply laboratory specimens (see *White (Arvin) v Metropolitan Police Commissioner* [1984] Crim. L.R. 687, "Miscellaneous circumstances" below).

21.19   Special reasons could not be found for not disqualifying a defendant who, having driven six miles, provided a roadside breath test which was negative, but one mile further on underwent a second (and unconnected) breath test which proved positive (*DPP v White* [1988] R.T.R. 267). It was well known that alcohol was released into the blood stream gradually and that levels could continue to rise for a time after ingestion had ceased; the defendant, having consumed alcohol, was at risk when he first drove and continued to be at risk notwithstanding the first negative breath test.

Where a defendant is liable to a minimum three-year period of disqualification because of a previous drink/driving conviction by virtue of s.34(3) of the 1988 Offenders Act, a court can only take into account special reasons which relate to the commission of the later offence (*Boliston v Gibbons* [1985] R.T.R. 176). An offender who escaped disqualification on the occasion of his first conviction cannot avoid the three-year minimum disqualification for a second offence within the 10-year period on the ground that he was not disqualified for the first (see also § 4.327).

Explanations for being unfit: charges under s.4

21.20   A defendant took a drug to soothe pain from an injured leg not knowing that this would make him more susceptible to the effects of alcohol. With reluctance, the court was prepared to hold that this could amount to special reasons: *Chapman v O'Hagan* [1949] 2 All E.R. 690. In *R. v Wickens* (1958) 42 Cr. App. R. 236, a defendant, who did not know that he was a diabetic, drank beer which, but for his illness, would not have affected his driving. This was held to be capable of amounting to a special reason. In *R. v Holt* [1962] Crim. L.R. 565, a defendant took Amytol tablets prescribed by a doctor who had failed to warn him of the effects of even a small quantity of alcohol; the full Court of Criminal Appeal held that this was capable of amounting to a special reason. It falls within the general proposition set out above that special reasons can be found where a defendant has been misled into committing an offence.

In *Brewer v Metropolitan Police Commissioner* [1969] 1 All E.R. 513, the defendant had absorbed fumes from a vat which made him unfit to drive after consuming a small quantity of alcohol. Quarter sessions found that he did not know, but ought to have known, that he had absorbed these fumes. The Divisional Court held that this was capable of amounting to a special reason.

It is not a special reason that the defendant's unfitness to drive has been **21.21** contributed to by a lack of food: *Archer v Woodward* [1959] Crim. L.R. 461. Nor is it a special reason that the defendant took the drugs which caused him to be unfit in an attempt at suicide: *Bullen v Keay* [1974] R.T.R. 559.

For mistakes as to the nature of the drink consumed, see below.

Explanations for having excess alcohol in the body: charges under s.5

In complete distinction to *R. v Wickens* and *R. v Holt* above, special reasons **21.22** cannot be found where the defendant has been affected by an illness or a drug of the effect of which he had no knowledge: see *R. v Scott* and *Goldsmith v Laver* above. This axiom was restated in *Kinsella v DPP* [2002] EWHC 545. There was expert evidence that indicated that, unknown to the appellant, he had an abnormal alcohol metabolism resulting in higher and more prolonged blood-alcohol than would be expected for a normal person. Had he had a normal alcohol metabolism, his blood and breath-alcohol levels, when the samples were taken, would have been well below the legal limit. The district judge who dealt with the matter at first instance correctly concluded that there was clear authority that special reasons are not available when an offender has been affected by an illness of which he has no knowledge. In breathalyser cases the test was objective, namely whether the blood-alcohol reading was over the prescribed limit, and the physical condition leading to the reading was a condition special to the offender not the offence. The defendant's condition was special to him, albeit unknown to him, but the defendant was aware that he had been drinking alcohol and, nevertheless, chose to drive.

This should be contrasted with the position of motorists who suffer from eructation, or regurgitated alcohol. Following *Zafar v DPP* [2004] EWHC 2468; [2005] R.T.R. 18 it is now settled law that "breath" in s.5(1) of the Road Traffic Act 1988 and s.15 of the Road Traffic Offenders Act 1988 did not have any special meaning and referred to any breath exhaled, regardless of whether it was infused with the alcohol contents of the defendant's stomach by way of oesophageal reflux. In *Woolfe v DPP* [2006] EWHC 1497; [2007] R.T.R. 16 it was confirmed that the word "consume" in s.15(3) of the Road Traffic Offenders Act 1988 did not include the regurgitating of the contents of the stomach into the mouth or upper oesophagus and reabsorbing them. However, this condition is capable of amounting to "special reasons" in relation to disqualification. In such a case, the bench must consider whether on the balance of probabilities the defendant has established: (1) that the amount of alcohol which the motorist had consumed was insufficient, without more, to exceed the prescribed limit; (2) whether, on each occasion when he provided specimens of breath for the Intoximeter, he had regurgitated alcohol from his stomach into his mouth; and (3) whether it was regurgitated alcohol that caused the readings to exceed the prescribed limit. If satisfied on a balance of probabilities as to those matters (and/or any of the matters advanced as special reasons), the court will have to consider as an exercise of discretion whether or not to disqualify or to disqualify for a shorter period. It is a two-stage process. This decision was followed in *O Sang Ng v DPP* [2007] EWHC 36; [2007] R.T.R. 35, which confirmed that the evidence on which the appellant sought to rely went directly to the commission of the offence. Thus it does not breach the principle, well established for over 60 years, that a special reason must be special to the offence and not the offender.

21.23   Special reasons have been found where the defendant did not know the nature of what he was drinking. The two types of situation in which this can arise are:

    (a) when the defendant does not know that he is drinking alcohol at all; and

    (b) where the defendant knows that he is drinking alcohol, but has been deceived or misled as to the nature of the drink.

It cannot be a special reason for a defendant to say simply that he was mistaken as to the amount of alcohol that he had drunk. In *Newnham v Trigg* [1970] R.T.R. 107, the defendant had been given whisky in bed by his wife, but by reason of his cold, could not tell how much he had drunk. It was held that ignorance of the exact quantity of drink cannot be a special reason, whereas a mistake as to the quality might be.

A defendant whose breath-alcohol level was 87µg/100ml contended that he was a Rastafarian who did not drink and that prior to being stopped he had attended a function at which he had drunk what he had assumed to be a non-alcoholic punch. His admitted feelings of tiredness he put down to a long day. The magistrates held that he was under a positive duty to make inquiries as to the content of the punch and therefore declined to find special reasons for not disqualifying him. Their decision was upheld by the Divisional Court in *Robinson v DPP* [2003] EWHC 2718; [2004] Crim. L.R. 670. A driver who assumed that a drink did not contain alcohol was taking a risk given that the purpose of the legislation was to ensure that people did not drive with excess alcohol. It was for the defendant to show in mitigation that he had done all that he could reasonably be expected to do to avoid the commission of an offence. In any event, given the high level of alcohol revealed by the breath analysis, the magistrates would have been entitled to find that they should not exercise their discretion in his favour notwithstanding that a special reason might otherwise have applied.

21.24   Ignorance of the fact that heavy evening consumption of alcohol can lead to a breath-alcohol level above the statutory limit the following morning cannot amount to a special reason for not disqualifying a defendant convicted of driving with excess alcohol. The Divisional Court so held in *DPP v O'Meara* [1989] R.T.R. 24 when allowing the prosecutor's appeal against a decision by justices not to disqualify a bus driver of some 16 years' experience who had drunk about eight cans of Long Life beer before retiring to bed and had breakfasted before resuming the road some 12 hours after his last drink. The offence concerned was an absolute one, and the fact that the defendant did not think or believe he would still be above the limit in the morning went to the *offender* rather than the *offence*, and accordingly could not qualify as a special reason.

It will usually be difficult for a defendant to establish that he did not know that he had been drinking alcohol at all; but clearly, if he can, this would be a special reason: see Lord Parker in *Newnham v Trigg* above.

The court is more often concerned with the defendant who alleges either that **21.25** his drink was "laced", or that he was in some other way deceived as to its strength.

In *Pugsley v Hunter* [1973] R.T.R. 284 it was held, following *R. v Shippam* [1971] Crim. L.R. 434, that where a defendant can establish that:

    (a) his drink was "laced";

    (b) he did not know or suspect that his drink was "laced"; and

    (c) if his drink had not been "laced" the alcohol level in his blood would not have exceeded the prescribed limit,

the court could be entitled to find special reasons, but that the defendant must establish head (c) with medical or scientific evidence unless it is obvious to a layman that the added drink explains the excess. No medical evidence was called for by the Bridport justices where special reasons were found because the defendant, whose blood-alcohol level was 81mg, had been taking cough medicine which unknown to him contained alcohol. In *R. v Cambridge Magistrates' Court Ex p. Wong* [1992] R.T.R. 382 a motorist's breath specimen indicated 40µg of alcohol in 100ml of breath. He was a regular consumer of cough linctus (which unbeknown to him contained alcohol) and on the occasion in question had taken 40ml thereof. Expert evidence indicated that this would have accounted for 1.7µg of the 40µg registered by the Lion Intoximeter. Had he not taken the linctus, he would have been below the level (40µg) at which the police prosecute. Such a fact was capable in law of constituting special reasons, but whether or not the discretion not to disqualify should be exercised was a matter for the justices. Special reasons could not be found for not disqualifying a driver who had not realised that he was drunk, but was aware of some effect, and drove whilst over the prescribed limit for alcohol because he had become addicted to a mouthwash (*DPP v Jowle, The Times*, December 13, 1997). The mouthwash in question was Listerine, which contained 26.9 per cent by volume of alcohol. The defendant knew that if he had taken Listerine it would give him a "lift" and his driving had been plainly erratic.

It would appear in the light of a number of cases decided by the Divisional **21.26** Court that the interpretation of the "obviousness to a layman" criterion in *Pugsley v Hunter* above is very much a matter of fact and degree, and that in the absence of perversity the decisions of lower tribunals are unlikely to be overturned. In *DPP v Younas (Note—1989)* [1990] R.T.R. 22, the defendant drank one and three quarter pints out of two pints of lager, each of which without his knowledge had been laced with a double Bacardi. Analysis of the defendant's breath specimen produced a reading of 72µg of alcohol per 100ml of breath. No medical evidence was adduced, but the justices were satisfied that, but for the rum, the defendant would not have been over the limit because it was obvious to them as laymen that one and three quarter pints of lager would not have taken him over the limit. In the view of the Divisional Court, each case depended upon its own facts and it was impossible to say that the justices' conclusion was perverse.

In *Smith v DPP* [1990] R.T.R. 17, however, the Crown Court on an appeal from justices felt disinclined to engage in detailed calculations as to whether the consumption of one and a half pints of lager would cause a person to be above the legal limit or to speculate on the dissipation rate applicable to the defendant, so that, in the absence of medical evidence, he had failed to establish that the alcohol he had unwittingly consumed (a fruit drink containing a single measure of vodka) was responsible for his being over the legal limit (86mg/100ml blood). His appeal against sentence by the Watford Justices was accordingly dismissed. In dismissing the defendant's appeal by way of case stated, the Divisional Court said that the Crown Court had applied the right test and it could not be said that its decision was perverse.

21.27   In order to meet the requirements of *Pugsley v Hunter* discussed above it is necessary to call relevant and admissible evidence. In *James v Morgan* [1988] R.T.R. 85 the only evidence available to the defendant was what he had been told some two weeks later by his workmates that they had put gin in his drinks; as that evidence was pure hearsay, it should not have been accepted by the justices. The Divisional Court held on an application for judicial review in *R. v Gravesham Magistrates' Court Ex p. Baker* [1998] R.T.R. 451 that it was in the interests of justice that a defendant who admitted driving with excess alcohol should have legal aid when arguing that there were special reasons for her not to be disqualified because her drink had been laced. In most such cases an expert witness was required to give an opinion on whether the applicant would have been over the limit if her drink had not been laced. Witnesses to the lacing would need to be traced and examined in court (not an easy task for an unrepresented defendant). It would not only be to the benefit of the applicant, but to the benefit of the court if legal aid were granted.

In *Smith v Geraghty* [1986] R.T.R. 222 it was held that in deciding whether or not special reasons for not disqualifying exist in a case where a defendant's drink has been "laced", justices have a discretion to entertain evidence which seeks to establish the defendant's blood-alcohol concentration at the time of his offence ("back calculation"); they should be wary, however, of allowing themselves to be drawn into considering detailed calculations, even when submitted as expert evidence. Consideration of the blood-alcohol level at the time of driving is practicable only when the evidence about it is reasonably clear, straightforward and relatively simple (see further § 4.169).

21.28   In *Williams v Neale* [1971] Crim. L.R. 598, the same approach was adopted where the defendant was charged with driving when unfit. He had drunk a fruit cup which, without his knowledge, had been "laced" with brandy. The burden of establishing that the added drink resulted in impairment is less onerous than that required to establish that the blood-alcohol level would have been below the limit.

However, it should, perhaps, be emphasised that even if special reasons have been established, the court must go on to consider whether or not to exercise its discretion in the defendant's favour. If the blood-alcohol level is high, or the impairment substantial, the court is bound to take into consideration the fact that whatever excuse the defendant may have had for drinking in the first place, he may have no proper excuse for driving or continuing to drive when he must or should have realised that he was affected by drink (*R. v Newton (David)* [1974] R.T.R. 451). A stipendiary magistrate was held to be wrong when he refused to allow a defendant, who had a blood analysis of 180mg of alcohol, to be asked if he realised that he was not in a fit state to drive (*Pridige v Gant* [1985] R.T.R. 196). It was again emphasised, following *R. v Newton (David)* above, that a court should first decide whether special reasons exist and then, in a case where the lacing of alcoholic or non-alcoholic drinks is relied on, whether the defendant should have realised that he was not fit to drive by reason of the alcohol he had in his body.

Pridige v Gant was considered and approved by the Divisional Court in *DPP v*   **21.29**
Barker [1990] R.T.R. 1. A woman who had drunk two or three glasses of wine
with dinner later went to a party where she consumed two or possibly three
tumblers of what she thought was orange juice, but which was in fact approximately one third vodka and two thirds orange juice. A breath specimen
taken from her following her arrest for a suspected offence under s.5 of the 1988
Act revealed an alcohol level in her breath of 109µg/100ml. She seldom drank
alcohol and had never previously consumed spirits; she remembered nothing after her first drink, save that the orange juice did not taste unusual to her. The justices were satisfied that but for the alcohol in the drinks consumed at the party the
defendant's breath-alcohol level would not have exceeded the prescribed limit
and that she suffered a total loss of knowledge of her actions and was not aware
that her condition was influenced by alcohol. They concluded that special reasons
existed and accordingly did not disqualify her. Dismissing the prosecutor's appeal against that finding, the Divisional Court pointed out that the question
deemed necessary of answer by the court in *Pridige v Gant*, namely should the
defendant have realised that she was not fit to drive due to alcohol, had been
answered satisfactorily by the justices in their findings of fact.

R. v Newton (David) above was held by the Divisional Court to have been correctly applied by justices in *Donahue v DPP* [1993] R.T.R. 156 when exercising
their discretion to disqualify, despite the existence of special reasons, a defendant
convicted of a s.5 offence. The defendant at a business function had asked for
alcohol-free wine but had in fact been served with alcoholic wine. When driving
away from the function he had left the road and collided with a hedge. A
subsequent breath test revealed an alcohol level of 99µg/100ml of breath. At the
scene he had repeatedly asked the police officer to forget the incident because his
licence was essential for his livelihood, but had made no mention of his belief
that he had drunk only alcohol-free wine. His doctor gave evidence that he might
have confused the effect of excess alcohol with fatigue induced by the previous
night of disturbed sleep as a result of attending to his sick father. The justices
found as a fact that the defendant, who was not an inexperienced or young man,
must have realised that he was not fit to drive through alcohol, and they had taken
account of the medical evidence put before them; accordingly there was no basis
upon which their discretion could be interfered with.

The defendant went for a drink with friends. Without her knowledge, one of   **21.30**
those friends added vodka to each of the two Smirnoff Ice drinks she bought for
her, believing the defendant would be travelling home by taxi and would appreciate the stronger drinks. Expert evidence was given to the effect that, given the
level of alcohol in the defendant's breath (twice the permitted limit), they would
have expected her to have been aware of being affected by alcohol. Although
surprising, the justices' finding that the defendant felt no effect of the additional
alcohol had led them to the conclusion that special reasons existed for not
disqualifying the defendant, and that conclusion on the facts as found was neither
perverse nor wrong in law (*DPP v Sharma* [2005] EWHC 879; [2005] R.T.R.
27).

In *Alexander v Latter* [1972] Crim. L.R. 646, the Divisional Court upheld a
finding that where a defendant was offered diabetic lager by a barman as an
alternative to ordinary lager without being informed that it was twice as strong,
this could amount to a special reason. But this case must be read with *Adams v*

Bradley [1975] Crim. L.R. 168 where a defendant drank strong lager without re-alising its strength, and the court declined to find special reasons. The distinction was found in the fact that in *Alexander v Latter* the defendant was misled by the barman, whereas in *Adams v Bradley* the defendant made no inquiries about the strength of the lager. The distinction between *Alexander v Latter* and *Adams v Bradley* was again adverted to in the case of *R. v Krebbs* [1977] R.T.R. 406. The Court of Appeal found special reasons for not disqualifying where the defendant had initially been given Harp Lager to drink but unknowingly was subsequently supplied with Lowenbraü, which was double the strength. In *Adams v Bradley* the mistake of the defendant as to the alcoholic strength of the beverage could not be said to have been induced by the action of a third party.

In *R. v Messom* [1973] R.T.R. 140, the Court of Appeal considered that special reasons existed where a defendant, having asked for a large ginger ale topped up with a small whisky, was in fact given a small ginger ale topped up with a large brandy. It is suggested that this is an example of a case where the defendant was misled.

Emergency

21.31   In *Brown v Dyerson* [1969] 1 Q.B. 45, it was stated that a sudden medical emergency could justify driving so as to be capable of amounting to a special reason. It has to be mentioned, however, that some new light has been thrown upon that decision by the words (admittedly obiter) of Simon Brown L.J. in *DPP v Whittle* [1996] R.T.R. 154 to the effect that whilst in earlier years it was envis-aged that a medical emergency was capable of amounting to a special reason, the better view might now be that any genuine such emergency would give rise to a complete defence, the defence of necessity, or as it is sometimes called, "duress of circumstances" (as delineated in *R. v Martin* [1989] R.T.R. 63: see § 5.83). Any risk to be averted less than that of serious injury could hardly justify imperil-ling the public by driving whilst over the alcohol limit. His Lordship expressed no concluded view upon the point, but mentioned it merely so that the inter-relation between special reasons and the full defence might be considered at some appropriate future time. Unless and until that consideration is given to the matter, however, and a proper determination made, it is submitted that the status accorded to a medical emergency by *Brown v Dyerson* still holds sway.

While the High Court have been willing to recognise that an emergency is capable of amounting to a special reason, in every case so far reported the High Court have emphasised that before an emergency can constitute a special reason, the defendant must first show that there was no alternative but for him to drive and that he had explored every reasonable alternative before driving. The emer-gency must be real, not nebulous, nor manufactured. It is not a sufficient emer-gency if it can be shown that the defendant should have anticipated the emer-gency arising.

21.32   In *R. v Baines* [1970] Crim. L.R. 590, the defendant drove to rescue his partner's frail, ailing and elderly mother stranded at night without petrol. It was held that he had not explored other avenues of rescue; and therefore it could not be said that the emergency necessitated his driving.

In *Evans v Bray* [1977] R.T.R. 24, the defendant was telephoned by his wife, who was away on a holiday, saying that she had forgotten tablets she required to control her blood pressure. The defendant, who had been drinking, drove over to her taking the tablets. The Divisional Court held that special reasons had not been established. He had not telephoned any of the emergency services. The question was not whether his action was understandable, but whether the defendant had no alternative but to drive as a result of the emergency.

In *DPP v Whittle* [1996] R.T.R. 154 (see also § 21.31) the defendant's wife **21.33** was driving him home after a night out when she complained of dizziness and blurred vision. He panicked because she was in pain and regarded the situation as a medical emergency even though he did not think she was in need of urgent medical attention, and he took over the driving from her. The Divisional Court held, applying *Taylor v Rajan* [1974] R.T.R. 304 (see § 21.35) that there was no evidence upon which the justices, had they applied the objective test required by the law, could have found that any reasonable person would have thought there was a medical emergency giving rise to a need for the defendant to drive.

The same principle applies when the emergency is non-medical. In *Jacobs v Reed* [1974] R.T.R. 81 where the defendant had been drinking at the airport awaiting a flight, when telephoned as a matter of emergency by his wife to say that their daughter had failed to turn up at school, as a result of which he drove home without considering alternative methods of transport.

It is not an emergency that the defendant was a detective constable engaged on **21.34** undercover operations which involved visiting licensed premises in plain clothes and had been given a £2 per day drinking allowance (*Vaughan v Duff* [1984] R.T.R. 376).

In *Park v Hicks* [1979] R.T.R. 259 the defendant had driven his wife away from a party where there was a disturbance. The justices held it to be a special reason for not disqualifying that his wife had had a brain haemorrhage and the disturbance had created a sudden medical emergency, namely a danger of a recurrence of a brain haemorrhage. Allowing an appeal from the justices' finding, the Divisional Court held that the evidence was too nebulous; unless full details of the special reasons relied on were given, a court could not exercise its discretion under what is now s.34(1) of the 1988 Offenders Act.

In *Powell v Gliha* [1979] R.T.R. 126 it was held not to be a special reason for a **21.35** wife to drive her paraplegic husband home in order that he might use a specially fitted lavatory. She and her husband had gone to a silver wedding anniversary party 30 miles from home and she was irresponsible in not having anticipated that her husband would need lavatory facilities while away from home.

Generally it cannot be an excuse amounting to a special reason for a doctor, paramedic or other member of emergency services to say that he was called out in an emergency; for to him it is routine. However, there may be circumstances in which he could properly say that he had no reasonable expectation of being summoned (e.g. where he was off duty and not on call, but a disaster required all available personnel, or, in the case of a doctor, where full and proper arrangements for covering emergencies had been made but for some unforeseen reason his services were essential). In this type of event it should be open to him to say that there are special reasons. It should be noted, however, that it will generally be considerably more difficult for him to establish special reasons in respect of a journey home after the emergency has been dealt with (*Taylor v Rajan* [1974] R.T.R. 304). This principle has been reinforced by the Divisional Court in *DPP v Waller* [1989] R.T.R. 112. In the court's view there was a distinct difference in the situation presented to a driver in respect of the outward and homeward journeys and accordingly the justices had erred in finding special reasons for not disqualifying a driver with excess alcohol in his body on his way home from attending an emergency. A similar conclusion was reached by the Divisional Court in *DPP v Feeney*, *The Times*, December 13, 1988; in that case the defendant was only 1,000yds from his home when the emergency had been dealt with, and the court saw no reason why he should not have left his car where it was and walked home. In *DPP v Goddard* [1998] R.T.R. 463 the defendant escaped his violent assailants by driving to his sister's house. Thereafter, having recalled that one of his attackers lived in the same square as his sister, he drove eight and a half miles to his own home. Although the justices were entitled to find that there had been an emergency in respect of the first journey, once the defendant had reached the relative safety of his sister's house a number of options were available to him, including calling the police. It was not reasonable for him to drive on to his own house, eight and a half miles away, having consumed more than the limit of alcohol; accordingly there were no special reasons for not ordering disqualification.

21.36   A mother left her young daughter in the care of a 14-year-old babysitter and drove her own car to a public house. She had previously received threatening telephone calls. During the evening she checked with the babysitter and all was well. However, when she telephoned home at 11pm she discovered to her consternation that a number of calls had been received in which the caller had threatened to use a knife. The babysitter was by then extremely frightened and implored the mother to return home. Having by then consumed at least a pint and a half of cider, the mother attempted (unsuccessfully) to call a taxi, and then went to another public house to try to contact some friends who might have been able to take her home; that effort also proved fruitless. In the circumstances she felt constrained to drive her own car home. She was stopped by the police and the lower of two specimens of breath provided at the police station revealed 44µg/100ml. At her trial she successfully pleaded special reasons for not being disqualified and the justices' decision on the facts was upheld by the Divisional Court in *DPP v Knight (Note—1988)* [1994] R.T.R. 374. What was clear was that the defendant had no intention at the material time of driving her car, but for the occurrence of the emergency, and that there was nothing untoward in the way in which she had behaved. On the facts found, the court was presented with a clear and compelling example of an emergency causing a person to drive who otherwise would not have done. The court was assisted in reaching its decision by reference to passages in Lord Widgery C.J.'s judgment in *Taylor v Rajan*, the "classic case" (per Leggatt J.) in which the principles to be applied in relation to emergencies were considered.

DPP v Knight was approved by the Divisional Court in *DPP v Upchurch* [1994] R.T.R. 366 when rejecting with some firmness the prosecutor's appeal against a finding by justices of special reasons for not disqualifying in an "emergency" case. The defendant and three of his friends had been innocently caught up in a serious disturbance involving some 200 people. His friends suffered head injuries and the defendant sought the assistance of a police officer to call an ambulance. He was told that no ambulances were available. As his friends seemed seriously unwell the defendant rang for a taxi but was informed that, because of the disturbance, the taxi would not come out. He decided to drive his friends the three miles to the hospital. He drove at twice the speed limit, but otherwise perfectly properly. He was stopped by a police officer who formed the view that, although the defendant's friends were not seriously hurt, their injuries were sufficiently serious to occasion the calling by him of an ambulance. The breath specimens subsequently provided by the defendant revealed a breath-alcohol content of 45µg/100ml. Blofeld J., delivering the first judgment, quoted, as particularly apt to describe the circumstances of the instant case, a passage in the judgment of Leggatt J. in *DPP v Knight* above in which he had described the circumstances of that case as "as clear and compelling an example as could be contemplated of a crisis or emergency".

Where a woman "blackmailed" a man into driving when over the alcohol limit **21.37** by threatening to report him for rape, that could amount in law to an emergency. The Divisional Court so held in *DPP v Enston* [1996] R.T.R. 324 when upholding a finding by justices that there were special reasons for not disqualifying him from driving. It could not be argued, because it was not sensible, that a personal crisis could not be a special reason.

A different conclusion was unsurprisingly reached, however, in *DPP v Doyle* [1993] R.T.R. 369 where a driver deliberately decided to drink when she knew that she would be driving. Having suffered an assault and damage to her car, the defendant drove to a friend's home and requested the police by telephone to meet her subsequently at her own home. She then consumed a quantity of brandy before driving to her home where she was breathalysed. The justices' finding of special reasons on the grounds of an emergency was overturned by the Divisional Court on the basis that the emergency had begun before the decision to drink was taken and that she had drunk the brandy in clear contemplation of driving to her own home thereafter.

The steward and keyholder of a club some 300yds from his home drove to that **21.38** club in response to a call around midnight from an intruder alarm company informing him that the alarm had been activated and that the police had been notified. In doing so he gave no thought to the amount of alcohol he had consumed, to alternative methods of transport or to the possibility of contacting other keyholders. His journey involved the use of only about 150yds of road and he had not come into contact with any other traffic. The Divisional Court in *DPP v Cox* [1996] R.T.R. 123 dismissed an appeal by the prosecutor against the finding by justices that in view of the shortness of the distance driven and the requirement for the prompt discharge of the duties of a keyholder, there were special reasons for not disqualifying the defendant, who had pleaded guilty to driving with excess alcohol. The situation at the club had not been stable but developing and could have been getting worse by the minute, so that the defendant could not have been sure how soon the police would arrive; in addition, the intruder or intruders might well have been vandals. Not without some hesitation, the court came to the conclusion that the justices were entitled to take the view they did.

Shortness of distance driven

The shortness of the distance driven is capable of amounting to a special rea- **21.39** son particularly where the defendant has only driven his car at the request of a third party. It cannot, however, amount to a special reason unless the shortness of the actual distance driven by the defendant is such that he is unlikely to be brought into contact with other road users and danger would be unlikely to arise.

In *James v Hall* [1968] Crim. L.R. 507, the shortness of the distance driven by the defendant was held to be capable of amounting to a special reason. This was followed in *R. v Agnew* [1969] Crim. L.R. 152 where a passenger was asked by the owner to move the car a matter of 6ft.

21.40   But the courts have been anxious to restrict any principle which may be gleaned from these cases to situations where the defendant is unlikely to be brought into contact with other road users and where, if this did happen, danger would be unlikely. In *Coombs v Kehoe* [1972] R.T.R. 224, justices were directed to disqualify a lorry driver who had driven 200yds through a busy street, colliding with cars as he attempted to park. And in *R. v Mullarkey* [1970] Crim. L.R. 406, the fact that a defendant drove 400yds after midnight in winter when there was little traffic about was held not to amount to a special reason.

Where a defendant, the worse for drink, but not intending to drive home, mistakenly and genuinely believed that he was being requested by a police constable to move his car a short distance, and did so, the court held that these were special reasons (*R. v McIntyre* [1976] R.T.R. 330). However, account has to be taken not only of the driving which has taken place at the constable's request, but also of the defendant's previous voluntary act of driving which preceded it. In *De Munthe v Stewart* [1982] R.T.R. 27 a constable saw the defendant park his car and walk away and asked him to move it as it was causing an obstruction. After the defendant had reparked, but before he had ceased to drive, the constable suspected he had excess alcohol and asked for a specimen of breath. The court held there was no special reason for not disqualifying. Similarly in a Scottish case, *Hutcheson v Spiers* 2004 S.L.T. 619, an erstwhile passenger with a breath-alcohol level of 89 μg/100ml, who at the request of a police officer drove an illegally parked car some 40m along a quiet road while the driver was in a shop, was held not to have established special reasons for non-disqualification. There was no reason why he should not have informed the officer that he believed himself to be unfit to drive and that the driver would soon return; furthermore he had merely been requested, not instructed, to move the vehicle.

21.41   In *Redmond v Parry* [1986] R.T.R. 146 it was held that special reasons for not disqualifying could be found in law where a defendant whose wife was reluctant to reverse their car out of a car park undertook the task himself, travelled only a few feet and collided with another car in the car park. The combination of shortness of distance driven, lack of intention to drive further and unlikelihood of danger to other road users was capable of amounting to a special reason.

That mere distance is not the only factor to be taken into account when deciding whether there are special reasons for not disqualifying a defendant convicted of driving with excess alcohol was re-emphasised by the Divisional Court in *Chatters v Burke* [1986] 3 All E.R. 168. According to the court there are seven matters to be considered. They are:

(1) how far the vehicle was driven;

(2) in what manner it was driven;

(3) the state of the vehicle;

(4) whether the driver intended to go further;

(5) the road and traffic conditions prevailing at the time;

(6) whether there was a possibility of danger by coming into contact with other road users or pedestrians;

(7) what the reason was for the car being driven.

Of these matters item (6) was in the court's mind the most important; distance driven was not of itself the determinant of special reasons. The facts of the case were that the defendant was a passenger in his car being driven by someone else who lost control of it. The car left the road, rolled over and ended up in a field. The defendant subsequently drove the vehicle from the field onto a road and stopped it there and apparently had no intention of driving it any further. Bearing in mind the minimal danger caused thereby to other road users the justices were entitled to find, as they did, that special reasons for not disqualifying the defendant had been made out. *Chatters v Burke* was applied by the Divisional Court in *DPP v Corcoran* [1991] R.T.R. 329. On the facts of the case (car driven approximately 40yds to a safe parking place; no actual or apprehended danger to other road users) the justices were entitled to find, as they did, that there were special reasons for not disqualifying the defendant.

Where an attempt had been made under the influence of excess alcohol to drive **21.42** a car, in establishing whether there were any special reasons why the motorist should not be disqualified it was necessary to look at what was intended and not merely at what was achieved. The Divisional Court so held in *DPP v Humphries* [2000] R.T.R. 52, when remitting a case to justices with a direction to disqualify. The defendant had been seen sitting in the driver's seat of a car. A friend was seen to get out of the car and start to push the vehicle forward by two lengths before it rolled back to its original position. The defendant was observed by police to be fiddling, knife in hand, with wires underneath the steering column. He was arrested and subsequently positively breathalysed. He stated in interview that he was extremely drunk, had been drinking all day and had to get home. Since he had no intention of walking he had decided to steal a car.

The justices considered the principles laid down in *Chatters v Burke* and concluded, inter alia, that there was an intention to drive the vehicle but the engine was never started, there was no possibility of danger by coming into contact with other road users or pedestrians, that the defendant had attempted to drive the vehicle home but was too intoxicated to get it started and was interrupted by the police. On the basis of the shortness of the distance driven they found that there were special reasons for not imposing a mandatory disqualification. It was submitted on behalf of the prosecution that the justices had overlooked the fact that it was the defendant's intention to drive home if he could. In considering an attempt, the court should look not only at what was actually achieved but also at what was intended. In the court's view the justices had lost sight of this point and had focused too heavily on what the defendant actually did. *Chatters v Burke* set out useful guidelines but did not compel any particular conclusion in any particular case. In the case in point what mattered was not the fact that the car was only driven a few feet but the fact that the driver intended to drive it on a public highway some considerable distance, when on his own admission he was unfit to drive. *Chatters v Burke* was also referred to in *DPP v Elsender (Pauline)* (1999) 19 W.R.T.L.B. [8], where a finding by justices of special reasons for not disqualifying a defendant who had driven for about half a mile with a breath-alcohol level more than double the prescribed limit was set aside. There might well have been traffic on the roads along which she drove, so it was not open to the justices properly to conclude that there was no possibility of danger to other road users; furthermore the distance covered was not insubstantial.

The Divisional Court in *DPP v Bristow* [1998] R.T.R. 100 stated that the key **21.43** question justices should ask themselves when assessing if special reasons existed and considering whether to exercise their discretion not to disqualify a drink/driver was what would a sober, reasonable and responsible friend of the defendant, present at the time, but himself a non-driver and thus unable to help, have advised in the circumstances; drive or not drive. On the facts, the defendant had drunk a good deal, and the court had to bear in mind the observations about exceeding the limit made in *Taylor v Rajan* [1974] R.T.R. 304 (see § 21.61). He was proposing to drive only 500yds in what the justices found was a well-maintained van on quiet, pedestrian-free roads. However, it was the prospective rather than actual state of the road which was important. Also the shorter distance could more readily be covered on foot. Several alternatives were open to the defendant. Applying the "sober, reasonable and responsible friend" test proposed by the court, the only sober advice possible was that the defendant had had far too much to drink and that there were other solutions. If the justices had applied that objective reasoning they would inevitably have come to the view that special reasons could not be found.

The defendant, having consumed alcohol so as to be over the limit, and being concerned about the safety of leaving tools in his van, drove for one fifth of a mile along a residential cul de sac from the pub to his home. It was held (unsurprisingly) in *DPP v Oram* [2005] EWHC 964 that the fact that he had only driven a short distance could not alone justify a finding of special reasons; otherwise in every case where a driver had attempted to drive whilst over the limit it could be said that there was a special reason not to disqualify. It was necessary to look at all the circumstances and to consider whether there had been some unforeseen emergency. There was no such emergency here; the defendant had known he had the tools with him when he started to drink, and the difficulty he found himself in was entirely of his own making. Furthermore, applying the test suggested in *DPP v Bristow* above, a reasonable and sensible friend would not have advised him to drive.

Miscellaneous circumstances

21.44   In *R. v Anderson* [1972] R.T.R. 113, the defendant was informed that he was not going to be prosecuted. As a result he destroyed the sample of blood which had been given to him for analysis. The prosecution analysis was 81mg. The Court of Appeal held that he had been deprived of a possible defence, particularly bearing in mind the finding of the prosecution analyst and that there were special reasons therefore for not disqualifying, but stated that the facts in the case were very unusual ("it is difficult to think that the facts of this case could ever be repeated ... or indeed that the conclusion of this court ... could ever be a precedent in any other case" (per Roskill L.J. at 117F)). In *Doyle v Leroux* [1981] R.T.R. 438 the defendant's blood analysis was 168mg. He kept his sample for over a fortnight in his refrigerator but destroyed it on receiving a letter from the police stating that he would not be prosecuted. The Crown Court disqualified him holding that these facts could not amount to special reasons. The Court of Appeal upheld the Crown Court's decision, holding that although *R. v Anderson* above established that such a defence could be, in law, a special reason, in this instance it was not such as would, or should, have led the Crown Court not to impose the normal disqualification. In *Harding v Oliver* [1973] R.T.R. 497, it was held that the loss of the defendant's sample could not itself amount to a special reason and in *Lodwick v Brow* [1984] R.T.R. 394 (where the defendant had no recollection because of post-traumatic amnesia of giving a specimen of blood or being offered a sample at hospital and when he knew about the sample some time after leaving hospital could not trace it) it was held that, following *Harding v Oliver*, the loss of the sample specimen could not be a special reason which related to the offence, because the taking of the specimen took place after the offence had been completed. It was also held that the decision in *Doyle v Leroux* that the loss of a specimen could amount to a special reason was decided *per incuriam* in view of the fact that *Harding v Oliver* was not cited to it.

In the view of the Divisional Court in *Daniels v DPP* [1992] R.T.R. 140 it was possible for a court to find that there were special reasons for not disqualifying a driver for failing to provide a specimen of breath for analysis even when it had held that the driver had not had a reasonable excuse for failing to provide a specimen. The facts of the case are somewhat unusual. The defendant had been in the car park of a public house helping another man "bump start" his motor cycle. The engine suddenly fired and the defendant rode the vehicle onto the highway to keep it going. He travelled no more than 35yds before stopping. He was stopped by police and questioned about the ownership of the motor cycle. He was arrested on suspicion of theft and taken to the police station.

21.45 At around midnight the owner of the motor cycle arrived to exculpate the defendant. No one told the defendant about that, however, and he remained in custody. At 12.55am he was asked to provide a specimen of breath for analysis; he refused. The Crown Court found that although the defendant had understood the warning about the consequences of failure to provide a specimen, his mind was still directed to the more serious allegation of theft and his refusal was based upon what seemed to him to be the relatively trivial nature of the allegation of unfitness to drive. It was implicit in the findings that if the defendant had not been so distracted he might have taken a different view. Bearing in mind that the courts had largely restricted "reasonable excuse" to physical or mental inability or risk to health (see *R. v Lennard* [1973] R.T.R. 252 at § 4.273), it was possible that matters could be regarded as special reasons which were not capable of being reasonable excuse. Any suggestion that a defendant could not have special reasons if the circumstances did not amount to reasonable excuse was not correct.

This decision appears to be in conflict with *Scobie v Graham* [1970] Crim. L.R. 589 but in accordance with *White (Arvin) v Metropolitan Police Commissioner* [1984] Crim. L.R. 687 in which it was held to be a "special reason" for reducing to 12 months the minimum three-year period for a second drink/driving offence in a case of refusing to supply two specimens of breath, contrary to what is now s.7(6) of the 1988 Act, that the defendant duly provided a first sample, which was below the prescribed limit namely 27µg. As it would appear from the report that the court did not have either of these previous cases drawn to its attention, it is impossible to predict with absolute certainty which line of authority is destined to be the more productive (particularly as it is also understood that the court in *White* did not have the then previous authorities headed by *Scobie* drawn to its attention). It is nevertheless submitted that the view of the law set out in *Daniels* is likely to prove the more lasting.

21.46 Further support for the *Daniels* approach may be gleaned from *DPP v Daley (No.2)* [1994] R.T.R. 107 in which *Daniels* was quoted with approval by the Divisional Court when upholding the prosecutor's appeal against a finding of special reasons for non-disqualification by the Crown Court on appeal from sentence by justices for an offence of failing to provide a specimen of breath for analysis. The Crown Court had sought to rely upon the original justices' finding that the defendant had "done his best" to provide breath specimens as the basis of its finding that special reasons existed. Although it was possible for circumstances which did not amount to a reasonable excuse for failing to provide a breath specimen for analysis to afford the foundation for a finding of special reasons, the court in such circumstances had to be in a position where it accepted the factual basis but found that the basis did not amount to a reasonable excuse. Unfortunately for the Crown Court, however, the Divisional Court when dealing earlier with a different question arising from the same case (see *DPP v Daley* [1992] R.T.R. 155 at § 4.276) had come to the clear conclusion that the factual basis of the finding that the defendant had a reasonable excuse could not be sustained, whether it was described as the defendant being "incapable" of providing the specimen or as the defendant "doing his best" to provide the same. Accordingly the special reasons found by the Crown Court were not, and could not have been, established.

A genuine fear of contracting Aids as a result of blowing into an Intoximeter mouthpiece was capable of amounting to special reasons for not disqualifying a driver who had refused to supply two specimens of breath for analysis, even though the defendant had not provided an explanation for his refusal at the time. The Divisional Court so held in *DPP v Kinnersley* [1993] R.T.R. 105 when dismissing the prosecution's appeal against a finding of special reasons by justices. Despite the obiter dictum of Forbes J. to the contrary in *Teape v Godfrey* [1986] R.T.R. 213 (see § 4.115), the duty to provide a specimen did not include the duty to inform the police of any medical condition which prevented the provision of a specimen (although a failure to provide an explanation might reflect on the bona fides of the defendant).

21.47   It is not a special reason to avoid disqualification for the defendant to have consumed alcohol after an accident when convicted of refusing to supply a specimen of blood or urine for laboratory testing, even though if he had consented he would have had a defence to a charge under s.6(1) of the Road Traffic Act 1972 prior to its amendment by the Transport Act 1981 (*Courtman v Masterson* [1978] R.T.R. 457).

The special reason proffered for failing to supply a specimen of blood or urine must relate to the failure to provide the specimen and not the circumstances in which the driver came to be driving in the first place (*Anderton v Anderton* [1977] R.T.R. 424).

21.48   In *McCormick v Hitchins* [1988] R.T.R. 182 *Note* it was held that where a defendant had no intention of driving the vehicle and he could not have been a danger on the road, there were special reasons for not endorsing the defendant's licence with the obligatory 10 penalty points in respect of a charge under what is now s.7(6) of the 1988 Act when not driving or attempting to drive. Whilst it is clear in the light of *McCormick v Hitchins* and *Bunyard v Hayes* [1985] R.T.R. 348 that the fact that a defendant charged with an offence under what is now s.7(6) of the 1988 Act was not *driving* at the material time is capable in law of amounting to a special reason, it is equally clear that courts still have a discretion under s.44(2) of the 1988 Offenders Act as to whether or not to order endorsement. The Divisional Court so held in *R. v Ashford & Tenterden Magistrates' Court Ex* *p. Wood, The Times*, May 8, 1987. On the particular facts of the case (defendant not driving only because so dissuaded by a friend) the justices were entitled to order, as they did, the endorsement of the statutory 10 penalty points upon the defendant's licence.

The offer by a defendant to provide a specimen of urine instead of the specimen of blood demanded by the police officer cannot amount to special reasons for not disqualifying. It is not a matter which ought properly to be taken into account when imposing sentence as to do so would mean that the proper exercise by a police officer of a discretion as to which sample the defendant should provide would in every such case amount to a special reason, a conclusion inconsistent with the law which provides for a conviction in such circumstances (*Grix v Chief Constable of Kent* [1987] R.T.R. 193).

Upon being required to provide a specimen of blood or urine at a police station, the defendant asked the arresting officer whether a failure to provide a specimen meant a definite disqualification and the officer replied that it did not. The defendant refused to provide a specimen. On appeal the Crown Court upheld his conviction, held that there were no matters capable of amounting to special reasons but nonetheless reduced the disqualification from 18 months to the minimum obligatory 12 months. The Divisional Court in *Bobin v DPP* [1999] R.T.R. 375 held that it was plain that the inaccurate information about disqualification given to the defendant could well be a mitigating or extenuating circumstance for the offence of failing to provide the specimen; that it did not amount to a defence; that, the Crown Court having found that the defendant's decision to refuse to provide the specimen had been affected by the erroneous information, it was directly concerned with the commission of the offence; that it was a matter that the court ought properly to take into account when considering sentence; and that, accordingly, the inaccurate information given to the defendant was capable of amounting in law to a special reason. The case was remitted to the Crown Court for it to consider whether the circumstances of the case did in fact give rise to a special reason justifying the imposition of a period of disqualification less than that normally prescribed. **21.49**

Dangerous and careless driving

In England and Wales, the triviality of the offence by itself cannot amount to a special reason (see § 21.07; see also *Nicholson v Brown*, ibid.). In Scotland, *Smith v Henderson* (see § 21.06) may still be followed, a fact which will produce an undesirable difference of view in two parts of the United Kingdom over the same statutory provision. **21.50**

The fact that the defendant was dealing with an emergency is capable of amounting to a special reason. In *R. v Lundt-Smith* [1964] 3 All E.R. 225, an ambulance driver conveying an urgent case to hospital crossed traffic lights at red, having, he thought, ensured that it was safe to do so. In fact, a motor cyclist was approaching and there was a collision in which the motor cyclist was killed. Although the ambulance driver pleaded guilty to the offence of causing death by dangerous driving, the judge found that the facts were capable of amounting to special reasons, absolutely discharged the driver, and did not disqualify him. Similarly, in *Wood v Richards* [1977] Crim. L.R. 295, the conviction by magistrates of a police officer, who was responding to an emergency call, of driving without due care and attention was upheld; no special exception or standard was to be applied for police officers. The magistrates' finding of special reasons in the case for not endorsing was approved. Where, however, a police officer on a training exercise which required him to maintain surveillance upon another police car crossed a red light and was involved in a collision, the Divisional Court declined to remove an endorsement for careless driving from his licence. Although the Crown Court had erred in not finding special reasons, the court's discretion would not be exercised in favour of the appellant since the safety of lawful users of the highway ought to take precedence over the need for realistic driver training (*Agnew v DPP* [1991] R.T.R. 144). The driver of a fire appliance answering an emergency call attempted to overtake two vehicles travelling in his direction but had to abort that manoeuvre when confronted with an oncoming vehicle. Unfortunately for him, the gap between the two vehicles he sought to overtake was shortened by the slowing down of the leading vehicle, and he was unable to pull into it without clipping that vehicle. He was convicted of careless driving. The High Court of Justiciary held in *Husband v Russell* (1997) 1998 S.L.T. 379 that special reasons could be found for not endorsing his licence. The driver had made a misjudgment, but the attempted overtaking was a manoeuvre on which he would probably not have embarked had he not been on an emergency journey.

21.51   It is axiomatic that a circumstance peculiar to an offender, as distinguished from an offence, cannot be a special reason (see *Whittal v Kirby* [1946] 2 All E.R. 552 at § 21.04). Thus a hypoglycaemic attack suffered by a driver who knew she was a diabetic could not amount to a special reason for not disqualifying her on a charge of dangerous driving (*Jarvis v DPP* (2001) 165 J.P. 15).

Traffic signs, pedestrian crossings, school crossings

21.52   Unless on public policy grounds the decisions in *Nicholson v Brown* and *Delaroy-Hall v Tadman* at § 21.07 are to be restricted to the particular offences with which they were concerned, the triviality of the infringement will not amount of itself to a special reason. If the submission is simply that the defendant passed, e.g. a red stop light extremely slowly, it will not be possible to point to any facts, other than those which constitute proof of the offence, as special reasons and therefore none could be found. However, if the offence was committed in circumstances where no danger was either caused or was likely to have been caused, particularly if the red lights had remained at red for an inordinate period and there was justification for a belief that these had jammed, those circumstances might be capable of amounting to special reasons on the same principle that the court applied in *James v Hall* and *R. v Agnew*, "Shortness of distance driven", §§ 21.39–43. In those cases, the shortness of the distance driven by drivers who were over the blood-alcohol limit was held to be capable, in very restricted circumstances, of amounting to a special reason. The words "capable of" must be emphasised. The Divisional Court is clearly concerned to restrict the ambit of special reasons. But, in principle, it would seem wrong to endorse the licence of a driver who, approaching a red traffic light in circumstances where he has ample visibility in both directions well before the junction, determines to proceed across when no danger or inconvenience could conceivably be caused in so doing.

The fact that the defendant was dealing with an emergency can amount to a special reason (see *R. v Lundt-Smith* above).

21.53   If a defendant has been misled by the actions of a police officer, or pedestrian or school crossing patrol, this could also be capable of amounting to a special

reason. The fact that a defendant was without fault in failing to accord precedence to a pedestrian on a pedestrian crossing might also be so capable. It is an
absolute offence: the facts showing that the defendant was without fault would
therefore be facts other than those constituting proof of the offence.

Speed limits

Special reasons can be found where the defendant exceeded a speed limit by   **21.54**
reason of an emergency (see Lord Goddard in *Whittal v Kirby* at § 21.04). In Police *Prosecutor v Humphreys* [1970] Crim. L.R. 234, the Divisional Court refused
to intervene when magistrates found special reasons in the fact that the defendant
was a solicitor's articled clerk hurrying to quarter sessions to instruct counsel,
having been delayed en route, in order that he should not hold up the business of
the court.

Police Prosecutor v Humphreys above was specifically not applied by the
Divisional Court in *Robinson v DPP* [1989] R.T.R. 42 when dismissing the
defendant's appeal against a refusal by the Crown Court to find special reasons
for not endorsing his licence. The defendant, a solicitor living in the Cheltenham
area, received a call at 5am from an inexperienced clerk of his in Bristol indicating that a situation had arisen which could give rise to serious trouble. Having
heard on his car radio of a fall of snow blocking the motorway ahead of him, he
deliberately increased his speed to 92mph in order to reach a junction. Traffic was
light and conditions excellent. After being stopped by police, the defendant
continued his journey to Bristol, arriving one and a half hours later than planned
(by which time the situation had been defused). Applying *Chatters v Burke* [1986]
R.T.R. 396 (see § 21.41 above), the court held that the defendant had driven fast
for a considerable distance with the intention of driving further, and that despite
the paucity of traffic on the road he was driving at such a speed that the possibility existed of contact with another road user.

While the fact that the 70mph motorway speed limit is only exceeded by   **21.55**
10mph cannot by itself amount to a special reason, the fact that the limit was
unintentionally exceeded can be (*Marks v West Midland Police* at § 21.08).

It is not a special reason that a road subject to a limit of 30mph was often
mistakenly thought to be subject to one of 40mph, nor that the defendant was the
last of a line of vehicles driving at the same speed in such an area: *Jones v Nicks*
[1977] R.T.R. 72. Ignorance of the fact that a 30mph area is normally created by
a system of street lights placed not more than 200yds apart, and therefore a failure to appreciate, in such an area, that there was such a limit cannot be a special
reason. Street lights are readily visible whether at night or day and a motorist
should be alerted by them to the existence of the limit: *Walker v Rawlinson* [1976]
R.T.R. 94. However, where a motorist came from a 40mph area to a 30mph area
and genuinely thought he was still in a 40mph area because there was no 30mph
sign when leaving the 40mph area, it was held that this could amount to a special
reason (*Burgess v West* [1982] R.T.R. 269).

Motorways

A finding by justices of special reasons for not endorsing the licences of   **21.56**
several motorists who had performed U-turns across the central reservation of a
motorway where, because of an apparent blockage, there was a long line of

stationary vehicles in the motorists' lane and there had been no traffic on the opposite carriageway for some considerable time, was upheld by the Divisional Court in *Fruer v DPP*, *Siba v DPP*; *Ward v DPP* [1989] R.T.R. 29. At the material time the motorway was not in what might be described as "normal use"; the traffic was already stationary and the defendants had ample time to examine the opposite carriageway before making their turns. In the circumstances there was unlikely to be contact with other road users and no danger was either caused or likely to be caused. The cases turned very much upon their own special facts, however, and the court's decision was not to be regarded as a licence to cross a central reservation when traffic was flowing normally.

Accidents

21.57   Where the failure to report an accident was as a result of an emergency, or because the defendant was misled, e.g. where both parties are apparently agreed that the incident is too trivial to be reported, then special reasons could be found, it is submitted.

It is also an offence under what is now s.170(2) of the 1988 Act for a driver involved in an accident to fail to give his name and address and also the name and address of the owners of the bus to a person who had reasonable grounds for so requiring. A bus driver had a slight impact with a car which had pulled out very suddenly in front of the bus. The driver of the car got out and asked the bus driver for his name and address (he was wearing his bus driver's identity disk in a prominent position on his uniform) which he omitted to give. The justices on his pleading guilty endorsed his licence with six penalty points holding that the fact that there were other means of identification available to the lady car driver did not relieve the bus driver of his responsibility and found no special reasons for not endorsing his licence. The Divisional Court disagreed and held that on the very special facts of the case there was material which could constitute special reasons and remitted the case to the justices but also said (per Croom-Johnson J.): "We wish to make it clear we are laying down no general rule which applies to all cases where the identification of the driver is obvious" (*Leeman v Walton*, October 8, 1984, unreported, DC).

Driving whilst disqualified

21.58   A disqualified driver appealed to the High Court of Justiciary and his disqualification was suspended pending the appeal. Unbeknown to him, his solicitor's failure to deliver the case stated in due time led to the deemed abandonment of the appeal and hence the reimposition of his disqualification. In genuine ignorance of that reimposition, the defendant drove whilst disqualified. The High Court held in *Robertson v McNaughton* 1993 S.L.T. 1143, applying *Brewer v Metropolitan Police Commissioner* [1969] 1 All E.R. 513 (discussed at § 21.20), that his ignorance of the fact that he was disqualified was capable of amounting to a special reason, and that since he was genuinely unaware that his disqualification had been reimposed, no good reason existed for not treating his unawareness as a special reason for ordering that his licence should not be endorsed.

Construction and Use Regulations

21.59   Section 48 of the Road Traffic Offenders Act 1988 provides that where a person is convicted of an offence under the Road Vehicles (Construction and Use) Regulations 1986, being an offence for which endorsement or disqualification is obligatory, the court *cannot* order endorsement or disqualification or a driving test if he establishes that he did not know and had no reason to suspect that the facts were such that an offence had been committed. This provision was first enacted in the Road Traffic (Amendment) Act 1967 s.7. All cases relating to special reasons in respect of such offences prior to 1968 must therefore be read with this more recent provision in mind. It is intended to deal with the cases where, e.g. an innocent employee or partner has been convicted; and, unlike special reasons, it does not simply give to the court a discretion to mitigate the normal consequences, but precludes the court from imposing them if the relevant facts are established. It will assist not only the innocent employee or partner, but also the employee who is without fault, the private car owner who has relied on his garage, even the member of the family who uses the family car reasonably believing it to be free of any defects. See further § 8.104.

It is obviously sensible for any employer who owns vehicles driven by employees to form a limited company to run the business. Otherwise he will be at risk of endorsement on his own licence or driving record in respect of defects in those vehicles, and therefore of disqualification under the penalty points provisions. Even though the provision referred to above provides some protection for him, it may not always be easy to satisfy a court that his maintenance and supervision have been adequate to establish that he was free of fault.

SPECIAL REASONS: PRACTICE AND PROCEDURE

Onus of proof, etc.

21.60 The onus of proof of establishing special reasons is on the defendant (*Jones v English* [1951] 2 All E.R. 853). The standard of proof is the balance of probabilities (*Pugsley v Hunter* [1973] R.T.R. 284). Special reasons must be supported by evidence, and not mere assertion by advocates (*Jones v English* above, *Brown v Dyerson* [1968] 3 All E.R. 39, *R. v Lundt-Smith* [1964] 2 Q.B. 167 and *MacLean v Cork* [1968] Crim. L.R. 507). It is a desirable practice that the defence should notify the prosecution in advance where special reasons are to be argued (per Lord Widgery C.J. in *Pugsley v Hunter* [1973] R.T.R. 284). Where a defendant sought upon conviction of an excess alcohol offence to advance special reasons why he should not be disqualified, but failed to give notice of his intention to the prosecution, the prosecution should cross-examine the defendant on his failure to give notice so that the tribunal could consider whether that failure reflected on his bona fides (*DPP v O'Connor* [1992] R.T.R. 66). The Divisional Court also took the opportunity to review and approve the authorities (in particular *R. v Newton (David)* [1974] R.T.R. 451 discussed in § 21.61 below and *Pugsley v Hunter* above) and to provide guidance on the general approach to special reasons.

Admissions made by the prosecution under s.10 of the Criminal Justice Act 1967 would suffice in theory. But the court should always examine the facts as thoroughly as it can; and admissions may not always be a satisfactory form of proof.

21.61 Once the court has found special reasons to exist it is then not bound not to disqualify or endorse; it merely means that the court has a discretion not to disqualify for the minimum period or not to endorse. Having found special reasons the court should then decide whether to exercise its discretion (*R. v Newton (David)* [1974] R.T.R. 451), where it was held that if the blood-alcohol level is high or the impairment substantial the court is bound to take into account the fact that, whatever excuse the defendant may have had for drinking in the first place, he may have no proper excuse for driving or continuing to drive when he must or should have realised that he was affected by drink.

In *R. v Mander (Avtar Singh)* [2008] EWCA Crim 1521 the defendant had been convicted by a jury of dangerous driving. He was fined and disqualified from driving for 12 months, thereafter to take an extended retest. He unsuccessfully appealed against disqualification. Mr Mander was a taxi driver. In the early hours of the morning he feared that he was not going to be paid by his passengers, young men who had been drinking. He therefore drove to the nearest police station. However, some of the passengers had already left the vehicle, and the driver failed to ensure that the nearside sliding passenger door had been properly secured before driving off. He had travelled for a distance of nine-tenths of a mile when one of the passengers decided to jump out of the taxi. The passenger leapt through the open door and subsequently died from his injuries. The Court of Appeal emphasised the two-stage process in considering first whether special reasons exist and secondly whether the court in its discretion should not disqualify or disqualify for less than 12 months. It first determined that special reasons existed. There was an extenuating circumstance. It did not amount in law to a defence. It was directly connected with the commission of the offence and the matter was one which the court ought properly to take into consideration. Nevertheless there was no basis for interfering with the trial judge's conclusion in the exercise of his discretion that in all the circumstances it was appropriate to impose the minimum period of disqualification, in a case where on the facts there was an over-reaction by the appellant to not being paid.

It was said by Lord Widgery C.J. in *Taylor v Rajan* [1974] R.T.R. 304, an "emergency" case, that the discretion where special reasons are found should only be exercised in clear and compelling circumstances, that in deciding whether to exercise their discretion the justices should have regard to the way in which the car was driven, and that they should have regard to the defendant's level of alcohol. "If the alcohol content exceeds 100 milligrammes per 100 millilitres of blood the justices should rarely if ever exercise their discretion in favour of the defendant driver" (*per* Lord Widgery at 310F). Applying *Taylor v Rajan* it was held in *Vaughan v Duff* [1984] R.T.R. 376 that justices should be directed to disqualify where the defendant (who was a detective constable on an undercover operation which involved visiting public houses for which he was paid £2 a day drinking allowance) was so drunk that he drove straight into a lamppost without any vehicle being involved and when breathalysed had a reading of 100µg, nearly three times the permitted limit.

21.62   Whether facts are, or are not, capable of amounting to special reasons is a matter of law, not of fact. Justices are well advised to consult their clerk and hear from the defence and the prosecution before deciding that special reasons exist. In *Barnes v Gevaux* [1981] R.T.R. 236 justices decided that the special circumstances of a careless driving offence amounted to a special reason for not endorsing the licence. The justices declined to state the special reasons or, at the clerk's suggestion, hear any submission from the prosecution and the defence. The Divisional Court held the justices to be wrong: although what is now s.47(1) of the 1988 Offenders Act is directory not mandatory, the justices should have allowed both the prosecutor and the defence to make submissions on the matter. It is well within the prosecutor's field "to bring to the justices' attention the jurisdictional limitations which exist on their power to decide whether to disqualify or to refrain from endorsing in a case which would otherwise be mandatory" (per Donaldson L.J. at 241).

The evidence upon which the court acts must be admissible evidence, not hearsay: *Flewitt v Horvath* (1972) 136 J.P. Jo. 164. Where it is suggested that the defendant's drink was "laced", medical or other expert evidence should be adduced to show that, but for the added drink, the defendant would not have been over the limit, unless this would be obvious to the layman: *Pugsley v Hunter* [1973] R.T.R. 284, § 21.25 above. If the defendant is intending to argue that special reasons exist by reason of the fact that his drink was "laced", he should inform the prosecution in sufficient time before the hearing for the police to make inquiries: ibid.

If the court finds special reasons established, the reason must be stated in open **21.63** court and, if in a magistrates' court, also entered in the court register: Road Traffic Offenders Act 1988 s.47. This requirement is directory and not mandatory and failure to comply is not of itself a ground of appeal by the prosecutor (*Brown v Dyerson* [1968] 3 All E.R. 39), but not where the justices refused to specify the special reasons (*Barnes v Gevaux* [1981] R.T.R. 236).

MITIGATING CIRCUMSTANCES

Penalty points disqualification

The *Report of the Inter-Departmental Committee on Road Traffic Law* **21.64** (HMSO, 1981) decided that the grounds on which courts may refrain from disqualifying should be restricted in view of the fact that, unlike the "totting-up" system, the penalty points system discriminates according to the seriousness of the offence. The committee recommended that a person liable to be disqualified under the penalty points system should be allowed to put forward mitigating circumstances in the same way as for "totting up", but recommended that none of the following circumstances should be allowed to be taken into account:

(a) any that are alleged to make the offence or any of the offences not a serious one;

(b) hardship, other than exceptional hardship; and

(c) any circumstances taken into account by a court when the offender escaped disqualification or was disqualified for less than the minimum period on a previous occasion when he was liable to be disqualified under s.35(1) of the 1988 Offenders Act.

These recommendations were accepted by the Government of the day and are embodied in what is now s.35(4) of the 1988 Offenders Act. One other useful and practical recommendation of the committee was either overlooked or rejected. This was that where mitigating circumstances were to be put forward advance notice should be given in order that there may be an opportunity for them to be challenged.

21.65   The general statutory formula which enables a court not to disqualify or to disqualify for a period less than the minimum period in s.35(1) of the 1988 Offenders Act is identical with the former words in s.93(3) of the 1972 Act and is *unless the court is satisfied, having regard to all the circumstances, that there are grounds for mitigating the normal consequences of the conviction.*

It should be noted that analysis of the words of s.35(1) seems to show the following two propositions:

(1) It is for the court to be satisfied that there are mitigating circumstances before the court can exercise its discretion not to disqualify for at least six months. It is suggested that the question the court might ask itself is "Are the mitigating circumstances sufficient to justify us in not disqualifying the offender for not less than six months?" *not* "Ought the offender to be disqualified?"

(2) Mitigating circumstances must be found if the court disqualifies for *less than six months*. Obviously the mitigating circumstances must be much greater to justify the court not disqualifying at all rather than merely reducing the period of disqualification. The more the period of disqualification is reduced, the greater should be the mitigating circumstances.

21.66   In *Lambie v Woodage* [1972] 2 All E.R. 462 the House of Lords held that the purpose of s.93(3) of the 1972 Act was to deal with the man who does not commit serious offences and that the subsection is aimed at the person who commits comparatively trivial offences frequently. It was held by the House of Lords in *Lambie v Woodage* that evidence that the previous convictions were for trivial offences was admissible. *Lambie v Woodage* does not apply to mitigating circumstances for the purposes of s.35(1) of the 1988 Offenders Act. One of the grounds now specifically excluded from consideration by a court is "any circumstances that are alleged to make the offence or any of the offences not a serious one" (s.35(4)(c)) (see below).

It was said in *Baker v Cole* [1971] 3 All E.R. 680 *Note* that anything which amounts to a special reason can be taken into account by the court under what is now s.35(1) of the 1988 Offenders Act and so can reasons special to the offender as well as those special to the offence, for the wording is intended to catch circumstances wider than those which constitute special reasons.

21.67   In *R. v Thomas* [1984] Crim. L.R. 49 the appellant aged 25 was convicted of two offences of driving while disqualified. He was disqualified for two years, the judge being bound by what is now s.35(2)(b) to impose a mandatory disqualification of two years by reason of previous disqualification. It was held that the general sentencing policy of not imposing a long term of disqualification on a persistent motoring offender who is sentenced to a term of imprisonment was a "ground for mitigating the normal consequences of conviction" and the Court of Appeal reduced the disqualification to 12 months.

In *R. v Preston* [1986] R.T.R. 136 the rehabilitation of a defendant was considered to be a mitigating circumstance *not* excluded by what is now s.35(4) of the 1988 Offenders Act. The case involved the theft of a motor car hired to the defendant under a hire-purchase agreement. The Court of Appeal was unable to find special reasons for not endorsing since the reasons advanced by the defendant (driving not specifically involved) applied to every case of theft by a hirer in such circumstances. The defendant already had eight points on his licence in respect of a car theft committed *before* the matter with which the court was dealing. The court (albeit with some hesitation) felt able, in the light of his previous record and with rehabilitation in mind (the defendant generally drove for a living), to mitigate the normal consequences of his conviction; accordingly his disqualification for six months was quashed. (It should be noted here that as a result of amendments made to the 1988 Offenders Act by the Road Traffic Act 1991, an offence of stealing a motor vehicle is not endorsable; see § 19.01.)

MITIGATING CIRCUMSTANCES: EXCLUDED GROUNDS

Circumstances alleged to make the offence not serious

Section 35(4)(a) of the 1988 Offenders Act excludes "any circumstances that are alleged to make the offence or any of the offences not a serious one". The effect of this exclusion seems clear: an advocate cannot avoid a penalty points disqualification by alleging that the particular offence or any of the offences do not justify the penalty points which have been imposed or would be imposed but for the disqualification. The exclusion seems to refer both to the instant offence or offences which brings the number of penalty points up to 12 and also to the offences for which previous penalty points were incurred. It is also clear that this exclusion does not prevent the advocate putting forward "special reasons" for not endorsing the offender's licence on the ground that the offence or offences are not serious. (As already explained, if special reasons for not endorsing an offender's licence are found, no penalty points are incurred.) Indeed, the effect of the exclusion is to force the advocate who wishes to avoid disqualification for his client because of the nature of the offence to confine his advocacy to special reasons for not endorsing in accordance with s.44(2) of the 1988 Offenders Act. Although triviality of the offence is not itself a special reason for not endorsing (see *Nicholson v Brown* at § 21.07), special reasons relate necessarily to the offence and not the offender (see § 21.04). The effect of this exclusion is to nullify the effect of *Lambie v Woodage* above.

21.68

Hardship other than exceptional hardship

The exclusion of "hardship, other than exceptional hardship" is contained in s.35(4)(b) of the 1988 Offenders Act. Almost every order of disqualification entails hardship for the person disqualified. It will be for the courts to interpret this phrase. For hardship to be "exceptional" it must be more than is normally suffered. Loss of employment, e.g. undoubtedly causes hardship, and many offenders lose their jobs if disqualified, but whether loss of employment amounts to "exceptional hardship" to the offender is a matter of fact and degree to be determined in each case. This was the question specifically considered by the High Court of Justiciary in *Brennan v McKay* (1996) 1997 S.L.T. 603. The appellant was a taxi driver who had faced a penalty points disqualification under s.35(1) of the 1988 Offenders Act as a result of a conviction for speeding. He had submitted that the loss of his licence would probably result in the loss of his job and that he would have difficulty in finding another; this would cause hardship to his family. He had been disqualified for six months. On his appeal the court referred to *Allan v Barclay* 1986 S.C.C.R. 111 and *Howdle v Davidson* 1994 S.C.C.R. 751 and held that, although the disqualification would cause hardship, this would not amount to "exceptional hardship" within s.35(4)(b) ibid.

21.69

It seems clear that the word "hardship" is not confined to the hardship that the disqualification will cause to the offender: often hardship will be caused to persons other than the offender who are wholly innocent and will suffer hardship if the offender is disqualified (see, e.g. *Cornwall v Coke* [1976] Crim. L.R. 519). It is submitted that a court may properly take more notice of hardship where it is caused either to the public or to the offender's employer, employees or family, and, depending on the degree of hardship, hardship to persons other than the offender may more readily be regarded as "exceptional hardship" than hardship to the offender himself. The offender's family or employees are innocent; the defendant himself, by definition, is not.

21.70   The phrase "exceptional hardship" in s.3(2) of the Matrimonial Causes Act 1973 (which enabled a petitioner to obtain leave to present a petition for divorce within three years of marriage) was considered by the House of Lords in *Fay v Fay* [1982] 2 All E.R. 922. Although many of the considerations adverted to in the case are irrelevant for the purpose of considering the meaning of "hardship, other than exceptional hardship" in a criminal statute, it is submitted that the approach to the problem as set out in the speech of Lord Scarman (who gave the only reasoned speech) is helpful to a court considering whether exceptional hardship exists for the purpose of s.35(4)(b) of the 1988 Offenders Act. The speech of Lord Scarman appears to show:

    (a) that in choosing the imprecise concept of "exceptional hardship" Parliament deliberately intended that what is or is not "exceptional hardship" should be a matter of fact for the judge at first instance to decide by making his own subjective value judgment;

    (b) that it would be wrong for an appellate court to attempt to define the concept of "exceptional hardship" with any precision or to attempt to lay down guidelines as to how the concept should be applied; and

    (c) that the decision of the judge at first instance should be treated as final unless it can be shown to be clearly wrong.

It is submitted that this approach is one which may be broadly applied by a criminal court in considering whether "exceptional hardship" exists.

21.71   The first consideration is that s.35(4)(b) requires the defendant to satisfy the court on the balance of probabilities that exceptional hardship other than ordinary hardship exists. The burden of establishing exceptional hardship is on the defendant. The court must disqualify the offender for the minimum period unless the court is satisfied exceptional hardship exists.

The second consideration is that what is exceptional hardship is a question of fact to be judged by the court on evidence. All that can be said with certainty is that the hardship must be something "out of the ordinary" (*per* Connor L.J. cited with approval by Lord Scarman at 926g). While the court in *Fay v Fay* was dealing with past as well as present and future suffering, a court in applying s.35(4)(b) is of necessity considering future suffering only. Nevertheless the principle stressed in *Fay v Fay* that there must be evidence of the degree of the circumstances relied on to show the character of the hardship to be exceptional seems to be equally applicable to a criminal court in deciding whether exceptional hardship exists.

21.72   The third consideration, namely that the appellate court will only intervene if the inferior court is clearly in the wrong, is no doubt correct when there is an appeal on law by way of case stated from the magistrates' court to the Divisional

Court. It does not seem to apply so cogently, however, to an appeal against sentence from the magistrates' court to the Crown Court which is by way of rehearing of the facts.

A defendant who had unsuccessfully pleaded exceptional hardship as a mitigating circumstance, both in the magistrates' court and at the Crown Court on appeal, applied for judicial review of the decision of the Crown Court on the ground that it had failed to provide reasons for its decision. It was held in *R. (on the application of Purnell) v Blackfriars Crown Court* [2002] EWHC 526 that, whilst a court was under a duty to give its reasons, where the only issue was exceptional hardship it was normally sufficient for the court to state that the facts advanced by the driver did not constitute such exceptional hardship. Article 6 of the European Convention on Human Rights required reasons to be given for a decision, but it did not require a written note of the reasons for the decision, provided that sufficient reasons were given (as they had been in the case in point).

Any circumstances previously taken into account

The exclusion regarding circumstances previously taken into account is set out **21.73** in s.35(4)(c) of the 1988 Offenders Act. Circumstances which were taken into account on an earlier occasion either for not disqualifying or for disqualifying for a lesser period of disqualification than the minimum are excluded by s.35(4)(c).

Oddly, the period during which circumstances are excluded differs between s.35(2) and s.35(4). Section 35(2) provides that the minimum period of disqualification is increased to 12 months (or two years if more than one) if a previous disqualification was imposed "within the three years immediately preceding the commission of the latest offence". The period for excluding circumstances under s.35(4) previously taken into account is "within three years immediately preceding the conviction". This difference could be slightly unfortunate. The effect is to encourage an unscrupulous offender in an appropriate case to endeavour to delay his conviction for an offence for which he will again be liable to a s.35(1) disqualification in order to try to get outside the three-year period and put forward similar circumstances to those put forward on the previous occasion.

The main difficulty, however, in the operation of s.35(4)(c) is to decide whether **21.74** or not circumstances put forward were put forward on the previous occasion. Although a court is required to state the grounds for not disqualifying and, if it is a magistrates' court, to enter the grounds in the register (s.47(1)), it often may be difficult to ascertain all the circumstances taken into account earlier. Even if an extract from the court register of the previous occasion is available, the full circumstances will rarely be disclosed in the register. It is likely that, for this reason, most courts will insist on the circumstances being fully set out. It would not be improper for the prosecution similarly to keep a record of the circumstances where an offender is not disqualified or is disqualified for less than the minimum period.

The evidential onus is on the defendant to show that the circumstances being put forward on a second occasion differ from those put forward and accepted by the court on the first occasion (*R. v Sandbach JJ. Ex p. Pescud* (1984) 5 Cr. App. R. (S) 177). He may do so by ensuring that a certified extract of the relevant court register is available to the court or he may do so by calling evidence. Should he be unable to do either of those things there and then, he may apply for an adjournment; whether such be granted is a matter for the court's discretion.

MITIGATING CIRCUMSTANCES: PRACTICE AND PROCEDURE

Onus of proof, etc.

21.75   As in the case of "special reasons", the onus of proof in establishing "mitigating circumstances" is on the defendant (*Owen v Jones* [1988] R.T.R. 102). Whilst in the vast majority of cases courts will require evidence upon which to satisfy themselves that, e.g. exceptional hardship has been made out, there may be circumstances in which a bench might rely upon information which they believed to be true based upon their own knowledge (ibid.). The facts of the case concerned were somewhat unusual. The defendant, who was liable to a penalty points disqualification, was a police officer. The justices did not hear evidence from the defendant or on his behalf as to mitigating circumstances although invited to do so by his solicitor. They heard instead a plea in mitigation from his solicitor which suggested that as a police officer he would be likely to lose both house and job if disqualified. That corresponded with the justices' own belief. They accordingly declined to disqualify him on grounds of exceptional hardship. The prosecutor's appeal was dismissed by the Divisional Court.

It is respectfully submitted that the decision in this case appears to arise from a laudable desire not to overturn a just decision of an inferior court and does not of itself establish any new principle of law. Indeed, Watkins L.J. delivering the leading judgment was at pains to point out that justices should not easily come to the conclusion that their belief was sufficient for such a purpose unless it was well founded on facts known to them; whilst it might prove to be so in exceptional cases, in the vast majority of cases evidence ought to be called.

21.76   If the court finds mitigating circumstances established they must be stated in open court and if in a magistrates' court entered in the court register (1988 Offenders Act s.47). It is particularly important that s.47 be fully complied with, in that once mitigating circumstances are found they may not be put forward again (see above). It was held in *Brown v Dyerson* [1968] 3 All E.R. 39 that the requirement in what is now s.47 is directory, not mandatory, and failure to comply with it is not appealable (*aliter* if the justices refuse to specify them (*Barnes v Gevaux* [1981] R.T.R. 236)).

CHAPTER 22

APPEALS

CONTENTS

" It is constantly said (although I am not sure that it is sufficiently remembered) that the function of a court of appeal is to exercise its powers when it is satisfied that the judgment below was wrong, not merely because it is not satisfied that the judgment was right. " (Lord Goddard C.J. in *Stepney Borough Council v Joffe* [1949] 1 K.B., at 602, 603, quoted with approval by Edmund Davies L.J. in *Sagnata Ltd v Norwich Corporation* [1971] 2 Q.B. 614.)

INTRODUCTION

Rights of appeal

Appeals from magistrates' courts lie to the Crown Court by the defendant against conviction or sentence or both and the High Court by the defendant or prosecutor against conviction or dismissal and, to a limited extent, sentence. The appeal to the High Court will be heard by a Divisional Court of the Queen's Bench Division.   **22.01**

Sections 35 and 36 of the Criminal Justice Act 1988 provide the Attorney General with a power to refer certain cases of what appears to him to be "unduly lenient" sentencing in the Crown Court to the Court of Appeal for review; on such a reference that court is empowered to quash the sentence of the lower court and pass in its place a more appropriate sentence (see § 22.45 below).

Part 9 (ss.57–74) of the Criminal Justice Act 2003 in so far as implemented, makes provision for the prosecution to have the right, in relation to trial on indictment, to appeal to the Court of Appeal in respect of the judge's rulings, including evidentiary rulings. Section 58 of the 2003 Act allows the prosecution to challenge rulings of the Crown Court which would otherwise bring proceedings in a particular case to an end, in such a way that, if the ruling in question were found to have been in error, it would be possible for the prosecution to continue. This provision applies to proceedings committed or sent for trial after implementation on April 4, 2005. Provision for appeals against evidentiary rulings which significantly weaken the prosecution case (2003 Act ss.62–67) were not in force as of the time of writing (March 2009). However, an "evidentiary" ruling within s.62 of the 2003 Act could also be a ruling "which relates to one or more offences   **22.02**

included within the indictment" within s.58 (*Prosecution Appeal (No.2 of 2008);*
R. v Y [2008] EWCA Crim 10; [2008] 2 All ER 484.

There is provision for any appeal under Pt 9 of the 2003 Act to be expedited by
the judge. A ruling may not be reversed by the Court of Appeal unless it was
wrong in law, or involved an error of law or principle, or was one that it was not
reasonable for the judge to have made.

Appeals generally

22.03   Where a sentence or order of a magistrates' court is clearly wrong or has been
made or imposed as a result of an obvious error, a defendant should be immediately advised to ask the court to rectify the mistake under s.142 of the Magistrates' Courts Act 1980. The powers of magistrates' courts to rectify mistakes
under s.142 were considerably widened as a result of the amendments made to
that section with effect from January 1, 1996 by s.26 of the Criminal Appeal Act
1995. Particular note should be taken of the removal of the former 28-day time-
limit for the reconsideration of cases; the court may reopen a case at any time
where it appears to the court that it is in the interests of justice to do so. The
court's powers may be exercised regardless of the defendant's plea, and there is a
requirement for the court to be constituted in a particular way. The powers may
not be exercised, however, where the Crown Court has already determined an appeal upon the matter or the High Court has determined a case stated arising from
it (see further § 2.188).

The Divisional Court emphasised the breadth of the discretion vested in justices under s.142 of the Magistrates' Courts Act 1980 in *R. v Newport JJ. Ex p.
Carey* (1996) 160 J.P. 613, a case where the decision of the justices concerned
was taken before the above-described amendments made to s.142 by the Criminal Appeal Act 1995 were brought into force. The justices were entitled to take
into account the fact that the defendant, through his own fault, had failed to appear and that witnesses would be inconvenienced by a retrial. In refusing to set
aside the defendant's conviction the justices were not finally shutting the door
upon the defendant since he retained an unfettered right of appeal to the Crown
Court under s.108 of the 1980 Act.

22.04   Where justices discovered subsequently to passing sentence that they had erred
in law in arriving at that sentence, s.142 of the Magistrates' Courts Act 1980
empowered them (subject at that time, of course, to the then 28-day time-limit) to
reconvene the court in order to reconsider, and, where appropriate, to increase
their sentence. The Divisional Court so held in *Jane v Broome, The Times,*
November 2, 1987, when dealing with a case in which justices had in the first
instance erroneously concluded that their findings of fact could amount in law to
special reasons for not disqualifying a defendant convicted of driving with excess
alcohol. The 12 months' disqualification imposed subsequently by the reconvened
court was accordingly a valid order.

A motorist was charged with dangerous and careless driving arising out of the
same incident. The justices dismissed the summons for dangerous driving but
convicted the defendant of careless driving. It was not until they had retired to
consider sentence that it was discovered that the summons in respect of the lesser
offence had been issued out of time. They accordingly set aside that conviction
under s.142 of the 1980 Act and convicted the defendant of careless driving
under the alternative verdict provisions of s.24 of the 1988 Offenders Act (see

§ 5.20). The Divisional Court in *R. v Haywards Heath JJ. Ex p. White* (2000) 164 J.P.N. 685 upheld that conviction as a valid exercise of their powers under s.142.

Justices have no power to reopen a case under s.142 of the Magistrates' Courts **22.05** Act 1980 where the prosecution has withdrawn the charges, since the defendant thereupon ceases to be an "offender" within the meaning of the statute. The Divisional Court so held in *Coles v Camborne JJ., The Times*, July 27, 1998 when allowing an appeal against the subsequent revocation by the justices of a defendant's costs order made in pursuance of s.16(1) of the Prosecution of Offences Act 1985.

A defendant's advisers should carefully consider the position where he wishes to appeal against conviction. If his case is strong on law and facts, the case will end completely if the Crown Court allows his appeal on the facts. If, however, the Crown Court decides the appeal in his favour on a point of law only, this gives to the prosecution the right to appeal to the High Court from the decision of the Crown Court, with consequent delay and further expense. Also, though a defendant can on an appeal to the Crown Court call additional witnesses or refrain from calling witnesses who were unhelpful before the magistrates, the prosecution can do the same in order to bolster up weaknesses in their own case. Quaere whether an appellant may appeal to the Crown Court and seek certiorari simultaneously.

If the defendant's case rests on law only, appeal by case stated may at first **22.06** sight appear to be the better course. Where the possible success of the appeal will depend largely on the facts as found by the magistrates, the appeal may have to be abandoned if, when the case is finally agreed, the facts as stated leave little room for argument on a point of law. Moreover, if a recognisance to prosecute the appeal to the High Court has been entered into, there is danger of its forfeiture, and, more important still, once a notice to state a case has been given any right of appeal to the Crown Court ceases (Magistrates' Courts Act 1980 s.111(4)). A late and accordingly statute-barred application to state a case is nevertheless an application for these purposes and will trigger the mechanism of the section (see *P & M Supplies (Essex) Ltd v Hackney* below). The right of appeal to the Crown Court ceases even if the application to state a case is subsequently abandoned (*R. v Winchester Crown Court Ex p. Lewington* [1982] Crim. L.R. 664). In *Fairgrieve v Newman* [1986] Crim. L.R. 47 the Divisional Court again drew attention to the difficulty for an appellant that an appeal to the High Court against the justices' decision to allow the amendment of an information precludes appeal to the Crown Court and an unsuccessful appeal to the Crown Court will prevent any appeal to the High Court. It would seem, however, that an appellant by way of case stated does not need the leave of the High Court to withdraw his appeal and apply instead to the justices to reopen his case in accordance with their powers under s.142 of the Magistrates' Courts Act 1980 (*Collett v Bromsgrove District Council* [1997] Crim. L.R. 206).

If there is a danger of time-limits for giving notices expiring or having expired it should also be borne in mind that, while the time-limit for giving notice to state a case to a magistrates' court cannot be extended, leave to appeal out of time to the Crown Court can be granted. Moreover the time-limit of 21 days which applies when asking the Crown Court to state a case can, unlike the notice to a magistrates' court for a case stated, be extended by the Crown Court (Criminal Procedure Rules 2005 r.63.2(3)).

22.07   Where a statute provided for the bringing of an appeal within 21 days, and the 21st day was one when the court offices were closed, filing of the request for entry of the appeal on the first working day thereafter came within the time-limit since it could only be effected when the offices were open. The Court of Appeal so held in *Aadan v Brent London Borough Council, The Times*, December 3, 1999, when considering the provisions of the CCR Ord.2 r.4. It should be noted in the context of appeals in criminal matters that time limits are generally capable of extension in any event where appropriate.

Suspension of disqualification pending appeal

22.08   By s.39(1) of the 1988 Offenders Act, a person who by virtue of an order of a magistrates' court is disqualified from driving may appeal against the order in the same way as against a conviction, and the court may, if it thinks fit, pending the appeal, suspend the operation of the order. The wording suggests that the disqualification may be suspended only if there is an appeal against the order of disqualification; a defendant wishing to appeal against his conviction should presumably include an appeal against the order of disqualification also in his notice of appeal and later abandon it if he fears that the Crown Court may increase the period of disqualification.

A defendant convicted of a number of motoring offences was sentenced inter alia to 12 months' disqualification from driving. He appealed against the convictions but did not apply to have his disqualification suspended pending the outcome of his appeal. Whilst awaiting the hearing of his appeal he was twice stopped whilst driving and charged inter alia with driving whilst disqualified. In due course his appeal against the convictions which had given rise to the order of disqualification was successful and those convictions were quashed. It was unsurprisingly held by the Divisional Court in *R. v Thames Magistrates' Court Ex p. Levy, The Times*, July 17, 1997, applying *R. v Lynn* [1971] R.T.R. 369 (discussed at § 11.77) that the defendant had been rightly convicted of driving whilst disqualified when, pending an appeal, he nevertheless drove a motor vehicle whilst an order of disqualification was lawfully in force.

22.09   When a statutory declaration under s.14 of the Magistrates' Courts Act 1980 was served upon a justices' clerk the earlier summons, the earlier proceedings and the disqualification became void from that time onwards, but not from any earlier point in time since, although the section provided in terms that the proceedings should be void, it did not suggest they should be void ab initio. Thus a driver who drove whilst subject to an order of disqualification on a date prior to the making by him of the statutory declaration was rightly convicted of driving whilst disqualified. The Divisional Court so held in *Singh v DPP* [1999] Crim. L.R. 914, and the decision is on all fours in analogical terms with that in *R. v Thames Magistrates' Court Ex p. Levy*, discussed above. (For the statutory declaration procedure, see § 2.76.)

There is an appeal, with the leave of the Court of Appeal, Criminal Division, to that court against an order of disqualification imposed by a Crown Court whether on conviction on indictment there or on dealing with a person committed for sentence (Criminal Appeal Act 1968 ss.9, 10(3), 11(1) and 50(1)). The time for appealing is 28 days but it may be extended with the Court of Appeal's leave.

22.10   Although it would appear from a reading of ss.39(1) and 40(2) of the 1988 Offenders Act that the Crown Court may suspend its own order of disqualification, the circumstances must be rare in practice in which it would be either proper or appropriate for application for suspension to be made to the Crown Court rather than to the Court of Appeal. It is submitted that an application to suspend any order of disqualification can only be made when there is an appeal pending or, in the case of a conviction by the Crown Court, when application has been made for leave to appeal. An appeal or application for leave to appeal can only be pending once notice in the appropriate form is served on the Registrar of the Court of Appeal in accordance with r.68.3 of the Criminal Procedure Rules 2005. Once notice has been so served, a single judge of the Court of Appeal has power to suspend the order of disqualification (Criminal Appeal Act 1968 s.31(2A)), and where he refuses an application, the applicant is entitled to have the application determined by the Court of Appeal (Criminal Appeal Act 1968 s.31(3)).

In Scotland, there is an appeal against a disqualification ordered by any court and the latter court may suspend it pending the appeal.

Until 1975 only the court which disqualified the offender could suspend the **22.11** disqualification, but by virtue of ss.40 and 41 of the 1988 Offenders Act appellate courts can suspend an order of disqualification imposed by the court of first instance. These sections were inserted in the Road Traffic Act 1972 (the relevant parts of which are now contained in the 1988 Offenders Act) by Sch.3 to the Road Traffic Act 1974 and enable all appellate courts other than the House of Lords to suspend an order of disqualification pending appeal. It is submitted that because an appeal to the Crown Court can only be commenced by giving notice in writing (see r.63.2(2) and r.63.3(1) of the Criminal Procedure Rules 2005) a court should not suspend an order of disqualification pending appeal until such notice has first been given. A Crown Court may suspend an order of disqualification pending the hearing of an appeal from a magistrates' court (s.40(2)); the High Court may do so on appeal by way of case stated from a magistrates' court or Crown Court (s.40(4)), or on application for certiorari or for leave to make such an application (s.40(5)); the Court of Appeal may do so on appeal or application for leave to appeal (s.40(2)). Similar powers apply to Scottish appellate courts (s.41). The Court of Appeal or the Divisional Court may suspend an order of disqualification on appeal, or after application has been made for leave to appeal to the House of Lords (s.40(3)). Disqualification must be endorsed on any licence held or to be held by the defendant (s.44) (except an order of disqualification under s.147 of the Powers of Criminal Courts (Sentencing) Act 2000 (see §§ 20.58–64)).

Disqualification is not suspended by notice of appeal alone (*Kidner v Daniels* (1910) 74 J.P. 127). Although a court is empowered by s.39 to suspend an order of disqualification of its own volition, in practice it would never do so unless the defendant had made an application (per Glidewell L.J. in *Taylor v Commissioner of Police of the Metropolis*, *The Times*, November 3, 1986).

There seems to be no appeal against refusal to suspend but if the court of first **22.12** instance has refused to suspend, application may be made to the appellate court and, seemingly, vice versa. A power to suspend also exists where the appeal is from the magistrates to the High Court. On suspending an order of disqualification pending appeal, the court suspending the order must notify the Department for Transport (1988 Offenders Act ss.40(7), (8) and 41(3), (4)). The power to suspend an order of disqualification pending appeal applies to an order of disqualification for use of a vehicle for crime (see §§ 20.58–64).

By s.43 of the 1988 Offenders Act in calculating the period for which a person is disqualified, by conviction or order, any time after conviction during which the disqualification was suspended or he was not disqualified shall be disregarded. Thus, if Jehu is convicted of driving under the influence of drink on July 1, 2009 and disqualified from driving for a year but immediately appeals and has the disqualification suspended the same day until the appeal is heard, the period of disqualification will run from the hearing of the appeal. If the Crown Court affirms the disqualification on October 1, 2009, he will be disqualified from then until the first moment of October 1, 2010. Again, if Toad is convicted of dangerous driving on August 1, 2009 and the magistrates omit to disqualify and the High Court, on appeal by the prosecutor, directs on December 4, 2009 that he be disqualified for a year, his disqualification will run from then until the first moment of December 4, 2010.

22.13   Days during which disqualification runs prior to suspension should be subtracted from the period running from the date of the appeal. Thus if Jehu was disqualified on July 1, 2009 for 12 months and appeals to the Crown Court who on August 1, suspend the disqualification pending hearing the appeal and on October 10, hear and dismiss Jehu's appeal, Jehu then again becomes disqualified on October 10, and remains disqualified until September 10, 2010.

Where an appeal is abandoned it would seem that an order of disqualification which is suspended pending the appeal will again come into effect as soon as the appeal is abandoned.

22.14   Any licence held by a person who is disqualified is revoked (unless the disqualification is for less than 56 days; 1988 Offenders Act s.37(1A)) and where the disqualification is suspended pending appeal the licence is treated as revoked on the day on which the disqualification ceases to be suspended (1988 Offenders Act s.37).

CROWN COURT

Scope of right and procedure

22.15   Appeals to the Crown Court from magistrates' courts are regulated by ss.108–110 of the Magistrates' Courts Act 1980 and rr.63.1–63.10 of the Criminal Procedure Rules 2005. The rules apply to appeals from the magistrates' court in a number of circumstances, including appeals under the Magistrates' Courts Act 1980 s.108, but also the Powers of Criminal Courts (Sentencing) Act 2000 Sch.3 para.10 and the Costs in Criminal Cases (General) Regulations 1986, and, giving effect to the decision in *Tucker and Haw v City of Westminster Magistrates' Court* [2007] EWHC 2960; [2008] Q.B. 888 (where it was held that a person convicted in a magistrates' court of contempt of court may appeal to the Crown Court against conviction and sentence under s.12(5) of the Contempt of Court Act 1981; there is no right of appeal against conviction or sentence to the High Court, although appeal could be taken there by case stated or judicial review), contempt of court. The appeal notice must be in writing and must specify a number of matters set out in r.63.3. The *Consolidated Criminal Practice Direction* [2002] 1 W.L.R. 2870 sets out a form of appeal notice for use in connection with r.63.3. Notice may be served as soon after the decision appealed against as the appellant wants, but not more than 21 days after sentence or the date sentence is deferred, whichever is the earlier (if the appeal is against conviction or against a finding of guilt), or sentence (if the appeal is against sentence) or the order or a failure to make an order about which the appellant wants to appeal (in any other case) (r.63.2). There is provision to apply for an extension of the time-limit. In *R. (on the application of Latimer) v Bury Magistrates' Court* [2008] EWHC 2213; (2008) 172 J.P.N. 773, a notice of appeal under the Town and Country Planning Act 1990 was sent by first class post to the magistrates' court, but at some stage the letter was lost. The court decided (acting on advice from its clerk) that the appeal had not been lodged in time. It was held on appeal to the High Court that the advice that because the letter could not be found, as a matter of law, no appeal was lodged in time, was not advice upon which the court could properly act. Its decision was quashed.

It would also seem that the Crown Court has an inherent jurisdiction to reinstate an appeal (*Hagon v Croydon LBC* [1976] Crim. L.R. 632).

22.16 Appeal lies against sentence only; "sentence" includes any order made on conviction by the magistrates, not being an order of conditional discharge, an order for payment of costs or "an order made in pursuance of any enactment under which the court has no discretion as to the making of the order or as to its terms" (Magistrates' Courts Act 1980 s. 108(3)(d)). An obligatory disqualification under s.34(1) or s.35(1) of the 1988 Offenders Act, it is submitted, comes within this definition and it is for this reason that statutory provision has been made (s.38(1)) specifically allowing an appeal to be made against such orders in the same manner as against a conviction. A discretionary order of disqualification under s.34(2) is appealable (*R. v Surrey Quarter Sessions Ex p. Commissioner of Police of the Metropolis* (1962) 126 J.P. 269) but, it is submitted, neither an endorsement nor an order for the payment of back-duty under s.30 of the Vehicle Excise and Registration Act 1994 may be appealable as both types of order appear to come within the definition under s.108(3)(d) above. There is a right of appeal in respect of the number of penalty points endorsed where the offence is one in which the court has a discretion as to the number of points to be imposed. Section 108(3)(d) only prohibits an appeal against sentence where the court has no discretion as to the order "on its terms". Quaere however as to whether "special reasons" gives a court discretion for the purpose of s.108. If it does not, why did Parliament enact s.38(1) (see above)? However, if an appeal is lodged against sentence generally, it would seem to be open to the Crown Court in considering sentence to review an order of endorsement or as to back-duty.

The Crown Court on an appeal against sentence has power to decide the factual basis of the sentence afresh and accordingly may determine the appeal on a basis of fact which differs materially from that adopted in the court below. That basis should be determined in precisely the same way as on a plea to an indictment. Where, however, the Crown Court decides not to accept the express view of the magistrates, it should make this clear to the appellant in question (*Bussey v DPP* [1998] Crim. L.R. 908).

22.17 Whether or not the appeal is against the whole of the decision, the Crown Court may increase or lessen the sentence provided the punishment is one which the magistrates' court might have awarded (Supreme Court Act 1981 s.48(4), (5)). On an appeal against disqualification from driving, however, it was wrong in principle for a court to quash the disqualification and make up for that by quadrupling the fine originally imposed by the justices: *R. v Maidstone Crown*

Court Ex p. Litchfield, The Times, June 30, 1992. Whilst it was open to the Crown Court to increase a fine, it was usual to give a defendant a warning and an opportunity to consider whether or not to pursue the appeal. In the light of *Dutta v Westcott* [1986] Crim. L.R. 677 and s.156 of the Criminal Justice Act 1988, the Crown Court may also deal with *all* matters which were adjudicated upon by the justices notwithstanding that the defendant has limited his appeal to one offence only (see further § 22.24). The court must not adjourn cases for sentence, however, in order to give itself increased sentencing powers if those powers would not have been available to the justices when *they* passed sentence (*Arthur v Stringer* [1987] Crim. L.R. 563; see further below). The same period of notice applies whether the appeal is against conviction, sentence or other order, and the other side and the magistrates' court officer must be notified.

A defendant appealed against the number of penalty points awarded against him for driving with excess alcohol where special reasons for not disqualifying him had been found by the magistrates, since the points concerned (11) had caused him in any event to be the recipient of a penalty points disqualification for six months as a result of the three points already endorsed on his licence. The Crown Court decided that in the light of the very high level of alcohol in the defendant's blood, the magistrates had wrongly exercised their discretion not to disqualify for special reasons, and accordingly increased the disqualification to a period of one year (presumably under s.34(1) of the 1988 Offenders Act). The Administrative Court held in *R. (on the application of Tottman) v DPP* [2004] EWHC 258 that it was not open to the Crown Court to extend the period of disqualification on the basis of extended findings of fact in circumstances where the court had not indicated that it was considering doing so and the defendant had had no opportunity to make submissions or give evidence. If the court had intended to follow that course it should have given a clear warning to that effect, since without such a warning there had been procedural unfairness.

22.18   If the defendant pleads guilty and the plea is unequivocal, there is no appeal to the Crown Court against conviction, but if the plea is equivocal, the case may be remitted by the Crown Court for hearing of a plea of not guilty. But a Crown Court has no jurisdiction to remit a case for rehearing on a plea of not guilty unless it has first made proper inquiries into the circumstance surrounding the guilty plea and has satisfied itself that the plea was equivocal (*R. v Manchester Crown Court Ex p. Anderton* [1980] Crim. L.R. 303). Provided that proper inquiry is made into the circumstances surrounding the defendant's plea before the justices, the Crown Court has the power to remit a case to the justices for rehearing on the basis that the defendant's plea was equivocal; in such an event the justices are bound to hear the case (*R. v Plymouth JJ. Ex p. Hart* [1986] 2 All E.R. 452). (See also § 2.151 as to equivocal pleas.)

The magistrates' court officer must, as soon as practicable, serve on the Crown Court officer: the appeal notice and any accompanying application served by the appellant; details of the parties including their addresses; a copy of each magistrates' court register entry relating to the decision under appeal and to any application for bail pending appeal; and any reports received for the purposes of sentencing (Criminal Procedure Rules 2005 r.63.4).

22.19   No recognisance is required for the appellant to prosecute an appeal to the Crown Court.

There is no appeal by the prosecutor to the Crown Court in road traffic prosecutions, unless there be one in an excise prosecution (Customs and Excise Management Act 1979 s.147(3)).

An appeal against conviction is a rehearing, and either side may call additional **22.20** witnesses or refrain from calling witnesses called before the justices. The prosecution call their evidence first and then the defence theirs. A defendant who is represented by counsel on his appeal to the Crown Court does not have to be physically present in court; he is *deemed* to be present in accordance with s.122 of the Magistrates' Courts Act 1980 (*R. v Croydon Crown Court Ex p. Clair* [1986] 2 All E.R. 716). The Crown Court may confirm, reverse or vary the justices' decision or remit it to them with their opinion, and exercise any power which the magistrates could have exercised. The Crown Court may not have regard to evidence given before the magistrates but not before it (*Bishop v Hosier, Guardian*, October 11, 1962). The Crown Court has no power to amend an information on appeal (*Garfield v Maddocks* [1973] 2 All E.R. 303). *Garfield v Maddocks* was followed by the Divisional Court in *Fairgrieve v Newman* [1986] Crim. L.R. 47. The appellant had originally been charged with a Pelican crossing offence; the justices allowed the prosecutor to amend the information to disclose a traffic signal offence instead. In dismissing the appeal, the court drew attention to the difficulty for an appellant that an appeal to the High Court against the justices' decision to allow the amendment precludes appeal to the Crown Court and an unsuccessful appeal to the Crown Court will prevent any appeal to the High Court.

Fairgrieve v Newman above was followed by the Divisional Court in *R. v Swansea Crown Court Ex p. Stacey* [1990] Crim. L.R. 260 in which it was stated that it is now settled law that the Crown Court has no jurisdiction to amend a defective information. Since, however, the defect in question was not such as to mislead the defendant (date of offence incorrectly stated as one day later than it should have been) the case was remitted to the Crown Court to continue with the unamended information.

Where a person convicted or sentenced by a magistrates' court desires to ap- **22.21** peal to the Crown Court, either court may order that a right to representation be granted to him (Access to Justice Act 1999 Sch.3).

Where the appeal is against conviction or sentence the Crown Court may increase or lessen the sentence, provided that the punishment is one which the magistrates' court might have awarded (Supreme Court Act 1981 s.48(4)). The court may not adjourn after convicting a person and before sentencing him in order that he may attain an age such that the court's sentencing powers in respect of him are altered; its sentencing powers on appeal are limited to those which the justices might have exercised when *they* passed sentence (*Arthur v Stringer* [1987] Crim. L.R. 563). The powers of the Crown Court contained in s.48 apply whether or not the appeal is against the whole of the magistrates' court's decision (s.48(5)) and by s.48(2)(c) the Crown Court may make "such other order in the matter as the court thinks just, and by such order exercise any power which the [magistrates' court] might have exercised".

Either party to the appeal to the Crown Court may, if dissatisfied with the de- **22.22** termination of the court as being erroneous in point of law, apply to have a case stated by the Crown Court for the opinion of the Divisional Court (Supreme Court Act 1981 s.28). The application must be made in writing to the Crown Court within 21 days of the decision but the Crown Court may extend the time for making application to state a case (Criminal Procedure Rules 2005 r.64.7(14)). A right to representation may be granted to an individual appellant or respondent under Sch.3 to the Access to Justice Act 1999. Appeal will lie from the High Court, with leave, to the House of Lords (Administration of Justice Act 1960 s.1), provided that the court below certifies that a point of law of general public importance is involved.

An application by the prosecution to the Crown Court to state a case to the Divisional Court out of time against the acquittal of a defendant (in the case in point, an acquittal on a charge of failing to supply a specimen of breath) may be dealt with by the Crown Court judge sitting on his own (*DPP v Coleman (Valerie)*, *The Times*, December 13, 1997). On any such application, however, the defendant must be given notice of the application and an opportunity to respond to all representations made on behalf of the prosecution. Such applications only rarely called for oral hearings.

22.23   Once notice of appeal has been given the appellate court, as well as the court of first instance, may suspend an order of disqualification pending appeal (see §§ 22.08–14).

Offences heard at the same time

22.24   The procedure as to appeal and suspension pending appeal (see §§ 22.08–14) is the same as for an appeal against any other obligatory disqualification with one qualification. This is caused by the fact that by virtue of s.35(3) of the 1988 Offenders Act not more than one order of disqualification under s.35(1) may be imposed where an offender is convicted on the same occasion of more than one offence. Section 35(3)(c) accordingly provides that for the purpose of any appeal any disqualification under s.35(1) will be treated as an order made on the conviction of each of the offences.

Section 48 of the Supreme Court Act 1981 was amended by s.156 of the Criminal Justice Act 1988 in order to give statutory effect to the Divisional Court decision of *Dutta v Westcott* [1986] 3 All E.R. 381. That case decided that where a defendant convicted of a number of offences committed on the same occasion appealed only in respect of the offence meriting the highest number of penalty points, the Crown Court was nevertheless empowered on a broad interpretation of s.48 as it then was to deal with the *whole* of the decision made by the justices and not merely the particular decision appealed against; therefore penalty points could be imposed as appropriate for other subsisting offences. The amendment introduced by the 1988 Act replaced the words "the decision appealed against" in s.48(2) with the words "any part of the decision appealed against, including a determination not to impose a separate penalty in respect of an offence".

Abandonment of appeal

22.25   The appellant may abandon an appeal without the Crown Court's permission by serving a notice of abandonment on the magistrates' court officer, the Crown Court officer, and every other party, before the hearing of the appeal begins. The former requirement to give notice not later than the third day before the hearing fixed for the appeal was removed with effect from October 6, 2008. However, once the hearing of the appeal begins, the appellant may abandon the appeal only with the Crown Court's permission. A notice of abandonment must be signed by or on behalf of the appellant. When an appellant who is on bail pending appeal abandons an appeal he must surrender to custody as directed by the magistrates' court officer, and any conditions of bail apply until then. When an appellant abandons an appeal to the Crown Court, both the Crown Court and the magistrates' court have power to make a costs order against that appellant in favour of the respondent (see s.52 of the Supreme Court Act 1981 and s.109 of the Magistrates' Courts Act 1980). Part 78 of the Criminal Procedure Rules 2005 contains rules on costs.

It was held in *R. (on the application of Hayes) v Chelmsford Crown Court* [2003] EWHC 73; *The Times*, January 30, 2003 that it was not open to the Crown Court to conclude that a defendant on bail who persistently failed to appear was wilfully frustrating the course of the proceedings and that his repeated failure to attend amounted to an abandonment of his appeal. Accordingly where it appeared that a defendant, who was obliged to attend, had deliberately absented himself, the court was obliged to hear the appeal in his absence.

If any period of disqualification has been suspended pending appeal, the period **22.26** of disqualification will commence to run as soon as the appeal is abandoned. If notice to abandon is not given in time, it would seem that the period of disqualification runs from any date upon which leave to abandon is given, or if no such leave has been given, upon dismissal of the appeal. Once a valid notice of abandonment has been given, the Crown Court cannot hear an appeal (*R. v Essex Quarter Sessions Ex p. Larkin* [1961] 3 All E.R. 930).

Where the appeal is abandoned or dismissed, the magistrates' court may issue process for enforcing their original decision (Magistrates' Courts Act 1980 ss.109 and 110). It would seem that if the licence has not been surrendered on abandonment or dismissal of the appeal, the magistrates' court has the power and duty to obtain the licence under ss.109 and 110 for the purpose of endorsement and sending to the Secretary of State. Any licence held by a person who is disqualified for 56 days or more is treated as revoked; where the disqualification is suspended pending an appeal, the licence is treated as revoked on the day on which the disqualification ceases to be suspended (1988 Offenders Act s.37(1A), (2)).

Constitution of the Crown Court

On the hearing of an appeal the general rule is that the Crown Court must **22.27** comprise a judge of the High Court, a circuit judge or a recorder and no less than two and no more than four justices of the peace, none of whom took part in the decision under appeal. If the appeal is from a youth court, each justice of the peace must be qualified to sit as a member of a youth court and the Crown Court must include a man and a woman. The Crown Court may include only one justice of the peace and need not include both a man and a woman if the presiding judge decides that otherwise the start of the appeal hearing will be delayed unreasonably, or one of the justices of the peace who started hearing the appeal is absent (Criminal Procedure Rules 2005 r.63.10).

HIGH COURT

Cases stated

Either side may appeal to the High Court from a decision of a magistrates' **22.28** court on the ground that it is wrong in law or in excess of jurisdiction (Magistrates' Courts Act 1980 s.111; Criminal Procedure Rules 2005 rr.64.1–6). The Divisional Court re-emphasised in *James v Chief Constable of Kent, The Times,* June 7, 1986 that an appeal by way of case stated is for an examination as to whether justices have erred on matters of law. The proper remedy for a defendant aggrieved by a decision of justices as to matters of fact is an appeal to the Crown Court. Written notice has to be given to the magistrates' court officer requiring the magistrates to state a case for the opinion of the High Court. It has to be given within 21 days from, and excluding, the day on which the justices finally disposed of the matter. The time for giving notice cannot be extended (*Michael v Gowland* [1977] 2 All E.R. 328). Sundays are included in the computation of the period (*Peacock v R.* (1858) 22 J.P. 403).

Rule 64.2(1) of the 2005 Rules places on the magistrates' court officer the responsibility for delivering the first draft of the case to the parties concerned. The intention is thereby to place on the magistrates' court officer the responsibility for preparing the initial draft unless the justices wish to assume the responsibility themselves. A detailed timetable is prescribed by the rules. A period of 21 days is allowed for delivery by the magistrates' court officer of the first draft to the parties (r.64.2(1)), a further period of 21 days is allowed for the parties to make representations after receiving the case and a final period of 21 days for the case to be settled by the court after having received the parties' observations. It was held in *Parsons v F.W. Woolworth & Co Ltd* (1980) 124 S.J. 775 that what is now r.64.2(1) is directory not mandatory. Rule 64.4 enables those time-limits to be extended but if there is a delay a written statement of the reasons for it must accompany the final case. Rule 64.1 requires the applicant to identify the point of law upon which the opinion of the High Court is sought or, where the point of law is that there was insufficient evidence to support the decision, r.64.1(2) provides that the application must identify the particular finding of fact which cannot be supported by the evidence. If the notice does not state the point of law it is a nullity, and the Divisional Court will not allow such a defective notice to be amended if the amendment is itself out of time (see (1980) 144 J.P. 303). But in *Robinson v Whittle* (1980) 124 S.J. 807 it was held that the requirement in (what is now) r.64.1(2) to state the point is directory not mandatory (the case referred to in 144 J.P. 303 was not, apparently, brought to the court's attention: *Robinson* is to be preferred, it is submitted).

22.29   It is not necessary for the justices in explaining their conclusions in any case stated to analyse every evidential issue that has arisen or to explain how they dealt with each of the conflicts between the witnesses, so long as their material findings on the important issues, together with their reasons for those findings, are sufficiently clear and comprehensible: *R. v Filmer* [2006] EWHC 3450; [2007] R.T.R. 28. On the other hand, the parties should ensure that the account of the evidence given in the draft case is sufficient, because it is impermissible to seek to supplement the case stated on the hearing of the appeal by reliance on notes of evidence taken at the hearing before the magistrates' court: *DSG Retail Ltd v Stockton on Tees Borough Council* [2007] A.C.D. 163 (38); [2007] C.L.W.25/2. This was reinforced in *Piggott v DPP* [2008] EWHC 305; [2008] R.T.R. 16 where it was said again that in an appeal by case stated the parties are bound by the terms of the case as stated by the magistrates. That applies with equal force to both the CPS and the defendant in the criminal proceedings. Other than documents referred to in the case stated, further evidence as to what the justices did or did not find is inadmissible. If either party is dissatisfied with the case as stated, then the appropriate remedy is to seek permission to apply for judicial review for an order of mandamus requiring the justices to amend or restate the case. "If that is not done, the parties, and this court, must simply do their best with the case as stated": [2008] EWHC 305 at [11], per Sullivan L.J.

Justices have no jurisdiction to state a case under s.111 unless and until they have reached a final determination on the matter before them. Similarly the Divisional Court has no jurisdiction to consider and determine such a case if justices nevertheless purport to state one (*Streames v Copping* [1985] R.T.R. 264). The proper course for a party aggrieved by a decision of justices *in medias res* might be, in a very special instance, to apply for judicial review with a view to obtaining an order of prohibition (see further §§ 22.35–44).

Justices are entitled, unless the application is by the Attorney General, to re-   **22.30**
fuse to state a case on the ground that the application is frivolous and if the applicant so requires shall give him a certificate to that effect (s.111(5)). In an appeal to the Court of Appeal the question for the court was whether the appeal was "frivolous or vexatious". The Court of Appeal held that the word frivolous in s.20 of the Criminal Appeal Act 1968 could not be intended to mean only foolish or silly, but must mean that the ground of appeal was one that could not possibly succeed on argument (*R. v Taylor* [1979] Crim. L.R. 649). It is submitted that "frivolous" in s.111(5) should be similarly interpreted.

Where justices refuse to state a case, the High Court on application by the person who applied for a case to be stated may by order of mandamus require a case to be stated (s.111(6)).

Hitherto the High Court has not been prepared to hear argument on any point   **22.31**
not raised before the magistrates' court. As the point of law is now required to be stated in the application, it may well be that the High Court will not be prepared to hear or consider any argument on any other point of law (other than a point of jurisdiction) unless it arises on the face of the facts stated in the case or upon a point of law which no evidence could alter. It was said in *Whitehead v Haines* [1964] 2 All E.R. 530 that on an appeal by case stated the High Court should entertain and determine a point of pure law open, on the facts found in the case, to an appellant convicted on a criminal charge, if that point of law was one which, if sound, might afford him a defence, notwithstanding that the point was not raised prior to his conviction.

Generally, the appellant must argue his point on the facts as found by the justices and indicated in their case. But the decisions of magistrates that certain facts did amount to obstruction and that other facts did not amount to dangerous driving were upset by the High Court in *Gill v Carson* (1917) 81 J.P. 250 and *Bracegirdle v Oxley* [1947] 1 All E.R. 126 respectively. The High Court can confirm, reverse or vary the magistrates' determination and can send back the case for further hearing with the High Court's ruling. The Divisional Court will not usually interfere with findings of fact by magistrates unless there was no evidence to support those findings or they were such that no reasonable magistrates, giving themselves proper directions and applying the proper considerations, could reach them. *Bracegirdle's* case above was an example of a successful appeal by the prosecutor against the dismissal of a dangerous driving charge. The well-established principle that the Divisional Court will not usually interfere with findings of fact by a magistrates' court unless there was no evidence to support those findings also applies to a ruling as to the admissibility of evidence of bad character. Unless the High Court concluded that no reasonable tribunal could have decided as a magistrates' court had done, an appeal would be unsuccessful: *DPP v Chand* [2007] EWHC 90; (2007) 171 J.P. 285.

22.32 Appeals by the prosecution against sentence on a point of law are sometimes brought where, e.g., an order of conditional discharge has been made and it is considered there has been an improper exercise of that power in view of the seriousness of the charge (*Gardner v James* [1948] 2 All E.R. 1069). They are frequently brought by prosecutors contesting a finding of special reasons.

Where the appellant abandons his appeal by way of case stated, there appears to be no statutory provision enabling the other party to obtain the costs incurred as a result. If, however, he has entered into a recognisance to prosecute his appeal, such recognisance can be forfeited. Although a forfeited recognisance is payable to the Crown and not to the respondent, it may be wise for a respondent, if he suspects that a case stated may be withdrawn by the appellant, to insist on a recognisance being entered into by the appellant. If this is done it is suggested that if the appellant wishes to withdraw his appeal the respondent should be able to request payment of his reasonable costs by the appellant or forfeit the appellant's recognisance. The conditions of an appellant's recognisance under s.114 of the Magistrates' Courts Act 1980 are to prosecute his appeal without delay, to submit to the judgment of the High Court and to pay any costs that the court may award.

22.33 Before requiring an applicant for a case to be stated to enter into a recognisance under s.114 of the 1980 Act to ensure that he prosecutes his appeal, justices must have due regard to the applicant's means in deciding whether to require a recognisance and, if so, its amount (*R. v Newcastle upon Tyne JJ. Ex p. Skinner* [1987] 1 All E.R. 349). Since the justices had clearly not taken means into account when requiring a recognisance of £500 from an applicant on supplementary benefit the case was referred back to them for reconsideration.

A right to representation may be granted to an individual appellant and/or respondent, as with other High Court proceedings, under the Access to Justice Act 1999 Sch.3.

22.34 Examining justices have no power to state a case (*Dewing v Cummings* [1971] R.T.R. 295, where the defendant elected trial on indictment on a charge under s.1(1) of the Road Safety Act 1967 (now s.5 of the 1988 Act), and the justices had found that there was no case to commit for trial). In the event of an unreasonable refusal to commit for trial, the prosecution can, if the facts warrant, apply to a judge of the High Court for a voluntary bill of indictment under the Administration of Justice (Miscellaneous Provisions) Act 1933 s.2. Examining magistrates do not come to a final decision when committing a defendant for trial and hence no case can be stated in respect of the decision to commit. Where however the magistrate is acting not as an examining magistrate, but deciding a preliminary issue as to jurisdiction, his ruling upon that is final and can properly be challenged by way of case stated or judicial review: *R. (on the application of Donnachie) v Cardiff Magistrates' Court* [2007] EWHC 1846; [2008] R.T.R. 2.

Appeal by either side will lie from the Divisional Court, with leave, to the House of Lords (Administration of Justice Act 1960, s.1), provided the Divisional Court certifies that a point of law of general public importance is involved.

The Divisional Court may suspend an order of disqualification pending hearing of an appeal by way of case stated, or on application for leave to apply for a writ of certiorari (see §§ 22.08–14).

Application for judicial review

Applications for judicial review must now comply with the Criminal Procedure Rules 2005, especially r.54.1. **22.35**

The textbooks will show the occasions for which an application by way of judicial review for orders of certiorari, mandamus and prohibition are appropriate. Where the error is obvious or undisputed, the situation can be rectified by an order under s.142 of the Magistrates' Courts Act 1980 (see § 22.03). In *R. v Kingston upon Thames JJ. Ex p. Khanna* [1986] R.T.R. 364 it was held that the writ of certiorari should issue to quash a conviction where the defendant had appealed to the Crown Court, who with the consent of both sides had remitted the case to the magistrates' court, who in turn had declined to hear the case, the justices holding themselves to be functi officio.

It should be noted that at the outset of the hearing of an application for judicial review an applicant who also has an appeal to the Crown Court pending should immediately inform the Divisional Court of that fact; failure so to do might well result in the matter being referred to the Crown Court as more suitable for determination there (*R. v Mid-Worcestershire JJ. Ex p. Hart*, *The Times*, December 17, 1988).

The House of Lords has held that the remedy of judicial review is concerned **22.36** not so much with the decision of which the review is sought but with the fairness of the decision-making process (*R. v Chief Constable of N Wales Police Ex p. Evans* [1982] 3 All E.R. 141). Where a defendant's previous drink/driving conviction was inadvertently disclosed to the Crown Court in the evidence produced by the respondents to his appeal against conviction of a similar offence, the defendant was entitled to an order of certiorari quashing the conviction. The Divisional Court so held in *R. v Cambridge Crown Court Ex p. Lindsey* [1991] R.T.R. 127. The previous conviction was both inadmissible and highly prejudicial and it could not be said by an objective observer that justice had been seen to be done.

A motorist and a woman gave perjured evidence to the Crown Court at the hearing of an appeal against conviction for not displaying "L" plates and driving with excess blood-alcohol, as a result of which convictions were set aside by the Crown Court. It was held that the Divisional Court had power on a hearing by way of judicial review to quash the decision of the Crown Court on appeal and thus restore the original conviction (*R. v Wolverhampton Crown Court Ex p. Crofts* [1983] R.T.R. 389).

R. v Wolverhampton Crown Court was followed in *Weight v Mackay* (1984) **22.37** 79 Cr. App. R. 324 where it was held that certiorari also lay to quash a decision of the Crown Court allowing an appeal not only where the Crown Court's decision had been obtained by fraud but also where the Crown Court had failed to comply with the rules of natural justice.

A defendant pleading not guilty to an alcohol-related offence wished to call two witnesses in his defence and witness summonses were issued for an adjourned hearing. At that hearing the witnesses failed to appear. The defendant's application for witness warrants was refused by the justices, and he was convicted. He applied for judicial review, which was successful, despite the fact that he also had a right of appeal to the Crown Court (*R. v Bradford JJ. Ex p. Wilkinson* (1990) 154 J.P. 225). Where there was, as here, an identifiable breach of natural justice it might well be appropriate to grant judicial review even though other remedies might be available.

22.38 *R. v Bradford JJ. Ex p. Wilkinson* was applied by the Divisional Court in *R. v Bristol Magistrates' Court Ex p. Rowles* [1994] R.T.R. 40 when granting an application for judicial review of a decision by justices to refuse the defendant's application for an adjournment for the attendance of two absent defence witnesses. The justices had proceeded under the misapprehension that the defendant had said he could go on without them. The Divisional Court stated that it had become the practice in accordance with *R. v Bradford JJ.* for cases involving the denial of natural justice to be accepted for judicial review without requiring the applicant to pursue an appeal to the Crown Court first; the proceedings were therefore properly launched. In *R. v Hereford Magistrates' Court Ex p. Rowlands*; *R. v Same Ex p. Ingram*; *R. v Harrow Youth Court Ex p. Prussia, The Times*, February 17, 1997 it was again emphasised that the existence of a right of appeal to the Crown Court did not preclude a person convicted of offences by the magistrates' court from seeking relief by way of judicial review where the complaint raised was of procedural impropriety, unfairness or bias.

It was held by the Divisional Court in *R. v Bolton Magistrates' Court Ex p. Scally* [1991] R.T.R. 84 that certiorari could be granted to quash convictions of motorists who had pleaded guilty to driving with excess alcohol in their blood without being aware that the blood tests on which the prosecution relied had been taken using cleansing swabs impregnated with alcohol. Although no dishonesty was involved, the process leading to conviction had been corrupted in a manner which was unfair and analogous to fraud, collusion or perjury. A free pardon would not be an appropriate remedy because it would not remove the conviction and the applicant would therefore be vulnerable to a minimum three-year disqualification if convicted of a further drink/driving offence within 10 years.

22.39 Seven applicants sought to challenge their convictions for offences of driving with excess alcohol on the basis that the police, in obtaining the relevant specimens as provided by ss.7 and 8 of the Road Traffic Act 1988, had failed to follow the relevant statutory procedure as subsequently laid down by the House of Lords in *DPP v Warren* [1992] 4 All E.R. 865 (see § 4.139). The Divisional Court held in *R. v Cheshire JJ. Ex p. Sinnott* [1995] R.T.R. 281 that the law as laid down in *Warren* was the law as it had always been, and it had been an error of law to allow the applicants to plead guilty; accordingly the court had jurisdiction to quash the convictions.

A quite contrary view was taken, however, by the Divisional Court in *R. v Dolgellau JJ. Ex p. Cartledge*; *R. v Penrith JJ. Ex p. Marks* [1996] R.T.R. 207, when holding that the court had no jurisdiction to quash a conviction which followed an unequivocal plea of guilty where no complaint was made of the conduct of the tribunal and where the conduct of the prosecution could not be fairly categorised as analogous to fraud. In both cases the police had taken specimens for analysis without following the procedure laid down in *DPP v Warren*. In reaching its conclusion the court drew upon the analysis of Buxton J. in *R. v Burton upon Trent JJ. Ex p. Woolley* [1995] R.T.R. 139 (see § 4.294) where he had said:

> "The jurisdiction is of a limited nature and there is no authority for recognising it as extending beyond conduct on the part of the prosecutor that can fairly be categorised as

analogous to fraud. It was, however, possible for conduct to be so categorised when there was no actual fraud or dishonesty ... Whether the conduct could be so categorised must be a matter of judgment for the court seised of the case looking at all the facts."

In *Cartledge's* case, which was decided before the decision of the House of **22.40** Lords in *Warren* was delivered, the prosecution could not be criticised for failing to anticipate that decision. The position in *Marks's* case was different, however, and it was submitted on his behalf that the prosecutor should have known of the decision in *Warren* and should have drawn the court's attention to it. Although there was some force in that argument, the circumstances of the case had not been put before the Divisional Court and it was possible that, if a plea of guilty had been indicated at an early stage, no further consideration would have been given to the question of the admissibility of the evidence of the analysis. In neither case had the conduct of the prosecution been "analogous to fraud". Furthermore, the court was satisfied that the motorists concerned had suffered no injustice. Unlike in cases where evidence which might have cast doubt upon guilt had been suppressed, there was in these cases no doubt as to their guilt. The court was not persuaded by the argument that had impressed the court in *Sinnott's* case, that since some people had had their convictions quashed without opposition from the Crown Prosecution Service it would be unfair to deny these motorists similar relief. The fact that some people had been so fortunate as to obtain an undeserved benefit did not mean that those who were not so lucky should have any justifiable sense of grievance or unfairness.

The divergence of view in the Divisional Court between *Sinnott's* case and *Woolley's* case, as examined by the court in the cases of *Cartledge* and *Marks*, is one which would undoubtedly benefit from the attention of the House of Lords. Prior to the occurrence of such a desirable event, however, it is cautiously submitted that *Woolley* is likely to prove the more fruitful authority.

The Divisional Court has jurisdiction to entertain an application for judicial **22.41** review of a forfeiture order made against the owner of property who was *not* a defendant in criminal proceedings, since the forfeiture order was not one relating to trial on indictment within the meaning of s.29(3) of the Supreme Court Act 1981. The words "matters relating to trial on indictment" were not to be read so widely as to deprive the applicant of a remedy in the event (as in the instant case) of an unjust order being made against him. The Divisional Court so held in *R. v Maidstone Crown Court Ex p. Gill* [1986] Crim. L.R. 737. (The facts of the case are set out at § 18.34 above.)

Costs on certiorari to remedy a mistake made by the magistrates should not be granted against them unless they have been guilty of deliberate misconduct (*R. v Amersham JJ. Ex p. Fanthorne* (1964) 108 S.J. 841). It was held that an order of certiorari cannot be used to quash a decision in order to introduce fresh evidence; but in *R. v Leyland JJ. Ex p. Hawthorn* [1979] R.T.R. 109 it was held that an order of certiorari could be made to quash a conviction by a magistrates' court on the grounds that there had been a denial of natural justice because the defendant had not been notified by the prosecution of the existence of witnesses known to the prosecution but whom the prosecution did not intend to call. In *R. v Wells St JJ. Ex p. Collett* [1981] R.T.R. 272 certiorari was refused where the defendant neither appealed to the Crown Court nor applied to the magistrates' court under what is now s.142 of the Magistrates' Courts Act 1980 and where it was not established there had been any fault on the part of the prosecution. In that case the defendant sold her car and subsequently was served with a request to serve a statutory statement of ownership under s.1(6) of the Road Traffic Act 1974. She was charged with failing to supply a statement and subsequently convicted in her absence. She sought certiorari on the ground she had posted a statement and had written saying that she had done so after receiving the summons.

22.42 An order of certiorari may be granted if the decision of the inferior tribunal was "harsh and oppressive" (*R. v St Albans Crown Court Ex p. Cinnamond* [1981] R.T.R. 139), or, to put it another way, the sentence is "so far outside the normal discretionary limits as to enable the court to say that its imposition must involve an error of law of some description, even if it may not be apparent at once what is the precise nature of that error" (per Donaldson L.J. at 144E). The applicant had been convicted by justices of driving with excess alcohol and of careless driving and was disqualified for a total of two years of which 21 months related to the excess alcohol charge. He appealed to St Albans Crown Court where the conviction for excess alcohol was quashed on technical grounds, but the sentence on the careless driving was varied from an order of disqualification of three months only for "totting up" to a disqualification of 18 months for the offence plus the consecutive period of three months for "totting up". An order of certiorari was granted and the disqualifications set aside, the court substituting an order of six months' disqualification for the offence and three months for "totting up". The *Cinnamond* principle was applied by the Divisional Court in *R. v Kingston Crown Court Ex p. Anderson* [1988] R.T.R. 368 in reducing a sentence for careless driving from a fine of £500 with £40 costs and 18 months' disqualification to one of a fine of £250 with no costs and three months' disqualification. The Crown Court had erred in allowing the fact that the defendant had provided a positive roadside breath test to influence its sentence, since such a test could not be relied upon to found a drink/driving conviction and the defendant had not been convicted of such an offence, nor of an offence of failing to provide a specimen for analysis. The Divisional Court has emphasised, however, in *Tucker v DPP* [1992] 4 All E.R. 901 that *R. v St Albans Crown Court Ex p. Cinnamond* should be regarded with circumspection in view of the narrowness of its application. A severe sentence imposed at the discretion of justices would only be varied if it appeared to be astonishing by any acceptable standards. The Divisional Court was not an appellate court. In all but the most exceptional circumstances the appropriate forum for those dissatisfied by a sentence imposed by magistrates was the Crown Court.

22.43 The view expressed in *Tucker v DPP* above to the effect that, in all but the most exceptional cases, the appropriate means of challenging a sentence imposed by justices was to appeal to the Crown Court, was endorsed by the Divisional Court in *R. v Ealing JJ. Ex p. Scrafield* [1994] R.T.R. 195. The court also pointed out the further drawback associated with the review procedure namely that on such an application (unlike an appeal by way of case stated) the court would not have the detailed facts or the justices' reasons before it. Although the matter under consideration was properly before the Divisional Court by leave of the court, that should not encourage other such applications when there was a right of appeal open and also a right to have a case stated to the Divisional Court. In the event, the 10-year disqualification imposed by justices upon a defendant who had pleaded guilty to driving with excess alcohol, driving whilst disqualified and without insurance was an appropriate sentence and the defendant's application for judicial review was refused.

An applicant is entitled to go to the Divisional Court from the Crown Court either by requiring the Crown Court to state a case under s.28 of the Supreme Court Act 1981 or by applying by way of judicial review for an order of mandamus, prohibition or certiorari under s.29. It was held in *R. v Ipswich Crown Court Ex p. Baldwin* [1981] 1 All E.R. 596 that the applicant may bring whichever proceeding is the more convenient in the circumstances, but where there is difficulty in obtaining the facts, the proper way to go to the Divisional Court is by way of case stated.

Where a defendant pleaded guilty by post before magistrates, any procedural **22.44** defect (such as a failure to have the defendant's mitigating circumstances read aloud to the court) might give rise to an application for judicial review; in such a case a declaration by the Divisional Court that the proceedings had been a nullity would have the effect of quashing the conviction but would not prevent a rehearing of the case before justices (*R. v Epping & Ongar JJ. Ex p. C Shippam*; *R. v Same Ex p. Breach* [1987] R.T.R. 233). It was not felt by the court that defendants should necessarily avoid the consequences of their plea of guilty.

REVIEWS OF SENTENCING

Sections 35 and 36 of, and Sch.3 to, the Criminal Justice Act 1988 provide the **22.45** Attorney General with a power to refer certain cases of what appears to him to be "unduly lenient" sentencing in the Crown Court to the Court of Appeal for review; on such a reference that court is empowered to quash the sentence of the lower court and pass in its place a more appropriate sentence. These sections provide that the power to review applies to sentences passed for offences triable only on indictment or such "either way" offences as may be specified by statutory instrument. The relevant statutory provisions are set out in Vol.2.

It should be noted that a decision to defer sentence is a sentence for the purposes of ss.35 and 36 and may as such be referred to the Court of Appeal as "unduly lenient" sentencing (*Att Gen's Reference No.22 of 1992 (Thomas)* [1993] Crim. L.R. 227; see further § 18.21).

ROYAL PARDON

Free pardon and remission of penalties

It sometimes happens that a defendant is convicted of an offence and afterwards **22.46** a decision of the High Court in another case shows that his conviction was wrong. In such circumstances he should be advised to apply to the Home Office for a royal pardon. If the defendant pleaded guilty on a mistake of fact (believing, e.g., that he was uninsured as his own policy did not cover him but subsequently finding that the car owner's policy covers him) he can apply to the Home Office for a *remission* under the Sovereign's royal prerogative. This has the effect of commanding the magistrates to remit the penalty imposed (Remission of Penalties Act 1859 s.1).

Appendices

DRINK/DRIVING

1A.01   See generally Chapter 4, Drink/Driving Offences. For evidential breath test devices, see §§ 4.175–195.

ALCOHOL CONCENTRATIONS

Conversion of breath-alcohol (µg/100ml) to blood/urine-alcohol (mg/100ml)

1A.02

Breath	Alcohol/ Blood	Urine	Breath	Alcohol/ Blood	Urine
26	60	80	83	190	254
27	62	83	85	195	260
28	64	86	87	200	267
29	67	89	89	205	274
30	69	92	91	210	280
31	71	95	94	215	287
32	74	98	96	220	294
33	76	101	98	225	300
34	78	104	100	230	307
35	80	107	102	235	314
37	85	113	105	240	321
39	90	120	107	245	327
41	95	127	109	250	334
43	100	133	111	255	341
45	105	140	113	260	347
48	110	147	115	265	354
50	115	153	118	270	361
52	120	160	120	275	367
54	125	167	122	280	374
56	130	173	65	150	200
59	135	180	67	155	207
61	140	187	70	160	214
63	145	193	72	165	220
74	170	227	124	285	381
76	175	234	126	290	387
78	180	240	129	295	394
80	185	247	131	300	401

To convert breath-alcohol readings outside of these figures, multiply breath-alcohol result by 2.3 and round to the nearest whole number to obtain the equivalent blood-alcohol reading; multiply by 3.06 for urine-alcohol reading.

TABLE OF METABOLIC LOSSES FOR BREATH AND BLOOD ANALYSES WITH TIME

(Annex A to cancelled Home Office circular of 1984)*

Breath (µg%)   **1A.03**

Blood (mg%)	15 min	30 min	45 min	60 min	75 min	90 min
35	33	31	30	28	26	25
80	76	72	68	65	61	57
40	38	36	35	33	31	30
92	88	84	80	77	73	69
45	43	41	40	38	36	35
103	99	95	91	88	84	80
50	48	46	45	43	41	40
115	111	107	103	100	96	92
55	53	51	50	48	46	45
126	122	118	114	111	107	103
60	58	56	55	53	51	50
138	134	130	126	123	119	115
65	63	61	60	58	56	55
149	145	141	137	137	130	126
70	68	66	65	63	61	60
161	157	153	149	146	142	138
75	73	71	70	68	66	65
172	168	164	160	157	153	149
80	78	76	75	73	71	70
184	180	176	172	169	165	161
85	83	81	80	78	76	75
195	191	187	183	180	176	172
90	88	86	85	83	81	80
207	203	199	195	192	188	184
95	93	91	90	88	86	85
218	214	210	206	203	199	195
100	98	96	95	93	91	90
230	226	222	218	215	211	207
105	103	101	100	98	96	95
241	237	233	229	226	222	218
110	108	106	105	103	101	100
253	249	245	241	238	234	230
115	113	111	110	108	106	105
264	260	256	252	249	245	241
120	118	116	115	113	111	110
276	272	268	264	261	257	253
125	123	121	120	118	116	115
287	283	279	275	272	268	264
130	128	126	125	123	121	120

| Breath (µg%) | | | | | | |
Blood (mg%)	15 min	30 min	45 min	60 min	75 min	90 min
299	295	291	287	284	280	276
135	133	131	130	128	126	125
310	306	302	298	295	291	287
140	138	136	135	133	131	130
322	318	314	310	307	303	299
145	143	141	140	138	136	135
333	329	325	321	318	314	310
150	148	146	145	143	141	140
345	341	337	333	330	326	322
155	153	151	150	148	146	145
356	352	348	344	341	337	333
160	158	156	155	153	151	150
368	364	360	356	353	349	345
165	163	161	160	158	156	155
379	375	371	367	364	360	356
170	168	166	165	163	161	160
391	387	383	379	376	372	368
175	173	171	170	168	166	165
402	398	394	390	387	383	379

1A.04   This table has been drawn up to aid persons who wish to compare breath and blood analysis, when the samples have been taken at different times.

When compiling the table, the following assumptions were made:

  (a) The subject has fully absorbed all of the alcohol consumed into his bloodstream.

  (b) The average metabolic rate of alcohol destruction by the body is 15mg/ 100ml/hour in the blood, and 6.5µg/100ml/hour in the breath.[1]

  (c) The blood/breath ratio is 2300:1.[2]

Each pair of numbers shows equivalent breath and blood concentrations, and each row is calculated to show how these values will decrease with the elapse of time in steps of 15 minutes.

For example, after 60 minutes have elapsed, a breath concentration of 70µg/ 100ml will, on average, drop to 63µg/100ml, and the corresponding blood concentration of 161mg/100ml will drop to 146mg/100ml.

Note. As a routine practice the Forensic Science laboratories make an allowance for analytical variation, by deducting 6 milligrammes from the blood analysis below 100 milligrammes per 100 millilitres, and 6% above this level, *before* they issue the certificate of analysis under the [*Road Traffic Offenders Act 1988*]. This table gives unadjusted figures. Thus the table shows that if a breath analysis of 50µg/100ml is obtained, the blood concentration at that time would be, on average, 115mg/100ml. A certificate of analysis of a blood sample taken an hour after this breath sample would, in a case of exact correspondence, show an alcohol concentration in the blood of not less than 94mg/100ml (94mg + 6mg FSS allowance + 15mg for time lapse = 115mg). Results will not always agree as exactly as this, due to variation in the metabolic rate and/or the blood/breath ratio between individuals.

References

[1] Walls H.J., Brownlie A.R. *Drink, Drugs and Driving* (Sweet & Maxwell, London, 1970).

[2] Isaacs M.D.J., Emerson V.J. et al., *8th International Conference on Alcohol, Drugs and Traffic, Safety* (Stockholm, 1980), p.442.

* It should be noted that the data collected for the *Report on Breath Alcohol Measuring Instruments* (HMSO, 1985) indicated a modal range of elimination of alcohol of 18–21mg/100ml per hour, a rate less favourable to accused persons than that set out in the table above; see further § 4.173.

1A.05   *Editorial note.*   The information reproduced below is exact, but the format is not the same because of technical difficulties in reproduction.

Camic Datamaster

OPERATIONAL SEQUENCE

1. Visual gas check. Gas module reading above 15 bar. No warning lights.

2. Fit new mouthpiece – check tube warm to touch. **Use a new mouthpiece for each subject.**

3. Press run.

4. Pick up print ticket and fill in details:
   Police Station
   Subject's name
   Date of Birth
   Operator's name

   Insert ticket.

5. If a keyboard is being used insert ticket and then, following the screen prompts, type in:
   Police Station ....Name
   Subject's name ................A.N. other
   Date of Birth ....27.03.1937 – if the subject will not give a date of birth it is acceptable to type in all zero's i.e. 00.00.0000.
   Operator's name ..............P.C. Smith

6. Wait for display to indicate "PLEASE BLOW" and sound pulsed tone.

7. Ask subject to blow until green light comes on.

8. Wait for second "PLEASE BLOW" request.

9. Ask subject to blow until green light comes on.

10. Wait for completed printout.

    Note.   1 Complete sequence aproximately 5 minutes.

    2 If pulsed tone restarts during a blow the subject needs to start again and blow a little harder.

    3 The subject has 3 minutes to provide each breath sample.

    4 If test is terminated before the end of normal cycle note error message and refer to Police procedures.

SAMPLE PRINTOUT

THIS SIDE DOWN

CAMIC DATAMASTER

RESULTS

INSTRUMENT SERIAL NO. 921061

MAY 04, 1995   16:59

POLICE STATION ....

SUBJECT'S NAME ....

DATE OF BIRTH ....

OPERATOR'S NAME ....

	ANALYSIS	G.M.T.
BLANK	0 µg/100ml	17:00
INTERNAL CHECK	OKAY	17:00
SIMULATOR CHECK 1	35 µg/100ml	17:00
BLANK	0 µg/100ml	17:01
BREATH SPECIMEN 1	45 µg/100ml	17:02
BLANK	0 µg/100ml	17:02
BREATH SPECIMEN 2	44 µg/100ml	17:03
BLANK	0 µg/100ml	17:03
SIMULATOR CHECK 2	36 µg/100ml	17:04

I certify that in this statement, reading one relates to the first specimen of breath provided by the subject named above and reading two to the second, at the date and time shown herein.

OPERATOR'S SIGNATURE ....

SUBJECT'S SIGNATURE ....

INTOXIMETER EC/IR

1A.07

Basic Operation

STEP	INSTRUCTION	DISPLAY
1.	Press ENTER key	TEST SUBJECT? (Y/N) Y
2.	Press ENTER.	OPERATOR
3.	Type in your name exactly as you did during your encodement. Capitals/lower case lettering must be reproduced exactly, or the code will not be accepted. Press ENTER.	OPERATOR ID
4.	Type in your ID NUMBER exactly as you did during you encodement. Press ENTER.	OPERATOR CODE
5.	Type in your operator code. Press ENTER.	SUBJ LAST NAME
6.	Type in the subject's last name (up to 20 characters). ENTER.	SUBJ FIRST NAME(S)
7.	Type in the subject's first name (up to 20 characters). ENTER.	SUBJ DOB (DD:MM:YY)
8.	Type in the subject's date of birth (two digits DAY, MONTH, YEAR). A valid entry is essential to enable the test to proceed. If no Date of Birth is available, follow force procedures. ENTER.	VERIFY DATA (Y/N)? N CHECKING SYSTEM
9.	If you wish to check your entries, type Y and ENTER Otherwise, ENTER. From this point until the end of the test, no entries are accepted from the keyboard. The display now moves through the sequence alongside. (It might appear to skip quickly to BLANK CHECK, as the sequence began during data entry.)	PURGING
		BLANK CHECK
		INTRODUCING STANDARD
		EVALUATING SAMPLE
		PURGING
		BLANK CHECK
		BLOW UNTIL IT BLEEPS

STEP	INSTRUCTION	DISPLAY

10. Unwrap a mouthpiece, taking care not to trap a part of the wrapping where it could enter the breath tube. Place the mouthpiece in the breath tube. The mouthpiece will only go in one way round and care must be taken not to touch the end to be presented to the subject except with the wrapping.

11. Instruct the subject to take a deep breath and blow into the mouthpiece as steadily and long as possible. Flowrate will be indicated by the *** characters. (If the subject does not submit a valid breath sample the unit will display SPECIMEN INCOMPLETE. Three minutes are allowed for a valid sample to be provided, failing which the test will be aborted and the printer will print all of the data gathered to that point followed by SPECIMEN 1 INCOMPLETE.) Leave the mouthpiece in place and rest the breath tube on the support clip.

   EVALUATING SAMPLE

   PURGING

   BLANK CHECK

   BLOW UNTIL IT BLEEPS

12. Instruct the subject to take a deep breath and blow into the mouthpiece as steadily and long as possible. Flowrate will be indicated by the *** characters. (If the subject does not submit a valid breath sample the unit will display SPECIMEN INCOMPLETE. Three minutes are allowed for a valid sample to be provided, failing which the test proceeds to a second simulator check and prints out a report followed by SPECIMEN 2 INCOMPLETE. See sample printouts in section 2.) Observe the subject test results on the instrument display. Remove the mouthpiece and discard, and return the breath tube to rest on the support clip.

   EVALUATING SAMPLE

   PURGING

   BLANK CHECK

   INTRODUCING STANDARD

   EVALUATING SAMPLE

   Spec. 1 [RESULT] µg/100ml.
   Spec. 2 [RESULT] µg/100ml.

   TEST NUMBER [NUMBER]

   PRINT ANOTHER COPY?
   (Y/N) N

13. Press Y and ENTER for another print copy. Otherwise, ENTER. Remove printouts.

   Instrument then returns to normal scrolling mode.

1A.08

Sample Printout

```
SUBJECT TEST

Intox EC/IR
SERIAL NUMBER:
01745

TEST NUMBER:
980212199
START DATE:
Thu 12 Feb 98
START TIME
08:57 GMT
LOCATION:
MIDDLETOWN POLICE
ANYTOWN

NAME:
JOHN
SMITH
DATE OF BIRTH:
08:10:44
SUBJECT SIGNATURE:
```

	Value µg/100ml	Time GMT
Blank	0	08:58
Simulator Check 1	35	08:59
Blank	0	09:00
Breath Specimen1	53	09:01
Blank	0	09:03
Breath Specimen2	54	09:04
Blank	0	09:06
Simulator Check 2	35	09:06
NO ERRORS		

I CERTIFY THAT IN THIS STATEMENT, READING ONE RELATES TO THE
FIRST SPECIMEN OF BREATH PROVIDED BY THE SUBJECT NAMED ABOVE
AND READING TWO TO THE SECOND, AT THE DATE AND TIME SHOW
HEREIN.

```
OPERATOR:
SGT JONES
OPERATOR SIGNATURE
```

LION INTOXYLIZER 6000UK

Sample Printouts

```
*********************************        *************************************
   BREATH ALCOHOL TEST RECORD              BREATH ALCOHOL TEST RECORD
     lion intoxylizer 6000UK                  lion intoxylizer 6000UK
  Serial Number: A0111 (UK 2.33)          Serial Number: A0111 (UK 2.33)

              TOWN                                   TOWN
            DIVISION                               DIVISION
             FORCE                                  FORCE

     Test Number: JJ/10019/97               Test Number: JJ/10001/97
       Thursday 8 May 1997                   Tuesday 15 April 1997

   Subject Name: GILES                    Subject Name: COLLINS
              Terence                               Phillip John Peter
  Date of Birth: 01-11-63 Sex: Male       Date of Birth: 12-03-45 Sex: Male
```

```
------------------------------------    -------------------------------------
   Subject Signature                       Subject Signature
TEST            BrAC      TIME - BST     TEST            BrAC      TIME - BST
                μg/100ml                                 μg/100ml
Blank 1         000       10:14:01       Blank 1         000       15:57:35
Simulator Check 1  036    10:14:30       Simulator Check 1  036    15:58:01
Blank 2         000       10:15:03       Blank 2         000       15:58:33
Breath Specimen 1  090    10:16:26       Breath Specimen 1  012    15:58:49
Blank 3         000       10:16:55       Blank 3         000       15:59:19
Breath Specimen 2  090    10:17:17       Breath Specimen 2  012    15:59:36
Blank 4         000       10:17:46       Blank 4         000       16:00:06
Simulator Check 2  036    10:18:15       Simulator Check 2  036    16:00:31
```

I certify that in this statement, reading one relates to the first specimen of breath provided by the subject named above and reading two the second, at the date and time shown herein.

    Operator Name: HIGGINBOTTOM JDE
        Rank: PC   PEN: 847621J

I certify that in this statement, reading one relates to the first specimen of breath provided by the subject named above and reading two the second, at the date and time shown herein.

    Operator Name: APPLETHWAITE PMJ
        Rank: INSP   PEN: 18234XT

```
------------------------------------    -------------------------------------
   Operator Signature                      Operator Signature
*********************************        *************************************
*********************************        *************************************
```

ENDORSEMENT AND SENTENCE CODES

2A.01   The information in the codes set out below is derived from the publication *DVLA Court Guidelines on Driver Notifications*, issued by the Driver and Vehicle Licensing Agency, Swansea (A671), as amended and from the Directgov website, see *http://www.direct.gov.uk/en/Motoring/DriverLicensing/index.htm* [Accessed May 5, 2009].

DVLA ENDORSEMENT CODES

	Code	Offence	Penalty points
2A.02			
		Accident offences	
	AC10	Failing to stop after an accident	5–10
	AC20	Failing to give particulars or to report an accident within 24 hours	5–10
	AC30	Undefined accident offences	4–9
		Disqualified driver	
	BA10	Driving while disqualified by order of court	6
	BA30	Attempting to drive while disqualified by order of court	6
		Careless driving	
	CD10	Driving without due care and attention	3–9
	CD20	Driving without reasonable consideration for other road users	3–9
	CD30	Driving without due care and attention or without reasonable consideration for other road users	3–9
	CD40	Causing death by careless driving when unfit through drink	3–11
	CD50	Causing death by careless driving when unfit through drugs	3–11
	CD60	Causing death by careless driving with alcohol level above the limit	3–11
	CD70	Causing death by careless driving then failing to supply specimen for analysis	3–11
	CD80	Causing death by careless or inconsiderate driving	3–11
	CD90	Causing death by driving unlicensed, disqualified or uninsured	3–11

Code	Offence	Penalty points
	Construction and Use offences	
CU10	Using a vehicle with defective brakes	3
CU20	Causing or likely to cause danger by reason of use of unsuitable vehicle or using a vehicle with parts or accessories (excluding brakes, steering or tyres) in a dangerous condition	3
CU30	Using a vehicle with defective tyre(s)	3
CU40	Using a vehicle with defective steering	3
CU50	Causing or likely to cause danger by reason of load or passengers	3
CU80	Breach of requirements as to control of vehicle, mobile telephones, etc.	3
	Reckless/Dangerous driving	
DD40	Dangerous driving	3–11
DD60	Manslaughter or culpable homicide while driving a motor vehicle	3–11
DD80	Causing death by dangerous driving	3–11
	Drink or drugs	
DR10	Driving or attempting to drive with alcohol concentration above limit	3–11
DR20	Driving or attempting to drive when unfit through drink	3–11
DR30	Driving or attempting to drive then failing to provide a specimen for analysis	3–11
DR40	In charge of a vehicle while alcohol level above limit	10
DR50	In charge of a vehicle while unfit through drink	10
DR60	Failure to provide a specimen for analysis in circumstances other than driving or attempting to drive	10
DR70	Failing to provide a specimen for breath test	4
DR80	Driving or attempting to drive when unfit through drugs	3–11
DR90	In charge of a vehicle when unfit through drugs	10
	Insurance offences	
IN10	Using a vehicle uninsured against third party risks	6–8
	Licence offences	
LC20	Driving otherwise than in accordance with a licence	3–6
LC30	Driving after making a false declaration about fitness when applying for a licence	3–6

Code	Offence	Penalty points
LC40	Driving a vehicle having failed to notify a disability	3–6
LC50	Driving after a licence has been revoked or refused on medical grounds	3–6

2A.03

Code	Offence	Penalty points
	Miscellaneous offences	
MS10	Leaving a vehicle in a dangerous position	3
MS20	Unlawful pillion riding	3
MS30	Play street offences	2
MS50	Motor racing on the highway	3–11
MS60	Offences not covered by other codes	As appropriate
MS70	Driving with uncorrected defective eyesight	3
MS80	Refusing to submit to an eyesight test	3
MS90	Failure to give information as to identity of driver, etc.	3
	Motorway offences	
MW10	Contravention of Special Roads Regulations (excluding speed limits)	3
	Pedestrian crossings	
PC10	Undefined contravention of Pedestrian Crossing Regulations	3
PC20	Contravention of Pedestrian Crossing Regulations with moving vehicle	3
PC30	Contravention of Pedestrian Crossing Regulations with stationary vehicle	3
	Speed limits	
SP10	Exceeding goods vehicle speed limits	3–6
SP20	Exceeding speed limit for type of vehicle (excluding goods or passenger vehicles)	3–6
SP30	Exceeding statutory speed limit on a public road	3–6
SP40	Exceeding passenger vehicle speed limit	3–6
SP50	Exceeding speed limit on a motorway	3–6
SP60	Undefined speed limit offence	3–6
	Traffic directions and signs	
TS10	Failing to comply with traffic light signals	3
TS20	Failing to comply with double white lines	3
TS30	Failing to comply with a "Stop" sign	3

Code	Offence	Penalty points
TS40	Failing to comply with direction of a constable/warden	3
TS50	Failing to comply with a traffic sign (excluding stop signs, traffic lights or double white lines)	3
TS60	Failure to comply with a school crossing patrol sign	3
TS70	Undefined failure to comply with a traffic direction sign	3

Totting disqualifications

| TT99 | Totting-up disqualification (12 penalty points within three years) | |

Theft or unauthorised taking

| UT50 | Aggravated taking of a vehicle | 3–11 |

Aiding, abetting, counselling or procuring
Offences as coded above, but with 0 changed to 2, e.g. IN10 becomes IN12.

Causing or permitting
Offences as coded above, but 0 is changed to 4, e.g. IN10 becomes IN14.

Inciting
Offences as coded above but 0 is changed to 6, eg IN10 becomes IN16.

Miscellaneous

NE96	Disqualification for non-payment of child support	
NE98	Disqualification for any offence under s.146, Powers of Criminal Courts (Sentencing) Act 2000	
NE99	Non-endorsable disqualification code. To be used where disqualification still relevant but endorsement no longer applicable.	

SENTENCE CODE

In the case of sentences other than fines or disqualification, the nature of the **2A.04** sentence is indicated on the driving licence by the following code which provides the first character of the endorsement:

A   Imprisonment
B   Detention in a place specified by the Secretary of State

C	Suspended sentence of imprisonment
D	Suspended sentence supervision order
E	Conditional discharge (max 3 years)
F	Bound over
G	Community punishment order (previously Probation)
H	Supervision order
I	No separate penalty
J	Absolute discharge
K	Attendance centre
L	Detention centre (Scottish courts only)
M	Community punishment order (previously Community service order)
P	Youth custody sentence (Scotland): Young offender institution (England and Wales)
Q	Parent or guardian order
R	Borstal (min 6 months, max 2 years)
S	Compensation order
T	Hospital or guardianship order
U	Admonition (Scottish courts only)
V	Young offender institution (Scottish courts only)
W	Care order
X	Total period of partially suspended prison sentence, i.e. period sentence served + period sentence suspended
#	Community punishment and rehabilitation order (previously Combination order) Curfew order
+	Action plan order
	Detention and training order
&	Reparation order
?	Drug treatment and training order
/	Curfew order with electronic monitoring

2A.05   If the first character of the endorsement is A, B, C, D, E, F, G, H, K, L, P, R, U, V or X, two digits and a character follow the initial character, indicating the duration of the sentence in hours, days, weeks, months or years (i.e. H, D, W, M or Y, respectively). For example, 18 months' imprisonment would be indicated by the code A 18 M. If no period is specified, the initial character is followed by three zeros.

If the first character of the endorsement is H, I, J, N, Q, S, T or W, three zeros follow the initial character. For example, absolute discharge would be indicated by the code J 000.

If the first character of the endorsement is M (community punishment order), three digits follow the initial character, indicating the number of hours' punishment (the letter H is not used). For example, 40 hours' community punishment would be indicated by the code M 040, 240 hours' by M 240.

If the first character of the endorsement is C (suspended prison sentence), two digits and a character follow the initial character, indicating the period the prison sentence has been suspended. For example, one month's prison suspended for one year would be indicated by A 01 M followed by C 01 Y.

If the first character of the endorsement is X (partially suspended prison sentence), the code is similar. Two digits and a character follow the initial character, indicating the period of prison sentence actually served. For example, four months' imprisonment with one month to be served would be indicated by A 04 M followed by X 01 M.

SENTENCING GUIDELINES

3A.01   In May 2008 the Sentencing Guidelines Council published the Magistrates' Court Sentencing Guidelines. The guidelines apply to all relevant cases appearing for allocation (mode of trial) or for sentence on or after August 4, 2008 and replace the guidelines which were effective from January 1, 2004. The new guidelines also supersede the part of the Practice Direction covering Mode of Trial Decisions (Pt V.51) in relation to offences contained within the guidelines. These definitive guidelines are available at *http://www.sentencing-guidelines.gov.uk* or can be obtained from the Sentencing Guidelines Secretariat at 4th Floor, 8–10 Great George Street, London SW1P 3AE.

Those parts of the Magistrates' Court Sentencing Guidelines that are most relevant to road traffic offences are published in this appendix with kind permission of the Sentencing Guidelines Council.

The Magistrates' Court Sentencing Guidelines have been a settled feature of magistrates' courts for many years. However, there is now for the first time a statutory obligation on every court to have regard to the new guideline in a relevant case and to give reasons when imposing a sentence outside the range identified.

The starting point for a guideline is for a first-time offender convicted after trial. Those who plead guilty, and in particular those who plead guilty at the first opportunity, receive a discount that in some cases can take the penalty below the range. Where there are previous convictions, and in particular where there are other aggravating features, the case can be sentenced above the range.

Most motoring offences are dealt with by a fine. The court will first identify the starting point from the relevant guideline. Then the court must identify aggravating and mitigating features that will move the seriousness of the offence up or down within the range. The detailed process for calculating a fine is set out from pp.145–155 of the guidelines (see pp.1256–1262 below). The guidelines take into account national prevalence.

Introduction
    [Not reproduced]   **3A.02**

User Guide

This user guide explains the key decisions involved in the sentencing process. A step-by-step summary
is provided on the pullout card.

1. Assess offence seriousness (culpability and harm)

Offence seriousness is the starting point for sentencing under the Criminal Justice Act 2003. The court's
assessment of offence seriousness will:

- determine which of the sentencing thresholds has been crossed;

- indicate whether a custodial, community or other sentence is the most appropriate;

- be the key factor in deciding the length of a custodial sentence, the onerousness of requirements
  to be incorporated in a community sentence and the amount of any fine imposed.

Effective from August 4, 2008

When considering the seriousness of any offence, the court must consider the offender's **culpability** in committing the offence and any **harm** which the offence caused, was intended to cause, or might forseeably have caused.[3] In using these guidelines, this assessment should be approached in two stages:

> ## 1. Offence seriousness (culpability and harm)
> ### A. Identify the appropriate starting point

The guidelines set out **examples** of the nature of activity which may constitute the offence, progressing from less to more serious conduct, and provide a **starting point** based on a **first time offender pleading not guilty.** The guidelines also specify a sentencing **range** for each example of activity. Refer to pages 145-146 for further guidance on the meaning of the terms 'starting point', 'range' and 'first time offender'.

Sentencers should begin by considering which of the examples of offence activity corresponds most closely to the circumstances of the particular case in order to identify the appropriate **starting point:**

- where the starting point is a fine, this is indicated as band A, B or C. The approach to assessing fines is set out on pages 148-155;

- where the community sentence threshold is passed, the guideline sets out whether the starting point should be a low, medium or high level community order. Refer to pages 160-162 for further guidance;

- where the starting point is a custodial sentence, refer to pages 163-164 for further guidance.

The Council's definitive guideline *Overarching Principles: Seriousness*, published 16 December 2004, identifies four levels of culpability for sentencing purposes (intention, recklessness, knowledge and negligence). The starting points in the individual offence guidelines assume that culpability is at the highest level applicable to the offence (often, but not always, intention). **Where a lower level of culpability is present, this should be taken into account.**

> ## 1. Offence seriousness (culpability and harm)
> ### B. Consider the effect of aggravating and mitigating factors

Once the starting point has been identified, the court can add to or reduce this to reflect any aggravating or mitigating factors that impact on the **culpability** of the offender and/or **harm** caused by the offence to reach a provisional sentence. Any factors contained in the description of the activity used to reach the starting point must not be counted again.

The **range** is the bracket into which the provisional sentence will normally fall after having regard to factors which aggravate or mitigate the seriousness of the offence.

However:

- the court is not precluded from going outside the range where the facts justify it;

- previous convictions which aggravate the seriousness of the current offence may take the provisional sentence beyond the range, especially where there are significant other aggravating factors present.

In addition, where an offender is being sentenced for multiple offences, the court's assessment of the totality of the offending may result in a sentence above the range indicated for the individual offences, including a sentence of a different type. Refer to page 147 for further guidance.

---

[3] Criminal Justice Act 2003, s.143(1)

Effective from August 4, 2008

The guidelines identify aggravating and mitigating factors which may be particularly relevant to each individual offence. These include some factors drawn from the general list of aggravating and mitigating factors in the Council's definitive guideline *Overarching Principles: Seriousness* published 16 December 2004, (reproduced on the pullout card). In each case, sentencers should have regard to the full list, which includes the factors that, by statute, make an offence more serious:

- offence committed while on bail for other offences;

- offence was racially or religiously aggravated;

- offence was motivated by, or demonstrates, hostility based on the victim's sexual orientation (or presumed sexual orientation);

- offence was motivated by, or demonstrates, hostility based on the victim's disability (or presumed disability);

- offender has previous convictions that the court considers can reasonably be treated as aggravating factors having regard to their relevance to the current offence and the time that has elapsed since conviction.

While the lists in the offence guidelines and pullout card aim to identify the most common aggravating and mitigating factors, **they are not intended to be exhaustive.** Sentencers should always consider whether there are any other factors that make the offence more or less serious.

2. Form a preliminary view of the appropriate sentence, then consider offender mitigation

When the court has reached a provisional sentence based on its assessment of offence seriousness, it should take into account matters of offender mitigation. The Council guideline *Overarching Principles: Seriousness* states that the issue of remorse should be taken into account at this point along with other mitigating features such as admissions to the police in interview.

3. Consider a reduction for a guilty plea

The Council guideline *Reduction in Sentence for a Guilty Plea*, revised 2007, states that the **punitive** elements of the sentence should be reduced to recognise an offender's guilty plea. The reduction has no impact on sentencing decisions in relation to ancillary orders, including disqualification.

The level of the reduction should reflect the stage at which the offender indicated a willingness to admit guilt and will be gauged on a sliding scale, ranging from a **recommended** one third (where the guilty plea was entered at the first reasonable opportunity), reducing to a **recommended** one quarter (where a trial date has been set) and to a **recommended** one tenth (for a guilty plea entered at the 'door of the court' or after the trial has begun). There is a presumption that the recommended reduction will be given unless there are good reasons for a lower amount.

The application of the reduction may affect the type, as well as the severity, of the sentence. It may also take the sentence below the **range** in some cases.

The court must state that it has reduced a sentence to reflect a guilty plea.[4] It should usually indicate what the sentence would have been if there had been no reduction as a result of the plea.

---

[4] Criminal Justice Act 2003, s.174(2)(d)

Effective from August 4, 2008

4. Consider ancillary orders, including compensation

Ancillary orders of particular relevance to individual offences are identified in the relevant guidelines; further guidance is set out on pages 168-174.

The court must **always** consider making a compensation order where the offending has resulted in personal injury, loss or damage.[5] The court is required to give reasons if it decides not to make such an order.[6]

5. Decide sentence
Give reasons

Sentencers must state reasons for the sentence passed in **every** case, including for any ancillary orders imposed.[7] It is particularly important to identify any aggravating or mitigating factors, or matters of offender mitigation, that have resulted in a sentence more or less severe than the suggested starting point.

If a court imposes a sentence of a different kind or outside the **range** indicated in the guidelines, **it must state its reasons for doing so.**[8]

The court should also give its reasons for not making an order that has been canvassed before it or that it might have been expected to make.

---

[5] Powers of Criminal Courts (Sentencing) Act 2000, s.130(1)
[6] ibid., s.130(3)
[7] Criminal Justice Act 2003, s.174(1)
[8] ibid., s.174(2)(a)

Effective from August 4, 2008

Arson (criminal damage by fire)

Criminal Damage Act 1971, s.1

Triable either way:
Maximum when tried summarily: Level 5 fine and/or 6 months
Maximum when tried on indictment: Life

Where offence committed in domestic context, refer to page 177 for guidance

Identify dangerous offenders
This is a serious offence for the purposes of the public protection provisions in the Criminal Justice Act 2003 – refer to page 187 and consult legal adviser for guidance

Offence seriousness (culpability and harm)
A. Identify the appropriate starting point
Starting points based on first time offender pleading not guilty

Examples of nature of activity	Starting point	Range
Minor damage by fire	High level community order	Medium level community order to 12 weeks custody
Moderate damage by fire	12 weeks custody	6 to 26 weeks custody
Significant damage by fire	Crown Court	Crown Court

Offence seriousness (culpability and harm)
B. Consider the effect of aggravating and mitigating factors
(other than those within examples above)
Common aggravating and mitigating factors are identified in the pullout card –
the following may be particularly relevant but **these lists are not exhaustive**

Factor indicating higher culpability 1. Revenge attack Factors indicating greater degree of harm 1. Damage to emergency equipment 2. Damage to public amenity 3. Significant public or private fear caused e.g. in domestic context	Factor indicating lower culpability 1. Damage caused recklessly

Form a preliminary view of the appropriate sentence, **then consider offender mitigation** Common factors are identified in the pullout card

Consider a reduction for a guilty plea

Consider ancillary orders, including compensation Refer to pages 168-174 for guidance on available ancillary orders

Decide sentence **Give reasons**

Effective from August 4, 2008

3A.04

Criminal damage (other than by fire)	Criminal Damage Act 1971, s.1(1)
Racially or religiously aggravated criminal damage	Crime and Disorder Act 1998, s.30

Criminal damage: triable only summarily if value involved does not exceed £5,000:
Maximum: Level 4 fine and/or 3 months

Triable either way if value involved exceeds £5,000:
Maximum when tried summarily: Level 5 fine and/or 6 months
Maximum when tried on indictment: 10 years

Racially or religiously aggravated criminal damage: triable either way
Maximum when tried summarily: Level 5 fine and/or 6 months
Maximum when tried on indictment: 14 years

Where offence committed in domestic context, refer to page 177 for guidance

Offence seriousness (culpability and harm)
A. Identify the appropriate starting point
Starting points based on first time offender pleading not guilty

Examples of nature of activity	Starting point	Range
Minor damage e.g. breaking small window; small amount of graffiti	Band B fine	Conditional discharge to band C fine
Moderate damage e.g. breaking large plate-glass or shop window; widespread graffiti	Low level community order	Band C fine to medium level community order
Significant damage up to £5,000 e.g. damage caused as part of a spree	High level community order	Medium level community order to 12 weeks custody
Damage between £5,000 and £10,000	12 weeks custody	6 to 26 weeks custody
Damage over £10,000	Crown Court	Crown Court

Offence seriousness (culpability and harm)
B. Consider the effect of aggravating and mitigating factors
(other than those within examples above)
Common aggravating and mitigating factors are identified in the pullout card –
the following may be particularly relevant but **these lists are not exhaustive**

Factors indicating higher culpability	Factors indicating lower culpability
1. Revenge attack 2. Targeting vulnerable victim	1. Damage caused recklessly 2. Provocation
Factors indicating greater degree of harm 1. Damage to emergency equipment 2. Damage to public amenity 3. Significant public or private fear caused e.g. in domestic context	

Form a preliminary view of the appropriate sentence
If offender charged and convicted of the racially or religiously
aggravated offence, increase the sentence to reflect this element
Refer to pages 178-179 for guidance

Consider offender mitigation
Common factors are identified in the pullout card

Consider a reduction for a guilty plea

Consider ancillary orders, including compensation
Refer to pages 168-174 for guidance on available ancillary orders

Decide sentence
Give reasons

Effective from August 4, 2008

Vehicle interference	Criminal Attempts Act 1981, s.9

Triable only summarily:
Maximum: Level 4 fine and/or 3 months

Offence seriousness (culpability and harm)		
A. Identify the appropriate starting point		
Starting points based on first time offender pleading not guilty		
Examples of nature of activity	**Starting point**	**Range**
Trying door handles; no entry gained to vehicle; no damage caused	Band C fine	Band A fine to low level community order
Entering vehicle, little or no damage caused	Medium level community order	Band C fine to high level community order
Entering vehicle, with damage caused	High level community order	Medium level community order to 12 weeks custody

Offence seriousness (culpability and harm)
B. Consider the effect of aggravating and mitigating factors (other than those within examples above)
Common aggravating and mitigating factors are identified in the pullout card – the following may be particularly relevant but **these lists are not exhaustive**

Factor indicating higher culpability 1. Targeting vehicle in dark/isolated location **Factors indicating greater degree of harm** 1. Emergency services vehicle 2. Disabled driver's vehicle 3. Part of series	

Form a preliminary view of the appropriate sentence, then consider offender mitigation
Common factors are identified in the pullout card

Consider a reduction for a guilty plea

Consider ancillary orders, including compensation
Refer to pages 168-174 for guidance on available ancillary orders
Consider disqualification from driving

Decide sentence
Give reasons

Effective from August 4, 2008

3A.06

Vehicle Excise and Registration Act 1994, s.44

Vehicle licence/registration fraud

Triable either way:
Maximum when tried summarily: Level 5 fine
Maximum when tried on indictment: 2 years

Offence seriousness (culpability and harm) A. Identify the appropriate starting point Starting points based on first time offender pleading not guilty		
Examples of nature of activity	**Starting point**	**Range**
Use of unaltered licence from another vehicle	Band B fine	Band B fine
Forged licence bought for own use, or forged/ altered for own use	Band C fine	Band C fine
Use of number plates from another vehicle; or Licence/number plates forged or altered for sale to another	High level community order (in Crown Court)	Medium level community order to Crown Court (Note: community order and custody available only in Crown Court)

Offence seriousness (culpability and harm)
B. Consider the effect of aggravating and mitigating factors
(other than those within examples above)
Common aggravating and mitigating factors are identified in the pullout card –
the following may be particularly relevant but **these lists are not exhaustive**

Factors indicating higher culpability 1. LGV, PSV, taxi etc. 2. Long-term fraudulent use Factors indicating greater degree of harm 1. High financial gain 2. Innocent victim deceived 3. Legitimate owner inconvenienced	Factors indicating lower culpability 1. Licence/registration mark from another vehicle owned by defendant 2. Short-term use

Form a preliminary view of the appropriate sentence,
then consider offender mitigation
Common factors are identified in the pullout card

Consider a reduction for a guilty plea

Consider ancillary orders
Refer to pages 168-174 for guidance on available ancillary orders
Consider disqualification from driving and deprivation of property
(including vehicle)

Decide sentence
Give reasons

Effective from August 4, 2008

Vehicle taking, without consent

Theft Act 1968, s.12

Triable only summarily:
Maximum: Level 5 fine and/or 6 months

May disqualify (no points available)

Offence seriousness (culpability and harm) A. Identify the appropriate starting point Starting points based on first time offender pleading not guilty		
Examples of nature of activity	Starting point	Range
Exceeding authorised use of e.g. employer's or relative's vehicle; retention of hire car beyond return date	Low level community order	Band B fine to medium level community order
As above with damage caused to lock/ignition; OR Stranger's vehicle involved but no damage caused	Medium level community order	Low level community order to high level community order
Taking vehicle from private premises; OR Causing damage to e.g. lock/ignition of stranger's vehicle	High level community order	Medium level community order to 26 weeks custody

Offence seriousness (culpability and harm)
B. Consider the effect of aggravating and mitigating factors
(other than those within examples above)
Common aggravating and mitigating factors are identified in the pullout card –
the following may be particularly relevant but **these lists are not exhaustive**

Factors indicating greater degree of harm	Factor indicating lower culpability
1. Vehicle later burnt 2. Vehicle belonging to elderly/disabled person 3. Emergency services vehicle 4. Medium to large goods vehicle 5. Passengers carried	1. Misunderstanding with owner **Factor indicating lesser degree of harm** 1. Offender voluntarily returned vehicle to owner

Form a preliminary view of the appropriate sentence,
then consider offender mitigation
Common factors are identified in the pullout card

Consider a reduction for a guilty plea

Consider ancillary orders, including compensation
Refer to pages 168-174 for guidance on available ancillary orders
Consider disqualification from driving

Decide sentence
Give reasons

Effective from August 4, 2008

3A.08

Theft Act 1968, ss.12A(2)(c) and (d)

Vehicle taking (aggravated)
Damage caused to property other than the vehicle in accident or damage caused to the vehicle

Triable either way (triable only summarily if damage under £5,000):
Maximum when tried summarily: Level 5 fine and/or 6 months
Maximum when tried on indictment: 2 years

- Must endorse and disqualify for at least 12 months
- Must disqualify for **at least** 2 years if offender has had two or more disqualifications for periods of 56 days or more in preceding 3 years – **refer to page 184 and consult your legal adviser for further guidance**

If there is a delay in sentencing after conviction, consider interim disqualification

Offence seriousness (culpability and harm) A. Identify the appropriate starting point Starting points based on first time offender pleading not guilty		
Examples of nature of activity	**Starting point**	**Range**
Exceeding authorised use of e.g. employer's or relative's vehicle; retention of hire car beyond return date; minor damage to taken vehicle	Medium level community order	Low level community order to high level community order
Greater damage to taken vehicle and/or moderate damage to another vehicle and/or property	High level community order	Medium level community order to 12 weeks custody
Vehicle taken as part of burglary or from private premises; severe damage	18 weeks custody	12 to 26 weeks custody (Crown Court if damage over £5,000)

Offence seriousness (culpability and harm) B. Consider the effect of aggravating and mitigating factors (other than those within examples above) Common aggravating and mitigating factors are identified in the pullout card – the following may be particularly relevant but **these lists are not exhaustive**	
Factors indicating higher culpability 1. Vehicle deliberately damaged/destroyed 2. Offender under influence of alcohol/drugs Factors indicating greater degree of harm 1. Passenger(s) carried 2. Vehicle belonging to elderly or disabled person 3. Emergency services vehicle 4. Medium to large goods vehicle 5. Damage caused in moving traffic accident	Factors indicating lower culpability 1. Misunderstanding with owner 2. Damage resulting from actions of another (where this does not provide a defence)

Form a preliminary view of the appropriate sentence, then consider offender mitigation Common factors are identified in the pullout card

Consider a reduction for a guilty plea

Consider ancillary orders, including compensation Refer to pages 168-174 for guidance on available ancillary orders

Decide sentence Give reasons

Effective from August 4, 2008

Vehicle taking (aggravated)
Dangerous driving or accident causing injury

Theft Act 1968, ss.12A(2)(a) and (b)

Triable either way:
Maximum when tried summarily: Level 5 fine and/or 6 months
Maximum when tried on indictment: 2 years; 14 years if accident caused death

- Must endorse and disqualify for at least 12 months
- Must disqualify for **at least** 2 years if offender has had two or more disqualifications for periods of 56 days or more in preceding 3 years – refer to page 184 and consult your legal adviser for further guidance

If there is a delay in sentencing after conviction, consider interim disqualification

Offence seriousness (culpability and harm)
A. Identify the appropriate starting point
Starting points based on first time offender pleading not guilty

Examples of nature of activity	Starting point	Range
Taken vehicle involved in single incident of bad driving where little or no damage or risk of personal injury	High level community order	Medium level community order to 12 weeks custody
Taken vehicle involved in incident(s) involving excessive speed or showing off, especially on busy roads or in built-up area	18 weeks custody	12 to 26 weeks custody
Taken vehicle involved in prolonged bad driving involving deliberate disregard for safety of others	Crown Court	Crown Court

Offence seriousness (culpability and harm)
B. Consider the effect of aggravating and mitigating factors
(other than those within examples above)
Common aggravating and mitigating factors are identified in the pullout card – the following may be particularly relevant but **these lists are not exhaustive**

Factors indicating higher culpability 1. Disregarding warnings of others 2. Evidence of alcohol or drugs 3. Carrying out other tasks while driving 4. Carrying passengers or heavy load 5. Tiredness 6. Trying to avoid arrest 7. Aggressive driving, such as driving much too close to vehicle in front, inappropriate attempts to overtake, or cutting in after overtaking **Factors indicating greater degree of harm** 1. Injury to others 2. Damage to other vehicles or property	

Form a preliminary view of the appropriate sentence, then consider offender mitigation
Common factors are identified in the pullout card

Consider a reduction for a guilty plea

Consider ordering disqualification until appropriate driving test passed
Consider ancillary orders, including compensation
Refer to pages 168-174 for guidance on available ancillary orders

Decide sentence
Give reasons

Effective from August 4, 2008

3A.10

Road Traffic Act 1988, s.3

> **Careless driving
> (drive without due care
> and attention)**

Triable only summarily:
Maximum: Level 5 fine

Must endorse and may disqualify. If no disqualification, impose 3 – 9 points

Offence seriousness (culpability and harm) A. Identify the appropriate starting point Starting points based on first time offender pleading not guilty		
Examples of nature of activity	**Starting point**	**Range**
Momentary lapse of concentration or misjudgement at low speed	Band A fine	Band A fine 3 – 4 points
Loss of control due to speed, mishandling or insufficient attention to road conditions, or carelessly turning right across on-coming traffic	Band B fine	Band B fine 5 – 6 points
Overtaking manoeuvre at speed resulting in collision of vehicles, or driving bordering on the dangerous	Band C fine	Band C fine Consider disqualification OR 7 – 9 points

**Offence seriousness (culpability and harm)
B. Consider the effect of aggravating and mitigating factors
(other than those within examples above)**
Common aggravating and mitigating factors are identified in the pullout card –
the following may be particularly relevant but **these lists are not exhaustive**

Factors indicating higher culpability	Factors indicating lower culpability
1. Excessive speed	1. Minor risk
2. Carrying out other tasks while driving	2. Inexperience of driver
3. Carrying passengers or heavy load	3. Sudden change in road or weather conditions
4. Tiredness	
Factors indicating greater degree of harm	
1. Injury to others	
2. Damage to other vehicles or property	
3. High level of traffic or pedestrians in vicinity	
4. Location e.g. near school when children are likely to be present	

**Form a preliminary view of the appropriate sentence,
then consider offender mitigation**
Common factors are identified in the pullout card

Consider a reduction for guilty plea

**Consider ordering disqualification until appropriate driving test passed
Consider ancillary orders, including compensation**
Refer to pages 168-174 for guidance on available ancillary orders

**Decide sentence
Give reasons**

Effective from August 4, 2008

Road Traffic Act 1988, s.2B	**Causing death by careless or inconsiderate driving**

Triable either way:
Maximum when tried summarily: Level 5 fine and/or 6 months
Maximum when tried on indictment: 5 years

Offence seriousness (culpability and harm)		
A. Identify the appropriate starting point		
Starting points based on first time offender pleading not guilty		
Examples of nature of activity	**Starting point**	**Range**
Careless or inconsiderate driving arising from momentary inattention with no aggravating factors	Medium level community order	Low level community order to high level community order
Other cases of careless or inconsiderate driving	Crown Court	High level community order to Crown Court
Careless or inconsiderate driving falling not far short of dangerous driving	Crown Court	Crown Court

Offence seriousness (culpability and harm)
B. Consider the effect of aggravating and mitigating factors (other than those within examples above)
Common aggravating and mitigating factors are identified in the pullout card – the following may be particularly relevant but **these lists are not exhaustive**

Factors indicating higher culpability	**Factors indicating lower culpability**
1. Other offences committed at the same time, such as driving other than in accordance with the terms of a valid licence; driving while disqualified; driving without insurance; taking a vehicle without consent; driving a stolen vehicle	1. Offender seriously injured in the collision
	2. The victim was a close friend or relative
2. Previous convictions for motoring offences, particularly offences that involve bad driving	3. The actions of the victim or a third party contributed to the commission of the offence
3. Irresponsible behaviour, such as failing to stop or falsely claiming that one of the victims was responsible for the collision	4. The offender's lack of driving experience contributed significantly to the likelihood of a collision occurring and/or death resulting
	5. The driving was in response to a proven and genuine emergency falling short of a defence
Factors indicating greater degree of harm	
1. More than one person was killed as a result of the offence	
2. Serious injury to one or more persons in addition to the death(s)	

Form a preliminary view of the appropriate sentence, then consider offender mitigation
Common factors are identified in the pullout card

Consider a reduction for a guilty plea

Consider ancillary orders, including disqualification and deprivation of property
Refer to pages 168-174 for guidance on available ancillary orders

Decide sentence
Give reasons

Effective from August 4, 2008

3A.12

Causing death by driving: unlicensed, disqualified or uninsured drivers – factors to take into consideration

This guideline and accompanying notes are taken from the Sentencing Guidelines Council's definitive guideline *Causing Death by Driving*, published 15 July 2008

Key factors

(a) Culpability arises from the offender driving a vehicle on a road or other public place when, by law, not allowed to do so; the offence does not involve any fault in the standard of driving.

(b) Since driving whilst disqualified is more culpable than driving whilst unlicensed or uninsured, a higher starting point is proposed when the offender was disqualified from driving at the time of the offence.

(c) Being uninsured, unlicensed or disqualified are the only determinants of seriousness for this offence, as there are no factors relating to the standard of driving. The list of aggravating factors identified is slightly different as the emphasis is on the decision to drive by an offender who is not permitted by law to do so.

(d) A fine is unlikely to be an appropriate sentence for this offence; where a non-custodial sentence is considered appropriate, this should be a community order.

(e) Where the *decision to drive was brought about by a genuine and proven emergency*, that may mitigate offence seriousness and so it is included as an additional mitigating factor.

(f) An additional mitigating factor covers those situations where an offender genuinely believed that there was valid insurance or a valid licence.

(g) Offender mitigation particularly relevant to this offence includes conduct after the offence such as where the offender gave direct, positive, assistance at the scene of a collision to victim(s). It may also include remorse – whilst it can be expected that anyone who has caused a death by driving would be remorseful, this cannot undermine its importance for sentencing purposes. It is for the court to determine whether an expression of remorse is genuine.

(h) Where an offender has a good driving record, this is not a factor that automatically should be treated as mitigation, especially now that the presence of previous convictions is a statutory aggravating factor. However, any evidence to show that an offender has previously been an exemplary driver, for example having driven an ambulance, police vehicle, bus, taxi or similar vehicle conscientiously and without incident for many years, is a fact that the courts may well wish to take into account by way of offender mitigation. This is likely to have even greater effect where the driver is driving on public duty (for example, on ambulance, fire services or police duties) and was responding to an emergency.

(i) Disqualification of the offender from driving and endorsement of the offender's driving licence are mandatory, and the offence carries between 3 and 11 penalty points when the court finds special reasons for not imposing disqualification. There is a discretionary power[1] to order an extended driving test/re-test where a person is convicted of this offence.

---

[1] Road Traffic Offenders Act 1988, s.36(4)

Effective from August 4, 2008

Road Traffic Act 1988, s.3ZB

Causing death by driving: unlicensed, disqualified or uninsured drivers

Triable either way:
Maximum when tried summarily: Level 5 fine and/or 6 months
Maximum when tried on indictment: 2 years

Offence seriousness (culpability and harm)
A. Identify the appropriate starting point
Starting points based on first time offender pleading not guilty

Examples of nature of activity	Starting point	Range
The offender was unlicensed or uninsured – no aggravating factors	Medium level community order	Low level community order to high level community order
The offender was unlicensed or uninsured plus at least 1 aggravating factor from the list below	26 weeks custody	High level community order to Crown Court
The offender was disqualified from driving OR The offender was unlicensed or uninsured plus 2 or more aggravating factors from the list below	Crown Court	Crown Court

Offence seriousness (culpability and harm)
B. Consider the effect of aggravating and mitigating factors
(other than those within examples above)
Common aggravating and mitigating factors are identified in the pullout card – the following may be particularly relevant but **these lists are not exhaustive**

Factors indicating higher culpability	Factors indicating lower culpability
1. Previous convictions for motoring offences, whether involving bad driving or involving an offence of the same kind that forms part of the present conviction (i.e. unlicensed, disqualified or uninsured driving)	1. The decision to drive was brought about by a proven and genuine emergency falling short of a defence
2. Irresponsible behaviour such as failing to stop or falsely claiming that someone else was driving	2. The offender genuinely believed that he or she was insured or licensed to drive
	3. The offender was seriously injured as a result of the collision
Factors indicating greater degree of harm	4. The victim was a close friend or relative
1. More than one person was killed as a result of the offence	
2. Serious injury to one or more persons in addition to the death(s)	

Form a preliminary view of the appropriate sentence, then consider offender mitigation
Common factors are identified in the pullout card

Consider a reduction for a guilty plea

Consider ancillary orders, including disqualification and deprivation of property
refer to pages 168-174 for guidance on available ancillary orders

Decide sentence
Give reasons

Effective from August 4, 2008

Dangerous driving	Road Traffic Act 1988, s.2

Triable either way:
Maximum when tried summarily: Level 5 fine and/or 6 months
Maximum when tried on indictment: 2 years

- Must endorse and disqualify for at least 12 months. Must order extended re-test
- Must disqualify for **at least** 2 years if offender has had two or more disqualifications for periods of 56 days or more in preceding 3 years – **refer to page 184 and consult your legal adviser for further guidance**

If there is a delay in sentencing after conviction, consider interim disqualification

Offence seriousness (culpability and harm)		
A. Identify the appropriate starting point		
Starting points based on first time offender pleading not guilty		
Examples of nature of activity	**Starting point**	**Range**
Single incident where little or no damage or risk of personal injury	Medium level community order	Low level community order to high level community order
		Disqualify 12 – 15 months
Incident(s) involving excessive speed or showing off, especially on busy roads or in built-up area; OR	12 weeks custody	High level community order to 26 weeks custody
Single incident where little or no damage or risk of personal injury but offender was disqualified driver		Disqualify 15 – 24 months
Prolonged bad driving involving deliberate disregard for safety of others; OR	Crown Court	Crown Court
Incident(s) involving excessive speed or showing off, especially on busy roads or in built-up area, by disqualified driver; OR		
Driving as described in box above while being pursued by police		

Offence seriousness (culpability and harm)	
B. Consider the effect of aggravating and mitigating factors	
(other than those within examples above)	
Common aggravating and mitigating factors are identified in the pullout card – the following may be particularly relevant but **these lists are not exhaustive**	
Factors indicating higher culpability	**Factors indicating lower culpability**
1. Disregarding warnings of others	1. Genuine emergency
2. Evidence of alcohol or drugs	2. Speed not excessive
3. Carrying out other tasks while driving	3. Offence due to inexperience rather than irresponsibility
4. Carrying passengers or heavy load	of driver
5. Tiredness	
6. Aggressive driving, such as driving much too close to vehicle in front, racing, inappropriate attempts to overtake, or cutting in after overtaking	
7. Driving when knowingly suffering from a medical condition which significantly impairs the offender's driving skills	
8. Driving a poorly maintained or dangerously loaded vehicle, especially where motivated by commercial concerns	
Factors indicating greater degree of harm	
1. Injury to others	
2. Damage to other vehicles or property	

Effective from August 4, 2008

Form a preliminary view of the appropriate sentence, then consider offender mitigation
Common factors are identified in the pullout card

Consider a reduction for guilty plea

Consider ancillary orders, including compensation and deprivation of property
Refer to pages 168-174 for guidance on available ancillary orders

Decide sentence
Give reasons

Effective from August 4, 2008

Drive whilst disqualified

Road Traffic Act 1988, s.103

Triable only summarily:
Maximum: Level 5 fine and/or 6 months

Must endorse and may disqualify. If no disqualification, impose 6 points

Offence seriousness (culpability and harm) A. Identify the appropriate starting point Starting points based on first time offender pleading not guilty		
Examples of nature of activity	**Starting point**	**Range**
Full period expired but retest not taken	Low level community order	Band C fine to medium level community order
		6 points or disqualify for 3 – 6 months
Lengthy period of ban already served	High level community order	Medium level community order to 12 weeks custody
		Lengthen disqualification for 6 – 12 months beyond expiry of current ban
Recently imposed ban	12 weeks custody	High level community order to 26 weeks custody
		Lengthen disqualification for 12 – 18 months beyond expiry of current ban

Offence seriousness (culpability and harm)
B. Consider the effect of aggravating and mitigating factors (other than those within examples above)
Common aggravating and mitigating factors are identified in the pullout card –
the following may be particularly relevant but **these lists are not exhaustive**

Factors indicating higher culpability	Factors indicating lower culpability
1. Never passed test	1. Defendant not present when disqualification imposed and
2. Planned long-term evasion	genuine reason why unaware of ban
3. Vehicle obtained during ban	2. Genuine emergency established
4. Driving for remuneration	
Factors indicating greater degree of harm	
1. Distance driven	
2. Evidence of associated bad driving	
3. Offender caused accident	

Form a preliminary view of the appropriate sentence, then consider offender mitigation
Common factors are identified in the pullout card

Consider a reduction for guilty plea

Consider ancillary orders, including deprivation of property
Refer to pages 168-174 for guidance on available ancillary orders

Decide sentence
Give reasons

Note

An offender convicted of this offence will always have at least one relevant previous conviction for the offence that resulted in disqualification. The starting points and ranges take this into account; any other previous convictions should be considered in the usual way – see pages 17 and 145.

Effective from August 4, 2008

Excess alcohol (drive/attempt to drive)

Road Traffic Act 1988, s.5(1)(a)

Triable only summarily:
Maximum: Level 5 fine and/or 6 months

- Must endorse and disqualify for at least 12 months
- Must disqualify for **at least** 2 years if offender has had two or more disqualifications for periods of 56 days or more in preceding 3 years – **refer to page 184 and consult your legal adviser for further guidance**
- Must disqualify for **at least** 3 years if offender has been convicted of a relevant offence in preceding 10 years – **refer to page 184 and consult your legal adviser for further guidance**

If there is a delay in sentencing after conviction, consider interim disqualification

Note: the final column below provides guidance regarding the length of disqualification that may be appropriate in cases to which the 3 year minimum applies. The period to be imposed in any individual case will depend on an assessment of all the relevant circumstances, including the length of time since the earlier ban was imposed and the gravity of the current offence.

Offence seriousness (culpability and harm) A. Identify the appropriate starting point Starting points based on first time offender pleading not guilty						
Level of alcohol			Starting point	Range	Disqualification	Disqual. 2nd offence in 10 years – see note above
Breath (mg)	Blood (ml)	Urine (ml)				
36 – 59	81 – 137	108 – 183	Band C fine	Band C fine	12 – 16 months	36 – 40 months
60 – 89	138 – 206	184 – 274	Band C fine	Band C fine	17 – 22 months	36 – 46 months
90 – 119	207 – 275	275 – 366	Medium level community order	Low level community order to high level community order	23 – 28 months	36 – 52 months
120 – 150 and above	276 – 345 and above	367 – 459 and above	12 weeks custody	High level community order to 26 weeks custody	29 – 36 months	36 – 60 months

Offence seriousness (culpability and harm) B. Consider the effect of aggravating and mitigating factors (other than those within examples above) Common aggravating and mitigating factors are identified in the pullout card – the following may be particularly relevant but **these lists are not exhaustive**	
Factors indicating higher culpability 1. LGV, HGV, PSV etc. 2. Poor road or weather conditions 3. Carrying passengers 4. Driving for hire or reward 5. Evidence of unacceptable standard of driving **Factors indicating greater degree of harm** 1. Involved in accident 2. Location e.g. near school 3. High level of traffic or pedestrians in the vicinity	Factors indicating lower culpability 1. Genuine emergency established * 2. Spiked drinks * 3. Very short distance driven * * even where not amounting to special reasons

Effective from August 4, 2008

**Form a preliminary view of the appropriate sentence,
then consider offender mitigation**
Common factors are identified in the pullout card

Consider a reduction for guilty plea

**Consider offering drink/drive rehabilitation course
Consider ancillary orders, including forfeiture or
suspension of personal liquor licence**
Refer to pages 168-174 for guidance on available ancillary orders

**Decide sentence
Give reasons**

Effective from August 4, 2008

Excess alcohol (in charge)

Road Traffic Act 1988, s.5(1)(b)

Triable only summarily:
Maximum: Level 4 fine and/or 3 months

Must endorse and may disqualify. If no disqualification, impose 10 points

Offence seriousness (culpability and harm)
A. Identify the appropriate starting point
Starting points based on first time offender pleading not guilty

Level of alcohol			Starting point	Range
Breath (mg)	Blood (ml)	Urine (ml)		
36 – 59	81 – 137	108 – 183	Band B fine	Band B fine 10 points
60 – 89	138 – 206	184 – 274	Band B fine	Band B fine 10 points OR consider disqualification
90 – 119	207 – 275	275 – 366	Band C fine	Band C fine to medium level community order Consider disqualification up to 6 months OR 10 points
120 – 150 and above	276 – 345 and above	367 – 459 and above	Medium level community order	Low level community order to 6 weeks custody Disqualify 6-12 months

Offence seriousness (culpability and harm)
B. Consider the effect of aggravating and mitigating factors
(other than those within examples above)
Common aggravating and mitigating factors are identified in the pullout card –
the following may be particularly relevant but **these lists are not exhaustive**

Factors indicating higher culpability	Factor indicating lower culpability
1. LGV, HGV, PSV etc. 2. Ability to drive seriously impaired 3. High likelihood of driving 4. Driving for hire or reward	1. Low likelihood of driving

Form a preliminary view of the appropriate sentence,
then consider offender mitigation
Common factors are identified in the pullout card

Consider a reduction for guilty plea

Consider ancillary orders, including forfeiture or
suspension of personal liquor licence
Refer to pages 168-174 for guidance on available ancillary orders

Decide sentence
Give reasons

Effective from August 4, 2008

3A.18

Road Traffic Act 1988, s.170(4)

Fail to stop/report road accident

Triable only summarily:
Maximum: Level 5 fine and/or 6 months

Must endorse and may disqualify. If no disqualification, impose 5 – 10 points

Offence seriousness (culpability and harm) A. Identify the appropriate starting point Starting points based on first time offender pleading not guilty		
Examples of nature of activity	**Starting point**	**Range**
Minor damage/injury or stopped at scene but failed to exchange particulars or report	Band B fine	Band B fine 5 – 6 points
Moderate damage/injury or failed to stop and failed to report	Band C fine	Band C fine 7 – 8 points Consider disqualification
Serious damage/injury and/or evidence of bad driving	High level community order	Band C fine to 26 weeks custody Disqualify 6 – 12 months OR 9 – 10 points

Offence seriousness (culpability and harm) B. Consider the effect of aggravating and mitigating factors (other than those within examples above) Common aggravating and mitigating factors are identified in the pullout card – the following may be particularly relevant but **these lists are not exhaustive**	
Factors indicating higher culpability 1. Evidence of drink or drugs/evasion of test 2. Knowledge/suspicion that personal injury caused (where not an element of the offence) 3. Leaving injured party at scene 4. Giving false details	Factors indicating lower culpability 1. Believed identity known 2. Genuine fear of retribution 3. Subsequently reported

Form a preliminary view of the appropriate sentence, then consider offender mitigation Common factors are identified in the pullout card

Consider a reduction for guilty plea

Consider ancillary orders, including compensation Refer to pages 168-174 for guidance on available ancillary orders

Decide sentence Give reasons

Effective from August 4, 2008

| Fail to provide specimen for analysis (drive/attempt to drive) | Road Traffic Act 1988, s.7(6) |

Triable only summarily:
Maximum: Level 5 fine and/or 6 months

- Must endorse and disqualify for at least 12 months
- Must disqualify for **at least** 2 years if offender has had two or more disqualifications for periods of 56 days or more in preceding 3 years – **refer to page 184 and consult your legal adviser for further guidance**
- Must disqualify for **at least** 3 years if offender has been convicted of a relevant offence in preceding 10 years – **refer to page 184 and consult your legal adviser for further guidance**

If there is a delay in sentencing after conviction, consider interim disqualification

Note: the final column below provides guidance regarding the length of disqualification that may be appropriate in cases to which the 3 year minimum applies. The period to be imposed in any individual case will depend on an assessment of all the relevant circumstances, including the length of time since the earlier ban was imposed and the gravity of the current offence.

Offence seriousness (culpability and harm)				
A. Identify the appropriate starting point				
Starting points based on first time offender pleading not guilty				
Examples of nature of activity	**Starting point**	**Range**	**Disqualification**	**Disqual. 2nd offence in 10 years**
Defendant refused test when had honestly held but unreasonable excuse	Band C fine	Band C fine	12 – 16 months	36 – 40 months
Deliberate refusal or deliberate failure	Low level community order	Band C fine to high level community order	17 – 28 months	36 – 52 months
Deliberate refusal or deliberate failure where evidence of serious impairment	12 weeks custody	High level community order to 26 weeks custody	29 – 36 months	36 – 60 months

Offence seriousness (culpability and harm)
B. Consider the effect of aggravating and mitigating factors
(other than those within examples above)
Common aggravating and mitigating factors are identified in the pullout card – the following may be particularly relevant but **these lists are not exhaustive**

Factors indicating higher culpability	Factor indicating lower culpability
1. Evidence of unacceptable standard of driving 2. LGV, HGV, PSV etc. 3. Obvious state of intoxication 4. Driving for hire or reward	1. Genuine but unsuccessful attempt to provide specimen
Factor indicating greater degree of harm 1. Involved in accident	

Form a preliminary view of the appropriate sentence,
then consider offender mitigation
Common factors are identified in the pullout card

Consider a reduction for guilty plea

Consider offering drink/drive rehabilitation course; consider ancillary orders
Refer to pages 168-174 for guidance on available ancillary orders

Decide sentence
Give reasons

Effective from August 4, 2008

3A.20

Road Traffic Act 1988, s.7(6)

Fail to provide specimen for analysis (in charge)

Triable only summarily:
Maximum: Level 4 fine and/or 3 months

Must endorse and may disqualify. If no disqualification, impose 10 points

Offence seriousness (culpability and harm)		
A. Identify the appropriate starting point		
Starting points based on first time offender pleading not guilty		
Examples of nature of activity	**Starting point**	**Range**
Defendant refused test when had honestly held but unreasonable excuse	Band B fine	Band B fine 10 points
Deliberate refusal or deliberate failure	Band C fine	Band C fine to medium level community order Consider disqualification OR 10 points
Deliberate refusal or deliberate failure where evidence of serious impairment	Medium level community order	Low level community order to 6 weeks custody Disqualify 6 -12 months

Offence seriousness (culpability and harm)	
B. Consider the effect of aggravating and mitigating factors	
(other than those within examples above)	
Common aggravating and mitigating factors are identified in the pullout card – the following may be particularly relevant but **these lists are not exhaustive**	
Factors indicating higher culpability 1. Obvious state of intoxication 2. LGV, HGV, PSV etc. 3. High likelihood of driving 4. Driving for hire or reward	**Factors indicating lower culpability** 1. Genuine but unsuccessful attempt to provide specimen 2. Low likelihood of driving

Form a preliminary view of the appropriate sentence, then consider offender mitigation
Common factors are identified in the pullout card

Consider a reduction for guilty plea

Consider ancillary orders
Refer to pages 168-174 for guidance on available ancillary orders

Decide sentence Give reasons

Effective from August 4, 2008

No insurance

Road Traffic Act 1988, s.143

Triable only summarily:
Maximum: Level 5 fine

Must endorse and may disqualify. If no disqualification, impose 6-8 points – see notes below.

Offence seriousness (culpability and harm)
A. Identify the appropriate starting point
Starting points based on first time offender pleading not guilty

Examples of nature of activity	Starting point	Range
Using a motor vehicle on a road or other public place without insurance	Band C fine	Band C fine 6 points – 12 months disqualification – see notes below

Offence seriousness (culpability and harm)
B. Consider the effect of aggravating and mitigating factors
(other than those within examples above)
Common aggravating and mitigating factors are identified in the pullout card –
the following may be particularly relevant but **these lists are not exhaustive**

Factors indicating higher culpability	Factors indicating lower culpability
1. Never passed test 2. Gave false details 3. Driving LGV, HGV, PSV etc. 4. Driving for hire or reward 5. Evidence of sustained uninsured use **Factor indicating greater degree of harm** 1. Involved in accident 2. Accident resulting in injury	1. Responsibility for providing insurance rests with another 2. Genuine misunderstanding 3. Recent failure to renew or failure to transfer vehicle details where insurance was in existence 4. Vehicle not being driven

Form a preliminary view of the appropriate sentence,
then consider offender mitigation
Common factors are identified in the pullout card

Consider a reduction for guilty plea

Consider ancillary orders
Refer to pages 168-174 for guidance on available ancillary orders

Decide sentence
Give reasons

Notes

Consider range from 7 points – 2 months disqualification where vehicle was being driven and no evidence that the offender has held insurance.

Consider disqualification of 6 – 12 months if evidence of sustained uninsured use and/or involvement in accident.

Effective from August 4, 2008

3A.22

Road Traffic Regulation Act 1984, s.89(10)

Speeding

Triable only summarily:
Maximum: Level 3 fine (level 4 if motorway)

Must endorse and may disqualify. If no disqualification, impose 3-6 points

Offence seriousness (culpability and harm)			
A. Identify the appropriate starting point			
Starting points based on first time offender pleading not guilty			
Speed limit (mph)	**Recorded speed (mph)**		
20	21 – 30	31 – 40	41 – 50
30	31 – 40	41 – 50	51 – 60
40	41 – 55	56 – 65	66 – 75
50	51 – 65	66 – 75	76 – 85
60	61 – 80	81 – 90	91 – 100
70	71 – 90	91 – 100	101 – 110
Starting point	Band A fine	Band B fine	Band B fine
Range	Band A fine	Band B fine	Band B fine
Points/disqualification	3 points	4 – 6 points OR Disqualify 7 – 28 days	Disqualify 7 – 56 days OR 6 points

Offence seriousness (culpability and harm)	
B. Consider the effect of aggravating and mitigating factors	
(other than those within examples above)	
Common aggravating and mitigating factors are identified in the pullout card –	
the following may be particularly relevant but **these lists are not exhaustive**	
Factors indicating higher culpability	**Factor indicating lower culpability**
1. Poor road or weather conditions	1. Genuine emergency established
2. LGV, HGV, PSV etc.	
3. Towing caravan/trailer	
4. Carrying passengers or heavy load	
5. Driving for hire or reward	
6. Evidence of unacceptable standard of driving over and above speed	
Factors indicating greater degree of harm	
1. Location e.g. near school	
2. High level of traffic or pedestrians in the vicinity	

**Form a preliminary view of the appropriate sentence,
then consider offender mitigation**
Common factors are identified in the pullout card

Consider a reduction for guilty plea

Consider ancillary orders
Refer to pages 168-174 for guidance on available ancillary orders

**Decide sentence
Give reasons**

Effective from August 4, 2008

Unfit through drink or drugs (drive/attempt to drive)

Road Traffic Act 1988, s.4(1)

Triable only summarily:
Maximum: Level 5 fine and/or 6 months

- Must endorse and disqualify for at least 12 months
- Must disqualify for **at least** 2 years if offender has had two or more disqualifications for periods of 56 days or more in preceding 3 years – **refer to page 184 and consult your legal adviser for further guidance**
- Must disqualify for **at least** 3 years if offender has been convicted of a relevant offence in preceding 10 years – **refer to page 184 and consult your legal adviser for further guidance**

If there is a delay in sentencing after conviction, consider interim disqualification

Note: the final column below provides guidance regarding the length of disqualification that may be appropriate in cases to which the 3 year minimum applies. The period to be imposed in any individual case will depend on an assessment of all the relevant circumstances, including the length of time since the earlier ban was imposed and the gravity of the current offence.

Offence seriousness (culpability and harm)
A. Identify the appropriate starting point
Starting points based on first time offender pleading not guilty

Examples of nature of activity	Starting point	Range	Disqualification	Disqual. 2nd offence in 10 years
Evidence of moderate level of impairment and no aggravating factors	Band C fine	Band C fine	12 – 16 months	36 – 40 months
Evidence of moderate level of impairment and presence of one or more aggravating factors listed below	Band C fine	Band C fine	17 – 22 months	36 – 46 months
Evidence of high level of impairment and no aggravating factors	Medium level community order	Low level community order to high level community order	23 – 28 months	36 – 52 months
Evidence of high level of impairment and presence of one or more aggravating factors listed below	12 weeks custody	High level community order to 26 weeks custody	29 – 36 months	36 – 60 months

Offence seriousness (culpability and harm)
B. Consider the effect of aggravating and mitigating factors
(other than those within examples above)
Common aggravating and mitigating factors are identified in the pullout card –
the following may be particularly relevant but **these lists are not exhaustive**

Factors indicating higher culpability	Factors indicating lower culpability
1. LGV, HGV, PSV etc.	1. Genuine emergency established *
2. Poor road or weather conditions	2. Spiked drinks *
3. Carrying passengers	3. Very short distance driven *
4. Driving for hire or reward	
5. Evidence of unacceptable standard of driving	* even where not amounting to special reasons
Factors indicating greater degree of harm	
1. Involved in accident	
2. Location e.g. near school	
3. High level of traffic or pedestrians in the vicinity	

Effective from August 4, 2008

> **Form a preliminary view of the appropriate sentence,
> then consider offender mitigation**
> Common factors are identified in the pullout card

> **Consider a reduction for guilty plea**

> **Consider offering drink/drive rehabilitation course
> Consider ancillary orders**
> Refer to pages 168-174 for guidance on available ancillary orders

> **Decide sentence
> Give reasons**

Effective from August 4, 2008

Unfit through drink or drugs (in charge)

Road Traffic Act 1988, s.4(2)

Triable only summarily:
Maximum: Level 4 fine and/or 3 months

Must endorse and may disqualify. If no disqualification, impose 10 points

Offence seriousness (culpability and harm)
A. Identify the appropriate starting point
Starting points based on first time offender pleading not guilty

Examples of nature of activity	Starting point	Range
Evidence of moderate level of impairment and no aggravating factors	Band B fine	Band B fine 10 points
Evidence of moderate level of impairment and presence of one or more aggravating factors listed below	Band B fine	Band B fine 10 points or consider disqualification
Evidence of high level of impairment and no aggravating factors	Band C fine	Band C fine to medium level community order 10 points or consider disqualification
Evidence of high level of impairment and presence of one or more aggravating factors listed below	High level community order	Medium level community order to 12 weeks custody Consider disqualification OR 10 points

Offence seriousness (culpability and harm)
B. Consider the effect of aggravating and mitigating factors
(other than those within examples above)
Common aggravating and mitigating factors are identified in the pullout card –
the following may be particularly relevant but **these lists are not exhaustive**

Factors indicating higher culpability	Factor indicating lower culpability
1. LGV, HGV, PSV etc. 2. High likelihood of driving 3. Driving for hire or reward	1. Low likelihood of driving

Form a preliminary view of the appropriate sentence, then consider offender mitigation
Common factors are identified in the pullout card

Consider a reduction for guilty plea

Consider ancillary orders
Refer to pages 168-174 for guidance on available ancillary orders

Decide sentence
Give reasons

Effective from August 4, 2008

3A.25

OFFENCES APPROPRIATE FOR IMPOSITION OF FINE OR DISCHARGE

Part 1: Offences concerning the driver

Offence	Maximum	Points	Starting point	Special considerations
Fail to co-operate with preliminary (roadside) breath test	L3	4	B	
Fail to give information of driver's identity as required	L3	6	C	For limited companies, endorsement is not available; a fine is the only available penalty
Fail to produce insurance certificate	L4	–	A	Fine per offence, not per document
Fail to produce test certificate	L3	–	A	
Drive otherwise than in accordance with licence (where could be covered)	L3	–	A	
Drive otherwise than in accordance with licence	L3	3 – 6	A	Aggravating factor if no licence ever held

Part 2: Offences concerning the vehicle

* The guidelines for some of the offences below differentiate between three types of offender when the offence is committed in the course of business: driver, owner-driver and owner-company. **For owner-driver, the starting point is the same as for driver; however, the court should consider an uplift of at least 25%.**

Offence	Maximum	Points	Starting point	Special considerations
No excise licence	L3 or 5 times annual duty, whichever is greater	–	A (1-3 months unpaid) B (4-6 months unpaid) C (7-12 months unpaid)	Add duty lost
Fail to notify change of ownership to DVLA	L3	–	A	If offence committed in course of business: A (driver) A* (owner-driver) B (owner-company)
No test certificate	L3	–	A	If offence committed in course of business: A (driver) A* (owner-driver) B (owner-company)
Brakes defective	L4	3	B	If offence committed in course of business: B (driver) B* (owner-driver) C (owner-company) L5 if goods vehicle – see Part 5 below
Steering defective	L4	3	B	If offence committed in course of business: B (driver) B* (owner-driver) C (owner-company) L5 if goods vehicle – see Part 5 below

Effective from August 4, 2008

Offence	Maximum	Points	Starting point	Special considerations
Tyres defective	L4	3	B	If offence committed in course of business: B (driver) B* (owner-driver) C (owner-company) L5 if goods vehicle – see Part 5 below Penalty per tyre
Condition of vehicle/accessories/equipment involving danger of injury (Road Traffic Act 1988, s.40A)	L4	3	B	Must disqualify for at least 6 months if offender has one or more previous convictions for same offence within three years If offence committed in course of business: B (driver) B* (owner-driver) C (owner-company) L5 if goods vehicle – see Part 5 below
Exhaust defective	L3	–	A	If offence committed in course of business: A (driver) A* (owner-driver) B (owner-company)
Lights defective	L3	–	A	If offence committed in course of business: A (driver) A* (owner-driver) B (owner-company)

Part 3: Offences concerning use of vehicle

* The guidelines for some of the offences below differentiate between three types of offender when the offence is committed in the course of business: driver, owner-driver and owner-company. **For owner-driver, the starting point is the same as for driver; however, the court should consider an uplift of at least 25%.**

Offence	Maximum	Points	Starting point	Special considerations
Weight, position or distribution of load or manner in which load secured involving danger of injury (Road Traffic Act 1988, s.40A)	L4	3	B	Must disqualify for at least 6 months if offender has one or more previous convictions for same offence within three years If offence committed in course of business: A (driver) A* (owner-driver) B (owner-company) L5 if goods vehicle – see Part 5 below
Number of passengers or way carried involving danger of injury (Road Traffic Act 1988, s.40A)	L4	3	B	If offence committed in course of business: A (driver) A* (owner-driver) B (owner-company) L5 if goods vehicle – see Part 5 below
Position or manner in which load secured (not involving danger) (Road Traffic Act 1988, s.42)	L3	–	A	L4 if goods vehicle – see Part 5 below

Effective from August 4, 2008

Offence	Maximum	Points	Starting point	Special considerations
Overloading/exceeding axle weight	L5	–	A	Starting point caters for cases where the overload is up to and including 10%. Thereafter, 10% should be added to the penalty for each additional 1% of overload Penalty per axle If offence committed in course of business: A (driver) A* (owner-driver) B (owner-company) If goods vehicle – see Part 5 below
Dangerous parking	L3	3	A	
Pelican/zebra crossing contravention	L3	3	A	
Fail to comply with traffic sign (e.g. red traffic light, stop sign, double white lines, no entry sign)	L3	3	A	
Fail to comply with traffic sign (e.g. give way sign, keep left sign, temporary signs)	L3	–	A	
Fail to comply with police constable directing traffic	L3	3	A	
Fail to stop when required by police constable	L5 (mechanically propelled vehicle) L3 (cycle)	–	B	
Use of mobile telephone	L3	3	A	
Seat belt offences	L2 (adult or child in front) L2 (child in rear)	–	A	
Fail to use appropriate child car seat	L2	–	A	

Part 4: Motorway offences

Offence	Maximum	Points	Starting point	Special considerations
Drive in reverse or wrong way on slip road	L4	3	B	
Drive in reverse or wrong way on motorway	L4	3	C	
Drive off carriageway (central reservation or hard shoulder)	L4	3	B	
Make U turn	L4	3	C	
Learner driver or excluded vehicle	L4	3	B	
Stop on hard shoulder	L4	–	A	
Vehicle in prohibited lane	L4	3	A	
Walk on motorway, slip road or hard shoulder	L4	–	A	

Effective from August 4, 2008

Part 5: Offences re buses/goods vehicles over 3.5 tonnes (GVW)

* The guidelines for these offences differentiate between three types of offender: driver; owner-driver; and owner-company. **For owner-driver, the starting point is the same as for driver; however, the court should consider an uplift of at least 25%.**

** In all cases, take safety, damage to roads and commercial gain into account. Refer to page 150 for approach to fines for 'commercially motivated' offences.

Offence	Maximum	Points	Starting point	Special considerations
No goods vehicle plating certificate	L3	–	A (driver) A* (owner-driver) B (owner-company)	
No goods vehicle test certificate	L4	–	B (driver) B* (owner-driver) C (owner-company)	
Brakes defective	L5	3	B (driver) B* (owner-driver) C (owner-company)	
Steering defective	L5	3	B (driver) B* (owner-driver) C (owner-company)	
Tyres defective	L5	3	B (driver) B* (owner-driver) C (owner-company)	Penalty per tyre
Exhaust emission	L4	–	B (driver) B* (owner-driver) C (owner-company)	
Condition of vehicle/accessories/equipment involving danger of injury (Road Traffic Act 1988, s.40A)	L5	3	B (driver) B* (owner-driver) C (owner-company)	Must disqualify for at least 6 months if offender has one or more previous convictions for same offence within three years
Number of passengers or way carried involving danger of injury (Road Traffic Act 1988, s.40A)	L5	3	B (driver) B* (owner-driver) C (owner-company)	Must disqualify for at least 6 months if offender has one or more previous convictions for same offence within three years
Weight, position or distribution of load or manner in which load secured involving danger of injury (Road Traffic Act 1988, s.40A)	L5	3	B (driver) B* (owner-driver) C (owner-company)	Must disqualify for at least 6 months if offender has one or more previous convictions for same offence within three years
Position or manner in which load secured (not involving danger) (Road Traffic Act 1988, s.42)	L4	–	B (driver) B* (owner-driver) C (owner-company)	
Overloading/exceeding axle weight	L5	–	B (driver) B* (owner-driver) C (owner-company)	Starting points cater for cases where the overload is up to and including 10%. Thereafter, 10% should be added to the penalty for each additional 1% of overload Penalty per axle

Effective from August 4, 2008

Offence	Maximum	Points	Starting point	Special considerations
No operators licence	L4	–	B (driver) B* (owner-driver) C (owner-company)	
Speed limiter not used or incorrectly calibrated	L4	–	B (driver) B* (owner-driver) C (owner-company)	
Tachograph not used/not working	L5	–	B (driver) B* (owner-driver) C (owner-company)	
Exceed permitted driving time/ periods of duty	L4	–	B (driver) B* (owner-driver) C (owner-company)	
Fail to keep/return written record sheets	L4	–	B (driver) B* (owner-driver) C (owner-company)	
Falsify or alter records with intent to deceive	L5/2 years	–	B (driver) B* (owner-driver) C (owner-company)	Either way offence

Effective from August 4, 2008

Explanatory Material

Meaning of 'range', 'starting point' and 'first time offender'

As in previous editions, and consistent with other Sentencing Guidelines Council guidelines, these guidelines are for a **first time offender** convicted after a trial. They provide a **starting point** based on an assessment of the seriousness of the offence and a **range** within which the sentence will normally fall in most cases.

A clear, consistent understanding of each of these terms is essential and the Council and the Sentencing Advisory Panel have agreed the meanings set out in paragraphs 1(a)-(d) below.

They are explained in a format that follows the structured approach to the sentencing decision which identifies first those aspects that affect the assessment of the seriousness of the offence, then those aspects that form part of personal mitigation and, finally, any reduction for a guilty plea.

In practice, the boundaries between these stages will not always be as clear cut but the underlying principles will remain the same.

In accordance with section 174 of the Criminal Justice Act 2003, a court is obliged to '*state in open court, in ordinary language and in general terms, its reasons for deciding on the sentence passed*'.

In particular, '*where guidelines indicate that a sentence of a particular kind, or within a particular range, would normally be appropriate and the sentence is of a different kind, or is outside that range*' the court must give its reasons for imposing a sentence of a different kind or outside the range.

Assessing the seriousness of the offence

1. a) These guidelines apply to an offence that can be committed in a variety of circumstances with different levels of seriousness. They apply to a **first time offender** who has been convicted after a trial.[1] Within the guidelines, a **first time offender** is a person who does not have a conviction which, by virtue of section 143(2) of the Criminal Justice Act 2003, must be treated as an aggravating factor.

    b) As an aid to consistency of approach, a guideline will describe a number of types of activity falling within the broad definition of the offence. These are set out in a column headed 'examples of nature of activity'.

    c) The expected approach is for a court to identify the description that most nearly matches the particular facts of the offence for which sentence is being imposed. This will identify a **starting point** from which the sentencer can depart to reflect aggravating or mitigating factors affecting the seriousness of the *offence* (beyond those contained in the description itself) to reach a **provisional sentence**.

    d) The range is the bracket into which the **provisional sentence** will normally fall after having regard to factors which aggravate or mitigate the seriousness of the offence. The particular circumstances may, however, make it appropriate that the **provisional sentence** falls outside the **range**.

2. Where the offender has previous convictions which aggravate the seriousness of the current offence, that may take the **provisional sentence** beyond the **range** given particularly where there are significant other aggravating factors present.

---

[1] This means any case in which there is no guilty plea including, e.g., where an offender is convicted in absence after evidence has been heard

Effective from August 4, 2008

Offender Mitigation

3. Once the **provisional sentence** has been identified (by reference to the factors affecting the seriousness of the **offence**), the court will take into account any relevant factors of **offender** mitigation. Again, this may take the provisional sentence outside the range.

Reduction for guilty plea

4. Where there has been a guilty plea, any reduction attributable to that plea will be applied to the sentence at this stage. This reduction may take the sentence below the **range** provided.

Fine band starting points and ranges

In these guidelines, where the starting point or range for an offence is or includes a fine, it is expressed as one of three fine bands (A, B or C). As detailed on page 148 below, each fine band has both a starting point and a range.

On some offence guidelines, both the starting point and the range are expressed as a single fine band; see for example careless driving on page 117 where the starting point and range for the first level of offence activity are 'band A fine'. This means that the starting point will be the starting point for fine band A (50% of the offender's relevant weekly income) and the range will be the range for fine band A (25-75% of relevant weekly income). On other guidelines, the range encompasses more than one fine band; see for example drunk and disorderly in a public place on page 55 where the starting point for the second level of offence activity is 'band B fine' and the range is 'band A fine to band C fine'. This means that the starting point will be the starting point for fine band B (100% of relevant weekly income) and the range will be the lowest point of the range for fine band A to the highest point of the range for fine band C (25%-175% of relevant weekly income).

Sentencing for multiple offences

The starting points and ranges indicated in the individual offence guidelines assume that the offender is being sentenced for a single offence. Where an offender is being sentenced for multiple offences, the overall sentence must be just and appropriate having regard to the totality of the offending; the court should not simply aggregate the sentences considered suitable for the individual offences. The court's assessment of the totality of the offending may result in an overall sentence above the range indicated for the individual offences, including a sentence of a different type.[1]

While concurrent sentences are generally to be preferred where the offences arose out of a single incident, consecutive sentences may be desirable in some circumstances. **Consult your legal adviser for further guidance.**

Offences not included in the guidelines

A number of offences are currently under consideration by the Council and will be included in the MCSG by way of an update when agreed. In the interim, the relevant guideline from the previous version of the MCSG has been included for ease of reference – **these do not constitute formal guidelines issued by the Council.**

Where there is no guideline for an offence, it may assist in determining sentence to consider the starting points and ranges indicated for offences that are of a similar level of seriousness.

When sentencing for the breach of any order for which there is not a specific guideline, the primary objective will be to ensure compliance. Reference to existing guidelines in respect of breaches of orders may provide a helpful point of comparison (see in particular page 43 (breach of community order) and page 83 (breach of protective order)).

Consult your legal adviser for further guidance.

---

[1] When considering whether the threshold for a community or custodial sentence is passed, ss.148(1) and 152(2) of the Criminal Justice Act 2003 confirm that the court may have regard to the combination of the offence and one or more offences associated with it

Effective from August 4, 2008

Approach to the assessment of fines

Introduction

1. The amount of a fine must reflect the **seriousness** of the offence.[1]

2. The court must also take into account the **financial circumstances** of the offender; this applies whether it has the effect of increasing or reducing the fine.[2] Normally a fine should be of an amount that is capable of being paid within 12 months.

3. The aim is for the fine to have an equal impact on offenders with different financial circumstances; it should be a hardship but should not force the offender below a reasonable 'subsistence' level.

4. The guidance below aims to establish a clear, consistent and principled approach to the assessment of fines that will apply fairly in the majority of cases. However, it is impossible to anticipate every situation that may be encountered and in each case the court will need to exercise its judgement to ensure that the fine properly reflects the **seriousness of the offence** and takes into account the **financial circumstances** of the offender.

Fine bands

5. For the purpose of the offence guidelines, a fine is based on one of three bands (A, B or C).[3] The selection of the relevant fine band, and the position of the individual offence within that band, is determined by the **seriousness** of the offence.

	Starting point	**Range**
Fine Band A	50% of relevant weekly income	25 – 75% of relevant weekly income
Fine Band B	100% of relevant weekly income	75 – 125% of relevant weekly income
Fine Band C	150% of relevant weekly income	125 – 175% of relevant weekly income

6. For an explanation of the meaning of starting point and range, both generally and in relation to fines, see pages 145-146.

Definition of relevant weekly income

7. The **seriousness** of an offence determines the choice of fine band and the position of the offence within the range for that band. The offender's **financial circumstances** are taken into account by expressing that position as a proportion of the offender's **relevant weekly income**.

8. Where an offender is in receipt of income from employment or is self-employed **and** that income is more than £100 per week after deduction of tax and national insurance (or equivalent where the offender is self-employed), the actual income is the **relevant weekly income**.

9. Where an offender's only source of income is state benefit (including where there is relatively low additional income as permitted by the benefit regulations) or the offender is in receipt of income from employment or is self-employed but the amount of income after deduction of tax and national insurance is £100 or less, the **relevant weekly income is deemed to be £100**. Additional information about the basis for this approach is set out on page 155.

10. In calculating relevant weekly income, no account should be taken of tax credits, housing benefit, child benefit or similar.

---

[1] Criminal Justice Act 2003, s.164(2)

[2] ibid., ss.164(1) and 164(4)

[3] As detailed in paras.36-38 below, two further bands are provided which apply where the offence has passed the threshold for a community order (Band D) or a custodial sentence (Band E) but the court decides that it need not impose such a sentence and that a financial penalty is appropriate

Effective from August 4, 2008

No reliable information

11. Where an offender has failed to provide information, or the court is not satisfied that it has been given sufficient reliable information, it is entitled to make such determination as it thinks fit regarding the financial circumstances of the offender.[4] Any determination should be clearly stated on the court records for use in any subsequent variation or enforcement proceedings. In such cases, a record should also be made of the applicable fine band and the court's assessment of the position of the offence within that band based on the seriousness of the offence.

12. Where there is no information on which a determination can be made, the court should proceed on the basis of an **assumed relevant weekly income of £350**. This is derived from national median pre-tax earnings; a gross figure is used as, in the absence of financial information from the offender, it is not possible to calculate appropriate deductions.[5]

13. Where there is some information that tends to suggest a significantly lower or higher income than the recommended £350 default sum, the court should make a determination based on that information.

14. A court is empowered to remit a fine in whole or part if the offender subsequently provides information as to means.[6] The assessment of offence seriousness and, therefore, the appropriate fine band and the position of the offence within that band is **not** affected by the provision of this information.

Assessment of financial circumstances

15. While the initial consideration for the assessment of a fine is the offender's relevant weekly income, the court is required to take account of the offender's **financial circumstances** more broadly. Guidance on important parts of this assessment is set out below.

16. An offender's financial circumstances may have the effect of increasing or reducing the amount of the fine; however, they are **not** relevant to the assessment of offence seriousness. They should be considered separately from the selection of the appropriate fine band and the court's assessment of the position of the offence within the range for that band.

Out of the ordinary expenses

17. In deciding the proportions of relevant weekly income that are the starting points and ranges for each fine band, account has been taken of reasonable living expenses. Accordingly, no further allowance should normally be made for these. In addition, no allowance should normally be made where the offender has dependants.

18. Outgoings will be relevant to the amount of the fine only where the expenditure is **out of the ordinary** and **substantially** reduces the ability to pay a financial penalty so that the requirement to pay a fine based on the standard approach would lead to **undue** hardship.

Unusually low outgoings

19. Where the offender's living expenses are substantially **lower** than would normally be expected, it may be appropriate to adjust the amount of the fine to reflect this. This may apply, for example, where an offender does not make any financial contribution towards his or her living costs.

---

[4] Criminal Justice Act 2003, s.164(5)

[5] For 2004-05, the median pre-tax income of all tax payers was £315 per week: HMRC Survey of Personal Incomes. This figure has been increased to take account of inflation

[6] Criminal Justice Act 2003, s.165(2)

Effective from August 4, 2008

Savings

20. Where an offender has savings these will not normally be relevant to the assessment of the amount of a fine although they may influence the decision on time to pay.

21. However, where an offender has little or no income but has substantial savings, the court may consider it appropriate to adjust the amount of the fine to reflect this.

Household has more than one source of income

22. Where the household of which the offender is a part has more than one source of income, the fine should normally be based on the income of the offender alone.

23. However, where the offender's part of the income is very small (or the offender is wholly dependent on the income of another), the court may have regard to the extent of the household's income and assets which will be available to meet any fine imposed on the offender.[7]

Potential earning capacity

24. Where there is reason to believe that an offender's potential earning capacity is greater than his or her current income, the court may wish to adjust the amount of the fine to reflect this.[8] This may apply, for example, where an unemployed offender states an expectation to gain paid employment within a short time. The basis for the calculation of fine should be recorded in order to ensure that there is a clear record for use in variation or enforcement proceedings.

High income offenders

25. Where the offender is in receipt of very high income, a fine based on a proportion of relevant weekly income may be disproportionately high when compared with the seriousness of the offence. In such cases, the court should adjust the fine to an appropriate level; as a general indication, in most cases the fine for a first time offender pleading not guilty should not exceed 75% of the maximum fine.

Offence committed for 'commercial' purposes

26. Some offences are committed with the intention of gaining a significant commercial benefit. These often occur where, in order to carry out an activity lawfully, a person has to comply with certain processes which may be expensive. They include, for example, 'taxi-touting' (where unauthorised persons seek to operate as taxi drivers) and 'fly-tipping' (where the cost of lawful disposal is considerable).

27. In some of these cases, a fine based on the standard approach set out above may not reflect the level of financial gain achieved or sought through the offending. Accordingly:

a. where the offender has generated income or avoided expenditure to a level that can be calculated or estimated, the court may wish to consider that amount when determining the financial penalty;

b. where it is not possible to calculate or estimate that amount, the court may wish to draw on information from the enforcing authorities about the general costs of operating within the law.

Reduction for a guilty plea

28. Where a guilty plea has been entered, the amount of the fine should be reduced by the appropriate proportion. See page 17 of the user guide for guidance.

---

[7] *R v Engen* [2004] EWCA Crim 1536 (CA)
[8] *R v Little* (unreported) 14 April 1976 (CA)

Effective from August 4, 2008

Other considerations

Maximum fines

29. A fine must not exceed the statutory limit. Where this is expressed in terms of a 'level', the maxima are:

Level 1	£200
Level 2	£500
Level 3	£1,000
Level 4	£2,500
Level 5	£5,000

Victims surcharge

30. Whenever a court imposes a fine in respect of an offence committed after 1 April 2007, it must order the offender to pay a surcharge of £15.[9]

31. Where the offender is of adequate means, the court must not reduce the fine to allow for imposition of the surcharge. Where the offender does not have sufficient means to pay the total financial penalty considered appropriate by the court, the order of priority is compensation, surcharge, fine, costs.

32. Further guidance is set out in *Guidance on Victims Surcharge* issued by the Justices' Clerks' Society and Magistrates' Association (30 March 2007).

Costs

33. See page 175 for guidance on the approach to costs. Where the offender does not have sufficient means to pay the total financial penalty considered appropriate by the court, the order of priority is compensation, surcharge, fine, costs.

Multiple offences

34. Where an offender is to be fined for two or more offences that arose out of the same incident, it will often be appropriate to impose on the most serious offence a fine which reflects the totality of the offending where this can be achieved within the maximum penalty for that offence. 'No separate penalty' should be imposed for the other offences.

35. Where compensation is being ordered, that will need to be attributed to the relevant offence as will any necessary ancillary orders.

Fine Bands D and E

36. Two further fine bands are provided to assist a court in calculating a fine where the offence and general circumstances would otherwise warrant a community order (band D) or a custodial sentence (band E) but the court has decided that it need not impose such a sentence and that a financial penalty is appropriate. See pages 160 and 163 for further guidance.

37. The following starting points and ranges apply:

	Starting point	**Range**
Fine Band D	250% of relevant weekly income	200 – 300% of relevant weekly income
Fine Band E	400% of relevant weekly income	300 – 500% of relevant weekly income

38. In cases where these fine bands apply, it may be appropriate for the fine to be of an amount that is larger than can be repaid within 12 months. See paragraph 43 below.

---

[9] Criminal Justice Act 2003, ss.161A and 161B

Effective from August 4, 2008

Imposition of fines with custodial sentences

39. A fine and a custodial sentence may be imposed for the same offence although there will be few circumstances in which this is appropriate, particularly where the custodial sentence is to be served immediately. One example might be where an offender has profited financially from an offence but there is no obvious victim to whom compensation can be awarded. Combining these sentences is most likely to be appropriate only where the custodial sentence is short and/or the offender clearly has, or will have, the means to pay.

40. Care must be taken to ensure that the overall sentence is proportionate to the seriousness of the offence and that better off offenders are not able to 'buy themselves out of custody'.

Consult your legal adviser in any case in which you are considering combining a fine with a custodial sentence.

Payment

41. A fine is payable in full on the day on which it is imposed. The offender should always be asked for immediate payment when present in court and some payment on the day should be required wherever possible.

42. Where that is not possible, the court may, in certain circumstances, require the offender to be detained. More commonly, a court will allow payments to be made over a period set by the court:

    a. if periodic payments are allowed, the fine should normally be payable within a maximum of 12 months. However, it may be unrealistic to expect those on very low incomes to maintain payments for as long as a year;

    b. compensation should normally be payable within 12 months. However, in exceptional circumstances it may be appropriate to allow it to be paid over a period of up to 3 years.

43. Where fine bands D and E apply (see paragraphs 36-38 above), it may be appropriate for the fine to be of an amount that is larger than can be repaid within 12 months. In such cases, the fine should normally be payable within a maximum of 18 months (band D) or 2 years (band E).

44. It is generally recognised that the maximum weekly payment by a person in receipt of state benefit should rarely exceed £5.

45. When allowing payment by instalments by an offender in receipt of earned income, the following approach may be useful. If the offender has dependants or larger than usual commitments, the weekly payment is likely to be decreased.

Net weekly income	Starting point for weekly payment
£60	£5
£120	£10
£200	£25
£250	£30
£300	£50
£400	£80

46. The payment terms must be included in any collection order made in respect of the amount imposed; see pages 156-157

SHOULD BE 220 mm wide for pullout

Effective from August 4, 2008

Assessment of fines: sentencing structure

1. Decide that a fine is appropriate

2. Offence seriousness
A. Identify the appropriate fine band

- In the offence guidelines, the starting point for a fine is identified as fine band A, B or C
- Each fine band provides a **starting point** and a **range** related to the **seriousness** of the offence expressed as a proportion of the offender's **relevant weekly income** – see paragraph 5 on page 148

2. Offence seriousness
B. Consider the effect of aggravating and mitigating factors

- **Move up or down from the starting point** to reflect aggravating or mitigating factors that affect the **seriousness** of the offence – this will usually be within the indicated **range** for the fine band but the court is not precluded from going outside the range where the facts justify it – see pages 145-146

3. Consider offender mitigation

- The court may consider it appropriate to make a further adjustment to the starting point in light of any matters of offender mitigation – see page 17 of the user guide

4. Form a view of the position of the offence within the range for the fine band then take into account the offender's financial circumstances

- Require the offender to provide a statement of **financial circumstances**. Obtain further information through questioning if necessary. Failure to provide the information when required is an offence
- The provision of financial information does not affect the seriousness of the offence or, therefore, the position of the offence within the range for the applicable fine band
- The initial consideration for the assessment of the fine is the offender's **relevant weekly income** – see paragraphs 7-10 on page 148
- However, the court must take account of the offender's financial circumstances more broadly. These may have the effect of **increasing or reducing** the amount of the fine – see paragraphs 15-25 on pages 149-150
- Where the court has **insufficient information** to make a proper determination of the offender's financial circumstances, it may make such determination as it thinks fit – see paragraphs 11-14 on page 149

5. Consider a reduction for a guilty plea

- Reduce the fine by the appropriate proportion – see page 17 of the user guide

6. Consider ancillary orders, including compensation

- Consider compensation in every case where the offending has resulted in personal injury, loss or damage – give reasons if order not made – see pages 165-167. Compensation takes priority over a fine where there are insufficient resources to pay both
- See pages 168-174 for guidance on available ancillary orders

7. Decide sentence
Give reasons

- **The resulting fine must reflect the seriousness of the offence and must take into account the offender's financial circumstances**
- Consider the proposed total financial penalty, including compensation, victims surcharge and costs. Where there are insufficient resources to pay the total amount, the order of priority is compensation, surcharge, fine, costs
- Give reasons for the sentence passed, including any ancillary orders
- State if the sentence has been reduced to reflect a guilty plea; indicate what the sentence would otherwise have been
- Explain if the sentence is of a different kind or outside the range indicated in the guidelines
- Expect immediate payment. If payment by instalments allowed, the court must make a collection order unless this would be impracticable or inappropriate – see pages 156-157

Effective from August 4, 2008

3A.30

Additional information: approach to offenders on low income

1. An offender whose primary source of income is state benefit will generally receive a base level of benefit (e.g. job seekers' allowance, a relevant disability benefit or income support) and may also be eligible for supplementary benefits depending on his or her individual circumstances (such as child tax credits, housing benefit, council tax benefit and similar).

2. If relevant weekly income were defined as the amount of benefit received, this would usually result in higher fines being imposed on offenders with a higher level of need; in most circumstances that would not properly balance the seriousness of the offence with the financial circumstances of the offender. While it might be possible to exclude from the calculation any allowance above the basic entitlement of a single person, that could be complicated and time consuming.

3. Similar issues can arise where an offender is in receipt of a low earned income since this may trigger eligibility for means related benefits such as working tax credits and housing benefit depending on the particular circumstances. It will not always be possible to determine with any confidence whether such a person's financial circumstances are significantly different from those of a person whose primary source of income is state benefit.

4. For these reasons, a simpler and fairer approach to cases involving offenders in receipt of low income (whether primarily earned or as a result of benefit) is to identify an amount that is deemed to represent the offender's relevant weekly income.

5. While a precise calculation is neither possible nor desirable, it is considered that an amount that is approximately half-way between the base rate for job seekers' allowance and the net weekly income of an adult earning the minimum wage for 30 hours per week represents a starting point that is both realistic and appropriate; **this is currently £100.**[1] The calculation is based on a 30 hour working week in recognition of the fact that many of those on minimum wage do not work a full 37 hour week and that lower minimum wage rates apply to younger people.

6. It is expected that this figure will remain in use until 31 March 2011. Future revisions of the guideline will update the amount in accordance with current benefit and minimum wage levels.

---

[1] With effect from 1 October 2007, the minimum wage is £5.52 per hour for an adult aged 22 or over. Based on a 30 hour week, this equates to approximately £149.14 after deductions for tax and national insurance. To ensure equivalence of approach, the level of job seekers' allowance for a single person aged 22 has been used for the purpose of calculating the mid point; this is currently £46.85

Effective from August 4, 2008

Road traffic offences

Disqualification

Obligatory disqualification

1. Some offences carry obligatory disqualification for a minimum of 12 months.[1] The minimum period is automatically increased where there have been certain previous convictions and disqualifications.

2. An offender must be disqualified for **at least two years** if he or she has been disqualified two or more times for a period of at least 56 days in the three years preceding the commission of the offence.[2] The following disqualifications are to be disregarded for the purposes of this provision:

- interim disqualification;

- disqualification where vehicle used for the purpose of crime;

- disqualification for stealing or taking a vehicle or going equipped to steal or take a vehicle.

3. An offender must be disqualified for **at least three years** if he or she is convicted of one of the following offences <u>and</u> has within the ten years preceding the commission of the offence been convicted of any of these offences:[3]

- causing death by careless driving when under the influence of drink or drugs;

- driving or attempting to drive while unfit;

- driving or attempting to drive with excess alcohol;

- failing to provide a specimen (drive/attempting to drive).

4. The individual offence guidelines above indicate whether disqualification is mandatory for the offence and the applicable minimum period. **Consult your legal adviser for further guidance.**

5. The period of disqualification may be reduced or avoided if there are special reasons.[4] These must relate to the offence; circumstances peculiar to the offender cannot constitute special reasons.[5] The Court of Appeal has established that, to constitute a special reason, a matter must:[6]

- be a mitigating or extenuating circumstance;

- not amount in law to a defence to the charge;

- be directly connected with the commission of the offence;

- be one which the court ought properly to take into consideration when imposing sentence.

6. **Consult your legal adviser for further guidance on special reasons applications.**

---

[1] Road Traffic Offenders Act 1988, s.34
[2] ibid., s.34(4)
[3] ibid., s.34(3)
[4] ibid., s.34(1)
[5] *Whittal v Kirby* [1946] 2 All ER 552 (CA)
[6] *R v Wickens* (1958) 42 Cr App R 436 (CA)

Effective from August 4, 2008

'Totting up' disqualification

7. Disqualification for a **minimum** of six months must be ordered if an offender incurs 12 penalty points or more within a three-year period.[7] The minimum period may be automatically increased if the offender has been disqualified within the preceding three years. Totting up disqualifications, unlike other disqualifications, erase all penalty points.

8. The period of a totting up disqualification can be reduced or avoided for exceptional hardship or other mitigating circumstances. No account is to be taken of hardship that is not exceptional hardship or circumstances alleged to make the offence not serious. Any circumstances taken into account in the preceding three years to reduce or avoid a totting disqualification must be disregarded.[8]

9. **Consult your legal adviser for further guidance on exceptional hardship applications.**

Discretionary disqualification

10. Whenever an offender is convicted of an endorsable offence or of taking a vehicle without consent, the court has a discretionary power to disqualify instead of imposing penalty points. The individual offence guidelines above indicate whether the offence is endorsable and the number or range of penalty points it carries.

11. The number of variable points or the period of disqualification should reflect the seriousness of the offence. Some of the individual offence guidelines above include penalty points and/or periods of disqualification in the sentence starting points and ranges; however, the court is not precluded from sentencing outside the range where the facts justify it. Where a disqualification is for less than 56 days, there are some differences in effect compared with disqualification for a longer period; in particular, the licence will automatically come back into effect at the end of the disqualification period (instead of requiring application by the driver) and the disqualification is not taken into account for the purpose of increasing subsequent obligatory periods of disqualification.[9]

12. In some cases in which the court is considering discretionary disqualification, the offender may already have sufficient penalty points on his or her licence that he or she would be liable to a 'totting up' disqualification if further points were imposed. In these circumstances, the court should impose penalty points rather than discretionary disqualification so that the minimum totting up disqualification period applies (see paragraph 7 above).

Disqualification until a test is passed

13. Where an offender is convicted of dangerous driving, the court must order disqualification until an extended driving test is passed.

14. The court has discretion to disqualify until a test is passed where an offender is convicted of any endorsable offence.[10] Where disqualification is obligatory, the extended test applies. In other cases, it will be the ordinary test.

15. An offender disqualified as a 'totter' under the penalty points provisions may also be ordered to re-take a driving test; in this case, the extended test applies.

16. The discretion to order a re-test is likely to be exercised where there is evidence of inexperience, incompetence or infirmity, or the disqualification period is lengthy (that is, the offender is going to be 'off the road' for a considerable time).

---

[7] Road Traffic Offenders Act 1988, s.35
[8] ibid.
[9] ibid., ss.34(4), 35(2), 37(1A)
[10] ibid., s.36(4)

Effective from August 4, 2008

Reduced period of disqualification for completion of rehabilitation course

17. Where an offender is disqualified for 12 months or more in respect of an alcohol-related driving offence, the court may order that the period of disqualification will be reduced if the offender satisfactorily completes an approved rehabilitation course.[11]

18. Before offering an offender the opportunity to attend a course, the court must be satisfied that an approved course is available and must inform the offender of the effect of the order, the fees that the offender is required to pay, and when he or she must pay them.

19. The court should also explain that the offender may be required to satisfy the Secretary of State that he or she does not have a drink problem and is fit to drive before the offender's licence will be returned at the end of the disqualification period.[12]

20. In general, a court should consider offering the opportunity to attend a course to all offenders convicted of a relevant offence for the first time. The court should be willing to consider offering an offender the opportunity to attend a second course where it considers there are good reasons. It will not usually be appropriate to give an offender the opportunity to attend a third course.

21. The reduction must be at least three months but cannot be more than one quarter of the total period of disqualification:

- a period of 12 months disqualification must be reduced to nine months;

- in other cases, a reduction of one week should be made for every month of the disqualification so that, for example, a disqualification of 24 months will be reduced by 24 weeks.

22. When it makes the order, the court must specify a date for completion of the course which is at least two months before the end of the reduced period of disqualification.

Disqualification in the offender's absence

23. A court is able to disqualify an offender in absence provided that he or she has been given adequate notice of the hearing and that disqualification is to be considered.[13] It is recommended, however, that the court should avoid exercising this power wherever possible unless it is sure that the offender is aware of the hearing and the likely imposition of disqualification. This is because an offender who is disqualified in absence commits an offence by driving from the time the order is made, even if he or she has not yet received notification of it, and, as a result of the disqualification, is likely to be uninsured in relation to any injury or damage caused.

New drivers

24. Drivers who incur six points or more during the two-year probationary period after passing the driving test will have their licence revoked automatically by the Secretary of State; they will be able to drive only after application for a provisional licence pending the passing of a further test.[14]

25. An offender liable for an endorsement which will cause the licence to be revoked under the new drivers' provisions may ask the court to disqualify rather than impose points. This will avoid the requirement to take a further test. Generally, this would be inappropriate since it would circumvent the clear intention of Parliament.

---

[11] Road Traffic Offenders Act 1988, s.34A
[12] Road Traffic Act 1988, s.94 and Motor Vehicles (Driving Licences) Regulations 1999, reg.74
[13] Magistrates' Courts Act 1980, s.11(4)
[14] Road Traffic (New Drivers) Act 1995

Effective from August 4, 2008

Annex B: Offences for which penalty notices are available

The tables below list the offences covered in the MCSG for which penalty notices are available and the amount of the penalty. **Consult your legal adviser for further guidance.**

Penalty notices for disorder

Offence	Legislation	Amount
Criminal damage (where damage under £500 in value, and not normally where damage over £300)	Criminal Damage Act 1971, s.1	£80
Disorderly behaviour	Public Order Act 1986, s.5	£80
Drunk and disorderly	Criminal Justice Act 1967, s.91	£80
Sale of alcohol to drunk person on relevant premises (not including off-licenses)	Licensing Act 2003, s.141	£80
Sale of alcohol to person under 18 (staff only; licensees should be subject of a summons)	Licensing Act 2003, s.146	£80
Theft from a shop (where goods under £200 in value, and not normally where goods over £100)	Theft Act 1968, s.1	£80

Fixed penalty notices

Offence	Legislation	Amount	Penalty points
Brakes, steering or tyres defective	Road Traffic Act 1988, s.41A	£60	3
Breach of other construction and use requirements	Road Traffic Act 1988, s.42	£60	3
Driving other than in accordance with licence	Road Traffic Act 1988, s.87(1)	£60	3
Failing to comply with police officer signal	Road Traffic Act 1988, s.35	£30	3
Failing to comply with traffic sign	Road Traffic Act 1988, s.36	£60	3
Failing to supply details of driver's identity	Road Traffic Act 1988, s.172	£120	6
No insurance	Road Traffic Act 1988, s.143	£200	6
No test certificate	Road Traffic Act 1988, s.47	£30	–
Overloading/exceeding axle weight	Road Traffic Act 1988, s.41B	£30	–
Pelican/zebra crossing contravention	Road Traffic Regulation Act 1984, s.25(5)	£60	3
Railway fare evasion (where penalty notice scheme in operation by train operator)	Railways (Penalty Fares) Regulations 1994	£20 or twice the full single fare to next stop, whichever is greater	–
Seat belt offences	Road Traffic Act 1988, s.14	£30	–
School non-attendance	Education Act 1996, s.444(1)	£50 if paid within 28 days; £100 if paid within 42 days	–
Speeding	Road Traffic Regulation Act 1984, s.89(1)	£60	3
Using hand-held mobile phone while driving	Road Traffic Act 1988, s.41D	£60	3
Using vehicle in dangerous condition	Road Traffic Act 1988, s.40A	£60	3

Effective from August 4, 2008

CAUSING DEATH BY DRIVING: DEFINITIVE GUIDELINE

The Sentencing Guidelines Council published its definitive guideline on causing death by driving on July 15, 2008. The guideline is available at *http://www.sentencing-guidelines.gov.uk* or can be obtained from the Sentencing Guidelines Secretariat at 4th Floor, 8–10 Great George Street, London SW1P 3AE. The guideline applies to the sentencing of offenders convicted of any of the offences dealt with in the guideline who are sentenced on or after August 4, 2008. It applies only to the sentencing of offenders aged 18 and older. A separate guideline setting out general principles relating to the sentencing of youths is planned.

The guidelines are reproduced with the kind permission of the Sentencing Guidelines Council.

4A.01

4A.02

CAUSING DEATH BY DRIVING

Introduction

1. This guideline applies to the four offences of *causing death by dangerous driving, causing death by driving under the influence of alcohol or drugs, causing death by careless driving and causing death by driving: unlicensed, disqualified or uninsured drivers.*

2. The Crown Prosecution Service's *Policy for Prosecuting Cases of Bad Driving* sets out the approach for prosecutors when considering the appropriate charge based on an assessment of the standard of the offender's driving. This has been taken into account when formulating this guideline. Annex A sets out the statutory definitions for dangerous, careless and inconsiderate driving together with examples of the types of driving behaviour likely to result in the charge of one offence rather than another.

3. Because the principal harm done by these offences (the death of a person) is an element of the offence, the factor that primarily determines the starting point for sentence is the culpability of the offender. Accordingly, for all offences other than *causing death by driving: unlicensed, disqualified or uninsured drivers*, the central feature should be an evaluation of the quality of the driving involved and the degree of danger that it foreseeably created. These guidelines draw a distinction between those factors of an offence that are intrinsic to the quality of driving (referred to as "determinants of seriousness") and those which, while they aggravate the offence, are not.

4. The levels of seriousness in the guidelines for those offences based on dangerous or careless driving alone have been determined by reference <u>only</u> to determinants of seriousness. Aggravating factors will have the effect of either increasing the starting point within the sentencing range provided or, in certain circumstances, of moving the offence up to the next sentencing range.[1] The outcome will depend on both the number of aggravating factors present and the potency of those factors. Thus, the same outcome could follow from the presence of one particularly bad aggravating factor or two or more less serious factors.

5. The determinants of seriousness likely to be relevant in relation to *causing death by careless driving under the influence* are both the degree of carelessness and the level of intoxication. The guideline sets out an approach to assessing both those aspects but giving greater weight to the degree of intoxication since Parliament has provided for a maximum of 14 years imprisonment rather than the maximum of 5 years where the death is caused by careless driving only.

6. Since there will be no allegation of bad driving, the guideline for *causing death by driving: unlicensed, disqualified or uninsured drivers* links the assessment of offender culpability to the nature of the prohibition on the offender's driving and includes a list of factors that may aggravate an offence.

7. The degree to which an aggravating factor is present (and its interaction with any other aggravating and mitigating factors) will be immensely variable and the court is best placed to judge the appropriate impact on sentence. Clear identification of those factors relating to the standard of driving as the initial determinants of offence seriousness is intended to assist the adoption of a common approach.

---

[1]   See page 8 for a description of the meaning of range, starting point etc. in the context of these guidelines.

A.   Assessing seriousness

(i)   Determinants of seriousness

8.   There are five factors that may be regarded as determinants of offence seriousness, each of which can be demonstrated in a number of ways. Common examples of each of the determinants are set out below and key issues are discussed in the text that follows in paragraphs 10–18.

Examples of the determinants are:

- **Awareness of risk**

(a) a prolonged, persistent and deliberate course of very bad driving

- **Effect of alcohol or drugs**

(b) consumption of alcohol above the legal limit

(c) consumption of alcohol at or below the legal limit where this impaired the offender's ability to drive

(d) failure to supply a specimen for analysis

(e) consumption of illegal drugs, where this impaired the offender's ability to drive

(f) consumption of legal drugs or medication where this impaired the offender's ability to drive (including legal medication known to cause drowsiness) where the driver knew, or should have known, about the likelihood of impairment

- **Inappropriate speed of vehicle**

(g) greatly excessive speed; racing; competitive driving against another vehicle

(h) driving above the speed limit

(i) driving at a speed that is inappropriate for the prevailing road or weather conditions

(j) driving a PSV, HGV or other goods vehicle at a speed that is inappropriate either because of the nature of the vehicle or its load, especially when carrying passengers

- **Seriously culpable behaviour of offender**

(k) aggressive driving (such as driving much too close to the vehicle in front, persistent inappropriate attempts to overtake, or cutting in after overtaking)

(l) driving while using a hand-held mobile phone

(m) driving whilst the driver's attention is avoidably distracted, for example by reading or adjusting the controls of electronic equipment such as a radio, hands-free mobile phone or satellite navigation equipment

(n) driving when knowingly suffering from a medical or physical condition that significantly impairs the offender's driving skills, including failure to take prescribed medication

(o) driving when knowingly deprived of adequate sleep or rest, especially where commercial concerns had a bearing on the commission of the offence

(p) driving a poorly maintained or dangerously loaded vehicle, especially where commercial concerns had a bearing on the commission of the offence

- **Victim**

(q) failing to have proper regard to vulnerable road users

9.   Issues relating to the determinants of seriousness are considered below.

(a)   **Alcohol/drugs**

10.   For those offences where the presence of alcohol or drugs is not an element of the offence, where there is sufficient evidence of driving impairment attributable to alcohol or drugs, the consumption of alcohol or drugs prior to driving will make an offence more serious. Where the drugs were legally purchased or prescribed, the offence will only be regarded as more serious if the offender knew or should have known that the drugs were likely to impair driving ability.

11.   Unless inherent in the offence or charged separately, failure to provide a specimen for analysis (or to allow a blood specimen taken without consent to be analysed) should be regarded as a determinant of offence seriousness.

12.   Where it is established to the satisfaction of the court that an offender had consumed alcohol or drugs unwittingly before driving, that may be regarded as a mitigating factor. However, consideration should be given to the circumstances in which the offender decided to drive or continue to drive when driving ability was impaired.

(b)   **Avoidable distractions**

13.   A distinction has been drawn between **ordinary** avoidable distractions and those that are more significant because they divert the attention of the driver for longer periods or to a greater extent; in this guideline these are referred to as a **gross** avoidable distraction. The guideline for *causing death by dangerous driving* provides for a gross avoidable distraction to place the offence in a higher level of seriousness.

14.   Any avoidable distraction will make an offence more serious but the degree to which an offender's driving will be impaired will vary. Where the reaction to the distraction is significant, it may be the factor that determines whether the offence is based on *dangerous* driving or on *careless* driving; in those circumstances, care must be taken to avoid "double counting".

15.   Using a hand-held mobile phone when driving is, in itself, an unlawful act; the fact that an offender was avoidably distracted by using a hand-held mobile phone when a causing death by driving offence was committed will always make an offence more serious. Reading or composing text messages *over a period of time* will be a *gross* avoidable distraction and is likely to result in an offence of causing death by dangerous driving being in a higher level of seriousness.

16.   Where it is proved that an offender was briefly distracted by reading a text message or adjusting a hands-free set or its controls at the time of the collision, this would be on a par with consulting a map or adjusting a radio or satellite navigation equipment, activities that would be considered an avoidable distraction.

(c)   **Vulnerable road users**

17.   Cyclists, motorbike riders, horse riders, pedestrians and those working in the road are vulnerable road users and a driver is expected to take extra care when driving near them. Driving too close to a bike or horse; allowing a vehicle to mount the pavement; driving into a cycle lane; and driving without the care needed in the vicinity of a pedestrian crossing, hospital, school or residential home, are all examples of factors that should be taken into account when determining the seriousness of an offence. See paragraph 24 below for the approach where the actions of another person contributed to the collision.

18. The fact that the victim of a causing death by driving offence was a particularly vulnerable road user is a factor that should be taken into account when determining the seriousness of an offence.

(ii) Aggravating and mitigating factors

(a) More than one person killed

19. The seriousness of any offence included in these guidelines will generally be greater where more than one person is killed since it is inevitable that the degree of harm will be greater. In relation to the assessment of culpability, whilst there will be circumstances in which a driver could reasonably anticipate the possible death of more than one person (for example, the driver of a vehicle with passengers (whether that is a bus, taxi or private car) or a person driving badly in an area where there are many people), there will be many circumstances where the driver could not anticipate the number of people who would be killed.

20. The greater obligation on those responsible for driving other people is not an element essential to the quality of the driving and so has not been included amongst the determinants of seriousness that affect the choice of sentencing range. In practical terms, separate charges are likely to be brought in relation to each death caused. Although concurrent sentences are likely to be imposed (in recognition of the fact that the charges relate to one episode of offending behaviour), each individual sentence is likely to be higher because the offence is aggravated by the fact that more than one death has been caused.

21. Where more than one person is killed, that will aggravate the seriousness of the offence because of the increase in harm. Where the number of people killed is high and that was reasonably foreseeable, the number of deaths is likely to provide sufficient justification for moving an offence into the next highest sentencing band.

(b) Effect on offender

22. Injury to the offender may be a mitigating factor when the offender has suffered very serious injuries. In most circumstances, the weighting it is given will be dictated by the circumstances of the offence and the effect should bear a direct relationship to the extent to which the offender's driving was at fault – the greater the fault, the less the effect on mitigation; this distinction will be of particular relevance where an offence did not involve any fault in the offender's standard of driving.

23. Where one or more of the victims was in a close personal or family relationship with the offender, this may be a mitigating factor. In line with the approach where the offender is very seriously injured, the degree to which the relationship influences the sentence should be linked to offender culpability in relation to the commission of the offence; mitigation for this reason is likely to have less effect where the culpability of the driver is particularly high.

(c) Actions of others

24. Where the actions of the victim or a third party contributed to the commission of an offence, this should be acknowledged and taken into account as a mitigating factor.

(d)   *Offender's age/lack of driving experience*

25.   The Council guideline *Overarching Principles: Seriousness*[2] includes a generic mitigating factor *"youth or age, where it affects the responsibility of the individual defendant"*. There is a great deal of difference between recklessness or irresponsibility – which may be due to youth – and inexperience in dealing with prevailing conditions or an unexpected or unusual situation that presents itself – which may be present regardless of the age of the offender. The fact that an offender's lack of driving experience contributed to the commission of an offence should be treated as a mitigating factor; in this regard, the age of the offender is not relevant.

(iii)   Personal mitigation

(a)   *Good driving record*

26.   This is not a factor that automatically should be treated as a mitigating factor, especially now that the presence of previous convictions is a statutory aggravating factor. However, any evidence to show that an offender has previously been an exemplary driver, for example having driven an ambulance, police vehicle, bus, taxi or similar vehicle conscientiously and without incident for many years, is a fact that the courts may well wish to take into account by way of personal mitigation. This is likely to have even greater effect where the driver is driving on public duty (for example, on ambulance, fire services or police duties) and was responding to an emergency.

(b)   *Conduct after the offence*

      – *Giving assistance at the scene*

27.   There may be many reasons why an offender does not offer help to the victims at the scene – the offender may be injured, traumatised by shock, afraid of causing further injury or simply have no idea what action to take – and it would be inappropriate to assess the offence as more serious on this ground (and so increase the level of sentence). However, where an offender gave direct, positive, assistance to victim(s) at the scene of a collision, this should be regarded as personal mitigation.

      – *Remorse*

28.   Whilst it can be expected that anyone who has caused death by driving would be expected to feel remorseful, this cannot undermine its importance for sentencing purposes. Remorse is identified as personal mitigation in the Council guideline[3] and the Council can see no reason for it to be treated differently for this group of offences. It is for the court to determine whether an expression of remorse is genuine; where it is, this should be taken into account as personal mitigation.

(c)   *Summary*

29.   Evidence that an offender is normally a careful and conscientious driver, giving direct, positive assistance to a victim and genuine remorse may be taken into account as personal mitigation and may justify a reduction in sentence.

---

[2]   *Overarching Principles: Seriousness*, paragraph 1.25, published 16 December 2004, www.sentencing-guidelines.gov.uk
[3]   ibid., paragraph 1.27

B. Ancillary orders

(i) Disqualification for driving

30. For each offence, disqualification is a mandatory part of the sentence (subject to the usual (very limited) exceptions), and therefore an important element of the overall punishment for the offence. In addition, an order that the disqualification continues until the offender passes an extended driving test order is compulsory[4] for those convicted of causing death by dangerous driving or by careless driving when under the influence, and discretionary[5] in relation to the two other offences.

31. Any disqualification is effective from the date on which it is imposed. When ordering disqualification from driving, the duration of the order should allow for the length of any custodial period in order to ensure that the disqualification has the desired impact. In principle, the minimum period of disqualification should either equate to the length of the custodial sentence imposed (in the knowledge that the offender is likely to be released having served half of that term), or the relevant statutory minimum disqualification period, whichever results in the longer period of disqualification.

(ii) Deprivation order

32. A general sentencing power exists which enables courts to deprive an offender of property used for the purposes of committing an offence.[6] A vehicle used to commit an offence included in this guideline can be regarded as being used for the purposes of committing the offence.

---

[4] Road Traffic Offenders Act 1988, s.36(1)
[5] ibid., s.36(4)
[6] Powers of Criminal Courts (Sentencing) Act 2000, s.143

4A.05

C.   Sentencing ranges and starting points

1.   Typically, a guideline will apply to an offence that can be committed in a variety of circumstances with different levels of seriousness. It will apply to a *"first time offender"* who has been **convicted after a trial**. Within the guidelines, a *"first time offender"* is a person who does not have a conviction which, by virtue of section 143(2) of the Criminal Justice Act 2003, must be treated as an aggravating factor.

2.   As an aid to consistency of approach, the guideline describes a number of levels or types of activity which would fall within the broad definition of the offence.

3.   The expected approach is for a court to identify the description that most nearly matches the particular facts of the offence for which sentence is being imposed. This will identify a **starting point** from which the sentencer can depart to reflect aggravating or mitigating factors affecting the seriousness of the offence (beyond those contained within the column describing the nature of the offence) to reach a **provisional sentence**.

4.   The **sentencing range** is the bracket into which the provisional sentence will normally fall after having regard to factors which aggravate or mitigate the seriousness of the offence. The particular circumstances may, however, make it appropriate that the provisional sentence falls outside the range.

5.   Where the offender has previous convictions which aggravate the seriousness of the current offence, that may take the provisional sentence beyond the range given particularly where there are significant other aggravating factors present.

6.   Once the provisional sentence has been identified by reference to those factors affecting the seriousness of the offence, the court will take into account any relevant factors of personal mitigation, which may take the sentence beyond the range given.

7.   Where there has been a guilty plea, any reduction attributable to that plea will be applied to the sentence at this stage. This reduction may take the sentence below the range provided.

8.   A court must give its reasons for imposing a sentence of a different kind or outside the range provided in the guidelines.

The decision making process

The process set out below is intended to show that the sentencing approach for offences of causing death by driving is fluid and requires the structured exercise of discretion.

1. Identify Dangerous Offenders

Offences under s.1 and s.3A of the Road Traffic Act 1988 are specified offences for the purposes of the public protection provisions in the 2003 Act (as amended). The court must determine whether there is a significant risk of serious harm by the commission of a further specified offence. The starting points in the guidelines are a) for offenders for whom a sentence under the public protection provisions is not appropriate <u>and</u> b) as the basis for the setting of a minimum term within an indeterminate sentence under those provisions.

2. Identify the appropriate starting point

Identify the level or description that most nearly matches the particular facts of the offence for which sentence is being imposed.

3. Consider relevant aggravating factors, both general and those specific to the type of offence

This may result in a sentence level being identified that is higher than the suggested starting point, sometimes substantially so.

4. Consider mitigating factors and personal mitigation

There may be general or offence specific mitigating factors and matters of personal mitigation which could result in a sentence that is lower than the suggested starting point (possibly substantially so), or a sentence of a different type.

5. Reduction for guilty plea

The court will then apply any reduction for a guilty plea following the approach set out in the Council's Guideline "Reduction in Sentence for a Guilty Plea" (revised July 2007).

6. Consider ancillary orders

The court should consider whether ancillary orders are appropriate or necessary.

7. The totality principle

The court should review the total sentence to ensure that it is proportionate to the offending behaviour and properly balanced.

8. Reasons

When a court moves from the suggested starting points and sentencing ranges identified in the guidelines, it should explain its reasons for doing so.

D. Offence guidelines

Causing death by dangerous driving

Factors to take into consideration

1. The following guideline applies to a *"first-time offender"* aged 18 or over convicted after trial (see page 8 above), who has **not** been assessed as a dangerous offender requiring a sentence under ss. 224-228 Criminal Justice Act 2003 (as amended).

2. When assessing the seriousness of any offence, the court must always refer to the full list of aggravating and mitigating factors in the Council guideline on Seriousness[7] as well as those set out in the adjacent table as being particularly relevant to this type of offending behaviour.

3. **Levels of seriousness**

   The 3 levels are distinguished by factors related predominantly to the standard of driving; the general description of the degree of risk is complemented by examples of the type of bad driving arising. The presence of aggravating factors or combinations of a small number of determinants of seriousness will increase the starting point within the range. Where there is a larger group of determinants of seriousness and/or aggravating factors, this may justify moving the starting point to the next level.

   Level 1 – The most serious offences encompassing driving that involved a deliberate decision to ignore (or a flagrant disregard for) the rules of the road and an apparent disregard for the great danger being caused to others. Such offences are likely to be characterised by:

   - A prolonged, persistent and deliberate course of very bad driving **AND/OR**
   - Consumption of substantial amounts of alcohol or drugs leading to gross impairment **AND/OR**
   - A group of determinants of seriousness which in isolation or smaller number would place the offence in level 2

   Level 1 is that for which the increase in maximum penalty was aimed primarily. Where an offence involves both of the determinants of seriousness identified, particularly if accompanied by aggravating factors such as multiple deaths or injuries, or a very bad driving record, this may move an offence towards the top of the sentencing range.

   Level 2 – This is driving that created a *substantial* risk of danger and is likely to be characterised by:

   - Greatly excessive speed, racing or competitive driving against another driver **OR**
   - Gross avoidable distraction such as reading or composing text messages over a period of time **OR**
   - Driving whilst ability to drive is impaired as a result of consumption of alcohol or drugs, failing to take prescribed medication or as a result of a known medical condition **OR**
   - A group of determinants of seriousness which in isolation or smaller number would place the offence in level 3

   Level 3 – This is driving that created a *significant* risk of danger and is likely to be characterised by:

   - Driving above the speed limit/at a speed that is inappropriate for the prevailing conditions **OR**
   - Driving when knowingly deprived of adequate sleep or rest or knowing that the vehicle has a dangerous defect or is poorly maintained or is dangerously loaded **OR**
   - A brief but obvious danger arising from a seriously dangerous manoeuvre **OR**
   - Driving whilst avoidably distracted **OR**
   - Failing to have proper regard to vulnerable road users

   The starting point and range overlap with Level 2 is to allow the breadth of discretion necessary to accommodate circumstances where there are significant aggravating factors.

4. Sentencers should take into account relevant matters of personal mitigation; see in particular guidance on **good driving record, giving assistance at the scene** and **remorse** in paragraphs 26-29 above.

---

[7] *Overarching Principles: Seriousness*, published 16 December 2004, www.sentencing-guidelines.gov.uk

Causing death by dangerous driving

Road Traffic Act 1988 (section 1)

THIS IS A SERIOUS OFFENCE FOR THE PURPOSES OF SECTION 224 CRIMINAL JUSTICE ACT 2003

Maximum penalty: 14 years imprisonment
> minimum disqualification of 2 years with compulsory extended re-test

Nature of offence	Starting point	Sentencing range
Level 1 The most serious offences encompassing driving that involved a deliberate decision to ignore (or a flagrant disregard for) the rules of the road and an apparent disregard for the great danger being caused to others	8 years custody	7–14 years custody
Level 2 Driving that created a *substantial* risk of danger	5 years custody	4–7 years custody
Level 3 Driving that created a *significant* risk of danger *[Where the driving is markedly less culpable than for this level, reference should be made to the starting point and range for the most serious level of causing death by careless driving]*	3 years custody	2–5 years custody

Additional aggravating factors	Additional mitigating factors
1. Previous convictions for motoring offences, particularly offences that involve bad driving or the consumption of excessive alcohol or drugs before driving 2. More than one person killed as a result of the offence 3. Serious injury to one or more victims, in addition to the death(s) 4. Disregard of warnings 5. Other offences committed at the same time, such as driving other than in accordance with the terms of a valid licence; driving while disqualified; driving without insurance; taking a vehicle without consent; driving a stolen vehicle 6. The offender's irresponsible behaviour such as failing to stop, falsely claiming that one of the victims was responsible for the collision, or trying to throw the victim off the car by swerving in order to escape 7. Driving off in an attempt to avoid detection or apprehension	1. Alcohol or drugs consumed unwittingly 2. Offender was seriously injured in the collision 3. The victim was a close friend or relative 4. Actions of the victim or a third party contributed significantly to the likelihood of a collision occurring and/or death resulting 5. The offender's lack of driving experience contributed to the commission of the offence 6. The driving was in response to a proven and genuine emergency falling short of a defence

4A.09

Causing death by careless driving when under the influence of drink or drugs or having failed without reasonable excuse either to provide a specimen for analysis or to permit the analysis of a blood sample

Factors to take into consideration

1. The following guideline applies to a *"first-time offender"* aged 18 or over convicted after trial (see page 8 above), who has **not** been assessed as a dangerous offender requiring a sentence under ss. 224-228 Criminal Justice Act 2003 (as amended).

2. When assessing the seriousness of any offence, the court must always refer to the full list of aggravating and mitigating factors in the Council guideline on Seriousness[8] as well as those set out on the facing page as being particularly relevant to this type of offending behaviour.

3. This offence can be committed through:

   (i) being unfit to drive through drink or drugs;

   (ii) having consumed so much alcohol as to be over the prescribed limit;

   (iii) failing without reasonable excuse to provide a specimen for analysis within the timescale allowed; or

   (iv) failing without reasonable excuse to permit the analysis of a blood sample taken when incapable of giving consent.

4. In comparison with *causing death by dangerous driving*, the level of culpability in the actual manner of driving is lower but that culpability is increased in all cases by the fact that the offender has driven after consuming drugs or an excessive amount of alcohol. Accordingly, there is considerable parity in the levels of seriousness with the deliberate decision to drive after consuming alcohol or drugs aggravating the *careless* standard of driving onto a par with *dangerous* driving.

5. The fact that the offender was under the influence of drink or drugs is an inherent element of this offence. For discussion on the significance of driving after having consumed drink or drugs, see paragraphs 10-12 above.

6. The guideline is based both on the level of alcohol or drug consumption and on the degree of carelessness.

7. The increase in sentence is more marked where there is an increase in the level of intoxication than where there is an increase in the degree of carelessness reflecting the 14 year imprisonment maximum for this offence compared with a 5 year maximum for causing death by careless or inconsiderate driving alone.

8. A refusal to supply a specimen for analysis may be a calculated step by an offender to avoid prosecution for driving when having consumed in excess of the prescribed amount of alcohol, with a view to seeking to persuade the court that the amount consumed was relatively small. A court is entitled to draw adverse inferences from a refusal to supply a specimen without reasonable excuse and should treat with caution any attempt to persuade the court that only a limited amount of alcohol had been consumed.[9] The three levels of seriousness where the offence has been committed in this way derive from the classification in the Magistrates' Court Sentencing Guidelines.

9. Sentencers should take into account relevant matters of personal mitigation; see in particular guidance on **good driving record, giving assistance at the scene** and **remorse** in paragraphs 26-29 above.

---

[8] *Overarching Principles: Seriousness*, published 16 December 2004, www.sentencing-guidelines.gov.uk

[9] *Attorney-General's Reference No. 21 of 2000* [2001] 1 Cr App R (S) 173

Causing death by careless driving when under the influence of drink or drugs or having failed either to provide a specimen for analysis or to permit analysis of a blood sample

Road Traffic Act 1988 (section 3A)

THIS IS A SERIOUS OFFENCE FOR THE PURPOSES OF SECTION 224 CRIMINAL JUSTICE ACT 2003

Maximum penalty: 14 years imprisonment;
          minimum disqualification of 2 years with compulsory extended re-test

The legal limit of alcohol is 35µg breath (80mg in blood and 107mg in urine)	Careless/ inconsiderate driving arising from momentary inattention with no aggravating factors	Other cases of careless/ inconsiderate driving	Careless/ inconsiderate driving falling not far short of dangerousness
71µ or above of alcohol/ high quantity of drugs OR deliberate non-provision of specimen where evidence of serious impairment	**Starting point:** 6 years custody **Sentencing range:** 5–10 years custody	**Starting point:** 7 years custody **Sentencing range:** 6–12 years custody	**Starting point:** 8 years custody **Sentencing range:** 7–14 years custody
51–70 µg of alcohol/ moderate quantity of drugs OR deliberate non-provision of specimen	**Starting point:** 4 years custody **Sentencing range:** 3–7 years custody	**Starting point:** 5 years custody **Sentencing range:** 4–8 years custody	**Starting point:** 6 years custody **Sentencing range:** 5–9 years custody
35–50 µg of alcohol/minimum quantity of drugs OR test refused because of honestly held but unreasonable belief	**Starting point:** 18 months custody **Sentencing range:** 26 weeks–4 years custody	**Starting point:** 3 years custody **Sentencing range:** 2–5 years custody	**Starting point:** 4 years custody **Sentencing range:** 3–6 years custody

Additional aggravating factors	Additional mitigating factors
1. Other offences committed at the same time, such as driving other than in accordance with the terms of a valid licence; driving while disqualified; driving without insurance; taking a vehicle without consent; driving a stolen vehicle 2. Previous convictions for motoring offences, particularly offences that involve bad driving or the consumption of excessive alcohol before driving 3. More than one person was killed as a result of the offence 4. Serious injury to one or more persons in addition to the death(s) 5. Irresponsible behaviour such as failing to stop or falsely claiming that one of the victims was responsible for the collision	1. Alcohol or drugs consumed unwittingly 2. Offender was seriously injured in the collision 3. The victim was a close friend or relative 4. The actions of the victim or a third party contributed significantly to the likelihood of a collision occurring and/or death resulting 5. The driving was in response to a proven and genuine emergency falling short of a defence

4A.11

Causing death by careless or inconsiderate driving

Factors to take into consideration

1. The following guideline applies to a *"first-time offender"* aged 18 or over convicted after trial (see page 8 above).

2. When assessing the seriousness of any offence, the court must always refer to the full list of aggravating and mitigating factors in the Council guideline on Seriousness[10] as well as those set out in the table below as being particularly relevant to this type of offending behaviour.

3. The maximum penalty on indictment is 5 years imprisonment. The offence is triable either way and, in a magistrates' court, statute provides that the maximum sentence is 12 months imprisonment; this will be revised to 6 months imprisonment until such time as the statutory provisions increasing the sentencing powers of a magistrates' court are implemented.[11]

4. Disqualification of the offender from driving and endorsement of the offender's driving licence are mandatory, and the offence carries between 3 and 11 penalty points when the court finds special reasons for not imposing disqualification. There is a discretionary power[12] to order an extended driving test where a person is convicted of this offence.

5. Since the maximum sentence has been set at 5 years imprisonment, the sentence ranges are generally lower for this offence than for the offences of *causing death by dangerous driving* or *causing death by careless driving under the influence*, for which the maximum sentence is 14 years imprisonment. However, it is unavoidable that some cases will be on the borderline between *dangerous* and *careless* driving, or may involve a number of factors that significantly increase the seriousness of an offence. As a result, the guideline for this offence identifies three levels of seriousness, the range for the highest of which overlaps with ranges for the lowest level of seriousness for *causing death by dangerous driving*.

6. The three levels of seriousness are defined by the degree of carelessness involved in the standard of driving. The most serious level for this offence is where the offender's driving fell *not that far short of dangerous*. The least serious group of offences relates to those cases where the level of culpability is low – for example in a case involving an offender who misjudges the speed of another vehicle, or turns without seeing an oncoming vehicle because of restricted visibility. Other cases will fall into the intermediate level.

7. The starting point for the most serious offence of *causing death by careless driving* is lower than that for the least serious offence of *causing death by dangerous driving* in recognition of the different standards of driving behaviour. However, the range still leaves scope, within the 5 year maximum, to impose longer sentences where the case is particularly serious.

---

[10] *Overarching Principles: Seriousness*, published 16 December 2004, www.sentencing-guidelines.gov.uk
[11] Criminal Justice Act 2003, ss.154(1) and 282; Road Safety Act 2006, s.61(5)
[12] Road Traffic Offenders Act 1988, s.36(4)

8. Where the level of carelessness is low and there are no aggravating factors, even the fact that death was caused is not sufficient to justify a prison sentence.

9. A fine is unlikely to be an appropriate sentence for this offence; where a non-custodial sentence is considered appropriate, this should be a community order. The nature of the requirements will be determined by the purpose[13] identified by the court as of primary importance. Requirements most likely to be relevant include unpaid work requirement, activity requirement, programme requirement and curfew requirement.

10. Sentencers should take into account relevant matters of personal mitigation; see in particular guidance on **good driving record, giving assistance at the scene** and **remorse** in paragraphs 26-29 above.

Causing death by careless or inconsiderate driving 4A.12

Road Traffic Act 1988 (section 2B)

Maximum penalty: 5 years imprisonment
minimum disqualification of 12 months, discretionary re-test

Nature of offence	Starting Point	Sentencing range
Careless or inconsiderate driving falling not far short of dangerous driving	**15 months custody**	**36 weeks–3 years custody**
Other cases of careless or inconsiderate driving	**36 weeks custody**	**Community order (HIGH)–2 years custody**
Careless or inconsiderate driving arising from momentary inattention with no aggravating factors	**Community order (MEDIUM)**	**Community order (LOW)–Community order (HIGH)**

Additional aggravating factors	Additional mitigating factors
1. Other offences committed at the same time, such as driving other than in accordance with the terms of a valid licence; driving while disqualified; driving without insurance; taking a vehicle without consent; driving a stolen vehicle 2. Previous convictions for motoring offences, particularly offences that involve bad driving 3. More than one person was killed as a result of the offence 4. Serious injury to one or more persons in addition to the death(s) 5. Irresponsible behaviour, such as failing to stop or falsely claiming that one of the victims was responsible for the collision	1. Offender was seriously injured in the collision 2. The victim was a close friend or relative 3. The actions of the victim or a third party contributed to the commission of the offence 4. The offender's lack of driving experience contributed significantly to the likelihood of a collision occurring and/or death resulting 5. The driving was in response to a proven and genuine emergency falling short of a defence

---

[13] Criminal Justice Act 2003, s.142(1)

4A.13

Causing death by driving: unlicensed, disqualified or uninsured drivers

Factors to take into consideration

1.   The following guideline applies to a *"first-time offender"* aged 18 or over convicted after trial (see page 8 above). An offender convicted of causing death by driving whilst disqualified will always have at least one relevant previous conviction for the offence that resulted in the disqualification. The starting point and range take this into account; any other previous convictions should be considered in the usual way.

2.   When assessing the seriousness of any offence, the court must always refer to the full list of aggravating and mitigating factors in the Council guideline on Seriousness[14] as well as those set out in the table below as being particularly relevant to this type of offending behaviour.

3.   This offence has a maximum penalty of 2 years imprisonment and is triable either way. In a magistrates' court, statute provides that the maximum sentence is 12 months imprisonment; this will be revised to 6 months imprisonment until such time as the statutory provisions increasing the sentencing powers of a magistrates' court are implemented.[15]

4.   Disqualification of the offender from driving and endorsement of the offender's driving licence are mandatory, and the offence carries between 3 and 11 penalty points when the court finds special reasons for not imposing disqualification. There is a discretionary power[16] to order an extended driving test where a person is convicted of this offence.

5.   Culpability arises from the offender driving a vehicle on a road or other public place when, by law, not allowed to do so; the offence does not require proof of any fault in the standard of driving.

6.   Because of the significantly lower maximum penalty, the sentencing ranges are considerably lower than for the other three offences covered in this guideline; many cases may be sentenced in a magistrates' court, particularly where there is an early guilty plea.

7.   A fine is unlikely to be an appropriate sentence for this offence; where a non-custodial sentence is considered appropriate, this should be a community order.

8.   Since driving whilst disqualified is more culpable than driving whilst unlicensed or uninsured, a higher starting point is proposed when the offender was disqualified from driving at the time of the offence.

9.   Being uninsured, unlicensed or disqualified are the only determinants of seriousness for this offence, as there are no factors relating to the standard of driving. The list of aggravating factors identified is slightly different as the emphasis is on the decision to drive by an offender who is not permitted by law to do so.

---

[14]   *Overarching Principles: Seriousness*, published 16 December 2004, www.sentencing-guidelines.gov.uk

[15]   Criminal Justice Act 2003, ss.154(1) and 282; Road Safety Act 2006, s.61(5)

[16]   Road Traffic Offenders Act 1988, s.36(4)

10.   In some cases, the extreme circumstances that led an offender to drive whilst unlicensed, disqualified or uninsured may result in a successful defence of 'duress of circumstances.'[17] In less extreme circumstances, where the *decision to drive was brought about by a genuine and proven emergency*, that may mitigate offence seriousness and so it is included as an additional mitigating factor.

11.   A driver may hold a reasonable belief in relation to the validity of insurance (for example having just missed a renewal date or relied on a third party to make an application) and also the validity of a licence (for example incorrectly believing that a licence covered a particular category of vehicle). In light of this, an additional mitigating factor covers those situations where an offender genuinely believed that there was valid insurance or a valid licence.

12.   Sentencers should take into account relevant matters of personal mitigation; see in particular guidance on **good driving record, giving assistance at the scene** and **remorse** in paragraphs 26-29 above.

Causing death by driving: unlicensed, disqualified or uninsured drivers   4A.14

Road Traffic Act 1988 (section 3ZB)

Maximum penalty: 2 years imprisonment
        minimum disqualification of 12 months, discretionary re-test

Nature of offence	Starting point	Sentencing range
The offender was disqualified from driving **OR** The offender was unlicensed or uninsured plus 2 or more aggravating factors from the list below	**12 months custody**	**36 weeks–2 years custody**
The offender was unlicensed or uninsured plus at least 1 aggravating factor from the list below	**26 weeks custody**	**Community order (HIGH)–36 weeks custody**
The offender was unlicensed or uninsured – no aggravating factors	**Community order (MEDIUM)**	**Community order (LOW)– Community order (HIGH)**

Additional aggravating factors	Additional mitigating factors
1. Previous convictions for motoring offences, whether involving bad driving or involving an offence of the same kind that forms part of the present conviction (i.e. unlicensed, disqualified or uninsured driving)	1. The decision to drive was brought about by a proven and genuine emergency falling short of a defence
2. More than one person was killed as a result of the offence	2. The offender genuinely believed that he or she was insured or licensed to drive
3. Serious injury to one or more persons in addition to the death(s)	3. The offender was seriously injured as a result of the collision
4. Irresponsible behaviour such as failing to stop or falsely claiming that someone else was driving	4. The victim was a close friend or relative

---

[17]   In *DPP v Mullally* [2006] EWHC 3448 the Divisional Court held that the defence of necessity must be strictly controlled and that it must be proved that the actions of the defendant were reasonable in the given circumstances. See also *Hasan* [2005] UKHL 22

4A.15

Annex A: DANGEROUS AND CARELESS DRIVING

Statutory definitions and examples

Dangerous driving

A person is to be regarded as driving dangerously if the standard of driving falls *far below* what would be expected of a competent and careful driver and it would be obvious to a competent and careful driver that driving in that way would be dangerous.

Examples of the types of driving behaviour likely to result in this offence being charged include:

- Aggressive driving (such as sudden lane changes or cutting into a line of vehicles) **or** Racing or competitive driving **or** Speed that is highly inappropriate for the prevailing road or traffic conditions
- Disregard of traffic lights and other road signs which, on an objective analysis, would appear to be deliberate
- Driving a vehicle knowing it has a dangerous defect or with a load which presents a danger to other road users
- Using a hand-held mobile phone or other hand-held electronic equipment when the driver was avoidably and dangerously distracted by that use
- Driving when too tired to stay awake or where the driver is suffering from impaired ability such as having an arm or leg in plaster, or impaired eyesight

Careless driving

Careless driving is driving that "falls *below* what would be expected of a competent and careful driver" and a person is to be regarded as driving without reasonable consideration for other persons "only if those persons are inconvenienced by his driving".[18]

Examples of the types of driving behaviour likely to result in an offence of *causing death by careless or inconsiderate driving* being charged are:

(i) Careless Driving

- overtaking on the inside or driving inappropriately close to another vehicle
- inadvertent mistakes such as driving through a red light or emerging from a side road into the path of another vehicle
- short distractions such as tuning a car radio

(ii) Inconsiderate Driving

- flashing of lights to force other drivers in front to give way
- misuse of any lane to avoid queuing or gain some other advantage over other drivers
- driving that inconveniences other road users or causes unnecessary hazards such as unnecessarily remaining in an overtaking lane, unnecessarily slow driving or braking without good cause, driving with un-dipped headlights which dazzle oncoming drivers or driving through a puddle causing pedestrians to be splashed

Depending on the circumstances, it is possible that some of the examples listed above could be classified as *dangerous* driving (see the revised CPS guidance). However, experience shows that these types of behaviour predominantly result in prosecution for *careless* driving.

A typical piece of *careless* driving may be that it is a momentary negligent error of judgement or a single negligent manoeuvre, so long as neither falls so far below the standard of the competent and careful driver as to amount to *dangerous* driving.

---

[18] 1988 Act, s.3ZA as inserted by the Road Safety Act 2006

STOPPING DISTANCES, ETC.

TABLE OF STOPPING DISTANCES   **5A.01**

*(taken, by permission, from the Typical Stopping Distances diagram,
Highway Code)*

Stopping distances—in metres and feet

mph	Thinking distance		Braking distance		Overall stopping distance		Car lengths*
	Metres/feet		Metres/feet		Metres/feet		
20	6	20	6	20	12	40	3
30	9	30	14	45	23	75	6
40	12	40	24	80	36	120	9
50	15	50	38	125	53	175	13
60	18	60	55	180	73	240	18
70	21	70	75	245	96	315	24

* Average car length = 4m.

Rule 126 of the Highway Code states: **5A.02**

"Drive at a speed that will allow you to stop well within the distance you can see to be clear. You should

- leave enough space between you and the vehicle in front so that you can pull up safely if it suddenly slows down or stops. The safe rule is never get closer than the overall stopping distance …

- allow at least a two-second gap between you and the vehicle in front on roads carrying faster-moving traffic. The gap should be at least doubled on wet roads and increased still further on icy roads

- remember, large vehicles and motorcycles need a greater distance to stop. If driving a large vehicle in a tunnel, you should allow a four-second gap between you and the vehicle in front.

If you have to stop in a tunnel, leave at least a five-metre gap between you and the vehicle in front."

(For use of the Highway Code and table, see §§ 5.69–73 and *R. v Chadwick* at § 5.70.)

5A.03

Conversion table

Miles per hour	Feet per second (to nearest foot)
20	29
30	44
40	59
50	73
60	88
70	103
80	117

Metric equivalents

km	miles/km	miles
16.093	10	6.214
32.185	20	12.428
48.278	30	18.642
64.371	40	24.856
80.463	50	31.070
96.556	60	37.284
112.649	70	43.498
128.742	80	49.712
144.834	90	55.926
160.927	100	62.140
177.020	110	68.354
193.112	120	74.568

1mm = 0.0397in.   1in. = 25.4mm

1m = 1.0936yd = 3.2808ft = 39.37in.

1kg = 2.205lb.   1lb = 0.454kg

1tonne = 1,000kg = 2,204.6lb.

(1ton = 20cwt = 2,240lb.)

5A.04

STANDARD SCALE FINES

Level on the standard scale	Amount on or after October 1, 1992
1	£200
2	£500
3	£1,000
4	£2,500
5	£5,000

See note on standard scale fines at § 18.07 and on the assessment and imposition of fines at §§ 18.08–10.

INDEX

This index has been prepared using Sweet and Maxwell's Legal Taxonomy. Main index entries conform to keywords provided by the Legal Taxonomy except where references to specific documents or non-standard terms (denoted by quotation marks) have been included. These keywords provide a means of identifying similar concepts in other Sweet & Maxwell publications and online services to which keywords from the Legal Taxonomy have been applied. Readers may find some minor differences between terms used in the text and those which appear in the index. Suggestions to *sweetandmaxwell.taxonomy@thomson.com*

All entries are to paragraph number.